The New York Times

CROSSWORD PUZZLE
DICTIONARY

The New York Times
CROSSWORD PUZZLE DICTIONARY

By

Tom Pulliam and Clare Grundman

A HUDSON GROUP BOOK

Portland House
New York

Produced in association with Morningside Associates.

Copyright 1974 by Thomas Pulliam and Clare Grundman. All rights
reserved, including the right to reproduce this book or portions thereof
in any form. Manufactured in the United States of America.

This 1986 edition published by Portland House, distributed by Crown
Publishers, Inc., 225 Park Avenue South, New York, New York 10003.

Library of Congress Catalog Card Number: 73-79912

ISBN 0-517-62605-5
h g f e d c b a

PREFACE

THE NEW YORK TIMES CROSSWORD PUZZLE DICTIONARY exceeds in completeness and scope all other puzzle dictionaries. No useful word has been omitted. Not only have puzzles themselves been combed for synonyms that are used over and over, but also a word-for-word reading of major unabridged dictionaries, both current and old, produced a thoroughly complete and extensive checklist.

Each of us has been solving and compiling puzzles for many years, and our chief purpose has been to design a practical and easy-to-use dictionary, in the belief that your needs and requirements for such a volume closely reflect our own. For example, the synonyms are arranged by the number of letters, and then alphabetized so you can quickly find the very word that fills the spaces in the puzzle. Another feature, one that seems obvious for a crossword puzzle dictionary but is not found in most of them, is that all words are printed in easy-to-read capital letters. The type has been chosen with great care for its legibility, and the three-column format not only provides a short line of type to scan, but also enables us to get a very large number of words on each page.

Synonyms of great length have been omitted to give room for the shorter, more useful words. The puzzler can always "fill in" the very long words provided he has a good supply of short common synonyms. We have placed, therefore, an arbitrary ceiling of eight-letter word-lengths, knowing this will satisfy almost all needs. Here and there, however, you will find occasional exceptions to this rule. These are synonyms of such frequent, interesting and normal usage that their omission might handicap the puzzler.

The "shaded boxes" scattered through the book are a notable and unique feature of THE NEW YORK TIMES CROSSWORD PUZZLE DICTIONARY. They collect under one heading a variety of categories and synonyms that you would have a hard time finding in other dictionaries. For example, when you are confronted by the clue "Brazilian river" merely turn to the shaded area marked BRAZIL, where you will find several excellent possibilities. Similarly, look for a "Philippine native" under PHILIPPINES, or a "Scottish measure" under SCOTLAND.

Another useful feature is the lavish listing of phrases. For instance, instead of being confronted by the simple clue "Sword," you may run up against "Double-edged sword." Under the entry word SWORD in this dictionary you will find ample phrases that qualify the entry word or more sharply specify its meaning. Also, given the definition "Turn aside," simply look under TURN and find that phrase, along with many others.

THE NEW YORK TIMES CROSSWORD PUZZLE DICTIONARY is a versatile reference book which you will want to keep on your desk or next to your chair for help, not only with crossword puzzles, but also for a large variety of other puzzles and contests. In addition, it will be invaluable for writers, speakers, and the like, for (with more than ½ million words) it is one of the largest books of synonyms ever published. Its simple arrangement makes it far easier to use than the standard thesauri.

Our hope is that you will come to use this new word book as we might. Get to know it and be adventuresome! If the first entry you consult does not corner the exact word you are seeking, let any listing at that spot lead you to a cross-reference. Follow this track until you have the right word "treed."

A project of this scope may well have been beyond the ability of only two to accomplish. We have required and welcomed top-flight support during our work. Although many might be named, special note must be given to the efforts of Richard Martz and David House of Dartmouth College, who were responsible for much of the computerization; also, to Gorton Carruth and Robert O'Brien of Morningside Associates. Each made his individual contributions, which we gratefully acknowledge.

Happy word hunting!

Tom Pulliam
Clare Grundman

The New York Times
CROSSWORD PUZZLE
DICTIONARY

A AN AY HA AIR ARY PER ALFA EACH
  ALPHA
  (EVER —) ARROW
AA LAVA
AAL AL MULBERRY
AARDVARK ANTEATER EDENTATE
AARDWOLF HYAENID
AARON (BROTHER OF —) MOSES
  (BURIAL PLACE OF —) HOR
  (FATHER OF —) AMRAM
  (SISTER OF —) MIRIAM
  (SON OF —) ABIHU NADAB ELEAZAR
AARONIC LEVITIC LEVITICAL
AB HATI
ABA ABAYAH
ABACÁ HEMP FIBER LUPIS LINAGA
  MANILA
ABACK SHORT
ABACUS SOROBAN
ABADDON PIT HELL ABYSS SATAN
  APOLLYON
ABAFT AFT BACK BAFT ABAFF
  ASTERN BEHIND REARWARD
  (— THE BEAM) LARGE
ABALONE EAR PAUA AWABI NACRE
  ORMER UHLLO ASSEIR MOLLUSK
ABANDON EGO CAST DROP FLEE
  JUNK QUIT SINK ALLAY DITCH
  EXPEL LEAVE PLANT REMIT SCRAP
  WAIVE YIELD ABJURE BANISH
  BETRAY DESERT DEVEST DISUSE
  DIVEST EXPOSE FOREGO FORHOO
  FORLET MAROON RECANT REFUSE
  REJECT RELENT RESIGN SLOUGH
  VACATE DEPLORE DISCARD FORFEIT
  FORSAKE SCUTTLE ABDICATE
  FORHOOIE FORSWEAR JETTISON
  RASHNESS RENOUNCE SURCEASE
  (WITH —) DESPERATELY
ABANDONED BAD LEFT LORN LOST
  WICKED CORRUPT FORLORN
  PROJECT DEPRAVED DERELICT
  DESERTED DESOLATE FLAGRANT
  FORSAKEN
ABANDONMENT BURIAL APOSTASY
  (— OF RESTRAINT) LETUP
ABASE SINK VAIL AVALE AVILE
  BLAME DEMIT DIMIT LOWER SHAME
  ABJECT BEMEAN DEBASE DEFAME
  DEJECT DEMEAN DEPOSE GROVEL
  HUMBLE LESSEN MEEKEN REDUCE
  DEGRADE DEPRESS MORTIFY
  DIMINISH DISGRACE DISHONOR
ABASED ABAISSE DEJECTED
ABASH AWE COW BASH BAZE DASH
  AVALE ESBAY SHAME HUMBLE
  CONFUSE MORTIFY BEWILDER
  BROWBEAT CONFOUND
ABASHED BLANK CHEAP SHAMED
  ASHAMED FOOLISH SHEEPISH
ABASHMENT VERGOYNE
ABATE EBB END LOW CALM CURB
  FAIK FALL MEND OMIT SLOW SOFT
  VOID WANE ALLAY ANNUL BREAK
  CHECK LOWER QUASH RELAX REMIT
  SLAKE SWAGE ASLAKE DEDUCT
  LESSEN PACIFY REBATE REDUCE
  RELENT ABOLISH ASSUAGE
  CASSARE CHANCER NULLIFY

QUALIFY SLACKEN SUBSIDE
  DECREASE DIMINISH MITIGATE
  MODERATE OVERBLOW PALLIATE
ABATEMENT DELF FALL ALLAY
  DELFT DELPH LETUP GUSSET
  MIOSIS DECREASE DISCOUNT
ABATIS OBSTACLE SLASHING
ABAXIAL DORSAL
ABBA FATHER
ABBE MONK CLERIC CURATE PRIEST
ABBESS AMMA VICARESS
ABBEY ABADIA ABBAYE PRIORY
  CONVENT NUNNERY CLOISTER
ABBOT ABBAS COARB
  (— OF MISRULE) BISHOP
ABBREVIATE CUT CLIP DOCK PRUNE
  DIGEST ABRIDGE BOBTAIL CURTAIL
  SHORTEN CONDENSE CONTRACT
  TRUNCATE
ABBREVIATED SHORT BOBTAIL
  CRYPTIC MUTILATE
ABBREVIATION LAPSE SIGLUM
  SYMBOL
  (PL.) SIGLA
ABC ALPHABET
ABDICATE CEDE QUIT DEMIT EXPEL
  LEAVE REMIT DEPOSE DISOWN
  FOREGO RESIGN RETIRE VACATE
  ABANDON DISCLAIM RENOUNCE
ABDICATION DRIFT
ABDOMEN BOUK WOMB ALVUS
  APRON BELLY MELON MIRAC PLEON
  THARM PAUNCH VENTER STOMACH
ABDOMINAL HEMAL CELIAC
  COELIAC VENTRAL VISCERAL
ABDUCT LURE TAKE STEAL ABDUCE
  KIDNAP RAVISH SPIRIT CAPTURE
ABDUCTION APAGOGE RAPTURE
ABDUCTOR SPIRIT
ABEAM ABREAST
ABECEDARIAN TYRO NOVICE
  LEARNER BEGINNER
ABECEDARIUS ABC
ABED SICK RESTING RETIRED
  SLEEPING
ABEL (BROTHER OF —) CAIN SETH
  (PARENT OF —) EVE ADAM
ABELMOSK MUSK MALLOW
ABERDEEN ANGUS BLACK DODDY
  DODDIE
ABERRANT WILD CLAMMY DEVIANT
  ABNORMAL STRAYING VARIABLE
ABERRATION SLIP WARP ERROR
  FAULT LAPSE MANIA DELIRIUM
  DELUSION INSANITY
ABESSIVE CARITIVE
ABET AID EGG BACK HELP BOOST
  COACH ASSIST FOMENT INCITE
  SECOND SUCCOR UPHOLD
  COMFORT CONNIVE ESPOUSE
  FORWARD FURTHER SUPPORT
  SUSTAIN ADVOCATE BEFRIEND
ABETO ACXOYATL
ABETTING CONFEDERATE
ABETTOR FAUTOR ADVOCATE
  PROMOTER
ABEYANCE ABEYANCY DORMANCY
ABEYANT LATENT
ABHOR UG IRK HATE SHUN AGRISE

DETEST LOATHE DESPISE DISLIKE
  EXECRATE
ABHORRENCE HATE ODIUM HATRED
  HORROR DISGUST DISLIKE
  AVERSION LOATHING
ABHORRENT UGSOM HATEFUL
  INFAMOUS
ABIDE BE WIN WON BEAR BIDE KEEP
  LAST LEND LENG LIVE REST STAY
  WAIT ABEAR AWAIT DELAY EXIST
  HABIT PAUSE STAND SWELL TARRY
  ENDURE HARBOR LINGER REMAIN
  RESIDE SUBMIT INHABIT SOJOURN
  SUBSIST SUSTAIN CONTINUE
  TOLERATE
  (— BY) HOLD
ABIDING FAST STABLE LASTING
ABIDINGNESS PERMANENCE
ABIES FIRS CONIFERS
ABIETATE SYLVATE
ABIGAIL MAID
  (HUSBAND OF —) DAVID NABAL
ABIGEUS ABACTOR
ABIJAH (FATHER OF —) DAVID
  (SON OF —) ASA
ABILITY G CAN MAY CLAY EASE
  FORM HAND CLASS FLAIR FORCE
  MIGHT POWER SKILL STUFF VERVE
  ENERGY ENGINE MAUGHT STROKE
  TALENT CALIBER CUNNING FACULTY
  POTENCY APTITUDE CAPACITY
  STRENGTH
  (— TO ENTER) ACCESS
  (— TO THROW) ARM
  (BATTING —) STICKWORK
  (CREATIVE —) IMAGINATION
  (INVENTIVE —) CONTRIVANCE
  (MENTAL —) INGENY BRAINPOWER
ABIPON CORONADO
ABJECT LOW BASE MEAN POOR
  SUNK VILE HELOT PALTRY SORDID
  SUPINE FAWNING FORLORN
  IGNOBLE SERVILE SLAVISH
  BEGGARLY CRINGING DEGRADED
  DOWNCAST LISTLESS WRETCHED
ABJOINT ABSTRICT
ABJURE DENY NITTE SPURN ESCHEW
  RECALL RECANT REJECT RESIGN
  REVOKE ABANDON DISAVOW
  EJURATE RETRACT ABNEGATE
  DISCLAIM FORSWEAR RENOUNCE
ABLAUT APOPHONY
ABLAZE ALOW AFIRE ALOWE
  ABLEEZE BURNING GLOWING
  RADIANT GLEAMING INFLAMED
ABLE APT BIG CAN FIT FERE ADEPT
  HABIL SMART THERE CLEVER
  EXPERT FACILE FITTED HABILE
  POTENT STRONG BASTANT
  CAPABLE DOUGHTY DEXTROUS
  POSSIBLE POWERFUL SKILLFUL
  SUITABLE TALENTED VIGOROUS
  (— TO WALK) FEERIE FEIRIE
ABLE-BODIED YAL YALD YAULD
ABLUTION BATH WIDU WUDU WUZU
  LOTION BAPTISM BATHING WASHING
ABNAKI WABANAKI
ABNEGATE DENY ABJURE FOREGO
  REFUSE REJECT DISAVOW DISCLAIM

FORSWEAR IMMOLATE RENOUNCE

ABNORMAL ENORM QUEER UTTER
ERRATIC UNUSUAL VICIOUS
ABERRANT ATYPICAL FREAKISH

ABNORMALITY ATAXY ATAXIA
LETHAL BROWNING DEMENTIA
ENORMITY
(CATTLE —) SAWDUST

ABOARD ON ONTO ACROSS
ATHWART

ABODE COT DAR HUT INN WON
BODE CELL FLAT HALL HOME NEST
OMEN REST SEAT TENT WOON
BEING BOWER DELAY HAUNT HOUSE
MANOR PITCH RESET SIEGE SUITE
ABIDAL BIDING ESTATE ADDRESS
COTTAGE HABITAT LODGING
MANSION SITTING CUNABULA
DOMICILE DWELLING RESIANCE
TENEMENT
(— OF DEAD) DAR AARU HELL
ARALU HADES ORCUS SHEOL
HEAVEN SHADES XIBALBA
(— OF DELIGHT) ELYSIUM
(— OF EVIL POWERS) ABYSS
(— OF GODS) MERU ASGARD
OLYMPUS
(— OF LOST SOULS) ABADDON
(— OF SOULS) LIMBO
(ANIMAL —) ZOO MENAGERIE
(CELESTIAL —) HEAVEN
(FILTHY —) STY STYE
(MISERABLE —) DOGHOLE
(SHELTERED —) SHADE

ABOLISH END BLOT KILL ABATE
ANNUL ERASE FORDO QUASH
CANCEL EFFACE FOREDO RECALL
REPEAL REVOKE VACATE DESTROY
NULLIFY RESCIND REVERSE
ABROGATE

ABOLITION EXTINCTION

ABOMA BOA BOM BOMA

ABOMASUM READ REED

ABOMINABLE VILE RUSTY ODIOUS
ROTTEN BEASTLY HATEFUL
HEINOUS MALEDICT

ABOMINABLY BEASTLY

ABOMINATE HATE ABHOR DETEST
LOATHE EXECRATE

ABOMINATION EVIL CRIME CURSE
HORROR PLAGUE DISGUST
AVERSION

ABONGO BABONGO

ABORAL DORSAL

ABORIGINAL ABO YAO FIRST NATAL
BINGHI NATIVE SAVAGE NATURAL
PRIMARY ORIGINAL
(— WOMAN) GIN

ABORIGINE KA KHA TODA ALFUR
BAIGA BLACK BOONG DASYU MAORI
MYALL ALFURO ARANDA ARANTA
ARUNTA BINGHI INDIAN KIPPER
KODAGA NATIVE SAVAGE ADIBASI
CHINHWAN WARRAGAL WARRIGAL

ABORT SLIP

ABORTION SLIP ABORT FAILURE
CASTLING FETICIDE MISBIRTH

ABORTIVE IDLE VAIN BLIND FUTILE

ABOUND SNY FLOW SNEE TEEM

COVER FLEET SWARM REDOUND
OVERFLOW

ABOUNDING RIFE FLUSH ROUTH
COPIOUS REPLETE TEEMING
ABUNDANT

ABOUT BY IN OF ON RE SAY AWAY
NEAR SOME UMBE UPON ANENT
ASTIR CIRCA ABROAD ACTIVE
ALMOST ANENST AROUND CIRCUM
TOWARD ENVIRON CIRCITER

ABOUT-FACE FLOP

ABOVE ON UP OER SUP ATOP OVER
PAST UPON ABEEN ABOON ABUNE
ALOFT SUPRA BEFORE BEYOND
HIGHER THEREUP OVERHEAD
SUPERIOR
(— GENERAL LEVEL) APART

ABRADE RAW RUB BARK FILE FRET
GALL RASP SAND WEAR CHAFE
ERASE GRATE GRAZE GRIND SCORE
TOUCH SCRAPE IRRITATE

ABRADER FILE RASP EMERY
SANDER ABRASER GRINDER
SCRAPER

ABRAHAM (BIRTHPLACE OF —) UR
(BROTHER OF —) HARAN NAHOR
(CONCUBINE OF —) HAGAR
(FATHER OF —) TERAH
(GRANDFATHER OF —) NAHOR
(GRANDSON OF —) ESAU
(NEPHEW OF —) LOT
(SON OF —) ISAAC MEDAN SHUAH
MIDIAN ZIMRAN ISHMAEL JOKSHAN
(WIFE OF —) SARAH KETURAH

ABRASION BURN GALL OUCH SCAR
SORE GRAZE BRUISE BLASTING

ABRASIVE SAND EMERY PUMICE
QUARTZ SILICA ALUNDUM ERODENT
ABRADANT CORUNDUM SCRUBBER

ABRAXAS GEM STONE AMULET
ABRASAX

ABREAST EVEN AFRONT BESIDE
HANGING

ABRET BREAD WAFER

ABRI SHED COVER DUGOUT SHELTER

ABRIDGE CUT DOCK LASK BRIEF
ELIDE LIMIT RASEE RAZEE BRIDGE
REDUCE SHRINK CURTAIL DEPRIVE
REWRITE SHORTEN ABSTRACT
BREVIATE COMPRESS CONDENSE
CONTRACT DIMINISH RETRENCH
SIMPLIFY

ABRIDGED TAIL

ABRIDGEMENT TAIL BRIEF DIGEST
PRECIS RESUME SKETCH COMPEND
EPITOME PANDECT SUMMARY
SUMMULA ABSTRACT BOILDOWN
BREVIARY SYNOPSIS

ABROAD OFF ASEA AWAY ABOUT
ASTIR FORTH ABREED AFIELD
ASTRAY WIDELY DISTANT OUTWARD
OVERSEA OFFSHORE

ABROGATE ANNUL QUASH REMIT
CANCEL REPEAL REVOKE VACATE
ABOLISH NULLIFY RESCIND
DISSOLVE OVERRULE

ABRUPT BOLD CURT DEAD FAST
RUDE BLUFF BLUNT BRIEF BRUSK
HASTY ICTIC QUICK ROUGH SHARP

SHEER SHORT STEEP STUNT SURLY
TERSE TOTAL CHOPPY CRAGGY
CRUSTY PROMPT RUGGED SUDDEN
ANGULAR BRUSQUE PRERUPT
VIOLENT HEADLONG VERTICAL
(NOT —) SOFT

ABRUPTLY BANG SHARP SHORT
STEEPLY SUDDENLY

ABSALOM (FATHER OF —) DAVID
(SLAYER OF —) JOAB

ABSAROKA CROW

ABSCESS BOIL MORO SORE ULCER
FESTER INCOME LESION QUINSY
VOMICA EXITURE GUMBOIL PARULIS
APOSTEME SQUINACY

ABSCISSA X COSINE

ABSCISSION APOCOPE

ABSCOND GO FLY RUN BOLT FLEE
HIDE QUIT ELOPE SCRAM SMOKE
DECAMP DEPART DESERT ELOINE
ESCAPE LEVANT WITHDRAW

ABSENCE CUT LACK VOID WANT
BLANK LEAVE DEFECT REMOVE
VACUUM DEFAULT FAILURE
VACANCY FURLOUGH
(— FROM DUTY) LIBERTY
(— FROM ONE'S COUNTRY) EXILE
(— OF AN ORGAN) AGENESIA
AGENESIS
(— OF BIAS) DETACHMENT
(— OF CEREMONY) FAMILIARITY
(— OF FAMILIARITY) DISTANCE
(— OF FEELING) APATHY
(— OF FEVER) APYREXY APYREXIA
(— OF FORM) ENTROPY
(— OF GOVERNMENT) ANARCHY
(— OF INHIBITIONS) ANIMALITY
(— OF LIGHT) BLACK DARKNESS
(— OF MARRIAGE) AGAMY
(— OF MIND) ABSTRACTION
(— OF NAILS) ANONYCHIA
(— OF PAIN) ANODYNIA
(— OF PIGMENTATION) ACHROMA
ACHROMIA
(— OF SKULL) ACRANIA
(— OF TAIL) ANURY
(— OF TASTE) AGEUSIA
(— OF TRUMPS) CHICANE
(— OF TRUTH) FALSEHOOD

ABSENT CUT OFF OUT AWAY AWOL
GONE LOST WANE DESERT MUSING
LACKING MISSING WANTING
ABSORBED DREAMING
(— IN MIND) ABSTRACT

ABSENTMINDED MUSING DISTRAIT
DREAMING

ABSENTMINDEDNESS STARGAZING

ABSINTHE AJENJO GENIPI

ABSOLUTE GOD ONE TAO TAT DEAD
DOWN FAIR FINE FREE MEAR MEER
MERE PLAT PLUM PURE RANK REAL
SELF TRUE VERY BLANK CLEAR
FIXED PLUMB SHEER STARK TOTAL
UTTER WHOLE ENTIRE SEVERE
SIMPLE SQUARE CERTAIN PERFECT
PLENARY ABSTRACT COMPLETE
DESPOTIC EVENDOWN EXPLICIT
IMPLICIT POSITIVE
(— TEMPERATURE) T

(NOT —) FINITE CONDITIONAL
ABSOLUTELY YEA YES AMEN BONE
COLD DEAD FAIR JUST PLAT SLAP
PLAIN PLUMB STARK BARELY
FAIRLY FLATLY SIMPLY WHOLLY
SHEERLY ENTIRELY EVENDOWN
ABSOLUTION EXCUSE PARDON
SHRIFT LOOSING SHRIVING
ABSOLUTISM CAESARISM
DESPOTISM
ABSOLVE FREE QUIT CLEAR LOOSE
REMIT ACQUIT ASSOIL EXCUSE
EXEMPT FINISH PARDON SHRIVE
UNBIND CLEANSE FORGIVE JUSTIFY
RELEASE DISPENSE LIBERATE
OVERLOOK
ABSORB EAT FIX SOP SUP SOAK
SUCK TAKE AMUSE DRINK MERGE
RIVET UNITE DEVOUR ENGAGE
ENGULF ENWRAP IMBIBE INGEST
INSORB INWRAP OCCUPY SPONGE
STIFLE COMBINE CONSUME
ENGROSS IMMERSE INVOLVE
OCCLUDE SWALLOW
ABSORBED DEEP GONE LOST RAPT
SUNK FIXED ABSENT BURIED
ENRAPT HIPPED INTENT PLUNGED
RIVETED WRAPPED IMMERSED
(— BY) ALL
ABSORBENT BASE FOMES SPONGY
ANTACID SORBENT ANTIACID
DRINKING
ABSORBER SNUBBER
(— OF MONEY) LICKPENNY
(SHOCK —) BUFFER DAMPER
ABSORPTION AUTISM
(— UNIT) SABIN
ABSTAIN DENY FAST KEEP STAY
AVOID CEASE SPARE SPURN WAIVE
DESIST DISUSE ESCHEW FOREGO
REFUSE REJECT FORBEAR REFRAIN
RESTRAIN TEETOTAL WITHHOLD
(— FROM) FAST FORGO LEAVE
ABJURE ESCHEW FOREGO
REFRAIN
ABSTAINER TOTE RECHABITE
ABSTEMIOUS SOBER ACETIC
SLENDER MODERATE
ABSTENTION CELIBACY CHASTITY
ABSTERGE WIPE BATHE CLEAN
PURGE RINSE
ABSTINENCE ENCRATY
ABSTINENT SOBER ABSTEMIOUS
ABSTRACT CULL DEED DRAW NOTE
PART PURE TAKE BRIEF IDEAL
STEAL ABSORB DEDUCT DETACH
DIVERT DOCKET PRECIS REMOVE
ABRIDGE COMPEND EXCERPT
ISOLATE PURLOIN SECRETE
SUMMARY VIDIMUS ABSTRUSE
ACADEMIC ARGUMENT BREVIATE
DISCRETE SEPARATE SYLLABUS
SYNOPSIS TABLEITY WITHDRAW
(NOT —) CONCRETE
(PL.) PARATITLA PARATITLES
ABSTRACTED REMOTE
ABSTRACTION STUDY ENTITY
ABSTRACT QUODDITY
ABSTRUSE DARK DEEP HIGH HIDDEN

MYSTIC REMOTE SECRET SUBTLE
CURIOUS OBSCURE RETIRED
ABSTRACT ACROATIC ESOTERIC
PROFOUND
ABSURD HOT RICH WILD DOTTY
DROLL FALSE INANE INEPT SILLY
SCREWY STUPID ASININE FATUOUS
FOOLISH LAPUTAN DOGGEREL
FABULOUS
ABSURDITY FATUITY FOOLERY
FOPPERY WALTROT MAGGOTRY
NONSENSE UNREASON
ABUNA METRAN
ABUNDANCE WON COPY FLOW
MORT SONS WONE CHEAP DEPTH
FOUTH POWER RIVER ROUTH
ROWTH SCADS SONSE STORE
WRECK BOUNTY FOISON GALORE
LAVISH OODLES PLENTY POWDER
RICHES TALENT UBERTY WEALTH
FLUENCY LASHINS SATIETY
BELLYFUL FULLNESS LASHINGS
OPULENCE PLEURISY RIMPTION
(IN —) APLENTY
ABUNDANT FAT OLD FREE LUSH
MUCH RANK RICH RIFE AMPLE
FLUSH HEFTY LARGE OPIME ROUTH
ROWTH STORE DEMOID GALORE
HEARTY ROUTHY APLENTY COPIOUS
FERTILE FULSOME LIBERAL
PROFUSE REPLETE TEEMING
UBERANT UBEROUS WEALTHY
AFFLUENT FRUITFUL GENEROUS
NUMEROUS
(NOT —) LIGHT SPARE
ABUNDANTLY RIFE WELL FREELY
LARGELY HEARTILY
ABUSE MAR MOB TAX BUSE CALL
DRUB FLAY GAFF HARM HURT LACK
MAUL RAIL RUIN SLAM TEEN VAIN
CRIME CURSE FAULT GRIEF SCOLD
SLANG SNASH SPOIL BERATE
DEFILE INJURE INSULT MALIGN
MISUSE MUMBLE PUNISH RAVISH
REVILE TANCEL TANSEL VILIFY
YATTER AFFRONT BACKJAW
BEDEVIL DECEIVE DESPITE FALSIFY
MISBEDE MISCALL MISNAME
OBLOQUY OUTRAGE PERVERT
PROFANE SLANDER TRADUCE
UPBRAID VIOLATE BALLARAG
BUSINESS DISHONOR FRUMPERY
LANGUAGE MALTREAT MISAPPLY
MISTREAT REPROACH SLAPDASH
ABUSED DOWNTROD DOWNTRODDEN
ABUSIVE FOUL DIRTY SHREWD
CORRUPT SATIRIC CHEATING
INSOLENT LIBELOUS
ABUT BUTT JOIN REST TOUCH
ADJOIN BORDER BUTTAL PROJECT
ABUTILON MALLOW
ABUTMENT CRIB PIER ALETTE
BUTTRESS
ABUTTING FLUSH ADJACENT
ABYSM ABIME BISME DOWNFALL
ABYSMAL DEEP DREARY PROFOUND
UNENDING WRETCHED
ABYSS PIT POT DEEP GULF HELL
VOID ABYSM CHAOS CHASM DEPTH

GORGE BOTTOM VORAGO ABADDON
GEHENNA SWALLOW DOWNFALL
INTERVAL
ABYSSAL ABYSMAL BASSALIAN
ABYSSINIA AXUM ETHIOPIA
ABYSSINIAN SIDI ABASSIN
(— BANANA) ENSETE
ACACIA GUM JAM BABUL GIDYA
MULGA MYALL SIRIS THORN TIMBE
VEREK ARABIC BABLAH BINDER
GIDGEA GIDGEE GIDYEA HASHAB
LEGUME LOCUST MIMOSA WATTLE
YARRAN BLUEBUSH BRIGALOW
CHAPPARO IRONWOOD ROSEWOOD
ACADEMIC IVY RIGID FORMAL
CLASSIC DONNISH ERUDITE
LEARNED POMPIER
ACADEMY LYCEE CRUSCA LYCEUM
MANEGE SCHOOL COLLEGE
SOCIETY YESHIVA SEMINARY
(RIDING —) MANAGE MANEGE
ACADIAN CAJUN
ACAJOU CAJU CAJOO CAJOU
ACALEPH MEDUSA MEDUSAN
ACANA ALMIQUE
ACANTHA FIN SPINE THORN PRICKLE
ACANTHON
ACAPU WALNUT WACAPOU
CHAPERNO
ACARID NYMPH NYMPHA OCTOPOD
DIBRANCH
ACAUDAL BOBBED ANUROUS
ECAUDATE TAILLESS
ACAULESCENT STEMLESS
ACCEDE LET AGREE ALLOW ENTER
GRANT YIELD ACCORD ASSENT
ATTAIN COMPLY CONCUR CONCEDE
CONFORM CONSENT
ACCELERATE GUN REV RUN HYPO
JAZZ RACE URGE DRIVE FAVOR
FORCE HURRY SPEED HASTEN
ADVANCE FORWARD FURTHER
QUICKEN ANTEDATE DISPATCH
EXPEDITE INCREASE THROTTLE
ACCELERATION SPEEDUP
(— OF REACTION) CATALYSIS
(— UNIT) STAPP
ACCELERATOR GAS SPEEDER
BETATRON THROTTLE
ACCENT BEAT BLAS BURR MARK
TONE ACUTE GRAVE ICTUS PITCH
PULSE SOUND THROB VERGE
BROGUE LENGTH RHYTHM STRESS
THESIS EMPHASIS
(DORIC —) PLATEASM
(IRISH —) BROGUE
(MUSICAL —) BEAT
(WITHOUT AN —) ATONIC
ACCENTED FZ SFZ TONIC STRONG
MARCATO MARCANDO SFORZATO
ACCENTUATE ACCENT
ACCENTUATION DECLAMATION
ENHANCEMENT
ACCEPT BUY EAT BEAR FANG HAVE
HOLD JUMP TAKE ADMIT ADOPT
AGREE ALLOW HONOR INFER
MARRY ASSENT ASSUME AVOUCH
POCKET APPROVE BELIEVE
CONCEDE EMBRACE ESPOUSE
RECEIVE

(— AS ONE'S OWN) NOSTRIFICATE
(— AT RANDOM) DRAW
(— BETS) BOOK
(— EAGERLY) LEAP
(— INHERITANCE) ADIATE
(— READILY) SWALLOW
(— WITHOUT QUESTION) ABIDE
ACCEPTABLE LIEF SIGHTLY
WELCOME GRACIOUS PASSABLE
PLEASANT
ACCEPTANCE PASS SNAFF ADITIO
TAQLID PASSAGE CREDENCE
CURRENCY
(— OF INHERITANCE) CERNITURE
(— OF ORDER) ALLOTMENT
ACCEPTED GOING VULGAR
POPULAR APPROVED CREDITED
ORTHODOX STANDARD
(WIDELY —) INVETERATE
ACCEPTOR BASE
ACCESS FIT WAY ADIT DOOR GATE
PATH ROAD ENTRY GOING ROUTE
ACCOST AVENUE COMING ENTREE
PORTAL STREET ADVANCE
APPROACH ENTRANCE PAROXYSM
RECOURSE
(— OF DISEASE) ATTACK
ACCESSIBILITY EXPOSURE
ACCESSIBLE NEAR OPEN HANDY
PATENT AFFABLE PRESENT
FAMILIAR PERVIOUS SOCIABLE
ACCESSION ENTER ALLUVIO
ILLAPSE ADDITION ALLUVION
ENTRANCE INCREASE
ACCESSORY HAT AIDE ALLY DOME
TOOL EXTRA SCARF HELPER
ABETTOR ADJUNCT ANCILLA
ENCLAVE FITTING FIXTURE ADDITIVE
HATSTAND
(PL.) ADDENDA FIXINGS STAFFAGE
ACCIACCATURA MORDENT
ACCIDENT HAP CASE LUCK EVENT
GRIEF CHANCE HAZARD INJURY
MISHAP FORTUNE QUALITY
CALAMITY CASUALTY DISASTER
FORTUITY INCIDENT
(EUCHARISTIC —S) SPECIES
ACCIDENTAL ODD CASUAL CHANCE
RANDOM EXTERNAL
ACCIPITER HAWK
ACCLAIM CRY CLAP FAME HAIL
LAUD ROOT CHEER CLAIM ECLAT
EXTOL SHOUT PRAISE APPLAUD
HOSANNA OVATION PLAUDIT
WELCOME APPLAUSE
(NOISY —) RIOT
ACCLAMATION CRY VOTE CHEER
SHOUT HOSANNA PLAUDIT
APPLAUSE
ACCLIMATE INURE HARDEN SEASON
ACCUSTOM
ACCLIMATIZE ADAPT HARDEN
SEASON
ACCLIVITY BANK BROW HILL RISE
GRADE PITCH SLANT SLOPE TALUS
ASCENT HEIGHT INCLINE
ACCOLADE EMMY KISS RITE SIGN
AWARD HONOR KUDOS MEDAL
OSCAR TOKEN SYMBOL EMBRACE

GARLAND CEREMONY
ACCOMMODATE AID BED BOW FIT
CAMP GIVE HELP HOLD LEND SORT
SUIT ADAPT BOARD DEFER FAVOR
HOUSE LODGE SERVE YIELD
ADJUST COMPLY FAVOUR OBLIGE
SETTLE CONFORM CONTAIN
FASHION ATTEMPER GARRISON
ACCOMMODATION LOAN BERTH
BERTHAGE GIFFGAFF
(— BILL) KITE
ACCOMPANIED FRAUGHT
ACCOMPANIMENT SON ALBA
BURDEN EXCORT OOMPAH ADJUNCT
DESCANT SUPPORT OBLIGATO
(PL.) FIXINGS
ACCOMPANIST JONGLEUR
ACCOMPANY SEE FARE FERE JOIN
LEAD TEND WAIT BRING PILOT
ASSIST ATTEND CONCUR CONVEY
CONVOY ESCORT FOLLOW SECOND
SQUIRE COEXIST CONDUCT
CONSORT SUPPORT CHAPERON
ACCOMPANYING FELLOW ADJUNCT
ACCOMPLICE PAL AIDE ALLY CHUM
BUDDY CRONY LOUKE SHILL TILER
BONNET COHORT FELLOW HELPER
ABETTOR FEODARY FEUDARY
HUSTLER PARTNER STEERER
ACCOMPLISH DO GO END WIN FILL
WORK ENACT EQUIP FETCH FORTH
SWING AFFORD ATTAIN EFFECT
FINISH FULFIL MANAGE ABSOLVE
ACHIEVE CHEVISE COMPASS
EXECUTE EXPLETE FULFILL FURNISH
OPERATE PERFECT PERFORM
REALIZE SUCCEED COMPLETE
CONTRIVE DISPATCH ENGINEER
OUTCARRY
ACCOMPLISHED APT ABLE DONE
ADEPT ENDED GREAT TERSE
BESEEN EXPERT HANDSOME
TALENTED
ACCOMPLISHMENT ART END DEED
FEAT PASS CRAFT SKILL EFFECT
TALENT EARNING QUALITY FRUITION
LEARNING
(PRIOR —) ANTICIPATION
ACCORD GIVE JIBE JUMP SUIT UNIT
AGREE ALLOW ATONE AWARD BEFIT
CHIME CHORD CORDE GRANT LEVEL
STAND TALLY UNITY ACCEDE
ADJUST ASSENT BESTOW BETEEM
COMPLY CONCUR SETTLE UNISON
COMPORT COMPOSE CONCEDE
CONCERT CONCORD CONSENT
CONSORT HARMONY RAPPORT
RESPOND UNANIME DIAPASON
SYMPATHY
(— WITH) SUIT
(IN —) ALONG
ACCORDANCE CONCERT CONSENT
(IN —) ALONG
ACCORDANT EVEN ATTUNED
AGREEING COHERENT SUITABLE
ACCORDING (— TO ART) SA
(— TO LAW) SL
(— TO) AD BY SEC EMFORTH
ENFORTH PURSUANT SECUNDUM

ACCORDINGLY SO THEN THUS
HENCE IGITUR
ACCORDION LANTUM FLUTINA
FLAUTINO
ACCOST BAIL HAIL MASH MEET
ABORD BOARD GREET SPEAK
ACCESS BROACH HALLOO SALUTE
ACCOAST ADDRESS SOLICIT
APPROACH GREETING
ACCOUCHEUR OBSTETRICIAN
ACCOUCHEUSE MIDWIFE
ACCOUNT TAB BILL BOOK DEEM
DRAW ITEM NICK NOTE RATE REDE
SAKE TAIL TALE TELL TEXT WORD
AUDIT BLAME CHALK COUNT JUDGE
SCORE STATE STORY VALUE
WORTH BATTEL CREDIT DETAIL
ESTEEM HORARY LEGEND PROFIT
REASON RECKON RECORD REGARD
RELATE RENDER REPORT REPUTE
TREATY ACCOMPT COMPOST
COMPUTE EXPLAIN JOURNAL
LEXICON NARRATE PROCESS
RECITAL TAILZIE BREVIARY
CONSIDER ESTIMATE TREATISE
(— FOR) SAVE EXPLAIN
(ACCURATE —) GRIFF GRIFFIN
(CREDIT —) TICK
(LONG —) ILIAD
(TRAVEL —) ITINERARY
ACCOUNTABILITY DETAIL LIABILITY
ACCOUNTABLE LIABLE AMENABLE
ACCOUNTANT CLERK SIRCAR
SIRKAR AUDITOR PESHKAR
PUTWARI KULKARNI MUTSUDDY
RECKONER
ACCOUNTANT-GENERAL DAFTARDAR
DEFTERDAR
ACCOUNTING TASK REASON
COSTING
ACCOUTER ARM RIG GIRD ARRAY
DRESS EQUIP ATTIRE CLOTHE
OUTFIT BEDIGHT FURNISH HARNESS
PROVIDE
ACCOUTERMENTS GEAR TIRE
DRESS ATTIRE GRAITH
ACCREDIT ALLOT VOUCH CREDIT
DEPUTE APPOINT APPROVE ASCRIBE
BELIEVE CERTIFY CONFIRM
ENDORSE LICENSE SANCTION
ACCRETION SUM GAIN GROWTH
DEPOSIT EXUDATE ADDITION
ADHESION INCREASE
(INJURIOUS —) RUST
ACCRUAL ACCRUE DEMERIT
ACCRUE ADD WIN EARN GAIN GROW
PILE ARISE ENSUE ENURE INCUR
INURE ISSUE MATURE RESULT
SPRING ACQUIRE COLLECT
REDOUND ACCRESCE CUMULATE
INCREASE
ACCUMULATE DRAW FUND GROW
HEAP HIVE MASS PILE SAVE AMASS
DRIFT HOARD STACK STORE TOTAL
ACCRUE GARNER GATHER MUSTER
SCRAPE COLLECT HARVEST
INCREASE
ACCUMULATION DRIP DUMP FUND
GAIN HEAP MASS PILE STACK

STORE ANLAGE BACKUP BUDGET
COLUMN DEBRIS GARNER BACKLOG
CUMULUS DEPOSIT DOSSIER
MORAINE DIVIDEND INTEREST
(— OF FLUID) EDEMA OEDEMA
ASCITES
(— OF FORCE) CHARGE
(— OF SNOW) ALIMENTATION
(— OF TRIFLES) FLOTSAM
(— ON CONCRETE) LAITANCE
ACCURACY NICETY FIDELITY
JUSTNESS
(HISTORICAL —) SYNCHRONISM
ACCURATE JUST LEAL NICE TRUE
CLOSE EXACT FLUSH RIGHT
NARROW PROPER SEVERE STRICT
CAREFUL CORRECT PRECISE
FAITHFUL PERQUEER PUNCTUAL
TRUTHFUL
(NOT —) IMPURE
(UNPLEASANTLY —) BRUTAL
ACCURATELY JUST FAIRLY JUSTLY
CLOSELY EXACTLY INSOOTH
ACCURSED FEY CURSED DAMNED
DOOMED FORBID SACRED WARIED
BLASTED MALEDICT
ACCUSATION BEEF WITE BLAME
CAUSE CRIME POINT WHITE APPEAL
ATTACK CHARGE THREAP THREEP
ACCUSAL SCANDAL DELATION
(FALSE —) SUGGESTION
ACCUSATORY WRAYFUL
ACCUSE TAX WRY CALL FILE NOTE
SHOW SLUR TASK WITE WRAY
ACOUP ARGUE BLAME PEACH TAINT
TOUCH WHITE APPEAL ATTACH
ATTACK BECALL BEWRAY CHARGE
DEFAME DELATE DETECT INDICT
INTENT MURMUR APPEACH ARRAIGN
ATTAINT CENSURE IMPEACH
IMPLEAD TRADUCE CHASTISE
DENOUNCE QUESTION REDARGUE
REPROACH
(— UNJUSTLY) SLANDER
ACCUSER CHARGER DELATOR
LIBELANT
ACCUSING CULPATORY
DENUNCIATORY
ACCUSTOM URE USE WIN WON
HAFT WONT ADAPT BREAK DRILL
ENURE FLESH HABIT HAUNT INURE
TRAIN ADDICT ADJUST CUSTOM
INDUCE SEASON CONSORT
EDUCATE TOUGHEN ACQUAINT
(— HORSE TO BIT) MOUTH
(— TO PASTURE) HAFT
ACCUSTOMED TAME USED WONE
WONT USANT USUAL INURED
CHRONIC CURRENT HABITED
CONSUETE
ACE AS ALS JOT ONE PIP TIB ATOM
CARD HERO MARK TOPS UNIT
ADEPT BASTO FLYER POINT BULLET
EXPERT AVIATOR BRISQUE
PARTICLE
(— OF CLUBS) BASTA BASTO
(— OF SPADES) SPADILLE SPADILLO
(— OF TRUMPS) TIB HONOR PUNTO
(THREE —S) GLEEK

ACEDIA SLOTH ACCIDIA ACCIDIE
ACEPHALOUS HEADLESS
ACER NEGUNDO
ACERB ACID HARD SOUR TART
ACRID HARSH SHARP BITTER
SEVERE
ACERBATE EMBITTER IRRITATE
ACERBITY ACRIMONY ASPERITY
SEVERITY TARTNESS
ACETABULUM PAN PYXIS CUPULE
ACETABLE HOLDFAST
ACETAL KETAL FORMAL KETATE
BUTYRAL
ACETALDEHYDE ETHYL ETHANAL
ALDEHYDE
ACETIC SOUR SHARP ZOONIC
ACETYLENE TOLAN ALKINE ALKYNE
ETHINE ETHYNE TOLANE
ACHE AKE NAG NIP ECHE GELL
HURT LONG PAIN PANG PINE RACK
WARK WERK HACHE SMART STANG
STOUN THROB THROE WARCH
DESIRE MISERY STITCH STOUND
TWINGE TWITCH ANGUISH EARACHE
SORENESS
ACHENE CYPSELA UTRICLE
ACHIEVE DO END GET WIN EARN
GAIN HACK HAVE MAKE FETCH
FORCE REACH SCORE AFFORD
ARRIVE ATTAIN EFFECT FINISH
OBTAIN CHEVISE COMPASS EXPLOIT
FULFILL PRODUCE REALIZE
SUCCEED TRIUMPH COMPLETE
CONCLUDE CONTRIVE
(— HARMONY) AGREE
(— ORIENTATION) ADJUST
ACHIEVEMENT ACT JOB DEED FEAT
WORK ACTION CAREER RESULT
EXPLOIT HARVEST FELICITY
ACHILLEA PTARMICA
ACHILLES PELIDES
(FATHER OF —) PELEUS
(FRIEND OF —) PATROCLUS
(HORSE OF —) XANTHUS
(MOTHER OF —) THETIS
(SLAYER OF —) PARIS
ACHIOTE OLEANA ACHUETE
ANNATTO ARNATTA ARNATTO
ACHRAS SAPOTA
ACHROMACYTE SHADOW
ACHROMATIC GRAY GREY NEUTRAL
ACICULAR SPLINTERY
ACID DRY YAR DIAL DOPA KEEN
PABA SOUR TART ACERB ACRID
ALGIN AMINO CERIN EAGER HARSH
LYSIN RHEIN SHARP ULMIC ABRINE
ALLIIN BITING BITTER GLYCIN
LYSINE PROLIN SERINE TWEAKY
VALINE ACERBIC ACETOSE CERASIN
FILICIN GLYCINE PROLINE STEARIN
VINEGAR
(NITRIC —) AQUAFORTIS
ACIDITY ACOR VERDURE ACERBITY
SOURNESS VERJUICE
ACKNOWLEDGE NOD OWN AVER
AVOW SIGN ADMIT ADOPT ALLOW
GRANT KITHE KYTHE THANK YIELD
ACCEDE ACCEPT AGNIZE ANSWER
ASSENT AVOUCH BEKNOW COUTHE

FATHER REWARD CONCEDE
CONFESS DECLARE OBSERVE
PROFESS DISCLOSE
ACKNOWLEDGEMENT GRANT
THANK AVOWAL CREDIT SHRIFT
APOLOGY AGNITION
ACLE AKLE IRUL JAMBA IRONWOOD
PYENGADU
ACLYS HURLBAT
ACME IT ACE CAP TOP APEX CULM
HIGH PEAK CREST PITCH POINT
STATE APOGEE CLIMAX COMBLE
CRISIS CULMEN HEIGHT HEYDAY
SUMMIT ZENITH CUMULUS SUBLIME
CAPSHEAF CAPSTONE PINNACLE
ACNE WHELK
ACOLYTE BOY HELPER NOVICE
SERVER LEARNER PATENER
ACOMIA BALDNESS
ACONITE BIKH ACONITUM NAPELLUS
ACORN NUT MAST GLAND OVEST
BELLOTA BELLOTE
(— CUPS) VALONIA
(PL.) MAST CAMATA PANNAGE
CAMATINA
ACORN-SHAPED BALANOID
ACOUSTICS SONICS PHONICS
ACQUAINT KNOW TELL TEACH
VERSE ADVISE INFORM NOTIFY
SCHOOL APPRISE APPRIZE POSSESS
RESOLVE
ACQUAINTANCE KITH HABIT
COUSIN FRIEND GOSSIP AFFINITY
FAMILIAR INTIMATE
(CLOSE —) HABIT INWARDNESS
(PRACTICAL —) PRACTICE PRACTISE
(PL.) KITH SOCIETY
ACQUAINTED ACQUENT VERSANT
ACQUIESCE BOW ABIDE AGREE
CHIME YIELD ACCEDE ACCEPT
ASSENT COMPLY CONCUR SUBMIT
CONCEDE CONFIRM CONFORM
CONSENT
ACQUIRE ADD BAG BUY GET WIN
EARN FORM GAIN GRAB HAVE MAKE
REAP ADOPT AMASS ANNEX BEGET
CHEVY CHIVY GLEAN LEARN REACH
SEIZE STEAL ATTAIN CHIVEY CHIVVY
DERIVE EFFECT GARNER OBTAIN
SECURE SNATCH COLLECT
CONQUER DEVELOP PROCURE
RECEIVE CONTRACT
(— DESIRABLE QUALITY) AGE
(— KNOWLEDGE) LERE
ACQUISITION WIN GAIN LUCRE
ACQUEST ACQUIST GETTING
CONQUEST
(DISHONEST —) GRAFT
ACQUIT PAY FREE QUIT CLEAR
QUIET ASSOIL BEHAVE BESTOW
EXCUSE PARDON ABSOLVE
COMPORT CONDUCT RELEASE
REQUITE LIBERATE OVERLOOK
UNCHARGE
ACQUITTAL EXCUSE
ACQUITTANCE QUIETUS RELEASE
ACRE AKER LAND ACKER FIELD
STANG ARPENT COLLOP FARMHOLD
(120 —S) HIDE

(2-3RDS —) COVER
(QUARTER —) ROOD
(PL.) ACREAGE
ACREMAN CARUCARIUS
ACRID HOT ACID BASK KEEN SOUR
HARSH ROUGH SHARP SURLY
BITING BITTER CAUSTIC PUNGENT
REEKING UNSAVORY VIRULENT
ACRIMONIOUS MAD ACID KEEN
ACRID ANGRY GRUFF HARSH IRATE
SHARP SNELL SURLY BITTER
CAUSTIC STINGING
ACRIMONY VIRUS PUNGENCY
SOURNESS
ACRISIUS (DAUGHTER OF —) DANAE
ACROBAT ZANY KINKER GYMNAST
TOPPLER TUMBLER BALANCER
ACROPOLIS FORT HILL POLIS
CADMEA CITADEL LARISSA
ACROSOME IDIOSOME IDIOZOME
ACROSS OVER SPAN YOND CROSS
ABOARD THWART ATHWART
OPPOSITE TRAVERSE
(CLEAN —) SHORT
ACROSTIC ABC AGLA DORA GAME
POEM TANAK PHRASE PUZZLE
TANACH
ACRYLIC PROPENOIC
ACT BE DO GO APE LAW LET ACTU
BILL COME DEAL DEED DORA FACT
FEAT HOCK JEST MAKE MOVE PART
PASS PLAY SKIT SLIM TAKE TURN
WORK ACTUS DRAMA EDICT EMOTE
ENTRY EXERT FEIGN GRACE KARMA
MODEL SCENE SHIFT STUNT ACTION
BEHAVE BESTIR DECREE DEMEAN
FACTUM MANAGE RAGMAN
COMPORT EXECUTE EXPLOIT
PERFORM PORTRAY PRETEND
STATUTE FUNCTION PRETENSE
SIMULATE
(— AFFECTEDLY) MIMP
(— AS WANTON) RIG
(— AWKWARDLY) HOCKER
(— BEFORE) ANTICIPATE
(— BLUNDERINGLY) BULL
(— DECEITFULLY) DOUBLE
(— DISHONESTLY) FUDGE
(— FOOLISHLY) FON FONNE FOLEYE
FOOTER FOOTLE
(— FRIVOLOUSLY) FRIVOL FRIBBLE
(— IN THEATER) GAFF
(— INDECISIVELY) DITHER
(— INDEPENDENTLY) SEVER
(— OF APPROVAL) EUGE
(— OF BEGGING) CADGE
(— OF CIVILITY) CURTSY DEVOIR
CURTSEY
(— OF KINDNESS) CARESS BENEFIT
(— OF LABOR) DILIGENCE
(— OF PRAYER) DEVOTION
(— OF STUPIDITY) BETISE
(— OF TRICKERY) COG
(— OUT) ENACT DRAMATIZE
(— PLAYFULLY) DALLY BANTER
(— QUICKLY) GIRD
(— RASHLY) RACKLE
(— SPORTIVELY) DAFF
(— SUDDENLY) FLASH

(— TIMIDLY) NESH
(— TOGETHER) AGREE COACT
CONCUR CONCORD
(— TRIFLINGLY) JANK
(— UP TO) EVEN
(— UPON) AFFECT HANDLE
(COMICAL —) JIG
(CONVENTIONAL —) AMENITY
(CORRUPT —) DEPRAVITY
(CRIMINAL —) INFAMY
(DARING —) ESCAPADE
(DECEITFUL —) ABUSE
(DECEPTIVE —) FEINT
(FAULTY —) PARAPRAXIS
(FOOLISH —) DIDO IDIOTISM
(FORBIDDEN —) CRIME
(FORMAL —) CEREMONY
(HABITUAL—) EXERCISE
(HASTY —) FLING
(HOSTILE —) BLOW
(INJURIOUS —) SPOIL
(LAUDATORY —) COUP
(LITURGICAL —) LAVABO
(LIVELY —) JIG
(MISCHIEVOUS —) DIDO CANTRAP
CANTRIP
(OFFENSIVE —) AFFRONT
(OFFICIAL —S) ACTA
(PLAYFUL —) RALLERY RAILLERY
(PRAISEWORTHY —) DEMERIT
(RUDE —) INCIVILITY
(SUDDEN VIOLENT —) BENSEL
BENSIL
(THOUGHTLESS —) FOLLY
(UNMANNERLY —) SOLECISM
(UNUSUAL —) STUNT
(VALOROUS —) WORSHIP
(VARIETY —) SKETCH
(WRONG —) DERELICT DERELICTUM
(PL.) DOINGS
ACTINAL ORAL
ACTING AGENT SERVING
(— AGAINST) ADVERSE
(— BY TURN) ALTERN
(— ODDLY) HAYWIRE
(— RAPIDLY) DRASTIC
(UNSKILLFUL —) BUNGLING
ACTINIAN OPELET VESTLET
ACTINOST RADIAL RADIALE
ACTINOZOAN SEAFLOWER
ACTION ACT AIR DAP JOB ACTO
CASE DEED FACT FRAY GEST PLAY
PLOY PUSH SHOW STEP SUIT WORK
ACTIO DOING EDICT FIGHT FLING
GESTE ISSUE THING TREAD VENUE
AFFAIR AGENCY BATTLE BEFOOT
COMBAT PRAXIS CONDUCT FACTION
GESTURE PROCESS TANQUAM
ACTIVITY BEHAVIOR BUSINESS
CONFLICT FUNCTION PRACTICE
PRACTISE
(— OF WIND) EOLATION
(ABSURD —S) BOSH
(ANTAGONISTIC —) ATOMISM
(BLAMEWORTHY —) WITE
(CAPRICIOUS —) FREAK
(COARSE —) HARLOTRY
(COOPERATIVE —) SYNERGISM
(COURT —) LAW SUIT ASSIZE

LAWSUIT QUERELA QUERELE
(CRUEL —) RUTH
(CUSTOMARY —) COURSE
(EXTEMPORE —) SCHEDIASM
(FINAL —) CATASTROPHE
(FOOLISH —) FOPPERY INEPTITUDE
(FRISKY —) FRISKIN
(FRIVOLOUS —) DALLIANCE
(IMPULSIVE —) STAMPEDE
(INITIAL —) LEADOFF INDUCTION
(JOINT —) COACTION
(LEGAL —) DEBT SUIT ACCOUNT
DETINET DETINUE
(MEAN —S) DOGGERY
(MILITARY —) SWEEP
(ODD —S) JIMJAMS
(PLAYFUL —) FUN FROLIC
(RASH —) HASTE
(REPEATED —) DRUM DOUBLE
(SUDDEN —) FLISK
(SYMBOLIC —) CHARADE
(TACTLESS —) GAUCHERIE
(UNAVOIDABLE —) FORCEPUT
(UNINTERMITTED —) HEAT
(VIOLENT —) HEAT AFFRAY
(WHIMSICAL —S) HUMORS
HUMOURS
(WILY —) WRINKLE
ACTIVATE SPARK ACTIFY ELICIT
ACTIVE UP YAL YAP YEP BUSY GAIN
LISH LIST PERT RASH SPRY TRIG
WHAT YALD YARE YEPE YERN
ABOUT AGILE ALERT ALIVE ASTIR
BRISK DEEDY FRESH LIGHT LINGY
LUSTY NIPPY PEART QUICK READY
SMART SNELL SPICY SPRIG STOUT
SWANK VIVID WIGHT YAULD YERNE
ACTUAL CLEVER DIRECT FEERIE
FEIRIE FIERCE HEARTY LIVELY
LIVING MOVING NIMBLE PROMPT
QUIVER SEMMIT SPEEDY SPRACK
SPROIL SPRUCE SPRUNT SWANKY
WIMBLE DASHING DEEDFUL DELIVER
DYNAMIC HOPPING HUMMING
KINETIC STHENIC THRODDY
YANKING ANIMATED ATHLETIC
BRAWLING DILIGENT SPIRITED
VIGOROUS
(NORMALLY —) ABOUT
ACTIVELY DOWN BUSILY DEEDILY
HEARTILY
ACTIVITY ACT ADO GOG VIR FIZZ
LIFE PLAY STIR BLAST CAPER
EVENT HEART RAJAS RALLY TRADE
VIGOR ACTION AGENCY BUSTLE
ENERGY HUSTLE SATTVA SPROIL
AGILITY CALLING BUSINESS
EXERCISE FUNCTION MOVEMENT
PARERGON STIRRING
(FUNCTIONAL —) SHOP
(MENTAL —) CONCEIT BRAINWORK
(SHARED —) COMMUNITY
(TROUBLESOME —) COIL
ACTON HOGTON HAQUETON
ACTOR HAM DOER HERO LEAD MIME
STAR AGENT COMIC DROLL EXTRA
HEAVY MIMIC PLANT SERIO SUPER
ARTIST COWBOY DISEUR FEEDER
FIDDLE MUMMER PLAYER PUPPET

STAGER TOMMER ARTISTE CABOTIN
DISEUSE HISTRIO PRIMOMO
ROSCIUS STORMER TROUPER
AISTEOIR COMEDIAN HISTRION
JUVENILE STROLLER THESPIAN
(INEPT —) HAM
(INFERIOR —) SHINE
ACTRESS DIVA STAR INGENUE
STARLET FARCEUSE THESPIAN
ACTUAL GOOD HARD REAL TRUE
VERY POSIT RIGHT BODILY FACTUAL
GENUINE CONCRETE DEFINITE
EXISTING MATERIAL POSITIVE
TANGIBLE
ACTUALITY FACT BEING VERITY
REALITY ENERGEIA REALNESS
ACTUALLY BUT DONE TRULY FAIRLY
ITSELF REALLY
ACTUATE ACT EGG RUN DRAW
MOVE URGE ENACT IMPEL ROUSE
START AROUSE COMPEL EXCITE
INCITE INDUCE AGITATE ANIMATE
ENLIVEN INSPIRE POINTED SHARPEN
MOTIVATE PERSUADE
ACUITY FINENESS
ACUMEN WIT INSIGHT CAPACITY
KEENNESS SAGACITY
ACUTE ACID FINE HIGH KEEN TART
HEAVY QUICK SHARP SMART SNACK
SNELL ARGUTE ASTUTE CRYING
SHREWD SHRILL SUBTLE TRELBE
URGENT CRUCIAL FEELING INTENSE
POINTED VIOLENT CRITICAL INCISIVE
POIGNANT
(MOST —) DIRE
(NOT —) SLOW GRAVE CHRONIC
ACUTENESS DEPTH SENSE ACUITY
ACUMEN NOSTRIL INCISION
SAGACITY SUBTLETY
(— OF SMELL) HYPEROSMIA
ACYCLIC SPIRAL ALIPHATIC
ADAD RAMMAN
ADAGE SAW DICT REDE TEXT WORD
AXIOM MAXIM MOTTO HOMILY
SAYING TRUISM WHEEZE BROMIDE
PRECEPT PROVERB APHORISM
APOTHEGM
ADAGIO ADAGE ADAGIETTO
ADAM ADE EDIE ADKIN
(GRANDSON OF —) ENOS ENOCH
(SON OF —) ABEL CAIN SETH
(TEACHER OF —) RAISEL
(WIFE OF —) EVE LILITH
ADAM-AND-EVE CRAWFOOT
ADAMANT FIRM GRIM HARD SOLID
STONY ADAMAS DIAMOND UNMOVED
OBDURATE SOLIDITY STUBBORN
ADAMANTINE FIRM BORON STONE
VAJRA ADAMANT
ADAMITE PICARD
ADAM'S APPLE GUZZLE
THROATBALL
ADAM'S NEEDLE YUCCA
ADAPT APT FIT PLY PUT EDIT MOLD
SORT SUIT AGREE HUMOR INURE
SHAPE ADJUST CHANGE COMPLY
DERIVE DOCTOR HUMOUR TEMPER
ARRANGE CONFORM CONVERT
PREPARE QUALIFY ATTEMPER

CONTRIVE EQUALIZE REGULATE
ADAPTABILITY FLUIDITY ELASTICITY
ADAPTABLE LABILE ELASTIC
PLIABLE FLEXUOUS
ADAPTED FIT FOR FITTED SUITED
ADAPTER KIT ARRANGER
ADAXIAL SUPERIOR
ADD AD EIK EKE SAY SUM TOT CAST
FOOT GAIN JOIN LEND PLUS TOTE
AFFIX ANNEX GIVEN TOTAL UNITE
ACCRUE ADJECT APPEND ATTACH
CONFER FIGURE RECKON SUPPLY
ACCRETE AUGMENT COMBINE
COMPILE COMPUTE ENLARGE
SUBJOIN SUMMATE INCREASE
(— ALCOHOL) SPIKE
(— FUEL) BEET
(— IN WRITING) ASCRIBE
(— TO) ADORN ENRICH AUGMENT
(— UP) SUM TOT COUNT TOTAL
AMOUNT
(— WORT TO BEER) KRAUSEN
ADDA SCINK SKINK LIZARD
ADDAX PYGARG PYGARGUS
ADDED AND EKE PLUS ADJUNCT
(— SOMETHING) TILLY
ADDEND SUMMAND
ADDER ATHER KRAIT VIPER ELAPID
NADDER NEDDER ELAPOID
HAGWORM HYPNALE
ADDER'S-TONGUE LILY LILIUM
COXCOMB ROOSTERS
ADDICT FAN BUFF DOPE DOPY HYPE
USER COKEY COKIE FIEND HOPPY
HOUND JUNKY SLAVE BOTARY
DEVOTE JUNKER JUNKIE DELIVER
DEVOTEE HABITUE HOPHEAD
SNIFTER ACCUSTOM DOPEHEAD
SNOWBIRD
ADDICTED GIVEN PRONE HOOKED
BIBULOUS
ADDICTION HABIT MONKEY
BIBACITY
ADDITION AND EIK EKE ELL TAB
TOO ALSO ELSE GAIN PLUS AFFIX
RIDER ACCRUE AUGEND ENCORE
GANSEL INCOME PREFIX ADJUNCT
ADVANCE AUCTARY CODICIL
JOINING PENDANT UNITING
ADDENDUM INCREASE MANTISSA
(— TO ARTICLE) SHIRTTAIL
(— TO BEEHIVE) IMP
(— TO MASS) FARCE FARSE
(— TO PRICE) ADVANCE
(TRIVIAL —) FILIP FILLIP
ADDITIONAL NEW ELSE MORE
ADDED EXTRA FRESH OTHER
TIDDER TOTHER ANOTHER BESIDES
FURTHER
ADDITIVE CUMOL CUMENE
ADDLE EARN HOME IDLE MIRE
AMAZE FILTH RIPEN SPOIL CURDLE
MUDDLE THRIVE AGITATE CONFUSE
BEFUDDLE BEWILDER
ADDLED ASEA EMPTY PUTRID
MUDDLED UNSOUND
ADDRA DAMA NANGER
ADDRESS AIM SUE WOO BACK CALL
EASE HAIL HOME MINT PRAY TACT

TALK TULK TURN ABODE APPLY
BOARD COURT DRESS ELOGE
GREET POISE SKILL SPEAK TREAT
ACCOST ADJUST APPEAL BOUNCE
CHARGE DEVOTE DIRECT EULOGY
MANNER PARLEY SALUTE SERMON
SPEECH BEHIGHT CONDUCT
CONSIGN ENTRUST LECTURE
ORATION TUTOYER APPROACH
DEDICATE DELIVERY DISPATCH
FACILITY HARANGUE INSCRIBE
PETITION
(— FAMILIARLY) TOM TUTOYER
(— SAUCILY) CHYAK CHYACK
(METHOD OF —) TONE
(PULPIT —) KHUTBA KHUTBAH
ADDUCE BEAR CITE GIVE NAME
ALLAY ARGUE BRING INFER OFFER
QUOTE ALLEGE ASSIGN OBJECT
ADVANCE COUNTER MENTION
PRESENT
ADE SQUASH
ADEPS FAT LARD
ADEPT ACE APT ABLE HANDY
ADROIT ARTIST CRAFTY DEACON
EXPERT MASTER VERSED ANCIENT
CAPABLE DABSTER MAHATMA
DEXTROUS SKILLFUL
ADEQUATE DUE FIT ABLE FAIR FULL
GOOD MEET WELL AMPLE DIGNE
EQUAL COMMON DECENT ENOUGH
PROPER CONDIGN SUITABLE
ADHERE HEW HUG CLAG CLAM GLUE
HOLD JOIN KEEP LINK AFFIX APPLY
CLEAM CLING STICK UNITE ATTACH
CEMENT CLEAVE COHERE FREEZE
ACCRETE ANNERRE PERSIST
ADHERENCE CLING ADHESION
ARIANISM FIDELITY
ADHERENT IST ITE AIDE ALLY JAIN
SIKH ADEPT BAHAI BLACK BONPA
DEIST JAINA SIDER SPIKE STOOP
FACTOR KIRKER VOTARY APRISTA
BAHAIST CHANIST FASCIST FLACIAN
GNOSTIC NICAEAN OWENIAN
SECTARY SEQUELA THOMIST
AGATHIST BELIEVER BUDDHIST
CABALIST DISCIPLE FAITHFUL
FATALIST FOLLOWER HUMANIST
HYLICIST IMPERIAL PARTISAN
RETAINER SERVITOR SOCINIAN
UPHOLDER
(PL.) FOLD FOLLOWING
ADHESION BLOCKING STICKAGE
SYNECHIA
ADHESIVE GUM WAX BOND CLAM
GLUE SIZE TAPE DABBY DAUBY
PASTE TACKY BINDER CEMENT
CLINGY GLUTEN MASTIC PLUCKY
SMEARY STICKY HOTMELT
MUCILAGE
ADHIBIT USE ADMIT AFFIX APPLY
ATTACH
ADIANTUM MAIDENHAIR
ADIEU ADEW ADDIO ADIOS LEAVE
FAREWELL
ADIPOSE FAT HARD SUET FATTY
OBESE PURSY SQUAT TALLOW
ADIT DOOR ENTRY SOUGH STULM

ACCESS TUNNEL PASSAGE APPROACH ENTRANCE

ADJACENT NEAR NIGH CLOSE FLUSH HANDY BESIDE NEARBY MEETING VICINAL ABUTTING TOUCHING

ADJECTIVE ADNOUN DIPTOTE EPITHET MONINAL MODIFIER

ADJOIN ADD ABUT BUTT JOIN LINE TACK COAST MARCH TOUCH UNITE ACCOST APPEND ATTACH BORDER CONTACT

ADJOURN END MOVE RISE STAY ARISE CLOSE DEFER DELAY RECESS SUSPEND DISSOLVE POSTPONE PROROGUE

ADJUDGE TRY DEEM FIND GIVE HOLD RATE ALLOT AREAD AREED AWARD GRANT JUDGE ORDER ADDEEM ADDICT ASSIGN DECERN DECIDE DECREE ORDAIN REGARD BEHIGHT CONDEMN SENTENCE
(— GUILTY) DAMN
(— NOT GUILTY) ABSOLVE

ADJUDICATE ACT TRY HEAR PASS RULE JUDGE DECIDE ESTEEM RECKON REGARD SETTLE ADJUDGE CONSIDER SENTENCE

ADJUNCT AID HELP PART WORD ANNEX DEVICE PHRASE ADJOINT ANCILLA EPITHET FITTING GARNISH PERTAIN TEACHER ADDITION ADDITIVE APPANAGE APPENDIX ORNAMENT

ADJURATION OATH APPEAL SWEARING

ADJURE ASK BEG BID BIND ETHE PRAY CRAVE PLEAD SWEAR APPEAL CHARGE BESEECH COMMAND CONJURE CONTEST ENTREAT REQUEST UNSWEAR

ADJUST FIT FIX SET CAST EASE FORM FREE GEAR JUST LINE PARE RATE SIZE SORT SUIT TRAM TRIM TRUE ADAPT ADMIT ALIGN ALINE ANGLE EQUAL FRAME PATCH RANGE RIGHT SHAPE ACCORD ATTUNE HAMMER JUSTEN SETTLE SQUARE TEMPER WANGLE ADDRESS ARRANGE BALANCE CHANCER COMPOSE CONCERT CONFORM CORRECT DISPOSE JUSTIFY PREPARE RECTIFY COMPOUND REGULATE
(— A LOOM) GATE
(— SAIL) FLATTEN

ADJUSTED KEYED

ADJUSTER FIXER FITTER ASSESSOR

ADJUSTMENT FIT GEAR TRIM FITNESS FITTING CHANCERY

ADJUTANT AIDE ALLY STORK ARGALA HELPER HURGILA MARABOU OFFICER

ADJUVANT AIDE HELPER ADJUNCT HELPFUL

AD-LIB FAKE

ADMAN HUCKSTER

ADMEASURE METE

ADMETUS (WIFE OF —) ALCESTIS

ADMINISTER DO RUN DEAL DEEM DOSE GIVE MOVE RULE APPLY SERVE TREAT DIRECT GOVERN MANAGE SETTLE SUPPLY TENDER ADHIBIT CONDUCE CONDUCT CONTROL EXECUTE EXHIBIT FURNISH HUSBAND DISPENSE MINISTER
(— FORCIBLY) HAND
(— SACRAMENT) BISHOP HOUSEL

ADMINISTRATION HELM RULE SWAY POLICY TAHSIL CONDUCT DIOCESE ECONOMY RECTORY REGIMEN CARRIAGE DISPOSAL MINISTRY
(— OF OATH) JURATION
(REVENUE —) HACIENDA

ADMINISTRATOR CAID HELM QAID GABBAI MANAGER TRUSTEE DIRECTOR EXECUTOR MINISTER PROVICAR
(INCA —) CURACA
(MORMON —) APOSTLE

ADMIRABLE FINE GOOD HIGH GRAND GREAT LUMMY PROUD DIVINE AMIABLE CAPITAL ELEGANT MIRANDA RIPPING

ADMIRAL FLAG AMREL AMRELLE FLAGMAN GENERAL

ADMIRATION FUROR GLORY ESTEEM LIKING WONDER CONCEIT WORSHIP
(— FOR BIGNESS) JUMBOISM

ADMIRE DIG LIKE LOVE ADORE EXTOL HONOR PRIZE VALUE ESTEEM MARVEL REGARD REVERE WONDER ADULATE APPROVE DELIGHT IDOLIZE RESPECT VENERATE

ADMIRER FAN BEAU LOVER SWAIN AMATEUR DEVOTEE FOLLOWER IDOLATOR
(PL.) FOLLOWING

ADMISSION FEE ADIT CALL ENTRY ACCESS CHARGE ENTREE TICKET APOLOGY CONSENT INGRESS ENTRANCE
(— TO BAR) CALL

ADMIT KEN LET OWN AVER AVOW BEAR TAKE AGREE ALLOW ENTER GRANT IMMIT INLET ACCEDE ACCEPT ADJUST ASSENT AVOUCH ENROLL INCUCT PERMIT SUFFER ADHIBIT CONCEDE CONFESS INCLUDE PROFESS RECEIVE SUFFICE INITIATE
(— AS MEMBER) INDUCT
(— AS VALID) SUSTAIN

ADMITTANCE ACCESS ADMITTY ENTRANCE

ADMIX DALLOP DOLLOP

ADMIXTURE DASH ALLOY BLEND SHADE SPICE TINGE DALLOP DOLLOP FLAVOR LEAVEN STREAK MIXTURE SOUPCON COMPOUND INFUSION

ADMONISH WARN CHIDE SCOLD ADVISE ENJOIN EXHORT NOTIFY REBUKE REMIND SCHOOL CAUTION

COUNSEL MONITOR REPROVE

ADMONITION ITEM ADVICE CAVEAT HOMILY CAUTION LECTURE REPROOF WARNING DOCUMENT REMINDER

ADNATE ADHERENT EPIGYNOUS
(— TO CALYX) INFERIOR

ADO DO COIL DEED FUSS ROUT STIR WORK HURRY TOUSE TOWSE BOTHER BUSTLE EFFORT FLURRY HUBBUB POTHER RUCKUS BLATHER BLETHER SPUTTER TROUBLE TURMOIL BUSINESS

ADOBE MUD CLAY DOBE DOBY SILT BRICK DOBIE TAPIA MUDCAP

ADOLESCENCE TEENS YOUTH NONAGE PUBERTY MINORITY

ADOLESCENT LAD YOUNG YOUTH IMMATURE TEENAGER

ADONIS ADON
(MOTHER OF —) MYRRH MYRRHA

ADOPT TAKE STEAL ACCEPT ASSUME ATTACH BORROW CHOOSE FATHER FOLLOW FOSTER MOTHER ACQUIRE EMBRACE ESPOUSE RECEIVE WELCOME ADVOCATE ARROGATE MAINTAIN

ADOPTION ESPOUSAL
(— OF DEBTS) ASSUMPTION

ADORABLE LOVELY LOVABLE CHARMING

ADORATION HOMAGE WORSHIP DEVOTION
(— OF GOD) LOVE

ADORE DOTE LAUD LOVE EXALT EXTOL HONOR WURTH ADMIRE ESTEEM PRAISE REVERE GLORIFY IDOLIZE WORSHIP VENERATE

ADORN DUB FIG GEM ORN SET BEAD BUSK DECK DILL DINK FOIL GAUD GILD LACE OUCH PICK PINK STUD SWAG TRIM ADORE ANORN ARRAY BEDUB BEGEM BELAY BRAVE CROWN DIGHT DRAPE DRESS FRONT GRACE HIGHT INLAY JEWEL MENSK PRANK PRICK PRIDE PRIMP PRINK ROUGE SPLAY SPRIG TRICK ATTIRE ATTRAP BECOME BEDECK BETRIM BLAZON BROOCH CLOTHE COLLAR DAMASK DIADEM EMBOSS ENAMEL ENRICH ENROBE FIGURE FINIFY FRIEZE FRINGE GRAITH INSTAL INVEST ORNIFY POUNCE QUAINT STATUE SUBORN TASSEL APPAREL BEDIGHT BEDIZEN COMMEND CORONET DEPAINT DIGNIFY EMPEARL FEATHER FOLIAGE FURNISH GARNISH GLORIFY GRATIFY IMPLUME SPANGLE VARNISH BEAUTIFY DECORATE EMBLAZON FLOURISH ORNAMENT SPLENDOR

ADORNED CLAD BESEEN DAEDAL ORNATE PICKED BRAIDED CLOTHED COLORED DAISIED FIGURED
(SHOWILY —) BEPRANKED

ADORNMENT TIRE ADORN DRESS PRIDE BEAUTY DECORE TAHALI TINSEL DECKING OUNDING

PRANKING TIREMENT

ADRIFT ASEA LOST AWAFT LIGAN LOOSE AFLOAT DERELICT FLOATING UNMOORED

ADROIT DEFT EASY FEAT GOOD NEAT SLIM ADEPT HANDY READY SMART SNACK TIGHT TRICK ARTFUL CLEVER EXPERT HABILE NIMBLE CUNNING DEXTROUS HANDSOME SKILLFUL

ADROITNESS ART EASE TACT KNACK SKILL ADDRESS FACILITY

ADSORBENT BASE EARTH SILICA

ADULATE FAWN LAUD GLOSS GLOZE PRAISE FLATTER

ADULATION GLOSE GLOZE PRAISE FLATTERY

ADULT MAN FULL MANLY MATURE EPHEBIC GROWNUP THRIVEN

ADULTERANT DOPE ALMEIDINA

ADULTERATE CUT MIX CARD DASH LOAD ABUSE ALLOY HOCUS TAINT DEACON DEBASE DEFILE DILUTE EXTEND MANAGE WEAKEN BASTARD CORRUPT FALSIFY VITIATE DENATURE IMPURIFY SPURIOUS

ADULTERATED CUT SHAM IMPURE CORRUPT SPURIOUS

ADULTEROUS ERRING

ADULTERY AVOUTRY CUCKOLDOM

ADUMBRATE IMAGE SHADE VAGUE OBSCURE SUGGEST INTIMATE

ADUMBRATION SHADE SHADOW PHANTASM

ADUNCOUS BENT HOOKED

ADUST BURNT FIERY GLOOMY SALLOW PARCHED SCORCHED SUNBURNT

ADVANCE GO AID PAY SOP WAY BULL CITE COME DASH GAIN HELP INCH LAUD LEND LIFT LOAN MARK MOVE NEAR NOSE PASS PUSH RISE SHOW STEP WORM AVANT BOOST BRING CREEP ENTER EXALT EXTOL FAVOR FORGE MARCH OFFER PLACE RAISE SERVE SPEED STAIR STAKE THROW ADDUCE ADMOVE ALLEGE AMOUNT ASSIGN ASSIST AVAUNT BETTER DEGREE EXTEND FAVOUR GROWTH HASTEN INCEDE INROAD PREFER PREPAY SCHOOL STRIDE STRIKE THRIVE VAUNCE BENEFIT DEVELOP ELEVATE ENHANCE FORTHGO FORWARD FURTHER HEADWAY IMPREST IMPROVE PROCEED PROCESS PROMOTE PROMOVE PROPOSE PROSPER PROVECT SUCCEED ADDITION DEVELOPE HEIGHTEN INCREASE PROGRESS

(— **BY CUTTING**) DRIVE

(— **BY LEAPS**) SALTATION

(— **IN LIFE**) WAY

(— **LABORIOUSLY**) STRIVE

(— **OBLIQUELY**) SIDLE

(— **ONE'S POINT**) TAKE

(— **SLOWLY**) INCH WORM CRAWL CREEP

(— **WAVERINGLY**) HOBBLE

(— **WITH EFFORT**) DRAG

(**DIFFICULT** —) SLOG

(**GRADUAL** —) ILLAPSE

(**STEADY** —) SWING

(**SUDDEN** —) SHOOT

(**VIGOROUS** —) SWING

(**PL.**) APPROACHES

ADVANCED FAR DEEP GONE HIGH LATE AHEAD OUTER FORWARD IMPREST LIBERAL VANWARD FOREMOST

(— **IN AGE**) DEEP ANTIQUATED

(— **IN YEARS**) SENIOR AGEABLE ELDERLY

(**MOST** —) EXTREME FARTHEST FOREMOST HEADMOST

(**WELL** —) AGED

ADVANCEMENT UP GOOD ASCENT INCREASE

ADVANTAGE AD BOT USE VAN BEST BOOT BOTE DRAW DROP EDGE GAIN GOOD HANK JUMP MEND NOTE ODDS PULL SAKE VAIL AVAIL BULGE BUNCE FAVOR FRAME FRUIT KINCH LAUGH SPEED START STEAD USAGE BEHALF BEHOOF BETTER CARROT EFFECT PROFIT ACCOUNT BENEFIT EXPLOIT FORDEAL FURTHER PROMOTE UTILITY VANTAGE HANDICAP INTEREST LEVERAGE OVERHAND OVERPLUS

(**ACCIDENTAL** —) FLUKE

ADVANTAGEOUS GOOD JOLI WELL JOLIE GOLDEN PLUMMY SPEEDY USEFUL ELIGIBLE

ADVENT COMING INCOME ARRIVAL APPROACH PAROUSIA

ADVENTITIOUS CASUAL FOREIGN STRANGE ACQUIRED EPISODIC

ADVENTURE GEST LARK RISK SEEK WAGE EVENT GESTE PERIL QUEST AUNTER AUNTRE CHANCE DANGER HAZARD EMPRISE EMPRIZE FORTUNE VENTURE ESCAPADE JEOPARDY

ADVENTURER ROUTIER ARGONAUT

ADVENTURESS DEMIREP DEMIMONDAINE

ADVENTUROUS RASH DARING ERRANT AUNTROUS RECKLESS

ADVERSARY FOE ENEMY RIVAL SATAN FOEMAN OPPONENT

(— **OF GOD**) DEVIL

ADVERSE FOE ILL EVIL CROSS LOATH THRAW AVERSE INFEST WITHER AWKWARD COUNTER DIVERSE FROWARD HOSTILE OPPOSED CONTRARY INIMICAL OF POSING OPPOSITE OVERWART THRAWART

ADVERSITY ILL WOE DECAY NIGHT MISERY SORROW WITHER ILLNESS TROUBLE CALAMITY DISTRESS

ADVERT HEED AVERT RECUR REFER ALLUDE ATTEND RETURN REVERT OBSERVE CONSIDER

ADVERTISE CRY BARK BILL CALL PLUG PUFF STAR WARN BLURB INFORM NOTIFY PARADE DECLARE

DISPLAY OBSERVE PLACARD PUBLISH ANNOUNCE PROCLAIM

ADVERTISED AFFICHE

ADVERTISEMENT AD BILL SIGN BLURB CHANT ADVERT CACHET DODGER NOTICE POSTER TEASER AFFICHE PLACARD STUFFER CIRCULAR HANDBILL

ADVERTISING BUSH BILLING PUFFERY

ADVICE AVIS AVYS LORE NEWS REDE AVYSE STEER ADVISO DEVICE NOTICE CAUTION COUNSEL OPINION TIDINGS GUIDANCE MONITION

(**PL.**) INFORMATION

ADVISABLE BOOK PROPER PRUDENT

ADVISE SAY READ REDE TELL VISE WARN WISE AREAD AREED COACH GUIDE WEISE WEIZE ADJURE ADVISO BEREDE CONFER DEVISE EXHORT INFORM PONDER REVEAL APPRISE APPRIZE COUNSEL ACQUAINT ADMONISH CONSIDER

(— **AGAINST**) DISSUADE

ADVISED DELIBERATE

ADVISER AIDE TOUT COACH COMES TUTOR DOCTOR EGERIA LAWYER NESTOR ADVISOR MONITOR STARETS TEACHER ATTORNEY CROUPIER DIRECTOR FIELDMAN PREACHER

ADVISORY URGING PRUDENT

ADVOCACY BOOM FAVOR AVOWRY FAVOUR ARIANISM

ADVOCATE PRO ABET BACK URGE VOGT ACTOR ADOPT FAVOR PLEAD ASSERT AVOWRY BACKER DEFEND IDEIST LAWYER PATRON SYNDIC ABETTOR APOSTLE DECLAIM ENDORSE ESPOUSE EXPOUND FASCIST GOLDBUG PATRIOT PLEADER PROCTOR SCHOLAR SUPPORT ATTORNEY CHAMPION CLUBBIST DEFENSOR HUMANIST PARTISAN PREACHER

(— **OF REVOLT**) ANARCH

ADVOWSON ADVOCACY TENEMENT

ADZ AX AXE ADZE EDGE ADDIS ADDICE EATCHE THIXLE HATCHET

AEACUS (FATHER OF —) ZEUS

(**SON OF** —) PELEUS TELAMON

AECIUM CAEOMA

AEETES (DAUGHTER OF —) MEDEA

AEGEAN SEA (ANCIENT PEOPLE OF —) PSARA PSYRA SAMIAN LELEGES SAMIOTE

(**GULF OF** —) SAROS

(**ISLAND OF** —) COS IOS KEOS NIOS RODI SCIO CHIOS LEROS MELOS NAXOS PAROS PATMO SAMOS SIROS TENOS THERA ANDROS IKARIA IMBROS LEMNOS LESBOS RHODES SKYROS

(**RIVER INTO** —) STRUMA VARDAR MARISTA

(**TOWN ON** —) CHIOS VATHY MYTILENE

AEGEON (WIFE OF —) AEMILIA

AEGIR HLER GYMIR

(WIFE OF —) RAN
AEGIRITE ACMITE
AEGIS EGIS SHIELD AUSPICE
DEFENCE DEFENSE
AEGISTHUS (FATHER OF —)
THYESTES
AEGYPTUS (BROTHER OF —)
DANAUS
(FATHER OF —) BELUS
AENEAS (COMPANION OF —)
ACHATES
(FATHER OF —) ANCHISES
(GREAT-GRANDSON OF —) BRUT
(MOTHER OF —) VENUS APHRODITE
(SON OF —) IULUS ASCANIUS
(WIFE OF —) CREUSA LAVINIA
AENGUS (MOTHER OF —) BOANN
AEOLUS (DAUGHTER OF —) CANACE
ALCYONE HALCYONE
(FATHER OF —) HIPPOTES
(SON OF —) SISYPHUS
AEON AGE EON ERA AION AEVUM
CYCLE KALPA PERIOD
(PAIR OF —S) SYZYGY
AEPYTUS (FATHER OF —)
CRESPHONTES
(MOTHER OF —) MEROPE
AERATE AERIFY CHARGE INFLATE
AERIAL AERY AIRY TWIN AERIE
LOFTY UNREAL ANTENNA ETHEREAL
AERIALIST FLIER FLYER
AERIE AERY AIRE AYRE EYRY NEST
AIERY BROOD EYRIE
AERIFORM UNREAL GASEOUS
AEROBE BACTERIUM
AERODROME AIRPORT AIRFIELD
AEROEMBOLISM BENDS
AEROLITE AEROLITH
AERONAUT PILOT SKYMAN
AERONAUTICS AVIATION
AEROSE BRASSY
AEROSTAT AIRSHIP BALLOON
AIRCRAFT
AERUGO RUST PATINA
AESON (BROTHER OF —) PELIAS
(FATHER OF —) CRETHEUS
(SON OF —) JASON
(WIFE OF —) ALCIMEDA
AESTHETIC ARTISTIC ESTHETIC
TASTEFUL
AETA ITA
AETOLUS (FATHER OF —) ENDYMION
(SON OF —) CALYDON PLEURON
(WIFE OF—) PRONOE
AFAR OFF AWAY SAHO FERNE
FERREN REMOTE YFERRE DANAKIL
DANKALI DISTANT
AFARA LIMBA
AFFABLE FAIR OPEN CIVIL FRANK
SUAVE BENIGN FACILE FORTHY
GENIAL URBANE AMIABLE CORDIAL
GENERAL LIKABLE CHARMING
FAMILIAR FRIENDLY GRACIOUS
PLEASANT SOCIABLE TOWARDLY
AFFAIR DO JOB PIE BLOW CASE
DUEL GEAR PLOY BRAWL CAUSE
EVENT FIGHT LEVEE PARTY THING
ACTION BATTLE BEHALF DOMENT
EFFEIR MATTER SETOUT SHAURI

BLOWOUT CONCERN FUNERAL
HOEDOWN JOURNEY LIAISON
PALAVER SHEBANG BUSINESS
COMETHER ENDEAVOR HYPOTHEC
INTRIGUE OCCASION
(CONFUSED —) SCHEMOZZLE
(CRITICAL —) KANKEDORT
(LOVE —) LOVE AMOUR INTRIGUE
(SOCIAL —) FORMAL JUNKET
SUPPER
(STATE —S) ESTATE
(PL.) SQUARES
AFFECT AIL AIR HIT BEAR MELT
MOVE POSE RINE SHAM STIR SWAY
ALLOT ALTER ANNOY COLOR DRIVE
FANCY FEIGN HAUNT IMPEL MINCE
SHOCK TOUCH ASPIRE ASSIGN
ASSUME CHANGE DESIRE MOLEST
SOFTEN STRIKE THRILL ATTAINT
ATTINGE BEWITCH CONCERN
EMOTION FEELING IMPRESS
OPERATE PASSION PRETEND
PROFESS ALLOCATE DISPOSED
FREQUENT INTEREST SIMULATE
(— BY HANDLING) TOUCH
(— FAVORABLY) LIKE
(— INJURIOUSLY) INTERESS
(— STRONGLY) HIT HOLD SURPRISE
AFFECTATION AIR POSE SHAM
FRILL GRACE MINCE CHICHI
DISPLAY FOPPERY FROUNCE
GRIMACE PIETISM FONDNESS
PRETENSE PUPPYISM
(PL.) LUGS
AFFECTED MOY AIRY FEAT AILED
APISH MOVED POSEY CHICHI
FALLAL FEISTY FORMAL QUAINT
SEIZED FEIGNED MINIKIN MISSISH
REACHED SMITTEN STILTED
TAFFETA TAFFETY TOUCHED
INVOLVED PRECIEUX
(— BY DECAY) DOTY
AFFECTING AIRIFIED POIGNANT
TOUCHING
AFFECTION LOVE WAFF ALOHA
AMOUR FLAME HEART CHERTE
DOTAGE ESTEEM HYDROA MALADY
REGARD THRUSH AILMENT CHARITY
EMOTION FEELING SYMPTOM
CHLOASMA DEARNESS DEVOTION
FONDNESS KINDNESS MELICERA
TENDENCY
(PARENTAL —) STORGE
(PL.) HEART HEARTSTRINGS
AFFECTIONATE DEAR FOND WARM
ARDENT DOTING LOVING TENDER
AMOROUS DEVOTED EARNEST
ZEALOUS ATTACHED PARENTAL
SISTERLY
AFFECTIVE SENSIBLE
AFFERENT BEAR ESODIC SENSORY
ADVEHENT INFERENT
AFFIANCE AFFY FAITH TRUST
ASSURE ENGAGE ENSURE FIANCE
PLEDGE PLIGHT SPOUSE BETROTH
PROMISE CONTRACT RELIANCE
AFFIANCED INTENDED
AFFIANT DEPONENT AFFIDAVIT
AFFIDAVIT DAVY OATH AFFIANT

AFFIDAVY AFFYDAVY
AFFILIATE ALLY UNIT ADOPT MERGE
UNITE ATTACH BRANCH RELATE
ASCRIBE CHAPTER CONNECT
FILIATE
AFFINITY KIN TELE FAMILY LIKING
AVIDITY CHEMISM KINDRED KINSHIP
RAPPORT ALLIANCE GOSSIPRY
HOMOLOGY RELATION SYMPATHY
AFFIRM PUT AFFY AVER AVOW TAKE
POSIT STATE SWEAR TRUTH VOUCH
ALLEGE ASSERT ATTEST AVOUCH
DEPOSE RATIFY SUBMIT THREAP
THREEP VERIFY ASSEVER CONFIRM
DECLARE PROFESS PROTEST
TESTIFY MAINTAIN
AFFIRMATION SAY VOW YES AMEN
OATH WORD DIXIT PONENT THESIS
AVERRAL AVERMENT
AFFIRMATIVE AY AYE NOD YAH YEA
YEP YES AMEN ATEN YEAH
DOGMATIC POSITIVE
AFFIX ADD FIX PEN PIN SET CASE
CLIP FAST JOIN NAIL SEAL SIGN
ANNEX INFIX STAMP UNITE ANCHOR
APPEND ATTACH FASTEN SETTLE
STAPLE ADHIBIT CONNECT ENTITLE
FORMANT IMPRESS PLASTER
SUBJOIN
AFFLATUS FURY FUROR FRENZY
VISION IMPULSE
AFFLICT AIL RUE TRY VEX COMB
FIRE HOLD HURT PAIN PINE RACK
TUKE ARRAY BESET CURSE GRILL
GRIPE HARRY PINCH PRESS SEIZE
SMITE TRYST VISIT WOUND BURDEN
GRIEVE HARASS HUMBLE INFECT
MOLEST PESTER REMORD SCORCH
STRAIN STRESS STRIKE CHASTEN
INFLICT OPPRESS SCOURGE
TORMENT TROUBLE DISTRESS
LACERATE STRAITEN
AFFLICTED JOB SAD SORRY AILING
WOEFUL GRIEVED HAUNTED
SMITTEN IMPAIRED STRICKEN
TROUBLED
AFFLICTION WOE EVIL LOSS PAIN
SORE TEEN TRAY ASSAY CROSS
GRIEF PRESS SMART STOUR
BUFFET DURESS MISERY PATHOS
PLAGUE SORROW STRESS THRONG
AILMENT DISEASE ILLNESS PASSION
PURSUIT SCOURGE TORTURE
TROUBLE CALAMITY DISTRESS
HARDSHIP SEVERITY SICKNESS
VEXATION
AFFLICTIVE SAD DIRE SORE SOUR
HEAVY SEVERE
AFFLUENCE EASE AFFLUX INFLUX
PLENTY RICHES WEALTH FORTUNE
OPULENCE
AFFLUENT FAT RICH FLUSH RIVER
STEAM BRANCH SPRUIT COPIOUS
FLOWING HALCYON OPULENT
WEALTHY ABUNDANT INFLUENT
AFFORD GO BEAR GIVE LEND GRANT
INCUR OFFER STAND THOLE YIELD
CONFER ENDURE MANAGE SUPPLY
ACHIEVE FORWARD FURNISH

FURTHER PRODUCE PROVIDE MINISTER

AFFRAY FEUD FRAY RIOT ALARM BRAWL BROIL CLASH FIGHT MELEE SCARE SPURN ATTACK BATTLE COMBAT EFFRAY ENFRAI FRIGHT STRIFE TERROR TUMULT ASSAULT CONTEST QUARREL SCUFFLE STARTLE FRIGHTEN STRUGGLE

AFFRIGHT COW FEAR AGAST ALARM DAUNT DOUBT DREAD SCARE AGRISE APPALL DISMAY CONFUSE STARTLE TERRIFY FRIGHTEN

AFFRONT CUT DEFY SLAP ABUSE BEARD PEEVE HARASS INJURE INSULT NETTLE OFFEND SLIGHT STRUNT ASSAULT OFFENCE OFFENSE OUTRAGE PROVOKE CONFRONT DISGRACE ILLTREAT IRRITATE

AFFUSION POURING INFUSION

AFGHAN RUG GHAN COVER DURANI HASARA HAZARA BLANKET PAKHTON PAKHTUN PUKHTUN ACHAKZAI COVERLET

AFGHAN FOX CORSAC CORSAK

AFGHANISTAN

CAPITAL: KABUL

COIN: PUL ABBASI AMANIA AFGHANI

LANGUAGE: DARI PASHTO PUSHTU BALOCHI BALUCHI

MEASURE: JERIB KAROH

MOUNTAIN: KOH SAFEO CHAGAI PAMIRS SULAIMAN HIMALAYAS

NATIVE: SISTANI

PARLIAMENT: SHURA

PROVINCE: GHOR FARAH HERAT KABUL KUNAR KUNUZ LOGAR ZABUL GHAZNI KAPISA PARWAN WARDAK

RIVER: LORA OXUS CABUL FARAH HARUT INDUS KABUL KHASH KUNAR KOKCHA KUNDUZ HELMUND MURGHAB

SEA: DARYA

TOWN: RUI JURM NANI WAMA ASMAR BALKH DOSHI KABUL KUNAR MARUF MATUN MUKUR PAHRA TULAK URGAN CHAMAN KUNDUZ NAUZAD PANJAO RUSTAK SANGAN SAROBI TUKZAR WASHIR BAGHLAN BAMIYAN DILARAM

TRIBE: SAFI TURK ULUS KAFIR TAJIK UZBEK BALOCH BALUCH HAZARA KIRGIZ PATHAN

WEIGHT: PAU PAW SER SIR KARWAR KHURDS

AFICIONADO FAN AMATEUR DEVOTEE FOLLOWER

AFIELD ABROAD ASTRAY

AFIRE ALOW ALOWE EAGER ABLAZE AFLAME ARDENT BURNING FLAMING

A-FLAT AS AIS

AFLOAT ASEA AWAFT AWASH ADRIFT BUOYED NATANT FLOODED

UNFIXED FLOATING

AFOOT ABOUT ASTIR ABROAD TOWARD WALKING

AFOREMENTIONED SAID SUCH

AFORESAID DITTO NAMED PRIOR PREVIOUS

AFORETIME ERE FORMER FORMERLY

AFRAID RAD REDE ADRAD FRAID REDDE TIMID AGHAST CRAVEN FEARED SCARED WROTHE AFEARED ALARMED ANXIOUS ASCARED FEARFUL GASTFUL COWARDLY GHASTFUL TIMOROUS

AFREET JINN AFRIT DEMON GIANT IFRIT JINNI AFRITE EFREET

AFRESH ANEW ANON OVER AGAIN NEWLY DENOVO ENCORE REPEATED

AFRICAN BOER AFRIC

AFRICAN MARIGOLD KHAKIBOS

AFRIKAANS TAAL DUTCH

AFT BACK REAR ABAFT AFTER ASTERN BEHIND
(**FARTHEST** —) AFTERMOST

AFTER A AB BY TO AFT EFT FOR SIN ANON NEXT PAST POST SYNE ABAFT APRES ARTER EFTER INFRA LATER SINCE ASTERN BEHIND BEYOND FOLLOW HINDER
(**— MEALS**) PC

AFTERBIRTH HEAM SOOTERKIN

AFTERBODY TONNEAU

AFTEREFFECT SEQUEL SEQUELA
(**PL.**) HANGOVER

AFTERGRASS FOG AFTERFEED

AFTERIMAGE SPECTRUM SENSATION
(**KIND OF** —) PURKINJE

AFTERMATH FOG ETCH LOSS ISSUE ROWEN ROWET TRAIL TRAIN ARRISH EDDISH EDGREW EDGROW EFFECT PROFIT RESULT ROWETT SEQUEL UPSHOT EAGRASS STUBBLE BACKWASH

AFTERMOST LAST HINDMOST

AFTERNOON AFTER TARDE UNDERN EVENING TEATIME

AFTERPIECE EPODE EXODE EXODIUM POSTLUDE

AFTERSONG EPODE

AFTERSWARM CAST SPEW SPUE CASTLING

AFTERTASTE FAREWELL

AFTERTHOUGHT FOOTNOTE

AFTERWARD EFT POST SITH THEN APRES LATER EFTSOON EFTSOONS

AGA AGHA LORD CHIEF
(**WIFE OF** —) BEGUM

AGAIN OR TO BIS EFT YET AGIN ANEW ANON AYEN AYIN BACK MORE OVER NEWLY AFRESH DENOVO ENCORE ITERUM EFTSOON FRESHLY FURTHER EFTSOONS MOREOVER
(**— AND AGAIN**) AND

AGAINST BY IN UP CON GIN NON AGIN ANTI GAIN INTO WITH AGAIN ANENT AYENS UNTIL ANENST AVERSE AYENST CONTRA GAINST UPTILL VERSUS FERNENT FORNENT OPPOSED ADVERSUS CONTRAIR

FORENENT FORNENST FORNINST
(**— HOPE**) AGLEE AGLEY

AGAL HEADROPE

AGALLOCH AGGUR ALOES GAROO GARROO GARROW TAMBAC LINALOE AGALWOOD CALAMBAC

AGAMA AGA AGHA GUANA AGAMID IGUANA LIZARD AGAMIAN

AGAMEMNON (**BROTHER OF** —) MENELAUS
(**DAUGHTER OF** —) ELECTRA IPHIGENIA
(**FATHER OF** —) PLISTHENES
(**GRANDFATHER OF** —) ATREUS
(**SON OF** —) ORESTES
(**WIFE OF** —) CLYTEMNESTRA

AGAMID AGA AGHA BALETE BALITI

AGAPANTHUS TULBAGHIA LOVEFLOWER

AGAPE LOVE OPEN FEAST GAPING YAWNING

AGAR MOSS GELOSE KANTEN GELOSIN GELOSINE

AGARIC BLEWITS BLUSHER FLYBANE LEPIOTA

AGASP EAGER GASPING

AGATE TAW ONYX RUBY ACHATE GAGATE MARBLE PEBBLE QUARTZ

AGATI SESBANIA

AGAVE ALOE LILY AGAUE AMOLE DATIL SISAL LILIUM MAGUEY MESCAL PULQUE ZAPUPE CANTALA KARATTO KERATTO TEQUILA HENEQUEN HENIQUEN JINIQUEN SOAPWEED
(**BROTHER OF** —) POLYDORUS
(**FATHER OF** —) CADMUS
(**HUSBAND OF** —) ECHION
(**MOTHER OF** —) HARMONIA
(**SISTER OF** —) INO SEMELE AUTONOE
(**SON OF** —) PENTHEUS

AGE ALD BIN DAY ELD EON ERA AEON EDGE OLAM TIME YUGA AETAT CYCLE EPOCH OLDEN RIPEN SECLE WORLD YEARS MATURE MELLOW PERIOD SIECLE WITHER CENTURY DEVELOP GLACIAL OLDNESS SECULUM SENESCE VORHAND ANCIENTY DURATION ETERNITY LIFETIME MAJORITY MATURITY
(**— OF 100 YEARS**) CENTENARY
(**— OF MOON**) EPACT
(**ADVANCED** —) DOTAGE
(**EARLY MIDDLE** —) SUMMER
(**GREAT** —) ANTIQUITY GRANDEVITY
(**OLD** —) CRUTCH SENIUM VETUSTY SENILITY

AGED AE AET AGY OLD RIPE ANILE HOARY OLDEN PASSE FEEBLE INFIRM MATURE OGYIAN SENILE WINTRY YEARED ANCIENT ELDERLY WINTERED
(**NOT** —) GREEN
(**WELL** —) STALE

AGEE AJEE AWRY AGLEY ASKEW

AGELESS ETERNAL TIMELESS

AGELONG SECULAR SAECULAR

AGENCY DINT HAND CHECK FORCE

LEVER MEANS MOYEN ORGAN
PROXY ACTION BUREAU MEDIUM
OFFICE ARBITER BENEFIT BROKERY
FACULTY LIBRARY MACHINE
ACTIVITY COMPTOIR COURTESY
MINISTRY
(PUBLIC —) AUTHORITY
(RESTORATIVE —) BALM
(SUPPOSITITIOUS —) ENTELECHY
AGENDUM SLATE DOCKET RECORD
RITUAL PROGRAM
AGENOR (BROTHER OF —) BELUS
(DAUGHTER OF —) EUROPA
(FATHER —) ANTENOR NEPTUNE
(MOTHER —) LIBYA
(SON OF —) CILIX CADMUS PHOENIX
(WIFE OF —) TELEPHASSA
AGENT SPY AMIN DOER ETCH GENE
ACTOR AMEEN BUYER CAUSE
ENVOY MEANS ORGAN PROXY
REEVE RIDER VAKIL WALLA ADUROL
ASSIGN ATOPEN BROKER BURSAR
COMMIS DEALER DEPUTY ENGINE
FACTOR FITTER KEHAYA LEDGER
MEDIUM MINION MUKTAR PESKAR
SELLER SYNDIC VAKEEL WALLAH
BAILIFF BLISTER CHANNEL
COUCHER DRASTIC FACIENT
FEDERAL HUSBAND LEAGUER
MOOKTAR MOUNTAR MUKTEAR
MUTAGEN OFFICER PESHKAR
PROCTOR SCALPER APPROVER
ATTORNEY AUMILDAR CATALYST
EMISSARY EXECUTOR GOMASHTA
GOMASTAH IMPROVER INCITANT
INSTITOR MINISTER MOOKHTAR
OPERATOR PROMOTER QUAESTOR
RESIDENT SALESMAN VIRUCIDE
(— OF CROMWELL) AGITATOR
(ANTIKNOCK —) ADDITIVE
ALKYLATE
(CLEANSING —) SOAP
(CONFIDENTIAL —) AMIN AMEEN
(DESTRUCTIVE —) DEVOURER
(EMPLOYMENT —) PADRONE
(ENFORCEMENT —) LAW
(ESPIONAGE —) COURIER
(FISCAL —) STEWARD
(MEDICINAL —) DRASTIC
(NARCOTIC —) GAZER
(PRESS —) FLACK
(PUBLICITY —) BEATER
(PURCHASING —) CIRCAR SIRCAR
SIRKAR
(STIMULATING —) FILIP FILLIP
(SUBVERSIVE —) STOOGE
(SWEETENING —) DULCIN
(VOLATILE —) SPIRIT
(WETTING —) SPREADER
AGGLOMERATE HEAP LUMP MASS
PILE SELF SLAG WIND CHAOS
GATHER CLUSTER COLLECT
AGGLOMERATION HORDE
CONGERY FAVELLA CONGERIE
AGGRANDIZE LIFT BOOST EXALT
RAISE ADVANCE AUGMENT DIGNIFY
ELEVATE ENLARGE MAGNIFY
PROMOTE INCREASE
AGGRAVATE IRK NAG VEX FEED

LOAD TWIT ANGER ANNOY TAUNT
TEASE BURDEN PESTER WORSEN
AGGREGE BEDEVIL ENHANCE
ENLARGE MAGNIFY PROVOKE
AGGRIEVE HEIGHTEN INCREASE
IRRITATE
AGGRAVATED ACUTE
AGGREGATE ADD ALL SET SUM
AUGE BAND BULK CLON CLUB
COMB DEME FLOC GOUT LATH
MASS BLOCK BUNCH CLASS CLONE
COVER CROWD FIELD GROSS
SHOOT TOTAL UNITE WHOLE
AMOUNT BALLAS DOMAIN PLUREL
VOLUME ASBOLAN COLLECT
ARCULITE ASBOLANE ASBOLITE
AXIOLITE COMPOUND COVERAGE
CUMULITE ENSEMBLE MANIFOLD
MULTEITY TOTALITY
(— OF MICA) BOOK
(— OF MINERALS) EYE
(— OF ORE) KIDNEY
(— OF POINTS) CELL
(— OF STATEMENTS) AUTHORITY
(— OF TISSUES) BODY
(MATHEMATICAL —) FIELD
SEQUENCE
AGGREGATION HEAD HERD CLUMP
CUTIN FLOCK GORGE GROUP LURRY
SWARM COLONY FAMILY NATION
SYSTEM CLUSTER CONGERY
GALLERY SORITES CONGERIE
EUMERISM
AGGRESSION WAR RAID ATTACK
INJURY ASSAULT OFFENSE
INVASION
AGGRESSIVE PUSHING
AGGRESSIVENESS CRUST
BELLICOSITY
AGGRIEVE TRY HARM HURT PAIN
HARRY WRONG INJURE AFFLICT
OPPRESS TROUBLE DISTRESS
AGGRIEVED SORE OFFENDED
AGHAST AGAST AFRAID
AGILAWOOD AGALLOCH
AGALLOCHUM
AGILE DEFT FAST LISH SPRY WIRY
ADEPT ALERT BRISK CATTY ELFIN
FLEET LITHE QUICK WANLE WITHY
ACTIVE ADROIT FEERIE FEIRIE
LIMBER LISSOM LITHER LIVELY
LUTHER NIMBLE QUIVER SUPPLE
WANDLE LISSOME SALIENT SPRINGE
SPRINGY ATHLETIC
AGILITY LEVITY SPROIL SLEIGHT
ACTIVITY LEGERITY SALIENCE
AGING BINNING
(PREMATURE —) GERODERMA
GERODERMIA
AGIO BATTA DISAGIO PREMIUM
DISCOUNT EXCHANGE
AGIST TAX FEED RATE GRAZE
PASTURE
AGITATE FAN IRK JAR VEX WEY
FRET FUSS MOVE PLOT RILE ROCK
SEEK STIR TEEM ALARM ALTER
BREAK BROIL CHURN DRIVE HARRY
IMPEL QUAKE ROUSE SHAKE
AROUSE BETOSS BUSKLE DEBATE

DEVISE EXCITE FOMENT HARASS
INCITE JABBLE JOSTLE JUMBLE
JUSTLE LATHER MANAGE RATTLE
RUFFLE SEETHE ACTUATE CANVASS
COMMOVE CONCUSS DISCUSS
DISTURB PERTURB REVOLVE
TEMPEST TROUBLE ACTIVATE
CONTRIVE CONVULSE DISQUIET
DISTRACT TRANSACT
(— A LIQUID) SPARGE
AGITATED STEWED STORMY YEASTY
AGITATO ESTUOUS UNQUIET
AESTUOUS FEVERISH FLURRIED
SEETHING
AGITATION GOG JAR JOG BOIL
FEAR FRET FURY GUST HEAT ITCH
JERK JOLT ALARM DANCE HURRY
QUAKE SHAKE STORM STOUR
TWEAK YEAST BUSTLE DITHER
ENERGY FIZZLE FLIGHT FLURRY
FRENZY JABBLE MOTION PUCKER
QUIVER RIPPLE SHAKES TREMOR
TUMULT EMOTION FERMENT
FLUSTER FLUTTER MADNESS
RAMPAGE STICKLE SWITHER
TEMPEST TURMOIL DISQUIET
PAROXYSM UPHEAVAL
(— AND PROPAGANDA) AGITPROP
AGITATOR HOG TREATER
AGLAIA (FATHER OF —) JUPITER
(MOTHER OF —) EURYNOME
(SISTER OF —) THALIA
EUPHROSYNE
AGLET TAB TAG LACE STUD PLATE
AIGLET PENDANT SPANGLE
HAWTHORN STAYLACE
AGLEY AWRY AGLEE ASIDE ASKEW
WRONG
AGLYCON GENIN NONSUGAR
AGNATE AKIN ALLIED COGNATE
KINDRED
AGNEL MOUTON
AGNOETE THEMISTIAN
AGNOMEN NAME ALIAS EPITHET
SURNAME COGNOMEN NICKNAME
AGNOSTIC ATHEIST DOUBTER
SKEPTIC NESCIENT
AGO BY SIN BACK ERST GONE PAST
SENS SYNE YGOE YORE ABACK
AGONE SINCE YGONE SINSYNE
BACKWARD
(LONG —) ANCIENTLY
AGOG AVID KEEN ASTIR EAGER
LIVELY EXCITED VIGILANT
AGONIZE BEAR RACK STRAIN
WRITHE
AGONIZING GRINDING HARROWING
AGONY ACHE PAIN PANG DOLOR
GRIEF GRIPE PANIC STOUR THRAW
THROE TRIAL ACHING ANGUISH
ANXIETY EMOTION TORMENT
TORTURE TRAVAIL DISTRESS
PAROXYSM
AGOUTI CAPA CAVY PACA ACUCHI
AGOUTY ACOUCHI
AGRARIAN RURAL PASTORAL
AGREE FAY FIT GEE HIT PAN YES
GIBE GREE JIBE JUMP MEET SIDE
SORT SUIT ADMIT ALLOW ATONE

BLEND CHECK CLICK CLOSE FADGE
GRANT HITCH JUTTY LEVEL MATCH
PIECE STAND TALLY UNITE YIELD
ACCEDE ACCORD ASSENT ASSORT
COMPLY CONCUR CONDOG COTTON
ENGAGE REWARD SETTLE SQUARE
SUBMIT ARRANGE BARGAIN
COMPORT CONCEDE CONFORM
CONGREE CONGRUE CONSENT
CONSIGN DARESAY PACTION
PROMISE COINCIDE COMPOUND
CONTRACT COVENANT QUADRATE
(— **MUTUALLY)** STIPULATE
(— **TO JOIN)** ADHERE
(— **TO)** ACCEPT
(— **UPON)** TAILYE TAILZEE TAILZIE
(— **WITH)** SIT LIKE SIDE TAIL
ANSWER
AGREEABLE AMEN EASY FAIR FINE
GOOD KIND LIEF NICE SOFT WEME
AMENE CANNY DULCE GRATE JOLIE
JOLLY LITHE LUSTY QUEME READY
SAPID SMIRK SUANT SUAVE SUENT
SWEET COMELY COWDIE DAINTY
DULCET KINDLY LIKELY SAVORY
SMOOTH SUITED ADAPTED AMABILE
AMIABLE COUTHIE DOUCEUR
TUNABLE WELCOME WILLING
WINSOME AMENABLE CHARMING
DELICATE GRATEFUL LIKESOME
LOVESOME OBLIGING PLACABLE
PLAUSIVE PLEASANT PLEASING
PURSUANT SOCIABLE SUITABLE
THANKFUL
(**NOT** —) ABHORRENT
(**UNPLEASANTLY** —) SACCHARINE
AGREEING CONNATE CONTENT
AGREEMENT GO FIT NOD AXIS
BOND DEAL FINE LINE MISE PACT
TACK TAIL TRUE ATONE COVIN
LEASE MATCH TERMS TOUCH
TRUTH TRYST UNITY ACCORD
ACTION ASSENT CARTEL CAUTIO
COMITY COVINE DICKER LEAGUE
PACTUM PLEDGE TREATY UNISON
BARGAIN CLOSURE COMPACT
CONCERT CONSENT CONSULT
ENTENTE HARMONY ONENESS
PACTION RAPPORT CONTRACT
DIAPASON SANCTION SORTANCE
SYMPATHY
(— **TO JOIN)** ADHESION
(**GRAMMATICAL** —) ATTRACTION
(**SECRET** —) CAHOOT CAHOOTS
AGRICULTURAL GEOPONIC
GEOPONICAL
AGRICULTURE FARMING GAINAGE
TILLAGE AGRONOMY
(— **SYSTEM)** KOLKHOZ
AGRICULTURIST THO FARMER
GROWER SANTAL PLANTER
RANCHER
AGRIMONY CLIVE BORWORT
HEMPWEED
AGRITO AGARITA MAHONIA
ALGERITO ASHBERRY
AGROUND SEWED ASHORE
BEACHED STRANDED
AGRYPHA LOGION
AGRYPNIA INSOMNIA

SLEEPLESSNESS
AGUACATE AHUACA AVOCADO
AGUAMAS PINGUIN
AGUE CHILL FEVER MALARIA
SHAKING SHIVERS
AGUE TREE SASSAFRAS
AGUEWEED BONESET
AH ACH
AHARTALAV YARROW MILFOIL
AHEAD ON UP ALEE FORE AFORE
ALONG DORMY BEFORE DORMIE
ONWARD ALREADY ENDWAYS
ENDWISE FORWARD LEADING
ADELANTE ADVANCED ANTERIOR
(— **OF TIME)** FAST
(**STRAIGHT** —) FORERIGHT
AHEM HUM
AHOY AVAST
AHUEHUETE CEDAR SABINO
CYPRESS
AID KEY ABET BACK BEET HAND
HELP PONY REDE ALLAY BOOST
COACH FAVOR GRANT SERVE
SPEED TREAT ASSIST FAVOUR
FRIEND PROFIT RELIEF REMEDY
RESCUE SECOND SUCCOR SUPPLY
UPHOLD ADVANCE AIDANCE
ANCILLA BACKING BENEFIT
COMFORT ENDORSE FORWARD
FURTHER INDORSE RELIEVE
SECOURS SERVICE SUBSIDY
SUPPORT ADJUVATE AUXILIUM
BEFRIEND SUFFRAGE
(— **A VESSEL)** HOVEL
(— **SECRETLY)** SUBAID
(**COMPLEXION** —) FUCUS
(**MORMON** —) COUNSELOR
COUNSELLOR
AIDE AID BEAGLE DEPUTY SECOND
OFFICER ORDERLY ADJUTANT
GALLOPER
(**BULLFIGHTER'S** —) CAPEADOR
AIGRETTE EGRET HERON PLUME
SPRAY AIGRET FEATHERS
AIL ILE AILD EILE EYLE FAIL PAIN
PINE AFFECT BOTHER FALTER
SUFFER AFFLICT DECLINE TROUBLE
COMPLAIN DISTRESS
AILANTHUS SUMAC SUMACH
AILING SICK CRAZY CRONK DONCY
DONSY SOBER DONSIE SICKLY
UNWELL CRAICHY CREACHY
AILMENT AIL ILL COUGH MALADY
DISEASE ILLNESS DISORDER
SICKNESS WEAKNESS
AIM END LAY TRY BEAD BEAM BENT
BUTT FINE GLEE GOAL HEAD HOLD
LEAD MARK MINT PLAN SEEK TEMP
VIEW VIZY WINK ACIES BLANK
DRIVE ESSAY ETTLE GUESS LEVEL
POINT PRICK SCOPE SIGHT TRAIN
VISIE VIZZY ASPIRE DESIGN DIRECT
ESTEEM INTEND INTENT OBJECT
SCHEME STRIVE ADDRESS ATTEMPT
CHIMERA MEANING PRETEND
PURPOSE RESPECT STAGGER
CHIMAERA CONSIDER ENDEAVOR
ESTIMATE PRETENSE STEERING
TENTAMEN
(— **A KICK)** FLING

(— **AT)** EYE AFFECT
(— **FURTIVELY)** STEAL
(— **INDIRECTLY)** GLANCE
AIMED FAST
(— **AT)** AFFECTED
AIMING LEVEL GUNLAYING
AIMLESS IDLE BLIND CHANCE
RANDOM DRIFTING
AIMLESSNESS FLANERIE
AIR AER PEW SKY AERE ARIA AURA
AYRE BROW DIRT FEEL LILT LOFT
MIEN PORT POSE SONG TELL TUNE
VENT WIND ETHER FRILL OZONE
UTTER VOICE AERATE AETHER
ALLURE ASPECT BROACH CACHET
MANNER MELODY OSTENT PIAFFE
REGARD REGION STRAIN VANITY
WELKIN WITHER BEARING DISPLAY
EXHIBIT EXPRESS FANFARE
MALARIA NEPHELE PIAFFER
ATTITUDE BEHAVIOR CARRIAGE
PRESENCE
(— **COOLED)** WATERLESS
(— **EXHALED)** BLAST
(— **IN MOTION)** BREATH
(— **PLANT)** LIFELEAF
(**BOASTFUL** —) PARADO
(**CONFIDENT** —) BRAVURA
(**COOL** —) FRESCO
(**COQUETTISH** —) MINAUDERIE
(**FETID** —) REEK
(**FOUL** —) DIRT
(**HAUGHTY** —**S)** ALTITUDES
(**MUSICAL** —) ARIA SOLO TUNE
BRAWL MELODY ARIETTA ARIETTE
MUSETTE
(**POMPOUS** —) SWELL
(**PUT ON** —**S)** PROSS
(**STALE** —) STEAM
(**STIFLING** —) SMORE
(**THE** —) GATE
(**WARM** —) OAM
(**PL.)** LUGS FRONT
AIRCRAFT KITE ABORT BLIMP CRAFT
FLYER PLANE GLIDER AEROBUS
AERONEF AIRSHIP BALLOON
AEROBOAT AERODYNE AEROSTAT
AIRLINER AIRPLANE AUTOGIRO
AUTOGYRO GYRODYNE
(**UNIDENTIFIED** —) UFO BOGY
BOGEY BOGIE
AIRCRAFTSMAN ERK
AIRCREWMAN KICKER AIREDALE
AIRFIELD AERODROME SATELLITE
AIRFOIL FIN FLAP SLAT BLADE
SURFACE AEROFOIL ELEVATOR
AIRILY JAUNTILY
AIRLINE FEEDER SKYWAY
AIRMAN FLIER FLYER BIRDMAN
WARBIRD WASTEMAN
AIRPLANE BUS CUB JET MIG BAKA
GYRO KILL KITE SHIP ZERO AVION
CRATE FLIER FLYER FRITZ GOTHA
HEINE JENNY LINER PLANE SCOUT
SNOOP BOMBER CANARD CHASER
COPTER FERRET FESSEL FIGHTER
GLIDER JENNIE SMOKER TANDEM
VESSEL AERONEF AVIATIK BIPLANE
CLIPPER FIGHTER FLIVVER FLYAWAY
HOTSHOT PENGUIN SNOOPER

SPOTTER TRACTOR WARBIRD
AEROSTAT ALBATROS KAMIKAZE
SEAPLANE SKYCOACH SKYCRAFT
SOCIABLE STRUTTER TRIPLANE
TURBOJET WARPLANE
(REMOTE-CONTROLLED —) DRONE
AIR PLANT LIFELEAF LIVELEAF
AIRPORT DROME AIRPARK JETPORT
SCUTTLE AIRDROME AIRFIELD
AIRSHIP (SEE ALSO AIRPLANE AND
AIRCRAFT) SHIP BLIMP GASBAG
AERONAT AEROSTAT PARSEVAL
ZEPPELIN
AIRSTREAM PEW DOWNWASH
AIRSTRIP LILY
AIRTIGHT SEALED AIRPROOF
HERMETIC
AIRWAY MONKEY RETURN SKYWAY
AIRWAVE WINDWAY WINDROAD
AIRY GAY COOL RARE THIN EMPTY
HUFFY LIGHT MERRY WINDY AERIAL
BREZZY FLUFFY JAUNTY JOCUND
LIVELY STARRY AIRLIKE AIRSOME
HAUGHTY JOCULAR SFOGATO
AFFECTED ANIMATED DEBONAIR
DELICATE ETHEREAL FLIPPANT
GRACEFUL SPARKISH TRIFLING
VOLATILE
AISLE ILE WAY YLE AILE LANE NAVE
WALK ALLEE ALLEY FEEDWAY
GANGWAY PASSAGE CORRIDOR
AIT OAT EYOT HOLM ISLE EIGHT
ISLET
AITCHBONE ICEBONE EDGEBONE
AJAR OPEN DISCORDANT
AJAX AIAS
(FATHER OF —) OILEUS TELAMON
(MOTHER OF —) ERIBOEA PERIBOEA
AJONJOLI SESAME
AJOWAN AJAVA AIWAIN
AKALI SHAHIDI
AKEAKE AKE HOPBUSH IRONWOOD
AKHA KAW
AKIMBO ANGLED AKEMBOLL
AKENBOLD
AKIN SIB LIKE NEAR NIGH ALIKE
CLOSE AGNATE ALLIED COUSIN
SIBBED TENDER COGNATE CONNATE
GERMANE RELATED SIMILAR
(— ON MALE SIDE) AGNATIC
(NOT —) UNSIB
AKRA ACCRA INKRA
AKU VICTORFISH
AL AAL AWL MULBERRY
ALA AXIL DRUM WING AXILLA
RECESS NOSEWING

ALABAMA
CAPITAL: MONTGOMERY
COUNTY: LEE BIBB CLAY DALE
PIKE COOSA HENRY LAMAR
MACON PERRY BLOUNT BUTLER
COFFEE DALLAS ELMORE
ETOWAH GENEVA GREENE
MARION MONROE MORGAN
SHELBY SUMTER WILCOX
CHILTON
MOUNTAIN: CHEAHA

NATIVE: LIZARD
RIVER: PEA COOSA CAHABA
MOBILE SIPSEY TENSAW
CONECUH SEPULGA TOMBIGBEE
STATE BIRD: YELLOWHAMMER
STATE FISH: TARPON
STATE FLOWER: CAMELLIA
STATE TREE: PINE LONGLEAF
TOWN: OPP PIPER SELMA ATHENS
CORONA LINDEN MARION
MOBILE SAMSON FLORALA
GADSDEN ANNISTON

ALABASTER GYPSUM TECALI
ONYCHITE
ALACK ALAS ALAKE
ALACRITY HASTE SPEED CELERITY
RAPIDITY
ALAMEDA MALL WALK
ALAN ALAND ALANT ALAUNT
ALANG-ALANG COGON KOGON
ALANS GHUZ OGHUZ
ALANTIN INULIN
ALAR PTERIC WINGED AXILLARY
WINGLIKE
ALARM COW DIN BELL FEAR FRAY
GAST LARM ALERT BROIL CLOCK
DAUNT FEEZE LARUM NOISE PANIC
ROUSE SCARE SIREN START STILL
UPSET AFFRAY ALARUM APPALL
AROUSE ATTACK BUZZER DISMAY
EXCITE FRIGHT OUTCRY SIGNAL
TERROR TOCSIN DISTURB GLOPNEN
GLOPPEN MOUNTEE STARTLE
TERRIFY TORPEDO WARNING
AFFRIGHT DISQUIET FRIGHTEN
SURPRISE
(FIRE —) STILL FIREBOX
ALARMED SCARY SCAREY FEARFUL
GASTFUL GHASTFUL SCAREFUL
STREAKED
ALARMER HUER
ALARMING SCARY SCAREY FEARFUL
SCAREFUL
ALAS AY ACH HEU LAS OCH VAE
WOE EHEU HECH OIME ALACK
HALAS HELAS OIMEE OCHONE
OTOTOI WAESUCK ULLAGONE
WAESUCKS WELLADAY WELLAWAY

ALASKA
CAPITAL: JUNEAU
ISLAND: ADAK ATKA ATTU UMNAK
KODIAK UNIMAK DIOMEDE
NUNIVAK
ISLAND GROUP: RAT ALEUTIAN
PRIBILOF ANDREANOF
LAKE: NAKNEK ILIAMNA
MOUNTAIN: BONA VETA SPURR
KATMAI PAVLOF FORAKER
MCKINLEY
MOUNTAIN RANGE: CRAZY
BROOKS KAIYUH CHUGACH
KILBUCK WRANGELL
NATIVE: ALEUT AHTENA ESKIMO
INGALIK KOYUKON TLINGIT
PENINSULA: KENAI SEWARD

RIVER: CHENA KOBUK YUKON
COPPER NOATAK TANANA
KOYUKUK SUSITNA CHULITNA
COLVILLE
STATE BIRD: PTARMIGAN
STATE FLOWER: FORGETMENOT
STATE TREE: SPRUCE
TOWN: EEK NOME KENAI SITKA
BARROW KODIAK NENANA
SKAGWAY KOTZEBUE
ANCHORAGE FAIRBANKS

ALASTRIM AMAAS
ALB ALBE AUBE CAMISIA CHRISOM
VESTMENT
ALBACORE TUNA TUNNY GERMAN
GERMON LONGFIN ALALONGA
ALALUNGA MACKEREL SCOMBRID

ALBANIA
ANCIENT PEOPLE: ILLYRIAN
CAPITAL: TIRANA TIRANE
COIN: LEK FRANC GUINTAR
KING: ZOG
LAKE: ULZE OHRIDSKO
MOUNTAIN: KORAB SHALA PINDUS
KORITNJK
REGION: EPIRUS
RIVER: MAT DRIN OSUM ERZEN
SEMAN VIJOSE SHKUMBI
TOWN: LIN FIER KLOS BERAT
DUKAT KORCE KRUJE PECIN
PEQIN QUKES RUBIC SPASH
VLONE VLORE AVLONA BITSAN
DARDHE DURRES PRESHE
VALONA DURAZZO KORITZA
SCUTARI SHKODER
TRIBE: GEG CHAM GHEG TOSK

ALBANIAN GEG GHEG GUEG
ARNAUT SKIPETAR
ALBATROSS GONY GOON GONEY
GOONY NELLY FABRIC GOONEY
GOONIE QUAKER SEABIRD
BLUEBIRD STINKPOT
ALBEIT ALL ALBE ALBEE ALLBE
THOUGH HOWBEIT
ALBINO LEUCAETHIOP
ALBIZZIA SIRIS
ALBUM ALBE BOOK RECORD
VOLUME REGISTER
ALBUMEN WHITE
ALBUMIN ALBUMEN PHASELIN
SYNTONIN
ALBUMINOID ELASTIN FIBROIN
KERATIN PROTEIN SERICIN
COLLAGEN GORGONIN
ALBURNUM SAP BLEA SPLINT
SAPWOOD
ALBUS BLANCO
ALCAEUS (FATHER OF —) PERSEUS
(SON OF —) AMPHITRYON
ALCAIDE CADE CAID QAID JUDGE
ALCADE
ALCESTIS (FATHER OF —) PELIAS
(HUSBAND OF —) ADMETUS
ALCHEMIST ADEPT ARTIST CHEMIC

CHEMICK CHEMIST HERMETIC
ALCHEMY ART MAGIC ALCUMY
CHYMIA SPAGYRIC
(GOD OF —) HERMES
ALCHORNEA DOVEWOOD
ALCINOUS (DAUGHTER OF —)
NAUSICAA
(FATHER OF —) NAUSITHOUS
(MOTHER OF —) PERIBOEA
(WIFE OF —) ARETE
ALCMAEON (FATHER OF —)
AMPHIARAUS
(MOTHER OF —) ERIPHYLE
(WIFE OF —) CALLIRHOE
ALPHESIBOEA
ALCMENE (FATHER OF —)
ELECTRYON
(HUSBAND OF —) AMPHITRYON
(SON OF —) HERCULES IPHICLES
ALCOHOL ALKY ETHAL ETHYL IDITE
LEDOL VINYL AMYROL ANDROL
CEDROL ELEMOL GLYCOL GUAIOL
HYDROL IDITOL LUPEOL LUTEIN
METHYL PHYTOL SPIRIT STERIN
STERNO STEROL TALITE ACRITOL
ADONITE ALDITOL ALKANOL ANISOIN
BORNEOL BUTANOL CAROTOL
DECANOL ETHANOL FENCHOL
HEPTITE HEXITOL INOSITE MENTHOL
PULEGOL QUINITE SCOPINE
SORBITE STETHAL STYRONE
TAGETOL TALITOL TROPINE XYLITOL
LINALOOL METHANOL
ALCOHOLATE SPIRIT ESSENCE
ALCOHOLIC ALKY
(NOT —) SOFT
ALCOHOLOMETER GENOMETER
VINOMETER
ALCOVE BAY NOOK BOWER NICHE
ORIEL STALL CARREL RECESS
CARRELL CUBICLE DINETTE
RETREAT SERVERY ALHACENA
SNUGGERY TABLINUM
ALDEHYDE ALDOL CITRAL ALKANAL
CHLORAL COGENER DECANAL
GLYOXAL HEXANAL ACROLEIN
CONGENER FURFURAL
ALDER ARN OLER ALNUS ELDER
OWLER SAGEROSE
ALDERMAN BAILIE SENIOR
HEADMAN
ALE MUM NOG BEER BOCK BREW
FLIP MILD NOGG PURL SCUD YELL
AUDIT CLINK DARBY JOUGH LAGER
NAPPY STOUT ALEGAR PORTER
STINGO SWANKY BITTERS
MOROCCO OCTOBER PHARAOH
HUGMATEE
**(— BREWED WITH BRACKISH
WATER)** TIPPER
(— MIXED WITH SWEETENER)
BRAGGET
(INFERIOR —) SWANKY SWANKEY
(NEW —) SWATS
(SOUR —) ALEGAR
(SPICED —) SWIG
(STRONG —) MUM HUFF BURTON
STINGO HUFFCAP
(WEAK —) TWOPENNY

ALEATORY HAZARDOUS
ALECOST COSTMARY
ALECTRYON TITOKI
ALEE AHEAD LEEWARD
ALEHOUSE PUB TAVERN BARROOM
MUGHOUSE POTHOUSE
ALEMBIC LIMBEC LIMBECK
CUCURBIT
ALERT APT GAY HEP HIP YAL YEP
FOXY GLEG KEEN LIVE PERT SNAP
WAKE WARN WARY YALD YEPE
ACUTE AGILE ALARM ALIVE AWAKE
AWARE BREME BRISK EAGER ERECT
LEERY MERRY PEART PEERT QUICK
READY SHACK SHARP SIREN SLICK
SWIFT TIGHT WAKER YAULD ACTIVE
ALARUM ARRECT BRIGHT DAPPER
LIVELY NIMBLE PROMPT SLIPPY
SPRACK SUDDEN TIPTOE TOCSIN
WACKER CAREFUL KNOWING
WAKEFUL WORKING PREPARED
THOUGHTY VIGILANT WAKERIFE
WATCHFUL
ALERTNESS NOUS SNAP APTNESS
APTITUDE
(MENTAL —) WIT
ALETTE WING ABUTMENT
ALEUT ATKA ORARIAN UNALASKA
**ALEUTIANS (ISLANDS AND ISLAND
GROUPS OF —)** FOX RAT ADAK
ATTU NEAR KISKA UMNAK KODIAK
(TOWN OF —) UNALASKA
(VOLCANO ON —) SHISHALDIN
ALEWIFE BANG ALLICE ALOOFE
BUCKIE ALEWHAP HERRING
OLDWIFE POMPANO WALLEYE
GRAYBACK GREYBACK SAWBELLY
SKIPJACK
ALEXANDER ALEX PARIS SAWNY
ELLICK SAWNEY SAWNIE ISKANDER
(BIRTHPLACE OF —) PELLA
(HORSE OF —) BUCEPHALUS
ALFA HALFA ESPARTO
ALFALFA HAY MEDIC FODDER
LEGUME LUCERN LUCERNE
ALFILARIA ERODIUM FILAREE
FILARIA PINWEED
ALFORJA BAG POUCH WALLET
ALFARGA ALFORGE
ALGA NORI ALGAL BROWN FUCUS
JELLY SLAKE SLOAK SLOKE DESMID
DIATOM FUNORI NOSTOC AMANORI
GULAMAN HAITSAI OARWEED
SEAWEED ANABAENA FERNLEAF
GELIDIUM HAIRWEED ROCKWEED
SEABEARD SILKWEED SPOROGEN
WHIPCORD ZOOGLOEA
ALGARROBA CAROB CALDEN
ALGEBRA LOGISTIC
ALGEBRAIC COSSIC
ALGENIB MIRFAK

ALGERIA

BERBER: KABYLE SHAWIA TUAREG
BERBER DIALECT: ZENATA
  SENHAJA
CAPITAL: ALGIERS
CAVALRYMAN: SPAHI SPAHEE

DEPARTMENT: ORAN ALGIERS
GRASS: ESPARTO
HILL: TELL
HOLY MAN: MARABOUT
MEASURE: PIK REBIS TARRI
  TERMIN
MONASTERY: RIBAT
MOUNTAIN: AISSA ATLAS AURES
  DAHRA TAHAT CHELIA AHAGGAR
  MOUYDIR DJURJURA
NAME: ALGERIE NUMIDIA
NATIVE: BERBER KABYLE
PIRATE: CORSAIR
RIVER: SHELIF CHELIFF MEDJERDA
RULER: BEY DEY BEVLERBEY
SECT: SUNNITE
SETTLER: COLON PIEDNOIR
SHIP: XEBEC
TOWN: BONE ORAN AFLOU ARZEW
  BATNA BLIDA MEDEA SAIDA
  SETIF TENES ABADLA ANNABA
  AUMALE BARIKA BECHAR BEJAIA
  BENOUD BISKRA BOUGIE
  DELLYS DJANET DJELFA DZIOUA
  FRENDA GUELMA SKIKDA
  BOGHARI MASCARA MILIANA
  NEGRINE NEMOURS OUARGLA
  TEBESSA TLEMCEN
WEIGHT: ROTL

ALGERINE COOLOOLY KOOLOOLY
ALGID COLD COOL CHILLY CLAMMY
ALGOLOGY VERATRIN
ALGONKIAN EOZOIC
(— ROCKS) UNKAR
ALIAS ELSE OTHER AYLESS
ASSUMED EPITHET
ALIBI PLEA EXCUSE APOLOGY
PRETEXT
ALIDADE INDEX DIOPTER
ALIEN GER DEED FREMD METIC
ALAUNT ALLTUD AUBAIN CONVEY
EXOTIC INMATE REMOTE ADVERSE
DENIZEN FOREIGN FRAMMIT
INVADER OUTLAND STRANGE
DETAINEE STRANGER TRANSFER
ALIENATE PART WEAN ALIEN AVERT
ANNALY CONVEY DEMISE DEVEST
FREEZE FORFEIT SUBVERT
AMORTIZE DISUNITE ESTRANGE
MORTMAIN SEPARATE STRANGER
TRANSFER WITHDRAW
ALIENATION GIFT DISTASTE
DISUNION DISUNITY DIVISION
DONATION INSANITY
ALIENIST PSYCHOPATH
PSYCHIATRIST
ALIGHT DROP LAND LEND REST
STOP LATCH LIGHT LODGE PERCH
ROOST STOOP SWOOP ARRIVE
SETTLE BURNING DESCEND
ALIGN LINE TRAM TRUE ALINE
ARRAY DRESS RANGE ADJUST
ARRANGE MARSHAL
(— PAPER) JOG
ALIGNED FAIR COLORED
ALIGNMENT KELTER KILTER
GROUPING

ALII ARIKI
ALIKE AKIN LIKE SAME EQUAL INLIKE SQUARE YLICHE EQUALLY SIMILAR UNIFORM
ALIMENT PAP FOOD FUEL BROMA MANNA VIANDS ALIMONY PABULUM RATIONS
ALIMONY ALIMENT
ALIPHATIC FATTY
ALIVE VIF BUSY KEEN SPRY VIVE AGILE ALERT ALIFE ASTIR AWARE BEING BRISK FRESH GREEN QUICK VITAL AROUND EXTANT LIVING SLIPPY ANIMATE VIBRANT ANIMATED EXISTENT SENSIBLE SWARMING
ALKALI LYE REH BASE BRAK KALI SALT SODA USAR BRACK CAUSTIC
ALKALOID BASE ERGOT ESERE ARICIN BRUCIN CEVINE CODEIN CONINE ACONINE ESERIN QUINIA QUININ ACONINE ARABINE ARICINE ATROPIA BOGAINE BOLDINE BRUCINE CAFFEIN COCAINE CODEINE CONIINE EMETINE HARMINE HYGRINE JERVINE KAIRINE NARCEIN NEOPINE PTOMAIN QUININE SCOPINE SINAPIN SOLANIN SOPHORA VIOLINE PIPERINE
ALKANE PARAFFIN
ALKANET BUGLOSS REDROOT
ALKANNIN ORCANET ANCHUSIN ORCHANET
ALKYD GLYPTAL
ALL A AL ANY SUM EACH FULL TOTE AUGHT EVERY GROSS OMNES OUGHT QUITE TOTAL TOTUM TUTTA TUTTO WHOLE ENTIRE SOLELY WHOLLY PLENARY ENTIRELY EVERYONE TOTALITY
(— BUT ABSOLUTELY) ALMOST
(— IN) ALTOGETHER
(— TOGETHER) COLLECTEDLY
(AND —) ANA
(AT —) AVA ANYWISE ANYTHING ANYWHERE
(OF —) AVA
ALLANITE CERINE CERITE ORTHITE
ALLAY AID LAY CALM CITE COOL EASE HELP HUSH STAY ABATE AGATE ALLOY CHARM CHECK DELAY QUELL QUIET SALVE SLAKE STILL ADDUCE LESSEN PACIFY QUENCH REDUCE SOFTEN SOLACE SOOTHE STANCH SUBDUE TEMPER APPEASE ASSUAGE COMFORT COMPOSE LIGHTEN MOLLIFY RELIEVE REPRESS STAUNCH MITIGATE PALLIATE
ALLAYED DEFERRED
ALLEGATION PLEA COUNT VOUCH CHARGE ESSOIN AVERRAL FICTION PROFERT SCANDAL SURMISE AVERMENT SCIENTER
ALLEGE LAY SAY AVER AVOW CITE SHOW URGE ALLAY CLAIM FEIGN INFER LEDGE OFFER PLEAD QUOTE STATE SWEAR VOUCH ADDUCE AFFIRM ASSERT ASSIGN CHARGE DEPOSE ESSOIN RECITE ADVANCE

ASCRIBE DECLARE LIGHTEN PRESENT PROFESS PROPOSE MAINTAIN
ALLEGED SUPPOSED SURMISED
ALLEGIANCE TIE DUTY FAITH HONOR FEALTY HOMAGE LYANCE LOYALTY SERVAGE SERVICE TRIBUTE CIVILITY DEVOTION FIDELITY LIGEANCE
ALLEGORICAL PARABOLIC SYMBOLICAL
ALLEGORICALLY SECRETLY
ALLEGORIZE TALMUDIZE
ALLEGORY MYTH TALE FABLE STORY EMBLEM PARABLE APOLOGUE METAPHOR
ALLELUIA AEVIA LAUDS
ALL-EMBRACING INFINITE SWEEPING
ALLERGEN INHALANT
ALLERGY ATOPY IDIOBLAPSIS
ALLEVIATE AID BALM CALM CURE EASE HELP ABATE ALLAY QUIET ALIGHT ALLEGE LENIFY LESSEN PACIFY SOFTEN SOLACE SOOTHE SUCCOR SUPPLE TEMPER ASSUAGE COMPOSE CONSOLE CORRECT LENIATE LIGHTEN MOLLIFY RELEASE RELIEVE DIMINISH MITIGATE MODERATE PALLIATE
ALLEVIATION ALAY SOLACE
ALLEY MIG ROW WAY CHAR LANE LEAD MALL MEWS PASS PATH VENT WALK WENT WIND WYND AISLE ALLEE BLIND BYWAY CHARE ENTRY TEWER WEENT PEEWEE TRANCE VENNEL PASSAGE
(BLIND —) LOKE STOP POCKET IMPASSE
ALLHALLOWTIDE HOLLANTIDE
ALLHEAL PANACEA WOUNWORT
ALLIANCE AXIS PACT UNION ACCORD FUSION LEAGUE LYANCE TREATY COMPACT ENTENTE SOCIETY AFFINITY AGNATION CACTALES COVENANT DREIBUND FEDERACY FUNGALES LILIALES TRIPLICE
(— IN WAR) SYMMACHY
ALLICE SHAD ALEWIFE POMPANO
ALLIED SIB AKIN AGNATE COUSIN JOINED LINKED UNITED COGNATE CONNATE FEDERAL GERMANE KINDRED RELATED SIMILAR RELATIVE
ALLIGATOR GATOR NIGER CAIMAN CAYMAN CROTCH JACARE LIZARD TRAVOY YACARE CRAWLER CREEPER LAGARTO TRAVOIS ALAGARTO LORICATE
(— PEAR) ZABOCA AVOCADO AGUACATE
(— TURTLE) LOGGERHEAD
(MALE —) BULL
ALLIGATORING WEBBING
ALL-INCLUSIVE GLOBAL
ALLITERATION LETTER
ALLITERATIVE LITERAL
ALLIUM LILY ONION GARLIC

ALLNESS OMNEITY OMNITUDE
ALLOCATE DEAL DOLE METE RATE ALLOT AWARD SHARE AFFECT ASSIGN OUTPLACE
ALLOCATION DRAW DESIGNATION
ALLOT FIX SET BILL CAST DEAL DOLE GIVE MARK METE PART RATE SORT ALLOW AWARD CAVEL GRANT SHARE ACCORD AFFECT ASSIGN BESTOW DEPUTE DESIGN DIRECT INTEND ORDAIN RATION ACCOUNT APPOINT DESTINE PRORATE QUARTER SPECIFY TRIBUTE ALLOCATE
(— QUARTERS) CANTON
ALLOTMENT CUT LOT DOLE CAVEL SHARE RATION SIZING LOTMENT LOTTERY PORTION DIVISION PITTANCE
ALLOW LET LOW BEAR GIVE HAVE LEND LOAN ADMIT DEFER GRANT LEAVE STAND THOLE YIELD ACCEPT ACCORD ASSIGN BESTOW BETEEM ENABLE ENDURE PERMIT SUFFER APPROVE CONCEDE CONFESS LICENCE LICENSE SUFFICE SUPPOSE SUSTAIN CONSIDER DISPENSE SANCTION TOLERATE
ALLOWABLE FREE LICIT LAWFUL
ALLOWANCE BOT FEE ICE AGIO BOTE DOLE EASE EDGE GIFT HIRE ODDS RATE SALT SIZE ARRAS BATTA CLOFF GRANT LEAVE SHARE STENT STINT BOUCHE BOUNTY CORODY FODDER MARGIN RATING REGAIN SALARY SEQUEL TANTUM ALIMENT ALIMONY CORODY DIETARY DIOBELY LEAKAGE LOWANCE PENSION PORTION PREBEND SCALAGE STIPENT TEARAGE APPENAGE APPROVAL BREAKAGE DISCOUNT DRAFTAGE ORDINARY QUANTITY SANCTION SOLATIUM VIATICUM
(— FOR EXPENSES) DIET
(— FOR MAINTENANCE) ALIMENT
(— FOR THICKNESS) BOXING
(— FOR WASTE) TRET
(— FOR WEIGHT) BUG TARE DRAFT DRAUGHT
(— OF ARROWS) SHEAF
(— OF FOOD) DIET BOUCHE DIETARY
(— OF TIME OR DISTANCE) LAW
(— TO COMPETITOR) LAW
(CLOTHING —) INLAY
(CORRECTIVE —) SALT
(NEGATIVE —) INTERFERENCE
ALLOWED VENIAL LICENTIATE
(NOT —) ILLICIT FORBIDDEN
ALLOY LAY LOY MIX AICH ASEM ALPAX BIDRI BIDRY BRASS CALIN DURAL FLINT INVAR MOKUM MONEL TERNE ALBATA ALNICO ALUMEL BIDREE BILLON BRONZE CERMET GARBLE ILLIUM LATTEN LEAVEN NIELLO OCCAMY OREIDE OROIDE PEWTER SOLDER TAMBAC TOMBAC TOMBAK ACIERAL ALCHEMY

AMALGAM BABBITT BIDDERY ELINVAR INCONEL MIXTURE PAKTONG RHEOTAN RHODITE SEMILOR SIMILOR TAENITE TUTANIA TUTENAG ALFENIDE ARGENTON ARSEDINE AWARUITE CALAMINE CARACOLI DORALIUM ELECTRUM EUTECTIC GUNMETAL HARDENER KAMACITE METALINE ROMANIUM STELLITE

ALL-PERVADING UNIVERSAL

ALL RIGHT OK YES OKAY AGREED OKEYDOKE

ALLSEED FLAXSEED BURSTWORT

ALL SOULS' DAY SOULMASS

ALLSPICE BUBBY PIMENTO

ALLTHORN JUNCO

ALLUDE HINT IMPLY POINT REFER ADVERT GLANCE RELATE CONNOTE MENTION SUGGEST INDICATE INTIMATE

ALLURE IT AIR COY WIN WOO BAIT DRAW LEAD LURE MOVE SWAY WILE ANGLE BRIBE CHARM COURT DECOY SNARE TEMPT ALLECT ENTICE ENTRAP ILLURE INDUCE INVITE SEDUCE ATTRACT BEGUILE ENSNARE BLANDISH INESCATE INVEIGLE PERSUADE SIRENING

ALLUREMENT BAIT CORD LURE ALLURE GLAMOR GUDGEON

ALLURING GREEN TAKING SIRENIC SUGARED TAKEFUL CATCHING ENTICING FETCHING

ALLUSION HINT TWIT TOUCH GLANCE REFLEX INKLING MENTION INNUENDO INSTANCE

ALLUSIVE CANTING

ALLUVIUM WASH

ALLY PAL AIDE JOIN RANGE UNION UNITE BACKER COXCOX FRIEND HELPER LEAGUE ALLIANT CONNECT PARTNER ADHERENT CONFEDER FEDERATE
(PL.) FOEDERATI

ALMANAC ORDO PADDY CALENDAR

ALMEMAR BEMA BIMA BIMAH

ALMIGHTY GOD GREAT CREATOR EXTREME JEHOVAH INFINITE POWERFUL PUISSANT

ALMOND DOE PILI BADAM CHUFA JORDAN KAMANI KANARI AMYGDAL BISCUIT TALISAY ALMANDER ALMENDRO·AMYGDALA ROSACEAN VALENCIA
(— BROWN) WOOD
(— SHAPED OBJECT) MANDORLA

ALMONRY AMBRY

ALMOST JUST LIKE MOST MUCH NEAR NIGH ABOUT ANEAR CLOSE AMAIST FECKLY MOSTLY NEARLY NIGHLY MUCHWHAT WELLMOST WELLNEAR

ALMS DOLE GIFT ALMOIN AUMOUS AWMOUS BOUNTY CORBAN MAUNDY RELIEF ALMOIGN CHARITY HANDOUT PASSADE DEVOTION DONATION GRATUITY OFFERING PITTANCE

ALMSHOUSE POORHOUSE WORKHOUSE

ALMUCE HOOD AMICE VAGAS TIPPET VAKASS VARKAS

ALODIUM ODAL ODEL ODHAL ESTATE PROPERTY

ALOE PITA AGAVE

ALOEUS (FATHER OF —) NEPTUNE
(SON OF —) OTUS EPHIALTES
(WIFE OF —) IPHIMEDIA

ALOFT UP HIGH ABOVE AHIGH UPWARD AHEIGHT SKYWARD OVERHEAD

ALONE ALL ONE BARE LANE LORN ONLY SOLE SOLO ALOOF APART SOLUS SIMPLY SINGLE SOLEIN SOLELY SULLEN UNIQUE ALONELY FORLORN UNAIDED DESOLATE DETACHED ISOLATED SEPARATE SOLITARY
(ALL —) LEELANE LEELONE

ALONG ON UP VIA AWAY LANG WITH YOND AHEAD LONGS BESIDE FORBYE FOREBY ONWARD ALONGST ENDLONG FORWARD PARALLEL TOGETHER
(— THE MARGIN) DOWN
(— WITH) AND
(WELL —) ENDWAYS ENDWISE

ALONGSIDE AT BY ASIDE CLOSE ABOARD BESIDE ABREAST FORNENT SIDLINS FORNENST PARALLEL

ALONSOA MASKFLOWER

ALOOF DRY SHY COLD COOL ABACK ALONE APART PROUD ABEIGH FROSTY OTIOSE REMOTE SILENT DISTANT REMOVED RESERVED

ALOPECIA PELADE ATRICHIA BALDNESS

ALOPECURUS FOXTAIL

ALPACA PACO

ALPENGLOW AFTERGLOW

ALPENSTOCK STOCK BERGSTOCK

ALPHABET ABC CUFIC KUFIC LATIN ONMUN ORDER BISAYA BRAHMI CIPHER GLAGOL HANGUL HANKUL KAITHI NAGARI PRIMER ROMAJI SARADA SCRIPT TAGALA VISAYA ALJAMIA FUTHARK KALEKAH LETTERS PESHITO ALJAMIAH CROSSROW GUJARATI GURMUKHI
(— SQUARE) TABLEAU

ALREADY EEN NOW DONE EVEN SINCE BEFORE

ALSACE-LORRAINE REICHSLAND

ALSINE ALLBONE

ALSO SO ALS AND EKE TOO YET ERST ITEM MORE PLUS ALONG DITTO BESIDES FURTHER THERETO LIKEWISE MOREOVER

ALTAR ARA BEMA BOMOS TABLE WEVED ACERRA AUTERE HAIKAL SHRINE TRIPOD VEDIKA CHANCEL CHANTRY ESCHARA SCROBIS THYMELE OMPHALOS REPOSOIR
(— BACK) TABLE
(— TOP) MENSA

ALTARPIECE ANCONA DIPTYCH TRIPTYCH

ALTAZIMUTH ABA

ALTER COOK DRAW EDIT GELD

MOVE RASE TURN VARY VEER WEND ADAPT AMEND BREAK ELIDE EMEND FORGE RESET SHAPE SHIFT ADJUST BUSHEL CENSOR CHANGE DEFORM IMMUTE JIGGER MODIFY MUTATE NEUTER REVISE TEMPER UNSAME CHAFFER COMMUTE CONVERT CORRECT CORRUPT DISTORT FASHION QUALIFY STRANGE ACTIVATE EXCHANGE
(— APPEARANCE) WRY
(— BOUNDARIES) DEACON
(— DIRECTION) BREAK
(— STANCE) CLOSE

ALTERATION DOWN CROSS ACTION CHANGE JANGLE DISEASE HEMIOLA MUTATION UPHEAVAL
(— OF BOUNDARY) ERUB ERUV

ALTERATIVE LAPPA FUMARIA

ALTERCATE JANGLE STICKLE WRANGLE

ALTERCATION SPAT TIFF TILT BRAWL BROIL CROSS FIGHT BARNEY BICKER FRACAS JANGLE STRIFE BRABBLE CONTEST DISPUTE PASSAGE QUARREL WRANGLE SQUABBLE

ALTERED BURNT BROKEN VARIED ANOTHER FEIGNED ADJUSTED

ALTERNATE ELSE SWAY VARY OTHER RECUR SHIFT ALTERN CHANGE RINGER ROTATE SECOND SEESAW SPIRAL EXCHANGE INTERMIT TRAVERSE
(— LEAPS AND DIVES) GREYHOUND

ALTERNATELY ABOUT RECIPROCALLY

ALTERNATION ADDITION

ALTERNATIVE OR FORK HORN CHOICE EITHER OPTION DISJUNCT ELECTION

ALTHAEA MALLOW
(FATHER OF —) THESTIUS
(HUSBAND OF —) OENEUS
(SON OF —) MELEAGER

ALTHORN SAX ALTO ALTUS SAXHORN

ALTHOUGH ALL EEN SET ALBE ALIF EVEN THAT WHEN WHILE ALBEIT THOUGH WHENAS DESPITE HOWBEIT WHEREAS

ALTITUDE APEX PEAK HIGHT LEVEL PITCH HEIGHT STATURE

ALTO MEAN ALTUS ALTHORN SAXHORN

ALTOGETHER ALL NUDE QUITE SHEER STICK AGREAT BODILY FREELY WHOLLY EXACTLY TOTALLY UTTERLY ALLTHING ENTIRELY

ALTRUISM OTHERISM

ALTRUISTIC HEROIC HEROICAL

ALUDEL POT LUDEL UDELL

ALULA LOBE WING ALULET SQUAMA TEGULA LOBULUS WINGLET CALYPTER

ALULIM ALOROS

ALUM AUM ALME ALUMEN MIGITE TSCHER STYPTIC HARDENER KALINITE

(FEATHER —) ALUNOGEN
ALUMINA ARGIL ALOXITE
ALUMNUS GRAD PUPIL GRADUATE
ALUMROOT HEUCHERA
ALUR LUR LURI
ALVEARY HIVE BEEHIVE
ALVEOLA FAVEOLUS
ALVEOLAR SPUMOID GINGIVAL
ALVEOLATE FAVOSE FAVOUS PITTED
ALWAYS O AY AYE EEN EER EVER
  SIMLE STILL ALWISE SEMPRE
  ALGATES FOREVER EVERMORE
ALYSSUM ALISON
AM M AME HAM
  (— NOT) NAM AINT AMNT
  (I —) CHAM CHYM
AMA CUP AMULA CRUET DIVER
  VESSEL CHALICE
AMABILE GENTLE TENDER
AMADAVAT WAXBILL TIGERBIRD
AMADOU PUNK TINDER
AMAH NURSE SERVANT
AMAIN GREATLY FORCIBLY
AMALA AMLAH
AMALGAM ALLOY MAGNESIA
AMALGAMATE MIX FUSE JOIN
  ALLOY BLEND MARRY MERGE UNITE
  BLUNGE MINGLE COMBINE
  COALESCE COMPOUND
AMALGAMATION MERGER ADDITION
AMALGAMATOR PLATEMAN
AMANORI NORI LAVER
AMANUENSIS PENMAN SCRIBE
  TYPIST RECORDER
AMARANTH JATACO FLORAMOR
  (PL.) LIGHTHOUSES
AMARILLO FUSTIC
AMARYLLIS LILY AGAVE CRINUM
AMASS HEAP HILL MASS PILE SAVE
  GROSS HOARD STACK STORE
  GATHER COLLECT COMPILE
  CONGEST ENGROSS ASSEMBLE
  OVERHEAP
AMATA (DAUGHTER OF —) LAVINIA
  (HUSBAND OF —) LATINUS
AMATEUR HAM TIRO TYRO NOVICE
  SUNDAY VOTARY ADMIRER
  DABBLER DEVOTEE FANCIER
  JACKLEG PATRIOT VARMENT
  VARMINT BEGINNER
AMATEURISH TYRONIC
AMATORY EROTIC LOVING TENDER
  AMOROUS GALLANT
AMAZE AWE MAZE STAM STUN
  ALARM FERLY ASTONY AWHAPE
  WONDER ASTOUND CONFUSE
  IMPRESS PERPLEX STAGGER
  STUPEFY ASTONISH BEWILDER
  CONFOUND DUMFOUND FRIGHTEN
  SURPRISE
AMAZED AGAZED BUSHED ASTONIED
AMAZEMENT STAM AMAZE FERLY
  GHAST FERLIE FRENZY WONDER
  MADNESS SURPRISE
AMBARI KANAF KENAF KANAFF
AMBASSADOR AGENT ELCHI ENVOY
  VAKIL DEPUTY ELCHEE LEDGER
  LEGATE NUNCIO VAKEEL EMBASSY
  LEAGUER CAPUCIUS DIPLOMAT
  MINISTER

AMBER GRIS LIME AUMER AWMER
  RESIN FUSTIC LAMMER SUCCIN
  YELLOW BURMITE AMBEROID
  ELECTRUM SUNSTONE
AMBERFISH JUREL CARANX KAHALA
  RUNNER CARANGID CARANGIN
  KINGFISH MACKEREL MEDREGAL
AMBERGRIS AMBER AMBRACAN
AMBERJACK ALMICORE CORONADO
AMBIENCE MILIEU AMBIANCE
AMBIGUITY AMBAGE PARADOX
AMBIGUOUS DARK VAGUE DOUBLE
  FORKED CRYPTIC DUBIOUS
  DOUBTFUL SLIPPERY SPURIOUS
  (NOT —) EXPRESS
AMBIT LIMIT SCOPE SPACE BOUNDS
  EXTENT SPHERE CIRCUIT COMPASS
  BOUNDARY PRECINCT
AMBITION ATE GOAL HOPE WISH
  GLORY DESIRE PURPOSE
AMBITIONLESS DRIFTING
AMBITIOUS AVID BOLD HIGH KEEN
  EAGER ETTLE SHOWY EMULOUS
  ASPIRING
AMBITUS TENOR
AMBIVALENCE BIPOLARITY
AMBIVALENT EQUIVOCAL
AMBLE FOOL GAIT MOOCH PADNAG
  MEANDER SAUNTER TRIPPLE
AMBLING TOLUTATION
AMBO DESK PULPIT
AMBOCEPTOR COPULA MEDIATOR
AMBOYNA LINGOA KIABOOCA
AMBROSIA AMBROSE KINGWEED
AMBROSIAL DIVINE FRAGRANT
AMBRY SAFE CHEST NICHE AUMRIE
  CLOSET PANTRY RECESS ALMONRY
  ARMOIRE ARMARIUM CUPBOARD
AMBULANCE AUXILIUM
AMBULATE GAD HIKE MOVE WALK
AMBULATORY WALK ALURE
  GALLERY PORTICO CLOISTER
  PERAMBLE
AMBUSCADE WATCH WAYLAY
  BUSHMENT
AMBUSH NAB LURE LURK TRAP
  WAIT AWAIT BLIND BUSSE CATCH
  COVER SHOMA SNARE STALE TRAIN
  WATCH INBUSH THREAT WAYLAY
  FORELAY SCUPPER DISGUISE
  ENBUSSHE
AMCHOOR AMHAR
AMELIORATE EASE HELP MEND
  AMEND EMEND BETTER REFORM
  IMPROVE PROMOTE
AMEN YEA TRULY ASSENT SOBEIT
  VERILY APPROVAL SANCTION
AMENABLE OPEN LIABLE PLIANT
  SUBJECT
AMEND END BEET HEAL MEND
  ALTER ATONE BEETE EMEND REDUB
  BETTER CHANGE DOCTOR REFORM
  REMEDY REPAIR REPEAL REVISE
  CONVERT CORRECT ENLARGE
  IMPROVE RECOVER RECTIFY
  REDRESS RESTORE CHASTISE
AMENDING COMPENSATION
AMENDMENT RIDER AMENDS
  SLEEPER

AMENDS BOOT MEND ASSETH
  ASSYTH REWARD APOLOGY
  REDRESS
AMENITY JOY COMITY FEATURE
  SUAVITY CIVILITY COURTESY
  MILDNESS
  (PL.) AGREMENS FROUFROU
  NICETIES
AMENT JUL CHAT IDIOT IULUS
  MORON CATKIN CACHRYS CATTAIL
  GOSLING IMBECILE NUCAMENT
AMERCE FINE MERCE MULCT TREAT
  AFFEER PUNISH SCONCE CONDEMN
  FORFEIT
AMERCEMENT MULCT UNLAW
  BLOODWIT
AMERICA INDIA
AMERICAN YANK GRINGO YANKEE
  YANQUI AMERICA WESTERN
  JONATHAN
AMERICANISM HECKERISM
AMETHYST ONEGITE CORUNDUM
AMIABILITY DOUCEUR
AMIABLE GOOD KIND WARM SWEET
  CLEVER GENIAL GENTLE LOVING
  MELLOW SMOOTH TENDER AFFABLE
  LOVABLE WINSOME CHARMING
  ENGAGING FRIENDLY PLEASING
AMICABLE KIND FRIENDLY
AMICE AMIT AMYS CAPE COWL
  HOOD EPHOD ALMUCE DOMINO
  TIPPET VAKASS AMICTUS VESTMENT
AMID IN OMEL AMELL AMONG
  AMIDST DURING IMELLE AMONGST
  BETWEEN
AMIDE LACTAM SULTAM ANILIDE
  ARYLIDE
AMINE ANILIN ANILINE
AMISS ILL MIS AWRY BIAS AGATE
  AGLEY ASKEW WRONG ACROSS
  AGRIEF ASTRAY FAULTY MISTAKE
  IMPROPER
AMITY PEACE ACCORD CONCORD
  HARMONY
AMMA ABBESS MOTHER
AMMONIA HARTSHORN
AMMONITE POLYPOD AMMONOID
  BACULITE CACULOID CERATITE
  SALIGRAM
AMMONIUM CARBONATE
  HARTSHORN
AMMUNITION AMMO AMMU ARMS
  SHOT BOMBS FODDER POWDER
  SHELLS BULLETS GRENADES
  MATERIAL MATERIEL ORDNANCE
  SHRAPNEL
AMNESIA LAPSE FORGETFULNESS
AMNESTY COWLE PARDON OBLIVION
AMNION SAC CAUL SEROSA
  INDUSIUM MEMBRANE
AMOBARBITAL AMYTAL
AMOEBA AMEBA AMEBULA AMOBULA
  PROTEUS RHIZOPOD
AMOK MAD AMUCK CRAZY CRAZED
  VIOLENT FRENZIED
AMOLE EMOL AMOULI AMOLILLA
  MANFREDA
AMONG IN MID AMID INTO MANG
  MONG OMEL WITH AMANG AMELL

MIDST AMIDST BIMONG IMELLE
WITHIN BETWEEN
(— **OTHER THINGS**) IA
AMOR EROS LOVE CUPID AMOROSO
AMORAL NEUTRAL NONMORAL
AMORITE CANAANITE
AMOROUS FOND GAMY SOFT WARM
CADGY JOLLY NUTTY ARDENT
COQUET EROTIC LOVELY LOVING
TENDER AMATIVE AMATORY
AMIABLE FERVENT GALLANT
JEALOUS SMICKER LOVESOME
VENEREAN
AMORPHOUS VAGUE HYALINE
DEFORMED FORMLESS RESINOUS
AMORT ALAMORT DEJECTED
LIFELESS
AMORTIZE DESTROY MORTISE
ALIENATE
AMOUNT GO GOB LOT SUM SUP TOT
ANTE BODY COME DOSE DRAW
FECK KIND LEVY MESS REAM RISE
SOUD SOWD UNIT WARE CHUNK
COUNT GROSS MOUNT PRICE
REACH STACK STORE STUFF TOTAL
WHOLE BUDGET DEGREE DOSAGE
EFFECT EXTENT FIGURE MATTER
NUMBER SUPPLY ADVANCE
FOOTING QUANTUM SCRUPLE
SIGNIFY SLATHER TODDICK
INCREASE QUANTITY SPOONFUL
SURMOUNT VALLIDOM
(— **BORNE BY BEAST**) SEAM
(— **CARRIED AT ONE TIME**) GANG
(— **DUE**) BILL SCORE
(— **HELD**) CAPACITY
(— **OF BASS**) BOOMINESS
(— **OF CONCRETE**) LIFT
(— **OF DYE**) STRIKE
(— **OF FLOW**) STRENGTH
(— **OF FREIGHT**) CARLOAD
(— **OF GAS**) BREATH
(— **OF HERRINGS**) CRANNAGE
(— **OF LEAKAGE**) SLIP
(— **OF LIQUOR**) SLUG
(— **OF MEDICINE**) DOSAGE
(— **OF MONEY**) BEAN BOND CASH
SCOT
(— **OF OIL**) ALLOWABLE
(— **OF PAYMENT**) FOOTAGE
(— **OF POWDER**) INCREMENT
(— **OF SOIL**) INTHROW
(— **OF WATER**) CATCHMENT
(— **OF WORK**) ASSIGNMENT
(— **OWED**) LIABILITY
(— **PAID**) COST
(— **TURNED BY SPADE**) GRAFT
(**APPRECIABLE** —) BEANS
(**COMPLETE** —) FULL
(**CONSIDERABLE** —) MIGHT HANTLE.
HATFUL
(**EXACT** —) NICK
(**EXTRA** —) BONUS
(**GREAT** —) MICKLE INFINITY
MOUNTAIN
(**GROSS** —) SLUMP
(**INADEQUATE** —) DEFICIENCY
(**INDEFINITE** —) BAIT SNAG SOME
(**INFINITESIMAL** —) IOTA

(**INSIGNIFICANT** —) SCRAT
(**LARGE** —) GOB LOB JUNT LUMP
MINT SNAG SWAG SIEGE SLASH
SPATE BOODLE SOMDEL BONANZA
SOMDIEL CARTLOAD MUCHNESS
SOMEDEAL
(**LAVISH** —) SLATHER
(**LEAST POSSIBLE** —) GRAIN
(**LIMITED** —) SPRINKLING
(**MINUTE** —) HAIR FLEABITE
(**RENT** —) GALE
(**SIZABLE** —) CHUNK SMART
(**SLIGHT** —) ADDED SNACK TILLY
(**SMALL** —) ACE BIT DAB DITE DOIT
DRAM DRIB FLOW HINT HOOT INCH
LICK SNAP SONG SPOT SPECK
SPURT TRACE DRAPPY PICKLE
SMIDGE TICKET CAPSULE DRAPPIE
GLIMMER KENNING SMIDGEN
SMIDGIN
(**SMALLEST** —) JOT STIVER
STEEVER STUIVER
(**TENFOLD** —) DECUPLE
(**USUAL** —) GRIST
(**WHOLE** —) ALL SUBSTANCE
(**YEARLY** —) ANNUITY
AMOUR DRURY DRUERY AMOURET
INTRIGUE PARAMOUR
AMPERSAND AND ALSO PLUS
AMPASSY IPSEAND
AMPHETAMINE BENZEDRINE
AMPHIBIA BATRACHIA
AMPHIBIAN EFT OLM FROG HYLA
NEWT RANA TOAD ANURA SIREN
SNAKE AMPHIB CAUDATE ERYOPID
PROTEUS TADPOLE AISTOPOD
AMPHIBOLE EDENITE ORALITE
URALITE ASBESTOS CROSSITE
AMPHICARPA FALCATA
AMPHIGASTRIUM UNDERLEAF
AMPHION (**BROTHER OF** —) ZETHUS
(**FATHER OF** —) ZEUS IASUS
JUPITER
(**MOTHER OF** —) ANTIOPE
(**WIFE OF** —) NIOBE
AMPHIPOD SHRIMP
AMPHITHEA (**DAUGHTER OF** —)
ANTICLEA
(**HUSBAND OF** —) AUTOLYCUS
AMPHITHEATER BOWL OVAL ARENA
CAVEA CIRCUS STADIUM THEATER
AMPHITRITE (**FATHER OF** —)
NEREUS OCEANUS
(**HUSBAND OF** —) NEPTUNE
POSEIDON
(**MOTHER OF** —) TETHYS
(**SON OF** —) TRITON
AMPHORA JUG URN VASE CADUS
DIOTA PELIKE
AMPLE BIG FAIR FULL GOOD MUCH
RICH SIDE WIDE BROAD GREAT
LARGE LUCKY PLUMP ROOMY
ROUND WALLY ENOUGH HEARTY
PLENTY PROLIX COPIOUS LIBERAL
OPULENT WEALTHY ABUNDANT
ADEQUATE BARONIAL GENEROUS
HANDSOME SPACIOUS
AMPLIFICATION GAIN
AMPLIFIED EXTENDED

AMPLIFIER BOOSTER REPEATER
AMPLIFY PAD FARCE FARSE SWELL
WIDEN DILATE EXPAND EXTEND
STRESS AUGMENT ENLARGE
STRETCH AMPLIATE HEIGHTEN
INCREASE LENGTHEN MULTIPLY
AMPLITUDE LATITUDE OPULENCE
AMPLY LARGE
AMPUTATE CUT LOP PRUNE SEVER
CURTAIL
AMPUTATION APOCOPE
AMRITA RASA
AMULA AMA VESSEL
AMULET GEM MET HAND JUJU MOJO
PLUM CHARM IMAGE MENAT SAFFI
SAFIE TOKEN FETISH GRIGRI
MASCOT SAPHIE SCROLL TABLET
AMALETT ICHTHUS ICHTHYS
PERIAPT GREEGREE HAGSTONE
LIGATURE ORNAMENT TALISMAN
AMULIUS (**BROTHER OF** —) NUMITOR
(**FATHER OF** —) PROCAS
(**NEPHEW OF** —) LAUSUS
AMURRU MARTU
AMUSE GAME LAKE ENJOY MIRTH
SHORT SPORT ABSORB DELUDE
DIVERT ENGAGE FROLIC PLEASE
POPJOY SOLACE TICKLE BEGUILE
DISPORT GRATIFY PASTIME
BEWILDER DISTRACT RECREATE
AMUSEMENT FAD FUN JEU GAME
JEST LAKE PLAY MIRTH SPORT
LAKING MUSERY PASTIME
COTTABUS LAUGHTER PLEASURE
(**PL.**) MIDWAY
AMUSING COMIC DROLL FUNNY
MERRY COMICAL FOOLISH KILLING
RISIBLE FARCICAL HUMOROUS
PLEASANT SPORTFUL
AMYGDALA TONSIL
AMYL AMYDON PENTYL ISOAMYL
AMYLASE PTYALIN DIASTASE
AMYMONE (**FATHER OF** —) DANAUS
(**HUSBAND OF** —) ENCELADUS
(**SON OF** —) NAUPLIUS
AMYTHAON (**BROTHER OF** —)
AESON PHERES
(**FATHER OF** —) CRETHEUS
(**MOTHER OF** —) TYRO
(**SON OF** —) BIAS MELAMPUS
(**WIFE OF** —) IDOMENE
AN ONE ARTICLE
ANA EVENTS OMNIANA SAYINGS
ANABAPTIST DIPPER ABECEDARIAN
ANABAS MARTINICO
ANABATIC DESCENDING
ANABO NABO ANABONG
ANABRANCH BRANCH TALLYWALKA
ANACHRONISM SOLECISM
ANACONDA BOA ABOLLA SUCURI
SUCURY CAMOUDIE SUCURUJU
ANACREONTIC TEIAN
ANACRUSIS UPBEAT
ANADEM CROWN DIADEM FILLET
WREATH CHAPLET CORONET
GARLAND
ANAGNOST LECTOR READER
ANAGOGICAL MYSTICAL
ANAGRAM REBUS PUZZLE
METAGRAM

(PL.) VERBARIUM
ANAGUA KNACKAWAY KNOCKAWAY
ANAL PODICAL
ANALABOS CLOAK
ANALGESIC ANTIPYRIN PHENALGIN
ANALOGICAL NORMAL
ANALOGOUS LIKE SIMILAR
ANALOGUE DFDT ANALOG
ANALOGY QIYAS
　(CLOSE —) PARITY
ANALYSIS TEST INDEX STUDY
　ANATOMY AUTOPSY SCANSION
　SOLUTION
　(ECONOMIC —) DYNAMICS
　(LOGICAL —) SYLLOGISM
ANALYTIC SUBTLE REGULAR
　(NOT —) SYNTHETIC SYNTHETICAL
ANALYTICAL CLINICAL DIVISIVE
ANALYZE RUN PART ASSAY BREAK
　PARSE SENSE STUDY WEIGH
　ASSESS DIVIDE REDUCE DISSECT
　EXAMINE ITEMIZE RESOLVE TITRATE
　UNPIECE APPRAISE CONSTRUE
　DIAGNOSE SEPARATE
　(— ACCOUNT) AGE
　(— VERSE) SCAN
ANAMITE TWINE
ANANAS ANANA PINGUIN
ANANIAS LIAR SIDRACH
ANANSI NANCY
ANAPEST ANTIDACTYL
ANARCHIST RED REBEL ANARCH
　NIHILIST REDSHIRT
ANARCHY RIOT CHAOS REVOLT
　LICENSE MISRULE DISORDER
ANASARCA DROPSY
ANASAZI PUEBLO PLATEAU
ANASCHISTIC EUMITOTIC
ANASTOMOSIS GLOMUS
ANASTROPHE INVERSION
ANATHEMA WO BAN MUD WOE
　OATH CURSE CENSURE
ANATHEMATIZE CURSE ACCURSE
　EXECRATE
ANATOMIZE ANALYZE DISSECT
ANATOMY TOPOLOGY
　(— OF HORSE) HIPPOTOMY
　(MICROSCOPIC —) HISTOLOGY
　(VEGETABLE —) PHYTOTOMY
ANAXIBIA (DAUGHTER OF —)
　PELOPEA ALCESTIS PISIDICE
　(FATHER OF —) BIAS
　(HUSBAND OF —) PELIAS
　(SON OF —) ACASTUS
ANCESTOR ION MIL ADAM EBER
　HETH ROOT SIRE DORUS ELDER
　STOCK APETUS ATAVUS AUTHOR
　BELDAM EPONYM FATHER MANNUS
　MILEDH PARENT STIPES ANCIENT
　BELDAME BELSIRE EPAPHUS
　FLEANCE FORBEAR IAPETUS
　ISHMAEL SAKULYA DARDANUS
　FOREBEAR FOREGOER MILESIUS
　MYRMIDON RELATIVE
　(— CULT) MANISM
　(—S OF GOTLANDERS) GEAT
　(MAORI —) TIKI TUPUNA
　(PL.) OLDERS ANCESTRY
ANCESTRAL AVAL AVITAL AVITIC

LINEAL FAMILIAL
ANCESTRY KIN RACE SEED ATHEL
　FAMILY ORIGIN PEOPLE SOURCE
　STRAIN DESCENT KINDRED LINEAGE
　BREEDING PEDIGREE
ANCHISES (FATHER OF —) CAPYS
　(MOTHER OF —) THEMIS
　(SON OF —) AENEAS
ANCHOR FIX BIND DRAG DRUG
　HOOK MOOR REST SLUG SPUD
　STOP AFFIX BERTH BOWER KEDGE
　RIVET SHEET STOCK ATTACH
　DROGUE FASTEN HERMIT KEDGER
　KELLEG SECURE STREAM CHAPLET
　CONNECT DEADMAN GRAPNEL
　GROUSER KILLICK MUDHOOK
　SUPPORT COCKBILL
　(— IN PLACE) ACOCKBILL
　(— RING) TORUS
　(AT —) ASTAY
　(BEAM —) WALL
ANCHORAGE DOCK STAY HARBOR
　REFUGE RIDING MOORAGE
　ABUTMENT BERTHAGE ROOTHOLD
ANCHORITE MONK HERMIT
　ACHORET ASCETIC EREMITE
　RECLUSE STYLITE
ANCHOVY NEHU BOCON SPRAT
　HERRING SARDINE
　(PL.) ALICI
ANCHUSA OXTONGUE
ANCIENT ELD OLD AGED AULD FERN
　HIGH HOAR IAGO YORE EARLY
　ELDER HOARY OLDEN BYGONE
　ENSIGN FORMER NOETIC PISTOL
　PRIMAL VETUST ANTIENT ANTIQUE
　ARCHAIC ARCHEAN CLASSIC
　OGYGEAN OGYGIAN HISTORIC
　NOACHIAN OBSOLETE PRIMEVAL
　PRISTINE
　(MOST —) ELDEST
ANCIENTLY OLD HIGH
ANCILLA HELPER ADJUNCT SERVANT
ANCON ELBOW CORBEL CONSOLE
AND N U AN ET SO ANT TOO ALSO
　PLUS BESIDES FURTHER MOREOVER
　(— SO FORTH) ETC USW
ANDAMAN MINCOPI MINKOPI
　MINCOPIE
ANDESITE BONINITE TIMAZITE
ANDIRON DOG CHENET COBIRON
　FIREDOG HESSIAN HANDIRON
　LANDIRON
ANDORRA (LANGUAGE OF —)
　CATALAN
　(NATIVE OF —) ANDOSIAN
　(RIVER OF —) VALIRA
ANDRADITE APLOME GARNET
ANDROCONIUM STIGMA PLUMULE
ANDROID ROBOT AUTOMATON
ANDROMACHE (FATHER OF —)
　EETION
　(HUSBAND OF —) HECTOR HELENUS
　(SON OF —) PIELUS ASTYANAX
　MOLOSSUS PERGAMUS
ANDROMEDA (FATHER OF —)
　CEPHEUS
　(MOTHER OF —) CASSIOPEA
　(RESCUER OF —) PERSEUS

ANDROMEDE BIELID
ANECDOTE GAG TOY JOKE TALE
　YARN EVENT STORY SKETCH
　HAGGADA EXEMPLUM HAGGADAH
ANECDOTAL LITERARY
ANECHOIC DEAD
ANEMIA SURRA SURRAH ANAEMIA
　HYPAEMA HYPHEMA HYPHEMIA
　ISCHEMIA SPANEMIA
ANEMIC LOW PALE WEAK WATERY
　LIFELESS
ANEMONE LILY CRASS EMONY
　OPELET BOWBELLS SNOWDROP
ANENT ON RE ABOUT ANENST
　BESIDE TOWARD AGAINST OPPOSITE
ANESTHESIA BLOCK CORYL SPINAL
ANESTHETIC GAS ETHER ACOINE
　OBTUSE OPIATE COCAINE DULLING
　MENTHOL PARAFORM SEDATIVE
ANESTHETIZE FREEZE ETHERIZE
ANEW OVER AGAIN NEWLY AFRESH
　ITERUM NEWLINS NEWLINGS
　RECENTLY
ANFRACTUOUS SPIRAL BENDING
　SINUOUS WINDING TORTUOUS
ANGEL MAH DEVA EBUS ANGLE
　ARDOR ARIEL DAEVA DULIA NAKIR
　YAKSA ABDIEL ARIOCH BACKER
　BELIAL CHERUB MONKIR MUNKAR
　NEKKAR SERAPH SPIRIT UZZIEL
　YAKSHA ANGELET EGREGOR
　ISRAFEL RAPHAEL SPONSOR
　WATCHER ZADKIEL ZOPHIEL
　APOLLYON GUARDIAN ITHURIEL
　SUPERNAL
　(— OF DEATH) AZRAEL SAMMAEL
　(FALLEN —S) HELL
　(GUARDIAN —) YAKSA YAKSHA
　YAKSHI
　(RECORDING —) SIJIL SIJILL
　(PL.) HOST FRAVASHI SERAPHIM
ANGELFISH MONK MUNK ANGEL
　QUOTT SQUAT MONACH FLATFISH
　KINGSTON MONKFISH SQUATINA
ANGELIC SAINTLY BEATIFIC
　CHERUBIC HEAVENLY SERAPHIC
ANGELICA JELLICA
ANGELIN PACAY ANGELEEN
ANGER ARR IRE IRK VEX BILE BURN
　CRAB FELL FUME FURY GALL GRIM
　HUFF MOOD RAGE RILE ROIL RUFF
　TEEN TIFF ANNOY BIRSE GRAME
　GRIPE HATEL IRISH PIQUE SPONK
　SPUNK THRAW WRATH BOTHER
　CHOLER DANDER ENRAGE EXCITE
　GRIEVE MONKEY NETTLE OFFEND
　RANCOR SPLEEN TALENT TEMPER
　WARMTH BURNING DESPITE
　DUDGEON EMOTION INCENSE
　INFLAME PASSION PROVOKE
　STOMACH ACRIMONY DISTRESS
　EBENEZER IRRITATE VEXATION
ANGERED SORE AGRAMED PELTISH
　INCENSED
ANGICO CURUPAY
ANGINA PRUNELLA
ANGIOSPERM HARDWOOD
　METASPERM
ANGLE IN BOB DIP ELL OUT TEE

WRO CANT COIN COOK DRAW FISH
FORK HADE KEEN KNEE LEAD NOOK
PEAK SITE WICK ANCON ARRIS
AXIAL BEVEL BIGHT CHOIL COIGN
DRAFT DRIFT ELBOW FLEAM GROIN
GUISE INGLE PHASE POINT QUOIN
SLANT ALLURE ANGULE ASPECT
CANTON CORNEL CORNER DIRECT
ENGHLE EPAULE HADING LAGGEN
LAGGIN OCTANT SCHEME SQUARE
TORNUS ANGLIAN ANGULUS
AZIMUTH BASTION DRAUGHT
GIMMICK KNUCKLE PERIGON
RAVELIN SALIENT ARGUMENT
DECALAGE DIHEDRAL FISHHOOK
INTRIGUE SHOULDER
(— OF BEVEL) FLEAM FLEEM
(— OF BOWSPRIT) STEEVE
STEEVING
(— OF CLUB HEAD) LIE
(— OF EYELIDS) CANTHUS
(— OF HAT BRIM) BREAK
(— OF HIPBONE) HOOK
(— OF LEAF) AXIL
(— OF RAFTER) HEEL
(— OF TIMBER KNEE) BREECH
(DRIFT —) LEEWAY
(OBTUSE —) HEEL BULLNOSE
(ROOF —) HIP FASTIGIUM
(ROUND —) PERIGON
(SALIENT —) ARIS ARRIS
ANGLED CANTED NOOKED
ANGULATE
ANGLER MONK FRIAR THIEF SLIMER
LOPHLID RODSTER SPINNER
WIDEGAB WIDEGAP ALLMOUTH
FROGFISH MONKFISH PISCATOR
TOADFISH
ANGLESMITH SLABMAN
ANGLEWORM ESS WORM
FISHWORM
ANGLICAN EPISCOPAL
ANGLO CAUCASIAN

ANGOLA
CAPITAL: LUANDA
COIN: MACUTA MACUTE
DISTRICT: CABINDA
KINGDOM: BAKONGO
LANGUAGE: BANTU KIMBUNDU
MOUNTAIN: LOVITI
PLATEAU: PLANALTO
PORT: LOBITO LUANDA
RIVER: CONGO CUITO COANZA
  CUNENE KUNENE KWANGO
  KWANZA
TOWN: LOBITO LUANDA
  BENGUELA MOSSAMEDES
TRIBE: BANTU KIKONGO

ANGORA CAT GOAT ANGOLA RABBIT
ANGRILY ANGERLY IRATELY
FUMINGLY
ANGRY MAD ASHY EVIL GRIM GRUM
HIGH RILY ROID ROSY SORE WARM
WAXY WILD WRAW CROOK CROSS
GRAME HUFFY IRATE IROUS MOODY
RATTY RILEY SNAKY STUNT VEXED
WEMOD WROTH BIRSIT CHAFED

CROUSE FRENZY FUMING FUMOUS
HEATED IREFUL LOADED SHIRTY
SNAKEY STUFFY FRETFUL FURIOUS
HOPPING IRACUND PAINFUL
SNAKISH SPLEENY CHOLERIC
INFLAMED RIGOROUS SPITFIRE
TEMPERED VEHEMENT WREAKFUL
(BE —) STEAM
ANGRY-LOOKING THUNDERY
ANGUISH WOE ACHE HARM HURT
PAIN PANG RACK TRAY AGONY
ANGST ANGUS DOLOR GRIEF THROE
MISERY REGRET SORROW ANGOISE
ANGWICH REMORSE TORMENT
TORTURE DISTRESS
ANGUISHED GRIEFFUL
ANGULAR BONE BONY EDGY LEAN
SLIM THIN GAUNT SHARP ABRUPT
POINTED SCRAWNY CORNERED
(NOT —) SOFT
ANGULARITY EDGINESS
ANGUS FORFAR FORFARSHIRE
ANHYDRIDE LACTAM SULTAM
FULGIDE LACTIDE SULTONE
GLUCOSAN MANNITAN SORBITAN
ANHYDROUS DRY DESICCATED
ANI WITCH CUCKOO JEWBIRD
KEELBILL KEELBIRD TICKBIRD
ANIMADVERSION BLAME REMARK
CENSURE COMMENT REPROOF
WARNING MONITION REPROACH
ANIMAL (LOOK ALSO UNDER
SPECIFIC HEADINGS) DEER BEAST
BIPED BLACK BRUTE GRADE GROSS
LUSTY STORE STRAY BRUTAL
CARNAL DAPPLE DESPOT FLESHY
KICKER MAMMAL RODENT SILVAN
SORREL SPONGE SYLVAN BEASTIE
BREEDER CARRION CRITTER
SENSUAL BURROWER CREATURE
EMIGRANT ORGANISM
(— COLLECTION) LARDER
(— FOR MARKET) STOCKER
(— INHABITED BY SPIRIT) GUACA
HUACA
(— OF LITTLE VALUE) SCALAWAG
SKALAWAG
(— RESEMBLING MAN) HOMINOID
(— SHOT) KILL
(— WITH BLACK COAT AND
MARKINGS) PARSON
(— WITH DOCKED TAIL) CURTAL
(—S AS RENT) CAIN
(2-HORNED —) BICORN BICORNE
(BEEF —) BONER GRASSER
(BOVINE —) BOSS BRUTE
(BROKEN-DOWN —) CROCK
(CARNIVOROUS —) SARCOPHILE
(CASTRATED —) SEG SEGG SPAY
SPADO GELDING
(COLD-BLOODED —) ECTOTHERM
(CREATED —) BARAMIN
(DOMESTIC —) DOER SCRUB
BESTIAL FOLLOWER SCRUBBER
(DRAFT —) AVER AIVER
(EMACIATED —) FRAME SKELETON
(FABULOUS —) KYLIN BUNYIP
DRAGON ACEPHAL GRIFFIN GRIFFON
GRYPHON UNICORN SEMITAUR
(FEMALE —) HEN SHE LADY JENNY
SHEDER

(FERAL —) CIMAROON CIMARRON
CIMMARON
(FLEA-RIDDEN —) FLEABAG
(FOOTLESS —) APOD APODE
(FREAKISH —) FERLY FERLIE
(GRASSHOPPER-EATING —)
WHANGAM
(GRAY —) GRIZZLE
(GRAZING —) HERBAGER
(GREEDY —) GORB
(HORNED —) HORN REEM
(HYPOTHETICAL —) PROAVIS
(IMAGINARY —) CATAWAMPUS
(LOWER —) BEAST CREATURE
(LUSTY OR PLUMP —) BILCH BILSH
(MALE —) HE TOM BUCK BULL JACK
STAG JOHNNY BACHELOR
(MARINE —) LANCELET
(MATURE —) SENIOR
(MEAT —) CHOPPER
(MISCHIEVOUS —) ELF
(MYTHICAL —) HODAG KYLIN
MOONACK
(ODD —) SPLACKNUCK
(PACK —) HUNIA SUMPTER
(PET —) CADE
(PURSUED —S) GAME
(ROASTED —) BARBECUE
BARBEQUE
(SADDLE —) LOPER
(SCRAWNY —) SCRAG
(SHORN —) SHEAR
(SKINNY —) SCRAE
(SLUGGISH —) DRUMBLE
(SPOTTED —) CALICO
(STOCKY —) BLOCK
(STUNTED —) SHARGAR SHARGER
(THICKSET —) NUGGET
(TOTEM —) EPONYM
(UNBRANDED —) SLICK
(UNCASTRATED —) ENTIRE
(UNDERSIZED —) DURGAN DURGEN
(UNHOUSED —) OUTLER OUTLIER
(UNWEANED —) SUCKER
(WANDERING —) STRAY ESTRAY
(WARM-BLOODED —) ENDOTHERM
HAEMATHERM
(WATER —) AQUATIC AQUATILE
(WEAK —) DRAG DOWNER
(WILD —) SAVAGE WILDLING
(WORNOUT —) KANCKER
(WORTHLESS —) CARRION
(YOUNG —) HOG BIRD HOGG JOEY
SHOT STORE JUNIOR PULLUS
FATLING LITTLIN KINDLING LITTLING
SUCKLING YOUNGLET
(PL.) ZOA FAUNA NECTON NEKTON
ANIMALCULISM SPERMISM
ANIMALITY HOGGERY
ANIMA MUNDI WELTGEIST
ANIMATE ACT PEP FIRE MOVE PERK
STIR URGE ALIVE BRISK CHEER
DRIVE FLUSH IMBUE IMPEL LIGHT
LIVEN QUICK ROUSE VITAL AROUSE
BRIGHT ENSOUL EXCITE INCITE
INDUCE INFORM KINDLE LIVING
PROMPT SPIRIT VIVIFY ACTUATE
COMFORT ENLIVEN INSPIRE
QUICKEN ACTIVATE ENERGIZE
INSPIRIT VITALIZE

(NOT —) BRUTE
ANIMATED UP GAY VIF GLAD VIVE
ALIVE ANIME BRISK QUICK VITAL
VIVID ACTIVE ARDENT BLITHE
BRISKY LIVELY LIVING SPARKY
SPUNKY BUOYANT JOCULAR
STHENIC BOUNCING LIFESOME
SPIRITED VIGOROUS
ANIME COPAL ELEMI RESIN ROSIN
ANIMATO
ANIMIKEAN LAWSON
ANIMISM NATURISM
ANIMOSITY HATE PIQUE SPITE
ANIMUS ENMITY HATRED MALICE
RANCOR DISLIKE
ANIMUS MIND ONDE WILL EFFORT
ENMITY SPIRIT TEMPER ATTITUDE
ANISE ANET DILL CUMEN UMBEL
FENNEL SIKIMI SHIKIMI
ANKH TAU
ANKLE COOT CUIT HOCK QUIT
ANCLE QUEET TALUS WRIST
TARSUS SHACKLE
(COCKED —S) KNUCKLING
ANKLEBONE TALUS ASTRAGAL
ANKLET SHOE SOCK BANGLE
FETTER SHACKLE
ANLAGE INCEPT PROTON INITIAL
BLASTEMA
ANNALIST WRITER RECORDER
ANNALS NIHONGI REGISTER
ANNAM (ALSO SEE VIETNAM)
VIETNAM
(BOAT OF —) GAYYOU GAYDIANG
(MEASURE OF —) LY GON NGU QUO
SAO TAT PHAN THAT SHITA THUOC
TRUONG
(TOWN OF —) HUE VINH TOURANE
QUANGTRI
(WEIGHT OF —) CAN BINH DONG
ANNATTO OTTER URUCU ORLEAN
SALMON ACHIOTE ACHUETE
ANNOTTO ARNATTO ORLEANS
ANNEAL BAKE FUSE HEAT SMELT
TEMPER INFLAME TOUGHEN
GRAPHITE
ANNEALER TUBER HEATER
ANNEALING LIGHTING
ANNELID NAID WORM LUGWORM
SERPULA ANNULATE SANDWORM
SERPULAN
ANNEX ADD ELL LAY JOIN AFFIX
SEIZE UNITE ADJECT ANNECT
APPEND ATTACH FASTEN ACQUIRE
CONNECT FIXTURE POSTFIX
SUBJOIN ADDITION ANNEXURE
DOCUMENT
ANNIHILATE END OUT KILL RAZE
RUIN SLAY ABATE ANNUL ERASE
WRECK DELETE DEVOUR NOUGHT
QUENCH REDUCE ABOLISH
DESTROY EXPUNGE DECIMATE
DISCREAT UNCREATE
ANNIHILATION FANA NEGATION
ANNIVERSARY FETE MASS EMBER
FEAST ANNUAL JUBILEE YEARDAY
BIRTHDAY FESTIVAL YAHRZEIT
(100TH —) CENTENNIAL
(150TH —) SESQUICENTENNIAL

(200TH —) BIMILLENARY
BIMILLENIUM
(25TH —) SEMIJUBILEE
(50TH —) JUBILEE SEMICENTENNIAL
ANNONA ATIS ATTA ATEES
ANNOTATE EDIT NOTE STET GLOSS
BENOTE NOTIFY POSTIL REMARK
APOSTIL COMMENT EXPLAIN
FOOTNOTE
ANNOTATION APOSTIL COMMENT
SCHOLION SCHOLIUM
ANNOTATOR NOTIST
ANNOUNCE BID CRY BODE CALL
DEEM MAKE SHOW SING TELL BRUIT
CLAIM KNELL STATE VOICE ASSERT
BLAZON BROACH DENOTE HERALD
INFORM PREACH REPORT REVEAL
SIGNAL SPRING STEVEN DECLARE
DIVULGE FORERUN GAZETTE
PUBLISH SIGNIFY DENOUNCE
FORETELL INTIMATE PROCLAIM
RENOUNCE SENTENCE
ANNOUNCEMENT BID CRY HAT
BILL CALL LEAD ALARM BANCO
BANNS BLURB EDICT ALARUM
DECREE DICTUM NOTICE GAZETTE
SENSING BULLETIN CIRCULAR
DECISION
ANNOUNCER NEBO PAGE CRIER
EMCEE CALLER HERALD NUNCIO
GONGMAN GRINDER SPIELER
NUNCIATE SPRUIKER
ANNOY ARR BUG DUN EAT EGG GET
GIG HOX IRE IRK NAG NOY NYE TRY
VEX BAIT BORE BURN FASH FRET
FUSS GALL GRIG HALE HARM HAZE
HUFF NARK PAIN RILE ROIL CHAFE
CHASE CHEVY CHIVY DEVIL GRAMY
GRATE HARRY PEEVE PIQUE SPITE
STURT TEASE THORN UPSET WEARY
WORRY BADGER BOTHER CADDLE
CHIVEY CHIVVY EARWIG ENRAGE
GRAVEL HAGGLE HARASS HECKLE
HECTOR INFEST INJURE MOLEST
NEEDLE NETTLE OFFEND PESTER
POTTER RATTLE REHETE RUFFLE
TICKLE BEDEVIL DISTURB HOTFOOT
JACKSON TERRIFY TROUBLE
DISTRESS IRRITATE
ANNOYANCE VEX FASH PEST WEED
CROSS GRIEF LOATH SPITE STALL
THORN INSECT PESTER DISGUST
FASHERY NOYANCE TROUBLE
UMBRAGE FASHERIE FLEABITE
NOISANCE NUISANCE PINPRICK
ANNOYED SORE INSULTED
ANNOYING TARE NOYOUS DISEASY
HATEFUL IRKSOME NOISOME
TARSOME FASHIOUS FRETSOME
SPITEFUL TIRESOME
ANNOYINGLY CONFOUNDED
CONFOUNDEDLY
ANNUAL BOOK BUGLE PLANT
FLOWER YEARLY ANNUARY
BUGSEED BUGWEED ETESIAN
GIFTBOOK PERIODIC YEARBOOK
(OLD WORLD —) WELD
ANNUITY CENSO CONSOL INCOME
PENSION TONTINE

ANNUL TOL CASS NULL TOLL UNDO
VOID ADNUL AVOID BLANK ELIDE
ERASE QUASH REMIT RETEX UNLAW
CANCEL FRIVOL NEGATE RECALL
REPEAL REVERT REVOKE UNLIVE
VACATE ABOLISH CASHIER CASSARE
CASSATE DESTROY NULLIFY
RESCIND RETRACT REVERSE
ABROGATE ARROGATE DEROGATE
DISANNUL DISSOLVE IMBECILE
OVERRULE
ANNULAR BANDED CYCLIC RINGED
ANNULATE CINGULAR CIRCULAR
ANNULARLY RINGWISE
ANNULET RING RIDGE FILLET
ANNULUS MOLDING
ANNULMENT UNDOING
ANNULUS RING ANNULE COLLAR
GYROMA INDUSIUM
ANNUNCIATION MARYMASS
ANNUNCIATOR TELLER INDICATOR
ANOA BUFFALO SAPIUTAN
ANODE PLATE ZINCOID
ANODIC ASCENDING
ANODYNE BALM ACOPON OPIATE
REMEDY EUGENOL SOOTHER
NARCOTIC SEDATIVE
ANOINT FAT OIL RUB BALM BEAT
CERE NARD ANELE ANOIL CREAM
CROWN ENOIL LATCH NUNCT
PRUNE SALVE SMEAR SMERL
CHRISM GREASE INUNCT SPREAD
THRASH MOISTEN UNGUENT
ANOINTMENT CHRISMATORY
ANOMALOUS ODD DIFFORM
STRANGE UNUSUAL ABERRANT
ABNORMAL ATYPICAL PECULIAR
ANOMALY CREEPER CYCLOPY
EPILOIA CYCLOPIA
ANON NAN ANEW ONCE SOON AGAIN
LATER AFRESH BEDEEN BEDENE
THENCE SHORTLY
ANONYMITY NOBODYNESS
ANONYMOUS UNKNOWN NAMELESS
UNAVOWED UNSIGNED
ANOPLURA PARASITA PEDICULINA
ANOTHER NEW THAT ALIAS FRESH
SECOND TIDDER TOTHER ANITHER
FURTHER
ANOXIA ASPHYXIA
ANSWER DO IT SAY SIT ECHO MEET
PLEA SUIT ATONE AVAIL COMES
COVER JAWAB REACT REPLY SERVE
LETTER REJOIN RESULT RETORT
RETURN RIPOST COUNTER DEFENCE
DEFENSE FULFILL RESPOND
SATISFY ANTIPHON COMEBACK
PLEADING REBUTTAL REPARTEE
RESPONSE SOLUTION
(— BACK) CHOP
(— FOR) FORM VANG
(— IN FUGUE) COMES
(— THE PURPOSE) DO FIT SUIT
AVAIL SERVE
(DECISIVE —) SOCKDOLAGER
SOCKDOLOGER
(LEGAL —) DUPLY
ANSWERABLE EQUAL LIABLE
FITTING ADEQUATE AMENABLE

ANSWERER USHABTI
ANT ANAI ANAY ANER ATTA GYNE
MIRE AMPTE EMMET KELEP MAXIM
MINIM NURSE SIAFU SLAVE AMAZON
DRIVER ERGATE NEUTER WORKER
BULLDOG FORAGER FORMICE
OUVRIER PISMIRE PISSANT PONERID
REPLETE SOLDIER TERMITE
ACULEATA DORYLINE FORMICID
GYNECOID HONEYPOT MICRANER
MYRMICID TAPINOMA
(— LION) DOODLEBUG
(— SHRIKE) BATARA
(— STUDY) MYRMECOLOGY
(— THRUSH) PITTA
(— TREE) WORMIGO
(WORKER —) ERGATE
ANTA PIER PARASTAS PEDESTAL
PILASTER
ANTACID SATURANT
ANTAGONISM WAR ANIMUS ENMITY
QUARREL AVERSION CONFLICT
(IN —) COUNTER
ANTAGONIST FOE ENEMY PARTY
RIVAL FOEMAN BATTLER WARRIOR
COPEMATE OPPONENT OPPOSITE
WRANGLER
ANTAGONISTIC ADVERSE COUNTER
HOSTILE ANTERGIC CONTRARY
INIMICAL OPPONENT OPPOSITE
(— TO GROWTH) ANTIBLASTIC
(NOT —) SYMPATHETIC
ANTAGONIZE CONTEST
ANT BEAR BEAR ERDVARK
AARDVARK ANTEATER EDENTATE
TAMANOIR
ANTE PAY STAKE
ANTEATER TAPIR NUMBAT ECHIDNA
TAMANDU AARDVARK AARDWOLF
DASYURID EDENTATE PANGOLIN
TAMANDUA TAMANOIR
ANTEBRACHIUM CUBIT CUBITAL
CUBITUS FOREARM
ANTECEDENT FORE CAUSE PRIOR
FORMER REASON WHENCE PREMISE
ANTERIOR PREVIOUS
(— OF CANON) GUIDA
ANTECHAMBER LIWAN
ANTEDATE PRECEDE PREDATE
FOREDATE
ANTEDATED FORETIMED
ANTELOPE GNU KID KOB RAM SUS
ASTE BISA BUCK DODA DUST GUIB
IBEX KOBA KUDU ORYX PUKU ROAN
SUNI TOPI TORA ADDAX BAIRA
BEIRA BEISA BEKRA BOHOR BONGO
BOVID BUBAL CHIRU ELAND GORAL
GUIBA IPETE LICHI NAGOR NYALA
ORIBI PEELE PERON SABLE SAIGA
SASIN SEROW TAKIN YAKIN
BAGWYN BHOKRA BUBALE CABREE
CABRET CABRIE CABRIT CHOUKA
DUIKER DUYKER DZERAN DZEREN
DZERIN DZERON GOORAL GRIMME
HEROLA IMPALA INYALA KOODOO
LECHWE LELWEL NAKONG NILGAI
NILGAU PALLAH POOKOO RHEBOK
ALGAZEL BLAUBOK BLESBOK
BUBALIS CHAMOIS CHIKARA

DEFASSA GAZELLE GEMSBOK
GERENUK GREENUK GRYSBOK
MADOQUA REDBUCK RHEEBOK
SASSABY STEMBOK AGACELLA
BLEEKBOK BLESBUCK BONTEBOK
BOSCHBOK BUSHBUCK KORRIGUM
LEUCORYX REEDBUCK STEENBOK
(YOUNG —) KID LAMB
ANTENNA DISH HORN LOOP PALP
TIER YAGI AERIAL DIPOLE FEELER
TACTOR DOUBLET WHISKER
PARABOLA RADIATOR
ANTENNATA INSECTA
ANTERIOR FORNE FRONT PRIOR
ATLOID BEFORE FORMER ANTICUS
PRORSAL VENTRAL ATLANTAL
INFERIOR PREVIOUS
ANTEROOM HALL FOYER LOBBY
ENTRANCE
ANTEWAR PREBELLUM
ANTHELION HALO NIMBUS ANTISUN
AUREOLE
ANTHELMINTIC CUNIC BRAYERA
EMBELIN
ANTHEM HYMN SONG AGNUS MOTET
PSALM INTROIT RESPOND
ASPERGES
(JAPANESE —) KIMIGAYO
ANTHER TIP CHIVE THECA
ANTHESIS BLOOM BLOSSOM
ANTHILL BANK TUMP
ANTHOCYANIN BETANIN PUNICIN
VIOLANIN
ANTHOLOGIST RHAPSODE
RHAPSODIST
ANTHOLOGY ANA POSY ALBUM
SYLVA CORPUS READER GARLAND
SYNTAGMA
ANTHOZOAN CORAL POLYP
ANEMONE GULINULA
ANTHRACONITE STINKSTONE
SWINESTONE
ANTHRAX CHARBON BLACKLEG
ANTHROPOLOGIST TOTEMIST
CULTURALIST
ANTHROPOPHAGITE CANNIBAL
ANTIAIRCRAFT ARCHIE
ANTIBALLOONER SEPARATOR
ANTIBIOTIC BIOTIC ABIOTIC
HUMULON CIRCULIN CITRININ
CLAVACIN CLAVATIN FRADICIN
HUMULONE NYSTATIN SUBTILIN
ANTIBODY REAGIN BLOCKER
GLUTININ
ANTIC TOY DIDO FOOL WILD CAPER
CLOWN COMIC DROLL MERRY
PRANK STUNT GAMBOL BUFFOON
CAPRICE GAMBADE GAMBADO
ANTICIPATE BALK BEAT HOPE JUMP
WISH ALLOT AUGUR AWAIT DREAD
SENSE STALL DIVINE EXPECT
THWART DEVANCE FORERUN
FORESEE OBVIATE PORTEND
PREPARE PREVENE PREVENT
PROPOSE RESPECT SUPPOSE
ANTEDATE FORECAST FOREFEEL
FORETAKE PROSPECT
ANTICIPATION ODIUM AUGURY
OPINION PROSPECT

ANTICLIMAX BATHOS
ANTICLINE ARCH DOME ISOCLINE
OVERFOLD
ANTICYCLONE HIGH
ANTIDOTE GUACO BEZOAR EMETIC
GALENA REMEDY THERIAC
DELETERY THERIACA
ANTIGEN N LYSOGEN BIOLOGIC
ANTIGONE (BROTHER OF —)
POLYNICES
(FATHER OF —) OEDIPUS
(MOTHER OF —) JOCASTA
ANTIGORITE SERPENTINE
ANTIMASK ANTIC ANTICK
ANTIMONIAL STIBIAL
ANTIMONY SB KOHL STIBIUM
ANTIMONY SULFIDE SURMA
SOORMA
ANTINOMIAN FIDUCIARY
ANTIOXIDANT SESAMOL
ANTIPATHY HATE ODIUM ENMITY
NAUSEA RANCOR DISGUST DISLIKE
AVERSION DISTASTE DYSPATHY
LOATHING
ANTIPHON GRADUAL GRADUALE
ANTIPHONALLY CHOIRWISE
ANTHEMWISE
ANTIPHONARY LEDGER
ANTIPODAL ANTARCTIC
ANTIPYRETIC SALOL MALARIN
THALLIN THALLINE
ANTIQUARY ARCHAIST ANTIQUARIAN
ANTIQUATED OLD AGED FUSTY
MOSSY PASSE FOSSIL VOIDED
ANCIENT ARCHAIC FOGYISH
NOACHIAN OBSOLETE OUTDATED
OUTMODED TIMEWORN
ANTIQUE ANTIC RELIC SIRUP SYRUP
VIRTU ANTICK NOETIC ANCIENT
NOACHIC NOACHIAN OUTMODED
ANTIQUITY ELD OLD PAST YORE
RELIC OLDNESS ANCIENCE
ANCIENCY
(PL.) ARCHEOLOGY ARCHAEOLOGY
ANTIRED WHITE
ANTI-SEMITISM JUDOPHOBIA
ANTISEPTIC CAVA EGOL KAVA SALT
AMIDO AMINE EUPAD EUSOL IODOL
SALOL AMADOL IATROL IODINE
KRELOS PHENOL PICROL ALCOHOL
ALUMNOL ARBUTIN ASEPTIC
COLYTIC LORETIN STERILE TACHIOL
TEUCRIN THALLIN CREOSOTE
ICHTHYOL KAVAKAVA METAPHEN
TEREBENE THALLINE
ANTISOCIAL HOSTILE ANARCHIST
ANTISPASMODIC KELLIN SAMBUL
SUMBAL SUMBUL KHELLIN
ANTISTROPHE REVERT
COUNTERTURN
ANTITHESIS AND CONTRAST
ANTITOXIN SERUM BIOLOGIC
ANTIVIVISECTIONIST BESTIARIAN
ANTLER DAG HORN KNOB RIAL TRAY
DAGUE RIGHT ROYAL SHOOT SPIKE
BOSSET SHOVEL TROCHE SPELLER
DEERHORN TROCHING
(— POINT) TROCHING
(PL.) HEAD ATTIRE

ANT LION DOODLEBUG
ANTSHRIKE BATARA
ANT THRUSH PITTA
ANT TREE HORMIGO
ANUS ASS ARSE BUNG VENT SIEGE
ANVIL BLOCK INCUS SNARL STAKE
  STITH TEEST STETHY STITHY
  ANFEELD BICKERN BEAKIRON
  (— SUPPORT) STOCK
  (MINIATURE —) STAKE STUMP
ANXIETY HOW CARE FEAR FRAY
  PAIN ALARM ANGOR DOUBT DREAD
  PANIC WORRY KIAUGH PUCKER
  ANGUISH CAUTION CHAGRIN
  CONCERN SCRUPLE TENSION
  THOUGHT TROUBLE DISQUIET
  SUSPENSE
ANXIOUS AGOG BUSY FOND TOEY
  EAGER FIRST UPSET AFRAID
  UNEASY CARKING EARNFUL
  FORWARD TIDIOSE UNQUIET
  DESIROUS RESTLESS THOUGHTY
  WATCHFUL
ANY A AN AY AIR ALL ARY ONI ONY
  AIRY EVER PART SOME WHAT
  (— WHATEVER) ALL
ANYBODY ANY ONE ANYONE
  SOMEONE
ANYHOW HOW NOWAY ALWAYS
  ANYWAY
ANYTHING THAT AUGHT OUGHT
ANYONE HE MAN ANYBODY
ANYWAY NOHOW ALWAYS
ANYWHERE EINWER OWHERE
  UBIQUE ANYPLACE
ANYWISE ANYHOW ANYWAY
  ANYWAYS
AOUDAD ARUI UDAD AUDAD SHEEP
  CHAMOIS
APACE FAST QUICK QUICKLY
  RAPIDLY SPEEDILY
APACHE YUMA PADUCA CIBECUE
  VAQUERO QUERECHO
APAGOGE ABDUCTION
APAP EPIPHI
APAR APARA BOLITA MATACO
APART BY OFF AWAY BOUT ELSE
  ALONE ALOOF AROOM ASIDE RIVEN
  SOLUS SPLIT YTWYN ABREID
  ATWAIN LONELY SUNDRY ASUNDER
  ENISLED REMOVED SEVERAL
  SEVERED SEPARATE
  (WIDE —) APAR
  (WIDELY —) ABROAD
APARTMENT BUT WON DIGS FLAT
  HALL ROOM STEW WENE WONE
  WOON ABODE BOWER OECUS ORIEL
  ROOMS SALON SOLAR SUITE
  ANDRON CLOSET DECKER DINGLE
  DUPLEX GROTTO LYCEUM SALOON
  SINGLE SOLLAR SPENCE STANZA
  BUTTERY CHAMBER COCKPIT
  GALLERY MANSION PRIVACY
  BUILDING EPHEBEUM SHOWROOM
  SOLARIUM TENEMENT THALAMUS
  (— FOR IDOL) TING
  (— IN CASTLE) BOWER
  (— OF WARSHIP) COCKPIT
  (OUTER —) BUT

(PRIVATE —) MAHAL
(RENTED —) LET
(PL.) GYNAECEUM
APATHETIC CALM COLD COOL DEAD
  DOWF DULL BLASE DOWFF INERT
  STOIC GLASSY SUPINE TORPID
  ADENOID PASSIVE UNMOVED
  LISTLESS SLUGGISH
APATHY SLOTH ACEDIA CAFARD
  PHLEGM TORPOR LANGUOR
  DOLDRUMS DULLNESS LETHARGY
  OMISSION STOICISM
APATITE IJOLITE MOROXITE
APAYAO ISNEG
APE KRA LAR PAN BOOR COPY DUPE
  FOOL MAHA MIME MOCK SHAM
  BEROK CLOWN MAGOT MIMIC
  ORANG PONGO PYGMY APELET
  BABOON GELADA GIBBON LANGUR
  MARTEN MARTIN MONKEY OURANG
  PARROT PONGID SIMIAN SIMIID
  BUFFOON COPYCAT EMULATE
  GORILLA IMITATE PORTRAY
  PRIMATE SIAMANG DURUKULI
  IMITATOR MANTEGAR SIMULATE
  (— STUDY) PITHECOLOGY
APEAK VERTICAL
APEIRON MATTER
APER BOAR MIME SNOB CLOWN
  MOCKER BUFFOON COPYCAT
APERCU DIGEST GLANCE PRECIS
  SKETCH INSIGHT OUTLINE
APERIENT LAX OPENER
APERIODIC DEADBEAT
APERITIF WHET CONZANO
  DUBONNET
APERTURE F EYE GAP OPE VUE
  BOLE BORE HOLE LEAK PASS PORE
  RIMA SLIT SLOT VENT BREAK
  CHASM CLEFT CRACK LIGHT MOUTH
  PUPIL STOMA CUTOUT HIATUS
  KEYWAY LOUVER WINDOW FISSURE
  KEYHOLE OPENING ORIFICE
  OSTIOLE PINHOLE SWALLOW
  TROMPIL APERTION FENESTRA
  LOOPHOLE OVERTURE SPIRACLE
APEX EPI PIN TIP TOP ACME AUGE
  CONE CUSP NOON PEAK RUFF
  CREST HIGHT PITCH POINT SPIRE
  APOGEE CLIMAX CRISIS CUPULA
  GENION HEIGHT SUMMIT TITTLE
  VERTEX ZENITH CACUMEN EVEREST
  PAPILLA PUNCTUM PINNACLE
  (— OF HELMET) CREST
APHAREUS (FATHER OF —)
  PERIERES
  (SON OF —) IDAS LYNCEUS
APHASIA ALALIA ALEXIA JARGON
  APHEMIA
APHID APHIS LOUSE APTERA BLIGHT
  COLLIER DIMERAN MIGRANS
  PUCERON BLACKFLY GREENFLY
  GYNOPARA HOMOPTER
APHORISM SAW ADAGE AXIOM
  GNOME MAXIM MOTTO SUTRA
  SUTTA DICTUM SAYING WISDOM
  EPIGRAM PRECEPT PROVERB
  APOTHEGM PISHOGUE
APHORISTIC GNOMIC

APHRODISIAC DEWTRY DAMIANA
  VENEREAL
APHRODITE VENUS CYPRIS URANIA
  ANTHEIA MYLITTA CYTHEREA
  PANDEMOS
  (FATHER OF —) JUPITER
  (HUSBAND OF —) VULCAN
  (MOTHER OF —) DIONE
  (SON OF —) EROS CUPID AENEAS
APIARIST SKEPPIST
APIARY HIVE SKEP BEEYARD
  BEEHOUSE
APICULTURE BEEKEEPING
APIECE UP ALL PER EACH SERIATIM
APIKORES BECORESH
APIO ARRACACH ARRACACHA
APIOS SOIA SOJA GLYCINE
APIS HAPI
APISH SILLY FOPPISH AFFECTED
APITONG BAGAC HAPITON KERUING
APIUM UMBEL
APLITE HAPLITE
APLOMB TACT NERVE POISE SURETY
  COOLNESS
APOCALYPSE SHOWING
  REVELATION
APOCRISIARY RESPONSAL
APOCRYPHAL SHAM FALSE UNREAL
  DOUBTFUL FABULOUS FICTIOUS
APODAL FOOTLESS
APOGEE ACME APEX AUGE PEAK
  CLIMAX ZENITH
APOGON AMIA CARDINAL
APOLLO SUN DELIUS AGYIEUS
  APOLLON LYKEIOS PATROUS
  PHOEBUS PYTHIUS CYNTHIUS
  PYTHAEUS
  (FATHER OF —) ZEUS JUPITER
  (MOTHER OF —) LETO LATONA
  (SISTER OF —) DIANA ARTEMIS
APOLLYON DEVIL SATAN ABADDON
APOLOGETIC SORRY
APOLOGUE MYTH FABLE STORY
  APOLOGY PARABLE ALLEGORY
APOLOGY PLEA ALIBI AMENDS
  EXCUSE PARDON REGRET SCRUPLE
  APOLOGIA
APOPHYGE SCAPE ESCAPE
APOPLEXY ESCA SHOCK STROKE
  POPLESIE
APOSTASY FALL LAPSE
APOSTATE RAT LAPSED CONVERT
  HERETIC PERVERT SECEDER
  DESERTER DISLOYAL RECREANT
  RENEGADE TURNCOAT
APOSTLE ESCAPE TEACHER
  DISCIPLE FOLLOWER PREACHER
  (BIBLICAL —) JOHN JUDE LEVI PAUL
  DENIS JAMES JUDAS PETER SIMON
  ANDREW PHILIP THOMAS DIDYMUS
  MATTHEW BARNABAS MATTHIAS
APOSTLE BIRD CATBIRD
APOSTROPHE TURNWAY TURNTALE
APOTHECARY CHEMIC SPICER
  CHEMICK DRUGGIST
APOTHECIUM CUP PELTA TRICA
  SHIELD ARDELLA LIRELLA PATELLA
APOTHEGM SAW DICT ADAGE AXIOM
  GNOME MAXIM SUTRA DICTUM

SAYING SUTTAH PROVERB
APHORISM SENTENCE
APOTHEOSIS DEIFICATION
CONSECRATION
APOTHEOSIZE DEIFY EXALT
ELEVATE GLORIFY CANONIZE
APPALL STUN APPAL DAUNT SHOCK
DISMAY REDUCE REVOLT WEAKEN
ASTOUND DEPRESS DISGUST
DISMISS HORRIFY TERRIFY
AFFRIGHT ASTONISH ENFEEBLE
FRIGHTEN OVERCOME
APPALLING AWFUL AWESOME
FEARFUL TERRIBLE TERRIFIC
APPANAGE GRANT ADJUNCT
APANAGE
APPARATUS BOX GUN LOG SET
ADON DRAG ETNA FAKE GEAR GRIP
HECK HELM LAMP LIFT STOW TIRE
TOOL BURET GANCH HOIST HORSE
LEECH RELAY SCUBA SHEAR SIREN
SONAR STILL STOVE SWING BUDDLE
BUFFER COILER COOKER DEVICE
DINGUS ENGINE FEEDER FILTER
FOGGER GADGET GEYSER GRAITH
LADDER LIFTER MILKER ORRERY
OUTFIT REFLUX SEESAW SHEARS
SMOKER SMUDGE TACKLE TIPPLE
TREMIE TROMPE AERATOR ALEMBIC
APPAREL AUTOMAT BAGGAGE
BALANCE BASCULE BURETTE
COVEYER DERRICK ECHELON
FURNACE GASOGEN GRILLER
HOISTER INHALER ISOTRON
MACHINE MEGAFOG PINCERS
PRESSER SOXHLET SPRAYER
STIRRER TELEPIX TREMOLO
TRIMMER UTENSIL AGITATOR
AQUALUNG BLOWDOWN CALUTRON
CONVEYOR CRYOSTAT DIALYZER
DIAPHOTE DIGESTER DRENCHER
DUMBBELL EOLIPILE EQUIPAGE
ERGOSTAT GASIFIER GAZOGENE
INJECTOR ISOSCOPE JACQUARD
OSMOGENE OZONISER PULMOTOR
PURIFIER RECORDER REDUCTOR
REHEATER SCRUBBER SOFTENER
STRIPPER
(— **IN STOMACH OF LOBSTER**) LADY
(**SEGMENTAL** —) BRAINSTEM
APPAREL DECK FARE GARB GEAR
ROBE SECT TIRE WEAR WEDE
ADORN ARRAY CLOTH DRESS EQUIP
HABIT TUNIC ATTIRE CLOTHE
GRAITH OUTFIT PARURE ROBING
CLOBBER COSTUME FURNISH
GARMENT HARNESS PREPARE
RAIMENT VESTURE CLOTHING
FOOTWEAR HEADWEAR WARDROBE
(**MILITARY** —) WARENTMENT
(**RICH** —) ARRAY
APPARENT OPEN BREEM BREME
CLEAR OVERT PLAIN FORMAL
PARENT PATENT PHANIC CERTAIN
EVIDENT GLARING OBVIOUS
SEEMING SHALLOW VISIBLE
DISTINCT ILLUSORY MANIFEST
PALPABLE PROBABLE SEMBLANT
APPARITION HUE HANT SHOW

DREAM FANCY FETCH GHOST
HAUNT IMAGE LARVA PHASM SHADE
SHAPE SPOOK ASPECT DOUBLE
IDOLUM SOWLTH SPIRIT SPRITE
STOUND SWARTH TAISCH THURSE
VISION WRAITH DISPLAY EIDOLON
FANTASY FEATURE PHANTOM
SPECTER SPECTRE EPIPHANY
ILLUSION PHANTASM PRESENCE
REVENANT SPECTRUM
APPARITOR BEADLE PARURE
PARITOR SUMMONER
APPEAL ASK BEG BID CRY CALL
CASE PLEA SEEK SUIT APPLY
CHARM CLEPE REFER SPEAK
ACCUSE ADJURE AVOUCH INVOKE
PRAYER SUMMON ADDRESS
CONJURE ENTREAT IMPLORE
REQUEST SOLICIT APPROACH
ENTREATY PETITION
(— **TO**) APPLY AVOUCH INVOKE
ARRAIGN
(**SEX** —) IT
APPEALING CUTE NICE CATCHY
CLEVER CUNNING SUGARED
PLEASANT
APPEAR BID CAR EYE GET COME
DAWN FARE LOOK LOOM MAKE
MEET PEER REAR RISE SEEM WALK
ARISE ENTER ISSUE KITHE KYTHE
OCCUR SOUND THINK ARRIVE
BESEEM EMERGE INFORM REGARD
SPRING BLOSSOM COMPEAR
DEVELOP RESEMBLE
(— **AND DISAPPEAR**) COOK
(— **BRIEFLY**) GLINT
(— **DIRECTLY BEFORE**) AFFRONT
(— **SUDDENLY**) BURST
(— **UNEXPECTEDLY**) BLOOM IRRUPT
APPEARANCE AIR CUT HUE CAST
FARE FORM GARB IDEA LATE LEEN
LOOK MIEN SHOW VIEW BLUSH
COLOR EIDOS FAVOR FRONT GUISE
HABIT PHASE PHASM SHAPE SIGHT
SOUND SPICE ASPECT EFFECT
FACIES FAVOUR MANNER OBJECT
OSTENT REGARD VISAGE ARRIVAL
DISPLAY FARRAND FASHION
FEATURE GLIMPSE RESPECT
SHOWING SPECIES ARTEFACT
ARTIFACT EPIPHANY ILLUSION
LIKENESS PRESENCE PRETENSE
(— **OF LIGHT ON HAIR**) HAG
(**CLOUDED** —) HAZE CHILL
(**CONSPICUOUS** —) FIGURE
(**DISTINCTIVE** —) AURA
(**FIRST** —) DAWN DEBUT SPRING
(**IMPOVERISHED** —) BEGGARY
(**MERE** —) INTENTIONAL
(**MOCK** —) SIMULACRUM
(**MOTTLED** —) ROE DAPPLE
(**MOTTLED SKY** —) BLINK
(**OUTWARD** —) FACE SEEM SHOW
APPAREL BALLOON SEEMING
SURFACE
(**PERSONAL** —) PRESENCE
(**STRIPED** —) ROE
(**SUPERNATURAL** —) APPARITION
(**SURFACE** —) TOUR BLOOM

(**UNGAINLY** —) ANGULARITY
(**VAGUE** —) BLUR
APPEASE LAY PAY CALM EASE
HUSH SATE ALLAY ALONE ATONE
MEASE PEACE PEASE QUIET SLAKE
STILL DEFRAY GENTLE MEEKEN
MODIFY PACIFY PLEASE SOFTEN
SOOTHE ASSUAGE CONTENT
DULCIFY GRATIFY MOLLIFY PLACATE
SATISFY STICKLE SUFFICE SWEETEN
MITIGATE
(— **APPETITE**) STAY
APPEASEMENT MUNICHISM
APPELLATION NAME TERM GODDY
STYLE TITLE APPEAL CALLING
EPITHET GOODMAN SURNAME
COGNOMEN METRONYM NICKNAME
APPEND ADD PIN TAG CLIP HANG
JOIN TACK AFFIX ANNEX ADJOIN
ATTACH FASTEN AUGMENT SUBJOIN
APPENDAGE ARM AWN FIN LEG TAB
TAG ARIL BARB CAUD FLAP HOOK
HORN LIMB LOBE SPUR TAIL AFFIX
BEARD CAUDA CERAS EXITE RIDER
SCALE TROLL WHISK CERCUS
CIRRUS CORONA ELATER ENDITE
LAGENA LIGULE PALPUS PAPPUS
STIPEL STYLET SUFFIX UROPOD
ADJUNCT ANTENNA AURICLE
CODICIL EARLOBE EMBLAST
FIXTURE FURCULA GONOPOD
HOUSING MALELLA PENDANT
STIPULE SWIMMER THIMBLE
TRAILER ADDITION ADHERENT
ASCIDIUM BRACHIUM EMPODIUM
FILAMENT GNATHITE PEDIPALP
PENDICLE PHYLLOID PREDELLA
RHABDITE SYNTROPE
(— **ON MOCCASIN**) TRAILER
(**EAR-SHAPED** —) AURICLE
(PL.) ADNEXA ANNEXA FORCEPS
APPENDIX EKE ANNEX LABEL
APPEND VERMIX AURICLE CODICIL
PENDANT ADDENDUM AURICULA
EPILOGUE
APPERTAIN LIE FALL REFER
BELONG RELATE CONCERN PERTAIN
APPETITE MAW YEN LUST PICA
TUCK URGE WILL ZEST BELLY
BLOOD GORGE GREED GUSTO
TASTE TWIST BULIMY DESIRE
FAMINE GENIUS GODOWN HUNGER
LIKING OREXIS RELISH STROKE
TALENT BULIMIA CRAVING EDACITY
LONGING PASSION STOMACH
SWALLOW WANTING CUPIDITY
FONDNESS GULOSITY TENDENCY
(— **LOSS**) ANOREXIA
(**ANIMAL** —) BLOOD
(**CANINE** —) PHAGEDENA
(**EXCESSIVE** —) GULOSITY
POLYPHAGIA
APPETIZER WET WHET SAUCE
CANAPE RELISH SAVORY CEVICHE
SASHIMI APERITIF COCKTAIL
DUBONNET
APPETIZING NICE GUSTY SAVORY
GUSTFUL GUSTABLE
APPLAUD CLAP LAUD ROOT RUFF

CHEER EXTOL HUZZA PRAISE
ACCLAIM APPROVE COMMENT
ENDORSE HOSANNA PLAUDIT
APPLAUSE CLAP HAND BRAVO
CHEER ECLAT HUZZA SALVO
HURRAH PRAISE ACCLAIM OVATION
CLAPPING
APPLE PIP CRAB OHIA POME COPEI
JAMBO BEEFIN BIFFIN CODLIN
DOUCIN ESOPUS GOLDIN KARELA
KAVIKA MACUPA MAKOPA PIPPIN
PUFFIN RENNET RUSSET BALDWIN
BEAUFIN CODLING COSTARD
FAMEUSE GOLDING PEELING
POMEROY RAMBURE RIBSTON
WAGENER WEALTHY WINESAP
AMPALAYA COCCAGEE CORTLAND
GREENING JONATHAN MCINTOSH
NONESUCH PARADISE PEARMAIN
POMANDER POROPORO QUEENING
REINETTE ROSACEAN WHITSOUR
(— OF PERU) JIMSON JIMPSON
SHOOFLY
(BITTER —) COLOCYNTH
(CRAB —) CRAB SCRAB WHARRE
POWITCH
(EMU —) COLANE
(GOLDEN —) BEL BAEL
(LIKE AN —) POMACEOUS
(PEELED —) DUMPLING
(SHRIVELED —) CRUMPLING
(SLICED DRIED —S) SNITS SNITZ
SCHNITZ
(SMALL —) CODLIN CODLING
(SMALL —S) GRIGGLES
(THORN —) MAD METEL
APPLEBERRY DUMPLING
APPLEJOHN DEUSAN DEUZAN
APPLE-POLISH BROWNNOSE
APPLIANCE GEAR GRAB IRON TOOL
BRACE CLAMP DEVIL FLIER FLYER
GLODE SHADE BONNET BREWER
DEVICE ENGINE FABRIC GADGET
GAITER JUICER SPLINT CHARGER
MACHINE SCRAPER STOPPER
UTENSIL BALANCER DEVIATOR
APPLICABLE APT FIT MEET PROPER
USEFUL FITTING PLIABLE APPOSITE
RELATIVE RELEVANT SUITABLE
(UNIVERSALLY —) CATHOLIC
(WIDELY —) BROAD
APPLICANT PROSPECT
APPLICATION USE DAUB FORM
BLANK TOPIC APPEAL EFFORT
ADDRESS EPITHEM REQUEST
EPITHEME LENITIVE PETITION
PRACTICE SEDULITY
(— OF KNOWLEDGE) PRACTICE
PRACTISE
(— TO WRONG PURPOSE) ABUSE
(MEDICINAL —) PLASTER DRESSING
FRONTING LENITIVE
(MENTAL —) INTENTION
APPLICATOR COLPOSTAT
APPLIED (CLOSELY —) ACCUMBENT
APPLIQUE DAG DAGGE ATTACH
DESIGN ORNAMENT
APPLY ASK LAY PLY PUT RUB SET
USE BEAR BEND CLAP DAUB GIVE

HOLD MOVE SEEK TOIL TURN WORK
ADAPT GRIND IMPLY LABOR LIKEN
REFER SMEAR ADDICT APPEAL
APPOSE BESTOW BETAKE BUCKLE
COMPLY DEVOTE DIRECT EMPLOY
EXTEND RESORT ADHIBIT COMPARE
CONFORM IMPRESS OVERLAY
PERTAIN REQUEST SOLICIT UTILIZE
DEDICATE DISPENSE MINISTER
PETITION
(— BRAKE) BUR
(— COSMETICS) DO POP
(— GRAPHITE) BLACKLEAD
(— GREASE) ARM
(— HOT CLOTHS) FOMENT
(— IMPROPERLY) ABUSE
(— ONESELF) ATTEND INTEND
MUCKLE
(— PIGMENT) DRAG
(— TO) CONSULT CONTACT
APPOGGIATURA BACKFALL
ACCIACCATURA
(DOUBLE —) FALL
APPOINT ARM FIX SET CALL DECK
GIVE MAKE NAME ALLOT ARRAY
AWARD CREST DIGHT ELECT ENACT
EQUIP INSET PITCH PLACE POINT
SHAPE SLATE ASSIGN ASSIZE
ATTACH CREATE DECREE DEPUTE
DETAIL DEVISE DIRECT ENTAIL
ORDAIN OUTFIT SETTLE STEVEN
TAILYE ARRAIGN CONFIRM DESTINE
DISPOSE FURNISH GAZETTE
RESOLVE TAILZIE DELEGATE
DEPUTIZE INDICATE NOMINATE
ORDINATE
(— A CLERIC) COLLATE
(— BEFOREHAND) STALL
APPOINTEE PLACEMAN
APPOINTMENT SET DATE BERTH
ORDER TRYST BILLET OFFICE
STEVEN COMMAND STATION
CREATION DELEGACY POSITION
(— OF HEIR) INSTITUTION
APPORTION LOT DEAL DOLE MARK
METE PART RATE ALLOT AWARD
CAVEL GRANT PARAL SHARE SHIFT
WEIGH APPLOT ASSESS ASSIGN
DIVIDE PARCEL RATION TAVERN
ARRANGE BALANCE QUARTER
ALLOCATE DESCRIBE
APPORTIONMENT DIVISION
APPOSITE APT PAT COGENT TIMELY
GERMANE INCIDENT RELATIVE
RELEVANT SUITABLE
APPRAISAL APPRIZAL
APPRAISE GAGE LOVE METE RATE
ASSAY GAUGE JUDGE PRICE PRIZE
VALUE ASSESS ESTEEM EVALUE
PONDER PRAISE SURVEY ADJUDGE
ANALYZE COMMEND ESTIMATE
EVALUATE
APPRECIABLE ANY SENSIBLE
APPRECIATE DIG FEEL LOVE JUDGE
PRIZE RAISE SAVOR TASTE VALUE
ADMIRE ESTEEM SAVOUR ADVANCE
APPRIZE APPROVE CHERISH
REALIZE INCREASE TREASURE
APPRECIATION EYE GUSTO SENSE
CONCEIT

APPRECIATIVE AWAKE GRATEFUL
(— OF BEAUTY) ESTHETIC
AESTHETIC
APPREHEND COP GET LAG NAB SEE
FEAR HEAR KNOW NOTE SCAN
TAKE VIEW CATCH DREAD GRASP
GRIPE INTUE SEIZE ARREST BEHOLD
DETAIN INTEND INTUIT BELIEVE
CAPTURE CONCEIT ENDOUTE
FORESEE IMAGINE REALIZE RECEIVE
SENSATE SUPPOSE CONCEIVE
DISCOVER OVERTAKE PERCEIVE
APPREHENDED GRIPPIT
APPREHENSIBLE NOETIC SENSATE
SENSIBLE
APPREHENSION FEAR FRAY PAIN
PANG SCAN WERE ALARM DOUBT
DREAD FANCY WORRY ARREST
DISMAY NOESIS ANXIETY CAPTURE
CONCERN PRESAGE SUSPECT
DISTRUST MISTRUST SUSPENSE
APPREHENSIVE APT JUMPY FEARED
MORBID ANXIOUS FEARFUL
JEALOUS NERVOUS STREAKY
DOUBTFUL
APPRENTICE CUB BIND BOOT SNOB
TYRO CADET DEVIL BURSCH
HELPER JOCKEY NOVICE BANKMAN
GROMMET LEARNER TRAINEE
WAISTER APRENDIZ BEGINNER
JACKAROO SERVITOR TURNOVER
APPRENTICESHIP SERVITUDE
APPRISE WARN LEARN TEACH
ADVISE INFORM NOTIFY REVEAL
APPRIZE ACQUAINT DISCLOSE
INSTRUCT
APPROACH TRY ADIT BUMP BURN
CHAT COME DRAW NEAR NERE
NIGH ROAD ABORD BOARD CLOSE
COAST ESSAY STALK VERGE
ACCEDE ACCESS ACCOST ADVENT
ANIMUS APPEAL BORDER BREAST
BROACH COMING GATHER IMPEND
PROACH TRENCH ADVANCE
AGGRESS APPULSE CONTACT
SEAGATE SUCCEED CONVERGE
NEIGHBOR ONCOMING
(— FROM WINDWARD) BEAR
(— GAME) DRAW
(— HOSTILELY) SWAY
(— NEAR) TOUCH
(— OF NIGHT) FALL
(— TENDENCY) ADIENCE
APPROACHABLE COMMON
APPROACHING LIKE COMING
TOWARD ONCOMING
APPROBATION TEST FAVOR PROOF
TRIAL ASSENT FAVOUR LOANGE
PRAISE REGARD REPUTE PLAUDIT
APPLAUSE APPROVAL SANCTION
APPROPRIATE ADD APT DUE FIT
LAY PAT AKIN CRIB FEAT GOOD
GRAB GRIP HELP JUST MEET SINK
SUIT TAKE ALLOT ANNEX FITTY
HAPPY RIGHT STEAL USURP ASSELF
ASSIGN ASSUME BORROW DECENT
DEVOTE DEVOUR DIGEST GATHER
GENTIL KINDLY PILFER PIRATE
PROPER TIMELY WORTHY APPROVE

APROPOS CABBAGE CONDIGN CONVERT FITTING GERMANE GRABBLE GRADELY IMPOUND PREEMPT PURLOIN RELATED SECRETE SWALLOW ACCROACH APPOSITE ARROGATE BECOMING DESERVED EMBEZZLE GRACEFUL HANDSOME IDONEOUS PROPERTY RELEVANT RIGHTFUL SUITABLE
(— **UNLAWFULLY)** HEIST STEAL
(**MOST** —) CHOICE

APPROPRIATENESS APTNESS DECENCY FITNESS APTITUDE
(**NICE** —) ELEGANCE

APPROPRIATION FUND VOTE DEVOTION
(**FRAUDULENT** —) CON EMBEZZLEMENT

APPROVAL AMEN ECLAT ASSENT ESTEEM APPROOF CONSENT PLAUDIT SUPPORT APPLAUSE BLESSING SANCTION SUFFRAGE

APPROVE DO OK BUY TRY HAVE LIKE OKAY OKEH PASS TEST VOTE ALLOW BLESS CLEAR FAVOR PROVE VALUE ACCEPT ADMIRE BISHOP CONCUR RATIFY APPLAUD CERTIFY COMMEND CONFIRM CONSENT ENDORSE EXHIBIT INDORSE SUPPORT ACCREDIT MANIFEST SANCTION

APPROVED TRYE EXPERT PROBAL ACCEPTED ORTHODOX

APPROVING HEARTY

APPROXIMATE NEAR ABOUT CIRCA CLOSE COAST ROUGH COARSE GENERAL APPROACH ESTIMATE

APPROXIMATELY SAY AWAY GAIN MUCH NIGH ABOUT ALMOST AROUND NEARLY TOWARD CRUDELY ROUGHLY

APPROXIMATING COMPARATIVE

APPROXIMATION CIRCA COUNTERFEIT

APPURTENANCE GEAR ANNEX ASSIGN EFFEIR ADJUNCT COMFORT APPANAGE PENDICLE
(PL.) ADDENDA

APRICOT COT UME ANSU MUME BLENHEIM
(**DRIED** —**S)** MEBOS MEEBOS

A PRIORI PURE

APRON BIB CAP BASE BOOT BRAT DICK RAMP SLOP TAYO TIER COVER EPHOD BARVEL BISHOP CANVAS DAIDLE DICKEY NAPRON RUNWAY SHIELD TARMAC TOUSER BRATTLE CANVASS DAIDLIE GREMIAL TABLIER LAMBSKIN PINAFORE PRASKEEN
(— **OF FURNITURE)** PETTICOAT
(— **OF SEAT)** FALL
(**CHILD'S** —) TIER BISWOP SLIPPER
(**LEATHER** —) DICK DICKY BARVEL DICKEY BARMFEL BARVELL BARMSKIN
(**MASON'S** —) LAMBSKIN
(**SILKEN** —) GREMIAL
(PL.) ARMITAS

APROPOS APT FIT PAT MEET TIMELY

RELEVANT SUITABLE

APSE APSIS NICHE CONCHA RECESS

APSIS APSE AUGE

APT FIT PAT YAP ABLE DEFT FAIN FEAT KEEN VAIN WONT ADEPT ALERT HAPPY PRONE QUICK READY ASPERT CLEVER DOCILE KITTLE LIABLE LIKELY SUITED TOWARD APROPOS CAPABLE FITTING IDONEAL WILLING APPOSITE DEXTROUS DISPOSED HANDSOME IDONEOUS INCLINED PRACTIVE PREPARED SKILLFUL SUITABLE
(— **TO TURN)** WALT

APTERYX KIWI RATITE KIVIKIVI KIWIKIWI

APTITUDE ART BENT GIFT HEAD TURN CRAFT FLAIR HABIT KNACK SKILL VERVE GENIUS TALENT ABILITY CONDUCT FACULTY FITNESS LEANING CAPACITY INSTINCT TENDENCY

APTNESS GIFT KNACK SKILL APTITUDE FELICITY

APUS CYPSELUS MICROPUS

AQUARIUS SKINKER

AQUEDUCT AQUA DUCT CANAL AQUAGE SPECUS CHANNEL CONDUIT PASSAGE
(— **OF SILVIUS)** ITER

AQUEOUS HYDATOID WATERISH

ARA MACAW

ARAB AHL AUS IBAD OMAN SLEB WAIF ARABY GAMIN NOMAD SAUDI TATAR SEMITE SLUBBI URCHIN ARABIAN BEDOUIN SARACEN SOLUBBI AZZAZAME KABABISH LARRIKIN SLOUBBIE YEMENITE

ARABIC CARSHUNI GARSHUNI KARSHUNI THAMUDIC
(— **ALPHABET)** BA FA HA RA TA YA ZA AYN DAD DAL JIM KAF KHA LAM MIM NUN QAF SAD SIN THA WAW ZAY ALIF DHAL SHIN GHAYN

ARABLE FERTILE PLOWABLE TILLABLE

ARACHNID CRAB MITE TICK TAINT ACARUS CARTER SPIDER CARTARE OCTOPOD PEDIPALP SCORPION SOLPUGID

ARAGONITE ALABASTER

ARAIN ARRAND

ARAKANESE MAGHI

ARAMAIC SYRIAC MANDAEAN
(— **TRANSLATION)** TARGUM

ARANEA EPEIRA

ARAPONGA BELLBIRD

ARAROBA ZEBRAWOOD

ARAUCANIAN AUCA PAMPA MAPOCHE MOLUCHE PAMPERO PICUNCHE

ARAWA AOTEA MATATUA

ARAWAK ARUA BARE URAN ARAUA BAURE CAMPA CHANE GUANA INERI SIUSI BAINOA BANIVA GUINAU IGNERI GOAJIRO IPURINA CAQUETIO CUSTENAU

ARBITER JUDGE CRITIC ÖDDMAN UMPIRE ADVISER DAYSMAN ODDSMAN OVERMAN REFEREE DICTATOR STICKLER

ARBITRAGE SHUNTING

ARBITRARY SEVERE THETIC WILLFUL ABSOLUTE DESPOTIC MASTERLY
(**NOT** —) FREE

ARBITRATE DECIDE MEDIATE

ARBITRATION DAYMENT

ARBITRATOR REF JUDGE UMPIRE ARBITER MUNSIFF REFEREE MEDIATOR

ARBOR BAR AXLE BEAM ABODE BOWER SHAFT STAFF STALK TRAIL ARBOUR BOWERY GARDEN HERBER PANDAL RAMADA VOIDER BERCEAU HARBOUR MANDREL MANDRIL ORCHARD PERGOLA RETREAT SPINDLE TRELLIS FRESCADE TONNELLE

ARBORVITAE AKEKI

ARBUTUS IVY

ARC BOW ARCH BEND FOIL HALO CURVE HANCE ORBIT SPARK SWING

FOGBOW FOLIUM OCTANT RADIAN
COMPASS RAINBOW FROSTBOW
(— OF HORIZON) AZIMUTH
AMPLITUDE
(ELECTRIC —) SPARK
ARCA BOX CHEST PATEN ARCULA
ARCADE ORB AVENUE LOGGIA
STREET GALLERY PORTICO
ARCATURE CLOISTER
ARCANE HIDDEN SECRET
ARCH ARC BOW COY SET SLY BACK
BEND COPE COVE DOME HARP
HOOP IRIS LEER OGEE PASS PEND
PERT SPAN ARCUS CHIEF CURVE
FAULD GREAT HANCE HUNCH
INBOW JOWEL OGIVE PAUKY PAWKY
POKEY PRIME ROACH SAUCY
SWEEP VAULT ARCADE BRIDGE
CALCAR CAMBER CLEVER DIADEM
FOGBOW FORNIX GIRDLE IMPISH
INVERT LANCET MANTEL SPRING
SUNBOW WICKET ZYGOMA
ARCHWAY CUNNING EMINENT
GATEWAY ROGUISH SEGMENT
SQUINCH SUPPORT TESTUDO
TRIUMPH WAGGISH ALVEOLAR
FOGEATER OVERCAST
(— OF SKY) FIRMAMENT
(DENTAL —) ARCADE
(LOGGING —) SULKY
(PL.) SUBARCUATION
ARCHAEOCYTE SORITE
ARCHAEOLOGIST POTHUNTER
ARCHAIC OLD ANCIENT ANTIQUE
HISTORIC OBSOLETE
ARCHANGEL SATAN URIEL GABRIEL
MICHAEL RAPHAEL
ARCHBISHOP HATTO PRELATE
PRIMATE ORDINARY
ARCHDEMON BELFAGOR BELFAZOR
ARCHDIOCESE EPARCHY
ARCHDUKE ERZHERZOG
ARCHED ARCHY CONVEX EMBOWED
VAULTED HOOPLIKE
(— IN) CONCAVE
ARCHEGONIUM CALYPTRA
OOANGIUM
ARCHEMORUS (FATHER OF —)
LYCURGUS
(MOTHER OF —) EURYDICE
(NURSE OF —) HYPSIPYLE
ARCHER BOW CLIM CLYM BOWER
BUTTY CUPID ROVER BOWBOY
BOWMAN BOWYER SHOOTER
(EQUIPMENT OF —) TACKLE
ARCHERY TOXOLOGY ARTILLERY
(— SPACE) PETTICOAT
ARCHETYPE IDEA MODEL FIGURE
SAMPLE ESSENCE EXAMPLE
PARAGON PATTERN EXEMPLAR
FRAVASHI ORIGINAL
ARCHIL CORKE CORCIR CORKER
PERSIS CUDBEAR LECANORA
ORCHILLA ORSEILLE
ARCHING CAMBER
ARCHITECT MAKER ARTIST ARTISAN
BUILDER CREATOR PLANNER
BEZALEEL DESIGNER SURVEYOR
ARCHITECTURAL TECTONIC
OECODOMIC

ARCHITECTURE DRAVIDA
ARCHITRAVE EPISTYLE PLATBAND
ARCHIVES TABULARY TABULARIUM
ARCHIVOLT RING ARCHBAND
HEADBAND
ARCHLUTE THEORBO
ARCHON RULER DIRECTOR OFFICIAL
ARCHWAY ARCH PEND ARCUS
PAILOO PAILOU
ARC LAMP MONOPHOTE
ARCOGRAPH BOW
ARCO SALTANDO SPICCATO
ARCTIC ICY COLD COOL GELID
POLAR BOREAL CHILLY FRIGID
GALOSH NORTHERN OVERSHOE
ARCTIUM LAPPA
ARCTOID URSINE
ARDENT HOT AVID FOND KEEN LIVE
WARM EAGER FIERY GLEDY RETHE
SHARP ABLAZE FERVID FIERCE
IGNITE STRONG TORRID AMOROUS
BURNING CORDIAL DEVOTED
EARNEST FEELING FERVENT
FLAMING FORWARD GLOWING
INTENSE SHINING ZEALOUS
DESIROUS EMPRESSE FEVERISH
FLAGRANT SANGUINE SCALDING
SPORTIVE VEHEMENT
ARDOR DASH EDGE ELAN FIRE
GLOW HEAT LOVE ZEST ESTRO
FLAME GUSTO HEART TAPAS VERVE
WRATH DESIRE FERVOR FOUGUE
METTLE SPIRIT SPLEEN WARMTH
ARDENCY EARNEST ENTRAIN
PASSION DEVOTION FEROCITY
VIOLENCE VIVACITY
ARDUOUS HARD LOFTY STEEP STIFF
SEVERE TRYING ONEROUS
EXACTING TIRESOME TOILSOME
ARE MU RE AIR ARN ARUN HARE
AREA BELT SIZE TREF ZONE BASIN
COAST COURT FIELD RANGE REALM
SCENE SCOPE SPACE TRACT
ACCENT AREOLA EXTENT GROUND
LOCALE MOARIA REGION SECTOR
SPHERE SPREAD VOLUME ACREAGE
AMENITY AREAWAY CIRCUIT
COMPASS COUNTRY ENVIRON
EXPANSE KINGDOM PURLIEU
SURFACE CAPACITY DISTRICT
ENCEINTE PROVINCE
(— AT INTERSECTION) CIRCUS
(— BETWEEN FILLETS) CANALIS
(— IN CARTOON) BALLOON
(— IN HOSTILE TERRITORY)
AIRHEAD
(— OF EXPERIENCE) BOOK
(— OF FLAG) CANTON
(— OF OLDER LAND) KIPUKA
(— OF RIDGES) BILO
(— OF TIMBERLAND) CHENA
(— ON MOON) MARE WANE
(— UNIT) TAN YOKE LABOR
VIRGATE PLETHRON PLOWGANG
PLOWGATE
(BLANK —) BITE HOLE
(COMBAT —) GLACIS
(CULTURAL —) HORIZON
(CURLING —) PARISH

(DENUDED —) BURN
(DIKED —) SLUSHPIT
(ELONGATED —) BELT
(ENCLOSED —) FOLD SEPT
(FENCED —) CAGE COMPOUND
(FERTILE —) HAMMOCK
(FLOORING —) SQUARE
(FORTIFIED —) BASTION ENCIENTE
(GATHERING —) MANDAPA
(HUNTING —) SURROUND
(INFESTED —) FLYBELT
(LOW-LYING —) GLADE SWALE
COULEE COULIE GUTTER
(LUMINOUS —) AUREOLA AUREOLE
(MINE —) SQUEEZE
(NUCLEAR —) HEARTH ECUMENE
(OPEN —) COURT LAUND CAMPUS
SQUARE HAGGARD
(OVERGROWN —) COGONAL
(PASTURE —) SOUM
(PAVED —) CAUSEY
(PLOWED —) BREAK
(RESIDENTIAL —) BANLIEU
BANLIEUE
(SLUM —) STEW
(SMALL —) AREOLA
(SMOKING —) BULLPEN
(STERN —) AFTERPART
(SUBURBAN —) ADDITION
FAUBOURG
(SUNKEN —) SAG
(SWAMPY —) SLASH
(TEST —) MILACRE
(TIDAL —) CLAMFLAT
(TRANSITION —) ECOTONE
(TREELESS —) SLICK
(TUMID —) CERE
(UNCLEARED —) BUSH
(VOLCANIC —) SOLFATARA
(WASTE —) FOREST
(WOODED —) HAG BOSK BOSQUE
ARECA ARAK ARCHA BETEL
ARENA AREA LIST OVAL RING RINK
COURT FIELD SCENE SCOPE SPACE
STAGE CIRCUS REGION SPHERE
COCKPIT STADIUM TERRAIN
THEATER BULLRING
ARENACEOUS SANDY GRITTY
SABULOUS
AREOLA PIT AREA RING SPOT SPACE
ARES MARS ENYALIUS GRADIVUS
QUIRINUS
(FATHER OF —) ZEUS JUPITER
(MOTHER OF —) ENYO HERA JUNO
(SON OF —) REMUS CYENUS
ROMULUS
ARGALA STORK MARABOU
ARGALI AMMON ARKAR AOUDAD
ARGAN IRONWOOD
ARGENT LUNA MOON PEARL WHITE
BLANCH SILVER CRYSTAL SHINING
SILVERY

ARGENTINA
CAPITAL: BUENOSAIRES
COIN: PESO CENTAVO ARGENTINO
DANCE: TANGO CUANDO GAUCHO
FALLS: GRANDE IGUAZU

INDIAN: LULE GUARANI
LAKE: VIEDMA CARDIEL FAGNANO MUSTERS
MEASURE: SINO VARA LEGUA CUADRA FANEGA LASTRE MANZANA
MOUNTAIN: TORO ANDES CHATO LAUDO POTRO CONICO PISSIS RINCON FAMATINA MURALLON OLIVARES TRONADOR ZAPALERI ACONCAGUA
PLAIN: PAMPA PAMPAS
PORT: ROSARIO
PROVINCE: CHACO JUJUY SALTA CHUBUT CORDOBA FORMOSA LARIOJA MENDOZA NEUQUEN TUCUMAN MISIONES PATAGONIA
REGION: CHACO PATAGONIA
RIVER: SALI ATUEL CHICO COYLE DULCE LIMAY NEGRO PLATA TEUCO BLANCO CHUBUT CUARTO FLORES GRANDE PARANA QUINTO SALADO BERMEJO DESEADO MENDOZA TERCERO TUNUYAN SENGUERR
TOWN: AZUL GOYA ORAN PUAN BAHIA JUNIN LANUS LUJAN METAN SALTA PARANA RUFINO ZARATE BOLIVAR CORDOBA DOLORES FORMOSA LABANDA MENDOZA POSADAS RAFAELA ROSARIO TUCUMAN
VOLCANO: LANIN MAIPO DOMUYO PETEROA
WEIGHT: LAST GRANO LIBRA QUINTAL TONELADA

ARGIL CLAY ALUMINA
ARGOL TARTAR
ARGOSY SHIP GALLEON RAGUSYE
ARGOT CANT FLASH LINGO SLANG JARGON PATOIS DIALECT
ARGUE JAW ARGY CHOP FUSS MEAN MOOT MOVE SPAR WORD ARGIE CAVIL ORATE PLEAD PROVE TREAT ACCUSE ADDUCE CAFFLE DEBATE EVINCE HASSLE REASON ARRAIGN CONTEND CONTEST COUNTER DISCUSS DISPUTE WRANGLE ERGOTIZE INDICATE MAINTAIN PERSUADE QUESTION TRAVERSE
(— DEDUCTIVELY) SYLLOGIZE
(— SUBTLY) DISTINGUISH
ARGUER JAW
ARGUMENT ROW AGON BEEF BLUE CASE FUSS MOOT PLEA SPAR TEXT CLASH DEBAT INDEX KNIFE LEMMA PROOF THEME TOPIC BARNEY COMBAT DEBATE DUSTUP ELENCH HASSLE MATTER TUSSLE APAGOGE CLAMPER DEFENCE DEFENSE DILEMMA DISPUTE ESSENCE FLUBDUB POLEMIC RHUBARB SOPHISM SUMMARY ABSTRACT CLINCHER COURSING EVIDENCE SPARRING TRILEMMA
(INVALID —) SOPHISM
ARGUMENTATION DEBATE DISPUTE ERGOTISM

ARGUMENTATIVE ERISTIC FRATCHY FORENSIC
ARGUSFISH SCAT
ARHAT MONK LOHAN RAKAN SAINT ARAHANT
ARIA AIR SOLO SONG TUNE MELODY SORTIE ARIETTA ARIETTE SORTITA
ARIADNE (FATHER OF —) MINOS
(HUSBAND OF —) THESEUS
(MOTHER OF —) PASIPHAE
ARIAN AGNOETE AGNOITE HOMOEAN ANOMOIAN EUSEBIAN
ARID DRY BALD BARE DULL LEAN BARREN DESERT JEJUNE MEAGER DROUTHY PARCHED STERILE THIRSTY DROUGHTY WITHERED
ARIDITY DROUTH DROUGHT SICCITY
ARIKARA REE
ARIL POD ARILLUS COATING ARILLODE
ARISE WAX COME FLOW FORM GROW LIFT REAR RISE SOAR STEM AWAKE BEGIN BUILD EXIST ISSUE MOUNT RAISE SPRAY STAND START SURGE TOWER WAKEN ACCRUE AMOUNT APPEAR ASCEND ATTAIN DERIVE EMERGE HAPPEN KITTLE SPRING DEVELOP EMANATE EXSURGE PROCEED REDOUND SOURDRE
ARISING LEVEE EMERGENT
ARISTOCRACY CLASS ELITE GENTRY ARISTOI SAMURAI NOBILITY OPTIMACY
ARISTOCRAT LORD NOBLE ARISTO GRANDEE PARVENU EUPATRID OPTIMATE
(PL.) ARISTOI
ARISTOCRATIC HIGH TONY NOBLE QUALITY CAVALIER
ARISTOTELIAN PERIPATETIC
ARITHMETIC SUM AUGRIM ALGORISM
ARITHMOMETER MULTIPLIER

ARIZONA
CAPITAL: PHOENIX
COUNTY: GILA PIMA YUMA PINAL APACHE MOHAVE NAVAJO COCHISE COCONINO MARICOPA
INDIAN: HOPI PIMA YUMA NAVAHO NAVAJO PAPAGO HUALAPAI
MOUNTAIN: BANGS GROOM LEMMON TURRET PASTORA HUALAPAI MERIDIAN
MOUNTAIN RANGE: GILA KOFA MOHAWK GALIURO AQUARIUS BUCKSKIN HUALAPAI
STATE BIRD: CACTUSWREN
STATE FLOWER: SAGUARO
STATE NICKNAME: OCOTILLO
STATE TREE: PALOVERDE
RIVER: GILA SALT ZUNI VERDE PUERCO COLORADO
TOWN: AJO ELOY MESA NACO YUMA GLOBE LEUPP TEMPE BISBEE MCNARY SALOME TOLTEC TUCSON CORTARO

KINGMAN MORENCI NOGALES SAFFORD FREDONIA

ARJUN KUMBUK
ARK BIN BOX BOAT SHIP BARGE CHEST HUTCH BASKET COFFER REFUGE WANGAN RETREAT SHELTER WANIGAN FLATBOAT
ARKANSAN ARKANSAWYER

ARKANSAS
CAPITAL: LITTLEROCK
COUNTY: CLAY DREW PIKE POLK POPE YELL CROSS DESHA IZARD SHARP STONE BAXTER
INDIAN: CADDO OSAGE QUAPAW CHOCTAW CHEROKEE
LAKE: CONWAY NIMROD GREESON NORFORK OUACHITA
MOUNTAIN: GAYLOR MAGAZINE
MOUNTAIN RANGE: OZARK OUACHITA
NATIVE: TOOTHPICK
RIVER: WHITE SALINE BUFFALO CURRENT COSSATOT OUACHITA
STATE BIRD: MOCKINGBIRD
STATE FLOWER: APPLEBLOSSOM
STATE TREE: SHORTLEAFPINE
TOWN: COY CUY KEO OLA ROE ULM ALMA BONO CASA DELL DIAZ MORO ENOLA PERLA RONDO ALICIA

ARKOSE ARENITE SANDSTONE
ARM FIN OAR TOE BOOM HEEL LIMB WING BLADE BOUGH CRANE EQUIP FENCE FIORD FIRTH FJORD FORCE GARDY INLET MIGHT OXTER POWER RIFLE SNORD STOCK BRANCH CRUTCH ENERGY FRETUM GIBBET MEMBER OUTFIT PINION RADIAL SLEEVE TAPPET WEAPON CATCHER DERRICK DRAWARM FLIPPER FOREARM FORTIFY FURNISH GARNISH HARNESS OCKSTER PREPARE PROTECT PROVIDE QUILLON SUPPORT ARMORIAL CROSSARM FOLLOWER FORELIMB PULLDOWN SOUPBONE STRENGTH TRANSEPT
(— HOLDING FLINT) HAMMER
(— OF BARNACLE) CIRRUS CIRRHUS
(— OF CHAIR) ELBOW
(— OF CRANE) JIB GIBBET RAMHEAD
(— OF GIN) START
(— OF PROPELLER) BLADE
(— OF SEA) COVE FLOW MEER MERE BRACE CANAL FIRTH FRITH GRAIN FRETUM ESTUARY
(— OF SPINNING MULE) SICKLE
(— OF WINDMILL) VANE WHIP
(— WITH GAFF) HEEL
(IRON —) CRANE
(LEVER —) SWEEP NIGGER
(PITCHING —) SOUPBONE
(PL.) ARMORY ARMAMENT

ARMADA NAVY FLEET FLOTILLA
ARMADILLO APAR PEBA TATU
  APARA POYOU TATOU BOLITA
  MATACO MATICO MULITA PELUDO
  TATOUAY TATUASU EDENTATE
  KABASSOU LORICATE PANGOLIN
ARMAMENT ARMADA BATTERY
ARMATURE ARMING KEEPER LIFTER
ARMBAND BRASSARD
ARMCHAIR BERGERE FAUTEUIL
ARMED FLUTE HEELED DAGGERED
  WEAPONED

ARMENIA
ANCIENT CAPITAL: ANI ARTASHAT
  ARTAXATA
CAPITAL: ERIVAN
FORTRESS: EREBUNI
HERO: ARA ARAM HAIK ARAME
  VARTAN
KING: ASHOT GAGIK TRDAT
  ZAREH DIKRAN ARTAKIAS
  ARTASHES TIGRANES ZARIADES
KINGDOM: URARTU VANNIC
  CILICIA SOPHENE ARDSRUNI
LAKE: VAN SEVAN URMIA
MOUNTAIN: ARA ALAGEZ ARARAT
  TAURUS ALADAGH ARAGATS
  KARABAKH
NATIVE: ARMEN GOMER
RIVER: KUR ARAS KURA ARAKS
  CYRUS HALYS ZANGA ARAXES
  RAZDAN TIGRIS EUPHRATES
SAINT: SAHAK MESROP
TOWN: VAN SIVAS BITLIS EREVAN
  ERIVAN ERZURUM TRABZON
  YEREVAN

ARMENIAN ERMYN HADJI
ARMFUL LOCK YAFFLE
ARMHOLE MAIL SCYE OXTER
  ARMSCYE ARMSEYE ARMSIZE
ARMISTICE LULL PEACE TRUCE
  INDUCIAE
ARMLET TABLET TORQUE ARMHOOP
ARMOR (AND SPECIFIC PIECES
  THEREOF) ARMS BACK BOOT EGIS
  JAMB MAIL TACE WEED ACTON
  AMURE BARDS BRACE CUISH CULET
  DORON GUARD GUIGE JAMBE PIECE
  PLATE PROOF SCALE STEEL TAPUL
  TASSE TRUSS ARMLET ARMOUR
  BEAVER BRINIE BRUNIE BYRNIE
  CAMAIL CORIUM COUTER CRANET
  CUISSE GORGET GRAITH GREAVE
  JAMBER POLEYN RONDEL SECRET
  SHIELD TASSET THORAX TONLET
  TUILLE VOIDER AILETTE ARMHOOP
  BESAGNE BROIGNE CORSLET
  CUIRASS DEFENSE EPAULET
  HARNESS HAUBERK JAZERAN
  KNEELET LAMBOYS PANOPLY
  PAUDRON PLACATE POITREL
  REREDOS ROUNDEL SABATON
  VENTAIL RAMENTUM VAMBRACE
(— ON TREE) TROPHY
(— PLATE) TUILLE
(ELBOW —) CUBITIERE

(FOOT —) SABATON SABBATON
  SOLLERET
(HEAD —) CASQUE HELMET PALLET
  SCONCE
(HORSE —) BARB BARD BARDE
  CRINET CRINIERE
(LEATHER —) CORIUM
(LEG —) BOOT JAMB CUISH JAMBE
  CUISSE GREAVE JAMBER TUILLE
  JAMBEAU
(NECK —) COLLAR GORGET
(PADDED —) GAMBESON
(SUIT OF —) CAST STAND
ARMOR-BEARER SQUIRE ARMIGER
  CUSTREL
ARMORED PANZER
ARMORER GUNSMITH ARTIFICER
ARMORICAN BRETON
ARMORY HERALDRY
ARMPIT ALA OXTER AXILLA
  ARMHOLE
ARMS TACKLE
ARMY FERD HERE HOST IMPI LEVY
  MAIN ARRAY CROWD FORCE HERSE
  HORDE POWER RANKS ZOMBI
  COHORT HONVED LEGION NUMBER
  THRONG TROOPS MILITIA CHIVALRY
  MILITARY
(HOSTILE —) FOE
(PL.) SABAOTH
ARMYWORM GRASSWORM
AROID APII ARAD TARO APIUM KRUBI
  TANIA KONJAK TANIER YAUTIA
  PINUELA CALADIUM CUNJEVOI
  MOCOMOCO
AROMA NOSE ODOR NIDOR SAVOR
  SCENT SMELL SNUFF SPICE FLAVOR
  BOUQUET PERFUME
(— OF WINE) BLOOM
AROMATIC BALMY SPICY SWEET
  MASTIC ODOROUS PIQUANT
  PUNGENT FRAGRANT REDOLENT
  SPICEFUL
AROUND NEAR UMBE ABOUT CIRCA
  CIRCUM ENVIRON
AROUSAL INDUCTION
AROUSE SOW CALL CITE FIRE GAIN
  HEAT MOVE REAR SPUR STIR WAKE
  WHET ADAWE ALARM ALERT AWAKE
  EVOKE FLESH PIQUE RAISE RALLY
  ROUSE ROUST SHAKE STEER
  WAKEN ABRAID AWAKEN ELICIT
  EXCITE FOMENT INCITE INDUCE
  KINDLE REVIVE SUMMON THRILL
  ACTUATE AGITATE CONNOTE
  INCENSE INFLAME INSPIRE
  PROVOKE SUGGEST INSPIRIT
(— DISPLEASURE) AGGRAVATE
(— ENMITY) ESTRANGE
(— WRATH) SPLEEN
ARPEGGIO SWEEP ROULADE
  FLOURISH
(— EFFECT) RASGADO
ARRACACHA APIO ARRA
ARRACK ARAK RACK ARAKI
  RACKAPEE
ARRAIGN TRY CITE ARGUE PEACH
  ACCUSE CHARGE IMPUTE INDICT
  INDITE SUMMON APPOINT IMPEACH
  DENOUNCE

ARRANGE DO FIX LAY RAY SET
  CAST COMB EDIT FILE FORM PLAN
  PLAT RAIL RULE SIDE SIZE SORT
  TIER TIFT WORK ADAPT AGREE
  ALIGN ALINE ARRAY BESEE CURRY
  DRAPE DRESS ETTLE FANCY FRAME
  GRADE RANGE SCORE SHAPE SHIFT
  SPACE STALL TRICK ADJUST
  BRANCH CODIFY DAIKER DESIGN
  DEVISE FETTLE INFORM ORDAIN
  SETTLE SOLUTE TAILYE ADDRESS
  APPOINT BESPEAK CATALOG
  COLLATE COMPONE COMPOSE
  CONCERT DISPOSE ENRANGE
  GRADATE MARSHAL PERMUTE
  PREPARE REDRESS SERIATE
  TAILZEE TAILZIE ALPHABET
  CLASSIFY CONCLUDE ORGANIZE
  REGULATE TABULATE
(— BEFOREHAND) FORLAY FORELAY
(— FANTASTICALLY) HARLEQUINIZE
(— FASTIDIOUSLY) PREEN
(— HAIR) SET TED COIF TRUSS
  COIFFE
(— HARMONIOUSLY) GRADATE
(— IN FLOCKS) HIRSEL HIRSLE
(— IN FOLDS) DRAPE
(— IN LAYERS) DESS TIER
(— IN ROW) RACE
(— STRAW) HAULM
(— SYSTEMATICALLY) DIGEST
(— WITH BEST AT TOP) DEACON
ARRANGEMENT FIX FLY LAY RAY
  DEAL FLOW PLAT RANK TIFF ARRAY
  BUILD DRAPE INDEX ORDER SETUP
  BORDER DESIGN HOOKUP LAYOUT
  SCHEME SETOUT SYNTAX SYSTEM
  TREATY BLEEDER INTERIM POSTURE
  TONTINE ATTITUDE CONTRACT
  DISPOSAL GROUPING POSITURE
  SEQUENCE
(— IN LOCK) DETECTOR
(— OF BRISTLES) CHAETOTAXY
(— OF CHESS PAWNS) CHAIN
(— OF DRAPERIES) CAST
(— OF FLOWERS) CASCADE
  CORSAGE
(— OF GRADES) CURVE
(— OF GUNS) ARMADA
(— OF HAIRDO) FORETOP
(— OF HAIRS) SCOPA
(— OF HOOKS) GIG
(— OF LOOM BARS) GRIFF GRIFFE
(— OF ROCKS) BEDDING
(— OF TACKLE) BURTON
(— OF TIMBER) ANCHOR
(— OF TROOPS) ECHELON
(CIRCULAR —) CYCLE
(DISHONEST —) CROSS
(GEOMETRICAL —) LATTICE
(TRADITIONAL —) AKOLUTHIA
  AKOLOUTHIA
ARRANGING ORDONNANT
ARRANT BAD THIEF OUTLAW
  ROBBER VAGRANT PRECIOUS
  RASCALLY
ARRAS ORRIS ARISTE DRAPERY
  TAPESTRY
ARRASTRA TAHONA

ARRAU JURARA
ARRAY DON DUB FIG ARMY BUSK DECK DOLL FYRD GALA GARB HOST POMP RAIL RANK ROBE VEST ADORN ALIGN ALINE ATOUR DRESS EQUIP HABIT HARKA HEDGE ORDER ADIGHT AGUISE ATTIRE ATTRAP BEDECK CLOTHE DEVISE FETTLE FINERY GRAITH INVEST MUSTER PLIGHT SERIES SETOUT SHROUD ADDRESS AFFAITE AFFLICT APPAREL ARRANGE BATTERY BEDIGHT COMPANY DISPLAY DISPOSE ENVELOP FURNISH FYRDUNG MARSHAL PANOPLY REPAREL ACCOUTER
(— OF CHEMICALS) ARA
(— OF GUNS) BROADSIDE
(— OF TROOPS) PAREL
(— OF WEAPONS) ARMORY
(— TASTELESSLY) DAUB
(BATTLE —) ACIES HERSE BATTALIA
ARRAYED HABITED ABULYEIT
ARREAR DEBT BEHIND UNPAID ARRIERE
(IN —S) BACK BEHIND
ARREST CAP COP FIX FOB LAG NAB NIP VAG BALK CURB FALL GLOM GRAB HALT HOLD JAIL KEEP NAIL NICK PULL REST SHOP SIST STAY STOP ARRET CATCH CHECK DELAY PINCH REEST SEIZE STILL STUNT ATTACH BRIDLE COLLAR DECREE DETAIN ENGAGE FINGER HINDER PLEDGE RETARD SLOUGH SNEEZE THWART CAPTION CAPTURE CUSTODY SUSPEND IMPRISON OBSTRUCT RESTRAIN
(— OF BLEEDING) HEMOSTASIS
(— OF DEVELOPMENT) ABORTION
ARRESTER (SPARK —) BONNET
ARRESTING BOLD SEIZING MAGNETIC PLEASING STRIKING
ARRET EDICT ARREST DECREE DECISION JUDGMENT
ARRHA HANDGELD
ARRIS PIEN ANGLE PIEND ARRIDGE
ARRIVAL COMER IKBAL VENUE ADVENT COMING INCOMING REACHING
(— TIME RECORD) OS
ARRIVE GO SEY COME FALL FLOW GAIN LAND LEND RIVE LIGHT OCCUR REACH WORTH APPEAR ATTAIN HAPPEN OBTAIN UPCOME COMPASS
(— AT) GET HIT FIND GAIN HENT MAKE BRING EDUCE FETCH GUESS SEIZE ATTAIN DERIVE ESTIMATE
ARRIVED-IN DONE
ARROBA ROVE
ARROGANCE PRIDE SWANK TUMOR BOWWOW HUBRIS BOBANCE CONCEIT DISDAIN EGOTISM HAUTEUR STOMACH BOLDNESS SUCCUDRY SURQUIDY
ARROGANT BOLD COXY HIGH MOOD COCKY GREAT HUFFY JOLLY LOFTY PROUD STOUT SURLY WLONK

ASSUME FIERCE LORDLY UPPISH UPPITY WANTON FORWARD FROSTED HAUGHTY HAUTAIN HUFFISH STATELY TOPPING AFFECTED ASSUMING CAVALiER FASTUOUS IMPUDENT SNUFFING SUPERIOR TUMOROUS
ARROGATE GRAB TAKE CLAIM SEIZE USURP ASSUME ADROGATE
ARROW FLO PIN ROD SEL BOLT DART REED SELF SELL SHOT VIRE BLUNT DEATH FLANE ROVER SHAFT ARCHER FLIGHT GANYLE GARROT QUARRY SPRITE TACKLE WEAPON BOBTAIL DOGBOLT MISSILE POINTER PROJECT QUARREL SAGITTA SPINNER FISHTAIL FORKHEAD
(— ARUM) TUCKAHOE
(— IN GRASS) GREEN SNAKE
(— IN LEG OF STAND) FOOT
(FIRE —) MALLEOLUS
(POISONED —) DERRID SUMPIT
(WOBBLING —) FISHTAIL
ARROWHEAD BUNT FORK HEAD PILE FLUKE POINT NEOLITH ARTIFACT CROWBILL FORKHEAD SPICULUM
ARROWROOT PIA ARUM MUSA SAGU ARARU CANNA TACCA TIKOR ARARAO CURCUMA
ARROWWORM SAGITTA CHAETOGNATH
ARROYO DRAW BROOK CREEK GULCH GULLY HONDO ZANJA RAVINE STREAM CHANNEL BARRANCA BARRANCO
ARSENAL ARMORY SUPPLY MAGAZINE
ARSHIN ARCHIN ALTSCHIN
(ONE-24TH OF —) PARMAK PARMACK
ARSIS BEAT ICTUS ACCENT RHYTHM UPBEAT DOWNBEAT
ARSON FIRE CRIME FELONY BURNING
ARSONIST ARSONITE
ARSPHENAMINE SIX SALVARSAN
ART WILE CRAFT KNACK KUNST MAGIC SKILL TRADE MISTER TECHNE ARTWORK CALLING CUNNING DESCANT DISCANT FACULTY FINESSE MYSTERY SCIENCE APTITUDE ARTIFICE BUSINESS LEARNING PRACTICE PRACTISE
(— OF APPLYING TESTS) DOCIMASY
(— OF BLAZONING) ARMORY
(— OF CALCULATING) ALGORISM ALGORITHM
(— OF DEFENSE) SKIRMISH
(— OF HEALING) LEECHCRAFT
(— OF HORSEMANSHIP) MANEGE
(— OF SPEECH) RHETORIC
(DIABOLIC —) DEVILRY DEVILTRY
(DRAMATIC —) STAGE
(LEG —) CHEESECAKE
(MAGIC —) WITHERCRAFT
(MYSTERIOUS —) CABALA KABALA

CABBALA KABBALA QABBALA CABBALAH KABBALAH QABBALAH
(OCCULT —) THEURGY
(SHODDY —) BONDIEUSERIE
ARTEMIS UPIS DELIA DIANA PHOEBE CYNTHIA AMARYSIA
ARTERY WAY PATH ROAD AORTA PULSE ROUTE COURSE DENTAL FACIAL RADIAL STREET VESSEL ANONYMA CAROTID COELIAC CONDUIT HIGHWAY SCIATIC VAGINAL CEREBRAL CERVICAL CORONARY DORSALIS EMULGENT PROFUNDA
ARTFUL APT FLY SLY FOXY WILY AGILE CRATY DOWNY SUAVE ADROIT CLEVER FACILE QUAINT SCHEMY SHREWD SMOOTH TRICKY CROOKED CUNNING KNOWING PLAITED POLITIC PRACTIC SUBTILE VULPINE DEXTROUS SCHEMING STEALTHY
ARTFULNESS ARTIFICE SUBTLETY
ARTHRITIS GOUT CARPITIS
ARTHROPOD GOLACH GOLOCH SPIDER CHILOPOD DIPLOPOD
ARTICHOKE BUR CANADA CYNARA CHOROGI CROSNES KNOTROOT
ARTICLE AN YE LOT ONE THE BOOK ITEM TERM BRIEF CHEAT ESSAY GEANE PAPER PIECE PLANK POINT STORY THEME THING CLAUSE DETAIL LEADER NOTICE OBJECT REPORT FEATURE BROCHURE CAUSERIE DOCTRINE POSTFACE TREATISE
(— OF CLOTHING) DUD DIDO APRON CLOUT DICKY FANCY THING CASUAL DICKEY GARMENT COINTISE CREATION
(— OF FOOD) CATE KNACK
(— OF FURNITURE) STICK
(— OF LITTLE WORTH) DIDO
(— OF SILK) SQUEEZE
(— OF TRADE) PADNAG
(— OF UNUSUAL SIZE) IMPERIAL
(—S OF FAITH) CREDENDA
(—S OF MERCHANDISE) CHAFFER
(CAST-IRON —S) KENTLEDGE
(CHEAP —) CAMELOT
(DECORATIVE —) LACKER LAQUER
(FANCY —) CONCEIT
(FIVE —S) HAND
(GENUINE —) GOODS
(HANDICRAFT —) BOONDOGGLE
(INFERIOR —S) SHODDY
(METAL —S) BATTERY
(MISCELLANEOUS —S) SUNDRIES
(NONDESCRIPT —) DODAD DOODAB DOODAD
(SECONDHAND —) JUNK
(SHOWY —) FRIPPERY
(VALUABLE —S) SWAG
(WORTHLESS —) TRANGAM
ARTICULATE BACK JOIN CLEAR FRAME JOINT SPEAK UNITE UTTER VOCAL ACCENT FLUENT VERBAL EXPRESS JOINTED DISTINCT
ARTICULATED BACK BLADE DENTAL

DORSAL LABIAL JOINTED ALVEOLAR
CEREBRAL
ARTICULATION JOINT VOICE
SUTURE ARTHRON JUNCTURE
SYNTAXIS
(DEFECTIVE —) LALLATION
LAMDACISM
ARTIFACT CELT DISC DISK BATON
GUACA HUACA AMGARN BRONZE
EOLITH FABRIC GORGET REJECT
RONDEL SAGAIE SKEWER ABRADER
ARTEFAC DISCOID RACLOIR
SCRAPER ARTEFACT DATEMARK
RONDELLE TRANCHET
(PL.) CACHE CERAUNIA
ARTIFICE ART GIN JET GAUD HOAX
JOUK PLAN PLOT RUSE TURN WILE
BLIND CHEAT COVIN CRAFT CROCK
CROOK DODGE DRAFT FEINT FETCH
FRAUD GUILE SHIFT SKILL STALL
TRAIN TRICK CAUTEL DECEIT
DEVICE DOUBLE ENGINE COMPASS
CUNNING DODGERY DRAUGHT
EVASION FINESSE SHUFFLE SLEIGHT
COZENAGE DISGUISE DOUBLING
INTRIGUE MANAGERY MANEUVER
PRACTICE PRACTISE PRETENSE
STRATEGY TRICKERY WINDLASS
(PL.) CABAL CRANS
ARTIFICER WRIGHT ARTIFEX
WORKMAN DAEDALUS LAPIDARY
MECHANIC OPIFICER TVASHTAR
TVASHTRI
ARTIFICIAL CUTE SHAM BOGUS
DUMMY FAKED FALSE ARTFUL
ERSATZ FORCED FORGED UNREAL
ASSUMED BASTARD FEIGNED
AFFECTED FABULOUS FALSETTO
POSTICHE POSTIQUE SPURIOUS
(NOT —) REAL NATURAL
(OVERLY —) ALEXANDRIAN
ARTILLERY (OR PIECE THEREOF)
ARMS GUNS DRAKE SAKER CANNON
MINION HEAVIES LANTACA LANTAKA
CANNONRY ORDNANCE
(— FIRE) STONK RAFALE
ARTILLERYMAN GUN GUNNER
LASCAR REDLEG LASHKAR
ENGINEER TOPECHEE
ARTISAN FEVER SMITH ARTIST
COOPER ARTIFEX TARKHAN
WORKMAN KAMMALAN LETTERER
MECHANIC OPIFICER
ARTISANSHIP FOLKCRAFT
ARTIST DAB NABI ACTOR ADEPT
BRUSH HILDA RAPIN DANCER
ETCHER EXPERT FICTOR MASTER
SINGER WIZARD ARTISAN ARTISTE
ARTSMAN FAUVIST OPERANT
PAINTER PONTIST SCHEMER
COLORIST FUSINIST IDEALIST
LADISLAW LETTERER MAGICIAN
MUSICIAN SCULPTOR SKETCHER
STIPPLER
(— SCHOOL) LUMINISM
(SIDEWALK —) SCREEVER
(PL.) SCHOOL
ARTISTIC ARTLY DAEDAL EXPERT
ESTHETIC

(— MATERIAL) KITSCH
(— QUALITY) VERTU VIRTU
ARTISTRY FOLKCRAFT
ARTLESS NAIF OPEN FRANK NAIVE
PLAIN SEELY CANDID RUSTIC
SIMPLE GIRLISH NATURAL
INNOCENT
ARTS TRIVIUM
ARTY CHICHI
ARUM ARAD TARO AROID CALALU
DRAGON TAWKEE WAMPEE
MANDRAKE TUCKAHOE
ARVIRAGUS CADWAL
ARYAN MEDE SLAV NORDIC
(NOT —) ANARYA
AS S SO ALS FOR HOW QUA ALSO
INTO LIKE SOME THAT THUS TILL
WHEN EQUAL QUOAD SINCE WHILE
BRONZE WHENAS BECAUSE
EQUALLY SIMILAR QUATENUS
(— FAR AS) TO INTO QUATENAS
(— IT WERE) FAIRLY
(— LONG AS) SOBEIT
(— MUCH) ALSMEKILL
(— SOON) ALSOON ASTITE ALSWITH
DIRECTLY
(— TO) QUOAD
(— WELL AS) FORBY FORBYE
(— WELL) EVEN
(— YET) HITHERTO
ASAFETIDA HING LASER FERULA
ASARABACCA HAZEL FOALFOOT
ASBESTOS ABBEST XYLITE AMIANTH
ABSISTOS ALBESTON AMIANTUS
WOODROCK
ASCEND UP STY RISE SOAR STYE
UPGO ARISE CLIMB MOUNT SCALE
STAIR TOWER AMOUNT ASPIRE
BREAST CLIMAX UPRISE CLAMBER
UPCLIMB ESCALATE PROGRESS
ASCENDANCY SWAY POWER
CONTROL MASTERY SUCCESS
DOMINION OWERANCE PRESTIGE
ASCENDANT MOUNTANT
ASSURGENT
ASCENDING ANODAL ANODIC
UPHILL UPWARD ANABATIC
ASPIRANT SUBERECT
(— WITHOUT A TURN) FLYING
ASCENSION APOTHEOSIS
ASCENT STY HILL RAMP RISE RIST
UPGO CLIMB GLORY GRADE MOUNT
SCEND SLOPE STEEP STEPS STILL
UPWAY SOURCE STAIRS UPCOME
UPGANG UPHILL UPRISE UPWITH
INCLINE SCALING UPGRADE
UPSWING EMINENCE GRADIENT
ASCERTAIN GET SEE SET TRY FEEL
FIND COUNT GLEAN LEARN PITCH
PROVE ASSURE ATTAIN FIGURE
ANALYSE ANALYZE APPRISE
APPRIZE COMPUTE MEASURE
UNEARTH DISCOVER
ASCETIC NUN MONK SOFI SUFI YATI
YOGI DANDY FAKIR FRIAR SADHU
SOFEE STOIC YOGIN CHASTE
ESSENE HERMIT SADDHU SEVERE
SOOFEE STRICT ADAMITE AUSTERE
BHIKSHU DEVOTEE EREMITE

RECLUSE SRAMANA STYLITE
TAPASVI AVADHUTA MARABOUT
SANNYASI
(PL.) THERAPEUTAE
ASCIDIAN POLYP CUNGEBOI
CUNGEVOI TETHYDAN TUNICATE
ASCIDIUM PITCHER VASCULUM
ASCOCARP ASCOMA
ASCOMA CUPULE
ASCRIBABLE DUE
ASCRIBE LAY ARET EVEN GIVE
BLAME COUNT GUESS IMPLY INFER
PLACE REFER TITLE ACCUSE
ALLEGE ARETTE ASSIGN ATTACH
CHARGE CREDIT IMPUTE PREFER
RECKON RELATE ASCRIVE ENTITLE
ACCREDIT ARROGATE DEDICATE
INSCRIBE INTITULE
ASCRIPTION LAUD CREDIT ADDITION
ASCUS BAG SAC THECA ASCELLUS
ASEA LOST ADDLED ADRIFT
PUZZLED SAILING CONFUSED
ASEXUAL AGAMIC
ASH AS ALS ASE ASS FIG RON COKE
SORB ARTAR ASHEN EMBER FRAIN
ROWAN CINDER CORPSE DOTTEL
DOTTLE WICKEN CLINKER RESIDUE
DOGBERRY FRAXINUS HOOPWOOD
WINETREE
(SILKY —) CEDAR
(PL.) ASE AXAN KELP SOIL ASHEN
VAREC WASTE BREEZE CINDERS
PULVERIN
ASHAMED MEAN NACE NAIS
ABASHED HANGDOG HONTOUS
ASH-COLORED CINEREAL
CINEREOUS
ASHEN WAN GRAY GREY PALE
WAXEN WHITE PALLID GHASTLY
BLANCHED CINEREAL
ASHKOKO CONY DAMAN HYRAX
ASHLAR ASELAR RANGEWORK
ASHORE ACOST ALAND AGROUND
BEACHED STRANDED
ASHTRAY SPITKID SPITKIT
ASHWEED GOUTWEED
ASHUR FEROHER
ASIDE BY BYE OFF AWAY GONE
NEAR PAST AGLEY ALOOF APART
FORBY ASLANT ASTRAY BESIDE
BEYOND BYHAND FORBYE FORTHBY
LATERAL PRIVATE WHISPER
OVERHAND RESERVED SECRETLY
SEPARATE SIDEWISE
ASININE DULL CRASS DENSE INEPT
SILLY ABSURD ASSISH OBTUSE
SIMPLE STUPID DOLTISH FATUOUS
FOOLISH IDIOTIC
ASK BEG SPY SUE FAND PRAY QUIZ
CLAIM CRAVE EXACT FRAYN PLEAD
QUERY SPEAK SPEER SPEIR SPELL
SPERE ADJURE DEMAND DESIRE
EXAMIN EXPECT FRAIST FRAYNE
INVITE BESEECH BESPEAK CONSULT
ENTREAT IMPLORE INQUIRE
REQUEST REQUIRE SOLICIT
PETITION QUESTION
(— ALMS) CANT THIG
(— FOR) BEG BID CRY DUN LAIT

SEEK BESPEAK INQUIRE REQUEST
(— **PAYMENT**) CHARGE
ASKANCE AWRY ASKEW ASKILE
CROOKED SIDEWAYS
ASKEW CAM AGEE ALOP AWRY
AZEW AGLEY AMISS ATILT CRAZY
GLEED ASKANT ASLANT ATWIST
FLOOEY SKEWED ASQUINT
CROOKED OBLIQUE BIASWISE
COCKEYED SIDELING
ASLANT ASIDE SLOPE
ASLEEP DEAD FAST IDLE LATENT
NUMBED DORMANT NAPPING
ASOCIAL EGREGIOUS
ASP ESP ASPIC ASPIDE URAEUS
ASPARAGUS LILY GRASS SPRUE
ASPERGE SPARAGE SPERAGE
(— **GARNISH**) PRINCESS
ASPECT AIR HUE WAY AURA FACE
HAND KIND LEER LOOK MIEN SIDE
VIEW VULT ANGLE COLOR DECIL
FACET GUISE IMAGE NORMA PHASE
SIGHT STAGE TRINE VISOR VIZOR
DECILE FACIES FIGURE GLANCE
MANNER PHASIS REGARD VISAGE
APPAREL BEARING ESSENCE
FEATURE MALEFIC OUTLOOK
RESPECT SEXTILE SHOWING
SPECIES CARRIAGE CONSPECT
FOREHEAD OUTSIGHT PROSPECT
QUINTILE
(— **OF CURVE**) INSIDE
(— **OF EMOTION**) AFFECT
(— **OF MOON**) CRESCENT
(— **OF MUSICAL NUANCES**)
AGOGICS
(**BALEFUL** —) DISASTER
(**CULTURAL** —) EMANATION
(**DETERMINING** —) HEART
(**FACIAL** —) EXPRESSION
(**LANGUAGE** —) DURATIVE
(**PRIMARY** —) HIGHWAY
(**QUARTILE** —) SQUARE
(**SECONDARY** —) BYWAY
ASPEN APS ASP ALAMO NITHER
POPLAR POPPLE QUAKER QUAKING
TREMBLE
ASPER AKCHA AKCHEH OTHMANY
ASPERGILLUM HYSSOP SPRINKLE
STRINKLE
ASPERITY IRE RIGOR ACERBITY
ACRIMONY TARTNESS
ASPERSE SKIT SLUR SPOT ABUSE
DECRY LIBEL SPRAY DEFAME
DEFILE MALIGN REVILE SHOWER
APPEACH BLACKEN DETRACT
LAMPOON SLANDER TARNISH
TRADUCE BESMIRCH FORSPEAK
SPRINKLE
ASPERSION SLUR BAPTISM
CALUMNY INNUENDO
ASPHALT BREA SLIME FILLER
MANJAK BITUMEN CUTBACK
MANJACK BYERLITE UINTAITE
ASPHALTUM CONGO
ASPHODEL KNAVERY AFFODILL
ASPHYXIA APNEA APNOEA
ACROTISM
ASPIC JELLY GELATIN GELATINE
LAVENDER

ASPIRATION GOAL IDEAL DESIRE
RECOIL SIGHTS AMBITION
ASPIRE AIM STY HOPE LONG MINT
RISE SEEK SOAR WISH ETTLE
MOUNT TOWER YEARN ASCEND
ATTAIN DESIRE PRETEND
ASPIRIN FEBRIFUGE
ASPIRING ASPIRANT
ASS DOLT FOOL JADE KHUR MOKE
BURRO CHUMP CUDDY DUNCE
EQUID GUDDA HINNY CUDDIE
DAPPLE DONKEY ONAGER ASINEGO
ASSHEAD JACKASS LONGEAR
MALTESE SOLIPED IMBECILE
(**FEMALE** —) JENNY JENNET
(**MALE** —**S**) JACKSTOCK
(**WILD** —) KIANG KULAN KYANG
KIYAND KOULAN ONAGER HEMIPPE
CHIGETAI GHORKHAR
(**PL**.) JACKSTOCK
ASSAI MANICOLE
ASSAIL WOO BEAT FRAY HOOT JUMP
PELT SAIL ASSAY BESET SHOCK
STONE WHACK WHANG ACCUSE
ATTACK BATTER BICKER BULLET
HURTLE IMPUGN INFEST INSULT
INVADE MALIGN MOLEST OFFEND
RATTLE SAILYE SCATHE STRIKE
ASSAULT ATTEMPT BELABOR
BESEIGE BOMBARD CATCALL
ENFORCE ASSEMBLE TOMAHAWK
ASSAILANT ONSETTER
ASSAM (**MOUNTAIN OF** —) JAPVO
(**STATE OF** —) KHASI MANIPUR
(**TOWN OF** —) IMPHAL SADIYA
GAUHATI SHILLONG
(**TRIBE OF** —) AO AKA AOR AHOM
GARO NAGA
ASSARACUS (**FATHER OF** —) TROS
(**SON OF** —) CAPYS
ASSART SART THWAITE
ASSASSIN THAG THUG BRAVE
BRAVO FEDAI FIDAI CUTTLE FIDAWI
KILLER SLAYER RUFFIAN STABBER
TORPEDO HACKSTER MURDERER
SICARIUS
ASSASSINATE KILL SLAY MURDER
REMOVE
ASSASSINATION THUGGEE
ASSAULT BEAT BLOW COSH FRAY
RAID SLUG ABUSE ALARM ASSAY
BRUNT HARRY ONSET POISE POUND
SHOCK SMITE STORM STOUR VENUE
AFFRAY ALARUM ASSAIL ATTACK
BREACH BUFFET CHARGE ENGINE
EXTENT HOLDUP INSULT INVADE
ONFALL STOUND STOUSH THRUST
YOKING ATTEMPT BOMBARD
DESCENT LAMBAST PURSUIT
RUNNING VIOLATE INVASION
OUTBURST
ASSAY RUN SAY TRY TEST ESSAY
PROOF PROVE TOUCH TRIAL ASSAIL
ATTACK EFFORT ANALYZE ATTEMPT
EXAMINE TASTING ANALYSIS
APPRAISE ENDEAVOR ESTIMATE
HARDSHIP
ASSAYER POTDAR TESTER
ASSEMBLAGE ARMY BODY CAMP

CLOT COMA CREW HERD HOST
MASS PACK RUCK BUNCH CHOIR
CROWD DRIFT DROVE FLOCK
GROUP LEVEE POSSE QUIRE SALON
SHOCK SWARM CONVOY GALAXY
HOOKUP RESORT SPREAD SYSTEM
THRONG CIRCUIT CLUSTER
COLLEGE COMPANY COMPLEX
CONVENT CULTURE SOCIETY
STATION STATUTE TABAGIE
ASSEMBLY AUDITORY CONGRESS
MULTIPLE
(— **OF FOSSILS**) COLONY
(— **OF INTEGERS**) IDEAL
(**CONFUSED** —) FARRAGO
ASSEMBLE FIT LAY POD SAM BULK
CALL HERD HOST KNOT MASS MEET
ROUT SAMM AMASS ASAME FLOCK
PIECE RALLY TROOP UNITE COUPLE
GATHER HUDDLE MUSTER SUMMON
COLLATE COLLECT COMPILE
CONVENE CONVOKE RECRUIT
CONGRESS
(— **CARDS**) BUNCH
ASSEMBLER BONDER
ASSEMBLY HUI SUM BAUD BEVY
BOGY DIET DRUM DUMA FEIS HOEY
MALL MOOT RAAD ROUT SEJM
SEYM TING AGORA BOGEY COURT
COVEN CURIA DOUMA FORUM
GROUP JUNTA LEVEE PARTY PRESS
SABHA SETUP SOBOR SYNOD THING
TROOP AENACH AONACH ASSIZE
BOBBIN BUSING CHAPEL COETUS
COVINE GEMOTE MAJLIS PARADE
PLENUM POWWOW SEIMAS SENATE
STEVEN CHAMBER CHAPTER
COLLEGE COMITIA COMMAND
COMPANY CONCION CONSORT
CONVENT COUNCIL DIETINE
EOTATES FOLKMOT HUSTING
LANDTAG MEETING PENSION
SERVICE SESSION SOCIETY
SYNAGOG SYNAXIS TEMPEST
TYNWALD ZEMSTVO AUDIENCE
CONCLAVE CONGRESS ECCLESIA
FOLKMOOT PLACITUM PORTMOTE
PRESENCE SEDERUNT SOBRANJE
TINEWALD TRIBUNAL VOLKSTAG
WARDMOTE
(— **HOUSE**) KASHIM
(— **OF BLESSED**) HEAVEN
(— **OF CONDUCTORS**) BUS
(— **OF WITCHES**) COVEN SABBAT
SABBATH
(**AFTERNOON** —) LEVEE
(**BOY SCOUT** —) JAMBOREE
(**CLOSED** —) CONCLAVE
(**FASTENER** —) SEMS
(**GRENADE** —) BOUCHON
ASSENT AYE BOW NOD YEA YES
AMEN SEAL SENT ADMIT AGREE
GRANT YIELD ACCEDE ACCEPT
ACCORD BELIEF CHORUS COMPLY
CONCUR SUBMIT UNISON APPROVE
CONCEDE CONFESS CONFORM
CONSENT ADHESION SANCTION
SUFFRAGE
ASSERT LAY BRAG SHOW VOICE

AFFIRM ALLEGE ASSURE AVOUCH
DEFEND DEPONE DEPOSE INTEND
INTENT THREAP UPHOLD ADVANCE
BETOKEN CONFIRM CONTEND
DECLARE PROTEST SUPPORT
ADVOCATE CHAMPION CONSTATE
MAINTAIN OUTSTAND POSITIVE
ASSERTION VOW FACT HOTI CLAIM
VOUCH AVERMENT
(BOASTFUL —) JACTATION
(DUBIOUS —) PLINYISM
ASSERTIVE BRASH DOGMATIC
POSITIVE
ASSESS LAY TAX CESS DOOM LEVY
MISE RATE SCOT TOLL CENSE
PRICE TEIND VALUE AFFEER ASSIZE
CHARGE EXTEND IMPOSE SAMPLE
MEASURE APPRAISE ESTIMATE
ASSESSMENT FEE LUG TAX CESS
DUTY LEVY SCOT TOLL CULET
JUMMA PRICE RATAL TITHE WORTH
EXTENT IMPOST PURVEY SURTAX
TARIFF SCUTAGE BRIGBOTE
TAXATION
ASSESSOR JUDGE MUFTI RATER
CESSOR LISTER TASKER AUDITOR
STENTOR TAXATOR
(PL.) FINTADORES
ASSET HONOR GETPENNY PROPERTY
RESOURCE STRENGTH
ASSETS GOODS MEANS MONEY
STOCK CREDIT WEALTH CAPITAL
EFFECTS ACCOUNTS PROPERTY
RESOURCE
ASSEVERATE SAY VOW AVER AVOW
STATE SWEAR AFFIRM ALLEGE
ASSERT ASSURE DECLARE PROTEST
ASSEVERATION VOW OATH
ASSIDUOUS BUSY GREAT ACTIVE
DEVOTED PENIBLE STUDIED
DILIGENT FREQUENT SEDULOUS
STUDIOUS
ASSIGN FIX LET SET CAST CEDE
DEAL DOLE DRAW GIVE METE RATE
SEAL SHOW SIGN ALLOT ALLOW
AWARD DIGHT ENDOW REFER SHIFT
TITLE ADDUCE AFFECT ALLEGE
CHARGE CONVEY DESIGN DIRECT
ENTAIL ORDAIN ACCOUNT APPOINT
ASCRIBE CONSIGN DISPOSE ENTITLE
SPECIFY STATION TRIBUTE
ALLOCATE ANTEDATE DELEGATE
INSCRIBE TRANSFER
(— QUARTERS) BILLET
(— TASK) STINT
ASSIGNATION DATE MEET TRYST
MEETING
ASSIGNMENT DECK DUTY TASK
GRIND STENT STINT TUNCA CESSIO
LESSON CESSION BUSINESS
HOMEWORK
ASSIGNOR CEDOR CEDENS CEDENT
ASSIMILATE MIX ONE FUSE ADAPT
ALTER BLEND LEARN MERGE
ABSORB DIGEST IMBIBE COMPARE
CONCOCT RESEMBLE
ASSIMILATION ECHOISM HOMEOSIS
(— OF FOOD) CONCOCTION
ASSINIBOIN HOHE

ASSIST AID ABET BACK HELP JOIN
AVAIL BOOST COACH FAVOR NURSE
SERVE SPEED STEAD ATTEND
ESCORT PROMPT SECOND SQUIRE
SUCCOR BENEFIT COMFORT
FURTHER RELIEVE SUPPORT
SUSTAIN ADJUVATE BEFRIEND
(— A READER) FESCUE
(— AT) STAY
ASSISTANCE AID ALMS CAST GIFT
HAND HELP LIFT BOOST FAVOR
HEEZE RELIEF REMEDY SUCCOR
SUPPLY ADJUTOR COMFORT
SECOURS SUBSIDY SUPPORT
AUXILIUM EASEMENT GIFFGAFF
LARGESSE
ASSISTANT CAD AIDE ALLY HAND
HELP MAID MATE PUNK SOUS ZANY
CLERK GROOM USHER VALET
AIDANT BUMPER COMMIS CURATE
DEPUTY FLUNKY HELPER LEGATE
SECOND TULTUL YEOMAN ABETTOR
ACOLYTE ADJOINT DOORMAN
DRESSER HOGGLER PADRINO
PARTNER PROVOST RUBBLER
SHIFTER STRIKER SWAMPER
ADJUTANT ADJUVANT FELDSHER
GOMASHTA LECTURER MINISTER
OFFSIDER PARASITE SERVITOR
SIDESMAN SUBPRIOR
(— TO ANIMAL SHOW JUDGE)
STEWARD
(AUCTIONEER'S —) SPOTTER
(DYEING —) CARRIER
(MASON'S —) GOUJAT
(MATADOR'S —) CHULO
(POLICE —) CORPORAL
(SURVEYOR'S —) CHAINMAN
(WAITER'S —) BUSBOY
ASSOCIATE MIX PAL AIDE ALLY
BAND CHUM HERD JOIN LINK MATE
MOOP MOUP PEER WALK WIFE
YOKE BLEND BUDDY CRONY HABER
MATCH TRAIN TROOP ASSORT
ATTACH ATTEND CHABER COHORT
COUSIN FASTEN FELLOW FRIEND
HELPER HOBNOB MARROW MEDDLE
MEMBER MINGLE PUISNE PUISNY
RELATE SOCIUS SPOUSE TRAVEL
ADJUNCT ASSOCIE BRACKET
COALITE COMMUNE COMPANY
COMPEER COMRADE CONNECT
CONSORT HUSBAND PARTNER
PEWMATE SOCIATE CONJOINT
CONVERSE COPEMATE FAMILIAR
FEDERATE FOLLOWER FREQUENT
GADSHILL IDENTIFY INTIMATE
PARTAKER
(— WITH) FRAT MOOP MOUP
(DEMON —) FLY
(PL.) ENTOURAGE
ASSOCIATION HUI BODY BOND
BUND CLUB GILD HONG HUNT TONG
ARTEL BOARD GUILD HANSA HANSE
SANGH TRUCK UNION CARTEL
CERCLE CHAPEL COMITY CONGER
GRANGE LEAGUE LEGION LYCEUM
PLEDGE SANGHA SCHOLA VEREIN
CIRCUIT COMPANY CONSORT

CONTACT CONVENT COU•ICIL
SOCIETY SOROSIS SYNOECY
AFFINITY ALLIANCE ASSEMBLY
ATHENEUM CONVERSE HABITUDE
INTIMACY SODALITY SYNOMOSY
TAALBOND
(— OF FOSSILS) FAUNULA FAUNULE
(ANTAGONISTIC —) ANTIBIOSIS
(BOOK-SELLERS' —) CONGER
(CLOSE —) HARNESS INTIMACY
(EMPLOYERS' —) GREMIO
(FARMERS' —) GRANGE
(IN —) ALONG
(LABOR —) ARTEL UNION
(RELIGIOUS —) SAMAJ
(SECRET —) CABAL
(STUDENTS' —) CORPS
ASSOIL RID SOIL ATONE CLEAR
SOLVE ACQUIT PARDON REFUTE
ABSOLVE DELIVER EXPIATE FORGIVE
RELEASE RESOLVE
ASSONANCE PUN RHYME
PARAGRAM
ASSORT BOLT CULL SUIT WINNOW
(— COINS) SHROFF
ASSORTED CHOW CHOWCHOW
ASSORTER FEEDER LOOKER
ASSORTMENT BAG LOT SET OLIO
BATCH GROUP SUITE MIXTURE
(— OF TYPE) BILL FONT
(COMPLETE —) STANDARD
ASSUAGE CALM EASE LIOS LISS
ABATE ALLAY CHARM DELAY LISSE
SALVE SLAKE STILL SWAGE LENIFY
LESSEN MODIFY PACIFY QUENCH
REDUCE SOFTEN SOLACE SOOTHE
TEMPER APPEASE COMFORT
MOLLIFY QUALIFY RELIEVE SATISFY
DIMINISH MITIGATE MODERATE
ASSUASIVE MILD LENIENT LENITIVE
SOOTHING
ASSUME DON PUT SAY SET BEAR
DARE FANG GIVE MASK PULL SHAM
SHIP TAKE ADOPT ANNEX CLOAK
ELECT FEIGN GUESS INDUE INFER
RAISE USURP ACCEPT AFFECT
BETAKE CLOTHE FIGURE ASSUMPT
BELIEVE PREMISE PRESUME
PRETEND RECEIVE SUBSUME
SUPPOSE SURMISE ACCROACH
ARROGATE SIMULATE
(— CHARACTER) ACT AFFECT
(— FORM) ENGENDER
(— OFFICE) ACCEDE
(— PAINTING STANCE) BACK
ASSUMED ALIAS FALSE GIVEN
FEIGNED AFFECTED
ASSUMING LOFTY UPPISH UPPITY
AFFECTED ARROGANT SUPERIOR
ASSUMPTION DONNEE THESIS
BALLOON FICTION SURMISE
HOMEOSIS MARYMASS PRETENCE
PRETENSE
(BASIC —) BEGINNING
(EMPTY —) IMAGINATION
ASSURANCE FACE GALL SEAL
BRASS FAITH NERVE TRUST
APLOMB BELIEF CAUTIO CREDIT
PLEVIN SAFETY COURAGE PROMISE

WARRANT AUDACITY BOLDNESS COOLNESS FIRMANCE FOREHEAD SECURITY SUREMENT

ASSURE AVER SURE CINCH HIGHT VOUCH AFFEER ASSERT AVOUCH ENSURE INSURE PLEDGE SECURE SEKERE SICCAR SICKER WITTER BETROTH CERTIFY COMFIRM DECLARE HEARTEN PROMISE PROTEST RESOLVE WARRANT AFFIANCE CONVINCE EMBOLDEN PERSUADE

ASSURED BOLD CALM COLD FIRM SURE BOUND SIKER SLUSH FACILE PROBAL SECURE SICCAR SICKER CERTAIN
(BLUNTLY —) KNOCKDOWN

ASSUREDLY AMEN SOON INDEED REDELY SICCAR SICKER SURELY VERILY HARDILY WITTERLY

ASSYRIA ASHUR ASSUR ASSHUR
(CAPITAL OF —) CALAH NINEVEH

ASSYRIAN NESTORIAN
(— PLUM) SEBESTEN

ASTER ARNICA COCASH AMELLUS BEEWEED BONESET EUASTER ASTROFEL COMPOSIT CYTASTER MONASTER STARWORT STOKESIA

ASTERISK MARK STAR ASTER ASTERISM WINDMILL
(THREE —S) ASTERISM

ASTERN AFT BAFT HIND REAR ABAFT APOOP BEHIND OCCIPUT BACKWARD

ASTEROID EROS HEBE IRIS JUNO CERES DIONE FLORA IRENE METIS VESTA ASTREA EGERIA EUROPA HYGEIA PALLAS PLANET PSYCHE THALIA THEMIS THETIS ELECTRA EUNOMIA FORTUNA LUTETIA CALLIOPE MASSALIA STARFISH STARLIKE VICTORIA

ASTHMA PHTHISIC

ASTHMATIC POUCY PURSY POUCEY WHEEZY PANTING PUFFING

ASTIR UP AGOG ABOUT AFOOT AGATE ALERT GOING ACTIVE AROUND ASTEER MOVING ROUSED ABROACH EXCITED STIRRING VIGILANT

ASTONISH AWE DAZE STAM AMAZE KNOCK SHOCK DAMMER MARVEL STOUND ASTOUND GLOPPEN IMPRESS STARTLE AMERVEIL BEWILDER CONFOUND SURPRISE

ASTONISHING AMAZING FABULOUS

ASTONISHMENT MUSE FERLY DISMAY FARLEY MARVEL STOUND WONDER SURPRISE

ASTOUND BEAT STUN AMAZE APPAL SHOCK STOUN APPALL STOUND STAGGER STUPEFY STUPEND TERRIFY ASTONISH CONFOUND SURPRISE

ASTOUNDING STUNNING

ASTRAGAL TALUS CHAPLET CORNICE

ASTRAKHAN BOKHARA

ASTRAL REMOTE STARRY STELLAR

ASTRAEAN SIDEREAL STARLIKE

ASTRAY AWRY LOST WILL AGLEY AMISS ASIDE GLEED WRONG ABROAD AFIELD ERRANT ERRING FAULTY DEPAYSE DEVIOUS FORLORN SINNING WILSOME MISTAKEN STRAYING

ASTRIDE ATOP ABOARD ACHEVAL SPANNING

ASTRINGENCY ACERBITY ACRIMONY

ASTRINGENT ACID ALUM COTO SOUR TART ACERB HARSH SAPAN STERN CORNUS MASTIC PONTIC SEVERE TANNIN ALUMNOL AUSTERE BINDING CATECHU PUCKERY RHATANY STYPTIC GERANIUM TRILLIUM

ASTROLOGER JOTI JOSHI ARTIST JOTISI MERLIN ZADKIEL SCHEMIST

ASTROLOGY STARCRAFT MATHEMATICALS

ASTRONOMER JOTI JOSHI JOTISI

ASTRONOMICAL FAR HUGE GREAT URANIC DISTANT IMMENSE URANIAN COLOSSAL INFINITE
(— INSTRUMENT) ARMILL

ASTRONOMY WAGON WAGONER WAGGONER

ASTUTE SLY FOXY KEEN WILY ACUTE CANNY QUICK SHARP SMART CLEVER CRAFTY NASUTE SHREWD CUNNING KNOWING SKILLED

ASUNDER ATWO APART SPLIT ATWAIN SUNDER SUNDRY DIVIDED DIVORCED YSOWNDIR

ASURA VARUNA

ASYLUM ARK HOME JAIL ALTAR COVER GRITH HAVEN BEDLAM HARBOR REFUGE ALSATIA COLLEGE HOSPICE RETREAT SHELTER BUGHOUSE MADHOUSE

ASYMMETRIC PEDIAL

AT A AL AU BY IN TO ALS TIL TILL UNTO ATTEN THERE HEREAT
(— ALL) ANY AVA EER EVER HALF OUGHT SOEVER HOWEVER

ATABAL DRUM TABOR ATTABAL

ATAMAN CHIEF JUDGE HETMAN HEADMAN

ATAVISM REVERSION

ATELIER SHOP STUDIO BOTTEGA WORKSHOP

ATEO WAKEA

ATES SWEETSOP

ATHAMAS (DAUGHTER OF —) HELLE
(FATHER OF —) AEOLUS
(SON OF —) PHRIXUS LEARCHUS PALAEMON
(WIFE OF —) INO NEPHELE

ATHANOR OVEN ATHENOR FURNACE

ATHAPASKAN HAW HARE HUPA KATO KASKA AHTENA BEAVER CHETCO GILENO LASSIK SARCEE SEKANI CARRIER CHILULA KOYUKON KUTCHIN

ATHEIST ZENDIK DOUBTER INFIDEL NASTIKA AGNOSTIC APIKOROS NETHEIST

ATHENA ALEA AUGE NIKE ALERA AREIA ERGANE HIPPIA HYGEIA

ITONIA PALLAS POLIAS AIANTIS MINERVA APATURIA

ATHENIAN ATTIC CHORAGUS CHOREGUS

ATHLETE PRO BLUE KEMP STAR BOXER COLOR CRACK CUTEY CUTIE TURNER ACROBAT AMATEUR GYMNAST STICKER TUMBLER VARMINT GAMESTER REPEATER WRESTLER

ATHLETIC AGILE BURLY LUSTY VITAL BRAWNY GYMNIC ROBUST SINEWY STRONG BOARDLY BOORDLY MUSCULAR POWERFUL VIGOROUS

ATHLETICS GAMES SPORT EXERCISE

ATHWART CROSS ABOARD ACROSS ASLANT OBLIQUE SIDEWISE TRAVERSE

ATLAS BOOK LIST MAPS TOME TITAN TELAMON MAINSTAY
(DAUGHTERS OF —) ATLANTIDES
(FATHER OF —) IAPETUS
(MOTHER OF —) CLYMENE
(WIFE OF —) PLEIONE

ATLE ETHEL

ATMAN ATMA ATTA SELF

ATMOSPHERE AIR SKY AURA FEEL LIFT MOOD TONE AROMA CLIME DECOR ETHER SMELL FROWST MIASMA NIMBUS SPHERE WELKIN FEELING HYALINE QUALIFY AMBIANCE AMBIENCE
(— OF DISCOURAGEMENT) CHILL
(NOXIOUS —) MIASMA
(SECTION OF —) SOLENOID
(STALE —) FROUST FROWST
(STUFFY —) FUG
(SUFFOCATING —) STIFLE

ATMOSPHERICS STATIC SPHERICS

ATOM ACE BIT ION JOT DIAD DYAD HAET HATE IOTA MITE MOTE WHIT ATOMY HENAD LABEL MONAD SHADE SPECK TINGE ADATOM BRIDGE CARBYL HEPTAD ISOBAR TETRAD ATOMIZE BODIKIN IONOGEN ISOTOPE RADICAL SPECIES FUNCTION ISOSTERE MOLECULE PARTICLE QUANTITY
(— TOTALITY) MATTER
(PL.) SMITHERS SMITHEREENS

ATOMIC TINY MINUTE NUCLEAR

ATOMIZER SPRAY SPARGE SCENTER SPRAYER AIRBRUSH ODORATOR PERFUMER

ATONE AGREE AMEND ACCORD ANSWER ASSOIL RANSOM REDEEM REPENT APPEASE EXPIATE RESTORE SATISFY
(— FOR) ABY BYE ABYE MEND ABIDE ABEGGE

ATONEMENT MEND MICHTAM PENANCE

ATOP ACOR

ATORAI DAURI

ATRABILIOUS GLUM ADUST GLOOMY MOROSE SULLEN

ATREUS (BROTHER OF —) THYESTES
(FATHER OF —) PELOPS
(HALF-BROTHER OF —) THYESTES

(MOTHER OF —) HIPPODAMIA
(SON OF —) MENELAUS
(WIFE OF —) AEROPE
ATRIP AWEIGH
ATRIUM HALL ATRIO COURT CAVITY
AURICLE CHAMBER PASSAGE
ATROCIOUS BAD DARK RANK VILE
AWFUL BLACK CRUEL GROSS
ATROCE BRUTAL ODIOUS SAVAGE
WICKED HEINOUS UNGODLY
VIOLENT FLAGRANT GRIEVOUS
HORRIBLE TERRIBLE
ATROPHIC AUANTIC
ATROPHY RUST STUNT TABES
MACIES SHRINK STARVE SWEENY
WITHER SWINNEY WASTING
STULTIFY
ATTACH ADD FIX SET SEW TAG TIE
BIND BOLT GLUE HANG JOIN LINK
SPAN TAKE VEST WELD ADOPT
AFFIX ANNEX BEWED FOUND HINGE
HITCH LATCH PASTE SCREW SEIZE
SPEND STICK TACHE TATCH UNITE
ACCUSE ADDICT ADHERE ADJOIN
APPEND ARREST CEMENT DEVOTE
ENGAGE ENTAIL ENTIRE FASTEN
FATHER INDICT SPLINE ADHIBIT
APPOINT ASCRIBE CONNECT
ESPOUSE SUBJOIN
(— TEMPORARILY) SECOND
ATTACHED FAST FOND DOTING
ADJUNCT BIGOTED SESSILE
ADSCRIPT INSERTED
ATTACHING INCIDENT ALLIGATION
ATTACHMENT ARM GAG BAIL BALE
DRUM FLAY HEAD HECK LOVE MOTE
SHIM SHOE AMOUR CHUCK CRUSH
DOBBY DODAD FENCE GUARD STRIG
AFFAIR BEATER BINDER BUMPER
DAMSEL DOBBIE DOCTOR DOODAD
DREDGE FELLER FETICH FETISH
HEMMER HILLER LAPPET LAYBOY
MARKER PACKER PICKUP SECTOR
SHIELD SIDING ADAPTOR AFFAIRE
BIGOTRY BRAIDER CREASER
DROPPER FAGOTER FITTING
GIGBACK HEADSET HOLDING
JOINTER KNOCKUP LEVELER
SPANNER SPRAYER DEVOTION
DINGDONG FASTNESS FIXATION
FONDNESS GOVERNOR HEADREST
ATTACK FIT HIT HOP SIC BAIT BOMB
BOUT CLAW COSH DINT FANG FORK
FRAY GANG GIVE HOOK JUMP PAIL
PANG RAID RISE RUSH SAIL SICK
SLOW TACK TURN WADE YOKE
ABUSE ALARM ASSAY BEGIN BESET
BLAST BLITZ BRASH BRUNT CATCH
CHECK DRIVE FIGHT FLUSH FORAY
FORCE GLIDE HARRY ICTUS ONSET
POISE PULSE SALLY SCUFF SMITE
SOUSE SPASM SPELL STORM
ACCESS ACCUSE ACTION AFFRAY
AFFRET ASSAIL ATTAME BATTLE
BICKER CHARGE CRISIS DOUBLE
ENVAYE EXPUGN EXTENT GRUDGE
INDICT INFEST INSULT INVADE
OFFEND ONFALL ONRUSH POUNCE
RUFFLE SAVAGE SHOWER SORTIE

STOUND STRIKE STROKE TACKLE
TAKING THRUST AGGRESS ASPERSE
ASSAULT ATTEMPT BARRAGE
BELABOR BELIBEL BESEIGE
BOMBARD CENSURE CRUSADE
DESCENT OFFENSE PICKOUT
POTSHOT RUNNING SCALING
SEIZURE STACKER CAMISADO
ENDEAVOR ESCALADE PAROXYSM
SKIRMISH SURPRISE TOMAHAWK
(— IN COCKFIGHT) SHUFFLE
(— OF ILLNESS) GO DWAM DWALM
(— OF SICKNESS) WHIP SEIZURE
(— TO ROB) THUG
(— WITH SHOUTS) HUE
(— WITH WORDS) STOUSH
(— ZEALOUSLY) CRUSADE
(CHESS —) FORK
(CRITICAL —) SLATING
(FENCING —) GLIDE
(LIGHT —) TOUCH
(SLIGHT —) WAFF
(SUDDEN —) ICTUS RAPTUS
SURPRISE
(SUICIDAL —) KAMIKAZE
(SURPRISE —) ALARM ALARUM
(VERBAL —) FIRE BLUDGEON
ATTACKER AGGRESSOR OFFENDANT
ATTAIN GO GET HIT WIN BUMP
COME EARN GAIN RISE SORT ARISE
CATCH COVER CROSS FETCH
PROVE REACH TOUCH ACCEDE
AMOUNT ARRIVE ASPIRE EFFECT
OBTAIN SECURE STRIKE ACHIEVE
ACQUIRE COMPASS PROCURE
SUCCEED OVERTAKE
(— TO ACCOMPLISH) FIND FORCE
ATTAINMENT ARRIVAL ADEPTION
ENERGEIA PURCHASE
(— OF NIRVANA) MOKSHA
(SCHOLARLY —) LETTERS
ATTAR ITR OIL ATAR OTTO ATHAK
OTTAR ESSENCE PERFUME
ATTEMPT GO PUT SAY SHY TRY
BOUT BURL DARE DASH FAND FIST
FOND HACK JUMP MIND MINT MIRD
OSSE SEEK SHOT SLAP STAB WAGE
WORK ASSAY BEGIN ESSAY ETTLE
FLING FRAME OFFER ONSET PRESS
PROOF PROVE START TEMPT TRIAL
WHACK ASSAIL ATTACK EFFORT
FRAIST STRIVE ENFORCE IMITATE
PRETEND PROFFER STAGGER
VENTURE CONATION ENDEAVOR
EXERTION PURCHASE TENTAMEN
(— TO AROUSE) AGITATE
(— TO BRIBE) APPROACH
(— TO INFLUENCE) AGITATION
(ABORTIVE —) FUTILITY
ATTEND GO HO HOA HOO SEE HEAR
HEED LIST MIND OYES OYEZ STAY
TEND WAIT WALK APPLY AUDIT
AWAIT GUARD LAKEY NURSE SERVE
TREAT VISIT WATCH ASSIST
CONVEY ESCORT FOLLOW HARKEN
INTEND LISTEN SECOND SHADOW
SQUIRE CONDUCT CONSORT
ESQUIRE HEARKEN LACQUEY
PERPEND RETINUE

(— A LADY) WAIT
(— FUNERAL) FOLLOW
(— REGULARLY) KEEP
(— TO) MIND TREAT FETTLE INTEND
(— UPON) TENT CHASE CHAPERON
ATTENDANCE GATE SUIT CHAPEL
NUMBER OFFICE REGARD SERVICE
PRESENCE
ATTENDANT BOY FLY LAD JACK
MAID MUTE PAGE PEON SYCE ZANY
CADDY COMES GILLY GROOM GUIDE
JAGER USHER VALET ALEXAS
CADDIE DACTYL DAMSEL EMILIA
ESCORT FRIEND GESITH HAIDUK
HOGMAN JAEGER MINION PORTER
SQUIRE STOCAH TUBMAN VARLET
VERGER WAITER YEOMAN ALIPTES
ARMORER BULLDOG CHOBDAR
COURIER CROSSER DAMOSEL
FAMULUS FENELLA FOOTBOY
GHILLIE HALLMAN HOSTESS
JACKMAN LINKMAN MYRIDON
ORDERLY PAGEBOY PIQUEUR
PRESSER SEQUENT SERVANT
SHIPBOY SPOUTER TRABANT
TRESSEL ATTENDEE BEACHBOY
CHASSEUR CORYBANT CRUTCHER
FEWTERER FOLLOWER GATHERER
HANDMAID HENCHBOY HENCHMAN
HOUSEMAN MINISTER OBSERVER
ROSALINE SERGEANT SERJEANT
STAFFIER TIPSTAFF WATERMAN
(— OF CYBELE) CORYBANT
(CROSSING —) GATEMAN
(KNIGHT'S —) SWAIN ESQUIRE
(PROCTOR'S —) BULLDOG
(YOUNG —) BOY LAD JACK PAGE
KNIGHT
(PL.) STAFF CORTEGE RETINUE
ATTENDED FRAUGHT
ATTENTION EAR CARE GAUM HEED
HIST MARK MIND NOTE RUSH SHUN
TENT FLOOR GUARD STUDY TASTE
DETAIL FAVORS NOTICE REGARD
ACCOUNT ACHTUNG ADDRESS
EARNEST HEARING RESPECT
THOUGHT AUDIENCE
(— FROM SUPERIOR) TASHRIF
TASHREEF
(— TO PETTY ITEMS) MICROLOGY
(AMOROUS —) GALLANTRY
(FIXED —) DHARANA
(FLATTERING —) HOMAGE
(PLEASING —) INCENSE
(SPECIAL —) ACCENT
ATTENTIVE WARY ALERT AWAKE
CIVIL CLOSE SHARP TENTY ARRECT
INTENT POLITE CAREFUL GALLANT
HEEDFUL LISTFUL MINDFUL
PRESENT DILIGENT OBEDIENT
STUDIOUS THOUGHTY VIGILANT
WATCHFUL
(— TO) IMMINENT
ATTENUATE SAP DRAW FINE THIN
WATER DILUTE LESSEN RAREFY
REDUCE WEAKEN SLENDER
AVIANIZE DECREASE DIMINISH
EMACIATE ENFEEBLE TAPERING
ATTENUATED GAUNT AERIAL

DILUTED SPINDLY FINESPUN
SMORZATO
ATTENUATION LOSS
ATTENUATOR PAD
ATTEST CHOP SEAL SIGN PROVE
STATE SWEAR VOUCH ADJURE
AFFIRM INVOKE RECORD WITTEN
CERTIFY CONFESS CONFIRM
CONSIGN TESTIFY WARRANT
WITNESS EVIDENCE INDICATE
MANIFEST
ATTESTATION DOCKET RECORD
ATTESTED SWORN CERTIFIED
ATTIC LOFT CELER SOLAR SOLER
GARRET TALLET GRENIER
COCKLOFT
(— SIDE) SKEELING
ATTIRE (ALSO SEE DRESS) BEGO
SUIT TIRE ADORN ARRAY BIGAN
DRESS HABIT AGUISE ENROBE
PLIGHT REVEST TOILET ADDRESS
APPAREL DUBBING PANOPLY
ACCOUTER CLEADING EQUIPAGE
FEATHERS
(FORMAL —) BALLDRESS
(SHINING —) SHEEN
ATTIRED TRICKSY
ATTITUDE AIR CUE SET BIAS MIEN
MOOD POSE SIDE ANGLE FRAME
HEART PHASE SHAPE SHELL SIGHT
SLANT STAND ACTION ANIMUS
ASPECT MANNER SPIRIT STANCE
BEARING FEELING GESTURE
POSTURE STATION STOMACH
BEHAVIOR CARAPACE CROTCHET
HABITUDE POSITION
(PREVAILING —) STREAM
ATTORNEY DOER AGENT PROXY
VAKIL DEPUTY FACTOR FISCAL
LAWYER LEGIST MUKTAR SYNDIC
VAKEEL PROCTOR ADVOCATE
ATTRACT BAIT CALL DRAW LURE
PULL TILL WIND BRING CATCH
CHARM COURT FETCH TEMPT
ALLURE ENGAGE ENLIST ENTICE
GATHER INVITE SEDUCE STRIKE
BEWITCH PROCURE INTEREST
(— FISH) CHUM
ATTRACTION BAIT CALL CARD
CLOU DRAW PULL CHARM DRAFT
SPELL TRACT APPEAL DESIRE
MAGNET BLOWOFF COITION
DRAUGHT GRAVITY INDRAFT
ADHESION AFFINITY COHESION
CONTRACT PENCHANT SIDESHOW
WITCHERY
ATTRACTIVE BRAW CHIC CUTE FAIR
GOOD BONNY FATAL JOLLY QUEME
SWEET COMELY FLASHY FRUITY
HEPPEN LOVELY PRETTY SAVORY
SNAZZY TAKING TRICKY AMIABLE
CIRCEAN CUNNING EYEABLE
EYESOME GRADELY WINNING
WINSOME ALLURING CHARMING
ENGAGING ENTICING FEATURED
FETCHING GRACEFUL GRACIOUS
HANDSOME INVITING SPECIOUS
VENEREAN
(NOT —) FOUL INCURIOUS

ATTRACTIVENESS CHARM GRACE
BEAUTY GLAMOR AMENITY GLITTER
AFFINITY HARLOTRY
ATTRIBUTABLE DUE
ATTRIBUTE FOX OWE GIVE MARK
SIGN TYPE ALLOT BADGE BLAME
CHARM PLACE POWER REFER
ALLEGE ALLUDE ASSERT ASSIGN
BESTOW CHARGE CREDIT IMPUTE
PREFER REPUTE SYMBOL ADJUNCT
ASCRIBE COUNTER ESSENCE
PERTAIN QUALITY ACCREDIT
GRANDITY INTITULE PROPERTY
PROPRIUM STRENGTH
(— WRONGFULLY) FOIST
(—S OF ROCKS) GEOLOGY
(PL.) SARIRA SHARIRA
ATTRIBUTION ACCENT THEORY
ANIMISM ETIOLOGY
ATTRITION WEAR GRIEF REGRET
SORROW ANGUISH ABRASION
BLASTING FRICTION
ATTUNE KEY TUNE ADAPT AGREE
ACCORD ADJUST TEMPER PREPARE
ATUA AKUA DEMON SPIRIT
ATYPICAL BIZARRE GROTESQUE
AUBERGE INN ALBERGO
AUBERGINE EGGPLANT
AUBURN ABRAM BLOND CACHA
CUTCH BLONDE CACHOU CATECHU
GOREVAN
AU COURANT CONTEMPORARY
AUCTION CANT ROUP SALE SELL
VEND COKER TRADE BARTER
BRIDGE HAMMER OUTCRY VENDUE
OUTROOP UNCTION DISPOSAL
KNOCKOUT PORTSALE
AUCTIONEER CRIER CRYER
OUTCRIER
AUDACIOUS BOLD BRASH BRAVE
FRACK HARDY SAUCY AUDACE
BRAZEN CHEEKY DARING FORWARD
ARROGANT FEARLESS IMPUDENT
INSOLENT INTREPID SPIRITED
(NOT —) CIVIL
AUDACITY CHEEK NERVE COURAGE
BOLDNESS TEMERITY
AUDIBLE RIFE ALOUD CLEAR HEARD
AUDIENCE EAR PIT FANS AUDIT
COURT FLOOR HOUSE PUBLIC
GALLERY HEARING ASSEMBLY
AUDITORY TRIBUNAL
AUDIT SCAN CHECK PROBE APPOSE
RECKON VERIFY ACCOUNT EXAMINE
INQUIRE INSPECT ESTIMATE
AUDITION HEARING
AUDITOR CENSOR HEARER APPOSER
AUDIENT PITTITE COUNTOUR
DISCIPLE LISTENER
AUDITORIUM HALL ROOM CAVEA
FRONT ODEUM THEATER AUDITORY
AUDITORY ORAL OTIC AURAL
AUDILE ACOUSTIC AUDITIVE
AUGER BIT BORE BORAL BORER
GRILL BORING GIMLET NAUGER
WIMBLE PIERCER TEREBRA
AUGHT ACHT EAWT AUCHT OWNED
CIPHER NAUGHT WORTHY NOTHING
VALIANT ANYTHING

AUGMENT ADD EKE FEED GROW
HELP URGE BOOST EXALT SWELL
APPEND DILATE EXPAND EXTEND
AMPLIFY BALLOON ENHANCE
ENLARGE IMPROVE INFLAME
MAGNIFY COMPOUND HEIGHTEN
INCREASE MAJORATE MULTIPLY
(— IN STRENGTH) INGROSS
AUGMENTATION RISE EKING SWELL
GROWTH AUCTARY ADDITION
AUGMENTED SHARP EXTREME
AUGUR BODE OMEN SEER SPEAK
AUSPEX DIVINE BETOKEN CONJECT
FORESEE OMINATE PORTEND
PREDICT PRESAGE PROMISE
PROPHET SIGNIFY DENOUNCE
FOREBODE FORESHOW FORETELL
FOREWARN INDICATE PROPHESY
AUGURY ORE OMEN RITE SIGN
SOOTH TOKEN HANSEL RITUAL
HANDSEL PRESAGE CEREMONY
AUGUST AWFUL GRAND NOBLE
KINGLY SERENE SOLEMN EXALTED
STATELY IMPOSING MAJESTIC
(FIRST DAY OF —) LAMMAS LUGNAS
LUGHNAS LUGNASAD
AUGUSTINIAN AUSTIN
ASSUMPTIONIST
AUHUHU HOLA
AUK FALK LOOM ARRIE DIVER LEMOT
MURRE NODDY SCOOT SCOUT
SKOUT MARROT PUFFIN ROTCHE
STARIK TINKER DOVEKEY DOVEKIE
PENGUIN PYGOPOD SEAFOWL
WILLOCK GAIRFOWL GAREFOWL
ROCKBIRD
AULA HALL COURT EMBLIC
AUNT TIA BAWD AUNTY NAUNT
TANTA TANTE AUNTIE GOSSIP
(— SALLY) STICKS
AURA AIR HALO ODOR AROMA
SAVOR SMELL BREEZE BUZZARD
ESSENCE FEELING
AUREATE GOLDEN ORNATE ROCOCO
YELLOW
AUREOLE HALO CROWN GLORY
LIGHT AREOLA CORONA GLORIA
NIMBUS VESICA GLORIOLE
MANDORLA
AUREUS (HALF —) SEMIS
AURICLE EAR PINNA ATRIUM EARLET
TRUMPET PAVILION
AURIGA WAGONER WAGGONER
AURIST OTOLOGIST
AUROCHS TUR UROX URUS BISON
WISENT BONASSUS
AURORA EOS DAWN DRAPERY
MORNING
AURORA BOREALIS DANCERS
AUSPICE CARE OMEN SIGN AUGURY
PORTENT GUIDANCE
(PL.) EGIS AEGIS
AUSPICIOUS FAIR GOOD TWINE
WHITE BRIGHT CHANCY DEXTER
CHANCEY FAVORING
AUSTERE BARE COLD HARD SOUR
BLEAK BUDGE GRAVE GRUFF
HARSH RIGID ROUGH SHARP STERN
STIFF STOUR BITTER CHASTE

FORMAL RUGGED SEVERE SIMPLE
SOMBER STRICT SULLEN TETRIC
ASCETIC EARNEST SERIOUS
GRANITIC RIGOROUS TETRICAL
AUSTERITY RIGOR CATOISM
AUSTRAL SOUTHERN

AUSTRALIA
ABORIGINE: MYALL
CAPE: HOWE
CAPITAL: CANBERRA
COIN: DUMP POUND SHILLING
DESERT: STURT GIBSON TANAMI
SIMPSON
ISLAND: CATO COCOS KOOLAN
CORINGA LACEPEDE ROTTNEST
TASMANIA
LAKE: EYRE COWAN FROME
BARLEE BULLOO AMADEUS
BLANCHE EVERARD TORRENS
GAIRDNER
LANGUAGE: YABBER
MEASURE: SAUM
MOUNTAIN: OLGA BRUCE LEGGE
CRADLE GARNET GAWLER
MAGNET STUART BONGONG
GREGORY CUTHBERT JUSGRAVE
MULLIGAN KOSCIUSKO
MOUNTAIN RANGE: DARLING
FLINDERS
NATIVE: MARA BINGE AUSSIE
DIGGER BILLIJIM KANGAROO
WARRAGAL WARRIGAL
JINDYWOROBAK
PENINSULA: EYRE
RIVER: DALY BULLO COMET ISAAC
PAROO ROPER SNOWY YARRA
BARCOO BARWON CULGOA
DAWSON DEGREY DARLING
FITZROY LACHLAN STAATEN
GEORGINA VICTORIA
SEA: CORAL TIMOR TASMAN
ARAFURA
SOLDIER: DIGGER SWADDY
BILLIJIM
STATE: TASMANIA VICTORIA
QUEENSLAND
TOWN: AYR YASS DUBBO PERTH
WAGGA ALBURY AUBURN
CAIRNS CASINO COBURG
DARWIN HOBART MACKAY
SYDNEY BENDIGO GEELONG
KOGARAH MILDURA MITCHAM
ADELAIDE BRISBANE ESSENDON
RANDWICK RINGWOOD
MELBOURNE TOOWOOMBA
VALLEY: GROSE JAMIESON
MEGALONG
WATER HOLE BILLABONG
WOMAN: LUBRA

AUSTRALIAN ANZAC AUSSIE DIGGER
AUSTRAL CURRENCY KANGAROO
WARRAGAL WARRIGAL
(— GIRL) LUBRA

AUSTRIA
ANCIENT PEOPLE: HUNS AVARS
RAETIANS SLOVENES
BAVARIANS
CAPITAL: WIEN VIENNA
CELTIC KINGDOM: NORICUM
COIN: DUCAT KRONE FLORIN
HELLER ZEHNER GROSCHEN
SCHILLING
DUCHY: STYRIA CARNIOLA
CARINTHIA
EMPEROR: CHARLES FRANCIS
FERDINAND
LAKE: ALMSEE FERTOTO
MONDSEE BODENSEE TRAUNSEE
CONSTANCE
MEASURE: FASS FUSS JOCH MASS
MUTH YOKE HALBE LINIE MEILE
METZE PFIFF PUNKT ACHTEL
BECHER SEIDEL DLAFTER
VIERTEL DREILING
MOUNTAIN: STUBAI EISENERZ
RHATIKON KITZBUHEL
NATIVE: STYRIAN TYROLEAN
NOBILITY: RITTER
PASS: LOIBL ARLBERG BRENNER
PLOCKEN
PROVINCE: TIROL TYROL STYRIA
VIENNA SALZBURG CARINTHIA
VORARLBERG
RIVER: INN MUR DRAU ENNS
KAMP LECH MURZ RAAB DONAU
MARCH SALZA THAYA TRAUN
DANUBE SALZACH
RIVER PORT: LINZ KREMS VIENNA
ROMAN PROVINCE: RAETIA
NORICUM PANNONIA
TOWN: ENNS GRAZ LECH LINZ
RIED WELS WIEN GMUND LIENZ
STEYR TRAUN LEOBEN VIENNA
BREGENZ MODLING SPITTAL
VILLACH DORNBIRN SALZBURG
INNSBRUCK
WEIGHT: MARC SAUM UNZE
DENAT KARCH PFUND STEIN
CENTNER PFENNIG VIERLING

AUTACOID HORMONE INCRETION
AUTARCHIC FREE
AUTHENTIC ECHT PURE REAL SURE
TRUE EXACT PUCCA PUCKA PUKKA
RIGHT VALID ACTUAL DINKUM
PROPER CORRECT CURRENT
GENUINE SINCERE CREDIBLE
OFFICIAL ORIGINAL RELIABLE
AUTHENTICATE SEAL PROVE
VOUCH ATTEST SIGNET VERIFY
APPROVE CONFIRM LEGALIZE
AUTHOR DOER JUDE SIRE JUDAS
MAKER RULER AUCTOR FACTOR
FORGER LOKMAN PARENT PENMAN
SCRIBE SOURCE WRITER ANCIENT
CLASSIC CREATOR ELOHIST
FOUNDER LOLLIUS ANCESTOR
BEGETTER COMPILER COMPOSER
IDEALIST IMMORTAL INVENTOR

JEHOVIST ORIGINAL PAYYETAN
PRODUCER
(PL.) SS
AUTHORITATIVE GRAVE CLASSIC
OFFICIAL ORACULAR POSITIVE
TEXTUARY
AUTHORITY LAW ROD SEE BALL
RULE SWAY ADEPT BOARD FAITH
POWER RICHE RIGHT STAMP SWING
TITLE ARTIST AUTHOR CREDIT
DANGER EMPERY EXPERT FASCES
REGENT REGIME SWINGE WEIGHT
AMITATE COMMAND CONTROL
DYNASTY FACULTY LEADING
LICENCE LICENSE SCEPTER
WARRANT DISPOSAL DOMINION
DOMINIUM HEGEMONY LORDSHIP
PRESTIGE SANCTION STRENGTH
(— OF SWITZERLAND) BUNDESRAT
(ARBITRARY —) ABOVE
(ROYAL —) SCEPTRE SOVRANTY
(SPIRITUAL —) KEYS KHILAFAT
(SUPREME —) SAY SIRCAR SIRKAR
(UNLIMITED —) AUTOCRACY
(PL.) ISNAD
AUTHORIZATION BARAT BERAT
PASSPORT SANCTION WARRANTY
AUTHORIZE LET LEAL VEST ALLOW
CLEAR CLOTHE PERMIT RATIFY
APPROVE EMPOWER ENDORSE
ENTITLE INDORSE JUSTIFY LICENSE
WARRANT ACCREDIT DELEGATE
LEGALIZE SANCTION
AUTHORIZED LEGAL OFFICIAL
AUTHORSHIP PENCRAFT PATERNITY
AUTO (ALSO SEE AUTOMOBILE)
CRATE CHUMMY LIZZIE
AUTOBIOGRAPHY VITA MEMOIR
AUTOCHTHONOUS NATIVE EDAPHIC
ENDEMIC
AUTOCLAVE DIGESTER DIGESTOR
AUTOCRACY MONARCHY
AUTOCRAT CZAR TSAR TZAR
MOGUL CAESAR DESPOT AUTARCH
MONARCH DICTATOR MONOCRAT
AUTOCRATIC ABSOLUTE
AUTO-DA-FE AUTO SERMO
AUTOGRAPH NAME SIGN MANUAL
INSCRIBE
AUTOMATIC MACHINE
AUTOMATON GOLEM ROBOT
AUTOMA ANDROID MACHINE
AUTOMOBILE BUG BUS CAR SIX
AUTO FOUR HEAP JEEP PONY TRAP
BUGGY COACH COUPE CRATE
EIGHT PONEY RACER SEDAN
BUCKET CHUMMY CUSTOM JALOPY
JUNKER SALOON AUTOCAR
COMPACT FLIVVER HACKNEY
HARDTOP MACHINE PHAETON
STEAMER TORPEDO VOITURE
CARRYALL DRAGSTER ELECTRIC
ROADSTER SQUADROL SUBURBAN
VICTORIA
(CONVERTIBLE —) DROPHEAD
(MIDGET —) DOODLEBUG
AUTONOMOUS FREE SEPARATE
AUTONOMY SOVEREIGNTY
SEPARATENESS

(— **OF GOD**) ASEITY ASEITAS
AUTOPSY NECROPSY
AUTUMN FALL KHARIF AUTOMPNE
FALLTIME MATURITY
AUXILIARY AID SUB AIDE ALLY
AIDING BRANCH DONKEY HELPER
ABETTER ABETTOR ADJUNCT
HELPING PARTNER ADJUTANT
(PL.) FOEDERATI
AVAIL DO AID DOW USE BOOT HELP
FADGE SERVE SKILL STEAD VALUE
MOMENT PROFIT BENEFIT BESTEAD
PREVAIL SERVICE SUCCEED SUFFICE
UTILIZE SUBSERVE
(— **ONESELF**) EMBRACE IMPROVE
SUBSERVE
AVAILABLE FIT FREE OPEN FLUSH
HANDY READY PATENT USABLE
PRESENT VISIBLE
AVALANCHE SLIDE LAWINE
VOLLEGE
AVANT-COURIER HERALD SCURRIER
AVANT-GARDE LITERATI
AVARICE GREED MISERY AVIDITY
CUPIDITY RAPACITY
AVARICIOUS CLOSE SLOAN GREEDY
HAVING HUNGRY SORDID STINGY
GRIPING GRIPPLE ITCHING MISERLY
COVETOUS GRASPING
AVATAR BALARAMA EPIPHANY
AVELLANEOUS HAZEL
AVENGE REPAY RIGHT VISIT WRACK
AWREAK PUNISH BEWREAK REQUITE
REVENGE SATISFY CHASTISE
AVENGER KANAIMA NEMESIS
WREAKER
AVENS GEUM BENNET BAREFOOT
AVENTURINE SUNSTONE
GOLDSTONE
AVENUE RUE WAY GATE MALL PIKE
ROAD ALLEE ALLEY DRIVE ENTRY
ACCESS ARCADE ARTERY RIDING
STREET AVENIDA OPENING
PASSAGE
AVER SAY AIVER CLAIM PROVE
STATE SWEAR AFFIRM ALLEGE
ASSERT ASSURE AVOUCH DEPOSE
VERIFY DECLARE JUSTIFY PROTEST
AVERAGE PAR SUM DUTY FAIR
MEAN NORM RULE RATIO USUAL
VALUE CHARGE MEDIAL MEDIAN
MEDIUM MIDDLE NORMAL TARIFF
ARRIAGE ESTIMATE MEDIOCRE
MIDDLING MODERATE ORDINARY
OVERHEAD QUANTITY STANDARD
(**NOT** —) BORDERLINE
AVERSE LOTH BALKY LOATH AFRAID
ADVERSE AGAINST OPPOSED
BACKWARD INIMICAL OPPOSITE
PERVERSE
(— **TO**) ABOVE
AVERSION TOY HATE DERRY ODIUM
ENMITY HATRED HORROR REGRET
DESPITE DISDAIN DISGUST DISLIKE
MISLIKE DISTASTE
(— **TO FOOD**) APOSITIA
(— **TO WORK**) ERGOPHOBIA
AVERT WRY BEND FEND MOVE SHUN
TURN WARD AVOID DETER DODGE

EVADE PARRY SHEER TWIST
DEFRAY DIVERT RETARD SHIELD
DECLINE DEFLECT EXPIATE
PREVENT ALIENATE ESTRANGE
FOREFEND WITHTURN
AVIARY CAGE HOUSE VOLARY
ORNITHON
AVIATOR ACE FLIER FLYER PILOT
AIRMAN FLYING ICARUS BIRDMAN
LOOPIST LUFBERY MANBIRD
SOLOIST
AVID AGOG KEEN WARM EAGER
ARDENT GREEDY HUNGRY JEJUNE
ANXIOUS ATHIRST CRAVING
LONGING THIRSTY DESIROUS
GRASPING
AVIDITY AVARICE CUPIDITY
AVIFAUNA BIRDS ORNIS BIRDLIFE
AVIKOM JACKS
AVOCADO COYO PEAR PALTA
AHUACA CHININ MARROW PERSEA
ZABOCA ABACATE ABBOGADA
AGUACATE ALLIGATO
AVOCET BARKER TILTER YELPER
SCOOPER
AVOID FLY SHY BALK FLEE HELP
MISS PASS QUIT SAVE SHUN VOID
WARE ABHOR ANNUL AVERT BURKE
DITCH DODGE ELUDE EVADE FEIGN
HEDGE PARRY SHIFT SHIRK SKIRT
SKULK SLACK SPAIR SPARE START
WANDE WONDE ABJURE BLENCH
BYPASS DETOUR ESCAPE ESCHEW
REFUTE REMOVE VACATE ABSTAIN
DECLINE EVITATE FORBEAR
FORSAKE REFRAIN
(— **A PUNCH**) SLIP
(— **COMMITMENT**) FUDGE
(— **EXPENSE**) HELP MISS SKIVE
(— **OVERWORKING**) FAVOR
(— **RESPONSIBILITY**) BLUDGE
AVOIDANCE DODGE OUTLET
EVASION ESCHEWAL
(— **OF RISK**) CAUTION
AVOUCH AVER ASSERT
AVOW OWN BIND WARE ADMIT
STATE AFFIRM ASSERT AVOUCH
DEPONE DEPOSE DEVOTE CONFESS
DECLARE JUSTIFY PROFESS
MAINTAIN
AVOWAL OATH WORD AVOURE
PROTEST
AVOWED FRANK SWORN STATED
DECLARED
AWAIT BIDE HEED KEEP PEND STAY
TEND WAIT ABIDE TARRY WATCH
ATTEND EXPECT IMPEND REMAIN
WAYLAY
(— **PAYMENT**) CARRY
AWAITING BEFORE BIDING
AWAKE DAW STIR WAKE ADAWE
ALERT ALIVE AWARE ROUSE ABRAID
ACTIVE AROUSE AWAKEN EXCITE
CAREFUL HEEDFUL STARTLE
VIGILANT
AWAKEN DAW STIR ALERT AROUSE
EXCITE KINDLE
AWAKENING REVIVAL WAKEFUL
AWARD LAW GIVE MARK MEED METE

WARD ALLOT GRANT MEDAL PRICE
PRIZE ACCORD ACTION ADDEEM
ASSIGN BESTOW BOUNTY CONFER
DECIDE MODIFY ADJUDGE APPOINT
CONSIGN CUSTODY KEEPING
ACCOLADE SENTENCE
(PL.) DESERTS
AWARE HEP RECK SURE WARE
WARY WISE ALERT ALIVE AWAKE
JERRY BEWARE KNOWING MINDFUL
APPRISED INFORMED SENSIBLE
SENTIENT VIGILANT WATCHFUL
AWARENESS EAR FEEL SENSE
FEELING INSIGHT
(— **OF WORTH**) APPRECIATION
AWAY BY TO AWA FRO OFF OUT VIA
WAY AFAR GONE PAST SCAT YOND
ALONG APART ASIDE FORTH HENCE
ABROAD ABSENT BEGONE ONWARD
THENCE DISTANT FROWARD
FAREWELL
(— **FROM HOME**) AFIELD OUTLAND
(— **FROM PORT**) AFLOAT
(— **FROM**) DOWN WITH ALONE
ALOOF APART BESIDE
(**FARTHER** —) BEYOND
AWE COW FEAR AMAZE DAUNT
DREAD SCARE FRIGHT HORROR
REGARD TERROR WONDER BUFFALO
RESPECT ASTONISH BEWILDER
OVERCOME RELIGION
AWE-INSPIRING GODFUL SOLEMN
AWESOME RELIGIO FEARSOME
OLYMPIAN
AWESOME EERY FELL HOLY AWFUL
EERIE WEIRD SOLEMN DREADED
GHOSTLY
AWESTRUCK SILENT
AWETO WERI
AWFUL DIRE FINE UGLY DREAD
GHAST AUGUST HORRID AWESOME
FEARFUL HIDEOUS SATANIC
DREADFUL SHOCKING TERRIBLE
AWFULLY AWFUL FIERCE
AWKWARD AWK CAR GAUM UNCO
CRANK FALSE FUDGY GAUMY
GAWKY GOATY INAPT INEPT SPLAY
STIFF UNCOW UNKED UNKID
CLUMSY GAUCHE RUSTIC STICKY
THUMBY UNEASY WOODEN
ADVERSE BOORISH CUBBISH
FROWARD HALTING LOUTISH
LUMPISH STILTED UNCANNY
UNCOUTH UNHANDY UNREADY
BUNGLING CLOWNISH FECKLESS
LUBBERLY PERVERSE UNGAINLY
UNTOWARD UNWIELDY
(— **PERSON**) TAWPY TUMFIE
(**NOT** —) FACILE
AWL BROD BROG NAIL NALL PROD
PROG BRODE ELSEN NALLE
BROACH DRIVER ELSHIN FIBULA
GIMLET BRADAWL SCRIBER
STABBER
AWN AIL EAR JAG BARB BEAK JAGG
PILE ARISTA BRISTLE
(— **OF BARLEY**) HORN
(— **OF OATS**) JAG JAGG
(PL.) BEARD

AWNING TILT BLIND SHADE VELUM CANOPY SEMIAN SHADER TIENDA TENTORY SEMIANNA SUNBLIND SUNSHADE VELARIUM

AWNLESS NOT NOTT HUMBLE HUMMEL POLLARD

AWRY CAM WRY AGEE BIAS SKEW AGLEY AMISS ASKEW GLEED GLEYD SNAFU WONKY WRONG ACROSS ASIDEN BLOOEY BLOOIE CAMMED FLOOEY ASKANCE ASQUINT ATHWART CROOKED OBLIQUE PERVERSE

AX ADZ AXE ADZE EAWT HACHE MATAX BIFACE PICKEL PIOLET POLEAX THIXLE TWIBIL BESAGUE BOUCHER BROADAX CHOPPER CLEAVER HATCHET JEDDING PULASKI TWIBILL FRANCISC

SUNDERER TOMAHAWK

(DOUBLE —) LABRYS

(HEADSMAN'S —) MANNAIA

(MASON'S —) CAVEL

(WOODEN —) MACANA

AXHAMMER CAVEL CAVIL KEVEL KNAPPER

AXIAL VENTRAL

AXIL ALA

AXILLA ALA AXIS ARMPIT SHOULDER

AXIOM SAW ADAGE MAXIM MOTTO BYWORD DICTUM SAYING TRUISM DIGNITY PRECEPT PROVERB APHORISM APOTHEGM DIGNITAS PETITION SENTENCE

AXIS AXE NUT AXLE STEM ARBOR HINGE STALK ARBOUR CAUDEX CENTER CHITRA RACHIS CAULOME

CORNCOB DENTATA POLAXIS SPINDLE SUCCULA SYMPODE TENDRIL AXLETREE MONOPODE

AXLE EX BAR COD PIN AXIS BOGY ARBOR BOGEY BOGIE EXTRE SHAFT AXTREE SLEEVE MANDREL SPINDLE SUCCULA

AYAH IYA CHAY EYAH MAID NURSE

AYE I AY EY EYE PRO YEA YES EVER ALWAYS ASSENT FOREVER

AYU AI SWEETFISH

AZALEA ERICA MINERVA CARDINAL

AZAZEL EBLIS

AZIMUTH ZN BEARING

AZTEC AZTECA MEXICA MEXICAN TENOCHCA

AZURE BICE BLUE HURT JOVE COBALT JOVIAL JUPITER CERULEAN SAPPHIRE

B SI BEE BAKER BRAVO
(— **FLAT**) ZA BEMOL
BA TRIPOS
BAA MAA MAE BLEAT
BABBAR UTU UTUO
BABBLE CHAT GASH KNAP TOVE
BABIL BLATE CLACK CLYDE GLOCK
HAVER PRATE TAVER WLAFF
CACKLE DITHER GABBLE GAGGLE
GLAVER GOSSIP JANGLE MURMUR
PALTER RABBLE TAIVER TUMULT
BLABBER BLATHER BLUSTER
CHATTER CHIPPER CLATTER
PRATTLE SMATTER TWADDLE
GLAISTER
BABBLER CACKLER BLATEROON
STIPITURE
BABEL DIN MEDLEY TUMULT
CHARIVARI CONFUSION
BABESIA APIOSOMA NUTTALIA
BABOON APE PAP PAPA DRILL
SPHINX BAVIAN CHACMA GIRRIT
PAPION BABUINA MANDRILL
HAMADRYAD
BABUL SANT SUNT ACACIA BABOOT
GARRAT GONAKE NEBNEB ATTALEH
GONAKIE
BABUSHKA SCARF KERCHIEF
BABY MOP BABA BABE CHAP DOLL
JOEY TOTO WEAN BAIRN CHILD
HUMOR SPOIL WAYNE CHRISM
CODDLE FONDLE INFANT MOPPET
PAMPER PUPPET SQUALL WEANIE
BAMBINO CHRISOM INDULGE
PAPOOSE WADDLER
BABY CARRIAGE PRAM BUGGY
WAGON GOCART STROLLER
BABYISH TIDDY PULING SIMPLE
PUERILE CHILDISH
BABYLONIAN (— **CYCLE**) SAROS
BABY'S BREATH GYP GYPSOPHILA
BACALAO MURRE SCAMP ABADEJO
CODFISH GROUPER GUILLEMOT
BACCATE BERRIED
BACCHANAL DEVOTEE REVELER
CAROUSER
BACCHANTE FROW MAENAD
BACCHUS LIBER LYAENS BROMIUS
DIONYSUS
(**AUNT OF** —) INO
(**FATHER OF** —) JUPITER
(**MOTHER OF** —) SEMELE
BACHELOR BACH SEAL BATCH
GARCON WANTER BACULERE
BENEDICT CELIBATE
BACILLUS GERM VIRUS MICROBE
BACK AID FRO TUB VAT ABET BAKE
BECK FULL HIND HINT NAPE NATA
REAR TAIL ABACK AGAIN ANGEL
BROAD CHINE DORSE NOTUM SPINE
SPLAT STERN VOUCH ASSIST
DORSUM HINDER SECOND SOOTHE
TERGUM TROUGH UPHOLD VERIFY
CISTERN ENDORSE FINANCE
RIGGING SPONSOR SUPPORT
SUSTAIN BACKWARD FULLBACK
HALFBACK MAINTAIN
(— **A ROWBOAT**) STERN
(— **OF ANIMAL**) RIG TERGUM

(— **OF ARCHERY TARGET**) BOSS
(— **OF AWNING**) RIDGEROPE
(— **OF BOOK**) DORSE SPINE
(— **OF BULL**) ROOF
(— **OF HAND**) OPISTHENAR
(— **OF HEAD**) NODDLE NIDDICK
OCCIPUT
(— **OF INSECT**) NOTUM
(— **OF NECK**) NAPE NUQUE SCRUFF
(— **OF PAGE**) FV
(— **OUT**) BEG JIB DUCK FLUNK
CRAWFISH
(— **TO BACK**) ADDORSED
(— **WATER**) STERN SHEAVE
(**SHOWING** —) TERGANT
BACKBITING DETRACTION
BACKBOARD BANK MONITOR
BACKBONE BACK GRIT GUTS CHINE
NERVE PLUCK RIDGE SPINA SPINE
LADDER METTLE SPIRIT GRISTLE
RIGBANE SPINULE STAMINA
VERTEBRA
(— **OF FISH**) GRATE
BACKCOUNTRY BUSH STICKS
BACKLAND BACKVELD BOONDOCKS
BACKDROP OLEO
BACKFIELD SECONDARY
BACKFIRE BOOMERANG
BACKFLASH GUTTER
BACKGAMMON IRISH LURCH TABLE
FAYLES GAMMON TABLES
BACKGAME TICKTACK
(— **MAN**) BLOT TABLEMAN
BACKGROUND FOND REAR GROUND
OFFING LINEAGE SETTING
BACKDROP DISTANCE EXTERIOR
OFFSCAPE TRAINING EDUCATION
(**MUSICAL** —) SUPPORT
BACKHANDED AWKWARD
BACKHOE PULLSHOVEL
BACKHOUSE PRIVY OUTHOUSE
BACKING AID EGIS AEGIS BACKUP
BEHIND LINING MUSLIN REFUSE
SUPPORT HEARTING FINANCING
(**LEGAL** —) STRENGTH
BACKLASH LASH SHAKE SLACK
BACKLOG RESERVE SURPLUS
BACKBRAND
BACKPIECE DOSSIERE
BACKPLATE REREDOS
BACKREST LAZYBACK
BACKROPE GOBLINE
BACKSEY SEY SIRLOIN
BACKSLIDE FALL LAPSE DESERT
REVERT RELAPSE
BACKSPIN DRAG UNDERCUT
UNDERSPIN
BACKSTITCH PURL PEARL
BACKSTOP BUTT
BACKWARD FRO JAY LAX YON
BACK CRAB DARK DULL LOTH
ABACK AREAR BLATE INAPT LOATH
THRAW UNAPT ARREAR ASTERN
AVERSE BYGONE POSTIC RETRAD
RETRAL STUPID BASHFUL LAGGARD
LAGGING REVERSE UPSTAGE
DILATORY IGNORANT LATEWARD
PERVERSE REARWARD TAILFIRST
BACKWARDNESS DARKNESS
BARBARISM

BACKWARDS YON AROUND
BACKWATER EBB COVE SLEW SLUE
BAYOU SHEAVE SLOUGH RETRACT
RETREAT BACKWASH BILLABONG
BACKWOODSMAN HICK WOODSY
BUCKSKIN HILLBILLY
BACKWORT COMFREY
BACON PIG BARD MEAT PORK
BARDE JAMON PRIZE SPECK FLITCH
GAMMON RUSTIC SAWNEY
GAMBONE SOWBELLY
BACOPA BRAMIA
BACTERIUM ROD COLI GERM
AEROBE CYTODE ANTHRAX
CHOLERA MICROBE PROTEUS
SARCINA VIBRION BACILLUS
LISTERIA BOTULINUS CYTOPHAGA
HEMOPHILE INFECTANT INFECTION
BAD BIG DUD ILL SAD EVIL FULL
HARD LEWD POOR PUNK QUED SICK
SOUR VILE WICK GAMMY NASTY
SORRY WEARY WORST WRONG
ARRANT FAULTY LITHER LUTHER
NOUGHT ROTTEN SEVERE SHREWD
SINFUL UNGOOD UNKIND WICKED
BALEFUL BANEFUL CORRUPT
FEARFUL HARMFUL HEINOUS
HURTFUL IMMORAL INUTILE
NAUGHTY SPOILED TAINTED
UNLUCKY UNMORAL UNSOUND
VICIOUS ANNOYING CRIMINAL
DEPRAVED DOGGEREL FIENDISH
FLAGRANT INFERIOR PRECIOUS
SINISTER UNSUITED
(— **MANNERS**) TROLLOPE
(**OUTRAGEOUSLY** —) GRIEVOUS
(**OUTSTANDINGLY** —) ARRANT
(**RATHER** —) INDIFFERENT
(**VERY** —) ALMIGHTY EXECRABLE
BADDERLOCKS MURLIN PURSES
HENWARE SEAWEED HONEYWARE
BADGE PIN MARK SIGN STAR COLOR
CREST CROSS FAVOR HONOR
ORDER PATCH TOKEN BUTTON
BUZZER COLLAR EMBLEM ENSIGN
FASCES GARTER GIGLIO PLAQUE
SHIELD SYMBOL TIPONI WEEPER
CHEVRON EPAULET FEATHER
BRASSARD INSIGNIA SCAPULAR
EPAULETTE
(**JAPANESE** —) MON KIRIMON
(**RUSSIAN** —) ZNAK
BADGER NAG PAT BAIT GRAY GREY
GRIS MELE PATE ANNOY BRACE
BROCK BRUSH CHEVY CHIVY
HURON MELES PAHMI RATED RATEL
TAXEL TAXUS TEASE WORRY
BAUSON BOTHER BRAROW CHIVVY
HAGGLE HARASS HAWKER HECKLE
KIDDER MELINE PESTER TELEDU
WOMBAT GRISARD TORMENT
BRAIREAU BULLYRAG CARCAJOU
HUCKSTER IRRITATE STINKARD
MISTONUSK
(— **STATE**) WISCONSIN
(**AUSTRALIAN** —) WOMBAT
(**COMPANY OF** —**S**) CETE
(**LIKE A** —) MELINE
BADINAGE FOOL JOKER BANTER

RAILLERY TRIFLING
BADLANDS MALPAIS
BADLY BAD ILL EVIL HARD ILLY SICK
SADLY EVILLY HARDLY POORLY
UNWELL FAULTILY WICKEDLY
VICIOUSLY
BADMINTON POONA
BADNESS MALICE PRAVITY UNVALUE
EVILNESS
BAD-TEMPERED FOUL ANGRY
STINGY GROUCHY
BAFFLE FOX GET BALK BEAT FOIL
LICK MATE POSE STOP UNDO
CHEAT CHECK ELUDE EVADE FLING
STICK STUMP BLENCH BOGGLE
DEFEAT DELUDE FICKLE INFAMY
OUTWIT PUZZLE RESIST THWART
BUFFALO CONFUSE DECEIVE
QUIBBLE STONKER BEWILDER
CONFOUND DISGRACE JUGGLING
BAFFLING SHREWD ELUSIVE
BAG COD KIT MAT NET PAD POD POT
SAC CELL DRAG GRIP LOBE MAIL
POCK POKE SACK TOOT TRAP
WOMB BELLY BOUGE BULSE CATCH
DILLI DILLY EMERY FLOAT HUSSY
PETER POUCH PURSE SCRIP SEIZE
SNARE STEAL BLOUSE BUDGET
CAVITY ENTRAP FOLLIS GASBAG
MATAPI PAGGLE POCKET POUNCE
SACHET SEABAG VALISE WALLET
ALFORJA BALLOON BEANBAG
BLISTER BUCKRAM CANTINA
CAPCASE CAPTURE CUSHION
GAMEBAG GOMUKHI HANDBAG
HOLDALL RETICLE SANDBAG
SARPIER SATCHEL TRAVOIS
CARRYALL CORNSACK ENTRAILS
ENVELOPE FOLLICLE KNAPSACK
MONEYBAG OVERSLIP RETICULE
RUCKSACK SUITCASE WINESKIN
MULTIWALL WEEKENDER
(— BULGING) SWAG
(— FOR LETTERS) MAIL POUCH
KAREETA MAILBAG POSTBAG
(— FOR TOOLS) WALLET
(— OF ANISEED) DRAG
(— WITH POCKETS) TIDE TIDY
(AUSTRALIAN —) SWAG DILLI SHIRT
SHAMMY
(GAS —) CELL
(GRAB —) FISHPOND
(HAWSE —) JACKASS
(LEATHER —) JAG JAGG ASKOS
BUDGE BOUGET MUSSUK
(NET —) SNOOD GARLAND
(SEWING —) HUSSY
(SLEEPING —) FUMBA FLEABAG
SLEEPER
(WATER —) CHAGAL CHAGEN
CHAGUL
BAGASSE BEGASS LINAGA MEGASS
BAGATELLE CANON TRUNK VERSE
CANNON TRIFLE
BAGGAGE ARMS GEAR MINX SWAG
CUTTY HUZZY NASTY SAMAN STUFF
TENTS TRASH WENCH HARLOT
REFUSE TRASHY TRUNKS CLOTHES
DUNNAGE EFFECTS FARDAGE

PLUNDER RUBBISH SALMARY
SUMPTER VALISES CARRIAGE
HARLOTRY RUBBISHY UTENSILS
BAGGAGE CAR WAGON FOURGON
BAGGER SACKER BATCHER
BAGGING SOUTAGE
BAGGY LOOSE POCKY PURSY
FLABBY PUFFED PURSIVE
BAGNIO BAIN BATH BAGNE PRISON
BROTHEL HOTHOUSE
BAGPIPE MUSE PIPE PIVA DRONE
TITTY BIGNOU BINIOU CHORUS
GEWGAW MUSETTE SAMBUKE
DULCIMER SYMPHONY ZAMPOGNA
CORNAMUTE CORNEMUSE
SYMPHONIA
BAGUETTE CHAPLET
BAH PO FOH PAH POH ROT RATS
FAUGH PSHAW NONSENSE
BAHAMAS (CAPITAL OF —) NASSAU
(ISLAND OF —) ABACO EXUMA
ANDROS BIMINI
BAHRAIN (CAPITAL OF —) MANAMA
(MONEY OF —) FILS DINAR
(TOWN OF —) RIFAA JIDHAFS
BAIL BOW DIP ANDI BALE BOND
HOOP LADE LAVE RING RYND YOKE
LADLE SCOOP THROW VOUCH
BUCKET HANDLE PLEDGE SECURE
SURETY VADIUM CUSTODY DELIVER
RELEASE REPLEVY BAILSMAN
BULWARKS SECURITY GUARANTEE
(— OUT) ABANDON
BAILEE LESSEE POSITOR
CONDUCTOR
BAILER SPOUCHER
BAILIFF GRAB HIND AGENT REEVE
SAFFO SCULT STAFF BAILIE BAILLI
BEADLE DEPUTY FACTOR GRIEVE
LOOKER OFFICE PORTER PREVOT
SCHOUT VARLET BUMTRAP GRIPPER
PROVOST PUTTOCK SHERIFF
STEWARD APPROVER HUISSIER
OVERSEER TIPSTAFF CONSTABLE
HUNDREDER PORTREEVE
SENESCHAL WAPENTAKE
BAILIWICK AREA FIELD DOMAIN
OFFICE PROVINCE
BAILOR LESSOR
BAIN NEAR LITHE READY SHORT
DIRECT LIMBER SUPPLE FORWARD
WILLING
BAIT BAD BOB COG DAP LUG BITE
CAST CHUM FEED HALT HANK LURE
PLUG TAIL DECOY HOUND LEGER
SHACK SLATE SQUID TEMPT TRAIN
WORRY ALLURE APPAST ATTACK
BADGER BERLEY ENTICE HARASS
HECKLE HECTOR KILLER LEDGER
REPAST SHRAPE SLIVER FULCRUM
GUDGEON PROVOKE TAGTAIL
TOLLING TORMENT CUNGEBOI
(— FOR BIRDS) SHRAP SHRAPE
(— FOR COD) CAPELIN
(GREASY —) ROGUE
(GROUND —) BERLEY
(MAGGOT —) GENTLE
(SCENTED —) DRAG
BAITING HANK

BAIZE BAY BAYES BAYETA DOMETT
BAKE DRY BURN COCT COOK FIRE
BATCH BROIL GRILL PARCH ROAST
ANNEAL HARDEN BISCUIT PISTATE
SCALLOP CLAMBAKE ESCALLOP
(— EGGS) SHIRR
(— THOROUGHLY) SOAK
BAKED (— IN EARTH OVEN) KALUA
(— PRODUCT) KICHEL
BAKER OVEN FIRER BAXTER BURNER
FURNER PISTOR FURNACE
OVENMAN ROASTER
BAKER BIRD HORNERO
BAKING CUIT BATCH COCTION
FURNAGE ASSATION
BAKONGO FIOT
BALACHONG NGAPI
BALANCE BEAM EVEN PEIS REST
SWAY TRIM COVER ERASE PEISE
POISE SCALE TRONE WEIGH WEIHE
ADJUST AUNCEL CANCEL EMBLEM
EQUATE KELTER KELVIN KILTER
LAUNCE OFFSET SANITY SQUARE
STRIKE DESEMER LIBRATE
OVERRUN RESIDUE TRABUSH
TRUTINE EQUALITY EQUALIZE
EQUATION SERENITY WESTPHAL
TREBUCHET
(— DUE) ARREAR
(— IN ACCOUNT) CREDIT
(— OF SAILS) ATRY
(MENTAL —) HEAD
BALANCED EVEN EQUAL LEVEL
APOISE KITTLE WEIGHED COMPLETE
QUADRATE
BALANCER HALTER ACROBAT
GYMNAST HALTERE
BALATA ICICA BULLACE BEEFWOOD
BORRACHA
BALCONY POY ORIEL PORCH STOOP
CIRCLE GAZEBO PIAZZA PODIUM
SOLLAR BALAGAN GALLERY
MIRADOR PERGOLA TERRACE
BRATTICE CANTORIA VERANDAH
BALD RAW BARE BASE BOLD CRUDE
DODDY NAKED PLAIN CALLOW
PALTRY PEELED PILLED SIMPLE
CALVOUS EPILOSE LITERAL
GLABROUS HAIRLESS
(— HEAD) PILGARLIC
(— SPOT) TONSURE
BALDACHIN CANOPY CIBORIUM
BALDER BALDR BALDUR BAELDAEG
(CHILD OF —) FORSETE FORSETI
(FATHER OF —) ODIN
(SLAYER OF —) HOTH LOKE HOTHR
(WIFE OF —) NANNA
BALDERDASH ROT GUFF TRASH
DRIVEL JARGON FLUBDUB
NONSENSE BALDUCTUM RIGMAROLE
BALDNESS ACOMIA CALVITY
ALOPECIA ATRICHIA OPHIASIS
BALDPATE ZUISIN POACHER
BALDRIC BELT LACE GIRDLE ZODIAC
BALTEUS SUPPORT NECKLACE
BALE NO GIB NOT WOE EVIL FIRE
HARM PACK PYRE BLOCK CRATE
DEATH FARDO SERON BALLOT
BUNDLE EMBALE SEROON SORROW

PACKAGE SARPLER
BALEARIC ISLANDS (ISLAND OF —)
IBIZA CABRERA MAJORCA MINORCA
CONEJERA
(MEASURE OF —) PALMO MISURA
QUARTA QUARTIN BARCELLA
(TOWN OF —) IBIZA MAHON PALMA
(WEIGHT OF —) CARGO CORTA
QUARTANO
BALEEN WHALEBONE
BALEFUL BAD EVIL DEADLY MALIGN
SACRED SULLEN MALEFIC NOXIOUS
RUINOUS SIDERAL SINISTER
WRETCHED
BALI (DANCE OF —) ARDJA BARIS
KRISS BARONG KETJAK MONKEY
DJANGER
(MOUNTAIN OF —) AGOENG
(MUSICAL INSTRUMENT OF —)
GAMELAN
(RICE FIELD OF —) SAWAII
(STRAIT OF —) LOMBOK
(TOWN OF —) SINGARADJA
BALINGHASAY ANAM ANAN
BALK GAG HUE JUB SHY BEAM BILK
BUCK BULL COND FOIL GORM HADE
HEAP LICK LOFT MISS OMIT PROP
SHUN SKIP SLIP STAY STOP AVOID
BAULK BLOCK CHECK CLAMP
DEMUR HUNCH MOUND REBEL
REEST RIDGE STAKE STICK WAVER
BAFFLE DEFEAT FALTER HINDER
IMPEDE OUTWIT RAFTER REFUSE
STRAIN THWART BLUNDER CODLING
GALLOWS ISTHMUS MISTAKE
(— IN FISHING) HUE COND
(HALF —) FLITCH
(PL.) MIDDLES
BALKAN (— COIN) NOVCIC
(— COUNTRY) GREECE SERBIA
ALBANIA RUMANIA BULGARIA
(— INSTRUMENT) GUSLA
(— RIVER) JIU OLT IBAR JIUL SAVA
TISA OLTUL DANUBE MORAVA
(— SEA) BLACK AEGEAN IONIAN
ADRIATIC
BALKER HUER CONNER
BALKY NAPPY STICK MULISH REESTY
RESTIVE CONTRARY STUBBORN
OBSTINATE
BALL IN BAL BOB FLY HOP NOB ORB
PEA TOY BEAD BOWL CLEW CLUE
KNOB KNOP KNUR PICK PILL POME
TRAP DANCE EDGER FAULT FLOAT
GLOBE GLOME HURLY ORBIT PEARL
PUPPY SHAPE SNACK SPORT TRUCK
BULLET BUTTON HOOKER HURLEY
MOONIE MUDDLE PEELEE PELLET
PELOTA POMMEL POMPON RONDEL
RUNDLE SPHERE SQUASH BALLOON
CONFUSE FLOATER GLOBULE
INCURVE INSHOOT KNAPPAN
LEATHER MANDREL PELOTON
RIDOTTO SLITTER BASEBALL
BISCAYEN FANDANGO FOOTBALL
GROUNDER HANDBALL QUENELLE
SOFTBALL SPHEROID TRAPBALL
(— AS SHIP'S SIGNAL) SHAPE
(— FOR MUSKET) GOLI SLUG

(— OF CLAY) KNICKER
(— OF RICE OR MEAT) PINDA
(— OF THREAD) CLEW CLUE GOME
BOTTOM WHARROW
(— OF THUMB) THENAR CUSHION
(— OF WASTE IRON) COBBLE
(— USED IN SHINTY) PEG
(—S OF MEDICI FAMILY) PALLE
(BILLIARD —) SPOT IVORY
SNOOKER
(BOWLED —) TICE CURVE SKYER
BAILER BUMPER FIZZER GOOGLY
KICKER POODLE YORKER CREEPER
SNORTER SPINNER BREAKBACK
CROSSOVER INSWINGER
(BOWLING —) DODO JACK
(CRICKET —) SNICK SHOOTER
(FIVES —) SNACK
(GOLF —) PUTTY
(HARD —) SNUG
(HOCKEY —) NUN NUR ORR
(INK —) PUMPET
(SKITTLE —) CHEESE
(TENNIS —) PALM
(WOODEN —) KNUR
BALLAD JIG LAI LAY LILT MELE
POEM SONG CAROL DERRY FANCY
BALLET BYLINA CARVAL SONNET
BALLANT CANZONE CORRIDO
GWERZIOU SINGSONG
BALLAST BED CRIB LOAD TRIM
METAL POISE STONE BOTTOM
BURDEN GRAVEL WEIGHT BALANCE
LASTAGE SANDBAG DRAGROPE
KENTLEDGE SABURRATE
BALLET BALLAD MASQUE BOURREE
PANTOMIME
(— MOVEMENT) VOLE TEMPS
APLOMB OUVERT POINTE RELEVE
RETIRE ALLONGE ARRONDI
ASSEMBLE ATTITUDE ARABESQUE
BALLHOOTER BRUTTER
BALLISTA SWEEP MANGONEL
BALLOON BAG BALL BLIMP EXPAND
GASBAG AIRSHIP DISTEND DRACHEN
INFLATE SAUSAGE SKYHOOK
AEROSTAT ENVELOPE DIRIGIBLE
(TRIAL —) KITE
BALLOONING BOSOMY
BALLOON VINE FAROLITO
HEARTPEA HEARTSEED
BALLOT BALE POLL PROX VOTE
ELECT PROXY VOICE BILLET CHOICE
POLICY TICKET SUFFRAGE
BALLROOM SALOON
BALLYHOO BALLY HOOPLA
BALM OIL BEEB BITO DAUB SALVE
ANOINT BALSAM EMBALM LOTION
RELIEF SOLACE SOOTHE ANODYNE
BESMEAR COMFORT PERFUME
UNGUENT OINTMENT
(— OF GILEAD) CANADA
OPOBALSAM
BALMY MILD SOFT BLAND DAFFY
MOONY SPICY SUNNY SWEET
GENTLE INSANE SERENE HEALING
LENIENT AROMATIC BALSAMIC
DRESSING FRAGRANT SOOTHING
BALONEY BUNK HOOEY BUSHWA
BUSHWAH

BALSA RAFT FLOAT GUANO POLAK
POLACK BOBWOOD CORKWOOD
BALSAM BALM RIGA TOLU UMIRI
COPALM GURJAN GURJUN STORAX
AMPALEA COPAIBA CREEPER
AMPALAYA BDELLIUM BENJAMIN
OINTMENT
BALSAM APPLE KARELA AMARGOSA
AMPALAYA BALSAMINE
BALSAM FIR SAPIN BAUMIER
BALSAM POPLAR BAUMIER
TACAMAHAC
BALSAMROOT SUNFLOWER
BALSAMWEED MOONSHINE
FEATHERWEED
BALT YOD ESTH LETT ESTONIAN
BALTIC (— GULF) RIGA DANZIG
BOTHNIA FINLAND
(— ISLAND) DAGO FARO OSEL
ALAND ALSEN OESEL OLAND
GOTLAND HIIUMAA BORNHOLM
(— PORT) KIEL RIGA MEMEL REVAL
DANZIG GDANSK TALINN LEIPAJA
(— RIVER) ODER ODRA DVINA
VIADUA
(— TOWN) MEMEL DANZIG GDANSK
LEIPAJA
BALUCHISTAN (— CULTURE)
QUETTA
BALUSTER SPOKE COLUMEL
BANISTER COLUMELLA
BALUSTRADE BARRER PARAPET
RAILING BALCONET BANISTER
BAMBOO DHA CANE REED BATAK
GLUMAL GUADUA TONKIN BATAKAN
WANGHEE WHANGEE
(SACRED —) NANDIN
(WOVEN —) SAWALI
BAMBOOZLE DUPE HAVE CHEAT
COZEN GRILL CAJOLE HUMBUG
BUFFALO DECEIVE DEFRAUD
MYSTIFY PERPLEX
BAN BAR WOE TABU VETO BANAL
BANUS BLOCK CURSE EDICT ORDER
TABOO BANISH CENSOR ENJOIN
FORBID HINDER INVOKE NOTICE
OUTLAW CONDEMN EXCLUDE
ANATHEMA DENOUNCE EXECRATE
PROHIBIT
BANAK UCUUBA
BANAL FLAT CORNY INANE SILLY
STALE TRITE VAPID JEJUNE INSIPID
TRIVIAL
BANANA FEI FIG MUSA SABA BERRY
ENSETE FINGER SAGING LACATAN
PLATANO SAGUING SUNBEAM
PLANTAIN
BAND BAR GAD HUB TIE TUB ZON
BEAD BELT BEND BOND CAME CASH
CORD CREW CUFF FALL FERD FESS
GANG GATE GIRT HOOD HOOP
KNOT LACE LIST RING SASH SHOE
TAPE WISP ZONA ZONE AMPYX
BANDY BRAID CHOIR CLAMP CORSE
COVEY COVIN CRAPE CROWN
FEMUR FLOCK FRAME GIRTH GORGE
GUARD JATHA LABEL MEINY NOISE
PANEL PATTE PRIDE QUIRE SABOT
SNOOD STRAP STRIP STROP TAPIS

TORSE TRACK TRIBE UNITE WERED WITHE ARMLET BENDEL BINDER BORDER BOYANG BRIDGE BUNDLE CIMBIA CLAVUS COHORT COLLAR COLLET COPULA COVINE CRANCE CRAVAT DECKLE FASCIA FETTER FILLET FRIEZE FRINGE FUNNEL GAMMON GARTER GASKET GIRDLE HYPHEN LEGLET MATRIX NIPPER NORSEL PLEDGE RADULA REGULA ROLLER SCREED STRAKE STRING STRIPE SWATHE TAENIA TETHER TISSUE WEEPER BINDING BLANKET CHAMBUL CIRCLET COMPANY ENOMOTY FERRULE FRONTAL GARLAND HATBAND HEADING NECKTIE ORPHREY PALLIUM PIGTAIL PROMISE SEQUELA SHACKLE SHOEING SWADDLE VINCULUM
(— ACROSS SUNSPOT) BRIDGE
(— IN BRAIN) LIGULA FRENULUM FUNICULUS
(— OF 13 WITCHES) COVEN
(— OF CLAY) COTTLE
(— OF COLOR) SOCK SLASH STRIA LACING
(— OF CRAPE) WEED SCARF
(— OF INDIANS) SHIVWITS
(— OF PILLAGERS) SKINNERS
(— OF PURPLE) CLAVUS
(— OF STRAW) GAD SIMMON
(— TOGETHER) BANDY
(ARMED —) JATHA POSSE
(ARMOR —) TONLET
(CIRCULAR —) HOOP RING ANNULE WREATH
(DANCE —) CHORO
(DECORATIVE —) PATTE LEGLET CORNICE
(IRON —) FRET GATE TRUSS FUNNEL STRAKE
(LACE —) SCALLOP
(MUSICIANS —) CONCERT
(RADIO —) CHANNEL
(RESONANCE —) FORMANT
(TRIBAL —) AIMAK
(PL.) GRIPES INTERLACERY
BANDAGE BAND BELT BIND TAPE BLIND BRACE CLOUT DRESS GALEA LINEN SLING SPICA SWARF SWATH TRUSS BINDER COLLAR CRAVAT FASCIA FETTLE FILLET LIGATE NIPPER ROLLER SWARTH SWATHE SWEATH REVERSE ROLLING SWADDLE TRUSSER ACCIPTER CAPELINE CINCTURE GAUNTLET LIGAMENT LIGATURE SCAPULAR STOCKING
(EYE —) MUFFLER
(FINGER —) HOVEL
(JAW —) FUNDA
(PL.) SWADDLING
BANDALORE QUIZ
BANDANNA WEB TURBAN BANDANA PULICAT PULICATE PULLICAT
BANDEAU BAND STRIP FILLET BRASSIERE
BANDICOOT RAT MARL BILBI BILBY BADGER BIELBY PINKIE QUENDA

BANDIT CACA TORY BRAVO THIEF BANISH HAIDUK HEYDUK OUTLAW ROBBER BANDIDO BRIGAND LADRONE TULISAN BUSHWACK MARAUDER MIQUELET PICAROON
(PL.) MANZAS
BANDLEADER MASTER MAESTRO CHORAGUS CONDUCTOR
BANDORE PANDURA
BANDSMAN WINDJAMMER
BANDSTAND KIOSK STAND
BANDY VIE BAND CART CHOP SWAP TRADE LEAGUE RACKET STRIVE CHAFFER CONTEND DISCUSS CARRIAGE EXCHANGE
(— WORDS) REVIE GIFFGAFF
BANE BAN WOE BONE EVIL HARM KILL PEST RUIN CURSE DEATH VENOM INJURY MURDER POISON SLAYER NEMESIS SCOURGE MISCHIEF MURDERER NUISANCE
BANEBERRY COHOSH REDBERRY TOADROOT GRAPEWORT
BANEFUL BAD ILL EVIL VILE SWART HARMFUL HURTFUL NOXIOUS RUINOUS VENOMOUS SINISTRAL
BANG POM RAP BAFF BEAT BLOW BOOT DASH DOCK DRUB POUF SCAT SLAM SWAP SWOP TANK BLAFF CLASH CRACK DRIVE EXCEL FORCE IMPEL POUND SLAKE SLUMP SOUND SPANG STRAM THUMP WHACK WHANG WHUMP BOUNCE CUDGEL ENERGY FRINGE STRIKE THRASH THUNGE THWACK SARDINE SURPASS THUNDER FORELOCK
(— ON HEAD) BRAIN
BANGLADESH (CAPITAL OF —) DACCA
(MONEY OF —) TAKA
(NATIVE OF —) BENGALI
(RIVER OF —) GANGES
BANG-UP SLAP CRACK TIPTOP
BANISH BAN FREE ABAND EJECT EXILE EXPEL FLEME WAIVE WREAK BANDIT DEPORT DISPEL DISTER FORSAY OUTLAW ABANDON CONDEMN CONFINE DISMISS DIVORCE EXCLUDE DISPLACE RELEGATE
BANISHED FUGITIVE
BANISHMENT EXILE BANNIMUS OUTLAWRY XENELASY OSTRACISM XENELASIA
BANISTER RAILING BALUSTER
BANJO BOX BANJORE BANJORINE
BANK BAR BAY COP JUG RIM ROW BINK BRAE BREW BUTT CAJA DIKE DUNE DYKE EDGE HEAD HILL LINK MASS PILE RAKE RAMP RIPA RIVE SAND SEAT SIDE TIER WEIR BANCO BENCH BLUFF BRINK COAST DITCH EARTH FENCE HOVER HURST LEVEE MARGE MOUND MOUNT RIDGE SAVER SHARE SHELF SHOAL SHORE SLOPE STACK STAGE TRUST BANQUE BORROW CAISSE CAUSEY CRADGE DEGREE DEPEND DOUBLE MARGIN RANDOM RECKON RIVAGE

STRAND ANTHILL BANKING CUSHION DEPOSIT LOMBARD POTTERY SANDBAG SHALLOW WINDROW BARRANCA PLATFORM TRAVERSE
(— A FIRE) REST
(— OF CANAL) BERM BERME HEELPATH
(— OF EARTH) COP DAM DITCH
(— OF RIVER) WHARF STRAND
(— OF SAND OR MUD) BAR SCALP
(— OF SNOW) WREATH SNOWDRIFT
(— OF TURF) SUNK
(OVERHANGING —) BREW HOVER
(RUSSIAN —) CRAPETTE
(STEEP —) HEUCH HEUGH WOUGH BARRANCA BARRANCO
BANKER BOOK SETH SETT FACTOR FINDER SAHKAR SHROFF SOUCAR SOWCAR LOMBARD MARWARI MONEYER SPONSOR TAILLEUR BANQUETER FINANCIER
BANKNOTE CRISP FLIMSY SCREEN
BANKRUPT SAP BUNG BUST RUMP BREAK BROKE DRAIN SMASH STRIP BROKEN BUSTED DYVOUR QUISBY CRACKED DEPLETE
BANKRUPTCY SMASH FAILURE SMASHUP
BANKSMAN LANDER HILLMAN
BANLIEUE LOWY ENVIRONS
BANNER FANE FLAG JACK SIGN COLOR ENSIGN FANNON PENNON LABARUM LEADING PENNANT SALIENT BANDEROL BRATTACH FOREMOST GONFALON ORIFLAMB STANDARD STREAMER VEXILLUM BEAUSEANT ORIFLAMME
(FUNERAL —) BANNEROL GUMPHEON GUMPHION
(PL.) ENSIGNRY
BANNOCK PANAK DIGGER JANNOCK
BANNS CRY BANS CRIES NOTICE SIBRET SIBRIT SIBREDE SPURRINGS
BANQUET FETE MEAL DIFFA FEAST DINNER JUNKET MANGER REGALE REGALO REPAST SEUDAH SPREAD AHAAINA CONVITO CONVIVE NAMGERY REGALIO CAROUSAL FESTIVAL SYMPOSIUM SYSSITION
BANQUETER CONVIVE SYMPOSIAST
BANQUETING EPULATION TRENCHERING
BANSHEE BOW SIDHE
BANTAM COCK GRIG BANTY DANDY SAUCY CHICKEN SEBRIGHT COMBATIVE
BANTENG OX TSINE BANTIN TEMADAU
BANTER COD KID RAG ROT CHIP FOOL JEST JOKE JOSH MOCK QUIZ RAIL RAZZ BORAK CHAFF DRAPE JOLLY QUEER RALLY ROAST TAUNT TRICK DELUDE DERIDE HAGGLE SATIRE BADINER STASHIE BADINAGE CHAFFING GIFFGAFF RAILLERY RIDICULE
BANTU ILA BULU GOGO GUHA HEHE YAKA ZULU DUALA KAFIR KAMBA KIOKO KONDE KONGO LAMBA

SHONA SWAZI BANYAI BASUTO
DAMARA HERERO KAFFIR NATIVE
THONGA WAGUHA YAKALA CABINDA
MASHONA SWAHILI WACHANGA
(— **LANGUAGE**) ILA RONGA THONGA
NYANAJA NYAMWEZI
BANYAN BUR BURR BANIYA BUNNIA
JAGUEY
BAOBAB MOWANA IMBONDO TEBELDI
CALABASH
BAPTISM CLEANSING IMMERSION
PALINGENY PERFUSION
BAPTISMAL FONTAL
BAPTIST DIPPER DIDAPPER
SEPARATE TRASKITE
BAPTIZE DIP DEPE FULL NAME
HEAVE VOLOW PLUNGE PURIFY
ASPERSE CLEANSE IMMERSE
CHRISTEN SPRINKLE
BAPTIZED ILLUMINATE
BAR BAN DAM FID FOX GAD LAW LEG
RIB ROD TAP AXLE BALK BAND
BANK BAUR BEAM BOLT BOOM
BULL CAKE CHAR CORE CROW
DRAG FLAT GATE HIDE JOKE LOCK
MAKE OUST POLE RACK RAIL REEF
SAVE SETT SHUT SKID SLAB SLAT
SLIP SLOT SNIB STOP TREE YARD
ARBOR BENCH BETTY BILBO BILCO
BLOCK BLOOM BRACE CATCH
CLASP CLOSE COURT CRAMP
CREEL DEBAR DETER DOLLY EASER
EMBAR ESTOP FENCE FORCE
GEMEL HEDGE HORSE HUMET
LEVER PERCH PILOT PINCH PITCH
RATCH SHADE SHAFT SHAPE SIGHT
SLOTE SNEEK SPELL SPOON SPRAG
STAFF STANG STAVE STRAP STRIP
STRUT SWIPE TRACE YAIRD
ANCONY BARRET BATTEN BILLET
BISTRO BODEGA BROOCH BUMPER
CRUTCH DOFFER DOLLEY DOLLIE
EVENER EXCEPT EYEBAR FASTEN
FORBAR FORBID FORCER FORSET
GRILLE HEAVER HINDER LADDER
MEAGRE NORMAN PEELER RABBLE
RADIAL RETURN RIFFLE SALOON
SHADES SHANTY STOWER STRIPE
TABLET TANGLE TILLER TOGGLE
BARRACE BARRAGE BARRIER
BOBSTAY BOLSTER BUVETTE
CHANNEL CHARIOT CONFINE
COUNTER DRAWBAR EXCLUDE
GALLOWS MANDREL MANDRIL
OVERARM PREVENT SCRATCH
SIDEBAR SNIBBLE SPINDLE
STEMMER TOMBOLO TOPRAIL
TRUNDLE WIREBAR ASTRAGAL
KNIFEWAY MURDERER PESSULUS
(— **FOR TAPPING FURNACE**) LANCET
(— **IN FABRIC**) BARRE
(— **IN RIVER**) CHAR SANDBAR
(— **IN SEA**) SWASH
(— **OF CULTIVATOR**) ARCH
(— **OF DOOR**) SLOT STANG
(— **OF ELECTRIC SWITCH**) BLADE
(— **OF GATE**) SPAR LEDGE
(— **OF HARROW**) BULL
(— **OF LOOM**) EASER SWORD

BATTEN BACKSTAY
(— **OF RAYS**) SHOOT
(— **OF STEEL**) BLOOM STIRRUP
(— **OF WAGON**) SHETH
(— **ON SIDE OF BOWSPRIT**)
WHISKER
(— **ON WINDMILL**) UPLONG
(— **WITH SPIKES**) HERISSON
(**HERALDIC** —) FESS FESSE HUMET
LABEL
(**JOINTED** —) CHILL
(**MINING** —) MOIL
(**NOTCHED** —) RISP SKEY
(**PAIR OF** —S) GEMEL GEMMEL
(**REFRESHMENT** —) CANTEEN
(**SOAP FRAME** —) SESS
(**STIRRING** —) CRUTCH
(**TAMPING** —) STEMMER
(**TYPEWRITER** —) BAIL BALE
SPACER SHUTTLE
(**WEAVING** —) TEMPLE
(**WHEEL** —) AXLE SPOKE
BARANI BRANDY
BARB AWN BUR JAG MOW BURR
CLIP FILE FLUE HAIR HERL HOOK
JAGG BEARD HORSE POINT RIDGE
SHAFT SPEAR PIGEON STRAIN
TIPPET WITTER BARBARY BARBULE
BRISTLE FILAMENT KINGFISH
(— **OF ARROW**) HOOK WING BEARD
WITTER
(— **OF FEATHER**) HARL HERL
RAMUS PINNULA FILAMENT
(— **OF HARPOON**) FLUE FLUKE
BARBADOS (**CAPITAL OF** —)
BRIDGETOWN
(**MOUNTAIN OF** —) HILLABY
(**NATIVE OF** —) BIM
BARBADOS CHERRY ACEROLA
BARBAREA CAMPE
BARBARIAN HUN BOOR GOTH RUDE
WILD ALIEN BRUTE SAVAGE VANDAL
RUFFIAN FOREIGNER UNTUTORED
BARBARIC GROSS ATROCIOUS
BARBARISM CANT DATISM
SAVAGISM SOLECISM
BARBARITY FERITY CRUELTY
FELLNESS FEROCITY RUDENESS
SAVAGERY BRUTALITY
BARBAROUS FELL RUDE WILD
CRUEL BRUTAL FIERCE GOTHIC
BESTIAL FOREIGN HUNNISH
INHUMAN SLAVISH UNCIVIL
IGNORANT CUTTHROAT FEROCIOUS
PRIMITIVE
BARBARY MAGOT MAGHRIB
MOGHRIB
(— **STATE**) TUNIS ALGIERS
MOROCCO TRIPOLI
BARBASCO CUBE JOEWOOD
BARBECUE ASADO BOCAN BUCCAN
BARBEL BEARD CIRRUS WATTLE
BARBLET CYPRINID
BARBER NAI FIGARO POLLER
SHAVER TONSOR SCRAPER
TONSURE
(— **FISH**) TANG
BARBET BARBION BARMKIN
DREAMER BARBICAN PUFFBIRD

WATERRUG IRONSMITH PEARLBIRD
THICKHEAD TIGERBIRD
BARBITAL VERONAL
BARD BHAT MUSE POET SCOP SWAN
DRUID OVATE RUNER SCALD SKALD
OSSIAN SHAPER SINGER BARDING
PENBARD MINSTREL MUSICIAN
TALIESEN DEMODOCUS
BARE DRY BALD LEAN MERE NUDE
POOR ALONE CRUDE EMPTY NAKED
PLAIN PLUME STARK STRIP WASTE
BARISH BARREN CALLOW DENUDE
DIVERT DIVEST EXPOSE HISTIE
MARGIN MEAGER MEAGRE PALTRY
PILLED REVEAL SCARRY SIMPLE
DIVULGE EXPOSED UNARMED
UNCOVER DENUDATE DESOLATE
DISCLOSE STRIPPED DESTITUTE
(— **TEETH**) TUCK
(**NOT** —) COOL
BAREFACED GLARING IMPUDENT
AUDACIOUS SHAMELESS
BARELY JIMP JUST ONLY FANIT
HARDLY MERELY POORLY SIMPLY
UNEATH UNNETH NAKEDLY
UNNETHE EDGEWAYS SCANTILY
SCARCELY SLIGHTLY
BARER NAVVY DELVER FEIGHER
MUCKMAN CALLOWER
BARFISH DORAB
BARGAIN GO BUY RUG WOD COPE
DEAL HUCK KOOP MART MISE PACT
PICK RUGG SALE SELL SNIP TROG
WHIZ CHEAP FIGHT PRICE STEAL
TROKE TRUCK WHACK WHIZZ
BARTER DICKER HAGGLE HIGGLE
NIFFER PALTER CHAFFER CHEAPEN
COMPACT CONTEND CONTEST
DISPOSE PACTION TRAFFIC
CONTRACT COVENANT PENNORTH
PURCHASE STRUGGLE WANWORTH
(— **HARD**) PRIG
(— **IN MINING**) STURT
BARGAINER NIP KITE COPER
COWPER CHAFFERER
(**SHARP** —) SCREW
BARGAINING MART ACHATE
CHAFFER CHEAPING HUCKSTERY
BARGE ARK BOX BOY HOY TOW TUB
BARK BOAT FUST LUMP PRAM RAFT
SCOW TROW BARCA CASCO DUMMY
FOIST LUNGE LURCH PRAAM SCOLD
SHREW VIXEN BARQUE BERATE
BUGERO DREDGE GALLEY GYASSA
PRAHAM REBUKE STUMPY TENDER
THRUST WHERRY BALLOON BIRLING
CHALANA DROGHER GABBARD
GABBART GONDOLA LIGHTER
OMNIBUS TOWBOAT TUMBLER
TUMBRIL BUDGEROW CARRIAGE
MOORPUNKY
(**COAL** —) KEEL
BARGEMAN PUG BARGEE BARGER
HOYMAN HUFFLER
BARGHEST PADFOOT
BARITE CAUK CAWK TIFF CAULK
BARYTES BARYTINE HEPATITE
BARK AGO BAG BAY OUF RUB TAN
WAP YAP YIP BAFF BOAT BOOF

COAT COTO DITA HOWL HUSK OPEN
PEEL PELT PILL REND RIND ROSS
SKIN SNAP TAPA WAFF YAFF YAWP
YELP AABEC BALAT BARCA BARGE
COUGH MOCHA NIEPA SHELL SHOUT
SPEAK STRIP TIMBE YABBA YAMPH
YOUFF ABRADE AGAMID AVARAM
BARKEY BOWWOW CASSIA CORNUS
CORTEX GIRDLE MASSOY SINTOC
TRANKY WAFFLE YAFFLE MALAMBO
MESENNA PERIERA PHLOEUM
SOLICIT TANBARK DOUNDAKE
EUONYMUS FRANGULA GRANATUM
MEZEREUM WOODSKIN
(AROMATIC —) CANELLA
CULILAWAN
(EXTERIOR OF —) ROSS
(LAVER OF —) HAT
BARKER BUFFER DOORMAN
GRINDER SPIELER SPUDDER
SPRUIKER CHARLATAN
BARKING BAY SPUD QUEST
LATRANT LATRATION
BARLEY BIG BEAR BENT BIGG GRAIN
SPRAT LICORN HORDEUM
WHITECORN
(AWN OF —) HORN
(GROUND —) TSAMBA
(HULLED —) PTISAN
(REFUSE —) SHAG FLINTS
BARN BYRE AMBAR LATHE STALL
GRANGE STABLE SKIPPER
COWHOUSE
(— OWL) LULU MADGE
(COW —) SAUR SHIPPON
BARNACLE BRAY BREY ACORN
LEPAS CYPRIS ANATIFA BALANID
LEPADID CIRRIPED GNATHOPOD
SACCULINA
BARNBURNER SOFT
BARNSTORM TOUR
BARNYARD PIGHTLE BACKSIDE
FARMYARD STRAWYARD
BAROMETER GLASS ANEROID
OROMETER
BARON DAIMIO BARONET FREEMAN
FREIHERR
(COURT —) HALLMOOT
BARONY HAN DOMAIN
BAROQUE GOTHIC ORNATE ROCOCO
GROTESQUE IRREGULAR
BAROTO VINTA
BARRACK CAMP BOTHY CASERN
CANNABA CUARTEL
BARRACUDA CUDA KAKU SPET
BARRY PELON SNAKE SNOEK
SNOOK BECUNA PICUDA SCOOTS
SENNET VICUDA KATONKEL
SCOOTERS
BARRAGE BAR ATTACK VOLLEY
BARRIER DRUMFIRE UMBRELLA
CANNONADE FUSILLADE
BARRAMUNDA SALMON CYCLOID
DIPNOAN FLATHEAD CERATODUS
BARRED CUCKOO RIBBED STRIPED
BARREL FAT HUB KEG TUN VAT
BUTT CADE CASK DRUM KANG TREE
BOWIE QUILL SHELL STAND UNION
FESSEL GIRNAL GIRNEL HOGGET

RUMBLE RUNLET TIERCE TUMBLE
VESSEL CALAMUS CISTERN
PACKAGE RATTLER RUNDLET
TUMBLER CYLINDER HOGSHEAD
KILDERKIN
(— OF FEATHER) CALAMUS
(— OF REVOLVER) CHAMBER
(— ROW) LONGER
(— WITH CRANKS) VANGEE
(CAPSTAN —) SPOOL
(CORE —) LANTERN
(HERRING —) CADE CRAN
(SMALL —) KEG KIT CADE KNAG
RUNLET BARRICO RUNDLET
BARRELHOUSE GUTBUCKET
BARREN DRY ARID BARE BOWY
DEAD DEAF DOUR DULL EILD GAST
GELD LEAN NUDE POOR SALT SECK
YELD YELL BLEAK BLUNT BOWEY
DRAPE DUSTY EMPTY GAUNT
GHAST GUESS NAKED STARK STERN
WASTE YEILD DESERT EFFETE
FALLOW HISTIE HUNGRY JEJUNE
MEAGER STUPID SAPLESS STERILE
DESOLATE IMPOTENT TEEMLESS
TREELESS
(NOT —) FACILE FECUND
(PL.) LANDES
BARRENNESS VACANCY EMPTINESS
BARRICADE BAR STOP BLOCK
CLOSE FENCE ABATIS PRISON
BARRAGE BARRIER DEFENSE
FORTIFY OBSTRUCT RAMFORCE
ROADBLOCK
(— OF TREES) ABATIS
BARRIER ALP BAR DAM BOMA CRIB
CROY DIKE DOOR DYKE FOSS GATE
LINE LOCK PALE STOP WALL WEIR
BOUND CHAIN FENCE FOSSE GRILL
HEDGE LIMIT STILE STUMP CORDON
GLACIS GRILLE HURDLE SCREEN
TREBLE BARRAGE CEILING CURTAIN
GALLERY PARAPET RAILING
RAMPART BOUNDARY FORTRESS
FRONTIER STOCKADE STRENGTH
TRAVERSE
(— ACROSS RIVER) STILL KIDDLE
(— IN TRUCK) HEADER
(ARTIFICIAL —) FOSS FOSSE
(TRAFFIC —) SEPARATOR
(PL.) BAIL
BARRING BUT SAVE CLOSED
BARRISTER COLT BARMAN JUNIOR
LAWYER TUBMAN COUNSEL
POSTMAN TEMPLAR ADVOCATE
ATTORNEY SERJEANT
BARROOM PUB CAFE HOUSE
SALOON CANTINA DOGGERY
GROCERY TAPROOM DRAMSHOP
DRINKERY EXCHANGE GROGGERY
GROGSHOP
BARROW HOD HOG BANK BIER DUNE
GALT HILL MOTE TUMP CARRY
GRAVE GURRY HURLY MOUND
BURROW GALGAL KURGAN NAVETA
HILLOCK TROLLEY TUMULUS
MOUNTAIN PUSHCART
BARRULET VIVRE
BARTENDER MIXER BARMAN

BARMAID SKINKER TAPSTER
BARTER CHAP CHOP COPE COUP
HAWK MANG MONG SELL SWAP
TROG VEND CORSE TRADE TROKE
TRUCK DICKER NIFFER SCORSE
BARGAIN CAMBIUM CHAFFER
PERMUTE TRAFFIC TRUCKLE
COMMERCE EXCHANGE
BARTERER COPER COWPER
TRUCKER
BASAL BASIC BASILAR RADICAL
BASALT MARBLE NAVITE DIABASE
GHIZITE KULAITE POTTERY
AUGANITE BANDAITE DOLERITE
ANAMESITE ARAPAHITE MELAPHYRE
SUDBURITE
BASE BED DEN HUB LOW TUT ANIL
CLAM EVIL FOOT FOUL HUBB LEWD
MEAN POOR RELY REST ROOT
SACK STAY STEM STEP VILE BASIS
BLOCK CHEAP DIRTY FIRST FLOOR
FOUND LACHE MUDDY PETTY SNIDE
SOCLE STAND STOOL WORSE
ABJECT BOTTOM BRASSY COARSE
COMMON DEMISS GROUND GRUBBY
HARLOT HUMBLE MENIAL NOUGHT
PALTRY PATAND PATTEN PERRON
PODIUM RASCAL SECOND SHABBY
SORDID VULGAR BASTARD CAITIFF
COMICAL CURRISH DEBASED
FOOTING HANGDOG HILDING
HOUSING IGNOBLE PEASANT
ROINISH SERVILE SLAVISH STADDLE
STANDER SUBBASE SUPPORT
CHURLISH COISTREL COISTRIL
DEGRADED DRAWHEAD HARLOTRY
HOLDFAST INFAMOUS INFERIOR
MECHANIC MESCHANT PEDESTAL
PEDIMENT RASCALLY SCULLION
SHAMEFUL STANDARD STEPPING
SUBSTRAT UNWORTHY WRETCHED
NIDDERING
(— IN QUALITY) LEADEN
(— OF CANNON) SOUL
(— OF OPERATIONS) BOOK HOME
(— OF PETAL) CLAW
(— OF PLANT) CAUDEX
(— OF POLLINIUM) DISC DISK
(— OF TUBER) HEEL
(CHEMICAL —) ACRIDAN ADENINE
ANSERIN CHOLINE GUANINE
ACRIDANE ACTININE AGMATINE
ALDIMINE ALKALOID ANSERINE
CONYRINE GALEGINE KETIMINE
LEPIDINE SEMIDINE
(HIDDEN —) LAIR
(HOME —) DEN
(LEAF —) FOVEA
(LOGARITHM —) E
(SECOND —) KEYSTONE
(STALKLIKE —) CNIDOPOD
BASEBALL PILL APPLE DUSTER
FLOATER INSHOOT LEATHER
BEANBALL HARDBALL HORSEHIDE
STICKBALL
(— PLAYER) YANNIGAN
BASEBOARD GRIN SKIRT PLINTH
EASEMENT MOPBOARD SKIRTING
WASHBOARD

BASE-DEALING BROKING
BASELESS IDLE UNFOUNDED
BASEMAN SACKER
BASEMENT BASE CELLAR
TAHKHANA
BASENESS FELONY VILITY BEGGARY
SQUALOR TURPITUDE
BASH BAT LAM BEAT BLOW DENT
MASH SWAT WHAM WHOP ABASH
SLOSH SMASH BRUISE STRIKE
BASHFUL COY SHY HELO SHAN
BLATE HELOE TIMID MODEST
PUDENT ASHAMED DAUNTED
BACKWARD BLUSHING DAPHNEAN
DISMAYED LOATHFUL PUDIBUND
RETIRING SACKLESS SHAMEFUL
SHEEPISH SKITTISH VERECUND
BASHFULNESS PUDOR SHYNESS
BASIC BASE BASAL VITAL BOTTOM
BEDROCK CANONIC CENTRAL
CLASSIC ZINCOUS CARDINAL
ULTIMATE ELEMENTAL ESSENTIAL
SUBSTRATE
BASIL TULASI
BASIN DOP PAN BOWL COMB COVE
DISH DOCK EWER FLOW FONT GULF
LAKE PARK SINK SLAD TALA TANK
COMBE LAVER SLAKE STOUP
BASSON BULLAN CHAFER CIRQUE
HOLLOW LAVABO LEKANE LOUTER
MARINA VALLEY VESSEL CUVETTE
PISCINA RECEIPT URCEOLE
CESSPOOL LAVATORY RECEPTOR
VANITORY WASHBOWL GEMELLION
(MOUNTAIN —) HOYA
(ROCK —) KEEVE KIEVE
BASIS BASE FOND FOOT FORM FUND
ROOT SILL AXIOM STOCK ANLAGE
BOTTOM GROUND ACCOUNT
BEDROCK FOOTING PREMISE
SUPPORT GRAVAMEN STRENGTH
AUTHORITY CRITERION FUNDAMENT
GROUNDSEL SUBSTANCE
BASK SUN BEEK WARM ACRID BATHE
ENJOY REVEL BITTER REJOICE
APRICATE
BASKET IE ARK COB FAN HOT KIT
LUG PAD PED PEG POT TAP TOP
BUCK CAUL COBB COOP CORB
CORF CRIB FLAT GOAL HOTT IEIE
KIPE KISH KIST KITT LEAP MAND
MAUN SKEP TAPE TILL TOUR TRUG
WEEL CABAS CASSY CESTA CHEST
CRAIL CRASH CRATE CREEL DEVIL
DILLI DILLY FRAIL GRATE MAUND
MOLLY NATTE RUSKY SCULL SWILL
WILLY BEACON BOKARK CASSIE
CLEAVE COFFIN COURGE CRADLE
DORSEL DORSER DOSSER FANNER
FASCET GABION HAMPER HOBBET
HOBBIT HOPPET JICARA JUNKET
KIBSEY KIPSEY MOCOCK MOLLIE
MURLIN PANIER PEGALL PETARA
POTTLE PUNNET SEQUIN TAPPET
TEANAL TOPNET VOIDER WINDEL
WINDLE WISKET ZEQUIN CANASTA
CORBEIL CRESSET FLASKET
HANAPER PANNIER PATTARA
PITARAH PRICKLE SCUTTLE SEEDLIP

SHALLOW SKEOUGH SKIPPET
WATTAPE WHISKET CALATHUS
CANISTER CHEQUEEN ZECCHINO
(— BOTTOM) SLATH
(— FOR CRUMBS) VOIDER
(— FOR EELS) BUCK COURGE
(— FOR FIGS) TAP CABAS FRAIL
TAPNET
(— FOR FRUIT) MOLLY CALATHOS
CALA
BASKET MAKER ANASAZI
BASKETRY UPSET
BASKETWORK TEE SLEW WALE
SLATH STAKE SLATHE STROKE
SLEWING
BASQUE VASCON EUSCARA
EUSCARO IBERIAN BISCAYAN
(— DIALECT) LABOURDIN
(PL.) VASCONA VASCONES
BAS-RELIEF PLAQUETTE
BASS LOW PES CHUB DEEP DRUM
FOOT ROCK BASSO DRONE HURON
ROCHE SWEGO VOICE BORDUN
BRASSE BURDEN CHERNA GROUND
JUMPER REDEYE SINGER STRIPE
ACHIGAN BARFISH BOURDON
BROWNIE GROWLER JEWFISH
STRIPER BACHELOR BIGMOUTH
BLUEFISH CABRILLA ROCKFISH
SPOTTAIL STREAKER CONTINUO
TALLYWAG WELSHMAN LINESIDES
(— DRUM) TAMBURONE
(— PART) ALBERTI
(GROUND —) OSTINATO
(THOROUGH —) BC
BASSOON CURTAL FAGOTT
FAGOTTE FAGOTTO
BASSWOOD LIN BASS WAHOO
LINDEN WICOPY DADDYNUT
WHITEWOOD
BAST LIBER RAMIE PHLOEM
NOSEBURN
BASTARD GET SOB BASE FALSE
CANNON COWSON GALLEY HYBRID
IMPURE MAMZER BYSPELL GETLING
LOWBRED MONGREL WOSBIRD
BANTLING BASEBORN MISBEGET
NAMELESS SPURIOUS WHORESON
BASTE SEW BEAT CANE COOK DRUB
LARD TACK FLAMB SAUCE CUDGEL
JIPPER PUNISH STITCH THRASH
BASTION JETTY MOINEAU
BAT CAT HIT WAD BACK BAKE BATE
BEAT CLUB FOWL GAIT JACK LUMP
MASS SWAT TRAP WINK BANDY
BATON BRICK CHUCK FUNGO HARPY
PIECE SPREE STICK ALIPED BACKIE
BASTON BEETLE CUDGEL DRIVER
KALONG POMMEL RACKET STRIKE
STROKE WILLOW BAUCKIE FLUTTER
JAVELIN NOCTULE VAMPIRE
BLUDGEON SEROTINE REREMOUSE
BATAK (— DIALECT) TOBA
BATCH LOT BAKE BREW CAST CROP
FINE MASS MESS SORT FLOOR
GROUP BAKING CHEESE MAKING
BOILING BREWING FORMULA
MIXTURE RAISING QUANTITY
(— OF EGGS) SETTING

(— OF GRAIN) GRIST
(— OF MAIL) SEPARATION
BATCHER BAGGER
BATE BAIT BEET PUER PURE GRAIN
BATELEUR BERGHAAN
BATEMAN DRENCHER
BATFISH ANGLER DIABLO MALTHE
DEVILFISH
BATH DIP TUB BAIN BATE PERT
TOSH BATHE LAVER STEEP THERM
DOUCHE LIQUOR MIKVAH PICKLE
PLUNGE SHOWER SPONGE
BALNEUM LAVACRE ABLUTION
BALNEARY
(FOOT —) PEDILUVIUM
(HOT —) STEW SCALD STUFE
THERM STUPHE THERME
(MUD —) ILLUTATION
(PHOTOGRAPHIC —) FIXER
(SITZ —) BIDET SITZBAD SEMICUPE
INSESSION
(SPINNING —) DOPE
(STEAM —) SAUNA
(TANNING —) BATE SOAK
(TURKISH —) HUMMUM HOTHOUSE
BATHE BAY TUB BAIN BASK DOOK
LAVE STEW WASH CLEAN DOUSE
DOWSE EMBAY SOUSE STEEP
ENWRAP FOMENT SHOWER SPLASH
EMBATHE IMMERSE PERVADE
SUFFUSE PERMEATE
BATHHOUSE SEW STEW SAUNA
STUFE CABANA HAMMAM STUPHE
BALNEARY
BATHING LAVACRE LAVEMENT
(— SUIT) SLIP TOGS MAILLOT
BATHSHEBA (HUSBAND OF —)
DAVID URIAH
(SON OF —) SOLOMON
BATHTUB TUB TOSH LAVACRE
BATON ROD BEND BURN WAND
STAFF STICK BAGUET BASTON
CUDGEL BOURDON SCEPTER
SCEPTRE BAGUETTE CROSSBAR
TRUNCHEON
BATSMAN BAT BATTER HITTER
SLOGGER SLUGGER STRIKER
BATTALION WARD CONREY
BATTEN END LAY RIB SLEY CLEAT
LEDGE BATTON BEATER ENRICH
FATTEN REEPER THRIVE FERTILIZE
(PL.) SPARRING
BATTER RAM BEAT DENT MAIM
CLOUR DINGE FRUSH PASTE POUND
SMASH BALLER BRUISE BUFFET
HAMMER HATTER HITTER PUMMEL
THRING TUMBLE BATSMAN
BOMBARD CRIPPLE DESTROY
FRITTER SHATTER SLUGGER
STRIKER DEMOLISH
BATTERCAKE WAFFLE
BATTERING BLAST LACING
BATTERY PILE SINK TIRE TROOP
RADEAU EXCITER SINKBOX
SINKBOAT
(GUN —) SWINGER
BATTLE WAR CAMP DUEL FEUD
FRAY MART MEET TILT TOIL UNDO
BRUSH FIELD FIGHT JOUST STOUR

ACTION AFFRAY CAMLAN COMBAT
SHOWER STRIVE CONTEND
CONTEST HOSTING JOURNAL
JOURNEY WARFARE CONFLICT
SKIRMISH STRUGGLE ENCOUNTER
NAUMACHIA THEOMACHY
BATTLE-AX WIFLE POLEAX SPARTH
TWIBIL BROADAX HALBERD TWIBILL
WHIFFLE FAUCHARD FRANCISC
BATTLE CRY CRY ENSIGN
GERONIMO BEAUSEANT
BATTLEFIELD BLAIR CHAMP TAHUA
CHAMPAIGN
BATTLEMENT KERNEL MERION
PINION CORNELLE
BATTLESHIP MAINE CARRIER
BATTY BATS BUGGY CRAZY SILLY
BATLIKE FOOLISH
BAUBLE BOW TOY BEAD GAUD
BUTTON GEWGAW TRIFLE MAROTTE
TRINKET GIMCRACK PLAYTHING
BAWD AUNT HARE DIRTY MADAM
DEFILE MADAME PANDER COMMODE
MACKEREL PROCURER PURVEYOR
BAWDY DIRTY SCARLET
BAWL CRY HOWL ROUT YAUP YAWP
BLORE GOLLY SHOUT BELLOW
BOOHOO OUTCRY GLAISTER
(— OUT) JUMP CRACK SCOLD
BAY ARM COD DAM RIA VOE BANK
BARK CHOP COVE GULF HOLE HOPE
HOWL LOCH ROAN TREE WICK
YAUP YAWP BAHIA BASIN BAYOU
BERRY BIGHT COLOR CREEK FIORD
FJORD FLEET HAVEN HORSE INLET
LOUGH MOUTH ORIEL QUEST SINUS
SPEAK TRAVE BABBLE HARBOR
LAUREL RECESS SEVERY WINDOW
BADIOUS BAYGALL ENCLOSE
ESTUARY MALABAR SILANGA
ULULATE BREWSTER CHESTNUT
(— OF BARN) GOAF SKEELING
SKILLING SKILLION
(— STATE) MASSACHUSETTS
(SWEET —) BREWSTER
BEAVERWOOD
BAYBERRY AUSU PIMIENTA
WAXBERRY
BAYOU SLEW SLOO SLUE BROOK
CREEK INLET RIVER OUTLET
SLOUGH STREAM RIVULET
BACKWATER
BAY WINDOW ORIEL MIRADOR
BAZAAR FAIR FETE SALE AGORA
BURSE CHAWK CHOWK MARKET
CANTEEN BOOKFAIR EMPORIUM
BEZESTEEN
BDELLIUM GUGAL GUGUL GOOGUL
BE ABE ARE BES BEEN BETH BIST
LIVE ABIDE EXIST OCCUR WORTH
REMAIN BREATHE CONSIST SUBSIST
CONTINUE
BEACH AIR BANK CHIP MOOR NARD
RIPA SAND SLIP COAST PLAGE
PLAYA PRAYA SHORE GROUND
SHILLA STRAND HARDWAY SEASIDE
SHINGLE LAKESHORE
(— RIDGE) FULL
(PROJECTING —) CUSP

BEACH APPLE CANAJONG
BEACHCOMBER SEASONER
STRANDLOOPER
BEACH FLEA SCUD SCREW
SANDBOY
BEACH GRASS STAR SPIRE
MARRAM BENTSTAR
BEACON MARK PIKE SIGN BAKEN
FANAL GUIDE PHARE RACON
ENSIGN PHAROS RAMARK SIGNAL
CRESSET SEAMARK WARNING
NEEDFIRE SIGNPOST STANDARD
BEAD NIB POT DROP FOAM GAUD
AGGRI AGGRY BUGLE FILET GRAIN
KNURL PEARL QUIRK SIGHT STAFF
ARANGO BAGUET BAUBLE BICUNE
BUBBLE CORNET FILLET PELLET
PIPPER PRAYER RONDEL WAMPUM
DEWDROP GLOBULE MOLDING
SPARKLE TRINKET AVEMARIA
CABOCHON
(ROSARY —) GAUD PATERNOSTER
(SHELL —S) SEWAN
BEADING VEINING
(PL.) TASBIH
BEADLE CRIER MACER POKER
USHER BEDRAL BUMBLE HARMAN
HERALD BAILIFF NUTHOOK OFFICER
SERVITOR SUMMONER APPARITOR
MESSENGER
BEADSMAN BEGGAR HERMIT
BLUEGOWN GOWNSMAN
BEAK NEB NIB BECK BILL CLAP
NOSE PIKE PROW LORUM SNOUT
SWORD TUTEL MASTER NOZZLE
SPERON WEAPON EMBOLON
EMBOLUM FOREBOW MOLDING
ROSTRUM BEAKHEAD MANDIBLE
CAPITULUM
(— OF SHELL) UMBO
(— OF SHIP) SPERON
(— OF SWORDFISH) SWORD
BEAKER CUP HORN TASS BIKER
BOCAL BOUSE GLASS BARECA
BEAM BAR LEG RAY TIE BALK BEAK
BOOM EMIT GLOW PLAT SILE SILL
SKID SPAR STUD ARBOR CABER
FLASH GLEAM GLEED JOIST LIGHT
RAYON SHAPE SHINE SHOOT SMILE
SPEAR STANG STOCK TRAVE
BINDER CAMBER CHEESE COLLAR
FLITCH GIRDER GLANCE HEADER
MANTEL NEEDLE RAFTER SUMMER
TIMBER TRABES TREVIS WALKER
BALANCE BUMPKIN CHANNEL
CHEVRON DORMANT DRAWBAR
FRIJOLE MADRIER PINRAIL RADIATE
SLEEPER SUPPORT TRANSOM
TRIMMER TYNDALL AXLETREE
BROWPOST HERISSON PADSTONE
PLOWHEAD ROOFTREE STENTREL
TEMPLATE
(— OF LIGHT) CHINK GLEED RAYON
SHAFT SIGNAL STREAM SUNBEAM
STRICTURE
(HIGH —) BRIGHTS
(LARGE —) BALK LACE BAULK
SUMMER
(LOW —) DIM

(SANIO'S —) CRASSULA
(WEAVER'S —) TRAM TAVIL
(PL.) CRANEWAY
BEAMER SCUDDER
BEAMING GAY ROSY BRIGHT
LUCENT MASSIVE RADIANT SHINING
BEAMY BROAD BRIGHT JOYOUS
LUCENT MASSIVE RADIANT
MIRTHFUL
BEAN BON NIB URD CHAP FABA
FAVA GRAM HABA HEAD LIMA POLE
SNAP TEKE TICK BRAIN CARAT
PULSE SIEVA SKULL CACOON
CASTER COLLAR FELLOW KIDNEY
LABLAB LENTIL NIPPLE NOGGIN
RUNNER RUTTEE SEEWEE STRIKE
TEPARY THRASH TRIFLE CALABAR
FRIJOLE PHASEMY SNAPPER
WINDSOR BONAVIST BONNYVIS
TICKBEAN TORNILLO
(— CURD) TOFU
(LOCUST —) CAROB
(MESCAL —) SOPHORA
(PL.) NIBS FASELS FESELS PODDER
PODWARE
BEANIE DINK
BEAN-SHAPED FABIFORM
BEANSHOOTER TRUNK
PEASHOOTER
BEAN TREE BOGUM
BEAN TREFOIL LABURNUM
BEAR GO CUB LUG BALU BERN
BORN CAST DREE DUBB FURE GEST
GIVE HAVE HOLD LIFT TEEM TOTE
URSA WEAR ABIDE ALLOW BALOO
BEGET BHALU BREED BRING BROOK
BROWN BRUIN CARRY DREIE DRIVE
GESTE ISSUE KOALA POLAR PRESS
SPARE STAND STICK THOLE THROW
WEIGH WIELD YIELD AFFORD
BEHAVE BRUANG CONVEY ENDURE
IMPORT INFANT KADIAK KINDLE
KODIAK PIERCE RENDER SUFFER
THRUST UPHOLD URSULA WOMBAT
WOOBUT ARCTOID BROWNIE
COMPORT CONDUCT EPHRAIM
FORBEAR GRIZZLY MUSQUAW
PRODUCE STOMACH SUPPORT
SUSTAIN UNDERGO FISSIPED
(— EXPENSES) DEFRAY
(— FLOWERS) FLOURISH
(— FRUIT) FRUCTIFY
(— INVESTIGATION) WASH
(— ON) CONCERN
(— OUT) PROPORT
(— PATIENTLY) DIGEST
(— UP) CAPE ENDURE SUSTAIN
(— WITH CREDIT) BROOK
(— WITNESS) TEEM SPEAK ATTEST
DEPOSE
(— YOUNG) FIND CALVE CHILD
(MALE —) BOAR
(SLOTH —) ASWAIL
BEARBERRY LARB WHORTLE
BILBERRY DOGBERRY FOXBERRY
CREASHAKS
BEARD ANE AWN AVEL BARB DEFY
FACE FUZZ NECK NOSE PEAK TUFT
ZIFFS ARISTA BEAVER GOATEE

TASSEL AFFRONT BARBULE
CHARLEY CHARLIE VANDYKE
IMPERIAL STILETTO WHISKERS
(— OF GRAIN) AIL AWN
(— TREATISE) POGONOLOGY
(SMALL —) BARBET
BEARDED AWNIE HAIRY BARBED
BARBATE HIRSUTE POGONIATE
WHISKERED
BEARDLESS NOT NOTT IMBERBE
POLLARD
BEARER NEWS HAMAL MACER
BEADLE HAMMAL HOLDER PACKER
PORTER ANCIENT CARRIER JAMPANI
PINCERN CHAPRASI ESCUDERO
PORTATOR STANDARD SUPPORTER
(— OF GREAT BURDEN) ATLAS
(ARMOR —) ESQUIRE
(BURDEN —) HAMAL HAMMAL
(CROZIER —) CROCIARY
(CUP —) SAKI COPPER
(PALANQUIN —) BOY SIRDAR
MUSAHAR
(SHIELD —) SQUIRE ESCUDERO
(STANDARD —) ANCIENT
(STRETCHER —) BRANCARDIER
(SWORD —) PORTGLAVE
PORTGLAIVE
BEARING AIM AIR COD BALL DUCT
GEST MIEN ORLE PORT RUBY BIRTH
FRONT GESTE HABIT JEWEL POISE
SETUP TENUE TREND ALLURE
APPORT ASPECT BILLET CHARGE
COURSE DEPORT GERENT GIGLIO
MANNER ORIENT SADDLE THRUST
VOIDER ADDRESS AZIMUTH
CONDUCT FASHION GESTURE
MEANING POSTURE PURPORT
RHODING SUPPORT AMENANCE
ATTITUDE BEHAVIOR BIRTHING
CARRIAGE DELIVERY DEMEANOR
FOOTSTEP PEDESTAL PRESENCE
PRESSURE RELATION STANDARD
TENDENCY TOURNURE YIELDING
(— FRUIT) FRUCTED
(— OUTWARD) EFFERENT
(ARROGANT —) HUFF
(HERALDIC —) GAD DELF ENTE
GORE MARK ORLE CROWN DELFT
DELPH FUSIL LAVER PHEON BILLET
DEVICE ENSIGN GOUTTE CHAPLET
CLARION DEMIVOL PLASQUE
QUARTER ORDINARY QUENTISE
(PERSONAL —) GARB
BEARLIKE URSINE
BEAR'S-EAR AURICULA
BEAR'S-FOOT OXHEAL PEGROOTS
BEARSKIN BUSBY
BEAR STATE ARKANSAS
BEAST BETE HOOF BRUTE VACHE
ANIMAL JUMENT MONSTER
MUSIMON VENISON BLIGHTER
OPINICUS
(— OF BURDEN) JUMENT SUMPTER
(3-HORNED —) TRICORN
(CASTRATED —) SPADO
(DEAD —) MORKIN
(FABULOUS —) YALE THRIS
BAGWYN TRICORN DINGMAUL

EPIMACUS GYASCUTUS
(HORNED —) RETHER ROTHER
(STURDY —) NUGGET
(WILD —) FERIN FERINE OUTLAW
UNBEAST
(WILD —S) ZIIM
BEASTLY GROSS PRONE ANIMAL
BRUTAL WICKED BESTIAL BRUTISH
INHUMAN SWINISH OFFENSIVE
BEAT BAT BUM COB DAD FAN FIB
LAM PIP PLY PUN RUN TAN TAP
TAW TEW TIE WAX BAFF BAIT BANG
BASH BATE BELT BEST BLOW BOLT
BRAY BUFF CANE CAST CHAP CLAP
CLUB COIL COLT COMB CRAB DAUD
DING DINT DRUB DUMP DUNT FELL
FIRK FLAP FLAX FLOG FRAM FRAP
FRAT GROW HAZE KILL LACE LAMP
LASH LICK LOUK LUMP LUSH MAUL
MELL MEND MILL PAIK PALE PANT
PELT POSS PRAT ROUT SCAT SLAM
SLAT SLOG SOCK SOLE SOWL STUB
SWAP SWOP TACK TAKE TICK TRIM
TUND TWIG WALK WARP WELT WHIP
WHOP WIPE BASTE BATON BERRY
BIRCH CHURN CLINK CREAM CURRY
DOUSE DRASH DRESS DRIVE FEEZE
FIGHT FILCH FLAIL FLANK FORGE
ICTUS INLAY KNOCK LABOR NEVEL
NOINT POUND PULSE ROUND SCATT
SCOOP SCOUR SKELP STAMP
STRAP SWACK SWING TARGE
THREP THROB THUMP TREAD
TRUMP UPEND WADDY WHACK
WHANG WORST ACCENT ANOINT
BAMBOO BATTER BENSEL BETTLE
BOUNCE BUFFET COTTON CUDGEL
DEFEAT DOWSEL FEAGUE FETTLE
HAMMER HAMPER JACKET KNEVEL
LARRUP LATHER NEAVIL NODDLE
OUTRUN PUMMEL RADDLE REBUKE
REESLE RHYTHM SCUTCH SQUASH
STOUND STOUSH STRIKE STRIPE
STROKE SUGGIL SWINGE SWITCH
TANSEL TEWTAW TEWTER THRASH
THREAP THREIP THREPE THRESH
TICKLE WAGGLE WALLOP WATTLE
ASSAULT BATTUTA BELABOR
BLATTER BLISTER CADENCE
CANVASS CONQUER CONTUSE
EXHAUST FATIGUE FLYFLAP
KNUCKLE LAMBACK LAMBAST
LOBTAIL LOUNDER PULSATE
REESHIE SHELLAC SURPASS
SWABBLE SWADDLE TROLLOP
TROUNCE VIBRATE
(— ABOUT) BUSK BANGLE
(— AGAINST THE WIND) LAVEER
(— AGAINST) BLAD
(— BARLEY) PAIL WARM
(— CLOTHES) BATTLE
(— COVERT) TUFT
(— DOWN) LAY FELL FULL ABATE
FLASH
(— EGGS) CAST
(— FIBERS) BRUSH
(— HIGH) LEAP
(— IT) LAM
(— OF HEART) DUNT STROKE

(— ON BUTTOCKS) COB
(— SEVERELY) DRUB LUMP SOAK
BASTE SOUSE LATHER
(— SMALL) CHAP
(— WINGS) BATE FLAP
(— WOODS) TUSK
(MUSICAL —) BOUNCE BATTUTA
BEATEN BEAT BETE BATTU PARTY
TRITE TRADED
BEATER RAB MAUL SEAL CANER
LACER STOCK DASHER DRIVER
MALLET TRIMMER THRESHER
SCUTCHER
BEATIFIC DEIFIC ELYSIAN
BEATIFY SAINT HALLOW HEAVEN
ENCHANT GLORIFY SANCTIFY
BEATING COB COBB LICK TUND
BEANS DOUSE JESSE PULSE STICK
HAZING HIDING ROPAND TATTOO
BASHING BATTERY BELTING
CLANKER DASHING DUSTING
LICKING SKELPIN WELTING WHALING
BIRCHING DRESSING DRUBBING
RIBROAST WHIPPING JACKETING
STRAPPADO
BEATITUDE JOY BLISS BENISON
MACARISM HAPPINESS
BEAU BEW BOY CHAP BLADE DANDY
FLAME LOVER SPARK SWELL
ESCORT FELLOW GARCON STEADY
SUITOR TATTLE ADMIRER AIMWELL
BRAVERY COURTER COXCOMB
CUPIDON GALLANT SPARKER
FOLLOWER
BEAU GREGORY COCKEYE
BEAUTIFUL FAIR FINE GLAD GOOD
MEAR MEER MERE WALY BELLE
BONNY KALON LUSTY SHEEN WLITY
WLONK BLITHE BONNIE COMELY
DECORE FREELY LOVELY POETIC
PRETTY VENUST ELEGANT
FORMOSE FORMOUS TEMPEAN
TOKALON CHARMING DELICATE
ESTHETIC FAIRSOME GORGEOUS
GRACEFUL HANDSOME LUCULENT
SPECIOUS
BEAUTIFY FAIR GILD ADORN GRACE
HIGHT PREEN PRIMP PRUNE BEAUTY
BEDECK DECORE ENAMEL QUAINT
ADONIZE ENHANCE GARNISH
GLORIFY DECORATE FAIRHEAD
EMBELLISH PULCHRIFY
BEAUTY FACE FAIR FORM GLEE
BEAUT BELLE CHARM FAVOR GLORY
GRACE PRIDE WLITE FINERY
LOOKER LOVELY POLISH DECORUM
FEATURE TOKALON SPLENDOR
FORMOSITY
(— OF FORM) SYMMETRY
(— OF STYLE) ELEGANCE
BEAVER BOOMER CASTOR RODENT
PRALINE MUSHROOM SEWELLEL
STARLING
(— SKIN) PLEW
(— STATE) OREGON
(DARK —) NUTMEG
BEBEERINE CURINE
BEBEERU SWEETWOOD
GREENHEART

BECAUSE AS SO FOR THAT BEING
CAUSE SINCE THERE FORWHY
THROUGH INASMUCH
BECCAFICO FIGEATER FIGPECKER
BECHE-DE-MER PIDGIN TREPANG
BECK RUN VAT BECON BROOK
(— **AND CALL**) DEVOTION
BECKEN CYMBALS
BECKET SQUILGEE SQUILLGEE
BECKON BOW NOD WAG BECK WAFT
WAVE CURTSY SUMMON BIDDING
COMMAND CURTSEY GESTURE
BECKONING WAFTURE
BECLOUD HIDE MASK BEDIM
DARKEN MUDDLE MYSTIFY
OBSCURE
BECLOUDED FOGGY
BECOME GO FIT GET RAX SET SIT
WAX COME FALL GROW LIKE PASS
SUIT TAKE TILL WEAR ADORN BEFIT
GRACE PROVE WORTH ACCORD
BEFALL BESEEM BETIDE CHANGE
IWORTH BEHOOVE FLATTER
PROCEED
(— **A PARTY**) ACCEDE
(— **AUDIBLE**) ARISE
(— **DAMP**) EVE
(— **DAZED**) DWAM DWALM
(— **DIM**) DASWEN
(— **DROWSY**) DOW
(— **FAT**) GRAZE
(— **FLUID**) FLOW FLUX LEACH
(— **KNOWN**) GO KITHE KYTHE
SPUNK
(— **MOLDY**) FUST MOUL FINEW
(— **MOROSE**) SOUR
(— **ROUND**) GLOBE
(— **SOUR**) FOX BLINK CARVE
BECOMING FIT FEAT GOOD BHAVA
FITTY RIGHT COMELY DUEFUL
GAINLY DECORUM FARRAND
FARRANT DECOROUS HANDSOME
SUITABLE WISELIKE
BECOMINGLY TALLY
BED COT HAY KIP PAD PAN TYE
BAND BASE BODY BUNK DOSS
DOWN FLOP FORM LAIR PLOT SACK
VEIN WADI WADY BERTH BOIST
COUCH FLASK FLOCK GRATE
GROVE LAYER THORE BORDER
BOTTOM COUCHE CRADLE GIRDLE
HOTBED LIBKEN LIBKIN LITTER
MATRIX OSIERY PALLET STRATA
CHANNEL CHARPOY FLEABAG
HAMMOCK LODGING QUARTER
REPOSAL SEEDBED SETTING
STRATUM SUBSOIL TRUCKLE
TRUNDLE BASSINET CAPSTONE
LENTICLE PLANCHER
(— **DOWN**) DOSS
(— **IN WAGON**) KATEL
(— **OF ANIMAL**) LAIR KENNEL
(— **OF COAL**) BRAT DELF SEAM
(— **OF EMBERS**) GRIESHOCH
(— **OF FURNACE**) HEARTH
(— **OF GUN-CARRIAGE**) FLASK
(— **OF HAND PRESS**) COFFIN
(— **OF REFUSE**) NITRIARY
(— **OF ROCK**) CAP PLUM

(— **OF ROSES**) ROSARY
(— **OF SEDIMENT**) WARP
(— **OF STREAM**) DRAW WASH
BILLABONG STREAMWAY
(**CREEK** —) COULEE COULIE
(**DRIED LAKE** —) CHOTT SHOTT
(**FEATHER** —) TIE TYE
(**FOLDING** —) SLAWBANK
(**LOW** —) LOWBOY
(**OYSTER** —) STEW LAYER SCALP
CLAIRE LAYING OYSTERAGE
(**RUBBLE** —) CALLOW
(**SEED** —) SEMINARY
(**WATER-BEARING** —) AQUAFER
AQUIFER
BEDAUB CLAG CLAT DAUB SOIL
SLAKE SMEAR SLAISTER
BEDBUG BUG CHINK CIMEX CHINCH
CHINTZ COREID PUNESE VERMIN
CIMICID PUNAISE REDCOAT
CONENOSE HEMIPTER HOUSEBUG
BEDCHAMBER BEDROOM CUBICLE
BEDCLOTHES COVER BEDDING
CLOTHES
BEDCOVER COMFORTER
PALAMPORE
BEDDING BEDROLL DOMESTICS
BEDECK GEM BEDO LARD TRAP
ADORN ARRAY DIGHT GRACE PRINK
ORNAMENT EMBELLISH
BEDECKED PRINKY
BEDEVIL ABUSE ANNOY BESET
WORRY HARASS MUDDLE PESTER
BEWITCH CONFUSE TORMENT
BEDEW DEW SHOWER IRRORATE
BEDIZEN DAUB ADORN ARRAY DIZEN
BEDAUB
BEDLAM RIOT NOISE RUDAS ASYLUM
TUMULT UPROAR MADNESS
MADHOUSE BETHLEHEM
BEDOUIN ABSI ARAB BEDU MOOR
NOMAD BADAWI BEDAWEE
SHAMMAR HOWEITAT
BEDQUILT POURPOINT
BEDRAGGLE TRACHLE
BEDRAGGLED FORLORN SHOPWORN
BEDRAIL RAVE RATHE
BEDRIDDEN ILL AILING BEDFAST
(**NOT** —) AFOOT
BEDROCK LEDGE NADIR SHELF
BOTTOM HARDPAN STONEHEAD
BEDROLL BINDLE
BEDROOM FLAT BERTH CABIN
BEDDER DORMER BOUDOIR
CHAMBER CUBICULO WARDROBE
GARDEROBE
BEDSORE DECUBITUS
BEDSPREAD ALEZE STRAIL
BEDCOVER COVERLET COVERLID
BEDSTEAD BED COT CRIB HATCH
STEAD STAPLE ANGAREP CHARPOY
BEDSTRAW CRUDWORT CURDWORT
FLEAWEED BEDFLOWER
CROSSWORT SCRAMBLER
BED TESTER SPARVER
BEDWARMER CURATE
BEE DOR FLY APIS BEVY KING RING
KARBI MASON NOMIA NURSE PARTY
DINGAR DRONEL DRONER FROLIC

INSECT NOTION TORQUE TSETSE
WORKER ANDRENA DEBORAH
KOOTCHA MELISSA RAISING
SERPENT STINGER SWERVER
TRIGONA ANDRENID ANGELITO
HONEYBEE QUILTING SCOPIPED
SHUCKING WAXMAKER GATHERING
(**QUEEN** —) KING
(**PL.**) BEEN BONE HIVE SPEW
SOCIALES
BEEBREAD CERAGO AMBROSIA
BEECH BUCK BIRCH MYRTLE
FLINDOSA FLINDOSY
BEECHNUT SPLITNUT
(**PL.**) BUCK MAST PANNAGE
BEEF JERK BEEVE BULLY GRIPE
JERKY VIFDA VIVDA CASSON
CUTTER CHARQUI TOPSIDE
COMPLAIN COMPOUND PASTRAMI
PIPIKAULA
(— **FOR SLAUGHTER**) MART
(**BOILED** —) BOUILLI
(**BROILED** —) CHURRASCO
(**CORN** —) BULLY
(**CUT OF** —) SEY LOIN RUMP SIDE
BARON CHINE CHUCK FLANK ROAST
ROUND SHANK STEAK ALOYAU
CUTLET SADDLE BRISKET KNUCKLE
QUARTER SIRLOIN EDGEBONE
SHOULDER AITCHBONE NINEHOLES
RATTLERAN
(**GROUND** —) HAMBURGER
(**INFERIOR** —) COMPOUND
(**JERKED** —) TASAJO BILTONG
CHARQUE CHARQUI
(**LEAN** —) LIRE
(**SALTED** —) JUNK VIFDA
BEEF BREAD SWEETBREAD
BEEFEATER OXBIRD OXBITER
OXPECKER TICKBIRD
BEEFWOOD TOA BELAH BELAR
FILAO
BEEFY HEAVY HEFTY SOLID BRAWNY
FLESHY
BEE GLUE PROPOLIS
BEEHIVE GUM BUTT GUME HIVE
SKEP PYCHE STAND STATE STOCK
SWARM APIARY HOPPET ALVEARY
SWARMER BEEHOUSE PRAESEPE
(— **STATE**) UTAH
(— **TOMB**) TREASURY
BEEKEEPER HIVER BEEMAN
BEEHERD APIARIST SKEPPIST
BEELZEBUB DEVIL
BEEN BE BON SEE BONE
BEE PLANT GUACO STINKWEED
BEER ALE MUM BIER BOCK BREW
FARO GAIL GROG GYLE HOPS KVAS
MALT MILD QUAS SCUD SUDS
BELCH CHANG CHICA GROUT KVASS
LAGER POMBE QUASS SCUDS
STOUT WEISS CHICHA DOUBLE
GATTER LIQUOR PORTER SPRUCE
STINGO SWANKY SWIPES WALLOP
ZYTHUM PANGASI PHARAOH
PILSNER TANKARD TAPLASH
TAPWORT CERVISIA
(**ADD TO** —) KRAUSEN
(**BAD** —) TACK TAPLASH

(HOT — AND GIN) PURL
(INFERIOR —) BELCH SWANKY
(SMALL —) TIFF GROUT
(SOUR —) BEEREGAR
(STRONG —) HUFF DOUBLE STINGO
(THIN —) PRITCH SWIPES
(TIBETAN —) CHANG
(WARM — AND OATMEAL) STORRY
(WEAK —) BEVERAGE
BEERHOUSE TIDDLYWINK
BEESWAX CAPPING
BEET CHARD MANGEL MANGOLD
STECHLING
(SUGAR —) BOLTER
BEETLE BAT BOB BUG JUT RAM
BEAT BUZZ FLEA FOWL GOGA
GOGO IPID MAUL MELL STAG TROX
TURK UANG AMARA ATLAS BORER
BULGE CAROB CHUCK DRIVE FIDIA
GOGGA HISPA LYCID MELOE SAGRA
TIGER CHAFER CLERID CUCOYO
CUCUYO ELATER GOLACH GOLOCH
HISTER JUTOUT KHAPRA LICTUS
MALLET MELOID PESTLE PRUNER
PTINID SAWYER SCARAB WEAVER
WEEVIL ADELOPS BRUCHID
BUZZARD CADELLE CARABID
CARABUS CUCUJID FIDDLER
FIREFLY GIRDLER GOLDBUG
LADYBUG LUCANID PAUSSID
PRIONID PROJECT SILPHID SKIPPER
SNAPPER SOLDIER TANBARK
TICKLER ATEUCHUS CALOSOMA
CETONIAN COCKTAIL CURCULIO
DYTISCID ENGRAVER EROTYLID
FIGEATER GLOWWORM HARDBACK
LADYBIRD LAMPYRID LOWERING
OVERHANG RUTELIAN SCOLYTID
SEARCHER SHARNBUD SHARNBUG
SKIPJACK SPHINDID SQUASHER
SQUEAKER SYMPHILE TOKTOKJE
WHIRLWIG DEDEMERID LONGICORN
OSTOMATID TUMBLEBUG TWIRLIGIG
WHIRLIGIG
(PL.) XYLOPHAGA
BEEWEED TONGUE
BEFALL HAP COME LIMP SORT TIDE
TIME CHEFE CHIVE OCCUR SHAPE
ASTART BECOME BETIDE HAPPEN
PERTAIN
BEFIT DOW SIT COME LONG SEEM
SORT SUIT BESET SERVE BECOME
BEHOVE BESEEM BETIDE BEHOOVE
BEFITTING FIT AFTER DECENT
PROPER WORTHY SEEMING THRIFTY
BECOMING DECOROUS SORTABLE
(PROFESSIONALLY —) ETHICAL
BEFOG GAUM CLOUD OBSANE
CONFUSE MYSTIFY
BEFOOL FON SOT BURN COLT CRAP
DOLT DUPE FODE JADE ASSOT
ELUDE FONNE DIDDLE TRIFLE
FOOLIFY
BEFORE OR TO AIR BUT ERE FOR
GIN TIL ANTE FORE SAID TILL YORE
AFORE AHEAD ANENT AVANT
CORAM FIRST FORBY FORNE FRONT
PRIOR SOPRA UNTIL FORBYE
FORMER RATHER SOONER TOFORE

WITHIN AGAINST ALREADY EARLIER
FORTHBY FORWARD
(— LONG) SOON ERELONG
(JUST —) TOWARD FORMERLY
BEFOUL FILE SLUT SOIL BERAY
DIRTY GRUFT BEMIRE DAGGLE
DARKEN DEFILE DRABBLE FEWMAND
POLLUTE SLUTTER BESQUIRT
ENTANGLE
BEFOULED SHARNY
BEFRIEND AID ABET HELP FAVOR
ASSIST BENFIT FOSTER FRIEND
SUCCOR SUPPORT SUSTAIN
BEFUDDLE BOX GAS ADDLE BESOT
MUDDLE BECLOUD CONFUSE
FLUSTER MYSTIFY STUPEFY
BEFUDDLED REE
BEG ASK BID CRY SUE WOO CANT
COAX KICK MUMP PRAY PRIG SEEK
SORN SUIT THIG TRAM CADGE
CRAVE MAUND MOOCH PLEAD
SCAFF TEASE YEARN ADJURE
BESEECH ENTREAT IMPLORE
MAUNDER REQUEST SKELDER
SOLICIT PETITION OBSECRATE
BEGET GET WIN BEAR HAVE KIND
SIRE BREED YIELD BIGATE CREATE
FATHER ACQUIRE ENGRAFF
CONCEIVE ENGENDER GENERATE
BEGETTER SIRE AUTHOR FATHER
MOTHER PARENT
BEGGAR BLOB RUIN ASKER HALFY
LAZAR RANDY ROGUE THRUM
TRAMP ARMINE BACACH BIDDER
CANTER DYVOUR MUMPER PARIAH
PAUPER SORNER WRETCH
ABRAHAM ALMSMAN BAIRAGI
BEGSTER JARKMAN LAZARUS
MAUNDER PARDHAN PROCTOR
RUFFLER SCAFFER SORNARI
STEMMER THIGGER ABRAMMAN
BADGEMAN BEADSMAN DUMMERER
GLASSMAN PALLIARD STROLLER
WHIPJACK SCHNORRER
(— DESCRIPTION) PASS
(PL.) GUEUX
BEGGARED PEELED
BEGGARLY MEAN POOR CHEAP
PETTY SORRY ABJECT PALTRY
PILLED PEGRALL BANKRUPT
INDIGENT HUNGARIAN
BEGGAR'S-LICE STICKWEED
BEGGAR-TICK CUCKOLD
(PL.) BOOTJACKS
BEGGARY THIG WANT INDIGENCE
PAUPERISM
BEGGING MAUND CRAVING
MENDICANT THOMASING
(— FOR FOOD) SCRANNING
(FRAUDULENT —) TRUANDISE
BEGHARD PICARD
BEGIN GIN GYN HIT FALL FANG
HEAD JUMP LEAD OPEN RISE TAME
YOKE ARISE ENTER FRONT START
ATTACK ATTAME INCEPT SPRING
STREAK COMMENCE INCHOATE
INITIATE
BEGINNER BOOT PUNK TIRO TYRO
ROOKY SOFTA GINNER NOVICE

ROOKIE SOPHTA AMATEUR
ENTRANT RECRUIT RUBBLER
STUDENT TRAINEE FRESHMAN
INCEPTOR NEOPHYTE NOVELIST
BEGINNING EGG DAWN EDGE GERM
HEAD RISE ROOT SEED ALPHA
BIRTH DEBUT ENTRY FIRST FRONT
ONSET START VAUNT AURORA
INCOME INSTIL ONCOME ORIGIN
OUTSET SETOUT SOURCE SPRING
CALENDS DAWNING GENESIS INCIPIT
INFANCY INITIAL INITION KALENDS
NASCENT OPENING SUNRISE
ENTRANCE EXORDIUM INCHOATE
OUTSTART RUDIMENT
(NEW —) EPOCH
(PL.) INCUNABULA
BEGONE OFF OUT VIA AWAY SCAT
SHOO SCOOT SCRAM AROINT
AVAUNT DEPART SKIDOO SKIDDOO
VAMOOSE
BEGONIA GAIETY GAYETY
BEGRIME COOM SOIL COLLY DITCH
GRIME BECOOM SMIRCH SMUDGE
BRUCKLE
BEGRIMED DIRTY GRIMY SMUDGY
CINDERY SMIRCHY
BEGRUDGE ENVY GRUDGE MALIGN
JALOUSE
BEGTI NAIR COCKUP
BEGUILE FOX COAX FODE FOIL
FOND GULL LURE VAMP WILE WISE
AMUSE CHARM CHEAT COZEN
ELUDE EVADE GUILE TRICK TROLL
TRYST WEIZE BRIGUE BUTTER
DELUDE DIVERT ENTRAP JUGGLE
VAMPEY DECEIVE ENSNARE
FLATTER FLUMMER MISLEAD
BEHALF HALF PART SAKE SIDE
FAVOR SCORE STEAD AFFAIR
MATTER PROFIT BENEFIT DEFENCE
SUPPORT INTEREST
BEHAVE DO ACT LET BEAR FARE
HAVE KEEP MAKE PLAY WALK
WORK CARRY REACT TREAT ACQUIT
DEMEAN DEPORT HANDLE COMPORT
CONDUCT CONTAIN DISPORT
GESTURE MANAGER FUNCTION
REGULATE RESTRAIN
(— AFFECTEDLY) MOP
(— AWKWARDLY) GAUM HOCKER
(— BOLDLY) GAUSTER
(— BRASHLY) HOOK
(— CHURLISHLY) CARL
(— EVASIVELY) DODGE
(— FOOLISHLY) DOLT
(— MISCHIEVOUSLY) LARK
(— NOISILY) HELL REHAYTE
(— OSTENTATIOUSLY) SWANK
(— VULGARLY) RAMP
BEHAVIOR AIR MIEN PORT RULE
THEW WALK FRONT GUISE HABIT
LATES USAGE ACTION COURSE
GOINGS MANNER ACTIONS BEARING
BIGOTRY COMPORT CONDUCT
DECORUM ERGASIA FACTION
FASHION HAVANCE HAVINGS
AMENANCE ATTITUDE BLINDISM
BREEDING BYRONICS CARRIAGE

FUNCTION MAINTAIN
(ARROGANT —) SIDE SWAGGER
(COURTEOUS —) COMITY
COURTESY
(DECENT —) CIVILITY
(FOOLISH —) SIMPLES SOTTISE
(LIVELY —) TITTUP
(LOUTISH —) BUFFOONRY
(RIOTOUS —) RAMPAGE
(SILLY —) SPOONISM
(STUDIED —) ART
BEHEAD NECK
BEHEST BID LAW HEST RULE ORDER
DEMAND BIDDING COMMAND
MANDATE
BEHIND AFT HINT PAST RUMP
ABACK ABAFF ABAFT AFTER AHIND
AREAR LATER PASSE TARDY
ARREAR ASTERN DERERE
BACKWARD DILATORY
BEHINDHAND TARDY LAGGARD
DILATORY HINDERLY
BEHOLD LA LO EYE SEE SPY ECCE
ESPY GAZE HOLD KEEP LOOK SCAN
STOP TOOT VIEW VISE WAIT HOLDE
OCULE SIGHT VOILA WATCH ASPECT
DESCRY MIRROR REGARD RETAIN
DISCERN OBSERVE SURVISE
WITNESS
BEHOLDEN OWING BOUNDEN
OBLIGED INDEBTED
BEHOOVE DOW FIT NEED SUIT THAR
BEFIT OUGHT THARF BELONG
PROPER REQUIRE
BEIGE HOP TAN ECRU HOPI GREGE
DORADO GREIGE STRING SUNBURN
BEING ENS ESSE FEAL SELF ENTIA
GNOME HUMAN SHAPE TROLL
ANIMAL ENTITY EXTANT LIVING
MORTAL PERSON SYSTEM ESSENCE
PRESENT REALITY VIVENCY
CREATURE EXISTENT ONTOLOGY
PRESENCE STANDING
(ANIMATE —) LIFE JAGAT
(CELESTIAL —) ANGEL CHERUB
SERAPH WATCHER DIVINITY
(DIMINUTIVE —) ELF GNOME
(DIVINE —) DEV DEVA DEMIGOD
(ESSENCE OF —) SAT
(ETERNAL —) EON AEON
(EVIL —) DEVIL GHOUL
(FABULOUS —) TENGU TORNIT
(HUMAN —) BODY BUCK JACK SOUL
BLADE HUMAN SLIME ANIMAL
ADAMITE CREATURE RATIONAL
CHRISTIAN
(IDEAL —) IMMORTAL
(ILL-FAVORED —) BLASTIE
(IMAGINARY —) SYLPH TERMAGANT
(INNER —) INWARD SPRITE INBEING
(INNERMOST —) HEART
(INTRINSIC —) ESSENCE
(LEGENDARY —) GIANT
(LIVING —) BLOOD WIGHT
(MATERIAL —) HYLIC
(PERFECT —) GOD
(PHYSICAL —) FLESH
(SEMIDIVINE —) SHEDU LAMASSU
(SMALL —) INCHLING

(SO —) SAEBEINS
(SUPERNATURAL —) DEV MAN AKUA
ATUA DEVA JANN ZEMI ADARO
BALAM DAEVA DEMON FAIRY TROLL
DAEMON GARUDA GODKIN SPIRIT
GODLING FOLLETTO HAMINGJA
(SUPREME —) DEITY MONAD
NYAMBE NZAMBI CREATOR
(TRUE —) OUSIA
BELABOR PLY BEAT DRUB LASH
WORK ASSAIL BOUNCE CUDGEL
HAMMER HAMPER THRASH THWACK
BELAY BESET BELAGE INVEST
WAYLAY BESEIGE
BELCH BOKE BOLK BURP GALP
RASP RIFT ERUCT FRUCT REBOKE
ERUCTATE
BELDAM HAG FURY CRONE RUDAS
ALECTO ERINYS RUDOUS VIRAGO
BELDAME JEZEBEL TISIPHONE
BELEAGUER BELAY BESET INVEST
ASSAULT BESEIGE LEAGUER
BLOCKADE SURROUND
BELEM PARA
BELEMNITE ARTIFACT KERAUNION
BELFRY SHED TOWER BEFFROY
CLOCHER CLOGHEAD BELLHOUSE

BELGIUM
CAPITAL: BRUSSELS BRUXELLES
CANAL: UNION ALBERT CAMPINE
GAUL TRIBE: REMI BELGAE NERVII
MEASURE: VAT AUNE LAST PIED
CARAT PERCHE BOISSEAU
MOUNTAIN: BOTRANGE
NAME: BELGIE BELGIQUE
PLATEAU: ARDENNES HOHEVENN
PORT: OSTEND ANTWERP
PROVINCE: LIEGE NAMUR
ANTWERP BRABANT HAINAUT
LIMBURG FLANDERS HAINAULT
RIVER: LYS DYLE LEIE MAAS
MARK YSER BOUCQ DEMER
LESSE MEUSE NETHE RUPEL
SENNE DENDER ESCAUT MANJEL
OURTHE SAMBRE SEMOIS
VESDRE WARCHE AMBLEVE
SCHELDT
TOWN: AS AAT ANS ATH HAL HUY
MOL SPA AATH AMAY ASSE
BOOM BREE DOEL GAND GEEL
GENK GENT HOEI LIER LOOZ
MONS VISE WAHA ZELE AALST
ALOST ARLON CINEY EEKLO
ESSEN EUPEN EVERE GENCK
GHENT HEIST IEPER JETTE
JUMET LIEGE NAMUR RONSE
TIELT UCCLE VORST WEZET
YNOIR YPRES AARLEN ANVERS
BERGEN BILZEN BRUGES
DEURNE IZEGEM LEUVEN LIERRE
MERXEM OPWIJK OSTEND
ANTWERP ARDOOIE BERCHEM
DOORWIK HERSTAL HOBOKEN
IXELLES LOUVAIN MECHLIN
ROULERS SERAING TOURNAI
BRUSSELS COURTRAI KORTRIJK
MOUSCRON TURNHOUT

VERVIERS WATERLOO
WEIGHT: LAST CARAT LIVRE
POUND CHARGE CHARIOT
ESTERLIN

BELIE BELONG DEFAME BESEIGE
FALSIFY PERTAIN SLANDER
TRADUCE DISGUISE STRUMPET
SURROUND
BELIEF CRY FAY ISM LEVE MIND
SECT TAKE TROW VIEW VOTE WEEN
CAUSE CREDO CREED DOGMA FAITH
OBEAH TENET TROTH TRUST
CREDIT GROUND CRIANCE FEELING
HOLDING OPINION TROWING
ARYANISM BITHEISM CREDENCE
DOCTRINE FINALISM HUMANISM
RELIANCE
(— IN DEVILS) DIABOLISM
(— IN GHOSTS) EIDOLISM
(FALSE —) DELUSION
(GROUNDLESS —) CANARD
(MORTAL —) HALL
(SHALLOW —) BALLOON
(SUPERSTITIOUS —) FREET
(TRADITIONAL —) ICON IKON EIKON
(UNFOUNDED —) FICTON
BELIEVE BUY WIS DEEM FEEL HOLD
TAKE TREW TROW WEEN CREED
FAITH FANCY GUESS JUDGE SEPAD
THINK TRUST ACCEPT CREDIT
ESTEEM EXPECT DARESAY SUPPOSE
ACCREDIT CONSIDER CREDENCE
(— ERRONEOUSLY) FEIGN
(— NAIVELY) SWALLOW
(— UNCRITICALLY) EAT
BELIEVER IST LEVER BOTARY KITABI
CREDENS ADHERENT ARMINIAN
BELITTLE DECRY DWARF SNEER
MINISH SLIGHT DETRACT DIMINUE
LIGHTLY MINIMIZE VILIPEND
DENIGRATE DISCREDIT DISPARAGE
BELITTLER ZOILUS
BELL HUB TOM CALL FAIR GONG
HUBB RING ROAR CHIME CLOAK
CLOCK CODON FLARE KNELL SWELL
TENOR BASKET BELLOW BUBBLE
CLOCHE CROTAL CURFEW PHONIC
SOCKET TAPPER TOCSIN TOLLER
TREBLE TRIPLE VESPER ANGELUS
BLOSSOM CAMPANA CAMPANE
COROLLA COWBELL JANGLER
JINGLER LOWBELL SKELLAT
SKILLET TAMBOUR TANTONY
TINKLER CASCABEL COCKBELL
DINGDONG DOORBELL HANDBELL
HAWKBELL MORTBELL PAVILLON
STARTLER TINGTANG
(ALARM —) TOCSIN
(CLOSED —) CROTAL
(EVENING —) CURFEW
(FUNERAL —) TELLER
(HAND —) CLAG
(LARGE —) SIGNUM
(LOWEST —) BORDON BOURDON
(PASSING —) KNELL
(SACRING —) SQUILLA
(SLEIGH —) GRELOT

BELLABELLA HAELTZUK HEILTSUK
BELLADONNA DWALE MANICON
  BANEWORT DAFTBERRY
  DWAYBERRY MYDRIATIC
BELLARMINE GRAYBEARD
  GREYBEARD LONGBEARD
BELLBIRD MAKO SHRIKE COTINGA
  ARAPUNGA KORIMAKO MAKOMAKO
  CAMPANERO
BELLBOY BUTTONS
BELLE SPARK TOAST
  (SPANISH —) MAJA
BELLEEK POTTERY CHAMPAGNE
BELLEROPHON (FATHER OF —)
  GLAUCUS
  (MOTHER OF —) EURYMEDE
BELLFLOWER RAMPION BELLWORT
  HASKWORT IVYBELLS MILKWORT
BELLHOP BELLBOY HALLBOY
  CHASSEUR
BELLICOSE MAD IRATE WARFUL
  HOSTILE WARLIKE MILITANT
BELLIGERENT BRISTLY HOSTILE
  WARLIKE CHOLERIC FIGHTING
  JINGOIST COMBATIVE IRASCIBLE
  LITIGIOUS WRANGLING
BELLOW CRY LOW MOO YAP BAWL
  BEAL BELL GAPE ROAR ROME ROUT
  YAUP YAWP BELVE BLART BLORE
  CROON ROUST SHOUT BULLER
  CLAMOR RUMMES BLUSTER
  RUMMISH ULULATE
BELLOWING ROUT ROUST BELLING
  BOATION MUGIENT
BELLOWS BELY LUNGS BULIES
  FEEDER SANDER WINKER SYLPHON
  WINDBAG EXPELLER
  (SMALL —) PLUFF
  (STORAGE —) RESERVOIR
BELLOWS FISH BUGLER SNIPEFISH
BELL RINGER TOLL YOUTH TOLLER
  CLINKUM
BELLWETHER MASTER
BELLY BAG COD GIE GUT MAW POD
  BOUK FILL KYTE MARY WAME WEAM
  WOMB BINGY BOSOM BULGE FRONT
  GORGE PLEON TABLE THARM
  THERM TRIPE BAGGIE BINGEE
  HUNGER PAUNCH VENTER ABDOMEN
  BALLOON STOMACH TUMBREL
  APPETITE
BELLYACHE COMPLAIN
  COLLYWOBBLES
BELLYBAND WANTY
BELLYING BUNTING PREGNANT
BELONG BE GO FIT LIE BEAR FALL
  RELY APPLY BELIE GROUP AFFEIR
  INHERE RELATE RETAIN BEHOOVE
  PERTAIN APPERTAIN SUBSCRIBE
BELONGINGS ALLS DUDS FARE
  GEAR GOODS TRAPS ASSETS
  DUFFEL DUFFLE ESTATE USINGS
  BAGGAGE EFFECTS CHATTELS
  PROPERTY PURPRISE FURNITURE
  HOUSEHOLD
BELOVED DEAR IDOL LIEF AIMEE
  BOSOM CHERI SWEET ADORED
  CHERIE MINION DARLING PRECIOUS
  (MOST —) ALDERLIEFEST

BELOW ALOW BAJO DOWN ABLOW
  AFTER INFRA NEATH SOTTO UNDER
  BEHIND BENEATH
BELT LAS AREA BAND BEAT BLOW
  CEST FELT GIRD LACE LIST MARK
  RING SASH ZONE GIRTH MITER
  MITRE PATTE STRAP STRIP SWATH
  TRACT WAIST WHACK ZONAR ZONIC
  BODICE CESTUS CINGLE FETTLE
  GIRDLE INVEST LUNGER REGION
  STRAIT STRIPE SWATHE ZONNAR
  ZONULE BALDRIC CIRCUIT PASSAGE
  BALTHEUS CEINTURE CINCTURE
  ELEVATOR ENCIRCLE MECHANIC
  SURROUND
  (ASTROLOGICAL —) CLIMATE
  (CONVEYOR —) HAUL
  (ENDLESS —) APRON CREEPER
  (GREEK —) ZOSTER
  (HINDU SWAMP —) TERAI
  (MACHINE —) SWIFTER
  (MINERAL —) RANGE
  (TREE —) BERM BERME
BELTED ZONATE GIRDLED
  CINCTURED
  (— WITH WHITE) SHEETED
BELUGA HUSE HUSO HAUSEN
  MARSOON WHITEFISH
BELVEDERE GAZEBO LOOKOUT
BEMIRE DAG SOIL JARBLE
BEMOAN MEAN MOAN SIGH MOURN
  PLAIN BEWAIL LAMENT DEPLORE
BEMUSE SOT BULL DAZE AMUSE
BEMUSED DOPY DOPEY
BENCH PEW BANC BANK BENK BERM
  BINK DAIS DEAS FORM MESA SEAT
  SILL STEP TRAM BASIN BASON
  BERME BREAK CABIN CHAIR FORME
  JUDGE PLANK STALL STOOL
  BANCUS BANKER SCONCE SEDILE
  SETTEE SETTLE SITTER COUNTER
  DRESSER REPOSAL SHAMBLE
  SITTING TRESTLE TRIBUNE
  ALEBENCH
  (— FOR DAIRY TUBS) TRAM
  (— FOR KNEADING DOUGH) BREAK
  (OUTDOOR —) EXEDRA EXHEDRA
  (PLAYER'S —) WOOD
  (ROWER'S —) BANK THOFT ZYGON
  THWART
  (SHOEMAKER'S —) FORME
  (WORKMAN'S —) SIEGE
BEND BOW NID NIP PLY SAG SET
  WIN WRY ABOW ARCH BENT BOOL
  BUCK COPE CURB DOME FAUD FLEX
  FOLD GENU HOOK KINK LEAN LOUT
  PLOY RUMP TURN VERT WEEP
  ANGLE BATON BIGHT BREAK COUDE
  COURB CRANK CRIMP CRINK CROOK
  CULGE CURVE DROOP FLECT FRESE
  HINGE HUNCH INBOW KNEEL PLICA
  QUIRL ROUND SCRAG SKELP SLANT
  STOOP TREND TWINE TWIST
  BOUGHT BUCKLE CAMBER CONVEX
  COTICE
BENDER BUM JAG LEG BUST DRUNK
  SPREE BRIDGE WHOPPER GUZZLING
  SIXPENCE BRANNIGAN INFLECTOR
BENDING BOW SAG KNEE KNOT

  CROOK CURVE LITHE TWIST PLIANT
  SUPPLE TWISTY ANFRACT FLEXION
  HOGGING SINUOUS BUCKLING
  FLECTION
  (— OF ROCK) DRAG
BENDY TREE MIRO MAHOE
BENEATH ALOW ANETH BELOW
  LOWER UNDER ANEATH
BENEDICITE BENISON CANTICLE
BENEDICTINE CLUNIAC
  CAMALDOLESE
BENEDICTION ABOT AMEN ABOTH
  NANDI AMIDAH BROCHO PRAYER
  BENISON BERAKAH BLESSING
BENEFACTION ALMS BOON GIFT
  PRESENT DONATION GRATUITY
BENEFACTOR AGENT ANGEL
  DONOR FRIEND HELPER PATRON
  SAVIOR MAECENAS PROMOTER
BENEFICE FEE FEU FEUD FIEF
  FAVOR SCARF CURACY LIVING
  BENEFIT PRELACY RECTORY
  TOTQUOT DONATIVE KINDNESS
  SINECURE VICARAGE
BENEFICENCE BOON GIFT GRACE
  BOUNTY CHARITY GOODNESS
  KINDNESS
BENEFICENT KINDLY AMIABLE
  GRACIOUS
BENEFICIAL GOOD USEFUL
  HEALTHY HELPFUL BONITARY
  SALUTARY SANATIVE SINGULAR
  AVAILABLE BENIGNANT DESIRABLE
  ENJOYABLE HEALTHFUL LUCRATIVE
  REWARDING WHOLESOME
BENEFICIARY HEIR USER DONEE
  CESTUI CESTUY USUARY VASSAL
  LEGATEE FEUDATORY
BENEFIT AID USE BOON BOOT GAIN
  GIFT GOOD HELP PROW SAKE AVAIL
  BOOST FRUIT SELTH STEAD VISIT
  ASSIST BEHALF BEHOOF BETTER
  FRINGE PROFIT SALUTE USANCE
  ADVANCE BESPEAK CONCERT
  DESERVE IMPROVE SERVICE UTILITY
  BEFRIEND INTEREST
BENEVOLENCE JEN GOODNESS
  GOODWILL HUMANITY
BENEVOLENT GOOD KING BENIGN
  KINDLY LOVING AMIABLE LIBERAL
  GENEROUS AVUNCULAR BENIGNANT
BENIGN BOON GOOD KIND MILD
  BLAND SWEET GENIAL GENTLE
  AFFABLE BENEDICT GRACIOUS
  INNOCENT SALUTARY FAVORABLE
  WHOLESOME
BENIGNANT KIND BLAND GENIAL
  LIBERAL GRACIOUS MERCIFUL
BENJAMIN (FATHER OF —) JACOB
  (MOTHER OF —) RACHEL
  (SON OF —) ARD EHI BELA GERA
  ROSH ASHBEL BECHER HUPPIM
  MUPPIM NAAMAN
BENNET CLOVEWORT
BENNISEED SESAME
BENO TUBA
BENT AIM BOW SET BIAS CAST GIFT
  TURN BOUND BOWED BOWLY
  COUDE CRANK CRUMP FLAIR

HUMOR KNACK LURCH PRONE
SQUAT SWING TASTE TREND
AKIMBO ANLAGE BENNET BIASED
BRACED COURBE COURSE CURVED
DOGLEG ENERGH GENIUS HOOKED
INTENT LIKING NECKED SQUINT
SWAYED TALENT BUCKLED
CROOKED CURVANT EMBOWED
FLEXION FLEXURE IMPETUS INTENSE
LEANING LEVELED PRONATE
PURPOSE STOOPED TENSION
APTITUDE ARCUATED CRUMPLED
DECLINED FLECTION IMMINENT
INFLEXED PENCHANT REFLEXED
TENDENCY
(— AT THE END) HAMATE HOGGED
GRYPANIAN
(— DOWNWARD) BOWED DECURVED
INCUMBENT RECLINATE
(— IN) INCAVATE
(— OF MIND) GEME AFFECTION
(EASILY —) LITHY
(NATURAL —) SWING
BEN-TEAK NANDI NANAWOOD
BENUMB NIP DAZE DUNT NUMB
STUN DAVER DOZEN SCRAM SHRAM
CUMBER DEADEN STOUND BINOMEN
FRETISH FRETIZE STIFFEN STUPEFY
TORPEDO
BENUMBED CHILL SCRAM CLUMSE
CLUMSY FROZEN TORPID CLUMPST
SHRAMMED
BENUMBING LEADEN
BENZENE PHENE BENZIN BENZOL
PHENENE
BENZOIN BENJOIN LINDERA
BENJAMIN FIXATIVE
BEQUEATH GIVE WILL ENDOW
LEAVE OFFER BESTOW COMMIT
DEMISE DEVISE LEGATE QUETHE
BEQUEST COMMEND TRANSMIT
BEQUEST GIFT WILL LEGACY
BEQUEATH HERITAGE PITTANCE
ENDOWMENT
BERATE JAW NAG DRUB LASH RAIL
ABUSE BASTE CHIDE SCOLD SCORE
SLATE REVILE CENSURE REPROVE
UPBRAID CHASTISE
BERBER RIF RIFF KABYL SHLUH
KABYLE SHILHA HARATIN MZABITE
SHILLUH HARRATIN MOZABITE
(— CHIEF) CAID
BERCEUSE CRADLESONG
WIEGENLIED
BEREAVE ROB STRIP WIDOW DIVEST
SADDEN DEPRIVE DESPOIL
BEREAVED BEREFT VIDUOUS
WIDOWED DESOLATE
BEREAVEMENT ORBITY ORBITUDE
VIDUATION
BEREFT ORB LORN LOST POOR QUIT
WIDOW ORBATE FORLORN
FORFAIRN DESTITUTE
BERG FLOE BARROW ICEBERG
FLOEBERG
BERGAMOT BOSE BERGAMA
BURGAMOT
BERIBERI KAKKE
BERITH BRIS BRISS BRITH

BERM BERME LISIERE HEELPATH
BERRY BAY DEW HAW ALEY BEAT
CRAN POHA RASP BACCA BLACK
FRUIT GRAIN GRAPE LANSA MOUND
SALAL SAVIN BURROW LANSAT
LANSEH SABINE THRESH CURRANT
ETAERIO HILLOCK ACROSARC
ALLSPICE COWBERRY DEWBERRY
HAWEBAKE
(ACID —) CURRANT
(COFFEE —) CHERRY
(DRIED —) PASA
(JUMPER —) ABHAL
(LAUREL —) BAY
(POISONOUS —) BANEBERRY
BERTH BED JOB BUNK DOCK SLIP
SOPT CABIN PLACE UPPER BILLET
OFFICE SECURE LODGING MOORING
SLIPWAY POSITION ANCHORAGE
BERYL EMERALD AEROIDES
HELIODOR GOSHENITE
BERYLLIA GLUCINA GLUCINE
BESEECH ASK BEG BID CRY SUE
WOO PRAY CRAVE HALSE PLEAD
ADJURE APPEAL OBTEST CONJURE
ENTREAT IMPLORE SOLICIT
IMPETRATE OBSECRATE
BESET PLY SET SIT BEGO SAIL STUD
ALLOT BELAY BIGAN HARRY PRESS
SIEGE SPEND STEAD ASSAIL
ATTACK HARASS INFEST OBSESS
WAYLAY ARRANGE BESIEGE
OVERSET PERPLEX BLOCKADE
ENCUMBER ENTHRONG OBSTRUCT
SURROUND BELEAGUER
BESHOW SKIL CUDDY CUDDEN
CUDDIE BADDOCK COALFISH
SKILFISH
BESIDE BY HEAR INBY ALONG
ANENT ASIDE FORBY ABREAST
AGAINST FORNENT ADJACENT
FORNENST
(— ONE ANOTHER) ABREAST
(— ONESELF) FEY
BESIDES BY TO AND BUT TOO YET
ALSO ELSE MORE OVER THEN UNTO
WITH ABOVE AGAIN FORBY SUPRA
BESIDE BEYOND EXCEPT FORBYE
WITHAL THERETO WITHOUT
LIKEWISE MOREOVER
BESIEGE GIRD GIRT BELAY BELIE
BESET SIEGE STORM ATTACK
OBSESS OBSIDE PESTER PLAGUE
COMPASS SOLICIT SURROUND
BELEAGUER
BESMEAR RAY BALM DAUB SOIL
APPLY COVER GRIME GRUFT MUDDY
SLAKE SMEAR SULLY TAINT BEDAUB
PLATCH BESLIME SMOTHER
BESMIRCH BESLUBBER
BESMIRCH DASH SLUR SOIL SMEAR
SULLY SLURRY SMIRCH ASPERSE
BLACKEN DRAGGLE TURPIFY
DISCOLOR
BESOM COW MAP DRAB BISME
BROOM SWEEP SLOVEN HEATHER
BESOT DULL ASOTE ASSOT MUDDLE
STUPID STUPEFY BEFUDDLE
BESPANGLE DOT STAR STUD

ADORN JEWEL SPRINKLE
BESPATTER BLOT DASH JAUP SOIL
SPOT MUDDY PLASH STAIN SULLY
BEGARY SPARGE ASPERSE
SCATTER SMOTTER REPROACH
SPRINKLE
BESPEAK CITE HINT SHOW ARGUE
IMPLY ORDER SPEAK TRYST
ACCOST ATTEST ENGAGE STEVEN
ADDRESS ARRANGE BENEFIT
BETOKEN DISCUSS EXCLAIM
RESERVE FORETELL INDICATE
BESPECKLE DASH
BESPRINKLE DROP POWDER
ASPERSE BESTREW BESPRING
SPRINKLE BEQUIRTLE
BEST O ACE BEAT GOOD LACE MOST
PICK TOPS WALE ELITE EXCEL
WORST CHOICE DEFEAT FINEST
FLOWER OUTWIT SUNDAY TIPTOP
UTMOST ARISTOS CONQUER
GARLAND LARGEST OPTIMUM
DAMNDEST GREATEST KOHINOOR
OUTMATCH OUTSTRIP POSSIBLE
VANQUISH
BESTIAL LOW VILE WILD BRUTE
FERAL PRONE BRUTAL FILTHY
BEASTLY BRUTISH INHUMAN
SENSUAL BELLUINE DEPRAVED
BESTIR STIR AWAKE SHIFT STEER
AROUSE HUSTLE
(— ONESELF) LEG
BEST MAN PARANYMPH
BESTOW ADD PUT USE CAST DEAL
DOTE GIVE SEND STOW TAKE WARE
ALLOT ALLOW APPLY AWARD BESET
GRANT INFER LODGE PLACE SPEND
THOLE WREAK ACCORD BETEEM
CONFER DEMISE DEVOTE DIVIDE
DONATE DOTATE EMPLOY ENTAIL
ESTATE EXTEND IMPART IMPOSE
RENDER SHOWER COLLATE
COMMEND DISPOSE ENLARGE
EROGATE INDULGE INSTATE
PARTAKE PRESENT QUARTER
TRIBUTE BEQUEATH
(— LAVISHLY) HEAP
(— UPON) GIFT
BESTOWAL DOLE DISPOSAL
COLLATION LARGITION
(— OF PRAISE) ACCOLADE
BESTRIDE HORSE STRIDE STRADDLE
BET GO UP BAS BOX LAY SET VIE
WAD ANTE BACK BRAG CHIP GAGE
HOLD JACK NOIR PAIR PLAY PLOT
PUNT RISK WAGE BOUND CARRE
HEDGE ROUGE SAVER SPORT
STAKE WAGER GAMBLE HAZARD
IMPAIR MANQUE MILIEU PLEDGE
DERNIER PREMIER
(— AGAINST) MILK COPPER
(— AT LONG ODDS) SKINNER
(— BOLDLY) BLUFF
(— CHIP) CHECK
(FARO —) SLEEPER
(HEDGING —) SAVER
(POKER —) BLIND
BETA AND GAMMA GUARDS
BETAKE GO GET HIE MOVE TAKE

APPLY CATCH GRANT ASSUME
COMMIT REMOVE REPAIR RESORT
COMMEND JOURNEY WITHDRAW
(— ONESELF TO MILL) SUE
(— ONESELF) BUN HIT BOUN MARK
PIKE TEEM AVOID FOUND HAUNT
REFER TRUSS YIELD
BETEL IKMO ITMO SERI SIRI SIRIH
PUPULO
BETEL LEAF PAN BUYO PAUN
PAWNE
BETEL NUT BONGA BONYA BUNGA
SUPARI
BETHABARA NOIBWOOD
GREENHEART
BETHEL BETHESDA
BETHINK TAKE THINK ADVISE
DEVISE RECALL REFLECT CONSIDER
REMEMBER RECOLLECT
(— ONE'S SELF) MIN MINE
UMBETHINK
BETHLEHEM BEDLAM
BETHROOT TRILLIUM
BETIDE HAP TIDE BEFIT OCCUR
TRITE WORTH BECOME BEFALL
CHANCE HAPPEN BETOKEN
PRESAGE
BETIMES ANON RATH SOON EARLY
RATHE TIMEOUS SPEEDILY
FORTHWITH
BETOKEN MARK NOTE SHOW SIGN
AUGUR TOKEN ASSERT BETIDE
DENOTE EVINCE IMPORT SHADOW
BESPEAK EXPRESS OBLIQUE
PORTEND PRESAGE SIGNIFY
FOREBODE FORESHOW INDICATE
BETONY BROOMWORT
BETRAY BLAB BLOW BOIL GULL
SELL SHOP SILE SING SPOT TELL
TRAY UNDO WRAY CROSS FALSE
PEACH ROUND SPILL SPLIT SWICK
SWIKE ACCUSE BEWRAY DELUDE
DESCRY DESERT QUATCH REVEAL
SEDUCE SNITCH SQUEAL BEGUILE
DECEIVE FALSIFY MISLEAD
PROMOTE TRAITOR DISCLOSE
DISCOVER
(— CONFIDENCES) SPILL
BETRAYAL RAP ACCUSE TREASON
GIVEAWAY PRODITION
BETRAYER RAT JUDAS SKUNK
SEDUCER TRAITOR DERELICT
RECREANT SQUEALER
BETRAYING TELLTALE
BETROTH AFFY EARL TOKEN TROTH
TRUTH ASSURE ENGAGE ENSURE
PLEDGE PLIGHT ESPOUSE PROMISE
AFFIANCE CONTRACT DESPOUSE
HANDFAST
BETROTHED SURE VOWED ASSURED
ENGAGED HANDFAST INTENDED
COMBINATE
BETTA PLAKAT
BETTER AID TOP BEET MEND AMEND
EMEND EXCEL SAFER WISER
BIGGER EXCEED REFORM ADVANCE
CHOICER CORRECT GREATER
IMPROVE PROMOTE RECTIFY
RELIEVE SUPPORT SURPASS

EMINENCE INCREASE SUPERIOR
(— A SCORE) BREAK
(— THAN ORDINARY) EXTRA
BETTING ACTION GAMBLING
(— SYSTEM) PAROLI ALEMBERT
BETTOR ORALER
BETTY JENNY COTBETTY JOCRISSE
MOLLYCOT WIFECARL
BETWEEN AMID EMEL AMELL
AMONG ENTRE TWEEN YTWYN
ATWEEN ATWIXT TWEESH AVERAGE
BETWIXT
BEUDANITE CORKITE
BEVEL BLOW CANT CONE EDGE
PUSH REAM ANGLE BEARD BEZEL
MITER MITRE SLANT SLOPE SNAPE
SPLAY ASLANT CIPHER RHYMER
CHAMFER INCLINE OBLIQUE
(— EDGES) BEARD
(WITHOUT —) FLAT
BEVERAGE ADE ALE CUP NOG POP
RUM SAP TEA BEER BREW CHIA
GROG MABI MATE MEAD MILK NIPA
SODA WHIG WINE CHOCA CIDER
CLARY COCOA DRAFT DRINK JULEP
LAGER LEBAN MORAT MULSE
NEGUS PUNCH SHRUB SMASH
TREAT TWIST WATER BISHOP
COFFEE EGGNOG LIQUID LIQUOR
NECTAR PORTER SPRUCE TISWIN
BUNNELL CASSINA LIMEADE
OENOMEL POTABLE STEPONY
TULAPAI ALEBERRY COCKTAIL
LEMONADE PIQUETTE POTATION
CALIBOGUS CHOCOLATE
GINGERADE POMPERKIN SOMETHING
SWITCHELL
(— FROM COW'S MILK) KEFIR
KEPHIR
(— FROM PEPPERS) KAVA
KAVAKAVA
(— FROM SAP) TUBA
(— OF BUTTERMILK AND WATER)
BLAND
(— OF CHAMPAGNE) POPE
(— OF HOT MILK) POSSET
(— OF PORT WINE) BISHOP
(— OF VINEGAR AND WATER)
POSCA
(ALCOHOLIC —) DEW ARAK SAKE
SAKI ARRAK BASIG SHRUB SNAPS
STUFF ARRACK FIREWATER
STIMULANT
(COLA —) DOPE
(EFFERVESCENT —) FIZZ
(FERMENTED —) BASI KUMYS
KUMISS
(FRUIT —) SMASH
(INSIPID —) WASH
(MEXICAN —) TEPACHE
(WEAK —) LAP
(PL.) WAIPIRO
BEVY HERD PACK COVEY DROVE
FLOCK GROUP SWARM FLIGHT
SCHOOL COMPANY
BEWAIL CRY RUE WEY KEEN MOAN
RAME SIGH WAIL WEEP MOURN
PLAIN BEMOAN GRIEVE LAMENT
PLAINT SORROW THROPE DEPLORE
COMPLAIN

BEWARE WAR CAVE GARE HEED
SHUN TENT WARD AVOID SPEND
ESCHEW WARNING
BEWILDER FOG FOX MAR BEAT
DAZE FOIL GAUM MAZE STUN
ABASH ADDLE AMAZE AMUSE
DEAVE DIZZY BAFFLE BEMIST
BEMUSE BOTHER DAZZLE DUDDER
MOIDER MOMBLE MUDDLE PUZZLE
WANDER WILDER BUFFALO
BUMBAZE CONFUSE FLASKER
MYSTIFY PERPLEX STAGGER
STUPEFY ASTONISH CONFOUND
DISTRACT ENTANGLE OVERMUSE
SQUATTER SURPRISE
BEWILDERED MAR ASEA LOST
MANG WILL AGAPE DAZED MAZED
BUSHED MAPPED STUPENT
WILSOME CONFUSED HELPLESS
WILLYARD PERPLEXED
BEWILDERMENT AWE FOG DAZE
MISMAZE STICKLE AMAZEMENT
CONFUSION
BEWITCH HEX WISH BLINK CHARM
MAGIC OBEAH SPELL WITCH
ENAMOR ENTICE GLAMOR GRIGRI
HOODOO STRIKE THRILL ATTRACT
BEDEVIL DELIGHT ENCHANT
GLAMOUR ENSORCEL FORSPEAK
GREEGREE OVERLOOK
BEWITCHED HAGGED
BEWITCHING SIREN
BEYOND BY FREE OVER YOND
ABOVE ASIDE AYOND FORBY ULTRA
BEHIND BEYANT YONDER BENEATH
BESIDES FORTHBY FURTHER
OUTGATE PASSING WITHOUT
OVERMORE SUPERIOR HEREAFTER
(— DOUBT) ASSURED
(— ORDINARY METHODS) AFIELD
(— THE MARK) GONE
(— THE SEA) ULTRAMARINE
(— THIS) STILL
BEZEL RIM TOP EDGE OUCH SEAL
BEVIL BEZIL CROWN FACET CHATON
FLANGE MARQUISE TEMPLATE
BEZIQUE PENCHANT
BEZOAR GOATSTONE HIPPOLITH
B-GIRL SITTER
BHAKTA BHAGAVATA
BHANG BANG BENG BENJ HASHISH
BHARAL TUR HALL NAHOOR
BURRHEL
BHIKSHU GELONG
BHUTAN (ASSEMBLY OF —)
TSONGDU
(CAPITAL OF —) THIMPHU
(CURRENCY OF —) PAISA RUPEE
(LANGUAGE OF —) DZONGKHA
(RIVER OF —) MACHU MANAS
AMOCHU
BHUTAN PINE KAIL
BIANNUAL BIYEARLY
BIAS PLY WRY AWRY BENT CANT
SWAY WARP AMISS COLOR FAVOR
POISE SLANT SLOPE SWING TWIST
BIGOTRY INCLINE OBLIQUE
SUGGEST CLINAMEN COLORING
DIAGONAL TENDENCY PREJUDICE

PROCEDURE SPECTACLE
BIASED SLANT COLORED PARTIAL
BIB SIP BRAT POUT APRON DRINK
FEEDER TIPPLE TUCKER BAVETTE
(CHILD'S —) BISHOP
(LEATHER —) DICK
BIBLE BOOK VULGATE SCRIPTURE
(— TEXT) MIKRA MIQRA
BIBLE LEAF COSTMARY
BIBULOUS DRINKING BIBACIOUS
BICKER JAR WAR BOWL SPAR TIFF
ARGUE BRAWL CAVIL FIGHT ASSAIL
ATTACK BATTLE CONTEND DISPUTE
PICKEER QUARREL WRANGLE
PETTIFOG SKIRMISH SQUABBLE
BICKERN ANVIL BEAKIRON
BICYCLE BIKE QUAD CYCLE HOBBY
MOUNT STEED WHEEL JIGGER
ORNARY SAFETY TANDEM ORDINAR
TRIPLET ORDINARY ROADSTER
BID GO BEG NAP BEDE BODE CALL
GIVE HEST HIST PRAY WISH CHEAP
CLEPE FRAGE OFFER ORDER
ADJURE CHARGE DIRECT ENJOIN
INVITE REVEAL SIMPLE SUMMON
TENDER BALANCE CHEAPEN
COMMAND DECLARE DROPVIE
ENTREAT PROFFER ANNOUNCE
PROCLAIM PROPOSAL
(— ADIEU) TEACH
(— AT AUCTION) CRY
(— IN CARDS) CUE FROG JUMP
SOLO FRAGE GRAND SHIFT BOSTON
DEFEND DEMAND DENIAL SMUDGE
BLUCHER COMMAND SHUTOUT
SUPPORT CONTRACT SCHMEISS
(SEALED —) TICKET
BIDDING AUCTION BIDDANCE
DIRECTIVE
BIDE FACE STAY WAIT ABIDE AWAIT
DWELL TARRY WATCH ENDURE
REMAIN SUFFER SOJOURN
CONTINUE TOLERATE
BIDENS CUCKOLD MANZANILLA
BIDET SITZBAD INSESSION
BIDRI VIDRY BIDDERY TUTENAG
BIER BEAR PYRE FRAME GRAVE
HANDY HORSE TABUT COFFIN
HEARSE LITTER SUPPORT
FERETORY FERETRUM
BIFURCATION WYE FORK SPLIT
BRANCH CROTCH FORKING DIVISION
DICHOTOMY
BIG FAT BARO BOLD HUGE MUCH
VAST BULKY CHIEF GAUCY GRAND
GREAT GROSS HUSKY LARGE
GAUCIE MIGHTY BIGGISH BUMPING
EMINENT HUMMING LEADING
MASSIVE POMPOUS UPRIGHT
VIOLENT BOASTFUL BOUNCING
ENORMOUS GENEROUS GIGANTIC
IMPOSING PLUMPING PREGNANT
SLAPPING SWANKING SWAPPING
THUMPING
(— WITH YOUNG) FULL GRAVID
(MARVELOUSLY —) TREMENDOUS
BIGHORN ARGAL AOUDAD ARGALI
CIMARRON
BIGHT BAY BEND BITE COIL GULF

LOOP ROVE ANGLE CURVE INLET
NOOSE CORNER HOLLOW POCKET
BIGOT CAFARD ZEALOT FANATIC
MUMPSIMUS
BIGOTED BIASED NARROW
HIDEBOUND ILLIBERAL SECTARIAN
BIGOTRY INTOLERANCE
BIGROOT MANROOT BITTERROOT
BIG SHOT MUCKAMUCK
BIG SKY COUNTRY MONTANA
BILE BOIL GALL HUMP VENOM
CHOLER GROWTH ATRABILE
BILGE PUMP SCUM BOUGE BULGE
BILLAGE THURROCK
BILIMBI CAMIAS KAMIAS CUCUMBER
BILINGUAL DIGLOT
BILIOUS GALLISH
BILIOUSNESS LIVER CHOLER
BILK DO GYP BALK HOAX CHEAT
COZEN TRICK DELUDE FLEECE
SWEDGE DECEIVE DEFRAUD
SWINDLE
BILL ACT DUN GET LAW NEB NIB TAB
BEAK CHIT CLAP GETT KITE NOTE
PECK SHOT CHECK ENTRY LIBEL
SCORE CARESS CHARGE DOCKET
INDICT LAWING PECKER PICKAX
POSTER STRIKE DERTRUM INVOICE
LAMPOON MATTOCK PLACARD
PROGRAM REMANET STATUTE
BILLHOOK DOCUMENT HEADLAND
INNOCENT PETITION TREASURY
(— OF ANCHOR) PEE PEAK
(— OF COMPLAINT) QUERELA
(— OF CREDIT) ANGEL
(— OF DIVORCE) GET GETT
(— OF EXCHANGE) SOLA HUNDI
DEVISE
(— OF FARE) MENU CARTE
(— OF PARCELS) FACTURE
(10-DOLLAR —) TEN TENNER
SAWBUCK
(100-DOLLAR —) CENTURY
(2-DOLLAR —) DEUCE
(5-DOLLAR —) FIN VEE FIVE FIVER
(COUNTERFEIT —S) STIFF
(DOLLAR —) BUCK SPOT SINGLE
FROGSKIN
(REVOLUTIONARY —) ASSIGNAT
BILLET BAR GAD HUT LAY LOG
LOOP NOTE PASS POST SPOT
BERTH ENROL HOUSE LODGE
ORDER SHIDE SPRAG STICK STRAP
BALLOT BULLET ENROLL HARBOR
LETTER LIBBET NOTICE TICKET
BEARING EPISTLE MISSIVE POLLACK
COALFISH DOCUMENT FIREWOOD
ORNAMENT POSITION QUARTERS
(— SOLDIERS) CESS
BILLET-DOUX CAPON
BILLETING LIVERY
BILLFISH GAR LONGJAWS SAILFISH
SPEARFISH
BILLHOOK BILL DHAW HOOK
PAWPAW SLASHER SNAGGER
SCIMITAR
BILLIARD BALL IVORY
BILLIARD CUE MACE MAST
(TIP OF —) LEATHER

BILLIARDS PILLS TRUCKS
(LAWN —) TROCO
BILLINGSGATE ABUSE SLAPDASH
BILLION MILLIARD
BILLON BAIOC VELLON BAJOCCO
BILLOW SEA BLOW WAVE BULGE
CLOUD FLOAT SURGE SWELL
RESACA RIPPLE ROLLER WALLOW
BREAKER UNDULATE
BILLY CAW CHAP CLUB GOAT MACE
MATE BATON FANNY NEDDY
CUDGEL FANNIE FELLOW BROTHER
COMRADE BILLIKIN BILLYCAN
BLUDGEON JACKSHAY BLACKJACK
TRUNCHEON
BIMAH ALMEMAR ALMEMOR
BIN ARK BOX CUB GUM BING BONE
CART CRIB VINA FRAME HUTCH
KENCH PUNGI STALL STORE WAGON
BASKET BUNKER GARNER HAMPER
MANGER POCKET TROUGH WITHIN
BLEACHER
(— FOR CEMENT) SILO
(— FOR FISH) KENCH
(— FOR GRAIN) ARK
BINARY HYDRIDE
BINATE DUAL DOUBLE PAIRED
COUPLED TWOFOLD GEMINATE
BINAURAL DIOTIC
BIND JAM LAP TIE WAP EARL FAST
FRAP GIRD GYVE HOLD HOOP KNIT
KNOT LASH MAIL NAIL TAPE YERK
BRACE CADGE CHAIN CINCH EDDER
GIRTH SNAKE STICK STRAP TRUSS
ATTACH BUNDLE COMMIT EMBIND
ENGAGE FETTER FREEZE GARTER
GIRDLE LIGATE OBLIGE STRAIN
SWATHE TETHER WRITHE ARTICLE
ASTRAIN BANDAGE CONFINE
EMBOUND ENCHAIN GRAPPLE
SHACKLE SWADDLE ASTRINGE
CONCLUDE FLIGHTER HANDFAST
INNODATE LIGATURE OBLIGATE
RESTRAIN
(— A FALCON) MAIL
(— BY LEASE) THIRL
(— BY PLEDGE) GAGE SWEAR
(— IN BUNDLE) KID BAVIN
(— INTO SHEAVES) GAVEL THRAVE
(— ONESELF) ADHERE
(— TO SECRECY) TILE
(— TOGETHER) LIME FAGOT SEIZE
CEMENT FAGGOT ASTRINGE
RELIGATE
(— UP) KILT BAVIN TRUSS UPBAND
ASTRICT REVOLVE
(— WITH THREAD) OOP
BINDER BAND BEAM BOND CORD
ROPE BALER COVER FRAME LEVER
FILLET FOLDER GIRDER HEADER
LIGNIN TARMAC HAYBAND
BONDSTONE BOOKMAKER
BINDING TAG BAND CORD GARD
HARD LEAR ROPE TAPE YAPP
COVER VALID CADDIS EDGING
RIBBON BOUNDEN CADDICE
GALLOON LAPPING MOUSING
WEBBING FAITHFUL LIGATIVE
LIGATORY STRINGENT

(— FAST) IRON
(— OF BOOK) FACE
(— OF GOLD) BISSET
(— ON DRESS) FENT
BINDWEED BINE WIRE CREEPER
TIEVINE BEARBIND BEARBINE
BELLBINE BINEWEED CORNBINE
HELLWEED MILKMAID WOODBINE
WITHYWIND
BINE WIRE
BINGE BAT BOW HIT BLOW BUST
SOAK BEANO PARTY SOUSE SPRAY
SPREE CRINGE BLOWOFF
CAROUSAL
BINGO KENO BEANO LOTTO BRANDY
SCREENO
BINNACLE PYX BITTACLE
BINOCULARS GLASS
BINOMIAL DIONYM BINOMEN
BIOGEOGRAPHY CHOROLOGY
BIOGRAPHER PLUTARCH
BIOGRAPHY BIO LIFE VITA MEMOIR
ACCOUNT HISTORY RECOUNT
(— OF SAINTS) HAGIOGRAPHA
HAGIOGRAPHY
BIOPHORE BIOGEN PLASOME
BIOPLAST MICELLA MICELLE
BIOTITE MICA ANOMITE MEROXENE
BIOTOPE STATION
BIPED DIPODE HINDQUARTERS
BIRCH COW BIRK CANE FLOG WHIP
ALDER ALNUS CANOE SWISH
BETULA BIRKEN TAWHAI HICKORY
BIRD ANI DAW DOG JAY NUN PIE TIT
COOT CROW DOVE FOWL IBIS JACK
KAGU KITE KNOT LARK QUIT RUFF
TERN TODY WING WREN BAKER
BRANT CHUCK CLEAR COVEY
EGRET FINCH FLIER FLYER GOOSE
HOBBY JUNCO LARID LIVER PEWEE
PEWIT RAVEN ROBIN SNIPE STILT
SWIFT TEREK TURCO TWITE VIREO
BULBUL DICKEY DIPPER DRIVER
DRONGO DUCKER DUNLIN FALCON
GROUSE GUINEA HOOPOE HOOTER
JACANA JAEGER LINNET MARTEN
MOCKER NESTER ORIOLE OSCINE
PHOEBE PLOVER SHRIKE SILVAN
SINGER SITTER SYLVAN THRUSH
TROGON TURNIX VERDIN WAYBUG
YAWPER ANTBIRD BABBLER
BLUEJAY BUNTING BUSTARD
BUZZARD CATBIRD CHIRPER
FEATHER FLAPPER FLICKER
FLIGGER FLOPPER GRACKLE
HALCYON HORNERO HURGILA
INCOMER IRRISOR JACAMAR
JACKDAW KINGLET MINIVET
MOULTER ORTOLAN PEACOCK
PERCHER QUILLER REDWING
SCRAPER SKINNER SKYLARK
SPARROW SUNBIRD SWALLOW
TANAGER TINAMOU TITLARK
TOMFOOL WARBLER WAXWING
ACCENTOR AIRPLANE AMADAVAT
ANNOTINE BLACKCAP BLACKNEB
BLUEBIRD BOATBILL BOBOLINK
BOBWHITE BUBBLING CAGELING
CARINATE COCKBIRD COCORICO

COTTINGA DREPANID FERNBIRD
FIREBIRD FIRETAIL GROSBEAK
GRUIFORM IBISBILL JUVENILE
KILLDEER KINGBIRD LOBEFOOT
OXPECKER PHEASANT PLUMIPED
POORWILL PREACHER REDSTART
SALTATOR SONGBIRD STARLING
SURFBIRD SWAMPHEN TAPACOLO
THRASHER THROSTLE TITMOUSE
TREMBLER UMBRETTE WHINCHAT
WOODCHAT WOODCOCK YEARBIRD
(— OF BRILLIANT PLUMAGE) TODY
JALAP ORIOLE TROGON JACAMAR
KIROMBO MINIVET TANAGER
(— OF INDIA) BAYA KALA SHAMA
(— OF OMEN) WAYBIRD
(— OF PREY) OWL HAWK KITE
EAGLE ELANT GLEAD GLEDE STOOP
EAGLET ELANET BUZZARD
GOSHAWK STOOPER VULTURE
(AFRICAN —) TAHA QUELEA
TOURACO UMBRETTE NAPECREST
(AUSTRALIAN —) EMU ROA LORY
ARARA LEIPOA BOOBOOK BUSTARD
FIGBIRD WAYBUNG BELLBIRD
LORIKEET LYREBIRD MANUCODE
(BIG-BEAKED —) BECARD HORNBILL
(CRESTED —) KAGU COPPY
HOATZIN TOPKNOT
(CROCODILE —) TROCHIL
(DECOY —) CALL STOOL
(DIVING —) AUK LOON GREBE
DOPPER DUCKER GRAYLING
PLUNGEON
(EUROPEAN —) ANI DAW MEW QUA
CIRL DARR KITE MALL MORO QUIS
ROOK STAG WHIM YITE AMSEL
BOONK GLEDE MAVIS MERLE OUSEL
OUZEL SACER SAKER SERIN TARIN
TEREK TERIN WHAUP AVOCET
COCKOO CUSHAT GAYLAG GODWIT
MARTEN MERLIN MISSEL REDCAP
WHEWER WINDLE WINNEL WRANNY
BITTERN BUSTARD HAYBIRD
KESTREL MOTACIL ORTOLAN
SAKERET STARNEL WHISKEY
WINNARD WITWALL BARGOOSE
CHEPSTER DOTTEREL GARGANEY
REDSTART WHEATEAR WHEYBIRD
WHIMBREL WRANNOCK YOLDRING
(EXTINCT —) MOA DODO JIBI KIWI
MAMO RUKH OFFBIRD
(FABULOUS —) ROC HALCYON
OOFBIRD
(FEMALE —) HEN JENNY
(FICTITIOUS —) JAYHAWK PHOENIX
(FISH-CATCHING —) OSPREY
CRABIER
(FLEDGLING —) SQUAB
(FLIGHTLESS —) EMU GOR MOA
DODO EYAS GORB GULL KAGU KIWI
CALLOW GORLIN APTERYX GORLING
NESTLER OSTRICH PENGUIN
BUBBLING NESTLING
(FRIGATE —) IOA IWA
(FRUIT-EATING —) COLY
(GALLOWS —) HEMPY HEMPIE
(GAME —) QUAIL SNIPE COLIMA
GROUSE INCOME FLAPPER INCOMER

(HAWAIIAN —) IO OO AVA IOA IWA
OOA IIWI JIBI KOAE MAMO MOHO
OMAO OOAA KAMAO PALILA
(HORN-HEADED —) KAMICHI
(INJURED —) CRIPPLE
(LARGEST —) LAMMERGEIER
(MADAGASCAR —) KIROMBO
(MECHANICAL —) ORTHOPTER
(MYTHICAL —) FUM ROC GANZA
SIMURG SIMURGH
(NEW ZEALAND —) KEA MOA OII
ROA HUIA KAKA KIWI KOKO KUKU
KULU PEHO RURU TITI WEKA
KAKAPO KOKAKO KUKUPA APTERYX
KORIMAKO MOREPORK NOTORNIS
(PASSERINE —) QUIT FINCH
SPARROW STARNEL SWALLOW
SYLVIID DREPANID FALCONET
FERNBIRD GRALLINA JACKBIRD
(PERTAINING TO —S) OSCINE
(RAPACIOUS —) JAEGER
(RASORIAL —) SCRATCHER
(RUNNING —) COURSER
(SAMOAN —) IAO
(SEA —) AUK ERN ERNE GONY
GULL SMEW TERN EIDER SOLAN
FULMAR GANNET HAGDON OSPREY
PETREL PUFFIN PELICAN SEAFOWL
MURRELET
(SHORE —) REE RAIL SORA SNIPE
STILT WADER AVOCET CURLEW
PLOVER WILLET WRYBILL
(SHORT-TAILED —) BREVE
(SINGING —) LARK WREN PIPIT
ROBIN VEERY VIREO CANARY
LINNET MOCKER ORIOLE OSCINE
SINGER THRUSH WARBLER
FAUVETTE REDSTART
(SMALL —) TIT TODY WREN DICKY
PEGGY PIPIT TYDIE VIREO DICKEY
LINNET SISKIN TOMTIT CREEPER
SPARROW TITLARK COCORICO
GNATSNAP STARLING WHEATEAR
(SOUTH AMERICAN —) GUAN MINA
MYNA RARA TOCA BAKER CHAJA
JOPIN TURCO BARBET BECARD
CHUNGA TOUCAN CARIAMA OILBIRD
BELLBIRD BOATBILL CARACARA
GUACHARO HOACTZIN PUFFBIRD
SCREAMER TAPACOLO TAPACULO
TERUTERO
(STYLIZED —) DISTELFINK
(TROPICAL —) ANI GUAN KOAE
TODY BOS'N BOSUN JALAP BARBET
BECARD MOTMOT TROGON
JACAMAR WIGTAIL LONGTAIL
SALTATOR
(WADING —) HERN IBIS RAIL SORA
CRANE HERON SNIPE STILT STORK
AVOCET GODWIT JACANA BOATBILL
FLAMINGO SHOEBILL SHOEBIRD
(WILD —S) GALLINAE
(YOUNG —) EYA GULL PIPER
FLAPPER NESTLER BIRDIKIN
NESTLING
(PL.) AVIFAUNA POLYMYODI
PRAECOCES
BIRD BOLT BURBOLT QUARREL
BIRD CAGE AVIARY PINJRA VOLARY

VOLERY PADDOCK
BIRDCATCHER FOWLER
BIRD CHERRY DOGWOOD
EGGBERRY HACKWOOD HAGBERRY
BIRDLIFE ORNIS
BIRDLIME GLUE LIME BELIME
VISCUM BIRDGLUE
BIRD OF PARADISE APUS
MANUCODE RIFLEBIRD
BIRD'S-FOOT FOWLFOOT
SERRADELLA
BIRD'S KNEE SUFFRAGO
BIRD'S MANTLE STRAGULUM
BIRI BIDI
BIRTH KIN BEAR FALL BLOOD
BURDEN GENTRY ORIGIN BEARING
BORNING DESCENT GENESIS
LINEAGE DELIVERY GENITURE
NASCENCY NATALITY NATIVITY
(FALSE —) SOOTERKIN
(GENTLE —) GENTILITY
(HONORABLE —) BLOOD
(OF LOW —) CRESTLESS
(OF NOBLE —) CORONETED
BIRTHMARK MOLE IMAGE NAEVE
NEVUS BLEMISH SPILOMA
SIGNATURE
BIRTHRATE NATALITY FERTILITY
BIRTHRIGHT KIND HERITAGE
BIRTHROOT BATHROOT BATHWORT
DEATHROOT DISHCLOTH
SQUAWROOT
BIRTHWORT GUACO ASARUM
BATHROOT
BISAYAN AKLAN CEBUAN AKLANON
CEBUANO
BISCUIT BUN NUT BAKE ROLL RUSK
SNAP WOOD BREAD SCONE WAFER
BISQUE COOKIE DODGER MUFFIN
SIMNEL CRACKER GALETTE PENTILE
PRETZEL RATAFIA RATIFIA
CRACKNEL HARDTACK ZWIEBACK
(BROKEN —S) DUNDERFUNK
(COLOR —) DOE PAWNEE
BISECT FORK CROSS HALVE SPLIT
CLEAVE DIVIDE MIDDLE SEPARATE
BISECTION MEDIATION
BISHOP EP ABBA EPUS LAWN PAPA
POPE ANGEL DENIS ARCHER
BUSTLE DESPOT EPARCH EXARCH
MAGPIE PRESUL PRIEST ROCHET
ROCKAT PONTIFF PRELATE PRIMATE
TULCHAN ANTISTES DIOCESAN
DIRECTOR ORDINARY OVERSEER
PONTIFEX
(— AND MARTYR) EM
(CHESS —) ALFIN ALPHYN ARCHER
BISHOP'S-WEED AMMI AMMEOS
KHELLA WILLIAM BOLEWORT
BULLWORT GOUTWEED TOOTHPICK
BISKOP BRUSHER STEENBRAS
BISMARK KRAPFE KRAPFEN
BISMUTH WISMUTH TINGLASS
BISON BUGLE BOVINE MITHAN
WISENT AUROCHS BONASUS
BUFFALO
BISTORT PATIENCE ADDERWORT
ASTROLOGE SNAKEWEED
SNAKEWORT

BISTRO BAR CAFE TAVERN
WINESHOP ESTAMINET NIGHTCLUB
BIT ACE FID FIP GAG JOT NIP ORT
PIP WEE ATOM BITE BITT CHIP
CROP CURB DITE DOIT DRIB FLAW
FOOD GRUE HAET HATE HOOT IOTA
ITEM LEVY MITE MOTE PART SLUT
SNAP SNIP SPOT TOOL WHIT AUGER
BLADE CHECK CRUMB DRILL GROAT
PATCH PEZZO PIECE POINT SCRAP
SHRED SMACK SNACK SPECK STEEK
TASTE THRUM WIGHT BITTIE BRIDLE
CANNON EATING MORSEL PELHAM
PICKLE SIPPET SMIDGE SPLICE
STITCH STIVER THOGHT TITTLE
TRIFLE BRADOON BRIDOON
CHILENO GLIMMER MORCEAU
PALLION PORTION SCATCHE
SMIDGEN SMIDGIN SMIGEON
SNAFFLE TRANEEN FISHTAIL
FRACTION FRAGMENT QUANTITY
SMITCHIN TWOPENNY
(— OF GOSSIP) HEARING
(— OF INFORMATION) GRIFF
GRIFFIN WRINKLE
(— OF KEY) WEB
(— OF LAND) CROOK
(— OF METAL) FLITTER
(— OF TOAST) SNIPPET
(— TO EAT) MUNGEY
(—S AND PIECES) GUBBINS
GUBBINGS
(—S OF COKE) BREEZE
(—S OF WRITING) EXCERPTA
(ONE-QUARTER —) GILL
(CUTTING —) CHASER
(DRILL —) CROWN
(FANCIFUL —) FLAM
(FIPPENY —) SIXPENCE
(FLORID —) FLOURISH
(HORSE'S —) KEVEL SNODE
CANNON PELHAM SCATCH SNAFFLE
BASTONET
(LEAST —) FIG JOT RAP HANG LICK
GHOST GROAT RIZZOM STITCH
(LITTLE —) PICK TOUCH BITTOCK
REMNANT SOUPCON
(SMALL —) BLEB GLIM SPUNK
(SMALL —S) SMATTER
(TINY —) SPECK DRIBBLE SCRINCH
TODDICK
(PL.) SMITHERS SMITHEREENS
BITCH DO GYP BICK LAMP SLUT
BRACH BROOD CHEAT GROUSE
COMPLAIN
BITE BIT CUT EAT JAW NIP BAIT
CHAM CHEW ETCH FOOD GASH
GNAP GNAW HOLD KNAP MEAL RIVE
SNAP TAKE CHACK CHAMM CHAMP
CHEAT GNASH PINCH SEIZE SMART
SNACK STING TOOTH TRICK
CRUNCH MORSEL NIBBLE PIERCE
SAVAGE BUGBITE CHEATER
CORRODE FORBITE IMPRESS
MORSURE MUNCHET PARTAKE
SHARPER SLANDER
(— AT) HIT
(— GREEDILY) HANCH
(— REPEATEDLY) CHAMP

BITING BIT HOT ACID HOAR KEEN
ACRID NIPPY QUICK SHARP SNELL
BITTER RODENT SEVERE SHREWD
STINGY TEETHY TWEAKY CAUSTIC
CUTTING MORDANT MORSURE
NIPPING PUNGENT SUBACID
DRILLING INCISIVE POIGNANT
SCALDING SCATHING STINGING
BITIS ECHIDNA
BITO BALM HAJILIJ
BITT BLOCK KNIGHT BOLLARD
(PL.) RANGEHEADS
BITTER AWA GAL ACID ACRE ASIM
BASK KEEN MARA RUDE SALT SORE
SOUR TART ACERB ACRID AMARA
ASPER BLEAK HARSH IRATE SHARP
BITING PICRIC SEVERE AUSTERE
CAUSTIC CRABBED CUTTING
FERVENT GALLING GALLISH PAINFUL
PUNGENT SATIRIC POIGNANT
STINGING SUBAMARE VIRULENT
BITTER APPLE COLOCYNTH
BITTER BIT SMALLPOX
BITTERBUSH SNAKEROOT
BITTER CLOVER YELLOWTOP
BITTERLY SOUR FELLY BITTER
ROUNDLY CURSEDLY
BITTERN BUMP SOCO BOONK BUTOR
HERON BITORE BUMBLE BUMMLE
BUTTAL KAKKAK BLITTER BUMMLER
ERICIUS DUNKADOO GRUIFORM
LONGNECK
(FLOCK OF —) SEDGE SIEGE
BITTERNESS RUE ACOR BILE FELL
GALL ATTER ENMITY MALICE
RANCOR AMARITY ACERBITY
ACRIDITY ACRIMONY FERVENCY
SEVERITY WORMWOOD
(EXTREME —) VIRULENCE
(WITH —) AMAREVOLE
BITTER PIT STIPPEN
BITTERROOT LEWISIA
TOBACCOROOT
BITTERS AMER
BITTER SPAR DOLOMITE
BITTERSWEET FELLEN DOGWOOD
LOBSTER SOLANUM WAXWORK
DULCAMARA FELONWOOD
FELONWORT FEVERTWIG
WITHYWIND WOLFBERRY
BITTER VETCH ERS
BITTERWEED RAGWEED
HORSEWEED
BITTERWORT FELWORT DANDELION
BITUMEN TAR CONGO PITCH SLIME
ASPHALT CARBENE ALKITRAN
ALCHITRAN ELATERITE
BIVALVE HEN CLAM SPAT PINNA
COCKLE DIATOM MUSSEL OYSTER
MOLLUSK NUCULID PANDORA
SCALLOP TOHEROA
BIVOUAC CAMP ETAPE WATCH
ENCAMP SHELTER
BIZARRE ODD ANTIC DEDAL OUTRE
QUEER QUAINT ANTICAL CURIOUS
FANCIFUL ECCENTRIC FANTASTIC
GROTESQUE
BLAB LAB CHAT BLART BLATE
CHEEP CLACK PEACH BABBLE

BETRAY GOSSIP REVEAL SQUEAL
TATTLE BLABBER CHATTER
CLATTER
BLACK DHU JET WAN CALO CROW
DARK EBON FOUL INKY NOIR PIKY
SOOT BUGLE COLLY DUSKY MURKY
NEGRO NOIRE RAVEN SABLE SOOTY
TARRY THICK ATROUS BRUNET
DISMAL ETHIOP GLOOMY MURREY
PITCHY SULLEN ABAISER AFRICAN
BLACKEN DIAMOND MELANIC
NEGRITO NIGRINE NIGROUS
PICEOUS SWARTHY UNCLEAN
MOURNFUL
(**— AND BLUE**) LIVID
(**— OUT**) CONK
(**BONE —**) SPODIUM
(**BROWNISH —**) LAVA
(**GREENISH —**) CORBEAU
(**IVORY —**) ABAISER
(**LIGHT-SKINNED —**) BROWN
(**RATHER —**) DUSKISH
(**VIOLET —**) CROW
BLACKAMOOR BLECK NEGRO
MORIAN NEGRESS ETHIOPIAN
BLACK ASH HOOPWOOD
BLACKBALL PIP PILL BALLOT
EXCLUDE HEEBALL OSTRACIZE
BLACK BASS HURON TROUT
ACHIGAN GROWLER OCHIGAN
BLACKBERRY AGAWAM LAWTON
DEWBERRY MULBERRY ROSACEAN
(**— BUSH**) MORE
BLACKBIRD ANI DAW PIE CROW
AMSEL COLLY MERLE OUSEL OUZEL
RAVEN BLACKY COLLEY MAIZER
BLACKIE COWBIRD GRACKLE
JACKDAW REDWING WOOFELL
TROOPIAL
BLACKBOARD CHALKBOARD
GREENBOARD
BLACKBREAM TARWHINE
BLACK-BROWED GLOOMY
BLACK BRYONY LILY LILIUM
OXBERRY BINDWEED MANDRAKE
BLACK BUCK SASIN
BLACKCAP GULL JACK PEGGY
HAYBIRD WARBLER MOCKBIRD
TITMOUSE JACKSTRAW RASPBERRY
BLACKDAMP STYTH STYTHE
CHOKEDAMP
BLACKDRINK YAPON YAUPON
BLACKEN INK TAR CHAR CORK SOIL
SOOT BLECK CLOUD COLLY JAPAN
SMOKE SULLY BEFOUL BLATCH
DARKEN DEFAME MALIGN SMEETH
SMIRCH VILIFY ASPERSE BENEGRO
NIGRIFY SLANDER SMOLDER
TRADUCE BESMIRCH
BLACKENED REECHY
BLACKEYE COWPEA
BLACKFELLOW BLACKBOY
YAMMADJI
BLACKFIN SESI CISCO
BLACKFISH GRIND TAUTOG
BORLASE DOGFISH GRAMPUS
POTHEAD HARDHEAD
BLACKFLY GNAT SIMULIID
BLACKFOOT BLOOD KAINAH PIEGAN

SIKSIKA SIHASAPA
BLACK GROUPER MERO AGUAJI
WARSAW GARRUPA
BLACKGUARD SHAG BLECK CATSO
GAMIN GUARD SNUFF SWEEP
ROTTER LADRONE VAGRANT
BLAGGARD CRIMINAL LARRIKIN
VAGABOND SCOUNDREL
BLACK GUILLEMOT CUTTY TYSTE
SCRABE DOVEKEY DOVEKIE
SCRABER PUFFINET
BLACK GUM TUPELO HORNPIPE
STINKWOOD
BLACK HAW SLOE BOOTS ALISIER
STAGBUSH VIBURNUM
BLACKHEAD COMEDO
BLACK HOREHOUND HENBIT
ARCHANGEL
BLACK HORSE SUCKER SUCKEREL
BLACKING LINK BLECK BLATCH
BLEACH ATRAMENT
BLACK IRONWOOD AXMASTER
AXEMASTER
BLACKISH DUSKY MOREL SWART
BLACKY
BLACKJACK OAK SAP CLUB COSH
DUCK FLAG JACK BETLE BILLY
JERKIN NATURAL BLUDGEON
BLACKLEG LEG FIRE SCAB SNOB
ANTHRAX GAMBLER JACKLEG
APOSTATE BLACKNEB BLACKNOB
SWINDLER KNOBSTICK
BLACK LETTER GOTHIC
BLACKLY SABLY
BLACK MAGIC DIABLERIE
BLACKMAIL BRIBE CHOUT COERCE
EXTORT TRIBUTE CHANTAGE
BLACKMAILER GHOUL BRIBER
LEECHER
BLACK MANGROVE COURIDA
BLACK MEDIC HOP TREFOIL
NONESUCH SHAMROCK
BLACKNESS GRIME DARKNESS
NIGRITUDE
BLACK NIGHTSHADE MOREL
DUSCLE SOLANUM BLUEBERRY
MOONSHADE TROMPILLO
BLACK OLIVE OXHORN
BLACK PEPPER PIMENTA
BLACK PINE MATAI
BLACK POISON WALNUT
BLACK RHINOCEROS BORELE
KEITLOA UPEYGAN
BLACK SALLY SALLEE
MUZZLEWOOD
BLACK SANICLE LUNGWORT
MASTERWORT
BLACK SHANK LANAS
BLACK SKIMMER CUTWATER
SHEARBILL
BLACKSMITH GOW SMUG LOHAR
SHOER SMITH PLOVER SMITHY
VULCAN BROOKIE FARRIER STRIKER
BURNEWIN IRONSMITH
BLACKSNAKE WHIP QUIRT RACER
ELAPID RUNNER COLUBRID
BLACK SPECK DARTROSE
BLACK SPURGE FLUXWEED
BLACKTAIL DASSY DASSIE

BLACK TERN DARR STARN
BLACKTHORN HAW SLOE SNAG
SCROG GRIBBLE SLOEBUSH
SLOETREE SNAGBUSH
BLACK-VARNISH TREE THEETSEE
BLACK VULTURE URUBU CORBIE
ZOPILOTE
BLACK WALNUT NOGAL
BLACKWATER STATE NEBRASKA
BLACK WIDOW POKOMOO
BLACK WOLF KARAKURT
BLACKWOOD BITI LIGHTWOOD
BLACKWORT COMFREY
BLADDER SAC VES VESICA AMPULLA
BLATHER BLISTER INFLATE
UROCYST UTRICLE VESICLE
(**AIR —**) POKE SWIM SOUND
SINGALLY
BLADDER-AND-STRING BUMBASS
BLADDER CAMPION BEHN BEHEN
SILENE COWBELL SNAPPER
RATTLEBOX
BLADDER KETMIE MODESTY
BLADDERNUT BAGNUT
BLADDERWORT POPWEED
BLADDER WRACK CUTWEED
KELPWARE
BLADE BIT FIN FOP OAR SAW WEB
BLOW BONE BOWL EDGE FLAG
HEAD LEAF LIMB TANG WEAK
BLOOD BRAND DANDY FLUKE GRAIN
GUIDE KNIFE LANCE SHEAR SPARK
SPEAR SPIRE SWORD BLUNGE
BUCKET BUSTER CUTTER DOCTOR
FOIBLE HEDDLE LAMINA PAGINA
RIPPER ROARER SCYTHE SICKLE
TOLEDO BAYONET CHIPPER
GALLANT POLESAW SCALPEL
SCAPULA SCRAPER SPINNER
MOLDBOARD PROPELLER
(**— OF FAN**) VANE
(**— OF GRASS**) PILE CHIRE SPEAR
SPIRE STRAP TRANEEN
(**— OF KNIFE**) TANG GRAIN
(**— OF LEAF**) LIMB LAMINA
(**— OF MORION**) COMB
(**— OF OAR**) PALM PELL WASH
(**— OF SCISSORS**) BILL
(**— OF YOUNG GRAIN**) SORAGE
(**CULTIVATOR —**) SWEEP DUCKFOOT
(**SKATE —**) RUNNER
(**SURGICAL —**) LEUCOTOME
BLAFFERT PLAPPERT
BLAIN RUBY SORE BULLA BLISTER
INFLAME PUSTULE
BLAKE MCKAY
BLAMABLE FAULTY CULPABLE
BLAME CALL CHOP HURT LACK
ONUS SAKE SPOT TWIT WITE CHIDE
FAULT GUILT ODIUM PINCH SHEND
SNAPE SWICK SWIKE TOUCH WHITE
ACCUSE ATTASK BUMBLE BURDEN
CHARGE DIRDUM PLIGHT REBUKE
REVILE SCANCE ASCRIBE CENSURE
CONDEMN CULPATE OBLOQUY
REPROOF REPROVE SLANDER
UPBRAID WITHNIM REPROACH
BLAMED BLINDING BLISTERING
BLAMELESS ENTIRE PERFECT

BLAMELESS INNOCENT SACKLESS SPOTLESS WITELESS RIGHTEOUS

BLAMEWORTHY GUILTY CRIMINAL CULPABLE REPROBATE

BLANCH FADE PALE BLENK CHALK SCALD WHITE APPALL ARGENT BIANCA BLEACH BLENCH FALLOW WHITEN ETIOLATE

BLANCHED ASHEN ETIOLATE BLOODLESS COLORLESS

BLANCMANGE FLUMMERY

BLAND COLD KIND MILD OILY OPEN SOFT SLEEK SUAVE BENIGN BREEZY GENIAL GENTLE SMOOTH URBANE AFFABLE AMIABLE LENIENT FAVONIAN GRACIOUS UNCTUOUS

BLANDISH COAX CHARM ALLURE BLANCH CAJOLE FONDLE SMOOTH FLATTER WHEEDLE HONEYFUG

BLANDLY CREAMILY

BLANK BARE BURR FLAN FORM SHOT VOID ANNUL BLIND BREAK CHASM CLEAN EMPTY FALSE RANGE SPACE WASTE WHITE COUPON VACANT ANTIQUE BRINDLE NONPLUS UNMIXED VACUOUS UNFILLED

BLANKED BLIND

BLANKET RUG BROT MAUD WRAP BLUEY COTTA COVER CUMLY LAYER MANTA PATTU QUILT SHEET SUGAN THROW AFGHAN COOLER CUMBLY GLOBAL KAMBAL MANTLE PALLET PONCHO PUTTOO SERAPE SOOGAN STIFLE STROUD TILPAH CHIRIPA DOUBLER SMOTHER WHITTLE COVERLET MACKINAW

(— A VESSEL) WRONG

(— WITH BOMBS) SATURATE

(BUSHMAN'S —) BLUEY

(QUILTED —) BROT

(SADDLE —) CORONA

BLANKETING DUFFEL DUFFLE

BLANKNESS VACUITY NEGATION

BLARE PEAL BLEAR BLART BLAST NOISE BLAZON SCREAM FANFARE TANTARA TRUMPET

BLARNEY CON BUTTER FLATTER WHEEDLE

BLASPHEME ABUSE CURSE DEFAME REVILE PROFANE

BLASPHEMOUS BAD RIBALD IMPIOUS PROFANE

BLASPHEMY CALUMNY CURSING IMPIETY ANATHEMA SWEARING

BLAST BUB NIP WAP BANG BLOW FRAP GALE GUST RUIN RUST SHOT TOOT WIND BLAME BLIST BLORE SPLIT STUNT ATTACK BLIGHT BUGGER FORBID NIDDER NITHER REBUFF VOLLEY WITHER BLUSTER DESPOIL EXPLODE SHATTER SHRIVEL DYNAMITE OUTBURST PROCLAIM WHIRLPUFF

(— OF WIND) GUST RISE PERRY PIRRIE VENTOSITY

(— ON HORN) TOOT PRYSE

(— WITH COLD) SNEAP

(FURIOUS —) SNIFTER

BLASTED BLAME BLAMED BLIGHTED BLINDING BLINKING

BLASTER FROSTER SHOOTER SHOTMAN

BLASTING SHOOTING STELLATION

(— METHOD) MUDCAP

BLASTULA PLACULA PLANULA PLANULAN

BLATANT GLIB LOUD BRASH GROSS NOISY SILLY VOCAL COARSE GARISH TONANT VULGAR BRAWLING STRIDENT

BLATHER STIR BLEAT BABBLE WAFFLE BLITHER PRATTLE NONSENSE

BLAUBOK ETAAC BLUEBUCK

BLAZE LOW BURN FIRE GLOW HACK LEAM LOWE MARK SHOT SPOT FLAME FLARE FLASH GLARE GLEAM GLORY INGLE RATCH SHINE STARE STEAM TORCH BLAZON BLEEZE BONFIRE PIONEER SPLENDOR

(— OUT) FLAP

BLAZING AFIRE FIERY FLAMY LIGHT FLAMING FLARING

BLAZING STAR LIATRIS GRUBROOT SNAKEROOT

BLAZON DECK SHOW ADORN BLARE BLAZE BOAST DEPICT SHIELD DECLARE DISPLAY EXHIBIT PUBLISH EMBLAZON INSCRIBE

BLAZONED ARMED BANNERED

BLEACH SUN WASH BLEAK CHALK CROFT POACH BLANCH BLENCH CHLORE PURIFY WHITEN DECOLOR LIGHTEN BLONDINE ETIOLATE PEROXIDE

(— PULP) POTCH

BLEACHER WHITSTER

BLEACHERS SCAFFOLD

BLEAK DIM RAW BLAE BLAY COLD DOUR GRAY PALE SPRAT STARK SWALE ALBURN BITTER BLEACH DISMAL DREARY FRIGID PALLID CUTTING DESOLATE CHEERLESS

BLEAT BAA BLAT BLEA YARM BLART BLATE BLATHER BLUSTER WHICKER

BLEATING BALANT

BLEB BLOB BULLA BUBBLE BLISTER PUSTULE VESICLE SWELLING

BLEED FLUX MILK WEEP BLOOD LEECH MULCT SWEAT SWINDLE TEICHER

BLEEDER STICKER

BLEEDING BLOODY SANGLANT

BLEEDING HEART EARDROP DICENTRA

BLEMISH MAR BLOT BLUR DENT FLAW GALL LACK MAIM MARK MOIL MOLE RIFT SAKE SCAR SLUR SPOT TASH VICE WANT AMPER BLAME BOTCH BRECK CLOUD CRACK FAULT FLECK MULCT NAEVE SPECK STAIN SULLY TACHE TAINT TOUCH BLOTCH BREACH DEFAME DEFECT IMPAIR INJURE MACULA MACULE MAYHEM SMIRCH STIGMA BUBUKLE CATFACE DEFAULT FAILING FISSURE SUNSPOT

(— IN CLOTH) AMPER SULLY

(— IN PAPER) FISHEYE

BLEMISHED BAD WEMMY

BLENCH FOIL SHUN WILE AVOID ELUDE EVADE QUAIL SHAKE SHIRK TRICK BAFFLE BLANCH BLEACH FLINCH RECOIL SHRINK DECEIVE

BLEND MIX RUN BLOT FADE FUSE JOIN MELT MENG MOLD ADMIX BLIND CREAM GRADE MERGE MOULD SHADE SMEAR SPOIL STAIN TINGE UNITE BLUNGE COMMIX CRASIS DAZZLE MINGLE TEMPER COMBINE CONFUSE CORRUPT DECEIVE GRADATE MIXTURE POLLUTE COALESCE CONCRETE IMMINGLE TINCTURE

(— OF NOISES) CHARM

(— OF SHERRY) SOLERA

(— OF WINES) CUVEE

BLENDE JACK SPHALERITE

BLENDED FONDU FUSED MIXED MERGED MINGLED CONFLATE CONFLUENT

BLENDING FUSION HOTCHPOT

BLENNY GUNNEL SHANNY EELPOUT JUGULAR KELPFISH SENORITA WOLFFISH WRYMOUTH QUILLFISH

BLESBOK NUNNI BLESBUCK

BLESS KEEP SAIN WAVE ADORE ANELE BENSH CROSS EXTOL FAVOR GUARD THANK VISIT WOUND CROUCH FAVOUR HALLOW PRAISE THRASH APPROVE BEATIFY EMBLISS GLORIFY PROTECT MACARIZE PRESERVE SANCTIFY

BLESSED HOLY BLEST HAPPY SEELY DIVINE JOYFUL SACRED SEELFUL BENEDICT BHAGAVAT BLISSFUL BLOOMING HALLOWED HEAVENLY

BLESSEDNESS BLISS FELICITY BEATITUDE HAPPINESS

BLESSING BOON GIFT SAIN BLISS DUKAN GRACE SORRA BARAKA DUCHAN PRAISE BENISON DARSHAN WORSHIP BERACHAH FELICITY BEATITUDE

BLEU DE ROI SEVRES

BLIGHT NIP FIRE RUIN RUST SMUT SOKA BLAST BRANT FROST SNEAP MILDEW NITHER TAKING WITHER DESTROY

BLIND BET POT ANTE BOMA DARK DEAD DULL HIDE HOOD SEEL BISME BLANK BLEND DUNCH SHADE STAKE STALL WAGER AMBUSH BISSON BLENDE DARKEN DAZZLE SCREEN SECRET AIMLESS ANTIQUE BANDAGE BATTERY BENIGHT ECLIPSE EYELESS OBSCURE PRETEXT RAYLESS SHUTTER ABORTIVE ARTIFICE BAYARDLY BLINDING EXCECATE HOODWINK IGNORANT INVOLVED JALOUSIE OUTSHINE PURBLIND UMBRELLA VENETIAN

(— IN ONE EYE) PEED GLEED GLEYD

(— MAN) MOLE

(HALF —) STARBLIND

(PL.) PERSIENNES

BLIND ALLEY LOKE STOP POCKET IMPASSE

BLINDER FLAP HOOD BLIND BLUFF LUNET WINKER BLINKER EYEFLAP LUNETTE HOODWINK BLINDFOLD

BLINDFOLD MOP DARK BLINK BLUFF SCARF MUFFLE BANDAGE BLINDER OBSCURE ENCLOSER HEEDLESS HOODWINK RECKLESS CONCEALED

BLINDING BISME BISSON

BLINDMAN'S BLUFF POST HOODWINK

BLINDNESS BISSON CECITY ABLEPSY ANOPSIA MEROPIA ABLEPSIA DARKNESS IGNORANCE

(— TO TRUTH) AVIDYA AVIJJA

(COLOR —) ACHROBIA

(DAY —) HEMERALOPIA

(NIGHT —) NYCTALOPIA

(PARTIAL —) MEROPIA HEMIOPSIA

(RED-GREEN —) DALTONISM

(SNOW —) CHIONABLEPSIA

(STUDY OF —) TYPHLOLOGY

(TEMPORARY —) MOONBLINK

BLINDSTITCH FELL

BLINDWORM SLOW ORVET ANGUID HAGWORM SLOWWORM

BLIND-YOUR-EYES GANGWA ALIPATA

BLINK BAT PINK SHUN WINK BLUSH CHEAT FLASH GLEAM SHINE TRICK GLANCE IGNORE OBTUSE WAPPER BLINTER CONDONE GLIMMER GLIMPSE NEGLECT NICTATE SPARKLE TWINKLE

BLINKER EYE BLINK BLUFF LIGHT SIGNAL WINKER BLINDER FLASHER GOGGLES COQUETTE HOODWINK MACKEREL

BLINTZE BLIN BLINTZ PANCAKE

BLIP ECHO

BLISS JOY EDEN KAIF SEIL BLESS GLORY ANANDA HEAVEN DELIGHT ECSTASY GLADDEN RAPTURE FELICITY GLADNESS PARADISE PLEASURE

BLISSFUL HOLY SEELY BLITHE BLESSED ELYSIAN UTOPIAN BEATIFIED GLORIFIED

BLISTER BEAT BLEB BLOB BLOW BOIL BURN LASH QUAT APTHA BLAIN BLIBE BULGE BULLA TOPIC VESIC APHTHA BUBBLE CUPOLA SCORCH SOTTER TETTER BLADDER BLUSTER SCALDER SKELLER VESICLE VESICATE

BLITHE GAY GLAD BONNY BUXOM HAPPY JOLLY MERRY BONNIE JOVIAL JOYOUS LIVELY GAYSOME JOCULAR WINSOME CHEERFUL GLADSOME SPRIGHTLY

BLIZZARD BLOW GALE WIND BURAN PURGA RETORT SNIFTER SQUELCHER

(— STATE) SD SDAK

BLOAT BLOW BLAST BLOWN FLOAT HOOVE HOVEN PUFFY SWELL

BOWDEN EXPAND TUMEFY DISTEND FERMENT INFLATE

BLOATED FOZY BLOAT BROSY CURED FOGGY HOVEN TUMID GOTCHY SODDEN TURGID POMPOUS REPLETE

BLOATER MOONEYE

BLOB LIP WEN BEAD BLEB BLOT BOIL CLOT DAUB DROP GLOB GOUT LUMP MARK MASS BUBBLE DALLOP DOLLOP PIMPLE SPLASH BLEMISH BLISTER BLOSSOM GLOBULE PUSTULE SPLOTCH

BLOC RING BLOCK CABAL PARTY UNION CLIQUE FACTION

BLOCK AME BAR COB COG DAM DIE DOG FID HOB HUB JAM KEY NOG ROW TOP VOL BALK BASE BEAR BILK BLOC BUCK BUNT CAKE CLOG CUBE DRUM FOIL FOUL FROG GLUT HEAD JAMB LEAD MASK MASS MOCK QUAR STAY STEP STOP TRIG BAULK BRICK CHAIR CHECK CHEEK CHUMP CLAMP CLEAT CLOSE COVER DETER DOLLY DUMMY EMBAR FLOAT HEART HORST JUMBO NUDGE PARRY PATCH SHAPE SPIKE SPOKE STOCK STUFF STUMP ASSIZE DENTIL DOLLEY DOMINO FIPPLE FORMER HAMPER HINDER IMPEDE KIBOSH MONKEY MUFFLE MUTULE OPPOSE OUTWIT QUERRE RIPPER SADDLE SCOTCH SNATCH SQUARE STREET STYMIE TAPLET THWART TROLLY WAYLAY BOLLOCK BOLSTER BUCKLER CONDEMN DEADEYE ERRATIC INHIBIT OUTLINE PREVENT QUADREL RAMHEAD STONKER TRIGGER TROLLEY BLOCKADE DEADHEAD ELECTRET FOLLOWER KEYSTONE MONOLITH OBSTACLE OBSTRUCT STOPPAGE WITHSPAR

(— A WHEEL) SCOTE

(— AT SPAR END) STEEVE

(— FOR SKIDDING LOGS) BICYCLE

(— IN SPEAKING) STAMMER

(— OF COAL) JUD JUDD

(— OF EARTH'S CRUST) HORST

(— OF GRANITE) SET

(— OF ICE) SERAC

(— OF LAND) FORTY

(— OF SEATS) CUNEUS

(— OF TIMBER) BOLT JUGGLE

(— SUPPORTING MAST) STEP

(— UP) BAR DAM QUIRT CONDEMN FORECLOSE

(— WITH HOLE IN IT) WAPP EUPHROE

(— WITH PROJECTING CORE) SETTLE

(—S OF STONE) DIMENSION

(ARCHITECTURAL —) DRUM STONE DENTIL IMPOST MUTULE PLINTH DOSSERET

(CHOPPING —) HACKLOG

(CLAY —) DRAWBAR

(FAULT —) MASSIF

(FELTED —) DAMPER

(FULCRUM —) GLUT

(FUSE —) CUTOUT

(IRON —) USE VOL BITT ANVIL CHAIR

(LOGGING —) LEAD JUMBO

(NAUTICAL —) CHOCK HEART STOCK SADDLE DEADEYE FAIRLEAD

(ORNAMENTAL —) BOSS

(PAVING —) SET CUBE SETT STONE WHEELER

(PLASTER —) BATTER

(POLISHING —) BUFF FLOAT

(PRINTING —) CUT QUAD RISER QUADRAT

(PULLEY —) CRAWL

(SANDSTONE —) SARSEN

(SQUARED —) MITCHEL

(STUMBLING —) HURTING

(TACKLE —) CALO TONGUE

(VAULTING —) BUCK HORSE

BLOCKADE DAM FERM BESET BLOCK EMBAR SIEGE WHISKY EMBARGO BLOCKAGE OBSTRUCT BARRICADE BELEAGUER

BLOCKAGE LOGJAM

BLOCKER CASER BRACER

BLOCKHEAD ASS LUG OAF BUST CLOT COOF COOT DAFF DOLT FOOL MOME NOWT STUB BLOCK CHUMP CUDDY GOLEM GOOSY IDIOT NINNY DIMWIT DISARD NOODLE TURNIP ASSHEAD DIZZARD DULBERT JACKASS LACKWIT MUDHEAD NOGHEAD TOMFOOL BEEFHEAD BONEHEAD CLODPATE CODSHEAD DULLHEAD DULLPATE DUMBHEAD DUMMKOPF GAMPHREL HARDHEAD JOLTHEAD LUNKHEAD

BLOCKHOUSE SPUR PUNTAL GARRISON

BLOCKING JAM JAMB DUNNAGE BLOCKADE CROSSING

BLOKE MAN CHAP COVE TOFF BLOAK JOKER FELLOW

BLOLLY BEEFWOOD CORKWOOD PORKWOOD

BLOND BAN FAIR LIGHT BLONDE FLAXEN GOLDEN YELLOW LEUCOUS BLONDINE

(AUTUMN —) FAWN

BLOOD KIN SAP GORE LIFE MASS MOOD RACE SANG SANK BLADE BLUDE BLUID CRUOR FLESH FLUID SERUM STOCK CLARET INDRED KAINAH SLUDGE GALLANT KINSHIP KINSMAN LINEAGE RELATION TROPHEMA

(CORRUPT —) YOUSTIR

(HALF —) DEMISANG

BLOODCURDLING GORY HORROR

BLOODFLOWER HIPPO REDHEAD BLOODWEED

BLOODHOUND LYM LYAM LYME HOUND LIMER SLOTH BANDOG LEAMER SLEUTH TIEDOG LYAMHOUND

BLOODIED BEBLED

BLOODLESS DEAD ANEMIC ANAEMIC INHUMAN TURNIPY LIFELESS UNFEELING

BLOODLETTER BLEEDER
BLOOD PHEASANT ITHAGINE
BLOODROOT PUCCOON REDROOT
BOLOROOT COONROOT CORNROOT
TURMERIC
BLOODSHED DEATH CARNAGE
VIOLENCE SLAUGHTER
BLOODSHOT RED INFLAMED
BLOODSTAINED GORY
BLOODSTONE SANGUINE
HEMACHATE
BLOODSUCKER LEECH SPONGER
VAMPIRE
BLOODTHIRSTY BLOODY CARNAL
TIGERISH FEROCIOUS MURDEROUS
BLOOD VESSEL VEIN COMES
HEMAD ARTERY CAPILLARY
BLOODWOOD AJHAR JAROOL
BLOODY GORY RUDE BLODE CRUEL
RUDDY BLUGGY CRUENT PLUCKY
CRIMSON BLEEDING DEATHFUL
HEMATOSE INFAMOUS SANGLANT
BUTCHERLY CRUENTOUS
FEROCIOUS MERCILESS
MURDEROUS
BLOODY BARK LANCEPOD
BLOOM DEW BLOW CAST HAZE
KNOT BLURT BLUSH CHILL BLOOTH
BLOWTH BLOSSOM BLOWING
ANTHESIS BLOOMING FLOREATE
FLOURISH
(— OF WILLOW) GULL
(— ON SHELL) CUTICLE
(— ON TREE) GOSLING
(METAL —S) HEAT
BLOOMER ERROR BLOWER
BLUNDER FAILURE
BLOOMERS KNICKERS PANTALETS
BLOOMERY FORGE HEARTH
FURNACE
BLOOMING PERT ROSY FLUSH
FRESH GREEN PRIME ABLOOM
FLORID BLOWING FLAMING
ROSEATE BLINKING
BLOOPER BLOOMER
BLOSSOM BUD BELL BLOB BLOW
CHIP SILK BLOOM LEHUA FLOWER
BLOWING BURGEON PROSPER
BOURGEON FLOURISH
(BLIGHTED —) BLAST
(HERALDIC —) FRASE FRAISE
(PL.) SET BLOSSOMRY
BLOSSOMING BLOWTH FLORAISON
FLORULENT
(— AFTER NOON) POMERIDIAN
BLOT MAR BLOB BLUR DAUB SOIL
SPOT BLACK BLANK BLEND BLOTE
ERASE SMEAR SPECK STAIN SULLY
BLOTCH CANCEL DAMAGE EFFACE
IMPAIR MACULA SHADOW SMIRCH
SMOUCH SMUDGE SMUTCH STIGMA
BLEMISH ECLIPSE EXPUNGE
INKBLOT OBSCURE SPLOTCH
TARNISH DISGRACE REPROACH
(— OUT) OUT ANNUL ERASE
CANCEL DELETE EXPUNGE
BLOTCH DAB BLOT DASH GOUT
MONK SPOT AMPER PATCH SMEAR
SPLAT STAIN MACULA MOTTLE

PLOTCH PURPLE SMIRCH SPLASH
STIGMA BLEMISH PUSTULE
SPLOTCH ERUPTION MACULATE
(PL.) BLIBE
BLOTCHED SCABBY MACULATE
SCABROUS SPLASHED
BLOTCHY SCOVY
BLOTTER BLAD
BLOUSE SHIRT SMOCK TUNIC
CAMISA GUIMPE JUMPER CASAQUE
VAREUSE CAMISOLE CASAQUIN
JIRKINET
(BUSHMAN'S —) BLUEY
BLOW BOB COB COP CUT DAB DAD
DUB FAN FIB HIT JAB JAR NAP ONE
PAT PEG POP RAP TAP TIP TIT WAP
ANDE BAFF BANG BASH BEAT BELT
BIFF BIRR BLAD BLAW BRAG BUFF
BULL BUMP BUTT CHAP CHOP CONK
COUP CRIG CUFF DASH DAUD DENT
DING DINT DIRD DOLE DRAW DRUB
DUNT DUSH FLAP FLAG FLIG FUFF
FUNK GALE GOWF GUST HACK HUFF
HURT JOLT KNAP KNEE LASH LEAD
LEFT LICK LOUK LUSH MINT ONER
PAIK PALT PANT PASS PICK PIRR
PLUG POLT PUCK PUFF PUSH SCUD
SLAM SLAP SLAT SLUG SOCK SPAT
STOP SWAP SWAT SWOP SWOT
THUD WELT WIND WIPE YANK BINGE
BLADE BLAST BLIZZ BLOOM BOAST
BRUNT BURST CLINK CLOUR CLOUT
CLUMP CLUNK CRUMP CRUNT
CURSE DEVEL DOUSE DOWSE
DUNCH FACER FILIP FLACK FLICK
FLIRT GOWFF ICTUS IMPEL KNOCK
OUTER PALMY PANDY PASTE PEISE
PLUNK PUNCH RIGHT SHAKE SHOCK
SKELP SKIRL SKITE SLASH SLIPE
SLOSH SMACK SMASH SMITE SNICK
SOUND SOUSE SPANK SPEND
STORM STRIP SURGE SWACK
SWEEP SWIPE THROW THUMP TRICE
WHACK WHANG WHIFF WHOOF
WHUFF BELTER BENSEL BENSIL
BETRAY BOUNCE BUFFET CONKER
DEPART DIRDUM DUNDER EXPAND
FILLIP FISTER FLOWER FROLIC
HANDER HUFFLE LARRUP REBUKE
SIFFLE STOUSH STRIPE STROKE
SWITCH THUNGE THWACK WALLOP
AFFLATE ASSAULT ATTAINT
BELLOWS BENSAIL BLOSSOM
BLOWOUT BLUSTER BOASTER
COUNTER CRUSHER DESTROY
INFLATE KNOCKER LAMBACK
LOUNDER MOUTHER PUBLISH
SHATTER SMACKER SPANKER
SQUELCH WHAMPLE WHIFFLE
WHITHER CALAMITY DISASTER
KNOCKOUT SASARARA SICKENER
(— ABRASIVES) BLAST
(— CEMENT) KIBOSH
(— GUSTILY) FLAW TUCK WINNOW
(— IN PUFFS) FAFF
(— NOSE) SNITE
(— OFF STEAM) SNIFT
(— ON HEAD) NOB CONK CLOUR
CONKER NOBBER TOPPER NOBBLER

(— ON NOSE) NOSER CANKER
NOZZLER SMELLER
(— SMOKE) NOSE
(— SOFTLY) BREATHE
(— UP) BOMB BLAST DYNAMITE
SUFFLATE
(— VIOLENTLY) STORM
(— WITH CUDGEL) DUB DRUB
CRUNT
(— WITH FIST) BOP BOX PEG BELT
HOOK CLOUT BUFFET
(— WITH FOOT) BOOT KICK SPURN
(GLANCING —) SCUFF
(HARD —) SLOG STOT YANK BEVEL
SWACK TWITCHER
(HEAVY —) DAD DONG DRUB DUNT
ONER SLAM SLUG CLOUT KNOCK
POISE SOUSE SQUAT STAVE SWASH
STOUND PLUMPER REEMISH
(MOCK —) FEINT
(NOISY —) DUNDER DUNNER
(RESOUNDING —) CLAP CRACK
(SHARP —) BAT NAP KNAP SLAP
SPAT CLICK FLICK FLEWIT STINGER
(SLIGHT —) SCLAFF
(SMART —) FLIP SKELP SKITE
YANKER
BLOWCASE EGG
BLOWER PAN DRIER DRYER WHALE
FANNER PUFFER BELLOWS
BLOOMER BOOSTER MUMBLER
BRAGGART OUTBURST
(GLASS —) GAFFER
BLOWGUN SUMPIT SUMPITAN
SARBACANE
BLOWHOLE BLOW GLOUP SPOUT
SPIRACLE
BLOWING ABLOW BLAST BLORE
GUSTY BLUSTER BLUSTERY
(— AT LOW SPEED) SLACK
(— AT RIGHT ANGLES) SIDE
(— OF WHALE) SPOUT
BLOWN STALE TIRED OPENED
WINDED BLOSSOM SWOLLEN
TAINTED BETRAYED FLYBLOWN
INFLATED
BLOWOUT BLOW FEED MEAL BURST
VALLEY FLAMEOUT
BLOWSY DOWDY BLOUSY BLOWZY
FROWZY
BLOWY DUSTY
BLUBBER CRY FAT BLUB FOAM WAIL
WEEP BIBLE MELON PIECE SPECK
SPICK SWELL THICK WHINE BUBBLE
FLITCH LIPPER LUBBER MEDUSA
NETTLE SEETHE BLABBER BLUSTER
SLOBBER SWOLLEN WHIMPER
(— AT WHALE'S NECK) CANT
(REFUSE —) FENKS FOOTING
FRITTERS
BLUDGEON BAT HIT SAP CLUB
MACE BILLY STICK TOWEL COERCE
COURSE TRUNCHEON
BLUE HAW LOW SAD SKY AQUA BICE
BLAE GLUM TEAL WOAD AZURE
BERYL LIVID NIKKO PERSE SMALL
WAGET COBALT GLOOMY INDIGO
LUPINE ORIENT PEWTER SEVERE
TRYPAN CELESTE CYANINE GENTIAN

GOBELIN HYPPISH LEARNED
LIBERTY LOBELIA MATELOT
MISTBLU MURILLO PEACOCK
QUIMPER REGATTA WATCHET
CERULEAN DEJECTED LABRADOR
LARKSPUR LITERARY MAZARINE
MIDNIGHT NATIONAL SAPPHIRE
WEDGWOOD POMPADOUR
(BLACKISH —) BLO BLOO
(DULL —) HAW
(ROYAL —) HATHOR
BLUEBELL CROWBELL HAREBELL
BLUEBERRY OHELO STONER
PALBERRY RABBITEYE VACCINIUM
BLUEBIRD (— GUIDE) LEADER
BLUE-BLACK BLO
BLUEBLOSSOM LILAC
BLUEBONNET CAP SCOT BLUECAP
BLUEBOTTLE BLUET BLAVER
BARBEAU BLAWORT BLOWFLY
BLUECAP BLUECUP BRUSHES
HARDOCK BLUEBLAW HYACINTH
CORNBINKS
BLUE CREEPER LOVE
BLUE CURLS FLEASEED FLEAWEED
BLUE-EYED GRASS PIGROOT
SATINFLOWER
BLUEFIN TUNNY
BLUEFISH ELF BASS ELFT SHAD
TUNA HORSE SAURY DARZEE
TAILER TAILOR FATBACK SKIPJACK
WEAKFISH
(YOUNG OF —) SNAPPER WHITEFISH
BLUEGILL BREAM SUNFISH
PONDFISH
BLUE GOOSE BALDHEAD
BLUEGRASS STATE KENTUCKY
BLUE GREEN VENICE
BLUE GUM FEVERGUM EUCALYPTUS
BLUE HEN STATE DELAWARE
BLUE HERON CRANE NAILROD
BLUEJACKET SAILOR DRAGMAN
BLUEJOINT REDTOP BLUETOPS
BLUE PETER ASK
BLUE PINE LIM
BLUE POINTER MAKO
BLUEPRINT MAP PLAN PLOT DRAFT
TRACE SKETCH DIAGRAM PROJECT
CYANOTYPE
BLUE RUNNER JUREL
BLUES MARE DUMPS CAFARD
DISMAL GLOOMS DISMALS
HORRORS HUMDRUM MEGRIMS
SADNESS DOLDRUMS DOLEFULS
BLUE SLATE SKAILLIE
BLUE SUCCORY CATNACHE
CUPIDONE
BLUET PISSABED EYEBRIGHT
INNOCENCE
BLUE TIT NUN STONECHAT
BLUE TITMOUSE YAUP TYDIE
TIDIFE BLUECAP
BLUETONGUE THICKHEAD
BLUE VERVAIN IRONWEED
BLUE VINNY DORSET
BLUEWEED ECHIUM IRONWEED
ADDERWORT
BLUFF ALTO BANK BRAG CURT FOOL
RUDE BLUNT BRAVE BURLY CLIFF

FRANK GRUFF SHORT SURLY WINDY
ABRUPT BOUNCE CRUSTY BLINDER
BLINKER BLUFTER BRUSQUE
DECEIVE UNCIVIL BARRANCA
BARRANCO CHURLISH HOODWINK
IMPOLITE
BLUISH-GRAY MERLE
BLUMEA PLACUS
BLUNDER ERR MIX BALK BONE
BUBU BULL DOLT FLUB GAFF ROIL
SKEW SLIP STIR BONER BOTCH
BREAK ERROR FAULT FLUFF GAFFE
LAPSE MISDO BOGGLE BUMBLE
BUNGLE ESCAPE FUMBLE GAZEBO
HOWLER MAFFLE MINGLE MUDDLE
BLOOMER BLOOPER CONFUSE
DERANGE FAILURE FLOATER
MISTAKE OVERSEE SOTTISE
STUMBLE SOLECISM
(— IN LANGUAGE) BULL
(— IN SPEECH) SOLECISM
(VERBAL —) SLIPSLAP SLIPSLOP
BLUNDERBUSS TRABU TRABUCO
TRABUCHO TROMBONE ESPINGOLE
BLUNDERER BUMBLER BUMMLER
KNOTHEAD LUMBERER
BLUNDERING AWKWARD BUMBLING
BLUNT BALD BATE BULL CURT DAMP
DULL FLAT MULL SNUB ABATE
BLATE BLUFF BRUSK DUBBY INERT
MORNE PLAIN PLUMP STUNT
CANDID CLUMSY DEADEN DIRECT
OBTUND OBTUSE REBATE RETUND
SHEATH STUBBY STUPID BRUSQUE
DISEDGE HACKNEY SHEATHE
SNUBBED SPADISH STUBBED
STUPEFY HEBETATE
BLUNTLY PLAT FLATLY CRUDELY
FRANKLY
BLUR DIM FOG HUM BLOB BLOT
FADE FUZZ MIST SLUR SOIL SPOT
BLEAR CLOUD FUDGE SHAKE
SMEAR STAIN SULLY MACKLE
MACULE SMUDGE STIGMA BLEMISH
CONFUSE FEATHER OBSCURE
TAILING
BLURB AD BOLT PUFF RAVE BRIEF
NOTICE
BLURRED FAINT FUZZY MUZZY
BLURRY SMUDGY SWIMMY WOOLLY
CLOUDED COMATIC EDGELESS
FLANNELLY
BLURT BLAT BOLT BLUNDER
EXCLAIM
BLUSH BLUE GLOW BLINK COLOR
FLUSH GLEAM PAINT ROUGE TINGE
CHANGE GLANCE MANTLE REDDEN
CRIMSON FLICKER LIKENESS
JOSEPHINE
BLUSHING RED ROSY ABLUSH
ROSEATE FLUSHING ROSACEOUS
BLUSTER BEEF BLOW DING HUFF
RAGE RANT BLAST BLEAT BLORE
BOAST BRACE BULLY NOISE STORM
SWANK BABBLE BELLOW BOUNCE
FRAPLE HECTOR HUFFLE TUMULT
WUTHER BLUBBER BRAVADO
FLUSTER GAUSTER ROISTER
SWAGGER WHITHER BOASTING

BULLYING THREATEN
BLUSTERER SWAG FLASH HECTOR
HUFFER FRAPLER HUFFCAP
TEARCAT
BLUSTERING BOG LOUD BRASH
VAPORS HUFFCAP VAPOURS
BULLYING
BOA BOM BOID BOMA ABOMA JIBOA
SCARF THROW ABOLLA ADJIGA
GIBOIA JOBOYA PYTHON ADJIGER
CAMOODI EMPEROR PEROPOD
ANACONDA CORALLUS
BOAR HOG APER SUID BRAWN SWINE
BARROW HOGGET TUSKER
BRAWNER SOUNDER SUIDIAN
VENISON WILRONE BRISTLER
SANGLIER HOGGASTER
(— CRY) FREAM
(— HEAD) HURE
(— IN 2ND YEAR) HOGGET
(— IN 3RD YEAR) HOGSTEER
HOGGASTER
(— STY) FRANK
(YOUNG —) GRISE SOUNDER
BOARD EAT LAG PAX TOE DAIL DEAL
DECK DIET EATS FARE FLIP HACK
JOIN KEEP LATH MEAT SHIP SIGN
SLAT TRAY TRIP BUIRD CHESE
CLEAR COARD COUCH COURT
ENTER FOUND HOUSE LODGE
MEALS PANEL PLANK RATCH SHIDE
STAGE STALL SWALE TABLE THEAL
ABACUS ACCOST COMMON PALLET
PLANCH RANDOM RIBBON SHIELD
SIDING TUCKER CABINET CHAMBER
COUNCIL CRIMPER DUOVIRI
ENPLANE ENTRAIN KNEELER
PALETTE PLANCHE SCRAPER
TABLING TRANSOM WHATMAN
APPROACH ASSEMBLY BOXBOARD
CUPBOARD EXCLUDER FETIALES
KEYBOARD LAPBOARD PEGBOARD
TRIBUNAL
(— FOR FALCON'S MEAT) HACK
(— OF BRIDGE) CHESS
(— OF LOOM) CARD
(— OF MILL WHEEL) AWE
(— ON CALF'S NOSE) BLAB
(— OVER) BERTH
(— WITH GROOVE) COULISSE
(— WITH HANDLE) CLAPPER
(— WITH NUMBER) SLATE
(— WITH PINS) RIDDLE
(— WITH TEETH) HACKLE RUFFER
(BLOCKHEAD —) DOLL
(CHANNEL —) PAN
(CHESS —) TABLER
(DRAWING —) COQUILLE
(EXHIBITION —) FRAME
(FLOOR —) KEY
(GAME —) HALMA
(HEART-SHAPED —) PLANCHET
(MORTAR —) HAWK
(NOTCHED —) HORSE
(OTTER —) DOOR
(POLING —) RUNNER
(PRESSED —S) FELT
(PULP-PRESSING —) COUCH
(RABBETED —S) SHIPLAP

(SHEATHING —S) SARKING
(STRIKE —) SCREED
(TANNING —) BEAM
(THIN —) SHIDE SARKING
(THIN —S) SLITWORK
(WARPING —) BARTREE
BOARDER MEALER TABLER GRAINER
PENSIONER SOJOURNER TRANSIENT
BOARDING LIVERY
BOARDINGHOUSE FONDA HOUSE
PENSION
BOARDWALK MARINA DUCKBOARD
BOARWOOD CHEWSTICK
BOAST BOG GAB JET BEEF BLAW
BLOW BRAG CROW POMP PUFF
RAVE VANT WIND WOST YELP
BLAST BRAVE CRACK CRAKE EXTOL
EXULT GLORY PRATE QUACK
ROOSE SCOLD SKITE VAPOR VAUNT
VOUST YOLPE AVAUNT BLAZON
BLEEZE BOUNCE CLAMOR FLAUNT
INSULT MENACE OUTCRY SPLORE
BLUSTER BRAVING CLAMOUR
DEVAUNT DISPLAY GLORIFY
SWAGGER FLOURISH THREATEN
VANTERIE VAUNTERY
BOASTER BLOW HUFF SKITE
CROWER GASCON PEDANT PRATER
SHAKER BOUNCER BRAGGER
BRAVADO CRACKER RUFFLER
BLOWHARD BRAGGART CACAFUGO
FANFARON GLORIOSO JINGOIST
RODOMONT TARTARIN WOUSTOUR
BOASTFUL BIG BRAG HIGH LARGE
BRAGGY PARADO JACTANT VAUNTIE
FANFARON GLORIOUS GASCONADE
THRASONIC
BOASTFULLY SIDE LARGE
BOASTFULNESS GLORY EGOTISM
WINDINESS
BOASTING BLOW HUFF YELP BOAST
CRACK PRATE ROOSE QUACKY
BOBANCE GASSING JACTANCE
JACTANCY QUACKISH VAUNTAGE
VENTOSITY
(EMPTY —) GAS
BOAT ARK BUM BUN CAT COG COT
DOW GIG MON TUB ACON BAIT
BARK BOOT BRIG CARV CHOP COCK
DHOW DINK DORY DUMP FLAT FOUZ
JUNK PAIR PLAT PRAM PUNT RAFT
SCOW SHIP SKAG TACK TODE TOPO
TROW WAKA YAWL YOLE ACCON
AVISO BANCA BARCA BARGE BARIS
BATEL BIDAR BOLIA BOYER BULLY
BUYER CANOE COBLE CRAFT DHONI
DINGY FERRY FOIST FORTY FUNNY
JOLLY KETCH LAKER LINER NADIR
OOLAK PIECE PILOT PRAAM RACER
SHELL SHOUT SIKAR SKIFF SKIFT
SMACK TOPPO UMIAK WAAPA WHIFF
XEBEC ZEBEC BAIDAK BANGKA
BATEAU BAWLEY BELLUM BILALO
BORLEY BOTTOM BOUTRE CAIQUE
CARVEL CAYUCO CHEBEC COCKLE
CRUISE CUTTER DINGHY DREDGE
DRIVER DROVER DUGOUT FLATTY
GALLEY GARVEY GAYYOU GLIDER
HOOKER JAGGER JIGGER KEELER

KICKER KUPHAR LERRET MAILER
NAGGAR NUGGAR PACKET PEAPOD
PEDULE PICARD PINKIE PLAYTE
PULWAR RANDAN ROCKER SANDAL
SCAPHE SCHOUW SCHUYT SETTEE
SINGLE SKERRY STRUSE TANKER
TENDER TIMBER TOGGER TORPID
TRANKY TROUGH VESSEL WAFTER
WHERRY ZEBECK AIRBOAT ALMADIA
ANGEYOK BALLOEN BALLOON
BAULEAH BUMBOAT CAISSON
CARRIER CATCHER CORACLE
CRUISER DOGBODY DRIFTER
DROGHER FLATTIE FLEETER
FLYBOAT FOYBOAT FRIGATE
GAIASSA GASBOAT GONDOLA
HOVELER HUFFLER KELLECK
LIGHTER MACHINE MASOOLA
NACELLE PEARLER PEDIWAK
PINNACE PIRAGUA POOKAWN
PUTELEE SCOOTER SCULLER
SHALLOP SHARPIE SHIKARA
SIKHARA SKAFFLE SKIPPET
SPONGER SPYBOAT STEAMER
TRAWLER TUCKNER TUMBREL
TUMBRIL VEDETTE WHIRREY
BALANGAY BARANGAY BILLYBOY
BOOMBOAT BULLBOAT BUMBARGE
CANALLER CHALOUPE CHEBACCO
CHELINGA CHELINGO COCKBOAT
DAHABEAH DUCKBOAT FIREBOAT
FLAGBOAT KEELBOAT LIFEBOAT
MACKINAW MONOXYLE NEWSBOAT
OYSTERER PALANDER PANCHWAY
PESSONER PESSULUS PULLBOAT
SAILBOAT SCHOKKER SCHOONER
SURFBOAT TONGKANG TRANSFER
(— OF MALTA) DGHAISA
(— WITH SAILS AND OARS)
LYMPHIAD
(3-OAR —) RANDAN
(6-OAR —) SEXERN
(8-OAR —) SHIP
(ABANDONED —) DERELICT
(CHEMICAL —) CAPSULE
(CHINESE —) JUNK SAMPAN
(CLUMSY —) HOOKER DROGHER
(DISPATCH —) AVISO PACKET
(ESKIMO —) KAMIK UMIAK OOMIAC
UMIACK
(FERRY —) BAC CUTT
(FISHING —) COG BOVO BUSS DONI
CANOA COBLE DHONI NOBBY
PYKAR SMACK VINTA BALDIE
BAWLEY DOGGER DROVER FISHER
KUPHAR NICKEY SANDAL SCAFFY
SEINER SEXERN TOSHER VOLYER
CARAVEL CRABBER DRAGGER
FOLLYER POOKAUN SHARPIE
SKAFFIE TRAWLER DRAGBOAT
GAROOKUH SHRIMPER
(FLAT-BOTTOM —) ARK BAC DORY
FLAT PLAT PRAM PUNT SCOW
BARGE COBLE DOREY FLOAT
MOSES PRAAM SHOUT BATEAU
BUGEYE GAYYOU PUTELI GONDOLA
LIGHTER FLATBOAT GUNDELOW
JOHNBOAT
(FLY —) BUSS FLUTE FLIGHT

(INCENSE —) NEF SHIP NAVICULA
(MORTAR —) PALANDER
(OPEN —) WHIFF LERRET SHALLOP
(PATROL —) SPITKID SPITKIT
(RACING —) SIX FOUR EIGHT SCULL
SHELL SINGLE TORPID SCULLER
(SHIP'S —) GIG MOSES DINGEY
DINGHY LAUNCH TENDER PINNACE
(SKIN —) BIDAR BAIDAR ANGEYOK
BIDARKA BULLBOAT
(WICKER —) KUFA GOOFA GOOFAH
CORACLE
(PL.) LIGHTERAGE
BOATBUILDING SETWORK
BOATHOOK STOWER HITCHER
BOATMAN DANDI DANDY PHAON
BARGER BOWMAN CHARON YAWLER
HOBBLER HOVELER HUFFLER
COBLEMAN VOYAGEUR WATERMAN
GONDOLIER
BOAT SEAT TAFT
BOAT SHELL YET SWEETMEAT
BOATSWAIN BOSN BOSUN SERANG
TINDAL
BOAZ (FATHER OF —) SALMA
SALMON
(SON OF —) OBED
(WIFE OF —) RUTH
BOB BAB BOW CUT DAB DIP HOD
JOG POP RAP TAP BALL BLOW
BUFF CALF CLIP CLOD COIN CORK
DUCK GRUB JEER JERK JEST KNOB
MOCK WORM BUNCH CHEAT DANCE
FILCH FLOAT FLOUT SHAKE TAUNT
TRICK BINGLE BOBBER BOBBLE
BUFFET CURTSY DELUDE HOBBLE
POMMEL POPPLE STRIKE WEIGHT
BOBSLED BOBTAIL CLUSTER
HAIRCUT PAGEBOY PENDANT
PLUMMET REFRAIN SHINGLE
SHILLING
(— UP) LOLLOP
BOBAC PAHMI TARBAGAN
BOBBER CORK DUCK FLOAT BOBFLY
BOBBIN PIN CONE CORD PIRN REEL
BRAID QUILL SPOOL BROCHE
HANGER SKREEL TAVELL WORKER
RATCHET SPINDLE TARELLE
TORCHON
(PL.) BONES
BOBBINET ILLUSION
BOBBLE ERROR
BOBOLINK DEER SUCKER
BUNTING MAYBIRD ORTOLAN
REEDBIRD RICEBIRD
BOBSLED BOB DRAY BOBLET
RIPPER TRAVERSE
BOBWHITE COLIN QUAIL PARTRIDGE
BOCACCIO TOMCOD
BOCCACCIO JACK TRECENTIST
BOCCARELLA NOSEHOLE
BOCE BOGUE OXEYE
BODE OMEN SIGN STOP AUGUR
OFFER HERALD MESSAGE PORTEND
PRESAGE FOREBODE FORECAST
FORESHOW FORETELL INDICATE
BODHISATTVA KWANNON MAITREYA
AVALOKITA PADMAPANI
BODICE JUPE CHOLI GILET JUMPS

WAIST BASQUE CORSET JELICK
LYFKIE CORSAGE OVERBODY
SLIPBODY
BODIERON BOREGAT
BODILY SOLID SOMAL ACTUAL
CARNAL FLESHLY SOMATIC
CORPORAL ENTIRELY EXTERNAL
MATERIAL PERSONAL PHYSICAL
SARKICAL VISCERAL CORPOREAL
(NOT —) INTERIOR
BODKIN AWL PIN POINT BROACH
DAGGER NEEDLE POPPER HAIRPIN
PONIARD STILETTO EYELETEER
BODO CACHARI
BODY BAND BELL BOLE BOOK BOUK
BUCK BULK CREW DEHA FORM
HEAD LICH MASS MOLD NAVE RIND
RUPA SOMA STEM ATOMY FLESH
FRAME HABIT MOULD SHANK STIFF
TORSO TRUNK CORPSE CORPUS
CUERPO EXTENT FUSEAU LICHAM
PERSON SARIRA AIRFOIL ANATOMY
CADAVER CARCASS COMPANY
ECONOMY QUANTUM SKINFUL
SUPTION TEXTURE CORSAINT
DEMARCHY EXTENSUM MAJORITY
QUARROME TENEMENT
(— OF 12 MEN) DOUZAINE
(— OF ARROW) SHAFT STELE
(— OF BELIEVERS) FAITH
(— OF CANONS) CHAPTER
(— OF CARDINALS) CONCLAVE
(— OF CHILDREN) INFANTRY
(— OF CHRISTIANS) KOINONIA
COMMUNION
(— OF DOCTRINES) DOGMA
(— OF ECHINODERM) DISC DISK
(— OF EVIDENCE) CASE CORPUS
(— OF FIBERS) FORNIX
(— OF HELMET) BELL
(— OF ISLAMIC CUSTOM) SUNNA
SUNNAH
(— OF KNOWLEDGE) STUFF
(— OF LAW) CODE SHAR HALAKA
SHARIA SHARIAT HALACHAH
(— OF MANKIND) HERD
(— OF MUSCLE) BELLY
(— OF NOTIONS) FOLKLORE
(— OF OFFICERS) BUREAU
(— OF ORE) BUNCH MANTO
(— OF PIGMENT) EYESPOT IMPASTO
(— OF POETRY) EPOS
(— OF ROCK) DIKE DYKE HORSE
STOCK BIOHERM MUDFLOW
INTRUSION
(— OF SINGERS) CHORUS
(— OF STUDENTS) CLASS
(— OF TEN) DECURY
(— OF TENANTS) GAVEL HOMAGE
(— OF THIEVES) SCHOOL
(— OF TRADITIONS) HADIT HADITH
(— OF TROOPS) FORCE AMBUSH
BATTLE CONREY SCREEN SQUARE
BRIGADE SUPPORT BATTALIA
GARRISON
(— OF TYPE) SHANK
(— OF VASSALS) BAN
(— OF WATER) BAY RIP SEA BAHR
FORD HEAD LAKE LAVE POND POOL

WAVE ABYSS BAYOU DRINK FLOOD
OCEAN SHARD SHERD SWASH
LAGOON NYANZA STREAM
FLOWAGE SWALLOW
(— OF WELLBORN MEN) COMITATUS
(— OF WRITINGS) SMRTI SMRITI
(— POLITIC) ESTATE
(— RIDDLED BY BULLETS) SIEVE
(CAROTID —) GLOMUS
(CART —) SIRPEA
(CELESTIAL —) SUN BALL COMET
PLANET SPHERE ELEMENT
ASTEROID SATELLITE
(COMPACT —) GLOBE
(CONDUCTING —) GROUND
(CORPORATE —) SOCIETY
(DEAD —) LICH MORT CADAVER
CARCASS CARRION SUBJECT
(ECCLESIASTICAL —) CLASSIS
(ELASTIC —) CUSHION
(EXTENDED —) LENGTH
(FAT —) EPIPLOON
(FRUITING —) CONK CLAVA
ASCOCARP
(GLOBULAR —) NOB KNOB
(GOVERNING —) KAHAL SYNOD
DURBAR SENATE DECARCHY
DIRECTORY
(HAT —) HOOD
(HEAVENLY —) SUN LAMP STAR
COMET LIGHT CANDLE
(HYALINE —) DRUSE
(IMMUNE —) DESMON
(JUDICIAL —) FORUM
(LEGISLATIVE —) CHAMBER
ASSEMBLY CONGRESS LAGTHING
(MAIN — OF ARMY) BATTLE
(MATHEMATICAL —) FILAMENT
(MORMON —) BISHOPRIC
(MORTAL —) KHET
(PRESBYTERIAN —) SESSION
JUDICATORY
(RELIGIOUS —) SECT CONVENT
(REPRODUCTIVE —) EGG GEMMA
SPORE GEMMULA
(SONOROUS —) PHONIC
(SPIRITUAL —) SAHU
(SWELLING —) BOSS
(WAGON —) BED BUCK PUNT
BODYGUARD THANE ESCORT
INWARD HUSCARL RETINUE
TRABANT THINGMAN WARDCORS
BOER TAKHAAR AFRIKANER
BOG BUG CAR DUB FEN GOG HAG
BOLD CARR CESS FLOW MIRE
MOOR MOSS OOZE SINK SLEW SLUE
SPEW STOG SUDS SYRT WASH
LETCH MARSH MIZZY SAUCY SLADE
SLOCK SWAMP MORASS MUSKEG
SLOUGH CRIPPLE FORWARD
PEATERY TURBARY QUAGMIRE
(PEAT —) CESS MOSS YARPHA
BOG ASPHODEL KNAVERY
BOGEY BUG COW HAG BOGIE BOGLE
DEVIL GNOME BOGGLE BOOGER
GOBLIN BOGGARD BOGGART
BUGABOO BUGBEAR SPECTER
SPECTRE
BOGGLE JIB SHY BALK FOIL STOP

ALARM BOTCH DEMUR SCARE
START STICK BAFFLE BUNGLE
GOBLIN SHRINK BAUCHLE BLUNDER
PERPLEX SCRUPLE STUMBLE
FRIGHTEN HESITATE
BOGGY WET DEEP MIRY SOFT
FENNY FOGGY GOUTY HAGGY
MOSSY SNAPY SPEWY MARSHY
QUAGGY SLOBBY SWAMPY WAUGHY
BOGGISH QUEACHY SQUASHY
BOGIER RIDER GEARMAN
BOGLAND SLADE
BOG MANGANESE WAD LAMPADITE
BOGO ABILO ABILAO
BOGOMILE PATARIN PATARINE
BOGUS FAKE SHAM FALSE PHONY
SPURIOUS
BOHEMIAN ARTY PICARD PICARO
ARTISTIC
(— RIVER) ELBE VLTAVA LUZNICE
BEROUNKA
(— TOWN) PISEK PLZEN PRAHA
TABOR PILSEN PRAGUE
BOHOR REEDBUCK
BOIL FRY PET STY BILE BLOB BOLL
BRAN BUCK BUMP COCT COOK
COWL LEEP PLAY PUSH QUAT RAGE
SEED SORE STEW STYE TEEM WALL
WALM WELL BOTCH BREDE STEAM
BETRAY BUBBLE BULDER BULLER
BURBLE DECOCT GALLOP PIMPLE
RISING SEETHE SIMMER TOTTLE
WABBLE WOBBLE ANTHRAX
BEALING BREEDER CATHAIR
ELIXATE ESTUATE INFLAME
AESTUATE EBULLATE FURUNCLE
PHLEGMON
(— IN LYE) BUCK
(— SYRUP) PEARL
(SAND —) BLOWOUT
BOILED SOD SODDEN
(— WITHOUT SAUCE) ANGLAISE
BOILER YET REEF STILL COPPER
KETTLE RETORT TEACHE ALEMBIC
CALDRON FURNACE
(SALT —) WELLER
BOILING WALM ABOIL FERVID
COCTION FERVENT SCALDING
SEETHING ELIXATION
BOISTEROUS GURL HIGH LOUD
RUDE WILD BURLY GURLY NOISY
ROUGH WINDY COARSE SHANDY
STOCKY STORMY STRONG UNRULY
FURIOUS MASSIVE ROARING
VIOLENT BIGMOUTH CUMBROUS
LARRIKIN STRIDENT VEHEMENT
BOLD BIG BOG YEP DERF HARD
KEEN PERT RASH RUDE TALL WHAT
YEPE APERT BARDY BIELD BRASH
BRAVE BRENT FRACK FREAK FRECK
GALLY HARDY JOLLY LARGE MANLY
NERVY PAWKY PEART POKEY
SAUCY STEEP STOUT WLONK
ABRUPT AUDACE BRASSY BRAZEN
CROUSE DARING FIERCE HEROIC
PLUCKY STRONG ASSURED
DASHING DEFIANT FORWARD
GRIVOIS HAUGHTY MASSIVE
VALIANT ARROGANT FAMILIAR

FEARLESS IMMODEST IMPUDENT
INTREPID MALAPERT POWERFUL
RESOLUTE TEMEROUS
(NOT —) GENTEEL
BOLDFACE BOLD BLACK FULLFACE
BOLDLY CRANK CROUSE HARDLY
HARDILY ROUNDLY STRONGLY
BOLDNESS BROW DARE FACE GALL
BIELD CHEEK NERVE PLUCK VIGOR
DARING BRAVERY COURAGE
FREEDOM AUDACITY TEMERITY
(— OF SPEECH) PARRHESIA
BOLDO NUTMEG
BOLE CLAY DOSE STEM BOLUS
CRYPT TRUNK RUDDLE TIMBER
BOLETUS CEPE
BOLIVIA PILE

BOLIVIA

CAPITAL: LAPAZ SUCRE
COIN: TOMIN CENTAVO
DEPARTMENT: LAPAZ ORURO
  PANDO ELBENI POTOSI TARIJA
INDIAN: URO INCA ITEN MOXO
  URAN ARAWAK AYMARA
  CHARCA CHICHA IXIAMA
  TACANA PUQUINA QUECHUA
  SIRIONE TUMUPASA
LAKE: POOPO COIPASA ROGAGUA
  AULLAGAS TITICACA
MEASURE: LEAGUE CELEMIN
MOUNTAIN: JARA CUSCO CUZCO
  PUPUYA SAJAMA SORATA
  ILLAMPU ANCOHUMA ILLIMANI
  ZAPALERI
MOUNTAINS: ANDES SUNSAS
  SANSIMON SANTIAGO
PANPIPE: SICU SIKU
PLATEAU: ALTIPLANO
RIVER: BENI YATA ABUNA APERE
  BOOPI LAUCA ORTON BAURES
  GRANDE ICHILO ITENEZ MADIDI
  MAMORE MIZQUE TARIJA
  YACUMA GUAPORE ITONAMA
  MACHUPO BENECITO INAMBARI
  PARAGUAY PARAPETI
SALT DEPOSIT: UYUNI EMPEXA
SWAMP: IZOZOG
TOWN: IVO ICLA ITAU MOJO POJO
  SAYA YACO YATA YURA CLIZA
  LAPAZ LLICA ORURO QUIME
  SUCRE UNCIA UYUNI ZONGO
  GUAQUI POTOSI TARIJA
VOLCANO: OLLAGUE
WEIGHT: LIBRA MARCO

BOLL BOW POD BULB KNOB SNAP
ONION BUBBLE CAPSULE
BOLLARD BITT KEVEL DOLPHIN
DEADHEAD
(—S AND BITTS) APOSTLES
BOLLER STRIPPER
BOLL WEEVIL PICUDO
BOLO MACHETE SUNDANG
BOLSHEVIST BOLO
BOLSHEVISM COMMUNISM
SOVIETISM
BOLSTER AID PAD JACK PILLOW
CUSHION HEADING STIFFEN

SUPPORT BACKSTOP BALUSTER
COMPRESS MAINTAIN
BOLT BAR JAG KEY LUE PEN PIN
ROD RUN BEAT BURR CRAM DART
DUMP FLEE GULP LOCK PAWL SHUT
SIFT SLOT SNIB SPAR STUD ARROW
BILBO CLOSE ELOPE FLASH FLOUR
GORGE LATCH RIVET SETUP SHAFT
STOCK ASSORT DECAMP DESERT
FASTEN FLIGHT GANYIE GARBLE
MOOTER PINTLE PURIFY QUARRY
REFINE SAFETY SEARCE SECURE
SNIBEL STREAK STRONG TOGGLE
WINNOW BAYBOLT DOGBOLT
EYEBOLT MISSILE QUARREL
SETBOLT SHACKLE SLABBER
THUNDER DRAWBOLT FASTENER
FISHBOLT FLATHEAD KINGBOLT
RINGBOLT SEPARATE STAMPEDE
(DOOR —) DRAWBOLT
(FIERY —) RESHEPH
(LIGHTNING —) SHAFT
(THUNDER —) FULMEN
BOLTER BOLT DRESSER MUGWUMP
BOMB DUD EGG ROC AZON BOOM
FRAG BLARE CRUMP RAZON SHELL
SQUIB ASHCAN SALUTE BALLOON
BOMBARD GRENADE MARMITE
FIREBALL WHIZBANG PINEAPPLE
(— RELEASE) TOGGLE
(TRENCH —) MINNIE
(PL.) STICK
BOMBARD BOMB CRUMP SHELL
ATTACK BATTER BOTTLE STRAFE
BOMBARDON TUBA NICOLO
POMMER BRUMMER
BOMBARDMENT BLITZ SIEGE
ATTACK RAFALE STRAFE BATTERY
SHELLING
BOMBAST GAS PAD PUFF RAGE
RANT RAVE STUFF TUMOR BLUSTER
FUSTIAN TYMPANY BOASTING
TURGIDITY
BOMBASTIC PUFFY TUMID VOCAL
WINDY FLUENT HEROIC MOUTHY
TURGID BOMBAST FLOWERY
FUSTIAN OROTUND POMPOUS
RANTING STILTED SWOLLEN
INFLATED SWELLING
(— STYLE) TYMPANY
BONACE TREE NOSEBURN
BONACI AGUAJI
BONA FIDE LEVEL GENUINE
AUTHENTIC
BONANZA STATE MONTANA
BONBON CANDY CREAM GOODY
DAINTY CARAMEL SNAPPER
CONFETTO
(PL.) CONFETTI
BOND BON DOG TIE VOW ANDI BAIL
BAND DUTY FIVE FOUR GLUE GYVE
HOLD KNOT LINK NOTE YOKE
BOUND CHAIN NEXUS SWATH
BINDER CEMENT CONNEX COUPLE
ENGAGE ESCROW FETTER LEAGUE
PLEDGE SOLDER SWATHE FOREIGN
HUSBAND LIAISON LIBERTY LINKAGE
MANACLE SHACKLE STATUTE
ADHESIVE CONTRACT COVENANT

LIGAMENT LIGATION LIGATURE
MORTGAGE SECURITY VADIMONY
VINCULUM
(PL.) IRON KHAKIS SHORTS
BONDAGE YOKE THRALL HELOTRY
SERFDOM SLAVERY BONDSHIP
THIRLING CAPTIVITY
BONDED CATTED ENGAGED
BONDMAN CARL ESNE PEON SERF
CHURL HELOT SLAVE STOOGE
SURETY THRALL VASSAL CHATTEL
PEASANT SERVANT VILLEIN
BONDSMAN
BONDSTONE BINDER BONDER
KEYSTONE
BONE OS DIB HIP RIB BANE ULNA
BLADE FEMUR HYOID ILIUM INCUS
JUGAL SLATE STONE TALUS TIBIA
UNION VOMER CANNON COCCYX
CONCHA COPULA CUBOID EPURAL
FIBULA NUCHAL PECTEN RADIAL
SPLINT STAPES TRIPOD UNGUIS
ZYGOMA
(ANKLE —) TALUS
(HIP —) HUGGIN
(SHIN —) CNEMIS
(THIGH —) FEMUR
BONEFISH OIO MACABI GRUBBER
BONYFISH LADYFISH
BONER BUBU FLUB ROCK ERROR
BRODIE STAYER STUMER BLOOMER
BLUNDER MISTAKE STEELER
STUMOUR
BONESET COMFREY AGUEWEED
EUPATORY HEMPWEEK
BONEYARD STOCK
BONFIRE BLAZE TANDLE TAWNIE
BALEFIRE BURNFIRE NEEDFIRE
BONGO DOR
BONING SAP
BONITO AKU ATU NICE COBIA
SARDA BONITA ROBALO ALBACORE
KATONKEL MACKEREL SCOMBRID
SKIPJACK
BONNET CAP HAT HOOD POKE POXY
SCON COVER DECOY SCONE SHAPE
TOQUE CAPOTE MOBCAP SLOUCH
CHAPEAU COMMODE CORONET
LEGHORN SOWBACK VOLUPER
BONGRACE HEADGEAR
BONNET MONKEY ZATI MUNGA
TOQUE MACACO RILAWA MACAQUE
BONNY GAY FINE MERRY PLUMP
BLITHE BONNIE PRETTY STRONG
HEALTHY BUDGEREE HANDSOME
BEAUTIFUL
BONTOK IGOROT
BONUS GIN TIP GIFT MEED AWARD
BRIBE BUNCE BUNTS PILON PRIZE
SPIFF REGALO REWARD CUMSHAW
DOUCEUR PREMIUM SUBSIDY
BOUNTITH DIVIDEND TANTIEME
LAGNIAPPE
BON VIVANT SPORT EPICURE
BON VIVEUR FLANEUR
BONY HARD LANK THIN LANKY STIFF
TOUGH OSTEAL SKINNY OSSEOUS
SCRAGGY SKELETAL
BONYFISH MENHADEN

BOOB ASS FOOL GOON GOOP
DUNCE GOONY NEDDY NITWIT
BOOBOOK OWL PEHO RURU
CUCKOO MOPOKE MOPEHAWK
MOREPORK
BOOBY GAWK GONY SULA DUNCE
IDIOT LOSER PRIZE SLEIGH STUPID
CAMANAY PIQUERO GOOSECAP
BOOBYALLA DOGWOOD
WATERBUSH
BOODLE SWAG CROWD GRAFT
BUDDLE NOODLE PLUNDER
CABOODLE
BOOGEYMAN PADFOOT
TANKERABOGUS
BOOJUM SNARK
BOOK MO LIL LOG CHAP CODE
FORM HEFT OPUS PAGE TEXT TOME
ALBUM ALDUS BIBLE CANON CANTO
CODEX DETUR DIARY DIVAN ENTER
FLETA FOLIO FROST GUIDE KITAB
LIBEL LIBER QUAIR QUIRE RAZEE
ZOHAR ALDINE ANONYM BODONI
CURSUS DOCKET HERBAL LEDGER
MAHZOR MANUAL MISSAL NUMBER
REBIND RECORD RITUAL SCHOOL
TICKET TROPER VOLUME BLOTTER
CATALOG COUCHER DIETARY
DISCARD FEODARY GARLAND
GRAMMAR JOURNAL LAWBOOK
LEXICON MANDALA OCTAPLA
OMNIBUS ORDINAL OUTBOOK
PEERAGE RECITER SAMHITA
SERVICE SLEEPER SPEAKER
SPELLER SYNAXAR TERRIER
TICKLER TRAVAIL TRIGLOT TYPICON
TYPICUM VESPERA WRITING
BANKBOOK BROCHURE CALCULUS
CASEBOOK CASHBOOK CHAPBOOK
COOKBOOK COPYBOOK DOCUMENT
FESTIVAL GIFTBOOK GOSPELER
HANDBOOK HARDBACK HERDBOOK
JESTBOOK JUVENILE LIBRETTO
PASTORAL POMANDER POSTBOOK
REGISTER SONGBOOK STUDBOOK
SYNAXARY TALEBOOK TRIODION
TWENTYMO
(— BACK) DORSE
(— FOR HARVARD GRADUATE)
DETUR
(— OF CHARTS) WAGONER
(— OF HERALDRY) ARMORY
ARMORIAL
(— OF MAPS) ATLAS
(— OF PSALMS) PSALTER TEHILLIM
(— OF RULES) HOYLE
(— OF SOLUTIONS) KEY
(—S KEPT IN PRINT) BACKLIST
(CHEAP —) BLOOD
(CHINESE —) CHING
(COMMONPLACE —) ADVERSARIA
(ELEMENTARY —) PRIMER
(FOLDED —) ORIHON
(JOKE —) JOE JESTBOOK
(MEMORANDUM —) AGENDA JOTTER
TICKLER
(MINIATURE —) BIBELOT
(PRAYER —) PORTAS SIDDUR
PORTASS PORTHORS

(RECORD —) LIBER TICKLER
(RELIGIOUS —) KITAB KORAN
QURAN GOSPEL HORARY KYRIAL
PROSAR GRADUAL KYRIALE
BREVIARY MEGILLAH ORDINARY
SYNAXARY
(SERVICE —) COMES GRAIL TEXTUS
(SLOW-SELLING —) PLUG
(STRANGE —S) CURIOSA
(UNBOUND —) CAHIER
(PL.) SHELF STUDY EROTICA
SCRIPTURE
BOOKBINDING STUB YAPP STRING
BOOKCASE DESK STAGE STALL
SCRINE PLUTEUS CREDENZA
BOOK COVER LID SIDE FOREL
RECTO VERSO FORREL REVERSE
REVERSO
BOOKISH BOOKY ERUDITE STUDIOUS
BOOKLET FOLDER NOVELET
BROCHURE
BOOKMAKER LAYER BOOKER
BOOKIE
BOOKMARK MARKER TASSEL
REGISTER
BOOK PALM TARA TALIERA
BOOKSHELF DESK PLUTEUS
(PL.) CLASSIS
BOOM JIB BEAM BOMB BUMP CRIB
POLE ROAR SPAR BRAIL CHAIN
CRANE CROON PROBE BUMPKIN
CATHEAD CURTAIN RESOUND
SUPPORT BOWSPRIT FLOURISH
(CRANE —) ARM GIB JIB
BOOMERANG KALIE KILEY KYLIE
WANGO ATLATL BOUNCE RECOIL
LEEWILL REBOUND WOMERAH
WOOMERA BACKFIRE HORNERAH
LEEANGLE RICOCHET TROMBASH
BOOMING HUMMING
BOOM IRON WITHE CRANCE
BOON GAY BENE GIFT GOOD KIND
BOUND FAVOR GRANT MERRY
ORDER BENIGN BOUNTY GOODLY
JOVIAL PRAYER BENEFIT COMMAND
PRESENT BLESSING INTIMATE
PETITION
BOOR CAD OAF BOER BORE CARL
HICK JACK KERN LOUT PILL RUNT
SLOB CHUFF CHURL CLOWN KERNE
SLAVE BUMKIN CARLOT CLUNCH
HOBLOB JOBSON JOSKIN LUBBER
LUMMOX RUSTIC BUMPKIN
CAUBOGE GROBIAN PEASANT
VILLAIN BOEOTIAN BOSTHOON
BOORISH ILL RUDE GAWKY ROUGH
RUNTY SURLY CLUMSY RUSTIC
SAVAGE SULLEN VULGAR WOOLEN
AWKWARD CRABBED HIRSUTE
HOBLIKE KERNISH LOUTISH PEAKISH
ROISTER UNCOUTH VILLAIN
WOOLLEN CARTERLY CHURLISH
CLODDISH CLOWNISH LUBBERLY
SWAINISH UNGAINLY
BOORISHNESS VILLAINY
GROBIANISM
BOOST AID LEG ABET BACK BOOM
HELP LIFT PLUG PUSH COACH
EXALT HOIST HOOSH RAISE ASSIST

ADVANCE COMMEND ELEVATE
ENDORSE PROMOTE INCREASE
BOOT PAC PAD USE CURE GAIN
HALF HELP HOOF KICK SHOE SOCK
AVAIL BOOTY EJECT JEMMY KAMIK
PEWEE SPOIL BOOTEE BUDGET
BUSKIN CASING CHUKKA CRAKOW
ENRICH FUMBLE GAITER GALOSH
INSHOE JOCKEY MUKLUK PEDULE
SHEATH BENEFIT BOTTINE COTHURN
COWHIDE CRUISER HESSIAN
HIGHLOW SEABOOT SHOEPAC
VANTAGE BALMORAL BOTTEKIN
CHASSURE COVERING FINNESKO
JACKBOOT LARRIGAN NAPOLEON
(— OF CARRIAGE) FOREBOOT
(— ON SADDLE) GAMBADE
GAMBADO
(HALF —) PAC BUSKIN COCKER
SKILTY
(HOB-NAILED —) BAT
(HORSE'S —) SCALPER
(LUMBERMAN'S —) CRUISER
(MARINE —) SKINHEAD
(RIDING —) JEMMY JIMMY JODHPUR
(SEALSKIN —) KAMIK
(STOUT —) STOGA STOGY
(TORTURE —) SQUEEZER
(PL.) OVERS HESSIANS
BOOTBLACK SHINER BLACKER
SHOEBOY
BOOTED OCREATE
BOOTES WAINMAN HERDSMAN
BOOTH BOX COOP DESK LOGE SHED
SHOP SOOK BOTHY CABIN CRAME
HOUSE KIOSK LIWAN LODGE PITCH
STALL STAND PAGODA PANDAL
PAYBOX SUCCAH SUKKAH TIENDA
BALAGAN COCKSHY TABERNA
BOOTLACE LACET
BOOTLEG SHY SLY ILLEGAL ILLICIT
BOOTY BOOT FANG GAIN LOOT PELF
PREY SWAG BUTIN CHEAT FORAY
GRAFT PRIZE CREAGH FLEECE
SPOILS DESPOIL PILLAGE PLUNDER
SPREATH STEALTH PURCHASE
SPUILZIE STEALAGE
BOOZE BOLL BOUT BUDGE DRINK
SPREE FUDDLE LIQUOR
BOOZY LIQUORY
BORAGE ANCHUSA
BORAX FLUX TINCAL
(— SOURCE) KERNITE
BORDER CUT HEM RIM TAB ABUT
BRIM CURB DADO EAVE EDGE LIMB
LINE LIST LOVE MARK NARK ORLE
RAND ROON RUND SIDE TRIM WELL
WELT BOARD BOUND BRAID BRINK
CHEEK COAST COSTA DRAFT FILET
FLANK FOREL FRAME FRILL GUARD
LIMIT MARCH MARGE MARLI PLAIT
SHORE SKIRT STRIP SWAGE TOUCH
VERGE ADJOIN EDGING FILLET
FORREL FRINGE IMPALE LACING
LIMBUS LISERE MARGIN ORFRAY
PURFLE QUADRA STRIPE TANIKO
WEEPER CONFINE DRAUGHT
FIMBRIA FLOROON MARGENT
SELVAGE VALANCE BOUNDARY

DOUBLING FRONTIER MARCHESE
NEIGHBOR OUTSKIRT PLATBAND
SKIRTING SURROUND TERMINUS
TRESSOUR TRESSURE
(— OF EXTERNAL EAR) HELIX
(— OF LACE) PICOT
(— OF ROCK) SALBAND
(— OF SAIL) DOUBLING
(— OF SHIELD) BORDURE
(— OF STREAM) ROND
(— ON) ABUT ACCOST AFFRONT
NEIGHBOR
(FLOWERED —) FLOROON
(ORNAMENTAL —) WAGE FRAME
FRINGE MATTING TRESSURE
(RIBBON —) FRILAL
(PL.) CONFINE CONFINES
BORDERED ORLE LIMBATE
BORDERING MARGENT FRONTIER
BORE BIT CUT EAT IRK JET TAP
DRAG FLAT HOLE JUMP PALL POKE
REAM RUSH SINK SIZE TIDE TIRE
TOOL ANNOY CHINK DRILL EAGRE
ENNUI GAUGE GOUGE OUGHT
PLONK PRICK PUNCH SUGUR TEWEL
TRICK VAPOR WEARY BEFOOL
CANNON GIMLET PIERCE THRILL
THRUST TUNNEL WIMBLE BROMIDE
CALIBER CALIBRE CONCAVE
CREVICE HUMDRUM NUDNICK
OPENING AIGUILLE CAPILLUS
DIAMETER DRAWBORE GRATIANO
POROROCA
(— OF CANNON) SOUL CHASE
BOREAS AQUILO AQUILON
(DAUGHTER OF —) CLEOPATRA
(FATHER OF —) ASTRAEUS
(MOTHER OF —) AURORA
(SON OF —) ZETES CALAIS
BORED WEARY ENNUYEE TEDIOUS
SATIATED
BOREDOM YAWN ENNUI TEDIUM
BORELE KEITLOA UPEYGAN
BORER MOLE BARDEE WIMBLE
HAGFISH TANBARK TERMITE
TERRIER FLATHEAD SHIPWORM
WOODWORM
BORING DIM DRY FLAT SLOW
BROACH STODGY STUPID TIRING
LUMPISH TEDIOUS PIERCING
TIRESOME
(— TOOL) AIGUILLE
BORN N NEE NATE INNATE NASCENT
NATURAL UTERINE ORIGINAL
(PREMATURELY —) SLINK ABORTIVE
(WELL —) FREE EUGENIC
BORNE RODE NARROW CARRIED
ENDURED
(— AFFRONTEE) CABOCHED
(— LOWER THAN USUAL) ABASED
(— ON WATER) AFLOAT

BORNEO
BAY: ADANG KUMAI SAMPIT
CAPE: ARU DATU LOJAR PUTING
SAMBAR SELATAN
MOUNTAIN: RAJA SARAN NIJAAN
TEBANG

MOUNTAINS: IRAN MULLER
SCHWANER
NAME: KALIMANTAN
NATIVE: DYAK DAJAK
RIVER: ARUT IWAN BAHAU BERAU
KAJAN PADAS PAWAN BARITO
KAPUAS SEBUKU KAHAJAN
MAHAKAM MENDAWI PEMBUANG
TOWN: KUMAI SAMBAS SAMPIT
MALINAU PAGATAN SANGGAU
SINTANG TARAKAN KETAPANG
TREE: KAPOR KAPUR
WEIGHT: PARA CHAPAH

BORO MARIANA
BORON BORAX ULEXITE
BORORO COROADO
BOROUGH BURG CITY TOWN WICK
BRUSH BURGH CASTLE COUNTY
CITADEL FORTESS VILLAGE
TOWNSHIP
BORROW BOT BITE COPY HIRE KICK
LOAN SHIN TAKE THIG ADOPT
STEAL TOUCH DESUME DUPLEX
PLEDGE STRIKE SURETY CHEVISE
HOSTAGE MUTUATE TITHING
BORROWER BOT CRIB MUTUARY
BOS OX NEAT TAURUS
BOSH END ROT JOKE SHOW TALK
TOSH TRASH BUSHWA FIGURE
FLAUNT HUMBUG TRIVIA TOSHERY
GALBANUM NONSENSE POPPYCOCK
BOSKY BUSHY TIPSY WOODY
FUDDLED
BOSNIA-HERZEGOVINA (RIVER OF
—) BOSNA DRINA NERETVA
(TOWN OF —) TUZLA MAGLAJ
MOSTAR VISOKO SARAJEVO
BOSOM LAP BARM CLOSE DICKY
HEART SINUS BREAST CAVITY
DESIRE DICKEY RECESS BELOVED
EMBRACE GREMIAL INCLOSE
INTIMATE
(— OF DRESS) SQUARE
(FALSE —) PLUMPER
BOSS BUR HUB MOP NOB ORB PAD
POP BAAS BEAD BOCE BUHR BURR
COCK CZAR KNOB KNOP KNOT NAIL
NULL STUD TSAR BULLA BULLY
BWANA CHIEF EMPTY JEWEL KNOSP
ORDER OWNER PEARL ANCHOR
BROOCH BUCKRA BUTTON CHEESE
DIRECT HOLLOW MANAGE MASTER
OCULUS PATERA PELLET SHIELD
BULLION CACIQUE CAPATAZ
CAPTAIN CUSHION FOREMAN
HASSOCK HEADMAN HOBNAIL
MANAGER PADRONE PHALERA
SPANGLE SPONSON DIRECTOR
DOMINEER MISERERE OMPHALOS
OVERSEER UMBILICUS
(— OF LOGGING CAMP) BULLY
(— OF SHIELD) UMBO
(FIRE —) GASMAN
(LEATHER —) BUTTON
(MINE —) SHIFTER SHIFTMAN
(POLITICAL —) CACIQUE CAUDILLO
(STRAW —) BULL LEADER

BOSTONIAN HUBBITE
BOTANY HERBARISM PHYTOLOGY
BOTCH MAR MUX BOIL BOSS MEND
MESS MULL SORE BITCH BODGE
BUTCH FLUFF FUDGE SPOIL STICK
BOGGLE BOLLIX BUMBLE BUNGLE
COBBLE JUMBLE MUCKER REPAIR
TINKER BLUNDER BUTCHER
SCAMBLE SCLATCH SLUBBER
SWELLING
BOTCHER GRILSE SALMON TINKER
BUNGLER BUTCHER CLOUTER
COBBLER
BOTCHERY PATCHERY
BOTE KINBOT MAGBOTE CARTBOTE
FRITHBOT PLOWBOTE WAINBOTE
BOTFLY BOTT GADBEE GADFLY
NITTER CANOPID OESTRID TORSALO
DIPTERAN OESTRIAN
BOTH BO ALL TWO BAITH EQUALLY
BOTHER ADO AIL BUG NAG VEX
FASH FAZE FUSS JADE WORK
ANNOY DEAVE KNOCK PHASE TEASE
TRADE WORRY BADGER BUSTLE
CUMBER DITHER FLURRY GRAVEL
HARASS MEDDLE MITHER MOIDER
MOLEST MUCKLE PESTER POTHER
POTTER PUTTER PUZZLE TAMPER
CONFUSE DISTURB FASHERY
GRIZZLE PERPLEX TERRIFY
TRACHLE TROUBLE BEWILDER
DISTRESS IRRITATE NUISANCE
BOTOCUDO BORUN AIMORE
AYMORO
BOTONEE TREFLEE FLEURONE
BO TREE PIPAL

BOTSWANA
CAPITAL: GABORONE GABERONES
COIN: RAND
DESERT: KALAHARI
LAKE: DOW NGAMI
LANGUAGE: BANTU CLICK
KHOISAN SETSWANA
MOUNTAIN: TSODILO
NATIVE: BANTU TSWANA
BUSHMAN
RIVER: NATA OKWA CHOBE
NOSOB CUANDO MOLOPO
SHASHI CUBANGO LIMPOPO
OKAVANGO
TOWN: KANYE ORAPA TSANE
SEROWE LOBOTSI MOCHUDI
PALAPYE THAMAGA
GABERONES

BOTTLE JUG BOSS SKIN VIAL VIOL
AMPUL ASKOS BETTY BOCAL BUIRE
BURET CADUS COOJA CROFT
CRUET CRUSE FIFTH FLASK GIRBA
GLASS GOURD HOUSE PHIAL SPLIT
VERRE ALUDEL BACBUC BUNDLE
CARAFE CARBOY CASTER CASTOR
CHAGUL CHATTY CREWET DORUCK
DUBBER FESSEL FIASCO FLACON
FLAGON GOGLET GUTTUS JORDAN
LAGENA MAGNUM MARINE MATARA
NURSER PACKER SIPHON VESSEL
WOULFF BALLOON BIBERON

BOMBARD BOMBOLA BURETTE
CANTEEN CARAFON COSTREL
DEADMAN FLACKET FLOATER
GRENADE INKHORN BOMBONNE
BORACHIO BUILDING CALABASH
DECANTER DEMIJOHN GARDEVIN
JEROBOAM MARIOTTE PRESERVE
REHOBOAM
(— IN WICKER) CARBOY DEMIJOHN
(18 —S OF WINE) RIDDLE
(EGYPTIAN —) DORUK DORUCK
(EMPTY —) MARINE
(HOT-WATER —) PIG
(LARGE —) KIT JEROBOAM
(LEATHER —) BOOT DUBBA BUDGET
DUBBER DUPPER MATARA BOMBARD
WHINNOCK WINESKIN
(OVERSIZED —) BALTHAZAR
(PAIR OF —S) GEMEL GEMMEL
(SMALL —) VIAL AMPUL PHIAL SPLIT
FLACON AMPOULE TICKLER
BOTTLE CAP CAPSULE
BOTTLE CARRIER FASCET
BOTTLE CASE CELLAR
BOTTLEHEAD DOEGLING
BOTTLER COOPER
BOTTOM ASS BED ARSE BASE DALE
DOUP FLAT FOND FOOT FUND HOLM
LEES ROOT ABYSS BASIS DREGS
FLOOR LAIGH NADIR BATHOS
FOUNCE FUNDUS GROUND GUTTER
LAAGTE LEEGTE BEDROCK
LOWLAND SUPPORT SURFACE
BUTTOCKS INTERVAL SEDIMENT
TETRAPOD
(— OF BENCH) TOE
(— OF CUPOLA) HEARTH
(— OF FURROW) SOLE
(— OF PAGE) TAIL
(— OF PISTOL GRIP) BUTT
(— OF POT) POTSTONE
(— OF PRINTER'S GALLEY) SLICE
(— OF PULLEY BLOCK) BREECH
(— OF SEA) GROUND BENTHOS
(— OF SOLE) NAUMK NAUMKEAG
(MARSHY —) SIKE
(ROCK —) HARDPAN
(PL.) HOLM HOLME
BOTTOM-DWELLING DEMERSAL
BOTTOMER FOOTMAN STATIONMAN
BOTTOMLAND STRATH
BOTTOMLESS ABYSMAL
BOTULISM LAMSIEKTE LAMZIEKTE
BOUDOIR ROOM CABIN BEDROOM
CABINET
BOUGH ARM LEG LIMB TWIG CHUCK
SHOOT SPRAY SPRIG BRANCH
RAMAGE SHROUD GALLOWS
PHYLLIS OFFSHOOT SHOULDER
(— ON TAVERN) BUSH
(PL.) RAMAGE DUNNAGE RAMMAGE
BOUGHT KEFT STORE ZEBINA
BOUGIE CANDLE COLLYRIE FILIFORM
BOULDER NOB KELK KNOB ROCK
STONE GIBBER BOOTHER DORNICK
ERRATIC GRAYBACK HARDHEAD
MEGALITH POTSTONE
BOULE BIRNE
BOULEVARD DRIVE PRADO AVENUE

STREET HIGHWAY TERRACE
BOULTER TRAWL SPILLER SPILLET
BOUNCE DAP HOP BANG BLOW
BRAG BUMP DING DIRD FIRE GATE
JUMP LEAP SACK STOT BOAST
BOUND BULLY CAROM CHUCK
EJECT KNOCK SCOLD THUMP VERVE
SPIRIT SPRING STRIKE ADDRESS
BLUSTER CHOUNCE DISMISS
REBOUND SWAGGER PROCLAIM
RICOCHET
BOUNCER CHUCKER SCROUGER
BOUNCING BIG BUXOM LUSTY
STOUT BOUNCY HEALTHY
(— OF TONGUE) FLAP
BOUND DAP END HOP LOP BENT
BIND BOND BONE BROW BUTT DART
GIRT JUMP LEAP LIST MERE RAMP
RISE SCUD SKIP STEM STOT SURE
TERM WALL AMBIT BOURN FIXED
GOING LIMIT READY SALLY START
STEND STING TILED VAULT VERGE
BORDER BOUNCE BOURNE BUTTAL
CAVORT CURVET DEFINE DOMAIN
FINISH GAMBOL GIRDED HURDLE
JETTED LIABLE LOLLOP OBLIGE
PRANCE SPRING BARRIER CERTAIN
CHAINED CLOSURE CONFINE
CONTAIN COSTIVE DELIMIT
DRESSED GAMBADO INCLUDE
REBOUND SALTATE SECURED
SUBSULT TERMINE TRUSSED
BOUNDARY CONFINED DESTINED
ENCLOSED FASCIATE FRONTIER
HANDFAST LANDMARK LIMITATE
OBLIGATE PINIONED PRECINCT
PREPARED RESTRICT SHACKLED
(— BY OATH) SWORN
(— BY OBLIGATION) AFFINED
(NOT —) SOLUTE
(RIGIDLY —) STATIC STATICAL
(PL.) AMBIT MOUND CLOSURE
COMPASS CONFINE PURLIEUS
BOUNDARY AHU END RIM DOLE
DOOL EDGE FINE FORM LINE LIST
MARK MEAR MEER MERE META
METE PALE SURF TERM TRIG WALL
AMBIT BOURN CLOSE FENCE FRAME
FRONT HEDGE LIMES LIMIT MARCH
MOUND SHORE VERGE BORDER
COLLET DEFINE OCTROI OCTROY
TROPIC BARRIER BOUNDER BUTTING
COMPASS FURLONG CURBLINE
FRONTIER LANDLINE LIMITARY
PRECINCT TERMINUS UMSTROKE
(PL.) ABUTTALS ENVIRONS
BOUNDLESS VAST UNTOLD
ENDLESS ETERNAL INFINITE
UNLIMITED
BOUNTEOUS BOON CROWNED
LIBERAL PLENTEOUS
BOUNTIFUL GOOD LUSH RICH
AMPLE FREELY LAVISH LIBERAL
PROFUSE ABUNDANT GENEROUS
BOUNTY BOON GIFT MEED AWARD
BONUS GRANT LARGE VALOR
WORTH BONTEE REWARD VIRTUE
LARGESS PREMIUM PRESENT
PROWESS SUBSIDY DONATIVE

GOODNESS GRATUITY KINDNESS
BOUQUET BOB AURA ODOR POSY
AROMA BLOOM CIGAR POSEY
SHEAF SPRAY BOWPOT BUSKET
SHOWER CORSAGE NOSEGAY
BOUGHPOT
(— GARNI) FAGOT FAGGOT
BOURGEOIS ORGON COMMON
STUPID BOORISH BURGHER
BOURSE BOLSA BORSE CAMBIO
BOURTREE ELDER
BOUT GO JOB BOOT FALL PULL
TURN BOOZE BRASH CRASH ESSAY
FIGHT MATCH PLUCK ROUND TRIAL
VENNY VENUE ATTACK COURSE
FRACAS YOKING ASSAULT ATTEMPT
CAROUSE CIRCUIT CONTEST
DEBAUCH OUTSIDE WITHOUT
CONFLICT
(DRINKING —) BAT BUST TIRL
BOOZE SPRAY SPREE SCREED
SPLORE CAROUSE GAEDOWN
WASSAIL POTATION
BOUTONNIERE BOUQUET
BUTTONHOLE
BOUW BAHU BAHOE
BOVATE OSKEN OXGANG OXGATE
OXLAND
(TWO —S) HUSBANDLAND
BOVINE OX BOS COW BOSS BULL
CALF DULL NEAT SLOW ZEBU
BEAST BISON STEER ANIMAL
COWISH HUMLIE HUMMEL OXLIKE
ROTHER BULLOCK TAURINE
BANGTAIL LEPTOBOS
BOW ARC LEG LUG NOD SAW TIE
YEW ARCH BAIL BECK BEND BENT
CURB DUCK FOLD FORE GORA
JOUK KNEE KNOT LATH LOUT MOVE
PROW SELF STEM SWIM TRUE TURN
WEND BINGE CLINE CONGE COQUE
COUCH CROOK CRUSH CURVE
DEFER GOURA HONOR KNEEL
NOEUD SHIKO STICK STOOP VENIE
YIELD ARCHER ASSENT BAUBLE
BUCKLE CONGEE CRINGE CROUCH
CURTSY FIDDLE FOGBOW RIBBON
SALAAM SALUTE SCRAPE SUBMIT
SWERVE TOURTE WEAPON DEPRESS
FOREBOW FORMBOW HANDBOW
INCLINE INFLECT LONGBOW
NECKTIE RAINBOW ARBALEST
COURTESY CRESCENT ENTRANCE
FOGEATER GREETING STONEBOW
TRUELOVE
(— DOWN) ALOUT HUMBLE
(— IN ONE PIECE) SELF
(— LOW) BINGE
(— OF VESSEL) HEAD PROW STEM
ENTRANCE
(— ON SCRAPER) BAIL BALE
(— ON SEA) ATRY
(— OUTWARD) CONVEX
(— SLIGHTLY) ADDRESS
(OVERHANGING —) SWIM
(VIOLIN —) STICK
BOWED ARCO BENT BANDY KNEED
ARCATE ARCATO CURVED BULGING
CURVANT SHAMBLE DOWNBENT

BOWELS GUT GUTS WOMB BELLY COLON ROPES VISCERA ENTRAILS
BOWER RUN BOOR JACK NOOK SALE ABODE ARBOR JOKER KNAVE ANCHOR BOWERY LEFSEL PANDAL BERCEAU CABINET CHAMBER COTTAGE EMBOWER ENCLOSE LEVESEL PERGOLA RETREAT SHELTER TRELLIS THALAMUS
(— **FOR SNAKES**) KISI
(**GARDEN** —) ALCOVE
BOWERBIRD CATBIRD COLLARBIRD
BOWFIN AMIA GANOID LAWYER MORGAY SAWYER CHOUPIC DOGFISH GRINDAL GRINDLE GRINNEL MUDFISH
BOWIE STATE ARKANSAS
BOWING FEATHERING
BOWL CAP CUP PAN TUN COUP ROLL TASS TRAY WOOD ARENA BASIN BOWIE DEPAS GUARD JORUM KITTY LAVER MAZER PHIAL PITCH ROGAN SCALE TANOA TAZZA TREEN TROLL BEAKER BICKER CHAWAN CLOSET COOTIE CRATER FESSEL JICARA KETTLE LEKANE MAZARD MORTAR TROUGH TUREEN VESSEL BRIMMER DITCHER DOUBLER DUGGLER SCYPHUS SKYPHOS SPILLER STADIUM TOUCHER TRINDLE TRUNDLE WHISKIN AQUARIUM BRIDECUP FISHBOWL LAVATORY MONTEITH REHOBOAM
(— **ILLEGALLY**) JERK
(— **OF PIPE**) STUMMEL
(— **ON PEDESTAL**) TAZZA SALVER
(— **OUT**) YORK
(— **THAT TOUCHED JACK**) TOUCHER
(— **WITH TWO HANDLES**) CAP DEPAS
(**DRINKING** —) TUN TASS
(**OBLONG** —) PITCHI
(**PUNCH** —) SNEAKER
(**SHALLOW** —) CAP COUPE WHISKIN
(**SMALL** —) JACK
(**SOUP** —) ECUELLE
(**SUGAR** —) SUGAR SUCRIER
(**TOILET** —) HOPPER
(**WOODEN** —) CAP BOWIE KITTY ROGAN BASSIE COOTIE
BOWLEG OUTKNEE
BOWLEGGED BANDY VALGUS
BOWLER POT DERBY KEGLER PINMAN SPINNER TRUNDLER
(**CRICKET** —**S**) ATTACK
BOWLINE BOWLIN FARGOOD
BOWLING BOWLS ATTACK KEGLING TENPINS
BOWLS RINK BOCCE BOCCIE
BOW-SHAPED ARCATE
BOWSTRING SERVING
BOWYER BOWER ARTILLER
BOX BED BIN CAR EAR FUR GIG KIT LOB LUG PIX PYX TYE ARCA BARK BODY BOOT CAGE CAJA CASE CIST CRIB CUFF CYST DRAB FLAT HEAD LOGE MILL PACK PUNG SCOB SEAT SLAP SLUG SPAR STOW TILL TRAY ARBOR BARGE BOIST BUXUS CADDY

CAPSA CHEST CLOUT CRATE FIGHT FRAME HUTCH LADLE POUCH PUNCH SHRUB STALL TRUNK ASCHAM BUFFET BUNKER CARTON CASKET COFFER COFFIN DRAWER GRILLE HAMPER HATBOX HAYBOX HOPPER ICEBOX MAROON MOCUCK PATRON PETARA PILLAR SAGGER SHRINE STRIKE TARBOX VANITY ARCANUM BANDBOX BATTERY BOXTREE BOXWOOD CABINET CAISSON CARRIER CASHBOX CASQUET CASSONE CONFINE COREBOX DICEBOX DREDGER DUSTBOX ENCLOSE EXHAUST FOSTELL FREEZER HANAPER JACKBOX PACKAGE PILLBOX PITARAH PRINTER SANDBOX SCATULA SHELTER TRUMMEL WHERRET BOXTHORN DOVECOTE DRAGEOIR JUNCTION LAVARIUM MATCHBOX POMANDER SHOWCASE SLIPCASE SOLANDER SWEATBOX
(— **FOR CUTLERY**) CANTEEN
(— **FOR FISH**) CAR NID
(— **FOR MONEY OFFERING**) ARCA LADLE
(— **FOR SALT**) DRAB
(— **FOR SEAL**) SKIPPET
(— **FOR SEED**) LEAP
(— **FOR TOBACCO**) BUTT DOSS CADDY SARATOGA
(— **IN TIMEPIECE**) BARREL
(— **IN WHEEL HUB**) FUR
(— **OF BIRCHBARK**) MOCUCK
(— **OF FIRE CLAY**) SAGGAR SAGGER
(— **OF ORGAN**) BOOT SWELL
(— **TO SHELTER BELL**) SCONCE
(— **USED AS DARKROOM**) TENT
(**BERRY** —) HALLOCK
(**BREAD** —) BARGE
(**CANDLE** —) BARK
(**CIRCULAR** —) THIMBLE
(**COMPASS** —) KETTLE BINNACLE
(**FANCY** —) ETUI ETWEE
(**FLOATING** —) CAISSON
(**FOUNDRY** —) FRAME
(**IRON** —) HANGER
(**JUGGLER'S** —) TRANKA
(**MONEY** —) CASH SAFE PIRLIE
(**PIVOTING** —) TOUR
(**PRINTING** —) TURTLE
(**REFRIGERATOR** —) COOLER
(**SHALLOW** —) FLAT BACKET HARBOR
(**SNUFF** —) MILL MULL
(**TEA** —) CADDY
(**TIN** —) TRUMMEL VASCULUM
BOX BRIER INDIGO INKBERRY
BOXCAR LOWRY STOCKCAR
BOX ELDER MAPLE NEGUNDO
BOXER CHAMP DARES BANTAM MILLER NOBBER TANKER WELTER BRUISER CRUISER FIGHTER SLUGGER SPARRER BUFFETER PUGILIST SOUTHPAW
BOXFISH CHAPIN COWFISH SHELLFISH TRUNKFISH
BOXING PLUG SAVATE PARINGS

SCIENCE SPARRING
(— **GLOVE**) MUFFLE
BOX TORTOISE COOTER
BOXWOOD KNYSNA DUDGEON
BOXY BLOCKY
BOY BO BUB FAG GUY HIM LAD PUR TAD BOYO CHAP LOON NINO PAGE PUER BILLY BUBBY BUDDY CHABO CHILD CRACK GAMIN GILPY GROOM KNAVE PUTTO ROGUE SWAIN VALET YOUTH BIRKIE BUTTON CALLAN CHOKRA GAFFER GARCON MANNIE MASTER NIPPER RASCAL SHAVER STIRRA UMFAAN URCHIN BOUCHAL CALLANT DRAWBOY GLEANER GOSSOON GRUMMET JACKBOY RUBBLER SERVANT SPADGER TRAPPER CLERGION HENCHBOY MUCHACHO SPALPEEN
(— **DRESSED AS WOMAN**) MALINCHE
(— **OF FREE BIRTH**) CAMILLUS
(**ALTAR** —) ACOLYTE THURIFER
(**AWKWARD** —) CUB CALF GRUMMET
(**BOLD** —) SPALPEEN
(**CHOIR** —) CHILD
(**CLEANING** —) BUSBOY
(**COLLIER'S** —) HODDER
(**EFFEMINATE** —) SISSY
(**HEAD** —) SENIOR CAPTAIN
(**ILL-MANNERED** —) CUB
(**MY** —) AVICK
(**NATIVE** —) MOWGLI
(**NON-JEWISH** —) SHEGETZ
(**OFFICE** —) DUFTRY DUFTERY
(**PERT** —) CRACK
(**POOR** —) HERO
(**ROGUISH** —) CRACK GAMIN URCHIN
(**SAUCY** —) NACKET
(**SERVING** —) KNAVE PEDEE CHOKRA MOUSSE FOOTBOY GOSSOON
(**SILLY** —) CALF
(**SMALL** —) BO BUDDY UMFAAN SPADGER
(**SPRIGHTLY** —) CRACK
(**STABLE** —) MAFU MAFOO MEHTAR
(**TOWN** —) CAD
(**YOUNG** —) LAD SONNY YOUTH NIPPER
(**PL.**) BOYHOOD
BOYCOTT MITE SHUN AVOID DEBAR BLACKBALL
BOYFRIEND BEAU STEADY
BRACE LEG MAN TIE TWO BEND BIND CASE FRAP GIRD JACK KNEE LACE MARK PAIR PROP SPUR STAY STEM STUD CLAMP CRANK DWANG GIRTH HOUND NERVE POISE RIDER SHORE STOCK STRUT ANKLET BINDER BRACHE CLENCH COLLAR COUPLE CRUTCH FASTEN FATHOM HURTER SPLINT STRING WIMBLE BOTTINE BRACKET EMBRACE REFRESH SPANNER STIFFEN SUPPORT ACCOLADE BITBRACE BITSTALK BITSTOCK BUTTRESS CROSSBAR ENCIRCLE
(— **ACROSS CABLE**) STUD
(— **AND HALF**) LEASH

(— BETWEEN FRAMES) TOM
(— FOR POST) SPUR
(— UP) ACCINGE SHARPEN
(PL.) BRIDGING
BRACED BENT
  (— ABACK) ABOX
BRACELET BAND RING ARMIL CHAIN
  ARMLET BANGLE GRIVNA ARMILLA
  CURCLET MANACLE POIGNET
  RACETTE WRISTER HANDCUFF
  MUFFETEE WRISTLET
  (SHELL —) SANKHA
BRACER TONIC SHORER BLOCKER
  ARMGUARD STIFFENER STIMULANT
BRACHIAL HUMERAL
BRACHIOPOD ATREMATE ATRYPOID
  SPIRIFER
BRACHIUM ARM
BRACING CRISP QUICK TONIC
  DUNNAGE
BRACKEN FERN BRAKE PLAID
BRACKET BIBB COCK CONK FORK
  GATE PUNK ANCON BELOW BRACE
  CLASS CONCH COUCH CRANE
  CRANK CROOK LEVEL SHELF STRUT
  TRUSS ANCONE BECKET BRIDGE
  CORBEL COUPLE GUSSET HANGER
  LADDER SADDLE SCONCE BECKETT
  CONSOLE DERRICK FEATHER
  FIXTURE GATELEG LOOKOUT
  POTENCE SPONSON SPOTTED
  BRAGWORT CATEGORY CROTCHET
  MISERERE SPECKLED STRADDLE
  (PL.) HOOKS CROOKS
BRACKISH YAR FOIST SALTY
  BRACKY SALINE BREACHY SALTISH
  NAUSEOUS
BRACT HUSK LEAF GLUME LEMMA
  PALEA PALET SCALE SPADIX
  SPATHE BRACTLET PHYLLARY
BRAD PIN NAIL PRIG RIVET SPRIG
BRAE BANK BRAY BROW HILL CLEVE
  SLOPE WOUGH CLEEVE VALLEY
BRAG JET BLAW BLOW CROW DEFY
  FACE HUFF PUFF WIND WOST YELP
  BLUFF BOAST CRACK FLIRD PREEN
  SKITE STRUT VAUNT BLEEZE
  BOUNCE INSULT SPLORE SPROSE
  SQUIRT DISPLAY GAUSTER ROISTER
  SWAGGER BRAGGART FLOURISH
  PRETENSE THREATEN
BRAGGART BRAG PUFF BOAST
  FACER BLOWER CROWER GASCON
  HECTOR POTGUN SKITER THRASO
  BLOWOFF BOASTER BOBADIL
  CRACKER RUFFLER SHALLOW
  VAPORER BANGSTER BLOWHARD
  CACAFUGO FANFARON PAROLLES
  PUCKFIST RENOWNER RODOMONT
  SKIPJACK
BRAGGARTISM COCKALORUM
BRAGGING ROOSE JACTANCE
  RODOMONT THRASONIC
BRAHMA KA SELF BRAMAH
BRAHMAN ARYAN HINDU PUNDIT
  SMARTA BRAHMIN
BRAID CUE BRAY GIMP JERK LACE
  PLAT TAIL TRIM BREDE FANCY
  FREAK JIFFY LACET MILAN ONSET

ORRIS PLAIT PLEAT QUEUE START
TAGAL TRACE TRADE TRESS TRICK
TWINE VOMIT WEAVE BOBBIN
BORDER CORDON EDGING GALLON
LACING MOMENT PLIGHT RIBBON
SENNET SNATCH STRING BANDING
BULLION CAPRICE ENTWINE
UPBRAID BRANDISH ORNAMENT
REPROACH SOUTACHE TRIMMING
  (— FOR HATS) SENNET SINNET
  (— OF WIG) SNAKE
  (LINEN —) INKLE
BRAIDER RATCHER
BRAIDING FROG BREDE
BRAIN MAD BEAN HARN MIND PATE
  UTAC WITS AXION HAIRN HAURN
  SKULL NODDLE PSYCHE FURIOUS
  SENSORY THINKER CEREBRUM
  (PL.) HARN PATE SCONCE HEADPICE
BRAINLESS SILLY STUPID FOOLISH
  WITLESS
BRAINPAN PAN HARNPAN PANNICLE
BRAIN SAND SABULUM
BRAIZE BECKER
BRAKE COW BULL BURR CAGE CLOG
  CURB DRAG FERN LOCK RACK SKID
  SLOW STAY TARA TRAP BLOCK
  CHECK COPSE DELAY DETER GRIPE
  SNARE SPOKE SPRAG VOMIT BRIDLE
  CONVOY HARROW HINDER REMORA
  RETARD STAYER WARABI BRACKEN
  DEADMAN DILEMMA SLIPPER
  STOPPER THICKET TRIGGER
  DRAGROPE RETARDER
BRAKEMAN GUARD SHACK SHAKE
  BRAKIE NIPPER DILLIER SNAPPER
  SWAMPER DILLYMAN INCLINER
  TRAINMAN
BRAMBLE WHIN BRIER RHAMN THIEF
  THORN BUMBLE JAGGER LAWYER
  STICKER DEWBERRY MAYBERRY
  NESSBERRY
BRAMBLE BUSH TUTU GRANJENO
BRAMBLING KATE SNOWHAMMER
BRAMBLY DUMAL SPINY THORNY
  PRICKLY
BRAN GRIT SEED DARAK TREAT
  CEREAL CHISEL POLLARD TOPPING
  BEESWING
  (— AND MEAL) SHORTS
  (CORNMEAL —) HUSK
  (FINE —) POLLEN
  (UNSORTED —) RUBBLES
BRANCH ARM BOW LAP LEG LOP
  RAY RUN BARB BROG BUSH CHAT
  FANG FORK LIMB PALM PART RAME
  RICE RISE SNAG SNUG SPUR STEM
  STUD TANG TWIG YARD AXITE
  BAYOU BOUGH BREAK BRIAR BRIER
  CREEK DRUPA GRAIN LAYER LULOV
  PLASH PRONG RAMUS REISE SCROG
  SHOOT SHRAG SPRAY SPRIG STICK
  TWIST VIMEN WITHE BUREAU
  CLADUS DIVIDE DRUKPA EXOPOD
  GERMEN GREAVE GROWTH LEADER
  MEMBER OFFSET OUTLET PHYLUM
  PORTIO RADDLE RAMAGE RAMIFY
  RUNNER SHROUD SPRANG STOLON
  STREAM TAPOUN CHAPTER DIALECT

DIVERGE ENDOPOD FURCATE
LATERAL PHYLLIS RAMULUS
TENDRIL TORRENT ANAPHYTE
BRONCHUS DISTRICT EFFLUENT
OFFSHOOT PEASTICK SCAFFOLD
SPRANGLE TRAILING
  (— OF ANTLER) SPELLER
ADVANCER
  (— OF COLONY) STIPE
  (— OF CRAFT) INDUSTRY
  (— OF FAMILY) SEPT
  (— OF FEATHER) BARB
  (— OF HORN) RIAL ANTLER
  (— OF IVY) BUSH
  (— OF LEARNING) ART STUDY
FACULTY KNOWLEDGE
  (— OF MATHEMATICS) ALGEBRA
CALCULUS
  (— OF THALLUS) STICHID
  (— OF TREASURY) FISCUS
  (DEAD —) FLAG
  (EVERGREEN —S) GREENS
  (LOCAL —) COURT
  (MINE —) LEADER
  (PALM —) LULAB
  (SMALL —) RICE
  (YOUNGER —) CADET
  (PL.) LOFT RAMI SKIRT SPRAY
RAMAGE CYPRESS DEADWOOD
BRANCHED FORKY FORKED RAMATE
  RAMOSE CLADOSE TROCHED
BRANCHIA GILL
BRANCHING ARMY RAMOSE
  FURCATE DICHOTOMY
BRANCHIOPOD SHRIMP
BRANCHLET RAMULUS SPILLER
BRAND BIRN BLOT BURN CHOP
  FLAW KIND MARK NOTE SEAR SMIT
  SMOT SORT VENT WIPE BUIST
  INURE LABEL SCEAR STAIN STAMP
  SWORD TAINT TORCH BARREL
  MARQUE STIGMA FLAMBEAU
BRANDING IRON BRAND CAUTER
  SEARER CAUTERY
BRANDISH WAG DART STIR WAVE
  WIND BLESS BRAID SHAKE SWING
  WIELD FLAUNT HURTLE QUAVER
  RUFFLE STRAIN WINNOW FLUTTER
  GLITTER SWAGGER VIBRATE
  FLOURISH VAMBRASH
BRANDY DOP BOOF FINE JACK
  MARC BINGO MOBBY NANTS PEACH
  RAKIA CINDER COGNAC GRAPPA
  KIRSCH PUPELO RAKIJA VISNEY
  ANISADO AQUAVIT QUETSCH
  ARMAGNAC CALVADOS SLIVOVIC
BRANK MUMPS BRIDLE PILLORY
BRANLE BRAWL
BRANT ROUT ERECT PROUD QUINK
  SHEER STEEP ROUGHT
BRASH GAY BOLD FACY RASH
  HASTY SAUCY STORM ATTACK
  RUBBLE BRITTLE FORWARD
  IMPUDENT TACTLESS
BRASQUE STEEP
BRASS CASH ALLOY MONEY NERVE
  BRAZEN BRONZE MASLIN ORMOLU
  OFFICER ORICHALC
  (— PLAYER) WINDJAMMER

BRASSIERE BANDEAU
BRAT BIB GET IMP BROT FILM SCUM
APRON BAIRN BILSH BROLL CHILD
CLOAK GAITT INFANT MANTLE
TERROR URCHIN GARMENT
BRATTICER AIRMAN CANVASMAN
BRAVADO POMP BRAVE PRIDE
STORM HECTOR BLUSTER BOMBAST
BRAVERY SWAGGER VAUNTERY
GASCONISM
BRAVE BOLD BRAW DARE DEFY
FACE FINE GAME GOOD PROW TALL
WILD ADORN BOAST BRAVO BULLY
FELON HARDY JOLLY MANLY
MOODY ORPED ROMAN STIFF
STOUT VAUNT WIGHT BRAWLY
BREAST DARING HEROIC MANFUL
PLUCKY STURDY BRAVADO
DOUGHTY GALLANT HAUTAIN
SOLDIER SWAGGER VALIANT
VENTURE WARRIOR CAVALIER
DEFIANCE EMBOLDEN FEARLESS
INTREPID LIONLIKE STALWART
SUPERIOR VALOROUS VIRTUOUS
BRAVELY BIG FINELY
BRAVERY GRIT VALOR SPIRIT
VIRTUE BRAVADO BRAVURA
COURAGE HEROISM JOLLITY
MANHEAD MANHOOD PROWESS
BOLDNESS
BRAVO OLE RAH EUGE THUG BRAVE
BULLY BANDIT CUTTER BRAVADO
SHABASH VILLAIN APPLAUSE
ASSASSIN
BRAWL DIN ROW BEEF CLEM FRAY
RIOT BLIND BROIL CHIDE CLASH
FIGHT MELEE REVEL SCOLD SCRAP
AFFRAY BICKER FRACAS HABBLE
REVILE RUFFLE RUMPUS SHINDY
STOUSH STRIFE TUMULT UPROAR
YATTER BOBBERY BRABBLE
DISCORD DISPUTE QUARREL
SCUFFLE WRANGLE COMPLAIN
SQUABBLE STRAMASH
BRAWLER FRATCH NICKER SQUARER
FRAMPLER NIGHTCAP OUTCRIER
BRAWLING NOISY BLATANT FLITING
SCAMBLING
BRAWN BEEF BOAR LIRE FLESH
FATTEN MUSCLE STRENGTH
(MOCK —) HEADCHEESE
BRAWNY BEEFY FLESHY ROBUST
SINEWY SQUARE STRONG STURDY
CALLOUS MUSCULAR POWERFUL
STALWART
BRAXY BRADSOT
BRAY CRY MIX RUB BEAT ROUT
TOOL CRUSH GRIND NOISE POUND
STAMP BRUISE HEEHAW OUTCRY
PESTLE THRASH WHINNY
BRAYERA KOSO CUSSO KOSSO
BRAZEN BOLD CALM HARD PERT
BRASS HARDY HARSH SASSY
AENEAN BRASSY BLATANT CALLOUS
FORWARD IMMODEST IMPUDENT
INSOLENT METALLIC
BRAZENFACED CHEEKY
BRAZIER HEARTH HIBACHI REREDOS
SCALDINO
BRAZIL ROSET

BRAZIL

BAY: MARAJO IGRANDE SEPETIBA
GUANABARA
BIRD: MITU MITUA
CAPE: FRIO BLANCO BUZIOS
GURUPY ORANGE SAOTOME
SAOROQUE
CAPITAL: BRASILIA
COIN: JOE REIS CONTO DOBRA
HALFJOE MILREIS CRUZEIRO
DAM: FURNAS PEIXOTO
DANCE: SAMBA MAXIXE
ESTUARY: PARA
FALLS: IGUAZU IGUASSU
INDIAN: ANTA ACROA ARARA
ARAUA BRAVO CARIB GUANA
ARAWAK CARAJA CARAYAN
JAVAHAI TARIANA BOTOCUDO
CHAMBIOA
ISLAND: MARACA MARAJO
BANANAL CARDOSO CAVIANA
MEXIANA COMPRIDA
LAKE: AIMA FEIA MIRIM
MEASURE: PE MOIO PIPA SACK
VARA BRACA FANGA LEGOA
MILHA PALMO PASSO TONEL
CANADA COVADO CUARTA
LEAGUE QUARTO TAREFA
ALQUIER GARRAFA ALQUEIRE
MOUNTAIN: URUCUM BANDEIRA
ITATIAIA
MOUNTAINS: MAR GERAL ORGAN
PIAUI ACARAI GURUPI ORGAOS
PARIMA AMAMBAI CARAJAS
GRADAUS RONCADOR
TOMBADOR
NATIVE: CABOCLO CURIBOCA
MAMELUCO PAULISTA
PORT: RIO PARA BAHIA BELEM
NATAL SANTOS PELOTAS
SALVADOR
STATE: ACRE PARA AMAPA BAHIA
CEARA GOIAS GOYAZ PIAUI
PARANA PIAUHY ALAGOAS
GUAPORE PARAIBA RORAIMA
SERGIPE AMAZONAS MARANHAO
PARAHIBA PARAHYBA RONDONIA
SAOPAULO
RIVER: APA ICA DOCE GEIO IVAI
JARI PARA PARU SONO TEFE
ABUNA ANAUA APORE CAPIM
CLARO CORUA ICANA IRIRI ITAPI
JURUA JUTAI MANSO NEGRO
PARDO PIAUI PRETO TIETE
TURVO URUBU VERDE XINGU
AJUANA AMAZON ARINOS
BALSAS BRANCO CANUMA
CONTAS CUIABA DEMINI GRAJAU
GRANDE GURUPI IBICUI IGUACU
JAPURA JAVARI MEARIM
MORTES MUCURI PARANA
PURPUS RONURO SANGUE
TACUTU TIBAGI UATUMA
UAUPES VELHAS CORUMBA
IGUASSU MADEIRA PARAIBA
SUCURIU TAPAJOS TAQUARI
TEODORO URUGUAI ARAGUAIA

PADAUIRI PARACATU PARAGUAI
PARNAIBA SOLIMOES TARAUACA
TOWN: ACU EXU ICO IPU ITU JAU
LUZ RIO UBA BAGE FARO IBIA
IJUI ITAI LAPA LINS PARA PIUI
TUPA UNAI BAHIA BAIAO BAURU
BELEM CEARA NATAL NEVES
CAMPOS CUIABA ILHEUS
MACEIO MANAOS MANAUS
OLINDA RECIFE SANTOS
ARACAJU CARUARU CITORIA
GOIANIA ITABUNA JUNDIAI
NITEROI PELOTAS TAUBATE
UBERABA ANAPOLIS BRASILIA
CAMPINAS CURITIBA LONDRINA
SALVADOR SOROCABA
TERESINA
TREE: ICICA UCUUBA ARARIBA
WEIGHT: BAG ONCA LIBRA
ARROBA OITAVA ARRATEL
QUILATE QUINTAL TONELADA

BRAZIL NUT JUVIA CASTANA
BRAZILWOOD VERZINO HYPERNIO
PEACHWOOD
BREACH GAP CHAP FLAW GOOL
RENT RIFT SLAP BRACK BRECK
BURST CHASM CLEFT CRACK PAUSE
SPLIT WOUND BRUISE HARBOR
HERNIA HIATUS INROAD SCHISM
SCREED SLUICE ASSAULT BLEMISH
DISPUTE FISSURE OPENING
QUARREL RUPTURE BREAKING
CREVASSE FRACTION FRACTURE
INTERVAL OUTBREAK SOLUTION
TRESPASS
(— IN DIKE) GOOL
(— IN SEAWAY) GOOL
(— OF DUTY) BARRATRY
(— OF ETIQUETTE) SOLECISM
(— OF FAITH) TREASON
(— OF MORALITY) SCAPE VAGARY
(— OF PEACE) FRACTION
(— OF UNITY) SOHISM
BREAD BAP BUN BODY BRAD DIET
FARE FOOD LOAF PAIN PONE RIMA
ROLL RUSH RUSK TOKE AZYME
BATCH BATON BOXTY CAPER CHEAT
KISRA LIMPA MICHE ROOTY TOMMY
CHAPON COCKET DAMPER DODGER
ENZYME HALLAH KANKIE MASLIN
MATZOS PANNAM SIMNEL TAMMIE
WASTEL YANNAM ALIMENT
BANNOCK EULOGIA MANCHET
POPOVER STOLLEN TOASTER
CORNCAKE HARDTACK SOFTTACK
ZWIEBACK
(— AND MILK) POBS PANADA
POBBIES
(— BOX) PANETIERE
(— QUALITY) PANEITY
(BATCH OF —) CAST
(BUTTERED —) CAPER
(DRY —) TOKE
(EUCHARISTIC —) BODY HOST
AZYME
(FANCY —) BRAID
(MAIZE —) PIKI

(OATMEAL —) ANACK JANNOCK
(POTATO —) FADGE
(QUICK —) SCONE
(S. AFRICAN —) DIKA
(SLICE OF —) TARTINE TRENCHER
(SMALL LOAF OF —) COB
(SMALL PIECE OF —) SIPPET
MEALOCK
(SOPPED —) MISER BREWIS BROWIS
(SWEET —) BUN BROWNIE STOLLEN
(TOASTED —) SIPPET
(UNLEAVENED —) AZYM AZYME
BANNOCK CHAPATTI
(WHEAT —) CHEAT HOVIS COCKET
MANCHET
BREADBOARD PANEL
BREADED ANGLAISE
BREADFRUIT MASI RIMA RIMAS
DUGDUG NANGCA CAMANSI
CASTANA ANTIPOLO BREADNUT
CHESTNUT
BREADNUT RAM
BREADWINNING GAP BOON BUST
DASH HINT KNAP PICK PLOW REND
RENT RIFT RIVE
BREAK GO CUT JAR LOP TEN ABRA
BUST CHIP DRAG FALL FLAW PART
RUIN RUSH SLIP SNAP STEP STOP
TEAR TURN UNDO WASH WORK
ALTER BLANK BURST CHECK CHINK
CLEFT COMMA CRACK CRAZE
DAUNT FALSE FRUSH LAPSE PAUSE
PLUCK ROUGH SEVER SMASH
SOLVE SPAWN SPELT STAVE SWING
WOUND BRUISE CABBLE CHANGE
CLEAVE CRANNY CUTOUT DEFEAT
HIATUS IMPAIR LACUNA PIERCE
SALTUS SHREND SPRING TEWTAW
TEWTER BLUNDER CAESURA
CRACKLE CRANKLE CREVICE
CRUMBLE DESTROY DISABLE
DISPART DISRUPT EXHAUST
FISSURE GRITTLE INFRACT INTERIM
OPENING RESPITE RUPTURE
SHATTER TAILING VARIATE
BREATHER CREVASSE DIERESIS
DIFFRACT FRACTION FRACTURE
FRAGMENT INFRINGE INTERVAL
SEPARATE SOLUTION STRAMASH
(— APART) SUNDER DISRUPT
SHATTER
(— AWAY) BOLT ESCAPE
(— BOULDERS) BULLDOZE
(— DOWN) CONK FAIL GIVE CRAZE
CROCK TRAIK BRUISE TUMBLE
ANALYZE FOUNDER REFRACT
COLLAPSE INFRINGE
(— FORCE) BAFFLE
(— FORTH) BOIL ERUPT EVENT
FLASH EXPLODE
(— FROM ICE MASS) CALVE
(— GLASS) SHREND DRAGADE
(— IN PIECES) CHAP DICE KNAP
CRASH CRAZE SMASH SMOKE
SHIVER CRUMBLE FRITTER SMATTER
DEMOLISH DIFFRACT DISJOINT
SPLINTER STRAMASH
(— IN WAVES) JABBLE
(— IN YARN) SMASH

(— IN) ENTER
(— INTO FOAM) COMB
(— INTO) BROACH IRRUPT
(— INWARD) STAVE
(— LANCE) TAINT
(— OF CONTINUITY) SALTUS
(— OFF) NUB DROP SNAP CEASE
LRAVE ABRUPT DIREMPT
(— OFF END) SNUB
(— OPEN) BUST CHOP FORCE
(— ORE) COB SPALL SPAWL
(— OUT) ERUPT START ASSURD
STRIKE
(— RANKS) DISMISS
(— SHARPLY) KNACK
(— SILENCE) QUATCH QUETCH
(— SKIN) GALL
(— SLATE) SCULP
(— STONE) CAVIL KEVEL
(— THE BACK) CHINE
(— THROUGH SHELL) PIP
(— THROUGH) BEAT FORCE
(— UP EARTH) HACK FALLOW
(— UP SIEGE) LEVY
(— UP) BUCK FALL MELT FLOUR
SEVER SPALE SPLIT STASH INCIDE
DEGRADE DIFFUSE DISBAND
DISSECT DISTURB REFRACT
SCARIFY SCATTER CROSSCUT
DISJOINT DISPERSE DISSOLVE
DISUNIFY FRAGMENT
(— WATER) FIN
(— WINDOWS) NICK
(STEM —) BROWNING
BREAKABLE BRITTLE BRUCKLE
FRIABLE DELICATE FRANGIBLE
BREAKAGE GRIEF
BREAKAX IRONWOOD
BREAKDOWN EDGER BURNOUT
DEBACLE HOEDOWN COLLAPSE
DILUTION
(— OF RIND) ADUSTIOSIS
(ELECTRIC —) AVALANCHE
BREAKER JUMP SURF WAVE BARECA
BEAKER BILLOW COMBER ROLLER
CRACKER SLEDGER LEDGEMAN
SCRAPPER
(— OF WORD) WARLOCK
(CIRCUIT —) CUTOUT
(ROCK —) ALLIGATOR
(PL.) BREACH
BREAKFAST BRUNCH DISJUNE
DISJEUNE
BREAKING BREACH BREAKUP
FRACTION FRACTURE SOLUTION
(— FORTH) ERUPTIVE
(— OFF) CHIPPING ABRUPTION
(— UP) DEBACLE ANALYSIS
BREAKSTONE SAXIFRAGE
BREAKWATER COB DAM COBB
CROY DIKE MOLE PIER PILE QUAY
JETTY GROYNE REFUGE BULWARK
STOCKADE
BREAM TAI BRIM CARP CHAD SCUP
SHAD ZOPE BROOM ROMAN BALEEN
BARWIN BRAISE SARGUS OLDWIFE
SUNFISH WAREHOU CYPRINID
FLATFISH STEENJIE TARWHINE
BREAST DUG BUMP CROP FACE

BOOBY BOSOM BRAVE BUBBY
CHEST HEART PETTO STALL
PECTUS POMMEL THORAX BRISKET
COUNTER KNOCKER FOREBOWS
(— OF HORSE) COUNTER
(PL.) BUST
BREASTBAND HORSE
BREASTBONE BREAST STERNUM
XIPHOID
BREASTHOOK CRUTCH FOREHOOK
BREASTPIECE RABAT RABBI
BREASTPLATE EGIS URIM AEGIS
BREAST GORGET LORICA ORACLE
SHIELD THORAX CUIRASS PALETTE
POITREL PECTORAL PLASTRON
BREASTWORK FORT REDAN
SANGAR SCHANZ SCHERM SUNGAR
BRATTLE PARAPET PLUTEUS
RAMPART BRATTICE
BREATH AIR ANDE GASP HUFF LIFE
ONDE PANT PECH PUFF SIGH WAFT
WIND BLAST PAUSE SCENT SMELL
VAPOR WHIFF BREEZE FLATUS
PNEUMA HALITUS INSTANT RESPITE
SPIRACLE
(— OF WIND) SPIRIT
(BAD —) OZOSTOMIA
(DIVINE —) NEPHESH
(LIFE —) PRANA SPIRIT
BREATHE ANDE LIVE ONDE PANT
PECH PUFF SIGH VENT EXIST EXUDE
SPEAK SPIRE UTTER ASPIRE
EXHALE INHALE WHEEZE AFFLATE
EMANATE RESPIRE SUSPIRE
(— HEAVILY) FOB PECH FNESE
SOUGH THROTTLE
(— LABORIOUSLY) GASP
(— NOISILY) SOUGH SNOTTER
(— UPON) FAN
BREATHING AIR ALIVE PNEUMA
SPIRIT GASPING SPIRITUS
SPIRATION
(— HEAVILY) SUSPIRIOUS
(LABORED —) ASTHMA
(SMOOTH —) LENE LENIS
BREATHLESSNESS TIFT
BREATHY HOLLOW ADENOID
BRED (WELL —) FREE
BREECH BORE BUTT DOUP BLOCK
BRICK CULOTTE DRODDUM
BUTTOCKS CYLINDER DERRIERE
BREECHBLOCK BLOCK VENTPIECE
BREECHCLOTH HIPPEN HIPPING
BREECHES HOSE CHAPS JEANS
LEVIS SLOPS STOCK TREWS
BRACAE BRAGAS BREEKS GASKIN
SMALLS TIGHTS TROUSE BOMBARDS
BREEKUMS JODHPURS KICKSIES
KNICKERS LEATHERS TROUSERS
PANTALOON
BREED GET ILK BEAR KIND RACE
REAR SORT BEGET BROOD CASTE
CAUSE CLASS FANCY HATCH ISSUE
RAISE STOCK STORE TRAIN CREATE
GENDER STRAIN EDUCATE NOURISH
PRODUCE PROGENY SPECIES
VARIETY ENGENDER GENERATE
INSTRUCT MULTIPLY
BREEDER RANCHER AURELIAN

HERDSMAN HORSEMAN
(FISH —) MILTER
BREEDING ORIGIN DESCENT
NURTURE TUPPING BEHAVIOR
CIVILITY PREGNANT TRAINING
(GOOD —) GENTRY
BREEZE AIR AURA BLOW FLAW GALE
GUST PIRR STIR WIND BLAST
RUMOR SLANT WALTZ BREATH
DOCTOR REPORT SLATCH SPIRIT
ZEPHYR FRESHEN MUZZLER
QUARREL VIRASON WHISPER
(COOL —) DOCTOR
(GENTLE —) AIR AURA ZEPHYR
(LAND —) TERRAL
(STIFF —) STOUR TIFTER
BREEZE FLY WHAME
BREEZY AIRY BRISK FRESH WINDY
AIRISH
BRETHREN IKHWAN
BRETON ARMORICAN
BREVE NOTE WRIT BRIEF MINIM
ORDER SHORT PRECEPT
BREVIARY ORDO CURSUS DIGEST
LEDGER PORTAS COUCHER
EPITOME SUMMARY ABSTRACT
PORTESSE PORTHORS
BREVITY SYNTOMY LACONISM
UNLENGTH BRIEFNESS SHORTNESS
TERSENESS
BREW ALE MIX BEER BOIL MAKE
PLOT POUR DRINK HATCH STOUT
BROWST DEVISE DILUTE FOMENT
GATHER LIQUOR SEETHE CONCOCT
INCLINE PREPARE CONTRIVE
(HOME —) SAMOGON
BREWER TUNNER
BREWING GAIL GYLE BROWST
BRIBE BUD FEE FIX OIL ROB SOP TIP
BAIT GIFT HAVE HIRE MEED MOIL
PALM VAIL WAGE BONUS CUDDY
GRAFT OFFER STEAL SUGAR TEMPT
TOUCH EXTORT GREASE NOBBLE
PAYOLA SQUARE SUBORN CORRUPT
DOUCEUR SWEETEN TICKLER
GRATUITY VENALIZE
BRIBERY MEED
BRIC-A-BRAC CURIO VERTU VIRTU
BIBELOT TROCKERY TRUMPERY
BRICK BAT GLUT MARL PAVE TILE
BLOCK QUARL SPLIT STOCK STONE
TOOTH CUTTER FELLOW HEADER
PAMENT PAVIOR BACKING CLINKER
FLETTON GRIZZLE PERPEND
SOLDIER BURNOVER
(— WALL) NECK
(CRACKED —) CHUFF SHUFF
(FINAL HALF —) JACK
(IMPERFECT —) BURNOVER
(PILE OF —S) HACK CLAMP
(PULVERIZED —) SOORKY SOORKEE
(SECOND-RATE —) GRIZZLE
(SOFT —) CUTTER RUBBER PICKING
(SQUARE —) QUADREL
(STACK OF —) LIFT
(SUN-DRIED —) BAT ADOBE
(UNBURNT —) ADOBE
(WOODEN —) DOOK
(PL.) CLAYWARE

BRICKLAYER BRICKY MASONER
BRICKMAKER MOLDER
BRICKWORK HOB BRICKING
BRIDAL NUPTIAL BRIDALTY
BRIDE KALLAH SPOUSE SHULAMITE
BRIDE-PRICE LOBOLA LOBOLD
BRIDESMAID PARANYMPH
BRIDEWELL MILLDOLL
BRIDGE WAY BRIG LINK NOSE PONS
PONT REST SPAN WIEN CROSS
SIRAT TOWIE GANTRY ISLAND
JIGGER RUNWAY SANGAR AUCTION
BASCULE BIFROST CONNECT
CULVERT EXOSTRA PASSAGE
PASSING PINNOCK PONCEAU
PONTOON PROPONS TRAJECT
TRESTLE VIADUCT CONTRACT
TRAVERSE DUPLICATE
(— OF MUSICAL INSTRUMENT)
MAGAS CHEVALET
(ARCADED —) RIALTO
(CONTRACT —) GHOULIE PLAFOND
(FLUE —) ALTAR
(GATEWAY —) GOUT
(HOSE —) JUMPER
(IMPEDANCE —) DIPLEXER
(NATURAL —) ARCH
(ROPE SUSPENSION —) JOOLA
BRIDGEMAKER PONTIFEX
BRIDGEMAN EBBMAN
BRIDGING ASTRIDE STRUTTING
BRIDLE BIT CURB REIN RULE BRAKE
BRANK BRIDE CHECK GUARD GUIDE
STRUT DIRECT GOVERN HALTER
MASTER SIMPER SUBDUE BLINDER
CONTROL LORMERY REPRESS
SNAFFLE SWAGGER CAVESSON
RESTRAIN SUPPRESS
BRIDLE PATH SPURWAY
BRIEF FEW CURT LIST RIFE WRIT
BLURB BREVE CHARM PITHY QUICK
SHORT TERSE ABRUPT COMMON
CURTAL FLYING HOURLY LETTER
LITTLE SNIPPY SUDDEN ABRIDGE
CAPSULE COMPACT COMPOSE
CONCISE CRYPTIC INVOICE LACONIC
MANDATE OUTLINE PRECEPT
SUMMARY BREVIATE CONDENSE
FLEETING FLITTING SNATCHED
SNIPPETY SUCCINCT SYLLABUS
BRIEF CASE FOLIO TASHIE
BRIEFLY BRIEF ENFIN SHORTLY
BRIER BARB PIPE BRIAR THORN
SMILAX BRUYERE INKBERRY
BRIER TREE PIPER
BRIG RIG JAIL PRISON GEORDIE
BRIGADE TERZO CAMPOO
BRIGAND THIEF USKOK BANDIT
LATRON PIRATE ROBBER CATERAN
KETTRIN LADRONE ROUTIER
SOLDIER PICAROON
(PL.) TCHETNITSI
BRIGANDINE PLACCATE
BRIGHT APT GAY NET FINE GILD
GLAD GLEG HIGH LIVE ROSY ACUTE
AGLOW ALERT ANIME BEAMY BRAVE
CLEAR CRISP EAGLE FLARY FRESH
GEMMY JOLLY LIGHT LUCID NITID
PRINT QUICK RIANT SHARP SHEEN

SHEER SHINY SMART SMOLT STEEP
SUNNY TINNY VIVID WHITE WITTY
BERTHA CHEERY CLEVER FLASHY
FLORID GARISH LIMPID LIVELY
LUCENT ORIENT SHRILL SILVER
BEAMISH DIAMOND DILUCID
FORWARD FULGENT LAMBENT
RADIANT RINGING SHINING
ANIMATED CHEERFUL FLASHING
GLEAMING LIGHTFUL LUMINOUS
LUSTROUS SPLENDID SPLENDOR
STARLIKE SUNSHINY
(BLINDINGLY —) GLARING
(NOT —) SOFT
(OFFENSIVELY —) GARISH
(SOFTLY —) LAMBENT
BRIGHTEN GILD LAMP BLOOM
CHEER CLEAR FLAME GLOZE LIGHT
LIVEN SHINE SNUFF CANTLE ENGILD
POLISH ANIMATE BURNISH EMBRAVE
ENLIVEN FURBISH LIGHTEN
SMARTEN ILLUMINE
BRIGHTENER FLUOROL
BRIGHTLY GAY CLEAR LIGHT SHEEN
BRIGHT FRESHLY SHEENLY
BRIGHTNESS SUN BLAZE BLOOM
ECLAT FLAME GLARE GLEAM GLINT
GLORY GLOSS LIGHT NITOR SHEEN
SHINE ACUMEN BRIGHT CANDOR
FULGOR LUSTER CLARITY GLISTEN
GLITTER LAMBENT NITENCY
SPARKLE RADIANCE SPLENDOR
(— OF TOBACCO) FLASH
(— UNIT) STILB
BRILLIANCE FAME BLARE BLAZE
ECLAT FLAME GLARE GLORY SHINE
VALUE KEENNESS RADIANCE
SPLENDOR VIVACITY
BRILLIANCY FIRE BLARE ECLAT
GLORY REFLET CLARITY GLITTER
ORIENCY RADIANCE SPLENDOR
BRILLIANT GAY GOOD KEEN SAGE
WISE BREME QUICK VIVID BRIGHT
CLEVER LIVELY PURPLE SIGNAL
BRITTLE EMINENT FLAMING
GLARING LAMBENT LAMPING
LOZENGE PRISMAL RADIANT
SHINING BLINDING DAZZLING
DIZZYING GLORIOUS INSPIRED
LUCULENT LUMINOUS SLASHING
SPLENDID
(TRANSIENTLY —) METEORIC
BRIM LIP RIM RUT SEA EDGE TURF
BLUFF BRINK MARGE OCEAN VERGE
WATER BORDER MARGIN TURNUP
COPULATE STRUMPET
(— OF HAT) FLAP LEAF POKE BRINK
TARFE
BRIMFUL TIPFUL TOPFUL CROWNED
BRIMMING BIG FULL ABRIM
BRIMSTONE SULFUR VIRAGO
SULPHUR BRINSTON SPITFIRE
BRINDLED TAWNY BRANDED
FLECKED STREAKED
BRINE SEA MAIN SALT BRACK LEACH
OCEAN TEARS PICKLE MARINADE
BRINER COBBERER
BRING DO LAY TEE WIN BEAR BUCK
CALL FIRK LEAD STOP TAKE TEEM

CARRY DRIVE ENDUE FETCH INCUR
APPORT ARRIVE CONVEY DEDUCE
CONDUCE CONDUCT EXHIBIT
PROCURE PRODUCE
(— **FORTH YOUNG**) EAN KID YEAN
(— **ABOUT CAPTURE**) ACCOUNT
(— **ABOUT**) DO SEE BREW MAKE
STAY TEEM CAUSE DIGHT FRAME
INFER MOVEN SHAPE SWING
CREATE EFFECT INVOKE SECURE
SPIRIT COMPASS CONDUCE INSPIRE
OPERATE PRODUCE CATALYZE
OCCASION TRANSACT
(— **BACK**) REFER EFFECT RECALL
REDUCE REDUCT RELATE RETURN
REVIVE REVOKE PRODUCE RESTORE
OCCASION RETRIEVE TRANSACT
(— **BEFORE**) HAUL
(— **CHARGE**) APPEACH
(— **DOWN STEER**) HOOLIHAN
(— **DOWN**) LAY DROP FALL FELL
STOP ABATE COUCH SOFTEN
DECLINE DESCEND DISMOUNT
(— **FORTH**) CAST FOAL GIVE MAKE
TEEM EDUCE HATCH ISSUE SPAWN
THROW PROFER DELIVER TRADUCE
ENGENDER
(— **FORWARD**) CITE LEAD INFER
ADDUCE ALLEGE ADJOUST
ADVANCE PROPOSE
(— **IN**) EARN INFER USHER IMPORT
INDUCE INVECT REPORT RETURN
ADHIBIT
(— **INTO BATTLE**) COMMIT
(— **INTO COURT**) SIST
(— **INTO DISGRACE**) FOUL
(— **LOW**) AVALE DEGRADE
SUPPLANT
(— **ON**) INFER INDUCE
(— **ONESELF**) GET
(— **OUT**) DRAW ACCENT ELICIT
DISINTER HEIGHTEN
(— **OVER**) CONVERT
(— **TO A HALT**) STICK
(— **TO AN END**) DO END FIT DOCK
DRAW REDD CEASE FORDO DECIDE
EXPIRE FINISH FOREDO FULFIL
DISJOIN INCLUDE COMPLETE
CONCLUDE DISSOLVE SURCEASE
(— **TO BAY**) CORNER
(— **TO BEAR**) EXERT
(— **TO HEEL**) FACE
(— **TO LIFE**) EVOKE ANIMATE
(— **TO LIGHT**) GRUB REAP DREDGE
ELICIT EXPOSE REVEAL UNEARTH
DISCLOSE DISCOVER
(— **TO NAUGHT**) DASH FOIL UNDO
NEGATE CONFUTE DESTROY
(— **TO PERFECTION**) RIPEN
(— **TO STOP**) CURB HALT ARREST
(— **TO THE GROUND**) GRASS
(— **TOGETHER**) JOIN AMASS RAISE
UNITE ADDUCT CONFER CORRAL
ENGAGE ENLINK GATHER SUMMON
COLLATE COLLECT COMPILE
COMPORT ASSEMBLE CONFLATE
ENSEMBLE
(— **UP**) REAR BREED NURSE RAISE
TRAIN NURSLE UPREAR EDUCATE
NOURISH

BRINGING-UP BREEDING EDUCATION
BRINJAL EGGPLANT
BRINK END EVE LIP RIM SEA BANK
BRIM EDGE FOSS MARGE SHORE
VERGE BORDER MARGIN MARGENT
BRINY BRACK SALTY SALINE
MURIATED
BRIOCHE ROLL STICH SAVARIN
BRISE-SOLEIL BLIND SUNBREAK
SUNSHADE
BRISK GAY BRAG BUSY FAST KEEN
PERK PERT RACY RASH SPRY TRIG
VIVE YERN AGILE ALERT ALIVE
BUDGE CANTY CRISP FRESH FRISK
KEDGE NIPPY PEART PERKY QUICK
ROUND ZIPPY ACTIVE BREEZY
COCKET CROUSE DAPPER FLICKY
LIVELY NIMBLE SNAPPY SPRUNT
TROTTY VIVACE ALLEGRO HUMMING
ANIMATED BRUSHING FRISKFUL
RATTLING SMACKING SPANKING
SPIRITED
BRISKLY YERN SHARP YERNE
BUSILY CROUSE ALLEGRO ROUNDLY
BRISKNESS ALACRITY VIRITOOT
BRISTLE AWN JAG RIB BARB HAIR
JAGG SETA TELA BIRSE BRUSH
PARCH PREEN STARE STRUT STYLE
TOAST CHAETA PALPUS RUFFLE
SETULA STIVER STRIGA STYLET
GLOCHIS SMELLER STUBBLE
WHISKER ACICULUM FRENULUM
SPICULUM VIBRISSA
BRISTLED HORRENT
BRISTLE-SHAPED STYLOID
BRISTLING ROUGH HISPID HORRID
SETOSE THORNY HORRENT
SCRUBBY SPINOUS
BRISTLY BIRSY PENNY SETOSE
STUBBY SCRUBBY STICKLE
BRITISH ENGLISH BRITANNIC
WHITEHALL
BRITISH HONDURAS (BAY OF —)
CHETUMAL
(**CAPITAL OF —**) BELMOPAN
(**FORMER CAPITAL OF —**) BELIZE
(**MOUNTAIN RANGE OF —**) MAYA
(**TOWN OF —**) CAYO STANN
COROZAL
BRITOMARTIS (FATHER OF —)
JUPITER
(**MOTHER OF —**) CARME
BRITON CELT SCOT BRYTHON
BRITTANY (NATIVE OF —) BRETON
BRITTLE DRY FROW WEAK BRASH
CANDY CRISP CRUMP EAGER FRAIL
FROWY FRUSH SHORT SPALT
CRISPY CRUMPY FEEBLE FICKLE
FROUGH GINGER IMFIRM SLIGHT
BRICKLE BRUCKLE CRACKLY
FRAGILE FRIABLE REDSEAR
SHIVERY SMOPPLE BRITCHEL
DELICATE SNAPPISH
BRITTLEBUSH ENCELIA
BROACH AIR AWL CUT PIN ROD TAP
OPEN OUCH SHED SPIT SPUR STAB
TAME VEER VENT BEGIN DRESS
DRIFT PRICK RIMER SPOOL START
VOICE ATTAME BORING BROOCH

DRIVER FIBULA LAUNCH PIERCE
REAMER RHYMER STRIKE ENLARGE
EXPRESS PUBLISH SPINDLE
SQUARER VIOLATE WIDENER
APPROACH DEFLOWER DRIFTPIN
INCISION PORPOISE
BROAD DEEP FREE VAST WIDE
AMPLE BEAMY DORIC GROSS LARGE
LARGO PLAIN ROOMY SPLAY SQUAB
STOUT THICK WOMAN COARSE
GLOBAL BELCHER EVIDENT
GENERAL GRIVOIS LIBERAL
OBVIOUS PLATOID SPACIOUS
TOLERANT
(— **AND FLAT**) PLATOID
(**NOT —**) STRAIT
BROADBILL GAYA RAYA GAPER
SCAUP BOATBILL SHOVELER
SWORDFISH
BROADCAST AIR SOW SEED SEND
CARRY RADIO STREW AIRING
SPREAD DECLARE DIFFUSE PUBLISH
SCATTER ANNOUNCE TELEVISE
TRANSMIT
BROADCLOTH CASTOR SUCLAT
TAUNTON
BROADEN BREDE WIDEN DILATE
EXPAND EXTEND SPREAD ENNOBLE
BROADHORN ARK
BROADNESS BIGNESS LIBERALITY
BROADSIDE BROAD GARLAND
BROADSWORD BILL KRIS GLAIVE
HANGER SPATHA CUTLASS
FERRARA CLAYMORE MONTANTO
SCIMITAR
BROBDINAGIAN HUGE
BROCADE ACCA BROCHE KINCOB
KINKHAB NISHIKI BAUDEKIN
DAMASSIN
BROCCOLI ASPARAGUS
BROCHURE TRACT BOOKLET
PAMPHLET TREATISE
BROCKET PITA STAG BROCK
SPITTER
BRODIAEA GRASSNUT
BROGAN STOGA STOGY BROGUE
STOGIE
BROIL ROW BURN CHAR FEUD FRAY
GRID HEAT TOIL ALARM BRAWL
GRILL MELEE SCRAP SWELT
AFFRAY BIRSLE BRAISE GRILLY
SPLORE SQUEAL TUMULT BRANDER
BRULYIE CARBONE CONTEST
DISCORD DISPUTE EMBROIL FRIZZLE
GARBOIL QUARREL SIMULTY
BARBECUE BLOODWIT CONFLICT
GRILLADE STRAMASH
BROILER GRILL SEARER CHICKEN
POUSSIN
BROKE HOG BUST STONY STONEY
CHICANE BANKRUPT
BROKEN DOWN RENT RUDE TORN
BLOWN BROKE BURST FRACT
GAPPY HAIRY ROMPU ROUGH
TAMED BRASHY HACKLY RUINED
SHAKEN CRACKED CRUSHED
FRACTED REDUCED SUBDUED
VICIOUS WHIPPED BANKRUPT
CONTRITE OUTLAWED RUPTURED

TATTERED WEAKENED
(— BUT NOT TRAINED) GREEN
(— IN HEALTH) CRAZY
(— IN) STOVEN
(— OFF) ABRUPT
(EASILY —) GINGER
BROKEN-DOWN HAYWIRE
DISJASKED DISJASKIT
BROKER AGENT CRIMP CORSER
DEALER FACTOR JOBBER BROGGER
CHANGER COURSER PEDDLER
REALTOR SCALPER HUCKSTER
INSTITOR MERCHANT
BROMATIUM KOHLRABI
BROME CHEAT
BROMEGRASS CHESS
BROMO ACID EOSIN EOSINE
BROMUS DRAWK
BRONCHITIS HUSK HOOSE HOOZE
BRONCO PONY PONEY CAYUSE
BRONCHO MUSTANG
BRONCOBUSTER BUSTER GINETE
BUCKAROO
BRONZE AES TAN BUST ALLOY
BROWN COWBOY ORMOLU STATUE
ASIATIC GUNMETAL
(— AGE CULTURE) UBAID
(ANTIQUE —) CACAO
(GILDED —) VERMEIL
(MEDAL —) CALABASH
BRONZEWING SQUATTER
BROOCH BAR PIN BOSS LACE OUCH
PRIN PROP CAMEO CLASP MORSE
PREEN SLIDE SPRAY SPRIG FIBULA
NOUCHE PLAQUE SHIELD FERMAIL
PETALON CROTCHET ORNAMENT
SUNBURST
BROOD EYE FRY NYE SET SIT MOPE
NEST NIDE RACE TEAM TRIP WEEP
AERIE BREED CLOCK COVER COVEY
FLOCK GLOOM GROUP HATCH
HOVER ISSUE SEDGE STOCK
WORRY YOUNG CLETCH CLUTCH
FAMILY KINDLE LITTER PONDER
PROGENY SPECIES COGITATE
INCUBATE KINDLING MEDITATE
(— OF BIRDS) AERY AERIE COVEY
EYRIE SEDGE SIEGE
(— OF PHEASANTS) EYE NID NYE
NIDE
BROODER HOVER MOTHER NURSERY
BROOK RUN BEAR BECK BURN GHYL
GILL LAKE RILL RUSH SIKE ABIDE
BAYOU BOURN CREEK GLIDE STAND
STELL TCHAI ARROYO CANADA
DIGEST ENDURE GUTTER RINDLE
RIVOSE RUNLET RUNNEL SICKET
STREAM SUFFER COMPORT
CONCOCT STOMACH QUEBRADA
TOLERATE
(RIPPLING —) PURL
(SALT —) LICK
BROOKLET BECK DOKE RILL RILLET
RUNNEL RILLOCK RIVULET
BROOM COW MOP FRAY SWAB
BESOM BISME BREAM BRUSH
SCRUB SPART SWEEP UALIS WHISK
GENISTA HAGWEED WHISKER
HACKWEED SPLINTER

(DYER'S —) GENET DYEWOOD
(NATIVE —) DOGWOOD
(TOPS OF —) SCOPARIUS
BROOMCORN HURL
BROOMCORN MILLET HIRSE PANIC
PANICLE KADIKANE
BROOMRAPE HELLROOT HERBBANE
BROOMROOT SACATON ZACATON
BROSE ATHOLE
BROTH SEW BREE BROO FOND KAIL
KALE SOUP GLAZE STOCK BREWIS
CULLIS JUSSAL JUSSEL LIQUOR
SKILLY CALDERA POTTAGE SOUCHIE
SUPPING BOUILLON CONSOMME
PISHPASH POSSODIE POWSOWDY
BROTHEL KIP CRIB STEW BAGNE
HOUSE BAGNIO BORDEL LUPANAR
BORDELLO CATHOUSE HOOKSHOP
HOTHOUSE JOYHOUSE SERAGLIO
BROTHER FR BUB FRA KIN PAL SIB
BHAI BRER EGIL FRAY MATE MONK
PEER BILLY BUBBY BUDDY CADET
FRERE FRIAR FELLOW FRAILE
FRATER GERMAN COMRADE SIBLING
FOSTERER
(HUSBAND'S —) LEVIR
(LAY —) SCOLOG
(WIFE'S —) AFFINE
(YOUNGER —) CADET
(PL.) FF BRETHREN CURIATII
HARLUNGEN
BROTHERHOOD GILD GUILD LODGE
ORDER PAPEY FRIARY BRATSVO
CHISHTI THIASOS THIASUS
BRODHULL SODALITY
(— OF FREEMASONS) CRAFT
(LITERARY —) FELIBRIGE
BROTHER-IN-LAW MAUGH
BROUGHAM PILLBOX CARRIAGE
BROUGHT BROCHT
(— FROM ELSEWHERE) DERIVED
(— TO BAY) CORNERED
(— TOGETHER) CONFLATE
(— UP BY HAND) CADE
BROW TOP BRAE EDGE MIEN SNAB
BOUND BRINK CREST EAVES FRONT
RIDGE SLOPE BOLDNESS FOREHEAD
BROWBEAT FACE ABASH BULLY
BOUNCE HECTOR DEPRESS
DUMBCOW OUTFACE SWAGGER
BROWBEATEN HACKED
BROWN (ALSO SEE COLOR) ART DUN
TAN ARAB COIN COOK DARK GOAT
LION SEAR ABRAM ACORN ARGUS
BRUNO DUSKY HAZEL KAFFA
MOSUL PABLO PENNY QUAIL SEDGE
SEPIA TAWNY TENNE TOAST UMBER
APACHE BEAVER BRUNET GLOOMY
MALAGA MANILA MASTIC MOHAWK
PALOMA PLOYER PONGEE RABBIT
RUSSET SENNET TANNED TURTLE
WIGWAM ASPHALT HARVEST
LIBERIA MUSCADE OAKWOOD
OXBLOOD POMPEII PRAIRIE
REDWOOD TANBARK TOBACCO
VESUVIN BRUNETTE MOCCASIN
MUSHROOM PHEASANT PERSIMMON
PYGMALION
(CONDOR —) TIFFIN

(DARK —) BURNET
(GRAYISH —) DUN
(HAIR —) ARGALI
(LIGHT —) ALOMA ALESAN STRING
(OLIVE —) BARK AUTUMN
(REDDISH —) BAY SORE SEPIA
AUBURN CROTAL GINGER RUSSET
SORREL AMBROSIA
(YELLOWISH —) AZTEC ALMOND
BAMBOO BLONDE BEESWAX
ALDERNEY
BROWNBACK DOWITCH DOWITCHER
BROWN HEART RAAN
BROWNIE ELK NIS COOKY DOBBY
NISSE URISK DOBBIE GOBLIN
URUISG
BROWNING SCALD SCORCH SUNTAN
BROWNISH UMBER BURNET
(— BLACK) LAVA
BROWNSTONE CHESTNUT
BROWSE BRUT CROP FEED GRAZE
FORAGE NIBBLE PASTURE
BRUISE JAM BASH BRAY BUBU DENT
DUNT HURT JAMB MAIM MAUL SORE
STUN TUND BLACK BREAK BRIZZ
CRUSH CURRY DELVE DINGE POUND
SQUAT BATTER BREACH HATTER
INJURY INTUSE MANGLE POUNCE
SHINER STOUND SUGGIL BATTERY
CONTUND CROWNER DAMMISH
DISABLE
BRUISED HURT LIVID FROISSE
BRUIT DIN FAME RALE ROAR TELL
NOISE RUMOR SOUND BLAZON
CLAMOR REPORT DECLARE
HEARSAY
BRUNEI (— WEIGHT) PARA CHAP'AH
(TOWN OF —) SERIA
BRUNET DARK BLACK BROWN GIPSY
GYPSY MORENA SWARTHY
BRUNETTE MORENITA
BRUNT JAR BLOW JOLT CLASH
FORCE ONSET SHOCK ATTACK
EFFORT IMPACT STRAIN STRESS
ASSAULT OUTBURST VIOLENCE
BRUSH DIP DUB PIG TIP CARD COMB
DUST FLAP FLAT FRAY KIYI SKIM
SWAB BROOM CHAPE CLEAN COPSE
FIGHT FITCH GRAZE LINER SABLE
SCOPA SCRUB SCUFF SWEEP
SWOOP WHISK BADGER BATTLE
BRIGHT BROSSE DABBER DAUBER
DUSTER MOGOTE PALLET PENCIL
PICKUP PUTOIS RIGGER RUBBER
SPONGE STROKE TEASEL CLEANSE
FOXTAIL GRAINER GROOMER
MOTTLER STIPPLE STRIPER THICKET
SCRUBBER SIFTENER SKIRMISH
STIPPLER TARBRUSH
(— ASIDE) SCUFF
(— IN DANCING) SCUFFLE
(— OF TWIGS) COW
(— TO CLEAN SHIP BOTTOM) HOG
(BLUNT —) BLENDER
(DENSE —) BUNDOCKS BOONDOCKS
(ELECTRIC —) DOCTOR
(EMPHASIZED —) SLAP
(FLESH —) SCRAPER STRIGIL
(GROWTH OF —) SYLVAGE

(POLLEN —) SCOPA SAROTHRUM
(SMALL —) TOOL FITCH FITCHEW
BRUSHER LIMBER LIPPER
BRUSH MAKER FLIRTY FLICKER
BRUSH SHUNT PIGTAIL
BRUSHWOOD HAG RICE RONE RUSH
BRAKE BRUSH COPSE FRITH REISE
SCROG SCRUB SPRAY COPPET
GARSIL MALLEE RAMMEL SCRUNT
SHROGS TINNET TINSEL COPPICE
ROUGHIE TEENAGE THICKET
WOODRIS BUSHWOOD
BRUSQUE CURT RUDE BLUFF BLUNT
GRUFF HASTY ROUGH SHORT
ABRUPT VIOLENT CAVALIER
IMPOLITE
BRUTAL CRUEL FERAL GROSS
CARNAL COARSE SAVAGE BEASTLY
BESTIAL BRUTISH CADDISH
INHUMAN BELLUINE INHUMANE
INSOLENT RUTHLESS
BRUTE BEAST GROSS YAHOO
ANIMAL BRUTAL SAVAGE BEASTLY
BESTIAL BRUTISH GORILLA RUFFIAN
BRUTISH FELL CRUEL BRUTAL
CARNAL FIERCE SAVAGE STUPID
BESTIAL INHUMAN SENSUAL
GADARENE
BRYONY HOP NEP ALRAUN COWBIND
MANDRAKE
(— FRUIT) OXBERRY
BRYOPHYTE ANOPHYTE LIVERWORT
BRYTHONIC CYMRIC KYMRIC
BRITTONIC
BUBBLE AIR BUB BEAD BELL BLEB
BLOB BOIL BOLL DUPE FOAM GLOB
SCUM SURBLE CAPER CHEAT EMPTY
VAPOR BURBLE DELUDE HOTTER
POPPLE SEETHE SOTTER TRIFLE
BLISTER BLUBBER DECEIVE
GLOBULE DELUSIVE
(— IN GLASS) BOIL REAM SEED
BLISTER
(PL.) SUDS
BUBBLING GAY BURBLY BOILING
GASSING EFFUSIVE
BUBINGA KEVAZINGO
BUBO EMEROD
BUCCANEER PIRATE RIFLER
ROBBER VIKING CORSAIR MARINER
SPOILER MAROONER PICAROON
BUCHMANITE GROUPER
BUCHU BUKA DIOSMA
BUCK FOB RAM BOIL BUTT DEER
DUDE MALE PRIG REAR SOAK STAG
TOFF WASH BLOOD DANDY PITCH
SASIN STEEP BASKET DOLLAR
OPPOSE RESIST STRIVE SAWBUCK
BUCKJUMP BUCKWASH
(— IN 1ST YEAR) FAWN
(— IN 2ND YEAR) PRICKET
(— IN 3RD YEAR) SORREL
(— IN 4TH YEAR) SORE
(— STEADILY) SUNFISH
(— UP) BRACE
BUCKBEAN BOGBEAN THREEFOLD
BUCKER DOLLYMAN
BUCKET SAY TUB BAIL BOOT BOWK
CAGE GRAB MEAL PAIL SKIP BOWIE

CHEAT SCOOP SKEEL STOOP STOUP
BAILER DIPPER DRENCH HOPPET
KIBBLE SITULA SUCKER VESSEL
FERMAIL GRAPPLE SNAPPER
SWINDLE CANNIKIN HEDGEHOG
PAINTPOT
(— ON MILL WHEEL) AW AWE EIE
(— ON WHEELS) SKIP
(GLASS-MAKING —) CUVETTE
(GRAVEL —) GRAB
(HOISTING —) HUDGE
(TWO —S OF WATER) GAIT
BUCKEYE STATE OHIO
BUCKLAW HAYSTON
BUCKLE BOW BEND CURL KINK
OUCH TACH TACK WARP BRACE
CLASP MARRY STRAP TACHE TWIST
FIBULA CONTEND FERMAIL GRAPPLE
FASTENER STRUGGLE
BUCKLER CRAB BLOCK SCUTE
TARGE SHIELD TAIRGE TARGET
BUCKLUM BUCKRAM ROTELLA
ROUNDEL SHUTTER
BUCKLING KINK UPSET
BUCK RAKE SWEEP
BUCKRAM STIFFENER
BUCKTHORN COMA RHAMN SCROG
WAHOO ALATERN CASCARA
BEARWOOD FRANGULA LOTEBUSH
WAYTHORN STINKWOOD
BUCKWHEAT BUCK CRAP BRANK
WRIGHT SARRAZIN
(PL.) FAGOPYRUM
BUCOLIC IDYL LOCAL NAIVE RURAL
FARMER RUSTIC SIMPLE COWHERD
ECLOGUE AGRESTIC HERDSMAN
PASTORAL
BUD BUR EYE GEM IMP PIP BULB
BURR CION FORM GERM GIRL
GROW KNOP KNOT WORK CAPOT
CHILD CLOVE GEMMA GRAFT SCION
SHOOT SPRIT SPURT YOUTH
BUDLET BUTTON FLOWER GERMIN
OCULUS OILLET SPROUT BLOSSOM
BROTHER CABBAGE GEMMULE
PLUMULE ROSEBUD TENDRON
BOURGEON BULBILLA
(BLIGHTED —) BLAST
(BROOD —) SOREDIUM
(UNDEVELOPED —) EYE
(PL.) CAPERS
BUDDHA FO FOH BUTSU JATAKA
GAUTAMA SRAMANA DAIBUTSU
(— STORY) JATAKA
BUDDHISM DAIJO FOISM KEGON
CHANISM LAMAISM HINAYANA
(— CODE) VINAYA
BUDDHIST (— DOCTRINE) ANATTA
TRIKAYA
(— FESTIVAL) WESAK
(— PATH) VEHICLE
(— SCHOOL) RITSU
(— SECT) SHIN TENDAI
BUDDLE TYE FRAME BODDLE SLIMER
STRIPE TROUGH
BUDDY BO BOY BUD PAL JACK MATE
DIGGER BROTHER COMRADE
COMPADRE TENTMATE
BUDGE FUR JEE BOGY MOVE STIR

BOOZE BRISK MUDGE STIFF THIEF
JOCUND LIQUOR SOLEMN AUSTERE
POMPOUS MOVEMENT
BUDGET BAG BOGY BOOT PACK
PLAN ROLL BATCH BOGEY BOGIE
BUNCH STOCK STORE BOTTLE
BUNDLE PARCEL SOCKET WALLET
PROGRAM
BUFF ASH BOB FAN TAN BLOW COAT
CURT FIRM SHINE SNUFF SPARK
BUFFET POLISH STURDY STAMMER
STUTTER NAUMKEAG
(TILLEUL —) ALABASTER
BUFFALO OX ANOA ARNA ARNI BUFF
STAG ARNEE BISON BUGLE BUFFLE
HAMPER KERBAU MURRAH WUNTEE
CARIBAO CARIBOU GAZELLE
OVERAWE TIMARAU ZAMOUSE
BEWILDER SAPIUTAN SELADANG
BUFFALO CHIPS BODEWASH
BUFFALO FISH SUCKER BUFFALO
BIGMOUTH GOURDHEAD
BUFFER DOG PAD FROG RACK
BUMPER FENDER HURTER PISTOL
CUSHION
BUFFET BAR BOB BOX BEAT BLAD
BLOW BUFF CUFF GOWF PLAT SCAT
SLAP TOSS FILIP KNOCK SCUFF
SCUFT SMITE STOOL ABACUS
BATTER FILLIP FLEWIT SERVER
SETOUT STRIKE STRIVE THRASH
COLPHEG CONTEND COUNTER
HASSOCK SMACKER SQUELCH
CREDENCE CREDENZA CUPBOARD
SPANGHEW
BUFFETING DIRD SKITE DUSTING
BUFFLEHEAD DUCK FOOL CLOWN
BUFFLE DIPPER DOPPER MARIONET
WOOLHEAD MERRYWING
BUFFOON DOR WAG WIT APER FOOL
JAPE MIME MOME VICE ZANY
ACTOR ANTIC BUFFO CLOWN COMIC
DROLE DROLL HARLOT JESTER
MUMMER STOOGE ANTIQUE
BOUFFON JUGGLER PLAYBOY
TOMFOOL BALATRON GRACIOSO
HUMORIST MACAROON MERRYMAN
OWLGLASS PLEASANT RIDICULE
PANTALOON
BUFFOONERY JAPERY ZANYISM
CLOWNERY
BUG (ALSO SEE INSECT) DOR FLAW
GERM IDEA MITE BOGEY BULGE
FIEND LYGUS ROACH ARADID
BEDBUG BEETLE BUGGER CAPSID
CHINCH COREID CORUCO ELATER
INSECT SALDID SCHEME TINGID
BELLIED BOATMAN BUGBEAR
CIMICID CORSAIR FORWARD
POMPOUS STRIDER BARBEIRO
CONENOSE HEMIPTER HOBBYIST
NAUCORID VINCHUCA
(RED —) CHIGGA CHIGGER
(SOW —) SLATER
BUGABOO BOGY FEAR GOGA GOGO
OGRE TURK ALARM BOGEY BOGIE
GOGGA BODACH GOBLIN BUGBEAR
SPECTER SPECTRE WORRICOW
BUGANDA (— KING) KABAKA

BUGBANE COHOSH BUGWORT RICHWEED HELLEBORE

BUGBEAR BUG COW BOGY BOGEY BOGIE CADDY MORMO POKER BOGGLE BOGGART BUGABOO FEARBABE SCAREBUG

BUGGER SOD CHAP BOOGER FELLOW PERSON RASCAL HERETIC

BUGGY CART SHAY TRAP NUTTY CALESA CABOOSE CALESIN FOOLISH VEHICLE DEMENTED INFESTED STANHOPE

BUGLE BEAD HORN BLACK BUFFALO BULLOCK CLARION HUTCHET TRUMPET
(— CALL) WARISON
(YELLOW —) IVA

BUGLER WINDJAMMER

BUGLOSS ALKANET ANCHUSA BLUEWEED OXTONGUE

BUILD BIG SET FORM LEVY MAKE REAR TELD CREAT DRIVE EDIFY ERECT FOUND FRAME HOUSE RAISE SHAPE THROW FABRIC GRAITH TAILLE TIMBER COMPILE EXTRUCT FASHION ASSEMBLE
(— FIRE) CHUNK
(— HASTILY) CLAP
(— NEST) AERIE NIDIFY
(— UP) AGGRADE
(BODY —) HABITUS

BUILDER EPEUS MAKER EPEIUS HANGER ERECTOR ENGINEER TECTONIC
(DAM —) DAMMER

BUILDING GIN CASA CRIB DOME FLAT HALL IGLU JAIL LAND PILE SHED SHOP SLAB SPOT TELD AEDES ARENA BLOCK COURT FOLLY FRAME HOTEL HOUSE IGLOO JAWAB STORE STUDY ARMORY BIGGIN BOTTLE CASING CHAPEL FABRIC GARAGE HAMMAM INSULA PALACE SCHOOL SUCCOR BREWERY BROODER CARBARN COLLEGE DIORAMA EDIFICE FACTORY FLATTOP FOUNDRY MANSION SALTERN STATION SYNAGOG ATHENEUM BAGHOUSE BASILICA BROCETTO CHANCERY DIPTEROS DRYHOUSE DWELLING DYEHOUSE ELEVATOR EPHEBEUM FIRETRAP GASHOUSE GINHOUSE HOTHOUSE ICEHOUSE MAGAZINE NYMPHEUM PANORAMA SERAPEUM STEMMERY TAXPAYER TENEMENT VELODROME
(— FOR AIRCRAFT) DOCK
(— GROUPS) HAM
(— OF STONE) KAABA CASHEL TRUDDO TRULLO
(— ON POSTS) PATAKA
(BUDDHIST —) TOPE
(CIRCULAR —) THOLE THOLOS ROTUNDA
(CRUDE —) SHANTY
(DILAPIDATED —) ROOKERY FIRETRAP
(EXHIBITION —) MUSEUM
(FARM —) BARN STABLE HACIENDA

(FORTIFIED —) CASTLE
(GRAIN —) GARNER
(JAI ALAI —) FRONTON
(MOVABLE —) TURRET
(ORNAMENTAL —) ALCOVE
(PUBLIC —) CASINO THEATER THEATRE COLISEUM
(QUADRANGULAR —) TETRAGON
(QUARANTINE —) LAZARET
(SACRED —) CHURCH MOSQUE TEMPLE SACRARY PANTHEON SARAPEUM
(SERIES OF —S) SWEEP
(SLIGHT —) SHED
(SMALL —) HUT COOP HOCK EDICULE
(SPORTS —) CAGE
(STATELY —) DOME
(STORAGE —) BARN HORREUM
(SUBSIDIARY —) ANNEX
(TRADE —) HALL
(UNCOMFORTABLE —) ARK
(PL.) FUNDUS

BUILT SET BOUKIT STACKED TIMBERED
(COMPACTLY —) CORKY
(HEAVILY —) BLOCKY
(LOOSELY —) GANGLING
(STRONGLY —) BURLY GROSS QUARRY
(WELL —) BUIRDLY

BUKIDNON MONTES BINOKID

BULB BUD SET BLUB CORM IXIA KNOB LAMP ROOT SEED SEGO CLOVE FLOAT GLOBE ONION SWELL TUBER BULBIL BULBUS CROCUS GARLIC SCILLA BABIANA GALTONIA SPARAXIS TRITONIA
(— OF PERCUSSION) CONCHOID
(LIGHT —) HELION
(ONION —) BUTTON
(PL.) SQUILL

BULBIL CHIVE BULBLET
(PL.) SPAWN

BULBLET CHIVE CORMEL BULBULE NUCLEUS PROPAGO

BULBUL KALA BUHLBUHL GREENBUL LEAFBIRD

BULGARIA

ASSEMBLY: SOBRANJE SOBRANYE
CAPE: EMINE SABLA KURATAN
CAPITAL: SOFIA
COIN: LEV LEW STOTINKA
GULF: BURGAS
COMMUNE: SLIVEN SLIVNO SISTOVA
MEASURE: OKA OKE KRINE LEKHE
MOUNTAIN: BOTEV SAPKA MUSALA VIKHREN
MOUNTAINS: PIRIN BALKAN RHODOPE
PEOPLE: SLAV TATAR BULGAR SLAVIC
RIVER: LOM VIT ARDA OSMA ISKER MESTA DANUBE MARICA OGOSTA STRUMA YANTRA MARISTA STRYAMA TUNDZHA
TOWN: RILA RUSE AYTOS BUTAN BYCLU ELENA ISKRA STARA VARNA BLEVEN BURGAS DULOVO LEVSKY PLEUNA SHUMEN SHUMLA SLIVEN SLIVNO WIDDIN YAMBOL ZAGORA GABROVO KARLOVO PLOVDIV SISTOVA TIRNOVA RUSTCHUK
WEIGHT: OKA OKE TOVAR

BULGARIAN POMAK

BULGE BAG BUG JUT SAG BUMP CASK HUMP KNOB LUMP PANT BILGE BLOAT BOUGE FLASK POUCH START STRUT SWELL BEETLE BILLOW COCKLE EXTEND PUCKER WALLET BLISTER PROJECT OVERHANG PROTRUDE SWELLING
(— OUT) TUT BELLY BOWDEN STRUNT
(OFFENSIVE —) SALIENT

BULGING FULL BOMBE BOWED BUGGY GOUTY PUDGY TUMID BAGGED CONVEX GOOGLY TOROSE GIBBOUS GOUTISH SWOLLEN BOUFFANT

BULK BODY BOUK HEAP HEFT HOLD HULK HULL LUMP MASS MOLE PILE SIZE BURLY CARGO GROSS MIGHT POWER SLUMP STALL SWELL CORPSE EXPAND EXTENT FIGURE VOLUME BIGNESS MAJORITY QUANTITY

BULKHEAD CHECK BATTERY PARTITION

BULKY BIG MAIN BURLY GROSS LARGE PUDGY STOUT CLUMSY STODGY HULKING LUMPING MASSIVE WEIGHTY UNWIELDY

BULL COP SEG APIS BEEF BILL JEST MALE ROAN SEAL SEGG SLIP STOT TORO ZEBU BACIS BEEVE BOBBY BONER BOVID BRUTE DRINK EDICT ERROR ANIMAL BOVINE BUSHWA LETTER PEELER TAURUS BULLOCK BUSHWAH CRITTER CRUSADE NOVILLO TAURINE CAJOLERY DOCUMENT FLATTERY
(— AREA) QUERENCIA
(— KILLING) VOLAPIE
(HORNLESS —) DODDY DODDIE
(HUMAN-HEADED —) SHEDU CAMASSU
(YOUNG —) STOT BUGLE MICKY STIRK STOTT BULLOCK
(PL.) BATTERY

BULLA BLEB BULL SEAL BLAIN BLISTER VESICLE

BULL CELL TORIL

BULLDOG BULL BULLER BULLDOZE

BULLDOZE COW RAM BULLY FORCE SCOOP COERCE BROWBEAT BULLYRAG RESTRAIN

BULLET GUN BALL LEAD PILL SHOT SLUG TOWEL CONOID DUMDUM PELLET PICKET SINKER TRACER DINGBAT MISSILE PELLOCK

PROJECT SPITZER MUSHROOM WADCUTTER (PL.) BALL LEAD STUFF

BULLETIN ITEM MEMO NOTICE POSTER REPORT SERIAL PROGRAM NEWSBILL

BULLFIGHT CORRIDA NOVILLADA

BULLFIGHTER TORERO MATADOR PICADOR CAPEADOR TOREADOR

BULLFIGHTING REJONEO

BULLFINCH ALP OLP HOOP MAWP MONK NOPE OLPH POPE HEDGE TANNY TAWNY MONACH REDBIRD REDHOOP SHIRLEY BLOODALP TONYHOOP

BULLHEAD CUR POUT

BULLIMONG FARRAGE

BULLION BILLOT

BULLISH STIFF

BULLOCK HOG HOGG NEAT NOWT STOT BUGLE KNOUT STEER STIRK BOVINE (DECOY —) COACH

BULL-ROARER BUZZ BUMMER BUZZER ROARER TUNDUN TURNDUN WHIZZER

BULL'S-EYE EYE BULL DUMP GOLD BLANK OXEYE WHITE TARGET ROUNDEL

BULL SNAKE GOPHER

BULL TROUT TRUFF

BULLY NUT BOAT BOSS FACE FINE GOOD HUFF MATE BRAVE BRAVO GREAT JOLLY SNOOL TIGER VAPOR BOUNCE CUTTER CUTTLE HARASS HECTOR HUFFER JOVIAL RUFFLE TYRANT BLUSTER BOUNCER BULLOCK DARLING DASHING GALLANT GAUSTER HUFFCAP ROISTER RUFFIAN RUFFLER SLASHER SOLDIER SWAGGER BANGSTER BARRATER BLUDGEON BROWBEAT BULLDOZE DOMINEER FRAMPLER NIGHTCAP RABIATOR (MASTIC —) ACOMA

BULLY TREE BALATA BULLACE GAUSTER BEEFWOOD

BULRUSH REED RISP RUSH TULE SEDGE BUMBLE GLUMAL AKAAKAI CATTAIL PAPYRUS SCIRPUS TUSSOCK

BULWARK BAIL FORT WALL FENCE JETTY MANTA MOUND TOWER WARDER BASTION DEFENCE DEFENSE PARAPET PROTECT RAMPART WEREWALL

BUM BEG DIN BOMB BOOM HOBO DRINK DRONE IDLER MOOCH SHACK STIFF TRAMP FROLIC GUZZLE SPONGE SQUEEF GUZZLER VAGABOND

BUMBLEBEE DOR CLOCK BUMBEE BUMBLE CARDER BUMBLER

BUMMER SKIDDER

BUMP CRY HIP HIT NOB BANG BLOW BOOM BUNK DIRD JOLT KNOB LUMP WHAP WHOP BULGE CLASH CLOUR CLOUT DUNCH KNOCK ORGAN THUMP BOUNCE CANNON IMPACT

JOUNCE NODULE STRIKE BITTERN COLLIDE CONFLICT SWELLING (— ON WHALE'S HEAD) HOVEL

BUMPER BOWL FINE GOOD FACER GLASS ROUSE BUFFER CASABE FENDER GOBLET HURTER KELTIE BRIMMER DINGMAN CARANGID (— GUARD) OVERRIDER

BUMPKIN JAY YAP BEAM BOOM BOOR CHAW CLOD GAWK HICK LOUT RUBE SWAB SWAD TIKE TYKE CHURL CLOWN ROBIN YAHOO YOKEL FARMER JOSKIN LUMMOX BUCOLIC CAUBOGE HAWBUCK

BUNCH BOB SET BALE BOSS CHOU CLEW CLUB CLUE COMA KICK KNOB KNOT PACK SWAD TUFT WISP BREAK CLUMP FAGOT FLOCK KNOLL PAHIL THUMP CLUTCH GAGGLE HUDDLE (— OF BANANAS) HAND STEM (— OF FLAX) HEAD STRICK (— OF FRUIT) HOG STRAP (— OF GRASS) WHISK (— OF GRAIN) RIP (— OF GRAPES) RAISIN (— OF HAIR) COB (— OF HERBS) BOUQUET (— OF IVY) BUSH (— OF TOBACCO LEAVES) HAND BREAK (— UP) SHRUG (SMALL —) WISP

BUNCHER BINDER

BUNCHY TRUSS

BUNCOMBE HOOEY BUNKUM

BUND BAND QUAY PRAYA LEAGUE SOCIETY

BUNDLE KID LOT PAD TOD WAD WAP BALE BAND BEAT BOLT BOOK BUNG DRUG DRUM GARB HANK HAUL HEAD KNOT LOCK PACK ROLL SWAG BLUEY BULTO BUNCH FADGE FAGOT GAVEL GLEAN GROUP LITCH NICKY PETER SHEAF SKEIN TARRY TRACE TRUSS TURSE WADGE BARSOM BATTEN BINDLE BOTTLE BUDGET DRIVER DUFTER FAGGOT FARDEL FASCES FUMBLE GATHER KNITCH LOGGIN NUMBER PACKET PARCEL SCROLL THRAVE DORLACH FASCINE GARBAGE MATILDA PACKAGE FASCICLE (— OF 60 SKINS) TURN (— OF BOARDS) BOLT (— OF FASCINES) ROULEAU (— OF FIBRILS) AXONEME (— OF FLAX) BEET HEAD (— OF HAIR) LEECH (— OF HAY, STRAW, ETC.) WAP WASE WISP GAVEL SHEAF BATTEN BOLTIN BOTTLE TIPPLE WINDLING (— OF HEATH) KID (— OF HIDES) KIP (— OF NERVE FIBERS) TRACT COLUMN (— OF PAPERS) SPUR DUFTER (— OF RODS) FASCES (— OF SACKS) BADGER

(— OF SACRED TWIGS) BARSOM (— OF THONGS) KNOUT (— OF TOBACCO) CARROT (— OF TWIGS) BIRCH BROOM FAGGOT (— OF WOOD) PIMP BAVIN FAGOT (— OF YARN) HAUL SLIP (BUSHMAN'S —) DRUM BLUEY

BUNG CORK PLUG SHIVE SPILE STOPPER

BUNGEY KIT

BUNGI-BUNGI STAVEWOOD

BUNGLE ERR GOOF MESS MUCK MUFF BLUNK BOTCH FAULT FLUFF FUDGE SPOIL STICK BOGGLE BOLLIX BUMBLE FOOZLE FUMBLE MOMBLE MUCKER MUDDLE TAILOR TOGGLE BAUCHLE BLUNDER BUTCHERY SHAMMOCK

BUNGLER LUMMOX PUDDLE TINKER BUMBLER BUMMLER FOOZLER DAUBSTER

BUNGLING FLUFF FUDGY INERT CLUMSY AWKWARD TINKERLY

BUNG START FLOGGER

BUNION ONION WYROCK

BUNJI-BUNJI CUDGERIE

BUNK BED CAR BLAA BLAH CASE JUNK SACK ABIDE BERTH BUNKO FRAME HOKUM HOOEY LEAVE LODGE SLEEP TRUCK BUNKUM TIMBER BALONEY BOLSTER CHICORY HEMLOCK TWADDLE BUNCOMBE NONSENSE

BUNKHOUSE BULLPEN

BUNKUM BLAH BUNK FUDGE HOKUM HOOPLA BALONEY BUNCOMBE

BUNTAL BURI BANGKOK

BUNTING EBB POP FLAG PAPE POPE CHINK DUMPY FINCH PLUMP COTTON STOCKY TOWHEE UNTIDY COWBIRD ETAMINE GARMENT OATFOWL ORTOLAN ROUNDED BELLYING BOBOLINK PRUSIANO RICEBIRD RINGBIRD SLOVENLY NONPAREIL

BUNTON DIVIDER

BUOY DAN WAFT BAKEN ELATE FLOAT LAGAN RAISE MARKER DOLPHIN SUSTAIN DEADHEAD LEVITATE MAKEFAST SONOBUOY

BUOYANCY BALON BALLON LEVITY SPRING ELATION

BUOYANT GAY CORKY HAPPY LIGHT BLITHE BOUNCY FLOATY LIVELY ELASTIC HOPEFUL JOCULAR LILTING SPRINGY ANIMATED CHEERFUL SANGUINE SPIRITED VOLATILE

BUR BUZZ TEAZEL STICKER

BURBARK AKONGE BOXBUSH BURRBARK

BURBOT COD CONY CUSK LING LOTA CONEY LOCHE LAWYER MORGAY DOGFISH EELPOUT GUDGEON BIRDBOLT

BURDEN TAX VEX BIRN CARE CARK CLAG CLOG DRAG DUTY FARE FOOT GANG LADE LOAD MUCK ONUS PORT SEAM TACK BIRTH CARGO

CROWD CRUSH DRONE HEAVY
LABOR MIDST CHARGE CUMBER
ENTAIL FARDEL HAMPER IMPOSE
LADING SADDLE THRACK WEIGHT
BALLAST BURTHEN CONVETH
FRAUGHT FREIGHT HAGRIDE
ONERATE OPPRESS REFRAIN
SUMPTER TROUBLE CAPACITY
CARRIAGE ENCUMBER ENGREGGE
HANDICAP OVERCOME QUANTITY
RUMBELOW MILLSTONE
(— OF SONG) WHEEL HOLDING
OVERTURN OVERWORD
(FINANCIAL —) EXPENSE
BURDENED HEAVY LADEN GRAVID
FRAUGHT HARASSED
BURDENER INCUBUS
BURDENSOME HEAVY IRKSOME
ONEROUS WEIGHTY CUMBROUS
GRIEVOUS GRINDING LOADSOME
BURDOCK DOCK GOBO CLITE CLOTS
DRAIN LAPPA BARDANE BURWEED
BUZZIES CADILLO CLOTBUR
HARDOCK HAREBUR CLEAVERS
HAULBACK
BUREAU DESK CHEST AGENCY
EXCISE OFFICE CENTRAL DRESSER
AGITPROP
BUREAUCRAT MANDARIN
BURFISH ATINGA
BURGEON BUD GROW ERUPT
SHOOT SPROUT
BURGESS CITIZEN FREEMAN
PORTMAN COMMONER GORGIBUS
(PL.) BURGWARE
BURG GRASS SANDBUR COCKSPUR
SANDSPUR
BURGLAR YEGG CRACK THIEF
GOPHER ROBBER RAFFLES
YEGGMAN PETERMAN PICKLOCK
BURGLARY BREAK CRACK THEFT
LARCENY ROBBERY STEALAGE
BURGUNDY POMMARD VOUGEOT
TONNERRE
BURIAL FUNERARY INTERMENT
(— MOUND) TOLA HUACA
BURIAL PLACE AHU TOMB GRAVE
BURIAL GIGUNU LAYSTOW PYRAMID
CATACOMB CEMETERY GOLGOTHA
LAYSTALL
BURIED HIDDEN HUMATE SEPULT
ABSORBED IMBEDDED
(NOT —) UNRESTED
(RECENTLY —) GREEN
BURIN GRAVER PLASTIC
BURL BURR KNAR KNOT LUMP
KNAUR PIMPLE PUSTULE
BURLAP GUNNY CROCUS BAGGING
HESSIAN SACKING WRAPPING
BURLER LECKER SPILER
BURLESQUE APE ODD COPY JEST
MIME BURLY DROLL FARCE REVUE
COMEDY OVERDO PARODY
BUFFOON JOCULAR MIMICRY
MOCKERY OVERACT DOGGEREL
RIDICULE TRAVESTY
BURLY FAT BLUFF BULKY GROSS
HEAVY HUSKY LARGE LUSTY NOBLE
OBESE STOUT THICK TRAMP

BOWERLY MASTIFF STATELY
IMPOSING

BURMA
BAY: BENGAL HUNTER HEANZAY
CAPITAL: RANGOON
GULF: MARTABAN
MEASURE: LY DHA GON LAN MAU
NGU SAO TAO TAT BYEE DAIN
PHAN SEIT TAUN TENG THAT
SALAY SHITA THUOC LAMANY
PALGAT TRUONG CHAIVAI
OKTHABAH
MONEY: KYAT
MOUNTAIN: POPA NATTAUNG
SARAMATI VICTORIA
MOUNTAINS: CHIN NAGA DAWNA
KACHIN KARENNI PEGUYOMA
NATIVE: AO VU WA LAI LAO MON
PYU TAI CHIN KADU KUKI LOLO
MIAO NAGA SEMA SHAN THAI
KAREN KHMER LHOTA BIRMAN
BURMAN KACHIN RENGMA
PALAUNG ARAKANESE
PORT: AKYAB BASSEIN HENZADA
MOULMEIN
SEA: ANDAMAN
TOWN: YE AVA PEGU AKYAB
BHAMO KATHA MINBU PAPUN
PROME TAVOY HSENWI HSIPAW
LASHIO MAYMYO MONYWA
SHWEBO BASSEIN HENZADA
PAKOKKU RANGOON MANDALAY
MOULMEIN
RIVER: HKA NMAI PEGU SALWIN
SHWELI KALADAN MALIKHA
MYITNGE SALWEEN SITTANG
CHINDWIN INDAWGYI
IRRAWADDY
WEIGHT: TA CAN MAT MOO PAI
VIS BINH DONG KYAT RUAY VISS
BAHAR BEHAR CANDY TICAL
TICUL ABUCCO PEIKTHA

BUR MARIGOLD BACLIN CUCKOLD
BURMESE KADU BIRMAN
ARAKANESE
BURN BREN BREW CHAR FIRE GLOW
PLOT RAZE RILL SEAR SERE TEND
TIND ADUST BLAZE BROIL BROOK
CENSE CHARK CLAMP FLAME FLARE
PARCH PLOUT QUICK ROAST SCALD
SCAUM SINGE SWEAL WASTE
WATER CROZLE IGNIFY NIGGER
SCORCH SIZZLE STREAM CHARPIT
COMBURE COMBUST CONSUME
CREMATE CROZZLE FLICKER
FRIZZLE INCENSE OXIDIZE RIVULET
SCOWDER SMOLDER FLAGRATE
SQUANDER
(— FEEBLY) GUTTER
(— FITFULLY) FLICKER
(— IN) INURE
(— MIDNIGHT OIL) LUCUBRATE
(— OUT) GUT
(— UP) ADUST EXUST
(— WITH LITTLE FLAME) SMUDGE
(LET —) BISHOP

BURNED ADUST
BURNER BEAK KORO BAKER PILOT
ARGAND BUNSEN CENSER
BATSWING CALCINER GASLIGHT
THURIBLE WELSBACH
BURNET SELFHEAL BLOODWORT
BURNING HOT FIRE LIVE AFIRE
ANGRY BLAZE CALID EAGER FIERY
FLAME GLEDY QUICK SCALD URENT
ABLAZE ARDENT FERVID FIRING
LIVING TORRID USTION ADURENT
CAUSTIC CAUTERY FERVENT
FLAMING GLARING GLOWING
MORDANT SCOWDER SHINING
ARDUROUS EXCITING FLAGRANT
INUSTION MUIRBURN PARCHING
SCOUTHER
(— BRIGHTLY) LIGHT
(— OF FORESTS IN INDIA) JHOOM
(MALICIOUS —) ARSON
(NO LONGER —) EXTINCT
BURNING BUSH WAHOO
BURNISH RUB GLAZE GLOSS INLAY
POLISH FURBISH
BURNISHER AGATE BUFFER GLAZER
FROTTON POLISHER
BURP BOKE BELCH BUBBLE
BURR NUT PAD BARB BIRR BOSS
BUZZ HALO KNOB PILE RING ROVE
SLUG WHIR BRIAR BURGH WHARL
WHIRR BANYAN CIRCLE CORONA
TEASEL TUNNEL WASHER CORONET
STICKER PARASITE
(— IN WOOD) GNAR KNAR
(— OF ANTLER) CORONET
(— ON TYPE) RAG
BURRO ASS DONKEY
BURROW BED DEN DIG SET BURY
HEAP HOLE MINE MOLE PIPE ROOT
TUBE BERRY COUCH EARTH MOUND
FURROW ROOTLE TUNNEL CLAPPER
GALLERY PASSAGE SHELTER
EXCAVATE WORMHOLE
(— AS EEL) MUD
(— IN) MOIL
(— OF BADGER) SET
(— OF OTTER) COUCH
(FOSSIL —) SCOLITE
BURROWS TOWN
BURSA SAC SACK POUCH CAVITY
BURSULA
BURSAR BOWSER PURSER TERRAR
BOUCHER CASHIER
BURSE CASE SHOP FOREL BAZAAR
BOURSE POCKET
BURST FIT FLY POP BLOW BUST
DASH GUSH GUST LOSS REND SCAT
TILT BLAST BLOUT BREAK CRACK
ERUPT FLAFF FLASH GRAZE REAVE
SALVO SCATT SHOUT SPASM SPLIT
START STAVE BROKEN DAMAGE
INJURY SPROUT EXPLODE IMPLODE
RUPTURE SHATTER AIRBURST
OUTBREAK SUNDERED
(— ASUNDER) OUTRIVE
(— FORTH) ERUPT SALLY EXPIRE
BALLOON
(— IN) IRRUPT IMPLODE
(— INTO FRAGMENTS) FLITTER

(— INTO LAUGHTER) BUFF
(— OF ACTIVITY) BRASH SPURT
SPRINT SPLURGE
(— OF ARTILLERY) GRAZE RAFALE
(— OF CHEERS) SALVO
(— OF ENERGY) BANG
(— OF FIRING) COUGH
(— OF HARMONIOUS SOUND)
DIAPASON
(— OF LIGHT) FLASH GLORY
(— OF SPEED) KICK FLUTTER
(— OF TEARS) BLURT
(— OF TEMPER) BOUTADE
(— OF WIND) FLAW
(— OPEN) UPBRAST
(— OUT) PRORUMP
(— THE HEART) RIVE
BURSTER GALE LUGGER CRACKER
BURSTING TUMID ABURST BLOWOUT
RUPTION ERUPTING

BURUNDI
CAPITAL: BUJUMBURA
COIN: FRANC
LAKE: RUGWERO TSHOHOHA
NATIVE: HUTU BANTU PYGMY
TUTSI WATUSI
RIVER: KAGERA RUVUVU RUZIZI
AKANYARU
TOWN: NGOZI BURURI KITEGA
MUYINGA BUJUMBURA

BURY URN CAMP HIDE MOOL RAKE
TURF VEIL CLOAK COVER EARTH
GRAVE INTER INURN VAULT WHELM
ENTOMB ENWOMB HEARSE INHUME
SEPULT SHROUD BEDELVE
CONCEAL ENGROSS IMMERSE
PITHOLE REPRESS SECRETE
FUNERATE SUBMERGE
BUS CAMION JITNEY JEEPNEY
BUSBOY OMNIBUS PICCOLO
BUSH TOD BUTT BOSCH BURSE
CLUMP GROVE PLASH SCRAY
SHRUB BRANCH TAVERN BOSCAGE
BOUCHON CLUSTER OUTBACK
THICKET BUSHLAND
(— SICKNESS) TAURANGA
(BLACKBERRY —) BRAMBLE
(STUNTED —) SCROG
(PL.) RUFFMANS
BUSH CLOVER HAGI
BUSH COW ZAMOUSE
BUSHEL FOO FOU GOB LOT MET
BUCKET STRICK
(1-4TH —) PECK
(1-HALF —) TOVET
(1-HALF TO 3-4THS —) CABOT
(1.6 —) FANEGA
(3 TO 5 —S) SACK
(3-4THS —) SKIPPLE
(41.28 —) WEY
(8 —S) SEAM
BUSHER SWAMPER
BUSHGRASS WOODREED
BUSHING BUSH COAK DRILL LINER
BOUCHE COLLET LINING SLEEVE
BOUCHON FERRULE GROMMET
PADDING

(HALF —) STEP
BUSHMAN GUNG BUSHY KHUAI
ABATOA ABATWA WHALER
BUSHBOY SWAGMAN NEGRILLO
(PL.) SAN SAAN
BUSHMASTER CURUCUCU
SURUCUCU
BUSHWHACKER PAPAW PAWPAW
BUSHY BOSKY SHOCK DUMOSE
DUMOUS BUSHMAN QUEACHY
BUSILY THRANG
BUSINESS ADO ART BIZ FAT JOB
PIE CARE FEAT FIRM FUSS GAME
GEAR LINE NOTE TASK WORK
CAUSE CRAFT TRADE TRUCK
AFFAIR CUSTOM EMPLOY ERRAND
MATTER METIER NEGOCE OFFICE
PIDGIN RACKET TURKEY ACCOUNT
CALLING CONCERN JOURNEY
PALAVER TRADING TRAFFIC
ACTIVITY AGIOTAGE BESOIGNE
COMMERCE FOLLOWER INDUSTRY
INTEREST VOCATION
(COMIC —) LAZZO
(MONKEY —) JOUKERY PAWKERY
(STAGE —) BYPLAY
BUSINESSMAN TYCOON POACHER
BOURGEOIS CONVERTER
BUSKIN BOOT SHOE CALIGA
BOTTINE COTHURN BRODEKIN
BUSSU UBUSSU TROOLIE
BUST BUMP FAIL RUIN TAME BOSOM
BREAK BURST BUSTO CHEST EDGAR
FLUNK SPREE BRONZE DEMOTE
REDUCE STATUE DEGRADE DISMISS
FAILURE PROTOME
(— SHAPE) TAILLE
BUSTARD KORI OTIS WATO PAAUW
TURKEY BEBILYA HOUBARA
KORHAAN FLORICAN GOMPAAUM
BUSTIC AUSUBO CASSADA
BUSTLE ADO BUZZ FIKE FRAY FUSS
JUMP STIR WHEW WHIR FRISK
HASTE HYPER KNOCK PAVIE STEER
WHIRL WHIRR BISHOP BUMBLE
ENERGY FISSLE FISTLE FLURRY
FUSTLE HUDDLE HUSTLE POTHER
RACKET TATTER THRONG TUMULT
UNREST UPROAR CLATTER CLUTTER
CONTEND LOUSTER SCOWDER
SCUFFLE SCUFTER SPUFFLE
ACTIVITY IMPROVER SPLUTTER
STRUGGLE TOURNURE
BUSTLING ADO BUSY FUSSY
SPOFFISH STIRRING
BUSY FAST FELL APPLY BRISK QUICK
ACTIVE EIDENT EMPLOY INTENT
LIVELY OCCUPY STEERY THRONG
UNIDLE ENGAGED HOPPING
HUMMING OPEROSE TROUBLE
WORKING DILIGENT EMPLOYED
EXERCISE OCCUPIED SEDULOUS
TIRELESS UNTIRING
(— ONESELF) STRAP
(NOT —) SLACK
BUSYBODY BUSY SNOOP EARWIG
SPOFFY ARDELIO MARPLOT
MEDDLER SNOOPER FACTOTUM
QUIDNUNC PRAGMATIC

BUT AC LO MA BIT SED YEA YET
MERE ONLY SAVE ARRAH STILL
ALWAYS EXCEPT UNLESS BESIDES
HOWBEIT HOWEVER
BUTCHER KILL SLAY BUTCH SPOIL
BUNGLE KIDDER LEGGER LEMMER
MURDER VENDOR BOTCHER
BRAINER BRITTEN FLESHER
MEATMAN PORKMAN KILLCALF
PIGSTICK SLAUGHTER
BUTCHERBIRD SHRIKE MATAGASSE
BUTCHER'S-BROOM RUSCUS
BRUSCUS
BUTCHERY MURDER CARNAGE
MASSACRE SHAMBLES SLAUGHTER
BUTEO BUZZARD
BUTLER SOMLER YEOMAN BOTELER
SERVANT SPENCER STEWARD
CELLARER CONSUMAH KHANSAMA
STEPHANO MAJORDOMO
BUTT JUR JUT MOT PIT PUT RAM
RUN TOY TUP BUCK BUNT BURT
BUSH CART CASK DISH DOSS FOOL
GOAD GOAL GOAT HORN JOLT
JURR POLL PUCK PUSH STUB TANG
TOPE TURR BOUND HINGE JOINT
MOUND ROACH SCOPE STOCK
STUMP BREECH TARGET THRUST
BEEHIVE BUTTOCK PARAPET
PROJECT REVERSE STUMMEL
ARIETATE FLATFISH FLOUNDER
RIDICULE SACKBUTT
(— FOR RIDICULE) GAME SPORT
STALE COCKSHY
(— OF CIGAR) DOCK SNIPE
(— OF HORSEHIDE) SHELL
(— OF JOKE) JEST SCOGGIN
JESTWORD
(CIGARETTE —) BUMPER
(HALF —) BEND
BUTTE HILL PICACHO
BUTTER SHEA CLART COCUM
BAMBUK BEURRE CAJOLE SPREAD
BLARNEY FLATTER
(— MEASURE) SPAN
(ARTIFICIAL —) BOSH OLEO BOSCH
MARGARINE
(BROWNED IN —) NOISETTE
(SEMIFLUID —) GHI GHEE
BUTTER-AND-EGGS RANSTEAD
TOADFLAX
BUTTERBUR CLEAT CLOTE ELDIN
GALON GALLON OXWORT GILTCUP
FLEADOCK
BUTTERCUP BOLT CYME CRAZY
ANEMONE CRAISEY CROWTOE
GILTCUP GOLDCUP KINGCOB
KINGCUP CRAWFOOT CROWFOOT
FROGWORT
BUTTERFISH GUNNEL POMPANO
WHITING PALOMETA SKIPJACK
BUTTERFLY IO BLUE ARGUS ELFIN
GHOST NYMPH QUEEN SATYR SWIFT
WHITE ZEBRA ALPINE APOLLO
CALIGO COPPER DANAID HOPPER
IDALIA JUGATE MORPHO PIERID
PROGNE SULFUR THECLA URSULA
VIOLET YELLOW ADMIRAL BUCKEYE
DIURNAL DOLPHIN EMPEROR

FRENATE MONARCH PIERINE
SATYRID SKIPPER SULPHUR
TUSSOCK VANESSA VICEROY
ARTHEMIS CECROPIA CRESCENT
GRAYLING HESPERID ITHOMIID
WANDERER
(— BREEDER) AURELIAN
BUTTERFLY FISH MOJARRA
FLATFISH
BUTTERFLY WEED FLUXROOT
MILKWEED WINDROOT
BUTTERMILK WHIG JOCOQUE
SOURDOOK
BUTTERSCOTCH TOFFY
BUTTERWORT BEANWEED
SHEEPWEED
BUTTERY BOTRY LARDER SPENCE
BUTLERY SPICERY
BUTTOCKS ASS BUM CAN FUD HAM
ARSE BUTT CULE DOCK DOUP DUFF
LEND POOP SEAT TAIL TOBY CROUP
FANNY NATES SLATS STERN TOUTE
BEHIND BOTTOM BREECH CURPIN
HEINIE HINDER CROUPON CRUPPER
DRODDUM HURDIES KEISTER
BACKSIDE DERRIERE NATIFORM
BUTTON BUD ZIP BOSS CHIN DOME
HOOK KNOB KNOP SPUR TUFT
BADGE CATCH GLIDE OLIVE PEARL
PRILL BAUBLE BUCKLE GLIDER
SHINER TOGGLE TROCHE DEWDROP
HORNTIP KNICKER PRESSEL
REGULUS DOORBELL FASTENER
OLIVETTE
BUTTONBUSH BUCKBRUSH
SWAMPWOOD
BUTTONHOLE EYE LOOP SLIT
BUTTON SNAKEROOT LIATRIS
SAWWORT

BUTTONWOOD COTONIER
BUTTRESS NOSE PIER PILE PROP
SPUR STAY BRACE BRICK OUTCAST
OUTSHOT SUPPORT TAMBOUR
ABUTMENT
(— MEMBER) TIRE
BUTYL TETRYL
BUXOM MILD AMPLE JOLLY PLUMP
PRONE SONSY BLITHE CRUMBY
CRUMMY FLORID FODGEL HUMBLE
PLIANT SONSIE BOWERLY
BOUNCING FLEXIBLE OBEDIENT
OBLIGING YIELDING JUNOESQUE
BUY CHAP COFF COUP GAIN HAVE
SHOP SNIP TAKE BRIBE CLAIM
TRADE ABEGGE MARKET RANSOM
REDEEM SECURE ACQUIRE CHAFFER
PURCHASE
(— BACK) REPRISE
(— OFF) APPEASE
(— UP STOCKS) COVER
BUYER CHAP AGENT CATER BEGGER
EMPTOR PATRON VENDEE CHAPMAN
SHOPPER ACHATOUR CUSTOMER
PROSPECT
(— OF CLOTH) REDUBBER
BUYING ACATE ACHATE EMPTION
(— MANIA) ONIOMANIA
BUZZ HUM BURR CALL DASH HISS
HUSS HUZZ RING WHIR FANCY
FLING PHONE RUMOR BUMBLE
NOTION WHISPER
BUZZARD AURA FOOL HAWK PERN
BUTEO GLADE GLEDE HARPY
STOOP BEETLE CURLEW PREYER
STUPID PUDDOCK PUTTOCK
VULTURE BROMVOEL
BUZZER BEE BELL ALARM HOWLER
SIGNAL WHIZZER

BY A P X AB AT OF TO AGO BYE GIN
PAR PER TIL ABUT ANON INTO
NEAR PAST TILL APART ASIDE
CLOSE FORBY BESIDE TOWARD
BESIDES THROUGH
(— AND BY) BELIVE BIMEBY
(— FAR) EASILY
(— HEART) PERQUEIR
(— HOOK OR CROOK) HABNAB
(— MEANS OF) PER MOYENANT
(— NO MEANS) NA
(— REASON OF THIS) HEREAT
(— STEALTH) STOWLINS
(— SURPRISE) ABACK
(— THE DAY) PD
(— THE ORDER OF) O
(— THE WAY) APROPOS
(— THIS TIME) ALREADY
(— WAY OF) VIA
(GONE —) AGO PAST
(NEAR —) GIN
BY-BIDDER FUNK CAPPER PUFFER
BY-CHANNEL BAYOU BRANCH
BYCOKET ABACOT ABOCOCKET
BYGONE PAST YORE OLDEN BYPAST
FORMER ANCIENT ELAPSED
BACKWARD DEPARTED FOREPAST
PRETERIT
BYPASS JUMP SHUN AVOID BURKE
EVADE SHUNT CUTOFF DETOUR
CIRCUIT OUTFLANK
BYPATH LANE BYWAY UNDERWALK
BY-PRODUCT SCRAP SHORTS
EFFLUVIUM
BYWAY LANE PATH ALLEY BYPATH
BYWALK OUTWAY SIDEWAY
BYWORD AXIOM MOTTO BYNAME
DIVERB PHRASE SAYING NAYWORD
PROVERB NICKNAME REPROACH

C DO CEE DOH COCA CHARLIE
HUNDRED
CAAMA FOX ASSE SILVER
CAB FLY KAB TAXI ARABA ARANA
CABIN GHARRI CRAWLER HACKNEY
SHOWFUL TAXICAB COUPELET
MOTORCAB
(2-PONY —) KOSONG
(4-WHEELED —) BOUNDE BOUNDER
GROWLER
(HINDU —) JUDKA
(LOW-HUNG —) HERDIC
CABAL PLOT RING JUNTA PARTY
BRIGUE CLIQUE SCHEME SECRET
CHATTER CONSULT COUNCIL
DISPUTE FACTION TALKING
INTRIGUE
CABALISTIC MYSTIC
CABARET CAFE TAVERN
CABASSOU XENURUS
CABBAGE CAB CHOU CRIB KALE
WORT CROUT FILCH SAVOY STEAL
STOCK PECHAY PILFER TAILOR
BOWKAIL OXHEART PAKCHOI
PALMITO PURLOIN BORECOLE
COLEWORT CRUCIFER CULTIGEN
DRUMHEAD KOHLRABI KERGUELEN
(STUFFED —) HOLISHKES
(PL.) WORTS
CABBAGE BARK ANGELIM ANGELIN
CABBAGE SOUP SHCHI STCHI
SHTCHEE
CABBAGE STALK CASTOCK
CABDRIVER HACK MUSH CABBY
CABMAN COCHER MUSHER
COCHERO HACKMAN
CABIN BOX CAB COT DEN HUT CAVE
CELL CREW SHED TILT BOOTH
CHOZA COACH CUDDY FELZE
HOVEL LODGE SHACK BOHAWN
CABANA CASITA LITTER REFUGE
SALOON SHANTY WIGWAM
BEDROOM BOUDOIR COTTAGE
HUDDOCK MUDSILL
(— ON SHIP'S DECK) TEXAS
(DOUBLE —) SADDLEBAG
(RUSS. LOG —) IZBA
CABINET BOX BUHL CASE FILE SINK
AMBRY BAHUT BOARD CABIN CHEST
BAFFLE BUREAU CLOSET ICEBOX
ALMIRAH BOUDOIR COMMODE
CONSOLE COUNCIL ETAGERE
FREEZER JUKEBOX WHATNOT
CELLARET CUPBOARD MINISTRY
SHOWCASE VARGUENO MONOCLEID
(FILING —) MORGUE
CABLE GUY TOW BOOM COAX CORD
FAST JUNK LINK ROPE STAY WIRE
CABLET GANGER STRAND TETHER
COAXIAL GUNLINE SKYLINE
CATENARY HIGHLINE TELEGRAM
(— WITH EYE AT EACH END) STRAP
(— WOUND) KECKLING
(CHAIN —) BOOM
(DERRICK —) BACKSTAY
(SPLICED —) SHOT
(SUSPENDED —) ROPEWAY
CABLE CAR TELFER TELPHER
CABLED RUDENTED

CABMAN IZVOZCHIK
CABOCHON CAB SHELL CARBUNCLE
CABOODLE KIT LOT CALABASH
CABOOSE CAB CAR VAN CRIB HACK
BUGGY CRUMMY GALLEY PALACE
BOUNCER COOKROOM DOGHOUSE
CABRILLA CONY GAPER GROUPER
CABSTAND HASARD HAZARD
CABUYA PITEIRA
CACAO BROMA COCOA ARRIBA
COCKER CRIOLLO FORASTIER
CACHARI BODA
CACHE BURY HIDE DEPOT STASH
STORE SCREEN CONCEAL DEPOSIT
TREASURE
CACHET SEAL STAMP WAFER
ESSENCE KONSEAL
CACIQUE BUNYAH CASSICAN
HANGNEST
CACKEREL MENDOLE
CACKLE CANK CONK CLACK LAUGH
BABBLE GABBLE GAGGLE GIGGLE
GOSSIP KECKLE TITTER CHACKLE
CHATTER SNICKER TWADDLE
LAUGHTER
CACKLING GOOSE GREASER
CACOMISTLE CIVET ARCTOID
RINGTAIL BASSARISK
CACOON SEGRA SEQUA
CACOPHONOUS HARSH RAUCOUS
JANGLING STRIDENT
CACTUS BLEO DILDO NOPAL
BAVOSO CARDON CEREUS CHAUTE
CHENDE CHINOA CHOLLA COCHAL
MESCAL PEYOTE PEYOTL TASAJO
AIRAMPO BISAGRE BISNAGA
SAGUARO ALICOCHE CHICHIPE
PITAHAYA XEROPHIL
(— FRUIT) MUYUSA
CAD CUR BOOR CHUM HEEL CHURL
MUCKER RASCAL ROTTER BOUNDER
DASTARD ASSISTANT
CADASTRAL UNIT YOKE
CADAVER BODY STIFF CORPSE
CARCASS SUBJECT SKELETON
CADAVEROUS PALE GAUNT LIVID
PALLID GHASTLY HAGGARD
CADDIE NACKET
CADDIS FLY DUN CADEW SEDGE
CADBIT
CADDISWORM PIPER
CADDO ADAI TEXAS EYEISH HAINAI
KICHAI HASINAI
CADE LAMB SOCK
CADENCE BEAT FALL IAMB LILT
PACE TONE CLOSE METER METRE
SOUND SWING THROB DACTYL
IAMBUS JINGLE RHYTHM BACCHIC
ANAPAEST CLAUSULA MOVEMENT
MEDIATION
CADENZA MELISMA BARIOLAGE
CADET SON DODO GOAT PLEBE
YOUTH EMBRYO JUNIOR SERGEANT
CADGE BEG BOT BUM TIE BIND
HAWK CARRY MOOCH PEDDLE
SPONGE SCROUNGE
CADGER BOT DEALER HAWKER
CARRIER PACKMAN SPONGER
HUCKSTER

CADGY KEDGY MERRY WANTON
AMOROUS LUSTFUL CHEERFUL
MIRTHFUL
CADMUS (DAUGHTER OF —) INO
AGAVE SEMELE AUTONOE
(FATHER OF —) AGENOR
(MOTHER OF —) TELEPHASSA
(SISTER OF —) EUROPA
(SON OF —) POLYDORUS
(WIFE OF —) HARMONIA
CADRE CORE FRAME
CADUCEUS WAND STAFF SCEPTER
SCEPTRE KERYKEION
CAECUM TYPHLON
CAESURA REST STOP BREAK PAUSE
INTERVAL DIAERESIS
CAFE BARROOM CABARET
ESTAMINET
(— AU LAIT) ALESAN
CAFE CREME SUEDE
CAFETERIA AUTOMAT
CAFFEINE THEIN THEINE
CAGAYAN IBANAG
CAGE BOX CAR GIG MEW PEN COOP
CORF CRIB GOAL BRAKE CAVEA
GRATE HUTCH AVIARY BASKET
BUCKET CHAPEL ENCAGE FLIGHT
PRISON CHANTRY CONFINE
ENCLOSE LANTERN SHELTER
TUMBREL TUMBRIL CARRIAGE
ELEVATOR IMPRISON LAVARIUM
RETAINER SCAFFOLD STRAINER
(— FOR HAWKS) MEW
(— FOR HENS) CAVEY CAVIE
(— OF MINE SHAFT) GIG
(— OF TRAM) CABIN
(BIRD —) AVIARY PINJRA VOLARY
BIRDCAGE
(FIRE —) CRESSET
(LOBSTER —) CORF CREEL
CAGED PENT CAPTIVE
CAGER ONSETTER
CAGEY CAGY WARY COONY
CAGMAG KEGMEG
CAGOT AGOTE
CAHITA YAQUI
CAHOT PITCHHOLE
CAIMAN CAYMAN JACARE
ALLIGATOR
CAINGANG COROADO AWEIKOMA
CORONADO
CAIRN MAN PIKE MOUND RAISE
GALGAL CATSTONE STONEMAN
CAIRNGORM MORION SMOKESTONE
CAISSON BOX PONT CAMEL CHEST
WAGON COFFER PONTON SAUCER
CAMAILE CHAMBER LACUNAR
PONTOON
CAITIFF BASE MEAN VILE COWARD
WICKED CAPTIVE COWARDLY
PRISONER WRETCHED
CAJOLE COG CON JIG COAX FLAM
FLUM PALP WORD CARNY CHEAT
CURRY DECOY FRAIK INGLE JOLLY
TEASE CARNEY DELUDE ENTICE
FRAISE HUMBUG WHILLY BEGUILE
FLATTER PALAVER SOOTHER
TWEEDLE WHEEDLE BLANDISH
CAJOLERY FRAIK SOOTH TAFFY

BUTTER FRAISE DAUBERY FLATTERY
CAKE BAR BUN NUT WIG BAKE BALL
FLAE FOOL LUMP MASS MOLE TART
ARVAL BATTY BLOCK BOXTY COOKY
CRUST CUPID FADGE KYAAK SCONE
SHIVE TORTE WAFER WEDGE
BARKLE CIMBAL COOKIE DAMPER
ECLAIR GATEAU HALLAH HARDEN
KICHEL KUCHEN NACKET PARKIN
PASTRY POPLIN SIMNEL TABLET
WASTEL ASHCAKE BANNOCK
BROWNIE CAKETTE CARAWAY
CROZZLE CRUMPET CUPCAKE
FAIRING GALETTE HOECAKE
MANCHET NUTCAKE OATCAKE
PANCAKE PLASTER POPADAM
CHRIMSEL CLAPCAKE KUGELHOF
MADELINE MARZIPAN SEEDCAKE
SOLIDIFY SOULCAKE TORTILLA
TURNPIKE
(— OF CLAY) PLATTEN
(— OF MEAL) DODGER
(— OF RUBBER) BISCUIT
(CREOLE RICE —) CALA
(FANCY —) SUNKET
(FLAT —) PLATE BUNUELO GALETTE
PLACENT CHRIMSEL
(FOURTH PART OF —) FARL FARLE
(FRIED —) WONDER CRULLER
DOUGHNUT
(GINGER —) BOLIVAR
(GRIDDLE —) LATKE FLIPPER
FRITTER FLAPJACK
(HOLIDAY —) SIMNEL
(HONEY —) LEKACH
(LAMB AND WHEAT —) KIBBE
KIBBEH
(LEAVENED —) BAP
(NEW YEAR'S —) HAGMENA
HOGMANAY
(OIL —) GRIT POONAC
(POTATO —) FADGE
(PRESS —) CACHAZA
(RUM —) BABA
(SEED —) WIG SEEDCAKE
(TEA —) LUNN SCONE
(THIN —) WAFER JUMBLE BANNOCK
TORTILLA
(YEAST —) KOJI
(PL.) AMSATH COLYBA
CAKED CLIT
CAKE PULLER KNOCKER
CALABA BIRMA GALBA
CALABASH GOURD CURUBA JICARA
CALABASH TREE JICARA HIGUERO
CALABOOSE JUG BRIG JAIL PRISON
CABOOSE BASTILLE
CALABUR TREE CAPULI CAPULIN
SILKWOOD
CALAMANCO MANKIE
CALAMINE CADMIA
CALAMITOUS BAD SAD DIRE EVIL
BLACK FATAL BITTER DISMAL
TRAGIC WOEFUL ADVERSE BALEFUL
DIREFUL HAPLESS RUINOUS
UNHAPPY UNLUCKY GRIEVOUS
TRAGICAL WRETCHED
CALAMITY ILL WOE BLOW DOOM
EVIL RUIN SLAP HYDRA STORM

WRACK MISERY ONCOME SORROW
EXTREME ACCIDENT DISASTER
DISTRESS FATALITY JUDGMENT
MISCHIEF
CALAMONDIN ORANGE CALAMANSI
CALAMUS PEN CANE REED QUILL
ACORUS RATTAN ROTANG
CALANGAY ABACAY COCKATOO
CALASH CALESA GALECHE
CALCANEUM FIBULARE
HYPOTARSUS
CALCAR OVEN SPUR FURNACE
CALCARIUM PREHALLUX
CALCEOLARIA FAGELIA IONIDIUM
CALCIFY CRETIFY
CALCINING BURNING
CALCINO MUSCADINE
CALCITE APHRITE CALCSPAR
ALABASTER ARGENTINE HISLOPITE
CALCIUM LIME
CALCIUM CARBONATE WHITING
DRIPSTONE
CALCULATE AIM SUM CALK CAST
PLAN RATE TELL COUNT FRAME
THINK CIPHER DESIGN EXPECT
FIGURE NUMBER RECKON ACCOUNT
AVERAGE CALLATE COMPUTE
PREPARE CONSIDER FORECAST
ESTIMATE
(— BY ASTROLOGY) ERECT
CALCULATED COLD
CALCULATING COLD WISE BRITTLE
CAUTIOUS
CALCULATION CARE SHARE
CALCUL ACCOUNT CAUTION
WORKING CALCULUS FORECAST
HINDCAST PRUDENCE
(PL.) FIGURES
CALCULATOR TABLE ABACUS
ABACIST SOROBAN CALCULER
COMPUTER ISOGRAPH
CALCULUS STONE UROLITH
ANALYSIS
CALDRON POT RED VAT LEAD
ALFET BOILER KELDER KETTLE
TRIPOD VESSEL CALDERA
CAULDRON
CALENDAR DIARY ALMANAC
CALENDS JOURNAL KALENDS
REGISTER SCHEDULE
(PL.) FASTI
CALENDER TABBY SCHREINER
CALENDERER CANROYER
SMOOTHER
CALENDS K KAL
CALF CA BOB BOX BOY LEG BUSS
DOLT VEAL VEAU BOBBY BOSSY
BUNCH DOGIE MOGGY PODDY
RANNY SOOKY YOUTH MUSCLE
VEALER WEANER BULCHIN FATLING
SLEEPER CALFLING
(LIKE A —) VITULINE
(PREMATURE —) SLINK
(UNBRANDED —) LONGEAR
SLEEPER
(YEARLING —) BUD DAIRT
(YOUNG —) DEACON
(PL.) CAURE
CALF'S-FOOT JELLY SULZE
FISNOGA

CALFSKIN COROVA VELLUM
GRASSER TULCHAN VEALSKIN
CALIBER BORE RANK DEGREE
TALENT ABILITY BREADTH COMPASS
QUALITY CAPACITY DIAMETER
(HIGH —) STATURE
CALIBRATED BRIX BEAUME BALLING
CALICHE CALCRETE TEPETATE
NITRATINE
CALICO BLAY PINTO SALLO CHINTZ
SALLOO CROYDON SPOTTED
GOLDFISH
CALICO ASTER WISEWEED
CALICOBACK STINKBUG
CALICO BASS CRAPPIE BACHELOR
CALICUT KOZHIKODE

CALIFORNIA
CAPITAL: SACRAMENTO
COLLEGE: MILLS POMONA
WHITTIER
COUNTY: INYO KERN MONO NAPA
YOLO YUBA MARIN MODOC
COLUSA LASSEN MERCED
PLACER PLUMAS SHASTA
SOLANO SONOMA SUTTER
TEHAMA TULARE ALAMEDA
VENTURA SISKIYOU CALAVERAS
INDIAN: HUPA POMO YANA YUKI
KAROK MAIDU MIWOK WAPPO
WIYOT YUROK PATWIN SHASTA
TOLOWA YOKUTS CHUMASH
LUISENO SALINAN SERRANO
DIEGUENO
LAKE: MONO SODA EAGLE OWENS
TAHOE SALTON TULARE
ALMANOR BERRYESSA
MOUNTAIN: MUIR LASSEN SHASTA
WHITNEY
NAME: ELDORADO
PARK: LASSEN SEQUOIA
YOSEMITE
PRESIDENT: NIXON
PRISON: ALCATRAZ
RIVER: EEL MAD PIT KERN OWENS
PUTAH STONY FEATHER
KLAMATH RUBICON TRINITY
SACRAMENTO
STATE BIRD: QUAIL
STATE FLOWER: POPPY
STATE NICKNAME: GOLDEN
STATE TREE: REDWOOD
TOWN: LODI AZUSA CHICO CHINO
INDIO BLYTHE CARMEL COVINA
EUREKA FRESNO LOMPOC
MERCED OXNARD POMONA
SONOMA TULARE ALAMEDA
BURBANK GARDENA NEEDLES
SALINAS VALLEJO VISALIA
ALTADENA BERKELEY
PASADENA REDLANDS
CUCAMONGA
UNIVERSITY: USC UCLA CALTECH
STANFORD

CALIPER JENNY ODDLEGS CALIPERS
CALIPH ABU ALI BEKR IMAM OMAR
CALIF OTHMAN ABBASID UMAYYAD
CALK JAG NAP COPY CORK FILL

STOP CAULK CLOSE HORSE ROUGH
CAREEN CALTROP CHINTZE
OCCLUDE SILENCE
CALKING OAKUM
CALL HO KA BAN BID CRY CUP DUB
HOY SAY SEE CITE COOP HAIL JERK
NAME NOTE PAGE PIST ROUP STOP
TERM TOOT YELL BEDUB CLAIM
CLEPE CLOCK ELECT HALLO HIGHT
HOLLA PHONE ROUSE SHOUT
SPEAK STYLE UTTER VISIT VOUCH
WAKEN YODEL ACCUSE APPEAL
AROUSE BECALL CHANGE DEMAND
HALLOA HALLOO INVITE INVOKE
MUSTER QUETHE SUMMON TEKIAH
TERUAH YELPER ACCLAIM ADDRESS
APPOINT BEHIGHT BETITLE COLLECT
COMMAND CONVENE CONVOKE
DECLARE ENTITLE IMPEACH INQUIRE
INSTYLE MOUNTEE WHISTLE
ANNOUNCE APPELATE ASSEMBLE
NOMINATE PROCLAIM VOCATION
(— A BET) STAY
(— ALOUD) COUNT
(— BACK) RECALL REVOKE
(— COARSELY) ROOP ROUP
(— DOWN) BRAWL DEVOCATE
IMPRECATE
(— FOR HELP) SOS
(— FOR HOGS) SOOK SOOEY
(— FOR) CRY TAKE CLAIM EXACT
DEMAND DESIRE COLLECT SOLICIT
(— FORTH) STIR EVOKE ELICIT
INDUCE INVOKE ATTRACT SUGGEST
(— HOUNDS) LIFT
(— IN ANGER) GREET
(— IN CHILDRENS' GAMES) FAN FEN
FIN VENTS
(— IN MARBLES) DUBS
(— INTO QUESTION) IMPUGN
(— LOUDLY) CRY HAIL ACCLAIM
(— MAN BY MAN) ARRAY
(— ON TELEPHONE) BUZZ
(— OUT) HAIL LURE ASCRY EVOKE
HALLO GOLLAR GOLLER HOLLER
HULLOO
(— TO ACCOUNT) AREASON
CONTROL
(— TO ARMS) ALARM ALARUM
RAPPEL
(— TO BELLBOY) FRONT
(— TO CAT) CHEET
(— TO COURT) ARRAIGN
(— TO COWS) SOOK COBOSS
SOOKIE
(— TO FOOD) SOSS
(— TO HORSE) HIE HUP WAY PROO
(— TO MIND) CITE MING RECORD
BETHINK REDOLLECT
(— TO PRAYER) AZAN
(— TO READINESS) ALERT
(— TO SPARROW) PHIPE PHIPPE
(— TO WITNESS) APPEAL
(— UPON) ASK SEE CITE GREDE
HALSE BECALL DEPOSE ENGAGE
SUMMON ADDRESS BESEECH
IMPLORE
(BIRD'S —) WEET
(BOATSWAIN'S —) WINDING

(BRIDGE —) DOUBLE
(BUGLE —) POST HALLALI STABLES
(CLOSE —) TOUCH
(DUCK —) SQUAWKER
(FRIENDLY —) CEILIDH
(HUNTING —) RECHATE RECHEAT
(MORNING —) MATIN
(NAUTICAL —) AHOY
(SHEPHERD'S —) OVEY
(SPORTSMAN'S —) HOICKS YOICKS
HALLALI
(SQUARE DANCE —) GEE HAW
(STAGE TRUMPET —) SENNET
SINNET
(TRUMPET —) BERLOQUE
CALLA LILY DRAGON MAYFLOWER
CALLBOY FRONT CALLER HALLBOY
CALLER FLOORMAN
CALLIGRAPHER PENMAN WRITER
COPYIST ENGROSSER
CALLIGRAPHY LETTERING
CHIROGRAPHY
CALLING ART JOB WAY CALL HAIL
RANK TRADE CAREER METIER
NAMING OUTCRY MISSION MYSTERY
PURSUIT STATION SUMMONS
WARNING BUSINESS FUNCTION
POSITION SHOUTING VOCATION
CALLIOPE (FATHER OF —) JUPITER
(MOTHER OF —) MNEMOSYNE
(SON OF —) ORPHEUS
CALLIRRHOE (FATHER OF —)
OCEANUS
(HUSBAND OF —) TROS ALCMAEON
(SON OF —) ILUS GANYMEDE
ASSARACUS
CALLISTO (FATHER OF —) LYCAON
(SON OF —) ARCAS
CALLITHRIX HAPALE JACCHUS
CALLOP YELLOWBELLY
CALLOSAL TRABAL
CALLOSITY SEG CALLUS SITFAST
TYLOSIS CHESTNUT
CALLOUS HARD HORNY TOUGH
BRAWNY OBTUSE SEARED TORPID
WAUKIT DEDOLENT OBDURATE
CALLOUSED BRAWNY
CALLOW BALD BARE CRUDE GREEN
SQUAB MARSHY IMMATURE
UNFORMED YOUTHFUL
CALLUS SEG POROMA TYLOMA
CALLOUS
CALM LAY LEE COOL DILL EASY
EVEN FAIR FLAT HUSH LOWN LULL
MEES MILD REST SOFT STAY ABATE
ALLAY CHARM LEVEL LITHE LOUND
MEASE PEACE QUELL QUIET SMOLT
SOBER STILL STOIC STREW DOCILE
GENTLE GLASSY IRENIC PACIFY
PLACID SEDATE SERENE SETTLE
SLATCH SLIGHT SMOOTH SOOTHE
STEADY APPEASE ASSUAGE
CALMATO COMPOSE GLACIAL
HALCYON MOLLIFY PACIFIC PATIENT
PLACATE QUALIFY QUIETEN
RESTFUL UNMOVED CALMNESS
COMPOSED DECOROUS PEACEFUL
PLACABLE RESTRAIN SERENITY
TRANQUIL UNRUFFLE

(INTERNAL —) HARMONY
(NOT —) BOISTEROUS
CALMLY COOLY COOLLY STILLY
CALMNESS CALM LULL POISE
PHLEGM REPOSE SERENE ATARAXY
COOLNESS SERENITY STILLNESS
CALNO KULLANI
CALOMEL TURPETH
CALORIC THERMOGEN
CALORIE THERM THERME
CALQUE LOANSHIFT
CALTROP CROWTOE GALTRAP
BULLHEAD CROWFOOT
CALUMNIATE BLOT SLUR TEEN
BELIE LIBEL ACCUSE ATTACK
BEFOUL DEFAME MALIGN REVILE
VILIFY ASPERSE BLACKEN SLANDER
TRADUCE
CALUMNIATION SATIRE ASPERSION
CALUMNY SLUR DEPRAVE OBLOQUY
CALVA CALOTTE SINCIPUT
CALVARIA SKULLCAP
CALVARY GOLGOTHA
CALVE FRESHEN
CALVINIST GENEVAN GOMARIAN
CALYCULUS CELL CALYX
CALYPTER ALULA SQUAMA
CALYPTRA CAP VEIL EPIGONIUM
CALYX CUP POP HULL HUSK LEAF
CULOT SEPAL SHUCK
CAM COG AWRY LOBE TRIG ASKEW
CATCH SNAIL WIPER LIFTER TAPPET
CROOKED TRIPPET KNOCKOFF
PERVERSE ROLLBACK
CAMACHILE INGA HUAMUCHIL
CAMAGON MABOLO
CAMAS LOBELIA
CAMBER SET ARCH SWEEP
ROUNDUP CROSSFALL

CAMBODIA

CAPE: SAMIT
CAPITAL: PNOMPENH PHNOMPENH
COIN: RIEL PUTTAN PIASTER
GULF: SIAM
LAKE: TONLESAP
MOUNTAIN: PAN AURAL
MOUNTAINS: DANGREK
CARDAMOM ELEPHANT
NAME: CAMBOJA CAMBODGE
NATIVE: CHAM KHMER
RIVER: SAN SEN BASSAC MEKONG
PORONG SREPOK SEKHONG
TONLESAP
RUINS: ANGKORWAT
TOWN: REAM TAKEO KAMPOT
KRATIE PURSAT KOHNIEH
KRACHEH ROVIENG SAMRONG
PNOMPENH SISOPHON
WEIGHT: MACE TAEL

CAME BAND CALM
CAMEL COLT OONT DELOUL
DROMED FENDER HAGEEN MEHARI
CAISSON TYLOPOD BACTRIAN
RUMINANT DROMEDARY
CAMEL GRASS SCHOENANTH
CAMELLIA JAPONICA
CAMEL LIP CHILOMA

CAMELOPARD GIRAFFE
CAMEO GEM GAMAHE CAMAIEU
CARVING PHALERA RELIEVO
ANAGLYPH
CAMERA KINO KODAK CHAMBER
MINICAM PANORAM ENLARGER
MINIATURE VERASCOPE
(— TUBE) VIDICON
CAMERAMAN LENSMAN
CAMEROON (CAPITAL OF —)
YAOUNDE
(RIVER OF —) DJA NYONG SANAGA
(TOWN OF —) POLI YOKO BAFIA
DOUALA
CAMISOLE WAISTCOAT
CAMLET MOHAIR BARRACAN
CAMOMILE OXEYE MORGAN
CAMOUFLAGE FAKE HIDE DAZZLE
MUFFLE SCREEN CONCEAL
DISGUISE
CAMOUFLET STIFLER
CAMP TAN PEST TENT DOUAR ETAPE
HORDE SIEGE TABOR CASTLE
LAAGER SUGARY BIVOUAC
HUTMENT LODGING MAHALLA
PALANKA ZAREEBA QUARTERS
(— OUT) MAROON OUTLIE
(HOBO —) JUNGLE
(LUMBER —) CHANTIER
CAMPA ANDA ANDI ANTI
CAMPAIGN BLITZ DRIVE PLAIN
WHOOP CANVASS CRUSADE
JOURNEY SERVICE SOLICIT
WARFARE
CAMPANA GUTTA
CAMPANERO COTINGA ARAPUNGA
BELLBIRD COTINGID
CAMPANILE TOWER BELFRY
CLOCHER STEEPLE CARILLON
CAMPESTRAL AGRARIAN
CAMPHOR ASARONE BORNEOL
MENTHOL
(ANISE —) ANETHOLE
CAMPHOR TREE KADUR KAPOR
CAMPING BIVOUAC
CAMPION ROBIN COWBELL
CAMPUS GATE QUAD YARD FIELD
CAN CUP JUG MAY MOW POT TIN
ABLE FIRE JAIL BILLY CADDY
COULD ESHIN OILER SHALL SKILL
BOTTLE VESSEL ABILITY BOMBARD
CANIKIN CAPABLE CREAMER
DISMISS GROWLER PIPETTE
BILLYCAN CONSERVE PRESERVE
(— FOR LIQUOR) JACK
(— ON WHEELS) DANDY
(BULGED —) SWELL FLIPPER
(DEFECTIVE —) SPRINGER
(LEAKY —) LEAKER
(MILK —) CHURN
(TIN —) DESTROYER
(TRASH —) DUSTBIN
CANAANITE ARKITE HIVITE AMORITE
HIVVITE JEBUSITE
CANACE (BROTHER OF —)
MACAREUS
(FATHER OF —) AEOLUS
(MOTHER OF —) ENARETE
(SON OF —) TRIOPAS

CANADA
BAY: JAMES HUDSON UNGAVA
GEORGIAN
CAPITAL: OTTAWA
INDIAN: CREE COMOX HAIDA
NISKA SARSI STALO MICMAC
NAHANE NOOTKA SARCEE
CARRIER NANAIMO SEKANEE
SHUSWAP SONGISH TAHLTAN
ALGONKIN COWICHON LILLOOET
MALECITE SQUAMISH TSATTINE
ISLAND: READ BANKS BYLOT
COATS DEVON SABLE BAFFIN
MANSEL VICTORIA ANTICOSTI
VANCOUVER
ISLANDS: PARRY BELCHER
BATHURST MAGDALEN
LAKE: BEAR CREE GARRY RAINY
SLAVE LOUISE SIMCOE ABITIBI
DUBAWNT NIPIGON KOOTENAY
OKANAGAN NIPISSING
MEASURE: MINOT PERCH ARPENT
CHAINON
MOUNTAIN: LOGAN ROYAL
ROBSON TREMBLANT
MOUNTAIN RANGE: SKEENA
CARIBOO STELIAS COLUMBIA
LAURENTIAN
NATIVE: CANUCK
PARK: YOHO BANFF ACADIA
JASPER
PENINSULA: GASPE BOOTHIA
MELVILLE
PROVINCE: QUEBEC ALBERTA
ONTARIO MANITOBA
NOVASCOTIA NEWFOUNDLAND
NEWBRUNSWICK SASKATCHEWAN
PROVINCIAL CAPITAL: QUEBEC
REGINA STJOHN HALIFAX
TORONTO EDMONTON VICTORIA
WINNIPEG CHARLOTTETOWN
RIVER: HAY RED BACK PEEL
PEACE SLAVE YUKON FRASER
NELSON OTTAWA SKEENA
THELON PETAWAWA SAGUENAY
MACKENZIE RICHELIEU
STRAIT: CABOT DEASE HECATE
HUDSON GEORGIA
SYMBOL: MAPLELEAF
TERRITORY: YUKON
TOWN: HULL BANFF LAVAL
GUELPH OSHAWA REGINA
SARNIA CALGARY HALIFAX
MONCTON NANAIMO SUDBURY
TORONTO WELLAND WINDSOR
KINGSTON MONTREAL VICTORIA
WINNIPEG SASKATOON
VANCOUVER
UNIVERSITY: MCGILL DALHOUSIE

CANADA BLUEBERRY SOURTOP
CANADA GOOSE HONKER BUSTARD
OUTARDE
CANADA JAY MEATBIRD MOOSEBIRD
CANADA LYNX PISHU LUCIVEE
CANADA PLUM CHENEY
CANADA VIOLET JUNEFLOWER

CANADIAN CANUCK
CANAILLE MOB FLOUR RABBLE
DOGGERY RIFFRAFF
CANAL CUT CANO DUCT LODE PIPE
SHAT TUBE BAYOU DITCH DRAIN
FOSSA GRAFF KLONG SCALA ZANJA
ESTERO GROOVE KENNEL STRAIT
TRENCH VAGINA ACEQUIA APHODUS
CHANNEL CONDUIT FOREBAY
RACEWAY SHIPWAY TOWPATH
AQUEDUCT EMISSARY IRRIGANT
MILLRACE PROSODUS VOLKMANN
(— LABORER) NAVIGATOR
(ALIMENTARY —) GUT ENTERON
INTESTINE
(ANATOMICAL —) SCALA MEATUS
(CARINAL —) LACUNA
CANARD DUCK HOAX RUMOR
GRAPEVINE
CANARY DICKY FRILL LIZARD
ROLLER CAYENNE CHOPPER
JONQUIL SQUEALER
(— HYBRID) MULE

CANARY ISLANDS
CAPITAL: SANTACRUZ
ISLAND: ROCA CLARA FERRO
LOBOS PALMA ROCCA GOMERA
HIERRO INFERNO GRACIOSA
TENERIFE LANZAROTTE
MEASURE: FANEGADA
MOUNTAIN: TEYDE LACRUZ
ELCUMBRE TENERIFE
PROVINCE: LASPALMAS
TOWN: LAGUNA ARRECIFE
VALVERDE

CANARY MOSS CORKIR
CANASTA SAMBA BOLIVIA
CANCEL BLOT DASH DELE OMIT
UNDO VENT WIPE ANNUL BELAY
CROSS ERASE QUASH REMIT SCORE
SCRUB DELETE EFFACE KILLER
RECALL REMOVE REVOKE STROKE
ABOLISH DESTROY EXPUNGE
NULLIFY RESCIND RETRACT
SCRATCH SUBLATE UNWRITE
ABROGATE
CANCELER BUMPER STAMPER
CANCELLATION GRID CANCEL
REVOKE SURRENDER
CANCER WOLF KASHYAPA
CANCERWORT FLUELLIN
CANDAREEN FAN FEN
CANDELABRUM PHAROS MENORAH
GIRANDOLE
CANDID FAIR JUST OPEN PURE
BLUNT CLEAR FRANK NAIVE PLAIN
HONEST ARTLESS JANNOCK
SINCERE EVENDOWN INNOCENT
SPLENDID STRAIGHT
CANDIDATE LEGACY ESQUIRE
NOMINEE ASPIRANT GRADUAND
PROSPECT
CANDIED GLACE
CANDLE DIP WAX GLIM SIZE SLUT
LIGHT SPERM TAPER TOLLY BOUGIE
CIERGE MORTAR PLANET SHAMUS

SLUSHY TALLOW TORTIS CANDELA
PERCHER PRICKET
(IMITATION —) JUDAS
(SQUARE —) QUARRIER
CANDLEFISH SKIL EULACHON
HOOLAKIN OOLACHAN SKILFISH
SABLEFISH
CANDLEHOLDER SPIDER
CANDLEMAKER CHANDLER
TALLOWER
CANDLEMAS TERM MARYMASS
CANDLENUT AMA LAMA BIABO
KUKUI IGUAPE KEMIRI LUMBANG
ABURAGIRI
CANDLESNUFFER DOUTER
CANDLESTAND TORCHERE
CANDLESTICK BUGIA DYKER JESSE
STICK CRUSIE LAMPAD MORTAR
SCONCE PASCHAL PRICKET
CHANDLER DICERION FLAMBEAU
STANDARD TRIKERION
CANDLEWICK MATCH SNAST
SHROUD
(CHARRED PART OF —) SNOT
SNUFF SNUFFING
CANDLEWOOD CIRIO OCOTILLO
TABANUCO
CANDOR PURITY FAIRNESS
KINDNESS INTEGRITY
CANDY DROP DUMP KISS PIPE ROCK
CREAM CRISP DULCE FUDGE GLACE
GUNDY LOLLY SPICE SQUIB SWEET
TAFFY BONBON COMFIT HUMBUG
NOGADA NOUGAT PATTIE PENIDE
BRITTLE CANDIEL CARAMEL
CONGEAL FLATTER FONDATE
GUMDROP SWEETEN SWEETIE
TORRONE ALPHENIG LOLLIPOP
STICKJAW
(PL.) CUTS CONFETTI
CANDYTUFT CRUCIFER
(PL.) IBERIS
CANE ROD BEAT CRAB DART FLOG
PIPE REED STEM TUBE WAND WHIP
BIRCH GIBBY GUNDY LANCE STAFF
STICK SWISH TOLLY WADDY
BAMBOO JAMBEE KEBBIE PUNISH
RATTAN CALAMUS HICKORY
KIPPEEN MALACCA SCOURGE
STADDLE TICKLER WHANGEE
GIBSTAFF
(BLACK —) JAPAN
(END OF —) FRAZE
(SPLIT —) CANEWORK
CANELLA WHITEWOOD
CANELO CIXO
CANESCENT HOARY
CANFIELD KLONDIKE
CANICULA SIRIUS
CANINE CUR DOG FOX PUP FISC
TUSH WOLF DOGLY DOGLIKE
LANIARY
CANING RATTAN BIRCHING
CANISTEL TIES EGGFRUIT
CANNA ACHIRA GOLDBIRD
CANNABIS BHANG GANJA GUAZA
GUNJA HEMPWORT
(— TOPS) TAKROURI
CANNEL BONE FURCULE

CANNEL COAL AMPELITE
CANNER CANMAN TINNER
CANNIBAL WINDIGO LESTRIGON
THYESTEAN
CANNON BIT EAR GUN BASE SHOT
TUBE ASPIC CRACK MOYEN PIECE
SACRE SACRI SAKER SHANK SLING
THIEF BICORN CURTAL FALCON
FOWLER JINGAL LICORN MORTAR
POTGUN BASTARD BOMBARD
BULLDOG CHAMBER HANDGUN
LOMBARD MOYENNE ROBINET
SERPENT STINGER UNICORN
BASILISK CULVERIN HOWITZER
MURDERER OERLIKON ORDNANCE
SPITFIRE ZUMBOORUK
(— OF BELL) EAR
(CARRIAGE OF —) NADRIER
(DISCHARGE OF —) TIRE
(DUMMY —) QUAKER
CANNONBALL GUN PILL BULLET
GUNSTONE
CANNON BOSS TRUNNION
CANNON PLUG TAMPION
CANNOT CANT CANNA DONNA
DOWNA UNABLE
CANNY SLY COZY SNUG WARY WILY
WISE COONY LUCKY PAWKY QUIET
CLEVER FRUGAL GENTLE SHREWD
STEADY CAREFUL CUNNING
KNOWING PRUDENT QUIETLY
THRIFTY CAUTIOUS SKILLFUL
WATCHFUL
CANOE AMA KIAK LISI PAHI PROA
WAKA AOTEA ARAWA BANCA BIRCH
BONGO BUNGO CANKA KAYAK
KOLEK PRAHU SKIFF TONEE UMIAK
VINTA WAAPA BAIDAR BALLAM
BAROTO CORIAL CUNNER DUGOUT
OOMIAK PAOPAO PITPAN PUNGEY
TAINUI TROUGH ALMADIA BIDARKA
BUCKEYE CANADER CASCARA
CORACLE CURIARA CURRANE
HOROUTA LAKATOI PIRAGUA
PIROGUE BALANGAY BARANGAY
FALTBOAT FOLDBOAT MONOXYLE
TAKITUMU THAMAKAU TSUKUPIN
WOODSKIN
CANON FEN LAW CODE FUGA HYMN
LAUD LIST RULE SONG AXIOM
GORGE GULCH MODEL NODUS
TABLE TENET ACTION DECREE
GNOMON LIBRARY PRECEPT
STATUTE DECISION STAGIARY
STANDARD
(BODY OF —S) CHAPTER
CANONICAL CANONIC ACCEPTED
ORTHODOX
(NOT —) APOCHRYPHAL
CANOPY SKY CEIL COPE DAIS HOOD
TILT CHUPA CROWN HOVEL SHADE
STATE VAULT AWNING BUBBLE
CELURE ESTATE FINIAL GABLET
HUPPAH SHADOW TESTER CEILING
HEAVENS MARQUEE SHELTER
SPARVER BASILICA CIBORIUM
COVERING OVERWOOD PAVILION
SEMIANNA
(— ABOVE THRONE) STATE

(— FOR LIVESTOCK) HOVEL
(— OF ALTAR) CIBORIUM
(— OF HEAVEN) VAULT
(— OVER BROODER) HOVER
(BED —) TESTER SPARVER
(HEARSE —) MAJESTY
CANT TIP COAX HEEL LEAN LIST
NOOK SING TILT TURN ARGOT
BEVEL CHANT DRIFT FLASH HIELD
LINGO LUSTY MERRY NICHE PITCH
SHARE SLANG SLANT SLOPE WHINE
CAREEN CASTER CORNER INTONE
JARGON LIVELY PATOIS PATTER
SNIVEL AUCTION DIALECT INCLINE
PORTION SINGING WHEEDLE
CHEERFUL PRETENSE VIGOROUS
CANTABRIGIAN CANTAB
CAMBRIDGE
CANTALA MAGUEY
CANTANKEROUS ILL CURSED
CUSSED ORNERY KICKISH
CANKERED CONTRARY PERVERSE
CANTATA SERENATA VILLANCICO
CANTEEN BAR FLASK BAZAAR
CANTINA
CANTER JOG RUN GAIT LOPE PACE
RACK AUBIN ROGUE BEGGAR
WHINER SNUFFLER VAGABOND
CANTERBURY BELL MILKWORT
CAMPANULA
CANTICLE ODE HYMN LAUD SONG
CANTO ANTHEM CANTIC HIRMOS
BRAVURA
CANTILEVER LOOKOUT SEMIBEAM
CARTOUCHE
CANTING CANT PIOUS SNUFFLING
CANTO AIR FIT BOOK DUAN PACE
SONG VERSE MELODY PASSUS
CANTON ANGLE UNION CORNER
VOLOST PORTION QUARTER
SECTION DISTRICT DIVISION
(HALF —) ESQUIRE
CANTOR HAZAN HAZZAN SINGER
CHANTER CHAZZAN SOLOIST
PSALMIST
CANVAS FLY PAT DUCK GLUT PATA
SAIL TARP TENT TEWK CLOTH
COAST SCRIM TOILE VITRY BURLAP
LINING MUSLIN PICTURE POLDAVY
SCUTAGE DRABBLER PAINTING
VANDELAS
(— FOR CONVEYING GRAIN) APRON
(OLD CONDEMNED —) RUMBOWLINE
(RUBBERIZED —) TOSH
(STUFFED —) BOLSTER
(TARRED —) COAT
CANVASBACK CAN DIVER CHEVAL
DUCKER POCHARD BULLNECK
CANVASS BEAT CASE DRUM HAWK
POLL SIFT RANDY STUDY DEBATE
PEDDLE SEARCH AGITATE DISCUSS
EXAMINE SOLICIT TROUNCE
CAMPAIGN CONSIDER
CANVASSER AGENT POLLER
ROADMAN
CANYON CAJON CHASM GORGE
GULCH ARROYO CANADA RAVINE
CAOUTCHOUC RUBBER ELATERITE
CAP CUP FEZ HAT LID PAD POT TAJ

TAM TIP TOP ACME COIF CORK
COWL DINK DOME DOWD ETON
GAGE HOOD HURE JOAN KEEP KEPI
MATE SHOE SHOW TOPI BERET
BOINA BUSBY CHIEF COVER CROWN
EXCEL FANON GALEA HOUVE KULAH
MATCH MUTCH OUTDO PHANO
PUNCH SEIZE SHAKO TOPEE TRUMP
ARREST BARRAD BARRET BEANIE
BIGGIN BIRRUS BONNET CALPAC
CLIMAX COCKUP CORNET GALERA
HELMET HUBCAP JINNAH MOBCAP
PILEUS PINNER PRIMER PUZZLE
SUMMIT TABARD TURBAN ALOPEKE
BIRETTA CALOTTE CAMAURO
CAPITAL CEREVIS CHAPEAU
CHECHIA CLOSURE COMMODE
FERRULE FLATCAP FORAGER
HEADCAP OVERLIE OVERTOP
PERPLEX PETASOS PILLBOX PILLION
SOWBACK SURPASS THIMBLE
TURNCAP ACROSOME BALMORAL
BEARSKIN BYCOCKET CAPELINE
COONSKIN ELECTRIC FOLLOWER
HEADGEAR PHRYGIUM SKEWBACK
SKULLCAP SURPRISE TARBOOSH
(— FOR PILEDRIVER) PUNCH
(— OF FLAGSTAFF) TRUCK
(— OF FOAM) HOOD
(— OF PYXIDIUM) LID
(— OF WATCH) DOME CROWN
(BISHOP'S —) HURA HURE
(HUNTER'S —) MONTERA MONTERO
(ICE —) BRAE CALOTTE
(JESTER'S —) COXCOMB FOOLSCAP
(MILITARY —) KEPI BUSBY SHAKO
(MOUNTAIN —) SCALP
(PERCUSSION —) CAPSULE
(PERUVIAN —) CHULLO
(POPE'S —) CAMAURO
(ROOT —) CALYPTRA
(WOMAN'S —) CAUL DOWD JOAN
KELL MUTCH COMMODE VOLUPER
BIGGONET
(WOOLEN —) BOINA TOQUE TUQUE
CAPABILITY STROIL ABILITY
CONDUCT FACULTY POTENCY
CAPACITY
CAPABLE APT CAN FIT ABLE GOOD
ADEPT CAPAX FENDY TIGHT EXPERT
SKILLED POWERFUL
(— OF BEING DEFENDED) TENABLE
(— OF BEING DRAWN OUT) DUCTILE
(— OF BEING SEVERED) SEVTILE
(— OF BEING THROWN) MISSILE
(— OF BEING UTTERED) EFFABLE
(— OF FLYING) VOLANT
(— OF SUBMISSION) AMENABLE
(NORMALLY —) ABOUT
CAPACIOUS FULL SIDE WIDE AMPLE
BROAD LARGE ROOMY GOODLY
ROOMFUL CAPTIOUS ROOMSOME
SPACIOUS
CAPACITOR CONDENSER
CAPACITY BACK BENT BIND DISH
GIFT GIVE SIZE TURN BLAST FLAIR
FORCE KNACK MODEL POWER SKILL
SPACE AGENCY BOTTOM BURDEN
ENERGY ENGINE EXTENT GENIUS

MODULE SPREAD TALENT VOLUME
ABILITY CALIBER CALIBRE CONTENT
FACULTY FITNESS QUALITY
APTITUDE INSTINCT STRENGTH
INFLUENCE
(— FOR EATING) STROKE
(— FOR ENDURANCE) STAY
(— FOR HIGHER KNOWLEDGE)
INTELLECT
(— OF LATHE) SWING
(— OF SHIP) BURDEN
(CIVIL —) CAPUT
(INNATE —S) STAMINA
(INTELLECTUAL —) BROW
(LOAD-PULLING —) DRAFT DRAUGHT
(MENTAL —S) BELFRY
(SPECIAL —) KNACK
(UNIT OF —) MUD MUID LAGEN
KISHEN MEDIMNUS KILDERKIN
(UNLIMITED —) INFINITY
CAPANEUS (FATHER OF —)
HIPPONOUS BELLEROPHON
(SLAYER OF —) JUPITER
(WIFE OF —) EVADNE
CAPARISON DECK TRAP HOUSE
COVERING TRAPPING
CAPE RAS COPE GAPE HEAD HOOK
LOOK NECK NESS TANG WRIT
AMICE CAPPA CLOAK FICHU ORALE
POINT SAGUM STARE STOLE TALMA
BERTHA BYRRUS CABAAN CHAPEL
DOLMAN MANTLE SONTAG TABARD
TIPPET LEATHER MANTEEL
MOZETTA SALIENT TANJONG
VANDYKE CIRCULAR COLLARET
HEADLAND LAMBSKIN MANTILLA
PELERINE SEALSKIN RAINPROOF
(— OF STRAW) MINO
(BULLFIGHTER'S —) CAPA
(DRESSING —) TOILET
(FEATHER —) AHUULA
(HOODED —) HUKE DOMINO
(LACE OR SILK —) VISITE
(LOW —) TANG
(PAPAL —) FANO FANON FANUM
ORALE PHANO
(RAIN —) CAPOTE
CAPE ANTEATER AARDVARK
CAPE ARMADILLO PANGOLIN
CAPE GOOSEBERRY POHA
CAPE HEN STINKER STINKPOT
CAPELIN SMELT ICEFISH
CAPE PIGEON PINTADO
CAPE POLECAT ZORIL MUISHOND
CAPER HOP JET DIDO HOIT JUMP
LEAP ROMP SKIP SKIT ANTIC BRANK
DANCE FLING FLISK FRISK PRANK
SAUCE SHRUB CAVORT CURVET
FRISCO FROLIC GAMBOL GAMOND
PRANCE SPRING TITTUP VAGARY
CORSAIR COURANT FRISCAL
GAMBADO PRANKLE CAPRIOLE
MARIGOLD
(— ABOUT) FLING CAVORT
(SILLY —) SHINE
CAPER SPURGE CATEPUCE
CAPE TOWN BOVENLAND
CAPHITE KIST
CAPITAL CAP CASH CITY FUND

GOOD LIMA MAIN RARE SEAT BASIC
CHIEF FATAL GREAT MAJOR MONEY
MUANG STOCK VITAL DEADLY
HEADLY IMPOST LETTER LISBON
MORTAL PRIMAL UNCIAL WEALTH
CENTRAL CHATTEL DRESDEN
LEADING RADICAL SERIOUS
WEIGHTY CABECERA CATALLUM
CHAPITER DOSSERET SWINGING
(— OF HEAVEN) AMARAVATI
(— OF HELL) PANDEMONIUM
(GAMBLER'S —) STAKE
(INADEQUATE —) SHOESTRING
CAPITATUM MAGNUM
CAPITELLUM KNOP
CAPITOL STATEHOUSE
CAPITOLINE SATURNIAN
CAPITULATION MUNICH TREATY
CAPITULUM HEAD KNOP
ANTHODIUM
CAPOTE HOOD CAPPO CLOAK
BONNET MANTLE TOPPER
CAPPER CORKER SEALER STEERER
CAPPY TALLOWY
CAPRICE FAD TOY KINK MOOD WHIM
ANTIC BRAID CRANK FANCY FREAK
HUMOR QUIRK CHANGE MAGGOT
NOTION SPLEEN TEMPER VAGARY
WHIMSY BOUTADE CONCEIT
CROCHET IMPULSE TANTRUM
WHIMSEY
CAPRICIOUS DIZZY DODDY FLUKY
MOODY CHANCY FICKLE FITFUL
KITTLE PLATTY WANTON COMICAL
ERRATIC FLIGHTY MAGGOTY
MOONISH PEEVISH VAGRANT
WAYWARD EPISODAL FANCIFUL
FREAKISH HUMOROUS SKITTISH
UNSTEADY VARIABLE VOLATILE
CROTCHETY FANTASTIC VAGARIOUS
CAPRICIOUSNESS FREAK
CAPRICORN GOAT
CAPRIPEDE SATYR
CAPRYL RUTYL DECANOYL
CAPSHEAF CAP HOOD
CAPSICUM AJI PEPPER
(— SAUCE) TABASCO
CAPSID MIRID
CAPSIZE COUP KEEL PURL UPSET
WRONG OVERTURN
CAPSTAN CRAB DRUM DANDY HOIST
LEVER NIGGER CYLINDER WINDLASS
CAPSTONE LECH TOPSTONE
CAPSULE CAP POD URN BOLL CASE
CYST PILL SEED PEARL PERLE
SHELL THECA WAFER AMPULE
BARROW CACHET OOCYST SHEATH
AMPOULE EYEBALL OTOCYST
SEEDBOX SILIQUE VANILLA
PERICARP PYXIDIUM
CAPTAIN BO BOH BAAS HEAD JOAB
RAIS REIS BARAK CHIEF LEADER
MASTER NAAMAN SOTNIK CAPITAN
FOREMAN HEADMAN MANAGER
PATROON SKIPPER FLUELLEN
GOVERNOR
(— OF CAVALRY) RITMASTER
(— OF CRICKET TEAM) SKIPPER
(— OF CURLING TEAM) SKIP

(— OF PRIVATEER) CAPER
(— OF SHIP) WAFTER
(STRICT —) SUNDOWNER
CAPTION TITLE LEADER LEGEND
CUTLINE HEADING SUBHEAD
CITATION HEADLINE SUBTITLE
CAPTIOUS CRAFY TESTY CRAFTY
SEVERE CARPING CYNICAL FRETFUL
PEEVISH TETTISH ALLURING
CATCHING CAVILING CONTRARY
CRITICAL
CAPTIOUSLY TUTLY
CAPTIVATE WIN TAKE CATCH
CHARM ALLURE ENAMOR PLEASE
RAVISH SUBDUE ATTRACT BEWITCH
CAPTIVE CAPTURE ENCHANT
ENTHRALL OVERTAKE SURPRISE
CAPTIVATED EPRIS EPRISE CAPTIVE
CAPTIVATING TAKING KILLING
WINNING WINSOME CATCHING
CAPTIVE SLAVE DANIEL ENAMOR
THRALL BRISEIS CAITIFF PRISONER
CAPTIVITY BOND IRON CHAINS
DURESS BONDAGE SERFDOM
SLAVERY
CAPTOR TAKER VICTOR CATCHER
CAPTURE BAG COP FIX GET NAB
NET WIN FALL FANG GRAB HOOK
LAND PREY SNIB TAKE TRAP TREE
CARRY CATCH FORCE PRIZE PURSE
RAVEN SEIZE SWOOP ARREST
COLLAR CORRAL ENTRAP GOBBLE
OBTAIN PIRACY REDUCE TAKING
CAPTIVE LOWBELL SEIZURE
WINNING EXCHANGE SURPRISE
UNDERNIM
(— BACKGAMMON PIECE) HIT
(— BIRDS) TOODLE
(— GAME) SATCHEL
(— OF ALL PRIZES) SWEEP
(— TROUT) TICKLE
CAPUCHIN MONKEY CAY SAI
CEPID SAJOU WEEPER SAPAJOU
CAPULIN CEREZA
CAPYBARA CAVY CARPINCHO
CAR BOX BUS PIG AUTO BOGY BUNK
DOLL DRAG DUMP GRIP JEEP RATH
TRAM ZULU BOGEY COACH DINER
DUMMY GURRY HUTCH JIMMY
RATHA SEDAN STOCK TRAIN TRUCK
WRONG BASKET BOXCAR BUFFET
CHIPPY DINGEY DINGHY DUPLEX
HOPPER JIGGER JINGLE SALOON
SETOFF SMOKER TOURER
AWKWARD CARROCH CHARIOT
COMBINE FLATCAR FREEZER
GIRAFFE GONDOLA HANDCAR
SIDECAR TELPHER TRAILER
TROLLEY VEHICLE HORSECAR
OUTSIDER QUADRIGA ROADSTER
SINISTER
(— FOR TRAIN CREW) CABOOSE
(— ON RAIL) TROLLEY
(BAGGAGE —) BLIND
(COAL —) HUTCH JIMMY WAGON
WAGGON
(ELECTRIC —) TELFER TELPHER
(ELEVATOR —) CAB CAGE
(EMPTY —) EMPTY IDLER

(JAUNTING —) SIDECAR
(LOG —) BUNK
(LOW-WHEELED —) HUTCH TRUCKLE
(MINE —) SKIP LARRY BARNEY
GIRAFFE GUNBOAT
(MONORAIL —) GYROCAR
(OBSERVATION —) BUGGY
(POLICE —) CRUISER
(TROLLEY —) SHORT
(USED —) DOG
CARABAO BUFF BUFFALO
CARACAL GORKUN SYAGUSH
CARACARA HAWK CARANCHA
CHIMANGO
CARACOLE FRISK CAREER
CARADOC BALA CRADOCK
CARAFE CROFT BOTTLE
CARAGUATA CHAGUAR
CARAJURA CHICA
CARAMBOLA BLIMBING BALIMBING
CARAMEL BLACKJACK
CARAPA CRAB CRAPPO CRABWOOD
CARAPACE CRUST SHELL LORICA
SHIELD CALAPASH
CARAVAN VAN TREK TRIP FLEET
TRAIN CAFILA COFFLE CONVOY
SAFARI TRAVEL JOURNEY VEHICLE
CONDUCTA
CARAVANSARY INN CHAN KHAN
HOTEL SERAI ZAYAT HOSTEL
IMARET CHOULTRY HOSTELRY
SERAGLIO
CARAWAY CARVY UMBEL
CARBINE STEN DRAGON MUSKET
DRAGOON ESCOPET
CARBOHYDRATE SUGAR AMYLAN
GELOSE STARCH FUCOSAN GLUCIDE
CELLULIN DEXTRINE DEXTROSE
GLYCOGEN GRAMININ PENTOSAN
TRITICIN CELLULOSE
CARBON COAL COKE COPY SOOT
NORIT CRAYON DIAMOND REPLICA
CHARCOAL GRAPHITE SCHUNGITE
CARBONADO BORT BOART BOORT
CARBON
CARBONATE BURN CHAR FIZZ
AERATE ALKALI ENLIVEN ENERGIZER
CARBONATOR GASMAN
CARBONIZER PICKLER
CARBORUNDUM EMERY ABRASIVE
CARBUNCLE RUBY PYROPE
ANTHRAX CHARBOCLE
CARBURETOR CARB DIFFUSER
VAPORIZER
CARCASS BEEF BODY BOUK CASE
CULL BLOCK MUMMY CORPSE
CARRION
(— OF WHALE) CRANG KRANG
KRENG
CARD ACE PAM WAG CLUB COMB
DRAW FACE FIVE FOUR JACK
KING MENU PLAN STOP BALOP
BLANK CARTE CHART CHECK DEUCE
DUMMY EIGHT ENTRY EQUAL FICHE
FLATS GREEN HEART JOKER LOSER
PIECE QUEEN SPADE STAMP STIFF
TAROT TEASE BENDER CARTEL
CONVEX FILLER KICKER KNIGHT
PIGEON READER SECOND TICKET

TOWSER BRAGGER BRISQUE
DIAMOND PROGRAM RELEASE
STARTER STOPPER TAROCCO
TRIUMPH BOOKMARK COMOQUER
DECKHEAD DRAWCARD SCHEDULE
SCRIBBLE SQUEEZER STRIPPER
TIMECARD
(— LAST IN BOX) HOCK HOCKELTY
(— WOOL) TUM ROVE
(3 —S IN SEQUENCE) TIERCE
FOURCHETTE
(3 ACE —S) CORONA
(3 FACE —S) GLEEK
(3 —S OF KIND) TRIO TRICON
PAIRIAL TRIPLET
(4 OF TRUMPS —) TIDDY
(5 FACE —S) BLAZE
(7, 8 AND 9 —S) VOIDS
(ACE OF CLUBS —) BASTA BASTO
MATADOR PUPPYFOOT
(ACE OF SPADES —) MATADOR
SPADILLE
(ACE OF TRUMPS —) TIB
(AVIATOR'S —) CARNET
(CLUB —) OAK
(COMPASS —) FLY ROSE
(DEAD —) SLEEPER
(DIAMOND —) PICK CARREAU
(DISCARDED —S) CRIB
(DRAWING —) BLOWOFF
(FARO —) SODA
(FOUR —) CATER QUATRE
(FOURTH —) CASE
(HIGHEST UNPAID —) COMMAND
(JOKER —) BRAGGER MISTIGRIS
(KING, QUEEN OR KNAVE —) COST
FACE
(KNAVE —) PAM TOM JACK BOWER
EQUES MAKER NODDY COQUIN
KNIGHT PICARO VARLET WENZEL
CUSTREL PEASANT VILLAIN
VARLETTO
(LAYOUT OF —S) TABLEAU
(LOW —) GUARD
(MARKED —) STAMP
(POSTAL —) COVER
(PULLING —S) TIRE
(QUEEN AND KNAVE —S) INTRIGO
INTRIGUE
(RUN OF —S) SEQUENCE
(SPADE —) PICK DIGGER
(STOCK —) TALON
(THIRD HIGHEST TRUMP —) BASTA
(THREE —) TREY THREE
(WILD —) FREAK
CARDAMOM KNOBWOOD
CARDBOARD CARD PALL BLANK
BOGUS CARTON BRISTOL
TAGBOARD
(TWO —S) SPHEROGRAPH
CARDER TOZER TEASER TUMMER
CARDIALGIA HEARTBURN
CARDIGAN CORGI FABRIC JACKET
WAMPUS SWEATER
CARDINAL MAIN BASIC CHIEF CLOAK
VITAL ALEPHA CLERIC DATARY
PRINCE RADICAL ALEFNULL
ALEFZERO CAMPEIUS
CARDINALATE PURPLE

CARDINAL BIRD CARNAL REDBIRD REDLEGS GROSBEAK REDSHANK
CARDINAL FISH FUCINITA ALFONCINO
CARDSHARP TRAMPOSO
CARDSHARPER GREEK SHARPER SPIELER
CARE DO DOW HOW CARK CURE DUTY FASH FRET HEED KEEP KEPE MIND PASS RECK SOIN TEND TENT WISH YEME COUNT GRIEF GUARD NURSE PAINS SORGE TRUST WORRY BURDEN CARIEN CHARGE CUMBER DESIRE GRIEVE LAMENT REGARD SORROW ANXIETY AUSPICE CAUTION CHERISH CONCERN CULTURE CUSTODY KEEPING RESPECT RUNNING SCRUPLE THOUGHT TUITION BUSINESS PERIERGY TENDMENT
(— FOR ONESELF) BACH
(— FOR) KNOW MIND RECK TEND WARD FORCE NURSE SAVOR FATHER MATTER REGARD CHERISH PROCURE
(— OF HOUSEHOLD) HUSBANDRY
(— OF LIVESTOCK) CHORE
(JUDICIOUS —) LEISURE
(WATCHFUL —) TENDANCE
CAREEN GIP CANT HEEL KEEL LIST TILT VEER LURCH SLOPE SWIFT INCLINE
CAREER RUN WAY LIFE ROAD TRADE CHARGE COURSE GALLOP CALLING PURSUIT
(MILITARY —) ARMS SERVICE
CAREFREE EASY FRANK HAPPY DEGAGE HOLIDAY DEBONAIR
CAREFUL BUSY WARY CANNY CHARY CLOSE EXACT HOOLY TENTY CHOICE DAINTY EIDENT EYEFUL FRUGAL NARROW TENDER ANXIOUS CURIOUS ENVIOUS GUARDED HEEDFUL PAINFUL PRUDENT THRIFTY ACCURATE CAUTIOUS CRITICAL DILIGENT DISCREET DREADFUL GINGERLY MOURNFUL PUNCTUAL TROUBLED VIGILANT WATCHFUL
CAREFULLY HOOLY NARROW CANNILY CHARILY TENTILY CHOICELY GINGERLY
CARELESS LAX COOL EASY LASH RASH SLACK CASUAL OVERLY RAKISH REMISS SECURE SLOPPY SUPINE UNTIDY UNWARY LANGUID SLIGHTY UNCANNY HEEDLESS LISTLESS MINDLESS RECKLESS SLATTERN SLIPSHOD SLOVENLY YEMELESS
CARELESSLY SLACK OVERLY SLACKLY SLIGHTLY
CARELESSNESS LACHES LAXITY INCAUTION
CARESS COY HUG PAT PET BILL CLAP DAUT DAWT KISS MUCH NECK INGLE NURSE CODDLE COSSET FONDLE PAMPER STROKE CHERISH EMBRACE FLATTER CANOODLE

CARETAKER KEEPER WARDER JANITOR
CARGO BULK LAST LOAD BURDEN LADING FREIGHT PACKAGE PORTAGE CARGASON PROPERTY SHIPLOAD SHIPMENT TRAFFICS
CARIAMA CHUNGA SERIEMA
CARIB GALIBI CALINAGO
CARIBBEAN (— GULF) DARIEN HONDURAS
(— ISLAND GROUP) LEEWARD ANTILLES WINDWARD
(— ISLAND) CUBA HAITI NASSAU TOBAGO CURACAO GRENADA JAMAICA DOMINICA
CARIBE PIRAI PIRANHA CHARACINE
CARIBOU STAG RANGIFER REINDEER
CARICATURE APE COPY MOCK SKIT FARCE LIBEL MIMIC SQUIB OVERDO PARODY SATIRE CARTOON TRAVESTY BURLESQUE
CARILLONNEUR CAMPANIST BELLMASTER
CARINA KEEL
CARMELITE EXTERN TERESIAN
CARMINATIVE GINGER CALAMUS CAMPHOR VALERIAN
CARMINE RED LAKE CRIMSON SCARLET
CARNAGE WAL MURDER POGROM STRAGE BUTCHERY MASSACRE BLOODSHED
CARNAL CROW LEWD GROSS ANIMAL BODILY SEXUAL BESTIAL BRUTISH EARTHLY FLESHLY SECULAR SENSUAL WORLDLY MATERILA PANDEMIC TEMPORAL
CARNATION JACK PINK FLAKE BIZARRE PICOTEE DAYBREAK DIANTHUS GRENADINE MALMAISON
CARNELIAN SARD COPPER
(BEAD OF —) ARANGO
CARNIVAL FETE SHOW CARNY CANVAS APOKREA CANVASS REVELRY FESTIVAL
CARNIVORE CAT DOG FOX BEAR COON LION LYNX MINK PUMA SEAL WOLF CIVET GENET HYENA OTTER PANDA PEKAN RATEL SABLE STOAT TIGER BADGER COUGAR ERMINE FELINE FERRET FISHER FOUSSA JACKAL JAGUAR MARTEN OCELOT POSSUM SERVAL WEASEL DASYURE GLUTTON LEOPARD MEERKAT POLECAT RACCOON TIGRESS MONGOOSE OPPOSSUM PREDACEAN ZOOPHAGAN
CAROB HUSK LOCUST ALGAROBA
CAROL LAY NOEL SING SONG DITTY YODEL WARBLE WASSAIL MADRIGAL AGUINALDO
CAROLINA ALLSPICE SHRUB
CAROLINE ISLANDS (— ISLAND GROUP) PALAU
(ISLAND OF —) YAP HALL PALU TRUK PELEW PULAP OROLUK PONAPE WOLEAI PELELIU
(TOWN OF —) LOT NIF RUNU KOROR MUTOK TOMIL PONAPE

MALAKAL GARUSUUN
CAROLINGIAN KARLING
CAROM SHOT BOUNCE CANNON GLANCE STRIKE REBOUND BILLIARD CARAMBOLE
CAROUSAL GELL LARK ORGY RIOT ROMP TOOT BINGE FEAST RANDY REVEL ROUSE SPRAY SPREE FROLIC SHINDY SPLORE BANQUET CAROUSE REVELRY WASSAIL DRINKING FESTIVAL JAMBOREE
CAROUSE JET BOUT HELL RANT TOOT BIRLE BOUSE DRINK QUAFF RANDY REVEL ROUSE SPREE TOAST COURANT JOLLIFY WASSAIL CAROUSAL
CAROUSER BACCHANAL
CAROUSING REVEL RAFFING
CARP KOI NAG BITE DRUM SING SNAG TALK YERK CAVIL PINCH PRATE SCOLD SPEAK CENSOR NIBBLE RECITE CENSURE CHATTER QUIBBLE COMPLAIN CYPRINID GOLDFISH
(CRUCIAN —) GIBEL
(LAKE —) DRUM LAKER
CARPAL ACTINOST
CARPEL CARPID COCCUS MERICARP CARPOPHYL
(PL.) CORE
CARPENTER ANT LOHAR FITTER FRAMER HOUSER JOINER PINNER WRIGHT BUILDER HOWSOUR WOODMAN INDENTER TECTONIC TIMBERER PITWRIGHT
(SHIP'S —) CHIPS
CARPENTRY WOODWORK WRIGHTRY
CARPER CRITIC
CARPET MAT RUG AGRA KALI KUBA HERAT KILIM SARUK SCOLD SUMAK TAPET TAPIS TEKKE USHAK AFGHAN FLOSSA FRIEZE KASHAN KIDDER KIRMAN LAVEHR NAMMAD RUNNER SAROUK SAXONY SELJUK SMYRNA TABRIZ VELVET WILTON DHURRIE GIORDES HAMADAN INGRAIN ISFAHAN ISPAHAN SHEMAKA TEHERAN AKHISSAR AMRITSAR BRUSSELS COVERING FOOTPACE KARABAGH MOQUETTE TAPESTRY TURCOMAN VENETIAN AXMINSTER
(HOLY —) KISWA
(PILELESS —) KILIM GELEEM
CARPETING FILLING
CARPET SHARK WOBBEGONG
CARPET SHELL EEROCK PULLET
CARPETWEED FICOID FICOIDAL
CARPING CRAB CAPTIOUS CAVILING CRITICAL
CARPSUCKER QUILLBACK
CARPUS WRIST CARPOPODITE
CARRAGEEN KILLEEN
CARREL STALL CUBICLE
CARRIAGE AIR CAB CAR FLY GIG RIG RUT SET VIS ARBA BIGA CART CHAR DUKE EKKA GAIT GARB HACK LOAD MIEN PORT RUTH SHAY TEAM TRAP WYNN ARABA BANDY BRAKE BREAK BRETT BUGGY CHAIR COACH

COUPE ESSED FRONT JUTKA MIDGE
PANEL POISE SADOO SETUP SULKY
TENUE TONGA TRUCK WAGON
BURDEN CALASH CHAISE CHARET
CISIUM CONVOY DENNET FIACRE
GHARRY GOCART HANSOM KOSONG
LANDAU MANNER MOTION PORTER
REMISE SADDLE SPIDER SURREY
TANDEM TELEGA TROIKA BAGGAGE
BEARING BERLINE BOUNDER
BRITSKA CALECHE CALESIN
CARAVAN CARIOLE CAROCHE
CHARIOT COACHEE CONDUCT
CROYDON DOGGART DOSADOS
DROSHKY FORECAR GESTURE
HACKMAN HACKNEY MINIBUS
PHAETON POSCHAY SHANDRY
SKYHOOK TALLYHO TARTANA
TILBURY TRANSIT TROLLEY
UNICORN VECTURE VEHICLE
VETTURA VOITURE VOLANTE
WAFTAGE BAROUCHE BEHAVIOR
BROUGHAM CARRYALL CLARENCE
CURRICLE DEARBORN DEMEANOR
DORMEUSE EQUIPAGE PORTANCE
PRESENCE ROCKAWAY SOCIABLE
STANHOPE TARANTAS TOURNURE
VICTORIA
(— OF HANDPRESS) COFFIN
(— OF HORSE) AIR
(AMMUNITION —) CAISSON
(ELEVATED —) LIFT
(INDIAN —) RUT EKKA BANDY
GHARRI GHARRY
(JAVANESE —) SADO SADOO
(LIVERY —) REMISE
(LOG —) DRAG
(PUBLIC —) FLY OMNIBUS
CARRIAGE HOUSE REMISE
CARRIER HOD BASE JEEP SHIP
TRAM BUGGY HAMAL KAHAR MACER
PLANE SABOT TAMEN TIGER BARKIS
BEARER CADGER COOLIE HAMMAL
HODMAN JAGGER PACKER PORTER
RUNNER TAILER WEASEL DRAYMAN
DROGHER FLATTOP POSTMAN
REMOVER TACULLI TROTTER
VEHICLE CARGADOR CARRYALL
PORTATOR RAILROAD TEAMSTER
SUBSTRATE
(COAL —) FLATIRON
(COLOR —) LUFIRIER
(ENDLESS —) TAILER
(FIRE —) PORTFIRE
(MAIL —) COURIER POSTMAN
(WATER —) BHISTI BHEESTY
CARRION KET VILE OFFAL CORPSE
HOODIE REFUSE ROTTEN CARCASS
CORRUPT DOGMEAT CROWBAIT
CARRION BIRD SCAVENGER
CARRION CROW DOWP HOODY
URUBU CORBIE HOODIE GERCROW
CARROT UMBEL CONIUM DAUCUS
CACHRYS SECRETE BUPLEVER
HILLTROT
(DEADLY —) DRIAS
(PERUVIAN —) ARRACACH
(PREPARED WITH —S) CRECY
CARROTING SECRETAGE

CARROUSEL RIDE WHIRLGIG
QUADRILLE
CARRY CAR HUG JAG LUG BEAR
BUCK CART DRAY FARE GEST HAVE
HOLD HUMP LEAD PACK PORT
SHOW TAKE TOTE TUMP BRING
BROOK CADGE CROSS FERRY
GESTE GUIDE POISE WALTZ WEIGH
BEHAVE CONVEY CONVOY DELATE
DEPORT DERIVE EXTEND COMPORT
CONDUCT CONTAIN ENTRAIN
PORTAGE PRODUCE SUPPORT
SUSTAIN UNDERGO BAJULATE
CONTINUE TRANSFER TRANSMIT
(— AWAY) FIRK DRAIN REAVE
SWEEP TRUSS ABLATE ASPORT
(— EFFIGY) GUY
(— FORWARD) EXTEND
(— IN OXCART) KURVEY
(— LIQUOR) BOOTLEG
(— OFF) HENT LIFE SACK FETCH
HEAVE RIFLE SCOUR SWOOP
ABDUCT ASPORT BRAZEN KIDNAP
SPIRIT
(— ON) DO RUN WAR HAVE LEAD
LEVY WAGE APPLY DRIVE ENSUE
FIGHT TRAIN CREATE DEMEAN
FOLLOW MANAGE OCCUPY
CONDUCT EXERCISE MAINTAIN
TRANSACT
(— ONESELF) HOLD
(— ONWARD) CONTINUE
(— OUT) DO ACT END GIVE LAST
HONOR AFFORD EFFECT ACHIEVE
EXECUTE FULFILL PERFORM
SATISFY
(— UPWARD) RAP ESCALATE
CARRYALL BUS CASE WAGON
CARRIAGE
CARRYING BURDEN GERENT
FRAUGHT
(— ON) GESTION
(— WEIGHT) EFFECTIVE
CART CAR POT RUT BUTT CHAR
COOP COUP DRAY HAUL JANG LEAD
LOAD PLOW PUTT RUTH TOTE WAIN
ARABA BANDY BOGEY BOGIE CADDY
CARRY DANDY DILLY DOLLY SULKY
TONGA TRUCK WAGON BARROW
CADDIE CHAISE CHARET CISIUM
CONVEY DOLLIE DUMPER GHARRI
GHARRY JIGGER JINKER KURUMA
LIMBER PLOUGH SPIDER CARRETA
CHARIOT DOGCART GUJERAT
HACKERY MORFREY SHALLOW
TROLLEY TRUNDLE TUMBLER
TUMBREL TUMBRIL VEHICLE
DUMPCART HANDCART PUSHCART
(— WITH TANK) TUMBLER
(2-PONY —) KOSONG
(2-WHEELED —) BANDY BUGGY
SULKY CARRETA TUMBREL
(3-WHEELED —) PORTER
(BULLOCK —) BANDY HACKERY
(COSTER'S —) TROLL
(COVERED —) JINGLE CARIOLE
(FARMER'S —) PUTT GAMBO
MORPHREY
(FREIGHT —) CARRETON

(LOG —) BUNK
(LUMBER —) GILL BUMMER
(MILKMAN'S —) PRAM
(OX —) RECKLA
(PARCELS —) FLY
(TIMBER —) CUTS
(TIP —) COOP COUP COUPE
(UNDERSLUNG —) FLOAT
CARTE MAP CARD LIST MENU CHART
CHARTER DIAGRAM
CARTE BLANCHE BLANK
CARTEL CARD DEFY PACT POOL
SHIP PAPER TRUST CORNER LETTER
TREATY CONTRACT SYNDICATE
CARTER CARMAN JAGGER LEADER
DRAYMAN LADEMAN TRUCKER
HORSEMAN TEAMSTER
CARTILAGE COPULA TISSUE
CRICOID EPIURAL GRISTLE RADIALE
STERNUM TARSALE THYROID
EPIPUBIS HYPOHYAL SESAMOID
TURBINAL
CARTILAGINOUS CHONDRIC
CARTOGRAPH MAP PLAT CHART
CARTOGRAPHER CHARTIST
CARTON BOX CASE SHELL
CARTOON EPURE ANIMATION
CARTOUCHE MESA OVAL DURANGO
CARTRIDGE
CARTRIDGE BAG CASE HULL BLANK
SHELL SHORT BULLET MAGNUM
PATRON CAPSULE TORPEDO
HANDLOAD SHOTSHELL
CARTULARY COUCHER
CARTWHEEL CLOGWHEEL
CARUCATE CARVE PLOWLAND
CARUNCLE COMB STROPHIOLE
CARVE CUT ALAY SIDE BEHEW
BREAK GRAVE KIRVE MINCE SHEAR
SPLAY SPOIL THIGH INCISE QUINSE
SCULPT THWITE TRENCH UNLACE
ENCHASE ENGRAIL ENGRAVE
DISJOINT MALAHACK SCULLION
(— A BIRD) WING
(— CHICKEN) FRUSH
(— GOOSE) REAR
(— HEN) SPOIL
(— PEACOCK) DISFIGURE
(— PLOVER) MINCE
(— SWAN) LIFT
CARVED CARVEN GLYPHIC INCISED
CARVER BODGER KIRVER CROPPER
FROSTER IVORIST CICELEUR
TRENCHER
CARVING CAMEO GLYPH IVORY
ENTAIL SCRIVE GLYPTIC MASKOID
NICKING INTAGLIO TRIPTYCH
CARYA HICORIA
CARYATID TELAMON CANEPHORA
(PART OF —) GAINE
CARYOCAR SOUARI
CARYOPHYLLUS JAMBOSA
CARYOPSIS SEED
CASCABEL POMMEL POMMELION
CASCADE LIN FALL LINN FORCE
SPOUT CATARACT
CASCARA BUCKTHORN WAHOO
SHITTIM

CASCARILLA CROTON GOATWEED
SWEETWOOD
CASE BAG BOX CUP HAP LEG POD
POT PYX BIND BOOT BUNK BURR
CASK COPE DEED DESK DOCK
DOME FILE PACK PAIR ROLL SUIT
TICK BRACE BRIEF BULLA BURSE
CADDY CASUS CAUSE CHAPE
COVER CRATE EVENT FOLIO FOREL
HUSSY HUTCH PRESS PYXIS SHELL
STATE THECA THING TRIAL ACTION
AFFAIR APPEAL BARREL BINDER
BOXING CARTON CASING CELLAR
CHANCE COFFIN COUPLE LOCKET
LORICA MATTER PATRON PENNER
PETARD POPPET QUIVER RIDDLE
SHEATH SHRINE STATOR SURVEY
TASHIE TWEEZE VALISE VANITY
CABINET CAMISIA CAPCASE
CAPSULE COUNTER CUSHION
DIECASE ENCLOSE ENVELOP
EXAMPLE GEARBOX HOLDALL
HOLSTER HOUSING HUMIDOR
INCLOSE LAWSUIT LUNETTE
PACKAGE REMANET SATCHEL
SHIPPER WARDIAN ACCIDENT
ARGUMENT BOOKCASE CARRYALL
CUPBOARD ENVELOPE EQUIPAGE
EXEMPLAR GARDEVIN INSTANCE
KNAPSACK PACKSACK PORTFIRE
SHOWCASE SITUATED SOLANDER
TANTALUS
(WICKER —) HASK BARROW
HANAPER
(— CONTAINING ELEVATOR BELT)
LEG
(— ENCLOSING CLOCK DIAL) HOOD
(— FOR CARDS) SHOE
(— FOR COMPASS) BINNACLE
(— FOR EXPLOSIVES) TRUNK
(— FOR JEWELS) TYE
(— FOR MOLD) COPE CHAPE
(— FOR MUMMY) SLEDGE
(— FOR PISTOL) HOLSTER
(— FOR PULLEY) BLOCK
(— FOR RIFLE) BOOT
(— FOR SEWING ITEMS) HUSSY
(— FOR TOOLS) TROUSSE
(— FOR TWEEZERS) BUBBLEBOW
(— FOR WRITING MATERIALS)
STANDISH
(— IN WATCH) DOME BARREL
(— OF FLOUR BOLTER) HUTCH
(— OF VENETIAN BLIND) HEADBOX
(— OF) A
(— WITH COMPARTMENTS) RIDDLE
(BONY —) CARAPACE
(COSMETIC —) COMPACT
(COURT —) LAWSUIT
(EGG —) OVISAC OOTHECA
(FIREWORKS —) LANCE
(GRAMMATICAL —) DATIVE ESSIVE
LATIVE ELATIVE FACTIVE ABLATIVE
EQUATIVE ERGATIVE GENITIVE
ILLATIVE LOCATIVE VOCATIVE
(HOPELESS —) GONER
(LUGGAGE —) IMPERIAL
(ORNAMENTAL —) ETUI
(PAPER —) COFFIN

(PILLOW —) SLIP
CASED BOUND
CASEMENT SASH LUKET WINDOW
CASHIER CASS CAST BREAK DEALER
POTDAR PURSER CHECKER DISMISS
CASHIERED BROKEN DEGOMME
CASHMERE KASHMIR PRUNELL
CASH REGISTER DAMPER REGEST
GREFFIER RECORDER REGISTER
CASING BODY BOOT BUNG CASE
CURB HULL SHOE SKIN TIRE APRON
BELLY DERMA EPHOD GAINE LINER
ROUND STOCK TRUNK BOXING
COFFIN COLLET JACKET KISHKE
LINING SCROLL SHEATH VOLUTE
FEEDBOX HOUSING MANHEAD
OUTCASE STAVING THIMBLE
CACHEPOT COVERING PLOWSHOE
SHIRTING WHEELBOX
(— FOR BRAIN) HARNPAN
CASK KEG TUB TUN VAT BOSS BUTT
CADE COWL DRUM KNAG PIPE RAPE
RIER SLIP TREE WOOD ANKER
BOWIE BULGE FOIST STAND UNION
BARECA BARREL CARDEL CASQUE
DOLIUM FIRKIN FOODER LONGER
OCTAVE TIERCE WINGER BARRICO
BREAKER FOSTELL RUNDLET
SACKBUT CASSETTE HOGSHEAD
PUNCHEON QUARDEEL ROUNDLET
(BREWING —) UNION
(LOCKED —) TANTALUS
(PERFORATED —) POT
(SMALL —) KEG TUB KNAG STOOP
STOUP
(WINE —) FAT TUN BOSS BUTT PIPE
TIERCE HOGSHEAD
(PL.) COOPERAGE
CASKET BOX PIX TYE CASE CASK
CIST TILL TOMB BUIST CHEST
ACERRA CHASSE COFFER COFFIN
SHRINE FOSTELL CASSETTE
CASQUE CASK HORN GALEA HELMET
CASSABANANA CURUBA
CASSANDRA (FATHER OF —) PRIAM
(HUSBAND OF —) AGAMEMNON
(MOTHER OF —) HECUBA
CASSAREEP CAXIRI
CASSAVA AIPI AIPIM YUCCA CASIRI
CAZIBI MANIOC TAPIOCA
CASSEROLE TUREEN COCOTTE
MARMITE TERRINE TZIMMES
CASSIA KEZIA SENNA SICKLEPOD
CASSIA FISTULA AMALTAS
CASSIMERE ZEPHYR
CASSITERITE TINSTONE
CASSITES KUSHSHU
CASSOCK GOWN SLOP VEST GIPPO
PRIEST PELISSE SOUTANE ZIMARRA
CASSOWARY EMU MURUP MOORUP
RATITE
CAST MEW PUT SET BILL DART HURL
MOLD MOLT PICK SHED SLAT SLIP
SPEW SWAK TINT TOSS TREE TURN
WHAP WHOP WURP BLOCK BRAID
CHUCK DEUCE DRIVE EJECT ERECT
FLING FLIRT FOUND FUSIL HEAVE
IMAGE KEIST PITCH SHADE SHOOT
SLING STAMP THROW TINGE

COLLAR INJECT NOSING STRIKE
STRIND THRILL AGARWAL CASHIER
DEPOSIT DISCARD VIBRATE
CASTLING CONSPECT OUTSLING
POLYTYPE TINCTURE
(— A SPELL) TAKE HOODOO
BESPELL BEWITCH FORSPEAK
(— ASIDE) DICE FLING
(— ASPERSIONS) SLUR SKLENT
APPEACH
(— AWAY) DUMP SHOVE DEJECT
REJECT
(— DICE) WHIRL
(— DISCREDIT) GLANCE
(— DOWN) DASH DUMP HURL SINK
ABASE AMATE AMORT AWARP
STREW ABJECT DECAST DEJECT
DEMISS THRING ECLIPSE RUINATE
DEJECTED
(— FORTH) SPEW SPUE WARP
BELCH BRAID LAUNCH
(— GLOOM) DUSK CLOUD DARKEN
DEPRESS
(— IN A MOLD) STRIKE
(— LOTS) CAVEL
(— METAL) YET
(— OF DICE) COUP DEUCE
(— OF HERRINGS) WARP
(— OF LANGUAGE) IDIOM
(— OF NET) SHOT SHOOT
(— OFF) DAFF JILT MOLT SHED
DITCH LOSSE SHAKE SLUFF WAIVE
CASTEN DEVEST REFUSE REJECT
SLOUGH ABDICATE RENOUNCE
(— ON GROUND) TERRE
(— OUT) EGEST EJECT EXPEL
BANISH ABANDON EXTRUDE
OSTRACIZE
(— SHADOW) ADUMBRATE
(— UP) SUM LEVY UPBRAID
(FRESHLY —) GREEN
(PLASTER —) CUIRASS
CASTANET KNACKER KNOCKER
SNAPPER TCHAPAN CROTALUM
CASTAWAY WAIF TRAMP CRUSOE
REJECT OUTCAST DERELICT
STRANDED
CASTE (OR CASTE MEMBER) DOM
MEO AHIR BHAR BHAT GOLA JATI
KOLI KORI MALI MINA PASI TELI
BAGDI BANIA DHOBY GOALA IRAVA
KAHAR KUMNI KUNBI KURMI LADHA
LOHAR MAHAR PALLI PUGGI SAMAR
SANSI SINGH SONAR SUDRA TANTI
VARNA ARORAS BAIDYA BALIJA
BANIAN BHANGI CHAMAR CHETTY
CHUHRA DHANUK DHOBIE DOSADH
DURZEE HOLEVA HOLIYA ILAVAN
JAJMAN KALWAR KAMBOH KHATRI
KUMHAR KURUBA LOHANA MADIGA
NATION PALLAR PRABHU PULAYA
PULIAN PURVOE RAJPUT VAISYA
AGARWAL BRAHMAN BRAHMIN
DHANGAR GADARIA HARIJAN
KAYASTH KOMATRI KURUMBA
NISHADA VELLALA KAMMALAN
KHANDAIT PARAIYAN POVINDAH
RAJBANSI VAKKALIGA
(LOWER —S) PANCHAMA

CASTER VIAL CRUET CRUSE PHIAL CASTOR HORRAL HURLER MASTER ROLLER FOUNDER PITCHER TRUCKLE TRUNDLE
(SURF —) SQUIDDER
CASTIGATE LASH EMEND SCARE SCORE BERATE PUNISH REVISE STRAFE SUBDUE CANVASS CENSURE CHASTEN CORRECT LEATHER REPROVE CHASTISE LAMBASTE FUSTIGATE
CASTIGATION HELL LASHING DRESSING
CASTING DIE PIG CAST FONT KEEP MOLD TYMP BLOCK CHOCK CHUCK FOUND MOULD BILLET BUMPER MATRIX MISRUN SPIDER COULAGE DARTING SEGMENT SEPARATOR
(— LOTS) SORTITION
(— OF HOROSCOPE) APOTELESM
(— OVERBOARD) JETTISON
(PL.) SPRAY FOUNDRY
CAST IRON YETLING
CASTLE BURY FORT HALL KEEP ROCK ROOK ABODE COURT MORRO PIECE CASBAH BASTILE BOROUGH CHATEAU CITADEL SCHLOSS UDOLPHO BASTILLE CASTELET CASTILLO FASTNESS FORTRESS STAROSTY TINTAGEL
(— IN CHESS) JUEZ ROOK TOUR JUDGE TOWER
(SMALL —) PEEL TOWER CASTLET CHATELET
CASTOR BEAVER LEATHER TRUCKLE TRUNDLE BARKSTONE
(— AND POLLUX) TWINS GEMINI DIOSCURI
CASTOR-OIL PLANT KIKI MAMONA PALMCRIST
CASTRATE CUT FIX GIB LIB GELD GLIB SPAY SWIG TRIM ALTER CAPON DESEX PRUNE STEER CHANGE EUNUCH NEUTER EVIRATE CAPONIZE MUTILATE SATURNIZE
CASTRATED CUT GIBBED UNPAVED
CASTRATO EUNUCH EVIRATO TENORINO
CASUAL GLIB STRAY BLITHE BYHAND CHANCE FOLKSY RANDOM CASALTY CURSORY LEISURE NATURAL OFFHAND RUNNING GLANCING INFORMAL
CASUALTY LOSS DEATH CADUAC CHANCE HAZARD INJURY MISHAP ACCIDENT DISASTER
CASUARINA BEEFWOOD
CASUIST JESUIST
CAT GIB RAT SOW TAB CHAT EYRA FLOG LION LYNX MISS PARD PUMA PUSS CHAUS CIVET FELID GATOL KITTY MANUL MEWER MOGGY OUNCE PUSSY SMOKE TABBY TIGER TILER WHITE ZIBET ANGORA COUGAR FELINE JAGUAR KITTEN KODKOD MALKIN MARGAY MAWKIN MIAUER MOUSER MUSION NEUTER OCELOT PAJERO PURRER SERVAL TIBERT TORTIE BURMESE CARACAL

CATHEAD CATLING CHEETAH KITLING KUICHUA LEOPARD LINSANG PANTHER PERSIAN SIAMESE TIGRESS WILDCAT WRAWLER BAUDRONS DASYURID FISSIPED PUSSYCAT RINGTAIL
(— CRY) WAW
(— GROUP) CLOWDER
(FEMALE —) QUEEN WHEENCAT
(MALE —) GIB TOM TOMCAT
(ROOF-PROWLING —) TILER
CATACHRESIS ABUSION
CATACLYSM FLOOD DELUGE DEBACLE DISASTER UPHEAVAL
CATACOMB TOMB CRYPT VAULT CEMETERY HYPOGEUM
(PL.) ARENARIAE
CATADROMOUS SEAGOING
CATALECTIC HEMIAMB TRUNCATED
CATALEPSY TRANCE SEIZURE CATATONY
CATALOG PIE PYE BILL BOOK LIST ROLL ROTA BRIEF CANON FLIER FLYER INDEX PINAX AUTHOR RAGGER RAGMAN RECORD ROSTER ARRANGE BEADROW DIPTYCH BEADROLL BULLETIN CALENDAR CLASSIFY REGISTER SCHEDULE CATALOGUE DIDASCALY INVENTORY
CATALUFA SCAD TORO BIGEYE
CATALYST CARRIER SAUSAGE ZIEGLER CATALYTE HOPCALITE
(NEGATIVE —) INHIBITER
CATAMARAN RAFT TROW BALSA FLOAT GUNBOAT JANGADA MONITOR AUNTSARY
CATAMITE INGLE GUNSEL NINGLE PATHIC BARDASH GANYMEDE
CATAMOUNT LYNX PUMA COUGAR
CATAPLASM POULTICE
CATAPULT GUN BIBLE SLING SWEEP THROW HURTLE LAUNCH ONAGER TREPAN ALACRAN BRICOLE PEDRERO TORMENT TRABUCH WARWOLF BALLISTA CROSSBOW DONDAINE LAUNCHER MANGONEL MARTINET SCORPION SPRINGAL STONEBOW
CATARACT LIN FALL LINN FALLS FLOOD PEARL DELUGE CASCADE NIAGARA CATADUPE OVERFALL VICTORIA
CATARRH MUR COLD MURR POSE RHEUM CORYZA
CATASTROPHE ACCIDENT CALAMITY DISASTER
CATCH BAG COB COP GET GIN KEP NAB NET DRAW FANG GLOM HASP HAUL HAWK HENT HOLD HOOK LAND MAKE MEET MESS NAIL PAWL SAVE SEAR SNAG SNAP SNIB STOP TAKE TRAP TREE VANG CLASP CLEEK CREEL FETCH GLOVE GRASP HITCH KETCH KNACK LASSO LATCH PLANT SEIZE SNARE SNICK SWOOP TRICK TROLL ARREST ATTAIN BUTTON CLUTCH CORNER CORRAL DETECT DETENT ENGAGE ENMESH ENTRAP IMMESH LOCKET NOBBLE

NOODLE SNATCH SPRENT TAIGLE TAKING TURNEL ATTRACT CAPTURE ENSNARE GIMMICK GRAPNEL RELEASE SPRINGE TRIGGER CONTRACT CRANNAGE ENTANGLE FASTNESS HOLDBACK HOLDFAST OVERTAKE SNAPHAAN SURPRISE
(— AT PROPER TIME) NICK
(— ATTENTION) FLAG
(— BIRDS) BATFOWL BIRDLIME
(— EELS) SNIGGLE
(— FIRE) SPUNK IGNITE KINDLE
(— FISH WITH HANDS) GUDDLE GRABBLE HANDFAST
(— FISH) JAB JIG GILL HANG GILLNET
(— IN VOICE) FETCH
(— OF DOOR) LATCH SNECK SNICK
(— OF FISH) FARE HAUL SHOT TACK TRIP SHACK
(— ONE'S BREATH) GASP CHINK
(— SIGHT OF) SPY ESPY SPOT DESCRY
(RATCHET —) CLICK
(SAFETY —) CLEVIS
CATCHER TAKER BIRDER FANGER LARKER RECEIVER
CATCHFLY SILENE FLYBANE
CATCHING CATCHY TAKING ALLURING ARRESTING
CATCHPOLE BAILIFF PUTTOCK
CATCHWEED CLEAVERS
CATCHWORD CUE TAG MOTTO BYWORD PHRASE SLOGAN STARTER CATCHCRY
CATCHY CATCHING APPEALING
CATECHISM GUIDE MANUAL CARRITCH QUESTIONS
CATECHU COTCH CUTCH KHAIR GAMBIER
CATECHUMEN PUPIL AUDIENT AUDITOR CONVERT BEGINNER NEOPHYTE COMPETENT
CATEGORICAL DIRECT ABSOLUTE EXPLICIT KNOCKDOWN
CATEGORIZE CODE HAVE
CATEGORY WAY KING RANK TALE CLASS FIELD GENRE GENUS ORDER STYLE FAMILY LEAGUE NUMBER RUBRIC SERIES SPECIES DIVISION
(— OF TENSES) INFECTUM
(HIGHEST —) IDEA
(PRIMARY —) SUBSTANCE
(TAXONOMIC —) FORM FORMA GENUS COHORT LEGION SUBCLASS SUBGENUS SUBFAMILY
CATER CUT FEED HUMOR SERVE TREAT PANDER PURVEY SUPPLY PROVIDE
CATERER ACATER
CATERPILLAR CAT MUGA AWETO ERUCA CANKER LOOPER PALMER PORINA RISPER TAILOR WOUBIT CUTWORM TRACTOR WEBWORM HANGWORM HORNWORM SILKWORM SKINWORM WORTWORM
CATERWAUL CRY WAIL MIAUL
CATFACE ARR SCAR
CATFISH MUD CUSK ELOD POUT

RAAD SHAL BAGRE DORAD RAASH
BARBER DOCMAC GLANIS GOONCH
GOUJON HASSAR MADTOM
BARBUDO CANDIRU COBBLER
FIDDLER PYGIDID SILURID WALLAGO
BULLHEAD BULLPOUT CORYDORA
FLATHEAD MATHEMEG PLOTOSID
SQUEAKER STONECAT
CATGUT THARM THAIRM CATLING
WHIPCORD
CATHARI BULGARI PATARINE
CATHARTIC ALOIN BRYONY PHYSIC
CALOMEL SCOURER EUONYMUS
EVACUANT HYDRAGOG KALADANA
LAPACTIC LAXATIVE SCAMMONY
SOLUTIVE SOLUTORY
CATHAYAN KITAN
CATHEDRA SEE
CATHEDRAL DOM SEE DUOMO
SOBOR MARTYRY MEMORIA
MINSTER BASILICA
CATHEXIS CHARGE
CATHODE K KA FILAMENT
ELECTRODE HYDROGODE
CATHOLIC BROAD GENERAL
LIBERAL TOLERANT
CATHOLICISM PAPISM POPERY
CATHOLICON PANACEA
CATKIN RAG TAG CHAT GULL AGLET
AMENT IULUS PUSSY CACHRYS
CATTAIL GOSLING
CATNIP NEP CATARIA CATMINT
CATWORT
CAT'S-CLAW LONGPOD ESCAMBRON
CAT'S CRADLE HEI
CAT'S-EAR GOSMORE CAPEWEED
FLATWEED
CAT'S EYE CHATOYANT
CAT'S-FOOT PUSSYTOE
CATTAIL DOD DODD FLAG MUSK
RUSH TULE AMENT BAYON BLECK
CLOUD RAUPO REREE WONGA
CATKIN GLADEN TOTORA BULRUSH
GLADDON MATREED BLACKCAP
CARBUNGI FLAXTAIL
CAT THYME HULWORT
CATTLE ZO BOW FEE GIR DHAN
GAUR KINE NEAT NOWT OXEN ZEBU
ZOBO DEVON STOCK ANKOLI
DURHAM GALYAK ONGOLE ROTHER
SINDHI SUSSEX BESTIAL NELLORE
REDPOLL COMPOUND OUTSIGHT
TUBICORN
(— CARRIED OFF) SPREATH
(BREED OF —) ANGUS BORAN
DEVON FJALL KERRY SANGA SANGU
ANGONI ANKOLI DEXTER DURHAM
FULANI JERSEY SUSSEX BAROTSE
BRAFORD BRAHMAN COASTER
CRIOLLA GUZERAT HARIANA
SAHIWAL ALDERNEY AYRSHIRE
CHARBRAY FRIBOURG FRIESIAN
GALLOWAY GUERNSEY HEREFORD
HOLSTEIN KANGAYAM LONGHORN
(DWARF —) NATA NIATA
(WILD YOUNG —) KANGAROO
CATTLE-BREEDER AHIR ALUR
CATTLE DEALER DROVER
CATTLEHIDE BUFF CROUPON

CATTLEMAN FAZENDEIRO
CATTLE MARKET SALEYARD
CATTLE PEN KRAAL
CATTLE RAID SPRAITH SPREAGH
CATTLE RUN STATION
CATTLE STEALER ABACTOR
ABIGEUS
CATTLE YARD CANCHA
CATTY KIN KATI
CAUCASIAN WHITE IRANIAN
EUROPEAN JAPHETIC PALEFACE
(— LANGUAGE) UDI UDIC UDIN
(PL.) MELANOI
CAUCHO ULE RUBBER
CAUDATA URODELA
CAUDEX STIPE
CAUGHT GRIPPIT ENTANGLED
CAUL HOW WEB KEEL KELL TRUG
VEIL GALEA HOUVE DORLOT
CREPINE KERCHER NETWORK
OMENTUM MEMBRANE SILLYHOW
TRESSOUR TRESSURE
CAULDRON KOHUA CALDRON
CAULICLE SCAPEL ROSTELLUM
CAULIFLOWER BROCCOLI
SNOWBALL CHOUFLEUR
CAULK CALK CORK FILL FLAG
CHINSE
CAUSAL GENETIC
CAUSE DO AIM GAR ISM KEY LET
WAY CASE CHAT FATE HOTI LEAD
MAKE MOVE ROOT SPUR SUIT
AGENT ARCHE BASIS BREED CAUSA
FRAME PARTY SKILL SLAKE WREAK
YIELD ADDICT CREATE EFFECT
ELICIT GOSSIP GROUND INDUCE
INVOKE MALADY MANNER MATTER
MOTIVE OBJECT ORIGIN PARENT
REASON RESORT SOURCE SPEECH
SPRING CHESOUN CONCERN
DISEASE LAWSUIT PROCURE
PRODUCE PROVOKE QUARREL
SUBJECT BUSINESS ENGENDER
GENERATE INSTANCE MOVEMENT
OCCASION WHEREFORE
(— A SORE) RANKLE
(— DAMAGE) DAMNIFY
(— FOR COMPLAINT) COMEBACK
(— OF RUIN) BANE
(— OF TERROR) AFFRIGHT
(— OF TROUBLE) TRACHLE
(— PAIN) URN
(— TO ARCH) ROACH
(— TO CONTRACT) PUCKER
(— TO CROUCH) COUCH
(— TO DESERT) DEFECT
(— TO END) ACHIEVE
(— TO MOVE RAPIDLY) GIG
(— TO PROJECT) JET
(— TO RESULT) ISSUE
(— TO STICK) MIRE
(— TO SWELL) BINGE EMBOSS
(— TO THICKEN) CURD
(FINAL —) END
(FORM-GIVING —) IDEA
(IMMEDIATE —) SIGNAL
(PRIMAL —) URGRUND
CAUSEWAY WAY DIKE ROAD
CHAUSSE HIGHWAY

CAUSTIC LYE ACID TART ACRID
QUICK SALTY SHARP SNELL BITING
BITTER SEVERE BURNING CAUTERY
CUTTING ERODENT MORDANT
NIPPING PUNGENT PYROTIC SATIRIC
ALKALINE DIERETIC SCATHING
SNAPPISH STINGING
CAUSTICITY ACRIMONY
CAUTERIZATION USTION INUSTION
CAUTERIZE BURN CHAR FIRE SEAR
BRAND INUST SINGE
CAUTION CARE FEAR HEED WARN
GUARD ADVICE CAUTEL CAVEAT
EXHORT ANXIETY COUNSEL
PRECEPT PROVISO WARNING
ADMONISH FORECAST FOREWARN
MONITION PRUDENCE WARINESS
CAUTIOUS SHY SAFE WARE WARY
ALERT CANNY CHARY SIKER FABIAN
HOOLIE SICKER TENDER TIPTOE
CAREFUL CURIOUS ENVIOUS
FEARFUL FERDFUL GUARDED
PRUDENT DISCREET SUSPENSE
VIGILANT
CAUTIOUSLY CANNY CANNILY
CHARILY EASYLIKE GINGERLY
TENDERLY
CAVALCADE RAID RIDE MARCH
TRAIN PARADE SAFARI COMPANY
JOURNEY PAGEANT
CAVALIER GAY CAVY CURT EASY
FINE BRAVE FRANK MOUNT RIDER
ESCORT KNIGHT BRUSQUE GALLANT
HAUGHTY OFFHAND SOLDIER
CAVALERO ROYALIST CHAMBERER
CHEVALIER COMMANDER
CAVALLA CERO JACK TORO ULUA
JUREL CARANX CARANGID
CREVALLE SCOMBRID
CAVALRY HORSE HEAVIES CHIVALRY
HORSEMEN YEOMANRY
CAVALRYMAN SOWAR SPAHI
SUWAR HUSSAR JINETE LANCER
ARGOLET COURIER DRAGOON
PLUNGER SABREUR TROOPER
GENDARME HORSEMAN STRADIOT
(PL.) FORAGERS
CAVE DEN TIP COVE HOLE LAIR MINE
REAR SINK TOSS WEEM ANTRE
CABIN CACHE CALVE CAVEA CRYPT
DELVE FOGOU SLADE SPEOS STORE
UPSET BEWARE CAVERN CAVITY
CELLAR DUGOUT GROTTO HOLLOW
LARDER LUSTER PANTRY PLUNGE
SHROUD MANSION RESERVE
SPELUNK CASTILLO COLLAPSE
OVERTURN MITHRAGUM
(— IN) COLT
CAVEAT BEWARE NOTICE CAUTION
WARNING
CAVE-DWELLER HORITE
TROGLODYTE
CAVE-DWELLING NATUFIAN
CAVEMAN NEANDERTHAL
CAVER SPELUNKER
CAVERN DEN CAVE COVE GROT
HOLE LAIR WEEM CROFT VAULT
ANTRUM CAVITY GROTTO HOLLOW
SPELUNK

CAVERNOUS ERECTILE
CAVESSON CHAIN
CAVETTO GULA GORGE
CAVIAR OVA ROE IKRA GARUM
   IKARY
CAVIL CARK CARP HAFT HAGGLE
   CAPTION CHICANE QUARREL
   QUIBBLE PETTIFOG QUIDDITY
   FORMALIZE
CAVILER CRITIC GIRDER HAFTER
   ZOILUS
CAVILING CAPTIOUS CRITICAL
   PICAYUNE
CAVITY BAG CUP PIT SAC ABRI AXIL
   CASE CAVE CELL DALK DENT DUCT
   HOLE MIND MINE VEIN VOID ABYSS
   BOSOM BURSA CRYPT DRUSE
   FOSSA GEODE GOUGE LUMEN
   MOUTH ORBIT SCOOP SINUS
   ANTRUM AREOLE ATRIUM AXILLA
   BORING CAECUM CAMERA CAVERN
   COELIA COELOM COTYLE CRATER
   DEBLAI GROTTO HOLLOW LACUNA
   POCKET SOCKET VACUUM VOMICA
   ABDOMEN CHAMBER CISTERN
   CYATHUS DIOCOEL KYATHOS
   LOCULUS MORTISE VACUITY
   VACUOLE VESICLE ALVEOLUS
   BROODSAC EPICOELE FOLLICLE
   WELLHOLE
   (— IN BONE) LACUNA
   (— IN CASTING) PIPE
   (— IN HEAD OF WHALE) CASE
   (— IN HILLSIDE) ABRI
   (— IN MINE) BAG
   (— MADE BY SEALS) IGLOO
   (— OF SEA-SHELL) FLUE
   (ALTAR —) TOMB
   (BODY —) GUT BELLY THORAX
   ABDOMEN STOMACH
   (CHEST —) THORAX
   (CRYSTAL-LINED —) VUGG DRUSE
   GEODE
   (GUN —) BORE
   (NASAL —) CAVUM
CAVORT PLAY BOUND CAPER
   CURVET GAMBOL PRANCE
CAVY PACA PONY AGOUTI APEREA
   CAYUSE CAPYBARA
   (FEMALE —) SOW
CAW KA CRY CALL CROAK QUARK
   QUAWK
CAYMAN JACARE
CAYUSE CAVY PONY BRONCO
   MUSTANG
CEASE HO BOW CUT DIE END LIN
   BALK BLIN DROP FINE HALT HOLD
   LIFT LISS QUIT REST SACE SHUT
   STAY STOP STOW AVAST CLOSE
   DOWSE LEAVE PAUSE PETER STINT
   SWICK WAIVE DESIST DEVALL
   EXPIRE FINISH FORGET ABSTAIN
   OUTGIVE REFRAIN SUSPEND
   INTERMIT OVERGIVE SURCEASE
   (— MILKING COW) SINE
   (— TEMPORARILY) LIFT
   (— TO ASSERT) ABANDON
CEASELESS EVER ENDLESS
   ETERNAL IMMORTAL UNENDING

CEASING CESSER CESSATION
CEBUS SAI
CECILIA SIS SISSU
CECROPS (DAUGHTER OF —) HERSE
   AGLAUROS PANDROSOS
   (WIFE OF —) AGLAURUS
CEDAR SUGI TOON SAVIN DEODAR
   SABINA TUMION CYPRESS JUNIPER
   WAXWING CALANTAS PAHAUTEA
CEDAR SWAMP GREENING
CEDAR WAXWING RECOLLET
CEDE CESS GIVE AWARD GRANT
   LEAVE WAIVE YIELD ASSIGN RESIGN
   SUBMIT CONCEDE RENOUNCE
   TRANSFER
CEDILLA TITTLE
CEIBA KAPOK BENTANG POCHOTE
CEIL LINE SYLE OVERLAY WAINSCOT
CEILING TOP DOME LACE LOFT
   CHUTT CUPOLA LINING SCREEN
   SOFFIT SYLING CURTAIN LACUNAR
   PLAFOND TESTUDO COVERING
   DECKHAND PANELING PLANCHER
   SEMIDOME
CELANDINE FICARY KILLWORT
   WARTWEED WARTWORT
   FELONWORT JEWELWEED
CELEBES (GULF OF —) BONE TOLO
   TOMINI
   (ISLAND OF —) MUNA BUTUNG
   PELENG SULAWESI
   (PEOPLE OF —) TORAJA
   (TOWN OF —) BUOL LUWUK
   MANADO MAKASAR
CELEBRATE FETE KEEP SING CHANT
   DITTY EXTOL HONOR REVEL SACRE
   SPEAK BESING CHAUNT EXTOLL
   PRAISE ELEGIZE EXECUTE GLORIFY
   MAFFICK OBSERVE EMBLAZON
   EULOGIZE PROCLAIM
   (— 2 MASSES) BINATE DUPLICATE
CELEBRATED KEPT FAMED NOTED
   FAMOUS EMINENT FEASTED
   RENOMME STORIED FABULOUS
   GLORIOUS NOTIFIED OBSERVED
   RENOWNED
CELEBRATION EED FETE GALA
   POPE RITE FESTA REVEL COOLIN
   CUSTOM DOMENT EASTER FIESTA
   POWWOW RENOWN SIMHAH
   BLOWOUT HOGMENA HOLIDAY
   JUBILEE PASCHAL SHINDIG SIMCHAH
   BINATION BIRTHDAY HOGMANAY
   MAKAHIKI OLYMPIAD POTLATCH
   SHIVAREE FESTIVITY HOOLAULEA
   JUNKETING
CELEBRATOR JUBILIST
CELEBRITY FAME LION NAME STAR
   CELEB ECLAT RENOWN REPUTE
CELERITY HASTE HURRY SPEED
   DISPATCH RAPIDITY VELOCITY
   SWIFTNESS
CELERY SIT ACHE STICK UMBEL
   KARPAS SALARY SMALLAGE
CELESTIAL HOLY DIVINE HEAVEN
   URANIC ANGELIC CHINESE ETHERED
   EMPYREAL ETHEREAL HEAVENLY
   OLYMPIAN
CELESTITE APOTOME

CELIBACY CHASTITY VIRGINITY
CELIBATE CLERK CHASTE SINGLE
   BACHELOR SPINSTER
CELL BOX EGG BAND BOOT CAGE
   CYTE DISC DISK GERM GONE HOLE
   JAIL KILL CABIN CAROL CLINK
   CRYPT CYTON FIBER FIBRE GHOST
   GLAND GROUP OOTID TMEMA TORIL
   VAULT ZOOID ANAXON CEPTOR
   COCCUS COOLER CYTODE GAMETE
   GONIUM INAXON PRISON SHIELD
   SIPHON SYPHON WESTON ZYGOTE
   AGAMETE AMEBULA APOCYTE
   CELLULE CHAMBER CLOCHAN
   CLOSTER COCCOID CUBICLE
   DIPLOID DUNGEON ELEMENT
   EPICYTE EUPLOID HAPLOID HEMATID
   INITIAL LOCULUS MYOCYTE
   OOBLAST PAPILLA PLASTID
   RENETTE SEGMENT SPORONT
   STEREID TRISOME UTRICLE VESICLE
   AMACRINE BASOCYTE BASOPHIL
   BIFORINE BIOPLAST CLOGHAUN
   DIKARYON FAVEOLUS GLIOCYTE
   GONIDIUM GONOCYTE HEMOCYTE
   HOLDOVER IDIOSOME LOCELLUS
   ORGANULE PROSORUS RECEPTOR
   SCLEREID SPERMULE SYNERGID
   TRACHEID TRIPLOID ZOOBLAST
   (— OF LEADERS) CADRE
   (BEE —) PIPE
   (DETENTION —) BULLPEN
   (PHOTOELECTRIC —) EYE
   (PRISON —) BING HOLE CABIN
   CLINK COOLER JIGGER
   (STAB —) BAND
   (THIN-WALLED —S) STOMIUM
   (VOLTAIC —) BATTERY
   (PL.) LAURA POTLINE SWEATBOX
CELLA NAOS
CELLAR CAVE VAULT BODEGA
   PALACE FAVISSA HYPOGEE
   BASEMENT HYPOGEUM MATAMORO
   VAULTAGE
CELLARET TANTALUS
CELLARMAN SOMMELIER
CELLULOID XYLONITE
CELLULOSE CRUMB AMYLOID
   LIGNOSE TAMIDINE
CELT GAEL GAUL KELT MANX IRISH
   WELSH BRETON BRITON EOLITH
   GOIDEL BRYTHON CORNISH
   PALSTAFF PALSTAVE
   (PL.) CYMRY KYMRY
CELTIC ERSE GAEL SCOTCH
CEMBALO DULCIMER ZIMBALON
CEMENT FIX KIT TIE GLUE HEAL
   JOIN KNIT LIME LUTE SLIP GROUT
   IMBED PASTE PUTTY SIMON STICK
   TABBY UNITE BINDER CHUNAM
   COHERE FASTEN FILLER GULGUL
   KIBOSH MALTHA MASTIC MORTAR
   OOGLEA SOLDER ASPHALT MIXTION
   ADHESIVE ALBOLITE ALBOLITH
   CEMENTUM HADIGEON SOLIDIFY
   SOLUTION
CEMENTER GLUER GLUEMAN
   SMEARER
CEMENT MIXER TEMPERER

CEMETERY HOWF KILL LAIR LITTEN CHARNEL BONEYARD CATACOMB GOLGOTHA URNFIELD
CENOBITE NUN MONK FRIAR ESSENE RECLUSE MONASTIC SYNODITE
CENOTAPH TOMB
CENSE THURIFY
CENSER INCENSER THURIBLE
CENSOR CRITIC SCREEN SYNDIC LAUNDER RESTRICT SUPPRESS
CENSORIOUS SEVERE BLAMING CARPING BLAMEFUL CAPTIOUS CRITICAL CULPABLE SLASHING
CENSORSHIP WRAPS ASSIZE CENSURE
CENSURABLE TAXABLE BLAMABLE CULPABLE
CENSURE BAN HIT NIP RAP TAP TAX WIG CALL CARP DEEM DRUB FLAY RATE SLAP TASK WITE BEANS BLAME CHIDE CURSE DECRY FAULT HOKER JUDGE PINCH SCOLD SLANG SLASH SLATE TAUNT TOUCH WHITE ACCUSE ATTACK BERATE CHARGE REBUFF REBUKE REFORM REMORD STRAFE TARGUE TIRADE BLISTER CHASTEN CONDEMN CONTROL DECRIAL DYSLOGY IMPEACH IMPROVE INVEIGH REPROOF REPROVE SCARIFY TRADUCE TROUNCE UPBRAID BACKBITE CHASTISE DISALLOW JUDGMENT LANGUAGE REPROACH SATIRIZE SENTENCE
CENSUS LIST POLL CENSE COUNT LUSTER LUSTRUM
CENT RED DUIT SANT BROWNIE CENTAVO STUIVER
(12 1-2 —S) LEVY
(ODD —S) BREAKAGE
CENTAUR CHIRON NESSUS HORSEMAN BUCENTAUR
CENTAURY BEHN BEHEN SABBATIA EARTHGALL
CENTENNIAL STATE COLORADO
CENTER COR EYE GIG HUB MID AXIS CORE NAVE SEAT SNAP YOLK FOCUS FOYER GLOME HEART MIDST PIVOT SPINE BOTTOM CENTRE MIDDLE PIPPER STAPLE TEMPLE CENTRUM ESSENCE LINEMAN NUCLEUS UMBILIC INCENTER OMPHALOS SNAPBACK
(— FOR SPINDLE) GIG
(— FOR TARGET) EYE PIN PINHOLE
(— OF ACTIVITY) HUB HIVE
(— OF ARCH) COOM
(— OF ASSURANCE) FORTRESS
(— OF ATTRACTION) FOCUS STAGE CYNOSURE
(— OF BASKET) SLATHER
(— OF CITY) DOWNTOWN
(— OF CULTIVATION) HOME
(— OF CULTURE) ATHENS
(— OF DIAMOND) WELL
(— OF FIGURE) CENTROID
(— OF FISHING NET) BUNT
(— OF FLOWER) EYE

(— OF HURRICANE) EYE
(— OF OPERATIONS) SHOP
(— OF POPULATION) CITY
(— OF POWER) SEE SIEGE
(— OF STAGE) LIMELIGHT
(— OF STRENGTH) GANGLION
(COLLECTION —) ENTREPOT
(COMMERCIAL —) MACHI EMPORIUM
(HARD —) KNOT
(INTIMATE —) BOSOM
(LATHE —) PIKE
(NERVOUS —) BRAIN
(NEURAL —) APPESTAT
(PROPAGANDA —) AGITPUNKT
(REHABILITATION —) HOSTEL
(TRADING —) BEACH EXCHANGE
(VITAL —) HEARTH HEARTBEAT
CENTERING COOM COOMB CENTRY FANTAIL
CENTERPIECE ROSACE DORMANT EPERGNE
CENTETES TENREC
CENTIARE LI
CENTIGRADE CELSIUS
CENTIME RAPPEN
CENTIMETER GAL
CENTIPEDE VEI VERI EARWIG GOLACH GOLOCH POLYPOD CHILOPOD MULTIPED MYRIAPOD SANTAPEE SCUTIGER
CENTRAL MID AXIAL BASIC CHIEF FOCAL MIXED PRIME MEDIAN MIDDLE CAPITAL CENTRIC LEADING NUCLEAR PIVOTAL PRIMARY CARDINAL DOMINANT

CENTRAL AFRICAN REPUBLIC
CAPITAL: BANGUI
COIN: FRANC
NATIVE: BAYA SARA BANDA BWAKA SANGO YAKOMA BANZIRI MANDJIA
RIVER: BOMU NANA CHARI KOTTO MBARI MPOKO OUAKA CHINKO LOBAYE UBANGI
TOWN: OBO IPPY BIRAO BOUAR KEMBE NDELE NGOTO PAOUA RAFAI ZEMIO BABOUA BAKALA BANGUI BOZOUM BAMBARI GRIMARI ZEMONGO

CENTRAL AMERICAN LADINO
(— TREE) TUNO TUNU
CENTRANTH SPURFLOWER
CENTRIFUGAL EFFERENT RADIATING
CENTRIFUGE CYCLONE SEPARATOR
CENTRIPETAL AFFERENT
CENTROSOME CENTRUM CENTRIOLE
CENTRUM CORE
CENTURIED SECULAR
CENTURY AGE SECLE SIECLE
CENTURY PLANT ALOE AGAVE MAGUEY CANTALA TEQUILA MONOCARP
CEPHALALGIA SODA HEADACHE
CEPHALIC CRANIAL ATLANTAL CEREBRAL

CEPHALOPOD SQUID CUTTLE INKFISH OCTOPUS SPIRULA DIBRANCH SCAPHITE
CEPHALUS (FATHER OF —) DEION
(MOTHER OF —) DIOMEDE
(WIFE OF —) PROCRIS
CERAMICS TILES POTTERY
CERATE WAX LARD SALVE UNGUENT OINTMENT
CERATOBRANCHIAL APOHYAL
CEREAL RYE BEAN BRAN CORN MUSH OATS RICE SAMP TEFF ARZUN GRAIN MAIZE SPELT WHEAT BARLEY BINDER FARINA HOMINY PABLUM OATMEAL SOYBEAN PORRIDGE
CEREAL LEAF FLAG
CEREBRAL CEPHALIC INVERTED
CEREBRATION THOUGHT
CEREBROSIDE KERASIN
CEREMENT SHROUD
CEREMONIAL FORM PRIM STIFF FORMAL RIALTY RITUAL SOLEMN PRECISE STUDIED TRIUMPH UPANAYA AVERSION SPLENDOR
CEREMONIOUS GRAND LOFTY STIFF FORMAL PROPER SOLEMN PRECISE STATELY STUDIED
CEREMONY BRIS FETE FORM GAUD HAKO ORGY POMP RITE SEAL SHOW SIGN SING BERIT DANCE STATE ACTION AUGURY BERITH BRIDAL BURIAL EXEQUY GOMBAY HOMAGE KERIAH MALKAH MAUNDY NIPTER OFFICE PARADE POWWOW REVIEW RITUAL SALUTE BAPTISM DISPLAY KIDDUSH MELAVEH OVATION PAGEANT PANAGIA PORTENT PRODIGY TAHARAH ACCOLADE APOLUSIS ASPERGES COEMPTIO CRIOBOLY ENCAENIA EXERCISE FUNCTION HABDALAH HAKAFOTH HERALDRY MARRIAGE OCCASION SKEYTING INAUGURAL INDUCTION
(HAZING —) CREELING
(MARRIAGE —) ESPOUSAL
(TEA —) CHANOYU
(PL.) DEGREE HOLIES AGENDUM FERALIA JUSTMENTS
CERES DEMETER
(DAUGHTER OF —) PROSERPINE PHERREPHATTA
(FATHER OF —) SATURN
(MOTHER OF —) VESTA
CERINTHE HONEYWORT
CERO SEARER SIERRA CAVALLA PINTADO KINGFISH
CERTAIN COLD COOL DEAD FAST FIRM FREE REAL SEAL SURE TRUE BOUND CLEAR EXACT FIXED PLAIN SIKER ACTUAL MEMORY SECURE SICKER STATED WITTER ASSURED PERFECT PRECISE SETTLED SRADDHA ABSOLUTE APPARENT CONSTANT OFFICIAL POSITIVE RELIABLE RESOLVED UNERRING CONFIDENT
CERTAINLY AY AYE WIS AMEN IWIS SOON SURE WHAT YWIS TRULY

CERTES INDEED PERDIE SICCAR SICKER SURELY VERILY HARDILY EVERMORE FORSOOTH SECURELY **(MOST —)** SO
CERTAINTY YEA CERT PIPE CINCH POLICY SURETY SURENESS CONSTANCY
(LACK OF —) SCRUPLE
CERTIFICATE BOND CHIT CHECK DEMIT JURAT LIBEL SCRIP TALON TITLE AMPARO ATTEST CEDULA COUPON INDENT PATENT POTTAH RETURN TICKET VERIFY CERTIFY CONSTAT DIPLOMA VOUCHER WARRANT WAYBILL AEGROTAT JUDGMENT KABBALAH NAVICERT REGISTER REGISTRY SECURITY TESCARIA TESTAMUR TEZKIRAH
(MARRIAGE —) LINES
(MINER'S —) LICENCE LICENSE
(PILOT'S —) BRANCH
(SERVANT'S —) CHIT
CERTIFICATION PASS STAMP APPROVAL HECHSHER CLEARANCE DISCHARGE
CERTIFIED SWORN
CERTIFY AVOW VISE SWEAR AFFIRM ASSURE ATTEST DEPOSE EVINCE VERIFY WITTER APPROVE ENDORSE LICENSE TESTIFY
CERTITUDE CERTAIN CONFIDENCE
CERULEAN BLUE AZURE COELIN CYANEAN CYANEOUS
CERUMEN WAX EARWAX
CESS BOG TAX CEDE DUTY LEVY LUCK RATE ABWAB SLOPE YIELD IMPOST MEASURE SURRENDER
(BAD —) SORRA
CESSATION HO END HOO BLIN HALT HUSH LISS LULL REST STAY STOP BREAK CEASE CLOSE DEVAL LETUP LISSE PAUSE SLACK STINT TRUCE CUTOFF DEMISE DISUSE OFFSET PERIOD RECESS CEASING CLOSURE RESPITE ABEYANCE BLACKOUT DESITION INTERVAL SHUTDOWN STOPPAGE SURCEASE SUSPENSE
(— OF HOSTILITIES) TRUCE INDUCIAE ARMISTICE
(— OF LIFE) DEATH
(— OF RESPIRATION) APNEA APNOEA
(— OF WORK) HARTAL
CESSPOOL SINK SUMP SINKER CISTERN JAWHOLE SINKHOLE SUSPIRAL
CESTRUM POISONBERRY
CESTUS CEST CESTON HURLBAT GAUNTLET WHIRLBAT
CETACEAN ORC CETE ORCA SUSU WHALE BELUGA COWFISH DOLPHIN GRAMPUS NARWHAL MUTILATE PORPOISE
CEYLON SERENDIP TAPROBANE

CEYLON
CAPITAL: COLOMBO
COIN: CENT
GULF: MANNAR
MEASURE: PARA PARAH AMUNAM PARRAH
POINT: PEDRO ,
STRAIT: PALK
TOWN: GALLE KANDY JAFFNA MANNAR MATARA BADULLA COLOMBO PUTTALAM
TREE: HORA PALU

CEYLONESE CEYLON BURGHER
CEYLON MOSS GULAMAN
CGS UNIT STILB STOKE
CHA TSIA CHAIS
CHACMA BAVIAN BOBBEJAAN

CHAD
CAPITAL: FORTLAMY
COIN: FRANC FRANCCFA
LAKE: CHAD
NATIVE: ARAB SARA KREDA MASSA TOUBOU KAMADJA MOUNDAN
PLATEAU: ENNEDI
RIVER: CHARI LOGONE BAHRAOUK
TOWN: ATI BOL LAI MAO FADA FAYA MONGO ARECHE BONGOR LARGEAU MOUNDOU MOUSSORO

CHADOR PHULKARI
CHAETOCHLOA SETARIA
CHAETOPOD SCALEBACK
CHAFE IRK RUB VEX FRET FRIG FROT FUME GALD GALL HEAT JOSH RAGE WARM WEAR ANGER ANNOY CHAFF GRIND SCOLD SNUFF WORRY WRING ABRADE BANTER EXCITE FRIDGE HARASS INJURY NETTLE RANKLE INCENSE INFLAME SNUFFLE FRICTION IRRITATE RAILLERY
CHAFER CRESSET
CHAFF GUY HAY PUG ROT BRAN CAFF CHIP GRIT GUFF JOSH PULU QUIZ RAZZ BORAK CHYAK DROSS GLUME HULLS HUSKS JOLLY SLACK STOUR STRAW TEASE TRASH BANTER BHOOSA REFUSE CAVINGS TAILING RAILLERY RIDICULE SHELLING
CHAFFER BANDY SIEVE WARES BUYING DICKER HAGGLE HIGGLE MARKET PALTER BARGAIN CHATTER SELLING TRAFFIC EXCHANGE
CHAFFINCH PINK CHINK SPINK TWINK ROBERD SCOBBY SHILFA SKELLY ROBINET SNABBIE WETBIRD
CHAFFY SCALY ACEROSE ACEROUS PALEATE
CHAFING GALLING IMPATIENCE
CHAGRIN ENVY SPITE VEXATION
CHAGRINED SICK ASHAMED
CHAIN FOB GUY NET ROW SET TEW TIE TOE TOW TUG TYE BIND BOND CURB FALL FAST FILE GYVE JOIN LINE LINK SEAL SOAM TEAM BRAIL CABLE GROUP GUARD LEASH

SHANK SHEET SLANG SLING SUITE TRACE TRAIN WRASE CARCAN CATENA COLLAR CORDON FASTEN FETTER GANGER HANGER HOBBLE JACKER JIGGER LINKER RACKAN SECURE SERIES STRING TETHER TOGGLE BOBSTAY CATFALL CHIGNON CONNECT EMBRACE ENSLAVE LASHING MANACLE NETWORK PAINTER PENDANT SAUTOIR SHACKLE TACKLER BACKROPE BRACELET CARCANET GLEIPNIR LINKWORK NECKLACE RECEPTOR RESTRAIN RIGWIDDY STROBILA WOOLDING
(— FOR ANCHOR) CATFALL PAINTER
(— FOR BINDING) JACKER TACKLER
(— FOR WRAPPING MAST) WOOLDING
(— OF AUTHORITIES) ISNAD
(— OF DUNES) SAIF SEIF
(— OF MOUNTAINS) RANGE
(— OF ROCKS) REEF
(— ON CONVICT'S LEG) SLANG
(— TO BIND CATTLE) SEAL
(DECORATIVE —) FESTOON
(ENDLESS —) CREEPER
(MAGIC —) GLEIPNIR
(SHORT —) SHANK
(SUSPENDED —) CATENARY
(WATCH —) FOB ALBERT
(PL.) IRONS CONVEYOR
CHAIN LINK SHUT COPULA SWIVEL
CHAINMAN CLASHY CLASHEE LINEMAN TAPEMAN
CHAIN-SHAPED CATENOID
CHAIR KEEP SEAT SHOP HORSE SEDAN STOOL ESTATE OFFICE PULPIT ROCKER SADDLE SITTER TONJON CACOLET COMMODE FANBACK GONDOLA SITTING VOYEUSE WINDSOR ARMCHAIR CARRIAGE CATHEDRA FAUTEUIL KANGAROO SGABELLO VOLTAIRE
(— OF STATE) THRONE
(— SLUNG FROM POLE) KAGO TALABON
(— WITH CANOPY) STATE
(BISHOP'S —) CATHEDRA FALDSTOOL
(EASY —) COGSWELL
(GREEK —) KLISMOS
(MINING —) DOG
(PORTABLE —) SEDAN
(SPRING —) PERCH
(THRONE —) SHINZA
CHAIRMAN HEAD CHAIR EMCEE PRESES SPEAKER CONVENER DIRECTOR
CHAISE GIG SHAY CHAIR CALESIN CARRIAGE
CHAISE LONGUE DAYBED DUCHESSE
CHALAZA TREAD TREADLE GALLATURE
CHALCEDONY ONYX OPAL SARD AGATE PRASE CATEYE JASPER QUARTZ CARNEOL ENHYROS OPALINE SARDINE SARDIUS

CHALCOPYRITE RUN
CHALDEAN KALDANI BABYLONIAN
(— **MEASURE**) CANE FOOT MAKUK
QASAB ARTABA GARIBA GHALVA
MANSION
(— **RIVER**) TIGRIS EUPHRATES
(— **TOWN**) UR
CHALICE AMA CUP BOWL CALIX
GRAIL REGAL GOBLET KRASIS
CHALK CAUK CORK PALE SCAR
TALC TICK CRETA FLOUR SCORE
BLANCH BLEACH CRAYON CREDIT
RUBBLE WHITEN ACCOUNT WHITING
(**GREEN** —) PRASINE
(**HARD** —) HURLOCK
(**RED** —) RUBRIC
(**SURVEYOR'S** —) KEEL
CHALKBOARD GREENBOARD
CHALKY CRETACIC
CHALLENGE VIE BRAG CALL DARE
DEFY FACE GAGE BANCO BLAME
BRAVE CLAIM QUERY STUMP
ACCUSE APPEAL BANTER CARTEL
CHARGE DACKER DAIKER DEMAND
DESCRY FORBID IMPUGN INFIRM
INVITE RECUSE SERDAB ARRAIGN
CENSURE IMPEACH PROVOKE
REPROVE SOLICIT SUMMONS
CHAMPION DEFIANCE GAUNTLET
QUESTION REPROACH
(— **A BULL**) CITE
CHALLENGING PIQUANT
BLOODSHOT
CHALYBEATE MARTIAL
CHAMBER ODA AGER CELL CIST
DOME FLAT FOLD HALL IWAN KIVA
ROOM SALE TOMB BOWER CAVUM
COURT GOMER HOUSE SENAT
SHAFT SOLAR SOLER STOVE
ATRIUM CAMARA CAMERA COFFER
HEADER HOLLOW MIHRAB SENADO
SENATE SOLLAR SPRING STANZA
WILSON BEDROOM CAISSON
CHALMAR CHANNEL CHAUMER
CONCAVE CUBICLE FAVISSA
FIREBOX GALLERY GEHENNA
MANSION RECEIPT CASEMATE
CYLINDER DIFFUSER FOUNTAIN
GROSSRAT SMOKEBOX SNEMOVNA
THALAMUS
(— **FOR MOLTEN GLASS**) FONT
(— **IN FURNACE**) SHAFT DOGHOUSE
(— **OF EAR**) SACCULE
(— **POT**) JORDAN JEROBOAM
(**AIR** —) SPONSON
(**BOMBPROOF** —) CASEMATE
(**FIRE** —) ARCH STOVE COCKLE
FIREBOX
(**FORTIFICATION** —) BUNKER
(**OPEN** —) LANTERN
(**ORGAN** —) SWELL
(**PRIVATE** —) CLOSET CONCLAVE
(**PUEBLO** —) KIVA ESTUFA
(**SLEEPING** —) BEDROOM
WARDROBE
(**SMALL** —) LOCULUS
(**SUPPLY** —) MAGAZINE
(**UNDERGROUND** —) CAVE CRYPT
CAVERN HYPOGEE

(**WATERTIGHT** —) CAISSON
CHAMBERLAIN EUNUCH FACTOR
SERVANT STEWARD PALATINE
POLONIUS
CHAMELEON ANOLE ANOLI LACERT
SAURIAN
CHAMFER BEVEL CHIMB CHIME
CHINE FLUTE CIPHER FURROW
GROOVE
CHAMOIS GEMS IZARD AOUDAD
SHAMMY
CHAMOMILE MAYWEED
CHAMP BITE CHAW FIRM HARD
MASH CHANK CHOMP FIELD GNASH
TRAMPLE
CHAMPAGNE AY BUBBLY SIMKIN
BELLEEK SILLERY
CHAMPION ACE AID FAN ABET BACK
BOSS DEFY HERO KEMP GHAZI
ASSERT ATTEND DEFEND KNIGHT
PATRON SQUIRE VICTOR ESPOUSE
FIGHTER PALADIN PROTECT
ADVOCATE DEFENDER PALMERIN
CHAMPIONSHIP TITLE LAURELS
ADVOCACY
CHAMPLEVE INLAID
CHANCE DIE HAP LOT CASE CAST
DINT DRAW FATE LINE LUCK ODDS
RISK SHOT SHOW TIDE BREAK
ETTLE STAKE WHACK BETIDE
CASUAL GAMBLE HAPPEN HAZARD
MISHAP RANDOM SQUEAK AIMLESS
FORTUNE STUMBLE VANTAGE
VENTURE ACCIDENT CASUALTY
EVENTUAL FORTUITY
(**ADVERSE** —) HAZARD
(**EVEN** —) TOSSUP
CHANCELLOR LOGOTHETE
CHANDELIER LUSTER PHAROS
PENDANT CHANDLER GASELIER
CHANDLER TALLOWER
CHANE OREJON
CHANGE MEW CHOP FLOP MOLT
MOVE ODDS PEAL TURN VARY VEER
WARP WEND ADAPT ALTER AMEND
BREAK COINS EMEND MOULT SHIFT
THROW ADJUST BECOME DIFFER
DIGEST IMMUTE MODIFY MUANCE
MUTATE REMOVE REVAMP REVISE
SWITCH WISSEL WRIXLE COMMUTE
CONVERT CUTOVER DEVIATE
FLUXION MORTIFY BECOMING
DENATURE EXCHANGE INNOVATE
LENITION REVISION TRANSFER
TRANSUME VARIANCE
(— **APPEARANCE**) DISGUISE
(— **COLOR**) TURN
(— **COURSE**) GYBE JIBE
(— **DIRECTION**) CUT CANT CHOP
HAUL KNEE VEER ANGLE BREAK
SHIFT
(— **FOR BETTER**) HELP
(— **FOR WORSE**) BEDEVIL
(— **FORM**) DEVELOP
(— **GAIT**) BREAK
(— **GRADUALLY**) PASS GRADUATE
(— **IN COURSE**) SHEER
(— **IN DIRECTION**) JOG KNEE STEP
(— **IN ELEVATION**) FORK

(— **IN SIZE**) ASTOGENY
(— **INTO VAPOR**) FLASH
(— **MONEY**) WISSEL
(— **OF FORM**) SET
(— **OF GEAR**) KICKDOWN
(— **OF MIND**) CAPRICE
(— **OF MOOD**) VARY
(— **OF PITCH**) MOTION INFLECT
(— **OF SEA LEVEL**) EUSTACY
(— **OF SOUND**) BREAKING
(— **OF WORD**) ANAGRAM
(— **ONE'S HEART**) REPENT
(— **POSITION**) STIR FLEET HOTCH
(— **QUICKLY**) FLY
(— **SHAPE**) DRAW CREEP DEFORM
(— **RESIDENCE**) FLIT
(**ABRUPT** —) DOGLEG SALTATION
(**ABNORMAL** —) LESION
(**GEAR** —) KICKDOWN
(**GRADUAL** —) DRIFT
(**PRESSURE** —) ALLOBAR
(**SHORT** —) FLUFF
(**SMALL** —) GROCERY
(**UNEXPECTED** —) SWITCH
(**PL.**) DOUBLES PLASTIQUE
CHANGEABLE EEMIS GIDDY IMMIS
LIGHT WINDY CHOPPY FICKLE
FITFUL GERFUL KETCHY LABILE
MOBILE MOTLEY MUABLE SHIFTY
BRUCKLE ERRATIC MUTABLE
PROTEAN UNSTAID VARIANT
VARIOUS VOLUBLE AMENABLE
CATCHING GLIBBERY MOVEABLE
TICKLISH UNSTABLE VARIABLE
VEERABLE VOLATILE WEATHERY
CHANGEABLENESS LEVITY
VIBRATION
CHANGED VARIED ANOTHER
CHANGEFUL FICKLE SHIFTY
MUTABLE RESTLESS
CHANGELESS CONSISTENT
CHANGELING AUF AWF OAF DOLT
FOOL CHILD DUNCE IDIOT WAVERER
IMBECILE KILLCROP RENEGADE
TURNCOAT
CHANGING FLUXIBLE ALTERNATE
(— **MONEY**) AGIO
(**CONTINUALLY** —) FLOATING
CHANK SANK CONCH
CHANNEL CUT GAT POD REE RUT
SOW CANO CAVA DEEP DIKE DUCT
DYKE FLUE GATE GOOL GOTE GOUT
GURT KILL KYLE LAKE LANE PACE
PIPE RACE SLEW SLOO VEIN WADI
WADY BAYOU CANAL CARRY CHASE
COWAL DITCH DRAIN DRILL FLUME
FLUTE GLYPH GUIDE INSET QUIRK
RIVER SINUS SLIDE STOOL STOVE
STRIA SWASH AIRWAY ALVEUS
ARROYO ARTERY BRANCH COURSE
CUTOFF ESTERO FURROW GROOVE
GULLET GUTTER HOLLOW KENNEL
KEYWAY LAGOON MEDIUM OFFLET
OILWAY RABBET RESACA RIVOSE
RUNWAY SLOUGH SLUICE SPECUS
STRAIT STRAND STREAM THROAT
TROUGH CHAMFER CONDUCT
CONDUIT CULVERT CUNETTE
EURIPUS OFFTAKE PASSAGE

RACEWAY RIVULET SHIPWAY
SILANGA STRIGIL THALWEG
TIDEWAY WASHOUT AQUEDUCT
FLOODWAY GUIDEWAY GUNKHOLE
RACELINE SCOURWAY SPILLWAY
(— FOR MOLTEN METAL) SOW GATE
RUNNER
(— IN CLOTH) FLUTE
(— IN ICE FIELD) LEAD
(— IN MOLD) SPRAY
(— OF AQUEDUCT) SPECUS
(— ON WHALE) SCARF
(ARTIFICAL —) GAT GOUT
(DRAINAGE —) GAW
(ENGLISH —) SLEEVE
(INCLINED —) SHOOT
(IRRIGATION —) AUWAI DROVE
(LYMPH —) CISTERNA
(SECONDARY —) BINNACLE
(SLOPING —) CHUTE SHUTE
CHANNELBILL RAINFOWL
CHANNELED FLUTED
CHANT CANT MELE SING SONG
TONE CAROL PSALM SOUGH
ANTHEM CANTUS INTONE LITANY
WARBLE CHORTLE INTROIT
PROSODE REQUIEM WORSHIP
ALLELUIA ANTIPHON SINGSONG
CHANTER STICK CANTOR SINGER
BAGPIPE SONGSTER CHALUMEAU
(— OF BAGPIPE) OBOE
CHANTERELLE CANTINO
CHANTING CHARM HAZANUT
ANTIPHONY CHAZZANUT
CHANTLATE SPROCKET
CHANTRY CAGE
CHAOS NU NUN PIE APSU GULF
HYLE MESS VOID ABYSS BABEL
CHASM JUMBLE MATTER TOPHET
ANARCHY MIXTURE DISORDER
SHAMBLES TAILSPIN TOHUBOHU
CHAOTIC MUDDLED CONFUSED
FORMLESS
CHAP BOY BUY DOG LAD MAN RAP
WAG BEAN BEAT BIRD BLOW CHIP
CHOP COVE DICK DUCK HIND JOHN
KIBE MASH MATE NABS SNAP BILLY
BLOKE BUCKO BULLY BUYER CHAFT
CHINK CLEFT CRACK FRUIT KNOCK
LOVER RUMMY SCOUT SPLIT SPORT
SPRAY SWIPE TRADE YOUTH
BARTER BOHUNK BREACH BUGGER
CALLAN CHOOSE CODGER CUFFIN
FELLOW FOUTER FOUTRA GAFFER
GEEZER JOSSER KIPPER SHAVER
STRIKE STROKE TURNIP BROTHER
CALLANT FISSURE HUSBAND
ROUGHEN BLIGHTER CUSTOMER
DIVISION MERCHANT
(— HANDS) RACK SPRAY
(— IN SKIN) KIN KIBE
(FINE —) BULLY
(OLD —) GEEZER
(QUEER —) GALOOT
(S.AFRICAN —) KEREL
(YOUNG —) GAFFER
(PL.) CHOPS
CHAPARRAL MONTE CHAMISAL
BUCKTHORN

CHAPARRO YAYA
CHAPBOOK CHAP GARLAND
CHAPE CRAMPET MORDANT
CHAPEL CAGE CAPE COPE COWL
HOOD CLOAK PORCH BETHEL
CHARRE CHURCH HAIKAL MORADA
SHRINE CAPELLA CHANTRY
CHARNEL CHHATRI GALILEE
MARTYRY MEETING MEMORIA
ORATORY SACRARY SERVICE
BETHESDA DEACONRY DIACONIA
FERETORY FERETRUM SACELLUM
SODALITY
(UNDERGROUND —) SHROUDS
CHAPERON HOOD ATTEND DUENNA
ESCORT MATRON GRIFFIN PROTECT
GUARDIAN TRAPPING
CHAPLAIN PADRE LEVITE CONDUCT
ALTARIST ORDINARY
CHAPLET BEAD ORLE STUD CROWN
ANADEM ANCHOR CIRCLE FILLET
JAMBER JAMMER ROSARY STAPLE
TROPHY WREATH CORONAL
CORONET GARLAND MOULDING
NECKLACE ORNAMENT
CHAPMAN CHAP BUYER DEALER
HAWKER TRADER COPEMAN
PEDDLER CUSTOMER MERCHANT
CHAPPIE JOCKEY
CHAPS FLEWS BREECHES LEGGINGS
OVERALLS
CHAPTER BODY CELL PACE POST
CAPUT COURT LODGE BRANCH
CABILDO CAPITAL CORRECT
COUNCIL MEETING SECTION
ASSEMBLY
(— OF BOOK) CAPITAL
(— OF KORAN) SURA SURAH
(— OF SOCIETY) CAMP CIRCLE
CHAR BURN CART COAL SEAR BROIL
CHARK CHORE SHARD SINGE TROUT
SCORCH BLACKEN CHARIOT
REDBELLY SAIBLING SALMONID
SANDBANK
CHARA MUSKGRASS
CHARACIN DORADO DOURADE
BLOODFIN
CHARACTER BALL BENT CARD CASE
CLAY CLEF DASH ECAD FLAT FOND
FORM HAIR KIND MAKE MARK MOLD
NOTE PART ROLE RUNE SIGN SORT
TONE TRIM TYPE BRAND COLOR
ETHIC ETHOS FIBER HABIT HEART
HUMOR INDEX SAVOR STAMP
TENOR TOKEN TRAIT WRITE
CARACT CIPHER COCKUP DAGGER
DIRECT EMBLEM FIGURE GENIUS
HANGER LETTER MANNER METTLE
NATURE REPUTE SIGLUM SPIRIT
STRIPE SYMBOL CLOTHES EDITION
ENGRAVE ESSENCE IMPRESS
QUALITY FRACTION IDENTITY
INFERIOR INSCRIBE LIGATURE
SELFHOOD SYLLABIC DESCENDER
(— IN DRAMA) CHORUS
(— IN PLAY) DAME BESSY
(— OF SOIL) LAIR
(ASSUMED —) ROLE FIGURE
INCOGNITO

(BAD —) DROLE BUDMASH
(BASIC —) BOTTOM
(CHINESE —) SHOU RADICAL
(COMMON —) COMMUNITY
(ESSENTIAL —) ALLOY
(FIRM —) BACKBONE
(GIVE — TO) TONE
(JAPANESE —S) HIBUNCI
(MENDELIAN —) ALLEL ALLELE
(PHYSICAL —) ARMENOID
(PRIME —) ESSENCE
(SHIFTLESS —) BEAT
(STOCK —) MACCUS
(TESTED —) ASSAY
(TRIED —) TOUCH
(VULGAR —S) ONMUN
(PL.) MANA
CHARACTERISTIC CAST COST
MARK MIEN ANGLE AROMA GRACE
POINT TACHE TOKEN TRAIT ACCENT
BEAUTY NATURE STIGMA STROKE
ADJUNCT AMENITY FEATURE
IMPRESS QUALITY SPECIES TYPICAL
ACTIVITY PECULIAR PROPERTY
SYMBOLIC
(— OF ANTIBODIES) AVIDITY
(ADVENTITIOUS —) ACCIDENT
(DISTINGUISHING —) SPECIES
HALLMARK BIRTHMARK
(PECULIAR —) IDIOPATHY
(PL.) CORNERS FACULTY
CHARACTERIZATION ELOGY
ELOGIUM
CHARACTERIZE MARK STYLE
DEFINE DEPICT TITULE ENGRAVE
ENTITLE IMPRINT PORTRAY
DESCRIBE INDICATE INSCRIBE
CHARADES GAME
CHARCOAL COAL CARBO CHARK
CARBON FUSAIN PENCIL BLACKEN
SPODIUM SCRIBBET
CHARGE FEE LAP LAY RAP TAX
BEEF BILL BUCK CALL CARE CARK
CAST COST CURE DUES DUTY FILL
GIBE KEEP LADE LIEN LOAD NICK
NOTE ONUS RACK RATE REST RUSH
SHOT SIZE SOAK SPAR TASK TOLL
WARD WIKE BLAME CAUSE CHALK
COUNT CRIME DEBIT EXTRA GYRON
ONSET ORDER PRICE REFER SCORE
SHOCK STICK STING THING TRUST
ACCUSE ADJURE ALLEGE APPEAL
ASSESS ATTACK BURDEN CAREER
CENSUS COURSE CREDIT DAMAGE
DEFAME DEMAND ENJOIN ENURNY
EXCESS IMPOSE IMPUTE METAGE
OFFICE PIPAGE REATUS SUMMIT
SURTAX TARIFF TOWAGE WEIGHT
ACIDIZE ANNULET ARRAIGN ARTICLE
ASCRIBE ASSAULT AVERAGE
BOATAGE CARTAGE CENSURE
CHEVRON CLAMPER COMMAND
CONCERN CONJURE CORKAGE
CORNAGE CUSTODY DOCKAGE
DRAYAGE EMBASSY EXPENSE
FLOTAGE HAULAGE IGNITER
IMPEACH KEEPING MANDATE
MILEAGE MISSION MIXTURE
MOORAGE PANNAGE QUAYAGE

REPRISE SIDEAGE SLANDER
SLIDAGE SURMISE WARPAGE
BILLBACK BRASSAGE CASUALTY
CHASTISE CRESCENT DELAYAGE
DENOUNCE LEGATION ORDINARY
OVERLOAD PLANKAGE POUNDAGE
PROVINCE QUESTION SLINGING
SPENDING STANDAGE TUTORAGE
VIGORISH COMPLAINT
(— AGAINST) TILT
(— BATTERY) SOAK BOOST
(— EXCESSIVELY) FLEECE
(— FALSELY) SURMISE
(— OF FIREARM) LOAD
(— OF METAL) HEAT
(— OF ORE) POST
(— TO BE PAID) LAW
(— UPON PROPERTY) LIEN
(— WITH CRIME) ACCUSE INDICT
ARTICLE ATTAINT IMPEACH
(— WITH GAS) AERATE
(AGGREGATE —S) BOOK
(CANNON —) GRAPE
(COVER —) COUVERT
(DEPTH —) CAN
(EXPLOSIVE —) CAP BLAST SNAKE
SQUIB TULIP BOOSTER BURSTER
IGNITER
(FALSE —) CALUMNY
(HERALDIC —) DROP GIRON GYRON
LABEL DRAGON GURGES BEARING
ESQUIRE
(MAILING —) FRANKAGE
(POWDER —) GRAIN
(SHAPED —) BEEHIVE
(SPIRITUAL —) CURE
(TEMPORARY —) CARE
(WINE —) CORKAGE
CHARGED UP HOT LADEN BELAST
BILLETY BILLETTE ELECTRIC
INSTINCT
(— WITH EMOTION) SWOLLEN
CHARGEHAND CLICKER
CHARGEMAN BLASTER
CHARGER DISH HORSE MOUNT
STEED ACCUSER COURSER
PLATTER
CHARILY FRUGALLY GINGERLY
CHARIOT CAR BIGA CART CHAR
RATH WAIN BUGGY CHAIR ESSED
RATHA TRIGA WAGON CHARET
QUADRIGA
CHARIOTEER AURIGA CARTER
DRIVER IOLAUS LEADER CARTARE
WAGONER MYRTILUS AUTOMEDON
CHARITABLE KIND BENIGN HUMANE
LENIENT LIBERAL GENEROUS
CHARITY ALMS DOLE GIFT LOVE
PITY RUTH MERCY BASKET BOUNTY
CARITAS HANDOUT LARGESS
LENIENCE TZEDAKAH
CHARIVARI BABEL SHALLAL
SERENADE SHIVAREE
CHARLATAN FAKE CHEAT FAKER
FRAUD QUACK CABOTIN EMPIRIC
IMPOSTER MAGICIAN SYCOPHANT
CHARLES II DAVID
CHARLIE MCCARTHY STOOGE
CHARLOCK KRAUT RUNCH HARLOCK

KEDLOCK KERLOCK MUSTARD
SINAPIS YELLOWS CHARDOCK
CHEDLOCK SKEDLOCK SKELLOCH
CHARM IT GBO KEY OBI CALM CHIC
HAND JINX JUJU JYNX LUCK MOJO
PLAY RUNE SNOW SONG TAKE TILL
ZOGO ALLAY BRIEF CATCH FAVOR
FREET FREIT GRACE LAMIN MAGIC
OBEAH SAFFI SAFIE SPELL VENUS
WANGA WEIRD ALLURE AMULET
BEAUTY CARACT DEASIL ENAMOR
ENGAGE ENTICE FETISH GLAMOR
GRIGRI INCANT MANTRA MELODY
PLEASE SAPHIE SCARAB SOOTHE
SUBDUE SUMMON VOODOO
ABRAXAS ASSUAGE ATTRACT
BEGUILE BEWITCH CANTION
CANTRIP CONJURE CONTROL
DELIGHT ENCHANT ENTHRAL
FLATTER HEITIKI PERIAPT PHILTER
PHILTRE SINGING SORCERY
BLESSING BRELOQUE COQUETRY
ENTHRALL ENTRANCE GLAUMRIE
GREEGREE PISHOGUE PRACTICE
TALISMAN
CHARMED CAPTIVE
CHARMER SIREN EXORCIST
MAGICIAN SORCERER ENCHANTER
CHARMING LEPID SWEET GOLDEN
WIZARD AMIABLE DARLING
EYESOME TEMPEAN WINNING
WINSOME ADORABLE DELICATE
GRACEFUL LOVESOME
CHARNEL GHASTLY CEMETERY
GOLGOTHA
CHARON (FATHER OF —) EREBUS
(MOTHER OF —) NOX
CHARPOY COT
CHARQUI JERKY XARQUE
CHART MAP BILL CARD PLAN PLAT
PLOT ROSE CARTE GRAPH STILL
RECORD SCHEME DIAGRAM
EMAGRAM EXPLORE ISOTYPE
OUTLINE PROJECT DOCUMENT
DOPEBOOK MERCATOR PLATFORM
(— BOOK) WAGONER
(— FROM AIR) AEROVIEW
(— MARK) VIGIA
(— OF A COURSE) RUTTER
(MARINER'S —) ROSE
(WEATHER —) ANALOGUE
CHARTER FIX LET BOND BOOK DEED
HIRE RENT CARTE CHART FUERO
GRANT LEASE SANAD CHARTA
PERMIT SUNNUD DIPLOMA
CONTRACT GRUNDLOV HEIRLOOM
LANDBOOK MONOPOLY PANCHART
CHARWOMAN CHARER CHARLADY
PORTRESS JANITRESS
CHARY SHY DEAR WARY CHERE
SCANT SPARE DAINTY FRUGAL
PRIZED SKIMPY CAREFUL CURIOUS
SPARING CAUTIOUS HESITANT
PRECIOUS RESERVED SPAREFUL
VIGILANT
CHASE FOG SIC SUE FALL HUNT
JERL SHAG SHOO SICK ANNOY
CATCH CHEVY CHIVY DRIVE HARRY
HOUND SCORE SHACK CACCIA

CHIVVY CHOUSE EMBOSS FOLLOW
FRIEZE FURROW GALLOP GROOVE
HALLOO HARASS HOLLOW INDENT
PURSUE QUARRY SCORSE TRENCH
CHANNEL ENGRAVE HUNTING
PURSUIT ORNAMENT PURCHASE
(— GAME) COURSE
(— HARD) RATTLE
CHASER RAM DRINK HOUND
FROGGER
(WOMAN —) SHEEPBITER
CHASM GAP KIN PIT GULF RIFT
YAWN ABYSS BLANK CANON CHAOS
CLEFT GORGE BREACH CANYON
HIATUS FISSURE MEGARON
SWALLOW VACANCY APERTURE
CREVASSE INTERVAL VACATION
CHASSE SLIP GLIDE SASHAY
CHASSEUR HUNTER BELLBOY
DOORMAN FOOTMAN HUNTSMAN
CHASSIS SASH FRAME FIGURE
CHASTE CAST PURE CLEAN ZONED
DECENT HONEST MODEST PROPER
SEVERE VESTAL VIRGIN CLEANLY
PUDICAL REFINED CELIBATE
INNOCENT VIRGINLY VIRTUOUS
CHASTEN RATE ABASE SMITE
SMOTE SNEAP SOBER HUMBLE
PUNISH REFINE SUBDUE TEMPER
AFFLICT CENSURE CORRECT
NURTURE CHASTISE MODERATE
RESTRAIN
CHASTISE BEAT FIRK FLOG LASH
SLAP TRIM WHIP AMEND BLAME
FEEZE SCOLD SPANK SPILL STRAP
TAUNT ACCUSE ANOINT BERATE
CHARGE PUNISH PURIFY REBUKE
REFINE SWINGE TEMPER THRASH
TICKLE CHASTEN CORRECT
REPROVE SCOURGE SHINGLE
SUSPECT
CHASTISEMENT ROD TOCO TOKO
CENSURE PAYMENT FLOGGING
(DIVINE —) WRATH
CHASTITY HONOR PURITY VIRTUE
HONESTY MODESTY CELIBACY
GOODNESS PUDICITY INNOCENCE
CHASUBLE CASULA DEACON INFULA
PLANET PAENULA PIANETA
VESTMENT
CHAT GAS JAW MAG BIRD CHIN
CONE COZE DISH GIST TALK TELL
TOVE TWIG YARN AMENT CAUSE
COOSE CRACK DALLY PITCH POINT
PRATE PROSE PROSS SPEAK SPIKE
VISIT BABBLE BRANCH CATKIN
CONFAB COURSE DEVICE GABBLE
GIBBER GOSSIP GOSTER HOBNOB
JABBER NATTER POTATO POTTER
SAMARA CHAFFER CHATTER
CAUSERIE CHATTERY CONVERSE
SPIKELET STROBILE
CHATEAU HOUSE TOWER CASTLE
MANSION SCHLOSS CHATELET
FORTRESS
CHATON BASIL BEZEL BEZIL STONE
COATING SETTING
CHATTEL CATTLE PLEDGE FIXTURE
CATALLUM PERSONAL

(DISTRAINT OF —S) NAAM
(PL.) STUFF FARLEU FARLEY
COMODATO HOUSEHOLD
CHATTER GAB JAW MAG YAP BLAB
CARP CHAT CHIN CLAP CLAT DISH
GASH HACK KNAP RICK TALK TEAR
YIRR CABAL CLACK GARRE HAVER
PRATE SHAKE BABBLE BRUDGE
CACKLE CLAVER GABBLE GIBBER
GOSSIP JABBER JANGLE JARGON
PALTER RATTLE SHIVER TATTER
TATTLE TINKLE YAMMER YATTER
BLABBER BRABBLE CHACKLE
CHAFFER CHIPPER CHITTER
CLACKET CLATTER CLITTER
NASHGOB PALAVER PRABBLE
PRATING PRATTLE SHATTER
SMATTER TRATTLE TWATTLE
TWITTER TWITTLE WHITTER
BABBLING LOLLYGAG SCHMOOSE
VERBIAGE
CHATTERBOX JAY MAG PIET BUCCO
CLACK CRYSTE GOSSIP MAGPIE
CHATTERER JAY CHUET CHEWET
GABBER MAGPIE RATTLE HAVERER
CHATTERING PIET BABBLY CHAVISH
POPPING TWITTER BABBLING
CHATTY CHIRRUPY GARRULOUS
CHAUFFEUR DRIVER SHOVER
TESTER
CHAUVINISM JINGOISM
CHAUVINIST JINGO JINGOIST
CHAW JAW VEX CHEW ENVY MULL
GRIND PONDER
CHAYOTE CHOCHO TALLOTE
HUISQUIL MIRLITON
CHEAP LOW BASE GAIN POOR VILE
BORAX CLOSE FLASH GAUDY
GROSS KITCH LIGHT MUCKY NASTY
PRICE SNIDE TATTY TIGHT TINNY
VALUE ABJECT BRUMMY CHEESY
COMMON CRUMBY CRUMMY LEADEN
PLENTY SHODDY SORDID STINGY
TAWDRY TRASHY UNDEAR BARGAIN
CHINTZY POPULAR TINHORN
BRUMMAGE INFERIOR PENNORTH
SIXPENNY TWOPENNY
(— ITEM) TWOFER
CHEAPEN DOCK STALE VILIFY
SMALLEN
CHEAP SKATE STIFF
CHEAT DO BAM BOB COG CON FOB
FOP FUB GIP GUM GYP JIG NIP
TOP BEAT BILK BITE BULL BURN
CLIP COLT CRIB DISH DUFF DUPE
FAKE FIRK FLAM FLUM GECK GULL
HAVE HOAX JILT JINK JOUK KNAP
LIAR MACE MUMP NAIL NICK NOSE
POOP PULL REAM ROOK SELL SHAM
SILE SKIN SLUR SNAP SWAP SWOP
TRIM WEED WIPE BITCH BLINK
BOOTY BUNCO BUNKO COZEN
CROOK CULLY DODGE FAKER FLING
FOIST FOURB FRAUD FUDGE GLEEK
GOUGE GUILE HOCUS KNAVE
LURCH MULCT PINCH PLOAT ROGUE
SCAMP SCREW SHARP SHORT
SLANG SPOIL STICK STIFF STING
SWICK SWIKE TOUCH TRICK VERSE

WELSH WRINK BAFFLE BLANCH
BUBBLE BUCKET CHIAUS CHISEL
CHOUSE CLOYNE COGGER DADDLE
DECEIT DELUDE DERIDE DIDDLE
DOODLE DUFFER EMUNGE EUCHRE
FIDDLE FLEECE GREASE HUMBUG
HUMMER HUSTLE ILLUDE JOCKEY
NIGGLE NOBBLE NUZZLE OUTWIT
RADDLE RENEGE SHAVER SHICER
SNUDGE SUCKER TWICER ABUSION
BEGUILE CHICANE DECEIVE
DEFRAUD ESCHEAT FAITOUR
FINAGLE FINESSE FOISTER
GUDGEON JUGGLER MISLEAD
PLUNDER QUIBBLE SHARPER
SHIFTER SKELDER SLICKER
SWINDLE VERNEUK ARTIFICE
BEJUGGLE CHALDESE CHISELER
DELUSION HOODWINK IMPOSTOR
INTRIGUE OUTREACH OVERTAKE
SHAMMOCK SWINDLER
CHEATED SOLD
CHEATER BITE GULL KNAVE BILKER
TOPPER SHARPER FINAGLER
TREACHER
CHEATING HOCUS BARRAT ODLING
ABUSIVE FUBBERY MICHERY
ROGUERY CHEATERY JUGGLING
TRICKERY
CHECK BIT DAM HAP LID NAB NIP
SAY SET TAB BAIL BALK BEAT BILK
BILL CHIP CHIT COOK CRIB CURB
DAMP FACE FOIL GAGE HURT ITEM
KITE PAWL REIN SKID SNEB SNIB
SNIP SNUB STAY STEM STOP STUB
TAKE TEST TICK TURN TWIT WERE
ABORT ALLAY ANNUL BLOCK BRAKE
CATCH CHIDE CHILL CHING CHOKE
CRACK CROOK DAUNT DELAY
DETER DRAFT EMBAR FACER FAULT
GAUGE LIMIT MODER PAUSE QUELL
REPEL SNAPE SPOKE STALL STILL
STUNT TALLY TAUNT THROW TOKEN
WAVER ARAYNE ARREST ATTACK
BAFFLE BOTTLE BRIDLE CHEQUE
COUPON DAMPEN DEFEAT DETAIN
DETENT DURESS GRAVEL HAFFET
HAFFIT HINDER IMPEDE OPPOSE
OUTWIT QUENCH RABBET REBATE
REBUFF REBUKE RETURN SCOTCH
STANCH STAYER STIFLE STYMIE
TICKET VERIFY ANSTOSS AWEBAND
BACKSET BECLOUD COMMAND
CONTAIN CONTROL COUNTER
CURTAIN DRAUGHT INHIBIT
MONITOR REFRAIN REPRESS
REPROOF REPROVE REPULSE
REVERSE SETBACK SNAFFLE
STAUNCH STOPPER TRAMMEL
TROUBLE BULKHEAD ENCUMBER
HOLDBACK OBSTRUCT PULLBACK
RESTRAIN WITHHOLD
(— ENTHUSIASM) DISMAY
(— GRADUALLY) CUSHION
(— GROWTH) BLAST STINT STUNT
(— IN GLASS) SPLIT
(— IN TIMBER) STARSHAKE
(— MOTION) SPRAG
(— OF HORSE) SACCADE

(— PASSER) PAPERHANGER
(— PROGRESS) DEFEAT
(FORGED —) STIFF STUMER
(HOLD IN —) COMPESCE
(RESTAURANT —) LAWING
(WORTHLESS —) DUD
CHECKED CHECK BEATEN CLOSED
CAPTIVE STOPPED
CHECKER DAM DICE FRET KING
CHECK FREAK FRECK PIECE WHITE
DAMPER DRAUGHT
CHECKERBERRY JINKS DRUNKARD
TEABERRY
CHECKERBOARD TABLE DAMBROD
DAMBOARD
CHECKERED PIED VAIR DICED PLAID
CHECKY MOTLEY
CHECKERS DRAFTS CHEQUERS
DRAUGHTS
CHECKERWORK TESSEL CHECKER
TESSERA
CHECKING REST BLOCK SETBACK
EBRILLADE
CHECKMATE LICK MATE STOP
UNDO BAFFLE CORNER DEFEAT
OUTWIT STYMIE THWART SUIMATE
CHECKSTONE CHUCK
CHEDDAR CHEESE
CHEEK CHAP CHOP GALL GENA
JAMB JOLE JOWL LEER SASS WANG
WANK BUCCA CHOKE CHYAK NERVE
SAUCE SHICK CHYACK HAFFET
HAFFIT OXCHEEK AUDACITY
TEMERITY
(— OF SPUR) SHANK
(— OF VISE) CHAP
CHEEKBONE MALAR ZYGOMA
CHEEP PIP YAP YIP CHIP HINT PEEP
PULE CHIRP CREAK TWEET SQUEAK
TATTLE
CHEER OLE RAH FARE FOOD MIND
ROOT VIVA YELL BRAVO CHIRK
ELATE ERECT FEAST HEART HUZZA
JOLLY MIRTH SHOUT SPORT TIGER
WHOOP CANTLE GAIETY HOORAY
HURRAH HUZZAH REHETE SOLACE
VIANDS ACCLAIM ANIMATE APPLAUD
CHERISH COMFORT CONSOLE
ENCHEER GLADDEN HEARTEN
JOLLITY LIGHTEN REFRESH REJOICE
SUPPORT UPRAISE APPLAUSE
BRIGHTEN HILARITY INSPIRIT
RECREATE VIVACITY
(BURST OF —S) SALVO
(GOOD —) WELFARE
(JAPANESE —) BANZAI
(SORRY —) PENANCE
CHEERFUL GAY CANT GLAD GLEG
GOOD HIGH ROSY CADGY CANTY
CHIRK DOUCE HAPPY JOLLY LIGHT
MERRY PEART READY SAPPY
SUNNY VAUDY BLITHE BRIGHT
CHEERY CHIRPY CROUSE GAWSIE
GENIAL HEARTY HILARY JOCUND
LIVELY BUOYANT CHERRLY CHIPPER
JOCULAR WINSOME CHEERING
CHIRRUPY EUPEPTIC FRIENDLY
GLADSOME HOMELIKE SANGUINE
SUNBEAMY SUNSHINE

CHEERFULLY GLADLY CANTILY CHEERLY JOLLILY CHEERILY GENIALLY

CHEERFULNESS JOY GLEE TAIT CHEER CHERTE GAIETY GAYETY LEVITY SPIRIT JOLLITY FESTIVAL GLADNESS HILARITY

CHEERING GLAD CORDIAL CHEERFUL CHIRPING

CHEERLESS SAD BLAE COLD DIRE DRAB GLUM GRAY BLEAK DREAR ELYNG WASTE DISMAL DREARY GLOOMY WINTRY DOLEFUL FORLORN JOYLESS SUNLESS DEJECTED DESOLATE LITHLESS

CHEER PINE CHIL

CHEERY BRIGHT GAYSOME

CHEESE OKA BLUE BRIE EDAM FETA HAND JACK TRIP APPLE BRICK COLBY CREAM DAISY DERBY GOUDA GRANA KENNO SWISS WHEEL ZIEGA ZIGER ASIAGO BARRIE BONDON BRYNZA CANTAL CASSAN DUNLOP GLARUS JUNKET MYSOST SAANEN SBRINZ TILSIT ZIEGER ANGELOT CHEDDAR CHEVRET COTTAGE FONTINA FROMAGE GJEDOST GRUYERE KEBBUCK PRIMOST PROVOLA SAPSAGO STILTON TRUCKLE AMERICAN CHESHIRE EMMENTAL LONGHORN MUENSTER PARMESAN PECORINO SLIPCOAT LEICESTER MOUSETRAP WILTSHIRE
(— FANCIER) TUROPHILE ·
(INFERIOR —) DICK
(LARGE —) KEBBOC

CHEESEPARING STINGY

CHEESE VAT CHESSEL CHESSART

CHEESEWOOD BONEWOOD WHITEWOOD

CHEETAH CAT YOUSE YOUZE GUEPARD

CHEF COOK SAUCIER CUISINIER

CHEFOO YENTAI

CHELA HAND MANUS PINCER

CHELATE COMPLEX

CHELICERA FALX FANG FALCER MANDIBLE

CHEMICAL (ALSO SEE SPECIFIC HEADINGS) ACID BASE SALT ALKALI BLEACH CHEMIC DODGER SAFENER ADDITIVE ALGICIDE CATALYST DEHORNER

CHEMIN-DE-FER SHIMMY

CHEMISE SHIFT SHIRT SIMAR SMOCK CAMISA SHIMMY LINGERIE

CHEMISETTE SHAM GUIMPE TUCKER PARTLET

CHEMIST ANALYST ASSAYER CHEMICK BENCHMAN COLORIST DRUGGIST

CHENDE CHINOA

CHENFISH KINGFISH

CHENILLE SNAIL

CHEQUEEN BASKET SEQUIN ZEQUIN CECCHINA ZECCHINO

CHERAW SARA

CHEREMIS MARI

CHERISH AID HUG PET BEAR DOTE HAVE HOPE LIKE LOVE SAVE ADORE BOSOM BROOD CHEER CLING COWER ENJOY NURSE PRIZE VALUE CARESS ESTEEM FADDLE FONDLE FOSTER GRUDGE HARBOR NESTLE NUZZLE PAMPER PETTLE REVERE COMFORT EMBOSOM EMBRACE INDULGE NOURISH NURTURE PROTECT SUPPORT SUSTAIN ENSHRINE INSPIRIT PRESERVE TREASURE

CHERISHED DEAR BOSOM DANDILY AFFECTED

CHEROOT TRICHI TRICHY

CHERRY BING CHOP DUKE FUJI GEAN MERRY MOREL CORNEL MAZARD BURBANK CAPULIN CHAPMAN LAMBERT MAHALEB MARASCA MAYDUKE MORELLO OXHEART PITANGA WINDSOR AMARELLE DURACINE EGGBERRY LUKEWARD NAPOLEON ROSACEAN

CHERRY-COLORED CERISE

CHERRY PLUM MYROBALAN

CHERRY STONE PAIP

CHERT BOONE WHINSTONE

CHERUB AMOR EROS ANGEL CUPID SERAPH SPIRIT AMORINO AMORETTO CHERUBIM

CHERVIL BUN KECK ARFOIL CERFOIL COWWEED HONEWORT MILKWEED RATSBANE

CHESS CHEAT SHOGI CHECKER SKITTLES
(— MOVE) ZUGZWANG

CHESSBOARD CHESS TABLE CHECKER

CHESSMAN PIN KING PIECE CHECKER CHEQUER
(— SET) MEINY MEINIE
(ANY — BUT PAWN) OFFICER
(BISHOP —) ALFIN ALPHIN ARCHER
(CASTLE —) JUEZ ROOK TOUR UDGE JUDGE LEDGE TOWER
(KNIGHT —) HORSE CHEVALIER
(PAWN —) PON POUNE
(QUEEN —) FERS FIERS PHEARSE

CHEST ARK BOX FIX KIT PIX PYX ARCA BUST CAJA CASH CIST CYST FUND KIST SAFE SCOB AMBRY BAHUT BUIST CADDY FRONT HOARD HUTCH RAZEE SISTA TRUNK ALMOIN BASKET BREAST BUNKER BUREAU CAISSE CAJETA CASKET COFFER COFFIN FORCER GIRNAL GIRNEL HAMPER JORDAN LARNAX LOCKER SCRINE SHRINE SPRUCE STRIPE THORAX WANGAN BRAZIER BRISKET CAISSON CAPCASE CASSONE COMMODE DEPOSIT DRAWERS DRESSER ENCLOSE HIGHBOY TOOLBOX WANIGAN WINDBAG CISTVAEN CUPBOARD FORCELET MANIFOLD STANDARD TREASURE TREASURY
(— FOR CUTLERY) CANTEEN
(— OF ORES) CAXON
(FRONT OF —) BREAST

CHESTNUT JOKE LING RATA BROWN HORSE CASTOR MARRON SATIVA CRENATA DENTATA
(HORSE —) CONKER
(POLYNESIAN —) RATA
(WATER —) LING

CHESTNUT-COLORED BAY ROAN

CHEVAL-DE-FRISE TURNPIKE

CHEVAL GLASS PSYCHE

CHEVALIER CADET NOBLE KNIGHT GALLANT CAVALIER HORSEMAN

CHEVIN CHUB CHEVESNE

CHEVRON BEAM MARK WOUND RAFTER STRIPE ZIGZAG

CHEVROTAIN MUSK NAPU DEERLET KANCHIL MEMINNA PLANDOK TRAGULE BOOMORAH PEESOREH RUMINANT

CHEW CUD EAT GUM TAW BITE CHAM CHAW GNAW QUID CHAMP CHONK GRIND MUNCH RUMEN CRUNCH MUMBLE CHUMBLE MEDITATE RUMINATE
(— UP NOISILY) CHANK GROUZE

CHEWINK FINCH JOREE TOWHEE GRASSET

CHEYENNE DOG

CHIAN SCIAN

CHIANTI FLORENCE

CHIASTOLITE MACLE ANDALUSITE

CHIBCHA MUISCA

CHIC PERT POSH TRIG TRIM KIPPY NATTY NIFTY SMART CHICHI DAPPER GIGOLO MODISH ELEGANT STYLISH

CHICAGO PORKOPOLIS

CHICANE DECEPTION

CHICANERY DIRT RUSE WILE FEINT TRICK ARTIFICE INTRIGUE TRICKERY DECEPTION

CHICK BIRD GIRL PEEP TICK CHILD NATTY POULET SCREEN SEQUIN SPROUT CHICKEN CHUCKIE

CHICKADEE BLACKCAP TITMOUSE

CHICKEN HEN KIP COCK FOWL BIDDY CAPON CHICK CHILD CHOOK CHUCK DEEDY FRYER LAYER MANOC POULT SILKY CHICKY PULLET SULTAN SUSSEX TURKEN ANCOBAR BOARDER BROILER DIBBLER POUSSIN ROASTER ROOSTER SCRATCH ARAUCANA COCKEREL PHASANID SPRINGER
(— SHELTER) MOTHER

CHICKEN COOP CAVY CAVIE

CHICKEN POX SOREHEAD VARICELLA

CHICK-PEA CHIT GRAM CHICH CICER COWGRAM SOWGRAM GARBANZO GARVANCE
(PL.) FASELS

CHICKWEED BLINK BLINKS SPURRY ALLBONE STARWORT

CHICO SAPODILLA

CHICORY BUNK CREPIS ENDIVE SUCCORY WITLOOF BLUEWEED COMPOSIT

CHIDE FUSS RAIL RATE BLAME CHECK FLITE FLYTE SCOLD SNEAP

BERATE REBUFF REBUKE SCHOOL
THREAP THREAT THREEP TONGUE
CENSURE REPROVE UPBRAID
WRANGLE ADMONISH LAMBASTE
REPROACH
CHIEF (ALSO SEE CHIEFTAIN) BO
AGA BIG BOH CAP CID COB DUX
MIR MOI TOP AGHA ALII ARCH ARII
BOSS CAID CHEF COCK DATO DEAN
DOEG DUCE DUKE HEAD HIER HIGH
INCA JARL JEFE KAID KHAN KING
MAIN MICO MOST NAIK ONLY QAID
RAIS RAJA REIS TYEE ALDER ALPHA
ARIKI DATTO ELDER FIRST GREAT
MAJOR MATAI NAYAK PRIMA PRIME
PRIMO RAJAH RULER THANE TITAN
VITAL ZAQUE ZIPPA ADALID CABEZA
DEPUTY FLAITH HEADLY INKOSI
KEHAYA KUBERA KUVERA LEADER
LULUAI MASTER MIRDHA NAIQUE
PENLOP PRABHU PRIMAL RECTOR
SACHEM SAYYID SHAYKH SHEIKH
SHERIF STAPLE SUDDER TOPMAN
TURNUS CAPITAL CAPTAIN CENTRAL
EMINENT FOREMAN GENERAL
HEADMAN INGOMAR LEADING
LEMPIRA MUGWUMP OVERMAN
PADRONE PALMARY POLYGAR
PRELATE PREMIER PRIMARY
SHEREEF STELLAR SUPREME
TOPSMAN TRIBUNE CABOCEER
CAPITANO CARDINAL DECURION
DIRECTOR DOMINANT ELDORADO
ESPECIAL FOREMOST GOVERNOR
HEADSMAN HIERARCH INTIMATE
MOKADDAM SAGAMORE SUBCHIEF
(— IN INDIA) PRABHU SIRDAR
(— OF 10 MEN) DEAN
(— OF ADVOCATES) BATONNIER
(— OF RELIGIOUS ORDER) GENERAL
(CHINOOK —) TYEE
(CLAN —) TOISECH
(INDIAN —) SUNCK SACHEM
SUNCKE CACIQUE SAGAMORE
(MOHAMMEDAN —) DATO DATTO
SAYID SAYYID
(SCHOOL —) DUX
(TIBETAN —) POMBO
(TURKISH —) AGA AGHA
CHIEFTAIN BEG CHAM EMIR HEAD
JARL KHAN ASTUR CHIEF EMEER
LEADER SIRDAR CAUDILLO
HIAWATHA
CHIEFTAINCY STOOL CHIEFRY
CHIEFTAINESS QUEEN
CHIFFCHAFF PEGGY CHIPCHAP
CHIPCHOP
CHIFFON SHEER
CHIFFONIER BUREAU CABINET
COMMODE
CHIGGER BICHO PIQUE CHIGGA
CHIGOE GIGGER JIGGER LEPTUS
WHEELWORM
CHIGNON COB KNOT COBBE TWIST
CHIGOE SIKA BICHO NIGUA PIQUE
SCREW CHIGGA ENIGUA JIGGER
SANDBOY SANDWORM
CHIH FU PREFECT
CHILBLAIN KIBE MULE BLAIN MOOLS

MOULS PERNIO
CHILD BEN BOY BUD ELF GET IMP
KID LAD SON SOT TAD TOT WAY
BABA BABE BABY BATA BIRD BRAT
CHIT CION FOOD GIRL GYTE PAGE
PUSS TIKE TINY TOTO TROT TYKE
WEAN BAIRN BIRTH BROLL BROWL
CHICK CHIEL COOKY ELFIN GAMIN
ISSUE KEIKI OLIVE POULT SCION
TIDDY TRICK WAYNE WENCH WHELP
CHERUB COOKIE ENFANT FILIUS
FOSTER INFANT MOPPET NIPPER
PLEDGE PROLES STUMPY TACKER
TODDLE URCHIN BAMBINO CHOOKIE
CHOPPER CHRISOM COCKNEY
DICKENS GANGREL GYTLING
KINCHIN KITLING LAMBKIN PAPOOSE
PROGENY STICHEL SUBTEEN
TIDDLER TODDLER TROTTIE
WRAWLER YOUNKER BANTLING
CHISELER DAUGHTER EPIGONUS
JUVENILE LITTLING NURSLING
PRATTLER RUNABOUT WEANLING
WHIMLING
(— OF THE WORLD) WELTKIND
(— UNDER 7 YEARS) INFANS
(BAD-MANNERED —) GOOP
(CHUBBY —) CHUNK
(ELF'S —) OAF CHANGELING
(FOSTER —) DAULT NORRY NURRY
FOSTER REARLING
(ILLEGITIMATE —) MISHAP BASTARD
(INNOCENT —) CHRISOM
(LAST-BORN —) DILLING
(LOVED —) JOY
(MERRY —) SUNBEAM
(MISCHIEVOUS —) IMP LIMB TIKE
DICKENS
(NAKED —) SCUDDY
(NEWBORN —) STRANGER
(PAUPER —) MINDER
(PLAYFUL —) ELF WANTON
(PLUMP —) FOB FUB
(PRECOCIOUS —) PRODIGY
(PURE —) DOVE
(ROWDY —) HOODLUM
(SMALL —) TAD TOT SPUD GAITT
KIDDY TIDDY TOTUM KIDLET
PEEWEE TACKER BAIRNIE
(SPOILED —) CADE COCKNEY
(STUNTED —) URF
(TROUBLESOME —) STICHEL
(UNMANNERLY —) SMATCHET
(YOUNG —) BABY JOEY INFANT
SQUIRT GANGREL NESTLER
TODDLER BANTLING INNOCENT
LITTLING SUCKLING
(YOUNGEST —) WRIG DILLING
CHILDBED JIZZEN
CHILDBIRTH LABOR CRYING INLYING
TRAVAIL OXYTOCIA
(— WOMAN) PUERPERA
CHILDHOOD INFANCY CHILDAGE
(2ND —) DOTAGE TWICHILD
CHILDISH TID WEAK DANSY NAIVE
PETTY SILLY YOUNG CHITTY PULING
SIMPLE WEANLY ASININE BABYISH
CHILDLY FOOLISH KIDDISH PEEVISH
PROGENY PUERILE UNMANLY

BAIRNISH BRATTISH IMMATURE
TOOTLING
CHILDLESS ORBATE
CHILDREN ISSUE PROLES STRAIN
PROGENY OFFSPRING
(NUMBER OF —) PARITY

CHILE

BAY: COOK EYRE NENA TARN
LOMAS OTWAY SARCO DARWIN
INUTIL MORENO STOKES
TONGOY DYNELEY INGLESA
SKYRING DESOLATE
CAPE: DYER HORN CHOROS
HORNOS QUILAN TABLAS
DESEADO BASCUNAN CARRANZA
CAPITAL: SANTIAGO
CHANNEL: ANCHO CHEAP BEAGLE
COCKBURN MORALEDA
COIN: PESO LIBRA CONDOR
ESCUDO
DESERT: ATACAMA
GULF: ANCUD GUAFO PENAS
ARAUCO
INDIAN: ONA AUCA INCA ONAN
ARAUCA CHANGO YAHGAN
MAPUCHE MOLUCHE PAMPEAN
PATAGON PUEGIAN RANQUEL
ALIKULUF PICUNCHE TSONECAN
ISLAND: LUZ PRAT BYRON GUAFO
HOSTE MOCHA NUEVA NUNEZ
VIDAL CHILOE DAWSON EASTER
LENNOX PIAZZI PICTON QUILAN
RIESCO STOSCH TALCAN
ANGAMOS CAMPANA HANOVER
REFUGIO TRANQUI CLARENCE
HUAMBLIN NALCAYEC NAVARINO
TRAIGUEN
ISLANDS: CHONOS HERMITE
PAJAROS CHAUQUES
ISTHMUS: OFQUI
LAKE: TORO RANCO YELCHO
PUYEHUE RUPANCO
MEASURE: VARA LEGUA LINEA
CUADRA FANEGA
MOUNTAIN: MACA TORO CHATO
MAIPO PAINE POTRO PULAR
TORRE YOGAN APIWAN BURNEY
CONICO JERVIS POQUIS RINCON
CHALTEL COPIAPO FITZROY
PALPANA VELLUDA COCHRANE
TRONADOR YANTELES
MOUNTAINS: ANDES DARWIN
ALMEIDA DOMEYKO
NATIVE: PATAGONIAN
PENINSULA: HARDY LACUY TAITAO
TUMBES
POINT: TORO GALLO LILES LOBOS
LOROS MORRO TALCA TETAS
VIEJA CACHOS GALERA MOLLES
ANGAMOS LAVAPIE
PORT: LOTA TOME ARICA
COQUIMBA
PROVINCE: AISEN ARICA AYSEN
MAULE NUBLE TALCA ARAUCO
BIOBIO CAUTIN CHILOE CURICO
OSORNO ATACAMA LINARES
MALLECO COQUIMBO OHIGGINS

SANTIAGO TARAPACA VALDIVIA
RIVER: LOA LAJA YALI ALHUE
AZAPA BRAVO BUENO ELQUI
ITATA LAUCA LLUTA MAIPO
MAULE PUELO RAHUE RAPEL
VITOR BIOBIO CAMINA CHOAPA
CHOROS CISNES COLINA
HUASCO LIMARI MORADO
PALENA POSCUA TOLTEN
COPIAPO VALDIVIA
SHRUB: LITRE
STRAIT: NELSON MAGELLAN
TOWN: BOCO CUYA LEBU LOTA
OCOA TOCO TOME ARICA TALCA
ARAUCO CURICO GATICO
OSORNO SERENA TEMUCO
VICUNA YUMBEL YUNGAY
CALDERA CHILLAN COPIAPO
COQUIMBO RANCAGUA
SANTIAGO VALDIVIA
TREE: RAULI
VOLCANO: LANIN MAIPO ANTUCO
LLAIMA OYAHUE TACORA
PETEROA SOCOMAP
WEIGHT: GRANO LIBRA QUINTAL
WIND: SURES

CHILE-BELLS COPIHUE LAPAGERIA
CHI-LIN KYLIN UNICORN
CHILL ICE RAW AGUE COLD COOL
DAZY ALGID ALGOR DAVER GELID
RIGOR SCHEL SHAKE FRAPPE
FREEZE FRIGID FROSTY SHIVER
SNELLY DEPRESS FRETISH FRISSON
MALARIA COLDNESS
CHILLED ACOLD CHILL FROZEN
STARVEN
CHILLING ICY COLD EERY BLEAK
EERIE CHILLY WINTRY GLACIAL
SHIVERY
CHILLY RAW COLD COOL LASH
ALGID BLEAK HUNCH AGUISH AIRISH
ARCTIC CRIMMY FROSTY FROZEN
LEEPIT
CHIMAERA BELUE DRAGON CATFISH
PLACOID RATFISH RATTAIL
DOODSKOP
CHIME DIN RIM BELL EDGE PEAL
RING SUIT TING AGREE CHIMB
CHINE PRATE ACCORD CLOCHE
CYMBAL JINGLE MELODY CONCORD
HARMONY SINGSONG
(PL.) BELL
CHIMER CYMAR SIMAR CHIMAR
TABARD
CHIMERA FANCY MIRAGE MOSAIC
POMATO ILLUSION
CHIMERICAL VAIN WILD INSANE
UTOPIAN DELUSIVE FANCIFUL
ROMANTIC IMAGINARY
CHIMNEY BAG LUM TUN FLUE LUMM
PIPE TUBE VENT GULLY STACK
TEWEL CHIMLA FUNNEL LOUVER
SMOKER TUNNEL FISSURE OPENING
ORIFICE FUMIDUCT
CHIMNEY CAP TURNCAP
CHIMNEY CORNER FIRESIDE
INGLENOOK

CHIMNEY COWL COW
CHIMNEY HOOD JACK
CHIMNEY PIECE PAREL
CHIMNEY PIPE TALLBOY
CHIMNEY POST SPEER
CHIMNEY SEAT SCONCE
CHIMNEY SWEEP SWEEP CHUMMY
FLUEMAN RAMONEUR
CHIMPANZEE APE CHIMP JACKO
JOCKO PIGMY PYGMY NCHEGA
PIGMEW PYGMEAN
CHIN JAW CHAT TSIN MENTUM
CHOLLER
(— POINT) MENTON POGONION
(DOUBLE —) BUCCULA CHOLLER
CHINA WARE JAPAN LENOX SPODE
CATHAY PARIAN SEVRES CERAMIC
CHEENEY DRESDEN LIMOGES
MEISSEN POTTERY CINCHONA
CROCKERY EGGSHELL

CHINA

ABORIGINE: YAO MANS MIAO
MANTZU YAOMIN MIAOTSE
AREA UNIT: MU MOU MOW
BAY: LAICHOW HANGCHOW
BUDDHA: FO
CAPE: OLWANPI
CAPITAL: PEKING TAIPEI PEIPING
CHANNEL: BASHI
COIN: PU CASH CENT MACE TAEL
TIAO YUAN SYCEE DOLLAR
DEPRESSION: TURFAN
DESERT: GOBI ORDOS SHAMO
ALASHAN TAKLAMAKAN
DIALECT: WU MIN AMOY HAKKA
CANTON HSIANG SWATOW
FOOCHOW WENCHOW
KANHAKKA MANDARIN
DRY LAKE: LOPNOR
DYNASTY: WU HAN SHU SUI WEI
YIN CHIN CHOU HSIA HSIN MING
SUNG TANG YUAN CHING
SHANG
GULF: POHAI CHIHLI TONKIN
PECHILI LIAOTUNG
ISLAND: AMOY FLAT MACAO
MATSU NAMKI CHUSAN HAINAN
PRATAS QUEMOY TAIWAN
YUHWAN FORMOSA HUNGTOW
TUNGSHA CHOUCHAN
KULANGSU STAUNTON
ISLANDS: PENGHU TACHEN
CHUSHAN MIAOTAO
LAKE: TAI CHAO KAOYU OLING
TELLI BAMTSO BORNOR EBINOR
ERHHAI KHANKA LOPNOR
NAMTSO POYANG CHALING
HUNGTSE KARANOR KOKONOR
HULUNNOR MONTCALM
TAROKTSO TELLINOR TIENCHIH
TSINGHAI TUNGTING
MEASURE: HO HU KO LI MU PU TO
TU FAN FEN PAU TOU TUN YIN
CHIH FANG KISH PARA QUEI
SHIH TSUN CHANG CHING
SHENG SHING CHUPAK KUNGHO
KUNGLI KUNGMU KUNGFEN

KUNGYIN KUNGCHIH
MOUNTAIN: OMI OMEI SUNG
KAILAS POBEDA EVEREST
MUZTABH SUNGSHAN
MOUNTAINS: ALTAY KUNLUN
ALASHAN KUENLUN MEILING
MINSHAN NANLING NANSHAN
TANGLHA BOGDOULA HIMALAYA
TAPASHAN TAYULING TIENSHAN
WUYLISHAN
NAME: CATHAY
NATIVE: PAT
PENINSULA: LEICHU LUICHOW
LIAOTUNG
PORT: AMOY WUHU AIGUN SHASI
ANTUNG CANTON CHEFOO
DAIREN ICHANG NINGPO PAKHOI
SWATOW SZEMAO WUCHOW
YOCHOW FOOCHOW HUNCHUN
MENGTSZ NANKING SAMSHUI
SANTUAO SOOCHOW WENCHOW
CHANGSHA HANGCHOW
KIUKIANG KONGMOON
LUNGCHOW SHANGHAI
TENGYUEH TIENTSIN TSINGTAO
WANHSIEN
PROVINCE: HONAN HOPEI HUNAN
HUPEI HUPEN JEHOL KANSU
KIRIN TIBET ANHWEI FUKIEN
SHANSI SHENSI TAIWAN YUNNAN
KIANGSI KWANGSI NGANHUI
CHEKIANG KWEICHOW LIAONING
MONGOLIA SHANTUNG
SZECHWAN TSINGHAI
MANCHURIA
RELIGION: JU SHINTO TAOISM
BUDDHISM
RESERVOIR: SUNGARI
RIVER: SI HAN ILI MIN NEN PEI
WEI AMUR HUAI LOHO TUNG
YALU YUAN YUEN ARGUN
FENHO MACHU PEIHO TARIM
TUMEN WEIHO CHUMAR DRECHU
DZACHU KHOTAN KUMARA
LIAOHO MANASS MEKONG
OCHINA URUNGU YELLOW
HOANGHO HWANGHO KERULEN
KIALING SALWEEN SIKIANG
SUNGARI TSANGPO WUKIANG
YANGTZE YARKAND YUKIANG
CHERCHEN HANKIANG
HUNGSHUI MINKIANG
RULER: WANG
SEA: ECHINA SCHINA YELLOW
STRAIT: HAINAN TAIWAN
FORMOSA
TOWN: BAI NOH AHPA AMOY ANSI
ANTA AQSU FUYU GUMA HAMI
HUMA IPIN KIAN KISI LINI LOHO
LUTA MOHO MOYU MULI NIYA
NOHO NURA OMIN OWPU RIMA
SAKA SIAN TALI TAYU WUHU
WUSU WUTU YAAN CHIAI FUSIN
HOFEI ICHUN JEHOL KIRIN
KOKLU LHASA MACAO PENKI
SHASI TAIAN TALAI TUTZE
TUYUN TZEPO WUHAN WUSIH

YENKI YULIN YUMEN ANSHAN
ANTUNG CANTON DAIREN
FUCHAU FUSHUN HANKOW
HANTAN HARBIN HOIHOW
KALGAN LOYANG LUSHUN
MUKDEN NINGPO PAOTOW
PEKING PENGPU SUCHOW
SWATOW TAINAN TAIPEI TALIEN
TSINAN YUNNAN CHUNGTU
FATSHAN FOOCHOW HANYANG
HUHEHOT KAIFENG KUNMING
KWEISUI LANCHOW NANKING
PAOTING PEIPING SOOCHOW
TAIYUAN TZEKUNG URUMCHI
WUCHANG YENPING CHANGSHA
CHAOCHOW CHENGTEH
CHINCHOW HANGCHOW
KIAOCHOW KWEIYANG
NANCHANG QARAQASH
SHANGHAI SHENYANG SIANGTAN
TANGSHAN TENGCHOW TIENTSIN
TSINGTAO TUNGCHOW
CHUNGKING
WEIGHT: LI TA FAN FEN HAO KIN
SSU TAN YIN CHEE CHIN DONG
MACE SHIH TAEL CATTY CHIEN
LIANG PICUL TCHIN HAIKWAN
KUNGFEN KUNGSSU KUNGCHIN

CHINABERRY LILAC AZEDARACH
CHINABALL SOAPBERRY
CHINA BLUE NIKKO
CHINA HAT HAELTZUK HEILTSUK
CHINAMAN CHOW JOHN JOHNNY
(PL.) TANKA
CHINA ROSE MANETTI HIBISCUS
CHINA STONE PETUNSE
CHINA TREE LILAC HAGBUSH
CHINCHILLA ABROCOME VIZCACHA
CHINE BACK IKAT CHINK CRACK
CREST GORGE RIDGE SPINE CLEAVE
RAVINE SPROUT CREVICE
CHINESE PAT BABA CHOW CERAI
CHINK SERES SERIC SINIC MANZAS
MONGOL ASIATIC CATAIAN CHINOIS
PIGTAIL SANGLEY
CHINESE ARTICHOKE CROSNE
CHOROGI CROSNES STACHYS
KNOTROOT
CHINESE CABBAGE PECHAY
PAKCHOI
CHINESE DATE JUJUBE
CHING TSING
CHINGPAW KACHIN SINGPHO
YAWYINS
CHINIOFON YATREN
CHINK GAP BORE CASH CHAP COIN
JINK KINK RENT RIFT RIME SCAR
BOORE CHECK CHINE CHUNK CLEFT
CRACK GRIKE KNACK MONEY
CRANNY SPRAIN CHINKLE CREVICE
FISSURE APERTURE
CHINPIECE BARBEL
CHINQUAPIN OAK BONNET
BONNETS CANDOCK CHESTNUT
WANKAPIN YOCKERNUT
CHINTZ PINTADO SALAMPORE
CHIONE (FATHER OF —) BOREAS

(HUSBAND OF —) NEPTUNE
(MOTHER OF —) ORITHYIA
DAEDALION
(SLAYER OF —) DIANA
(SON —) EUMOLPUS AUTOLYCUS
PHILAMMON
CHIOT SCIOT
CHIP BIT CUT DIB GAG HEW NIG
BONE CHAP CLIP HACK KNAP KNOP
NICK PARE SAND SKIN SNIP SNUB
BEACH CHECK CRACK FLAKE PIECE
SCRAP SKELF SLICE SPALE SPALL
SPALT SPAWL SPELL SPOON WASTE
BORING CHISEL GALLET MARKER
NOODLE COUNTER SHAVING
CHIPPING COSSETTE FRAGMENT
SPLINTER WHITLING
(— OF SOLDER) LINK
(— OF WOOD) SPOON
(— OUT) DESEAM
(BUFFALO —S) BODEWASH
(CORN —S) FRITOS
(POTATO —) CRISP
(SUPPLY OF —S) STACK
CHIPMAN SCRAPMAN
CHIPMUNK CHIPPY GOPHER GRINNY
HACKEE GRINNIE SQUIRREL
CHIPPENDALE AFGHAN
CHIPPER GAY SPRY CHIRP PERKY
BABBLE COCKEY FIERCE HACKER
KIPPER LIVELY CHATTER CHEERFUL
CHIRRUP TWITTER
CHIPPINGS SWARF
CHIRO BONYFISH FRANCESCA
CHIROGRAPHY WRITING
CHIRON (— AS CONSTELLATION)
SAGITTARIUS
(FATHER OF —) SATURN
(MOTHER OF —) PHILYRA
CHIROPODIST PEDICURE
CORNCUTTER
CHIRP PEW PIP PEEK PEEP PIPE
TWIT WEAK CHEEP CHELP CHIRK
CHIRL CHIRM CHIRT TWEET TWINK
CHIPPER CHIRRUP CHITTER REJOICE
SHATTER TWEEDLE TWITTER
WHEETLE WHITTER
CHIRR PITTER
CHIRU SUS
CHISEL BUR CUT GAD CHIP ETCH
FORM MOIL PARE SEAT SETT TANG
TOOL BRUZZ BURIN CARVE CHEAT
DROVE GOUGE HARDY POINT
SCOOP SLICK STIFF BROACH
CHESIL FIRMER FORMER GRAVEL
HAGGLE POMMEL QUARRY REAMER
TOOLER BARGAIN BOASTER
CHIPPER ENGRAVE GRADINE
GRUBBER POINTER QUARREL
SCOOPER SCORPER SHINGLE
CROSSCUT SPLITTER
(BLACKSMITH'S —) HARDY HARDIE
(FLINT —) TRANCHET
(ICE —) SPUD
(JEWELER'S —) SCAUPER SCORPER
(PREHISTORIC —) CELT
(STONEMASON'S —) TOOL DROVE
POMMEL TOOLER SPLITTER
(TOOTHED —) GRADINE

(TRIANGULAR —) BUR BURR
(WHEELWRIGHT'S —) BRUZZ
CHISELER CHEAT CROOK COYOTE
GOUGER
CHIT DAB BILL NOTE DRAFT LETTER
VOUCHER
CHITARRONE ARCHLUTE
CHITCHAT GASH GUFF TALK
BANTER GOSSIP GOSSIPRY
BAVARDAGE
CHITINOUS SHELLY
CHITON EXOMIS DIPLOIS EXOMION
CHITTAMWOOD IRONWOOD
CHIVALROUS BRAVE CIVIL NOBLE
PREUX GENTLE POLITE GALLANT
GENTEEL VALIANT WARLIKE
KNIGHTLY
CHIVE CIVE SIVE CIVET SITHE
ALLIUM
CHIVY RUN VEX BAIT HUNT RACE
CHASE CHEVY TEASE BADGER
CHIVVY FLIGHT HARASS PURSUE
PURSUIT SCAMPER TORMENT
MANEUVER
CHLOASMA MOTH
CHLOR LEMON
CHLORIDE BUTTER CALOMEL
MURIATE ALEMBROTH
CHLORINE OXYGEN
CHLORION SPHEX
CHLORIS (FATHER OF —) AMPHION
(HUSBAND OF —) NELEUS
(MOTHER OF —) NIOBE
(SON OF —) NESTOR
CHLORITE AMESITE
CHOANA COLLAR
CHOBDAR USHER CHOPDAR
CHOCK COG PAD BLOCK BRACE
CHUCK CLEAT SPOKE SPRAG
WEDGE SCOTCH
(PL.) STOWWOOD
CHOCOLATE BUD CANDY COCOA
NORFOLK JACOLATT
CHOGAK SHOQ
CHOICE BET ODD TRY BEST FINE
FORE GOOD MIND PICK RARE WALE
WEAL WILL CREAM ELITE PRIME
VOICE CHOSEN DAINTY DESIRE
FLOWER OPTION PICKED PLUMMY
SELECT DILEMMA ELEGANT
EXCERPT PERMISS DELICATE
ELECTION EXIMIOUS UNCOMMON
VOLITION
(FAVORITE —) STANDBY
(FREE —) SWING DRUTHERS
CHOIR KERE QUIRE CHAPEL CHORUS
CHORALE CONCERT KAPELLE
PSALMODY
CHOIRBOY CLERGEON CHORISTER
CHOIR LEADER CANTOR CHORAGUS
CHORISTER PRECENTOR
CHOKE DAM GAG GOB CLOG DAMP
PLUG QUAR STOP WARP CHECK
CHOCK CLOSE GRAIN GRANE
SCRAG WORRY HINDER IMPEDE
STIFLE SWARVE CONGEST QUACKLE
QUEAZEN QUERKEN REPRESS
SILENCE SMOLDER SMOTHER
OBSTRUCT QUEASOME SCUMFISH

STOPPAGE STRANGLE SUPPRESS
THROTTLE
(— OFF) BESET
(— UP) CLOY GORGE STUFF
CHOKEBERRY DOGBERRY
SOAPBERRY
CHOKED FOUL WOOLY WOOLLY
CLOTTED
CHOKEDAMP STYTHE BLACKDAMP
CHOKERMAN CHAINER CHAINMAN
CHOKWE KIOKO
CHOLER IRE BILE FURY RAGE
ANGER WRATH SPLEEN TEMPER
DISTEMPER
CHOLERIC MAD ANGRY CROSS
FIERY HUFFY TESTY FUMISH IREFUL
TOUCHY BILIOUS ENRAGED
IRACUND PEEVISH PEPPERY
WASPISH WRATHFUL IMPATIENT
CHOLIAMB SCAZON
CHONDRIOME CYTOME
CHOOSE OPT TRY CHAP CULL LIKE
LIST LOVE LUST PICK TAKE VOTE
WALE WEAL ADOPT ELECT PRICK
ANOINT DECIDE PLEASE PREFER
SELECT EMBRACE ESPOUSE
EXTRACT SEPARATE
CHOOSY CHOICY FINICAL
CHOP AX AXE CUT HAG HEW JAW
LOP CHAP CHIP DICE GASH HACK
HASH HOWL RIVE SLIT CARVE
CLEFT CRACK KNOCK MINCE NOTCH
SLASH STAMP TRADE TRUCK
WHANG BARTER CHANGE CLEAVE
INCISE EXCHANGE
(— OFF) SNIG
(— SMALL) DEVIL MINCE
(— UP) HACKLE
(— WITH DULL AX) BUTTE
(PORK —) GRISKIN
CHOPINE CIOPPINO PANTOFLE
CHOPPED CUT CHAPPED
CHOPPER MINCER SLASHER
TRANCHET
CHOPPINESS CHOP JABBLE
CHOPPING BLOCK HACKLOG
CHOPPING TOOL (— CULTURE)
SOAN SOHAN
CHOPPY BUMPY LOPPY LUMPY
PECKY ROUGH SHORT POPPLY
CHORAL (— SOCIETY) ORPHEON
CHORD CORD DYAD ROLL TONE
CORDE NERVE TRIAD TRINE
ACCORD STRING TENDON TETRAD
CADENCE CONCORD HARMONY
ARPEGGIO DIAMETER FILAMENT
CHORDATA VERTEBRA
CHORE JOB JOT CHAR DUTY TASK
CHARE KNACK STINT ERRAND
BUSINESS
CHOREA JUMP JERKS
CHOREOGRAPHY TERPSICHORE
CHORION SEROSA
CHORISTER SINGER CHANTER
CHOIRBOY
CHORUS SONG CHOIR DRONE QUIRE
ACCORD ASSENT BURDEN UNISON
CHORALE HOLDING REFRAIN
RESPONSE THYMELICI

(— IN PLAY) GREX
CHOSEN ELECT ELITE SORTED
ELECTED FANCIED AFFECTED
SELECTED
CHOUGH COW CHANK CHEWET
CORBIE CHOCARD
CHOWRY COWTAIL
CHRISM CREAM CREME MURON
MYRON
CHRIST X KING LORD TRUE JUDGE
RANSOM VERITY MESSIAH SAVIOUR
DRIGHTEN PARAMOUR
(INFANT —) BAMBINO
CHRISTEN NAME KIRSEN BAPTIZE
CHRISTENING GOSSIPING
CHRISTIAN XN XT XTIAN UNIATE
GENTILE THOMEAN CHRISTEN
GALILEAN MELCHITE NAZARENE
ORIENTAL STONEITE TRADITOR
COLOSSIAN
(JEWISH —) JUDAIZER
(PL.) FLOCK LAPSED ACEPHALI
FAITHFUL
CHRISTIANIA CRISTY
CHRISTIANITY WAY XTY XNTY
CHRISTMAS NOEL YULE HOLIDAY
NATIVITY YULETIDE MIDWINTER
CHRISTMAS ROSE BEARFOOT
LUNGWORT MELAMPOD PEDELION
CHRIST'S-THORN NABK JUJUBE
ZIZYPHUS
CHROMA COLOR QUALITY
CHROMATIC HUEFUL FLAMING
SEMITONAL
CHROMATOPHORE ALLOPHORE
LIPOPHORE UNIVALENT
CHROMOSOME DIAD DYAD
HOMOLOG ALLOSOME AUTOSOME
IDIOSOME KARYOMERE LEPTONEMA
PLANOSOME
(PL.) GEMINI
CHROMOSPHERE SIERRA
CHRONIC FIXED SEVERE INTENSE
CONSTANT STUBBORN
CHRONICLE BRUT ANNAL DIARY
ENACT RECORD ACCOUNT HISTORY
RECITAL CORNICLE REGISTER
(PL.) ANNALS ARCHIVE
CHRONICLER WRITER CHRONIST
COMPILER RECORDER HISTORIAN
CHRONOLOGICAL TEMPORAL
CHRONOMETER DIAL HACK CLOCK
TIMER WATCH
CHRYSAL FRET
CHRYSALIS KELL PUPA AURELIA
CHRYSANTHEMUM MUM KIKU
SPOON BRUTUS POMPON KIKUMON
KIRIMON AZALEAMUM
CHRYSIN FLAVONE
CHRYSOBERYL CATEYE CHRYSOPAL
CYMOPHANE
CHRYSOLITE OLIVINE PERIDOT
CHRYSOPAL
CHTHONIAN INFERNAL
CHUB DACE DOLT FOOL KIYI LOUT
POLL CHOPA CHEVIN SHINER
CYPRINID FALLFISH MACKEREL
HORNYHEAD
CHUBBY FAT CHUFF FUBSY PLUMP

CHOATY CHUFFY PLUMPY ROTUND
ROLYPOLY
CHUB MACKEREL TINK TINKER
HARDHEAD SCOMBRID
CHUCK HEN LOG PIG CHUG GRUB
HURL JERK LUMP TOSS CHOCK
CLUCK PITCH THROW BOUNCE
CHUCKY COLLET CHUCKLE DISCARD
CHUCK-A-LUCK SWEAT HAZARD
BIRDCAGE
CHUCKER CROZER
CHUCK-FARTHING CHUCK KNICKER
CHUCKHOLE CAHOT CHUGHOLE
CHUCKLE CHUCK CLUCK EXULT
LAUGH GIGGLE GIZZEN KECKLE
SMUDGE TITTER CHORTLE
CHUD VEPS VEPSE
CHUDDAR PHULKARI
CHUFA SEDGE GLUMAL CYPRESS
EARTHNUT GALANGAL TIGERNUT
GROUNDNUT
CHUM CAD PAL BAIT MATE PARD
TOLE TOLL BUDDY BUTTY CRONY
AIKANE CHUMMY COBBER COPAIN
FRIEND PARDNER ROOMMATE
(— AROUND) HOBNOB
CHUMMY GREAT PALLY FAMILIAR
CHUMP ASS DOLT HEAD BLOCK
PUMPKIN ENDPIECE
CHUNCHO CHAMA
CHUNK DAB DAD FID GOB PAT WAD
JUNK JUNT SLUG CHOCK CHUCK
CLAUT PIECE THROW WHANG
WHANK DORNICK KNUCKLE
LUNCHEON
CHUNKY LUMPY PLUMP SQUAT
STOUT THICK TRUSS BLOCKY
CHUBBY STOCKY CHUNKED
CHURCH DOM SEE DOME FANE
FOLD HIGH KILL KIRK KURK TERA
ABBEY AUTEM FAITH FLOCK KOVIL
SAMAJ TITLE CHAPEL CHARGE
HIERON SPOUSE TEMPLE EDIFICE
FANACLE IGLESIA LATERAN
MEMORIA MINSTER RECTORY
STATION TEMPLET BASILICA
EBENEZER ECCLESIA PECULIAR
(— BOOK) TRIODION
(CHRISTIAN —) BODY ISRAEL
HERITAGE
CHURCHMAN KIRKMAN
(HIGH —) PUSEYIST PRELATIST
(LOW —) SIM LOWBOY SIMEONITE
CHURCH SERVICE HEARING
TENEBRAE
CHURCHWARDEN STRAW WARDEN
WARNER
CHURCHYARD HAW LITTEN
CEMETERY KIRKYARD
CHURL CAD MAN BOOR CARL GNOF
HIND LOUT SERF CARLE CEORL
CHUFF GNOFF KNAVE MISER
BODACH CARLOT HARLOT LUBBER
RUSTIC VASSAL YEOMAN BONDMAN
FREEMAN HASKARD HUSBAND
NIGGARD PEASANT VILLAIN VILLEIN
CHURLISH MEAN BLUFF GRUFF
ROUGH RUNTY SURLY URSAL
CRABBY RUSTIC SORDID SULLEN

VULGAR BOORISH CARLAGE
CARLISH CRABBED INCIVIL PEEVISH
VIOLENT

CHURN BEAT BOIL KIRN MOIL STIR
DRILL SHAKE BUBBLE SEETHE
AGITATE BARATTE TRUNDLE

CHUTE RUSH SLIP TUBE FLUME
HURRY RAPID SHOOT SLIDE
HOPPER TROUGH DECLINE DESCENT
DOWNFALL STAMPEDE TELEGRAPH
(MINING —) PASS TELEGRAPH

CIBOL SYBO ONION SYBOW SHALLOT

CIBORIUM PIX PYX CANOPY CIVORY
COFFER CIMBORIS

CICADA CAD CIGALE JARFLY
LOCUST TETTIX LYREMAN
HOMOPTER

CICATRICE FESTER

CICATRICLE TREAD GALLATURE

CICATRIX EYE MARK SCAB SCAR
SEAM

CICATRIZE FESTER SCARIFY

CICELY MYRRH

CICERO TULLY

CICERONE GUIDE PILOT MENTOR
ORATOR COURIER SIGHTSMAN

CICERONIAN TULLIAN

CID HERO CAMPEADOR

CIDER PERRY PERKIN SWANKY
SYDDIR POMMAGE BEVERAGE
COCCAGEE
(HARD —) APPLEJACK
(INFERIOR —) SWANKY

CIGAR PURO TOBY WEED BREVA
CLARO SEGAR SHUCK SMOKE
CONCHA CORONA HAVANA MADURA
MADURO MANILA STOGIE TWOFER
BOUQUET CHEROOT CULEBRA
LONDRES REGALIA TRABUCO
COLORADO LOCOFOCO PANATELA
PERFECTO PICKWICK PURITANO

CIGARETTE CIG FAG BIRI BUTT KING
PILL SKAG CUBEB JOINT SHUCK
SMOKE GASPER REEFER CIGARITO
(— BUTT) ROACH
(MARIHUANA —) STICK

CIGARFISH SCAD QUIAQUIA

CILIUM HAIR LASH EYELASH
UNCINUS BARBICEL CILIOLUM

CILLOSIS LIFEBLOOD

CIMBALOM CEMBALON DULCIMER

CIMEX BEDBUG ACANTHIA

CINCH BELT GIRD GRIP PIPE SNAP
GIRTH GRAVY BREEZE CINCHA
FASTEN PIANOLA SINECURE

CINCHONA CHINA QUINA

CINCINNATI PORKOPOLIS

CINCTURE BAND BELT GIRD HALO
LIST RING ZONE GIRTH CENTER
CESTUS COLLAR FILLET GIRDLE
BALDRIC COMPASS ENCIRCLE
SURCINGLE

CINDER ASH TAP COAL GRAY SCAR
SLAG CHARK DROSS EMBER
DANDER SCORIA CLINKER FOXTAIL
RESIDUE
(REFUSE —) BREEZE
(VOLCANIC —) LAPILLUS
(PL.) GLEEDS

CINEMATIZE FILMIZE

CINEMATOGRAPH KINO VERISCOPE
VITAGRAPH

CINERARIA SENECIO

CINGULUM BAND RIDGE GIRDLE

CINNAMON CANEL SPICE CASSIA
SANELA STACTE BARBASCO
(WILD —) BAYBERRY

CINNAMONROOT FLYBANE
FLEAWORT

CINNAMON STONE GARNET
ESSONITE

CINQUEFOIL FRASIER COWBERRY
HARDHACK ROSACEAN QUINTFOIL

CINYRAS (DAUGHTER OF —)
MYRRHA
(FATHER OF —) APOLLO
(SON OF —) ADONIS

CION BUD IMP SECT SLIP GRAFT
SCION SHOOT UVULA SARMENT
GRAFTING

CIPHER KEY NIL CODE NULL ZERO
ALBAM AUGHT OUGHT DECODE
DEVICE FIGURE LETTER NAUGHT
NOUGHT NUMBER SYMBOL
ATHBASH NULLITY MONOGRAM
VIGENERE NOTHINGLY

CIRCASSIAN ADIGHE KABARD
CHERKESS KABARDIN

CIRCE SIREN TEMPTER
(BROTHER OF —) AEETES
(FATHER OF —) SOL
(LOVER OF —) ULYSSES
(MOTHER OF —) PERSE
(SON OF —) TELEGONUS

CIRCLE DOT LAP ORB RED SET
CLUE CULT DISK GYRE HALO HOOP
IRIS LOOP MARU ORBE RING RINK
ROLL TOUR TURN ZONE BLACK
CAROL CLASS CROWN CYCLE
FETCH FRAME GROUP KREIS MONDE
PEARL REALM RHOMB RIGOL
ROUND ROWEL SWIRL TWIRL
BEZANT BROUGH CIRCUS CIRQUE
CLIQUE COLLET COLURE CORDON
CORONA DIADEM EQUANT GIRDLE
RONDEL ROTATE RUNDLE SPIRAL
SYSTEM TROPIC AZIMUTH CHUKKAR
CHUKKER CIRCLET CIRCUIT
COMPANY COMPASS CORONET
COTERIE ENCLOSE HORIZON
MONTHON REVOLVE RINGLET
DEFERENT ECLIPTIC FROSTBOW
SURROUND
(— AROUND ORGAN) ANNULET
(— IN BULL'S-EYE) CARTON
(— OF HELL) MALEBOLGE
(— OF MONOLITHS) CROMLECH
(— TRACED BY HORSE) VOLT
(ASTRONOMICAL —) EQUANT
EPICYCLE
(DANCE —) GALLEY
(FAIRY —) RINGLET
(GREAT —) EQUATOR ECLIPTIC
MERIDIAN
(IMAGINARY —) CYCLE DEFERENT
(INNER —) BOSOM
(PARHELIC —) FROSTBOW
(QUARTER —) ARC

(STONE —) CAROL HURLER
GORSEDD
(TRAVERSE —) RACER
(TWO —S) CACHET

CIRCLET BAND HALO HOOP RING
CROWN VERGE BANGLE CIRQUE
CORONA CIRCUIT CORONET
VALLARY BRACELET HEADBAND

CIRCUIT LAP AREA BOUT EYRE ITER
LOOP TOUR WEND ZONE AMBIT
CHAIN CYCLE ORBIT ROUND ROUTE
VIRON AMBAGE BUFFER DETOUR
DOUBLE SPHERE UMGANG ZODIAC
ADAPTER ADDRESS COMARCA
COMPASS COUNTER DIOCESE
ACCEPTER DIPLEXER DISTRICT
PERIPLUS PROGRESS
(BRANCH —) LEG
(ELECTRIC —) LEG LOOP DOUBLER
SQUELCH SECONDARY
(ELECTRONIC —) GATE

CIRCUITOUS MAZY CURVED
CROOKED DEVIOUS OBLIQUE
SINUOUS TWISTED VAGRANT
WINDING FLEXUOUS INDIRECT
RAMBLING TORTUOUS DECEITFUL
DEVIATING WANDERING
(— METHOD) WINDLASS

CIRCULAR O BILL FLIER FLYER
LIBEL ORBAL ORBED ROUND
DODGER FOLDER RINGED WHEELY
ANNULAR COMPASS CYCLOID
DISCOID DISLIKE HANDOUT PERFECT
COMPLETE DOPEBOOK ENCYCLIC
GLOBULAR INFINITE PAMPHLET
DOPESHEET

CIRCULAR-KNIT SEAMLESS

CIRCULATE GO AIR MIX MOVE PASS
RISE TURN WALK WIND TROLL
CANARD ROTATE SCURRY SPHERE
SPREAD WANDER CANVASS
CONVECT DIFFUSE PUBLISH
CONVOLVE

CIRCULATING WAIF AFLOAT
CURRENT

CIRCULATION ISSUE COURSE
COVERAGE CURRENCY

CIRCUMCISER MOHEL

CIRCUMCISION BRITH PERITOMY

CIRCUMFERENCE ARC AUGE AMBIT
APSIS GIRTH VERGE BORDER
BOUNDS CIRCLE LIMITS COMPASS
BOUNDARY SURROUND
(— OF SHELL) LIMBUS

CIRCUMFERENTOR PLANCHETTE

CIRCUMFLEX DOGHOUSE
(INVERTED —) HACEK

CIRCUMLOCUTION AMBAGE
CIRCUIT WINDING VERBIAGE

CIRCUMSCRIBE BOUND FENCE
LIMIT DEFINE CAPTURE CONFINE
ENCLOSE ENVIRON ENCIRCLE
RESTRAIN RESTRICT SURROUND
CONSCRIBE

CIRCUMSCRIBED NARROW INSULAR
LIMITED

CIRCUMSPECT SHY WARY WISE
ALERT CHARY CAREFUL GUARDED
PRUDENT CAUTIOUS DISCREET

VIGILANT WATCHFUL

CIRCUMSPECTION RESPECT PRUDENCE WARINESS

CIRCUMSTANCE GO FIX CASE FACT ITEM NOTE EVENT PHASE POINT START STATE THING AFFAIR DETAIL FACTOR PICKLE CALLING ELEMENT EPISODE INCIDENT INSTANCE POSITION
(CRITICAL —S) EXTREMES
(EXECRABLE —) ATROCITY
(LUDICROUS —) JEST
(PL.) CIRCS STATE TERMS ESTATE FORTUNE

CIRCUMSTANTIAL EXACT FORMAL MINUTE PRECISE DETAILED ITEMIZED

CIRCUMSTANTIATE SUPPORT EVIDENCE

CIRCUMVENT BALK BEAT DUPE FOIL CHEAT CHECK COZEN EVADE OUTGO TRICK BAFFLE DELUDE ENTRAP NOBBLE OUTWIT THWART CAPTURE DECEIVE DEFRAUD ENSNARE PREVENT SURROUND UNDERFONG

CIRCUS RING SHOW ARENA CANVAS CIRCLE CIRQUE CARNIVAL
(— LOT) TOBER
(— RING) TAN

CIRQUE CWM CIRC BASIN CIRCLE CIRCUS CORRIE RECESS CIRCLET EROSION

CIS SYN NERAL NORMAL

CISCO KIYI BLOAT BLOATER BLUEFIN LONGJAW MOONEYE BLACKFIN GRAYBACK TULLIBEE WHITEFIN

CISSA SIRGANG

CISSUS TREEBINE

CIST BOX KIST TOMB CHEST CISTA QUOIT CASKET CHAMBER KISTVAEN

CISTERN BAC FAT SAC TUB URN VAT BACK PANT SUMP TANK URNA WELL LAVER CAVITY CAISSON CHULTUN CUVETTE STEEPER FEEDHEAD

CITADEL ARX FORT HALL ALAMO BURSA BYRSA TOWER CASTLE BOROUGH CHESTER KREMLIN FASTNESS FORTRESS TOOTHILL

CITATION CITAL NOTICE MENTION SUMMONS MONITION AUTHORITY EVOCATION

CITE CALL NAME SIST TELL ALLAY EVOKE QUOTE REFER ACCITE ACCUSE ADDUCE ALLEGE AROUSE AVOUCH EXCITE INVOKE NOTIFY RECITE REPEAT SUMMON ADVANCE ARRAIGN BESPEAK CONVENT EXCERPT EXTRACT IMPEACH MENTION INDICATE INSTANCE REHEARSE

CITHARA CITHER PHORMINX

CITHERN ZITTERN

CITIZEN CIT ALLY VOTER NATIVE BURGESS BURGHER CITOYEN CLERUCH DENIZEN ELECTOR FLATCAP FREEMAN OPPIDAN SUBJECT TOWNMAN AMERICAN

CIVILIAN COMMONER CONSCIVE DOMESTIC NATIONAL OCCUPANT RESIDENT
(— OF SECOND CLASS) KNIGHT HIPPEUS
(—S OF MEDINA) ANSAR
(FOREIGN-BORN —) ALIEN
(PL.) SUBJECT PERIOECI CITIZENRY

CITIZENRY COUNTRY SUBJECT

CITRAL GERANIAL

CITRON LIME CEDRA LEMON CEDRAT ETHROG YELLOW

CITTERN LAUD CITHERN PENORCON

CITY FU WON BURG DORP TOWN URBS WOON ZION BURGH CALNO EKRON JEBUS LILLE MANOA PIECE PLACE POLIS SETTE STEAD VILLE CALNEH CENTER CIUDAD CUTHAH GILEAD JAMNIA JEBUSI LAGADO NAGARA PITHOM STAPLE BABYLON CAMBALU CHESTER ELLASAR FREEDOM JABNEEL MECHLIN CABECERA ELDORADO MAGAZINE PALENQUE
(— LIFE) ASHCAN
(ANCIENT —) PERGAMUM
(CHIEF —) CAPITAL CABECERA MEGAPOLIS
(RICH —) MAGAZINE
(TREASURE —) RAAMSES
(WICKED —) BABYLON

CITY-STATE POLIS CIVITAS

CIVET CAT CIT GENET RASSE ZIBET BONDAR FOUSSA MUSANG PAGUMA ZIBETH CIVETTA FOSSANE LINSANG NANDINE POLECAT ZIBETUM ZINSANG FANALOKA MONGOOSE TANGALUNG

CIVIC LAY CIVIL SUAVE URBAN POLITE URBANE CIVICAL SECULAR

CIVIL FAIR HEND HENDE SUAVE POLITE URBANE AFFABLE AMIABLE COURTLY ELEGANT GALLANT POLITIC REFINED SECULAR DISCREET GRACIOUS OBLIGING POLISHED WELLBRED

CIVILIAN CIT CIVIE CIVIL CIVVY PEKIN MOHAIR CITIZEN TEACHER CIVILIST GOWNSMAN
(— ENTERTAINING SOLDIER) PYKE

CIVILITY BONTE COMITY NOTICE AMENITY COURTESY URBANITY GENTILITY
(PL.) HONORS HONOURS

CIVILIZATION ISLAM KULTUR POLICE CULTURE ECUMENE CIVICITY
(GREEK —) HELLENISM

CIVILIZE TAME TEACH TRAIN POLISH REFINE EDUCATE HUMANIZE URBANIZE

CIVILIZED CHRISTIAN

CLABBER LOP MUD MIRE CURDLE LOPPER CLAUBER

CLACKDISH CLICKET

CLAD DREST ROBED BESEEN CLEDDE DECKED ADORNED ARRAYED ATTIRED CLOTHED COVERED DRESSED SHEATHED
(— IN PURPLE) PORPORATE

(SCANTILY —) SINGLY

CLADOSE RAMOSE CLADINE BRANCHED

CLAIM ASK DUE AVER AVOW CALL CASE DIBS LIEN MINE NAME PLEA COLOR DRAFT EXACT PLEAD RIGHT SHOUT TITLE ASSERT DEMAND DESIRE ELICIT EQUITY INTEND RECKON ACCLAIM COLLECT DERECHO DRAUGHT PRETEND PRETEXT PROFESS RECLAIM REQUIRE SOLICIT ARROGATE INTEREST MAINTAIN PRETENCE PRETENSE PROCLAIM SUBCLAIM
(— IN BUSINESS) CAPITAL
(— TO BE BELIEVED) AUTHORITY
(FALSE —) JACTATION
(INDIAN LEGAL —) HAK HAKH

CLAIMANT CLAIMER USURPER PRETENDER

CLAIRE PARK

CLAIRVOYANCE INSIGHT VOYANCE LUCIDITY SAGACITY TELOPSIS

CLAIRVOYANT FEY SEER OMENER PROPHET SEERESS

CLAM MYA BASE CLOG DAUB GLAM HUSH MEAN BLUNT CLAMP CRASH GAPER GLAUM GRASP GROPE PAHUA RAZOR SHELL SMEAR SOLEN SPOUT STICK VENUS ADHERE CLUTCH GWEDUC QUAHOG STICKY BIVALVE CLANGOR COQUINA MOLLUSK STEAMER ADHESIVE BULLNOSE SHIPWORM NANNINOSE

CLAMBAKE BAKE RALLY CLAMAROO SQUANTUM

CLAMBER CLIMB SCALE CLAVER SCRAWM SPRAWL RAMMACK SCRABBLE SCRAMBLE SPRACHLE STRUGGLE

CLAMMY DAMP DANK SOFT WACK MOIST SAMMY STICKY WAUGHY SQUIDGY CLAMMISH

CLAMOR CRY DIN HUE BERE BUNK GAFF RANE RERD ROAR ROUP ROUT SONG UTAS WAIL BLARE BOAST BRUIT CHIDE CHIRM NOISE OUTAS RERDE RUMOR SHOUT BELLOW BOWWOW HUBBUB OUTCRY QUETHE RACKET TUMULT UPROAR YATTER CLAMOUR EXCLAIM ORATION STASHIE NORATION PILILLOO PULLALUE SHOUTING
(— AGAINST) DECRY

CLAMOROUS NIP LOUD NOISY VOCAL BLATANT CLAMANT DINSOME YELLING BRAWLING DECRYING

CLAMP DOG HOG LUG NIP PIN SET BAIL BALE BEND BOLT BURY CLAM GLAM GRIP JACK MUTE NAIL VISE YOKE BLOCK BRACE CLASP CRAMP GLAND GLAUM HORSE CLINCH FASTEN MOPHEAD STIRRUP FASTENER HOLDFAST
(— FOR BASS DRUM) SPUR
(— FOR CORK) AGRAFE AGRAFFE
(— FOR FLASK) GLAND
(STORAGE —) GRAVE

CLAMSHELL CLAM GRAB SHUCK
CLAN ATI HAN KIN SET SIB CULT
GENS HAPU NAME RACE SECT SEPT
SIOL UNIT AIMAK AYLLU CLASS
GENOS GROUP HORDE PARTY TRIBE
ABUSUA CLIQUE FAMILY SENAAH
ABIEZER KINDRED PHRATRY
SATSUMA SOCIETY ZADRUGA
CALPULLI DIVISION
(— **SUBDIVISION**) OBE
CLANDESTINE BYE SLY FOXY
HEDGE PRIVY QUIET SNEAK COVERT
HIDDEN SECRET BOOTLEG FURTIVE
ILLICIT BACKDOOR HIDLINGS
STEALTHY
CLANG DIN DING PEAL RING TONK
CLANK CLASH NOISE JANGLE
TIMBRE
CLANGOR DIN CLAM ROAR CLANG
HUBBUB UPROAR
CLANGOROUS BRAZEN PLANGENT
CLANGULA HARELDA
CLANK RING RACKLE
CLAP BANG FLAP PEAL SLAP SPAT
TACK CHEER CLINK CRACK SMITE
POSTER STRIKE STROKE APPLAUD
CHATTER CLAPPER PLAUDIT
HANDCLAP
(— **OF THUNDER**) DINT
(— **ON**) CRACK
CLAPBOARD KNAPPLE CLAPHOLT
CLAPNET DAYNET
CLAPPER CLAP CLACK RATTLE
TONGUE JINGLET KNACKER
KNOCKER
(— **OF BELL**) TONGUE
(**PL.**) BONES
CLAPTRAP TRASH BLAGUE BUNKUM
DEVICE EYEWASH FUSTIAN
BUNCOMBE NONSENSE TRICKERY
CLARE MINORESS
CLARENCE GROWLER
CLARET TERSE LAFITTE BORDEAUX
BADMINTON
CLARIAS HARMOOT KARMOUTH
CLARIFIED PURED LAUTER
CLARIFY CLAY FINE CLEAN CLEAR
PURGE SNUFF PURIFY REFINE
RENDER SERENE SETTLE CLEANSE
DESPUME EXPLAIN GLORIFY
DEFECATE DEPURATE ELIQUATE
SIMPLIFY
CLARIN ACOCOTL
CLARINET BEN BIN BON BEEN BONE
REED AULOS CLARY PUNGI
CLARONE LAUNEDDAS
CLARION REST CLARE CLARY CLEAR
CLARINO SUFFLUE TRUMPET
CLARITY GLORY SPLENDOR
STRENGTH CLEARNESS
CLARY CLARRE SALVIA
CLASH JAR BANG BOLT BUMP DASH
FRAY NEWS SLAM BRAWL BRUNT
CHECK CRASH FIGHT FRUSH KNOCK
OCCUR PRATE SHOCK AFFRAY
DIFFER GOSSIP HURTLE IMPACT
JOSTLE STRIFE STRIKE TATTLE
THRUST THWART COLLIDE DISCORD
SCANDAL ARGUMENT CONFLICT

CLASHING HARSH CONFLICT
FRICTION COLLISION
CLASP HUG PIN CLIP DOME FOLD
GRAB GRIP HASP HOLD HOOK HOOP
KEEP OUCH STAY TACH BRACE
CATCH CLING GRASP MORSE PREEN
SEIZE SLIDE SPANG TACHE ACCOLL
AGRAFE AMPLEX BECLIP BROOCH
BUCKLE CLENCH CLUTCH ENFOLD
ENWRAP FASTEN FIBULA GIMMER
GIMMOR INCLIP INFOLD JIMMER
STRAIN TASSEL AGRAFFE AMPLECT
EMBRACE ENTWINE FERMAIL
HOLDING MOUSING TENDRIL
BARRETTE CORSELET FASTENER
SURROUND
(— **HANDS**) SHAKE WRING
CLASS ILK BRAN CHOP FORM KIND
RACE RANK RATE SECT SORT SUIT
TYPE YEAR BREED CASTE GENRE
GENUS GRADE GROUP ORDER
RANGE TRIBE VARNA VERGE
ASSORT CIRCLE CLINIC DECURY
FAMILY GENDER LEAGUE MISTER
NATION PHYLUM RATING RECKON
REMOVE RUBRIC STRAIN STRIPE
CATALOG FACTION LECTURE
REGIMEN SEMINAR SPECIES
VARIETY CATEGORY DESCRIBE
DIVISION GENOTYPE GEOMOROI
(— **OF BARDS**) THULIR
(— **OF GOODS**) BRAND
(— **OF OUTCASTS**) ETA
(— **OF PEOPLE**) FOLK SALARIAT
(— **OF SECURITIES**) LEGAL
(— **OF SHASTRAS**) SRUTI SHRUTI
(— **OF SOUNDS**) ENDING
(— **OF TEASELS**) KINGS
(**ARISTOCRATIC** —) ARISTOI
(**CHOICEST** —) ROBUR
(**DEPRESSED** —) PANCHAMA
(**FIRST** —) GAY
(**HEREDITARY** —) CASTE
(**JAPANESE** —) HEIMIN KWAZOKU
(**LABORING** —) PARAIYAN
(**LEARNED** —) VATES CLERISY
(**LOWER** —) BELOW GENTE
(**LOWEST** —) LAG SCUM
(**PEASANT** —) JACQUERIE
(**SLAVEHOLDING** —) CHIVALRY
(**SOCIAL** —) ESTATE SHIZOKU
(**WORKING** —) TOIL
CLASSIC VINTAGE
CLASSICAL PURE ATTIC GREEK
LATIN ROMAN CHASTE CLASSIC
ACADEMIC HELLENIC MASTERLY
(**NOT** —) BASE
CLASSICALLY IDEALLY
CLASSIFICATION FILE RANK RATE
SORT CODEN GENRE GENUS GRADE
ORDER TAXIS RATING SYSTEM
ANALYSIS CATEGORY DIVISION
TAXONOMY BREAKDOWN
CLASSIFIED SECRET
CLASSIFIER COUNTER SEPARATOR
CLASSIFY CODE LIST RANK RATE
SIZE SORT SUIT TAPE TYPE BREAK
CLASS DRAFT GRADE GROUP LABEL
RANGE TRIBE ASSORT CODIFY

DIGEST DIVIDE IMPOST TICKET
ACCOUNT ARRANGE BRACKET
BRIGADE CATALOG DISPOSE
DRAUGHT GRAMMAR MARSHAL
SUBSUME REGISTER
(— **TOGETHER**) SLUMP
CLASSIS CONFERENCE
CLATHRATE LATTICED
CLATTER DIN JAR CLACK NOISE
RUMOR BABBLE GABBLE GOSSIP
HURTLE RACKLE RATTLE TATTLE
BLATTER CHATTER CLUNTER
CLUTTER PRATTLE REESHLE
SHATTER SLAMBANG
CLATTERING CLATTERY SLITHERING
CLAUSE ITEM PART CLOSE COMMA
JOKER PLANK RIDER TROPE
MEMBER PHRASE ARTICLE
COMMATA PASSAGE PROVISO
SLEEPER PETITION REDDENDO
SENTENCE TENENDAS TENENDUM
NOVODAMUS
(— **IN WRIT**) TESTE
(— **OF WILL**) DEVISE
(**ADDITIONAL** —) RIDER
CLAVACIN PATULIN
CLAVER PRATE CLOVER GOSSIP
CHATTER CLABBER CLAIVER
CLAMBER
CLAVICHORD CLAVIER MANICORD
UNICHORD CLARIGOLD MONOCHORD
CLAVICLE FURCULE COLLARBONE
CLAVIER MANUAL KLAVIER
CLAVUS CORN BUNION HELOMA
CLAW DIG PEG CLEE CRAB FANG
FAWN HAND HOOK NAIL PULL SERE
TEAR UNCE CHELA CLOOF CLUFE
COURT GRASP GRIFF ONGLE SCLAW
SEIZE TALON UNCUS CLUNCH
CLUTCH CRATCH NIPPER POUNCE
SCRAPE SINGLE UNGUAL UNGUIS
UNGULA WEAPON CRUBEEN
FALCULA FLATTER SCRATCH
SHUTTLE WHEEDLE SCRABBLE
(**PL.**) CLUTCH
CLAY BAT COB PUG WAD WAX BASS
BEND BODY BOLE BOTT GALT GLEY
LOAM LUTE MARL MIRE PAPA SMIT
TILL ARGIL BRICK CLOAM EARTH
GAULT LOESS OCHRE PASTE RABAT
TASCO BINDER CLEDGE CLUNCH
KAOLIN PUDDLE SAGGER DAUBING
MOULDER RASHING CAMSTANE
FIRECLAY GUMBOTIL LATERITE
LIFELESS SINOPITE
(— **FOR MELTING POTS**) TASCO
(— **IN GLASS**) TEAR
(— **IRON**) BULL
(— **LAYER**) VARVE
(**3-ARMED, HARD-FIRED** —) STILT
(**COVERED WITH** —) LUTOSE
(**HARD** —) BEND
(**HARDENED** —) METAL
(**INDURATED** —) BASS CLUNCH
(**PIECE OF FIRED** —) TILE
(**PIPE** —) CAMSTANE CAMSTONE
(**POTTER'S** —) SLIP ARGIL
(**REMOVE** —) UNLUTE
(**SURPLUS** —) SPARE

(TOUGH —) LECK

CLAYEY BOLAR HEAVY MALMY
MARLY CLEDGY LUTOSE ARGILLIC

CLAYMORE FERRARA

CLAY PIGEON BIRD CLAY

CLAYSTONE LECK

CLAYWARE GLOST

CLEADING CLOTHING

CLEAN DO FAY FEY HOE MOP NET
DRUM DUST FAIR NEAT PURE REDD
RIPE SIDE SMUG SWAB TRIM WASH
WIPE CLEAR CURRY EMPTY FEIGH
GRAVE SCOUR SCRUB SMART
SWEEP TERSE TOSHY BARREL
CHASTE CLEVER KOSHER PURIFY
SPANDY APINOID BANDBOX
CHAMOIS CLEANLY CLEANSE
CLEARLY FURBISH PERFECT
SWINGLE ABSTERGE BACKWASH
BRIGHTLY DEXTROUS ENTIRELY
RENOVATE SCAVENGE SPOTLESS
UNSOILED

(— A FUR) DRUM

(— A QUILL) DUTCH

(— BOAT) CAREEN

(— BY SCRAPING) GRAVE

(— BY SMOKE) SMEEK

(— CANNON) SCALE

(— FIREARM) WORM

(— FLAX) SWINGLE

(— IN ACID) BLANCH

(— OUT) USH SPEAR

(— SHIP'S BOTTOM) HOG BREAM
GRAVE

(— UP) DISPATCH

(RITUALLY —) KOSHER

CLEAN-CUT CRISP

CLEANED BRIGHT

CLEANER SOAP BORAX PURER
FOLDER GUMMER RAMROD
FLUEMAN SPOTTER CLEANSER

(AIR —) CAN

(GRAIN —) KICKER

CLEAN-LIMBED CLEVER

CLEAN-LINED SPRUCE

CLEANLY PURE CLEAN ADROIT
ARTFUL CHASTE FAIRLY SPANDY
CORRECT ELEGANT INNOCENT
SKILLFUL

CLEANNESS PURITY

CLEANSE FAY BRAN CARD COMB
FARM HEAL PICK SOAP WASH
BROOM BRUSH CLEAN CLEAR DIGHT
DRESS FEIGH FLAME FLUSH PURGE
RINSE SCOUR SCRUB SNUFF
BOTTOM CAREEN EMUNGE PICKLE
PURIFY REFINE SPONGE WILLOW
BAPTIZE CLARIFY DEBRIDE
DETERGE EXPIATE LAUNDER
MUNDIFY SWEETEN ABSTERGE
DEPURATE OFFSCOUR RENOVATE
SCAVENGE SPRINKLE

CLEANSER LYE SOAP CLEANER
PURIFIER DETERGENT DETERSIVE

CLEANSING BATH FLUSH ABLUENT
CLYSMIC WASHING ABLUTION
CLEANING LAVATION DETERGENT

(CEREMONIAL —) LAVABO
PURGATION

CLEANUP KILLING SWEEPUP

CLEAR HOT JAM NET RID WAY CAST
EASY FAIR FINE FLAT FREE GAIN
GRUB JUMP NEAT OPEN OVER PURE
PUTE QUIT REDD RIFE SHUT SLAM
VOID ACUTE ATRIP AZURE BREAK
BREME BRENT BROAD CHUCK
CLEAN CRISP DRIVE LIGHT LUCID
NAKED PLAIN PRINT PRUNE SCOUR
SHARP SMOLT SUNNY SUTEL
SWEEP UNTIE VIVID ACQUIT AERIAL
ASSOIL BRIGHT CANDID CLEVER
EXCUSE EXEMPT FLUTED LAUTER
LIMPID LIQUID LUCENT PATENT
PURIFY SERENE SETTLE SHRILL
SMOOTH UNSTOP ABSOLVE CAPITAL
CLARIFY CLARION CRYSTAL
DELIVER DILUCID EVIDENT EXPLAIN
EXPRESS GLARING GRAPHIC
LIGHTEN OBVIOUS PERVIAL
RELEASE SILVERY ACCREDIT
APPARENT BRIGHTEN BULLDOZE
DEFINITE DISTINCT EXPLICIT
LUCULENT LUMINOUS MANIFEST
PELLUCID REVELANT

(— AWAY) FAY FEY FEIGH BANISH
DISPEL DISCUSS

(— FROM) ALOOF

(— LAND) CURE BRUSH SLASH
DEADEN

(— OF GROUND) ATRIP AWEIGH

(— OF MUD) SLUTCH

(— OF SCUM) SKIM

(— OF TUFTS) HOB

(— OUT) BLOW HOOK SWAMP
SKIDDOO HIGHTAIL DISCHARGE

(— PATH) FRAY HACK BUSHWACK

(— THROAT) HOICK HOUGH

(— UP) SOLVE ASSOIL RESOLVE
DISSOLVE UNSHADOW

(NOT —) DULL DUSKY FOGGY
INEVIDENT

CLEARANCE CHOP ROOM RUNBY
BACKLASH ALLOWANCE

CLEAR-CUT LUCID SHARP DIRECT
CONCISE DECIDED CHISELED
DEFINITE DISTINCT INCISIVE
TRENCHANT

CLEARING FIELD FRITH GLADE
SHADE TRACT ALCOVE ASSART
RIDING RIDDING SLASHING

CLEARLY FAIR CLEAR LIGHT REDLY
FAIRLY FRANKLY WITTERLY

CLEAR-MINDEDNESS LUCIDITY

CLEARNESS CLARITY FINESSE
EVIDENCE FINENESS

CLEARWEED RICHWEED

CLEAT BITT STUD BLOCK CHOCK
KEVEL LEDGE RANGE WEDGE
BATTEN RIFFLE BOLLARD COXCOMB
GROUSER SIRMARK SUPPORT
SURMARK

CLEAVAGE RIFT CLEFT WASSIE
FISSION FISSURE WEDGING DIVISION
SCISSION

CLEAVE CUT RIP CHOP HANG HOLD
JOIN LINK PART RELY REND RIFT
RIVE SLIT TEAR BREAK CARVE
CHAWN CHINE CLAVE CLEFT CLING

CLOVE CRACK SEVER SHALE SHARE
SHEAR SLIVE SPLAT STICK ADHERE
BISECT COHERE DIVIDE FURROW
PIERCE SLEAVE SUNDER DISPART
FISSURE SEPARATE

(— OFF) SCIND

CLEAVER CLIVE CLEAVE FROWER
CHOPPER PARANGI

CLEAVERS GRIP CLOTE CLOTS
CLITHE HAIRIF HAIRUP BURHEAD
LOVEMAN PIGTAIL BIRDLIME

CLEAVING DYSTOME FISSION
DYSTOMIC

(— READILY) EUTOMOUS

CLECHE URDE URDY URDEE

CLEF KEY CLIVE CHIAVETTA

CLEFT CUT GAP CHAP CHOP FENT
FLAW GASH NOCK REFT RIFT RILL
RIMA RIVE SLIT BREAK CHASM
CHAWN CHINK CLOVE CRACK
CREEK CRENA GULCH RILLE RIVEN
SINUS SPLIT BREACH CHAPPY
CLEAVE CLOUGH CLOVEN CRANNY
CROTCH DIVIDE LISSOM PARTED
RECESS RICTUS STIGMA BLASTED
CHIMNEY CREVICE DIVIDED FISSURE
OPENING SLIFTER APERTURE
FRACTURE INCISION INCISURA
MULTIFID SCISSURA SCISSURE

(— IN HOOF) SEAM

(— IN THE POSTERIORS) NOCK

(— OF BUTTOCKS) CREASE

CLEMATIS PIPESTEM CURLYHEAD

CLEMENCY ORE PITY GRACE
MERCY LENITY QUARTER KINDNESS
LENIENCY MILDNESS

CLEMENT MILD SOFT WARM GENTLE
LENIENT MERCIFUL

CLENCH FIST GRIP GRIT HOLD NAIL
BRACE CLASP CLENK CLINT CLOSE
GRASP CLINCH CLUTCH DOUBLE

(— FIST) GRIPE

CLEPE CLUPIEN

CLEPSYDRA GURRY GHURRY

CLERGY CLOTH CRAPE CHURCH
CLERISY MINISTRY

(BODY OF —) PULPIT

CLERGYMAN ABBA ABBE DEAN
PAPA CANON CLERK FROCK PADRE
PILOT PRIOR RABBI VICAR BISHOP
CLERIC CURATE DEACON DIVINE
DOMINE PAROCH PARSON PASTOR
PRIEST RECTOR SUPPLY CASSOCK
PRELATE CARDINAL CHAPLAIN
CLERICAL DIOCESAN EMERITUS
LECTURER MINISTER ORDINARY
PREACHER REVEREND SQUARSON
PRESBYTER

CLERIC ABBE CLERK FROCK
DEACON GALLAH LEVITE PRIEST
ACOLYTE ANAGNOST

CLERICAL BLACK CLERIC CLERKISH
PARSONIC PARSONLY

CLERK NUN BABU MONK AGENT
AWARD BABOO CLARK FILER RALPH
WRITE BILLER CHASER CLERIC
COMMIS GRADER HERMIT KITMAN
LAYMAN MAPPER MASTER MUNSHI
PANDIT PENMAN PRIEST PUNDIT

RALPHO SCRIBE TELLER WRITER
YEOMAN ACOLYTE ACTUARY
BOOKMAN CARCOON COMPOSE
DOPSTER GOMASTA PIARIST
SCHOLAR SHIPPER SHOPMAN
STUFFER CLERGEON CLERGION
CLERKESS EMPLOYEE GREFFIER
MUTSUDDY PENCLERK RECORDER
SALESMAN
(— OF ST PAUL) BARNABITE
(HOTEL —) DESKMAN
CLERKLY LEARNED SCRIBAL
CLERGIAL SCHOLARLY
CLEVE BRAE CLIFF CLEEVE HILLSIDE
CLEVER APT SLY ABLE CUTE DEFT
FEAT FELL FINE FOXY GNIB GOOD
HEND KEEN SLIM SPRY AGILE
ALERT CANNY CLEAN CLEAR CUNNY
FALSE FEATY FENDY HANDY HEADY
HENDE LITHE QUICK SHARP SLICK
SMART SNACK WITTY ACTIVE
ADROIT ARTFUL ASTUTE BRIGHT
CRAFTY EXPERT HABILE HEPPEN
KITTLE KNACKY NEATLY NIMBLE
PRETTY SHREWD SPIFFY STALKY
SUBTLE AMIABLE CUNNING GNOSTIC
PARLISH PARLOUS VARMENT
VARMINT DEXTROUS HANDSOME
OBLIGING SKILLFUL TALENTED
CLEVERLY SLICK FEATLY TIDELY
SMARTLY ASTUTELY
CLEVERNESS CAN CHIC NOUS TACT
SKILL ESPRIT INDUSTRY DEXTERITY
CLEVIS COP DEE HAKE CLEVY
COPSE BRIDGE BRIDLE MUZZLE
SHACKLE PLOWHEAD
CLEW BALL CLUE HINT GLOBE
GLOME SKEIN BOTTOM HURDLE
THREAD
CLICHE COMMONPLACE
CLICK DOG DOT DASH PAWL SLAP
TICK AGREE CATCH FORGE SNECK
SNICK DETENT PALLET RATCHET
(HEEL —S) BELLS
(TELEGRAPH —) DASH
CLICK BEETLE ELATER
CLIENT CEILE JAJMAN PATRON
PATIENT CUSTOMER HENCHMAN
RETAINER
CLIENTELE PUBLIC CLIENTRY
CLIFF HOE NIP CRAG HILL KLIP
ROCK SCAR BLUFF CLEVE CLINT
HEUCH HEUGH KRANS SCARP
SHORE SLOPE STEEP CLEEVE
HEIGHT KRANTZ PISKUN CLOGWYN
HILLSIDE PALISADE TRAVERSE
(BROKEN —) CRAG
(ICE —) ICEBLINK
(LINE OF —S) PALISADE
CLIFFY SCARRY
CLIMATE SKY SUN MOOD CLIME
HEAVEN REGION TEMPER ATTITUDE
(SCIENCE OF —) PHENOLOGY
CLIMAX CAP TOP ACME APEX HEAD
NEAR PEAK SHUT CREST CROWN
MOUNT SCALE TIGHT APOGEE
ASCEND FINISH HEIGHT SHINNY
SUMMIT ZENITH BLOWOFF EVEREST
CAPSHEAF CAPSTONE EPIPLOCE

CLIMB GAD STY COON RAMP RISE
SHIN SKIN SOAR STYE CREEP
GRIMP MOUNT SCALE SKLIM SPEED
SPEEL SWARM TWINE ASCEND
ASCENT BREAST SCLIMB SCRAWM
SHINNY SWARVE SWERVE CLAMBER
SCRAMBLE TRAVERSE
(— ABOARD). HOP
(— DOWN) LIGHT UNSCALE
(— IN MOUNTAINEERING) CHIMNEY
(— OVER) SURMOUNT
CLIMBER CUBE AKALA AKELA KAIWI
RIGGER SCALER CRAMPON
CREEPER
(MOUNTAIN —) ALPINIST
CLIMBING SCANDENT
(MOUNTAIN —) ALPINISM
CLIMBING FERN NITO AGSAM
CLIMBING IRON SPUR PRICK
CRAMPET CRAMPIT CRAMPON
CREEPER PRICKER CRAMPBIT
CLIMBING PALM RATTAN
CLIMBING PEPPER BETEL
CLIMBING ROSE SCRAMBLE
CLINCH FIX GET HUG TOE BIND GRIP
LOCK NAIL SEAL CLAMP CLING
CLINK CLINT GRASP RIVET SEIZE
CLENCH CLUTCH FASTEN SECURE
SNATCH CONFIRM EMBRACE
GRAPPLE SCUFFLE COMPLETE
CONCLUDE HOLDFAST
CLING HUG BANK HANG HOLD RELY
CLASP HITCH STICK TRUST ADHERE
CLEAVE CLINCH COHERE DEPEND
FASTEN SHRINK WITHER CHERISH
EMBRACE SHRIVEL CONTRACT
CLINGER LIMPET
CLINGFISH SUCKER TESTAR TETARD
SUCKFISH
CLINGING CLUNG HUGGING
ADHAMANT ADHERENT OSCULANT
CLINK ALE JUG PUT RAP BEAT
BLOW BRIG CASH CLAP COIN JAIL
MOVE RING SLAP KLINK LATCH
MONEY RHYME SEIZE CLINCH
JINGLE LOCKUP MOMENT PRISON
STRIKE TINKLE INSTANT JINGLING
CLINKER BUR BUHR BURR SCAR
SLAG WASTE HOLLANDER
CLINKER-BUILT SHINGLED
LAPSTRAKE
CLINOMETER TRIMMER
CLINTONIA BLUEBEAD DOGBERRY
COWTONGUE
CLIP BAT BOB CUT DOD HUG LIP
LOP MOW NIG NIP BARB BEAK CHIP
COLL CROP DOCK DODD FLAG
HOLD PACE PARE POLL SNIP TRIM
BRUSH CLASP DRESS FORCE LUNET
MINCE PRUNE SHAVE SHEAR SHRIP
STEEK CLUPPE CLUTCH CRUTCH
FASTEN GADGET HINDER HOLDER
LACING CALIPER CURTAIL CURTAIN
EMBRACE HICKORY LUNETTE
SCISSOR SHORTEN DIMINISH
ENCIRCLE RETAINER
(— A COIN) SHORTEN
(— WOOL) CRUTCH
(CARTRIDGE —) CHARGER

(HAIR —) BARRETTE
(SPRING —) JACK
CLIPPED TONSURED
CLIPPER BOAT SHIP DOCKER SLICER
CHAINER CLAMMER CLEANER
GRABMAN GRIPPER SHEARER
SNAPPER
CLIPPING BOB SCROW CUTTING
SNIPPING
(—S OF METAL) SCISSEL
(PL.) BRASH SHORTS EXCERPTA
CLIQUE COT MOB SET BLOC CLAN
CLUB GANG KNOT RING CABAL
CROWD GROUP JUNTO WRITE
CIRCLE CLETCH SCHISM COTERIE
FACTION CONCLAVE SODALITY
CLITELLUM GIRDLE SADDLE
CINGULUM
CLOAK ABA HAP BRAT CAPA CAPE
COPE HIDE HUKE IZAR MANT MASK
PALL RAIL ROBE VEIL WRAP BURKA
CAPOT CHOGA COVER GREGO
GUISE JELAB MANTA MANTO SAGUM
SHUBA TILMA ABOLLA AHUULA
ASSUME BAUTTA CAMAIL CAPOTE
CASTER CHAMMA CHAPEL CHIMER
DOLMAN JOSEPH MANTLE MANTUA
PHAROS PONCHO RHASON SCREEN
SERAPE SHIELD SHROUD TABARD
VISITE ALICULA BAVAROY CASSOCK
CHLAMYS CONCEAL COURTBY
GARMENT MANTEAU PAENULA
PELISSE PELLARD PRETEXT
SHELTER SURCOAT ZIMARRA
ALBORNOZ BURNOOSE CAPUCHIN
DISGUISE INTRIGUE MANTILLA
PALLIATE
(— OF FEATHERS) MAMO AHUULA
(— WITH CROSSES) ANALABOS
(HOODED —) HUKE CAPOT BAUTTA
BIRRUS BAVAROY CARDINAL
(RED —) CAPE
(SOLDIER'S —) SAGUM
(WATERPROOF —) GOSSAMER
CLOAKED PALLIATE
CLOAKROOM VESTIARY
CLOAM DAUB CLOMB CROCKERY
CLOCHE BELL
CLOCK NEF BELL CALL DIAL GOER
GONG TIME WRAP BUNDY CLUCK
GURRY HATCH HURRY KNOCK
METER QUIRK STYLE VERGE WATCH
BEETLE CROUCH GHURRY ORLAGE
TICKER SKELPER STRIKER TATTLER
HOROLOGE INCUBATE ORNAMENT
RECORDER SOLARIUM TELLTALE
(— IN FORM OF SHIP) NEF
(— ON STOCKING) QUIRK GUSHET
GUSSET
(— WITH PENDULUM) PENDULE
(TIME —) BUNDY
(WATER —) GURRY GHURRY
SOLARIUM CLEPSYDRA
CLOCKER SIZER TIMER RAILBIRD
CLOCKWISE DEASIL DESSIL
SUNWISE POSITIVE
CLOD SOD CLAT CLOT DOLT DULL
LOUT LUMP SLOB TURF CLOUT
CLOWN DIVOT EARTH GLEBE GROSS

KNOLL YOKEL CLATCH GROUND
STUPID BUMPKIN
CLODDISH GROSS STUPID BOORISH
CLODHOPPER BOOR CLOD SHOE
RUSTIC HOBNAIL PLOWMAN
CLODIA LESBIA
CLODPATE CLOT DOLT FOOL
RAMHEAD CLODPOLE CLODPOLL
IMBECILE
CLOG FUR GUM JAM LOG BALL
CLAG CLAM CLOY CURB DRAG
GLUB LEAD LOAD LUMP SHOE SKID
STOP BLIND BLOCK CHECK CHOKE
DANCE SABOT SPOKE TRASH
ADHERE BURDEN CHOPIN COBCAB
DAGGLE ENCLOG FETTER FREEZE
GALOSH HAMPER HOBBLE IMPEDE
PATINE PATTEN REMORA SANDAL
SECQUE WEIGHT CONGEST
CREEPER ENGLEIM FETLOCK
PERPLEX SHACKLE SPANCEL
TRAMMEL TRIGGER BEDAGGLE
COALESCE ENCUMBER OBSTRUCT
OVERSHOE RESTRAIN
(— A FILE) PIN
(WOODEN —S) GETA GETAS
CLOG ALMANAC STAFF
CLOGGED FOUL FURRY PINNY
FROZEN CLOTTED BEGUMMED
CLOGGING CLOGGY FOULING
CUMBROUS
CLOGGY DULL HEAVY LUMPY
STICKY
CLOISONNE SHIPPO
CLOISTER HALL STOA ABBEY AISLE
ARCADE FRIARY IMMURE PIAZZA
PRIORY CLOSTER CONVENT
NUNNERY MONASTERY
CLOISTERED RECLUSE
CLOSE BY IN CAP END GUM HAW
HOT TYE AKIN BUNG CHOP CLAP
CLIT DAUB FAST FILL FINE FIRM
GRIP HARD HIDE LOUK MEET NEAR
NIGH QUIT SEAL SHUT SLAM SNUG
SPAR STOP TINE WINK WYND ZERO
ANEAR BLOCK BREAK CEASE CHEAP
CHIEF COAPT DENSE FENCE FINIS
FLIRT GARTH GROSS ISSUE MUGGY
SNECK SOLID STEEK STICK STIVY
THICK TIGHT BUCKLE BUTTON
CLAUSE CLENCH CLUTCH DOUBLE
EFFECT EXPIRY FINALE FINISH
INSTOP INWARD NARROW NEARBY
PERIOD SECRET SETTLE SILENT
STANCH STINGY STITCH STRAIT
STRICT STUFFY THRONG ADJOURN
BOROUGH CLOSING CLOSISH
COMPACT CONDEMN CONTEXT
COSTIVE EXTREME GRAPPLE
MISERLY OCCLUDE POCKETY
PUTHERY RAMPIRE RECLUDE
SHUTTER SIMILAR STAUNCH
STOPPER ACCURATE ADJACENT
BLOCKADE CLAUSULA COMPLETE
COMPRESS CONCLUDE ENCEINTE
ESPECIAL FAMILIAR FINALIZE
HAIRLINE IMMINENT INTIMATE
PARCLOSE PRECLUDE
(— BY) FORBY AROUND BESIDE

FOREBY HEREBY FORTHBY
SISTERING
(— EYES OF HAWK) SEEL
(— IN ON) TAKE
(— IN) BESET ENCLOSE INCLOSE
(— THE MOUTH) STOPPLE
(— TO BATSMAN) SILLY
(— TO COMMUNICATION) CORDON
(— TO QUARRY) HOT
(— TO THE HEART) DEAR
(— TO THE WIND) SHARP
(— TO) BY INBY NEAR NIGH ANEAR
INBYE ALMOST AGAINST
(— TOGETHER) COLLAPSE
(— UP) DIT CORK DITT FILL FOLD
STOP SERRY UPCLOSE
(— WITH A CLICK) SNECK
(— WITH) BIND
(PARTIALLY —) HOOD
(VERY —) CHIEF STINGY
CLOSE-COUPLED COMPACT
CLOSED DARK DOWN SHUT CLOSE
LUCKEN UNOPEN BLOCKED
COVERED
(— AT ONE END) BLIND
CLOSEFISTED MEAN NEAR FISTY
TIGHT SNIPPY STINGY MISERLY
HANDFAST
CLOSE-FITTING FIT HARD MEET
SNUG THEAT THEET TIGHT THIGHT
SUCCINCT
CLOSE-KNIT TRUSSED
CLOSE-LIPPED SILENT
CLOSELY FAST JUST NEAR WELL
SADLY ALMOST BARELY HARDLY
NARROW NEARLY JUNCTLY
STRICTLY
CLOSEMOUTHED SECRET SILENT
(NOT —) LEAKY
CLOSENESS DENSITY SECRECY
FIDELITY INTIMACY NEARNESS
PARSIMONY
CLOSER VAMPER CLOSURE
CLOSEST NEXT NEAREST
CLOSESTOOL STOLE
CLOSET ARK EWRY ROOM SAFE
AMBRY CUBBY CUDDY PRESS
LOCKER PANTRY SECRET CABINET
CONCEAL PRIVATE CONCLAVE
CUPBOARD GARDEVIN WARDROBE
CLOSING FLY SLAM SNAP CLOSURE
CLOTURE CLAUDENT BUTTONING
CLOSURE END GAG BOLT SEAL
BOUND LIMIT ATRESIA CLOTURE
FERRULE TENSION CLAUSURE
FINALITY KANGAROO
CLOT DOT GEL CLAG CLAT GOUT
JELL LUMP MASS MOLE SHED
CLART GRUME BALTER COTTER
LAPPER LOPPER CLODDER
EMBOLUS THICKEN CLODPATE
COAGULUM CONCRETE SOLIDIFY
CLOTH DAB RAG BLUE COAT DRAB
DRAP ECRU FELT FILE PALL SEAM
WARE WOOF BEIGE BLUET CABAN
CLOUT DITTO FOULE GOODS GREEN
LODEN LUNGI MOORY PRINT STUPE
TAMMY TAWNY TIBET TOILE TWEED
TWILL ALPACA AWNING BENGAL

BYSSUS CANAMO CANVAS CHADOR
CLAITH CLERGY COVERT DORSEL
DOSSAL DOSSER DRAPET DUSTER
FABRIC LIVERY LONGYI LOWELL
MELLAY MULETA NAPKIN RENGUE
REXINE SARONG SURNAP TILLOT
WITNEY ACETATE BOULTEL
CHADDAR CHRISOM COATING
CRIMSON DRAPERY DUSTRAG
FALDING GARMENT JACONET
ORLEANS PANUELO RAIMENT
SACKING SURNAPE TEXTILE
WATCHET WORSTED BATSWING
CHRISMAL COMPRESS CORPORAL
CRAMOISY DWELLING FROCKING
HOMESPUN LAMBSKIN MATERIAL
PHULKARI RADEVORE SHAATNEZ
SHEETING THICKSET TOILINET
(— OF GOLD) SONERI
(— FOR BELT) SHROUD
(— FOR WIPING TABLE) FILE
(— FOR WRAPPING FABRICS) TILLET
(— FOR WRAPPING THE DEAD)
CEREMENT
(— HANGING FROM WAISTBAND)
LANGOOTY
(— OF SINGLE WIDTH) STRAITS
(— REMAINING AFTER CUTTING)
CABBAGE
(— WORN LIKE KILT) LAVALAVA
(ALTAR —) TOWEL PENDLE PALLIUM
VESPERAL CATASARKA
(ARABIAN —) HAIK CABAN CABAAN
(BARK —) TAPA TAPPA
(BED —) COVER SPREAD
(BLACK —) KISWA KISWAH
(COARSE —) DOZEN DUROY
CANGAN DOWLAS DOZENS FORFAR
FRIEZE HODDEN KERSEY KHARVA
KHARWA STAMIN STROUD TAPALO
CAMBAYE COTONIA DRUGGET
FORFARS RAPLOCH RUGGING
SARPLER SOUTAGE FLUSHING
RADEVORE SARCILIS
(COMMUNION —) FANON SINDON
CORPORAL
(COTTON —) JEAN TOBE ADATI
BLUET CAFFA CRASH DURRY JEANS
KHADI KHAKI SURAT BEAVER
CALICO CANGAN DOWLAS DURRIE
GANZIE HUMHUM KALMUK NANKIN
PENANG CAMBAYE FUSTIAN
GALATEA GINGHAM JACONET
KHADDAR LASTING NANKEEN
REGATTA BOGOTANA DOMESTIC
MUSLINET
(CRIMSON —) CRAMASIE CRAMOISY
(DECORATIVE —) SCARF
(EMBROIDERED —) SAMPLER
(GLASS —) DORON
(GOAT-WOOL —) SLING
(GREEN —) KENDAL
(GUNNY —) TAT
(HAIR —) ABA ABBA CILICE
(HEMP —) PINAYUSA
(HOMESPUN —) KELT KHADI PATTU
PUTTOO HEADING KHADDAR
(LAP —) GREMIAL
(LINEN —) BRIN LINE GULIX

DOWLAS FORFAR BRABANT
LOCKRAM SILESIA BLANCARD
CORPORAL GAMBROON GHENTING
LINCLOTH
(LONG —) LUNGI WHITE LUNGEE
(ORNAMENTAL —) TRAP DOSSAL
DOSSEL
(PACK —) MANTA
(PACKING —) SOUTAGE
(PIECE OF —) APRON CLOUT
GODET LANGOOTY
(RICH —) SCARLET
(SADDLE —) PANEL
(SILK —) CAFFA BENGAL PATOLA
(SOAKED —) BUCK
(SOFT —) RUGINE
(STAGE —) BACKDROP
(STARCHED —) GUIMPE
(STRIPED —) RAY
(STRONG —) CANVAS DURANCE
(TWILLED —) JANE JEAN
GAMBROON
(UNDYED —) HODDEN
(WASHING —) SHAMMY CHAMOIS
(WAX —) MUMJUMA
(WET —) DAB
(WOOL —) SAY DRAB PUKE BEIGE
BUREL DOZEN DUROY LAINE STARA
TAMIS TAMMY DOZENS DUFFEL
HODDEN KENDAL KERSEY MEDLEY
MELTON MUSTER SAXONY STAMIN
TAMINY TARTAN BASTARD BLANKET
DUNSTER FLANNEL RAPLOCH
ROPLOCH RUGGING BEARSKIN
BUCKSKIN FLORENCE SARCILIS
VENETIAN
(WORSTED —) RASH SHAG
BOMBAZET
CLOTHE DON DUB HAP LAP RIG TOG
DECK GARB GIRD GOWN ROBE VEST
ADORN ARRAY CLEAD CLEED
DRESS ENDOW ENDUE FLESH
FROCK HABIT INDUE ATTIRE
BEWRAP SHRIDE SHROUD SWATHE
ADDRESS APPAREL FEATHER
RAIMENT VESTURE ACCOUTER
ACCOUTRE
CLOTHED CLAD BECLAD HABITED
CLOTHES CASE DUDS GARB GEAR
GORE KAPA SUIT TACK TOGS WEAR
BRAWS DUCKS HABIT ATTIRE
FARDEL SHROUD TROGGS APPAREL
BAGGAGE COSTUME IRONING
RAIMENT REGALIA TOGGERY
VESTURE WEARING CLOTHING
FEATHERS FRIPPERY GARMENTS
INDUMENT
(CASTOFF —) FRIPPERY
(DRESS —) WAMPUM
(FINE —) BRAWS
(HANDSOME —) BRAVERY
(MOURNING —) DOLE
(SHOWY —) LUGS
(SOAKED —) BUCK
CLOTHES DRYER AIRER TUMBLER
CLOTHESPIN PEG
CLOTHESPRESS ARMOIRE TALLBOY
WARDROBE
CLOTH FOLDER CUTTLER

CLOTHING (ALSO SEE CLOTHES)
BACK BLUE BRAT COAT GARB GEAR
SEAM WEAR ARRAY BUREL CLOTH
DRESS GREEN HABIT JABOT STUFF
ATTIRE FARDEL ROBING VESTRY
APPAREL CLOBBER CLOTHES
CRIMSON DRAPERY OUTWALL
RAIMENT VESTURE WEEDERY
INDUMENT KNITWEAR ORNAMENT
SLOPWORK VESTIARY VESTMENT
(BLACK —) SABLE
(COARSE —) BUREL
(LOWER —) LAP
(MUSLIM —) IHRAM
(NAUTICAL —) SLOPS
(SHEER —) FLIMSIES
(SHOWY —) SHEEN FINERY
(WOMEN'S —) FRILLIES
(WORK —) FATIGUES
CLOTHING DEALER HOSIER
CLOTHWORKER FULLER
CLOTTED GORY CLOTTY CLOUTED
GARGETY GRUMOUS LIVERED
CLOTURE GAG CLOSURE
CLOUD DOG FOG NUE SKY BLUR
DAMP DARK DUST FOOL HAZE HELM
HIDE MIST REEK SMUR ARCUS
BEDIM BEFOG BLOOM DRIFT GLOOM
MUDDY NUBIA OXEYE SHADE STAIN
SULLY SWARM TAINT VAPOR
CIRRUS DAMAGE DARKEN DEEPEN
DEFAME FUNNEL MUDDLE NEBULA
NIMBUS PILEUS POTHER SCREEN
SHADOW STIGMA BLACKEN
CONFUSE CUMULUS ECLIPSE
FUMULUS GRANULE OBSCURE
POOTHER STRATUS SUNSPOT
TARNISH CLOUDCAP CLOUDLET
COCKTAIL NIGHTCAP NUBILATE
OVERCAST WOOLPACK
(— OF DUST OR VAPOR) STEW
SMOTHER
(— OF MIST) SOP
(— OVER MOUNTAIN) HELM
(HIGH —) CIRRUS
(HORIZONTAL —) STRATUS
(MASS OF HIGH —S) RACK
(MASSY —) CUMULUS
(NUCLEAR —) FIREBALL
(RAIN —) NIMBUS
(PL.) SCUD SOUP CARRY GASHES
CLOUDBERRY AKPEK MOLKA
AVERIN
(FRUIT OF —) NOOP
CLOUDED HAZY DIRTY DUSTY FILMY
JASPE MUCKY SHADY ACLOUD
GLOOMY TURBID INFUMATE
NEBULOUS
CLOUDINESS FAIR HAZE GLOOM
MUDDLE
CLOUDING DAPPLE
(— OF EYE) CATARACT
CLOUDLESS AZURE CLEAR BRIGHT
CLOUDY DIM DARK DULL HAZY
BLEAR FILMY FOGGY MISTY MURKY
SHADY GLOOMY LOWERY OPAQUE
SMURRY VEILED BLURRED CLOUDED
NEBULAR OBSCURE CONFUSED
NUBILOUS OVERCAST VAPOROUS

CLOUGH CLUF CLEFT CLOES
CLEUCH CLEUGH RAVINE VALLEY
CLOUT BAT BOX DAB HIT BEAT
BLOW BUMP CLOD CLUB CUFF JOIN
MEND NAIL SLAP SLUG SWAT
PATCH SMITE KLOWET STRIKE
TARGET THRASH WASHER BANDAGE
BOSTHOON
CLOVE GAP NAIL CHIVE CLEFT GILLY
BUTTON CLEAVE RAVINE SHERRY
GILLIVER
CLOVEN CLEFT SPLIT DIVIDED
BISULCATE
CLOVEN-FOOTED SLIT FISSIPED
CLOVE PINK GELOFER GRENADIN
CLOVER RED HAGI SEED HUBAM
LOTUS MEDIC NARDU PUSSY ALSIKE
BERSIM LADINO LEGUME LUXURY
NARDOO ALFALFA BERSEEM
BERSINE CLAIVER COMFORT
LUCERNE MELILOT SAPLING
TREFOIL TRIFOLY COWGRASS
HAREFOOT NAPOLEON PUSSYCAT
SHAMROCK SUCKLING YELLOWTOP
CLOVER DODDER AILWEED
EPITHYME HAILWEED HAIRWEED
HALEWEED
CLOWN HOB OAF PUT APER BOOR
FOOL GAUM GOFF JOEY LOUT MIME
MOME SWAD ZANY ANTIC BUFFO
CHURL COMIC FESTE IDIOT MIMER
PATCH PUNCH WAMBA ZANNI
AUGUST BODACH HOBBIL JESTER
LUBBER RUSTIC STOOGE AUGUSTE
BODDAGH BUFFOON BUMPKIN
CHARLEY COSTARD KOSHARE
LAVACHE LOBSTER MUDHEAD
PEASANT PIERROT PLAYBOY
SCOFFER TOMFOOL COVIELLO
KOYEMSHI MERRYMAN WHITEFACE
CLOWNISH RAW RUDE ZANY GAWKY
ROUGH CLUMSY COARSE RUSTIC
AWKWARD BOORISH HOBLIKE
KERNISH LOBBISH LOUTISH UNCIVIL
VILLAIN CLUBBISH SWADDISH
UNGAINLY
CLOY CLOG GLUT NAIL PALL SATE
GORGE PRICK ACCLOY PIERCE
SATIATE SATISFY SURFEIT
SATURATE
CLOYER SNAP
CLOYING GOOEY SWEET VANILLA
CLOYSOME LUSCIOUS
CLUB BAT DOG HIT HUI SET BEAT
CANE JOIN MACE MALL MAUL MERE
POLT TEAM BAFFY BANDY BATON
BILLY BUNCH CLOUT HURLY KEBBY
LODGE MASHY ORDER STAFF STICK
TOWEL UNITE YOKEL ZONTA
BULGER CERCLE CLIQUE CUDGEL
HURLEY KEBBIE LIBBET MACANA
MASHIE MENAGE MUCKLE NULLAH
PRIEST STRIKE TAIAHA VEREIN
WEAPON WHITES CAMBUCA
COLLEGE COUNCIL HETAERY
HETAIRY SOROSIS ATHENEUM
BLUDGEON CATSTICK SODALITY
SORORITY SPONTOON TERTULIA
KNOBKERRY

(— IN PLAYING CARDS) OAK
(— OF ANTENNA) CLAVUS
(BASEBALL —) FARM
(GOLF —) IRON WOOD BAFFY
CLEEK MASHY SPOON STICK
BRASSY BULGER DRIVER JIGGER
LOFTER MASHIE PUTTER BLASTER
MIDIRON NIBLICK PITCHER
(MAORI —) MERE MERAI MARREE
(POLICEMAN'S —) SAP BILLY
PANTOON SPONTON SPONTOON
(POLITICAL —) ROTA HETAERY
HETAIRY
(WAR —) WADDY
(WOMEN'S —) SOROSIS SORORITY
CLUB CARRIER CLAVIGER
CLUBFOOT TALUS VARUS TALIPES
CYLLOSIS POLTFOOT
CLUB MOSS MOSS FOFEET
LYCOPOD PILIGAN CROWFOOT
FERNWORT
CLUBROOT CLUB ANBURY HANBURY
CLUBBING CLUBFOOT
CLUB RUSH RUSH SEDGE GLUMAL
DEERHAIR
CLUCK HEN FUSS CHUCK CLACK
CLICK CLOCK CLOOK
CLUE KEY TIP BALL CLEW HINT IDEA
LEAD GUIDE TWINE BOTTOM
THREAD INNUENDO
CLUMP SOP TOD BLOW BUSH CLOT
HEAP KNOT LUMP MASS MOSS
MOTT TOPE TUFT TURB BLUFF
BUNCH CLAMP GROUP GROVE
HOUSE PATCH PLUMP STUMP
TREAD WUDGE CLUNCH DOLLOP
LUMPER CLUMPER CLUSTER
THICKET
(— OF BRIERS OR ROSES) ROAN
RONE
(— OF CELLS) SLUDGE
(— OF SHRUBS) BUSH
(— OF SPORANGIA) SORUS
(— OF TREES) BLUFF HOUSE HURST
HYRST BOSQUE
CLUMSILY SOUSE GREENLY
GAUCHELY
CLUMSY AWK FLOB LEWD NUMB
RUDE BLUNT BULKY GAUMY GAWKY
HOGGY HULKY INAPT INEPT SCRAM
SPLAY STIFF STOGY GAUCHE
LUBBER NOGGEN THUMBY
AWKWARD BOORISH CHOCKLE
CHUCKLE UNHANDY UNREADY
BENUMBED BUNGLING CLOWNISH
FOOTLESS HANDLESS LUMBERLY
TACTLESS UNGAINLY UNWIELDY
(NOT —) FINE
CLUSTER BOB BOG BUSH CLOT
COMA CONE CYME KNOT LUMP
TUFT BUNCH CLUMP DRUSE GROUP
PLUMP SHEAF CENTER COLONY
GATHER MORULA PLEIAD REGIME
BOUROCK CLUTHER DOLPHIN
ENVIRON FOLIAGE FASCICLE
NUCLEATE SURROUND
(— AS BEES) BALL KNIT
(— OF BANANAS) HAND
(— OF BRANCHES) SPRAY

(— OF CRYSTALS) DRUSE
(— OF FEATHERS) MUFF
(— OF FIBERS) NEP
(— OF FLOWERS) CYME CORYMB
ANTHEMY
(— OF HAIRS) MYSTAX
(— OF METAL BALLS) GRAPE
(— OF NODULES) GRAPES
(— OF PILES) DOLPHIN
(— OF PLANTS) BED
(— OF RAYS) AIGRETTE
(— OF SPORES) SORUS
(— OF STARS) PRAESEPE
(— OF TINES) TROCHE
(CONFUSED —) SPLATTER
(SUSPENDED —) SWAG
CLUSTER BEAN GUAR
CLUSTERED TUFTED RACEMOSE
AGGREGATE
CLUTCH HUG NAB SET CLAM CLAW
CLEM CLIP FIST GLAM GRAB GRIP
NEST BROOD CATCH CLASP CLAUT
CLEEK CLICK GLAUM GRASP GRIPE
GRISP HATCH LEVER POWER SEIZE
TALON CLEACH CLENCH CLETCH
CLINCH CUTOUT FASTEN RETAIN
SNATCH CONTROL CRAMPON
COUPLING
(— OF EGGS) SET LAWTER LAYING
SETTING SITTING LAUGHTER
CLUTCHING GRIP GRIPING
CLUTTER MESS STUFF BUSTLE
CUMBER CLATTER DISORDER
CONFUSION
CLUTTERED CLATTY CLOTTED
CLYMENE (FATHER OF —) OCEANUS
(HUSBAND OF —) IAPETUS
(MOTHER OF —) TETHYS
(SON OF —) ATLAS PHAETHON
MENOETIUS
CLYPEUS NASUS EPISTOME
PRELABRUM
CLYSTER LAVEMENT INJECTION
CLYTEMNESTRA (FATHER OF —)
TYNDAREUS
(HUSBAND OF —) AGAMEMNON
(MOTHER OF —) LEDA
(SON OF —) ORESTES
COACH BUS CAR FLY DRAG HACK
HELP ARABA BRIEF CABIN FLIER
FLYER PILOT PRIME STAGE TEACH
TRAIN TUTOR ADVISE DIRECT
FIACRE JARVEY SALOON ADVISER
CHARIOT COACHER CONCORD
GONDOLA PREPARE RATTLER
TALLYHO CARRIAGE DORMEUSE
PUPILIZE
(3-WHEELED —) TRICYCLE
(FAST —) FLIER FLYER
(HACKNEY —) FIACRE JARVEY
(HEAVY —) DRAG
(SLOW —) SLOWPOKE
COACHMAN FLY FISH JEHU WHIP
PILOT COACHY DRIVER COACHEE
COACHER YAMSHIK YEMSCHIK
COACTION EXPLOITATION
COADJUTOR PRIOR
COAGULANT CURD RENNET
STYPTIC COAGULUM GELATINE

COAGULATE GEL SET CAKE CLOD
CLOT CURD JELL QUAIL YEARN
COTTER CURDLE LAPPER LOBBER
LOPPER POSSET CLABBER CLOTTER
CONGEAL PECTIZE THICKEN
COAGULUM CONCRETE SOLIDIFY
COAGULATED CRUDY CURDY
LIVERED
COAGULATION GOUT CLOTTER
COAGULUM CLOT THROMBUS
COAL RIB BASS DUFF FUEL SWAD
BLOCK CHARK EMBER GHOST
GLEED STOKE BARING BRAZIL
BURGEE CANNEL CARBON CINDER
FIRING SPLINT BACKING BOGHEAD
BRIGHTS BYERITE COBBLES LIGNITE
RATTLER VITRAIN AMPELITE
LANDSALE
(— IN PLACE) SOLID
(— PILLAR) STOOK
(— SLAB) SKIP
(BAD —) SMUT
(DIRTY —) RASH
(FINE —) DUFF SCREENINGS
(IMPURE —) SWAD
(LARGE BLOCK OF —) JUD JUDD
(LIVE OR GLOWING —) GLEED
GLEYD
(REFUSE —) BREEZE
(SIZE OF —) EGG NUT PEA LUMP
RICE SLACK STOVE BARLEY
BROKEN CHESTNUT WALLSEND
BUCKWHEAT
(SLATY —) BASS BONE BONY
(SMALL LUMP OF —) NUBBLING
(SMALL PORTION OF UNCUT —)
PANEL
COAL BED SEAM
COALBIN BUNKER
COAL BROKER CRIMP
COAL CAR JIMMY
COAL CHUTE DOCK
COAL DUST COOM CULM SMUT
COOMB
COALESCE MIX CLOG FUSE JOIN
BLEND MERGE UNITE EMBODY
MINGLE COMBINE
COALESCENCE UNION FUSION
LEAGUE CAPTURE SYNANTHY
COALFISH SEY PARR CUDDY SEITH
BESHOW BILLET CUDDEN PODLER
SAITHE BADDOCK GLASHAN
GLASSIN PILTOCK POLLACK
(YOUNG —) PODLER PODLEY
COMAMIE POODLER SILLOCK
GRAYFISH
COALITION FRONT TRUST UNION
FUSION LEAGUE MERGER ENTENTE
ALLIANCE
COAL OIL KEROSENE
COALRAKE HOE FREGGIN FRUGGAN
SCRAPPLE
COAL WORKER GEORDIE HURRIER
COAL YARD REE
COAMING CURB LEDGE COMBING
COARSE FAT LOW RAW BASE BULL
DANK FOUL HARD HASK LEWD
LOUD RANK RUDE SOUR VILE
BAWDY BRASH BROAD CRASS

CRUDE DIRTY GREAT GROFF GROSS
HARSH HASKY HEAVY LARGE
LOOSE PLAIN RANDY ROUGH ROUTH
ROWTY STOGY STOUR THICK
UNORN BLOWSY BRAZEN BRUTAL
CALLOW COMMON DUDGEN EARTHY
IMPURE INCULT RANDIE RIBALD
ROUDAS RUDOUS RUSSET RUSTIC
SULTRY UNFELE VULGAR BLATANT
CARLAGE CARLISH FULSOME
GOATISH LOUTISH OBSCENE
RAPLOCH RAUCOUS ROINISH
SENSUAL CLOWNISH HOMESPUN
IMMODEST INDECENT PLEBEIAN
STUBBORN UNCHASTE
COARSE-FIBERED STRONG
COARSE-GRAINED DRY GRUFF
COARSELY BROADLY HARSHLY
COARSEN HACKNEY
COAST BANK LAND RIPA BEACH
CLIFF SHORE SLIDE WARTH ADJOIN
BORDER RIVAGE STRAND BOBSLED
SEASIDE APPROACH SEABOARD
SEASHORE
COASTER MAT SLED DOLLY TROUT
CRADLE CREEPER TOBOGGAN
COASTLAND MAREMMA
COAT FUR LAY PEE SAC TOG BARK
BLUE BUFF CONY DAUB FOIL FOLD
HIDE HUSK JACK JAMA JUPE PINK
RIND SACK SCAB SEAL TOGE ZINC
BENNY CLOTH CONEY COVER
CRUST FLASH FROCK GLACE GLAZE
HABIT JAMAH JEMMY LAYER OILER
PAINT PLATE QUYTE SAQUE SHELL
TERVE ALPACA BYRNIE COATEE
DUSTER ENAMEL EXTIMA GROUND
HACKLE INTIMA INVEST JACKET
JOSEPH KIRTLE LACKER MANTLE
MELOTE PARGET PELAGE RABBIT
REEFER SEALER SILVER SLOUGH
STUCCO TABARD VENEER BEESWAX
BOBTAIL CASSOCK COATING
COURTBY CRISPIN CUTAWAY
GARMENT GROGRAM INCRUST
KARAKUL LACQUER OILCOAT
OVERLAY PALETOT PELISSE
PLASTER SHELLAC SHOOTER
SPENCER STRATUM SUBCOAT
SURCOAT SURTOUT SWAGGER
TOGEMAN TOPCOAT VESTURE
BENJAMIN COURTEPY GRAPHITE
INTONACO MACKINAW MEMBRANE
ROCKELAY SEALSKIN SHERWANI
SILICATE TEGUMENT TRENCHER
(— FOOD) DREDGE
(— LENS) BLOOM
(— OF ARMS) CREST BLAZON
BEARINGS
(— OF BIRD SKINS) TEMIAK
(— OF CARIBOU SKINS) KOOLETAH
(— OF DEFENSE) JACK
(— OF EYE) CHOROID
(— OF EYEBALL) SCLERA
(— OF GRAVEL) BLOTTER
(— OF MAIL) FROCK BRINIE BYRNIE
SECRET HAUBERK
(— OF ORGAN) INTIMA
(— OF PLASTER) SET ARRICCIO

BROWNING INTONACO
(— OF SEED) BRAN
(— OF WOOL) FLEECE
(— WITH ALLOY) TERNE
(— WITH PITCH) PAY
(DEER'S WINTER —) BLUE
(FIRST — OF TIN) LIST
(HAIR —) MELOTE
(HOODED —) GREGO CAPOTE
(LONG —) JIBBA JIBBAH KAPOTE
DJIBBAH
(LOOSE —) CASSOCK PALETOT
INVERNESS
(MILITARY —) TUNIC BLOUSE
BUFFCOAT
(RIDING —) JOSEPH
(SEALSKIN —) NETCHA
(SHEEPSKIN —) ZAMARRA
ZAMARRO
(SHORT —) PEA SACK JERKIN
REEFER PEACOAT
(THREE-QUARTER LENGTH —)
ACHKAN
(WATERPROOF —) BURSATI SLICKER
(WOMAN'S —) CARACO DOLMAN
COATED GLACE BACKED FURRED
LOADED CANDIED
COAT HANGER SHOULDER
COATI NASUA TEJON NARICA PISOTE
ARCTOID
COATING (ALSO SEE COAT) FUR
GUM ARIL DOPE DRAB FILM FLOR
HAIR HOAR SKIN BLOOM FLASH
GLACE GLAZE ICING SCALE BEAVER
CHATON COVERT FINISH JACKET
PATINA VENEER BACKING DIPCOAT
FURRING GILDING LACQUER
PLATING TINNING ACIERAGE
CAMBOUIS CLADDING EMULSION
FLOODING MUCILAGE PERIDIUM
(— OF BACTERIA) SLIME
(— OF GLASS) MOILES FOLIATION
(— OF GLUE) ENAMEL
(— OF ICE) GLAZE
(— OF SEED) TESTA
(— OF TONGUE) ATTER
(CORROSION —) RUST
(POWDERY —) DOWN
(PRUINOUS —) FARINA
(WALL —) GROUT
COATTAIL LABIE LAPPET
COAX BEG COY PET CANT DUPE
FAGE FAWN LURE URGE JOLLY
TEASE BANTER CAJOLE CUITLE
CUTTER ENTICE FLEECH SEDUCE
BEGUILE CROODLE CROWDLE
CRUDDLE FLATTER IMPLORE
SOOTHER WHEEDLE BLANDISH
COLLOGUE INVEIGLE PERSUADE
COAXIAL CONCENTRIC
COB EAR LOB MEW COBB
COBBERER ROARER ROUSER
COBBLE DARN MEND PAVE BOTCH
PATCH BUNGLE COGGLE REPAIR
COBBLER PIE SNOB SHEEP SOLER
SUTOR ARTIST COZIER SOUTER
BOTCHER CATFISH CRISPIN
POMPANO SADDLER CHUCKLER
SCORPION SNOBSCAT

COBBLERFISH COBBLER SUNFISH
SHOEMAKER
COBBY STOUT HEARTY LIVELY
STOCKY COMPACT
COBLE MULE KOBIL
COBNUT COB OUABE HOGNUT
PIGNUT
COBRA ASP NAG HAJE NAGA NAJA
KRAIT VIPER ELAPID URAEUS
COBWEB NET TRAP SNARE WEVET
GOSSAMER
COCA CUCA KHOKA TRUXILLO
COCAINE COKE SNOW
(— MIXED WITH HEROIN)
SPEEDBALL
COCASH ASTER SWANWEED
COCCOID BERRYLIKE
COCCULUS CEBATHA FISHBERRY
COCHE MOCOA
COCHINEAL GRAIN BLANCO
COCCUS GRANILLA
COCHINEAL FIG NOPAL
COCHINEAL INSECT VERMIL
VERMEIL VERMILION
COCK COX TAP BANK BOOT COIL
FOWL HEAP KORA PILE RICK SPAN
COCKY COQUE FIGHT FUGIE GALLO
SHOCK STACK STRUT VALVE YOWLE
CRAVEN FAUCET HAMMER HEELER
LEADER CONTEND GORCOCK
PETCOCK ROOSTER SWAGGER
ASTROLOG COCKBIRD COCKEREL
COXBONES GAMECOCK JERMONAL
STOPCOCK
(— GUNLOCK) NAB
(— OF HAY) HIPPLE
(— OF THE WALK) KINGFISH
(— WITHOUT COURAGE) CRAVEN
(— WITHOUT SPURS) MUCKNA
(FIGHTING —) FUGIE HEELER
TURNPOKE
(TURKEY —) STAG
(WATER —) KORA
(WEATHER —) FANE VANE
COCKADE KNOT BADGE COCKARD
ROSETTE
COCKATIEL QUARRION
COCKATOO ARA ARARA COCKY
GALAH MACAW ABACAY COCKIE
PARROT CORELLA JACATOO
CALANGAY GANGGANG
COCKATOO BUSH BLUEBERRY
COCKBOAT COG COCK COGBOAT
COCKCHAFER OAKWEB BUZZARD
HUMBUZZ
COCKED HAT SCRAPER RAMILLIE
COCKER CODDLE COGGER QUIVER
SPANIEL
COCKEREL COCK SLIP BANTAM
COCKINESS SWAGGER
COCKLE COCK GALL GITH KILN
OAST BULGE KAKEL SHELL STOVE
DARNEL NUCULA PALOUR PUCKER
RIPPLE WABBLE ZIZANY CUCKOLD
WRINKLE HARDHEAD
COCKLEBUR COTS CLOTE COCKLE
BURDOCK BURWEED CADILLO
CLOTBUR CUCKOLD CLOTWEED
DITCHBUR

COCKNEY ORTHERIS LONDONESE
COCKPIT PIT RING RINK WELL
ARENA CABIN FIELD GALLERA
COCKROACH BUG DRUM ROACH
BEETLE BLATTID DRUMMER
KNOCKER
COCKSCOMB CREST COXCOMB
COCKSPUR FINGRIGO GARABATO
COCKTAIL SOUR ZOOM BRONX
CRUSTA GIBSON MARTINI SAZERAC
SIDECAR STINGER SWIZZLE
APERITIF DAIQUIRI
COCKY PERK PERT CRANK CROUSE
FARMER JAUNTY COCKING
ARROGANT
COCO KOKO BROMA COCOA COKER
YUNTIA
COCOA MAHAL PATASHTE
COCONUT COCO COCKER NARGIL
COCOANUT
COCONUT FIBER COIR KAIR KYAR
CAYAR
COCONUT MEAT COPRA
COCONUT PALM KOKO NIOG
COCOON POD CLEW CLUE KELL
SCAB SHED SHELL BOTTOM
DOUPION FOLLICLE
COCO PLUM ICACO HICACO
COCOWOOD KOKRA
COCUSWOOD KOKRA
COD BAG BIB COR KID POD AXLE
BANK CUSK FOOL GADE HOAX
HUSK POOR ROCK BELLY DROUD
GADID POUCH SCROD SHALE SHAUP
TORSK BURBOT CODGER CULTUS
ESCROD FELLOW MULVEL PILLOW
POCKET TOMCOD WACHNA
BACALAO CODFISH CODLING
CUSHION KEELING KILLING MILWELL
SCROTUM CABELIAU DOLEFISH
KABBELOW KLIPFISH
(BUFFALO —) LING
(CURED —) DUNFISH
(DRIED —) STOCK
(PILE OF DRIED —) YAFFLE
(SALTED —) COR KLIPFISH
HABERDINE
(YOUNG —) SPRAG
CODA CAUDA RONDO EPILOG FINALE
CODETTA EPILOGUE
CODDLE PET BABY CADE COOK
MUCH HUMOR NURSE SMALM SPOIL
CARESS COCKER COSSET COTTON
FONDLE PAMPER PTISAN QUADLE
PARBOIL
CODE LAW FLAG CANON CODEX
DOGMA FUERO CIPHER DIGEST
SECRET SIGNAL MULTEKA PRECEPT
DOOMBOOK
(— OF CHIVALRY) BUSHIDO
(— OF LAWS) ADA ADAT PANDECT
DOOMBOOK
(— OF RULES) VINAYA
(— OF WHAT IS FITTING) DECORUM
CODETTA CONDUIT
CODEX ALEF CODE ALEPH ANNAL
CODFISH POOR SPRAG TORSK
KEELING
CODGER COD CUFF CHURL CRANK

MISER FELLOW NIGGARD
CODICIL ANNEX LABEL SCRIPT
CODIFY INDEX DIGEST CLASSIFY
CODLING HAKE
CODOL RETINOL
COEFFICIENT CUMULANT
AUSTAUSCH
COELENTERATE POLYP MEDUSA
ACALEPH RADIATE ACALEPHE
COENOBIUM COLONY
COENOCYTE SYMPLASM SYMPLAST
SYNCYTIUM
COENZYME COFACTOR
COERCE COW CURB MAKE BULLY
CHECK DRIVE FORCE ORDER
COHERT COMPEL HIJACK CONCUSS
ENFORCE REPRESS SANDBAG
BLUDGEON BULLDOZE DISTRAIN
RESTRAIN RESTRICT
COERCION HEAT FORCE DURESS
COMMAND
COEUR D'ALENE SKITSWISH
COFFEE JO JOE RIO CAFE COHO
COHU JAVA MILD MOCHA BOGOTA
BRAZIL CAUFLE CHAOUA JAMOKE
SANTOS TRIAGE ARABICA BOURBON
MELANGE SUMATRA ESPRESSO
MAZAGRAN MEDELLIN TRILLADO
COFFEE BEAN QUAKER
COFFEEBERRY JOJOBA CASCARA
SOYBEAN PEABERRY
COFFEE CAKE KUCHEN
COFFEEHOUSE INN CAFE CAFENER
CAFENET
COFFEEMAKER SILEX
COFFEE TREE BONDUC CHICOT
VIRGILIA
COFFER ARK BOX DAM PYX CHEST
HUTCH TRUNK CASKET FORCER
FORCET SPRUCE TRENCH CAISSON
CASHBOX CASSOON COFFRET
LACUNAR LAQUEAR CIBORIUM
STANDARD
COFFIN BIER CASE CIST KIST MOLD
PALL SHELL BASKET CASING
CASKET COFFER HEARSE TROUGH
THROUGH
(LEADEN —) COPE
COG CAM LIE CAUK COCK GEAR
JEST CATCH CHEAT CHOCK CHUCK
COGUE COZEN TENON TOOTH
TRICK WEDGE WHEEL CAJOLE
COGGING DECEIVE PRODUCE
QUIBBLE WHEEDLE
COGENT GOOD PITHY VALID POTENT
STRONG TELLING FORCIBLE
POWERFUL
COGITATE MULL MUSE PLAN THINK
PONDER CONNATE MEDIATE
REFLECT CONSIDER
COGNATE KIN AKIN ALIKE ALLIED
COGENER KINDRED RELATED
SIMILAR BANDHAVA RELATIVE
APOPHONIC
COGNITION GNOSIS NOESIS
KENNING KNOWLEDGE
COGNITIVE KNOWING EPISTEMIC
COGNIZANCE KEN WIT HEED MARK
BADGE CREST EMBLEM NOTICE

BEARING COCKADE KNOWING
PRIVITY WITTING
COGNIZANT WARE WISE AWAKE
AWARE GUILTY KNOWING SENSIBLE
(BE —) DEEM
COGNOMEN NAME BYNAME
AGNOMEN SURNAME NICKNAME
PATRONYM
COGON ILLUK KUNAI LALANG
COGWOOD CERILLO
COHABIT LIVE DWELL ADHERE
OCCUPY COMPANY ACCUSTOM
COHERE FIT BOND GLUE SUIT
AGREE CLING SEIZE STICK UNITE
ADHERE CEMENT CLEAVE CONNECT
COINCIDE
COHERENCE UNION CONSENT
CONTEXT COHESION STRENGTH
COHERENT SERRIED
COHESION BOND ADHESION
HARDNESS STRENGTH
COHESIVE FATTY TENACIOUS
COHESIVENESS TENACITY
COHOBA PARICA
COHOSH SQUAWROOT
PAPOOSEROOT
COHUNE COROJO COROZO
COIF CAP HOW HOOD HOUVE
BEGGIN BURLET HAIRDO QUAIFE
ARRANGE CALOTTE BIGGONET
COIFFURE SKULLCAP
COIFFURE COIF HEAD HAIRDO
TUTULUS TRESSURE
COIL ADO WIN WIP ANSA CLEW
CURL FAKE FANK FURL FUSS HANK
LINK LOOP ROLL TUFT WIND ENROL
FLAKE HELIX QUERL QUILE ROUND
SPIRE TENSE TESLA TWINE TWIRL
TWIST WHORL WRING BOBBIN
BOTTOM BOUGHT DIMMER ENROLL
GLOMUS HEATER RENDER RUNDLE
SPIRAL TEASER TUMULT UPWIND
VOLUME WINDUP WREATH ENTRAIL
HAYCOCK INVOLVE PRIMARY
RINGLET SNAKING TICKLER
TROUBLE WREATHE COFUSION
ENCIRCLE INDUCTOR OVERCOIL
(— IN STILL) SCROLL
(— INTO BALL) WIRE
(— OF CAPILLARIES) TUFT
(— OF HAIR) BUN PUG
(— OF SNAKE) FOLD
(— OF WIRE) BOBBIN SOLENOID
(INDUCTION —) JIGGER
COILED GYRATE TORTILE WRITHEN
COILER FLARER
COILING SPIRY
COIN AS BU PU AVO BAN BIT BOO
COB DAM DIE DUB ECU FIL JOE KIP
LAT LEK LEU LEV LEY ORI PUL SEN
SOL TRA WEN WON ABAS ANNA
ATTE BAHT BATZ BESA CASH CENT
CHIP CHON DEMY DIME DOIT DONG
DOTT DUMP DURO FELS FILS GILL
GROS GROT HARP HOON HWAN
JACK JANE KRAN KYAT LEVY LION
MAIL MAKE MILL MINT MITE MULE
OBAN ONZA OORD PARA PAUL
PESA PESO PICE POND POUL QUAN

RAND RIAL ROCK RYAL SCAD SENT
SINK SIZE SLUG TAEL TARA TARE
TARI TARO TIAO TREY TYPE UNIT
ACKEY AGNEL AKCHA ALBUS ALTIN
ALTUN AMANI ANGEL ANGLE ASPER
BAIOC BAIZA BATTE BEKAR BELGA
BETSO BEZZO BISTI BLANC BLANK
BODLE BROAD BROWN CHINK CLINK
COIGN CONTO COROA CROSS
CROWN CUNYE DARIC DINAR DISME
DOBLA DUCAT EAGLE EYRIR FANAM
FANON FODDA FRANC GAZET
GRANO GROAT GROSZ HALER
HECTE JACOB JULIO JUSTO KOBAN
KRONA KRONE KROON LIARD LIBRA
LITRA LOUIS MEDAL MEDIN MEDIO
MILAN MOHUR MOPUS NOBLE
NOMOS OBANG ORKEY ORKYN
PAISA PAOLO PARDO PENNY PERAU
PESSA PIECE PLACK PLATE POALI
POALO PROOF QUART QUINE RAPPE
REBIA RIDER RIYAL ROYAL RUBLE
RUPIA SAIGA SAPEK SCEAT SCUDO
SCUTE SEMIS SHAHI SICCA SMASH
SOLDO STAMP STYCA SUCRE TALER
TANGA TANKA TEMPO THRIP TICAL
TRIME UNCIA UNITE WHITE ABASSI
ABBASI AFGHAN AHMADI ARGENT
ASSARY AUREUS AZTECA BALBOA
BAUBEE BAWBEE BEAVER BEZANT
BIANCO BLANCO BOGACH BRONZE
CARLIN CENTAS CHAISE COBANG
CONDOR COPPER CORONA CUARTO
CUNZIE DECIME DENARY DENIER
DERHAM DINDER DIOBOL DIRHAM
DIXAIN DIZAIN DOBLON DODKIN
DOLLAR DOPPIA DOUBLE ESCUDO
FILLER FLORIN FOLLIS FORINT
GEORGE GIULIO GOURDE GRIVNA
GROSSO GUINEA GULDEN HARPER
HELLER ICHIBU ITZEBU JUSLIK
KLIPPE KOPECK KORONA KORUNA
LAUREL LEPTON MACUTA MAHBUB
MAIDEN MANCUS MEDINO MISKAL
NICKEL NORKYN OCHAVO OCTAVE
ONGARO PADUAN PAGODA PARDAO
PATACA PATART PHILIP QUEZAL
ROSARY SALUNG SALUTE SATANG
SEQUIN SESKIN SHEKEL SHIELD
SIGLOS SINKER SIXAIN SOMALO
SOVRAN STATER STELLA STIVER
TALENT TARGET TESTAO TESTER
TESTON THALER THOMAN TOSTON
TRIENS TUMAIN TUNGAH TURNER
TURNEY TURTLE UNGARO VINTEM
XERIFF YUZLIK ZECHIN ZEHNER
ZEQUIN ALFONSO ALTILIK ANGELET
ANGELOT ANGOLAR ANGSTER
BAIOCCO BAJOCCO BARBONE
BOLIVAR CARDECU CARLINE
CARLINO CAROLIN CAROLUS
CENTAVO CHALCUS CHALKOS
CORDOBA COUNTER CRUSADO
DAMPANG DRACHMA DUCATON
DUPLONE ESCALAN JACOBUS
JOANNES KASBEKE KREUZER
LEMPIRA LEONINE LEOPARD
LUIGINO MANGOUR MARENGO
MOIDORE MONARCH MUZOONA

NOUMMOS ONCETTA PAHLAVI
PARISIS PATACAO PATAGON
PATAQUE PENNING PFENNIG
PISTOLE QUADRIN QUARTER
QUATTIE QUETZAL QUINYIE
REDDOCK RUDDOCK RUSPONE
SANTIMS SCRUPLE SEXTANS
SILIQUA SIZEINE SOLIDUS SPECIES
STAMPEE STOOTER STUIVER
SULTANE TALLERO TEECALL
THRYMSA TORNESE TRIOBOL
UNICORN XERAFIN ALBERTIN
AMBROSIN AQUILINO AUGUSTAL
AUKSINAS BAETZNER BAGATINE
BECHTLER BLAFFERT BLANKEEL
BLANKILO BROCKAGE CAVALIER
CHINKERS CHUCKRAM COLONIAL
COURONNE CROCKARD CRUZEIRO
DECUSSIS DENARIUS DIDRACHM
DIOBOLON DOUBLOON EQUIPAGA
FARTHING FILIPPIC FREDERIK
GAZZETTA GENOVINO GIGLIATO
GIUSTINA GROSCHEN HARDHEAD
HYPERPER IMPERIAL ISABELLA
JOHANNES KREUTZER LUSHBURG
MACARONI MAJIDIEH MARCELLO
METALLIK MILESIMA PATACOON
PAVILION PICAYUNE PIEDFORT
PISTOLET PLAPPERT PORTAGUE
QUADRANS QUADRINE QUARTINE
QUINCUNX RESTRIKE RIGMAREE
RISDALER RIXDALER SCUDDICK
SEMUNCIA SESTERCE SHILLING
SIXPENCE SKILLING SLEEPING
SOLIDARE STERLING STOTINKA
SULTANIN TENPENNY TETROBOL
THIRTEEN TWOPENCE ZECCHINO
(— AROUND NECK) TALI
(— IMPERFECTLY MINTED)
BROCKAGE
(— OF TRIFLING VALUE) RAP
(BASE —) SHAND SHEEN SINKER
(COUNTERFEIT —) GRAY GREY SLIP
SHEEN SHOFUL STUMER STUMOR
(PLUGGED —) PLUG
(SMALL THICK —) DUMP
(PL.) CHANGE CHINKS SERIES
COINAGE
COINAGE FICTION GALUMPH
MINTAGE
COINCIDE FIT GEE JIBE JUMP
AGREE TALLY CONCUR
COINCIDENT EVEN TOGETHER
COINCIDING CONGRUENT
COINER MONIER MONEYER
COITION SOIL VENERY MEETING
CONGRESS
COKE ASK COAL COLK CORE DOPE
CHARK COCAINE
COL GAP HALS JOCH PASS HALSE
SWIRE SADDLE
COLANDER SIEVE STRAINER
COLCOTHAR SAFFRON TUSCANY
COLD FLU ICY MUR NIP COOL DEAD
DULL HARD HASK HOAR MURR
ROUP SOUR ACALE ACOLD ALGID
BLEAK CHILL CRISP FISHY FRORE
GELID GLACE GLARE OORIE OURIE
PARKY POOSE RHEUM SHARP

STONY VIRUS ARCTIC BITTER
BOREAL CHILLY CLAMMY CRIMMY
FREDDO FRIGID FRIGOR FROSTY
GLASSY MARBLY STECKY WAIRCH
WINTRY BRITTLE CATARRH CHILLED
COLDISH COSTIVE DISTANT
FROSTED GLACIAL INHUMAN
MORFOND SHIVERY STRANGE
FREEZING MORFOUND PIERCING
RESERVED RHIGOSIS STANDOFF
UNHEATED
(— IN HEAD) POSE POOSE CORYZA
CATARRH GRAVEDO SNIVELS
SNIFFLES SNIFTERS
(BITTER —) ARCTIC
(VERY —) FRIGID PEEVISH
COLD-BLOODED BRUTAL LEEPIT
COLD CUTS ASSIETTE
COLD-HEARTED COLD FROZEN
BLOODLESS
COLDLY DRILY DRYLY
COLDNESS COLD FROST STEEL
PHLEGM DISTANCE FROIDEUR
COLDONG FRIARBIRD
COLE CALE KAIL KALE COLZA
FRIGOR COLEWORT
COLEUS KOORKA
COLEWORT COLE KALE RIBE STOCK
CABBAGE
(SPROUT OF —) STOVEN
COLIC BATS FRET BATTS GUTTIE
BELLYACHE
COLICROOT UNICORN ALOEROOT
HUSKROOT HUSKWORT STARWORT
COLIMA TAPA IRONWOOD
COLISEUM HALL STADIUM THEATER
COLOSSEUM
COLL HUG CLIP CULL POLL PRUNE
EMBRACE
COLLABORATE AID ASSIST
COOPERATE
COLLAPSE CAVE FALL FLOP FOLD
GIVE SINK CRASH SLUMP WRECK
BUCKLE SHRINK TUMBLE CAPSIZE
CROPPER CRUMBLE CRUMPLE
DEBACLE DEFLATE FAILURE
FLUMMOX FOUNDER SMASHUP
CONTRACT DOWNFALL TAILSPIN
COLLAPSED QUAT CLUNG
COLLAPSIBLE FOLDING
COLLAPSING FAILURE COLLABENT
COLLAR CAP FUR NAB BAND ETON
FALL FANO GILL GRAB POKE RING
RUFF CHAIN DICKY FANON FANUM
FICHU PHANO RUCHE SEIZE STOCK
TRASH WHISK BERTHA CARCAN
CHOKER COLLET COLLUM DICKEY
GORGET PARRAL PARREL RABATO
REBATO SADDLE SLEEVE TACKLE
TORQUE TUCKER TURNUP BOBACHE
BOBECHE CAPTURE CHIGNON
CIRCLET PANUELO PARTLET
POTHOOK REBATER SHACKLE
STICKUP VANDYKE CARCANET
CINCTURE NECKBAND NECKLACE
RABATINE STARCHER TURNDOWN
(— FOR HORSE) BARGHAM
BRECHAM
(HIGH —) GILLS

(IRON —) JOUG JOUGS CARCAN POTHOOKS
(LACE —) SCALLOP
(MAGISTRATE'S —) GOLILLA
(ROMAN —) RABAT
(WHEEL-SHAPED —) RUFF
(WOODEN —) CANG CANGUE
COLLAR BEAM SPANNER SPANPIECE
COLLARBONE CLAVICLE
COLL'ARCO ARCATO
COLLARED ACCOLLE ACCOLLEE TORQUATE
COLLAR PAD AFTERWALE
COLLATE BESTOW CONFER VERIFY COMPARE
COLLATERAL SIDE MARGIN OBLIQUE INDIRECT PARALLEL SECURITY
COLLATION TEA MEAL LUNCH REPAST SERMON ADDRESS READING DEJEUNER HOTCHPOT TREATISE
COLLEAGUE AIDE ALLY UNITE DEPUTY SOCIUS ADJUNCT COLLEGE COMPEER CONSORT PARTNER CONFRERE CONSPIRE
COLLECT JUG SAM TAX CALL CARD CULL DRAW HEAP LEVY LIFT PICK PILE POOL REAR SAMM SAVE AMASS CROWD GLEAN GROUP HOARD RAISE STORE SWEEP ACCOIL ACCRUE CENTER CONFER GARNER GATHER MUSTER PRAYER SEMBLE SHEAVE UPTAKE ARCHIVE CLUSTER COMPILE CONGEST ENGROSS IMPOUND RAMMASS RECUEIL SCAMBLE SYNAPTE ASSEMBLE CONFLATE CONTRACT CUPBOARD INGATHER RESEMBLE SCRAMBLE SCROUNGE
(— AND DRIVE INTO ENCLOSURE) WEAR
(— FOOD) FORAGE
(— GRAIN) GAVEL
(— INTO COVEY) JUG
(— MONEY) NOB
(— WAGES) UPLIFT
COLLECTED CALM COOL SOBER SERENE PRESENT COMPOSED
COLLECTION ANA BAG KIT SET BAND BEVY BOOK CLAN CROP FILE HEAD HEAP KNOT LEVY OLIO RAFT SORT ALBUM ANNEX BATCH BUDGE DEPOT FLOCK GLEAN GROUP HOARD KITTY SHEAF STORE SUITE SWATH BUNDLE CONGER CORPUS FARDEL MISHNA PARCEL RAGBAG RECULE SORITE SPRING SWATHE TUMBLE ACCOUNT COLLECT CONGERY EXHIBIT FERNERY FISTFUL FLUTTER GALLERY QUOTITY RECUEIL SAMHITA SMATTER SMYTHIE SYLLOGE TERRIER ASSEMBLY CABOODLE CONGERIE COSTOMAL FASCICLE GATHERUM GLOSSARY ROMESCOT ROMESHOT SYNTAGMA
(— AT FOX HUNT) CAP
(— OF 24 SHEETS) QUIRE

(— OF ANIMALS) ZOO HEAD
(— OF BOOKCASES) STACK
(— OF BOOKS) SET BIBLE CANON LIBRARY
(— OF CONIFERS) PINETUM
(— OF DATA) GROUND
(— OF FORMULAS) CODEX
(— OF FOUR) TETRAD
(— OF LAWS) CODE
(— OF MAPS) ATLAS
(— OF OBJECTS) AFFAIR
(— OF OPINIONS) SYMPOSIUM
(— OF PERSONS) BOODLE
(— OF PLANTS) SERTULE
(— OF POEMS) DIVAN DIWAN SYLVA ANTHOLOGY
(— OF PUS) HYPOPYON
(— OF REVENUES) TAMSIL TEHSIL
(— OF ROCKS) SUITE
(— OF RULES) SUTRA SUTTA
(— OF SAMPLES) SWATCH
(— OF SAYINGS) ANA
(— OF SPECIMENS) CABINET
(— OF STAFFS) SYSTEM
(— OF STORIES) LEGEND
(— OF TOOLS) LAYOUT
(— OF TREES) SERINGAL
(— OF UNWANTED ANIMALS) LARDER
(CONFUSED —) CLUTTER
(MISCELLANEOUS —) OLIO FARDEL SMYTRIE
(VAST —) CLOUD
COLLECTIVE GROUP AGGREGATE
COLLECTIVIST COMMUNIST SOCIALIST
COLLECTOR COMB CAMEIST CURIOSO DUSTMAN FURIOSO UPTAKER ANTIQUER COUNTOUR GATHERER STAMPMAN VIRTUOSO ZAMINDAR
(— ITEMS) RARIORA
(— OF BUTTERFLIES) AURELIAN
(— OF HERBS) SIMPLER
(— OF REVENUE) AUMIL AUMILDAR TALUKDAR ZAMINDAR
(CUSTOMS —) HOPPO CUSTOMER
(TAX —) CAID QAID GABBAI TAHSILDAR
COLLECTORATE TALUK
COLLEEN GIRL LASS MISS BELLE CAILIN DAMSEL
COLLEGE TOL HALL AGGIE HOUSE LYCEE CAMPUS COLAGE SCHOOL SIWASH ACADEMY MADRASA SEMINARY
COLLEGER TUG
COLLET BAND NECK RING CHUCK CULET CASING CIRCLE COLLAR COLLUM FLANGE BUSHING
COLLIDE HIT RAM BUMP DASH FRAY HURT CLASH CRASH KNOCK SHOCK SMITE WRECK HURTLE STRIKE THRUST
(— WITH) IMPINGE
COLLIE BEARDIE
COLLIER MINER PLOVER GEORDIE COILYEAR FLATIRON SCUTCHER
COLLIQUATION SYNTEXIS

COLLISION HIT FOUL CLASH CRASH SHOCK HURTLE IMPACT JOSTLE SMASHUP CLASHING CONFLICT
COLLOCATE SET PLACE ARRANGE
COLLOID GEL
COLLOQUIAL FAMILIAR INFORMAL
COLLOQUIUM INDUCEMENT
COLLOQUY CHAT TALK PARLEY DIALOGUE
COLLOTYPE ARTOTYPE HELIOTYPE
COLLUDE PLOT SCHEME CONNIVE COLLOGUE CONSPIRE
COLLUM NECK
COLLUSION DECEIT CAHOOTS SECRECY PRACTICE PRACTISE
COLLUSIVE COVINOUS COLLUSORY

COLOMBIA

CAPE: VELA AGUJA MARZO AUGUSTA
CAPITAL: BOGOTA
CAY: VELA VIGIA RONCADOR
COIN: PESO REAL CONDOR PESETA CENTAVO
FORMER NAME: DARIEN NEWGRANADA
GULF: URABA CUPICA DARIEN TIBUGA TORTUGAS
INDIAN: BORO CUNA HOKA MACU MUZO PAEZ CARIB CATIO CHOCO COFAN COGUI CUBEO GUANE PIJAO SEONA ARAWAK BETOYA CALIMA INGANO SALIVA TAHAMI TUCANO TUNEBO YAHUNA ACHAGUA ANDAQUI CHIBCHA CHIMILA GUAHIBO GUAJIRO PANCHES PUINAVE PUITOTO QUECHUA TAIRONA GUARAUNO MOTILONE
INLET: TUMACO
ISLAND: BARU NAIPO FUERTE GORGONA CUSACHON
MEASURE: VARA AZUMBRE CELEMIN
MOUNTAIN: CHITA HUILA PURACE TOLIMA
MOUNTAINS: ABIBE ANDES BAUDO COCUY AYAPEL PERIJA TUNAHI CHAMUSA ORIENGAL
PLAINS: LLANOS
POINT: CRUCES LACRUZ SOLANO CARIBANA GALLINAS
PORT: LORICA CARTAGENA
PROVINCE: META CAUCA CHOCO HUILA VALLE ARAUCA BOYACA CALDAS NARINO TOLIMA VAUPES BOLIVAR CAQUETA GUAJIRE VICHADA AMAZONAS PUTUMAYO
RIVER: UVA BITA META MUCO SINU TOMO UPIA YARI BAUDO CAUCA CESAR ISANA MESAI NECHI PATIA PAUTO SUCIO AMAZON ARAUCA ARIARI ATRATO CAGUAN VAUPES YAPURA APAPOIS CAQUETA GUAINIA INIRIDA TRUANDO VICHADA CASANARE GUAVIARE

PUTUMAYO MAGDALENA
TOWN: TEN ANZA BUGA CALI MITU
MUZO PAEZ SIPI TADO TOLU
YARI BELLO CHINU GUAPI NEIVA
PASTO TUNJA BOGOTA CUCUTA
IBAGUE QUIBDO SANGIL
CARTAGO LETICIA PALMIRA
PEREIRA POPAYAN GIRARDOT
MEDELLIN MONTERIA
CARTAGENA
TREE: ARBOLOCO
VOLCANO: PURACE
WEIGHT: BAG SACO CARGA LIBRA
QUILATE QUINTAL

COLON CROWN POINT HEMISTICH
MESYMNION
COLONIAL OVERSEA OVERSEAS
COLONIST BOOR COLON FATHER
CUTHEAN PIONEER PLANTER
SETTLER EMIGRANT
(AUSTRALIAN —) STERLING
(PL.) DEHAITES DEHAVITES
COLONIZE ECIZE FOUND PLANT
GATHER SETTLE MIGRATE
COLONIZER OECIST OEKIST
COLONNADE ROW STOA PORCH
PARVIS PIAZZA GALLERY PERGOLA
PORTICO TERRACE CHOULTRY
COLONNETTE COLUMELLA
COLONY STATE STOCK SWARM
CENOBE CORMUS APOIKIA COLONIA
CENOBIUM GANNETRY
(— OF BEES) HIVE SKEP SWARM
(BRYOZOAN —) ESCHARA
COLOR DIP DYE HUE BLEE CAST
FAKE FLAG PUKE SUIT TINT TONE
BADGE BLUSH GLAZE GLOSS GRAIN
PAINT SHADE STAIN TAINT TASTE
TENNE TINCT TINGE BANNER
BLEACH BOTTOM BRIDGE CHROMA
ENSIGN INFECT LOCKET MANTLE
RADDLE REDDEN STREAK TEMPER
COULEUR DEPAINT DISTORT
ENGRAIN PENNANT PIGMENT
SPECKLE COLORING STANDARD
TERTIARY TINCTURE
(— IMPARTED TO HERRINGS)
GILDING
(— LOSS) POLIOSIS
(— OF BIRD) SMUT
(— OF BODY) HEAT
(— OF EYES OF FOWLS) DAW
(— OF HUMAN FLESH) CARNATION
(— OF ROCK) STONE
(BLUE —) FOG JAY SKY WAD AQUA
BICE CIEL CYAN DELF DELP DUSK
IRIS NAVY PAON SAXE WADE WOAD
ZINC AZURE BERYL BLUET CADET
CAPRI CHING COPEN DELFT DIANA
DRAKE EMAIL GRAPE METAL NIKKO
ORION PEARL ROYAL SLATE SMALT
SMOKE VANDA CANTON CENDRE
COELIN ENSIGN GROTTO HATHOR
INDIGO LUPINE MARINE MASCOT
MIGNON ORIENT PENSEE ROMANY
SEVRES VENICE ZENITH CELESTE
CERAMIC CHICORY DUSTBLU

GOBELIN HORIZON LIBERTY LOBELIA
LOGWOOD MATELOT PEACOCK
PETUNIA RAMESES SISTINE SIXTINE
ABSINTHE BLUEBIRD BLUEWOOD
BRITTANY CAESIOUS CATTLEYA
CERULEAN CERULEUM DUCKLING
ELECTRIC GENDARME HYACINTH
INFANTRY LABRADOR LARKSPUR
MASCOTTE MAZARINE MIDNIGHT
MOONBEAM NATIONAL SAPPHIRE
TWILIGHT WEDGWOOD
(BROWN —) BAY ELK FOX OAK TAN
ARAB BARK BOLE BRAN BURE CAIN
CLAY CORK CUBA DATE DEER DRAB
DUST ECRU FAON FAWN GOAT
GOLD HOPI IRON LAMA LION MAST
MESA MUSK SEAL SIAM TEAK
ACORN ADUST ALOMA AZTEC BEIGE
BISON BLOND BLUSH BOLUS BRIAR
BRICK BRIER BROWN BUNNY CACAO
CAMEL CANNA CLOVE COCOA
CONGO EAGLE FRIAR FUDGE GIPSY
GRAIN GYPSY HAZEL HENNA KAFFA
KHAKI LIVER MAHAL MALAY MECCA
MINIM MUMMY NEGRO OTTER
PABLO QUAIL SABEL SEDGE SEPIA
SIENA SIRUP SNUFF SUDAN SUEDE
SUMAC SYRUP TABAC TAFFY TENNE
TOAST TOPAZ AFGHAN ALESAN
ALMOND APACHE ARGALI AUBURN
BAMBOO BEAVER BISQUE BISTER
BISTRE BLONDE BRONCO BRONZE
BURNET COCHIN COFFEE CONDOR
COOKIE COWBOY CROTAL DORADO
ESKIMO FALLOW GINGER GRAVEL
GROUSE HAVANA ISABEL LOUTRE
MAROON MERIDA MOHAWK MUFFIN
NUTMEG ORIOLE PAWNEE PLOVER
PUEBLO RABBIT RACKET RUDDLE
RUSSET SAHARA SANTOS SHERRY
SORREL SPHINX SPONGE STRING
STUCCO SUMACH SUNTAN THRUSH
TIFFIN TURTLE ASPHALT BADIOUS
BEESWAX BITUMEN BRACKEN
BRONCHO CALDRON CATTAIL
CIGARET COCONUT COTRINE
CRACKER DOGWOOD DURANGO
FEUILLE FILBERT GAZELLE
GOREVAN HARVEST LEATHER
LIBERIA MALABAR MIRADOR
MORDORE MOROCCO MUSCADE
MUSTANG NORFOLK OAKWOOD
PERIQUE PRALINE RACQUET
ROSARIO SABELLA SUNBURN
SUNDOWN TALLYHO TANBARK
TOBACCO TUSCANY ALDERNEY
ALGERIAN AMBROSIA BISMARCK
BOBOLINK CALABASH CARTOUCH
CAULDRON CINNAMON CLAYBANK
CORDOVAN DOUBLOON ETRUSCAN
EUCHROME HAZELNUT ISABELLA
KOLINSKY LEAFMOLD MANDALAY
MOCCASIN MOLESKIN MOROCCAN
MUSHROOM NOISETTE PHEASANT
SAUTERNE SHAGBARK STARLING
TAMARACK TEAKWOOD TERRAPIN
TORTOISE WOODBARK
(DEEP —) DARK
(FAST —) GRAIN

(GREEN —) BOA FIR IVY ALOE BICE
FERN JADE LEEK MOSS NILE SAGE
ALOES CEDRE CHLOR DRAKE FAIRY
HOLLY KELLY LOVAT OLIVE SPRAY
CANNON EMPIRE HUNTER JASPER
LAUREL LIERRE LIZARD MEADOW
MOUSSE MYRTLE SPRUCE VERDET
CELADON CITRINE CORBEAU
CRESSON CYPRESS EMERALD
INGENUE JADEITE JUNIPER
MESANGE NEPTUNE OLIVINE
PERIDOT SEAFOAM SERPENT
TILLEUL VERDURE BAYBERRY
CHASSEUR COPPERAS EMERAUDE
GLAUCOUS GLOWWORM PARAKEET
PERRUCHE PISTACHE POPINJAY
SHAMROCK TARRAGON VIRIDIAN
WOODLAND
(GRIZZLED —) AGOUTI AGOUTY
(OTHER —S) OR ASH BAT DOE DUN
JET TEA CHIP CORN CROW DAWN
DOVE GRAY GREY GULL HEMP LAVA
LEAD MODE MOLE NICE NUDE PLUM
PORT ROAN RUST SAND SOOT
WOOD AMBER BEACH BLACK
CAMEO CERES CHILE CHILI COPRA
CRANE CRASH CREAM DWALE
EBONY FLESH GRAPE GREBE
GREGE MAUVE MOUSE PANSY
PHLOX PLOMB PRAWN PRUNE
PUTTY RIFLE SABLE SPICE STEEL
THYME TWINE ANATTO AURORA
AUTUMN CASTOR CINDER COLLIE
CORCIR DAHLIA DAMSON DENVER
EVEQUE FIESTA FUSTIC GAMBIA
GRIEGE KASPER MALLOW MODENA
NAVAHO NAVAJO NIMBUS NUTRIA
ONDINE ORCHID OXFORD OYSTER
PEANUT PEBBLE PIGEON QUAKER
RAISIN RESEDA ROUCOU SEASAN
SILVER TUSCAN VANITY VESTAL
VIOLET WALNUT ADMIRAL ANNATTO
ARBUTUS ARDOISE ARNATTA
BEGONIA BERMUDA BLOSSOM
BRINDLE CARAIBE CARAMEL
COTRINE COWSLIP CRACKER
CRUISER MORELLO MURILLO
NATURAL OPHELIA PELICAN
PONTIFF POPCORN PRELATE
PUMPKIN QUIMPER REGATTA
ROSEBUD SAKKARA SANDUST
SPARROW SUNBEAM THISTLE
TUSSORE VERVAIN VIOLINE
WEIGELA WHEATEN ALUMINUM
AMETHYST BLONDINE CARMETTA
CHARCOAL CLEMATIS COCOBOLO
COQUETTE CREVETTE CYCLAMEN
EGGPLANT EMINENCE FELDGRAU
FLAMINGO GILLIVER GRAPHITE
GUNMETAL HONEYDEW IMPERIAL
JACINTHE LAVENDER MARATHON
MORILLON MULBERRY PALMETTO
ROSEWOOD SAUTERNE SQUIRREL
SUNBURST WIRELESS WISTARIA
WISTERIA CARNELIAN
(RED —) DAWN FLEA GOLF GOYA
HEBE LAKE MIST PUCE RUBY TULY
WINE AGATE BRASS BRICK CANNA
CANON CEDAR CORAL CUTCH

EMBER FLAME FLASH GULES LILAC
MELON NYMPH PEACH PEONY
POPPY ROSET SIENA SPARK TOTEM
ACAJOU ARCHIL AURORE AUTUMN
AZALEA BRAZIL CANYON CARROT
CATSUP CERISE CHERRY CHERUB
CLARET COGNAC DAMASK FRAISE
GAIETY GARNET GAYETY GRANET
JOCKEY KERMES MADDER MALAGA
MIKADO MURREY NECTAR ORCHIL
PATISE SALMON SANDIX SHRIMP
SIERRA SULTAN TITIAN TOMATO
AFRICAN ANAMITE ANEMONE
BEGONIA BISCUIT BOKHARA
CARMINE CATAWBA CATCHUP
CATECHU CRIMSON CURRANT
FIREFLY FUCHSIA FUCHSIN
GRANATE GRANITE HEATHER
INDIANA KETCHUP LACQUER
LOBSTER MAGENTA MASCARA
NACARAT OXBLOOD PAPRIKA
POMPEII PONCEAU REDWOOD
ROSETAN ROSETTE RUBELLE
SAFFLOR SARAVAN SCARLET
SINOPLE STAMMEL SULTANA
VERMEIL ALKERMES AMARANTH
ARCHILLA BISMARCK BORDEAUX
BURGUNDY CAMELLIA CARDINAL
CHAUDRON CHEROKEE CHERUBIM
CHESTNUT COCOANUT CONFETTI
DAMONICO DIANTHUS DUBONNET
EVENGLOW GERANIUM GRENADIN
GRIDELIN MAHOGANY MANDARIN
MAROCAIN NACARINE TOREADOR
(SOLID —) SOLID
(TONE —) TIMBRE
(YELLOW —) HAY RAT WAX BEAR
BUFF CLAY CORN CUIR ECRU FLAX
GOLD LARK LIME MOTH WELD
WOLD ACIER ALOMA AZTEC BEIGE
BLAKE BRASS CRASH CREAM GRAIN
HONEY IVORY LEMON MAIZE MAPLE
SHELL STRAW TAUPE WOULD
ACACIA ALMOND BANANA CANARY
CATHAY CHROME CITRON CITRUS
CROCUS DORADO FALLOW MANILA
MASTIC MIMOSA NANKIN NUGGET
OXGALL SULFUR SUNRAY SUNSET
ANTIQUE APRICOT BISCUIT CAVALRY
CHAMOIS GAMBOGE JASMINE
JONQUIL LEGHORN MEXICAN
NANKEEN PRAIRIE RHUBARB
SAFFRON SULPHUR SUNGLOW
ANTELOPE CALABASH CAPUCINE
COCKATOO DAFFODIL EGGSHELL
GENERALL GOLDMIST MARIGOLD
ORPIMENT PRIMROSE SNOWSHOE
(PL.) FLAG
COLORABLE SPECIOUS

COLORADO
CAPITAL: DENVER
COLLEGE: REGIS
COUNTY: BACA MESA YUMA
OTERO OURAY ROUTT GILPIN
CHAFFEE
MOUNTAIN: LONGS PIKES ELBERT
MOUNTAIN RANGE: ROCKY
NATIVE: ROVER
PARK: ESTES
RIVER: YAMPA DOLORES
APISHAPA ARIKAREE GUNNISON
PURGATOIRE
STATE FLOWER: COLUMBINE
STATE NICKNAME: CENTENNIAL
STATE TREE: SPRUCE
TOWN: ASPEN DELTA LAMAR
GOLDEN PUEBLO SALIDA
ALAMOSA BOULDER DURANGO
GREELEY GUNNISON LOVELAND
TRINIDAD

COLORATION BLEE PILE FLASH
CLOUDING COLORISM SCHILLER
COLORATURA GORGIA SOPRANO
COLOR-BLINDNESS DALTONISM
COLORED FAW HUED MALE BIASED
DEPAINT STAINED
(— IN RED) RUBRIC
(— LIKE PIPE BOWL) TROUSERED
(BRILLIANTLY —) SUPERB FLAMING
(HIGHLY —) CHROMATIC
(PARTI —) PIED PIEBALD
(UNIFORMLY —) HARD
COLORFUL GAY BRAVE JUICY VIVID
COLORY GOLDEN FREAKED
GORGEOUS
COLORING BLEE TINT PAINT TINGE
TINGENT BRONZING PAINTING
TINCTURE
(— MATTER) TINCTION
COLORLESS WAN DRAB DULL PALE
ASHEN BLAKE BLANK PLAIN
MOUSEY PALLID HUELESS NEUTRAL
ACHROMIC ACHROOUS BLANCHED
ETIOLATE LIFELESS
COLOSSAL BIG HUGE VAST GREAT
LARGE IMMENSE TITANIC
ENORMOUS GIGANTIC MONSTROUS
COLOSSUS GIANT TITAN STATUE
COLOSSO MONOLITH
COLOSTRUM FOREMILK AFTERINGS
COLT FOAL STAG FILLY POTRO
STAIG HOGGET POLEYN STAGGIE
EQUULEUS
COLTER LAVER COOTER COULTER
FOREIRON
COLTSFOOT DOCK CLOTE HOOFS
CLEATS FARFARA LAGWORT
SOWFOOT BULLFOOT CLAYWEED
FOALFOOT
COLUGO COBEGO
COLUMBATE NIOBATE
COLUMBIA SINKIUSE
COLUMBINE AQUILEGE BLUEBELL
CHUCKIES ROCKBELL
COLUMBITE DIANITE NIOBITE
COLUMELLA STALACE
COLUMN COG LAT ROW FILE FUST
GOAL LINE POLE POST PROP STUB
BAGUE SHAFT STELA STELE TORSO
TRUNK WURTZ ASOKAN CORNER
GNOMON PILLAR SCAPUS STAPLE
STRING TSWETT SUPPORT VIGREUX
CYLINDER PILASTER
(— IN EAR) MODIOLUS

(— OF FIGURES) SUM
(— OF FILAMENTS) SYNEMA
(BUDDHIST —) LAT
(FIGURE USED AS —) ATLAS
TELAMON
(ROCK —) HOODOO
(ROULETTE —) DERNIER
(SPINAL —) HORN SPINE BACKBONE
(STRUCTURAL —) LALLY
(TWISTED —) TORSO
COLUMNAR TERETE STELENE
COLUMNAL VERTICAL
COLUMNIST WRITER ANALYST
COLY MOUSEBIRD
COLZA SARSON
COMA TUFT BUNCH CARUS SLEEP
STUPOR SUBETH TORPOR TRANCE
SEMICOMA CHEVELURE
COMATOSE OUT DROWSY
LETHARGIC
COMB CARD GILL KAME LASH RACK
RAKE REDD REED SEEK TOZE
BREAK BRUSH CAMBE CLEAN
CREST CTENE CURRY FLISK RAVEL
TEASE HACKLE SMOOTH CUSHION
HATCHEL WRAITHE BEATILLE
CARUNCLE TORTOISE
COMBAT WAR BLOW BOUT COPE
DUEL FRAY MEEK MEET RUSH TILT
CLASH FIGHT JOUST REPEL STOUR
ACTION AFFRAY BATTLE MEDLEY
OPPOSE RESIST SHOWER STRIFE
CONTEND CONTEST COUNTER
DERAIGN DISPUTE EXPLOIT SCUFFLE
SERVICE ARGUMENT CONFLICT
STRUGGLE
(— BETWEEN KNIGHTS) JOUST
(FUTILE —) SCIAMACHY
(SINGLE —) DUOMACHY
COMBATANT DUELER BATTLER
FIGHTER CHAMPION GLADIATOR
COMBATIVE BANTAM MILITANT
BELLICOSE DEPENDENT
COMBED CRESTED
COMBER WAVE HANDER BREAKER
KEMPSTER
COMBINATION KEY BLOC GANG
PACT POOL RING CABAL COMBO
GROUP JUNTO PARTY TRUST UNION
CARTEL CLIQUE CORNER CRASIS
FUSION LEAGUE MEDLEY MERGER
AMALGAM COMBINE CONSORT
COTERIE FACTION HARMONY
JOINING MIXTURE ADDITION
ALLIANCE ENSEMBLE MONOPOLY
(— OF 10) DECUPLET
(— OF CARDS) SET BUILD FLUSH
SPREAD STRAIGHT
(— OF CIRCUMSTANCES) ACTION
(— OF COLORS) HARLEQUIN
(— OF FACES) FORM
(— OF FIRMS) TRUST
(— OF INTAGLIO FORMS) GRYLLI
(— OF NUMBERS) GIG SADDLE
(— OF TACKLES) JEERS
(— OF TONES) CHORD
(DANCE —) SEQUENCE
(HARMONIOUS —) CONCORD
(NOSE-JAW —) LAYBACK

(SCORING —) IMPERIAL

COMBINE ADD FIX MIX WED BIND BLOC CLUB JOIN NICK POOL BLEND GROUP JOINT MARRY MERGE TOTAL UNITE ABSORB CONCUR LEAGUE MEDDLE MERGER MINGLE SPLICE ACCRETE AMALGAM COMPACT CONJOIN CONJURE MACHINE COALESCE COMPOUND CONCRETE CONDENSE CONFLATE CONSTRUE CONTRACT CUMULATE FEDERATE

(— AGAINST) BOYCOTT

(— WITH GAS) AERATE

(— WITH WATER) AQUATE

COMBINED GUM BOUND FIXED JOINT UNITED CONJOINT

COMBUSTIBLE FUEL FIERY ARDENT CINDER PICEOUS BURNABLE

COMBUSTION FIRE HEAT FLAME THERM TUMULT BURNING BACKFIRE

COME BE GET LAY COOP DRAW FALL GROW HAUL PASS WHEN ARISE CHIVE FETCH ISSUE LIGHT OCCUR REACH ACCRUE ADVENE APPEAR ARRIVE BECOME BEFALL EMERGE HAPPEN OBTAIN SPRING ADVANCE DEVELOP EMANATE PROCEED APPROACH PRACTICE

(— ABOUT) ARISE CHANCE

(— AFTER) SUE FOLLOW

(— APART) FRAY SHED BREAK STAVE

(— BEFORE) FORERUN PREVENE ANTECEDE ANTEDATE

(— DOWN) SWOOP ALIGHT DESCEND SUCCEED DISMOUNT

(— FORTH) EMIT BREAK ISSUE ACCEDE FORTHGO FURNACE

(— FORWARD) ACCEDE

(— IN CONTACT) ATTINGE

(— INTO BLOOM) BURST BLOSSOM

(— INTO COLLISION) MEET CLASH COLLIDE

(— INTO EXISTENCE) FORM BEGIN ACCRUE HAPPEN SPRING

(— INTO POSSESSION) ACQUIRE INHERIT

(— OF AGE) MAJORIZE

(— OFF) HARL

(— OUT) ISSUE APPEAR EMERGE EMANATE

(— TO BELIEVE IN) ADOPT

(— TO CONCLUSION) DECIDE

(— TO DIE) DO DIE SET DROP EXPIRE FINISH SURCEASE

(— TO GRIEF) FOUNDER

(— TO HAND) OFFER

(— TO LIGHT) SPUNK DEVELOP

(— TO MIND) OCCUR STRIKE

(— TO PASS) SORT BREAK LIGHT BEFALL BETIDE HAPPEN

(— TO PERFECTION) RIPEN

(— TO TERMS) AGREE TRYST ACCORD BARGAIN COMPOSE COMPOUND

(— TO) TOUCH ADVENE STRIKE RECOVER REVERSE

(— TOGETHER) ADD HERD JOIN MEET AMASS CONCUR COUPLE

GATHER COLLECT COMBINE CONVENE ASSEMBLE

(— UNDER) SUBVENE

(— UPON) FIND CROSS INVENT STRIKE

(FULLY —) EXPIATE

COMEBACK RALLY ANSWER RETORT RETURN REBOUND HAULBACK RECOVERY REPARTEE

COMECRUDO CARRIZO

COMEDIAN WAG WIT CARD ACTOR ANTIC CLOWN COMIC GAGMAN JESTER BUFFOON FUNSTER COMOEDUS FUNMAKER FUNNYMAN PATTERER

COMEDO BLACKHEAD

COMEDOWN BATHOS DESCENT LETDOWN

COMEDY SOCK DRAMA FARCE LAZZO REVUE COMEDIA TEMACHA COMOEDIA TRAVESTY BACCHIDES SLAPSTICK

(HEROIC —) NATAKA

COMELINESS GRACE DECORUM FEATURE VENUSTY

COMELY FAIR GOOD HEND PERT TALL TIDY WEME BONNY HENDE QUEME SONCY SONSY TIGHT DECENT FORMAL GOODLY LIKELY LIKING LOVELY PRETTY PROPER SEEMLY SONSIE VENUST FARRANT FORMFUL SIGHTLY BECOMING DECOROUS FEATURED GRACEFUL HANDSOME PLEASING SUITABLE

COMET STAR METEOR XIPHIAS

(— HEAD) COMA

COMEUPPANCE REBUKE DESERTS BUSINESS

COMFIT CANDY SUCKLE CONFECT PRALINE CONSERVE PRESERVE

COMFORT AID EASE REST STAY BIELD CHEER LIGHT SOOTH VISIT ENDURE RELIEF REPOSE SOLACE SOOTHE SUCCOR ANIMATE ASSUAGE CHERISH CONFIRM CONSOLE ENLIVEN GLADDEN REFRESH RELIEVE SUPPORT SUSTAIN INSPIRIT NEPENTHE PLEASURE REASSURE

COMFORTABLE RUG BEIN BIEN COSH COSY COZY EASY FEEL FEIL LIKE SNUG TRIG CANNY COMFY COUTH CUSHY LITHE QUEME QUILT SCARF SONCY COUTHY HEPPEN PENTIT SONSIE RELAXED RESTFUL CHEERFUL DELICATE EUPHORIC HOMELIKE WRISTLET

COMFORTABLY SWEETLY

COMFORTED CONSOLATE

COMFORTER PUFF COVER EIDER NAHUM QUILT SCARF TIPPET CHEERER PACIFIER

COMFORTING TOSY TOSIE FRIENDLY

COMFORTLESS DREARY FORLORN UNCOUTH DESOLATE EITHLESS

COMFREY DAISY BONESET BACKWORT KNITBACK

COMIC DROLL FUNNY STRIP

BUFFONE COMIQUE THALIAN COMEDIAN FARCICAL

COMICAL LOW BASE BUFFO DROLL FUNNY MERRY QUEER STRIP WITTY BOUFFE AMUSING CARTOON JOCULAR RISIBLE STRANGE TRIVIAL HUMOROUS TICKLISH SPLITTING

COMING DUE COME NEXT VENUE ADVENT FUTURE TOWARD ARRIVAL FOOTING FORWARD BECOMING DESERVED PAROUSIA

(— AFTER) LATTER

(— AND GOING) FITFUL

(— INTO BEING) BIRTH GENESIS

(— NEAR) ACCESSION

(— OUT) ISSUE EGRESS

(— TO OFFICE) ACCESS

(— TO) ADIT

(— TOGETHER) SEANCE CONGRESS COUPLING GATHERING

COMMA POINT VIRGULE

(SCRATCH —) DIAGONAL

COMMAND DO BID SAW SOH BECK BODE BOON CALL COME EASY FIAT HEST HETE MAND RATE RULE SWAY WARN WILL WISH WORD BEKEN CHECK COVER EDICT EXACT FORCE HIGHT ORDER POWER SWEEP UKASE ADJURE BEHEST CHARGE COMPEL DEGREE DEMAND DEVICE DIRECT ENJOIN GOVERN HOOKUM IMPOSE MASTER ORACLE ORDAIN STEVEN SUMMON APPOINT BEHIGHT BIDDING CONCERN CONTROL DICTATE JUSSION JUSSIVE LEADING MANDATE OFFICER PRECEPT REQUIRE SKIPPER WARRANT BIDDANCE DOMINEER IMPERATE INSTRUCT RESTRAIN

(— OF ARMY) CONDUCT

(— TO HORSE) GEE HAW HUP HUPP WHOA GIDDAP HUDDUP

(— TO TURN RIGHT) GEE HUP HUPP

(MAGICIAN'S —) PRESTO

COMMANDANT GOVERNOR KILLADAR

COMMANDED IMPERATE

COMMANDEER PRESS

COMMANDER CID DUX DUKE EMIR HEAD JEFE CHIEF EMEER ADALID LEADER MASTER RAMMER TARTAN ALCALDE CAPTAIN CROWNER DECARCH DEKARCH DRUNGAR EMPEROR GENERAL KHALIFA MARSHAL NAVARCH OFFICER VAIVODE HERETOGA HIPPARCH LOCHAGER LOCHAGUS MYRIARCH PHYLARCH RISALDAR SERASKER TAXIARCH TETRARCH VINTENER

(— IN CHIEF) SIRDAR TARTAN TURTAN ADMIRAL GENERAL

COMMANDING DOMINANT IMPERANT IMPERIAL IMPOSING

COMMANDMENT LAW RULE ORDER COMMAND MITZVAH PRECEPT BODEWORD

(DIVINE —) LAW

(TEN —S) DECALOG DECALOGUE

COMMANDO RAIDER RANGER
FEDAYEE
COMMELINA DEWFLOWER
COMMEMORATE FETE KEEP FEAST
REMENE EPITAPH MEMORATE
MONUMENT REMEMBER
COMMEMORATION AWARD MEDAL
COMMEM PLAQUE JUBILEE
MEMORIA MENTION SERVICE
EBENEZER MEMORIAL
COMMEMORATIVE HONORARY
COMMENCE FALL FANG FILE MOVE
OPEN ARISE BEGIN FOUND START
ARRAME EMBARK INCEPT LAUNCH
SPRING STREAK STREEK INITIATE
COMMENCEMENT ONSET ORIGIN
KICKOFF OPENING ENTRANCE
COMMENCING INITIAL NASCENT
INCIPIENT
COMMEND KEN PAT GIVE LAUD
ADORN ALOSE BEKEN BOOST
EXTOL GRACE OFFER BESTOW
BETAKE COMMIT PRAISE RESIGN
APPLAUD APPROVE BESPEAK
BETEACH DELIVER ENTRUST
INTRUST BEQUEATH
COMMENDABLE GOOD WORTHY
LOVABLE LOWABLE LAUDABLE
COMMENDATION LAUD PRAISE
CITATION
(EFFUSIVE —) SLAVER
(MARKED —) APPLAUSE
COMMENSAL EPIZOON MESSMATE
COMMENSALISM SYNOECY
SYMPHILY COMMUNISM
COMMENSURATE EVEN EQUAL
ENOUGH ADEQUATE RELEVANT
COMMENT BARB BRAG GIBE JIBE
NOTE TALK WORD ASIDE BREAK
DUNCE GLOSS GLOZE CUTTER
DILATE GAMBIT NOTATE POSTIL
REMARK SCANCE CAPTION
DESCANT DISCUSS EXPLAIN
EXPOUND ADDENDUM SCHOLION
SCHOLIUM DISPRAISE
(— DISAPPROVINGLY) HARRUMPH
(CAUSTIC —) SATIRE
COMMENTARY GLOSS GEMARA
MEMOIR SATIRE ACCOUNT
COMMENT MEKILTA POSTILS
FOOTNOTE GLOSSARY TREATISE
COMMENTATOR CRITIC GLOZER
ANALYST GLOSSIST SCHOLIAST
COMMERCE TRADE BARTER
CHANGE TRAFFIC BUSINESS
EXCHANGE MERCATURE
COMMERCIAL STORE TRADY
TRADAL MERCHANT TRADEFUL
(— ESTABLISHMENT) HONG
COMMERCIALISM HUCKSTERISM
COMMINGLE MIX FUSE JOIN BLEND
IMMIX MERGE UNITE MINGLE
COMBINE COMINGE EMBROIL
COMEDDLE
COMMINUTE MILL CRUSH GRIND
POUND POUNCE POWDER
COMMINUTED FINE
COMMISERATE PITY
COMMISERATION PITY EMPATHY
SYMPATHY

COMMISSION PLAT SEND TASK
BOARD PRESS TRUST BRANCH
BREVET CHARGE DEMAND DEPUTE
ERRAND LEGACY OFFICE ORDAIN
PERMIT COMMAND CONSIGN
DUOVIRI EMPOWER FITTAGE
GOSPLAN MANDATE MISSION
SQUEEZE WARRANT CORNETCY
DELEGATE ENCHARGE POUNDAGE
(— AS CAPTAIN) POST
COMMISSIONAIRE CADDY CADDIE
DUBASH
COMMISSIONER ENVOY TRIER
LEDGER ARRAYER OFFICER
PRISTAW DELEGATE
COMMISSURE VINCULUM
COMMIT DO GIVE PULL STOW TAKE
ALLOT ARRET HIGHT LEAVE REFER
TEACH ARETTE ASSIGN BETAKE
ENGAGE PERMIT REMAND BEHIGHT
BETEACH COMMAND COMMEND
COMMISE CONFIDE CONSIGN
DELIVER DEPOSIT ENTRUST
INTRUSE INTRUST BEQUEATH
DEDICATE DELEGATE IMPRISON
RELEGATE
(— ERROR) SNAPPER
(— MONEY) INVEST
(— TO BATTLE) LAUNCH
(— TO JAIL) JUG
(— TO MEMORY) CON LEARN
MEMORIZE
(— VIOLENCE) TOUCH
COMMITTAL COMPROMISE
COMMITTEE BODY JURY RUMP
BOARD GROUP JUNTA TABLE
BUREAU SOVIET COUNCIL
DELEGACY SYNDICATE
COMMIXTURE MIXTURE CONFUSION
IMMISSION
COMMODE CAP CHEST STOOL
TOPKNOT CUPBOARD FONTANGE
COMMODIOUS FIT AMPLE ROOMY
PROPER USEFUL SPACIOUS
SUITABLE CAVERNOUS
COMMODITY ITEM WARE GOODS
STUFF EXPORT FUTURE STAPLE
ARTICLE SHIPMENT
(— SOLD SHORT) BEAR
(UNSALABLE —) DRUG
(PL.) KIND SPOTS CHANDLERY
COMMON LAY LOW NOA TYE BASE
MEAN TOWN VILE BANAL BRIEF
CHEAP EJIDO EXIDO GREEN GRIMY
GROSS JOINT LEASE OFTEN SLACK
STALE TRITE USUAL COARSE
DEMOID FAMOUS MODERN MUTUAL
ORNERY PROPIO PUBLIC SIMPLE
VULGAR AVERAGE CURRENT
DEMOTIC GENERAL GENERIC
IGNOBLE NATURAL POPULAR
RAFFISH REGULAR TRIVIAL
UNNOBLE VILLAIN BANAUSIC
EPIDEMIC FAMILIAR FREQUENT
HABITUAL MECHANIC MEDIOCRE
ORDINARY PANDEMIC PLEBEIAN
TRIFLING
(— OF ESTOVERS) BOT BOTE
(IN —) ALIKE

(NOT —) UNTRADED
(PL.) COMMUNE
COMMONER SNOB CEORL PLEBE
SIMPLE BURGESS CITIZEN STUDENT
ROTURIER
COMMONLY VULGO FAMILIARLY
COMMONNESS IDIOTISM
COMMUNITY VULGARITY
COMMON PEOPLE VULGUS
COMMONPLACE DULL FADE WORN
BANAL DAILY PLAIN PROSE STALE
TOPIC TRIPY TRITE USUAL COMMON
GARDEN HOMELY MODERN TRUISM
FADAISE HUMDRUM INSIPID PROSAIC
TEDIOUS TRIVIAL BANALITY
EVERYDAY ORDINARY RUMTYTOO
COMMONPLACENESS BATHOS
HUMDRUM
COMMON SENSE WIT NOUS SALT
GUMPTION
COMMONWEAL WEAL REPUBLIC
COMMONWEALTH POLIS STATE
ESTATE PUBLIC WEALTH COMONTE
COUNTRY COMMONTY
(IDEAL —) UTOPIA
COMMOTION DO ADO DIN BREE
DUST FRAY FUSS HEAT RIOT STIR
TOSS WHIR ALARM FLARE FUROR
HURRY STORM STOUR WHIRL
BUSTLE CATHRO FISSLE FISTLE
FLURRY FRACAS FURORE GARRAY
HOOPLA MOTION MUTINY PHRASE
POTHER RUFFLE SHINDY SPLORE
SQUALL STEERY TUMULT UNREST
UPSTIR WELTER BLATHER BLUSTER
CATOUSE CLATTER KIPPAGE
SHINDIG TAMASHA TEMPEST
TURMOIL DISORDER ERUPTION
REMOTION STIRRAGE STRAMASH
TIRRIVEE UPHEAVAL UPRISING
COMMUNAL EJIDAL
COMMUNE AREA DEME TALK ARGUE
REALM SHARE TREAT ADVISE
CONFER DEBATE IMPORT PARLEY
REVEAL CONSULT DISCUSS DIVULGE
COMMERCE CONVERSE DISTRICT
STANITZA TOWNSHIP
COMMUNICABLE OPEN FRANK
CATCHING SOCIABLE
COMMUNICATE SAY GIVE SHOW
SIGN TELL BREAK DRILL SPEAK
YIELD BESTOW COMMON CONVEY
IMPART INFECT INFORM REVEAL
SIGNAL ADDRESS BREATHE
DECLARE DICTATE DIVULGE
CONVERSE DESCRIBE INTIMATE
(— BY ALLUSION) IMPLY
COMMUNICATION CALL NOTE
WORD CABLE FAVOR LETTER
SPEECH ADDRESS DIVULGE
GALLERY MESSAGE COMETHER
LANGUAGE TELEGRAM
COMMUNICATIVE FREE SOCIABLE
EXPANSIVE
COMMUNION CULT HOST MASS
SECT TALK CREED FAITH SHARE
UNITY CHURCH HOMILY COMMUNE
CONCORD NAGMAAL SYNAGOG
ANTIPHON COMMERCE CONVERSE

KOINONIA VIATICUM
(— **SERVICE**) ACTION
COMMUNISM LENINISM SOVIETISM
COMMUNIST RED COMMIE SOVIET
COMRADE
COMMUNITY MIR BODY BURG CITY
CLAN DESA MARK MURA DESSA
FIRCA STATE THORP CENOBY
CLIMAX COLONY FAMILY HAMLET
MILLET NATION POLITY PUBLIC
SOCIES ANTHILL BOHEMIA
COMMUNE COMONTE CONVENT
HERONRY KINGDOM PHALANX
SOCIETY VILLAGE ZADRUGA
AUTONOMY COMMONTY DISTRICT
LIKENESS PRIORATE PROVINCE
SODALITY SWEEPDOM TOWNSHIP
(— **OF INTERESTS**) KINSHIP
(— **OF NATURE**) RACE
(— **OF ORGANISMS**) GAMODEME
(— **OF TURKS**) KIZILBASH
(**JEWISH** —) JEWRY KOLEL ALJAMA
SHTETL JUDAISM SHTETEL
SYNAGOG KEHILLAH
(**MAORI** —) KAIK KAIKA
(**PERUVIAN** —) AYLLU COMUNIDAD
(**PLANT** —) HEATH FOREST ALTERNE
ENCLAVE
(**RELIGIOUS** —) CENOBY SAMGHA
SANGHA CONVENT CENOBIUM
(**RUSSIAN** —) MIR
(**VILLAGE** —) IKHWAN
COMMUTATE COMMUTE UNDIRECT
COMMUTATOR BREAK BREAKER
RHEOTROPE
COMMUTE ALTER CHANGE TRAVEL
CONVERT EXCHANGE
COMPACT BALL BOND CASE FAST
FIRM HARD KNIT PACK PACT PLOT
SNUG TRIM TRUE BRIEF CLOSE
COVIN CROWD DENSE GROSS
HARDY HORNY MATCH PITHY SOLID
SPISS TERSE THICK TIGHT BEETLE
COMART HARDEN LEAGUE SHRINK
SPISSY STOCKY VANITY BARGAIN
CONCISE CONCORD CROWDED
NUGGETY PACTION SERRIED
ALLIANCE CONDENSE CONTRACT
COVENANT FLAPJACK HEAVYSET
SOLIDIFY SUCCINCT
COMPACTED SAD CROWDED
COMPACTNESS BODY DENSITY
FASTNESS SOLIDITY INTENSITY
COMPANION PAL SOC CHUM FERE
MAKE MATE PEER TWIN WIFE BILLY
BUDDY BULLY BUTTY CHINA COMES
CRONY CULLY DARES GREEK
MATCH MATEY MAUGH RIVAL SPORT
ATTEND BILLIE BROLGA COBBER
COHORT COMATE CUMMER DUENNA
EGERIA ESCORT FELLOW FRIEND
GESITH GOSSIP KIMMER MARROW
PANION SHADOW SPOUSE STEADY
TROJAN ACHATES COMPANY
COMPEER COMRADE CONSORT
ELPENOR HUSBAND PARTNER
SOCIATE SOCIETY SPECIAL
BEAUPERE COMPADRE CORRIVAL
EPHESIAN EPHESINE FAITHFUL

FAMILIAR HELPMATE PARALLEL
PLAYFERE SYNODITE
(**ARCHER'S** —) BUTTY
(**DRINKING** —) CUPMATE
(**POT** —) ALEKNIGHT
(**READING** —) LECTRICE
(**TABLE** —) CONVICTOR
(**PL.**:) SOCIETY
COMPANIONABLE FERE MATEY
SOCIAL CORDIAL FELLOWLY
GRACIOUS SOCIABLE
COMPANIONSHIP FERE SHIP HAUNT
COMPANY SOCIETY AFFINITY
COMPANY CRY MOB SET BAND
BEVY BODY CORE CREW CRUE
FARE FERE FIRM GANG GEST GING
HERD HOST MANY PUSH ROUT
SORT TEAM TURM AERIE COVEN
COVEY CROWD FLOCK FLOTE
GESTE GROUP GUEST HORDE
JATHA MEINY PARTY SQUAD SUITE
TROOP TURMA CIRCLE CLIQUE
COHORT COVINE CURNEY DECURY
LOCHUS RESORT THRONG TROUPE
TWENTY VOLLEY BATTERY COLLEGE
CONDUCT CONSORT HOLDING
JIMBANG MANIPLE SOCIETE
SOCIETY THIASOS THIASUS VISITOR
ASSEMBLY FAISCEAU FOLKMOOT
JINGBANG
(— **OF BADGERS**) CETE
(— **OF DANCERS**) COMPARSA
(— **OF HERDSMEN**) BOOLY BOOLEY
(— **OF HORSEMEN**) TROOP
(— **OF MARTENS**) RICHESSE
(— **OF SINGERS**) CHOIR QUIRE
CHORUS
(— **OF THE FAITHFUL**) FOLD
(— **OF TRAVELERS**) CAFILA
CAVALCADE
(— **OF WOMEN**) GAGGLE
(**EXCLUSIVE** —) CROWD
(**FINANCIAL** —) FACTOR
(**FIRE** —) SQUAD
(**MILITARY** —) WATCH DECURY
VENLIN PELOTON VEXILLUM
(**RECORDING** —) LABEL
(**SUITABLE** —) BESORT
COMPARABLE LIKE SAME SIMILAR
COMPARE VIE EVEN LIKE SIZE
APPLY EQUAL LIKEN MATCH SCALE
TALLY ALLUDE CONFER PARIFY
RELATE SEMBLE BRACKET COLLATE
EXAMINE SENIBLE SIGNIFY
ASSEMBLE CONFRONT CONTRAST
ESTIMATE RESEMBLE SIMILIZE
(— **WITH**) TO
COMPARISON SIMILE ANALOGY
BALANCE COMPARE PARABLE
DISIMILE LIKENESS LIKENING
METAPHOR PARALLEL
COMPARTMENT BAY BIN BOX CAB
POD CELL DECK FLUE PANE PART
SLOT WELL ABODE CABIN HATCH
HUTCH PANEL STALL VOLET
ABACUS ALCOVE BUNKER GARAGE
HOPPER MUFFLE REGION SEVERY
SMOKER ALVEOLE CABINET
CAPSULE CELLULE CHAMBER

FIREBOX HOUSING KITCHEN
MANSION ROTONDE SECTION
ALVEOLUS COALHOLE DIVISION
FOREPEAK GRINTERN LOCELLUS
STEERAGE TRAVERSE
(— **FOR COAL**) BUNKER
(— **FOR TREATING ORE**) KITCHEN
(— **IN BARN**) BAY
(— **IN STOVE**) BROILER
(— **OF COACH**) IMPERIAL
(— **OF ROOF**) SEVERY
(— **OF WINDOW**) LIGHT
(— **ON GAMEBOARD**) STORE
(— **ON ROULETTE WHEEL**) EAGLE
(**CARGO** —) HOLD
(**GAS-TIGHT** —) BALLONET
(**GUNNER'S** —) BLISTER
(**REFRIGERATOR** —) CHILLER
(**SLEEPING** —) CUBICLE
(**STAGECOACH** —) COUPE
(**STORAGE** —) BOOT
COMPASS BOW AREA DIAL GAIN
ROOM ROSE SIZE TOUR AMBIT
FIELD GAMUT RANGE REACH SCOPE
SWEEP TENOR WHEEL ARRIVE
ATTAIN BOUNDS CIRCLE DEGREE
DEVICE DIACLE EFFECT EXTENT
MERIST MODULE SPHERE SPREAD
VOLUME ACHIEVE AZIMUTH CALIBEF
CIRCUIT CONFINE DIVIDER EMBRACE
ENCLOSE ENVIRON HORIZON
IMAGINE PELORUS PURVIEW
TRAMMEL BOUNDARY CINCTURE
CIRCUITY DIAPASON PRACTICE
PRACTISE SURROUND
(— **IN SHIP'S CABIN**) TELLTALE
(— **NEEDLE END**) LILY
(— **OF MELODY**) AMBITUS
(— **OF TONES**) DIAPASON
(— **OF VOICE**) GAMUT SCALE
(— **POINT**) RHUMB
(**BELL-MAKING** —) CROOK
COMPASS BOX KETTLE
COMPASS CARD ROSE PEDRERO
PERRIER
COMPASSION RUE PITY RUTH
GRACE HEART MERCY PIETY SORRY
KARUNA LENITY REMORSE
STOMACH CLEMENCY HUMANITY
KINDNESS SYMPATHY
COMPASSIONATE RUTH SOFT
HUMAN GENTLE TENDER CLEMENT
PIETOSO PITEOUS PITIFUL
GRACIOUS MERCIFUL
COMPASS PLANT PILOTWEED
ROSINWEED
COMPASS QUARTER PLAGE
COMPASS SIGHT VANE
COMPATIBLE AKIN CIVIL ARTISTIC
SUITABLE
COMPATRIOT NATIVE PATRIOT
SYNETHNIC
COMPEL GAR MAKE MOVE URGE
BRING CAUSE COACT DRIVE EXACT
FORCE IMPEL PRESS SHOVE
COERCE ENJOIN EXTORT INCITE
OBLIGE THREAT ACTUATE AFFORCE
ATTRACT COMMAND DRAGOON
ENFORCE NECESSE REQUIRE
VIOLENCE

(— TO GO) HALE

(— TO PAY) STICK

COMPELLED HAS FAIN MUST BOUND FORCED ENFORCED

COMPELLING COGENT STRONG TELLING BRUISING FORCEFUL

COMPELLINGLY BADLY

COMPENDIOUS BRIEF SHORT DIRECT COMPACT CONCISE SUMMARY SUCCINCT

COMPENDIUM LIST BRIEF APERCU DIGEST PRECIS SKETCH SURVEY CATALOG COMPEND EPITOME LEXICON MEDULLA OUTLINE PANDECT SUMMARY SYLLOGE ABSTRACT BREVIARY BREVIATE LANDSKIP SYLLABUS SYNOPSIS

COMPENSATE PAY JIBE AGREE ATONE COVER REPAY TALLY OFFSET RECOUP REDEEM REWARD SQUARE COMMUTE CORRECT PLASTER REDRESS REPRISE REQUITE RESTORE SATISFY COMPENSE DISPENSE EQUALIZE

COMPENSATION BOT FEE PAY UTU HIRE MEND TOLL BONUS LOWER WAGES AMENDS ANGILD GERSUM OFFSET REWARD SALARY SETOFF DAMAGES FREIGHT PAYMENT REDRESS SALVAGE STIPEND BREAKAGE DONATIVE EARNINGS INTEREST OCTOGILD PITTANCE REQUITAL SOLATIUM

(— FOR KILLING MAN) MANBOT MANBOTE

(MEAGER —) PITTANCE

(WORKER'S —) COMPO

COMPENSATORILY EVEN

COMPETE PIT VIE COPE KEMP TEND CLASH MATCH RIVAL STRIVE CONTEND CONTEST EMULATE CORRIVAL

(— WITH) BUCK

COMPETENCE SKILL ABILITY FACULTY CAPACITY

COMPETENCY MAY CAPACITY

COMPETENT UP APT CAN FIT ABLE GOOD HOME MEET SANE ADEPT CAPAX SMART SWEET TIGHT INTACT LAWFUL WORTHY CAPABLE ENDOWED SKILLED ADEQUATE SUITABLE

COMPETITION VIE DRAW GAME HEAT JUMP MATCH PRIZE TRIAL WAGER CONTEST PARAGON RIVALRY CONCOURS CONFLICT

(— AMONG REAPERS) KEMP

COMPETITOR FOE ENEMY MATCH RIVAL WAGER COUSIN PLAYER ENTRANT CORRIVAL FAVORITE GAMESTER OPPONENT

COMPILATION ANA BOOK CODE CENTO DIGEST CASEBOOK DIRECTORY GATHERING

COMPILE ADD EDIT AMASS GATHER SELECT ARRANGE COLLECT COMPOSE PREPARE

COMPILER AUTHOR EDITOR GATHERER GLOSSIST SCISSORER

COMPLACENT CALM SMUG FATUOUS PRIGGISH

COMPLACENTLY FATLY

COMPLAIN AIL YIP BEEF CARP CRIB FRET FUSS GREX KEEN KICK KREX MEAN MOAN MOOT MUTE RULE WAIL YELP YIRN BITCH BRAWL CRAKE CROAK CROON GRIPE GROWL GRUMP GRUNT PINGE PLAIN WHINE BEWAIL CHARGE COTTER CREATE GRIEVE GROUSE GRUTCH HOLLER MURMUR PEENGE REPINE SQUAWK THREAP THROPE YAMMER CHUNNER DEPLORE GRIZZLE GRUMBLE INVEIGH PROTEST

COMPLAINANT ACTOR ASKER ACCUSER PLAINER QUERENT RELATOR

COMPLAINING PULY LATRANT QUERENT DOLEANCE

COMPLAINT RAP BEEF FUSS HOWL MEAN MOAN WAIL BITCH GRIPE GROWL WHINE CHESON GROUCH GROUSE GRUDGE GRUTCH HOLLER LAMENT MALADY PLAINT REPINE SQUAWK AILMENT DISEASE GRUMBLE ILLNESS PROTEST QUARREL QUERELE RECLAMA TRAGEDY COMPLAIN DISORDER DOLEANCE GRAVAMEN JEREMIAD

COMPLAISANCE AMENITY SUAVITY FACILITY URBANITY

COMPLAISANT BON ABLE EASY KIND BUXOM CIVIL SUAVE BONAIR POLITE SMOOTH SUPPLE URBANE AFFABLE AMIABLE BOWABLE LENIENT GRACIOUS OBLIGING PLEASING

COMPLEMENT CREW GANG FORCE TALLY ALEXIN AMOUNT COUSIN ADJUNCT OBVERSE

(MILITARY —) STRENGTH

COMPLETE DO ALL END BLUE DASH DEAD DEEP FAIR FILL FINE FULL JUST PASS PURE RANK CLOSE CROWN EVERY GROSS LARGE PLAIN PLUMB POINT PUCCA PUKKA QUITE RIPEN ROUND SOUND TOTAL UTTER WHOLE CHOATE DAMPEN DEADLY EFFECT ENTIRE FINISH GLOBAL HOLLOW INTACT MATURE PROPER SINGLE STRICT ACHIEVE CONFIRM EXECUTE EXPLETE FULFILL GERMANE PERFECT PLENARY REALIZE REPLETE SPHERAL ABSOLUTE BLINKING CIRCULAR CONCLUDE FINALIZE IMPLICIT INTEGRAL OUTRIGHT OVERCOME PRECIOUS PROFOUND THOROUGH BODACIOUS

(— CARELESSLY) HUDDLE

(REMARKABLY —) SPLENDID

COMPLETED PAU OVER CLOSED SUMMED COMPLETE FINISHED

(NOT —) DURATIVE

COMPLETELY ALL JAM BARE BUCK FAIR FLAT GOOD SLAM SLAP SPAN BLACK CLEAN CLOSE FULLY PLUMB QUITE SHEER SMACK SPANG STICK

STOCK UTTER BODILY ENTIRE GAINLY HOLLOW PURELY SPANDY WHOLLY ALGATES BLANKLY THROUGH CLEVERLY DIRECTLY ENTIRELY HEARTILY OUTRIGHT

COMPLETENESS DEPTH ALLNESS FULLNESS RIPENESS INTEGRITY

COMPLETION END FINISH

COMPLEX HARD MAZY BEING ETHOS FIELD HYOID MIXED ADDUCT DESERT KNOTTY SYSTEM CULTURE NETWORK SAMKARA SINUOUS TANGLED TWISTED COMPOUND EQUATION EXCHANGE INVOLVED MANIFOLD SAMSKARA SYNDROME

(— OF DIALECTS) HINDI

(— OF HORMONES) CALINE

(— OF IDEAS) EGO SYSTEM

(BASEMENT —) FLOOR

(NOT —) SIMPLE

COMPLEXION HUE RUD BLEE CAST LEER LOOK RUDD TINT COLOR HUMOR STATE TENOR TINGE ASPECT TEMPER COLORING

(BAD —) DYSCHROA

COMPLEXITY SCHEME INTRIGUE

COMPLIANCE TRUE ASSENT MUNICH CESSION CONSENT HARMONY OBSEQUY ABIDANCE CIVILITY FACILITY FORMALITY

COMPLIANT EASY OILY SOFT BUXOM FACILE PLIANT SUPPLE COMMODE DUCTILE DUTIFUL WILLING OBEDIENT TOWARDLY YIELDING

COMPLICATE INTORT PUZZLE TANGLE EMBROIL INVOLVE PERPLEX BEWILDER INTRIGUE INTRICATE

COMPLICATED HARD KNOTTY PROLIX COMPLEX GORDIAN SNARLED TANGLED INVOLVED PLEXIFORM

COMPLICATION KNOT NODE PLOT NODUS SNARL INTRIGUE

COMPLIMENT GIFT LAUD EXTOL EULOGY PRAISE SALAAM SALUTE ADULATE APPLAUD BOUQUET COMMEND DOUCEUR FLATTER TRIBUTE ENCOMIUM FLUMMERY GRATUITY GREETING

COMPLY PLY CEDE OBEY ABIDE ADAPT AGREE APPLY YIELD ACCEDE ACCORD ASSENT ENFOLD SUBMIT CONFORM EMBRACE OBSERVE

(— WITH) OBEY SERVE OBSERVE SATISFY

COMPONE GOBONE GOBONY

COMPONENT KEY DRAG FORM ITEM PART UNIT GIVEN FACTOR MEMBER SIMPLE ELEMENT FORMANT CONJUNCT INTEGRAL

(— OF ARMY) CAVALRY

(— OF CELL WALLS) CALLOSE

(ELECTRIC —S) CIRCUITRY

(PRINCIPAL —) BASIS

COMPORT ACT BEAR HAVE HOLD JIBE KEEP SUIT AGREE BROOK CARRY TALLY ACCORD ACQUIT BEHAVE DEMEAN ENDURE SQUARE CONDUCT

COMPORTMENT CONDUCT DEALING
BEHAVIOR DEMEANOR
COMPOSE BAT PEN SET CALM
COMP DITE FORM LULL MAKE
ALLAY BREVE BRIEF CLERK CLINK
COUCH DIGHT DRAFT FRAME ORDER
PATCH PIECE SPELL STICK WRITE
ACCORD ADJUST CREATE DESIGN
GRAITH INDITE RECITE REDACT
SETTLE SOOTHE STEADY ARRANGE
COMPACT COMPILE COMPONE
CONCOCT CONFORM DICTATE
DISPOSE DRAUGHT FASHION
PATIENT PRODUCE TYPESET
COMPOUND COMPRISE REGULATE
(— **POETRY**) SING
COMPOSED SET CALM COOL QUIET
SOBER WROTE DEMURE DIGEST
PLACID SEDATE SERENE COMPACT
WRITTEN COMPOUND DECOROUS
TRANQUIL
(— **IN METER**) FOOTED
(**ILL** —) LAME
COMPOSEDNESS SOSSIEGO
COMPOSER BARD POET LYRIC
ODIST AUTHOR LYRIST PENMAN
WRITER CONTEUR ELEGIST
FANTAST MAESTRO COLORIST
ELEGIAST IDYLLIST ILIADIST
MELODIST MONODIST MUSICIAN
PHANTAST TUNESMITH
COMPOSITE HYBRID ITALIC MOTLEY
COMPLEX COMPOSED CONCRETE
INTEGRAL
COMPOSITION ANA DITE MASS
OPUS WORK CENTO DITTY DRAMA
FUGUE GETUP MURKY PIECE POESY
STUCK THEME ACCORD EULOGY
FILLER HAIKAI LESSON MAGGOT
MONODY THESIS THREAD VULGUS
ARTICLE COMPOST CONSIST
DISPLAY EBURINE EPISTLE MIXTURE
PICTURE STOPPER WRITING
ACROSTIC CAUSERIE COMPOUND
DIALOGUE DIAPENTE EXERCISE
FANTASIA FROTTAGE HEELBALL
(— **FOR BILLIARD BALLS**) COMPO
(— **TO BE ACTED**) PLAY DRAMA
(— **TO FILL LEATHER**) STUFF
(**AMOROUS** —) EROTIC
(**ARTISTIC** —) COLLAGE
(**BUILDING** —) STAFF
(**CHORAL** —) MOTET CANTATA
ORATORIO
(**GUMMY** —) GROUND
(**HAND** —) CASEWORK
(**HUMOROUS** —) BURLA
(**INSTRUMENTAL** —) AIR GATO
FANCY RONDO GROUND SKETCH
SONATA TIENTO CANZONE
BERCEUSE CONCERTO FANTASIA
RHAPSODY SYMPHONY
(**IMPERFECT** —) SOOTERKIN
(**LITERARY** —) BOOK CENTO DEBAT
ESSAY PIECE COMEDY SATIRE
SKETCH THESIS TREATISE
(**MAGIC** —) HELLBROTH
(**MUSICAL** —) DUET GLEE IDYL
OPUS SOLO SONG TRIO BURLA

CANON DANCE ELEGY ETUDE
FUGUE GAZEL IDYLL NONET SCORE
STUDY ADAGIO ARIOSO ENTREE
GHAZEL HOCKET HOQUET SEPTET
SEXTET BALLADE BOURREE
BOUTADE BRAVURA QUARTET
SCHERZO TOCCATA CAVATINA
CHACONNE CLAUSULA CONCERTO
INNOMINE SERENADE SINFONIA
STANDARD SYMPHONY ANTIPHONY
(**NARRATIVE** —) BALLAD
(**PLASTIC** —) CEMENT
(**POETIC** —) GLOSS KAVYA
(**RAMBLING** —) SATIRE
(**RELIGIOUS** —) MOTET ANTHEM
HYMNIC CANTATA ORATORIO
(**RUBBER** —) GUM
(**VEDIC** —) GAYATRI
(**VITREOUS** —) ENAMEL
(**VOCAL** —) ARIA SOLO SONG
CANON ANTHEM ELEVATIO
CONDUCTUS
(PL.) JUVENILIA LITERATURE
COMPOSITOR COMP TYPO ADMAN
SETTER BANKMAN CASEMAN
PRINTER STONEMAN
COMPOST PELF SOIL MINGLE
COMPOTE MIXTURE COMPOUND
DRESSING
COMPOSURE BOND MIEN QUIET
UNION REPOSE TEMPER BALANCE
POSTURE CALMNESS SERENITY
COMPOTATION SYMPOSIUM
COMPOTE BOWL COMPORT
COMPOST
COMPOUND MIX BASE FILL JOIN
MIXT SOUR ALKYL ALLOY AMIDE
AMINE BLEND ESTER FURIL UNION
ADJUST ALKIDE BORANE COPULA
IODIDE JUMBLE KETONE MEDLEY
PHENOL POLYOL PTERIN PYRONE
SETTLE TEMPER URACIL URAMIL
AGATHIN ALCOHOL ALLICIN
ALLOXAN AMALGAM AMIDATE
AMIDINE AMINATE AMMONIA
COMBINE COMPLEX COMPONE
COMPOSE COMPOST DVANDVA
KAMPONG KHELLIN PHORBIN
PREPARE SPIRANE STEROID
AGLUCONE AGLYCONE ALIZARIN
ALKOXIDE AMMONATE ANTIPODE
APIGENIN BRAZILIN CEROMIDE
COMPOSED FUCHSONE GARDENIN
GENTISIN GOSSYPOL IODOFORM
ISOLOGUE STYRACIN
(**ADHESIVE** —) SALVE
(**POISONOUS** —) KETENE CACODYL
GLYCINE HELENIN STIBINE
(**SYNTHETIC** —) ANDROGEN
SORBITAN
COMPOUNDED CONCRETE
COMPOSITE
COMPOUNDER TANKER
COMPOUNDING INTIMACY
COMPREHEND GET SEE KNOW
TAKE TWIG COVER GRASP IMPLY
LATCH REACH SAVVY SEIZE SENSE
SKILL SMOKE SPELL ATTAIN DIGEST
EMBODY FATHOM FOLLOW PIERCE

UPTAKE COMPASS CONTAIN
DISCERN EMBRACE ENCLOSE
IMAGINE INCLUDE INVOLVE REALIZE
RECEIVE SWALLOW COMPRISE
CONCEIVE CONCLUDE PERCEIVE
COMPREHENSIBLE EXOTERIC
INCLUDED SENSABLE SCRUTABLE
COMPREHENSION HOLD SABE
GRASP SAVVY SENSE ESPRIT
FATHOM NOESIS UPTAKE EPITOME
INSIGHT KNOWING SUMMARY
BEARINGS
COMPREHENSIVE BIG FULL WIDE
BROAD GRAND LARGE GLOBAL
SCOPIC CAPABLE CONCISE
GENERAL GENERIC CATHOLIC
ENCYCLIC SPACIOUS
COMPREHENSIVENESS SCOPE
EXTENT BREADTH WIDENESS
LARGENESS
COMPRESS NIP TIE BALE BIND FIRM
LACE WRAP CLING CRAMP CROWD
CRUSH PINCH PRESS SMASH
BUNDLE DEFORM DIGEST GATHER
SHRINK STRAIN THRONG ABRIDGE
BOLSTER CABBAGE COMPACT
CURTAIL DEFLATE EMBRACE
FLATTEN REPRESS SQUEEZE
SQUINCH ASTRINGE CONDENSE
CONTRACT LAMINATE PEMMICAN
RESTRAIN SUPPRESS
(— **WOOL**) DUMP
(**MEDICAL** —) BOLSTER PLEDGET
COMPRESSED STRICT CROWDED
SUCCINCT
COMPRESSION CRUSH SQUEEZE
PRESSURE THLIPSIS
COMPRESSOR PUMP ROTARY
CONDENSER
COMPRISE HOLD COVER IMPLY
SEIZE ATTACH CONFER EMBODY
EMPLOY MUSTER COMPOSE
CONTAIN EMBRACE ENCLOSE
INCLUDE INVOLVE CONCEIVE
PERCEIVE
COMPROMISE FINE TRIM COMMIT
INTERIM COMPOUND ENDANGER
PALLIATO
COMPROMISING FALSE
COMPULSION NEED URGE FORCE
PRESS DURESS STRESS IMPULSE
COACTION COERCION DISTRESS
EXACTION PERFORCE
COMPULSORY COERCIVE FORCIBLE
COMPUNCTION QUALM REGRET
SORROW REMORSE SCRUPLE
COMPURGATOR COJUROR
COSWEARER
COMPUTATION COMPOT ACCOUNT
COMPUTE CALCULUS COMPUTUS
ESTIMATE
COMPUTE ADD SUM CAST ITEM
RATE COUNT TALLY VALUE ASSESS
CIPHER FIGURE NUMBER RECKON
ACCOUNT BALANCE SUPPUTE
ESTIMATE
COMPUTER ENIAC MANIAC
COMRADE PAL ALLY CHUM MATE
PEER BILLY BUDDY CRONY HABER

HAVER TOWNY BURSCH CHABER
CHAVER COPAIN COUSIN DIGGER
ENGIDU FELLOE FRATER FRIEND
GOSSIP HEARTY BROTHER
COMPEER CONVIVE BEAUPERE
CAMARADA CAMARADE COMORADO
CONFRERE COPEMATE TOVARICH
(— AT TABLE) CONVIVE
(PL.) SOCE

CON DO RAP ANTI KNOW LEAD LOOK
PORE QUIN READ SCAN CHEAT
CUNNE GUIDE KNOCK LEARN STEER
STUDY DIRECT PERUSE REGARD
VERSUS AGAINST DECEIVE EXAMINE
INSPECT OPPOSED SWINDLE

CONCAVE CAVE VOID CAMUS MINUS
ARCHED DISHED HOLLOW SIMOUS
VAULTY VAULTED CRESCENT
INCURVED

CONCAVITY COVE CONCHA HOLLOW
VENTER KNEEPAN

CONCEAL MEW WRY BURY DERN
FEAL HIDE KEEP LENE MASK SCUG
SILE VEIL VEST WRAP BLIND BOSOM
CACHE CLOAK COUCH COVER FEIGN
LAYNE PLANT SHADE BURROW
CLOSET DOCTOR ELOIGN EMBOSS
HUDDLE HUGGER IMBOSK OCCULT
POCKET SCREEN SHADOW SHIELD
SHROUD STIFLE ABSCOND ENVELOP
OPPRESS PLASTER SECRETE
BESCREEN DISGUISE ENSCONCE
PALLIATE PRETENCE PRETENSE
WITHHOLD
(— A FUGITIVE) HARBOR
(— A TRAIL) TRASH
(— INFORMATION) LAYNE

CONCEALED DERN SCUG SNUG
BLIND PRIVY BURROW COVERT
HIDDEN LATENT OCCULT PERDUE
SECRET VEILED COVERED LARVATE
WRAPPED ABSTRUSE CRYPTOUS
HIDEAWAY
(— BY) BENEATH

CONCEALING DESIGNING
OBVELATION

CONCEALMENT MEW LAIN COVER
FRAUD NIGHT SECRECY CELATION
VELATION
(IN —) DOGGO

CONCEDE OWN CEDE GIVE ADMIT
AGREE ALLOW GRANT WAIVE YETTE
YIELD ACCORD ASSENT BETEEM
CONFESS OTTROYE BEGRUDGE
(— AS ADVANTAGE) SPOT

CONCEIT EGO TOY IDEA SIDE
CRANK FANCY KNACK PRIDE QUIRK
BABERY DEVICE NOTION VAGARY
VANITY BIGHEAD CAPRICE EGOTISM
OUTRAGE TYMPANY CONCETTO
FLIMFLAM

CONCEITED BUG BRAG COXY FESS
VAIN CHUFF COCKY FLORY HUFFY
PENSY PROUD SAUCY CLEVER
BIGGETY BIGGITY ARROGANT
DOGMATIC NOSEWISE PENSEFUL
PRIGGISH SNOBBISH

CONCEIVABLE EARTHLY POSSIBLE
CONCEIVE FORM HOLD MAKE PLAN

TEEM WEEN BEGIN BRAIN CATCH
DREAM FANCY FRAME GUESS IMAGE
THINK DESIGN DEVISE IDEATE
INTEND PONDER SETTLE GESTATE
IMAGINE REALIZE SUPPOSE
SUSPECT COMPRISE CONTRIVE
ENVISAGE

CONCENTRATE AIM FIX MASS PILE
COACT EXALT FOCUS PURSE UNIFY
ARREST ATTEND CENTER CITRIN
DECOCT DISTIL FIXATE GATHER
SINGLE COMPACT CONGEST DISTILL
ENGROSS ESSENCE EXTRACT
THICKEN ABSOLUTE APPROACH
ASSEMBLE CONDENSE CONTRACT
FOCALIZE GRADUATE
(— ORE) STRAKE

CONCENTRATED HARD DENSE
FIXED INTENT STRONG EXALTED
INTENSE
(NOT —) DIFFUSE

CONCENTRATION BRIX CENTER
BALLING SAMADHI ACTIVITY
FIXATION PELMANISM
(— OF ARTILLERY FIRE) STONK
(— OF ENERGY) EXCITON
(— OF PLANTS) BED

CONCEPT GUT GUTS IDEA FANCY
IMAGE BEGRIFF CONCEIT OPINION
THOUGHT ABSOLUTE CATEGORY

CONCEPTION ENS IDEA VIEW EIDOS
FANCY FETUS IMAGE BELIEF DESIGN
EMBRYO ENTITY NOTION CONCEIT
CONCEPT PROJECT PURPOSE
CATEGORY ESTHETIC NOTATION
RATIONAL
(— OF IDEA) HENT
(— OF ONESELF) BOVARISM
BOVARYSM
(ABSTRACT —) ARCHETYPE
(FALSE —) IDOL DELUSION
(QUICKNESS OF —) PREGNANCY

CONCEPTUAL IDEAL
CONCEPTUALISM SERMONISM
CONCERN BUG BEAR CARE FEAR
FIRM GEAR HAND PART RECK SAKE
APPLY CAUSE DRIVE EVENT GRIEF
HEART SORGE STAND TOUCH
WORRY AFFAIR AFFECT BEHOLD
CHARGE DIRECT EMPLOY FINGER
IMPORT MATTER REGARD ANXIETY
ARTICLE BOTTLER COMPANY
DISTURB FUNERAL INVOLVE
PERTAIN RESPECT SHEBANG
SOLICIT TROUBLE BUSINESS
HYPOTHEC INTEREST JEALOUSY
(— ONESELF) DEAL PASS TOUCH
INTERMIT
(INDUSTRIAL —) COLOSSUS
(PRUDISH —) COMSTOCKERY
(SPECIAL —) ACCENT
(WORLDLY —S) EARTH

CONCERNED INTENT ANXIOUS
WORRIED ATWITTER BOTHERED

CONCERNING BY OF ON RE TO FOR
TIL TILL ABOUT ANENT ANENST
APROPOS TOUCHING

CONCERT POP PLAN RECK UNITE
ACCORD DEVISE SMOKER ARRANGE

BENEFIT CONCENT CONCORD
CONSORT CONSULT HARMONY
POPULAR RECITAL

CONCERTINA ORGAN LANTUM
SQUIFFER BANDONION MELOPHONE

CONCESSION BOON FAVOR GRANT
LEASE STOOP ASSENT GAMBIT
OCTROY CESSION EPITROPE
MYNPACHT ADMISSION ALLOWANCE
PRIVILEGE

CONCESSIONAIRE GRIFTER

CONCH CONK PUNK SHELL COCKLE
MUSSEL STROMB STROMBUS

CONCIERGE PORTER SUISSE
WARDEN JANITOR

CONCILIATE GET CALM EASE GAIN
ATONE HONEY THING ADJUST
PACIFY SOFTEN ACQUIRE APPEASE
CONCILE MOLLIFY PLACATE SATISFY

CONCILIATOR ARBITRATOR

CONCILIATORY MILD SOFT GENTLE
GIVING IRENIC LENIENT PACIFIC
WINNING IRENICAL LENITIVE
TREATABLE

CONCISE CURT NEAT TRIG BRIEF
CRISP PITHY SHORT TERSE COGENT
CUTTED COMPACT LACONIC
POINTED PRECISE SERRIED
SUMMARY MUTILATE PREGNANT
SUCCINCT

CONCISELY PRESSLY ELLIPTICALLY

CONCISENESS BREVITY ECONOMY
SYNTOMY FASTNESS SYNTOMIA

CONCLAVE SOBOR CLOSET
CHAMBER MEETING AREOPAGY
ASSEMBLY

CONCLUDE BAR END FINE REST
TAKE CLOSE DRIVE ESTOP INFER
JUDGE LIMIT CLINCH DECIDE
DEDUCE EXPIRE FIGURE FINISH
GATHER INDUCE PERIOD REASON
RECKON SETTLE ACHIEVE ARRANGE
COLLECT CONFINE EMBRACE
ENCLOSE RESOLVE SUPPOSE
COMPLETE DISPATCH ESTIMATE
GRADUATE PARCLOSE RESTRAIN

CONCLUDED OVER COMPLETE

CONCLUDING LAST DESITIVE

CONCLUSION END AMEN CODA
ERGO FINE LAST TERM CLOSE
ENVOY EVENT FINIS ISSUE LOOSE
POINT ENDING FINALE FINISH
PERIOD RESULT SEQUEL THIRTY
UPSHOT CLOSURE CURTAIN FINDING
OUTCOME SEQUELA APODOSIS
DECISION EPILOGUE FINALITY
FRUITION GODSPEED ILLATION
ILLATIVE JUDGMENT PARCLOSE
SENTENCE
(— OF ARIA) CABALETTA
(FINAL —) ISSUE
(RANDOM —) SURMISE
(PL.) COLLATION

CONCLUSIVE LAST FINAL VALID
COGENT CERTAIN EVIDENT
EXTREME TELLING DECISIVE
DEFINITE ULTIMATE

CONCOCT MIX BREW COOK FAKE
PLAN PLOT VAMP FRAME HATCH

THINK DECOCT DEVISE DIGEST
INVENT MINGLE REFINE SCHEME
COMPOSE CONFECT PERFECT
PREPARE COMPOUND INTRIGUE
CONCOCTION PLAN PLOT MUMMY
DEVICE MUMMIA BREWING MIXTURE
SNEEZER BUSINESS COMPOUND
CONCOMITANT SEQUELA INCIDENT
ACCESSORY ASSOCIATE ATTENDANT
ATTENDING COMPANION CONJOINED
COOPERANT SATELLITE
CONCORD PART AGREE AMITY
PEACE TERMS UNION UNITY TREATY
UNISON COMPACT CONCENT
CONCERT HARMONY ONENESS
QUARTER COVENANT SYMPATHY
COMMUNITY
(— OF SOUNDS) SYMPHONIA
CONCORDANT UNISON TUNABLE
TUNEFUL HARMONIC UNISONAL
UNISONOUS
CONCOURSE CROWD HAUNT PLACE
POINT REPAIR RESORT THRONG
COMPANY ASSEMBLY FREQUENCE
(INFERNAL —) HELL
CONCRETE CLOT FIRM HARD REAL
BETON GROUT SOLID UNITE ACTUAL
CEMENT COMBINE CONGEAL
SPECIAL COALESCE COMPOUND
POSITIVE TANGIBLE AEROCRETE
CONCRETION CLOT KNOT MESS
FLINT FUSIL PEARL STONE BEZOAR
NODULE TOPHUS LITHITE OTOLITH
CALCULUS POTSTONE SEBOLITH
(— IN BAMBOO) TABASHIR
TABASHEER
CONCUBINAGE KARAO KAREWA
HETAERISM
CONCUBINE DASI HAGAR RIZPAH
BEDMATE ODALISK MISTRESS
CONCUPISCENCE DESIRE
CONCUPISCENT ANTSY
CONCUR HAND JIBE JOIN AGREE
CHECK CHIME UNITE ACCEDE
ACCORD ASSENT CONDOG APPROVE
COMBINE CONSENT CONVENT
COINCIDE CONSPIRE CONVERGE
(— IN) SUBSCRIBE
CONCURRENCE UNION ASSENT
BESTOW CONSENT CONSORT
MEETING ADHESION SYNDROME
ADMISSION
CONCURRENT COEVAL UNITED
MEETING COPIJNCTAL
CONCUSSION BUMP SHOCK IMPACT
ICEQUAKE COMMOTION
CONDEMN BAN CAST DAMN DEEM
DOOM FILE FINE HISS BLAME BLESS
DECRY JUDGE AMERCE ATTAIN
AWREAK BANISH DETEST ADJUDGE
CENSURE CONVICT DENOUNCE
FORJUDGE REPROACH SENTENCE
CONDEMNATION DOOM BLAME
CENSURE DECRIAL BRICKBAT
CONDEMNATORY SEVERE ADVERSE
CONDEMNED FATAL DAMNED
CONDENSATION BAN STORY
DIGEST CAPSULE BOILDOWN
CONDENSE CUT JIG BRIEF UNITE

DECOCT DIGEST HARDEN LESSEN
NARROW REDUCE SHRINK ABRIDGE
CAPSULE COMBINE COMPACT
DEFLATE DENSATE DISTILL
SHORTEN SQUEEZE THICKEN
COMPRESS CONTRACT DIMINISH
PEMMICAN SOLIDIFY
CONDENSED CURT BRIEF CAPSULE
COMPACT CONCISE ABSORBED
CONDENSER ALUDEL REFLUX
BALANCER CAPACITOR
CONDER HUER
CONDESCEND DEIGN FAVOR GRANT
STOOP ASSENT OBLIGE SUBMIT
CONCEDE DESCEND
CONDESCENDING AVUNCULAR
CONDESCENSION STOOP DISDAIN
COURTESY DIGNATION
CONDIGN DUE FIT FAIR JUST
SEVERE WORTHY ADEQUATE
SUITABLE
CONDIMENT SOY HERB KARI MACE
SAGE SALT CAPER CURRY DULCE
DULSE SAUCE SPICE THYME AIWAIN
AJOWAN CATSUP CLOVES GARLIC
PEPPER RELISH SAMBAL TAMARA
CANELLA CHUTNEY KETCHUP
MUSTARD OREGANO PAPRIKA
VINEGAR ALLSPICE BALACHAN
BLATJANG DRESSING SEASONER
TURMERIC
CONDITION IF AND FIG PLY WAY
CASE FORM MODE PASS RANK
ROTE TERM TIFF TRIM ANGLE BIRTH
CAUSE CLASS COLOR COVIN ESTRE
FACET JOKER PLACE POINT SHAPE
STAGE STATE THEAT WHACK
AGENCY DEGREE DONNEE ESTATE
FETTLE GENTRY MORALE MUSCLE
PLIGHT STATUS STRING ARTICLE
CALLING FEATHER FOOTING
PREMISE PROVISO STATION
SUSPEND COVENANT OCCASION
POSITION PROTASIS STANDING
(— OF ANXIETY) CARK
(— OF BODY) HEAT AFFECTION
(— OF FATIGUE) FRAZZLE
(— OF FLUCTUATION) EURIPUS
(— STATED BEFOREHAND) PREMISE
(CHANCE —) ACCIDENT
(DEBASED —) CACHEXY CACHEXIA
(DEPRESSED —) DOWNBEAT
(DETERMINING —) GROUND
(DIRTY —) CLAT
(DISEASED —) DIEBACK
(DISGRACEFUL —) IGNOMINY
(DRUNKEN —) BUN
(FLOURISHING —) HEALTH
(GENERAL —) VOGUE
(HABITUAL —) TENOR
(MISERABLE —) SQUALOR
(MORBID —) HOLDOVER
(MOST APPROPRIATE —) CHECKER
(NECESSARY —) MEAN
(NEUROTIC —) LATAH
(ORDERLY —) DECENCY
(PAINFUL —) CRICK
(PERMANENT —) HEXIS
(PROPER —) KILTER

(PROTECTIVE —) CALLUS CALLOUS
(SCURFY —) BUCKSKIN
(STATIONARY —) JIB
(SUBLIME —) HEAVEN
(SURROUNDING —) AIR
(TRUE —) SIZE
(UNEQUAL —) ODDS
(UNPROSPEROUS —) ILLTH
(WEATHER —S) ELEMENTS
(PL.) HAND TERMS STRINGS
CONDITIONAL EVENTUAL
CONNEXIVE QUALIFIED
CONDITIONED FINITE LIMITED
CONDITIONER DEGGER
CONDITIONING EDUCATION
HYPOTHESIS
CONDOLENCE PITY RUTH EMPATHY
SYMPATHY
CONDONE BLINK REMIT ACQUIT
EXCUSE FORGET IGNORE PARDON
ABSOLVE FORGIVE OVERLOOK
CONDOR TIFFIN BUZZARD VULTURE
CONDUCE GO AID HELP HIRE LEAD
TEND BRING GUIDE CONFER EFFECT
ENGAGE ADVANCE CONDUCT
FURTHER REDOUND
CONDUCT ACT CON RUN USE WIN
BEAR CALL COND CONN DEED FACT
FARE FIRK FORM GARB GEST HAND
KEEP LEAD MIEN PLAY QUIT RULE
SHOW TAKE WAGE WALK BATON
CARRY DRESS DRIVE FETCH GESTE
GUARD GUIDE HABIT MAYNE SITHE
TRADE TRAIN USAGE USHER ACTION
ATTEND BEHAVE COLORS CONVEY
CONVOY COURSE DEDUCE DEMEAN
DEPORT DIRECT ESCORT GOVERN
INDUCT MANAGE MANNER SQUIRE
ACTIONS BEARING CHANNEL
COMPERE COMPORT CONDITE
CONDUCE CONDUIT CONTAIN
CONTROL EXECUTE GALLANT
GESTION OFFICER OPERATE
WIREWAY ARRIVISM BEHAVIOR
CARRIAGE CHAPLAIN COURTESY
DEMEANOR GUIDANCE REGULATE
SHEPHERD TRANSACT
(— ONESELF) DO ACT ACQUIT
BEHAVE BESTOW DEMEAN DEPORT
COMPORT CONTAIN DISPORT
ENTREAT MAINTAIN
(APPROPRIATE —) DHARMA
(BRASH —) FACE
(CONVENTIONAL —) PRAXIS
(DISORDERLY —) RANDAN
(DORMANT —) LATENCY
(ETHICAL —) HONOR
(PROPER —) CRICKET
(RECKLESS —) DEVILRY DEVILTRY
(RIGHT —) TE TAO
(SAFE —) KOWL COWLE
(SHOWY —) BRAVADO
(SLOPPY —) SWASH
(VAINGLORIOUS —) HEROICS
(WANTON —) RUFF
(WEAK —) FOLLY
CONDUCTANCE G
(— UNIT) MHO
CONDUCTION COURSING

CONDUCTOR CON BOND CADE LEAD MAIN BRUSH GUARD SHUNT SPOUT TRUNK BRIDGE BUSMAN CARMAN CONVOY COPPER ESCORT FEEDER LEADER OFFSET RETURN CAPTAIN CATHODE MAESTRO MANAGER AQUEDUCT BATONIST CICERONE CONVEYOR DIRECTOR EMPLOYEE FILAMENT STICKMAN
(ELECTRIC —) FILAMENT
(OMNIBUS —) CAD
(PL.) SERVICE
CONDUIT BOSS DUCT GOUT MAIN PIPE SINK TUBE WIRE CABLE CANAL CUNDY SEWER STACK HEADER SLUICE TROUGH CARRIER CHANNEL CHIMNEY CONDITE CONDUCT CULVERT CUNDITE EXHAUST FOGGARA LATERAL LAUNDER PASSAGE WIREWAY AQUEDUCT OLEODUCT PENSTOCK WASTEWAY
(PL.) LIMBERS
CONDYLOMA SYCOMA
CONE CAP YOW CHAT KING PINA TOOT CONUS CRACK SCREW SHAPE SPIRE YOWIE BOBBIN CONOID MONTRE PASTIL CLUSTER CONELET CONIOLE FISSURE FRUSTUM PROLONG PYRAMID STROBIL THIMBLE CANNELON DUMPLING GALBULUS PASTILLE STROBILE STROBILUS
(— OF CLOTH) VANE
(— OF FIR) YOW YOWIE STROBIL STROBILE STROBILUS
(— OF GUNPOWDER) PEEOY
(— OF HOP PLANT) BUR BURR
(— OF SILVER AMALGAM) PINA
(— ON LOG END) CAP
(— ON SHOE) CLEAT
(— STRUCTURE) NURAGHE
(HALF —) FORME NAPPE
(ICE CREAM —) ICE CORNET
(INVERTED —) HOPPER
(PAPER —) SPILL COFFIN
(TOP CUT FROM —) UNGULA
(PL.) HOPS
CONENOSE BEDBUG BARBEIRO
CONESTOGA WAGON CARAVAN
CONEY CONY HYRAX HYRACID GUATIBERO
CONFAB CHAT TALK POWWOW CONFLAB PRATTLE
CONFECTION CHOW MOSS CANDY DULCE MEBOS SWEET BONBON COCKLE COMFIT DAINTY DRAGEE HALVAH JUNKET MAJOON NOUGAT SWEETY CARAMEL CONFECT FONDANT MIXTURE POMFRET PRALINE SEATRON SUCCADE ANGELICA CHOWCHOW CODINIAC COMPOUND CONSERVE DELICACY MARZIPAN PRESERVE SUBTLETY
CONFECTIONERY CIMBAL CONFISERIE
CONFEDERACY BUND COVIN CREEK KEDAR UNION COVINE LEAGUE COMPLOT ALLIANCE COVENANT FEDERACY ILLINOIS BLACKFOOT

CONFEDERATE AID PAL REB ALLY BAND PUFF REBEL STALL UNITE LEAGUE SANTAR ABETTER ABETTOR CONJURE FEDARIE FEDERAL FEODARY PARTNER STEERER CONSPIRE FEDERARY FEDERATE
(— SOLDIER) CONFED JOHNNY GRAYBACK GRAYCOAT GREYBACK
(PICKPOCKET'S —) STALL
CONFEDERATION BODY BUND UNION LEAGUE COMPACT HASINAI SOCIETY ALLIANCE COVENANT
CONFER DUB GIVE MEET TALK AWARD ENDOW FEOFF GRANT INFER SPEND TREAT ADVISE BESTOW COMMON CONFAB DONATE ENTAIL HUDDLE IMPARL IMPART INVEST PARLEY COLLATE COMMUNE COMPARE CONDUCE CONSULT CONTACT COUNSEL DISCUSS INSTATE PRESENT COLLOGUE COMPRISE CONVERGE
(— DEGREE UPON) CAP
(— KNIGHTHOOD UPON) DUB
CONFERENCE DIET TALK SYNOD TREAT TRUST CAUCUS CONFAB HUDDLE INDABA KORERO PARLEY PARVIS POWWOW SUMMIT CIRCUIT COUNCIL MEETING PALAVER PARLING SEMINAR COLLOQUE COLLOQUY CONCLAVE CONGRESS PRACTICE PRACTISE TUTORIAL
CONFERRING GRANT DATION
CONFESS OWN AVOW FESS KNOW SING ADMIT GRANT KITHE ACKNOW ATTEST AVOUCH BEKNOW COUTHE RENDER REVEAL SHRIFT SHRIVE SQUEAK CONCEDE DIVULGE PROFESS DISBOSOM DISCLOSE DISCOVER MANIFEST
CONFESSION ALHET CREDO CREED GRANT AVOWAL SHRIFT SHRIVE VIDDUI ASHAMNU FORMULA PECCAVI COGNOVIT
(MUTUAL —) SHARING
CONFESSIONAL SHRIFT MALCHUS
CONFESSOR FATHER SHRIFT SHRIVER
CONFIDANT PRIVY FRIEND INWARD PRIVADO INTIMATE
CONFIDE AFFY RELY TELL TRUST COMMIT DEPEND LIPPEN BELIEVE CONSIGN ENTRUST INTRUST
(— IN) VENTURE
CONFIDENCE FACE HARK HOPE BIELD CHEEK FAITH STOCK TRUST APLOMB BELIEF CREDIT FIANCE FIDUCE METTLE MORALE SECRET SPIRIT SURETY COUNSEL COURAGE PRIVITY AFFIANCE BOLDNESS CREDENCE RELIANCE SECURITY SURENESS
CONFIDENT BOLD SMUG SURE CRANK HARDY SIKER CROUSE SECURE SICKER TRAIST ASSURED CERTAIN HOPEFUL RELIANT CONSTANT FEARLESS FIDUCIAL IMPUDENT POSITIVE SANGUINE TRUSTFUL

CONFIDENTIAL BOSOM PRIVY CLOSET COVERT HUSHED INWARD SECRET PRIVATE ESOTERIC FAMILIAR INTIMATE
CONFIDING TRUSTY CREDENT RELIANT TRUSTFUL CONFIDENT
CONFIGURATION FORM SHAPE FIGURE BANDING CONTOUR DIAMOND GESTALT OUTLINE GEOMETRY POSITURE
(CELESTIAL —) SYZYGY
CONFINE BAR BOX CUB DAM HEM NUN PEN PIN STY TIE BAIL BIND BOOM CAGE COOP CRIB FOLD HASP JAIL KEEP LACE LOCK PEND SEAL SHUT SPAN STEW STOP STOW BOUND CABIN CHAIN COART CRAMP CROWD DELAY FENCE HOUSE LIMIT MARCH PINCH POUND STICK STINT BORDER BOTTLE COARCT CORRAL EMBANK FETTER FORBAR HAMPER HURDLE IMMURE IMPALE IMPARK INTERN KENNEL PINION POCKET PRISON STRAIN TETHER ASTRICT CHAMBER COMPASS CONTAIN IMPOUND INCLUDE MANACLE PINFOLD POISTER RECLOSE SECLUDE SHACKLE TRAMMEL BASTILLE BOUNDARY CLOISTER CONCLUDE DISTRAIN FOCALIZE IMPRISON RESTRAIN STRAITEN
CONFINED ILL FAST PENT BOUND CAGED CLOSE CRAMP BEDRID IMPALE IMPENT PENTIT SEALED CAPTIVE CRAMPED CRIBBED LIMITED SQUEEZY IMPENDED IMPLICIT INTERNED
(— TO CERTAIN AREA) ENDEMIC
(— TO SELECT GROUP) ESOTERIC
CONFINEMENT MEW BOND HOLD JAIL WARD CRYING GATING DURANCE INLYING JANKERS WARDING CLAUSURE FIRMANCE GROANING SOLITARY
CONFINING NARROW
CONFIRM FIX SET FIRM SEAL PROVE VOUCH AFFEER AFFIRM ASSENT ASSURE ATTEST AVOUCH BISHOP CLINCH FASTEN HARDEN RATIFY REABLE SECOND SETTLE STABLE VERIFY APPROVE COMFORT CONSIGN ENDORSE FORTIFY JUSTIFY PROPORT SUPPORT SUSTAIN THICKEN ACCREDIT CONVINCE CORROBER ENTRENCH INSTRUCT SANCTION STRENGTH VALIDATE
CONFIRMATION PROOF SANCTION
CONFIRMED SET FIXED SWORN ARRANT STABLE CERTAIN CHRONIC HABITUAL HARDENED RATIFIED
CONFISCATE GRAB SEIZE USURP CONDEMN CONFISK PUBLISH DISTRAIN
CONFISCATION ESCHEAT INCENSION
CONFLAGRATION FIRE BLAZE FEVER BURNING INFERNO
CONFLICT JAR WAR BOUT BUMP

DUEL FRAY MEET MUSS RIFT
AGONY BROIL BRUSH CLASH FIGHT
GRIPS STOUR ACTION BATTLE
COMBAT MUTINY OPPOSE SCRAPE
SHOWER STRIFE CONTEND
CONTEST DISCORD SCUFFLE
WARFARE ANTIMONY DISAGREE
MILITATE SKIRMISH STRIVING
STRUGGLE
(DRAMATIC —) AGON
(FINAL —) ARMAGEDDON
CONFLICTING ADVERSE
ABHORRENT
CONFLUENCE FORK CROWD INFALL
CONFLUX MEETING JUNCTION
CONFORM DO GO FIT HEW LEAN
OBEY SORT SUIT ADAPT AGREE
APPLY SHAPE YIELD ACCEDE
ADJUST ASSENT COMPLY CONFER
SETTLE SQUARE SUBMIT COMPOSE
CONFIRM
(— TO) KEEP MEET ANSWER
BEHAVE SATISFY
CONFORMABLE DONE SUING
SUITED CONFORM PURSUANT
QUADRANT
CONFORMATION FORM BUILD
(MENTAL —) SAMSKARA
CONFORMING FAIR SAME COMELY
DECENT CORRECT CONGRUOUS
CONFORMIST BOY COMPLIER
CONFORMITY FIT ACCORD DHARMA
EQUITY HARMONY JUSTICE KEEPING
ACCURACY AFFINITY JUSTNESS
LIKENESS SYMMETRY FORMALITY
(— TO LAW) DECENCY LEGALITY
CONFOUND MIX BLOW DASH MATE
MAZE ROUT STAM STUN WHIP
ABASH ADDLE AMAZE BLAST FOUND
SHEND SPOIL STUMP WASTE
AWHAPE BAFFLE COMMIT DISMAY
DUDDER MINGLE MUDDLE RABBIT
RATTLE ASTOUND CONFUSE
CONFUTE CORRUPT DESTROY
FLUMMOX FORLESE PERPLEX
STUMBLE STUPEFY ASTONISH
BABELIZE BEWILDER DISTRACT
DUMFOUND SURPRISE
CONFOUNDED MATE BLAME
BLAMED DEUCED BLASTED MURRAIN
PEEVISH DUMMERED SWITCHED
CONSARNED
(BE —) ABAVE ABAWE
CONFRATERNITY BODY UNION
SOCIETY CONFRAIRY
CONFRONT DARE DEFY FACE MEET
NOSE BEARD BRACE BRAVE CROSS
FRONT STAND ACCOST ASSAIL
BREAST OPPOSE RESIST VISAGE
AFFRONT COMPARE PROPOSE
ENVISAGE THREATEN
CONFRONTING BEFORE ADVERSE
CONFRONT
CONFUSE BOX FOX MIX BALL DASH
DAZE DOIT DOZE DUST GAUM HARL
MAZE MUSS ROUT ABASH ADDLE
AMAZE BEFOG BITCH BLEND CLOUD
DEAVE DIZZY SHEND SHENT SNARL
STEER TWIST UPSET BAFFLE

BEDAZE BEMUSE BOTHER BURBLE
CADDLE COMMIT CORPSE DUDDER
DUDDLE FLURRY FUDDLE GRAVEL
JUMBLE MADDLE MAFFLE MAMMER
MASKER MIZZLE MOMBLE MUDDLE
PUZZLE RAFFLE RATTLE TWITCH
WIMPLE BECLOUD BEDEVIL
BLUNDER BUMBAZE DERANGE
DIFFUSE EMBROIL FLUSTER
GARBOIL GIDDIFY MYSTIFY
NONPLUS PERPLEX SCATTER
SHUFFLE STUPEFY UNRAVEL
BEFUDDLE BEWILDER CONFLATE
CONFOUND DISORDER DISTRACT
DUMFOUND ENTANGLE MISORDER
SQUATTER
(— AN ACTOR) CORPSE
(— BY NOISE) DUDDER
CONFUSED ASEA LOST ADDLE
DIZZY FOGGY FUZZY HEAVY MISTY
MUDDY MUZZY VAGUE WESTY
WOOLY BLOTTO CLOUDY DOILED
DOITED DRUMLY JUMBLY MEDLEY
MOPISH MUSHED SHAGGY TAVERT
WOOLLY BLURRED CHAOTIC
CLOUDED CONFUSE DIFFUSE
OBSCURE RATTLED STUPENT
COCKEYED DERANGED FLURRIED
INVOLVED
CONFUSING DIZZY MAZEFUL
BAFFLING BLINDING DIZZYING
CONFUSION PI DIN PIE COIL DUST
FUSS HARL MESS MOIL RIOT AMAZE
ATAXY BABEL CHAOS CHEVY CHIVY
DERAY FRASE HAVOC HURLY LARRY
SNAFU SNARL STROW ATAXIA
BABBLE BAFFLE BALLUP BEDLAM
CHIVVY FRAISE HABBLE HOBBLE
HUBBUB HUDDLE JABBLE JUMBLE
MASTIC MUCKER MUDDLE POTHER
RABBLE RUFFLE RUMPUS THRONG
TOPHET TUMULT UPROAR WELTER
ANARCHY BLUNDER BLUSTER
CLUTTER COBWEBS FARRAGE
FLUTTER GARBOIL HURLING
KIPPAGE LOUSTER MISRULE
MISMAZE ROOKERY RUMMAGE
SCADDLE SCOWDER TOPHETH
TURMOIL WHEMMEL WIDDRIM
BABELISM DISARRAY DISORDER
EQUIVOKE HOOROOSH SCOUTHER
SHAMBLES SPLUTTER TOHUBOHU
CONFUTATION DISPROOF
CONFUTE DENY EVICT REBUT
EVINCE EXPOSE REFUTE FALSIFY
IMPROVE SILENCE SUBVERT
CONCLUDE CONFOUND CONVINCE
DISPROVE INFRINGE OVERCOME
REDARGUE
CONGEAL GEL ICE SET GEAL JELL
CANDY COTTER CURDLE FREEZE
HARDEN STIFFEN STORKEN THICKEN
CONCRETE SOLIDIFY
(— INTO HOARFROST) RIME
CONGEALED FROZEN
CONGELATION FROST
CONGENER BEAVER DOTTREL
DOTTEREL
CONGENIAL SIB BOON HAPPY

NATAL NATIVE AMIABLE CONNATE
KINDRED
CONGENITAL INNATE CONNATE
CONNATAL GENETOUS
CONGERIES CALCULARY
COLLECTION
CONGEST STUFF IMPACT
CONGESTED INJECTED
CONGESTION JAM HEAP LAMPAS
LAMPERS CROWDING STOPPAGE
CONGLOMERATE HEAP MASS PILE
ROCK STACK BANKET PSEPHITE
NAGELFLUH
CONGLOMERATION HUDDLE
GLOMMOX IMBROGLIO
CONGO MUMMY ASPHALTUM

CONGO
CAPITAL: BRAZZAVILLE
COIN: FRANC FRANCCFA
LAKE: MWERU TUMBA UPEMBA
  LEOPOLD
NATIVE: SUSA VILI MANTU PYGMY
  BATEKE MBOCHI WABUMA
  BAKONGO BANGALA
PLATEAU: BATEKE
RIVER: CONGO KWILU LULUA
  NGOKO NIARI SANGA WAMBA
  KWENGE LOANGE UBANGI
  KOUILOU LUBILASH
TOWN: EWO EPENA HOLLE JACOB
  OKOYO SEMBE MAKOUA
  OUESSO ZANAGA DOLISIE
  ENYELLE SOUANKE DJAMBALA
  BRAZZAVILLE
TRIBUTARY: LOMAMI UBANGI
  ARUWIMA LUALABA LUAPULA
  ITIMBITI

CONGOU KEEMUN
CONGRATULATE HUG JOY LAUD
GREET SALUTE FLATTER MACARIZE
CONGRATULATION PARABIEN
(PL.) GRATTERS
CONGREGATE HERD MASS MEET
PACK TEEM GROUP SWARM TROOP
GATHER MUSTER COLLECT
CONVENE ASSEMBLE
CONGREGATION PEW BODY FOLD
HERD HOST MASS FLOCK SAMAJ
SWARM CHURCH PARISH COMPANY
MEETING SYNAXIS ASSEMBLY
BRETHREN CHAPELRY
(— OF WITCHES) COVEN
(JEWISH —) KOLEL ALJAMA
SYNAGOG
(PL.) CHARGE
CONGRESS MOD DAIL DIET SYNOD
UYEZD OBLAST OUYEZD POWWOW
COUNCIL GORSEDD MEETING
ASSEMBLY CONCLAVE
CONGRESSMAN SENATOR
DOUGHFACE
CONGRUITY ACCORD CONCORD
FITNESS HARMONY KEEPING
SYMMETRY COHERENCE
CONGRUOUS CONGRUE HARMONIC
SUITABLE ACCORDING

CONICAL CONIC TAPER COPPED COPPLED TAPERING

CONIFER FIR YEW PINE CEDAR LARCH SPRUCE SOFTWOOD EVERGREEN

CONIFERAE PINALES

CONIUM HEMLOCK

CONJECTURE AIM CAST PLOT ROVE SHOT VIEW AUGUR ETTLE FANCY GUESS OPINE THINK BELIEF DIVINE THEORY CONJECT IMAGINE OPINION PRESUME SUPPOSE SURMISE SUSPECT HINDCAST SUPPOSAL

CONJOIN JOIN KNIT ATTEND EMPALE IMPALE

CONJOINED JOINED JUGATE LINKED JUGATED CONJUNCT TOUCHING

CONJOINTLY JUNCTLY TOGETHER

CONJUGAL SPOUSAL CONNUBIAL

CONJUGATE YOKED JOINED UNITED COUPLED INFLECT

CONJUGATION SYNGAMY ZYGOSIS CYTOGAMY ENDOGAMY SYNOPSIS

CONJUNCTION AS ET IF OR AND BUT NOR TIE THAN JOINT SINCE SYNOD UNION UNITY THOUGH COITION CONSORT JOINDER CONJUNCT RATIONAL

CONJUNCTURE SEASON

CONJURATION ART CHARM MAGIC SPELL VOODOO EXORCISM

CONJURE PRAY WISH CHARM HALSE ADJURE ENJOIN INVENT INVOKE SUMMON BESEECH COMBINE ENTREAT IMAGINE CONSPIRE CONTRIVE EXORCIZE

CONJURE MAN CUNJAH CUNJER GOOFER GUFFER

CONJURER MAGE PELLAR POWWOW SHAMAN WIZARD JUGGLER WARLOCK WIELARE JONGLEUR MAGICIAN PYTHONIC SORCERER

CONJURING JADU JADOO CONJURY VOODOOISM

CONK FAIL HEAD KONK NOSE FAINT KNOCK STALL BRACKET

CONNECT COG PUT TIE ALLY BIND BOND GEAR GLUE JOIN KNIT KNOT LINK AFFIX CHAIN MARRY NITCH UNITE ATTACH BRIDGE CEMENT COHERE COMMIT RELATE COUPLE ENLINK FASTEN RELATE SPLICE COMBINE ENCHAIN INVOLVE APPARENT CATENATE CONTINUE DOVETAIL INTERTIE
(— TREADLE) CORD

CONNECTED ALLIED CONNEX AFFINED COUPLED HANGING
(ELECTRICALLY —) ALIVE
(NOT —) FOREIGN ASYNARTETE
(SYNTACTICALLY —) ABSOLUTE

CONNECTICUT
CAPITAL: HARTFORD
COLLEGE: TRINITY
COUNTY: TOLLAND WINDHAM
INDIAN: PEQUOT MOHEGAN
  NIANTIC

STATE BIRD: ROBIN
STATE FLOWER: LAUREL
STATE NICKNAME: NUTMEG
STATE TREE: OAK
TOWN: AVON BETHEL CANAAN
  COSCOB DARIEN MYSTIC
  SHARON STORRS DANBURY
  MERIDEN NIANTIC NORWALK
  NORWICH TOLLAND WINDSOR
  NEWHAVEN SIMSBURY
  WESTPORT GREENWICH
UNIVERSITY: YALE WESLEYAN

CONNECTING BETWEEN SYNDETIC

CONNECTION Y HUB TAP TIE BOND LINK HITCH NEXUS UNION BUCKLE CLEVIS FAMILY GROUND REPORT SUTURE SWIVEL BEARING BOLSTER CONTACT DESCENT FERRULE HOLDING KINSHIP LIAISON SIAMESE SIBNESS SOCIETY AFFINITY ALLIANCE COMMERCE CONNEXUS INTIMACY JUNCTION LIGATION RELATIVE SYNDETIC
(ELECTRICAL —) GROUND
(FORKED —) BRANCH
(MECHANICAL —S) LEADOUT

CONNECTIVE IZAFAT SUTURAL JUNCTION LIGATIVE SYNDETIC VINCULAR

CONNING TOWER SAIL

CONNIVANCE CAHOOT CAHOOTS

CONNIVE ABET PLOT WINK BLINK CABAL ASSENT FOMENT INCITE COLLUDE
(— AT MEDICAL TREATMENT) COVER

CONNOISSEUR JUDGE CRITIC EXPERT CAMEIST EPICURE GOURMET CIDERIST DILETANT LAPIDARY

CONNOTATION DEPTH INTENT MEANING

CONNUBIAL MARITAL CONJUGAL DOMESTIC

CONQUER GET WIN BEAT BEST DOWN FIRK GAIN LICK ROUT TAME WHIP CRUSH DAUNT DEBEL EVICT DEBELL DEFEAT EVINCE HUMBLE IMPORT MASTER REDUCE SUBDUE VICTOR ACQUIRE PREVAIL SUBJECT SURPASS TRIUMPH OVERCOME OVERGANG SURMOUNT VANQUISH

CONQUEROR HERO VICTOR WINNER TRIUMPHER

CONQUEST MASTERY SCALING TRIUMPH VICTORY WINNING

CONSANGUINEOUS AKIN CARNAL KINDRED NATURAL RELATED

CONSANGUINITY BLOOD NASAB KINSHIP AFFINITY

CONSCIENCE WORD DAENA HEART INWIT SENSE SCRUPLE THOUGHT

CONSCIENTIOUS FAIR JUST EXACT RIGID EIDENT HONEST STRICT DUTIFUL UPRIGHT FAITHFUL

CONSCIENTIOUSNESS RELIGION

CONSCIOUS KEEN WARE ALIVE AWAKE AWARE JERRY GUILTY FEELING KNOWING WITTING RATIONAL SENSIBLE SENTIENT CONSCIENT

CONSCIOUSNESS EGO HEART SENSE SPIRIT ANOESIS FEELING SENTIENT AWARENESS

CONSCRIPT LEVY CHOCO DRAFT ENROL ENLIST MUSTER DRAFTEE DRAUGHT RECRUIT JEANJEAN

CONSCRIPTION LEVY

CONSECRATE VOW FAIN HOLY SAIN SEAL BLESS DEIFY HEAVE SACRE ANOINT DEVOTE HALLOW ORDAIN SACRATE CONSACRE DEDICATE SANCTIFY

CONSECRATED BLEST OBLATE SACRED VOTARY VOTIVE BLESSED SACRATE HALLOWED HIERATIC

CONSECRATION IHRAM SACRE SACRY SACRING HOLINESS

CONSECUTIVELY TOGETHER

CONSECUTIVENESS SEQUENCE

CONSENT HEAR AGREE ALLOW GRANT YIELD ACCEDE ACCORD ASSENT BETEEM COMPLY CONCUR PERMIT APPROVE GOODWILL

CONSENTIENT UNANIMOUS

CONSEQUENCE AND END BORE EVENT FORCE FRUIT ISSUE SUITE WORTH BROWST CHARGE EFFECT ENTAIL FIGURE GROWTH IMPORT MOMENT REPUTE RESULT SEQUEL WEIGHT CONCERN OUTCOME PRODUCE SEQUELA SEQUENT AFTERING INTEREST MISCHIEF OCCASION
(DONE IN —) PURSUANT
(HARMFUL —) EVIL
(PL.) AFTERINGS

CONSEQUENT COMES THESIS ADJUNCT

CONSEQUENTIAL HEAVY POMPOUS COROLLARY

CONSEQUENTLY SO ERGO THEN THUS HENCE LATER PURSUANT PRESENTLY

CONSERTAL SUTURAL

CONSERVATION HUSBANDRY

CONSERVATISM BOURBONISM

CONSERVATIVE SAFE TORY FUSTY STAID FABIAN HUNKER STABLE BOURBON DIEHARD MODERATE UNIONIST

CONSERVATORY STOVE SCHOOL ACADEMY

CONSERVE CAN JAM SAVE GUARD GUMBO JELLY DEFEND SECURE SHIELD UPHOLD HUSBAND PROTECT SEATRON SUSTAIN MAINTAIN PRESERVE
(GRAPE —) UVATE

CONSIDER AIM BAT LET SEE CALL CAST DEEM GAUM GIVE HASH HEED HOLD MULL MUSE RATE SEEM TAKE TALE VIEW VISE WISE ALLOW BESEE COUNT ENTER ETTLE JUDGE PANSE POISE SPELL STUDY THINK VERSE VOLVE WEIGH ADVERT ADVISE

BEHOLD DEBATE DEVISE DIGEST
ESTEEM EXPEND FIGURE IMPUTE
PONDER REASON RECKON REGARD
REWARD SURVEY ACCOUNT BELIEVE
BETHINK CANVASS CONSULT
EXAMINE INSPECT PREPEND
REFLECT RESPECT REVOLVE
SUPPOSE COGITATE ESTIMATE
MEDITATE PERPENSE RUMINATE
(— **FAVORABLY**) CREDIT
(— **PROS AND CONS**) ARGUE
(— **SEPARATELY**) SPECIALIZE
CONSIDERABLE GAY GEY FAIR
GOOD CANNY GEYAN GREAT LARGE
SMART STARK GOODLY PRETTY
GOODISH HEALTHY INTENSE
NOTABLE SEVERAL HANDSOME
POWERFUL SENSIBLE UNLITTLE
CONSIDERABLY GAY GEY WELL
GEYAN PRETTY SMARTLY
CONSIDERATE KIND MILD NICE
GENTLE TENDER CAREFUL HEEDFUL
PRUDENT SERIOUS DELICATE
GRACIOUS
CONSIDERATENESS GRACE
(**MUTUAL** —) SHU
CONSIDERATION GUT GUTS SAKE
COUNT PRICE STUDY TOPIC ADVICE
ASPECT COMITY DEBATE ESTEEM
MOMENT MOTIVE NOTICE REASON
REFLEX REGARD SURVEY ACCOUNT
INSIGHT PREMIUM RESPECT
THOUGHT ALTRUISM COURTESY
DELICACY EMINENCE EMPHASIS
GRATUITY SANCTION
(**BASIC** —) BEDROCK
(**ETHICAL** —) SCRUPLE
(**THOUGHTFUL** —) THEORIA
CONSIDERED ADVISED DELIBERATE
CONSIDERING IF FOR SINCE SEEING
CONSIGN DOOM GIVE MAIL SEND
SHIP ALLOT AWARD CHECK DIGHT
REMIT SHIFT YIELD ASSIGN COMMIT
DESIGN DEVOTE REMAND RESIGN
ADDRESS BETEACH CONFIDE
DELIVER DEPOSIT ENTRUST
INTRUST BEQUEATH DELEGATE
RELEGATE TRANSFER
(— **FOR DESTRUCTION**) ACCURSE
(— **TO OBLIVION**) BURY EXPUNGE
(— **TO PERDITION**) DAMN CONDEMN
CONSIGNEE AGENT FACTOR
SHIPPER RECEIVER
CONSIGNMENT INVOICE FOREDOOM
SHIPMENT
(— **OF TEA**) BREAK
CONSIST LIE HOLD RELY REST
DWELL EXIST STAND INHERE RESIDE
CONTAIN EMBRACE COMPRISE
CONSISTENCY BODY UNION
DEGREE CONCENT CONCORD
HARMONY KEEPING COMPAGES
EVENNESS FIRMNESS SOLIDITY
SYMMETRY
CONSISTENT EVEN FIRM STEADY
DURABLE LOGICAL UNIFORM
COHERENT ENDURING SUITABLE
(— **WITH NATURE**) KIND KINDLY
(**BE** —) ACCORD

(**MAKE** —) CLEAR
CONSOLATION SOP FINE RELIEF
SOLACE COMFORT SPIRITING
CONSOLE CALM ALLAY ANCON
CHEER ORGAN TABLE SOLACE
SOOTHE BRACKET CABINET
COMFORT RELIEVE SUPPORT
SUSTAIN CARTOUCH
CONSOLER PARACLETE
CONSOLIDATE COG MIX KNIT MASS
POOL WELD BLEND CLOSE MERGE
UNIFY UNITE HARDEN MINGLE
SETTLE COMBINE COMPACT
ANKYLOSE COALESCE COMPRESS
CONDENSE ORGANIZE SOLIDIFY
CONSOLIDATED CONFLATE
CONSOLS GOSCHENS
CONSONANCE ACCORD UNISON
HARMONY DIAPASON DIAPENTE
SYMPATHY SYMPHONY
CONSONANT WAW MUTE STOP
DENTAL FORTIS LABIAL LETTER
LIQUID SONANT UNISON LATERAL
MUTABLE PALATAL SPIRANT UNIFIED
ALVEOLAR ASPIRATA ASPIRATE
BILABIAL EJECTIVE GEMINATE
HARMONIC SUITABLE
(**CONSECUTIVE** —**S**) CLUSTER
(**SMOOTH** —) LENE LENIS
(**TENSE AND STRONG** —) FORTIS
(**VOICELESS** —) SPIRATE
CONSORT COT AIDE ALLY JOIN
MATE WIFE YOKE GROUP UNITE
ACCORD ATTEND ESCORT MINGLE
SPOUSE COMPANY COMRADE
CONCERT DAMKINA EMPRESS
HUSBAND PARTNER ACCUSTOM
ASSEMBLY PRINCESS
CONSPECTUS LIST APERCU SURVEY
OUTLINE THEATER THEORIC
SPECTRUM SYNOPSIS
CONSPICUOUS BIG BOLD CLEAR
FAMED PLAIN STARY EXTANT
FAMOUS MARKED PATENT SIGNAL
BLATANT EMINENT GLARING
NOTABLE OBVIOUS POINTED
SALIENT SIGHTLY VISIBLE
APPARENT EMPHATIC FLAGRANT
KENSPECK MANIFEST STRIKING
CONSPIRACY COUP PLAN PLOT
RING CABAL COVIN JUNTO PARTY
COVINE SCHEME COMPACE
COMPACT COMPLOT INTRIGUE
CONSPIRATOR PACKER PLOTTER
SCHEMER
CONSPIRE ABET PACK PLOT UNITE
LEAGUE SCHEME COLLUDE
COMPLOT CONJURE CONNIVE
CONTRIVE
CONSTABLE COP BULL PEON SLOP
BEADLE BEAGLE HARMAN KAVASS
KEEPER WARDEN BAILIFF CORONER
DOZENER NUTHOOK OFFICER
STALLER SUBASHI ALGUAZIL
DOGBERRY TIPSTAFF
CONSTANCY ZEAL ARDOR FAITH
TRUTH FEALTY HONESTY LOYALTY
ONENESS DEVOTION FIDELITY
CONSTANT K SET EVEN FIRM JUST

LEAL TRUE FIXED LOYAL SOLID
STILL TIGHT TRIED ITHAND STABLE
STEADY CERTAIN CHRONIC
DURABLE FOREVER LASTING
REGULAR STAUNCH UNIFORM
DEFINITE ENDURING FAITHFUL
POSITIVE RESOLUTE SEDULOUS
STANDING
CONSTANTLY AWAY EVER ALWAYS
THRONG
CONSTELLATION ARA CUP FLY FOX
LEO APUS ARGO COLT CROW CRUX
DOVE GOAT GRUS HARE HARP LION
LYNX LYRA MAST PAVO PLOW SIGN
SWAN TAUR URSA VELA WAIN WOLF
ALTAR ARIES CAMEL CETUS CLOCK
CRANE DRACO EAGLE GROUP
HYDRA INDUS LEPUS LIBRA LUPUS
MALUS MENSA MUSCA NORMA
ORION PYXIS RAVEN TABLE VIRGO
WAGON WHALE ANTLIA AQUILA
AURIGA BOOTES CAELUM CANCER
CARINA CORVUS CRATER CYGNUS
DIPPER DORADO FORNAX GEMINI
HYDRUS INDIAN LIZARD OBELUS
OCTANS OKNARI PICTOR PISCES
PISCIS PLOUGH PUPPIS SCALES
SCUTUM TAURUS TIGRIS TOUCAN
TUCANA VOLANS ALGEBAR
CEPHEUS CLUSTER COLUMBA
COMPASS DOLPHIN FURNACE
GIRAFFE LACERTA MONARCH
OETAEUS PATTERN PEACOCK
PEGASUS PERSEUS PHOENIX
RHOMBUS SAGITTA SCORPIO
SERPENS SERPENT SEXTANS
SEXTANT XIPHIAS AQUARIUS
ASTERISM CHAMPION CIRCINUS
CYNOSURE EQUULEUS ERIDANUS
HERCULES HERDSMAN KASHYAPA
QUADRANS REINDEER RETICULE
SCORPION SCORPIUS SCULPTOR
TRIANGLE
CONSTERNATION FEAR ALARM
PANIC DISMAY FRIGHT HORROR
TERROR TREPIDITY
CONSTITUENCY BOROUGH
CONSTITUENT ATOM ITEM PART
PIECE VOTER DETAIL FACTOR
FUSAIN MATTER MEMBER SIMPLE
ELECTOR ELEMENT FEATURE
TAGMEME INTEGRAL
(— **OF BLOOD SERUM**) OPSONIN
(— **OF CLINKER**) ALITE CELITE
(— **OF COAL**) DURAIN FUSAIN
(— **OF DURAIN**) ATTRITUS
(—**S OF BEER**) EXTRACT
(**NECESSARY** —) ESSENCE
(**PL.**) MATTER BIOSESTON
CONSTITUTE BE FIX SET FORM
MAKE ENACT ERECT FORGE FOUND
SHAPE SPELL CREATE DEPUTE
GRAITH ORDAIN APPOINT COMPOSE
FASHION STATION COMPOUND
COMPRISE
CONSTITUTION LAW SET CODE
SETT BEING CANON FRAME HUMOR
SETUP STATE CHARTE CRASIS
CUSTOM DESIGN ESTATE HEALTH

NATURE TEMPER CHARTER HABITUS
SYNODAL GRONDWET GRUNDLOV
HABITUDE PHYSIQUE POLITEIA
(— **STATE**) CONNECTICUT
(**BODILY** —) HABIT SPIRITS
(**GERMINAL** —) HEREDITY
CONSTITUTIONAL WALK HECTIC
INNATE RIKKEN EXERCISE
CONSTITUTIVE FORMAL
CONSTRAIN ART PUT TIE ARCT
BEND BIND CURB DOOM FAIN HALE
HOLD LEAD URGE CHAIN CHECK
CLASP COART CRAMP DETER DRIVE
FORCE IMPEL LIMIT PRESS COERCE
COMPEL EVINCE OBLIGE RAVISH
SECURE STRAIN THRAST ASTRICT
CONFINE CONJURE ENFORCE
OPPRESS REPRESS VIOLATE
COMPRESS CONCLUDE DISTRESS
PERFORCE POUNDAGE RELIGATE
RESTRAIN
CONSTRAINED FAIN TIED VAIN
BOUND FORCED FORMAL UNEASY
COACTED
CONSTRAINING UNEASY
COMPELLENT
CONSTRAINT BOND CRAMP FORCE
DURESS STRESS RESERVE STRAINT
COERCION DISTRESS PRESSURE
CONSTRICT TIE BIND CURB GRIP
CHOKE CRAMP LIMIT STRAP
HAMPER SHRINK STRAIN STRAIT
ASTRICT DEFLATE SQUEEZE
STIFFEN TIGHTEN ASTRINGE
COMPRESS CONDENSE CONTRACT
DISTRAIN RESTRICT
CONSTRICTED STRAIT STRICT
ADENOID
CONSTRICTION KNOT CHOKE
ISTHMUS STENOSIS
CONSTRICTOR BOA ABOMA
GUAVINA
CONSTRUCT UP BIG ATOM FORM
IDEA LEVY MAKE REAR BUILD
CRAFT DIGHT EDIFY ERECT FRAME
MODEL BURROW DEDUCE DESIGN
DEVISE FABRIC ARRANGE CARPENT
COMBINE COMPILE COMPOSE
CONCEPT CONFECT CONTOUR
EXTRUCT FASHION CONSTRUE
ENGINEER PRACTISE
(— **ARCH**) TURN
CONSTRUCTED BUILT EDIFICATE
(**CAREFULLY** —) CLEVER
(**HASTILY** —) GIMCRACK JIMCRACK
CONSTRUCTION BOOM ALTAR
FRAME FABRIC MONSTER SYNESIS
APPROACH BUILDING DWELLING
ERECTION
(— **OF NAME**) ABSTRACTION
(**ABSTRACT** —) STABILE
(**GRAMMATICAL** —) SYNESIS
APPOSITION
(**POINTED** —) BEAK
CONSTRUCTIVE FACTIVE HELPFUL
VIRTUAL CREATIVE IMPLICIT
INFERRED
CONSTRUCTOR ENGINEER
CONSTRUE INFER PARSE STRUE

INTEND RENDER ANALYZE CONSTER
DISSECT EXPLAIN EXPOUND
RESOLVE
CONSUL SUFFECT
CONSULT LOOK SEEK TALK ADVISE
CONFER EMPARL IMPARL COUNSEL
RESOLVE
CONSULTANT EXPERT ADVISER
COUNSEL
CONSULTATION ADVICE COUNCIL
COUNSEL
CONSUME EAT SUP USE BOLT BURN
CHEW FANG FARE FEED FRET GULP
IDLE KILL RUST TAKE TUCK WEAR
DALLY DRINK FLAME LURCH RAVEN
SHIFT SPEND TOOTH WASTE
ABSORB BEZZLE BROWSE CANKER
DEVOUR ENGAGE EXPEND FINISH
IMBIBE INHALE PERISH PUNISH
VANISH CORRODE DESTROY
DWINDLE ENGROSS EXHAUST
SWALLOW CONTRIVE SQUANDER
(— **TOTALLY**) KILL
(— **VORACIOUSLY**) HOG
CONSUMED ALL PAU DOWN BURNT
SPENT COMBUST OUTWORN
CONSUMING EATING SACRED
BURNING FLAMING
CONSUMMATE END FINE FULL RIPE
CLOSE IDEAL SHEER ARRANT
EFFECT FINISH FULFIL RATIFY
ACHIEVE CONSUME CROWNED
FULFILL PERFECT PERFORM
ABSOLUTE COMPLETE MERIDIAN
THOROUGH
CONSUMMATION PERIOD UPSHOT
CONSUMPTION USE DECAY WASTE
EXPENSE WASTING PHTHISIS
SPENDING
CONSUMPTIVE LUNGY HECTIC
PREDATORY
CONTACT ABUT JOIN KISS MEET
SLED CROSS TOUCH TRUCK UNION
ARRIVE IMPACT SYZYGY EPHAPSE
HOLDING MEETING TACTION
JUNCTION TANGENCY TOUCHING
(— **OF TELEGRAPH KEY**) ANVIL
(**3-POINT** —) OSCNODE
(**ELECTRICAL** —) HUB HUBB
(**EVIL** —) CONTAGION
(**FLEETING** —) BRUSH
(**FORCIBLE** —) IMPACT
CONTAGION POX TAINT VIRUS
MIASMA POISON
CONTAGIOUS TAKING NOXIOUS
SMITTLE CATCHING EPIDEMIC
CONTAIN RUN HAVE HOLD KEEP
STOW TAKE CARRY CHECK CLOSE
COVER HOUSE EMBODY ENFOLD
ENSEAM HARBOR RETAIN COMPILE
EMBRACE ENCLOSE INCLUDE
INVOLVE RECEIVE SUBSUME
SUSTAIN COMPRISE RESTRAIN
CONTAINED IN
CONTAINER BAG BOX CAN CUP HAT
JAR JUG KEG LUG NIN PAN POD
POT TIN TUB URN VAT BAIL BOMB
CAGE CASE CASK CRIB DRUM EWER
FILE FLAT JACK SACK SALT SILO

SINK SKIP TANK TUBE VASE ALBUM
BASIN BILLY CADDY CHEST CRATE
CRUET DEWAR EMPTY FLASK GLASS
GOURD POUCH SCOOP SCRAY
STAND STOOP STOUP BARREL
BASKET BOTTLE BUCKET BUSHEL
CARBOY CARTON CASTER CASTOR
COOLER CRADLE DUSTER HAMPER
HATBOX HOLDER INKPOT PICNIC
RABBIT RIDDLE SHAKER WITJAR
AEROSOL BANDBOX BLADDER
CAPSULE COASTER COSTREL
CRISPER FEEDBOX HANAPER
HOLDALL INKWELL PACKAGE
SEEDLIP SHIPPER STEEPER
CANISTER DECANTER DEMIJOHN
ENVELOPE HOGSHEAD HONEYPOT
INHOLDER KNAPSACK PUNCHEON
SLIPCASE
(— **FOR BEER**) GROWLER
(— **FOR COINS**) BANK
(— **FOR EXPLOSIVE CHARGE**) CAP
(— **FOR GOLD DUST**) SHAMMY
(— **FOR HOLY OIL**) STOCK
(— **FOR PLANTS**) BAND
(— **MADE OF HOLLOW LOG**) GUM
(**5-GALLON** —) JERICAN JERRICAN
(**COFFEE** —) INSET
(**EARTHENWARE** —) STEAN
(**FIRECLAY** —) SETTER
(**RAILROAD** —**S**) BUNKER
(**SHELVED** —) CABIN
(**SHIPPING** —) KIT
(**SNUFF** —) WEASAND
(**TOBACCO** —) SARATOGA
(**VENTILATED** —) CHIP
(PL.) CONVEYER CONVEYOR
CONTAMINATE FOUL HARM SLUR
SMIT SOIL STAIN SULLY TAINT
BEFOUL DEBASE DEFILE INFECT
INJURE POISON ATTAINT CORRUPT
DEBAUCH FLYBLOW POLLUTE
TARNISH VITIATE DISHONOR
CONTAMINATED DIRTY DEGRADED
INFECTED
CONTAMINATION INFECTION
TAINTMENT
(— **IN GLASS**) STONE
CONTE TALE CRAYON
CONTEMN HATE FLOUT SCORN
SPURN REJECT SLIGHT DESPISE
DISDAIN CONTEMPT INDIGNIFY
CONTEMPLATE FACE MUSE PLAN
SCAN VIEW DEIGN STUDY THINK
WEIGH DESIGN PONDER REGARD
SURVEY CHERISH PROPOSE
REFLECT CONSIDER ENVISAGE
ENVISION MEDITATE
CONTEMPLATION MUSE STUDY
DHYANA MUSING PRAYER REGARD
THEORY INSIGHT MOONING
REQUEST THEORIA PETITION
CONTEMPLATIVE BROODY PENSIVE
THEORIC STUDIOUS
CONTEMPORANEOUS COEVAL
LIVING MODERN CURRENT EXISTING
CONTEMPORARY EQUAL COEVAL
FELLOW CURRENT PRESENT
YEALING EXISTENT

CONTEMPT PRUT SCORN SHAME
SNEER SLIGHT CONTEMN DESPECT
DESPITE DISDAIN HETHING
MOCKERY DEFIANCE DERISION
DESPISAL DISGRACE MISPRIZE
CONTEMPTIBLE LOW BASE MEAN
VILE BALLY CHEAP DIRTY DUSTY
LOUSY MANGY MUCKY PETTY
POCKY RUDDY SCALD SORRY
ABJECT BLOODY GRUBBY MEASLY
PALTRY SCABBY SCUMMY SCURVY
SHABBY SNOTTY SORDID YELLOW
BROKING LIGHTLY PEEVISH PITIFUL
SCALLED SCORNED SHITTEN
SLAVISH SQUALID BAUBLING
BEGGARLY FRIPPERY INFAMOUS
INFERIOR PITIABLE SNEAKING
UNWORTHY WRETCHED
CONTEMPTIBLENESS BEGGARY
CONTEMPTUOUS SLIGHT SNOOTY
HAUGHTY LIGHTLY SLIGHTY
SPITOUS ARROGANT FLOUTING
INSOLENT SCOFFING SCORNFUL
CONTEND TUG VIE WAR WIN CAMP
COCK COPE DEAL FRAB KEMP PLEA
RACE WAGE ARGUE BANDY BRAWL
CHIDE CLAIM FIGHT FLITE PRESS
ASSERT BATTLE BICKER BREAST
BUCKLE BUFFET BUSTLE COMBAT
DEBATE DIFFER JOSTLE JUSTLE
MEDDLE OPPOSE REASON STRIVE
BARGAIN COMPETE CONTEST
COUNTER DISPUTE PROPUGN
QUARREL SCUFFLE STICKLE
SUSTAIN WRESTLE CONFLICT
CONTRAST CONTRIVE MAINTAIN
MILITATE SQUABBLE STRUGGLE
CONTENT PAY CALM EASE GIST
GLAD PAID RATH APPAY HAPPY
HUMOR RATHE SERVE AMOUNT
CUBAGE PLEASE APPEASE
CONTENU GRATIFY REPLETE
SATIATE SATISFY SUFFICE WILLING
BLISSFUL CAPACITY CONTINEU
WILCWEME
(**—S OF STOMACH**) COOKIES
(**ENERGY —**) STRENGTH
(**HEAT —**) ENTHALPY
(**SUPERFICIAL —S**) AREA
(**PL.**) LINING
CONTENTED COZY FAIN VAIN QUIET
SATED CONTENT PLEASED
CHEERFUL
CONTENTION WAR BAIT BATE FEUD
PLEA RIOT TIFF TOIL BROIL CHEST
STRUT BICKER COMBAT DEBATE
ESTRIF JANGLE STRIFE CHIDING
CONTEKE CONTEST DISCORD
DISPUTE OPINION QUARREL
RIVALRY WRANGLE ARGUMENT
CONFLICT SQUABBLE STRUGGLE
VARIANCE
CONTENTIOUS CROSS BATEFUL
PEEVISH PERVERSE
CONTENTMENT EASE BLISS
HEAVEN PLEASURE
CONTERMINOUS NEXT ADJACENT
FRONTIER PROXIMAL
CONTEST GO IT BEE FIX RUN SUE

TRY VIE AGON BOUT CAMP COPE
DUEL FEUD FRAY GAME HOLD KEMP
LAKE MART PULL RACE SHOW SPAR
TIFF TILT TURN YOKE AGONY
ARGUE BROIL CLASH DERBY EVENT
FIGHT MATCH PLATE PRIZE ROLEO
SCRUB SPORT TRIAL WAGER
ACTION ADJURE AFFRAY BATTLE
BISLEY COMBAT DEBATE DEFEND
FLIGHT OPPOSE RESIST RUBBER
SEESAW STRIFE STRIVE TUSSLE
YOKING BARGAIN BRABBLE CLASSIC
COMPETE CONTECK CONTEND
DERAIGN DISPUTE GRAPPLE
PROTEST SHUTOUT TOURNEY
WARFARE ARGUMENT CONCOURS
CONFLICT DOGFIGHT HANDICAP
LITIGATE SKIRMISH SLUGFEST
STRIVING STRUGGLE WALKAWAY
WALKOVER
(**— IN WORDS**) SPAR
(**— NARROWLY WON**) SQUEAKER
(**DRAWN —**) TIE DRAW STALEMATE
(**MOCK —**) SCIAMACHY
(**RACING —**) DRAG
(**REAPING —**) KEMP
CONTESTANT VIER RIVAL WAGER
PLAYER AGONIST ENTRANT
SCRATCH FINALIST PROSPECT
CONTIGUOUS NEXT NIGH NEARBY
TANGENT ABUTTING ADJACENT
TOUCHING
CONTIGUITY ADJACENCY CONFINITY
IMMEDIACY
CONTINENT ASIA MASS SOBER
AFRICA CHASTE EUROPE CONTENT
CAPACITY MAINLAND MODERATE
ABSTINENT
CONTINGENCY BOOK CASE EVENT
CHANCE ADJUNCT CONTACT
VENTURE ACCIDENT CASUALTY
FORTUITY INCIDENT JUNCTURE
PROSPECT
CONTINGENT CASUAL CHANCE
DOUBTFUL EVENTUAL INCHOATE
TOUCHING
CONTINUAL STILL HOURLY ENDLESS
ETERNAL LASTING REGULAR
UNDYING UNIFORM CONSTANT
ENDURING UNBROKEN
CONTINUALLY AY AYE EVER STILL
ALWAYS EVERLY HOURLY STEADY
ENDLESS ETERNAL FOREVER
MINUTELY
CONTINUANCE STAY WHEN DELAY
LEASE SEQUEL DURANCE LASTING
ABIDANCE DURATION SURVIVAL
CONTINUANT OPEN LIQUID
DURATIVE
CONTINUATION SEQUEL DURATION
(**— OF DOUBLET**) BASQUE
CONTINUE BE DO ABY SUE BIDE
DURE HOLD JUMP KEEP LAST LIVE
STAY TIDE ABIDE CARRY EXIST
PERGE STICK UNITE ABEGGE
BELEVE ENDURE EXTEND PURSUE
REMAIN RESUME BELEAVE CONNECT
CONTUNE PERSIST PROCEED
PROLONG SUBSIST SURVIVE

SUSTAIN PROTRACT
(**— UNALTERED**) TARRY
CONTINUED STILL SERIAL CHRONIC
CONSTANT
CONTINUING DURABLE DURATIVE
(**— FOR LONG TIME**) CHRONIC
(**— TO BE**) YET
CONTINUITY TRACT SCRIPT
COHESION SCENARIO CONTINUUM
CONTINUOUS RUN EVEN ANEND
EIDENT ENTIRE EYDENT STEADY
CHRONIC ENDLESS RUNNING
UNBROKEN
CONTINUOUSLY AWAY EVER FAST
ANEND OUTRIGHT
CONTORT WRY BEND COIL CURL
TURN WARP GNARL SCREW TWIST
WREST CRINGE DEFORM WRITHE
DISTORT PERVERT SQUINCH
WREATHE OBVOLUTE
CONTORTED WRY WRIED KNOTTY
CRISPED KNOTTED SCREWED
WRITHEN OBVOLUTE
CONTORTION SCREW STITCH
WRITHE MURGEON WORKING
CONTOUR FORM LINE CURVE
GRAPH SHAPE SWEEP AMOEBA
FIGURE OUTLINE PROFILE
CARTOUCH CONTORNO MANDORLA
PLANFORM TOURNURE
(**— ON SHIP**) HANCE
CONTRA CONTRE AGAINST COUNTER
OPPOSED
CONTRABAND HOT GOODS ILLEGAL
ILLICIT SMUGGLED UNLAWFUL
CONTRABASS BASS OCTOBASS
CONTRACT GET BOND DRAW FARM
FORM HALE KNIT PACT SALE TACK
CATCH CLOSE COACT COUCH
CRAMP FEVER INCUR LEASE LIMIT
NEXUM PINCH SHRUG SNURP
CARTEL COCKLE COMMIT CRINGE
ENGAGE FUTURE GATHER HIRING
INDENT LESSEN MUTUUM NARROW
PLEDGE POLICY PROMPT PUCKER
REDUCE SHRIMP SHRINK SUBLET
TREATY ABRIDGE BARGAIN
BUMMERY CHARTER COMPACT
CRUMPLE CURTAIL DEFLATE
FIDUCIA MANDATE PROMISE
SCRUNCH SHORTEN SHRIVEL
SOCIETY WRINKLE ASSIENTO
BOTTOMRY CONDENSE COVENANT
HANDFAST HARDNESS LOCATION
RESTRICT STEELBOW STRAITEN
SYNGRAPH
(**— BROW**) FROWN
(**— INTO WRINKLES**) KNIT
(**BRIDGE —**) SOLO AUCTION
(**MARRIAGE —**) KETUBA AFFIANCE
HANDFAST BETROTHAL SPONSALIA
CONTRACTED BOXY CRAMP
BOOKED ASTRICT INGROWN
INSULAR SCREWED CONTRACT
CONTRACTILITY MOTILITY
CONTRACTION HM ANT NIP TIC TIS
AINT CANT ISNT KNIT MAAM WONT
CRAMP HADNT HASNT NISUS SPASM
CRASIS GATHER INTAKE MUSTNT

SHRINK TWITCH ELISION EPITOME
WOULDNT APNEUSIS TRACTION
(— OF HEART) SYSTOLE
(— OF SYLLABLES) SYNIZESIS
(PL.) TREPPE

CONTRACTOR KHOT BUTTY
BUILDER REMOVER SUPPLIER

CONTRADICT DENY BELIE CROSS
REBUT FORBID IMPUGN NEGATE
OPPOSE RECANT REFUTE COUNTER
GAINSAY REVERSE WITHSAY
CONTRARY DISPROVE DOWNFACE
NEGATIVE OUTSTAND

CONTRADICTION DENIAL PARADOX
WITHSAW ANTILOGY ANTIMONY
ANTILOQUY

CONTRADICTORY OPPOSE
ANTINOME OPPOSITE THWARTING

CONTRAPTION RIG TOOL DEVICE
GADGET JIGGER CONCERN MACHINE

CONTRARILY BACKWARD
CRISSCROSS

CONTRARIWISE CROSS CONTRA
CONTRARY

CONTRARY BALKY KICKY SNIVY
AVERSE CONTRA ORNERY SNIVEY
ADVERSE COUNTER CRABBED
FROWARD HOSTILE INVERSE
OPPOSED PEEVISH RESTIVE
REVERSE WAYWARD ABSONANT
ANTIPODE CAPTIOUS CONTRAIR
INIMICAL OPPOSITE PERVERSE
PETULANT SINGULAR
(— TO HAPPINESS) ILL
(— TO REASON) SILLY
(— TO) BESIDE AGAINST ATHWART

CONTRAST CLASH STRIFE COMPARE
CONTEND DISCORD ANTIMONY
DIVISION DYNAMICS OPPOSITE

CONTRAVENE DEFY DENY HINDER
OPPOSE THWART DISPUTE VIOLATE
INFRINGE OBSTRUCT

CONTRAVENTION SIN VICE CRIME
BREACH OFFENSE

CONTRETEMPS SLIP BONER HITCH
MISHAP SCRAPE ACCIDENT
INCIDENT

CONTRIBUTE AID ANTE FORK GIVE
HELP MAKE TEND CAUSE ENTER
GROUT SERVE ASSIST BESTOW
CONCUR CONFER DONATE PUNGLE
SUPPLY TENDER ANIMATE CONDUCE
FURNISH FURTHER PROVIDE

CONTRIBUTION BIT SUM TAX ALMS
BOON GIFT SCOT SHOT ESSAY
INPUT SHARE IMPOST SYMBOL
ARTICLE LARGESS PAYMENT
PRESENT RENEWAL WRITING
DONATION EXACTION OFFERING
ROMESHOT

CONTRITE WORN SORRY HUMBLE
RUEFUL PENITENT SORROWFUL

CONTRITION SORE SORROW
PENANCE

CONTRIVANCE (ALSO SEE DEVICE)
ART BOW FLY GIN JET JIG LEG
DROP GEAR HARP JACK KITE LURE
PLAN PLOT RASP REED TOOL
CARRY CHECK DOLLY DRAFT FLOAT

FRAME GUIDE HICKY KNACK MIXER
QUIPU SHIFT SNARE STOCK
ANCHOR DAMPER DECEIT DESIGN
DEVICE DOCTOR DOLLIE ENGINE
FABRIC FANGLE GABION GADGET
GIMBAL HANGER HARROW HEATER
HICKEY HOLDER JIGGER JINKER
MARKER MORTAR MUZZLE POLICY
RATTLE SCHEME SLUICE SPIDER
TEASEL WEIGHT WHEEZE WINDAS
WRENCH BOLSTER CLEANER
CLEARER CONCERN COUPLER
CUNNING DINGBAT DRAUGHT
FICTION FISHWAY HUMIDOR
KNOCKER MACHINE PAGEANT
PROJECT REDUCER ROASTER
SCRAPER SHEBANG SPANNER
STOPPER TOASTER TRIPPER
VOLVELL ADAPTION ARTIFICE
CROTCHET DUTCHMAN EUPYRION
FAKEMENT FORECAST GOVERNOR
INDUSTRY MOLITION OXIDATOR
REGISTER RESOURCE SCISSORS
SQUEEZER SUBTLETY WITCRAFT

CONTRIVE GET LAY BREW CAST
DRAW FIND FIRK MAKE PLAN PLOT
WORK FRAME FUDGE HATCH SHAPE
STAGE WEAVE AFFORD DESIGN
DEVISE DIVINE ENGINE FIGURE
INVENT MANAGE SCHEME WANGLE
ACHIEVE AGITATE COMMENT
COMPASS CONCOCT CONJURE
CONSULT CONTEND FASHION
IMAGINE MACHINE PROCURE
PROJECT REPAREL CONSPIRE
ENGINEER FORECAST INTRIGUE
PURCHASE

CONTRIVED SLICK STAGED
TIMBERED

CONTRIVER DAEDAL DAEDALUS
ENGINEER

CONTRIVING FASHION SCHEMERY

CONTROL BIT LAP LAW MAN POT
RUN CONN CURB EGIS GRIP HAND
HANK HAVE HOLD REDE REIN RULE
STAY SWAY WIND AEGIS BOOST
CHARM CHECK COACT DAUNT
DUMMY GRASP GUIDE LEASH
ORDER POWER STEER SWING
THEAT TREAT VERGE WIELD
BANDON BRIDLE CHARGE CLUTCH
COERCE CORNER DANGER DIRECT
EMPERY GOVERN HANDLE MANAGE
POCKET TEMPER AMENAGE
COMMAND CONDUCT CONTAIN
CUSTODY FORBEAR MASTERY
QUALIFY STRINGS COACTION
DOMINATE DOMINIUM IMPERIUM
MODERATE REGULATE SERVOTAB
(— A BULL) MANDAR
(— OF RESOURCES) HUSBANDRY
(ABSOLUTE —) BECK
(FIRE —) BLANKET
(GOVERNMENT —) SQUADRISM
(NONCLERICAL —) LAICISM LAICITY

CONTROLLED STEADY SERVILE
CONTAINED

CONTROLLER FENCER MASTER
STARTER

(SPEED —) GOVERNOR RHEOCRAT

CONTROLLING MASTER LEADING
DOMINANT HEGEMONIC

CONTROVERSIAL ERISTIC POLEMIC

CONTROVERSIALIST ERISTIC
POLEMIC DISPUTANT GLADIATOR

CONTROVERSY PLEA SPAT SUIT
CHEST FUROR BATTLE COMBAT
DEBATE FURORE HASSEL HASSLE
HOORAH HURRAH STRIFE TUSSLE
DISPUTE POLEMIC QUARREL
WRANGLE ARGUMENT TRAVERSE
(ART OF —) POLEMICS

CONTROVERT DENY FACE MOOT
ARGUE DEBATE DEFEND OPPOSE
OPPUGN REFUTE CONTEST DISPUTE
GAINSAY DISPROVE

CONTUMACIOUS UNRULY RIOTOUS
CONTUMAX INSOLENT MUTINOUS
PERVERSE STUBBORN

CONTUMELY ABUSE SCORN INSULT
CONTECK DISDAIN REPROOF
UPBRAID CONTEMPT RUDENESS

CONTUSE BEAT POUND THUMP
BRUISE INJURE SQUEEZE

CONTUSION POUND BRUISE

CONUNDRUM PUN WHIM ENIGMA
PUZZLE RIDDLE CONCEIT
CROTCHET

CONURE ARATINGA

CONVALESCE MEND GUARISH
RECOVER

CONVENANCE FORM

CONVENE SIT CALL HOLD MEET
UNITE GATHER MUSTER SUMMON
CONVENT CONVOKE ASSEMBLE
CONVERGE

CONVENIENCE GAIN URINAL
LEISURE COMMODITY

CONVENIENT FIT GAIN HEND HANDY
HENDE READY CLEVER FITTED
PROPER SUITED USEFUL ADAPTED
AVENANT COMMODE HELPFUL
BECOMING EXPEDITE SUITABLE

CONVENIENTLY HANDILY CLEVERLY

CONVENT ABBEY TEKKE TEKYA
CENOBY COVENT FRIARY PRIORY
CONVENT MEETING RECLUSE
CLOISTER LAMASERY

CONVENTION DIET FEIS FORM MISE
RULE TABU SYNOD TABOO USAGE
CARTEL CAUCUS CUSTOM TREATY
DECORUM MEETING ASSEMBLY
ASSIENTO CONCLAVE CONGRESS
CONTRACT COVENANT PRACTICE
(LONG-ESTABLISHED —) TRADITION
(STAGE —) ASIDE
(PL.) DECENCIES

CONVENTIONAL MORE NOMIC
RIGHT TRITE USUAL DECENT
FORMAL MODISH PROPER CORRECT
REGULAR ACADEMIC ACCEPTED
CUSTOMARY

CONVENTIONALITY FORM
ACADEMISM FORMALITY GRUNDYISM

CONVENTIONALIZE STYLIZE

CONVERGE JOIN MEET FOCUS
CONCUR CORNER DESCEND
APPROACH FOCALIZE

CONVERSANT ADEPT BUSIED EXPERT VERSED SKILLED FAMILIAR OCCUPIED

CONVERSATION SAY CALL CHAT CHIN RUNE TALE TALK CRACK PROSE CACKLE CONFAB DEVICE GOSSIP PARLEY POWWOW SPEECH YABBER CEILIDH COMMUNE CONDUCT PALAVER PURPOSE BACKCHAT BEHAVIOR CAUSERIE CHITCHAT COLLOGUE COLLOQUY DIALOGUE GIFFGAFF HARANGUE PARLANCE QUESTION
(— **BETWEEN WHALERS**) GAM

CONVERSATIONALIST TALKER CAUSEUR

CONVERSE CHAT CHIN LIVE MOVE TALK DWELL SPEAK CACKLE CONFER DEVISE HOMILY PARLEY REASON COMMUNE CONVERT DISCUSS OBVERSE PROPOSE REVERSE COLLOQUE EXCHANGE OPPOSITE QUESTION

CONVERSION CHANGE EXCHANGE
(— **INTO VAPOR**) FLASH
(— **OF IRON**) FINING

CONVERT TAW TURN WEND ALTER AMEND APPLY MAULA RENEW CHANGE DECODE DETECT DIRECT MAWALI NOVICE SHAIKH SOUPER COMMUTE CONCOCT RESOLVE RESTORE REVERSE ACTIVATE CONVERSE DISCIPLE NEOPHYTE PERSUADE
(— **COTTON**) LAP
(— **INTO LEATHER**) TAN TAW
(— **INTO LIQUID**) BREW
(— **INTO SOAP**) SAPONIFY
(— **INTO STEEL**) ACIERATE
(— **INTO STONE**) LAPIDIFY
(— **SOAP**) CLOSE
(— **TO CARBON**) CHAR

CONVERTER ROTARY SELECTOR

CONVERTIBLE AUTO DROPHEAD

CONVEX BOWED ARCHED CAMBER CURVED BULGING EMBOWED GIBBOUS ROUNDED

CONVEY JAG BEAR BOOK CART CEDE DEED DUCT HAVE LEAD MEAN PASS SEND SIGN TAKE TOTE WAIN WILL BRING CARRY DRIVE FETCH GRANT GUIDE HURRY STEAL ARRIVE ASSIGN CONVOY DEDUCE DELATE DEMISE DEVISE ELOIGN GIGGIT IMPART IMPORT REMOVE YMMOTE AUCTION CHANNEL CHARIOT CHARTER CONDUCT DELIVER DERRICK DISPONE DISPOSE LIGHTER RESTORE ALIENATE BEQUEATH DESCRIBE TRANSFER TRANSMIT
(— **AN ESTATE**) DEMISE
(— **BY ALLUSION**) IMPLY
(— **FORCIBLY**) HUSTLE
(— **LEGALLY**) DEED GRANT LEASE DEMISE ELOIGN DISPONE
(— **NEARER**) BRING
(— **SECRETLY**) CRIM

CONVEYANCE BUS CAR AUTO CART DEED DRAG GIFT LOAD SLED TAXI TRAM GRANT SEDAN STAGE TAUGA THEFT TRAIN WAGON DEMISE JINGLE CHARTER CONDUCT COURIER MACHINE RATTLER TRAILER TRAJECT TRANSIT TROLLEY VECTURE VEHICLE WAFTAGE CARRIAGE CARRYING CONVEYAL DELATION FERRIAGE STEALING TRANSFER

CONVEYOR LIFT WORM DRAPER LADDER SHAKER CARRIER CREEPER HURRIER SCRAPER CAROUSEL CONVEYER ELEVATOR

CONVICT LAG CAST FIND STAR ARGUE EXILE FELON LIFER PROVE TAINT ATTAIN FORCAT LAGGER TERMER TRUSTY APPROVE ATTAINT CAPTIVE CONDEMN CULPRIT EXPIREE IMPEACH REPROVE CRIMINAL JAILBIRD PRISONER REDARGUE SENTENCE

CONVICT FISH MANINI HINALEA

CONVICTION CREDO CREED DOGMA FAITH SENSE TAINT TENET BELIEF CREDIT CONCERN OPINION SENTENCE

CONVINCE EVICT FETCH ASSURE EVINCE REPROVE RESOLVE SATISFY CONCLUDE
(— **OF ERROR**) CONVICT

CONVINCED FIRM SOLD SURE CERTAIN ABSOLUTE POSITIVE

CONVINCING SOUND VALID COGENT POTENT EVIDENT TELLING FORCIBLE POWERFUL PREGNANT

CONVIVIAL GAY BOON FESTAL GENIAL JOVIAL SOCIAL FESTIVE HOLIDAY JOCULAR REVELING

CONVIVIALITY REVEL FESTIVAL

CONVOCATION DIET SYNOD CALLING COUNCIL MEETING SUMMONS ASSEMBLY CONGRESS VOCATION

CONVOKE CALL HOLD GATHER SUMMON CONVENE ASSEMBLE

CONVOLUTE COIL ROLL WIND TWIST TANGLE WRITHE CONTORT INVOLUTE OBVOLUTE

CONVOLUTED GYRATE

CONVOLUTION COIL CURL FOLD TURN WRAP GYRUS SWIRL TWINE TWIRL TWIST WHORL CUNEUS GYROMA VOLUME VOLUTION

CONVOLVE TURN WIND TWIST ENFOLD ENWRAP INFOLD WRITHE

CONVOLVULUS BINDWEED SCAMMONY

CONVOY LEAD WAFT CARRY GUARD GUIDE PILOT TRADE WATCH ATTEND CONVEY ESCORT MANAGE CONDUCT WAFTAGE

CONVULSE ROCK STIR SHAKE EXCITE AGITATE DISTURB

CONVULSION FIT SHRUG SPASM THROE ATTACK TUMULT UPROAR CONVULSE LAUGHTER PAROXYSM COMMOTION

CONVULSIVE FITFUL EPILEPTIC

CONY DAS HARE PIKA CONEY CUNNY DAMAN DASSY GANAM HUTIA HYRAX BURBOT CONEEN DASSIE GAZABO GAZEBO RABBIT WABBER ASHKOKO BOOMDAS HYRACID KLIPDAS HYRACOID KLIPDACH

COO CROO CURR WOOT CHIRR CHIZZ CROOD MURMUR CROODLE CRUDDLE

COOK DO FIX FRY BAKE BOIL CHEF COCT MAKE SEAR STEW BROIL CUSIE FRIZZ GRILL POACH ROAST SCALD SHIRR STEAM BRAISE CODDLE COOKIE COOPER DECOCT DIGEST PORTER SAUTEE SEETHE SIMMER ARTISTE BROILER FRIZZLE GRIDDLE PASTLER PERCOCT POTAGER PREPARE PROCESS SERVANT SMOTHER SWAMPER BAWARCHI BOBACHEE COCINERO CUSINERO GRILLADE MAGIRIST PASTERER
(— **UP**) BUILD
(**BULL** —) FLUNKY FLUNKEY GREASER
(**SHIP'S** —) DOCTOR SLUSHY SKILLET SLUSHER

COOKED DONE FRIED BOILED
(— **WITH SUGAR**) CANDIED

COOKEE FLUNKY HASHER FLUNKEY

COOKER CANNER HAYBOX DIGESTER

COOKERY CURY CUISINE KITCHEN MAGIRICS

COOKHOUSE GALLEY

COOKIE CAKE ROCK SNAP COOKY HERMIT KIPFEL BISCUIT BROWNIE OATCAKE PLACENT CRESCENT SEEDCAKE

COOL AIR FAN ICE CALM COLD KEEL AKELE ALGID ALLAY CHILL EVENT FRESH GELID NERVY QUEEL SOBER STAID WHOLE AIRISH CALLER CHILLY PLACID QUENCH SEDATE SERENE TEMPER UNWARM COOLISH REFROID UNMOVED CARELESS CAUTIOUS COMPOSED MITIGATE MODERATE TRANQUIL
(— **IN WATER**) SLACK SLACKEN
(— **OF EVENING**) SERENE

COOLED COLD FRAPPE

COOLER ICER JAIL KEEL OLLA SINK ICEBOX LOCKUP PRISON SINKER KEELFAT KEELYAT ALCOGENE
(**WINE** —) GLACIER

COOLIE CHANGAR MADRASI MAZDOOR

COOLNESS COOL FROST NERVE SWALE APLOMB PHLEGM SERENITY

COOM CULM GAUM SMUT SOOT COOMB GRIME SLACK

COONTIE SAGO ZAMIA COMPTIE

COOP COT CUB CUP MEW PEN POT RIP CAGE COOB COTE JAIL CRAMP HUTCH BASKET CORRAL CONFINE
(— **UP**) PEN IMMEW INCOUP
(**HEN** —) CAVEY CAVIE BARTON

COOPER BUNGS COPER COWPER HEADER HOOPER TUBBER TUBBIE TUBMAN

COOPERATE HAND TEND AGREE COACT UNITE CONCUR COMBINE CONDUCE CONNIVE COADJUTE CONSPIRE

COOPERATION SOCIETY COURTESY TEAMWORK

COOPERATIVE COOP SOCIAL SYNERGIC

COORDINATE SINE ADAPT EQUAL ADJUST ARRANGE SYNTONY ABSCISSA CLASSIFY ENSEMBLE

COORDINATION BOND SKILL HARMONY LIAISON

COORG KADAGA

COOT CUIT DUCK RAIL QUEET SMYTH BELTIE GORHEN PELICK SCOTER HENBILL LOBIPED PULLDOO LOBEFOOT RAILBIRD SWAMPHEN

COP BAG NAB ROB BANK BLOW BULL HEAD HEAP JOHN LIFT PILE TRAP TUBE CATCH CREST FILCH MOUNT QUILL SHOCK SNARE STEAL STOCK SWIPE BOBBIN COPPIN PEELER SPIDER STRIKE CAPTURE

COPA YAYA COPITA

COPAL BOEA LOBA ANIME CONGO KAURI KAURY RESIN COWRIE CHAKAZI

COPE VIE WAR CAPE DUTY FACE LIFT MEET CAPPA CLOAK COVER DRESS EQUAL FIGHT MATCH NOTCH RIVAL VAULT WIELD BARTER CANOPY CHAPEL COMBAT MANTEL MUZZLE OPPOSE SEMBLE STRIKE STRIVE ANABATA CONTEND CONTEST GRAPPLE MANDYAS PLUVIAL COMPLETE EXCHANGE FACTABLE SEMICOPE STRUGGLE VESTMENT

COPEHAN WINTUN

COPEPOD CALANID CAYENNE DIAPTOMID

COPIAPITE MISY MISSY IHLEITE

COPIER COPIST SCRIBE JOHNSONIAN

COPING CAP COPE FLUE SKEW CORDON CAPSTONE FACTABLE

COPING STONE TABLET TABLING

COPIOUS FREE FULL GOOD LUSH RANK RICH AMPLE LARGE FLUENT LAVISH DIFFUSE FLOWING FULSOME LENGTHY PROFUSE REPLETE TEEMING UBEROUS ABUNDANT AFFLUENT FRUITFUL GENEROUS NUMEROUS

COPIOUSNESS COPY PLENTY

COPPER AES COP BULL CENT BOBBY METAL PENNY VENUS CUPRUM PEELER VELLON BLISTER CARNELIAN
(GILDED —) VERMEIL
(OF —) AEN

COPPERAS COPEROSE INKSTONE

COPPERHEAD REDEYE MOCCASIN

COPPERSMITH TINKERBIRD

COPPER SULFATE BLUESTONE

COPPER SULFIDE FERRETTO COVELLINE COVELLITE

COPPERY CUPREOUS

COPPICE COP BROW WOOD COPPY

COPSE FIRTH FRITH GROVE COVERT FOREST GROWTH SPROUT THICKET ARBUSTUM

COPSE CUT HAG HASP HEWT HOLT MOTT SHAW TRIM DROKE HURST CLEVIS SPINNY COPPICE LOWWOOD SHACKLE SPINNEY ARBUSTUM COPEWOOD

COPULA BAND LINK UNION

COPY APE CALK CAST ECHO EDIT MIME MOCK NICK DITTO DUMMY GROSS IMAGE MIMIC MODEL REVIE STICK STUFF TRACE CALQUE DOUBLE ECTYPE EFFIGY FILLER FLIMSY FOLLOW MATTER RECORD REFLEX SAMPLE SHADOW EDITION EMULATE ENGROSS ESTREAT EXTRACT IMITATE PATTERN REDRAFT REPLICA REPRINT RUBBING TRACING VIDIMUS APOGRAPH EXEMPLAR EXSCRIBE EXSCRIPT LIKENESS MANIFOLD POROTYPE PORTRAIT RESEMBLE SPECIMEN
(— EDITOR) SLOT
(— OF DOCUMENT) EXTRACT PROTOCOL
(— OF DRESS) FORD
(EXACT —) TENOR
(PRINTING —) KILL BOGUS
(UNREMUNERATIVE —) LEAN
(WORTHLESS —) BALAAM

COPYING MIMICRY INSINUATION

COPYIST COPIER SCRIBE COPYCAT SCRIVENER

COPYREAD EDIT SUBEDIT

COQUET TOY COPPY DALLY FLIRT TRIFLE BLINKER CELIMENE

COQUILLE SHELL

COQUINA DONAX

CORA NAYARIT

CORACLE SCOW CURAGH CURRANE

CORAL RED PINK AKORI BLOOD POLYP ALCYON PALULE PORITE FUNGIAN OCULINA ACROPORE ASTRAEAN CORALLUM FAVOSITE POLYPITE STAGHORN TUBIPORE ZOOPHYTE

CORAL BEAN SOPHORA FRIJOLILLO

CORAL-BELLS HEUCHERA

CORALBERRY BUCKBUSH

CORALFISH DOLLFISH

CORALROOT ORCHID CRAWLEY

CORAL SNAKE ELAPID ROLLER ELAPOID

CORAL TREE GABGAB ERYTHRINA

CORBEIL PANNIER

CORBEL KNOT ANCON CORBET TIMBER BRAGGER RESPOND CARTOUCH SPRINGER

CORBELING SQUINCH

CORBIESTEP CATSTEP CROWSTEP

CORCIR CORKE ARCHIL CORKER ORCHIL ARCHILLA

CORD AEA RIB AGAL BAND BIND BOND FILE LACE LASH LINE ROPE WELT BRAID CHORD FUNIS GUARD LEASH LIGNE MATCH NERVE OLONA TWINE TWIST BINDER BOBBIN BRIDLE BUNGEE CATGUT CHORDA CORDON FIADOR GIRDLE LASHER LISERE RACHIS SENNET STRING TENDON TOGGLE AMENTUM BOWYANG BULLION CORDING FUNICLE LANIARD LANYARD MACRAME SEAMING SEIZING SKIRREH TIEBACK URACHUS BELLPULL CHENILLE DRAWCORD HAIRLINE SHOELACE WHIPCORD
(— AROUND BOWSTRING) SERVING
(— FOR PIPING) BOBBIN
(— OF CANDLENUT BARK) AEA
(CROCHETING —) CORDE
(ELECTRIC —) FLEX
(EMBROIDERY —) ARRASENE
(FRINGED —) LLAUTU
(HAMMOCK —S) CLEW
(MASON'S —) SKIRREH
(ORNAMENTED —) AGLET AIGLET
(PARACHUTE —) SHROUD
(SACRED —) KUSTI
(SPINAL —) EON AEON NUKE
(TWISTED —) TORSADE

CORDAGE DA COIR ERUC FERU HEMP IMBE JUTE KYAR ROPE HAMBER SENNIT RIGGING
(LENGTH OF —) CATENARY

CORDATE HEARTED

CORDED TIED JETTED REPPED RIBBED WELTED TWILLED

COR-DE-NUIT PASTORITA

CORDER RUFFER

CORDIAL REAL WARM CREAM ARDENT CASSIS DEVOUT ELIXIR GENIAL HEARTY CORDATE DIAMBER LIQUEUR PERSICO ROSOLIO SINCERE ZEALOUS ANISETTE FRIENDLY GRACIOUS PERSICOT VIGOROUS
(NOT —) DISTANT STANDOFF
(PL.) SWEETS

CORDIERITE IOLITE FAHLUNITE

CORDON BLEU BENGALEE

CORDONNET CRESCENT

CORDWOOD BODYWOOD

CORE AME COB HUB NUT BONE COKE COLK GIST KNOT NAVE PITH BLOCK FOCUS HEART NOWSE RUMPF SPOOL BARREL CENTER CENTRE HEATER KERNEL MATRIX MIDDLE NODULE POCKET STAPLE CENTRUM CHEMISE COMPANY CORNCOB ESSENCE NUCLEUS FILAMENT HEARTING
(— OF COAL) STOCK
(— OF COLUMN) BELL HEART
(— OF CRICKET BALL) QUILT
(— OF LOG) PITH
(WATER —) GLASSINESS

CORE ARBOR STALK

COREE CORANINE

CORELIGIONIST BROTHER

COREMIUM SYNEMA SYNNEMA

COREOPSIS TICKSEED TICKWEED LEPTOSYNE

CORF TUB CAGE CAWF COFF CORB SKIP CREEL BASKET DOSSER

CORGI CARDIGAN PEMBROKE

CORIUM CUTIS DERMA LAYER DERMIS

CORK PLUG FLOAT SHIVE SUBER BOBBER BOUCHON CRINKLE PHELLEM SOBERIN STOPPER STOPPLE

CORKER WHIZ RAKER WHIZZ CUTTER HUMDINGER

CORKSCREW WORMER

CORKWOOD BALSA GUANO HAREFOOT

CORM SET BULB SEED CORMEL CORMUS FREESIA UINTJIE

CORMEL BULBLET
(PL.) SPAWN

CORMORANT SHAG CRANE GORMA NORIE SCARF SCART DUIKER DUYKER GORMAW GUANAY SCARFE SCARTH GLUTTON SHAGLET

CORN ZEA DANA DENT SALT SAMP GRAIN MAIZE SPIKE WYROK AGNAIL CALLUS CLAVUS HELOMA INDIAN KERNEL MEALIE NOCAKE NUBBIN POWDER WYROCK FORMITY FRUMENT FRUMENTY PRESERVE SAUTERNE
(— SPURREY) YARR
(CROW —) COLICROOT
(CRUSHED —) STAMP
(DECORATED EAR OF —) TIPONI
(EAR OF —) ICKER
(GUINEA —) DURRA DHURRA
(INDIAN —) MAIZE INDIAN NOCAKE
(PARCHED —) ROKEE NOCAKE YOKAGE GRADDAN ROKEAGE YOKEAGE
(STRING OF —) TRACE
(UNRIPE EAR OF —) TUCKET

CORNAGE HORNGELD

CORN BREAD PONE KANKIE BANNOCK

CORN COCKLE GITH COCKLE POPPLE COCKWEED HARDHEAD MELANTHY

CORNCRACKER STATE KENTUCKY

CORNCRAKE RAIL CORNBIRD

CORN CROWFOOT JOY GOLDWEED HELLWEED JACKWEED

CORNEL DOGWOOD REDBRUSH

CORNEOUS HORNLIKE KERASINE

CORNER IN GET OUT WRO BEND CANT COIN HALK HERN JAMB NOOK POOL TRAP TREE WICK ANCON ANGLE BIGHT CATCH COIGN ELBOW HERNE INGLE JAMBE NICHE QUOIN TRUST BOTTLE CANTLE CANTON COLLAR CORNEL CRANNY RECESS SQUARE QUINYIE TURNING MONOPOLY
(— IN A DRIFT) ARRAGE
(— OF EYE) CANTHUS
(— OF GUNSTOCK) TOE
(— OF MOLDBOARD) SHIN
(— OF SAIL) CLEW CLUE TACK GOOSEWING
(LOWER —) CLEW CLUE
(ROUNDED —) FILET FILLET
(SECRET —) CREEK
(TIGHT —) BOX

CORNERPIECE BUMPER CANTLE

CORNERSTONE COIN BASIS COIGN HEADSTONE

CORNET HORN ZINK TWIST ZINKE ZINCKE CORONET CORNETTO

CORNETFISH FLUTEMOUTH HEMIBRANCH

CORNFIELD MOW

CORN FLAG LEVERS

CORNFLOWER BLUET BLAVER BARBEAU BLUECAP BLUECUP BLAEWORT

CORN GROMWELL SALFERN

CORNHUSK CAP

CORNHUSKER STATE NEBRASKA

CORNHUSKING SHUCKING

CORNICE CAP BAND DRIP EAVE JOPY ANCON CROWN JOWPY DETAIL GEISON PELMET ANTEFIX MOLDING SURBASE ASTRAGAL SWANNECK
(UNDER SIDE OF —) PLANCIER

CORNICLE SIPHON SYPHON

CORNISHMAN CELT KELT

CORN MARIGOLD GOLD GOOLS BODDLE BOODLE BUDDLE GOWLAN GOLDING GOLLAND

CORN MEAL MASA SAMP ATOLE HOECAKE

CORN PARSLEY UMBEL

CORN POPPY BLAVER CANKER COCKLE COPROSE EARACHE PONCEAU REDWEED SOLDIER

CORN SALAD FETTICUS MILKGRASS

CORN STACK HOVEL

CORNSTALKS KARBI

CORNSTARCH BINDER

CORNU HORN THYROHYAL

CORNUCOPIA HORN CORNU COFFIN

CORNUS CORNIN REDBRUSH

CORN VIOLET SPECULARIA

CORN WOUNDWORT STACHYS

CORNY BANAL STALE TRITE MICKEY BUCKEYE

COROADO BORORO

CORODY CONRED

COROLLA CUP BELL COROL CUPULE LIGULE PERIANTH

COROLLARY DOGMA PORISM RESULT TRUISM ADJUNCT THEOREM

COROMANDEL COLCOTHAR

CORONA BUR BURR CIGAR CROWN GLORY AURORA FILLET ROSARY WREATH AUREOLE CIRCLET CORONET GARLAND SCYPHUS

CORONAL CRONET CORONEL CROWNAL

CORONATION ABHISEKA CROWNMENT

CORONER ELISOR CROWNER EXAMINER SEARCHER

CORONET BAND BURR CROWN TIARA ANADEM CIRCLE CRONET DIADEM TIMBRE WREATH CHAPLET CORONAL CROWNAL CROWNET GARLAND CROWNLET

CORONOPUS CARARA

CORPORAL NYM FANO NAIG NAIK FANON FANUM NAYAK PHANO BODILY EXEMPT GUNNER NAIGUE NAIQUE SINDON TINDAL

CORPORATE UNITED COMBINED

CORPORATION BODY CITY FIRM POUCH TRUST SCHOLA BOROUGH COLLEGE FREEDOM GUILDRY SOCIETY SPONSOR

CORPOREAL REAL HYLIC SOMAL ACTUAL BODILY CARNAL FLESHLY SOMATIC MATERIAL PHYSICAL TANGIBLE

CORPOSANT HERMO

CORPS CORE ORDU VELITES SERAGLIO
(— DE BALLET) ENSEMBLE

CORPSE BIER BODY DUST LICH MORT GHOST MUMMY RELIC STIFF TRUCK ZOMBI CORPUS DEADER ZOMBIE ANATOMY CADAVER CARCASS CARRION CROAKER DEADMAN FLOATER
(— WASHING) TAHARAH

CORPSMAN BEARER

CORPULENCE FAT FATNESS STOUTNESS

CORPULENT FAT BULKY BURLY FATTY GROSS HUSKY OBESE PLUMP STOUT FLESHY GREASY PORTLY ROTUND ADIPOSE BELLIED WEIGHTY

CORPUSCLE CELL GHOST GLOBULE HEMATID HAEMATID HEMOCYTE

CORRAL PEN STY COOP ATAJO POUND TAMBO CONFINE ENCLOSE STOCKAGE SURROUND
(ELEPHANT —) KRAAL

CORRECT DUE FIT FIX TIC BEET BOOK EDIT JUST LEAL LEAN MARK MEND NICE OKAY SMUG TRUE AMEND CHECK CLEAN EMEND EXACT ORDER RIGHT SOUND SPILL ADJUST BETTER CHANGE INFORM PROPER PUNISH REBUKE REFORM REMEDY REPAIR REVAMP REVISE STRICT ADDRESS CHAPTER CHASTEN CORRIGE ELEGANT IMPROVE PERFECT PRECISE RECLAIM RECTIFY REDRESS REGULAR REPROVE SINCERE ACCURATE CHASTISE DEFINITE EMENDATE EQUALIZE REGULATE RIGOROUS STRAIGHT TRUTHFUL
(GRAMMATICALLY —) CONGRUE

CORRECTABLE CORRIGIBLE

CORRECTION YARD CENSURE FLEXURE IMPRINT REDRESS FUGACITY

CORRECTIVE SALT REMEDY

CORRECTLY JUST RIGHT ARIGHT RIGHTLY SOUNDLY PROPERLY

CORRECTNESS TRUTH DECORUM FITNESS JUSTICE ACCURACY JUSTNESS VERACITY

CORRELATE HARMONIZE

CORRELATIVE OR NOR THEN EQUAL STILL EITHER MUTUAL NEITHER ANALOGUE CONJOINT REDDITIVE

CORRESPOND FIT GEE JIBE SUIT AGREE MATCH TALLY WRITE

ACCORD ANSWER CONCUR SQUARE COMPORT RESPOND COINCIDE PARALLEL QUADRATE
(— IN SOUND) ASSONATE
(— TO) ENSUE
CORRESPONDENCE MAIL TALLY ANALOGY CONSENT HARMONY KEEPING LETTERS TRAFFIC FUNCTION HOMOGENY HOMOLOGY SYMMETRY SYMPATHY
(INCOMPLETE —) ASSONANCE
CORRESPONDENT QUADRATE RELEVANT STRINGER SUITABLE STRINGMAN
CORRESPONDING LIKE SIMILAR CONGRUENT
CORRESPONDINGLY SORTLY SIMILARLY
CORRIDA BULLFIGHT
CORRIDOR HALL AISLE ORIEL VISTA ARCADE COULOIR GALLERY PASSAGE COULISSE HALLCIST TRESANCE
CORRIE CIRQUE
CORRIGENDUM ERRATUM
CORROBORATE PROVE SECOND APPROVE COMFORT CONFIRM SUPPORT SUSTAIN ROBORATE
CORRODE EAT BITE BURN ETCH FRET GNAW RUST DECAY ERODE EXEDE TOUCH WASTE BEGNAW CANKER IMPAIR CONSUME GRAPHITE
CORRODING BITE RODENT ESURINE
CORROSION EROSION EMBAYMENT
CORROSIVE ACID ACRID ARDENT BITING CORSIE EATING CAUSTIC EROSIVE ESURINE FRETFUL MORDANT DIERETIC
CORRUGATE CRIMP CRISP FURROW RUMPLE CRINKLE CRUMPLE WRINKLE
CORRUGATED PLAITED WRINKLY FURROWED WRINKLED
CORRUGATION BAT FOLD GILL REED CREASE PUCKER CRINKLE WRINKLE
CORRUPT BAD ILL LOW ROT WEM EVIL RANK SICK SOIL VILE BLEND BRIBE FALSE SPOIL STAIN SULLY TAINT VENAL VENOM WEMMY AUGEAN CANKER DEBASE DEFILE FESTER IMPURE INFECT PALTER POISON PUTRID RAVISH ROTTEN SEPTIC ABUSIVE ATTAINT BEDEVIL BEGRIME BESHREW CARRION CORRUMP CROOKED DEBAUCH DEFINED DEGRADE DEPRAVE ENVENOM FALSIFY IMMORAL PECCANT PERVERT POLLUTE PUTREFY SUBVERT TRADING VIOLATE VITIATE CONFOUND DEPRAVED EMPOISON PERVERSE POLLUTED PRACTICE PRACTISE SINISTER VITIATED
CORRUPTED SICK
CORRUPTION DIRT SOIL VICE DECAY SPOIL TAINT JOBBERY PRAVITY SQUALOR ADULTERY INFECTION

CORSAC ADIVE KARAGAN
CORSAGE WAIST BODICE BOUQUET CANEZOU
CORSAIR BUG CAPER PIRATE ROBBER CURSARO PICAROON ROCKFISH
CORSELET THORAK ALLECRET HALECRET
CORSET BELT BUSK STAY STAYS GIRDLE SUPPORT
CORSICA (CAPITAL OF —) AJACCIO
(HARBOR OF —) BASTIA
(MOUNTAIN OF —) CINTO ROTONDO
(RIVER OF —) GOLO TARAVO GRAVONE
(TOWERLIKE STRUCTURES OF —) TORRI
(TOWN OF —) CALVI CORTE ALERIA BASTIA AJACCIO SARTENE
(VEGETATION OF —) MAQUIS
CORSICAN PINE LARCH
CORTEGE POMP SUITE TRAIN PARADE RETINUE
CORTEX BARK PEEL RIND MANTLE PALLIUM PERIBLEM PERIDIUM
CORUNDUM RUBY SAND EMERY ADAMAS ALUMINA ABRASIVE AMETHYST CORINDON SAPPHIRE BARKLYITE
(SYNTHETIC —) EMERALD
CORUSCATE BLAZE FLASH GLEAM SHINE GLANCE GLISTEN GLITTER RADIATE SPARKLE BRANDISH
CORVEE POLO
CORYZA COLD
COSCET COTTAR COTARIUS COTSETLE
COSMETIC WASH CREAM FUCUS HENNA LINER PAINT PETER ROUGE BLANCH CERUSE CRAYON ENAMEL POMADE POWDER MASCARA STIBIUM LIPSTICK STIBNITE
COSMIC VAST MUNDANE ORDERLY CATHOLIC INFINITE
COSMOLABE PANTACOSM
COSMOPOLITAN URBAN ECUMENIC PANDEMIC AMPHIGEAN
COSMOS EARTH GLOBE ORDER REALM WORLD FLOWER HEAVEN HARMONY UNIVERSE
COSSACK TURK TATAR ATAMAN HETMAN TARTAR ZAPOROGUE
COSSET MUD PET LAMB CARESS CODDLE CUDDLE FONDLE PAMPER TIDDLE
COSSETTE CHIP SLICE STRIP SCHNITZEL
COST SIT GAFF LOSS PAIN SOAK BASIS PRICE SPEND STAND VALUE CHARGE DAMAGE OUTLAY SCATHE EXPENSE REPRISE ESTIMATE SPENDING

COSTA RICA
CAPE: ELENA VELAS BLANCO
CAPITAL: SANJOSE
COIN: COLON CENTIMO
DANCE: PUNTO TORITO
GULF: DULCE NICOYA PAPAGAYO
INDIAN: BORUCA GUAYMI
ISLAND: COCO
LAKE: ARENAL
MEASURE: VARA CAFIZ CAHIZ FANEGA TERCIA CAJUELA CANTARO MANZANA
MOUNTAIN: BLANCO CHIRRIPO
PENINSULA: OSA NICOYA
POINT: QUEPOS CAHUITA GALONOS LLERENA
PORT: LIMON PUNTARENAS
RIVER: POAS IRAZU MATINA SIXAOLA TENORIA TARCOLES
TOWN: CANAS NICOYA VESTA BORUCA NICOYA BAGACES CARTAGO GOLFITO HEREDIA LIBERIA NEGRITA ALAJUELA COLORADO GUAPILES
VOLCANO: POAS IRAZU
WEIGHT: BAG CAJA LIBRA

COSTERMONGER COSTER HAWKER NIPPER PEARLY PEDDLER BARROWMAN
COSTIVE BOUND EMPLASTIC
COSTLINESS DEARTH DEARNESS
COSTLY DEAR FINE HIGH RICH SALT DAINTY LAVISH SILVER COSTFUL COSTLEW GORGEOUS PLATINUM PRECIOUS PRODIGAL SPLENDID
COSTMARY TANSY ALECOST MAUDLIN ROSEMARY
COSTREL KEG HEAD FLASK BOTTLE COYSTREL
COSTUME RIG GARB ROBE SARI SUIT BURKA DRESS GETUP HABIT SHAPE TRUSS ATTIRE DOMINO FORMAL SETOUT TOILET APPAREL BLOOMER CLOTHES POLLERA RAIMENT SCARLET UNIFORM CHARSHAF CLOTHING ENSEMBLE TOILETTE VENETIAN
(ACADEMIC —) GUISE
COSTUSROOT PACHAK
COSY FEEL FEIL
COT BED HUT MAT PEN BOAT COOP COTE FOLD ABODE BOTHY CABIN COUCH COVER HOUSE STALL COTEEN CRADLE GURNEY PALLET SHEATH TANGLE CHARPAI CHARPOY COTTAGE SHELTER BEDSTEAD COTHOUSE DWELLING STRETCHER
COTERIE SET RING CABAL JUNTO MONDE CIRCLE CLIQUE GALAXY SETOUT CENACLE CIRCUIT COLLEGE PLATOON SOCIETY
COTHURNUS BOOT BUSKIN COTHURN
COTILLION GERMAN
COTO OREJON
COTTA KATHA STOLE MANTLE BLANKET SURPLICE VESTMENT
COTTAGE BOX COT HUT BACH BARI COSH CRIB SHED WALK BOWER CABIN HOUSE HOVEL LODGE SHACK BOHAWN CABANA CHALET SHELTER BUNGALOW COTHOUSE SHEELING

SHIELING THALTHAN
COTTAGE CHEESE SKYR
SMEARCASE
COTTER KEY MAT PIN VEX CLOT
BOWPIN COTMAN FASTEN MAILER
POTTER PUCKER SHRINK TOGGLE
WITHER CONGEAL COTTIER
PEASANT SHRIVEL VILLEIN
COTARIUS COTTAGER COTTEREL
ENTANGLE FORELOCK LINCHPIN
COTTON SAK BEAT DRAB FLOG
PIMA AGREE BAYAL BOLLY DERRY
MATTA SAKEL SURAT BROACH
CODDLE COMBER DHURRY FABRIC
MAARAD MALLOW NANKIN PEELER
STAPLE ALGODON BENDERS
BOMBACE DHURRIE GARMENT
GINNING SILESIA SUCCEED
(**— SQUARE**) TZUT TZUTE
(**BOLL OF —**) SNAP
(**NAPPED —**) LAMBSKIN
(**PAINTED —**) INDIENNE
(**PIECE OF —**) SPONGE
(**PRINTED —**) SARONG
(**RAW —**) LINT BAYAL
(**SILK —**) FLOSS
(**STRIPED —**) BENGAL
(**TREE —**) MACO
(**TWILLED —**) JEAN SALLO SALLOO
(**WAD OF —**) TAMPON
(**WASTE —**) GRABBOTS
COTTON GRASS CANNA CANNACH
DRAWLING
COTTON PLANT LAMB
(**— FLOWER**) SQUARE
COTTON TREEE SIMAL
COTYLEDON BUTTON PICHURIM
COUCH BED COT KIP LAY LIE HIDE
LAIR LURK SOFA SUNK DIVAN INLAY
LODGE PRESS SKULK SLINK SNEAK
SNOOP SQUAB SQUAT UTTER
BURROW CLOTHE DAYBED LITTER
PALLET PLINTH SETTEE CONCEAL
EXPRESS HAMMOCK OTTOMAN
OVERLAY RECLINE TRANSOM
(**NUPTIAL —**) THORE
COUCH GRASS CUTCH KUTCH
QUACK QUICK TWICH QUITCH
SCOTCH SCUTCH STROIL QUICKEN
WITHVINE
COUGAR CAT PUMA PAINTER
PANTHER CARCAJOU
COUGH YEX YOX BAFF BARK HACK
HOST CROUP HOAST HOOSE HOOZE
TUSSIS
COUGH DROP PASTIL TROCHE
LOZENGE PASTILLE
COUGH SYRUP LINCTUS
COULEE DRAW GORGE GULCH
COOLEY RAVINE
COULOMB WEBER
COUMA SORVA HYAHYA
COUNCIL BODY BULE DAEL DIET
DUMA FONO RAAD REDE YUAN
BOARD BOULE BUNGA CABAL
CAPUT DIVAN DIWAN DOUMA JIRGA
JUNTA JUNTO SABHA SOBOR STATE
SYNOD THING JIRGAH LUKIKO
MAJLIS POWWOW QUORUM SENATE

SOVIET TARYBA CABILDO CABINET
CHAMBER CONSULT GERUSIA
HUSTING MEETING PENSION
WHITLEY ASSEMBLY CONCLAVE
CONGRESS FOLKMOOT FOLKMOTE
HEEMRAAD HEEMRAAT MINISTRY
PLACITOM RIGSRAAD
COUNCILLOR RAT VIZIR ENDUNA
INDUNA VIZIER FAIPULE SENATOR
WISEMAN
COUNSEL RAD LORE REDE RULE
RUNE SILK WARD WARN AREED
CHIDE DEVIL GUIDE ADVICE ADVISE
CONFER LEADER ABOGADO
CAUTION COUNCIL LECTURE
ADMONISH ADVOCATE PRUDENCE
(**JUNIOR LEGAL —**) DEVIL
(**KING'S —**) SILK
(**SACRED —**) TORAH
COUNSELOR RAT SAGE WITE
CONSUL LAWYER MENTOR NESTOR
ADVISER ADVISOR COUNSEL
ECHEVIN GONZALO PROCTOR
STARETS ADVOCATE ATTORNEY
REDESMAN UCALEGON
COUNT ADD GAN SUM TOT BANK
CAST EARL FOOT GANO GRAF NAME
RELY RIME SIZE TALE TELL TOTE
COMES COMPT COMTE GRAVE
JUDGE RHYME SCORE TALLY WEIGH
CENSUS CONSUL COUNTY DEPEND
ESTEEM FIGURE IMPUTE NUMBER
RECKON TOTTLE ACCOUNT ARTICLE
ASCRIBE COMPUTE GANELON
ADNUMBER NUMERATE SANCTION
(**— IN BILLIARDS**) DOUBLE
(**— OF A FIBER**) GRIST
(**— OF SHEEP OR CATTLE**) BREAK
(**— ON**) LITE RELY
(**— UNIT**) WARP
COUNTABLE DISCRETE
COUNTENANCE AID MUG OWN RUD
ABET BROW FACE GIZZ LEER MIEN
PUSS SHOW VULT CHEER FAVOR
FRONT GRACE ASPECT ENDURE
UPHOLD VISAGE APPROVE BEARING
CONDUCT ENDORSE FEATURE
PROFFER SUPPORT BEFRIEND
DEMEANOR FOREHEAD SANCTION
COUNTER BAR DIB LOT BANK BUCK
CENT CHIP DESK DUMP EDDY FISH
JACK KIST PAWN STOP CAROM
CHECK FORCE HATCH JETON PIECE
SHELF STALL STAND TABLE TOTER
BUFFET COMBAT GEIGER ISLAND
JETTON MARKER OPPOSE SQUAIL
ADVERSE BUTTOCK CONTEND
CURRENT FANTAIL SHAMBLE
CONTRARY MAHOGANY OPPOSITE
TELLTALE
(**— TO**) AGAINST
(**LEADEN —**) DUMP
(**LUNCH —**) PLACE
COUNTERACT CHECK CANCEL
OPPOSE RESIST THWART BALANCE
CORRECT DESTROY NULLIFY
ANTIDOTE NEGATIVE
COUNTERACTION DEADLOCK
COUNTERACTIVE REMEDY
ADVERSE

COUNTERBALANCE COVER WEIGH
CANCEL SETOFF BALANCE
COUNTERCLOCKWISE DIRECT
DIRECTLY
COUNTERCURRENT BACKSET
COUNTEREARTH ANTICHTHON
COUNTERFEIT ACT BASE COIN
COPY DAUB DUFF FAKE IDOL MOCK
SHAM BELIE BOGUS DUMMY FALSE
FEIGN FLASH FORGE FUDGE GAMMY
MIMIC PHONY QUEER SNIDE AFFECT
ASSUME CHEMIC ERSATZ FORGED
PSEUDO TINSEL CHEMICK DUFFING
FALSIFY FASHION FEIGNED
FORGERY IMITANT IMITATE
DEFORMED POSTICHE POSTIQUE
RESEMBLE SIMILIZE SIMULATE
SPURIOUS SUPPOSED
COUNTERFEITER COINER JACKMAN
JARKMAN SCRATCHER
COUNTERFEITING COINING FICTION
POSTICHE POSTIQUE
COUNTERFOIL FOIL STUB CHECK
COUNTERFORT SCONCE BUTTRESS
COUNTERION GEGENION
COUNTERIRRITANT MOXA GINGER
IODINE PEPPER MUSTARD
CANTHARIS
COUNTERMAND STOP ANNUL
CANCEL FORBID RECALL REVOKE
ABOLISH RESCIND REVERSE
UNORDER ABROGATE PROHIBIT
COUNTERMOVE DEMARCHE
COUNTERMOVEMENT BACKFIRE
COUNTERPANE PANE LIGGER
BEDSPREAD
COUNTERPART COPY LIKE MATE
SPIT TWIN FETCH IMAGE MATCH
MORAL SHELL TALLY COUSIN
DOUBLE SHADOW BALANCE
COUNTER OBVERSE PENDANT
SIMILAR ANTIPART PARALLEL
RESCRIPT
(**SPEECH —**) A
COUNTERPOINT FOIL DESCANT
CONTRAST
COUNTERPOISE POISE OFFSET
BALANCE EQUALIZE
COUNTERPOISON ORVIETAN
COUNTERSIGN BACK MARK SEAL
SIGN SIGNAL CONFIRM ENDORSE
PASSWORD SANCTION
COUNTERSINK DISH REAM BEVEL
CHAMFER
COUNTERSTATEMENT ANSWER
COUNTERSUN ANTHELION
COUNTERWEIGHT TARE
COUNTERWORD ANIMAL COUNTER
COUNTESS OLIVIA COMTESSE
CONTESSA
COUNTLESS INFINITE
COUNTRIFIED JAY BUCOLIC
LOBBISH HOBNAILED
COUNTRY SOD DESH EARD HICK
HOME KITH LAND PAIS SOIL ADDLE
EARTH FAIRY FRITH MARCH PLAGE
REALM STATE TRACT WEALD
GROUND KINTRA KINTRY NATION
PEOPLE REGION STICKS UPLAND

IMAMATE KWINTRA MONKERY
MUFASAL DISTRICT DOMINION
ELDORADO LANDWARD MAGAZINE
MOFUSSIL REGALITY
(— OF ETHIOPIA) SEBA
(— OF ORIGIN) HOMELAND
(— OF PERFECTION) EUTOPIA
(— ON SEA) SEABOARD
(— STYLE) PAYSANNE
(ANCIENT —) ARAM
(CABIN —) LOBBY
(FRONTIER —) BORDER
(IMAGINARY —) LILLIPUT
(MARITIME —) MAREMMA
(MYTHICAL —) UTOPIA LEONNOYS
SVITHIOD SWITHIOD TEUTONIA
(OPEN —) BLED VELD FIELD VELDT
WEALD CAMPAIGN
(PETTY —) TOPARCHY
(ROUGH —) BOONDOCK BUNDOCKS
COUNTRYMAN HOB BOOR HIND
KERN TIKE CHURL CLOWN HODGE
KERNE SWAIN YOKEL GAFFER
GIBARO JIBARO GRANGER HAYSEED
LANDMAN PAISANO PEASANT
PLOWMAN LANDSMAN
(PL.) KITH
COUNTRYSIDE BLED BOCAGE
MOFUSSIL
COUNTY AMT LAN SEAT FYLKE
SHIRE DOMAIN PARISH BOROUGH
COMITAT NORFOLK DISTRICT
COUP BUY BLOW DEAL PLAN PLAY
COUPE FAULT SCOOP UPSET
ATTACK BARTER REFAIT STRIKE
STROKE CAPSIZE TRAFFIC
OVERTURN
COUP DE POING BOUCHER
HANDSTONE
COUPE CUT CABRIOLET LANDAULET
COUPED HUMETTY HUMETTEE
COUPLE DUO TIE TWO BOND CASE
DYAD JOIN LINK MATE PAIR SPAN
TEAM TWIN YOKE BRACE LEASH
MARRY TWAIN UNITE GEMINI SPLINE
SWINGE BRACKET CONNECT
COUPLER COUPLET DOUBLET
SHACKLE TWOSOME VOLTAIC
ACCOUPLE ASSEMBLE COPULATE
COUPLED GEMEL YOKED JOINED
WEDDED GEMELED COPULATE
GEMINATE
COUPLER LINK RING BOBBER
COPULA JANNEY LINKER SUTURE
UNITER DRAGBAR DRAWBAR
REDUCER SHACKLE SNAPPER
TIRASSE DRAGBOLT DRAWBOLT
DRAWGEAR SHACKLER
COUPLET BAIT COPLA ELEGIAC
COUPLING HUB HICKY UNION
CLUTCH HICKEY NIPPLE SHACKLE
SHACKLER
COUPON TWOFER
COURAGE BIEL FIRE GRIT GUTS
MIND MOOD PROW SAND SOUL
BIELD CREST HEART HONOR NERVE
PLUCK SPUNK VALOR DARING
DAUBER METTLE PECKER SPIRIT
VIRTUE VIRTUS BRAVERY COJONES

CORAGIO HEROISM MANHEAD
MANHOOD MANSHIP PROWESS
VENTURE AUDACITY BOLDNESS
FIRMNESS TENACITY
(— OF CONVICTION) STAMINA
(MORAL —) STRENGTH
COURAGEOUS BOLD GAME GOOD
TALL BRAVE GUTSY HARDY LUSTY
MANLY STOUT DARING HEROIC
MANFUL PLUCKY SPUNKY CORIAUS
GALLANT SPARTAN STAUNCH
VALIANT FEARLESS GENEROUS
INTREPID VALOROUS
COURAGEOUSLY BIG BRAVELY
COURANT ROMP CAPER DANCE
LETTER CORANTO CURRENT
GAZETTE RUNNING
COURBARIL JATOBA LOCUST
GUAPINOL CUAPINOLE
COURIER NEWS POST GUIDE SCOUT
KAVASS NEWING POSTER ESTAFET
ORDERLY PATAMAR POSTBOY
POSTMAN SOILAGE CICERONE
CURSITOR DRAGOMAN HORSEMAN
ORDINARY PATTAMAR
COURLAN LIMPKIN
COURONNE CROWN
COURSE FLY LAP RUN WAY BEAT
BENT FLOW GAGE GAME GANG
GATE HEAT HUNT LANE LINE LODE
MESS MODE PACE PATH RACE
RACK RAND RILL RING RINK ROAD
ROTA ROTE WENT CLASS COURS
CRUST CURRY CURVE CYCLE DRAFT
DRIFT DRIVE EMBER GAUGE GREAT
LAPSE LAYER LEDGE MARCH
MOYEN ORBIT PLATE POINT ROUTE
SENSE SITHE SPACE STEPS SWELT
SWING TENOR TRACK TRACT TRADE
TRAIL TREND WEENT ARTERY
CAREER COPING CURSUS DROMOS
FURROW GALLOP GIRDER GUTTER
HONORS MANNER METHOD MOTION
RESACA SCHOOL SERIES SPHERE
STREAM STREET SYSTEM TRIPOS
ZODIAC AZIMUTH BEELINE CHANNEL
CIRCUIT CONDUCT DIAULOS
DRAUGHT HIGHWAY LECTURE
PASSADE PASSAGE PATHWAY
PROCESS ROUTINE RUNNING
SEMINAR SERVICE STRETCH
SUBJECT SUCCESS TIDEWAY
TRAJECT TRUNDLE CURRENCY
CURRICLE DISTANCE ELECTIVE
PROGRESS RECOURSE SEQUENCE
STEERAGE TENDENCY
(— OF A ROPE) LEAD
(— OF ACTION) LARK TROD VEIN
DANCE CUSTOM ROUTINE
DEMARCHE
(— OF ACTIVITY) SIDELINE
(— OF BOAT) LEG
(— OF BRICK) BED ROWLOCK
SCINTLE CREASING
(— OF FEEDING) DIET
(— OF KNITTING) BOUT
(— OF LIFE) GOINGS
(— OF LUCK) FORTUNE
(— OF MASONRY) BAHUT STILT

COPING HEADING SKEWBACK
(— OF NATURE) TAO
(— OF PROCEDURE) RULE
(— OF PROCEEDING) FORE
(— OF PURSUIT) SCENT
(— OF ROADBED) SUBCRUST
(— OF STONES) BED PLINTH
(— OF STUDY) DEBATE COLLEGE
LECTURE SEMINAR ELECTIVE
(— OF SUN) JOURNEY
(— OF TREATMENT) CURE
(— OF WALL) CORNICE
(— WITH GREYHOUNDS) GREW
(BELL-RINGING —) HUNT
(CIRCULAR —) SWEEP CHUKKAR
CHUKKER COMPASS
(CURVING —) SWING
(CUSTOMARY —) GUISE
(DOWNWARD —) DIP DECLINE
TOBOGGAN
(EASY —) PIPE
(EXACT —) BEAM
(FIRST —) ANTEPAST
(FREE —) FORTH
(IRREGULAR —) ERROR
(LAST —) VOID
(MIDDLE —) MIDS TEMPER
(NATURAL —) RITA
(OBLIQUE —) SKEW
(OVERHANGING —) JET
(PREDETERMINED —) DESTINY
(ROUNDABOUT —) DETOUR
WINDLASS
(SETTLED —) BIAS GROOVE
(SKIING —) SCHUSS
COURSER HORSE RACER STEED
CUSSER CHARGER
COURSING CURSIVE
COURT BAR BID SEE SUE WOO AREA
BAIL BODY CLAW FUSS GATE GIRL
LEET QUAD ROTA SEAT SEEK SUIT
TOWN WALE WARD WYND YARD
ARENA BENCH BUREO CURIA CURRY
DAIRI DIVAN FAVOR FORUM FUERO
GARTH JUDGE PATIO SHIRE SPACE
SPARK SPOON SWEET TEMPT THING
THINK TOURN TRAIN YAMEN
ADALAT ALLURE ATRIUM BAILEY
COUNTY DARGAH DURBAR DURGAH
GEMOTE HOMAGE INVITE PALACE
PARVIS SPLUNT SUITOR TOLSEY
ADAWLUT ADDRESS ASSIZES
ATTRACT BARMOTE DUOVIRI
EPHETAE FOREIGN HELIAEA
HUSTING JUSTICE RETINUE SOLICIT
TEMENOS TOURNEL AUDIENCE
BURHMOOT CHANCERY FOUJDARY
LAWCOURT MARKMOOT MARKMOTE
QUARANTY SERENADE SESSIONS
SWANMOTE TRIBUNAL WOODMOTE
(— FAVOR) FAWN
(— OF A HUNDRED) MALL MALLUM
MALLUS
(— OF CIRCUIT JUDGES) EYRE
(— OF FORTRESS) PEEL
(— OF MIKADO) DAIRI
(— ORDER) VACATUR
(— THE GREAT) LEVEE
(ECCLESIASTICAL —) ROTA CURIA

SYNOD COLLOQUY AUDIENCIA
(EXERCISE —) EPHEBEUM
(FORTIFIED —) BAWN
(INNER —) PATIO
(MUSLIM —) DIVAN DIWAN
(REFORMED —) CLASIS
(SMALL —) WIND WYND
(SUPREME —) SUDDER
(TURKISH —) GATE
COURTEOUS FAIR HEND BUXOM
CIVIL GENTY SUAVE BONAIR
GENTLE POLITE SMOOTH URBANE
AFFABLE CORDIAL GALLANT
GENTEEL GENTILE REFINED
DEBONAIR FAMILIAR GRACIOUS
OBLIGING
COURTEOUSLY FAIR FAIRLY
GENTLY KINDLY AFFABLY
COURTESAN MADAM QUAIL THAIS
WHORE COURTY GEISHA LALAGE
MADAME PLOVER AMOROSA
CANIDIA PUCELLE DEVADASI
(PL.) DEMIMONDE
COURTESY MENSK COMITY EXTENT
GENTRY MANSHIP TASHRIF
CALIDORE CORTEISE ELEGANCE
GENTRICE GRATUITY URBANITY
(PL.) HONORS
COURTHOUSE CUTCHERY
COURTIER CURAN OSRIC WOOER
OSRICK COURTER IACHIMO
COURTMAN POLONIUS
COURTING SUING SPLUNT
COURTLY HEND AULIC CIVIL HENDE
POLITE AULICAL ELEGANT REFINED
STATELY POLISHED DIGNIFIED
COURT-NOUE RONCET
COURTSHIP SUIT AMOUR DRURY
SPARKING
COURTYARD AREA WYND CURIA
PATIO TRANCE CORTILE TETRAGON
COUSIN COZ KIN AKIN HERO ALLIED
NEPHEW
COVE CO BAY DEN CAVE CHAP FILE
GILL HOLE NOOK PASS SUMP BASIN
BAYOU BIGHT CREEK INLET COVING
FELLOW HOLLOW RECESS VALLEY
MOLDING CALANQUE GUNKHOLE
COVENANT BIND BOND BRIS MISE
PACT TRUE AGREE BERIT BRITH
TOUCH ACCORD BERITH CARTEL
COMART CONAND ENGAGE INDENT
LEAGUE PATISE PLEDGE TREATY
BARGAIN COMPACT CONCORD
PROMISE ALLIANCE CONTRACT
DOCUMENT HANDFAST TREATISE
COVENANTER HILLMAN
COVER DO CAP COT HAP LAP LAY
LID NAP TOP TUP WRY BIND CEIL
CLAD COAT COOM CURE DAUB
DECK FACE FADE FALL FURL GARB
GATE HEAD HEAL HEEL HIDE HILL
HOOD LATH LEAD LEAP LINE MASK
PAVE ROOF SILE SPAN TELD TICK
TIDE TILT VEIL APRON BATHE
BOARD CLOAK CLOUT COPSE
CROWN DRAPE DRESS FENCE
FLESH FLOOD GUISE HATCH KIVER
MOUNT RECTO SCARF SERVE

SHADE STREW STUDY THEAK THEEK
TOWEL TREAD VERSO WELME
WHALM AWNING BATTER BINDER
BLAZON CANOPY CHALON CLOTHE
DOUBLE EARLAP ENAMEL ENCASE
ENFOLD ENTIRE ENVEIL FOLDER
HACKLE IMMASK INVEST JACKET
KIRTLE MANTLE OVERGO POTLID
RUNNER SCONCE SCREEN SHADOW
SHEATH SHIELD SLEEVE SPREAD
SPRING SWATHE TOILET TOPPER
WHAUVE APPAREL ASPHALT
BANDAGE BESTREW BLANKET
CAPSULE CONCEAL CONTECT
COUVERT ELYTRON EMBRACE
ENCRUST FASCINE HEADCAP
HOUSING INCRUST KNEECAP
MANHEAD OBSCURE OMNIBUS
OVERLAY PRETEXT SHEATHE
SHELTER SHUTTER TAMPION
THIMBLE BEDCOVER COMPRISE
COVERCLE DEBRUISE ENCLOTHE
ENSCONCE HOODWINK IMMANTLE
OVERHAIL OVERSILE OVERWEND
PALLIATE PRETENCE PRETENSE
SLIPOVER SURPOOSE
(— A FIRE) DAMP
(— AROUND FLOWER) CYMBA
(— BRICKS) SCOVE
(— FOR ALEMBIC) HEAD
(— FOR CHALICE) PALL
(— FOR DIAPER) SOAKER
(— FOR ENGINE) COWLING
(— FOR FOOD) BELL
(— FOR GUN) TAMPION
(— FOR MILITARY CAPE) HAVELOCK
(— FOR PISTON) FOLLOWER
(— FOR POWDER PAN) HAMMER
(— FOR WIRES) BOOTLEG
(— GROUND) HEAT
(— HEARTH) FETTLE
(— OF BALL) CARCASS
(— OF BOILER) VOMIT
(— OF COFFIN) COOM
(— OF HAWSEHOLE) BUCKLER
(— OF MINE CAGE) BONNET
(— OF RIFLE MAGAZINE) GATE
(— OF SPORANGIUM) EPIGONE
(— OF VEGETATION) GROWTH
(— OPPRESSIVELY) SMOTHER
(— OVER) RAKE WELME WHELM
QUELME SHEUGH BECLOUD
OVERDECK WITHHELE
(— PLANTS) BAG
(— PROTECTIVELY) SHROUD
SHEATHE
(— ROAD) BLIND
(— SOIL WITH CLAY) GAULT
(— UP) HAP BELY FOLD BELIE
SALVE SLEEK HUDDLE
(— WITH ASHES) SOIL
(— WITH BACON) BARD
(— WITH CLAY) CLOAM
(— WITH COWL) MOB
(— WITH CRUMBS) BREAD
(— WITH DOTS) CRIBBLE
(— WITH DROPS) DAG
(— WITH EARTH) BURY HEAL INTER
(— WITH FILM) SKIM

(— WITH FLESH) INCARN
(— WITH FOAM) EMBOSS
(— WITH GOLD) GILD
(— WITH MEAL) MELVIE
(— WITH MUD) BEMUD BELUTE
(— WITH OAKUM) FOTHER
(— WITH PITCH) PAY
(— WITH PLASTER) PARGET
(— WITH SHEATH) GLOVE
(— WITH SOLDER) SPLASH
(— WITH STONE) ASHLAR
(— WITH STRAW) THATCH
(— WITH TIN) BLANCH
(— WITH TOPSOIL) KELLY
(— WITH WATER) DOUSE DOWSE
FLOOD WHELM
(— WITH WAX) CERE
(— WITH WEAVING) GRAFT
(— WITH WINGS) BROOD
(BED —S) HEALING
(BEEHIVE —) QUILT
(BOOK —) CASE SIDE
(GLASS —) STRIKE
(PACK —) MANTA
(POSTAL —) ENTIRE
(POT —) BRED
(SADDLE —) PILCH HOUSING
(SLIDING —) BRIDGE
(TABLE —) BAIZE
(WING — OF BEETLE) SHARD
COVERALL GOWN JUMPER
COVERED CLAD FULL SHOD TECT
BLIND MOSSY CLOSED COVERT
HIDDEN ENCASED OBTECTED
SCREENED
(— WITH CRYSTALS) DRUSY
(— WITH FEATHERS) HIRSUTE
(— WITH FOREST) HYLEAN
(— WITH HAIRS) COMATE VILLOUS
(— WITH PROTUBERANCES) HUMRY
(— WITH SCALES) SCUTATE
(— WITH SEAWEED) TANGLY
(THINLY —) BARISH
COVERED WAGON WHITETOP
BUCKWAGON
COVERER DECKER
COVERING (ALSO SEE COVER) BOX
COT FUR HAP KEX ARIL BARB BARK
BOOT CASE CAUL CUFF DECK FILM
HAME HEAD HOOD HULL HUSK KELL
MASK OVER PALL PUFF ROBE ROOF
SLIP SPAT TARP TILE TILT TRAP
VEIL APRON ARMOR BRAID BURSE
CRUST DRESS GLOBE GLOVE
HATCH QUILT SCALE SHELL SKIRT
STALL SWARD TESTA TUNIC TWEEL
WREIL ARMING AWNING BANCAL
BANKER CANOPY CANVAS COVERT
DRAPET EMBRYO ENAMEL FACING
FENDER GAITER GANOIN HACKLE
HATCAP HELMET JACKET MUZZLE
PELAGE SADDLE SCREEN SHEATH
SHROUD SINDON VERNIX BUFFONT
CAMISIA CAPSULE CEILING COATING
COWLING EARFLAP ENVELOP
EXCIPLE GRATING HAPPING
HEALING HEELCAP HOUSING
MUFFLER OVERLAY PURPORT
SARPLER SHADING SHELTER

SHOEING SLIPPER TECTURE
TEGMENT VESTURE WRAPPER
ARMGUARD BLAZONRY BOARDING
CASEMENT CLEADING CLOTHING
COMPRESS COVERLET EGGSHELL
EPISPORE INDUMENT INDUSIUM
MANTELET MANTLING OVERCAST
PAVILION PERICARP SETATION
UMBRELLA
(— FOR BENCH) BANKER
(— FOR BOXERS' HANDS) CESTUS
(— FOR NECK) TUCKER
(— FOR ROOF APEX) EPI
(— FOR SHOULDERS) STOLE
(— FOR SKI) SKIN
(— FOR STIRRUP) HOOD
(— OF BED) TIKE
(— OF BELL ROPE) GRIP
(— OF BIRD) INDUMENT
(— OF BOW HANDLE) ARMING
(— OF CASH SHORTAGE) LAPPING
(— OF FEATHERS) DOWN
(— OF NUTMEG) MACE
(— OF ROPE) SERVICE
(— OF VEGETATION) FLEECE
(CAST —S) EXUVIAE
(CHIMNEY —) COWL
(CLOTH —) TOILET
(COARSE —) CADDOW TILLET
(DEFENSIVE —) ARMOR KICKER
(EAR —) EARLAP EARFLAP
EARMUFF OREILET
(EYE —S) GOGGLES
(FLOOR —) RUG TILE CRASH
CARPET LINOLEUM OILCLOTH
(FOUL —) SCUM
(HEAD —) CAP HAT WIG HAIR HIVE
HOOD BONNET HELMET BIRETTA
CHAPEAU CHAPERON HAVELOCK
HEADRAIL TROTCOZY
(LEG —) BOOT HOSE STOCK GAITER
LEGGIN PEDULE KNEELET LEGGING
STOCKING
(LIGHT —) GRIMING
(LINEN —) BARB
(OUTER —) BARK HIDE HULL HUSK
CRUST TESTA JACKET CARAPACE
(PROTECTIVE —) APRON ARMOR
SHELL COCOON
(SLIGHT —) CYMAR
(STAGE —) HEAVENS
(STERILE —) DRAPE
(STICKY DAMP —) GLET
(THIN —) FILM SCRUFF WASHING
COVERLET PANE HELER HOUSE
QUILT REZAI THROW AFGHAN
CADDOW CHALON COLCHA LIGGER
SPREAD BLANKET BUFFALO
COVERLID DAGSWAIN
COVER-SHAME SAVIN SAVINE
COVERT DEN LAY LIE SLY LAIR
VERT EARTH NICHE PRIVY ASYLUM
HARBOR HIDDEN LATENT MASKED
MYSTIC REFUGE SECRET COVERED
DEFENSE PRIVATE SHELTER
TECTRIX THICKET DISGUISE
INVOLVED
(PL.) CRISSUM
COVERTLY CLOSE CLOSELY

COVET ACHE ENVY PANT WANT
WISH CRAVE YEARN YISSE DESIRE
GRUDGE HANKER
COVETOUS AVID GAIR GARE EAGER
FRUGAL GREEDY SORDID STINGY
ENVIOUS GRIPPLE MISERLY
DESIROUS GRASPING
COVETOUSNESS GREED MISERY
AVARICE YISSING COVETISE
PLEONEXIA
COVEY BEVY FALL BROOD FLOCK
HATCH COVERT COMPANY
COVIN BAND CREW FRAUD COVINE
COMPANY CONVENE ASSEMBLY
TRICKERY
COW AWE KEY NOT BEEF BOGY
BOSS COWL CUSH FAZE MOIL MULL
NOTT ROAN RUNT VACA ABASH
ALARM BEEVE BOSSY BROCK BULLY
CUSHA DAUNT DOMPT DRAPE
MOGGY QUAIL SCARE SNOOL
VACHA BOVINE BULLER COLLOP
CRUMMY GOBLIN HAWKEY HAWKIE
HEIFER MAILIE MILKER MULLEY
SUBDUE BOARDER BUGBEAR
BULLOCK CRITTER CRUMMIE
DEPRESS MESTENO MILCHER
OVERTOP SQUELCH TERRIFY
ALDERNEY AUDHUMLA BROWBEAT
COWBRUTE DISPIRIT FRIGHTEN
STRIPPER THREATEN
(— ABOUT 3 FEET HIGH) GYNEE
(— BEFORE CALVING) SPRINGER
(BARREN —) DRAPE BARRENER
(DRY —) KEY SEW
(HORNLESS —) NOT MOIL NOTT
DODDY MULEY DODDIE HUMLIE
MAILIE HUMBLIE POLLARD
MOULLEEN
(PREGNANT —) CALVER INCALVER
(WHITE-FACED —) HAWKEY HAWKIE
(YOUNG —) STIRK HEIFER
(PL.) KINE DAIRY
COWARD COW COOF DAFF FUNK
FUGIE LACHE PIKER CRAVEN
FUNKER PIGEON CAITIFF CHICKEN
COUCHER DASTARD MEACOCK
NITHING PANURGE QUITTER
NIDERING POLTROON RECREANT
TURNBACK TURNTAIL
COWARDICE DASTARDY LASHNESS
COWARDLY SHY ARGH FAINT LACHE
TIMID AFRAID COWARD COWISH
CRAVEN TURPID YELLOW CAITIFF
CHICKEN GUTLESS HILDING
FACELESS NIDERING POLTROON
RECREANT SNEAKING
COWBARN BYRE SAUR SHIPPON
VACCARY
COWBIRD BECCO BUNTING
CUCKOLD OXBITER COKEWOLD
LAZYBIRD
COWBOY HAZER RIDER ROPER
SCREW WADDI WADDY CHARRO
GAUCHO GINETE HERDER JINETE
COWHAND COWHERD COWPOKE
GRAZIER HERDBOY LLANERO
PANIOLO PUNCHER REFUGEE
VAQUERO BUCKAROO DALLYMAN

JACKAROO NEATHERD NOWTHERD
OUTRIDER PASTORAL RANCHERO
SWINGMAN WRANGLER
COWCATCHER GUARD PILOT
FENDER
COWED HANGDOG DOWNCAST
COWER HUG COUR FAWN RUCK
HOVER QUAIL SHRUG SNOOL SQUAT
STOOP TOADY WINCE COORIE
CRINGE CROUCH HURKLE SHRINK
CROODLE CRUDDLE
COWFISH TORO BECCO CUCKOLD
MANATEE SIRENIA
COWHAGE KIWACH
COWHAND PEELER FLANKER
STOCKMAN
COWHERB COCKLE SOAPWORT
COWHERD HERDSMAN NEATHERD
COWHOUSE BYRE SHIPPEN SHIPPON
COWL CAP COW LID SOE TUB COUL
HOOD MONK MITER BONNET
CUCULE CAPUCHE SCUTTLE
CAPUCHIN
COW PARSNIP MADNEP CADWEED
HOGWEED PIGWEED BEARWORT
BUNDWEED
COWPEA SITAO FRIJOL FRIJOLE
TOWCOCK BLACKEYE BLACKPEA
COWPEN CUPPEN CUPPIN
COWPOX PAPPOX KINEPOX VACCINA
VACCINIA
COWRIE COWRY VENUS ZIMBI
CYPRAEID
COWSLIP PAIGLE PRIMULA SHOOTER
AURICULA CYCLAMEN MARIGOLD
PRIMROSE
COXA HIP HAUNCH
COXCOMB FOP NOB BUCK DUDE
FOOL TOFF CLEAT DANDY HINGE
PRINCOX POPINJAY PRINCOCK
COXCOMBRY FOPPERY
COY PAL SHY ARCH COAX NICE
ALOOF CHARY DECOY QUIET SQUAB
STILL ALLURE CARESS DEMURE
MODEST PROPER BASHFUL DISTANT
PEEVISH STRANGE RESERVED
SKITTISH
COYNESS SHYNESS
COYO CHININ
COYOL COROJO COROZO
COYOTE VARMINT
(— STATE) SOUTHDAKOTA
COYPU DEGU NUTRIA
COZEN COG CON BILK GULL POOP
CHEAT TRICK CHISEL GREASE
BEGUILE DECEIVE DEFRAUD
SWINDLE HOODWINK
COZENER SNAP SNECKDRAW
COZENING SIMILATE
COZIER CADGER CODGER COSIER
COZY RUG BEIN BIEN COSY EASY
HOMY SAFE SNUG BIELD CANNY
CUSHY HOMEY CHATTY PENTIT
SECURE TOASTY COVERING
FAMILIAR HOMELIKE SOCIABLE
CRAB GIN UCA BOCO JUEY MAJA
ZOEA ANGER ARROW AYUYU BLUEY
MAIAN MAIID MAJID RACER SANDY
THIEF WINCH BUSTER CANCER

GROUSE HARPER HERMIT KABURI
NIPPER PARTAN PEELER PUNGAR
PUNGER RACING SPRITE BUCKLER
BUCKLUM BURSTER CABOUCA
CANCRID FIDDLER GRUMBLE
INACHID OCYPODE PANFISH
POLYPOD SHEDDER SOLDIER
SPECTER SPECTRE SURIQUE
ARACHNID CRABFISH DORIPPID
GRAPSOID HORSEMAN IRRITATE
LIMULOID LITHODID OCHIDORE
OXYSTOME PORTUNID RANININAN
TRAVELER WINDLASS
(MATING —) DOUBLER
CRAB APPLE CRAB SCRAB SCROG
COLING
CRABBED SOUR UGLY CABBY
CROSS SURLY TESTY BITTER
COPPED CROOSE CROUSE CRUSTY
MOROSE RUGGED SULLEN TEETHY
TRYING BOORISH CANKERY
CRABBIT CRAMPED CRONISH
CROOKED FRABBIT GNARLED
KNOTTED OBSCURE PEEVISH
CHURLISH CONTRARY CRABBISH
LIVERISH PETULANT VINEGARY
CRABBEDNESS ACRIMONY
ASPERITY
CRABCATCHER CRABIER
CRABER VOLE AGOUARA
CRABGRASS DRAWK FONIO PANIC
DARNEL PANICLE CRABWEED
ELEUSINE
CRAB LOUSE CRAB MORPION
MOREPEON
CRAB PLOVER DROME
CRAB TREE GRIBBLE
CRABWOOD ANDIROBA
POISONWOOD
CRACK GAG KIN POP BANG BLOW
CHAP CHIP CHOP CLAP CONE DOKE
FENT FLAW GAIG JEST JIBE JOKE
KIBE LEAK LICK QUIP REND RIFT
RIME RIVE SCAR SLAT SNAP YERK
BRACK BREAK CHARK CHECK CHICK
CHINE CHINK CLACK CLEFT CRAKE
CRAZE FLAKE FLANK FLASH GRIKE
KNACK KNICK SCORE SHAKE SLASH
SPANG SPLIT CLEAVE CRANNY
SLITER SPIDER SPRING BLEMISH
CRACKLE CREVICE FISSURE SLIFTER
SLITHER FRACTURE HAIRLINE
STRAMASH
(— A WHIP) YERK FLANK
(— IN FLESH) KIN CHAP KIBE
(— IN FLOOR) STRAKE
(— IN INGOT) SPILL
(— IN MAST) SPRING
(— IN ROCK) GRIKE JOINT
(— IN SEA ICE) RIFTER
(— IN STEEL) CHECK SPILL
(— OPEN) SEAM
(— PETROLEUM) BURN
(— WHILE FIRING) DUNT
(PL.) CRAZE
CRACKAJACK NAILER NAILING
CRACKBRAINED CRAZY NUTTY
CRACKY ERRATIC
CRACKED FLED NECKED CHAPPED

COMICAL TOUCHED CRACKERS
CRACKER BAKE LIAR WAFER
POPPER BISCUIT BOASTER
BREAKER BURSTER COSAQUE
REDNECK SALTINE SNAPPER
(— STATE) GEORGIA
(BOILED —S) CUSH
(BROKEN —S) DUNDERFUNK
CRACKERJACK TRUMP
CRACKING CRAZE SHIVERING
(PL.) SCRAP
CRACKLE SNAP BREAK CRACK
CRISP BRUSTLE CRINKLE SPARKLE
SPUTTER
CRACKLING CRISP GREAVE SNAPPY
CRACKEL CRACKLE CREMANT
GREAVES CRACKNEL CRITLING
(PL.) SCRAPS GRIEBEN
CRACKNEL SIMNEL CRACKLING
CRACKPOT CRACK ERRATIC
LUNATIC CRANKISH
CRACKSMAN YEGG BURGLAR
PETEMAN
CRADLE BED COT CRIB REST ROCK
WOMB CRATE FRAME CRECHE
MATRIX ROCKER TROUGH BERCEAU
SHELTER BASSINET CUNABULA
(— FOR SHIP) BED SLEE
(— FOR VATS) STILLING STILLION
(— IN ARCHERY) PURSE
(CERAMICS —) CHUM
(GRAIN —) CADAR CADER
(PL.) CHOCKS
CRADLESONG BERCEUSE
CRADLING BRACK
CRAFT ART BARK BOAT SAIL FRAUD
GUILE SKILL TRADE BARQUE
BATEAU DECEIT DROGER METIER
MISTER POLICE ROADER STRUSE
TALENT VESSEL ABILITY CUNNING
DROGHER MYSTERY PANURGY
SLEIGHT APTITUDE ARTIFICE
BASKETRY VOCATION
(ANTIQUATED OR CLUMSY —)
HOOKER
CRAFTILY FOXILY
CRAFTINESS DESIGN SLEIGHT
SLYNESS
CRAFTSMAN CARL HAND CARLE
CRAFT NAVVY ARTIST WRITER
ARTISAN TOHUNGA WORKMAN
LETTERER MECHANIC
CRAFTY SLY ARCH DEEP DERN FINE
FOXY SLIM WILY WISE ADEPT
COONY SLAPE SLEEK ADROIT
ARTFUL ASTUTE CALLID QUAINT
SHREWD SOLERT SUBTLE TRICKY
CUNNING SLEEKIT SLEIGHT SUBTILE
VAFROUS VERSUTE VULPINE
CAPTIOUS DEXTROUS ENGINOUS
FETCHING JESUITIC SLEIGHTY
CRAG TOR CRAW KNEE NECK ROCK
SCAR SPUR ARETE BRACK CLIFF
CLINT CRAIG HEUCH HEUGH
THROAT
CRAGGY ROUGH ABRUPT CLIFFY
CLIFTY KNOTTY PAMPER RUGGED
CRAGGED KNAGGED
CRAKE CROW RAIL ROOK RAVEN

CORNBIRD RAILBIRD
CRAKOW BEAKER CRACOWE
POULAINE
CRAM MUG RAM WAD BONE FILL
GLUT LADE PACK PANG PORR PURR
STOW TUCK URGE CROWD CRUSH
DRIVE FARCE FORCE FRANK GORGE
GRIND LEARN PRESS SCRAM STECH
STUDY STUFF TEACH AGROTE
CROMME PESTER STEEVE THRACK
CRAMMED PANG STODGY
CHOCKFUL
CRAMMER CRAM FEEDER
CRAMMING GAVAGE
CRAMP ART ARCT COOP CRIB KINK
PAIN TUCK CRICK CRIMP CROWD
DOWEL PINCH STUNT TRAMP
AGRAFE DOGTIE HAMPER HINDER
KNOTTY PESTER CONFINE CRAMPER
CRAMPET COMPRESS CONTRACT
RESTRAIN RESTRICT
CRAMPED CRIMP CRIMPED SQUEEZY
CRAMPFISH TORPEDO
CRAMPING UNEASY
CRAMPON CRAMP CRAMPET
CRAMPOON
CRANBERRY BERRY CRANE ERICAD
BOGWORT PEMBINA ACROSARC
BILBERRY BOGBERRY COWBERRY
FENBERRY FOXBERRY
(— BUSH) PIMBINA
CRANBERRY TREE PEMBINA
SNOWBALL VIBURNUM
CRANE JOB GRUS HOOK SWAY
CYRUS DAVIT HERON HOIST JENNY
RAISE SARUS TITAN WADER
BROLGA COOLEN JIGGER KULANG
SAHRAS COOLUNG CRAWLER
DERRICK GOLIATH KAIKARA
WHOOPER GRUIFORM TRAVELER
(— FOR FIREPLACE) COTTREL
COTTEREL
CRANE ARM GIB JIB GIBBET
RAMHEAD COTTEREL
CRANESBILL ALUMROOT DOVEFOOT
FLUXWEED
CRANIUM PAN HEAD CRANE CRANY
SKULL BRAINPAN
CRANK NUT WIT BENT SICK WALT
WEAK WHIM WIND BRACE LOOSE
ROGUE SHAKY THROW WALTY
WINCH AILING BOLDLY CRANKY
EVENER GROUCH HANDLE INFIRM
AWKWARD BRACKET FANATIC
LUSTILY
(SOMEWHAT —) TENDER
CRANKCASE SUMP
CRANKINESS ANGULARITY
CRANKY UGLY CRAZY CRONK
CROSS LUSTY SHAKY TESTY AILING
CRANNY FIFISH INFIRM SICKLY
CROOKED GROUCHY PERVERSE
TORTUOUS
CRANNY HOLE NOOK CHINK CLEFT
CRACK CORNER CRANNEL CREVICE
FISSURE
CRANTARA TARIE
CRANTS WREATH CORANCE
GARLAND

CRAPE BAND CURL FRIZ CREPE CRIMP DRAPE GAUZE SHROUD MOURNING

CHAPE MYRTLE JAPONICA ASTROMEDA

CRAPPIE BACH SHAD BATCH CALICO CROPPIE BACHELOR BACULERE NEWLIGHT SACALAIT TINMOUTH CHINKAPIN

CRAPS CRAP HAZARD

CRASH BASH FAIL FALL RACK BLAST BURST CLOTH CRUSH FRUSH PRANG SHOCK SMASH SOUND FIASCO FRAGOR HURTLE FAILURE SHATTER STENTER COLLAPSE ICEQUAKE SPLINTER STRAMASH (— **OF THUNDER**) CLAP

CRASHING ROPAND SMASHING

CRASH-LAND DITCH

CRASS RAW DULL LOUD RUDE CRUDE DENSE GROSS ROUGH THICK COARSE OBTUSE STUPID

CRASSNESS SQUALOR

CRATCH CRIB RACK CRITCH MANGER GRATING

CRATE BOX CAR CASE CRIB FLAT PLANE SERON BASKET CRADLE ENCASE HAMPER HURDLE CACAXTE CANASTA CARRIER PACKAGE VEHICLE (**EMPTY** —) EMPTY

CRATER CUP PIT CONE HOLE DINOS FOVEA NICHE CELEBE HOLLOW CALDERA (— **FORMED BY STEAM**) MAAR (**LUNAR** —) LINNE

CRAUNCH CRANCH SCRANCH

CRAVAT TIE TECK ASCOT FRONT SCARF STOCK CHOKER GRAVAT BANDAGE NECKTIE OVERLAY SOUBISE CRUMPLER

CRAVE ASK BEG GAPE ITCH LONG NEED PRAY SEEK WISH COVET GREED YEARN DESIRE HANKER HUNGER LINGER THIRST YAMMER BESEECH ENTREAT IMPLORE REQUEST REQUIRE SOLICIT APPETITE

CRAVEN AFRAID COWARD SCARED DASTARD COWARDLY DEFEATED OVERCOME POLTROON RECREANT SNEAKING

CRAVING AVID ITCH WANT LETCH DESIRE HUNGER THIRST LONGING APPETITE LIKEROUS TICKLING APPETENCE (— **FOR LIQUOR**) DRY (— **FOR UNNATURAL FOOD**) PICA (**ABNORMAL** —) BULIMY BULIMIA BOULIMIA

CRAW MAW CRAG CROP STOMACH

CRAWFISH KREEF

CRAWL LAG COON DRAG FAWN INCH LOOP RAMP SHUG SWIM CREEP KRAAL SLIDE SLIME SNAKE TRAIL BUSTLE CRINGE GROVEL SCRAWL SCRIDE CLAMBER SLITHER SNIGGLE TRUDGEN INCHWORM

CRAWLY CREEPY

CRAYFISH DAD CRAB YABBY YABBIE CAMARON CRAWDAD LOBSTER CAMBARUS CRABFISH CRAWFISH

CRAYON KEEL PLAN CHALK CONTE SAUCE PASTEL PENCIL SKETCH SANGUINE

CRAZE BUG FAD FLAW MAZE MODE RAGE BREAK CRACK CRUSH FEVER FUROR MANIA VOGUE DEFECT IMPAIR MADDEN MADDLE WEAKEN WHIMSY DERANGE DESTROY FASHION SHATTER WHIMSEY DISTRACT

CRAZED MAD REE AMOK LOCO WILD WOOD WOWF ZANY BALMY BATTY DAFFY DOTTY GIDDY MANIC NUTTY POTTY WACKY COOCOO DOTTLE INSANE LOONEY BERSERK FANATIC LUNATIC DATELESS DELEERIT DEMENTED DERANGED

CRAZINESS CRAZE LUNACY DEMENTIA

CRAZY (ALSO SEE CRAZED) OFF REE WET BUGS GYTE HITE LOCO WILD ZANY BATTY BEANY DAFFY DOTTY GOOFY LOONY POTTY CRANKY CUCKOO DOTTLE FRUITY INSANE LOCKET MENTAL SCATTY SCREWY CRACKED LUNATIC PEEVISH SCRANNY BUGHOUSE COCKEYED CRACKERS DERANGED HALLICET HALUCKET MESHUGGA

CREAK GIG GEIG GIRG JARG RASP YIRR CHARK CHEEP CHIRK CRAIK CRANK CROAK GRIND GROAN FRATCH SCREAK SCRIKE SCROOP SKRAIK SQUEAK COMPLAIN

CREAKING JARG SCREAK SCRIKE

CREAKY ARTHRITIC

CREAM DIP BEAT BEST FOOL HEAD REAM CREME ELITE FROTH REAME SAUCE BONBON CHOICE TRIFLE COLOGNE FATNESS EMULSION OINTMENT

CREAMING MANTLING

CREAM PUFF PUFF DUCHESSE

CREAMY RICH REAMY ACREAM SMOOTH LUSCIOUS

CREASE GAW CLAM FOLD LINE LIRK RUCK RUGA SEAM BLOCK CRESS CRIMP PLAIT PLEAT PRESS SCARF SCORE FURROW SCARPA SUTURE WREATH CRUMPLE CRUNKLE WRIMPLE WRINKLE (**SERIES OF** —S) BREAK (PL.) RASCETA

CREASED CRUMPLED ACCORDION

CREATE COIN CREE FORM MAKE PLAN BUILD CAUSE ERECT FORGE IMPEL RAISE SHAPE WRITE AUTHOR DESIGN IMPOSE INVENT COMPACT COMPOSE CONJURE FASHION IMAGINE PRODUCE COMPOUND GENERATE CONSTRUCT (— **A DISTURBANCE**) RIOT (— **CONFUSION**) GARBOIL

CREATION WORLD COSMOS EFFECT NATURE POETRY EDITION FACTURE FASHION POIESIS PRODUCT SHAPING BERESHIT BUSINESS CREATURE UNIVERSE (**MENTAL** —) FANTASY PHANTASY (**VISIONARY** —) DREAM

CREATIVE FERTILE FORMFUL PLASTIC POIETIC FORGEFUL GERMINAL NATURING POMATIVE

CREATOR MAKER AUTHOR FATHER FORMER VARUNA WORKER KHEPERA TAGALOA DESIGNER INVENTOR OPERATOR PRODUCER TANGALOA

CREATURE MAN FOOD TOOL BEAST BEING DABBA JOKER SLAVE THING TRICK WIGHT ANIMAL FELLOW MINION PERSON WRETCH CRITTER GANGREL MINIKIN MINIMUS SHAPING CRAYTHUR CREATION HELLICAT (— **OF LITTLE VALUE**) SHOT (3 —S **OF A KIND**) LEASH (**CANNIBALISTIC** —) WENDIGO WINDIGO (**DISORDERLY** —) ROIT ROYT (**DWARF** —) FAIRY GNOME (**ELFLIKE** —) PERI (**EVIL** —) HELLICAT (**FABLED** —) LUNG SIREN MERMAN WIVERN ALBORAK MERMAID (**LITTLE** —) MITING (**MANGY** —) RONION RONYON (**MANLIKE** —) HOMINID HOMONID HOMINIAN (**MEAN** —) LEFT (**MECHANICAL** —) GOLEM (**MISERABLE** —) SNAKE (**NONSENSE** —) SNARK (**SILLY** —) GOOSE (**SMALL** —) ATOM GRIG BEASTIE (**SPRY** —) WHIPPET (**STUNTED** —) WIRL URLING WIRLING (**SUPERNATURAL** —) MAN DRAGON (**TINY** —) ELF ATOMY (**UNDERDEVELOPED** —) SLINK (**USELESS** —) HUSHION (**VICIOUS** —) DEVIL (**WORTHLESS** —) SCULPIN SNIPJACK (**WRETCHED** —) ARMINE (PL.) CREATION

CRECHE CRIB PUTZ MANGER NURSERY

CREDENCE FAITH TRUST BELIEF BUFFET CREDIT CREANCE CREDENZA

CREDENTIAL VOUCHER CREDENCE

CREDENZA NICHE SHELF TABLE BUFFET SERVER CREDENCE CUPBOARD

CREDIBILITY FAITH CREDIT

CREDIBLE LIKELY CREDENT FAITHFUL PROBABLE TROWABLE

CREDIT LOAN TICK ASSET CHALK ENDOW FAITH HONOR IZZAT MENSK MERIT STRAP TENET TRUST BELIEF CHARGE ESTEEM IMPUTE RENOWN REPUTE TICKET WEIGHT ACCOUNT ASCRIBE BELIEVE CREANCE JAWBONE OPINION WORSHIP ACCREDIT CREDENCE HEADMARK (**HOCKEY** —) ASSIST

CREDITABLE HONEST CREDIBLE REPUTABLE

CREDITOR DEBTEE SHYLOCK TRUSTER ADJUDGER APPRIZER CRANSIER CREANCER
(TROUBLESOME —) DUN

CREDO FAITH

CREDULITY EASINESS

CREDULOUS FOND SIMPLE SPOONY SPOONEY CREDIBLE GULLIBLE

CREED ISM LAY CULT SECT CREDO DOGMA FAITH TENET BELIEF KELIMA SYMBOL CREANCE KALIMAH TROWING DOCTRINE SYMBOLUM

CREEK BAY CUT GEO GIO GUT RIA RIO RUN VLY VOE BURN COVE HOPE KILL PILL RILL SLEW SLUE VLEI VLEY WASH WICK BACHE BAYOU BIGHT BOGUE BROOK CRICK DRAFT FLEET INLET ZANJA ARROYO BRANCH BREACH CANADA ESTERO SLOUGH STREAM DRAUGHT ESTUARY RIVULET ZANJONA MUSKOGEE
(AUSTRALIAN —) COWAL
(TIDE —) SLAKE

CREEK SEDGE THATCH

CREEL RIP CAUL CAWL HASK JACK KELL RACK TRAP HARSK BASKET JUNKET
(— FOR BOBBINS) BANK

CREELER TUBER LIGGER

CREEP COON FAWN INCH RAMP CRAWL CROPE DRIFT GLIDE PROWL SKULK SLINK SMOOT STEAL TRAIL CRINGE GROVEL SCRIDE SPRAWL CRAMBLE CRAMMEL SNIGGLE TAURANGA
(— AS IVY) RIZZLE
(PL.) WILLIES

CREEPER IVY JITI SHOE VINE WORM CREEP CROPE SNAKE COWAGE CRADLE IPECAC REPENT ROMPER TECOMA CLAMPER CLIMBER COWHAGE COWITCH CRAWLER REPTANT REPTILE RUNNING TRAILER FOXGLOVE GUITGUIT PICUCULE WOODBINE

CREEPING SLOW REPTANT REPTILE SERVILE

CREEPING CROWFOOT SITFAST CRAWFOOT

CREEPING SNOWBERRY MOXA TEABERRY

CREESE KRIS STAB CRESS CRISE SWORD DAGGER

CREMATE BURN

CRENEL LOOP CORNEL KERNEL CRENELT

CREOLE PATOIS CRIOLLO DIALECT HAITIAN MESTIZO
(— STATE) LOUISIANA

CREON (DAUGHTER OF —) GLAUCE
(FATHER OF —) MENOECEUS
(SISTER OF —) JOCASTA HIPPONOME

CREOSOTE BUSH LARREA

CREPE CRAPE FRIZZED NACARAT PANCAKE CHIRIMEN CRINKLED WRINKLED

CREPITATE SNAP GRATE RATTLE CRACKLE

CRESCENT HORN LUNE MOON ROOL CURVE LUNAR LUNOID LUNULE MOONED SICKLE WAXAND LUNETTE DEMILUNE MENISCUS
(END OF —) CUSP HORN

CRESCENTLIKE BICORN

CRESCENT-SHAPED MOONY LUNATE LUNATED

CRESOL FROTHER

CRESS EKER KERSE CUCKOO MADWORT CRUCIFER WHITETOP

CRESSET TORCH BASKET BEACON SIGNAL CRISSET FLAMBEAU

CREST COP TIP TOP ACME APEX COMB EDGE HOOD KNAP PEAK SEAL TUFT CHINE CROWN PLUME RIDGE COPPLE CREASE CRISTA CUMBRE FINIAL HEIGHT HELMET SUMMIT TIMBER TIMBRE BEARING FEATHER TOPKNOT CENTROID CRESTING ECTOLOPH METALOPH PINNACLE WHITECAP
(— OF BREAKER) SEEGE
(— OF HELMET) COMB
(— OF HILL) KNAP
(— OF MINERAL VEIN) APEX
(— OF MOUNTAIN RANGE) ARETE SAWBACK
(— OF RIDGE) EDGE
(— ON BIRD) CROWN ECKLE COPPLE
(IMPERIAL —) KIKUMON
(WAVE —) FEATHER WHITECAP

CRESTED COMBED MUFFED TAPPET TAPPIT COPPLED CRISATE CROWNED PILEATED

CRESTED GREBE CARGOOSE

CRESTED QUAIL COPPY

CRESTFALLEN COWED DEJECTED

CRESTING CHENEAU

CRETACEOUS CHALKY

CRETAN KEFTI MINOAN CANDIOT

CRETAN SPIKENARD PHU

CRETE

BAY: SUDA KANCA KISAMO MESARA
CAPE: BUZA LIANO SALOME SIDERO SPATHA STAVROS LITHINON SIDHEROS
GULF: KHANIA MERABELLO
MOUNTAIN: IDA DIKTE JUKTAS LASITHI THEODORE
MOUNTAINS: PHINO MADARAS
TOWN: HAG LATO CANEA KHORA SITIA ZAKRO ANOYIA CANDIA KHANIA KISAMO RETIMO KASTELLI HERAKLION

CRETIN IDIOT

CREUSA GLAUCE GLAUKE

CREUSA (FATHER OF —) CREON PRIAM
(HUSBAND OF —) AENEAS
(KILLER OF —) MEDEA
(SON OF —) ION ASCANIUS

CREVALLE JACK JUREL

CREVASSE CHASM SPLIT SCHRUND CLEAVAGE

CREVICE KIN BORE LEAK NOOK PEEP SEAM VEIN BREAK CHINE CHINK CLEFT CRACK CREEK CUNNE GRIKE CRANNY STRAKE CRANNEL FISSURE GUNNIES KRAVERS OPENING SLIFTER CREVASSE PEEPHOLE

CREW LOT MEN MOB SET BAND GANG GING HERD OARS SHIP TEAM COVIN EIGHT HANDS MEINY PARTY SQUAD STAFF COVINE MEINIE SEAMEN THRONG AIRCREW COMPANY FACULTY MANNING MEMBERS RETINUE EQUIPAGE
(— OF SHEARERS) BOARD

CREWEL CRUEL CADDIS CADDICE

CRIB BED BIN BOX CAB COT CUB HUT KEY BOOM CRUB CURB DIVE JACK PONY RACK RAFT SKIN BOOSE BOOSY CHEAT CRATE FRAME HOVEL STALL STEAL BUNKER CRATCH CRECHE CRITCH MANGER PIGSTY PILFER CABBAGE ENGLISH PURLOIN BASSINET CORNCRIB CRIBBAGE CRIBBING CRIBWORK

CRIBBER SHORER STUMPSUCKER

CRICK KINK CREEK HITCH SPASM TWIST

CRICKET GRIG MOLE SNOB CHANGA SADDLE GRYLLID TWIDDLER
(— HIT) SLOG

CRICKETER CUT COLT PLAYER RABBIT GENTLEMAN

CRIER HUER CRYER BEADLE HERALD WAILER BELLMAN MUEZZIN WRAWLER OUTCRIER

CRIME ACT SIN EVIL FACT LACK ABUSE ARSON BLAME CAPER FOLLY LIBEL WRONG FALSUM FELONY INCEST MURDER PIACLE FORFEIT FORGERY MISDEED OFFENCE OFFENSE INIQUITY SABOTAGE VILLAINY
(ORGANIZED —) GANGLAND

CRIMINAL BAD SORE YEGG CROOK FELON APACHE BASHER DACOIT GUILTY GUNMAN INMATE KILLER NOCENT SLAYER WARGUS WICKED CONVICT CULPRIT HEINOUS HOODLUM ILLEGAL NOXIOUS SEVENER VAUTRIN CRIMEFUL CULPABLE GANGSTER GAOLBIRD HABITUAL HARDCASE JAILBIRD SCELERAT
(PETTY —) ROUNDER
(VIOLENT —) DESPERADO
(PL.) AMALAITA

CRIMINATE IMPEACH

CRIMP BEND CURL FOLD FRIZ POKE POTE WAVE WEAK CLAMP CRISP FLUTE FRILL FRIZZ PINCH PLAIT BUCKLE GOFFER RUFFLE CRIMPER CRIMPLE CRINKLE FRIABLE GAUFFER WRINKLE OBSTACLE

CRIMSON LAC RED PINK GRAIN

BLOODY JOCKEY MAROON MODENA
CARMINE SCARLET CRAMOISY
CRIMSON CLOVER NAPOLEON
CRINED MANED
CRINGE BOW BEND CURB CURR
DUCK FAWN JOUK BINGE COWER
CRAWL CREEP QUAIL SNEAK SNOOL
STOOP WINCE YIELD BUCKLE
CROUCH GROVEL SHRINK SUBMIT
CRINKLE DISTORT SCRINGE
TRUCKLE
CRINGING ABJECT HANGDOG
SERVILE SPANIEL
CRINKLE BEND CURL KINK TURN
WIND CREPE CRISP PUCKER RIPPLE
RUMPLE RUSTLE CRACKLE
CRANKLE FRIZZLE WRINKLE
CRINKLED CRIMP CURLY BUCKLED
ENCOMIC CRISPATE
CRINKLY CREPY CREPEY
CRINOID POLYP CRINITE CAMERATE
COMATULA
(BODY OF —) CROWN
CRINOLINE CRIN HOOP
CRIPPLE MAR CRIP GIMP HARM
HURT LAME MAIM BACACH HOBBLE
IMPAIR INJURE SCOTCH WEAKEN
CRAPPLE CRUMPET DISABLE
LAMETER LAMIGER LAMITER
HANDICAP LAMESTER MUTILATE
PARALYZE
(PL.) LAMZIEKTE
CRIPPLED GIMPY COUPLED
DISABLED
CRIPPLING MAIM MAYHEM
CRISIS FIT ACME CRUX FLAP HEAD
JUMP PASS TURN CARDO CRISE
PANIC PERIL PINCH POINT STATE
STORM TRIAL STRAIT DUNKIRK
DECISION JUNCTURE MOUNTAIN
CRISP NEW COLD CURL FRIZ FROW
HARD BRISK CLEAR CRIPS CRUMP
CURLY FRESH FRIZZ NIPPY PITHY
SHARP SHORT SPALT STIFF TERSE
BITING BRIGHT CRISPY LIVELY
SNAPPY BRACING BRITTLE CONCISE
CRACKLY CRUNCHY CUTTING
FRIABLE FRIZZLE SMOPPLE INCISIVE
CRISPED FUZZY FRIZZLY CRISPATE
CRISPNESS SNAP
CRISSCROSS AWRY CROSS
NETWORK CONFUSED
CRITERION LAW NORM RULE TEST
TYPE AXIOM CANON CHECK GAUGE
MODEL PROOF TOUCH CRISIS
METRIC INDICIA MEASURE PLUMMET
STANDARD
CRITIC MOME BOOER JUDGE MOMUS
CARPER CENSOR CORNER EXPERT
PUNDIT SLATER SYNDIC ZOILUS
STYLIST COLLATOR CRITIQUE
DEBUNKER OVERSEER REVIEWER
THONGMAN
CRITICAL EDGY HIGH ACERB ACUTE
CHILLY CRITIC SEVERE URGENT
ACERBIC ADVERSE CARPING
EXIGENT NERVOUS PARLOUS
CAPTIOUS CARDINAL CAVILING
DECISIVE EXACTING JUDICIAL

SLASHING TICKLISH
CRITICISM RAP FIRE GAFF SLAM
BLAME KNOCK SLATE CRITIC
REVIEW CENSURE COMMENT
DESCANT SLASHER SLATING
ZOILISM BLUDGEON CRITIQUE
DIATRIBE JUDGMENT
CRITICIZE HIT PAN RAP RIP CARP
CRAB FLAY FLOG SKIN SLAM SLUR
TIDE YELP BLAME BLAST CAVIL
DECRY GRIPE JUDGE KNOCK ROAST
SCORE SLASH SLATE BERATE
CRITIC REBUKE REVIEW CENSURE
COMMENT CONDEMN CRITIZE
EXAMINE CRITIQUE DENOUNCE
TOMAHAWK
(— SEVERELY) FLAY JUMP
(— SLASHINGLY) SLASH SLATE
CRITIQUE CRITIC REVIEW CRITICISM
CRO CROY PAYMENT
CROAK CAW DIE GASP KILL PORK
ROUP CREAK CRONK PLUNK QUALM
QUARK SPEAK CROAPE GRUMBLE
COMPLAIN FOREBODE
CROAKER SPOT RONCO CROCUS
RONCHO TOMCOD BUBBLER
CABEZON CORBINA CORVINA
CABEZONE HARDHEAD KINGFISH
SCIAENID
CROAKING CROAKY HOARSE
RANARIAN COAXATION
CROAT CHORWAT CHROBAT
SYRMIAN
(PL.) HRVATI HERVATI
CROCARD BRABANT SCALDING
SLEEPING
CROCHET HOOK KNIT BRAID PLAIT
WEAVE CROTCHET
CROCK JAR PIG POT SMUT SOIL
SOOT STEAN STEEN STOOL CHATTY
CRITCH GOOLAH PANMUG SMUDGE
CRAGGAN TERRINE POTSHERD
CROCKERY CHINA CLOAM DISHES
PIGGERY POTWARE CLAYWARE
CROCODILE GOA CROC GATOR
CAYMAN GAVIAL JACARE LIZARD
MUGGER YACARE CRAWLER
CREEPER DIAPSID REPTILE SAURIAN
SERPENT LORICATE
CROCODILE BIRD SICSAC TROCHIL
MESSMATE
CROCUS IRID LILY SAFFRON
CROFT FARM TORP CRAFT CRYPT
FIELD GARTH VAULT BLEACH
CAVERN PARROCK
CROMLECH QUOIT CIRCLE DOLMEN
CROMMEL GORSEDD
CROMORNA CREMONA KRUMHORN
CRONE HAG AUNT CRONY WITCH
BELDAM RIBIBE BELDAME
CRONY PAL CHUM BILLY GOSSY
NETOP GIMMER GOSSIP
CROOK BEND HOOK TURN WARP
CHEAT CHINK CLEEK CRANK CROMB
CROOM CRUMP CURVE HUNCH
NIBBY PEDUM STAFF THIEF TRICK
CRUMMY INDENT TWICER CAMBUCA
CROSIER CROZIER CRUMMIE
INCURVE POTHOOK SLICKER

ARTIFICE CHISELER CRUMMOCK
SWINDLER
(— IN BRANCH) KNEE
(— OF HEAD) HEEL
(SHEPHERD'S —) CROTCH
CROOKBACKED CROUCHIE
CROOKED CAM WRY AGEE AWRY
BENT GAME WOGH AGLEY ASKEW
BOWLY CRUMP FALSE GLEED KINKY
SNIDE THRAW WRONG ACROOK
AKIMBO ARTFUL ASLANT CAMMED
CRABBY CRAFTY CRANKY CURVED
DOGLEG HURLED THRAWN TRICKY
WEEWAW WEEWOW ZIGZAG
ASKANCE ASQUINT CORRUPT
CRABBED CURVOUS OBLIQUE
TURNING TWISTED WINDING
CAMSHACH THRAWART TORTUOUS
CROOKEDNESS PRAVITY RHEBOSIS
CROOKNECK CASHAW CUSHAW
CROON HUM LOW BOOM LULL SING
WAIL CHIRM CRONY WHINE LAMENT
MURMUR TEEDLE COMPLAIN
CROP BOB COW CUT MAW SET TOP
CLIP CRAP CRAW KNAP MINE REAP
SETT STOW TRAP TRIM WHIP FRUIT
GRAZE PLANT QUIRT SHAVE SHEAR
SHIFT SWATH TILTH TRASH BURDEN
DECERP GATHER GEBBIE SILAGE
BEARING BURTHEN CRAPPIN
CURTAIL CUTTING HARVEST
MAMMONI MASHLUM TILLAGE
GLEANING PROFICHI TRASHIFY
INGLUVIES
(— CANDLEWICK) SNUFF
(— OF A HAWK) GORGE
(— OF FRUIT) HANG
(— OF GRASS) LEA LEY SWATH
SWARTH SWATHE
(— OF OYSTERS) SET
(— OF POTATOES) GARDEN
(— OUT) BASSET
(GREEN —S) SOILAGE
(INDIAN —) RABI KHARIF
(LARGE —) HIT
(RIDING —) ROP
(SECOND-GROWTH —) ROWEN
(PL.) FEED TILLAGE
CROPPED GOTCH SHAVED GOTCHED
CROPPER CARVER MUCKER PURLER
GRINDER PLUMPER
CROPPING EARMARK
CROQUET ROQUE BOMBARD
CROQUETTE CECIL OYSTER
KROMESKI KROMESKY
CROSIER BAGLE CROCE CROOK
PEDUM STAFF POTENT BACULUS
CAMBUCA CROZIER PASTORAL
CROSS GO CAM CUT MIX TAU ANKH
CRUX FORD FUNK MARK PASS
ROOD SIGN SOUR SPAN TREE
WOOD ANGRY CANGY CHUFF
CORSE GAMMY GURLY SURLY
TEATY TESTY THRAW TRAVE TRIAL
YAPPY BISECT CHUFFY CRABBY
CRANKY CROUCH DENIAL EMBLEM
GIBBET GROUTY GRUMPY HIPPED
OUTWIT PATCHY SIGNUM SNAGGY
SNASTY SULLEN SYMBOL TEETHY

THWART TOUCHY WICKED WOOLLY
ATHWART BECROSS CALVARY
CRABBED CROSIER CROZIER
CRUSADE CRUSADO FRABOUS
FRETFUL FROWARD OBLIQUE
PASSAGE PATIBLE PEEVISH PETTISH
POTENCE SALTIER SALTIRE
CAMSHACH CRANTARA CROCIATE
CROISADE CROSSLET CROTCHED
CRUCIFIX DEBRUISE DEMISANG
FRAMPOLD FRATCHED FRUMPISH
PECTORAL PETULANT PHRAMPEL
SNAPPISH SWASTIKA THUNDERY
TRAVERSE VEXILLUM WINDMILL
(— BY PLANE) HOP
(— ONESELF) SAIN
(— OVER) SPAN TRAJECT
(DOUBLE —) BUSINESS
(MALTESE —) FIREBALL
CROSSARM WISHBONE
CROSSBAR CROWN JUGUM DRIVER
TRANSOM
(— IN GATE) SWORD
(— IN SHAFT) STEMPEL STEMPLE
(— OF BALANCE) BEAM
(— OF WINDOW) LOCKET
CROSSBEAM BAR BUNK SPUR
TRAVE GIRDER BOLSTER TRANSOM
TRAVERSE
CROSSBEARER SPREADER
CROSSBILL FINCH
CROSSBOW PROD RODD BRAKE
LATCH PIECE PRODD TILLER
SLURBOW ARBALEST BALLISTA
STEELBOW STOCKBOW STONEBOW
CROSSBREED HUSKY METIS SANGA
SANGU HYBRID
CROSS CARRIER CRUCIFER
CROSSCURRENT SURGING
CROSSCUT DRIFT OFFSET TUNNEL
COUPURE
CROSSCUT SAW BRIAR
CROSSCUTTER BUCKER
CROSSE STICK
CROSSED ACROSS SQUINT WOOFED
CRUCIAL THWARTING
CROSSER STICKER
CROSSETTE EAR ANCON ELBOW
ANCONE CROSET
CROSS-EYE ESOTROPIA
CROSS-EYED SQUINT
CROSS-FERTILIZATION ALLOGAMY
PHYTOGAMY
CROSS FORM URDE URDY
CROSS-GRAINED UGLY NURLY
GNARLED HICKORY CONTRARY
CROSSHEAD YOKE
CROSSING XG PASS CROSS LACED
MIXTURE PASSAGE TRAJECT
CRUCIATE OPPOSING TRAVERSE
CROSSOVER
CROSSPATCH BEAR CRAB CRANK
GROUCH
CROSSPIECE BAR BAIL SPAR STEP
YOKE BEARD GLAND GRILL ROUND
STOCK THWART TOGGEL TOGGLE
BOLSTER TRANSOM CROSSARM
CROWFOOT FOOTRAIL HEADRAIL
TRAVERSE CHOPSTICK

(PL.) CROSSTREE
CROSS-QUESTION TARGE TAIRGE
CROSSROAD LEET VENT WENT
WEENT CAREFOX CARFOUR
COMPITUM CROSSWAY
(PL.) TRIVIA
CROSSRUFF SAW SEESAW
CROSS-SHAPED CRUCIAL CRUCIATE
CROSS-STAFF CROSS RADIUS
CROSIER CROZIER
CROSS STROKE BIND
CROSS-TEMPERED FRUMPISH
CROSSWISE CROSS ACROSS
ATHWART ACROSTIC DIAGONAL
OVERWART TRAVERSE WEFTWISE
CROSSWAYS
CROSSWORT MAYWORT MUGWEED
MUGWORT
CROTALUM CROTAL CYMBAL
CROTCH FORK POLE POST CLEFT
NOTCH STAKE CRATCH CRUTCH
GRAINS CROTCHET
CROTCHET FAD HOOK KINK WHIM
CRANK FANCY FREAK VAGARY
CORCHAT CRANKUM
CROTCHETY KINKY CRANKY
CROUCH HUG BEND CLAP COOK
CURB DARE DROP FAWN FORM
ROOK RUCK COWER HOVER SQUAT
STOOP COORIE CRINGE CROOCH
HUDDLE HUNKER HURKLE HURTLE
SCOOCH SCOUCH CROODLE
CROWDLE SCROOCH SCRUNCH
SQUATTER
CROUCHING SQUAT CROUCHANT
CROUD SCROUGE
CROUP CRUP HIVES CRUPPER
CROUPIER DEALER TOURNEUR
CROUTON DIABLOTIN
CROW AGA CAW CRY DAW BRAG
BRAN CRAW DOWP ROOK AYLET
BOAST CRAKE CROWD EXULT
HOODY KELLY RAVEN VAUNT
CARNAL CORBIE CORVUS HOODIE
KOKAKO GORCROW GRAPNEL
JACKDAW SWAGGER ABSAROKA
BALDHEAD BLACKNEB GAVELOCK
GRAYBACK GREYBACK
CROWBAR PRY SET CROW BETTY
JEMMY JIMMY LEVER SETUP SWAPE
FORCER GABLOCK PITCHER
GAVELOCK HANDSPEC
CROWBERRY HEATH HEATHER
CROWD FRY HUG JAM MOB SET TIP
BIKE CRAM CRUT FARE HEAP HERD
HOST JOSS MONG PACK PAVE PILE
PUSH ROCK ROTE ROUT RUCK
SERR SLUE SORT STOW SWAD
TURB WOOD BUNCH CLOUD COHUE
COVEY CRAMP CRUSH CRWTH
DROVE FLOCK GROUP HORDE
HURRY PLUMP POSSE PRESS ROTTA
SERRY SHACK SHOAL STECH STIVE
STUFF SWARM THREE VOLGE
WEDGE BOODLE CHORUS CLIQUE
HUBBLE HUDDLE HUSTLE IMPACT
JOSTLE MITHER MOIDER PESTER
RABBLE RESORT SCRUZE THRAVE
THREAD THRIMP THRONG THRUST

TOURBE TYMPAN VOLLEY BOUROCK
CHROTTA COMPANY CONGEST
IMPRESS JIMBANG SCROOGE
SCROUGE SQUEEZE THICKEN
THRUTCH ENTHRONG FREQUENT
JINGBANG SANDWICH SATURATE
VARLETRY GATHERING
(— ABOUT) FLOCK
(— AROUND) BESIEGE
(— OUT) DISPLACE
(— TOGETHER) HUG HOTTER
HOWDER HUDDLE CLUTTER
CONTRUDE
(CONFUSED —) HURRY
(MOVING —) DROVE
(NOISY —) ROUT
CROWDED CLOSE DENSE SPISS
STIFF THICK FILLED SPISSY THRONG
BUNCHED COMPACT OPPLETE
POPULAR SERRIED STIPATE
STUFFED TEEMING NUMEROUS
POPULOUS
CROWFOOT JOY PAGLE EXOGEN
PAIGLE EELWARE GOLDCUP
GOLLAND GOWLAND BANEWORT
CRAWFOOT GOLDWEED HELLWEED
CROWING COCK
CROWN CAP TAJ TIP TOP BULL COIN
GULL HELM PATE PEAK POLL RIGO
TIAR ADORN BASIL BEZEL BEZIL
CREST MITER MITRE MURAL POLOS
REGAL ROUND ROYAL TIARA
ANADEM CANTLE CIRCLE CLIMAX
CORONA DIADEM DOLLAR FILLET
INVEST LAUREL POTONG REWARD
SUMMIT TIMBER TROPHY UPWARD
VALLAR VERTEX WREATH AUREOLE
CHAPLET CORNICE CORONAL
CORONET FORETOP GARLAND
INSTALL PSCHENT STEPHEN
TONSURE CORONATE CORONULE
ENTHRONE PINNACLE SURMOUNT
TURNPIKE
(— OF CHICORY) ENDIVE
(— OF EGYPT) ATEF PSCHENT
(— OF HEAD) PATE SKULL CANTLE
POMMEL FORETOP
(— OF HILL) KNAP
(— OF LAUREL) BAY
(HALF —) GEORGE ALDERMAN
(PIECE OF —) BULL
(PLANT —) STOOL
CROWNED CORONATE LAURELED
(— WITH ROSES) ROSATED
CROW SHRIKE MAGPIE SQUEAKER
CROW'S NEST LOOKOUT
CROZER CHUCKER
CRUCIAL ACUTE PIVOT NEEDLE
SEVERE TRYING PIVOTAL SUPREME
TELLING CRITICAL DECISIVE
CRUCIAN CARP GIBEL
CRUCIBLE POT DISH ETNA SHOE
TEST CRUCE FOYER CRUSET
HEARTH MONKEY RETORT FURNACE
CROSSLET
CRUCIFIX PAX ROOD CROSS
CRUCIFIXION CROSS RANSOM
CRUCIFY VEX HANG KILL HARRY
MORTIFY TORMENT TORTURE
CRUCIATE

CRUDE ILL RAW BALD BARE RUDE BRUTE CRASS GREEN GROSS HAIRY HARSH ROUGH TACKY CALLOW COARSE DOUGHY INCULT KUTCHA SAVAGE UNRIPE VULGAR ARTLESS GLARING SQUALID UNCOUTH IGNORANT IMMATURE IMPOLITE INDIGEST
(NOT —) DELICATE
CRUDELY HARSHLY GAUCHELY
CRUDITY CRASSNESS GAUCHERIE ROUGHNESS
CRUEL ILL FELL GRIL GRIM HARD BLACK BREEM BREME BRUTE FELON HARSH RETHE SADIC STERN WROTH BITTER BLOODY BRUTAL DIVERS DREARY FIERCE IMMANE SAVAGE SEVERE UNJUST UNKIND UNMEEK UNMILD UNRIDE BESTIAL BOARISH BRUTISH GRIMFUL INHUMAN NERONIC SCADDLE SPITOUS WILROUN BARBARIC DIABOLIC FELONOUS FIENDISH INHUMANE PITILESS RUTHLESS SADISTIC TYRANNIC
CRUELLY FELL HARD CRUEL FELLY HARSHLY
CRUELTY RIGOR DURESS SADISM DEVILRY DEVILTRY FELLNESS SEVERITY
CRUET AMA JAR JUG VIAL BURET CRUSE BOTTLE CASTER CREVET CREWET GUTTUS AMPULLA BURETTE URCEOLE
CRUISE SAIL TRIP JUNKET STOOGE
(— AS A PIRATE) BUSK
CRUISER SHIP VALUER VESSEL WARSHIP ESTIMATOR
CRULLER WONDER OLYCOOK OLYKOEK TWISTER DOUGHNUT
CRUMB BIT ORT MURL PIECE LITTLE MORSEL CRIMBLE CRUMBLE MEALOCK MURLACK REMNANT FRAGMENT
(PL.) PANADA PANURE MOOLINGS
CRUMBLE ROT CRIM MURL MUSH BREAK BROCK CRUSH DECAY RAVEL SLAKE SPALL SPOIL BUCKLE MOLDER MYRTLE PERISH SLOUGH CORRADE CRIMBLE MOULDER COLLAPSE
(— DOWN) GRUSH
(— UNDER OVERWEIGHT) FLUSH
CRUMBLED UNDURE
(EASILY —) CRIMP BRUCKLE CRUMBLY
CRUMBLING SAMEL SAMMEL
CRUMBLY MURLY CRUMBY CRUMMY FRIABLE
CRUMPET CAKE MUFFIN PIKELET
CRUMPLE FOLD MOOL MUSS ROOL WISP CRUSH SCREW BUCKLE CREASE FURROW RAFFLE RUCKLE RUMPLE CRIZZLE CRUNKLE FRUMPLE SCRUNCH WRINKLE COLLAPSE CONTRACT SCRUMPLE
CRUNCH BITE CHEW CHOMP CRASH CRUMP CRUSH GNASH GRIND MUNCH PRESS RUNCH CRANCH

CRINCH GRANCH GROWSE CRAUNCH SCRUNCH
CRUPPER CROUP CURPEL CURPIN TAILBAND
CRUSADE WAR JEHAD JIHAD CROISEE CAMPAIGN CROCIATE
CRUSADER PILGRIM TEMPLAR EQUITIST REFORMER
(PL.) CROISES
CRUSH BOW HUG JAM BEND BORE BRAY CASE CHEW CRAM DASH MASH MILL MULL PASH RAVE STUB BRAKE BREAK BRIZZ CHAMP CRASH CRAZE CREEM CROWD FORCE FRUSH GRIND GRUSH PRESS QUASH QUELL SMASH SMUSH SQUAB SQUAT STAMP TREAD UNMAN BRUISE BURDEN CRUNCH DEFOIL DEFOUL KNATCH KNETCH SCOTCH SCRUSH SCRUZE SQUASH SQUISS SUBDUE THRING THRONG THWACK ACCABLE BECRUSH CONQUER CRACKLE CRUMPLE DEPRESS DESTROY OPPRESS OVERRUN REPRESS SCRUNCH SCRUNGE SHATTER SQUEEZE SQUELCH SUCCUMB TRAMPLE COMPRESS FORBREAK OVERCOME SQUABASH SUPPRESS
(— BEANS) NIB
(— HAT) BONNET
(— IN) STAVE
(— ROCK) DOLLY DOLLEY DOLLIE
(— SPIRIT) BREAK
CRUSHABLE QUASHY
CRUSHED TAME BROKEN ECRASE MUSHED CONTRITE
CRUSHER NIBBER
CRUSHING FIERCE BRUISING SMASHING SQUABASH
CRUST FUR CAKE HULL RIND SCAB SHELL SKULL COFFIN CRUSTA ESCHAR GRATIN HARDEN RONDLE SCRUFF ABAISSE CALICHE COATING ENCRUST INCRUST CARAPACE PELLICLE SCUTULUM WINEBALL DURICRUST
(— ON WINE) ARGAL ARGOL
(PIE —) HUFF COFFIN
(PL.) SORDES
CRUSTA PES
CRUSTACEAN BUG APUS CRAB FLEA SCUD ZOEA ALIMA CARID LOUSE PRAWN SCREW SCROW CYPRID ENDITE ISOPOD SHRIMP SLATER SQUILL ARTEMIA COPEPOD CRAYLET DAPHNID DECAPOD GRIBBLE HAYSEED LOBSTER SQUAGGA SQUILLA BARNACLE CRAYFISH GAMMARID LERNAEAN MONOCULE SQUILLID
CRUSTADE DARIOLE
CRUSTY CURT BLUFF BLUNT RUSTY TESTY MOROSE SULLEN CRABBED PEEVISH PETTISH STARCHY SNAPPISH
CRUTCH FORK STILT CLUTCH CRATCH CROTCH POTENT SADDLE SCATCH STADDLE

CRUX NUB GIST HALF PITH CROSS POINT PUZZLE RIDDLE PROBLEM
CRUX ANSATA ANKH
CRWTH ROTA ROTE CROWD CRUTH ROTTA ROTTE CROUTH CHROTTA
CRY HO BOO CAW CRI FAD HOA HUE OLE PIP SOB YIP BAWL BELL BUMP CALL COWL CROW EVOE FALL GLAM GOWL HAIL HAWK HOOT HOWL KEEN MEWL NOTE OYES OYEZ PULE RAGE RAME RANE REEM RERD SCRY SIKE TOOT WAIL WEEP YELL YELP BARLA BLART BLORE CHEVY CLEPE CRAKE CROUP CRUNK GREDE GREET GROAN QUEAK RUMOR SHOUT SOUND TROAT UTTER VOGUE WHEWL WHINE WHULE WRAWL BARLEY BELLOW BOOHOO CHIVVY CLAMOR DEMAND ENSIGN LAMENT OUTCRY QUETHE SCREAM SHRIEK SLOGAN SNIVEL SQUALL SQUAWL SQUEAL TONGUE WIMICK YAMMER EXCLAIM FASHION HOSHANA SCREECH SPRAICH GARDYLOO PROCLAIM SCRONACH
(— ALOUD) BLART GREDE
(— AT SIGHT OF WHALE) FALL
(— DOWN) DOWNCRY BERATTLE
(— FOR TRUCE) BARLA BARLY BARLEY
(— HOARSELY) CROUP
(— LIKE ELEPHANT) BARR TRUMPET
(— LIKE PIG) WRINE
(— OF A BAT) CHIP
(— OF ABORIGINES) COOEE
(— OF BACCHANALS) EVOE
(— OF BIRD) CAW COO PEW BOOM CAWK CLANG BIRDCALL
(— OF BITTERN) BILL
(— OF CAT) MEW MEWL MIAOU MIAOW MIAUL MIAUW CALLING
(— OF CONTEMPT) BOO
(— OF DEER) BELL
(— OF ENTHUSIASM) BANZAI
(— OF GOOSE) HONK YANG
(— OF GUINEA HEN) POTRACK
(— OF HOUND) MUTE MUSIC
(— OF JACKAL) PHEAL PHEALE PHEEAL
(— OF MOURNING) KEEN TANGI
(— OF NEWBORN CHILD) VAGITUS
(— OF RAVEN) QUALM
(— OF SHEEP) BAA BLAT BLEAT
(— OF SNIPE) SCAPE
(— OF SORROW) ULLAGONE
(— OF SURRENDER) KAMERAD
(— OF WATCHMAN) WATCH
(— OUT) BAY BAWL BRAY GALE GAPE HOOT HOWL JERK SCRY BLORE CHIRM CLAIM ESCRY SHOUT HALLOO HOLLER SCREAM SHRIEK THREAP THROPE BREATHE EXCLAIM RECLAIM DISCLAIM PROCLAIM
(— TO CLEAR PASSAGE) HALL
(— TO COMBATANTS) BAILE
(— UP) CRACK
(BATTLE —) CRY ENSIGN MONTJOY GERONIMO MONTJOYE

(DRINKING —) RIVO
(HOARSE —) CROAK
(HUNTING —) TIVY CHEVY CHIVY CHEVVY STABOY YOICKS TALLYHO PILILLOO
(PROLONGED —) RANE
(RALLYING —) SLOGAN
(RAUCOUS —) CATCALL
(SHRILL) SKIRL SQUEAK SQUEAL SCREECH YALLOCK
(WAR —) DIN ALALA SLOGAN
(WORDLESS —) KEEN ULULU
CRYING PIPING URGING CLAMANT HEINOUS VAGIENT PRESSING RECREANT
(— OF HOUND) BELLING
CRYPT PIT CRAFT CROFT CROWD VAULT CAVERN GROTTO RECESS SHROUD CHAMBER FOLLICLE
CRYPTIC DARK VAGUE HIDDEN OCCILT SECRET OBSCURE ELLIPTIC MYSTICAL SIBYLLIC
CRYPTOGRAM CODE CRYPT CIPHER
CRYPTOGRAPH GEMATRIA
CRYPTOGRAPHER VIGENERE
CRYPTORCHID RIDGLING
CRYSOPHANIC RHEUMIC
CRYSTAL XL ICE DIAL DOME HARD IRIS SEED XTAL CLEAR GLASS GRAIN LUCID LUNET TABLE GLASSY LIMPID MIRROR NEEDLE PEBBLE QUARTZ TABLET ACICULA DIAMOND DIPLOID GLASSIE LUNETTE ORTHITE TWOLING ULEXITE YAJEINE ZOISITE FIVELING FOURLING PELLUCID TRICHITE TRILLING
(— FOREIGN TO ROCK) XENOCYST
(FINE —) BERYL
(ICE —S IN WATER) FRAZIL
(NEEDLE-SHAPED —S) RAPHIDES
(ROCK —) BRISTOL
(TWIN —) TWIN MACLE TWINDLE TWOLING FOURLING
(PL.) DRUSE GRAIN
CRYSTAL GAZE SCRY
CRYSTAL GAZER SEER SCRYER SKRYER
CRYSTALLINE PURE CRYSTAL PELLUCID
CRYSTALLITE BELONITE TRICHITE BACILLITE SCOPULITE
CRYSTALLIZE FIX FIRM JELL CANDY SUGAR NEEDLE CONGEAL SOLIDIFY
CRYSTALLOGRAPHY LEPTOLOGY
C-SHAPED SIGMATE
CTENIDIUM COMB
CTENOPHORE RIB NUDA CYDIPPID JELLYFISH
CUADRA MANZANA
CUB FRY PEN BEAR CHIT COOP SHED TOTO STALL WHELP LIONET NOVICE CODLING REPORTER
(— SCOUT) WEBELOS

CUBA
BAY: NIPE PIGS
CAPE: CRUZ MAISI LUCRECIA
CAPITAL: HAVANA
CIGAR: HAVANA
COIN: PESO CENTAVO CUARENTA
DANCE: CONGA RUMBA DANZON RHUMBA GUARACHA PACHANGA
FALLS: TOA AGABAMA CABURNI
GULF: MEXICO ANAMARIA BATABANO
INDIAN: CARIB TAINO ARAWAK
ISLAND: PINES
ISLANDS: SABANA CAMAGUEY
MEASURE: VARA BOCOY TAREA CORDEL FANEGA
MOUNTAIN: TURQUINO
MOUNTAINS: CRISTAL MAESTRA ORGANOS TRINIDAD
PROVINCE: HAVANA ORIENTE CAMAGUEY MATANZAS
RIVER: ZAZA CAUTO
SWAMP: ZAPATA
TOWN: COLON MANES BAYAMO GUINES HAVANA BARACOA HOLGUIN PALMIRA ARTEMISA CAMAGUEY GUAYABAL MATANZAS SANTIAGO
TREE: JIQUE JIQUI
WEIGHT: LIBRA TERCIO

CUBAN LILY SCILLA
CUBBYHOLE NOOK CUBBY
CUBE CUT DIE NOB KNOB BLOCK EIGHT SOLID TIMBO BABASCO CUBELET TESSELA TESSERA BARBASCO QUADRATE
(— OF BREAD) CROUTON
(MEAT —S) CABOB KABOB KEBOB
(PL.) DICE
CUBIC SOLID CUBOID CUBICAL
CUBICALLY DIEWISE
CUBIC CENTIMETER FLUIGRAM
CUBIC METER STERE
CUBICLE BAY CELL ROOM BOOTH CABIN NICHE STALL ALCOVE CARREL CARRELL
CUBIT ELL CODO HATH COVID HASTA COUDEE
CUB SHARK LAMIA GALEID REQUIEM
CUCKING STOOL THEW TUMBLER TUMBREL TUMBRIL
CUCKOLD TUP HORN BECCO VULCAN WITTOL ACTAEON CORNUTE CORNUTO HORNIFY RAMHEAD COKEWOLD
CUCKOLDED FORKED UNICORN
CUCKOLDRY HORNWORK
CUCKOO ANI COWK CUCK FOOL GOUK GOWK KOEL KOIL CLOCK CRAZY KOKIL SILLY COUCAL DIDRIC HUNTER KOBIRD BOOBOOK CHATAKA DIEDRIC KOWBIRD SIRKEER CHOWCHOW PICARIAN RAINBIRD RAINFOWL
CUCKOOFLOWER HEAD PAGLE SPINK CUCKOO PAIGLE HEADACHE MILKMAID
CUCKOOPINT ARUM RAMP AARON BOBBIN DRAGON BUCKRAM OXBERRY MANDRAKE
CUCKOO SPIT WOODSERE

CUCULLATE COWLED HOODED COVERED
CUCUMBER CUKE PEPO GOURD CONGER CUCURB PEPINO PICKLE GHERKIN PICKLER CUCURBIT PEPONIDA PEPONIUM
(BITTER —) COLOCYNTH
(SHRIVELED —) CRUMPLING
(WILD —) CREEPER
CUCURBIT BODY FLASK GOURD CUCURB ALEMBIC MATRASS
CUD CHEW QUID BOLUS QUEED RUMEN CUDGEL
CUDBEAR CORK PERSIO PERSIS CUDWEED
CUDDLE HUG LAP PET CARESS COSSET FONDLE HUGGLE KIDDLE KIUTLE NESTLE PETTLE CROODLE CRUDDLE EMBRACE SMUGGLE SNOOZLE SNUGGLE
CUDDLESOME HUGGABLE
CUDDY ASS LOUT BRIBE CABIN DONKEY GALLEY PANTRY CUDEIGH
CUDGEL BAT CUD BEAT CANE CLUB CRAB DRUB KENT MACE RACK RUNG TREE BASTE BATON DRIVE KEBBY KEVEL LINCH LINGE SHRUB STAFF STAVE STICK THUMP TOWEL ALPEEN BALLOW BASTON BILLET GIBBET KEBBIE LIBBET THRASH WASTER BELABOR BOURDON DRUBBER SWADDLE SWINGLE TROUNCE BLUDGEON SHILLALA THWACKER
CUDWEED ENAENA CATFOOT
CUE QU NOD TAG TIP HINT MAST TAIL WINK BRAID CLUFF PLAIT QUEUE TWIST PROMPT SIGNAL PIGTAIL
(BILLIARD —) MAST STICK
(SHUFFLEBOARD —) SHOVEL
(TIP OF —) LEATHER
CUFF BOX BANK BLOW GOWF SLAM SLAP SLUG SWAT TURF CLOUT FIGHT GOWFF MISER SCUFF SCUFT SMITE SOUSE BUFFET CODGER FENDER MITTEN STRIKE TURNUP COLPHEG SCUFFLE WHERRET GAUNTLET HANDBLOW HANDCUFF TURNBACK
CUIR DORADO
CUIRASS CURACE CURATE CURIET LORICA THORAX
CUIRASSIER LOBSTER
CUISINE FOOD MENU TABLE COOKERY KITCHEN
CUITLATEC TECO
CUL-DE-SAC POCKET STRAIT IMPASSE
CULL OPT CAST COIL DUPE GULL PICK PIKE SIFT SORT ELECT GLEAN PLUCK ASSORT CHOOSE GARBLE GATHER REMOVE SELECT CULLING SEPARATE
CULLET SCRAP
CULM COOM HAULM SLACK COOMBE REFUSE DEPOSIT
(PL.) SIRKI SIRKY
CULMINATION END ACME APEX

AUGE CULM NOON ROOF BLOOM CREST CROWN HIGHT POINT APOGEE CLIMAX CULMEN CUMBLE HEIGHT PERIOD SUMMIT VERTEX ZENITH BLOWOFF

CULPABILITY BLAME GUILT DEMERIT

CULPABLE FAULTY GUILTY LACHES SINFUL IMMORAL BLAMABLE CRIMINAL

CULPRIT FELON CONVICT CRIMINAL OFFENDER

CULT CLAN DADA SECT CREED KUKSU CHURCH CULTUS DOMNEI MANISM NUDISM RITUAL SCHOOL SHINTO AMIDISM DADAISM ICONISM MYALISM MYSTERY WORSHIP DEVILISM HUMANISM SATANISM

CULTCH CUTCH STOOL SCULCH

CULTIVATE EAR HOE CROP DISC DISK FARM GROW PLOW REAR TEND TILL WORK DRESS EARTH LABOR NURSE RAISE STUDY TRAIN AFFECT FOSTER FURROW HARROW MANAGE MANURE PLOUGH RATOON SARCLE SCHOOL ACQUIRE CHERISH CONTOUR CULTURE EDUCATE EMBRACE EXPLOIT HUSBAND IMPROVE NOURISH PREPARE SCRATCH CIVILIZE
(— FAVOR) BOOTLICK

CULTIVATED ABAD TAME CIVIL GROWN POLITE SATIVE TOILED POLITIC REFINED CULTURED
(ARTIFICIALLY —) HOTHOUSE

CULTIVATION CROP TILTH FINISH GROWTH CULTURE TILLAGE TILTURE LABORAGE MANURAGE
(— IN MANNERS) FINISH
(MENTAL —) HUMANITY

CULTIVATOR JAT KMET RYOT ILAVA SULKY FARMER GADABA HARROW ILAVAN MAMOTY MILLER RIDGER TILLER FLORIST GRUBBER HUSBAND MEADOWER ROSARIAN SCUFFLER
(— GANG) RIG
(PL.) LAETI

CULTURAL HUMANIST

CULTURE ART AGAR STAB KULLI NASCA NAZCA SHAKE SLANT SLOPE TAJIN TASTE TILTH JHUKAR KULTUR POLISH STREAK WILTON ABASHEV ANANINO AZILIAN IRANISM JHANGAR KAYENTA SOCIETY STARTER TILLAGE HUMANISM LEARNING
(ESKIMO —) DORSET
(MEXICAN —) MAZAPAN

CULTURED CIVIL LETTERED

CULVERIN SLING CULVER LANTACA PELICAN SPIROLE

CULVERT FOX GOUT DRAIN SLUIT BRIDGE CONDUIT CULBERT PINNOCK PONCEAU OVERPASS

CUMBER BURDEN CUMMER SHACKLE

CUMBERSOME GOURD HEAVY CLUMSY UNRIDE AWKWARD LUGSOME ONEROUS WEIGHTY CUMBROUS UNWIELDY

CUMMER GIRL LASS WOMAN KIMMER

CUMMERBUND BAND BELT SASH

CUMULATE HEAP GATHER COMBINE

CUMULATIVE CHAIN SUMMATIVE

CUNA CUEVA DARIEN

CUNEIFORM ULNARE WEDGED

CUNNER CANOE NIPPER WRASSE BURGALL CHOGSET GOLDNEY NIBBLER BERGGYLT BLUEFISH CORKWING GILTHEAD

CUNNING ART OLD SHY SLY WIT ARCH CUTE DEEP FAST FINE FOXY KEEN SLIM SNOD TRAP WILY WISE CANNY CRAFT DOWNY FAVEL GUILE LOOPY PAUKY PAWKY POKEY SHARP SMART ADROIT ARTFUL ASTUTE CALLID CLEVER CRAFTY DAEDAL DECEIT ENGINE FOXERY PRETTY SHREWD SUBTLE SUPPLE TRICKY WISDOM COMPASS CRAFTLY CURIOUS FINESSE KNOWING PARLISH PARLOUS POLITIC PRACTIC SLEIGHT SUBTILE VARMINT VULPINE CONTOISE DEXTROUS MANAGERY QUENTISE SKILLFUL SLEIGHTY STEALTHY YEPELEIC

CUNNINGLY YEPLY YEPELY

CUP AMA BOX CAN DOP MUG NOG POT TOT TUN TYG CELL DOPP HORN LOTA PECE SHOE SKEW TASS TOSS BOUSE CALIX CHARK COGUE COPPE CRUSE CYLIX DEPAS GLASS GODET GRAIL KITTY PHIAL SCALE STEIN STOOP STOUP TAZZA THECA BEAKER BICKER BUCKET BUMPER CAPPIE CHOANA COTYLA CRATER CUPULA DOBBIN EGGCUP EYECUP FALSIE FESSEL FINJAN GOBLET JICARA KOTYLE MAZARD NAGGIN NOGGIN OXHORN POTION RUMKIN TASSIE VESSEL BRIMMER CAPSULE CHALICE CHEERER CYATHUS GODDARD KYATHOS QUONIAM SCYPHUS SHERBET STIRRUP THIMBLE TRINKET VENTOSE BRIDECUP GRADUATE STANDARD TJANTING
(— FOR HOLDING DIAMOND) DOP DOPP
(— FOR PERFUMES) CONCH
(— FOR YEAST) SKEP
(— IN SAUCER OF ALCOHOL) ETNA
(— OF FLOWER) BELL
(— OF TEA) DISH SPEED OYSTER
(— ON BULLET) GASCHECK
(— WITH COVER) HANAP
(ASSAYING —) CUPEL
(DRINKING —) CAN MUG NUT TIG TUN TYG CANN HORN TASS TOSS GODET BEAKER GOBLET HOLMOS RUMMER CHALICE GODDARD TRINKET
(FAIRY —) COOLWORT
(FILLED —) BUMPER
(IRON —) CULOT MUSHROOM
(LARGE —) FACER
(LEATHER —) WELL GISPIN
(LONG-HANDLED —) CYATH DIPPER CYATHUS KYATHOS
(NAUTICAL —) THIEF

(ORNAMENTAL —) TAZZA
(PAPER —) DIXIE
(PASTRY —) DARIOLE
(PRIZE —) PEWTER
(SACRED —) GRAIL
(SHALLOW —) CYLIX TAZZA TASTER CAPSULE
(SMALL —) DOP NOG TOT DOPP TASS DOBBIN NAGGIN NOGGIN TASSIE
(SQUARE —) MADDER METHER
(STIRRUP —) BONAILIE
(WOODEN —) COG COGUE CAPPER CAPPIE METHER QUAICH
(PL.) VALONIA

CUPBEARER HEBE SAKI CUPPER GANYMEDE

CUPBOARD CUB KAS BOLE CASE COIN SAFE AMBRY CHEST CUBBY CUDDY HUTCH PRESS ABACUS BUFFET CLOSET LARDER LOCKER PANTRY SPENCE ARMOIRE CABINET DRESSER SKIBBET ALHACENA CREDENCE CREDENZA TROSTERA
(ARCHERY —) ASCHAM

CUPEL TEST

CUPFUL CUP CAROUSE

CUP HOLDER ZARF

CUPID DAN AMOR EROS LOVE PUTTO CHERUB AMORINO AMOURET
(PL.) PUTTI

CUPIDITY LUST GREED DESIRE AVARICE AVIDITY LONGING APPETITE RAPACITY

CUPOLA DOME KILN TYPE VAULT BELFRY TURRET CALOTTE FURNACE LANTERN LOOKOUT CIMBORIO COCKLOFT

CUPOLAMAN HEATER

CUPPING GLASS VENTOSE

CUPSEED NUTSEED

CUP-SHAPED PEZIZOID SCYPHATE

CUPULE CUP BOLSTER CYATHUS THUMBMARK

CUR DOG YAP FICE FIST FYCE MUTT TIKE TYKE FEIST KEOUT MESSAN MESSIN BOBTAIL MONGREL WHAPPET

CURARE URARE URARI OORALI WOORALI

CURASSOW MITU COPPY HOCCO MITUA PAUXI

CURATE ABBE CURA AGENT VICAIRE MINISTER

CURATIVE HEALING IATRICAL PHYSICAL REMEDIAL SALUTARY SANATIVE

CURATOR KEEPER STEWARD GUARDIAN OVERSEER

CURB BIT LID CRUB FOIL KERB REIN SKID SNIP SNUB BRAKE CHECK CRIMP CURVE GUARD LIMIT MOUND ARREST BRIDLE COERCE COLLAR DECKLE GOVERN HAMPER STIFLE STRAIN SUBDUE THWART CONTROL CURBING INHIBIT REFRAIN REPRESS SHACKLE ATTEMPER COMPESCE MODERATE RESTRAIN RESTRICT WITHHOLD

(OFFICIAL —) LID
(WELL —) PUTEAL
CURCULIO TURK WEEVIL
CURD CRUD DAHI CHEESE CURDLE
CASEINE CLABBER CONGEAL
COAGULUM
(— IN MILK) ZIEGA
(—S AND WHEY) SLIP PINJANE
(BEAN —) TOFU
(PL.) FLEETINGS
CURDLE CAP LOP RUN SAM SET
CRIM CURD EARN LEEP QUAR SAMM
SOUR TURN WHIG YERN CARVE
QUAIL QUARL SPOIL YEARN CAILLE
LAPPER LOBBER LOPPER POSSET
QUARLE CLABBER CONGEAL
CRIDDLE CRUDDLE THICKEN
CONDENSE
CURDLED CURDLY QUARRED
SHOTTEN
(NOT —) UNCRUDDED
CURE DIP DRY DUN FIX BEEF BOOT
CARE CORN HEAL HEED HELP JERK
MEND SALT SANE SAVE AMEND
BLOAT BOTEN LEECH REEST SMEEK
SMOKE CHARGE CURATE KIPPER
PHYSIC PRIEST RECURE REMEDY
SEASON SUCCOR TEMPER WARISH
BESMOKE RECOVER RESTORE
THERAPY TREACLE ANTIDOTE
BARBECUE CURATION GUERISON
PRESERVE RECOVERY
(— BY SMOKING) GAMMON SMUDGE
(— FISH) DUN ROUSE
(— GRASS) HAY
(— HAY) WIN
(— HERRINGS) BLOAT
(— IN SUN) RIZZAR
(— SKINS) DRESS
(COUGH —) SAPA SAPE
CURE-ALL BALM AVENS ELIXIR
REMEDY PANACEA THERIAC
CURED SALT BLOATED
CURIOSITY CURIO INTEREST
(— OF SMALL VALUE) GABION
(—S OF THE CITY) LIONS
(PL.) CURIOSA
CURIOUS ODD NOSY RARE SELI
QUEER SELLE SELLY PRYING
QUAINT SNOOPY CUNNING STRANGE
UNUSUAL FREAKISH MEDDLING
PECULIAR SINGULAR
CURL BOB BEND COIL FEAK FURL
KINK LOCK PURL ROLL WAVE WIND
ACKER CANON CRIMP CRISP DILDO
FRILL FRIZZ QUIRL SPIRE TRESS
TWIRE TWIST BERGER BUCKLE
CANNON CRUCHE CURDLE FROWSE
MULLET RIPPLE SPIRAL WRITHE
CRIDDLE CRIMPLE CRINKLE
CROCKET CRUDDLE EARLOCK
FLEXURE FRIZZLE FROUNCE
RINGLET SERPENT TENDRIL
WHISKER FAVORITE LOVELOCK
SQUIGGLE
(— HAIR) CROOK
(— OF WIG) SNAKE
(— ON FOREHEAD) CRUCHE
CROUCHE

(— OVER) BREAK
(— UP) CRUMP HUNCH SNIRL
HUDDLE SHRINK SNUGGLE
(FRINGE OF —S) FRISETTE
FRIZETTE
(METAL —) CHIP
(SMALL —) CROCK
CURLED CRISP FUZZY KINKY SPIRY
CIRRATE COCKLED CRISPED
FRIZZLY SAVOYED WREATHY
CRISPATE GAUFFRED GOFFERED
HELICINE SCROLLED
CURLER GOFFER TEASER CRIMPER
FRIZZER MULLETS
CURLEW FUTE JACK SPOW KIOEA
SNIPE SPOWE WHAAP WHAUP
DIKKOP MARLIN SMOKER BANKERA
BUSTARD DOEBIRD BLUELEGS
WHIMBREL
CURLICUE ESS CAPER CURVE
CASSIS PARAPH SQUIRL FLOURISH
PURLICUE SCRIGGLE SQUIGGLE
CURLING MARK TEE
CURLING MATCH SPIEL
CURLING STONE IRON STONE
LOOFIE GRANITE
(— SPIN) RAISE
CURLY WAVY CRISP CRULL OUNDY
RIPPLED CRINKLED
(— HAIR) VEDDOID
CURMUDGEON CRAB CHURL MISER
GLEYDE GROUCH NIGGARD
CURMUDGEONLY STINGY
CURRANT PASA BERRY CASSIS
RAISIN RIZZAR RIZZLE CORINTH
(PL.) RIBES SPICE
CURRANT BUN WIG WIGG
CURRAWONG SQUEAKER STREPERA
CURRENCY CASH COIN PASS BILLS
CATER MONEY SCRIP SERIES
SPECIE PASSAGE WILDCAT
(FRACTIONAL —) SPONDULIX
(SHELL —) UHLLO
CURRENT NOW WAY EDDY FLOW
FLUX FORD RACE RIFE TIDE VEIN
WAFT ALIVE DRIFT GOING RAPID
ROUST SCOUR SWIFT TENOR TESLA
TREND USUAL ACTUAL COEVAL
COMMON COURSE DOUCHE DURANT
FLUENT LIVING MOTION MOVING
OFFSET OUTSET RECENT RULING
SLUICE STRAND STREAM TONGUE
VOLANT COUNTER DRAUGHT
FLOWING FRESHET GENERAL
INDRAFT INSTANT PASSANT
PRESENT RUNNING STICKLE
THERMAL TORRENT CURRANCE
DOWNCAST FREQUENT MILLRACE
PASSABLE TIDERACE TODAYISH
UNDERTOW
(— IN SPEECH) WAIF
(AIR —) DRAFT SHEET SPLIT
BREEZE DRAUGHT DOWNCAST
DOWNFLOW
(ELECTRIC —) STRAY
(HOT —) BACK
(JAPAN —) KUROSHIO KUROSIWO
(RAPID —) SWIFT TONGUE
(SOUND —) DISTORTION

(STRONG —) GALE ROOST ROUST
CURRENTLY ANYMORE
CURRISH BASE CYNICAL DOGGISH
IGNOBLE SNARLING
CURRY COMB DRUB KARI CLEAN
DRESS GROOM BRUISE CAJOLE
CARREE POWDER PREPARE
TARKEEAN
(— FAVOR) HUG NUT QUILL COTTON
SMOOGE SMOODGE
CURSE BAN BANE BLOW CUSS DAMN
OATH PIZE WARY BLAST BLESS
CORSE SHREW SPELL SWEAR
WEARY WINZE DETEST DEVOTE
GOOFER GUFFER MAKUTU MALIGN
MAUGER MAUGRE BESHREW
MALISON ANATHEMA EXECRATE
FORSPEAK
CURSED DASH CUSSED DAMNED
DASHED ACCURSED
CURSER WARIER
CURSING BLESSING BLASPHEMY
CURSIVE RUNNING
CURSORY FAST BRIEF HASTY QUICK
SHORT FITFUL ROVING SPEEDY
PASSANT PASSING SHALLOW
CARELESS RAMBLING
CURT BUFF RUDE TART BLUFF
BLUNT BRIEF BRUSK SHORT SQUAB
TERSE ABRUPT CURTAL CUTTED
SNIPPY BRUSQUE CONCISE CRYPTIC
LACONIC CAVALIER SNAPPISH
SNIPPETY SUCCINCT
CURTAIL CUT LOP CLIP CROP DOCK
PARE STOP ABATE ELIDE SHORT
SLASH STUNT TRUNK DECURT
LESSEN REDUCE ABRIDGE BOBTAIL
CRACKLE SHORTEN DIMINISH
MINORATE RETRENCH
CURTAILED TAIL SHORT STUNT
CURTAL BOBTAIL CONCISE
ABRIDGED
CURTAIN END BOOM DROP IRIS
MASK VEIL WALL BLIND DRAPE
SCENE SHADE SHEET VELUM
COSTER HANGER PURDAH SCREEN
SHROUD CEILING CONCEAL
CORTINE DRAPERY HANGING
VITRAGE· ASBESTOS PORTIERE
TRAVERSE
(CHURCH —) RIDDEL ENDOTYS
ENDOTHYS
(THEATRE —) SCRIM TEASER
TRAVELER TORMENTER
CURTAIN ROD TRINGLE
CURTAIN STRETCHER SCRAY
STRAINER
CURTAL CRAPE COURTAL CURTLAX
CURTSY BOB BOW DIP DOP BECK
DROP JOUK KNEE CONGE HONOR
CURCHY
CURUBA CASSA BANANA
CURVATED STUNT HOOKED
CURVATURE ARC PLY ARCH BENT
BOOL CURL CURVE SHEER SINUS
CAMBER CURVITY ADUNCITY
APOPHYGE CYRTOSIS GRYPOSIS
KYPHOSIS LORDOSIS
(— OF DECK) SHEER

(— **OF LEGS**) RHEBOSIS
(— **OF SHOE SOLE**) SWING
(— **OF SPINE**) KYPHOSIS SCOLIOSIS
(— **OF STOMACH**) FUNDUS
(— **OF STRAKE**) SPILING
CURVE ARC BOW CUP ESS SAG
ARCH BEND BOUT COME CURB
FADE HOOK KNEE LINE OGEE TURN
VEER WIND AMBIT BIGHT BREAK
CONIC CROOK CRUMP CUBIC HELIX
NONIC OGIVE PEDAL POLAR QUIRK
SLICE SWEEP SWIRL TARVE TREND
TWIST WITCH BOUGHT CAMBER
CIRCLE DEFLEX JORDAN SOLVUS
SPIRAL SPRING TOROID WIMPLE
ADIABAT BRACKET CAUSTIC CIRCUIT
CISSOID COMPASS CONCAVE
CONTOUR COSEISM CURVITY
CYCLOID ELLIPSE ENVELOP
FESTOON FLEXURE INCURVE
INFLECT LIMACON PHUGOID
PROFILE SCALLOP SINUATE
SOLIDUS CARDIOID CATENARY
CONCHOID DYGOGRAM ELASTICA
EXTRADOS FADEAWAY INTRADOS
INVOLUTE LIGATURE LIQUIDUS
OPHIURID PARABOLA SINUSOIS
TONOGRAM TRACTRIX
(— **DESCRIBED BY GRAPH**) GRAM
(— **IN HANDRAIL**) KNEE
(— **IN PLANKING**) HANG
(— **OF ARCH**) INTRADOS
(— **OF BALL**) DROP
(— **OF BIT**) LIBERTY
(— **OF FINGERNAIL**) GRYPOSIS
(— **OF HORSE'S NECK**) CREST
(— **OF PLANK**) SNY
(— **OF SHIP'S BOW**) FLAIR FLARE
(— **OF TIMBER**) CUP
(— **SATISFYING EQUATION**) BRANCH
(— **SPACE**) KNOT
(— **WHEN DRAWN**) COME
(**BASEBALL** —) SNAKE
(**CRICKET** —) SWERVE
(**DOUBLE** —) CIMA CYMA
(**VERTICAL** —) RAMP
CURVED BENT SOFT ADUNC CORBE
CURVE CURVY ROUND WOUND
CONVEX CURVEY GYRATE HAMATE
TURNED ARCUATE ARRONDI
CONCAVE CROOKED CURVANT
EMBOWED FALCATE SIGMOID
ADUNCOUS ANCHORAL AQUILINE
ARCIFORM CRUMPLED CYGNEOUS
DECURVED EXCURVED SCROLLED
ARCHIFORM
CURVET HOP LEAP LOPE SKIP TURN
BOUND CAPER FRISK PRANK VAULT
CAVORT CROUPE FROLIC GAMBOL
PRANCE PANNADE CORVETTA
CROUPADE
CURVING SPIRY SIMOUS TWISTY
AQUILINE DRAWDOWN
(— **IN**) CONCAVE
(**SMOOTHLY** —) FAIR
CUSH-CUSH CARA YAMPEE
CUSHION BAG COD MAT PAD PIG
BALL BANK BOSS PUFF SEAT SUNK
TRIM GADDI GADHI PANEL SQUAB

TRUSH BUFFER INSOLE JOCKEY
MUSNUD PILLOW SACHET BOLSTER
BRIOCHE COSSHEN HASSOCK
KNEELER MUFFLER PILLION
REPOSAL ROOTCAP CUTIDURE
OREILLER PULVINAR
(**LACE-MAKERS** —) BOTT
(**PIN** —) PRINCOD
(**SEAT** —) BANKER
(**TAILOR'S** —) HAM
CUSHIONING DUNNAGE
CUSHIONLIKE PULVINAR
CUSHION PLANT POLSTER
CUSHIONY PADDY
CUSHITIC NUBIAN
CUSK TUSK TORSK BURBOT CATFISH
CUSP APEX CONE HORN PEAK
ANGLE POINT STYLE TOOTH
CORNER SPINODE ENTOCONE
HYPOCONE METACONE PARACONE
CUSPIDOR GABOON CRACHOIR
SPITTOON
CUSSO KOSO KOUSSO BRAYERA
BRAZERA
CUSTARD FLAN FOOL FLAWN
DOUCET DOWCET CHARLET PARFAIT
FLUMMERY DIABLOTIN
CUSTARD APPLE ANONA ANNONA
PAWPAW CORAZON SWEETSOP
CUSTODIAN HACK GUARD BAILEE
CUSTOS KEEPER SEXTON WARDEN
WARDER CURATOR JANITOR
CERBERUS CLAVIGER GUARDIAN
CONCIERGE
CUSTODY LAP BAIL CARE HOLD
KEEP WARD TRUST ARREST
CHARGE SAFETY YEMSEL CONTROL
DURANCE KEEPING TUITION
COMMENDA CUSTODIA HANDFAST
SECURITY
CUSTOM FAD LAW MOS PAD TAX
URE USE ASAL DUTY FORM GARB
MODE MORE RITE ROTE RULE THEW
TOLL WONE WONT FUERO GUISE
HABIT HAUNT RITUS STYLE SUNNA
TRADE TREAD TRICK USAGE VOGUE
BYRLAW DASTUR DHARMA GROOVE
IMPOST MANNER MINHAG MONTEM
PRAXIS SUNNAH USANCE COSTUME
DUSTOOR DUSTOUR FASHION
FORMULA HALAKAH TRIBUTE
USAUNCE WARNOTH BUSINESS
ENDOGAMY HABITUDE PRACTICE
(**BINDING** —) LAW
(**BUSINESS** —) TRADE GOODWILL
(**CHURCH** —) COMITY
(**CORRUPT** —) ABUSE
(**FESTIVAL** —) HOCKING
(**OUTMODED** —) ARCHAISM
(**PRIMITIVE** —) COUVADE
(**RURAL** —) HEAVING
(**SECRET** —) SANDE
(**TEMPORARY** —) FAD VOGUE
(**PL.**) MORES MOEURS HAIKWAN
FOLKLORE
CUSTOMARILY USUALLY CUSTOMLY
CUSTOMARY PER RIFE TAME USED
NOMIC USUAL COMMON SOLEMN
VULGAR WONTED CLASSIC

GENERAL USITATE EVERYDAY
FAMILIAR HABITUAL ORTHODOX
(**NOT** —) INSOLENT
CUSTOMER CHAP BUYER CLIENT
PATRON SUCKER ACCOUNT
CALLANT CHAPMAN PATIENT
SHOPPER MERCHANT PROSPECT
(**PRINTER'S** —) AUTHOR
(**TOUGH** —) HARDCASE
(**PL.**) CUSTOM CLIENTELE
CUSTOMHOUSE ADUANA DOGANA
DOUANE
CUSTOM-MADE BESPOKE
BESPOKEN
CUSTOMS OFFICER SHARK WAITER
CUT AX ADZ AXE BOB DAG DAP DIE
HAG HEW KIT LOP MOW NIP RIT
SAW SNY TAP ADZE BANG BITE
BOLO BOLT BUZZ CHIP CHOP CLIP
CROP DADO DOCK FACE FELL FILE
GASH GIRD HACK HASH HEWN JERK
KNAP LIMB MAKE MODE MUSH NICK
OCHE PARE RACE RASH RAZE REAP
SIDE SKIN SLIT SLOT SMIT SNEE
SNEG SNIP SNUB STOW SUMP SWAP
SWOP TAME TRIM VELL VIDE BEVEL
BLOCK BREAK CANAL CANCH
CARVE CHIVE CLEFT COPSE COUPE
CRIMP DRESS FLICK FRAZE FRITH
GOUGE GRAVE GRIDE GROOP
HOWEL KITTE KNIFE LANCE LATHE
MINCE NOTCH PLATE PRUNE RAZEE
SABER SABRE SCALP SCARP SCIND
SCORE SEVER SHARE SHEAR SHIVE
SHRED SKICE SKISE SLASH SLICE
SLICK SLISH SLIVE SNICK SPLIT
STAMP SWEEP SWIPE SWISH TOUCH
TWITE VOGUE WHITE ABLATE
AJOURE BARBER BISECT BROACH
CAMBER CHISEL CLEAVE CORNER
CUTTED DIVIDE EXCISE FIGURE
FLETCH FLITCH FRENCH GROOVE
GULLET HACKLE HAGGLE IGNORE
INCIDE INCISE INDENT LESSEN
MANGLE OUTPUT RASURE REDUCE
RIPPLE SCORCH SCOTCH SCRIBE
SCYTHE SLIGHT SLIVER SNATHE
STRAIT STREAK SULLET SWINGE
TAILYE THWITE TRENCH AFFRONT
CONVERT CURTAIL CUTTING
DIACOPE DISSECT DRAWCUT
ENGRAVE FASHION FRITTER
HATCHET SCALPEL SCISSOR
SCUTTLE SECTILE TAILZEE WHITTLE
DISSEVER FRACTION INCISION
INCISURE INTAGLIO LACERATE
MALAHACK RETRENCH THWITTLE
(— **A THREAD**) CHASE
(— **AN OPENING**) BREACH
(— **AT ANGLE**) CANT BEVEL
(— **AT RANDOM**) SLASH
(— **AWAY**) COPE SLIT UNDO ABATE
CONCISE
(— **BACK**) HEAD SPUR
(— **BARK**) CHIP
(— **BEAM**) KERF
(— **CARS**) LIFT
(— **CHEESE**) HARP
(— **CLAY**) SLING

(— **CORNERS**) SKIRT CHAMFER CHAMPHER
(— **CRUST**) CHIP
(— **DEEPLY**) DIG SHANK
(— **DIAGONALLY**) CATER SLANT
(— **DOWN**) MOW FELL STAG STUB RAZEE SCARP ABRIDGE SHORTEN RETRENCH
(— **FANCY FIGURE**) DASH
(— **FISH**) SOLAY STEAK
(— **FOR FODDER**) CHAFF
(— **FROM STACK**) DESS
(— **GEAR TEETH**) RATCH
(— **GLASS**) SPLIT
(— **GRAIN**) BAG FAG CRADLE SWINGE
(— **IN A TREE**) FACE
(— **IN BARREL STAVE**) HOWEL
(— **IN EXCAVATIONS**) GULLET
(— **IN RELIEF**) ENCHASE
(— **IN SOFT ROCK**) CAVATE
(— **IN SQUARES**) CHECK
(— **IN**) INSECT INCISED
(— **INTO SLIPS**) ZEST
(— **INTO STRIPS**) JERK FLETCH FLITCH JULIENNE
(— **INTO TREE**) BOX
(— **JAGGEDLY**) HACK SNAG
(— **LEDGES**) BENCH
(— **LOGS**) LUMBER
(— **OF FISH**) JOWL
(— **OF GEM**) STAR
(— **OF GRAIN**) MELL
(— **OF MEAT**) ARM SEY CROP HOCK SHIN SIDE CHUCK SHANK STEAK BRISKET FORESEY ICEBONE SIRLOIN EDGEBONE FORERIBS
(— **OF RIFLING**) GROOVE
(— **OFF BY BITS**) DRIB
(— **OFF END**) BUTT
(— **OFF WOOL**) DOD DODD
(— **OFF**) BOB LOP CLIP CROP DOCK KILL PARE SHUT SLIT STAG BELEE CROSS ELIDE PRUNE SCIND SEVER SHAVE SHEAR SKIVE SLIPE SPIKE COUPED DECIDE EXEMPT FORCUT RESECT SHIELD STIFLE SWATCH ABSCIND ABSCISE ABSCISS CURTAIL EXSCIND ISOLATE PRECIDE RESCIND AMPUTATE CLEIDOIC DESECATE RESECATE RETRENCH TRUNCATE
(— **OPEN**) SPLAY
(— **OUT**) DESS DINK CLICK BROACH EXCIDE EXCISE EXSECT
(— **PATH**) FRAY
(— **SALMON**) CHINE
(— **SHEEP**) TOMAHAWK
(— **SHORT**) BOB COW HOG LOP BANG CROP DOCK JIMP SNIB BOBBED HOGGED BOBTAIL CONCISE SCANTLE PRESCIND
(— **TENDONS**) ENERVATE
(— **THE THROAT**) JUGULATE
(— **THE WAVES**) SNORE
(— **THINLY**) CURL
(— **TO PIECES**) CHOP DICE MINCE BRITTLE FRITTER
(— **TO SIZE**) TAIL
(— **TURF**) VELL

(— **UNDER**) KIRVE
(— **UNEVENLY**) CHATTER
(— **UP SWAN**) LIFT
(— **UP**) TUSK CARVE CHINE JOINT PRANK SPOIL TRAIN GOBBET COLLOPED
(— **WHALE BLUBBER**) LEAN
(— **WITH BACKWARD SLOP**) COOT
(— **WITH DIE**) DINK BLANK
(— **WITH SHEARS**) SHIRL
(— **WITH SICKLE**) BAG REAP
(**COLD** —S) ASSIETTE
(**CREW** —) BUTCH FLATTOP
(**DEEP NARROW** —) JAD
(**FENCING** —) STRAMAZON
(**LARGE** — **OF FOOD**) DODGE
(**NOT** —) UNCORVEN
(**SHORT** —) ATAJO
(**SLIGHT** —) SNICK SCOTCH
(**THIN** —) TARGET
CUT-AND-DRIED CANNED
CUTANEOUS DERMAL
CUTCH GAMBIR CATECHU GAMBIER
CUTE COY KEEN COONY DINKY DUCKY SHARP CLEVER PRETTY SHREWD CUNNING DARLING
CUTICLE DERM HIDE SKIN SHUCK THECA MEMBRANE PELLICLE
(— **OF EGGSHELL**) BLOOM
CUTLASS SWORD CURTAL DUSACK HANGER TESACK CURTAXE MACHETE SHABBLE CAMPILAN
CUTLASS FISH HIKU SAVOLA KALKVIS MACHETE HAIRTAIL
CUTLET SCHNITZEL
CUTOVER COUPE
CUTPURSE THIEF HORNTHUMB
CUTTER DIE BEEF BOAT IRON MILL PONE SLED BRAVO FACER FRAZE SLOOP SMACK BAYMAN CHERRY COLTER COTTER DOCKER EDITOR FRAZER MINCER SLEIGH SLICER CLIPPER COULTER DROMOND INCISOR RUFFIAN KNIFEMAN REVENUER SCHOKKER SHEPSTER
(— **OF STONES**) LAPIDARY
(**BRICK** —) RUBBER
(**PEAT** —) PINER
(**WIRE** —) SECATEUR
CUTTERHEAD WABBLER WOBBLER
CUTTHROAT BRAVO CUTTER RUFFIAN SWORDER
CUTTHROAT TROUT MYKISS
CUTTING CUT HAG RAW SET ACID CARF CURT KEEN KERF SETT SLIP TART TWIG ACUTE BLEAK CHECK CRISP EAGER EDGED GRIDE SCION SCRAP SCROW SHARP SMART BITING BITTER BORING ENTAIL GODOWN GORING JAGGED PHYTON PIPING SECANT SEVERE SNITHE BURNING CAUSTIC GRIBBLE INCISAL MORDANT NICKING OVERCUT PAINFUL PIQUANT POLLING SARMENT SATIRIC SECTION SLICING CHILLING CLEARING INCISIVE PIERCING POIGNANT QUICKSET SCISSION SNAPPISH WOUNDING
(— **FOR DIRT-CAR TRACK**) GULLET

(— **FOR WATER**) TAJO
(— **FROM PLANT**) SLIP SHROUD TRUNCHEON
(— **OF DEER**) SAY
(— **OF TREES**) HAG
(— **OFF**) AVULSION
(— **SHORT**) ABORTIVE
(**DRILL** —S) MUD
(**OBLIQUE** —) BARBING
(**SECOND** —) ROWEN
(**WASTE** —) SELVAGE SELVEDGE
CUTTLEBONE SEPIA SEPION SEPIUM GLADIUS SEPIARY
CUTTLEFISH SEPIA SHELL SQUID CUDDLE CUTTLE SCRIBE CATFISH DECAPOD INKFISH MOLLUSK OCTOPUS SCUTTLE
CUVETTE POT TUB TANK BASIN BUCKET TRENCH CISTERN
CYANIDE NITRILE CYANURET
CYANITE SAPPARE DISTHENE
CYANOGEN PRUSSIN PRUSSINE
CYBELE RHEA KYBELE AGDISTIS
(**DAUGHTER OF** —) JUNO
(**FATHER OF** —) URANUS
(**HUSBAND OF** —) SATURN
(**MOTHER OF** —) GAEA
(**SON OF** —) JUPITER NEPTUNE
CYCAD BANGA CICAD ZAMIA COONTIE CYCADITE
CYCLAMEN BACCHAR PRIMWORT SOWBREAD
CYCLE AGE EON ERA AEON BIKE EPOCH KALPA PEDAL PRIME ROUND SAROS SECLE WHEEL BAKTUN CIRCLE COURSE CYCLUS PERIOD BICYCLE CIRCUIT DICYCLE TRICYCLE
(— **OF WORK**) JOURNEY
(—**S CAUSED BY KARMA**) SAMSARA SANSARA
(**BUSINESS** —) JUGLAR KITCHIN
(**LUNAR** —) SAROS
(**ONE** — **PER SECOND**) HERTZ
(**SECONDARY** —) EPICYCLE
CYCLIC CYCLAR ANNULAR CYCLICAL
CYCLIST CYCLER WHEELER WHEELMAN
CYCLOLITH CROMLECH
CYCLOMETER ODOGRAPH
CYCLONE GALE GUST WIND BLAST STORM BAGUIO TORNADO TWISTER TYPHOON SECONDARY
CYCLOPEAN HUGE VAST STRONG MASSIVE COLOSSAL GIGANTIC
CYCLOPS ARGES BRONTES COPEPOD STEROPES
CYCLORAMA CYKE PANORAMA
CYCLOSIS STREAMING
CYCLOSTOME HAGFISH
CYLINDER CAN EKE GIG TIN BEAM BOMB BURR CAGE CANE DRUM LEAD MUFF PIPE PRIM ROLL SLUG TUBE WELL BLOCK CORER DRAIN FIBER FIBRE FUDGE SCREW SHELL SPOOL STELA STELE SWIFT BARREL BOBBIN BUTTON COLUMN COPPER DECKER DOFFER DUSTER FILTER GABION PISTON PLATEN ROLLER

SCREEN TIPITI TUMBLE URCHIN WORKER CUTCHER SLEEVER SUCCULA FOLLOWER GRADUATE NEURAXIS SPARKLET
(— AROUND MOLD) COTTLE
(— OF STEAM WHISTLE) BELL
(— OF TISSUE) CORTEX
(— OF YARN) CAKE
(— ON LOOM) BEAM
(— WITH PERFORATIONS) FLUSHER
(—S PULLED THROUGH DUCT) MANDREL
(ARMORED —) BARBETTE
(GLASS —) MUFF
(HOLLOW —) PIPE TUBE
(MARKING —) LEAD
(NAPPING —) GIG
(RELAY —) BATON
(REVOLVING —) BEATER ROLLER
(TOOTHED —) SPROCKET
CYLINDRICAL ROUND TERETE TOROSE CENTRIC TUBULAR TERETIAL
CYMA GOLA GULA OGEE DOUCINE MOLDING CYMATIUM
CYMA REVERSA HEEL
CYMBA YET
CYMBAL ZEL CHIME TARGET CROTALUM KYMBALON (PL.) TAL BECKEN PIATTI
CYMBIUM MELO
CYME CYMULE BOSTRYX
CYMLING SIMNEL CYMBLIN SCALLOP PATTYPAN
CYMOSE DEFINITE SYMPODIAL
CYMRY KYMRI WELSH
CYNIC SATYR TIMON DOUBTER APEMANTUS

CYNICAL CYNIC SULLEN CURRISH DOGGISH DOGLIKE CAPTIOUS SARDONIC SNARLING JAQUESIAN
CYNOCEPHALUS AANI
CYNOSURE SHOW LODESTAR
CYPRESS CULL SABINO SIPERS FIREBALL AHUEHUETE BELVEDERE
CYPRESS SPURGE BALSAM NAPOLEON
CYPRIPEDIUM CYP DUCK NERVINE

CYPRUS
CAPE: GATA GRECO ANDREAS ARNAUTI ZEVGARI
CAPITAL: NICOSIA
COIN: PARA
MEASURE: OKA OKE PIK CASS DONUM KOUZA GOMARI KARTOS MEDIMNO
MOUNTAIN: TROODOS
TOWN: POLIS PAPHOS KYRENIA LARNACA MORPHOU NICOSIA LIMASSOL
WEIGHT: OKA OKE MOOSA KANTAR

CYRILLA TITI
CYRUS KORESH
CYST BAG SAC WEN POUCH CYSTUS RANULA DERMOID HYDATID HYGROMA VESICLE DACRYOPS MUCOCELE STEATOMA
CYSTOPTERIS FILIX
CYTOME SPHEROME
CYTOPLASM MASSULA OOPLASM DIASTEMA

CZAR CSAR IVAN TSAR TZAR PETER NICHOLAS
CZARDAS CSARDAS
(SECTION OF —) FRISS LASSU FRISZKA
CZECH CECH TSECH TSCEKH BOHEMIA

CZECHOSLOVAKIA
BEER: PILSEN
CAPITAL: PRAHA PRAGUE
CASTLE: HRADCANY
COIN: CROWN DUCAT HALER HELLER KORUNA
DANCE: POLKA REDOWA FURIANT
MEASURE: LAN SAH MIRA KOREC LATRO STOPA MERICE STRYCH
MOUNTAIN: ORE TATRA SUDETEN
PROVINCE: BOHEMIA MORAVIA SLOVAKIA
RIVER: UH MZE VAG VAH DYJE EGER ELBE GRAU HRON IPEL ISAR ISER LABE NISA ODER OHRE OLSE WAAG BECVA DUNAJ MARCH NITRA SLANA TISZA DANUBE MOLDAU MORAVA ONDAVA SAZAVA TORYSA VLTAVA LABOREC LUZNICE BEROUNKA
TOWN: AS ASCH BRNO CHEB EGER MOST BRUNN OPAVA PLZEN TABOR TUZLA AUSSIG BILINA KLADUS PILSEN PRESOV VSETIN ZVOLEN BUDWEIS JIHLAVA OSTRAVA TEPLITZ

D DE DEE DOG DELTA

DAB DAP DOB DOT DUB HIT PAT BLOW CHIT DAUB LICK LUMP PECK SPOT CLOUT DHABB DIGHT SMEAR BLOTCH EXPERT STRIKE DABSTER PORTION SPLOTCH FLATFISH FLOUNDER MARYSOLE SANDLING

DABBER BALL PROD TAMPON

DABBING PICKING

DABBLE DAB DIB MESS DALLY DIBBLE MEDDLE MUDDLE PADDLE POTTER SOSSLE SPLASH TAMPER TRIFLE DRABBLE MOISTEN PLOUTER PLUTTER SMATTER SPATTER DELIBATE SPRINKLE
(— WITH BLOOD) ENGORE

DABBLER AMATEUR DABSTER

DABCHICK GREBE DIPPER DOBBER DOPPER PUFFER HENBILL DIDAPPER DOPCHICK

DACE CHUB DARE DART CYPRINID GRAYLING

DACHSHUND DACHS BADGERER

DACOIT DAKU DAKOO ROBBER CRIMINAL

DACTYLOPODITE POLLEX

DACTYLOZOOID PALPON

DACTYLUS DACTYL DIGITUS

DAD BEAT BLOW DAUD HUNK LUMP PAPA KNOCK THUMP FATHER STRIKE

DADDY BABBO DEDDY

DADDY LONGLEGS SPINNER LONGLEGS PHALANGID

DADO DIE GROOVE SOLIDUM

DAEDALUS (ANCESTOR OF —) ERECHTHEUS
(NEPHEW OF —) TALUS
(SON OF —) ICARUS

DAEMON (ALSO SEE DEMON) GHOST DAIMON PYTHON EUDAEMON MISTRESS
(PL.) CURETES

DAFFODIL GLEN LILY DAFFY DILLY JONQUIL ASPHODEL BELLWORT CROWBELL

DAFT GAY WILD BALMY CRAZY DAFFY GIDDY LOONY POTTY SILLY INSANE FOOLISH IDIOTIC IMBECILE

DAG JAG DAGG STAB SLASH DAGGLE PIERCE DAGGING DAGLOCK PRICKET

DAGAME SALAMO MADRONA LEMONWOOD

DAGGER DAG SAX DIRK ITAC KRIS SAEX SNEE SPUD STAB TANG CRISE DAGUE KATAR KREES POINT PRICK SKEAN STEEL ANLACE BODKIN COUTEL CREESE DIESIS HANGER KIRPAN KUTTAR PANADE PINKER POPPER SKHIAN STYLET BALARAO BASLARD BAYONET COUTEAU DUDGEON HANDJAR KANDJAR KHANJAR OBELISK PONIARD SLASHER STABBER PUNCHEON PUNTILLA STILETTO
(— AS CERAMICS COVER) HILLER
(— REFERENCE MARK) SPIT
(— WITH WAVY BLADE) KRIS

CREESE KREESE
(DOUBLE —) DIESIS
(SACRED —) KIRPAN

DAGOMBA DAGBANE DAGBANI

DAH DAO DOW DHAO

DAHLIA JICAMA POMPON

DAHOMEY (CAPITAL OF —) PORTONOVO
(PEOPLE OF —) FON FONG
(RIVER OF —) NIGER OUEME
(TOWN IN —) KANDI NIKKI ABOMEY OUIDAH COTONOU

DAILY ADAY DIARY DIURNAL

DAINCHA NARDOO

DAINTIES EST ESTE SOCK CATES DIABLOTIN

DAINTILY CHOICELY GINGERLY MINIONLY

DAINTINESS FLUTTER DELICACY

DAINTY CATE FINE NICE RARE TEAR ACATE DAINT DENTY FRILL GENTY NAISH BONBON CHOICE COSTLY FRIAND MIGNON MINION PICKED REGALO SCARCE SPICED SUNKET CURIOUS ELEGANT FINICAL FINICKY MINIKIN REGALIA TAFFETA TAFFETY DAINTITH DAINTREL DELICACY DELICATE ETHEREAL LIKEROUS MIGNIARD TRYPHOSA

DAIRY TAMBO LACTARY VACCARY CREAMERY DEYHOUSE
(— PRODUCTS) MILCHIGS

DAIRYMAID DEE DEY DEYWOMAN MILKMAID

DAIRYMAN AHIR MILKMAN

DAIS PACE SEAT BENCH LEWAN STAGE TABLE CANOPY ESTATE LISSOM PODIUM PULPIT SETTLE ESTRADE TERRACE TRIBUNE CHABUTRA FOOTPACE HALFPACE HATHPACE HUSTINGS PLATFORM

DAISY BULL GOLD DANDY GOWAN OXEYE BENNET MORGAN SHASTA BONESET BOWWORT COMFREY DOGBLOW BACKWORT BONEWORT COMPOSIT HEXAFOIL KNITBACK PISSABED MOONPENNY

DAISY CUTTER GRUB

DAISY FLEABANE ERIGERON SCABIOUS

DAKOTA SIOUX LAKOTA

DALE HAW DELL DENE GLEN VALE SPOUT BOTTOM DINGLE TROUGH VALLEY

DALEA PAROSELA

DALLES DELLS RAPIDS

DALLIANCE TOY CHAT PLAY TALK SPORT GOSSIP TOUSEL TOUSLE TRIFLE COLLING

DALLIER PINGLER

DALLY TOY CHAT DAFF FOOL IDLE JAKE JAUK PLAY SWAN WAIT DELAY FLIRT SPORT TARRY COQUET DABBLE DAWDLE LINGER LOITER TRIFLE WANTON DRINGLE SLIDDER

DALLYING COQUETRY SISSETON

DALMATIC TUNICLE

DAM BAR BAY PEN REE DAME HEAD POND SADD SPUR STAY STEM STOP SUDD WEIR BLOCK CAULD CHECK CHOKE GARTH MOUND POUND STANK ANICUT CAUSEY HINDER MOTHER PARENT ANNICUT BARRAGE BARRIER MILLDAM PENHEAD RAMPIRE TAPPOON ABOIDEAU BLOCKADE GRANDDAM OBSTACLE OBSTRUCT RESTRAIN

DAMAGE MAR BLOT BURN COST HARM HURT JEEL LOSS RUIN SKIN TEEN BLITZ BURST CLOUD CRACK HAVOC PRANG SPOIL WOUND WRONG BATTER CHARGE DANGER DEFACE DEFECT HINDER IMPAIR INJURE INJURY INSULT SCATHE SORROW AFFLICT DAMNIFY DEGRADE DISTURB EXPENSE FOUNDER OFFENCE OFFENSE PAYMENT SCRATCH SCUTTLE SHATTER ACCIDENT BUSINESS DISSERVE FRACTURE FRETTING MISCHIEF SABOTAGE

DAMAGED HURT CRAZY LESED BROKEN CRACKED INJURED

DAMAGES INTEREST HAMESUCKEN

DAMAGING HARMFUL HURTFUL

DAMAN DAS CONY CONEY CUNNY DASSY GANAM HYRAX DASSIE WABBER ASHKOKO CHEROGRIL

DAMA PADEMELON TAMMAR WALLABY

DAMASCENED WATERED

DAMASCENE WORK KOFTGARI

DAMASK LINEN DARNEX DORNIC DORNICK DAMASSIN DRAWLOOM

DAME DINT LADY DAMIE WOMAN MATRON

DAME'S VIOLET EVEWEED

DAMMARA AGATHIS

DAMN DEE DEM DOG RAT BLOW BURN DANG DARN DASH DING DRAT DUMB DURN BLAME BLANK BLAST BLESS CURSE FETCH WHOOP BEDAMN BUGGER DEMPNE DEVOTE GODDAM CONDEMN CONSARN DOGGONE GODDAMN GOLDARN GOLDURN CONFOUND EXECRATE

DAMNABLE DAMNED ODIOUS ACCURSED INFERNAL

DAMNABLY DEUCED CURSEDLY DEUCEDLY

DAMNATION NATION PERDITION

DAMNED DEE DAMN DARN DEED DURN LOST BALLY DOOMS BLOODY DARNED DASHED DURNED GODDAM GORMED TARNAL BLESSED CONSARN DOGGONE ETERNAL GOLDARN GOLDURN MUCKING ACCURSED BLANKETY BLINKING DASHEDLY INFERNAL JIGGERED

DAMP DEG FOG RAW WAK WET CLAM DANK DEWY DULL MIST ROKY SOFT WACK BLUNT DABBY HUMID JUICY MALMY MOCHY MOIST MOOTH MUGGY MUNGY MUSTY RAFTY RAINY RAWKY SAPPY SOBBY SOGGY THONE WAUGH WEAKY CLAMMY DAMPEN DEADEN MUFFLE QUENCH STUPOR BEDEWED

DAMPISH DEPRESS MOISTEN SQUIDGY DEJECTED DISPIRIT HUMIDIFY HUMIDITY MOISTURE
(— **OF EVENING)** SERENE
(**CHOKE —)** STYTHE
DAMPEN DEG DAMP MOIL CHILL CRAMP FREEZE SPONGE MOISTURE
DAMPENER MULLER
DAMPER DAMP MUTE BREAD CHECK CHECKER REGISTER
DAMPNESS DAMP HUMIDITY
DAMSEL GIRL WENCH MAIDEN MOPPET DAMOSEL DAMOZEL PUCELLE DONZELLA PRINCESS
DAMSELFISH PINTANO
DAMSELFLY NAIAD
DAN GI DEN
DANAKIL AFAR
DANAUS ANOSIA
DANCE BAL BOB HOP JIG MAI SON BALL DRAG DUET DUMP FISH FOOT FRUG HEEL HOOF HORA JAZZ JIVE JUBA KOLO LEAP LOPE MASK MILL MOVE PROM REEL SAIL SHAG SKIT STEP BAILE BAMBA BONGO BRAWL CANON CAPER CAROL CONGA DANZA ENTRY FLING FLISK FRIKE FRISK GOPAK LASYA MAMBO PAVAN POLKA RINKA RUMBA SALLY SAMBA STOMP SWING TANGO TRACE TREAD TWIST VOLTA WALTZ ALTHEA AREITO BALLET BALTER BOLERO BOOGIE BOSTON BRANLE CANARY CANCAN CEBELL CORDAX DANZON DIDDLE DREHER FADING FORMAL FROLIC GERMAN HORMOS MASQUE MINUET MOBBLE MONKEY MORRIS NRITTA PASSAY RACKET RHUMBA SHIMMY TODDLE TRESCA TUMBLE VALETA ANTHEMA BEGUINE CALINDA CANTICO COURANT CZARDAS DANSANT FADDING FARRUCA FOOTING FOXTROT FURLANA GAVOTTE MORISCO PATTERN SALTATE SARDANA SHUFFLE TEMPETE TRESCHE TRIPPLE VOLTIZE ZIGANKA ANGLAISE AURRESCU BAMBOUJA BAMBOULA CACHUCHA CAKEWALK CHACONNE COMPARSA COONJINE COTILLON ENTRACTE ESTAMPIE FANDANGO FANTASIA FLAMENCO GALOPADE GUARACHA HABANERA HEYDEGUY HORNPIPE KOLATTAM MATELOTE
(— **ART)** NATYA ORCHESIS
(— **ATTENDANCE)** LACKEY LACQUEY
(— **CLUMSILY)** BALTER
(— **DRAMA)** NO NOH
(— **FACE TO FACE)** SET
(— **FORM)** PIVA
(— **IN CIRCLE)** JIGGER
(— **METHOD)** LABAN
(— **NIMBLY)** CANARY
(— **RESEMBLING THE POLKA)** BERLIN
(— **STEP)** RIFF PICKUP
(— **STYLE)** ABHINAYA
(— **TYPE)** TANDAVA

(**ACROBATIC —)** ADAGIO
(**AFRICAN —)** SHOUT
(**ARGENTINE —)** CUANDO
(**AUSTRIAN —)** LANDLER
(**BALINESE —)** KEBYAR LEGONG
(**BALLROOM —)** SON CONGO COTILLON
(**BOHEMIAN —)** REDOWA FURIANT
(**CARNIVAL —)** COOCH FOLIA COOTCH
(**CEREMONIAL —)** AREITO CANTICO DUTUBURI
(**COQUETTISH —)** PURPOSE
(**COUNTRY —)** HAY CONFESS ANGLAISE
(**COURTSHIP —)** CUECA BATUQUE LEZGIBKA
(**DANISH —)** SEXTUR
(**FIESTA —S)** AKRIEROS
(**FLAMENCO —)** ALEGRIAS
(**FRENCH —)** BAL BOREE BRAWL GAVOT BRANLE BOURREE BOUTADE BRANSLE GAVOTTE LAVOLTA
(**GAY —)** RANT GAILLARD GALLIARD
(**GESTURE —)** SIVA
(**GREEK —)** CORDAX KORDAX SIKINNIS
(**GYPSY —)** FARRUCA
(**HAITIAN —)** JUBA
(**HOBBYHORSE —)** CALUSAR
(**HOLIDAY —)** PATTERN
(**HUNGARIAN —)** KOS
(**INDIAN —)** IRUSKA KATHAK
(**IRISH —)** FADING
(**ITALIAN —)** FORLANA FURLANA
(**JAPANESE —)** BUGAKU KAGURA
(**JAVANESE —)** SERIMPI
(**LIVELY —)** JIG REEL GALOP GIGUE POLKA RUMBA BOLERO CANARY RHUMBA SPRING BOURREE FURLANA HOEDOWN GALLIARD GALOPADE HORNPIPE
(**MAORI —)** HAKA
(**MEXICAN —)** DARABE HUAPANGO SANDUNGA
(**MOURNFUL —)** DUMP
(**NORWEGIAN —)** HALLING
(**OLD ENGLISH —)** CEBELL MORRIS ARGEERS ANGLAISE
(**OLD-FASHIONED —)** LOURE
(**PEASANT —)** JOTA DANZON BALITAO
(**PERUVIAN —)** CUECA KASWA CACHUA
(**POLISH —)** KUJAWIAK
(**POLYNESIAN —)** HULA
(**PORTUGUESE —)** FADO
(**ROUND —)** RAY BRAUL CAROL WALTZ CAROLE MAXIXE
(**RUSTIC —)** HAY HEY HAYMAKER
(**SPANISH —)** JOTA POLO JALEO BOLERO JARABE CHACONNE FLAMENCO GUARACHA
(**SPEAR —)** BARIS
(**SQUARE —)** SQUARE ARGEERS HOEDOWN LANCERS QUADRILLE
(**STATELY —)** PAVAN PAVANE EMMELEIA SARABAND
(**SWORD —)** BACUBERT MATACHIN

(**VENEZUELAN —)** JOROPO
(**WEDDING —)** CANACUAS
DANCER PONY CLOWN PONEY ARTIST CORNER HOOFER HOPPER MAENAD APSARAS CLOGGER DANSEUR PASCOLA PRANCER PRANKER SAILOUR STEPPER TODDLER BALADINE BAYADERE DANSEUSE DEVADASI FIGURANT MORRICER
(**BALLET —)** ETOILE SOLISTE CORYPHEE
(**EGYPTIAN —S)** GHAWAZI GHAWAZEE
(**JAVANESE —)** SERIMPI
(**JAVANESE —)** BEDOYO
(**MASKED —S)** GAHE
(**SQUARE —S)** FLOOR
(**SWORD —)** MATACHIN
(**ZUNI —)** SHALAKO
DANCING SWING ADANCE BALLET CHANGE FROLIC MORRIS SALTANT SURGING STEPPING TRIPSOME
(— **MANIA)** TARANTISM
DANDELION BLOW BLOWER CANKER DINDLE CHICORY HAWKBIT BLOWBALL COMPOSIT PISSABED
DANDELION HEAD PUFF CLOCK BUFFBALL BULLFICE BULLFIST PUFFBALL
DANDER ANGER DUTCH SCURF STROLL TEMPER WANDER HACKLES PASSION SAUNTER DANDRUFF
DANDIFIED SPRUCE BUCKISH ADONIZED
DANDIFY ADONIZE DANDYIZE
DANDLE DANCE DIDDLE FADDLE FONDLE PAMPER
DANDRUFF SCURF DANDER FURFUR
DANDY FOP JAY ADON BEAU BUCK DAND DUDE FINE JAKE MAJO PRIG TOFF TRIG YAWL BLOOD DILDO JEMMY SWELL ADONIS MIZZEN BUCKEEN CAPSTAN COXCOMB ELEGANT FOPPISH JESSAMY MACARONI SAILBOAT
DANDY HORSE HOBBY DRAISINE
DANDYISM BUCKISM
DANE DANSKER LOCHLIN DUBHGALL
DANEWORT EBULUS LOCHLIN DANEBALL DANEWEED DEADWORT WALLWORT
DANGER FEAR RISK DOUBT PERIL WATHE HAZARD PLIGHT EXTREME PITFALL VENTURE DISTRESS JEOPARDY
DANGEROUS BAD HOT ILL RUM DEAR FOUL GRAVE NASTY RISKY FICKLE KITTLE SCATHY SHREWD UNSURE AWKWARD FEARFUL PARLOUS UNCANNY DOUBTFUL INSECURE PERILOUS UNCHANCY
DANGLE LOP HANG LOLL DROOP SWING DANDLE SHOGGLE SHOOGLE SUSPEND TROLLOP
DANGLIN DANLI
DANK WET DAMP DONK HUMID MOIST CLAMMY COARSE DAMPEN

DANKISH DRIZZLE WETNESS
MOISTURE
DANSEUSE DANCER BALLERINA
DANZIG GDANSK
　(**— LIQUEUR**) RATAFIA
DAPPER NEAT TRIM NATTY SPRUCE
FINICAL FOPPISH SPARKISH
DAPPLE COVER FLECK FRECK
DAPPLED BLOCKY DOTTED POMELY
FLECKED MOTTLED SPOTTED
FRECKLED
DARBHA KUSA KUSHA
DARDANUS (**FATHER OF** —) JUPITER
(**MOTHER OF** —) ELECTRA
DARE OSS DAST DEFU FACE OSSE
RISK BRAVE STUMP ASSUME
BANTER DACKER ATTEMPT
BRAVADE FASHION PRESUME
VENTURE
　(**— NOT**) DASSNT DAURNA DASSENT
DAREDEVIL MADCAP HARDYDARDY
DARING BOLD DARE DERF PERT
RASH WILD BRAVE HARDY MANLY
NERVE PREST FELONY HEROIC
COURAGE DAIROUS DAREFUL
BOLDNESS DEVILISH FEARLESS
DARIOLE MADELINE
DARK DIM DUN MUM SAD WAN BASE
BLAE DEEP DERK DERN DUSK EBON
HARD MALE MIRK MURK BLACK
BLIND BROWN CLOUD DINGY DUSKY
FAINT MIRKY MURKY SHADY SOOTY
SWART UMBER UNLIT VAGUE
CLOSED CLOUDY CYPRUS DIMPSY
DISMAL DRUMLY GLOOMY OPAQUE
SOMBER SOMBRE SWARTH WICKED
DARKISH DUSKISH MELANIC
OBSCURE PITMIRK RAYLESS
STYGIAN SUNLESS SWARTHY
THESTER UNCLEAR ABSTRUSE
DARKLING DARKSOME GLOOMFUL
GLOOMING IGNORANT LOWERING
SINISTER
DARK-COLORED SAD SWART
SOMBER SOMBRE SWARTH
SWARTHY
DARKEN DIM DUN BLUR DULL DUSK
BEDIM BLIND CLOUD GLOAM GLOOM
POCHE SHADE SULLY SWART
UMBER DEEPEN ENDARK SHADOW
BECLOUD BENIGHT BLACKEN
ECLIPSE EMBROWN OBSCURE
OPACATE PERPLEX SLUBBER
TARNISH OVERCAST
　(**— HAIR**) BLEND
DARKENED SABLE CLOUDY BLINDED
LAMPLESS
DARKENING SCURF
DARK HORSE MOREL
DARKISH DIM
DARKLY DARK CLOSE SABLY
MISTILY
DARKNESS DARK DERN DUSK MIRK
MURK BLACK GLOOM NIGHT SHADE
TAMAS SHADOW DIMNESS PITMIRK
PRIVACY SECRECY TENEBRA
GLOAMING INIQUITY MIDNIGHT
TENEBRES TWILIGHT
DARLING JO JOE PET CHOU CONY

DEAR DUCK LIFE LOVE NOBS PEAT
ROON AROON ARUIN BULLY CHERI
DEARY DUCKS LIEVE SWEET WHITE
CHERIE DAUTIE DAWTIE MINION
MOPPET OCHREE ACUSHLA
BUNTING CUSHLAM DILLING MINIKIN
PIGSNEY PINKENY QUERIDA
STOREEN DEARLING DUMPLING
FAVORITE LIEBCHEN LOVELING
MACUSHLA PRECIOUS SWEETING
DARLING PEA INDICO INDIGO
DARN DOG BLOW DERN DURN MEND
PATCH BUGGER REPAIR DOGGONE
DARNED BLAME BLAMED DEUCED
DURNED BLESSED BLINDING
DOWNGONE
DARNEL RAY CRAP TARE WEED
CHEAT CHESS DRANK DRAWK
DRUNK EAVER GRASS IVRAY NEELE
COCKLE EGILOPS AEGILOPS
DART JET POP BOLT BUZZ CANE
CHOP COLP FLIT JOUK LEAP LICK
PILE PLAN PLAY ROUT ARROW
BOUND FLAME FLING FLIRT GLEAM
GLINT LANCE SCAMP SCOOT SHAFT
SHOOT SKITE SKIVE SPEAR SPEED
SPRIT START ANCHOR BULTEN
DARTLE ELANCE GLANCE LANCET
LAUNCH METHOD SCHEME SPRING
SQUIRT STRIKE SUMPIT THRUST
JAVELIN MISSILE STRALET VERUTUM
BRANDISH GAVELOCK JACULATE
SPICULUM
　(**— ABOUT**) SPRINKLE
　(**— OF LIGHTNING**) STREAK
　(**— OF MOLDING**) ANCHOR
　(**— REPEATEDLY**) DARTLE
DARTER SPECK
DARTING SALLY ARROWY
DARTLIKE SPICULAR
DASH DAD DAH PEP ZIP BANG BOLT
CAST DING DIVE ELAN GIFT HINT
HURL LASH LINE LUSH PASH PELT
POSS RACE RASH RUIN RULE RUSH
SHOW SLAM SOSH TICK VEIN WHAP
WHOP ABASH ARDOR BLANK BREAK
CHAFE CLASH CRASH CRUSH DRIVE
ECLAT FLASH FLING FRUSH KNOCK
PLASH PLOUT SKITE SLASH SLOSH
SMASH SPEED SPEND SPICE SPURN
START STYLE SWASH SWELL TASTE
THROW TOUCH TRICK BEDASH
DALLOP DASHEE DOLLOP ENERGY
HURTLE HYPHEN RELISH SHIVER
SPIRIT SPLASH SPRINT STRAIN
STROKE THRUST BRAVURA
BREENGE COLLIDE DEPRESS
DISPLAY HUNDRED IMPINGE
SHATTER SPATTER SPLOTCH
TANTIVY CONFOUND GRATUITY
SPLINTER
　(**— ABOUT WILDLY**) GAD REEL
　(**— AGAINST**) BEAT
　(**— DOWN**) QUELL STRAM
STRAMASH
　(**— IN PIECES**) CRASH
　(**— OF SPIRITS**) LACE LACING
　(**— OUT**) QUELL
　(**— TOGETHER**) COLLIDE

　(**— UP**) FLURR
　(**— WITH WATER**) JAW BLASH
SLASH
DASHBOARD DASH FACIA DASHER
FASCIA
DASHED SWITCHED
DASHER DASH BEATER PLUNGER
DASHING BOLD BULLY DASHY
DOGGY SHOWY SMART SWASH
JABBLE SPANKY SWANKY VELOCE
DOGGISH GALLOWS LARKING
STYLISH SWAGGER VARMINT
SLASHING SPANKING SPIRITED
DASTARD CAD SOT DAFF SNEAK
COWARD CRAVEN DULLARD
WITHING POLTROON
DASTARDLY FOUL VILLAIN
COWARDLY POLTROON SNEAKING
DASYLIRION SOTOL
DASYPUS TATU
DASYURE TIGER YABBI DAPPLE
DATA DOPE FACTS IMPUT INPUT
MATERIAL
DATE AGE DAY ERA DRAG FARD
FUSS DATUM EPOCH FARDH FRUIT
SAIDI CUTOFF FRIEND HALAWI
JUJUBE RECKON GALLANT
ANTEDATE ASHARASI DEADLINE
　(**— FIXED UPON**) TERM
　(**— RIPENING**) KIMRI RUTAB KHALAL
DATED GIVEN PASSE OUTMODED
DATE PLUM LOTUS SAPOTE ZAPOTE
DATOLITE BAKERITE HUMBOLDTITE
DATUM FACT ITEM GIVEN
DATURA DUTRA STRAMONY
TOGUACHA
DAUB DAB DOB MUD BALM BLOB
BLOT CLAG CLAM CLAT CLAY COAT
GAUM MOIL SOIL TEER CLAIK
CLART CLEAM COVER DITCH FLICK
PAINT SLAKE SLAUM SMEAR
BEDAUB CLATCH GREASE LABBER
SMUDGE SPLASH BESMEAR DRIBBLE
PLASTER SCLATCH SLUBBER
SPLATCH SPLOTCH SLAISTER
DAUBED GAUMY
DAUBING DUBBING MOILING
DAUBY BLOTTY
DAUGHTER ANAC BINT DAME GIRL
CHILD FILLE FILLY KIBEI REGAN
ALUMNA CADETTE DOCHTER
GONERIL CORDELIA
　(**PANTALOON'S** —) COLUMBINE
DAUNT AWE COW DAW ADAW DARE
DAZE FAZE MATE STUN TAME
ABASH ACCOY AMATE BREAK
CHECK DETER DOMPT DANTON
DISMAY SUBDUE CONQUER
CONTROL OVERAWE REPRESS
STUPEFY TERRIFY DISPIRIT
OVERCOME
DAUNTLESS BOLD GOOD BRAVE
AWELESS FEARLESS INTREPID
DAVENPORT DESK SOFA COUCH
DIVAN
DAVID TAFFY DAWKIN
DAVIDIST JORIST
DAVIT CRANE
DAW DA DAWN DRAB DAUNT MAGPIE

DAWPATE JACKDAW SLATTERN SLUGGARD

DAWDLE LAG IDLE JAUK MUCK MULL POKE TOIT DALLY DELAY DRILL KNOCK DADDLE DAIDLE DIDDLE DOODLE DRETCH FADDLE LINGER LOITER MUCKER PICKLE PIDDLE PINGLE POTTER PUTTER TANTLE TRIFLE DRIDDLE FINNICK QUIDDLE SAUNTER LALLYGAG LOLLYGAG SHAMMOCK SLUMMOCK

DAWDLER DAWDLE MUSARD LOUTHER

DAWN DAW ROW EOAN MORN BREAK CREEK LIGHT PRIME SHINE SUNUP AURORA MORROW ORIENT SPRING UPRISE DAWNING GREKING MORNING SUNRISE COCKCROW DAYBREAK

DAY DA DEI ERA SUN YOM DATE DIEM DIES DIET TIME EPOCH LIGHT FRIDAY MONDAY PERIOD SUNDAY JOURNEY TUESDAY LIFETIME SATURDAY THURSDAY WEDNESDAY
(— AND NIGHT) KALPA
(— BEFORE) EVE
(— OF JUDGMENT) INQUEST DOOMSDAY
(— OF ORIGIN) BIRTHDAY
(— OF REST) SABBATH
(— OF ROMAN MONTH) IDES NONES CALENDS KALENDS
(5 NAMELESS —S) UAYEB
(60TH OF —) GHURRY
(8TH — AFTER FEAST) UTAS
(DOG —S) CANICULE
(EVERY —) ALDAY
(EVIL —S) DISMAL
(FAST —) ASHURA FASTEN
(FIRST — OF AUGUST) LAMMAS
(FIRST — OF MAY) BELTANE BEALTINE
(HOLY —) FEAST HOLIDAY
(HOT —) BROILER ROASTER
(LAST — OF FESTIVAL) APODOSIS
(MARKET —) NUNDINE TIANGUE
(NO FLESH —) MAIGRE
(PATRON SAINT'S —) PATTERN
(QUARTER —) TERM
(TWELFTH —) EPIPHANY
(WEEK —) FERIA
(WORK —) WARDAY

DAYAK DYAK IBAN BAHAU DUSUN KAYAN KENYA KENYAH KELABIT

DAYBOOK BOOK DIURNAL JOURNAL

DAYBREAK DAWN MORN SUNUP DAWNING DAYDAWN DAYLIGHT

DAYDREAM DWAM MUSE DREAM DWALM FANCY VISION FANTASY REVERIE PHANTASY

DAYFLOWER COHITRE

DAYLIGHT DAY LIGHT DAYSHINE
(BROAD —) FUIRDAYS

DAYWORKER DILKER

DAZE FOG DAMP DARE MAZE STUN DAUNT DAVER DIZZY DOZEN SWOON ASTONY BEDAZE BEMUSE BENUMB DAZZLE DEAFEN MUDDLE TRANCE CONFUSE PETRIFY

STUPEFY TORPIFY ASTONISH BEWILDER DUMFOUND PARALYZE

DAZED MAD ASEA DAMP ASSOT DIZZY DOYLT SILLY TOTTY CUCKOO DOILED GROGGY ROTTEN BEMUSED DONNERT SPOILED WITLESS ASTONIED BESOTTED DITHERED DONNERED WITHERED

DAZEDLY GROGGILY

DAZZLE DARE DAZE BLEND BLIND DROWN GLAIK SHINE FULGOR ECLIPSE BEWILDER OUTSHINE SURPRISE

DAZZLED BLINDED

DAZZLING FLARE FLASH FLASHY GARISH ADAZZLE FLARING FULGENT GLARING RADIANT DIZZYING GORGEOUS

DDT TDE DICOPHANE

DEACON ADEPT CLERIC DOCTOR LAYMAN LEVITE MASTER PHILIP MINISTER

DEACONESS WIDOW

DEAD FEY LOW AWAY BUNG COLD DEAF DOWD DULL FLAT GONE MORT NUMB POKY SURE TAME ADEAD AMORT BLIND DEEDS INERT NAPOO POKEY QUIET SLAIN STARK VAPID ASLEEP BYGONE FALLEN LAPSED NAPOOH REFUSE DEADISH DEFUNCT EXACTLY EXPIRED EXTINCT INSIPID SAINTED STERILE TEDIOUS ABSOLUTE COMPLETE DECEASED DEPARTED INACTIVE LIFELESS OBSOLETE
(— AT TOP) RAMPICK

DEAD-ARM NECROSIS

DEAD-DRUNK BLIND

DEADEN DAMP DULL DUMB KILL MULL MUTE NUMB SEAR STUN BLUNT SLAKE BENUMB DAMPEN MUFFLE OBTUND OPIATE RETARD STIFLE WEAKEN MORTIFY PETRIFY REPRESS SLUMBER SMOTHER AMORTIZE ASTONISH ENFEEBLE
(— A SCENT) FOIL

DEAD END PLACE

DEADENED DEAD DEAF SEAR SERE

DEADENING PUGGING

DEADHEAD SINK BOBBER SINKER

DEADHOUSE MORGUE MORTUARY

DEAD LETTER NIX

DEADLINE DATELINE

DEADLINESS LETHALITY

DEADLOCK TIE LOGJAM IMPASSE STANDOFF STOPPAGE

DEADLY WAN DIRE FELL MORT FATAL FERAL TUANT DEATHY LETHAL MORTAL CAPITAL DEATHLY FATEFUL RUINOUS MORTIFIC VENOMOUS VIRULENT

DEADLY CARROT DRIAS THAPSIA

DEAD NETTLE HENBIT

DEADS MULLOCK

DEAF SURD DUNCH DUNNY SORDA SORDO

DEAFEN DIN DORR DEAVE DEADEN

DEAFENING DEEVEY

DEAF-MUTE FENELLA SURDOMUTE

DEAFNESS ASONIA SURDITY ANACUSIA ANACUSIS COPHOSIS

DEAL GO END JOB DAIL DOLE LEND PART SALE TALE WHIZ ALLOT BOARD BROKE FETCH PLANK SERVE SEVER SHAKE SHARE SHIFT TRADE TREAT TROKE TRUCK WIELD YIELD BATTEN BESTOW DIVIDE HANDLE MEDDLE NUMBER PARCEL BARGAIN DELIVER INFLICT PIANOLA PORTION SCATTER TRUCKLE WRESTLE DISPENSE SEPARATE
(— CARDS) DRAW TALLY
(— CLANDESTINELY) TRINKET
(— IN A TRIFLING WAY) PIDDLE
(— IN BRIDGE) BOARD
(— IN GRAIN) SWALE
(— OF CARDS) COUP SPOIL GOULASH
(— SHREWDLY) JOCKEY
(— WITH) HAND COVER DIGHT TREAT BUCKET CUSTOM DEMEAN HANDLE ENTREAT
(GREAT —) MORT LOADS MIGHT SIGHT JUGFUL SKINFUL
(POLITICAL —) DICKER

DEALER BANK CHAP AGENT COPER BADGER BANKER BROKER CADGER EGGLER GROCER JOBBER JUNIOR MONGER SELLER TRADER BUTCHER CHAPMAN KEELMAN YOUNGER CHANDLER MERCHANT OCCUPIER OPERATOR STICKMAN TAILLEUR
(— IN CATTLE) COUPER COWPER DROVER
(— IN CHEMICALS) SALTER DRYSALTER
(— IN DRY GOODS) DRAPER
(— IN GRAIN) SWALER
(— IN OLD CLOTHES) FRIPPER
(— IN PAINTS) COLORMAN
(— IN TEXTILES) MERCER
(CARDS —) FARMER
(COAL —) COLLIER
(HORSE —) COPER COUPER COWPER CHANTER SCORSER
(SLAVE —) MANGO
(STOCK —) STAG JOBBER OUTSIDER

DEALFISH VAAGMAR VAAGMAER

DEALING DOLE PRICE TRUCK TRADING TRAFFIC EXCHANGE
(BUSINESS —S) TROKE
(JUST —) DOOM
(TRICKY —) BROKING
(PL.) DEAL TRAFFIC BUSINESS COMMERCE PRACTICE PRACTISE

DEAN DECAN DOYEN DEANER SENIOR VERGER PREFECT PROVOST SUBDEAN ARCHDEAN PRAEFECT

DEAR JO GRA HON JOE PET AGRA CARA CHER CONY FAIR FOND GOOD HIGH LAMB LIEF LOVE NEAR NOBS SALT BOSOM CHARY CHERE CHUCK DEARY HONEY LOVED SWEET TIGHT COSTLY DAUTIE DAWTIE DEARIE DEARLY POPPET SCARCE SEVERE SQUALL TENDER WORTHY BELOVED DARLING LOVABLE PIGSNEY

QUERIDA SPECIAL TOOTSIE
ESPECIAL ESTEEMED GLORIOUS
PRECIOUS VALUABLE
DEARLY DEAR ALIFE DEEPLY
KEENLY RICHLY HEARTILY
DEARNESS CHERTE DEARTH
DEARTH LACK WANT CHERTE
FAMINE PAUCITY POVERTY
DEARNESS SCARCITY SOLITUDE
DEATH DEE END BALE BANE DEAD
DOOM EXIT FAIL FATE KILL MORS
MORT OBIT PASS REST WINK
ANKOU DECAY GRAVE GRUEL
LETHE NIGHT SLEEP CHAROS
CHARUS DEMISE DEPART ENDING
EXITUS EXPIRY MURDER PERIOD
REAPER WAGANG CURTAIN
DECEASE FUNERAL PARTING
PASSAGE QUIETUS SILENCE
BIOLYSIS CASUALTY FATALITY
NECROSIS RAWBONES THANATOS
(— **ANGEL**) AZRAEL
(— **BY HANGING**) HALTER
(— **OF TISSUE**) GANGRENE
DEATH ADDER ELAPID ELAPOID
DEATH CAMASS LOBELIA
DEATHLESS ETERNAL UNDYING
IMMORTAL
DEATHLIKE DEATHLY GHASTLY
MACABRE GHASTFUL MORIBUND
MORTUOUS
DEATHLY DEAD FATAL DEADLY
MORTAL GHASTLY STYGIAN
DEATHFUL MORTALLY
DEATH'S-HEAD SKULL
DEBAR DENY TABU CROSS ESTOP
REPEL TABOO DISBAR FORBID
HINDER REFUSE BOYCOTT DEPRIVE
EXCLUDE OUTSHUT PREVENT
SECLUDE SUSPEND PRECLUDE
PROHIBIT
DEBARK LAND
DEBARRED FROZEN OUTSHUT
DEBASE SINK ABASE ALLOY AVILE
DIRTY LOWER STOOP BEMEAN
DEFILE DEMEAN DILUTE EMBASE
IMPAIR NIDDER NITHER REDUCE
REVILE VILIFY CORRUPT DEBAUCH
DECLINE DEGRADE DEPRAVE
PERVERT TRADUCE VILLAIN VITIATE
DEBASED BASE VILE BASTARD
CORRUPT SQUALID CANKERED
DEGRADED DEROGATE
DEBASEMENT TARNISH
DEBASING DOWNWARD
DEBATABLE MOOT DISPUTABLE
DEBATE AGON BEAT FRAY MOOT
ARGUE FIGHT PLEAD STUDY
ARGUFY HASSEL HASSLE REASON
STRIFE AGITATE CANVASS CONTEND
CONTEST DISCEPT DISCUSS
DISPUTE EXAMINE MOOTING
PALAVER QUARREL WRANGLE
ARGUMENT CONSIDER CONTRARY
MILITATE PARLANCE QUESTION
DEBATER PICADOR
DEBAUCH BOUT FILE SPREE TAINT
WHORE DEBASE DEBOSH DEFILE
GUZZLE MISUSE SEDUCE SPLORE

VILIFY CORRUPT DEBOISE DEPRAVE
MISLEAD POLLUTE VIOLATE
DISHONOR SQUANDER STRUMPET
STUPRATE
DEBAUCHED LEWD RAKELY
DEBOIST DEBOSHED RAKEHELL
DEBAUCHEE RIP RAKE ROUE
HOLOUR LECHER RAKEHELL
DEBAUCHERY RAKERY DEBAUCH
PRIAPISM
DEBENTURE SECURITY
DEBENZOLIZE STRIP
DEBILITATE SINK
DEBILITATED WEAK SEEDY FEEBLE
INFIRM SAPPED ASTHENIC
DEBILITY ATONY ASTHENY LANGUOR
ASTHENIA WEAKNESS
DEBIT DEBT LOSS CHARGE
DEBONAIR AIRY JAUNTY POLITE
CAVALIER GRACEFUL GRACIOUS
DEBOUCH FALL MOUTH
DEBOUCHMENT INFLUX INFLUXION
DEBRIS GUCK SLAG DECAY FRUSH
TRADE TRASH WASTE REFUSE
RUBBLE RUDERA CRUMBLE ELUVIUM
RUBBISH SLIDDER DETRITUS
(— **IN WOOL**) BUR BURR
(— **OF INSECTS**) FRASS
(— **OF ROCKS**) HEAD DRIFT TALUS
ELUVIUM
(**FLUFFY** —) FLUE
(**FOREST** —) SLASH
DEBT DUE SIN POST DEBIT FAULT
STOCK ARREARS DEBITUM
JUDGMENT TRESPASS
(**PL.**) OBLATA WANIGAN ARREARAGE
DEBTOR OWER SKIP DYVOUR
DEBITOR YIELDER
DEBUT OPENING ENTRANCE
DEBUTANTE BUD DEB DEBBY
INGENUE ROSEBUD
DECADENT EFFETE DECAYED
HOTHOUSE OVERRIPE
DECAHYDRATE SODA
DECALOGUE WITNESS
DECAMP GUY PUT BOLT HIKE KITE
ELOPE MOSEY SCOOT SCOUR
VAMOS DEPART ESCAPE LEVANT
MIZZLE MORRIS POWDER VAMOSE
ABSCOND DISCAMP VAMOOSE
DECAMPING GUY
DECAN DECURION
DECANT EMIT POUR UNLOAD
TRANSFER
DECANTER CARAFE CARAFON
URCEOLE GARDEVIN INGESTER
DECAPITATE BEHEAD DECOLLATE
DECAPITATION DECOLL HEADING
DECAPOD BUSTER
DECARBONIZE DECOKE
DECATING SPONGING
DECAY EBB ROT ROX BLET CONK
DOAT DOTE DOZE FADE RUIN SEED
WANE WEAR CROCK DEATH FAILL
SHANK SLOOM SLOUM SPOIL
WASTE CARIES FADING MARCOR
MILDEW MOLDER MOSKER SICKEN
WITHER CRUMBLE DECLINE FAILURE

MORTIFY PUTREFY DECREASE
FORDWINE
(— **IN WOOD**) CONK DOZE
(**INCIPIENT** —) BLET
DECAYED BAD DEAF DOZY ROXY
FRUSH SEEDY DAISED MARCID
PUTRID ROTTEN SPAKED RUINOUS
SNAGGLED
DECAYING COLD DOTY SHABBY
CARIOUS
DECEASE DIE FAIL OBIT PASS
DEATH DEMISE PASSAGE
DECEASED DEAD PARTED DEFUNCT
EXTINCT UMWHILE DEPARTED
UMQUHILE
DECEIT GAB DOLE FLUM GAFF GULL
RUSE SHAM TRAP TRAY WILE COVIN
CRAFT DOLUS FRAUD GUILE SARAB
SWICK SWIKE CAUTEL FELONY
WOIDRE CUNNING DISSAIT FAITERY
FICTION ARTIFICE FALSEDAD
INTRIGUE SPOOFERY SUBTLETY
TRICKERY TRUMPERY WILINESS
DECEITFUL BLIND BRAID FALSE
GAUDY JANUS LOOPY SLAPE
ARTFUL COVERT CRAFTY DOUBLE
FICKLE HOLLOW TRICKY CUNNING
EVASIVE FICTIVE SIRENIC SLEEKIT
SLIDDER UNWREST WINDING
COVINOUS GUILEFUL ILLUSIVE
INDIRECT SHAMMISH TORTUOUS
DECEITFULLY DOUBLE FALSELY
DECEITFULNESS SHAM DECEIT
FALSITY
DECEIVE BOB COG CON DOR FOB
FUB GAB GAS GUM KID LIE BILK
BRAG BUNK CRAP DUPE FAKE FLAM
FOOL GAFF GULL HAVE HOAX JILT
JOUK MOCK SELL SHAM SILE SNOW
TURN WILE ABUSE AMUSE BLEAR
BLEND BLENK BLIND BLINK BLUFF
CATCH CHEAT COZEN CROSS
CULLY DODGE DORRE FEINT GLEEK
GLOZE HOCUS LURCH PATCH
SPOOF SWICK SWIKE TRICK TROIL
TRUFF TRUMP TRYST BAFFLE
BEDOTE BEFLUM BEFOOL BETRAY
BLANCH BUBBLE CAJOLE CLOINE
CLOYNE DELUDE DIVERT EUCHRE
GAMMON HUMBUG ILLUDE JUGGLE
MISUSE NIGGLE SUCKER WIMPLE
BEGUILE DEFRAUD MISLEAD
OVERSEE TRAITOR BEJUGGLE
FLIMFLAM HOODWINK OUTREACH
DECEIVER ANGLE CHEAT HOCUS
COGGER FAITOR FALSER GUILER
MOCKER TRAPAN TREPAN FALSARY
ILLUSOR JUGGLER SHARPER
SPOOFER TRUMPER WARLOCK
WERNARD IMPOSTOR LOSENGER
LOTHARIO MAGICIAN
DECELERATE SLOW
DECENCY GRACE DECORUM
HONESTY MODESTY CHASTITY
DECENNIUM DECADE
DECENT FAIR CHASTE COMELY
HONEST MODEST PROPER SEEMLY
FITTING GRADELY JANNOCK
SHAPELY SIGHTLY DECOROUS

GRAITHLY WISELIKE
DECENTLY WHITE
DECEPTION BAM COG DOR GAG LIE
DOLE FLAM FLUM GAFF GULL HOAX
MAZE RIDE RUSE SELL SHAM WILE
ABUSE BLIND CHEAT COVIN CRAFT
CURVE DOLUS DORRE FAVEL FRAUD
GLEEK GUILE MAGIC SNARE SPOOF
TRICK BARRAT CAUTEL DECEIT
DUPERY HUMBUG JUGGLE ABUSION
BLAFLUM CHICANE CUNNING
EVASION FALLACY FALSERY FICTION
GULLAGE GULLERY KNAVERY
PRETEXT SLYNESS ARTIFICE
DISGUISE FALSEDAD FLIMFLAM
ILLUSION INTRIGUE PHANTASM
PRESTIGE SUBTLETY TRICKERY
TRUMPERY WILINESS
DECEPTIVE FLAM FALSE ARTFUL
SIRENIC TRICKSY DELUSIVE
DELUSORY FLIMFLAM ILLUSORY
IMPOSING SHAMMISH UNSICKER
DECEPTIVENESS FANTASTRY
DECIBEL (10 —S) BEL
DECIDE FIX CAST DEEM HOLD RULE
TELL WILL AWARD JUDGE PATCH
PITCH DECERN DECISE DECREE
FIGURE REWARD SETTLE ADJUDGE
DERAIGN RESOLVE CONCLUDE
SENTENCE
(— UPON) SET ELECT CHOOSE
TERMINE
DECIDED FIRM FLAT MAIN FORMED
SETTLED DECISIVE RESOLUTE
DECIDEDLY DIRECTLY DISTINCTLY
DECIDUA CADUCA
DECIGRAM LI
DECIMA TENTH TITHE
DECIMAL DENARY REPEATER
(— PART) MANTISSA
DECIMATE TENTH DESTROY
DECIPHER READ SOLVE CIPHER
DECODE DETECT REVEAL DECRYPT
DISCOVER INDICATE UNPUZZLE
DECIPHERING EPIGRAPHY
DECISION ACT END CALL DOOM
FIAT GRIT ARRET AWARD CANON
FAITH ISSUE PARTY PLUCK POINT
ACTION CHOICE CRISIS DECREE
DIKTAT RULING ACUERDO CONSULT
INTERIM PRACTIC VERDICT FINALITY
JUDGMENT PLACITUM SENTENCE
SUFFRAGE UMPIRAGE
(— OF COURT) HOLDING
(EXISTENTIAL —) LEAP
(FINAL —) ISSUE
DECISIVE FINAL CRISIC PAYOFF
VIRILE CRUCIAL DECIDED CRITICAL
CRUSHING DECRETAL POSITIVE
DECISIVELY FINALLY
DECK FIG TOG BANK BUSS DAUB
DINK FLAT HEAP PINK POOP PROW
TRIG ADORN ARRAY COVER DIZEN
DRESS EQUIP FLOOR HATCH PRANK
PRINK STORE AWNING BEDECK
BLAZON CLOTHE ENRICH FETTLE
FOCSLE LAUREL APPAREL BEDIGHT
BEDIZEN FEATHER FLOUNCE
GEMMATE BEAUTIFY DECORATE

EMBLAZON PLATFORM
(— OF CARDS) BOOK
(— OUT) BARB TIFF DIZEN SPICK
BEDECK FANGLE FINIFY BEDIGHT
(HIGH —) POOP
(LOWEST —) ORLOP
DECKED CLAD BESEEN ARMORIED
LAURELED
(— OUT) SPIFFED
DECKHAND BOATMAN TRIMMER
BARGEMAN
DECKHOUSE CABOOSE CAMBOOSE
DECKLE DECKEL FEATHEREDGE
DECKMAN TRIPPER LEVERMAN
DECLAIM GALE RANT RAVE ROLL
MOUTH ORATE SPEAK SPOUT
BLEEZE RECITE ELOCUTE INVEIGH
DENOUNCE DISCLAIM HARANGUE
PERORATE SINGSONG
DECLAIMER BARD SPEECHIFIER
DECLAMATION FROTHING
HARANGUE SPOUTING
DECLARATION BILL CALL DICK
NARR TALE WORD COUNT FUERO
LIBEL PAROL AVOWAL DECEIT
MISERE ORACLE PAROLE PLACET
SAYING EXPRESS PROMISE
RESOLVE MANIFEST PLATFORM
(— IN BRIDGE) MAKE AUCTION
(— OF HOSTILITIES) DEFIANCE
(OFFICIAL —) AUTHORITY
DECLARE BID KEN LAY SAY VOW
AVER AVOW DENY MAKE READ
SHOW SNUM SWAN TROW VOTE
AREAD AREED BRUIT KEETH KITHE
KYTHE POSIT SNORE SOUND SPEAK
STATE TRUTH VOUCH AFFIRM
ALLEGE ASSERT ASSURE AUTHOR
AVOUCH BLAZON COUTHE DEPONE
DESCRY EXPONE HERALD INDICT
NOTIFY PATEFY RELATE SPRING
UPGIVE ACCLAIM BEHIGHT DISCUSS
EXPRESS OUTTELL PROFESS
PROTEST PUBLISH SIGNIFY TERMINE
TESTIFY ANNOUNCE DENOUNCE
DESCRIBE INDICATE INTIMATE
MAINTAIN MANIFEST NUNCIATE
PROCLAIM RENOUNCE
(— A SAINT) CANONIZE
(— ARBITRARILY) GAVEL
(— INVALID) ANNUL
(— PUBLICLY) CRY
(— UNTRUE) DENY
(— WAR) DEFY
(SOLEMNLY —) AFFY SWEAR
DECLARED AVOWED STATED
DECLARER LAWMAN VIVANT
DECLINATION BIAS DECAY SLOPE
REGRET DECLINE DESCENT
REFUSAL SOUTHING SWERVING
DECLINE BEG DIP EBB SAG SET
BALK BEND BUST DENY DIVE DOWN
DROP FADE FAIL FALL FLAG FLOP
HELD SINK SLIP TURN VAIL WANE
WELK BAULK CHUTE DECAY DROLL
DROOP DWINE FAINT HEALD HIELD
LAPSE LOWER QUAIL REPEL SLACK
SLOPE SLUMP SPURN STOOP STRAY
TABES WAIVE DEBASE FALTER

REFUSE REJECT RENEGE SICKEN
WEAKEN ATROPHY DESCEND
DESCENT DETRECT DEVIATE
DISAVOW DWINDLE ECLIPSE
FAILURE FALLOFF FORBEAR
INFLECT LETDOWN SINKAGE
DECREASE DOWNBEAT DOWNTURN
FOREBEAR LANGUISH TOBOGGAN
WITHDRAW
(— IN MARKET PRICE) SPILL
(— IN POPULATION) CRASH
DECLINING DOWN AWANE BEARISH
FALLING WESTERN DECADENT
DECLIVITY BENT BREW FALL HANG
SIDE SKUG CLIFF COAST DEVEX
PITCH SCARP SLENT SLOPE CALADE
HANGER DECLINE DESCENT
HANGING DOWNHILL
DECLIVOUS PRONE SLOPING
DECOCT BOIL COOK SMELT EXCITE
KINDLE REFINE EXTRACT
DECOCTION BANG OOZE SAVE
BHANG APOZEM CREMOR PTISAN
TISANE APOZEMA DECOCTUM
DECOHERER TAPPER
DECOLLETE LOW
DECOMPOSE ROT FOUL FRIT DECAY
ATTACK DIGEST DEGRADE DISSOLVE
DECOMPOSED PUTRID
DECOMPOSITION DECAY BREAKUP
BIOLYSIS EXCHANGE
DECORATE DO BIND CHIP CITE
DECK EDGE FRET GAUD PINK RAIL
RULE TIFF TIRE TRIM ADORN DRESS
FLOCK FRILL GRAIN INLAY MENSE
PANEL POKER TRAIL TRICK BEDECK
BUTTON DAIKER DAMASK DECORE
EMBOSS FLOWER FRESCO PARGET
POUNCE PURFLE SPONGE SUBORN
BECROSS CORONET ENCHASE
FESTOON FURNISH GADROON
GARNISH HISTORY IMPASTE
INWEAVE MINIATE PERFORM
BELETTER FLOURISH ORNAMENT
OVERWORK TITIVATE
DECORATED GIDDY LACED AJOURE
FLAMBE ORNATE ADORNED
DAMASSE FROGGED INCISED
WROUGHT COCKADED DISTINCT
FLORETED
DECORATING LIMNERY
DECORATION KEY BUHL FALL FUSS
IKAT BOULE DECOR DODAD HONOR
MEDAL PRIDE BOULLE DECKER
DECORE DESIGN DOODAB DOODAD
FINERY FLORET FRIEZE GOTHIC
NIELLO PLAQUE SETOFF TINSEL
ARTWORK BARBOLA DECKING
EPERGNE FLUTING GARNISH
TRACERY BAYADERE DENTELLE
DIAMANTE ESCALLOP FLOURISH
FRETTING FRETWORK INTARSIA
ORNAMENT
(— IN GUEST CHAMBER) XENIUM
(— OF LEAVES) VIGNETTE
(— OF MONKEYS) SINGERIE
(— TECHNIQUE) PLANGI
(BOOK-COVER —) DENTELLE
(CUTOUT —) APPLIQUE

(FESTIVE —) GALA
(INESSENTIAL —) SPINACH
(MURAL —) TOPIA
(MUSICAL —) GRACE
(PORCELAIN —) KAKIEMON
(POTTERY —) BRODERIE
(WALL —S) TENTURE
(PL.) COLORS BUNTING GREENERY
DECORATIVE FANCY FIKIE
DECOROUS CALM DONE GOOD NICE
PRIM DOUCE GRAVE QUIET SOBER
STAID CHASTE DECENT DEMURE
MODEST POLITE PROPER SEDATE
SEEMLY SERENE STEADY BECOMED
FITTING ORDERLY REGULAR
SETTLED BECOMING COMPOSED
MANNERLY
DECOROUSLY FITLY
DECOROUSNESS CHASTITY
POLITESSE
DECORTICATE FLAY HULL HUSK
PARE PEEL PILL SKIN STRIP
DENUDE
DECORUM DECENCY DIGNITY
FITNESS MODESTY
DECOY COY BAIT CALL GOAD LURE
TOLE TOLL CRIMP DRILL PLANT
ROPER SHILL STALE STALL STOOL
TEMPT TRAIN ALLURE BUTTON
CALLER CAPPER ENTICE ENTRAP
PIGEON SEDUCE TOLLER TREPAN
BARNARD BERNARD DECOYER
INVEIGLE SQUAWKER
(— FOR GAMBLERS) CAPPER
(— FOR SWINDLERS) BARNARD
BERNARD
(AUCTIONEER'S —) BUTTON
DECREASE EBB BATE DROP FALL
LOSS SINK WANE WELK WILK ABATE
CROCK DECAY LAPSE SWAGE
TAPER WANZE WASTE CHANGE
DECESS DECREW IMPAIR LESSEN
NARROW REDUCE SHRINK ATROPHY
CUTDOWN DECLINE DWINDLE
SHORTEN SLACKEN SUBSIDE
DECIMATE DIMINISH DOWNTURN
MODERATE RETRENCH
(— IN FORCE) LAY
(— IN VOLUME) ABLATION
(— OF EFFICIENCY) FATIGUE
(— STITCHES) FASHION
DECREE ACT DIT LAW SAW SET
DOOM FIAT REDE RULE WILL WITE
AREAD AREED ARRET CANON EDICT
ENACT FIANT GRACE HATTI IRADE
JUDGE ORDER POINT SHAPE TENET
UKASE WRITE ARREST ASSIZE
DECERN DICTUM FIRMAN INDICT
MODIFY ORDAIN PLACIT RECESS
ADJUDGE APPOINT BESLUIT
COMMAND CONSULT DECREET
DICTATE DIVORCE ESCRIPT
GEZERAH MANDATE SETNESS
STATUTE WORKING DECISION
DECRETUM JUDGMENT PLACITUM
PSEPHISM RESCRIPT ROGATION
SANCTION SENTENCE
(— BEFOREHAND) DESTINE

(ECCLESIASTICAL —) CANON
SYNODICAL
(JUDICIAL —) AUTO
(MOHAMMEDAN —) IRADE
(OFFICIAL —) RESCRIPT
DECREPIT LAME WEAK UNORN
BEDRID CREAKY FEEBLE INFIRM
SENILE FAILING INVALID FORFAIRN
DECRY BOO SLUR LOWER ROGUE
DESCRY LESSEN ASPERSE BARRACK
CENSURE CONDEMN DEBAUCH
DEGRADE DETRACT BELITTLE
DEROGATE MINIMIZE
DECRYPT BREAK DECODE
DECURRENT DEFLUENT
DECUSSATION CHIASMA
DEDANS HAZARD
DEDICATE VOW VOTE DEVOW
SACRE SACRI DEVOTE DEVOVE
DIRECT HALLOW OBLATE ASCRIBE
ENTITLE CHRISTEN INSCRIBE
INTITULE SEPARATE
DEDICATED HOLY OBLATE SACRED
VOTIVE
DEDICATION CULT WAKF DEVOTION
DEDUCE PUT DRAW LEAD TAKE
BRING DRIVE FETCH GUESS INFER
TRACE DEDUCT DERIVE ELICIT
EVOLVE GATHER COLLECT EXPLAIN
EXTRACT SUBSUME CONCLUDE
DEDUCT BATE DOCK TAKE ABATE
ALLOW SHAVE DEFALK REBATE
RECOUP REDUCT REMOVE CURTAIL
SUBDUCT TRADUCE ABSTRACT
DISCOUNT SEPARATE SUBTRACT
DEDUCTION AGIO SALT CREDIT
DEDUCT REBATE BEAMAGE
DOCKAGE IMPRESS OFFTAKE
REPRISE DISCOUNT ERGOTISM
ILLATION STOPPAGE
DEDUCTIVE DOGMATIC
DEE DUANT
DEED DO ACT BILL BOOK CASE FACT
FAIT FEAT FIAT GEST HARD JEST
TURN WORK ACTUM ACTUS BROAD
CHART DOING GESTE ISSUE SANAD
THING TITLE ACTION CONVEY
ESCROW FACTUM POTTAH REMISE
SASINE SUNNUD TAILYE CHARTER
EXPLOIT FACTION TAILZIE CHIVALRY
HEIRLOOM PARERGON PRACTICE
PRACTISE TRANSFER
(BRUTAL —) ATROCITY
(CHARITABLE —S) ALMS
(GOOD —) BENEFIT MITZVAH
(HEBREW —) STARR
(PART OF —) HABENDUM
(VALIANT —) VALIANCE
(WICKED —) ILL
(PL.) DOINGS SERVICE MUNIMENTS
DEEM LET SAY SEE GIVE HOPE RECK
SEEM TELL JUDGE OPINE THINK
ESTEEM EXPECT ORDAIN RECKON
REGARD ACCOUNT ADJUDGE
BELIEVE RECOUNT RESPECT
SURMISE ANNOUNCE CONSIDER
JUDGMENT PROCLAIM
DEEMSTER DOOMSMAN
DE-ENERGIZE KILL CLEAR

DEEP LOW SAD SEA BOLD DUAT
HOLL HOWE NEAL RAPT ABYSS
BROAD DEWAT GRAVE GREAT
GRUFF HEAVY OCEAN STIFF STOOR
STOUR HOLLOW INTENT STRONG
SULLEN ABYSMAL INTENSE SERIOUS
UNMIXED ABSORBED ABSTRUSE
COMPLETE POWERFUL PROFOUND
THOROUGH
DEEP-DYED ENGRAINED
DEEPEN CLOUD DARKEN DREDGE
ENHANCE THICKEN HEIGHTEN
DEEPEST INMOST DEEPMOST
DEEPLY DEEP ADEEP DEARLY
SOUNDLY DEVOUTLY GROUNDLY
INWARDLY
DEEP-SEA DIPSY BATHYL DIPSEY
BATHYAL
DEEP-SEATED DEEP INTIMATE
PROFOUND INGRAINED
DEEP-TONED STOUR
DEER ELK RED ROE AXIS BUCK DAIM
HART HIND MILU MUSK OLEN PARA
PUDU RUSA SHOU SIKA STAG WILD
BROCK GEMUL MARAL MOOSE
SABIR SPADE STAIG CERVID CHITAL
CHITRA FALLOW GUEMAL HANGUL
HEARST HUEMUL PARRAH RASCAL
SAMBAR SAMBUR THAMIN VENADA
BROCKET BROWZER CARIBOU
CERVINE CERVOID CHEETAL
DEERLET FANTAIL GUAZUTI
KASTURA MUNTJAC PLANDOK
SAMBHAR THAMENG VENISON
BOBOLINK ELAPHURE RUMINANT
(— IN 3RD YEAR) SPAY SOREL
SPAYAD SPAYARD
(— UNDER 1 YEAR) KID
(2-YEAR OLD —) KNOBBER
(CASTRATED —) HAVIER
(FEMALE — IN 2ND YEAR) TEG
HEARST
(FEMALE —) DOE ROE HIND
(HINDQUARTERS OF —) FOUCH
FOURCHE
(MALE — IN 2ND YEAR) PRICKET
(MALE — IN 4TH YEAR) SORE
STAGGARD STAGGART
(MALE — OVER 5 YEARS) HART
STAG
(RED —) OLEN MARAL BROCKET
(RUSINE —) AXIS
(YOUNG —) KID FAWN SPITTER
DEER BUSH SOAPBUSH
DEER FERN HARDFERN
DEERFLY TABANID
DEERHAIR SEDGE BULRUSH
DEERHOUND DEERDOG BUCKHOUND
DEERSKIN BUCK DEER
DEFACE MAR FOUL RUIN SCAR
ERASE SHAME SPOIL CANCEL
DAMAGE DAMASK DEFAME DEFOIL
DEFORM DEFOUL EFFACE INJURE
INJURY DESTROY DETRACT DISTORT
SLANDER DISGRACE DISHONOR
MALAHACK MUTILATE OUTSHINE
DEFACED FOUL
DEFACING DIMINUTION
DEFALCATE DRIB DEFALK

DEFAMATION LIBEL DEFAME DEFAMY DEPRAVE SCANDAL SLANDER

DEFAME FOUL ABASE BELIE CLOUD LIBEL NOISE SMEAR ACCUSE CHARGE DEFACE DEFOIL DEFOUL FORGAB INFAME INJURE MALIGN SUGGIL VILIFY ASPERSE BLACKEN BLEMISH DEBAUCH DETRACT DIFFAME PUBLISH SCANDAL SLANDER SPATTER TRADUCE DISHONOR INFAMIZE

DEFAMER SYCOPHANT

DEFAULT FAIL FLAW LOSS MORA ERROR FAULT OFFEND BLEMISH FAILURE MISTAKE NEGLECT OFFENSE OMISSION
(— **ON DEBT**) LEVANT

DEFEASANCE DEFEAT UNDOING

DEFEASIBLE IMPERFECT

DEFEAT EAT PIP WIN BALK BEAT BEST BOWL CAST DING DOWN DRUB FOIL HAVE JINK KILL LACE LICK LOSS ROUT RUIN RUSH SINK SKIN STOP TOLL TOSS TRAP TRIM UNDO WHIP AVOID BREAK CHECK FACER FALSE FLING FLOOR OUTDO PASTE SKUNK SWAMP THROW WASTE WHACK WORSE WORST WRACK BAFFLE CUMBER DEROUT EUCHRE LARRUP MASTER MURDER STOUSH THWACK THWART WAGGLE WEAKEN CONQUER DEPRIVE DESTROY LICKING OVERSET PEREMPT REVERSE SCOMFIT SETBACK SHELLAC SNOOKER SUBVERT TROUNCE INFRINGE IRRITATE OVERCOME VANQUISH WATERLOO
(— **COMPLETELY**) SKUNK
(— **DECISIVELY**) EAT DRUB SACK BLAST CLEAN FLATTEN SHELLAC
(— **IN BRIDGE**) SET
(— **IN LAWSUIT**) CAST
(**DECISIVE** —) CLEANUP CLEANING
(**INTO** —) DOWN
(**UTTER** —) MATE ROUT DEROUT

DEFEATED DOWN LOST KAPUT BEATEN CRAVEN WHIPPED

DEFEATIST BOLO FATALIST

DEFECT BUG FLAW LACK MAIM TWIT VICE WANE WANT BOTCH CLOUD CRAZE ERROR FAULT MINUS MULCT TOUCH DAMAGE DESERT INJURY LACUNA MALADY MAYHEM PLIGHT VICETY VITIUM ABSENCE BLEMISH DEMERIT FAILING MISPICK PEELING PINHOLE COLOBOMA CRESCENT DRAWBACK WEAKNESS
(— **IN CRYSTAL**) HOLE
(— **IN ENAMEL**) SCAB SAGGING SCUMMING
(— **IN FABRIC**) GOUT SCOB BARRE BRACK SMASH
(— **IN GLASS**) KNOT TEAR STONE THREADS
(— **IN IRON**) SEAM
(— **IN MARBLE**) TERRAS TERRACE TERRASSE

(— **IN METAL**) SNAKE
(— **IN PRINTING PLATE**) HICKY HICKEY
(— **IN STEEL**) LAP
(— **IN TIMBER**) LAG SHAN COLLAPSE
(— **IN YARN**) SINGLING CORKSCREW
(— **OF CHARACTER**) HOLE SHADE HAMARTIA
(**LINT** —) SPOT
(**SPEECH** —) CLUTTERING
(**TELEVISION** —) FLOPOVER

DEFECTION LETDOWN DESERTION

DEFECTIVE BAD ILL EVIL FOXY LACK LAME MANK POOR SICK BAUCH BAUGH BLIND FALSE FLAWY PASUL COMMON FAULTY FLAWED MANGUE MEAGER MEAGRE RAGGED HALTING TOMFOOL VICIOUS DISGENIC DYSGENIC MUTILOUS VITIATED

DEFEND FEND HOLD KEEP SAVE WARD WARN WEAR COVER GUARD SHEND WATCH ASSERT FORBID SCREEN SECURE SHIELD UPHOLD WARISH BUCKLER CONTEST DERAIGN ESPOUSE EXPOUND FLANKER JUSTIFY PREVENT PROPUGN PROTECT SHELTER SUPPORT WARRANT ADVOCATE CHAMPION CONSERVE GARRISON MAINTAIN PRESERVE PROHIBIT

DEFENDANT REA REUS ACCUSED AVOWANT APPELLEE

DEFENDER FENDER PATRON ADVOCATE ASSERTER ASSERTOR CHAMPION GUARDIAN UPHOLDER

DEFENSE EGIS FORT WALL WEAR AEGIS ALIBI FENCE GRITH ANSWER BEHALF COVERT FRAISE SCONCE BARRACE BULWARK CONTEST DEFENCE OUTWORK RAMPART SHELTER BOUNDARY SECURITY SEPIMENT SPOLOGIA PALE ROCK WARD GUARD TOWER ABATIS BARRIER COUNTER DILATOR PARADOS WARDING WARRANT FRONTIER GALAPAGO GARRISON MUNITION

DEFENSELESS BARE COLD NAKED SILLY UNARMED HELPLESS

DEFENSIBLE TENABLE JUSTIFIABLE

DEFER BOW RISE STAY WAIT DELAY DRIVE HONOR REFER REMIT TARRY TRACK WAIVE YIELD ESTEEM HUMBLE RETARD REVERE SUBMIT ADJOURN SUSPEND CONSIDER INTERMIT POSTPONE PROROGUE PROTRACT SUSPENSE

DEFERENCE VAIL COURT HONOR CRINGE ESTEEM HOMAGE REGARD RESPECT WORSHIP CIVILITY

DEFERENT ECCENTRIC

DEFERENTIAL DUTIFUL OBEISANT

DEFERMENT STAY

DEFERVESCENCE LYSIS DECLINE

DEFIANCE DARE DEFI DEFY GAGE BRAVE DEFIAL

DEFIANT BOLD BARDY BRAVE STOUT

DARING STOCKY INSOLENT STUBBORN

DEFICIENCY FAIL LACK WANT ANOIA ERROR FAULT MINUS DEARTH DEFECT INLAIK ULLAGE ABSENCE ANOESIA BLEMISH DEFICIT FAILING FAILURE DELETION SCARCITY SHORTAGE
(— **OF NERVOUS ENERGY**) ANEURIA
(— **OF OXYGEN**) ASPHYXIA
(**CARBON DIOXIDE** —) ACAPNIA
(**MENTAL** —) IDIOCY AMENTIA
(**PL.**) SHORTS

DEFICIENT BAD LEAN WANE BLUNT MINUS BARREN FEEBLE MEAGER MEAGRE SCARCE SCRIMP SKIMPY BOBTAIL DISGENIC DYSGENIC INDIGENT
(— **IN TURGOR**) FLACCID
(**MENTALLY** —) SOFT

DEFICIT SHORTAGE UNDERAGE

DEFILE GUT RAY ABRA BAWD BEDO FILE FOIL FOUL GATE GOWL HALS LIME MOIL MUCK PACE PASS SLIP SLUT SMUT SOIL ABUSE BERAY CLEFT CROCK DIRTY FILTH GLACK GORGE HALSE NOTCH SMEAR STAIN SULLY TAINT BEWRAY DEBASE GULLET IMBRUE INFECT RAVISH SMOUCH SMUTCH CORRUPT DEBAUCH DEPRAVE DISTAIN PASSAGE POLLUTE PROFANE SMATTER TARNISH VIOLATE DISHONOR MACULATE

DEFILED DIRTY IMPURE SPOTTY UNCLEAN MACULATE

DEFILEMENT MOIL SOIL SULLAGE TAINTURE

DEFILING PIKY PITCHY

DEFINE END FIX SET MERE TERM BOUND LIMIT DECIDE CLARIFY DELIMIT EXPLAIN EXPOUND DESCRIBE DISCOVER

DEFINED FORMED
(**SHARPLY** —) HARD

DEFINITE SET FIRM HARD SURE CLEAR FINAL FIXED SHARP FINITE FORMED LIQUID STRAIT CERTAIN EXPRESS LIMITED POINTED PRECISE DISTINCT EMPHATIC EXPLICIT LIMITING POSITIVE PUNCTUAL SPECIFIC

DEFINITELY BUT WELL FAIRLY EVERMORE

DEFINITION GLOSS CLARITY
(— **OF FORM**) SFUMATO

DEFINITIVE LAST FINAL GRAND ORISTIC DEFINITE

DEFLATE EMPALE IMPALE CONTRACT

DEFLATED FLAT

DEFLATING SETDOWN

DEFLATION HANGOVER

DEFLECT CUT WRY BEND COCK SWAY WARP PARRY WREST WRING BAFFLE DETOUR DIVERT SWERVE DEVIATE DIVERGE INFLECT REFLECT REFRACT

DEFLECTION DROOP SWEEP
WINDAGE
(— **ON METER**) KICK
DEFLOWER FRAY DEFOIL DEFOUL
FORLIE RAVAGE RAVISH DEFLORE
DESPOIL VIOLATE UNMAIDEN
UNVIRGIN
DEFORM MAR FLOW WARP GNARL
DEFACE BLEMISH CONTORT
DISFORM DISTORT DIFFORME
DISGUISE DISHONOR MISSHAPE
DEFORMATION CREEP SPRING
STRAIN FLEXURE FLOWAGE
DEFORMED GAMMY WRONG INFORM
PAULIE CROOKED HIDEOUS
MISBORN FORMLESS UNMACKLY
DEFORMITY GALL VICE BLEMISH
HARELIP PRAVITY CLUBFOOT
CLUBHAND FLATFOOT WANSHAPE
DEFRAUD ROB BEAT BILK FAKE
GULL NICK ROOK TRIM WIPE CHEAT
COZEN GOUGE MULCT SLICK STICK
TRICK WRONG BOODLE CHOUSE
CHOWSE DECEIVE SWINDLE
DEFRAY PAY BEAR AVERT COVER
EXPEND PREPAY APPEASE REQUITE
SATISFY DISBURSE
DEFT GAIN NEAT TALL TRIM AGILE
HANDY QUICK SLICK ADROIT
EXPERT HEPPEN NIMBLE SPRACK
SPRUCE DELIVER DEXTROUS
SKILLFUL
DEFTEST EFTEST
DEFTLY SLICKLY DELIVERLY
DEFTNESS SLEIGHT
DEFUNCT DEAD EXTINCT DECEASED
DEPARTED FINISHED
DEFY BRAG DARE DEFI FACE MOCK
BEARD BRAVE STUMP TEMPT
CARTEL FORBID MAUGER MAUGRE
REJECT AFFRONT BRAVADE
DESPISE DISDAIN OUTDARE
OUTFACE CHAMPION DEFIANCE
OUTSCOUT RENOUNCE
DEGENERATE ROT SINK DEBADE
EFFETE UNKIND DEGENER DEGRADE
DEPRAVE DESCEND DEGENDER
(— **IN IDLENESS**) RUST
(— **TOWARD BARBARISM**) WILDER
DEGENERATION WALLER ATROPHY
ADIPOSIS
DEGRADATION FALL WOHL SHAME
DECLINE DESCENT ADULTERY
DEPOSURE IGNOMINY
DEGRADE BUST SINK ABASE BREAK
DECRY LOWER SHAME SHEND
STOOP STRIP UNMAN DEBASE
DEMEAN DEMOTE DEPOSE EMBASE
HUMBLE LESSEN REDUCE VILIFY
CORRUPT DECLINE DEPRESS
IMBRUTE REGRADE VILLAIN
DIMINISH DISGRACE DISHONOR
DISMOUNT DISPLUME SUPPLANT
DEGRADED BASE SEAMY ABJECT
DEMISS FALLEN DEBASED DEGREED
GRIECED OUTCAST
DEGRADING BASE MENIAL
SHAMEFUL
DEGRAS MOELLON

DEGREE PEG PIP POL BANK CAST
DEAL FORM GREE HEAT PEEP POLL
RANK RATE RUNG STEP TERM TIER
CLASS GRADE GRADO GRECE GRICE
HONOR LEVEL NOTCH ORDER PITCH
PLACE POINT PRICK SHADE STAGE
STAIR EXTENT GRIECE LENGTH
MEDIUM SOEVER DESCENT DIGNITY
MEASURE SAENGER STATION
ACCURACY AEGROTAT QUANTITY
STANDING STRENGTH
(— **OF CLOSENESS**) FIT
(— **OF COMBINING POWER**)
VALENCE
(— **OF CONTRAST**) GAMMA
(— **OF DEVIATION**) LEEWAY
(— **OF ELEVATION**) ASCENT
(— **OF ENGAGEMENT**) DEPTH
(— **OF FLAWLESSNESS**) CLARITY
(— **OF FORCE**) KICK
(— **OF HEIGHT**) GRADE
(— **OF IMPORTANCE**) CALIBER
CALIBRE
(— **OF INFESTATION**) BURDEN
(— **OF INTOXICATION**) EDGE
(— **OF KNOWLEDGE**) SCIENTER
(— **OF LIGHTNESS**) VALUE
(— **OF MIXTURE**) ALLOY
(— **OF OPACITY**) DENSITY
(— **OF PLENTIFULNESS**)
ABUNDANCE
(— **OF SLOPE**) SPLAY
(— **OF STREAMLINING**) FAIRNESS
(— **OF THE SOUL**) RUACH
(— **OF WATER HARDNESS**) GRAIN
(— **OF WHITENESS**) BLEACH
(10 —**S OF LONGITUDE**) FACE
(15 —**S**) HOUR
(**EXCESSIVE** —) EXTREME
(**GREATEST** —) UTMOST
(**HIGHEST** —) PINK SUMMIT
SUPREME SUBLIMITY
(**INDEFINITE** —) SEEM
(**MINUTE** —) DROP SHADE
(**MUSICAL** —) SPACE SUBTONIC
(**RABINNICAL** —) SEMICHA SEMIKAH
CEMICHAH
(**SMALL** —) ACE HAIR INCH IOTA
SHADOW GLIMMER
(**SOME** —) BIT
(**UTMOST** —) SUM ACME HEIGHT
EXTREME EXTREMITY
DEGU OCTODONT
DEGUM STRIP
(— **SILK**) SOUPLE
DEHGAN SWAT SWATI
DEHORN SNUB DISBUD
DEHWAR DEHKAN
DEHYDRATE DRY DESICCATE
DEIANIRA (BROTHER OF —) TYDEUS
MELEAGER
(**FATHER OF** —) OENEUS
(**HUSBAND OF** —) HERCULES
(**MOTHER OF** —) ALTHAEA
DEIDAMIA HIPPODAMIA
(**FATHER OF** —) LYCOMEDES
(**LOVER OF** —) ACHILLES
(**SON OF** —) PYRRHUS
NEOPTOLEMUS

DEIFY GOD BEGOD DIVINE GODDIZE
DIVINIFY DIVINIZE
DEIGN STOOP VOUCHSAFE
DEIPHOBUS (BROTHER OF —) PARIS
HECTOR
(**FATHER OF** —) PRIAM
(**MOTHER OF** —) HECUBA
(**WIFE OF** —) HELEN
DEITY (ALSO SEE GOD AND
GODDESS) EA EL KA RA RE SU ABU
BEL GAD GOD RAN SHU SOL AKAL
AMEN AMON BAAL CAGN DEVA
FAUN FURY GWYN MIND MORS
RANA SIVA SOBK ALALA ALALU
AMIDA AMITA AMMON DAGAN
DAGON HOBAL HORUS HUBAL
INUUS JANUS MIDER MITRA MONAD
SATYR SEBEK SHIVA SIRIS SURYA
ZOMBI ASHIMA ATHTAR BATALA
BUNENE CAISSA FATHER FAUNUS
IASION MARDUK MOLOCH NIBHAZ
OANNES ORISHA ORMAZD ORMUZD
RIMMON SOMNUS SUCHOS SYLVAN
VARUNA ZOMBIE ALASTOR FORSETE
FORSETI GODDESS GODHEAD
GODLING GODSHIP HERSHEF
IAPETUS KHEPERA MANITOU
NINURTA NISROCH PHORCUS
PHORKYS RESHEPH SETEBOS
SILENUS TAGALOA TARANIS VIRBIUS
BAALPEOR BEELPEOR BELFAGOR
DEVARAJA DIVINITY ELAGABAL
GOVERNOR HACHIMAN MELKARTH
MERODACH PICUMNUS PILUMNUS
SEILENOS SILVANUS TANGALOA
TUTELARY ZEPHYRUS ZOOMORPH
(**AVENGING** —) ALASTOR
(**HEATHEN** —) IDOL
(**INFERIOR** —) GODKIN GODLING
DEMIURGE PETTYGOD
(**SHINTO** —) KAMI
(**SUPREME** —) HANSA
(**TUTELARY** —) NUMEN GENIUS
(PL.) CABIRI
DEJECT ABASE LOWER HUMBLE
LESSEN FLATTEN DISPIRIT
DOWNCAST
DEJECTA EGESTA
DEJECTED BAD LOW SAD DAMP
DOWN GLUM POOR SUNK AMORT
MUDDY WAPED ABASED DEJECT
DEMISS DROOPY GLOOMY PINING
SOMBER SOMBRE DUMPISH
HANGDOG HANGING HUMBLED
LUMPISH UNHAPPY DOWNCAST
DOWNWARD REPINING WOBEGONE
WRETCHED
DEJECTEDLY HEAVILY
DEJECTION DAMP GLOOM SLOTH
DISMAY DISMALS HUMDRUM
SADNESS
DEJEUNER LUNCH BREAKFAST
COLAZIONE COLLATION
DEL NABLA

DELAWARE
CAPITAL: DOVER

COUNTY: KENT SUSSEX
NEWCASTLE
INDIAN: LENAPE
STATE FLOWER: PEACH
STATE BIRD: BLUEHEN
STATE NICKNAME: DIAMOND
STATE TREE: HOLLY
TOWN: LEWES SMYRNA ELSMERE
CLAYMONT WILMINGTON

DELAY LAG LET BLIN BODE HOLD
HONE LENG LING LITE MORA SIST
SLOW SLUG STAY STOP WAIT ABIDE
ABODE ALLAY BLINE CHECK DALLY
DEFER DEMUR DETER DRIFT DWELL
FRIST REPRY SLOTH STALL STENT
STICK STINT TARDY TARRY TRACT
ARREST ATTEND BACKEN BELATE
DAWDLE DETAIN DILATE DILUTE
DRETCH ESSOIN FUTURE HINDER
HOLDUP IMPEDE LINGER LOITER
QUENCH REMORE RETARD TAIGLE
TARROW TEMPER WEAKEN
ADJOURN ASSUAGE BARRACE
CONFINE DRUTTLE FORSLOW
PROLONG RESPECT RESPITE
SLACKEN SOJOURN DEMURRAL
DILATION FORESLOW FOURCHER
HANGFIRE HESITATE MACERATE
MITIGATE MORATION OBSTRUCT
POSTPONE REPRIEVE STOPPAGE
(— TRIAL) TRAVERSE
(LEGAL —) DILATOR INDUCIAE
(UNDUE —) LACHES
DELAYED LATE TARDY LAGGED
BELATED OVERDUE
DELAYING TRAIN DILATORY
DELECTABLE TASTY DESIROUS
PLEASING BEAUTIFUL EXQUISITE
DELEGATE NAME SEND ASSIGN
COMMIT DELATE DEPUTE DEPUTY
LEGATE NUNCIO APPOINT CONSIGN
EMPOWER ENTRUST EMISSARY
RELEGATE TRANSFER
DELEGATION MISSION DELEGACY
(ATHENIAN —) DELIA
DELETE DELE EDIT OMIT BLACK
ERASE PURGE SLASH CANCEL
CENSOR DELATE REMOVE STRIKE
DESTROY EXPUNGE STONKER
CASTRATE
DELETERIOUS BAD PRAVE HARMFUL
HURTFUL NOXIOUS PRAVOUS
DAMAGING DELETERY
DELIBERATE COOL PORE RUNE
SLOW STUDY THINK ADVISE
CONFER DEBATE PONDER REGARD
ADVISED BALANCE BETHINK
CONSULT COUNCIL COUNSEL
DELIBER DELIVER REFLECT
RESOLVE STUDIED WILLING
CONSIDER DESIGNED MEASURED
MEDITATE PERPENSE PREPENSE
PROPENSE STUDIOUS
DELIBERATELY COOLY COOLLY
APURPOSE ADVISEDLY
DELIBERATENESS MATURITY
DELIBERATION ADVICE COUNCIL

COUNSEL LEISURE THOUGHT
VISEMENT
DELICACY BIT ROE CATE EASE NORI
TACT ACATE FRILL KNACK TASTE
CAVIAR DAINTY DELICE JUNKET
LUXURY NICETY REGALO FINESSE
REGALIA TENUITY AIRINESS
DAINTITH DAINTREL DELICATE
KICKSHAW LEGERETE NICENESS
PLEASURE SUBTLETY
(PL.) CATES ACATES
DELICATE SLY AIRY FINE LACY
NESH NICE SOFT TEAR ZART DELIE
DORTY ELFIN FRAIL LIGHT SILKY
TEWLY CASHIE CHOICE DAINTY
FLIMSY GENTLE GINGER INCONY
KITTLE MINION PASTEL PETITE
PULING QUEASY SILKEN SLIGHT
SUBTLE TENDER TICKLE TWIGGY
ELEGANT EPICENE FINICAL FRAGILE
MINIKIN REFINED SLIMMER SUBTILE
SUMMERY TAFFETA TAFFETY
TENUOUS TIFFANY WILLOWY
ARANEOUS CHARMING ETHEREAL
FEATHERY GOSSAMER GRACEFUL
HOTHOUSE LUSCIOUS MIGNIARD
PINDLING PLEASANT SENSIBLE
SUMMERLY TICKLISH UNLUSTIE
(— IN APPEARANCE) HUNGRY
DELICATELY FINE SMALLY FAIRILY
DELICATESSEN GASTRONOME
CHARCUTERIE
DELICIOUS DAINTY FRIAND
DELICATE
DELIGHT JOY GLEE GUST LITE LOVE
SEND TAKE BLISS CHARM EXULT
FEAST GRACE GUSTO MIRTH REVEL
SAVOR SMACK ADMIRE ARRIDE
DELICE DIVERT LIKING PLEASE
RAVISH REGALE RELISH DISPORT
ECSTASY ENCHANT GLADDEN
GRATIFY JOYANCE JOYANCY
LECHERY RAPTURE REJOICE
DELICATE ENTRANCE GLADNESS
PLEASURE SAVORING
(— IN) LOVE SAVOR
(PL.) DELICIAE
DELIGHTED GLAD
DELIGHTFUL NICE GREAT JAMMY
JOLLY MERRY SOOTH DREAMY
SAVORY ELYSIAN LEESOME
ADORABLE DELICATE DELITOUS
GLORIOUS GORGEOUS HEAVENLY
LUSCIOUS
DELIMER DRENCHER
DELIMIT FIX DEFINE SUBTEND
DELIMITED MERED MEERED
DELINEATE MAP DRAW ETCH LIMN
LINE CHALK CHART FENCE IMAGE
PAINT STELL TABLE TOUCH TRACE
TRICK BLAZON CIPHER DELINE
DEPICT DESIGN DEVISE SKETCH
SURVEY DEPAINT EXPRESS LINEATE
OUTLINE PICTURE PORTRAY
DECIPHER DEFIGURE DESCRIBE
TRAVERSE
DELINEATION DRAFT DESIGN
SKETCH SURVEY DRAUGHT
DELINQUENCY FAULT GUILT

FAILURE MISDEED OFFENSE
OMISSION
DELINQUENT CRIMINAL
(PL.) KALANG
DELIQUESCE MELT LIQUEFY
DISSOLVE
DELIRIOUS FEY MAD OFF REE GYTE
LIGHT MANIC INSANE RAVING
FLIGHTY FRANTIC LUNATIC
BRAINISH DELEERIT DELIERET
DERANGED FRENETIC FRENZIED
DELIRIUM FURY MAZE MANIA
FRENZY LUNACY RAVERY MADNESS
DELIRACY IDLENESS INSANITY
DELIRIUM TREMENS JUMP
HORRORS JIMJAMS JIMMIES
POTOMANIA
DELIVER DO HIT LAY LET RID BAIL
BORN DEAL FREE GIVE LEND REDD
SAVE SELL SEND TAKE BEKEN
BRING COUGH LIVER SERVE SPEAK
UTTER ADDICT ASSIZE ASSOIL
BETRAY COMMIT CONVEY EXEMPT
PREACH RANSOM REDEEM RENDER
RESCUE RESIGN SUCCOR UNBIND
BETEACH BITECHE COMMEND
CONSIGN DECLAIM DICTATE
OUTTAKE PRESENT RECOVER
RELEASE RELIEVE DISPATCH
EXORCISE EXORCIZE LIBERATE
(— BALL) BOWL
(— BLOW) LEND SEND
(— BLOWS ON HEAD) NOB
(— CHILD) LIGHT
(— FORCEFULLY) FASTEN
(— LOGS) STOCK
(— MERCHANDISE) UTTER
(— OVER) BETAKE CONSIGN
(— RHETORICALLY) DECLAIM
(— SPEECH) ADDRESS
DELIVERANCE BOOT ESCAPE
RESCUE SAVING DELIVERY
RIDDANCE SOLUTION VOIDANCE
SALVATION
DELIVERED LANDED
(— FREE) FRANCO
(PRECISELY —) FLUSH
DELIVERER SOTER DRAYMAN
SAOSHYANT
DELIVERY FLY BAIL FLIER FLYER
ISSUE RESCUE ADDRESS AIRDROP
BAILMENT SHIPMENT
(— IN SPEAKING) DICTION
(— OF BALL) BOWL
(— WAGON) FLY
(MAIL —) TAPPALL TAPPAUL
DELL DEN HOW DALE DEAN DENE
DILL DRAB GLEN VALE SLACK
SLADE TRULL WENCH DINGLE
RAVINE VALLEY
(PL.) DALLES
DELPHINIUM DAUPHIN DOLPHIN
LARKSPUR
DELUDE BOB JIG BILK DUPE FOOL
HOAX MOCK AMUSE CHEAT COZEN
ELUDE EVADE GLAIK SPOOF TRICK
BAFFLE BANTER BEFOOL BUBBLE
DIDDLE ILLUDE BEGUILE DECEIVE
ENCHANT MISLEAD OVERSEE

BEJUGGLE HOODWINK INVEIGLE
OVERSILE
DELUGE SEA FLOW FLOOD SWAMP
DILUVY CATARACT INUNDATE
OVERFLOW SATURATE SUBMERGE
DELUNDUNG LINSANG ZINSANG
VIVERRINE
DELUSION MAZE MOHA ABUSE
DWALE FRAUD TRICK MIRAGE
VISION CHIMERA FALLACY FANTASM
PHANTOM WANHOPE ILLUSION
NIHILISM PHANTASM
DELUSTER DULL
DELVE DEN DIG DIP PIT CAVE DINT
MINE DITCH PLUMB BRUISE
BURROW EXHUME FATHOM INDENT
IMPRESS EXCAVATE INSCRIBE
DEMAGNETIZE DEPERM
DEPOLARIZE
DEMAGOGUE CLEON LEADER
ORATOR ROUSER DEMAGOG
SPEAKER TRIBUNE JAWSMITH
DEMAND ASK CRY TAX USE CALL
NEED RAME SALE CLAIM CRAVE
DRAFT EXACT GAVEL ORDER QUERY
SIGHT BEHEST CHARGE DESIRE
ELICIT EXPECT SNATCH SUMMON
ARRAIGN COMMAND CONSIST
DRAUGHT INQUIRE MANDATE
REQUEST REQUIRE SOLICIT
INSTANCE QUESTION
(— PAYMENT) DUN CALL
(— RECOGNITION) CLAIM ASSERT
(PL.) EXIGENCE EXIGENCY
DEMANDABLE DUE EXIGIBLE
DEMANDED COMPULSORY
DEMANDING HEFTY EXIGENT
(— ATTENTION) ACUTE
DEMANTOID EMERALD OLIVINE
DEMARCATE DELIMIT SEPARATE
DEMARCATION CELL
DEMEAN ABASE CARRY LOWER
BEHAVE DEBASE DEPORT CONTAIN
DEGRADE DESCEND MALTREAT
DEMEANOR AIR GARB MIEN PORT
FRONT HABIT ACTION HAVIOR
BEARING CONDUCT DISPOSE
FASHION CARRIAGE PORTANCE
DEMENTED MAD BUGGY CRAZY
NUTTY INSANE SKEWED FATUOUS
DEMENTIA FATUITY INSANITY
DEMERIT MARK FAULT DESERT
BROWNIE
(PL.) GIG
DEMESNE MANOR PLACE REALM
DOMAIN ESTATE REGION DISTRICT
DEMETER CERES MISTRESS
DEMIGOD HERO YIMA ADAPA SATYR
TRITON GODLING
(PL.) NEPHILIM
DEMIGODDESS URD NORN HEROINE
DEMILUNE RAVELIN
DEMISE WILL DEATH CONVEY
DECEASE BEQUEATH
DEMISED LETTEN
DEMIT LOWER HUMBLE RESIGN
ABDICATE
DEMOCRACY POPULACY
COMMONALTY

DEMOCRAT DEMO DANITE HUNKER
SNAPPER DEMOCRAW LOCOFOCO
POPOCRAT
(CONSERVATIVE —) HARD
DEMODULATE DETECT
DEMOISELLE KULM CRANE COOLEN
KAIKARA
DEMOLISH RASE RAZE RUIN ABATE
BREAK ELIDE LEVEL WASTE WRECK
BATTER SLIGHT DESTROY RUINATE
SHATTER SUBVERT UNBUILD
DOWNCAST STRAMASH
DEMOLITION END FALL
DEMON ALP DEV HAG IMP NAT OKI
AITU ATUA BADB BALI BHUT DEVA
DOOK OGRE OKEE PUCK RAHU
SURT WADE ASURA DEVIL DHOUL
FIEND GENIE GHOST JUMBY LAMIA
LESHY LESIY OTKON SATAN SATYR
SHEDU SURTR TAIPO WITCH ABIGOR
AFREET ARIOCH BILWIS DAEMON
DAIMON DAITYA GENIUS JUMBIE
MAMMON PILWIZ PISACA THURSE
VRITRA YAKSHA YAKSHI ASMADAI
ASMODAY DEMONIO HARPIER
PISACHA VILLAIN WARLOCK
ALICHINO ASHMODAI ASMODEUS
BAALPEOR BEELPEOR CURUPIRA
EUDAEMON OBIDICUT SUCCUBUS
WATERMAN
(— OF WOODS) LESHY LESIY
LESHEY
(ARABIC —) AFRIT AFREET AFRITE
EFREET
(EVIL —) SHEDU
(FEMALE —) HAG LAMIA PISACHI
SUCCUBUS
(NATURE —) GENIUS
(PETTY —) IMP
(PL.) DASYUS
DEMONIAC DEMONIC LUNATIC
SATANIC DEVILISH DIABOLIC
FIENDISH INFERNAL
DEMONIACAL DEMONIAC INFERNAL
DEMONSTRATE GIVE SHOW CLEAR
PROVE SPEAK CONVICT DISPLAY
PORTRAY CONVINCE INSTANCE
MANIFEST
DEMONSTRATION SHOW SIGN TIME
PROOF APODIXIS BALLYHOO
DARSHANA MANIFEST
(OSTENTATIOUS —) SPLURGE
DEMONSTRATIVE THAT THIS THESE
THOSE EFFUSIVE EVINCIVE
DEMOPHON (FATHER OF —) CELEUS
THESEUS
(MOTHER OF —) PHAEDRA
METANIRA
DEMORALIZE WEAKEN CONFUSE
CORRUPT DEPRAVE PERVERT
DEMORALIZING INFECTIOUS
SHATTERING
DEMOTE BUMP BUST REDUCE
UNRANK DEGRADE DISRATE
DEMOTIC POPULAR ENCHORIAL
DEMOTION BUMP
DEMULCENT MANNA SALEB SALEP
BORAGE GINSENG EMULSION
SOOTHING

DEMUR COY GIB JIB SHY BALK STAY
DELAY DOUBT PAUSE STICK
BOGGLE LINGER OBJECT STRAIN
DEMEORE SCRUPLE STICKLE
STUMBLE SUSPEND DEMURRER
HESITATE SUSPENSE
DEMURE COY MIM SHY MURE PRIM
GRAVE SPAKE STAID SUANT SUENT
MODEST SEDATE PRENZIE PRIMSIE
COMPOSED DECOROUS
DEN MEW CAVE COVE DEAN DELL
DIVE GLEN HOLE HOLT HUNK LAIR
LAKE NEST ROOM SHED SINK BIELD
CABIN CAVEA COUCH DELVE HAUNT
LODGE SLADE STUDY BURROW
CAVERN COVERT GROTTO HOLLOW
KENNEL RAVINE SHROUD RETREAT
SPELUNK HIDEAWAY SNUGGERY
WORKROOM
(— OF BEAR) WASH
(— OF INIQUITY) DOMDANIEL
(FOUL —) SPITAL
(GAMBLING —) DEADFALL
DENARIUS DENAR PENNY DINDER
DENIAL NO NAY WARN DENAY
DENIER NAYSAY DEFENSE DEMENTI
REFUSAL REPULSE CONTRARY
TRAVERSE
(— OF AUTHORITY) ANARCHY
(— OF TRUTH) HERESY
DENIED LOST
DENIER DINERO NEGATOR DENARIUS
DINHEIRO
(HALF —) MAIL MAILLE
DENIGRATE BEFOUL CRUCIFY
DENIM DUNGAREE
DENIZEN CITIZEN RESIDENT
(— BY BIRTH) NATIVE
(— OF HELL) HELLION

DENMARK
CAPITAL: COPENHAGEN
CHEESE: SAMSO
COIN: ORA ORE KRONE
COUNTY: AMT RIBE SORO VEJLE
AARHUS MARIBO ODENSE
TONDER VIBORG AALBORG
RANDERS AABENRAA
BORNHOLM
INLET: ISE LIM FJORD VEJLE
NISSUM ODENSE HORSENS
LOGSTOR MARIAGER
ISLAND: OE ALS FYN MON AARO
AERO FANO FOHR MORS ROMO
BAAGO FAERO FAROE LAESO
SAMSO SANDO AMAGER SEJERO
SUDERO FALSTER SEELAND
ZEALAND
MEASURE: ELL FOD MIL POT ALEN
FAVN RODE ALBUM KANDE
LINJE PAEGL TOMME ACHTEL
PAEGL SKEPPE LANDMIL
OLTONDE SKIEPPE VIERTEL
FJERDING
PARLIAMENT: RIGSRAD FOLKETING
LANDSTING
PENINSULA: JUTLAND

POSSESSION: FAROE ICELAND GREENLAND
RIVER: ASA HOLM OMME STOR GUDEN SKIVE SUSAA VARDE GELSAA STORAA VORGOD GUDENAA LILLEAA LONBORG
SETTLERS: OSTMEN
STRAIT: KATTEGAT SKAGERRAK
TOWN: ARS HOV HALS KOGE NIBE SORO VRAA FARUM HOBRO SKIVE AARHUS DRAGOR KORSOR NYBORG ODENSE SKAGEN STRUER VIBORG AALBORG HERNING HORSENS KOLDING RANDERS BALLERUP ELSINORE GENTOFTE GLOSTRUP ROSKILDE HELSINGOR COPENHAGEN
TRIBE: DANES JUTES ANGLES CIMBRI TEUTONS
TRIBUNAL: RIGSRAD RIGSRET
WEIGHT: ES LOD ORT VOG LAST MARK PUND UNZE CARAT KVINT POUND QUINT TONDE CENTNER LISPUND QUINTIN LISPOUND SKIPPUND

DENOMINATE CALL NAME STYLE TITLE DENOTE CHRISTEN INDICATE NOMINATE
DENOMINATION CULT NAME SECT CLASS FAITH TITLE VALUE CHURCH SCHOOL SOCIETY CATEGORY
DENOMINATIONAL SECTARIAN CONFESSIONAL
DENOTATION SIGN TOKEN EXTENT NOTION SPHERE AMBITUS BREADTH
DENOTE GIVE MARK MEAN NAME NOTE SHOW SOUND IMPORT NOTIFY BETOKEN CONNOTE EXPRESS SIGNIFY DENOTATE DESCRIBE INDICATE
DENOUEMENT END ENVOY ISSUE OUTCOME SOLITION
DENOUNCE BAN WRAY ASCRY BASTE BLAST DECRY TAUNT ACCUSE DELATE DESCRY DETEST MENACE SCATHE ARRAIGN CONDEMN DECLAIM DECLARE UPBRAID EXECRATE PROCLAIM THREATEN
DENOUNCEMENT DELATION
DENSE SAD FAST FIRM CLOSE CRASS DUNCH FOGGY GROSS HEAVY MASSY MURKY SILLY SOLID SOUND SPISS STIFF THEET THICK TIGHT WOOFY OBTUSE OPAQUE SPISSY STUPID THICKY THIGHT COMPACT CROWDED INTENSE SERRIED CONDENSE
(NOT —) TENUOUS
DENSITY FOG CANDY FASTNESS GAUSSAGE SOLIDITY
DENT BASH BURT DINT DOKE DUNT FAZE NICK CLOUR DELVE DINGE NOTCH STOVE TOOTH BATTER DUNTLE HALLOW INDENT BLEMISH DEPRESS

(— OF REED) SPLIT
(PL.) BEER
DENTAL POINT
DENTICULATE SERRATE SERRATED
DENTICULATION JAG JAGG
DENTIFRICE WASH
DENTIL DENTEL DENTELLO DENTICLE
DENTINE IVORY DENTIN
DENTIST ODONTIST OPERATOR
DENTURE PLATE BRIDGE
DENUDE BARE SCALP SHAVE STRIP DIVEST NUDATE DESPOIL DENUDATE
DENUNCIATION THREAT THUNDER ANATHEMA DIATRIBE
DENY NAY NAIT NICK NITE WARN BELIE DEBAR NITTE RENAY REPEL WERNE ABJURE DISOWN FORBID IMPUGN NEGATE REFUSE REFUTE REJECT RENEGE CONFUTE DEPRIVE DISAVOW DISPUTE FORSAKE GAINSAY PROTEST SUBLATE WITHSAY ABNEGATE DENEGATE DISALLOW DISCLAIM FORSWEAR NEGATIVE RENOUNCE TRAVERSE WITHHOLD
(— ACCESS) CLOSE
(— RECOGNITION) BLINK
DEOXIDIZE REDUCE
DEPART GO DIE MOG OFF WAG BLOW EXIT FLIT HOOK MOVE PACK PART PASS PIKE QUIT SHED STEP VADE VARY VOID WALK WEND WITE AVOID BREAK FOUND LEAVE MOSEY SEVER SHAKE SHIFT START TRUSS AVAUNT BEGONE DECAMP DECEDE DEMISE DESIST DIVIDE PERISH RECEDE REMOVE RETIRE SKIDOO SUNDER SWERVE WANDER ABSCOND DEVIATE DISCEDE FORSAKE RETREAT SKIDDOO VAMOOSE DISCOAST FAREWELL SEPARATE TRESPASS WITHDRAW
(— FROM HARBOR) SORTIE
(— FROM LIFE) DECEASE
(— IN HASTE) BREEZE
(— IN HURRY) SKIVE LAMMAS
(— SECRETLY) ABSCOND
(— SUDDENLY) FLEE DECAMP
(— WITH SPEED) VAMOOSE
DEPARTED DEAD BYGONE DEFUNCT DECEASED DECEDENT
DEPARTMENT END PART OKRUG REALM AGENCY BRANCH BUREAU EXCISE MEMBER OKROOG SPHERE FOUNDRY HANAPER PORTION REVENUE SPICERY AGITPROP CHANCERY DIVISION INDUSTRY NOMARCHY PROVINCE SCULLERY
(— IN CHINA) FU
(NEWSPAPER —) COLUMN FEATURE
(TREASURY —) CAMERA
DEPARTURE BUNK EXIT BREAK DEATH EXODE GOING LEAVE OUTGO CHANGE CONGEE DEPART EGRESS EXODUS HEGIRA SETOFF WAGANG WAYING DECEASE EASTING OUTGANG PARTING PARTURE RETREAT SAILING TRUNDLE WAYGATE DEPARTER FAREWELL

OFFGOING REMOTION
(— FROM CORRECTNESS) ATROCITY
(— FROM SUBJECT) ASIDE
(— FROM THEME) CADENZA
(— OF SHIP) SORTIE
(EMERGENCY —) BAILOUT
(GEOLOGICAL —) ANOMALY
(SECRET —) GUY SLIP
DEPEND BANK HANG LEAN PEND RELY REST RIDE STAY TURN COUNT FOUND HINGE TRUST CONFIDE
DEPENDABILITY SECURITY
DEPENDABLE GOOD SURE SIKER SOLID SOUND THERE SECURE SICCAR SICKER STANCH STEADY CERTAIN STAUNCH RELIABLE SILVENDY SUREFIRE
DEPENDENCE MAINSTAY RELIANCE SERVILITY
DEPENDENCY TALUK COLONY APANAGE APPANAGE
DEPENDENT CHILD CLIENT HANGBY MINION SPONGE VASSAL FEODARY FEUDARY PRONEUR RELIANT SERVILE SPONGER SUBJECT WRAPPED BEHOLDEN CLINGING CREATURE ENCLITIC EVENTUAL FOLLOWER RETAINER
(— ON) ILLATIVE
DEPENDING ATTENDANT
(— ON UNCERTAIN EVENTS) ALEATORY
DEPICT HUE DRAW ETCH LIMN PICT UNDO ENTER IMAGE PAINT SPEAK WRITE BLAZON SHADOW DEPAINT DISPLAY EXPRESS IMPAINT PICTURE PORTRAY DESCRIBE EMBLAZON RESEMBLE
DEPICTED DEPAINT
(— AS BROKEN) ROMPU
DEPICTION SCHEMA
DEPILATION PSILOSIS
DEPILATORY RUSMA EPILATOR PELADORE PSILATRO
DEPLETE DRAIN EMPTY PUNISH REDUCE UNLOAD EXHAUST BANKRUPT DIMINISH
DEPLETED WASTE BANKRUPT
DEPLETION DRAIN EROSION
DEPLORABLE SAD WOFUL WOEFUL DOLOROUS GRIEVOUS WAILSOME WRETCHED
DEPLORABLY SADLY
DEPLORE RUE MOAN SIGH WAIL MOURN BEMOAN BEWAIL GRIEVE LAMENT REGRET COMPLAIN
DEPLOY UNFOLD DISPLAY
DEPLOYMENT FORMATION
DEPOLYMERIZE DEGRADE
DEPONE SWEAR DEPOSE TESTIFY
DEPONENT AFFIANT DEPONER EXAMINATE
DEPOPULATE RAVAGE DESOLATE DISPEOPLE
DEPORT BEAR EXILE EXPEL BANISH BEHAVE DEMEAN BEARING CONDUCT DISPORT RELEGATE
DEPORTMENT AIR GEST MIEN PORT GESTE HABIT ACTION DEPORT

HAVING MANNER ADDRESS BEARING
COMPORT CONDUCT GESTURE
HAVANCE BREEDING CARRIAGE
DEMEANOR MAINTAIN
DEPOSE AVER ABASE PRIVE SWEAR
AFFIRM ASSERT BANISH DEPONE
DIVEST REDUCE REMOVE DEGRADE
DEPOSIT DESTOOL TESTIFY
DETHRONE DISCROWN DISPLACE
DEPOSIT FUR LAY SET ADHI BANK
CAKE CAST CRUD DROP DUMP
FUND HIDE HOCK PAWN BLOOM
CHEST COUCH COVER DEPOT
LODGE PLACE SCURF STORE TOSCA
BESTOW DEPONE DEPOSE ENTOMB
ESCROW FLYSCH GARNER IMPOSE
INHUME PLEDGE REPOSE SALINE
SCORIA SCROLL SETTLE SINTER
TOPHUS ASHFALL CONSIGN
HORIZON DILUVIUM FOULNESS
SANDBANK
(— BALLOT) CAST
(— DRIFT-SAND) SUD
(— EGGS) BLOW SPAWN
(— FOR COPYRIGHT) ENTER
(— IN CHAMPAGNE) GRIFFE
(— IN EARTH) INTER INHUME
(— IN GUN BORE) FOULING
(— IN WINE CASK) CRUST TARTAR
(— OF DEBRIS) BRECCIA
(— OF LOAM) LOESS
(— OF ORE) BANK FLAT
(— OF PEBBLES AND SAND) BEACH
CASCALHO
(— OF SALT WATER) SOAK
(— ON LEATHER) BLOOM
(— ON LEAVES) HONEYDEW
(— STOLEN ARTICLES) FENCE
(— USED AS FERTILIZER) FALUN
(ALLUVIAL —) APRON DELTA
(ARCHAEOLOGICAL —) LENS LENSE
(BANK —S) CASH
(BLACK —) STUPP
(CORNEA —) ARCUS
(EARTHY —) GUHR MARL
(GEOLOGIC —) BLANKET HORIZON
(GLACIAL —) TILL DRIFT ESKAR
ESKER SHEET PLACER MORAINE
(GRAVEL —) LEAD
(KIDNEY —) GRAVEL
(MASS OF SEDIMENTARY —S) GOBI
(MINERAL —) FLAT LODE CARBONA
(MUDDY —) SLUDGE SLUMGULLION
(SEDIMENTARY —) SILT
(SHOAL-WATER —) CULM
(SKELETAL —) CORAL
(TARRY —) GUM
(WELDING —) TACK
DEPOSITARY POSITOR SEQUESTER
DEPOSITION PAD BURIAL DEPOSIT
OPINION SILTING DEPOSURE
SEDIMENT
DEPOSITORY BANK DROP SAFE
ATTIC VAULT DEPOSIT OSSUARY
SENTINE DEPOSITO ESCROWEE
OSSARIUM
DEPOT BANK BASE GARE AURANG
AURUNG STAPLE STATION
MAGAZINE TERMINAL TERMINUS

DEPRAVE TAINT DEBASE DEFILE
INFECT MALIGN REVILE BESHREW
CORRUPT PERVERT VITIATE
DEPRAVED BAD EVIL UGLY VILE
PRAVE ROTTEN SHREWD WICKED
BESTIAL CORRUPT IMMORAL
PRAVOUS VICIOUS
DEPRAVITY VICE ABYSS ILLNESS
PRAVITY VILLAINY
DEPRECATE PRAY INVOKE BESEECH
DEPRECIATE FALL LACK ABASE
AVILE DECRY SLUMP DEBASE
EMBASE LESSEN MINISH REDUCE
SHRINK CHEAPEN DEBAUCH
DEGRADE DEPRAVE DEPRESS
DETRACT SLANDER SMALLEN
BELITTLE DEROGATE DISCOUNT
DISPRIZE DISVALUE MINIMIZE
PEJORATE VILIPEND
DEPRECIATION AGIO DECRIAL
DISCOUNT
DEPREDATION PREY PILLAGE
DEPRESS BOW COW HIP LOW BATE
BEAR BORE DAMP DASH DENT FALL
FLAT SINK SUMP ABASE APPAL
BREAK CHILL COUCH CRUSH FAINT
LOWER SLUMP VAPOR WEIGH
APPALL DAMPEN DEBOSS DISMAY
HUMBLE INDENT LESSEN MURDER
SADDEN SETTLE SICKEN STRIKE
WEAKEN DECLINE DEGRADE
DESTROY FLATTEN OPPRESS
REPRESS BROWBEAT DIMINISH
DISPIRIT DOWNBEAR ENFEEBLE
DEPRESSANT HELLEBORE
DEPRESSED LOW SAD BLUE DAMP
DULL FLAT SICK SUNK WROTH
BROODY DISHED GLOOMY HIPPED
HOLLOW LONELY OBLATE SOMBER
TRISTE LETDOWN DEJECTED
DOWNCAST DOWNSOME
(— AT THE POLES) OBLATE
(ECONOMICALLY —) HARD
DEPRESSING SAD BLUE COLD
BLEAK CHILL DREAR DUSKY MUZZY
OURIE DREARY GLOOMY SOMBER
SOMBRE TRISTE
DEPRESSION COL DIP EYE GAT PAN
PIT BUST CROP DAMP DELK DENT
DOKE DOWN FALL FOSS GASH GLEN
HOLL HOWE SLEW SLOT SLUE WELL
ATRIO BASIN BLUES BOSOM CANON
COWAL CRYPT DELVE DINGE FOSSA
FOSSE FOVEA GLOOM GROIN NADIR
NAVEL ORBIT POLJE SALAR SCOOP
SELLA SINUS SLUMP SWALE AMPHID
BUCKLE CAFARD CANYON CAVITY
CRATER CUPULE DIMPLE DISMAY
FURROW GROOVE GULLEY GUTTER
INDENT RAVINE SAUCER SLOUGH
SPLEEN VALLEY WALLOW ALVEOLA
BLOWOUT BOGHOLE CHAGRIN
CLAYPAN CONCAVE COUNTER
FOSSULA FOSSULE FOVEOLA
JIMMIES SADNESS SALTPAN
SINKAGE SINKING VARIOLE
BOTHRIUM DOLDRUMS DOWNBEND
FAINTING FOLLICLE FOREDEEP
FOSSETTE FOSSULET PUNCTURE

SINKHOLE SOAKAWAY EPHIPPIUM
(— BEHIND COW'S SHOULDERS)
CROP
(— BETWEEN BREASTS) CLEAVAGE
(— BETWEEN HILLS) SWIRE
(— IN BOARD) SKIP
(— IN BOTTLE BOTTOM) KICK
(— IN DOG'S FACE) STOP
(— IN FRUITS) EYE
(— IN GROUND) DALK DELK SWAG
WELL SWALE CHARCO
(— IN MILLSTONE) BOSOM
(— IN NILE VALLEY) KORE
(— IN RANGE) PASS
(— IN RIDGE) COL
(— IN SNOW) SITZMARK
(— IN VELD) COMITJE KOMMETJE
(— OF EAR) SCAPHA
(— OF SPIRITS) JAWFALL
(— PRONE) VAPORISH
(ARTICULAR —) GLENE
(OBLONG —) CIRCUS
(SMALL —) DENT DIMPLE LACUNA
FOLLICLE
DEPRIVATION COST LOSS MAIM
WANT MAYHEM AMOTION MISTURE
DEPRIVAL
(— OF SIGHT) DARKNESS
DEPRIVE BAR ROB BATE DENY DOCK
EASE GELD TWIN ABATE BENIM
BREAK DEBAR EMPTY EXUTE PREVE
SPOIL STRIP WRONG AMERCE
DEFEAT DENUDE DEPOSE DEVEST
DISMAY DIVEST FAMISH FORBAR
HINDER HUSTLE REMOVE ABRIDGE
BEGUILE BEREAVE CASHIER
CURTAIL DECEIVE DEFORCE
DEPRAVE DESPOIL DESTROY
DISABLE EXHAUST FOREBAR
GUDGEON PRIVATE UNDRESS
BANKRUPT DENATURE DESOLATE
DISANNUL EVACUATE
(— BY TRICKERY) NOSE MULCT
(— FRAUDULENTLY) GUDGEON
(— OF BRILLIANCE) DEADEN
(— OF COURAGE) UNNERVE
(— OF FREEDOM) FETTER
(— OF INDIVIDUALITY) FORDIZE
(— OF LIFE) DEADEN
(— OF OFFICE) DEPOSE
(— OF POSSESSIONS) FLAY
(— OF REASON) DEMENT
(— OF SENSATION) BENUMB
(— OF SENSE) INEBRIATE
(— OF SIGHT) SEEL
(— OF STRENGTH) ENERVATE
(— OF VIRGINITY) DEFLOWER
DEPRIVED REFT SANS BANKRUPT
DESOLATE
DEPTH DIP BURY DEEP DROP MOHO
ABYSS MIDST SIDTH FATHOM
HEIGHT ALTITUDE DEEPNESS
PROFOUND SOUNDING STRENGTH
(— OF NIGHT OR WINTER) HOLL
HOWE
(— OF SAIL) HOIST
(— OF SHIP) GAGE GAUGE
(— OF SIN) SLOUGH
(— OF SPADE) SPIT GRAFT

(— OF WATER) DRAFT DRAUGHT
(LOWEST —) GROUND
(MORAL —) ABYSS
(PL.) MUD HEART
DEPUTATION MISSION THEORIA
LEGATION
DEPUTE SEND ALLOT ASSIGN
DEVOTE APPOINT DELEGATE
DEPUTY AIDE AGENT ENVOY NABOB
PROXY VICAR ANGELO COMMIS
CURATE DEPUTE EXARCH FACTOR
KEHAYA LEGATE MINION ADJOINT
BAILIFF ESCALUS QAMAQAM
SUBDEAN CAIMACAM DELEGATE
ORDINARY PYLAGORE TENIENTE
VICARIAN
DERAIL TOAD DERAILER THROWOFF
DERANGE TURN CRAZE UNWIT
UPSET HAMPER RUFFLE CONFUSE
DERAIGN DISEASE DISTURB
PERTURB UNSHAPE DISORDER
DISPLACE UNSETTLE
DERANGED OUT GYTE CRAZY
CRAZED FRANTIC FURIOUS
BUGHOUSE DEMENTED DETRAQUE
INFORMAL
DERANGEMENT MANIA UPSET
FRENZY LUNACY DISEASE MADNESS
PHRENSY RUMMAGE DELIRIUM
DISORDER INSANITY
DERBY POT CADY KATY RACE
BOXER CADDY DICER KELLY SHIRE
BOWLER
DERELICT STREET FAILURE
BETRAYER CASTAWAY
DERELICTION FAILURE RELICTION
DERIDE BOO GECK GIBE HOOT JAPE
JEER JIBE LOUT MOCK TWIT DRAPE
FLEER FLOUT KNACK LAUGH RALLY
SCOFF SCORN SCOUT TAUNT
EXPOSE ILLUDE IRRIDE CATCALL
LOWBELL RIDICULE
DERIDER IRRISOR
DERISION GECK JEER MOCK HOKER
SCORN SPORT MOWING ASTEISM
MOCKERY CONTEMPT IRRISION
RIDICULE
DERISIVE JEERY SNIDE MOWING
SATANIC DERISORY IRRISORY
SARDONIC SCOFFING
DERIVATION ORIGIN DESCENT
PEDIGREE
DERIVATIVE FURAN LININ SLOPE
ACOINE ACYLAL BORANE FURANE
INDOLE PHENOL RETENE ALKYLOL
ANALGEN DERIVED ENOLATE
FLAVONE FLUXION FULGIDE
FULVENE GERMANE SUCRATE
ALBUMOSE ANALGENE FLAVONOL
FORMAZAN HEMATINE INDAZOLE
STANNANE
DERIVE GET DRAW STEM TAKE
BRING CARRY DRIVE FETCH INFER
TRACE BORROW CONVEY DEDUCE
DESUME ELICIT EVOLVE GATHER
OBTAIN SPRING DESCEND EXTRACT
PROCEED RECEIVE TRADUCE
DERMA LAYER CORIUM DERMIS
KISHKE

DERMATITIS ICH ICK CASCADO
CUTITIS
DERMIS DERM CUTIS DERMA
CORIUM
DERNIER LAST FINAL DARREIN
DERNIER CRI FASHION
DEROGATE ANNUL DECRY LESSEN
REPEAL DETRACT SLANDER
RESTRICT WITHDRAW
DEROGATORY BAD
DERRICK JIB RIG LIFT SPAR CRANE
DAVIT HOIST TACKLE ERECTER
ERECTOR GALLOWS HANGING
HANGMAN STIFFLEG JINNYWINK
DERRIS TUBA DEGUELIA
DERVISH AGIB FAKIR FAKEER
SADITE SANTON DARWESH WHIRLER
CALENDER
DESALT DEIONIZE
DESATURATE SADDEN
DESCANT SING SONG COPULA
MELODY REMARK WARBLE
COMMENT QUINIBLE
DESCEND DIP SYE DIVE DROP DUCK
FALL SHED SINK SKIN VAIL AVALE
LIGHT LOWER SQUAT STOOP
SWOOP ALIGHT DERIVE DEVALL
DEVAUL SETTLE DECLINE DELAPSE
DEVOLVE SUBSIDE SUCCEED
DISMOUNT
(— INTO HELL) HARROW
DESCENDANT SON CION GHUZ HEIR
SEED SLIP CHILD GHUZZ SCION
BRANCH LINEAL DESCENT
AARONITE ASHERITE DAUGHTER
EPIGONUS
(— OF IMMIGRANTS) BRAVA
(— OF JEW) CHUETA
(— OF MOHAMMED) EMIR
(— OF NOAH) AD
(—S OF MOHAMMED) ASHRAF
(INSIGNIFICANT —) TAG
(PL.) SEED DONMEH DUNMEH
STRAIN PROGENY OFFSPRING
POSTERITY
DESCENDING FALL CADENT
DOWNWARD
(— FROM COMMON ANCESTOR)
AKIN
DESCENT JET KIN SET DIVE DOWN
DROP FALL KIND VAIL BIRTH BLOOD
CANCH CHUTE ISSUE SCARP SHUTE
SLOPE STOCK CLEUCH CLEUGH
ESCARP RAPPEL STRAIN ASSAULT
DECLINE DISSENT EXTRACT
FALLOUT INCLINE KINDRED LINEAGE
PROGENY ANCESTRY BREEDING
COMEDOWN DOWNCOME DOWNFALL
DOWNGATE DOWNHILL GLISSADE
INVASION PEDIGREE
(— IN MOUNTAINEERING) ABSEIL
(— OF AIRPLANE) LETDOWN
APPROACH
(— OF BIRD) STOOP
(— OF DEITY) AVATAR AVATARA
(— OF LIQUID) DRIBBLE
(— OF MASS) SLIDE
(— OF RIVER) LEAP
(FAMILIAR —) HAVAGE

(OVERWHELMING —) AVALANCHE
(PARACHUTE —) JUMP BAILOUT
(PLUNGING —) SPIN
DESCHAMPIA AIRA
DESCRIBE GIVE READ TELL BLAZE
IMAGE PAINT POINT STYLE WRITE
DEFINE DENOTE DEPICT DEVISE
DILATE RELATE REPORT SKETCH
TITLE DECLARE DEPAINT DISPLAY
EXPLAIN EXPRESS NARRATE
OUTLINE PICTURE PORTRAY
PRESENT RECOUNT STORIFY
DESCRIVE INSCRIBE REHEARSE
(— A LINE) CUT
(— AS) CALL
(— BRIEFLY) KODAK
(— GRAMMATICALLY) PARSE
DESCRIPTION KIN IMAGE BLAZON
SKETCH SURVEY ACCOUNT DICTION
DISPLAY PICTURE LANDSKIP
RELATION TREATISE
(— OF A COUNTRY) FACE
(— OF VISION) AISLING
(BRIEF —) LEGEND
(RUSTIC —) IDYL IDYLL
DESCRY SEE SPY ESPY MAKE SCRY
ASCRY SIGHT BEHOLD BETRAY
DETECT REVEAL DISCERN DISPLAY
DENOUNCE DESCRIBE DISCLOSE
DISCOVER PERCEIVE
DESECRATE ABUSE DEFILE
POLLUTE PROFANE VIOLATE
TEMERATE UNHALLOW
DESERT DUE ERG RAT RUN AREG
ARID BOLT FAIL FLEE MEED SAND
SERT TURN VAST GUILT LEAVE
LURCH MERIT PLANT SERIR START
WAIVE WASTE WORTH BARREN
BETRAY DEFECT EXPOSE LONELY
RENEGE REWARD SHRINK THIRST
WESTEN ABANDON ABSCOND
CHICKEN DEMERIT FORSAKE
HORNADA OVERRUN WASTERN
WASTINE DESOLATE RENOUNCE
SOLITARY SOLITUDE WASTABLE
(PL.) GUILT
DESERTED DEAD WYSTY LONELY
FORLORN DESOLATE FORSAKEN
SOLITARY
(— WOMAN) AGUNAH
DESERTER RAT BOLTER BUGOUT
APOSTATE BUSHWACK FUGITIVE
RECREANT RENEGADE TURNTAIL
DESERTION BUGOUT RATTERY
APOSTASY
DESERT LEMON KUMQUAT
DESERVE EARN MEED RATE MERIT
REPAY SERVE ASSERVE BENEFIT
DEMERIT DISSERVE PROMERIT
DESERVED JUST COMING WORTHY
CONDIGN
DESERVING WORTHY WORTHFUL
ADMIRABLE
DESICCATE DRY ARID SEAR SERE
DRAIN DEHYDRATE
DESICCATION XERANSIS
DESIDERATUM NEED DESIRE
DESIGN AIM END MAP CAST DRAW
GOAL IDEA MARK MEAN PLAN PLAT

PLOT TREE WORK ALLOT CHECK
DECAL DECOR DODAD DRAFT DRIFT
ETTLE FANCY MODEL MOTIF NOTAN
QUILT SHAPE STAMP STUDY
BOWPOT CACHET CORNER CREATE
DEVICE DEVISE DOODAD DOODLE
EMBLEM FIGURE FLORAL FLOWER
INCUSE INTEND INTENT INVENT
LAYOUT MODULE OBJECT OBTENT
PROJET SCHEME SKETCH SYSTEM
VERVER ALLOVER BOSCAGE
CARTOON CARVING CHASING
COMPOSE COUNSEL CROQUIS
DESTINE DIAGRAM DRAUGHT
ETCHING FANTASY FASHION
OUTLINE PATTERN PRETEND
PROJECT PROPOSE PURPORT
PURPOSE REVERSE SCALLOP
SLEIGHT APPLIQUE BAYADERE
BOUGHPOT CONTRIVE CYMATION
CYMATIUM ENGINEER FILIGREE
FLOCKING FORECAST GRAFFITO
GROOVING INTAGLIO PHANTASY
PLATFORM REMARQUE SINGERIE
STRIPING SUNBURST GOFFERING
(**— AS TITLE PAGE**) VIGNETTE
(**— ON CARPET**) MEDALLION
(**— ON COIN**) BEADING
(**— ON FABRIC**) BATIK BATTIK
(**BOOK —**) FILET FILLET
(**CUP-SHAPED —**) HUSK
(**EMBLEMATIC —**) IMPRESS
(**ESSENTIAL —**) BONES
(**FASHION —**) FORD
(**OUTLINE —**) KEYSTONE
(**PERFORATED —**) POUNCE
(**STRIPED —**) STRIA STRIE
(**TESSELLATED —**) MOSAIC
(**TEXTILE —**) STRIPE HAIRLINE
DESIGNATE SET HAIL MARK MEAN
NAME SHOW ELECT LABEL SPEAK
STYLE TITLE ANOINT ASSIGN
DENOTE DESIGN FINGER INTEND
SETTLE APPOINT EARMARK ENTITLE
EXPRESS SPECIFY SURNAME
ALLOCATE DESCRIBE IDENTIFY
INDICATE NOMINATE
DESIGNATION NAME STYLE TITLE
CAPTION HOMONYM ADDITION
(**— OF PLACE**) ADDRESS
DESIGNED PREPENSE SUPPOSED
DESIGNER FANCIER PLANNER
PLOTTER SCHEMER COLORIST
ENGINEER MEDALIST
(**PL.**) COUTURE
DESIGNING ARTFUL CUNNING
JESUITIC PLANNING PLOTTING
SCHEMING
DESIRABLE FAIR GOOD KEEN
WORTH PLUMMY AMIABLE GRADELY
HEALTHY OPTABLE WELCOME
WISHFUL DESIROUS ELIGIBLE
ENVIABLE PLEASING SALUTARY
DESIRE YEN ACHE CARE ENVY EROS
FAIN HAVE HOPE ITCH KAMA KEEP
LEST LIST LOAD LUST MIND NEED
PANT URGE WANT WILL WISH WIST
ARDOR BOSOM BRAME COVET
CRAVE FANCY GIMME GREED

GROAN HEART MANGE MANIA NISUS
QUEST STUDY TANHA TASTE WILNE
YEARN YISSE AFFECT APPETE
ASPIRE BEHEST DEMAND DEVICE
HANKER HUNGER OREXIS POTHOS
PREFER TALENT THIRST UTINAM
YAMMER AVARICE AVIDITY
CONATUS COURAGE CRAVING
EROTISM FANTASY HIMEROS
INKLING LONGING PASSION
STOMACH VOLUNTY WILLING
AMBITION APPETITE COVETISE
CUPIDITY PLEASING
(**— FOR LIFE**) TANHA
(**— WITH EAGERNESS**) ASPIRE
(**ARDENT —**) THIRST
(**IRRITATING —**) ITCH
(**STRONG —**) CUPIDITY SLAVERING
(**UNCONTROLLABLE —**) CACOETHES
DESIROUS AVID FAIN FOND LIEF
VAIN EAGER FRACK FRECK LUSTY
ARDENT WILFUL ANXIOUS WILLFUL
WILLING WISHING APPETENT
COVETOUS LIKEROUS SPIRITED
DESIST HO LIN EASE HALT QUIT
REST SIST STOP WHOA CEASE
LEAVE SPARE STINT SWICK SWIKE
WONDE DEPART ABANDON
FORBEAR FORFEIT RESPITE SUBSIST
SURCEASE
(**— FROM**) CUT LEAVE REMIT
FORBEAR
DESK PEW AMBO SCOB BOARD
DESSE TABLE BUREAU CAISSE
PULPIT CONSOLE LECTERN
PLUTEUS COPYDESK STANDISH
VARGUENO
DESMA CLON CLONE
DESMAN MOLE SQUASH MUSKRAT
ONDATRA
DESMANTHUS ACUAN
DESOLATE SAD BARE LORN RUIN
SACK SOLE VAST WILD ALONE
BLEAK DREAR GAUNT GUBAT STARK
UNKED UNKET UNKID WASTE WASTY
WYSTY BARREN DESERT DISMAL
DREARY GLOOMY GOUSTY LONELY
RAVAGE DESTROY FORLORN
GOUSTIE HOWLING LACKING
UNCOUTH WIDOWED WILSOME
DEPRIVED DESERTED FORSAKEN
SOLITARY WASTEFUL WOBEGONE
DESOLATION WOE RUIN GLOOM
GRIEF HAVOC WASTE RAVAGE
SADNESS
DESPAIR GLOOM UNHOPE WANHOPE
DESPAIRING HOPELESS
DESPERADO BRAVO BADMAN
BANDIT RUFFIAN CRIMINAL
RESOLUTE
DESPERATE MAD DIRE RASH
DESPERT EXTREME FORLORN
FRANTIC HEADLONG HOPELESS
PERILOUS RECKLESS
DESPERATELY BONE
DESPICABLE BASE MEAN ORRA VILE
CHEAP DIRTY FOUTY SCALY ABJECT
PALTRY SHABBY SORDID CAITIFF
IGNOBLE PITIFUL REPTILE PITIABLE

UNWORTHY WRETCHED
DESPICABLY DIRTILY
DESPISE DEFY HATE SCORN SCOUT
SPISE SPURN DETEST FORHOO
LOATHE SLIGHT VILIFY CONTEMN
DESPITE DISDAIN DISPRIZE
MISPRIZE VILIPEND
DESPITE BY VEX SPITE MALGRE
DESPISE
DESPOIL ROB PELF PILL POLL RAID
RAPE RUIN SKIN BOOTY HARRY
PLUME REAVE RIFLE SPOIL STRIP
STRUB TRICE DIVEST FLEECE
HESPEL HUSPEL RAVAGE RAVISH
REMOVE BEREAVE DEPRIVE
DISROBE PILLAGE PLUNDER
UNSPOIL DEFLOWER DISARRAY
SPOLIATE SPUILZIE UNCLOTHE
DESPOINA KORE PERSEPHONE
DESPONDENCY DUMP BLUES
DUMPS GLOOM ATHYMY MISERY
ATHUMIA ATHYMIA DESPAIR
DESPOND
DESPONDENT SAD BLUE GLOOMY
FORLORN DEJECTED DOWNCAST
HOPELESS
DESPOT CZAR TSAR TZAR ANARCH
SATRAP TYRANT AUTARCH
MONARCH AUTOCRAT
DESPOTIC LORDLY ABSOLUTE
DOMINANT
DESPOTISM TYRANNY SULTANISM
DESQUAMATE PEEL
DESSERT ICE PIE CAKE FOOL SKYR
SNOW VOID BETTY BOMBE COUPE
DOLCE FRUIT GLACE GRUNT JELLY
LACTO SLUMP AFTERS ECLAIR
JUNKET MOUSSE PASTRY SPONGE
SWEETS TRIFLE BAKLAVA BANQUET
PARFAIT PUDDING SHERBET
SOUFFLE SPUMONE STRUDEL
SUPREME DUMPLING FLUMMERY
FRUMENTY NAPOLEON SILLABUB
DESTINATION END GOAL PORT
BOURN BILLET BOURNE
DESTINE DOOM EURE FATE MARK
ALLOT SHAPE SLATE WEIRD DEPUTE
DESIGN DEVOTE INTEND ORDAIN
APPOINT PURPOSE SENTENCE
DESTINY LOT DOLE DOOM EURE
FATE SORT KARMA MOIRA STARS
WEIRD KHARMA KISMET DESTINE
FORTUNE PORTION FOREDOOM
DESTITUTE BARE NACE POOR SANS
VOID CLEAN EMPTY NAKED NEEDY
WASTE BEREFT DEVOID VACANT
WASTED FORLORN LACKING
NAUGHTY VIDUATE WANTING
BANKRUPT BEGGARED DEFEATED
DEPRIVED DESOLATE FORSAKEN
HELPLESS INDIGENT INNOCENT
VIDUATED
(**— OF FEATHERS**) DEPLUMATE
(**— OF LEAVES**) APHYLLOUS
(**— OF LIGHT**) DARK
(**— OF TEETH**) EDENTATE
(**— OF WATER**) ANHYDROUS
(**— OF**) BUT
DESTITUTION NEED WANT FAMINE

PENURY BEGGARY DEFAULT
POVERTY

DESTROY BAG EAT END GUT RID
BLOW CHEW FRAP FULL KILL NULL
RASE RAZE RUIN RUSH SINK SLAY
SMIT STRY TINE UNDO VOID BREAK
CRACK CRAZE DECAY ELIDE ERASE
ERODE FORDO HAVOC MISDO
PRANG QUADE QUAIL QUELL SHEND
SHOOT SMASH SMITE SPEED SPEND
SPILL SPLIT SPOIL STROY SWAMP
WASTY WRACK WRECK BLIGHT
CANCEL CUMBER DEFACE DEFEAT
DELETE DEVOID DEVOUR EFFACE
FAMISH FOREDO MURDER PERISH
QUENCH RANKLE RAVAGE STARVE
UNMAKE UNPILE UNWORK UPROOT
UPTEAR ABOLISH CONSUME
CORRODE DEPRIVE DISTURB
ENECATE EXPUNGE FLATTEN
FORFARE FORLESE MORTIFY
NULLIFY OVERRUN PEREMPT
RUINATE SHAMASH SHATTER
SMOTHER SUBVERT TERRIFY
UNBUILD WHITTLE AMORTIZE
CONFOUND DECIMATE DEMOLISH
DESOLATE DESTRUCT DISANNUL
DISPLANT DISSOLVE FRACTURE
FRAGMENT IMMOLATE INFRINGE
MUTILATE OVERTURN SABOTAGE
STRAMASH
(— **BARK**) GIRDLE
(— **BY FIRE**) CONSUME
(— **FERTILITY**) EXHAUST
(— **SELF-POSSESSION**) ABASH
(— **TOTALLY**) SMASH SWEEP
CUMBER SCUTTLE

DESTROYED FLAT BLOWN KAPUT
KAPUTT

DESTROYER CAN HUN DEATH
TINCAN UNDOER VANDAL VICTOR
FLIVVER STROYER UNMAKER
WARSHIP DEVOURER SABOTEUR

DESTROYING FELL

DESTRUCTIBLE FRAIL

DESTRUCTION BAR END HEW BANE
DOGS DOOM FIRE LOSS RACK RUIN
STRY TALA CRUSH DEATH DECAY
GRAVE HAVOC STRIP STROY WASTE
DEFEAT DISMAY ENDING EXPIRY
WONDER ABADDON CARNAGE
EROSION UNDOING COLLAPSE
DELETION DISPOSAL DOWNFALL
EVERSION EXCISION SHAMBLES
SMASHERY
(— **OF BONES**) CARIES
(— **OF SHIP'S PAPERS**) SPOLIATION
(**CELL** —) LYSIS
(**GRADUAL** —) CORROSION
(**MALICIOUS** —) SABOTAGE

DESTRUCTIVE FELL FATAL DEADLY
MORTAL BALEFUL DEATHLY EXITIAL
FATEFUL HARMFUL HUMLIKE
HURTFUL NOISOME NOXIOUS
RUINOUS ANERETIC DEATHFUL
EXITIOUS WASTEFUL WRACKFUL
WREAKFUL ANAERETIC

DESUETUDE BREACH DISUSE

DESULTORY IDLE HASTY LOOSE

ROVING AIMLESS CURSORY
RAMBLING UNSTEADY WAVERING
IRREGULAR

DETACH CUT DRAFT LOOSE SEVER
LOOSEN UNBIND UNGLUE UNWORK
CRACKLE DISJOIN DRAUGHT
ISOLATE UNHINGE UNRIVET UNSEIZE
ABSTRACT DISSOLVE DISUNITE
PRESCIND SEPARATE UNFASTEN
WITHDRAW

DETACHABLE SLIP

DETACHED CUT COLD FREE ALONE
ALOOF DEADPAN INSULAR PORTATO
SCIOLTO ABSTRACT CLINICAL
DISCRETE ISOLATED SEPARATE
SPICCATO UNBIASED

DETACHMENT POSSE ATARAXY
OUTPOST ATARAXIA AVULSION
OUTGUARD

DETAIL CREW ITEM DODAD POINT
ACCENT ASSIGN DOODAB DOODAD
NICETY PARCEL RELATE RETAIL
ACCOUNT APPOINT ARTICLE ITEMIZE
MINUTIA NARRATE NULLING
RESPECT SEVERAL SPECIFY
INSTANCE REHEARSE SALIENCE
(—**S OF MAP**) CULTURE
(**CLIMACTIC** —) BEAUTY
(**PETTY** —) CHICKEN
(**PL.**) DOPE FROUFROU FURNITURE

DETAILED PROLIX CLOSEUP SPECIAL
PUNCTUAL TIRESOME

DETAIN BAIL HOLD KEEP STAY STOP
CHECK DELAY TARRY ARREST
ATHOLD COLLAR HINDER RETARD
TAIGLE IMPRISON RESTRAIN
WITHHOLD

DETECT SEE SPY ESPY FIND NOSE
SPOT CATCH SCENT SENSE SMOKE
DESCRY DIVINE EXPOSE REVEAL
DEVELOP DISCERN UNCOVER
DECIPHER DISCOVER OVERTAKE

DETECTIVE EYE TEC BULL BUSY
DICK TRAP PLANT SNOOP BEAGLE
MOUSER RUNNER SHADOW SHAMUS
SLEUTH TAILER TRACER GUMSHOE
SCENTER SNOOPER SPOTTER
TRAILER DETECTOR FLATFOOT
HAWKSHAW HOUSEMAN OPERATOR
SHERLOCK PINKERTON

DETECTOR COHERER REAGENT
SFERICS SPHERICS

DETENT DOG PALL PAWL CATCH
CLICK RATCH PALLET RATCHET

DETENTION DELAY ARREST
CAPTURE DETINUE DETAINER
STOPPAGE

DETER BAR FEAR BLOCK BLUFF
CHECK DELAY DEHORT HINDER
RETARD PREVENT TERRIFY
DISSUADE PRECLUDE RESTRAIN

DETERGE PURGE CLEANSE MUNDIFY

DETERGENT SOAP SYNDET
ABLUENT PURGING RHYPTIC
SMECTIC SOLVENT CLEANSER
GARDINOL

DETERIORATE GO FAIL GIVE SLIP
SOUR WEAR DECAY ERODE SPILL
WORST APPAIR APPERE DEBASE

IMPAIR SICKEN DECLINE PERVERT
FIREFANG

DETERIORATING DECADENT

DETERIORATION DECAY IMPAIR
MALADY DECLINE EROSION FAILURE
DOLDRUMS

DETERMINABLE FIXED DEFINITE
DEFINABLE GAUGEABLE

DETERMINANT CYTOGENE
JACOBIAN CIRCULANT WRONSKIAN

DETERMINATE CERTAIN ORISTIC
DEFINITE RESOLUTE RESOLVED
SPECIFIC

DETERMINATION ACT HEST WILL
ASSAY BLANK CAUSE ADVICE
BEARING CONSULT PURPOSE
RESOLVE ANALYSIS BACKBONE
BIOASSAY DECISION DIVISION
FIRMNESS FORECAST JUDGMENT
JUDICIAL SENTENCE VOLITION

DETERMINATIVE FINAL FORMANT
SHAPING LIMITING
(**MOST** —) DOMINANT

DETERMINE END FIT FIX GET RUN
TEST WILL ASSAY AWARD JUDGE
PITCH WIELD ADJUST ASSESS
ASSIGN DECERN DECIDE DECREE
DEFINE DESCRY DETECT DETERM
DEVISE FIGURE GOVERN PERFIX
SETTLE ACCOUNT ADJUDGE
ANALYZE APPOINT ARRANGE
COMPUTE DELIMIT DERAIGN
DISPOSE RESOLVE TERMINE
COGNOSCE CONCLUDE DISCOVER
INFLUENCE
(— **FINENESS**) SET SETT
(— **RATE**) ASSESS
(— **ROOT**) EXTRACT

DETERMINED SET BENT DERN FIRM
GRIM GIVEN STOUT UPSET BITTER
DOGGED GRITTY INTENT MULISH
STURDY DECIDED SETTLED
DECISIVE FOREGONE PERVERSE
RESOLUTE RESOLVED STUBBORN

DETERMINER GENE CHANCE

DETERMINIST JABARITE

DETEST DAMN HATE ABHOR CURSE
LOATHE CONDEMN DESPISE DISLIKE
DENOUNCE EXECRATE

DETESTABLE FOUL HORRID ODIOUS
BLASTED HATABLE HATEFUL
HELLISH HIDEOUS ACCURSED
DAMNABLE HATEABLE INFAMOUS
INFERNAL

DETESTATION ODIUM HATRED
HORROR LOATHING ANTIPATHY

DETHRONE DEPOSE DIVEST
UNCROWN

DETONATE FIRE BELCH BLAST
SHOOT EXPLODE DETONIZE

DETONATION BLAST KNOCK
AMBITUS PINGING PINKING

DETONATOR CAP FUSE FUZE FUSEE
FUZEE SQUIB TORPEDO INITIATOR

DETOUR BYPASS CIRCUIT DIVERSION

DETRACT TAKE DECRY DEDUCT
DEFAME DETRAY DIVERT VILIFY
ASPERSE TRADUCE BELITTLE
DEROGATE DIMINISH DISTRACT

MINIMIZE PROTRACT SUBTRACT WITHDRAW

(— FROM) IMPEDE

DETRACTION CALUMNY SCANDAL SLANDER ZOILISM

DETRIMENT COST HARM HURT LOSS SORE WOUND DAMAGE DAMNUM DENIAL INJURY BEATING EXPENSE JACTURE DISFAVOR MISCHIEF

DETRIMENTAL ADVERSE CAPITAL HARMFUL HURTFUL LOSSFUL DAMAGING INVIDIOUS

DETRITUS OUTWASH SHINGLE SHEETWASH

DEUCALION (FATHER OF —) PROMETHEUS

(WIFE OF —) PYRRHA

DEUCE DIANTRE DICKENS

(WILD —) FREAK

DEUCEDLY BLAME BLAMED

DEUTERIUM H

DEUTEROGAMY DIGAMY

DEUTOMALA LABIUM

DEVA DEV DEWA SURA ANGEL DEITY

DEVASTATE EXILE HARRY HAVOC WASTE DEVAST RAVAGE ATOMIZE DESTROY PILLAGE PLUNDER SCOURGE DEMOLISH

DEVASTATED WASTE

DEVASTATION RUIN EXILE HAVOC WASTE HARASS RAVAGE SACCAGE SACKAGE SACCADGE

DEVASTATING DEADLY LETHAL SAVAGE CRUSHING FEROCIOUS

DEVELOP BUD RUN BOOM COOK FORM GROW STEM TILL ARISE BREAK BREED BUILD ERECT RIPEN SHOOT APPEAR BRANCH DETECT EVOLVE EXPAND FLOWER FULFIL MATURE REVEAL UNFOLD UNFURL BURGEON BURNISH EDUCATE ENLARGE EVOLUTE EXPOUND FULFILL UNCOVER DEVELOPE DISCLOSE DISCOVER DISVELOP ENGENDER GENERATE INCUBATE MANIFEST

(— A HEAD) HEART

(— BULB) BOTTOM

(— COLOR) AGE

(— CRACKS) ALLIGATOR

(— WELL) COTTON

DEVELOPABLE TORSE

DEVELOPED DEEP FORWARD

(— AFTER BIRTH) ACQUIRED

(FULLY —) BOLD ADULT FLORID FORMED SUMMED

(GREATLY —) ADVANCED

(IMPERFECTLY —) ABORTIVE

(INCOMPLETELY —) SEED

DEVELOPER ELON SOUP ORTOL AMIDOL GLYCIN KACHIN BUILDER GLYCINE RODINAL

DEVELOPMENT WAX DRIFT EVENT HATCH ESTATE GROWTH DESCENT GENESIS PROCESS STATURE BREEDING INCREASE PEDIGREE UPGROWTH UPSPRING

(— OF SEX) DIOECISM

(FULL —) BLOW MATURITY

(HIGHEST —) BLOOM

(NORMAL —) APHANISIA

(SUBSEQUENT —) SEQUEL

(THEMATIC —) CONTINUITY

(UNEXPECTED —) ACCIDENT

DEVI UMA KALI DURGA GAURI CHANDI SHAKTI BHAVANI BHOWANI HIMAVAT MAHADEVI HAIMAVATI

DEVIANT ABERRANT DIVERGENT

DEVIATE ERR RUN WRY YAW LEAN MISS VARY VEER BEVEL BREAK DRIFT LAPSE SHEER SPORT START STRAY WAIVE CHANGE DEPART DETOUR DIVERT RECEDE SQUINT SWERVE WANDER DECLINE DEFLECT DIGRESS DIVERGE INCLINE REFLECT ABERRANT DEROGATE

(— FROM VERTICAL) HADE

DEVIATING SKEW DEVIANT DEVIOUS ERRATIC SINUOUS ABERRANT INDIRECT

DEVIATION BOW HELM JUMP SKEW TURN DRIFT LAPSE QUIRK SHEER TWIST ABRASH BATTER CHANGE DETOUR FIGURE SPREAD ANOMALY BRISURE LICENCE LICENSE ACCURACY DRIFTAGE LATITUDE SOLECISM VARIANCE

(— OF COLOR) ABRASH

(STANDARD —) SIGMA

DEVICE (ALSO SEE INSTRUMENT) ARM ART DIE DOG DOP EYE FAN FLY FOB GAG GIN GUN HOG JIG KEY MOP MOT PEN SET TIP TUP WAY WIT ARCH BELL BOND BOOM BUFF COIN COMB COUP DARE DOPP DRAG DRIP FAKE FIRE FLAG FORK FROG FUSE FUZE GAGE GATE GOBO GRAB GRIP GYRO HASP HAUL HEAD HECK HORN IRIS IRON JACK KEEP KITE LAMP LENS LOCK MOVE MULE MUTE NAIL PACE PAGE PAWK PLOW POKE PUMP REEL SEAL SHOE SHUT SIGN SLAY SLEY SLUR SNAP SPUD STOP STUD SUMP TOOL TRAP TRIP VICE WEIR WHIM WHIP WIND WING WOLF ALARM APRON BADGE BALUN BITCH BLOCK BREAK BRUSH CHECK CLAMP CODER COVIN CRAMP CROSS DODGE DRIER DRIFT DRYER DUMMY FADER FANCY FLAIL FLARE FLASH FLIRT FLOAT GAUGE GLAND GORGE GRIPE GUARD GUIDE GUILE HICKY HINGE HOKUM IMAGE KAZOO KEYER LADLE LASER LATCH LEVEL MATCH OTTER PARER PLATE PUNKA SCREW SHADE SHANK SHIFT SIEVE SIGHT SIGIL SIREN SIZER SKATE SLAVE SLICK SLIDE SLING SONDE SPOOL SPOUT SQUIB STAMP STILL STOOL STOVE SWEEP SWELL TABLE TABUT TAMER THIEF TIMER TORCH TRUER TUNER UNION VERGE AGRAFE AIRWAY ALARUM ALINER ANCHOR ARREST BAILER BASTER BEACON BEATER BECKET BEDDER BEEPER BINDER BLOWER BOBBIN BOOMER BRIDLE BROOCH BUCKLE BUFFER BULLEN BUMPER BUNGEE BUNTER BURNER BUTTON CIPHER COOKER DASHER DECEIT DERAIL DESIGN DIMMER DOFFER DOTTER DRIVER DROGUE DUMPER EMBLEM ENGINE EVENER FABRIC FALLER FEEDER FENDER FILLER FILTER FINDAL FINDER FORMER GADGET GLAZER GOFFER GOGGLE GRADER GRATER GRISLY GUIDER HANGER HEATER HICKEY HOLDER HOOTER INVENT JIGGER JOGGER KEEPER KICKER LAYBOY LETOFF LIFTER LOOPER MARKER MIRROR MODULE MORTAR MOTHER NIPPLE NONIUS NOTION PACKER PEELER PLAYER PLOUGH PORTER POTEYE PULLER PUNKAH REROLL RINGER ROCKET ROLLER ROOTER ROTULA ROUTER SACKER SADDLE SAFETY SANDER SCALER SCHEME SCREEN SEALER SEEKER SENSOR SETTER SHAKER SHIELD SIFTER SIGNAL SINKER SIPPER SLEIGH SLICER SLIDER SLIMER SLOPER SLUICE SOCKET SOLION SORTER SPACER SPRING STONER STYLUS SUCKER SWITCH TACTIC TAGGER TAPPER TELLER TEMPLE TESTER TILLER TRACER TUCKER TUNNEL TURNER WARMER WASHER WEANER WEEDER WHEEZE WINDER WINNOW WORKER ADAPTER ADJUNCT AERATOR AGRAFFE ALIGNER BALANCE BECKETT BIMETAL BIMORPH BINDING BLEEDER BLENDER BLINKER BLOCKER BLOWOFF BLOWOUT BOOKEND BOOSTER BREAKER CALTROP CHIPPER CLAPPER COMPASS DASHPOT DISHMOP DIVISOR DRAWOFF DRESSER DRINKER EARPICK EDUCTOR EJECTOR EMPRESA EXCITER FACEBOW FASHION FETLOCK FICELLE FICTION FITMENT FIXTURE FLASHER FLIPPER FLUSHER FLYFLAP FRISKET GAUFFER GIMMICK GLASSES GRAINER GRENADE GRIDDLE GRILLER GRINDER GRIPPER GRIZZLY GROMMET GROOVER GROWLER GUDGEON GUZZLER HATCHER HELIDON IGNITER IMAGINE IMPRESA IMPRESS INFUSER INHALER IRONMAN KICKOFF KNOTTER LIGHTER MACHINE MUFFLER OOGRAPH PIGTAIL PLOTTER POINTER PRESSER RATCHET RATTLER RECEDER REDUCER RELEASE ROASTER ROSETTE SAMPLER SCALPER SCANNER SCOGGAN SCRAPER SCUPPER SERVANT SETBACK SETOVER SETWORK SHACKLE SHEDDER SHIFTER SHIPPER SHOOFLY SHUTTER SHUTTLE SINKBOX SKIMMER SLAPPER SLEEVER SLINGER SLITTER SLUDGER SLUSHER SNAPPER SNIFFER SNIGGLE SNORKEL SNUBBER

SNUFFER SNUGGER SONOVOX
SOUNDER SPARGER SPEEDER
SPLICER SPOTTER SPRAYER
SQUEEZE STACKER STAPLER
STARTER STEMMER STENTER
STIRRER STOPPER STRIKER
STRIPER SUCTION SWATTER
SWEEPER SYRINGE TAMBOUR
TENDRIL TENSION THEORIC
THINNER TICKLER TREADLE
TRINDLE TRIPPER TRIPPET
TUMBLER TURNOUT TWISTER
WASHOUT WRINGER ABSORBER
ADJUSTER AQUASTAT BACKSTAY
BAROSTAT BIOMETER BLOCKING
BOOTJACK BRAILLER BREATHER
BRONTEUM BUSINESS BUSYBODY
CATAPULT CATHETER CONTOISE
COUPLING CROTCHET CRYOTRON
DAMPENER DEHORNER DERAILER
DIFFUSER DIRECTOR DISPOSER
DOORSTOP DROPHEAD DUPLEXER
EARPHONE ESPRESSO EXPLODER
FAIRLEAD FAKEMENT FASTENER
FLASHGUN FLYBRUSH FUELIZER
GASCHECK GATHERER GIMCRACK
GUNSTICK GYROSTAT HALLMARK
HANDTRAP HEADGEAR HOLDBACK
IMPROVER INKSTAND IRENICON
IRISCOPE ISOLATOR KNOCKOUT
LAUNCHER LEEBOARD LOXOCOSM
LUNARIUM MNEMONIC MOLITION
NEOSTYLE ODOGRAPH OVERLIFT
PACIFIER PARAVANE PENWIPER
PINWHEEL PULSATOR PYROSTAT
QUADRANT QUENTISE REFILTER
REHEATER REPEATER RETARDER
REVERSER SCORCHER SCOTCHER
SCRAWLER SCUTCHER SELECTOR
SHRINKER SILENCER SILVERER
SINKBOAT SMOOTHER SNOWPLOW
SNOWSHOE SPLITTER SPREADER
SPROUTER SQUEEGEE SQUEEZER
STOPWORK STRAINER STRINGER
STRIPPER STROPPER SURFACER
SWEATBOX TELETYPE TELLTALE
TERMINAL THROWOFF THROWOUT
TRAVELER TRAVERSE TRIANGLE
(— FOR BENDING PIPE) HICKEY
(— FOR BORING WELLS) TIGER
(— FOR CONCENTRATING ORE)
JIGGER
(— FOR PUTTING IN GEAR) STRIKER
(— IN LOOM) FEELER TEMPLE
(— ON FLAG) UNION
(— PLACED OVER CHIMNEY) JACK
(— PROTECTING DENTIST'S HAND)
THIMBLE
(— TO RETAIN COFFEE GROUNDS)
GRECQUE
(CENTRIFUGAL —) CYCLONE
(CLEVER —) COUP KNACK
(DISTINGUISHING —) SPOT
(GAMBLING —) HOLDOUT
(GLASSBLOWER'S —) DUMMY
(HAMPERING —) HOBBLES
(HEATING —) ETNA
(HERALDIC —S) ARMS
(LITERARY —) FRAME

(MAGICIAN'S —) FAKE FEKE CRAFT
(MIXING —) CRUTCHER
(POLISHING —) WAGWAG
(PYROTECHNIC —) FOUNTAIN
(SIGHTING —) ALIDADE
(SIGNALLING —) CRICKET
(SKILLFUL —) ART
(SPEECH —) ITALICS
(THEATRICAL —) SLOAT SLOTE
(TIMEKEEPING —) HOROLOGE
(WATER-RAISING —) JANTU SWEEP
CHURRUS
(WEAVING —) BOAT
(PL.) ENGINERY
DEVIL DEL IMP BENG BHUT BOGY
DEIL HAZE MAHU NICK PUCK QUED
WOLF WOND ANNOY BOBBY BOGEY
BOGIE CHORT CLOOT DEMON
DEUCE EBLIS FIEND HARRY SATAN
SCRAT SHEDU TAIPO TEASE
AMAMON DAEMON DIABLE DIABLO
HORNIE NICKIE PESTER RAGMAN
SORROW THURSE AMAIMON
ANHANGA CLOOTIE DIANTRE
DICKENS GREMLIN LUCIFER
MAHOUND RUFFIAN SERPENT
SHAITAN TORMENT WARLOCK
WENDIGO WINDIGO APOLLYON
BAALPEOR BEELPEOR BELFAGOR
CAGNAZZO CURUPIRA DEVILING
DEVILKIN DIABOLUS MEPHISTO
MISCHIEF OBIDICUT PLOTCOCK
WORRICOW
(BLUE —S) MARE
DEVILFISH RAY MANTA
DEVILISH DARING DEUCED DEVILY
RAKISH WICKED DEMONIC EXTREME
FIENDLY HELLISH INHUMAN SATANIC
DEMONIAC DIABOLIC FIENDISH
INFERNAL SATURNINE
DEVILISHLY DEUCED DEUCEDLY
DEVIL'S CLUB FATSIA
DEVIL'S COACHHORSE DARDAOL
DEVIL'S-MILK WARTWEED
WARTWORT
DEVIL'S-TREE DITA
DEVIOUS DEEP ERRING LOUCHE
ROVING SHIFTY SUBTLE TRICKY
OBLIQUE PLAITED VAGRANT
WINDING HAVERING INDIRECT
RAMBLING SCHEMING TORTUOUS
DEVISE AIM CAST COOK FIND GIVE
PLAN PLOT WARP WILL ARRAY
FANCY FRAME FUDGE IMAGE LEAVE
SHAPE WEAVE ADVISE CONVEY
DECOCT DESIGN DEVICE DIVIDE
DIVINE INVENT SCHEME AGITATE
APPOINT ARRANGE BETHINK
COMMENT COMPASS CONCERT
CONCOCT CONSULT IMAGINE
PREPARE PROJECT BEQUEATH
CONTRIVE
DEVISER FINDER ARTIFICER
DEVISING DEVICE DEVISAL FORGERY
DEVITALIZE DULL DEADEN
DEVITALIZED DEGENERATE
DEVITRIFIED AMBITTY
DEVOID FREE VOID EMPTY BARREN

EXPERT VACANT SINCERE WANTING
DESOLATE
(— OF HELP) AIDLESS
(— OF KINDNESS) CRUEL
(— OF MERCY) BRUTAL
(— OF MIND) AMENTAL
(— OF VALUE) HOLLOW
(— OF) BOUT EMPTY
DEVOLUTION DESCENT
DEVOLVE FALL PASS RESULT
BLOSSOM SUCCEED OVERTURN
TRANSFER TRANSMIT
DEVOTE VOW ALLY AVOW DOOM
GIVE LEND TAKE TURN APPLY
DEVOW ADDICT ATTACH BESTOW
DEPUTE DESIGN DEVOVE DIRECT
EMPLOY INTEND RESIGN ADDRESS
CONSIGN DESTINE DEDICATE
VENERATE
(— TIME) BOTHER
DEVOTED MAD HIGH TRUE LIEGE
LOYAL PIOUS ARDENT DEVOUT
DOOMED ENTIRE FERVID OBLATE
VOTARY VOTIVE ADORING ARDUOUS
JEALOUS SERIOUS ZEALOUS
ADDICTED ATTACHED CONSTANT
FAITHFUL
(— TO COUNTRY) PATRIOTIC
(— TO ENJOYMENT) APOLAUSTIC
(OVERLY —) SUPERSTITIOUS
DEVOTEE CAT FAN NUN BUFF MONK
YATI ADEPT JNANI ADDICT BHAGAT
BHAKTA DEVOTO DEVOUT HEPCAT
VOTARY VOTEEN ZEALOT ADMIRER
AMATEUR BOPPIST BOPSTER
CINEAST FANATIC HEPSTER HIPSTER
SHAVIAN TARTUFE AMOURIST
BURNSIAN CABALIST DEVOTARY
FOLLOWER IBSENITE PARTISAN
PRIAPIAN SAVOYARD SIMPLIST
TARTUFFE VOTARESS VOTARIST
ALLIGATOR
DEVOTION CULT ZEAL ARDOR PIETY
BHAKTI NOVENA ANGELUS ARABISM
CULTISM LOYALTY FIDELITY
IDOLATRY JEALOUSY KAVVANAH
KAWWANAH RELIGION
(— OF ONESELF) VOW
(— TO HUMAN WELFARE)
HUMANISM
(FERVENT —) ADORATION
(PARENTAL —) PROGENITY
(PL.) HOLIES
DEVOTIONAL SOLEMN
DEVOUR EAT JAW FRET GULP SWAP
SWOP VOUR GORGE RAVEN WASTE
AFRETE ENGULF CONSUME
ENGORGE FRAUNCH SWALLOW
(— GREEDILY) SWILL
DEVOURING PREY EATING GREEDY
VORANT EDACIOUS
DEVOUT GOOD HOLY WARM FROOM
GODLY GRACY PIOUS HEARTY
INWARD SOLEMN CORDIAL DEVOTED
GODLIKE PITEOUS SAINTLY SINCERE
REVERENT PIETISTIC
(NOT —) LINK
DEVOUTNESS PIETY DEVOTION
DEW DAG RIME BLOOM FROST

MOISTEN REFRESH MOISTURE
(— **METER**) PAGOSCOPE
DEWBERRY MAYES
DEWDROP PEARL
DEWLAP JOWL GULLET JOLLOP
CHOLLER WATTLES
(— **OF MALE MOOSE**) BELL
DEWY DAMP RORY MOIST RORAL
RORIC RORID GENTLE ROSCID
DEXTERITY ART CHIC CRAFT KNACK
SKILL STROIL ABILITY ADDRESS
AGILITY APTNESS CUNNING FINESSE
SLEIGHT APTITUDE DEFTNESS
FACILITY
(— **IN ARMS**) CHIVALRY
DEXTEROUS APT FLY DEFT FEAT
HEND WISE ADEPT CANNY CLEAN
FEATY HANDY HAPPY HENDE JIMMY
QUICK READY SMART TIGHT ADROIT
ARTFUL CLEVER DRAFTY CUNNING
SLEIGHT DEXTROUS HANDSOME
SKILLFUL SLEIGHTY
DEXTEROUSLY YARELY HANDILY
DEXTRAN GLUCOSAN
DEXTROROTATORY POSITIVE
DEXTRORSE EUTROPIC
DEXTROSE AME CERELOSE
DHAK DAK PALAS PULAS
DHAVA BAKLI
DHOLE KOLSUN
DHOW BUGALA LATEEN SAMBUK
SAMBOUK LATEENER
DHYANA JHANA
DIABASE OPHITE DOLERITE
THOLEITE
DIABOLICAL CRUEL WICKED
DEMONIC HELLISH INHUMAN
SATANIC VIOLENT DEMONIAC
DEVILISH DIABOLIC FIENDISH
INFERNAL
DIABOLISM SATANISM
DIACETATE ACETIN
DIACONATE DEACONRY
DIACONICON PARABEMA
DIACRITIC HACEK TILDE UMLAUT
MODIFIER
DIAD DIGONAL TWOFOLD
DIADEM MIND CROWN TIARA
ANADEM CIRCLE EMBLEM FILLET
CORONET HEADBAND
DIAERESIS CESURA CAESURA
DIALYSIS
DIAGNOSE ANALYZE IDENTIFY
KNOWLEDGE
DIAGONAL BIAS SLANT SLASH
COUNTER SOLIDUS VIRGULE
BENDWISE DIAGONIC
DIAGONALLY BIAS BENDWAYS
BENDWISE
DIAGRAM MAP PLAN PLOT TREE
CARTE CHART EPURE GRAPH
DESIGN FIGURE SCHEMA SCHEME
SYMBOL YANTRA ISOGRAM ISOTYPE
SECTION VIAGRAM
DIAGRAMMATIC GRAPHIC
DIAGRAPH OE
DIAL NOB FACE KNOB WATCH
DIACLE JIGGER AZIMUTH CRYSTAL

DECLINER HOROLOGE INCLINER
RECLINER
DIAL BIRD DAYAL DHYAL
DIALECT (ALSO SEE LANGUAGE) HO
KA WU GEG GIZ KHA LAI SAC TWI
AMOY CANI CANT EFIK EGBA EPIC
GEEZ GHEG GONA GUEG IOWA ITZA
KORA MANX NAMA NORN OGAM
PALI SAUK SHOR SOGA TALK TCHI
TOSK TUBA ALTAI ARGOT ASURI
ATTIC CONOY DORIC FANTI GHEEZ
GHESE HAKKA IDIOM IONIC IOWAY
IRAQI KANSA KAREL KOINE LADIN
LINGO MAZUR MOPAN MUKRI
NGOKO OGHAM PARSI PUNIC SABIR
SAXON SCOTS SLANG TIGRE TSCHI
VALVE VOGUL ZMUDZ AEOLIC
AGNEAN ASANTE ATSINA AWADHI
BADAGA BROGUE CANTON CREOLE
DEBATE DUNGAN FAEROE FANTEE
FURLAN GASCON GULLAH GUTNIC
HARARI HARAYA IBANAG ISINAI
ITAVES JARGON KANSAS KHAMIR
KORANA KVITSH LADAKI LAHULI
LALLAN LIBYAN PARSEE PATOIS
PATTER PICARD SANTEE SCOTCH
SHARRA SKAGIT SPEECH SUDANI
SWATOW SYRIAC SZEKEL TAVAST
TONGUE TUSCAN YANKEE ZENAGA
ACADIAN AEOLIAN AMOYESE
ASHANTI BHOTANI BHUTANI
BUNDELI CHILULA CHUVASH
CLATSOP COCKNEY CORNISH
CUZCENO CYPRIOT FAYUMIC
FOOCHOW GEECHEE GHEGISH
GUTNISH JAIPURI KARAITE KITKSAN
KONKANI LADAKHI LALLAND
LEONESE LESBIAN MALTESE
MARSIAN MARWARI MIDLAND
MULTANI MUNDARI OLONETS
PANAYAN PRAKRIT SAHIDIC SANPOIL
SHORTZY SOKOTRI SPOKANE
SQUAXON SWABIAN SZEKLER
TIGRINA VAUDOIS ABANEEME
ACHMIMIC AKHMIMIC ALGERINE
ARCADIAN ASSYRIAN BAVARIAN
BHOJPURI BISCAYAN BOEOTIAN
BOHAIRIC CLAKAMAS COLVILLE
CORSICAN CYPRIOTE FALERIAN
FALISCAN FAROEISH FRANCIEN
FRIULIAN GARHWALI HARARESE
IZCATECO KANESIAN KARELIAN
KERMANJI KICKAPOO KINGWANA
LACANDON LANGUAGE LAWLANTS
MAGHREBI MAGHRIBI MAITHILI
MANDAEAN MANDARIN MANISIAN
MAZATECO MAZURIAN MEMPHITE
NABATEAN NEENGATU PANAYANO
PEKINESE RABBINIC SALTEAUX
SOULETIN SOUTHERN TAUNGTHU
TIGRINYA TIRHUTIA TUNISIAN
VENERIAN VIENNESE
(**STRANGE** —) GIBBERISH
(PL.) WU ANGLIAN
DIALECTIC PILPUL
DIALOGUE ION CRITO DIALOG
EPILOG PATTER PHAEDO TIMAEUS
COLLOQUY DUOLOGUE EPILOGUE
EXCHANGE PHAEDRUS

(—**S OF BUDDHA**) SUTRA SUTTA
(**COMIC** —) LAZZO
DIAMETER BORE GAGE GEAR MOOT
GAUGE WIDTH MODULE
(— **OF BULLET**) CALIBER CALIBRE
(— **OF PELVIS**) CONJUGATA
(— **OF PUPIL**) APERTURE
(— **OF WIRE**) GAGE GAUGE
DIAMOND GEM ICE BORT LASK PICK
ROCK ROSE BAHIA BOORT BORTZ
DORJE FANCY FIELD JAGER JEWEL
LOZEN MELEE POINT RHOMB RIVER
SANCY SPARK TABLE VAJRA
ADAMAS CANARY CARBON JAEGER
LASQUE ORLOFF PENCIL REGENT
RONDEL SHINER TABLET ADAMANT
BRIOLET CARREAU CRYSTAL
FISHEYE INFIELD LOZENGE PREMIER
RHOMBUS SPARKLE CORUNDUM
KOHINOOR RONDELLE SPARKLER
(— **CUT TOO THIN**) FISHEYE
(— **MOLDER**) DOP
(— **STATE**) DELAWARE
(— **USED FOR ENGRAVING**) SHARP
(**BLACK** —) CARBONADO
(**FLAT** —) LASQUE
(**GLAZIER'S** —) QUARREL
(**IMITATION** —) SCHLENTER
(**INFERIOR GRADE OF** —) FLAT
(**PERFECT** —) PARAGON
(**PURE WHITE** —) RIVER
(**SINGLE** —) SOLITAIRE
(**TRANSPARENT** —) CRYSTAL
(**YELLOW** —) CANARY
(PL.) MELANGE
DIAMOND BIRD PARDALOTE
DIAMORPHINE HEROIN
DIANA LUCINA TRIVIA ARTEMIS
(**BROTHER OF** —) APOLLO
(**FATHER OF** —) JUPITER
(**MOTHER OF** —) LATONA
DIANA MONKEY ROLOWAY
DIAPASON MONTRE DIAPASE
DIAPAUSE BLOCK
DIAPER FUR DIDY CLOUT DIDIE
NAPPY HIPPEN HIPPIN NAPKIN
NAPPIE DIAPERY
DIAPHANOUS CLEAR SHEER
FRAGILE DIAPHANE
DIAPHONY ORGANUM TRIPHONY
DIAPHORETIC BUCCO BUCHU
BUCKU BORAGE DIAPNOIC HIDROTIC
SUDATORY
DIAPHRAGM IRIS RIFF SLIT APRON
PHREN SKIRT WAFER DECKER
PLATEN MIDRIFF PHRAGMA
SKIRTING TRAVERSE TYMPANUM
DIAPHRAGMATIC PHRENIC
DIARRHEA LAX FLUX LASK GURRY
RELAX SCOUR SPRUE PURGING
SQUIRTS LIENTERY
DIARY LOG RECORD DAYBOOK
DIURNAL JOURNAL REGISTER
EPHEMERIS
DIASKEUAST EDITOR REVISER
DIASPORA GALUT GOLAH GALUTH
DIASPORE MIGRULE
DIASTASE MALT ENZYME AMYLASE

DIATOM BRITTLEWORT ASTERIONELLA

DIATONIC ACHROMATIC

DIATRIBE SCREED HARANGUE INVECTIVE

DIB DAP DIP DIBBLE DIBSTONE

DIBBLE DAP DIB DABBLE DIBBER KIPPIN TRIFLE DIBBLER KIPPEEN

DIBS COCKAL

DICAST HELIAST JURYMAN

DICE CHOP CUBE DEES BONES CRAPS FLATS LOWMEN REJECT CHECKER IVORIES
(**— GAME**) SET RAPHE MUMCHANCE
(**— HAVING FOUR SPOTS**) QUATRE
(**2, 3, OR 12 ON 1ST —**) MISSOUT
(**FALSE —**) GOAD TATS GOURD GRAVIERS SQUARIER STOPDICE
(**HIGHEST THROW AT —**) APHRODITE
(**LOADED —**) TOPS DOCTOR
(**LOWEST THROW AT —**) AMBSACE
(**PAIRED NUMBERS AT —**) DUPLET DOUBLETS

DICE PLAYER THROWSTER

DICER DERBY GAMBLER GRAINER

DICERION DYKER

DICHONDRA LAWNLEAF

DICHOTOMY DUALITY

DICKENS HECK DEUCE

DICKER ICRE SWAP DAKER BARTER HAGGLE BARGAIN CHAFFER EXCHANGE

DICKEY POOP WEAK DICKY FRONT GILET SHAKY DONKEY RUMBLE VESTEE HADDOCK PLASTRON

DICKIE SHAM DICKY FRONT SQUARE TUCKER STARCHER

DICLINOUS IMPERFECT

DICTATE SAW SAY DITE TELL UTTER WRITE DECREE DICTUM ENJOIN IMPOSE INDITE OCTROY ORDAIN SCHOOL COMMAND DELIVER REQUIRE SUGGEST WARRANT DICTAMEN

DICTATION DICTAMEN

DICTATOR CZAR DUCE TSAR CAESAR PENDRAGON

DICTATORIAL BOSSY LORDLY CZARIST POMPOUS TSARIST ARROGANT DOGMATIC ORACULAR POSITIVE

DICTION STYLE TERMS PHRASE IMAGERY LANGUAGE PARLANCE VERBIAGE
(**BAD —**) CACOLOGY

DICTIONARY GRADUS CALEPIN LEXICON GLOSSARY WORDBOOK THESAURUS

DICTUN SAY ADAGE AXIOM EDICT DECREE SAYING DICTATE EFFATUM OPINION APOTHEGM PRINCIPLE STATEMENT

DID D CAN DED DEDE DYDE
(**— NOT**) DIDNA DIDNT

DIDACTIC DRY PREACHY SERMONIC

DIDO ANTIC CAPER TRICK
(**BROTHER OF —**) PYGMALION
(**FATHER OF —**) BELUS
(**HUSBAND OF —**) SICHAEUS

(**LOVER OF —**) AENEAS

DIE GO BED DEE DOD END HOB HUB PIP ROT SIX TAT BOSS COIN CONK CUBE DADO DEAD DICE DROP EXIT FADE FAIL FALL FINE FIVE FLIT KICK MARK MOLD PART PASS PIKE PILE SEAL TATT TINE WANE CROAK FORCE FUDGE GHOST IVORY NAPOO PATAY PRINT PUNCH QUAIL SHAPE SNUFF SOUGH SPILL STALL STAMP STOCK SWELT CHANCE DEMISE DEPART DOCTOR EXPIRE FAMISH FINISH FORCER FORMER FULLAM MATRIX MULLAR PATRIX PERISH ROLLER STARVE STRIKE TORFEL TORFLE TRANCE VANISH WITHER BLOCKER DECEASE SUCCUMB TESSERA INTAGLIO LANGUISH MISCARRY PUNCHEON TRESPASS TRUSSELL
(**— AWAY**) FAIL SWOON
(**— BY HANGING**) SWING
(**— DOWN**) FLIT SINK
(**— FOR DRAWING WIRE**) WHIRTLE WHORTLE
(**— FOR MAKING DRAINPIPE**) DOD
(**— FOR MOLDING BRICK**) KICK
(**— FROM HUNGER**) AFFAMISH
(**— OF COLD**) STARVE
(**— WITH 4 SPOTS**) QUATRE
(**— WITH 6 SPOTS**) CISE SICE SISE SIZE
(**COINING —**) SICCA
(**FRAUDULENT —**) FULHAM FULLAM FULLOM
(**HOLLOW —**) GOURD
(**IMPROPER —**) FLAT
(**LOADED —**) TAT DOCTOR FULHAM HIGHMAN LANGRET
(**LOWER —**) BED
(**REVOLVING —**) DREIDEL

DIEBACK STAGHEAD EXANTHEMA

DIED DYDE WRATE

DIEHARD TORY BLIMP

DIESIS FEINT

DIET BANT FARE FAST FOOD SEIM SEYM BOARD HOFTAG REDUCE SEIMAS VIANDS VICTUS DIETINE LANDTAG REGIMEN RIKSDAG CONGRESS KREISTAG VOLKSTAG

DIETARY (**— LAWS**) KASHRUTH

DIETETICS SITOLOGY

DIETHER APIOL APIOLE DIOXANE

DIETING BANTING

DIFFER VARY RECEDE SQUARE COMPARE DISCORD DISSENT DIVERGE DISAGREE

DIFFERENCE SHED CHASM CLASH FAVOR BREACH CHANGE DIFFER ANOMALY BRISURE DISCORD DISPUTE QUALITY VARIETY DISTANCE DIVISION IMPARITY VARIANCE
(**— IN ELEVATION**) HEAD
(**— IN LATITUDE**) SOUTHING
(**— IN LONGITUDE**) EASTING
(**— IN PITCH**) COMMA INTERVAL
(**— IN PRESSURE**) DRAFT DRAUGHT
(**— IN WIDTH**) BILGE

(**— OF OPINION**) DISSENT ARGUMENT
(**— OF VESSEL'S DRAFT**) DRAG
(**ANGULAR —**) EXPLEMENT
(**GRADED —**) GRADIENT
(**MINUTE —**) SHADE
(**PRICE —**) BASIS
(**SMALL —**) HAIRLINE

DIFFERENT FAR MANY SERE FRESH OTHER PARTY DIVERS SCREWY SUNDRY UNLIKE ANOTHER DISTANT DIVERSE SEVERAL STRANGE UNALIKE UNUSUAL VARIANT VARIOUS CONTRARY DISTINCT MANIFOLD SEPARATE

DIFFERENTIA MARK LIMIT

DIFFERENTIAL FLUXION

DIFFERENTIATE APLITE DIFFER DISCERN HAPLITE CONTRAST SPECIATE

DIFFERENTIATION ANABOLY DEVIATION DICHOTOMY

DIFFERING DIVERSE SINGULAR DIVERGENT

DIFFICULT ILL HARD WICK CRAMP CRANK GREAT HEAVY SPINY STIFF AUGEAN CRABBY CRANKY KNOTTY SEVERE STICKY STRAIT STRONG TICKLE TRAPPY UNEASY UNEATH UPHILL WENETH WICKED ARDUOUS AWKWARD BRITTLE CRABBED DIFFUSE LABORED NERVOUS OBSCURE PAINFUL PERPLEX PRACTIC SERIOUS STICKLE UNNETHE ABSTRACT CUMBROUS FIENDISH PUZZLING SCABROUS STRUGGLE STUBBORN
(**— TO BEAR**) BITTER
(**— TO COMPREHEND**) STRANGE
(**— TO FOLLOW**) DIRTY
(**— TO GRASP**) FUGITIVE
(**— TO HANDLE**) SPINOUS
(**— TO MANAGE**) SURLY STURDY
(**— TO OBTAIN**) CLOSE
(**— TO PLEASE**) CURIOUS
(**— TO RAISE**) DORTY
(**— TO SATISFY**) CHOOSY CHOOSEY
(**— TO UNDERSTAND**) DEEP HIGH SUBTLE CRABBED ABSTRACT ABSTRUSE ESOTERIC

DIFFICULTY ADO BAR ILL JAM RUB BUMP CLOG COIL HEAT JAMB KNOT LOCK NODE PAIN PINE SNAG SORE WERE CHECK DOUBT GRIEF NODUS PRESS RIGOR STAND STOUR TRADE APORIA BOGGLE BUNKER HABBLE HOBBLE PLIGHT PLUNGE RUBBER SCRAPE STRAIT TIFTER BARRIER DICKENS GORDIAN PITFALL PROBLEM SQUEEZE ASPERITY HARDNESS HARDSHIP OBSTACLE SEVERITY STRUGGLE
(**UNEXPECTED —**) SNAG
(**WITH —**) SCARCELY

DIFFIDENCE DOUBT MODESTY RESERVE SHYNESS DISTRUST HUMILITY TIMIDITY

DIFFIDENT SHY BLATE CHARY MODEST BACKWARD RESERVED

RETIRING SHEEPISH
DIFFUSE FULL SHED BLEED EXUDE
LARGE STREW WORDY DEFUSE
DERIVE DILATE DIVIDE EXPAND
EXTEND OSMOSE PROLIX SPREAD
SPRING COPIOUS DIALYSE DIALYZE
DIFFUND PERPLEX PERVADE
PUBLISH RADIATE SCATTER
SPARKLE SPRAWLY SPRENGE
SUFFUSE VERBOSE CONFUSED
DIFFUSED DIOSMOSE DISPERSE
PATULENT PATULOUS SPRANGLE
(NOT —) STRICT COMPACT
DIFFUSION SPREAD OSMOSIS
BLEEDING DEFUSION
DIG HOE JOB NIP CLAW DIKE DYKE
GIRD GORE GRUB HOWK MINE
MOOT PION POKE PROD ROOT SINK
SMUG SPIT SPUD SUMP SWOT
DELVE DITCH DWELL GAULT GRAFT
GRAVE LODGE POACH PROBE
SNOUT SPADE START STOCK
BURROW DREDGE EXHUME GRAVEL
HOLLOW PLUNGE SHOVEL THRUST
TUNNEL BEDELVE COSTEAN
SPUDDLE UNEARTH EXCAVATE
(— OUT CREVICES) FOSSICK
(— OUT) SCOOP STUMP EXHUME
(— PEAT) SHEUGH
(— POTATOES) LIFT
(— TRENCHES) GRIP COSTEAN
COSTEEN
(— UP) CAST GRUB STUB SPADE
STOCK EXHUME UPGRAVE DISINTER
(— WITH NAILS) SCRAPE
(— WITH SNOUT) GROUT
DIGAMMA VAU
DIGEST COCT CODE DEFY ENDEW
ENDUE INDUE RIPEN CODIFY
DECOCT DOCKET MATURE SEETHE
CONCOCT EPITOME PANDECT
SUMMARY CONDENSE SYLLABUS
DIGESTION PEPSIS COCTION
EUPEPSY EUPEPSIA
DIGESTIVE PEPTIC DIGERENT
DIGGER DIG PAL PLOW MINER
BANKER BILDAR DRUDGE PLOUGH
COMRADE PEATMAN PIONEER
PLODDER TRENCHER
(POST HOLE —) LOY
DIGGING DIG DIKAGE DYKAGE
STRIPPING
DIGHT DAB RUB DECK DINK DITE
WIPE ADORN DICHT DRESS EQUIP
ORDER RAISE TREAT MANAGE
REPAIR WINNOW APPOINT CONSIGN
PERFORM PREPARE
DIGIT TOE UNIT DOIGT POINT THUMB
FIGURE FINGER HALLUX MEDIUS
NUMBER DEWCLAW DIGITAL
(BINARY —) BINIT
(EXTRA —) PREPOLLEX
DIGITAL KEY MANUAL
DIGITATE DIGITAL FINGERED
DIGNIFIED GRAND LOFTY MANLY
NOBLE STAID AUGUST LORDLY
SEDATE SOLEMN COURTLY EXALTED
STATELY TOGATED ELEVATED
ENNOBLED MAJESTIC

DIGNIFY DUB ADORN CROWN EXALT
GRACE HONOR RAISE ELEVATE
ENNOBLE PROMOTE
DIGNITARY DON WIG RAJA RAJAH
PRIEST SHERIF DIGNITY HUTUKTU
PRELATE SHEREEF HUTUKHTU
VESTIARY
DIGNITY DOG CHIC FACE RANK
BENCH DINES HONOR IZZAT PRIDE
STATE AFFAIR BARONY LAUREL
REPOSE BARONRY BEARING
DECORUM DUKEDOM EARLDOM
FITNESS GRAVITY MAJESTY
SHAHDOM STATION WORSHIP
CHIVALRY EARLSHIP GRANDEUR
NOBILITY
(— OF BISHOP) LAWN
(ACCIDENTAL —) JOY HAYZ
(PAPAL —) TIARA
DIGRAPH CH OE PH RH TH RRH
BIGRAM LIGATURE DIPHTHONG
DIGRESS VEER EXCUR DIVERT
SWERVE WANDER DEVIATE DIVERGE
EXCURSE DISGRESS DIVAGATE
DIGRESSION ASIDE VAGARY
DIGRESS ECBASIS EPISODE
EXCURSE PASSAGE TANGENT
DISGRESS EXCURSUS SIDESLIP
(RHETORICAL —) ECBOLE
DIKE BAR RIB BANK BUND DICE DICK
DYKE POND POOL DIGUE DITCH
LEVEE CAUSEY CRADGE CHANNEL
DIKELET POWDIKE CAUSEWAY
ESTACADE SPREADER
DIKER COWAN COWEN
DIKETONE BENZIL BIACETYL
DIMEDONE
DILACTONE LACTIDE ANEMONIN
DILAPIDATE DESTROY
DILAPIDATED BAD BEATEN CREAKY
RAGGED RUINED SHABBY WRECKY
CRAICHY CREACHY RUINOUS
DESOLATE TATTERED WOBEGONE
DILAPIDATION RUIN DECAY
DECREPITY DISREPAIR
DILATATION BULB SINUS VARIX
JARBOT SPREAD AMPULLA ECTASIA
ECTASIS ANEURISM DILATION
DILATE DELAY PLUMP SWELL WIDEN
DELATE EXPAND EXTEND SPREAD
AMPLIFY BROADEN DESCANT
DIFFUSE DISTEND ENLARGE INFLATE
PROLONG STRETCH DISPERSE
INCREASE LENGTHEN PROTRACT
DISCOURSE
DILATOR DIOPTER DIOPTRA DIOPTRY
DIVULSOR SPECULUM
DILATORY LATE SLOW SLACK
SPARE TARDY FABIAN REMISS
DILATOR LAGGARD LATREDE
TEDIOUS BACKWARD DELAYING
INACTIVE SLUGGISH
DILEMMA FIX FORK LOCK NODE
BRIKE CHOICE PLUNGE CORNUTE
SNIFTER JEOPARDY QUANDARY
DILETTANTE LOVER SUNDAY
ADMIKER AMATEUR DABBLER
DABSTER ESTHETE AESTHETE
DILIGENCE HIE CARE HEED DILLY

EFFORT CAUTION HORNING
BUSINESS INDUSTRY ASSIDUITY
DILIGENT BUSY HARD TIDY ACTIVE
EIDENT ITHAND STEADY CAREFUL
EARNEST HEEDFUL OPEROSE
PAINFUL WORKFUL CAUTIOUS
CONSTANT LABOROUS SEDULOUS
STUDIOUS
DILL ANET CALM SOYA ANISE UMBEL
PICKLE SOOTHE DILLWEED
DILLYDALLY LAG TOY LOAF DELAY
DILLY STALL LOITER TRIFLE
DILOGY ECHO
DILUENT CARRIER VEHICLE
DILUTE CUT BREW FUSE LEAN THIN
WEAK ALLAY BLUNT DELAY WATER
RAREFY REDUCE WEAKEN WHITISH
DIMINISH LENGTHEN WATERISH
(— LIQUOR) BREW SPLIT
(— WINE) GALLIZE
(VERY —) SMALL
DILUTED WASHY DILUTE REMISS
DIM DIP WAN BLUR DARK DULL FADE
GRAY HAZY MIST PALE PALL VEIL
BEDIM BLEAK BLEAR BLIND DUSKY
DUSTY FAINT FOGGY MISTY STAIN
BEMIST BLEARY CLOUDY DARKEN
DASWEN DIMPSY GLOOMY OBTUSE
SHADOW TWILIT DARKISH DISLIMN
ECLIPSE OBSCURE OPACATE
SHADOWY TARNISH DARKLING
OVERCAST
(NOT —) FRESH
DIME HOG HOGG DISME TENPENCE
TENPENNY
(HALF —) PICAYUNE
DIMEDON METHONE
DIMENHYDRINATE DRAMAMINE
DIMENSION BODY BULK SIZE SCOPE
WIDTH ASSIZE DEGREE EXTENT
HEIGHT LENGTH MOISON BREADTH
(COLOR —) CHROMA
(TYPE —) EM EN
(PL.) GAGE SIZE GAUGE GIRTH
EXTENT SIDING MEASURE
DIMIDIATE HALVED
DIMINISH GO CUT EBB SAP BATE
BURN CHOP DAMP DROP EASE
FADE FAIL FINE FRET MELT PARE
PINK SINK WANE WEAR ABATE
ALLAY BREAK CLOSE DRAFT DWARF
ELIDE ERODE LOWER MINCE PETER
SLACK SMALL TAPER DAMPEN
DEBATE DECOCT DEDUCT DILUTE
IMPAIR LESSEN MINISH REBATE
REDUCE SLOUGH VANISH WITHER
ABRIDGE ASSUAGE CORRODE
CURTAIL DEGRADE DEPLETE
DEPRESS DETRACT DIMINUE
DRAUGHT DWINDLE FRITTER INHIBIT
QUALIFY REFRACT RELIEVE
TARNISH ADMINISH AMOINDER
CONDENSE DECREASE DIMINUTE
DISCOUNT MINORATE MITIGATE
MODERATE RETRENCH
(— FRONT) PLOY
DIMINISHED SLACK GRAYED
DIMINUTE

DIMINISHING TAPER CRITICAL
FLAGGING
(— **IN LOUDNESS**) CALANDO
DIMINUTION FALL WASTE
DECREASE
DIMINUTIVE TOY WEE BABY TINY
BANTY DWARF PETTY RUNTY SMALL
YOUNG BANTAM LITTLE PETITE
POCKET MANIKIN MIDGETY MINIKIN
SHRIMPY EXIGUOUS
(— **OF BAR**) SCARP CLOSET
SCARPE
DIMLY DULLY DARKLY FEEBLY
SHADOWY
DIMMED BLEARY CLOUDY GRAYED
BLEARED
DIMMING GRAYOUT
DIMNESS DIM HAZE MIST SLUR
GLOOM CALIGO DARKNESS
DIMPLE DOKE AHMADI AHMEDI
RIPPLE GELASIN FOSSETTE
DIM-SIGHTED PURBLIND
DIN BUM DUN RERD RIOT ALARM
BABEL BRUIT CHIME CHIRM CLANG
DEAVE DEEVE FRUSH NOISE RERDE
ALARUM BELDER CLAMOR FRAGOR
HUBBUB RACKET RATTLE STEVEN
TUMULT UPROAR CLANGOR
CLATTER DISCORD TURMOIL
DINGDONG TINTAMAR
DINAR DENARE MARAVEDI
DINDLE RING QUIVER THRILL TINGLE
TINKLE TREMOR STAGGER VIBRATE
DINE EAT SUP FARE FEAST REGALE
DINER EPICURE GOURMAND
DING DIN BEAT DANG DASH KICK
PUSH RING WHIP CLANG DRIVE
EXCEL FLING KNOCK PITCH POUND
PUNCH THUMP STROKE THRASH
THRUST
DINGE DENT DINT BATTER BRUISE
TARNISH
DINGHY SKIFF DINGEY ROWBOAT
SHALLOP SNOWBIRD
DINGLE DEN DALE DELL GLEN VALE
DIMBLE DUMBLE HOLLOW VALLEY
DINGMAN BUMPER
DINGO WARRAGAL WARRIGAL
DINGUS GADGET DOOHICKEY
DINGY DUN DARK DIRTY DUSKY
GRIMY OURIE SMOKY DINGHY
SUBFUSC SMIRCHED
DINING CENATION
DINING ROOM TRICLINIUM
DINKA JANGHEY
DINNER DINE HALL KALE MEAL
MEAT NOON BEANO FEAST DINING
REPAST BANQUET PUCHERO
FUNCTION
(**CEREMONIAL** —) SEDER
DINOSAUR DIAPSID SAURIAN
DUCKBILL NODOSAUR SAUROPOD
TROODONT
DINT BEAT BLOW DENT DUNT NICK
CLOUR DELVE DINGE FORCE NOTCH
ONSET POWER PRESS SHOCK
ATTACK CHANCE EFFORT STRIKE
STROKE IMPRINT EFFICACY
STRIKING

DIOCESAN EPISCOPAL
DIOCESE SEE EPARCHY DISTRICT
BISHOPRIC
DIODE KENOTRON
DIOLEFIN DIENE ALLENE HEXADIENE
DIOMEDES (FATHER OF —) MARS
TYDEUS
(**MOTHER OF** —) CYRENE DEIPYLE
(**WIFE OF** —) AEGIALE
DIONYSUS BACCHUS BROMIOS
BROMIUS LENAEUS LIKNITES
DIOPSIDE VIOLAN ALALITE
PYROXENE
DIORITE CORSITE DIABASE ORNOITE
APPINITE
DIOSCURI ALCIS ANACES ANAKES
CASTORES
DIOXIDE SILICA BINOXIDE
DIP DAP DIB DOP SOP BAIL DROP
DUCK DUNK LADE LAVE SINK SOAK
BATHE DELVE LADLE LOWER MERSE
PITCH SCOOP SLOPE SOUSE
SWOOP TAINT CANDLE HOLLOW
PLUNGE BAPTIZE DECLINE IMMERGE
IMMERSE INCLINE MOISTEN
DIPSTICK SUBMERGE
(— **AND THROW**) BAIL BALE
(— **IN DANCING**) CORTE
(— **INTO**) SAMPLE
(— **OUT**) KEACH
DIPENTENE CINENE CAJUPUTENE
DIPHTHONG BIVOCAL
DIPHTHONGIZED BROKEN
DIPLOIDIZE SPERMATIZE
DIPLOMA SANAD DEGREE SUNNUD
CHARTER CODICIL
DIPLOMACY TACT POLICE TREATY
DIPLOMAT DEAN ENVOY CONSUL
ATTACHE MINISTER
DIPLOMATIC SUAVE FECIAL FETIAL
DIPLOPIA POLYOBA AMBIOPIA
DIPNOAN DIPNOID MUDFISH
DIPODY METER METRE DIIAMB
SYZYGY
DIPPER BAIL GAWN PIET PLOW
GOURD HANDY LADLE SCOOP
SPOON BUCKET DUNKER PIGGIN
PLOUGH TUNKER DUNKARD PICKLER
CALABASH
(**ASTRONOMICAL** —) WAGON
WAGGON
DIPSOMANIA ENOMANIA POTOMANIA
DIPTERAN SYRPHID
DIPTERON DIPTER
DIPTEROUS BIALATE
DIRDUM BLOW BLAME DURDUM
OUTCRY REBUKE TUMULT UPROAR
SCOLDING
DIRE DERN EVIL FELL AWFUL FATAL
DEADLY DISMAL DREARY FUNEST
TRAGIC WOEFUL DIREFUL DOLEFUL
DRASTIC FEARFUL DREADFUL
FUNESTAL HORRIBLE TERRIBLE
ULTIMATE
DIRECT AIM BID CON KEN SAY SET
WIS AGYE AIRT BAIN BEAM BEND
BOSS CAST DEAD EDIT EVEN FLAT
FULL GAIN HEAD HELM HOLD LEAD
NEAR NIGH OPEN REIN SEND SOON

SWAY TELL TURN WAFT WEND WILL
WISE AIRTH APPLY AREAD AREED
BLANK BOUND BURLY COACH
DRESS ETTLE FLUSH FRAME FRANK
GUIDA GUIDE HIGHT INDEX LEVEL
ORDER PLUMP POINT REFER RIGHT
SPEED STEER TEACH TRAIN UTTER
WEISE WRITE ADVERT ARRECT
CUSTOS DEVOTE ENJOIN ENSIGN
FASTEN GOVERN GRAITH HANDLE
HOMELY HONEST IMPART INDITE
INFORM INTEND LINEAL MANAGE
MASTER MOSTRA REFORM SQUARE
STEADY STRECK TEMPER WITTER
ADDRESS APPOINT COMMAND
CONDUCT CONTROL CONVERT
DEICTIC DESTINE EXECUTE EXPRESS
FRONTAL GENERAL INSTANT
MARSHAL OFFICER PRESIDE
SPADISH ABSOLUTE CONVERSE
DEDICATE DIRECTOR HOMESPUN
IMMEDIAL INSTRUCT INTIMATE
MANUDUCE MANUDUCT MINISTER
OUTRIGHT REGULATE STRAIGHT
(— **AGAINST**) LAUNCH
(— **ATTENTION**) ATTEND
(— **BLOW**) MARK
(— **DOGS**) BLOW
(— **FALL OF TREE**) GUN
(— **HELMSMAN**) CON CONN
(— **HORSE**) HUP
(— **ITSELF**) TENT
(— **ONE'S COURSE**) HIT
(— **PROCEEDINGS**) PRESIDE
(— **SECRETLY**) STEAL
(— **SIDEWAYS**) SKLENT
(— **TO GO**) ADDRESS
(— **UPWARD**) MOUNT
DIRECTED FAST COMPULSORY
(— **FORWARD**) ANTRORSE
(— **TOWARD GOAL**) HORMIC
(— **UPWARD**) ERECT
DIRECTING AIM LEADING PRINCIPAL
DIRECTION AIM RUN WAY AIRT
BENT CARE DUCT EAST EGIS GATE
HAND LEFT PART ROAD RULE WEST
WORD YARD AEGIS ANGLE COAST
DRIFT EAVER KIBLA NORTH ORDER
PARTY POINT QIBLA RANGE ROUTE
SENSE SOUTH TENOR TREND
ASPECT COURSE DESIGN ADDRESS
BEARING BIDDING CHANNEL
COMMAND CONDUCT CONTROL
COUNSEL DICTATE HEADING
HELMAGE MANDATE PRECEPT
STRETCH BEARINGS CALENDAR
DELEATUR DIAGONAL GUIDANCE
STEERAGE STEERING TENDENCY
(— **OF CURRENT**) AXIS
(— **OF FLOW**) SET
(— **OF ROCK CLEAVAGE**) GRAIN
(— **OF WIND**) EYE CORNER
(— **OUTWARD**) BEAM
(—**S FOR DELIVERY**) ADDRESS
(**DANCE** —) CALL
(**HORIZONTAL** —) COURSE AZIMUTH
(**OBLIQUE** —) SKEW
(**OPPOSITE** —) EYE COUNTER
(**SINGING** —) GIMEL GYMEL

DIRECTIVE DICTATE CIRCULAR
DIRECTLY DUE BANG BOLT DEAD
FLAT GAIN JUST MEAN PLAT PLUM
SLAP SOON PLAIN PLUMB POINT
ROUND SHEER SOUSE SPANG
STANG ARIGHT CLEVER SIMPLY
SQUARE RIGHTLY SHEERLY
OUTRIGHT PROMPTLY SLAPDASH
STRAIGHT
DIRECTNESS CLARITY IMMEDIACY
DIRECTOR BOSS HEAD COACH
GUIDE PILOT STAFF ARCHON
BISHOP LEADER MASTER RECTOR
WARDEN CURATOR DESKMAN
MANAGER PREFECT STARETS
STERNER TRAINER ACCENTOR
DISPOSER GOVERNOR PRAEFECT
PRODUCER TETRARCH
DIRECTORY PIE BOOK
DIRGE KEEN SONG ELEGY KINAH
LINOS LINUS QINAH TANGI HEARSE
LAMENT MONODY THRENE EPICEDE
REQUIEM CORONACH THRENODY
ULLAGONE
DIRIGIBLE BLIMP AIRSHIP
DIRK SNEE SKEAN SWORD DAGGER
SKHIAN SKIVER
DIRT FEN MUD PAY DUST GORE
GUCK MUCK NAST SOIL SUMP
EARTH FILTH GRIME GROUT SEUCH
SEUGH TRASH GRAVEL GROUND
REFUSE MULLOCK MUCKMENT
DIRTINESS GRIME JAKES
DIRTY LOW BASE CLAT DIRT FOUL
MUSS SOIL WORY BAWDY BLACK
CABBY DINGY FOGGY GRIMY GUSTY
HORRY MUDDY NASTY POUSY SOILY
SULLY BEMIRE CLARTY CLATTY
DEFILE DIRTEN FILTHY FULYIE
FULZIE GREASY GRUBBY IMPURE
MUSSED POUCEY SCRIMY SLASHY
SLURRY SMUTTY SOILED SORDID
STORMY BEGRIME BROOKED
BROOKIE BRUCKLE CLOUDED
GRUFTED IMBROIN MUDDIED
ROYNOUS SLOTTER SMUTCHY
SQUALID SULLIED TARNISH
UNCLEAN SLOBBERY SLOTTERY
SOAPLESS
DISABLE OUT HOCK LAME MAIM
BREAK CHINK CROCK GRUEL UNFIT
WRECK BRUISE DISMAY UNABLE
WEAKEN CRIPPLE
(— CANNON) SPIKE
(— TANK) BELLY
DISABLED LAME INVALID
DISABLING BUM
DISACCHARIDE BIOSE LACTOSE
MALTOSE SUCROSE
DISACCUSTOM DISUSE
DISACKNOWLEDGE DISCLAIM
DISADVANTAGE HURT MISS RISK
LURCH WORRY DAMAGE DENIAL
INJURY STRIKE DICKENS PENALTY
UNSELTH UNSPEED DISAVAIL
DISFAVOR HANDICAP
DISADVANTAGEOUS HURTFUL
INCONVENIENT
DISAFFECT DEBAUCH ESTRANGE

DISAFFECTED FALSE UNTRUE
DISEASED DISLOYAL FORSWORN
PERJURED RECREANT
DISAFFECTION DECEIT MUTINY
DISEASE DISGUST DISLIKE
DISORDER HOSTILITY
DISAFFIRM DENY ANNUL REVERSE
DISCLAIM
DISAGREE VARY ARGUE DIFFER
DISCEPT DISCORD DISSENT
QUARREL CONFLICT
DISAGREEABLE BAD ILL ACID EVIL
FOUL PERT SOUR UGLY VILE AWFUL
CROSS HARSH NASTY STIFF
GREASY PUTRID ROTTEN SNUFFY
STICKY UNEASY UNGAIN CHRONIC
COMICAL GHASTLY HATEFUL
INGRATE IRKSOME NAUGHTY
UNLUSTY CHISELLY KINDLESS
TERRIBLE UNGENIAL UNLIKELY
UNLOVELY UNSAVORY
DISAGREEABLENESS ILLNESS
ASPERITY
DISAGREEABLY HARSHLY
DISAGREEING ODD DISSENTIVE
DISAGREEMENT BREE CLASH
CROSS FIGHT BREACH FRATCH
DISCORD DISGUST DISPUTE DISSENT
FISSURE MISLIKE QUARREL
WRANGLE ARGUMENT DISTANCY
DIVISION FRICTION SQUABBLE
VARIANCE
(IN —) APART
DISALLOW FORBID REJECT
CENSURE DISCLAIM DISPROVE
PROHIBIT
DISAPPEAR DIE FLY DROP FADE
FALL FLEE LIFT PASS SINK WEND
WHOP CLEAR FAINT LAPSE SLIDE
SNUFF REMOVE RETIRE VANISH
EVANISH IMMERGE DISSOLVE
EVANESCE
(— GRADUALLY) ELY FADE DRAIN
EVANESCE
(— SUDDENLY) COOK DUCK BURST
MIZZLE
DISAPPEARANCE ECLIPSE
FADEAWAY
DISAPPOINT BALK BILK FAIL FALL
MOCK SOUR UNDO CHEAT SNAPE
BAFFLE DEFEAT DELUDE OUTWIT
THWART BEGUILE DECEIVE
DESTROY FALSIFY NULLIFY
DISPOINT
DISAPPOINTED OUTED THROWN
SOREHEAD
DISAPPOINTING FIERCE
FALLACIOUS
DISAPPOINTMENT RUE BALK SUCK
BAULK LURCH DENIAL LETDOWN
COMEDOWN
DISAPPROBATION ODIUM DISLIKE
DISAPPROVAL BAN BOOH HISS
VETO CATCALL CENSURE DISFAVOR
DISGRACE
DISAPPROVE GROAN REJECT
RESENT CENSURE CONDEMN
DISLIKE MISTAKE PROTEST
DISALLOW DISPROVE

DISAPPROVED DISTASTED
DISAPPROVER WOWSER
DISARM SUBDUE UNSTEEL
DISARRANGE MUSS DEFORM
GARBLE RUFFLE TIFFLE UNTIDY
UNTUNE CLUTTER CONFUSE
DERANGE DISTURB RUMMAGE
SLATTER TROUBLE COCKBILL
DISHEVEL DISORDER UNSETTLE
(— TYPE) SQUABBLE
DISARRANGEMENT DISARRAY
DISARRAY MESS STRIP CADDLE
DISRAY FUFFLE HUDDLE DESPOIL
UNDIGHT DISHEVEL DISORDER
DISARRAYED UNKEMPT
DISASSEMBLE STRIP DEMOUNT
DISMOUNT
(— CASK) SHAKE
DISASSEMBLY TAKEDOWN
TEARDOWN
DISASSOCIATE SEVER SEPARATE
DISASTER ILL WOE BALE BLOW EVIL
FATE RUIN GRIEF MISHAP STROKE
REVERSE ACCIDENT CALAMITY
CASUALTY EXIGENCY FATALITY
DISASTROUS BAD ILL FATAL WEARY
SINISTER
DISAVOW DENY DEVOW ABJURE
DISOWN RECANT REFUSE DECLINE
RETRACT ABNEGATE DISCLAIM
DISVOUCH RENOUNCE
DISAVOWAL DENIAL
DISBAND BREAK REDUCE REFORM
ADJOURN CASHIER DISMISS
RELEASE SCATTER DISSOLVE
DISBAR EXCLUDE
DISBELIEF ATHEISM SCRUPLE
DISBELIEVE DOUBT REJECT
SUSPECT DISCOUNT DISCREDIT
DISBELIEVER ATHEIST HERETIC
INFIDEL
DISBURDEN RID EASE CLEAR
UNLOAD DELIVER DISLOAD RELIEVE
DISBURSE SPEND DEFRAY EXPEND
OUTLAY DEBURSE
DISC (ALSO SEE DISK) DIAL DISK
BLANK MEDAL PATEN PLATE QUOIT
COLTER RECORD RONDEL COULTER
DISCOID PLATTER TROCHUS
(— FOR PRESSING HERRINGS)
DAUNT
DISCANT HOCKET
DISCARD CAST DECK JILT JUNK
MOLT OMIT OUST SHED CHUCK
DITCH FLING SCRAP SHUCK SLUFF
THROW CHANGE DECARD DISUSE
DIVEST EXCUSS REJECT SLOUGH
ABANDON CASHIER DISMISS
EXPUNGE FORSAKE ABDICATE
JETTISON
(— IN BRIDGE) ECHO
DISCARDED DORMANT
DISCARDING DISPOSAL
DISCERN KEN SEE SPY WIT DEEM
ESPY KNOW READ SCAN JUDGE
SIGHT BEHOLD DESCRY DETECT
DEVISE NOTICE PIERCE SCERNE
DIGNOSCE DISCOVER PERCEIVE
DISCERNIBLE EVIDENT VISIBLE

APPARENT MANIFEST

DISCERNING SAGE WISE SHREWD
SAPIENT

DISCERNMENT EYE DOOM GOUT
TACT FLAIR SENSE SKILL TASTE
ACUMEN INSIGHT ELECTION
JUDGMENT SAGACITY

DISCHARGE AX DO AXE CAN GUN
LET RUN BOLT BOOT CASS DUMP
EMIT FIRE FLOW FLUX FREE GIVE
KICK PASS POUR QUIT RIFF SACK
SEND SHOT VENT VOID BLAST
BLEED BRUSH CLEAR DRAIN EJECT
EMPTY EXPEL EXUDE FRUSH GLEET
GRASS ICHOR ISSUE LOOSE OZENA
PURGE RHEUM SHOOT SPEED
START VOMIT WHIFF YIELD ACQUIT
ASSOIL BOUNCE DEFRAY EFFECT
EXCERN EXEMPT EXHALE FEEDER
LOCHIA OZAENA TICKET UNLADE
UNLOAD ABSOLVE CASHIER
DEBOUCH DEFEASE DEHISCE
DELIVER DERAIGN DISBAND DISMISS
EXCRETE EXHAUST MISSION
PAYMENT PERFORM QUIETUS
RELEASE RELIEVE SATISFY SKITTER
SOLUTIO CATAPULT COMPOUND
DEFECATE DESPATCH DISGORGE
DISPATCH DISPLACE DISPLODE
EMISSION EVACUATE MITTIMUS
OUTSHOOT PERSOLVE SEPARATE
SOLUTION STREAMER
(— **ARROW**) TWANG
(— **BULLET**) DRIVE
(— **CARGO**) STRIKE
(— **DEBT**) MEET CLEAR LOOSING
(— **DUTY**) SERVE
(— **FROM HORSE'S FOOT**) FRUSH
(— **FROM RESERVOIR**) HUSHING
(— **MATTER**) WEEP
(— **OF DEBT**) SETOFF
(— **OF GAS**) FEEDER
(— **OF STREAM**) FALL SPOUT
(— **SUDDENLY**) HIKE
(**BLOODY** —) SHOW SANIES
(**CANNON** —) TIRE CANNON
(**CONCENTRATED** —) BARRAGE
(**DISHONORABLE** —) BOBTAIL
(**ELECTRIC** —) SPARK LEADER
EFFLUVE STREAMER LIGHTNING
(**ELECTRIC** —S) STATIC
(**HEAVY** —) STORM
(**SIMULTANEOUS** —) SALVO
BROADSIDE FUSILLADE

DISCHARGED SPED SATISFIED

DISCHARGER EXCITATOR

DISCHARGING LABILE

DISCIPLE SON JOHN MARK CHELA
JUDAS MURID PETER PUPIL TEACH
TRAIN ANANDA DISPLE DORCAS
HEARER PUNISH APOSTLE AUDITOR
MATTHEW OVIDIAN SCHOLAR
SECTARY SRAVAKA STUDENT
ADHERENT FOLLOWER GALENIST
SECTATOR

DISCIPLINARIAN RAMROD TRAINER
MARTINET

DISCIPLINARY STRICT

DISCIPLINE THEW WHIP BREAK

DRILL INURE TEACH TRAIN CHURCH
ETHICS FERULA FERULE GOVERN
INFORM PUNISH SEASON TAIRGE
VIRTUE CHASTEN CORRECT
CULTURE EDUCATE FURNACE
NURTURE SCOURGE DISCIPLE
DOCTRINE EXERCISE INSTRUCT
LEARNING MATHESIS PEDAGOGY
REGULATE RESTRAIN TEACHING
TRAINING TUTORING
(**MENTAL** —) YOGA
(**RELIGIOUS** —) CHURCH PENANCE
SADHANA

DISCIPLINED INURED STEADY

DISCLAIM DENY DEVOW ABJURE
DISOWN REFUSE DISAVOW
ABDICATE ABNEGATE DISALLOW
RENOUNCE

DISCLOSE OPE RIP BARE BLOW
CALL KNOW OPEN TELL BREAK
COUGH UNRIP UNWRY UTTER
BETRAY BEWRAY DESCRY DIVINE
EVOLVE EXPOSE IMPART REVEAL
SHRIVE UNBURY UNCASE UNHASP
UNHIDE UNLOCK UNROLL UNSEAL
UNSHUT UNVEIL UNWRAP CONFESS
DEVELOP DISCUSS DISPLAY
DIVULGE EXHIBIT EXPLAIN UNCLOSE
UNCOVER DISCOVER INDICATE
MANIFEST UNBUNDLE UNKENNEL
UNSECRET UNTHATCH

DISCLOSED OUT

DISCLOSURE REVEAL SHRIFT
COLORING DESCRIAL DISCLOSE
OVERTURE

DISCOLOR FOX BURN FADE SPOT
BLACK SMOKE STAIN TINGE SMIRCH
STREAK DISTAIN TARNISH
BESMIRCH

DISCOLORATION CORN BLEED
SCALD SPECK STAIN TINGE FOXING
LIVEDO MILDEW ARGYRIA BURNING
MELASMA BRONZING BROWNING
CHLOASMA CYANOSIS DYSCHROA
SCALDING
(— **OF FRUIT**) SUNBURN
(— **OF TURKEYS**) BLUEBACK
(— **ON CHOCOLATE**) BLOOM
(— **ON CURED FISH**) RUST
(**SMALL** —) FRECKLE

DISCOLORED HAW FOUL DINGY
FOXED RUSTY STAINED SCORCHED
USTULATE
(— **BY DECAY**) DOTY FOXED

DISCOMFIT MATE ROIT ABASH
ABAVE AFLEY SHEND SHENT UPSET
WORST BAFFLE DEFEAT FEAGUE
SQUASH CONFUSE CONQUER
DISTURB

DISCONCERT BASH BOWL FAZE
FUSS HACK ABASH BLANK DAUNT
FEEZE PHASE UPSET WORRY
BAFFLE BLENCH MISPUT PUZZLE
RATTLE SQUASH CONFUSE DISTURB
FLUMMOX NONPLUS PERTURB
SQUELCH BROWBEAT DISORDER

DISCONCERTED BLANK ASHAMED
RATTLED CONFUSED

DISCONNECT UNDO SEVER DIVIDE

UNYOKE DISJOIN DISSOLVE
DISUNITE SEPARATE UNCOUPLE

DISCONNECTED LOOSE ABRUPT
BROKEN CHOPPY CURSORY
DECOUSU RAMBLING STACCATO

DISCONSOLATE SAD GLOOMY
WOEFUL DOLEFUL FORLORN
UNCOUTH DEJECTED DESOLATE
DOWNCAST HOPELESS

DISCONTENT ENVY DISQUIET
SOURNESS

DISCONTENTED DUMPY

DISCONTINUANCE BREAK LAPSE
DEMISE CUTBACK DISUNION
SHUTDOWN

DISCONTINUE END DROP HALT
QUIT STOP BREAK CEASE CLOSE
LETUP DESIST DISUSE SUNDER
DISRUPT SUSPEND INTERMIT
SURCEASE

DISCONTINUITY JAR BREAK

DISCONTINUOUS BROKEN
DISJUNCT SALTATORY

DISCORD DIN JAR BROIL JANGLE
SCHISM STRIFE DISLIKE FACTION
FISSURE JARRING MISTONE
CONFLICT DISTANCE DIVISION
FRACTION MISCHIEF UNSAUGHT
VARIANCE

DISCORDANT AJAR RUDE CRONK
HARSH FROWZY HOARSE JANGLY
HIDEOUS JARRING SQUAWKY
ABSONANT CONTRARY JANGLING

DISCOUNT AGIO BATTA SHAVE
REBATE REDUCE DISCOMPT

DISCOURAGE CARP DAMP CHILL
DAUNT DETER FROST DAMPEN
DEJECT DISMAY FREEZE STIFLE
DEPRESS FLATTEN INHIBIT DISPIRIT
DISSUADE

DISCOURAGEMENT COLD DAMP
DAUNT LETDOWN PUTBACK

DISCOURAGING CHILL DREARY

DISCOURSE SAW CARP RANT READ
TALE TALK TELL WORD DROOL
FABLE ORATE PAPER SPEAK SPELL
THEME TRACT TREAT COMMON
DILATE EULOGY HOMILY PARLEY
PREACH REASON SCREED SERMON
THESIS TREATY ACCOUNT ADDRESS
COMMENT CONTEXT DECLAIM
DELIVER DESCANT DIETARY
DISCANT DISCUSS DISSERT
ENTREAT EXPOUND GRAMMAR
LECTURE NARRATE ORATION
PRATING PRELECT PURPOSE
TALKING ARGUMENT COLLOQUY
CONVERSE EXERCISE LOCUTION
LOQUENCE PARLANCE SPEAKING
SPELLING TRACTATE TREATISE
(— **OF LITTLE VALUE**) STUFF
(**LAUDATORY** —) PANEGYRIC
(**LONG** —) SCREED
(**PROLONGED** —) DIATRIBE
(**SERIOUS** —) HOMILY
(**SIMPLE** —) PAP
(**UNIMAGINATIVE** —) PROSE
(**PL.**) EXOTERICS

DISCOURTEOUS RUDE SCURVY

UNCIVIL UNHENDE IMPOLITE
UNGENTLE
DISCOURTESY CUT SLIGHT
DISCOVER RIP SEE SPY WIT ESPY
FEEL FIND PICK TWIG CATCH LEARN
SPELL DEFINE DESCRY DETECT
DIVINE EXPOSE IMPART INVENT
LOCATE OVERGO REVEAL STRIKE
UNHIDE CONFESS DESCURE
DEVELOP DISCERN DISCURE
DISPLAY DIVULGE EXHIBIT EXPLORE
UNCOVER UNEARTH CONTRIVE
DECIPHER DESCRIBE DISCUREN
MANIFEST UNKENNEL
DISCOVERABLE VISIBLE
DISCOVERER SPY SCOUT
COLUMBUS EXPLORER INVENTOR
DISCOVERY FIND TROVE DESCRY
ESPIAL STRIKE DESCRIAL
DISCREDIT FOUL DECRY DOUBT
REFEL DEFACE DEFECT ASPERSE
BLEMISH DESTROY IMPEACH
SCANDAL SUSPECT BELITTLE
DISGRACE DISHONOR DISTRUST
REPROACH UNCREDIT
DISCREDITABLE BLACK UNHONEST
DISCREET WARY WISE CIVIL
HUSHED POLITE SILENT CAREFUL
GUARDED POLITIC PRUDENT
CAUTIOUS RESERVED RETICENT
DISCREETLY SENSIBLY
DISCREPANCY VARIANCE
DISCREPANT VARIANT CONTRARY
DISSONANT
DISCRETE ETERNAL DISTINCT
DISCRETION TACT WISDOM
CONDUCT RETENUE COURTESY
JUDGMENT PRUDENCE
DISCRIMINATE PART SEVER
SECERN DISCERN PERCEIVE
SEPARATE
DISCRIMINATED DISTINCT
DISCRIMINATING GOOD NICE
ACUTE SHARP ASTUTE CHOICE
SELECT CHOOSEY CRITICAL
EXPLICIT
DISCRIMINATINGLY CHOICE FINELY
DISCRIMINATION EYE DOOM TACT
TASTE ACUMEN CHOICE FINESSE
RESPECT DELICACY SAPIENCE
(SYMBOL OF —) HANSA
DISCURSIVE ROVING CURSORY
RAMBLING DESULTORY
DISCURSIVELY WIDE
DISCUS DISC DISK QUOIT DISKOS
DISCOID
DISCUSS AIR MOOT RUNE TALK
ARGUE BANDY COVER DANDY
TRACT TREAT COMMON CONFER
DEBATE DICKER EMPARL EXCUSS
IMPARL PARLEY AGITATE BESPEAK
CANVASS COMMENT CONSULT
DESCANR DESCANT DISCANT
DISCEPT DISCUTE DISPUTE DISSERT
EXAMINE NARRATE TRAVERSE
(— AT LENGTH) BAT
(— CASUALLY) MENTION
(— EXCITEDLY) AGITATE
(— LIGHTLY) BANDY

(— QUICKLY) SKIP
(— SECRETLY) ROUN
(— TERMS) CHAFFER
(— THOROUGHLY) EXHAUST
DISCUSSION MOOT DEBAT FORUM
COMMON CONFAB DEBATE HASSEL
HOMILY HUDDLE PARLEY TREATY
BARGAIN CANVASS COMMENT
COUNSEL DISCUSS DISPUTE
MOOTING PRIBBLE ARGUMENT
CAUSERIE CHINFEST COLLOQUY
DIATRIBE ENTREATY EXCURSUS
QUESTION
(CONTROVERSIAL —) DISPUTE
(DIDACTIC —) HARANGUE
DISDAIN TUT DAIN DEFY PRIDE
SCORN SDAIN SPURN SDEIGN
SLIGHT CONTEMN DESPISE
CONTEMPT
DISDAINFUL COY DIGNE SAUCY
TOSSY SCORNY SLIGHT SNIFFY
SNUFFY DAINFUL HAUGHTY
ARROGANT DEIGNOUS SCORNFUL
SNIFFISH TOPLOFTY
DISDAINFULLY SMALL SNIFFILY
DISEASE BUG FLU MAL ROT BATS
COTH CRUD EVIL FLAW GOUT GRIP
NOMA PEST PHOS SORE AGROM
BATTS BEJEL BENDS CAUSE COTHE
CROUP DECAY DOLOR FEVER GRIEF
LUPUS PHOSS PINTA PINTO SCALL
SHAKE SPRUE SURRA AINHUM
ANGINA CANCER CARATE CORYZA
COURAP DENGUE GRAVEL GRIPPE
HERPES MALADY MORBUS PALMUS
PIEDRA POPEYE SCURVY SICKEN
SURRAH UROSIS ZOOSIS AILMENT
ALASTIM CHOLERA COXALGY
DECLINE ENDEMIC ENTASIA
LANGUOR LEPROSY MALEASE
MISLIKE MYCOSIS MYIASIS PATHEMA
RAPHANY SCOURGE SEQUELA
SERPIGO SIBBENS SORANCE
SYCOSIS XERASIA ZYMOTIC
ATHEROMA BERIBERI COXALGIA
CRIPPLER CYNANCHE DIAMONDS
ENZOOTIC JAUNDICE LEUKEMIA
PALUDISM PANDEMIC PELLAGRA
RAPHANIA SCABBADO SICKNESS
SMALLPOX SORRANCE STAGGERS
SYPHILIS UNHEALTH XANTHOMA
ZOONOSIS
(— OF ANIMALS, GENERAL) ROT
CLAP CORE FIRE GOUT HUSK LICK
WEED APTHA CLEFT CLING CLOSH
COTHE CROOK DRUSE FARCY
FLAPS NENTA NGANA PAINS SPEED
SWEAT TAINT APHTHA AVIVES
BROSOT CANKER CARNEY CREEPS
FARCIN GARGET GRAPES LAMPAS
NAGANA ROUGET SPAVIN SURRAH
WOBBLE ANTHRAX BIGHEAD
CALCINO CALORIS CARCEAG
DOURING EARWORM EQUINIA
FASHION FISTULA FOUNDER
FROUNCE KETOSIS LAMPERS
MURRAIN MURRINA QUITTER
QUITTOR SLOBBER SOLDIER
TAKOSIS BULLNOSE CRATCHES

CRIPPLES FERNSICK FOOTHALT
HORSEPOX HYSTERIA MAWBOUND
SLOBBERS SNUFFLES THWARTER
VACCINIA EPIZOOTIC
(— OF APPLES) CORK BLOTCH
(— OF BANANAS) SIGATOKA
SQUIRTER
(— OF BARLEY) STRIPE
(— OF BEES) SACBROOD
(— OF BEETS) HEARTROT
(— OF BIRDS) GOUT
(— OF BLUEBERRY) BLUESTEM
(— OF CABBAGE) CLUBROOT
(— OF CATERPILLARS) WILT
FLACHERY
(— OF CATTLE) TURN BLAIN CLOSH
FARCY HOOZE COWPOX GARGET
GRAPES HAMMER HEAVES ANTHRAX
BLACKLEG
(— OF CEREALS) ERGOT
(— OF CHICKEN) PIP CORYZA
(— OF COTTON) HYBOSIS CYRTOSIS
STENOSIS
(— OF DUCKLING) KEEL
(— OF EYES) WALL GLAUCOMA
SYNECHIA TRACHOMA
(— OF FIGS) SMUT
(— OF FINGERNAILS) FLAW
(— OF FLAX) BROWNING
(— OF FOWLS) PIP CRAY ROUP
GAPES SOREHEAD
(— OF GRAIN) ILIAU ICTERUS
(— OF GRAPES) COLEUR ERINOSE
ROUGEAU ROUGEOT SHELLING
(— OF HAWKS) RYE CRAY CROAK
CROAKS FROUNCE
(— OF HORSES) HAW CLAP MOSE
MULE WEED FARCY LEUMA SCALMA
DOURINE SARCOID AZOTURIA
GLANDERS HORSEPOX STRANGLES
(— OF LAMB) SWAYBACK
(— OF LETTUCE) STUNT
(— OF NARCISSUS) SMOLDER
SMOULDER
(— OF ONION) SMUDGE
(— OF ORANGE) LEPROSIS
(— OF PALMS) KOLERUGA
(— OF PLANTS, GENERAL) POX ROT
BUNT CORK DROP FIRE GOUT KNOT
PULP SMUT BLAST DWARF EDEMA
ERGOT FLECK FLOCK GRUBS SCALD
SCALE SCURF SEREH SPIKE STUNT
TUKRA TWIST AUCUBA BLIGHT
BLOTCH BLUING BRAUNE CALICO
CANKER COLEUR GIRDLE OEDEMA
OIDIUM PETECA SMUDGE STREAK
STRIPE VIROSE BLISTER BLUEING
BRINDLE CRINKLE DIEBACK ERINOSE
EYESPOT FROGEYE HYBOSIS
MEASLES PRURIGO ROSETTE
SHATTER SMOLDER STIPPEN
TIPBURN TOMOSIS VIRUELA
WALLOON BLUESTEM BREAKING
BROWNING BUCKSKIN CLUBROOT
CYRTOSIS DARTROSE EXANTHEM
FLYSPECK GUMMOSIS KOLEROGA
LEPROSIS MELANOSE MELAXUMA
POLEBURN PSOROSIS SMOULDER

STENOSIS VIROSITY WHIPTAIL
WILDFIRE
(— OF POTATO) CURL HAYWIRE
(— OF RABBITS) SNUFFLES
(— OF RICE) BLAST SPECK
(— OF SHEEP) CAW COE GID MAD
ROT BANE BELT CORE HALT WIND
BLAST BLOOD BRAXY GILLAR
OVINIA PINING STURDY ANTHRAX
BRADSOT DAISING RUBBERS
SCRAPIE THWARTER WILDFIRE
(— OF SILKWORM) UJI CALCINO
GATTINE PEBRINE FLACHERY
(— OF SUGARCANE) ILIAU SEREH
EYESPOT
(— OF SWINE) GARGET
(— OF TOBACCO) ETCH CALICO
BRINDLE FROGEYE
(— OF TOMATO) FERNLEAF
GRAYWALL
(— OF TREES) KNOT
(— OF TULIPS) SHANKING
(— OF UNKNOWN ORIGIN) AINHUM
ACRODYNIA
(CAISSON —) CHOKES
(FOOT-AND-MOUTH —) AFTOSA
(FUNGUS —) PECK
(KIDNEY —) RIPPLE
(LUNG —) CON
(MUSHROOM —) FLOCK
(SKIN —) ACNE SCAB FAVUS HIVES
LEPRA MANGE PSORA SCALL TINEA
ECZEMA LICHEN TETTER EXORMIA
PORRIGO PURPURA SERPIGO
VERRUGA IMPETIGO MILIARIA
MYCETOMA SHINGLES VERRUGAS
VITILIGO
(VENEREAL —) BURNING SYPHILIS
(WINE —) GRAISSE
DISEASED BAD EVIL SICKLY
MORBOSE PECCANT VICIOUS
MORBIFIC
DISEMBARK LAND ALIGHT DEBARK
UNBARK UNBOAT DISBOARD
DISEMBARRASS EXTRICATE
DISEMBODIED SEPARATE
DISBODIED FLESHLESS
DISEMBODIMENT SOUL SPIRIT
DISEMBOGUE MOUTH
DISEMBOWEL GUT HULK PAUNCH
DEBOWEL EMBOWEL GARBAGE
UNTRIPE GRALLOCH
DISEMIC DIMORIC DICHRONOUS
DISENCHANT DISMAY
DISENCHANTED SOUR
DISENCUMBER RID FREE REDD
UNCUMBER
DISENGAGE FREE CLEAR EDUCE
UNTIE DETACH EVOLVE LOOSEN
CUTOVER DISGAGE RELEASE
UNRAVEL LIBERATE UNCLUTCH
DISENTANGLE CARD COMB FREE
REED TOSE TOZE CLEAR LOOSE
RAVEL TEASE EVOLVE SCUTCH
SLEAVE UNMAZE UNMESH RESOLVE
UNRAVEL UNREAVE UNTWINE
UNTWIST OUTTWINE UNTANGLE
DISENTANGLEMENT SOLUTION
DISESTEEM UMBRAGE DISVALUE

DISFAVOR DUTCH ODIUM DISLIKE
OFFENCE OFFENSE UMBRAGE
MALGRACE
DISFIGURE MAR BLUR FOUL MAIM
SCAR DEFACE DEFEAT DEFORM
INJURE MANGLE BLEMISH DISGRACE
DISGUISE MUTILATE
DISFIGURED FOUL DEFET DEFEIT
DEFORMED
DISFIGUREMENT SCAR BLEMISH
CATFACE DEFORMITY
DISGORGE SPEW VENT EJECT
EMPTY VOMIT
DISGRACE BLOT FOIL FOUL HISS
LACK SLUR SMIT SOIL SPOT TASH
ABASE CRIME ODIUM SCORN SHAME
SHEND SPITE STAIN TAINT BAFFLE
BEFOUL BISMER HUMBLE INFAMY
REBUKE STIGMA VILIFY AFFRONT
ATTAINT DEGRADE OBLOQUY
OFFENCE OFFENSE REPROOF
SCANDAL SLANDER UMBRAGE
CONTEMPT DISHONOR IGNOMINY
REPROACH SHENDING UNWORTHY
VILLAINY
DISGRACEFUL MEAN SOUR FILTHY
INDIGN IGNOBLE CRIMINAL
DEFAMOUS INHONEST SHAMEFUL
DISGRUNTLED SORE PEEVISH
DISGUISE DAUB FACE HIDE LAIN
LEAN MASK VEIL BELIE CLOAK
COLOR COUCH COVER FEIGN
GLOZE GUISE SHADE VISOR VIZOR
COVERT DEFORM IMMASK MANTLE
MASQUE VIZARD CONCEAL
OBSCURE PRETEND PURPORT
COLORING DISLIKEN MISGUISE
PALLIATE PRETENCE PRETENSE
TRAVESTY UMBRELLA
(— INFORMATION) LAYNE
DISGUISED COVERT FUCATE GILDED
LATENT MYSTIC FEIGNED PALLIATE
TRAVESTY
DISGUST IRK LOATH REPEL SHOCK
STALL DEGOUT HORROR NAUSEA
OFFEND REVOLT SICKEN STOMACH
SURFEIT AVERSION DISTASTE
KREISTLE LOATHING NAUSEATE
SICKNESS
DISGUSTED IRK SICK IRKSOME
DISGUSTING FOUL PERT VILE
LOUSY MUCKY NASTY FILTHY
SCRIMY SICKLY BEASTLY FULSOME
HATEFUL LOATHLY MAWKISH
NOISOME OBSCENE SHITTEN
FOULSOME LOATHFUL NAUSEOUS
SHOCKING
DISH CAP CAUP CUSH DISC DISK
FOOL MEAT MOLD PLAT SOLE
BASIN BATEA COMAL DEVIL MOULD
NAPPY PATEN PINAX PLATE SHAPE
BASQUE BASSIE BICKER BLAZER
BUTTER CHAFER CRITCH CUSCUS
ENTREE FONDUE LUGGIE OLIVES
PADDLE PANADA PATERA PATINA
PHIALE RECIPE SAUCER SUNDAE
TAMALE TUREEN BALANCE
BOBOTEE BOBOTIE CEVICHE
CHARGER COCOTTE COMPORT

COMPOTE CRESSET DORMANT
DOUBLER EPERGNE PAPBOAT
PATELLA PLATEAU PLATTER
RAMEKIN SCUTTLE SUPREME
TERRINE TIMBALE AMATORIO
CIOPPINO CLAPDISH COQUILLE
COUSCOUS GALATINE KEDGEREE
MAZARINE POWSODDY STANDARD
ENTREMETS
(— IN PYRAMID STYLE) BUISSON
(BAKING —) SCALLOP SCOLLOP
(BRAISED —) HASLET
(CHAFING —) CHAFER CHOFFER
(FANCY —) SURPRISE
(FLAT —) COMAL CHARGER
(HIGH-FLAVORED —) HOGO
(JEWISH —) CHOLENT
(PHILIPPINE —) BURO
(PIE —) COFFIN
(PILE OF —S) BUNG
(ROMAN —) LANX PATERA PATINA
(SAILOR'S —) SCOUSE
(SCOTTISH —) BROSE
(SIDE —) OUTWORK
(SWEET —) JUNKET FLUMMERY
(TASTY —) MORSEL
(WOODEN —) CUP CAUP BOWIE
GOGGAN LUGGIE KICKSHAW
(PL.) GARNISH BAKEWARE
FLATWARE ENTREMETS
DISHABILLE MOB DISARRAY
DISORDER NEGLIGEE
DISHARMONY SCHISM ADHARMA
FRACTION
DISHCLOTH DISHRAG
DISHCLOTH GOURD LOOFAH
PATOLA DISHRAG
DISHEARTEN AMATE DAUNT FAINT
DEJECT DEPRESS FLATTEN
UNHEART UNNERVE DISHEART
DISPIRIT
DISHEARTENED DULL GLOOMY
DOWNCAST DEPRESSED
DISHEARTENING GLOOMY
DESOLATE
DISHEVEL MUSS TOWZE RUFFLE
TOUSEL TOUSLE TUMBLE TRACHLE
DISARRAY DISORDER
DISHEVELED ROOKY BLOUSY
BLOWZY FROWZY TUMBLED
UNKEMPT FROWZLED SHEVELED
SLIPSHOD TATTERED
DISHONEST FOUL LEWD CRONK
FALSE LYING QUEER SNIDE TWISTY
UNFAIR UNJUST CORRUPT
CROOKED KNAVISH INDECENT
INDIRECT SHAMEFUL SINISTER
UNCHASTE UNHONEST
DISHONESTLY DOUBLY FALSELY
DISHONESTY IMPROBITY
DISHONOR FILE FOUL ABASE ABUSE
ODIUM SHAME SPITE STAIN WRONG
DEFAME DEFILE DEFORM INFAMY
VILIFY DEGRADE DISTAIN OBLOQUY
SLANDER VIOLATE DISGLORY
DISGRACE DISPLUME IGNOMINY
REPROACH VILLAINY
DISHONORABLE BASE FOUL MEAN
BLACK NASTY SHABBY YELLOW

IGNOBLE SHAMEFUL UNHONEST
UNWORTHY
DISHONORED DEFAMED
DISHPAN KEELER
DISHRACK FIDDLE
DISHWASHER SWILLER
DISILLUSION SOUR DISMAY
DISINCLINATION NILL UNLUST
UNWILL DISLIKE QUARREL
AVERSION DISTASTE
DISINCLINED LOTH LOATH AFRAID
AVERSE HESITANT
(— TO) ABOVE
DISINFECT SCRUB SEASON
CLEANSE SWEETEN
DISINFECTANT IODINE PHENOL
CREOLIN EUGENOL TACHIOL
FUMIGANT HALAZONE PARAFORM
DISINGENUOUS FALSE UNFAIR
OBLIQUE
DISINHERIT DEPRIVE DISHEIR
ABDICATE DISHERIT
DISINTEGRATE BEAT DUST MELT
BREAK DECAY ERODE GRUSH
SLAKE SPLIT MOLDER CRUMBLE
DISBAND RESOLVE SHATTER
COLLAPSE DISSOLVE SEPARATE
DISINTEGRATING SCHIZOID
DISINTEGRATION DECAY BREAKUP
EROSION BIOLYSIS COLLAPSE
HEARTROT
DISINTER EXHUME UNBURY UNTOMB
UNGRAVE
DISINTERESTED FAIR CANDID
APATHETIC IMPARTIAL
DISJOIN PART UNDO SEVER DETACH
SUNDER UNTACK UNYOKE DISSOLVE
DISUNITE SEPARATE
DISJOINED SEJOINED DIAZEUTIC
DISK (ALSO SEE DISC) EYE NOB ORB
PAN SAW WAX WEB BURR CHAD
DIAL DISC FLAN FLAT KNOB PALM
PUCK STAR TUFT CAKRA DAUNT
MEDAL PATEN PLATE ROUND SABLE
SABOT SPILL TOKEN TRUCK WAFER
WHEEL WHORL BEZANT BOTTOM
BUCKET BUMPER BUTTON CACHET
CARTON CHAKRA CONCHA CONCHO
CORONA DISCUS GHURRY HARROW
PALLET PELLET RECORD RIFFLE
RONDEL SEQUIN SHEAVE SQUAIL
WASHER WEIGHT ZEQUIN ACETATE
BLOTTER BOBECHE CHECKER
CHIPPER CLIPEUS DIOPTER DISCOID
GOGGLES KNICKER MEDALET
PHALERA ROSETTE SLITTER
SPINNER SPOTTER TONDINO
DIFFUSER EYEPIECE HOLDFAST
PLANCHET RONDELLE ROUNDLET
ZECCHINO
(— FOR BARRELING HERRING)
DAUNT
(— FOR CHEESE) FOLLOWER
(— FOR STRIKING HOURS) GHURRY
(— OF JELLYFISH) BELL
(— OF WAX) AGNUS
(— ON WOODEN ROD) SPILL
(BULL'S-EYE —) CARTON
(COIN-MAKING —) FLAN PLANCHET

(ECCENTRIC —) SHEAVE
(FLESHY —) SARCOMA
(HANDLED —) RIFFLE
(MEDICATED —) LAMELLA
(METAL —) SLUG MEDAL
(ORNAMENTAL —) BANGLE
SPANGLE
(PADDED IRON —) SPINNER
(PAPER —S) CONFETTI
(POTTER'S —) BAT
(REVOLVING —) WAFTER
(ROTATING —) SCANNER
(SOLAR —) ATEN ATON
(SUN —) CAKRA CHAKRA
(TROCHAL —) CORONA
(WINGED —) FEROHER
DISLIKE DOWN HATE LOTH MIND
DERRY LOATH SPITE DETEST
REGRET SPLEEN UNLIKE DESPISE
MISLIKE QUARREL SCUNDER
SCUNNER STOMACH AVERSION
DESPISAL DISFAVOR DISTASTE
(— OF CHILDREN) MISOPEDIA
(FOOLISH —) TOY
DISLOCATE LUX SLIP BREAK SPLAY
UNSET LUXATE DISLOCK UNWREST
DISJOINT DISPLACE
DISLOCATED SHOTTEN DISLOCATE
DISLOCATION BREAK SHIFT SLIDE
THROW
(PL.) SETTLEMENTS
DISLODGE BEAT BOLT BUCK BUMP
EXPEL SHAKE SHIFT SWOOP
REMOVE DISROOT UNHORSE
UNHOUSE UNLODGE DISHABIT
(— BY BLASTING) BRUSH
DISLODGING BULLING
DISLOYAL FALSE FELON UNTRUE
DISLEAL
DISLOYALTY SWICK SWIKE
UNLEWTY UNTRUTH
DISMAL SAD WAN DARK DIRE DOWF
DREE DULL EERY GASH GLUM GRAY
GREY BLACK BLEAK DOWFF DREAR
EERIE LURID OURIE SABLE SORRY
SURLY SWART WASTE WISHT
DREARY DREICH DREIGH GLOOMY
GOUSTY SULLEN TRISTE DIREFUL
DOLEFUL FUNERAL GASHFUL
GHASTLY GOUSTIE JOYLESS
OMINOUS POCOSIN UNCOUTH
UNHAPPY DESOLATE DOLESOME
DOLOROUS FUNEREAL GROANFUL
LONESOME NOVEMBRY WEARIFUL
DISMAL-LOOKING GASH
WOBEGONE
DISMALLY DERNLY DIRELY
DISMANTLE RASE RAZE STRIP
DIVEST STRIKE DEPRIVE DESTROY
UNCLOAK DISMOUNT
DISMAY BOWL FEAR RUIN ALARM
AMATE APPAL DAUNT DREAD FLUNK
APPALL ASTONY CHASSE FRIGHT
SUBDUE TERROR DEPRESS DEPRIVE
FOUNDER HORRIFY TERRIFY
AFFRIGHT CONFOUND
DISMAYED ASTONIED
DISMAYING HIDEOUS
DISMEMBER LIMB MAIM PART REND

SEVER MANGLE UNLIMB DISCERP
DISLIMB DISSECT QUARTER
DISJOINT MUTILATE
DISMISS AX AXE CAN PUT BOOT
BUMP BUST CASH CAST DROP
DRUM FIRE KICK OUST QUIT SACK
SEND SHAB SWAP SWOP TURN VAIK
VOID AMAND AMOVE BREAK BRUSH
CHUCK DEMIT DIMIT DITCH EJECT
EXPEL FLIRT FLUNK LOOSE SCOUT
BANISH BOUNCE CONGEE DISMIT
DISOWN REJECT REMOVE SHELVE
CASHIER DISBAND DISCARD
LICENCE LICENSE DISGRACE
DISPATCH DISPOINT RELEGATE
WITHDRAW
DISMISSAL AX BOOT SACK BRUSH
CHUCK CONGE SHAKE AVAUNT
KICKAXE REMOVAL DISPATCH
MITTIMUS
(UNCEREMONIOUS —) CONGE
CONGEE
DISMISSED DEGOMME
DISMOUNT AVALE AVOID LIGHT
ALIGHT DEVOID DESCEND FLYAWAY
UNHORSE UNMOUNT DISHORSE
UNSTRIDE
DISOBEDIENCE CONTEMPT
DISOBEDIENT BAD FORWARD
FROWARD NAUGHTY UNBUXOM
UNGODLY WAYWARD MUTINOUS
DISOBEY SIT REJECT
DISOBLIGE OFFEND REFUSE
AFFRONT NEGLECT
DISOBLIGING MEAN UNBAIN
UNBANE
DISORDER ILL MUX PIE CRUD FLAW
MESS MUSS RIOT RUFF STIR TOUT
CHAOS CRACK DERAY GRIME
HAVOC REVEL SNAFU SPLIT TOUSE
TUKRA UPSET BURBLE CHOREA
DESRAY HUDDLE JUMBLE LITTER
MALADY MASTIC MUCKER MUDDLE
RUFFLE TOUSLE TROPPO TUMULT
UNTIDY WALTER AILMENT CLUTTER
COBWEBS CONFUSE DERANGE
DISEASE DISTURB EMBROIL
FERMENT FLUTTER GARBOIL
ILLNESS MISDEED MISRULE
OUTRAGE PERTURB SHATTER
TROUBLE UNRAVEL UNSHAPE
DISARRAY DISHEVEL EPILEPSY
MISORDER ROWDYISM SICKNESS
UNSETTLE
(— OF EYES) HIPPUS
(— OF VISION) DIPLOPIA
(— OF WINES) CASSE
(COMPLETE —) CHAOS
(MENTAL —) INSANITY PARANOIA
(SPEECH —) LALOPATHY
DISORDERED ILL SICK CRAZY
GAUMY LIGHT MESSY UNRID
BLOTTO FROUZY FROWSY FROWZY
INCULT INSANE MUSSED CHAOTIC
CLOUDED FORLORN TUMBLED
UNSIDED CONFUSED DERANGED
DISEASED FEVERISH FLURRIED
INCHOATE
DISORDERING CRIMP

DISORDERLY RAND RANDY RABBLE UNRULY BUNTING LAWLESS ROARING CONFUSED FAROUCHE LARRIKIN SLIPSHOD SLOVENLY SLUTTISH

DISORGANIZE SHOCK UPSET CONFUSE CONTUSE DERANGE DISBAND DISRUPT DISORDER DISSOLVE

DISOWN DENY RENAY UNOWN REJECT DISAVOW RETRACT ABDICATE DISALLOW DISCLAIM RENOUNCE

DISPARAGE LACK SLUR ABUSE DECRY LOWER DEBASE LESSEN SLIGHT BACKCAP DEBAUCH DEGRADE DEMERIT DEPRESS DETRACT DISABLE DOWNCRY IMPEACH BELITTLE DEROGATE DIMINISH DISCOUNT DISHONOR DISPRIZE MINIMIZE MISLIKEN VILIPEND

DISPARAGEMENT DIASYRM SNIDERY WASHWAY

DISPARAGING SNIDE SLIGHTING

DISPARATE UNEQUAL SEPARATE

DISPARITY DISSENT DISTANCE IMPARITY

DISPASSIONATE CALM COOL FAIR STOIC SEDATE SERENE CLINICAL COMPOSED MODERATE

DISPATCH RID FREE KILL MAIL NOTE POST SEND SLAY WING BRIEF ENVOY FLASH HASTE HURRY SHOOT SPEED DIRECT EMPLOY HASTEN ADDRESS COMMAND DELIVER DISPEED EXPRESS HATCHET BREVIATE CELERITY CONCLUDE DESPATCH EXPEDITE TELEGRAM

DISPATCH BOAT AVISO PACKET

DISPATCHER STARTER

DISPEL FRAY SHOO CHASE BANISH DISCUSS SATISFY SCATTER DISPERSE

DISPENSATION LAW LILA GRACE LIVERY ECONOMY FACULTY QUIENAL TOTQUOT DISPOSAL

DISPENSE DEAL DOLE HELP WEIGH EFFUSE EXCUSE EXEMPT FOREGO MANAGE SPREAD ABSOLVE ARRANGE DISPEND DRIBBLE MINISTER

(— WITH) MISS WANT SPARE SUSPENSE

DISPENSER BOMB MANAGER STEWARD

DISPERSE DOT SOW FRAY MELT PART ROUT SHED LOOSE SCALE SEVER SKAIL STREW BAFFLE DEFEAT DILATE DISPEL SPARSE SPERSE SPREAD UNKNIT VANISH WINNOW DIFFUSE DISBAND DISJECT DISMISS DRIBBLE FRITTER SCATTER SHATTER SPARKLE SPARPLE SPERPLE DISSOLVE DISTRACT SEPARATE SQUANDER STAMPEDE

DISPERSING SCALE

(— SHADOWS) SCIALYTIC

DISPERSION CUT FOAM STAIN

SPREAD DEBACLE SCATTER DIASPORA EMULSOID SOLUTION STAMPEDE

DISPIRIT COW DAMP MATE MULL CHILL DAUNT DEJECT DEPRESS FLATTEN

DISPIRITED DOWY DOWIE ABATTU ABATTUE LETDOWN SHOTTEN DOWNCAST DOWNSOME SACKLESS UNHEARTY WOBEGONE

DISPIRITING COLD CHILL DISMAL

DISPLACE BUMP EDGE MOVE STIR BANISH DEPOSE MISLAY REMOVE WINKLE DERANGE SWALLOW UNHINGE UNPLACE ANTEVERT DISLODGE DISPLANT MISPLACE SUPPLACE SUPPLANT UNSETTLE

(— LATERALLY) HEAVE

DISPLACED ATOPIC DEPAYSE

DISPLACEMENT BUMP SLIP HEAVE SCEND SHIFT START CUBAGE UPSLIP FALLING EVECTION

DISPLAY ACT AIR BRAG DASH GAUD ORGY POMP SHOW SIGN STAR WEAR AGONY ARRAY BINGE BLAZE BOAST DERAY ECLAT EMOTE FLASH PRIDE SCENE SHINE SIGHT SPLAY SPORT STAGE VAUNT BLAZON DEPLOY DESCRY ESTATE EVINCE EXPOSE EXTEND FLAUNT MUSTER OSTENT OUTLAY PARADE REVEAL RUFFLE SETOUT SPLASH SPRANK SPREAD UNCASE APPROVE BALLOON BRAVERY ETALAGE EXHIBIT EXPRESS FANFARE FLUTTER GAUDERY PAGEANT PRESENT SHOWING SPLURGE TRADUCE UNCOVER BEEFCAKE BLAZONRY BOOKFAIR CEREMONY DISCLOSE DISCOVER EMBLAZON EQUIPAGE EVIDENCE EXERCISE EXPOSURE FLOURISH INDICATE MANIFEST PARAFFLE SPLENDOR TINSELRY

(— EXCITEMENT) FAUNCH
(— OF EMOTION) GUSH
(— OF SKILL) APPERTISE
(BOASTFUL —) JACTATION
(EMPTY —) GAUD EYEWASH
(FLORAL —) BLOW BLANKET
(IMPRESSIVE —) SWELL
(OSTENTATIOUS —) DOG GAUDERY SWAGGER
(RADAR —) SCAN

DISPLAYED SPLAY EXPANDED

DISPLEASE VEX MIFF ANGER ANNOY PIQUE MISPAY MISSET OFFEND DISLIKE DISSUIT MISLIKE PROVOKE IRRITATE

DISPLEASED GLUM UNEASY UNFAIN

DISPLEASING BAD DRY PUTRID IRKSOME TEDIOUS UNLOVELY

DISPLEASURE IRE ANGER MUMPS PIQUE INJURY STRUNT UNLUST UNWILL DISLIKE OFFENSE TROUBLE UMBRAGE UNTHANK DISFAVOR DISGRACE DISTASTE

DISPORT PLAY AMUSE FRISK SPORT DIVERT FROLIC GAMBOL DISPLAY

DISPOSAL SALE BANDON CLEANUP PROPINE BESTOWAL DEVOTION DISPATCH

(QUICK —) WASHWAY

DISPOSE APT SET BEND CAST DUMP GIVE MIND TRIM YARK ARRAY BRUSH DIGHT ORDER PLACE POSIT ADJUST ATTIRE BESTOW DIGEST SETTLE TEMPER APPOINT ARRANGE DISPONE GESTURE INCLINE PREPARE RESOLVE DISPATCH REGULATE

(— OF) JOB SELL SCRAP FINISH HANDLE

DISPOSED APT FIT SET SIB LIEF GIVEN PRONE READY WRAST MINDED MINDFUL SUBJECT WILLING ADDICTED PROCLIVE PROTENSE TALENTED

(— AT INTERVALS) ALTERNATE
(— TO ACTION) ACTIVE
(— TO ASSOCIATE WITH ONE GROUP) CLANNISH
(— TOWARD) AFFECTED
(FAIRLY —) CANDID
(WELL —) FAIN INCLINED

DISPOSITION BENT BIAS MAKE MIND MOOD RACE SORT TRIM TURN DRIVE ETHOS FRAME GRAIN HABIT HEART HUMOR SPITE TACHE AFFECT ANIMUS DESIGN GENIUS HEALTH KIDNEY NATURE PTYXIS SPIRIT SPRITE STRIND TALENT TEMPER CONCEPT COURAGE DISPOSE FACULTY STOMACH APTITUDE ATTITUDE DISPOSAL POSITURE

(— OF DRAPERIES) CAST
(— OF PAWNS) SKELETON
(— TO ANGER) CHOLER
(— TO RESIST) DEFIANCE
(GENEROUS —) HEART
(KINDLY —) CHARITY HUMANITY
(NATURAL —) KIND GRAIN TARAGE INDOLES
(ORNAMENTAL —) DECOR
(ULTIMATE —) FATE

DISPOSSESS OUST EJECT EVICT EXPEL STRIP WRONG DEPOSE DIVEST BEREAVE CASHIER DEPRIVE DISSEIZE SEPARATE

DISPOSSESSED LUMPEN

DISPRAISE BLAME CENSURE

DISPROOF ELENCH REFUTE IMPROOF REPROOF

DISPROPORTIONATE UNEQUAL

DISPROVE BREAK REBUT REFEL NEGATE REFUTE CONFUTE EXPLODE IMPROVE REPROVE DISALLOW REDARGUE

DISPUTABLE MOOT VAGUE UNSURE DUBIOUS FALLIBLE

DISPUTANT FENCER POLEMIC WRANGLER

DISPUTATION PARVIS PILPUL POLEMIC PROBLEM WRANGLE ARGUMENT COURSING DEBATING EXERCISE

DISPUTE JAR TAX CALL CHOP DENY

FEUD FRAY FUSS HOLD MOOT ODDS
RIOT SAKE SPAR SPAT TILT ARGUE
BRAWL BROIL CABAL CHEST FLITE
FLYTE HURRY PLEAD SPUTE SQUIB
ARGUFY BARNEY BICKER CAMPLE
CANGLE DABBER DACKER DAIKER
DEBATE DIFFER FITTER FRATCH
HAGGLE HASSLE IMPUGN MATTER
NAGGLE SHARRY SQUALL SQUEAL
THREAP BRABBLE CONTEND
CONTEST DERAIGN DISCUSS
DISSERT FACTION GAINSAY PRIBBLE
QUARREL WRANGLE ARGUMENT
CATFIGHT CONTRARY POLEMIZE
QUESTION SKIRMISH SPARRING
SPLUTTER SQUABBLE
(POETICAL —) FLYTING PARTIMEN
DISQUALIFY DEBAR UNFIT OUTLAW
DISABLE
DISQUIET VEX FEAR FRET PAIN
TOSS UNRO EXCITE UNCALM
UNEASE UNREST AGITATE ANXIETY
DISREST DISTURB INQUIET SOLICIT
TROUBLE TURMOIL UNPEACE
UNQUIET
DISQUIETED UNEASY
DISQUIETUDE CHAGRIN WANREST
WANRUFE
DISRAELI DIZZY
DISREGARD BY SIT BLOW MOCK
OMIT PASS WANE BELAY FLING
WAIVE FORGET HUBRIS IGNORE
SLIGHT UNHEED CASHIER DESPISE
FORHEED LICENCE LICENSE
NEGLECT OVERSEE DISCOUNT
DISFAVOR DISPENSE DISVALUE
EASINESS OVERHALE OVERLOOK
OVERPASS UNREGARD
DISRELISH DISLIKE DISTASTE
DISREPUTABLE LOW BASE GAMY
HARD WAFF GAMEY SEAMY SHADY
SHODDY RAFFISH SHAMEFUL
UNHONEST
DISREPUTABLENESS BEGGARY
DISREPUTE DISFAME DISFAVOR
DISHONOR REPROACH
DISRESPECT AFFRONT CONTEMPT
RUDENESS
DISRESPECTFUL HARM SAUCY
UNCIVIL IMPOLITE IMPUDENT
INSOLENT
DISROBE STRIP CHANGE DIVEST
DESPOIL UNDRESS
DISRUPT GASH REND TEAR BREAK
CROSS HAMPER DISRUMP DISTRACT
DISRUPTED BROKEN DISRUPT
DISRUPTION BREACH BREAKUP
DEBACLE RUPTURE SOLUTION
DISSATISFACTION PAIN DISTASTE
VEXATION
DISSATISFIED UNEASY
DISSATISFY MISPAY
DISSECT BAR ANALYZE DISJOIN
SCALPEL UNPIECE
DISSECTED MATURE
DISSECTION ANATOMY ANALYSIS
DISSEMBLE ACT FOX HIDE MASK
CLOAK FEIGN BOGGLE SEMBLE

CONCEAL DISGUISE SIMULATE
SIMULIZE
DISSEMBLER SIMULAR
DISSEMBLING SLY IRONIC FICTION
AESOPIAN IRONICAL
DISSEMINATE SOW BEAR BLAZE
STREW EFFUSE SPREAD DIFFUSE
PUBLISH SCATTER SPARPLE
DISPERSE SEMINATE
DISSENSION JAR ODDS DEBATE
STRIFE DISCORD DISLIKE DISSENT
FACTION MISLIKE BROILERY
DISPEACE DISTANCE DISUNION
DISUNITY DIVISION FRACTION
FRICTION SEDITION
DISSENT VARY DIFFER HERESY
CONTEND PROTEST DISAGREE
DISSENTER HERETIC SECTARY
RECUSANT SEPARATE RASKOLNIK
(PL.) SEPARATION
DISSEPIMENT REPLUM SEPTUM
PHRAGMA
DISSERTATION ESSAY THEME
TRACT DEBATE MEMOIR SCREED
THESIS DESCANT LECTURE
MEMOIRS EXCURSUS EXERCISE
TRACTATE TREATISE
(— ON TEA) TSIOLOGY
DISSERVICE HARM DAMAGE INJURY
MISCHIEF
DISSIDENT FRONDEUR
DISSIMILAR UNLIKE DIFFORM
DIVERSE UNLIKEN
DISSIMILATE UNLIKEN
DISSIMULATION IRONY DECEIT
DISSIPATE BURN FRAY SPEND
WASTE BANISH DISPEL EXPEND
CONSUME DIFFUSE DISCUSS
FRITTER RESOLVE SCATTER
SHATTER SWATTLE TARNISH
DISPERSE DISSOLVE EMBEZZLE
EVANESCE SQUANDER
DISSIPATED FAST HIGH LOST
SPORTY OUTWARD RACKETY
DISSOLUTE LAX LEWD WILD LOOSE
SLACK RAKELY RAKISH SUBURB
UNTIED WANTON IMMORAL
LAWLESS VICIOUS DESOLATE
RAKEHELL RECKLESS RESOLUTE
SUBURBAN UNCURBED
DISSOLUTION END RUIN DECAY
BREAKUP DECEASE DIVORCE
DIALYSIS
DISSOLVE CUT END DEFY FADE
FUSE MELT SOLV THAW BREAK
FLEET LOOSE SOLVE UNFIX DIGEST
DISTIL RELENT SOLUTE UNBIND
UNGLUE UNKNIT ADJOURN DESTROY
DISBAND DISJOIN DISTILL DIVORCE
LIQUEFY RESOLVE DISCANDY
DISUNITE SEPARATE
(— OUT) LEACH
DISSOLVED SOLUT REMISS SOLUTE
RESOLUTE
DISSONANCE WOLF DISCORD
DIAPHONY
DISSONANT HARSH RAGGED
GRATING JARRING JANGLING
DISSUADE BLUFF DETER DEHORT

DIVERT RETIRE
DISTAFF ROCK
DISTANCE DX WAY BLUE GAIT GATE
LOOK PIPE SPAN STEP DEPTH
DRAFT RANGE SPACE GROUND
HEIGHT LENGTH SPREAD STANCE
STITCH BOWSHOT BREADTH
DRAUGHT FARNESS JOURNEY
MILEAGE MILEWAY RESERVE
STRETCH YARDAGE COLDNESS
COSECANT DIAMETER FOOTSTEP
HANDSPAN INTERVAL LATITUDE
OFFSCAPE OUTSTRIP
(SAFE —) BERTH
(— ALONG TRACK) LEAD
(— BETWEEN BATTENS) GAG
(— BETWEEN MASTS) INTERVAL
(— BETWEEN RAILS) GAGE GAUGE
(— BETWEEN RIVET-HEADS) GRIP
(— FOR PUTTING COAL) RENK
(— FROM BELLY TO BACK) BODY
(— FROM EQUATOR) HEIGHT
(— FROM LOCK FACE) BACKSET
(— FROM THE EYE) DEPTH
(— IN ADVANCE) START
(— OF ARCHERY RANGE) BUTT
(— OF BOW SHOT) CAST
(— OF HAUL) LEAD LEADAGE
(— OF TURNING SHIP) ADVANCE
(— OF VISION) KEN
(— ON FISHHOOK) BITE
(— ON GEAR WHEEL) ADDENDUM
(— OVER WHICH WIND BLOWS)
FETCH
(ANGULAR —) ANOMALY
(AT A —) LARGE
(GREAT —) INFINITY
(INTERVENING —) GAP
(PERPENDICULAR —) DROP CAMBER
ALTITUDE
(SEA —) OUTING STEAMING
(SHOOTING —) SHOOT
(SHORT — AWAY) OUTBYE
(SHORT —) INCH SPIT STEP SPELL
FOOTSTEP
(SMALL —) HAIR STEP
(UNIT OF —) LI YOJAN PARASANG
DISTANT DX COY FAR OFF AFAR
AWAY BACK COLD SIDE YOND
ALOOF CHILL FERNE HENCE FERREN
REMOTE YONDER FARAWAY
FOREIGN FROSTED REMOVED
STRANGE RESERVED
(— IN TIME) EARLY
(— PART) OFFSCAPE
(MORE —) YOND YONDER ULTERIOR
DISTASTE HATE DEGOUT UNLUST
DISGUST DISLIKE MISLIKE AVERSION
MISTASTE
DISTASTEFUL SOUR AUGEAN
BITTER BEASTLY HATEFUL
BRACKISH NAUSEOUS SHOCKING
UNSAVORY
DISTEMPER SOAK STEEP CHOLER
DILUTE GARGET GARGIL GARGLE
MALADY PANTAS AILMENT DISEASE
ILLNESS DISORDER DYSCRASE
SICKNESS UNSETTLE
(— OF COLT) STRANGLES

DISTEND BAG BLOW FILL GROW HEFT BLOAT PLUMP STRUT SWELL WIDEN DILATE EXPAND EXTEND INTEND SPREAD BALLOON ENLARGE INFLATE STRETCH

DISTENDED FULL PENT TAUT TRIG WIDE BLOWN POOCH TUMID GRAVID BLOATED DISTENT SWOLLEN INFLATED PATULENT PATULOUS

DISTENTION BLOAT DISTENT TYMPANY

DISTHENE CYANITE KYANITE

DISTICH SLOKA PROODE COUPLET

DISTILL DROP ELIX EMIT RATE STILL DISTIL EXTILL INFUSE ALEMBIC LIMBECK TRICKLE

DISTILLATE GUNDY ROSIN BENZIN BENZINE

DISTILLATION RUN DESCENT

DISTILLER ABKAR STILLER

DISTILLERY STILL JIGGER STILLERY

DISTINCT HOT FAIR FREE VIVE BREME BRISK CLEAR PLAIN SHARP VIVID PLUCKY PROPER SECRET SUNDRY ANOTHER ASUNDER DIVERSE EVIDENT LEGIBLE OBVIOUS PRECISE SEVERAL SPECIAL APPARENT DISCRETE DIVIDUAL PALPABLE PECULIAR SEPARATE

DISTINCTION MARK NOTE RANK SHED TEST CLASS GLORY HONOR FIGURE LAUREL LUSTER LUSTRE RENOWN QUALITY QUILLET ACCESSIT DIVISION GRANDEZA SUBTLETY
(ACADEMIC —) HONORS HONOURS
(WITHOUT —) COMMON

DISTINCTIVE JUICY DIRECT PROPER SIGNAL PECULIAR PHONEMIC SEPARATE SPANKING TALENTED

DISTINCTIVENESS EMPHASIS

DISTINCTLY CLEAR REDLY FAIRLY CLEARLY

DISTINCTNESS PLUCK CLARITY SEVERALTY
(LACKING —) SMUDGY

DISTINGUISH DEEM KNOW MARK SORT BADGE JUDGE LABEL SEVER SKILL STAMP DECERN DEFINE DESCRY DEVISE DIVIDE ENSIGN SECERN SINGLE CONCERN DISCERN DESCRIBE PERCEIVE SEPARATE

DISTINGUISHED CLEAR GREAT NOTED SWELL BANNER FAMOUS GENTLE MARKED SOLEMN EMINENT INSIGNE NOTABLE SIGNATE SPECIAL DISTINCT LAUREATE RENOWNED SPLENDID

DISTINGUISHING BETWEEN

DISTORT WRY SKEW CLOUD COLOR FUDGE SCREW TWIST WREST WRING CRINGE DEFACE DEFORM DETORT GARBLE SHEVEL WRITHE BLUBBER CONTORT FALSIFY GRIMACE PERVERT SHACHLE SHACKLE SLANDER OUTIMAGE WIREDRAW

DISTORTED WRY AWRY SKEW ASKEW CRANK SKEWED WARPED CROOKED DISTORT GNARLED LOXOTIC WRITHEN CAMSHACH DEFORMED DEGRADED STRAINED TORTIOUS

DISTORTING CONVULSION

DISTORTION HOG SAG WOW WREST STRAIN FLUTTER GRIMACE GARBLING SKEWNESS
(— IN WOOD) DIAMONDING

DISTRACT MAD AMUSE CRAZE STROY BEMUSE DETRAY DIVERT HARASS INSANE MADDEN MITHER MOIDER PUZZLE TWITCH AGITATE CONFUSE DETRACT DISTURB EMBROIL PERPLEX SCATTER BEWILDER CONFOUND

DISTRACTED GYTE CRAZY STRACT FRANTIC SCRANNY

DISTRACTION ALARM BLIND ALARUM ESCAPE FRENZY TUMULT ECSTASY

DISTRAIN NAM NAAM DRIVE POIND STRAIN STRESS DISTRESS POUNDAGE

DISTRAINT NAM NAAM POIND

DISTRAUGHT MAD CRAZED FRANTIC DERANGED DISTRACT DISTRAIT STRAUGHT

DISTRESS AIL ILL MAR BITE CARK HURT MOAN NEED PAIN PORT TEEN AGONY ANGER ANNOY DOLOR GRATE GRIEF GRILL GRIPE LABOR PINCH PRESS SMART TRYST TWEAK WORRY WOUND BARRAT DANGER DURESS GRIEVE GRUDGE HARASS HARROW LAMENT MISERY SORROW STRESS THRONG WORRIT AFFLICT ANGUISH ANXIETY CHAGRIN DAYMARE DESTROY DISEASE EXTREME HERSHIP MISEASE OPPRESS PASSION PENANCE PERPLEX STURBLE TORMENT TORTURE TROUBLE UNQUERT AGGRIEVE CALAMITY DARKNESS DISTASTE DISTRAIN FORHAILE PRESSURE SORENESS STRAITEN WANDRETH GRIEVANCE

DISTRESSED WRUNG DOWNGONE

DISTRESSFUL STRAIT

DISTRESSING BAD HOT SAD GRIM HARD SORE BLEAK CHARY CRUEL DIRTY SHARP BITTER SEVERE SHREWD THORNY CARKING FEARFUL GRIPING PAINFUL GRIEVOUS

DISTRIBUTE DOT SOW CAST DEAL DOLE GRID METE SEED SORT TAME ALLOT CLASS DIVVY ISSUE SHARE SHIFT SPEND ASSIGN ASSORT DEPART DEVISE DIGEST DIVIDE EXPEND IMPART PARCEL REPART SPARSE SPREAD ARRANGE DISPEND DISPOSE EROGATE PRORATE SCATTER ALLOCATE CLASSIFY DESCRIBE DISBURSE DISPENSE DISPERSE SEPARATE SPRINKLE
(— GUNFIRE) SEARCH
(— SEED) SOW SEED DRILL
(— TYPE) THROW

DISTRIBUTED BALANCED DISPERSE

DISTRIBUTION DOLE SALE ARRAY DIVVY DETAIL DIVIDE PARTING DISPOSAL DIVIDEND

DISTRIBUTIVELY EACH APIECE

DISTRIBUTOR SOWER SHARER CARRIER ZANJERO

DISTRICT DO AMT GAU LAN SOC WON AREA COIL FARM HUNT LEET LIWA PALE PART SIDE SLUM SOKE TEMA WARD WENE WICK WOON AIMAK ANNEX COILA EXURB HARSH JAGIR JEWRY MAHAL OKRUG PAGUS PARTY SHIRE SOKEN TALUK TEMAN TRACT VICUS AGENCY BARRIO BOWERY CANTON CERCLE CIRCLE COUNTY FOREST JAGHIR MARKAZ MEMBER MERINA OKROOG PARAMO PARISH POLLAM REGARD REGION SIRCAR STAPLE STREET SYSSEL VINTRY ZILLAH CALABAR CIRCUIT CLASSIS COMARCA COMMUNE COUNTRY CURRAGH DEMESNE DIOCESE ENCLAVE FREEDOM LIBERTY MAHALLA MALACCA MAYFAIR MELIZKI MISSION PIMLICO PURLIEU QUARTER SEASIDE SLUMDOM THANAGE THEBAID UPRIVER CHAPELRY CIMARRON DISTRITO DIVISION FAUBOURG GILDABLE LEGATION MACASSAR MAGAZINE MONTANAS PRECINCT PROVINCE REGIMENT
(— BORDERING RIVER) WATER
(— OF COURT) LEET
(— OF JAPAN) DO KEN
(BROTHEL —) STEW
(BURNED —) QUEMADO
(CHINESE —) HIEN
(ECCLESIASTICAL —) SYNOD CLASSIS DIOCESE
(HUNTING —) WALK
(ICELANDIC —) SYSSEL
(JUDICIAL —) CIRCUIT
(POOR —) SLUM SLUMS
(POSTAL —) RAYON
(RURAL —) WAYBACK
(RURAL —S) STICKS
(RUSSIAN —) STANITSA STANITZA
(TENANT —) THIRL
(TRIBAL —) GAU
(TURKISH —) ORDU SANJAK
(PL.) GAELTACHT

DISTRUST FEAR DOUBT DREAD STRIFE DIFFIDE SUSPECT UNFAITH UNTRUST DEFIANCE DISFAITH MISFAITH MISTRUST WANTRUST

DISTRUSTFUL SHY LEERY JEALOUS

DISTURB VEX BUSY FAZE FRET FUSS JOLT RILE ROIL STIR TOSS ALARM ANNOY BRASH DROVE FEEZE KNOCK PHASE ROUSE SHAKE STEER UPSET BOTHER HARASS JOSTLE MOLEST RUFFLE SQUEAK UNCALM UNEASE AGITATE COMMOTE COMMOVE DERANGE DISREST DRUMBLE FRAZZLE GARBOIL INQUIET MISMAKE PERTURB SCUFFLE SOLICIT STURBLE

TEMPEST TROUBLE CONVULSE
DISJOINT DISORDER DISQUIET
DISTRACT DISTRESS FRIGHTEN
(— **BY HANDLING**) TOUCH
(— **SUDDENLY**) START
(— **THE PEACE**) RIOT INQUIET
DISTURBANCE VEX BOIL BREE CAIN
COIL DUST RIOT ROUT STIR WIND
WORK ALARM BRAWL BROIL DERAY
FUGUE FUROR HURRY SHINE SHOCK
STEER STORM STROW STURT
TOUSE AFFRAY BOTHER BREEZE
CATHRO DESRAY FRACAS FRAISE
FURORE HUBBUB KICKUP POTHER
RUMBLE RUMPUS SHINDY SQUALL
STATIC TUMULT TURNUP UPROAR
BLUNDER BOBBERY BRULYIE
BRULZIE CHAGRIN CLATTER
CLUTTER DISTURB EMOTION
FERMENT GRINDER MADNESS
ROOKERY TROUBLE TURMOIL
BROILERY BUSINESS DISORDER
FOOFARAW INCIDENT REELRALL
STRAMASH TRAVALLY
(— **OF OCEAN**) SEA
(**ATMOSPHERIC** —) STORM GRINDER
(**DIGESTIVE** —) BLOAT
(**MENTAL** —) FRENZY PHRENSY
DELIRIUM
(**SEISMIC** —) SEAQUAKE
DISTURBED CRACKED INQUIET
MAKADOO TROUBLE AGITATED
FLURRIED STREAKED
DISTURBING BREAK HAUNTING
DISUNION DIVORCE
DISUNITE RIP PART SEVER UNTIE
DETACH DIVIDE SUNDER UNKNIT
UNLIME DISBAND DISJOIN DISLINK
DISSENT DIVORCE UNRAVEL
ALIENATE DISSEVER DISSOLVE
ESTRANGE SEPARATE UNSOLDER
DISUNITY DISCORD DISUNION
DIVISION
DISUSE MISUSE OUTAGE ABANDON
DISCARD DISUSAGE MISAPPLY
DISUSED DEAD WASTE DESUETE
EXOLETE
DITCH GAW RUT SAP SOW DELF
DICK DIKE DYKE FOSS GOOL GOUT
GRIP GURT HOLL LEET MOAT SEEK
SICK SIKE SINK TRIG CANAL CLAUD
DELFT DELVE FENCE FLEAM FOSSA
FOSSE GRAFF GRAFT GRAVE GRIPE
GROOP GULLY PUDGE RHEEN RHINE
SEWER SHORE SLONK SLUIT SOUGH
STANK STELL ZANJA GUTTER
GUZZLE HOLLOW RELAIS SHEUCH
SHEUGH TRENCH ZANJON ABANDON
ACEQUIA CHANNEL GRINDLE
GRIPPLE LATERAL VANFOSS
ZANJONA WATERING
(**MUDDY** —) LETCH
(**NARROW** —) RELAIS
(**OPEN** —) STELL
DITCH GRASS ENALID
DITCH MILLET HUREEK PASPALUM
DITCH REED SPIRE BENNEL
DITHER SHAKE BOTHER LATHER
SHIVER TROUBLE

DITROCHEE DIPODY
DITTO SAME REPEAT LIKEWISE
DITTY DIT LAY DITE DYTE POEM
SING SONG THEME VERSE SAYING
DICTATE VINETTA
DIURETIC ZEA CAVA KAVA BUCCO
BUCHU LAPPA PICHI SABAL NASROL
DROSERA EMICTORY
DIVER AMA LOON DUCKER PEARLER
PLUNGER PLUNGEON
DIVERGE LEAVE BRANCH DIFFER
DIVIDE RAMIFY SPREAD SQUARE
SWERVE DEVIATE DIGRESS DIVERSE
DISAGREE DIVAGATE
DIVERGENCE DIP ERROR CHANGE
SPREAD VAGARY CONTRAST
DIVERGENT OFF APART REMOTE
TANGENT VARIANT
(**MORE** —) FARTHER
DIVERS EVIL MANY CRUEL SUNDRY
SEVERAL VARIOUS PERVERSE
DIFFERING
DIVERSE EVIL SERE MOTLEY
SUNDRY UNLIKE VARIED ADVERSE
SEVERAL VARIOUS DISTINCT
PERVERSE SEPARATE VARIETAL
DIVERSIFIED EXTENDED
DIVERSIFY DOT FRET VARY CHECK
FRECK BEGARIE VARIATE SPRINKLE
DIVERSION JEU GAME MASK PLAY
ALARM FEINT FRISK HOBBY SPORT
ATTACK DEDUIT DIVERT LAUGHS
SCHEME SOLACE DISPORT PASTIME
ESCAPISM PLEASURE SIDESHOW
VARIORUM
(— **OF STREAM**) CAPTURE
DIVERSITY CHANGE DISCORD
DISSENT VARIETY CONTRAST
DIVERT SWAY AMUSE BLANK RELAX
SHUNT SPORT WRING DERAIL
DERIVE DETURN SIPHON SWITCH
SYPHON TICKLE BEGUILE CELIGHT
DECEIVE DEFLECT DETRACT
DISPORT PASTIME PERVERT
REFLECT ABSTRACT DISSUADE
DISTRACT ESTRANGE RECREATE
(— **ATTENTION**) COVER
(— **HEADWATERS**) BEHEAD
(— **STREAM**) CAPTURE
(— **WATER**) FLUME
DIVERTED MERRY AMUSED
DISTRACT
DIVERTICULUM UTERUS OLEOCYST
DIVERTING DROLL AMUSING
FOOLISH PLEASANT SPORTFUL
LAUGHABLE
DIVEST BARE DOFF REFT TIRL
EMPTY EXUTE REAVE SHEAR SPOIL
STRIP DELAWN DENUDE DEPOSE
DEVEST DISMIT UNVEST BEREAVE
DEPRIVE DESPOIL DISROBE
UNCOVER UNDRESS DENATURE
DETHRONE UNCLOTHE
(— **OF ARMOR**) DEMAIL
(— **OF VALUE**) DEVALUE
(— **OF**) ABDICATE
DIVIDE CUT LOT CAST DEAL FORK
MERE PART RIFT SHED SLIP ZONE
BREAK CARVE CLASS CLEFT DIVVY

GAVEL JOINT SCALE SCIND SEVER
SHARE SHIFT SLICE SNACK SPACE
SPLIT SPRIT WHACK BEPART BISECT
BRANCH CANTLE CANTON CLEAVE
COTEAU DEPART DEVISE DIFFER
DOMIFY INDENT PARCEL RAMIFY
SECTOR SEJOIN SLEAVE SUNDER
ALIQUOT ANALYZE ATOMIZE
AVERAGE BRITTEN COMPART
DIFFUSE DIREMPT DISCIDE DISPART
DISSECT DIVERGE FISSURE FRITTER
PARTAKE PRORATE ALLOCATE
CLASSIFY CROSSCUT DISCRETE
DISSEVER DISTRACT DISUNITE
FRACTION FRAGMENT GRADUATE
HEMISECT MEDISECT SEPARATE
STRATIFY UNSEEDER
(— **BEEF**) BLOCK
(— **FILAMENTS**) SLEAVE
(— **INTO 2 PARTS**) HALVE BISECT
(— **INTO 4 PARTS**) QUARTER
(— **INTO DISTRICTS**) CANTON
(— **INTO MEASURES**) BAR
(— **INTO PIECES**) GOBBET
(— **LAND**) STINT
(— **NATURALLY**) FALL
(— **SMALL**) SCANTLE
DIVIDED ENTE REFT SIDE CLEFT
FORKY SPLIT ATOMIC CLOVEN
PRONGY FISSATE FOURCHE
GYRONNY PARTITE SEPTATE
AEROLATE CAMERATE DIVIDUAL
FOURCHEE
(— **IN TWO**) FOURCHE DIMIDIATE
(— **INTO 4 PARTS**) PALY
QUARTERED
(**NOT** —) GLOBAL
DIVIDEND BONUS SHARE
DIVIDER BUNTON MERIST SHARER
BUNTING COMPASS SEVERER
DIVIDANT
DIVI-DIVI LIBIDIBI
DIVINATION OMEN SORS SORT
AUGURY MANTIC SCRYING SORCERY
GEOMANCY TAGHAIRM
(— **SCIENCE**) MANTIC
DIVINE HOLY SORT SPAE TWIG
AREAD AREED DIVUS GUESS PIOUS
DEIFIC DETECT DEVISE GODFUL
HALSEN PRIEST SACRED BLESSED
FORESEE GODLIKE PORTEND
PREDICT PRESAGE ARIOLATE
CONTRIVE FOREBODE FOREKNOW
FORETELL HEAVENLY IMMORTAL
MINISTER PERCEIVE UBIQUIST
DIVINER SEER AUGUR SIBYL
ARUSPEX AUGURER PROPHET
HARUSPEX
DIVING BELL NAUTILUS
DIVING BOARD RISE
DIVING SUIT GANGAVA
DIVINING ROD TWIG DOWSER
DIVINITY (ALSO SEE GOD AND
GODDESS) JOSS LLEU LLEW TIEN
AHURA DEITY HYBLA NUADA NUADU
NYMPH POWER ATHTAR VEDUIS
GLAUCUS GODDESS GODHEAD
GODSHIP HYBLAEA TARANIS VIRBIUS
TEUTATES VEDIOVIS

(— **CIRCUIT BINDING**) YAPP
(PL.) ELOHIM
DIVISIBLE SECABLE DIVIDUAL
PARTIBLE
(— **BY 2**) AIM
DIVISION BAY BOX CUT DAG FIT LEG
CHAP CLAN DOLE FARM FAUN FORK
GELD GELT GORE HOLD LITH NEAT
PACE PANE PART RANK RAPE RIFT
CAPUT CHASM CLASS CLEFT CURIA
DIGOR DIVVY DULAN DULAT FIELD
FIGHT GENOS GRANT GROUP IJORE
MURUT PERES REALM SHARD
SHARE SUBAH TAXIS THEME TOMAN
WHEEN CANTON DECADE DECURY
DEGREE DIVIDE EOGAEA HAWIYA
IMAHAL JHURIA PORTIO SCHISM
SEASON SECTOR SUNDER VOLOST
ZILLAH BREAKUP COMARCA
CUSTODY DIOCESE DUALISM
ENOMOTY FISSURE FURLONG
HASHIYA KINGDOM KITSKAN
NATUARY PARTAGE PARTING
ROULADE SECTION SEGMENT
SUBRACE ARPEGGIO CATEGORY
CLEAVAGE DECANATE DIERESIS
DISTRICT FASCICLE MEROTOMY
PARGANNA PRECINCT SCISSION
SCISSURE SHEDDING SQUADRON
SUBCLASS
(— **BETWEEN PIERS**) BAY
(— **BETWEEN STALLS**) BAIL
(— **FOR TAXATION**) GELD
(— **IN DENMARK**) AMT
(— **IN HUNGARY**) COMITAT
(— **IN MINING BED**) CLEAVE
(— **OF ANGELS**) CHOIR
(— **OF ARMY**) BATTLE LOCHUS
(— **OF BEJA**) BISHARIN
(— **OF BOOK**) CHAPTER FASCICLE
(— **OF BUILDING**) STORY STOREY
(— **OF CHARIOTEERS**) FACTION
(— **OF CONTEST**) HEAT INNING
(— **OF COUNTY**) RAPE BARONY
HUNDRED
(— **OF CROPLAND**) FLAT
(— **OF DISCOURSE**) HEADING
(— **OF DRAMA**) ACT SCENE
(— **OF FAMILY**) BRANCH
(— **OF FIELD**) RIG
(— **OF FOOT**) SEMEION
(— **OF FOREST**) WARD
(— **OF GEOLOGICAL TIME**) EPOCH
(— **OF GRASS**) SPRIG
(— **OF GREAT HORDE**) DULAN
DULAT KANGLA KANGLI
(— **OF HEADLINE**) BANK DECK
(— **OF LAND**) LAINE KONOHIKI
(— **OF LEGION**) COHORT HASTATI
MANIPLE TRIARII
(— **OF LOG LINE**) KNOT
(— **OF MANCHU ARMY**) BANNER
(— **OF MANKIND**) RACE
(— **OF MEAL**) COURSE
(— **OF NIGHT**) WATCH
(— **OF ORANGE**) LITH
(— **OF POEM**) FIT DUAN CANTO
STANZA STROPHE
(— **OF PROCESS**) STAGING

(— **OF ROCKS**) SYSTEM
(— **OF ROSARY**) DECADE
(— **OF SOCIETY**) CASTE ATOMISM
(— **OF SONG**) FIT
(— **OF STOPE**) FLOOR
(— **OF STRUCTURE**) STAGE
(— **OF TREF**) RANDIR
(— **OF UTTERANCE**) COLON
(— **OF WINDOW**) DAY
(— **OF ZODIAC**) SIGN DECAN
(— **OVER ISSUE**) BREACH
(**ADMINISTRATIVE** —) FU LATHE
CHARGE CIRCLE COUNTY EYALET
CUSTODY DIOCESE TOWNSHIP
(**ANTHROPOLOGICAL** —) STOCK
(**ARMY** —) MORA
(**ASTROLOGICAL** —) FACE
(**CELL** —) AMITOSIS
(**ECCLESIASTICAL** —) SCHISM
SOCIETY PRECINCT
(**GEOLOGICAL** —) ERA LIAS MALM
LUDIAN SERIES LARAMIE ARNUSIAN
RICHMOND
(**HINGED** —) LEAF
(**ISLE OF MAN** —) SHEADING
(**MUSICAL** —) ALLEGRO
(**NUCLEAR** —) FISSION
(**PHILIPPINE** —) ATO
(**POLICE** —) TANA THANA
(**POLITICAL** —) ATO CITY LATHE
STATE COUNTY PARISH BOROUGH
HUNDRED SURPLUS DISTRICT
PURCHASE
(**POPULATION** —) STRATUM
(**SOCIAL** —) HORDE
(**TRIBAL** —) CLAN
DIVORCE GET GETT AHSAN HASAN
KHULA SEVER TALAK SUNDER
ASUNDER DISBAND DISMISS
MUBARAT UNMARRY DISSOLVE
DISUNION DISUNITE SEPARATE
DIVOT CLOD TURF
DIVULGE BARE CALL SHOW TELL
BLURT BREAK SPILL UTTER VOICE
BEWRAY EVULGE IMPART REVEAL
SPREAD UNFOLD PROPALE PUBLISH
UNCOVER DISCLOSE DISCOVER
EVULGATE PROCLAIM
DIZZINESS HILO SWIM DINUS TIEGO
MEGRIM VANITY MERLIGO SCOTOMY
VERTIGO SWIMMING WILLNESS
DIZZY DUNT CRAZY FAINT GIDDY
LIGHT TOTTY WESTY FICKLE STUPID
FOOLISH SWIMMING UNSTEADY
DO D ACT DIV FAY TRY BILK BURN
CHAR COME DEAL DOST MAKE
PASS SUIT AVAIL BITCH CHEAT
EXERT GUISE SERVE SHIFT TRICK
ANSWER COMMIT NOBBLE RENDER
ACHIEVE EXECUTE PERFORM
PRODUCE SATISFY SUFFICE
TRANSACT
(— **AWAY WITH**) BURK ABATE
BURKE FORDO BANISH FOREDO
ABOLISH AMOLISH CASHIER
CONSUME ABROGATE DEMOLISH
DISSOLVE IMBOLISH RETRENCH
(— **BUSINESS**) CHAFFER
(— **CARELESSLY**) SLIM

(— **CASUAL WORK**) GRASS
(— **FOR**) FIX GET JACK SINK FETCH
NAPOO DIDDLE
(— **IMPERFECTLY**) HUDDLE
(— **IN SLOVENLY WAY**) SLUBBER
(— **INJURY**) BANE
(— **NOT**) DONT DINNA
(— **PENANCE**) SATISFY
(— **PIECEWORK**) DACKER
(— **SMARTLY**) LINK
(— **THOROUGHLY**) FLOOR
(— **WITHOUT**) LACK SPARE
FORBEAR DISPENSE
(— **WRONG**) ERR SIN MISCARRY
(— **YE**) DEE
DOABLE AGIBLE
DOBLON ISABELLA
DOBRA JO JOE OCTAVE
DOCENT TUTOR TEACHER
LECTURER
DOCILE CALM MEEK TALL TAME
TAWIE FACILE GENTLE DOCIOUS
DUCTILE DUTIFUL BIDDABLE
TOWARDLY
DOCK BOB CUT BANG CLIP MOOR
PIER QUAY RUMP SCUT BASIN
SHORE WHARF CAMBER COFFER
DOCKEN FIDDLE HAMBLE MARINA
SORREL STRUNT BOBTAIL CURTAIL
PARELLA PARELLE SHORTEN
CANAIGRE PATIENCE SHIPSIDE
DOCKAGE BERTHAGE
DOCKMACKIE VIBURNUM
DOCKYARD ARSENAL
(— **WORKMAN**) MATEY
DOCTOR DOC COOK DOPE DOSE
FAKE BRUJO HAKIM LEECH SUGAR
TREAT CROCUS DEACON EXTERN
HAIKUN HEALER INTERN MAULVI
POWWOW CROAKER KORADJI
TEACHER MEDICATE
(— **OF CANON LAW**) JCD
(— **OF LAWS**) JD
(— **UP**) COOK FAKE EYEWASH
(**PLAY** —) FIXER
(**QUACK** —) CROCUS
(**WITCH** —) BOCOR BOKOR GOOFER
GUFFER WIZARD WITCHMAN
DOCTRINAIRE ISMY
DOCTRINE ISM DOXY LEAR RULE
CREDO CREED DOGMA LIGHT MAXIM
TABLE TENET ZOISM AHIMSA
BABISM BELIEF DHARMA EGOISM
EROTIC GOSPEL HOLISM MALISM
MONISM NOETIC THEORY ACROAMA
AMIDISM ANIMISM ARTICLE ATAVISM
ATHEISM ATOMISM BAHAISM
DUALISM EGOTISM EVANGEL
KARAISM KRYPSIS MISHNAH
NEOLOGY NOETICS OPINION
PEELISM PRECEPT PROGRAM
REALISM SENSISM TRIKAYA
ACTIVISM AGATHISM ANALYTIC
ARIANISM ARYANISM BAJANISM
CHILIASM CYNICISM DARBYISM
DEVILISM DOCETISM DYNAMISM
ENERGISM FATALISM FINALISM
GOBINISM HEDONISM HYLOLOGY
IDENTISM IDEOLOGY ISLAMISM

NIHILISM PAJONISM PAMNESIA
PEJORISM POSITION POSOLOGY
PSYCHISM REGALISM RHEMATIC
SIDERISM SOLIDISM SPHERICS
TYPOLOGY UBIQUITY VITALISM
(BUDDHIST —) ANATTA ANATMAN
(CONTRARY —) HERESY
(ESOTERIC —) CABALA QABBALA
CABALISM
(EVIL —) MOLOCH
(PL.) ESOTERY SCOTISM CREDENDA
DONATISM LABADISM SCRIBISM
DOCUMENT DOC GET BILL BOND
BOOK CALL DEED FORM GETT OLLA
SEAL WRIT CHART DEMIT DIMIT
GRIEF LEASE PAPER PROOF SCRIP
SCRIT STIFF TARGE TEACH TITLE
BILLET BREVET CADJAN CAJANG
CEDULA COCKET DOCKET PATENT
RAGMAN SCHOOL SCRIPT SOURCE
SURVEY TICKET VOLUME ARCHIVE
CONDUCT DIPLOMA ELOHIST
ESCRIPT EXHIBIT INQUEST LICENSE
MISSIVE PLACARD PRECEPT
WARRANT WAYBILL WHEREAS
WRITING CONTRACT COVENANT
FURLOUGH INSTRUCT MORTGAGE
SCHEDULE SECURITY TRANSIRE
(CONDITIONAL —) SCRIP
(COPY OF —) VIDIMUS
(PL.) BUMF ARCHIVE ARCHIVES
PALAPALA
DODDER SCAD SCALD SHAKE
DODDLE DOTHER FIDEOS TOTTER
TREMBLE FLAXDROP HAIRWEED
HALEWEED HELLWEED MULBERRY
DODDERING OLD INANE INFIRM
SENILE FOOLISH
DODDER LAUREL WOEVINE
MISTLETOE
DODDIE HUMLIE
DODECANESE (— **ISLAND)** KOS
SYME KASOS LEROS TELOS KHALKE
LIPSOS PATMOS NISYROS
KALYMNOS
DODGE SHY BILK DUCK GAME JINK
JOUK LURK RUSE AVOID CHEAT
ELUDE EVADE FENCE FUDGE GLOSS
LURCH PARRY SHIFT SHIRK SHUNT
STALL TRICK ESCAPE WHEEZE
DECEIVE EVASION PROFFER
ARTIFICE CROTCHET GILENYIE
MALINGER SIDESTEP
DODGER FLIER FLYER HAGGLER
HANDBILL
(DRAFT —) BUSHWACK
DODGING JINK
DOE DA ROE TEG FAUN HIND NANNY
ALMOND BISCUIT
(— IN 1ST YEAR) FAWN
(BLUE —) FLIER FLYER
DOER ACTOR AGENT MAKER
AUTHOR FACTOR FEASOR WORKER
FACIENT MANAGER ATTORNEY
EXECUTOR
(— OF ODD JOBS) JACK
DOES S DOTH DUSE
(— NOT) DONT DISNA DOESNT
DOFF OFF DAFF VAIL AVALE DOUSE

DOWSE STRIP DIVEST REMOVE
UNDRESS
DOFFER DRUM DUFFER
DOFFING CAP
DOG CUR MUT PUG PUP YAP ALAN
ALCO CHOW DANE FAUS GOER KIYI
MONG MUTT PAWL STAG TIKE TRAY
TYKE ALAND ALANT ARGOS BAWTY
BEDOG BESET BOUCH BOXER
CALEB CANID CORGI DERBY DODGE
HOUND HUSKY LIMER PELON
POOCH PUPPY RACHE RAKER
RATCH SLING SPITZ STALK WHELP
AFGHAN BANDOG BASSET BAWTIE
BEAGLE BELTON BORZOI BOSTON
BOWWOW BRIARD BUFFER CANINE
COCKER COLLIE COONER DANCER
DETENT DRIVER ESKIMO FINDER
GUNDOG HEADER HEELER HUNTER
JOWLER KELPIE KENNET MISSET
POODLE RANGER RATTER SALUKI
SEIZER SETTER SHOUGH SIRIUS
SUSSEX TALBOT TOLLER TOWSER
VIZSLA YAPPER YAUPER YELPER
BASENJI BOARDER BULLDOG
CARRIER COURSER CRAMPON
CREEPER DOGGESS DROPPER
GRIFFON HARRIER LURCHER
MALTESE MASTIFF MONGREL
OWTCHAR POINTER SCOTTIE
SKIRTER SLEUGHI SPANIEL
SPORTER STARTER TERRIER
TUMBLER WHIPPET YAPSTER
AIREDALE ALEUTANT ALSATIAN
CERBERUS CYNHYENA DEMIWOLF
DOBERMAN ELKHOUND FISSIPED
FOXHOUND KEESHOND LABRADOR
LANDSEER LONGTAIL MALEMUTE
MALINOIS PAPILLON PEKINESE
SAMOYEDE SEALYHAM SHEPHERD
SIBERIAN SPRINGER TURNSPIT
VERMINER WATCHDOG WATERRUG
(— OF LATHE) DRIVER
(— TRAINED AS DECOY) TOLLER
(BIRD —) BOLTER
(CHAINED —) BANDOG
(ESKIMO —) HUSKY SIWASH
(FARM —) KOMONDOR
(FEMALE —) GYP SLUT BITCH
DOGGESS
(FOXLIKE —) COLPEO
(HOUSE —) WAP WAPP
(HUNGARIAN —) KUVASZ
(HUNTING —) ALAN BRACH RACHE
RATCH ALAUND BASSET HUNTER
KENNET LUCERN RACCHE SALUKI
SEIZER SETTER SLOUGH COURSER
DROPPER HARRIER POINTER
STRIKER
(JAPANESE —) AKITA
(LAP —) MESSAN SHOUGH
(LARGE —) DANE TOWSER MASTIFF
KOMONDOR
(LIKE A —) CYNIC
(LONG-HAIRED —) ALCO SHOCK
(MONGREL —) CUR DEMIWOLF
(NON-BARKING —) BASENJI
(PARTI-COLORED —) PIE PYE
(PET —) MINX LAPDOG MOPPET

(PUG —) MOPS
(PUNCH'S —) TOBY
(SHAGGY —) RUG OWTCHAH
(SHEEP —) CUR COLLIE KELPIE
BEARDIE MALINOIS SHEPHERD
(SMALL —) TOY FICE FIST DOGGY
FEIST PIPER DOGGIE AMERTOY
SPANIEL PAPILLON PEKINESE
(VICIOUS —) TAEPO
(WATCH —) CUR GARM GARMR
(WILD —) ADJAG DHOLE DINGO
GUARA JACKAL AGOUARA
CIMARRON
(YELPING —) WAPPET
(PL.) DOGGERY
DOGBANE KENDIR KENDYR ECHITES
FLYTRAP ALSTONIA MILKWEED
DOGBOAT PIG
DOGCART GADDER TUMTUM
BOUNDER GADABOUT
DOG COLLAR TRASH
DOG DAYS CANICULE
DOG EAR LEATHER
DOG FENNEL HOGWEED
DOGFIGHT SCRAMBLE
DOGFISH DOG HOE HUSS TOPE
FLAKE HOUND HURSE MANGO
TOPER DAGGAR GALEID MORGAY
BONEDOG GABBACK SPURDOG
TRIAKID GRAYFISH SEAHOUND
DOGGED DOUR SULLEN DOGGISH
DOGLIKE STUBBORN
DOGGEREL NOMINY TRIVIA DIGGREL
SINGSONG
DOGGONE BLESSED DOWNGONE
DOGIE LEPPY STRAY
DOG KEEPER FEWTERER
DOGLIKE CYNIC CYNOID DOGGED
DOGMA CREED TENET DICTUM
DOCTRINE DOCUMENT
DOGMATIC POSITIVE CONFIDENT
DOGMATISM BOWWOW
DOGMATIST PHILODOX
DOG POUND GREENYARD
DOG ROSE BUCKY CANKER
BEDEGUAR DOGBERRY
DOG SALMON CHUM KETA MORGAY
DOGFISH
DOGSHORE DOG DAGGER
DOG'S MERCURY SAPWORT
DOG SNAPPER JOCU
DOGSTAIL BENT
DOGWOOD OSIER SUMAC CORNEL
CORNUS GAITER WIDBIN BARBASCO
FISHWOOD
DOILY MAT TIDE TIDY NAPKIN
DOING ACT DEED FACT STIR EVENT
ACTION FUNCTION PRACTIVE
(PL.) FARE GEAR
DOIT DODKIN
DOLE LOT ALMS DEAL DOOL GIFT
GOAL METE PART VAIL ALLOT
FRAUD GRIEF GUILE MOURN SHARE
DECEIT GRIEVE RELIEF SORROW
CHARITY DEALING DESTINY
HANDOUT PAYMENT PORTION
BOUNDARY DIMENSUM DISPENSE
DIVISION GRATUITY LANDMARK
PITTANCE

DOLEFUL SAD DOWY DOWIE DREAR HEAVY DISMAL DOOLFU DREARY FUNEST RUEFUL FLEBILE DOLESOME DOLOROUS FUNESTAL MOURNFUL TRAGICAL

DOLL TOY BABE BABY MOLL ARRAY DOLLY PUPPE DOLLIE KEWPIE MAIDEN MAUMET MOPPET MUNECA POPPET POUPEE PUPPET KACHINA KATCINA KATCHINA MISTRESS **(— UP)** SWANK **(PASTEBOARD —)** PANTINE

DOLLAR BALL BEAN BONE BUCK CASE DURO FISH ROCK SCAD SKIN SPOT ADOBE BERRY DALER EAGLE PLONK PLUNK WHEEL GOURDE PATACA DAALDER SMACKER FROGSKIN PATACOON SIMOLEON **(SILVER —)** SINKER **(SPANISH —)** COB DURO COBBE **(THOUSAND —S)** GEE THOU GRAND

DOLLARFISH SHINER MOONFISH STARFISH

DOLLY DRAB HOBBY PEGGY PUNCH SWAGE MAIDEN FOLLOWER MISTRESS SLATTERN

DOLLYMAN BUCKER

DOLLYWAY DOCK

DOLMEN SENAM TOLMEN CROMMEL CROMLECH MEGALITH

DOLOMITE ANKERITE PEARLSPAR

DOLOR CALOR GRIEF SORROW ANGUISH SADNESS DISTRESS MOURNING

DOLOROUS SAD DISMAL DOLEFUL GRIEVOUS PATHETIC

DOLPHIN INIA SUSU BOUTO WHALE DORADO KILLER PALACH TURSIO BOLLARD COWFISH PELLOCK PULLOCK SNUFFER CETACEAN MAHIMAHI MUTILATE PORPOISE

DOLT ASS OAF PUT ASSE CALF CHUB CLOD COOF DULT FOOL GOFF MOKE PEAK STUB CHUMP DOBBY DUMMY DUNCE FUNGE IDIOT NUMPS PATCH THICK BEFOOL CUDDEN DOODLE DULTIE HOBBIL OXHEAD BLUNTIE DAWCOCK DULLARD JACKASS SCHNOOK BONEHEAD BOSTHOON CLODPATE DUMBBELL IMBECILE LUNKHEAD MACAROON MOONCALF NUMSKULL

DOLTISH DULL STUPID FOOLISH PEAKISH SOTTISH TOMFOOL BESOTTED BLOCKISH DOLTLIKE

DOMAIN LAND BOUND BOURN REALM SCOPE STATE WORLD BARONY BOURNE COUNTY DEMAIN EMPERY EMPIRE ESTATE SPHERE DEMESNE EARLDOM BIRTHDOM DOMINION LORDSHIP PROVINCE SEIGNORY STAROSTY **(— OF SULTAN)** SOLDAN **(— OF THE UNCONSCIOUS)** SHADOWLAND **(MATHEMATICAL —)** FIELD **(NETHER —)** HELL **(TRANSCENDENT —)** HEAVEN **(WOMAN'S —)** DISTAFF

DOMBEYA ASSONIA

DOME CAP CIMA TYPE CROWN VAULT COCKLE CUPOLA THOLOS CALOTTE EDIFICE CIMBORIO HEMIDOME **(— OVER TOMB)** WELI **(BUDDHIST —)** TOPE **(OBSERVATION —)** BLISTER **(SNOW-CAPPED —)** CALOTTE

DOMER CLASPER

DOMESTIC HIND HOME MAID MOZO DOMAL TABBY FAMILY HAMEIL HAMELT HEYDUC HOMELY HOMISH HOUSAL INLAND INMATE INWARD MENIAL NATIVE FAMILIC HEYDUCK SCALDER SERVANT FAMILIAR HOMEBRED HOMEMADE INTIMATE **(PL.)** FOLK

DOMESTICALLY ONSHORE

DOMESTICATE TAME ENTAME AMENAGE RECLAIM CIVILIZE

DOMESTICATED TAME GENTLE INWARD DOMESTIC FAMILIAR

DOMICILE CRIB HOME SHED ABODE HOUSE MENAGE DWELLING

DOMINANCE SWAY INFLUENCE

DOMINANT BOSSY CHIEF FIFTH TENOR RULING SOVRAN CENTRAL REGNANT SUPREME DOMINULE SUPERIOR

DOMINATE TOP HAVE RULE CHARM REIGN COERCE DIRECT GOVERN VASSAL BEWITCH COMMAND CONTROL ENVELOP BESTRIDE DOMINEER OVERSWAY OVERTONE

DOMINATING SUPERIOR BREATHLESS

DOMINATION EMPIRE CONTROL STRINGS BOVARISM BOVARYSM DOMINION

DOMINEER BOSS BRAG LORD RULE BULLY FEAST REVEL TOWER COMPEL COMMAND SWAGGER DOMINATE OVERBEAR OVERLEAD OVERLORD **(— OVER)** RIDE HECTOR

DOMINEERING SURLY LORDLY HAUGHTY ARROGANT DESPOTIC MASTERLY

DOMINICAN JACOBIN JACOBITE PREACHER PREDICANT

DOMINIE MASTER PASTOR

DOMINION RULE SWAY CROWN REALM REIGN DITION DOMAIN EMPERY EMPIRE REGNUM CONTROL DIOCESE DYNASTY KHANATE POUSTIE REGENCY CALIFATE IMPERIUM LORDSHIP SEIGNORY SIGNORIA SOVRANTY **(PL.)** DUCHY

DOMINO DIE BONE CARD FIVE MASK TILE BLANK JETON STONE DOUBLE JETTON MATADOR VENETIAN **(FIRST — PLAYED)** SET **(PL.)** BONEYARD

DOM PEDRO SNOOZER

DON WEAR ARRAY DRESS ENDUE INDUE THROW ASSUME CLOTHE INVEST ADDRESS NOBLEMAN

DONATE GIE GIFT GIVE BESTOW PRESENT

DONATION GIFT GRANT DONATIO PRESENT DONATIVE **(—S RECEIVED BY SINGERS)** CARL

DONE GAR DEEN OVER BAKED ENDED GIVEN COOKED THROUGH FINISHED **(— BY WORD OF MOUTH)** PAROL PAROLE **(— CARELESSLY)** SCAMBLING **(— FOR)** GONE SUNK KAPUT KAPUTT FINISHED **(— IN FAITH)** AF **(— IN PLAIN SIGHT)** BRAZEN **(— POORLY)** BOTCHY **(— TOGETHER)** CONCERTED **(— WITH)** BY **(— WITHOUT DELIBERATION)** SNAP **(— WRONG WAY)** AWK **(TO BE —)** PASS

DONEE DONATOR HERITOR RECEIVER

DONJON KEEP ROCCA DUNGEON

DONKEY ASS BUSS DONK FUSS MOKE BURRO CHUMP CUDDY DICKY EQUID GENET GUDDA HINNY HORSE JENNY NEDDY CUDDLE DICKEY JENNET ONAGER ASINEGO BUSSOCK FUSSOCK JACKASS LONGEAR

DONKEY ENGINE DOCTOR DONKEY ROADER YARDER DOLLBEER

DONOR GIVER DONATOR

DO-NOTHING DONNOT DONOUGHT FAINEANT

DONUM GIVER DEUNAM

DOODAD DODAD DOODAB DOFUNNY GIMCRACK JIMCRACK

DOOM KER LAW LOT DAMN FATE

RUIN CURSE DEATH JUDGE DECREE
DEVOTE STEVEN CONDEMN DESTINE
DESTINY FORTUNE STATUTE
DECISION FOREDOOM SENTENCE
DOOMED FEY DEAD DONE FATAL
DAMNED FORLORN ACCURSED
FINISHED
DOOM PALM DOUM
DOOMSMAN LAWMAN
DOOR LID DROP EXIT FOLD GATE
HECK SHUT TRAP ENTRY HATCH
JANUA VALVE JIGGER PORTAL
RADDLE WICKET BARRIER
DOORWAY INGRESS OPENING
OUTDOOR PASSAGE POSTERN
ANTEPORT ENTRANCE FOREDOOR
POSTICUM SERVIDOR STOPPING
TRAVERSE
(— IN MINE) STOPPING
(— OF ASH PIT) ARCH
(— OF MASONIC LODGE) TILE
(AIRPLANE —) CLAMSHELL
(HALF —) HECK HATCH
(ROMAN —S) FORES
(SLIDING —) SHUT SHOJI FUSUMA
TRAVERSE
(STORM —) DINGLE
(STRONG —) OAK
(TRAP —) SLOT SCRUTO VAMPIRE
VAMPYRE
DOORFRAME BUCK
DOORHEAD DERNER
DOORKEEPER TILER TILIA USHER
DURWAN PORTER WARDEN
DOORMAN JANITOR OSTIARY
DOORWARD HUISSIER JANITRIX
PORTRESS WISKINKY
DOOR KNOCKER HAMMER RAPPER
DOOR LATCH SNECK HAGGADAY
DOORMAN FOOTMAN HALLMAN
DOORWARD
DOORMAT COCOMAT
DOORPOST DURN JAMB PIER POST
ALETTE POSTEL
DOORSILL SOIL
DOORSTOP BUMPER HOLDBACK
DOORWAY DOOR EXIT PORTAL
OPENING
DOPATTA UPARNA DOOPUTTY
DOPE HOP BOOB DRUG GOFF GOON
GOOP BOOBY OPIUM PASTE HEROIN
INSIDE OPIATE LOWDOWN PREDICT
STUPEFY NARCOTIC
DOPER GREASER
DOR BEE DORR JOKE MOCK BONGO
CLOCK DORRE JOKER SCOFF TRICK
BEETLE DRONER BUFFOON DECEIVE
MOCKERY
DORADO CUIR XIPHIAS GOLDFISH
DORBEETLE DOR CLOCK DRONER
BUZZARD BUMCLOCK
**DORIS (BROTHER AND HUSBAND OF
—)** NEREUS
(FATHER OF —) OCEANUS
(MOTHER OF —) TETHYS
DORMANCY TORPOR ABEYANCE
DORMANT FIXED ASLEEP LATENT
TORPID RESTING SLEEPER INACTIVE
SLEEPING CONNIVENT

DORMER WINDOW LUCOMB
MEMBER DORMANT EYEBROW
LUCARNE LUTHERN
DORMITORY DORM HALL HOUSE
DORMER DORTER HOSTEL BULLPEN
COLLEGE DORTOUR CUBATORY
QUARTERS
DORMOUSE LOIR DRYAD LEROT
GLIRID SLEEPER
DORNICK DONEY LINEN DARNEX
DONACK DONNICK
DORPER DORSIAN
DORSAL NOTAL DORSER DOSSER
TERGAL ABAXIAL HANGING
SUPERIOR
DORSUM BACK
DOSAGE (SCIENCE OF —)
POSOLOGY
DOSE BOLE DOST SHOT BROMO
DATIO DOSIS DRAFT STORE TREAT
DATION DOCTOR DOSAGE DRENCH
POTION BOOSTER BROMIDE
CAPSULE DRAUGHT QUANTITY
(NARCOTIC —) LOCUS BINDLE
LOCUST
DOSS BOW DOS KNOT TUFT BUNCH
DOSSERET PULVINO
DOT SET CLOT DOTE LUMP MOTE
PECK SPOT STAR TICK COVER
DOWER DOWRY POINT PRICK SPECK
BULLET CENTER CENTRE DOTLET
PERIOD STIGME TITTLE TOCHER
PUNCTUM PUNCTUS SPECKLE
SPOTTLE STIPPLE FLYSPECK
PARTICLE SPRINKLE
(— IN CODE) DIT
(— ON FOREHEAD) BOTTU
**(— ON PATCH OF DIFFERENT
COLOR)** ISLET
(BLACK —) DARTROSE
(PL.) LEADERS
DOTAGE DOTE FOLLY DRIVEL
SENILITY TWICHILD
DOTARD DOTER SILLY DOTANT
SENILE DOTTREL DOTTEREL
IMBECILE LIRIPIPE LIRIPOOP
DOTCHIN STEELYARD
DOTE ROT DOVE DOZE FOND LIKE
LOVE ADORE DECAY ENDOW
BESTOW DOTAGE DOTARD DRIVEL
STUPOR IMBECILE
DOTING FON FOND GAGA DOTAGE
PAWING
DOTTED SEME SEMEED TICKED
TOUCHY SPOTTED PUNCTATE
SPECKLED STIPPLED STELLATED
(— SWISS) LAPPET
DOTTER SPOTTER
DOTTEREL DUPE GULL WIND
PLOVER DOTTREL MORINEL
DOTTY TOTY CRAZY TOTTY FEEBLE
SPOTTY
DOUBLE KA BOW PLY DUAL FOLD
SORE TWIN CRACK DUPLE FETCH
ROUND SOSIE BIFOLD BINARY
BINATE DOPPIO DUPLEX MIDDLE
DIPLOID DOUBLET TWOFOLD
BIVALENT GEMINATE
(— IMPRESSION) MACKLE

(— IN POKER) STRADDLE
(— MUSICAL NOTES) AUGMENT
(— UP) BUCK JACKKNIFE
(PHANTOM —) FETCH
DOUBLE BASSOON FAGOTTONE
DOUBLE CHIN CHOLLER
DOUBLECROSS BITCH CHEAT
BETRAY DECEIVE SWINDLE
BUSINESS
DOUBLE-CROSSER RAT HEEL
DOUBLED GEMEL GEMINOUS
DOUBLE DAGGER DIESIS
DOUBLE-DEALING DECEIT
DUPLICITY
DOUBLE FLUTE DIAULOS
DOUBLENESS DUALITY PLENITUDE
DOUBLE-RIPPER BOBSLED
BOBSLEIGH
DOUBLE-RUNNER SKATE
DOUBLET SNIFF DOUBLE DUPLET
PALTOCK PLACCATE POURPOINT
DOUBLETREE EVENER SPREADER
DOUBLING LAP FOLD HEAD LOOP
(— OF THE BLIND) STRADDLE
DOUBLOON ONZA
DOUBT FEAR WEIR DEMUR DREAD
DWERE QUERY WAVER BALANCE
DIFFIDE DUBIATE DUBIETY SCRUPLE
SKEPSIS SUSPECT SWITHER
UMBRAGE DISTRUST DUBITATE
HESITATE MISTRUST QUESTION
STAGGERS MISLIPPEN
DOUBTER CYNIC SKEPTIC
DUBITANTE
DOUBTFUL JUBUS DOUBTY UNSURE
DUBIOUS FEARFUL JEALOUS
PERHAPS WILSOME BOGGLISH
DREADFUL JUBEROUS PERILOUS
WAVERING
DOUBTING DUBIOUS DUBITANT
DOUBTLESS WITTERLY
DOUCEUR BONUS POURBOIRE
DOUCHE RINSE EYEWASH
DOUGH CASH DUFF CRUST DAIGH
MONEY PASTE PUPPY CHANGE
HALLAH NOODLE SPONGE BRIOCHE
MANDLEN TEIGLACH
(BISCUIT —) CAKE
(BREAD —) SPONGE
(FERMENTING —) LEAVEN
(FRIED —) SPUD
(NOODLE —) FARFEL FERFEL
DOUGHNUT NUT SINK DONUT
CYMBAL SINKER CRULLER FATCAKE
NUTCAKE OLYCOOK OLYKOEK
SIMBALL TWISTER BISMARCK
FASNACHT
(SHAPED LIKE —) TOROIDAL
DOUGHTY FELL PREU TALL BRAVE
VALIANT INTREPID
DOUGHY DUNCH SODDEN
DOUR DERN GLUM GRIM HARD SOUR
ROUGH STERN GLOOMY MOROSE
SEVERE STRONG SULLEN OMINOUS
TACITURN
DOUSE BEAT BLOW DOFF DUCK
QUIT STOW CEASE DOWSE RINSE
SOUSE DRENCH PLUNGE SLUICE

STRIKE STROKE IMMERSE
DOWNPOUR
DOUZEPER ANSEIS PALADIN
DOVE DOO DOW DOZE KUKU JONAH
CULVER CUSHAT JEMIMA PIGEON
COLUMBA DOVELET LAUGHER
NAMAQUA SLUMBER DOVELING
RINGDOVE
(— SOUND) CURR
(GROUND —) ROLA
(RING —) TOOZOO
(ROCK —) SOD
(SCALE —) INCA
DOVECOTE DOOCOT LOUVER
DOVECOT DOWCOTE PIGEONRY
DOVEKIE AUK ALLE BULL ROTCH
ROTGE DOVEKEY BULLBIRD
DOVELIKE
DOVETAIL COG JAG JAGG TENON
DOWDINESS FRUMPERY
DOWDY POKY FRUMP POKEY TACKY
BLOWZY SHABBY STODGY UNTIDY
FRUMPISH SLOVENLY
DOWEL PEG PIN COAK STUD SPRIG
JOGGLE PINTLE DULEDGE
DOWER DOS DOWRY ENDOW
TOCHER DOARIUM PORTION
HERITAGE MARITAGE
DOWITCHER SNIPE DRIVER SLEEPER
GRAYBACK GREYBACK LONGBEAK
DOWN HUP BETE CAST DOON DOWL
FELL FLIX FLUE FUZZ HILL LINT
SOUR ADOWN BELOW DOWLE EIDER
FLOOR FLUFF BEDOWN FRIEZE
LANUGO PAPPUS HANDOUT HILLOCK
PLUMAGE DOWNLAND
(— AND OUT) QUISBY
(— AT THE HEEL) SLIPSHOD
(— THAT WAY) DOWNBY DOWNBYE
(— THE LINE) ALONG
(FAR —) DEEP DEEPLY
(FARTHEST —) BOTTOMMOST
(STRAIGHT —) DOWNRIGHT
DOWNBEAT THESIS
DOWNCAST BAD SAD DOWN ABJECT
GLOOMY HANGING DEJECTED
HOPELESS
DOWNFALL PIT FALL FATE RUIN
TRAP ABYSS FINISH DESCENT
ECLIPSE UNDOING COLLAPSE
DOWNCOME
DOWNFEED OVERHEAD
DOWNFLOW VAIL DEFLUX
DOWNFOLD SADDLE DOWNWARP
DOWNHILL DOWNDALE
DOWNPOUR POUR RAIN DOUSE
DOWSE FLOOD SPILL SPOUT
DELUGE TORRENT CATARACT
DOWNRIGHT FAIR FLAT PURE RANK
BLANK BLUNT PLAIN PLUMB ROUND
SHEER STARK ARRANT DIRECT
FAIRLY STURDY ABSOLUTE
EVENDOWN POSITIVE THOROUGH
DOWNSPOUT SPOUT DOWNPIPE
DOWNTAKE
DOWNSTAIRS BELOW
DOWNSTROKE DOWNBEAT
DOWNSWING DOLDRUMS
DOWNWARD ADOWN BELOW LOWER

PRONE DEORSUM DOWNWITH
(— ON ONE SIDE) SIDEWAYS
DOWNWIND LEEWARD
DOWNY SOFT FLUEY MOSSY NAPPY
PILAR PLUMY QUIET CALLOW
FLEDGY FLOSSY FLUFFY PILARY
PLACID COTTONY CUNNING
KNOWING SOOTHING
DOWRY DOS DOT GIFT DOWER
SULKA DOWAGE TALENT PORTION
DOWSE WITCH
DOXOLOGY GLORIA KADDISH
DOXY WENCH HARLOT
DOYEN DEAN DOYENNE
DOZE NAP NOD ROT DORM DOTE
DOVE DECAY DOVER SLEEP SLOOM
CATNAP DROWSE MUDDLE SNOOZE
MEMENTO PERPLEX SLUMBER
SNOOZLE STUPEFY
DOZEN DIZZEN DOSAIN
(FIVE —) TALLY
(TWO —) THRAVE
DOZING DOGSLEEP
DRAB BOX DAW FOX SAD DELL
DRUG DULL BESOM BLEAK DINGY
DOLLY GRAVE GRAZE HEAVY
WENCH WHORE FRUMPY MALKIN
POISON STODGY PROSAIC SUBFUSC
DOLLYMOP EVERYDAY POMPLESS
(CHAETURA —) BEAR
DRABBLE DRAGGLE
DRACHM DRAM
DRACO ANGUIS DRAGON
DRAFT NIP SIP CHIT DOSE DRAG
DRAM DRAW GLUT GULF GUST ITEM
LEVY PLAN PLOT SUCK SWIG TOOT
WORK BLAST CHECK DRINK EPURE
SLOCK SWILL SWIPE TAPER WRITE
DESIGN DRENCH GODOWN MINUTE
POTION REDACT RETURN SCHEME
SCROLL SKETCH WAUCHT WAUGHT
ABBOZZO DRAUGHT DRAWING
OUTLINE PATTERN PROJECT
BEVERAGE POTATION PROTOCOL
(— OF A VESSEL) GAGE GAUGE
(— OF AIR) COOKE
(— OF COMPOSITION) SCORE
(— OF LAW) BILL
(— OF PATTERN) STRIP
(— OFF) SHED
(HEAVY —) WHITTER
(LARGE —) SCOUR CAROUSE
(MIDDAY —) NOONING
(ORIGINAL —) PROTOCOL
(ROUGH —) BROUILLON SCANTLING
(SLEEPING —) DORTER
(SMALL —) NIP SIP SUCK TIFF TIFT
DRAFTER HORSER
DRAFTSMAN DRAWER TRACER
TIPPLER
DRAG DOG LAG DRUG HONE HOOK
KITE SHOE SKID SLUR TOLE TOLL
CREEP DEVIL DRAWL DRIFT FLOAT
LURRY NOWEL PLUCK RALLY SLIDE
SNAKE SWEEP TEASE TRAIL TRAIN
TRAWL TRICE DAGGLE DROGUE
LINGER REMORA SCHOOL TAIGLE
TRAYNE DRAGBAR DRAGGLE
GRAPNEL GRAPPLE SCHLEPP

SKIDPAN ARRASTRA DRAGSHOE
(— ALONG) LUG CRAWL SHOOL
TRAYNE TRACHLE TRAUCHLE
(— CARELESSLY) HIKE
(— DOWN) DEGRADE
(— FEET) SLODGE
(— FORCIBLY) SNAKE
(— HOME CARCASS OF GAME)
TUMP
(— IN DEEP WATER) CREEP
(— JERKILY) SNIG
(— LOGS) SKID
(— OFF) HARRY
(— OUT) DRAWL
(PLANK —) RUBBER
DRAGGING LEADEN
(— DEAD BULL FROM RING)
ARRASTRE
DRAGGLE LAG DRAIL DAGGLE
DRABBLE
DRAGNET FLUE TRAIN TRAWL
DRAWNET TRAINEL
DRAGON AHI LUNG WORM DRAKE
RAHAB NIDHOG VRITRA WYVERN
BASILISK DRAGONET NIDHOGGR
NITHHOGG
(— WITH 7 HEADS) HYDRA
(SEA —) QUAVIVER
DRAGONET FOX ILLECK FOXFISH
GOWDNIE GURNARD JUGULAR
SCULPIN LORICATE QUAVIVER
DRAGONFLY NAIAD SKIMMER
LIBELLULA
DRAGON TREE DRACAENA
DRAGROPE DRAG GUSS
DRAIN DRY FRY GAN GAW SAP SEW
TOP BUZZ COUP DAIL DALE DELF
DIKE DRAG DRAW GOUT GRIP GURT
LADE LODE MILK SIKE SINK SOAK
SUFF SUMP TEEM TILE BLEED
BUNNY CANAL DELFT DRAFT DREEN
DRILL DROVE EMPTY FLEET GROOP
GULLY LEECH RHINE SEUCH SEUGH
SEWER SHORE SIVER STELL
EMULGE FILTER FURROW GUZZLE
RIGGOT SHEUCH SHEUGH SIPHON
SPONGE SWOUGH SYPHON TRENCH
TROGUE TROUGH ZANJON ACEQUIA
ALBERCA CAROUSE CARRIER
CHANNEL CULVERT DEPLETE
DRAUGHT EXHAUST GRINDLE
GRIPPLE SCUPPER ZANJONA
CANALIZE CARRIAGE SINKHOLE
SUBDRAIN THURROCK
(— DRY) JIB
(— IN FEN) LEAM
(— IN MINE) SOUGH
(— IN STABLE) GROOP
(COVERED —) THURROCK
(OPEN —) SIVER STELL
(SMALL —) TRONE
DRAINAGE ADIT SAUR SOCK
SULLAGE SUMPAGE
DRAINAGEWAY DRAW
DRAINING SEEPAGE DRAINAGE
EMULGENT
DRAINPIPE SINK SHELL WHELM
LEADER QUELME
DRAKE STAG STAIG DRAKELET

DRAM GO NIP MITE SLUG TIFT
DRAFT DRINK SOPIE CALKER
DRACHM JIGGER CAULKER SNIFTER
MERIDIAN POTATION QUANTITY
(— **OF LIQUOR**) TOT SLUG SNIFTER
(— **OF SPIRITS**) NOBBLER
DRAMA RAS AUTO MIME PLAY LEGIT
OPERA COMEDY NATAKA SCENES
SOAPER TRAGIC ATELLAN COMEDIA
HISTORY PROVERB THEATRE
TRAGEDY DUODRAMA MONODRAM
OPERETTA PASTORAL
(**DANCE** —) KATHAKALI
(**JAPANESE** —) NO KABUKI
(**MUSICAL** —) OPERA SAYNETE
OPERETTA
DRAMATIC WILD VIVID SCENIC
THESPIAN
(— **REPRESENTATION**) WAYANG
DRAMATIST OG ACTOR IBSENITE
DRAMSHOP GROGSHOP
DRAPE HANG ADORN COVER CRAPE
WEAVE CURTAIN FESTOON HANGING
VALANCE
DRAPED BEHUNG
DRAPER TAILOR LINENMAN
DRAPERY SWAG BAIZE DRAPE
SCENE CURTAIN REREDOS VALANCE
MOURNING
(— **ON BEDSTEAD**) PAND
(**PIECE OF** —) HANGING
DRAPING BLOUSE DRAPERY
DRASTIC DIRE HARSH EXTREME
RADICAL RIGOROUS
(**NOT** —) BLAND
DRAT RABBIT DOGGONE
DRATTED BLESSED
DRAUGHT (ALSO SEE DRAFT) SLUG
OENOMEL
DRAVIDIAN GOND KOTA TODA TULU
ARAVA COORG GONDI KHOND KLING
MALTO ORAON TAMIL ANDHRA
BADAGA BIRHOR BRAHUI KODAGU
KURUKH TELEGU TELUGU COLLERY
DRAVIDA TAMILIC KANARESE
TAMILIAN
DRAW LUG TEE TIE TOW TUG DRAG
DUCT HALE HAUL LADE LIMN LINE
LURE PULL RAKE SPAN TILL TIRE
TOLL TREK VENT CATCH DRAFT
DRILL EDUCE ENDUE EXACT HEAVE
PAINT SKINK TRACE TRAIN TRECK
ALLURE BUCKET DEDUCE DEPICT
DERIVE DESIGN DEVISE ELICIT
ENGAGE ENTICE INDUCE INHALE
SELECT SKETCH STRIKE ATTRACT
BEGUILE CONTOUR DETRACT
DOGFALL DRAUGHT EXTRACT
INSPIRE PORTRAY SCUMBLE
INSCRIBE INVEIGLE OUTBRAID
STANDOFF
(— **A CARD**) CUT
(— **AIR**) BREATHE
(— **ALONG**) TRACK TRAIN
(— **APART**) REAM DIVEL DIDUCE
DIVERGE
(— **AT A PIPE**) SHOOH SHAUGH
(— **AWAY**) ARACE DRAFT ABDUCT
ARACHE DRAUGHT ENTRAIN

DISTRACT
(— **AWKWARDLY**) SCRAWL
(— **BACK FROM**) BLENCH FLINCH
TORFEL TORFLE DETRECT
(— **BACK LIPS**) GRIN
(— **BACK**) FADE REVEL START
WINCE ARREAR RETIRE REVOKE
SHRINK CRINKLE RECLAIM WITHTEE
(— **BOLT**) SLOT
(— **BY SUCTION**) ASPIRATE
(— **DEEP BREATH**) SUSPIRE
(— **DRINK**) BIRL
(— **EARTH AROUND**) HILL
(— **FORTH**) EDUCE FETCH ELICIT
DEPROME EXHAUST
(— **ON**) INDUE INDUCE SOLICIT
(— **OUT**) MILK SLUB EXACT SKINK
TRACT ELICIT EXHALE EXTEND
PRODUCE PROLONG LENGTHEN
(— **TIGHT**) FRAP THRAP STRAIN
(— **TOGETHER**) COWL LACE COART
GATHER
(— **UP**) FORM MAKE HUCKLE INKNIT
UPHALE
DRAWBACK OUT LETDOWN
TAKEOFF DISCOUNT PULLBACK
DRAWBAR DRAGBAR BULLNOSE
DRAWLINK SLIPRAIL
DRAWBRIDGE PONTLEVIS
DRAWEE ACCEPTER
DRAWER TILL LIMNER LOCKER
TILLER ENTERER INTAKER SHUTTLE
(— **OF WATER**) GIBEONITE
(**COAL** —) PUTTER
(**TYPEWRITER** —) BED
DRAWER-DOWN KNOBBLER
DRAWER-IN ENTERER HEALDER
HEDDLER
DRAWER-OFF RACKER
DRAWERS PANTS SHORTS LININGS
PANTIES SHALWAR CALSOUNS
CALZOONS SHINTYAN SHULWAURS
DRAWGATE SLACKER
DRAWING DRAW CHALK DRAFT
ENVOI EPURE SEPTA TUSHE
CRAYON DESIGN DETAIL FIGURE
FUSAIN SKETCH CARTOON CROQUIS
DIAGRAM DRAUGHT HAULING
ISOTYPE PULLING TOUSCHE
CHARCOAL CROSSING DOODLING
FREEHAND FROTTAGE HATCHING
LINEWORK SANGUINE SPECULUM
STICKMAN TRACTION TRANSFER
TRICKING
(— **IN**) INDRAFT
(— **OF LOTS**) BALLOT
(— **OUT**) BATTUE
(**COMIC** —) CARTOON DROLLERY
(**SIDEWALK** —) SCREEVE
DRAWING-IN DRAW ENTERING
DRAWKNIFE SHAVE JIGGER
DRAWL DRANT DRATE DRUNT TRAIN
LOITER PROLATE
DRAWN DRAFT STREIT DRAUGHT
GRAPHIC HAGGARD
(— **APART**) DISTRACT
(— **AWAY**) ABSTRACT
(— **CLOSE**) STRICT
(— **OFF**) DRAINED

(— **OUT**) DREE DREICH DREIGH
EXTENDED
DRAWPLATE AGATE FLATTER
DRAWSHEET TYMPAN
DRAWSTRING LATCH STRING
DRAY CART LORRY SCOOT SLOOP
WAGON CAMION JIGGER SLOVEN
WHEERY
DREAD AWE DREE FEAR FRAY FUNK
WARD WERE ANGST AWFUL DOUBT
GRISE TIMOR ADREAD AGRISE
DISMAY ESCHEW HORROR TERROR
ANXIETY DISMISS DRIDDER
REDOUBT AFFRIGHT DREDDOUR
GASTNESS MISDREAD TERRIBLE
DREADED AWESOME BEDREAD
DREADFUL DIRE AWFUL CRUEL
DISMAL GRISLY HORRID AWESOME
CAREFUL DIREFUL DRIDDER
FEARFUL GHASTLY GRIMFUL
HIDEOUS UNCOUTH DOUBTFUL
DOUBTOUS GHASTFUL HORRIBLE
HORRIFIC PERILOUS SCAREFUL
SHOCKING TERRIBLE TERRIFIC
DREADFULLY DIRELY GRISLY
ABYSMALLY
DREADNOUGHT TANK DAREALL
WARSHIP FEARLESS
DREAM METE MOON MUSE REVE
FANCY SWEVEN VISION AISLING
AVISION CHIMERA FANTASY IMAGINE
NIRVANA REVERIE ROMANCE
CHIMAERA DAYDREAM PHANTASM
SOMNIATE
DREAMER POET METER MUSARD
FANTAST IDEALIST PHANTAST
DREAMINESS LANGUOR
DREAMING ADREAM TRAUMEREI
DREAMTIME ALCHERA
DREAMY KEF SOFT MOONY VAGUE
POETIC FARAWAY LANGUID ONEIRIC
PENSIVE DREAMFUL FANCIFUL
SOOTHING
DREAR DERN DISMAL GLOOMY
DOLEFUL
DREARY SAD DIRE DOWY DREE
DULL FLAT GLUM BLEAK CRUEL
DOWIE DRURY OURIE WASTE WISHT
DISMAL ELENGE GLOOMY GOUSTY
LONELY DOLEFUL GOUSTIE
HOWLING WILSOME GRIEVOUS
WEARIFUL
DREDGE MOP DRAG DREG SIFT
SCOOP TRAIN DEEPEN DRUDGE
SCRAPE SPONGE GANGAVA
SCALLOP EXCAVATE SPRINKLE
DREDGER DUSTER HEDGEHOG
DREDGING JILLING
DREGS LAG MUD CRAP FAEX LAGS
LEES SCUT SILT SUDS TAIL DRAFF
DREST DROSS DRUGS FECES FOOTS
GROUT JAUPS MAGMA BOTTOM
DRAINS DUNDER MOTHER REFUSE
SORDES SORDOR ULLAGE DRIBBLE
GROUNDS GRUMMEL HEELTAP
OUTWALE RESIDUE RINSING
GRUMMELS REMNANTS SEDIMENT
SETTLING
(— **OF LIQUOR**) TAPLASH

(— **OF MOLTEN GLASS**) DRIBBLE
(— **OF SOCIETY**) WASH
DREIBUND TRIPLICE
DREIDEL TRENDEL
DRENCH DOSE HOSE SIND SINK
SOAK TOSH BLASH DOUSE DOWSE
DRAFT DRINK DROKE DROUK
DROWN SLOCK SLUSH SOUSE
STEEP SWILL BUCKET DELUGE
DOUCHE IMBRUE INFUSE POTION
SLUICE DRUNKEN EMBATHE
IMMERSE INDRENCH PERMEATE
SATURATE SUBMERGE
DRENCHED DRUNKEN
DRENCHER INFUSER
DRENCHING DOUSE DOWSE
DOWNPOUR
DRESS AX AXE BED DON DUB FIG
FIT HOE KIT RAG RAY RIG TOG
BARB BEGO BOWN BUSK BUSS
CLAY COAT COMB DESK DILL DINK
GALA GARB GEAR GORE GOWN
HONE HUKE KNAP MILL RAIL ROBE
SUIT TIFF TIRE TRIM TUBE TUCK
VEST WEAR ADORN ARRAY BIGAN
CLEAN CLOTH CRUMB CRUSH
CURRY DIGHT DIZEN EQUIP FLOAT
FROCK GUISE HABIT IHRAM MAGMA
PREEN PRICK PRIMP PRINK PRUNE
SHAPE THING TRICK AGUISE ATTIRE
BARBER BROACH CLOTHE ENROBE
FANGLE FETTLE FRAISE GRAITH
INVEST JELICK JUMPER KIRTLE
MAGPIE MULLET MUUMUU OUTFIT
PLIGHT REVEST SARONG SHEATH
SHROUD TOILET ADDRESS AFFAITE
APPAREL BANDAGE BEDIZEN
CHEMISE CLOTHES COSTUME
DALLACK DUBBING GARMENT
GARNISH HARNESS HATCHEL
RAIMENT TOGGERY VESTURE
ACCOUTER CLEADING CLOTHING
DECORATE FEATHERS HANDMADE
ORNAMENT SUNDRESS TAILLEUR
VESTMENT EMBELLISH
(— **A SKIN**) WHEEL
(— **DOWN**) BRACE
(— **ELEGANTLY**) DINK
(— **FISH**) CALVER
(— **FLAX**) TED
(— **FLINT**) NAP KNAP
(— **FOOD**) SAUCE
(— **FOR FELTING**) CARROT
(— **HAIR**) TIRE TRUSS BARBER
(— **HIDES**) BEAM
(— **HURRIEDLY**) HUDDLE
(— **IN FINE CLOTHES**) DIKE
(— **MEAT**) LARD SHROUD
(— **NEGLIGENTLY**) MOB
(— **ORE**) VAN
(— **OVER**) STOP
(— **SHEEPSKINS**) TAW
(— **SMARTLY**) DALLACK
(— **STONE**) DAB NIG DAUB DRAG
FACE GAGE HACK GAUGE NIDGE
POINT SCABBLE SCAPPLE
(— **TAWDRILY**) BEDIZEN
(— **UNTIDILY**) MAB
(— **UP**) BUSK DILL ADORN ARRAY

PRANK PRIMP PRINK SPICK WATER
FETTLE TOGGLE BECLOUT BEDRESS
(— **VULGARLY**) DAUB
(— **WITH CHISEL**) DROVE
(— **WITH TROWEL**) STRIKE
(— **WORN BY MAN**) DRAG
(— **WOUND**) PANSE BANDAGE
(**COAT** —) SIMAR SYMAR SIMARRE
(**EVENING** —) FORMAL
(**FESTIVE** —) GALA
(**INCOMPLETE** —) DISARRAY
(**LOOSE** —) SACK SACQUE
(**MORNING** —) PEIGNOIR
(**PECULIAR** —) LIVERY
(**POPLIN** —) TABINET TABBINET
(**RUSSIAN NATIONAL** —) SARAFAN
(**STYLE OF** —) GETUP
DRESSED CLAD DONE BOUND
BECLAD COATED COMBED HABITED
GOFFERED
(— **GAILY**) FRESH SPARKISH
(— **IN WHITE**) CANDIDATE
(**LOOSELY** —) DISCINCT
(**RICHLY** —) BROCADED
(**ROUGHLY** —) HEWN
(**SHOWILY** —) BEPRANKED
(**STYLISHLY** —) SMART
(**WELL** —) BRAW GASH
DRESSER ROBER TAWER BUREAU
FRAMER MODISTE CUPBOARD
(**LEATHER** —) LEVANTER
DRESSING CAST GRAVY BEATING
BLANKET IODOFORM RAVIGOTE
REMOLADE SCOLDING STUFFING
(— **FOR WOUNDS**) LINT SPONGE
(— **OF STONE**) SKIFFLING
(**HAIR** —) LACKER LACQUER
DRESSING ROOM SHIFT VESTRY
CAMARIN VESTUARY
DRESSMAKER SEWER SEAMER
MODISTE STITCHER COUTURIER
TIREWOMAN
DRESS RACK FRIPPERY
DRESSY SHARP
DRIBBLE DRIB DRIP DROP CARRY
DRIVEL DRIBLET DRIPPLE DRIZZLE
DRIBLET CLOT PIECE
(**PL.**) SMALLS
DRIED SEAR SERE ADUST GIZZEN
TORRID WIZENED GIZZENED
DRIFT FAN JET SAG DENE DUNE
FORD HERD PLOT SILT TIDE TILL
DRIVE DROVE FLEET FLOAT FLOCK
IOWAN SENSE SLIDE SLOOM SLOUM
TENOR TREND BROACH COURSE
DESIGN DEVICE DRIVER OFFSET
PODGER SCHEME STREAM TUNNEL
WINDLE CURRENT DIPHEAD DRIBBLE
GALLERY HEADING IMPETUS
IMPULSE LATERAL OUTWASH
PASTURE PROCESS PURPORT
SETBOLT DILUVIUM DRIFTPIN
TENDENCY
(— **LANGUIDLY**) SWOON
(— **OF CLOUDS**) CARRY
(— **OF SAND OR SNOW**) WREATH
(— **SIDEWISE**) CRAB
(— **WITH ANCHOR DOWN**) CLUB
(**DOWNWARD** —) DROOP

(**GLACIAL** —) CARY TILL IOWAN
(**RUBBLE** —) HEAD
DRIFTER DROVER
DRIFTING ADRIFT DRIFTAGE
DRIFT PLUG DUMMY
DRIFTWAY DROVE
DRIFTWOOD WAFTURE
DRILL GAD JAR JIG RIG SOW TAP
BORE CORE SPUD AUGER BORER
CHARK CHURN DECOY DREEL
PADDY THIRL TRAIN TUTOR TWIRL
WHIRL ALLURE BROACH ENTICE
FURROW JUMPER PIERCE SCHOOL
SEEDER SINKER STOPER THRILL
CHANNEL DRIFTER JANKERS
PLUGGER STARTER EXERCISE
INSTRUCT
(— **SYSTEM**) MARTINET
DRILLMAN STOPER
DRINK GO ADE ALE BIB BUM FIX GIN
HUM LAP MOP PEG POT RUM RYE
SIP SUP TEA TOT WET BALL BEER
BEND BENO BOLL BOSA BOZA
BREW BULL CHIA COKE COLA DRAG
DRAM FIZZ FLIP GROG HAVE HORN
JAKE LUSH MEAD NIPA NOGG PULL
PURL SHOT SIND SLUG SOAK SOMA
SOPE SPOT SWIG TIFF TOOT TOPE
WHET AIRAH BEVER BLAND BOMBO
BOOZE BOUSE BOZAH BUBUD
BUMBO CRUSH DAISY DRAFT FLOAT
GLOGG HAOMA JULEP LAGER
MORAT NEGUS PAINT POSCA PUNCH
QUAFF ROUSE SETUP SKINK SLING
SLOCK SMACH SMASH SMILE
SMOKE SNIFF SNORT SOPIE SOUSE
SWATS SWILL THING TOAST TODDY
VODKA WHIFF ZOMBI ABSORB
BEZZLE BRACER BRANDY BUMPER
CALKER CASIRI CATLAP CAUDLE
CHASER COFFEE COOPER DIBBLE
DRENCH EGGHOT EGGNOG FUDDLE
GIMLET GODOWN GUGGLE GUZZLE
HOOKER IMBIBE MESCAL POSSET
POTION PTISAN RICKEY SCREED
SHANDY SIPPLE SIRPLE SWANKY
SWINGE TACKLE TAMPOY TASTER
TIPPLE VELVET WAUCHT WAUGHT
ZOMBIE BRAGGET BRIMMER
CAROUSE CHEERER CHIRPER
COBBLER COLLINS CONSUME
CORDIAL DILUENT DRAUGHT
EXHAUST FLANNEL GUARANA
GUARAPO MORNING NOONING
PROPOMA SHERBET SIDECAR
SNEEZER SNIFTER SUCTION
SUPPAGE SWALLOW TANKARD
TRILLIL APERITIF BEVERAGE
BRIDECUP COCKTAIL HIGHBALL
LIBATION MAHOGANY POTATION
QUENCHER REFRESCO RUMBARGE
SANGAREE SPRITZER SYLLABUB
TEQUILA
(— **AT DRAFT**) TOP
(— **EXCESSIVELY**) TOPE BIBLE
SOUSE BEZZLE BIBBLE SWIZZLE
(— **FROM FERMENTED MILK**) AIRAN
(— **GREEDILY**) SLOP SWACK SWILL
GUTTLE GUZZLE

(— **HEAVILY**) TOOT SWINK
(— **INTOXICATING LIQUOR**)
IRRIGATE
(— **LIQUOR**) TIP DRAM SOAK BOOZE
PAINT
(— **NOISILY**) SLURP
(— **OF BEER**) BUTCHER
(— **OF IMMORTALITY**) SOMA
(— **OF INDIA**) SOMA SHRAB
(— **OF LIQUEUR**) FRAPPE
(— **OF LIQUOR**) WET DRAM SHOT
SPOT WHET SETUP WHIFF CALKER
JIGGER TASTER WETTING HIGHBALL
NIGHTCAP
(— **OF MOLASSES**) SWITCHEL
(— **OF THE GODS**) NECTAR
(— **OF VINEGAR AND WATER**)
POSCA
(— **OFF**) COUP
(— **SOCIALLY**) BIRL HOBNOB
(— **SPARINGLY**) BLEB
(— **TO LAST DROP**) BUZZ
(— **UP**) CRUSH EPOTE CAROUSE
EXHAUST
(**ADDITIONAL** —) EIK EKE
(**ALCOHOLIC** —) BENO BINO NIPA
BOMBO BUDGE BUMBO DRAIN
JOUGH SHRAB SLING SNORT
SNIFTER
(**BRAZILIAN** —) ASSAI ASSAHY
(**BUTTERMILK AND WATER** —)
BLAND
(**DRUGGED** —) HOCUS
(**FARINACEOUS** —) PTISAN
(**FERMENTED** —) BOSA MEAD
BALCHE MUSHLA CASSIRI GUARAPO
(**FREE** —) SHOUT
(**HALF-SIZED** —) CHOTAPEG
(**HEADY** —) HUFFCAP
(**HOT** —) COPUS SALOP TODDY
BISHOP EGGHOT PLOTTY SALOOP
CARDINAL
(**INCLINED TO** —) OUTWARD
(**INSIPID** —) SLUM
(**INTOXICATING** —) GROG SUCK
BOOZE KUMISS SCOTCH DRAPPIE
PAIWARI SWIZZLE SKOKIAAN
(**INTOXICATING —S**) SAUCE BOTTLE
(**LONG** —) SWIPE HIGHBALL
(**MEAN** —) LAP
(**MIDDAY** —) NOONING MERIDIAN
(**NON-ALCOHOLIC** —) GAZOZ
COOLER
(**PARTING** —) BONAILIE
(**POISONOUS** —) DRENCH
(**RUSSIAN** —) OBARNE OBARNI
(**SACRED** —) HOMA AMRIT HAOMA
AMRITA
(**SACRIFICIAL** —) HOMA SOMA
(**SMALL** —) PEG DRAM SOPIE
DALLOP WETTING
(**STRONG** —) BUB HUM BENO SICER
FUDDLE
(**TASTELESS** —) SLOP
(**THIN** —) SLOSH
(**WEAK** —) LAP BOOL BULL CATLAP
DRINKER SOT TANK POTER TOAST
TOPER BARFLY BENDER CUPMAN
LUSHER SOAKER SPONGE IMBIBER

INTAKER QUAFFER DRUNKARD
(**EXCESSIVE — OF TEA**) THEIC
(**WATER —**) HYDROPOT
DRINKING BEVER DRAFT DRINKY
GUZZLE DRAUGHT POTTING
CAROUSAL POTATION
DRIP LIP SIE SYE DROP LEAK SEGE
SILE WEEP CANAL DRILL EAVES
LABEL STILL DRIBBLE DRIPPLE
LARMIER TRICKLE TRINKLE TRINTLE
(— **WITH TINKLING SOUND**) PINK
DRIPPING ADRIP STAXIS WEEPING
DRIPSTONE BAT DING LABEL
HOODMOLD
DRIVE CA CAW COT FOG JOG AUTO
BANG BEAR BEAT BUTT CALL CRAM
DING DRUB DRUM FIRE FIRK FLOG
GOAD HACK HERD HUNT HURL
JASM JEHU KICK LASH PICK PILE
POSS PUSH RIDE SEND SERR SINK
SLOG SPUR STAB STUB TOOL TOUR
TURN URGE BRAWL CHASE CHECK
COACT CROWD DRIFT DROVE FEEZE
FLAIL FORCE HORSE HURRY IMPEL
INFER LODGE POACH PRESS PULSE
PUNCH REPEL ROUST SHOVE SLASH
SMITE SPANK SWEEP TEASE
ATTACK BATTER BEETLE BENSEL
CHARGE COMPEL CUDGEL DEDUCE
DERIVE FERRET HAMMER HASTEN
IMPACT JARVEY JOSTLE PLUNGE
PROPEL BLUSTER ENFORCE
IMPULSE OVERTAX SETDOWN
TRAVAIL CATAPULT CONATION
SHEPHERD TENDENCY
(— **A BALL**) LACE SEND
(— **A HORSE ONWARD**) WHIG
(— **AIR**) BLOW
(— **ANIMALS**) HAZE
(— **AT TOP SPEED**) CAREER
(— **AWAY**) RID FIRK HUSH SHOO
BANDY EXILE FEEZE FLEME REPEL
SMOKE SWEEP AROINT BANISH
DEFEND DISPEL ENCHASE DISPLACE
EXORCISE
(— **BACK AND FORTH**) TENNIS
(— **BACK**) RUSH REBUT REPEL
CULBUT DEFEND REBATE REBUFF
RETUND REPULSE REFRINGE
(— **BEFORE STRONG WIND**) SPOON
(— **BRISKLY**) JUNE
(— **CRAZY**) BUG
(— **DISTRACTED**) BEDEVIL
(— **FORTH**) ISH
(— **HARD**) SWEAT HACKNEY
(— **HURRIEDLY**) BUM BUCKET
(— **IN**) CRAM DINT PILE TAMP
INJECT
(— **IN A PARK**) TOUR
(— **INTO THE GROUND**) STUB
(— **INTO WATER**) ENEW
(— **LOGS**) SPLASH
(— **OFF STAGE**) EXPLODE
(— **OFF**) KEEP LIFT EXCOCT
(— **OUT**) BOLT FIRE DEPEL DROWN
EJECT EXPEL KNOCK WREAK
EXTURB ABANDON DISLODGE
EXORCISE PROPULSE
(— **RECKLESSLY**) COWBOY

(— **ROUGHLY**) CHOUSE
(— **SLANTINGLY**) TOE
(— **TO BAY**) EMBOSS
(— **TO MADNESS**) FRENZY
(— **VIOLENTLY**) THUD SMASH
HURTLE
(— **WITH BLOWS**) SKELP COURSE
(— **WITH SHOUTS**) HOY HUE
DRIVEL DOTE DRIP DROOL SLUSH
DOTAGE DRUDGE FOOTLE HUMBUG
MENIAL SLAVER DRIBBLE EYEWASH
SLABBER TWADDLE NONSENSE
SALIVATE
DRIVELING SLAVERY FOOTLING
IMBECILE SLOBBERY
DRIVEPIPE POINT
DRIVER MUG HACK JEHU MUSH WHIP
DRABI URGER CABMAN CALLER
COWBOY DROVER FLYMAN HAULER
JARVEY JOCKEY MALLET MUSHER
PONIER STAGER VANMAN WAINER
CATCHER COCHERO FLANKER
HACKMAN HOODLUM HURRIER
JITNEUR PHAETON SPANKER
SPEEDER SUMPTER TOPSMAN
TRUCKER WHIPMAN BANDYMAN
BULLOCKY CALESERO CAMELEER
COACHMAN DRAGSMAN ENGINEER
GALLOWAY GOADSMAN IMPULSOR
JITNEUSE MOTORMAN OVERSEER
TEAMSTER WHIPSTER
(— **OF ANIMALS**) DROVER SKINNER
(— **OF ELEPHANT**) MAHOUT
(— **OF OMNIBUS**) PIRATE
(**CAMEL** —) SARWAN CAMELEER
(**FAST** —) JEHU SPEEDER
(**FIELD** —) HAYWARD
(**PACK-HORSE** —) SUMPTER
(**SKILLFUL** —) REINSMAN
(**TOWPATH** —) HOGGY HOGGEE
DRIVEWAY DRIVE SWEEP AVENUE
DRIFTWAY
DRIVING PELTING COACHING
SLASHING
(— **ALONG**) SCUD
(— **OF GAME**) BATTUE
(— **OF WIND**) GUST
(— **TOGETHER**) DRIFT
(— **TOWARD**) APPULSE
DRIZZLE DEG MUG DANK DRIP
DROW HAZE LING RAIN SMUR STEW
DRISK MISLE SMURR MIZZLE
DRISSEL SCOUTHER SPRINKLE
(— **OF RAIN**) SKEW
DRIZZLY SOFT DRIPPY
DROGUE DRAG DRUG
DROLL ODD COMIC DROLE FUNNY
MERRY QUEER JESTER JOCOSE
AMUSING BUFFOON COMICAL
JOCULAR STRANGE WAGGISH
FARCICAL HUMOROUS
DROLLERY WIT JEST FARCE HUMOR
DROLERIE
DROMEDARY OONT CAMEL DELUL
DELOUL HAGEEN HAGEIN HYGEEN
MEHARI CAMAILE CAMELUS
DROMOND
DRONE BEE BUM HUM DRUM SLUG
DRANT DROLL IDLER SNAIL BUMBLE

BURDEN CHORUS DRAUNT DRONEL
DRONET LUBBER BAGPIPE
BUMBARD BUMBASS HUMMING
SHIRKER SLEEPER SOLDIER
SPEAKER LOITERER SLUGGARD
DRONE BASS FOOT
DRONING HUMMING
DRONISH SLOW INDOLENT
SLUGGISH
DRONGO FORKTAIL
DROOL FLAT DRIVEL SLAVER
DRIBBLE SLABBER SLOBBER
SALIVATE
DROOP FAG LOB LOP SAG BEND
DROP FADE FLAG HANG LAVE LOLL
PINE SINK SWAG WEEP WILT DAVER
DREEP DROWK FLACK HEALD HIELD
MOURN BANGLE BLOUSE DANGLE
DEPEND NUTATE SLOUCH CURTAIN
DECLINE FLITTER LANGUISH
DROOPING LOP DRAG FLAG LANK
LAZY LIMP GOTCH ADROOP
DROOPY FLAGGY NUTANT SLOUCH
SOPITE GOTCHED HANGING
LANGUID NODDING POPPIED
CERNUOUS TRAILING
(— OF EARS) LAVE
(— OF EYELID) PTOSIS
DROOPY DREEPY SLIMPSY
DROP DAP DIP SIE SYE BEAD BEDE
BLOB CAST DRIB DRIP DUMP FALL
GLOB GOUT OMIT SEGE SHED SILE
SINK SPOT STOP TEAR BREAK
CLOTH DROOG FLUMP GUTTA LAPSE
LOWER MINIM PEARL PLUMP PLUNK
SLUMP STILL SWOOP CANCEL
DISTIL DRAPPY EXTILL FUMBLE
GOBBET GOUTTE PLUNGE SINKER
SLOUGH SPRINK TUMBLE ABANDON
CURTAIN DESCENT DEWDROP
DISCARD DISMISS DISTILL DRAPPIE
DRIBBLE DRIBLET DROPLET
EXPUNGE FORSAKE GLOBULE
GUTTULA GUTTULE INCURVE
LETDOWN MELDROP PLUMMET
RELEASE SPATTER DECREASE
DROPLING
(— ANCHOR) SLIP
(— ARGENT) LARME
(— AS SEEDS FROM A POD) ROSE
(— AWAY) DESERT
(— BAIT IN WATER) DAP
(— BY DROP) DROPWISE GUTTATIM
(— DOWN) VAIL
(— IN) STOP HAPPEN INSTIL INSTILL
(— OF GIN) DAFFY
(— OUT) FLOUNCE
(THEATRICAL —) TAB SCRIM
(UNEXPECTED —) DOYST
(PL.) GTT GUTT
DROP-CURTAIN GREENY
DROP ELBOW PIERDROP
DROPLET GLOBULE
(PL.) DEW
DROPLIGHT PENDANT
DROPPER SINK BOBBER SINKER
PIPETTE
DROPPING FALL SCAT SKAT SHARD
COWSHARD

(— ABRUPTLY) BOLD
(— SHARPLY) ABRUPT
(PL.) SOIL SPOOR FLYINGS
DROPSICAL PUFFY EDEMIC
DROPSIED HYDROPIC
DROPSY EDEMA ANASARCA
DROPWORT HORSEBANE
DEADTONGUE
DROSS KISH LEES SCUM SLAG
CHAFF DREGS DRUSH SPRUE
WASTE GARBLE REFUSE SCORIA
SCRUFF SHRUFF SINTER CINDERS
LEAVING OFFSCUM
DROSSEL SLUT HUSSY DRAZEL
DRAZIL
DROUGHT DRYTH DROUTH THIRST
ARIDITY DRYNESS
DROVE MOB SENT ATAJO CROWD
DRIFT FLOCK MANADA BOASTER
DISTURB TROUBLE DRIFTWAY
DROVER DEALER DRIVER TOPMAN
TOPSMAN WHACKER HERDSMAN
DROWN DEAFEN DRENCH STIFLE
ADRENCH DRUNKEN INDRENCH
INUNDATE OVERTONE
DROWNED ADRENT
DROWNING NOYADE
DROWSE NOD SOG DOZE DOVER
DRONE SLEEP SNOOZE SLUMBER
DROWSINESS DULLNESS LETHARDY
DROWSING DORMANT
DROWSY DOZY DULL LOGY HEAVY
NODDY SLEEPY SNOOZY SOPITE
STUPID SUPINE SWOONY DORMANT
LULLING NODDING POPPIED
COMATOSE COMATOUS OSCITANT
SLUGGISH
DRUB TAP BANG BEAT BLOW DRUM
ARRAY CURRY STAMP THUMP
WHALE CUDGEL THRASH BELABOR
SHELLAC
DRUBBING LICKING SACKING
DRUDGE DIG FAG TUG DROY DRUG
GRUB HACK MOIL PLOD TOIL DROIL
GRIND SCRAT SCRUB SLAVE SWEAT
DIGGER DRIVEL ENDURE JACKAL
MOILER SCODGY SLAVEY SLUDGE
SUFFER GRUBBER HACKNEY
PLODDER SLAVERY SWEATER
TRACHLE
DRUDGERY FAG MOIL SLOG TOIL
WORK LABOR SWEAT SWINK
FAGGERY SLAVERY TRACHLE
TURMOIL DRUDGISM
DRUG HOP ALOE ALUM CURE DOPE
DRAB DULL HEMP LOAD NUMB SINA
HOCUS JALAP LOCUS MECON
OPIUM SALOL SENNA SPECE SULFA
TONGA TRUCK COOLER DEWTRY
FINGER HEROIN IPECAC JAMBUL
LOCUST MYOTIC NOBBLE OPIATE
PEYOTE PEYOTL PITURI POTION
SIMPLE SULPHA ANODYNE ATEBRIN
BOTANIC CUSHION DAMIANA
DILATER ECBOLIC ETHICAL HASHISH
JAMBOOL PHILTER PHILTRE
QUASSIA STUPEFY STYPTIC
SURAMIN ZEDOARY ADJUVANT
AROMATIC ASPIDIUM ATARAXIC

HYPNOTIC KOROMIKO LAXATIVE
MEDICATE MEDICINE NARCOTIC
NEPENTHE SALIVANT SEDATIVE
SPECIFIC TOXICANT ZERUMBET
ATARACTIC
(— USER) JOYPOPPER
(VEGETABLE —) FINGER
(PL.) DRUGGERY
DRUGGED POPPIED
DRUGGIST CHEMIST DRUGGER
GALLIPOT
DRUGSTORE APOTHEC PHARMACY
DRUID SARONIDE
DRUM GIN GOO BOWL CAGE DRUB
LALI ROUT SKIN SPOT TOPH TRAP
BONGO CONGA CRAWL DRONE
GUMBE GUMBY SHAPE SNARE
SWASH TABOR THRUM TOMBE
ATABAL BARREL CROCUS RIGGER
TABRET TAMBOR TIMBRE TUMBLE
TUMMER TYMPAN ANACARA
BUBBLER CROAKER FRUSTUM
GRUNTER RATTLER REDFISH
SNUBBER TABORIN TAMBOUR
TEMPEST TIMBREL TUMBLER
BAMBOULA BARBUKKA CANISTER
CYLINDER DERBUKKA DRUMFISH
HUEHUETL MOULINET TYMPANUM
(— AS SHIP'S SIGNAL) SHAPE
(— FOR WINDING ROPE) CAGE
(— IN WINCH) GIPSY GYPSY
(— MADE FROM HOLLOW TREE)
GUMBE GUMBY
(— ON WINDLASS) WILDCAT
(— UP BUSINESS) HUSTLE
(— UP INTEREST) BALLYHOO
(HEATED —) DRIER DRYER
(IGOROT —) GANGSA
(REVOLVING —) GURDY RATTLER
(SUMERIAN —) ALA ALAL
DRUMBEAT DUB FLAM RUFF TUCK
MARCH RUFFLE BERLOQUE
BRELOQUE
(— SOUND) TUCK
DRUMFISH SPOT CROCUS BUBBLER
CROAKER DRUMMER DRUMSLER
SCIAENID
DRUMLIN DRUM SOWBACK
DRUMMER DRUM TABOR STICKS
TABRET ROADMAN SWASHER
TAMBOUR TUMMLER DRUMSLER
SALESMAN
DRUM ROLL DIAN DIANA
DRUMSTICK LEG STICK BAGUET
TAMPON BAGUETTE
DRUNK CUT FOU REE WET GONE
HIGH LUSH NASE PAID RIPE SOSH
BLIND BOOZE BOSKY CLEAR DRINK
LUMPY LUSHY MALTY OILED QUEER
SHICK STIFF TIGHT TIPSY BAGGED
BLOTTO BOILED BUZZED CANNED
FLUFFY GROGGY JAGGED LOADED
LOOPED MORTAL SLOPPY SODDEN
SOSHED SOZZLY SPONGY SPRUNG
STEWED STINKO STONED TIDDLY
UPPISH UPPITY BLOTTER CROCKED
DRUNKEN JINGLED MAUDLIN
SCREWED SHICKER SLOPPED
SOZZLED SQUIFFY SWACKED

COCKEYED GLORIOUS MUCKIBUS
PLEASANT SQUIFFED STINKING
BLITHERED

DRUNKARD SOT SOAK BLOAT DIPSO
DRUNK GULCH RUMMY SOUSE
TOPER LUSHER SOAKER SPONGE
DRUNKER FUDDLER POTSHOT
SHICKER STEWBUM TIPPLER
TOSSPOT BORACHIO HABITUAL
SWILLTUB

DRUNKEN REE GONE WINY BLIND
BOUSY DROWN DRUNK BLOTTO
FLUFFY SODDEN DRUCKEN PICKLED
SOTTISH WHIPCAT DRENCHED
SATURATE SQUIFFED VINOLENT
WOODSERE

DRUNKENNESS BUN IVRESSE
POTSHOT

DRUPE TRYMA DRUPEL DRUPELET
DRUPEOLE

DRUPELET GRAIN ACINUS

DRUPE STONE NUTLET

DRY EBB KEX SEC TED WIN ADRY
ARID BAKE BLOT BRUT DULL EILD
GELD HASK KEXY KILN PINE SAVE
SERE SOUR WIPE AREFY CORKY
DRAIN FROST GUESS HASKY JUSKY
PARCH PROSY SANDY SECCO
SMEEK SWEAT VAPID WIZEN
BARKEN BARREN BIRSLE BORING
CHIPPY ENSEAR GIZZEN HISTIE
JEJUNE SCORCH STARKY AREFACT
BRUSTLE INSIPID SAPLESS SICCATE
SQUALID STERILE THIRSTY
TORREFY XEROTIC BARBECUE
DROUGHTY INFUMATE TIRESOME
WOODSERE
(— **HERRINGS**) DEESE
(— **IN SUN**) RIZZAR
(— **OF MILK**) SEW EILD
(— **PARTLY**) SAMMY
(— **UP**) SERE WELK WITHER
AREFACT FORWELK SKELLER
(— **WOOD**) BEATH SWEAT SEASON
(**NOT** —) SWEET

DRYAD DRYAS NYMPH CAISSA
YAKSHA YAKSHI WOODMAID

DRYER DRIER STOVE SIROCCO

DRY GOODS DRAPERY

DRYING SICCANT

DRYING RACK CRIB

DRYNESS DROUTH ARIDITY
DROUGHT SICCITY XEROSIS
XEROTES HASKNESS

DUAL TWIN BINARY DOUBLE DUALIST
TWOFOLD

DUALISM DVAITA

DUALITY DUAD TWINE TWONESS

DUANT DE DEE

DUB DIB RUB ADUB BLOW CALL
NAME POOL ADORN ARRAY DRESS
STYLE THUMP CLOTHE KNIGHT
PUDDLE SMOOTH STRIKE ENTITLE
BEGINNER DRUMBEAT ORNAMENT

DUBBIN DAUBING

DUBIOUS DICKY FISHY JUBUS
DOUBTY BEARISH DOUBTFUL
DOUBTING JUBEROUS
(**NOT** —) EXPRESS

DUCHY DUCATUS DUCHERY
DUKEDOM PARMESAN

DUCK AIX BOB BOW CAN DIG DIP
DOP MIG PET WIO CHAP COLK
COOT DIVE DOGS DOGY DOKE
DUKW JOUK LADY LORD PATO
ROOK SMEE SMEW TEAL TEUK
BOOBY BUNTY CRICK DILLY DODGE
DOUSE DOWSE DUCKY EIDER
HOUND MOMMY NODDY PADDY
POKER ROUEN SCAUP SHIRK SOUSE
SPIKE SPRIG STOOL BOBBER
CALLOO CALLOW CANARD CANNET
DUCKIE FELLOW GARROT PEKING
PERSON PLUNGE QUANDY RUNNER
SCOTER SMETHE BARWING BLACKIE
BOWSSEN BUMMALO CANETTE
CRACKER DABBLER DARLING
DRABBET DUCKING DUCKLET
DUNBIRD FIDDLER FLAPPER
GADWALL GEELBEC GREASER
MALLARD OLDWIFE PENTAIL
PINKEYE PINTAIL POCHARD
REDHEAD REDLEGS REDWING
SCOOTER SLEEPER SPATTER
WADDLER WIDGEON YAGUAZA
BLUEBILL BLUEWING BOATBILL
BULLNECK DUCKLING DUCKWING
GARGANEY GRAYBACK GREYBACK
HARDHEAD IRONHEAD MOONBILL
MORILLON PIKETAIL REDSHANK
RINGBILL RINGNECK SHOVELER
SHUFFLER SQUEALER WIRETAIL
(— **EGGS**) PIDAN
(**MALE** —) DRAKE
(**STUFFED** —) DUMPOKE
(**YOUNG** —) CANETON FLAPPER
FLOPPER

DUCKBILL OOTOCOID PLATYPUS
TAMBREET

DUCKWEED GLIT GRAIN LEMNAD
LENTIL DIGMEAT DUCKMEAT
FROGFOOT

DUCT VAS MAIN PIPE TUBE CANAL
ALVEUS BUSWAY DUCTUS MEATUS
URETER CHANNEL CONDUIT
DUCTULE DUCTURE LACTEAL
LEADING PASSAGE TRACHEA
AQUEDUCT CALIDUCT DOWNTAKE
EFFERENT EMISSARY EXHALANT
GONADUCT GUIDANCE OLEODUCT

DUCTILE SOFT DOCILE FACILE
PLIANT PLASTIC PLIABLE TENSILE
FLEXIBLE TRACTILE

DUD FLOP LEMON STUMER STUMOR
FAILURE

DUDE FOP DANDY DUDINE JOHNNY
COXCOMB JACKEEN

DUE HAK OWE BACK CENS DEBT
FAIR FARM FLAT HAKH JUST MEED
OWED TOLL DROIT ENDOW ENDUE
FATED MERIT OWING COMING
CUSTOM DESERT EXTENT LAWFUL
MATURE PROPER UNPAID CONDIGN
EXACTLY FALDFEE FITTING JETTAGE
TALLAGE ADEQUATE DIRECTLY
HEREGELD HEREZELD RIGHTFUL
SUITABLE TRUNCAGE

DUEL TILT FENCE FIGHT AFFAIR

COMBAT DUELLO CONTEST
MEETING CONFLICT DUELLIZE
HOLMGANG

DUELIST FIGHTER SPADASSIN

DUENNA DRAGON CHAPERON

DUES TOLLS DROITS CHIEFRY
INWARDS JETTAGE PAYMENT
PENSION QUAYAGE ALTARAGE
HAVENAGE SOUNDAGE THIRLAGE

DUET DUO TWO DUETTO TWOSOME
(**BALLET** —) ADAGIO

DUFF ALTER BRAND CHEAT FLOOR
PUDDING

DUFFER DUB MUFF SHAM CHEAT
BUFFER HAWKER SHICER PEDDLER

DUG (— **UP**) HOWKIT

DUGONG SEACOW YUNGAN
COWFISH HALICORE MUTILATE
SIRENIAN

DUGOUT ABRI BOAT BURY CAVE
BANCA BONGO BUNGO CANOE
DONGA DUNGA SHELL BAROTO
BUNKER CAYUCA CAYUCO CORIAL
TROUGH BANTING PIRAGUA
PIROGUE SHELTER BLINDAGE
LIPALIPA

DUIKER IPITI DUYKER BLAUBOK

DUKE DUC DUX KNEZ PEER AYMON
CHIEF KNIAZ HERZOG LEADER
ORSINO AUMERLE GORLOIS
SOLINUS STEENIE HERETOGA
PROSPERO

DUKEDOM DUCHY DUCATAS

DULCET SWEET DULCID SIRUPY
SYRUPY SOOTHING

DULCIAN CURTAL

DULCIMER CANUN CITOLE SANTIR
CEMBALO MAGADIS SANTOUR
CYMBALOM PANTALON ZIMBALON

DULIA ADORATION

DULL DIM DOW DRY FAT LAX MAT
SAD BLAH CLOD COLD DAMP DEAD
DILL DOWD DOWF DOWY DRAB
DREE DRUG DUMB FLAT GRAY
GREY LOGY MOPE MULL POKY
SLOW TAME THIN TURN BESOT
BLAND BLATE BLEAR BLIND BLUNT
BRUTE CRASS DENSE DINGY DOWFF
DOWIE DOWLY DREAR DUBBY
DUNCH DUNNY DUSTY FISHY FOGGY
GLAZY GRAVE GROSS HEAVY INERT
LOURD MATTE MORON MOSSY
MUDDY MUSTY MUZZY NOOSE
PLUMP POKEY PROSE PROSY
SHADE SLACK SOGGY STARY STILL
SULKY TERNE THICK UNAPT VAPID
WASTE BARREN BLEARY BOVINE
CLOUDY DAMPEN DARKEN DEADEN
DISMAL DRAGGY DREARY DRIECH
DRIEGH DROWSY EARTHY FRIGID
FRUMPY GLASSY HEBETE JEJUNE
LEADEN LOURDY MUFFLE OBTUND
OBTUSE OPAQUE REBATE SLEEPY
SLOOMY SODDEN SOMBER SOMBRE
STODGY STOLID STUFFY STUPID
SULLEN TIMBER TORPID TRISTE
TURBID URLUCH WOODEN ADENOID
BLUNTED CONFUSE DEADISH
DISEDGE DOLTISH DOWFART

DRAINED DULLISH DUMPISH
HUMDRUM INSIPID IRKSOME
LANGUID LUMPISH MUMPISH
PEAKISH PINHEAD PROSAIC
SHEATHE SOTTISH STUPEFY
TEDIOUS UNLUSTY VACUOUS
BACKWARD BANAUSIC BEFUDDLE
BLOCKISH BOEOTIAN BROMIDIC
COMATOSE COMATOUS DIDACTIC
DISCOLOR DULLSOME EDGELESS
FRUMPISH GAUMLESS HEBETATE
INFICETE LIFELESS LISTLESS
LOURDISH OVERCAST PLODDING
SLOTTERY SLUGGISH STAGNANT
TIRESOME
(— EDGE OF) ABATE
(— IN MOTION) LOGY
(— SCENT) FOIL
(— WITH LIQUOR) SEETHE
(BECOME —) PALL RUST
(MENTALLY —) DOPY DOPEY
BARREN
DULLARD DOLT DUNCE IDIOT
MORON DODUNK STUPID BROMIDE
DASTARD DOLDRUM DULBERT
POTHEAD DULLHEAD
DULLED EMPTY HEAVY JADED
BROKEN CLOUDY GRAYED SODDEN
STUPID BLEARED
DULLISH DIRTY
DULLNESS DRAB HAZE YAWN
TAMAS PHLEGM DIMNESS DOLDRUM
DULLITY DUNCERY FATUITY
LANGUOR OPACITY DUMBNESS
HEBETUDE SLOWNESS VAPIDITY
DULL-SPIRITED MUZZY
DULL-WITTED FOZY WITLESS
BESOTTED
(— PERSON) MOREPORK
DULLY FLATLY HEAVILY
DULSE DILLESK DILLISK SEAWEED
DULY DUE FITLY RIGHT RITELY
PROPERLY
DUMB DULL MUTE STONY SILENT
STONEY STUPID
DUMBBELL DUMMY DUNCE HALTER
KNOTHEAD
DUMBFOUND DAZE STUN AMAZE
CONFUSE CONFOUND SURPRISE
DUMBFOUNDED STUPENT
DUMBNESS APHRASIA
DUMBWAITER LIFT DUMMY
DUMMY COPY DOLT MUTE SHAM
DUMBY FAGOT EFFIGY FAGGOT
PONTIC SHADOW SILENT PHANTOM
DUMBBELL
(SWORDSMAN'S —) PEL
DUMP SUM TIP BEAT CASH COIN
COUP FALL HOLE JAIL MUSE NAIL
TOOM EMPTY HOUSE SHOOT
GRIEVE PLUNGE TIPPLE UNLOAD
BOGHOLE COUNTER DEPOSIT
REVERIE SADNESS STORAGE
(PL.) SUDS MOPES SADNESS
DUMPCART DUMPER TUMBREL
TUMBRIL
DUMPER TIPMAN
DUMPLING COB CRUST KNODEL
KNAIDEL NOCKERL DOUGHBOY

QUENELLE
(PL.) KLOSSE GNOCCHI
DUMPY DUNCH GROSS PUDGY
SQUAB SQUAT DUMPTY STOCKY
SQUATTY
DUN BUM TAN FORT KICK URGE
ANNOY BROWN CRAVE CROWD
DINGY FAVEL MOUND SEPIA
DUNNER LEADEN PESTER PLAGUE
DUNNISH SWARTHY
DUNCE ASS DOLT DULT GABY GONY
BOBBY BOOBY DOBBY IDIOT NINNY
DULTIE HOBBIL PEDANT DULLARD
SOPHIST NUMSKULL STUNPOLL
TOMNODDY WISEACRE
DUNDERHEAD OAF DOLT DUNCE
DUNE BAR DENE MEAL MOUND
TOWAN TWINE BARKAN BARCHAN
BARKHAN
(SAND —) DRAB SAIF SEIF
DUNG MIS CACK CHIP DOLL FIME
GORE MERD MUCK MUTE SOIL TATH
ARGAL ARGOL FECES FILTH FUMET
MIXEN SCARN SHARN BILLET
CASSON FIANTS LESSES MANURE
ORDURE SCUMBER SCUMMER
TREDDLE COWSHARD DROPPING
STALLAGE
(— AS FUEL) ARGOL CASSON
CASSONS
(— OF BEAST OF PREY) LESSES
(— OF DEER) FUMET FEWMET
(COW —) UPLA COWSHARD
COWSHARN
(OTTER'S —) SPRAINTS
(SHEEP —) BUTTONS TREDDLE
TROTTERS
DUNGEON PIT CELL HELL HOLE
LAKE VAULT CACHOT DONJON
PRISON CONFINE OUBLIET
REVOLVER
DUNGHILL MIXEN MIDDEN MIXHILL
DUNGON DONGON SUNDARI
DUNK DIP SOP SOAK STEEP
IMMERSE MOISTEN
DUNKER DIPPER TAUFER TUNKER
DUMPLER DUNKARD TUMBLER
DUNLIN STIB OXEYE PURRE STINT
DORBIE OXBIRD REDBACK
LEADBACK
DUODECIMO TWELVEMO
DUPE APE FOB FOP MUG BOOB
COAX CONY CULL DUST FOOL GECK
GULL HOAX LAMB ROOK TOOL
CHEAT CHUMP COKES CONEY
CULLY HEALD MOOTH MOUTH
SLANG STALE TRICK BEFOOL
BUBBLE CHOOSE CHOUSE COUSIN
DELUDE DERIDE MONKEY PIGEON
PLOVER SQUARE SUCKER VICTIM
CATSPAW CHICANE DECEIVE
GUDGEON MISLEAD SAPHEAD
SWINDLE YOUNKER DOTTEREL
HOODWINK RODERIGO
DUPERY RAMP
DUPLE BINARY DOUBLE TWOFOLD
DUPLEX DOUBLE TWOFOLD
DUPLEXITY EQUIVOKE
DUPLICATE BIS COPY DUPE ALIKE

DITTO SPARE TALLY DOUBLE
FLIMSY REPEAT COUNTER ESTREAT
MISLEAD REPLICA TWOFOLD
LIKENESS
DUPLICATION DISOMATY
DUPLICITY ART GUILE DECEIT
TRICKERY
DUPONDIUS BRONZE
DURABILITY WEAR FIBER FIBRE
STEEL DURANCE STAMINA
DURABLE FIRM HARD LASTY STOUT
STABLE STAPLE LASTING SERVICE
CONSTANT ENDURING LIVELONG
DURABLENESS DURATION
DURAMEN HEARTWOOD
DURANCE DURANT DURESS
CUSTODY
DURANGO CARTOUCH
DURATION AGE DATE LAST LIFE
SPAN TERM TIME WHEN DUREE
KALPA SPACE LENGTH PERIOD
DURANCE LASTING INFINITE
LIFETIME STANDING
(— BREEZE) SLATCH
(BOUNDLESS —) INFINITE
(INFINITE —) ETERNITY
DURESS FORCE DANGER CRUELTY
DURANCE COERCION HARDNESS
PRESSURE
DURGA CHAMUNDA
DURIAN JAK JACK JAKFRUIT
DURING IN ON BIN AMID OVER TIME
AMONG INTRA WHILE AMIDST
WHILST WITHIN AMONGST DURANTE
PENDING ENDURING
DURRA DARI DURA MILO JOWAR
CHOLUM DHURRA JONDLA
SORGHUM FETERITA
DUSACK TESACK
DUSK DIM EVE DARK DIMPS GLOAM
GLOOM DIMMET DIMPSY DIMNESS
DUCKISH DARKNESS GLOAMING
OWLLIGHT TWILIGHT
DUSKY DIM SAD WAN DARK DUSK
ADUSK BROWN DINGY GRIMY
MOORY TAWNY GLOOMY SMUTTY
SOMBER SOMBRE SWARTH DARKISH
DARLING OBSCURE SUBFUSC
SUBFUSK SWARTHY BLACKISH
DUST ROW COOM DIRT FOGO MUCK
MULL PILM SMUT BRISS CLEAN
COOMB FLOUR POUCE STIVE STOUR
DREDGE FILLER KITTEN POLLEN
POWDER SMEECH BEFLOUR
EBURINE REMAINS SAWDUST
SMEDDUM TURMOIL ANTELOPE
BULLDUST PUMICITE
(— IN FLOUR MILLS) STIVE
(— IN QUARTZ MILL) SLICKENS
(BLOOD —) HEMOCONIA
(COAL —) COOM CULM COOMB
(COKE —) BREEZE
(COSMIC —) STARDUST
(DIAMOND —) SEASONING
(FIBER —) FLOCK
(FLAX —) POUCE POUSE
DUST CLOUD STEW
DUST COVER WRAPPER

DUSTER DEVIL WILLOW ZEPHYR
DUSTCOAT
DUSTY ADUST MOTTY MOTTLE
POUCEY STOURY POWDERY
UNDUSTED
DUTCH (SEE NETHERLANDS) HOGEN
HOLLAND
DUTCH FOIL ORSEDE ORSEDUE
DUTCH GOLD CLINQUANT
DUTCHMAN HANS HOGEN BLANDA
DUTCHY BELANDA DUTCHER
MYNHEER BATAVIAN
DUTCHMAN'S-BREECHES
DICENTRA
DUTIFUL DOCILE LAWFUL DEBTFUL
DUTEOUS OBEDIENT OFFICIAL
REVERENT
DUTY DO END JOB LOT TAX CALL
CARE FYRD ONUS PART PROW
ROLE TAIL TASK TOLL WIKE CHORE
DEVER ERMIN LADLE OUGHT PREST
RIGHT STINT WIKEN BLANCH
BURDEN CHARGE COCKET DEVOIR
DHARMA EXCISE EXITUS HERIOT
IMPOSE IMPOST INGATE OFFICE
RIVAGE TARIFF AVERAGE BAILAGE
BOOMAGE FOSSAGE FURDUNG
GRANAGE INDULTO KEELAGE
LASTAGE PONTAGE PRIMAGE
ROYALTY SCAVAGE SERVICE
STATION TONNAGE TRIBUTE
TROWAGE TUNNAGE BALLIAGE
BUSINESS FUNCTION MALIKANA
MALTOLTE REDDENDO WEIGHAGE
(— FOR LEAD ORE) COPE
(FEUDAL —) HERIOT
(IMPORT —) ERMIN INDULTO
(MILITARY —) STABLES
(TIRING —) FATIGUE
(PL.) CUSTOMS INGATES ACTIVITY
DUX CHIEF LEADER SUBJECT
HERETOGA
DWARF ELF PUG URF AETA CRUT
GRIG GRUB NANA RUNT CRILE
CROWL GALAR GNOME KNURL
MIDGE PIGMY PYGMY SCRUB STUNT
TROLL ABLACH ALVISS CONJON
DROICH DURGAN DURGEN MIDGET
SHRIMP ANDVARI ANDWARI BLASTIE
CONGEON MANIKIN OVERTOP
PACOLET WRATACK ALBERICH
BELITTLE HOMUNCIO HOMUNCLE
HUCKMUCK KNURLING MENEHUNE
NANANDER
(PL.) CERCOPES NIBLUNGS
NIBELUNGS
DWARF DANDELION KRIGIA
DWARFED STUNTY STUNTED
DWARFING BRACHYSM
DWARFISH ELFIN PIGMY PYGMY
GRUBBY KNURLY NANOID RUNTISH
STUNTED
DWARFISHNESS NANISM
DWARFISM ATELIOSIS
DWARF MALLOW CHEESE PELLAS
DWARF RASPBERRY PLUMBOG
DWELL BIG COT DIG SIT WIN WON
BIDE BIGG HAFT HARP LIVE STAY
TELD WINE WONT ABIDE BIELD

BOWER BROOD BUILD DELAY
HOUSE LODGE PAUSE SHACK STALL
TARRY LINGER REMAIN RESIDE
TENANT CLIMATE COHABIT INHABIT
CONVERSE
(— IN) BIG BIGG BEDWELL INHABIT
(— IRRITATINGLY) GRATE
(— ON) HARP BROOD GLOAT
DWELLER TENANT WONNER
DENIZEN PALEMAN DOWNSMAN
HABITANT OCCUPANT RESIDENT
(— BY SEA) PARALIAN
(BUSH —) HATTER
(CAVE —) CAVEMAN TROGLODYTE
(CITY —) SLICKER
(COAST —) BUFFALO ORARIAN
(LAKE —) LACUSTRIAN
(PL.) HUTHOLD
DWELLING DAR HUT INN SEE WON
CASA FARM FLAT FORT HAFT HALL
HOME NEST ROOF SLUM TENT WIKE
WONE ABODE CABIN DOMUS HOTEL
HOUSE HOVEL JOINT MANSE MOTEL
CASTLE DUGOUT DUPLEX HOMING
MALOCA SHANTY TEEPEE WIGWAM
WONING COTTAGE LODGING
MANSION SALTBOX TRAILER
TRIPLEX WONNING BUILDING
BUNGALOW DOMICILE TENEMENT
(— IN UNDERWORLD) CHTHONIC
(— PLACE) HOWF HOWFF
(— WITH ANOTHER) INMATE
(ATTRACTIVE —) BOWER
(CRUDE —) SHED SHEBANG
(LAKE —) PALAFITTE
(MEAN —) SHANTY
(MISERABLE —) BURROW
(NAVAJO —) HOGAN
(NEOLITHIC —) TERRAMARA
(ONE-ROOM —) CELL
(RAMSHACKLE —) HUMPY
(RUDE —) BOTHY BOTHIE
(SUBTERRANEAN —) WEEM
(SWISS —) CHALET
(PL.) HOUSING
DWINDLE FADE FAIL FINE MELT PINE
WANE DECAY DRAIN PETER TAPER
TRAIL WASTE MOLDER SHRINK
CONSUME DECLINE FRITTER
MOULDER DECREASE DIMINISH
FORDWINE
DWINDLING DOWN FLAGGING
DYBBUK GILGUL
DYE (ALSO SEE DYESTUFF) AAL DIP
LIT ANIL BLUE COLOR EMBUE
FUCUS IMBUE LOKAO STAIN SUDAN
TINCT VENOM ARCHIL INFECT
MADDER TINGER ENGRAIN INTINCT
LACMOID LOGWOOD ZAMBESI
AMARANTH COLORANT DYESTUFF
FUGITIVE INDIGOID TINCTURE
(— FUR) FEATHER
(— NOT FAST) FUGITIVE
(BLACK —) GUAKO
(BLUE —) RUM ROOM WOAD
CYANINE DICYANINE
(BROWN —) CACHOU
(GENERAL —S) NIL NILL AZINE
BROWN EOSIN GREEN DIANIL

EOSINE ISAMIN ORANGE PURPLE
VIOLET CYANINE FUCHSIN METANIL
PONCEAU PRIMULA ALIZARIN
AURANTIA CIBACRON DICYANIN
EURHODOL FUCHSINE HYPERNIC
INDULINE TURNSOLE VIRIDINE
SAFRANINE
(HAIR —) RASTIK
(ORANGE —) KAMALA
(PURPLE —) CASSIUS GALLEIN
(RED —) AAL AURIN EOSIN GRAIN
HENNA RUBIN AURINE CERISE
EOSINE RELBUN RUBINE CORINTH
CRIMSON MAGENTA PONCEAU
SAFFLOR ALIZARIN AMARANTH
BORDEAUX CORALLIN CROCEINE
(SCARLET —) TULY GRAIN
(VIOLET —) MAUVE ARCHIL ORCHIL
LACMOID ARCHILLA
(YELLOW —) ARUSA FLAVIN
CHRYSIN FISETIN FLAVINE LAWSONE
WONGSHY AURAMINE
DYED INGRAIN
(PERMANENTLY —) FAST
DYEING TINCTION
DYER LISTER TINGER TINTER
DYESTER FIELDER SKEINER
TAINTOR TINTIST
DYERMA ZARMA ZAREMA
DYERS' MULBERRY FUSTIC
DYERS'-WEED SOLIDAGO
DYESTUFF (ALSO SEE DYE) DYE LIT
WELD WOAD LOKAO WOULD
ANATTO LITMUS ORCEIN RELBUN
ALKANET ARNATTO CUDBEAR
DYEWARE SAFFRON
DYEWEED WOODWAX
DYEWOOD FUSTET FUSTIC
BARWOOD CAMWOOD HYPERNIC
DYING FEY DEATH MORENDO
PARTING MORIBUND
(— AWAY) CALANDO DILUENDO
MANCANDO PERDENDO SMORZATO
DYNAMIC POTENT DRIVING KINETIC
FORCEFUL
DYNAMITE BLAST DUALIN SAWDUST
RENDROCK GELIGNITE
DYNAMO EXCITER TORNADO
DYNASTY (OR MEMBER THEREOF)
KIN SUI WEI YIN CHIN CHOU HSIA
RACE SUNG TANG YUAN BUYID
CHING PIAST REALM RULER SHANG
HAFSID PRINCE SAFAVI SELJUK
ALMOHAD ARSACID ATTALID
AYUBITE AYYUBID BOUIDES FATIMID
HAFSITE IDRISID JAGELLO LAKHMID
MONARCH OMAYYAD ROMANOV
SAADIAN SAFAWID SAMANID
TULUNID AGHLABID AGLABITE
ASMONEAN BUWAIHID CAPETIAN
CHALUKYA DOMINION EDRISITE
GOVERNOR IDRISITE JAGIELLO
LORDSHIP SAFFARID SARGONID
SASANIAN SELEUCID SOFFARID
SASSANIDE
DYSENTERY FLUX SCOUR MENISON
TOXEMIA DIARRHEA
DYSPHORIA FIDGET
DYSSODIA BOEBERA

E EASY ECHO
EA HEA ENKI
EACH A EA UP ALL ILK THE UCH
ILKA UCHE EVERY APIECE EITHER
EVERYONE
EAGER HOT RAD YAN ACID AGOG
AVID EDGY FAIN FELL FOND FREE
GAIR HIGH KEEN RATH SOUR TARE
THRO VAIN WARM WAVE YARE
YERN AFIRE AGASP ANTSY BRIEF
FIRST FRACK FRECK HASTY HIGRE
ITCHY PRIME READY SHARP SNELL
YIVER ARDENT FIERCE GREEDY
HETTER INTENT STRONG TIPTOE
ANXIOUS ATHIRST BRITTLE BURNING
EXCITED FERVENT FORWARD
ITCHING PROVOKE DESIROUS
IRRITATE SPIRITED VIGOROUS
YEARNING
(— IN PURSUIT) SHARP
(WILDLY —) CRAZY
EAGERLY FAST FELL YERN HOTLY
BELIVE TIPTOE YARELY YEPELY
PRESTLY HUNGRILY INTENTLY
EAGERNESS GOG ELAN GARE ZEAL
ARDOR DESIRE FERVOR ARDENCY
AVIDITY ALACRITY CUPIDITY
DEVOTION FAINNESS FERVENCY
EAGLE AAR ERN CROW ERNE GIER
TERN HARPY AQUILA BERGUT
EAGLET FALCON FORMAL FORMEL
RAPTOR ALLERION BATALEUR
BEARCOOT BERGHAAN RINGTAIL
(SEA —) ERN ERNE PYGARG
PYGARGUS
EAGLE OWL KATOGLE
EAGLESTONE AETITES
EAGLET BIRD LAIGLON
EAGLEWOOD AGALLOCH
EAGRE BORE WAVE AEGIR HYGRE
EAR LUG NEB CLIP HEAR HEED
HOOK LIST OBEY PLOW TILL AURIS
BRACE PINNA SENSE SOUSE SOWSE
SPIKE CANNON CONCHA CROSET
EARLET LISTEN AURICLE HEARING
SENSORY AUDIENCE RECEPTOR
(— OF BELL) CANON CANNON
(— OF CORN) COB ICKER NUBBIN
CORNCOB
(— OF GRAIN) RISOM SPIKE RIZZOM
(— OF WHEAT) SPICA WHEATEAR
(—S OF GRAIN) CAPES EARHEAD
(UNRIPE — OF CORN) TUCKET
EARACHE OTALGY OTALGIA
EARCOCKLE PURPLES
EARDRUM TABOR TABOUR TYMPAN
DRUMHEAD TYMPANUM
EARFLAP LUG EARLAP EARTAB
EARMUFF
EARL EORL GRAF LORD PEER
COMES NOBLE CONSUL SIWARD
(— OF COVENTRY)
SNIPSNAPSNORUM
EARLDOM DERBY COUNTY
EARLIER ERE OLD ERST FORE
ELDER UPPER BEFORE FORMER
HITHER RATHER SOONER FIRSTER
FURTHER PIONEER PREMIER
PREVIOUS

EARLIEST ERST FIRST ELDEST
MAIDEN RATHEST FURTHEST
PRIMROSE
EAR LOBE LUG EARLAP
(— PEOPLE) OREJON
EARLY AIR ERE OLD GOOD HIGH
RARE RATH SOON FORME PRIMY
RATHE VERTY REARLY SUDDEN
TIMELY ANCIENT BETIMES ERLICHE
FORWARD YOUTHFUL
EARMARK BIT CROP SPLIT LUGMARK
OVERBIT SLEEPER ALLOCATE
OVERCROP UNDERBIT
EAR MUFF OREILET
EARN GET WIN FANG GAIN TILL
VANG ADDLE ETTLE GLEAR MERIT
GARNER HUSTLE OBTAIN ACHIEVE
ACQUIRE CHEVISE DEMERIT
DESERVE
(— BY LABOR) ADDLE SWINK
BESWINK
EARNEST ARRA DEAR DERN HARD
PAWN ARLES GRAVE SMART SOBER
STAID ARDENT ENTIRE HANSEL
HEARTY INTENT SEDATE SOLEMN
EMULOUS ENGAGED FERVENT
FORWARD HANDSEL INTENSE
SERIOUS SINCERE ZEALOUS
DILIGENT EMPHATIC STUDIOUS
(IN —) AGOOD
EARNESTLY HARD DEARLY WISHLY
EARNEST DEVOUTLY DINGDONG
ENTIRELY HEARTILY INTENTLY
INWARDLY
EARNESTNESS GLOW FERVOR
WARMTH GRAVITY DEVOTION
DILIGENCE
EARNINGS GET MAKING ADDLINS
PICKING ADDLINGS
EARPIECE BUTTON
EARPLUG STOPPLE TEMBETA
EARSPOOL
EARRING DROP GRIP EARBOB
EARLET PENDLE EARCLIP EARDROP
PENDANT EARSCREW
EAR SHELL ORMER ABALONE
EARSHOT SOUND HEARING
EARREACH
EARTH ERD ORB SET BALL BANK
BURY BYON CLAY CLOD DIRT DUST
FLAG FOLD GRIT LAND LOAM MARL
MASS MEAL MOLD MOOL MUCK
ROCK SOIL SORY STAR VALE YIRD
ADOBE CRUMB FLOSS GLEBE
GLOBE GROOT INTER LOESS MOULD
REGUR TERRA TRASS UMBER
WORLD CENTER CENTRE COARSE
GROUND YACATA KOKOWAI
MIDGARD TERRENE TIERRAS
TOPSOIL TRIPOLI MAGNESIA
MIDGARTH
(— PROVIDING OCHER) KOKOWAI
(— SUITABLE FOR CULTIVATION)
LAYER
(BLACK —) MUCK SORY KILLOW
AMPELITE
(BLUE —) KIMBERLITE
(BROWN —) UMBER
(CLAYEY —) LAME LOAM

(DRY —) MOOL GROOT
(FULLER'S —) CRETA
(GEM-BEARING —) BYON
(LOOSE —) CRUMB GEEST
(MOIST —) SLIME
(POOR —) RAMMEL
(REFUSE —) MURGEON
(RIVER-BANK —) GREWT
(SMALL —) TERRELLA
(SOAP —) SOAPROCK
(STRAW-YELLOW —) BISMITE
(SUN-DRIED —) SWISH
(VITRIFIED —) FLOSS
(VOLCANIC —) TRASS TARRASS
EARTHEN FICT DIRTEN EARTHLY
YARTHEN
EARTHENWARE POT DELF CHINA
CLOAM CROCK DELFT CLAYEN
JASPER ASTBURY BISCUIT FAIENCE
POTTERY TICKNEY BUFFWARE
CROCKERY TALAVERA
(BROKEN PIECE OF —) CROCK
EARTHINESS SALT TERREITY
EARTHKIN TERRELLA
EARTHLY LAIRY CARNAL EARTHY
MORTAL EARTHEN GLEBOUS
MUNDANE SECULAR TERRAIN
TERRENE WORLDLY SUBLUNAR
TEMPORAL
EARTHNUT ARNUT CHUFA HOGNUT
JARNUT PEANUT PIGNUT HARENUT
HAWKNUT TRUFFLE
EARTH PIG ERDVARK AARDVARK
EARTHQUAKE QUAKE SEISM SHAKE
SHOCK TEMBLOR SEAQUAKE
EARTHSTAR GEASTER
EARTHWALL TRINCHERA
EARTHWORK BANK RATH AGGER
CASTLE RAMPART TERRACE
EARTHWORM ESS MAD WORM
ANNELID DEWWORM IPOMOEA
MADDOCK ANGLEDOG BRANDLIN
EACEWORM FISHWORM RAINWORM
TWATCHEL LUMBRICID
EARTHY GROSS SALTY WORMY
VULGAR EARTHLY TERRENE
BARNYARD TERREOUS VISCERAL
EAR TICK PINOLEA
EAR TRUMPET CORNET
EARWAX CERUMEN
EARWIG GOLACH GOLOCH
TOUCHBELL
EARWORM BOLLWORM
EASE CALM COSY COZY EASY REST
ALLAY KNACK PEACE QUIET RELAX
SLAKE LOOSEN PACIFY REDUCE
RELIEF REPOSE SAUGHT SMOOTH
SOFTEN SOOTHE APPEASE
ASSUAGE COMFORT CONTENT
FACULTY FLUENCY FREEDOM
LEISURE LIBERTY LIGHTEN RELIEVE
SLACKEN SUBSIDE DIMINISH
FACILITY MITIGATE MODERATE
PALLIATE PLEASURE SECURITY
UNBURDEN
(— OF A BURDEN) LIGHT
(— OFF) FLOW CHECK START
SLOUGH
(APATHETIC —) INDOLENCE

(AT —) OTIOSE
(CAREFREE —) ABANDON
EASEL FRAME SUPPORT SCAFFOLD
EASEMENT EASE EASING RELIEF
  HERBAGE TURBARY SERVITUS
  WAYLEAVE
EASE-TAKING PICKTOOTH
EASIEST EFTEST
EASILY EASY EATH WELL LIGHT
  EATHLY GENTLY GLIBLY HANDILY
  LIGHTLY READILY SLIGHTLY
  SMOOTHLY
EASINESS GRACE FACILITY
EASING DETENTE
EAST ASIA MORN LEVANT ORIENT
  SUNRISE EASTWARD
  (— OF) FOLLOWING
EAST AFRICA (— TREE) PODO
EASTER PT PACE PASCH EOSTRE
  PASCHA PASQUE
EASTERN LEVANT ORTIVE AURORAL
  ORIENTAL
EASTERNER DUDE
EAST INDIAN (— TREE) SAL TEAK
  KOKAN LANSA MAHUA MOHWA
  NIEPA ROHAN ROHUN SALAI SIMAL
EASTLAND ESTRICHE
EASTWARD EAST EASEL EASSEL
EASY CALM COZY CRIP EATH EITH
  GAIN GLIB MILD RIFE SNAP SOFT
  CUSHY JAMMY LARGE LIGHT PRONE
  ROYAL SUAVE YEZZY CASUAL
  COMODO FACILE FLUENT FRUITY
  GENTLE GENTLY SECURE SIMPLE
  SMOOTH UNHARD ARTLESS
  GRADUAL LENIENT NATURAL
  CAREFREE CARELESS CAVALIER
  EXPEDITE FAMILIAR GRACEFUL
  HOMELIKE MODERATE TRANQUIL
  UNFORCED
  (— IN MIND) SECURE
  (— TO HANDLE) HANDSOME
  (— TO USE) CLEVER
EASYGOING LAX DEGAGE
EAT FOG KAI SUP BITE CHOW DINE
  FARE FEED FRET GNAW GRUB HAVE
  HEYT MAKE PECK RUST TUCK
  ERODE FEAST GRAZE MANGE
  MUNCH SCOFF STOKE TASTE
  WASTE ABSORB BEGNAW DEVOUR
  INGEST NIBBLE RAVAGE CONSUME
  CORRODE DESTROY SWALLOW
  VICTUAL
  (— A MEAL) GRUB
  (— AS HOGS) SLUICE
  (— AWAY) GNAW ERODE RANKLE
  CORRODE
  (— BIG MEAL) STOKE
  (— CRUNCHINGLY) GROUZE
  (— GLUTTONOUSLY) GUDGE STUFF
  (— GREEDILY) GAMP GAWP SLAB
  SLOP TUCK CHAUM MOOCH SCOFF
  GOBBLE GOFFLE GUTTLE GUZZLE
  RAUNGE GLUTTON GOURMAND
  (— HEARTILY) THORN
  (— IN GULPS) LAB
  (— MINCINGLY) PICK PICKLE PIDDLE
  (— NOISILY) SLOP GULCH SLURP
  GUTTLE SLOTTER

(— OUT) EXEDE
(— RUDELY) TROUGH
(— SLOVENLY) SLUP MUMMICK
(— SPARINGLY) DIET
(— TO EXCESS) COLF BEZZLE
(— UP) DEMOLISH
(— VORACIOUSLY) CRAM WORRY
(— WITH GUSTO) SMOUSE
(— WITHOUT CHEWING) BOLT
EATABLE FOODY COOKER EDIBLE
  ESCULENT
EATEN CANKERED
(HALF —) SEMESE
EATER PECKER DEVOURER
(GREEDY —) GOURMAND
EATING BIT FOOD ESURINE
  (— BETWEEN MEALS) TIFFIN
  (— COARSE FOOD) FOUL
  (— INTO) CANKEROUS
  (— OUT) EXESION
EAVES EASE EASING
EAVESDROP DARK HARKEN
  HEARKEN
EAVESDROPPER EARWIG
  DRAWLATCH
EAVES TROUGH CHENEAU
EBB FAIL FALL SINK WANE ABATE
  DECAY RECEDE REFLOW REFLUX
  RETIRE TIDING DECLINE SUBSIDE
  DECREASE DIMINISH
  (— AND FLOW) ESTUS AESTUS
  FLUIDITY
EBBING AWANE REFLUENT
  REFLUOUS
  (— AND FLOWING) TIDAL
EBLIS JANN IBLIS
EBONY EBON BLACK GABON
  GABOON WAMARA HEBENON
  IRONWOOD
EBULLIENCE OVERFLOW ELEVATION
EBULLIENT BRASH FERVID BOILING
EBULLIOSCOPE ZEOSCOPE
EBULLITION SEETHE FERMENT
  OUTBURST
ECAD ECOPHENE
ECCENTRIC ODD CARD DOER
  CRANK DOTTY KINKY QUEER WIPER
  CRANKY LOCOED OUTISH PSYCHO
  SCREWY SHAGGY BIZARRE CURIOUS
  DEVIOUS ERRATIC STRANGE
  TOUCHED ABNORMAL FITIFIED
  PECULIAR SINGULAR
ECCENTRICITY KINK FERLY ODDITY
  CROTCHET QUIDDITY
  (— OF CURVE) E
ECCLESIASTES KOHELETH
  QOHELETH
ECCLESIASTIC ABBE ABBOT CLERK
  VICAR ARCHON FATHER LEGATE
  PRIEST KIRKMAN PRELATE SECULAR
  EPISTLER SUBDEACON
ECCLESIASTICAL CHRISTIAN
  SPIRITUAL
ECHEVIN SCABINE SCABINUS
ECHIDNA NODIAK ANTEATER
  EDENTATE PORCUPINE
ECHINODERM CYSTID CRINOID
  BLASTOID STARFISH
ECHINOPANAX FATSIA

ECHINO-SOREX GYMNURA
ECHION (FATHER OF —) MERCURY
  (MOTHER OF —) ANTIANIRA
  (SON OF —) PENTHEUS
  (WIFE OF —) AGAVE
ECHO ECO RING SING CHORUS
  REPEAT REVERB SECOND IMITATE
  ITERATE RESOUND RESPEAK
  RESPOND REVOICE RESPONSE
ECLAT FAME GLORY RENOWN
  ACCLAIM SCANDAL APPLAUSE
  FACILITY PRESTIGE SPLENDOR
ECLECTIC BROAD LIBERAL
ECLIPSE DIM BIND BLOT HIDE BLIND
  CLOUD SHADE STAIN SULLY
  DARKEN DAZZLE DEFECT EXCEED
  OCCULT DEFAULT OBSCURE
  PRODIGY TRAVAIL OUTRIVAL
ECLOGUE IDYL IDYLL BUCOLIC
ECOLOGIST BIONOMIST
ECOLOGY BIOLOGY BIONOMY
  MESOLOGY
ECONOMICAL WARY CHARY FENDY
  FRUGAL SAVING CAREFUL PRUDENT
  SPARING THRIFTY SCREWING
ECONOMICS PLUTONOMY
ECONOMIST HUSBAND MANAGER
ECONOMIZE HAIN SAVE SKIMP
  STINT SCRIMP HUSBAND UTILIZE
  RETRENCH
ECONOMY SPARE SAVING SYSTEM
  THRIFT MANAGERY
ECSTASY JOY BLISS POWER SWOON
  TRANCE DELIGHT EMOTION
  MADNESS RAPTURE
ECSTATIC HOT RAPT PYTHIAN
  GLORIOUS
ECTENE IRENICON
ECTODERM EXODERM EPIBLAST
ECTOMORPHIC LINEAR ASHENIC
  LEPTOSOME
ECTROPION EVERSION
ECU SCUTE SHIELD

ECUADOR
ANCIENT NAME: QUITO
CAPE: ROSA PASADO PUNTILLA
CAPITAL: QUITO
COIN: SUCRE CONDOR CENTAVO
INDIAN: CARA INCA PALTA
  CANELO JIVARO
ISLAND: PUNA WOLF MOCHA
  PINTA BALTRA CHAVES DARWIN
  PINZON WENMAN ISABELA
ISLANDS: COLON GALAPAGOS
LANGUAGE: JIBARO QUECHUA
  SPANISH
MEASURE: CUADRA FANEGA
MOUNTAIN: ANDES SANGAY
  CAYAMBE ANTISANA COTOPAXI
NATIVE: MONTUVIO
PROVINCE: LOJA AZUAY CANAR
  COLON ELORO CARCHI GUAYAS
  MANABI BOLIVAR LOSRIOS
  COTOPAXI IMBABURA
RIVER: COCA MIRA NAPO DAULE
  PINDO TIGRE GUAYAS TUMBES
  ZAMORA CURARAY PASTAZA

AGUARICO BOBONAZA NARANJAL PUTUMAYO
TOWN: JAMA LOJA MERA NAPO PUYO TENA CANAR GUANO MANTA PAJAN PINAS PIURA QUITO YAUPI AMBATO CUENCA IBARRA PUJILI TULCAN ZARUMA AZOGUES CAYAMBE GUAMOTE MACHALA PELILEO PILLARO SALINAS BABAHOYO GUARANDA RIOBAMBA
WEIGHT: LIBRA

ECUMENE HEARTH
ECUMENICAL LIBERAL CATHOLIC
ECZEMA TETTER EARWORM MALANDERS
EDACITY GREED APPETITE VORACITY
EDDA SAGA
EDDISH ETCH ARRISH EEGRASS
EDDO TARO COCOYAM
EDDY CURL GULF PURL WASH WEEL WELL ACKER GURGE SHIFT SWIRL TWIRL WHIRL SWOOSH VORTEX WIRBLE BACKSET WREATHE
EDDYING WALE
EDEMA BRAXY TUMOR DROPSY BIGHEAD HYDROPS ANASARCA SWELLING
EDEMATOUS BLOATED HYDROPIC
EDEN ADEN HEAVEN UTOPIA ARCADIA ELYSIUM PARADISE
EDENTATA BRUTA
EDENTATE SLOTH ANTEATER
EDGE AGE BIT HEM JAG LIP RIM BANK BERM BRIM BROW CURB DRAW FACE KANT LIMB LIST RAND SIDE TRIM WELL WHET ARRIS BERME BEVEL BLADE BOARD BRINK CHIMB CHIME CREST EAVES FRILL KNIFE LABEL LEDGE MARGE PEARL RULER SHARP SIDLE SPLAY VERGE BORDER DECKLE FLANGE FORAGE IMPALE LABRUM MARGIN NOSING PLANGE MARGENT SELVAGE SHARPEN VANDYKE BOUNDARY EMBORDER KEENNESS MAJORITY OUTSKIRT SELVEDGE STICKING UMSTROKE
(— FORWARD) CREEP
(— IN MINING DRIFT) ARRAGE
(— OF BASKET) FOOT
(— OF BED) STOCK
(— OF BIRD'S BILL) TOMIUM
(— OF BOOK COVER) FLAP
(— OF BOOK) FERRULE BACKBONE
(— OF BRILLIANT) GIRDLE
(— OF CASK) CHIME CHINE
(— OF COAL PILE) RUN
(— OF DAM) CREST
(— OF DUMP) TOE
(— OF FLAG) HOIST
(— OF MESA) CEJA
(— OF MINERAL VEIN) APEX
(— OF ROADWAY) SHOULDER
(— OF RUDDER) BEARDING
(— OF RUFFLE) HEADING

(— OF SAIL) FOOT HEAD LEACH LEECH
(— OF SAW) SAFE
(— OF SHELL) HINGE
(— OF STRATUM) BASSET
(— OF STREAM) HAG
(— OF TOOL) BEZEL BEZIL
(— OF TOOTH) SCALPRUM
(— OF TROUSERS) CREASE
(— OF VAULT) GROIN
(— OF WOOD) WOODRIME
(—S OF COAT) LAP
(BEVELED —) CHAMFER
(CUTTING —) SHOE
(DOUBLE —) FLAT
(EMBROIDERED —) SURFLE SURPHUL
(EXTERIOR —) AMBITUS
(FRONT — OF BOOK) FACE
(ORNAMENTAL —) FRILL
(RAGGED —) RAG
(ROUGH —S) FASH
(SHARP —) ARRIS BEARD
(UNPLOWED — OF FIELD) RAND
(UNTRIMMED —) DECKLE
EDGED EDGY EROSE SHARP CRENATE CUTTING
(— BY ARCS) INVECTED
EDGER WHETTER STRANDER
EDGING HEM CURB EDGE LACE LIST FILET FRILL LEDGE PICOT BORDER FILLET FRINGE BEADING BINDING GIMPING HAMBURG COQUILLE FRILLING PUNTILLA RICKRACK SKIRTING SURROUND
EDGY EAGER SHARP ANGULAR CRITICAL SNAPPISH
EDIBLE EDULE EATABLE ESCULENT
EDICT ACT BAN LAW BULL FIAT TYPE ARRET BANDO BULLA IRADE ORDER SANAD UKASE ASSIZE DECREE DICTUM NOTICE COMMAND EMBARGO PLACARD PROCESS PROGRAM STATUTE ECTHESIS
EDIFICE DOME CHURCH TURBEH BUILDING ERECTION TETRAGON
EDIFY GROW BUILD FAVOR TEACH BENEFIT IMPROVE PROSPER CONVINCE INSTRUCT ORGANIZE
EDIFYING HIGH SAVORY ELEVATED
EDIT CUT EMEND DIRECT REDACT REVIEW REVISE ARRANGE COMPILE CORRECT PREPARE PUBLISH REWRITE COPYREAD
EDITION KIND EXTRA FINAL FIRST ISSUE PRINT STAMP ALDINE DIGLOT SOURCE AUSGABE BULLDOG HEXAPLA OCTAPLA VERSION PRINCEPS VARIORUM
(FIRST —) PRINCEPS
EDITOR AUTHOR OVERSEER REDACTOR
EDITORIAL LEADER
EDO BENI BINI
EDUCATE REAR BREED TEACH TRADE TRAIN EXPAND INFORM SCHOOL DEVELOP NURTURE INSTRUCT
EDUCATED BRED CIVIL TAUGHT

TRAINED INFORMED LETTERED LITERATE
EDUCATION NURTURE BREEDING LEARNING NORTELRY TRAINING
(LIBERAL —) HUMANITY
(PHYSICAL —) GYM
EDUCATOR TEACHER
EDUCE DRAW EVOKE ELICIT EVOLVE EXTORT EXTRACT
EEL ELE GRIG LING OPAH SNIG TUNA ELVER MORAY SIREN APODAN CARAPO CONGER FAUSEN MOREIA MURENE CONGRIO KWATUMA LAMPREY MURAENA SNIGGLE WRIGGLE CONGEREE GYMNOTID KINGKLIP
(25 —S) STICK SWARM
(YOUNG —) ELVER OLIVER YELVER
EELGRASS DREW WRACK ENALID
EELPOUT BARD LING POUT QUAB BURBOT CONGER GUFFER YOWLER LYCODOID
EELSKIN (10 —S) TIMBER
EELSPEAR PILGER
EELWORM EEL NEMA
EERIE EERY SCARY TIMID WEIRD WISHT CREEPY DISMAL GLOOMY GOUSTY SPOOKY AWESOME GHOSTLY GOUSTIE MACABRE STRANGE UNCANNY ELDRITCH GHOULISH POKERISH
EFFACE BLOT DASH DELE RASE RAZE WEAR ERASE CANCEL DEFACE SPONGE STRIKE DESTROY DISLIMN EXPUNGE NULLIFY UNPAINT
EFFECT DO SEE DENT DOES FECK HAVE PRAY PREY TEEM WORK CAUSE CLOSE ECLAT ENACT ETTLE EVENT FORCE FRUIT ISSUE STAMP ENERGY GROWTH INDUCE INTENT OBTAIN RESULT SECURE SEQUEL STEREO UPSHOT ACHIEVE ACQUIRE ARRANGE COMPASS CONDUCE EMOTION EXECUTE FULFILL IMPRESS IMPRINT OPERATE OUTCOME PERFORM PROCURE PRODUCE PURPORT REALIZE CAUSATUM COMPLETE CONCLUDE CONTRIVE FRUITAGE
(— OF PAST EXPERIENCE) MNEME
(BLURRED —) FUZZ
(COUNTERBALANCING —) STANDOFF
(DAZZLING —) ECLAT
(DECORATIVE —) CHIPPING
(ELECTRICAL —) STRAY
(ESTHETIC —) ATMOSPHERE
(FALSE —) FACADE
(FINAL —) AMOUNT
(ILL —) EVIL
(INTENSE —) STRESS
(MOTTLED —) SPRINKLE
(MUSICAL —) BEND SHADING
(PAINFUL —) JAR
(PAINTING —) STIPPLE
(PENETRATING —) SEARCH
(PERNICIOUS —) BLAST
(PERSONAL —S) DUNNAGE
(SHATTERING —) BRISANCE

(THEATRICAL —) CURTAIN
(TO HAVE —) MILITATE
(TOTAL —) ENSEMBLE
(TOXIC —S) THEISM
(TREMOLO —) BEBUNG
(VISIBLE —) TOUCH
EFFECTIVE ABLE HOME REAL ALIVE
GREAT HAPPY SIKER VALID ACTIVE
ACTUAL CAUSAL DEADLY DIRECT
FRUITY POTENT SEVERE SICKER
SOVRAN CAPABLE FECKFUL
TELLING VIRTUAL ADEQUATE
FORCEFUL POWERFUL SMASHING
STRIKING VIGOROUS
EFFECTIVELY NAITLY
EFFECTIVENESS AIM BANG EDGE
VOLTAGE EFFICACY LEVERAGE
EFFECTUAL TOOTHY ADEQUATE
POWERFUL MAGISTRAL
EFFECTUATE FULFIL FULFILL
COMPLETE
EFFEMINATE NICE MILKY SAPPY
BITCHY FEMALE LYDIAN NIMINY
SILKEN TENDER WANTON WEAKLY
CITIZEN EPICENE WOMANLY
FEMINATE FEMININE LADYLIKE
OVERSOFT WOMANISH
EFFERENT EXODIC
EFFERVESCE FIZZ HUFF KNIT
BUBBLE SPARKLE
EFFERVESCENCE FRET CRACKLE
SPARKLE
EFFERVESCENT UP BRISK FIZZY
QUICK BUBBLY ELASTIC BUBBLING
EFFERVESCING BRISK
EFFETE SERE SPENT BARREN
DECADENT ETIOLATE MORIBUND
EFFICACIOUS VALID MIGHTY
POTENT FORCIBLE POWERFUL
SINGULAR VIGOROUS VIRTUOUS
EFFICACY DINT FECK DEVIL FORCE
GRACE MIGHT POWER DEGREE
VIRTUE POTENCY
EFFICIENCY POWER SKILL AGENCY
ABILITY FACULTY DISPATCH
EFFICACY
EFFICIENT ABLE GOOD SMART
VALID POTENT CAPABLE FECKFUL
POWERFUL SPEEDFUL
EFFIGY GUY IDOL POPE SIGN
DUMMY IMAGE LIKENESS
MONUMENT
EFFLORESCE GERMINATE
EFFLORESCENCE RASH BLOOM
BLOSSOM ROSEOLA ANTHESIS
ERUPTION WHITEWASH
EFFLUENCE ISSUE EFFLUX ELAPSE
EMANATE
EFFLUVIA SCENT
EFFLUVIUM AURA MIASMA FLUXION
SPECIES APORRHEA EMISSION
OUTGOING EMANATION
EFFLUX OUTGO OUTFLOW EFFUSION
EFFORT JOB TRY TUG DINT FIST
HUMP JUMP MINT SHOT TOIL ASSAY
BRUNT BURST CRACK DRIVE ESSAY
FLING LABOR NISUS PAINS POWER
REACH STUDY THROE TRIAL ANIMUS
DEVOIR FAVORS FIZZLE FUFFLE

PINGLE STRAIN STROKE THRIFT
ATTEMPT CONATUS MOLIMEN
NITENCY SPLURGE STRETCH
TENSURE TROUBLE WORKING
ENDEAVOR EXERTION GOODWILL
INDUSTRY MOLITION REACHING
STRIVING STRUGGLE
(— FOR ONESELF) FEND
(ABORTIVE —) FIZZLE
(AGONIZED —) THROE
(ARTICULATIVE —) ACCENT
(EARNEST —) STUDY
(EFFECTIVE —) LICK
(FINAL —) CHARETTE
(INITIAL —) ASSAY
(MAXIMUM —) BEST
(SALVATIONIST —) ATTACK
(SINGLE —) HEAT TRICE
(STRENUOUS —) HASSEL HASSLE
(UNSUCCESSFUL —) ATTEMPT
(UTMOST —) DEVOIR BUSINESS
(VIOLENT —) BURST STRAIN
OUTRAGE STRUGGLE
EFFORTLESS EASY
EFFORTLESSNESS EASE
EFFRONTERY BROW FACE GALL
FRONT BRONZE AUDACITY
BOLDNESS FOREHEAD TEMERITY
EFFULGENCE BLAZE GLORY
RADIANT RADIANCE SPLENDOR
EFFULGENT BRIGHT FULGENT
RADIANT SHINING
EFFUSE GUSH SHED FLING EFFUND
EMANATE DISPENSE
EFFUSION EFFLUX FOISON SPILTH
STREAM
EFFUSIVE GOOEY GUSHY LAVISH
SLOPPY GUSHING BUBBLING
EFFUSIVENESS SLOP
EFT ASK EVET NEWT LIZARD TRITON
EGAD ADAD ECOD IGAD SGAD
EGEST VOID EXCRETE ELIMINATE
EGG AI ABET GOAD GOOG OVUM
PROD SEED SPUR URGE CHECK
OVULE SPORE DARNER INCITE
OOCYTE PEEWEE ZYGOTE ACTUATE
COKENEY OOPLAST OOSPERM
PROTOVUM
(— CASE) POD
(— CLUTCH) LAUGHTER
(— OF FISH OR LOBSTER) BERRY
(— ON) HAG EDGE GOAD URGE
(— PRODUCT) ZOON
(—S OF BEES) BROOD
(—S OF SILKWORM) GRAINE
(ACID —) SLOWCASE
(CRACKED —) CHECK CRACK
LEAKER
(DRIED —S) AHUATLE
(DUCK —S) PIDAN
(FLY'S —) BLOW FLYBLOW
(FOSSIL —) OVULITE
(GOLDEN —S) SUNCUP
(GOOSE —) BLOB
(HUNT BIRDS' —S) OOLOGIZE
(INFERTILE —) CLEAR
(SMALL —) OVULE OVULUM
(PL.) OVA ROE SEED EYREN SPAWN
CLUTCH ETTING AHUATLE

EGG AND DART ECHINUS
EGGFRUIT LUCUMA CANISTEL
EGGHEAD HIGHBROW INTELLECTUAL
EGGNOG NOG ADVOCAAT
EGGPLANT BRINJAL SOLANUM
BRINGELA EGGFRUIT
EGG-SHAPED OOID OVAL OVATE
OVOID OOIDAL OBOVOID OVALOID
OVIFORM
EGGSHELL SHARD CASCARON
EGG WHITE GLAIR ALBUMEN
EGG YOLK YELLOW VITELLUS
EGO I SELF ATMAN EGOITY FYLGJA
CONCEIT SUBJECT
EGOCENTRIC INSEEING
EGOISM PRIDE ONEISM VANITY
CONCEIT EGOTISM OWNHOOD
SELFNESS
EGOTISM EGO PRIDE EGOISM
VANITY CONCEIT EGOMANIA
EGREGIOUS FINE GROSS CAPITAL
EMINENT FLAGRANT PRECIOUS
SHOCKING
EGREGIOUSLY BEASTLY
EGRESS EXIT ISSUE OUTGO OUTLET
EXITURE EXEMION OUTGATE
PASSAGE REGRESS OUTGOING
EGRET HERON PLUME GAULIN
KOTUKU AIGRETTE GAULDING
EGYPT MIZRAIM

EGYPT

BAY: FOUL
CALENDAR: AHET APAP TYBI
PAYNI SHEMU THOTH CHOIAK
HATHOR MECHIR MESORE
PAOPHI PACHONS
CANAL: SUEZ
CAPE: BANAS RASBANAS
CAPITAL: CAIRO ELQAHIRA
CHRISTIAN: COPT COPTIC
COIN: FILS DINAR GIRSH POUND
DIRHAM GUINEA JUNAYH
PIASTER MILLIEME
DAM: ASWAN
DESERT: LIBYAN
GOVERNORATE: SUEZ CAIRO
CANAL SINAI BAHARIYA
BAHRIYAH ALEXANDRIA
GULF: AQABA
ISTHMUS: SUEZ
KING: AY IB KA ITI ITY TUT DJER
DJET HUNY PAMI PEPI SETI
TEOS TETI UNIS ARSES BEBTI
FOUAD ITETI KEBEH KHUFU
KNIAN MENES NEBKA NECHO
NEFER UDIMU ZEMTI ZOSER
CHEOPS DARIUS FAROUK
KHAFRE NARMER RANSES
SENEDJ XERXES MENKURE
PHARAOH PTOLEMY RAMESES
SALADIN CHEPHREN THUTMOSE
LAKE: EDKU IDKU MARYUT
MOERIS MANZALA BURULLUS
MAREOTIS
LAKES: BITTER
MEASURE: APT DRA HEN PIK ROB
DRAA KHET ROUB THEB ABDAT

ARDAB CUBIT FARDE KELEH
KILAH SAHME ARTABA AURURE
FEDDAN KEDDAH ROBHAH
SCHENE CHORYOS DARIBAH
MALOUAH ROUBOUH TOUMNAH
KASSABAH KHAROUBA
MOUNTAIN: SINAI GHARIB
KATHERINA
NAME: UAR
NATIVE: ARAB COPT NILOT
BERBER MUSLIM NUBIAN
OASIS: SIWA DAKHLA KHARGA
FARAFRA BAHARIYA
PENINSULA: SINAI
PORT: TOR SUEZ ATTUR DUMYAT
QUSEIR RASHID SAFAGA
SALLUM ROSETTA DAMIETTA
HURGHADA PORTSAID
ALEXANDRIA
PROVINCE: GIZA QENA QINA
ASWAN ASYUT MINYA SOHAG
DUMYAT FAIYUM SAWHAJ
TAHRIR ALJIZAH BEHEIRA
BENISUEF DAMIETTA GHARBIYA
MINUFIYA SHARQIYA
RESERVOIR: ASWAN
RIVER: NILE
RUINS: ABYDOS SPHINX THEBES
MEMPHIS PYRAMIDS
SUN GOD: RA RE TEM ATMU
ATUM
TOWN: NO MUT DUSH GIZA IDFU
ISNA QENA SAIS SIWA SUEZ
ZOAN ASWAN ASYUT BENHA
BULAQ CAIRO ELTUR FAYID
GIRGA GIZEH LUXOR NAKHL
SALUM SOHAG TAHTA TANIS
TANTA ABYDOW AKHMIN
DUMYAT ELQASR HELWAN
KARNAK RASHID THEBES
BURSAID ROSETTA ZAGAZIG
BENISUEF DAMIETTA ISMAILIA
WEIGHT: KAT KET OKA OKE HEML
KHAR OKIA ROTL ARTAL ARTEL
DEBEN KERAT MINAE MINAS
OKIEH POUND RATEL UCKIA
HAMLAH KANTAR DRACHMA
QUINTAL
WELL: BIRTABA
WIND: KAMSIN SIROCCO
KHAMSEEN

EGYPTIAN ARAB COPT GIPPY GYPPY
TASIAN PHARIAN BADARIAN
MEMPHIAN
EIDER COLK WAMP DIVER EDDER
DUCKER SHOREYER
EIDOLON ICON GHOST IMAGE
IDOLUM PHANTOM LIKENESS
EIGHT ETA ECHT AUGHT CHETH
OCTAD OCTET OCTAVE OGDOAD
OCTONARY
EIGHTH AUGHT
EIGHTH NOTE UNCA CROMA
CHROMA QUAVER
EIRE (SEE IRELAND)
EITHER ANY EDDER ITHER OTHER
WHETHER

EJACULATE BELCH BLURT EJECT
FLING EXCLAIM EMISSION
EJACULATION HOW COADS ZOWIE
BEGORRA UTTERING
(MYSTIC —) OM
EJACULATORY SPUTTERY
EJECT OUT BLOW BOOT CAST EMIT
FIRE HOOF OUST SHED SPAT SPEW
SPIT VOID WARP AVOID BELCH
CHUCK ERUCT ERUPT EVICT EXPEL
SHAKE SHOOT SPOUT SPURT VOMIT
BANISH BOUNCE SQUIRT DEFORCE
DISMISS EXCLUDE EXTRUDE
OBTRUDE DISGORGE OUTBRAID
EJECTION BLOW OUSTER OUTING
EVICTION
EJECTOR LIFTER EDUCTOR
EKE IMP ALSO YEKE AUGMENT
ENLARGE HUSBAND STRETCH
APPENDIX INCREASE LENGTHEN
LIKEWISE UNDERLAY
ELABORATE FIKIE GREAT LABOR
DELUXE DRESSY ELABOR ORNATE
QUAINT REFINE CURIOUS DEVELOP
ENLARGE LABORED PERFECT
ELABORATED WROUGHT
ELABORATELY FANCILY
ELABORATENESS FINENESS
CURIOSITY
ELAMITE SUSIAN ANZANITE
ELAN DASH ARDOR DRIVE GUSTO
VERVE SPIRIT WARMTH POTENCY
ELAND IMPOFO
ELAN VITAL ZOISM
ELAPS MICRURUS
ELAPSE GO RUN PASS ROLL SLIP
GLIDE SPEND EXPIRE
ELAPSING CURRENT
ELASTIC QUICK GARTER RUBATO
SPONGY BUOYANT SPRINGY
STRETCH CHEVEREL CHEVERIL
FLEXIBLE STRETCHY VOLATILE
ELASTICITY GIVE LIFE ELATER
SPRING STRETCH
ELATE BYOU CHEER EXALT EXULT
FLUSH LOFTY RAISE ELATED EXCITE
PLEASE THRILL ELEVATE GLADDEN
INFLATE SUBLIME SUCCESS
ELEVATED HEIGHTEN INSPIRIT
JUBILATE
ELATED RAD HIGH RADE CHUFF
ELATE HAPPY PROUD VAUDY VOGIE
WLONK CHUFFY JOVIAL UPPISH
UPPITY EXCITED EXULTED JOCULAR
SUBLIME EXULTANT GLORIOUS
INFLATED JUBILANT PRIDEFUL
UPLIFTED
ELATER BEETLE CRINULA SKIPJACK
ELATION JOY GLEE RUFF BUOYANCY
ELBOW ELL BEND ANCON JOINT
NUDGE SHOVE CROSET ELBUCK
JOSTLE JUSTLE SPRING PIERDROP
ELCAJA MAFURA
ELDER AIN IVA AINE WITE ELLER
OLDER PRIOR MAHANT SENIOR
ANCIENT NEGUNDO STAROST
TRAMMON ANCESTOR BOUNTREE
BOURTREE CARELESS DANEWORT
ELDERMAN

ELDERLY AGED GRAY ALDER
ELDERN SENILE BADGERLY
ELDEST AYNE EIGNE OLDEST
ELECAMPANE INULA CANADA
ELFWORT SCABWORT
ELECT CALL PICK VOICE ASSUME
CHOOSE CHOSEN DECIDE ISRAEL
PREFER SELECT
ELECTION PROXY CHOICE LECTION
ELECTIONEERING HUSTINGS
ELECTIVE OPTION
ELECTOR VOTER ELISOR CHOOSER
ELIGENT INTRANT ELECTANT
ELECTORATE PEOPLE COUNTRY
ELECTRA LAODICE
(BROTHER OF —) ORESTES
(DAUGHTER OF —) IRIS
(FATHER OF —) ATLAS AGAMEMNON
(HUSBAND OF —) PYLADES
(MOTHER OF —) PLEIONE
CLYTEMNESTRA
(SON OF —) DARDANUS
ELECTRICIAN GAFFER JUICER
BOARDMAN
ELECTRICITY JUICE PYROGEN
ELECTRIC GALVANISM
ELECTRIFY EXCITE THRILL STARTLE
ELECTROCUTE BURN EXECUTE
ELECTRODE DE DEE GRID ANODE
PLATE DYNODE CATHODE IGNITER
CROWFOOT REOPHORE
(PL.) ELEMENT
ELECTRODEPOSIT STRIKE
REGULINE
ELECTROLYTE STRIKE IONOGEN
ELECTROMAGNETIC **(— UNIT)**
OERSTED ABAMPERE
ELECTRON ION POLARON
ELECTRONIC RADIONIC
ELECTRONOGRAPHY ONSET
ELECTRON TUBE TRIODE
ELECTROPHONE MARTENOT
ELECTROPLATE SILVER
ELECTROTYPE PATCH CLICHE
WORKER ELECTRO
ELECTRUM AMBER ELECTRE
ORICHALC
ELECTRYON (DAUGHTER OF —)
ALCMENE
(FATHER OF —) PERSEUS
(MOTHER OF —) ANDROMEDA
ELECTUARY DIASCORD LECTUARY
THERIACA
ELEGANCE CHIC GARB LUXE CLASP
GRACE STYLE SWANK TASTE
FINERY GAIETY GAYETY LUXURY
NICETY POLISH COURTESY
EUPHUISM FINENESS FRIPPERY
GRANDEUR SPLENDOR
ELEGANT CHIC DINK FAIR FEAT FINE
FIXY GENT POSH CIVIL COMPT
FANCY SHARP SLEEK SWANK
CHOICE CLASSY DAINTY DELUXE
DRESSY FACETE MINION QUAINT
SUPERB SWANKY URBANE VENUST
CAPITAL CLEANLY COURTLY
FEATISH FEATOUS GENTEEL MINIKIN
REFINED SMICKER DELICATE
GINGERLY GRACEFUL GRAZIOSO

HANDSOME POLISHED TASTEFUL
ELEGANTLY FINE TALLY FAIRLY
GENTLY GINGERLY
ELEGIAC MOURNFUL EPICEDIAL
ELEGY POEM SONG DIRGE KINAH
QINAH LAMENT MONODY EPICEDE
ELEMENT AIR ATOM DIAD DYAD
RECT WOOF BEARD ETHER FIBER
FIBRE METAL MONAD PUNCT STUFF
AETHER ARTIAD COSTAL FACTOR
HEPTAD LOSSER MATTER MOMENT
SIMPLE ACTINON ADAPTER
BUNCHER CARRIER CATCHER
ESSENCE FEATURE ACTINIDE
BACKBONE CEREBRAL EQUATION
PERISSAD RUDIMENT SELECTOR
THERBLIG
(— IN GRAPH) SPIKE
(— IN WAVE) DART
(— IN WORD GROUP) KOINON
(— OF ALCHEMIST) AIR FIRE EARTH
WATER
(— OF EXISTENCE) DHARMA
(— OF MACHINE) HORN SPIDER
(— OF WEALTH) COMMODITY
(ALIEN —) ALLOY
(ARCHITECTURAL —) SLAB
(BINDING —) CEMENT
(CHEMICAL —) TIN GOLD IRON
LEAD NEON ZINC ARGON BORON
RADON XENON BARIUM CARBON
CERIUM CESIUM COBALT COPPER
CURIUM ERBIUM HELIUM INDIUM
IODINE MURIUM NICKEL OSMIUM
OXYGEN RADIUM SILVER SODIUM
SULFUR ARSENIC BISMUTH BROMINE
CADMIUM CALCIUM FERMIUM
GALLIUM HAFNIUM HOLMIUM
IRIDIUM KRYPTON LITHIUM
MERCURY NIOBIUM RHENIUM
RHODIUM SILICON TERBIUM
THORIUM THULIUM URANIUM
WOLFRAM YTTRIUM ANTIMONY
ASTATINE CHLORINE CHROMIUM
EUROPIUM FLUORINE FRANCIUM
HYDROGEN LUTETIUM MASURIUM
NITROGEN NOBELIUM PLATINUM
POLONIUM RUBIDIUM SAMARIUM
SCANDIUM SELENIUM TANTALUM
THALLIUM TITANIUM TUNGSTEN
VANADIUM
(COMMUNION —) GIFT
(CRIMINAL —) GANGLAND
(DECORATIVE —S) ART
(DOMINANT —) CAPSHEAF
(ELECTRIC —) IMPEDOR
(ESSENTIAL —) CORPUS
(EUCHARISTIC —S) HAGIA SPECIES
(FATAL —) BANE
(FUNDAMENTAL —) STAMEN
(HEATING —) CALANDRIA
(HYPOTHETICAL —) CORONIUM
(INTERFERING —) CRIMP
(LAMP —) GLOWER
(LEADING —) HEAD
(LINGUISTIC—) SERVILE INTENSIVE
(MILITARY —) SUPPORT
(MODIFYING —) LEAVENING
(MORAL —) DAENA

(MOST IMPORTANT —) CAPSTONE
(PRIMAL —) GUNA SALT ARCHE
(PRINCIPAL —) STAPLE
(SKELETAL —) SCLERE
(STRUCTURAL —) ARCUALE
(SUPPOSED —) WELSIUM VICTORIUM
(SUSTAINING —) BREAD STAPLE
(TRANSITORY —S) SKANDHAS
(UNITING —) BOND
(PL.) DETAIL ALPHABET
ELEMENTAL PURE BASIC PRIMAL
SIMPLE PRIMARY ULTIMATE
ELEMENTARY SIMPLE INITIAL
INCHOATE ULTIMATE
ELEMI ANEMI ANIME MATTI RESIN
CONIMA
ELEPHANT COW BULL CALF HINE
PUNK HATHI HATTY JUMBO ROGUE
MUCKNA TUSKER KOOMKIE
AIRAVATA LOXODONT MASTODON
OLIPHANT
ELEPHANT FISH JOSEF JOSUP
JOSEPH
ELEPHANTIASIS TYRIASIS
ELEPHANTINE HUGE ENORMOUS
ELEPHANT'S-EAR TARO
ELEPHANT SHREW JUMPER
ELEUT KALMUK KALMYK KALMUCK
ELEVATE HAIN JUMP LIFT REAR RISE
EDIFY ELATE ENSKY ERECT EXALT
EXTOL GRIMP HEAVE HOIST MOUNT
RAISE TOWER REFINE UPLIFT
ADVANCE DIGNIFY ENHANCE
ENNOBLE GLORIFY PROMOTE
SUBLIME UPRAISE HEIGHTEN
INSPIRIT
ELEVATED EL FINE HIGH GREAT
LOFTY NOBLE RISEN STEEP
AMOTUS ELATED RAISED RISING
WINGED ELEVATO EXALTED
MOUNTED STILTED MAJESTIC
UPLIFTED
(— IN CHARACTER) HIGH
(NOT —) COMICAL
ELEVATION UP ARM BAND BANK
DOME DRUM GLEE HIGH HILL HUMP
LIFT RISE SPUR TOFT TOOT UMBO
BULLA GRADE KNOLL MOUND PITCH
RAISE RIDGE SHOAL SWELL TOWER
WHEAL CONULE CRISTA HEIGHT
PAPULE UPLIFT DIGNITY FURCULA
MAJESTY UPRIGHT ALTITUDE
EMINENCE EVECTION HIGHNESS
LEVATION MOUNTAIN SWELLING
(— OF CARTILAGE) ANTHELIX
(— OF CUTICLE) BLEB
(— OF SKIN) BLISTER
(— ON TOOTH) STYLE
(— SEPARATING CREEKS) BUGOR
(GUN —) RANDOM
(TURRET —) HOOD
ELEVATOR BIN CAGE LIFT SILO
HOIST BRIDGE LIFTER TEAGLE
HOISTER STACKER UPTAKER
UPLIFTER UPRAISER
ELEVENTH ELFT
ELF FAY HAG HOB IMP OAF PUG
DROW FANE OUPH PERI PIXY
DWARF ELFIN FAIRY GNOME OUPHE

PIGMY PIXIE ELFKIN GOBLIN SPIRIT
SPRITE URCHIN BLASTIE BROWNIE
INCUBUS SUCCUBUS
ELFIN ELF FEY CHILD ELFIC ELFISH
URCHIN
ELFISH ELFIN ELVAN ELVISH IMPISH
URCHIN ELFLIKE TRICKSY
ELICIT DRAW MILK PUMP CLAIM
EDUCE EVOKE EXACT FETCH WREST
WRING DEDUCE DEMAND ENTICE
EXTORT INDUCE EXTRACT SOLICIT
ELIDE OMIT SKIP ANNUL IGNORE
DESTROY NULLIFY DEMOLISH
SUPPRESS
ELIGIBILITY FITNESS
ELIGIBLE FIT ACTIVE WORTHY
SUITABLE
ELIMINATE FAN COMB EDIT KILL
EDUCE EXPEL SCRUB DELETE
EFFACE EXCEPT IGNORE REMOVE
SCREEN WINNOW BLANKET
BRACKET DIVULGE EXCLUDE
EXCRETE RELEASE SCISSOR
SILENCE SUBLATE SEPARATE
ELIMINATION STRIP
ELISION SYNCOPE
ELITE BEST LITE PINK CIRCLE
CHOICE FLOWER GENTRY SELECT
PERFECTI
ELIXIR AMRITA SPIRIT AMREETA
ARCANUM CORDIAL CUREALL
ESSENCE PANACEA MEDICINE
ELK ALCE DEER LAMA LOSH ALAND
ALCES ELAND LOSHE MOOSE
CERVID SAMBAR WAPITI SAMBHUR
WAMPOOSE
(— HIDE) LOSH
(YOUNG —) DEACON
ELK BARK BIGBLOOM
ELL ULNA ELBOW ALNAGE ADDITION
ELLIPSE OVAL
ELLIPSIS BRING ELLIPSE
ELLIPSOGRAPH TRAMMEL
ELLIPSOID CONOID ELLIPTIC
SPHEROID
ELLIPTICAL OVAL OVATE OBLONG
ELLOBIUM AURICULA
ELM ULME ELVEN ULMUS WAHOO
MEZCAL CHEWBARK ORHAMWOOD
ELOCUTION SPEECH DICTION
ORATORY
ELOCUTIONIST READER RECITER
ELOIGN CONVEY REMOVE ABSCOND
CONCEAL
ELONGATE EXTEND REMOVE
STRETCH LENGTHEN PROTRACT
ELONGATED LANK LONG LINEAR
OBLONG PROLATE SLENDER
HAIRLIKE PRODUCED
ELOPE DECAMP ESCAPE ABSCOND
ELOQUENCE FACUND FLUENCY
ORATORY
ELOQUENT VOCAL DISERT FACUND
FERVID FLUENT SILVER RENABLE
SPEAKING

EL SALVADOR
CAPITAL: SANSALVADOR

COIN: PESO COLON CENTAVO
DANCE: PASILLO
GULF: FONSECA
INDIAN: PIPIL
LAKE: GUIJA ILOPANGO
MEASURE: VARA CAFIZ CAHIZ
FANEGA TERCIA BOTELLA
CAJUELA CANTARO MANZANA
POINT: REMEDIOS
PORT: CUTUCO ACAJUTLA
RIVER: JIBOA LAPAZ LEMPA
RUINS: TAZUMAL
TOWN: CUTUCO IZALCO CORINTO
METAPAN ACAJUTLA USULUTAN
VOLCANO: IZALCO
WEIGHT: BAG CAJA LIBRA

ELSE OR ENS ENSE OTHER BESIDES
INSTEAD
ELSEWHERE ALIBI EXCEPT THENCE
(FROM —) ALIUNDE
ELUCIDATE CLEAR LUCID EXPLAIN
SIMPLIFY
ELUDE BEAT FLEE FOIL MISS MOCK
SLIP AVOID DODGE EVADE BAFFLE
BEFOOL DELUDE DOUBLE ESCAPE
BEGUILE DECEIVE HEDGEHOP
ELUSIVE EELY LUBRIC SHIFTY
SUBTLE TRICKY TWISTY EVASIVE
BAFFLING FUGITIVE SLIPPERY
ELYSIUM EDEN ANNWIN PARADISE
ELYTRON HUSK SCUTE SHARD
SHERD SHEATH
ELYTRUM SHARD TEGMEN
EM EMMA
(HALF —) EN
EMACIATED LEAN POOR EMPTY
GAUNT MEAGER PEAKED SKINNY
WASTED WASTREL SKELETAL
EMACIATING MARCID
EMACIATION NITON TABES MACIES
ATROPHY POVERTY MARASMUS
EMANATE FLOW ARISE EMANE
EXUDE ISSUE DERIVE EFFUSE
EXHALE OUTRAY SPRING BREATHE
OUTCOME PROCEED RADIATE
EMANATING EFFLUENT
EMANATION FUG AURA BEAM BLAS
GLORY NITON AZILUT BREATH
EFFLUX ELAPSE EIDOLON OUTCOME
PROCESS SEPHIRA EMISSION
(— FROM A MEDIUM) ECTOPLASM
(PL.) SCENT
EMANCIPATE FREE MANUMIT
RELEASE LIBERATE UNFETTER
EMANCIPATION FREEDOM RELEASE
(FINAL —) NIRVANA
EMASCULATE GELD SOFTEN
EVIRATE CASTRATE ENERVATE
EMBALM BALM CERE MUMMY SPICE
BALSAM SEASON CONDITE MUMMIFY
EMBANK BUND
EMBANKMENT BAY BAND BANK
BUND DIKE DYKE FILL QUAY ARGIN
DIGUE LEVEE MOUND REVET
BUNKER STAITH BACKING BANKING
PILAPIL RAMPART RAMPIRE
SEAWALL APPROACH STRENGTH

EMBARGO EDICT ORDER IMBARGE
BLOCKADE STOPPAGE
EMBARK BANK SAIL SHIP ENGAGE
ENLIST INSHIP INVEST LAUNCH
IMBARGE
EMBARRASS SET CHAW CLOG FAZE
HACK LAND ABASH ANNOY SHAME
UPSET BOGGLE CUMBER GRAVEL
HAMPER HINDER HOBBLE IMPEDE
PLUNGE PUZZLE RATTLE CONFUSE
ENTRIKE FLUMMOX INVOLVE
NONPLUS BEWILDER CONFOUND
DUMFOUND ENCUMBER ENTANGLE
HANDICAP IMPESTER OBSTRUCT
STRAITEN
EMBARRASSED FLURRIED SHEEPISH
EMBARRASSING HIDEOUS
EMBARRASSINGLY AWKWARDLY
EMBARRASSMENT FIX GENE LURCH
SHAME STAND CADDLE HOBBLE
PUZZLE
EMBASSY SAND ERRAND AMBASSY
MESSAGE MISSION INBASSAT
LEGATION
EMBATTLED BATTLED CRENELE
BRETESSE CRENELEE
EMBAY BATHE DETAIN ENCLOSE
SHELTER SUFFUSE ENCIRCLE
SURROUND
EMBAYMENT FIORD FJORD
EMBED BED SET BOND IMBED
STAMP CHARGE ENGAGE EMBOWEL
IMMERSE
EMBEDDED INNATE ENGAGED
IMMERSED
EMBELLISH GEM DECK GILD TRIM
ADORN DRESS FUDGE GRACE
BEDECK BLAZON EMBOSS ENRICH
FIGURE FLOWER APPAREL BEDRAPE
EMBLAZE GARNISH MYSTIFY
VARNISH BEAUTIFY DECORATE
FLOURISH ORNAMENT
EMBELLISHED FLORID GESTED
ORNATE COLORED FUCUSED
BROCADED SPLENDID
EMBELLISHMENT FILIP GRACE
FILLIP RELISH AGREMEN GARNISH
GILDING WINDING AGREMENT
FLOURISH MOUNTING ORNAMENT
PARERGON TRAPPING TRICKING
PASSAGGIO
(MUSICAL —) ARABESQUE
(PL.) FIXINGS
EMBER ASH COAL AIZLE GLEED
IMBER CINDER
(RED-HOT —S) BAGA
EMBEZZLE STEAL PECULATE
SQUANDER
EMBEZZLEMENT THEFT
EMBITTER SOUR BITTER CURDLE
ACIDIFY ENVENOM ACERBATE
EMPOISON VERJUICE
EMBITTERED SOURED ACERBATE
EMBLAZON LAUD ADORN EXTOL
BLAZON DISPLAY EMBLAZE EXHIBIT
GLORIFY
EMBLAZONED CLOUE CLOUEE
CRINED CRESTED BRISTLED
(— WITH ANTLERS) ATTIRED

(— WITH BEARD) BARBED
EMBLAZONMENT HERALDRY
EMBLEM BAR ANKH ATEN MACE
ORLE SEAL SIGN STAR TYPE
AWARD BADGE CREST CROSS
EAGLE FAVOR IMAGE TIARA TOKEN
DEVICE DIADEM ENSIGN FIGURE
KAHILI SABCAT SHIELD SIGNAL
SYMBOL TRISUL CHARACT IMPRESA
IMPRESE SCEPTER SCEPTRE
ALLEGORY CADUCEUS COLOPHON
INSIGNIA
(— OF CUCKOLD) HORN
(— OF IRELAND) SHAMROCK
(— OF WALES) LEEK
(PRINTING —) COLOPHON
(SACRED —) HIEROGRAM
EMBLEMATIC TYPAL FIGURAL
TYPICAL SYMBOLIC
EMBLIC AMLA AULA MYROBALAN
EMBODIMENT MAP SON SELF
AVATAR GENIUS EPITOME IMAGERY
BODIMENT
EMBODY BODY UNITE INBODY
CONTAIN EXPRESS COALESCE
ORGANIZE
EMBOLDEN BOLD BIELD BRAVE
ERECT NERVE ASSURE BOWDEN
ENHARDY HEARTEN STOMACH
EMBOLUS CLOT STYLE
EMBOSOM BOSOM FOSTER CHERISH
ENCLOSE IMBOSOM SHELTER
SURROUND
EMBOSS BOSS HIDE KNOB KNOT
ADORN BLOCK CHASE GOFFER
INDENT POUNCE ANTIQUE CONCEAL
ENCLOSE EXHAUST GAUFFER
INFLATE ORNAMENT
EMBOSSED BOSSED RAISED
ANTIQUE CHAMPED
EMBOSSING CELATURE
EMBOUCHURE LIP CHOPS LIPPING
EMBOWER BOWER
EMBOWERED ARBORED
EMBRACE ARM HUG CLIP COLL
FOLD LOVE NECK PLAT SIDE ZONE
ADOPT BOSOM BRACE CHAIN CLASP
CLING CRUSH ENARM GRASP HALCH
HALSE INARM OXTER TWINE
ABRAZO ACCEPT ACCOLL AMPLEX
BECLIP CARESS CLINCH COMPLY
CUDDLE ENFOLD FATHOM HUDDLE
INCLIP INFOLD PLIGHT SHRINE
AMPLECT CHERISH CONTAIN
ENCLOSE ESPOUSE INCLUDE
INVOLVE ACCOLADE AMPLEXUS
COMPLECT COMPRESS COMPRISE
CONCLUDE ENCIRCLE
EMBRACING COLLING OSCULANT
EMBRASURE LOOP PORT VENT
CRENEL CRENELLE PORTHOLE
EMBROCATION ARNICA EMBROCHE
LINIMENT
EMBROIDER RUN TAT DARN FRET
LACE BROUD COUCH FAGOT PANEL
SMOCK BEWORK EMBOSS FAGGOT
FRIEZE PURFLE STITCH SURFLE
TISSUE BROIDER TAMBOUR
ORNAMENT

EMBROIDERED BRODE BRODEE BROWDEN BROCADED
EMBROIDERER SPRIGGER
EMBROIDERY KANT LACE OPUS WORK BREDE ASSISI BONNAZ CREWEL EDGING HEDEBO APPAREL CHICKEN CUTWORK ORPHREY SETWORK TAMBOUR ARRASENE BRODERIE BROIDERY FAGOTING LISTWORK PHULKARI SMOCKING TAPESTRY
EMBROIL BROIL JUMBLE INVOLVE PERPLEX TROUBLE DISORDER DISTRACT ENTANGLE
EMBRYO GERM CADET FETUS OVULE FOETUS EMBRYON NEURULA ACANTHOR BLASTULA GASTRULA PRINCIPE
EMBRYONIC GERMINAL
EMCEE HOST
EME AUNT YEME UNCLE FRIEND NEIGHBOR
EMEND (ALSO SEE AMEND) EDIT MEND ALTER AMEND BETTER REFORM REPEAL REVISE CORRECT IMPROVE RECTIFY REDRESS EMENDATE
EMERALD BERYL GREEN EMRAUD EMERANT PRASINE SMARAGD
EMERALD FISH ESMERALDA
EMERGE BOB DIP BOLT LOOM PEER RISE BREAK ERUPT EXUDE ISSUE START APPEAR BECOME PLUNGE SPRING DEBOUCH EXTRUDE
(— FROM EGGSHELL) HATCH ECLOSE
(— FROM SLEEP) AWAKE
EMERGENCE NEED BIRTH EGRESS GROWTH PRICKLE BECOMING DEBOUCHE ECLOSION EMERSION ERUPTION EXIGENCE TENTACLE
(— FROM DARKNESS) BREAK
EMERGENCY NEED PEND PUSH PINCH CRISIS STRAIT SUDDEN EMERGENT EXIGENCY JUNCTURE
EMERGENT RISING
EMERGING EMANANT EMERGENT
EMERITA HIPPA
EMERY EMERIL SMIRIS ABRASIVE CORUNDUM
EMETIC ALUM PICK PUKE PUKER VOMIT EVACUANT VOMITIVE VOMITORY
EMIGRANT EMIGRE EXODIST PATARIN SETTLER COLONIST PATERINE STRANGER
(— FROM MECCA) COMPANION
EMIGRATE MOVE REMOVE MIGRATE
EMIGRATION EXODUS HEGIRA HEJIRA SWARMING
EMINENCE DUN BALL BERG CRAG KNOT MONS MOTE NOTE POLE RANK RISE SCAR TOOT CHIEF HOYLE KNOLL PERCH STATE WHEAL WORTH ASCENT HEIGHT KRANTZ RENOWN RIDEAU ALTITUDE GRANDEUR TUBERCLE
(— OF HAND) SUBVOLA
EMINENT BIG ARCH HIGH CHIEF

GRAND GREAT LOFTY NOBLE NOTED FAMOUS MARKED SIGNAL EXCELSE GLORIOUS RENOWNED SINGULAR TOWERING
EMIR AMIR AMEER NOBLE RULER LEADER PRINCE ADMIRAL GOVERNOR
EMISSARY SPY AGENT SCOUT LEGATE DELEGATE
EMISSION FUME GUST VENT
EMISSIVE EMITTENT EXHALANT
EMIT RUN BARK BEAM CAST DRIP GIVE GUSH HURL LASH MOVE OOZE PASS POUR REEK SEND SHED SPIT VENT VOID WARP AVOID BELCH EJECT ERUCT EXERT EXUDE FLASH FLING ISSUE UTTER YIELD DECANT DONATE EVOLVE EXHALE EXPIRE SPREAD BREATHE DISTILL EMANATE EXHAUST OUTSEND RADIATE REFLAIR ERUCTATE TRANSMIT
(— FOAM) SPURGE
(— FORCEFULLY) FIRE
(— IN PUFFS) PLUFF
(— LIGHT) GLOW
(— OUTCRIES) CHUNNER CHUNTER
(— PLAY OF COLORS) OPALESCE
(— RAYS) RADIATE IRRADIATE
(— SMOKE) SMEECH
(— SOUND) BUFF MOVE
(— SPARKS) SNAP
(— ODOR) REEK STEAM
EMITTING EMISSIVE SOUNDING
EMMENAGOGUE ALOE SAFFRON GROUNDSEL
EMMER SPELTZ AMELCORN
EMMET ANT ENEMY PISMIRE FORMICID
EMOLLIATE SOFTEN
EMOLLIENT LENIENT ICHTHYOL LENITIVE MALACTIC MOLLIENT SUPPLING
EMOLUMENT FEES WAGES INCOME PROFIT SALARY BENEFIT STIPEND
EMOTION IRE LOVE ONDE STIR AGONY ANGER CHORD GRIEF HEART SHAME AFFECT EFFECT MOTION RAPTUS SNIVEL SPLEEN ECSTASY FEELING PASSION VULTURE GRAMERCY MOVEMENT SURPRISE
(CONTROLLING —) LEITMOTIF LEITMOTIV
(EVIL —) DEMON DAEMON
EMOTIONAL DRIPPY EMOTIVE
(UNDULY —) SPOONY SPOONEY
EMOTIONLESS COLD
EMPATHY SYMPATHY
EMPEROR I IMP CZAR INCA KING TSAR AKBAR RULER TENNO CAESAR DESPOT KAISER SULTAN BAGINDA MONARCH VIKRAMA AUGUSTUS IMPERIAL PADISHAH
EMPERY DOMAIN EMPIRE EMPIRY DOMINION
EMPHASIS ANGLE ACCENT STRESS WEIGHT EMPIRISM SALIENCE
EMPHASIZE HIT CLICK PINCH PRESS ACCENT BETONE CHARGE STRESS

EMPHATIC STRONG EARNEST MARCATO SERIOUS ENFATICO FORCIBLE MARCANDO POSITIVE
EMPHATICALLY FLATLY STRONGLY POINTEDLY
EMPHYSEMA HEAVES
EMPIRE RULE SWAY POWER REALM REIGN STATE DIADEM DOMAIN EMPERY CONTROL KINGDOM IMPERIUM
(— STATE OF SOUTH) GEORGIA
(— STATE) NEWYORK
(SELJUK —) RUM ROUM
EMPIRIC QUACK IMPOSTOR
EMPIRICIST VIRTUOSO
EMPLACEMENT BATTERY GALLERY PLATFORM
EMPLOY FEE PAY USE BUSK BUSY HIRE PLOY TAKE WAGE WISE ADOPT APPLY BESET IMPLY SPEND BESTOW ENGAGE ENLIST INFOLD INVOKE OCCUPY SUPPLY CONCERN CONDUCT ENCLOSE IMPROVE INVOLVE SERVICE UTILIZE PRACTICE
(— FLATTERY) COLLOGUE
(— ONESELF ABOUT) TOSS
(— SHIFTS) CHICANE
EMPLOYED APPLIED ENGAGED
EMPLOYEE HAND HELP BOOTS CLERK FACTOR LEADER BELLBOY BOOTBOY CALLBOY CARRIER SERVANT CHASSEUR CIVILIAN FLOORMAN IMPROVER
EMPLOYER JOSS BLOKE GAFFER ENGAGER MANAGER GOVERNOR
(SMALL —) CORK
EMPLOYMENT FEE JOB USE CALL HIRE NOTE TASK TOIL USER WORK CRAFT TRADE TREAD USAGE MISTER THRIFT CALLING PURPOSE SERVICE USAUNCE BUSINESS EXERCISE RETAINER VOCATION
(CASUAL —) GRASS
EMPORIUM MART SHOP BAZAR STORE BAZAAR EMPORY MARKET STAPLE MONOPOLE
EMPOWER POWER ENABLE ENTITLE DELEGATE DEPUTIZE
EMPRESS IMPX EMPERESS IMPERIAL KAISERIN
EMPTIED DRAINED
EMPTILY TOOMLY
EMPTINESS VAIN VOID INANE ANEMIA VACUUM VANITY ANAEMIA INANITY VACANCY VACUITY LEERNESS
(— OF SPIRIT) ENNUI
EMPTY DRY FAT RID TIM AIRY BARE BOSS BUZZ CANT DEAF DUMP EMPT FALL FARM FREE GLIB HOWE IDLE LEER NEAR POUR ROOM TEEM TOOM VAIN VIDE VOID ADDLE AVOID BLANK BLEED CLEAN CLEAR DRAIN EQUAL EXPEL HUSKY INANE LEERY MOUTH SCOOP SHOOT STARK START STRIP SWAMP TINNY WINDY BARREN BUBBLE CHAFFY DEVOID HOLLOW JEJUNE STRIKE SWASTY UNEMPT UNLOAD VACANT VACATE

DELIVER DEPLETE EXHAUST EXPRESS UNTAKEN VACUATE VACUOUS DISGORGE EVACUATE EVANESCE NEGATION UNFILLED (— AN EGG) BLOW

EMPTY-HEADED VAIN DOLLISH

EMPTYING EVACUANT (ACT OF —) KENOSIS

EMPTY-SOUNDING TOOM

EMPUSA MONSTER SPECTER SPECTRE

EMPYREAN ETHER AETHER HEAVENS EMPYREUM

EMU EMEU RHEA RATITE

EMU APPLE COLANE

EMU BUSH BERRIGAN

EMULATE APE VIE COPY EMULE EQUAL EXCEL RIVAL COMPETE IMITATE

EMULATION STRIFE CONTEST PARAGON RIVALRY

EMULATOR RIVAL

EMULOUS EMULATE ENVIOUS

EMULOUSLY AVIE

EMULSIFIABLE SOLUBLE

EMULSION PAP LATEX

EMU WREN STIPITURE

EN NUT

ENABLE ABLE EMPOWER ENTITLE QUALIFY INHABILE

ENACT LIVE MAKE PASS ADOPT DECREE EFFECT ORDAIN ACTUATE APPOINT PERFORM PORTRAY

ENACTMENT LAW DOOM ENACT NOVEL ASSIZE DECREE MEASURE PASSAGE STATUTE ENACTION ENACTURE

ENAMEL AMEL FLUX SLIP EMAIL GLAZE GLOSS PAINT SLUSH AUMAIL SHIPPO SMALTO DENTINE LIMOGES SCHMELZ

ENAMOR LOVE CHARM SMITE CAPTIVE

ENAMORED FOND EPRIS EPRISE MASHED AMOROUS CHARMED SMITTEN (VAINLY —) FOOLISH

ENCAMP TELD TENT LODGE PITCH INCAMP LAAGER BIVOUAC LEAGUER

ENCAMPMENT CAMP DOUAR SIEGE LAAGER BIVOUAC CASTRUM HUTMENT TOLDERIA

ENCASE CASE HOUSE SHELL INCASE ENCHASE INCLOSE ENCAPSUL SURROUND

ENCELIA INCIENSO

ENCEPHALON CEREBRUM

ENCHAIN FETTER INCHAIN

ENCHANT CHARM DELUDE GLAMOR INCANT ATTRACT BESPELL BEWITCH DELIGHT GLAMOUR BEDAZZLE ENSORCEL

ENCHANTED RAPT HAGGED CAPTIVE

ENCHANTER MAUGIS CHARMER MAGICIAN MALAGIGI

ENCHANTING WIZARD HEAVENLY SPELLFUL

ENCHANTMENT HEX TAKE CHARM

FAIRY MAGIC SPELL SPOKE CARACT CHANTRY DEVILRY GRAMARY SORCERY SORTIARY WITCHERY

ENCHANTRESS CIRCE FAIRY MEDEA ACRASIA URGANDA

ENCHARGE ENJOIN ENTRUST

ENCHASE INFIX ENRICH ENGRAVE

ENCHIRIDION MANUAL HANDBOOK TREATISE

ENCHORIAL NATIVE DEMOTIC DOMESTIC

ENCIPHER CODE CIPHER ENCRYPT

ENCIRCLE ORB BAND BELT BIND CLIP COIL GIRD GIRT HALO HOOP PALE RING RINK STEM WIRE ZONE BELAY BRACE CLASP CROWN EMBAY EMBOW GIRTH HEDGE INORB ROUND TWINE TWIST BECLIP CIRCLE EMBALL ENGIRT ENLACE ENRING ENWIND FATHOM GIRDLE IMPALE SWATHE WRITHE BETREND COMPASS EMBRACE ENCLAVE ENCLOSE ENTWINE ENVIRON ENWHEEL SERPENT WREATHE CINCTURE CORSELET ENSPHERE IMMANTLE SURROUND

ENCIRCLED GIRT CINCT BELTED SUCCINCT

ENCIRCLEMENT EMBRACE

ENCIRCLING AROUND EMBRACE CORONARY ENCYCLIC

ENCLAVE INLIER

ENCLOAK MANTLE

ENCLOSE IN BAY BOX CAN HEM LAP MEW ORB PAR PEN PIN RIM BANK BUNG CAGE CASE COOP FORT GIRD HAIN HOOP PALE SPAR TINE WALL WARD YARD BOSOM BOUND BOWER BRICK CHEST CLOSE DITCH EMBAR EMBED EMBOX FENCE FRAME GRIPE HEDGE HOUSE IMBED INURN BOUGHT CARTON CASTLE CAVERN CIRCLE CORRAL EMBANK EMBOSS EMPALE EMPARK EMPLOY ENCASE ENCYST ENFOLD ENGULF ENLOCK FASTEN IMMURE IMPALE IMPARK INCASE INCLIP INHOOP INSACK INWALL JACKET PICKET POCKET TACKLE APPROVE CAPSULE COMPASS CONFIDE CONTAIN CURTAIN EMBOSOM EMBOWEL EMBOWER EMBRACE ENCHASE ENCLAVE ENGLOBE ENHEDGE ENVELOP HARNESS IMBOSOM IMMERSE IMPOUND INBOUND INCLUDE INFIELD PARROCK PINFOLD SHEATHE BULKHEAD COMPRISE COMPRIZE CONCLUDE CONVOLVE EMBORDER ENCIRCLE ENSHRINE ENSPHERE IMPRISON LANDLOCK PALISADE PARCLOSE SURROUND (— IN ARMOR) EMPANOPLY (— LOGS) CRIB

ENCLOSED BOUND CLOSED OBTECT INGROWN INTERNAL

ENCLOSING LIMITARY

ENCLOSURE HAG HAW HOK MEW PAR PEN REE STY TYE BAWN BOMA BYTH CAGE CAVE CELL COOP DOCK

FOLD HAIN HOCK KILN LIST PEEL SEPT SKIT SLOT TIGH TOWN WALL WEIR YARD ALTIS ATAJO BASIN BLIND BOOLY BOOTH BOSOM CAROL CLOSE COURT CRAWL CREEP CUBBY FENCE FRANK GARTH GOTRA HOARD KENCH KRAAL LOBBY MARAI PLECK POUND REEVE STALL STELL AVIARY BOOLEY BOXING CANCHA CARREL CORRAL COWPEN CRUIVE DRYLOT GARDEN HURDLE INTAKE KENNEL OUTSET PALING PRISON SERAIL TAMBOR TEOPAN TINING VIVARY WARREN BELLOWS BOROUGH BULLPEN CLOSURE COCKPIT EMBRACE GALLERY GONDOLA HENNERY HOUSING HUMIDOR LANTERN PADDOCK PIGHTLE PUDDOCK SEVERAL STUFFER TAMBOUR AEDICULA CASEMATE CHIPYARD CINCTURE CLAPNEST CLAUSURE CLOISTER COMPOUND DELUBRUM ENCHASER PARADISE POUNDAGE PRECINCT PURPRISE SEPIMENT SERAGLIO SKIRTING STOCKADE VIVARIUM (— ABOUT ALTAR) BEMA (— FOR BOWLING) ALLEY (— FOR COCKPIT) CANOPY (— FOR FISH) CROY YAIR YARE KENCH SPILLER SPILLET (— FOR JURY) BOX (— FOR KNIGHTLY ENCOUNTERS) BARRACE (— FOR LIGHT) LANTERN (— FOR ROASTING ORE) STALL (— OF HOUSE) BAWN (— SURROUNDED BY DITCH) COP (ELEPHANT —) KEDDAH (OBLONG —) CIRCUS (POULTRY —) HENNERY (SACRED —) SECOS SEKOS

ENCOLPION PANAGIA

ENCOMIAST EULOGIST

ENCOMIUM ELOGE ENCOMY EULOGY PRAISE PLAUDIT TRIBUTE

ENCOMPASS BEGO BELT CLIP GIRD PALE RING SPAN WALL WRAP BELIE BERUN BESET BIGAN CLOSE CROWN ROUND BEGIRD BEGIRT CIRCLE ENGIRD COMPASS EMBOWEL EMBRACE ENCLOSE ENVIRON INCLUDE SUBSUME UMBESET ENCIRCLE ENGIRDLE PURPRISE SURROUND (— WITH ARMS) FATHOM

ENCOMPASSED AMID BAYED AMIDST BEGIRT

ENCOMPASSING ROUND AMBIENT CINCTURE PROFOUND INCLUSIVE

ENCORE BIS AGAIN ANCORA RECALL REPEAT

ENCOUNTER BIDE BUMP COIL COPE FACE FIND KEEP MEET MOOT RINK BRUSH FIGHT FORCE GREET INCUR OCCUR ONSET SHOCK STOUR VENUE ACCOST AFFRAY ANSWER ASSAIL ATTACK BATTLE BREAST

CAREER COMBAT JOSTLE JUSTLE
OPPOSE ADDRESS AFFRONT
CONTEST COUNTER DISPUTE
HOSTING JOINING PASSAGE
CONFLICT CONFRONT CONGRESS
REANSWER RECONTER SKIRMISH
(— HOSTILELY) CROSS
(HOSTILE —) CLOSE
(PUGILISTIC —) MILL
ENCOURAGE DAW EGG ABET BACK
FIRM URGE BOOST CHEER ERECT
FAVOR FLUSH HEART IMPEL NERVE
SERVE STEEL ADVISE ASSURE
EXHORT FOMENT FOSTER HALLOO
HARDEN INCITE INDUCE INVITE
NUZZLE REHETE SECOND SPIRIT
UPHOLD ADVANCE ANIMATE
CHERISH COMFORT CONFIRM
CONSOLE ENFORCE ENLIVEN
FLATTER FORTIFY FORWARD
HEARTEN INSPIRE PROMOTE
STOMACH UPCHEER UPRAISE
EMBOLDEN INSPIRIT REASSURE
ENCOURAGED BUCKED CONFIRMED
ENCOURAGEMENT BOOST FLUSH
HURRAH FOMENTO IMPETUS
BLESSING SANCTION
ENCOURAGING HELPFUL FAVORING
ENCRATITE TATIAN AQUARIAN
ENCROACH JET PINCH POACH
IMPOSE INVADE TRENCH IMPINGE
INTRUDE SHINGLE ENTRENCH
INFRINGE INTRENCH TRESPASS
ENCROACHING INVASIVE
ENCROACHMENT BREACH INROAD
ENCROACH INVASION
ENCRUST CAKE CANDY BARKEN
BARKLE INCRUST
ENCRUSTED SCABROUS
ENCUMBER CLOG LOAD PACK
BESET CHECK CROWD TRASH
BEMOIL BURDEN FELTER HAMPER
HINDER IMPEDE LUMBER MITHER
MOIDER RETARD SADDLE WEIGHT
BEPAPER INVOLVE OPPRESS
ACCUMBER ENTANGLE HANDICAP
OBSTRUCT OVERCOME OVERLOAD
ENCUMBERED HEAVY CONGESTED
ENCUMBRANCE CLOG LIEN LOAD
CLAIM BURDEN CHARGE CUMBER
TROUBLE MORTGAGE
ENCYCLICAL PASCENDI
ENCYCLOPEDIA TOME
(GAME —) HOYLE
ENCYSTED CYSTIC SACCATE
SACCATED
END EN AIM DAG EAR FAG TIP BUTT
DATE DOUP FACE FATE FINE FOOT
GOAL HALT HEEL LAST MAIN MARK
SAKE STOP TAIL TERM VIEW AMEND
ARTHA BLOCK BREAK CAUSE CEASE
CLOSE DEATH ENSUE EVENT FINIS
ISSUE LIMIT LOOSE NAPOO OMEGA
POINT PRICK RAISE SCOPE SCRAP
START STASH THULE DEFINE
DESIGN EFFECT EFFLUX ENDING
EXITUS EXPIRE EXPIRY FINALE
FINISH INTENT NAPOOH OBJECT
PERIOD RESULT THIRTY UPSHOT

UTMOST WINDUP ABOLISH ACHIEVE
CLOSURE CURTAIN DESTROY
FANTAIL FINANCE LINEMAN OUTGIVE
PURPOSE REMNANT BOUNDARY
COMPLETE CONCLUDE DESITION
DISSOLVE FINALITY SURCEASE
TERMINAL TERMINUS ULTIMATE
(— DEBATE) CLOTURE
(— OF ANTENNA) CLAVA
(— OF ANVIL) BICKIRON
(— OF ARCHERY PILE) STOPPING
(— OF ARROW) NOCK
(— OF BEEF LOIN) BUTT
(— OF BLANKET) DAGON
(— OF BONE) EPIPHYSIS
(— OF BOOM) JAW
(— OF BOW) EAR
(— OF BRICK) HEADING
(— OF BRISTLE) FLAG
(— OF BUILDING) GABLE
(— OF CAN) BREAST
(— OF CANE) FRAZE
(— OF CART) TIB
(— OF CRESCENT) HORN
(— OF EGG) DOUP
(— OF EXISTENCE) DEMISE
(— OF FABRIC) FENT
(— OF FISHHOOK) SPEAR
(— OF FLAG) FLY
(— OF FROG) TOE
(— OF HALTER) CAPITULUM
(— OF HAMMER) CLAW POLL
(— OF HAMMERHEAD) PEEN
(— OF HORSE-COLLAR) GULLET
(— OF INGOT) CROP
(— OF KEEL) GRIPE
(— OF LEVER) FORK
(— OF LOAF) HEEL
(— OF MINE TUNNEL) FACE
(— OF MINING LEVEL) DEAN
(— OF MUZZLE) MUFFLE
(— OF NAIL) CLENCH
(— OF ONE'S LIFE) DOOM
(— OF PIER) CUTWATER
(— OF PIPE) TAFT SPIGOT
(— OF POCKETKNIFE HANDLE)
BOLSTER
(— OF RAILROAD CAR) BEND
(— OF ROAD) ROADHEAD
(— OF ROD) FORKHEAD
(— OF SHEEP SHEARING) CUTOUT
(— OF SHIP) STERN
(— OF SPINE) ACRUMION
(— OF TENON) HAUNCH
(— OF TOOL) BUTT
(— OF UTERUS) FUNDUS
(- OF WORLD) PRALAYA
(— OF YARD) ARM YARDARM
(— ON POND) FOREBAY
(—S OF RIBBONS) FATTRELS
(—S OF SATURN'S RINGS) ANSA
(CANDLE —) DOUP SNUFF
(DOMINO —) ACE
(FAG —) RUMP
(HANGING —) DAG DAGGE
(JAGGED —) SHRAG
(NARROWED —) NEB
(NORTH — OF COMPASS NEEDLE)
LILY

(POINTED —) APEX
(POSTERIOR —) BOTTOM
(REEF —S) DEADMAN
(ROPE'S —) FEAZE PIGTAIL
FEAZINGS
(SPECIAL —) SAKE
(TAPERING —) POINT
(TATTERED —) FRAZZLE
(ULTIMATE —) SUM TELOS
(UNPLEASANT —) GRIEF
(UPPER —) HEAD
(WARP —S) ACCIDENTAL
ENDANGER DANGER HAZARD
IMPERIL
ENDANGERED BESTED BESTEAD
FRAUGHT
ENDANGERER MARPLOT
ENDEARMENT LOVE CARESS
ENDEAVOR DO AIM PUT TRY WIN
BEST MINT SEEK WORK ASSAY
ESSAY ETTLE EXERT OFFER STUDY
TEMPT TRIAL AFFAIR ASSAIL
DEVOIR EFFORT INTEND STRIFE
STRIVE AFFORCE ATTEMPT
CONATUS CULTURE EMPRISE
EMULATE IMITATE MOLIMEN
NITENCY WORKING EXERTION
PURCHASE STRUGGLE
(— TO CONCLUSION) STUDY
(BEST —) DEVOIR
(EARNESTLY —) FEND
ENDED DONE OVER PAST FINISHED
(— BY CONSONANT) CHECKED
ENDEMIC LOCAL ENDEMIAL
ENDING END CLOSE DEATH GRAVE
FINALE BREAKUP FINANCE DESITION
(NERVE —) SPINDLE
ENDIVE CHICORY WITLOOF
ESCAROLE SCARIOLE
ENDLESS ANANTA ETERNE ETERNAL
FOREVER UNDYING UNENDED
UNENDLY DATELESS FINELESS
IMMORTAL INFINITE UNENDING
ENDMOST TIPMOST FARTHEST
REMOTEST
ENDOCARP STONE PYRENA
PUTAMEN
ENDOGENOUS INNATE AUTOGENIC
ENDOMORPHIC PYCNIC PYKNIC
ENDOPITE PETASMA
ENDOPLEURA TEGMEN
ENDORSE BACK SIGN ADOPT BOOST
DOCKET ENDOSS SECOND APPROVE
CERTIFY INDORSE SUPPORT
ADVOCATE SANCTION
ENDORSEE HOLDER
ENDORSEMENT FIAT FORM VISA
RIDER BACKING APPROVAL
HECHSHER SANCTION
ENDOSPERM FARINA ALBUMEN
ENDOSPORIUM INTINE
ENDOW DOW DUE DOTE GIFT RENT
VEST BLESS CROWN DOWER ENDUE
EQUIP FOUND INDUE SEIZE STATE
STUFF ASSIGN CLOTHE DOTATE
ENABLE ENRICH ENSOUL ESTATE
INVEST CHARTER ENLARGE FURNISH
INSTATE APPANAGE BENEFICE
BEQUEATH ENTALENT
(— WITH FORCE) DYNAMIZE

ENDOWED ABLE GIFTED FAVORED
ENDOWMENT CLAY FINE GIFT WAKF
  WAQF DOWER DOWRY GRACE
  CORPSE GENIUS TALENT APANAGE
  CHANTRY CHARISM FACULTY
  APPANAGE DOTATION
  (NATURAL —S) BUMP DOTES
  TALENT
  (PL.) ALTARAGE
ENDPAPER FLYLEAF
ENDPIECE BRACE CHUMP
  (— OF STETHOSCOPE) BELL
ENDUE DUE ENDOW INDUE TEACH
  CLOTHE INVEST INSTRUCT
ENDURABLE LIVABLE BEARABLE
  LIVEABLE
ENDURANCE GAME LAST TACK
  PLUCK BOTTOM COMFORT
  DURANCE GRANITE LASTING
  STAMINA BEARANCE DURATION
  GAMENESS HARDSHIP PATIENCE
  STRENGTH
ENDURE GO ABY SIT VIE ABYE BEAR
  BIDE DREE DURE HOLD KEEP LAST
  TAKE TIDE WEAR ABEAR ABIDE
  ALLOW BROOK CARRY DRIVE
  POUCH SPARE STAND STICK STOUT
  THOLE TOUGH WIELD ABROOK
  ACCEPT DRUDGE HARDEN REMAIN
  SUFFER COMFORT FORBEAR
  PERSIST SUPPORT SUSTAIN
  SWALLOW TOUGHEN UNDERGO
  WEARING CONTINUE FOREBEAR
  TOLERATE
ENDURING FAST SURE STOUT
  BIDING DURING STABLE STURDY
  DURABLE ETERNAL LASTING
  PATIENT IMMORTAL REMANENT
  STUBBORN
ENDWAYS ANEND ENDWISE
ENEMA CLYSMA CLYSTER LAVEMENT
ENEMY FOE AXIS BOYG FEID DEVIL
  FIEND SATAN FOEMAN HOSTILE
  CONTRARY OPPONENT
  (— OF MANKIND) DEVIL FIEND
  SATAN
  (PERSONAL —) HATER
ENERGETIC FAST FELL HARD LIVE
  RASH BRISK DASHY LUSTY STOUT
  TIGHT VITAL YAULD ACTIVE HEARTY
  HUSTLE LIVELY SPROIL ACTIOUS
  ANIMOSO ARDUOUS DASHING
  DRIVING DYNAMIC ENERGIC
  FURIOUS PUSHFUL PUSHING
  EMPHATIC ENERGICO FORCEFUL
  FORCIBLE HUSTLING VIGOROUS
  (— PERSON) TOWSER
ENERGETICALLY MANLY
  FURIOUSLY
ENERGIZE EXCITE ANIMATE
ENERGIZING KINETIC VIRTUAL
ENERGY U W GO PEP VIM ZIP BANG
  BENT BIRR DASH EDGE JASM LIFE
  SAKT SNAP TUCK ZING ARDOR
  ECLAT FORCE INPUT NERVE POWER
  STEAM VIGOR EFFORT FOISON
  INTAKE ORGONE OUTPUT SPIRIT
  SPRAWL SPRING SPROIL STARCH
  VIRTUE POTENCY SPIRITS ACTIVITY

AMBITION DYNAMISM ENERGEIA
MOTIVITY PRAKRITI STRENGTH
VIVACITY
(— PEAK) NUCLEUS
(EMOTIONAL —) LIBIDO
(LIBINAL —) CATHEXIS
(LIFE —) JIVA SAKTI SHAKTI
(LIGHT —) RAD
(MENTAL —) DOCITY PSYCHURGY
(POTENTIAL —) ERGAL
(RADIANT —) SOUND ACTINISM
  EINSTEIN
(VITAL —) HORME PANZOISM
ENERVATE SAP COOK FLAG MELT
  SOFTEN WEAKEN MOLLIFY UNNERVE
  UNSINEW ENFEEBLE
ENERVATED BEDRID EFFETE
  LANGUID BEDRIDDEN
ENERVATING DREARY
ENERVATION COLLAPSE
ENFEEBLE NUMB FAINT SHAKE
  APPALL DEADEN FEEBLE IMPAIR
  SOFTEN WEAKEN DEPRESS
  UNSINEW AFFEEBLE ENERVATE
  IMBECILE UNSTRONG
ENFEEBLED FEY NUMB
ENFOLD (ALSO SEE INFOLD) LAP
  FURL WRAP CLASP COVER DRAPE
  ENROL IMPLY COMPLY ENLACE
  ENROLL ENWIND ENWRAP INFOLD
  INWIND SHADOW SWATHE WATTLE
  EMBRACE ENCLOSE ENVELOP
  ENVIRON INCLUDE INVOLVE
  UMBELAP CONVOLVE
ENFORCE BULL LEVY EXACT FORCE
  PRESS COERCE COMPEL EFFECT
  FOLLOW INVOKE EXECUTE IMPLANT
ENFORCED COMPULSORY
ENFORCER EXECUTOR MUSCLEMAN
ENFRAMEMENT CARTOUCH
ENG AGMA
ENGAGE DIP WED BOOK BUSY GAGE
  HAVE HIRE JOIN LIST MESH RENT
  SIGN TAKE WAGE AGREE AMUSE
  CATCH ENTER LEASE PITCH TRADE
  TRYST ABSORB ARREST EMBARK
  EMPLOY ENLIST INDUCE OBLIGE
  OCCUPY PLEDGE PLIGHT BESPEAK
  BETROTH CONCERN CONDUCE
  CONSUME ENGROSS IMMERSE
  INVOLVE PROMISE AFFIANCE
  CONTRACT COVENANT ENTANGLE
  INTEREST INTRIGUE PERSUADE
  (— DEEPLY) DROWN
  (— IN ARGUMENT) BALK BAULK
  (— IN COMBAT) DEBATE STRIKE
  (— IN DEBATE) STONEWALL
  (— IN DISCUSSION) CONTEND
  (— IN PRANKS) LARK
  (— IN TILT) JUST JOUST
  (— IN) GO CUT SUE HAVE JOIN
  LEAD
  (— WHOLLY) ABSORB CONSUME
  IMMERSE
ENGAGED BENT BUSY FAST GONE
  HIRED ACTIVE BONDED BOOKED
  MESHED ASSURED BESPOKE
  EARNEST ENTERED PLEDGED
  TOKENED VERSANT ABSORBED

ATTACHED EMBEDDED EMPLOYED
INSERTED INTEREST INVOLVED
OCCUPIED PROMISED
(— IN CONTROVERSY) DISPUTANT
(— IN) ABOUT
(MENTALLY —) VERSANT
(WARMLY —) ZEALOUS
ENGAGEMENT AVAL DATE COWLE
  SPURN ACTION AFFAIR BATTLE
  COMBAT ESCROW PLIGHT STANZA
  SURETY BARGAIN BOOKING
  DUSTING SERVICE CONFLICT
  RETAINER SKIRMISH WARRANTY
  (— TO MARRY) TRYST
  (MILITARY —) DO SHOW
  (SHORT —) SNAP
  (SINGLE —) GIG
  (THEATRICAL —) SHOP
  (WRITTEN —) COWLE
ENGAGING SOFT SAPID SWEET
  TAKING
ENGENDER BEGET BREED CAUSE
  EXCITE GENDER DEVELOP PRODUCE
  GENERATE INGENDER OCCASION
ENGIDU EABANI
ENGINE GAS JET SIX FOUR GOAT
  TANK EIGHT JINNY MOTOR OILER
  STEAM BANKER DIESEL DOCTOR
  DUDLER DUDLEY INGENE JORDAN
  KICKER PUFFER RADIAL ROADER
  YARDER MACHINE POACHER
  POTCHER SKIDDER STEAMER
  TRACTOR TURBINE BULLGINE
  COMPOUND DOLLBEER EXPANDER
  GASOLINE IMPULSOR
  (— FOR HAULING LOGS) DUDLER
  DUDLEY
  (— FOR THROWING MISSILES) GIN
  SPRINGAL
  (— OF TORTURE) GIN RACK
  (— OF WAR) RAM SWEEP HELEPOLE
  (DONKEY —) DOCTOR
  (FIRE —) TUB
  (JET —) ATHODYD
  (MILITARY —) BOAR TOWER FABRIC
  TREPAN DONDINE PERRIER
  TORMENT WARWOLF BALLISTA
  DONDAINE MANGONEL MARTINET
  SCORPION
  (RAILROAD —) HOG GOAT YARDER
  SWITCHER
ENGINEER PLAN GUIDE DRIVER
  FANNER HOGGER MANAGE SAPPER
  HOGHEAD PLANNER PLOTTER
  CONTRIVE DESIGNER INGENIER
  INVENTOR MANEUVER
ENGINEMAN HOISTER HOISTMAN
ENGINERY TIRE
ENGIRDLED CINCT
ENGLAND HOME ALBION LOGRIA
  BLIGHTY BRITAIN LOEGRIA
  HOMELAND

ENGLAND		
AIRFORCE: RAF		
BAY: TOR LYME WASH START		
MOUNTS BIGBURY BIDEFORD		
CARDIGAN FALMOUTH		

TREMADOC WEYMOUTH
CAPITAL: LONDON
CHANNEL: SOLENT BRISTOL
ENGLISH SPITHEAD
CHANNEL ISLAND: HERM SARK
JERSEY ALDERNEY GUERNSEY
COIN: ORA RIAL RYAL ACKEY
ANGEL CROWN GROAT NOBLE
PENCE PENNY POUND SPRAT
UNITE BAWBEE FLORIN GUINEA
SESKIN TESTON ANGELET
CAROLUS HAPENNY TUPPENY
FARTHING SHILLING SIXPENCE
TUPPENCE
CONSERVATIVE: TORY
COUNTY: KENT DEVON ESSEX
HANTS SALOP WIGHT DORSET
DURHAM LONDON SURREY
SUSSEX NORFOLK RUTLAND
SUFFOLK CHESHIRE CORNWALL
SOMERSET
DANCE: MORRIS
FIRTH: SOLWAY
FOREST: ARDEN EXMOOR
DARTMOOR SHERWOOD
HEAD: SPURN BEACHY FORMBY
LIZARD CEMMAES TREVOSE
HILLS: MENDIP BRENDON CHEVIOT
CHILTERN COTSWOLD
INVADER: DANE PICT ROMAN
SAXON NORMAN
ISLAND: MAN HOLY LUNDY WIGHT
COQUET MERSEA THANET
TRESCO WALNEY BARDSEY
HAYLING IRELAND SHEPPEY
ANGLESEA ANGLESEY
FOULNESS HOLYHEAD
ISLANDS: FARNE SCILLY CHANNEL
KING: HAL LUD BRAN BRUT CNUT
COLE KNUT LEAR HENRY JAMES
SWEYN ALFRED BLADUD
BRUTUS CANUTE EDWARD
EGBERT GEORGE ARTEGAL
ELIDURE RICHARD WILLIAM
GORBODUC
LAKE: CONISTON
LIBERAL: WHIG
MEASURE: CUT ELL LEA MIL PIN
ROD RUN TON TUN VAT ACRE
BIND BOLL BUTT CADE COMB
COOM CRAN FOOT GILL GOAD
HAND HANK HEER HIDE INCH
LAST LINE MILE NAIL PACE
PALM PECK PINT PIPE POLE
POOL ROOD ROPE SACK SEAM
SPAN TRUG TYPP WIST YARD
YOKE BODGE CABOT CHAIN
COOMB CUBIT DIGIT FLOAT
FLOOR FLUID HUTCH JUGUM
MINIM OUNCE PERCH POINT
PRIME QUART SKEIN STACK
TRUSS BARREL BOVATE BUSHEL
CRANNE FATHOM FIRKIN
GALLON HOBBET HOBBIT
LEAGUE MANENT OXGANG
POTTLE RUNLET SECOND
SQUARE STRIKE SULUNG
THREAD TIERCE AUCHLET

FURLONG KENNING QUARTER
RUNDLET SEAMILE SPINDLE
TERTIAN VIRGATE CARUCATE
CHALDRON HOGSHEAD
LANDYARD PUNCHEON
QUADRANT QUARTERN
STANDARD
MOUNTAIN: PEAK SCAFELL
SKIDDAW SNOWDON
MOUNTAINS: BLACK PENNINE
SNOWDON CAMBRIAN CUMBRIAN
NAME: ALBION BRITAIN BRITANNIA
PENINSULA: PORTLAND
POINT: NAZE LYNAS MORTE
SALES DODMAN LIZARD PRAWLE
HARTLAND LANDSEND
GIBRALTAR
POLICEMAN: BOBBY COPPER
PEELER
RACE TRACK: ASCOT
RESORT: BATH BRIGHTON
BLACKPOOL
RIVER: CAM DEE DON ESK EXE
LEA NEN URE WYE AIRE AVON
EDEN LUNE NENE NIDD OUSE
PENK TAME TEES TILL TYNE
WEAR YARE ANKER COLNE
DEBEN STOUR SWALE TAMAR
TAWAR TRENT TWEED HUMBER
KENNET MERSEY RIBBLE
ROTHER SEVERN THAMES
WENSUM WHARFE WITHAM
DERWENT PARRETT WAVENEY
WELLAND TORRIDGE
ROCKS: MANACLES
ROYAL HOUSE: YORK TUDOR
STUART HANOVER WINDSOR
LANCASTER PLANTAGENET
SCHOOL: ETON RUGBY HARROW
SEA: IRISH NORTH
SETTLER: JUTE PICT ANGLE
SAXON NORMAN
SOLDIER: TOMMY REDCOAT
FUSILEER
STRAIT: DOVER
TOWN: ELY BATH DEAL HULL
RYDE WARE YORK BLYTH
BRENT DERBY DOVER ERITH
FLINT LEEDS RIPON TRURO
WIGAN BARNET BOLTON
BOOTLE CAMDEN DURHAM
EALING EXETER HANLEY
JARROW LEYTON LONDON
OLDHAM OXFORD YEOVIL
BRISTOL BROMLEY BURNLEY
CHELSEA CROYDON ENFIELD
GRIMSBY HALIFAX HORNSEY
IPSWICH LAMBETH NEWPORT
NORWICH PRESTON SALFORD
SEAFORD WESTHAM BRADFORD
BRIGHTON CORNWALL
COVENTRY DEWSBURY
HASTINGS PLYMOUTH
ROCHDALE WALLASEY
WALLSALL GREENWICH
LIVERPOOL SHEFFIELD
BIRMINGHAM MANCHESTER
TRIBE: ICENI

UNIVERSITY: LONDON OXFORD
CAMBRIDGE
VALLEY: COOM EDEN TEES TYNE
COMBE COOMB COQUET
WEIGHT: BAG KIP TOD TON KEEL
LAST MAST MAUN BARGE
FAGOT GRAIN MAUND POUND
SCORE STAND STONE TRUSS
BUSHEL CENTAL FANGOT FIRKIN
FOTHER FOTMAL POCKET
QUARTER QUINTAL SARPLER

ENGLISH SAXON AUSTRAL BRITISH
ENGLAND SAXONISH SOUTHRON
STANDARD
(IN —) ANGLICE
ENGLISHMAN SAXON BRITON
GODDAM GRINGO JOHNNY
MACARONI SOUTHRON ENGLISHER
ENGLISHWOMAN INGLESA
ENGORGE GLUT GORGE DEVOUR
SWALLOW
ENGRAFT INSET
ENGRAM TRACE
(— PATTERN) MEANING
ENGRAVE CUT ETCH RIST CARVE
CHASE GRAVE HATCH PRINT SCULP
CHISEL INCISE SCULPT CRIBBLE
ENCHASE EXARATE IMPRESS
IMPRINT INSCULP STIPPLE INSCRIBE
ORNAMENT
ENGRAVED GRAVEN GRAPHIC
INCISED
ENGRAVER POINT CHASER ETCHER
GRAVER ARTISAN INSCULP BURINIST
MEDALIST SCULLION WRIGGLER
(— OF STONES) LAPIDARY
ENGRAVING CUT PRINT SCULP
STAMP GRAVERY GRAVING
GRAVURE WOODCUT AQUATINT
DRYPOINT HATCHING INTAGLIO
LINEWORK
ENGROSS BURY SINK SOAK AMASS
GROSS ABSORB ENGAGE ENROLL
ENWRAP OCCUPY SCROLL COLLECT
CONSUME IMMERSE INVOLVE
ENGROSSED DEEP FULL RAPT
INTENT WRAPPED ABSORBED
IMMERSED
ENGULF GULF ABYSM ABYSS SOUSE
SWAMP WHELM ABSORB DEVOUR
INVADE QUELME SLOUGH ENGORGE
SWALLOW SUBMERGE
ENHANCE FOIL LIFT BUILD ENARM
ENDOW EXALT RAISE DEEPEN
AUGMENT ELEVATE ENLARGE
EXHANCE GREATEN IMPROVE
SHARPEN HEIGHTEN INCREASE
ENHANCEMENT SAKE
ENHYDRA LATAX
ENIGMA WHY EGMA GRIPH REBUS
PUZZLE RIDDLE SPHINX GRIPHUS
MYSTERY PROBLEM PROVERB
ENIGMATIC HUMAN MYSTIC
CRYPTIC OBSCURE ELLIPTIC
MYSTICAL PUZZLING RIDDLING
ENJAMBMENT OVERFLOW
ENJOIN BID JOIN WILL ENIUN ORDER

CHARGE DECREE DIRECT FORBID
COMMAND DICTATE REQUIRE
ADMONISH PROHIBIT

ENJOY GO JOY FAIN HAVE LIKE
BROOK FANCY PROVE SAVOR
TASTE WIELD ADMIRE DEVOUR
RELISH DELIGHT
(— ONESELF) FEAST LAUGH

ENJOYABLE GOOD FRUITY AMIABLE
BLESSED CAPITAL GLORIOUS
SAVOROUS SPLENDID

ENJOYING FRUITIVE

ENJOYMENT FUN JOY USE BASK
BOOT EASE GUST KAMA PLAY ZEST
GUSTO LIKING RELISH COMFORT
DELIGHT JOLLITY JOYANCE
JOYANCY FELICITY FRUITION
PLEASURE SKITTLES

ENKINDLE WARM INCENSE INFLAME

ENLARGE ADD EKE BORE GROW
HONE HUFF OPEN REAM ROOM
BUILD FARCE LARGE SWELL WIDEN
BIGGEN BRANCH BROACH DIDUCE
DILATE EXPAND EXTEND FRAISE
GATHER LARGEN OMNIFY SPREAD
AMPLIFY AUGMENT DISTEND
ENHANCE GREATEN IMPROVE
INGREAT MAGNIFY STRETCH
AMPLIATE CUMULATE FLOURISH
INCREASE
(— COAL MINE) SNUB

ENLARGED BLOATED SWELLED
SWOLLEN AMPLIATE CAPITATE
EXPANDED EXTENDED VARICOSE

ENLARGEMENT BULB DISC DISK
KNOP CLAVA SWELL BLOWUP
BUNION GIBBER GROWTH SCYPHA
ENLARGE FOOTING SCYPHUS
STATION INCREASE SWELLING
(— IN MINE SHAFT) STATION
(— OF GLAND) GOITER GOITRE
(— OF GULLET) CROP
(— OF MOLD) RAPPAGE
(— OF NERVE FIBER) BOUTON
(— OF ORGAN) STRUMA
(BONY —) SPAVIN SPAVINE

ENLARGING EVASE SWELLING

ENLIGHTEN OPEN CLEAR EDIFY
TEACH ILLUME INFORM UNSEEL
EDUCATE LIGHTEN ENKINDLE
INSTRUCT

ENLIGHTENED WISE LUMINOUS

ENLIGHTENMENT BODHI LIGHT
SATORI WISDOM CULTURE SAMADHI

ENLIST DRUM JOIN LEVY SOUD
ENROL ENTER HITCH PREST
ENGAGE ENROLL INDUCT IMPRESS
RECRUIT REGISTER

ENLISTMENT LEVY HITCH PREST
LISTING

ENLIVEN DASH JAZZ WARM BRACE
BRISK CHEER QUICK ROUSE KITTLE
REVIVE ANIMATE COMFORT INSPIRE
REFRESH SMARTEN BRIGHTEN
INSPIRIT

ENLIVENING GENIAL LIVELY VIVIFIC
CHIRPING

ENMESH TRAP CATCH SNARL
IMMESH ENSNARE ENTANGLE

ENMITY WAR FEUD SPITE WRAKE
ANIMUS HATRED MALICE RANCOR
STRIFE FOEHOOD AVERSION

ENNOBLE LORD EXALT HONOR
NOBLE RAISE GENTLE UPLIFT
DIGNIFY ELEVATE GLORIFY
GREATEN NOBLIFY

ENNUI BORE TEDIUM BOREDOM
DOLDRUM

ENORMITY GRAVITY

ENORMOUS BIG GOB HUGE REAM
VAST ENORM GREAT HEROIC
MIGHTY UNRIDE IMMENSE
ABNORMAL COLOSSAL FLAGRANT
GIGANTIC WHAPPING WHOPPING

ENOS (FATHER OF —) SETH
(GRANDFATHER OF —) ADAM
(SON OF —) CAINAN

ENOUGH BAS ENOW WELL WHEN
AMPLE ASSAI BASTA ANEUCH
PLENTY APLENTY SUFFICE
ADEQUATE
(HARDLY —) SKIMP

ENOUNCE STATE UTTER AFFIRM
DECLARE PROCLAIM

ENRAGE RAGE ANGER GRIEVE
MADDEN INCENSE INFLAME
STOMACH

ENRAGED MAD ASHY WODE WOOD
ANGRY IRATE SAVAGE AGRAMED
BERSERK CHOLERIC INCENSED
MADDENED

ENRAPTURE RAVISH TRANCE
ECSTASY ENCHANT ENRAVISH
ENTRANCE

ENRAPTURED RAPT ENRAPT
TRANCED ECSTATIC

ENRICH FAT BOOT FEED FRET LARD
RICH ADORN CROWN ENDOW
GUANO BATTEN FATTEN INVEST
FEATHER FORTIFY FURNISH
GUANIZE INCREASE ORNAMENT
TREASURE
(— A GAS) CARBURET
(— A MINE) SALT
(— FUEL MIXTURE) CHOKE

ENRICHED FLORID

ENRICHMENT DITATION

ENROLL BEAR JOIN LIST POLL
ENROL ENTER WRITE ATTEST
BILLET ENFOLD ENLIST INDUCT
MUSTER RECORD ASCRIBE IMPANEL
INITIATE INSCRIBE REGISTER

ENROLLMENT LISTING REGISTRY

ENROOT ENRACE IMPLANT

ENSCONCE HIDE COVER SETTLE
CONCEAL SHELTER

ENSEMBLE CORPS DECOR WHOLE
COSTUME
(— OF ARMS) ARMORY

ENSHEATHE EMBOSS

ENSHRINE SAINT SHRINE ENCHASE
ENTEMPLE

ENSHROUD WRAP

ENSIFORM ENSATE XIPHOID
GLADIATE

ENSIGN FLAG IAGO SIGN BADGE
COLOR SENYE AQUILA BANNER
BEACON PENNON PISTOL SIGNAL

SYMBOL ALFEREZ ANCIENT INSIGNE
DANEBROG GONFALON ORIFLAMB
PAVILION STANDARD
(—S ARMORIAL) ARMS
(IMPERIAL —) TUT
(JAPANESE —) SUNBURST
(PL.) ENSIGNRY HERALDRY

ENSILE SILO SILAGE

ENSLAVE THEW CHAIN SLAVE THIRL
ENTHRAL NESLAVE SLAVISH
ENTHRALL

ENSLAVED SLAVE THRALL

ENSLAVEMENT DULOSIS SLAVERY

ENSNARE NET WEB GIRN LACE LIME
MESH TOIL TRAP WRAP BENET
CATCH NOOSE SNARE SNARL
ALLURE ATTRAP ENGINE ENMESH
ENTOIL ENTRAP TANGLE TREPAN
BEGUILE DECEIVE ENGLEIM SNIGGLE
SPRINGE BIRDLIME INVEIGLE
OVERTAKE SURPRISE

ENSNARL ENTANGLE

ENSPHERE INORB SPHERE

ENSUE FOLLOW RESULT SUCCEED
(— UPON) SUE

ENSUING NEXT SUING SEQUENT

ENSURE ASSURE INSURE SECURE
BETROTH ESPOUSE WARRANT
AFFIANCE

ENTADA LENS

ENTAIL TAIL INCUR IMPOSE CONTAIN
INVOLVE REQUIRE TAILZIE

ENTAILED AYNE TAIL EIGNE

ENTAMOEBA LOSCHIA

ENTANGLE ELF LAP MAT TAT WEB
CAST COLL FOUL HARL KNIT KNOT
LIME MESH MIRE TOIL WRAP BROIL
CATCH HALCH RAVEL SNAFU SNARE
SNARL TWIST BEFOUL COTTER
ENGAGE ENLACE ENMESH ENTRAP
ENWRAP FANKLE FELTER HAMPER
HANKLE HATTER INMAZE INMESH
PESTER PUZZLE RAFFLE RANGLE
TACKLE TANGLE WRAPLE CONFUSE
EMBRAKE EMBROIL ENSNARL
ENTRIKE IMBRIER INVOLVE PERPLEX
TRAMMEL BEWILDER ENCUMBER
IMPESTER INTRIGUE STRAPPLE

ENTANGLED DEEP FOUL COTTY
TANGLY COMPLEX KNOTTED
IMPLICIT

ENTANGLEMENT FOUL KNOT TWIT
HITCH BUNKER HEDGEHOG
OBSTACLE

ENTASIS SWELL

ENTENTE TREATY ALLIANCE

ENTER BOX DIP SET BEAR BOOK
JOIN POST ADMIT BEGIN BOARD
BREVE ENROL INCUR PROBE SHARE
START ACCEDE APPEAR BILLET
ENGAGE ENLIST ENROLL ENTRER
INCEPT INVADE PIERCE RECORD
SPREAD INGRESS INTRUDE
COMMENCE ENCROACH INITIATE
INSCRIBE NOMINATE REGISTER
(— BY FORCE) BREAK IRRUPT
INTRUDE
(— HASTILY) BULGE
(— IN ATTACK) FORCE

(— **IN BOOKS**) ACCRUE
(— **INTO**) JOIN INTERN
(— **SLOWLY**) SEEP
(— **UNNOTICED**) CREEP
(— **UPON CAREER**) INCEPT
(— **UPON DUTIES**) ASSUME
(— **WITHOUT RIGHT**) ABATE
ENTERING ENTRY INGOING INGRESS
INTRANT INCOMING
ENTEROTOXEMIA STRUCK
ENTERPRISE FIRM IRON PUSH TOGT
DRIVE ESSAY ACTION EMPIRE SPIRIT
VOYAGE ATTEMPT EMPRISE
HOLDING PROJECT VENTURE
BUSINESS CARNIVAL GUMPTION
VIRITOOT
(**CRIMINAL** —) JOB
(**HARD** —) DIFFICULTY
(**REMEDIAL** —) CRUSADE
(**SPECULATIVE** —) ADVENTURE
(**UNPROFITABLE** —) SINKHOLE
ENTERPRISING BOLD FORTHY
PUSHFUL PUSHING
ENTERTAIN INN BEAR BUSK EASE
FETE HAVE HOLD HOST AMUSE
ENJOY FEAST GUEST SPORT TREAT
DIVERT FROLIC GESTEN HARBOR
JUNKET RECULE REGALE RETAIN
SOLACE BEGUILE CHERISH DISPORT
KITCHEN CONSIDER INTEREST
(— **WITHOUT CHARGE**) DEFRAY
ENTERTAINED OUGHT
ENTERTAINER BHAT HOST ACTOR
AMUSER ARTIST BUSKER DANCER
FIDDLE HARLOT SINGER ACTRESS
ARTISTE GLEEMAN HETAERA
HOSTESS REGALER SPEAKER
BEACHBOY COMEDIAN HOSTELER
MAGICIAN MINSTREL
ENTERTAINING GOOD RICH TREAT
PRETTY AMUSING BEDSIDE
GUESTING SPORTFUL
ENTERTAINMENT BASH BILL FARE
FETE GALA GLEE PLAY SHOW
BOARD CHEER FEAST GAUDY
OPERA REVUE SPORT CIRCUS
DIVERT DOMENT GAIETY GAYETY
HOSTEL INFARE KERMIS NAUTCH
SETOUT SHIVVO WATTLE BANQUET
BENEFIT BUMMACK BUMMOCK
BURLESK CEILIDH CONCERT
COSHERY FESTINE FESTINO JOLLITY
KERMESS PASTIME RIDOTTO
CAKEWALK COMMORTH DROLLERY
EASEMENT ENTREATY ENTREMES
FUNCTION GESTNING GESTONIE
GUESTING HOGMANAY JONGLERY
MUSICALE WAYZGOOSE
(**FAREWELL** —) FOY
ENTHALPY H
ENTHRALL SEND CHARM THIRL
THRALL ENSLAVE ENTHRAL
ENTHRONE CROWN EXALT STALL
ENSEAT THRONE THRONIZE
ENTHUSIASM BUG ELAN FIRE FURY
ZEAL ZEST ZING ARDOR ESTRO
FEVER FLAME FUROR HEART MANIA
VERVE FERVOR HURRAH SPIRIT
WARMTH ABANDON ARDENCY

AVIDITY MADNESS MUSTARD
DEVOTION LYRICISM
(— **IN BATTLE**) EARNEST
(**CONTAGIOUS** —) FUROR FURORE
(**EXCESSIVE** —) MANIA
(**WILD** —) DELIRIUM
ENTHUSIAST BUG FAN NUT BUFF
BIGOT ROOTER VOTARY ZEALOT
DEVOTEE EUCHITE FANATIC
FANCIER FOLLOWER VOTARESS
VOTARIST
(PL.) ARDITI
ENTHUSIASTIC GAGA KEEN WARM
HAPPY NUTTY RABID ARDENT
HEARTY CRACKED FERVENT
GLOWING CRACKERS
(**EXCESSIVELY** —) FANATIC
(**VAINLY** —) FOOLISH
ENTICE COG COY PUT WIN BAIT
COAX DRAW DRIB LEAD LOCK LURE
TICE TOLE TOLL WILE CHARM
DECOY DRILL LATHE SIREN SLOCK
STEAL TEMPT TRAIN TROLL TULLE
ALLECT ALLURE ATTICE CAJOLE
ENLURE INCITE INDUCE INVITE
SEDUCE ATTRACT BEWITCH SOLICIT
SUGGEST INVEIGLE PERSUADE
ENTICEMENT BAIT CORD LURE TICE
ENTICING SIREN ALLURING
ENTIRE ALL DEAD EVEN FULL HALE
MEAR MERE SOLE CLEAN EVERY
GROSS PLAIN QUITE ROUND SOUND
STARK TOTAL TUTTO UTTER WHOLE
VERSAL PERFECT PLENARY
ABSOLUTE COMPLETE ENDURING
GLOBULAR INTEGRAL LIVELONG
OUTRIGHT TEETOTAL UNBROKEN
ENTIRELY DEAD DEIN FAIR FULL
PURE CLEAN CLEAR FULLY PLAIN
QUITE STARK WHOLE BODILY
WHOLLY EXACTLY QUITELY
THROUGH CLEVERLY
ENTIRETY WHOLE ENTIRE TOTALITY
ENTITLE DUB CALL NAME TERM
AFFIX STYLE ENABLE CAPTION
EMPOWER QUALIFY INTITULE
NOMINATE
ENTITLED APPARENT ELIGIBLE
ENTITY ENS BODY FORM UNIT BEING
HABIT OUSIA SPACE THING ENERGY
ESSENCE INTEGER TOTALITY
ENTOMB BURY TOMB INTER INURN
ENCAVE HEARSE IMMURE INHUME
SHRINE
ENTOMOLOGY BUGOLOGY
ENTOMOPHTHORA EMPUSA
ENTOTROPHI DIPLURA
ENTOURAGE TRAIN COMITES
RETINUE
ENTRACTE INTERACT INTERVAL
ENTRAIL BOWEL TRAIL INTRAIL
ENTRAILS GUT GUTS DRAFT TRIPE
FIBERS GIBLET HALLOW INWARD
JAUDIE MUGGET PAUNCH QUARRY
QUERRE UMBLES INSIDES NUMBLES
CHAWDRON GRALLOCH
ENTRANCE ADIT BOCA CUSP DOOR
GATE HALL BOCCA CHARM DEBUT
ENTER ENTRY FOYER GORGE INLET

MOUTH PORCH STULM THIRL TORAN
ACCESS ATRIUM ENTREE INFAIR
INGANG INGATE INROAD PORTAL
RAVISH TORANA TRANCE ZAGUAN
DELIGHT GATEWAY HALLWAY
INGOING INGRESS INITIAL INTRADO
INTROIT PASSAGE POSTERN
ENTRESSE FOREGATE VOMITORY
(— **TO VALLEY**) CHOPS
(**ASTROLOGICAL** —) CUSP
(**CELLAR** —) ROLLWAY
(**FORCIBLE** —) INROAD
(**FORMAL** —) DEBUT
(**HARBOR** —) BOCA
(**HOSTILE** —) INVASION
(**HURRIED** —) BOUT
(**PRIVATE** —) POSTERN
ENTRANCED RAPT CHARMED
TRANCED ECSTATIC
ENTRANCEMENT SPELL
ENTRANCING ORPHIC
ENTRANT INTRANT STARTER
BEGINNER
ENTRAP BAG EBB NET HOOK SNIB
TOIL TRAP CATCH CRIMP DECOY
NOOSE SNARE ALLURE AMBUSH
ATTRAP ENGAGE ENTOIL TAIGLE
TANGLE TREPAN BEGUILE ENSNARE
PITFALL ENTANGLE INVEIGLE
ENTRAPPED (— **IN SEDIMENT**)
CONNATE
ENTREAT ASK BEG BID SUE WOO
PRAY PRIG SEEK URGE CRAVE
HALSE PLEAD PRESS TREAT
ADJURE APPEAL DESIRE INVOKE
BESEECH CONJURE EXORATE
IMPLORE PREVAIL PROCURE
REQUEST SOLICIT PERSUADE
PETITION
ENTREATING TREAT CRAVING
ENTREATY DO CRY PLEA SUIT
APPEAL DEESIS PRAYER TREATY
BESEECH BIDDING ENTREAT
PURSUIT REQUEST URGENCY
PETITION PLEADING
ENTREE ENTRY ACCESS BOUDIN
OSTIUM ENTRADA INTRADA
SOUFFLE ENTRANCE FRICANDO
MAZARINE
ENTREMES SAINETE SAYNETE
ENTRENCH INVADE SCONCE
TRENCH ENCROACH TRESPASS
ENTRENCHMENT CLOSURE
LODGMENT
ENTROPY S
ENTRUST ARET FIDE GIVE STOW
BEKEN TRUST CHARGE COMMIT
CREDIT LIPPEN ADDRESS BEHIGHT
COMMEND CONFIDE CONSIGN
DEPOSIT INTRUST BEQUEATH
DELEGATE ENCHARGE
(— **TO DEPUTY**) DEVIL
ENTRY ADIT HALL ITEM STET BREAK
CLOSE DEBIT AUTHOR CREDIT
DOCKET ENTREE POSTEA RECORD
RINGER TRANCE ENTRADA INGRESS
INTRADO PASSAGE ENTRANCE
ENTRESSE ENTRYWAY NOTANDUM
REGISTER VOCATION

ENTWINE FOLD LACE WIND BRAID
CLASP IMPLY PLASH TWINE TWIST
WEAVE ENLACE INWIND ENTWIST
INVOLVE SERPENT WREATHE
ENTWINED ACCOLLE BRAIDED
INWOVEN ACCOLLEE
ENUMERATE POLL TELL COUNT
SCORE DETAIL NUMBER RECITE
RECKON RELATE COMPILE
COMPUTE ITEMIZE RECOUNT
ESTIMATE REHEARSE
ENUMERATION LIST TALE COUNT
SCORE CENSUS ACCOUNT CATALOG
RECITAL CITATION
ENUNCIATE SAY UTTER DECLARE
DELIVER ENOUNCE ANNOUNCE
PROCLAIM
ENUNCIATION DICTION DELIVERY
(IMPERFECT —) LALLATION
ENVELOP BUR FOG LAP LOT POD
WEB BURR CASE COMA FOLD HUSK
MAIL BRACE CLOUD COVER KNIFE
ROUND BEGIRD BEGIRT BEMIST
BINDLE CLOTHE COCOON CORONA
ENFOLD ENGIRT ENTIRE ENWRAP
FARDEL FOLDER INFOLD INVEST
JACKET MANTLE MUFFLE POCKET
SHEATH SHROUD STIFLE SWATHE
WRIXLE CALYMMA CAPSULE
CHORION ENCLOSE ENVIRON
INVOLVE SWADDLE SWALLOW
VESTURE WRAPPER ENSPHERE
ENVELOPE MANTLING PERIANTH
PERIDIUM POCHETTE SURROUND
WRAPPAGE
(— IN SMOKE) ENFUME
(GLASS —) BULB
(LUMINOUS —) CORONA
(NEBULOUS —) CHEVELURE
(OPEN —) JACKET
(PAY —) PACKET
(STAMPED —) ENTIRE
(VEGETABLE —) COD
ENVELOPED WOMPLIT
ENVELOPING AMBIENT
ENVENOM VENOM CORRUPT VITIATE
EMBITTER EMPOISON
ENVIOUS YELLOW EMULOUS
JEALOUS ENVIABLE
ENVIRON HEM BEGO GIRD BIGAN
LIMIT VIRON ENVIRE GIRDLE
SUBURB COMPASS ENVELOP
INCLOSE INVOLVE PURLIEU
DISTRICT ENCIRCLE SURROUND
(PL.) SKIRT UMLAND BANLIEU
SUBURBS PRECINCT
ENVIRONMENT HOTBED MEDIUM
MILIEU AMBIENT CONTEXT ELEMENT
HABITAT SETTING TERRAIN
AMBIANCE CINCTURE PRECINCT
(— OF NURTURE) LAP
(DOMESTIC —) INTERIEUR
(NORMAL —) HOME
ENVISAGE FACE CONFRONT
ENVISION
ENVOY AGENT ELCHI ENVOI DEPUTY
ELCHEE LEGATE LENVOY NUNCIO
EMBASSY TORNADA ABLEGATE
LEGATION METATRON

ENVY CHAW ONDE COVET GRUDGE
EMULATE BEGRUDGE GRUDGERY
JEALOUSY
ENWRAP FOLD ROLL CLASP IMPLY
ENFOLD INFOLD KIRTLE ENGROSS
ENVELOP OBVOLVE CONVOLVE
ENVELOPE INSWATHE
ENZOOTIC RABIES
ENZU SIN
ENZYME ASE ZYM ZYMO RENIN
CYTASE KINASE LIPASE LOTASE
MUTASE OLEASE PAPAIN PEPSIN
RENNIN UREASE ZYMASE ACYLASE
ADENASE AMIDASE AMINASE
AMYLASE APYRASE CASEASE
DIATASE EMULSIN ENOLASE
EREPSIN FERMENT GUANASE
HYDRASE INULASE LACCASE
LACTASE MALTASE MYROSIN
OXIDASE PECTASE PEPSINE
PHYTASE PRUNASE TANNASE
TRYPSIN ALDOLASE ARGINASE
BROMELIN CATALASE CATALYST
CYTOLIST DIASTASE ELASTASE
ERAPTASE ESTERASE FUMARASE
INVERTIN NUCLEASE PROTEASE
RACEMASE SEMINASE TRYPTASE
EOS MORNING
EPAULET KNOT SWAB SWOB WING
SCALE SHELL
EPENDYTES HAPLOMA
EPHELIS FRECKLE
EPHEMERAL BRIEF VAGUE HORARY
DIURNAL PASSANT PASSING
EPISODAL EPISODIC FUGITIVE
MUSHROOM STAYLESS
EPHEMERIS DIARY TABLE RECORD
ALMANAC JOURNAL CALENDAR
EPHIPPIUM SADDLE
EPHTHALITE HAITHAL
EPI PEAK SPIRE FINIAL PINNACLE
EPIBLAST ECTODERM
EPIC EDDA EPOS SAGA GRAND ILIAD
NOBLE BYLINA EPOPEE HEROIC
BEOWULF EPYLLION RAMAYANA
EPICALYX CALYCLE
EPICARP HUSK RIND EXOCARP
EPICENE SEXLESS
EPICURE FRIAND FEASTER GLUTTON
GOURMET GOURMAND PALATIST
EPICUREAN APICIAN SENSUOUS
EPIDEMIC FLU PLAGUE POPULAR
PANDEMIA PANDEMIC
EPIDERMIS SKIN CUTICLE ECDERON
VELAMEN
EPIDOTE SCORZA
EPIGLOTTIS FLAP WEEZLE
EPIGRAM POEM ENGLYN EPITAPH
EPIGRAMMATIC LACONIC POINTED
EPIGRAPH EPIGRAM IMPRINT
EPILEPTIC FITIFIED
EPILOGUE CLOSE APPENDIX
EPIMANIKION CUFF
EPINAOS POSTICUM
EPINEPHRINE ADRENINE
EPIPACTIS SERAPIAS
EPIPHANY TWELFTH
EPIPHARYNX PALATE EPIGLOTTIS
EPIPHRAGM TYMPANUM

EPIPHYTE KARO EPIPHYLL
EPIPHYTOTIC EPIDEMIC
EPIRUS (KING OF —) PYRRHUS
EPISCOPACY BISHOPRIC PRELATISM
EPISCOPAL PRELATIC
EPISODE GAG EPOCH EVENT SCENE
STORY AFFAIR INCIDENT SEQUENCE
(COMIC —) BURLA
(MUSICAL —) COUPLET
EPISPASTIC VESICANT
EPISPERM TESTA
EPISTAXIS NOSEBLEED
EPISTLE CANON JAMES LETTER
PISTLE MISSIVE WRITING DECRETAL
EPISTLER SUBDEACON
EPISTOLOGRAPHIC DEMOTIC
EPISTROPHE EPODE ABGESANG
EPISTYLE PLATBAND
EPITHELIUM ENDODERM
EPITHET AKAL GOOD NAME TERM
LABEL SMEAR TITLE BYWORD
MONETA PHRASE AGNOMEN
JAPHETIC MULCIBER
(PL.) LANGUAGE
EPITOME MAP SUM FLETA DIGEST
PRECIS SCHEME COMPEND PITOMIE
SUMMULA ABSTRACT BREVIARY
LANDSKIP SYLLABUS SYNOPSIS
EPITOMIZE RESUME CURTAIL
ABSTRACT COMPRESS CONDENSE
CONTRACT DIMINISH
EPITONIUM SCALA
EPIZOA PARASITA
EPOCH AGE ERA DATE ECCA TIME
DWYKA EVENT EOCENE PERIOD
CLINTON
EPONYM LIMMU ANCIENT
EQUABLE EVEN JUST EQUAL SUANT
SMOOTH STEADY UNIFORM
TRANQUIL
EQUAL AEQ PAR TIE COPE EGAL
EVEN FERE JUST LIKE MAKE MATE
MEET PEEL PEER SAME ALIKE
LEVEL MATCH PARTY RIVAL TOUCH
DOUBLE EQUATE EVENLY FELLOW
MARROW PAREIL ABREAST
BALANCE COMPEER EMULATE
EQUABLE IDENTIC PAREGAL
UNIFORM ADEQUATE EQUALIZE
EVENHAND PATCHING TRANQUIL
(— IN MEANING) BE
(— QUANTITY) ANA
(— TO) ANOTHER
(NOT —) UNMEET UNMETE
EQUALING TO
EQUALITY PAR TIE EQUITY OWELTY
PARAGE PAREIL PARITY BALANCE
EGALITE EGALITY ISOTELY
EQUATION EVENHAND EVENNESS
FAIRNESS
(— BEFORE THE LAW) ISONOMY
(— OF ELEVATION) ISOMETRY
(— OF POWER) ISOCRACY
(— STATE) WYOMING
EQUALIZATION EQUATION
DISCHARGE
EQUALIZE EVEN KNOT EQUAL LEVEL
EQUATE BALANCE ADEQUATE
EQUALIZER EVENER

EQUALLY AS BOTH LIKE ONCE SAME
ALIKE EGALLY EVENLY JUSTLY
EMFORTH
EQUANIMITY POISE PHLEGM
TEMPER BALANCE EGALITY
CALMNESS EVENNESS SERENITY
EQUATE EQUAL BALANCE EQUALIZE
EQUATING COMPARISON
EQUATION CUBIC IDENTITY
EQUATOR LINE GIRDLE EQUINOX
(— CROSSER) POLLIWOG
EQUES KNIGHT
EQUIDISTANT CENTRAL HALFWAY
EQUILIBRIUM POISE APLOMB
BALANCE STATION EQUATION
EVENHAND ISOSTASY
(— OF FLUID) LEVEL
EQUINE COLT FOAL MARE FILLY
HORSE ZEBRA EQUOID EQUINAL
HORSELY
EQUINIA MALLEUS
EQUIP ARM FIT IMP KIT RAY RIG
ABLE BEAM DECK FEAT FIND GEAR
GIRD GIRT HEEL REEK TRIM ARRAY
DIGHT DRESS ENARM ENDOW POINT
SPEED STUFF ATTIRE BUCKLE
ORDAIN OUTFIT SUBORN APPAREL
APPOINT BEDIGHT FORTIFY
FRAUGHT FURNISH GARNISH
HARNESS PLENISH PREPARE
QUALIFY ACCOUTER ACCOUTRE
(— FOR ACTION) ARM
EQUIPAGE RIG CREW SAMAN SUITE
TRAIN SUPPLY RETINUE TURNOUT
UNICORN CARRIAGE
EQUIPMENT KIT FARE GEAR TIRE
STOCK STUFF ATTIRE CONREY
DUFFEL DUFFLE FITOUT GRAITH
OUTFIT SETOUT TACKLE APPAREL
BAGGAGE FITMENT HARNESS
PANOPLY ARMAMENT EQUIPAGE
MATERIAL MATERIEL MOUNTING
SUPELLEX
(— FOR CATCHING FISH) CRAFT
(— FOR JOURNEY) FARE
EQUIPOISE POISE BALANCE
EQUIPOTENTIAL LEVEL
EQUIPPED ARMED BODEN THERE
EQUIPT ARMORED INSTRUCT
WEAPONED
(FULLY —) SUMMED
(INADEQUATELY —) HAYWIRE
(LIGHTLY —) EXPEDITE
EQUISETUM CANDOCK
EQUITABLE EVEN FAIR JUST EQUAL
RIGHT EVENLY HONEST EQUABLE
UPRIGHT BONITARY RIGHTFUL
EQUITY LAW EPIKY MARGIN EPIKEIA
HONESTY JUSTICE EQUALITY
EVENHAND FAIRNESS
EQUIVALENT KIND SAME EQUAL
COUSIN UNISON ANALOGUE
EVENHAND
(— IN MONEY) CHANGE
(— OF TWO BUSHELS) HUTCH
EQUIVOCAL SHADY DOUBLE
FORKED DUBIOUS EVASIVE
HALFWAY OBSCURE DOUBTFUL
HAVERING PUZZLING SIBYLLIC

EQUIVOCATE LIE DODGE EVADE
SHIFT ESCAPE PALTER TRIFLE
WEASEL QUIBBLE SHUFFLE
EQUIVOCATION QUIP QUIRK
EVASION SHUFFLE EQUIVOKE
EQUULEUS FOAL
ERA AGE AEON DATE TIME EPOCH
STAGE PERIOD CENOZOIC
(EMPEROR'S —) KIMIGAYO
(HINDU —) SAMVAT
(MUSLIM —) HEGIRA HEJIRA
ERADICATE DELE ROOT SLAY WEED
CROSS ERASE STAMP DELETE
EFFACE REMOVE UNROOT UPROOT
ABOLISH DESTROY EXPUNGE
OUTROOT SUPPLANT
(— HAIR) EPILATE
ERADICATOR ERASER
ERAL MOINE
ERASE BLOT DASH DELE RACE RASE
RASH RAZE ANNUL PLANE CANCEL
DEFACE DELETE EFFACE EXCISE
REMOVE SCRAPE SPONGE DESTROY
EXPUNGE OUTRAZE SCRATCH
UNWRITE
ERASER RASER RUBBER
ERASURE RASURE ERASION
DELETION EXCISION
ERD SHREW RANNY
ERE OR AIR SOON EARLY PRIOR
BEFORE EREWHILE FORMERLY
EREBUS (FATHER OF —) CHAOS
(SISTER OF —) NOX
(SON OF —) CHARON
ERECHTHEUS (DAUGHTER OF —)
CREUSA PROCRIS CHTHONIA
ORITHYIA
(FATHER OF —) PANDION
(SLAYER OF —) JUPITER
(SON OF —) MERION CECROPS
PANDORUS
(WIFE OF —) PRAXITHEA
ERECT BIG SET BIGG LEVY REAR
RECT STEP STEY SWAY TELD
AREAR BRANT BUILD DRESS EXALT
FRAME MOUNT RAISE SETUP STAND
ARRECT UPLIFT UPREAR ADDRESS
BRISTLE ELEVATE STATELY UPRAISE
UPRIGHT UPSTART STANDING
STRAIGHT VERTICAL
(NOT —) LAZY COUCHED
ERECTED UPSET
ERECTION DOME HARD FABRIC
CHORDEE MACHINE
ERELONG ANON SOON
EREMITE HERMIT ASCETIC RECLUSE
ANCHORET
EREWHILE ERE WHILOM
ERG REG EROGON
(PL.) AREG
ERGO SO ARGO ARGAL HENCE
ERGOT SPUR CLAVUS ECBOLIC
(STAGE OF —) SPHACELIA
ERICHTHONIUS (FATHER OF —)
VULCAN DARDANUS
(MOTHER OF —) ATTHIS
(SON OF —) PANDION
ERIDANUS (FATHER OF —) OCEANUS
(MOTHER OF —) TETHYS

ERIE WENRO
ERIGONE (FATHER OF —) ICARIUS
AEGISTHUS
(MOTHER OF —) CLYTEMNESTRA
ERINYS FURY ALECTO MEGAERA
(PL.) DIRAE FURIAE SEMNAE
EUMENIDES
ERIOPHORUM DRAWLING
ERISTIC DIALECTIC
ERMINE VAIR VARE STOAT WEASEL
ERMELIN FUTERET FUTTRAT
MINIVER CLUBSTER WHITRACK
WHITTRET
ERODE EAT COMB ETCH GNAW GULL
WEAR CLIFF GULLY SCOUR ABRADE
DENUDE CORRODE DESTROY
ERODIUM HERONBILL
EROS AMOR CUPID AENGUS POTHOS
EROSE ERODED UNEVEN
EROSION PIPING CHIMNEY NIVATION
SCOURING
EROTIC LOVING AMATORY AMOROUS
CURIOUS LESBIAN THERMAL
EROTICA CURIOSA FACETIAE
ERR MAR SIN FAIL MISS SLIP ABERR
LAPSE MISGO STRAY BUNGLE
FORVAY WANDER BLUNDER DEVIATE
MISPLAY MISTAKE SCRITHE
STUMBLE MISCARRY MISJUDGE
ERRAND CHORE ENVOY JOURNEY
MISSION LEGATION
(— BOY) LOBBYGOW
ERRANT STRAY ASTRAY ERRING
DEVIOUS PRICKANT
ERRATIC WILD CRAZY HUMAN
QUEER WACKY CRANKY WHACKY
STRANGE TANGENT VAGRANT
ACROSTIC ERRABUND FITIFIED
PLANETAL PLANETIC TRAVELED
VAGABOND
ERRATUM ERROR
ERRING ASTRAY ERRANT DEVIOUS
ERRINGLY FALSE
ERRONEOUS AMISS FALSE WRONG
UNTRUE ERRATIC MISTAKEN
STRAYING WRONGFUL
ERRONEOUSNESS FALLACY
ERROR X HOB SIN BUBU BULL FLUB
HELL MUFF SLIP TRIP BEARD BEVUE
BONER DEVIL FAULT FLUFF LAPSE
SCAPE BOBBLE FUMBLE GARBLE
HOWLER LAPSUS MISCUE NAUGHT
SPHALM BLOOMER BLUNDER
DEFAULT ERRATUM FALLACY
FALSITY LITERAL MISPLAY MISSTEP
MISTAKE OFFENSE RHUBARB
SNAPPER STUMBLE DELUSION
HAMARTIA MISPRINT MISSMENT
SOLECISM
ERS VETCH KERSANNE
ERSE ERSCH IRISH CELTIC GAELIC
SCOTTISH
ERST ONCE FORMERLY RECENTLY
ERSTWHILE ONCE FORMER
FORMERLY
ERUCT RASP BELCH
ERUCTATION BELCH
ERUDITE LEARNED CLERGIAL
DIDACTIC

ERUDITION WIT LORE WISDOM
LETTERS LEARNING
ERUPT BOIL BELCH BURST EJECT
IRRUPT
ERUPTING ACTIVE
ERUPTION ITCH RASH REEF RUSH
AGRIA BURST RUPIA SALVO STORM
BLOTCH HYDROA NIRLES ACTERID
BLOWOUT ECTHYMA MORPHEA
MORPHEW PUSTULE SAWFLOM
SUDAMEN EMPYESIS ENANTHEM
OUTBREAK OUTBURST
(CUTANEOUS —) HUMOR
ERVUM LENS LENTILLA
ERYSICHTHON (FATHER OF —)
CECROPS TRIOPAS
(MOTHER OF —) AGRAULOS
(SISTER OF —) IPHIMEDIA
ERYSIPELAS POX ROSE BLAST
WILDFIRE
ERYTHROBLASTOSIS HYDROPSY
ERYX (FATHER OF —) BUTES
(MOTHER OF —) VENUS
(SLAYER OF —) HERCULES
ESAU EDOM
(FATHER OF —) ISAAC
(MOTHER OF —) REBEKAH
(SON OF —) JEUSH KORAH REUEL
JAALAM ELIPHAZ
(WIFE OF —) ADAH BASHEMATH
ESCALADE SCALE SCALADE
SCALADO ESCALADO
ESCAPADE CAPER PRANK SALLY
SCHEME RUNAWAY
ESCAPE FLY GUY LAM RUN BAIL
BALE BEAT BLOW BOLT FLEE GATE
HISS JINK JUMP LEAK MISS SHUN
SKEW SLIP VENT AVOID BREAK
CHAPE DODGE ELOPE ELUDE EVADE
FLANK ISSUE SCAPE SHIFT SKIRT
SMOKE SPILL ASTERT DECAMP
ESCHEW OUTLET POWDER SQUEAK
ABSCOND AVOLATE BLOWOUT
ELUSION EXHAUST GETAWAY
LEAKAGE MISTAKE OUTFLOW
SCRITHE SQUEEZE WILDING
BLOWBACK ESCAPADE ESCAPAGE
EXSHEATH OUTSCAPE OVERSLIP
RIDDANCE WITHSLIP
(— FROM WORK) SNIB
(— FROM) FLY SHUN ILLUDE
(— NOTICE) ELUDE
(— OF FLUID) EFFUSION
(NARROW —) SHAVE
ESCAPEMENT SCAPE CRUTCH
ESCAPE FOLIOT VIRGULE KARRUSEL
ESCARGOT SNAIL
ESCAROLE ENDIVE SCAROLA
ESCARPMENT EDGE
ESCHAR SCAB CRUST ASCHER
ESCHAROTIC CAUSTIC
ESCHEAT FALL LAPSE REVERT
EXCHEAT FORFEIT
ESCHEW SHUN AVOID FORGO
ESCAPE FOREGO ABSTAIN
ESCOLAR PALU ROVET OILFISH
ROVETTO MACKEREL
ESCORT MAN SEE SET TRY BEAR
BEAU COND LEAD SHOW TEND WAIT

BRING CARRY GUARD USHER
ATTEND CONVEY CONVOY FOLLOW
SQUIRE COLLECT CONDUCT
CONSORT ESQUIRE GALLANT
CAVALIER CHAPERON SHEPHERD
(PAID —) GIGOLO
ESCRITOIRE DESK BUREAU
LECTERN
ESCULENT EDIBLE EATABLE
ESCUTCHEON CREST SHIELD
ESKER AS OS OSE KAME ESKAR
HOGBACK
ESKIMO ITA HUSKY INUIT INNUIT
AGOMIUT AMERIND ANGAKOK
KUNMIUT OKOMIUT ORARIAN
AGLEMIUT ESQUIMAU IKOGMIUT
KIDNELIK KINIPETU MAGEMIUT
MALEMIUT NUGUMIUT SINIMIUT
(— ASSEMBLY HOUSE) KASHIM
(— CULTURE) PUNUK
(— TENT) TUPEK TUPIK
ESOPHAGUS GULLET SWALLOW
WEASAND
ESOTERIC INNER MYSTIC ORPHIC
SECRET PRIVATE ABSTRUSE
ESPADON ESPADA SPADON
SPADROON
ESPALIER CORDON LATTICE RAILING
TRELLIS PALISADE
ESPARTO ALFA HALFA SPART STIPA
ATOCHA
ESPAVE CARACOLI
ESPECIAL VERY CHIEF SPECIAL
PECULIAR UNCOMMON
ESPECIALLY SUCH EXTRA RATHER
CHIEFLY OVERALL SPECIAL
ESPIAL SPY ESPY SCOUT NOTICE
ESPINAL MONTE
ESPIONAGE SPYING
ESPLANADE WALK DRIVE MAIDAN
MARINA
ESPOUSAL CEREMONY SPOUSAGE
BETROTHAL
ESPOUSE WED AFFY MATE ADOPT
MARRY DEFEND ENSURE SPOUSE
BETROTH EMBRACE HUSBAND
SUPPORT ADVOCATE MAINTAIN
ESPUNDIA UTA
ESPY SEE ASPY SPOT ASCRY SIGHT
WATCH BEHOLD DESCRY DETECT
LOCATE NOTICE DISCERN OBSERVE
DESCRIBE DISCOVER
ESQUIRE RADMAN ARMIGER
ESCUDERO SERGEANT
ESSAY TRY SEEK ASSAY CHRIA
OFFER PAPER PROVE TASTE THEME
TRACT TRAIL CASUAL EFFORT
MEMOIR SAILYE SATIRE SCREED
THESIS ARTICLE ATTEMPT PROFFER
VENTURE WRITING ENDEAVOR
EXERCISE EXERTION TRACTATE
TREATISE TURNOVER
ESSE BEING
ESSENCE ENS NET ATAR BASE
BONE CORE CRUX DRAW ESSE GIST
GUTS KIND ODOR OTTO PITH QUID
RASA SOUL YOLK ATTAR BASIC
BASIS BEING EIDOS FIBER FIBRE
FUMET HEART JUICE OTTAR OUSIA

STUFF BOTTOM EFFECT ENTITY
FLOWER INWARD MARROW NATURE
SPRITE ALCOHOL ELEMENT
EXTRACT FUMETTE GODHEAD
INBEING MEDULLA PERFUME
BERGAMOT CONCRETE ESSENTIA
(— OF BEING) SAT
(— OF FLOWERS) CONCRETE
(— OF GOD) SPIRIT DIVINITY
(— OF MEAT) BLOND
(— OF TEA) DRAW
(— OF VITAL MATTER) GLAME
(INNERMOST —) ATMAN
(UNIVERSAL —) FORM
(VITAL —) STAMINA
ESSENE ESSEE ASCETIC
ESSENTIAL REAL BASAL BASIC
VITAL ENTIRE FORMAL INWARD
CENTRAL CRUCIAL NEEDFUL
CARDINAL CRITICAL INHERENT
MATERIAL
(— TO LIFE) BIOGENOUS
ESSENTIALLY AUFOND
ESSONITE GARNET HYACINTH
ESTABLISH BED FIX PUT SET BASE
FAST FIRM FOOT MAKE REAR REST
SEAT BUILD DEFIX EDIFY ENACT
ERECT EVICT FOUND PLANT PROVE
RAISE SEIZE SETUP START STATE
STELL ATTEST AVOUCH BOTTOM
CEMENT CLINCH CREATE ENROOT
FASTEN FICCHE GROUND INVENT
INVEST LOCATE ORDAIN RATIFY
SETTLE STABLE VERIFY ACCOUNT
APPOINT APPROVE CONFIRM
ENSTATE INSTALL INSTATE INSTORE
POSSESS PREEMPT SUSTAIN
COLONIZE CONSTATE CONTRACT
ENSCONCE ENTRENCH IDENTIFY
INITIATE INSTRUCT RADICATE
REGULATE STABLISH VALIDATE
(— FACT) APPROVE
(— FIRMLY) INDURATE
(— MORALS) ETHIZE
(— TRUMP) PITCH
ESTABLISHED SAD FAST FIRM SURE
LEGAL SEATED SICCAR STABLE
STAPLE STATED STRONG CERTAIN
SETTLED STANDING
ESTABLISHMENT HONG MILL SHOP
STAB DAIRY FORGE JOINT PLANT
SALON STORE AGENCY CAISSE
CENOBY ECESIS LAYOUT MENAGE
SALOON SCHOOL ARSENAL ATELIER
BROTHEL COENOBY CONCERN
DOUNSET DOWNSET FACTORY
FISHERY FOUNDRY FUNDUCK
SHEBANG AQUARIUM AVERMENT
BUSINESS CHEESERY CREAMERY
ERECTION HACIENDA
(— IN NEW HABITAT) ECESIS
(— OF COLONY) DEDUCTION
(DOMESTIC —) MENAGE
(DRINKING —) STUBE SALOON
BARROOM SHEBEEN
(GAMBLING —) HOUSE TRIPOT
(HORSE-BREEDING —) HARAS
(MONASTIC —) CLOISTER
ESTAFETTE COURIER STAFETTE

ESTATE FEE ALOD COPY FEOD FIEF
HOME LAND POMP RANK ACRES
ALLOD DAIRA DOWER DOWRY
ESTER ESTRE ETHEL FINCA FUNDO
HABIT HOUSE MANOR STATE TALUK
ABBACY DEMISE DOMAIN ENTAIL
GROUND LIVING MISTER QUINTA
TALUKA ALODIUM CHATEAU
COMMONS DEMESNE DIGNITY
DISPLAY FORTUNE HAVINGS
MAJORAT ALLODIUM BENEFICE
COPYHOLD DOMINION EXECUTRY
FREEHOLD HACIENDA JOINTURE
LIFEHOLD LONGACRE MESNALTY
POSITION PROPERTY SENASORY
STANDING
(— OF REBEL) FISC FISK
(— WITH SERFS) HAM
(HINDU —) CHAK
(PORTION OF —) LEGITIM
(REAL —) FUNDUS
(PL.) AMANI
ESTEEM AIM LET USE DEEM HOLD
TALE ADORE COUNT FAVOR HONOR
PRICE PRIDE STEEM THINK VALUE
WEIGH WORTH ADMIRE CREDIT
EXTIME REGARD REPUTE REVERE
TENDER WONDER ACCOUNT
CONCEIT OPINION RESPECT
SUSPECT APPRAISE CONSIDER
ESTIMATE VENERATE
ESTEEMED DEAR
ESTER BIXIN ETHER OLEIN SARIN
TABUN BORATE CAPRIN ERUCIN
HUMATE LAURIN MALATE OLEATE
ACETATE ADIPATE ANISATE
AZELATE CINERIN ELAIDIN FORMATE
FUROATE GALLATE HEPARIN
INDICAN LACTATE LACTONE
LAURATE MALEATE MELLATE
NITRATE OCTOATE OXALATE
OXAMATE PECTATE PEPSIDE
PICRATE SORBATE STEARIN
SULTONE ABIETATE ACRYLATE
ARSENATE ARSENITE ARSONATE
BEHENATE BENZOATE CAFFEATE
CONGENER DIPHENAN ESTOLIDE
FLUORIDE FUCOIDIN KETIPATE
LINOLATE LINOLEIN MALONATE
MARGARIN MYRISTIN NUCLEATE
PALMITIN PIMELATE PIPERATE
RACEMATE SEBACATE SELENATE
SILICATE SINAPATE STEARATE
SUBERATE TARTRATE
ESTIMABLE GOOD SOLID WORTH
GENTLE HONEST WORTHY THRIFTY
VALUABLE
ESTIMATE AIM SET CALL CAST
GAGE RANK RATE READ RECK
ASSAY AUDIT CARAT CENSE COUNT
GAUGE GUESS JUDGE MOUNT
PLACE PRIZE SCALE STOCK TALLY
VALUE WEIGH ASSESS BUDGET
ESTEEM RECKON REGARD SURVEY
ACCOUNT AVERAGE BALANCE
CENSURE COMPUTE MEASURE
APPRAISE CONSIDER CRITIQUE
(— OF ONE'S SELF) OPINION
(— TOO HIGHLY) OVERRATE

ESTIMATION AIM EYE CESS FAME
NAME ODOR PASS RATE COUNT
HONOR PRICE SIEGE VALUE CHOICE
ESTEEM REGARD REPUTE OPINION
JUDGMENT
(HIGH —) CONCEIT
(LOW —) DISREPUTE
ESTIMATOR CRUISER
ESTOC STOCK SWORD
ESTOILE STAR ETOILE

ESTONIA
CAPITAL: TALLINN
COIN: SENT KROON ESTMARK
DIALECT: TARTU
ISLAND: DAGO OESEL SAARE
 HIIUMAA
LAKE: PEIPUS
MEASURE: TUN ELLE LIIN PANG
 SUND TOLL TOOP FADEN VERST
 SAGENE VERSTA KULIMET
 VERCHOC TONNLAND
NATIVE: ESTH AESTI
PROVINCE: SAARE
RIVER: EMA NARVA
TOWN: NARVA PARNU REVAL
 TARTU TALLINN
WEIGHT: LOOD NAEL PUUD

ESTONIAN ESTH
ESTOP BAR FILL PLUG STOP DEBAR
PREVENT
ESTRANGE PART WEAN ALIEN
AVERT DIVERT ALIENATE DISUNITE
STRANGER
ESTRANGEMENT STANCE DISTASTE
ESTRAY STRAY WANDER
ESTREAT COPY FINE EXACT RECORD
STREET EXTRACT EXTREAT
ESTREPEMENT STRIP
E STRING QUINT
ESTRIOL THEELOL
ESTRONE THEELIN
ESTRUS HEAT SEASON
ESTUARY PARA WASH CREEK FIRTH
FLEET FRITH INLET LIMAN ESTERO
ETCETERA ETC KTL
ETCH BITE FROST ENGRAVE
AQUATINT INSCRIBE
ETCHED FROSTED
ETCHER POINT
ETCHING ETCH AQUATINT
ETEOCLES (BROTHER OF —)
POLYNICES
(FATHER OF —) OEDIPUS
(MOTHER OF —) JOCASTA
ETERNAL ETERNE TARNAL AGELESS
ENDLESS LASTING UNAGING
ENDURING IMMORTAL TIMELESS
UNCAUSED
ETERNALLY AKE EER EVER ALWAYS
ETERNE FOREVER
ETERNITY AGE EON AEON OLAM
GLORY ETERNE ETERNAL EWIGKEIT
INFINITY
ETESIAN ANNUAL PERIODIC
ETHANE DIMETHYL
ETHER AIR SKY APIOL ESTER PINOLE

ANISOLE ASARONE EPOXIDE
ETHYLIN HARMINE SAFROLE
SESAMIN SESAMOL SOLVENT
ACACETIN ELEMICIN EMPYREAN
GUAIACOL
ETHEREAL AERY AIRY SKYEY
AERIAL SKYISH AIRLIKE ETHERIC
FRAGILE SLENDER DELICATE
HEAVENLY SUPERNAL VAPOROUS
ETHICAL ETHIC MORAL HONORABLE
ETHICS HEDONICS

ETHIOPIA
CAPITAL: ADDISABABA
COIN: BESA AMOLE GIRSH
 DOLLAR TALARI ASHRAFI
 PIASTER
DEPRESSION: DANAKIL
FALLS: TISISAT BLUENILE
ISLANDS: DAHLAK
LAKE: ABE TANA ABAYA SHOLA
 ZEWAY RUDOLF STEFANIE
LANGUAGE: GEEZ TIGRE SOMALI
 AMHARIC GALLINYA TIGRINYA
MARRIAGE: DAMOZ QURBAN
 SEMANYA
MEASURE: TAT KUBA SINJER
 SINZER FARSAKH FARSANG
MOUNTAIN: BATU GUGE GUNA
 TALO
MOUNTAINS: AHMAR CHOKE
NAME: ABYSSINIA
NATIVE: AFAR GALLA ABIGAR
 AMHARA ANNUAK HAMITE
 SEMITE SOMALI TIGRAI CUSHITE
 DANAKIL FALASHA
PORT: ASSAB MASSAWA
PRINCE: RAS
RIVER: OMO WEB BARO DAWA
 GILA ABBAI AKOBO AWASH
 FAFAN TAKKAZE
TOWN: EDD GOBA GORE THIO
 ADOLA ADUWA AKSUM ASSAB
 AWASH DIMTU HARAR JIMMA
 MOJJO ASMARA DESSYE
 DUNKUR GONDAR MAKALE
 GARDULA MASSAWA NAKAMTI
 DIREDAWA LALIBALA MUSTAHIL
VALLEY: RIFT
WEIGHT: KASM NATR OKET ALADA
 NETER WAKEA WOGIET
 FARASULA

ETHIOPIAN SIDI HAMITE HARARI
AETHIOP AFRICAN CUSHITE
FALASHA
ETHIOPIC GIZ GEEZ GHEEZ
ETHNIC (— GROUP) ACHANG
ETHOS MANNER
ETHYLENE ELAYL ETHENE ETHERIN
ETIQUETTE FORM DECORUM
MANNERS
(— OF DRINKING TEA) CHANOYU
ETRUSCAN TUSCAN RASENNA
ETRURIAN TYRRHENE
(PL.) TURSENOI TYRRHENI
ETUDE STUDY
ETUI CASE ETWEE TWEEZE TWEEZER
EQUIPAGE RETICULE

ETYMOLOGY ORIGIN DERIVATION
ETYMON RADIX
EUBOEANS ABANTES
EUCALYPT GUM YATE APPLE BIMBIL
  CARBUN JARRAH MALLEE MYRTAL
  CARBEEN CUTTAIL MESSMAN
  IRONBARK MESSMATE WHITETOP
  YERTCHUK
EUCALYPTOLE CINEOL CINEOLE
EUCALYPTUS EUCALYPT WHIPSTICK
EUCHARIST HOUSEL MAUNDY
  SUPPER MYSTERY VIATICUM
EUCHARISTIC (— ELEMENTS) HAGIA
EUCHITE SATANIST ADELPHIAN
  MESSALIAN
EUCHRE LOVE
  (— HAND) JAMBONE JAMBOREE
EUDAEMONIA HAPPINESS
EUDOCIMUS GUARA
EULALIA NETI
EULENSPIEGEL OWLGLASS
EULOGIST PRAISER LAUREATE
EULOGISTIC EULOGIC EPENETIC
  MAGNIFIC LAUDATORY
EULOGY PRAISE TONGUE ADDRESS
  ELOGIUM ORATION ENCOMIUM
  PANEGYRE
EUMOLPUS (FATHER OF —)
  NEPTUNE
  (MOTHER OF —) CHIONE
  (SON OF —) ISMARUS
EUNUCH CAPON SPORUS WETHER
  GELDING HALFMAN CASTRATE
EUPHAUSID SHRIMP
EUPHEMISM DEE FIB GEE GOR
  DASH GOSH GOLES GOLLY LAWKS
  DIANTRE DICKENS GRACIOUS
EUPHONIOUS TUNEFUL
EUPHORIA ELATION
EUPHROSYNE JOY
EUPHUISM GONGORISM
EURASIAN BURGHER FERINGI
EURO WALLAROO
EUROPE BELAIT CONTINENT
EUROPEAN FRANK SAHIB BOHUNK
  EUROPE FRINGE INDIAN FERINGI
  TOPIWALA
  (— IN INDIES) BLIJVER
  (WESTERN —) FRANK
EUROPEAN BARRACUDA SPET
EUROPEAN BASS BRASSE
EUROPEAN BISON AUROCHS
EUROPEAN CLOVER ALSIKE
EUROPEAN GULL MEW
EUROPEAN HERRING SPRAT
EUROPEAN JUNIPER CADE
EUROPEAN KITE GLEDE
EUROPEAN LAVENDER ASPIC
EUROPEAN LINDEN TEIL
EUROPEAN MINT HYSSOP
EUROPEAN OAK DURMAST
EUROPEAN PERCH RUFF RUFFE
EUROPEAN POLECAT FITCHEW
EUROPEAN PORGY BESUGO
EUROPEAN RABBIT CONY
EUROPEAN SHARK TOPE
EUROPEAN SPARROW WHITECAP
EUROPEAN STARLING STARNEL
EUROPEAN SWALLOW MARTIN

EUROPEAN THRUSH MAVIS OUZEL
EUROPEAN WIDGEON WHIM
  WHEWER
EUROPEAN WREN STAG
EURYPTERID SERAPHIM
EURYPYLUS (FATHER OF —)
  NEPTUNE TELEPHUS
  (MOTHER OF —) ASTYOCHE
  (SLAYER OF —) PYRRHUS
  HERCULES
EURYSACES (FATHER OF —) AJAX
  (MOTHER OF —) TECMESSA
EURYSTHEUS (FATHER OF —)
  STHENELUS
  (MOTHER OF —) NICIPPE
  (SLAYER OF —) HYLLUS
EUTECTIC STEADITE
EUTERPE (FATHER OF —) JUPITER
  (MOTHER OF —) MNEMOSYNE
EUXANTHONE PURRONE
EUXOA AGROTIS
EVACUATE PASS VENT VOID AVOID
  EMPTY EXPEL STOOL VACATE
  DEPRIVE EXCRETE EXHAUST
  NULLIFY VACUATE PERSPIRE
EVACUATION OFFICE DUNKIRK
EVADE BEG GEE BILK DUCK FLEE
  FOIL JOUK JUMP SHUN SLIP VOID
  AVERT AVOID BLINK DALLY DODGE
  ELUDE FENCE FLANK PARRY SHIRK
  SKIRT BAFFLE BLENCH BYPASS
  DELUDE ESCAPE ILLUDE BEGUILE
  FINESSE OUTSLIP QUIBBLE
  HEDGEHOP LEAPFROG SIDESTEP
  (— LEGAL PROCESS) ABSCOND
  (— PAYMENT) BILK
  (— WORK) JOUK
EVADNE (FATHER OF —) NEPTUNE
  (HUSBAND OF —) CAPANEUS
  (MOTHER OF —) IPHIS
  (SON OF —) IAMUS
EVALUATE RATE ASSESS PONDER
  RECKON DISSECT APPRAISE
  ESTIMATE
EVALUATION STOCK ESTIMATE
EVANDER (FATHER OF —) HERMES
  (MOTHER OF —) CARMENTA
EVANESCE FADE VANISH
EVANESCENCE ANICCA
EVANESCENT FLEET EVANID
  BRITTLE CURSORY EVASIVE
  FRAGILE DELICATE FLEETING
  FLITTING FUGITIVE STAYLESS
EVANGELICAL GOSPEL
  (— ACTIVITY) WARFARE
EVANGELIST LUKE MARK EVANGEL
  GOSPELER
EVAPORATE DRY EXHALE AVOLATE
  CONDENSE VAPORIZE
EVAPORATOR BOILER EFFECT
EVASION JINK SLIP DODGE QUIRK
  SALVE SHIFT ESCAPE SNATCH
  ELUSION OFFCOME SHUFFLE
  TWISTER ARTIFICE ESCAPISM
  VOIDANCE
EVASIVE SLY EELY DODGY SHIFTY
  TWISTY ELUSIVE ELUSORY TRICKSY
  SLIPPERY SLIPSKIN
EVE DUSK EREB EREV EVEN VIGIL

SUNSET SUNDOWN
  (NEW YEAR'S —) HAGMENA
  HOGMANAY
EVEN ALL DEN EEN TIE YET FAIR
  HUNK JUST PAIR TILL ALINE EQUAL
  EVERY EXACT FLUSH GRADE HUNKY
  LEVEL MATCH PLAIN RIVAL STILL
  SUANT SUENT SWEET DIRECT
  ITSELF PLACID SILKEN SMOOTH
  SQUARE STEADY ABREAST
  BALANCE EQUABLE FLATTEN
  REGULAR UNIFORM UPSIDES
  EQUALIZE MODERATE PARALLEL
  (— NUMBERS) PAIR
  (— OFF) LEVEL
  (— THOUGH) IF ALTHO ALBEIT
  ALTHOUGH
  (MAKE —) WEIGH STEADY
EVENING DEN EVE EREB EVEN
  ABEND TARDE SUNSET VESPER
  EVENTIDE VESPERAL
  (AT —) TEEN
  (YESTERDAY —) STREEN
EVENING PRIMROSE SUNCUP
  SCABIOUS
EVENING STAR VENUS HESPER
  VESPER EVESTAR HESPERUS
EVENLY FAIR PLAIN FLATLY
  EQUALLY
EVENNESS EQUALITY
EVENT HAP CASE FACT FATE FEAT
  TILT CASUS DOING EPOCH FRAME
  ISSUE THING ACTION EFFECT
  FACTUM RESULT TIDING TIMING
  EPISODE FIXTURE MIRACLE
  PORTENT TRAGEDY INCIDENT
  OCCASION
  (AMUSING —) COMEDY
  (CHANCE —) ACCIDENT FORTUITY
  (EXTRAORDINARY —) MIRACLE
  (FORTUITOUS —) HAZARD
  (GRAVE —) CALAMITY
  (HAPPY —) GODSEND
  (IMPORTANT —) ACE ERA
  (PAST —S) HISTORY
  (SET OF —S) EPISODE
  (SIGNIFICANT —) CRISIS
  (SKI —) DOWNHILL
  (SOCIAL —) BENEFIT
  (SPORTING —) STAKE
  (THEATRICAL —) DRAW
  (TURNING-POINT —) LANDMARK
  (UNEXPECTED —) STUNNER
  AFTERCLAP
  (YEARLY —) ANNUAL
EVENTFUL NOTABLE
EVENTIDE VESPER EVENING
EVENTUAL LAST FINAL ULTIMATE
EVENTUALITY EVENT
EVENTUALLY YET FINALLY
EVENTUATE GO LEAD ISSUE
  RESULT SUCCEED ULTIMATE
EVENUS (DAUGHTER OF —)
  MARPESSA
  (FATHER OF —) MARS
EVER O AY SO AYE EER ONCE STILL
  ALWAYS ETERNE FOREVER
EVERGLADE STATE FLORIDA
EVERGREEN BOX FIR IVY YEW ASIS

BAGO ILEX PINE TAWA BOLDO
CAROB CEDAR HEATH HOLLY
LARCH SAVIN THUYA TOYON
BAUERA COIGUE DAHOON LAUREL
MASTIC SPRUCE BANKSIA BARETTA
BEBEERU BILIMBI GOWIDDE
HEMLOCK JASMINE TARATAH
BOXTHORN CALFKILL CARAUNDA
IRONWOOD TILESEED
(PL.) CHRISTMAS
EVERLASTING ETERNE AEONIAL
AEONIAN AGELONG DURABLE
ENDLESS ETERNAL FOREVER
LASTING TEDIOUS ENDURING
IMMORTAL INFINITE TIMELESS
EVERLASTINGLY ALWAYS FOREVER
EVERSION BLOWOUT BEARINGS
EVERT UPSET EVERSE SUBVERT
OVERTURN
EVERY ALL ANY ILK THE EACH EVER
ILKA ENTIRE EVERICH COMPLETE
(— DAY) QD QUOTID
(— HOUR) QH
(— NIGHT) QN
EVERYBODY ALL EACH EVERYMAN
EVERYONE
EVERYDAY USUAL HOMELY PROSAIC
ORDINARY WORKADAY
EVERYTHING ALL ATHING
EVERYWHERE PASSIM UBIQUE
ALGATES AYWHERE OVERALL
ALLWHERE
EVICT OUST EJECT EXPEL
EVIDENCE MARK SHOW SIGN TEST
PROOF SCRIP SMOKE TOKEN TRACE
TRIAL ATTEST RECORD REVEAL
CHARTER EXHIBIT HEARSAY
SHOWING SUPPORT ARGUMENT
DISPROOF DOCUMENT EVICTION
INDICATE MANIFEST MONUMENT
MUNIMENT WARRANTY
(— OF DISEASE) SYMPTOM
(— OF FRESHNESS) BLOOM
(— OF WRONGDOING) GOODS
(POSITIVE —) CONSTAT
EVIDENT LOUD OPEN PERT APERT
BROAD CLEAR FRANK GROSS PLAIN
EXTANT LIQUID PATENT WITTER
EMINENT GLARING OBVIOUS
PROBATE VISIBLE APPARENT
DISTINCT FLAGRANT LUCULENT
MANIFEST PALPABLE
EVIL BAD DER ILL SIN BALE BASE
DIRE HARM LEWD PAPA POOR SORE
VICE VILE WICK YELL CRIME CURSE
DEVIL FELON FOLLY MALUM QUEDE
SORRY WATHE WRONG CANCEL
DIVERS INJURY MALIGN MENACE
NAUGHT ROTTEN SHREWD SINFUL
UNFEEL UNFELE UNGOOD UNWELL
WICKED WONDER ADVERSE
BALEFUL CORRUPT DISEASE
DIVERSE HEINOUS HURTFUL
IMMORAL MISDEED NOXIOUS
SATANIC UNHAPPY UNSOUND
VICIOUS CALAMITY DEPRAVED
DEVILISH DISASTER GANGRENE
IMPROPER INIQUITY MISCHIEF
QUEDSHIP SINISTER

(— BEING) MARE
(— OF MANY PHASES) HYDRA
(— SPIRIT) JUMBIE
(IMAGINARY —) WINDMILL
(IMPENDING —) MENACE IMMINENCE
(SOCIAL —) SCOURGE
(SPIRITUAL —) SCAB
EVILDOER SLASHER
EVIL EYE DROCHUIL MALOCCHIO
EVINCE SHOW ARGUE PROVE
SUBDUE BREATHE CONQUER
DISPLAY EXHIBIT EVIDENCE
INDICATE MANIFEST
EVISCERATE GUT DRAW BOWEL
PAUNCH GARBAGE
EVOCATION SADHANA
EVOKE FIT MOVE STIR EDUCE
AROUSE ELICIT SUMMON EVOCATE
SUGGEST
EVOLUTION DRIFT GROWTH
BIOGENY DIOECISM HOROTELY
MANEUVER BRADYTELY
(PL.) AEROBATICS
EVOLUTIONISM DARWINISM
EVOLVE COOK EMIT EDUCE DERIVE
UNFOLD UNROLL BLOSSOM
DEVELOP EVOLUTE CONCEIVE
UNPLIGHT
EWE KEB TEG CROCK CRONE DRAPE
SHEEP GIMMER LAMBER RACHEL
THEAVE CHILVER
(— AND LAMB) COUPLE
(OLD —) BIDDY CROCK CRONE
BIDDIE
(YOUNG —) THEAVE
EWER JUG CREW LAIR BASIN UDDER
PITCHER URCEOLE
EXACERBATE SOUR ENRAGE
FERMENT EMBITTER IRRITATE
EXACERBATION PAROXYSM
EXACT ASK DUE DEAD EVEN FINE
FLAT HAVE JUMP JUST LEVY NICE
TRUE VERY PRESS SCREW WREAK
WREST COMPEL DEMAND ELICIT
EVINCE EXTORT FORMAL GRAITH
MINUTE NARROW PROPER SEVERE
SQUARE STRAIT STRICT CAREFUL
CERTAIN COLLECT COMMAND
CORRECT ENFORCE ESTREAT
EXPRESS EXTRACT LITERAL
PARTILE PERFECT POINTED PRECISE
PRECISO REFINED REGULAR
REQUIRE ACCURATE CRITICAL
EXPLICIT FAITHFUL RIGOROUS
SPECIFIC
(— BY FINE) ESTREAT
(— SATISFACTION) AVENGE
(NOT —) PLATIC
EXACTING NICE HARSH STERN STIFF
TIGHT SCREWY SEVERE STRAIT
ARDUOUS EXIGENT FINICKY
CRITICAL IMPOSING IRONCLAD
PRESSING SCREWING
(— EXCLUSIVE DEVOTION) JEALOUS
EXACTION TAX MART GOUGE GRIPE
(— OF PROVISIONS) CESS COYNE
COIGNY
(UNDUE —) EXTORTION
EXACTLY DUE BANG DEAD EVEN

FLAT FLOP FULL JUMP JUST VERY
PLUMB QUITE RIGHT SHARP SPANG
TRULY ARIGHT EVENLY ITSELF
JUSTLY NICELY PERFECT SLAPDAB
DIRECTLY MINUTELY
EXACTNESS RIGOR TRUTH NICETY
ACCURACY DELICACY DISPATCH
FIDELITY IDENTITY JUSTNESS
SAPIENCE SEVERITY
(FUSSY —) FIKE
EXAGGERATE GAB MORE CHARGE
EXTEND OVERDO AMPLIFY ENHANCE
ENLARGE MAGNIFY OUTLASH
ROMANCE STRETCH INCREASE
OVERDRAW OVERLASH OVERTELL
(— OPENING OF MOUTH) CHINK
EXAGGERATED SLAB TALL
COLORED FUSTIAN FABULOUS
INFLATED OVERSHOT
EXAGGERATING ARROGANT
EXAGGERATION REACHER
HYPERBOLE
EXALT HAUT REAR AREAR BUILD
DEIFY ELATE ERECT EXTOL HEAVE
HEEZE HONOR MOUNT RAISE
TOWER ALTIFY ASCEND EXHALE
PREFER REFINE UPREAR WORTHY
ADVANCE AUGMENT DIGNIFY
ELEVATE ENHANCE ENNOBLE
FEATHER GLORIFY GREATEN
INSPIRE MAGNIFY PROMOTE
SUBLIME DIVINIZE ENTHRONE
GRADUATE HEIGHTEN INHEAVEN
PEDESTAL
EXALTATION LAUD AVATAR ELATION
RAPTURE ERECTION
EXALTED HAUT HIGH ELATE GRAND
LOFTY NOBLE SHEEN SKYEY SOARY
ASTRAL TIPTOE TOPFUL HAUGHTY
SUBLIME ELEVATED EXALTATE
EXALTING HUMAN
EXAMINATION EX MAY EXAM FACE
QUIZ TEST ASSAY AUDIT BOARD
CHECK FINAL GREAT POINT PROBE
STUDY TRIAL BIOPSY EXAMEN
REVIEW SCHOOL SEARCH SURVEY
TRIPOS AUTOPSY BEARING
CANVASS CHECKUP DIVVERS
EXAMINE HEARING INQUEST INQUIRY
MIDYEAR OPPOSAL TUGGERY
ANALYSIS CRITIQUE EXERCISE
NECROPSY RESEARCH SCANNING
SCRUTINY
(PL.) HOURS
EXAMINE ASK CON FAN SEE SPY
TRY BOLT CASE COMB FEEL LAIT
LINE LOOK OGLE QUIZ RIPE SCAN
SEEK SIFT TEST VIEW ASSAY AUDIT
CHECK ENTER GROPE PROBE
QUEST QUOTE SAMEN SENSE
SOUND STUDY VISIT APPOSE
BEHOLD CANDLE DEBATE PERUSE
PONDER REVIEW SCREEN SEARCH
SURVEY ANALYZE CANVASS
COLLATE DISCUSS EXPLORE
INQUIRE INSPECT OVERSEE
PALPATE RUMMAGE CONSIDER
OVERHAUL
(— BY TOUCH) PALPATE

(— CAREFULLY) SCAN SIFT PONDER
(— LAND) SOUM
EXAMINER POSER TRIER CENSOR
CONNER SABORA ANALYST
APPOSER AUDITOR CORONER
PROBATOR SEARCHER
EXAMPLE A CASE CAST COPY LEAD
NORM TYPE BEAUT BYSEN ESSAY
LIGHT MODEL PIECE EMBLEM
PRAXIS SAMPLE BOUNCER LEADING
LECTURE PATTERN PURPOSE
SAMPLER THEATER CALENDAR
ENSAMPLE EXEMPLAR EXEMPLUM
FORBYSEN FOREGOER INSTANCE
PARADIGM SPECIMEN
(DISGRACEFUL —) BIZEN BYSEN
BYZEN
(EXTREME —) CAUTION
(INFERIOR —) EXCUSE
(INSTRUCTIVE —) LESSON
(OLDEST —) DOYEN
(SUPERLATIVE —) BLINGER
EXANTHEMA DIEBACK ERUPTION
EXASPERATE IRE IRK MAD BAIT
GALL HEAT URGE ANNOY BLOOD
ENRAGE EXCITE NETTLE EXASPER
INFLAME PROVOKE ROUGHEN
ACERBATE IRRITATE
EXASPERATED SNAKY WROTH
SNAKEY SNAKISH
EXASPERATION GALL HEAT WRATH
EXCAVATE CUT DIG PIT HOLE HOWK
MINE MOLE MUCK PION SINK DELVE
DRILL DRIVE GRAVE NAVVY SCOOP
STOPE BURROW DREDGE EXCAVE
GULLET HOLLOW QUARRY
EXCAVATION CUT DIG PIT HOLE
MINE REDD SINK SUMP BERRY
DELFT DELPH DITCH GRAVE PILOT
STOPE BURROW CAVITY DUGOUT
GROOVE TRENCH BREAKUP
CUTTING PADDOCK TUTWORK
WORKING DENEHOLE SLUSHPIT
EXCAVATOR DIG BILDAR CLEOID
DIGGER DIPPER DRIFTER HATCHET
PIONEER
EXCEED COW TOP BEST PASS
EXCEL OUTDO OUTGO BETTER
OUTRUN OUTVIE OVERDO OVERGO
ECLIPSE OUTPASS OVERRUN
OVERTAX PRECEDE SURPASS
OUTRANGE OUTSTRIP OVERCOME
OVERGANG OVERSTEP OVERWEND
SURMOUNT
(— THE RESOURCES) BEGGAR
EXCEEDING VILE
EXCEEDINGLY ALL DONE PURE
TRES VERY AMAIN BLAME BLAMED
MASTER PURELY AWFULLY LICKING
PARLOUS PASSING HEARTILY
HEAVENLY HORRIBLE PROPERLY
EXCEL CAP COB TOP BANG BEAT
BEST DING FLOG MEND PASS
BLECK OUTDO OUTGO SHINE
BETTER EXCEED MASTER OUTRAY
OVERDO OVERGO PRECEL ECLIPSE
EMULATE OUTPEER SURPASS
OUTCLASS OUTRANGE OUTRIVAL
OUTSHINE OUTSTRIP OVERPEER
SUPERATE SURMOUNT

EXCELLENCE ARETE MERIT PRICE
VIRTU WORTH BEAUTY DESERT
HEIGHT VIRTUE DIGNITY PROWESS
GOODNESS SPLENDOR
(— OF QUALITY) STRIKE
(MORAL —) GRACE
(PL.) SANCTITIES
EXCELLENT GAY RUM BEST BRAW
COOL FINE GOOD HEND HIGH PURE
RARE RIAL SLAP TALL TRIM ATHEL
BONNY BONZA BRAVE BULLY BURLY
GREAT JOLLY PIOUS PRIME SOLID
SUPER SWELL TRIED WALLY BONNIE
BONZER BOSKER CHEESY CHOICE
CLASSY FAMOUS FREELY GENTLE
GOODLY PRETTY PROPER SELECT
SPIFFY WICKED WIZARD WORTHY
YANKEE BLIGHTY BOSHTER CAPITAL
CORKING CURIOUS ELEGANT
GALLANT IMMENSE QUALITY
SNIFTER STAVING TOPPING
CLIPPING EXIMIOUS GENEROUS
KNOCKOUT STUNNING SUPERIOR
VALUABLE VIRTUOUS WAUREGAN
YNGOODLY
(— IN QUALITY) FRANK
(MOST —) BEST
EXCELLENTLY BRAWLY CLEVER
FINELY FREELY PROUDLY DIVINELY
FAMOUSLY
EXCELLING BEST PASSANT
EXCEPT BAR BUT CEP NOT BATE
BOUT OMIT ONLY SAVE FORBY
SEVER EXEMPT FORBYE NOBBUT
SAVING SCUSIN UNLESS BESIDES
EXCLUDE OUTCEPT OUTTAKE
OUTWITH RESERVE WITHOUT
FORPRISE OUTTAKEN RESERVED
EXCEPTING BATING EXCEPT SAVING
UNLESS
EXCEPTION DEMUR SALVO SAVING
DISSENT OFFENSE DEMURRER
FALLENCY FORPRISE INSTANCE
EXCEPTIONAL RARE EXEMPT
STRANGE UNUSUAL ABERRANT
ABNORMAL ESPECIAL SINGULAR
UNCOMMON
EXCEPTIONALLY AMAZING
SPANKING
EXCERPT CITE PATCH QUOTE
SCRAP EXTRACT OFFPRINT
(— FROM SONG) SNATCH
EXCESS OVER PLUS RIOT FLOOD
INORD LUXUS PRIDE ACRASY
ACRASIA BALANCE DEBAUCH
EXTREME MISRULE NIMIETY
OUTRAGE OVERAGE OVERSET
PROFUSE RIOTISE SURFEIT
SURPLUS EXCEDENT GLUTTONY
INTEREST OVERLASH OVERMUCH
OVERPLUS PLETHORA PLEURISY
(— OF LOGS) BANK
(— OF METAL) FEEDHEAD
(— OF SOLAR MONTH) EPACT
EXCESSIVE TOO OVER RANK ENORM
FANCY STEEP STIFF UNDUE DEADLY
WOUNDY EXTREME FURIOUS
NIMIOUS SURFEIT ABNORMAL
CRIMINAL DEVILISH ENORMOUS
HORRIBLE INSOLENT OVERMUCH

TERRIBLE TERRIFIC
EXCESSIVELY TOO SUPER DEADLY
OVERLY STRONG UNDULY PARLISH
PARLOUS PASSING PLAGUEY
WOUNDLY DEVILISH PLAGUILY
EXCHANGE RAP SET CASH CAUP
CHOP CODE COPE COUP KULA
MART SELL SWAP SWOP BANDY
BOARD BOLSA CORSE SHIFT STORE
TRADE TROKE TRUCK BARTER
BOURSE CAMBIO CHANGE DICKER
EXCAMB MARKET NIFFER RESALE
RIALTO SCORSE SHOPPE TOLSEL
TOLZEY VALUTA WISSEL WRIXLE
BARROOM CAMBIUM CHAFFER
COMMUTE CONVERT DEALING
PERMUTE TRAFFIC COMMERCE
TRUCKAGE
(— IN CHECKERS) CUT SHOT
(— OF BLOWS) HANDPLAY
(— OF PRISONERS) CARTEL
(— OF SYLLABLES) ANACLASIS
(— SMALL TALK) CHAFFER
(— THOUGHTS) CONVERSE
(— VISITS) GAM
(DANCE —) CROSSOVER
(FAIR —) GIFFGAFF
(FOREIGN —) DEVISE
(POETICAL —) FLYTING
(POST —) CANTEEN
(TELEPHONE —) CENTRAL
EXCHEQUER FISC PURSE COFFER
KHALSA CHECKER FINANCE
TREASURY
EXCIPIENT OXYMEL
EXCISE TAX CROP DUTY GELD TOLL
SLASH EXCIDE EXSECT IMPOST
RESECT EXSCIND ALCABALA
RETRENCH
EXCISEMAN GAGER GAUGER
EXCISOR
EXCISION CUT ERASURE
EXCITABLE NERVOUS
EXCITATION LASH
EXCITE HOT CITE FIRE HEAT HYPO
SEND SPUR STIR URGE WAKE WHET
WORK YERK ALARM AMOVE ANGER
CHAFE ELATE ERECT FLAME FLUSH
IMPEL PIQUE RAISE ROUSE SCALD
SPOOK AROUSE AWAKEN BOTHER
DAZZLE DECOCT FLURRY FOMENT
IGNITE INCEND INCITE INVOKE
JANGLE KINDLE LATHER PROMPT
SALUTE TICKLE UPREAR WECCHE
AGITATE ANIMATE COMMOVE
ENCHAFE FERMENT INCENSE
INFLAME PHILTER PROVOKE
QUICKEN STARTLE WHITTLE
DISQUIET ENGENDER EXCITATE
IRRITATE
(— MIRTH) DIVERT
EXCITED UP GAY HOT AGOG GYTE
PINK CADGY EAGER RANTY SKEER
BLEEZY ELATED HEATED STEAMY
ATHRILL FEVERED HAYWIRE
SKEERED WAKENED AGITATED
ATWITTER ELEVATED FEVERISH
FLURRIED FRENETIC STARTLED
(EASILY —) KITTLE
EXCITEMENT ADO GOG BUZZ FUSS

GLOW HEAT KICK STIR TOSS UNCO
FEEZE FEVER FUROR LARRY MANIA
SETUP STOUR UNCOW FRENZY
SPLASH WARMTH FERMENT
FRISSON NERVISM TAMASHA
WIDDRIM BROUHAHA DELIRIUM
INTEREST RACKETRY
(FILLED WITH —) HECTIC
(GREAT —) FEVER
(MENTAL —) WIDDRIM
(PLEASANT —) SUSPENSE
(VIOLENT —) GARE
EXCITING HOT HIGH HECTIC
AGACANT BURNING RACKETY
ROUSING EXCITANT EXCITIVE
PATHETIC STIRRING TERRIFIC
(— HORROR) DIRE DIREFUL
EXCLAIM CRY HOWL BLURT ESCRY
SNORT CLAMOR OUTCRY BESPEAK
EXCLAMATION O AH AI AY BO EH
EY HA HI HO LA LO MY OH OW SO
ST YO AHA AIE BAH BAM BOO FEN
FIE FOH GEE GIP GRR GUP HAI HAW
HAY HEM HEP HEY HIC HOY HUH
NOW OCH OFF OHO OUF OUT PAH
PEW POH POX ROT SEE SUZ TCH
TCK TUT UGH VOW WEE WOW YAH
YOW AHEM ALAS AVOY BUFF DEAR
DRAT EGAD EVOE FAST GARN
GOOD HAIL HECH HECK HIST HOLA
HUFF HUNH HUSH HYKE OONS
OUGH PHEW PHOO PHUT PIFF PISH
POOH PRUT PUGH RATS RIVO SCAT
SIRS SOFT SOHO TCHU TUSH WALY
WEEK WEET WELL WHAM WHAT
WHEE WHEW WHIR WHIT WUGG
YOOP YULE ALACK BRAVO EWHOW
FAINS FANCY FAUGH FEIGH GLORY
GOODY HEIGH HELLO HOLLA HUFFA
HULLO HUMPH HUZZA JOSSA
OHONE PSHAW RIGHT SALVE SHISH
SKOAL SORRY SUGAR TEREU
WAUGH WELOO WHING WHISK
WHIST WHOOP WIRRA WOONS
CARAJO CLAMOR ENCORE HALLOO
HEYDAY HOOTAY HURRAH INDEED
OUTCRY PERFAY QUOTHA RATHER
RIGHTO SHUCKS STEADY WALKER
WHOOSH CARAMBA DOGGONE
GODSAKE HOSANNA JIGGERS
KERCHOO KERWHAM NICHEVO
PRITHEE RUBBISH SALAMAT
TANTIVY THUNDER WELCOME
WHOOPEE FAREWELL WAESUCKS
WELLAWAY
(— OF DISGUST) AUH FIE FOH PAH
UGH AUGH AVOY PHEW PISH POOT
PSHA PUGH FAUGH FEICH FEIGH
PSHAW WELOO
(— OF DISTRESS) AI AIE HARO
HARROW
(— OF DOUBT) HUM HUMPH
(— OF IMPATIENCE) GIP PHEW
(— OF INCREDULITY) AHEM INDEED
WALKER
(— OF REPUGNANCE) UGH
(— OF SURPRISE) HA OW GIP LAW
HEIN HUNH LACK LAND LAWK LORD
ODSO BABAI HEUGH LAWKS

CRIMINE CRIMINY HEAVENS JUCKIES
GORBLIMY GRAMERCY
(— OF TRIUMPH) AH IO GRIG
HEUCH HOOCH HURRAH
(PROFANE —) BAN
EXCLAMATION POINT BANG
SHOUT SCREAMER
EXCLUDE BAR SHUT SINK CLOSE
DEBAR EJECT EXPEL FENCE BANISH
DISBAR EXCEPT EXEMPT FORBAR
FORBID REJECT BLANKET DEFAULT
EXPUNGE FOREBAR FOREIGN
OUTTAKE OUTWALL REPULSE
SECLUDE SUSPEND
EXCLUDED EXEMPT FOREIGN
EXCLUDING BAR BUT LESS
BARRING
EXCLUSIVE ALL ONLY RARE SOLE
ALONE ELECT WHOLE NARROW
SELECT ENTIRELY
(— OF) BEFORE
EXCLUSIVELY ALL ALONE SINGLY
ENTIRELY
EXCOGITATE CONSIDER
EXCOMMUNICATE CURSE
UNCHURCH
EXCOMMUNICATION BAN CURSE
HEREM EXCISION
EX-CONVICT LAG LAGGER
EXCORIATE FLAY GALL SCORE
STRIP ABRADE SCORCH BLISTER
LAMBASTE
EXCREMENT LEE CRAP DIRT DREG
DUNG FRASS JAKES HOCKEY
ORDURE REFUSE VOIDING
CROTTELS
(— OF EARTHWORM) CAST
(— OF HARES) CROTTELS
(— OF INSECTS) FRASS
(PL.) DEJECTA
EXCRESCENCE NOB PIN WEN BURL
BURR GALL HORN KNOB KNOT
KNUR LUMP WART FUSEE FUZEE
KNURL THORN EXCESS HURTLE
MORULA NUBBLE PIMPLE BOLSTER
PUSTULE RATTAIL SPINACH
CARUNCLE EPITHEMA TUBERCLE
(— ON HORSE'S FOOT) FIG
(— ON WHALE'S HEAD) BONNET
EXCRETA EGESTA
EXCRETE EGEST SWEAT EXCERN
DEFECATE PERSPIRE
EXCRETION SORDES ECRISIS
EXCRUCIATE RACK GRIND AGONIZE
TORMENT TORTURE
EXCRUCIATING GRINDING
EXCULPATE FREE CLEAR REMIT
ACQUIT EXCUSE PARDON ABSOLVE
FORGIVE JUSTIFY RELEASE
PALLIATE
EXCULPATION EXCUSE
EXCURSION DIP HOP ROW DIET
RIDE SAIL SPIN TOUR TRIP ESSAY
JAUNT RANGE SALLY START TRAMP
CANTER CRUISE FLIGHT JUNKET
OUTING PASEAR RAMBLE SASHAY
VAGARY VOYAGE JOURNEY
OUTLOPE OUTRIDE OUTROAD
CAMPAIGN ESCAPADE

EXCURSIONIST TRIPPER
EXCUSABLE VENIAL
EXCUSE FAIK PLEA ALIBI COLOR
GLOSS PLANE REMIT SALVO SCUSE
ACQUIT ESSOIN EXEMPT PARDON
REFUGE SCONCE SECURE SUNYIE
ABSOLVE APARDON APOLOGY
CONDONE ESSOIGN EXCUSAL
FORGIVE OFFCOME PRETEXT
DISPENSE OCCASION OVERLOOK
PALLIATE PRETENCE
(CONSCIENTIOUSLY —) SCRUPLE
EXCUSS SHAKE DISCARD DISCUSS
EXECRABLE BAD CURST CURSED
DAMNED HEINOUS ACCURSED
DAMNABLE WRETCHED
EXECRATE BAN DAMN ABHOR
CURSE DEVOTE
EXECRATION CURSE
EXECUTE DO ACT CUT TOP BURN
DASH FILL GIVE HANG HAVE KILL
OBEY PASS PLAY SLAY FRAME
GANCH LYNCH SCRAG YIELD
DESIGN DIRECT EFFECT FINISH
FULFIL GARROT GIBBET MANAGE
CONDUCT ENFORCE FULFILL
GAROTTE PERFORM STRETCH
COMPLETE DISPATCH EXPEDITE
PRACTICE PRACTISE
(— BOW) WREATHE
(— POORLY) DUB
(— SUCCESSFULLY) COMPLETE
EXECUTED GIVEN
(— EXQUISITELY) CURIOUS
(— WITH CARE) ACCURATE
(CRUDELY —) DAUBY
EXECUTION GANCH TOUCH EFFECT
FACTURE GARROTE HANGING
TECHNIC CARRIAGE GARROTTE
PRACTICE
(— BY BURNING) STAKE
(— OF WILL) FACTUM
EXECUTIONER BURRIO HEADER
TORTOR BUTCHER HANGMAN
HEADMAN LOCKMAN CARNIFEX
EXECUTOR HEADSMAN
EXECUTIVE BOSS DEAN MAYOR
WARDEN CASHIER MANAGER
PODESTA PREMIER GOVERNOR
OFFICIAL
EXECUTOR DOER AGENT ALBACEA
SECUTOR ENFORCER MINISTER
EXEGESIS ANAGOGE ANAGOGY
MIDRASH HAGGADAH
EXEMPLAR MODEL FATHER MIRROR
MODULE EIDOLON EXAMPLE
PARABLE PATTERN
EXEMPLARY LAUDABLE
EXEMPLIFICATION SOUL EXAMPLE
EXEMPLIFY SAMPLE SATISFY
ENSAMPLE MODELIZE
EXEMPT EXON FREE EXEEM EXEME
FRANK SEVER SPARE EXPERT
FIDATE IMMUNE EXCLUDE RELEASE
DISPENSE EXCEPTED
EXEMPTION GRACE CHARTER
FREEDOM LIBERTY SWEATER
BLOODWIT IMMUNITY IMPUNITY
EXEQUATUR PLACET

EXERCISE ACT AIR DIP PLY URE USE BEAR HAVE DRILL ETUDE EXERT HALMA LATIN LONGE SWEAT AIRING BREATH CAREER EMPLOY EXERCE LESSON MANUAL PARADE PRAXIS SCHOOL AUFGABE BREATHE DISPLAY ENHAUNT PROBLEM ACTIVITY EXERTION FORENSIC PALESTRA PRACTICE PRACTISE
(— **CONTROL**) BOSS PRESIDE
(— **HORSE**) BREEZE
(**ACADEMIC** —) PRACTICUM
(**CAVALRY** —) MELEE
(**MUSICAL** —) ETUDE SOLFEGE VOCALISE
(**STRONG** —) INTENSION
(**UNWARRANTED** —) STRETCH
(**PL.**) ALLEGRO ATHLETICS

EXERT DO PLY PUT DRAW EMIT HUMP STIR DRIVE SPEND SWING EXTEND REVEAL STRAIN AFFORCE ENFORCE IMPRESS CHARETTE ENDEAVOR EXERCISE
(— **A SPELL**) TAKE
(— **POWER**) ACT BEAR
(— **PRESSURE**) SQUEEZE
(— **TRACTION**) HAUL

EXERTING (— **POWER**) AGENT

EXERTION HEFT BURST ESSAY LABOR TRIAL WHILE ACTION EFFORT MOTION STRESS STRIFE ATTEMPT TROUBLE ENDEAVOR EXERCISE STRUGGLE
(**EXCESSIVE** —) STRAIN
(**STRENUOUS** —) HUMP

EXFOLIATE SCALE
EXFOLIATION FURFUR
EXHALATION AURA FUME REEK STEAM BREATH EXPIRY MIASMA HALITUS MALARIA FUMOSITY MEPHITIS

EXHALE CAST EMIT REEK EXUDE STEAM WHIFF EXPIRE BREATHE FURNACE REFLAIR RESPIRE EXHALATE PERSPIRE
EXHALED SFOGATO

EXHAUST DO FAG SAP BEAT BURN COOK COWL EMIT FAIL FLAG FLOG JADE KILL MATE SOAK TIRE TUCK BLAST BREAK CLEAN DRAFT DRAIN EMPTY FORDO GRUEL LEECH PETER SHOOT SPEND SWINK WASTE WEARY ABRADE BETOIL BOTTOM BUGGER EMBOSS FINISH FOREDO HARASS HATTER OVERDO TAIGLE TUCKER BREATHE CONSUME DEPLETE DEPRIVE DRAUGHT EXTRACT FATIGUE OUTWEAR SCOURGE SURREIN DISTRESS EDUCTION EVACUATE FORSPEND FORWEARY OVERWEAR

EXHAUSTED TAM BEAT DEAD DONE DUNG GONE WEAK WORN BLOWN EMPTY JADED SPENT STANK TIRED BARREN BEATEN BUSHED EFFETE GROGGY MARCID PLAYED TOILED TRAIKY ATTAINT DRAINED EMPTIED FORDONE FORSUNG FORWORN TEDIOUS WHACKED BANKRUPT

CONSUMED FOREDONE FOREWORN FORFAIRN FORSPENT FOUGHTEN HARASSED OUTSPENT OVERWORN
(— **OF AIR**) HIGH
EXHAUSTING ARDUOUS IRKSOME PREYING
EXHAUSTION EXHAUST FATIGUE SELLOUT SOOREYN GONENESS
EXHAUSTIVE FULL MINUTE THOROUGH

EXHIBIT AIR PEN FAIR HAVE SHEW SHOW TURN WEAR SPORT STAGE BLAZON DEMEAN EVINCE EXPOSE OPPOSE OSTEND PARADE REVEAL APPROVE CONCENE DIORAMA DISPLAY EXPRESS MONSTER PERFORM PRESENT PRODUCE PROJECT PROPOSE TRADUCE BOOKFAIR BRANDISH CONCEIVE DISCLOSE DISCOVER EMBLAZON EVIDENCE FORTHSET MANIFEST SHOWCASE
(— **ALARM**) GLOFF
(— **DOGS**) BENCH
(— **IN SNARLING**) GRIN

EXHIBITION FAIR SALE SHOW DROLL ENTRY SALON SIGHT ANNUAL PARADE SALARY DISPLAY EXHIBIT PAGEANT PENSION PRESENT SHOWING STAGERY EXERCISE
(— **OF DOGS**) BENCH
(— **ON STAGE**) STAGERY
(**PUBLIC** —) SPECIES
(**RIDING** —) CAROUSEL

EXHIBITIONER SERVITOR
EXHIBITIONIST HAM HAMFATTER
EXHIBITOR SHOWER
EXHILARATE AMUSE CHEER ELATE ANIMATE ELEVATE ENLIVEN GLADDEN
EXHILARATED RAD GLAD HAPPY HEADY ELEVATED
EXHILARATION GAIETY JOLLITY GLADNESS HILARITY
EXHORT URGE WARN CHARM ADHORT ADVISE CHARGE DEHORT ENGAGE INCITE PREACH CAUTION ADMONISH DISSUADE
EXHORTATION ADVICE EXHORT HOMILY COUNSEL PROPHECY
EXHORTER HORTATOR PREACHER
EXHUME DIG DELVE UNBURY UNTOMB UNEARTH DISINTER EXHUMATE
EXIGENCY NEED WANT EXIGENT URGENCY JUNCTURE OCCASION PRESSURE
EXIGENT DIRE VITAL URGENT CRITICAL EXACTING PRESSING
EXIGUITY PAUCITY
EXILE EXUL POOR RUIN THIN EXPEL GALUT WREAK BANISH DEPORT GALUTH OUTLAW SCANTY WRETCH EXULATE GERSHOM OUTCAST PILGRIM REFUGEE SLENDER DIASPORA FUGITIVE OUTLAWRY
EXILED FOREIGN FUGITIVE
EXIST AM BE IS ARE LIE COME

GROW LIVE MOVE PASS DWELL CONSIST
(— **IN FULL SUPPLY**) FLOW
EXISTENCE ENS ESSE LIFE SEIN BEING DASEIN ENTITY IDEATE INESSE ESSENCE IDEATUM REALITY ENERGEIA IDENTITY SURVIVAL
(— **AFTER DEATH**) AFTERLIFE
(**DULL** —) DEATH
(**ETERNAL** —) SAT
(**EVER-CHANGING** —) SAMSARA SANSARA
(**IN** —) GOING AROUND EXTANT
(**PERMANENT** —) INHERENCE
(**WAKING** —) JAGRATA
EXISTENT HARD REAL ALIVE BEING ACTUAL EXTANT EXISTING
(— **IN DIFFERENT FORMS**) ALLOTROPIC
(**CONTINUALLY** —) STUBBORN
EXISTING GOING ACTUAL EXTANT EXISTENT
(— **IN NAME ONLY**) DUMMY
EXIT ISH DOOR GATE VENT GOING ISSUE LEAVE EGRESS EXITUS OUTLET OUTWAY EXITION OUTGATE OUTPORT PASSAGE DEBOUCHE
(**HURRIED** —) BOUT
EXITE BRACT
EX LIBRIS BOOKPLATE
EXOCYCLIC IRREGULAR
EXODUS EXODY EXITUS HEGIRA HEJIRA EXODIUM
EXON EXEMPT
EXONERATE FREE ALIBI CLEAR ACQUIT EXCUSE EXONER UNLOAD ABSOLVE RELIEVE
EXOPODITE EXOPOD SQUAMA
EXORABLE PRAYABLE
EXORBITANT STEEP UNDUE ABNORMAL
EXORDIUM PREFACE PRELUDE
EXOSKELETON CORSLET CORSELET
EXOSPORIUM EXINE EXTINE EXOSPERM
EXOSTOSIS POROMA SPLINT OSSELET
EXOTIC ALIEN FOREIGN STRANGE
EXOTOSPORE BLAST
EXOTROPIA WALLEYE
EXPAND OPE WAX BLOW BULK FLAN FLUE FOAM GROW HUFF OPEN FARCE FLASH RETCH SPLAY SWELL WIDEN DIDUCE DILATE EXTEND INTEND SPREAD SPROUT UNFOLD UNFURL AMPLIFY BALLOON BLOSSOM BOLSTER BROADEN BURGEON DEVELOP DIFFUSE DISPAND DISPLAY DISTEND EDUCATE ENLARGE EXPANSE EXPLAIN INFLATE STRETCH DISPREAD INCREASE LENGTHEN OUTREACH
(— **AS A VESSEL**) FLAN
(— **FEATHERS**) PRIDE
(— **INTO PODS**) KID
EXPANDED NOWY OPEN OVERT DILATE SPREAD DILATED SWOLLEN INFLATED PATULENT PATULOUS

EXPANDER EXTENDER
EXPANDING BOSOMY
EXPANSE AREA ROOM BURST FIELD
REACH TRACT EXTENT LENGTH
SPREAD COUNTRY STRETCH
DISTANCE EXPANSUM SEPARATE
(— OF ICE) SHEET
(— OF SEA ICE) FIELD
(BROAD —) ACRE MAIN
(IMMEASURABLE — OF TIME)
ETERNITY
(IMMENSE —) OCEAN
(INDEFINITE —) VAGUE
(VAST —) SEA
(WIDE —) BREADTH
EXPANSIBILITY ELATER
EXPANSION ALA BULB WING FLUSH
SPLAY GROWTH SPREAD ECTASIA
ECTASIS EXPANSE HASTULA
ACROCYST COQUILLE DIASTOLE
DILATION INCREASE SWELLING
(— IN SEEDS) ALA WING
(— OF RIVER) BROAD
(FOLIOSE —) LAMINA
(LITURGICAL —) EMBOLISM
EXPANSIVE FREE WIDE BROAD
GENIAL ELASTIC LIBERAL
GENEROUS SPACIOUS SWELLING
EXPATIATE DWELL DILATE EXPAND
SPREAD AMPLIFY BROADEN
DESCANT DIFFUSE ENLARGE
SATISFY
EXPATRIATE EXILE EXPEL BANISH
OUTLAW OUTCAST
EXPATRIATION EXILE
EXPECT ASK DEEM HOPE LITE LOOK
STAY TEND TROW WAIT WEEN
ABIDE AWAIT THINK ATTEND
DEMAND INTEND LIPPEN RECKON
PRESUME REQUIRE SUPPOSE
SUSPECT
EXPECTANT ATIPTOE CHARGED
HOPEFUL INCHOATE
EXPECTANTLY TIPTOE
EXPECTATION HOPE VIEW WAIT
WEEN EXPECT FUTURE ESPEIRE
OPINION SUPPOSE THOUGHT
WEENING PROSPECT
EXPECTED DUE SUPPOSED
EXPECTORANT CINEOL STORAX
CINEOLE EMETINE CREOSOTE
GUAIACOL TEREBENE
EXPECTORATE SPIT
EXPECTORATION EMPTYSIS
EXPEDIENCE ARTIFICE
EXPEDIENT FIT WISE ATAJO CRAFT
DODGE JOKER KNACK SHIFT DEVICE
RESORT STRING DODGERY POLITIC
STOPGAP ARTIFICE RESOURCE
DESIRABLE
EXPEDITATE LAW
EXPEDITATION LAWING
EXPEDITE HIE EASY FREE HURRY
SPEED EXPEDE GREASE HASTEN
QUICKEN DISPATCH
EXPEDITION CAMP FARE ROAD
TREK DRAVE HASTE HURRY RANGE
SCOUT TRADE SAFARI VOYAGE
CARAVAN CRUSADE ENTRADA

JOURNEY OUTLOPE SERVICE
WARFARE WARPATH COMMANDO
HEADHUNT PROGRESS
(FISHING —) DRAVE
(HUNTING —) SAFARI
(MILITARY —) HARKA CRUSADE
JOURNEY WARPATH
EXPEDITIOUS FAST HASTY QUICK
RAPID READY SHORT PROMPT
SPEEDY
EXPEL CAN OUT USH BLOW BOLT
DRUM DUMP FIRE OUST VOID WARP
AVOID CHASE CHECK DEPEL EJECT
ERUPT EVICT EXILE KNOCK SPURT
BANISH BOUNCE DEBOUT DEPORT
DEVOID DISBAR DISOWN OUTPUT
OUTRAY REFUSE ABANDON
EXCLUDE EXPULSE EXTRUDE
OBTRUDE SCRATCH SECLUDE
SUSPEND DISLODGE DISPLACE
EVACUATE FORJUDGE
(— AIR) COUGH
(— FROM MEMBERSHIP) HAMMER
(— GAS) BELCH
(— SUDDENLY) SLIRT
EXPEND USE LEND SPEND SPORT
WASTE WREAK DEFRAY IMPEND
OCCUPY PONDER CONSUME
DISPEND EROGATE EXHAUST
OVERUSE DISBURSE SQUANDER
EXPENDITURE COST OUTGO PENSE
CHARGE OUTLAY EXPENSE PENSION
SPENDING
(— OF ENERGY) EFFORT
EXPENSE EX COST GAFF LOSS
BATTA PRICE SUMPT CHARGE
DAMAGE GERSUM ONCOST OUTLAY
OUTSET OVERHEAD SUMPTURE
(— OF CARRYING) CARRIAGE
(— OF TREAT) SAM
(PL.) BATTA COSTS MISES
EXPENSIVE DEAR HIGH SALT STIFF
COSTLY LAVISH LIBERAL THRIFTY
EXPERIENCE SEE TRY FEEL FIND
HAVE HENT HOLD KNOW LIVE TEST
ASSAY EVENT PROOF PROVE SKILL
TASTE TRIAL USAGE BEHOLD
EXPERT FRAIST ORDEAL SAMPLE
SUFFER APPROVE CALVARY
CONTACT FEELING FURNACE
KNOWING REALIZE SUSTAIN
UNDERGO ESCAPADE
(— GOOD OR ILL FORTUNE) SPEED
(— OF INTENSE SUFFERING)
CALVARY
(— WITH BITTERNESS) BEAR
(CALAMITOUS —) ADVERSITY
(ORDINARY —) USE
(PAINFUL —) FIT
(PARTIAL —) GUST
(TRYING —) ORDEAL
EXPERIENCED HAD MET OLD USED
SALTY EXPERT SALTED TRADED
ANCIENT PRACTIC THRIVEN
VETERAN WEIGHED SEASONED
(— INTENSIVELY) ACUTE
(ACTUALLY —) SPECIOUS
EXPERIENTIAL EMPIRIC
EXPERIMENT SHY TRY TEST ASSAY

ESSAY TRIAL ATTEMPT CONTROL
EXPERIMENTAL SAMPLE
(NOT —) STANDARD
EXPERT ACE DAB DEFT FULL GOOD
PERT ADEPT FLASH READY SHARP
SWELL ADROIT ARTIST CLEVER
FACILE HABILE KAHUNA PANDIT
PERTLY QUAINT SUBTLE WIZARD
ARTISTE ATTACHE CAPABLE
DABSTER SKILLED DEXTROUS
GAINSOME SKILLFUL SPEEDFUL
VIRTUOSO
(— IN JEWISH LAW) DAYAN
(— ON DRIVING LOGS) LAKER
(BANK —) SHROFF
(GREAT —) ONER
(SCIENTIFIC —) BOFFIN
EXPERTNESS SAVVY SKILL FACILITY
HABILITY
EXPIATE ABY SKUG ATONE AVERT
ASSOIL RANSOM
EXPIATORY PIACULAR
EXPIRATION END DEATH BREATH
EFFLUX ELAPSE EXPIRE EXPIRY
(SPASMODIC —) SNEEZE
EXPIRE DIE END EMIT FALL EXPEL
GHOST LAPSE ELAPSE EXHALE
INLAIK OUTRUN PERISH
EXPIRED UP DEAD
EXPIRING DYING
EXPIRY ISH CLOSE DEATH EFFLUX
EXPLAIN OPEN RECE SAVE SCAN
UNDO WISE AREAD AREED CLEAR
GLOSS GLOZE PLANE RECHE SOLVE
SPEED TOUCH DEFINE EXPAND
EXPLAT EXPONE REMENE RIDDLE
UNFOLD ABSOLVE ACCOUNT
AMPLIFY CLARIFY COMMENT
CONTRUE DECLARE DEVELOP
DISCUSS EXHIBIT EXPOUND JUSTIFY
RESOLVE CONSTRUE DESCRIBE
MANIFEST SIMPLIFY UNPLIGHT
UNWONDER
EXPLAINER EXPONENT
EXPLAINING EXPONENT
EXPLANATION KEY NOTE GLOSS
SALVE SALVO ANSWER CAVEAT
ACCOUNT APOLOGY ADDENDUM
EXEGESIS INNUENDO NOTATION
SOLUTION
EXPLETIVE AND GEE BOSH EGAD
GOSH OATH BEGAD MODAL BEHEAR
SDEATH TUNKET DAMMISH
MORBLEU GOODYEAR GRACIOUS
EXPLICATE OPEN CLEAR EXPAND
UNFOLD ACCOUNT EXPLAIN
EXPLICATION CRIB ANALYSIS
EXPLICIT OPEN CLEAR EXACT FIXED
PLAIN EXPRESS PRECISE ABSOLUTE
DEFINITE IMPLICIT POSITIVE
PUNCTUAL SPECIFIC
EXPLICITLY DIRECT FORMALLY
EXPLODE POP BLOW FIRE BELCH
BLAST BURST CRUMP ERUPT PLUFF
SHOOT SQUIB SPRING BACKFIRE
DETONATE DISPLODE
EXPLOIT ACT DEED FEAT GEST JEST
MILK WORK GESTE GOUGE STUNT
PERFORM SUCCESS CHIVALRY

PARERGON PROPERTY

EXPLORATION SPY PROBE SEARCH
EXPLORE

EXPLORATORY FRONTIER

EXPLORE DO DIP MAP SPY DIVE
DRAG FEEL VIEW CHART COAST
DELVE RANGE SCOUT SOUND
SEARCH EXAMINE PALPATE
BOTANIZE DISCOVER

EXPLORER CAVEMAN PIONEER
COLUMBUS

EXPLOSION POP BLOW BLAST
BURST CRUMP SALVO BLOWUP
BOUNCE REPORT PLOSION INCIDENT
OUTBURST
(FUEL —) BACKFIRE
(SLIGHT —) PLUFF

EXPLOSIVE EGG TNT MINE AMVIS
AMATOL JOVITE LIMPET POWDER
TETRYL TONITE TORPEX TOUCHY
TRITON ABELITE AMMONAL AZOTINE
DUNNITE LIGNOSE LYDDITE PLOSIVE
PUDDING SHIMOSE THORITE
CHEDDITE DYNAMITE ECRASITE
ERUPTIVE GELATINE MELINITE
PYROLITE ROBURITE
(CHARGE OF —) TULIP RESPONDER

EXPOLIATE SCALE SPALL SPAWL

EXPONENT INDEX

EXPORT OUTCARRY

EXPORTATION EXPORT OUTPORT

EXPOSE AIR BARE GIVE OPEN RISK
SHOW STRIP BEWRAY DEBUNK
DETECT EXPONE GIBBET OBJECT
OPPOSE REVEAL UNHUSK UNMASK
DISPLAY EXHIBIT EXPOUND PILLORY
PROPINE PUBLISH SUBJECT
UNCOVER UNEARTH UNTRUSS
BRANDISH DISCLOSE DISCOVER
MUCKRAKE RIDICULE SATIRIZE
UNCLOTHE UNSHROUD
(— FOR BLEACHING) CROFT
(— ORE) HUSH
(— PLAYING CARD) BURN
(— SELF TO) WAGE
(— SUDDENLY) FLASH
(— TO AIR) AERATE
(— TO DANGER) JUMP COMMIT
SUBMIT
(— TO HEAT) AIR
(— TO INFAMY) GIBBET
(— TO MOISTURE) RET
(— TO SCORN) PILLORY
(— TO SULFUR DIOXIDE) STOVE
(— TO SUN AND AIR) FIELD
(— TO SUN) INSOLATE SOLARIZE

EXPOSED AIRY BARE OPEN BLEAK
LIABLE UNSAFE SUBJECT VEILLESS
(— TO DANGER) INSECURE
(— TO) AGAINST

EXPOSITION FAIR GECK SHOW
ZEND TRACT EXPOSE METHOD
SURVEY ACCOUNT EXPOSAL
MIDRASH ANALYSIS EXEGESIS
EXPOSURE EXTHESIS HAGGADAH
TREATISE
(— OF FEAST) SYNAXARY

EXPOSITORY EXEGETIC

EXPOSTULATE ARGUE DISCUSS

EXAMINE PROTEST

EXPOSTULATION PROTEST

EXPOSURE ASPECT EXPOSE
EXPOSAL FLASHING FRONTAGE
PROSPECT
(— OF CARDS) SPREAD
(— OF KING) CHECK
(— TO AIR) AERATE AIRING
(BODY —) FLASH

EXPOUND OPEN UNDO GLOZE
SENSE TREAT DEFINE EXPONE
EXPOSE DEVELOP DISCUSS EXPLAIN
EXPOSIT EXPRESS CONSTRUE
SIMPLIFY

EXPOUNDER MUFTI MULLAH
EXPRESS EXPONENT HERMETIC

EXPRESS AIR BID PUT SAY CAST
EMIT PASS POST VENT COUCH
EMOTE FRAME OPINE SPEAK STATE
UTTER VOICE WIELD BROACH
DEMEAN DENOTE DIRECT EVINCE
IMPORT PHRASE ABREACT BREATHE
DECLARE DICTATE EXPOUND
EXPREME TESTIFY DEFINITE
DESCRIBE DISPATCH EXPLICIT
INTIMATE MANIFEST
(— APPROVAL) AGREE ACCEDE
APPLAUD
(— AS LANGUAGE) LAY
(— BY GESTURE) BECK
(— BY LAUGHTER) LAUGH
(— CONCERN) CLUCK
(— DISAPPROVAL) BOO CHIDE
DECRY GROAN CATCALL
(— DISDAIN) TUT
(— EFFERVESCENTLY) CHORTLE
(— FOLLY) EXPAND
(— GRATITUDE) THANK AGGRATE
(— GRIEF) DEPLORE
(— IN WORDS) SAY DRAW SPEAK
PHRASE
(— NUMERICALLY) EVALUATE
(— ONE'S FEELINGS) FLOW
(— SORROW) LAMENT COMPLAIN
(— WILLINGNESS) CONSENT

EXPRESSION DIT HIT SAY CAST
EUGE FACE FORM POSE SHOW SIGN
TERM VULT WORD ADIEU GLIFF
IDIOM SNEER TOKEN VOICE
BYWORD DILOGY DIVERB EFFECT
FACIES ORACLE PHRASE SPEECH
SYMBOL COMMENT DESCANT
EPITHET EXPRESS GRIMACE
ALLEGORY AUSDRUCK DANICISM
FELICITY LACONISM MONOMIAL
(— IN FEW WORDS) BREVITY
(— OF ANNOYANCE) SOH
(— OF APPROVAL) EUGE PLACET
(— OF ASSENT) CONTENT
(— OF BEAUTY) ART
(— OF CHOICE) VOTE
(— OF DISPLEASURE) FROWN
(— OF DISTASTE) FACE
(— OF HOMAGE) OVATION
(— OF JOY) GREETING
(— OF OPINION) EDITORIAL
(— OF RESPECT) DUTY
(— OF SADNESS) SHADE
(— OF SCORN) GECK

(— OF SINGLE IDEA) RHEME
(APT —) FELICITY
(CHEMICAL —) EQUATION
(COMMONPLACE —) BROMIDE
(CORRECT —) SUMPSIMUS
(CURT —) LACONIC
(FACIAL —) GRIN CHEER SCOWL
SMILE
(INCONGRUOUS —) BULL
(LOUD —) CLAMOR
(MATHEMATICAL —) INDEX SERIES
BINOMIAL EQUATION FUNCTION
INTEGRAL
(MOCKING —) SCOFF
(PECULIAR —) IDIOM
(PET —) CANT
(PUERILE —) BOYISM
(SARCASTIC —) GIBE JIBE
(SERIOUS —) EARNEST
(SINCERE —) CANDOR
(SYMBOLIC —) FORMULA
(TENDER —) LANGUISH
(TRITE —) CLICHE
(UNRESTRAINED —) EFFUSION
(VERBAL —) LETTER
(WISE —) ORACLE

EXPRESSIONLESS STONY LEADEN
SODDEN VACANT WOODEN
TONELESS

EXPRESSIVE POETIC TONGUED
ELOQUENT EMPHATIC SPEAKING

EXPRESSIVENESS DICTION
DELICACY TOURNURE ELOQUENCE

EXPRESSLY NAMELY EXPRESS
PRESSLY FORMALLY

EXPRESSWAY FREEWAY SPEEDWAY

EXPROBATE CENSURE UPBRAID

EXPULSION EXILE BOUNCE
BANNIMUS EJECTION EXCISION

EXPUNGE BLOT DELE ERASE SLASH
CANCEL DELETE EFFACE EXCISE
SCRAPE DESTROY SCRATCH
DISPUNGE

EXPURGATE GELD PURGE
CASTRATE

EXPURGATION BOWDLERISM

EXQUISITE FOP DUDE FINE NICE
PERT PINK RARE DANDY EXACT
CHOICE DAINTY CAREFUL ELEGANT
GEMLIKE PERFECT REFINED
AFFECTED DELICATE ETHEREAL
MACARONI

EXQUISITELY CHOICELY

EXSCIND CUT SEVER EXCISE

EXTANT ALIVE BEING LIVING VISIBLE
EXISTING MANIFEST

EXTEMPORE SUDDEN OFFHAND
IMPROVISO

EXTEND GO EKE LIE RUN BEAR
BUSH COME DATE DRAW GROW
LAST OPEN PASS RISE ROLL SPAN
SPIN BREDE BULGE CARRY COVER
FARCE REACH RENEW RETCH SEIZE
SHOOT STENT VERGE WIDEN
AMOUNT DEEPEN DEPLOY DILATE
EXPAND INTEND OUTLIE SPREAD
SPRING STRAIN STREAK THRUST
TRENCH AMPLIFY BROADEN
DIFFUSE DISPLAY DISTEND ENLARGE

OVERLAP OVERRUN PORRECT PORTEND PRODUCE PROFFER PROJECT PROLONG PROMOTE PROTEND RADIATE STRETCH CONTINUE ELONGATE INCREASE LENGTHEN OUTREACH PROROGUE PROTRACT PROTRUDE
(— **ACTIVITIES**) BRANCH
(— **AROUND**) GIRTH
(— **IN SPACE**) DURE
(— **IRREGULARLY**) TRAIL
(— **OVER**) SPAN COVER CROSS CONTAIN OVERLAP
(— **SAIL**) SHEET
(— **THE FRONT**) DEPLOY
(— **TO**) LINE REACH
EXTENDED FAT LONG OPEN BROAD EXTENT SPREAD EXTENSE LENGTHY PROLATE SPLAYED EXPANDED INTENDED
EXTENDER INERT FILLER LIGNIN
EXTENDING BROAD
(— **OVER**) ASTRIDE
EXTENSION ARM EKE ELL AREA CAPE SCOPE POCKET SATTVA SPHERE SPREAD BREADTH STRETCH ADDENDUM ADDITION DURATION INCREASE PROTENSE
(— **OF BUILDING MATERIAL**) APRON
(— **OF CREDIT**) DATING
(— **OF MINERAL VEIN**) FLAT
(— **OF RACE TRACK**) CHUTE SHUTE
(— **OF SHELL**) LAPPET
(— **OF TIME**) RESPITE
(— **OF WAGON FRAME**) THRIPPLE
(**BALLET** —) BATTEMENT
EXTENSIVE HUGE VAST WIDE AMPLE BROAD LARGE EXTENSE IMMENSE EXPANDED INFINITE SWEEPING
EXTENT DUE RUN TAX AREA BODY BULK DEAL GAGE LEVY PASS SIZE WRIT AMBIT DEPTH FIELD GAUGE LIMIT RANGE REACH SCOPE SPACE STENT SWEEP TRACK AMOUNT ASSIZE ATTACK DEGREE LENGTH SPREAD STREEK ACREAGE ASSAULT BREADTH COMPASS EXPANSE SEIZURE STRETCH VARIETY DISTANCE INCREASE LATITUDE QUANTITY STRAIGHT
(— **OF FRONT**) FRONTAGE
(— **OF LAND**) HEIGHT CONTINENT
(— **OF SPACE**) ROOM
(**BROAD** —) SWEEP
(**SOME** —) BIT
(**UNLIMITED** —) INFINITY
(**UTMOST** —) FULL
(**VAST** —) DEEP
(**VERTICAL** —) ALTITUDE
EXTENUATE THIN GLOZE MINCE EXCUSE LESSEN SOOTHE WEAKEN DIMINISH PALLIATE
EXTERIOR CRUST ECTAD ECTAL OUTER SHELL EXTERN OUTSIDE OUTWARD SURFACE EXOTERIC EXTERNAL OUTLYING
EXTERMINATE WIPE EXPEL UPROOT ABOLISH DESTROY
EXTERNAL OUT OUTER EXTERN

OUTSIDE OUTWARD STRANGE EXOTERIC EXTERIOR INCIDENT
EXTERNALITY OUTNESS
EXTERNALLY OUTWARD WITHOUT
EXTINCT DEAD BYGONE DEFUNCT QUENCHED
(— **MAN**) KANJERA
EXTINCTION DOOM FINE DEATH EXPIRY DELETION
EXTINGUISH OUT DAMP DOUT REDD STUB ANNUL CHOKE CRUSH DOUSE DOWSE DROWN QUELL REPEL SLAKE SNUFF STAMP QUENCH STANCH STIFLE BLANKET DESTROY ECLIPSE EXPIATE EXTINCT OBSCURE OPPRESS SLOCKEN STAUNCH SUPPRESS
(— **CIGARETTE**) SNUB
EXTINGUISHED OUT DEAD EXTINCT
EXTINGUISHER DOUTER STAUNCH BACKPACK QUENCHER STANCHER
EXTIRPATE DELE STUB ERASE EXPEL STAMP STOCK EXCISE EXTIRP UPROOT DESTROY EXSCIND OUTROOT SUPPLANT
EXTIRPATION ROOTAGE EXCISION
EXTOL CRY FETE HYMN LAUD BLESS CRACK EXALT KUDOS ROOSE SPEAK EXTOLL PRAISE ADVANCE APPLAUD COLLAUD COMMEND ELEVATE ENHANCE GLORIFY RESOUND UPRAISE EMBLAZON EULOGIZE
EXTOLMENT PRECONY
EXTORT PEEL PILL BRIBE EDUCE EXACT FORCE PINCH WREST WRING COMPEL ELICIT SPONGE STRAIN WRENCH WRITHE EXTRACT OUTWREST
EXTORTION CHOUT GOUGE EXTORT HOLDUP SCOTAL BRIBERY PILLAGE CHANTAGE EXACTION RAPACITY
EXTORTIONATE HARD CRIMINAL GRINDING
EXTORTIONER BRIBER POLLER SHAVER VAMPIRE
EXTORTIONIST POLLER
EXTRA ODD MORE ORRA OVER PLUS ADDED SPARE SPECIAL SURPLUS SUPERIOR
EXTRACT DIG PRY CITE DRAW KINO KOLA PULL SOAK ANIMA BLEED CUTCH DRAFT EDUCE ELUTE EXACT KUTCH KYPOO QUOTE RENES RUSOT SCRAP STEEP WRING CORTIN CURARE DECOCT DEDUCE DERIVE DEWTRY DISTIL ELICIT ELIXIR EVULSE EXTORT GOBBET GUACIN MULIUM OVARIN REMOVE RENDER RUSWUT TRIPOS UZARON ABORTIN AMALTAS ARCANUM CATECHU DESCENT DISTILL DRAUGHT ERGOTIN ESSENCE ESTREAT EXCERPT EXHAUST FUMARIA INTRAIT LIMBECK MONESIA PASSEWA SUMMARY VANILLA ACETRACT AMBRETTE GINGERIN HYPERNIC INFUSION LICORICE PERICOPE SEPARATE TIKITIKI

TINCTURE WITHDRAW
(— **BY BOILING**) DECOCT ELIXATE
(— **BY DIGGING**) GRUB
(— **FORCIBLY**) EVULSE
(— **FROM ACACIA**) KATH CASHOO CATECHU
(— **FROM BERBERIS**) RUSOT RUSWUT
(— **OF GINGER**) JAKE JAKEY
(— **ORE**) STOPE
(**TANNING** —) AMALTAS
EXTRACTION KIN BIRTH STOCK ORIGIN DESCENT EDITION ESSENCE EXTRACT EXTREAT BREEDING TINCTURE
(— **OF ROOTS**) EVOLUTION
(— **OF STEAM**) BLEEDING
EXTRACTIVE AGAR BANG BHANG AMAROID CARAGEEN
EXTRADITE BANISH
EXTRANEOUS OUTER EXOTIC FOREIGN OUTLYING SPURIOUS
EXTRAORDINARILY BYOUS
EXTRAORDINARY ODD FREM ONCO RARE BYOUS ENORM SMASH DAMNED EXEMPT MIGHTY RAGING SIGNAL CORKING CURIOUS HUMMING NOTABLE SPECIAL STRANGE UNUSUAL ABNORMAL EXIMIOUS FORINSEC SINGULAR SMASHING UNCOMMON
EXTRARETINAL PAROPTIC
EXTRAVAGANCE FRILL PRIDE WASTE LUXURY EXPENSE RAMPANCY SQUANDER UNTHRIFT WILDNESS
(**MENTAL** —) MADNESS
EXTRAVAGANT MAD HIGH WILD FANCY FISHY FOLLE LARGE OUTRE COSTLY GOTHIC HEROIC LAVISH SHRILL WANTON BAROQUE BIZARRE COSTLEW FANATIC FLAMING FURIOUS NIMIOUS PROFUSE RAMPANT VAGRANT INSOLENT PRODIGAL RECKLESS ROMANTIC UNTHRIFT WANDERER WASTEFUL
EXTRAVAGANTLY LARGE
EXTRAVAGATION VIBEX
EXTRAVASATION EFFUSION
EXTREME BLUE DEEP DIRE HIGH LAST RANK SORE VILE ACUTE BLACK CLOSE CRUEL DENSE DIZZY FINAL GREAT LIMIT PITCH STEEP ULTRA UNDUE UTTER ARDENT ARRANT BRAZEN DEADLY FIERCE HEROIC LENGTH MORTAL SAVAGE SEVERE STRONG UTMOST WOUNDY DRASTIC FEARFUL FORWARD FRANTIC HOWLING INTENSE OUTWARD PROFUSE RADICAL SURFEIT VIOLENT ALMIGHTY DEVILISH DREADFUL EGYPTIAN ENORMOUS FABULOUS FARTHEST GREATEST MERCIFUL SPENDFUL TERRIBLE TERRIFIC ULTIMATE EXQUISITE
(**NOT** —) SWEET
(**PL.**) PASO
EXTREMELY SO BIG DOG TOO WAY

BONE DEAD EVER FULL MAIN RANK
SELI THAT UNCO VERY AWFUL
BLACK BULLY BYOUS CRAZY CRUEL
EXTRA HEAPS RIGHT SELLE SOWAN
SUPER BITTER DAMNED DEADLY
DEUCED HIGHLY MIGHTY NATION
POISON SORELY SURELY UNCOLY
APLENTY AWFULLY BOILING
CRUELLY EXTREME GALLOWS
HOPPING INNERLY SOPPING
STAVING ALMIGHTY ENORMOUS
MORTALLY PRECIOUS PROPERLY

EXTREMISM JACOBINISM

EXTREMIST JACOBIN RADICAL

EXTREMITY END TIP HEAD NEED
PUSH TAIL CLOSE LIMIT SHIFT
START VERGE BORDER FINGER
EXIGENT EXTREME ACROSTIC
ALTITUDE DISASTER JUNCTURE
OUTRANCE TERMINAL
  (— OF MOON) HORN
  (— OF TENDRIL) HOLDFAST
  (— OF TOOTH ROOT) APEX
  (REMOTEST —) CORNER

EXTRICATE FREE HELP CLEAR
LOOSE RESCUE SQUIRM OUTWIND
EXPEDITE LIBERATE UNTANGLE
  (— ONESELF) WANGLE

EXTRINSIC ALIEN EVERY FOREIGN
OUTWARD EXTERNAL OUTLYING

EXTROVERT SYNTONIC

EXTRUDE BEAR SPEW EJECT EXPEL
SHOOT PROJECT PROTRUDE

EXUBERANCE PRICE EXCESS
LUXURY PLENTY ABANDON
LAUGHTER OVERFLOW RAMPANCY

EXUBERANT BOUNCY FEISTY LAVISH
COPIOUS FERTILE GLOWING
PROFUSE RAMPANT EFFUSIVE

EXUDATE GUM SPEW SPUE MANNA
DIKAMALI GUAIACUM HONEYDEW
SARCOCOL

EXUDATION DIP GUM LAC SAP TAR

BALM COPAL PITCH RESIN ROSIN
SUDOR MASTIC SANIES GALIPOT
MOCHRAS SPEWING BLEEDING
EXUDENCE LAITANCE MOISTURE

EXUDE GUM DRIP EMIT OOZE REEK
SPEW BLEED STILL SWEAT EXTILL
STRAIN STREAM EXUDATE GUTTATE
SCREEVE SECRETE SWELTER
PERSPIRE

EXULT JOY CROW LEAP BOAST
GLOAT GLORY INSULT SPRING
REJOICE TRIUMPH

EXULTANT ELATED

EXULTATION JOY OVATION
RAPTURE

EXULTING EXULTANT JUBILANT

EYALET VILLAYET

EYAS NESTLING

EYE O EE HE ORB SPY DISC GAZE
GLIM LAMP LOOP MIEN OGLE SCAN
UVEA VIEW GLARE GLASS GLENE
NAVEL OPTIC SENSE SHANK SIGHT
TOISE WATCH BEHOLD COLLAR
EUCONE EYELET GOGGLE OCULAR
OCULUS OILLET PEEPER POPEYE
REGARD ROLLER SHINER STEMMA
VISION WINDOW WINKER BLINKER
EUCONIC EXOCONE EYEBALL
EYEHOLE OBSERVE OCELLUS
PIERCER PIGSNEY PINKANY PINKENY
SENSORY WITNESS LATCHING
NOISETTE OMMATEUM RECEPTOR
  (— AMOROUSLY) OGLE
  (— FORMED BY ROPE) TONGUE
  (— IN BIGHT) COLLAR
  (— IN EGYPTIAN SYMBOLISM) UTA
  (— OF BEAN) HILUM
  (— OF FRUIT) NOSE
  (— OF HINGE) GUDGEON
  (— OF INSECT) STEMMA
  (— OF RA) SEKHET
  (— SORENESS) LIPPITUDE
  (BLACK —) SHINER

  (EVIL —) DROCHUIL MALOCCHIO
  (METAL —) HONDA
  (PL.) EEN EES NIE YEN YES EYNE
LAMPS LIGHTS SEEING GOGGLES
KEEKERS GLAZIERS GLIMMERS

EYEBALL EYE BALL GLASS GLOBE
  (— MOVEMENT) VERGENCE

EYEBOLT SPRIG RINGBOLT
  (INTERLOCKING —S) SNIBEL

EYEBRIGHT EYEWORT EUPHRASY

EYEBROW BREE BROW EEBREE
WINBROW WRIGGLE

EYE-CATCHING BOLD

EYECUP EYEGLASS

EYEGLASS QUIZ NIPPER MONOCLE

EYEGLASSES GLIMS SPECS LENSES
GLASSES LORGNON NIPPERS
BIFOCALS

EYEHOLE EYELET EYEPIT

EYELASH BREE LASH CILIUM
WINKER EYEBREE
  (LOSS OF —S) MADAROSIS
  (PL.) CILIA EAVES

EYELET MAIL PINK OELET AGRAFE
OILLET POUNCE AGRAFFE CRINGLE
GROMMET PEEPHOLE

EYELID HAW LID BREE WINDOW
EYEBREE PALPEBRA
  (PL.) EAVES

EYEPIECE OCULAR EYEGLASS
  (— OF TELESCOPE) POWER

EYESHADE OPAQUE

EYESHOT RANGE REACH EYESIGHT

EYESIGHT VIEW LIGHT SIGHT

EYE SOCKET ORBIT

EYESORE DESIGHT

EYESPOT EYEDOT STIGMA EYEHOLE
OCELLUS EYEPOINT

EYESTALK STIPES

EYETOOTH CUSPID DOGTOOTH

EYEWASH COLLYRIE EYEWATER

EYOT AIT EIGHT ISLET

EYRE AIR ITER

F EF FF EFF FOX DIGAMMA FOXTROT
FABA VICIA
FABLE MYTH TALE FEIGN STORY
LEGEND TRIFLE FICTION PARABLE
POETIZE UNTRUTH ALLEGORY
APOLOGUE FABULATE FABULIZE
(— OF GOLD COAST) NANCY
(MORAL —) EMBLEM
FABRIC ACCA CORD DUCK GOLD
GROS HAIR HUCK IKAT SILK SUSI
TAPA TARS TUKE CHECK CREPE
DHOTI DOBBY DYNEL FANCY MOIRE
NINOW PRINT RUMAL SCRIM SPLIT
STUFF SUPER SURAH SURAT TABBY
TAMMY TARSE TERRY TEWKE
TWEED TWILL UNION VICHY VOILE
WEAVE AGARIC ALACHA BENGAL
BROCHE BYSSUS CAFFOY CARPET
COTTON CREPON CYPRUS DACRON
DAMASK DIAPER DOBBIE EPONGE
ESTRON FLEECE HARDEN LAPPET
LUSTER LUSTRE MARBLE MASHRU
MURREY POODLE SENNIT STRIPE
TAMINY TANJIB TARTAN TRICOT
TUSSAH VELURE VELVET WADMAL
WINCEY ZENANA ACETATE ALEPINE
ALLOVER BANDALA BANDING
BELTING BEWPERS BINDING
BUCKRAM CANILLE CHALLIS
CHEKMAK CHINON CYPRESS
DAMASSE DOESKIN DRABBET
EDIFICE ELASTIC EPINGLE FACONNE
FUSTIAN MIXTURE MORELLA
PAISLEY PLUMBET SAYETTE
SEGATHY SILESIA SUITING TABARET
TABINET TAFFETA TEXTILE TIFFANY
VESSETS AGABANEE BARRACAN
BOCASINE BOURETTE CAMELINE
CANNELLE CASEMENT CHAMBRAY
CRETONNE DUCHESSE HAIRLINE
HANDMADE HARATEEN JACQUARD
KNITTING LUSTRINE MATERIAL
MOLESKIN OSNABURG SHANTUNG
SHIRTING SICILIAN SKIRTING
SWANSKIN TAPESTRY TARLATAN
VALENCIA
**(— CONTAINING GOLD OR SILVER
THREAD)** ACCA TASH TASS
(— FOR STIFFENING) WIGAN
(— OF TWO OR MORE MATERIALS)
UNION
(— RESEMBLING TOWELING)
AGARIC
(— WITH INWOVEN SCENES) ARRAS
(ABSORBENT —) HUCK
(BROCADED —) LAME LAMPAS
(COARSE —) TAT CRASH HAIRE
DUFFEL RATINE STAMIN BAGGING
BOCKING DRABBET SACKING
STAMMEL DAGSWAIN
(CORDED —) REP DUCAPE POPLIN
OTTOMAN
(COTTON —) CREA DUCK JEAN
LENO LINO SUSI BAIZE BASIN DENIM
DRILL RUMAL SUPER SWISS VICHY
WIGAN BURRAH CALICO CANVAS
CATGUT CHILLO CHINTZ COUTIL
COVERT DIMITY MADRAS MUSLIN
PENANG SATEEN BLANKET BUSTIAN

CANTOON DAMASSE ETAMINE
FLANNEL GALATEA GINGHAM
HICKORY HOLLAND JACONET
PERCALE TICKING BUCKSKIN
COTELINE COUTILLE CRETONNE
DRILLING DUNGAREE INDIENNE
SHEETING
(DECORATED —) DIAMANTE
(DELICATE —) HUSI JUSI
(DURABLE —) SCRIM SERGE
(ELASTIC —) GORING ELASTIC
(EMBOSSED —) CLOKY CLOQUE
(EMBROIDERED —) BALDAQUIN
(FIGURED —) BROCADE BROCATEL
(FINE —) PIMA SILK SUSI LINEN
DIMITY MERINO MOHAIR PERCALE
(GAUZELIKE —) BAREGE GOSSAMER
(GLAZED —) CIRE
(GLOSSY —) SATIN GLORIA SATEEN
(GOAT'S-HAIR —) TIBET
(HEAVY —) GROS CRASH DENIM
DRILL BURLAP CATGUT FRIEZE
LINENE TOBINE WHITNEY
(JUTE —) BALINE BURLAP
(KNITTED —) SUEDE BOUCLE
JERSEY TRICOT CHIFFON
(LIGHTWEIGHT —) GLORIA BUNTING
DELAINE FORTISAN
(LINEN —) SINDON BEWPERS
BUCKRAM CAMBRIC DRABBET
HOLLAND CRETONNE
(MOTTLED —) CHINE
(MOURNING —) ALMA
(MUSLIN —) TANJIB
(OPENWORK —) LACE SKIPDENT
(ORNAMENTAL —) GIMP LACE
LAMPAS GALLOON
(PEBBLY-SURFACED —) ARMURE
(PILED —) TERRY KRIMMER
CHENILLE
(PRINTED —) BATIK CALICO
ALLOVER PERCALE TOURNAY
(RIBBED —) CORD GROS COTELE
FAILLE SOLEIL CORDUROY
MAROCAIN MOGADORE WHIPCORD
(ROUGH —) TERRY HOPSACK
HOMESPUN
(SATIN —) CAMLET ETOILE
(SHEER —) LAWN SHEER SWISS
DIMITY BATISTE SOUFFLE VALENCE
GOSSAMER
(SHORT-NAPPED —) RAS
(SILK —) ACCA ALMA FUGI FUJI
GROS IKAT MOFF ATLAS CARDE
PEKIN RAJAH RUMAL SATIN SHIKH
SURAH TIRAZ ARMORE BROCHE
CAMACA CHAPPE CREPON DIAPER
DUCAPE FAILLE KHAIKI MANTUA
SENDAL ALACHAH ALAMODE
BROCADE EPINGLE GROGRAM
SCHAPPE YESTING DUPPIONI
EOLIENNE IMPERIAL ORMUZINE
SHAGREEN SIAMOISE
(SOFT SILK —) KASHA BARATHEA
(SOFT-NAPPED —) PANNE DUVETYN
(STRIPED —) ABA STRIPE
BAYADERE MERALINE
(THIN —) CRISP GAUZE VOILE
PONGEE TAMISE HERNANI MARABOU

PERSIAN
(TWILLED —) SAY DENIM KASHA
SERGE SURAH COUTIL BOLIVIA
ESTAMIN FLANNEL ZANELLA
CAMELINE CASHMERE CORDUROY
DIAGONAL SHALLOON VENETIAN
(UNBLEACHED —) DRABBET
(UNGLAZED —) CRETONNE
(UPHOLSTERY —) FRIEZE BROCATEL
MOQUETTE
(VELVETY —) TRIPE DUVETYN
(WOOLEN —) REPP BAIZE DOILY
OSSET SERGE TWEED BUFFIN
BURNET COTTON DJERSA DUFFEL
FRISCA MANTLE MOREEN MOTLEY
PERPET SAXONY SHODDY STAMIN
TAMISE VICUNA WADMAL WITNEY
BATISTE BOCKING BOLIVIA CHEVIOT
CHEYNEY CRYSTAL DELAINE
DRUGGET FRISADO HEATHER
RATTEEN STAMMEL ALGERINE
BATSWING BURBERRY CASHMERE
CATALOON CHIVERET HARATEEN
LAMBSKIN PRUNELLA RATTINET
SHALLOON SHETLAND WOOLENET
ZIBELINE
(WORSTED —) TABBY COBURG
ESTAMIN ETAMINE SAGATHY
(WOVEN —) LENO TWEED TWILL
SOLBIL TISSUE GROGRAM TEXTURE
VALENCIA
FABRICATE COIN COOK FAKE FORM
MAKE MINT VAMP WARP BUILD
FORGE FRAME FRUMP WEAVE
DEVISE INVENT CONCOCT FASHION
IMAGINE PRODUCE CONTRIVE
(— CLOTH) DRAPE
(— PAPER) CONVERT
FABRICATION LIE WEB TRIFLE
CHIMERA FICTION FINGURE
FORGERY UNTRUTH BASKETRY
PRETENSE
(PL.) INVENTARY
FABRICATOR LIAR COINER FORGER
FABULIST LIAR AESOP FABLER
FABULOUS FEIGNED MYTHICAL
ROMANTIC
FACADE FACE FRONT FUCUS
FRONTAL FRONTLET
FACE JIB MAP MUG NEB PAN BIDE
CHIV CLAD COPE DARE DEFY DIAL
GIZZ HEAD LEER LINE MASK MEET
MOUE MUNS PHIZ PUSS SIDE ABIDE
BEARD BRAVE BRICK BRUNT CASTE
CHECK CHEER COVER FACET FAVOR
FRONT GUARD INDEX REVET STAND
STONE VISOR VIZOR BRAZEN
FACADE FACIES KISSER MAZARD
MUZZLE OPPOSE PHIZOG VENEER
VISAGE COMMAND DIGLYPH
FASHION FEATURE GRIMACE
GRUNTLE PROPOSE RESPECT
REVERSE SURFACE UPRIGHT
CONFRONT ENVISAGE EXTRADOS
FEATURES FROGFACE FRONTAGE
FRONTIER PROSPECT SEMBLANT
(— DOWN) DEFACE
(— IN DEFIANCE) AFFRONT
(— OF ANIMAL) MASK

(— OF CUBE) SQUARE
(— OF CUTTING TOOL) BEZEL BEZIL
(— OF GLACIER) SNOUT
(— OF STUMP) SCARF SCARPH
(— ONE'S DANCING PARTNER) SET
(— TO FACE) AFRONT BEFORE
FACIAL DIRECTLY
(— WITH MARBLE) PIN
(— WITH STONE) BATCH
(CLOCK —) DIAL TABLE WATCH
(CURVED —) EXTRADOS INTRADOS
(DIE —) ACE
(FANTASTIC —) ANTIC
(HALF DOMINO —) END
(HAVING SHORT BROAD —)
LATERAL
(INNER —) CONCAVE
(MADE-UP —) MOP
(MINING —) BANK BREAST
FOREHEAD LONGWALL
(MOCKING —) MOE MOWE
(ROCK —) CLIFF
(UPPER —) BROW
(WRY —) MOUTH GRIMACE
FACE-ARBOR KNIFE
FACE GUARD FRONTAL
FACEMAN HAGGER WINNER
FACEPLATE FRONT DOGPLATE
FACER BUMPER DRIFTER TANKARD
FACET PANE STAR BEZEL CULET
PHASE COLLET STEMMA FACETTE
LOZENGE TEMPLET
FACETIAE CURIOSA
FACETIOUS FUNNY MERRY SMART
WITTY FACETE JOCOSE JOCULAR
HUMOROUS POLISHED
FACILE ABLE EASY QUICK READY
EXPERT FLUENT GENTLE AFFABLE
DUCTILE LENIENT
FACILITATE AID EASE HELP FAVOR
SPEED ASSIST GREASE EXPEDITE
FACILITY ART EASE FEEL HELP
ECLAT KNACK SKILL ADDRESS
COMMAND FREEDOM EASINESS
(PL.) ADDITIONS
FACING DADO HARL FRONT HARLE
LAPEL LINER PANEL SKIRT BEFORE
TOWARD VENEER AGAINST
FORNENT SURFACE BLACKING
CAMPSHOT CONFRONT COVERING
FACEWORK FORNENST OPPOSITE
PITCHING
(— AGAINST GLACIER) STOSS
(— AHEAD) FULL
(— APEX) ACROSCOPIC
(— AUDIENCE OBLIQUELY) EFFACE
(— EACH OTHER) AFFRONTE
AFFRONTY
(— INWARD) INTRORSE
(— OUTWARDS) EXTRORSE
FACSIMILE COPY MODEL REPLICA
AUTOTYPE
FACT CASE DEED FAIT DATUM EVENT
SOOTH TRUTH DONNEE EFFECT
FACTUM COMPERT FORMULA
GENERAL INDICIA KEYNOTE
LOWDOWN REALITY
(CONCLUSIVE —) CRUSHER
(DECISIVE —) CLINCHER

(FUNDAMENTAL —) KEYNOTE
(TRUE —S) STRENGTH
(PL.) DATA FEAT
FACTION BLOC NERI PART SECT
SIDE WING CABAL JUNTO PARTY
BRIGUE CLIQUE SCHISM BIANCHI
DISPUTE PINFOLD QUARREL
INTRIGUE SPLINTER
(PARTY —) STASIS
FACTITIOUS SHAM WHIPPED
KRITRIMA
FACTOR GEN DOER GENE ITEM
AGENT ALLEL CAUSE MAKER
ALLELE AUTHOR CENTER DETAIL
BAILIFF CONTROL COUCHER
CUSHION ELEMENT ENTROPY
FACTRIX ISOLATE STEWARD
ADHERENT AUMILDAR COFACTOR
DOMINANT EQUATION GOMASHTA
INCIDENT INCITANT
(—S IN EVOLUTION) ANTICHANCE
(CYTOPLASMIC —) KAPPA
(DECISIVE —) CAPSTONE
(ECOLOGICAL —) INFLUENT
(ENVIRONMENTAL —) GEOGEN
(HEREDITY —) GENE INSTINCT
(INTELLIGENCE —) G
(PERSONALITY —) SURGENCY
(RESTRICTIVE —) BARRIER
FACTORY HONG MILL SHOP PLANT
USINE AURANG AURUNG FABRIC
SUGARY CANNERY HATTERY
HOSIERY OFICINA SOAPERY
BUILDING COMPTOIR FABRIQUE
FILATURE OFFICINA STAMPERY
WORKSHOP
FACTOTUM COMPRADOR
FACTUAL HARD REAL TRUE ACTUAL
BEDROCK EARTHLY EMPIRIC
LITERAL
(INSUFFICIENTLY —) ABSTRACT
FACTUALLY INSOOTH
FACULTY ART WIT BOOM EASE GIFT
WILL FANCY SENSE BREATH BUDDHI
GIFTIE SEEING TALENT ABILITY
COLLEGE COUNSEL HABITUS
APTITUDE CAPACITY FELICITY
(— OF EXPRESSION) LANGUAGE
(CRITICAL —) JUDGMENT
(MENTAL —) HEADPIECE
(POETIC OR CREATIVE —) IDEALITY
PRINCIPLE
(REASONING —) DISCOURSE
(PL.) INDULTS
FAD BUG FIKE RAGE WHIM CRAZE
FANCU HOBBY FOIBLE CROCHET
FASHION WRINKLE
FADE DIE DIM DOW FLY WAN BRIT
CAST FATE FLAT GIVE PALE PEAK
PINE PINK VADE WELK WILK WILT
BLANK DAVER DECAY FLEET PASSE
PETER QUAIL SWING SWOON
DARKLE PERISH VANISH WITHER
DECLINE INSIPID LIGHTEN DIMINISH
DISCOLOR DISSOLVE EVANESCE
LANGUISH
(— AWAY) DOW BREAK FLEET
WALLOW

FADED PASSE SHABBY EXOLETE
SHOPWORN
FADGE FAY FIT SUIT
FADING FUGITIVE SWINGING
FAG FLAG JADE TIRE TOIL DROOP
WEARY DRUDGE HARASS MENIAL
EXHAUST FATIGUE FRAZZLE
FAGGED TASKIT
FAGGOT BROSNA CHUMPA FAGALD
FAGOT KID BUNT PILE PIMP FADGE
NICKY NITCH FAGGOT KNITCH
GARBAGE
FAIL GO CUT EBB ERR BANK BUST
CONK CALL FLAG FLOP FOLD LACK
LOSE MISS SINK SKEW SPIN WANE
APPAL BREAK BURST CRACK FAULT
FLUFF FLUKE FLUNK PETER QUAIL
SLAKE SPILL VAILE APPALL BETRAY
DEFAIL DEFECT DESERT FALTER
FIZZLE REPINE WINDER DECLINE
DEFAULT EXHAUST FALSIFY FLICKER
FLUMMOX FOUNDER MISFARE
MISGIVE SCANTLE LANGUISH
(— AT) FLUB
(— IN DUTY) LAPSE
(— IN EARLY STAGES) ABORT
(— IN HEALTH) SINK BREAK
(— IN STUDIES) BILGE
(— ON RIFLE RANGE) BOLO
(— TO GROW) MISS
FAILING BAD ILL BLOT FAULT
FOIBLE BLEMISH FAILURE FRAILTY
ABORTIVE WEAKNESS
FAILURE DUD BALK BUST FAIL FLOP
FLUB FOIL LACK LOSS MISS MUFF
TRIP BAULK BILGE CRASH DECAY
ERROR FAULT FLUKE FLUNK FROST
GRIEF GUILT LAPSE LEMON PLUCK
SMASH BRODIE FIASCO FIZZLE
STUMER STUMOR BLOOMER
CROPPER DEBACLE DECLINE
DEFAULT FLIVVER FLUMMOX
NEGLECT STUMBLE ABORTION
COLLAPSE DISASTER FAILANCE
FLOPEROO OMISSION
(— OF DAM) BLOW
(— OF FIREARM) STOPPAGE
(— OF MILK SECRETION) AGALAXY
AGALAXIA
(— OF MUSCLE) ACHALASIA
(— OF PAVEMENT) BLOWUP
(— OF PRIMER) HANGFIRE
(— OF VITALITY) DELIQUIUM
(— TO RAISE OAR) CRAB
(FLAT —) DUD
(RIDICULOUS —) FIASCO
FAIN FOND GLAD LIEF EAGER
PLEASED WILLING DESIROUS
INCLINED
FAINEANT IDLE LAZY
FAINT GO DIM WAN WAW COLD
CONK COOL DARK PALE PALL SOFT
THIN WEAK LIGHT QUEAL QUEER
SHADY SWELT SWOON TIMID WAUFF
WAUGH WERSH EVANID FEEBLE
REMISS SICKLY WAMBLY FEIGNED
FORGONE LANGUID OBSCURE
SWITHER SYNCOPE WEARISH
COWARDLY DELICATE LANGUISH

LISTLESS SLUGGISH TIMOROUS
(— FROM HEAT) SWELTER
(— FROM HUNGER) LEERY
(— OF SCENT) COLD WAUGH
FAINTHEARTED TIMID COWARD
CRAVEN COWARDLY UNHEARTY
FAINTHEARTEDNESS QUALM
FAINTING AFAINT SYNCOPE
DELIQUIUM
(— SPELL) DROW DWAM DWALM
FAINTLY DIMLY FAINT SMALL
FAINTNESS TENUITY GONENESS
WEAKNESS
FAINT-VOICED INWARD
FAIR GAY GEY MOP BEAU BELL
CALM EVEN FINE GAFF GALA GOOD
HEND JUST MART PLAY TIDE TIDY
BAZAR BLOND CLEAN CLEAR EQUAL
FERIA HENDE LARGE RIGHT ROUND
SHEER TRYST WHITE AONACH
BAZAAR BLONDE CANDID COMELY
DECENT DINKUM HONEST KERMIS
PRETTY SQUARE EXHIBIT JANNOCK
KERMESS STATUTE BOOKFAIR
DISTINCT FESTIVAL HORNFAIR
MIDDLING STRAIGHT UNBIASED
(— AND CALM) SETTLED
(— AND SQUARE) DINKUM
(HINDU —) MELA
(VILLAGE —) WALK
FAIRER SHIPWRIGHT
FAIRING SPAT SPINNER FAIRLING
FAIR-LEAD WAPP
FAIRLY WELL GAILY GAYLY GEYAN
EVENLY JUSTLY MEANLY HANDILY
PLAINLY RIGHTLY PROPERLY
SUITABLY
FAIRNESS FAIR CANDOR EQUITY
HONESTY JUSTICE EQUALITY
EVENNESS FAIRHEAD FAIRHOOD
FAIRWAY HOLE WATERWAY
FAIR-WEATHER SUNSHINE
FAIRY ELF FAY HOB IMP FAIN PERI
PIXY PUCK SHEE VILA OUPHE
PECHT PIXIE SIDHE WIGHT COURIL
FAERIE HATHOR KEWPIE SPIRIT
SPRITE YAKSHA YAKSHI ARGANTE
BANSHEE ORIANDA SHEOGUE
SYLPHID URGANDA FOLLETTO
MELUSINA
(IRISH —) SHEE SIDHE
(TRICKSY —) PUCK
(PL.) GENTRY
FAIRY BELL FOXGLOVE
FAIRYFOLK SHEE SIDHE
FAIRYLAND ANNWN ANNWFN
ELFLAND
FAITH DIN FAY FOY LAW LAY VAY
FACK FEGS SLAM TROW CERTY
CREED HAITH STOCK TOUCH TROTH
TRUST TRUTH BELIEF CERTIE
CREDIT GOSPEL FACKINS AFFIANCE
RELIANCE RELIGION
(BAD —) DUPLICITY
(RELIGIOUS —) SRADH SRADDHA
SHRADDHA
FAITHFUL FAST FEAL FIRM GOOD
JUST LEAL LIKE REAL TRIG TRUE
FALSE HEMAN LIEGE LOYAL PIOUS

SWEER TIGHT TREST TRIED ARDENT
ENTIRE FIDELE HONEST LAWFUL
PISTIC STANCH STEADY TRUSTY
DEVOTED SINCERE STAUNCH
ACCURATE CONSTANT RESOLUTE
SPEAKING
FAITHFULNESS HSIN FEALTY
VERITY LOYALTY FIDELITY
TRUENESS
FAITHLESS FALSE PUNIC FICKLE
HOLLOW UNJUST UNTRUE ATHEIST
APOSTATE DELUSIVE DISLOYAL
SHIFTING UNSTABLE
FAITHLESSNESS FALSITY PERFIDY
UNTRUTH
FAKE DUD DUFF FEKE HOAX HOKE
SHAM BOGUS CHEAT FALSE FEIGN
FLAKE FRAUD FUDGE PHONY
WANGLE DUFFING FALSIFY FURBISH
GUNDECK PRETEND SWINDLE
SIMULATE SPURIOUS
(— OF STOWED ROPE) FLEET
FAKER FAKIR QUACK HUMBUG
CAMELOT PEDDLER
FAKIR FAKIH FAQUIR DERVISH
FALCHION FALX
FALCON EYAS HAWK SORE BESRA
HOBBY SAKER STOOP GENTLE
JAGGER JUGGER LANNER LUGGAR
LUGGER MERLIN MUSKET PREYER
RAPTOR SHAHIN TERCEL KESTREL
SAKERET BERIGORA BOCKEREL
FALCONET PEREGRIN SOREHAWK
(— BOARD) HACK
(— IN FIRST YEAR) SORE
SOREHAWK
(FEMALE —) FORMAL FORMEL
LANNER
(MALE —) TASSEL TERCEL SAKERET
(SMALL —) HOBBY MERLIN KESTREL
(WHITE —) ICELANDER
FALCONER HAWKER OSTREGER
FALCONRY HAWKING
FALDSTOOL ORATORY
FALL GO EBB SAG SYE TIP BACK
BAND COME COUP DIVE DRIP DROP
DUNT FLOP HANG PICK PLOP RASH
RUIN RUSE SHED SILE SINK SLIP
SWAK SWAP SWAY SWOP TILT
WHAP WHOP ABATE CHUTE CLOIT
CRASH DROOP HANCE INCUR JABOT
LAPSE LIGHT LODGE PITCH PLUMB
PLUMP RAPID SAULT SHAKE SHOOT
SKITE SLIPE SLUMP SPILL SQUAB
SQUAT THROW TRACE TWINE
ALIGHT AUTUMN BRODIE DEVALL
DOUNCE DRYSNE FOOTER HAPPEN
HEADER JOUNCE PERISH PLUNGE
RECEDE SEASON SLOUGH STREEK
STRIKE TOPPLE TUMBLE CASCADE
CROPPER CROWNER DECLINE
DEGRADE DEPRESS DESCEND
DEVOLVE DRIBBLE ESCHEAT
ILLAPSE PLUMMET RELAPSE
RETREAT SQUELCH STUMBLE
SUBSIDE CATARACT COLLAPSE
COMMENCE DECREASE DOWNCOME
(— ABRUPTLY) DUMP
(— APART) BREAK SHIVER

COLLAPSE DISUNITE
(— AWAY) DEFECT
(— BACK) RECEDE RESORT
(— BEHIND) LAG
(— DIZZILY) SPIN
(— DOWN) CAVE FLOP SWAP SLUMP
REVERSE SWITHER
(— DUE) BEFALL
(— FAST) HOP
(— FLAT) PLAT FLIVVER
(— FORWARD) PECK PITCH
PROLAPSE
(— FROM A HORSE) PURL
(— FROM UNDERMINING) CALVE
(— FROM VIRTUE) LAPSE
(— GRADUALLY) EBB SAG
(— HEAVILY) DING LUMP SOSS
CLOIT CLYTE GULCH PLOUT PLUMP
SOUSE SWACK THROW
(— ILL) TRAIK
(— IN DROPS) DRIP STILL DRIBBLE
(— IN FLURRIES) SPIT
(— IN FOLDS) BLOUSE
(— IN RIVER) SAULT
(— IN WITH) INCUR
(— IN) CAVE FOUNDER
(— INTO ERROR) SLIP STUMBLE
(— INTO FAINT) DWAM DWALM
(— INTO RUIN) DECAY
(— INTO SLUMBER) DROWSE
(— INTO TRAP) DECOY
(— INTO WATER) DOP
(— INTO) STRIKE
(— OF DEW) SEREIN SERENE
(— OF RAIN) SKIFF SKIFT SHOWER
(— OF SNOW) SKIFF SKIFT ONCOME
SCOUTHER SNOWFALL
(— OF WICKETS) ROT
(— OFF) BATE SLIP SLACK
(— ON BACK) BACKER
(— ON SUCCESSIVE DAYS) CONCUR
(— ON THE NOSE) NOSER
(— OUT) LIGHT FORTUNE QUARREL
(— PRONE) GRABBLE
(— RAPIDLY) SKID
(— SHORT) DROP FAIL FAULT
(— SLOWLY) SETTLE
(— SUDDENLY) BOLT PLOP SLUMP
(— THROWING HORSE AND RIDER)
CRUMPLER
(— TO NOTHING) DISSOLVE
(— TO PIECES) BUCKLE CRUMBLE
(— UPON) WARP
(— VIOLENTLY) BEAT
(BAD —) BUSTER
(HEAVY —) PASH POUR SWAG
CLOIT GULCH SKELP SOUSE SQUAT
MUCKER
(INCOMPLETE WRESTLING —) FOIL
(SOFT —) SCLAFF
(SUDDEN —) HANCE SQUAT SQUASH
FALLACIOUS SLY WILY ABSURD
CRAFTY UNTRUE DELUSIVE
GUILEFUL ILLUSORY
FALLACY IDOL ERROR FALLAX
IDOLUM SOPHISM EQUIVOKE
ILLUSION
FALLEN DOWN FAUN FLAT SHED
LAPSED DECLASSE

(— IN) SUNKEN
FALLER GILL FLATHEAD
FALLFISH CHUB DACE CORPORAL
FALL HERRING TAILOR
FALLIBLE HUMAN ERRANT ERRABLE
FALLING SIT CADENT CAVING
PROLAPSE WINDFALL
(— BACK) ESCHEAT
(— DOWN) RUIN
(— INTO) INFALL
(— OF MINE ROOF) SIT
(— OF RAIN) SPIT
(— OFF) CADUCE LEEWAY
CADUCOUS
(— ON SOMETHING) INCIDENT
(— OUT) DIFFICULTY
(— SHORT) DEFICIT
FALLOPIAN TUBE TUBAL
FALLOVER OSTREGER
FALLOW LEA PALE HOBBY BARREN
VALEWE
FALLOW DEER DAMINE DAPPLE
FALLOWING ARDER
FALSE DEAD FAKE FLAM SHAM
BOGUS FAUSE LYING PASTE PHONY
WRONG FICKLE HOLLOW LUTHER
PSEUDO UNTRUE ASSUMED
BASTARD CROOKED FEIGNED
DISLOYAL ILLUSIVE RECREANT
SPECTRAL SPURIOUS
FALSE BEACHDROPS PINESAP
FALSE CRAWLEY PINEDROPS
FALSE FOXGLOVE FEVERWEED
FALSE HELLEBORE EARTHGALL
FALSEHOOD COG FIB LIE BUNG
CRAM FLAM TALE CRACK ERROR
FABLE STORY FALSET UNFACT
YANKER CRAMMER CRETISM
FALSAGE FALSERY FALSITY FIBBERY
FICTION LEASING PERFIDY
PHANTOM ROMANCE UNTRUTH
FALSHEDE ROORBACK STRAPPER
FALSE MERMAID FLOERKEA
LIMNANTH
FALSENESS SHAM
FALSE WINTERGREEN PYROLA
FALSEWORK CENTERING
FALSIES CHEATERS
FALSIFIER FALSER FORGER
FALSARY
FALSIFY LIE COOK FAKE WARP
ABUSE BELIE FEINT FORGE BETRAY
DOCTOR GUNDECK VIOLATE
EMBEZZLE
FALSITY LIE ERROR VANITY
UNTRUTH INVERITY
FALTER FAIL HALT PAUSE WAVER
BOGGLE FLINCH TOTTER FRIBBLE
STAMMER STUMBLE TREMBLE
HESITATE
FALTERING HINK HALTING
FALX FALCULA
FAME BAY CRY LOSE NAME STAR
WORD BRUIT ECLAT GLORY HONOR
KUDOS PRICE RUMOR VOICE
ESTEEM LAUREL RENOWN REPORT
REPUTE TONGUE HEARSAY
WORSHIP
(EVIL —) INFAMY

FAMED RIFE KNOWN NOTED
EMINENT RENOMEE RENOWNED
FAMILIAR FLY BAKA BOKO BOLD
COZY EASY FREE FULL HOMY TAME
TOSH CLOSE CONNU GREAT HOMEY
KNOWN PRIVY THICK USUAL
BEATEN CHUMMY COMMON ENTIRE
FOLKSY GERMAN HOMELY INWARD
KENNED STRAIT THRONG VERSED
AFFABLE FAMULAR FOLKSEY
POPULAR FREQUENT HABITUAL
INTIMATE SOCIABLE STANDARD
(— WITH) KNOWING
(MAKE —) POST
(PRESUMPTUOUSLY —) INSOLENT
FAMILIARITY HABIT FREEDOM
LIBERTY PRIVACY PRIVITY TRAFFIC
HABITUDE INTIMACY
FAMILIARIZE HAFT VERSE
ACCUSTOM ACQUAINT FREQUENT
FAMILIARLY HOMELY
FAMILY ILK KIN AIGA CLAN GING
KIND LINE NAME RACE TEAM TRIP
CINEL CLASS FLESH GOTRA GROUP
HOUSE MEINY STIRP STOCK CLETCH
FAIMLY PARAGE STEMMA STIRPS
STRAIN ZEGRIS DYNASTY KINDRED
LINEAGE ORLEANS PROGENY
CATEGORY FIRESIDE
(COSMOPOLITAN —) FELIDAE
FABACEAE
(FIRST —) FF
(LANGUAGE —) CHON BANTU CLICK
COCHE CUNAN KADAI STOCK
AIMARA ATALAN AYMARA CHOLON
GILIAK HUARPE LENCAN SERIAN
BOTOYAN CADDOAN CATIBAN
CHINOOK CHOLONA CHUMASH
COPEHAN ESSELAN KARTHLI
KARTVEL KERESAN SHASTAN
ATAKAPAN CHANGOAN
(LARGE —) QUIVERFUL
(ONE-PARAMETER —) PENCIL
(SUPER —) APINA APOIDEA
FAMINE LACK PINE WOLF DEARTH
HUNGER SCARCITY
FAMISH KILL STARVE DESTROY
ENFAMISH
FAMOUS MERE BREME FAMED
GRAND NOBLE NOTED FAMOSE
NAMELY EMINENT NAMABLE
NOTABLE RENOWNED
FAMULUS WAGNER SERVANT
FAN ONE RUN VAN BEAT BUFF COOL
WASH DELTA PUNKA WHIFF BASKET
BLOWER CHAMAR COLMAR FANNER
FLABEL FLIGHT PUNKAH ROOTER
SHOVEL SPREAD VENTOY WINNOW
ADMIRER DEVOTEE FLABRUM
FLYFLAP MPANGWE PAHOUIN
WHISKER EVENTAIL FOLLOWER
(— FOR BLOWER) WAFTER
(ALLUVIAL —) CONE APRON DELTA
(FOOTBALL —) GRIDDER
(WINNOWING —) SAIL LIKNON
(PL.) FOLLOWING
FANALOKA FOSSA FOUSSA
FANATIC MAD BIGOT CRAZY FIEND
RABID ULTRA ZEALOT DEVOTEE

FURIOSO PHANTIC PULAHAN
PULIJAN BABAYLAN FRENETIC
FANATICAL RABID ULTRA EXTREME
FURIOUS
FANCIED UNREAL DREAMED
AFFECTED
FANCIFUL ODD IDEAL QUEER VIEWY
DREAMY QUAINT UNREAL BIZARRE
FANCIED LAPUTAN STRANGE
WHIMSIC FANCICAL FILIGREE
ROMANTIC
FANCY BEE FAD GIG IDEA ITEM LIKE
LOVE MAZE TROW WEEN WHIM
BRAID BRAIN DREAM FREAK GUESS
HUMOR SHINE AFFECT BEGUIN
FIGURE FLOSSY IDEATE LIKING
MEGRIM NOTION ORNATE SHINDY
VAGARY VISION WHIMSY CAPRICE
CHIMERA CONCEIT CONCEPT
CROCHET FANCIED FANCIFY
FANTASY PROPOSE ROMANCE
SUSPECT WRINKLE CHIMAERA
CONCEIVE CROTCHET DAYDREAM
ILLUSION PHANTASM PHANTASY
(FOOLISH —) CHIMERA CHIMAERA
(PASSING —) FIKE
(PERVERSE —) CROTCHET
(WILD —) TOY MAZE
(PL.) DREAMERY
FANDANGO MURCIANA
FANE FLAG BANNER FANACLE
FANFARE TUSCH HOORAY HURRAH
TUCKET TANTARA FANFARON
FLOURISH
FANFARONADE BLUSTER FANFARE
SWAGGER BOASTING
FANFLOWER TACCADA
FANG FAN EARN FALX TAKE TANG
TUSK VANG BEGIN PRONG SEIZE
SNARE TOOTH ASSUME OBTAIN
PANGWE CAPTURE PAHOUIN
PROCURE
FANON CAPE ORALE PHANO FANNEL
MANIPLE
FAN PALM YARAY ERYTHEA
FANTREE TALIPOT
FAN-SHAPED ALARY
FANTAIL COMET SHAKER WAGTAIL
FAN-TAN PARLIAMENT
FANTASIA FANTASY QUODLIBET
FANTASTIC ODD ANTIC LUCIO
QUEER ABSURD GOTHIC ROCOCO
TOYISH UNREAL ANTICAL BIZARRE
WHIMSIC FANCIFUL FREAKISH
ROMANTIC SINGULAR
(— PERSON) KICKSHAW
FANTASY IDEA DREAM FANCY
DESIRE VISION CAPRICE CHIMERA
PHANTOM ROMANCE CHIMAERA
PHANTASM PHANTASY
FAR AWAY LONG MUCH ROOM SIDE
WELL WIDE CLEAN SIZES WIDEN
REMOTE DISTANT FARAWAY
ROOMWARD
(— AND AWAY) STREETS
(— OFF) OUTBYE
(— ON) ADVANCED
FARCE MIME DROLL EXODE FORCE
STUFF COMEDY GARLIC SOTTLE

EXODIUM MOCKERY TEMACHA
DROLLERY FARCETTA
(RELATING TO —) ATELLAN
FARCEUR WAG JOKER FORCER
FARCICAL BUFFO COMIC DROLL
ATELLAN
FARCTATE STUFFED
FARCY FARCIN EQUINIA FASHION
FARE DO GO EAT TRY COME DIET
FEND FOOD PATH RATE TIME WEND
CHEER CHEFE CHIVE FRAME GOING
LIGHT PRICE SPEED TABLE TOKEN
TRACK VIAND COMMON FARING
FETTLE HAPPEN TRAVEL CARFARE
JOURNEY PASSAGE PROCEED
PROSPER WAFTAGE WAYFARE
FERRYAGE PROGRESS
(— FOR FERRY) NAULUM FERRYAGE
(— WELL) SPEED
(COARSE —) HAWEBAKE
FAREWELL AVE VALE ADIEU ADIOS
ALOHA CONGE FINAL LEAVE
CHEERO BONALLY CHEERIO
GOODBYE LEAVING PARTING
FARFETCHED FARFET FORCED
DEVIOUS STRAINED EXQUISITE
FAR-FLUNG EXTENDED
FARINA MEAL FLOUR FARINE
POLLEN STARCH
FARKLEBERRY BLUET
FARL PARLY FARREL
FARM FEU CROP TACK TILL TORP
TOWN WALK CROFT DAIRY EMPTY
FIRMA HARAS MAINS MILPA PLACE
RANCH RANGE STEAD BARTON
BOWERY CHACRA ESTATE FURROW
GRANGE RANCHO TYDDEN TYDDYN
CLEANSE HENNERY KOLKHOZ
MAILING POTRERO POULTRY
SOVKHOS VACCARY ESTANCIA
HACIENDA HATCHERY LABORING
LOCATION STEADING TOWNSHIP
(— OUT) DIMIT ARRENT
(COLLECTIVE —) KIBBUTZ KOLKHOZ
(COMMUNAL —) KVUTZA KVUTZAH
(DAIRY —) WICK
(LARGE —) RANCH BARTON
(RENTED —) MAILING
(SMALL —) CHACRA
(STOCK —) ESTANCIA
(STUD —) STUD HARAS
FARMER HOB CARL FARM HOBB
KHOT KYLE RYOT TATE AILLT AUMIL
BOWER CARLE CEILE CLOWN
COLON HODGE KISAN COCKIE
GROWER HOGMAN JIBARO TILLER
YEOMAN BUCOLIC BUSHMAN
BYWONER COTTIER CROFTER
GRANGER HAYSEED HUSBAND
LANDMAN PLANTER PLOWMAN
RANCHER SCULLOG TILLMAN
TRUCKER COCKATOO PRODUCER
PUBLICAN RURALIST SELECTOR
(AUSTRALIAN —) SELECTOR
(NORWEGIAN —) BONDER
(POOR —) PIKE
(PROSPEROUS —) KULAK
(SMALL —) BOOR
(TENANT —) AILLT GEBUR SIRDAR

COLONUS SHAREMAN
FARMHAND HAND HELP
FARMHOLD CROFT
FARMHOUSE FARM TOWN ONSET
GRANGE QUINTA CASERIO ONSTEAD
STEADING
FARMING SOIL FARMERY
HUSBANDRY
(— SYSTEM) METAYAGE
FARMLAND ACREAGE
FARMSTEAD TOWN WICK STEAD
FARMERY
FARMYARD WERF CLOSE BARTON
RICKYARD
FARO MONTE STUSS TIGER
PHARAOH
(— CARD) SODA
FARO BANK TIGER
FAR-OFF DISTANT
FAR-REACHING GREAT FARGOING
FARRIER SHOER SMITH MARSHAL
FARROW PIG ROW RAKE DRAPE
LITTER
FARSIGHTED SHREWD SIGHTY
FARTHER YOND AHEAD STILL
LONGER FURTHER REMOTER
THITHER
FARTHEST ULTIMA ENDMOST
EXTREME FARMOST LONGEST
OUTMOST DOWNMOST FURTHEST
REMOTEST ULTIMATE
FARTHING RAG GRIG JACK QUAD
FADGE FERLING QUARTER
QUADRANS QUADRANT
(HALF —) CUE
(THREE —S) GILL
FARTHINGALE FERDEGEW
VERTUGAL
FASCIA BAND SASH FACIA FILLET
BANDAGE MOLDING LIGATURE
FASCICLE BUNDLE PHALANGE
FASCICULUS HEFT BUNDLE COLUMN
TRACTUS
FASCINATE DARE CHARM SEIZE
WITCH ALLURE ENAMOR ATTRACT
BEWITCH ENCHANT ENGROSS
GLAMOUR PHILTER PHILTRE
ENSORCEL ENTRANCE INTEREST
INTRIGUE SIRENIZE
FASCINATED BESOTTED
FASCINATING NUTTY SIRENIC
CHARMING FETCHING MESMERIC
FASCINATION CHARM SPELL
WITCHERY
FASCINE FAGOT FAGGOT SAUCISSE
FASCIOLA DISTOMA DISTOMUM
FASCIOLE SEMITA
FASCIST BLACK FASCISTA
FASHION GO CRY CUT FAD LAT TON
WAY CHIC FEAT FORM GARB GATE
KICK MAKE MODE MOLD RAGE RATE
SORT TURN TWIG WEAR WISE BUILD
CRAZE FEIGN FORGE FRAME GUISE
MODEL MOULD SHAPE STYLE
VOGUE WEAVE ASSIZE BUSTLE
CAMBER CREATE CUSTOM DESIGN
FANGLE INVENT MANNER METHOD
ALAMODE COMPOSE IMAGERY
PORTRAY QUALITY CONTRIVE

(LATEST —) KICK
(PREVAILING —) CRY
(SPECIAL —) TOUCH
FASHIONABLE CHIC PINK DASHY
DOGGY DOSSY SMART SWELL
SWISH VOGUE GIGOLO JAUNTY
MODISH TIMISH TONISH DASHING
GALLANT GENTEEL STYLISH
SWAGGER
(NOT —) DEMODE
FASHIONABLY SMARTLY
FASHIONED HUED CARVED SHAPED
WROUGHT FEATURED
FASHIONING FINGENT
FASHION PLATE SWELL
FASSAITE PYRGOM
FAST HOT HUT COLD FIRM HARD
LENT SOON SURE WIDE AGILE
APACE BRISK CHEAP FIXED FLASH
FLEET HASTY QUICK RAPID ROUND
SADLY STUCK SWIFT TIGHT TOSTO
CARENE ESTHER FASTLY LIVELY
SECURE SPEEDY SPORTY STABLE
STARVE ABIDING EXPRESS
HOTSHOT HURRIED PROVISO
RASPING SETTLED SIKERLY STATION
TAANITH ENDURING FAITHFUL
SPINNING SPORTING WIKIWIKI
(— DAY) ASHURA
FAST-DYED INGRAIN
FASTEN BAR DOG FAY FIX GAD GIB
KEY LAG PEN PIN SEW TAG TIE YOT
BELT BEND BIND BOLT BRAD CLIP
FRET GIRD GIRT GLUE GRIP HANG
HANK HASP HOOK HOOP HORN KILT
KNIT KNOT LACE LASH LINK LOCK
MOOR NAIL ROPE SEAL SNIB SOUD
SPAN SPAR STAY WELD WIRE AFFIX
ANNEX BELAY BIGHT BRACE CABLE
CATCH CHAIN CINCH CLAMP CLASP
CLING COPSE DEFIX GIRTH HALSH
HITCH INFIX LATCH PASTE RIVET
SCREW SEIZE SLOUR SNECK STEEK
STICK STRAP TRUSS WITHE
ANCHOR ATTACH BATTEN BUCKLE
BUTTON CEMENT CLINCH COTTER
COUPLE ENGAGE ENTAIL FATHER
GARTER HAMPER HANKLE INKNOT
PICKET SECURE SKEWER SOLDER
STAPLE STITCH STRAIN TETHER
BRACKET CONFINE CONNECT
EMBRACE GRAPPLE GROMMET
PADLOCK BARNACLE FORELOCK
INTERTIE OBLIGATE TRANSFIX
(— A SAIL) CROSS
(— ABOUT) THRAP
(— ANCHOR) SCOW
(— AS SPURS) SPEND
(— IN) EMBAR
(— TO) TAG
(— TOGETHER) COAPT SEIZE
SPLICE CONNECT
(— WINGS ON) IMP
(— WITH A GIRTH) WARRICK
(— WITH NOTCHES) GAIN
FASTENED FAST SHUT BOUND FIXED
BOUNDEN
FASTENER BAR GIB GIN NUT PIN
AGAL BOLT DOME FAST FROG HASP

LOCK NAIL SNAP TACK CATCH
CLAMP CLASP LATCH RIVET SCREW
SPIKE STRAP TATCH THONG
BUCKLE BUTTON HATPIN STAPLE
ZIPPER FIXATOR LATCHET PADLOCK
SNAPPER TENDRIL FASTNESS
STAYLACE
FASTENING TEE TIE FROG HASP
SEAL SNAP SNIB STAY TACK
BUCKLE CLINCH LACING MUZZLE
STRIKE TINGLE BINDING CLOSURE
LATCHET MOUSING PINNING SEIZING
FORELOCK KNITTING
(— **FOR HAWK'S WING**) BRAIL
(— **ON HARPOON IRON**) HITCH
(**HOOK AND LOOP** —) AGRAFE
AGRAFFE
(PL.) GRIPES
FASTIDIOUS FINE NICE CHARY
DONCY FEEST FUSSY NAISH NATTY
PAWKY CHOICE CHOICY CHOOSY
DAINTY DONSIE MOROSE PICKED
QUAINT QUEASY SPRUCE CHOOSEY
CURIOUS ELEGANT FINICAL FINICKY
HAUGHTY PICKING REFINED
TAFFETA TAFFETY CRITICAL
DELICATE EXACTING GINGERLY
OVERNICE PICKSOME PRECIOUS
SCORNFUL
(**NOT** —) GROSS
(**OVERLY** —) SAUCY
FASTIDIOUSNESS DAINTY NICETY
DELICACY
FASTING RAMADAN
FAST-MOVING SUDDEN
FASTNESS FORT CASTLE CITADEL
RETREAT FORTRESS
FAST-WORKING HOTSHOT
FAT GHI OIL TUB FOZY GHEE LARD
LIPA MORT RICH SAIM SUET ADEPS
BROSY CETIN CHUFF COCUM ESTER
FLECK FLICK FOGGY GROSS JUICY
KEDGE KOKUM LARDY LIPID LIPIN
LUSTY OBESE PLUMP PODGY
PORKY PUDDY PUDGY PURSY
SAAME SPICK SQUAB STOUT SUMEN
THICK WASTY AXUNGE BLOWSY
CHOATY CHUBBY CHUFFY DEGRAS
FATTED FINISH FLESHY GREASE
LIPIDE PLUFFY PORTLY PUBBLE
PUNCHY PYKNIC ROTUND STOCKY
STUFFY TALLOW UCUUBA ADIPOSE
BLOATED BLUBBER CEROTIN
FATNESS FERTILE FLESHLY
FULSOME LANOLIN OPULENT
PINGUID PURSIVE REPLETE STEARIN
EXTENDED FRUITFUL MARROWED
MURUMURU UNCTUOUS
(— **AROUND WHALE'S NECK**) KENT
(— **MEAT**) SPECK
(— **OF HIPPOPOTAMUS**) SPECK
(— **PERSON**) SQUAB
(**ANIMAL** —) GLOR SAIM SUET
ADEPS GLORE GREASE TALLOW
(**FLOATING** —) FLOT
(**LARD** —) FLARE FLECK FLICK
(**LUMP OF** —) KEECH
(**NATURAL** —) ESTER
(**POULTRY** —) SCHMALZ SCHMALTZ

(**SOLID** —) LARD KIKUEL STEARIN
FATAL FEY DIRE MORT FERAL VITAL
DEADLY DISMAL DOOMED FUNEST
LETHAL MORTAL CAPITAL DEATHLY
EXITIAL FATEFUL KILLING OMINOUS
RUINOUS UNSONSY BASILISK
DESTINED EXITIOUS FUNESTAL
MORTIFIC
FATALITY DOOM ACCIDENT
CALAMITY DISASTER
FAT-BELLIED GUTTY
FATE DIE END KER LOT CAST DOLE
DOOM EURE NORN RUIN SORT STAR
CAVEL EVENT GRACE KARMA MOIRA
MORTA WEIRD WHATE WRITE
ANANKE CHANCE KISMET DESTINY
FORTUNE OUTCOME PORTION
DOWNFALL FATALITY
(**INEXORABLE** —) HEAVEN
(**ONE OF** —S) NONA PARCA CLOTHO
DECUMA ATROPOS LACHESIS
FATED DUE FEY FATAL DOOMED
DECREED DESTINED
FATEFUL FATAL FATED DEADLY
DOOMFUL OMINOUS DOOMLIKE
FATHEAD REDFISH
FATHEADED FOZY
FATHEADEDNESS FOZINESS
FATHER BU DA PA ABU AMA DAD
POP TAT ABBA ABOU AMBA ANBA
ATEF BABA BAPU DADA PAPA PERE
SIRE ADOPT BABBO BEGET DADDY
FRIAR PADRE PATER VADER
PARENT PRIEST SUBORN ELKANAH
GENITOR TATINEK BEAUPERE
GENERATE GOVERNOR
(**CHURCH** —) APOLOGIST
(**SEMIDIVINE** —) PITRI
(**SIDE OF** —) AGNATE
(PL.) PP
FATHERLAND KITH HOMELAND
FATHER-LASHER GUNDIE SCULPIN
BULLHEAD LORICATE
FATHERLESS ORBATE SIRELESS
FATHOM BRACE BRASS DELVE
FADME PLUMB SOLVE SOUND
TOUCH BOTTOM MEASURE
PLUMMET
FATIGUE FAG HAG TEU BEAT COOK
JADE TASH TIRE TRAY SPEND
STALL TARRY THRIE TRAIK TRASH
WEARY HARASS OVERDO TAIGLE
TUCKER EXHAUST FATIGATE
VEXATION
FATIGUED BEAT GONE JADED TIRED
WEARY TASKIT OUTWORN WEARIED
FATIGATE HARASSED TUCKERED
FATIGUING HARD IRKSOME
FATLIKE LIPOID
FATNESS BLOOM GREASE
FATTEN FAT BEEF LARD SOIL
BRAWN FARCE FLESH FRANK PROVE
SMEAR STALL BATTEN ENRICH
FINISH TALLOW THRIVE PINGUEFY
SAGINATE
FATTENING FRANK BATTEL
BATTABLE
FATTY SUETY BACONY GREASY
ADIPOSE ADIPOUS FATLIKE PINGUID

SEBIFIC LIPAROID LIPAROUS
UNCTUOUS
FATUOUS DOPY DOPEY INANE SILLY
SIMPLE STUPID UNREAL FATUATE
FOOLISH IDIOTIC WITLESS
DEMENTED ILLUSORY IMBECILE
FAUCES JAWS
FAUCET BIB TAP BIBB COCK QUILL
SPOUT VALVE CUTOFF DOSSIL
DOZZLE OFFLET SPIGOT BIBCOCK
HYDRANT PETCOCK TURNCOCK
(**WOODEN** —) HORSE
FAUGH BAH FOH VAH
FAUJDAR PHOUSDAR
FAULT BUG RUB SIN CLAG COUP
DEBT FAIL FLAW FLUB HOLE LACK
LAST MOLE SAKE SLIP SPOT VICE
WANT WITE ABUSE AMISS BLAME
BREAK CULPA ERROR FLUFF GUILT
LAPSE SCAPE SHIFT SLIDE SWICK
TACHE BLOTCH DEFECT FOIBLE
RUNNER THRUST VICETY VITIUM
BLEMISH BLISTER BLUNDER
DEFAULT DEMERIT EYELAST FAILING
FAILURE FRAILTY MISTAKE NEGLECT
OFFENSE FAULTING PECCANCY
WEAKNESS
(— **IN BADMINTON**) SLING
(**MINING** —) COUP LEAP CHECK
HITCH
(PL.) FAULTAGE
FAULTFINDER MOMUS CARPER
CRITIC MOMIST CAPTION KNOCKER
NAGSTER
FAULTFINDING CARPING CAPTIOUS
CRITICAL
FAULTILY BADLY
FAULTLESS PURE CLEAN RIGHT
CORRECT PERFECT PRECISE
FLAWLESS
FAULTY BAD ILL SICK AMISS UNFIT
WRONG FLAWED FAULTED PECCANT
VICIOUS BLAMABLE CULPABLE
SPURIOUS
FAUN SATYR WOODMAN WOODWOSE
FAUNA FAUNULA FAUNULE ZOOLOGY
(**FOSSIL** —) BIOCHRON
FAUSSEBRAIE VAMURE VAUMURE
FAUX PAS GAFF SLIP BONER ERROR
GAFFE FLOATER MISSTEP MISTAKE
SNAPPER
FAVOR AID FOR ORE PRO BOON
ESTE FACE GREE HEAR HELP LIKE
MAKE BLESS BRIBE GRACE LEAVE
MENSK SERVE SPARE SPEED THANK
TREAT ASSIST ERRAND ESTEEM
FAVOUR LETTER NOTICE PENCEL
UPHOLD ADVANCE AGGRACE
ENFAVOR FEATURE FORWARD
GRATIFY INDULGE RESPECT
SUPPORT ADVOCACY BEFRIEND
COURTESY FAVORIZE GOODWILL
KINDNESS RESEMBLE SYMPATHY
FAVORABLE HOT BOON FAIR FREE
GOOD HIGH KIND ROSY TIDY CIVIL
CLEAR HAPPY LARGE MERRY TRINE
WHITE WILLY BENIGN DEXTER
GENIAL GOLDEN KINDLY TOWARD
BENEFIC EXALTED OPTIMAL

POPULAR PRESENT FRIENDLY
GRACIOUS PLEASING PROPENSE
SPEEDFUL TOWARDLY
(— TO PURCHASER) KEEN
(NOT —) INFAUST
FAVORABLY FAIR WELL HIGHLY
FAVORED WELL FAURD HAPPY
FAURED GIFTED BLESSED
FAVOURED
FAVORER FAUTOR FRIEND FAVORITE
FAVORING FAVONIAN
FAVORITE BOY PET POT PEAT
CHALK GREAT INGLE WHITE MINION
DARLING FANCIED MINIKIN POPULAR
SPECIAL GRACIOSO WHITEBOY
FAVORITISM BIAS FAVOR NEPOTISM
FAVUS WHITECOMB
FAWN COG BUCK CLAW DEER FAON
JOUK ROOT COWER CRAWL CREEP
GLOZE HONEY TOADY WHELP
CRINGE CROUCH GROVEL KOWTOW
SHRINK SLAVER ADULATE CROODLE
CRUDDLE FLATTER FLETHER
HANGDOG SERVILE SPANIEL
TOADEAT TRUCKLE WHEATEN
BOOTLICK
(— UPON) SUCK SMOOGE ADULATE
FAWNING SLEEK CRINGE GREASE
SLEEKY SURPLE FLETHER GLOZING
HANGDOG SERVILE SPANIEL
FLATTERY
FAWNSKIN NEBRIS
FAY ELF FEY FAIRY FEIGH
FAZE DAUNT FEEZE PHASE WORRY
FEALTY FEE FEWTE HOMAGE
LOYALTY SERVICE TREWAGE
FIDELITY
FEAR UG AWE DREE FLAY FUNK
WARD ALARM DOUBT DREAD JELLY
PANIC ALARUM DANGER DISMAY
FRIGHT HORROR PHOBIA TERROR
ANXIETY SUSPECT AFFRIGHT
DISQUIET DISTRUST EERINESS
MISDOUBT VENERATE
FEARFUL ARGH DIRE AWFUL PAVID
TIMID WINDY WROTH AFRAID
COWISH FRIGHTY GHASTLY
NERVOUS PANICKY WORRIED
CAUTIOUS DOUBTFUL DREADFUL
GREWSOME GRUESOME HORRIBLE
HORRIFIC SHOCKING SKITTISH
TERRIBLE TERRIFIC TIMOROUS
FEARLESS BOLD BRAVE DARING
HEROIC AWELESS IMPAVID INTREPID
FEASIBLE FIT LIKELY POSSIBLE
PROBABLE SUITABLE
FEAST (ALSO SEE FESTIVAL) EAT
FOY SUP DINE FARM FETE LUAU
MEAL TUCK UTAS AZYME CHEER
CHOES CITUA DIRGY FESTA FESTY
GAUDY REVEL TREAT ARTHEL
AVERIL DEVOUR DINNER DOUBLE
INFARE JUNKET MAUNDY REGALE
REPAST SIMPLE SMOUSE SPREAD
AHAAINA BANQUET BRIDALE
DELIGHT FESTINO GRATIFY
GREGORY LAMBALE LEMURIA
SHEVUOS SYNAXIS ANALEPSY
CAROUSAL DOMINEER EPIPHANY

FESTIVAL GESTNING GESTONIE
HANUKKAH KOIMESIS PASSOVER
POTLATCH SHABUOTH VESTALIA
(— BEFORE JOURNEY) FOY
(— OF BOOTHS) SUCCOS SUKKOTH
(— OF LANTERNS) HON
(— OF LOTS) PURIM
(— OF WEEKS) SHEVUOS
SHABUOTH
(— PLACE) IDGAH
(DRINKING —) BANQUET
(FUNERAL —) ARVAL ARVEL DIRGY
DIRGIE DREDGIE
(HARVEST —) BUSK
(JEWISH —) SENDAH
(RELIGIOUS —) CANAO KANYAW
(VILLAGE —) TANSY
FEASTER CONVIVE
FEASTING FEAST CARNIVAL
FEAT ACT KIP DEED FATE GEST
WORK GESTE SPLIT STUNT TRICK
CRADDY CUTOFF EXPLOIT MASTERY
MIRACLE WORSHIP DEXTROUS
(CRICKETER'S —) DOUBLE
(TUMBLING —) SCISSORS
(PL.) DAGS
FEATHER BOO PEN TAB DECK DOWN
FLAG HERL SETA STUB VANE
ADORN AXIAL PENNA PINNA PLUMA
PLUME QUILL REMEX CLOTHE
COVERT CRINET FLEDGE FLETCH
FLIGHT HACKLE MANUAL PINION
SARCEL SICKLE TIPPET TONGUE
AXILLAR BRISTLE FLEMISH IMPLUME
PRIMARY RECTRIX REMICLE STIPULE
TERTIAL TOPPING AXILLARY
SCAPULAR STREAMER TERTIARY
(BRISTLELIKE —) VIBRISSA
(HAWK'S —S) BRAIL BRAILS
(HORSE —) SPEAR
(NEW —) STIPULE
(OSTRICH TAIL —) BOO
(PINION —) SARCEL
(TAIL —) SICKLE RECTRIX
(YELLOW —S) HULU
(PL.) GIG BOOT CAPE DOWN FLUE
MAIL BRAIL CRISSUM CUSHION
FLIGHTS PLUMAGE REMIGES
SPURIAE
FEATHER BED TYE
FEATHER CLOAK AHUULA TEMIAK
FEATHERED FLEDGE FLEDGY
PENNATE PINNATE FLIGHTED
FEATHERING STOCKING
FEATHER KEY FIN STOP SPLINE
FEATHER
FEATHER-LEGGED COOTY COOTIE
FEATHERLIKE PINNATE
FEATHERY PLUMY FLEDGY FLUFFY
PLUMOSE PLUMEOUS
FEATLY NEATLY FOOTINGLY
FEATURE WAY FACE ITEM NOTE
STAR BREAK FAVOR GRACE MOTIF
TOKEN TRACT TRAIT TREAT ASPECT
CACHET FAVOUR SPLASH AMENITY
OUTLINE HALLMARK SALIENCE
(— OF WORD FORM) ASPECT
(ATTRACTIVE —) AMENITY
(DETERMINING —) LIMIT

(DISTINGUISHING —) TRAIT STROKE
HALLMARK
(FATAL —) BANE
(LINGUISTIC —) ISOGLOSS
SURVIVAL
(MAIN —) CRUX
(MOST COGENT —) BEAUTY
(OBJECTIONABLE —) DISCOUNT
DRAWBACK
(SALIENT —) MOTIF
(TOPOGRAPHIC —) ARC
(TOPOGRAPHIC —S) LIE
(PL.) LAY FACE CONTOUR FASHION
GEOLOGY
FEAZE FRAY FAIZE ROUGHEN
FEBRIFUGE PEREIRA
FEBRILE PYRETIC FEVERISH
FECES DRAST HOCKEY ORDURE
FECKLESS WEAK FEEBLE
FECULENCE DREG
FECULENT DREGGY
FECUND FERTILE FRUITFUL PROLIFIC
FED FAT MEATED
FEDERATION BUND CROM UNION
LEAGUE NATION COUNCIL ALLIANCE
FEDERACY TRIALISM
FEE FEU DUES DUTY FEAL FEUL FIEF
FIER HIRE RATE WAGE CAULP
EXTRA HANSE PRICE RIGHT ALNAGE
AMOBER BARONY CHARGE DASTUR
EMPLOY EXCISE REWARD SALARY
SHEKEL BUOYAGE DASTURI
DUMPAGE DUSTOOR FIRNAGE
FURNAGE GAOLAGE GARNISH
GRATIFY GUIDAGE HALLAGE
HOUSAGE JAILAGE MULTURE
PAYMENT PINLOCK PREFINE
STIPEND STORAGE TALLAGE
TRIBUTE VANTAGE BOOTHAGE
BOUNTITH CHUMMAGE EXACTION
FAREWELL GRATUITY MALIKANA
POUNDAGE REREFIEF RETAINER
SHIPPAGE WHARFAGE
(— TO LANDOWNER) TERRAGE
(— TO TEACHER) MINERVAL
(CUSTOMARY —) DASTUR
(CUSTOMS —) LOT
(ENTRANCE —) HANSA HANSE
INCOME
(INITIATION —) FOOTING
(PHYSICIAN'S —) SOSTRUM
(UNAUTHORIZED —) GARNISH
(PL.) EXHIBITS
FEEBLE WAN FLUE LAME MEAN PALE
POOR PUNY SOFT WEAK DONCY
DOTTY FAINT SEELY SILLY SOBER
UNORN WANKY WASHY WONKY
CADUKE DEBILE DONSIE DOTAGE
FAINTY FLABBY FLIMSY FOIBLE
INFIRM PAULIE PUISNE SCANTY
SEMMIT SICKLY SIMPLE TANGLE
UNFIRM WANKLE WEANLY DWAIBLY
DWEEBLE FRAGILE INVALID LANGUID
QUEECHY RICKETY SAPLESS SHILPIT
SLENDER SLIMPSY UNWIELD
UNWREST DECREPIT DROGHLIN
FEATLESS IMBECILE IMPOTENT
INFERIOR MALADIVE RESOLUTE
THEWLESS THOWLESS UNSTRONG

UNWIELDY WATERISH YIELDING
FEEBLE-MINDED ANILE DOTTY
DOTTLE FOOLISH MORONIC
WANTING IMBECILE
FEEBLENESS DOTAGE FEEBLE
POVERTY CADUCITY DEBILITY
WEAKNESS
FEED EAT HAY BAIT BEET BRAN
CROP DIET DINE FILL FOOD GLUT
GRUB MEAL MEAT OATS SATE
AGIST FLESH FLUSH GORGE GRASS
GRAZE NURSE SERVE STOKE TABLE
BROWSE FODDER FOSTER INFEED
NOODLE REFETE REPAST SUCKLE
SUPPLY BLOWOUT FURNISH
GRATIFY HERBAGE INDULGE
KEEPING NOURISH NURTURE
PASTURE PROVENT SATIATE
SATISFY SUBSIST SURFEIT SUSTAIN
VICTUAL
(— ABUNDANTLY) STOKE
(— ANIMAL) SORT SERVE
(— AT NIGHT) SUP
(— FOR CATTLE) FODDER STOVER
TACKLE
(— FORCIBLY) CRAM
(— GLUTTONOUSLY) BATTEN
(— GREEN FOOD TO CATTLE) SOIL
(— HIGH) FRANK
(— IN STUBBLE) SHACK
(— ON FLIES) SMUT
(— RAVENOUSLY) FRAUNCH
(— STOCK) FOG SOIL SOILING
(— TO REPLETION) ENGORGE
(— TO THE FULL) SATIATE
(— WELL) BATTLE
(GROUND —) CHOP
(POULTRY —) SCRATCH
(RED —) HAYSEED
(STOCK —) BRAN
(WHALE —) GRIT
FEEDBOARD DECK
FEEDER HOGGER HOPPER PECKER
STOCKER
(YARN —) CARRIER
FEEDHEAD RISER FEEDER SINKHEAD
FEEDING RELIEF FOLDAGE PANNAGE
(— GROUND FOR FISH) MEADOW
(— THROUGH TUBE) GAVAGE
(FREE-CHOICE —) CAFETERIA
FEEL FIND PALP GROPE SENSE
THINK TOUCH FIMBLE FINGER
HANDLE RESENT EXAMINE EXPLORE
FEELING SENSATE PERCEIVE
(— ACUTELY) SUFFER
(— AVERSION FOR) HATE LOATHE
(— CHILLY) CREEM
(— COMPASSION) PITY YEARN
(— DEJECTION) REPINE
(— FEAR) UG GRUE UGGE TREMBLE
(— GRIEF) GRIEVE DEPLORE
(— HAPPY OR BETTER) LIGHT
(— NAUSEA) WAMBLE
(— OF CLOTH) HAND
(— ONE'S WAY) GROPE FUMBLE
GRAMMEL
(— OUT) SOUND
(— PAIN) URN
(— REPUGNANCE) ABHOR

(— SHAME) BLUSH
(— WANT OF) MISS
FEELER DRAW KITE PALP SNIFF
PALPUS TACTOR ANTENNA SMELLER
PROPOSAL TENTACLE
FEELING FEEL PITY TACT VIEW
CHEER HEART HUMOR SENSE
SORGE TOUCH AFFECT CEMENT
MORALE CONSENT EMOTION
OPINION PASSION VELUNGE
ATTITUDE SENTIENT
(— ILL) HOWISH
(— MIRTH) JOCUND
(— OF ACCORD) SYMPATHY
(— OF AMUSEMENT) CHARGE
(— OF ANTIPATHY) ALLERGY
(— OF ANXIETY) ANGST
(— OF CONTEMPT) DISDAIN
(— OF DISGUST) UG
(— OF HORROR) CREEP CREEPS
(— OF HOSTILITY) ANIMUS
(— OF JOY) GLOAT
(— OF OPPOSITION) KICK
(— OF RESENTMENT) GRUDGE
(— OF ROMANCE) STARDUST
(— OF UNEASINESS) MALAISE
(— OF WEARINESS) ENNUI
(— OF WELL-BEING) EUPHORIA
(ANGERED —) DUDGEON
(BODILY —) TABET
(CONCEITED —) SWELLING
(ILL —) HARDNESS
(INTUITIVE —) HUNCH
(KINDLY —) GOODWILL
(REPRESSION OF —) STOICISM
(STRONG —) STAB
(PL.) HEART WITHERS
FEET DOGS TONGS STAMPS
WALKERS GUNBOATS TRILBIES
(— WASHING) MAUNDY
(BOARD —) FOOTAGE
(LARGE —) GUFFINS
FEIGN ACT FAKE MINT MOCK SEEM
SHAM VEYN AVOID FABLE FALSE
FORGE PAINT SHAPE SHIRK AFFECT
ASSUME GAMMON INVENT POSSUM
CONCEAL FALSIFY FASHION IMAGINE
POETIZE PRETEND ROMANCE
DISGUISE SIMULATE
(— ASSENT) COLLOGUE
(— IGNORANCE) CONNIVE
(— ILLNESS) MALINGER
FEIGNED SHAM FALSE FEINT POETIC
PSEUDO ASSUMED COLORED
FICTIVE FICTIOUS SIMULATE
FEIGNING FICTION FORGERY
FEIJOA ANDRE
FEINT FAKE MINT RUSE APPEL FAINT
SHIFT SPOOF TRICK FALSIFY
FEIGNED FEINTER FINCTURE
PRETENSE REVIRADO
FELDSPAR AMBITE GNEISS CELSIAN
SYENITE ANDESINE FELSPATH
SANIDINE
FELICIA AGATHAEA
FELICITATE HUG BLESS MACARIZE
FELICITOUS FIT HAPPY
FELICITOUSLY HAPPILY
FELICITY JOY BLISS SONSE HEAVEN

FELINE CATTISH
FELL CUR FEN HEW DOWN DROP
FALL HIDE HILL MOOR PELT RUIN
SKIN VERY CRUEL EAGER FIELD
GRASS GREAT SHARP DEADLY
FIERCE FLEECE INTENT MIGHTY
SAVAGE SHREWD TUMBLE BRUTISH
CRASHED DOUGHTY HIDEOUS
INHUMAN STRETCH TUMBLED
MOUNTAIN SPIRITED VIGOROUS
(— A TREE) HEW LODGE
FELLER GIDEON
FELLING FALL CUTTING
FELLOE BOD FELF FALLY
FELLOW S BO BOY COD DON EGG
FOX GUY JOE LAD MAC MAN MUN
NUT WAG WAT YOB BALL BEAN
BEAU BIRD BOZO BUFF CARL CHAL
CHAP COVE CUSS DEAN DICK DUCK
DULL GENT GILL GINK HIND HUSK
JACK JAKE JOHN LOON MATE NABS
PEER PRIG SNAP BILLY BIMBO
BLOKE BROCK BUDDY BULLY CARLE
CHIEL COVEY FRUIT GROOM GUEST
JOKER MATCH PARTY SCOUT SKATE
SLAVE SPORT SPRIG SWIPE
BEGGAR BILLIE BIRKIE BOHUNK
BOOGER BUDDIE BUFFER BUGGER
BUSTER CALLAN CHIELD CODGER
CUFFIN CUTTER FELLER FOOTER
FOUTER FOUTRA GALOOT GAZABO
HOMBRE JASPER JOCKEY JOHNNY
JOSSER KIPPER PERSON SHAVER
SINNER SIRRAH SISTER SOCIUS
TURNIP BASTARD BROTHER
CALLANT CHAPPIE COMRADE
CULLIES CULLION CUSTRON
KNOCKER PARTNER SCROYLE
SNOOZER BLIGHTER CONFRERE
DOTTEREL MERCHANT NEIGHBOR
SYNODITE
(AWKWARD —) OAF CLUB GAWK
CLOWN LOOBY GALOOT SLOUCH
(BASE —) CARL CARLE CULLION
(BASHFUL —) SHEEP
(BOLD —) HEARTY
(BRUTAL —) CLUBFIST
(CLOWNISH —) COOF BAYARD
LOBLOLLY
(CLUMSY —) FILE CAMEL FARMER
LUBBER
(COMMON —) JACK LOUT
(CONCEITED —) JEMMY DALTEEN
(CONTEMPTIBLE —) DOG SCUT
SMAIL SNAKE RABBIT SMATCH
PEASANT
(CONTENTIOUS —) SQUARER
(CORPULENT —) POMPION
(COUNTRY —) JAKE JASPER
(CRUDE —) STIFF
(DASHING —) BUCK BLADE
(DASTARDLY —) HOUND
(DESPICABLE —) FOUTER FOUTRA
HANGDOG SMATCHET
(DIRTY —) SCAB BROCK
(DISAGREEABLE —) GLEYDE
(DISSOLUTE —) RAKE ROUE
RAKEHELL
(DROLL —) CARD

(DROWSY —) LUNGIS
(DULL —) BUFF DRIP FOGY LUNGIS HUMDRUM
(FAT —) HIND GULCH GLUTTON
(FIERCE-LOOKING —) KILLBUCK
(FINE —) BAWCOCK
(FOOLISH —) SOP GABY GOFF ZANY GANDER JACKSON WIDGEON
(GOOD —) BRICK BULLY TRUMP HEARTY
(GOOD-FOR-NOTHING —) JACKEEN
(GREEDY —) SLOTE
(IDLE —) FANION FOOTER STOCAH LOLLARD SKULKER
(IGNORANT —) GOBBIN
(ILLBRED —) LARRIKIN
(IMPERTINENT —) JACK WHISK
(INSIGNIFICANT —) SQUIB
(JOLLY —) VAVASOR VAVASOUR
(LAZY —) BUM LUSK TOOL LENTO
(LOW —) RAG WAFF SWEEP LIMMER VARLET MECHANIC WHORESON
(MEAN —) CAD DOG BOOR BOUCH BUCKO CAVEL CHURL SCURF RASCAL CULLION COISTREL SNEAKSBY SPALPEEN STINKARD
(NIGGARDLY —) SNUDGE
(NOISY —) MOUTH
(OLD —) GLYDE GAFFER GEEZER
(OLD-FASHIONED —) FOGY
(OVERBEARING —) GRIMSIR
(PROSAIC —) PRUNE
(PUNY —) SMAIK
(QUARRELSOME —) HECTOR
(QUEER OLD —) GEEZER
(RESIDENTIAL —) DON
(ROGUISH —) DOG
(RUDE —) JACK ROUGH
(SHABBY —) SHAB SQUEEF
(SHEEPISH —) SUMPH
(SHIFTLESS —) PROG SHACK PROGGER
(SHREWD —) COLT
(SILLY —) TOT GUMP ZANY SHEEP SMAIK DOTTEREL MUSHHEAD
(SIMPLE —) DOODLE
(SLOVENLY —) SLUTE
(SLY —) FOX
(SNEAKING —) SNUDGE
(SORDID —) HUNKS
(SOUTH AFRICAN —) KEREL
(SPORTY —) PLAYBOY
(STRANGE —) CODGER
(STRAPPING —) SWANKY SWANKIE
(STUPID —) ASS CLOD COOF DAFF DOLT GUMP HASH MUFF SIMP BOOBY DUNCE MORON STIRK BAYARD FARMER FOOZLE GANDER DOWFART CODSHEAD SOCKHEAD
(SULLEN —) GLUMP
(TRICKISH —) HUMBUG
(TRICKY —) ROOK GREEK KNAVE SCAMP DODGER RASCAL
(UNCIVIL —) RUDESBY
(UNCOUTH —) JAKE KEMP TIKE
(VILE —) RAT SKUNK
(VULGAR —) TIGER
(WORTHLESS —) BUM CUR DOG HASH PROG WAFF JAVEL ROGUE

SCAMP SHOAT SNAKE BROTHEL BUDMASH PROGGER VAURIEN TARTARET
(WRETCHED —) DEVIL DOGBOLT
(YOUNG —) BILLY BUCKO CADIE CADDIE
FELLOWMAN BROTHER
FELLOWSHIP GUILD HAUNT UNION FAMILY COMPANY ALLIANCE SODALITY
(CHRISTIAN —) KOINONIA
FELLY RIM FELF FELLOE KEENLY CRUELLY BITTERLY FIERCELY SAVAGELY TERRIBLY
FELO-DE-SE SUICIDE
FELON WILD CRUEL FETLOW FIERCE WICKED CONVICT CULPRIT PANARIS VILLAIN WHITLOW PHLEGMON RUNROUND
FELONY ARSON CRIME OFFENSE
FELT JIG PLAIT FILTER SENSED SOLEIL VELOUR DOUBLER FELTING PANNOSE
(— INTENSIVELY) ACUTE
(— THROUGH SENSES) SENSATE
(DEEPLY —) CORDIAL INTENSE
(PERSONALLY —) CONSCIOUS
(PL.) CLOTHING
FELTWORK NEUROPIL
FEMALE DOE EWE HER SHE SOW DAME GIRL GYNE LADY MORT ADULT JENNY SMOCK SQUAW WOMAN WAHINE WEAKLY DISTAFF FEMINAL WOMANLY DAUGHTER FEMININE GYNAECIC LADYLIKE WOMANISH
(— ANCESTOR) TAPROOT
(IMPERFECT —) FREEMARTIN
(PARTHOGENETIC —) AMAZON
FEMININE FAIR SOFT WEAK WOMAN FEMALE TENDER WAHINE FEMINAL WOMANLY WOMANISH
FEMININITY MUSLIN FEMINITY
FEMME FATALE SIREN
FEMORAL CRURAL
FEMUR THIGH
FEN BOG CARR FAIN FELL FOWL MERE MOOR WASH BROAD FAINS MARSH SNIPE SWAMP VENTS MORASS QUAGMIRE
FENCE BAR HAW HAY BANK DIKE DUEL DYKE HAHA HAIN PALE PLAY RAIL STUB WALL WEIR WIRE BEARD DODGE FRITH GUARD HEDGE MOUND PALIS STICK STUMP DETENT FENDER GLANCE HURDLE LEADER PALING PICKET RADDLE RASPER SCHERM SCRIME TIMBER BARRIER BULWARK CYCLONE DEFENSE ENCLOSE FENCING FENSURE IMPALER PASSAGE RAILING SWAGMAN BACKSTOP ENCHASER ENCLOSER GRAFFAGE HOARDING PALISADE PALISADO SEPIMENT SKIRMISH
(— AROUND BULLRING) BARRERA
(— CLOSING DITCH) WOLF
(— OF LOCK) STUB
(— OF LOGS) GLANCE

(CATTLE —) WIPE SKERM SCHERM
(FISH —) WEIR LEADER
(METAL —) RAIL RAILING
FENCER DUELIST IMPALER PARRIER PROVOST SCRIMER SWORDER FOILSMAN BACKSWORD
FENCE RAIL DRAWBAR
FENCE SECTION PANE
FENCE-SITTER MUGWUMP
FENCING WIRE FENCE PALING ESCRIME PASSAGE SCIENCE SWORDING
FEND WARD PARRY SHIRK DEFEND FORBID RESIST SUPPORT
FENDER SKID WING CAMEL GUARD SKATE BUFFER BUMPER SHIELD DOLPHIN PUDDING BOWGRACE SPLASHER
(— FOR FIREPLACE) CURB KERB
(— NEAR HOLE) TELLTALE
FENDER SKID GLANCER
FENESTRA FORAMEN
FENGHUANG FUM PHOENIX
FENKS FRITTERS
FENMAN WEBFOOT
FENNEC ZERDA
FENNEL ANIS DILL HEMP SOYA FERULE FINKEL COWBANE HOGWEED SPINGEL FINOCHIO FLORENCE CAROSELLA
FENNER ZERDA
FENSTER WINDOW
FENUGREEK BAUMIER MELLILOT
(SEEDS OF —) HELBEH
FERAL WILD BRUTAL DEADLY FERINE SAVAGE BESTIAL UNTAMED FUNEREAL UNBROKEN
FER-DE-LANCE BONETAIL JARARACA
FERMATA HOLD PAUSE TENOR CORONA
FERMENT FRY LOB ZYM BARM FRET HEAT SOUR TURN WORK ZYME FEVER SWEAT YEAST DANDER ENZYME FLOWER FOMENT SEETHE SIMMER TUMULT UPROAR AGITATE QUICKEN TURMOIL DISORDER
FERMENTATION SWEAT CUVAGE FERMENT MOWBURN WORKING ZYMOSIS
FERMENTED SOD
(IMPROPERLY —) FOXY
FERMENTING WORKING
FERN HEII NITO PULU TARA WEKI BRAKE DUGAL EKAHA FROND NARDO PITAU PONGA ULUHI WHEKI AMAMAU DOODIA NARDOO OSMUND PTERIS ACROGEN ATERACH BOGFERN BRACKEN SYNANGE WOODSIA ADIANTUM ASPIDIUM BUCKHORN BUNGWALL CETERACH DAVALLIA DENDRITE FERNWORT FILICITE GOLDBACK HARDFERN KOLOKOLO MOONWORT MULEWORT PARAREKA PILLWORT POLYPODY SPOROGEN STAGHORN
FERN LEAF FROND CROSIER
FERNLIKE FERNY PTEROID
FEROCIOUS ILL FELL GRIM RUDE

WILD CRUEL FERAL BLOODY
BRUTAL FEROCE FIERCE GOTHIC
RAGING SAVAGE ACHARNE INHUMAN
OMINOUS VIOLENT WOLFISH
PITILESS RAVENOUS RUTHLESS
TARTARLY

FEROCITY FERITY SAVAGERY
VIOLENCE

FERRARA ANDREW

FERRET HOB MONK TAPE PADOU
MONACH WEASEL POLECAT
(— **OUT**) FOSSICK
(**FEMALE** —) GIL GILL JILL BITCH
(**MALE** —) HOB HOBB

FERRIAGE WAFTAGE

FERRIC OXIDE CROCUS

FERROTYPE GLAZE TINTYPE

FERROUS SIDEROUS

FERRULE CAP TIP CUFF RING SHOE
VIRL COLLET PULLEY RUNNER
VERREL VIROLE ARMGARN BUSHING
CRAMPET

FERRY FORD PASS PONT SCOW
PASSAGE TRAJECT TRANSFER

FERRYBOAT BAC PONT FERRY

FERRYMAN CHARON FERRIER
WATERMAN

FERTILE FAT GOOD RANK RICH
GLEBY BATFUL BATTLE FECUND
HEARTY STRONG TEEMING
ABUNDANT BATTABLE FRUITFUL
GENEROUS PREGNANT PROLIFIC
SPAWNING

FERTILITY HEART FATNESS
(**PATRON OF** —) YAKSHA

FERTILIZATION ENDOGAMY
POROGAMY

FERTILIZE FAT DUNG FISH LIME
MARL CHALK BATTEN ENRICH
FRUCTIFY

FERTILIZER FAT MARL GUANO
HUMUS ALINIT FLOATS MANURE
POLLEN POTASH CARRIER
COMPOTE KAINITE NITRATE
TANKAGE AMMONITE CINEREAL
NITROGEN

FERULA NARTHEX

FERULE ROD RULER COLLET FENNEL
FERULA PALMER

FERVENCY WARMTH CANDENCY

FERVENT HOT KEEN WARM EAGER
FIERY ARDENT BITTER FERVID
FIERCE INWARD RAGING SAVAGE
BOILING BURNING GLOWING
INTENSE PECTORAL VEHEMENT

FERVID HOT ARDENT TROPIC
BOILING BURNING FERVENT
GLOWING ZEALOUS UNCTUOUS
VEHEMENT

FERVOR FIRE HEAT RAGE SOUL
ZEAL ARDOR WARMTH PASSION
CANDENCY DEVOTION STRENGTH
VIOLENCE
(— **IN PRAYER**) KAVVANAH
KAWWANAH

FESCUE VESTER

FESS BAR BAND PERT DANCE HUMET

FESTAL GAY GALA GAUDY FESTIVE
FESTUAL FEASTFUL

FESTER ROT BEAL RANK SCAR
RANKLE PUSTULE PUTREFY

FESTERING FRETTY

FESTIVAL (ALSO SEE FEAST) ALE
BON PWE BUSK FAIR FEIS FETE
GALA HOLI MELA TIDE UTAS WAKE
DELIA FEAST FERIA FESTA GAUDY
HALOA PURIM REVEL ROUSE SEDAR
BAIRAM BRIDAL CARNEA DEWALI
DIASIA DIPALA FIESTA HOHLEE
HUFFLE KERMIS LAMMAS LENAEA
OPALIA PONGOL POOJAH SUCCOS
AGONIUM AGRANIA BANQUET
BELTANE DASAHRA EQUIRIA
FESTIAL HILARIA KERMESS MATSURI
SUKKOTH THIASOS TOXCATL
UPHELYA VINALIA AGRIONIA
AIANTEIA APATURIA ATHENAEA
BEALTINE BRUMALIA CARNIVAL
COTYTTIA DASAHARA DIIPOLIA
DIONYSIA DUSSERAH ENCAENIA
FASNACHT FLORALIA HANUKKAH
HIGHTIDE KALENDAE MARYMASS
MATRALIA MITHRIAC MUHARRAM
MUNYCHIA NATIVITY NEOMENIA
POTLATCH STAMPEDE
(**PL.**) MOED VOTA

FESTIVE GAY GALA JOLLY FESTAL
GENIAL JOYOUS FEASTLY HOLIDAY
JOCULAR CONVIVAL FEASTFUL
MIRTHFUL SPORTIVE

FESTIVITY GALA UTAS UTIS FEAST
MIRTH RANDY REVEL GAIETY
GAYETY SPLORE HOLIDAY JOLLITY
JOYANCE PATTERN FESTIVAL
FUNCTION

FESTOON SWAG WREATH GARLAND
DECORATE
(**PL.**) ENCARPUS

FETCH FET FESH GASP GIVE SHAG
TACK TAKE TEEM WAIN BRING
SWEEP TRICK DOUBLE STROKE
WRAITH ACHIEVE ATTRACT ARTIFICE
FETCHING INTEREST

FETCHED FOSH

FETCHING SWEET CRAFTY CUNNING
ALLURING PLEASING SCHEMING

FETE FAIR GALA FEAST HONOR
BAZAAR FIESTA HOLIDAY

FETID OLID RANK MUSTY PUTID
ROTTEN VIROSE NOISOME

FETIDLY FOULLY

FETISH OBI IDOL JUJU OBIA ZEME
ZEMI ZOGO ANITO ASCON CHARM
GUACA HUACA OBEAH OBIAH
TOTEM FETICH GRIGRI NAGUAL
VOODOO SHINTAI SORCERY
FETISHRY GREEGREE TALISMAN

FETLOCK COOT FOOTLOCK

FETTER BAND BEND BOLT BOND
FIND GYVE IRON SPAN BASIL BEWET
BILBO CHAIN SWATH ANKLET
GARTER HALTER HAMPER HOBBLE
HOPPLE IMPEDE LANGEL RACKAN
SWATHE CLINKER CONFINE ENCHAIN
FETLOCK GARNISH MANACLE
SHACKLE SPANCEL TRAMMEL
RESTRAIN
(**PL.**) IRONS LINKS DARBIES

GARNISH GARTERS

FETTERBUSH PIPESTEM PIPEWOOD

FETTLE BEAT DECK FUSS MULL TIDY
VEIN DRESS GROOM WHACK YARAK
GIRDLE REPAIR SETTLE STRIKE
ARRANGE BANDAGE FEATHER
HARNESS

FETTLER BILLYER NOBBLER

FETTLING FIX FETTLE FIXING

FETUS BIRTH CHILD YOUNG AMELUS
BREECH EMBRYO FOETUS ABORTUS
CYCLOPS FEATURE AMORPHUS

FEUD FIEF FRAY BROIL AFFRAY
ENMITY FEODUM FEUDUM STRIFE
CONTEST DISPUTE QUARREL
VENDETTA

FEUDATORY FIEF VASSAL ZAMINDAR
ZEMINDAR

FEUILLE MORTE PHILAMOT

FEVER AGUE FIRE ARDOR CAUMA
DANDY LEUMA OCTAN CAUSUS
DENGUE FEBRIS HECTIC SEPTAN
SEXTAN SODOKU TYPHIA TYPHUS
AMAKEBE FERMENT FEVERET
HELODES MALARIA PINKEYE
PYREXIA QUARTAN TERTIAN
TYPHOID SYNOCHUS TERTIANA
TYPHINIA
(— **OF HORSE**) SCALMA
(**BRAIN** —) PHRENITIS
(**MALARIAL** —) TAP
(**MARSH** —) HELODES
(**TEXAS** —) TRISTEZA

FEVERED DISEASED

FEVERFEW MAYWEED MUGWORT

FEVERISH HOT FIERY FEVERY
HECTIC EXCITED FEBRILE FRANTIC
RESTLESS

FEVERLESS APYREXIA

FEVERROOT GENSON

FEVER TREE BITTERBARK

FEVERWEED FITWEED

FEW LIT CURN LESS SOME SCANT
THREE WHEEN WHONE CURRAN
PICKLE LIMITED EXIGUOUS

FEWER LESS

FEWNESS PAUCITY

FEY DEAD DYING ELFIN FATAL
UNLUCKY

FEZ TARBOOSH

FIADOR THEODORE

FIANCE TRUST SPOUSE FIANCEE
PROMISE AFFIANCE

FIASCO CRASH FLASK FROST FIZZLE
FAILURE DISASTER

FIAT EDICT ORDER DECREE
COMMAND DECISION SANCTION

FIB LIE YED FLAW WHID SLANT
STORY FITTEN PUMMEL SKLENT

FIBBER LIAR

FIBER TAL ADAD BASS BAST COIR
ERUC FERU FLAX HARL HEMP IMBE
JUTE LINE PITA SILK SUNN TULA
ABACA AGUST AZLON CAJUN
CAROA CHOEL ERIZO FIBRE GRAIN
HARLE ISOTE FIBRE IXTLE IZOTE
KENAF KITUL MURVA OAKUM RAMIE
RAPHE SIMAL SISAL STRAW TERAP
TOSSA TUCUM VIVER AMIRAY

BINDER BUNTAL BURITI CABUYA
CATENA DACRON EMBIRA FIBRIL
FIMBLE HINOKI KANAFF KENDIR
KOHEMP MUCUNA NYTRIL RAFFIA
SALAGO STAPLE STRAND STRING
SUTURE THREAD TUCUMA TURURI
VINYON YACHAN ZAPUPE ACETATE
ACRYLIC ANONANG ARAMINA
BASSINE CANTALA CASCARA
CHANDUL CHINGMA COQUITA
ESPARTO FILASSE GEBANGA
GRAVATA GUAXIMA GUMIHAN
HUARIZO KERATTO KITTOOL
MOCMAIN PALMITE PANGANE
PAUKPAN POCHOTE SABUTAN
CANAPINA CURRATOW FILAMENT
HARAKEKE HENEQUEN PIASSAVA
TOQUILLA TRONADOR
(— FROM PEACOCK FEATHERS)
MARL
(— OF PALM) DOH LIF ERUC COYOL
COROZO GOMUTI COQUITA
GEBANGA
(—S OF FLAX) HARE
(CLUSTER OF —S) NEP
(COARSE —) KEMP
(COCONUT —) COIR KYAR
(COTTON —) LINT STAPLE
(KNOT OF —) NOIL
(MANUFACTURED —) DYNEL
ESTRON SPANDEX
(MATTED —) SHAG
(MINERAL —) ASBESTOS
(MUSCLE —) RHABDIUM
(NERVE —) EFFERENT DEPRESSOR
(PULVERIZED —) FLOCK
(SILKY —) KAPOK KUMBI YACHAN
CASTULI
(TWISTED —S) STRAND
(WASTE —) FLY GOUT
(WASTE —S) FLOSS
(WOODY —) BAST GRAIN SCUTCH
(PL.) FUZZ KERATTO
FIBRIL AXONEME DESMOSE
MYONEME MYOPHAN
FIBRIN GLUTEN MYOSIN
FIBROCARTILAGE FABELLA
MENISCUS
FIBROID DESMOID
FIBROMA INOMA FIBROID
FIBROUS FIBROSE STRINGY
NEMALINE
FIBULA LACE CLASP BROOCH
BUCKLE SPLINT
FICKLE GERY DIZZY FALSE GIDDY
LIGHT UNSAD HARLOT KITTLE
MOBILE PUZZLE SHIFTY VOLAGE
WANKLE WANKLY CASALTY
CASELTY FLATTER MOVABLE
MUTABLE VAINFUL VARIANT
VOLUBLE GOSSAMER MOVEABLE
SKITTISH STIRRING UNSTABLE
UNSTEADY VARIABLE VOLATILE
WAVERING
FICKLENESS LEVITY EASINESS
FICKLETY VARIANCE
FICO FIG FIGO TANTI
FICTION TALE FABLE FALSE NOVEL
ROMAN STORY DECEIT DEVICE

FABULA FITTEN LEGEND COINAGE
FANTASY FIGMENT FORGERY
MARCHEN NOVELRY ROMANCE
ROMANZA KAILYARD PHANTASY
FICTITIOUS BOGUS DUMMY FALSE
PHONY FABLED POETIC ASSUMED
FEIGNED FABULOUS FICTIOUS
MYTHICAL ROMANTIC SIMULATE
SPURIOUS LEGENDARY
FICUS PYRULA
FID PRICK NORMAN PRICKER
SPLICER
FIDDLE BOW BOX GIG SAW VIOL
CHEAT CROWD GEIGE GIGUE
GUDOK CHORUS FITHEL POTTER
TRIFLE URHEEN VIOLIN CHROTTA
SWINDLE HUMSTRUM
(— STRING) THAIRM
(— WITH) TWIDDLE
FIDDLER CRAB VIOLER VIOLIN
CROWDER SCRAPER SIXPENCE
FIDDLER CRAB RACER FIDDLER
OCYPODE SOLDIER
FIDDLESTICKS PSHAW FIDDLE
FIDELITY TRUE ARDOR FAITH PIETY
TROTH TRUTH FEALTY HONESTY
LOYALTY ADHESION DEVOTION
RELIGION VERACITY
FIDGET MOP FIKE FIRK FUSS ROIL
FIDGE FITCH HOTCH SHRUB SHRUG
WORRY BREVIT FIGGLE FISSLE
FISTLE FRIDGE FUSSER HIRSEL
JIFFLE JIGGET NESTLE NIBBLE
NIGGLE TIDDLE TRIFLE VIGGLE
WORRIT NERVOUS RESTLESS
TWITCHET
(— ABOUT TRIFLES) SPOFFLE
(STATE OF —) FANTAD FANTOD
(PL.) JUMPS
FIDGETY FIKIE FUSSY ITEMY FEISTY
FIGENT FLISKY KITTLE UNEASY
RESTIVE TWITCHY RESTLESS
FIDUCIARY TRUSTEE TRUSTFUL
FIE SISS FAUGH
FIEF FEE HAN FEUD FEOFF TIMAR
ZIAMET SATSUMA SUBFIEF
BENEFICE
(— HOLDER) TIMARIOT
FIELD LEA LOT ACRE AGER AREA
BENT CAMP FELL FLAT HADE INAM
LAND LIST MEAD PALE PARK RAND
TOWN WONG BRECK CAMPO CHAMP
CLOUR CROFT EARTH GLEBE INNAM
LAYER MILPA NILPA PADDY RANGE
ROWEN SAWAH TILTH VELDE
ARRISH CAMPUS CAREER CHAMPE
DOMAIN FURROW GARDEN GROUND
MACHAR MATTER MEADOW PINGLE
SHIELD SPHERE CHARMEL COMPASS
CULTURE DIAMOND FERRING
GARSTON INFIELD MOWLAND
NEWTAKE PADDOCK PARROCK
PIGHTLE PURVIEW QUILLET TERRAIN
THWAITE TILLAGE CLEARING
PROVINCE
(— ADJOINING HOUSE) CROFT
(— AT CRICKET) SCOUT
(— OF ACTIVITY) GAME ARENA
BARONY SPHERE TERRAIN

(— OF BATTLE) PLAIN
(— OF BLOODSHED) ACELDAMA
AKELDAMA
(— OF CONTROL) DOMAIN
(— OF ENDEAVOR) BUSINESS
(— OF SNOW) NEVE SNOWPACK
(— OF STUDY) GROUND
(— ON WHICH GRASS IS GROWN)
MEAD MEADOW
**(— SOWN FOR TWO SUCCESSIVE
YEARS)** HOOK
(ENCLOSED —) AGER TOWN CLOSE
CROFT
(FOOTBALL —) GRIDIRON
(FRUITFUL —) CHARMEL
(GRASSY —) LEA PEN GARSTON
(HOP —) HOPYARD
(LAVA —) PEDREGAL
(LITTLE-KNOWN —) BYWAY
(NEW GOLD —) RUSH
(PLOWED —) FURROW
(RICE —) SAWAH
(SMALL —) HAW CROFT PADDOCK
(STUBBLE —) HIRSH ROWEN ARRISH
GRATTEN GRATTON
(TILTING —) LISTS
(TOBACCO —) VEGA
(UNEXPLOITED —) FRONTIER
(UNPLOWED EDGE OF —) RAND
(PL.) FIELDEN
FIELD BALM SHEEPMINT
FIELD CAMOMILE OXEYE
FIELDER GLOVEMAN
(CRICKET —) SLIP COVER FIELD
GULLY SCOUT GULLEY INFIELDER
FIELDFARE FELT JACK REDLEG
FELLFARE HILLBIRD JACKBIRD
REDSHANK SNOWBIRD VELTFARE
FIELD MADDER SPURWORT
FIELD MOUSE VOLE MIGALE
FIELDPIECE GUN AMUSETTE
GALLOPER
FIELD SCABIOUS BLUECAP
FIELDWORK LUNET REDAN LUNETTE
FIEND FEN FOE PUG FEND FYND
DEMON DEVIL ENEMY SATAN TRULL
WIZARD SHAITAN SUCCUBA TITIVIL
BARBASON SUCCUBUS
FIENDISH CRUEL WICKED DEMONIC
FIENDLY SATANIC DEMONIAC
DEVILISH DIABOLIC INFERNAL
FIERCE ILL BOLD FELL GRIM KEEN
RUDE THRO ASPER BREME CRUEL
EAGER FELON HATEL ORPED RETHE
SHARP SMART STARK STERN
STOUR STOUT WROTH ARDENT
FEROCE GOTHIC HETTER IMMANE
RAGING RUGGED SAVAGE STURDY
UNMEEK UNMILD WICKED BRUTISH
FERVENT FURIOSO FURIOUS
GRIMFUL INHUMAN MANKIND
RABIOUS RAMPANT SCADDLE
VIOLENT STERNFUL TIGERISH
FIERCE-EYED WALLEYED
FIERCELY FELL HARD FELLY FIERCE
FIERCENESS FURY FEROCITY
FIERY HOT RED ADUST FIRED QUICK
SHARP ARDENT FLASHY IGNITE
BURNING FERVENT FLAMING

FURIOUS GLOWING HOTHEAD
IGNEOUS PARCHED PEPPERY
VIOLENT ADUSTIVE CHOLERIC
FEVERISH FRAMPOLD INFLAMED
PHRAMPEL SPIRITED SPITFIRE
VEHEMENT

FIESTA FETE FERIA PARTY HOLIDAY
(— **COSTUME**) POLLERA

FIFE STICK PIFERO PIFFERO

FIFTEEN FIVE

FIFTEENTH DOUBLETTE

FIFTH QUINT QUINTIN

FIFTY (— **YEAR ANNIVERSARY**)
JUBILEE

FIFTY-FIFTY EVEN

FIG RIG FICO ARRAY BREBA DRESS
ELEME ELEMI PIPAL SABRA TANTI
BALETE BALITI FOUTER FOUTRA
GINGER LOBFIG PEEPUL TRIFLE
FURBISH GONDANG SICONUS
SYCONUS WARINGIN
(— **CROP**) MAMME

FIG BASKET CABAS

FIGHT BOX MIX WAP WAR WIN BEAT
BEEF BLUE BOUT CAMP CLEM COCK
COPE COWP CRAB CUFF DUEL FLOG
FRAY LAKE MEET MELL MILL SHOW
SLUG SPAR TILT WAGE YOKE
BRAWL CLASH FIELD FLOLT HURRY
JOUST MATCH MELEE SCRAP SHINE
SPURN STOUR TOUSE AFFAIR
AFFRAY BARNEY BATTLE BICKER
COMBAT DEBATE FEUCHT FRACAS
FRAISE HASSLE IMPUGN MEDDLE
OPPOSE RELUCT REPUGN RESIST
RIPPIT RUFFLE SHOWER STOUSH
STRIFE STRIKE STRIVE TOUSEL
TURNUP BARGAIN BRABBLE
CONTEND CONTEST COUNTER
JOURNEY QUARREL RUCTION
SIMULTY TUILYIE WARFARE
CONFLICT DOGFIGHT DUOMACHY
FINISHER GUNFIGHT MILITATE
SKIRMISH SQUABBLE STRUGGLE
TIRRIVEE TIRRWIRR TRAVERSE
(— **AGAINST**) BUCK
(— **BETWEEN TWO**) DUEL
DUOMACHY
(— **FOR**) SERVE CHAMPION
(— **WITH CLUB**) TIMBER
(**FIST** —) RIPPIT TURNUP
(**SEA** —) NAUMACHY
(**STREET** —) HABBLE

FIGHTER PUG VAMP BOXER COCKER
BATTLER DUELIST SLUGGER
SOLDIER WARRIOR ANDABATA
BARRATER BARRATOR CHAMPION
GUERILLA PUGILIST SCRAPPER
(**FIRE** —) EXEMPT HOTSHOT

FIGHTING BLOW AFFRAY DEBATE
WARLIKE CONFLICT MILITANT
(— **WITH SHADOW**) SCIAMACHY

FIGHTING FISH PLAKAT

FIG MARIGOLD SAMH MESEM
FICOID FOXCHOP FICOIDAL

FIGMENT IDEA FICTION

FIGPECKER BECCAFICO

FIGURATE FLORID FIGURAL FIGURED
FIGURATO

FIGURATION FORM SHAPE DESIGN
OUTLINE

FIGURATIVE FLORID FIGURAL
FIGURED FLOWERY TYPICAL
ALLUSIVE TROPICAL

FIGURE HUE VOL BOSH DOLL FORM
IDEA SIGN STAR ANGLE ANTIC
DATUM DIGIT FLIRT FRAME IMAGE
MAGOT MOTIF SHAPE SPADE SPRIG
BABOON CHANGE CIPHER COCKUP
CUTOUT DEVICE EFFIGY EMBLEM
ENTAIL FIGGER GOOGOL INCUSE
NUMBER PERSON SCHEME SYMBOL
TAILLE TATTOO CHASSIS CHEVRON
CHIFFER CHIFFRE COMPUTE
CONTOUR DRAWING GESTALT
IMPRESS NUMERAL OUTLINE
STATURE DIHEDRAL FIGURATE
GRAFFITO HEXAGRAM LIKENESS
SEMBLANT
(— **FORMED BY INTERSECTING**
LINES) KNOT
(— **IN PRAYER**) ORANT
(— **IN WOOD GRAIN**) BURL FLAKE
(— **MADE OF 3 LINES**) TRIGRAM
TRIANGLE
(— **MADE OF CORN**) KNACK
(— **OF SPEECH**) IMAGE IRONY
TROPE APORIA CLIMAX FLOWER
SCHEME SIMILE VISION ANALOGY
IMAGERY METAPHOR METONYMY
(— **OUT**) BOTTOM
(— **UP**) ITEM
(— **USED AS COLUMN**) ATLAS
TELAMON CARYATID
(— **USED AS MAGIC SYMBOL**)
PENTACLE
(—**S OF SPEECH**) COLORS
(**ANATOMICAL** —) ECORCHE
(**ARTIFICIAL** —) GOLEM
(**BIBLICAL** —) ANGEL CHERUB
(**CARVED** —) GLYPH FIGURINE
(**CENTRAL** —) HERO
(**CIRCULAR** —) HOOP
(**COMIC** —) BILLIKEN
(**CONSPICUOUS** —) MARK
(**CRESCENT-SHAPED** —) LUNE
(**DANCE** —) SWING TRACE SQUARE
PURPOSE ASSEMBLE
(**DOMINANT** —) CAPTAIN
(**FEMALE** —) ORANTE
(**GEOMETRICAL** —) BODY CONE
CUBE LUNE PRISM RHOMB SOLID
CIRCLE GNOMON ISAGON ISOGON
OBLONG SECTOR SQUARE DIAGRAM
ELLIPSE LOZENGE PELCOID
RHOMBUS SECTION HEXAFOIL
SPHEROID
(**GREEK** —) KOUROS
(**GROTESQUE** —) MAGOT BABCON
MAXIMON
(**IDEAL** —) EIDOLON
(**IMAGINARY** —) BOGEYMAN
(**INCISED** —) INTAGLIO
(**MUMMYLIKE** —) USHABTI
(**MUSICAL** —) IDEA LICK
(**ODD** —) MAUMET
(**OVAL** —) SWASH ELLIPSE
(**PREHISTORIC** —) CHACMOL

CHACMOOL
(**QUADRILLE** —) POULE
(**QUEER** —) GIG
(**RHYTHMIC** —) SNAP
(**SHADOW** —) SKIAGRAM
(**SKATING** —) SPIRAL BRACKET
COUNTER
(**SPINDLE-SHAPED** —) FUSEE FUZEE
(**STUFFED** —) DUMMY
(**SYLLOGISTIC** —) SCHEMA
(**SYMBOLIC** —) MORAL EMBLEM
(**TRIANGULAR** —) TRIQUET
(**UNDRAPED** —) NUDE
(**WINGED** —) ANGEL EIDOLON
(**PL.**) SPILING

FIGURED FIGURY FACONNE

FIGUREHEAD DUMMY FRONT
SCROLL

FIGURINE TANAGRA CRIOPHORE

FIGWORT BARTSIA PILEWORT

FIJI

BAY: MBYA NATEWA NGALOA
SAVUSAVU
CAPITAL: SUVA
EASTERN GROUP: LAU
ISLAND: ELD KIA ONO AIWA KIOA
KORO MALI NGAU VIWA WAIA
AGATA MANGO MOALA NAIAU
RAMBI MAMOLO MATUKU
MBENGA MBULIA NAIRAI NAVITI
NGAMEA OVALAU TOTOYA
YASAWA YENDUA KAMBARA
LAKEMBA TAVEUNI VITILEVU
MOUNTAIN: NARARU MONAVATU
NIECE OR NEPHEW: VASU
POINT: VUYA
TOWN: MAU MBA MOMI REWA
SUVA TUVU THUVU ETUMBA
NALOTO NAMOLI NARATA
NASALA NAVOLA SAGARA

FIJIAN VITIAN

FILAGO GIFOLA

FILAMENT BRIN DOWL HAIR HARL
NEMA PILE SILK CHIVE CHORD
FIBER FIBRE FILUM TWIRE CIRRUS
ELATER HEATER MANTLE STRAND
THREAD CIRRHUS FLIMMER RHIZOID
TEXTILE PARANEMA PHACELLA
STERIGMA
(— **OF FEATHER**) DOWL DOWLE
(— **OF MINERAL**) STRINGER
(— **OF SILK**) BRIN
(—**S OF FLAX OR HEMP**) HARL
(**TWISTED** —**S**) STRAND
(**PL.**) HACKLE

FILAMENTOUS STRINGY HAIRLIKE

FILANDERS BACKWORM

FILARIASIS MUMU

FILBERT HAZEL COBNUT HAZELNUT
(**SIEVE OF** —**S**) PRICKLE

FILCH BOB FUB NIM ROB BEAT FAKE
PILK PRIG SMUG SNIP FETCH LURCH
PILCH SNAKE SNEAK STEAL CLOYNE
PILFER SMOUCH STRIKE CABBAGE
PURLOIN

FILE BOX ROW BARB DECK LINE LIST
RANK RASP RATE RISP ROLL SLIP

STUB EMERY ENTER FLOAT FOUND
GRAIL INDEX LABEL RIFLE TRACK
TRAIN ACCUSE ANSWER BEFOUL
CARLET DEFILE FILACE RASCAL
RUBBER STRING TOPPER ARCHIVE
ARRANGE CHOILER CONDEMN
DOSSIER EXHIBIT GRAILLE QUANNET
TICKLER DRAWFILE
(— **DOWN SAW TEETH**) JOINT
(— **OF SIX SOLDIERS**) ROT
(— **OFF**) DEFILE
(— **USED BY COMBMAKERS**) GRAIL
TOPPER GRAILER GRAILLE
(**COARSE** —) RAPE
(**CURVED** —) RIFFLER
FILE BOX SOLANDER
FILEFISH LIJA UNIE TURBOT
UNICORN BALISTIS FOOLFISH
FILIAL PIUS SONLY
FILIBUSTER FLIBUTOR STONEWALL
FILING RASION LIMATION
(PL.) LEMEL LIMAIL
FILIPENDULA ULMARIA
FILIPINO KALINGA KANKANAI
FILL EKE HIT PAD BUNG CLOY CRAM
FEED GLUT HOLD LADE LINE MEET
PANG QUAR SATE STOP TEEM
BELLY BLOAT BULGE CHOKE ESTOP
FLOCK GORGE KEDGE PITCH STORE
STUFF CHARGE FULFIL INFUSE
OCCUPY QUERRE SUPPLY AGGRADE
DISTEND ENLARGE EXECUTE
FILLING FRAUGHT FULFILL IMPLETE
INFLATE INVOLVE PERFECT
PERFORM PERVADE PLENISH
SATIATE SATISFY SUFFUSE
COMPLETE COMPOUND FREQUENT
PERMEATE
(— **COMPLETELY**) SATURATE
(— **CUP TO BRIM**) BRIM CROWN
BUMPER
(— **FULL**) FARCE STUFF
(— **IN CHINKS**) LIP
(— **IN WITH RUBBLE**) HEART
(— **IN**) NOG KILL STOP SLUSH
INFILL BALLAST
(— **INTERSTICES**) BLIND
(— **LEATHER WITH OIL**) FAT
(— **OUT**) BUNCH SWELL
(— **TO EXCESS**) CROWD FLOOD
CONGEST SURFEIT
(— **TO OVERFLOWING**) FLOW
THWACK
(— **UP HOLE**) STIFLE
(— **UP**) STOP BRICK CHOKE CLOSE
ESTOP STOAK FULFIL IMPACT
STODGE PLENISH
(— **WITH ALE**) RACK
(— **WITH ANXIETY**) ALARM ALARUM
(— **WITH CARGO**) STOW
(— **WITH CLAY**) CAT
(— **WITH FEAR**) APPAL APPALL
(— **WITH HORROR**) ABHOR
(— **WITH LIGHT**) GLUT
(— **WITH LIQUOR**) TUN SKINK
(— **WITH METAL**) BACK
(— **WITH MORTAR**) GROUT
(— **WITH ODORS**) EMBALM

(— **WITH RUBBISH**) BASH
(— **WITH TERROR**) AMAZE
(— **WITH**) SWILL
(**ONE'S** —) SLITHERS
FILLED BIG ALIVE FLUSH QUICK
SATED SOLID GRAVID LOADED
CROWDED HAUNTED IMPLETE
OPPLETE REPLETE SWOLLEN
FREQUENT INSTINCT POPULOUS
(— **OUT**) BOLD FULL
(— **TO EXCESS**) FLOWN
(— **WITH EXCITEMENT**) ABUZZ
(— **WITH FEAR**) AFRAID
(— **WITH INTERSTICES**) AREOLAR
(— **WITH MOISTURE**) FAT
(— **WITH PRIDE**) YNPRIDID
FILLER GARA BOGUS SILEX SILKA
SQUIB BALAAM LIGNIN FILLING
LOADING WRAPPER
FILLET BAND BONE GIRT LIST ORLE
ORLO SOLE TAPE AMPYX CROWN
FACET FILET GORGE LABEL LEDGE
MITER MITRE QUIRK SCROD SNOOD
STRAP STRIA TIARA VITTA ANADEM
BENDEL BINDER CIMBIA COMBLE
CORONA DIADEM FASCIA INFULA
LISTEL NORSEL POTONG QUADRA
REGULA RIBBON ROLLER TAENIA
TURBAN TURBOT ANNULET
BANDAGE BANDEAU CLOISON
CORONET EYEBROW FACETTE
FRONTAL GARLAND LAMBEAU
MOLDING TRESSON TRINGLE
BANDELET CINCTURE FRONTLET
HAIRLACE HEADBAND PLATBAND
TRESSOUR TRESSURE UNDERCUT
FILLIFORM CATENOID
FILL-IN MODESTY
FILLING GOB FILL MODE PLUG WEFT
WOOF INLAY STUFF FILLER
STOPPING STUFFING
(— **OF GAPS**) CONFAB
(— **UP**) CLOSURE RIPIENO
(**BASKET** —) SLEW
(**DENTAL** —) INLAY
(**SILK** —) SHIKII
FILLIP BLOW FLIP SNAP TOSS URGE
FILIP FLASH FLIRT FLISK IMPEL
BUFFET INCITE MOMENT PROJECT
FILLY COLT FOAL GIRL
FILM H BRAT HAZE HULL KELL MIST
SCUM SKIM SKIN VEIL WEFT BLEAR
COVER FLAKE GLAZE LAYER PEARL
PLATE SCALE SHOOT SHORT
BUBBLE MOTHER PATINA SCRUFF
CUTICLE FEATURE PHILOME
TAFFETA TOPICAL TRAILER
BEESWING FIRECOAT NEGATIVE
PELLICLE
(— **OF OIL**) SLICK
(— **OF TARTAR**) SCALE
(— **ON COPPER**) PATINA
(— **ON PORRIDGE**) BRAT
(— **ON WINE**) BEESWING
(**DISCARDED** —) OUTTAKE
(**X-RAY** —) BITEWING
FILMY FINE HAZY GAUZY MISTY
WISPY CLOUDY CLOUDED TIFFANY
FILMLIKE GOSSAMER

FILTER CLAY RAPE SIFT SILE DRAIN
SEITZ SIEVE BOUGIE CANDLE
COLATE LAUTER MEDIUM PURIFY
REFINE STRAIN BAGHOUSE
FILTRATE INFILTER STRAINER
FILTERER CLARIFIER
FILTH FEN KET DIRT DUNG GORE
MUCK NAST SLUT SOIL SUDS ADDLE
DRECK GLEAM GLEET JAKES POUCE
SWILL DEFILE FULYIE FULZIE
IMMUND ORDURE SORDES VERMIN
SLOTTER SQUALOR SULLAGE
FOULNESS MUCKMENT SNOTTERY
WORTHING
FILTHINESS MUCOR SQUALOR
SULLAGE CENOSITY
FILTHY LOW FOUL MIRY VILE DIRTY
DROVY DUNGY GROSS LAIRY
MUCKY NASTY BAWDRY CRUMBY
CRUMMY CRUSTY DIRTEN IMMUND
IMPURE SORDID BESTIAL HOGGISH
OBSCENE PIGGISH SQUALID
UNCLEAN ORDUROUS SLUTTISH
FILTRATE MALLEIN
FILTRATION BAGGING
FIN ARM RAG RIB ANAL BURR FANG
HAND KEEL SAIL FLASH PINNA
CAUDAL FINLET ACANTHA FEATHER
FLIPPER PINNULE VENTRAL
FORELIMB PECTORAL
FINAGLE CHEAT TRICK REVOKE
DECEIVE FENAGLE
FINAL LAST UTTER FINIAL LATTER
RUNOFF ULTIMA UTMOST DARREIN
DERNIER EXTREME FINALIS
OUTMOST PARTING SUPREME
ABSOLUTE DECISIVE DECRETAL
DEFINITE EVENTUAL FAREWELL
ULTIMATE
(— **STANZA**) ENVOI
FINALE END CODA FINIS ENDING
CLOSING
FINALITY END ERGO
FINALLY YET LAST AFINE LASTLY
FINANCE TAX BACK BANK FUND
GOODS REVENUE TAXATION
TREASURE
FINANCIAL FISCAL MONETARY
FINANCIER MONEYMAN
FINBACK WHALE FINNER GIBBAR
FINFISH RORQUAL JUBARTAS
FINCH FINK MORO PAPE JUNCO
SERIN TERIN BURION CANARY
CITRIL LINNET PALILA SISKIN
TOWHEE BUNTING CHEWINK
PEEWEEP REDHEAD REDPOLL
SENEGAL SPARROW TANAGER
WAXBILL AMADAVAT COMBASOU
FIRETAIL GOULDIAN GROSBEAK
HAWFINCH SNOWBIRD
(— **FLOCK**) CHARM
FIND GET RUG MEET CATCH INVENT
LOCATE STRIKE ADJUDGE FINDING
DISCOVER SCROUNGE
(— **FAULT**) CARP BARGE BLAME
CAVIL GRONT KNOCK PINCH SCOLD
NATTER ARRAIGN
(— **GUILTY**) ATTAINT CONVICT
(— **OUT**) AFIND CHECK ESSAY

LEARN SPELL TROVE DETECT
CONTRIVE DECIPHER DISCOVER
(— **REFUGE**) BIEL BIELD
(— **SOLUTION**) SOLVE
(— **THE SUM**) SUMMATE
(— **TIME**) EEM
FINDER SIGHT SEEKER FOUNDER
FINDING TROVER INQUEST VERDICT
FINE CRO GAY RUM TAX BEIN BIEN
BRAW CAIN CROP DIRE ERIC FAIR
GENT GOOD HUNK JAKE LEVY NICE
PURE RARE SEPT SLAP TALL TEAR
TINE TRIM ABWAB BONNY BRAVE
BULLY CHECK DAISY DANDY DELIE
DUCKY FRAIL GAUDY GRAND GREAT
HUNKY ISSUE KELTY MULCT NOBLE
RORTY SHARP SHEER SMALL SPALE
SWEET UNLAW WALLY WHITE
AMENDE AMERCE BONNIE BRAWLY
BRIGHT CHEESY CHOICE CLEVER
COSTLY CRAFTY DAINTY FACETE
FINISH FLUTED GERSUM HUNGRY
ORNATE PRETTY PROPER RANSOM
SARAAD SCONCE SERENE SILKEN
SLIGHT SPIFFY TENDER CLARIFY
CONDEMN CORKING CUNNING
ELEGANT ESTREAT FERDWIT
FINICAL FORFEIT FRAGILE GALANAS
GALLANT GALLOWS GRADELY
IMMENSE MARCHET MERCHET
MURDRUM ORFGILD PENALTY
PERFECT REFINED SCUTAGE
STAVING TENUOUS TOPPING
VALIANT ABSOLUTE BLOODWIT
BUDGEREE CAVALIER CLINKING
DELICATE DUSTLIKE FLITWITE
FOOTGELD HANDSOME LASHLITE
MARITAGE PENALIZE PESHKASH
PLEASANT SKILLFUL SPLENDID
SUPERIOR WARDWITE WIRESPUN
(— **AGAINST SERVANTS**) CHECK
(— **FOR KILLING**) BOTE
(— **IN LIEU OF FLOGGING**) HIDE
(**BLOOD** —) ERIC WITE
(**OSTENTATIOUSLY** —) GAUDY
(**PRINTING OFFICE** —) SOLACE
(**VERY** —) BUNKUM SPLENDID
(**PL.**) SILT FLOUR
FINE-DRAW RANTER
FINE-LOOKING SPICY SPIFFY
FINELY FINE GAILY GAYLY BRAGLY
RARELY SMALLY BRAVELY SMICKLY
SWEETLY
FINENESS ALLOY GRAIN TRICK
DENIER FINERY PURITY THREAD
EXILITY FINESSE DELICACY
(— **AS RECKONED BY CARATS**)
TITLE
(— **OF FABRIC**) CUT GAGE GAUGE
(— **OF METAL**) STANDARD
(— **OF PITCH**) COUNTS
FINERY GAUD WALY ARRAY BRAWS
WALLY BAUBLE BAWDRY BEAUTY
FEGARY GAIETY GAYETY TAWDRY
BRAVERY GAUDERY REGALIA
BEAUETRY ELEGANCE FINENESS
FOFARRAW FOLDEROL FOOFARAW
FRIPPERY ORNAMENT RIBANDRY
FINESPUN HAIR THIN TWITTERY

FINESSE ART CHEAT SKILL TRICK
PURITY SERENE CUNNING ARTIFICE
DELICACY SUBTLETY THINNESS
FINFOOT SUNBIRD
FINGER TOY PAUT PLAY DIGIT INDEX
PINKY DACTYL HANDLE MEDDLE
MEDIUS PILFER PINKIE POLLEX
ANNULAR DIGITAL MINIMUM
MINIMUS PURLOIN DIGITIZE
THRIMBLE
(— **INFECTION**) FELON
(**FORE** —) INDEX
(**LITTLE** —) PINKIE PIRLIE MINIMUS
AURICULAR
(**RING** —) RINGMAN ANNULARY
(**PL.**) HOOKS
FINGERFLOWER FOXGLOVE
FINGERING DOIGTE
FINGERLING PARR TROUTLET
FINGERNAIL DIGGER
(**RELATING TO** —) ONYCHOID
FINGERPRINT ARCH LOOP WHORL
LATENT
FINGERROOT FOXGLOVE
FINIAL EPI NOB TEE TOP CROP
KNOB KNOP KNOT BUNCH CREST
CROWN FINAL POPPY PRICKET
ORNAMENT PINNACLE
FINICAL NICE FUSSY CHOOSY
DAINTY DAPPER JAUNTY PRETTY
PRISSY SPRUCE CHOOSEY FINICKY
FINIKIN FOPPISH MINCING PICKING
SMICKER DELICATE
FINICALLY SMICKLY GINGERLY
FINICKY DINKY FIKEY FIKIE PRISSY
FINICAL FINIKIN
FINISH DO DIE END CHAR EDGE
FACE FINE MILL OVER PASS SINK
SNUG STOP BLOOM BOUND CEASE
CHARE CHEVE CLOSE CROWN
FEEZE GLACE GLAZE LIMIT SPEED
UPPER BOTTOM BUSHEL FULFIL
FULLDO PLISSE SETTLE WINDUP
ABSOLVE ACHIEVE DEPETER
EXECUTE FLUTING FULFILL PERFECT
SURFACE COMPLETE CONCLUDE
DEPRETER DRESSING FINALIZE
FROSTING TERMINAL
(— **CAREFULLY**) NEATEN
(— **CLOTH**) BURL CONVERT
(— **OF FABRIC**) CIRE HOLLAND
(— **OF PAPER**) STIPPLE
(— **OFF**) DASH CRUSH
(— **STONE**) COMB BOAST DROVE
(— **WITH A SEAM**) FELL
(— **WORK**) FLOOR
(**CALENDERED** —) CHASING
(**DULL** —) MAT MATTE
(**GLAZED** —) GLACE LACKER
LACQUER
(**STUCCO** —) SPATTER
(**SUPERFICIAL** —) BLAZONRY
FINISHED BY DID OER PAU DONE
DOWN FINE GONE OVER RIPE SHOT
ENDED EXACT KAPUT NAPOO
ROUND CLOSED NAPOOH ORNATE
PERFECT REFINED ROUNDED
STOPPED BANKRUPT CLIMAXED
GOFFERED LUSTERED POLISHED

(— **IN NATURAL COLOR**) FAIR
(— **WITH NAP**) BRUSHED
(**ABSOLUTELY** —) SUNK
(**HIGHLY** —) SUAVE
(**IMPERFECTLY** —) RUDE
FINISHER EYER ENDER GAFFER
BEETLER CEMENTER ENAMELER
FINISHING CRUSHING
FINITE LIMITED

FINLAND
CAPITAL: HELSINKI HELSINGFORS
COIN: PENNI MARKKA
DIVISION: IJORE VILLIPURI
GOD: TAPIO JUMALA
ISLAND: ALAND KARLO AALAND
HAILUTO VALLGRUND
ISTHMUS: KARELIA
LAKE: JUO MUO KEMI KIVI NASI
OULO PURU PYHA SIMO ENARE
HAUKI INARI KALLA LAPPA LESTI
PUULA LENTUA SAIMAA SOUNNE
SYVARI KOITERE NILAKKA
PIELIEN
LANGUAGE: AVAR LAPP UGRIC
MAGYAR OSTYAK TARAST
SAMOYED ESTONIAN
MEASURE: KANNU TUNNA VERST
FATHOM SJOMIL OTTINGER
SKALPUND TUNNLAND
MOUNTAIN: HALTIA
NAME: SUOMI
PARLIAMENT: EDUSKUNTA
PROVINCE: HAME KYMI LAPPI
VAASA
RIVER: II KALA OULU SIMO TENO
IVALO LOTTA OUNAS SIIKA
IIJOKI LAPUAN MUONIO PASVIK
TORNIO KITINEN KOKEMAKI
TOWN: ABA ABO KEM KEMI OULU
PORI VASA ENARE ESPOO
KOTKA LAHTI TURKU VAASA
IMATRA KUOPIO MIKKELI
TAMPERE HELSINKI
TRIBE: HAME VEPS VEPSE UGRIAN
KARJALAISET SUOMALAISET

FINLET PINNULE
FINN FIOUN INGER OSTIAK OSTYAK
TAVAST INGRIAN CHEREMIS
INGERMAN SWEKOMAN
(**PL.**) SUOMI
FIORD FJORD INLET
FIORIN KNOTGRASS
FIPPLE FLUTE RECORDER
FIR VER LARCH SAPIN BAUMIER
LASHORN PINABETE
FIR CLUB MOSS FOXFEET
FIRE CAN FEU LOW AGNI APOY BALE
BRIO BURN HEAT KILN LOWE POOP
SWAP SWOP ZEAL ARDOR ARSON
BLAST BLAZE BREAK BURST EMPTY
FEVER GLEED INGLE LIGHT LOGHE
LOOSE LOUGH PLUFF SERVE SHOOT
SQUIB STOKE AROUSE ENGHLE
EXCITE FERVOR IGNITE INCITE
KINDLE SMUDGE SPIRIT SPLEEN
VULCAN ANIMATE BONFIRE BURNING

BURNOUT CHIMNEY DISMISS
EMITTER EXPLODE FURNACE
GLIMMER INFLAME INSPIRE
SMOLDER BACKFIRE BALEFIRE
CAMPFIRE DETONATE HELLFIRE
ILLUMINE IRRITATE NEEDFIRE
SMOULDER VIVACITY
(— A REVOLVER) FAN
(— ON) AFIRE
(— THE CHARGE) HIT
(— TWO ROUNDS) DOUBLE
(— UPON) GUN SPRAY
(CROSS —) GANTLET GAUNTLET
(DAMPENED —) SMOTHER
(FOREST —) BREAK
(LITTLE —) SPONK SPUNK
(MASSED —) ARTILLERY
(PEAT —) GREESAGH
(RUNNING-OUT —) DANDY
(SIGNAL —) BALE BEACON
BALEFIRE
FIRE ALARM FIREBOX
FIREARM ARM GUN IRON SHOT
TUBE FIRER ORGAN PIECE RIFLE
JEZAIL MAGNUM MAUSER MUSKET
PISTOL POPPER BOMBARD CARBINE
CURRIER DEMIHAG HANDGUN
PINFIRE SHOOTER SPANNER
ARQUEBUS BROWNING CULVERIN
EXPELLER EXPLODER PETRONEL
REVOLVER
(PL.) HARDWARE ARTILLERY
FIRE ARROW MALLEOLUS
FIREBACK REREDOS MACARTNEY
FIRE BEETLE COCUYO CUCUYO
ELATER ELATERID
FIREBOAT PALANDER
FIREBRAND BLAZE BRAND BLEERY
BOUTEFEU
FIREBRICK QUARLE
(PL.) GROG
FIREBUG BUG ARSONIST
FIRE CARRIER PORTFIRE
FIRECLAY THILL
FIRE COVER CURFEW CURPHEW
FIRECRACKER DEVIL SQUIB PETARD
SALUTE CRACKER SNAPPER
FIREWORK WHIZBANG
FIRE-CURED DARK
FIREDAMP GAS FOULNESS WILDFIRE
FIREDART PHALARICA
FIREDOG DOG
FIRE ENGINE RIG TUB MANUAL
FIRE EXTINGUISHER SQUIRT
EXTINCTOR
FIRE FIGHTER EXEMPT HOTSHOT
FIREFLY CUCUYO FIREBUG GLOWFLY
LAMPFLY FIREWORM GLOWWORM
LAMPYRID
FIREGUARD FENDER
FIRELINE GUTTER
FIRELOCK FUSEE FUZEE SPANNER
FIREMAN VAMP FIRER FUELER
STOKER TEASER TIZEUR FIREBOY
HOSEMAN BAKEHEAD FURNACER
FIREPLACE FOCUS FOGON FORGE
FOYER GRATE INGLE TISAR HEARTH
CHIMNEY CHEMINEE
(— AND CHIMNEY) STACK

(— **STONE**) MANTEL
(**PORTABLE** —) BARBECUE
BARBEQUE
FIREPLUG PLUG HYDRANT
FIRER STOKER BLASTER
FIRESIDE SMOKE HEARTH
FIRESTAND HASTER HASTENER
FIRE THORN PYRACANTH
FIREWEED FIRETOP PILEWEED
PILEWORT
FIREWOOD FIRE LENA SLAB WOOD
CHUNK FAGOT BILLET BILLOT
ELDING FIRING TALWOOD FIREBOTE
TALLWOOD TALSHIDE
FIREWORK JET SUN GERB DEVIL
GERBE PEEOY SAXON SHELL WHEEL
FIZGIG MAROON PETARD ROCKET
SALUTE SHOWER TRACER CASCADE
SERPENT SPARKER TORPEDO
FOUNTAIN SPARKLER
(PL.) FUN FIRE
FIRE WORSHIPPER PARSI GHEBER
GHEBRE PARSEE
FIRING FIRE FUEL COUGH SALVO
BURNING DRUMFIRE
FIRKIN VESSEL
FIRM HUI BUFF FAST HARD IRON
NASH SURE TAUT TRIG TRIM CHAMP
CORKY CRISP DENSE FIRMA FIXED
HARDY HOUSE LOYAL RIGID SOLID
SOUND STARK STIFF STITH STOUT
SWITH TIGHT HARDEN HEARTY
SECURE SETTLE SICCAR SICKER
SINEWY STABLE STANCH STEADY
STEEVE STOLID STRONG STURDY
ADAMANT CERTAIN COMPACT
COMPANY CONCERN CONFIRM
CONTEXT DECIDED DURABLE
STAUNCH UNMOVED CONSTANT
FAITHFUL FIDUCIAL OBDURATE
RESOLUTE SUBSTANT UNSHAKEN
(— **BUT EASILY CUT**) SEMISOFT
(**NOT** —) FUZZY
FIRMAMENT SKY DEEP POLE CARRY
CANOPY HEAVEN EXPANSE
EMPYREAN EMPYREUM EXPANSUM
FIRMLY BUFF FAST FIRM HARD
SADLY STARK TIGHT HARDLY
SQUARE SURELY SOLIDLY
SECURELY STRONGLY
FIRMNESS BODY GRIT IRON ETHAN
PROOF FIXURE COURAGE FIRMITY
GRANITE BACKBONE DECISION
FASTNESS SECURITY SOLIDITY
STRENGTH TENACITY
FIRST ERST FUST GULE HEAD HIGH
MAIN ALPHA CHIEF FORME NIEVE
PRIMA PRIME PRIMO MAIDEN
PRIMAL PRIMUS VIRGIN FIRSTLY
HIGHEST INITIAL LEADING PRIMARY
EARLIEST FOREHAND FOREMOST
FORMERLY ORIGINAL PARAVANT
PREMIERE PRINCEPS
(— **PRIZE**) BLUE
(— **SERGEANT**) TOP
(— **STATE**) DELAWARE
FIRSTBORN AYNE EIGNE ELDEST
FIRST-CLASS GAY TOP BOSS FLASH
PRIME BUNKUM STUNNING

FIRST-FRUITS ANNATES
FIRSTHAND DIRECT PRIMARY
ORIGINAL
FIRST-RATE BOSS BRAG GOOD JAKE
MAIN SLAP BULLY DANDY LUMMY
PRIME SLEEK SLICK SUPER SWELL
BONSER BONZER BOSKER CHEESY
FAMOUS TIPTOP BLIGHTY BOSHTER
CAPITAL SKOOKUM STELLAR
TOPPING CHAMPION CLINKING
CLIPPING TOPNOTCH
FIRTH KYLE FRITH INLET COPPICE
ESTUARY
FISCAL BURSAL MONETARY
FISH AU ID AKU AWA AYU BIB CAT
COD DAB DAP DIB EEL FIN GAR GIG
GOO HEN IDE IHI JIG JUG ORF RAY
SAR TAI UKU BANK BARB BASS
BOCE BOGA CARP CAST CERO
CHUB CHUG CHUM CLOD CRAB
CUSK DACE DORY DRAG DRAW
DRUM ERSE FUGU GADE GHOL
GOBY GRIG HAKE HIND HUCH HUSO
JACK JUNK LINE LING LOTE MADO
MERO MOLA OPAH PEAL PEGA PIKE
POOR POUT PRIM QUAB RAIL RUDD
RUFF SCAD SCUP SEER SHAD SOLE
SPET SPIN SPOT TILE TORO TUNA
ACARA AHOLE AKULE ANGLE ATULE
BEGTI BINNY BLEAK BOLTI BOLTY
BREAM BULLY BULTI CABIO CATLA
CHIRO CISCO COBIA CONEY DANIO
DORAB DRAIL DRIFT DRIVE ELOPS
ERIZO FLOAT FLUKE FOGAS FRIAR
GADID GRUNT HILSA HUCHO JUREL
KILLY LAKER LANCE MANTA MIDGE
MINIM MORAY OTTER PERCH PIABA
PORGY POWAN POWER REINA
ROACH SAIDE SARGO SAURY SEINE
SHARK SKATE SMELT SNOEK
SNOOK SPRAT SQUID SULEA SWEEP
TENCH TRABU TROLL TROUT TUNNY
UMBRA VIUVA VORAZ WAHOO WHIFF
AIMARA ALEVIN ANABAS ANGLER
BARBEL BARBER BENNET BISKOP
BLENNY BONITO BOWFIN BUMPER
BURBOT CALLOP CANDIL CAPLIN
CARANX CARIBE COELHO COTTID
CREOLE CUCHIA CUNNER DARTER
DASSIE DENTEX FISHET GANOID
GINNEL GULPER GUNNEL HAMLET
HAPUKU HILSAH HUSSAR INANGA
KOKOPU LAUNCE LEDGER LIGGER
LOUVAR MAIGRE MARLIN MENISE
MILTER MINNOW MOLOID MULLET
NONNAT PHOEBE PLAICE POMPON
PUFFER PUNECA REDFIN REMORA
ROBALO ROUGHY RUNNER SABALO
SALELE SALEMA SALMON SAPSAP
SARDEL SAUGER SAUREL SERRAN
SHINER SIERRA SIMARA SPARID
SUCKER TAILER TAIMEN TANDAN
TARPON TAUTOG TESTAR TETARD
TINOSA TOMCOD TURBOT VENDIS
WALLER WEAVER WIRRAH WRASSE
ZINGEL ALEWIFE ALFIONA ANCHOVY
BACALAO BARBUDO BATFISH
BEARDIE BERYCID BIRCHIR BOXFISH
BRAGGLE BUFFALO CABEZON

CANDIRU CAPELIN CAPLING CATFISH
CAVALLA CAVALLY CHIMERA
CHROMID CICHLID CLUPEID CONVICT
CORVINA COWFISH CRAPPIE
CROAKER CUTLIPS CYCLOID
DRABBLE DREPANE DRUMMER
EELPOUT ESCOLAR FATHEAD
FINFISH GALJOEN GEELBEC
GEELBEK GOBIOID GOGGLER
GOLDEYE GOURAMI GRAYSBY
GROUPER GRUNTER GUAPENA
GUAVINA GUDGEON GULARIS
GURNARD GWYNIAD HADDOCK
HAGFISH HALIBUT HARMOOT
HERRING HINALEA HOGFISH
HOUTING ICEFISH ICHTHUS INCONNU
JAWFISH JEWFISH JUGULAR
LABROID LAGARTO LONGFIN
MACHETE MAHSEER MAYFISH
MOJARRA MOONEYE MORWONG
OARFISH OLDWIFE OQUASSA
PEGASUS PIGFOOT PINTADO
PIRANHA POISSON POLLACK
POMFRET POMPANO RONQUIL
SANCORD SARDINE SAUROID
SAVELHA SAWFISH SCALARE
SCAROID SCHELLY SCULPIN
SENNETT SILURUS SLEEPER
SMUTTER SNAPPER SOLDIER
SPAWNER STERLET SUNFISH
TELEOST TOMTATE TOPKNOT
TORPEDO TUBFISH UMBRANA
UNICORN VENDACE VIAJACA
WAREHOU WAUBEEN WHAPUKA
WHAPUKU WHITING ALBACORE
ALFONSIN APOGONID ARAPAIMA
ATHERINE BAITFISH BALISTID
BIGMOUTH BILLFISH BLENNOID
BLUEBACK BLUEFISH BOARFISH
BONEFISH BRISLING BROTULID
BULLHEAD CACKEREL CANCHITO
CARANGID CARANGIN CARDINAL
CATALINA CATALUFA CHANCITO
CHIMAERA CHOANATE CHROMIDE
CORACINE CROSSOPT CYPRINID
DEALFISH DIPNEUST DITREMID
DONCELLA DRAGONET DRUMFISH
DUMBFISH ECHENEID ELEOTRID
EPISCATE FALLFISH FILEFISH
FLAGFISH FLATFISH FLATHEAD
FLOUNDER FOOLFISH FROGFISH
FUNDULUS GAMBUSIA GEELBECK
GILTHEAD GOATFISH GOLDFISH
GRAINING GRAYFISH GRAYLING
GREYSKIN HAIRFISH HALFBEAK
HANDFISH HANDLINE HAPLOMID
HARDHEAD HARDTAIL HOMOCERC
HORNFISH HORSEMAN JACKFISH
JUMPROCK KABELJOU KARMOUTH
KELPFISH KINGFISH LADYFISH
LUMPFISH MACKEREL MENHADEN
MILKFISH MOONFISH PICKEREL
PILCHARD PORKFISH QUERIMAN
ROBALITO ROCKFISH ROCKLING
ROSEFISH SAILFISH SALANGID
SANDFISH SANDGOBY SCIAENID
SCOMBRID SCOTSMAN SEERFISH
SKILFISH SKIPJACK SOAPFISH
STUDFISH STURGEON TALLYWAG

TARWHINE TERAGLIN TILEFISH
TOADFISH TREEFISH TREVALLY
WARMOUTH WEAKFISH WHISTLER
WRYMOUTH
(— BY TROLLING) DRAIL
(— FOR EELS) GRIG SNIGGLE
(— FOR SALMON) SNIGGER
(— NETTED) LIFT
(— NOT UNDERSIZED) COUNT
KEEPER
(— TAPE) SNAKE
(— THROUGH ICE) CHUG
(— UNDERWATER) GOGGLE
(25 LBS. OF —) STICK
(BLIND —) PINKFISH
(CURED —) DUNFISH
(FABLED —) MAH
(FEMALE —) RAUN SPAWNER
(FIGHTING —) PLAKAT
(HAWAIIAN —) AU
(HERALDIC —) CHABOT
(INDIAN —) ROHU
(NUMBER OF —) SCHOOL
(OLD —) MOSSBACK
(QUANTITY OF —) MAZE
(RAW —) SASHIMI
(REFUSE —) CHUM SHACK
(SALTED —) COR
(SPLIT —) KLIPFISH
(THIN —) RACER
(YOUNG —) FRY ALEVIN
FISH BASKET POT CAUL CREEL
SLATH
FISH BOX TRUNK
FISH BRINER COBBERER
FISH CLEANER GILLER
FISH DRESSER IDLER
FISHER MART EELER PEKAN SABLE
SOBOL TAIRA TAYRA MARTEN
SEINER WEJACK MARTRIX TRAWLER
TROLLER
(SPONGE —) HOOKER
FISHERMAN (ALSO SEE ANGLER)
TOTY EELER ANGLER GIGMAN
GILLER KEDGER MAIMUL SEINER
WORMER ADMIRAL DORYMAN
DRAGMAN PRAWNER RODSTER
SHANKER SMELTER STRIKER
TRAWLER TROTTER TROWMAN
PETERMAN PISCATOR SEASONER
SHRIMPER
FISHERY FISHING PISCARY SEALERY
FISHGARTH WEIR
FISHHOOK FLY GIG HOOK LARI
ANGLE DRAIL KIRBY LARIN SLEEK
ANGULE SPROAT KENDALL
ABERDEEN BARBLESS CARLISLE
LIMERICK
(PL.) PULLDEVIL
FISHING PIKING ANGLING BANKING
BASSING GRAINING SNOEKING
(— TOOL) OVERSHOT
FISHING GROUNDS HAAF
FISHING ROD GAD
FISHING TACKLE TEW LEDGER
FISHLINE GIMP TROT SNELL TRAWL
DIPSEY LIGGER BOULTER GANGION
OUTLINE SETLINE TRIMMER
HAIRLINE TROTLINE

FISH LOUSE GISLER
FISHMONGER PESSONER
FISH NEST REDD
FISHNET FLUE SEINE SETNET
FISHPOND VIVER PISCINA VIVARIUM
FISHPOUND MADRAGUE
FISH SPEAR GRANES WASTER
LEISTER
FISHTAIL UROSOME
FISHWAY PASS RACEWAY
FISHY DULL FUNNY GLASSY VACANT
FISSION BREAKING CLEAVAGE
CLEAVING GAMOGENY SCISSION
FISSURE GAP CHAP CONE FLAW
GOOL GULL LEAK LOCH LODE RENT
RIFT RIMA RIME SEAM SLIT VEIN
VENT CHASM CHINE CHINK CLEFT
CRACK FLAKE PIPER PORTA SHAKE
SPLIT ZYGON CLEAVE CRANNY
DIVIDE LESION RICTUS RIMULA
SPRING SULCUS BLEMISH CREVICE
FISSURA OPENING SWALLET
APERTURE BLOWHOLE CLEAVAGE
COLOBOMA CREVASSE INCISURE
QUEBRADA SCISSURA TRAVERSE
(— IN BUILDING STONE) DRY
(— IN HEEL) GAUG
(— IN MAST) SPRING
(— IN PLATEAU) ABRA
(PL.) RHAGADES
FISSURED RIMATE CHAPPED
CLEFTED FISSATE
FIST JOB DUKE NAVE NEIF NIEF
FOIST GRASP INDEX NIEVE CLENCH
CLUTCH DADDLE EFFORT MAULER
MAULEY PINKER STRIKE ATTEMPT
CLUBFIST FISTNOTE PUFFBALL
TIGHTWAD
FISTFIGHT TURNUP
FISTICUFF BOX NEVEL FISTIFY
FISTULA EGILOPS
FISTULOUS TUBULAR
FIT GO APT FAY GEE PAN RIG SIT
ABLE AGUE FEAT FURY GOOD HARD
KINK MEET PANG RIPE SORT SUIT
TURN WELL WHIM ADAPT ADEPT
APPLY BESIT CHINK CLICK DIGNE
EXIES FADGE FANCY FITLY FRAME
FRISK FUROR HAPPY ICTUS MATCH
PITCH QUEME QUIRK READY RIGHT
SERVE SPASM SPELL START STOUR
SWOON TALLY ACCESS ADJUST
ANSWER ATTACK BECOME BEHOVE
BESORT DUEFUL FINISH FITTEN
HABILE HEPPEN LIABLE PROPER
SEASON SEEMLY SPLEEN SQUARE
STREAK STROKE STRONG SUITED
WORTHY ADAPTED BEHOOVE
CAPABLE CONDIGN CONFORM
CORRECT DESPAIR FASHION FITTING
HEALTHY PREPARE QUALIFY
SEIZURE TANTRUM WIDDRIM
ADEQUATE BECOMING DOVETAIL
ELIGIBLE GLOOMING IDONEOUS
OUTBREAK PAROXYSM PASSABLE
SUITABLE SYNCOPES
(— CLOSELY) FAY CHOCK
(— CORNER TO CORNER) BUTT
(— FOR THE GALLOWS) WIDDIFOW

(— **IN**) GO
(— **INTO SOCKET**) FANG
(— **LOOSELY**) SLOP
(— **OF ANGER**) FRAP FUME HUFF
RAGE TIFF FLING RAVERY SPLEEN
(— **OF DEPRESSION**) HUMP
(— **OF ILL HUMOR**) TIG FUNK TOUT
GRUMPS
(— **OF ILL TEMPER**) TANTRUM
(— **OF ILLNESS**) DROW TOUT FLING
(— **OF LAUGHTER**) GIRD KINK
(— **OF NERVOUSNESS**) TWITCHET
(— **OF RESENTMENT**) PIQUE SNUFF
(— **OF SHIVERING**) AGUE GROOSE
(— **OF SULKS**) GEE STRUM
(— **OF SULLENNESS**) DOD
(— **OF TEMPER**) WAX BAIT HISSY
TETCH GROUCH SPLEEN SQUALL
BRAINGE
(— **OF WEEPING**) CRY
(— **OF YAWNING**) GAPE
(— **ONE WITHIN ANOTHER**) NEST
(— **OUT**) ARM BUSK BEFIT EQUIP
ASTORE CLOTHE OUTFIT APPAREL
APPOINT FURNISH HABILLE
ACCOUTER
(— **RIFLE BARREL**) BED
(— **TIGHTLY**) STUFF
(— **TO BE DRUNK**) SORBILE
(— **TOGETHER**) MESH COAPT JOINT
COHERE ASSEMBLE
(— **UP**) RIG
(— **WITH COMPACTNESS**) BOX
(— **WITH FETTERS**) GARNISH
(**RITUALLY** —) KOSHER
(**PL.**) LUNES
FITCH LINER
FITFUL GERY CATCHY GERFUL
GLEAMY CURSORY FLIGHTY
RESTLESS UNSTABLE VARIABLE
FITLY FIT PAT DULY FEATLY GLADLY
MEETLY TIDELY APROPOS HAPPILY
PROPERLY SUITABLY
FITNESS FORM APTNESS DECENCY
DECORUM DIGNITY APTITUDE
CAPACITY IDONEITY JUSTNESS
PROPERTY
FITTED APT ABLE ADAPT KEYED
SUITED ADAPTED ENGAGED
ADJUSTED ASSORTED ELIGIBLE
FITTER TUBER GASMAN
FITTING TO APT CAP DUE LUG PAT
BUTT FAIR FEAT FORK HARP JUMP
JUST KIND MEET CLEAT HAPPY
QUEME WORTH BECOME CLENCH
CLEVIS LEADER PROPER SADDLE
SEEMLY WASHER ADAPTER
CONGRUE PENDANT SERVING
SHACKLE SUCTION TACTFUL
CONDULET DECOROUS GRACEFUL
RIGHTFUL SUITABLE
(— **TIGHTLY**) CLOSE
(**PIPE** —) CROSS ELBOW
(**PL.**) BRASS COVER REPAREL
FITMENTS
FIVE CINQ FUNF CINQUE EPSILON
QUINQUE
(— **CENTS**) JITNEY NICKEL

(— **HUNDRED DOLLARS, POUNDS**)
MONKEY
(— **IN CRAPS**) PHOEBE
(— **OF TRUMPS**) PEDRO
(— **YEARS**) LUSTRUM
(**TWO** —**S**) QUINAS
FIVES BALL SNACK
FIVESTONES SNOBS
FIX BOX JAM PEG PIN SET FAST FIRM
GAFF GLUE HOLD HOLE JAMB LOCK
MEND MOOR NAIL PICK RELY SEAL
SPOT STAY AFFIX ALLOT DEFIX
FOUND GRAFT GRAVE IMBED INFIX
LIMIT PLACE PLANT POINT POSIT
SEIZE STATE STEEK STELL TRYST
ADJUST ANCHOR ARREST ASSIGN
ASSIZE ATTACH CEMENT CLINCH
DEFINE ENROOT ENTAIL FASTEN
FICCHE FIXATE FREEZE GROUND
IMPALE REPAIR REVAMP SETTLE
SQUARE TEMPER APPOINT
ARRANGE CALCIFY CONFIRM
DELIMIT DESTINE DILEMMA GRAPPLE
IMPLANT IMPRESS IMPRINT
PREPARE STATION RENOVATE
TRANSFIX
(— **AMOUNT**) AFFEER
(— **ATTENTION**) NAIL
(— **FIRMLY**) SEAL FREEZE IMPACT
INCUBE RAMPIRE
(— **PRICE**) ASSIZE CHARGE SETTLE
(— **UPON**) CHAP AFFIX
FIXATION FETICH FETISH
FIXATIVE FIXER SKATOLE AMBRETTE
EUDESMOL HYRACEUM LABDANUM
FIXED PAT PUT SAD SET SOT FAST
FIRM FLAT HARD GIVEN SIKER
STAID UPSET FINITE FROZEN INTENT
MENDED SICKER STABLE STATED
STEADY STRONG CERTAIN
DORMANT EMPIGHT HABITED
LIMITED SETTLED SITFAST STATARY
STATIVE STELLED ACCURATE
ARRANGED ATTACHED CONSTANT
DEFINITE EXPLICIT FASTENED
IMMOBILE IRONCLAD MOVELESS
RESIDENT RESOLUTE STANDING
STUBBORN
(**NOT** —) FLUID SHIFTY FUGITIVE
FIXEDLY SAD FAST FIRM FIXLY
INTENTLY
FIXEDNESS FASTNESS
FIXER PATCH
FIXTURE ANNEX EVENT GUARD
FAUCET SHIELD BRACKET CREEPER
KNOCKER THIMBLE
(**LIGHTING** —) SCONCE
(**STORE** —) GONDOLA
FIZZING FIZZY GASSING
FIZZLE FLOP FUSS BARNEY FAILURE
FLIVVER
FLABBINESS MYATONIA
FLABBY LAX FOZY LASH LIMP WEAK
BAGGY FLASH FOGGY FRUSH SAPPY
WOOZY CASHIE DOUGHY FEEBLE
FLAGGY FLAPPY LIMBER QUAGGY
WATERY FLACCID YIELDING
FLACCID LIMP WOOZY FLABBY

FLAGGY EMARCID FLACKED
YIELDING
FLAG FAG LAG SAG SOD FAIL FANE
FLAT HOOK JACK JADE LECK PINE
TURF WAFT WAIF WILT CREST
DROOP FAINT FLAKE SEDGE SLAKE
UNION VEXIL WHEFT WHIFF BANNER
BOUGEE BURGEE COLORS CORNET
EMBLEM ENSIGN FANION GUIDON
LEVERS PENCEL PENNON SIGNAL
TABARD WIMPLE ANCIENT BEEWORT
CALAMUS CATTAIL CURTAIN
DECLINE DRAPEAU FANACLE
LABARUM PENDANT PENNANT
SCOURGE BANDEROL BRATTACH
GONFALON HANDFLAG LANGUISH
PAVILION STANDARD STREAMER
TRICOLOR VEXILLUM WATCHMAN
(— **CORNER**) UNION
(— **OF DENMARK**) DANEBROG
(— **OF TRANSVAAL**) VIERKLEUR
(— **OF TRUCE**) KARTEL
(— **OF U.S.**) GRIDIRON
(**BLUE** — **WITH WHITE SQUARE**)
PETER
(**CAVALRY** —) STANDARD
(**KNOTTED** —) WAFT
(**PIRATE** —) ROGER
(**SERPENT-LIKE** —) DRACO ANGUIS
(**SHIP'S** —) DUSTER
(**TURKISH** —) ALEM
(**WATER** —) SAG
FLAG BEARER GUIDON ANCIENT
FLAGELLANT WHIPPER SCOURGER
(**PL.**) ALBI
FLAGELLATE MONAS
FLAGELLUM WHIP RUNNER
KONSEAL WHIPLASH
FLAGEOLET PIPE ZUFOLO BASAREE
LARIGOT SIBILUS ZUFFOLO
MONAULOS
FLAGGING WEAK LANGUID
FLAGITIOUS WICKED CORRUPT
HEINOUS CRIMINAL FLAGRANT
GRIEVOUS
FLAGON GUN STOUP BOTTLE
VESSEL FLACKET FLAGONET
REHOBOAM
FLAGRANT BAD RED RANK GROSS
ODIOUS STRONG WANTON WICKED
GLARING HATEFUL HEINOUS
SCARLET VIOLENT SHAMEFUL
FLAGSHIP FLAG ADMIRAL
FLAGSTONE FLAG LECK SLAB
FAVUS
FLAIL BEAT FLOG WHIP DRASH FRAIL
THRAIL THRASH THRESH SWINGLE
SWIPPLE STRICKLE
FLAIR RAY BENT NOSE ODOR SMELL
GENIUS LEANING
FLAKE CHIP FILM FLAG FLAW RACK
SNOW FLANK FLECK FLOCK LAMIN
SCALE SLATE SPALL SPAWL STRIP
APHTHA HURDLE LAMINA PALING
FLAUGHT SHAVING FLOCCULE
FRAGMENT
(— **OF METAL**) FLITTER
(— **OF SNOW**) FLAG
FLAKY SCALY SHIVERY

FLAMBE JUBILEE
FLAMBEAU TORCH
FLAMBOYANCE BLARE PANACHE
FLAMBOYANT FLORID GARISH
ORNATE BUCKEYE FLAMING
GORGEOUS
FLAME LOW FIRE GLOW LOWE
ARDOR BLAZE FLARE FLASH GLARE
GLEED INGLE LIGHT RESEPH
TONGUE BURNING FLAMELET
INKINDLE
(ACETYLENE —) CALCIUM
(SMALL —) SPUNK FLAMELET
FLAMMULE
(PL.) GLEED
FLAME TREE KURRAJONG
FLAMING LIVE AFIRE FIERY FLAMY
VIVID AFLARE ARDENT BLAZING
BURNING FLARING FLAGRANT
FLAN PLANCHET
FLANGE BEAD BOSS BEZEL COLLAR
COLLET FLANCH SHROUD FEATHER
DUCKBILL FOLLOWER
(WITHOUT —) BALD
FLANGER FLAYER GOUGER
FLANK LEER LISK SIDE WING CHEEK
SKIRT THIGH BORDER FLITCH
FLANNEL LANA DOMETT SAXONY
STAMIN WHITTLE MOLLETON
SWANSKIN
FLAP FAN LUG ROB TAB TAG TAP
WAP BATE BEAT BLOW CLAP FLIP
FLOG FLOP GILL LOBE LOMA SLAM
SLAT WAFF WELT ALARM APRON
FLACK FLAFF FLICK BALLUP
BANGLE LAPPET LIBBET STRIKE
TONGUE WAFFLE WINNOW AILERON
BLINDER CLICKET FLAPPET FLICKER
FLOUNCE FLUTTER SWINDLE
VALANCE AVENTAIL BACKFLAP
COATTAIL CODPIECE TURNOVER
(— OF BOOTEE) FLY
(— OF GARMENT) LAP
(— OF HAT OR CAP) VALANCE
(— OF HINGE) LEAF
(— ON HOLSTER) FLOUNCE
(— ON SADDLE) SKIRT JOCKEY
(— VIOLENTLY) FLOG SLAT
(CARDIAC —) CUSP
(FLESHY —) GILL
(TROUSERS' —) FALL
FLAPPER FLAP FLOPPER SNICKET
FLAPPING WAFF WHUTTER
FLARE BELL FLUE BLAZE FLAME
FLASH FLECK FUSEE LIGHT SPIRT
TORCH FLANCH SIGNAL SPREAD
FLICKER TRUMPET OUTBURST
(— ON SHIPBOARD) DUCK
(— UP) KINDLE
FLARING BELL FLUE EVASE GAUDY
AFLARE FLAMING GLARING
SWAGGER BOUFFANT DAZZLING
FLASH DOT BEAT DASH LAIT LAMP
LASH LEAM POOL SHOT STAB WINK
BLASH BLAZE BURST FLAME FLARE
FLOSH FLUFF GLADE GLAIK GLEAM
GLENT GLINT LEVIN MARSH SPARK
STEAM BOTTLE FILLIP GLANCE
QUIVER FLAUGHT FOULDRE

GLIMMER GLIMPSE GLISTEN
GLITTER INSTANT LIGHTEN QUICKEN
SHIMMER SPARKLE TWINKLE
SPLINTER SUNBURST
(— FORTH) OUTRAY
(HOT —) FLUSHING
(NEWS —) FUDGE
FLASHBACK THROWBACK
FLASHING CURB FLASH STEEP
BRIGHT FLASHY FORWARD LAMPING
SHINING CREASING METEORIC
SLASHING SNAPPING
FLASHLIGHT BUG GLIM FLASH
TORCH PENLITE
FLASHY GAY FLAT GAUD LOUD
BAVIN FIERY GAUDY SHOWY SLEEK
FLOSSY FROTHY GARISH SLANGY
SPORTY STUNTY INSIPID RAFFISH
TINHORN DAZZLING FLASHING
SPORTING TIGERISH VEHEMENT
FLASK BOX PIG BODY HEAD HELM
JACK OLPE SNAP BETTY BULGE
FRAME GIRBA GOURD BOTTLE
FIASCO FLACON GUTTUS HELMET
LAGENA AMPULLA BOMBOLA
CANTEEN FLASKET MATRASS
TICKLER WARBURG CHRISMAL
CUCURBIT
(POCKET —) TICKLER
FLAT DEAD DOWD DULL EVEN FADE
PLAT SLOB ABODE AFLAT BANAL
BLAND BLUNT DUSTY LEVEL MOLLE
MUSTY PLAIN PLANE PRONE ROOMS
SEBKA SLAKE VAPID WALSH
AGRUFE BORING DREARY FLASHY
JEJUNE LEADEN QUATCH SEBKHA
SILENT SIMOUS DECIDED FLIPPER
INSIPID INSULSE PLATOID PROSAIC
SHILPIT TABULAR UNIFORM
DIRECTLY LIFELESS UNBROKEN
WATERISH
(— AND CIRCULAR) DISCOID
(— AND SHORT) CAMUS CAMUSE
(— IN MUSIC) BEMOL MOLLE
(— OF SWORD) PLAT
(MUD —) SLOB CORCASS
(NOT —) BRISK
(SALT —) SALINA
(THEATRICAL —) JOG
FLATBOAT ARK SCOW PULLBOAT
FLATCAR FLAT IDLER LORRY
(ON A —) PIGGYBACK
FLATFISH DAB RAY BUTT DACE KITE
SLIP SOLE TONG BREAM BRILL
FLUKE QUIFF WHIFF ACEDIA CARTER
PLAICE TURBOT HALIBUT SUNFISH
TORPEDO FLOUNDER MARYSOLE
FLATHEAD SALISH
FLATIRON IRON GOOSE STEEL
SADIRON
FLATNESS BATHOS SILENCE
EVENNESS KURTOSIS
(— OF NOSE) SIMITY
FLATTEN BEAT COMB DECK EVEN
PLAT CRUSH LEVEL PLUSH SPLAT
BEETLE CLINCH DEJECT SMOOTH
SPREAD SQUASH DEPRESS EXPLAIN
PANCAKE SUBSIDE SURBASE
COMPRESS DISPIRIT

FLATTENED ECRASE OBLATE
DILATED PLANATE
FLATTER BULL CLAW COAX DAUB
FAGE FUME PALP SOAP WORD
CHARM FLOAT GLOZE HONEY PAINT
ROOSE SLEEK SMALM BECOME
BUTTER CAJOLE FICKLE FLEECH
FRAISE GLAVER KITTLE PEPPER
PHRASE SAWDER SLAVER SMOOGE
SOOTHE STROKE ADULATE BEGUILE
BLARNEY FLETHER FLUTTER
INCENSE PALAVER SOOTHER
SWEETEN WHEEDLE BESLAVER
BLANDISH BOOTLICK COLLOGUE
FLATTERER FLOIT COGGER DAUBER
EARWIG GLOZER JENKINS PRONEUR
SOOTHER BOOTLICK CLAWBACK
COURTIER DAMOCLES LOSENGER
SLAVERER SMOOTHER
FLATTERING SOAPY SMARMY
SMOOTH BUTTERY CANDIED
COURTLY GLAVERING
FLATTERY BULL BUNK DAUB FLUM
MUSH SOAP FRAIK GLOZE SALVE
TAFFY BUTTER CARNEY FLEECH
GREASE PHRASE SAWDER SLAVER
BLARNEY DAUBING EYEWASH
FAWNING FLETHER INCENSE
PALAVER CAJOLERY
FLATULENCE VAPOR
FLATULENT GASSY WINDY TURGID
POMPOUS VENTOSE FLATUOUS
INFLATED
FLATWARE SILVER
FLATWORM ACOEL FLUKE PLATODE
RADIATE POLYCLAD
FLAUNT BOSH SHOW WAVE BOAST
STOUT VAUNT PARADE DISPLAY
FLUTTER TRAIPSE BRANDISH
FLOURISH
FLAUNTING GAUDY PURPLE
FLAGGERY
FLAVONE CHROMONE
FLAVOR GAMY GOUT MASK ODOR
RASA SALT TANG ZEST AROMA
ASSAI CURRY DEVIL SAPID SAPOR
SAUCE SAVOR SCENT SPICE TASTE
TINGE ASARUM ASSAHY INFUSE
RANCIO RELISH SEASON TARAGE
FLAVOUR PERFUME SUPTION
HAUTGOUT PIQUANCY
(HIGH —) HOGO
(SPECIAL —) GUST
(UNPLEASANT —) TACK
FLAVORED SPICY TINCT SPICED
FLAVORFUL SAVOROUS
FLAVORING DIP ALMOND MIREPOIS
FLAVORLESS STALE SILENT
WATERISH
FLAW BUG FIB GAP LIE MAR RUB
WEM BANE BLOT FLEE GALL HOLE
RASE RIFT SPOT WIND BOTCH
BRACK BURST CHICK CLEFT CRACK
CRAZE FAULT FLAKE PLUME SPECK
BLOTCH BREACH DEFECT FOIBLE
LACUNA LESION BLEMISH BLISTER
DEFAULT EYELAST FEATHER
FISSURE NULLIFY SUNSPOT VIOLATE
WHITLOW FRACTURE FRAGMENT

GENDARME WINDFLAW
(— **IN CASTING**) BUCKLE
(— **IN CLOTH**) BRACK
(— **IN DIAMOND**) GENDARME
(— **IN MARBLE**) TERRACE
(— **IN METAL**) SNAKE
(— **IN PRECIOUS STONE**) FEATHER
(— **IN STEEL**) STAR
(— **IN STONE**) DRY
(**MORAL** —) SMIRCH
FLAWED CRACKED
FLAWLESS CLEAN SOUND PERFECT
FLAX LIN POB TOW CARD FLIX HARL
LINE LINT ROCK GRAIN HURDS
BREADS KORARI PEANUT PEBBLE
SCUTCH LINSEED FLAXWORT
HARAKEKE
(— **DISEASE**) PASMO
FLAXEN FLAXY BLONDE
FLAXWEED TOADFLAX
FLAY SKIN STRIP FLEECE UNCASE
CENSURE PILLAGE REPROVE
SCARIFY
FLEA LOP SCUD FLECH FLECK PULEX
TUNGA CHEGRE CHIGOE VERMIN
PULICID SANDBOY
(— **INFESTED**) PULICOSE
FLEABANE SKEVISH SCABIOUS
WHITETOP
FLEA BEETLE THRIPS
FLEAM BEVEL
FLEAWORT CAMMOCK FLEASEED
PSYLLIUM
FLECHE SPIRELET
FLECK FLAKE FREAK DAPPLE
FLEECE POUNCE STREAK STIPPLE
FLEDGED FLUSH FLIGGED
FLEDGLING SQUAB FLIGGER
BIRDLING
FLEE FLY LAM RUN BOLT FLEG LOUP
SCUR SHUN TURN ELOPE ELUDE
SKIRR SPEED ESCAPE VANISH
ABANDON ABSCOND FORSAKE
SCAMPER LIBERATE
FLEECE JIB KET TEG BUCK CAST
FELL GAFF MORT SKIN TEGG TEGS
FLICK PASHM PLOAT SHAVE SHEAR
SHEEP SWEAT PASHIM PIGEON
PUSHUM TOISON SHEARING
(— **OF MEDIUM GRADE**) SUPER
(**POOREST PART OF** —) ABB
FLEEING FUGIENT HOTFOOT
RUNNING FUGITIVE
FLEER GIBE JIBE LEER FLIRE FLOUT
SCOFF SNEER
FLEET BAY FAST FLIT NAVY SAIL
SKIM SWIM CREEK DRAIN DRIFT
EVAND FLOAT FLOTA HASTY INLET
POWER QUICK RAPID SWIFT
ARGOSY ARMADA FLIGHT HASTEN
NIMBLE SPEEDY CARAVAN
COMPANY FLOTILLA WARCRAFT
FLEETING BRIEF CADUCE FLYING
VOLAGE FLIGHTY PASSING POSTING
SHADOWY VOLATIC CADUCOUS
FUGITIVE VOLATILE
FLESH KIN BEEF BODY FELL GAME
LAMB LIRE MEAT RACE WEED
SLATE STOCK FAMILY MUSCLE

SEASON CARNAGE KINDRED
MANKIND NATURAL HUMANITY
MOONLIGHT
(— **ABOUT CHIN AND JAWS**) GILL
(— **OF CALF**) SLINK
(— **OF GOAT**) CHEVON
(— **OF KID**) CABRITO
(— **OF SHEEP**) TRAIK
(— **ON LOWER JAW**) CHOLLER
(— **OUT**) CLOTHE
(— **UNDER SKIN**) FELL
(**ANIMAL** —) BRAWN
(**DEAD** —) MURRAIN
(**HORSE** —) JACK
(**LIFELESS** —) MUMMY
(**PUTREFYING** —) CARRION
(**SUN-DRIED** —) TAPA
(**SUPERFLUOUS** —) LUMBER
FLESHBRUSH STRIGIL
FLESH-COLORED SARCOLINE
FLESHER LINING
FLESHINESS FULLNESS
FLESHLY CARNAL FLESHY SENSUAL
SARKICAL
FLESHY FAT BEEFY LUSTY OBESE
PLUMP PULPY STOUT ANIMAL
BODILY BRAWNY CARNAL BUNTING
CARNOSE SARCOUS
FLETCH WING FLIGHT
FLEUR-DE-LIS LIS LYS LILY LUCY
FLEUR
FLEX BEND
FLEXED PENCHE
FLEXIBILITY WHIP FLUIDITY
FLEXIBLE LIMP LUSH SOFT BUXOM
LIMSY LITHE WANDY WITHY FLOPPY
LIMBER LITHER PLIANT SUPPLE
DUCTILE ELASTIC FINGENT FLEXILE
FLEXIVE LISSOME PLIABLE SPRINGY
WILLOWY WINDING WRIGGLE
BENDSOME YIELDING
FLEXURE ARCH BEND BENT CURL
FOLD CURVE TWIST SIGMOID
WINDING
FLICK FLIP CLICK FLACK FLANK
FLECK FLIRT FLISK
FLICKER FAIL FLIT LICK WINK BLINK
FLAME FLARE FLICK FLUNK WAVER
BICKER FITTER SHIVER YUCKER
BLINTER FLIMMER FLITTER FLUTTER
SKIMMER TREMBLE TWINKLE
WHIFFLE FLICHTER HIGHHOLE
FLICKERING FLICKY FLUTTER
LAMBENT FLEXUOUS UNSTEADY
FLICKERTAIL STATE
NORTHDAKOTA
FLIER ACE KIWI FLYER PILOT
AIRMAN AVIATOR
FLIGHT FLY HOP LAM BOLT LAKE
PAIR ROUT WING CHEVY FLOCK
GLIDE GRICE SCRAP VOLEE CHIVVY
EXODUS FUGACY HEGIRA HEJIRA
JOYHOP SPIRAL BOUQUET EVASION
FLAUGHT FLYOVER MIGRATE
MISSION SCAMPER STEPWAY
REGIFUGE STAMPEDE SWARMING
(— **OF BALL**) HOOK DRIVE SLICE
(— **OF BIRDS**) VOLARY VOLERY
VOLLEY

(— **OF FANCY**) SALLY
(— **OF SNIPE**) WISP
(— **OF STEPS**) RISE TRAP GRECE
PITCH SCALE STOOP PERRON
STAIRS STEPWAY STAIRWAY
(— **OF WILD FOWL**) SKEIN
(**ABORTIVE** —) ABORT
(**HASTY** —) TIFT
(**HAWK'S** —) CAREER
(**HIGH** —) TOWER
(**IN** —) ALOFT
(**SUDDEN** —) START STAMPEDE
(**UNAUTHORIZED** —) BUGOUT
(**UPWARD** —) SOAR
FLIGHTY ANILE BARMY GIDDY LIGHT
SWIFT FITFUL GARISH UNFIRM
VOLAGE WHISKY FLYAWAY FOOLISH
GIGGISH MOONISH ROCKETY
FLEETING FREAKISH
(— **PERSON**) TRIVVET
FLIMSINESS INANITY
FLIMSY LIMP THIN VAIN WEAK FRAIL
GAUDY JERRY FEEBLE PALTRY
SLEAZY SLIGHT SLIMSY HAYWIRE
SHALLOW TENUOUS TIFFANY
GIMCRACK GOSSAMER JIMCRACK
TWITTERY
FLINCH FUNK GAME JARG BLUNK
BUDGE FEIGN SHUNT START WINCE
WONDE BLANCH BLENCH FALTER
FLENSE RECOIL SHRINK SCRINGE
SCUNNER SQUINCH
FLINCHER VELLINCH
FLINDER FLITTER SMITHERS
FLINDERSIA SILKWOOD
FLINDOSA CUDGERIE
FLING SHY BUZZ CAST DART DASH
DING EMIT FLAP FLEG GIBE HURL
KICK LASH PECK PICK SLAT TOSS
WARP BRAID CHEAT DANCE FLIRT
LANCE PITCH SHOOT SLING SNEER
SWING THROW WHANG BAFFLE
EFFUSE HURTLE LAUNCH PLUNGE
REBUFF SPIRIT ENFORCE FLOUNCE
REPULSE SARCASM SCATTER
SWINDLE SHYLANCE SPANGHEW
(— **MISSILES**) CHUNK
(— **UPWARD**) HAUNCH
(**HIGHLAND** —) WALLOCH
FLINT CORE BLANK CHERT MISER
SILEX EOLITH QUARTZ REJECT
ESLABON FURISON SCRAPER
GRATTOIR GUNFLINT
FLINTINESS HEART
FLINTLOCK FUSEE FUSIL FUZEE
MUSKET SPANNER FIRELOCK
MIQUELET SNAPHAAN
FLINTWOOD WHITETOP
FLIP SKY TAP FLAP SNAP TOSS TRIP
FLANK FLICK FLIRT SLIRT SMART
FILLIP FLITCH LIMBER NIMBLE
PLIANT PROPEL
FLIPPANT AIRY FLIP GLIB FLUENT
LIMBER NIMBLE
FLIPPER ARM FIN PAW HAND SWELL
PADDLE FLAPPER SPRINGER
FLIRT TOY FIKE FLIP MASH TICK
FLICK ROVER SLIRT JILLET MASHER

TRIFLE GALLANT PICKEER TWINKLE
COQUETTE
FLIRTATION FIKE PASSADE
COQUETRY PHILANDER
FLIT DART FLOW SCUD FLECK FLEET
FLICK FLIRT FLOAT FLURR HOVER
QUICK SCOOT SKIFF SWIFT NIMBLE
FLICKER FLUTTER
FLITCH FLICK GAMMON LONGWOOD
MIDDLING
FLOAT BOB FLY KIT SEA BOOM
BUOY CORK DRAG FLOW FLUX
HAWK HONE HOVE LIVE PONT RAFT
RIDE SAIL SCOW SOAR SWIM TILT
WAFT WAVE BALSA BLADE CAMEL
DERBY DRIFT DRIVE FLEET FLOOD
FLUSH GRAIL HOVER LADLE QUILL
SHOAD SWOON BILLOW BOBBER
BUCKET BUNGEY CANNEL DOBBER
PADDLE PONTON RADEAU STREEL
TOPPER CAISSON DRINGLE FLATTER
FLOTTER FRESHEN OROPESA
PAGEANT PLANKER PLUMMET
PONTOON SLICKER LEVITATE
PICKOVER
  (— **AIMLESSLY**) DRIFT
  (— **DELIGHTFULLY**) COWD
  (— **FOR HERRING NET**) BOWL
  (— **FOR RING BUOY**) LEMON
  (— **LOGS**) DRIVE
  (— **OF REEDS**) KELEK LIGGER
  (— **PAST**) GLACE
  (— **PROPERLY**) WATCH
  (**CANOE** —) AMA
  (**FISHLINE** —) BOB CORK BOBBER
  DOBBER
  (**PLASTERER'S** —) DARBY
FLOATBOARD BLADE FLOAT LADLE
FLOATER STIFF
FLOATING FREE WAFT AWASH
LOOSE ADRIFT AFLOAT FLYING
NATANT BUOYANT FLYAWAY
PENDENT DRIFTING FLUITANT
SHIFTING UNFUNDED
FLOCCILATION TILMUS
FLOCK MOB POD BAND BANK BEVY
FOLD GAME GANG HERD MANY
PACK ROUT SAIL SORT TEAM TRIP
WISP BROOD BUNCH CHARM COVEY
CROWD DRIFT DROVE FLAKE FLECK
GROUP PLUMP SEDGE SHOAL
SWARM TRIBE TROOP COVERT
FLIGHT GAGGLE HIRSEL MANADA
MEINIE RAFTER SCHOOL SCURRY
VOLERY COMPANY GOOSERY
THICKEN PADDLING
  (— **OF BIRDS**) POD BANK HERD
  TEAM WISP BROWN COVEY SEDGE
  SIEGE TRIBE FLIGHT VOLERY
  (— **OF BITTERNS**) SEDGE SIEGE
  (— **OF FINCHES**) CHARM
  (— **OF GEESE**) GAGGLE
  (— **OF HERONS**) SEDGE SIEGE
  (— **OF LARKS**) EXALTATION
  (— **OF LIONS**) PRIDE
  (— **OF MALLARDS**) SORD SUTE
  (— **OF NIGHTINGALES**) WATCH
  (— **OF PARTRIDGE**) COVEY
  (— **OF PEACOCKS**) MUSTER

  (— **OF PIGEONS**) KIT LOFT
  (— **OF ROOKS**) ROOKERY
  (— **OF SANDPIPERS**) FLING
  (— **OF SHEEP**) FOLD HIRSEL
  (— **OF SWANS**) BANK GAME MARK
  (— **OF TURTLE-DOVES**) DOLE
  (— **OF WIDGEONS**) COMPANY
  (— **OF WILDFOWL**) SKEIN
  (— **TOGETHER**) RAFT
  (**SMALL** —) SPRING
FLOCKING REPAIR
FLOG CAT TAN TAW BEAT CANE
CHOP HIDE LASH LICK LUMP TOCO
WALE WARM WELK WHIP YANK
BIRCH EXCEL FIGHT FLAIL HORSE
KNOUT LINGE QUILT SAUCE SKEEG
SWISH COTTON LARRUP LATHER
STRIKE SWITCH THRASH WALLOP
WATTLE BALEISE BELABOR
COWHIDE SCOURGE SJAMBOK
TROUNCE CARTWHIP CHAWBUCK
SLAISTER URTICATE VAPULATE
  (— **WATER**) SCRINGE
FLOGGER HORSING SWISHER
FLOGGING TOCO TOKO TANNING
BIRCHING WHIPPING
FLOOD SEA BORE BUOY FLOW FLUX
POUR TIDE EAGRE FLOAT FLUSH
SPATE SWAMP SWILL WATER
DELUGE EXCESS RAVINE SLUICE
SPLASH DEBACLE FLOTTER
FRESHET NIAGARA TORRENT
ALLUVION CATARACT INUNDATE
OVERFLOW SURROUND
FLOODED AWASH AFLOAT
FLOODGATE CLOW DRAG GOLE
HATCH SLUICE STAUNCH CATARACT
PENSTOCK
FLOODING UP PROUD FLOWAGE
DILUVIAL FLOATING
FLOODLIGHT OLIVET
FLOODPLAIN BENCH DAMBO
FLOOR BECK DROP FLAT LAND PAVE
SEAT BOARD FLOAT GRASS PIANO
PIECE SOLAR STAGE STORY BELFRY
FLIGHT GROUND SOLLAR PLANCHE
BARBECUE FLOORING HALFPACE
PAVEMENT SUBFLOOR
  (— **OF COAL MINE**) SOLE THILL
  (— **OF COAL SEAM**) SILL
  (— **OF FORGE**) HEARTH
  (— **OF GLASS FURNACE**) SIEGE
  (— **OF OCEAN**) SEABED
  (— **OF SPORTS RING**) CANVAS
  (— **OF WOOLSHED**) BOARD
  (**FOREST** —) SEEDBED
  (**GROUND** —) TERRENO BASEMENT
  (**OPENWORK** —**S**) GRATINGS
  (**RAISED** —) LEEWAN HALFPACE
  (**THRESHING** —) MOWSTEAD
FLOORBOARD FOOTLING
FLOORING STAGE PARQUET
TERRAZZO
FLOORMAN CALLBOY
FLOP DOG SWOP WHOP SQUAB
TURKEY TRAGEDY
FLORA FLORULA
  (— **AND FAUNA**) BIOTA
FLORAL TREE LEAF

FLORENCE FLASK BETTY
FLORENCE IRIS ORRIS TREOS
FLORID FINE HIGH BUXOM FRESH
RUDDY ORNATE ROCOCO ASIATIC
FLOWERY TAFFETA BLOOMING
FIGURATE RUBICUND SPLENDID
VIGOROUS

FLORIDA
BAY: APALCHEE BISCAYNE
  WACCASASSA
CAPITAL: TALLAHASSEE
COLLEGE: ROLLINS
COUNTY: DADE GUFF ALACHUA
  BREVARD BROWARD MANATEE
  OSCEOLA VOLUSIA PINELLAS
  SARASOTA
INDIAN: AIS OCALE UTINA CALUSA
  CHATOT POTANO TIMUCUA
  SEMINOLE
ISLANDS: KEYS
KEY: WEST LARGO BISCAYNE
LAKE: DORA APOPKA HARNEY
  JESSUP NEWNAN LEDWITH
  ARBUCKLE KISSIMMEE
  OKEECHOBEE
NATIVE: CONCH CRACKER
RIVER: BANANA INDIAN AUCILLA
  MANATEE SCAMBIA SUWANEE
  OCHLAWAHA
STATE BIRD: MOCKINGBIRD
STATE FLOWER: ORANGE
STATE NICKNAME: SUNSHINE
STATE TREE: PALMETTO
TOWN: TICE COCOA MIAMI OCALA
  TAMPA ORLANDO PALATKA
  SEBRING SARASOTA
  PENSACOLA
UNIVERSITY: STETSON
WETLANDS: GLADES

FLORIDIAN CRACKER
FLOSS FLUFF SKEIN WASTE CADDIS
SLEAVE CADDICE
FLOSSER FANNER
FLOSS-SILK TREE SAMOHU
FLOTSAM JETSAM WILSAM WAFTURE
WAVESON DRIFTAGE FLOATAGE
FLOUNCE FLAP HUFF SKIT SLAM
FLING FRILL RUCHE RIPPLE ROBING
ROUNCE RUFFLE VOLANT FALBALA
FALBELO FROUNCE RUCHING
FLOUNDER FURBELOW STRUGGLE
FLOUNDER DAB GAD BUTT KEEL
POLE ROLL TOSS BREAM FLUKE
SLOSH WITCH WRELE GADOID
GROVEL MEGRIM MUDDLE PLAICE
TURBOT WALLOP WALLOW WARSLE
BLUNDER FLASKER FLOUNCE
PLOUNCE STUMBLE SUNFISH
TOPKNOT VAAGMAR ANACANTH
FLATFISH FOOLFISH PLUNTHER
SANDLING
FLOUR AMYL ATTA DUST CONES
HOVIS BINDER CLEARS FARINA
FLOWER PATENT POLLEN SICKEN
TSAMBA WHITES BOXINGS CRIBBLE
CANAILLE

(— OF MALT) SMEDDUM
(COARSE —) THIRD CHISEL
BOXINGS CRIBBLE
(FINE —) CONES SUJEE
(LOW-GRADE —) TAIL
(PARTICLE OF —) CHOP
(POTATO —) FROW
(UNSORTED —) ATTA
FLOURISH TAG WAG BOOM BRAG
FUSS GROW LICK RIOT RISE SHOW
WAVE ADORN BLOOM BOAST CHEVE
GLOSS QUIRK REIGN SHAKE SWASH
SWING TUSCH VAUNT CATTER
PARADE PARAPH QUAVER SQUIRL
THRIVE BLOSSOM BURGEON
CADENZA DISPLAY ENLARGE
FANFARE GAMBADE GAMBADO
PASSAGE PROSPER ROULADE
SUCCEED TRIUMPH ARPEGGIO
BRANDISH CURLICUE INCREASE
ORNAMENT SKIRMISH
(— OF BAGPIPE) WARBLER
(— OF TRUMPET) TUCKET
FLOURISHING FAR FRIM FRUM PERT
GREEN PALMY PEART VITAL
BLOOMY FLORID GOLDEN FLORENT
HEALTHY VERNANT THRIVING
VEGETOUS
FLOURY MEALY
FLOUT BOB GIBE JEER JERK JIBE
LOUT MOCK FLEER FLITE FRUMP
SCOFF SCOMM SCORN SCOUT
SNEER TAUNT DERIDE INSULT
BETONGUE
FLOW GO EBB ERN JET PUT RUN
SET SUE BORE COMB FLIT FLUX
FUSE GUSH HALE LAVA LAVE MELT
PASS POUR RAIL ROLL SEND SHED
SILE SLIP SOAK SWIG TAIL TEEM
TIDE WELL AVALE DRAIN DRIFT
EAGRE EXUDE FLEAM FLEET FLOAT
FLOOD FLUSH FRESH GLIDE ISSUE
QUELL RIVER SCOOT SLIDE SPEND
SPILL SPURT SWILL TRILL ABOUND
AFFLUX COURSE CURSUS DELUGE
GUGGLE GUTTER RECEDE RINDLE
SPRING STREAM CURRENT DEVOLVE
DISTILL DRIBBLE EMANATE
FLOWAGE FLUTTER FLUXION
ILLAPSE INDRAFT MEANDER
SPURTLE TRINKLE TRINTLE
ALLUVION BACKWASH CURRANCE
CURRENCY DOWNFLOW EMISSION
FOUNTAIN INUNDATE
(— AGAINST) LAP LAVE BATHE
(— BACK) EBB
(— BEYOND BANKS) DEBORD
SURROUND
(— DOWN) AVALE
(— IN RILLS) DRILL
(— IN RIVULETS) GUTTER
(— IN SPURTS) SALTATION
(— IN) INFLOW INFLOOD
(— INTERMITTENTLY) HEAD
(— OF AIR) SIDEWASH
(— OF ELECTRICITY) BOLT
(— OF METAL) CREEP
(— OF RADIO SIGNAL) BEAM
(— OF SOUNDS) CADENCE

(— OUT) EMIT ISSUE EFFUSE
SPREAD EXHAUST RESOLVE
(— OVER) BERUN
(— SLOWLY) SEEP EXUDE GLEET
(— TOGETHER) CONCUR CONFLOW
(— WITH) FLEET
(CONTINUOUS —) LAPSE
(COPIOUS —) HALE RIVER
(RHYTHMICAL —) LILT
(TIDAL —) BORE AEGIR EAGER
EAGRE
FLOWER (ALSO SEE PLANT AND
HERB) BUD GAY BEST BLOW FLAG
IRIS IXIA PINK POLE POSY ROSE
ARROW ASTER BLOOM BREAK
DAISY ELITE FANCY FLOOR GOWAN
LILAC PANSY PHLOX TRUSS TULIP
TUTTY AZALIA CHOICE CORYMB
CROCUS CYMULE DAHLIA DATURA
FLORET MAYPOP ORCHID SCILLA
SEASON SHOWER SINGLE STEVIA
UNFOLD AMELLUS ANEMONE
ARBUTUS BLETHIA BLOSSOM
BOSTRYX DEVELOP ESSENCE
FLEURET FLOSCLE GAZANIA
GENTIAN GERBERA IPOMOEA
PETUNIA PICOTEE TORENIA
BELAMOUR CAMELLIA CYCLAMEN
DAFFODIL DIANTHUS GARDENIA
GERANIUM HEPATICA HIBISCUS
HYACINTH PRIMROSE SPARAXIS
(— STATE) FLORIDA
(— WITH 6 SEGMENTS) SEXFOIL
(COTTON —) SQUARE
(DEFORMED —) BULLHEAD
(DOUBLE —) BURSTER
(DRIED —S) BRAYERA
(IMAGINARY —) AMARANTH
(STRIPED —) BIZARRE
(UNFADING —) AMARANTH
(PL.) BOUQUET
FLOWERFLY SYRPHID
FLOWERING AFLOWER FLOWERY
ANTHESIS BLOOMING
FLOWERING GLUME LEMMA
FLOWER-OF-AN-HOUR SHOOFLY
FLOWER-PECKER KAKAWAHIE
FLOWERPOT POT CACHEPOT
FLOWERY BLOWN BLOOMY FLORID
POSIED FLORENT PRIMROSE
FLOWING FAIR FLUX LAVE SIDE
AFLOW FLOAT FLUID FLUOR QUICK
TIDAL AFFLUX DEFLUX FLUENT
FUSILE LIVING COPIOUS CURRENT
CURSIVE EMANANT FLUXING
FLUXION FLUXIVE RUNNING SLIDING
DEFLUENT DILUENDO FLUVIOSE
(— AT LOW SPEED) SLACK
(— BACK) EBB
(— IN) INFLUX INFLUENT INFLUXION
(— OF GLAZE) STREAMING
(— OF TIDE) FLOOD
(— OUT) ELAPSE EFFLUENT
FLOWOFF RUNOFF
FLUCAN SELVAGE SELVEDGE
FLUCTUATE SWAY VARY VEER
FLEET SWING WAVER BALANCE
VIBRATE WAMPISH UNDULATE
UNSTEADY

FLUCTUATING WAVY HECTIC LABILE
RUBATO ERRATIC FLUXIVE
WAYWARD UNSTABLE UNSTEADY
FLUCTUATION CYCLE FADING
JIGGLE FLICKER FLUTTER VIBRATO
FLUE NET BARB DOWN OPEN PIPE
THIN VENT FLARE FLUFF FLUKE
FUNNEL TUNNEL UPTAKE CHIMNEY
PASSAGE DOWNTAKE
FLUE-CURED BRIGHT
FLUENCY SKILL
FLUENT GASH GLIB FLUID READY
FACILE LIQUID SMOOTH STREAM
COPIOUS CURRENT FLOWING
FLUIDIC RENABLE VERBOSE
VOLUBLE ELOQUENT FLIPPANT
FLUFF LINT PUFF BEARD WHEEL
FLUFFING WHEELING
FLUFFY SOFT DOWNY DRUNK FILMY
FLUEY FUZZY LIGHT LINTEN PLUFFY
FEATHERY UNSTEADY
(NOT —) CLOSE
FLUID INK SAP MASS RASA BLOOD
FLUOR HUMOR JUICE LATEX SERUM
SPERM SWEAT WATER FLUENT
LIQUID WATERY FLOWING FLUIBLE
FLUXILE GASEOUS SYNOVIA
EMULSION FLOATING FLUXIBLE
FORESHOT
(ANIMAL —) SERUM
(EGYPTIAN PRIMEVAL —) NU NUN
(ETHEREAL —) ICHOR
(LIVER —) BILE
(LUBRICATING —) SYNOVIA
(MAMMARY —) MILK
(SOLDERING —) FAKE
(THICK VISCOUS —) GRUME
(WATERY —) LYE SANIES SEROSITY
(WORKING —) AIR
FLUIDITY LENGTH
(— UNIT) RHE
FLUKE FLUE PALM BLADE GRASP
PLAICE DISTOME PLATODE
SCRATCH FLATWORM FLOUNDER
(— OF ANCHOR) HOOK
(— OF WHALE'S TAIL) BLADE
FLUME CHUTE DITCH SHUTE SLUICE
FLUMMERY SOWENS WASHBREW
FLUNK BUST FAIL SKEW SPIN
FLICKER
FLUNKY SNOB TOADY COOKEE
JEAMES LACKEY FOOTMAN
SERVANT STEWARD
FLUORESCENCE BLOOM
FLUORINE PHTOR PHTHOR
FLUORITE CAND FLUX FLUOR
FLURRY ADO FIT FACT FRET GUST
PIRR SPIT STIR TEAR HASTE SKIFF
SKIRL BOTHER BUSTLE SCURRY
SQUALL CONFUSE FLUSKER
FLUSTER FLUTTER FOOSTER
SWITHER WHITHER SPITTING
FLUSH JET EVEN GLOW HUSH JUMP
POOL ROSE BLOOM BLUSH COLOR
ELATE FLASH FLUSK FRESH KNOCK
LEVEL RAISE ROUGE START VIGOR
AFLUSH EXCITE HECTIC LAVISH
MANTLE MORASS REDDEN RUDDLE
SLUICE SPRING THRILL ANIMATE

BOBTAIL CRIMSON SUFFUSE
ABUNDANT AFFLUENT PRODIGAL
ROSINESS
(— **GAME**) SERVE
(— **IN SKY**) SUNGLOW
(**NOT** —) FLAT

FLUSHED RED ROSY BEAMY FIERY
FLOWN FLORID FLUSHY HECTIC
CRIMSON

FLUSTER PAVIE SHAKE BOTHER
FLURRY FUDDLE MUDDLE POTHER
RATTLE CONFUSE FLUSKER
FOOSTER SWITHER BEFUDDLE
FLOWSTER FLUSTRUM

FLUTE NAY FIFE FUYE PIPE AULOS
CRIMP CUENA PUNGI QUENA STICK
STYKE TIBIA TWILL CANNEL DOUCET
FLAUTO GEWGAW GOFFER POOGYE
ZUFOLO CHAMFER DIAULOS
FLAMFEW FLUTING GAUFFER
HEMIOPE MAGADIS MATALAN
PICCOLO SIBILUS SIFFLOT TONETTE
TRANGAM WHISTLE ZUFFOLO
FLAUTINO MONAULOS RECORDER
(— **OF A COLUMN**) STRIGA
CHANNEL
(— **STOP**) VENTAGE
(**CHINESE** —) TCHE
(**EAST INDIAN** —) MATALAN
(**EUNUCH** —) KAZOO
(**JAPANESE** —) FUYE
(**LYDIAN** —) MAGADIS
(**MOSLEM** —) NAY
(**PHOENICIAN** —) GINGRAS
(**PL.**) NEHILOTH

FLUTED QUILLED
FLUTEMOUTH CORNETFISH
FLUTE PLAYER AULETE FLUTER
FLUTIST TIBICEN TOOTLER
AULETRIS FLAUTIST

FLUTING STRIX FULLER GADROON
STRIGIL COULISSE QUILLING

FLUTTER BAT FAN BATE BLOW BUZZ
FLAP FLIT FLOW PLAY WAFF WAVE
FLACK FLAFF FLARE FLECK FLICK
FLURR HOVER SHAKE WAVER
BANGLE FLAUNT FLURRY RUFFLE
SWIVET WAFFLE WALLOP FLACKER
FLAFFER FLASKER FLATTER
FLAUGHT FLICKER FLITTER
FLUSKER SKIMMER WAGTAIL
WHIFFLE FLICHTER SQUATTER
VOLITATE
(**IN A** —) PITAPAT

FLUTTERING AWING FLITTY
WHUTTER AFLUTTER FLICKERY
FLUTTER-TONGUING GROWL
FLUX FLOW FUSE LASK MELT BORAX
FLOAT FLOOD ISSUE RESIN ROSIN
SMEAR SMELT FUSION CURRENT
EURIPUS FLOWING LEAKAGE
OUTFLOW
(— **UNIT**) WEBER MAXWELL

FLY BEE FAG FAN GAD HOP RUN
FIRK FLEA FLEE FLEG FLIT GNAT
KITE KIVU LASH LEAP MELT RACK
RAKE SAIL SCUD SMUT SOAR SOLO
WHEW WHIR WHIZ WIND WING ZIMB
AGILE ALERT EMPID FLEET FLIER

FLOAT FLURR FLUSH FLYER GLIDE
LATCH MIDGE MUSCA OXFLY PERLA
PHORA PILOT QUICK SEDGE SHARP
SKIRL SKIRR STOUR WHAME WHIRR
ZEBUB ASILID AVIATE BANGLE
BLOWER BOTFLY BREEZE DAYFLY
ESCAPE FLIGHT FLYBOY GADFLY
GORFLY JARFLY LEPTID NIMBLE
PALMER PHORID PUNKIE RANDON
ROBBER SEPSID SEROOT SPRING
TIPULA TSETSE VANISH VERMIN
WINNOW AVIGATE AVOLATE
CANOPID CHALCID CONOPID
FORMATE GRANNOM KNOWING
ORTALID PYRALIS SCIARID TYRPHID
AIRPLANE BIBIONID BRACONID
COACHMAN DIPTERAN DROPPING
EPHYDRID EULOPHID GLOSSINA
HORSEFLY HOUSEFLY RUBYTAIL
SIMULIID TACHINID TATUKIRA
VOLITATE
(— **AFTER GAME**) RAKE
(— **AIMLESSLY**) BANGLE
(— **ALOFT**) SOAR TOWER
(— **AWAY**) CARRY
(— **CLUMSILY**) FLIGHTER
(— **ERRATICALLY**) GAD
(— **INTO RAGE**) FUFF RARE
(— **LOW**) DICE DRAG HEDGEHOP
(— **OUT**) EXPIRE
(— **RAPIDLY**) SCUR SKIRR
(— **TOO HIGH**) SCUD
(— **WIDE**) MISS
(**FISHING** —) BEE DUN OAK BUZZ
GNAT HARL HERL SMUT WASP ZULU
ABBEY ALDER BAKER FAIRY NYMPH
SEDGE BADGER BOBFLY CADDIS
CAHILL CANARY CLARET DOCTOR
HACKLE MILLER ORIOLE WILLOW
BABCOCK BUTCHER CADDICE
COLONEL DROPPER DUBBING
GRANNOM HUZZARD SPINNER
WATCHED WATCHET BUCKTAIL
CATSKILL COACHMAN FERGUSON
GOVERNOR STREAMER WOODRUFF
WRENTAIL
(**MAY** —) DUN DRAKE
(**SHEEP** —) FAG KED
(**STONE** —) SALLY

FLYBLOWN BLOWN STRUCK
FLYBOAT FLUTE FLIGHT
FLYCATCHER TODY PEWEE PEWIT
CHEBEC COBWEB MILLER PEEWEE
PHOEBE PIPIRI RAFTER TYRANT
YETAPA ELEPAIO FANTAIL GRIGNET
GRINDER PITIRRI TOMFOOL TYRANNI
BEAMBIRD FIREBALL FIREBIRD
FLYEATER FORKTAIL GERYGONE
KINGBIRD KISKADEE PITANGUA
WALLBIRD

FLYING AWING FLIGHT VOLANT
WAVING FLOTANT VOLATIC
AVIATION FLOATING
(— **MANEUVER**) LUFBERY
FLYING FISH SKIPPER VOLADOR
FLYING FOX KALONG PTEROPID
FLYING GURNARD ANGLER
BATFISH LATCHET LOPHIID
VOLADOR

FLYING LEMUR COBEGO COLUGO
KUBONG
FLYING MACHINE AVIATOR
AEROSTAT
FLYING PHALANGER CUSCUS
SQUIRREL
FLYING SQUIRREL TAGUAN
ASSAPAN
FLYWHEEL FLY FLIER FLYER WHORL
WHARVE
FLYMAN LOFTMAN
FLYSCH MACIGNO
FOAL CADE COLT FILLY PODDY
SLEEPER
FOAM FOB SUD BARM BEES BOIL
FUME HEAD KNIT REAM SCUD SCUM
SUDS WORK CREAM FROST FROTH
SPUME YEAST BUBBLE FLOWER
FLURRY FREATH IMBOST LATHER
SEETHE BLUBBER DESPUME
MELDROP
FOAMING AFOAM NAPPY YEASTY
SPUMOUS MANTLING
FOAMY BARMY SPUMY SUDSY
FROTHY SPUMOSE
FOB FUB SPUNG POCKET
FOCAL POINT OMPHALOS
FOCUS FIX PUT POINT PURSE TRAIN
CENTER CLIMAX DIRECT FASTEN
FIXATE HEARTH TEMPLE NUCLEUS
CONVERGE FOCALIZE GANGLION
FODDER HAY FEED FOOD SOIL VERT
GOOMA MANGE FORAGE FOTHER
PODDER SILAGE STOVER FARRAGE
PODWARE ENSILAGE ROUGHAGE
FODDERCAGE TUMBREL
FODDERER FOGGER
FOE ENEMY FIEND RIVAL FOEMAN
HOSTILE OPPOSER OPPONENT
FOG FF DAG RAG DAMP DAZE HAAR
HAZE MIST MOKE MOSS MURK PRIG
RACK ROKE SMOG SMUR SOUP
BEDIM BRUME CLOUD GRASS
HUMOR MUDDY SMIRR SPRAY
STOUR VAPOR MUDDLE NEBULA
SALMON STUPOR FOGGAGE
OBSCURE POGONIP SMOTHER
BEWILDER MOISTURE
(— **OF THE NILE**) QOBAR
(**FROZEN** —) BARBER
(**LIGHT** —) GAUZE
(**SEA** —) HAAR HARR
FOGBOW DOG FOGDOG SEADOG
MISTBOW FOGEATER
FOGDOG DOG STUBB FOGBOW
SEADOG FOGEATER
FOGGINESS CLOUDING
FOGGY DIM DULL HAZY MIRK MOKY
MURK ROKY DENSE DIRTY GROSS
MISKY MISTY MURKY ROOKY ROUKY
SPEWY CLOUDY GREASY GROGGY
MARSHY MILKEN SMURRY BRUMOUS
MUDDLED OBSCURE CONFUSED
NUBILOUS VAPOROUS
FOGHORN SIREN TYFON RIPPER
MEGAFOG
FOGY FOGEY FOGRAM FOOZLE
STODGER MOSSBACK
FOGYISH MUSTY

MAST PROG RAID FORAY BREVIT
RUSSUD ZACATE GOITCHO
BOOTHALE SCROUNGE
FORAGER OUTRIDER
FORAMEN PORE EXOSTOME
METAPORE
FORAY RAID MELEE FURROW
INROAD RAVAGE RAZZIA SORTIE
CHAPPOW HERSHIP PILLAGE
SPREAGH SPREATH
FORBEAR LET BEAR HELP HOLD
SHUN SIRE AVOID FORGO SPARE
WAIVE DEPORT DESIST ENDURE
PARENT RETAIN ABSTAIN DECLINE
REFRAIN RESPITE ANCESTOR
FOREBEAR WITHDRAW
(— PROSECUTION) COMPOUND
FORBEARANCE MERCY LENITY
NONACT QUARTER MILDNESS
PATIENCE
FORBEARING CLEMENT LENIENT
PATIENT MERCIFUL TOLERANT
FORBID BAN BAR DEFY DENY FEND
TABU VETO WARN DEBAR TABOO
BANISH DEFEND ENJOIN IMPEDE
OPPOSE REFUSE SHIELD FORFEND
FORWARN GAINSAY INHIBIT
WITHSAY DISALLOW FORSPEAK
PRECLUDE PROHIBIT
FORBIDDANCE BAN VETO FORBODE
FORBIDDEN TABU TABOO BANNED
DENIED VERBOTEN
FORBIDDING DOUR GRIM HARD
BLACK GAUNT STERN FIERCE
GLASSY GLOOMY GRISLY ODIOUS
STRICT FORBODE GRIZZLY
FORCE GAR GUT HAP JAM LID VIM
VIS ZIP BANG BEAR BEAT BEND
BIRR BODY CLIP CRAM DINT DOOM
DRAG EDGE FECK FOSS GRIP GUTS
HEAD JAMB JINX MAIN MAKE MANA
SOCK ABATE AGENT ARDOR BRAWL
BRING BRUSH CLAMP COACT CRAFT
CROWD CRUSH DEMON DRAFT
DRIVE EXACT EXERT FOHAT GAVEL
IMPEL KARMA MIGHT PAINT PEISE
POACH POINT POWER PRESS PRIZE
PUNCH REPEL SHEAR SHOVE SINEW
STEAM STUFF THROW WAKAN
WREST CHARGE COERCE COMPEL
CUDGEL DURESS EFFECT EFFORT
ENERGY EXTORT HIJACK HOTBED
IMPACT IMPOSE JOSTLE OBLIGE
POWDER RAVISH SHAKTI STRAIN
WRENCH ABILITY AFFORCE
BLUSTER CASCADE CONCUSS
DRAUGHT DYNAMIC IMPETUS
IMPRESS IMPULSE OPPRESS
REQUIRE SQUEEZE TORMENT
VIOLATE WAKANDA ACTIVITY
ADHESION AFFINITY BULLDOZE
COACTION COERCION DYNAMISM
EFFICACY HOTHOUSE MOMENTUM
PRESSURE STRENGTH VALIDITY
VIOLENCE VIRILITY
(— AIR UPON) BLOW
(— AN ENTRANCE) RANDOM
THRUST
(— APART) SUNDER DISPART

(— BACK) REPEL RAMBARRE
(— BY THREAT) SWAGGER
(— DOWN) CLEW CLUE DETRUDE
DISMOUNT
(— IN) INJECT INTRUDE
(— OPEN) BURST JIMMY SPORT
RANFORCE
(— OUT) SPEW EJECT ERUPT EVICT
EXPEL KNOCK EXTUND EXPRESS
(— PASSAGE) SQUEEZE
(— WAY) CROWD WRING
(— WITH LEGAL AUTHORITY) POSSE
(ALLEGED —) OD
(ARMED —) CREW HEAD CONREY
ARMAMENT
(CONCENTRATED —) PITH
(CONFINING —) LID
(CONSTRAINING —) STRESS
(COSMIC —) EVIL
(CREATIVE —) NATURE
(DRIVING —) STEAM SWINGE
(HYPOTHETICAL —) FORTUNE
(LIFE —) SHAKTI
(MAIN —) BRUNT
(MILITANT —) SWORD
(MILITARY —) FYRD LEGION WERING
(NAVAL —) FLEET
(PHYSICAL —) NERVE
(PREPONDERATING —) SWAY
(PROTECTIVE —) CONVOY
(RELIGIOUS —) SANCTITY
(SACRED —) KAMI
(SPIRITUAL —) SOUL
(UNRESTRAINED —) FURY
(UPWARD —) BUOYANCY
(PL.) ARMY WILL COLORS
FORCED LABORED ENFORCED
FALSETTO SPURIOUS STRAINED
FORCEFUL GREAT GUTSY STIFF
STOUT MIGHTY PUNCHY STRONG
VIRILE DYNAMIC VIOLENT BRUISING
ELOQUENT EMPHATIC ENFATICO
FORCIBLE VIGOROUS
FORCEFULNESS EMPHASIS
FORCEMEAT FARCE BOUDIN
GODIVEAU QUENELLE STUFFING
FORCEPS DOG FURCA TONGS
TENAIL BULLDOG CLAMMER
PINCERS PINSONS CROWBILL
DENTAGRA PINCETTE VULSELLA
FORCIBLE VIVE STOUT VALID
COGENT MIGHTY POTENT STRONG
FORCIVE NERVOUS VIOLENT
WEIGHTY EMPHATIC FORCEFUL
POWERFUL PREGNANT PUISSANT
VIGOROUS
FORCIBLY AMAIN SADLY HARDLY
MAINLY HEAVILY STRONGLY
FORD PASS RIFT WADE WATH DRIFT
STREAM CURRENT FORDING
PASSAGE PASSING CROSSING
(PAVED —) STEAN STEENING
FORE VAN WAY AFORE AHEAD
FRONT PRIOR FORMER FURTHER
FOREARM CUBIT CUBITAL CUBITUS
FOREBEAR ANCESTOR
FOREBODE BODE GIVE OMEN
ABODE AUGUR CROAK BETIDE
DIVINE BETOKEN MISBODE OMINATE

PORTEND PREDICT PRESAGE
FORETELL
FOREBODING OMEN BLACK FATAL
AUGURY BODING DISMAL GLOOMY
ANXIETY BALEFUL BANEFUL
DRUTHER OMINOUS PRESAGE
BODEMENT SINISTER
FOREBODINGLY DIRELY
FOREBRAIN CEREBRUM
FORECAST BODE CAST SCHEME
CAUTION FORESEE FORESET
PREDICT FOREDEEM FOREDOOM
FORETELL PROPHESY
FORECASTLE FOCSLE ISLAND
FOREDOOM JINX DESTINY
FOREFACE CUSHION
FOREFATHER AYEL SIRE ELDER
PITRI PARENT ANCESTOR
FOREBEAR
FOREFINGER INDEX
FOREFOOT PAW PUD GRIPE
FOREFOOTING MANGANA
FOREFRONT VAN FRONT VAWARD
FOREGO FORGO WAIVE ESCHEW
ABSTAIN NEGLECT PRECEDE
REFRAIN ABNEGATE DISPENSE
RENOUNCE
FOREGOING PAST ABOVE ANTERIOR
PREVIOUS
FOREHEAD BROW FRONS FRONT
FRONTLET SINCIPUT
(— INDENTATION) STOP
(— MARK) KUMKUM
(HIGH —) LEPTENE
FOREHEARTH SETTLER
FOREIGN UNCO ALIEN FREMD
WELSH ALANGE EXILED EXOTIC
FRENCH REMOTE UNKIND DISTANT
ECDEMIC EPIGENE EXCLUDE
FRAMMIT HEATHEN OUTBORN
OUTLAND OUTWARD STRANGE
BARBARIC EPIGENIC EXTERIOR
EXTERNAL FORINSEC OVERSEAS
PEREGRIN STRANGER
(— TO) DEHORS
FOREIGNER ALIEN HAOLE ALLTUD
GRINGO PAKEHA GREENER
OUTBORN OUTLAND PARDESI
OUTSIDER PEREGRIN PORTUGEE
STRANGER MLECHCHHA
FOREKNOW DIVINE FORESEE
FOREWIT
FOREKNOWLEDGE PRESAGE
FORELOCK TOP BANG QUIFF
COTTER TOUPET FORETOP TOPPING
FOREBUSH
FOREMAN BOSS BULL CORK JOSS
LUNA PUSH CHIEF DOGGY GAFFER
GANGER LEADER RAMROD SIRDAR
TENTER CAPATAZ CAPORAL
CAPTAIN FOUNDER HEADMAN
MANAGER MANDOER OVERMAN
SHOOFLY SKIDDER STEWARD
FOREHAND GANGSMAN OVERSEER
FOREMOST TOP HEAD HIGH MAIN
CHIEF FIRST FORME FRONT GRAND
BANNER FORMER LEADING
SUPREME VANMOST CHAMPION
(— PART) VAWARD

FOREORDAIN FATE SLATE DESTINE
FORESAY PREDOOM FORECAST
FOREORDINATION FATE
FOREPART FRONT FOREHEAD
(— **OF FACE**) CHAP
(— **OF SHIP**) STEM FORWARD
CUTWATER ENTRANCE
FOREPOLE LATH SPILE SPILING
FORERUN HERALD OUTRUN
PRECEDE PRELUDE ANNOUNCE
FORESHOT
FORERUNNER OMEN SIGN USHER
AUGURY HERALD ANCESTOR
FOREGOER FOURRIER PRODROME
FORERUNNING PRECURSE
FORESADDLE RACK
FORESEE SEE READ DIVINE PURVEY
PREVISE PROVIDE ENVISAGE
ENVISION FORECAST FOREKNOW
PROSPECT
FORESHADOW HINT FIGURE HERALD
FORERUN PATTERN PRELUDE
UMBRATE FORETYPE
FORESHORE HARD SHORE
HARDWAY SEASHORE
FORESHOW BODE ABODE AUGUR
BETOKEN PORTEND SIGNIFY
FORETELL PROPHESY
FORESIGHT FEAR VISION FOREWIT
FORECAST FORELOOK PROSPECT
PRUDENCE
FORESIGHTED CAGY CAGEY CANNY
FOREST BUSH GAPO MATA RUKH
WOLD WOOD FIRTH GLADE GUBAT
MATTA MATTO SYLVA TAIGA WASTE
WEALD JUNGLE TIMBER BOSCAGE
CALYDON COPPICE CAATINGA
WOODLAND
(— **CITY**) PORTLAND SAVANNAH
CLEVELAND
(— **FOR DEER**) FIRTH
(**IMMENSE** —) MONTANA
(**RAIN** —) SELVA
(**SIBERIAN** —) URMAN
(**STUNTED** —) CAATINGA
KRUMMHOLZ
FORESTAGE APRON
FORESTALL BEAT HELP STALL
DEVANCE FORERUN OBVIATE
PREVENE PREVENT FORSTEAL
FORESTALLER GROSSER
FORESTAYSAIL JUMBO
FORESTER FOSTER WALKER
MONTERO TINEMAN TREEMAN
WOODMAN WOODSMAN
FORETASTE GUST HANSEL TEASER
EARNEST HANDSEL ANTEPAST
PROSPECT
FORETELL BODE ERST READ SPAE
AUGUR INSEE WEIRD DIVINE
HALSEN HERALD BESPEAK FORESAY
PORTEND PREDICT PRESAGE
ANNOUNCE FOREBODE FORECAST
FORESHOW PROPHESY SOOTHSAY
FORETELLING PROPHESY
FORETHOUGHT CAUTION FORECAST
PREPENSE PRUDENCE
FORETOKEN OMEN PORTEND

PROMISE FORECAST FORESHOW
FORESIGN
FOREVER AY AKE AYE EVER ETERN
ALWAYS ETERNE ENDLESS
ETERNITY EVERMORE
FOREWARNING HINT PORTENT
FOREWING PRIMARY
FOREWORD PROEM PREFACE
PREAMBLE
FORFEIT WED FINE LOSE TINE WITE
CRIME DEDIT FORGO LAPSE
FOREGO DEFAULT ESCHEAT
FORWORK PENALTY FORFAULT
FORFEITURE FINE BLIND MULCT
TINSEL ESCHEAT FORFEIT PENALTY
FORGE FOGE MINT TILT WELL CLICK
FALSE FEIGN SMITH STOVE HAMMER
SMITHY STEADY STITCH STITHY
SWINGE CHAFERY FALSIFY FASHION
BLOOMERY
FORGED BOGUS SPURIOUS
FORGER SMITH FALSER FALSARY
LEVERMAN
FORGERY SHAM FALSUM FICTION
BLOOMERY
FORGET LOSE OMIT WANT FLUFF
BILEVE UNKNOW UNMIND NEGLECT
OVERLOOK
FORGETFULNESS SWIM FLUFF
LETHE AMNESIA AMNESTY OBLIVION
FORGET-ME-NOT MYOSOTE
FORGING HOOP CLICK JACKET
FORGIVE REMIT SPARE ASSOIL
EXCUSE PARDON ABSOLVE
CONDONE OVERLOOK
FORGIVENESS GRACE PARDON
FORGIFT
FORGIVING GRACE HUMANE
CLEMENT MERCIFUL
FORGOTTEN DERELICT UNMINDED
FORINT FLORIN
FORK CROC EVIL HOOK TANG TINE
CLEFT CLOFF FURCA GLACK GRAIN
GRAIP PRONG TWIST BISECT
BRANCH CLITCH CROTCH DIVIDE
FEEDER GAFFLE HACKER OFFSET
TWISEL BIPRONG FOURCHE
FRUGGIN HAYFORK TOASTER
CROTCHET EQUULEUS GRAINING
(— **OF BODY**) SHARE
(— **OF PENNON**) FANON
(**THATCHER'S** —) GROM
(**TUNING** —) DIAPASON
FORKED BIFID FORKY FURCAL
PRONGY DIVIDED FURCATE LITUATE
BIFORKED BRANCHED FOURCHEE
SUBBIFID
FORKING STAR
FORLORN LORN LOST REFT ALONE
ABJECT FORFAIRN FORSAKEN
HELPLESS HOPELESS PITIABLE
WITLOSEN
FORM AME DIG FIG HEW HUE SET
BLEE BODY CASE CAST CAUL DOME
FLOW GARB IDEA KERN KITE MAKE
MODE MOLD PLAN RITE SEAT THEW
TURN BENCH BLANK BLOCK BOARD
BUILD BUNCH CHART CHECK CRUSH
DUMMY EIDOS ERECT FORGE

FORMA FORME FRAME GALBE GUISE
IMAGE MATCH MEUSE MODEL
SHAPE SPELL STAMP THROW
USAGE ADJUST COUPON CREATE
CUSTOM DEVISE DOCKET FIGURE
FILLER HANGER INVENT MANNER
REMOVE RITUAL SCHEMA SCHOOL
SPONGE STRIKE SYSTEM TAILLE
AGENDUM ARRANGE COMPOSE
CONFECT CONTOUR DEVELOP
FASHION FEATURE FORMULA
GESTALT IMPANEL INVOICE LITURGY
MAKEDOM OUTLINE PATTERN
PORTRAY PORTURE PRODUCE
PROFILE SPECIES STATURE
BILLHEAD CEREMONY COMPOUND
CONCEIVE CONTRIVE FORMWORK
INSTRUCT LIKENESS ORGANIZE
(— **A HEAD**) POME
(— **A RING**) ENVIRON
(— **ASSUMED AFTER DEATH**)
KAMARUPA
(— **BRANCHES**) BREAK
(— **BY CUTTING OFF**) ABJOINT
(— **CONNECTION**) ALLY
(— **FOR BELL FOUNDING**) SWEEP
(— **FOR CONCRETE**) BOXING
(— **FOR HOLDING BARREL**) SQUAW
(— **FOR MOLD**) JACKET
(— **FOR PRESSING VENEERS**) CAUL
(— **FRUIT**) KNIT
(— **INTO A CHAIN**) CATENATE
(— **INTO BALL**) CONGLOBE
(— **INTO RINGLETS**) CRISP
(— **LEATHER**) CRIMP
(— **MOUND**) TUMP
(— **OF GOVERNMENT**) ESTATE
KINGSHIP
(— **OF PREDICATION**) CATEGORY
(— **POLITICAL SUCCESSION**) CAVE
(— **WITH PLASTER**) RUN
(— **YARN INTO THREAD**) CABLE
(**ANCESTRAL** —) BLASTAEA
STEMFORM
(**CONVENTIONAL** —) AMENITY
(**DEXTROROTATORY** —) CAMPHOR
(**IMPERFECT** —) SEMIFORM
(**ISOMETRIC** —) DIPLOID
(**LINGUISTIC** —) FOSSIL GERUND
(**LITERARY** —) KNACK
(**LYRICAL** —) SESTINA
(**MUSICAL** —) SUITE
(**POINTED** —) ANGLE
(**SCHOOL** —) SHELL
(**SHOE** —) LAST FILLER
(**SONG** —) BAR
(**SPECTRAL** —) SHADOW
(**SPEECH** —) LEXEME
(**SPIRAL OR CIRCULAR** —) GYRE
(**TOP** —) GROOVE
(**VERB** —) FUTURE CONATIVE
DEFINITE DURATIVE
(**VERSE** —) EPODE BALLAD SONNET
KYRIELLE LIMERICK
(**VISIBLE** —) RUPA
(**WILD** —) AGRIOTYPE
(**WORD** —) ETYMON ANOMALY
FORMAL SET BOOK PRIM BUDGE
CHILL COURT EXACT STIFF SOCIAL

SOLEMN STOCKY BOOKISH LOGICAL
ORDERLY OUTWARD PRECISE
REGULAR SOLWARD STARCHY
STATELY STILTED ABSTRACT
ACADEMIC AFFECTED ELEVATED
FORMULAR OFFICIAL PUNCTUAL
STARCHED

FORMALDEHYDE FORMAL MONOSE
HARDENER METHANAL

FORMALIST PEDANT

FORMALISTIC COURT ACADEMIC

FORMALITY FORM SASINE STARCH
BUCKRAM DECENCY WIGGERY
CEREMONY

FORMALIZE STIFFEN

FORMALLY FORMLY STARCHLY

FORMAT SIZE GETUP SHAPE STYLE

FORMATION FORM RANK SPUR
BIOME FLIGHT GROWTH HARROW
MASSIF SPREAD POTENCE
BOTRYOID
(— ENCLOSING MINE WORKING)
GROUND
(— ENCOUNTERED IN DRILLING)
STRAY
(— OF BRANCHES) CANOPY
(— OF CRYSTAL) SHOOT
(— OF JOINT) ANKYLOSIS
(— OF PLANES) JAVELIN
(— ON TOAD) SPADE
(— RESEMBLING ICICLE) STIRIA
(BATTLE —) HERSE
(CLOUD —) NUBECULA
(DANCE —) SET
(DIAGONAL —) HARROW
(DRIPSTONE —) COLUMN
(ECOLOGICAL —) BIOME
(FLIGHT —) SQUADRON
(GEOLOGIC —) BOEL CULM CHICO
STRAY MARKER MEDINA CURTAIN
MANLIUS MATAWAN POTOMAC
TERRAIN AQUIFUGE FERNANDO
KOOTANIE KOOTENAI LOCKPORT
TOPATOPA YORKTOWN
(HABIT —) FIXATION
(INDENTED —) CLEFT
(INFANTRY —) TERTIA ECHELON
(LAND —) BOOTHEEL
(MILITARY —) SNAIL FLIGHT
(NAVAL —) SCREEN
(POINTED —) BEAK

FORMATIVE PLASTIC DEMIURGIC

FORMED BUILT BOOKIT DECIDED
MATURED SETTLED WROUGHT
TIMBERED
(— AT BASE OF MOUNTAIN)
PIEDMONT
(— INTO STEPS) GRADY
(— ON SURFACE OF EARTH)
EPIGENE
(IMPERFECTLY —) ABORTIVE
(STURDILY —) BUXOM

FORMEE PATE PATTEE

FORMER DIE OLD ERER ERST FERN
FORE LATE ONCE PAST ELDER
FORME GAUGE GUIDE MAKER PRIOR
BYGONE RATHER WHILOM ANCIENT
ANOTHER CREATOR EARLIER
FIRSTER FURTHER ONETIME PRIDIAN

QUONDAM TEMPLET UMWHILE
PRETERIT PREVIOUS SOMETIME
STRICKLE UMQUHILE

FORMERLY ERE NEE OLD ERST
FORE ONCE THEN YORE GRAVE
WHILOM WHILST ONETIME
QUONDAM SOMETIME UMQUHILE

FORMIDABLE MEAN FEARFUL
ALARMING DREADFUL MENACING
TERRIBLE FEROCIOUS
(— PERSON) TARTAR

FORMLESS ARUPA DOUGHY ANIDIAN
CHAOTIC DEFORMED INDIGEST

FORMOSA (SEE TAIWAN)

FORMULA LAW MIX DATE FIAT FORM
RULE CANON CREED DHIKR GRAPH
INDEX LURRY KEKULE MANTRA
METHOD RECIPE THEORY RECEIPT
APOLYSIS CLAUSULE DOXOLOGY
EXORCISM
(— OF FAITH) KELIMA
(MAGICAL —) CARACT
(PL.) RAKA RAKAH

FORMULARY SYMBOL

FORMULATE PUT CAST DRAW
FRAME DEVISE CAPSULE COMPOSE
FORMULE PLATFORM

FORMULATED STATED WRITTEN

FORMULATION (— OF A TRUTH)
COUNT CREED DOGMA APHORISM
APOTHEGM DOCTRINE

FORMWORK SHUTTERING

FORNIX VAULT PSALIS

FORSAKE DENY DROP FLEE QUIT
SHUN ABAND AVOID FORGO LEAVE
WAIVE DEFECT DEPART DESERT
FOREGO FORHOO FORLET REFUSE
REJECT ABANDON DISCARD
FORLESE DESOLATE FORHOOIE
RENOUNCE WITHDRAW

FORSAKEN LORN FORLORN
DESERTED DESOLATE LASSLORN

FORSOOTH EVEN QUOTH

FORSWEAR DENY ABJURE REJECT
ABANDON PERJURE ABNEGATE
MANSWEAR RENOUNCE

FORT PA DUN LIS PAH LISS PEEL
SHEE SPUR WORK COTTA REDAN
SIDHE CASTLE SANGAR SCHERM
SCONCE STRONG BASTION
BULWARK CITADEL CLOSURE
REDOUBT BASTILLE CASTILLO
FASTHOLD FASTNESS FORTRESS
MARTELLO PRESIDIO
(FAIRY —) LIS LIOS LISS SHEE
SIDHE
(RUINS OF —) ZIMBABWE
(SMALL —) GURRY FORTIN BASTIDE
FORTLET FORCELET

FORTE FORT STARK STRONG
EMINENCY STRENGTH

FORTESCUE COBBLER SCORPION

FORTH OUT AWAY FURTH

FORTHRIGHT BURLY GUTTY CANDID

FORTHRIGHTLY FRANKLY

FORTHWITH NOW ANON AWAY
BEDENE DIRECT BETIMES FORTHON
DIRECTLY

FORTIFICATION BOMA FORT MOAT

WALL REDAN TOWER ABATIS
CASTLE GLACIS BASTION BULWARK
CITADEL DEFENCE DEFENSE
PARAPET PILLBOX RAMPART
RAVELIN REDOUBT FORTRESS
MUNITION RONDELLE STRENGTH
(LINE OF —S) TROCHA

FORTIFIED ARMED CONFIRMED

FORTIFY ARM MAN BANK FORT LINE
WALL WARD SPIKE STANK BATTLE
IMMURE MUNIFY MUNITE BULWARK
COMFORT DEFENSE GARNISH
RAMPIRE BASTILLE EMBATTLE
FORTRESS RAMFORCE STOCKADE

FORTITUDE GRIT GUTS SAND FIBER
FIBRE PLUCK METTLE BRAVERY
COURAGE HEROISM STAMINA
BACKBONE PATIENCE STRENGTH

FORTNIGHTLY BIWEEKLY

FORTRESS (ALSO SEE FORT) BURG
KEEP KASBA PIECE PLACE ROCCA
CASBAH CASTLE ALCAZAR BARRIER
BOROUGH CASTRUM CHATEAU
CITADEL KREMLIN ZWINGER
ALCAZAVA BASTILLE FASTNESS
STRENGTH

FORTUITOUS CASUAL CHANCE
RANDOM FORTUIT FORTUNEL

FORTUITY LUCK CHANCE

FORTUNATE EDI FAT HAP SRI GOOD
SHRI WELL CANNY FAUST HAPPY
LUCKY RIGHT WHITE DEXTER
EUROUS BLESSED FAVORED
WEIRDLY GRACIOUS

FORTUNATELY FAIR HAPPILY

FORTUNE DIE HAP LOT URE BAHI
DOOM FALL FARE FATE HAIL LUCK
PILE STAR EVENT GRACE ISSUE
LINES SONSE SPEED WEIRD WHATE
CHANCE ESTATE MISHAP RICHES
WEALTH DESTINY SUCCESS
THEEDOM VENTURE ACCIDENT
CASUALTY FELICITY STOCKING
(GOOD —) SELE SONSE SPEED
THRIFT FURTHER GOODHAP
BONCHIEF FELICITY
(ILL —) DOOM THRAW

FORTUNE-TELLER SEER SIBYL
SYBIL SPAEMAN SORTIARY
SPAEWIFE
(PL.) CHALDAEI

FORUM COURT PLATFORM TRIBUNAL

FORWARD ON TO AID BOG BUG GAY
ABET BAIN BOLD FORE FREE HELP
PERT SEND SHIP STEP AHEAD
ALONG BARDY BRASH CAGER
EAGER FAVOR FORTH FRACK FRECK
FRONT HASTY PAWKY READY
RELAY REMIT SAUCY SERVE SPACK
ULTRA AFFORD ARDENT AVAUNT
BEFORE BRIGHT COMING DEVANT
FORRIT FORTHY HASTEN NUZZLE
ONWARD PROMPT ROUDAS SECOND
TOWARD ADVANCE EARNEST
EXTREME FURTHER PROMOTE
PUSHING RADICAL SOLICIT
ADELANTE ARROGANT FROMWARD
IMMODEST IMPUDENT ONCOMING
PERVERSE PETULANT TELLSOME

TOWARDLY TRANSMIT
(MOST —) HEADMOST
FORWARDNESS IMMODESTY
FOSSA FOSS FOVEA GALET TRENCH
VALLIS FOSSULA FOSSETTE
FOSSE DITCH GRAFF
FOSSIL CYCAD CYSTID DOLITE
FUCOID ICHITE PINITE AMBRITE
BICHRON BLASTID CHAMITE CRINITE
ICHNITE JUNCITE LITUITE NEREITE
OVULITE TYLOPOD ZOOLITE
ZOOLITH AISTOPOD AMMONITE
ANCODONT ASTROITE BALANITE
BLASTOID BUFONITE CALAMITE
CERATITE CONCHITE CONODONT
ECHINITE EOHIPPUS FAVOSITE
FILICITE FUSULINA GEDANITE
GYROLITH MIMOSITE PEUCITES
POLYPITE SALIGRAM SCAPHITE
SERAPHIM SPONGOID SYNAPSID
TARSIOID
FOSTER REAR NURSE COCKER
HARBOR NUZZLE SUCKLE CHERISH
DEPOSIT EMBOSOM GRATIFY
INDULGE NOURISH NURTURE
BEFRIEND
FOSTERAGE NURSERY
FOSTERER NORRY
FOUL BAD BASE EVIL HORY RANK
ROIL VILE BAWDY BLACK DIRTY
DITCH FUNKY GRIMY GURRY HORRY
KETTY MUDDY MUSTY NASTY
RUSTY SULLY WEEDY CLARTY
DEFAME DIRTEN DREGGY FILTHY
GREASY IMPURE MALIGN ODIOUS
PUTRID ROTTEN SOILED SORDID
UNFAIR ABUSIVE DEFACED FULSOME
HATEFUL ILLEGAL IMBROIN
NOISOME OBSCENE PROFANE
SMEARED SQUALID TETROUS
UNCLEAN VICIOUS AMURCOUS
ENTANGLE FECULENT INDECENT
SLOTTERY STAGNANT STINKING
TRAUCHLE WRETCHED
(— UP) BOTCH
FOULMOUTHED ROUDAS ABUSIVE
OBSCENE PROFANE
FOULNESS FEDITY PRAVITY
(— OF MOUTH) SABURRA
FOUL-SMELLING FUNKY
FOUND FIX TRY YET BASE CAST
REST STAY BEGIN BOARD BUILD
ENDOW ERECT START ATTACH
BOTTOM DEPART GROUND INVENT
EQUIPPED PRACTICE PROVIDED
SUPPLIED
FOUNDATION BED BASE BODY FIRM
FUND GIST ROOT SILL SOLE BASIS
FOUND STOCK STOOL ANLAGE
BOTTOM CRADLE GROUND LEGACY
MATRIX PODIUM RIPRAP BEDDING
BEDROCK CHANTRY COLLEGE
MORTISE PINNING RADICAL
ROADBED SUBBASE WARRANT
BACKBONE DONATION MATTRESS
MIRAPOIX PEDESTAL PLATFORM
STANDARD UNDERLAY
(— FOR WIG) CAUL
(— OF BASKET) SLATH SLARTH

(FLOATING —) CRIB
(PRECARIOUS —) STILT
FOUNDED FUSILE
FOUNDER FAIL IMAM AUTHOR
CASTER DYNAST EPONYM HELLEN
YETTER AFOUNDE STUMBLE
BELLETER MISCARRY
FOUNT FONS FONT SOURCE
FOUNTAIN URN AQUA FOND HEAD
KELD PANT PILA SYKE WELL DIRCE
FOUNT GURGE QUELL SURGE
ORIGIN PHIALE PIRENE SOURCE
SPRING BUBBLER CONDUIT
SPRUDEL AGANIPPE SALMACIS
UPSPRING WELLHEAD
(INK —) DUCT
(SODA —) SPA
FOUNTAINHEAD ORIGIN SOURCE
FOUNTAIN PEN STICK STYLO
FOUR MESS CATER DELTA DALETH
FEOWER TETRAD QUARTET
QUATRAL MURNIVAL QUADRATE
(— OF ANYTHING) GUNDA
(— OF TRUMPS) TIDDY
(— TIMES A DAY) QD QID
(— YEAR PERIOD) PYTHIAD
FOURCHETTE FORGET SIDEWALL
WISHBONE
FOURFOLD FOURBLE QUATERN
FOURIERISM SOCIALISM
FOUR-O'CLOCK FRIARBIRD
FOURPENNY BIT JOE FLAG JOEY
GROAT
FOURTEENER SEPTENAR
FOURTH DELTA QUART FARDEL
FORPIT FERLING QUARTER
QUADRANT
(— HOUR) SEXT
(— OF BAHMIN EMPIRE) TARAF
(— OF CAKE) FARL FARLE
(— OF YEAR) RAITH
(AUGMENTED —) TRITONE
FOUSSA CIVET GALET
FOVEOLA VARIOLE
FOWL HEN RED COCK GAME GRIG
JAVA ROCK SLIP BIDDY CHUCK
CLUCK COPPY MALAY MANOC
MARAN SILKY ANCONA ASHURA
BANTAM BRAHMA CAMBAR COCHIN
HOUDAN LAMONA LEGBAR POLISH
REDCAP SULTAN SUSSEX BUFFBAR
CAMPINE CHICKEN CORNISH
DORKING FRIZZLE HAMBURG
LEGHORN MINORCA OKLABAR
POULTRY ROOSTER SPANISH
SUMATRA COCKEREL CUBALAYA
DELAWARE DUCKWING DUNGHILL
GAMECOCK LANGSHAN SHANGHAI
SHOWBIRD VOLAILLE
(5-TOED —) SILKY SILKIE
(AGGREGATION OF —) RAFT
(CASTRATED —) CAPETTE
(CRESTED —) TOPKNOT
(GUINEA —) KEEL COMEBACK
(MALE —) STAG
(STUFFED —) FARCI
(TAILLESS —) RUMKIN
FOWLER BIRDMAN
FOX DOG KIT PUG TOD ASSE FOOL

STAG WILD ADIVE CAAMA SWIFT
TRICK VIXEN ZORRO ARCTIC
BAGMAN CANDUC COLFOX CORSAC
FENNEC LOWRIE OUTWIT RENARD
BEGUILE CHARLEY CHARLIE
KARAGAN REYNARD STUPEFY
VULPINE CUSTOMER MUSKWAKI
OUTAGAMI PLATINUM
FOX-AND-GEESE MERELS
FOXGLOVE POPPY POPDOCK
THIMBLE FLAPDOCK POPGLOVE
FOX GRAPE ISABELLA LABRUSCA
FOXHOUND WALKER
FOX HUNTER PINK
FOXTAIL CAUDA CHAPE COUGH
KNEED TWITCH SETARIA GAMELOTE
FOXY SLY WILY COONY SHREWD
CUNNING VULPINE DEXTROUS
FOYER HALL LOBBY
FRACAS BOUT BRAWL MELEE MUSIC
BICKER RUMPUS SHINDY UPROAR
QUARREL SHINDIG FRACTION
INCIDENT
FRACTION BIT CUT PYO FLUX PART
BREAK PIECE SCRAP BREACH
LITTLE MOIETY DECIMAL GLUTOSE
WETNESS
(— OF RADIATION) ALBEDO
(NAPHTHA —) LIGROIN
FRACTIONAL ALIQUOT FRACTED
PARTIAL
FRACTIOUS MEAN UGLY CROSS
UNRULY CRABBED PEEVISH
WASPISH PERVERSE SNAPPISH
FRACTURE BUST FLAW REND BILGE
BREAK CLEFT CRACK FAULT JOINT
BREACH DEFORM HACKLE DIACOPE
FISSURE RUPTURE DIACLASE
FRACTION
FRACTURED SPLIT BROKEN
FRACTURING SLIP STRAIN FAILURE
FRAGILE FINE FROW WEAK FRAIL
FROWY LIGHT SWACK FEEBLE
FROUGH INFIRM SLIGHT TENDER
BRICKLE BRITTLE FROUGHY
SLENDER TIFFANY DELICATE
EGGSHELL ETHEREAL FRACTILE
SLATTERY
FRAGILITY DELICACY
FRAGMENT BIT ORT ATOM BLAD
CHIP DRIB FLAW GROT MOIT MOTE
PART RUMP SHED SNIP WISP ANGLE
BRACK BREAK BROKE CATCH
CHUNK CLOUT CRUMB FRUST
GIGOT PIECE RELIC SCRAP SHARD
SHERD SHIVE SHRED SPALL SPELL
SPLIT FARDEL FILING GOBBET
MORSEL REMAIN SCREED SHIVER
SIPPET SLIVER CANTLET EXCERPT
FLINDER FLITTER FRITTER FRUSTUM
MACERAL MAMMOCK REMANIE
REMNANT SEGMENT SHATTER
SHAVING CHIPPING DETRITUS
FRACTION POTSHERD SKERRICK
SPLINTER
(— CUT OFF) CANTLE
(— OF BONE) SEQUESTER
(— OF BRICK) BRICKBAT
(— OF DIAMOND) CLEAVAGE

(— OF ICE) CALF
(— OF LAVA) FAVILLA LAPILLUS
(— OF MELODY) LAY
(— OF ROCK) CRAG AUTOLITH
(— OF SAIL) HULLOCK
(— OF SOD) TAB
(— OF STONE) SCABBLING
(— OF UNFINISHED WORK) TORSO
(— OF VEIN MATERIAL) SHOAD
SHODE
(—S OF CLOUD) SCUD
(—S OF SAND) FINES
(CAST IRON —) POTLEG
(JAGGED —) BROCK
(MASS OF —S) BRASH
(PLANT —) SHIVE
(SHELL —S) SHRAPNEL
(WOODY —S FOUND IN FOOD) CHAD
(PL.) FRUSH SCRAPS CINDERS
FITTERS GUBBINS SMATTER
FLINDERS LEFTOVER SMITHERS
FRAGMENTARY HASHY SNIPPY
SCRAPPY DIVIDUAL
FRAGRANCE BALM ODOR AROMA
SCENT SMELL SWEET FLAVOR
FRAGOR BOUQUET INCENSE
PERFUME SUAVITY
FRAGRANT NOSY RICH BALMY
OLENT SPICY SWEET SAVORY
SPICED ODORANT ODOROUS
PERFUMY SCENTED AROMATIC
FLAGRANT NECTARED ODORIFIC
REDOLENT
FRAIL FINE PUNY WEAK CRAZY
REEDY SEELY SILLY BASKET
BROTEL CROCKY FLIMSY INFIRM
SICKLY SINGLE SLIGHT SLIMSY
SQUEAL TICKLE TOPNET BRITTLE
BRUCKLE FRAGILE SLENDER
UNHARDY DELICATE PINDLING
FRAILTY FAULT FOIBLE INVENT
FAILING DELICACY WEAKNESS
(HUMAN —) ADAM
FRAMBESIA PIAN YAWS BUBAS
FRAME BED BIN BOW BOX FLY GYM
MAT SET BAIL BEAM BIER BUCK
BULK BUNK CANT CASE CAUM CELL
CLAM CRIB CURB DESK DRAG FORM
FROG GATE GILL HACK HARP HECK
JACK MOLD PORT RACK SASH SLEY
SOLE STEP BANJO BLADE BLIND
BLOCK BUILD CADRE CHASE CLEAT
CRATE CROOK DRAFT EASEL FLAKE
FLASK FLEAK FLOAT GRATE HERSE
HORSE MOUNT OXBOW PERCH
SCRAY SHAPE STAND STATE STEAD
STOCK STOOL TRAIL BATTEN
BINDER BUCCAN BUCKET CASING
CHEVAL COFFIN CRADLE CRATCH
CRUTCH DECKLE DREDGE FABRIC
FENDER GANTRY GRILLE HANGER
HARROW HOTBED HURDLE PERSON
PILLAR QUADRA REDACT REEDER
SCREEN SETTLE SLEDGE SPIDER
SQUARE STAPLE TANGLE TENTER
TESTER ARMRACK BREAKER
CABINET CARRIER CASEBOX
CHASSIS COAMING COASTER
CRAMPON CRIMPER DRAUGHT

DROSSER FASHION FRAMING
FRISKET GALLOWS GARLAND
GATEWAY GIGTREE GRATING
HAYRACK HOUSING ICEBOAT
MACHINE MONTURE OXBRAKE
PORTRAY SETTING STADDLE
TRANSOM TRESTLE TRIBBLE
BARBECUE BOWGRACE CARRIAGE
CONCEIVE CONTRIVE DOORCASE
GRAFFAGE GRIDIRON GRILLAGE
HALBERDS HOGFRAME PLOWHEAD
RAILROAD RECEIVER RETAINER
SKELETON THRIPPLE TRIANGLE
TURNPIKE
(— FOR ARCH) COOM COOMB
(— FOR BEEHIVE) SECTION
(— FOR CANDLES) HEARSE
(— FOR CARRYING STRAW) KNAPE
(— FOR CASK) GANTRY STALDER
(— FOR CATCHING FISH) HATCH
(— FOR CLOTHES DRYING) AIRER
(— FOR CONFINING HORSE) TRAVE
TRAVAIL
(— FOR COW'S HEAD) BAIL
(— FOR DRYING FISH) HACK HAIK
(— FOR DRYING SKINS) HERSE
(— FOR FISHING LINE) CADAR
CADER
(— FOR GLAZING LEATHER) BUCK
(— FOR HAWKS) CADGE
(— FOR KILLING PIGS) CREEL
(— FOR LENS) BOW
(— FOR ROLLER BEARINGS) CAGE
(— FOR SMOKING MEAT) BOUCAN
BUCCAN
(— FOR STACK) HAYRACK STADDLE
(— OF A VESSEL) HULL
(— OF MIND) HAZE SPITE SPIRIT
FEELING
(— OF PIER) JETTY
(— OF SAW) HUSK
(— OF SPINNING MULE) SQUARE
(— OF STRAW) SIME
(— OF TINWORK) MARQUITO
(— ON STAGE) CEILING
(— TO CATCH STARFISH) TANGLE
(— TO CLEAN SHIP'S BOTTOM) HOG
(2-WHEELED —) GILL
(BELL —) SWEEP
(CARRIAGE —) BRAKE BREAK
(DIVING —) LUNET LUNETTE
(EMBROIDERY —) TABORET
TAMBOUR
(FISHING —) DREDGE
(GLAZIER'S —) FRAIL
(HARNESS —) HEALD
(LOOM —) SLAY SLEY SLEIGH
(MINING —) APRON
(PHOTOGRAPHY —) BUTTERFLY
(PORTABLE —) BIER CACAXTE
(PRINTING —) PRESS
(SHIP'S —) CANT
(SLUBBING —) BILLY
(STRETCHING —) TENT SLEDGE
TENTER
(TANNING —) BEAM
(WINDOW —) CHESS
(PL.) PROFILE
FRAMED NATE NATED ENGAGED

FRAMEWORK BED BENT BIER BONE
BUCK CAGE CRIB DURN GRID RACK
SASH BONES CADRE CHUTE COPSE
CREEL FLAKE SHELL STOCK BELFRY
BRIDGE BUSTLE CABANE CRADLE
DESIGN FABRIC GOCART GUARDS
HARROW HEARSE REBATO SHIELD
STROMA WATTLE CABINET CARCASS
CLIMBER COMMODE DERRICK
FRAMING FULCRUM JACKBOX
LATTICE PANNIER REBATER
RETABLE STADDLE TRESTLE
BARBECUE BEDSTEAD BULKHEAD
CARRIAGE CRADLING CRIBWORK
GRIDIRON GRILLAGE OSSATURE
SCAFFOLD SHELVING SHOWCASE
SKELETON
(— FOR PEAL OF BELLS) CAGE
(— OF REFERENCE) SCHEMA
(— TO EXPAND SKIRTS) BUSTLE
PANNIER
(EMPTY —) HUSK
(SCULPTOR'S —) ARMATURE
FRAMING CURB LEAD BELFRY
ARMATURE BEDPLATE

FRANCE
BAY: BISCAY ARACHON
CAPE: HAGUE
CAPITAL: PARIS
CHEESE: BLEU BRIE BONBEL
BOURSIN MUNSTER CAMEMBERT
MARCILLAT ROQUEFORT
COIN: ECU SOL SOU GROS AGNEL
BLANC BLANK FRANC LIARD
LIVRE LOUIS OBOLE SAIGA
SCUTE BLANCA BLANCO DENIER
DIZAIN TESTON AGNEAUX
CENTIME TESTOON CAVALIER
NAPOLEON
DANCE: GAVOT BRANLE CANARY
CANCAN BOUTADE GAVOTTE
DEPARTMENT: AIN LOT VAR AUBE
AUDE CHER EURE GARD GERS
JURA NORD OISE ORNE TARN
AISNE
DIVISION, ANCIENT: ARLES
PERCHE NEUSTRIA AQUITAINE
AQUITANIA
DYNASTY: CAPET VALOIS
BOURBON ORLEANS CAPETIAN
MEROVINGIAN
FOOD: PATE CREPE CANAPE
MOUSSE QUICHE BRIOCHE
SOUFFLE ESCARGOT PIPERADE
POTAUFEU TOURNEDO
ISLAND: RE YEU CITE CORSE
GROIX HYERE OLERON USHANT
CORSICA
KING: ODO EUDES PEPIN CLOVIS
LOTHAIR
LAKE: ANNECY CAZAUX
MEASURE: POT SAC AUNE LINE
MINE MUID PIED VELT ARPEN
CARAT LIEUE LIGNE MINOT
PERCH PINTE POINT POUCE
TOISE VELTE ARPENT HEMINE
LEAGUE QUARTE SETIER

CHOPINE HEMINEE POISSON
SEPTIER BOISSEAU QUARTAUT
ROQUILLE QUARTERON
MILITARY ACADEMY: STCYR
SAINTCYR
MOUNTAIN: PUY DORE BLANC
CINTO FOREZ PELAT COTEDOR
MOUNIER VENTOUX VIGNEMALE
CHAMBEYRON
MOUNTAIN RANGE: ALPS ECRINS
VOSGES CEVENNES PYRENEES
MARITIMES
NAME: GAUL GAULE GALLIA
NATIONAL ANTHEM: MARSEILLAISE
NATIVE: CELT GAUL FRANK
BASQUE BRETON GASCON
NORMAN PICARD CATALAN
GALLOIS LORRAIN FRANCIEN
LIGURIAN PROVENCAL
BURGUNDIAN
PORT: CAEN BREST CALAIS
TOULON LEHAVRE BORDEAUX
CHERBOURG DUNKERQUE
MARSEILLE
PROTESTANT: HUGUENOT
PROVINCE: FOIX ANJOU AUNIS
BEARN ALSACE ARTOIS COMTAT
POITOU AUVERGNE BRETAGNE
BRITTANY LIMOUSIN LORRAINE
PROVENCE TOURAINE
RACE TRACK: AUTEUIL
LONGCHAMPS
REPUBLIC CALENDAR: NIVOSE
FLOREAL VENTOSE BRUMAIRE
FERVIDOR FRIMAIRE GERMINAL
MESSIDOR PLUVIOSE PRAIRIAL
FRUCTIDOR THERMIDOR
VENDEMIAIRE
RESORT: PAU NICE CANNES
MENTON RIVIERA
RIVER: AIN LOT LUY LYS VAR
AIRE AUBE AUDE CHER DRAC
EURE GARD GERS LOIR OISE
ORNE TARN VIRE ADOUR AISNE
AULNE DROME INDRE ISERE
LOIRE MARNE MEUSE RHONE
RISLE SAONE SEINE SOMME
VIAUR YONNE ALLIER ARIEGE
ESCAUT SAMBRE SCARPE
VEZERE VIENNE DURANCE
GARONNE GIRONDE MAYENNE
MOSELLE CHARENTE
DORDOGNE
STOCK EXCHANGE: BOURSE
STRAIT: BONIFACIO
TOWN: AY EU AIX DAX GEX PAU
AGDE AGEN ALBI AUBY AUCH
BRON CAEN LAON LOOS METZ
NICE OPPY ORLY RIOM SENS
SETE STLO UZES VAUX VIMY
VIRE ARLES ARRAS BLOIS
BREST DIJON DINAN DOUAI
ERNEE LAVAL LILLE LISLE
LYONS NANCY NERAC NESLE
NIMES ORNES PARIS REIMS
ROUEN SEDAN TOURS TULLE
VICHY AMIENS ANGERS CALAIS
LEMANS LONGWY NANTES

PANTIN RENNES RHEIMS SARLAT
SENLIS SEVRES TARARE TARBES
TOULON TROYES VALOIX
VERDUN BAREGES CASTRES
LIMOGES ORLEANS ROUBAIX
VALENCE BORDEAUX CLERMONT
GRENOBLE MULHOUSE
ROCHELLE TOULOUSE
MARSEILLE STRASBOURG
TRIBE: REMI AEDUI ARVERNI
SALUVII ALLOBROGES
VERSE FORM: LAI ALBA AUBADE
RONDEL BALLADE DESCORT
RONDEAU VIRELAI VIRELAY
WEIGHT: GROS MARC ONCE
CARAT LIVRE POUND TONNE
TONNEAU ESTERLIN
WIND: MISTRAL
WINE: MACON MEDOC GRAVES
CHABLIS POMEROL BORDEAUX
BURGUNDY MUSCADET
SAUTERNE CHAMPAGNE
WINE DISTRICT: MEDOC ALSACE
BORDEAUX BURGUNDY
CHAMPAGNE

FRANCHISE SOC SOKE VOTE CHASE
FERRY HONOR INFANG CHARTER
FREEDOM LIBERTY CONTRACT
FREELAGE SUFFRAGE TENEMENT
FRANCOLIN COQUI TETUR TITAR
REDWING PHEASANT
FRANCOPHILE GALLOMAN
FRANGIPANI SHAKEWOOD
FRANK FREE OPEN RANK BLUFF
BLUNT BURLY LUSTY NAIVE PLAIN
BRAZEN CANDID DIRECT FORTHY
HONEST SALIAN ARTLESS GENUINE
LIBERAL PROFUSE SINCERE
CAREFREE CAVALIER GENEROUS
STRAIGHT VIGOROUS
FRANKINCENSE THUS OLIBAN
OLIBANUM
FRANKLY FREELY OPENLY PLAINLY
CANDIDLY
FRANKNESS CANDOR FREEDOM
OPENNESS
FRANKPLEDGE BORROW FRIBORG
FRANTIC MAD WOOD RABID INSANE
MANIAC FURIOUS LUNATIC VIOLENT
DERANGED FEVERISH FRENETIC
FRENZIED MANIACAL
FRAPPE ICE GRANITE
FRATERCULA MORMON
FRATERNAL BROTHERLY DIZYGOTIC
FRATERNITY FRAT FRARY HOUSE
ORDER FRATRY QUALITY SOCIETY
SODALITY
FRATERNIZE FRAT COTTON
FRAUD GYP DOLE FAKE GAFF GAUD
GULL JAPE JUNT LURK RUSE SHAM
SKIN WILE CHEAT COVIN CRAFT
DOLUS FAKER FAVEL GLAIK GUILE
HOCUS LURCH SHARK SHIFT SWICK
SWIKE TRICK BROGUE DECEIT
FULLAM HUMBUG INTAKE STUMER
WRENCH FLIVVER KNAVEFY
ROGUERY STUMOUR SWINDLE

BOODLING COZENAGE IMPOSTER
OPERATOR SUBTLETY TRUMPERY
FRAUDULENT SKIN WILY CRONK
COGGED CRAFTY QUACKY ABUSIVE
CROOKED CUNNING KNAVISH
CHEATING COVINOUS FRAUDFUL
GUILEFUL QUACKISH SINISTER
SPURIOUS
FRAXINELLA DITTANY RUEWORT
FRAY FRET BROIL BROOM FEAZE
MELEE RAVEL AFFRAY BUSTLE
CHAUVE FRIDGE TIFFLE CONTEST
FRAZZLE
FRAYED WORN FLAGGY RAVELED
FRAZER FINNER
FREAK FIRK FLAM WHIM FANCY
HUMOR LUSUS MOODS SCAPE
SPORT MEGRIM SPLEEN WHIMSY
CAPRICE CROTCHET ESCAPADE
FLIMFLAM WHIMWHAM
(CRAZY —S) LUNES
FREAKISH FREAKY FLIGHTY
MAGGOTY WHIMSIC CRANKISH
FRECKLE CHIT EPHELIS FRECKEN
LENTIGO SUNSPOT
FRECKLED FRECKLY FLECKLED
FREE LAX LET RID BOLD EASE LISS
OPEN REDD SHED SHUT CLEAN
CLEAR FLUID FRANK LARGE LISSE
LOOSE READY SCOUR SLAKE SPARE
ACQUIT DEGAGE DEVOID EXEMPT
FACILE FLUENT FREELY GRATIS
IMMUNE LOOSEN SOLUTE UNSLIP
VACANT VAGILE CLEANSE DELIVER
GRIVOIS INEXACT LASKING LIBERAL
MANUMIT RELEASE SCIOLTO
UNBOUND UNSLAVE UNTWIST
WILLING ABSOLUTE AUTARKIC
EASINESS EXPEDITE FACILITY
FREEHAND GRIVOISE INDIGENT
LAXATIVE LIBERATE UNBRIDLE
(— AND EASY) GLIB FAMILIAR
(— BROOK OF WEEDS) RODE
(— FROM ABIGUITY) HOMELY
DECIDED
(— FROM ACCUSATION) SACKLESS
(— FROM ACIDITY) DULCIFY
(— FROM ANXIETY) CONTENT
(— FROM ARTIFICIAL) ARTLESS
(— FROM BIAS) CANDID
(— FROM CARE) EASY CARELESS
(— FROM CHARGE) FDD PURGE
FRANCO
(— FROM CONSTRAINT) CASUAL
(— FROM DEDUCTIONS) NET
(— FROM DEFECT) HAIL HALE
SOUND
(— FROM DIRT) BRIGHT
(— FROM DOUBT) RESOLVE
(— FROM ELECTRICAL CHARGE)
DEAD
(— FROM ERROR) LEAL SOUND
CORRECT ACCURATE
(— FROM EVIL) RESCUE
(— FROM EXTREMES) EQUABLE
(— FROM FLAWS) GOOD
(— FROM FROST) FRESH
(— FROM IMPURITIES) FINE DRESS
DEFECATE DEPURATE

(— FROM KNOTS) ENODE ENODATE
(— FROM MARKS) BLANK
(— FROM MICROORGANISMS)
ASEPTIC STERILE
(— FROM OBLIGATION) ACQUIT
EXCUSE
(— FROM PENALTY) ABSOLVE
(— FROM STONES) CHESSOM
(— FROM) EX REDD DEVOID
DISPATCH
(— OF DIFFICULTIES) AFLOAT
(— OF FAT) ENSEAM
(— OF TAR) WRECK
(— ONE'S SELF) SOLVE
(— PLUNGER) ARM
(— THROW AREA) KEYHOLE
FREEBOARD QUICKSIDE
FREEBOOTER TORY RIDER THIEF
PIRATE CATERAN CORSAIR
PILLAGER RAPPAREE SNAPHANCE
FREEBORN INGENUOUS
FREEDMAN LEYSING TITYRUS
(PL.) LAET
FREEDOM RUN EASE FRITH LARGE
ACCESS STREET APATHIA BREADTH
LEISURE LIBERTY LICENCE LICENSE
RELEASE AUTONOMY FREELAGE
FREENESS IMMUNITY IMPUNITY
LARGESSE WITHGATE
(— FROM BIAS) CANDOR
(— FROM CONSTRAINT) ABANDON
(— FROM DANGER) SECURITY
(— FROM ERROR) ACCURACY
(— FROM GUILT) SHRIVE
(— OF ACCESS) ENTREE
(— OF ACTION) SWINGE LATITUDE
(— OF SPEECH) PARISIA
(— TO PROCEED) HEAD
FREEHOLD BARONY
FREEHOLDER SWAIN BONDER
YEOMAN FRANKLIN
FREEING LIVERY ACQUITAL
FREE LANCE ROUTIER
FREELY FREE LIEF LARGE LARGELY
READILY HEARTILY
FREEMAN BUR AIRE BARON CEORL
HAULD BONDER FRANKLIN
ROTURIER
FREEMASON FRATER MORGAN
NOACHITE
(ONE NOT A —) COWAN
FREESTONE HAZEL
(— STATE) CONNECTICUT
FREETHINKER INFIDEL SKEPTIC
AGNOSTIC
FREEZE ICE RIME CATCH CHILL
FROST CURDLE FRAPPE HARDEN
STARVE STEEVE CONGEAL
GLACIATE
FREEZING COLD FREEZY FRIGID
FROSTY GLACIAL GELATION
FREIGHT LOAD CARGO GOODS
ASTRAY LADING FRAUGHT HOTSHOT
PLUNDER PORTAGE TRUCKAGE
(— CAR) TRUCK
FREMD FRAIM FRAMMIT
FRENCH CREOLE FRANCO GALLIC
GALLIAN GALLICAN
FRENCH GUIANA (CAPE OF —)
ORANGE

(CAPITAL OF —) CAYENNE
(RIVER OF —) MARONI
(TOWN OF —) MANA KOUROU
FRENCH HONEYSUCKLE SULLA
FRENCH LAVENDER STECHADOS
FRENCHMAN GAUL PICARD
FRENCHY MONSIEUR
PARLEYVOO
FRENCH MULBERRY SOURBUSH
FRENCH REPUBLIC MARIANNA
MARIANNE
FRENULUM TENDON
FRENUM BRIDLE FRAENUM
FRENULUM VINCULUM
FRENZIED RABID RAMAGE BERSERK
FANATIC FRANTIC FRENETIC
FURIBUND
FRENZY AMOK FURY GERE MOON
MUST RAGE AMUCK FUROR MANIA
MUSTH FURORE MADNESS OESTRUS
SWIVVET DELIRIUM INSANITY
FREQUENCY HERTZ CREBRITY
FREQUENT USE BANG KEEP HAUNT
HOWFF OFTEN AFFECT COMMON
HOURLY INFEST RESORT ENHAUNT
OFTTIME CREBROUS FAMILIAR
PRACTICE
FREQUENTLY OFT OFTEN HOURLY
UNSELDOM
FRESH GAY HOT NEW WET FLIP
GOOD RACY SMUG WARM BRISK
CRISP GREEN MOIST QUICK RUDDY
SASSY SMART SOUND SWEET VIVID
CALLER CALVER FLORID LIVELY
MAIDEN STRONG UNUSED VIRENT
VIRGIN ANOTHER NOUVEAU
UNFADED NOUVELLE ORIGINAL
SPANKING YOUTHFUL
FRESHEN BRACE FRESH RENEW
BREEZE CALLER REVIVE CHOUNCE
PEARTEN REFRESH SWEETEN
FRENCHEN
FRESHENER BRACER
FRESHET TIDE FLOOD FRESH SPATE
TORNADO
FRESHMAN FOX BEJAN FROSH
BEJANT GREENY FRESHER
FRESHNESS VERD NOVELTY
VERDURE VIRIDITY
FRET DIK NAG ORP RUB RUX VEX
CARK FASH FRAY FUSS GALL GNAW
RAGE STEW YIRM CHAFE CRAKE
CRISP FLISK GRATE PIQUE WORRY
WREAK ABRADE CORSIE CRYSAL
HARASS MUCKLE NETTLE PLAGUE
REPINE RIPPLE RUFFLE CHRYSAL
GRECQUE GRIZZLE MEANDER
SCRUPLE SQUINNY ALIGREEK
IRRITATE
FRETFUL GIRNY ORPIT TEATY TEENY
TESTY FRETTY PENCEY SULLEN
TATCHY TWISTY FRECKET PEEVISH
PETTISH SPLEENY CAPTIOUS
CRANKOUS FRETSOME FROPPISH
PETULANT PINDLING
FRETTED FRETTY MAGGED
FRETTING FRET EATING
FREY FREYR YNGVI
FRIABLE CRIMP CRISP CRUMP FLAKY
FRUSH MEALY SHORT CRUMBY

CRUMMY FLUFFY PUTRID CHESSOM
CRUMBLY MOLDERY POWDERY
RESOLUTE ROTTENLY SHATTERY
(NOT —) SAD
FRIAR FRATE FREER MINIM MINOR
BHIKKU FRATER GELONG GOSAIN
LISTER BHIKSHU JACOBIN LIMITER
SERVITE BREVIGER CAPUCHIN
JACOBITE MINORIST MINORITE
PREACHER
FRIARBIRD COLDONG PIMLICO
MONKBIRD
FRIAR SKATE DOCTOR
FRICANDEAU GRENADINE
FRICASSEE POTPIE
FRICATIVE BUZZ HISS OPEN YOGH
DURATIVE
FRICTION BUZZ DRAG HISS CHAFE
WINDAGE
FRICTIONLESS SMOOTH
FRIED FRIT SAUTE
FRIEDCAKE WONDER CRULLER
FATCAKE DOUGHNUT
FRIEND AME AMI AMY BOR CAD EME
PAX BHAI CHUM NABS OPPO WINE
AMIGO BUDDY INGLE NETOP TROUT
AIKANE BELAMY COUSIN CUMMER
GOSSIP INWARD KIMMER PRINCE
QUAKER ACHATES COMRADE
SOCIETY COCKMATE COMPADRE
DEMOPHIL FEDERATE HICKSITE
INTIMADO INTIMATE TILLICUM
(—S NOT SPEAKING) CUTS
(CLOSE —) PRIVY COBBER
COMPADRE
(DIVINE —) SOCIUS
(FAMILIAR —) CRONY GREMIAL
SPECIAL
(GIRL —) DOXY DRAG DONEY DOXIE
STEADY
(INTIMATE FEMALE —) CUMMER
(PRIVATE —) PRIVADO
(WOMAN —) GIMMER
(PL.) FOLK KITH SOCE FOLKS
SOCIETY
FRIENDLESS FORLORN
FRIENDLINESS AMITY AFFINITY
BONHOMIE GOODWILL
FRIENDLY COSH GOOD HOLD HOMY
KIND CHIEF COUTH GREAT HOMEY
THICK AMICAL CHATTY FOLKSY
FORTHY HOMELY KINDLY SMOOTH
AMIABLE AMICOUS COUTHIE
AMICABLE HOMELIKE INTIMATE
SOCIABLE
FRIENDSHIP PAX AMITY AMOUR
FRIEZE KELT FRISE CUSHION
FALDING FRISADO FRIEZING
FRIGATE ZABRA
FRIGATE BIRD IOA IWA ALCATRAS
FRIGATE MACKEREL BONITO
TASSARD
FRIGG FREA FRIJA
FRIGHT COW BOOF FEAR FLEG FRAY
ALARM GHAST GLIFF GLOFF PANIC
SCARE AFFRAY GASTER GLIFFY
SCHRIK TERROR STARTLE SWITHER
FRIGHTEN GASTNESS GLIFFING
FRIGHTEN AWE COW FLY SHY SOB
BAZE BREE DOSS FEAR FLEG FLEY

FRAY FUNK HARE HAZE SHOO
AFEAR AFLEY ALARM APPAL BLUFF
GALLY GHOST GLIFF HAZEN SCARE
SHORE SPOOK AFFRAY ALARUM
APPALL BOGGLE BOOGER COWARD
FLAITE FLIGHT FRIGHT GALLEY
GALLOW AFFREUX FRECKEN
SCARIFY STARTLE TERRIFY
AFFRIGHT MISTRYST
(— BIRDS) KEEP
FRIGHTENED RAD EERY FRIT GAST
EERIE GHAST AFRAID AGHAST
SCARED SCAREY STURTIN
GHASTFUL
(EASILY —) TIMID SKITTISH
FRIGHTENING EERY DREAD EERIE
GOURY HAIRY FRIGHTY GHASTLY
SHIVERY DREADFUL FLEYSOME
FRIGHTFUL WAN GRIM UGLY AWFUL
FERLY HORRID UGSOME AFFREUX
DIREFUL FEARFUL GASHFUL
GHASTLY HIDEOUS ALARMING
DREADFUL ELDRITCH FEARSOME
GHASTFUL HORRIBLE HORRIFIC
TERRIBLE TERRIFIC
FRIGID DRY ICY COLD BLEAK FISHY
ARCTIC FROSTY FROZEN WINTRY
GLACIAL FREEZING SIBERIAN
FRIGIDITY GLARE
FRILL DIDO PURL JABOT RUCHE
RUFFLE ARMILLA FLOUNCE SPINACH
SPINAGE CHITLING CRIMPING
FRILLERY FURBELOW
(— OF HAIR) APRON
(PL.) PUFFERY FOOFARAW FRILLERY
FRILLINESS CHICHI
FRILLING SWEEPER
FRILLY CHICHI
FRINGE WLO EDGE GILL LOMA RUFF
WELT BEARD THRUM BORDER
EDGING MARGIN TASSEL BULLION
CREPINE EYELASH FEATHER
FIMBRIA SELVAGE TRAILER
VALANCE WHISKER CILIELLA
FRISETTE INDUSIUM SELVEDGE
TRIMMING
(SOFT —S) THRUM
(PL.) ZIZITH
FRINGED JUBATE
FRINGEFOOT UMA
FRINGEPOD LACEPOD
FRINGETAIL VEILTAIL
FRINGE TREE SHAVINGS
FRIPPERY FLIPPERY TRINKUMS
(PL.) GAUDERY
FRISK COLT FISK PLAY ROLL SKIP
WHID CAPER SKICE CAREER
CAVORT FRISCO FROLIC TITTUP
WANTON FRISCAL FRISKLE
FRISKY GAY PERT FRISK CROUSE
FEISTY KIPPER LIVELY COLTISH
JIGGISH PLAYFUL SPORTIVE
FRISON KNUB
FRIT FRETT CALCINE
FRITTER FOOL FRIT TEAR BOLLO
DRILL BANGLE DRIVEL LOUNGE
BEIGNET DRIBBLE FLITTER
SLATTERN
FRIVOLITY LEVITY FRIBBLE INANITY

ITEMING FUTILITY NONSENSE
NUGACITY
FRIVOLOUS GAY DAFT GIDDY INANE
LIGHT PETTY SILLY WASHY FLIMSY
FRILLY FRIVOL FROTHY FUTILE
TOYISH YEASTY FATUOUS FRIBBLE
LIGHTLY NIDGETY SHALLOW TRIVIAL
GIMCRACK JIMCRACK SKITTISH
TRIFLING
FRIVOLOUSNESS FUTILITY
FRIZZ FRIZ FRIZE FRIZZLE FROUNCE
FRIZZED CRISPY
FRIZZLY FUZZY CRIMPY FRIZZY
FRIZZY FUZZY CRIMPY FRIZZLY
FROCK DUD JAM GOWN JUMP SLIP
WRAP LAMMY SMOCK TRUSS TUNIC
CLERIC JERSEY LAMMIE MANTLE
ROCHET SUKKENYE
FROCK COAT CRISPIN
FROG PAD POD KICK FROSH FROSK
FROUD PADDO PADDY RONCO
ANURAN PEEPER TOGGLE CHARLIE
CRAWLER CREEPER CROAKER
CUSHION FRESHER FROGLET
PADDOCK PODDOCK QUILKIN
BULLFROG FERREIRO FROGGING
PLATANNA REPLACER
(— IN LOOM) HEATER
(— OF HORSE'S HOOF) FRUSH
CUSHION
FROG CRAB RANINIAN
FROGFISH SLIMER TOADFISH
FROGGER CHASER TRAILER
ZOOGLER
FROGGY RANARIAN
FROGHOPPER HOPPER CERCOPID
FROGMOUTH MOREPORK
PODARGUE
FROLIC BUM GAY RIG BLOW COLT
GAME GELL HAZE JINK LAKE LARK
ORGY PLAY PLOY RANT REEK ROMP
CAPER FREAK FRISK MERRY PRANK
RANDY ROUSE SPORT SPREE
CURVET FRATCH GAMBOL PLISKY
POWWOW PRANCE ROLLIX SHINDY
SPLORE VAGARY WANTON DISPORT
GAMMOCK MARLOCK PLISKIE
SCAMPER SKYLARK SPANIEL
STASHIE WASSAIL CAROUSAL
JAMBOREE
FROLICSOME GAY DAFT ROID ANTIC
FRISK GILPY LARKY FRISKY LIVELY
WANTON ANTICAL JOCULAR
LARKING LARKISH WAGGISH
ESPIEGLE FRISKFUL FROLICKY
GAMESOME LARKSOME PRANKISH
SPORTFUL SPORTIVE
FROLICSOMENESS HEYDAY
FROM A AB DE EX OF FAE FRA FRO
VAN VON THROM AGAINST
(— A DISTANCE) ALOOF
(— BEGINNING TO END) THROUGH
(— ELSEWHERE) ALIUNDE
(— OFF) AFFA
(— SIDE TO SIDE) OVER CROSS
ATHWART
(— THIS PLACE) HENCE
FROND FERN TRESS CROSIER
FRONDLET

FRONT BOW VAN BROW FACE FORE
HEAD PROW THIN AFORE VAUNT
BEFORE DEVANT FACADE FACING
FORMER OPPOSE SECTOR ADVANCE
FORWARD FRONTAL FURTHER
OBVERSE PREFACE RESPECT
SLENDER FOREHEAD FOREMOST
FOREPART FORESIDE FRONTAGE
(— OF ASTROLABE) WOMBSIDE
(— OF BARN) FOREBAY
(— OF BIRD'S NECK) GUTTUR
(— OF BODY) GROUF
(— OF HEAD) VISAGE FORETOP
(— OF HELMET) VENTAIL
(— OF WATERWHEEL BUCKET)
START
(— UPON) AFFRONT
FRONTAL FRONT SINDON FRONTON
METOPIC FRONTLET SUFFRONT
FRONTIER BOUND COAST FRONT
MARCH BARRIER FRONTURE
OUTLYING
(FORTIFIED —) LIMES
FRONTING OBVIOUS
FRONTISPIECE FRONT UNWAN
FRONTIS
FRONTLET TIARA FRONTAL
CHAMFRON
FRONTPIECE GORE
FROST ICE COLD HOAR RIME RIND
FROSTING ICING DIVINITY
FROSTWEED ROCKROSE
FROSTY ICY COLD RIMY CHILL CRISP
FRORE GELID GLARY HUNCH
BOREAL FRIGID FROREN CHILLING
INIMICAL PRUINOUS
(NOT —) OPEN
FROTH FOB BARM FOAM REAM
SCUM SUDS WORK CREAM SPUME
YEAST FLOWER FREATH LATHER
SPURGE
FROTHER CREOSOTE
FROTHING HUMMING MANTLING
FROTHY FOAMY REAMY SPEWY
SPUMY SUDSY FLASHY YEASTY
SPUMOSE SPUMOUS WHIPPED
FROWARD RANK CROSS AWKWARD
PEEVISH WAYWARD CONTRARY
FROPPISH PERVERSE PETULANT
PROTERVE SHREWISH UNTOWARD
FROWN GLUM LOUR GLOOM GLOUT
GLUMP LOWER SCOWL GLOWER
GLUNCH FROUNCE FRONTLET
FROWNING GLUM GLUNCH
FROWZY BLOUSY BLOWSY BLOWZY
RAFFISH FROWZLED SCABROUS
SLOVENLY
FROZEN FAST FIXED FRORE FRORY
GELID GLARY FRAPPE FROREN
FRUCTOSE ACROSE
FRUGAL EASY MILD CANNY CHARY
ROMAN SCANT SPARE SAVING
SCARCE SCOTCH CAREFUL
PRUDENT SLENDER SPARING
THRIFTY
FRUGALITY SPARE THRIFT
ECONOMY PARCITY MANAGERY
FRUGALLY HARD CHARILY SAVINGLY
FRUIT BEL FIG HAW UVA BAEL COYO

DATE DIKA DROP GEAN JACK LIME NOOP PEAR PLUM POME SEED SLOE SNAP SORB AKENE ANISE APPLE BERRY CLING COUMA DRUPE GENIP GOURD GRAPE GUAVA HAZEL ILAMA LEMON LIMON MANGO MELON OLIVE PAPAW PEACH RIPER SORVA ACHENE ALMOND BANANA BUTTON CEDRON CEREZA CHERRY CITRON CITRUS COBNUT COCHAL COCONA DAMSON DURIAN EMBLIC EMBOLO GUARRI JUJUBE KEEPER LEGUME LONGAN LOQUAT MARANG MAYPOP MUYUSA ORANGE PAPAYA PAWPAW PELLAS POMATO RESULT SAPOTA SQUASH UVALHA WESTME ZAPOTE APRICOT ATEMOYA AVOCADO AZAROLE BILIMBI BLOATER CARAWAY CHAYOTE CHECKER CIRUELA COCONUT CURRANT DESSERT GEEBUNG GENIPAP GHERKIN KUMQUAT PIGFACE PRODUCT RIPENER SERVICE SHALLON SOURSOP TANGELO ACHENIUM BAYBERRY BELLERIC BILBERRY CALABASH CANISTEL CAPSICUM CARDAMUM CITRANGE CUCUMBER DEWBERRY DOGBERRY EGGFRUIT FOLLICLE FRUITAGE FRUITERY FRUITLET GOLKAKRA INKBERRY LIMEQUAT OSOBERRY PIEPRINT PODOCARP RAMBUTAN SEBESTEN SEEDBALL SHADDOCK SWEETSOP
(— OF CACTUS) SABRA
(— OF CAPER) CAPOT
(— OF CITRON) ETROG ETHROG
(— OF HEMLOCK) CONIUM
(— OF PALM) SALAK
(— OF ROSE) HEP HIP BUTTON
(— ON TREES) HANG
(—S COOKED IN SYRUP) COMPOTE
(AGGREGATE —) ETAERIO DRUPETUM HETAERIO
(ASTRINGENT —) GAB GAUB CHEBULE
(AVOCADO-LIKE —) ANAY
(CANDIED —) CONSERVE
(CARMINATIVE —) BADIAN
(COILED —) STROMBUS
(COLLECTIVE —) SYNCARP
(DRIED —) PASA CUBEB MUMMY SABAL OREJON CAPSULE EMBELIA
(EARLY —) PRIMEUR HASTINGS
(FALLEN —) SHEDDER
(FIRST —S) ANNATES BIKKURIM PRIMICES
(FLESHY —) SYCONIUM
(GOURD —) PEPO
(GRAPEFRUIT-LIKE —) SUHA
(GRAPELIKE —) WAMPEE
(HAWTHORN —) PEGGLE
(IMPERFECT —) SPECH NUBBIN
(MASHED —) FOOL
(MEDICINAL —) AIWAIN AJOWAN EMBELIA
(ONE-SEEDED —) AKENE ACHENE
(PALMYRA —) PUNATOO
(PLUMLIKE —) CARISSA CIRUELA

(PRESERVED —) SUCCADE CONFITURE
(PRICKLY —) HEDGEHOG
(SELF-FERTILIZED —) AUTOCARP
(SLICED DRIED —) SNITS SNITZ SCHNITZ
(SPURGE —) TAMPOE
(SUPERIOR —) TOPPER
(UNRIPE OAK —) CAMATA
(WINGED —) SAMARA
(WOODY —) XYLOCARP
FRUIT BAT KALONG
FRUIT-BEARING FERTILE
FRUIT DOVE KUKU
FRUITFUL FAT FOODY BATTEL FECUND FRUITY GRAVID FERTILE TEEMFUL UBEROUS ABUNDANT CHILDING FRUITIVE PREGNANT PROLIFIC
FRUITFULNESS UBERTY FATNESS
FRUITGROWER FRUITIST
FRUITLESS DRY GELD VAIN ADDLE BARREN FUTILE STERILE USELESS ABORTIVE BOOTLESS
FRUIT PIGEON KUKU LUPE KUKUPA MANUMA MANUTAGI
FRUIT STONE COB PYRENE PUTAMEN
FRUSTRATE BALK BILK DASH DISH FOIL LAME BLANK BLOCK CHECK CROSS ELUDE SMEAR THRAW WRECK BAFFLE BLIGHT DEFEAT DELUDE KIBOSH OUTWIT SCOTCH THWART ANIENTE DECEIVE FALSIFY PREVENT CONFOUND INFRINGE STULTIFY
FRUSTRATER MARPLOT
FRUSTRATING BOOTLESS
FRUSTRATION FOIL SUCK DEFEAT FIASCO
FRUSTULE TESTULE HYPOTHECA
FRY SILE BROOD FRIZZ KRILL SAUTE FRIZZLE GREYFISH
FRYER FRIER FRIZZER SPRINGER
FRYING PAN FRYPAN SPIDER CREEPER SKILLET
FUCHSIA CORREA KONINI FUCHSIN EARDROPS
FUCHSIN ROSEINE SOLFERINO
FUCHSINE RUBIN RUBINE MAGENTA
FUDDLE FUZZLE FLUSTER
FUDDLED FAP REE DOPY BOSKY DOPEY SWASH TIPSY MAUDLIN
FUDGE HUNCH SNUDGE PENUCHE DIVINITY
FUEL GAS OIL POB COAL COKE FIRE PEAT UPLA ARGOL ACETOL ELDING FIRING SHRUFF TIMBER COALITE SYNTHOL FIREBOOT FIREBOTE GASOGENE GAZOGENE
FUGITIVE HOT FLEME FLYER FUGIE SCAMP OUTLAW FLEEING LAMSTER REFUGEE RUNAWAY FLEETING RUNAGATE UNSTABLE
  (PL.) MANZAS
FUGUE FUGA
  (— THEME) DUX
  (PART OF —) STRETTA
FULA PEUL PEUHL FELLANI FELLATA

FULANI PEUL PEUHL
FULCRUM BAIT GLUT
FULFILL FILL FULL KEEP MEET HONOR ANSWER COMPLY FULFIL REDEEM SATISFY COMPLETE COMPLISH
FULFILLMENT PASS EFFECT FUNCTION
  (— OF GOD'S WILL) KINGDOM
  (IMAGINARY —) FANTASY
FULGURATION BLICK
FULL BAD BIG FAT FOW COOL DEEP FAIR GOOD JUST PANG RANK TRIG TUCK AMPLE AWASH BROAD CLEAR FLUSH LARGE LUCKY PIENO PLAIN PLENY ROUND SATED SOLID TIGHT TOTAL WHOLE ENTIRE GOGGLE HONEST STRONG BAPTIZE BRIMFUL COPIOUS DESTROY DIFFUSE FULFILL FULSOME LIBERAL OROTUND PERFORM PLENARY REPLETE TEEMING TRAMPLE WEALTHY ABSOLUTE ADEQUATE BOUFFANT BRIMMING CHOCKFUL COMPLETE EXTENDED FREQUENT RESONANT THOROUGH
  (— CLOTH OR YARN) WALK
  (— OF AIR) LIGHT
  (— OF BLANKS) LACUNOSE
  (— OF CHINKS) RIMOSE
  (— OF DELAY) MOROSE
  (— OF DEVILTRY) HEMPY HEMPIE
  (— OF DIRT) FOUL
  (— OF EGGS) GRAVID
  (— OF ENERGY) STOUT SWANK
  (— OF FLAWS) CRAZY
  (— OF FUN) FROLIC
  (— OF HAPPINESS) SUNSHINY
  (— OF INTEREST) AGOG
  (— OF IRON) SIDEROSE
  (— OF LIFE) SPUNKY ANIMATE
  (— OF LOOPS) KINKY
  (— OF MATTER FOR THOUGHT) MEATY
  (— OF RUSHES) SPRITTY
  (— OF SAND) ARENOSE
  (— OF SLEEP) SOPOROSE
  (— OF SMALL OPENINGS) POROSE POROUS
  (— OF SPIRIT) GENEROUS
  (— OF VIGOR) FLUSH GREEN LUSTY ANIMATED SPIRITED
  (— OF ZEST) RACY
FULL-BLOWN JUICY
FULLBODIED FAT LOFTY HEARTY
FULL-BOSOMED BUXOM
FULLER GAG HARDY HARDIE ROLLER TUCKER WALKER BLOCKER CREASER THICKER CLOTHIER
FULL-FACED AFFRONTE AFFRONTY
FULL-FLAVORED BOLD RACY
FULL-FLEDGED SUMMED
FULL-GROWN RIPE GROWN MATURE SEEDED
FULLNESS BODY FLAIR FLARE FULTH PLENUM FULNESS PLEROMA SATIETY
FULLY ALL DOWN EVEN INLY WELL AMPLY LARGE ENOUGH FAIRLY

THRICE WHOLLY CLEARLY LARGELY
UTTERLY CLEVERLY ENTIRELY
INWARDLY MATURELY
FULMAR HAG NELLY NODDY
HAGDON NELLIE MALDUCK
MALMOCK STINKER
FULMINATE BLOW FULMINE
FULSOME SUAVE FOULSOME
FUMARIC BOLETIC LICHENIC
FUMBLE BOOT MUFF MULL PIRL
BOBBLE FAFFLE MUMBLE PRODDLE
MISFIELD THRUMBLE
FUMBLER STUMER STUMOUR
FUMBLING HALTING
FUME FUFF RAGE REEK EWDER
SMOKE STIFE SNUFFLE FUMIGATE
FUMID SMOKY SMOKEY
FUMIGATE SMEEK SMOKE PASTIL
CYANIDE PASTILLE
FUMIGATION GASSING
FUMIGATOR AERATOR
FUMITORY FUMARIA FUMEROOT
FUMEWORT
FUN GIG GAME GELL JEST JOKE
LAKE PLAY BORAK BOURD HUMOR
KICKS MIRTH MUSIC SPORT FROLIC
GAIETY GAYETY DAFFERY DAFFING
GAMMOCK WHOOPEE
(UNRESTRAINED —) HELL
FUNCTION ACT JOB RUN USE DUTY
FORM ROLE WORK ACTION AGENCY
MATRIX MISTER OFFICE SQUASH
CONCEPT FACULTY ISOLATE
SERVICE WORKING ACTIVITY
BUSINESS MINISTRY PROVINCE
(— EFFECTIVELY) AVAIL
(—S OF JUDGES) ERMINE
(APPARENT —) STUDY
(ESSENTIAL —) DHARMA
(MATHEMATICAL —) DEL FORM
INVERSE
(SPECIAL —) CEREMONY
FUNCTIONAL DYNAMIC
FUNCTIONARY FLUNKY CAPTAIN
FLUNKEY CHAPRASI
FUNCTIONING AFLOAT
FUNCTIONLESS OTIOSE
FUND BOX BANK FOND MASS CHEST
KITTY MOUNT SLUSH STOCK STORE
ESCROW CHALUKA JACKPOT
RESERVE HALUKKAH PECULIUM
(PL.) CAJA COFFER
FUNDAMENT NOCK TAIL BOTTOM
FUNDUS
FUNDAMENTAL BASAL BASIC
KLANG PRIME VITAL BOTTOM
SIMPLE BASILAR BEDROCK ORGANIC
PRIMARY RADICAL ABSOLUTE
ORIGINAL RUDIMENT SUBSTRAT
FUNDAMENTALLY AUFOND
FUNDUS FORNIX
FUNERAL TANGI BURIAL EXEQUY
BURYING CORTEGE FUNEBRE
FUNERARY MORTUARY
FUNERAL DIRECTOR BLACKMAN
FUNEREAL FERAL DISMAL SOLEMN
FUNEBRE FUNERAL DIRGEFUL
EXEQUIAL MOURNFUL
FUNGICIDE NABAM ZINEB FERBAM
CALOMEL BORDEAUX DICHLONE

FUNGOID MYCOID FUNGOUS
FUNGUS MOLD SMUT BRAND ERGOT
FUNGE HYPHO MOREL MOULD
PHOMA SPUNK SWARD TRUFF
VALSA VERPI AGARIC BOLETE
FUNGAL MILDEW OIDIUM AMANITA
BOLETUS CHYTRID FUNGOID
GEASTER LEPIOTA TRUFFLE
AECIDIUM CLATHRUS CORNBELL
EUMYCETE FUSARIUM HELVELLA
MUCEDINE MUSHROOM OOMYCETE
OTOMYCES PHALLOID POLYPORE
PUFFBALL SAPROGEN SPOROGEN
TREMELLA TUCKAHOE
(UNICELLULAR —) BEES EAST
YEAST
FUNK FUNG NESH
FUNNEL CAST STACK TEWEL TRUNK
FILLER FUMMEL SIPHON SYPHON
TUNNEL TUNNER TRUMPET TUNDISH
HYPONOME WINDSAIL
FUNNY ODD GOOD COMIC DROLL
MERRY QUEER COMICAL JOCULAR
RISIBLE STRANGE HUMOROUS
(VERY —) SPLITTING
FUR FOX BEAR CALF COON FLIX FOIN
GRAY GREY GRIS MINK PEAN PELF
PELL SEAL VAIR BUDGE COYPU
CROSS FITCH FLICK GENET GRISE
OTTER PAHMI SABLE SCARF SHUBA
BADGER BEAVER COUGAR DESMAN
ERMINE FISHER GALYAC JACKET
MARTIN NUTRIA PELAGE POTENT
RABBIT SPRING SUSLIK CALABER
CARACAL FITCHET FITCHEW
FURRURE MINIVER TOPCOAT
CACOMIXL ERMINOIS KOLINSKI
(— OF LAMBSKIN AND WOOL)
BUDGE
(— RESEMBLING PERSIAN LAMB)
KRIMMER
(BEAVER —) WOOM CASTOR
(GRAY —) GRAY GREY GRIS GRISE
CRIMMER LETTICE
(NUMBER OF — SKINS) TIMBER
TIMMER
(RABBIT —) CONY SCUT CONEY
FLICK LAPIN HATTER SEALINE
ERMILINE
(SQUIRREL —) CALABAR
(SQUIRREL OR MARTIN —) AMICE
POPEL
(STONE MARTEN'S —) FOIN
(PL.) PELTRY FURRIERY
FURBEARER PLATINUM
FURBELOW DIDO FALBALA
FURBISH DO FIG RUB FAKE FINE
VAMP CLEAN SCOUR FINIFY POLISH
BURNISH VARNISH RENOVATE
FURCATE FORKY BRANCH FURCAL
FURCULA SPRING FURCULUM
FURCULUM WISHBONE
FURFOOZ GRENELLE
FURIOUS MAD GRIM WOOD ANGRY
BRAIN GIDDY IRATE RABID SHARP
FIERCE FURIAL FURIED INSANE
RENISH STORMY FRANTIC HOPPING
MADDING MANKIND PELTING
RAGEOUS REDWOOD RUSHING
TEARING VIOLENT FRENZIED

VEHEMENT VESUVIAN WRATHFUL
FURIOUSLY CRAZY ANGERLY
TEARING
FURL FOLD HAND ROLL STOW WRAP
FRESE TRUSS FARDEL FURDLE
FURLED IN
FURLONG SHOT STADE
FURLOUGH LEAVE BLIGHTY
FURNACE ARC KILN OVEN TANK
BENCH CUPEL DRIER DRYER FORGE
MOUTH TISAR BURNER CALCAR
CUPOLA HEATER ATHANOR
CHAFERY CRESSET FIREPOT
PUDDLER ROASTER BESSEMER
BLOOMERY CALCINER FIREWORK
IRONCLAD LIMEKILN PRODUCER
REFINERY TRYWORKS
(— DOOR) TWEEL
(ALMOND —) ALMAN
(ARC —) HEROULT
(GLASS-HEATING —) TISAR
(PORTABLE —) DANDY CRESSET
FURNACEMAN BUSTLER DROSSER
SMELTER IMPROVER REHEATER
FURNISH ARM SOW DECK FEAT
FEED FILL FRET FRUB GIVE LEND
TRIM VEST ARRAY ENDOW EQUIP
FRAME INDUE PITCH POINT SERVE
SPEED STOCK STORE STUFF
AFFORD GRAITH INSURE INVEST
OUTFIT RENDER SUPPLY ADVANCE
APPAREL APPOINT BRACKET
GARNISH INSTORE PERFORM
PLENISH PRESENT PRODUCE
PROVIDE SUFFICE ACCOUTER
DECORATE FRUBBISH MINISTER
(— ABUNDANTLY) FREQUENT
(— ANALYSIS) ACCOUNT
(— FULLY) CHARGE
(— REFRESHMENT) EASE
(— WITH DRINK) BIRL BYRL
(— WITH MEALS) BOARD
(— WITH STEEP SLOPE) ESCARP
(— WITH STRENGTH) MAN
(— WITH WINGS) IMP
(— WITH) BESEE
FURNISHED ARMED BODEN GARNI
(COMFORTABLY —) BEIN
FURNISHING ADVANCE FITMENT
(PL.) STUFF BAGGAGE PENATES
FURNITURE ADAM TIRE SAMAN
STOOL STUFF GRAITH FITMENT
MEUBLES MOVABLE EQUIPAGE
ORNAMENT SUPELLEX TACKLING
(CHEAP —) BORAX
(SHIP'S —) HARNESS
FURORE FUROR BROUHAHA
FURRED PURED LOADED
FURRING PACKING
FURROW FUR GAP GAW RIB RUT
FURR GRIP HINT LINE PLOW RAIN
RILL ROUT RUCK SEAM SULK
CHASE DRAIN DRILL EARTH FIELD
RIGOL SCORE SEUGH STRIA
GROOVE GUTTER INDENT SULCUS
SUTURE TRENCH BREAKER
CHAMFER CHANNEL CRUMPLE
FEERING PLOWING QUILLET
SCRATCH WINDROW WRINKLE
CARRIAGE NOTAULIX THOROUGH

FURROWED SEAMED EXARATE FURROWY SULCATE TRENCHED

FURROWING KNOT DRESS

FURRY SHAGGY

FUR SEAL URSAL

FURTHER MO AID YET HELP YOND ADDED AGAIN FRESH SPEED SUPRA BEYOND EXTEND SECOND ADVANCE DEVELOP FARTHER FORWARD PROMOTE MOREOVER REMANENT ULTERIOR

FURTHERMORE BESIDES FURTHER OVERMORE

FURTIVE SLY PRIVY CLAMMY SECRET SHIFTY SNEAKY HANGDOG MEACHING MYSTICAL SNEAKING STEALTHY

FURTIVELY SLILY SLYLY SIDELINS

FURTIVENESS STEALTH

FURUNCLE BOIL

FURY HAG IRE WAX BURN RAGE ANGER BRETH DREAD FUROR IRISH RIGOR WRATH BELDAM CHOLER FRENZY FURORE MADNESS WIDDRIM DELIRIUM FEROCITY VIOLENCE WOODNESS

FURZE FUN FUZZ LING ULEX WHIN GORSE WHINCOW

FUSE RUN CAKE FLOW FLUX FRIT FUZE MELT BLEND FOUND FUSEE FUZEE QUILL SMELT SQUIB SWAGE TRAIN UNITE MINGLE SPITTER CONCRETE CONFLATE COPULATE PORTFIRE SAUCISSE

FUSED CONNATE

FUSEE FUZEE SPINDLE VESUVIAN VESUVIUS

FUSELAGE BODY (— **MEMBER**) LONGERON

FUSIFORM FUSATE SPINDLE

FUSIL (DIVIDED INTO —S) PLUMETE

FUSION ZYG FLUX FUSURE CHIASMA FLUXION CYTOGAMY MITAPSIS

FUSS DO ADO ROW TEW COIL FAFF FIKE FIRK FIZZ FRET ROUT SONG STIR TIME TOUSE TOWSE TRADE WHAUP BOTHER CADDLE DIRDUM FANTAD FETTLE FISSLE FISTLE FIZZLE FRAISE FUFFLE FUSTLE HOORAY HURRAH PHRASE POTHER SETOUT STROTH TURNUP FOOSTER FRIGGLE FUSSIFY NAUNTLE POOTHER SPUFFLE SPUTTER TAMASHA BUSINESS FOOFARAW SCRONACH

FUSSBUDGETY SPOFFISH

FUSSINESS DAINTY FADDLE FIKERY FOOSTER

FUSSING BOTHER

FUSSY FIKY FIXY FUDGY FIDFAD PROSSY SPOFFY SPRUCE STICKY FIDGETY SPOFFISH

FUSTET ZANTE FUSTIC

FUSTIAN HOLMES PILLOW BOMBAST TWADDLE MOLESKIN

FUSTIC LIME MORA FUSTET DYEWOOD AMARILLO

FUSTINESS FOIST

FUSTY FOIST MOLDY MUSTY FOISTY FROWSTY

FUTILE IDLE VAIN OTIOSE USELESS FOOTLESS FUTILOUS HELPLESS

FUTILITY VANITY NUGACITY

FUTTAH WHATA

FUTURE LATER SKULD COMING ONWARD OPTION TOCOME TOWARD LAVENIR FUTURITY (— **TIME**) MANANA

FUZZ LINTERS

FUZZY LOUSY MUZZY WOOLY WOOLLY

G GEE GOLF GEORGE
GA AKRA ACCRA INKRA
GAB GOB YAP BLAB CHINFEST
GABBLE WAB CANK CHAT CONK
JAVER BABBLE GAGGLE HABBLE
RABBLE TATTER YABBLE CLATTER
JAUNDER TWADDLE TWITTER
SLIPSLOP
GABBRO BOJITE NORITE EUCRITE
GABION KISH KEESH BASKET
WALING CORBEIL
GABLE GAVEL GOFOL DETAIL
DORMER GABLET KENNEL MEMBER
PINION AILERON PEDIMENT
GABON (CAPITAL OF —) LIBREVILLE
(LAKE OF —) ANENGUE AZINGUO
(MOUNTAIN OF —) MPELE
(NATIVE OF —) FANG ADOUMA
ECHIRA OKANDE
(RIVER OF —) OGOUE ABANGA
IVINDA NGOUNIE
(TOWN OF —) OYEM BONGO KANGO
MITZIC OMVANE MAKOKOU
GABOON OKOUME
GABRIELINO TOBIKHAR
GAD GAR RUN GAUD JAZZ RAKE
JINKET GADLING TRAIPSE
(— ABOUT) HAIK ROLL STRAM
GALLANT TROLLOP
(FATHER OF —) JACOB
GADABOUT GAD GADDER TRAIPSE
GADFLY GAD CLEG GLEG CLEGG
STOUT WHAME BOTFLY BREEZE
GADBEE OESTRID HORSEFLY
GADGET DODAD GISMO GIZMO
HICKY DINGUS DOODAD GILGUY
HICKEY JIGGER JIMJAM WIDGET
CONCERN DOFUNNY GIMMICK
BUSINESS GIMCRACK JIMCRACK
(PL.) GIBBLES GUBBINS GADGETRY
GADUS MORRHUA
GADWALL RODGE VOLANT GADWELL
REDWING SHUTTLE
GAEL CELT KELT SCOT GOIDEL
GAEDHEAL
GAELIC ERSE IRISH
GAFF CLIP SPAR SPUR YARD GAFFLE
GABLOCK GAFFLET SLASHER
GAVELOCK
(— MACKEREL) GAMBEER
GAG BOFF GEGG JOKE PONG SCOB
HEAVE KEVEL SCOBE AGUAJI
MUZZLE WHEEZE
GAGE (ALSO SEE GAUGE) LAY PAWN
WAGE GAUGE JEDGE NORMA
WAGER FEELER PLEDGE SPIDER
SCANTLE STANDARD UDOMETER
GAIETY JOY GALA JEST CHEER
MIRTH BAWDRY FROLIC GAYETY
LEVITY BAUDERY BEGONIA DAFFERY
DAFFING GAYNESS JOLLITY
JOYANCE ROLLICK FESTIVAL
HILARITY VIVACITY
GAILY GAY GAYLY BRAVELY LIGHTLY
GAIN BAG DAP GET NET POT WIN
BEAR BOOT DRAW GROW HAVE
LAND MAKE PELF SACK TILL ADDLE
BOOTY CATCH LATCH LUCRE
REACH SCORE ARRIVE ATTAIN

CHIEVE DERIVE GATHER INCOME
OBTAIN PROFIT STRAIN CAPTURE
CONQUER EMBRACE GAYMENT
GETTING HARVEST POSSESS
PROCURE REALIZE VANTAGE
WINNING CLEANING CONQUEST
PURCHASE
(— ADMISSION) ENTER
(— ADVANTAGE) GLEEK
(— ASCENDANCY) PREVAIL
(— BY EXTORTION) SQUEEZE
(— BY FORTUNE) DRAW HAZARD
(— COMMAND OF) MASTER
(— KNOWLEDGE) EDIFY LEARN
(— OVER) ENGAGE
(— UNDERSTANDING) SMOKE
(— WITHOUT DEDUCTION) CLEAR
(DISHONEST —) MEED
(ESTIMATED —) ESTEEM
(ILL-GOTTEN —) PELF
(MATERIAL —) PUDDING
(UNEXPECTED —) BUNCE
(PL.) PICKING PLUNDER GANANCIAS
GAINFUL LUCROUS GAINSOME
GAINSAY DENY FORBID IMPUGN
OPPOSE REFUTE RESIST DISPUTE
RECLAIM WITHSAY AGAINSAY
GAIT BAT JOG GANG LOPE PACE
RACK SKIP STEP TROT VOLT WALK
AMBLE AUBIN GOING STALK TRAIN
ALLURE CANTER GALLOP LOUNGE
SLOUCH SWINGE TODDLE WADDLE
WALLOW WAMBLE WOBBLE
DOGTROT HICKORY SAUNTER
SCUTTLE SHAMBLE SHUFFLE
WALKING WAUCHLE
(— OF ILL-BROKEN HORSE) CHACK
(4-BEAT —) AMBLE
(DEFECTIVE —) WINDING
(UNSTEADY —) STAGGER
GAITER SPAT VAMP STRAD BONNET
BRAGAS COCKER GASKIN GUETRE
HOGGER HUGGER LEGGIN PUTTEE
GAMBADE GAMBADO LEGGING
STARTUP BOOTIKIN CUTTIKIN
(PL.) UPPERS GASKINS GAMASHES
GRAMOCHES
GAIZE MALMSTONE
GAJO GORGIO
GALACTITE MILKSTONE
GALACTOSIDE IDEIN IDAEIN
GALAGO LEMUR LEMUROID
GALANAS GAINES
GALATEA (FATHER OF —) NEREUS
(LOVER OF —) ACIS
(MOTHER OF —) DORIS
GALAX COLTSFOOT
GALAXY NEBULA SPIRAL
GALBANUM FERULA GALBAN
ALBETAD
GALCHA PAMIR
GALE BLOW GELL HELM WIND
GAGEL PERRY STOUR BUSTER
EASTER BAYBUSH BURSTER
GALEAGE TEMPEST FLEAWOOD
GALEWORT NORWESTER
GALEA MITRA HELMET
GALGA INGUSH
GALIBI CARIBI KALINA

GALINGALE CYPRESS WANHORN
CHINAROOT
GALIPOT BARRAS GALLIPOT
TACAMAHAC
GALJOEN BLACKFISH
GALL GA GAW BAIT FELL FRET
WRING COCKLE HARASS BEDEGAR
GALLNUT KNOPPER NUTGALL
BEDEGUAR CECIDIUM FLEASEED
IRRITATE OAKBERRY SEEDGALL
SPURGALL TACAHOUT
(SAND —) SALT NATRON SANDIVER
(PL.) PURPLES
GALLANT GAY BEAU PROW BLADE
BRAVE BULLY CIVIL JOLLY LOVER
NOBLE PREUX SHOWY SPARK
SWAIN DONZEL ESCORT HEROIC
POLITE RUTTER SPARKY SQUIRE
SUITOR AMATORY AMORIST
AMOROUS CONDUCT GALANTE
GREGORY SPARKER STATELY
TOPPING YOUNKER CAVALIER
CICISBEO FEMALIST GALLIARD
HANDSOME POLISHED
GALLANTRY GAME DRURY DRUERY
BRAVERY COURAGE PROWESS
PARAMOUR
GALLBERRY INKBERRY
GALLED RAW
GALLEON CARAC CARRACK
GALLOON
GALLERY POY SAP COOP GODS
JUBE LOFT PAWN ALURE BOYAU
ORIEL PRADO ARCADE BURROW
DEDANS NARROW PIAZZA SCHOOL
SOLLAR SUBWAY TUNNEL BALCONY
GALERIE HEADWAY TERRACE
VERANDA BRATTICE CANTORIA
CORRIDOR HOARDING PARADISE
PERAMBLE SCAFFOLD TRAVERSE
VERANDAH
(— IN BAZAAR) PAWN
(— IN HOUSE OF COMMONS)
VENTILATOR
(— MADE BY INSECT) MINE
(CHURCH —) JUBE LAFT LOFT
(MINE —) BORD BROW SLOVAN
(MINSTREL'S —) ORIEL
(OPEN —) LOGGIA
(UNDERGROUND —) HYPOGEE
HYPOGEUM
GALLEY FUST CUDDY DRAKE FOIST
STICK BIREME GALIOT HEARTH
ZYGITE BASTARD CABOOSE
DROMOND GALLIOT HEXERIS
LYMPHAD TRIREME UNIREME
CAMBOOSE COOKROOM CROMSTER
GALLEASS RAMBERGE
(— BOTTOM) SLICE
(CHIEFTAIN'S —) BIRLING BIRLINN
(PHILLIPINE —) CALAN
(VIKING —) AESC DRAKE
GALLEY SLAVE FORSADO
SFORZATO
GALLFLY CYNIPID
GALLINAE RASORES
GALLINAZO VIRU VULTURE
GALLING BITTER
GALLINULE COOT KORA MOHO RAIL

GORHEN PUKEKO SKITTY MOORHEN STANKIE SULTANA DABCHICK HYACINTH MANUALII RAILBIRD RICEBIRD SWAMPHEN
GALLIVANT KITE GALLANT
GALLON GAWN CONGIUS
(**— OF ORE**) DISH
(**128 —S**) LEAGUER
(**EIGHTH —**) OCTARIUS
GALLOON ORRIS
GALLOP FOG RUN AUBIN PRICK CANTER CAREER COURSE TITTUP WALLOP TANTIVY
GALLOWS NUB CRAP DROP FORK TREE BOUGH CHEAT FURCA WIDDY GIBBET DERRICK FORCHES JUSTICE POTENCE STIFLER WARYTREE
GALLOWS BIRD HEMPY WIDDY HEMPIE HEMPSEED WIDDIFOW CRACKROPE
GALOSH ARCTIC ZIPPER EXCLUDER OVERSHOE
GALUTH GOLUS GOLAHI
GALVANIC VOLTAIC
GALVANIZE ZINCIFY
GALVANOMETER DETECTOR REOMETER
GAMBESON WAMBAIS
GAMBIA (**CAPITAL OF —**) BANJUL
(**LANGUAGE OF —**) JOLA WOLOF FULANI MALINKE
(**MONEY OF —**) DALASI
(**NATIVE OF —**) JOLA PEUL WOLOF DIOLAS FULANI MANDINGO SERAHULI
(**TOWN OF —**) MANSA BINTANG KUNTAUR
GAMBIA POD BABLOH
GAMBIER CATECHU
GAMBIT MANEUVER
GAMBLE BET DICE GAFF GAME NICK PLAY PUNT RISK SPORT STAKE WAGER CHANCE GAMMON HAZARD PLUNGE FLUTTER
(**— AGAINST**) BUCK
GAMBLER PIKER SPORT CARROW DEALER PLAYER PUNTER HUSTLER PLAYMAN PLUNGER SLICKER THROWER BLACKLEG GAMESTER HAZARDER
GAMBLING GAMING HAZARDRY
(**— DEVICE**) PACHINKO
GAMBLING HOUSE HELL TRIPOT
GAMBO GOOSE SPURWING
GAMBOL HOP PLAY CAPER FRISK KEVEL PRANK CAREER CAVORT FROLIC GAMBADO
GAMBREL CAMMOCK SPREADER
GAME COB FUN JEU JIG GAMY LAKE MAIL PLAY DANCE GAMEY PARTY SPIEL SPORT WATHE BATTUE MORRIS QUARRY RAMSCH VENERY JENKINS KNICKER BREATHER FIGHTING FOREGAME
(**— FOR FISHERMEN**) SKISH
(**— LIKE HANDBALL**) FIVES
(**— LIKE HOCKEY**) DODDART
(**— NARROWLY WON**) SQUEAKER
(**— OF CAT**) BILLET

(**— OF FOOTBALL**) BOWL CAMP
(**— OF FORFEITS**) KEN
(**— OF HOCKEY**) BANDY SHINNY
(**— OF MARBLES**) TAW BOWL BONCE GULLY KEEPS KNUCKS MIGGLES
(**— OF MENTAL SKILL**) GO CHESS CHECKERS
(**— OF NINEPINS**) KAILS KAYLES
(**— OF PRISONER'S BASE**) CHEVY CHIVVY
(**— WITH BOOMERANG**) BRIST
(**— WITH COUNTERS**) DUMPS GOOSE
(**— WITH SHUTTLECOCK**) TAHYING
(**BACKGAMMON —**) HIT IRISH
(**BALL —**) CAT TUT SNOB CATCH RUGBY SOCCER SQUASH TENNIS CRICKET KNAPPAN BASEBALL FOOTBALL HANDBALL SLUGFEST SOFTBALL
(**CARD —**) AS HOC LOO MAW NAP PAM PIT PUT SET BRAG CENT FARO FISH FROG GRAB JASS LANT PINK POOL POPE POST RUFF SANT SKAT SLAM SNAP SOLO STUD VINT BEAST BUNCO BUNKO CARDS CARIE CHICO CINCH COMET CRIMP DECOY GILET GLEEK GRAND LEAST MONTE OMBER OMBRE PEDRO PITCH POKER PRIME RUMMY SCOPA STOPS STUSS TRUMP WHIST BASSET BIRKIE BOODLE BOSTON BRIDGE CASINO CHEMMY COMMIT ECARTE EIGHTS EUCHRE FARMER FLINCH HEARTS HOWELL LOADUM PANFIL PIQUET QUINZE RAMSCH ROUNCE SLOUGH SMUDGE SPIDER TOURNE AUCTION AUTHORS BELOTTE BEZIQUE CANASTA CASSINO CAYENNE CHICAGO COONCAN GARBAGE HUNDRED JACKPOT REVERSI RONTOON SCOPONE SETBACK TRIUMPH VINGTUN VITESSE BACCARAT BASEBALL BRISCOLA COMMERCE CONQUIAN CONTRACT CRIBBAGE FREAKPOT HANDICAP IMPERIAL NAPOLEON PATIENCE PENCHANT PENNEECH PINOCHLE SHOWDOWN SKINBALL SKINNING SLAPJACK TREDILLE TRESILLO VERQUERE VIDERUFF
(**CARNIVAL —**) HOOPLA
(**CHILDREN'S —**) TAG DIBS JACKS KICKBALL
(**CONFIDENCE —**) RAMP BIGMITT
(**COURT —**) SQUASH TENNIS HANDBALL
(**DICE —**) FARE BINGO CRAPS NOVUM RAPHE HAZARD BARBUDI ADDITION BARBOTTE CAMEROON HOOLIGAN
(**DRAWN —**) SPOIL REFAIT
(**DRINKING —**) HIJINKS
(**EGYPTIAN —**) SENT SENIT
(**GAMBLING —**) TAN FARO HAND PICO BOULE CRAPS MACAO MONTE POKER PROPS RONDO STUSS

BRELAN HAZARD RONDEAU ROULETTE
(**GENERAL —**) HEI HIT HOB TAG TIG BALL BASE BULL BUZZ CENT DIBS DUCK FARE GOLF HOLE JOWL KENO MALL POLO POOL SLAM SNOB TICK BANDY BINGO BONCE BOULE CHESS CHUBA CHUNK CLOSH DARTS DOLOS FIVES GOOSE HALMA HOUSE IRISH JACKS LOTTO LURCH NOVUM NULLO PITCH PUSSY RUGBY SALTA SALVO SCRUB TROCO WHOOP BEAVER CAROMS CHIVVY CHUNKY CLUMPS COBNUT COCKAL COOTIE CRAMBO FEEDER GOBANG GRACES HAZARD HOOPLA HUBBUB JEREED KAYLES MERELE PELOTA PLUMPS RAGMAN RINGER SEESAW SHINNY SIPPIO SKILLO STICKS TENNIS TIGTAG TIPCAT TIVOLI TRIGON TRUCKS BALLOON BEANBAG BEEBALL BOWLING COBBLER CONKERS CROQUET CURLING DIABOLO DODDART DOUBLES DREIDEL ENDBALL GOGGANS HANGMAN HURLBAT LOGGATS MAHJONG MATADOR MUGGINS NETBALL PALLONE PASSAGE PEEVERS PUSHPIN QUINTET RINGTAW SARDINE SQUAILS STATUES TENPINS TOMBOLA ANAGRAMS BALKLINE BASEBALL CHARADES CHECKERS CHOUETTE DOMINOES DOUBLETS DRAUGHTS DUCKPINS FIVEPINS FOOTBALL FORFEITS GIVEAWAY HARDHEAD KICKBALL LEAPFROG PARCHESI PEEKABOO PURPOSES PUSHBALL PYRAMIDS RINGTOSS ROULETTE ROUNDERS SCRABBLE SKITTLES STOBBALL STOWBALL TRAPBALL VERQUERE
(**GUESSING —**) LOVE MORA CANUTE
(**INDIAN —**) CHUNKY HUBBUB
(**INFERIOR —**) CHECK
(**NUMBERS —**) BUG
(**OUTDOOR —**) GOLF POLO HURLY ROQUE RUGBY SOCCER CROQUET HURLING BASEBALL FOOTBALL LACROSSE
(**PROGRESSIVE —**) DRIVE
(**REHEATED —**) SALMI SALMIS
(**SWISS —**) JASS
(**THREE BOWLING —S**) SERIES
(**TRAPSHOOTING —**) SCOOT
(**WAR —**) BARRIERS
(**WORD —**) GHOST ANAGRAMS
GAMECOCK STAG STAIG
GAMEKEEPER GAMIE KEEPER WALKER WARNER WARRENER
GAMESTER DICER PLAYER GAMBLER PLAYMAN SHARPER HAZARDER TABLEMAN
GAMETE SPERM OOCYTE ZYGOTE GAMETOID OOGAMETE OOSPHERE
GAMETOCYTE GAMONT CRESCENT GONOCYTE
GAMETOPHYTE GERMLING

GAMIN TAD ARAB URCHIN
GAVROCHE
GAMMA AGMA
GAMUT GAMME RANGE SCALE
SERIES COMPASS DIAGRAM
GANDER STEG STAIG GANNER
(— AND GEESE) SET
GANESA GUNPUT GANAPATI
GANG MOB SET BAND BUND CORE
CREW GING PACK PAIR PUSH TEAM
GROUP HORDE SPELL CHIURM
COFFLE GAGGLE LAYOUT MOHOCK
SCHOOL COMPANY
(— MEMBER) WHYO
(— OF FISHHOOKS) PULLDEVIL
(— OF MINERS) CORE
GANGLING GAWKY GANGLY
GANGLION TUMOR CEREBRUM
GANGPLANK BROW GANGWAY
GANGRENE CANKER GANGER
SPHACEL
GANGSTER HOOD WHYO BANDIT
COWBOY CHOPPER
GANGUE MATRIX LODESTUFF
VEINSTONE
GANGWAY ROAD SLIP LOGWAY
TUNNEL CATWALK COULOIR
GATEWAY
GANJA GUNJAH CANNABIS
GANNET BOOBY GAUNT SOLAN
PIQUERO SEAFOWL
GANTRYMAN DROPMAN
GANYMEDE (BROTHER OF —) ILUS
ASSARACUS
(FATHER OF —) TROS
(MOTHER OF —) CALLIRRHOE
GAP SAG FLAW GAPE GOWL GULF
MUSE NICK SLAP SLOP WANT
BREAK BRECK CHASM CHAUM
CHAWN CLOVE FRITH MEUSE MUSET
NOTCH SHARD SHERD VUIDE
BREACH GULLET HIATUS LACUNA
SPREAD THROAT VACUUM CLOSING
OPENING VACANCY VACUITY
APERTURE DIASTEMA ENTREFER
INTERVAL MULTIGAP QUEBRADA
(— IN BANK OF STREAM) GAT
(— IN MEMORY) AMNESIA
(— SERVING AS PASS) COL
GAPE GAN GAP GANT GAUP GAWK
GAWP GAZE GOVE GRIN YAWN
CHAUN HIATE STARE RICTUS
DEHISCE INHIATE
GAPING GALP AGAPE HIANT CHAPPY
CHASMA GAWISH MOUTHED
RINGENT
GAR HOUND SNOOK AGUJON
CHERNA GARFISH GARPIKE BILLFISH
GOREFISH GURDFISH HORNFISH
HORNKECK LONGJAWS LONGNOSE
GARAGE HANGAR LOCKUP SIDING
GARRIDGE
(ROW OF —S) MEWS
GARAVANCE CARAUNA GARBANZO
GARB (ALSO SEE APPAREL AND
DRESS) COWL GEAR TOGA VEST
DRESS GUISE HABIT APPAREL
CLOTHES COSTUME RAIMENT
GARBAGE GASH SLOP OFFAL TRASH

WASTE GIBLET REFUSE SCRAPS
GARBAGEMAN DUSTMAN
GARBLE GELD JUMBLE MANGLE
DISTORT GARBLING MUTILATE
GARDANT AFFRONTE
GARDEN HAW EDEN KNOT YARD
ARBOR GARTH CIRCLE POMACY
POMARY QUINTA SHAMBA VERGER
VIHARA ACADEMY HERBARY
OLITORY ORCHARD ROCKERY
TOPIARY CHINAMPA FLORETUM
HORTYARD KALEYARD LEIGHTON
PARADISE POTAGERE ROSARIUM
(— CITY) CHICAGO
(— STATE) NEWJERSEY
GARDENER MALI PONICA CROPPER
PLANNER BOSTANGI
GARDEN HELIOTROPE VALERIAN
GARDENIA TIARA
GARDENING TOPIARY
GARDEN ROCKET EVEWEED
GARDEN WARBLER JACK HAYBIRD
BECAFICO FAUVETTE FIGEATER
GARFISH (SEE GAR)
GARGANEY TEAL CRICK
GARGANTUAN HUGE VAST GIANT
HOMERIC TITANIC ENORMOUS
GIGANTIC HOMERIAN
GARGLE GURGLE COLLUTORY
GARGOYLE BOSS
GARIBALDI GOLDFISH
GARISH GAUDY GIDDY SHOWY
CRIANT GLARING
GARISHNESS GLARE
GARLAND BAY LEI CROWN VITTA
ANADEM CORONA CRANTS ROSARY
WREATH CHAPLET CORANCE
CORONAL FESTOON
GARLIC AJO MOLY CHIVE PORET
ALLIUM PORRET RAMSON
GARMENT DUD TOG BACK BRAT
COAT GOWN PELL PELT RAIL ROBE
SARK SHAG SILK SLIP SLOP SULU
VEST WEED ABAYA BUREL CENTO
CLOAK CLOTH COTTE CYMAR
DRESS FROCK HABIT HAORI JOSEY
JUPON KHAKI MANGA NABOB
SHAWL SHIFT SHIRT SIMAR SKIRT
STOLE WRIEL ALPACA ATTIRE
BARROW BLOUSE CAFTAN CAMLET
CAPOTE CHAMMA COTTON CYCLAS
ERMINE EXOMIS FECKET HUIPIL
JACKET JERSEY JUMPER KERSEY
KIRTLE MOHAIR MOTLEY SARONG
SHORTY SHROUD STROUD TAMEIN
ZIZITH AMICTUS BROIGNE BUNTING
CAMBLET CHIRIPA CRAWLER
CUCULLA CULOTTE DOUBLET
FALDING FLOCKET GROGRAM
PALETOT PELISSE RAIMENT
SHORTIE SURCOAT SWEATER
VESTURE WRAPPER BATHROBE
CAMELINE CAPUCHIN CHAUSSES
COLOBIUM CORSELET COVERALL
DEERSKIN EPIBLEMA GAMBESON
GUERNSEY HIMATION INDUMENT
PADUASOY SCAPULAR SEALSKIN
SLIPOVER SNOWSUIT VESTMENT
WEARABLE STROUDING

(— OF HERALD) TABARD
(— OF HIGH PRIEST) EPHOD
(— OF PATCHES) CENTO
(BABY'S —) BARROW CRAWLER
CREEPER
(BADLY-MADE —) DRECK
(BLUE —) MAZARINE
(BURIAL —) SHROUD
(COARSE —) BRAT STROUD
(DEFENSIVE —) JACK BROIGNE
GAMBESON
(ECCLESIASTICAL —) STOLE
RHASON CASSOCK
(ETHIOPIAN —) CHAMMA
(HINDU —) SARI SAREE
(INFANT'S —) DIAPER BUNTING
SLEEPER
(JAPANESE —) HAORI
(LEATHER —) BUFF
(LINEN —) LINE
(LONG —) JIBBA STOLE JIBBEH
MANDYAS PELISSE HIMATION
(MEDIEVAL —) ROCHET CHAUSSES
DALMATIC GAMBESON
(MONK'S —) SCAPULAR
(MOURNING —) SABLE
(OUTER —) BRAT COAT GOWN HAIK
HYKE SLOP WRAP FROCK HAORI
NABOB PALLA PILCH SMOCK
DOLMAN ROCHET CHEMISE GALABIA
PALETOT SURCOAT SWEATER
HIMATION OVERSLOP
(PADDED —) TRUSS
(SLEEVELESS —) ABA CAPE COWL
VEST MANTLE CUCULLA GANDURAH
(SQUARE —) KAROSS
(THIN —) GOSSAMER
(TIGHT-FITTING —) HOSE COTTE
LEOTARD
(WOMAN'S —) IZAR BURKA CYMAR
NABOB SIMAR BURKHA CHITON
JOSEPH PEPLOS PEPLUM VISITE
BURNOUS
(PL.) GEAR COSTUME GARNISH
FLANNELS
GARNER REAP STORE GATHER
IMBARN COLLECT
GARNET GRENAT PYROPE ANTHRAX
GRANATE OLIVINE VERMEIL
ESSONITE MELANITE ROSOLITE
YANOLITE
GARNISH LARD TRIM ADORN DRESS
EQUIP MENSE STICK FURNISH
TOPPING CHUMMAGE DECORATE
DUXELLES ORNAMENT
GARNISHED GARNI
GARNISHEE CHECK FACTOR
GARNISH
GARRET ATTIC SOLAR SOLLAR
MANSARD COCKLOFT
GARRISON WARD STUFF PRESIDY
WARNISON
GARRULITY POLYLOGY
GARRULOUS GABBY TALKY WORDY
BABBLY TONGUY VOLUBLE
GARTER GARTEN LEGLET ELASTIC
STRAPPLE
GARTH CORTILE OUTGARTH
GARUM LIQUAMEN

GAS DAMP XENON FLATUS GENAPP LEAVEN OXYGEN PETROL EXHAUST KRYPTON YPERITE AFTERGAS ETHERION FIREDAMP HYDROGEN STANNANE VESICANT
(— CONSTANT) R
(COLORLESS —) OXAN OXANE KETENE GERMANE STIBINE
(NERVE —) SARIN
(NONCOMBUSTIBLE —) INERT
(POISONOUS —) ARSINE CYANOGEN PHOSGENE
GASCONADE BRAG CROW BOAST BLUSTER
GASEOUS AERIFORM GASIFORM VOLATILE
GASH CUT CHOP LASH BLASH CRIMP GANCH GRIDE SCORE SLASH SLISH SCOTCH SLUICE TRENCH INCISION INCISURE
(— A FISH) RIM
GASKET LUTE CASKET GASKIN GROMMET SCISSIL
GASKIN BRAGAS
GASOLINE GAS AVGAS JUICE PETROL BENZINE NATURAL
GASP FOB BLOW GAPE KINK PANK PANT CHINK CROAK FETCH THRATCH
GASTRONOME EPICURE
GASTROPOD SLUG DRILL HARPA OLIVA SNAIL BUCKIE NERITE ABALONE MOLLUSK TOXIFER UNIVALVE VELUTINA
GATE BAB BAR JET HEAD LIFT PORT SASH SLAP YETT ENTRY HATCH JANUA SALLY SPRAY STICK TORAN ENAJIM ESCAPE FENDER FUNNEL HARROW INGATE LIGGAT PADDLE PORTAL RUNNER TIMBER TORANA WICKET ZAGUAN BARRIER CLICKET FIVEBAR GATEWAY LIDGATE POSTERN SHUTTER ABOIDEAU ANTEPORT DECUMANA ENTRANCE FOREGATE GURDWARA PENSTOCK TOLLGATE TOWNGATE TRIMTRAM TURNPIKE
(— OF CASTLE) BAR
(BACK —) POSTERN
(CUSTOMS —) BARRIER
(IRRIGATION —) CHECK TAPON TAPPOON
(LICH —) SCALLAGE TRIMTRAM
(RUNNING —) FUNNEL
(SAW —) FRAME
(SAWMILL —) SASH
(SLALOM —S) HAIRPIN
(SLUICE —) HATCH VALVE
(WATER —) SLUICE
GATEADO DIOMATE
GATEHOUSE BAR LODGE
GATEKEEPER WARDEN CERBERUS GATEWARD PORTITOR STILEMAN
GATEMAN GUARD
GATEPOST DURN HARR HEEL PIER POST SHAFT POSTEL
GATEWAY DAR DOOR GATE LOKE TORU PYLON TORAN TORII BARWAY GOPURA TORANA PROPYLON

GATHER GET LEK POD WIN BAND BREW CLAN CLOT CROP CULL FURL HERD HIVE HOST PICK REAP RELY TUCK AMASS BANGE BROOM BUNCH FLOCK GLEAN GUESS INFER LEASE PLUCK RAISE SWEEP ACCRUE COMPEL CORRAL DECERP DERIVE GARNER HUDDLE HUSTLE IMBARN MUSTER RAMASS SCRAPE CLUSTER COLLATE COLLECT COMPILE CONGEST CONVENE CONVOKE HARVEST RAMMASS RECRUIT ASSEMBLE CUMULATE SHEPHERD
(— AS ARMY) HOST
(— BY SCRAPING) SCRATCH
(— GRASS SEED) STRIP
(— HEADWAY) SET
(— HERBS) SIMPLE
(— IN A HEAP) HATTER
(— IN RAGS) TAT
(— SEWING) GAGE GAUGE
(— UP) KILT
GATHERED KILTED CUMULATE
GATHERER GEDDER TUCKER RUFFLER CHICLERO PLICATOR PUCKERER
GATHERING HUI LED LEK SUM FAIR FEST KNOT SING SIVA LEVEE SHINE TRYST INDABA MUDDLE PLISSE POWWOW RUELLE SMOKER COLLECT COMMERS COMPANY FUNFEST HARVEST HOSTING HUSKING JOLLITY KLATSCH MEETING MOOTING NYMPHAL ROCKING TURNOUT ASSEMBLY CONCLAVE JUNCTION JAMBOREE PANIONIA POTATION RECOURSE SINGSONG SOCIABLE STAMPEDE
(— OF ANIMALS) DRIVE
(— OF ARMED MEN) HOSTING
(— OF CLOTH) SHIRR SHIRRING
(— OF FILM) CISSING
(— OF SCOUTS) CAMPOREE JAMBOREE
(— PLACE) LESCHE
(FORMAL —) HALL
(RELIGIOUS —) SHOUT
(SOCIAL —) BEE FRY BAKE BALL CLUB DRUM STAG WINE BAILE BINGE BINGO DANCE MIXER SHIVOO SMOKER CANTICO KLATSCH SHINDIG SQUEEZE BARBECUE CAMPFIRE CLAMBAKE TALKFEST SYMPOSIUM
GAU BANT
GAUCHE CLUMSY AWKWARD
GAUD GAY GAUDY FANGLE VANITY TRINKET
GAUDINESS GLARE GLITTER
GAUDY GAY LOUD CHEAP FLARY SHOWY VAUDY BRAZEN FLASHY FLIMSY FLORID GARISH GAWISH SKYRIN TAWDRY TINSEL BRANKIE CHINTZY FLARING GAUDISH GLARING
GAUGE (ALSO SEE GAGE) BORE GAGE MOOT PLUG SIZE TRAM GADGE NORMA RANGE DENTIN FEELER FORMER GABARI DEPTHEN

TEMPLET TRAMMEL ESTIMATE INDICANT MEASURER STANDARD SURFACER TEMPLATE
(— FOR SLATES) SCANTLE
(RAIN —) UDOMETER
GAUGER SURVEYOR
GAUL GALLIA
(PL.) PICTONES
GAUNT BONY GRIM LANK LEAN SLIM THIN PINED SPARE THIRL BARREN HAGGED HOLLOW MEAGER MEAGRE SHELLY HAGGARD SLENDER DESOLATE RAWBONED
GAUNTLET TOP CUFF GLOVE GANTLET GAINPAIN GANTLOPE
GAUR BISON SELADANG
GAUZE LISSE MARLI MARLY UMPLE CYPRUS CYPRESS TIFFANY CARBASUS
GAUZY FILMY
GAVE GIN GUV YAF YAFE
GAVEL HAMMER GAVELAGE
GAVIAL NAKOO LIZARD GHARIAL LORICATE
GAVOTTE MUSETTE
GAWK GAWKY GAWNEY LUMPKIN RAMMACK
GAWKY GOWKIT AWKWARD GAWKISH
GAY MAD AIRY BOON DAFT GLAD GLEG HIGH RORY TRIM WILD BONNY GAUDY JOLLY LIGHT MERRY RORTY SUNNY VAUDY WLONK ALEGER BLITHE CHEERY FLASHY FRISKY FROLIC GARISH JOCUND JOVIAL JOYFUL JOYOUS KIPPER LIVELY SPORTY CHIPPER FESTIVE GALLANT GIOJOSO GLEEFUL LARKING RACKETY SMICKER TITTUPY WINSOME CAVALIER FROHLICH GAMESOME PLEASANT PRIMROSE SPARKISH SPLENDID SPORTIVE
GAY-FEATHER LIATRIS
GAYWINGS MAYWINGS
GAZE EYE PRY CAPE GAPE GOUK GOWK LEER LOOK MOON OGLE PEER PORE SCAN TOOT GLAIK GLARE GLOAT GLORE SIGHT STARE TWIRE VISIE WLITE ASPECT GLOWER REGARD
GAZELLE AHU GOA ADMI AOUL CORA DAMA MOHR ADDRA ARIEL KORIN DZEREN GROUSE ALGAZEL CHIKARA CORINNE DIBATAG TABITHA CHINKARA
GAZELLE HOUND SALUKI
GAZETTE COURANT JOURNAL
(— OF CRIMES) HUE
GE TAPUYAN
GEAN MERRY MURIE MURRY GUIGNE GASKINS
GEAR KIT SPUR TACK TRIM IDLER TOOTH FOURTH GRAITH HYPOID PINION TACKLE CLOBBER GEARING HARNESS REVERSE RIGGING SEGMENT TRILOBE HEADGEAR
(— OF DIVER) ARMOR
(CHAFING —) SCOTCHMAN
(DEFENSIVE —) ARMORY

(RUNNING —) CARRIAGE
(TRANSMISSION —) HIGH FIRST
SPEED FOURTH SECOND REVERSE
GEARED GIRT
GEARWHEEL UNILOBE WABBLER
WOBBLER
GEB KEB SEB
GECKO FANFOOT TARENTE
GEKKONID LACERTID
GEELBEC SALMON TERAGLIN
GEEPOUND SLUG
GEESE SET
GEIGER TREE ALOEWOOD
SEBESTEN
GEL JELL JELLY LIVER GELATE
ALCOGEL
GELATIN GLUE COLLIN GLUTIN
GLUTOID HAITSAI NORGINE
ISINGLASS
GELATINOUS MUCULENT JELLYLIKE
GELD LIB GELT ALTER CASTRATE
GELDING HORSE SPADE SPADO
GEM GIM JADE ONYX OPAL RUBY
AGATE BERYL CAMEO JAZEL JEWEL
PEARL SPARK STONE TOPAZ ZIMME
AMULET BAGUET CRUSTA GARNET
JASPER PEBBLE PYROPE RONDEL
ZIRCON CITRINE DIAMOND DOUBLET
EMERALD JACINTH KUNZITE
ONEGITE PERIDOT SPARKLE
ACHROITE AMATRICE AMETHYST
BAGUETTE HYACINTH INTAGLIO
MARQUISE ORIENTAL RONDELLE
SAPPHIRE SARDONYX HIDDENITE
(— CARVED IN RELIEF) CAMEO
INTAGLIO
(— ENGRAVED WITH CHARM)
ABRAXAS
(— OF IMPERFECT BRILLIANCY)
LOUPE
(— REFLECTING LIGHT IN 6 RAYS)
ASTERIA
(— STATE) IDAHO
(IMITATION —) PASTE
(UNCUT —) ROUGH CABOCHON
GEMMA BUD GEMMULE SOREDIUM
GEMMULE SPORE BROODSAC
GEMMY EMERALD
GEMSBOK ORYX KOKAMA
GEMSBUCK
GEMSTONE JADE STAR CHEVEE
SPINEL EMERALD FISHEYE
CROSSCUT HYALITHE
GENA CHEEK
GENDER SEX KIND CLASS FEMININE
GENE GEN ALLEL AMORPH FACTOR
LETHAL PRIMER CYTOGENE
MODIFIER
GENERAL MAIN MOST BROAD
GROSS COMMON VULGAR CURRENT
GENERIC MARSHAL SUMMARY
AUFIDIUS CANIDIUS CATHOLIC
ECUMENIC ENCYCLIC OVERHEAD
PANDEMIC PUFIDIUS STRATEGE
BRIGADIER
GENERALITY CREDO GENERALE
GENERALIZATION LAW AXIOM
BROMIDE
GENERALIZE WIDEN EXTEND

SPREAD BROADEN
GENERALIZED GROSS GLOBAL
GENERALLY BROADLY LARGELY
ROUNDLY MOSTWHAT
GENERATE MAKE SIRE TEEM BEGET
BREED IMPEL SPAWN STEAM
CREATE FATHER GENDER IMPOSE
KITTLE DEVELOP INBREED PRODUCE
ENGENDER
(— PUS) DIGEST
GENERATION AGE KIND TIME
WORLD STRAIN STRIND DESCENT
DIPLOID GETTING KINDRED
GAMOBIUM GENITURE SAECULUM
THEOGONY TRIPLOID UPSPRING
OFFSPRING
GENERATIVE GENIAL GAMETIC
GENESIC GENETIC SEEDFUL
PROLIFIC
GENERATOR BUZZER DYNAMO
RULING ELEMENT DIPHASER
GENERANT
GENEROSITY GRACE LARGE
BOUNTY GENTRY BREADTH
FREEDOM HONESTY COURTESY
GOODNESS KINDNESS LARGESSE
GENEROUS BIG FREE OPEN SOFT
FRANK HEFTY LARGE NOBLE
LIBERAL GRACIOUS HANDSOME
INSORDID LARGEOUS MAGNIFIC
GENEROUSLY LUCKY MANLY
KINDLY FRANKLY
GENESIS BIRTH ORIGIN BERESHIT
GENETICS
GENET BERBE CIVET DAPPLE
VIVERRINE
GENIAL BEIN BIEN WARM DOUCE
SONSY DOULCE FORTHY FURTHY
HEARTY KINDLY MELLOW MENTAL
CHEERFUL GRACIOUS PLEASANT
GENIALITY BONHOMIE
GENICULATE KNEED ELBOWED
GENIE GENIUS HATHOR SANDMAN
GENII XIN JANN
GENIN BUFAGIN
GENIP GINEP JAGUA IRONWOOD
GENIPAP GENIP JAGUA GUENEGE
GENISTA FURZE RETAMA
GENITAL SECRET
(PL.) HARNESS PRIVITY GENITURE
GENIUS FIRE GIFT HAPI KALI TURN
ANGEL BRAIN DEMON GENIO NUMEN
DAEMON INGENY INGINE TALENT
WIZARD DUSTMAN DUAMUTEF
EINSTEIN FRAVASHI SILVANUS
(— OF LANGUAGE) IDIOM
GENOA GEANE
GENOTYPE BIOTYPE LOGOTYPE
GENOUILLERE KNEELET
GENRE EPIC KIND SORT TYPE CLASS
STYLE FABLIAU SPECIES CATEGORY
GENS HOUSE
GENTEEL NICE GENTY GENTIL
JAUNTY POLITE STYLISH GRACEFUL
GENTIAN BIT FELWORT AGUEWEED
GALLWEED BALDMONEY
GENTILE GOI GOY ARIAN ARYAN
GOYISH HEATHEN
GENTILITY GENTRICE

GENTLE MOY CALM DEFT DEWY
FAIR HEND KIND MEEK MILD MURE
NESH SLOW SOFT SOOT TAME
BLAND CANNY LIGHT LITHE MILKY
QUIET SMALL SOBER SWEET
BONAIR CADISH DOCILE FACILE
MODEST PLACID REMISS SILKEN
SILVER SOFTLY TENDER AMABILE
CLEMENT GRADUAL SOAKING
SUBDUED DEBONAIR DOVELIKE
EGGSHELL LAMBLIKE LENITIVE
MAIDENLY MANSUETE MODERATE
PEACEFUL SARCENET TOWARDLY
TRANQUIL
(— AS OF THE WIND) LOOM
GENTLEFOLK GENTRY GENTILITY
GENTLEMAN NIB SIR BABU GENT
BABOO CURIO DORAY SAHIB SENOR
GEMMAN MILORD SENHOR SIGNOR
YONKER BRAVERY GALLANT
GENTMAN MYNHEER CAVALIER
MIRABELL SEIGNEUR SEIGNIOR
SQUIREEN
(— COMMONER) HAT
(— TRAINING FOR KNIGHTHOOD)
DONZEL
(COUNTRY —) SQUIRE
(GIPSY —) RYE
(MILITARY —) CADET
(WOULD-BE —) SHONEEN
(PL.) HERREN CHIVALRY
GENTLEMANLY JAUNTY
GENTLENESS FLESH LENITY
AMENITY DOUCEUR KINDNESS
GENTLY SOFT CANNY SOAVE EASILY
FAIRLY LIGHTLY EASYLIKE PRETTILY
TENDERLY
GENTRY COUNTY GENTRICE
SQUIRAGE SZLACHTA
GENUFLECTION VENIE KNEELING
GENUINE ECHT GOOD LEAL REAL
TRUE VRAI PLAIN PUKKA SOLID
ACTUAL ARRANT DINKUM DIRECT
HONEST KOSHER PISTIC CURRENT
GERMANE GRADELY SINCERE
VERIDIC GRAITHLY STERLING
(NOT —) TIN SHAM BOGUS
(SEEMINGLY —) COLORABLE
GENUINENESS VERIDITY
GENUS KIND CLASS ANALOG
GENDER GENERAL
(— OF ALGAE) DASYA FUCUS
BANGIA CHORDA CODIUM HYPNEA
NOSTOC PADINA DIATOMA LEMANEA
LIAGORA PTILOTA VALONIA
ZYGNEMA ANABAENA BRYOPSIS
CAULERPA CERAMIUM CHONDRUS
CONFERVA CUTLERIA DICTYOTA
DUMONTIA GELIDIUM GOMONTIA
HALIMEDA LERAMIUM LESSONIA
NEMALION OOCYSTIS PALMELLA
PORPHYRA STRIARIA TAONURUS
ULOTHRIX
(— OF AMOEBA) CHAOS
(— OF AMPHIBIAN) HYLA RANA
SIREN PROTEUS AMPHIUMA
NECTURUS
(— OF ANT) ATTA ECITON LASIUS
PONERA TERMES FORMICA

PHEIDOLE TAPINOMA
(— OF ANTELOPE) ORYX KOBUS
GAZELLA MADOQUA REDUNCA
ANTILOPE EGOCERUS
(— OF APE) PAN PONGO SIMIA
(— OF APHID) ADELGES CHERMES
(— OF ARACHNID) ACARUS
GALEODES
(— OF ARMADILLO) DASYPUS
XENURUS
(— OF ASCIDIAN) CIONA MOLGULA
BOLTENIA PYROSOMA
(— OF ASCLEPIAD) STAPELIA
(— OF AUK) ALCA ALLE
(— OF BABOON) PAPIO
(— OF BACTERIA) VIBRIO EIMERIA
ERWINIA GAFFKYA PROTEUS
SARCINA BACILLUS BRUCELLA
SERRATIA SHIGELLA
(— OF BADGER) MELES ARCTONYX
HELICTIS
(— OF BARNACLE) LEPAS BALANUS
ELMINIUS
(— OF BASIDIOMYCETE) BOVISTA
(— OF BAT) EUDERMA PETALIA
DESMODUS DIPHYLLA MOLOSSUS
MORMOOPS NOCTILIO NYCTERIS
PLECOTUS PTEROPUS VAMPYRUM
(— OF BEAR) URSUS EUARCTOS
MELURSUS
(— OF BEAVER) CASTOR
(— OF BEE) APIA APIS BOMBUS
ANDRENA TRIGONA COLLETES
HALICTUS MELIPONA
(— OF BEETLE) AMARA FIDIA HISPA
LAMIA LARIA LYTTA MELOE SAGRA
ALTICA ASILUS CLERUS ELATER
LYCTUS PTINUS SILPHA ACILIUS
ADELOPS AGRILUS ANOBIUM
ANOMALA BRUCHUS CARABUS
CASSIDA EPITRIX PRIONUS SAPERDA
SITARIS ADORETUS AGRIOTES
APHODIUS CALOSOMA CATORAMA
CYBISTER DERMETES DYNASTES
DYTISCUS EPICAUTA EUMOLPUS
HARPALUS LAMPYRIS MEGASOMA
PASSALUS POPILLIA SCOLYTUS
SPHINDUS TENEBRIO
(— OF BIRD) ARA ALCA APUS CRAX
CREX GYPS JYNX MIRO MITU MOHO
OTIS PICA RHEA SULA TYTO XEMA
AJAJA ANOUS ANSER ARDEA ARGUS
ASTUR BUCCO FALCO GAVIA GOURA
GUARA GYGIS IRENA JUNCO LARUS
LERWA LOXIA MIMUS MITUA MUNIA
PIPRA PITTA SITTA TODUS UPUPA
VIDUA VIREO ALAUDA ALCEDO
ANHIMA ANTHUS AQUILA BONASA
BRANTA CAPITO CIRCUS COLIUS
CORVUS DACELO ELANUS FULICA
GALLUS JACANA LANIUS LEIPOA
LIMOSA MARECA MENURA MEROPS
MILVUS MONASA NESTOR NUMIDA
PASSER PASTOR PERDIX PERNIS
PROGNE QUELEA RALLUS SAPPHO
SCOPUS SIALIA SPINUS STERNA
SYLVIA TETRAO TRERON TRINGA
TROGON TURDUS TURNIX VULTUR
ANHINGA APTERYX ARTAMUS

BUCEROS CACICUS CAPELLA
CARIAMA CERTHIA CHIONIS CICONIA
CINCLUS COLINUS COLUMBA
COLYBUS COTINGA CUCULUS
ELAENIA GALBULA GARRUPA
HALCYON HIRUNDO IBYCTER
ICTERUS KAKATOE LAGOPUS
LOPHURA LYRURUS MALURUS
MANACUS MESITES MILVAGO
MOMOTUS ORIOLUS PANDION
PAROTIA PIRANGA PITYLUS
PLAUTUS PLOCEUS PORZANA
REGULUS SEIURUS SERINUS
STURNUS TANAGRA TIMALIA
TOTANUS XENICUS ZENAIDA
ACCIPTER ACREDULA AFROPAVO
AGELAIUS AMIZILIA BOTAURUS
BUCORVUS BURHINUS CHAETURA
CORACIAS COTURNIX DELICHON
DIATRYMA DINORNIS DIOMEDEA
DREPANIS EMBERIZA EUPHONIA
EURYPYGA FULMARUS GARRULUS
GEOSPIZA GERYGONE GLAREOLA
GRALLINA GYPAETUS IONORNIS
LUSCINIA MACHETES MYCTERIA
NEOPHRON NOTORNIS NUMENIUS
OREORTYX PENELOPE PHAETHON
PITANGUS PLATALEA PLEGADIS
PODARGUS PRIONOPS PRUNELLA
PUFFINUS RUPICOLA SALTATOR
SAXICOLA SCOLOPAX SPEOTYTO
SPIZELLA STRUTHIO TRAGOPAN
TYRANNUS
(— OF BIVALVES) MYA PINNA
ANOMIA MACTRA NUCULA ETHERIA
MYTILUS PANDORA COLYMBUS
HINNITES PISIDIUM SAXICAVA
SPHAERUM TRIDACNA XYLOTRYA
(— OF BOWFIN) AMIA
(— OF BRACHIOPOD) ATRYPA
CRANIA ATHYRIS DISCINA SPIRIFER
(— OF BRYOZOAN) BUGULA
ESCHARA FLUSTRA RETEPORA
(— OF BUG) ANASA CIMEX EMESA
CORIXA TINGIS
(— OF BUTTERFLY) CALIGO COLIAS
DANAUS MORPHO PIERIS THECLA
EURYMUS JUNONIA KALLIMA
LYCAENA PAPILIO STRYMON
VANESSA ARGYNNIS HESPERIA
LEMONIAS MELITAEA SPEYERIA
(— OF CABBAGE) COS
(— OF CACTUS) CEREUS NOCALEA
OPUNTIA HARRISIA
(— OF CAT) FELIS ACINONYX
HEMIGALE
(— OF CEPHALOPOD) SEPIA
SPIRULA
(— OF CETACEAN) INIA
(— OF CHINK) LACUNA
(— OF CHIPMUNK) EUTAMIAS
(— OF CILIATE) COLPODA
CHILODON EUPLOTES
(— OF CIVET) FOSSA PAGUMA
(— OF CLAM) ENSIS GEMMA SOLEN
SPISULA
(— OF COCKLE) CHIONE
(— OF COCKROACH) BLATTA
(— OF CORAL) ASTREA FUNGIA

OCULINA PORITES ACROPURA
MAEANDRA TUBIPORA
(— OF CRAB) UCA MAIA BIRGUS
CANCER GRAPSUS OCYPODE
PAGURUS LITHODES PORTUNUS
(— OF CRANE) GRUS
(— OF CRAYFISH) CAMBARUS
(— OF CRICKET) ACHETA GRYLLUS
(— OF CRUSTACEAN) APUS HIPPA
JASUS LIGIA MYSIS CYPRIS LIGYDA
SELLUS TRIOPS ARGULUS ARTEMIA
ASTACUS BOPYRUS CALAPPA
CHELURA DAPHNIA EMERITA
HOMARUS IDOTHEA LERNAEA
NEBALPA SQUILLA CAPRELLA
ESTHERIA GAMMARUS LEUCIFER
LIMNETIS LIMNORIA NEPHROPS
PHRONIMA
(— OF CTENOPHORE) BEROE
CESTUM
(— OF DEER) AXIS DAMA PUDU
RUSA CERVUS MAZAMA MOSCHUS
RUCERVUS
(— OF DIATOM) DIATOMA SYNEDRA
MERIDION NAVICULA
(— OF DODO) DIDUS
(— OF DOG) CUON CANIS LYCAON
(— OF DORMOUSE) GLIS
(— OF DRAGONFLY) AESCHNA
(— OF DUCK) AIX ANAS AYTHYA
MERGUS NYROCA NETTION
SPATULA CLANGULA FULIGULA
(— OF EAGLE) AQUILA
(— OF ECHINODERM) ASTERIAS
(— OF EDENTATE) MANIS
(— OF EEL) CONGER ECHIDNA
MURAENA ANGUILLA GYMNOTUS
MORINGUA
(— OF FERN) FILIX TODEA ANEMIA
AZOLLA DOODIA CYATHEA ISOETES
ONOCLEA OSMUNDA PELLAEA
WOODSIA ADIANTUM ASPIDIUM
ATHYRIUM BLECHNUM CETERACH
CIBOTIUM CLEMATIS DAVALLIA
LYGODIUM MARATTIA SALVINIA
SCHIZAEA VITTARIA
(— OF FIREFLY) LAMPYRIS
(— OF FISH) AMIA ESOX HURO
LOTA MOLA RAJA ZEUS ALOSA
BADIS BERYX BETTA DORAS ELOPS
GADUS GOBIO HUCHO LATES
MANTA MUGIL PERCA SALMO
SARDA SOLEA UMBRA ALBULA
ANABAS APOGON BAIGRE BARBUS
BELONE CARANX CLUPEA COTTUS
DIODON GERRES GOBIUS HIODON
KUHLIA LABRUS LATRIS MOBULA
MYXINE NOMEUS PAGRUS PSETTA
REMORA SCARUS SPARUS TRIGLA
TRUTTA TURSIO ABRAMIS ALOPHAS
ALOPIAS ARACANA ASPREDO
BROTULA CARAPUS CLARIAS
DREPANE ECHIDNA GARRUPA
GIRELLA GYMNORA LEPOMIS
LIMANDA LUCANIA LYCODES
OSMERUS PEGASUS PRISTIS
SCIAENA SCOMBER SEPIOLA
SERIOLA SIGANUS SILLAGO SILURUS
SPHYRNA SQUALUS SYNODUS

THUNNUS TORPEDO TOXOTES
TRIODON XIPHIAS ZOARCES
AMEIURUS ANABLEPS ANGUILLA
ARAPAIMA ASTYANAX ATHERINA
BALISTES BODIANUS CARANGUS
CHIMAERA CLADODUS CTENODUS
CYPRINUS DAPEDIUS DIPLODUS
DIPTERUS DOROSOMA ECHENEIS
ETRUMEUS FUNDULUS GADOPSIS
GALAXIAS GAMBUSIA GOBIESOX
HAEMULON ICOSTEUS KYPHOSUS
LEBISTES LUTIANUS MEGALOPS
MORMYRUS MUSTELUS NOTROPIS
OPHIDION PALOMETA PANTODON
PHOCAENA POLYODON PYGIDIUM
SERRANUS SQUATINA COREGONUS
MYCTOPHUM
(— OF FLAGELLATE) COCOS
GONIUM OPHION SYNURA VOLVOX
ATTALEA CARYOTA EUGLENA
GIARDIA BORASSUS CERATIUM
EUDORINA HEXAMITA HYDRURUS
(— OF FLEA) PULEX BOSMINA
(— OF FLY) DACUS MUSCA MYMAR
PERLA PHORA ASILUS CEPHUS
FANNIA PIMPLA RHYSSA SCIARA
TIPULA CALIROA CHALCIS DIOPSIS
EPHYDRA HYLEMYA MIASTOR
ORTALIS OSCINIS PANORPA
TACHINA THEREVA ACROCERA
AGROMYZA ANOMALON APHIDIUS
BORBORUS CHELONUS CHRYSOPA
CHRYSOPS GLOSSINA PSYCHODA
SCHEDIUS SIMULIUM STOMOXYS
(— OF FLYING SQUIRREL) BELOMYS
(— OF FOSSIL) AMPYX ERYON
ADAPIS ATRYPA BAIERA ERYOPS
GEIKIA HYENIA KLUKIA MAMMUT
OLENUS ORTHIS RHYNIA ANDRIAS
ANTEDON APTIANA ASAPHUS
CAYONIA DICERAS EXOGYRA
GANODUS HAMITES HYBODUS
KNORRIA LESKEYA LESLEYA
LOXOMMA MESONYX MOROPUS
MYGODON OTOZOUM PHACOPS
PHIOMIA PROAVIS PROETUS
WALCHIA AGLASPIS AGNOSTUS
AMYNODON APHELOPS ARCHELON
BIRKENIA BRONTOPS CALIPPUS
CALYMENE CERATOPS CLYMENIA
CTENODUS DAPEDIUS DEINODON
DIATRYMA DINOHYUS DIPLODUS
DIPTERUS ENCHODUS ENCRINUS
EODISCUS EOHIPPUS EOSAURUS
EUSMILUS GORDONIA GRYPHAEA
HALLOPUS HELIGMUS ILLAENUS
LANARKIA LEBACHIA LECROSIA
LEGUATIA LESTODON LITUITES
MACLUREA MARRELLA METOPIAS
OLDHAMIA PLACODUS PORTHEUS
RUTIODON SMILODON SPIRIFER
STEGODON STEGOMUS TAONURUS
THELODUS XIPHODON ZAMICRUS
CONULARIA
(— OF FOX) ALOPEX VULPES
UROCYON
(— OF FROG) RANA ANURA
HYLODES
(— OF FUNGUS) FOMES IRPEX

PHOMA TUBER VALSA VERPA
ALBUGO BREMIA CAEOMA EMPUSA
FUMAGO HYDNUM ISARIA OIDIUM
PEZIZA TORULA ZYTHIA ACRASIA
AMANITA BOLETUS CANDIDA
CHALARA CYATHUS ELSINOE
ERYSIBE FABRAEA GEASTER
LEPIOTA MONILIA NECTRIA OZONIUM
PACHYMA PYTHIUM RHIZINA
RUSSULA SIMBLUM STEREUM
STICTIS STILBUM TYPHULA XYLARIA
ACHORION AECIDIUM AGARICUS
BOTRYTIS CALVATIA CLATHRUS
CLAVARIA COLLYBIA COPRINUS
CORYNEUM CYPHELLA CYTTARIA
DAEDALEA DIPLODIA ENDOTHIA
ENTOLOMA ENTYLOMA ERYSIPHE
EXOASCUS FUSARIUM GEASTRUM
GNOMONIA GRAPHIUM HELOTIUM
HELVELLA LENZITES MERULIUS
MYCOGONE PAXILLUS PHOLIOTA
PUCCINIA RHIZOPUS RHYTISMA
SEPTORIA SORDARIA SPICARIA
TAPHRINA TERFEZIA TRAMETES
TREMELLA TROCHILA USTILAGO
USTULINA VENTURIA CORDICEPS
(— OF GALLFLY) CYNIPS
(— OF GASTROPOD) FICUS HARPA
LIMAX OLIVA EBURNA PATELLA
TENEBRA SCYLLAEA STROMBUS
(— OF GEESE) CHEN ANSER
NETTAPUS
(— OF GNAT) SCIARA
(— OF GOAT) IBEX CAPRA
OREAMNOS
(— OF GRASS) POA ZEA AIRA COIX
AVENA BRIZA ORYZA STIPA APLUDA
ARUNDO BROMUS ELYMUS HOLCUS
LOLIUM LYGEUM MELICA MILIUM
NARDUS PHLEUM SECALE UNIOLA
ZOYSIA BAMBUSA BUCHLOE
CHLORIS CYNODON FESTUCA
HILARIA HORDEUM LAGURUS
LEERSIA MELINIS MOLINIA PANICUM
SETARIA SORGHUM ZIZANIA
AEGILOPS AGROSTIS ARISTIDA
AXONOPUS BULBILIS CENCHRUS
DACTYLIS ELEUSINE GLYCERIA
GYNERIUM IMPERATA PASPALUM
PHALARIS SPARTINA SPINIFEX
TRISETUM TRITICUM
(— OF GRASSHOPPER) LOCUSTA
(— OF GULL) XEMA LARUS
(— OF HAWK) BUTEO CIRCUS
(— OF HERB) GYP IVA AMMI ARUM
BETA GEUM GLAX HEBE LENS MEUM
MUSA OLAX RUTA SIDA SIUM ADOXA
AJUGA APIOS APIUM CALLA CANNA
CAREX CARUM CICER DALEA DRABA
ERUCA ERVUM FEDIA GALAX GAURA
GILIA GLAUX HOSTA INULA LAPPA
LAVIA LAYIA LEMNA LINUM LOASA
LOTUS LUFFA MADIA MALVA NAPEA
PANAX PARIS PHACA PHLOX PILEA
RHEUM RHOEO RUBIA SEDUM
TACEA URENA VICIA VIGNA VINCA
VIOLA ZIZIA ACAENA ACNIDA
ACORUS ACTAEA ADONIS ALISMA
ALLIUM ALSINE AMOMUM ANOGRA

ARABIS ARALIA ARNICA ASARUM
ATROPA BACOPA BAERIA BASSIA
BELLIS BIDENS BLITUM BLUMEA
BORAGO CAKILE CALTHA CASSIA
CELSIA CICUTA CISTUS CLEOME
CNICUS COLEUS CONIUM COPTIS
COSMOS CRAMBE CREPIS CRINUM
CROCUS CROTON CUNILA CYNARA
DAHLIA DATURA DAUCUS DIODIA
DONDIA ECHIUM ELODES ELODIA
EMILIA EUCLEA FILAGO GALEGA
GALIUM GIFOLA GYNURA ISATIS
ISMENE KOCHIA KRIGIA KUHNIA
LAMIUM LECHEA LUZULA MALOPE
MENTHA MIMOSA MONTIA MUCUNA
MUILLA NERINE NERIUM NESLIA
ONONIS OTHAKE OXALIS PICRIS
PISTIA PYROLA RESEDA RESTIO
RHEXIA RIVINA RUPPIA SAGINA
SALVIA SCILLA SESBAN SESELI
STEVIA SUAEDA THALIA TULIPA
VIORNA ZINNIA ABRONIA ADLUMIA
AETHUSA ALEGRIA ALETRIS
ALKANNA ALPINIA ALTHAEA
ALYSSUM AMORPHA AMSONIA
ANCHUSA ANEMONE ANETHUM
ANYCHIA APHANES ARACHIS
ARCTIUM ARNEBIA ARUNCUS
BABIANA BARTSIA BEGONIA
BOEBERA BUTOMUS CACALIA
CAJANUS CALYPSO CARLINA
CELOSIA CHELONE CIRCAEA
CIRSIUM CLARKIA COMARUM
CROOMIA CURCUMA CUSCUTA
CYTINUS DATISCA DECODON
DERINGA DIASCIA DROSERA
ELATINE EOMECON EPISCIA
ERODIUM FELICIA FICARIA FRASERA
FREESIA FUMARIA GAZANIA
GERBERA GLECOMA GLYCINE
GUNNERA HALENIA HECHTIA
HEDEOMA HOMERIA HUGELIA
HYPOXIS IRESINE JASIONE KICKXIA
KNAUTIA KOELLIA LACTUCA
LAPPULA LAPSANA LEWISIA LIATRIS
LINARIA LINNAEA LOGANIA LOPEZIA
LUNARIA LUPINUS LYCHNIS
LYTHRUM MARANTA MEDEOLA
MIMULUS MITELLA MOLLUGO
MONESES MUSCARI NEMESIA
NIGELLA OTHONNA PAEONIA
PAPAVER PAVONIA PEGANUM
PETUNIA PLUCHEA PRIMULA
RORIPPA ROTALIA RUELLIA
SALSOLA SAMOLUS SCANDIX
SENECIO SESAMUM SHORTIA
SILYBUM SINAPIS SOLANUM
SONCHUS STACHYS STATICE
SUCCISA SWERTIA TAGETES
TALINUM TELLIMA THAPSIA THESIUM
THLASPI THURNIA TORENIA TORILIS
TOVARIA TRILISA URGINEA VALLOTA
VERBENA ZEBRINA ACALYPHA
ACANTHUS ACHILLEA ACONITUM
AGALINIS AGERATUM ALLIARIA
ALLIONIA ALOCASIA AMBROSIA
AMMODIUM ANDRYALA ANGELICA
ANTHEMIS ANTICLEA APOCYNUM
ARCTOTIS ARENARIA ARGEMONE

ARISAEMA ASPERULA ATRIPLEX
BAPTISIA BARBAREA BARTONIA
BERGENIA BERTEROA BETONICA
BISTORTA BOLTONIA BORRERIA
BRASSICA BRUNONIA BUCHNERA
CALATHEA CAMASSIA CAMELINA
CANNABIS CAPSICUM CERINTHE
CLEMATIS COCHARUS COLLOMIA
COLUMNEA COMANDRA COOPERIA
CRASSULA CUBELIUM DENTARIA
DIANTHUS DICENTRA DIPSACUS
DISPORUM DYSSODIA ECHINOPS
EPIFAGUS ERANTHIS EREMURUS
ERIGENIA ERIGERON ERYNGIUM
ERYSIMUM EUCHARIS EUTHANIA
FITTONIA FLAVERIA FLOERKEA
FRAGARIA GALACTIA GENTIANA
GERARDIA GESNERIA GILLENIA
GLAUCIUM GLECHOMA GLORIOSA
GLOXINIA GOODENIA GRATIOLA
GUZMANIA HELENIUM HELONIAS
HEPATICA HESPERIS HEUCHERA
HIBISCUS HIPPURIS HOSACKIA
HOTTONIA HUDSONIA HYDROLES
HYSSOPUS IONIDIUM ISNARDIA
JATROPHA JUSSIAEA JUSTICIA
KNEIFFIA KOHLERIA LAPORTEA
LAVATERA LEONOTIS LEONURUS
LEPIDIUM LEPTILON LIMONIUM
LOPHIOLA LYCOPSIS MACLEAYA
MANFREDA MANTISIA MEDICAGO
MEIBOMIA MYOSOTIS MYOSURUS
OBOLARIA OENANTHE OPOPANAX
ORONTIUM PAROSELA PHACELIA
PHORMIUM PHYMOSIA PHYSALIS
PHYSARIA PLANTAGO PLUMBAGO
POLYGALA POLYMNIA POTERIUM
PRUNELLA PSORALEA RAPHANUS
RHAGODIA SABBATIA SAMBUCUS
SANICULA SARCODES SAROTHRA
SATUREIA SCABIOSA SCOLYMUS
SESBANIA SESUVIUM SEYMERIA
SIDALCEA SILPHIUM SOLIDAGO
SPERGULA SPIGELIA SPINACIA
STOKESIA TAENIDIA THASPIUM
TIARELLA TRIBULUS TRILLIUM
TROLLIUS TUECRIUM UVULARIA
VACCARIA VALERIAN VANELLUS
VERATRUM VERNONIA VERONICA
VISCARIA WATSONIA XANTHIUM
(— OF HERON) ARDEA EGRETTA
(— OF HORSE) EQUUS CALIPPUS
EOHIPPUS
(— OF HYDROZOAN) DIPHYES
PHYSALIA
(— OF HYENA) HYAENA CROCUTA
(— OF INSECT) NEPA APHIS EMESA
JAPYX SIREX BOREUS CICADA
COCCUS CORIXA EMPUSA ICERYA
KERMES MANTIS PHASMA PODURA
SIALIS THRIPS CHALCIS FORMICA
FULGORA LEPISMA ORYSSUS
RANATRA STYLOPS VEDALIA
BACILLUS CAMPODEA EPHEMERA
LABIDURA LACCIFER LECANIUM
LYONETIA MACHILIS MANTISPA
NERTHRUS REDUVIUS
(— OF ISOPOD) IDOTEA IDOTHEA
CIROLANA

(— OF JAY) GARRULUS
(— OF JELLYFISH) CYANEA AURELIA
AEQUOREA
(— OF JERBOA) DIPUS
(— OF KELP) AGARUM
(— OF LANGUR) SIMIAS
(— OF LEAFHOPPER) AGALLIA
EMPOASCA
(— OF LEECH) HIRUDO HAEMOPIS
(— OF LEMUR) INDRI GALAGO
(— OF LIANA) BAUHINIA
(— OF LICE) APHIS PSYLLA
ARGULUS ONISCUS BOVICOLA
ERIOSOMA GONIODES LIPEURUS
(— OF LICHEN) CORA USNEA
STICTA EVERNIA GRAPHIS LECIDEA
LOBARIA PHYSCIA CETRARIA
CLADONIA LECANORA PARMELIA
ROCCELLA STRIGULA
(— OF LIMPET) ACMAEA
(— OF LIZARD) UTA AGAMA DRACO
GEKKO AMEIVA ANGUIS ANOLIS
IGUANA EUMECES LACERTA
PYGOPUS SCINCUS ACONTIAS
CHIROTES COLEONYX LYGOSOMA
RHINEURA
(— OF LOCUST) TETRIX TETTIX
(— OF MACAW) ARA
(— OF MAMMAL) BOS SUS HOMO
LAMA ALCES BISON CAPRA TAYRA
DUGONG FRISON AELURUS AILURUS
BUBALUS GALIDIA GYMNURA
LINSANG OTOCYON AUCHENIA
CYCLOPES CYNOGALE SURICATA
TRAGULUS
(— OF MAPLE) ACER
(— OF MARSUPIAL) DASYURUS
MACROPUS POTOROUS TARSIPES
(— OF MARTEN) MARTES MUSTELA
(— OF MEDUSA) SARSIA GERYONIA
(— OF MICROSPORIDIAN) GLUGEA
(— OF MILDEW) ERYSIPHE
UNCINULA
(— OF MILLIPEDE) JULUS
(— OF MINT) ICIMUM NEPETA
MELISSA PERILLA PHLOMIS
ORIGANUM
(— OF MITE) ACARUS ACERIA
LEPTUS DEMODEX ACARAPIS
(— OF MOLD) MUCOR FULIGO
MELIOLA
(— OF MOLE) TALPA SCALOPS
SCALOPUS
(— OF MOLLUSK) ARCA DOTO LEDA
LIMA CHAMA DONAX EOLIS FICUS
HARPA LIMAX MUREX OLIVA VENUS
AEOLIS ANOMIA BANKIA CASSIS
CHITON LEPTON LUCINA OSTREA
PECTEN PHOLAS PYRULA SEMELE
TEREDO TETHYS ACTAEON ASTARTE
ATLANTA CARDITA CARDIUM
CYPRAEA CYPRINA DOSINIA
ETHERIA EXOGYRA LINGULA
TELLINA BUCCINUM GRYPHAEA
HALIOTIS LIMACINA LUTRARIA
MODIOLUS NAUTILUS PINCTADA
SCYLLAEA STROMBUS
(— OF MONGOOSE) GALIDIA
(— OF MONKEY) AOTES AOTUS

CEBUS ATELES MACACA CACAJAO
COLOBUS NASALIS SAIMIRI PITHECIA
(— OF MOOSE) ALCES
(— OF MOSQUITO) AEDES CULEX
(— OF MOSS) BRYUM CHILO EUXOA
MNIUM SAMIA SESIA TINEA ACTIAS
ALYPIA ARCTIA BOMBYX COSSUS
DATANA HYPNUM LESKEA PLUSIA
PSYCHE SPHINX THYRIS URANIA
AGROTIS ALABAMA APATELA
ARCHIPS ATTACUS BARBULA
CRAMBUS FUNARIA GRIMMIA
PHASCUM PRONUBA PYRALIS
SESAMIA TORTRIX ZEUZERA
ZYGAENA ANDREAEA CATOCALA
DAWSONIA DIATRAEA DICRANUM
ENDROMIS EPHESTIA EUPREPIA
GALLERIA GELECHIA HEPIALUS
PLUTELLA PRODENIA PYRAUSTA
SATURNIA SPHAGNUM THUIDIUM
(— OF MOUSE) MUS APODEMUS
(— OF MUSKRAT) FIBER ONDATRA
(— OF NARWHAL) MONODON
(— OF NEMATODE) ACUARIA
ALAIMUS ANGUINA NECATOR
(— OF NUDIBRANCH) GLAUCUS
(— OF OATS) AVENA
(— OF OPOSSUM) MARMOSA
(— OF ORCHID) DISA VANDA BLETIA
LAELIA PHAJUS ACINETA AERIDES
ANGULOA BRASSIA CORDULA
EUCOSIA IBIDIUM ISOTRIA LIPARIS
LISTERA MALAXIS POGONIA VANILLA
ANGRECUM ARETHUSA BLETILLA
CALANTHA CATTLEYA CYTHEREA
FISSIPES GOODYERA MILTONIA
ONCIDIUM PERAMIUM SERAPIAS
SOBRALIA TRIPHORA
(— OF OTTER) LUTRA
(— OF OWL) BUBO NINOX STRIX
KETUPA NYCTEA AEGOLIUS
SPEOTYTO
(— OF OXEN) BIBOS
(— OF PALM) NIPA ARECA ASSAI
COCOS HOWEA SABAL ARENGA
ELAEIS INODES KENTIA RAPHIA
RHAPIS ATTALEA BACTRIS CALAMUS
CARYOTA CORYPHA ERYTHEA
EUTERPE GEONOMA LATANIA
LICUALA PHOENIX SERENOA
THRINAX BORASSUS HYPHAENE
IRIARTEA LODOICEA MAURITIA
(— OF PARASITE) STRIGA CUSCOTA
HYDNORA OLPIDIUM CASSYTHIA
(— OF PARRAKEET) ARATINGA
(— OF PARROT) AMAZONA KAKATOE
(— OF PEACOCK) PAVO
(— OF PENGUIN) EUDYPTES
(— OF PHALANGER) DROMICIA
(— OF PIGEON) GOURA DUCULA
COLUMBA
(— OF PLANT) ALOE ARUM COLA
DION FABA IRIS IXIA PUYA SOJA
ADOXA AGAVE ASTER BATIS CANNA
CHARA DIOON DRYAS INULA NAIAS
PIPER RUMEX TRAPA TYPHA XYRIS
YUCCA ZILLA ABROMA ACACIA
AIZOON ALBUCA ANANAS CACTUS
CUPHEA DATURA EXACUM FERULA

IBERIS JAMBOS JUNCUS LICHEN
LILIUM MAYACA MORAEA NUPHAR
PHRYMA RICCIA SILENE SMILAX
STRIGA URTICA VISCUM ALONSOA
ASTILBE BALLOTA CABOMBA
CUCUMIS CYPERUS DIONAEA
DROSERA ENCELIA EPACRIS
EPIGAEA EURYALE FAGELIA
GLYCINE GODETIA HELXINE
HOOKERA ISOETES ISOLOMA
KARATAS LYCOPUS MANIHOT
MONARDA NELUMBO NITELLA
RAOULIA RICINUS STEMONA
SYRINGA TRIURUS TURNERA
WOLFFIA WYETHIA ZOSTERA
ABUTILON ADIANTUM ANABASIS
ANTHYLIS BRASENIA BRODIAEA
BROMELIA CALADIUM CAPSICUM
CYCLAMEN FORCRAEA FURCRAEA
GALTONIA GASTERIA GERANIUM
LATHRAEA LATHYRUS MARSILEA
MONSTERA NYMPHAEA PANDANUS
PEDALIUM PELVETIA PERESKIA
SAURURUS SPARAXIS THEVETIA
TIGRIDIA TRITONIA VELLOZIA
VICTORIA ZINGIBER
(— OF POLYZOAN) LEPRALIA
LOXOSOMA
(— OF POPLAR) ALAMO
(— OF PORCUPINE) COENDU
HYSTRIX
(— OF PORPOISE) INIA
(— OF PRAWN) PALAEMON
(— OF PROTOZOAN) BODO HYDRA
MONAS ADELEA AMOEBA ACINETA
ARCELLA EIMERIA STENTOR
DIDINIUM EUGLYPHA ISOSPORA
UROGLENA
(— OF RABBIT) LEPUS
(— OF RAT) ANISOMYS
(— OF RHIZOPOD) AMOEBA GROMIA
LAGENA HATTERIA PELOMYXA
(— OF RODENT) MUS CAVIA DIPUS
LEPUS ZAPUS GEOMYS LEMMUS
SPALAX CYNOMYS DINOMYS
ECHIMYS LEGGADA MERINES
NESOKIA ZYZOMYS ALACTAGA
ARVICOLA CAPROMYS CITELLUS
CRICETUS HAPLODON HYDROMYS
LAGIDIUM MICROTUS MYOTALPA
ORYZOMYS
(— OF ROTIFER) HYDATINA
PEDALION
(— OF RUST) UREDO HEMILEIA
UROMYCES
(— OF SALAMANDER) ANDRIAS
EURYCEA STREDON TRITURUS
(— OF SCALE) KERMES LECANIUM
(— OF SCALLOP) HINNITES
(— OF SCORPION) BUTHUS
SCORPIO CHELIFER
(— OF SEA ANEMONE) MINYAS
ACTINIA
(— OF SEA FAN) GORGONIA
(— OF SEA OTTER) ENHYDRA
(— OF SEA SLUG) ELYSIA
(— OF SEA URCHIN) ARBACIA
CIDARIS DIADEMA ECHINUS
(— OF SEAL) PHOCA HYDRURGA

MIROUNGA ZALOPHUS
(— OF SEAWEED) ULVA ALARIA
(— OF SEDGE) FUIRENA SCIRPUS
SCLERIA SCHOENUS
(— OF SHARK) LAMNA GALEUS
ISURUS ACRODUS ALOPIAS
SPHYRNA SQUALUS CLADODUS
MENASPIS SQUATINA
(— OF SHELL) PUPA LAMBIS
EXOGYRA LATIRUS MALLEUS
TROCHUS HAMINOEA MACLUREA
OLIVELLA TRIGONIA UMBRELLA
(— OF SHREW) SOREX BLARINA
(— OF SHRIMP) CRAGO CRANGON
(— OF SHRUB) IVA ACER BIXA BRYA
HOYA ILEX INGA ITEA MABA OLEA
RHUS ROSA SIDA THEA ULEX ALNUS
ANONA BIOTA BUTEA BUXUS CATHA
DALEA DIRCA ERICA EURYA FICUS
HAKEA IXORA LEDUM MALUS
OCHNA PADUS RIBES RUBUS SABIA
SALIX TAXUS THUJA TREMA UNONA
URENA VITEX ABELIA ACAENA
ADELIA ALHAGI AMYRIS ANNONA
ARALIA ARONIA AUCUBA AZALEA
BAPHIA BAUERA BETULA BLUMEA
BYBLIS CANTUA CASSIA CELTIS
CERCIS CISTUS CITRUS CLEOME
CLUSIA COFFEA CORDIA COREMA
CORNUS CORREA CROTON DAPHNE
DATURA DERRIS DIOSMA DONDIA
DRIMYS ECHIUM EVODIA FATSIA
FEIJOA GARRYA GNETUM GREWIA
GUAREA KALMIA KERRIA LARREA
LIPPIA LITSEA LUCUMA LYCIUM
MIMOSA MYRCIA MYRICA MYRTUS
OCOTEA OLINIA OPILIA PENAEA
PERSEA PIERIS PROTEA PTELEA
PUNICA QUIINA RAMONA RANDIA
ROCHEA ROYENA RUSCUS SALVIA
SAPIUM SCHIMA SELAGO SESBAN
SORBUS STEVIA STYRAX SUAEDA
TECOMA AECULUS AMORPHA
ARBUTUS ARDISIA ARMERIA ASIMINA
ASSONIA BANKSIA BAROSMA
BENZOIN BORONIA BUMELIA
BURSERA CALLUNA CARISSA
CASASIA CERASUS CESTRUM
CLETHRA CNEORUM COLUTEA
CORYLUS COTINUS CUNONIA
CYRILLA CYTISUS DEUTZIA
DOMBEYA DURANTA EHRETIA
ENCELIA EPACRIS EPHEDRA
EUCHLEA EUGENIA EURSERA
FABIANA FUCHSIA GENISTA GMELINA
GYMINDA HAMELIA HOVENIA
KARATAS LAGETTA LANTANA
MAHONIA MERATIA MONUMIA
MORINDA MUTISIA MYRRHIS
NANDINA NEMESIA OLEARIA
OTHONNA PAVETTA PAVONIA
PENTZIA PIMELEA PISONIA PURSHIA
QUASSIA QUERCUS RAPANEA
REMIJIA RHAMNUS RHODORA
ROBINIA ROMNEYA RUELLIA
SALSOLA SENECIO SKIMMIA
SOLANUM SOPHORA SPIRAEA
SURIANA SYRINGA TAMARIX
TELOPEA VERNICA XIMENIA XYLOPIA

XYLOSMA ZELKOVA ACALYPHA
ALANGIUM ALSTONIA ANAGYRIS
ATRIPLEX BALOCHIA BAUHINIA
BERBERIS BORRERIA BUCKLEYA
BUDDLEIA CAMELLIA CAPPARIS
CAPSICUM CARAGANA CASSIOPE
CASTANEA CODIAEUM COLLETIA
CONDALIA CONNARUS COPROSMA
CORIARIA CRATAEVA DAVIESIA
DENDRIUM DILLENIA DODONAEA
DOVYALIS DRACAENA DUBOISIA
EMPETRUM EUONYMUS EUPTELEA
EXOSTEMA FRAXINUS GALACTIA
GOODENIA GORDONIA GUAIACUM
HIBISCUS HIRTELLA IONIDIUM
JASMINUM JATROPHA JUSTICIA
KNIGHTIA KRAMERIA LABURNUM
LAVATERA LAWSONIA LEONOTIS
MAGNOLIA MAYTENUS MENZIESA
MICHELIA MYOPORUM NOTELAEA
PALIURUS PAROSELA PHILESIA
PHOTINIA PHYMOSIA PLUMIERA
POLYGALA POTERIUM PROSOPIS
PSORALEA RHAGODIA ROLLINIA
RORIDULA RUSSELIA SAMBUCUS
SATUREIA SAURAUIA SESBANIA
SOLANDRA SORBARIA SPARTIUM
TABEBUIA TORRUBIA TRECULIA
VARRONIA VERNONIA VIBURNUM
VOCHYSIA WITHANIA ZIZYPHUS
(— OF SILKWORM) BOMBYX
(— OF SKUNK) MEPHITIS
(— OF SLOTH) BRADYPUS
(— OF SLUG) DOTO ARION DORIS
LIMAX ELYSIA GLAUCUS
(— OF SNAIL) HUA PILA CONUS
FUSUS GALBA HELIX MITRA OVULA
PHYSA THAIS TURBO CERION
EULIMA NATICA NERITA RISSOA
TRITON ANCYLUS BITTIUM BULINUS
BUSYCON CYMBIUM LATIRUS
LITIOPA LYMNARA MELANIA
MODULUS PURPURA RANELLA
VALVATA VERTIGO VITRINA ZONITES
ACHATINA ALOCINMA ELLOBIUM
FOSSARIA GYRAULUS HELICINA
HELISOMA JANTHINA KATAYAMA
LITORINA NERITINA OLEACINA
SUCCINEA
(— OF SNAKE) BOA ERYX NAIA
NAJA ASPIS BITIS BOIGA ECHIS
ELAPS CAUSUS DABOIA ELAPHE
HURRIA ILYSIA LIGUUS NATRIX
PYTHON VIPERA ATHERIS BOAEDON
COLUBER ECHIDNA MEHELYA
OPHIDIA ZAMENIS BOTHROPS
BUNGARUS CERBERUS CROTALUS
DEMANSIA EUNECTES FARANCIA
LAVHESIS MICRURUS STORERIA
TYPHLOPS
(— OF SPIDER) ARANEA LYCOSA
MYGALE AGALENA ARGIOPE
ATTIDAE NEPHILA PHOLCUS
LINYPHIA ULOBORUS
(— OF SPIROCHETE) BORRELIA
(— OF SPONGE) SYCON GEODIA
SCYPHA ASCETTA CHALINA
GRANTIA SPONGIA SYCETTA
LEUCETTA

(— **OF SPOROZOAN**) NOSEMA
(— **OF SQUID**) LOLIGO SEPIOLA
(— **OF SQUIRREL**) SCIURUS
(— **OF SUBSHRUB**) LECHEA
ARMERIA ASCYRUM BEGONIA
FELICIA ATRIPLEX COLUMNEA
(— **OF SWAN**) OLOR CYGNUS
(— **OF TAKIN**) BUDORCAS
(— **OF TAPEWORM**) BERTIA LIGULA
DAVAINEA HARRISIA
(— **OF TAYRA**) GALERA GALICTIS
(— **OF TELEDU**) MYDAUS
(— **OF TERN**) GYGIS STERNA
(— **OF THISTLE**) CARDUUS
(— **OF TICK**) ARGAS ARGUS IXODES
HYALOMMA
(— **OF TOAD**) BUFO HYLA PIPA
ALYTES XENOPUS ASCAPHUS
(— **OF TREE**) ACER BIXA BRYA
COLA HURA ILEX INGA MABA OLAX
OLEA RHUS THEA ABIES AEGLE
ALNUS ANIBA BIOTA BUTEA BUXUS
CARYA CEIBA CYCAS DURIO EURYA
FAGUS FICUS HAKEA HEVEA HOPEA
IXORA KHAYA LARIX MALUS MELIA
MESUA MORUS NYSSA OCHNA
PADUS PICEA PINUS PYRUS SALIX
TAXUS THUJA TILIA TOONA TREMA
TSUGA ULMUS UNONA VITEX XYLIA
ACHRAS AKANIA AMOMIS AMYRIS
ANDIRA ANNONA ARALIA AZALEA
BAPHIA BETULA BOMBAX CANTUA
CARAPA CARICA CASSIA CEDRUS
CELTIS CERCIS CITRUS CLUSIA
COFFEA CORDIA CORNUS DATURA
DRIMYS EPERUA EPERVA EUCLEA
EVODIA FEIJOA GARRYA GENIPA
GINKGO GNETUM GREWIA GUAREA
IDESIA ILLIPE LAURUS LITCHI LITSEA
LUCUMA LYCIUM MAMMEA MIMOSA
MYRCIA MYRICA OCOTEA OLNEYA
OSTRYA OWENIA PAPPEA PARITI
PERSEA PRUNUS PTELEA QUIINA
RANDIA ROYENA SAPIUM SAPOTA
SCHIMA SENCIO SESBAN SHOREA
SIMABA SORBUS STYRAX TECOMA
AGATHIS ARBUTUS ARDISIA ASIMINA
ASSONIA BANKSIA BUMELIA
BURSERA CANELLA CASASIA
CATALPA CEDRELA CERASUS
CLETHRA COPAIVA CORYLUS
COTINUS CUNONIA CUPANIA
CYDONIA CYRILLA DOMBEYA
ECHINUS EHRETIA EPACRIS EUGENIA
FERONIA GMELINA GUAZUMA
GYMINDA HAGENIA HALESIA
HICORIA HOVENIA HUMIRIA ILLICUM
JUGLANS KADELIA KOKOONA
LAGETTA LICANIA LINGOUM
MACLURA MICONIA MORINDA
MORINGA MURRAYA OCHROMA
OLEARIA PANGIUM PIMENTA PISONIA
PLANERA POPULUS PROTIUM
PSIDIUM QUASSIA QUERCUS
RAPANEA REMIJIA RHAMNUS
ROBINIA SCHINUS SENECIO SEQUOIA
SLOANEA SOLANUM SOPHORA
SURIANA SYRINGA TAMARIX
TECTONA TELOPEA TORREYA

TROPHIS VATERIA XIMENIA XYLOPIA
XYLOSMA ZELKOVA AESCULUS
ALANGIUM ALBIZZIA ALSTONIA
ANTIARIS AVERRHOA BALANOPS
BALOGHIA BAUHINIA BRABEJUM
BROSIMUM BUDDLEIA CABRALEA
CAMELLIA CANANGIA CANARIUM
CAPPARIS CAROGANA CARPINUS
CARYOCAR CASEARIA CASTANEA
CASTILLA CECROPIA CINCHONA
CODIAEUM CONDALIA CYBISTAX
DILLENIA DIPTERYX DODONAEA
DOVYALIS DRACAENA DUBOISIA
EUCOMMIA EUONYMUS EUPTELEA
EXOSTEMA FITZROYA FRAXINUS
FUNTUMIA GARCINIA GARDENIA
GORDONIA GUAIACUM HIBISCUS
HIRTELLA HOMALIUM HYMENAEA
JATROPHA KANDELIA KNIGHTIA
LABURNUM LAPORTEA LAVATERA
LECYTHIS LEUCAENA LYSILOMA
MAGNOLIA MALLOTUS MAYTENUS
MESPILUS MICHELIA MIMUSOPS
MYOPORUM NOTELAEA PHOTINIA
PISCIDIA PISTACIA PLATANUS
PLUMIERA PONCIRUS PROSOPIS
QUILLAJA RAVENALA ROLLINIA
SAMADERA SAMBUCUS SANTALUM
SAPINDUS SAURAUIA SESBANIA
SIMARUBA SPONDIAS SWARTZIA
TABEBUIA TAXODIUM TORRUBIA
TRECULIA VARRONIA VERONICA
VIBURNUM VIRGILIA VOCHYSIA
(— **OF TUNICATE**) SALPA ASCIDIA
DOLIOLUM
(— **OF TURTLE**) EMYS AMYDA
CHELUS CHELYS CARETTA CHELONE
CLEMMYS TESTUDO TRIONYX
ARCHELON CHELONIA CHELYDRA
PELUSIOS
(— **OF TWINER**) STEMONA
(— **OF UNIVALVE**) DOLIUM
(— **OF VINE**) ROSA ABRUS ABUTA
PISUM TAMUS UNONA VIGNA VITIS
AKEBIA CISSUS COBAEA DERRIS
ENTADA HEDERA MUCUNA PETREA
POTHOS SICANA SICYOS SOLLYA
VIORNA ARAUJIA BASELLA
BOMAREA BRYONIA ECHITES
EMBELIA EPACRIS FALCATA
HUMULUS IPOMOEA MIKANIA
PISONIA SECHIUM UNCARIA
ZANONIA ANAMIRTA ATRAGENE
BIGNONIA CLEMATIS COCCULUS
DEGUELIA DOLICHOS EUONYMUS
JASMINUM KENNEDYA PANDOREA
PUERARIA SECAMONE SERJANIA
TACSONIA WISTARIA
(— **OF WALRUS**) ODOBENUS
(— **OF WASP**) SPHEX VESPA
BEMBEX CYNIPS SCOLIA TIPHIA
CHRYSIS EUMENES MASARIS
MUTILLA ANDRICUS CHLORION
ODYNERUS POLISTES POMPILUS
SPHECIUS
(— **OF WEASEL**) MUSTELA
(— **OF WEED**) CAPSELLA
(— **OF WEEVIL**) APION HYPERA
SITONA CLEONUS CALANDRA

CALENDRA CURCULIO
(— **OF WHALE**) CETE ARETA KOGIA
BALAENA ORCINUS ZIPHIUS
PHYSETER
(— **OF WOLVERINE**) GULO
(— **OF WORM**) DERO SPIO ALARIA
EUNICE KERRIA MERMIS NEREIS
SYLLIS ACHAETA ACHOLOE ASCARIS
DUGESIA EISENIA FILARIA GLYCERA
GORDIUS HESIONE LEODICE
POLYNOE SABELLA SAGITTA
SERPULA SETARIA SPIRURA TUBIFEX
ARABELLA ASCAROPS BIPALIUM
BONELLIA COOPERIA DOCHMIUS
ECHIURUS FASCIOLA GEOPLANA
PHORONIS SPADELLA SUBULURA
SYNGAMUS SYPHACIA
(— **OF ZORIL**) ICTONYX
GEODE DRUSE
GEOMETRIC CUBIST CUBISTIC
GEOMETRY EUCLID SPHERICS
GEOPHAGY PICA

GEORGIA

CAPITAL: ATLANTA
COLLEGE: SPELMAN MOREHOUSE
COUNTY: BIBB COBB TIFT RABUN
  TROUP DEKALB FULTON TALBOT
  LAURENS GWINNETT MUSCOGEE
INDIAN: GUALE YUCHI CHIAHA
  OCONEE YAMASEE
LAKE: LANIER MARTIN HARDING
  NOTTELY BANKHEAD HARTWELL
  SINCLAIR
MOUNTAIN: STONE KENNESAW
NATIVE: CRACKER
RIVER: PEA FLINT ETOWAH
  OCONEE PIGEON CONECUH
  SATILLA ALTAMAHA OCMULGEE
STATE BIRD: THRASHER
STATE NICKNAME: PEACH
STATE TREE: LIVEOAK
TOWN: JESUP MACON AUGUSTA
  CONYERS DECATUR VIDALIA
  MARIETTA MOULTRIE SAVANNAH
  VALDOSTA WAYCROSS
UNIVERSITY: EMORY GATECH
  MERCER

GEORGIAN ADZHAR CRACKER
GEORGIA PINE LONGLEAF
GEPHYREAN STARWORM
GER STRANGER
GERANIUM DOVEFOOT FLUXWEED
SHAMEFACE
GERANIUM LAKE SPARK NACARAT
GERBIL JIRD
GERIANOL ISOLATE
GERM BUG CHIT SEED SPARK
SPAWN SPERM GERMEN GERMULE
MICROBE SEMINAL SEEDLING
SEMINARY SEMINIUM
(— **CELL**) GONE
GERMAN HUN BALT HANS MUFF
ALMAN BOCHE FRITZ HEINE JERRY
ALMAIN DUTCHY HEINIE TEUTON
SAUSAGE TEDESCO COTILLON
GERMANIC TUDESQUE

GERMANDER POLY BETONY
FOXTAIL SOVENEZ SCORDIUM
GERMANE GERMAN PERTINENT
GERMANIC GOTHIC GOTHONIC
TEUTONIC
GERMAN SHEPHERD ALSATIAN

GERMANY

ANCIENT: ALMAIN ALMAINE
ANCIENT TRIBESMAN: JUTE
TEUTON VISIGOTH OSTROGOTH
CANAL: KIEL WESER LUDWIG
CAPITAL: BONN BERLIN
CHEESE: MUENSTER TILSITER
LIMBURGER
COAL REGION: RUHR SAAR SARRE
COIN: MARK KRONE TALER
GULDEN KRONEN THALER
PFENNIG GROSCHEN
DIALECT: KOLSCH KOELSCH
BALTISCH HESSISCH
DYNASTY: HOHENSTAUFEN
HOHENZOLLERN
FOOD: WURST KNODEL SPATZLE
STRUDEL MARZIPAN ROULADEN
HANSEATIC CITY: KOLN LUBECK
COLOGNE HAMBURG LUEBECK
ISLAND: USEDOM WOLLIN
FEHMARN FRISIAN
LAKE: DUMMER WURMSEE
AMMERSEE BODENSEE
CHIEMSEE MURITZEE
CONSTANCE
LANGUAGE: DEUTSCH
MEASURE: AAM IMI OHM FASS
FUSS LAST RUTE SACK STAB
CARAT EIMER KANNE KETTE
LINIE MAASS METZE RUTHE
SIMRI MASSEL MORGEN OXHOFT
SEIDEL STRICH JUCHART
KLAFTER TAGWERK SCHEFFEL
SCHOPPEN STUBCHEN VIERLING
MOUNTAIN: FELDBERG WATZMANN
MOUNTAIN RANGE: ORE ALPS
HARZ RHON HARDT HUNSRUCK
NAME: REICH ASHKENAZ
GERMANIA DEUTSCHLAND
NATIVE: GOTH SAXON TEUTON
RESORT: EMS BADEN AACHEN
TRIBAL REGION: GAU GAUE GAUS
UNIVERSITY TOWN: FREIBURG
HEIDELBERG
PORT: EMDEN BREMEN HAMBURG
ROSTOCK STETTIN
RIVER: ALZ EMS INN EDER EGER
ELBE ISAR LAHN LECH MAIN
NAAB NAHE ODER OKER REMS
RUHR SAAR SIEG ALLER DONAU
EIDER FULDA HAVEL HUNTE
ILLER LEINE LIPPE MOSEL
MULDE PEENE REGEN RHEIN
RHINE SAALE SAUER SPREE
UCKER WERRA WESER DANUBE
ELSTER KOCHER NECKAR
NEISSE RANDOW TAUBER
VECHTE WARNOW ALTMUHL
JEETZEL PEGNITZ SALZACH
UNSTRUT

STATE: BADEN LIPPE BAYERN
BREMEN HESSEN SAXONY
BAVARIA HAMBURG PRUSSIA
SAARLAND BRUNSWICK
TOWN: AUE EMS HOF ULM BONN
GERA GOCH HAAR HAMM JENA
KIEL KOLN LAHR AALEN AHLEN
EMDEN ESSEN FURTH GOTHA
HAGEN HALLE HERNE MAINZ
MOLLN NEUSS PIRNA TRIER
AACHEN ALTENA ALTONA
BARMEN BERLIN BREMEN
CASSEL DACHAU DESSAU
ERFURT KASSEL LINDEN
LUBECK MUNICH PLAUEN
TREVES BAMBERG BRESLAU
COBLENZ COLOGNE CREFELD
DRESDEN GORLITZ HAMBURG
HANOVER LEIPZIG MAYENCE
MUNCHEN MUNSTER POTSDAM
ROSTOCK SPANDAU ZWICKAU
AUGSBURG CHEMNITS
DORTMUND DUISBURG
FREIBURG LIEGNITZ MANNHAIM
NURNBERG WURSELEN
WURZBURG DARMSTADT
KARLSRUHE MAGDEBURG
NUREMBERG OSNABRUCK
STUTTGART WUPPERTAL
DUSSELDORF HEIDELBERG
OBERHAUSEN
WEIGHT: LOT GRAN LOTE LOTH
UNZE LOTHE PFUND STEIN
PRUNDE DRACHMA ZENTNER
VIERLING
WINE: MOSELLE RIESLING

GERMICIDE KRELOS
GERMINABLE PREGNANT
GERMINATE BUD HIT CHIP CHIT
GERM SHOOT SPIRE SPRIT BRAIRD
SPROUT STRIKE
GERMINATION CATCH
GESAN TAPUYAN CHAVANTE
GESTATION GOING BREEDING
GESTICULATE GESTURE
GESTURE CUT FIG BECK BERE GEST
SIGN FILIP GESTE HONOR SANNA
BECKON BREATH CUTOFF FILLIP
MOTION SALUTE SIGNAL CURTSEY
FASHION FLICKER MURGEON
ACCOLADE CEREMONY
(— **OF DERISION)** SNOOK
(AFFECTED —) GAATCH
(USELESS —) FUTILITY
GET COP GIT WIN FALL GAIN GRAB
HAVE HENT TAKE TILL AFONG
ANNEX CATCH COVER FETCH LATCH
DERIVE OBTAIN SECURE ACQUIRE
CONQUER PROCURE PRODUCE
RECEIVE PERCEIVE
(— **ABOARD)** FLIP
(— **ABOUT)** BEGO
(— **ALONG)** DO GEE FARE FEND
AGREE FADGE FODGE SPEED
FETTLE
(— **AROUND)** BYPASS COMPASS
FINESSE FLUMMER

(— **AT)** ATTAIN
(— **AWAY)** LAM RYNT SLIP EVADE
CHEESE ESCAPE
(— **BACK)** REDEEM RETIRE
RECOVER
(— **BETTER OF)** WAX BEST DING
DOWN DAUNT FLING SHEND SHENT
STICK STING JOCKEY OVERGO
RECOVER SURMOUNT
(— **BY ARTIFICE)** WIND
(— **BY ASKING)** KICK
(— **BY CUNNING)** WHIZZLE
(— **BY EXTORTION)** GRATE
(— **BY FLATTERY)** COG
(— **CLEAR OF)** STRIP
(— **DISHONESTLY)** FIRK
(— **DOWN)** ALIGHT
(— **ON WELL)** LIKE
(— **ON)** FARE BOARD CHEFE CHEVE
FRAME SHIFT EXPLOIT
(— **OUT)** LEAK SCRAM CHEESE
OUTWIN VOETSAK
(— **PAST)** BEAT HURDLE
(— **POSSESSION)** CARRY
(— **READY)** GET PARE RANK BRACE
FRAME FETTLE ORDAIN APPAREL
(— **RID)** CAST DISH DUMP FREE
JUNK SHAB TOSS ERASE SHAKE
SHIFT SHOOT SLOUGH UNLOAD
DELIVER DISCARD EXTRUDE
DISPATCH DISSOLVE
(— **SURREPTITIOUSLY)** SNEAK
(— **THE POINT)** SAVVY
(— **TO BOTTOM OF)** FATHOM
(— **UNDER CONTROL)** RAIM
(— **UP)** ARISE HUDDUP UPRISE
HAIRPIN
GETA SABOT
GET-TOGETHER DO DRINK HOBNOB
BAMBOCHE POTLATCH
GETUP SETOUT
GEWGAW DIE TOY WALY KNACK
WALLY BAUBLE FANGLE FEGARY
JIGGER FLAMFEW TRANGAM
TRINKET FOLDEROL GIMCRACK
JIMCRACK TRIMTRAM
GEYSER BORE JETTER

GHANA

CAPITAL: ACCRA
DAM: AKOSOMBO
LAKE: VOLTA BOSUMTWI
LANGUAGE: GA EWE TWI FANTI
HAUSA DAGBANI DAGOMBA
MONEY: NEWCEDI
MOUNTAIN: AFADJATO
NATIVE: GA EWE AHAFO BRONG
FANTI ASHANTI DAGOMBA
MAMPRUSI
RIVER: OTI PRA DAKA TANO
AFRAM VOLTA ANKOBRA
KULPAWN
TOWN: HO WA ODA AXIM FIAN
KETA TALA TEMA ACCRA
BAWKU ENCHI LAWRA LEGON
SAMPA YAPEI DUNKWA KARAGA
KPANDU KUMASI NSAWAM
OBUASI SWEDRU TAMALE

TARKWA WASIPE ANTUBIA
DAMONGO MAMPONG PRESTEA
SEKONDI SUNYANI WINNEBA
AKOSOMBO KINTAMPO
TAKORADI
WIND: HARMATTAN

GHARRY SHIGRAM
GHASTLY WAN GRIM PALE BLATE
GHAST LURID UNKET UNKID DISMAL
GOUSTY GRISLY PALLID CHARNEL
DEATHLY FEARFUL GASHFUL
GRIZZLY GRUGOUS HIDEOUS
MACABRE DREADFUL GRUESOME
HORRIBLE SHOCKING TERRIBLE
GHAWAZI BARAMIKA
GHERKIN CUCUMBER
GHETTO JEWRY JUDAISM
GHIBELLINE WAIBLING
GHOST HAG KER BHUT HANT JUBA
WAFF BUGAN CADDY DUFFY DUPPY
FETCH GAIST GUEST HAUNT JUMBY
LARVA PRETA SHADE SPOOK
UMBRA CHUREL SOWLTH SPIRIT
SPRITE TAISCH ANTAEUS ANTAIOS
BOGGART BUGGANE GYTRASH
PHANTOM SPECTER SPECTRE
VAMPIRE BARGHEST GUYTRASH
PHANTASM REVENANT
GHOSTFISH WRYMOUTH
GHOSTLY EERY EERIE GOUSTY
SHADOWY UNCANNY WEIRDLY
CHTHONIC GHASTFUL SPECTRAL
GHOST MOTH SWIFT HEPIALID
GHOST-WRITER SPOOK
GHOULISH SATANIC
GHUZ OGHUZ
GIAI NHANG
GIANT ORC ETEN HUGE OGRE OTUS
WATE YMER YMIR AFRIT BALOR
CACUS HYMIR JOTUN MIMAS MIMER
THRYM TITAN TROLL AFREET
ALBION FAFNIR GIGANT GOEMOT
PALLAS THJAZI THURSE TITYUS
WARLOW ANTAEUS CYCLOPS
GOLIATH WARLOCK ASCOPART
BELLERUS COLBRAND GIGANTIC
GOEMAGOT GOGMAGOG MASTODON
MORGANTE ORGOGLIO TYPHOEUS
(1-EYED —) CYCLOPS
(100-HANDED —) GYGES COTTUS
BRIAREUS
(1000-ARMED —) BANA
(PL.) ANAK ANAKIM COTTUS
ALOADAE REPHAIM NEPHILIM
ZAMZUMMIM
GIANTESS NORN ARGANTE
GIANT FULMAR NELLY STINKER
STINKPOT
GIANT GRASS OTATE
GIANT HERON GOLIATH
GIANT LILY FIGUE MAGUEY
GIANT PUFFBALL FUZZ FUZZBALL
GIARDIA LAMBLIA
GIB JIB SHOE DEMUR SLIPPER
GIBBAR GIBBERT JUBARTAS
GIBBER CHAT CHATTER
GIBBERISH GREEK JABBER JARGON
CHOCTAW

GIBBET STOB TREE CROOK JEBAT
GALLOWS POTENCE EQUULEUS
GIBBON LAR WAWA UNGKA WUYEN
CAMPER HULOCK HOOLOCK
SIAMANG
GIBBOUS CONVEX HULCHY HUMPED
GIBE (ALSO SEE JIBE) BOB RUB GIRD
JAPE JEST JIBE PROG QUIB QUIP
SKIT WIPE FLEER FLING FLIRT
FRUMP GLEEK KNACK SCOFF
SCOMM SCORN SLANT SNEER
DERIDE GLANCE HECKLE BROCARD
SARCASM RIDICULE
GIBING SNASH
GID DUNT GIDDY STURDY GOGGLES
POTHERY VERTIGO
GIDDINESS LUNACY SOORAWN
GIDDY GLAKY LIGHT WESTY GIGLET
GLAKED GOWKED GOWKIT SHANNY
STURDY VOLAGE GLAIKET LARKING
HALUCKET HELLICAT
GIFT BOX FOY QUO SOP BENT BOON
DASH ENAM MEED SAND BONUS
BRIBE CAULP CUDDY DONUM
GRANT KNACK TOKEN CADEAU
DASHEE DONARY GENIUS GERSUM
GIFTIE GIVING HANSEL LEGACY
RECADO REGALO TALENT XENIUM
APTNESS BENEFIT CHARISM
CHARITY DEODATE DONATIO
DOUCEUR ETRENNE FACULTY
GIFTURE HANDSEL PRESENT
PROPINE REGALIO SUBSIDY TASHRIF
TRIBUTE AMATORIO APTITUDE
BENEFICE BESTOWAL BLESSING
COURTESY DONATION DONATIVE
GARRISON GIVEAWAY GRATUITY
MORTUARY OBLATION OFFERING
POTLATCH SPORTULA
(— FROM HUSBAND TO WIFE)
ARRAS
(— OF GOD) GRACE
(— OF MONEY) POUCH BAKSHISH
(— OF NATURE) DOWER DOWRY
(CHARITABLE —) ALMS ENAM
PITTANCE
(COMPULSORY —) SIXENIA
(LIBERAL —) LARGESSE
(NATURAL —) TALENT
(NEW YEAR'S EVE —) HAGMENA
HOGMANAY
(SPIRITUAL —) CHARISM CHARISMA
(PL.) OBLATA MISSILES
GIFTBOOK ANNUAL KEEPSAKE
GIG TUB BANDY CHAIR GIGGE
CHAISE DENNET WHISKY CALESIN
TILBURY STANHOPE
GIGANTIC HUGE GIANT MAMMOTH
TITANIC COLOSSAL ENORMOUS
GIGANTAL
GIGGER TEASELER
GIGGLE KECKLE SNICKER TWITTER
GIGLET JIG
GILD GILT BEGILD ENGILD ORFGILD
GILDED GILT AURATE INAURATE
GILDER TRACER
GILGAMESH IZDUBAR
GILL JILL QUAD GHYLL PLICA GILLIE
LAMELLA BRANCHIA QUADRANT

(—S OF BIVALVE) BEARD
(PL.) GINNERS CHOLLERS
GILLAR PITTO
GILLIE GILLY HENCHMAN
GILLYFLOWER STOCK GILVER
GELOFRE GILLIVER
GILTHEAD CONNER MELANURE
GIMBAL GEMEL JEMBLE
GIMCRACK QUIP BAUBLE GEWGAW
JIMJAM TRIFLE TRANGAM TRINKET
JIMCRACK WHIMWHAM
GIMLET SCREW WIMBLE PIERCEL
PIERCER
GIMMICK GAFF
GIMP TAR ORRIS GUIMPE GIMPING
GIN MAX CRAB GRIN LACE RUIN
TAPE CLEAN JACKY SNARE SNARL
DIDDLE GENEVA JAMBER JAMMER
SPRINGE TITTERY EYEWATER
HOLLANDS SCHIEDAM SCHNAPPS
(DROP OF —) DAFFY
GINGER PEPPER RATOON AROMATIC
ZINZIBER COLTSFOOT
GINGERBREAD SPICE PARKIN
GINGERLY GINGER WARILY CHARILY
EDGINGLY
GINGERROOT HAND RACE
(PL.) ASARUM
GINGHAM CHAMBRAY
GINKGO ICHO
GINSENG SANG FATIL PANAX
ARALIA IVYWORT REDBERRY
GIRAFFE OONT CAMEL DAPPLE
KAMEEL SERAPH CAMAILE
RUMINANT
GIRD BELT BIND GIRR GIRT HASP
YERK CLOSE SCOFF ENGIRD
FASTEN GIRDLE SECURE ACCINGE
ENVIRON CINCTURE SURROUND
GIRDER BEAM GIRD GIRT GIRTH
TABLE TRUSS BINDER SUMMER
WARREN GIRDING TWISTER
BUCKSTAY STRINGER
GIRDING CINCTURE
GIRDLE OBI ZON BARK BELT CEST
GIRD HOOP SASH ZONA ZONE
CEINT GIRTH MITER PATTE SARPE
WAIST BODICE CESTUS CINGLE
CIRCLE MOOCHA TISSUE ZODIAC
ZONULA ZOSTER BALDRIC BALTEUS
CENTRUM CENTURE COMPASS
GIRDING SHINGLE CEINTURE
CINCTURE CINGULUM SURROUND
(— FOR HELMET) TISSUE
(— OF DIATOM) HOOP
(BRIDE'S —) CEST CESTUS
(LITTLE —) ZONULE ZONELET
(ROYAL —) MALO
(SACRED —) KUSTI
GIRDLED RUNG
GIRL BIT GAL HER KIT POP SHE SIS
TIB TID TIT BABE BABY BINT BIRD
DAME DEEM DELL GILL JANE JILL
JUDY LASS MARY MOPS MORT PERI
SLUT WREN BEAST FILLY GUIDE
KITTY LUBRA QUEAN SISSY SKIRT
TIDDY TITTY TRULL BURDIE CALICO
CLINER CUMMER DALAGA DAMSEL
DEEMIE FEMALE FIZGIG GEISHA

GIRLIE LASSIE LOVELY MAGGIE
NUMBER PIGEON SHEILA SISTER
SUBDEB TOMATO CAMILLA COLLEEN
DAMOSEL MADCHEN MAUTHER
TENDREL BONNIBEL FARMETTE
FEMININE GRISETTE MUCHACHA
(AGILE —) YANKER
(AWKWARD —) HOIT
(BEATIFIED —) BEATA
(BEAUTIFUL —) BELLE
(BOLD —) HOIDEN HOYDEN
(CAMP FIRE —) ARTISAN
(CHORUS —) CHORINE CORYPHEE
(COUNTRY —) MEG JOAN
(DANCING —) DASI KISANG KISAENG
DEVADASI
(DANCING —S) GHAWAZI
(DEAR —) PEAT
(FLIGHTY —) GOOSECAP
(FLIRTATIOUS —) JADE JILLET
(FLOWER —) NYDIA
(FORWARD —) STRAP
(FROLICSOME —) GILPY
(GIDDY —) GIG GIGLET GIGLOT
JILLET
(GREEK —) HAIDEE
(GYPSY —) GITANA
(HIRED —) BIDDY BIDDIE
(IMPUDENT —) STRAP
(JAPANESE —) GEISHA
(LITTLE —) SIS COOKY SISSY
COOKIE LASSOCK
(MISCHIEVOUS —) CUTTY HUSSY
(MODEST —) BLUSHET
(NAIVE —) INGENUE
(NON-JEWISH —) SHIKSE SHICKSA
(PERT —) MINX HUSSY
(PRETTY —) PRIM CUTEY CUTIE
(ROMPING —) STAG TOMBOY
(SAUCY —) SNIP
(SERVANT —) SLUT
(SILLY —) SKIT
(SINGING —) ALMA ALMEH
(SLENDER —) SYLPH
(SMALL —) PINAFORE
(SPIRITED —) FILLY
(UNATTRACTIVE —) FRUMP
(UNMARRIED —) MOUSME TOWDIE
MUSUMEE
(WANTON —) GIG FILLOCK
(WILD —) BLOWZE
(WORKING —) ORISETTE
(WORTHLESS —) HUSSY
(YOUNG —) BUD MODER TITTY
MAIDEN MOTHER BAGGAGE
COLLEEN FLAPPER GIRLEEN
ROSEBUD
(PL.) GIRLERY GIRLHOOD
GIRT CINCT
GIRTH GIRD GIRT TAPE CINCH
GARTH GIRSE GRETH WANTY
CINGLE WARROK GIRDING SHINGLE
WEBBING
GIST JET NET NUB SUM CHAT CORE
GITE KNOT PITH GREAT HEART
JOIST SENSE BURDEN KERNEL
PURPORT SUMMARY STRENGTH
GITH MELANTHY
GIVE ADD GIE HOB TIP BEAR DEAL

DOLE HAND METE SELL TAKE WEVE
WHIP ALLOW AWARD COUGH GRANT
REFER YIELD ACCORD AFFORD
BESTOW CONFER DEMISE DOTATE
FASTEN IMPART IMPOSE IMPUTE
RENDER SUPPLY CONSIGN DELIVER
FORGIVE FURNISH PRESENT
BEQUEATH DISPENSE
(— A BOOST) BOLSTER
(— A PLACE TO) SITUATE
(— A REMEDY) MINISTER
(— ADHERENCE) ASSENT
(— ADMITTANCE) ACCEPT
(— ADVICE) READ ADVISE
(— AN ACCOUNT) TELL RELATE
REPORT
(— AND TAKE) GIFFGAFF
(— ANYTHING NAUSEOUS TO) DOSE
(— APPROVAL) CONSENT
(— AS CONCESSION) YETTE
(— AS EXPLANATION) ASSIGN
(— ASSURANCE) EFFRONT
(— ATTENTION TO) HEED
(— AUTHORITY) ENABLE EMPOWER
ACCREDIT
(— AWAY) PART
(— BACK) REFUND RETURN
RESTORE
(— BIRTH) KIT BEAR BORN DROP
FIND MAKE BEGET BREED ISSUE
WORLD FARROW KINDLE LITTER
DELIVER FRESHEN
(— BY WILL) DEVISE
(— CARE) NURSE
(— CLAIM TO) REMISE
(— COUNSEL) AREAD AREED
(— CREDIT FOR) FRIST
(— CURRENCY TO) PASS
(— EAR) HARK HARKEN LISTEN
HEARKEN
(— EXPRESSION TO) EMOTE FRAME
VOICE
(— FORM) CUT
(— FORTH) WARP YIELD AFFORD
CONCEIVE
(— GROUND) RETIRE
(— HEED) LOOK ATTEND
(— IN EXCHANGE) SWAP SWOP
(— IN MARRIAGE) BESTOW SPOUSE
(— IN) BOW COLLAPSE
(— INFORMATION) WARN
(— INSTRUCTION) LEAR
(— NAME TO) BAPTIZE
(— NOTICE TO APPEAR) GARNISH
(— NOTICE) WARN HERALD APPRISE
PUBLISH ANNOUNCE INTIMATE
(— OBLIQUE EDGE) CANT
(— OFF) EMIT SEND SHED FLING
DIVIDE EFFUSE EVOLVE EXHALE
EXPIRE EXCRETE SEPARATE
(— ONE'S SELF OVER TO) ADDICT
(— ONE'S WORD) PROMISE
(— OUT) BOOM LEAK EXUDE ISSUE
PETAL EVOLVE EMANATE OUTGIVE
(— PAIN) AGGRIEVE
(— PLACE) VAIL BACCARE
(— PLEDGE) GAGE
(— PROMINENCE TO) FEATURE
(— RELUCTANTLY) BEGRUDGE

(— SATISFACTION) ABY ABYE
ABEGGE
(— SPARINGLY) INCH
(— STRENGTH TO) NERVE
(— SUPPORT) ASSIST ANIMATE
(— TEMPORARILY) LEND
(— TIP) TOUT
(— TONGUE) CRY YEARN
(— UP) PUT BURY DROP PART
CHUCK DEMIT DEVOW FORGO
LEAVE REMIT SHOOT SPARE SPEND
ABJURE ADDICT BETRAY DESERT
DEVOTE FOREGO MIZZLE REFUSE
RELENT RENDER RESIGN VACATE
ABANDON DEPOSIT DESPAIR
FLUMMOX FORBEAR FORGIVE
REFRAIN RELEASE ABDICATE
RENOUNCE
(— VENT TO) EMIT ISSUE
DISCHARGE
(— VOICE) BOLT ACCENT
(— WARNING) ALERT
(— WAY) GO FAIL FOLD KEEL SINK
VAIL BREAK BUDGE BURST FAINT
SLAKE YIELD BUCKLE FALTER
RELENT SWERVE FOUNDER RECLAIM
SUCCUMB
(— WITNESS) DEPOSE
GIVEN APT DONEE NATHAN PROMPT
(— TO) ALL AFTER
GIVER DONOR
(— OF LIFE) APHETA
(NAME —) EPONYM
GIVING DOLE BOUNTY DATION
REMISE
(— HELP) ADJUTANT
(— MILK) FRESH
(— NO MILK) YELD YELL
(— TROUBLE) CUMBROUS
GIZZARD GIGERIUM
GIZZARD SHAD SKIPJACK
GLABROUS SMOOTH GLABRATE
LEVIGATE
GLACIATION MINDEL
(— STAGE) RISS WURM
GLACIER BRAE ICECAP STREAM
CALOTTE ICEBERG PIEDMONT
GLACIOLOGY CRYOLOGY
GLACIS ESPLANADE
GLAD GAY FAIN LIEF VAIN CANTY
HAPPY PROUD BLITHE FESTUS
GLADLY JOCUND JOYFUL JOYOUS
GLADFUL GLEEFUL JOCULAR
ANIMATED CHEERFUL CHEERING
FESTIVAL GLADSOME PLEASING
GLADDEN JOY GLAD BLISS CHEER
EXULT MIRTH BLITHE COMFORT
GLADIFY LIGHTEN REJOICE
GLADE LAWN LAUND SLADE SHRADD
SUNGLADE SUNSCALD
GLADIATOR THRAX RETIARY
SAMNITE SECUTOR ANDABATA
GLADIOLUS GLAD IRID LILY LEVERS
LILIUM GLADIOLA
GLADLY GLAD LIEF FAINLY LIEFLY
LOVELY HAPPILY
GLADNESS JOY GLAD GLEE BLISS
MIRTH BLITHE FAINNESS GLADSHIP
PLEASURE

GLAGA KASA KUSA TALTHIB
GLAMORIZE POT GLORIFY
GLAMOROUS EXOTIC ALLURING
CHARMING
GLANCE EYE RAY SEE BEAM CAST
GLIM LEER PEEK SCRY SKEG VIEW
WINK BLENK BLINK BLUSH CAROM
FLASH GLEEK GLENT GLIDE GLIFF
GLINT GLISK GRAZE PRINK SCREW
SIGHT SKIME SLANT SQUIZ ASPECT
CARROM GANDER REGARD SCANCE
STRIKE VISION EYEBEAM EYESHOT
EYEWINK GLIMPSE BELAMOUR
GLIFFING OEILLADE
(— OFF) GLACE
(— THROUGH) SAMPLE
(MELANCHOLY —) DOWNCAST
(SHARP —) DART
(SIDELONG —) SHEW SLENT SKLENT
(SLY —) GLEG GLIME GLOAT
GLAND MILT NOIX SETA CLYER
CRYPT GONAD LIVER MAMMA
BREAST KERNEL THYMUS ADRENAL
CRUMENA NECTARY PAROTID
PAROTIS TEARPIT THYROID
ENDOCRIN FOLLICLE FOLLOWER
GANGLION GLANDULA GLANDULE
HOOFWORM PROSTATE SCIRRHUS
SPERMARY
GLANDERS FARCY MALLEUS
GLANDULAR EARTHY INNATE
SEXUAL PHYSICAL
GLANS NUT GLAND
GLARE BEAT GAZE BLARE BLAZE
BLOOM FLAME GLAZE STARE
GLITTER ICEBLINK RADIANCE
GLARING HARD RANK GLARY
AGLARE GARISH BURNING FLARING
STARING FLAGRANT
GLASS CUP VER CALX FLAT FLUX
FRIT JENA MOIL PONY VITA CHARK
FACER FLINT GLAZE STOOP STOUP
VERRE VITRE CALGON CEMENT
CULLET SPECKS VITRUM ALEYARD
BIFOCAL BRIMMER CHIRPER
CRYSTAL PERLITE SCHMELZ
TALLBOY VITRITE FROSTING
OBSIDIAN SCHOPPEN
(— IN STATE OF FUSION) METAL
(— OF A MIRROR) STONE
(— OF BEER) BREW
(— OF BRANDY) SNEAKER
(— OF WHISKY) KELTY RUBDOWN
(— OF WINE) APERITIF
(— STICKING TO PUNTY) COLLET
(BEER —) SHELL SEIDEL
(BELL-SHAPED —) CUP CLOCHE
(BURNING —) SUNGLASS
(CHEVAL —) PSYCHE
(COLORED —) SMALT SMALTO
TINTER SCHMELZ
(COLORED —S) GOGGLES
(CUPPING —) VENTOSE
(CURVED —) LENS
(DESSERT —) COUPE
(DRINKING —) GOBLET RUMKIN
PILSNER PIMLICO SCUTTLE
TUMBLER SCHOONER
(EXAMINATION —) SLIDE
(FULL —) BUMPER

(FUSIBLE —) FLUX
(HALF —) SPLIT
(ICE CREAM —) SLIDER
(LEAD —) STRASS
(LIQUEUR —) PONY PONEY
(LIQUOR —) GUN
(MAGNIFYING —) LOUPE
(MASS OF MOLTEN —) PARISON
(OPALESCENT —) OPALINE
(OPAQUE —) HYALITHE
(PIECE OF HOT —) BIT
(PULVERIZED —) FROSTING
(REFUSE —) CALX CULLET
(RUSSIAN —) CHARK
(SHERBET —) SUPREME
(SMOKED —) SHADE
(STAINED —) VITRAIL
(TALL —) RUMMER
(VOLCANIC —) PUMICE PERLITE
(WINDOW —) PANE
(PL.) SHELLS
GLASSBLOWER MUMBLER
GLASS CRAB SPECTER SPECTRE
GLASSHOUSE STOVE HOTHOUSE
GLASS-LIKE VITRIC
GLASSWARE AGATA AURENE
BURMESE FAVRILE OPALINE
STEUBEN VITRICS AMBERINA
GLASSWORK GLAZING GLAZIERY
GLASSWORKER GANGMAN GLAZIER
SNAPPER GLASSMAN SERVITOR
GLASSWORT KALI KELPWORT
SALTWORT SAMPHIRE
GLASSY GLIB FILMY GLAZY GLAZEN
GLASSEN HYALINE HYALOID
VITREAL VITREOUS
GLAUCE (FATHER OF —) CREON
(HUSBAND OF —) JASON
GLAUCUS (FATHER OF —) MINOS
SISYPHUS
(MOTHER OF —) MEROPE PASIPHAE
GLAZE DIP LEAD SIZE SLIP GLASS
SLEET SMEAR ENAMEL QUARRY
CELADON COPERTA EELSKIN
GLASSEN GLAZING GLIDDER
COUVERTE TIGEREYE
(— OF ICE) GLARE
GLAZED FILMY GLACE GLASSEN
GLOSSED
GLAZED WARE GLOST
GLAZIER (TOOL OF —) SPRIG
LADKIN
GLEAM RAY BEAM GLOW LEAM
WAFT WINK BLENK BLINK BLUSH
FLASH GLAIK GLEEN GLENT GLINT
GLISK GLIST GLOSE SHINE SKIME
SPUNK STARE STEEM TWIRE
GLANCE SCANCE FOULDRE
GLIMMER GLITTER SHIMMER
(— FAINTLY) SHIMMER
(— OF LIGHT) LEAM PINK GLAIK
SCANCE
(FAINT —) SCAD
GLEAMING FAW GLOW CLEAR GLINT
STEEP ABLAZE BRIGHT GLEAMY
ADAZZLE SHINING GLOOMING
GLEAN CULL EARN REAP LEASE
GATHER COLLECT SCRINGE
GLEANER STIBBLER
GLEANING CROP GATHERING

(LITERARY —S) ANALECTA
ANALECTS
GLEBE SOD CLOD LAND SOIL
TERMON KIRKTOWN
GLEE GLY JOY SONG MIRTH SPORT
GAIETY DELIGHT ELATION WASSAIL
HILARITY MADRIGAL
GLEEFUL GAY MERRY JOYOUS
JOCULAR GLEESOME
GLEEMAN SONGMAN MINSTREL
GLEN DEN GILL GLYN GRIFF HEUCH
HEUGH KLOOF SLACK SLADE TEMPE
CANADA DINGLE POCKET
GLIADIN GLUTIN PROLAMIN
GLIB PAT FLIP SLICK CASUAL
GLOSSY OFFHAND RENABLE
SHALLOW VOLUBLE FLIPPANT
GLIDE GO SKI FLOW SAIL SILE SKIM
SLIP SLUR SOAR SWIM COAST
CREEP DANCE FLEET GLACE GRAZE
LAPSE MERGE SCOOP SHIRL SKATE
SKIFF SKIRR SLADE SLEEK SLICK
SLIDE SLIPE STEAL GLANCE GLIDER
SASHAY SNOOVE ILLAPSE SCRIEVE
SCRITHE SKITTER SLITHER
AIRPLANE GLISSADE VOLPLANE
(— AWAY) ELAPSE
(— BY) PASS FLEET
(— OFF) EXIT
GLIDER SCOOTER
GLIDING TRAIL SLIDING
(— OF THE VOICE) DRAG
(— OVER) LAMBENT
GLIMMER FIRE GLIM GLOW LEAM
STIM BLINK FLASH GLEAM GLOOM
STIME SIMPER BLINTER FLIMMER
GLIMPSE GLITTER SHIMMER
SPARKLE TWINKLE SUNBLINK
GLIMMERING GHOST AGLIMMER
GLOOMING
GLIMPSE IDEA WAFF WAFT BLINK
BLUSH FLASH GLIFF GLINT GLISK
SIGHT STIME TINGE TRACE WHIFF
GLANCE LUSTER SCANCE GLIMMER
INKLING
(BRIEF —) APERCU
(FLEETING —) SHIM SNATCH
GLINT PEEP FLASH GLEAM GLENT
GLANCE SPARKLE
GLIS MYOXUS
GLISSANDO GLISS SMEAR GLISSADE
GLISTEN FLASH GLISK GLISS GLIST
SHINE GLISTER GLITTER SHIMMER
SPANGLE SPARKLE
GLISTENING SHINY AGLISTEN
GLITTER FLASH GLARE GLEAM
GLEIT GLINT GLORE SHEEN SHINE
SKYRE STARE LUSTER SCANCE
GLIMMER GLISTEN GLISTER SKINKLE
SPANGLE SPARKLE TWINKLE
BRANDISH RADIANCE
(FALSE —) GILT
GLITTERING GEMMY SHEEN SHINY
STEEP FULGID SPANGLY AGLITTER
GLITTERY
GLOAMING EVE DUSK GLOAM
GLOOMING TWILIGHT
GLOAT GAZE GLUT TIRE EXULT
GLOBE ORB BALL BOWL CLEW CLUE
POME AGGER GEOID MONDE ROUND

SPHERE COMPASS GEORAMA
GLOBULE GRENADE AQUARIUM
GLOBEFISH FUGU TOBY TOADO
ATINGA BOTETE PUFFER BLAASOP
BURFISH OOPUHUE
GLOBEFLOWER BOLT GOLLAND
GOWLAND CORCHORUS
GLOBE THISTLE ECHNOPS
GLOBOSE COCCOID COCCOUS
CAPITATE GLOBULAR
GLOBULAR GLOBED GLOBATE
GLOBOSE GLOBICAL
GLOBULE BEAD BLOB DROP GLOB
PEARL BUBBLE BUTTON REGULUS
GLOBULET SPHERULE
(— OF TAPIOCA) FISHEYE
GLOBULIN MAYSIN MYOSIN VIGNIN
ARACHIN CORYCIN EDESTIN
LEGUMIN TUBERIN VICILIN
ANTIBODY BIOLOGIC EXCELSIN
GLYCININ MUSCULIN ORYZENIN
GLOCKENSPIEL BELL LYRA
CARILLON
GLOMERULE GLOME FASCICLE
GLOOM DUSK MURK CLOUD DREAR
FROWN SOMBER DESPAIR DIMNESS
GLOOMTH SADNESS DARKNESS
MIDNIGHT
GLOOMY DUN SAD WAN BLUE COLD
DARK DOUR DREE DULL EERY GLUM
MURK ADUSK ADUST BLACK BROWN
DOWFF DREAR DUSKY EERIE FERAL
GUMLY HEAVY LURID MOODY
MORNE MUDDY MUNGY MUSTY
SABLE SORRY STERN SULKY SURLY
SWART TRIST CLOUDY DREARY
DREICH DROOPY DRUMLY GLUMMY
MOROSE SOLEMN SOMBER SULLEN
TETRIC THRAWN OBSCURE STYGIAN
THESTER DESOLATE DOLESOME
DOWNBEAT DOWNCAST FUNEREAL
GLOOMING LOWERING OVERCAST
GLORIA GLORY AUREOLE
GLORIFY HERY LAUD BLESS DEIFY
EXALT EXTOL HERSE HONOR PRIDE
WURTH KUDIZE PRAISE CLARIFY
ELEVATE MAGNIFY DIVINIZE
EMBLAZON EULOGIZE STELLIFY
GLORIOUS SRI DEAR DERE MERE
SHRI GRAND BRIGHT EMINENT
RENOWNED
GLORY JOY ORE SUN FACE FAME
GLOR HALO HORN BLAZE BOAST
EXULT HONOR KUDOS PRIDE
WULDER AUREOLA CLARITY
GARLAND GLORIFY RADIANCE
SPLENDOR WORTHING
GLOSS GILL COLOR DUNCE GLASS
GLAZE GLOZE JAPAN SHEEN SHINE
BLANCH LUSTER LUSTRE POSTIL
REMARK VENEER BURNISH
EXPOUND VARNISH FLOURISH
PALLIATE POLITURE
(— OVER) FARD HUSH SALVE SLEEK
SOOTHE
GLOSSA LINGUA
GLOSSARY GLOSS CLAVIS
GLOSSIPHONIA CLEPSINE
GLOSSY GLOZE NITID SHINY SILKY
SLICK SATINY SMOOTH

GLOVE KID CUFF GAGE MITT COFFE
BERLIN MITTEN CHEVRON DANNOCK
GANTLET GOMUKHI GAUNTLET
(— FOR RUBBING SKIN) STRIGIL
(BISHOP'S —) GWANTUS
(BODY OF —) TRANK
(HEDGER'S —) DANNOCK
(HUSKING —) HUSKER
GLOVEMAKER DOMER GLOVER
CLASPER FINGERER
GLOVER TRANKER
GLOW ARC LOW AURA BURN FIRE
LEAM LOOM LOWE BLAZE BLOOM
BLUSH FLAME FLASH FLUSH GLAZE
GLEAM GLEED GLORY GLOSS
GLOZE SHINE STEAM CORONA
KINDLE WARMTH FLUSTER LIGHTEN
(— OF PASSION) ESTUS AESTUS
(— WITH INTENSE HEAT) IGNITE
GLOWER GAZE GLOW GLARE
GLOOM GLORE
GLOWING HOT LIVE WARM AGLOW
FIERY LIGHT QUICK RUDDY VIVID
ABLAZE ARDENT ORIENT BURNING
CANDENT FERVENT RADIANT
SHINING FLAGRANT
GLOWWORM FIREFLY FIREWORK
GLOWBIRD LAMPYRID
GLOZE FAWN PAINT SMOOTH
FLATTERY
GLUCOSE AME GLYCOSE DEXTROSE
GLUCOSIDE GEIN APIIN RUTIN TUTIN
ADONIN BINDER CORNIN DURRIN
FRAXIN FUSTIN IRIDIN PICEIN
UZARIN ACACIIN ARBUTIN DAPHNIN
DIOSMIN ESCULIN ESTEVIN GITALIN
GITONIN GITOXIN HEDERIN HELECIN
INDICAN LOGANIN LOTUSIN LUPININ
ONABAIN POPULIN ROBININ SALICIN
TABACIN TEUCRIN ADONIDIN
CARTHAME ERICOLIN GENISTIN
GOSSYPIN MORINDIN NARINGIN
PARIGLIN PARILLIN PRUNASIN
QUINOVIN SAPONINE SCILLAIN
SINIGRIN SYRINGIN THEVETIN
VERNONIN VIBURNIN VICIANIN
GLUE PAD MOUNT STICK BEGLEW
CEMENT FUNORE FUNORIN STICKER
TAUROCOL
GLUEY GLUISH STICKY STRINGY
VISCOUS ADHESIVE
GLUM CLUM DOUR GRUM SURLY
GLOOMY GLUMPY MOROSE SULLEN
GLUMALES POALES
GLUME PILE FLIGHT
(FLOWERING —) LEMMA
(PL.) CHAFF
GLUSIDE SACCHARIN
GLUT CLOY FILL GULP QUAT SATE
CHOKE DRAFT GORGE BATTEN
ENGLUT EXCESS MARROW PAMPER
PAUNCH ENGORGE GLUTTON
SATIATE SURFEIT SWALLOW
OVERFEED SATURATE
GLUTEAL NATAL
GLUTELIN AVENINE ORYZENIN
GLUTENIN AVENIN ZYMOME
ZYMOMIN
GLUTINOUS ROPY SIZY ROPEY
SLIMY TOUGH STICKY VISCID

GLUTTED QUAT GORGED SATIATED
GLUTTER VEER
GLUTTON PIG GLUT GORB GUTS
GULCH MIKER GLOTUM HELLUO
MACCUS EPICURE GUTLING
LURCHER MOOCHER RAVENER
SWILLER DRAFFMAN GOURMAND
GULLYGUT
(STUPID —) GRUB
GLUTTONIZE BIZLE BEZZLE
GLUTTONOUS GREEDY GLUTTON
HOGGISH GOURMAND
GLUTTONY GULE SURFEIT
GLYCERIDE BUTYRIN
GLYCINE SOJA
GLYCOL CARBOWAX
GLYCOPROTEIN MUCIN MUCOID
GLYCOSIDE APIIN CROCIN ACACIIN
CYMARIN DIGOXIN GITALIN GITOXIN
HEDERIN HYPERIN LOGANIN
LOTUSIN SAPONIN ALDESIDE
ANDROSIN ANTIARIN HOLOSIDE
KETOSIDE
GNARL NOB KNOB KNUR KNARL
KNURR SNIRL WARRE DEFORM
GNARLED GNARLY KNARRY KNOTTY
CRABBED KNOTTED KNURLED
GNASH TUSK CHAMP CRASH GANCH
GRASH GRATE KNASH
GNAT KNAW SMUT MIDGE STOUT
KNATTE SCIARA SCIARID SCINIPH
BLACKFLY DIPTERAN GNATLING
GNATCATCHER SYLVIID
GNATHION MENTON
GNAW EAT NAB BITE FRET TIRE
CHELE GNARL MOUSE SHEAR
ARRODE BEFRET BEGNAW CHAVEL
NATTLE NIGGLE ROUNGE CHIMBLE
CHUMBLE CORRODE
GNAWING EATING RODENT FRETFUL
ARROSION ROSORIAL
GNOME NIS NISSE PECHT PYGMY
KOBOLD VAKSHA YAKSHI GNOMIDE
GREMLIN HODEKEN ERDGEIST
GNOMON COCK INDEX STILE STYLE
FESCUE STYLUS
GNOSTIC CLEVER SHREWD
KNOWING PERATES EBIONITE
MANDAEAN SEVERIAN SIMONIAN
SIMONITE
GNU KOKOON BRINDLE
GO BE DO ACT GAE HOP ISH LAY
NIM PEP TEE WAG BANG BEAR BING
BOWN BUSK DRAW FAND FARE
FOND GANG HARK HAUL HUMP
MOVE QUIT ROAM ROLL SEEK SHOT
SILE SLAP SNAP STEP TAKE
TEEM TOUR WADE WANE WEAR
WEND WEVE WIND WISE WORK
YEDE AMBLE BOUND CARRY CHEVE
DEMON DRESS FETCH FRAME
HAUNT KNOCK LEAVE MOSEY
PLUCK REACH SCRAM SHAKE
SLOPE SPEED TOUCH TRACE TRACK
TRENE TRINE TRUSS WHIZZ YONGE
BECOME BETAKE CHIEVE CRUISE
DEPART EXTEND QUATCH QUETCH
REPAIR RESORT RESULT RETIRE
SASHAY STRAKE STRIKE TODDLE
TRAVEL WEAKEN JOURNEY SCRITHE
DIMINISH WITHDRAW

(— **ABOUT DEJECTEDLY**) PEAK
(— **ABOUT GOSSIPING**) COURANT
(— **ABOUT**) JET BEGO BIGAN
(— **AHEAD**) HOLD
(— **AIMLESSLY**) ERR
(— **ALONG**) PATH
(— **AROUND**) SKIRT BYPASS CIRCUE
(— **ASHORE**) LAND
(— **ASTRAY**) ERR MAR WRY MANG
WILL MISGO DELIRE FORVAY
MISWEND DEROGATE MISCARRY
(— **AWAY**) AGO HOP BEAT BUNK
HIKE NASH PART SHOO VADE
CLEAR HENCE IMSHI LEAVE SCRAM
SHIFT BEGONE BUGGER DEPART
REMOVE VACATE SKIDDOO
ELONGATE
(— **BACK IN TIME**) MOUNT
(— **BAD**) SOUR
(— **BEFORE**) LEAD FOREGO
PRECEDE ANTECEDE PREAMBLE
(— **BEYOND**) SURPASS FOREPASS
(— **BRISKLY**) JUNE
(— **BROKE**) BUST
(— **COURTING**) WENCH
(— **DOWN**) SET SINK DROOP SOUND
DESCEND
(— **EASILY**) AMBLE
(— **ERRATICALLY**) KICK
(— **FAST**) HURRY SPLIT BEELINE
(— **FORTH**) AGO DEPART FORTHGO
(— **FORWARD**) HUP HUPP ADVANCE
AGGRESS PROCEED
(— **FOWLING**) AUCUPATE
(— **FURTIVELY**) SLINK SNEAK STEAL
(— **HANG**) SNICK
(— **HEAVILY**) LOB LAMPER
(— **IN HASTE**) LEN LAMMAS
(— **IN HURRY**) SCOFFLE
(— **IN PURSUIT**) SUE
(— **IN**) ENTER INGRESS
(— **INTO BUSINESS**) EMBARK
(— **LAME**) FOUNDER
(— **LEISURELY**) BUMMEL JIGGET
JIGGIT
(— **LIGHTLY**) TIPTOE
(— **MAD**) CRAZE MADDLE
(— **NEAR**) APPROACH
(— **NOISILY**) LARUM
(— **OFF**) MOG DISCHARGE
(— **ON BOARD**) BOARD EMBARK
ENTRAIN
(— **ON FOOT**) SHANK
(— **ON TO SAY**) ADD
(— **ON**) DO GARN LAST PASS
PERGE FURTHER PROCEED
(— **OUT**) EXIT ISSUE SLOCK EGRESS
EXEUNT QUENCH SORTIE
(— **OVER AGAIN**) RENEW REVISE
RETRACE
(— **OVER**) KNEE REVOLT SURPASS
OVERGANG
(— **PROSPEROUSLY**) COTTON
(— **QUICKLY**) GET HIE BUZZ LAMP
PIKE SCAT SPEED
(— **RAPIDLY**) LAMP SPLIT
(— **SHARES**) SNACK
(— **SLOWLY**) CRAWL CREEP
(— **SLUGGISHLY**) SHACK
(— **SMOOTHLY**) SLIP

(— **STEALTHILY**) SHIRK SLINK
SNEAK GUMSHOE
(— **SUDDENLY**) SCOOT
(— **SWIFTLY**) SCOOT SKISE STRIP
HIGHBALL
(— **THE ROUNDS**) PATROL
(— **THROUGH WATER**) SQUATTER
(— **THROUGH**) SUFFER
(— **THROUGHOUT**) COAST
(— **TO BED**) KIP FLOP SNUG
(— **TO EXCESS**) DEBORD
(— **TO HARBOR**) VERT
(— **TO PIECES**) SNURP
(— **TO SCHOOL**) SCOLEY
(— **TO SLEEP**) HUSHABY
(— **TO WAR**) RISE
(— **UP**) CLIMB AMOUNT ASCEND
(— **WEARILY**) HAGGLE
(— **WITH EFFORT**) HIKE
(— **WRONG**) MISS FAULT CURDLE
MISFARE
GOAD EGG GAD GIG HAG BAIT BROD
BROG DARE EDGE GAUD LASH
MOVE PROD SPUR URGE WHIP YERK
ANKUS HARRY IMPEL PIQUE PRICK
PROGG PUNGE STING VALET INCITE
OXGOAD ANKUSHA HOTFOOT
INFLAME PROVOKE IRRITATE
SLAPJACK STIMULUS
GOADMAN GADMAN GAUDSMAN
GOADSTER
GOAL BYE DEN END BASE BUTT
DOLE HAIL HALE MARK METE PORT
BOURN FINIS IDEAL SCOOP SCOPE
SCORE STING DESIGN OBJECT
SIGHTS DESTINY HORIZON
TERMINUS
(— **IN GAMES**) HUNK
(**FIELD** —) BASKET
(**REMOTE** —) THULE
(**UNATTAINABLE** —) STAR
GO-ASHORE KOHUA
GOAT TUR IBEX TAHR BEDEN BILLY
BOVID EVECK SEROW ALPINE
ANGORA AOUDAD CAPRID CHAMAL
JEMLAH MAZAME NUBIAN PASANG
SAANEN WETHER CHAMOIS
AEGAGRUS CAPRIPED MARKHOOR
(**DOMESTIC** —) HIRCUS
(**FEMALE** —) NANNY DOELING
(**MALE** —) BUCK BUCKLING
(**YOUNG** —) KID KIDDY TICCHEN
GOATLING
GOAT ANTELOPE GORAL SEROW
GOORAL
GOATEE TUFT
GOATFISH MOANO
GOATHERD DAMON
GOAT-LIKE GOATISH HIRCINE
GOAT MOTH COSSID
GOATSBEARD ROSACEAN
GOATSKIN CRUST CASTOR
CHEVRETTE
GOATSUCKER PUCK PEWKE POTOO
EVEJAR DORHAWK GRINDER
SPINNER DOORHAWK EVECHURR
NIGHTJAR PAURAQUE
GOB CLOT GOAF SWAB SWOB
WASTE GOBBET SWABBY
GOBBLE MOP BOLT SLOP GOFFLE
GORBLE

GOBBLEDYGOOK PEDAGESE
GO-BETWEEN BAWD FIXER MEANS
BROKER DEALER PANDAR CONTACT
MEDIATOR
GOBLET DINOS GLASS HANAP
POKAL SKULL STOOP STOUP
HOLMOS RUMKIN CHALICE SNIFTER
TALLBOY JEROBOAM STANDARD
STEMWARE
GOBLIN (ALSO SEE HOBGOBLIN)
COW HAG NIS BHUT BOGY MARE
BOGEY NISSE OUPHE POOKA
BODACH BOGGLE BOOGER CHUREL
FOLIOT SPRITE BOGGART BROWNIE
BUGBEAR KNOCKER PADFOOT
BARGHEST BOGEYMAN FOLLETTO
GOBY MAPO BULLY BIGHEAD
CHALACO GOBIOID GUAVINA
GUDGEON MUDFISH BULLHEAD
PINKFISH SANDGOBY
GOCART SULKY WALKER STROLLER
GOD (ALSO SEE DEITY) EA EL ER RA
VE BEL BES COG DAD DES DEV DIS
DOD EAR GAR GAW GEB GOG GOL
GOM GUM ING KEB LAR LOK MEN
MIN ODD ORO SEB SUN TEM TYR
ULL UTU VAN AITU AMEN AMON
ARES ASUR ATEO ATUA ATYS BAAL
BEER BRAN BURE CHAC COCK
DEUS DEVA DIEU ESUS FONS FREY
GAWD GOSH HAPI HOLY HOTH INTI
JOVE KANE KING LIFE LLEU LOKE
LOKI LOVE LUGH MARS MIND NABU
NEBO NUDD ODIN PTAH SHEN SOMA
SOUL TANE THOR TIKI ULLR UTUG
VAYU XIPE YAMA ZEUS ARAWN
ASHUR ASURA ATTES ATTIS COMUS
DAGDA DEITY DEOTA DUVEL DYAUS
DYLAN EBISU ELOAH FREYR GHOST
GOLES GOLLY GRAVE GUACA
HESUS HIEMS HORUS HOTHR
HUACA HYMEN INDRA JUDGE KINGU
LADON LIBER LLUDD MENTU MIDER
MOMUS NJORD NUMEN PALES SILEN
TAMUZ THOTH TINIA TRUTH TYCHE
URASH WAKEA WODIN WOTAN
ZOMBI ADITYA ADONAI ADONAY
ANSHAR ANUBIS APOLLO ASEITY
AUTHOR CHAMOS CONSUS DEVATA
DHARMA ELATHA ELOHIM FATHER
FAUNUS GANESA HEAVEN HERMES
HOENIR METZLI MILCOM MITHRA
NEREUS NERGAL OSIRIS PATRON
PENEUS PLUTUS PUSHAN SESHAT
SOCIUS SOURCE SPIRIT SUTEKH
SYLENE TAAROA TAMMUZ TARTAK
TERAPH TRITON TRIVIA VARUNA
VEDUIS VERITY VISHNU VULCAN
WISDOM YAKSHA YAKSHI ZOMBIE
ABRAXAS ADRANUS ALPHEUS
ANTEROS BELENUS CHEMOSH
DAIKOKU DELLING ETERNAL
GODHEAD HANUMAN IAPETUS
JEHOVAH JUPITER KANALOA
MERCURY MITHRAS MUTINUS
NEPTUNE NJORTHR PROTEUS
PRYDERI REMPHAN ROBIGUS
SAVITAR SERAPIS TRIGLAV VATICAN
VEJOVIS ZAGREUS ALMIGHTY
ASTRAEUS BISHAMON CAMAXTLI

DEMIURGE DEVOTION DIVINITY GUCUMATZ INFINITE JIUROJIN KUKULKAN MIXCOATL MORPHEUS POSEIDON SABAZIOS SUMMANUS TANGAROA TERMINUS TUTELARY VEDIOVIS ZEPHYRUS
(— OF AGRICULTURE) PICUS URASH FAUNUS AMAETHON NINGIRSU
(— OF ARTS) SIVA
(— OF ATMOSPHERE) HADAD
(— OF COMMERCE) MERCURY
(— OF CORN) CAT
(— OF DAY) HORUS
(— OF EARTH) BEL GEB KEB SEB DAGAN
(— OF EVIL) SET FOMOR FOMORIAN
(— OF FIRE) AGNI GIRRU NUSKU RUDRA VULCAN
(— OF FLOCKS) PAN
(— OF HAPPINESS) HOTEI JUROJIN
(— OF HEAVENS) ANU JUMALA
(— OF JUSTICE) FORSETE FORSETI
(— OF LEARNING) IMHOTEP
(— OF LOVE) AMOR ARES EROS KAMA BHAGA CUPID AENGUS
(— OF MOON) SIN ENZU NANNAR
(— OF NATURE) MARSYAS
(— OF POETRY) BRAGE BRAGI
(— OF RAIN) PARJANYA
(— OF SEA) LER VAN AEGIR DYAUS NEPTUNE PROTEUS PALAEMON POSEIDON
(— OF SKY) ANU GWYDION
(— OF SLEEP) HYPNOS HYPNUS MORPHEUS
(— OF SOUTHEAST WIND) EURUS
(— OF STORM) ZU ADAD ADDA ADDU MARUT RUDRA TESHUP
(— OF SUN) RA RE SHU SOL TEM TUM UTU AMON ATMU ATUM BAAL LLEU UTUG SAMAS SEKER SURYA APOLLO HELIOS SOKARI KHEPERA PHOEBUS SHAMASH PHAETHON TONATIUH
(— OF THUNDER) THOR DONAR PERUN PERKUN PEROUN TLALOC HURAKAN TARANIS
(— OF UNDERWORLD) DIS GWYN YAMA HADES ORCUS PLUTO
(— OF VEGETATION) ATYS ATTIS
(— OF WAR) ER IRA ORO TIU TYR ARES COEL IRRA MARS MENT ODIN THOR MONTU NINIB MEXITL SKANDA CAMULUS MEXITLI NINURTA ENYALIUS NINGIRSU QUIRINUS
(— OF WEALTH) BHAGA KUBERA KUVERA PLUTUS
(— OF WIND) ADAD ADDA ADDU VAYU MARUT AEOLUS BOREAS EECATL
(— OF WISDOM) TAT THOTH
(— WILLING) DV
(BLIND —) HOTH HOTHR
(FALSE —) BAAL IDOL MAUMET
(FEMALE —) GODDESS
(HAWAIIAN —) AUMAKUA
(PAGAN —) DEMON
(RAM-HEADED —) AMON KHNUM KHNEMU
(TUTELARY —) LAR

(UNKNOWN —) KA
(WOOD —) SILEN SILENUS
(PL.) DI DII AESIR IGIGI SUPERI PANTHEON TRIMURTI
GODDESS (ALSO SEE DEITY) AI NU ANA ANU ATE AYA DEA DON NUT OPS UNI VAC ANTA BADB BODB CACA DANA DANU ERIS ERUA FRIA HELA HERA JORD JUNO MAIA MEDB NIKE NINA NONA PELE SAGA SATI TARA UPIS ALLAT AMENT ANATH ANTUM ARURU BAUBO CERES CHLOE DEESS DIANA DIANE DIRGA DOLMA DOMNU EPONA FRIGG HYBLA IAMBE ISTAR KOTYS MAEVE NANAI NINTU PAKHT PALES PARCA SALUS SEDNA SKADI TANIT TYCHE USHAS VENUS VESTA ADEONA AESTAS ANATUM ANUKIT APHAIA ATHENA BELILI BENDIS BOOPIS BRIGIT CYRENE EOSTRE FRIGGA GEFJON HELENA HESTIA HYGEIA INNINA KISHAR LIBERA MOTHER NINGAL PEITHO PHOBOS POMONA PRORSA RUMINA SEKHET SEMELE SKATHI SOTHIS TANITH TEFNUT TRIVIA URANIA VACUNA YDGRUN ANAHITA ANAITIS ARTEMIS ASHERAH DEMETER DERCETO FERONIA FJORGYN GODHEAD LARENTA LARUNDA MAJAGGA MAJESTA MINERVA MORNING MORRIGU MYLITTA NEKHEBT NEMESIS PALATUA PARBATI PARVATI SALACIA ADRASTEA AGLAUROS ANGERONA BELISAMA CARMENTA CENTEOTL COCAMAMA DESPOINA DICTYNNA GULLVEIG MORRIGAN NEPHTHYS PARBUTTY PRAKRITI RHIANNON SEFEKHET THOUERIS VICTORIA
(— OF AGRICULTURE) BAU OPS DEMETER CENTEOTL
(— OF AIR) AURA
(— OF BEAUTY) VENUS LAKSHMI
(— OF BURIAL) LIBITINA
(— OF CHILDBIRTH) LEVANA LUCINA
(— OF DAWN) EOS USAS USHAS AURORA MATUTA
(— OF DEW) HERSE
(— OF DISCORD) ATE ERIS
(— OF EARTH) GE LUA SEB ERDA GAEA GAIA TARI ARURU DIONE JORTH TERRA SEMELE TELLUS THEMIS DAMKINA PERCHTA
(— OF FERTILITY) MA ISIS MAMA NERTHUS
(— OF FLOWERS) FLORA CHLORIS
(— OF FORTUNE) TYCHE FORTUNA
(— OF GRAIN) CERES
(— OF HEALING) EIR GULA
(— OF HEALTH) DAMIA HYGEIA VALETUDO
(— OF HEARTH) VESTA HESTIA
(— OF HISTORY) SAGA
(— OF HOPE) SPES
(— OF INFATUATION) ATE
(— OF JUSTICE) DIKE MAAT ASTRAEA NEMESIS JUSTITIA
(— OF LEGISLATION) EUNOMIA

(— OF LOVE) ATHOR FREYA VENUS FREYJA HATHOR
(— OF MAGIC) HECATE
(— OF MARRIAGE) HERA
(— OF MATERNITY) APET
(— OF MERCY) KWANNON
(— OF MOTHERHOOD) ISIS
(— OF NIGHT) NOX NYX
(— OF OCEAN) NINA
(— OF OVENS) FORNAX
(— OF PEACE) PAX IRENE NERTHUS
(— OF PLEASURE) BES
(— OF RAINBOW) IRIS
(— OF SEASONS) DIKE HORA
(— OF THE DEAD) HEL HELA
(— OF THE HUNT) DIANA VACUNA ARTEMIS
(— OF THE MOON) LUNA MOON DIANA SELENA TANITH ARTEMIS
(— OF THE SEA) INO RAN DORIS BRANWEN EURYNOME
(— OF TRUTH) MAAT
(— OF VEGETATION) OPS CERES COTYS COTYTTO
(— OF VENGEANCE) ARA NEMESIS
(— OF VICTORY) NIKE
(— OF WAR) ENYO ANATH ANATU ANUNIT BELLONA
(— OF WATER) ANAHITA
(— OF WEALTH) LAKSHMI
(— OF WISDOM) ATHENA MINERVA
(— OF YOUTH) HEBE JUVENTAS
(3-HEADED —) HECATE
(COW-HEADED —) ISIS
(ESKIMO —) SEDNA
(SUBORDINATE —) DEMIURGE
(THUNDER-SMITTEN —) SEMELE KERAUNIA
(PL.) MATRIS POINAE ASYNJUR
GO-DEVIL TRAVOIS ALLIGATOR
GODFATHER GOSSIP GODPAPA PADRINO SPONSOR GODPHERE
GODHEAD DEITY GODHOOD DIVINITY
GODLESS WICKED ATHEIST IMPIOUS PROFANE UNGODLY
GODLESSNESS ATHEISM
GODLIKE DEIFIC DIVINE IMMORTAL OLYMPIAN
GODLINESS SANCTITY
GODLING DEVATA GENIUS GODKIN GODLET PANISC DEMIGOD PANISCUS
GODLY HOLY PIOUS DEVOUT GRACIOUS
GODMOTHER CUMMER GOSSIP SPONSOR GODMAMMA MARRAINE
GODPARENT SPONSOR
GOD'S S
GODSON FILLEUL GODCHILD
GOD TREE CEIBA
GODWIT PICK PRINE BARKER MARLIN SCAMMEL YARWHIP RINGTAIL SHRIEKER SPOTRUMP YARDKEEP YARWHELP
GOFFER FULLER GAUFFER
GO-GETTER HUSTLER
GOGGLER SCAD
GOGLET COOJA SERAI MONKEY SURAHI GURGLET SURAHEE

GOING FARE GAIT BOUND AGOING WAYING PASSADO SLEDDING
(— **ABOUT**) AROUND
(— **BEYOND OTHERS**) ULTRA
(— **IN**) INEUNT INFARE INGOING
(— **ON**) FARE AGATE TOWARD
(— **OUT**) EGRESS
(— **UP**) ANABASIS
GOITER WEN GLANS GOITRE STRUMA
GOITERED ANTELOPE ZENU
GOITROUS STRUMOUS
GOLD OR ORO RED SOL DORE GILT GULL ALTUN AURUM GUILD METAL OCHER OCHRE RIDGE SHINY GOLDEN OBRIZE ORMOLU YELLOW BULLION SPANKER
(— **PIECE**) TALI
(**GREENISH** —) AENEUS AENEOUS
GOLDBEATER (**TOOL OF** —) WAGON
GOLDCREST MOON TIDLEY MUDDLER TROCHIL
GOLDEN RED DORE GOLD BLEST DURRY GOLDY SUNNY AUREAL BLONDE GILDEN GILTEN AUREATE AUREOUS HALCYON AURULENT DEAURATE
(— **STATE**) CALIFORNIA
GOLDEN CHAIN LABURNUM
GOLDEN CLUB TAWKEE TAWKIN TUCKAHOE
GOLDEN EAGLE RINGTAIL
GOLDENEYE CUR GARROT COBHEAD GOWDNIE BULLHEAD IRONHEAD MORILLON WHIFFLER WHISTLER
GOLDEN ORIOLE PIROL WITWALL
GOLDEN PLOVER KOLEA FROGSKIN SQUEALER WHISTLER
GOLDEN RAGWORT LIFEROOT
GOLDENROD BONEWORT SOLIDAGO JIMMYWEED
GOLDENSEAL EYEBALM EYEROOT ICEROOT PUCCOON
GOLDEN SHINER CHUB DACE WINDFISH
GOLDFINCH JACK FINCH GOLDY GOWDY CANARY REDCAP FLAXBIRD GRAYPATE
GOLDFINNY GOLDNEY CORKWING
GOLDFISH FUNA MOOR COMET CALICO FANTAIL CYPRINID VEILTAIL
GOLD-OF-PLEASURE FLAX MADWORT OILSEED
GOLDSMITH SONAR AURIFEX
GOLFER TEER
GOMUTI EJOO IROK ARENG KITTUL SAGWIRE SAGOWEER
GONAD GERMEN
GONCALO ALVES KINGWOOD
GONDOLA GON BARGE GUNDALOW
GONE AWAY LOST NAPOO
(— **BY**) AGO DONE PAST AGONE PASSE BEHIND BYGONE
(— **OUT OF USE**) EXTINCT
(— **TO PIECES**) HAYWIRE
GONG BELL CLOCK GANGSA DOORBELL
(**SERIES OF** —**S**) BONANG
GONGORISM CULTISM

GONOPHORE MEDUSOID SPOROSAC
GOOD BON GAY TOP TRY ABLE BEAU BEIN BIEN BOON BRAW FINE GAIN HEND NICE NOTE PROW SAKE BONUM BRAVE BULLY CANNY FRESH GWEED JELLY KAPAI PAKKA PUKKA SEELY SOUND VALID BENIGN BRAWLY BUCKRA DIVINE EXPERT FACTOR FORBYE HONEST MABUTI PRETTY PROFIT PROPER WEALTH BENEFIT COPIOUS CORKING FAIRISH FORTHBY GODLIKE GRADELY HELPFUL LIBERAL SNIFTER STAVING TRAINED UPRIGHT BUDGEREE GRAITHLY INTEREST LAUDABLE PLEASING SALUTARY SKILLFUL SUITABLE
(**EXCEPTIONALLY** —) SLAMBANG
(**EXTREMELY** —) SLICK
(**HOLD** —) BEAR
(**INFINITELY** —) HOLY
(**MIGHTY** —) SKOOKUM
(**NO** —) NAPOO NAPOOH
(**PRETTY** —) FAIR TIDY
(**RELATIVELY** —) SMOOTH
(**SUPERLATIVELY** —) BRAG BEAUTIFUL
(**SUPREMELY** —) IMMENSE GORGEOUS
(**SURPASSINGLY** —) SUPERIOR
(**VERY** —) HOT TOP DANDY DICTY GRAND NIFTY NAILING SPLENDID SWINGING
GOOD-BYE BY BYE TATA ADIEU ADIOS LULLABY FAREWELL SAYONARA
GOOD-FOR-NAUGHT LOSEL
GOOD-FOR-NOTHING BUM ORRA SLIM SLINK KEFFEL RIBALD BRETHEL FUSTIAN SCROYLE SHOTTEN SKEEZIX SKYBALD WOSBIRD VAGABOND
GOOD-KING-HENRY BLITE ALLGOOD MARKERY MERCURY CHENOPOD
GOOD-LOOKING FAIR BONNY GAWSY COMELY PRETTY SEEMLY EYESOME GRADELY WINSOME GOODLIKE HANDSOME STUNNING
GOODLY BOON PROPER GOODLIKE
GOOD-NATURED SONSY CLEVER AMIABLE
GOODNESS BONTE BONUM MENSK PROOF BONITY BOUNTY SATTVA VIRTUE KINDNESS
GOODS FEE GEAR KIND PELF CARGO STUFF TRADE WORLD WRACK ADVANCE CAPITAL CHATTEL EFFECTS FINANCE HAVINGS INSIGHT TRAFFIC CHAFFERY HIGGLERY PROPERTY
(— **BARTERED**) DICKER
(— **CAST OVERBOARD**) JETSAM
(— **SUNK IN SEA**) LAGAN LIGAN LAGEND
(**DRY** —) DRAPERY
(**HOUSEHOLD** —) INSIGHT
(**IMPERFECT** —) FENT
(**INFERIOR** —) BRACK
(**PIECE** —) CUTTANEE

(**SECONDHAND** —) BROKERY
(**SLOW-SELLING** —) JOBS
(**STOLEN** — **THROWN AWAY**) WAIF
(**SURPLUS** —) OVERAGE
(**VALUABLE** —) SWAG
GOOD-SIZED HEFTY GAWSIE
GOOD-TASTING DAINTY
GOODWILL GREE
GOODY-GOODY PI
GOOEY CLARTY
GOOF BOOB GOOFER
GOOGLY BOSEY WRONGUN
GOON MUSCLEMAN
GOOSANDER JACKSAW RANTOCK
GOOSE ELK LAMA NENE BRANT BRENT EMDEN HANSA HOBBY ROMAN SOLAN WAVEY CAGMAG CANADA EMBDEN GALOOT GANDER GOSLET HISSER HONKER SOLAND AFRICAN BLACKIE BUSTARD GAGGLER GOSLING GRAYLAG GREASER GREYLAG OUTARDE WIDGEON BALDHEAD BARNACLE BERGOOSE BERNICLE SPURWING TOULOUSE
(**MYTHICAL** —) GANZA
GOOSEBERRY BLOB FABE FAPE POHA BRAGAS GOBLIN GOZILL GROZER DOWNING GASKINS GROZART CARBERRY CATBERRY DOGBERRY EATBERRY FEABERRY GOOSEGOG HOUGHTON INDUSTRY
(**PL.**) THAPES
GOOSE EGG DUCK
GOOSEFOOT BASSIA KOCHIA ALLSEED PIGWEED
GOOSEGIRL GOSSARD
GOOSE GRASS HERIF HARIFFE CLEAVERS
GOOSEHERD GOZZARD GOOSEBOY
GOOSENECK ROOSTER
GOPHER TUZA GAUFFRE GEOMYID MUNGOFA QUACHIL SALAMICH TUCOTUCO
(— **STATE**) MINNESOTA
GOPHERMAN SWAMPER
GOPHERWOOD FUSTIC
GORE CLY CLOY GARE HIKE HIPE HOOK HORN PICK PIKE SHOT CRUOR GODET STICK GORING GUSSET
GOREVAN AUBURN
GORGE GAP JAM FILL GASH GAUM GLUT JAMB KHOR RENT BREAK CAJON CANON CHASM CHINE CLUSE DRAFT FARCE FLUME GULLY GURGE KLOOF PONGO POUCH STECH STRID STUFF TANGI CANYON DEFILE NULLAH RAVINE STODGE STRAIT THROAT COULOIR DATIATE DRAUGHT ENGORGE SATIATE SLABBER QUEBRADA
GORGED ACCOLLE
GORGEOUS VAIN GRAND SHOWY COSTLY DAZZLING GLORIOUS SPLENDID
GORGERIN NECK NECKING
GORGING STODGE
GORGON MEDUSA STHENO EURYALE
GORILLA APE PIGMY PYGMY

GORING CORNUPETE
GORMANDIZE STECH STEGH
GUTTLE
GORMANDIZER HELLUO GLUTTON
GORSE ULEX WHIN FURZE GORST
GORY BLOODY
GOSHAWK GOS ASTUR TERCEL
GOSLING GULL
GOSPEL SPELL DHARMA EVANGEL
KERUGMA KERYGMA SYNOPTIC
(— OF REDEMPTION) CROSS
(PL.) TEXT
GOSSAMER MOUSEWEB STARDUST
GOSSIP EME GUP PIE AUNT BUZZ
CANT CLAT CONK COZE DIRT NEWS
TALK CAUSE CLACK CLASH CLYPE
COOSE CRACK FERLY FRUMP
GOSSY SIEVE BABBLE CADDLE
CALLET CAMPER CLAVER FERLIE
JANGLE NORATE TATTLE TITTLE
CLATTER COMPERE GOSTHER
HASHGOB NASHGAB SCANDAL
TATTLER TRATTLE CHITCHAT
GOSSIPRY QUIDNUNC
GOSSIPY BUZZY
GOTH GOTHIAN SUIOGOTH VISIGOTH
GOTHIC OGIVAL
GOUGE DIG PUG BENT SCUFF
CHISEL FLUKAN GOUGER HOLLOW
SCRIBE FLOOKAN SCORPER
SELVAGE SELVEDGE STICKING
(— OUT) BULLDOZE
(V-TYPE —) VEINER
GOUGER CHISELLER
GOURD MATE PEPO LUFFA ABOBRA
JICARA PATOLA ANGURIA DISHRAG
HECHIMA CALABASH CUCURBIT
PEPONIDA PEPONIUM
GOURMAND EPICURE GLUTTON
GORMAND
GOURMET PALATE EPICURE
GOURMAND
GOUT GUT CLOT DROP SPLASH
PODAGRA PODAGRY
GOUTTE DROP ICICLE
GOUTWEED AXWEED ASHWEED
ACHEWEED AISEWEED BOLEWORT
GOATWEED GOUTWORT
GOUTY PODAGRAL PODAGRIC
GOVERN RUN WIN CURB KING LEAD
REDE REIN RULE SWAY WALD WARD
WIND YEME GUIDE JUDGE REGLE
STEER TREAT WIELD BRIDLE DIRECT
MANAGE ORDAIN POLICE POLICY
TEMPER COMMAND CONDUCT
CONTROL PRESIDE REFRAIN
DISPENSE DOMINATE IMPERATE
MODERATE OVERRULE OVERSWAY
POLICIZE REGULATE RESTRAIN
GOVERNESS ABBESS DUENNA
FRAULEIN MISTRESS
GOVERNING REGENT REGITIVE
GOVERNMENT GATE LAND RULE
KREIS POWER STATE STEER
DURBAR HAVANA POLICY RULING
CABINET CZARISM DIARCHY
DYARCHY RECTION REGENCY
REGIMEN TSARISM CIVILITY
ENDARCHY GOBIERNO HEGEMONY
ISOCRACY ISOCRYME KINGSHIP

STEERING
(— BY 10) DECARCHY
(— BY 2) DIARCHY DUARCHY
(— BY GOD) THEONOMY
(— BY WOMEN) GYNARCHY
(— OF CEYLON) DISSAVA
(— OF TURKEY) GATE PORTE
(INDIAN —) CIRCAR SIRCAR
(MALAYSIAN —) KOMPENI
(MOROCCAN —) MAGHZEN
MAKHZAN
GOVERNMENTAL ARCHICAL
GOVERNOR BAN BEY DEY EARL
KAID LORD NAIK TUTU VALI BANUS
CLEON DEWAN DIWAN HAKIM
NABOB NAZIM SHEIK SUBAH TUPAN
AUTHOR DYNAST GRIEVE LEGATE
MOODIR MYOWUN NAIGUE NAIQUE
PATESI PENLOP RECTOR REGENT
SACHEM SATRAP SHEIKH SHERIF
TUCHUN WARDEN CATAPAN
DAROGHA LEONATO PODESTA
SHEREEF TOPARCH TSUNGTU
VICEROY WIELDER AUTOCRAT
BURGRAVE ETHNARCH HOSPODAR
LANDVOGT MISTRESS RESIDENT
SUBAHDAR TETRARCH
(— OF ALGIERS) DEY
(— OF BURMA) WUN WOON
(— OF CEYLON) DISAWA
(— OF EGYPT) MUDIR
(— OF TAMMANY) SACHEM
(BYZANTINE —) EXARCH CATAPAN
(GERMAN —) LANDVOGT
(GREEK —) ETHNARCH
(JAPANESE —) SHOGUN TYCOON
(PAPAL —) LEGATE
(ROMAN —) TETRARCH
(SELJUK —) ATABEG ATABEK
(SPARTAN —) HARMOST
(TURKISH —) BEY WALI KEHAYA
GOVERNOR-GENERAL VALI
GOWK CUCKOO
GOWN GOR SAC GITE GORE HUKE
JAMA RAIL SACK SILK TOGA BANIA
DRESS FROCK GOUND HABIT JAMAH
MANTO TABBY TOOSH BANIAN
BANIYA CAFTAN CAMISE CANDYS
CHITON JESUIT JOHNNY KIMONO
KIRTLE KITTEL LEVITE MANTUA
ARISARD CASSOCK GARMENT
JOHNNIE SULTANA SULTANE
WRAPPER GANDOURA PEIGNOIR
(HAWAIIAN —) HOLOKU
GOYA CURRANT
GOYIM GENTES
GRAB NAB NAP RAP GLAM GOPE
GLAUM SCRAB COLLAR CRATCH
DIPPER NIPPER SNATCH CRAPPLE
GRABBLE GRAPNEL GRAPPLE
NIPPERS
GRABEN TROUGH
GRACE EST ORE BEAT ESTE GARB
HELD SWAY ADORN COULE HONOR
MENSE MENSK MERCY SLIDE THANK
VENUS BEAUTY BECOME BEDECK
CHARIS POLISH RELISH THALIA
AGGRACE CHARISM COMMEND
DIGNITY FINESSE GRATIFY MELISMA
MORDENT BACKFALL BEAUTIFY

BLESSING DECORATE EASINESS
ELEGANCE FELICITY GRATUITY
LEVATION ORNAMENT
(— OF FORM) FLOW SWAY
TOURNURE
GRACEFUL AIRY FEAT GENT GENTY
GRATE COMELY FEATLY FELINE
FLUENT GAINLY QUAINT SEEMLY
SILKEN VENUST ELEGANT FITTING
GENTEEL GRACILE SYLPHID
WILLOWY CHARMING DELICATE
GRACIOUS LEGGIERO MACEVOLE
SWANLIKE SYLPHISH
GRACEFULNESS JOLLITY
ELEGANCE
GRACEFULLY FAIR FEATLY HAPPILY
LEGGIERO
GRACELESS AWKWARD
GRACES CHARITES
GRACIOUS GOOD HEND HOLD KIND
MILD CIVIL GODLY HAPPY LUCKY
SUAVE WINLY BENIGN GENIAL
GENTLE GOODLY KINDLY AFFABLE
CORDIAL WINSOME BENEDICT
DEBONAIR GENEROUS HANDSOME
MERCIFUL PLEASING SOCIABLE
GRACIOUSLY FAIR SWEETLY
GRACIOUSNESS GRACE MENSK
FACILITY GRATUITY
GRACKLE BEO JACKDAW BOATTAIL
TINKLING TROOPIAL
GRADATION HUE CLIMAX NUANCE
GEOCLINE STRENGTH
GRADE CUT BANK CHOP EVEN FORM
MARK RANK SIZE STEP GLIDE LEVEL
ORDER PLANE SCORE SIEGE STAGE
ASCENT DEGREE RATING STAPLE
TRIAGE FAILURE INCLINE INSPECT
DEMISANG GRADIENT GRADUATE
MERIDIAN STANDARD
(— DOWN) FAULT
(— LUMBER) SURVEY
(— OF BEEF) GOOD CUTTER
(— OF LUMBER) CULL
(— OF OAK) WAINSCOT
(— OF OFFICER) CORNET
(— ROAD) IMPROVE
(ABLAUT —) GUNA
(SUPERIOR —) SUPER
(THIRD —) FAIR
GRADER PLANER CLASSER SCRAPER
GRADIENT GRADE LAPSE SLOPE
ASCENT INCLINE DOWNHILL
GRADIN GRADINO PREDELLA
GRADUAL EASY FLAT SLOW GRAIL
GENTLE LENTOUS STEPWISE
GRADUALLY GENTLY EDGINGLY
GRADATIM INCHMEAL
GRADUATE GRAD GRADE ALUMNA
DIVIDE FELLOW ALUMNUS GRADATE
BACHELOR
GRADUATED SCALAR MEASURED
GRADUATION CLICK
GRAFT BUD IMP CION WORK GRAFF
GRAVY INEYE BOODLE INARCH
SPLICE ENGRAFT IMPLANT JOBBERY
SQUEEZE TOPWORK APPROACH
BOODLING GRAFTING INSITION
GRAFTED ENTE
GRAFTER BOODLER

GRAFTING GRAFTAGE INSITION
GRAIL CUP GRAAL CHALICE
SANGRAAL
GRAIN JOT RUN RYE WAY CORN
CURN DANA KERN PILE RICE SAND
SEED WALE WOOD EMMER FIBER
FIBRE FUNDI GAVEL GLEBE GRIST
PANIC SCRAP SPARK STUFF TRACE
WHEAT ANNONA BARLEY BRAINS
CEREAL CURRAN GROATS KERNEL
FRUMENT GRANULE PANICLE
VICTUAL GRAINING PARTICLE
STRAIGHT SWEEPAGE
(— FOR MUSH) KASHA
(— FROM MASH TUN) DRAINS
(— LEFT AFTER HARVEST) GAVEL
SHACK
(— MEASURE) THRAVE
(— OF BOARD) BEAT
(— OF GOLD) PIPPIN
(— OF WOOD) BATE
(CHAFF OF —) BRAN
(COARSE —) THIRD
(COARSELY GROUND —) MEAL
GRITS KIBBLE
(DAMAGED —) SALVAGE
(EAR OF —) SPIKE RISSOM RIZZON
(GERMINATED —) MALT
(GROUND —) GRIST
(HANDFUL OF —) REAP
(HULLED —) GRITS GROUT GROATS
SHELLING
(HUSKED —) SHEALING SHILLING
(MIXED —) MASLIN
(MIXED —S) DREDGE
(PARCHED —) GRADDAN
(REFUSE —) SHAG DRAFF
(SACRIFICIAL —) ADOR
(SHOCK OF —) COP
(STACK OF —) HOVEL
(PL.) PICKLES RAGGING
GRAIN BEETLE CADELLE
GRAINER DICER BOARDER
GRAINSMAN THROWER DRAFFMAN
GRAIN SORGHUM DURRA SHALLU
GRAM KHESARI
(MILLIONTH —) GAMMA
GRAMMAR SYNTAX GRAMARY
PRISCIAN
GRAMMARIAN PRISCIAN
GRAMPUS ORC COWFISH DOLPHIN
SPRINGER
GRANARY GOLA GUNJ SILO GOLAH
GUNGE LATHE GARNER GIRNEL
GRANGE HORREUM RESERVE
CORNLOFT GRAINERY
GRAND OLD AIRY EPIC MAIN TALL
CHIEF GREAT LOFTY NOBLE PROUD
SHOWY SWELL WLONK ANDEAN
AUGUST COSMIC EPICAL FAMOUS
GLOBAL KINGLY LORDLY SIGHTY
SUPERB SWANKY EXALTER
IMMENSE STATELY SUBLIME
COSMICAL FOREMOST GLORIOUS
GORGEOUS IMPOSING MAJESTIC
SPLENDID
GRAND CANYON STATE ARIZONA
GRANDCHILD OE OY OYE
(GREAT —) IEROE
GRANDDAUGHTER NIECE

GRANDEE DON GRAND OMRAH
BASHAW GRANDO MAGNATE
GRANDEUR POMP STATE ESTATE
FIGURE PARADE MAJESTY
ELEGANCE GRANDEZA HAUTESSE
SPLENDOR VASTNESS
GRANDFATHER AIEL NONO BOBBY
GRAMP ATAVUS GRAMPS BELSIRE
GRANDAD GRANDPA GRANDFER
GUIDSIRE
(GREAT —) NONO
(GREAT-GREAT-GREAT —)
QUATRAYLE
GRANDILOQUENT TALL HEROIC
TURGID BOMBAST MAGNIFIC
GRANDIOSE GRAND COSMIC TURGID
COSMICAL IMPERIAL
GRANDMOTHER GRAM GRAN
LUCKY GRANNY GUDAME LUCKIE
BELDAME NOKOMIS BABUSHKA
GRANDAME
GRANDPARENT TUTU TUPUNA
GRAND SLAM VOLE
GRANDSON NEPHEW NEPOTE
GRANITE MOYITE RUNITE GREISEN
SYENITE ALASKITE RAPAKIVI
(— STATE) NEWHAMPSHIRE
(DECOMPOSED —) GROWAN
GRANITEWARE GRAYWARE
GRANNY TUTU BABUSHKA
GRANT AID FEU BOOK BOON CEDE
ENAM GALE GIFT GIVE HEAR LEND
LOAN MISE SEND STOW YARK
ADMIT ALLOT ALLOW AWARD
BONUS CHART COWLE FLOAT
FUERO LEASE SEIZE SPARE TITHE
YETTE YIELD ACCEDE ACCORD
AFFORD ASSENT BESTOW BETAKE
BETEEM BOUNTY CONFER DESIGN
EXTEND FIRMAN IMPART JAGEER
NOVATE OCTROI PATENT PERMIT
REMISE ADJUDGE COLLATE
CONCEDE CONSENT DISPONE
INDULGE LICENSE PRESENT
PROMISE SUBSIDY TRIBUTE
APPANAGE BESTOWAL CONTRACT
DONATION EXCHANGE MONOPOLY
PITTANCE TRANSFER
(— AS PROPER) ACCORD
(— OF LAND) FEU ENAM GALE PATA
SASAN CASATE
(— PERMISSION) ALLOW DISPENSE
(— RELIEF) FORGIVE
(INDIAN —) ENAM COWLE SASAN
JAGEER JAGHIR
(PL.) PORK
GRANTING IF ALTHO REMISE
ALTHOUGH
GRANTOR LESSOR
GRANULAR OPEN GRAINY
GRANULATE CORN KERN GRAIN
SUGAR
GRANULATED CORN GRANULAR
GRANULATION SUGARING
GRANULE GRIT GRANUM LUCULE
NODULE BIOBLAST GONIDIUM
GRANULET
(ALTMANN'S —S) BIOPLAST
(ICE —S) FRAZIL
GRAPE UVA VINE BERRY GRAIN

PINOT TOKAY ACINUS AGAWAM
ISABEL MALAGA MONICA MUSCAT
RAISIN VERDEA WORDEN CATAWBA
CONCORD HAMBURG MISSION
NIAGARA SULTANA VINIFER
CABERNET DELAWARE GRAPELET
ISABELLA LABRUSCA MALVASIA
MORILLON MOUNTAIN MUSCATEL
NUCULANE RIESLING SLIPSKIN
SYLVANER THOMPSON
(PL.) RAPE
GRAPEFRUIT POMOLO POMMELO
TORONJA
GRAPE HYACINTH MUSK
GRAPE JUICE MUST SAPA STUM
GRAPENUTS TERRAPIN
GRAPEROOT BERBERIS
GRAPH CHART CURVE OGIVE TRACE
CONTOUR DIAGRAM PROFILE
ISOPLETH
GRAPHITE WAD KISH LEAD WADD
KEESH PENCIL PLUMBAGO
GRAPNEL CROW DRAG GRAB CREEP
CREEPER GRABBLE GRAPPLE
SNIGGER GRABHOOK
GRAPPLE DOG CLOSE GRASP GRIPE
LATCH BUCKLE GRABBLE GRAPNEL
GRIPPLE SNIGGER SNIGGLE
WRESTLE
(— QUARRY) BIND
GRAPPLING IRON CLIP DRAG
CLASP CRAMP CORVUS CRAMPER
CRAMPON CREEPER GRAPNEL
GRAPPLE HARPAGO
GRAPTOLITHA XYLINA
GRASP HUG NAP SEE CLAM CLAW
CLUM FAKE FANG FIST GLAM GRAB
GRIP HAND HENT HOLD SNAP SPAN
TAKE VICE CATCH CINCH CLAMP
CLASP CLAUT CLEUK GRIPE GROPE
LATCH SAVVY SEIZE SENSE SHAKE
SPEND CLINCH CLUTCH COLLAR
FATHOM GOUPEN CLAUGHT
COMPASS ENCLOSE GRAPPLE
GRIPPLE SMITTLE CONCEIVE
HANDFAST HOLDFAST
(— FULLY) SWALLOW
(— MENTALLY) ENVISAGE
(— OF REALITY) EPIPHANY
GRASPING HARD NIPPY SNACK
GRABBY GREEDY GRIPPY HAVING
TAKING BROKING PUGGING
COVETOUS HANDGRIP
GRASS BON FAG FOG POA RAY
BENT COIX DISS DOOB GAMA HERB
ICHU KANS KUSA MUNJ MUSK RAGI
TORE ANKEE BARIT BROME COGON
COUCH CROFT DRAWK DRINN
FLAWN FUNDI GARSE GIRSE GLAGA
GRAMA HARIF HAVER HICHU ILLUK
KOGON KUSHA KWEEK PANIC QUILA
REESK ROOSA SEREH SPIRE STIPA
SUDAN ZORRA BARLEY BHABAR
BHARTI DARNEL EMOLOA FESCUE
GLUMAL QUITCH RAGGEE REDTOP
RIPGUT SCUTCH TOETOE TWITCH
ZACATE AMOURET CANNACH
DOGFOOT ESPARTO EULALIA
FESTUCA FINETOP FOXTAIL
GALLETA GOLDEYE HERBAGE

HORDEUM JARAGUA MATWEED
MUSCOVY PANICLE PASTURE
PIGROOT SETARIA SORGHUM
TIMOTHY TOCUSSO TUSSOCK
VETIVER ZACATON AEGILOPS
BLUESTEM BROWNTOP CALFKILL
CAMALOTE CELERITY COCKSPUR
DOGSTAIL DRAWLING DROPSEED
EELGRASS ELEUSINE FINEBENT
GAMELOTE MANGRASS MATGRASS
PASPALUM SANDBURR SANDSPUR
SANDSTAY SPANIARD SPARTINA
SPINIFEX SWEEPAGE TEOSINTE
WHITETOP
(— AMONG GRAIN) DRAWK
(— FOR STOCK) EATAGE
(— FOR THATCHING) BANGO
(— ON BORDER OF FIELD) RAND
(— READY FOR REAPING) SWATH
SWATHE
(AROMATIC —) KHUS CUSCUS
KHUSKHUS
(BEACH —) STAR
(BERMUDA —) DOOB SCUTCH
(COARSE —) FAG RISP TATH
COGON REESK SNIDDLE
(COUCH —) CUTCH KWEEK QUITCH
SCUTCH STROIL SQUITCH
(CURED —) HAY
(DEAD —) FOG FOGGAGE
(DITCH —) ENALID
(GOOSE —) CLIVERS CLEAVERS
(MEADOW —) POA
(NUT —) COCO COCOA
(ORCHARD —) DOGFOOT
(PASTURE —) TORE GRAMMA
(POVERTY —) HEATH
(QUAKING —) SHAKER
(REED —) CARRIZO
(REEDLIKE —) BENT DISS
(SUDAN —) GARAWI
GRASSERIE JAUNDICE
GRASSHOPPER GRIG CICADA
HOPPER QUAKER SAWYER TETTIX
ACRIDID CRICKET KATYDID SKIPPER
ACRIDIAN LANGOSTA
GRASSLAND HAM LEA RAKH VELD
VELDT BOTTOM MEADOW PATANA
LEYLAND PASTURE SAVANNA
(TRACT OF —) PRAIRIE
(PL.) SCHII
GRASS PEA LANG KHESARI
GRASSQUIT QUAT QUIT CIVITE
GRASS TREE BLACKBOY
GRASSY HERBY
GRATE JAR FRET GRIT RASP CHARK
DANDY DEVIL GRIND RANGE STOVE
ABRADE CHAFER SCRAPE SCREAR
SCREEK SCROOP GRATING
MANGRATE
(FALSE —) DANDY
GRATEFUL KIND WELCOME
THANKFUL
GRATEFULNESS GRATUITY
GRATIFICATION GLUT GUST
LUXURY RELISH REWARD SATIETY
DELICACY GRATUITY PLEASURE
TICKLING
GRATIFIED GLAD PROUD CHARMED
CONTENT PLEASED

GRATIFY PAY BABY FEED LUST
AMUSE FEAST FLESH GRACE
HUMOR MIRTH QUEME SAVOR
SERVE STILL WREAK ARRIDE
FOSTER OBLIGE PAMPER PLEASE
SALUTE TICKLE AGGRATE CONTENT
DELIGHT FLATTER GLADDEN
INDULGE SATISFY PLEASURE
(— THE PALATE) SEASON
GRATIFYING GOOD COMELY
DELICATE GRATEFUL
GRATING GRID HACK HARP HECK
JACK RACK CRATE CRUDE GRILL
HARSH RANGE TRAIL BAFFLE
CRATCH GITTER GRILLE HOARSE
WICKET BAFFLER ECHELLE
ECHELON BABRACOT CATAPULT
GRIDIRON SCRANNEL STRIDENT
GRATIS FREE FREELY BUCKSHEE
GRATITUDE THANK THANKS
GRATUITY
GRATUITOUS FREE WANTON
BASELESS NEEDLESS
GRATUITY FEE TIP DASH VAIL PILON
SPIFF SPILL CUMSHAW DASTURI
DOUCEUR PRESENT PRIMAGE
BAKSHISH BONAMANO BUCKSHEE
COURTESY DUSTOORI GRATUITO
REAPDOLE
(PL.) LARGESSE
GRAVE BED DRY LOW PIT SAD URN
BALK BIER CELL CIST DEEP DELF
FOSS GRIT HIGH HOME KIST LAIR
LAKE MOLD MOOL RUDE SADE
SAGE TOMB URNA DELFT FOSSE
GRAFF GROVE HEAVY MOULD
SHEOL SOBER STAID STIFF SUANT
VAULT BURIAL DEMURE GRIEVE
HEARSE SEDATE SEVERE SOLEMN
SOMBER SOMBRE STEADY AUSTERE
EARNEST FUNERAL PITHOLE
SERIOSO SERIOUS SOBERLY
DECOROUS MATRONAL SERMONIC
GRAVECLOTHES LINEN
GRAVEDIGGER BURIER FOSSOR
PITMAN
GRAVEL GRIT ARENA GEEST GRAIL
CHESIL RANGLE SAMMEL SHILLA
BALLAST CALICHE CHANNEL
RATCHEL STANNER BLINDING
(— AND SAND) DOBBIN
(— DEPOSIT) LEAD
(— IN KIDNEYS) ARENA
(LOOSE —) SLITHER
(SCREENED —) HOGGINS
GRAVELLY HASKY CHISELLY
GLAREOUS
GRAVELY SADLY DEEPLY
GRAVE MOUND TUMULUS
GRAVER BURIN STYLE PLASTIC
SCORPER
GRAVESTONE BAUTA PLANK STELA
STELE STONE TABLE CIPPUS
JUMPER THROUGH
GRAVEYARD CEMETERY
GRAVID HEAVY WOMBED PREGNANT
GRAVIMETER DOODLEBUG
GRAVITATIONAL UNIT SLUG
GRAVITY WEIGHT DIGNITY EARNEST
SOBRIETY

GRAVY JUS SOP BREE FOND LEAR
BLANC BUNCE JIPPER
GRAY ASH BAT FOG ASHY BEAR
BLAE BLUE DOVE DUSK GREY GRIS
GULL HOAR IRON LEAD SALT ACIER
CAMEL CRANE HOARY LYART
MOUSE STEEL WHITE CASTOR
CINDER DENVER FROSTY FRUSTY
GREIGE GRISLY LEADEN NICKEL
NUTRIA PEWTER QUAKER STRING
BLUNKET CRUISER GRANITE
GRIZARD GRIZZLE GRIZZLY
HUELESS MURINUS NEUTRAL
PELICAN PILGRIM SARKARA
SPARROW ALUMINUM CHARCOAL
CINEREAL CINEROUS EVENGLOW
PLATINUM PLYMOUTH
(DARKEST —) BLACK
(GOOSE —) LAMA
(MOLE —) TAUPE
(MOTH —) SHEEPSKIN
GRAYBACK DOWITCH GRAYCOAT
GREYBACK
GRAY CRANE COOLEN COOLUNG
GRAYLING PINK OMBRE UMBER
HERRING UMBRANA BLUEFISH
SALMONID
GRAY PARROT JAKO
GRAYNESS CANITIES
GRAYSBY CONY CONEY
GRAY WHALE RIPSACK GRAYBACK
HARDHEAD
GRAZE BITE CROP FEED SKIM AGIST
BRUSH GRASS GRIDE RANGE
SCAMP SCUFF SHAVE SKIFF STOCK
BROWSE CREASE FODDER GLANCE
RIPPLE SCRAPE SCRASE PASTURE
GRAZIER PASTURER SQUATTER
TREKBOER
GRAZING BIT FEED GRASS COLLOP
RASANT FOLDING PASCUAGE
GREASE COOM SAIM ADEPS BLECK
COOMB SMEAR SPICK ARMING
AXUNGE CREESH ENSEAM LIQUOR
POMATE ALEMITE SAINDOUX
(— IN HARD CAKES) SEAK
(PIG'S —) MORT
(WOOL —) YOK DEGRAS LANOLIN
GREASE-HEELS GRAPES
GREASER DOPER
GREASEWOOD CHICO CHEMIZO
GREASY FAT GLET OILY RICH FATTY
PORKY YOLKY SMEARY TRAINY
CREESHY TALLOWY UNCTUOUS
GREAT BIG FAR FAT FIT OLD BARO
DEEP DREE FELL FINE GONE GURT
HUGE KEEN MAIN MUCH RIAL TALL
UNCO VAST VILE AMPLE BURRA
CHIEF FELON GRAND LARGE MEKIL
STOUR SWEET SWELL YEDER
FIERCE GAPING HEROIC MICKLE
NATION STRONG CAPITAL EMINENT
EXTREME GALLOWS HOWLING
IMMENSE INTENSE STAVING TITANIC
VIOLENT VOLUMED ALMIGHTY
CRACKING ELEVATED ENORMOUS
FAVORITE GALACTIC GALAXIAN
GIGANTIC HORRIBLE INFINITE
(— LAND) ALASKA
(IMMEASURABLY —) ABYSMAL

(VERY —) MAIN SORE AWFUL STEEP ARDENT DEADLY IMMANE INGENT MORTAL EXTREME FRANTIC GHASTLY HOWLING SUBLIME DREADFUL MOUNTAIN

GREAT AUK PENGUIN PINWING GAREFOWL

GREAT BRITAIN (SEE ENGLAND)

GREATCOAT GREGO JEMMY JOSEPH OVERCOAT

GREATER SUPERIOR

GREATER STITCHWORT HEAD SNAPPER HEADACHE SNAPJACK SNAPWORT

GREATER YELLOWLEGS YELPER

GREATEST UTMOST EXTREME MAXIMAL

(— POSSIBLE) ALL SUPREME

GREAT-GRANDCHILD IEROE

GREAT GRANDFATHER NONO BESAIEL GRANDSIR

GREAT LAKE ERIE HURON ONTARIO MICHIGAN SUPERIOR

GREATLY FAR MUY FELL MUCH AMAIN SWITH FINELY MAINLY STRONG SWYTHE SWEETLY WOUNDLY

GREAT MOLE RAT ZEMMI ZEMNI

GREATNESS FORCE GRANDEUR GRANDEZA MUCHNESS

GREAT RAGWEED KINGHEAD

GREAT TITMOUSE SHARPSAW

GREAVE JAMB JAMBE JAMBEAU

(PL.) CRAP HOSE GRAVES

GREBE LEAD LOON DIVER GAUNT WITCH DIPPER DOBBER DUCKER FINFOOT HENBILL PYGOPOD ARSEFOOT CARGOOSE DABCHICK DIDAPPER GRUIFORM

GRECE GRICE DEGREE GRISSEN

GREECE

ANCIENT LOCATION: ELIS DORIS PYLOS ACHAEA ACTIUM ATTICA DELPHI EPIRUS HELLAS LOCRIS PHOCIS SPARTA THEBES TIRYNS BOEOTIA CORINTH EPEIROS LACONIA MACEDON MEGARIS MYCENAE PAESTUM

ARMY UNIT: TAXIS

BAY: ELEUSIS SALAMIS PHALERON

CAPE: KRIOS MALEA SPADA AKRITAS MATAPAN SIDEROS DREPANON GRAMBYSA TAINARON

CAPITAL: ATHENS ATHENAI

COIN: OBOL HECTE DIOBOL LEPTON STATER DRACHMA DIOBOLON

COLUMN: DORIC IONIC CORINTHIAN

DANCE: PYRRHIC ROMAIKA

DIALECT: COAN ATTIC DORIC ELEAN EOLIC IONIC AEOLIC MELIAN THERAN ACHAEAN ARCADIAN

DISTRICT: ARTA ELIS CANEA CHIOS CORFU CRETE DRAMA

EVROS KHIOS PELLA SAMOS ZANTE ACHAEA ACHAIA ATTICA EPIRUS EUBOEA KILKIS KNANIA KOZANE LARISA LESBOS LEUKAS PHOCIS PIERIA SERRAI THRACE XANTHE AETOLIA ARCADIA ARGOLIS BOEOTIA CORINTH KAVALLA LACONIA LARISSA LASETHI MTATHOS PREVEZA RHODOPE CYCLADES IOANNINA KARDITSA KASTORIA MAGNESIA MESSENIA PHLORINA RETHYMNE SALONIKA THESSALY TRIKKALA MACEDONIA

GULF: VOLOS ATHENS MESARA PATRAI PATRAS ARGOLIS CORINTH KAVALLA KNANION LACONIA LEPANTO MESSINI RENDINA SARONIC STRIMON MESSENIA SALONIKA SINGITIC THERMAIC TORONAIC

HOME OF GODS: OLYMPUS

ISLAND: DIA IOS KEA KOS NIO CEOS KEOS MILO SYME SYRA CHIOS CORFU CRETE DELOS KASOS KHIOS LEROS MELOS MILOS NAXOS PAROS PAXOI PAXOS PSARA RODOS SAMOS SARIA SYROS TELOS TENOS THERA THIRA TINOS ZANTE ANAPHE ANDROS CANDIA CERIGO CHALKE EUBOEA EVVOIA GAVDOS IKARIA ITHACA ITHAKI LEMNOS LESBOS LEUKAS LEVKAS PATMOS RHENEA RHODES SIFNOS SKYROS THASOS AMORGOS CIMOLUS CYTHERA KERKYRA KIMOLOS KYTHERA KYTHNOS LEVITHA MYKONOS NISYROS SALAMIS SIPHNOS KALYMNOS MYTILENE SANTORIN SERIPHOS

ISLANDS: IONIAN CYCLADES SPORADES DODECANESE STROPHADES

LAKE: KARLA VOLVE COPAIS KOPAIS PRESPA TOPOLIA KASTORIA TACHINOS VISTONIS

LETTER: MU NU PI XI CHI ETA PHI PSI RHO TAU BETA IOTA ZETA ALPHA DELTA GAMMA KAPPA OMEGA SIGMA THETA LAMBDA EPSILON OMICRON UPSILON

MARKET PLACE: AGORA

MEASURE: PIK BEMA PIKI POUS BARIL CADOS CHOUS CUBIT DIGIT MARIS PEKHE PODOS PYGON XYLON ACAENA BACHEL BACILE BARILE COTULA DICHAS GRAMME HEMINA KOILON ORGYIA PALAME PECHYS SCHENE AMPHORA CHENICA CHOENIX CYATHOS DIAULOS HEKTEUS METRETA STADION STADIUM STREMMA CONDYLOS DAKTYLOS DEKAPODE DOLICHOS MEDIMNOS METRETES PALAISTE PLETHRON

PLETHRUM SPITHAME STATHMOS

MOUNTAIN: IDA IDHI OSSA ATHOS PAROS ELIKON PARNON PELION PILION WITSCH HELICON OLYMPUS VURANON KRAGNOVO SMOLIKAS TAYGETOS PARNASSUS

MOUNTAINS: OETA OTHRYS PINDUS RODOPI RHODOPE HYMETTOS TAYGETUS

NAME: ELLAS HELLAS

PENINSULA: ACTE AKTE AKTI MOREA SITHONIA PELOPONNESE

PORT: SYRA CORFU PYLOS SYROS VOLOS MEGARA PATRAI PATRAS KAVALLA KERKYRA PIRAEUS SALONIKA

RIVER: IRI ARDA ARTA AURO AXIOS DOONA EVROS LERNA ALFIOS NESTOS PENEUS PINIOS STRUMA VARDAR ALPHEUS EUROTAS EVROTAS ILISSOS PENEIOS ROUFIAS SARANTA STRIMON ACHELUOS AKHELOOS ALIAKMON KEPHISOS RHOUPHIA

RUINS: DELOS PELLA SAMOS CORINTH ELEUSIS ELEVSIS ACROPOLIS

SEA: CRETE AEGEAN IONIAN MIRTOON

STATE: PHOCIS

TOWN: IOS KEA KOS ARTA ELIS KYME PETA SYME YDRA ADREA AGYIA ARGOS CANEA CHIOS CORFU DRAMA KARYA MELOS NAXOS NEMEA PELLA POROS PSARI PYLOS PYRGI SAMOS SYROS TENOS VAMOS VATHY VOLOS VYRON ZANTE ACTIUM ATHENS CANDIA DAPHNI DELPHI EDESSA ITHACA JANINA KOZANE LARISA MEGARA NIKAIA PATRAS RHODES SERRAI SERRES SPARTA THEBES TIRYNS XANTHE ATHENAI CORINTH ELEUSIS KERKYRA LARISSA MYCENAE PIRAEUS IOANNINA KOMOTINE MARATHON PHARSALA SALONIKA TRIKKALA

VALLEY: NEMEA

VERNACULAR: DEMOTIC

WEIGHT: MNA OKA OKE MINA OBOL LITRA LIVRE MANEH POUND DIOBOL DRAMME KANTAR OBOLOS OBOLUS STATER TALENT CHALCON CHALQUE DRACHMA DIOBOLON TALANTON

WOMEN: THYIAD

GREED AVARICE AVIDITY HOGGERY CUPIDITY

GREEDINESS AVARICE AVIDITY GULOSITY

GREEDY AVID GAIR GORB YELP EAGER GUTTY YIVER GRABBY GUNDIE KITISH STINGY GLUTTON

GRIPPLE HOODOCK MISERLY
PIGGISH COVETOUS ESURIENT
GRASPING RAVENOUS
GREEK GREW ATTIC HADJI KOINE
METIC ARGIVE IONIAN KLEPHT
ACHAIAN GRECIAN GRIFFON
HELLENE GRECANIC HELLENIC
ITALIOTE SICELIOT
GREEN LEEK VERD VERT CRUDE
FRESH CALLOW VIRENT VORENT
NOUVEAU SINOPLE UNFIRED
VERDANT BAYBERRY IMMATURE
NOUVELLE VAGABOND VIRIDIAN
WEDGWOOD WOODLAND
(— MOUNTAIN STATE) VERMONT
(COOKED —S) SALAD
(NILE —) BOA
(PALE —) ALOE ALOES
(YELLOWISH —) GLAUZY ABSINTHE
GLAUCOUS
GREEN AMARANTH REDROOT
GREENBACK FROGSKIN
(PL.) GREEN LETTUCE
GREEN CORMORANT SHAG
GREENFISH BLUEFISH
GREENHEART BIBIRU BEBEERU
GREEN HERON KIALEE
GREENHORN JAY YAP JAKE IKONA
GREENY SUCKER SOFTHORN
GREENHOUSE STOVE GREENERY
HOTHOUSE ORANGERY COOLHOUSE

GREENLAND

AIR BASE: THULE
BAY: DISKO BAFFIN MELVILLE
CAPE: JAAL GRIVEL WALKER
BISMARCK BREWSTER
FAREWELL LOWENORN
CAPITAL: GODTHAAB
DISCOVERER: ERIC
MOUNTAIN: FOREL PAYER
KHARDYU
STRAIT: DAVIS DENMARK
TOWN: ETAH NORD THULE
UMANAK GODHAVN IVIGTUT
GODTHAAB

GREENLING BOREGAT BODIERON
LORICATE
GREEN MONKEY GUENON
GREENNESS VERD VERT VERDURE
VERDANCY VIRIDITY
GREEN PIKE JACK
GREENROOM FOYER
GREENSHANK TATTLER
GREENSTONE POUNAMU
GREEN SUNFISH REDEYE
GREENWEED WOODWAX
GREEN WOODPECKER ECCLE
SPRITE YOCKEL YUKKEL HEWHALL
HEWHOLE SNAPPER SPEIGHT
YAFFLER WOODHACK WOODWALL
GREET CRY JOY CROW HAIL HALSE
ACCOST HERALD SALUTE ADDRESS
RECEIVE WELCOME
GREETING HOW HIYA ALOHA GREET
HELLO HOWDY KOMBO ACCOST
CHEERO SALAAM SALUTE SHALOM
ADDRESS CHEERIO COMMEND
SLAINTE WELCOME

GREGARIOUS GREGAL SOCIAL
GREGE NUTRIA
GRENADE EGG TROMBE GRENADO
FIREBALL PINEAPPLE
GRENADIER RATTAIL WHIPTAIL
GRENADINE FLORENCE
GREY (SEE GRAY)
GREYHOUND GREW BANJARA
SAPLING WHIPPET
GRID BOOCAN BUCCAN GRIDDLE
GRIDIRON
GRIDDLE COMAL GRILL GIRDLE
GRILLE BRANDER
GRIDDLE CAKE AREPA LATKE
CHAPATTY CORNCAKE FLAPJACK
SLAPJACK
GRIDIRON GRID GRILL TRAIL
BRANDER BROILER GRIDDLE
GRIEF WOE CARE DILL DOLE DOOL
DREE HARM HURT MOAN MOOD
PAIN RUTH SORE TEEN TINE AGONY
DOLOR GRAME RUING TRIAL
WRONG BARRAT DESIRE MISHAP
REGRET SORROW STOUND WONDER
ANGUISH CHAGRIN EMOTION
FAILURE OFFENSE SADNESS
THOUGHT TROUBLE WAESUCK
WAYMENT DISASTER DISTRESS
HARDSHIP
(— STEM) KELLY
(SECRET —) CANKER
GRIESEN ZWITTER
GRIEVANCE BEEF GRIEF BURDEN
BYGONE GRAVAMEN HARDSHIP
GRIEVE CARE DOLE DUMP EARN
ERME HURT PAIN PINE SIGH WAIL
GRAME GRIPE MOURN SORRY
WOUND YEARN ATHINK CORSIE
LAMENT SORROW AFFLICT CHAGRIN
CONDOLE GRIZZLE TROUBLE
WAYMENT COMPLAIN DISTRESS
GRIEVED WOE GRAME SORRY
GRIEVING SORRY
GRIEVOUS SAD DEEP DERF HARD
SORE CHARY DIRTY GRIEF HEAVY
SORRY WEARY BITTER DREARY
SEVERE SHREWD HEINOUS WEIGHTY
DOLOROUS
GRIEVOUSLY FOULLY SORELY
HEAVILY
GRIFFE SPUR
GRIFFIN GRIPE GRYPHON EPIMACUS
GRILL REJA BRACE BROIL DEVIL
TRAIL AFFLICT BROILER GRILLADE
GRILLE FACE REJA HAZARD
GRILLROOM GROOM
GRILSE PEAL FINNAC GRAWLS
BOTCHER FORKTAIL
GRIM GASH SOUR BLEAK CRUEL
GAUNT STERN GRIMLY GRISLY
HORRID SULLEN TORVID GHASTLY
GRIZZLY HIDEOUS TORVOUS
PITILESS RUTHLESS
GRIMACE MOP MUG POT FACE GIRN
IRPE MOUE MUMP YIRN FLEER
MOUTH SNEER SNOOT GIMBLE
SHEYLE STITCH MURGEON SIMAGRE
GRIME DIRT SMUT COLLY SMOUCH
SMUTCH
GRIMME COQUETOON

GRIMNESS TORVITY
GRIMY DINGY GRUBBY SCABROUS
GRIN DRAD GIRN MUMP FLEER
SNEER SIMPER GRIZZLE
GRIND DIG SAP BONE BRAY CHEW
FILE GRUN MILL MULL MUZZ SMUG
SWOT CRUSH FLOAT FLOUR GRATE
GRIDE GRIST QUERN CRUNCH
DRUDGE POWDER EMERIZE GRISTLE
SWOTTER LEVIGATE
(— COARSELY) KIBBLE
(— SMALL) BRAY
(— TEETH) GNASH GRATE GRINT
GRISBET
GRINDER CRASH MULLER BRUISER
GRINDING BREAK MOLAR ABRASION
(— OF MEAL) BREAK GRIST
GRINDSTONE MANO PAVER STONE
GRIP BITE BURR CLIP FANG FIST
HOLD HOLT TAKE VICE CHOKE
CINCH CLAMP CLASP GRASP GRIPE
PINCH SALLY SEIZE BARREL CLINCH
CLUTCH CRADLE FREEZE EMBRACE
HANDBAG HOLDING SEIZURE
ADHESION FOOTLOCK HANDFAST
HANDGRIP HANDHOLD
(— OF A SWORD) FUSEAU
(— OF BELL ROPE) SALLY
(— TO A SPAR) DOG
GRIPE FRIB BITCH CREATE HOLLER
NATTER SNATCH GRIZZLE
COMPLAIN
GRIPER GRIZZLER
GRIPES TORMINA
GRIPING GRIPPLE PINCHING
GRIPPER KEEPER NIPPER
GRIPPING STONY STONEY
GRIQUA BASTARD BASTAARD
GRISLY GRIM GHASTLY GRIZZLY
HIDEOUS GRUESOME
GRISON HURON GALICTIS
GRIST PABULUM
GRIT SAND GRIND BOTTOM BRAVERY
DECISION GRITROCK RUBSTONE
(PL.) CUTLINGS
GRITH MUND GYRTH
GRITTY SANDY SHARP GRISTY
CHISELLY SABULINE SABULOUS
GRIVET TOTA WAAG GEUNON
NISNAS
GRIZZLED GRISLY STREAKED
GRIZZLY BEAR (— STATE)
CALIFORNIA
GROAN MOAN ROME GRANK GRUNT
STECH COMPLAIN
GROAT BIT FLAG GILL HARP
GROCER SPICER EPICIER PEPPERER
GROCERY PULPERIA
GROG RUMBO TEMPER CHAMOTTE
GROGGERY SHANTY GROGSHOP
GROGGY SHAKY UNSTEADY
WAVERING
GROGSHOP SHANTY DOGGERY
GROGGERY
GROIN LISK PIER SHARE CLITCH
INGUEN GRUNZIE
GROMMET BECKET COLLAR EYELET
CRINGLE GARLAND
GROMWELL REDROOT GRAYMILL

GROOM LAD MAFU NEAT SYCE CURRY DRESS MAFOO STRAP SWIPE TIGER BARBER FETTLE FOGGER GUINEA MEHTAR OSTLER HOSTLER MARSHAL COISTREL GROOMLET STRAPPER

GROOVE RUT BEAD DADO GAIN KERF LUCE PORT RAKE SLOT CANAL CHASE CROZE FLUTE GLYPH GORGE GOUGE GUIDE JOINT QUIRK REGAL RIFLE RIGOL SCARF SCORE STRIA SWAGE CREASE CULLIS FULLER FURROW GUTTER KEYWAY RABBET RAGGLE RAGLET REBATE RIFFLE RUNNER SCROBE SULCUS THROAT TRENCH CHAMFER CHANNEL GARLAND KEYHOLE PLOWING SULCATE BOTHRIUM GROOVING PHILTRUM

(— **IN AUGER**) POD

(— **IN COLUMN**) FLUTE

(— **IN MASONRY**) RAGGLE

(— **IN STAVES**) CROZE

(— **IN STONE**) JAD

(— **IN TIRE**) SIPE

(— **ON UPPER LIP**) PHILTRUM

(— **ON WEEVIL**) SCROBE

(— **ON WHALE**) SCARF

(— **UNDER COPING**) GORGE

(—**S ON ROCK**) LAPIES

GROOVED FLUTED EXARATE SULCATE

GROOVER FLUTER

GROPE CLAM CLAW FEEL POKE GLAUM GRAIP FUMBLE GUDDLE GRABBLE GRAPPLE GROPPLE GRUBBLE SCRABBLE

GROSBEAK FINCH HAWFINCH

GROSGRAIN ROYALE

GROSS FAT DULL FOUL RANK CRASS FOGGY GREAT GUTTY LARGE THICK WHOLE ANIMAL COARSE EARTHY FILTHY GREASY SORDID STRONG BLOATED FULSOME CLODDISH FLAGRANT INDECENT SLUTTISH

GROSSO MATAPAN

GROTESQUE ANTIC WOOZY BIZARRE CROTESCO FANCIFUL

GROTTO CAVE GROT SPEOS CAVERN

GROUCH SULK CRANK GROUSE SOURBALL SOURPUSS

GROUND SEW SOD SUE BASE CLOD DIRT FOLD FOND GIST LAND MOLD REST ROOT SOIL STAY WOLD EARTH FIELD FIRTH FOUND MOULD PLACE SCORE TRAIN TUTOR VENUE CREASE MATTER REASON SMACKED FORELAND INITIATE

(— **AT TOP OF SHAFT**) BANK

(— **COVERED WITH RUBBLE**) TITI

(— **FOR COMPLAINT**) BEEF

(— **OF FLAG**) FIELD

(— **OF LACE**) FOND

(— **OVERLYING TIN DEPOSIT**) BURDEN

(**BOGGY** —) SOG SNAPE

(**BROKEN** —) HAG

(**BURYING** —) CEMETERY

(**CAMPING** —) AUTOCAMP

(**COLLEGE** —**S**) CAMPUS

(**DUMPING** —) TIP TOOM

(**FALLOW** —) BRISE

(**FEEDING** —) HAUNT

(**FIRM-HOLDING** —) LANDFANG

(**FISHING** —) HAAF

(**FROZEN** —) TJAELE

(**GRASSY** —) LAWN CLOWRE

(**HARD** —) HARDPAN

(**HUNTING** —) CHASE

(**LOW** —) INCH SWALE TALAO

(**MIDDLE** —) LIMBO

(**NEW ENCLOSED** —) TINING

(**ORIGINAL** —) URGRUND

(**PASTURE** —) HIRSEL

(**RECREATION** —) PARK

(**RISING** —) HURST HYRST

(**SLOPING** —) CLEVE

(**SOLID** —) HILL

(**SPONGY** —) BOG

(**SWAMPY** —) PUXY CRIPPLE

(**UNCULTIVATED** —) JUNGLE

(**UNUSED** —) AREA

(**WET WASTE** —) MOOR

(**PL.**) GROUT STOCK

GROUND HEMLOCK SHINWOOD

GROUND HOG MARMOT

GROUND IVY GILL HEWE HOVE JILL YARROW ALEHOOF CATFOOT GAGROOT MILFOIL TUNHOOF FOALFOOT

GROUNDLESS IDLE FALSE BASELESS

GROUNDLINE SETLINE

GROUNDMAN GRUNT

GROUNDMASS PASTE CEMENT MATRIX

GROUNDNUT GOBBE PEANUT PIGNUT

GROUND PINE FOXTAIL STAGHORN

GROUNDSEL SIMSON DOGBUSH SENCION SENECIO BINDWEED BIRDSEED

GROUNDSMAN CURATOR

GROUND SQUIRREL GOPHER GRINNY SUSLIK SCIURID SOUSLIK SCIURINE

GROUND THRUSH PITTA

GROUNDWORK BASE FOND FUND BASIS FUNDUS

GROUP MOB SET BAND BEVY BODY CREW DECK FOLD GANG KNOT PAIR RING SECT SORT STEW TREF ARRAY BATCH BREED CLASS CLUMP COVEY FIRCA FLOCK GENUS GLOBE PLUMP SABHA SKULK SQUAD STACK TALLY WHEEN CLUTCH COHORT FAMILY GRUPPO PARCEL RUBRIC AGGROUP BATTERY BOILING BOUROCK BRACKET COLLEGE COMPANY CONSORT FELLOWS FLUTTER QUOTITY SECTION SEVERAL SOCIETY ALLIANCE CATEGORY CLASSIFY DIVISION FAISCEAU FLOTILLA GROUPING

(— **OF 10 NOTES**) DECUPLET

(— **OF 1000**) CHILIAD

(— **OF 12**) DOZEN

(— **OF 2 VOWELS**) DIGRAM DIGRAPH

(— **OF 40 THREADS**) BEER BIER

(— **OF 60 PIECES**) SHOCK

(— **OF ANGELS**) FLIGHT

(— **OF ARTIFACTS**) CACHE

(— **OF BADGERS**) CETE

(— **OF BUILDINGS**) BLOCK

(— **OF CASTINGS**) SPRAY

(— **OF CATS**) CLOWDER

(— **OF CELLS**) GLAND ISLET CENTER CORONA EPITHEM SEMILUNE

(— **OF DECOYS**) STOOL

(— **OF DEITIES**) CABEIRI

(— **OF DIALECTS**) AEOLIC

(— **OF EELS**) SWARM

(— **OF EIGHT**) OCTAD OCTET OCTETTE

(— **OF FAMILIES**) FINE

(— **OF FIVE**) PENTAD CINQUAIN

(— **OF FOUR**) MESS QUARTET

(— **OF FRIENDS**) BUNCH

(— **OF FURNISHINGS**) ENSEMBLE

(— **OF HAITIANS**) COMBITE COUMBITE

(— **OF HOUSES**) BOROUGH

(— **OF HUTS**) BUSTI KRAAL BUSTEE

(— **OF ISOGLOSSES**) BUNDLE

(— **OF KINDRED**) SIOL

(— **OF KINSMEN**) AHL

(— **OF LAYMEN**) COFRADIA

(— **OF LIONS**) PRIDE

(— **OF LISTENERS**) AUDIENCE

(— **OF MARTENS**) RICHESSE

(— **OF MILITARY VEHICLES**) DEADLINE

(— **OF MOLDINGS**) DANCETTE

(— **OF NINE**) ENNEAD NONARY

(— **OF NUCLEONS**) SHELL

(— **OF OFFSPRING**) CLUTCH

(— **OF ORGANISMS**) FORM STRAIN

(— **OF PARACHUTISTS**) STICK

(— **OF PERSONS**) BAG CLUB KNOT SWAD CROWD DROVE CIRCLE GAGGLE KENNEL

(— **OF RETORTS**) BENCH SETTING

(— **OF SCULPTURE**) MORTORIO

(— **OF SEVEN**) HEPTAD SEPTET HEBDOMAD

(— **OF SIX**) HEXAD SENARY

(— **OF SLAVES**) COFFLE

(— **OF SOILS**) LATERITE

(— **OF SOLDIERS**) DRAFT COHORT

(— **OF STARS**) ASTERISM

(— **OF STRATIFIED BEDS**) FACIES

(— **OF STUDENTS**) SEMINAR

(— **OF SYLLABLES**) FOOT

(— **OF SYMBOLS**) FORMULA

(— **OF SYMPTOMS**) SYNDROME

(— **OF TEN**) DECADE DENARY

(— **OF TENTS**) CAMP CANVAS

(— **OF THEATERS**) CIRCUIT

(— **OF THREE**) TRIO GLEEK TRIAD TRINE

(— **OF TRAITS**) COMPLEX

(— **OF TROUT**) HOVER

(— **OF VERSES**) SYSTEM

(— **OF WINGS**) RUFFLE

(— **OF WIRES**) DROP

(— OF WORDS) ACCENT GENITIVE
(ASSISTANCE —) AINI
(ATOMIC —) LIGAND
(AUTHORITATIVE —) CONCLAVE
(CONFUSED —) SNARL
(CORE —) CADRE
(ECOLOGICAL —) GUILD
(ETHNIC —) LI ACHANG BALAHI
BATTAK ETHNOS CHINGPAW
(ETHNOLOGICAL —) ISLAND
(EXCLUSIVE —) ELECT
(FAMILY —) GWELY
(HARMONIOUS —) DOVECOTE
(INTIMATE —) COTERIE
(KINSHIP —) SUSU
(LIVELY —) GALA
(NON-MOSLEM —) MILLET
(PAGAN —) BATAK BATANGAN
(PHILOSOPHICAL —) CENACLE
(POLITICAL —) BLOC PARTY
COMMONS
(SEGREGATED —) GHETTO
(SOCIAL —) KITH SEPT TRIBE
FAMILY INGROUP
GROUPED AGMINATE
GROUPER GAG HIND MERO GUASA
HAMEL SCAMP AGUAJI BONACI
CHERNA GROPER HAMLET WARSAW
BACALAO GARLOPA GARRUPA
GOURAMI JEWFISH REDFISH
LAPULAPU REDBELLY ROCKFISH
SCIRENGA SERRANID
(YOUNG —) SNAPPER
GROUPING KIND ARRAY BATTERY
KINDRED DIVISION GROUPAGE
SODALITY SYNTAGMA
(— OF POTTERY) SERIES
GROUSE CRAB BITCH GANGA
GORHEN GROUCH HOOTER
ATTAGEN CHEEPER GAZELLE
GORCOCK PINTAIL COMPLAIN
MOORBIRD MOORFOWL
(YOUNG —) POULT SQUEALER
GROUT GROOT LARRY SLUSH
GROUTING
GROUTER GUNITER
GROVE CAMP HEWT HOLT MOTT
SHAW TOFT TOPE WONG ALTIS
BLUFF COPSE GLADE HURST HYRST
GARDEN GREAVE GROVET ISLAND
OLIVET SPRING ACADEMY ARBORET
BOSCAGE COPPICE THICKET
WOODING SERINGAL WODELEIE
(— OF ALDERS) CARR
(— OF MANGO TREES) TOPE
(— OF OAKS) ENCINAL
(— OF OSIERS) HOLT
(— OF SUGAR MAPLES) CAMP
(SACRED —) ALTIS SARNA
(SMALL —) SHAW
GROVEL FAWN ROLL CREEP CRINGE
TUMBLE WALLOW WELTER GRABBLE
FLOUNDER
GROVELING WORMY HANGDOG
REPTILE
GROW AGE BUD GET HIT ICH WAX
BOLL COME CROP ECHE ITCH MAKE
RISE SEED THEE THRO WEAR EDIFY
ISSUE PLANT PROVE RAISE SHOOT

SWELL ACCRUE BATTEN BECOME
DOUBLE EXPAND EXTEND GATHER
SPRING SPROUT THRIVE AUGMENT
BROADEN BURGEON DEVELOP
DISTEND ENLARGE IMPROVE
NOURISH ADOLESCE FLOURISH
HEIGHTEN INCREASE THRODDEN
(— ANGRY) STIVER
(— BETTER) IMPROVE
(— DARK) GLOAM GLOOM NIGHT
DARKEN DARKLE
(— FAINT) DIE APPAL APPALL
(— FAT) FEED BATTEN
(— IN LENGTH) ELONGATE
(— IRREGULARLY) SCRAMBLE
(— LESS) SLAKE ASSUAGE
DECREASE
(— LIGHT) DAWN
(— LUXURIANTLY) THRIVE
(— MAD) WOOD
(— MILD) GIVE
(— OLD) AGE OLD SENESCE
(— OVER) INVADE
(— PLUMP) PLIM
(— RICH) FATTEN
(— SOUND) HEAL
(— SPIRITLESS) FLAG
(— STILL) HUSH
(— STRONG) FORTIFY STORKEN
(— THIN) PEAK
(— TO HEAD) CABBAGE
(— TO STALK) SPINDLE
(— TOGETHER) KNIT ACCRETE
CONCREW COOSIFY COALESCE
(— UNDER GLASS) GLASS
(— UP) STEM ACCRUE
(— WEAK) FAINT
GROWING GROWY CRESCENT
CRESCIVE
(— ANGRY) IRASCENT
(— IN CLUSTERS) RACEMOSE
(— IN GRAIN FIELDS) SEGETAL
(— IN HEAPS) ACERVATE
(— IN MEADOW) PRATAL
(— IN PAIRS) BINATE
(— IN WATER) AQUATIC
(— ON A STEM) CAULINE
(— OUT) ENATE
(— RAPIDLY) BOOMING
(— THICKLY) HOUSY
(— VIGOROUSLY) THRIFTY
(— WILD) SAVAGE AGRARIAN
AGRESTAL
GROWL YAR GNAR GURL GURR
NARR RASE ROIN ROME WIRR YARR
YIRR GARRE GNARL GNARR GROIN
SNARL GOLLAR HABBLE GRUMBLE
MAUNDER
GROWLER CLARENCE
GROWLING GROIN SURLY
GROWN THRIVEN
(— COLD) DEAD
(— HIGH) LOGGY
(— TOGETHER) ADNATE ACCRETE
(FULL —) GREAT MATURE
(WELL —) THRODDY
GROWN-UP ADULT GROWN
GROWTH FUR WAX BUSH COAT
CORN FILM GROW JUBA RISE SPUR

SUIT DUVET FLUSH GUMMA MAQUI
STAND STOCK STOOL SWELL
BUTTON CALLUS CANCER CLAVUS
EATAGE EPULIS FRINGE FUNGUS
LANUGO SCREEN SPROUT TYLOSE
UPCOME WASTME AUXESIS
BRACKEN COPPICE ERINEUM
FUNGOID MACCHIE SARCOID
STATURE TYLOSIS BEARDING
CARUNCLE ENDOGENY INCREASE
SETATION SWELLING UPSPRING
(— IN EYE) FILM
(— OF BEARD) DOWN
(— OF HAIR) SUIT
(— OF HORN) BUTTON SPIDER
(— OF TREES) BOSQUE BOSCAGE
COPPICE SHINNERY
(— ON HORSE'S LEG) FUSEE FUZEE
(— ON VESSEL'S BOTTOM) GARR
(2ND — OF GRASS) FOG
(ABUNDANT —) FLUSH
(DENSE —) BRUSH FOREST
SHINNERY
(DOWNY —) LANUGO
(GREEN —) GREENTH
(HARD —) STONE
(LUXURIANT —) FLOURISH
(ROUGH —) STUBBLE
(RUDIMENTARY —) STUB STUMP
(SIDE —) SPRIG
(SPARSE —) SCRAGGLE
(SUPERFICIAL —) MILDEW
(TRANSPARENT —) DRUSE
(VIGOROUS —) THRIFT
(WOODY —) BURL
GRUB BOB DIG EATS HUHU MOIL
MOOT STUB WORM CHUCK GROUT
MATHE SCRAN SNOUT WROTE
ASSART ESSART GRUGRU MUZZLE
ROOTLE NEASCUS PIGROOT
FLAGWORM GRUBWORM
MUCKWORM SKINWORM
GRUBROOT STARWORT
GRUDGE DOWN ENVY DERRY PEEVE
SCORE SPITE GROUCH GRUNCH
GRUTCH SPLEEN DESPITE EYELAST
SIMULTY
GRUDGING JEALOUSY
GRUEL SLOP BLEERY BURGOO
CONGEE CROWDY SOFKEE
BROCHAN CROWDIE LOBLOLLY
WANGRACE
GRUESOME UGLY GRISLY HORRID
SORDID FEARFUL GHASTLY
HIDEOUS MACABRE
GRUFF BLUFF ROUGH CLUMSE
SULLEN AUSTERE BEARING
BRUSQUE CLUMPST
(PL.) TAILINGS
GRUIFORMES GRALLAE
GRUMBLE GIRN GREX HONE KREX
ROIN BROCK CROAK DRUNT GROIN
GROWL GRUMP GRUNT MUNGE
GROUCH GROUSE GRUDGE GRUNCH
MUMBLE MUNGER MURMUR MUTTER
NOLLER PEENGE REPINE RUMBLE
SQUEAL TARROW YAMMER
CHANNER CHUNNER CHUNTER
GNATTER GRIZZLE GRUNTLE

MAUNDER MURGEON QUADDLE
SWAGGER COMPLAIN
GRUMBLER GROUCH QUADDLE
GROGNARD
GRUMBLING BITCH DRUNT GRIPE
GROIN GRUDGE MURMUR MURGEON
GRUMPY ILL CROSS GLUMPY
GLUMPISH GRUMPISH
GRUNION SMELT
GRUNT BURRO GROIN HUMPH
RONCO SARGO GRUMPH RONCHO
BURRITO CROAKER GRUNTER
GRUNTLE PIGFISH PINFISH TOMTATE
KNORHAAN KOORHAAN PORKFISH
REDMOUTH RONCADOR
GUACHARO FATBIRD OILBIRD
GUAICURU CADUVEO
GUAMA INGA PACAY
GUAN JACU ORTALIS PHEASANT
GUANA CHANE
GUANABANA SOURSOP
GUANCHE CANARIAN
GUANO OSITE
GUAPENA SERRAN SERRANA
AGUAVINA
GUARANTEE (ALSO SEE GUARANTY)
BAIL BAND SEAL CINCH COVER
AVOUCH ENGAGE ENSURE INSURE
RATIFY SECURE SURETY CAUTION
CERTIFY HOSTAGE WARRANT
AWARRANT GUARANTY PRESTATE
SECURITY WARRANTY
GUARANTEED ASSURED CERTIFIED
FOOLPROOF
GUARANTOR ENGAGER GRANTOR
GUARAND GUARANTY
GUARANTY (ALSO SEE GUARANTEE)
ANDI AVAL PAWN SEAL CAUTIO
PLEDGE WARRANT SECURITY
WARRANTY
GUARD BOW LEG NIT PAD SEE CARE
CURB HERD HOLD KEEP KNOW
LOOK REDE SAVE STOP STUB TENT
TILE WAIT WEAR WERE WITE YEME
ASKAR AWARD BLESS BLOCK
CHECK COVER FENCE FORAY
HEDGE HINGE PILOT SCREW SKIRT
TUTOR WAKEN WATCH ASKARI
BANTAY BASKET BRACER BRIDLE
BUMPER BUTTON CONVOY DEFEND
DRAGON ESCORT FENDER GHAFIR
GUNMAN JAILER KAVASS KEEPER
MIDDLE POLICE SCREEN SECURE
SENTRY SHIELD SHROUD WAITER
WARDER YEMING CHERISH
ESGUARD FRONTAL GHAFFIR
GHATWAL GUARDER KEEPING
PANDOUR PRESIDY PROTECT
SOULACK TRABANT WARDAGE
WARRANT CHAPERON GARRISON
MUDGUARD OUTGUARD PEDESTAL
PILOTMAN PRESERVE SECURITY
SENTINEL SHEPHERD SPLASHER
WARDSMAN WATCHMAN
(— ON FOIL) BUTTON
(AXLE —) HOUSING
(COACH —) SHOOTER
(CONSULAR —) KAVASS
(IMPERIAL —) BOSTANGI BOSTANJI

(KEYHOLE —) LAPPET
(MOUNTED —) SHOMER
(NECK —) CAMAIL
(ON —) AWARE
(PRISON —) HACK SCREW CHASER
JAILER
(SWORD —) BOW TSUBA
(PL.) HEAVIES
GUARDED WARY IMMUNE MANNED
GUARDEDLY GINGERLY
GUARDHOUSE BRIG CLINK BULLPEN
HOOSEGOW
GUARDIAN HERD ANGEL ARGUS
TUTOR YEMER CUSTOS KEEPER
MIMING PASTOR PATRON SHOMER
WARDEN CURATOR GARDANT
GARDEEN BARTHOLO BELLERUS
CERBERUS CREANCER DEFENDER
ECKEHART FRAVASHI GOVERNOR
GUARDANT PROTUTOR TUTELARY
(— OF HOME) SIF
(WORLD —) LOKAPALA MAHARAJA
(PL.) SELLI SELLOI
GUARDIANSHIP WARD TUTELA
CUSTODY KEEPING TUITION
WARDAGE WARDING CUSTODIA
GUARDAGE TUTELAGE WARDENRY
WARDSHIP
GUARDROOM WARDROOM
GUARDSMAN GUARDEE
GUASA MERO

GUATEMALA

CAPITAL: GUATEMALACITY
COIN: PESO CENTAVO QUETZAL
DANCE: ELSON GUARIMBA
GULF: HONDURAS
INDIAN: MAM CHOL ITZA IXIL
MAYA XINCA CARIBE QUICHE
POCOMAM
LAKE: DULCE GUIJA PETEN IZABAL
ATITLAN
MEASURE: VARA CUARTA FANEGA
TERCIA CAJUELA MANZANA
MOUNTAIN: AGUA FUEGO PACAYA
TACANA ATITLAN TOLIMAN
TAJAMULCO
PORT: OCOS BARRIOS LIVINGSTON
RIVER: AZUL BRAVO DULCE LAPAZ
BELIZE CHIXOY NEGINO PASION
SAMALA CHIAPAS MOTAGUA
SARSTUN POLOCHIC
RUINS: TIKAL
TOWN: OCOS COBAN VIEJA
CHAHAL CHISEC CUILCO
FLORES IZTAPA JALAPA SALAMA
SOLOLA TACANA TECPAN
YALOCH ZACAPA ANTIGUA
CUILAPA JUTIAPA SANJOSE
PROGRESO
VOLCANO: AGUA FUEGO ATITLAN
WEIGHT: CAJA LIBRA

GUAVA ARACA MYRTAL GUAYABA
GUAYABO GOIABADA
GUAYCURU MBAYA
GUDDLE GUMP NOODLE HANDFISH
GUDGEON PIN QUAB CHALDER
TRUNNION

GUELDER-ROSE GAITER OPULUS
DOGWOOD WHITTEN DOGBERRY
SNOWBALL VIBURNUM
GUENON GRIVET NISNAS VERVET
TALAPOIN TALLAPOI MOUSTACHE
GUEREZA COLOBIN COLOBUS
GUERRILLA COWBOY GORILLA
JAYHAWK SKINNER BUSHWACK
FELLAGHA KOMITAJI
GUESS AIM CALL HARP REDE SHOT
WEEN AREAD COUNT ETTLE FANCY
INFER TWANG DEVISE DIVINE
RECKON IMAGINE SURMISE
SUSPECT
(— CORRECTLY) TOUCH
GUEST COME GOER HOST DINER
INVITEE VISITOR SYMPHILE VISITANT
(— AT RANCH) DUDE
(UNINVITED —) SHADOW
(PL.) LEVEE COMPANY
GUFA KUFA GOOFAH KUPHAR
GUFFAW GAFF HEEHAW
GUIDANCE AIM DUCT EGIS AEGIS
STEER CONDUCT GUIDAGE
HELMAGE LEADING WISSING
AUSPICES ENGINERY REGIMENT
STEERAGE
GUIDE GUY LAY PIR TIP AIRT BEAD
CURB GAGE GATE LEAD PASS REIN
RULE SWAY CARRY CHARM DRESS
FRAME GAUGE LIGHT MAHDI MOROC
PILOT STEER TEACH WEISE ADALID
BARKER BEACON BEDWAY CONVOY
DIRECT ESCORT FORMER GILLIE
GOVERN INFORM LEADER MANAGE
POPPET CONDUCE CONDUCT
COURIER GHILLIE INSPIRE MARSHAL
MERCURY PIONEER SHIKARI
STERNER TRACKER CALENDAR
CICERONE DIRECTOR DRAGOMAN
ENGINEER FAIRLEAD LODESMAN
PEDESTAL POLESTAR PRACTICO
REPEATER SHIKAREE SIGNPOST
(SPIRITUAL —) PIR GURU BISHOP
DIVINE
(TRAFFIC —) MUSHROOM
GUIDEBOOK ABC GUIDE WAYBOOK
BAEDEKER HANDBOOK ROADBOOK
GUIDELINE SLUG
GUIDEPOST GUIDE PARSON
WAYMARK WAYPOST SIGNPOST
GUIDEWAY SLAY SLEY SLEIGH
SLIDEWAY SWANNECK
GUIDING POLAR BEHIND HOMING
LEADING
GUILD HUI GILD HOEY HONG YELD
CRAFT HANSA HANSE GREMIO
GUIDRY SCHOLA BASOCHE
COLLEGE COMPANY MYSTERY
GUILE DOLE WILE CHEAT CRAFT
FRAUD TRAIN DECEIT HUMBUG
CUNNING FALLACY ARTIFICE
GUILELESS PLAIN CANDID HONEST
ARTLESS ONEFOLD IGNORANT
INNOCENT UNNOOKED
GUILLEMOT AUK COOT LARY LAVY
LOOM QUET TURR URIA ARRIE
CUTTY FROWL MURRE SCOUT TOIST
TYSTE GRYLLE LUNGIE MAGGIE

MARROT SCRABE TINKER DOVEKEY
DOVEKIE SKIDDAW TARROCK
WILLOCK PUFFINET ROCKBIRD
SCUTTOCK SPRATTER

GUILT SIN SAKE WITE BLAME CULPA
FAULT PIACLE PLIGHT NOCENCE
OFFENSE HAMARTIA INIQUITY

GUILTLESS FREE PURE CLEAN
UNSAKED INNOCENT SACKLESS

GUILTY FAULTY NOCENT WICKED
CORREAL HANGDOG NOXIOUS
BLAMEFUL CRIMINAL CULPABLE
GUILTFUL
(— OF ERROR) LAPSED

GUINEA

CAPE: VERGA
CAPITAL: CONAKRY
COIN: SILY FRANC
ISLAND: TOMBO TRISTAO
MEASURE: JACKTAN
MOUNTAIN: TAMGUE
MOUNTAINS: LOMA NIMBA
NATIVE: SUSU TOMA KISSI FULANI
   GUERZI MALINKE KOURANKE
   LANDUMAN
RIVER: NIGER BAFING FALEME
   SENEGAL KONKOURE TINKISSO
TOWN: BOKE FRIA KADE LABE
   BENTY BEYLA COYAH KOULE
   MAMOU DABOLA DALABA
   DOUAKO FABALA KANKAN
   KINDIA BOFOSSO CONAKRY
   FARANAH KONFARA KOUMBIA
   OUASSOU SIGUIRI KEROUANE
WEIGHT: AKEY PISO UZAN BENDA
   SERON QUINTO AGUIRAGE

GUINEA MEG BEAN QUID QUEED
GEORGE SHINER GEORDIE
(HALF —) SMELT

GUINEA FOWL KEEL KEET PEARL
MEBACK GALEENY PINTADO
COMEBACK GALLINEY
(SOUND OF —) POTRACK

GUINEA GRASS PANIC PANICLE
SACATON ZACATON GAMELOTE

GUINEA PEPPER PIMENTO

GUINEA PIG CAVY
(MALE —) BOAR BUCK

GUINEA RUSH ADRUE

GUISE HUE FORM GARB COLOR
COVER SHAPE MANNER PERSON
APPAREL CLOTHES GUISARD
LIKENESS

GUITAR BOX KIT PIPA JAMON KITAR
SITAR TIPLE GIMBRI KITTAR
SANCHO SATTAR CITHERN CITTERN
MACHETE UKULELE CHARANGO
CHITARRA

GUITARFISH RAY BATOID PURAQUE

GUITGUIT PITPIT

GULANCHA GILO GILOE

GULCH GULLY SLUIT CANYON
RAVINE

GULDEN FLORIN GUILDER
(100,000 —) TUN

GULES MARS RUBY TORTEAU

GULF SINE CHAOS GULPH VORAGE
VORAGO
(BOTTOMLESS —) ABYSM ABYSS

GULFWEED SARGASSO

GULL COB COX MEW COBB CONY
COOT CULL DUPE FOOL GOLL LARI
MALL PINT PIRR SELL SKUA XEME
ALLAN ALLEN ANNET BOSUN CHEAT
CHUMP COBBE COKES CROCK
CULLY HOODY JAGER LARID LARUS
PEWIT SCULL SMELT YAGER BONXIE
BUBBLE CHOUSE COUSIN JOCKEY
PIGEON SIMPLE TEASER TULIAC
VICTIM WAGGEL WHILLY CROCKER
DECEIVE MEDRICK PICKMAW
POPELER SCAURIE SEABIRD
SEAFOWL SWARBIE TARROCK
TRUMPIE BLACKCAP DIRTBIRD
DOTTEREL DUNGBIRD SEEDBIRD
(LIKE A —) LAROID

GULLET MAW GULE LANE GORGE
GARGLE PECHAN THROAT KEACORN
STOMACH SWALLOW WEASAND
GURGULIO

GULLIBLE GOOFY GREEN SIMPLE
CULLIBLE

GULLIVER GRILDRIG

GULLY BOX GUT DRAW GULL RAIK
RAKE SICK SIKE DONGA DRAFT
GOYLE GULCH SLAKE SLUIT ZANJA
ARROYO GULLET GULLEY GUTTER
NULLAH SHEUCH SHEUGH CHIMNEY
COULOIR DRAUGHT BARRANCA

GULP BOLT GAUP GLUT GULL POOP
SOPE SWIG GULCH QUILT SLOSH
SWIPE ENGLUT GLUTCH GOBBLE
GOLLOP PAUNCH SLABBER
SWALLOW SWATTLE
(— NOISILY) SLORP

GUM AMRA BLOB FILL GOOM LOAD
TUNO AMAPA BABUL CUMAY DHAVA
CHICLE KARAYA TOUART TUPELO
CARANNA CARAUNA GINGIVA
GUMWOOD BORRACHA CARABEEN
DRESSING FEVERGUM
(ACACIA —) GEDDA
(AROMATIC —) MYRRH
(ASTRINGENT —) KINO
(CHEWING —) WAX
(FRAGRANT —) BUMBO
(RED —) JARRAH
(UNGRADED —) SORTS
(WOOD —) XYLAN
(PL.) ULA

GUM ARABIC KIKAR ACACIA ACACIN

GUMBO OKRA

GUMBOIL PARULIS

GUMBO-LIMBO JOBO BIRCH
GOMART MASTIC NEGRITO
ALMACIGO ARCHIPIN

GUMDROP GUM JUJUBE

GUMMER BIDDY BIDDIE SCRAPER
SCUFFER SCUFFLER SCUPPLER

GUMMY GLUEY CLAGGY MASTIC
GUMMOUS

GUMPTION SENSE SPRAWL

GUM SUCCORY HOGBITE

GUM TREE KARI KARRI TOOART
TOUART TUPELO EUCALYPT

GUMWEED GRINDELIA SUNFLOWER

GUN GAT POP BREN HAKE PIAT
ROER TUBE BARIL FIFTY FIRER
FUSEE FUZEE RAKER REWET RIFLE
ARCHIE BERTHA CANNON CHASER
CULVER DUCKER INCHER JEZAIL
MINNIE QUAKER RANDOM SWIVEL
TUPARA CALIVER FIREARM
HACKBUT HANDGUN JINGALL
LANTACA MUZZLER AMUSETTE
ARQUEBUS CHAUCHAT CULVERIN
FIRELOCK GALLOPER SHAGBUSH
TROMBONE
(BOAT —) BASE
(LOWER-DECK —) BARKER
(MACHINE —) CHOPPER GATLING
(TOY —) SPARKLER
(PL.) FLAK CHASE ARTILLERY

GUNA RAJAS TAMAS SATTVA

GUNBOAT SKIP BARCA GONDOLA
TINCLAD

GUN CARRIAGE PANEL MADRIER
GALLOPER

GUNCREWMAN PLUGMAN

GUNFLINT STONE

GUNITE SHOTCRETE

GUNLOCK ROWET FIRELOCK

GUNMAN HOOD GUNSEL GUNSMAN
TORPEDO ENFORCER GANGSTER

GUNNEL BLENNY SWORDICK

GUNNER GUN POPPER FIREMAN
SHOOTER ENGINEER

GUNNY TAT BURLAP BAGGING
SACKING

GUNNYSACK CORNSACK

GUNPOWDER SULFUR SULPHUR

GUNSIGHT VISIE HAUSSE

GUNSTOCK BLANK TIPSTOCK

GUNSTONE OGRESS PELLET

GUNWALE GUNNEL PORTOISE

GUNZ SCANIAN

GUPPY MILLIONS BELLYFISH

GUR GOOR KHAUR JAGGERY
VOLTAIC

GURGLE GLOX QUARK SLOSH
BURBLE GOLLER GUGGLE

GURGLINGLY TRILLIL

GURJUN YANG

GURNARD CUR TUB PIPER ELLECK
ROCHET BATFISH CAPTAIN
GRUNTER LATCHET SOLDIER
TRIGLID TUBFISH VOLADOR
HARDHEAD KNORHAAN LORICATE

GURO KWENI

GUSH JET BOIL FLOW FOAM HUSH
RAIL SLOP WALM BELCH SLUSH
SMALM SMARM SPIRT SPURT STOUR
SWOSH BURBLE PHRASE SWOOSH
WALLOW WHOOSH SLOBBER

GUSHING SLOPPY SMARMY
EFFUSIVE

GUSSET GORE MITER MITRE QUIRK
PIECETTE

GUST BUB FLAN GALE GUSH WAFF
WAFT WIND BLAST FRESH SLANT
FLURRY HUFFLE SQUALL WILLIWAW
WINDFLAW
(— OF RAIN) SKIT
(— OF WIND) FLAM FLAN FUFF

GALE GUSH PIRR SCUD TIFT BERRY BLAST FLAFF THODE SQUALL WINDELAW

GUSTATION TASTE

GUSTO GUST ZEST RELISH

GUSTY DIRTY PUFFY BLASHY BLASTY FRETFUL GUSTFUL SQUALLY

GUT GIB BOWEL CECUM CLEAN CAECUM CATGUT HOLLOW STRING ELISION GRALLOCH
(FISH —) GIP GILL
(TWISTED —) THARM THERM
(PL.) BOWELS COJONES PUDDING ENTRAILS

GUTTA SOH DROP PUAN SIAK SUSU DUJAN GERIP SANGE SUNDIK CAMPANA JANGKAR SEMARUM TRENAIL TRUNNEL HANGKANG KETAPANG

GUTTER GRIP SIKE GRIPE GULLY SIVER SPOUT SWEAL BOTTOM CANNEL CULLIS GROOVE GUZZLE KENNEL RIGGOT STRAND TROUGH VENNEL CHANNEL CHENEAU GRIZZLE

(— OF STREET) KENNEL
(MINING —) BOTTOM HASSING
(ROOF —) RONE
(PL.) LIMBERS

GUTTERMAN SWAMPER

GUTTURAL GRUM BURRY HARSH THICK

GUY BOD CAT EGG JOE NUT BIRD BOZO GENT GINK HUSK JACK JOHN COOKY JOKER SCOUT SPOOF BUFFER COOKIE GAZABO GAZEBO GAZOOK GILGUY HOMBRE JASPER JIGGER MALKIN MAUMET MAWKIN KNOCKER BLIGHTER

GUY ROPE STAY VANG

GUZ GAZ GEZ ZAR ZER GUDGE

GUZERAT KANKREJ

GUZZLE BUM GUM SOT TUN BEND GULL SLOSH SWILL GOOZLE GUDDLE SWATTLE SWIZZLE

GUZZLER BENDER

GWYNIAD SCHELLY

GYASCUTUS PROCK

GYMNASIUM GYM PALESTRA TURNHALL

GYMNAST SOKOL BENDER TURNER ACROBAT TUMBLER

GYMNASTIC (— SOCIETY) SOKOL

GYNOECIUM BRUSH APOCARP

GYNOPHORE PODOGYN

GYPSUM GYP GYPS YESO GESSO LUDIAN PARGET GYPSITE SATINITE SELENITE ALABASTER

GYPSY CALO APTAL CAIRD GIPSY ROMNI BOSHAS GITANO ROMANY TINKER AZUCENA CZIGANY MOONMAN TINKLER TZIGANE ZINGARO BOHEMIAN EGYPTIAN FLAMENCO ZIGEUNER
(NON —) GORGIO
(SEA —) BAJAU
(PL.) ROMANESE

GYRATE GYRE SPIN TURN TWIRL WHIRL CURVET INGYRE ROTATE REVOLVE SQUIRREL

GYRATORY GIDDY GYRAL

GYRFALCON JERKIN

GYRON GIRON ESQUIRE

H HOW AITCH HOTEL ASPIRATE
HABERDASHERY TOGGERY
HABERGEON HAUBERK
HABILIMENT GARB HABIT APPAREL
RAIMENT CLOTHING
(PL.) CLOTHES EQUIPAGE
HABILITATE ENABLE
HABIT LAW PAD SET USE COAT
GARB GATE SUIT THEW WONT
FROCK HAUNT TACHE TRADE TRICK
USAGE CUSTOM GROOVE MANNER
PRAXIS TALENT CLOTHES FOLKWAY
HABITUS WONTING CROTCHET
HABITUDE PHYSIQUE PRACTICE
PRACTISE
(— OF GRINDING TEETH) BRUXISM
(BAD —) HANK VICE MISTETCH
(SPEECH —S) ACCENT
(PL.) DAPS
HABITABLE BIGLY
HABITAT ECE HOME RANGE PATRIA
STATION LOCALITY
HABITATION HOLD TELD TENT
ABODE BIELD HABIT HOUSE WONING
DOMICILE DWELLING PANTHEON
TENEMENT RESIDENCE
(— SITE) YACATA
(QUIET —) SHADE
(UNDERGROUND —) HOLE
HABITUAL USUAL COMMON HECTIC
CHRONIC REGULAR FREQUENT
ORDINARY
HABITUATE USE HOWF ENURE
FLESH HABIT INURE ADDICT SEASON
HACKNEY ACCUSTOM ACQUAINT
OCCASION
HABITUATED WONT SEASONED
HABITUDE HABIT SCHESIS
HABITUE DENIZEN COURTIER
HABRONEMIASIS BURSATI
BURSATTEE
HACEK WEDGE
HACK HAG HEW BOLO CHIP HAKE
DEVIL HATCH DRUDGE FIACRE
HACKLE HAGGLE HODMAN JOBBER
MANGLE HACKNEY MATTOCK
VETTURA MUTILATE
(LITERARY —) GRUB DEVIL
HACKBERRY EGGBERRY HACKTREE
HAGBERRY ONEBERRY
HACKBUT HAGBUT DEMIHAG
HACKBUSH
HACK GHARRI SHIGRAM
HACKLE COMB RUFF HECKLE
NAPPER RUFFER HATCHEL
ROUGHER
HACKNEY HACK MIDGE NODDY
HACKNEY CARRIAGE MIDGE
FIACRE JARVEY VETTURA
HACKNEYED HACK WORN HOARY
TRITE CANNED CLICHE COMMON
FOREWORN
HAD D HED HEDDE
(— NOT) HADNA HADNT
HADDOCK GADE GADID SCROD
DICKEY HADDIE
(DRIED —) CRAIL RIZZAR SPELDING
SPELDRIN
HADE UNDERLIE

HADES PIT HELL AIDES ORCUS
PLUTO SHEOL SHADES TARTAR
AIDONEUS TARTARUS
(FATHER OF —) SATURN
(WIFE OF —) PROSERPINA
HAECCEITY THISNESS
HAFNIUM CELTIUM
HAFT HEFT HOVE HELVE DUDGEON
HAFTER HANDLER
HAG ATE MARE REBEC RUDAS
VECKE WITCH BELDAM HECATE
ROUDAS BELDAME HAGGARD
HELLCAT HARRIDAN
HAGAR (SON OF —) ISHMAEL
HAGBOAT HOGGET HOGGIE
HAGFISH HAG BORER VECKE
MYZONT SUCKER PLACOID
MYXINOID
HAGGARD PALE THIN GAUNT WISHT
HAGGED
HAGGLE CHOP PRIG DODGE BADGER
BANTER BOGGLE DICKER HACKER
HIGGLE HUCKLE NAGGLE PALTER
SCOTCH THREEP BARGAIN CHAFFER
HUCKSTER
HAGGLER DODGER
HAGGLING BARGAIN CHAFFER
HAGIOGRAPHA KETUBIM
HAGIOSCOPE SQUINT SQUINCH
HAIDA SKITTAGET
HAIL AVE HOY HALE GREET SALVE
SPEAK STORM ACCOST BAYETE
HAGGLE HALLOO HERALD SALUTE
(SOFT —) GRESIL GRAUPEL
HAILSTONE STONE
HAINAI IONI
HAIR FAX JAG RIB WIG BARB CROP
FLUE GLIB HEAD KEMP PELF PILE
SETA WIRE BEARD CRIMP CRINE
FRIZZ FRONT PILUS QUIFF ANGORA
BRILLS BRUTUS CRINET FIBRIL
FROWZE MERKIN SETULA THATCH
TRAGUS CULOTTE ELFLOCK
GLOCHIS TOPKNOT WHISKER
CAPILLUS COLLETER PALPOCIL
TENTACLE TRICHODE TRICHOME
VIBRISSA
(— BROWN) ARGALI
(— OF ANIMALS) FUR PELF
(— OF HORSES OR COWS) CERDA
(— OF TERRIER) FALL
(— ON LEAF) GLAND
(— ON TEMPLES) HAFFET HAFFIT
(— ON THIGHS) CULOTTE
(— OVER EYES) BROW GLIB
EYELASH
(BARBED —) GLOCHIS
(BRAID OF —) QUEUE PIGTAIL
(BUNDLE OF —) LEECH
(CAMEL'S —) DEER
(COARSE —) KEMP BRISTLE
(CURLED —) FRIZZ
(CUTDOWN —) STUMPS
(FALSE —) WIG JANE FRONT
PERUKE
(FRIZZED —) FROWZE
(GRAY —) GRIZZLE
(LOCK OF —) TUZ FEAK TATE
FLOCK TRESS

(LONG HEAVY —) MANE
(LOOSE —) COMBINGS
(MATTED —) SHAG ELFLOCK
(MOP OF —) TOUSLE
(NOSE —) VIBRISSA
(PLANT —) COLLETER
(ROOT —) FIBRIL
(SNARL OF —) TANGLE
(SOFT —) DOWN LANUGO
(STINGING —) STING STIMULUS
(STRAY LOCK OF —) TAG
(TUFT OF —) PLUME KROBYLOS
(WAVING LOCK OF —) WIMPLER
(WHITE —) SNOW SNOWS
(PL.) COWAGE COWHAGE HACKLES
HAIRBREADTH HERMELE WHISKER
HAIRBRUSH TOILETRY
HAIRCLOTH HAIR CILICE
HAIRCUT BOB CUT CROP BUTCH
SHINGLE DUCKTAIL
HAIRDO FRISURE
HAIRDRESSER WAVER FRISEUR
COIFFEUR
HAIRDRESSING FRISURE
HAIR FRAME PALISADE
HAIRINESS PILOSISM PILOSITY
HAIRLESS PELON CALLOW ATRICHIC
DEPILOUS
HAIRLIKE TRICHOID
HAIRLINE WHISKER
HAIRPIN ACUS BODKIN SKEWER
HAIRSPLITTING FINE PILPUL
HAIRWORM GORDIID GORDIOID
HAIRY FAXED MOSEY ROUGH
COMATE COMOUS PILARY PILINE
CRINOSE HIRSUTE PILEOUS VILLOUS
UNSHAVEN

HAITI
CAPE: FOUX
CAPITAL: PORTAUPRINCE
CHANNEL: SUD STMARC
COIN: GOURDE
DEITY: LOA
INDIAN: TAINO
ISLAND: VACHE GONAVE TORTUE
NAVASSA TORTUGA
ISLAND GROUP: ANTILLES
CAYMITES
LAKE: SAUMATRE
MAGIC: OBI OBEAH
MOUNTAIN: NORD CAHOS NOIRES
LAHOTTE LASELLE TROUDEAU
PLAIN: NORD CAYES JACMEL
LEOGANE ARCAHAIE CULDESAC
GONAIVES
PRIEST: BOCOR HOUNGAN
RIVER: GUAYAMOUL ARTIBONITE
SPIRIT: LOA BAKA BOKO
TOWN: AQUIN CAYES FURCY
LIMBE HINCHE JACMEL JEREMIE
LEOGANE SALTROU GONAIVES
KENSCOFF

HAKAM CACAM HAHAM CHOCHEM
KHAKHAM
HAKE GADE HAIK LING GADOID
CODLING HADDOCK WHITING

ANACANTH QUODLING
HAKENKREUZLER SWASTIKA
HALBERD BILL PIKE GLAIVE GLEAVE
  POLEARM PARTISAN
HALBERDIER DRABANT
HALCYON CALM ALCYON GOLDEN
HALE YELL FRACK FRECK TRAIL
  ROBUST STRONG HEALTHY
  VIGOROUS
HALER HELLER
HALF M ARF ELF DEMI HAUF HOVE
  SEMI SIDE MEDIO HALFEN HALFLY
  MOIETY MEDIETY
  (— GALLON) POTTLE
  (— OF DRAW) BRACKET
  (— OF EM) EN
  (— OF INNING) BOTTOM
  (— OF MOLD) VALVE
  (FRUIT —S) SLABS
HALFBEAK GAR IHI BALAO PIPER
  BALLYHOO
HALF-BLOOD DEMISANG
HALF BOOT BUSKIN
HALF-BREED BREED METIF METIS
  SAMBO MUSTEE RAMONA CABOCLO
  MESTIZO METISSE DEMISANG
  HARRATIN MIXBLOOD
HALF-CASTE TOPAZ TOPASS
HALF-CRAZY FIFISH
HALF CROWN GEORGE ALDERMAN
HALF DENIER MAILE MAILLE
HALF DOBRA PECA
HALF-EATEN SEMESE
HALF-FARTHING CUE MITE MINUTE
HALF GAINER ISANDER
HALF-GROWN HALFLIN
HALF-GUINEA SMELT
HALF HITCH ROLLING
HALF MASK LOUP DOMINO
HALF-MOON LUNETTE DEMILUNE
HALF NOTE MINIM
HALFPENCE GROCERY
HALFPENNY OB MAG MEG DUMP
  GRAY GREY MAIL MAKE MEKE OBOL
  SOUSE STAMP BAUBEE MAILLE
  HAPENNY STUIVER
  (COUNTERFEIT —) RAP GRAY
  (THICK —) DUMP
HALF-PIKE SPONTON DEMIPIKE
  SPONTOON
HALF-PINT CUP JACK CUPFUL
HALF REST SOSPIRO
HALF SOLE TAP
HALF STEP CHROMA
HALFTONE DROPOUT
HALF TURN DEMIVOLT
HALF-WIT DOLT DUNCE HAVEREL
  TOMFOOL STAUMREL UNDERWIT
HALF-WITTED SOFT DOTTY SIMPLE
  HALUCKET IMBECILE STAUMREL
HALIBUT BUT BUTT FLITCH TURBOT
  FLATFISH
HALIFAX BALLYHACK
HALIOTIS ABALONE
HALIRRHOTHIUS (FATHER OF —)
  NEPTUNE
  (MOTHER OF —) EURYTE
  (SLAYER OF —) MARS
HALL HA AULA HELL IWAN SALA

AIWAN ATREO ATRIO BALAI BURSA
CURIA DIVAN ENTRY FOYER HOUSE
OECUS SALLE SALON ATRIUM
CAMERA DURBAR GARDEN LESCHE
SALOON SCHOOL SENATE TOLSEY
TRANCE APADANA CHAMBER
DANCERY GALLERY HALLWAY
KURHAUS KURSAAL MEGARON
PASSAGE VINGOLF ANTEROOM
ARCHEION ASSEMBLY CHOULTRY
COLISEUM CORRIDOR FOREHALL
HASTROND HOSPITAL RAADZAAL
TOLBOOTH VALHALLA
(— FOR PERFORMANCES) ODEON
ODEUM
(— WITH STATUES) VALHALLA
(DINING —) COMMON
(LECTURE —) SCHOLA
(MISSION —) CITADEL
(MUSIC —) GAFF
(TOWN —) CABILDO RATHAUS
TRIBUNAL
(UNIVERSITY —) BURSA
HALLMARK CROWN SHOPMARK
HALLOO HO HOO LOO ALEW LURE
  WHOOP ACCOST TALLYHO
HALLOW BLESS HALWE DEDICATE
  SANCTIFY
HALLOWED HOLY SACRED BLESSED
HALLUCINATION DWALE ACOASMA
  ACOUASM ACOUSMA FANTASY
  PHONEME DELUSION ILLUSION
  PHANTASY ZOOSCOPY
HALLUX TALON
HALLWAY ENTRY FOYER TRANCE
HALMA HOPPITY
HALMALILLE PETWOOD
HALO DOG BURR GLOR NIMB GLORY
  SHINE AREOLA CIRCLE CORONA
  GLORIA NIMBUS SUNDOG AREOLET
  AUREOLE BOROUGH CINCTURE
HALT HO HOP ALTO BAIT BALK HOLD
  LIMP SKID STAY STOP TRIP WAIT
  BAULK BLOCK BREAK CEASE CHECK
  HILCH HITCH STAND ARREST
  BARLEY SCOTCH STANCE CONTAIN
  CRIPPLE STATION STOPPAGE
  (— GAME) CALL
  (— TO DOGS) TOHO
HALTER EVIL SOLE BRANK TRASH
  WANTY WIDDY WITHE POISER
  CAUSSON CAVESON JAQUIMA
  POINTEL BALANCER NECKLACE
HALTING BODE LAME ZOPPA
  CRIPPLE LIMPING
HALVE DIMIDIATE
  (PL.) HALVERS
HALVING HAPLOSIS
HAM PIG GAMMON JAMBON JARRET
  PESTLE GAMBONE
  (FATHER OF —) NOAH
  (PICNIC —) CALA CALI
  (SON OF —) CUSH CANAAN
HAMATUM UNCIFORM
HAMESUCKEN HAMFARE
HAMITE BORAN BORANA DANAKIL
  DANKALI
HAMLET KOM DORP TOWN TREF
  VILL CASAL HAMEL SITIO STEAD

THORP VICUS ALDEIA BUSTEE
THORPE CLACHAN KAMPONG
KIRKTON KIRKTOWN
HAMMER AX AXE BIT DOG PEG SET
  CALL COCK DROP HORN MALL
  MASH MAUL MELL SETT TILT CAVIL
  KEVEL KNOCK MADGE POUND SMITE
  THUMP BEETLE BUCKER CLOYER
  DRIVER FALLER FULLER MALLET
  MARTEL NOPPER OLIVER PLEXOR
  SCUTCH SLEDGE TACKER TILTER
  KNAPPER KNOCKER MALLEUS
  PLESSOR STRIKER CRANDALL
  MALLEATE MJOLLNIR SCUTCHER
  TREMBLER
  (— FOR DRESSING STONE) KEVEL
  (— OF GUNLOCK) DOG COCK
  DOGHEAD
  (— OUT) ANVIL
  (BRICKLAYER'S —) SCOTCH SCUTCH
  SCUTCHER
  (LEADEN —) MADGE
  (MINER'S —) BULLY
  (PAVING —) REEL
  (PNEUMATIC —) GUN BUSTER
  (STEAM —) IMPACTER IMPACTOR
  (TUNING —) KEY
HAMMERED BEATEN WROUGHT
HAMMERHEAD CORNUDA
HAMMERKOP UMBER UMBRETTE
HAMMERLOCK BAR ARMLOCK
HAMMERMAN STRIKER
HAMMOCK SACK HUMMOCK
  (— CARRIED BY BEARERS) DANDY
  (— SLUNG ON POLE) MACHILA
  (WOODEN —) KATEL KARTEL
HAMPER BIN COT MAR PED TUB
  BEAT BIND CLOG CURB FLAT HURT
  LOAD SLOW TUCK BLOCK CRAMP
  CRATE MAUND RUSKY SERON
  BASKET BURDEN FETTER HALTER
  HINDER HOBBLE HOPPLE IMPEDE
  BUFFALO CONFINE HANAPER
  MANACLE PANNIER PERPLEX
  SHACKLE TRAMMEL ENCUMBER
  ENTANGLE OBSTRUCT RESTRAIN
  RESTRICT STRAITEN
HAMPERING STIFLING DIFFICULT
HAMSTER CRICETID
HAMSTRING HOX HOCK LAME
  HOUGH ENERVATE
HANAPER HAMPER
HAND M CAT DAB FAM FIN HAN PAW
  PUD CLAW DEAL DUKE GIVE GOLL
  HALF JACK LOOF MAIN MANO MITT
  PART PASS SPAN CAMAY CLAUT
  CLEUK FLUSH GLAUM GRASP GRIPE
  INDEX MANUS MAULY NIEVE POWER
  SHARE STIFF STOCK BRIDGE
  CLUNCH CLUTCH DADDLE DOUBLE
  FAMBLE GOWPEN HANDLE MINNIE
  STAGER WORKER CLAWKER
  FAMELEN FLAPPER FLIPPER
  POINTER WORKMAN GRAPPLER
  MORTMAIN
  (— COUNTING ZERO) BACCARA
  BACCARAT
  (— DOWN) DEVOLVE TRADUCE
  BEQUEATH TRANSMIT

(— GESTURES) MUDRA
(— IN POKER) FULL SKIP BLAZE
FLUSH SKEET TIGER BICYCLE
JACKPOT SKIPPER IMMORTAL
STRAIGHT
(— IN WHIST) MORT TENACE
(— ON) BUCK
(— OVER) GIVE REACH BETEACH
BITECHE DELIVER
(— UP STRAW) SERVE
(— WITH 5 HIGHEST TRUMPS)
JAMBOREE
(BABY'S —) SPUD
(BIG AND UNGAINLY —) MAIG
(BRIDGE —) BID DUMMY DOUBLE
LAYDOWN
(CLENCHED —) FIST
(COLD —S) SHOWDOWN
(CURSIVE —) CIVILITE
(DECK —) HAWSEMAN
(DUMMY —) BOARD
(ELDEST —) EDGE SENIOR
(EXTRA — IN LOO) MISS
(FRENCH —) COULEE
(GRASPING —) CLAUT
(GREEN —) FARMER JACKEROO
(LEFT —) SINISTRA
(LONE —) JAMBONE
(PERSIAN —) SHIKASTA
(POKER —S) BOARD
(RANCH —) COWBOY
(REEL —) SPINDLER
(RIGHT —) DEXTER
(ROUND —) RONDE
(SECTION —) SNIPE
(SKILLFUL —) DAB
(SPARE — IN CARDS) CAT
JAMBOREE
(UNSKILLED —) DABSTER
(UPPER —) BULGE EMINENCE
(WEAK CARD —) BUST
HANDBAG BAG CABA NEIF CABAS
PURSE SATCHEL ENVELOPE
GRIPSACK POCHETTE RETICULE
HANDBALL PALM
HANDBARROW BIER HANDY TRUCK
BARROW
HANDBELL SKELLAT TANTONY
HANDBILL BILL FLIER FLYER LIBEL
DODGER
HANDBOOK VADY GRADUS MANUAL
BAEDEKER
HANDBOW STONEBOW
HANDCAR DRAG
HANDCART PRAM DANDY HURLY
TRUCK GOCART TROLLY TROLLEY
HANDCUFF CUFF STAY LINKER
NIPPER STAYER MANACLE TRAMMEL
WRISTER BRACELET HANDBOLT
HANDLOCK LIGAMENT SNITCHER
WRISTLET
(PL.) IRONS SNAPS DARBIES
NIPPERS
HANDER-IN INGIVER
HANDFUL M MAN GRIP LOCK WISP
YELM CLAUT GRIPE LITCH GOUPIN
GOWPEN HANTLE YAFFLE FISTFUL
MANIPLE
(— OF GRAIN) REAP SINGLE
SONGLE

(— OF LEAVES) PATRIN
(DOUBLE —) GOWPEN
(LAST — OF HARVEST) KIRN
HANDGRIP TUFFING
HANDGUN HAKE CALIVER HANDARM
HANDICAP START BURDEN DENIAL
HAMPER HINDER IMPEDE STRIKE
ENCUMBER PENALIZE
HANDICAPPED CRIMP CRIMPED
HANDICRAFT MYSTERY MECHANIC
HANDCRAFT
HANDICRAFTSMAN ARTISAN
HANDILY HANDY GAINLY
HANDINESS YARAGE
HANDIWORK MACHINE
HANDKERCHIEF WIPE CLOUT
FOGLE HANKY STOOK WIPER
HANKIE MADRAS NAPKIN SUDARY
TIGNON BANDANA BELCHER
FOULARD KERCHER MANIPLE
SNEEZER BANDANNA KERCHIEF
MOCKETER MONTEITH MOUCHOIR
SUDARIUM VERNACLE VERONICA
HANDLE BOW EAR FAN NIB NOB PAD
PIN PLY USE ANSA BAIL BALE BOOL
BUTT CROP FEEL FIST GAUM GRIP
HAFT HALE HAND HANK HILT KILP
KNOB LIFT RAPE RUNG STOP
GRASP GRIPE GROPE HELVE MOUNT
SHAFT SPOKE STAIL STALE START
STEAL STELE STOCK SWING TREAT
WIELD BECKET FETTLE FINGER
FUSEAU HANGER LIFTER MANAGE
MANURE POMMEL ROUNCE TILLER
CONDUCT DUDGEON WOOLDER
BEERPULL BELLPULL BITSTALK
BITSTOCK DISPENSE HANDGRIP
HANDHOLD HANDLING MOPSTICK
STAGHORN
(— AWKWARDLY) FUMBLE THUMBLE
(— BADLY) ILLGUIDE
(— CLUMSILY) PAW FUMBLE
(— IMPROPERLY) GAUM
(— MODISHLY) GALLANT
(— OF AXE) HELVE
(— OF BENCH PLANE) TOAT TOTE
(— OF DAGGER) DUDGEON
(— OF KETTLE) BAIL
(— OF LADLE) SHANK
(— OF OAR) GRASP
(— OF PLOW) HALE STAFF START
STILT PLOWTAIL
(— OF PRINTING PRESS) ROUNCE
(— OF RAKE) STALE
(— OF SCYTHE) TACK SNATH
SNEAD THOLE SNATHE SNEATH
(— OF SWORD) HAFT HILT
(— OF WHIP) CROP
(— RECKLESSLY) FOOL
(— ROUGHLY) MALL MAUL TOWSE
MUZZLE GRABBLE
(— VIOLENTLY) BOUNCE
(CRANK —) WINK
(CROSSBOW —) TILLER
(CURVED —) BOOL BOUL
(DETACHABLE —) KILP
(LIFTING — OF GUN) DOLPHIN
(PUMP —) BRAKE SWIPE
(ROPE —) SHACKLE

(WOODEN —) TREE
(PL.) HALES
HANDLED (EASILY —) BANTAM
HANDLER DOCKHAND
(AIRPLANE —) AIREDALE
HANDLING USE CONTROL
(SKILLFUL —) CONDUCT
(UNSKILLFUL —) BUNGLING
HANDMAID ANCILLA
HANDOUT DOWN
HANDRAIL BAR RAIL MANROPE
BANISTER EASEMENT MOPSTICK
TOADBACK
HANDSHAKE SHAKE SHRUG
HAND-SHAPED PALMATE
HANDSOME BRAW FAIR FINE PERT
TALL BONNY FETIS FITTY FUSOM
LUSTY ADONIC BRAWLY CLEVER
FARAND GOODLY HEPPEN LIKELY
PROPER SEEMLY ADONIAN AVENANT
ELEGANT FEATISH FEATOUS
FEWSOME GALLANT LIBERAL
SMICKER GOODLIKE STUNNING
VENEREAN WEELFARD
HANDSOMELY FAIRLY HANDSOME
HANDSTONE MANO
HAND STRAP TOGGEL TOGGLE
HANDSTROKE TALLY
HANDWORK TOOLING
HANDWRITING PAW FIST HAND
WRITE DUCTUS NIGGLE SCRIPT
SCRIVE BATARDE WRITING
BACKHAND HANDWRIT
HANDY DAB DEFT GAIN WEME
JEMMY LUSTY QUEME READY TIGHT
CLEVER HEPPEN KNACKY
DEXTROUS EXPEDITE HANDSOME
SKILLFUL
HANDYMAN MOZO JUMPER
GREASER SWAMPER
HANG NUB TOP CRAP DRAG FALL
HANK KILT PEND TREE TUCK DRAPE
DROOP HOVER KETCH NOOSE
STRAP SWING TRINE TRUSS TWIST
ANHANG APPEND DEPEND GIBBET
HALTER IMPEND SLOUCH STRING
TALTER DOGGONE HANGING
LANTERN STRETCH SUSPEND
(— ABOUT) DRING HOVER
(— AROUND) KNOCK HANKER
SLINGE
(— BACK) LAG BOGGLE
(— BEHIND) PLOD
(— CRIMINAL) STRAP TOTTER
(— DOWN) DIP LOP LAVE DROOP
DEPEND FESTOON PROPEND
(— HEAVILY) SWAG
(— LOOSELY) BAG SAG FLAG FLOW
LOLL BANGLE DANGLE PAGGLE
(— ONE'S HEAD) SLINK
(— OUT) LILL
(— OVER) WAUVE IMPEND WHAUVE
(— PICTURE NEAR CEILING) SKY
(— SOGGILY) TROLLOP
(— WITH TAPESTRY) TAPIS
HANGAR DOCK GARAGE AIRDOCK
HANGER PASSIVE SHABBLE
WHINYARD
(— FOR CARCASSES) STANG

(COAT —) SHOULDER
(CRANK —) BRACKET
(LACE-MAKING —) WORKER
(SWORD —) CARRIAGE
HANGER-ON BUR BURR SPIV LEECH
  TOADY HANGBY HEELER LACKEY
  LACQUEY PENDING PARASITE
HANGING FLAG HEMP TURN ARRAS
  BAGGY DRAPE SWING CELURE
  DORSEL DOSSER DERRICK DRAPERY
  PENDENT PENSILE ANTEPORT
  HANGMENT
  (— LOOSE) LOPPY BAGGED
  (— LOW) SIDE
  (— THREATENINGLY) IMMINENT
  (LIMPLY —) FLAGGY SLIMPSY
  (WALL —) CEILING TENTURE
  (PL.) TAPIT TAPPET DRAPERY
  PARAMENT
HANGMAN KETCH HANGER HANGIE
  TOPMAN DERRICK GREGORY
  TOPSMAN VERDUGO CARNIFEX
  SCRAGGER
  (HALTER OF —) TOW
HANGMAN'S DAY FRIDAY
HANGNAIL AGNAIL
HANGOUT JOINT SCATTER
HANGOVER HOLDOVER RESIDUUM
HANK HASP SKEIN BOBBIN
  SELVAGEE
  (— OF FLAX) HEAD
  (— OF TWINE) RAN
  (— OF YARN) SLIP
HANKER HANK LONG LINGER
HANKERING ITCH HANKER
HANKUL ENMUN ONMUN
HANSOM CAB SHOFUL SHOWFUL
HANUMAN ENTELLUS
HAP REDE CHANCE FORTUNE
  HAPPING
HAPHAZARD CASUAL CHANCE
  CHANCY RANDOM BUCKEYE
  SCRATCH CARELESS SCRAMBLY
  SLAPDASH
HAPHAZARDLY ANYHOW
HAPLESS POOR UNLUCKY
HAPLY HAPS HAPPILY
HAPPEN BE DO GO HAP COME COOK
  FALL FARE GIVE LUCK PASS TIDE
  TIME BREAK EVENE EVENT LIGHT
  OCCUR SHAPE ARRIVE BECOME
  BEFALL BETIDE CHANCE TUMBLE
  FORTUNE STUMBLE SUCCEED
  BECHANCE OVERCOME
  (— TOGETHER) CONCUR
HAPPENING HAP FACT EVENT THING
  CHANCE TIDING TIMING INCIDENT
  OCCASION
  (ACTUAL —) FACT
  (UNEXPECTED —) ACCIDENT
HAPPILY FAIN FITLY GLADLY
  JOYOUSLY
HAPPINESS JOY WIN GLEE SELE
  SONS WEAL BLISS GLORY MIRTH
  SOOTH FELICE WEALTH DELIGHT
  ECSTASY FELICIA RAPTURE UTILITY
  FELICITY GLADNESS HILARITY
HAPPY FIT COSH FAIN GLAD GLEG
  SELI WELY BONNY FAUST FELIX

LIGHT LUCKY MERRY PROUD SEELY
  SONSY SUNNY WHITE BONNIE
  JOYFUL COMICAL GLEEFUL
  HALCYON JOCULAR PERFECT
  SEELFUL WEALFUL WEIRDLY
  BLISSFUL CAREFREE DISPOSED
  FROHLICH GRACIOUS SUNSHINE
HARA-KIRI SEPPUKU
HARANGUE ORATE CONCIO PATTER
  SERMON SPEECH ADDRESS
  DECLAIM EARBASH DIATRIBE
  PERORATE
HARASS FAG GIG HAG HOX MAG
  NAG RAG TAW VEX BAIT CARK
  FRAB FRET GALL GNAW HAKE HALE
  HARE HAZE HOCK JADE PAIL RIDE
  SEEK TIRE TOIL TOSS WORK ANNOY
  BESET BULLY CHAFE CHASE CHEVY
  CHIVY CURSE FLISK GRIND GRIPE
  HARRY HURRY TARGE TEASE
  WEARY WORRY BADGER BOTHER
  CHOUSE CUMBER FERRET HATTER
  HECKLE HECTOR HESPEL HOORAY
  HURRAH INFEST MOLEST MURDER
  OBSESS PESTER PLAGUE POTHER
  PURSUE AFFLICT AGITATE BEDEVIL
  DRAGOON HAGRIDE HARRAGE
  OPPRESS PERPLEX PROVOKE
  TERRIFY TORMENT TRAVAIL
  TROUBLE TURMOIL BULLYRAG
  DISTRACT DISTRESS EXERCISE
  FORHAILE IRRITATE SPURGALL
  SUPPRESS
  (— MENTALLY) GRUDGE
HARASSED BESTEAD HARRIED
  HAUNTED
  (— BY) BEFORE
HARASSING WARM
HARBINGER ANGEL USHER HERALD
  FORAGER FORAYER FURRIER
  PRODROME
  (— OF SUMMER) SWALLOW
HARBOR REE BEAR DOCK HOLD
  PIER PORT BASIN BAYOU CHUCK
  CREEK HAVEN HITHE SLADE
  BREACH BUNDER COTHON FOSTER
  OUTPORT PORTLET SEAPORT
  SHELTER CARENAGE ENHARBOR
  SHIPRADE
  (— A CRIMINAL) RESET
HARBOR SEAL DOTANT DOTARD
  RANGER SEALCH TANGFISH
HARD DRY FIT ILL COLD DEAR DOUR
  DURE FAST FIRM IRON MEAN NASH
  OPEN CHAMP CLOSE CORKY HARSH
  HORNY ROCKY SMART SNELL SOLID
  SOUND STERN STONY STOOR
  STOUT TIGHT BOARDY BRAWNY
  COARSE FLINTY GLASSY KITTLE
  KNOBBY KNOTTY ROBUST RUGGED
  SEVERE STARKY STINGY STRICT
  STRONG UNEATH UNNETH ARDUOUS
  AUSTERE CALLOUS HARDWAY
  ONEROUS SUBDURE CORNEOUS
  DILIGENT HARDBACK HARDENED
  IRONHARD OBDURATE PETROSAL
  RIGOROUS SCLEROID SCLEROSE
  TOILSOME
  (— BY) FORBY FORTHBY

(— TO BEAR) FIERCE
(— TO MANAGE) SALTY
(— TO PLEASE) FINICKY CONCEITY
(— TO REACH) CUMBROUS
(— TO READ) BLIND
(— TO SATISFY) EXIGENT EXIGEANT
(— TO SELL) STICKY
(— TO UNDERSTAND) DIFFUSE
HARD-BILL SEEDEATER
HARD-BITTEN GNARLED
HARDEN SET TAW BAKE BEEK CAKE
  FIRM HARN KERN SEAR BRAZE
  ENURE FLESH INURE STEEL STONE
  ENDURE FREEZE OBDURE POTASH
  SEASON TEMPER CALCIFY
  EMBRAWN STIFFEN THICKEN
  CONCRETE ENHARDEN INDURATE
  SOLIDIFY
  (— QUILL) DUTCH
  (CASE —) STEEL
HARDENED DRAW HARD LOST
  SALTED CALLOUS CRUSTED
  FIBROUS INDURATE OBDURATE
HARDENING SET POROMA
  SCLEROMA
HARDHACK SPIREA IRONBUSH
  WHITECAP
HARDHEAD LION BOCHE
HARDHEARTED STERN STONY
  OBDURATE
HARDIHOOD PLUCK COURAGE
  AUDACITY
HARDLY ILL SCANT BARELY RARELY
  SCARCE UNEATH SCARCELY
HARDNESS SEG GRAIN PROOF
  RIGOR STEEL DURESS DURITY
  ADAMANT HARDSHIP SEVERITY
  SOLIDITY
  (— OF CHARACTER) HEART
HARD-OF-HEARING DULL DUNCH
  DEAFISH
HARDPAN PAN CLAYPAN MOORPAN
  ORSTEIN MOORBAND ORDSTEIN
HARDSHIP HARD GRIEF RIGOR
  STOUR THRONG UNWEAL SQUEEZE
  ASPERITY HARDNESS
  (PL.) EXTREMES
HARDTACK PANTILE
  (— AND MOLASSES) BURGOO
HARDWARE TRIM IRONWARE
HARDWOOD HARD BREAKAX
  LEAFWOOD
HARDWORKING EIDENT
HARDY DOUR HARD WIRY LUSTY
  MANLY STOUR STOUT TOUGH
  GARDEN INURED RUGGED STURDY
  SPARTAN STUBBED GAILLARD
  GALLIARD STUBBORN
HARE PUG WAT BAWD CONY PUSS
  SCUT BAWTY CUTTY LEPUS PUSSY
  MALKIN MAUKIN BELGIAN LEPORID
  VENISON KLIPHAAS LEPORINE
  (— IN FIRST YEAR) LEVERET
  (— TRACK) PRICK
  (FEMALE —) DOE
  (GREAT —) MANABOZHO
  (LITTLE CHIEF —) CONY PIKA
  (MALE —) BUCK
  (SIBERIAN —) TOLAI
  (PL.) FLICK

HAREBELL THIMBLE BLAEWORT
BLUEBELL
HAREBRAINED GIDDY WINDY
HARELIP LAGOSTOMA
HAREM SERAI ZENANA ANDERUN
HAREMLIK SERAGLIO
HARE'S-EAR MODESTY
HARIJAN PANCHAMA
HARL WHIRL
HARLEQUIN DUCK SQUEALER
(FEMALE —) LADY
(MALE —) LORD
HARLOT PUG DRAB SLUT HIREN
PAGAN QUEAN RAHAB STRAP
TWEAK WHORE RIBALD TOMBOY
DELILAH MERMAID WAGTAIL
MERETRIX MISWOMAN STRUMPET
HARLOTRY PUTAGE BITCHERY
HARM NEY NOY NYE WEM ARME
BALE BANE DERE HURT SORE TEEN
WERD GRAME HERME LOATH
QUALM SHEND SPOIL TOUCH
WATHE WEMMY WOUGH WOUND
WRAKE WREAK WRONG DAMAGE
DAMNUM DANGER GRIEVE INJURE
INJURY SCATHE SORROW WONDER
DESPITE DISEASE FORFEIT IMPEACH
TROUBLE UNQUERT BUSINESS
DISAVAIL DISSERVE ENDAMAGE
MISCHIEF NOCUMENT NUISANCE
(— REPUTATION) DEFAME
(DO —) ENVY
HARMFUL BAD EVIL HARM NASTY
NOXAL NOCENT NOCIVE NOYFUL
UNSELY BANEFUL HURTFUL
NOISOME NOXIOUS DAMAGING
INIMICAL SINISTER
HARMFULNESS VICE MALICE
HARMLESS SAFE SELI TAME SEELY
WHITE DOVISH FEARLESS HURTLESS
INNOCENT SACKLESS UNHARMED
HARMONIA (DAUGHTER OF —) INO
AGAVE SEMELE AUTONOE
(FATHER OF —) MARS
(HUSBAND OF —) CADMUS
(MOTHER OF —) VENUS
(SON OF —) POLYDORUS
HARMONICA HARP SYRINX AEOLINE
PANPIPE ARMONICA ZAMPOGNA
HARMONIOUS HAPPY SWEET
COSMIC SILKEN UNITED MUSICAL
SPHERAL TUNEFUL BALANCED
CHARMING HARMONIC PEACEFUL
HARMONITE RAPPIST RAPPITE
HARMONIUM ORGAN VOCALION
HARMONIZE GO FIT GEE KEY JIBE
SORT TUNE AGREE ATONE BLEND
CHORD GROUP HITCH ACCORD
ASSORT COTTON COMPORT
CONCENT CONCORD CONSORT
ORDINATE
HARMONIZING HENOTIC
HARMONY SUIT TUNE CHIME CHORD
UNITY ACCORD ATTUNE COSMOS
HEAVEN MELODY UNISON BALANCE
CONCERT CONCORD CONSENT
CONSORT KEEPING RAPPORT
DIAPASON SYMPATHY SYMPHONY
HARNESS TUG GEAR HAME LEAF

REIN BRACE CROWN DRAFT FRONT
GEARS SLING TRACE COLLAR
FETTLE GULLET INSPAN TACKLE
DRAUGHT GEARING GIGTREE
LORMERY SIMBLOT TOGGERY
DRAWGEAR ENCLOSER HEADGEAR
TACKLING TURNBACK
(— FOR LOOM) LEAF HEALD
MOUNTING
(DECORATIVE —) CAPARISON
(WEAVING —) HEADLE HEDDLE
HARNESSED ANTELOPE GUIB
GUIBA BOSCHBOK BUSHBUCK
HARNESS MAKER KNACKER
WHITTAW
HAROLD I HAREFOOT
HARP ARPA FORK VINA NABLA
NANGA HARPER SABECA CHROTTA
DECHORD SAMBUKE AUTOHARP
CLARSACH
(CELTIC —) TELYN
(FINNISH —) KANTELA KANTELE
(ICELANDIC —) LANGSPIL
(JAPANESE —) KOTO
(JEW'S —) TRUMP
(PERSIAN —) SANG
(TRIANGULAR —) TRIGON TRIGONON
HARPOON IRON FIZGIG GRAINS
FISHGIG PARPAGO STRIKER
HARPAGON
HARPOONED FAST
HARPOONER STRIKER
HARP SEAL HARP BEATER SADDLER
HARPSICHORD SPINET CEMBALO
CLAVIER CLAVECIN HASPICOL
HARPY HAG AELLO CELAENO
OCYPETE PODARGE
HARQUEBUS HAGBUT CALIVER
HACKBUT ARQUEBUS
HARQUEBUSIER CARABIN
HARRIER HAWK KAHU FALLER
MILLER PUTTOCK HARROWER
HARROW COG CHIP DISC DISK DRAG
HARO TINE BRAKE BREAK HERSE
DREDGE DRUDGE FALLOW LADDER
SPADER CUTAWAY LACERATE
OXHARROW
HARROWED HAGGARD
HARROWING TINE TINING TEARING
HARRY HAG BRACE CHIVEY CHIVVY
FERRET HARASS CRUCIFY
HARSH ILL ACID BULL DOUR FOUL
HARD HASH HASK IRON RUDE SOUR
ACERB ACRID ASPER BRUTE CRONK
CRUDE GRILL GRUFF HEAVY HUSKY
RASPY ROUND RUVID SHARP SNELL
STARK STERN STIFF STOUR STOUT
BRUTAL COARSE FLINTY GRAVEL
GRISLY HOARSE RAGGED RASPED
RUGGED SEVERE SHREWD STURDY
SULLEN TETRIC UNKIND UNRIDE
AUSTERE RASPING RAUCOUS
SQUAWKY ACERBATE ASPERATE
ASPEROUS CATONIAN CLASHING
DRACONIC GRAVELLY GRINDING
GUTTURAL JANGLING OBDURATE
RIGOROUS SCABROUS SCRANNEL
STRIDENT STROUNGE STUBBORN
TETRICAL UNGENTLE UNKINDLY

(— OF VOICE) STEER
HARSHLY HARD HARSH SHORTLY
HARSHNESS WOLF RIGOR DURESS
CATOISM CRUDITY CRUELTY
DUREZZA ACERBITY ASPERITY
FELLNESS HARDNESS HASKNESS
SEVERITY
HART SPADE VENISON
HARTEBEEST ASSE TORA TORI
BUBAL CAAMA KAAMA KONZE
LECAMA BUBALIS CONGONI
KONGONI
HART'S-TONGUE LONGLEAF
HARUSPEX ARUSPEX ARUSPICE
EXTISPEX
HARVEST IN WIN CROP HEAP RABI
REAP SLED SNAP FOISON GATHER
HAIRST RUBBEE COMBINE GRABBLE
INGATHER SHEARING
HARVEST FISH WHITING MOONFISH
STARFISH
HARVEST HOME KIRN MELL
HOCKEY HORKEY
HARVESTING SLEDDING
HARVESTMAN CARTER CARTARE
HAS S AS HATH
(— NOT) NAS AINT
HAS-BEEN WUZZER
HASH RAPE MINCE HACHIS
HASHISH HEMP ASSIS
HASID ASSIDEAN
HASKALAH (FOLLOWER OF —)
MASKIL
HASP COP HAPS COPSE SPRENT
HASSAR DORAD
HASSOCK TUT BOSS PESS TOIT
TRUSH BUFFET TUFFET
HASTE HIE POST RACE RAGE RAPE
CHASE FEVER HASTY HURRY SPEED
BUSTLE FLURRY SWIVET DISPATCH
RAPIDITY STROTHER
(HEADLONG —) SPURN
(IN —) HOTFOOT
(IN GREAT —) AMAIN
HASTEN HIE RAP RUN BUSK DUST
FIRK PELL PLAT POST RACE RAPE
RUSH SPUR URGE CATCH CHASE
DRIVE FLEET HASTE HURRY PRESS
PREST SLATE SPEED STEER EXPEDE
SCURRY STREAK SWITHE ADVANCE
FORWARD HACKNEY HOTFOOT
PREVENT QUICKEN SLITHER
SWIFTEN WITHHIE DISPATCH
EXPEDITE
(— AWAY) FLEE SHERRY SQUIRR
HASTILY HOTLY RAPELY RASHLY
FOOTHOT HOTFOOT HYINGLY
HEADLONG
HASTY FAST RAPE RASH FLEET
QUICK FLYING RAPELY CURSORY
HOTHEAD HURRIED TEARING
HASTEFUL HEADLONG SUBITANE
(TACTLESSLY —) BRASH
HAT DIP FEZ LID NAB ATTE BAKU
COIF DISC DISK FELT FLAT HIVE
HOOD KNAB MOAB SLOP TILE TOPI
BEANY BENJY BENNY BERET BOXER
CADDI CORDY DERBY DICER GIBUS
JERRY KELLY MILAN MITER MITRE

SHELL TARAI TOPEE TOQUE TRUSH
ABACOT BEANIE BEAVER BOATER
BOWLER BRETON BUMPER CASQUE
CLAQUE CLOCHE COCKUP COIFFE
FEDORA HELMET PANAMA PILEUS
RAFFIA SAILOR SHOVEL SLOUCH
TOPPER TURBAN VIGONE BANDEAU
BANGKOK BRIMMER BYCOKET
CATSKIN CAUBEEN CHAPEAU
FANTAIL HATTING HATTOCK
HOMBURG LEGHORN PETASOS
PILLBOX PLATEAU PLATTER
SALACOT SCRAPER SHALLOW
SKIMMER SMASHER BONGRACE
CAPELINE GOSSAMER HEADGEAR
JIPIJAPA MONTABYN MUSHROOM
NABCHEAT RAMILIES REHOBOAM
ROUNDLET SOMBRERO
(— BLOCKER) ROPER
(3-CORNERED —) TRICORN
(BEAVER —) CASTOR
(CLERGYMAN'S —) SHOVEL
(COCKED —) BICORNE RAMILIE
SCRAPER
(COWBOY —) STETSON
(FABRIC —) TOQUE
(FELT —) DERBY JERRY TARAI
TERAI ALPINE BOWLER TRILBY
(HIGH —) KYL TILE TOPPER
(IRON —) GOSSAN GOZZAN
(MILITARY —) BUSBY BEARSKIN
(OILSKIN —) SQUAM
(OPERA —) GIBUS CLAQUE
(PITH —) TOPI TOPEE
(SILK —) KYL BEAVER SHINER
CATSKIN
(STIFF —) TILE DERBY KELLY
BOATER BOWLER SAILOR
(STOVEPIPE —) CAROLINE
(STRAW —) BAKU FLAT HOOD KADY
KATY BENJY BENNY CADDY STRAW
BOATER PANAMA LEGHORN
(TOP —) PLUG TOPPER
(UNBLOCKED —) CONE
(WIDE-BRIMMED —) FLAT BENJY
TARAI SUNDOWN
HATBAND BAND WEED WEEPER
HAT BRIM LEAF TARFE TURNUP
HATCH HECK BROOD CLECK CLOCK
COVEY GUICHET UNSHELL
DISCLOSE INCUBATE
HATCHERY CHICKERY
HATCHET MOGO HACHE GWEEON
THIXIE FRANCISC TOMAHAWK
HATCHING CLETCH BREEDING
ECLISION
HATCHWAY HATCH SCUTTLE
HATE FIRE TEEN ABHOR SPITE
DETEST HATRED LOATHE UNLOVE
DESPITE
HATEFUL FOUL LOTH BLACK CURST
DIRTY HATEL LOATH CURSED
ODIOUS HEINOUS HIDEOUS
FLAGRANT
HATER ULYSSES
HATH MOOLUM
HAT MONEY TAMPANG
HATRED DOSA ENVY HATE HELL

ONDE HAINE ODIUM SPITE ENMITY
RANCOR AVERSION
(— OF CHILDREN) MISOPEDIA
(— OF MARRIAGE) MISOGAMY
(— OF MEN) MISANDRY
(— OF NEW IDEAS) MISCAINEA
(— OF WOMEN) MISOGENY
HATTER GADGER HURRER
HAUBERK BYRNIE
HAUGHTILY BIGLY
HAUGHTINESS AIR PRIDE HEIGHT
MORGUE ORGUIL HAUTEUR
STOMACH HAUTESSE
HAUGHTY DAIN HIGH RANK STAY
DIGNE DORTY HUFFY LOFTY LUSTY
POTTY PROUD STOUT SURLY TAUNT
FEISTY FIERCE HAUGHT QUAINT
DISTANT HAUTAIN HONTISH
PAUGHTY STATELY SUBLIME
ARROGANT CAVALIER DEIGNOUS
FASTUOUS GLORIOUS IMPERIAL
INSOLENT ORGULOUS PRIDEFUL
SCORNFUL SNIFFISH SUPERIOR
TOPLOFTY
HAUL KEP LUG RUG TEW TOW TUG
DRAG DRAW DRAY HALE HURL
JUNK PULL SKID TAKE TOTE TRAM
BOUSE DRAVE HEAVE LIGHT ROUSE
SNAKE TRACT TRAVOY DRAUGHT
SCHLEPP CORDELLE HANDBANK
(— AFT) TALLY
(— DOWN) STRIKE
(— IN) GATHER
(— LOGS) TODE SLOOP SWAMP
SIWASH HANDBANK
(— OF FISH) TACK DRAVE
(— OF NET) LIFT
(— SAIL) BUNT CLEW CLUE
(— SHIP) SPRING
(— TO DECK) BOARD
(— UP AND FASTEN) TRICE
(— WITH TACKLE) BOUSE
HAULAGE DOOK
HAULAGEWAY GANGWAY
HAULING HALE CARTAGE
HAUNCH HIP HOOK HUCK HANCE
HUCKLE
(PL.) GRUG HUNKERS
HAUNT DEN HANT HOME HOWF KEEP
NEST WALK GHOST HOWFF SPOOK
STALK INFEST OBSESS OUTLAY
REPAIR PURLIEU FREQUENT
PRACTICE
(— OF ANIMALS) LIE HOME
(FAMILIAR —) SLAIT
HAUNTED SPOOKY
HAUNTING SPOOKY BESETTING
HAUSTELLATE GLOSSATE
HAUSTORIUM SINK SINKER SUCKER
HAUTBOY OBOE WAIT
HAUTEUR HEIGHT
HAVE A AN OF OWN HOLD BOAST
ENJOY OUGHT WIELD POSSESS
HAVEN HOPE PIER PORT HITHE
HARBOR HAVENET
HAVOC HOB HELL WASTE RAVAGE
HAW HOI HECK SLOE WIND WYND
BOOTS PEGGLE ALISIER

HAWAII
BAY: POHUE HALAWA KIHOLO
MAMALA KAMOHIO KANEOHE
WAIAGUA KAWAIHAE MAUNALUA
BEACH: WAIKIKI
CAPITAL: HONOLULU
CHANNEL: AUA KAIWI KALOHI
PAILOLO
COUNTY: MAUI KAUAI HAWAII
HONOLULU
CRATER: KILAUEA
DESERT: KAU
DISTRICT: KONA PUNA
FISH: ULUA AKULE MOANO
HARBOR: PEARL
HEAD: DIAMOND
ISLAND: MAUI OAHU KAUAI KAULA
LANAI NIIHAU MOLOKAI
MOUNTAIN: KAALA KOHALA
KAMAKOU MAUNAKEA
LANAIHALE
MOUNTAIN RANGE: KOHALA
KOOLAU WAIANAE
NATIVE: KANAKA
STATE BIRD: GOOSE
STATE FLOWER: HIBISCUS
STATE NICKNAME: ALOHA
STATE TREE: CANDLENUT
TOWN: EWA AIEA HANA HILO LAIE
PAIA KAPAA LIHUE MAILI KAILUA
KEKAHA KAHULUI KANEOHE
WAHIAWA WAIANAE WAILUKU
HONOLULU
TREE: KOA NAIO WILIWILI
VALLEY: MANOA
VOLCANO: MAUNALOA

HAWAIIAN KANAKA KAMAAINA
HAWFINCH KATE GROSBEAK
HAWK IO EYAS KITE ALLAN BATER
BUTEO CADGE EYESS HOICK HOUGH
REACH RIVER STOOP BAWREL
FALCON FOOTER HIGGLE MERLIN
MUSKET OSPREY PALLET PEDDLE
RAMAGE RAPTOR RIFLER SHIKRA
VERMIN BUZZARD GOSHAWK
HAGGARD HARRIER HERONER
LENTNER SWOOPER BRANCHER
CARACARA HARROWER LENTINER
PASSAGER ROUGHLEG SPARHAWK
TALENTER TARTARET
(— FIGHT) CRAB
(CROP OF —) GORGE
(FEMALE —) FORMAL FORMEL
(MALE —) JACK TASSEL TERCEL
(YOUNG —) EYAS NIAS BRANCHER
HAWKER CRIER CRYER BADGER
CADGER COSTER DUFFER JOWTER
PEDDER PETHER CAMELOT
CHAPMAN HIGGLER MERCURY
PEDDLER CRATEMAN GLASSMAN
HUCKSTER
HAWKEYE STATE IOWA
HAWKING FALCONRY
HAWK PARROT HIA
HAWKWEED DINDLE BUGLOSS
FIREWEED
HAWSE BAG JACKASS

HAWSER FAST WARP HEADLINE
HAWTHORN HAW MAY QUICK
THORN AIGLET MAYBUSH
COCKSPUR MAYBLOOM MAYTHORN
QUICKSET
(**FRUIT OF —**) HAZEL PEGGLE
HAY HEI RIP MATH RAKH RISP
FETTLE STOVER WINDLIN
SWEEPAGE
(**— CUT FINE**) CHAFF
(**— PUT IN BARN**) END
(**BUNDLE OF —**) TRUSS
(**PILE OF —**) TUMBLE
(**ROW OF —**) WINDROW
(**SECOND-GROWTH —**) EDDISH
(**SMALL LOAD OF —**) HURRY
(**SMALL PIECE OF —**) TATE
HAYCOCK MOW COIL HOVEL QUILE
SHOCK DOODLE HIPPLE LAPCOCK
HAYSHOCK
HAYFIELD PARK RAKH MOWING
HAYFORK PIKE PICKEL
HAYLOFT LOFT TALLET SCAFFOLD
HAYMAKER PICKMAN
HAYMOW GOAF HAYLOFT OVERDEN
OVERHEAD
HAYRACK HECK HAYRIG THRIPPLE
HAYSTACK COB PIKE RICK HOVEL
HAYRICK STACKAGE
HAYSUCK EYSOGE
HAY SWEEP BUCK
HAYWARD MEADSMAN
HAZAN CANTOR CHAZZAN
HAZARD DIE LAY LOT JUMP PAWN
RISK WAGE JENNY LOSER PERIL
CHANCE DANGER BALANCE IMPERIL
VENTURE ENDANGER JEOPARDY
HAZARDOUS RISKY CHANCY
QUEASY RISQUE UNSAFE UNSURE
PERILOUS
HAZARDOUSLY CHANCILY
HAZE FOG URE FILM GLIN MIST REEK
SMOG TRUB DEVIL GAUZE HAZLE
SMEETH
HAZEL AGLET AIGLET COBNUT
MUFFIN FILBERT HAZELNUT
NOISETTE
(**— FOR THATCHING**) SPRAYS
HAZEL HOE PULASKI
HAZELNUT NIT HAZEL FILBERT
HAZEL TREE AVELLANO
HAZILY DIMLY
HAZINESS HAZE GRAYOUT
HAZY DIM FOGGY MISTY SMOKY
THICK VAGUE CLOUDY DREAMY
OBSCURE SMUISTY NEBULOUS
HE A E HI HO HEH HEY HIM HYE SHE
ILLE THON CESTUI
(**— DIED**) OB
(**— GAVE AND DEDICATED**) DDD
(**— MADE**) F FEC
(**— PAINTED IT**) PNXT
(**— READS**) LEG
(**— WAS NOT FOUND**) NEI
HEAD BIT BUT COP DON FAT MIR
NAB NOB PEN POW TOP BEAN BOSS
CAPE COCO CONK COSP CROP
DATU DEAN DOME HELM JOLE JOWL
KAID KNOB LEAD MASK NOLL PASH

PATE POLL RAIS TURN YEAD ALDER
ATTIC BLADE BLOCK CHIEF CHUMP
CROWN DATTO MAZER ONION RISER
SCALP SHODE SKULL START TIBBY
TROPE BELFRY BLANCH CABEZA
CENTER CHAULE COBBRA COCKER
DAROGA EXARCH GARRET GATHER
HEADER KAISER MAHANT MAZARD
NAPPER NODDLE PALLET RUBRIC
SCONCE CAPITAL CAPTAIN
COCONUT COSTARD COSTREL
COXCOMB CRUMPET CUPHEAD
GENARCH HEADING HEGUMEN
NUCLEUS PRELATE TOPKNOT
CALABASH CEPHALON DECURION
DIRECTOR DUFFADAR FOUNTAIN
HEADLINE INITIATE PHYLARCH
POINTING TOPPIECE
(**— IN PARTICULAR DIRECTION**)
STEM
(**— OF 10 MONKS**) DEAN
(**— OF ABBEY**) ABBOT
(**— OF ALEMBIC**) MITER MITRE
(**— OF BEAR, WOLF OR BOAR**) HURE
(**— OF CABBAGE**) LOAF
(**— OF CEREAL**) EAR
(**— OF CHAIR**) MAKER
(**— OF CLOVER**) COB SUCKER
(**— OF COMET**) COMA
(**— OF CONVENT**) ABBESS
SUPERIOR
(**— OF DRILL BRACE**) CUSHION
(**— OF FAMILY**) ALDER GOODMAN
(**— OF FISH**) JOWL
(**— OF GANG**) TINDAL
(**— OF GOVERNMENT**) MUKHTAR
(**— OF GRAIN**) ICKER
(**— OF HAIR**) SUIT CRINE FLEECE
(**— OF HARPOON**) BOMB
(**— OF HERRING**) COB
(**— OF JEWISH ACADEMY**) GAON
(**— OF LANCE**) MORNE MOURNE
(**— OF LOOM**) JACQUARD
(**— OF MONASTERY**) HEGUMEN
(**— OF MUSICAL INSTRUMENT**)
SCROLL
(**— OF NUNNERY**) DAME
(**— OF ORDER**) MURSHID
(**— OF RING**) CHATON
(**— OF RIVET**) BULLHEAD FLATHEAD
SNAPHEAD
(**— OF STATE**) PRINCEPS
(**— OF TAPEWORM**) SCOLEX
(**— OF TREE**) COMA
(**— ON**) SQUARE
(**— PREMATURELY**) BUTTON
(**— USED AS TARGET**) SARACEN
(**BAKED SHEEP'S —**) JAMES JEMMY
(**BALD —**) PILGARLIC
(**BARBED —**) FLUKE
(**DRAGON'S —**) RAHU
(**FLOWER —**) DAISY ARNICA BUTTON
PINBALL
(**FLOWER —S**) CURD ANTHEMIS
(**NAIL —**) ROSEHEAD
(**POPPY —**) POST
(**PRINTED —**) BOXHEAD
(**SEED — OF FLAX**) HOPPE

(**SHRUNKEN —**) TSANTSA
(**PL.**) GEONIM
HEADACHE HEAD SODA BUSTHEAD
HEADWARK MIGRAINE
HEADBAND MITER MITRE VITTA
CARCAN DIADEM TAENIA CIRCLET
GARLAND CARCANET FOOTBAND
STEPHANE
HEADBOROUGH VERGES
HEADCAP SETHEAD
HEADDRESS FLY TOP TOY APEX
COIF FRET HEAD HORN PARE POUF
TETE TIRE TOUR AEGIS AMPYX
CROWN GABLE LAUTU PASTE
POLOS PSHEM SHAKO TIARA
TOWER VITTA ALMUCE ATTIRE
ATTOUR BONNET CASQUE CORNET
FAILLE HENNIN KENNEL KULLAH
MOBCAP PINNER TIRING TUINGA
BANDORE COMMODE FLANDAN
MORTIER PSCHENT STEEPLE
TABLITA THERESE TRESSON
TUTULUS BILIMENT BINNOGUE
BYCOCKET CAPRIOLE COIFFURE
HEADGEAR HEADTIRE KAFFIYEH
MASKETTE STEPHANE TRESSURE
(**— OF DOGES**) TOQUE
(**— WITH LONG LAPPET**) PINNER
(**HIGH —**) TOWER STEEPLE
(**WIDOW'S —**) BANDORE
HEADED KNOTTED
(**— OUT**) RIZZOMED
HEADER BINDER NOBBER SADDLE
KNOBBER HEADSMAN STRETMAN
HEADFAST HEADROPE
HEADFIRST HEADLONG
HEADFOREMOST TOPSAIL
HEADFRAME POPPET GALLOWS
HEADGEAR (ALSO SEE HEADDRESS)
HIVE PASTE BONNET BRIDLE
HEADWEAR
HEADHUNTER LAKHER TAIYAL
ATAIYAL QUIANGAN
HEADING END HEAD STOW PILOT
TROPE WICKET CAPTION DIPHEAD
HEADILY STENTON WITCHET
FOREHAND STENTING
HEADLAND KOP PEN RAS BILL HEAD
MULL NAZE NESS NOOK PEAK
SCAW THRUM FORELAND
HEADLINE HEAD LABEL BANNER
CAPTION DROPLINE SCREAMER
STREAMER
HEADLONG FULL RANK HASTY
PRONE STEEP SUDDEN RAMSTAM
TANTIVY GADARENE HEADLING
RECKLESS
HEADMAN JARL CHIEF DATTO MALIK
PATEL POMBO VIDAN ATAMAN
CABEZA HETMAN INDUNA LOWDAH
LULUAI POTAIL TOPMAN KOMARCH
ALDERMAN CABOCEER CAPITANO
HEADSMAN KONOHIKI MALGUZAR
MOKADDAM PENGHULU PRINCEPS
STAROSTA TENIENTE
HEADMASTER HEAD REGENT
HEADMOST FOREMOST
HEADNOTE SYLLABUS
HEADPIECE CAP POT BASKET

CASQUE HELMET PALLET TESTER TREMOR CASQUET CHAMFRON TESTIERE

HEADPIN KINGPIN

HEADQUARTERS DEPOT YAMEN AGENCY FONDACO EXCHANGE BATTALION

HEADROPE BALK BAULK HEADLINE

HEADSET PHONES

HEADSHIP CHIEFTY

(SPIRITUAL —) KHALIFAT

HEADSPACE OUTAGE

HEADSTALL HALTER BRADOON BRIDOON JAQUIMA

HEADSTOCK POPPET

HEADSTRONG RASH COBBY RACKLE STOCKY UNRULY HOTSPUR RAMSTAM VIOLENT WAYWARD

HEADWAITER CAPTAIN

HEADWAY WAY DENT SEAWAY WAYGATE HEADROOM

HEADWORD ENTRY

HEADY BOLD NAPPY HUFFCAP

HEAL CURE HALE MEND SAIN AMEND COVER LEECH SALVE SOUND WHOLE PHYSIC RECURE SUPPLE TEMPER WARISH CLEANSE GUARISH RECOVER REDRESS RESTORE MEDICATE

(— OVER) INCARN

HEALD CAMB DUPE HAVEL

HEALER CURER ALTHEA SHAMAN POWWOWER

HEALING IATRIC POWWOW BALSAMIC CURATION IATRICAL SANATION

HEALTH SAP HAIL HEAL SONS QUART SALEW LIKING PLEDGE SALUTE SANITY EUCRASY SLAINTE EUCRASIA TONICITY VALETUDE

(GOOD —) PLIGHT VERDURE

(ILL —) SICKNESS

(NORMAL —) USUAL

HEALTHFUL HEALTHY HYGIENIC SALUTARY SANATORY SANITARY

HEALTHY FIT FIER FIRM HALE IRON SAFE SANE TIDY WELL BONNY HODDY QUART SOUND STOUT VALID ENTIRE HEARTY ROBUST BOUNCING LAUDABLE SALUTARY SANITARY VEGETOUS VIGOROUS

HEAP COP CUB HOT MOW PIE SOW TON BALE BING BULK DECK DESS HILL HOTT LEET PILE POKE POOK REEK RUCK SESS TASS TUMP AMASS CLAMP CLUMP COUCH CROWD SHOCK STACK WOPSE BURROW HIPPLE HOTTER ISLAND MEILER OODLES QUARRY RICKLE RUCKLE SCRAPE SORITE TOORIE BOUROCK CUMULUS ENDORSE HAYCOCK HAYRICK HURROCK TOOROCK TUMMELS WINDROW BASURALE

(— HAY) UNCOCK

(— OF DEAD BODIES) CARNAGE

(— OF GAME) QUARRY

(— OF ORE) PANEL

(— OF PRODUCE) BURY CLAMP

(— OF REFUSE) BURROW BASURAL

(— OF RUBBISH) GAGING

(— OF SILVER ORE) TORTA

(— OF STONES) AHU MAN CAIRN SCRAE SCREE HURROCK MONTJOY

(— OF VEGETABLES) HOG

(— REPROACHES) KICK

(— TOGETHER) AGGEST HOWDER LUMBER CUMULATE

(— UP) HILL SACK AGGEST ACERVATE AGGERATE OVERHEAP

(COMBUSTIBLE —) PYRE

(MANURE —) HOTT MIXEN

(PROMISCUOUS —) RAFF

HEAR EAR LIST OYES OYEZ LEARN LITHE HARKEN LISTEN HEARKEN

(— DIRECTLY) IMPINGE

HEARD AUDIBLE

(EASILY —) CLEAR

HEARER AUDIENT AUDITOR

HEARING EAR LIST OYER AUDIT SOUND ASSIZE AUDIENCE AUDITION

HEARKEN HARK HEAR HEED LIST TEND LITHE ATTEND HARKEN INTEND

HEARSAY REPORT ACCOUNT

HEARSE HACK CATAFALCO

HEART AB COR CORE GIST HATI RAAN SOUL YOLK BOSOM BOWEL CHEER QUICK BREAST CENTER CENTRE DEPTHS HASLET MIDDLE TICKER VISCUS COURAGE EMOTION ESSENCE FEELING

(— OF DIXIE) ALABAMA

(DEAR —) DILIS

HEARTACHE SORROW

HEARTBEAT STROKE

HEARTBURN PYROSIS

HEART CHERRY GASKINS

HEARTEN BIELD CHEER HEART SPIRIT EMBOLDEN INSPIRIT

HEARTFELT DEAR DEEP REAL TRUE INFELT INWARD CORDIAL GENUINE SINCERE

HEARTH EARD SOLE TEST ASTRE CUPEL EARTH FOCUS FOGON FOYER SMOKE CHIMNEY

(— GODDESS) VESTA

HEARTILY INLY AGOOD DEARLY FREELY WARMLY SHEERLY DINGDONG INWARDLY STRONGLY

HEARTINESS GOODWILL

HEARTTHROB DUNT

HEARTWOOD HEART SAPAN SPINE GUAYAB BUBINGA DURAMEN TRUEWOOD

HEARTY REAL WARM COBBY FRECK HEAVY STOUT DEVOUT ENTIRE ROBUST STANCH BOBBISH CORDIAL EARNEST HEALTHY RAFFING SINCERE HEARTFUL VIGOROUS

HEAT HET HOT RUT SUN TAP BOIL FIRE GLOW SALT WARM ARDOR BROIL CALOR CAUMA CHAFE FEVER PRIDE PROUD STECH TEPOR TRIAL ACHAFE ANNEAL DEGREE DIGEST FERVOR HEATEN IGNITE SCORCH SEASON SPARGE WARMTH CALCINE CALORIC ENCHAFE FERMENT

FLUSTER INCENSE INFERNO PASSION SWELTER UPERIZE CALIDITY

(— GENTLY) SOAK

(— OF BATTLE) PRESS

(— SCRAP IRON) BUSHEL

(— SWEETEN, AND SPICE) MULL

(— TOBACCO) SAP

(SCORCHING —) EWDER

HEATED WARM FIERCE STEAMY

HEATER FIRE COCKLE SMOKER CHAFFER CHOFFER LATROBE

HEATH BENT YETH BESOM BRIAR BRIER ERICA ERICAD COMMONS HEATHER

HEATHEN AKKUM PAGAN ETHNIC GENTILE PROFANE SARACEN GENTILIC

HEATHENISM ODINISM OTHINISM PAGANISM

HEATHER BENT GRIG LING BROOM ERICA HEATH HADDER

HEATHERY LINGY

HEATH PEA CARMELE

HEATING BAKEOUT BURNING

HEATLESS ATHERMIC

HEAVE GAG BUNG HEFT HOVE KECK LIFE QUAP FETCH HOIST SCEND SURGE BUCKLE KECKLE POPPLE ESTUATE

HEAVEN SKY HIGH ABOVE BLISS DYAUS ETHER GLORY CANAAN HIMMEL SVARGE SWARGA URANUS WELKIN KINGDOM OLYMPUS DEVALOKA EMPYREAL EMPYREAN PARADISE SVARLOKA

(12TH PART OF —) HOUSE

(PL.) ARCH LIFT LANGI HEIGHT REGION SPHERE ELEMENT TENGERE EMPYREAN KAMALOKA

HEAVENLY ABOVE DIVINE ANGELIC URANIAN ETHEREAL OLYMPIAN

HEAVENWARD ZIONWARD

HEAVER COALY DANNER HEFTER

HEAVILY SOSS CLOIT CLYTE HEAVY SADLY SOUSE SWACK

HEAVINESS HEFT GLOOM POISE WEIGHT GRAVITY

HEAVY FAT HOT SAD CLIT DEEP DULL HARD BEEFY BURLY DENSE DOWFF DUNCH GRAVE GREAT GROSS HEFTY HOGGY STIFF THARF THERF WROTH CHARGE CLUMSY DOUGHY DRAGGY HEARTY LEADEN LIVERY LOGGER SODDEN STODGY STRONG STUPID INSIPID LABORED LIVERED LUMPING MASSIVE ONEROUS WEIGHTY CUMBROUS GRIEVOUS PERSANTE PREGNANT THUMPING

HEAVY-FOOTED SOGGY LEADEN INFICETE

HEBDOMADARY WEEKLY

HEBE (FATHER OF —) JUPITER

(HUSBAND OF —) HERCULES

(MOTHER OF —) JUNO

HEBREW RABBINIC

HECATE TRIVIA

(FATHER OF —) PERSES

(MOTHER OF —) ASTERIA
HECKLE BAIT GIBE HACK BADGER
HARASS HECTOR HATCHEL
HECTIC ETIK SEPTIC HECTIVE
FEVERISH FRENETIC FRENZIED
HECTOLITER VAT
(5.82 —S) LEAGUER
HECTOR BAIT HUFF BULLY HARRY
WORRY HARASS HECKLE BLUSTER
BRAVADO BROWBEAT
(FATHER OF —) PRIAM
(MOTHER OF —) HECUBA
(WIFE OF —) ANDROMACHE
HECUBA (DAUGHTER OF —)
POLYXENA
(FATHER OF —) DYMAS CISSEUS
(SON OF —) PARIS HECTOR
POLYDORUS
HEDDLE CAMB DOUP HAVEL HEALD
(PL.) CAAM
HEDGE BAR HAW HAY HYE OXER
SAVE BEARD EDDER FENCE FRITH
FUDGE HOVER MOUND QUICK
COPPER FRIGHT RADDLE ENCLOSE
QUICKSET RUFFMANS SEPIMENT
SURROUND THICKSET
HEDGE BINDWEED CREEPER
HELLWEED WOODBINE
HEDGEHOG ORCHEN URCHIN
ECHINUS ERICIUS YLESPIL
HEDGEPIG HERISSON
HEDGE LAUREL TARATA
HEDGE MUSTARD BANKWEED
FLUXWEED
HEDGE NETTLE STACHYS
HEDGE PARSLEY HOGWEED
HEDGE-PRIEST PATRICO
HEDGE SPARROW DICKY DONEY
DICKEY EYSOGE PHILIP CHANTER
DUNNOCK HAYSUCK PINNOCK
TITLING ACCENTOR
HEDGEWOOD LAYER
HEED CARK COME CURE GAUM HEAR
KEEP LOOK MIND NOTE RECK TEND
TENT VISE WARE YEME AWAIT
TASTE VALUE ATTEND INTENT
NOTICE REGARD REMARK REWARD
CAUTION OBSERVE RESPECT
SUSPECT THOUGHT
HEEDFUL WARE ATTENT DILIGENT
HEEDLESS RASH BLIND DIZZY GIDDY
BLITHE REMISS UNWARY LANGUID
UNHEEDY CARELESS LISTLESS
MINDLESS RECKLESS WISTLESS
HEEDLESSLY BLIND HEADLONG
HEEL TIP BUTT CALX FROG HIELD
SPIKE TALON DOTTLE INCLINE
BOOTHEEL
(— IN) SHOUGH
(— OF GATE) HARR
(— OF HORSESHOE) SPONGE
(— OF SWORD BLADE) TALON
RICASSO
(— OVER) SEEL TILT CAREEN
HEEL BEVEL RAND
HEEL PLATE SHOD CLEAT
HEFT WEIGHT
HEFTY HEAVY
HEIFER IO QUI QUEE QUEY QUOY

BULLER STOCKER
(— IN 2ND YEAR) STIRK
(YEARLING —) BURLING
HEIGH-HO HECH
HEIGHT SUM ACME ALTO APEX FELL
HIGH LOFT MOTE PINK TUNE CREST
HICHT STATE ALTURE INCHES
SUMMIT CEILING COMMAND
HEIGHTH STATURE SUPREME
ALTITUDE EMINENCE HAUTESSE
SIDENESS VERTICAL ACROPOLIS
(— OF FASHION) GO
(— OF PROSPERITY) GLORY
(— OF ROOM) STUD STUDDING
(— OF SAIL) HOIST
(GREATEST —) SUMMIT ZENITH
(ROCKY —) KNOT
HEIGHTEN ENDOW EXALT FORCE
RAISE ACCENT BOLSTER ENHANCE
SUBLIME
(— FLAVOR) PETUNE
HEINOUS SWART CRYING WICKED
SCARLET FLAGRANT GRIEVOUS
HEIR SCION SPRIG COHEIR HERITOR
APPARENT PARCENER
(— APPARENT) ATHELING ETHELING
(FEMALE —) DISTAFF
HEIRESS BEGUM PORTIA FORTUNE
HERITRIX
HEIRLOOM (PL.) CIMELIA
HELENUS (FATHER OF —) PRIAM
(MOTHER OF —) HECUBA
(SON OF —) CESTRINUS
(WIFE OF —) ANDROMACHE
HELIANTHEMUM SUNROSE
HELICAL SPIRAL
HELICOPTER COPTER CHOPPER
WINDMILL
HELIOPOLIS ON
HELIOS HYPERION PHAETHON
(FATHER OF —) HYPERION
(MOTHER OF —) THEIA
HELIOSIS SUNBURN
HELIOTROPE HELIO BENNET
SETWALL GIRASOLE TURNSOLE
HELIPORT SKYPORT
HELIX COIL SPIRAL
HELIXIN HEDERIN
HELL PIT POT HECK PAIN ABYSS
AVICI BLAZE DEUCE HADES SHEOL
BLAZES NARAKA TARTAR TOPHET
TUNKET ABADDON GEHENNA
HELLBOX INFERNO TARTARUS
BARATHRUM
HELLBENDER TWEEG
HELLE (FATHER OF —) ATHAMAS
(MOTHER OF —) NEPHELE
(SISTER OF —) PHRIXUS
HELLEBORE POKE BUGBANE
ITCHWEED LINGWORT LUNGWORT
NOSEWORT POKEROOT VERATRUM
EARTHGALL
HELLEN (FATHER OF —) DEUCALION
(MOTHER OF —) PYRRHA
(SON OF —) DORUS AEOLUS
XUTHUS
(WIFE OF —) ORSEIS
HELLER HALER HALERZ
HELLERI SWORDTAIL

HELLGRAMMITE DOBSON SIALID
CLIPPER CRAWLER SPRAWLER
HELLISH HELLY SATANIC STYGIAN
DEVILISH INFERNAL TOPHETIC
HELLO HALLO HILLO HULLO HILLOA
HELM KEY STEER STERN TIMON
HELMET TIMBER STEERAGE
HELMET CAP POT CASK HELM HOOD
ARMET CREST GALEA MAZER
MOUND BARBEL BEAVER CASQUE
CASTLE GALERA HEAUME MORION
PALLET SALADE SALLET TESTER
BASINET CASQUET GALERUM
GALERUS AVENTAIL BURGONET
HEADGEAR KNAPSCAP SCHAPSKA
SKULLCAP TARNHELM TESTIERE
(— PART) VENTAIL
(PITH —) TOPI TOPEE
HELMET-SHAPED GALEATE
HELMSMAN PILOT STEER GLAUCUS
TIMONEER
HELP AID BOT ABET BACK BOOT
CAST LIFT STOP AVAIL FAVOR
FRITH HEEZE RESET SPEED START
STEAD YELDE ASSIST HELPER
RELIEF REMEDY SECOND SUCCOR
UPTAKE BENEFIT BESTEAD CHEVISE
COMFORT FORWARD FURTHER
HELPING IMPROVE PRESIDY
PROMOTE REDRESS RELIEVE
SUPPORT SUSTAIN ADJUMENT
BEFRIEND SUFFRAGE
(— FORWARD) FRANK FURTHER
(— ON) ADVANCE
(— ONWARD) FORWARD
(— OUT) FIRK
(HIRED —) LABOR
HELPER AID CAD FOAL HELP MATE
PAGE ANSAR AIDANT BARBOY
COOKEE DIENER FLUNKY JUMPER
NIPPER TENTER WAITER ADJOINT
ADJUTOR ANCILLA CASHBOY
GALOPIN SUMPMAN SWAMPER
HELPMATE OFFSIDER SCULLION
TROUNCER
(— IN GLASSWORKS) SNAPPER
(BLACKSMITH'S —) STRIKER
(CHIMNEY SWEEP'S —) CHUMMY
(COOK'S —) SLUSHY
(COOPER'S —) TUBBIE
(HORSESHOER'S —) FLOORMAN
(PICKPOCKET'S —) BULKER
(YOUNG —) FOAL
HELPFUL GOOD AIDANT AIDFUL
HELPLY SECOND SPEEDY USEFUL
ADJUVANT HELPSOME OBLIGING
SINGULAR
HELPING HELP AIDANT PORTION
SERVING ADJUTORY ADJUVANT
HELPLESS NUMB SILLY ABJECT
UNABLE AIDLESS FORLORN
FECKLESS HAVELESS REDELESS
HELTER-SKELTER TAGRAG
PELLMELL
HELVE HELM SHAFT
HELVE HAMMER OLIVER
HEM HUM WLO FELL SLIP WELT
HEDGE SPLAY PURFLE TURNUP
HEMMING TURNING SURROUND

(— AND HAW) HAVER
(— GLOVE) WRIST
(— IN FISH) EBB
(— IN) BOX LAP BEBAY BESET
IMPALE BESIEGE COMPASS
ENCLOSE ENVIRON STRAITEN
SURROUND
(— OF SAIL) TABLING
(— OF TROUSERS) CUFF
HEMATITE ORE OLIGIST SANGUINE
HEMICRANIA MIGRAINE
HEMIEPES ENOPLION
HEMIMORPHITE CALAMINE
HEMIOLIC SESCUPLE
HEMISTICH SECTION
HEMLOCK BUNK CASH KELK
BENNET CICUTA COWBANE DEATHIN
SHINWOOD
HEMOPHILIAC BLEEDER
HEMORRHAGE STAXIS APOPLEXY
BLEEDING HEMOPTOE PETECHIA
HEMOSTATIC ERIGERON
HEMP IFE KEF KIF TOW BANG CARL
POOA RINE SUNN ABACA BHANG
DACHA DAGGA FIQUE GANJA HURDS
MURVA SABZI SISAL AMBARY
CABUYA FIMBLE LIAMBA NALITA
SINAWA AMYROOT CABULLA
GAGROOT NIYANDA PANGANE
PITEIRA SOSQUIL BIRDSEED
CANNABIS CHUCKING LOCOWEED
NECKWEED NEPENTHE
HEMP AGRIMONY EUPATORY
HEMPWEED
HEMPEN NOGGEN
HEMP NETTLE IRONWORT
HEMPWEED BONESET DUCKBLIND
HEN FOWL BIDDY CHUCK LAYER
BROODY MABYER PULLET HOVERER
PARTLET
(— THAT HAS NOT LAID) TOWDIE
(— WITH CHICKENS) CLUCK
(— WITH SHORT LEGS) GRIG
(1-YEAR-OLD —) YEAROCK
(BROODY —) SITTER
HENBANE HEBENON CHENILLE
HENCE AWAY ERGO HYNE THUS
AVAUNT HETHEN HEREOUT
HENCEFORTH YET HENCE
HENCHMAN FELLOW SATRAP
FOLLOWER
HEN COOP CAVY CAVIE
HENGEST (BROTHER OF —) HORSA
(KINDOM FOUNDED BY —) KENT
(SON OF —) AESC
HEN HARRIER FALLER KATABELLA
(IMMATURE —) RINGTAIL
(MALE —) MILLER
HENNA MENDY ALCANNA ALHENNA
CAMPHIRE
HENNIN STEEPLE
HENRY QUAD HAWKIN SECOHM
HEINRICH QUADRANT
HEP (NOT —) ICKY
HEPATICA AI TRINITY
HEPATITIS JAUNDICE
HEPHAESTUS LEMNIAN
(FATHER OF —) ZEUS
(MOTHER OF —) HERA
(WIFE OF —) CHARIS

HER A ARE SHE HARE HERS HURE
HERA JUNO
(FATHER OF —) KRONOS
(HUSBAND OF —) ZEUS
HERALD BODE USHER BEADLE
DECLARE FORERUN PREFACE
STENTOR BLAZONER PRECURSE
PROCLAIM ROTHESAY
HERALDIC FECIAL FETIAL
HERALDRY ARMORY
HERB ANU APE PIA RUE UDO WAD
ALOE ANET ANYU ARUM COUS DILL
HEMP IRID LEEK MINT MOLY POLY
RAPE SAGE SOLA WOAD WORT
YAMP YARB AWIWI BLITE BRUSH
CREAT CROUT DAGGA DAISY DRABA
GALAX GAURA GILIA GRASS HOSTA
LOASA LUFFA MEDIC MUNGO NANCY
SEDGE SOLAH STOCK SULLA THYME
ZIZIA ALLIUM ARALIA ARNICA
AXSEED BAGPOD BAMBAN BANANA
BLINKS BORAGE CANCER CATGUT
CATNIP CENIZO CICELY CISTUS
CLOVER COCASH COLEUS CONIUM
COWISH COWPEA ELODEA ENDIVE
ERYNGO FENNEL GALAXY GINGER
HARMEL HYSSOP KOCHIA KRIGIA
KRIGLA LOOFAH LOVAGE RAMTIL
RATTLE ROBERT SESAME SESELI
SHEVRI WASABI ABRONIA ALPINIA
ALTHAEA ALYSSUM AMORPHA
AMSONIA ANCHUSA ANEMONE
ANGELON ARACHIS BABIANA
BABROOT BARTSIA BIRDEYE
BLINKER BONESET BUGSEED
BUGWEED CHICORY CUDWEED
CULVERS DEWDROP DYEWEED
EPISCIA ERODIUM FREESIA FROGBIT
FUMMORY GERBERA GINSENG
GOITCHO GOSMORE GOUAREE
GUAYULE GUNNERA HARMALA
HEDEOMA HENBANE HERBLET
IRESINE ISOLOMA JONQUIL LABIATE
LEWISIA LINNAEA MARANTA
MIMULUS MUDWEED MUDWORT
MULLEIN MUSTARD NAILROD
NEMESIA NIEVETA PAVONIA PETUNIA
PINESAP PINWEED PUCHERA
ROSELLE SAFFLOR SALSIFY
SEEDBOX SKIRRET SOWBANE
SPIGNEL STACHYS ABELMUSK
ACANTHUS ACONITUM AGERATUM
ALOCASIA ALUMROOT AMBROSIA
AMMOBIUM ANGELICA ARGEMONE
ASPHODEL BEDSTRAW CALATHEA
CAPEWEED CARELESS CENTAURY
CHENILLE COLLOMIA COSTMARY
COWWHEAT CRASSULA CROMWELL
DANEWEED DEERWEED DROPWORT
ECHINOPS EGGPLANT EREMURUS
ERIGERON EUCHARIS FEVERFEW
FLEABANE FOWLFOOT GAYWINGS
GERARDIA GESNERAD GESNERIA
GHETCHOO GLOXINIA GOATROOT
GUZMANIA HAREBELL HEPATICA
HEUCHERA HIBISCUS HOLEWORT
HONEWORT HOROKAKA HUDSONIA
IRONWEED LICORICE LOCOWEED
MANDRAKE MANFREDA MANYROOT

MARJORAM MARTYNIA MURRNONG
PHACELIA PINKROOT PLUMBAGO
SACALINE SAINFOIN SALICORN
SAMPHIRE SANDBURR SCABIOUS
SHINLEAF SMALLAGE SNOWDROP
SOAPROOT SOAPWORT STAPELIA
SUNDROPS TETRIFOL TOCALOTE
WOODRUFF
(— COUNTERACTING POISON)
CANCER
(— OTHER THAN GRASS) FORB
(AROMATIC —) MINT ANISE CLARY
CATNIP CAAPEBA CHERVIL DITTANY
(BIENNIAL —) LEEK PARSLEY
ANGELICA
(BULBOUS —) LILY CANNA ALLIUM
CRINUM GARLIC NERINE SQUILL
BABIANA SHALLOT DOGTOOTH
SLANGKOP
(FABULOUS —) MOLY PANAX
PANACE
(FLOATING —) FROGBIT
(FORAGE —) FITCHES GOITCHO
(POISONOUS —) CONIUM HEMLOCK
(PL.) POTAGERIE
HERBAGE HAY BITE GRASS GRAZE
PICHI ADONIS SACATE ZACATE
GRAZING
HERB EVE IVA IVY
HERB GRACE RUE
HERBICIDE IPE
HERB IMPIOUS DOWNWEED
HOARWORT
HERB PARIS TRUE ONEBERRY
TRUELOVE
HERB ROBERT JENNY ROBIN
ROBERT
HERCULEAN HUGE
HERCULES ERCLES ALCIDES
HERSHEF OETAEUS OVILLUS
HERAKLES
(BROTHER OF —) IPHICLES
(FATHER OF —) JUPITER
(MOTHER OF —) ALCMENA
(WIFE OF —) HEBE MEGARA
DEIANIRA
HERCULES ALLHEAL OPOPANAX
HERCULES-CLUB ARALIA IVYWORT
RUEWORT SHOTBUSH
HERD BOW GAM MOB BAND CREW
GAME GANG HEAD RACE ROUT TAIL
TEAM TRIP DROVE FLOCK HEARD
TROOP CAVIYA CHOUSE HIRSEL
HUDDLE MANADA MEINIE REMUDA
SPREAD THRAVE CREAGHT
RANGALE SHEPHERD
(— CATTLE) TAIL WRANGLE
(— OF CATTLE) FLOTE
(— OF COLTS) RAG
(— OF HORSES) RACE HARAS
HARRAS
(— OF SEALS) PATCH
(— OF WHALES) GAM
(— OF WILD SWINE) SOUNDER
HERDBOY BOUCHAL
HERDER DROVER FEEDER HERDBOY
HERDSMAN AMOS SENN GAUCHO
HERDER LOOKER PASTOR HERDBOY
LLANERO THYRSIS VAQUERO

BEASTMAN DAMOETAS GARTHMAN
NEATHERD PASTORAL PASTURER
RANCHERO SWANHERD WRANGLER
HERE READY WHERE HEREAT HITHER
PRESENT
(— AND THERE) ABOUT ABROAD
AROUND PASSIM SPARSIM
HEREAFTER BEYOND
HEREDITAMENT LAND
HEREDITARY INBORN INNATE
KINDLY LINEAL
HEREIN WITHIN
HERESY KETZEREI MISBELIEF
HERETIC BUGGER KETZER ZINDIQ
LOLLARD PATARIN PROFANE
SECTARY JUDAIZER
HERETICAL HERETIC HETERODOX
MISCREANT
HERETO HITHER
HERETOFORE ERST BEFORE
ERENOW EREWHILE FORMERLY
HERITAGE HEIRDOM HEIRSHIP
HERMA MERCURY
HERMAPHRODITE MOPH SCRAT
HERMAPHRODITIC BISEXED
BISEXUAL
HERMAPHRODITISM GYNANDRY
HERMAPHRODITUS (FATHER OF —)
MERCURY
(MOTHER OF —) VENUS
HERMES MERCURY AGORAIOS
CYLLENIUS
(FATHER OF —) ZEUS
(MOTHER OF —) MAIA
HERMIONE (FATHER OF —)
MENELAUS
(HUSBAND OF —) PYRRHUS
(MOTHER OF —) HELEN
HERMIT ARME MUNI HANIF MINIM
ANCHOR SANTON SULLEN ASCETIC
EREMITE RECLUSE TAPASVI
ANCHORET MARABOUT SOLITARY
HERMITAGE ASHRAM ASHRAMA
RECLUSE
HERNIA BURST RAMEX BREACH
RUPTURE MEROCELE
HERO KIM RAB AJAX EGIL IDAS MAUI
NALA NATA OFFA RINK YIMA ADAPA
BERNE DEBON ETANA FAUST GHAZI
HODER HOTHR IRAYA KIPPS MARKO
ORSON TASSO TIMON VOTAN
EGMONT FIGARO GIDEON GOLIAS
HEROIC IASION IOLAUS MAUGIS
MINYAS OSSIAN PELHAM PENROD
RIENZI ROLAND RUSTAM SIGURD
TARZAN USHEEN VATHEK ALCESTE
BOGATYR DEMIGOD FAUSTUS
GLUSKAP INGOMAR JAMSHID
MACBETH MANRICO MARMION
MAZEPPA ORLANDO OTHELLO
PALADIN RAFFLES TANCRED
THALABA THESUES TROILUS
ULYSSES VOLPONE WERTHER
WIDSITH WIELAND ACADEMUS
ARGONAUT FANSHAWE FERUMBAS
FRITHJOF GAEDHEAL GILGAMES
LAMMIKIN MALAGIGI MORGANTE
OROONOKO PALMERIN PARSIFAL
PERICLES RASSELAS RODOMONT

SUPERMAN TRISTRAM WAVERLEY
(LOVER OF —) LEANDER
(TRIBAL —) JUDGE
HEROIC EPIC FELL GREAT NOBLE
EPICAL FEATLY EXTREME GALLANT
VALIANT FEARLESS HEROICAL
HOMERIAN INTREPID
HEROIN JUNK HORSE
HEROINE AIDA EMMA MIMI RUTH
JULIE MEDEA NORMA SEDNA THAIS
ESTHER FEDORA GUDRUN HELENA
JUDITH JULIET MARTHA MIGNON
PAMELA PHEDRE RAMONA ROMOLA
SALOME SILVIA TRILBY UNDINE
ERMINIA EVELINA GALATEA GINEVRA
GRAINNE HEROESS MONIMIA
SHIRLEY ZENOBIA ZULEIKA
ATALANTA ISABELLA MARGARET
PATIENCE POMPILIA ROSMUNDA
SOFRONIA
HEROISM VALOR BRAVERY
COURAGE
HERON QUA POKE SOCO CRAIG
CRANE EGRET FRANK HERNE
PADDY QUAWK YABOA AIGRET
KIALEE KOTUKU QUAKER SQUAWK
BITTERN CRABIER GOLIATH
HANDSAW QUABIRD SQUACCO
BOATBILL GAULDING HERONSEW
UMBRETTE
(— FLOCK) SIEGE
HERON'S-BILL ERODIUM
HERPES TETTER
HERPES ZOSTER ZONA SHINGLES
HERRING ALEC BRIT CHUB SILD
BLOAT CAPON CISCO DORAB HILSA
MARAY MATIE SPRAT KIPPER
TAILOR BLOATER CLUPEID NAILROD
ROLLMOP SHADINE BLUEBACK
BRISLING BUCKLING CROPSHIN
GRAYBACK QUODDIES SCUDDAWN
STRADINE
(— SEASON) DRAVE
(— UNIT) LAST MAZE
(2, 3 OR 4 —S) WARP
(FEMALE —) RAUN
(LAKE —) KIYI CISCO
(RED —) CAPON SOLDIER
(SMOKED —) BLOATER
(YOUNG —) COB BRIT SILE SILL
SOIL WILE COBBE MATIE SPRAT
SARDINE SPERLING
HERS HERN SHISN
HERSE (FATHER OF —) CECROPS
(SISTER OF —) AGLAUROS
(SON OF —) CEPHALUS
HERSELF HI HER SELF ITSELF
HERSHEF ARSAPHES
HESHVAN BUL CHESHVAN
HESIONE (FATHER OF —)
LAOMEDON
(HUSBAND OF —) TELAMON
(RESCUER OF —) HERCULES
HESITANCY HANG
HESITANT SHY CAGY CHARY
GROPING HALTING SUSPENSE
(NOT —) FACILE
HESITATE COY HEM STAY STOP
CHECK CRANE DEMUR DOUBT

FORCE PAUSE STAND STICK SUSSY
WAVER BOGGLE FALTER HANKER
LINGER MAMMER RELUCT SCOTCH
TARROW TARTLE BALANCE
PROFFER SCRUPLE STAGGER
STAMMER SWITHER THRIMBLE
(— IN SPEAKING) HACKER
HESITATING JUBUS HALTING
BACKWARD DOUBTFUL JUBEROUS
TIMOROSO
HESITATION HANG HINK WAND
PAUSE STAND STICK SUSSY
SWITHER
HESSIAN BURLAP
HESTIA (FATHER OF —) KRONOS
(MOTHER OF —) RHEA
HETAERA LAIS THAIS PHRYNE
MISTRESS
HETERODOX HERETIC SINISTRAL
HETERODOXY HERESY CACODOXY
HETEROGENEOUS MIXED MOTLEY
UNLIKE DIVERSE PIEBALD
ASSORTED
HETEROMYS SACCOMYS
HETEROTROPHIC HOLOZOIC
HETEROXENOUS INDIRECT
HETEROZYGOUS CROSS SPLIT
IMPURE
HETMAN ATAMAN
HEW CUT HAG CHIP SNAG STUB
SHRED SLICE
(— OUT) CARVE
(— STONE) CHAR
HEWER JOEY GETTER GIDEON
FACEMAN
HEX WITCH VOODOO WHAMMY
HEXAGON SEXANGLE
HEXAGONAL HEX DIMETRIC
HEXAGRAM PENTACLE
HEXAMETER MIURUS
(DACTYLIC —) EPOS HEROIC
HEXOBARBITAL EVIPAL
HEXOSAN MANNAN GLUCOSAN
MANNOSAN
HEYDAY MAY HIGHDAY
HEZEKIAH (FATHER OF —) AHAZ
HIATUS GAP BREAK CHASM BREACH
HIATAL LACUNA
HIBERNATE SHACK WINTER
SLUMBER
HIBERNATING LATITANT
HIBERNIA JUVERNA
HIBERNIAN IRISHMAN IVERNIAN
HICCUP YEX YOX HICK HOCKET
HOQUET SINGULTUS
HICK BOOR HIND JAKE BACON
BUSHMAN CORNBALL
HICKORY NOGAL PIGNUT BULLNUT
SHAGBARK
HICKORY NUT TRYMA PIGNUT
BULLNUT KISKITOM
HICKWALL ECCLE HECKLE HICKWAY
HIDDEN HID SHY DEEP DERN LOST
TECT BLIND DUSKY PERDU PRIVY
ARCANE BURIED COVERT INNATE
LATENT MASKED MYSTIC OCCULT
SECRET VEILED BOSOMED COVERED
CRYPTIC OBSCURE RECLUSE
SUBTILE ABDITIVE ABSTRUSE

CRYPTOUS HIDEAWAY PALLIATE
SCREENED SECLUDED SNEAKING
HIDE HOD WRY BUFF BURY CASE
CROP DARK DERN FELL FELT HILL
HOOD JOUK LEAN MASK PELL PELT
SCAB SKIN SKUG SNUG STOW VEIL
WELL BELIE BELLY BLIND CACHE
CLOAK CLOUD COUCH COVER
DITCH EARTH FLANK GLOSS LAYNE
LOSHE MANSE PLANT SHADE SPOIL
STASH STEER TAPIS BURROW
BUSHEL CASATE EMBOSS ENCAVE
ENWOMB FOREST HUDDLE IMBOSK
MANENT PELAGE SCREEN SHADOW
SHIELD SHROUD CONCEAL COWHIDE
EMBOWEL OBCLUDE OVERLAY
SECLUDE SECRETE SPREADY
CARUCATE DISGUISE ENSCONCE
HIDELAND HOODWINK PALLIATE
PLOWLAND SQUIRREL SUPPRESS
(— AS AN EEL) MUD
(— IN WOODS) WOOD BUSHWACK
(— UNDER) BUSHEL
(CALF'S —) DEACON
(DRESSED —S) LEATHER
(HALF OF —) BEND
(HAVING SOFT —) MELLOW
(SHEEP'S —) SLAT
(TANNED —) CROP
(THICKEST —S) BACKS
(UNDRESSED —) KIP
(PL.) KIP JUFTI JUFTS
HIDE-AND-GO-SEEK BOGLE WHOOP
BOGGLE
HIDEAWAY MEW LAIR
HIDEBOUND BORNE NARROW
BIGOTED
HIDEOUS FELL GRIM UGLY AWFUL
TOADY DEFORM GRIMLY GRISLY
HORRID ODIOUS OGRISH GHASTLY
DEFORMED DREADFUL FIENDISH
GRUESOME HORRIBLE SHOCKING
TERRIBLE
HIDEOUSLY FOULLY
HIDING MICHING SECRECY ABDITIVE
HIDEAWAY
HIEMAL WINTRY
HIERACIUM DINALE HAWKWEED
HIERARCHY SATRAPY
HIEROGLYPH CIPHER
(PL.) SIGNARY
HIGGLE HUCK HAGGLE
HIGH UP ALT AIRY DEAR HAUT MAIN
MUCH TALL ACUTE ALOFT BRENT
CHIEF CLOSE FIRST GREAT LOFTY
MERRY NOBLE SHARP STEEP
COSTLY SHRILL EMINENT EXALTED
HAUGHTY SUBLIME TOPPING
VIOLENT ELEVATED FOREMOST
PIERCING TOWERING
(— AND MIGHTY) HOGEN
(— IN CHROMA) STRONG
(— IN PITCH) ALT ACUTE
(— IN RANK) MUCH
(— PITCH) ORTHIAN
(MOST —) SERENE
(PRETTY —) STIFFISH
(VERY —) TAUNT
HIGHBORN NOBLE GENEROUS

HIGHBOY TALLBOY
HIGHBRED SOFT REFINED
HIGHBROW EGGHEAD
HIGH-CLASS CLASSY UPSTAGE
HIGH-CLIMBER TOPPER
HIGH-COLORED BLOWSY BLOWZY
HIGHER ABOVE SENIOR SUPERIOR
HIGHEST TOP HEXT FIRST EXTREME
MAXIMAL SUPREME BUNEMOST
HIGHMOST OVERMOST
(— IN DEGREE) LAST
HIGHFALUTIN PAUGHTY
HIGH-FED BEANY
HIGH-FLAVORED GAMY
HIGH-FLOWN TALL TUMID
HIGH-HANDED CAVALIER
HIGHLAND RAND CERRO
HIGHLANDER GAEL TARTAN
NAINSEL PLAIDMAN REDSHANK
TREWSMAN UPLANDER
(PL.) TREWS TARTAN
HIGHLIGHT ADORN HEIGHTEN
SALIENCE
HIGHLY THRICE
HIGH-MINDED HAUGHT
HIGHNESS ALTESSE ALTEZZA
ALTITUDE
(— OF PRICE) DEARTH
HIGH-PITCHED PROUD PIPING
TREBLE SHRIEKY
HIGH-POWERED MAGNUM
HIGH-PRICED DEAR
HIGH-RIGGER TOPPER
HIGH-SOUNDING BIG BOMBAST
MAGNIFIC SONORANT SONOROUS
SOUNDING
HIGH-SPIRITED CRANK FIERY
FIERCE LIVELY GALLANT GINGERY
RAMPANT CAVALIER VASCULAR
HIGH-SPIRITEDNESS SPLEEN
HIGH-STRUNG TENSE NERVOUS
HIGH-TONED TONY DICTY DICKTY
HIGHWAY VIA WAY BELT ITER PATH
PIKE ROAD TOBY BOLOS ARTERY
CAUSEY COURSE RUMPAD SKYWAY
STREET BELTWAY CALZADA
FREEWAY RAMPIRE ARTERIAL
BROADWAY CAUSEWAY CHAUSSEE
HIGHROAD SPEEDWAY
(— ROBBERY) TOBY
(LOCATED OFF THE —) DEVIOUS
HIGHWAYMAN PAD RIDER SCAMP
CUTTER PADDER RODMAN FOOTPAD
LADRONE PRANCER RODSMAN
TOBYMAN BIDSTAND DAMASTES
HIGHTOBY HIJACKER LANCEMAN
OUTRIDER
HIGH-WROUGHT INTENSE
HIKE MUSH MARCH TRAMP RAMBLE
HILARIOUS MAD JOVIAL JOCULAR
CHIRPING GLORIOUS
HILARITY GIG JOY GLEE LAUGH
MIRTH GAIETY GAYETY DEVILRY
JOLLITY WHOOPEE
HILL BEN DEN HOE HOW KOP LOW
PUY VAN ALTO BANK BERG BRAE
BULT BUMP COTE DAGH DENE
DOWN DRUM FELL HIGH HONE KNAP
LOMA LUMP MESA MOOR MOTE

NOUP PAHA TOFT ZION BARGH
BUTTE CERRO CLIFF COAST HEUGH
KNOCK KNOLL KOPJE MORRO
MOUND MOUNT STILL SWELL TELLE
WATCH ASCENT BARROW BEACON
COBBLE COLLIS COPPLE CUESTA
HEIGHT HEUVEL LOMITA SPRUNT
STRONE CAELIAN CAPITOL COLLINE
DRUMLIN HILLOCK NUNATAK
PICACHO SOWBACK VIMINAL
AREOPAGY CATOCTIN DRUMLOID
FOOTHILL MONTICLE QUIRINAL
(— OF SAND) DENE DUNE
(— OF STRATIFIED DRIFT) KAME
(— UP) MOLD
(BROAD-TOPPED —) LOMA
(CONICAL —) LAW
(CRAGGY —) TOR
(FORTIFIED —) RATH
(HIGH —) BEN
(ISOLATED —) HUM TOFT BARGH
BUTTE
(LAST —) STRONE
(LOW —) HOW BAND WOLD
SOWBACK
(NIPPLELIKE —) PAP
(NORTH AFRICAN —) JEBEL DJEBEL
(RESIDUAL —) CATOCTIN
(ROUNDED —) DODD HONE
(SHARP-POINTED —) KIP KIPP
(SMALL —) KNAP KNOLL KOPJE
KOPPIE HILLOCK MOLEHILL
(STEEP —) BREW BROW STILL
(STONY —) ROACH
(SUGAR-LOAF —) SPITZKOP
(WOODED —) HOLT HURST
HILLOCK HOW LOW NOB BOSS BULT
DOWN KAME KNOB TERP TUMP
BERRY HEAVE HURST KNOCK
KNOLL KOPJE MOUND TOMAN
BURROW COPPET HILLET HUMMOCK
TUMMOCK TUMULUS MOLEHILL
HILLSIDE BENT BRAE COTE EDGE
CLEVE FALDA SLADE FELLSIDE
SIDEHILL
HILLTOP PIKE KNOLL
HILLY KNOBBY
HILT HAFT POIGNET HANDGRIP
(— OF DAGGER) DUDGEON
(PART OF —) LANGUET
HILUM EYE HILUS PORTA NUCLEUS
CICATRIX
HIM A EN HE HEM HIN MUN
HIMATION PALLION PALLIUM
HIMSELF HIM IPSE SELF HISSEL
ITSELF HERSELF HISSELF
HIND ROE CONY HINE HINT CONEY
HEARST HINDER VENISON CABRILLA
HINDER BAR DAM KEP LET MAR ROB
CLOG HELP SLOW SLUG STAY STOP
TENT WARN AFTER BLOCK CHEAT
CHECK CHOKE CRAMP DEBAR
DELAY DETER EMBAR ESTOP HEDGE
SLOTH THROW TRASH ARREST
CUMBER DETAIN FORBID FORLET
HAMPER HARASS HINNER IMPEDE
IMPEND INJURE RETARD SCOTCH
TAIGLE UNHELP ABSTAIN DEPRIVE
FORELAY IMPEACH INHIBIT PREVENT

TRACHLE ENCUMBER HANDICAP
IMPEDITE OBSTRUCT PRECLUDE
PROHIBIT
HINDERED FOUL
HINDERER LETTER
HINDERMOST LAG ACHTER
HINDQUARTER HIND HAUNCH
(**HALF** —) LEG
(PL.) FOUCH CRUPPER HAUNCHES
HINDRANCE BAR LET RUB BALK
CURB REIN SLUG STAY STOP
BLOCK CHECK DELAY HITCH TRASH
ARREST CUMBER DENIAL HINDER
OBJECT UNHELP UNSPEED
DISCOUNT DRAWBACK HOLDBACK
OBSTACLE PULLBACK
HINDU BABU BABOO SUDRA BABHAN
GENTOO JAJMAN KALWAR KHATRI
NAYADI SHUDRA THAKUR VAISYA
MUSAHAR VAIRAGI
(**— ASCETIC**) SADHU
(**— ASSOCIATION**) SANGH
(**— CASTE**) TELI VARNA
(**— CUSTOM**) SATI SUTTEE
(**— ENERGY**) SAKTI SHAKTI
(**— IDOL**) SWAMI
(**— INTERJECTION**) OM AUM
(**— PHILOSOPHY**) VEDANTA
(**— PRACTICE**) PURDAH
(**— RITE**) PUJA POOJA
(**— SAGE**) RSI RISHI
(**— VARNA MEMBER**) SUDRA
(**— WORSHIPER**) SAKTA
(**— WRITINGS**) SMRTI TANTRA
(**TWICE-BORN** —) KSATRIYA
HINDUSTANI URDU HINDI OORDOO
DAKHINI
HINGE RUN BAND BUTT FLAP HARR
TRIM TURN CARDO CROOK GEMEL
JOINT MOUNT NODUS SKELL SKEWL
TWIST DEPEND GARNET GEMMEL
GIMMER HANGLE JIMMER SNIBEL
CHARNEL COXCOMB FULCRUM
HOLDBACK
(**— OF BIVALVE, SHELL**) CARDO
(**— OF HELMET**) CHARNEL
(**— TOGETHER**) SCISSOR
(**HALF OF** —) FLAP
(**PHILATELIC** —) STICKER
HINGED SWING
HINNY BURDON FUNNEL JENNET
HINT CUE ASTE ITEM MINT WINK
CHEEP IMPLY INFER POINT SPELL
STEER TOUCH TRACE WHIFF
ALLUDE GLANCE OFFICE SMATCH
WHEEZE INKLING LEADING
MEMENTO SUGGEST UMBRAGE
WHISPER WRINKLE ALLUSION
INDICATE INNUENDO INTIMATE
TELLTALE
HINTERLAND BLED BACKLAND
HIP HEP COXA HUCK PITCH SHOOP
HAUNCH HUCKLE HIPBERRY
(**— JOINT**) THURL
(**— OF ROSE**) BERRY CHOOP SHOOP
(**— OF TARGET**) SPOT
HIPBONE FINBONE EDGEBONE
SIDEBONE
HIPPEUS KNIGHT

HIPPOCAMPUS ERGOT HIPPO
HIPPOCOON (**BROTHER OF** —)
TYNDAREUS
(**FATHER OF** —) OEBALUS
(**MOTHER OF** —) GORGOPHONE
(**SLAYER OF** —) HERCULES
HIPPODAMIA (**FATHER OF** —)
ADRASTUS OENOMAUS
(**HUSBAND OF** —) PELOPS
PEIRITHOUS
(**SON OF** —) ATREUS TROEZEN
PITTHEUS THYESTES
HIPPOLYTUS (**FATHER OF** —)
THESEUS
(**MOTHER OF** —) HIPPOLYTE
(**STEPMOTHER OF** —) PHAEDRA
HIPPONACTEAN SCAZON
HIPPOPOTAMUS HIPPO ZEEKOE
BEHEMOTH BUNODONT
HIPPOTRAGUS OZANNA EGOCERUS
HIRE FEE JOB HAVE MEED RENT
SIGN WAGE PREST WAGES EMPLOY
ENGAGE RETAIN SALARY BESPEAK
CHARTER CONDUCE CONDUCT
FREIGHT STIPEND
(**— CATTLE**) TACK
HIRED PAID TEEKA TICCA WAGED
HIRELING HACK VENAL HACKNEY
MYRMIDON WAGELING MERCENARY
HIRSUTE HAIRY SHAGGY
HIS S AS ES IS HISN
HISPID STRIGOSE STRIGOUS
HISS BLOW FUFF HISH HIZZ QUIZ
SISS SIZZ GOOSE WHISS FISSLE
FIZZLE SIFFLE WHOOSH WHISTLE
SIBILATE
(**— OF SWORD**) SOUGH
HISSING BIRD SIBILANT
HISTONE GLOBIN
HISTORIAN MORONI STORIER
ANNALIST
HISTORICAL GENETIC
HISTORIOGRAPHER SCALD SKALD
HISTORY STORY ANNALS LEGEND
SURVEY ACCOUNT ANCESTRY
PROPHECY RELATION
(**— OF EXPERIENCES**) MEMOIRS
(**— OF JAPAN**) KOJIKI
(**LIFE** —) COURSE
HISTRIONIC ACTORY ACTORISH
ACTRESSY
HIT BAT BOP BOX DOT GET HAT JOB
PEG PIP WOW BASH BEAN BEAT
BELT BLOW BOFF BUST CHOP CONK
DONG FOUR GOLD NAIL PINK PUCK
PUNT RUFF SLAM SOCK SWAT SWIP
TAKE TANK TUNK WART WIPE
ANGLE CHECK CLOUT CLUNK
CROWN FIVER FLICK GOUFF KNOCK
POTCH PRANG PUNTA PUNTO
SCORE SLASH SLOSH SMITE SNICK
SWIPE TAINT TOUCH VENUE ATTAIN
DOUBLE FOURER HURTLE SCLAFF
STRIKE VOLLEY ATTAINT BOFFOLA
CONNECT MUZZLER SANDBAG
WHERRET BLUDGEON BOUNDARY
LENGTHER STRICKEN
(**— A KEY**) STRIKE
(**— BALL**) CUR FLY DINK DRIVE

SHOOL SNICK
(**— BUNT**) DRAG
(**— GAME**) STOP
(**— GENTLY**) BABY
(**— GOLF BALL**) CAN BLAST
EXPLODE
(**— HARD**) DUMP SLOG SLUG SOUSE
STOUSH STONKER
(**— IN BOXING**) LEADOFF
(**— IN FIELD HOCKEY**) CORNER
(**— IN TILTING**) TAINT
(**— IT OFF**) CLICK
(**— LIGHTLY**) KISS
(**— ON BULL'S-EYE**) GOLD
(**— POORLY**) DUB
(**— TOGETHER**) CLASH
(**— UPON**) FIND
(**— WITH FOOT**) KICK SPURN
(**BASE** —) BINGLE DOUBLE SAFETY
SINGLE TRIPLE SCRATCH SMOTHER
(**CRICKET** —) SLOG BOUNDARY
(**EASILY** —) SITTING
(**FENCING** —) HAI HAY
(**SHARP** —) LICK
(**SMASH** —) SOCKEROO
HITCH JET TUG HALT HIKE ITCH
KNOT PULL CATCH HOTCH SPELL
TRACE HIRSLE INSPAN MAGNUS
(**NOSE** —) BOZAL
HITCHHIKE HOP THUMB
HITCHING KNOT SHRUG
HITHER HERE
HITHERTO YET BEFORE
HIT-OR-MISS CASUAL CHANCE
HOBNOB CARELESS
HITTER SWATTER
HITTING BATTING SLOGGING
HITTITE HATTI KHATTI TABALIAN
HIVE GUM BIKE SKEP PYCHE STAND
STATE STOCK SWARM APIARY
ALVEARY BEEHIVE SWARMER
(**— PLACED OVER ANOTHER**) SUPER
HLORRITHI THOR THORR
HOAR GRAY RIME HOARY
HOARD HEAM POSE SAVE AMASS
HUTCH MISER STOCK COFFER
MAGPIE MUCKER STOUTH GENIZAH
HUSBAND SQUIRREL TREASURE
HOARDER MUCKER STORER
HUSBAND
HOARFROST RAG HOAR RIME RIND
HOARINESS HOAR MUCOR
HOARSE RAW FOGGY GRUFF HEAZY
HUSKY RAWKY ROKEY ROUGH
ROUPY STOUR CROAKY RASPED
ROUPIT GRATING RAUCOUS
HOARSENESS FROG ROUP QUACK
HASKNESS
HOARY GRAY GREY HOAR WHITE
FROSTY ANCIENT HOARISH
INCANOUS
HOATZIN ANNA HANA HOACTZIN
HOAX BAM COD FUN GAG HUM KID
RAG RIG BILK DUPE FAKE GAFF
GEGG GUNK QUIZ RAMP RUSE SELL
SHAM SKIT CHEAT FRAUD GREEN
SHAVE SPOOF TRICK WINDY
CANARD DIDDLE HUMBUG STRING
BLAFLUM DECEIVE FLIVVER
ARTIFICE

HOB HUB PUNCH MATRIX
HOBBER LEANER
HOBBLE GIMP LOCK SPAN BUNCH
HILCH HITCH STILT STUMP HABBLE
HIRPLE HOPPLE LANGLE LANKET
TOLTER CRAMBLE CRAMMEL
CRIPPLE SHACKLE SHAFFLE
SPANCEL STAGGER SIDELINE
HOBBLEBUSH DOGWOOD
HOBBY BUG FAD HOBBLER
AVOCATION
HOBBYHORSE HOBBY PLAYMARE
HOBBYIST BUG
HOBGOBLIN (ALSO SEE GOBLIN)
COW HAG HOB PUG BOGY PUCK
BOGEY BUCCA BUGAN POKER
SCRAT SPOOK BOODIE BOWSIE
BUGANE EMPUSA SPOORN
BUGABOO RAWHEAD BOGGLEBO
COLTPIXY POPLEMAN PUCKEREL
WORRICOW
HOBNAIL HOB HUB PUNCH TACKET
HOBNAILED TACKETY
HOBO BO BOE BUM STIFF
HOCK HAM HOX HEEL HOUGH HUXEN
SINEW SKINK JARRET GAMBREL
HOCKSHIN SUFFRAGO
HOCKEY HURLY HORKEY HURLEY
SHINNY CAMMOCK HURLBAT
HOCKEY STICK HOOKY HURLY
STICK BULGER SHINNY CAMBUCA
CAMMOCK DODDART HURLBAT
HOCUS-POCUS HUMBUG FLIMFLAM
QUACKERY
HOD TRAY
HOD CARRIER PADDY
HODGEPODGE CHOW HASH MESS
OLIO RAFF SALAD BOLLIX JUSSEL
MAGPIE MEDLEY CHIVAREE
CHOWCHOW HOTCHPOT KEDGEREE
MISHMASH PASTICHE PORRIDGE
SCRAMPUM
HOE BROD CHIP CLAT HACK HOWE
SHIM LARRY THIRD CHONTA
HACKER PAIDLE SARCLE GRUBBER
PULASKI SCRAPER SCUFFLE
GRIFFAUN
(— HANDLE) STAIL
(HORSE —) NIDGET NIGGET
HOECAKE CORNCAKE
HOG BEN SOW BOAR GALT GILT
PORK DUROC GRUNT SHOAT
BARROW HOGGET HOGGIE PORKER
PORKET YORKER BACONER
BUTCHER GRUNTER HOGLING
MONTANA BABIRUSA BENODONT
BUNODONT HEREFORD LANDRACE
VICTORIA
HOGBACK FLATIRON HOGFRAME
HOGCHOKER SOLE
HOGFISH CAPITAN LADYFISH
LORICATE SCORPION
HOGGER HUGGER HOGHEAD
HOGGISHNESS GRILL GRYLL
HOGNOSE SNAKE ADDER
FLATHEAD
HOG PLUM AMRA JOBO
HOGSHEAD CASK CARDEL
HOG'S-MEAT TOSTON HOGWEED

HOG-TIE HAMPER
HOGWASH DRAFF SWASH SWILL
PIGWASH
HOIST FID HEFT KILT LIFT SWAY
SWIG WHIM WHIP ERECT HEAVE
HEEZE HEIST HOICK HOOSH HORSE
RAISE WEIGH JAMMER LAUNCH
LIFTER TUGGER WHIMSY DERRICK
(— A LOG) CANNON
(— FISH) BRAIL
(— FLUKES) FISH FANCHER
HOISTED (— TIGHT) ATRIP
HOISTMAN CAGEMAN
HOKUM BLAA BLAH HOKE JUNK
HOLD HOD OWN BULK DEEM FEEL
FILL GAUM GIVE GRIT HANK HAVE
HELD HEND HILT HOLE HOLT HOOK
KEEP LOCK NAIL RELY STOW
AFONG AHOLD AHOLT CARRY CINCH
CLAMP CLING GRASP GRIPE LATCH
LEASE PAUSE ROCCA STORE
WOULD ADHERE ADSORB ARREST
CLUTCH DETAIN HANDLE INTERN
MANURE OCCUPY REGARD REPUTE
RETAIN ADJUDGE CAPTURE
CONFINE CONTAIN ENCLOSE
FERMATA GRAPPLE HOLDING
RECEIVE SEIZURE SUBSIST
SUSPEND COMPRISE FOOTHOLD
FOREHOLD HANDFAST HANDHOLD
HEADLOCK HOLDFAST PURCHASE
THURROCK
(— A BELIEF) SUPPOSE
(— AS PRECIOUS) TREASURE
(— AS TRUE) ACCEPT
(— AT BAY) DOMPT
(— BACK ON LEASH) TRASH
(— BACK) STOP WELL BELAY
LAYNE BOGGLE DETAIN FLINCH
HINDER RETIRE SHRINK CONTAIN
DETRACT FORBEAR INGIBIT
RECLAIM REFRAIN SLACKEN
HESITATE SUPPRESS WITHDRAW
(— CLOSELY) CRADLE CUDDLE
(— CONSULTATION) ADVISE
(— CORONER'S INQUEST) CROWN
(— DEAR) CHERISH
(— DOWN) PINION CONTAIN
(— FAST) FIX BAIL BITE CLING
SNARL CLENCH CLINCH SECURE
STABLE
(— FIRMLY) INSIST
(— FOR FOOD) COZY COSEY
(— GOOD) SERVE
(— IN CHECK) REIN GOVERN
REPRESS COMPESCE
(— IN CONTEMPT) SMILE DISPRIZE
(— IN PLACE) ANCHOR
(— OF PLASTER) KEY
(— ON COURSE) STEM FETCH
STAND
(— ON FINAL NOTE) TENOR
(— ON SHORE) LANDFAST
(— OUT) DREE LAST STAY OFFER
EXTEND PROTEND STRETCH
SUSTAIN
(— PROTECTIVELY) LAP
(— TIGHTLY) CLIP STICK
(— TOGETHER) BOND COHERE
CONSIST

(— UP BY LEADING STRINGS) DADE
(— UP TO CONTEMPT) FLEER
(— UP TO PUBLIC NOTICE) GIBBET
(— UP) BEAR HALT STAY ERECT
HEIST IMPEDE UPHOLD RUMPADE
SUPPORT SUSTAIN TRADUCE
(SHIP'S —) HOLE HOLL FISHHOLD
(WRESTLING —) CROTCH KEYLOCK
CHANCERY HEADLOCK SCISSORS
SIDEHOLD
HOLDER WYE HAVER STOCK DIPPER
SOCKET CRACKER JAGIRDAR
(— FOR CARRYING GLASS) FRAIL
(— FOR COIL) SPOOL
(— FOR CUP) ZARF
(— FOR TOOLS) TURRET
(— OF GRANT) ENAMDAR
(CANDLE —) SPIDER GIRANDOLE
(LAMP —) BODY
(PL.) GRIPPERS
HOLDFAST CLINCH HAPTERON
HOLDIKEN HADDIN
HOLDING HAL COPY COTE HOLD
TAKE GRASP HONOR HADDIN
POFFLE TENANT TENURE TENANCY
COMMENDA
(— DIFFERENT OPINIONS) APART
(— FAST) IRON
(— OF SECURITIES) CARRY
(PL.) FLOCKS PROPERTY
HOLDUP HEIST STICKUP
HOLE CAN CUP EYE GAP PIT TAP
BORE BURY LEAK MAIL MUSE PECK
PINK POCK PUKA WANT CHINK
DITCH FLOSS FOSSE MEUSE SINUS
SLACK SPRUE SQUAT TEWEL THURL
BURROW CAVITY CENTER CENTRE
CRANNY CRATER EYELET HOLLOW
LACUNA OBTAIN OILLET PIERCE
POCKET POUNCE WEEPER
BLOWOUT BOGHOLE BOTHROS
DIBHOLE EYEHOLE KEYHOLE
MORTICE MORTISE OILHOLE
OPENING PINHOLE POTHOLE
SCUTTLE SWALLET VENTAGE
ACCEPTER APERTURE BLOWHOLE
BOREHOLE COALHOLE CRABHOLE
FUMAROLE HANDHOLE KNOCKOUT
KNOTHOLE OVERTURE PEEPHOLE
POSTHOLE PUNCTURE WELLHOLE
WINDHOLE
(— CAUSED BY LEAK) GIME
(— FOR WIRE) HUB HUBB
(— IN BANK OF STREAM) GAT
(— IN GARMENT) FRACK
(— IN GUILLOTINE) LUNET LUNETTE
(— IN HEDGE) SMEUSE
(— IN KEEL) RUFFLE
(— IN KIVA) SIPAPU
(— IN STREAM BED) DUMP
(— IN WIND INSTRUMENT) LILL
(— INTO MOLD) SPRUE
(AIR —) SPIRACLE
(DEEP —) POT GOURD
(FOX —) KENNEL
(GOLF —) CUP DOGLEG
(MELON —) GILGAI
(SAND —) BUNKER
(SINK —) SOAKAWAY

(TO —) GOBBLE HAZARD
(VOLCANIC —) FUMAROLE
(WATER —) DUB CHARCO
(WELL-LIKE —) CASCAN
HOLIDAY HOL PLAY TIDE WAKE
FERIE FESTA MERRY FIESTA JOVIAL
FESTIVE HALEDAY PLAYDAY
YEARDAY SHABUOTH WAYGOOSE
(HALF —) REMEDY
(PL.) FERIA
HOLINESS PIETY HALIDOM SANCTITY
HOLLA SOLA
HOLLAND (ALSO SEE NETHERLANDS)
FROGLAND
HOLLANDAISE GULASH GOULASH
HOLLANDER DUTCHMAN
HOLLANDS GIN GENEVA
HOLLER HALLO HOLLO HALLOO
KYOODLE
HOLLO SOLA
HOLLOW DEN DIP KEX BOSS BOWL
CAVE COMB COOM COVE DALK
DELL DENT DINT DISH DOCK DOKE
FOLD GORE HOLE HOLL HOWE
KEXY SINK SLOT THIN VOID WAME
BASIN BIGHT CAVUM CHASE CLEFT
CUPPY DELVE DOWFF EMPTY
GAUNT GOYLE GULCH GULLY
HEUCH LAIGH NOTCH SCOOP SINUS
SLOCK SWAMP WOMBY BULLAN
CAVITY CORRIE DIMPLE HOLLER
INDENT KETTLE MATRIX POCKET
SOCKET SUNKEN VACANT WALLOW
BOXLIKE CONCAVE UNSOUND
VACUITY CAVITARY CHELIDON
CRUCIBLE FISTULAR FOSSETTE
NOTCHING SPECIOUS
(— AMONG HILLS) SWAG SLOCK
(— IN COIL OF CABLE) TIER
(— IN HILL) COOM CLASH COOMB
CORRIE
(— IN TILE) KEY
(— OF ARM) LEAD ARMPIT
(— OF HANDS) GOUPEN GOWPEN
(— OF HORSE'S TOOTH) MARK
(— OF KNEE) HAM
(— OUT) CUT DIG BORE HOWK
KERF CAVERN EXCISE
(LONG —) GROOVE
(NOT —) SOLID FARCTATE
(PASSING —) CRESCENT
(SECLUDED —) GLEN
(SPRINGY —) GAW
(WOODED —) GULLY
HOLLOWED HOWKIT CONCAVE
SPOUTED
HOLLOWNESS VANITY INANITY
VACUITY
HOLLY HOLM HULL ILEX MATE
DAHOON HOLLIN HULVER TOLLON
YAUPON CATBERRY INKBERRY
MILKMAID
HOLLYHOCK HOCK ALTHEA
MALLOW
HOLOTHURIAN TREPANG
HOLY SRI SHRI HUACA SAINT SANTO
DEVOUT DIVINE SACRAL SACRED
BLESSED PERFECT SAINTLY
SINLESS BLISSFUL INNOCENT
REVEREND

(— MAN) SADHU
(— OF HOLIES) ADYT ADYTUM
(ALL —) PANAGIA
HOLY BASIL TULCE TOOLSY
HOLY STONE BEAR BIBLE
HOLY WOOD LIGNUM
HOMAGE FEE COURT HONOR YMAGE
FEALTY MANRED INCENSE LOYALTY
MANRENT MANSHIP OVATION
SERVICE TREWAGE EMINENCE
(SUPREME —) LATRIA
HOME BYE DEN HAM HAME HUNK
WIKE ABODE ASTRE BEING DOMUS
FOYER HAUNT SMOKE HEARTH
BLIGHTY SHELTER DOMICILE
FIRESIDE ROOFTREE
(— FOR THE POOR) HOSPICE
(— OF THE BLESSED) GIMLE
(FUNERAL —) CHAPEL
(HARVEST —) KERN KIRN MELL
HOCKEY
(REST —) FARM HOSTEL
HOMELAND HAVAIKI
HOMELESS ROOFLESS VAGABOND
HOMELIKE HOMEY HAMEIL HAMILT
HOMISH HOMESOME
HOMELINESS YEOMANRY
HOMELY FOUL UGLY PLAIN DUDGEN
PLAINLY EVERYDAY FAMILIAR
HOMELIKE
HOME PLATE RUBBER
HOMER KOR CHOMER
HOME RUN SWAT SWOT
HOMESICKNESS HEIMWEH
NOSTALGIA
HOMESPUN KERSEY RUSSET
HOMESTEAD TOFT TREF ONSET
PLACE WORTH TYDDYN FARMERY
ONSTEAD STEADING
HOMESTEADER NESTER
HOMETHRUST HAI HAY
HOMEWORK PREP
HOMICIDE DEATH MORTH KILLING
HOMILETIC KERYSTIC
HOMILY PRONE OMELIE POSTIL
SERMON
HOMINY SAMP NASAUMP
HOMOEOMERY GERM SEED
(PL.) SPERMATA
HOMOGENEITY SAMENESS
HOMOGENEOUS LIKE SOLID
GLOBAL SIMPLE COMPACT SIMILAR
HOMOGENOUS ENTIRE
HOMOLOGUE CYANINE HOMOTYPE
HOMOPHONY MONODY
HOMORGANIC COGNATE
HOMOZYGOUS PURE ISOGENIC

HONDURAS

CAPITAL: TEGUCIGALPA
COIN: PESO CENTAVO LEMPIRA
GULF: FONSECA
INDIAN: MAYA PAYA SUMO ULVA
CARIB LENCA PIPIL TAUIRA
JICAQUE MISKITO MOSQUITO
ISLAND: ROATAN
ISLANDS: BAY BAHIA
LAKE: CRIBA YOJOA BREWER

MEASURE: VARA MILLA MECATE
TERCIA CAJUELA MANZANA
MOUNTAINS: PIJA AGALTA
CELAQUE
PORT: LACEIBA TRUJILLO
RIVER: COCO SICO ULUA AGUAN
LEMPA NEGRO TINTO WANKS
PATUCA SULACO GUAVAPE
OLANCHO SEGOVIA SANTIAGO
RUINS: TENAMPUA
TOWN: TELA YORO COPAN LAPAZ
ROATAN GRACIAS LACEIBA
TRUJILLO YUSCARAN JUTICALPA
WEIGHT: CAJA LIBRA

HONE HO STROKE
HONEST FAIR GOOD TRUE AFALD
FRANK ROUND SOUND WHITE
CANDID DEXTER DINKUM ENTIRE
PROPER RUSTIC SINGLE SQUARE
SINCERE UPRIGHT RIGHTFUL
STRAIGHT
HONESTLY TRULY DINKUM HONEST
INDEED SINGLY SQUARE SQUARELY
HONESTY FAITH HONOR SATIN
EQUITY LUNARY REALTY VERITY
JUSTICE LUNARIA PROBITY
BOLBONAC FAIRNESS FIDELITY
MOONWORT SATINPOD YEOMANRY
HONEY MEL MELL HINNY HONEYBUN
(— BEVERAGE) MULSE
HONEYBEE (ALSO SEE BEE) BEE
GYNE KING DRANE DRONE QUEEN
DINGAR DRONER EGATES CYPRIAN
DEBORAH DESERET KOOTCHA
MELISSA STINGER ACULEATE
ANGELITO
HONEY BUZZARD PERN
HONEYCOMB COMB FRAME
WAXCOMB
HONEYCREEPER IIWI MAMO PALILA
DREPANID GUITGUIT
HONEYDEW MILDEW
HONEY EATER OO IAO TUI MOHO
MINER TENUI MANUAO MAOMAO
ROSTER BELLBIRD WURRALUH
HONEYED SWEET HYBLAN SUGARY
SUGARED HYBLAEAN LUSCIOUS
HONEY GUIDE MOROC
HONEY MESQUITE ALGAROBA
HONEYPOD
HONEY PLANT HOYA HUAJILLO
HONEYSUCKLE VINE SUCKLE
WEIGELA BINDWEED SUCKLING
WOODBINE

HONG KONG

BAY: SHEKO REPULSE
CAPITAL: VICTORIA
COIN: CENT DOLLAR
DISTRICT: WANCHAI
GARDENS: TIGERBALM
ISLAND: LANTAO
MOUNTAIN: CASTLE VICTORIA
PENINSULA: KOWLOON

HONK KONK YANG CRONK

HONOR BAY ORE FAME FETE HORN
ADORE GLORY GRACE HERRY IZZAT
MENSE MENSK SPEAK TREAT
CREDIT DECORE ENHALO ESTEEM
HOMAGE HONOUR LAUREL PRAISE
REVERE SALUTE WORTHY DIGNITY
EMBLAZE GLORIFY HONESTY
MANSHIP RESPECT WORSHIP
DECORATE GRANDEZA TASHREEF
(PL.) ACES
HONORABLE DEAR FREE GOOD
DIGNE NOBLE OPIME WHITE GENTLE
HONEST HONORA LORDLY SQUARE
UPRIGHT GENEROUS HANDSOME
HONORARY
HONORABLENESS HONESTY
HONORABLY GENTLY
HONORARIUM SALARY DOUCEUR
ALTARAGE HONORARY
HONORED GOOD FAMOUS LAUREL
LAURELED
HONORIFIC MAGNIFIC
HOOD HOW COIF COWL HEAD HUDE
JACK AMICE ALMUCE BIGGIN
BONNET BURLET CALASH CAMAIL
CANOPY CAPOTE CUTOFF DOMINO
FUNNEL MANTLE RAFFIA BANGKOK
BASHLYK CALOTTE CAPUCHE
BLINDAGE CAPUTIUM CHAPERON
CUCULLUS FOOLSCAP LIRIPIPE
LIRIPOOP MAZARINE TROTCOZY
(— AND CAPE COMBINED)
FALDETTA
(— OF BOILER) VOMIT
(— OF CARRIAGE) HEAD
(— OF MAIL) COIF CAMAIL COIFFE
(— OF VEHICLE) TOP CAPOTE
(— ON CUPBOARD) TREMOR
(— ON HORSES) BLINKER
(LENS —) SUNSHADE
(MONK'S —) COWL
(STIRRUP —) TAPADERO
(STRAW —) JAVA
(WOMAN'S —) SURTOUT VOLUPER
HOODED COWLED GALEATE
HOODED CROW HOODIE GRAYBACK
GREYBACK
HOODED MERGANSER SMEW
SNOWL SPIKE TADPOLE TOWHEAD
MOSSHEAD
HOODED SEAL WIG HOOD
HOODCAP
HOODLUM HOOD BADDY BADDIE
SKOLLY LURCHER HOOLIGAN
LARRIKIN
HOODOO JINX
HOODWINK MOP DUPE FOOL BLEAR
BLIND BLUFF CHEAT CLOYNE
DELUDE GAMMON WIMPLE AVEUGLE
BEGUILE BLINKER DECEIVE MISLEAD
INVEIGLE
HOOEY BUSHWAH
HOOF CLOOF CLOOT COFFIN UNGUIS
UNGULA CLOOTIE HOOFLET
FOREHOOF
HOOK DOG GAB JIG PEW TUG CLIP
DRAG FLAG GAFF HAKE HUCK KILP
MEAK NOCK PRIN PUGH SETT SKID
STAY TACK CATCH CLEEK CLICK

CRAMP CROME CROOK DRAIL
HAMUS ONCIN PREEN SARPE SPOON
TACHE UNCUS BECKET DETENT
HANGLE HINGLE PINTLE TENTER
AGRAFFE GAMBREL GRUNTER
HAMULUS HITCHER HOOKLET
KNUCKLE NUTHOOK PELICAN
PENNANT PINHOOK POTHOOK
RAMHEAD SNIGGLE SPERKET
UNCINUS BOATHOOK CROTCHET
GRABHOOK PORTHOOK PULLBACK
VULSELLA WEEDHOOK
(— FISH) FOUL HANG SNAG DRAIL
HITCH STRIKE SNIGGLE FISHHOOK
(— FOR BACON) COMB
(— FOR KETTLE) KILP HANGLE
TRAMMEL
(— FOR POT) DRACKEN POTHOOK
SLOWRIE
(— FOR TWISTING HEMP) WHIRL
WHIRLER
(2 —S FASTENED AT SHANKS)
DOUBLES
(BENCH —) JACK
(BOAT —) HITCHER
(BOXING —) CROSS
(COUPLING —) JIGGER
(LONG-HANDLED —) HOCK MEAK
(MUSICAL —) FLAG PENNANT
(PRUNING —) SARPE CALABOZO
(REAPING —) HINK TWIBILL
(SAFETY —) CLEVIS
(SKIDDING —S) GRAB
HOOKAH KALIAN
HOOKED ADUNC UNCOUS FALCATE
HAMATED HAMULAR ADUNCATE
AQUILINE HAMIFORM UNCINATE
HOOKEDNESS ADUNCITY
HOOKER-OUT STICKMAN
HOOK-SHAPED ANKYROID
HOOKUP CIRCUIT
HOOKWORM STRONGYL
HOOLIGAN GOONDA
(PL.) AMALAITA
HOOP RIB BAIL BAND BOND BOOL
CLIP GIRD GIRR PASS RING TIRE
GARTH GIRTH FRETTE HOOPLE
LAGGIN WICKET CIRCLET GARLAND
TRUNDLE
(— FOR A SPAR) BANGLE
(— FOR BARREL) BAND GIRD GIRTH
(— FOR LAMPSHADE) HARP
(— FOR ORE BUCKET) CLEVIS
(— FOR WINNOWING GRAIN)
WEIGHT
(— NET) TRUNK
(— TO STRENGTHEN GUN) FRETTE
(HALF —) BAIL BALE
HOOPED RUNG
HOOPOE HOOP UPUPA WHOOP
IRRISOR DUNGBIRD PICARIAN
HOOPSKIRT TUBTAIL
HOOP SNAKE WAMPUM
HOOSE HUSK
HOOSIER STATE INDIANA
HOOT CURR WHOO WHOOT EXPLODE
ULULATE
HOP HIP NIP FLIP JUMP LEAP BOUND
HITCH SWINE FLIERS GAMBOL

SPRING TITTUP CROWHOP HOPBIND
HOPVINE LUPULUS SKIPPER
HOPBUSH AKE AKEAKE
HOP CLOVER SHAMROCK SUCKLING
HOPE WON DEEM SPES TROW THINK
TRUST DESIRE EXPECT PERDUE
ESPEIRE THOUGHT SPERANZA
VELLEITY
(VAIN —) PIPE WANHOPE
HOPEFUL FOND SANGUINE
WENLICHE
HOPELESS DULL ABJECT FORLORN
DOWNCAST
HOPELESSNESS DESPAIR
HOP HORNBEAM DEERWOOD
HARDHACK IRONWOOD
HOPI MOKI MOQUI
HOP-LIKE LUPULINE
HOPPER CURB JACK CLOSET
HAPPER MACARONI
HOPPLE HOBBLE PASTERN
SIDELANG
HOPS SHATTER
(— BETWEEN 2 AND 4 YEARS) OLDS
HOPSCOTCH POTSY HOPPERS
PALLALL PEEVERS
HOP TREE RUEWORT WINGSEED
HORDE ARMY CAMP CLAN PACK
CROWD GROUP SWARM LEGION
THRONG
(INNER —) BUKEYEF
HOREHOUND HENBIT MARVEL
WONDER MARRUBE
HORIZON LAYER COMPASS FINITOR
ORTERDE SKYLINE
HORIZONTAL LEVEL LINEAR NAIANT
ACLINAL STRAIGHT
HORIZONTALLY FLATLY BARWAYS
BARWISE ENDLONG FESSWAYS
FESSWISE
HORMIGO QUIRA
HORMONE CORTIN LUTEIN EQUILIN
ESTRIOL ESTRONE GASTRIN INSULIN
RELAXIN THEELIN THEELOL
ANDROGEN ENDOCRIN ESTROGEN
FLORIGEN GALACTIN LACTOGEN
OESTRIOL SECRETIN CORTISONE
HORN BEAK BATON BUGLE CONCH
CORNO CORNU SHOOT ANTLER
CLAXON KLAXON OXHORN TOOTER
ALPHORN ALTHORN BUFFALO
CLARONE FOGHORN HELICON
HUTCHET OUTHORN PRICKET
SHOPHAR UNICORN BEAKIRON
BUCKHORN CLAVICOR CORNICLE
OLIPHANT SLUGHORN STAGHORN
WALDHORN
(— NOTE) MORT
(— OF CRESCENT MOON) CUSP
(— OF DILEMMA) PIKE
(— OF DRINK) SLOSH
(— OF YOUNG STAG) BUNCH
(BUDDING —) SHOOT
(DRINKING —) RHYTON
(ENGLISH —) CA
(FRENCH —) CORNO
(GREY —) COLUMN
(HUNTER'S —) HUTCHET
(INSECT'S —) ANTENNA

(RAM'S —) SHOPHAR
(RUDIMENTARY —) SLUG
(STUNTED —) SCUR
HORNBEAM HARDBEAM HARDHACK
HORNWOOD IRONWOOD
HORNBILL TOCK CALAO TOUCAN
HOMURAI BROMVOEL PICARIAN
YEARBIRD
HORNBLENDE SIDERITE
HORNED FORKED
HORNED DACE CHUB
HORNED POUT CATFISH
HORNED SCREAMER ANHIMA
KAMACHI UNICORN
HORNED VIPER WAMPUM
CERASTES
HORNET VESPA VESPID STINGER
HORNGELD CORNAGE
HORNLESS NAT NOT MOIL POLL
DODDY MULEY POLEY DODDED
HUMBLE HUMMEL MAILIE MULLEY
POLLED ACEROUS
HORNPIPE MATELOTE
HORN POPPY SQUATMORE
HORNSTONE KERALITE
HORNTAIL SIREX ORYSSID
UROCERID WOODWORM
HORNWORT COONTAIL HORNWEED
HORNY WAUKIT CALLOUS CERATOID
CORNEOUS KERASINE KERATOID
HORNYHEAD CHUB
HOROSCOPE SCOPE THEME FIGURE
GENESIS NATIVITY
HORRIBLE DIRE GRIM UGLY GREAT
GRISLY HORRID GEARFUL GHASTLY
HIDEOUS HORRENT UNSLOGH
DREADFUL GRUESOME HORRIFIC
SHOCKING TERRIBLE
HORRID GRIM UGLY AWFUL ROUGH
RUGGED SNUFFY UGSOME WICKED
HIDEOUS DREADFUL GRUESOME
HORRIBLE SHOCKING
HORRIFIC FEARFUL
HORRIFIED AGHAST GHASTLY
HORRENT
HORRIFY DISMAY ENHORROR
HORROR FEAR DREAD TERROR
(PL.) JIMJAMS
HORS D'OEUVRE CANAPE RELISH
OUTWORK ZAKUSKA
(PL.) ASSIETTE
HORSE BAY CUT DUN GEE GRI NAG
PAD POT RIP TIT ARAB AVER BARB
DOON GOER GROG HACK HAND
HOSS JADE MARE MOKE PRAD
PROD QUAD RACK RIDE ROAN ROIL
SKIN STUD TEAM TURK WEED YAWD
ZAIN AIVER ARION ARVAK BEAST
BIDET BLACK BROCK CAPLE CAPUL
CHUNK CREAM CROCK DUMMY
EQUID FAVEL GLYDE GRANI HAIRY
HOBBY MILER MOREL PACER PINTO
PIPER POLER PUNCH RACER ROGUE
RUNSY SCREW SHIER SHIRE SKATE
SOMER STEED STIFF TACKY WALER
WIDGE ALEZAN AMBLER BANKER
BOLTER BRONCO BRUMBY BUCKER
BUSSER CABBER CALICO CASTER
CHEVAL COLLOP CURTAL CUSSER

DAPPLE DOBBIN DRIVER ENTIRE
EQUINE FENCER FILLER GANGER
GARRON GLEYDE GRULLA HUNTER
JUMPER KEFFEL LEADER MAIDEN
MORGAN NUBIAN ORLOFF OUTLAW
PELTER PLATER POSTER PULLER
ROARER ROUNCY RUNNER SAVAGE
SORREL STAGER TARPAN TRACER
TURKEY VANNER WARPER WEAVER
ALSVINN ALSVITH ARABIAN
BARBARY BELGIAN BOARDER
CABALLO CHARGER CLICKER
CLIPPER COACHER COCOTTE
COURSER CRIBBER CRIOLLA
CRITTER DRAFTER FLEMISH
GALATHE GELDING GIGSTER
GRUNTER HACKNEY KNACKER
LEEFANG MONTURE MUSTANG
NEIGHER PACOLET PALFREY
PIEBALD PRANCER PRANKER
RATTLER REESTER REFUSER
REMOUNT RUNAWAY SADDLER
SLEDDER SLEEPER SPANKER
STAGGIE STEPPER SUFFOLK
SUMPTER TRAPPER TRESTLE
TROOPER TROTTER WHEELER
ARDENNES BATHORSE BUCKSKIN
CHESTNUT CHEVALET COCKTAIL
COLICKER CREATURE CYLLAROS
DEMISANG DESTRIER EOHIPPUS
FOOTROPE FRIPPERY GALLOPER
GALLOWAY HRIMFAXI KADISCHI
MACHINER OUTSIDER RIDGLING
ROADSTER SKEWBALD STIBBLER
TRIPPLER WHISTLER YARRAMAN
(— ACT) MANAGE
(— CERTAIN NOT TO WIN) STIFF
(— ESTABLISHMENT) HARAS
(— LOSING FIXED RACE) STUMER
STUMOUR
(— OF UNIFORM DARK COLOR) ZAIN
(— RACE) WALKOVER
(—S RUNNING BEHIND) RUCK
(2-YEAR OLD —) TWINTER
(3 —S ABREAST) TROIKA
(3 —S ONE BEHIND ANOTHER)
RANDOM
(4 —S ABREAST) QUADRIGA
(ARABIAN —) ARAB KOHL ARABIAN
(BALKY —) JIBBER
(BROKEN-DOWN —) JADE CROCK
SCREW DURGAN GARRAN
(CALICO —) PINTO
(CASTRATED —) GELDING
(CLUMSY —) STAMMEL
(DECREPIT —) SKATE GLEYDE
(DRAFT —) HAIRY PUNCH SHIRE
BEETEWK BELGIAN SUFFOLK
(DROVE OF —S) ATAJO
(EASY-PACED —) PAD
(FALLOW —) FAVEL
(FAMILY —) DOBBIN
(FAST —) GANGER
(FEMALE —) MARE FILLY
(FLEMISH —) ROIL
(GRAY —) SCHIMMEL
(HIGH-SPIRITED —) STEPPER
(IMAGINARY —) AULLAY
(IMMUNIZED —) BLEEDER

(INFERIOR —) PLUG PLATER
(JUMPING —) LEPPER
(MALE —) STALLION
(NEAR —) HAND
(OLD —) JADE PROD AIVER CROCK
(PACK —) BIDET SUMPTER
(RANGE —) FANTAIL
(SHAFT —) SHAFTER THILLER
(SHAGGY —) ALTAI
(SLUGGISH —) HOG
(SMALL —) NAG TIT BIDET GENET
HOBBY JENNET GALLOWAY
(STOCKY —) COB
(TEAM OF —S) CARTWARE
(TEAM OF 3 —S WITH LEADER)
UNICORN
(TRICK —) SIMON
(UNBROKEN —) BRONCO
(VICIOUS —) LADINO
(WILD —) FUZZY BRUMBY KUMRAH
TARPAN JUGHEAD BANGTAIL
FUZZTAIL WARRIGAL
(WINGED —) PEGASUS
(WORN-OUT —) HACK GARRAN
KNACKER CROWBAIT
(WORTHLESS —) JADE SHACK
KEFFEL
(YOUNG —) TIT COLT FOAL STAG
STOT STAGGIE
(PL.) MANADA STABLE UNICORN
HORSE BALM KNOBWEED
KNOTROOT RICHWEED
HORSE BLANKET RUG MANTA
HORSE BOY TRACER
HORSE CHESTNUT CONKER
HORSECLOTH HOUSE HOUSING
HORSE DEALER COPER CHANTER
COURSER
HORSE-EYE JACK XUREL
HORSE FENNEL SESELI
HORSEFLESH JACK
HORSEFLY BOT GAD CLEG CLEGG
STOUT BOTFLY BREEZE GADBEE
GADFLY BULLDOG DEERFLY
TABANID
HORSEHAIR SETON
HORSELAUGH GUFFAW
HORSELEECH ALUKAH
HORSELOAD SEAM
HORSE MACKEREL TUNNY SAUREL
HORSEMAN RIDER CHARRO
COWBOY HUSSAR KNIGHT RUTTER
COURIER PICADOR PRICKER
GALLOPER
(PL.) HORSE CAVALRY
HORSEMANSHIP CAVALRY
HORSEMINT RIGNUM
HORSE MUSHROOM WHITECAP
HORSE NETTLE SOLANUM
HORSEPLAY HIJINKS
HORSEPOWER SOUP
HORSEPOX GREASE
HORSE-RADISH MAROR MOROR
REDCOLL
HORSE-RADISH TREE BEHN BEHEN
HORSESHOE TIP SHOE PLATE
HOBBER LUNETTE
HORSETAIL TAIL PRELE TOADPIPE
HORSETAIL LICHEN TREEHAIR

HORSETAIL TREE AGOHO AGOJO
HORSEWEED COCASH COWTAIL
　HOGWEED FIREWEED SCABIOUS
HORTATORY EMOTIVE
HORUS SEPT SOPT SEPTI
　HORMAKHU
　(FATHER OF —) OSIRIS
HOSACKIA ACMISPON
HOSE LINE VAMP HOSEN GASKIN
　BROGUES BULLION HOSIERY
　HANDLINE HOSEPIPE
HOSIERY HOSE KNITWEAR
　(— WORKER) LOOPER
HOSPICE IMARET DIACONIA
　HOSPITAL
HOSPITABLE DOUCE CLEVER
　DOULCE SOCIAL CORDIAL FRIENDLY
HOSPITAL BEDLAM CRECHE SPITAL
　COLLEGE LAZARET
HOSPITALITY SALT MENSE
　XENODOCHY
HOSPODAR VOIVOD GOSPODAR
HOST SUM ARMY FYRD WARE
　CROWD JASON MAKER POWER
　SWARM WERED LEGION LODGER
　NATION THRONG BALEBOS
　COMPANY FYRDUNG SACRING
　VIANDER LANDLORD PARTICLE
　(— OF INVADERS) HERE
　(EUCHARISTIC —) LAMB SACRING
　(PL.) SABAOTH
HOSTA NIOBE FUNKIA
HOSTAGE BORROW PLEDGE SURETY
　RANSOMER
HOSTEL INN ENTRY HOSTAGE
　KINGDOM HOSPITAL
HOSTESS TAUPO LANDLADY
HOSTILE FOE HARD ALIEN BLACK
　ENEMY FREMT HATEL STOUT
　DEADLY FRIGID INFEST ADVERSE
　ASOCIAL FIENDLY OPPOSED
　UNQUERT WARLIKE CONTRARY
　INIMICAL OPPOSITE
HOSTILITY WAR FEID FEUD HATE
　ANIMUS ENMITY HATRED RANCOR
　SCHISM DAGGERS RUPTURE
　(PL.) WAR ARMS ARMOR WARFARE
HOSTLER NAGMAN OSTLER
　HORSEBOY
HOT WARM CALID EAGER FIERY
　ARDENT ESTIVE FERVID IGNITE
　SULTRY TORRID ANIMOSE ANIMOUS
　BOILING BURNING FERVENT
　PEPPERY THERMAL CAYENNED
　FEVERISH SEETHING SIZZLING
　(— WATER) SOUP
HOTBED BED HOTHOUSE
HOT-BLOODED VASCULAR
HOTBOX SMOKER STINKER
HOTEL INN SPA FLOP FONDA HOUSE
　HYDRO HOSTEL HOTTLE POSADA
　FLEABAG FONDACO FUNDUCK
　GASTHOF HOSTELRY
HOTELKEEPER HOTELIER
HOT-HEADED BRAINISH MADBRAIN
HOTHOUSE STEW STOVE PINERY
　FRUITERY
HOT ROD DRAGSTER
HOT-TEMPERED PEPPERY

CHOLERIC SPITFIRE
HOTTENTOT TOTTY HOTNOT
　KOKANA WITBOOI QUAEQUAE
　(PL.) BALAO BALAWU
HOUND DOG PIE BAIT HARL HUNT
　MUTE BRACE BRACH ENTRY HARRY
　LEASH LIMER SLATE AFGHAN
　BASSET BEAGLE HUNTER LEAMER
　LUCERN SLEUTH TUFTER CURTISE
　ENTRADA GELLERT REDBONE
　SKIRTER BARUKHZY BLUETICK
　BRATCHET COURSING FOXHOUND
　(BITCH —) BRACH
　(CRY OF —) MUSIC
　(RELAY OF —S) VANLAY
　(SLEUTH —) TALBOT
　(SPECTRAL —) SHUCK
　(PL.) RACHES
HOUND'S-TONGUE TORYWEED
HOUR URE TIDE TIME CURFEW
　GHURRY
　(6 —S) QUADRANT
　(CANONICAL —) NONE SEXT PRIME
　MATINS TIERCE VESPERS COMPLINE
　EVENSONG
　(HALF —) BELL
　(KILOWATT —) KELVIN
　(LAST —S) DEATHBED
　(STUDY —) PREP
HOURLY HORAL HORARY
HOUSE BOX KEN CASA CRIB DOME
　DUMP FIRM FLET HALL HELL HOLE
　HOME RACE ROOF STOW ABODE
　ADOBE AERIE BAHAY BANDA COVER
　DACHA DOMUS HOOSE JACAL
　LODGE MEESE STAGE WHARE
　BIGGIN BOTTLE CAMARA CASITA
　CASTLE CHEMIS CLOTHE DUPLEX
　FAMILY HEARTH MAISON PALACE
　PARISH SINGLE STABLE WIGWAM
　BASTIDE BIGGING CABOOSE
　CASSINE EUDEMON FAZENDA
　HOGGERY HOUSING MESUDGE
　QUARTER SHELTER AEDICULA
　BARADARI BUNGALOW DOMICILE
　DOVECOTE DWELLING MEDSTEAD
　MESSUAGE TENEMENT
　(— AND 5 ACRES) COTE
　(— AND LAND) DEMESNE
　(— FOR DOGS) KENNEL
　(— FOR WOMEN) HAREM
　(— IN BOROUGH) HAW
　(— OF A MARABOUT) KOUBA
　(— OF LEGISLATURE) CHAMBER
　ASSEMBLY
　(— OF PARLIAMENT) COMMONS
　(— OF PROSTITUTION) CRIB BAGNIO
　(— OF THIEVES) KEN
　(— OF WORSHIP) BETHEL CHURCH
　(APARTMENT —) INSULA
　(ASTROLOGICAL —) ANGLE
　(AUSTRALIAN —) HUMPY
　(CHANGE —) DRY
　(CHAPTER —) CABILDA
　(CLAY —) ADOBE TEMBE
　(COACH —) REMISE
　(COMMUNAL —) MORONG
　(COUNTRY —) PEN DACHA CASINO
　GRANGE QUINTA BASTIDE CHATEAU

　(COW —) VACCARY
　(DAIRY —) WICK
　(EATING —) COOKSHOP
　(ESKIMO —) IGLU IGLOO TOPEK
　KASHGA KASHIMA
　(FIJI —) BURE
　(FORTIFIED —) GARRISON
　(GAMBLING —) BANK HELL
　(GOVERNMENT —) KONAK
　(GRINDING —) HULL
　(HAWAIIAN —) HALE
　(LODGING —) INN KIP HOST ENTRY
　HOTEL HOSTEL
　(LOG —) TILT
　(MANOR —) HAM HALL COURT
　PLACE SCHLOSS
　(PLANETARY —) TOWER
　(POULTRY —) ARK HENNERY
　(PUBLIC —) INN HOSTEL SNUGGERY
　(RANCH —) HUT
　(RELIGIOUS —) CELL CONVENT
　KELLION
　(RENTED —) LET
　(REST —) DAK KHAN SERAI
　(RETREAT —) CENACLE
　(ROOMING —) DOSS FLOP FLEABAG
　(ROYAL —) AERIE
　(SMALL —) COT HUT BACH CELL
　CABIN HOVEL SHACK CASITA
　COTTAGE
　(SOD —) SODDY
　(STILT —) CHIKEE CHICKEE
　(SUMMER —) TRELLIS
　(TENEMENT —) LAND CHAWL
　(THATCHED —) BANDA
　(TOY —) COBHOUSE
　(TURKISH —) KONAK
HOUSEBOAT BARGE HOUSER
　WANGAN DAHABEAH
HOUSEBREAKER MILL JACOB
　MILLKEN
HOUSEBREAKING CRACK
HOUSECARL THINGMAN
HOUSECOAT DUSTER
HOUSEFINCH BURION LINNET
　REDHEAD
HOUSEHOLD HIRED HOUSE FAMILY
　HOUSAL MEINIE MENAGE FIRESIDE
　MAINFAST
HOUSEHOLDER ASTRER GOODMAN
　GUIDMAN NAUKRAR FRANKLIN
HOUSEKEEPER HUSSY MATRON
HOUSELEEK JUBARB AYEGREEN
　HOMEWORT SENGREEN SILGREEN
HOUSEMATE DOMESTIC
HOUSEWARMING INFARE
HOUSEWIFE DAME FRAU FROW
　WIFE HUSSY VROUW BUSHWIFE
　HAUSFRAU
　(MEAN —) NIP
HOUSING BOX BASE CASE DRUM
　TRAP BANJO BLIMP GLOBE HOUSE
　KIOSK BARREL RADOME SHIELD
　HOUSAGE SHELTER DOGHOUSE
　PADCLOTH PECTORAL PEDESTAL
　(HORSE'S —) BASE
　(RADAR —) BLISTER
　(PL.) HOLSTERS
HOVA IMERINA

HOVEL COSH CREW CRIB CRUE HELM HULK HULL CHOZA HUTCH LODGE BURROW CRUIVE PONDOK

HOVELER HOBBLER HUFFLER

HOVER BAIT FLIT HANG HOVE BROOD FLUTTER HOVERER

HOW AS FOO HOO HOWE HOWEER HOWEVER QUOMODO WHEREBY

HOWDAH TOWER AMBARI AMBAREE

HOWEVER BUT THO YET HOWSO STILL THOUGH

HOWITZER HOWITZ LICORN UNICORN

HOWITZER SHELL OBUS

HOWL WAP WOW BAWL GOWL GURL HURL WAUL WAWL YAWL YOLL YOUT YOWL TIGER WHEWL WRAWL BEHOWL STEVEN ULULATE (— VOCIFEROUSLY) TONGUE

HOWLER ERROR ARAGUATO

HOWLER MONKEY MONO ARABA HOWLER GUARIBA GUEREBA STENTOR ALOUATTE

HOWLING ULULANT

HOY TJALK CRUMSTER

HOYDEN MEG BLOWZE RIGSBY TOMBOY

HREIDMAR (SON OF —) REGIN FAFNER

H-SHAPED ZYGAL

HUAMUCHIL INGA

HUAVE WABI HUABI

HUB HOB BOSS NAVE STOCK CENTER CENTRE FAUCET HUBBLE SOCKET SPIDER OMPHALOS (— AND SPOKES) SPEECH

HUBBLE-BUBBLE CALEAN CALAHAN

HUBBUB DIN STIR CLAMOR FRAISE HUBBLE RACKET TUMULT BOBBERY CLUTTER BROUHAHA HUBBABOO ROWDYDOW SPLATTER

HUCHEN HUSO

HUCHNOM TATU

HUCKLEBERRY HURT ERICAD CRACKERS

HUCKSTER BADGER CADGER KIDDER HAGGLER KIDDIER TRUCKER OUTCRIER

HUDDLE RUCK HUNCH CRINGE FUMBLE HOWDER HURTLE SCRUMP SHRIMP SHRINK CROODLE SCRINCH SCROOCH SCRUNCH SHUFFLE

HUE RUD BLEE BLUE COND CYAN CHLOR COLOR GREEN LEMON TAINT TINCT (DULL —) DRAB (SOMBER —) DARK

HUELESS GRAY GREY

HUFF DOD BLOW RUFF DRUNT SNUFF

HUFFY FUFFY SHIRTY

HUG CLIP COLL COUL MOLD CREEM CRUSH HALSE CUDDLE HUDDLE HUGGLE STRAIN CHERISH EMBRACE SQUEEZE

HUGE BIG FELL MAIN VAST ENORM GIANT GREAT JUMBO LARGE STOUR HEROIC IMMANE BANGING BUMPING DECUMAN IMMENSE MASSIVE MONSTER TITANIC COLOSSAL ENORMOUS GALACTIC GIGANTIC MOUNTAIN PYTHONIC SLASHING SWAPPING THWACKING

HUGENESS ENORMITY

HUISACHE WABI AROMO CASSIE POPINAC OPOPANAX

HULK CHOP HULL CORSE

HULL HUD POD BODY BULK HULK HUSK PILL BURSE CASCO SWELL (— OF COTTON BOLL) BUR BURR (— OF SHIP) BODY HULK BOTTOM

HULLABALOO DIN FLAP CLAMOR HUBBUB RACKET BROUHAHA

HUM BUM BLUR BRUM BUZZ HUSS TUNE CHIRM CROON DRONE FEIGN SOUGH SOWFF HUMBLE TEEDLE FREDDON TRUMPET

HUMAN BEING MANLY FINITE FLESHY HUMANE MORTAL MANNISH HOMININE HUMANIST

HUMAN BEING MAN WIGHT MORTAL PERSON ADAMITE CREATURE RATIONAL

HUMANE CIVIL KINDLY TENDER MERCIFUL

HUMANELY MANLY

HUMANITY FLESH MENSK WORLD MANHEAD MANHOOD MANSHIP SPECIES ADAMHOOD HUMANISM KINDNESS LENITUDE

HUMBLE LOW HOWE MEAN MILD MURE POOR TAME VAIL ABASE ABATE BUXOM DEMIT DIMIT LOWER LOWLY PLAIN SILLY SMALL SOBER WORMY ATTERR DEJECT DEMISS EMBASE HONEST MASTER MODEST REDUCE SIMPLE SLIGHT UNPUFF AFFLICT DEGRADE DEPRESS FOOLISH IGNOBLE MORTIFY OBSCURE CONTRITE DISGRACE (— ONESELF) STOOP GROVEL

HUMBLED SMALL ABASED DEJECTED

HUMBLENESS HUMILITY

HUMBLER INFERIOR

HUMBLING SETDOWN

HUMBLY SIMPLE

HUMBUG GAS GUM HUM KID FLAM GAME GUFF JAZZ SHAM CHEAT FRAUD FUDGE GUILE JOLLY SPOOK TRICK BLAGUE GAMMON FLUMMER VERNEUK FLIMFLAM FLUMMERY HUCKMUCK IMPOSTER NONSENSE

HUMDINGER DOOZY DINGER HUMMER SNORTER

HUMDRUM IRKSOME PROSAIC

HUMERUS ARM

HUMID WET DAMP DANK MOIST SOGGY STICKY SULTRY WETTISH HUMOROUS

HUMILIATE ABASE ABASH SCALP SHAME NIDDER NITHER DEGRADE MORTIFY UNPLUME DISGRACE

HUMILIATED SMALL ASHAMED

HUMILIATION DUST COMEDOWN DISGRACE

HUMILITY MODESTY MEEKNESS MILDNESS

HUMIN MELANIN

HUMMEL FALTER

HUMMING AHUM BROOL SINGING

HUMMINGBIRD RUBY STAR MANGO SYLPH TENUI TOPAZ AMAZON COQUET HERMIT HUMMER ROSTER SAPPHO COLIBRI EMERALD HUMBIRD JACOBIN RAINBOW SNOWCAP TROCHIL WARRIOR CALLIOPE COQUETTE FIRETAIL FROUFROU MIMOTYPE PICARIAN SAPPHIRE WHITETIP

HUMMOCK HUMP CHENIER HAMMOCK TUSSOCK

HUMOR CUE PIN TID WIT BABY BILE CANT MOOD TIFF VEIN WHIM FRAME IRONY TUTOR MEGRIM PHLEGM SANIES SOOTHE SPLEEN SPRITE TEMPER FOOLING GRATIFY INDULGE VITREUM VITRINA ARCHNESS DISHUMOR DROLLERY EYEWATER FUMOSITY SANGUINE VITREOUS (BAD —) BATS THROW (ILL —) BILE DUDGEON (QUIET —) DRYNESS (SLIMY —) HIPPOMANES

HUMORIST JOKER FUNSTER FUNMAKER FUNNYMAN

HUMOROUS DROLL FUNNY QUEER JOCOSE COMICAL GIOCOSO PLAYFUL WAGGISH PLEASANT SARDONIC

HUMP BOSS HUNK BULGE BUNCH CROUP CRUMP HULCH HUNCH GIBBER GIBBUS HUMMIE GIBBOUS

HUMPBACK LORD CRUMP PUNCH

HUMPBACKED HUMPED HUMPTY GIBBOSE GIBBOUS

HUMPBACKED SALMON HADDO HOLIA

HUMPED HULCH HUMPY HUTCH HUMPTY HUNCHY

HUMUS MOR MOLD MULL HUMIN MOULD

HUNCH HUMP HUNK HULCH HUNCHET SCRUNCH

HUNCHBACK URCHIN HUMPBACK

HUNDRED RHO CENT CENTUM HUNDER HUNNER CANTRED CENTARY (— THOUSAND) LAC LAKH (5 —) D

HUNDREDFOLD CENTUPLE

HUNDREDTH (— OF INCH) POINT (— OF RIGHT ANGLE) GRAD GRADE

HUNDREDWEIGHT CENT CENTAL CENTENA CENTNER HUNDRED QUINTAL

HUNGARIAN HUN KUMAN MAGYAR

HUNGARY

CANAL: SIO SARVIZ
CAPITAL: BUDAPEST
COIN: GARA BALAS LENGO FILLER FORINT KORONA
DANCE: CZARDAS
DYNASTY: ARPAD ANGEVIN
FOREST: BAKONY
GYPSY: SZIGANE TZIGANI

KING: BELA GEZA IMRE ARPAD
  ISTVAN KALMAN MATTHIAS
LAKE: FERTO BALATON VELENCE
  BLATENSEE
MEASURE: AKO HOLD JOCH YOKE
  ANTAL ITCZE MAROK METZE
  HUVELYK MERFOLD
MOUNTAIN: KEKES BAKONY
  MECSEK BORZSONY KORISHEGY
MOUNTAIN RANGE: BUKK MATRA
  MECSEK CARPATHIAN
MUSICAL INSTRUMENT:
  TAROGATO
NATIVE: HUN SERB CROAT GYPSY
  MAGYAR SLOVAK UGRIAN
PLAIN: PUSZTA
REGIME: KADAR
RIVER: DUNA MURA RAAB RABA
  SAJO ZALA BODVA DRAVA
  DRAVE IPOLY KAPOS KOROS
  MAROS RABCA TARNA TISZA
  DANUBE HENRAD POPRAD
  SZAMOS THEISS ZAGYVA
  VISTULA BERRETYO
TOWN: ABA ACS OZD VAC BUDA
  EGER GYOR MAKO PAPA PECS
  PEST TATA ZIRC KOMLO
  CEGLED MOHACS SOPRON
  SZEGED DBRECEN MISKOLC
  SZENTES DEBRECEN SZEGEDIN
WEIGHT: VAMFONT VAMMAZSA
WINE: EGER TOKAJ TOKAY
  SZEKSZARD

HUNGER BELL CLEM WANT ACORIA
  DESIRE FAMINE CRAVING
HUNGRY YAP HOWE KEEN LEER
  EMPTY THIRL HOLLOW JEJUNE
  PECKISH YAPPISH ANHUNGRY
  ESURIENT
HUNK DAD DAUD JUNK MOUNTAIN
  (— OF BREAD) TOMMY
HUNT DOG GUN JAG MOB RUN
  GREW JACK LARK PUMP SEAL SEEK
  SHOP CHASE CHEVY DRIVE HOUND
  REVAY TRACK TRAIL BATTUE
  BEAGLE BREVIT CHEVVY COURSE
  FALCON FERRET SEARCH SHIKAR
  VANLAY ENCHASE AUCUPATE
  PIGSTICK SCROUNGE
  (— BIG GAME) GHOOM
  (— DEER) FLOAT
  (— DOWN) QUARRY
  (— DUCKS) TOLL
  (— FOX) CUB
  (— WITH HAWK) FLY
  (— WITH SPEAR) STICK
HUNTER GUN HUNT PINK JAGER
  BIRDER CHASER GUNNER JAEGER
  NIMROD THERON ACTAEON
  BUSHMAN CATCHER COURSER
  MONTERO SHIKARI SHOOTER
  SKIRTER STALKER TRAILER
  VENERER CEPHALUS CHASSEUR
  FIELDMAN HUNTSMAN TRAILMAN
  (— ON SNOW) CRUSTER
  (BUFFALO —) CIBOLERO

(MYTHOLOGICAL —) GWYN ORION
(RING OF —S) TINCHEL TINCHILL
HUNTING DRAG HANK AHUNT
  WATHE SHIKAR VENERY CUBBING
  GUNNING BEAGLING PURCHASE
  SHOOTING SURROUND VENATION
  (— SIGNAL) SEEK
HUNTSMAN WHIP HUNTER JAEGER
  ACTAEON CATCHER COURSER
  MONTERO SCARLET VENATOR
  VENERER CHASSEUR
HURDLE TRAY FLAKE FRITH PANEL
  STALE STICK DOUBLE RADDLE
  SLEDGE WATTLE
HURDS TOW
HURDY-GURDY LIRA ROTA LANTUM
  VIELLE SAMBUKE HUMSTRUM
  SYMPHONY
HURL BUN CAST CLOD DASH DUST
  FIRE PASH PELT PICK SLAT SOAK
  SOCK DRIVE FLING HEAVE LANCE
  PITCH SLING SMITE SPANG SWING
  THIRL THROW WHIRL THRILL
  HURLBAT SWITHER WHITHER
  JACULATE
HURLY-BURLY HURL UPROAR
HURRAH HAIL HUZZA HOORAY
  HURRAY
HURRICANE PRESTER FURACANA
  FURICANE WILDWIND
HURRIED HASTY THRONG HASTEFUL
  SNATCHED
HURRY ADO FOG NIP RAP RUB RUN
  DUST HUMP PELL PLAT POST RAPE
  RESE RUSH STIR TIFT TROT URGE
  WHIR CHASE CROWD HASTE HYPER
  LURRY PRESS SESSA SKIRT SPEED
  STAVE STOUR WHIRL BUCKET
  BUNDLE BUSTLE HASTEN HUSTLE
  POWDER STROTH TATTER WHORRY
  HOTFOOT QUICKEN SCUDDLE
  SKELTER SLITHER WHITHER
  DISPATCH EXPEDITE SPLUTTER
  (— A HORSE) SPUR
  (— ABOUT) SCOUR
  (— AWAY) FLEE BUNCH SCREW
  SKIRT
  (— CLUMSILY) TAVE TEAVE
  (— NOISILY) SPLUTTER
  (— OFF) DUST
  (— UP) BUSK
HURT CUT HOT DERE FIKE GALL
  HARM ABUSE BLAME GRIEF GRIPE
  SORRY SPITE THORN WATHE
  WOUND BRUISE DAMAGE GRIEVE
  IMPAIR INJURE INJURY LESION
  MIFFED MITTLE PAINED SCATHE
  STRAIN STROKE WINGED AFFLICT
  HURTING OFFENCE OFFENSE
  MISCHIEF NUISANCE
  (— EASILY) FROISSE
  (— FEELINGS) CUT TOUCH
  (— REPUTATION) LIBEL
  (— SEVERELY) KILL
  (EASILY —) GINGER
HURTFUL BAD ILL EVIL MALIGN
  NOCENT NOCIVE NOUGHT SHREWD
  TAKING BANEFUL HARMFUL
  MALEFIC NOCUOUS NOXIOUS

UNQUERT GRIEVOUS HURTSOME
  SCATHFUL
HURTLE HURL FLING THIRL
HUSBAND EKE MAN WER BOND
  CHAP FERE KEEP LORD MAKE MATE
  SAVE SIRE BARON CHURL HOARD
  HUBBY MATCH STORE MANAGE
  MASTER MISTER SPOUSE CONSORT
  GOODMAN GUIDMAN HENPECK
  PARTNER CONSERVE
  (— OF ADULTRESS) CUCKOLD
  (AFFIANCED —) FUTURE
  (PL.) PUNALUA
HUSBANDMAN BOND BOOR CARL
  CLOWN COLON TILLER ACREMAN
  HUSBAND PLOWMAN TILLMAN
  AGRICOLE
HUSBANDRY GAINER GAINOR
  THRIFT ECONOMY MANAGERY
HUSH SH HSH MUM PAX HESH HOOT
  LULL BURKE SHUSH STILL WHISH
  WHIST WHUSH HUDDLE HUSHABY
  SILENCE
HUSHED QUIET STILL GENTLE
  WHISHT
HUSK BUR COD HUD KEX SID BARK
  BURR COAT COSH HOSE HUCK
  HULK SEED SHIV SKIN HOOSE
  SCALE SHACK SHALE SHAUP SHELL
  SHILL SHOOD SHUCK SHUDE
  COLDER DEHUSK FLIGHT SLOUGH
  BOLSTER CARCASS CASCARA
  (— OF NUT) SHACK BOLSTER
  (— OF OATS) SHUD SHOOD FLIGHT
  (CORN —) HOJA
  (PL.) BHUSA CHAFF BHOOSA
  HULKAGE SHELLING
HUSKY HUSK CODDY FOGGY
  FURRED BUIRDLY HULKING
  BOUNCING SIBERIAN
HUSSITE TABORITE
HUSSY MINX SLUT BESOM CUTTY
  GIPSY GYPSY MADAM STRAP HIZZIE
  LIMMER DROSSEL
HUSTLE FAN HUMP JUMP BLITZ
  SKELP BUCKET BUNDLE BUSTLE
  JOSTLE RUSTLE SCUFTER
HUSTLECAP PINCH
HUSTLER HUSTLE PEELER BUSTLER
  FIREBALL
HUT COE COT BARI BUTT COSH
  COTE CREW CRIB HALE HULK HULL
  ISBA IZBA SHED SKEO TENT BASHA
  BENAB BOHIO BOTHY CABIN CHAWL
  CHOZA HOVEL HUMPY HUTCH
  JACAL KRAAL LODGE SCALE SETER
  SHACK SHIEL TOLDO TOPEK WHARE
  WURLY BOHAWN CANABA CHALET
  GUNYAH GUNYEH MIAMIA PONDOK
  RANCHO REFUGE SAETER SCONCE
  SHANTY SHELTY WIGWAM WIKIUP
  BALAGAN BARRACK BOUROCK
  CAMALIG COTTAGE GOONDIE
  HUDDOCK HUTMENT SHEBANG
  YAKUTAT BARABARA CHANTIER
  RONDAWEL SHIELING THOLTHAN
  TUGURIUM
  (— FOR TEMPORARY USE) CORF
  (— OVER MINING SHAFT) COE

(ABORIGINAL —) MIMI WURLY
GUNYAH MIAMIA WURLEY GOONDIE
(FISHERMAN'S —) SKEO
(HEATED —) HOTHOUSE
(HERMIT'S —) CELL
(NAVAJO —) HOGAN
(POULTRY —) IGLOO
(SAMOYED —) CHUM
(SIBERIAN —) JURT
(SOUTH AFRICAN —) STRUIS
HUTCH ARK RABBITRY
HUTIA UTIA JUTIA PILORI
HYACINTH LILY MUSK LILIUM
CROWTOE FLOATER GREGGLE
JACINTH BLUEBELL CROWFOOT
HAREBELL JACOUNCE
HYACINTH BEAN LABLAB BONAVIST
BONNYVIS DOLICHOS
HYACINTHUS (FATHER OF —)
AMYCLAS
(MOTHER OF —) DIOMEDE
HYALOGEN NEOSSIN
HYBRID DZO ZHO MULE ZOBO
CROSS GRADE HINNY LIGER
COYDOG GALYAK MOSAIC MULISH
SPLAKE TURKEN BASTARD BIGENER
CATTALO PLUMCOT ZEBRASS
ZEBRULA ZEBURRO CARIDEER
KAFERITA LIMEQUAT ZEBRINNY
HYBRIDIZE CROSS
HYDRANT CHUCK FIREPLUG
HYDRANTH SIPHON SYPHON
HYDRATE SLAKE
HYDRAZINE DIAMIDE
HYDRAZOATE AZIDE
HYDRIA KALPIS
HYDROCARBON ARENE CUMOL
FREON GUTTA IDRYL INDAN IRENE
TOLAN XYLOL ALKANE ALKYNE
ALLENE BUTANE BUTYNE CARANE
CETANE CETENE CYMENE DOCANE
ETHANE ETHENE HEXINE INDANE
INDENE MELENE NONENE OCTANE
OCTENE OCTINE PICENE PYRENE
RETENE TOLANE TOLUOL XYLENE
AMYLENE AZULENE BENZENE
CHOLANE CYCLENE DECALIN
ETHERIN FULVENE HEPTANE
HEPTENE HEPTYNE LYCOPIN
MUCKITE MYRCENE OLEFINE
PENTINE PENTYNE PROPANE
STYRENE TETROLE TOLUENE
BIPHENYL CADALENE CADINENE
CARBURAN CEROTENE CETYLENE

CHRYSENE CORONENE CUMULENE
DECYLENE DIOLEFIN DOCOSANE
DYSODILE EICOSANE ETHYLENE
EUDALENE FLUORENE HEXYLENE
ILLIPENE ISOPRENE LYCOPENE
MENTHENE NONYLENE OCTYLENE
PARAFFIN PRISTANE PYRACENE
RUTYLENE SABINENE SQUALENE
STILBENE
HYDROCYANIC PRUSSIC
HYDRODAMALIS RHYTINA
HYDROEXTRACTOR BUZZER
WHIZZER
HYDROFLUORIC PHTHORIC
HYDROGEN HYDRO
HYDROHEMATITE TURGITE
HYDROID POLYP OBELIA ACALEPH
ZOOPHYTE
HYDROLEA NAMA
HYDROMEL ALOJA
HYDROMETER SPINDLE
HYDROPERITONEUM ASCITES
HYDROPHOBIA LYSSA RABIES
HYDROPHOBIC LYSSIC
HYDROPHYLLIUM BRACT
HYDROXIDE ALKALI HYDRATE
HYDRIDE
HYDROZINCITE CALAMINE
HYENA HINE DABUH SIMIR HYAENID
HYGIENIC SANITARY
HYGRODEIK PAGOSCOPE
HYLLUS (FATHER OF —) HERCULES
(MOTHER OF —) DEIANIRA
(SLAYER OF —) ECHEMUS
(WIFE OF —) IOLE
HYLOZOIST PHYSICIST
HYMEN CHERRY BRIDEGOD
HYMENIUM THECIUM
HYMENOCALLIS ISMENE
HYMN ODE FUGE LAUD SING DIRGE
GATHA PAEAN PSALM YASHT
YMPNE ANTHEM CARVAL CHORAL
HIMENE HIRMOS MANTRA ORPHIC
THEODY VESPER CHORALE EXULTET
HEIRMOS INTROIT CANTICLE
DOXOLOGY ENCOMIUM PSALMODY
SEQUENCE
(— COLLECTION) MENAION
(MEXICAN —) ALABADO
(PL.) HYMNODY
HYMNAL HYMNARY HYMNBOOK
HYPERCORACOID RADIAL SCAPULA
HYPERCRITICAL NICE CAPTIOUS
CRITICAL

HYPERDULIA ADORATION
HYPEREMIA RUBOR
HYPEREMIC CONGESTED
HYPERICUM TUTSAN
HYPERION (DAUGHTER OF —)
AURORA
(FATHER OF —) URANUS
(MOTHER OF —) GAEA
(WIFE OF —) THEA
HYPEROPIC FARSIGHTED
HYPERSENSITIVITY ATOPY
HYPHA STOLON
HYPHEN BAND
(PL.) LEADERS
HYPNOTIC AMYTAL BARBITAL
HYPNOTISM DEVIL BRAIDISM
HYPNOSIS MESMERISM
HYPNOTIST OPERATOR SVENGALI
HYPOBLAST ENDODERM HYPODERM
HYPOCHONDRIA HIP HYP HYPO
MEGRIM
HYPOCHONDRIAC ARGAN HIPPY
HIPPIST
HYPOCOTYL RADICLE TIGELLA
TIGELLUS
HYPOCRISY SHAM POPEHOLY
HYPOCRITE CANT BIGOT CHEAT
FACER FRAUD BLIFIL CAFARD
HUMBUG MAWWORM CHADBAND
DECEIVER TARTUFFE
HYPOCRITICAL FALSE SLAPE
DOUBLE CANTING PLASTER
POPEHOLY SPECIOUS
HYPOCYCLOID ASTROID
HYPODERMIS SKIN
HYPOPHARYNX LINGUA LABIELLA
HYPOSTASIS PERSON
HYPOSTATIZE ENTIFY
HYPOTENUSE SUBTENSE
HYPOTHESIS SYSTEM THEORY
WEGENER SUPPOSAL
HYPOTHETICAL IDEAL
HYPOTRACHELIUM GORGERIN
HYPTIS OREGANO
HYRAX DAS CONY CONEY DAMAN
WABUR DASSIE WABBER ASHKOKO
KLIPDAS HYRACOID
HYSTERIA MOTHER PIBLOKTO
TARASSIS
(PRONE TO —) VAPORISH
(RELIGIOUS —) LATA
HYSTERICAL SHRIEKY

I Y HI HY ICH ISS SHE ITEM UTCH
INDIA UTCHY
  (— **AM**) ISE CHAM ICHAM
  (— **HAD**) CHAD
  (— **WILL**) CHILL ICHULLE
  (— **WOULD**) CHUD
IALEMUS (FATHER OF —) APOLLO
  (**MOTHER OF —**) CALLIOPE
IAMB IAMBIC IAMBUS
  (**DOUBLE —**) DIIAMB
IAPETUS (FATHER OF —) URANUS
  (**MOTHER OF —**) GAEA
  (**SON OF —**) ATLAS MENOETIUS
  (**WIFE OF —**) ASIA CLYMENE
IAPYGIANS MESSAPII
IATROCHEMICAL SPAGYRIC
IATROCHEMISTRY SPAGYRIC
IBANAG CAGAYAN
IBEX KYL TEK TUR ZAC KAIL BEDEN
EVECK IZARD JAELA EVICKE
SAKEEN
IBIS GUARA GANNET HADADA JABIRU
TURKEY CICONIID IRONHEAD
ICARIUS (DAUGHTER OF —) ERIGONE
PENELOPE
  (**FAITHFUL DOG OF —**) MOERA
  (**FATHER OF —**) OEBALUS
ICE YS GEAL FROST GLACE CRYSTAL
VERGLAS
  (— **IN ROUGH BLOCKS**) RUBBLE
  (**ANCHOR —**) FRAZIL
  (**DRIFTING FRAGMENT OF —**) PAN
CALF
  (**PATCH OF —**) RONE
  (**PINNACLE OF —**) SERAC
  (**RIDGE OF —**) HAMMOCK HUMMOCK
  (**SEA —**) GLACON SLUDGE
  (**SHORE —**) FAST
  (**SLUSHY —**) SISH
  (**SOFT —**) SLOB LOLLY
  (**THIN NEW —**) DISH PANCAKE
  (**THIN OR FLOATING —**) FLOE GRUE
BRASH
  (**WATER —**) SHERBET
ICEBERG BERG GROWLER
FLOEBERG
ICEBOAT SKEETER
ICE CREAM BISK CREAM GLACE
AUFAIT BISQUE NOUGAT TASTER
SPUMONI TORTONI
ICE CREAM CONE CORNET
ICED COLD GLACE FRAPPE
ICEFISH SALANGID
ICEHOUSE (— **WORKER**) AIRMAN

ICELAND
BALLAD: RIMUR
CAPITAL: REIKJAVIK REYKJAVIK
COIN: AURAR EYRIR KRONA
DISH: SKYR SVIO BLOOMOR
  HAROFISK
EPIC: EDDA SAGA
FIRST SETTLER: ARNARSON
GEYSER: GRYLA
GIANT: ATLI
GLACIER: HOFSJOKULL
  LANGJOKULL VATNAJOKULL

HERO: BELE ERIC LEIF
  SIGUROSSON
LAKE: MYVATN THORISVATN
MEASURE: SET ALIN LINA ALMUD
  TURMA ALMENN ALMUDE
  FERFET POTTUR FATHMUR
  FERALIN FERMILA OLTUNNA
  SJOMILA
MOUNTAIN: JOKUL
PARLIAMENT: ALTHING
REPUBLIC: LYOVELDIO
RIVER: HVITA JOKULSA THJORSA
TOWN: AKRANES AKUREYRI
  KEFLAVIK KOPAVOGUR
VOLCANIC ISLAND: SURTSEY
VOLCANO: LAKI ASKJA HEKLA
WATERFALL: GULLFOSS
  DETTIFOSS
WEIGHT: PUND POUND

ICHNEUMON URVA NYMSS VANSIRE
ICHOROUS GLEETY
ICHU HICHU STIPA
ICICLE ICARY ICKLE YOKEL TANGLE
SHOGGLE SHOOGLE COCKBELL
ICINESS GLARE
ICING ICE PIPING FROSTING
MERINGUE
ICON IKON EIKON IMAGE DEESIS
ICONOCLAST DEBUNKER
ICONOSTASIS DIASTYLE
ICTEROHEMATURIA CARCEAG
ICTONYX ZORILLA
ICTUS ACCENT DOWNBEAT
ICY GELID BOREAL FRIGID WINTRY
GLACIAL
ID ES ORF GARDON SYPHILID

IDAHO
CAPITAL: BOISE
COUNTY: ADA GEM BUTTE LATAH
  POWER TETON CARNAS CASSIA
  BENEWAH KOOTENAI
DAM: OXBOW BROWNLEE
INDIAN: BANNOCK KALISPEL
  NEZPERCE SHOSHONI
LAKE: BEAR GRAYS PRIEST
MOUNTAIN: RYAN BORAH RHODES
  TAYLOR BIGBALDY BLUENOSE
MOUNTAIN RANGE: CABINET
  SELKIRK
NICKNAME: GEM
RIVER: SNAKE LOCHSA SALMON
  PAYETTE
SPRINGS: SODA HOOPER
  LAVAHOT
STATE BIRD: BLUEBIRD
STATE FLOWER: SYRINGA
TOWN: BUHL MALAD NAMPA
  MOSCOW REXBURG POCATELLO

IDAS (BROTHER OF —) LYNCEUS
  (**FATHER OF —**) APHAREUS
  (**WIFE OF —**) MARPESSA
IDE ORFE
IDEA EGG GIG KINK EIDOS IMAGE
THING ANONYM DHARMA ECTYPE

FIGURE INTENT NOTICE NOTION
RECEPT THREAP THROPE BEGRIFF
CONCEIT CONCEPT GIMMICK
GLIMPSE MAROTTE OPINION
PROJECT SPECIES SURMISE
THOUGHT GIMCRACK NOTIONAL
  (—**S OF LITTLE VALUE**) STUFF
  (**CENTRAL —**) ARGUMENT
  (**CONSERVATIVE —S**) FOGYISM
  (**DULL STUPID —S**) STODGE
  (**FAINT —**) GLIMMER
  (**FALSE —**) FALLACY
  (**FANTASTIC —**) VAPOR
  (**FAVORITE —**) HORSE
  (**FIXED —**) TICK
  (**FUNDAMENTAL —**) KEYNOTE
  (**IRRATIONAL —**) FOLLY
  (**MUSICAL —**) SENTENCE
  (**ODD —**) FREAK
  (**OVERWORKED —**) CLICHE
  (**PLATONIC —**) ESSENCE
  (**RECURRING —**) BURDEN
  (**STALE —S**) BILGE
  (**SUPERSTITIOUS —**) FREIT
  (**TRANSCENDENT —**) FORM
  (**PL.**) THOUGHT
IDEAL ISM IDEA DREAM AERIAL
BEAUTY DOMNEI DREAMY MENTAL
UNREAL PATTERN PERFECT
UTOPIAN ABSTRACT FANCIFUL
IDEALITY QUADRATE
  (— **OF BEAUTY**) KALON
IDEALISM IDEOLOGY
IDEALIST IDEIST UTOPIAN FICHTEAN
UTOPIAST
IDENTICAL LIKE SAME SELF VERY
ALIKE EQUAL EVENLY PROPER
CORRECT IDENTIC NUMERIC
SELFSAME
IDENTIFICATION IDENT DOCUMENT
EQUATION
IDENTIFIED SIGNATE
IDENTIFIER BIRDER
IDENTIFY MARK NAME RANK SPOT
IDENT TALLY FINGER DISCERN
DIAGNOSE
  (— **WITH**) ENTER
IDENTITY UNITY IPSEITY ONENESS
EQUALITY SAMENESS
IDEOGRAPH CHARACTER
  (**PL.**) KANJI
IDEOGRAPHIC REAL
IDEOLOGICAL MENTAL
IDIOBLAST SPHERE IDIOSOME
IDIOCY ANOIA ANOESIA FATUITY
IDIOTRY MOROSIS IDIOTISM
IDIOM CANT ARGOT JUANG DORISM
IFUGAO JARGON MEDISM SPEECH
AEOLISM ANOMALY GRECISM
TURKISM DANICISM DORICISM
IDIOTISM IONICISM LANGUAGE
LOCALISM RURALISM
IDIOMORPHIC EUHEDRAL
IDIOPHONE RATTLE
IDIOSOME SPHERE
IDIOSYNCRASY WAY IDIASM
RUMNESS
IDIOT FON OAF SOT DAFF DOLT
FOOL AMENT BOOBY DUNCE FONNE

HOBBIL NIDGET NIDIOT DULLARD
NATURAL OMADAWN PINHEAD
IMBECILE INNOCENT
IDIOTIC DAFT ZANY IDIOT FATUOUS
FOOLISH WANTWIT IMBECILE
IDLE COLD DEAD HACK HAKE HANG
HULL JAUK LAKE LAZE LAZY LUSK
MUZZ SOFT SORN TICK VAIN VOID
DALLY EMPTY SHOOL SLIVE THOKE
WASTE COOTER DANDER DREAMY
FOOTER GAMMER LOUNGY OTIANT
OTIOSE SLIMSY TEETER TIDDIE
TIFFLE TRUANT UNUSED VACANT
IDLEFUL IDLESET LOAFING SAUNTER
SHACKLE SLUMBER SLUTHER
UNLUSTY VACUOUS WHIFFLE
WORLESS BASELESS FAINEANT
INACTIVE INDOLENT SHAMMOCK
SLAISTER SLOTHFUL TRIFLING
(TO BE —) SLOTH
IDLENESS LAZE RUST SLOTH IDLETY
IDLESET IDLESSE IGNAVIA VACANCY
FLANERIE IDLEHOOD INACTION
(— PERSONIFED) LAURENCE
LAWRENCE
(LIVE IN —) MAROON
IDLER BUM GAUM HAKE JAUK KERN
DRONE BADAUD BUMBLE IDLEBY
LUBBER PLAYER QUISBY RODNEY
STALKO BLELLUM BUCKEEN
DAWDLER FAITOUR FRANION
IDLESBY LOUNGER LOUTHER
LURDANE SLOUNGE TRIFLER
DOLITTLE FAINEANT IDLESHIP
LAZARONE UNWORKER WHIFFLER
IDLE WHEEL IDLER RUNNER
IDLY TOOMLY VAGUELY
IDMON (FATHER OF —) APOLLO
(MOTHER OF —) CYRENE ASTERIA
IDOCRASE EGERAN CYPRINE
VESUVIAN
IDOL GOD BAAL ICON JOSS TIKI ZEMI
ANITO BESAN EIKON GUACA HOBAL
HUACA IMAGE STOCK SWAMI
IDOLET IDOLUM MAUMET MINION
PAGODA POPPET PUPPET TERAPH
EIDOLON MAHOMET BAPHOMET
MAUMETRY PANTHEUM
(HEATHEN —) DEVIL
IDOLATER AKKUM HEATHEN IDOLIST
IDOLATROUS PAGAN IDOLISH
IDOLATRY BAALISM IMAGERY
ADULTERY MAUMETRY
IDOLIZE GOD IDOL ADORE ADMIRE
WORSHIP
IDUMAEAN EDOMITE
IDYL IDYLL BUCOLIC ECLOGUE
IDYLLIC PASTORAL
IF AN AND GIF GIN THO GEVE IFFEN
SOBEIT THOUGH PROVIDED
(— EVER) ONCE
(— NOT) BUT ELSE NISI
IGNEOUS PLUTONIC
IGNIS FATUUS WISP SPUNKIE
WILDFIRE
IGNITE FIRE TIND FLASH LIGHT
SHOOT ILLUME KINDLE CALCINE
LIGHTEN
IGNITED LIVING BURNING

IGNITER SPARKER
IGNITION FIRE LIGHTING
IGNOBLE LOW BASE MEAN VILE
ABJECT GRUBBY SORDID CURRISH
SERVILE UNNOBLE BASEBORN
SHAMEFUL
IGNOBLY BASELY
IGNOMINIOUS BASE INFAMOUS
SHAMEFUL
IGNOMINY SHAME REBUKE SCANDAL
DISGRACE DISHONOR
IGNORAMUS IDIOT IGNARO SIMPLE
AMHAAREZ
IGNORANCE IRONY TAMAS AGNOSY
AVIDYA AVIJJA BETISE NICETY
RUDITY UNSKILL DARKNESS
IDIOTISM
(FEIGNED —) IRONY
IGNORANT LAY DARK NICE RUDE
VAIN GREEN GROSS SILLY INGRAM
SIMPLE ARTLESS SECULAR
UNAWARE UNCOUTH UNKNOWN
IMPERITE INNOCENT INSCIENT
INSCIOUS NESCIENT UNTAUGHT
IGNORANTLY SIMPLY
IGNORE BALK BLOW SINK SNUB
VAIN BAULK BLINK ELIDE BYPASS
MISKEN SLIGHT DESPISE MISKNOW
CONFOUND OVERJUMP OVERLEAP
OVERLOOK
IGOROT BONTOK NABALOI KANKANAI
IGUANA GUANA GUANO LEGUAN
IJO DJO BONI BONNY
ILAIRA (FATHER OF —) LEUCIPPUS
(SISTER OF —) PHOEBE
ILEUS MISERERE
ILIA RHEA
(FATHER OF —) NUMITOR
(SON OF —) REMUS ROMULUS
ILIONE (FATHER OF —) PRIAM
(HUSBAND OF —) POLYMNESTOR
ILK KIN
ILL BAD EVIL ILLY SICK AEGER
DONCY FUNNY WISHT GROGGY
INJURY POORLY SICKLY UNWELL
SICKISH VICIOUS MISCHIEF
PHYSICAL
(— AT EASE) ASHAMED AWKWARD
ILL-ADVISED FOOLISH
ILL-BEHAVED UNTHEWED
ILL-BEING ILLTH
ILL-BODING DIRE DISMAL
ILL-BRED HOYDEN CADDISH
CHURLISH PLEBEIAN
ILL-CHOSEN UNSORTED
ILL-CONSIDERED HASTY
ILL-DEFINED BLIND VAGUE
ILLEGAL BLACK LAWLESS
UNLAWFUL WRONGOUS
(NOT —) COLD
ILLEGALITY UNLAW
ILLEGIBLE BLIND
ILLEGITIMACY BASTARDY
ILLEGITIMATE BASE BASTARD
BOOTLEG NATURAL NOTHOUS
MISBEGOT UNLAWFUL WRONGFUL
ILL-FATED UNHAPPY UNSONCY
UNCHANCY
ILL-FAVORED UGLY UNSONCY

ILL-FORMED SCRAWLY INFORMED
ILL HUMOR TID BILE DRUNT GRUMP
THRAW FANTEE SPLEEN DUDGEON
FANTIGUE
ILL-HUMORED FOUL GLUM CROOK
DUDDY GRUMPY MOROSE STUFFY
SULLEN CROOKED FRETFUL
PEEVISH
ILLIBERAL LITTLE NARROW INSULAR
GRUDGING
ILLICIT SLY BLACK ILLEGAL
UNLAWFUL
ILLIMITABLE INFINITE

ILLINOIS
CAPITAL: SPRINGFIELD
COLLEGE: AURORA EUREKA
OLIVET QUINCY SHIMER
COUNTY: BOND CASS COOK KANE
OGLE COLES MACON BUREAU
DUPAGE GRUNDY HARDIN
MASSAL PEORIA IROQUOIS
MACOUPIN SANGAMON
FRENCH SETTLEMENT: CAHOKIA
HILLS: SHAWNEE
INDIAN: FOX SAUK
LAKE: MICHIGAN
NICKNAME: PRAIRIE
RIVER: OHIO ROCK WABASH
ELKHORN MACKINAW
SANGAMON
STATE BIRD: CARDINAL
STATE FLOWER: VIOLET
STATE TREE: OAK
TOWN: PANA ALTON FLORA
OLNEY PEKIN ALBION CANTON
HERRIN JOLIET PEORIA SKOKIE
CHICAGO DECATUR GENESCO
MENDOTA NOKOMIS ROCKFORD

ILLINOISIAN SUCKER
ILLIPE BASSIA VIDORICUM
ILLITERATE UNREAD IGNORANT
MUSELESS UNTAUGHT
ILL-MADE AWKWARD
ILL-NATURED UGLY SURLY CRABBY
SNARLY SULLEN CANKERY PEEVISH
ILLNESS DROW TOUT BRASH CHILL
TRAIK MORBUS PLUNGE DISEASE
SICKNESS
(MINOR —) HURRY
(MOMENTARY —) DROW
(SUDDEN —) WEED SWEAM
ILL-NOURISHED SHELLY
ILLOGICAL SPURIOUS
ILL-OMENED DISMAL UNLUCKY
ILL-SHAPED WEEDY
ILL-SMELLING FUSTY STINKING
ILL-TEMPERED ILL FESS MEAN
PUXY CHUFF NURLY CAMMED
CHUFFY GIRNIE SHRILL SNAGGY
RAMPANT VICIOUS CAMSHACH
LUNGEOUS SHREWISH VIXENISH
ILL-TREAT FOB HOIN MISDO
AFFRONT
ILLUMINATE FIRE LIMN CLEAR
LIGHT ENLIMN ILLUME KINDLE
BESHINE CLARIFY EMBLAZE

LIGHTEN MINIATE RADIATE EMBRIGHT FLOURISH ILLUMINE LUMINATE
(— FAINTLY) TWILIGHT
ILLUMINATION E GLIM GLORY LIGHT SHINE LIGHTING LUMINARY
(— INCREASE) WOMP
(— UNIT) PHOT
ILLUMINE SUN FIRE CLEAR LUMINE ENLIGHT
ILL-USAGE ABUSE
ILLUSION DEATH ERROR FAIRY FANCY FLESH TRICK MATTER CHIMERA ELUSION FALLACY FICTION MOCKERY PHANTOM RAINBOW ZOLLNER DELUSION PHANTASM PRESTIGE
ILLUSORY FALSE EVANID FATUOUS APPARENT ILLUSIVE SPECTRAL
ILLUSTRATE INSTANCE
ILLUSTRATION CUT GAY ICON IKON SHOW SPOT INSET FIGURE COMPARE DISIMILE EXEMPLUM INSTANCE VIGNETTE
ILLUSTRATIVE CLASSIC
ILLUSTRIOUS GRAND NOBLE NOTED SHEEN BRIGHT CANDID HEROIC EMINENT EXALTED GLORIED SHINING GLORIOUS HEROICAL LUCULENT MAGNIFIC PRECLARE RENOWNED SPLENDID STARLIKE
ILL WILL SPITE ENMITY GRUDGE MALICE MAUGER MAUGRE RANCOR DESPITE AMBITION
ILL-WISHER FOE
ILUS (FATHER OF —) TROS
(MOTHER OF —) CALLIRRHOE
(SON OF —) LAOMEDON
ILVAITE YENITE LIEVRITE
ILYSIA TORTRIX
IMAGE DAP GOD MAP FORM ICON IDOL IKON JOSS MAKE SEAL SIGN SPIT TIKI AGNUS DITTO EPHOD FANCY HERMA IMAGO MEDAL MORAL PAINT PRINT SAMMY SANTO SHAPE SIGIL SWAMI SWAMY TOTEM AGALMA ALRAUN EFFIGY EMBLEM FIGURE MAUMET MODULE POPPET RECEPT REFLEX SHRINE SPHINX STATUE SVAMIN TERAPH VISAGE WEEPER EIDOLON EXPRESS FANTASY GODLING IMAGERY KATCINA PICTURE PROPOSE CONCEIVE DAIBUTSU OPTOGRAM PORTRAIT SURPRINT ZOOMORPH
(— IN CHINESE COSTUME) MANDARIN
(— OF CHRIST) SUDARIUM
(— OF DEITY) SWAMI GODKIN SVAMIN GODLING
(— OF SAINT) BULTO SAINT SANTO GEORGE SANTON
(— OF WOOD) XOANON
(— RECALLED BY MEMORY) IDEA
(CULT —) JOSS
(FALSE —) GHOST
(GOOD-LUCK —) ALRAUN ALRUNA
(HEAVENLY —) FRAVASHI
(LINGERING —) SHADE

(MENTAL —) FANCY IMAGO RECEPT CONCEPT FANTASY SPECIES PHANTASM
(RADAR —) BLIP
(REFLECTED —) SHADOW SPECIES
(SEQUENCE OF —S) REVERIE
(VAGUE —S) FRINGE
(PL.) IMAGERY TERAPHIM
IMAGERY ICONISM
IMAGINARY IDEAL AERIAL FEIGNED FICTIVE SHADOWY CHIMERAL CHIMERIC FANCIFUL FICTIOUS MYTHICAL NOTIONAL QUIXOTIC ROMANTIC SCENICAL VISIONAL
IMAGINATION CHIC BRAIN FANCY FLAME NOTION FANTASY PROJECT THOUGHT
(DROLL —) HUMOR
IMAGINATIVE FORMFUL CREATIVE FANCIFUL POETICAL
IMAGINE SEE WIS REDE WEEN DREAM FANCY FEIGN FRAME GUESS IMAGE THINK DEVISE FIGURE IDEATE INVENT COMPASS CONCEIT CONJURE FANCIFY FANTASY FEATURE PICTURE PORTRAY PROJECT PROPOSE SUPPOSE SURMISE SUSPECT CONCEIVE DAYDREAM JEALOUSE
IMAGINED FANCIED SUPPOSED
IMAGINER FANCIER
IMAGINING FICTION PHANTOM
IMAM IMAUM MAHDI
IMBALANCE DRIVE DYSCRASIA
IMBECILE MAD DOTE FOOL AMENT DAFFY IDIOT CRANKY DOTARD DOTING DOTISH CONGEON FATUOUS
IMBECILITY FATUITY
IMBIBE DRINK SMACK ABSORB SPONGE INHAUST SWALLOW IRRIGATE
IMBIBING SUCTION
IMBIBITORY SPONGY
IMBRUE EMBREW INSTEEP
IMBUE SOAK STEW COLOR CROWN EMBUE INDUE SCENT STEEP TINCT ENSOUL IMBIBE INFUSE LEAVEN SEASON ANIMATE INGRAIN INSENSE INSTILL SATURATE TINCTURE
IMBUED INSTINCT REDOLENT
IMIDE LACTIM SACCHARIN
IMITATE APE COPY ECHO MIME MOCK ZANY ENSUE FORGE IMAGE MIMIC ANSWER FOLLOW SEMBLE COPYCAT EMULATE PAGEANT PASTICHE RESEMBLE SIMULATE
IMITATION COPY FAKE SHAM DUMMY IMAGE MIMIC ALPACA ANSWER BUMPER ECTYPE SHADOW CAMBLET FOULARD IMITANT MIMESIS MOCKAGE MOCKERY CHENILLE PARROTRY PASTICHE POSTIQUE
(— OF COIN) COUNTER
(BURLESQUE —) TRAVESTY
(EXAGGERATED —) BURLESQUE
(UNSUBSTANTIAL —) GHOST
IMITATIVE ARTY MIMIC ARTFUL ECHOIC SHODDY MIMETIC SIMULAR

SLAVISH APATETIC EPIGONAL
IMITATOR APE MIME ZANY MIMIC COPIER COPYIST EPIGONE EMULATOR EPIGONUS HOMERIST
IMMACULATE CLEAN CANDID CHASTE BLOTLESS SPOTLESS UNSOILED
IMMANENCE INBEING
IMMATERIAL MENTAL SLIGHT ETHEREAL FORMLESS SEPARATE TRIFLING
IMMATURE RAW CRUDE GREEN SAPPY SMALL VEALY YOUNG BOYISH CALLOW JEJUNE LARVAL NEANIC TENDER GIRLISH HALFLIN IMPUBIC LADDISH NOUVEAU UNBAKED JUVENILE NEPIONIC UNWEANED
IMMATURITY NONAGE
IMMEASURABLE UNTOLD INFINITE
IMMEDIACY HERE
IMMEDIATE DIRECT MODERN PARATE SUDDEN INSTANT PRESENT PROXIMAL SYNECTIC
IMMEDIATELY TIT ANON AWAY FAST JUST ONCE SOON PLUMB RIGHT ASTITE DIRECT PRESTO SUBITO DIRECTLY HEREUPON OUTRIGHT STRAIGHT
IMMEDIATENESS INSTANCY
IMMEMORIAL DATELESS
IMMENSE HUGE VAST GRAND GREAT LARGE UNMEET UNRIDE TITANIC ENORMOUS GIGANTIC INFINITE SLASHING WHOOPING
IMMENSELY EVER
IMMENSITY VAST IMMANE IMMENSE ENORMITY GRANDEUR HUGENESS
IMMERSE DIP SINK SOAK COVER DOUSE MERGE MERSE SOUSE STEEP DRENCH PLUNGE BAPTIZE BOWSSEN DEMERGE EMBATHE ENSTEEP IMMERGE DISSOLVE
IMMERSED DEEP INNATE
IMMERSION DIP DUNKING MERSION
IMMERSIONIST DIPPER
IMMIGRANT LAG BALT ISSEI JIMMY METIC POMMY GUINEA HALUTZ CHALUTZ INCOMER PILGRIM COMELING
IMMINENCE INSTANCY
IMMINENT TOWARD PENDING
IMMOBILE FIXED STILL FROZEN DORMANT GLACIAL TRANCED MOVELESS
IMMOBILIZATION FUSION FIXATION
IMMOBILIZE FREEZE SPLINT STIFFEN
IMMOBILIZED STIFF
IMMODERATE FREE DIZZY UNDUE LAVISH UNMETH EXTREME
IMMODERATENESS EXCESS
IMMODEST FREE BRAZEN OBSCENE INDECENT PETULANT UNCHASTE
IMMORAL BAD ILL EVIL IDLE LOOSE WRONG WANTON CORRUPT VICIOUS CULPABLE DEPRAVED INDECENT SLIPPERY
IMMORTAL DIVINE ENDLESS

ETERNAL GODLIKE UNDYING
ENDURING UNDEADLY
IMMORTALITY ATHANASY ETERNITY
IMMOVABLE PAT SET FAST FIRM
FIXED RIGID ADAMANT SITFAST
CONSTANT IMMOBILE IMMOTIVE
OBDURATE
IMMUNE FREE SALTED
IMMUNITY SOC CHARTER FREEDOM
LIBERTY WOODGELD
IMMURE MURE WALL CONFINE
CLOISTER IMPRISON
IMMUTABILITY ONENESS
IMMUTABLE ETERNAL
IMP PUG LIMB DEVILET DEVILING
DEVILKIN FOLLETTO
IMPACT HIT JAR BEAT BITE BLOW
BUMP DASH JOLT SLAM BRUNT
CLASH FEEZE PEISE POISE PULSE
SHOCK SKITE GLANCE STROKE
CONTACT IMPULSE
IMPAIR MAR BLOT HARM HURT
MANK SOUR WEAR ALLOY CLOUD
CRACK CRAZE DECAY ERODE QUAIL
SPOIL TAINT ACRAZE DAMAGE
DEADEN DEFACE HINDER INJURE
LABEFY LESSEN REDUCE SICKEN
WEAKEN WORSEN BLEMISH DISABLE
IMPEACH REFRACT SHATTER
STRETCH VITIATE DECREASE
ENFEEBLE IMBECILE IMPERISH
INFRINGE LABEFACT
(— BY INACTIVITY) RUST
(— ESSENTIALLY) RUIN
IMPAIRED HURT STALE CROCKY
FLYBLOWN
(— BY AGE) FUSTY
(— IN TONE) BREATHY
IMPAIRMENT FAULT SPOIL DOTAGE
IMPAIR INJURY LESION BEATING
DEFICIT DISEASE EROSION WEARING
AKINESIA PAIRMENT
(— OF CONSCIOUSNESS) ABSENCE
IMPALA PALLA PALLAH REDBUCK
ROODEBOK
IMPALE BAIT SPIT GANCH GANSH
SPEAR SPIKE STAKE STICK STING
SKIVER TRANSFIX
IMPALPABLE ELUSIVE
IMPART GIVE SHED TELL BREAK
DRILL SHARE YIELD BESTOW
COMMON CONFER CONVEY DIRECT
IMPUTE INSTIL PARTEN REVEAL
DELIVER DIVULGE PURPORT
DISCOVER INSTRUCT INTIMATE
(— TONE) TONE
(— ZEST) ANIMATE
IMPARTIAL EVEN FAIR JUST EQUAL
LEVEL NEUTER UNBIASED
IMPARTIALITY CANDOR EQUITY
EQUACITY EVENNESS
IMPARTIALLY FAIRLY EQUALLY
IMPASSABLE WICKED PASSLESS
IMPASSE LOGJAM DEADLOCK
IMPASSION COMMOVE
IMPASSIONED ARDENT FERVID
FERVENT FEVERISH
IMPASSIVE FROZEN STOLID PASSIVE
STOICAL

IMPASSIVENESS APATHY MORGUE
STOICISM
IMPATIENT HOT ANTSY EAGER
HASTY SHARP TESTY FRETFUL
PEEVISH TIDIOSE CHOLERIC
PETULANT
IMPATIENTLY HASTILY
IMPEACH CALL ACCUSE CHARGE
INDICT ARRAIGN CENSURE IMPLEAD
TRAVERSE
IMPECCABLE SINLESS
IMPECUNIOUS POOR
IMPEDE BOG DAM GUM JAM LET
MAR CLOG GRAB JAMB KILL SLUG
SNAG ANNOY BLOCK CHECK CHOKE
DELAY EMBAR ESTOP HITCH SLOTH
SPOKE FETTER FORBID FORSET
HAMPER HARASS HINDER HOBBLE
PESTER RETARD STYMIE IMPEACH
PREVENT SHACKLE ENCUMBER
HANDICAP OBSTRUCT PRECLUDE
IMPEDIMENT BAR RUB CLOG SNAG
STOP BLEAR BLOCK HITCH SPOKE
STICK RUBBER SCOTCH BLINDER
EMBARGO OBSTACLE OBSTANCY
(— IN SPEECH) HAAR
IMPEDIMENTA STUFF
IMPEDING CATCH HEAVY FOULING
IMPEL PAT PUT BEAR BEAT CALL
CAST GOAD HURL MOVE SEND
URGE WHIP CARRY DRIVE FEEZE
FORCE KNOCK PRICK PULSE
COMPEL EXCITE INCITE INDUCE
PROPEL DESTINE INSPIRE INSTINCT
MOTIVATE
(— TO GREATER SPEED) GATHER
IMPELLER RUNNER
IMPEND BREW HANG DEPEND
IMPENDING PENDENT PENDING
IMMINENT MENACING
IMPENETRABLE HARD DENSE
MURKY PROOF THICK AIRTIGHT
HARDENED
IMPENITENT HARDENED OBDURATE
IMPERATIVE VITAL PRESSING
IMPERCEPTIBLE OCCULT SUBTLE
IMPERFECT ILL HALF POOR AMISS
BLIND FUZZY ROUGH FAULTY
PLATIC STICKIT UNWHOLE VICIOUS
INPARFIT MUTILOUS
IMPERFECTED INCHOATE
IMPERFECTION BUG RUB WEN
FLAW KINK MOLE SLUR VICE ERROR
FAULT BLOTCH DEFECT FOIBLE
BLEMISH CRUDITY DEFAULT
DEMERIT FAILING FRAILTY
WEAKNESS
(— IN BOTTLE) HEELTAP
(— IN GLASS) STRIA STREAK
(— IN LEATHER) FRIEZE
(— IN SILK) CORKSCREW
(— IN WICK) THIEF WASTER
IMPERFECTIVE ATELIC
IMPERFECTLY ILL HALF AMISS
IMPERFORATION ATRESIA
IMPERIAL TUFT ROYAL KINGLY
PURPLE MAJESTIC
IMPERIL RISK EXPONE EMPERIL
ENDANGER JEOPARDY

IMPERIOUS SURLY LORDLY
HAUGHTY DESPOTIC IMPERIAL
MASTERLY PRESSING
IMPERISHABLE ETERNAL UNDYING
ENDURING IMMORTAL
IMPERMANENCE ANICCA
IMPERMANENT FLEETING
IMPERSONAL COLD DEADPAN
INHUMAN ABSTRACT
IMPERSONATE ACT POSE TYPIFY
PERSONIFY
IMPERSONATION GENIUS
IMPERSONATOR ACTOR CACHINA
KACHINA KATCINA
IMPERTINENCE PAWK SNASH
AUDACITY
IMPERTINENT GAY FREE RUDE
FRESH SASSY SAUCY IMPERENT
IMPUDENT
IMPERTURBABILITY ATARAXY
ATARAXIA SANGFROID
IMPERTURBABLE COOL PLACID
GLACIAL TRANQUIL
IMPERVIOUS DEAD GASTIGHT
HARDENED HERMETIC
IMPETUOSITY FURY HASTE WRATH
FOUGUE POWDER RANDOM SPLEEN
IMPETUOUS HOT RAMP RUDE
BRASH EAGER FIERY FRECK HASTY
HEADY SHARP ARDENT BROTHE
FIERCE FLASHY LAVISH RACKLE
STRONG BUCKISH FURIOUS
HOTHEAD HOTSPUR BRAINISH
EMPRESSE HEADLONG SLAPDASH
VEHEMENT
IMPETUS BIRR FARD SEND DRIFT
GRACE SWING YMPET BENSEL
IMPACT POWDER RAVINE SWINGE
SWOUGH IMPULSE MOMENTUM
IMPINGE FALL IMPACT ASSAULT
CROSSCUT
IMPINGEMENT IMPACT
IMPIOUS UNHOLY ATHEIST ATHEOUS
GODLESS UNGODLY DOWNWEED
HOARWORT NEFANDOUS
IMPISH IMPY ELFISH WARLOCK
IMPLACABLE STOUT DEADLY
IMPLACABLY FATALLY
IMPLANT FIX IMP SOW HAFT ROOT
GRAFT INFIX INLAY ENRACE
ENROOT FASTEN INFUSE INSTIL
ENFORCE IMPRESS INSPIRE
ENTRENCH INSTINCT
IMPLANTED INBORN INSITE
IMPLEMENT (ALSO SEE TOOL) AX
AXE BAT CARD DISC DISK FORK
GRAB HACK HONE HOOK LOOM
PLOW SPUD SPUR TOOL CROOK
DRILL FLINT LANCE SCRUB SHEAR
SLICK SPADE SPOON STEEL STICK
TRIER AMGARN BEAMER BLADER
BROACH COLLAR COOLER DIBBLE
DREDGE DRIVER DUSTER EOLITH
FLAKER FLUTER HACKER HARROW
INVOKE LADDER LIPPER LUNATE
MARKER MEALER PACKER PADDLE
PALLET PESTLE PLOUGH RIMMER
SCREEN SCYTHE SEATER SEEDER
SERVER SHEARS SHOVEL SICKLE

SLICER SMOOTH BREAKER
CHOPPER CLEANER CLEAVER
ENFORCE FLESHER FLYFLAP
GAROTTE GRUBBER HARPOON
HUSTLER KNAPPER MATTOCK
NUTPICK SKIMMER SLABBER
SLASHER SLEEKER SLICKER
SPATTLE SPATULA SPITTLE
SPURTLE STAMPER STICKER
SWATHER UTENSIL AGITATOR
BUSHWACK MEASURER SCUTCHER
SEARCHER SHREDDER SKETCHER
SPLITTER SPREADER STRIPPER
TERRACER THWACKER TOLLIKER
TRANCHET TWEEZERS WARKLOOM
WORKLOOM
(— FOR CUTTING CHEESE) HARP
(— FOR HANGING POT) HALE
(— TO PREVENT MALT FROM
OVERFLOWING) STROM
(—S OF HUSBANDRY) WAINAGE
(ANCIENT —) POINT SLICE AMGARN
EOLITH NEOLITH RACLOIR
(BAKER'S —) PEEL
(CLIMBING —) CREEPER
(ESKIMO —) ULU
(GARDENING —) HOE RAKE SEEDER
SICKLE
(HEDGING —) TRAMP
(IRRIGATION —) CROWDER
(LOGGING —) TODE
(POTTER'S —) PALLET SPATTLE
(PREHISTORIC —) CELT FLAKER
(SHOVEL-LIKE —) SCOOP
(SOLDERING —) DOCTOR
(TORTURE —) ENGINE
(UPROOTING —) MAKE
(WINNOWING —) FAN
(PL.) GEAR CUTLERY GAINAGE
FLAUGHTS
IMPLICATE DIP ENWRAP CONCERN
EMBROIL INCLUDE INVOLVE
IMPLICATION CLAIM IMPLIAL
INNUENDO
IMPLICIT COVERT
IMPLIED TACIT IMPLICIT
IMPLORATION PETITION
IMPLORE ASK BEG CRY PRAY
CHARM CRAVE PLEAD INVOKE
BESEECH CONJURE ENTREAT
SOLICIT ENTREATS
IMPLY HINT ARGUE CARRY COUCH
INFER EMPLOY ENTAIL IMPORT
INDUCE CONNOTE CONTAIN
INCLUDE INVOLVE SIGNIFY SUGGEST
SUPPOSE
IMPOLITE RUDE UNCIVIL
IMPOLITENESS CRUDITY
IMPONDERABLE FRIGORIC
IMPORT SAY WIT BEAR BODY TOUR
DRIFT FORCE IMPLY MORAL SCOPE
SENSE SOUND SPELL VALOR
AMOUNT CHARGE DENOTE INGATE
INTENT MATTER BETOKEN MEANING
PRETEND SIGNIFY CARRIAGE
INDICATE
(PL.) INWARDS
IMPORTANCE BORE MARK PITH
FORCE POISE WORTH CHARGE

IMPORT MATTER MOMENT REMARK
STRESS STROKE WEIGHT ACCOUNT
ESSENCE GRAVITY VALENCY
EMPHASIS
IMPORTANT DEAR DREE HIGH MAIN
REAL GRAVE GREAT GAPING
NEEDLE STRONG URGENT VALOUR
CAPITAL CRUCIAL EMINENT
MATTERY SERIOUS EVENTFUL
MATERIAL
IMPORTER MILLINER
IMPORTUNATE URGENT INSTANT
DEVILING EXIGEANT PRESSING
IMPORTUNE BEG BEAT BONE TOUT
TEASE BESIEGE INSTANT SOLICIT
TERRIFY INSTANCE
IMPORTUNITY BRASS URGENCY
IMPOSE LAY SET TOP CLAP GIVE
LEVY MUMP POLE SORN ABUSE
APPLY INPUT STAMP TRUMP
BURDEN CHARGE ENJOIN ENTAIL
FASTEN FATHER IMPONE IMPUTE
BLAFLUM DICTATE INFLICT
IRROGATE
(— UPON) FOB GAG HUM LAY DUPE
SELL CULLY TRAIL BLUDGE DELUDE
EXCISE HUMBUG NUZZLE DECEIVE
HOODWINK
IMPOSED BOUNDEN
IMPOSING BIG EPIC BUDGE BURLY
GRAND HEFTY NOBLE PROUD
AUGUST EPICAL FEUDAL PORTLY
HAUGHTY POMPOUS STATELY
HANDSOME SONORANT SONOROUS
(— UPON) PRACTICE PRACTISE
IMPOSITION BAM COD HUM LEVY
SELL TAIL GOUGE IMPOT CHOUSE
GAMMON INTAKE TAILLE IMPOSAL
ARTIFICE IMPOSURE
(MILITARY —) CESS
IMPOSSIBLE HOPELESS
IMPOST LAY TAX CAST LEVY TAIL
TASK TOLL ABWAB ANNALE AVANIA
EXCISE GABELLE POUNAMU
TALLAGE TONNAGE TRIBUTE
CHAPTREL SPRINGER
(PL.) CUSTOMS
IMPOSTOR FOB FAKE GULL IDOL
CHEAT FAKER FRAUD GOUGE
QUACK BUNYIP FOURBE HUMBUG
MUMPER EMPIRIC FAITOUR
PROCTOR SHAMMER PHANTASM
IMPOSTURE GAG FAKE HOAX SHAM
CHEAT FRAUD TRICK DECEIT
HUMBUG JUGGLE ARTIFICE
DELUSION JUGGLERY
IMPOTENCE ACRATIA UNMIGHT
WEAKNESS
IMPOTENCY UNWELTH
IMPOTENT WEAK FRIGID PAULIE
UNABLE STERILE UNMIGHTY
IMPOUND FIND POUND INTERN
IMPOVERISH PILL CLOUD BEGGAR
IMPOOR SICKEN DEPLETE DEPRESS
EMPOVER BANKRUPT POVERISH
IMPOVERISHED POOR OBOLARY
BANKRUPT INDIGENT
IMPRACTICAL CRAZY FECKLESS
IMPRECATE WISH

IMPRECATION DASH OATH PIZE
WISH BLAME CURSE DAMME
DAMMIT CONSARN ANATHEMA
IMPREGNABILITY STRENGTH
IMPREGNABLE FAST PROOF
IMPREGNATE BIG HOP DOPE FILL
LIME MILT BREED IMBUE STOCK
STUFF TINCT AERATE CHARGE
INFORM INFUSE LEAVEN SEASON
ASPHALT ENVENOM IMPREGN
CHROMATE CONCEIVE CREOSOTE
FRICTION FRUCTIFY GRAPHITE
MEDICATE PERMEATE SATURATE
SILICATE TINCTURE
IMPREGNATED BRED COATED
IMPRESS FIX BITE COIN DING DINT
ETCH MARK AFFIX BRAND CLAMP
CRIMP DRIVE GRAVE GRILL INFIX
PRESS PRINT REACH SEIZE STAMP
STEAD WRITE AFFECT ENSEAL
FASTEN INCUSE INDENT SALUTE
STRIKE ANTIQUE ENGRAVE
ENSTAMP IMPLANT IMPREST
IMPRINT INSENSE INSCRIBE
NEGATIVE
(— DEEPLY) DELVE ENGRAVE
(— SUDDENLY) SMITE
(— WITH FEAR) AFFRIGHT
IMPRESSED BLIND ANTIQUE
INDENTED
IMPRESSIBLE WAXY
IMPRESSION CUT HIT AURA CAST
CHOP DENT DINT IDEA MARK MOLD
SEAL STEP STIR FANCY GOUGE
IMAGE MOULD STAMP STATE
ECTYPE EFFECT ENGRAM FIGURE
INCUSE OFFSET SIGNET STRIKE
EOPHYTE ETCHING FANTASY
IMPRESS MOULAGE OPINION
SEALING SQUEEZE STENCIL
TOOLING BLANKING ENGRAMMA
PRESSION PRESSURE STAMPAGE
TOOLMARK
(— ON COIN) CROSS
(— WITHOUT INK) ALBINO
(AUDITORY —) SOUND
(DOUBLE —) MACKLE MACULE
(IMMEDIATE —) APERCU
(MENTAL —) GRAVING
(STRONG —) HUNCH
(VIVID —) SPLASH
IMPRESSIONABLE SOFT WAXY
WAXEN TENDER PLASTIC PASSIBLE
IMPRESSIONIST LUMINIST
IMPRESSIVE BIG FAT EPIC AWFUL
GRAND NOBLE PROUD EPICAL
PESANTE STATELY TEARING
WEIGHTY FORCIBLE IMPOSING
SMASHING SONORANT SONOROUS
STUNNING
IMPRINT DINT ETCH SIGN STEP
PRESS STAMP CUTOFF FASTEN
STRIKE ENGRAVE ENSTAMP
IMPRESS APREYNTE EPIGRAPH
PRESSION PRESSURE STAMPAGE
(— ON CHEEK) FASTEN
IMPRISON JUG LAG NUN BOND
GAOL HULK JAIL SEAL SHOP WARD
CROWD EMBAR GRATE COMMIT

IMMURE JIGGER PRISON SLOUGH
CONFINE INTOWER BASTILLE
IMPRISONED FAST
IMPRISONMENT BAND BOND
ARREST CHAINS DURESS PRISON
CUSTODY DURANCE
IMPROBABLE FISHY UNLIKE
UNLIKELY
IMPROMPTU GLIB SUDDEN OFFHAND
IMPROPER BAD PAH PAW AMISS
LARGE UNDUE UNFELE UNJUST
ILLICIT INDECENT TORTIOUS
UNSEEMLY WRONGOUS
IMPROPRIETY SOLECISM
IMPROVE FIX GAIN GOOD GROW
HELP MEND AMEND EDIFY EMEND
GRADE MOISE SMART TOUCH
BETTER ENRICH PROFIT ADVANCE
BENEFIT CORRECT ELEVATE
PROMOTE RECTIFY UPSWING
(— APPEARANCE OF HORSE)
BISHOP
(— APPEARANCE OF TEA) FACE
(— CONDUCTIVITY) AGE
IMPROVED BETTER
IMPROVEMENT AMENDS PICKUP
POLICY PROFIT REDRESS UPSWING
IMPROVIDENT PRODIGAL WASTEFUL
(— PERSON) MICAWBER
IMPROVISATION THEME CALYPSO
IMPROVISE JAM COOK FAKE PONG
VAMP FANTASY
IMPRUDENCE FOLLY
IMPRUDENT FESS RASH FALSE
UNWARY FOOLISH RECKLESS
IMPUDENCE GALL BRASS CHEEK
MOUTH SLACK BRONZE PUPPYISM
IMPUDENT BOLD COXY FACY RUDE
BANTY BARDY BRASH FRESH GALLY
LIPPY SASSY SAUCY BRASSY
BRAZEN CHEEKY STOCKY BIGGETY
CHUNKED FORWARD GALLOWS
PERKING INSOLENT MALAPERT
IMPUDENTLY COOLY COOLLY
FRESHLY
IMPUGN DENY FALSE DISPUTE
IMPEACH
IMPULSE FIT BIAS RESE SEND URGE
DRIVE SPEND START DESIRE
MOTIVE SIGNAL SPLEEN YETZER
CALLING CONATUS IMPETUS
INSTINCT MOVEMENT STIRRING
(BLIND —) ATE
(ELECTRICAL —) KICK
(SPONTANEOUS —) ACCORD
(SUDDEN —) SPLEEN
(SUPERNATURAL —) AFFLATUS
IMPULSION SWING IMPULSE
IMPULSIVE QUICK FITFUL HEADLONG
IMPURE DRY FOUL LEWD GROSS
HORRY FILTHY TURBID UNPURE
UNCLEAN VICIOUS INDECENT
MACULATE
IMPURITY CRUD DONOR DROSS
FEDITY ACCEPTER FOULNESS
(— IN LINT) SHALE
(— IN MINERAL) GANG GANGUE
(PL.) SCUM GARBLE SLUMMAGE
IMPUTATION SCANDAL

IMPUTE LAY RET ARET EVEN WITE
COUNT REFER CHARGE FASTEN
IMPOSE OBJECT RECKON REPUTE
ASCRIBE ENTITLE IMPEACH
IN A I N Y AT TO BAJO INBY INTO
UPON ALONG INTIL
(— A FAINT) AWAY
(— A SERIES) SERIATIM
(— A STATE OF ACTION) ENERGIC
(— ACCORDANCE) AFTER
(— ADDITION) EKE TOO ALSO
ABOVE AGAIN ALONG FORBY STILL
BEYOND BESIDES FARTHER
FURTHER MOREOVER OVERPLUS
THERETIL
(— ADVANCE) AHEAD FORTH
BEFORE
(— ANY CASE) EVER HOWEVER
(— BEHALF OF) PRO
(— CASE THAT) AUNTERS
(— CIRCULATION) ABROAD
(— CONNECTION WITH) FORNENT
FERNINST
(— EARNEST) AGOOD
(— EXCESS OF) OVER
(— FACT) SOOTH TRULY INDEED
ITSELF MERELY VERILY ACTUALLY
VERAMENT
(— FAITH) IVADS EFECKS YFACKS
(— FRONT) FORE AFACE FORNE
AGAINST PARAVANT
(— FULL) ALONG
(— GOOD SEASON) BETIMES
(— GOOD SPIRITS) BOBBISH
(— GRACEFUL MANNER) ADAGIO
(— JEST) AGAME
(— NO MANNER) NOWISE NAEGATES
(— ONE DIRECTION) ANON
(— ORDER) FOR ATAUNT ATAUNTO
(— PLACE OF) FOR WITH INSTEAD
(— POSSESSION) WITHIN
(— PROGRESS) AFOOT TOWARD
(— PROPER MANNER) DULY
(— RESPECT TO) ANENT
(— RETURN FOR) AGAINST
(— ROTATION) ABOUT
(— SO FAR AS) AS QUA
(— SOLE CONTROL) ABSOLUTE
(— SOOTH) PARFEY PERFAY
(— SPITE OF) FOR ALTHO MALGRE
AGAINST DESPITE MALGRADO
(— SUSPENSE) PENDING
(— THE DOING OF) WITH
(— THE FIRST PLACE) IMP IMPRIMIS
(— THE FUTURE) HENCE
(— THE MORNING) MANE
(— THE REAR) AREAR ASTERN
(— THE REGIONS OF UNBELIEVERS)
IPI
(— THE SAME PLACE) IBID IBIDEM
(— THE SAME WAY) AS
(— TOWARD) INOWER
(— TRUTH) MARRY SOOTH CERTES
INDEED VERILY SOOTHLY
FORSOOTH
(— VAIN) WASTELY
(— VIEW OF THE FACT THAT)
SEEING
(— WHAT MANNER) HOW QUOMODO

INABILITY (— TO FEED) APHAGIA
(— TO MASTICATE) AMASESIS
(— TO SPEAK) ALOGIA ANEPIA
DUMBNESS
(— TO WALK) ABASIA
INACCESSIBLE COY REMOTE
UNGAIN WICKED SHADOWY
INACCESSIBILITY FASTNESS
INACCURATE SOUR FALSE LOOSE
FAULTY UNJUST INEXACT IMPROPER
SLIPSHOD
INACHUS (DAUGHTER OF —) IO
(FATHER OF —) OCEANUS
(MOTHER OF —) TETHYS
(SON OF —) PHORONEUS
INACTION RUST
INACTIVATE MOTHBALL
INACTIVE LAX DEAD DRUG FLAT
IDLE LAZY MESO SLOW HEAVY
INERT NOBLE SLACK SULKY ASLEEP
SUPINE CESSANT DORMANT
PASSIVE RESTIVE COMATOSE
COMATOUS DEEDLESS DILATORY
FAINEANT SLOTHFUL SLUGGISH
INACTIVITY SLOTH ANERGY
ANERGIA ABEYANCE IDLENESS
CESSATION
INADEQUACY DEFECT FRAILTY
SCARCITY
INADEQUATE BAD BARE POOR THIN
INEPT SHORT SLACK FEEBLE STRAIT
FOOLISH INVALID SLENDER
HIGHLAND INFERIOR
INADEQUATELY BADLY SLACK
SLACKLY
INADVERTENCE LAPSUS
INADVERTENT CARELESS
INAJA JAGUA
INALIENABLE INHERENT
INAMORATA AMORADO AMORETTO
INANE DIZZY EMPTY JERKY SILLY
VAPID JEJUNE VACANT FATUOUS
FOOLISH INSIPID VACUOUS IMBECILE
SLIPSLOP TRIFLING
INANGA MINNOW
INANIMATE DEAD DULL BRUTE
INERT DEADLY STOLID STUPID
LIFELESS
INANITY FATUITY VACUITY
INAPPLICABLE SPURIOUS
INAPPROPRIATE INEPT UNAPT
UNDUE FOREIGN UNHAPPY
INAPT BACKWARD FOOTLESS
INARTICULATA LYOPOMA
INARTICULATE DUMB LAME THICK
INARTISTIC ARTLESS
INATTENTION ABSENCE NEGLECT
APROSEXIA
INATTENTIVE DEAF SLACK ABSENT
REMISS SUPINE DREAMSY UNTENTY
CARELESS DISTRAIT HEEDLESS
MINDLESS
INAUDIBLE SECRET
INAUDIBLY INWARDLY SECRETLY
INAUGURATE AUGUR BEGIN
HANDSEL INITIATE
INAUSPICIOUS BAD ILL EVIL FOUL
ADVERSE OBSCENE OMINOUS
UNHAPPY UNLUCKY SINISTER

INAUTHENTIC SPURIOUS
INBORN GENIAL INBRED INNATE
  NATIVE CONNATE NATURAL
  HABITUAL INHERENT
INBRED INBORN INNATE
INBREED SELF
INBREEDING ENDOGAMY
INCA INGUA OREJON
INCALCULABLE UNTOLD SUMLESS
  UNKNOWN
INCA MAGIC FLOWER CANTUT
  CANTUTA
INCANDESCENCE GLOW
INCANDESCENT BRIGHT
INCANTATION CHARM DAWUT
  SPELL CARMEN FETISH MANTRA
  CANTION CHANTRY GREEGREE
INCAPABLE DEAD NUMB UNABLE
  HANDLESS
INCAPACITATE NAPOO UNFIT
  NOBBLE UNABLE DISABLE
INCAPACITATED FLAT DISABLED
  STRICKEN
INCARCERATE IMMURE CONFINE
  IMPRISON
INCARNATE BODIED EMBODY
  CARNATE ENFLESH HUMANIFY
INCARNATION IMAGE ADVENT
  AVATAR GENIUS MNEVIS TERTON
  HUTUKTU EPIPHANY
INCAUTIOUS RASH UNWARY
  UNCHARY UNTENTY CAREFREE
  RECKLESS
INCENDIARY FIREBUG ARSONIST
  BOUTEFEU
INCENSE CENSE INFLAME KETURAH
  PROVOKE IRRITATE THYMIAMA
  (**— INGREDIENT**) ONYCHA
  (**— VESSEL**) SHIP
INCENSED RAW IRATE WROTH
  WRATHFUL
INCENTIVE BROD GOAD SPUR PRICK
  MOTIVE IMPETUS IMPULSE INCITIVE
  STIMULUS
INCEPTION ORIGIN ANCESTRY
INCESSANT STEADY ENDLESS
  CONSTANT
INCESSANTLY FOREVER
INCH UNCH PRIME UNCIA
  (**100TH OF —**) POINT
  (**4 —S**) HANDFUL
  (**48TH OF —**) IRON
  (**9 —S**) SPAN
  (**ABOUT 7 —S**) FISTMELE
INCHOATE FORMLESS
INCIDENT GO EVENT LIABLE
  CAUTION EPISODE PASSAGE
  SUBJECT ACCIDENT CASUALTY
  OCCASION
  (**AMUSING —**) BREAK
  (**LITERARY —**) BIT
INCIDENTAL BY BYE SIDE STRAY
  CASUAL EPISODIC GLANCING
  INCIDENT
INCIDENTALLY BYHAND OBITER
  APROPOS
INCINERATE COMBUST CREMATE
INCINERATOR BURNER
INCIPIENCE BUD

INCIPIENT INITIAL GERMINAL
  INCHOATE
INCISE CHOP RASE INCIDE CHANNEL
  ENGRAVE
INCISION CUT GASH SLIT SNIP
  ISSUE SCORE BROACH SCOTCH
  STREAK CUTDOWN DIACOPE
  APLOTOMY CECOTOMY COLOTOMY
INCISIVE ACID KEEN CRISP SHARP
  BITING BRUTAL CUTTING ACULEATE
INCISOR CUTTER NIPPER GATHERER
INCITE EGG HIE HOY PUT SIC TAR
  ABET BUZZ EDGE FIRE GOAD LASH
  MOVE PROD SICK SNIP SPUR STIR
  URGE AWAKE CHIRK IMPEL PRICK
  PROKE SPARK SPURN STING TEMPT
  AROUSE ENTICE EXCITE EXHORT
  FOMENT HALLOO INDUCE KINDLE
  NETTLE PROMPT UPSTIR ANIMATE
  COMMOVE INCENSE INSPIRE
  PROMOVE PROVOKE QUICKEN
  SOLICIT INCITATE MOTIVATE
  (**— SECRETLY**) SUBORN
  (**— TO ATTACK**) SET HIRR SOOL
INCITEMENT GOAD PROD SPUR
  STING MOTIVE EGGMENT STIRRING
  (**— OF LITIGATION**) BARRATRY
INCITER FEEDER MONITOR
  INCENSOR INCENTOR
INCLEMENCY RIGOR CRUELTY
  TYRANNY ASPERITY HARDNESS
  SEVERITY
INCLEMENT RAW HARD RUDE SOUR
  GURLY STARK COARSE SEVERE
  UNFINE UNKINDLY
  (**NOT —**) OPEN CIVIL
INCLINATION DIP GEE MAW PLY
  SET BENT BIAS BROO CANT CARE
  DRAG DRAW EDGE FALL GUST
  HANG LEAN LIKE LIST LOVE LUST
  MIND SLEW TURN VEIN WILL BEVEL
  BOSOM DRAFT DRIFT FANCY GRAIN
  HABIT HIELD HUMOR KNACK LURCH
  PITCH POISE SLANT SLOPE STUDY
  SWING TASTE THEAT TREND
  AFFECT ANIMUS ANLAGE ASCENT
  DESIRE DEVICE GATHER GENIUS
  INTENT LIKING MOTION NOTION
  PONDUS RELISH SQUINT TALENT
  YETZER APTNESS CONATUS
  COURAGE CURRENT DESCENT
  DRAUGHT FANTASY INKLING
  LEANING STOMACH VERSANT
  WILNING APTITUDE DEVOTION
  GRADIENT PENCHANT TENDENCY
  VELLEITY VERGENCY WOULDING
  (**— DOWNWARD**) DIP DESCENT
  HANGING
  (**— OF OARSMAN'S BODY**) LAYBACK
  (**PREDOMINATE —**) STRENGTH
INCLINE APT BOW DIP TIP WRY
  BEND BIAS BREW CANT CAST DOCK
  DOOK DOOR DROP GIVE HANG HEEL
  HELD HILL LEAN LIKE LIST PEND
  RAKE STAY SWAY TILT TURN BEVEL
  CLIMB CLINE DROOP FLECT HIELD
  JINNY OFFER SHAPE SLANT SLOPE
  SOUND VERGE AFFECT GLACIS
  INTEND SHELVE STEEVE UPBROW

  DECLINE DESCEND GANGWAY
  PROPEND PROCLINE PROCLIVE
  (**— SKI**) EDGE
INCLINED APT SIB BENT CANT FAIN
  RIFE VAIN ARAKE GIVEN PRONE
  READY COUCHE MINDED PROMPT
  SLOPED SUPINE FORWARD HANGING
  OBLIQUE PRONATE STUDIED
  AFFECTED DISPOSED ENCLITIC
  PROPENSE SIDELING TALENTED
  (**— TO DRINK**) BIBULOUS
INCLINING HILLY SHELVY SLOPING
  CERNUOUS SIDELING
INCLUDE ADD LAP HAVE TAKE
  ANNEX COUCH COVER IMPLY
  EMPLOY ENSEAM RECKON BELOUKE
  COLLECT CONTAIN EMBRACE
  IMMERSE INVOLVE RECOUNT
  SUBSUME COMPRISE CONCLUDE
  (**— IN LIST**) ENGROSS
INCLUDING TO CUM
INCLUSIVE GRAND CAPABLE
  CATHOLIC
INCLUSIVELY BROADLY
INCLUSUS RECLUSE
INCOHERENT FUZZY BROKEN
  RAVING INCHOATE
INCOHERENTLY IDLY
INCOMBUSTIBLE APYROUS
  ASBESTIC
INCOME GAIN PORT RENT LIVING
  PEWAGE PEWING PROFIT SALARY
  FACULTY INTRADO INTRATE
  PRODUCE REVENUE STIPEND
  INTEREST PROCEEDS
  (**ANNUAL —**) RENTE
  (**UNFORESEEN —**) GRAVY
INCOMMENSURATE UNEQUAL
INCOMMODE VEX ANNOY MOLEST
  PLAGUE TROUBLE DISQUIET
INCOMPARABLE ALONE
INCOMPATIBILITY SOLECISM
  ANTIPATHY
INCOMPETENT INEPT UNFIT
  SLOUCH UNABLE UNMEET FECKLESS
  HANDLESS HELPLESS SPLITTER
INCOMPLETE WANE BLIND ROUGH
  BROKEN UNDONE DIVIDED LACKING
  PARTIAL IMMATURE INCHOATE
INCOMPLETELY BADLY HALVES
INCOMPOSITE PRIME
INCOMPREHENSIBLE PARTIAL
  COCKEYED
INCONCLUSIVE FUZZY
INCONGRUITY JAR SOLECISM
INCONGRUOUS ALIEN ABSURD
INCONNU CONY NELMA CONNIE
  SHEEFISH
INCONSIDERABLE LIGHT PETTY
  LITTLE
INCONSIDERATE RASH UNKIND
  ASOCIAL RECKLESS
INCONSISTENCY HOLE
INCONSPICUOUS OBSCURE
INCONSTANCY CHANGE LEVITY
INCONSTANT FICKLE BRUCKLE
  FLUXILE SLIDING VARIOUS FLUXIBLE
  MOVEABLE VARIABLE
INCONTESTABLE SURE CLEAN
  CERTAIN

INCONTINENCE ENURESIS
INCONTINENT LOOSE LAXATIVE
INCONTROVERTIBLE GRAND
INCONVENIENCE FASH BOTHER
CUMBER STRESS SQUEEZE
DISQUIET
INCONVENIENT UNKED CLUMSY
UNBANE UNGAIN AWKWARD
UNHANDY ANNOYING UNCHANCY
UNTOWARD
INCOORDINATION ASTASIA
INCORPORATE MIX FOLD FUSE JOIN
ANNEX KNEAD MERGE UNITE
ABSORB EMBODY ENGRAIN ENTRAIN
INWEAVE INCORPSE
(**— IN WALL**) ENGAGE
INCORPOREAL AERY BODILESS
ASOMATOUS
INCORRECT BAD ILL FALSE WRONG
PECCANT UNRIGHT UNSOUND
VICIOUS
INCORRIGIBLE HARD
INCORRUPTIBLE IMMORTAL
INCREASE UP ADD EIK EKE IMP WAX
BUMP ECHE GAIN GROW HELP HIKE
ITCH JACK JUMP MEND MORE MUCH
PLUS PUSH RISE SOAR THEE THRO
BOOST BUILD BULGE CLIMB CROWD
FLUSH FRESH HEAVE LARGE RAISE
SPURT SWELL ACCENT ACCESS
BETTER BIGGEN CHANGE CREASE
DEEPEN DOUBLE EXPAND EXTEND
EXTENT GATHER GROWTH SPREAD
SPRING ADVANCE AMPLIFY AUCTION
AUGMENT AUXESIS BALLOON
DISTEND ELEVATE ENGROSS
ENHANCE ENLARGE GREATEN
IMPROVE INFLATE MAGNIFY
STEEPEN SURCRUE ACCRESCE
ADDITION COMPOUND FLOURISH
HEIGHTEN LENGTHEN MAJORATE
MAXIMATE MAXIMIZE MULTIPLY
THRODDEN
(**— AT USURY**) OCKER
(**— HEAT OF KILN**) RUSTLE GLISTER
(**— IN PAY**) FOGY FOGIE
(**— IN STRENGTH**) FRESHEN
(**— KNOWLEDGE**) ENRICH
(**— POWER**) SOUP
(**— PRICE BY BIDDING**) CANT
(**— SPEED**) JAZZ
(**— STITCHES**) FASHION
(**— SUDDENLY**) LEAP
(**PRICE —**) RIST
(**SHORT-TERM —**) BOOMLET
INCREASING GROWING CRESCENT
CRESCIVE DILATANT SWELLING
(**— RAPIDLY**) BOOMING
INCREDIBLE TALL STEEP DAMNED
FABULOUS
INCREDULITY UNBELIEF
INCREDULOUS INFIDEL
INCREMENT DOSE DELTA INCREASE
INCRIMINATE ACCUSE
INCRUST FOUL
INCRUSTATION CRUD MOSS CRUST
SCALE TARTAR FOULING FURRING
INCUBATE SIT BROOD CLOCK
COVER HATCH

INCUBATOR FURNACE HATCHER
COUVEUSE ISOLETTE
INCUBUS DUSE MARE DUSIO
NIGHTMARE
INCULCATE BREED INFIX INCULK
INFUSE IMPLANT IMPRESS INSTILL
INCULCATED BRED
INCUMBENT COARB BEARER
INCUR RUN BEAR GAIN WAGE
CONTRACT
INCURABLE BOOTLESS HOPELESS
INCURRENT INHALANT
INCURSION RAID ROAD FORAY
INFALL INROAD RAZZIA DESCENT
HOSTING INBREAK INCURSE
INVASION
INCUS AMBOS ANVIL
INDEBTED DEBTFUL BEHOLDEN
INDEBTEDNESS DEBT SCORE
INDECENCY IMPURITY PRIAPISM
RIBALDRY
INDECENT PAW FOUL LEWD RANK
BAWDY GROSS NASTY SAUCY
GREASY IMPURE PAWPAW SMUTTY
GRIVOIS IMMORAL OBSCENE
IMMODEST IMPROPER SHAMEFUL
UNCOMELY
INDECISION DEMUR DOUBT MAYBE
POISE SWITHER
INDECISIVE DRAWN HALTING
INDECISIVENESS SUSPENSE
INDECOROUS RUDE COARSE
FORWARD UNCIVIL IMMODEST
IMPOLITE IMPROPER INDECENT
UNSEEMLY UNTOWARD
INDEED SO ARU WIS YEA AWAT
DEED EVEN IWIS JUST SURE QUOTH
TIENS ITSELF SURELY FAITHLY
FRANKLY FORSOOTH VERAMENT
INDEFATIGABLE TIRELESS
INDEFENSIBLE INVALID
INDEFINITE HAZY FUZZY GROSS
LOOSE VAGUE DIVERS INEXACT
AORISTIC
INDEFINITELY IN
INDELIBLE FAST FIXED
INDELICATE RAW FREE WARM
BROAD GROSS COARSE GREASY
IMPOLITE IMPROPER UNSEEMLY
INDEMNIFICATION RELIEF
INDEMNIFY PAY RECOUP SATISFY
WARRANT
INDENT JAG BRIT DENT GIMP MUSH
CHASE DELVE NOTCH STAMP
TOOTH WHEEL BRUISE ENGRAIL
GAUFFER
INDENTATION CHOP DENT DINT
DOKE FOIL KINK SCAR BOSOM
BULGE CLEFT CRENA DINGE NOTCH
SINUS DIMPLE FURROW GROOVE
INDENT IMPRESS CRENELLE
TOOTHING
(**— IN BOTTLE**) KICK
(**— IN DOG'S FACE**) STOP
(**— IN SHELL**) EYE
INDENTED WAVED NOTCHED
INDENTURE BIND INDENT ESCALLOP
SYNGRAPH
INDEPENDENCE AUTARKY

FREEDOM AUTARCHY
(**— OF GOD**) ASEITY ASEITAS
(**POLITICAL —**) SWARAJ
INDEPENDENT FREE PROUD
SEEKER BIGGITY DIVIDED MUGWUMP
SECTARY ABSOLUTE PECULIAR
SEPARATE
INDEPENDENTLY APART
INDESCRIBABLE TERMLESS
INEFFABLE
INDETERMINATE AORISTIC
FORMLESS INFINITE
INDEX PIE FIST HAND ARNETH
ELENCH PIGNET TONGUE POINTER
ALPHABET REGISTER

INDIA

CAPE: COMORIN
CAPITAL: NEWDELHI
CASTE: JAT MAL AHIR GOLA JATI
MALI DHOBI SANSI SUDRA
VARNA DACOIT DHANUK
LOHANA VAISYA AGARWAL
BRAHMAN DHANGAR
COAST: MALABAR
COIN: LAC PIE ANNA FELS LAKH
PICE TARA ABIDI CRORE PAISA
RUPEE
COLLEGE: TOL
DESERT: THAR
DISTRICT: SIBI NASIK PATNA
SIMLA ZILLAH MALABAR
NELLORE MOFUSSIL
GULF: KUTCH CAMBAY MANNAR
ISLAND: CHILKA
LAKE: WULAR CHILKA COLAIR
DHEBAR SAMBAHR
LANGUAGE: URDU HINDI TAMIL
TELUGU SANSKRIT
MEASURE: ADY DHA GAZ GUZ
JOW KOS LAN SER BYEE COSS
DAIN DHAN HATH JAOB KUNK
MOOT PARA RAIK RATI SEIT
TAUN TENG TOLA AMUNA BIGHA
CAHAR COVID CROSA DANDA
DRONA GARCE GIREH HASTA
PALLY PARAH RATTI SALAY
YOJAN ADHAKA ANGULA
COVIDO CUDAVA CUMBHA
GEERAH LAMANY MOOLUM
MUSHTI PALGAT PARRAH
ROPANI TIPREE UNGLEE YOJANA
ADOULIE DHANUSH GAVYUTI
KHAHOON NIRANGA PRASTHA
VITASTI OKTHABAH
MOUNTAIN: MERU GHATS KAMET
MASTUJ TANKSE KALAHOI
SIWALIK VINDHYA SULEIMAN
MOUNTAIN RANGE: SATPURA
VINDHYA ARAVALLI HIMALAYA
NATIVE: HINDU TAMIL
PROVINCE: HAR ASSAM BIHAR
ANDHRA BENGAL KERALA
MADRAS MYSORE ORISSA
PUNJAB GUJARAT HARYANA
KASHMIR MANIPUR
REGION: MALABAR
RIVER: AI DOR SON TEL KOSI KUSI

NIRA REHR SIND BETWA BHIMA
DAMOH GOGRA INDUS JAWAI
RAPTI SANKH SONAR TAPTI
TUNGA CHENAB GANGES KISTNA
PENNER SUTLEJ WARDHA
CAUVERY CHAMBAL IRAWADI
KRISHNA NARMADA NARMEDA
HEMAVATI HYDASPES MAHANADI
NERBUDDA VINDHYAS
SEAPORT: DAMAN BOMBAY
  COCHIN MADRAS CALCUTTA
STRAIT: PALK
TOWN: DIU AGRA DAMA GAYA
  PUNA REWA ADONI AKOLA
  ALWAR ARCOT BHERA DACCA
  DATIA DELHI GIROT KALPI
  MYSOR PATAN PATNA POONA
  SALEM SIMLA SURAT TEHRI
  AJMERE AMBALA BARELI
  BARODA BHOPAL BOMBAY
  CHAMBA COCHIN DUMDUM
  HOWRAH INDORE JAIPUR
  KANPUR LAHORE MADIRA
  MADRAS MADURA MEERUT
  MULTAN MUSORE MUTTRA
  NAGPUR RAMPUR UJJAIN
  ALIGARH BENARES BIKANER
  CALICUT CAWNPUR DINAPIR
  GWALIOR JODHPUR KARACHI
  KURNOOL LASWARI LUCKNOW
  RANGOON RANGPUR AMRITSAR
  BHATINDA BHATPARA CALCUTTA
  DINAPORE JABALPUR KOLHAPUR
  MANDALAY MIRZAPUR
  PESHAWAR SHOLAPUR
  SRINAGAR VARANASI
TRIBE: AO GOR BHIL BADAGA
  SHERANI
WEIGHT: MOD PAI SER VIS DHAN
  DRUM KONA MYAT PALA PANK
  PICE RAIK RATI RUAY SEER
  TANK TOLA YAVA ADPAD BAHAR
  CANDY CATTY HUBBA MASHA
  MAUND PALLY POUAH RATTI
  RETTI RUTEE TICAL TICUL TIKAL
  ABUCCO DHURRA KARSHA
  CHITTAK PEIKTHA

INDIAN LO RED ROJO INJUN
TAWNY INDISH BHARATI HOSTILE
NAIKPOD REDSKIN LONGHAIR
(AMERICAN —) AIS AUK FOX HOH
KAW OTO SAC SIA UTE WEA ZIA
ADAI COOS CREE CROW DOEG ERIE
EYAK HANO HOPI HUPA IOWA KATO
KOSO MOKI MONO OTOE OTTO PIMA
PIRO SAUK TANO TAOS TEWA TIOU
TOAG UTAH WACO YUMA ZUNI
ACOMA ALSEA BANAK BIDAI CADDO
CHAUI COMOX CONOY COREE
CREEK HANIS HOOPA HUECO
HURON JEMEZ KANIA KANSA KAROK
KERES KIOWA KOROA KUSAN
LENCA LIPAN MAKAH MANSO MIAMI
MINGO MODOC MOQUI NAMBE
OMAHA OSAGE OSTIC OZARK
PECOS PINAL PIUTE PONCA SAMBO
SARSI SEWEE SIOUX SITKA SKIDI

SLAVE SNAKE SOOKE TETON TEXAS
TIGUA TONTO TWANA TYIGH UINTA
UNAMI WAPPO WASCO WASHO
WIYOT YAMEL YAZOO YUCHI YUROK
AGAWAM AHTENA APACHE ATSINA
ATUAMI AVOYEL BILOXI CALUSA
CAYUGA CAYUSE CHATOT CHERAW
CHETCO COOSUC CUPENO DAKOTA
DIGGER EYEISH FARAON GILENO
HAINAI HAISLA ISLETA KAIBAB
KAINAH KANSAS KICHAI KOSIMO
KUITSH LAGUNA LENAPE MANDAN
MAUMEE MAYEYE METOAC MICMAC
MIKMAK MOHAVE MOHAWK MUNSEE
NASHUA NATICK NAUSET NAVAHO
NAVAJO NEUTER NOOTKA OGLALA
ONEIDA OREJON OTTAWA PAIUTE
PAPAJO PATWIN PAWNEE PEORIA
PEQUOD PEQUOT PIEGAN PODUNK
PUEBLO QUAPAW QUERES RIKARI
SALISH SAMISH SANTEE SAPONI
SATSOP SENECA SHASTA SILETZ
SIOUAN SIWASH SKAGIT SOKOKI
SUMASS SUMDUM SUTAIO SYLVID
TAPOSA TENINO TOHOME TOLOWA
TONGAS TUNICA TUTELO UNPQUA
WALAPI WAPATO WATALA WAXHAW
WEANOC WIKENO WINTUN YAKIMA
YAMASI YAVAPA ZUNIAN ABENAKI
ALABAMA ALIBAMU AMERIND
ANDARKO ANDASTE ARIKARA
ATAKAPA AYAHUCA BANNOCK
CAHOKIA CAHUILA CALOOSA
CATAWBA CHILCAT CHILULA
CHINOOK CHOCTAW CHUMASH
CHUMAWI CIBECUE CLALLAM
CLATSOP COCHITI COLCINE
COWLITZ DEADOSE DHEGIHA
DWAMISH ESSELEN GOSHUTE
HELLELT HIDATSA HUCHNOM
HUICHOL INGALIK JUANENO
KANAWHA KLAMATH KOASATI
KOHUANA KOPRINO KUNESTE
KUTCHIN KUTENAI LUISENO
MASHPEE MASKOKI MOHEGAN
MOHICAN MONACAN MONSONI
MONTAUK MOUSONI NANAIMO
NASCAPI NATCHEZ NIANTIC NIMKISH
NIPMUCK OJIBWAY PACIFID
PADUCAH PAMLICO PICURUS
QUAITSO SALINAN SANETCH
SANFOIL SERRANO SHAPTAN
SHAWANO SHAWNEE SIKSIKA
SIUSLAW SONGISH SPOKANE
SQUAXON STIKINE TAMAROA
TESUQUE TIMUCUA TLINGIT
TONKAWA TUALATI TULALIP
TUTUTNI UGARONO WAILAKI
WALPAPI WAMESIT WANAPUM
WASHAKI WEWENOC WHILKUT
WICHITA WISHOSK WITUMKI
WYANDOT YANKTON YAQUINA
YOJUANE YONKALA ABSAROKA
ACHOMAWI ACHUMAWI ALGONKIN
AMERICAN AMOSKEAG APALACHI
ARIVAIPA ARKANSAS ASTAKIWI
ATFALATI ATSUGEWI CAHINNIO
CAHUILLA CANARSIE CHAWASHA
CHEHALIS CHEMAKUM CHEROKEE

CHEYENNE CHIMAKUM CHOPTANK
CHOWANOC CLACKAMA COLUMBIA
COLVILLE COMANCHE COQUILLE
COYOTERO DELAWARE DIEGUENO
ETCHIMIN FLATHEAD HITCHITI
HUNKPAPA ILLINOIS IROQUOIS
KALISPEL KAWAIISU KICKAPOO
KIKATSIK KLASKINO KLIKITAT
KONOMIHU LAMANITE MALECITE
MASKOTIN MENOMINI MIKASUKI
MINITARI MISSOURI MOGOLLON
MUSCOGEE MUSKWAKI NEHANTIC
NESPELIM NOTTOWAY OKINAGAN
ONONDAGA PAMUNKEY PANAMINT
PATUXENT PAVIOTSO PENACOOK
PISHQUOW POWHATAN PUYALLUP
QUATSINO QUERECHO QUILEUTE
QUINAULT ROCKAWAY SAHAPTIN
SAULTEUR SAVANNAH SEMINOLE
SHIVWITS SHOSHONE SIHASAPA
SINGSING SINKIUSE SINKYONE
SINTSINK SISSETON SOUHEGAN
SQUAMISH SQUEDUNK TLAKLUIT
TOBIKHAR TOPINISH TSIHALIS
TUSHEPAW TUSKEGEE UMATILLA
WABANAKI WACHUSET WAHPETON
WETUMPKA YAHUSKIN YAMACRAW
DOUSTIONI SQUAWTITS
(BRAZILIAN —) BUGRE
(CANADIAN —) DENE COMOX HAIDA
SLAVE TINNE DOGRIB HAISLA
LASSIK SARSEE BEOTHUK GOASILA
KHOTANA KOYUKON CHISEDEC
COEICHAN HEILTSUK KIMSQUIT
KWAKIUTL LILLOOET SALTEAUX
(FEMALE —) SQUAW KLOOCH
(MALE —) BUCK SANNUP
(MEXICAN —) MAM OVA CHOL CORA
JOVA MAYA MAYO ROTO SERI TECA
TECO XOVA AZTEC CHIZO CHORA
HUABI HUAVE KAMIA NAHUA OPATA
OTOMI YAQUI ZOQUE CAHITA
CHOCHO CONCHO EUDEVE KILIWI
NEVOME OTONIA PAKAWA TARASC
TOLTEC ZOTZIL ACOLHUA AKWAALA
AMISHGO CHATINO CHINCHA
CHINIPA CHONTAL COTONAM
COUHIMI GUASAVE HUASTEC
HUAXTEC MAZATEC MISTECA
MIXTECA NAYARIT SINALOA
TEGUIMA TEHUECO TEPANEC
TEPEHUA TZENTAL TZOTZIL
ZACATEC ZAPOTEC CHANABAL
CHAPANEC CHUCHONA COLOTLAN
COMANITO CONICARI GUASAPAR
HUASTECO IRRITILA JACALTEC
JANAMARE LACANDON LAGUNERO
TARUMARI TECPANEC TEXCOCAN
TEZCUCAN TOTONACO TZAPOTEC
YUCATECO
(OTHER —) GE ITE ONA URO URU
YAO AGAZ ANDE ANTA ANTI AUCA
BABU CAME CANA CARA CHUJ
COTO CUNA DENE DIAU DUIT INCA
ITEN ITZA IXIL MOJO MOXO MURA
MUSO MUZO PEBA PIRO RAMA
TAMA TAPE TATU TOBA TRIO TUPI
TUPY ULUA ULVA ACROA ARARA
ARAUA ARUAC AUETO BAURE BETOI

BRAVO BUGRE CAITE CAMPA CANCA
CARIB CHANE CHIMU CHITA CHOKO
CHOLA CHOLO CHONO COCTO
COLAN CUEVA DIRIA GUANA GUATO
HUARI JAVAH KASKA LENCA MOCOA
MOZCA OPATA OYANA PALTA
PAMPA PASSE PETEN PINTO PIOJE
PIOXE PIPIL POKAN POKOM QUITU
SENCI SIUSI SMOOS TAINO UAUPE
UMAUA VEJOZ WAURA XINCA
YAGUA YAMEO YUNCA YUNGA
AGUANO AIMARA AKAVAI AKAWAI
AMORUA ANDOKE ANTISI APANTO
APARAI APIACA ARAWAK AROACO
ATORAI AYMARA BABINE BANIVA
BETOYA BORORO BRIBRI BRUNKA
CAHETE CAIGUA CANCHI CANELO
CARAHO CARAJA CARAYA CARIRI
CAUQUI CAVINA CAYAPA CHAIMA
CHARCA CHAYMA CHICHA CHISCA
CHOCOI CHORTI COCAMA COCOMA
COCORA COFANE COLIMA COTOXO
CUCAMA CULINO CUMANA DOGROB
DORASK GALIBI GOYANA GUAIMI
GUAQUE GUAYMI HUARPE HUBABO
IGNERI INCERI IXIAMA JIVARO
JUCUNA JUMANA JURUNA KARAYA
KEKCHI KUCHIN LENGUA LUCAYO
MACUSI MAKUSI MANGUE MANIVA
MIRANA MUYSCA NAHANE NASCAN
OMAGUA OTOMAC PAPAGO
PKOMAM PURUHA QUICHE SABUJA
SACCHA SALIBA SALIVA SAMUCU
SEKANE SETIBO SIPIBO SUERRE
TACANA TAGISH TAHAMI TAMOYO
TAPAJO TAPUYA TARUMA TECUNA
TICUNA TIMOTE TOTORO TUCANO
TUNEBO UIRINA UITOTO VILELA
WAIWAI WITOTO WOOLWA YAHGAN
YAHUNA YARURO YURUNA ZAPARA
ACHAGUA ACKAWOI AKAMNIK
ANDAQUI ANGAITE APALAII APINAGE
ARECUNA ARHUACO BEOTHUK
BILQULA CACHIBO CAINGUA
CALIANA CAMACAN CARANGA
CARIBAN CARIBEE CARRIER
CASHIBO CHARRUA CHIBCHA
CHIMANE CHIMILA CHIRINO
CHONCHO CHOROTE CHUMULU
CHUNCHO CHURAPA CHUROYA
CIBONEY CJACOGO COROADO
FRENTON FUEGIAN GITKSAN
GOAHIVO GOAJIRA GUARRAU
GUAHIVO GUARANY GUARANI
GUARAYO GUARUAN GUATUSO
GUETARE HUANUCO HUATUSO
ITONAMA JACUNDA JICAQUE
KALIANA KOPRINO KULIANA
LUCAYAN MAIPURE MONGOYO
MORCOTE NICARAO PAMPERO
PAYAGUA PEDRAZA PIARROA
POKOMAM PUELCHE PUQUINA
QUECHUA QUEKCHI RANQUEL
SARIGUE SATIENO SHUSWAP
SINSIGA SIRIONE TAHLTAN TALUCHE
TALUHET TAMANAC TARIANA
TARRABA TAYRONA TELEMBI
TIMBIRA TIRRIBI TSONECA UARAYCU
UCAYALE VOYAVAI WOYAWAY

YUSTAGA ZUTUHIL AGUARUNA
AHOUSAHT AKIYENIK ALACALUF
AMAHUACA APOLISTA ARAQUAJU
AWISHIRA BOTOCUDO CAINGANG
CALINAGO CANAMARY CANOEIRO
CAQUETIO CARIBISI CARIJONA
CARIPUNA CAYUBABA CHAMBOIA
CHANDALA CHAVANTE CHIQUITO
CHIRIANA COLORADO COMIAKIN
CONCHUCO CORABECA CUSTENAU
GUAYAQUI GUAYCURU JAVITERO
KANHOBAL KLASKINO LOROKOTO
MACARANI MAYORUNA MISSKITO
MOSQUITO NIQUIRAN OCHOZOMA
OROTINAN PACAVARA PALENQUE
PARUKUTU PINALENO POIGUARA
POKONCHI POPOLOCO POTYUARA
PUPULUCA QUATSINO QUERENDY
QUIMBAYA SHIRIANA SNONOWAS
SUBTIABA TADOUSAC TAPACURA
TENAKTAK TOCOBAGA TOROMONA
TSATTINE TUMUPASA UAREKENA
URUKUENA USPANTEC YURUCARE
(SPANISH-AMERICAN —) CHOLO

INDIANA
CAPITAL: INDIANAPOLIS
COLLEGE: BALL BETHEL DEPAUW
GOSHEN MARIAN PURDUE
WABASH
COUNTY: JAY CASS VIGO JASPER
TIPTON DAVIESS
INDIAN: MIAMI SHAWNEE
LAKE: MONROE MANITOU
WAWASEE MICHIGAN
NATIVE: HOOSIER
RIVER: OHIO WHITE WABASH
STATE BIRD: CARDINAL
STATE FLOWER: PEONY
STATE TREE: TULIP
TOWN: GARY PERU BRAZIL
GOSHEN JASPER KOKOMO
MUNCIE WABASH

INDIAN BEECH KURUNJ
INDIAN BREAD TUCKAHOE
INDIAN CORN KANGA MAIZE
CHOLUM JAGONG MEALIES
INDIAN FIG SABRA
INDIAN FISH FLATFISH
INDIAN GOOSEBERRY EMBLIC
INDIAN HEMP KEF KIF DAGGA SABZI
AMYROOT DOGBANE
INDIANIAN HOOSIER
INDIAN JALAP TURPETH
INDIAN LICORICE JEQUIRITY
INDIAN MADDER MUNJEET
INDIAN MALLOW SIDA DAGGA
PIEPRINT
INDIAN MILLET JONDLA
INDIAN MULBERRY AL AAL ACH
ALROOT
INDIAN PIPE FITROOT EYEBRIGHT
WAXFLOWER
INDIAN SHOT ALIIPOE
INDIAN TOBACCO GAGROOT
LOBELIA PUKEWEED SOURBUSH
INDIAN YELLOW PIOURY PURREE

INDIC (— LANGUAGE) URDU VEDIC
INDICATE RUN SAY BODY CITE HINT
LOOK MAKE MARK READ SHOW
ARGUE INDEX INFER POINT PROVE
SPEAK ALLUDE ATTEST BETRAY
DENOTE DESIGN EVINCE FINGER
IMPORT NOTIFY REVEAL BESPEAK
BETOKEN CONNOTE DECLARE
DISPLAY SIGNIFY SPECIFY
ADMONISH ANNOUNCE DECIPHER
DISCLOSE EVIDENCE MANIFEST
OUTPOINT REGISTER
(— BY SOUNDING) STRIKE
(— WILLINGNESS) AGREE
INDICATION BECK CLEW CLUE HINT
LEAD MARK NOTE SHOW SIGN
CURVE INDEX PROOF SCENT TOKEN
AUGURY BEACON INDICE REMARK
SAMPLE SIGNAL AUSPICE MENTION
PROFFER SYMPTOM ALLUSION
ARGUMENT EVIDENCE MONITION
MONUMENT NOTATION SIGNANCE
TELLTALE
(— OF APPROVAL) CACHET
(— OF CONTROL) COLLAR
(— OF LIGHT) AUREOLE
(— OF OFFICE) SEAL
(OBSCURE —) SHADOW
(VAGUE —) GLIMMER
(PL.) INDICIA
INDICATOR PIN HAND SIGN FLOAT
INDEX LITMUS SHOWER STYLUS
TARGET LACMOID POINTER
DETECTOR TELLTALE
(— OF BALANCE) COCK
(— OF HOUR) GNOMON
INDICT DITE CRIME PANEL ACCUSE
ATTACH CHARGE INDITE ARRAIGN
ARTICLE IMPEACH TROUNCE
WARRANT
INDICTMENT CHARGE DITTAY
INDIFFERENCE APATHY PHLEGM
DISDAIN COLDNESS EASINESS
FROIDEUR
INDIFFERENT COLD COOL DEAD
DRAM EASY SOSO ALOOF BLASE
EQUAL SOBER CASUAL DEGAGE
FRIGID SUPINE CALLOUS NEUTRAL
DETACHED LISTLESS LUKEWARM
MEDIOCRE RECKLESS SUPERIOR
UPSITTEN
INDIFFERENTIST POLITIC
INDIFFERENTLY DRYLY HUMDRUM
INDIGENCE NEED WANT PENURY
BEGGARY POVERTY TENUITY
INDIGENE ENDEMIC
INDIGENOUS DESI NATIVE
DOMESTIC HOMEBORN
INDIGENT POOR BEGGARLY
INDIGESTION APEPSY APEPSIA
DYSPEPSY
INDIGNANT ANGRY WROTH
ANNOYED INCENSED
INDIGNATION IRE ANGER WRATH
DESPITE DISDAIN JEALOUSY
INDIGNITY CUT SLUR SCORN INSULT
SLIGHT AFFRONT OFFENCE
INDIGO ANIL NILL SHOOFLY
INDIRECT SIDE DEVIOUS OBLIQUE

CIRCULAR GLANCING OVERHEAD
OVERWART SIDELONG SIDEWAYS
SIDEWISE
(— **WAY**) AMBAGE
INDIRECTION CIRCUITY
INDISCREET RASH HASTY SILLY
WITLESS CARELESS HEEDLESS
INDISCRETION FOLLY FREDAINE
INDISCRIMINATE MIXED MINGLED
SWEEPING
INDISCRIMINATELY PELLMELL
INDISPENSABLE NEEDFUL CRITICAL
INDISPOSED ILL MEAN SICK ILLISH
UNWELL
INDISPOSITION AIL MALADY
AILMENT SICKNESS
(— **TO MOTION**) INERTIA
INDISPUTABLE SURE CERTAIN
EVIDENT MANIFEST POSITIVE
INDISTINCT DIM DARK DULL HAZY
FAINT FUZZY INNER LIGHT MISTY
MUDDY SHADY THICK VAGUE
CLOUDY DREAMY INWARD SLURRY
WOOLLY BLEARED BLURRED
OBSCURE SHADOWY UNCLEAR
(— **IN UTTERANCE**) CHOKING
INDISTINCTNESS BLUR
INDITE DITE DRAW
INDIVIDUAL GEE MAN ONE HEAD
SORT UNIT BEING MONAD THING
PROPER SINGLE SPIRIT APOMICT
ATAVISM AZYGOTE BIONTIC DIPLOID
EIDETIC ISOLATE MONADIC NUMERIC
SEVERAL SPECIAL EVERYONE
IDENTITY SEPARATE SINGULAR
SOLITARY SPECIMEN
(**COUNTRIFIED** —) HOBNAIL
(**DESPICABLE** —) HEEL
(**DULL** —) BOEOTIAN
(**FOOLISH** —) SOP
(**HAUGHTY** —) POT
(**IMMATURE** —) ADULTOID
(**IMPUDENT** —) BOLDFACE
(**IRRITABLE** —) SNAPPER
(**LEADING** —) KEY
(**MOSAIC** —) GYNANDER
(**MUTANT** —) SALTANT
(**PHYSIOLOGICAL** —) BION
(**ROUGH-LOOKING** —) BOHUNK
(**SKILLED** —) ADEPT
(**SLOVENLY** —) GROBIAN
(**STUPID** —) HOBBIL
(**TRICKY** —) BILK
(**UNDERSIZED** —) KIT KITT
(**WINGED** —) ALATE
(**YOUNG** —) KID
(PL.) FRY
INDIVIDUALITY SEITY QUALITY
SELFDOM HECCEITY IDENTITY
SELFHOOD
INDIVIDUALIZE ATOMIZE
INDIVIDUALLY APART APIECE
SINGLY PROPERLY
INDIVIDUATION AHANKARA
INDIVISIBLE PUNCTUAL
INDO-CHINESE SERIFORM
INDOCTRINATE BRIEF INSTRUCT
INDO-EUROPEAN ARIAN ARYAN
INDOLE KETOLE

INDOLENCE SLOTH LANGUOR
IDLESHIP MUSARDRY SLUGGING
(— **PERSONIFIED**) LAURENCE
LAWRENCE
INDOLENT IDLE LAZY FAINT INERT
SWEER DROWSY OTIOSE SUPINE
DRONISH LABGUID WILSOME
FAINEANT INACTIVE LISTLESS
LOUNGING SLOTHFUL SLUGGISH
PICKTOOTH
INDO-MALAYAN (— **TREE**) SUPA

INDONESIA
CAPITAL: DJAKARTA
COIN: RUPIAH
GULF: BONE TOLO TOMINI
ISLAND: ALOR BALI BURU JAVA
CERAM IRIAN SUMBA WETAR
BANGKA BAWEAN BORNEO
BUTUNG FLORES KOMODO
LOMBOK MADURA PELENG
CELEBES SALAJAR SUMATRA
SUMBAWA BILLITON SULAWESI
KALIMANTAN
ISLAND GROUP: EWAB SUNDA
BANJAK NATUNA ANAMBAS
MOLUCCA TABELAN SABALANA
LANGUAGE: BAHASA MALAYAN
LAKE: RANAU TOWUTI
MOUNTAIN: BULU NIUT RAJA
DEMPO MURJO NIAPA LEUSER
SLAMET MENJAPA OGOAMAS
SAMOSIR KATOPASA KERINTJI
MAHAMERU RINDJANI TALAKMAU
MOUNTAINS: MULLER BARISAN
QUARLES SCHWANER
RIVER: HARI MUSI DIGUL KAJAN
PAWAN BARITO KAMPAR
KAPUAS MAHAKAM
SEA: JAVA BANDA CERAM TIMOR
FLORES ARAFURA CELEBES
STRAIT: SUNDA LOMBOK
MAKASSAR
TOWN: MEDAN MALANG MANADO
BANDUNG MAKASAR SEMARANG
SURABAJA
VOLCANO: SLAMET
WEIGHT: CATTY OUNCE THAIL

INDONESIAN NESIOT SADANG
INDOORS WITHIN
INDRA SAKKA SAKRA
INDUBITABLE SURE EVIDENT
APPARENT MANIFEST UNIVOCAL
INDUCE GET DRAW LEAD MOVE
URGE WORK ARGUE BRIBE BRING
CAUSE IMPEL INFER TEMPT WEIGH
ADDICT ADJURE ALLURE ENGAGE
ENTICE IMPORT INCITE INVITE
OBTAIN REDUCE SEDUCE SUBORN
PREVAIL PROCURE SOLICIT
MOTIVATE PERSUADE WIREDRAW
(— **BY BRIBERY**) FIX
INDUCEMENT MOTIVE REASON
FEATURE
INDUCT STALL INSTAL INITIATE
INDUCTANCE HENRY
INDUCTION EPAGOGE

INDULGE PET BABY CADE CANT
FEED GLUT HUMOR JOLLY SPOIL
TUTOR WALLY WREAK COCKER
FOSTER PAMPER PETTLE DEBAUCH
GRATIFY
(— **IN PRIDE**) PRIDE
(— **TO EXCESS**) PAMPER DEBAUCH
SURFEIT
INDULGED CADE
INDULGENCE LAW BINGE FAVOR
FOLLY MERCY SPREE EXCESS
INDULT PARDON PATENT JUBILEE
QUIENAL SURFEIT COURTESY
DELICACY EASINESS GLUTTONY
POCULARY
(**SEXUAL** —) LECHERY
INDULGENT FOND GOOD MEEK MILD
SPOONY LENIENT TOLERANT
INDURATE HARDEN INDURE
INDURATED SCLEROID SCLEROUS
INDURATION SCLEROMA
INDUSTRIOUS BUSY DEEDY EIDENT
PAINFUL DILIGENT SEDULOUS
VIRTUOUS WORKSOME
INDUSTRY TOIL LABOR SCREEN
VIRTUE CERAMICS SEDULITY
INDWELLING IMMANENT INHERENT
INEBRIATE SOUSE EBRIATED
INEBRIATED DRUNK DRINKY
INEFFACEABLE INBURNT INDELIBLE
INEFFECTIVE DUD WEAK CLUMSY
DREEPY FLABBY FUTILE FLACCID
HALTING STERILE BUMBLING
INEFFECTIVELY ILL BADLY FEEBLY
INEFFECTUAL WAN DEAD IDLE
TAME VAIN VOID JERKY FUTILE
SPINDLY USELESS FAINEANT
FIDDLING NUGATORY
INEFFICIENT ILL LAME POOR
CLUMSY DOLESS UNABLE SLOUCHY
USELESS FECKLESS HANDLESS
INELEGANT RUDE HOYDEN
AWKWARD
INELOQUENT WANMOL
INEPT INAPT ABSURD AWKWARD
FOOTLESS
INEQUAL ROUGH
INEQUALITY ODDS CAHOT ANOMALY
EVECTION IMPARITY NUTATION
INEQUITABLE HARD
INERADICABLE LASTING IDELIBLE
PERMANENT
INERT DEAD DULL LAZY SLOW
HEAVY NOBLE SULKY LEADEN
SODDEN STUPID SUPINE TORPID
PASSIVE INACTIVE INDOLENT
LIFELESS SLOTHFUL SLUGGISH
STAGNANT
INERTIA TAMAS
INESCAPABLE DEAD
INESTIMABLE SUMLESS PRICELESS
INEVITABILITY FINALITY
INEVITABLE DUE DIRECT CERTAIN
FATEFUL
INEXACT FREE ROUGH CLOUDY
INEXHAUSTIBLE INFINITE
INEXORABLE STERN STONY STRICT
RIGOROUS
INEXPEDIENCY IMPOLICY

INEXPEDIENT UNWISE
INEXPENSIVE CHEAP
INEXPERIENCED RAW PUNY CRUDE
FRESH YOUNG UNSEEN KITLING
STRANGE INEXPERT INSOLENT
PRENTICE UNTRADED
INEXPERT ILL RUDE CRUDE GREEN
SIMPLE
INEXPLICABLE FELL
INFAMOUS BASE RUDDY BLOODY
NOTOUR ODIOUS BLEEDING
FLAGRANT NIDERING SHAMEFUL
INFAMY STAIN BAFFLE DEFAME
SHONDE DISHONOR IGNOMINY
INFANCY CRADLE BABYHOOD
INFANT BABE BABY TINY WEAN
CHILD MINOR PREMIE CHRISOM
MILKSOP BALDLING BANTLING
(NAKED —) SCUDDY
(NEWLY-BORN —) NEONATUS
(VORACIOUS -) KILLCROP
INFANTILE BABYISH
INFANTRY FOOT FANTERIE
FOOTFOLK
INFANTRYMAN ASKAR ZOUAVE
DOGFACE DRAGOON DOUGHBOY
PIOUPIOU SOREFOOT
INFATUATE FOOL ASSOT
INFATUATED MAD FOND GONE
ASSOT CRAZY DOTTY ENGOUEE
FOOLISH BESOTTED
INFATUATION ATE RAVE CRUSH
FOLLY BEGUIN
(TRANSIENT —) CRAZE
INFECT SMIT TAINT CANKER DEFILE
EMPEST ENTACH INFEST POISON
CORRUPT DISEASE POLLUTE
SMITTLE
INFECTED FUNGUSED
(NOT —) BLAND
INFECTION COLD DOSE FELON
TAINT FUNGUS
INFECTIOUS TAKING SMITTLE
CATCHING SMITABLE SMITTING
VIRULENT
INFER DRAW PICK TAKE GUESS
JUDGE DECIDE DEDUCE DEDUCT
DERIVE DIVINE GATHER INDUCE
REASON COLLECT INCLUDE
PRESUME SURMISE CONCLUDE
CONSTRUE
INFERENCE EDUCT SEQUEL
ANALOGY SEQUELA ILLATION
SEQUENCE SEQUITUR
INFERIOR BAD BUM DOG ILL LOW
SAD EVIL LESS MEAN PUNK SLIM
SOUR WAFF BASER BAUCH BELOW
DOGGY GROSS LOWER PETTY PLAIN
SCALY SCRUB WORRY BEHIND
CAGMAG COMMON CRAPPY FEEBLE
FEMALE IMPURE LESSER MEASLY
PEDARY PUISNY ROTTEN SECOND
SHABBY WOODEN BADDISH CRIPPLE
HUMBLER NAGGISH POPULAR
SCRUBBY SUBJECT ABNORMAL
ANTERIOR DEROGATE ORDINARY
INFERIORITY LESSNESS MEANNESS
INFERNAL AVERNAL ETERNAL
HELLISH SATANIC SHEOLIC STYGIAN

CHTHONIC DAMNABLE DEVILISH
PLUTONIC
INFERTILE DEAD DEAF DOUR LEAN
POOR THIN CLEAR STERILE
INFEST COE VEX BESET INFECT
PESTER PLAGUE OVERRUN
TORMENT
INFESTATION SCALE PLAGUE
STRIKE LOAIASIS
INFESTED MITY BLOWN BROOD
BUGGY FLUKY FLUKED GRUBBY
HAUNTED FLYBLOWN
INFIDEL DEIST GIAOUR PAYNIM
ATHEIST SARACEN SKEPTIC
AGNOSTIC
INFIDELITY PERFIDY ADULTERY
TRAHISON
INFIELD INTOWN DIAMOND
INFILTRATE FILTER CRETIFY
COLONIZE
INFILTRATION SEEPAGE ADIPOSIS
INFINITE CHAOS COSMIC ENDLESS
ETERNAL IMMENSE
INFINITENESS ETERNITY
INFINITESIMAL PUNCTUAL
INFINITIVE SUPINE VERBID
INFINITY OLAM ANANTA ETERNITY
INFIRM LAME WEAK ANILE CRAZY
CRONK SHAKY CRANKY FEEBLE
SICKLY UNFIRM UNSURE CASALTY
CRAICHY DOWLESS DWAIBLE
FRAGILE INVALID SAPLESS UNFEARY
DODDERED FIRMLESS INSECURE
RESOLUTE UNSTRONG
INFIRMITY WOE CRAZE DOTAGE
FOIBLE UNHEAL DISEASE FAILING
FRAILTY UNMIGHT DEBILITY
SICKNESS WEAKNESS
INFIX INLAY INSET ENGRAVE
IMPLANT INGRAIN
INFIXED INHERENT
INFLAME BURN FIRE GOAD HEAT
STIR ANGER BLAIN FLAME SCALD
SHAME AROUSE ENAMOR EXCITE
FESTER IGNITE INCEND KINDLE
MADDEN RANKLE EMBRASE
FLUSTER INCENSE ESCHAUFE
INFLAMED RED ANGRY FIERY
ABLAZE FRETTY TORRID FLAGRANT
INFLAMMABLE FIERY ARDENT
TOUCHY PICEOUS TINDERY
INFLAMMATION FIRE ANGER FELON
GLEET SCALD SEBEL AGNAIL
BLIGHT CANKER DEFLUX GREASE
IRITIS AORITIS CATARRH CECITIS
CHAFING COLITIS COXITIS FISTULA
GONITIS ILEITIS QUITTOR SUNBURN
ADENITIS ANGIITIS BURSITIS
CHILITIS CYCLITIS CYSTITIS
SHINGLES
INFLATE HOVE HUFF KITE PLIM
BLOAT BOLNE HEAVE SWELL DILATE
EMBOSS EXPAND HUFFLE INBLOW
TUMEFY BLADDER BOMBAST
DISTEND FORBLOW OUTSWELL
SUFFLATE
INFLATED BLOWN FLOWN GASSY
PUFFY TUMID TURGID BOMBAST
FUSTIAN STILTED SWOLLEN

TURGENT BLADDERY OUTBLOWN
TUMOROUS VANITOUS
INFLATION FLATUS CADENCE
TYMPANY
INFLECT COMPARE DECLINE
INFLECTION SIGN ACCENT FLEXION
LATINISM
INFLECTIONAL FORMAL
INFLEXIBILITY ACAMPSIA
INFLEXIBLE ACID DOUR FIRM HARD
IRON EAGER SOLID STERN STIFF
STONY STOUR SEVERE STRICT
STUFFY ADAMANT RESTIVE
GRANITIC IRONCLAD OBDURATE
PREFRACT RESOLUTE RIGOROUS
STIFFISH STUBBORN
INFLICT DO ADD SET GIVE SEND
INFER YIELD IMPOSE RAMROD
STRIKE
(— CHASTISEMENT) WREAK
(— HURT) BRUISE
(— INJURY) AGGRIEVE
(— PAIN) LAY CHASTISE
INFLORESCENCE CHAT CYME
AMENT ARROW BRUSH SPIKE
UMBEL CORYMB FLOWER RACEME
SPADIX TASSEL PANICLE THYRSIS
CYATHIUM FASCICLE
INFLOW INSET INCOME INFLUX
INCOURSE
INFLUENCE IN WIN BEND BIAS COAX
DRAG DRAW HANK HEFT LEAD
MOVE PULL PUSH RULE SUCK SWAY
BRIBE CHARM COLOR ENACT FORCE
GRACE IMPEL MOYEN POWER
REACH SPELL VAPOR VOGUE WEIGH
AFFECT ALLURE CREDIT EFFECT
GOVERN IMPORT INDUCE INFLOW
INFLUX MOTIVE OBSESS PONDUS
SALUTE SHADOW STROKE WEIGHT
ATTINGE ATTRACT BEARING
BEWITCH BLARNEY BOSSDOM
CAPTURE CONCUSS CONTROL
DISPUTE ENCHANT GRAVITY
IMPRINT INCLINE INSPIRE MASTERY
TENDRIL DOMINION HEGEMONY
INTEREST LEVERAGE MEDICINE
PRESTIGE SANCTION STRENGTH
CAPTIVATE
(— BY GIFTS) GREASE
(— CORRUPTLY) BRIBE
(— OF GODS) MANA
(— OF THE STARS) BLAS
(— UNREASONABLY) OBSESS
(BENIGN —) UNCTION
(CONTROLLING —) SWAY
(CORRUPTING —) SMOUCH SMUTCH
(DEPRESSING —) CHILL
(DIABOLICAL —) DEVILDOM
(DISRUPTIVE —) GREMLIN
(DOMINANT —) GENIUS STREAM
(DULLING —) DAMPER
(ELEVATING —) LIFT
(HARMFUL —) UPAS GRUDGE
(INJURIOUS —) RUST
(MALEVOLENT —) DISASTER
(MALIGN —) TAKING
(PERNICIOUS —) BALE BLAST
(SINISTER —) MALICE

(SOOTHING —) SALVE
(SURROUNDING —) AIR
INFLUENCING INFUSIVE
INFLUENTIAL GRAVE POWERFUL
INFLUENZA FLU LEUMA GRIPPE
PINKEYE
INFLUX STORM INCOME INFLOW
INRUSH ILLAPSE
(— IN A MINE) COURSE
(— OF TIDE) INSET
INFOLD WRAP IMPLY TWINE EMPLOY
INWRAP ENVELOP INVOLVE
CONVOLVE
INFORM KEN BEEF BLOW FINK NOSE
POST SHOP SHOW TELL WARN WISE
LEARN PEACH ADVISE ASSURE
DELATE DETECT NOTIFY PREACH
SNITCH WITTER APPRISE EDUCATE
IMPEACH INSENSE PARTAKE
POSSESS RESOLVE SIGNIFY
SUGGEST ACQUAINT DENOUNCE
INFORMED INSTRUCT SPARSILE
INFORMAL BREEZY CASUAL CHATTY
COMMON FOLKSY TWEEDY
INTIMATE SLIPSHOD SOCIABLE
INFORMANT AUTHOR INFORMER
SYCOPHANT
INFORMATION AIR GEN OIL WIT
CLEW CLUE DOPE INFO LORE NEWS
NOTE TALE WIRE WORD DATUM
GRIFF SCOOP SKILL ADVICE INSIDE
LIGHTS NOTICE APPRISE PEMICAN
TIDINGS WITTING BRIEFING
NOTITION PEMMICAN
(BODY OF —) DIGEST
(SECRET —) ARCANUM
INFORMED UP HEP WISE AWARE
WITTY KNOWING LEARNED
INFORMER FINK NARK NOSE PIMP
STAG RUSTY SPLIT CANARY FINGER
SETTER SNITCH TELLER DELATOR
TANQUAM APPROVER PROMOTER
SQUAWKER SQUEAKER SQUEALER
TELLTALE
INFORTUNE MARS SATURN
INFRACTION BREACH OFFENCE
TRESPASS
INFRARED ULTRARED
INFREQUENCY SELDOMCY
INFREQUENT RARE SELDOM
FUGITIVE UNCOMMON
INFRINGE IMPOSE INVADE TRENCH
IMPINGE INFRACT INTRUDE
ENCROACH REFRINGE TRESPASS
INFRINGEMENT FOUL BREACH
TRESPASS VIOLENCE
INFRINGER PIRATE
INFULA FANON LABEL LAPPET
HEADBAND
INFUNDIBULUM FUNNEL PAVILION
INFURIATE ENRAGE ENFELON
INFUSE DRAW IMBUE IMMIT SPOIL
STEEP AERATE AERIFY IMMISS
INFLOW INFORM INFUND INVEST
LEAVEN BREATHE DISTILL ENGRAIN
IMPLANT INFOUND INSPIRE INSTILL
SUFFUSE SATURATE
(— TEA) TRACK
(— WITH HATRED) TURN

INFUSED SHOT
INFUSION SHADE CARDIN INCOME
TISANE HORDEATE
(— OF MALT) WORT GROUT
INFUSORIAN LEPOCYTE
INGA GUAVA
INGATE GATE LEDGE TEDGE
INGATHERING HARVEST
INGENIOUS SLY CUTE FAST FEAT
FINE ACUTE SHARP SMART ADROIT
BRAINY CLEVER CRAFTY DAEDAL
GIFTED KNACKY PRETTY SUBTLE
CUNNING SKILLFUL
INGENUITY ART WIT ENGINE
ADDRESS COMPASS ARTIFICE
CONTOISE INDUSTRY QUENTISE
INGENUOUS FREE FRANK NAIVE
PLAIN HONEST ARTLESS SINCERE
INNOCENT
INGENUOUSNESS NAIVETE
INGEST EAT INCEPT ENGLOBE
SWALLOW
INGESTION SLURP
INGOT GAD SOW WEDGE LINGOT
NIGGOT CROPHEAD
(— OF BRASS) STRIP
(— OF SILVER) SHOE TING SCHUYT
(SILVER —S) SYCEE
(SOAKING —S) HEAT
INGRAIN GRAIN INFUSE ENFLESH
INGRAINED INWORN
INGRATE SNAKE
INGRATIATE FLATTER
INGRATIATING BLAND SILKY SLEEK
SLICK SOAPY SILKEN SMOOTH
INGRATITUDE UNTHANK
INGREDIENT FACTOR BINDING
ELEMENT ADJUVANT
(ACTIVE —) ANIMA
(FUNDAMENTAL —) BASIS
(FUSIBLE —) BOND
(MAIN —) BASE
INGRESS ENTRY ENTRANCE
INGROWTH APODEMA
INGUEN GROIN
INHABIT BIG WIN WON COVER
DWELL HABIT BEDWELL INDWELL
POSSESS
INHABITANT INMATE BURGHER
CITIZEN DENIZEN DWELLER
PEOPLER BORDERER CONFINER
DEMESMAN HABITANT INCOLANT
INHOLDER
(— OF ALASKA) SOURDOUGH
(— OF BORDER REGION) MARCHER
(— OF CITY) CIT CITIZEN
(— OF INDIA) BHARATA
(— OF JUNGLE) JUNGLI
(— OF SWISS ALPS) GRISON
(— OF TORRID ZONE) ASCIAN
(— OF VIRGINIA) COOHEE
(— OF WISCONSIN) BADGER
(PL.) SIDE WARE
INHALATION SNUFF BREATH
INHALE DRAW TAKE SMOKE SNIFF
ATTRACT BREATHE INHAUST
INSPIRE RESPIRE ASPIRATE
INHALER SNIFTER
INHARMONIOUS ABSURD

INHERE CONSIST INEXIST
INHERENCE INBEING
INHERENT KIND INBORN INNATE
INWARD NATIVE PROPER INGENIT
HABITUAL IMMANENT INTEGRAL
INTERNAL RESIDENT
INHERIT HEIR SUCCEED
INHERITANCE KIND ENTAIL
HEIRDOM HEIRSHIP HEREDITY
HERITAGE LANDFALL VACANTIA
(— OF CATTLE) ERF
INHERITED INBORN INNATE
INHIBIT COOP CURB SNUB CRIMP
DETER FORBID STIFLE SUPPRESS
INHIBITED COLD
INHIBITION AKINESIS
INHIBITORY COLYTIC
INHOSPITABLE STERN DESERT
INHUMAN FELL CRUEL BRUTAL
FIERCE IMMANE SAVAGE BESTIAL
MANLESS DEVILISH KINDLESS
INHUMANE WANTON
INHUMANITY CRUELTY
INHUME BURY INTER ENTOMB
INIMICAL BAD FROSTY HOSTILE
INIQUITOUS ILL DARK WRONG
SINFUL WICKED
INIQUITY SIN EVIL VICE CRIME GUILT
DARKNESS MISCHIEF
INITIAL LETTER VIRGIN ASPIREE
(INTERWOVEN —S) CIPHER
(PL.) PERFINS
INITIATE HEAD MYST OPEN ADMIT
BEGIN BREAK ENTER EPOPT FOUND
START GROUND INDUCE INDUCT
INVENT LAUNCH MYSTES ORPHIC
BAPTIZE INSTALL INSTATE OPERATE
ORPHEAN SYMMIST COMMENCE
ESOTERIC INCHOATE
INITIATION DIKSHA OPENING
ENTRANCE
(— OF GROWTH) BUDBREAK
INITIATIVE PEP LEAD GETUP ACTION
AMBITION GUMPTION
INJECT DRIVE IMMIT
INJECTION HYPO SHOT BOOSTER
CLYSTER
INJUDICIOUS UNWISE
INJUDICIOUSNESS ACRISY
INJUNCTION HEST BEHEST CHARGE
IMPOSE BIDDING DICTATE EXPRESS
MANDATE PRECEPT
INJURE DO GAS ILL MAR BURN
CHEW ENVY GALL HARM HURT
MAUL TEEN WERD ABUSE BLAST
CRAZE DIRTY MISDO SCALD SHEND
SMITE SPOIL STEER WOUND WRONG
BRUISE DAMAGE DEFACE DEFECT
DEPAIR GRIEVE HINDER IMPAIR
INJURY MANGLE RANKLE SCATHE
SCOTCH STRAIN AFFLICT AFFRONT
CONTUSE DAMNIFY DESPITE
FORWORK MISBEDE TERRIFY
DISASTER DISSERVE IMPERISH
INTERESS MISCHIEF MISGUIDE
MUTILATE PREJUDGE SPURGALL
(— BY ASPERSION) SPATTER
(— BY FALSE REPORT) SLANDER
(— BY GLANCE OF BASILISK)
STRIKE

(— BY TREADING UPON) FITTER
(— SCENT) STAIN
(— SERIOUSLY) DO KILL SPOIL
(— SLIGHTLY) ANNOY
(— THE BACK) CHINK
INJURED HURT LESED BLASTED
INJURIOUS BAD ILL EVIL NOYANT
NOYFUL SHREWD ABUSIVE
HARMFUL HURTFUL NOXIOUS
DAMAGING GRIEVOUS SINISTER
TORTIOUS TORTUOUS WRACKFUL
WRONGFUL
INJURIOUSLY HEAVILY
INJURY ILL JAM MAR BANE BURN
EVIL HARM HURT JEEL LOSS RUIN
TEEN TORT WITE ABUSE BLAME
CHAFE CRUSH GRIEF SCALD SCORE
SPITE SPOIL TOUCH WATHE WRACK
WRONG BREACH BRUISE DAMAGE
DANGER IMPAIR LESION SCATHE
STRAIN STROKE TRAUMA BEATING
DESPITE EXPENSE OFFENSE
PAYMENT SCADDLE SCRATCH
SORANCE BUSINESS CASUALTY
CREPANCE INTEREST MISCHIEF
NUISANCE
(— OF HORSES) TREAD
(— OF PLANTS) SUNSCALD
(CHIEF —) FOCUS
(SERIOUS —) MAYHEM
INJUSTICE WRONG INJURY INJURIA
UNRIGHT HARDSHIP INEQUITY
(GROSS —) INIQUITY
INK BEAT COLOR ARNEMENT
ATRAMENT
INK-BALL DABBER PUMPET
INKER SLOSHER
INKING PAD TOMPION
INKLE SPINEL
INKLING HINT ITEM SCENT GLIMMER
GLIMPSE
INKSTAND STANDISH
INKWELL FOUNT INKSTAND
INLAID PIQUE CONTISE
(— WORK) KOFTGARI
INLAND MAUKA INMORE INWARD
MIDLAND INTERIOR
INLAY PICK PIKE COUCH HATCH
INLET PIQUE SPELL CRUSTA
ENAMEL IMPAVE INDENT NIELLO
TARSIA ENCHASE ENCRUST
INCRUST COMMESSO
INLAYING TARKASHI
INLET ARM BAY CUT GEO RIA VOE
COVE DOCK HOPE MERE SLEW
WICK BAYOU BRACE CHUCK CREEK
FIORD FJORD FLEET HAVEN LOGAN
LOUGH STOMA ESTERO HARBOR
INFALL SLOUGH DOGHOLE INDRAFT
SUCTION CALANQUE SEAPOOSE
(— OF THE SEA) EA
(MUDDY —) SUMP
(TIDAL —) GAP
INLIER WINDOW
INLYING INNERLY
INMATE FISH LODGER TENANT
BEADSMAN DOMESTIC PRISONER
INMOST SECRET RETIRED
INN PUB KHAN STOP VENT ANGEL

FONDA HOTEL MESON TAMBO
VENTA CABACK HARBOR HOSTEL
HOSTRY IMARET POSADA PUBLIC
SHANTY ALBERGE AUBERGE
BOLICHE CAFENEH CAFENET
FONDACO FONDOUK HOSTAGE
LOCANDA OSTERIA SOJOURN
SURAHEE CHOULTRY GASTHAUS
HOSTELRY ORDINARY SERAGLIO
WAYHOUSE
INNARDS GIZZARD INWARDS
STUFFING
INNATE BORN KIND INBORN INBRED
CONNATE INGRAIN NATURAL
INSTINCT
(— QUALITY) LARGESS
INNER BEN ENTAL INSIDE INWARD
INWITH MENTAL INTERIOR INTERNAL
PECTORAL
(— LIGHT) SEED
INNERMOST UPPER INMOST
INTIMATE
INNINA ISHTAR
INNING END HAND HEAD FRAME
(PL.) KNOCK
INNKEEPER HOST DUENA TAPPER
VENTER GOODMAN HOSTESS
HOSTLER PADRONE BONIFACE
(PL.) CAUPONES
INNOCENCE BLUET WHITE CANDOR
PURITY
INNOCENT SOT FREE PURE CLEAR
SEELY WHITE CHASTE DOVISH
HONEST SIMPLE CHRISOM LAMBKIN
UPRIGHT HARMLESS IGNORANT
PASTORAL PRIMROSE SACKLESS
UNGUILTY ZACCHEUS
INNOCUOUS HARMLESS INNOCENT
INNOVATE NOVELIZE
INNOVATION NOVEL NOVELTY
INNOVATOR HERETIC
INNUENDO HINT SLUR SLIPE
INNUMERABLE MYRIAD
INO (FATHER OF —) CADMUS
(HUSBAND OF —) ATHAMAS
(MOTHER OF —) HARMONIA
INOCULATE SEED PLANT INFUSE
ENGRAFT EQUINATE
INOCULUM STAB STREAK
INOFFENSIVE HARMLESS
INOPERATIVE OFF DEAD NUGATORY
INOPPORTUNE UNTIMELY
INORDINATE WILD UNDUE
ENORMOUS
INORGANIC MINERAL
INOSITOL DAMBOSE
INPOURING INFLUX
INQUEST CROWN QUEST ASSIZE
OFFICE INQUIRY
INQUIET UNEASY
INQUILINE GUEST
INQUIRE ASK AXE SEEK QUERY
SPERE DEMAND FRAYNE SEARCH
EXAMINE HEARKEN QUESTION
INQUIRER ASKER QUERENT
INQUIRY PROBE QUERY THANK
TRIAL DEMAND EXAMEN TRACER
DOCIMASY QUESTION RESEARCH
SCRUTINY SPEERING

INQUISITION CUSTOM INQUIRY
QUAESTIO
INQUISITIVE NOSY PEERY PRYING
CURIOUS MEDDLING
INROAD RAID BREACH INBREAK
INVASION
INSALUBRIOUS NOXIOUS
INSANE MAD WUD DAFT WOOD
BALMY BATTY BUGGY CRAZY DIPPY
QUEER WRONG CRANKY LOCOED
SCREWY FLIGHTY FRANTIC FURIOUS
LUNATIC WITLESS BUGHOUSE
DEMENTED DERANGED DISTRACT
INSANITY RAGE CRACK CRAZE
FOLIE MANIA FRENZY LUNACY
MADNESS VESANIA DELIRIUM
DEMENTIA WOODNESS PSYCHOSIS
INSATIABLE GREEDY
INSCRIBE DELVE ENTER WRITE
BLAZON DOCKET INDITE LEGEND
LETTER SCRIBE SCRIVE SCROLL
ASCRIBE ENDORSE ENGROSS
DEDICATE DESCRIBE EMBLAZON
ENSCROLL INTITULE
INSCRIBED INWRIT WRITTEN
DESCRIPT
INSCRIPTION HEAD ELOGY CACHET
LEGEND LETTER ELOGIUM EPIGRAM
EPITAPH MENTION TITULUS WRITING
COLOPHON EPIGRAPH GRAFFITO
INSCRIPT SCRIBING
(— ON TOMBSTONE) ELOGE
ELOGIUM
(3-LETTER —) TRIGRAM
INSCRUTABLE EQUIVOCAL
INSECT ANT BEE BUG DOR DUN ELF
FLY NIT ANER FLEA GNAT GOGO
GYNE MOTH PELA PEST PUPA SPIT
WASP WETA ZIMB APHID APHIS
BICHO BORER FLYER GOGGA GUEST
IMAGO LOUSE MINER ROACH SCALE
BEETLE BLIGHT CALLOW CICADA
CIXIID EARWIG EMBIID HAWKER
HOPPER INSTAR MANTIS NITTER
PODURA SAPPER SAWFLY THRIPS
VERMIN WALKER WEEVIL ATTACUS
BLATTID BOATMAN BUZZARD
CRAWLER CREEPER CRICKET
CYNIPID DEALATE DRUMMER
EARWORM FIREBUG FIREFLY
GALLFLY GIRDLER GRAYFLY
HEXAPOD JAPYGID KATYDID
SANDBOY SCINIPH SKIPPER
SPECTRE STAINER STYLOPS
TERMITE VAGRANT WEBWORM
ALDERFLY ALKERMES BLACKFLY
BRACONID FIREBRAT FULGORID
GLOWWORM HOMOPTER HORNTAIL
LACEWING LECANIUM PRONYMPH
SEMIPUPA SEXUPARA SPHECOID
STINKBUG STYLOPID SYMPHILE
INSECTICIDE DDD DDT DIP CUBE
FLIT ALDRIN DERRIS ENDRIN
CALOMEL ISODRIN LINDANE OVICIDE
CHLORDAN CULICIDE DIELDRIN
SCHRADAN
INSECTIVORE MOONRAT ALAMIQUI
INSECURE DICKY EEMIS LOOSE
SHAKY INFIRM TICKLE UNFAST

UNSAFE UNSURE CASALTY
INSEMINATE BREED
INSENSATE SURD FATUOUS
INSENSIBILITY DAMP APATHY
TORPOR
INSENSIBLE DEAR DULL LOST NUMB
BRUTE DENSE SEARED DATELESS
INSENSITIVE BLUNT STONY STUPID
BOORISH
INSEPARABLE WRAPPED
INSERT SLIP SPUD STOP BOTCH
DICKY ENROL ENTER FUDGE IMMIT
INFER INFIX INLET INSET STUFF
COLLET GUSSET INWORK INWEAVE
GATEFOLD INTROMIT SANDWICH
SLASHING SUBTRUDE THROWOUT
(— **IN SHOE**) CUSHION
(— **SURREPTITIOUSLY**) FOIST
INSERTION FLOWER BEADING
INSET GODET INSERT
INSHEATHE EMBOSS
INSIDE IN BEN ATHIN INBYE INNER
INWITH KEYHOLE INTERIOR
(— **OF ANGLE BAR**) BOSOM
(— **OF OUTER EAR**) BUR BURR
INSIDIOUS SLY SNARY COVERT
SUBTLE GUILEFUL
INSIGHT KEN SIGHT APERCU
THEORY NOSTRIL
INSIGNIA ORDER SIGNS COLLAR
GEORGE CADUCEUS COMMENDA
HERALDRY OPINICUS
INSIGNIFICANT NULL POOR PUNY
DINKY FOOTY PETIT PETTY POTTY
SMALL HUMBLE NAUGHT PALTRY
PUISNE SIMPLE SLIGHT FOOLISH
NAUGHTY NIFLING PELTING PIMPING
SCRUBBY TENUOUS TRIVIAL
BAUBLING INFERIOR PEDDLING
PITIABLE SNIPPING TRIFLING
TRIPENNY
INSINCERE FALSE DOUBLE FEIGNED
INSINCERITY ARTIFICE DISGUISE
INSINUATE HINT MINT WIND CRAWL
SCREW TWIST ALLUDE GLANCE
INFUSE INSTIL WRITHE IMPLANT
INNUATE
INSINUATING SNIDE SILKEN
SMARMY
INSINUATION HINT INKLING
INSIPID DRY WAW DEAD FADE FLAT
FOND FOZY TAME BANAL BAUCH
BLAND FLASH INANE PROSY STALE
VAPID WALSH WAUGH FLASHY
FRIGID JEJUNE SWASHY THREEP
WAIRSH WALLOW EXOLETE
FATUOUS INSULSE PROSAIC
SAPLESS SHILPIT WEARISH WEERISH
LIFELESS UNSAVORY WATERISH
INSIST AVER CONSIST
(— **PEEVISHLY**) CRAIK
(— **UPON**) SOLICIT
INSISTENCE URGENCY INSTANCY
INSISTENT ADAMANT INSTANT
EMPHATIC FRENZIED IMPOSING
INSOLE CUSHION SLIPSOLE
INSOLENCE CHEEK PRIDE SNASH
DISDAIN AUDACITY SURQUIDY
INSOLENT FACY PERT RUDE WISE

BARDY LUSTY LORDLY WANTON
ABUSIVE DEFIANT PAUGHTY
ARROGANT IMPUDENT PETULANT
SCORNFUL
INSOLUBLE HOPELESS
INSOMNIA AHYPNIA AGRYPNIA
INSOUCIANT CAVALIER
INSPECT SEE VET CASE ESPY LOOK
BRACK CHECK SIGHT VISIT INLOOK
PERUSE SURVEY EXAMINE OVERSEE
CONSIDER OVERLOOK OVERVIEW
(— **CASUALLY**) BROWSE
(— **COINS**) SHROFF
(— **MERCHANDISE IN BALTIC**)
BRACK
INSPECTION EYE PRY VIEW CHECK
SIGHT REVIEW SURVEY BEDIKAH
CHECKUP INSIGHT INSPECT
PERUSAL VIDIMUS OVERVIEW
SCRUTINY
INSPECTOR SAYER SNOOP BISHOP
CENSOR CONNER JUMPER LOOKER
VIEWER GRAINER MOOCHER
PERCHER SAMPLER SNOOPER
VEADORE EXAMINER SEARCHER
(— **OF COAL**) KEEKER
(— **OF COTTON LOOMS**) TACKLER
(— **OF ELECTRIC LAMPS**) AGER
INSPIRATION FIRE SIGH POESY
ANIMUS SPIRIT SPRITE IMPULSE
MADNESS AFFLATUS INFLATUS
INSPIRE FIRE MOVE CHEER ELATE
EXALT SPARK BEACON INBLOW
INCUSS INDUCE INFORM INFUSE
KINDLE PROMPT ACTUATE ANIMATE
EMBRAVE ENFORCE ENLIVEN
HEARTEN IMPLANT PREMOVE
QUICKEN SUGGEST CATALYZE
ENTALENT INSPIRIT MOTIVATE
SUFFLATE
INSPIRED AFFLATED ENTHEATE
VISIONED
INSPIRER SOUL
INSPIRING INFUSIVE STIRRING
INSPIRIT CHEER HEART ROUSE
SPIRIT ANIMATE CHERISH COMFORT
ENLIVEN HEARTEN INSPIRE QUICKEN
ALACRIFY
INSPISSATE STIFFEN THICKEN
INSPISSATED STIFF THICK
INSTABILITY SLIDDER FLUIDITY
INSTALL SEAT CHAIR STALL INDUCT
INVEST ENSTOOL POSSESS
ENTHRONE INITIATE
INSTALLATION INDUCTION
(— **OF MINISTER**) INFARE
(**MILITARY** —) GARRISON
INSTALLMENT KIST SERIAL
EARNEST CONTRACT
(— **OF WAGES**) COMPO
(— **SELLER**) TALLYMAN
(**FIRST** —) HANDSEL
(**NEXT** —) SEQUEL
INSTANCE CASE PINK SAMPLE
EXAMPLE PURPOSE ENSAMPLE
EXEMPLAR
(**EXTREME** —) CAPSHEAF
INSTANT POP HINT WHIP WINK
BLICK CLINK CRACK FLASH GLENT

GLIFF GLISK JIFFY POINT SHAKE
SOUND START TRICE WHIFF WIGHT
BREATH FLIFFY MINUTE MOMENT
SECOND PRESENT CLIFFING
(**PRECISE** —) TIME
INSTANTANEOUS PRESTO
DIRECTLY
INSTANTLY SLAP SWITH SWITHE
DIRECTLY MOMENTLY
INSTAR STAGE
INSTEAD EITHER
INSTEP WRIST TARSUS
INSTIGATE EGG ABET GOAD MOVE
SPUR URGE IMPEL ATTICE ENTICE
EXCITE FOMENT INCITE INDUCE
INVOKE PROMPT SPIRIT SUBORN
INCENSE INSTINCT
INSTIGATION MOTION MOTIVE
EGGMENT INSTANCE INSTINCT
INSTIGATOR AUTHOR MOTIVE
SOURCE MONITOR
INSTILL GRAFT INFIX IMPART INFUSE
INSTIL BREATHE IMPLANT
INSTINCT KIND FILLED CHARGED
IMPULSE CAPACITY TENDENCY
INSTINCTIVE INNATE NATURAL
INHERENT ORIGINAL
INSTITUTE BRING ERECT FOUND
RAISE STUDY INVENT KINDLE
ORDAIN ACTIVATE
(— **MEMBER**) PIARIST
INSTITUTION BANK CAMP FOLD
CLINIC FRIARY SCHOOL ACADEMY
CHARITY COLLEGE GALLERY
JUBILEE LIBRARY SHELTER STATION
VERITAS SEMINARY
(— **FOR INSANE**) ASYLUM
(**CHARITABLE** —) SPITTLE
DEACONRY HOSPITAL
(**DRUIDICAL** —) GORSEDD
INSTRUCT KEN REAR SHOW WISE
COACH DRILL EDIFY ENDUE GUIDE
TEACH TRAIN CHARGE DIRECT
GROUND INDUCE INFORM LESSON
PREACH REFORM SCHOOL
COMMAND EDUCATE INSENSE
POSSESS DOCUMENT
INSTRUCTED SCIENCED
INSTRUCTION LORE ADVICE ASSIZE
CHARGE LESSON COUNSEL
PRECEPT TUITION WISSING
COACHING DOCTRINE DOCUMENT
MONITION PEDAGOGY PROPHECY
TEACHING TUTELAGE
(**DIVINE** —) LAW
(**SACRED** —) TORAH
(**PL.**) BRIEFING
INSTRUCTIVE DOCENT DIDACTIC
INSTRUCTOR DON SOAK SCREW
TUTOR MENTOR REGENT ACHARYA
CRAMMER TEACHER BEACHBOY
CHAIRMAN ELDERMAN
INSTRUMENT (ALSO SEE MUSICAL
INSTRUMENT) DEED TOOL WRIT
AGENT SLANG THEME FACTUM
UTENSIL SYNGRAPH
(— **NOT UNDER SEAL**) PAROL
(— **OF DESTRUCTION**) SWORD
(— **OF DIVINATION**) EPHOD

(— OF TORTURE) BOOT RACK
BRAKE BRANK FURCA GADGE
WHEEL TUMBREL BARNACLE
SQUEEZER
(—S OF WAR) ENGINERY
(FINANCIAL —) ITEM
(LEGAL —) DEED GRANT FACTUM
SASINE SCRIPT CHARTER CODICIL
DUPLICATE
(NEGOTIABLE —) HUNDI HOONDEE
(OFFICIAL —) SLANG
(PREHISTORIC —) CELT
(SCIENTIFIC OR OTHER —) AWL FAN
HOE KEY MET RAX SAX BROG
COMB DIAL DRAG FILE FORK GAGE
HOOK PLOW RACK RING SPAR
ARMIL BEVEL BLADE BRACE BRAKE
CHAIN CLAMP DATER DOLLY DRILL
FLAIL FLOAT FLUKE GAUGE GLASS
INDEX KNIFE LADLE LEVER METER
PILOT RAZOR SCALE SCOPE SLATE
SLICE SLING SPADE SPEAR SPRAY
STAMP STEEL SWIFT THROW TONGS
TUNER WHISK ABACUS BEETLE
BODKIN BRIDGE CIRCLE DOUCHE
ENGINE ERASER FERULE FOLDER
GRATER LEAPER MORTAR NEEDLE
PESTLE PICKER PLOUGH PULLER
PUMPER RAMMER RASPER RATTLE
RUBBER SCALER SCORER SCRIBE
SCUTCH SCYTHE SHEARS SQUARE
SQUIRT STADIA STRAIK STROBE
STYLET STYLUS TACKLE TICKER
WIMBLE ALIDADE BELLOWS
BREAKER CADRANS CLEAVER
COMPASS DIOPTER DOLABRA
DOUBLER FISTUCA GRAFTER
GRAINER GRAPPLE HATCHEL
LAYOVER MEASURE MEASURE
OOMETER OOSCOPE PAVIOUR
PELORUS PIERCER PINCERS
PRICKER PRINTER PYROPEN
QUADRAT SCRAPER SEXTANT
SHOCKER SHUTTLE SLITTER
SOUNDER SPLAYER SPRAYER
STRIGIL SUNDIAL SWINGLE
TRAMMEL TRIMMER WHISTLE
ANALEMMA ATOMIZER BIRDCALL
BLOWPIPE BUTTERIS CALLIPER
COALRAKE DECAPPER DETECTOR
DIAGRAPH DIPMETER DIVIDERS
EQUULEUS ERGMETER EXPLORER
FATHOMER GEOPHONE HOROLOGE
IMPINGER ISOGRAPH ISOSCOPE
JOVILABE MESOLABE MHOMETER
ODOMETER OHMMETER PHOTOMER
QUADRANT RECORDER RINGHEAD
RUMMAGER SCISSORS SEARCHER
SQUEEGEE STILETTO STRICKLE
TJANTING TRIANGLE VELLINCH
VIAGRAPH YAWMETER
(SURGICAL OR MEDICAL —) GAG
HOOK SPUD FLEAM PROBE SCOOP
SNARE SOUND STAFF STYLE BILABE
BOUGIE BROACH GORGET LANCET
SEEKER TREPAN TROCAR UNGULA
VECTIS XYSTER AIRDENT DILATER
FORCEPS HARPOON LEVATOR
LIGATOR MYOTOME PELICAN

PLUGGER RONGEUR SCALPEL
SOUNDER SYRINGE TRACTOR
TRILABE TURNKEY ANOSCOPE
AURILAVE AXOMETER BISTOURY
DIRECTOR DIVULSOR ECRASEUR
ELEVATOR EXSECTOR HEMOSTAT
KERATOME MYOGRAPH SPECULUM
TREPHINE
INSTRUMENTAL MEDIATE ORGANIC
SERVILE SERVIENT
INSTRUMENTALIST KLEZMER
SIDEMAN
INSTRUMENTALITY HAND MEANS
AGENCY MEDIUM CHANNEL COUNCIL
MINISTRY
(— FOR ACQUISITION OF
KNOWLEDGE) ORGANON
(NAVAL —S) BEACH
INSUBORDINATE FACTIOUS
MUTINOUS UNWIELDY
INSUBORDINATION MUTINY
INSUBSTANTIAL AIRY INANE
FROTHY SLENDER SPECTRAL
INSUBSTANTIALITY FRAILTY
INSUFFICIENCY PAUCITY
INSUFFICIENT POOR WANE SHORT
SCANTY
INSUFFICIENTLY BARELY FEEBLY
THINLY
INSULATE ISLE ISLAND ISOLATE
INSULATION LAGGING ISOLATION
INSULATOR NOB KNOB TAPLET
VITRITE MEGOHMIT
(PL.) STRING
INSULT CAG FIG JOEY RUMP SLAP
ABUSE CHECK FLOUT FRUMP SLANG
INJURE INJURY OFFEND OUTRAY
RUFFLE SCRAPE ABUSION AFFRONT
OFFENCE OUTRAGE BRICKBAT
DISHONOR CONTUMELY
INSULTING RUDE ARROGANT
INSOLENT
INSULTINGLY FOULLY
INSURANCE LINE CHOMAGE
COVERAGE INDEMNITY
(— AGENT) TWISTER
(UNEMPLOYMENT —) DOLE
INSURE COVER ASSURE ENSURE
FURNISH
INSURGENT REBEL RISER CHOUAN
OAKBOY TAIPING BARRABAS
CAMISARD STEELBOY
INSURRECTION RIST MUTINY
REVOLT UPROAR OUTBREAK
SEDITION UPRISING
INSURRECTO GUGU
INTACT SOUND WHOLE ENTIRE
INTAGLIO ENTAIL DIAGLYPH
(PART OF —) INCAVO
INTANGIBLE VAGUE SUBTLE
AERIFORM SLIPPERY
INTEGER SUM NORM TOTITIVE
INTEGRAL FLUX NEEDFUL
INTEGRANT ELEMENT
INTEGRATE FUSE PIECE COMBINE
FULFILL
INTEGRATED FUSED INTEGRAL
INTEGRATION BALANCE HARMONY
INTEGRITY HONOR TRUTH HONESTY

JUSTICE PROBITY CHASTITY
STRENGTH
INTEGUMENT KEX SKIN TESTA
TUNIC SWATHE CUTICLE ENVELOP
EPIDERM EXODERM PRIMINE
TUNICLE EPISPERM PERISARC
SCABBARD
INTELLECT MIND HEART INWIT
MAHAT SKILL BRAINS NOTICE
REASON SPIRITS THINKING
(HIGHEST —) NOUS
INTELLECTUAL BLUE GAON IDEAL
BOOKSY MENTAL SOPHIC BRAHMIN
EGGHEAD GNOSTIC CEREBRAL
LONGHAIR SOPHICAL DIANOETIC
INTELLIGENCE AIR CIT SAT CHIT
KNOW MIND NEWS NOTE WORD
AGIEL SENSE ADVICE BRAINS
ESPRIT INGENY NOTICE WITTING
(— IN EGYPTIAN LORE) CHU
(— OF PLANET JUPITER) JOPHIEL
(LIVELY —) WIT
INTELLIGENT APT GASH PERT
ACUTE ALERT SMART SPACK
AKAMAI BRAINY BRIGHT CLEVER
MENTAL SPRACK WITFUL KNOWING
INFORMED LUMINOUS RATIONAL
SKILLFUL
INTELLIGENTSIA CLERISY
INTELLIGIBLE CLEAR PLAIN
LUMINOUS PELLUCID PERVIOUS
REVELANT
INTELLIGIBLY SIMPLY
INTEMPERANCE ACRASY EXCESS
ACRASIA OUTRAGE
INTEMPERATE SHRILL SURFEIT
(NOT —) SWEET
INTEND GO AIM FIX CAST MEAN
MIND MINT PLAN PLOT TEND ALLOT
ALLOW ETTLE TIGHT ATTEND
DESIGN RECKON BEHIGHT DESTINE
FORELAY PRETEND PROPOSE
PURPORT PURPOSE FOREMIND
MEDITATE PRETENSE
INTENDED SUPPOSED
INTENSE HOT ACID COLD DEEP
HARD HIGH KEEN BLANK DENSE
GREAT HEAVY QUICK SHARP TENSE
VIVID ARDENT BRAZEN FIERCE
INTENT PITCHY STRONG BURNING
CHARGED CHRONIC CUTTING
EXTREME FERVENT FRANTIC
FURIOUS VIOLENT EGYPTIAN
GRIEVOUS POWERFUL SEETHING
VEHEMENT
INTENSELY STIFF HIGHLY ACUTELY
CURSEDLY FERVIDLY SHREWDLY
INTENSIFIED ACUTE
INTENSIFY RISE URGE EXALT RAISE
ACCENT DEEPEN BOLSTER
ENFORCE ENHANCE IMPROVE
INFLAME SHARPEN THICKEN
CONDENSE HEIGHTEN INCREASE
INTENSION INTENT MEANING
INTENSITY EDGE HEAT ARDOR
DEPTH DRIVE FEVER FIELD DEGREE
DOSAGE FERVOR FRENZY STRESS
CURRENT FEROCITY STRENGTH
VIOLENCE

INTENSIVE HARD HIGH EXTENDED
INTENSIVELY HARD SOLIDLY
INTENT SET DEEP DOLE FELL HENT
MIND TENT BEADY CAUSE DRIFT
ETTLE FIXED HEART PRICK SCOPE
TENOR TENSE EFFECT SPIRIT
COUNSEL INTENSE PRESENT
STUDIED WISTFUL
(**CRIMINAL —**) DOLE
(**EVIL —**) DOLUS
INTENTION AIM END GOAL HENT
MIND WILL HEART SCOPE ANIMUS
ATTENT DESIGN DEVICE EFFECT
INTENT OBJECT REGARD COUNSEL
COURAGE EARNEST FORESET
MEANING PROPOSE PURPORT
PURPOSE SUPPOSE PRETENSE
INTENTIONAL SET WILLFUL WILLING
WITTING INTENDED
INTENTLY BUSILY WISHLY EAGERLY
FIXEDLY
INTER BURY EARTH ENTER GRAVE
PLANT ENTOMB INHUME INEARTH
INTERACTION COUPLING
INTERAGENT MEDIUM MIDDLER
INTERBREED CROSS
INTERBREEDING APOGAMY
MIXTURE PANMIXY CROSSING
INTERCALATE INSERT
INTERCALATION EMBOLISM
INTERCEPT KEP HEAD KEEP STOP
CATCH NORMAL TRAMMEL
GAINCOPE INTERPEL RETRENCH
INTERCEPTION CUTOFF
INTERCESSION MOYEN DIPTYCH
PLEADING
INTERCESSOR MEANS PLEADER
ADVOCATE MEDIATOR
INTERCHANGE CHANGE ANAGRAM
COMMUTE PERMUTE COMMERCE
EXCHANGE
(**— OF OPINION**) COUNSEL
(**— OF WORDS**) SPEECH
INTERCHANGEABLE FUNGIBLE
INTERCOLUMNIATION EUSTYLE
SYSTYLE DIASTYLE
INTERCOMMUNICATION LIAISON
INTERCONNECTED SYNDETIC
INTERCONNECTION BONDING
INTERCOURSE GAM DEAL MANG
MONG TRADE TRUCK TURGY
BAWDRY HOBNOB NEGOCE COITION
DEALING MIXTURE QUARTER
SOCIETY TRAFFIC BUSINESS
COMMERCE CONVERSE RECOURSE
INTERDICT BAN TABU TABOO
FORBID UTRUBI INHIBIT PROHIBIT
SUPPRESS
INTERDICTION VETO
INTEREST BUG DIP FAD USE BENT
GOOD HAND HOLD PART CLOSE
COLOR DRIVE FAVOR FETCH GAVEL
HOBBY RIGHT STAKE STUDY USAGE
USURA USURY BEHALF ENGAGE
EQUITY ESTATE FAENUS FERVOR
FINGER INCOME USANCE ATTRACT
CONCERN RESPECT USAUNCE
CONTANGO INCREASE VIGORISH
(**— OF HUSBAND**) CURTESY

(**— ON LAND**) CLOSE
(**ACTIVE —**) SYMPATHY
(**LEGAL —**) EASEMENT
(**POLITICAL —**) FENCE
(**SECURITY —**) LIEN
(**SPECIAL —**) ANGLE
INTERESTED HIPPED ENGAGED
SERIOUS
INTERESTING FRUITY CURIOUS
STORIED
INTERFERE CUT MAKE ANNOY
BLOCK CHECK HITCH POACH
BAFFLE HAMPER HINDER HOBBLE
IMPEDE MEDDLE STRIKE TAMPER
INTRUDE INTROMIT
(**— SLIGHTLY**) BRUSH
(**— WITH**) AIL JOLT HECKLE
BLANKET DISTURB
INTERFERENCE BALK CHOKE
THUMP HINDER JOSTLE MEDDLE
CONFLICT FREINAGE
INTERFERING CUT
INTERFEROMETER ETALON
INTERFLUVE DOAB
INTERIM BREAK VACANCY
INTERIOR BEN BELLY BOSOM INNER
ENTIRE INLAND INWARD INWITH
MIDDLE GIZZARD ENTRAILS
INTERNAL
(**— OF CUPOLA**) CALOTTE
(**— OF TEMPLE**) CELLA
(**— OF VESSEL**) HOLD
(**— PART**) MANTLE
INTERJECT ENTER SQUIB INJECT
THRUST
INTERJECTION AW ER HA LO FIE
GEE GIP HAH HEH HEY AHEM AHOY
ALAS EGAD FORE GOSH HECH HOLA
JOVE GOODY HEIGH MAFEY SUGAR
TENEZ EUREKA HARROW OUTCRY
LACKADAY
INTERLACE LACE WARP BRAID
WEAVE ENLACE PLEACH INWEAVE
WREATHE
INTERLACED BRACED FRETTED
PLEACHED
INTERLACEMENT KNOT
INTERLACING TWINY
INTERLINING DOUBLER
INTERLOCK KNIT LOCK PITCH
ENGAGE FINGER TANGLE DOVETAIL
INTERLOPE INTRUDE
INTERLUDE JEST COMEDY VERSET
TEMACHA TRIUMPH ENTRACTE
ENTREMES RITORNEL VERSETTE
(**ROMANTIC —**) IDYL IDYLL
INTERMEDDLER STRANGER
INTERMEDDLING GESTION
INTERMEDIARY MEAN AGENT
MOYENER MEDIATOR TRAMPLER
INTERMEDIATE MEAN MESNE
FILLER ISATIN MEDIAL MEDIUM
MIDDLE MIDDLING
INTERMEDIATOR BROKER
INTERMENT BURIAL BURYING
DEPOSIT HUMATION
INTERMINABLE ETERNAL INFINITE
TIMELESS UNENDING
INTERMINGLE MIX BRAID IMMINGLE

INTERMIT INTERMIX
INTERMINGLED AMONG AMONGST
INTERMISSION REST WAIT BREAK
DWELL PAUSE DEVALL RECESS
NOONING RELACHE RESPITE
INTERVAL SURCEASE VACATION
(**— OF PAIN**) SABBATH
INTERMISSIVE CESSANT
INTERMIT CEASE DEFER DEVAUL
SUSPEND
INTERMITTENT BROKEN FITFUL
PERIODIC
INTERMIX MEDLEY MINGLE
INTERMIXTURE INTIMACY
INTERNAL INLY INNER ENTIRE
INLAND INNATE INSIDE INWARD
DOMESTIC
INTERNALLY INLY INSIDE INWARD
INWARDLY
INTERNODE ROSETTE
INTERPELLATION FLOWER
INTERPENETRATED SHOT
INTERPLAY AUSPICE
INTERPOLATE FARCE FARSE FOIST
FUDGE INSERT THRUST
INTERPOLATION GAG FARSE
INTERPOSE BAR CHOP DEMUR
OBJECT THRUST THWART MEDIATE
INTERPRET MAKE OPEN READ SCAN
TAKE AREAD AREED FANCY GLOSS
GLOZE RECHE DEFINE DIVINE
INTEND CLARIFY COMMENT
DECLARE ENGLISH EXPLAIN
EXPOUND CONSTRUE DECIPHER
SIMPLIFY
INTERPRETATION REDE GLOSS
SENSE GOSPEL STRAIN ANAGOGE
BARAITA COMMENT EPIKEIA
CABALISM EXEGESIS INNUENDO
SOLARISM SOLUTION
INTERPRETER BROKER DUBASH
UNDOER EXEGETE LATINER
MUNCHEE CABALIST DRAGOMAN
EXPONENT LINKSTER TRUCHMAN
(**— OF SCRIPTURE**) TROPIST
(**PL.**) HAHAM SELLI SELLOI
CHOCHEM HAKAMIM
INTERRELATED INTIMATE
INTERRELATIONSHIP ACCORD
LIAISON COMMERCE
INTERROGATE ASK TARGE DEBRIEF
EXAMINE INQUIRE
INTERROGATION EROTESIS
QUESTION
INTERRUPT CUT MAR NIP CHOP
STOP TAKE BREAK CHECK CRACK
EMBAR ARREST DERAIL DERANGE
DISRUPT FORBREAK INTERMIT
INTERPEL OBSTRUCT
INTERRUPTED BROKEN CHOPPY
SNATCHY
INTERRUPTER BUZZER
INTERRUPTION CESS JUMP STOP
BLOCK BREAK CHECK DWELL LAPSE
PAUSE BREACH HIATUS HOCKET
HOQUET ISLAND CAESURA CUTBACK
DIASTEM BLOCKING BREAKAGE
SOLUTION STOPOVER
(**WITHOUT —**) FLUSH

INTERRUPTOR TIKKER BREAKER
CHOPPER RHEOTOME
INTERSECT CUT CROSS BISECT
INCISE CROSSCUT
INTERSECTING CRUCIAL COMPITAL
INTERSECTION LEET CHINE CROSS
CURVE CHIASMA CROSSING
CROSSWAY JUNCTION
INTERSEXUAL EPICENE
INTERSEXUALITY GYNANDRY
INTERSPACE SPACE POCKET
INTERSPERSE DOT SALT SHED
MEDDLE THREAD CHECKER
INTERSOW SPRINKLE
INTERSTICE PORE SEAM CHINK
GRATE AREOLA RIFFLE CELLULE
VACUITY
(PL.) CANCELLI
INTERSTRATIFY INTERBED
INTERTWINE KNIT LACE WARP
TWINE FELTER TANGLE WAMPLE
WARPLE WRITHE ENSNARL
COMPLECT INTERTEX
INTERTWINED INWOUND
INTERVAL GAP LAG CENT GULF
REST SAND SEXT SPOT STEP BLANK
BREAK COMMA CYCLE FIFTH LAPSE
QUINT SIXTH SPACE SWING TENTH
THIRD BREACH DECIMA DEGREE
DIESIS DITONE FOURTH MERLON
SECOND SYSTEM ADVANCE
DIASTEM DISCORD HEADWAY
HEMIOLA INTERIM PASTIME RESPITE
SCHISMA SETTIMO STADIUM
TRITONE DIAPASON DIAPENTE
DISTANCE ELEVENTH ENTRACTE
FONTANEL
(— **BETWEEN FINGERS**) SUBVOLA
(— **OF BRIGHTNESS**) FLICKER
(— **OF FAIR WEATHER**) SLATCH
(— **OF HARSH WEATHER**) SNAP
(— **OF SEMITONE**) APOTOME
(**REST** —) SOB
(**SHORT** —) STREAK
(**TIME** —) HEADWAY
INTERVALE BOTTOM
INTERVENE CHOP STEP STRIKE
MEDIATE OBVIATE STICKLE
INTERCUR
INTERVENING MESNE MIDDLE
MEDIANT
INTERVIEW BUZZ CONTACT
AUDIENCE CONGRESS
INTERWEAVE MAT PLAT CRISP
PLAIT PLASH RADDLE TANGLE
WATTLE ENTWINE TEXTURE TRELLIS
COMPLECT ENTANGLE IMPLEACH
INTERTEX
INTERWEAVING BREDE CROWN
INTIMATE
INTERWOVEN INWOVEN IMPLICIT
INTIMATE
INTESTINAL INNER ENTERAL
ENTERIC
INTESTINE GUT ROPE BOWEL INNER
THARM INWARD MIDDLE
(**PORTION OF** —) JEJUNUM
(PL.) VISCUS INGANGS CHITLINS
INTHROW RIDGE

INTIMACY LIAISON PRIVACY
AFFINITY CHUMMERY GOSSIPRY
INTRIGUE
(**UNDUE** —) LIBERTY
INTIMATE SIB BOON GRIT HINT
HOME HOMY KIND NEAR NEXT PACK
TOSH BOSOM CHIEF CLOSE GREAT
PALLY PRIVY THICK ALLUDE ENTIRE
FRIEND HOMELY INTIME INWARD
NOTICE SECRET STRAIT STRICT
THRANG THRONG CHAMBER
CLOSEUP GREMIAL INNERLY
INNUATE KEYHOLE PRIVADO
PRIVATE SIGNIFY SPECIAL SUGGEST
COCKMATE ESPECIAL FAMILIAR
FREQUENT FRIENDLY INDICATE
INTIMADO
(**MOST** —) MIDMOST
(PL.) FOLKS
INTIMATELY INLY TOSH WELL
COZILY CLOSELY INWARDLY
INTIMATION CUE HINT ITEM WARN
WIND SCENT NOTICE OFFICE
GLIMMER INKLING INNUENDO
MONITION
INTIMIDATE COW HAZE ABASH
BULLY COWER DAUNT DETER
HECTOR TERRIFY BROWBEAT
BULLDOZE BULLYRAG FRIGHTEN
INTO IN INTIL WITHIN
INTOLERANCE BIGOTRY
INTOLERANT CLOSED BIGOTED
INTONATION FALL ITALICS
INTONE CANT SING TONE CHANT
CHAUNT ENTUNE MODULATE
INTOXICATE FOX TIP TOX FLAW
GOOF SOAK TODDY FUDDLE
MUDDLE SOZZLE SPRING TIPSIFY
DISGUISE OVERTAKE SPRINKLE
INTOXICATED CUT FAP LIT WET
HIGH LUSH RIPE SHOT SOSH TOFT
TOSY BOSKY BUFFY DRUNK FRESH
FRIED FUNNY HEADY LACED NAPPY
PIPED TIGHT BOILED GROGGY
LOADED MELLOW PIPPED QUAINT
SCREWY SKEWED SLEWED SLOPPY
SODDEN SOSHED SOZZLE STEWED
TANKED UPPISH UPPITY EBRIATE
EXALTED FLECKED JINGLED
POTSHOT SCREWED SLOPPED
SMASHED SPIFFED SQUIFFY
UNSOBER BESOTTED COCKEYED
DELEERIT ELEVATED OVERSEEN
OVERSHOT PLEASANT SQUIFFED
TEMULENT TOXICATE
INTOXICATING HARD HEADY STARK
HUFFCAP
INTOXICATION WINE FUDDLE
IVRESSE LOCOISM DISGUISE
EBRIOSITY
(— **OF ANIMALS**) DUNZIEKTE
INTRACTABLE BAD HARD SALTY
STACK SURLY FIERCE SULLEN
THWART UNRULY CRABBED
HAGGARD RESTIVE ROPABLE
WAYWARD CHURLISH INDOCILE
MUTINOUS OBDURATE PERVERSE
SHREWISH
INTRADOS SOFFIT

INTRANSITIVE NEUTER
INTREPID BOLD BRAVE HARDY
HEROIC PRETTY SAVAGE DOUGHTY
VALIANT RESOLUTE
INTREPIDITY GAME COURAGE
INTRICACY KNOT INTRIGUE
INTRICATE HARD MAZY BLIND
DAEDAL IMPLEX KNOBBY KNOTTY
TANGLY TRICKY COMPLEX CRABBED
CURIOUS GORDIAN PERPLEX
PUZZLED SINUOUS INVOLUTE
INVOLVED
INTRIGUE PLOT ANGLE CABAL
CLOAK STORY AFFAIR AMOUNT
BRIGUE DECEIT SCHEME CONNIVE
FACTION FINAGLE JOBBERY
TRINKET TRINKLE ARTIFICE
CHEATING COLLOGUE PRACTICE
PRACTISE STRATEGY TRIPOTER
INTRIGUER JESUIT SCHEMER
DESIGNER
INTRIGUING EXCITING SCHEMING
INTRINSIC REAL TRUE INBORN
INBRED INNATE INWARD NATIVE
GENUINE NATURAL ABSOLUTE
IMMANENT INHERENT INTERNAL
INTIMATE
INTRINSICALLY PROPERLY
INTRODUCE READ DEBUT ENTER
FRONT IMMIT INFER PLANT START
USHER BROACH HERALD INDUCE
INDUCT INFUSE INJECT INSERT
INVECT INVOKE LAUNCH PREFER
FORERUN IMPLANT INSTILL INVEIGH
PRECEDE PREFACE PRELUDE
PRESENT SHUFFLE SPONSOR
ACQUAINT INNOVATE INTROMIT
WIREDRAW
(— **AIR INTO**) AERATE
(— **AS FIRST ACT**) INITIATE
(— **FROM WITHOUT**) IMPORT
(— **SURREPTITIOUSLY**) FOIST
INTRODUCTION LASSU PROEM
PRONE INTRADA INTROIT ISAGOGE
MENTION PREFACE ENTRANCE
EXORDIUM PREAMBLE PROLOGUE
(— **INTO STOMACH**) GAVAGE
(— **OF DRAMA**) PROTASIS
(— **OF NOVELTY**) CHANGE
(**MUSICAL** —) INTRO INTRADA
INTRODUCTORY EXORDIAL
LIMINARY PROTATIC SYSTATIC
INTROIT REQUIEM
INTRORSE ANTICAL
INTROSPECTION INLOOK REFLEX
INTRUDE JET ABATE CRASH POACH
BOTHER CHISEL INGYRE INJECT
INVADE IRRUPT THRUST OBTRUDE
ENCROACH INFRINGE TRESPASS
INTRUDER INTRUS INCOMER
INVADER STRANGER
INTRUSION INVASION
INTRUSIVE FRESH SPURIOUS
INTUITION HUNCH INSTINCT
INTUITIONIST EIDETIC
INULIN ALANTIN
INUNDATE FLOW DROWN FLOOD
INUND SWAMP DELUGE OVERFLOW
SUBMERGE SURROUND

INUNDATION FLOW FLOOD WATER
DELUGE ALLUVIO FRESHET
ALLUVION FLOODAGE OVERFLOW
INURE URE BREAK ENURE STEEL
HARDEN SCHOOL SEASON
ACCUSTOM INDURATE
INVADE ASSAIL INTRUDE ENCROACH
INTRENCH TRESPASS
INVADER HUN PICT
INVADING INGRUENT
INVAGINATION GULLET
INVALID BAD BUM NULL NUGATORY
INVALIDATE AVOID BREAK CANCEL
INFIRM IMPROVE INVALID VITIATE
INVALUABLE COSTLY PRECIOUS
INVARIABLE STEADY UNIFORM
CONSTANT
INVARIABLENESS ONENESS
INVARIABLY EVER ALWAYS
INVASION RAID INROAD DESCENT
INBREAK INJURIA
INVECTIVE ABUSE HOKER RAILING
DIATRIBE REPROACH
INVEIGH INVECT DECLAIM
DENOUNCE
INVEIGLE COAX ROPE CHARM
DECOY SNARE ALLURE ENTICE
SEDUCE
INVENT COIN FIND FORM MINT VAMP
FEIGN FRAME FRUMP CREATE
DESIGN DEVISE IDEATE CONCOCT
CONJURE CONTRIVE DISCOVER
INVENTION FANCY DEVICE FINDAL
NOTION FANTASY FICTION FIGMENT
FORGERY WITCRAFT
(DRAMATIC —) IBSENISM
INVENTIVE ADROIT FERTILE
CREATIVE MECHANIC ORIGINAL
PREGNANT
INVENTIVENESS WIT ARTIFICE
INVENTOR TALOS COINER FINDER
FRAMER MINTER CREATOR
MINTMAN ENGINEER
INVENTORY BILL LIST STOCK
ACCOUNT INVOICE TERRIER
ANAGRAPH REGISTER SCHEDULE
INVERSION WALDEN CHIASMUS
ENTROPION
INVERT CANT TURN REVERT
REVERSE
INVERTASE SUCRASE
INVEST DON DUB PUT BELT FUND
GARB GIFT GIRD GIRT GOWN LOCK
SINK VEST WRAP BELAY BLOCK
ENDOW ENDUE FEOFF INDUE
CLOTHE EMBODY ENROBE FORSET
OCCUPY COMPASS ENFEOFF
ENVELOP INSTATE OBSERVE
BENEFICE BLOCKADE SURROUND
(— ONESELF) COVER ASSUME
(— WITH AUTHORITY) SCEPTER
ACCREDIT
(— WITH ENERGY) CATHECT
(— WITH SOVEREIGN DIGNITY)
ENTHRONE
(— WITH) INFEFT
INVESTED GARTERED
INVESTIGATE SPY SIFT CHECK
PROBE SOUND STUDY EXCUSS

FATHOM SEARCH DISCUSS EXAMINE
EXPLORE INQUIRE INDAGATE
SCRUTATE
(— QUICKLY) SKIP
INVESTIGATION CHECK PROBE
TRIAL EXAMEN PILPUL SEARCH
DELVING INQUEST INQUIRY
LEGWORK ZETETIC ANALYSIS
QUESTION RESEARCH SCRUTINY
SOUNDING
INVESTIGATOR SNOOP TRIER
SLEUTH GUMSHOE SPOTTER
FIELDMAN
INVESTITURE VESTURE INDUMENT
INVESTMENT DOG FLIER CUTICLE
CATHEXIS
INVETERATE BLACK SWORN
ROOTED CHRONIC HARDENED
INVIDIOUS ENVIOUS HATEFUL
INVIGORATE BRACE CHEER RAISE
RENEW VIGOR VIVIFY COMFORT
ENFORCE ENLIVEN FORTIFY
INNERVE INSINEW REFRESH INSPIRIT
INVIGORATING BRISK CRISP FRESH
TONIC VITAL HEARTY BRACING
CORDIAL VEGETANT
INVIOLABILITY SANCTITY
INVIOLABLE SECURE STYGIAN
INVIOLATE SACRED
INVISIBLE HID SECRET UNSEEN
VIEWLESS
INVITATION BID CALL CARD INVITE
BIDDING CALLING
(— TO CONTEND) DARE
INVITE ASK BID WOO BEAR CALL
LURE PRAY TOLL CLEPE COURT
LATHE TRYST ALLURE DESIRE
ENTICE INDITE ATTRACT CONVITE
PROVOKE REQUEST SOLICIT
INVITING ADORABLE HOMELIKE
INVOCATION WISH DAWUT NANDI
BISMILLAH
INVOICE BILL BRIEF CHALAN
FACTURE MANIFEST
INVOKE WISH CLEPE EVOKE APPEAL
ATTEST OBTEST CONJURE ENTREAT
PROVOKE SOLICIT INVOCATE
INVOLUCRE HULL HUSK CUPULE
EPICALYX
INVOLUNTARY FORCED HELPLESS
INVOLUTE INVOLVED
INVOLUTED SCREWY
INVOLUTION ATRESIA
INVOLVE DIP LAP MIX MIRE WRAP
BROIL CARRY COUCH IMPLY RAVEL
DIRECT EMPLOY ENGAGE ENTAIL
HANKLE INWRAP TANGLE COMPORT
CONCERN CONNOTE EMBRACE
EMBROIL ENSNARE ENTWINE
ENVIRON IMMERSE INCLUDE
ENCUMBER ENTANGLE INTEREST
(— IN DIFFICULTY) STEAD
INVOLVED IN DEEP GONE BLIND
KNOTTY COMPLEX ENGAGED
PLAITED IMPLICIT INVOLUTE
INWARD ENTAD INNER INWITH
BENWARD INNERLY HOMEFELT
INWICK INRING
IO (BROTHER OF —) PHORONEUS

(FATHER OF —) INACHUS
(SON OF —) EPAPHUS
IOLE (FATHER OF —) EURYTUS
(HUSBAND OF —) HYLLUS
IOLITE IBERITE PELIOMA
ION ACID ADION ANION CATION
ISOMER KATION LIGAND AMPHION
HYDRION OXONIUM SPECIES
(— DURATION) LIFETIME
(FATHER OF —) XUTHUS
(MOTHER OF —) CREUSA
IONIZATION BURST
IOTA JOT WHIT GHOST SCRUPLE
IOU MARKER

IOWA
CAPITAL: DESMOINES
COLLEGE: COE DORDT LORAS
CORNELL PARSONS GRINNELL
WARTBURG
COUNTY: IDA SAC LINN TAMA
ADAIR KEOKUK KOSSUTH
OSCEOLA
LAKE: CLEAR STORM SPIRIT
NICKNAME: HAWKEYE
PRESIDENT: HOOVER
RIVER: CEDAR SKUNK BIGSIOUX
MISSOURI
STATE BIRD: GOLDFINCH
STATE FLOWER: WILDROSE
STATE TREE: OAK
TOWN: MASON PERRY SIOUX
ALGONA KEOKUK LEMARS
MARION ANAMOSA OTTUMWA
WATERLOO DAVENPORT

IOWAN HAWKEYE
IPECAC ITOUBOU
IPHICLUS (BROTHER OF —)
HERCULES
(FATHER OF —) PHYLACUS
AMPHITRYON
(MOTHER OF —) ALCMENA
IPHIGENIA (BROTHER OF —)
ORESTES
(FATHER OF —) AGAMEMNON
(MOTHER OF —) CLYTEMNESTRA
(SISTER OF —) ELECTRA
IPHIS (FATHER OF —) LIGDUS
(MOTHER OF —) TELETHUSA
(WIFE OF —) IANTHE
IPHITUS (FATHER OF —) EURYTUS
(SLAYER OF —) HERCULES
IPIL VESI
IPOMOEA NIL NILL BATATAS
MANROOT SCAMMONY
IPSEITY SELFHOOD
IRACUND IREFUL

IRAN
CAPE: HALILEH
CAPITAL: TEHRAN TEHERAN
COIN: PUL ASAR CRAN LARI RIAL
BISTI DARIC DINAR LARIN SHAHI
TOMAN STATER ASHRAFI
KASBEKE PAHLAVI
DESERT: KERMAN

FORMER NAME: PERSIA
LAKE: NIRIS NIRIZ TASHT TUZLU URMIA SAHWEH SISTAN MAHARLU NEMEKSER URUMIYEH
LANGUAGE: ZEND PAHLAVI
MEASURE: GAZ GUZ MOV ZAR ZER CANE FOOT GAREH JERIB KAFIZ MAKUK QASAB ARTABA CHARAC CHEBEL GARIBA GHALVA OUROUB CAPICHA CHENICA FARSAKH FARSANG MANSION MISHARA PARASANG PIAMANEH SABBITHA STATHMOS
MOUNTAIN: CUSH KUSH HINDU KHOSF ARARAT HAMUNT BINALUD KHORMUJ SABALAN DEMAVENO
MOUNTAIN RANGE: ELBURZ SIAHAN ZAGROS JAGATAL
PEOPLE: LUR KURD MEDE SART KAJAR MUKRI PERSE TAJIK HADJEMI PERSIAN
PORT: JASK BUSHIRE PAHLEVI
RIVER: MAND MUND SHUR ARAKS JAGIN KARUN RABCH SEFID BAMPUR GORGAN HALIRI TIGRIS KARKHEH MASHKEL SAFIDRUD ZAYENDEH EUPHRATES
STRAIT: HORMUZ
TOWN: FAO KOM AMOL YAZD AHVAZ KHVOY NIRIZ RESHT ABADAN DEZFUL GORGAN KASVIN KERMAN MASHAD MESHED SHIRAZ TABRIZ TAURIS HAMADAN ISFAHAN SANANDAJ
WEIGHT: SER DRAM DUNG ROTL SANG SEER ABBAS ARTEL MAUND PINAR RATEL BATMAN DIRHEM GANDUM KARWAR MISCAL NAKHOD NIMMAN ABBASSI TCHEIREK

IRANIAN TAT SART GALCHA SHUGNI BACTRIAN BARTANGI
(— SOVEREIGN) SHAH

IRAQ
CAPITAL: BAGDAD BAGHDAD
COIN: DINAR
DISTRICT: BASRA KURDISTAN
FORMER NAME: MESOPOTAMIA
MOUNTAINS: ZARGOS KURDISTAN
OASIS: MANIYA
PEOPLE: ARAB KURD
PORT: BASRA
RIVER: ZAB TIGRIS EUPHRATES
TOWN: AMARA BASRA MOSUL NAJAF HILLAH KIRKUK KARBALA

IRASCIBILITY BILE CHOLER
IRASCIBLE WARM ANGRY CROSS FIERY GASSY HASTY IRATE SHARP TECHY TESTY CRANKY IREFUL SPUNKY TETCHY TOUCHY BILIOUS FRETFUL IRACUND PEEVISH WASPISH CAPTIOUS CHOLERIC

PETULANT SNAPPISH STOMACHY
IRATE ANGRY HEATED CHOLERIC WRATHFUL
IRE FURY ANGER WRATH
IREFUL ANGRY JEALOUS

IRELAND
BAY: MAL CLEW SLIGO BANTRY DINGLE GALWAY TRALEE DONEGAL DUNDALK KILLALA BLACKSOD DROGHEDA
CAPE: CLEAR
CAPITAL: TARA DUBLIN
COIN: RAP REAL
COUNTY: CORK DOWN LEIX MAYO CAVAN CLARE KERRY LOUTH MEATH SLIGO ANTRIM ARMAGH CARLOW GALWAY OFFALY TYRONE ULSTER DONEGAL KILDARE LEITRIM WEXFORD WICKLOW KILKENNY LIMERICK MONAGHAN
ISLAND: ARAN TORY SALTEE RATHLIN
LAKE: DOO KEY REE TAY CONN DERG MASK CARRA GOWNA LEANE RAMOR BODERG COOTER ENNELL DROMORE OUGHTER SHEELIN
MEASURE: MILE BANDLE
MOUNTAIN: OX CAHA ANTRIM GALTEE KEEPER MOURNE MULREA DONEGAL ERRIGAL KENNEDY KIPPURE WICKLOW LEINSTER
MOUNTAIN RANGE: GALTY STACKS COMERAGH
OTHER NAME: EIRE ERIN BANBA IERNE IRENA ULSTER BOGLAND HIBERNIA INISFAIL
PEOPLE: CELT ERSE GAEL CELTIC HIBERNIAN
PERTAINING TO: CELTIC GAELIC
POINT: CAHORE CARNSORE
PROVINCE: ULSTER MUNSTER LEINSTER CONNAUGHT
RIVER: LEE BANN DEEL ERNE NORE SUIR BOYNE CLARE FEALE FLESK FOYLE LAUNE BANDON BARROW LIFFEY KENMARE MUNSTER SHANNON
TOWN: CORK ADARE DUBLIN LURGAN LIMERICK TIPPERARY

IRENE (FATHER OF —) JUPITER
(MOTHER OF —) THEMIS
IRENIC CALM HENOTIC PEACEFUL
IRENICA AITESIS
IRIDESCENCE LUSTER LUSTRE
IRIDESCENT SHOT IRISED IRIDINE IRISATE PAVONINE
IRIS EYE SET FLAG LILY LUCE LUCY SEGG AZURE IREOS ORRIS SEDGE FLAGON LEVERS LILIAL LILIUM SHADOW SUNBOW ALCAZAR BABIANA FLAGGER GLADDON FLAGLEAF

(FATHER OF —) THAUMAS
(MOTHER OF —) ELECTRA
IRISH ERSE EIRANN IRISHRY MILESIAN
(— KING) RIG
(ILLITERATE —) KEELMAN
IRISHMAN MAC PAT CELT GAEL KELT SCOT GREEK IRISH PADDY YREIS TEAGUE GRECIAN IRISHER MILESIAN ORANGEMAN
(LEARNED —) OLLAMH
IRISH MOSS SLOKE CHONDRUS
IRISHWOMAN HARP
IRK BORE ITCH ANNOY WEARY BOTHER
IRKSOME DULL WARM WEARY HUMDRUM OPEROSE TEDIOUS ANNOYING TIRESOME
IROKO ODUM ODOOM MUVULE KAMBALA
IRON BIT DOG IRE MARS WIRE ANGLE ANVIL BASIL BRAND DRAIL DRIFT FLOSS HORSE NEGRO SPIKE STEEL WAVER ANCONY BEATER CALKER CAUTER FERRUM GAGGER GOFFER JAGGER OSMUND CAUTERY COBIRON CRAMPER FERRITE FURISON GAMBREL GAUFFER PRICKER SADIRON FLATIRON TRICOUNI
(— FOR CLOSING STAVES) HORSE
(— OF MILLSTONE) RIND RYND
(— ORE) LIMNITE
(— PIECES) POTLEG
(— PLATE) TRAMP
(— SUPPORTING SPIT) COBIRON
(— TO SUPPORT BEAM) TORSEL
(8 PIGS OF CAST —) FODDER
(ANGLE —) LATH STIFFENER
(BASKETWORK —) BEATER
(BOOM —) WITHE WYTHE
(BRANDING —) BURN
(CAST —) METAL YETLIN SPIEGEL YETLING SEMISTEEL
(CLIMBING —) GAFF SPUR CREEPER
(CRUDE CASTING OF —) PIG
(DRIVING —) CLEEK
(GLASSBLOWING —) BAIT
(GOLF —) JIGGER
(GRAPPLING —) CRAMPON CRAMPOON
(HATTER'S —) SLUG
(MASS OF WROUGHT —) BLOOM
(METEORIC —) SIDERITE
(PASTY —) SPONGE
(PIG —) SPIEGEL KENTLEDGE
(PRIMING —) DRIFT
(RUSSIAN —) SABLE
(SHEET —) TERNE
(SOLDERING —) COPPER
(SPECULAR —) HEMATITE
(TAILOR'S —) GOOSE
(TAMPING —) DRIVER
(PL.) GARTERS
IRONBARK MUGGA
IRON BROWN NEGRO
IRONCLAD ARMORED IRONSIDE
IRON HAT GOSSAN

IRONIC ACERB ACERBIC SATIRIC
IRONICAL CRUEL
IRON-LIKE MARTIAL
IRON MAN TALUS
IRONMONGERY HARDWARE
IRONSMITH FERRER
IRONSTONE DOGGER
IRONWEED FLATTOP VERNONIA
  WINGSTEM
IRONWOOD TITI COLIMA MOPANE
  MOPANI PURIRI WAMARA CYRILLA
  JOEWOOD AXMASTER BURNWOOD
  FIREWOOD
IRONWORKER LOHAR MOSCHI
IRONWORT SIDERITE
IRONY SATIRE ASTEISM SARCASM
  RIDICULE
IROQUOIS HURON MINGO CAYUGA
  MENGWE
IRRADIATE XRAY ENBEAM
IRRATIONAL REE SURD WILD SILLY
  RAVING STUPID BESTIAL FOOLISH
IRREDUCIBLE BASIC
IRREGULAR DUMB WILD BUMPY
  EROSE FANCY MIXED WOPSY
  ATYPIC CATCHY FITFUL RAGGED
  RUGGED SPOTTY UNEVEN UNLIKE
  WEEWAW ANAXIAL ATACTIC
  BAROQUE CATERAN CRABBED
  CROOKED CURSORY DEVIOUS
  DIFFORM ERRATIC FRECKET
  MUTABLE SCRAWLY UNEQUAL
  WAYWARD ABNORMAL ATYPICAL
  DOGGEREL INFORMAL PINDARIC
  SCRAGGLY SCRAMBLY UNLAWFUL
  UNSTABLE UNSTEADY VARIABLE
IRREGULARITY SNAG DEFECT
  RUFFLE ANOMALY ACCIDENT
  (— IN YARN) SNICK
IRREGULARLY UNDULY
IRRELIGIOUS PAGAN WICKED
  HEATHEN IMPIOUS PROFANE
  SENSUAL
IRREMEDIABLE HELPLESS
  HOPELESS
IRREPROACHABLE SPOTLESS
IRRESISTIBLE MESMERIC
IRRESISTIBLY FATALLY
IRRESOLUTE FICKLE INFIRM
  UNSURE WANKLE DOUBTFUL
  UNSTABLE
IRRESPONSIBLE WILDCAT
  CAREFREE FECKLESS SKITTISH
IRRESPONSIVE LEADEN
IRRETRIEVABLE HOPELESS
IRREVERENCE IMPIETY
IRREVERENT ATHEIST AWELESS
  IMPIOUS PROFANE
IRREVOCABLE DEAD
IRREVOCABLY FATALLY FINALLY
IRRIGATE FLOAT WATER SYRINGE
IRRIGATION KAREZ
IRRIGATOR FLOATER
IRRITABILITY ERETHISM SORENESS
  VAGOTONY
IRRITABLE BAD EDGY BIRSY CROOK
  FIERY FUSSY HASTY HUFFY JUMPY
  MUSTY NAGGY TETTY TILTY TOITY

CRANKY GROWLY NETTLY SPUNKY
STOCKY TEETHY TETCHY TOUCHY
FRATCHY FRETFUL HORNETY
HUFFISH KICKISH PECKISH PEEVISH
SPLEENY TEDIOUS TWITCHY
WASPISH PETULANT SNAPPING
SNAPPISH STOMACHY
IRRITATE BUG EAT GET IRE IRK NAG
  RUB TAR TEW TRY VEX BURN CRAB
  FIRE FRET GALL GOAD GRIG GRIT
  ITCH NARK RILE ROIL SOUR TEEN
  ANGER ANNOY CHAFE EAGER
  FRUMP GRATE GRILL GRIPE PEEVE
  PIQUE STING TARRY ABRADE
  BOTHER FRIDGE GRAVEL HARASS
  HECTOR NETTLE RUFFLE AFFRONT
  INCENSE INFLAME NERVOUS
  PROVOKE STOMACH ACERBATE
IRRITATED RILY SORE HUFFY
  MUFFED SHIRTY EMPORTE
  FRATCHED SOREHEAD
  (EASILY —) TESTY
IRRITATING ACRID HARSH CORSIE
  ELVISH GRAVEL FRETFUL GALLING
  IRKSOME PUNGENT RASPING
  ANNOYING FRETSOME GRAVELLY
  NETTLING SCRATCHY SPITEFUL
  STINGING TIRESOME
IRRITATION FRET TEEN BIRSE PIQUE
  STEAM RUFFLE TEMPER WARMTH
  ANTPRICK FLEABITE PINPRICK
  VEXATION
IRRUPTION BREAK INROAD INBURST
  ERUPTION INVASION
IS S YS BEES
  (— NOT) NIS AINT ISNT
ISAIAH ESAY ESAIAS
ISCHEMIA ANEMIA
ISCHIAL SCIATIC
ISHPINGO CINNAMON
ISHSHAKKU PATESI
ISHTAR NINNI
ISINGLASS LEAF PIPE KANTEN
ISIS (BROTHER OF —) OSIRIS
  (FATHER OF —) SATURN
  (MOTHER OF —) RHEA
ISLAM ABBASID
ISLAMIC (— CUSTOM) SUNNA
ISLAND CALF CAYO HOLM INCH ISLE
  JAVA POLO ENNIS MALTA MAYDA
  AVALON ITHACA OGYGIA REFUGE
  RIALTO CIPANGO JAMAICA MADEIRA
  TOWHEAD BLEFUSCU CALAURIA
  DOMINICA GUERNSEY LILLIPUT
  LUGGNAGG
  (— IN EVERGLADES) HAMMOCK
  (— OF REIL) INSULA
  (ARTIFICIAL —) CRANNOG
  (CORAL —) ATOLL
  (FABLED —) MERU UTOPIA
  (FLOATING —) HOVER
  (FLYING —) LAPUTA
  (LEGENDARY —) BRAZIL OBRAZIL
  (LITTLE —) AIT KAY KEY ISLET
  (LOW —) KEY
  (ROCKY —) SKERRY
  (SANDY —) BEACH BARRIER
  (SMALL —) CAY ISLE ISLET

SANDKEY
ISLANDER KANAKA ISLEMAN
  INSULARY
ISLE IZLE ISLET SKERRY
ISLET OE AIT CAY KEY EYOT HAFT
  HOLM ILOT MOTU ROCK ISLOT
  STACK NUBBLE
ISMENE (FATHER OF —) OEDIPUS
  (MOTHER OF —) JOCASTA
  (SISTER OF —) ANTIGONE
ISOBAR MEIOBAR MESOBAR
  PLEIOBAR
ISOLATE ISLAND DISSECT SECLUDE
  COLONIZE INSULATE SEPARATE
  SEQUESTER
ISOLATED POCKET UNIQUE
  SOLITARY STRANDED
ISOLATION HERMITRY LONENESS
  SOLITUDE
ISOMER PYRAN TOSYL XYLENE
  CUMIDINE DECOSANE DODECANE
ISOMERIC ISO ALLO
ISOMETRIC CUBIC REGULAR
  TESSULAR
ISOPLETH GEOTHERM
ISOPOD SLATER ASELLUS BOPYRID
  GRIBBLE EPICARID
ISOTOPE IONIUM CARRIER
ISOTYPE COTYPE SYNTYPE
ISPAGHUL SPOGEL
ISPAHAN HERAT HERATI

ISRAEL
CAPITAL: JERUSALEM
COIN: POUND
COLLECTIVE FARM: KIBBUTZ
DESERT: NEGEV
FORMER NAME: CANAAN
  PALESTINE
LAKE: HULEH TIBERIAS
MEASURE: CAB HIN KOR LOG
  BATH EPHA EZBA OMER REED
  SEAH CUBIT EPHAH HOMER
  KANEH QANEH
MOUNTAIN: NAFH SAGI HARIF
  MERON RAMON TABOR ATZMON
  CARMEL
RIVER: FARIA MALIK SOREQ
  JORDAN QISHON SARIDA
  YARKON LAKHISH
SEA: DEAD GALILEE
SEAPORT: ASHDOD TELAVIV
TOWN: ACRE RAMA HAIFA HOLON
  JAFFA JENIN JOPPA RAMLA
  SAFAD BATYAM HEBRON
  NABLUS JERICHO NATANYA
  TELAVIV TULKARM NAZARETH

ISRAELI SABRA
  (— STUDY CENTER) ULPAN
ISRAELITE JEW SAINT HEBREW
  JACOBITE
  (PL.) ZION
ISSUE END ISH COME EMIT FALL
  FLOW GIVE GUSH HEAD MISE REEK
  TERM VENT ARISE COUNT EVENT
  FRUIT LOOSE OUTGO SETON SOURD

UTTER EFFECT EFFUSE EGRESS
EMERGE ESCAPE EXITUS MUTTON
RESULT SEQUEL SETTER SPRING
UPPING BALLOON DEBOUCH
DESCENT DRIZZLE EMANATE
ESSENCE EXSURGE OUTCOME
PROCEED PROGENY REDOUND
REFLAIR SUCCESS EXPEDITE
FONTANEL INCREASE ISSUANCE
KINDLING OUTGOING
(— **AND ORDER**) BID
(— **SLOWLY**) EXUDE
(— **SPASMODICALLY**) BELCH
(— **SUDDENLY**) SALLY
(— **WITH FORCE**) SPOUT
(**BOND** —) CONSOL
(**FAVORABLE** —) SPEED FORTUNE
(**FINAL** —) UPSHOT UTMOST
(**NUMEROUS** —) SPAWN
ISSUED OUT
ISSUING EMANANT JESSANT
· MANATION
ISTHMUS BALK STRAIT TARBET
ISTLE PITA IXTLE JUAMAVE
GUAPILLA
IT A HE HIT MUN TAGGER
(— **FOLLOWS**) SEQ SEQU
(— **HAS BEEN SWORN**) JURAT
ITALIAN ITALIC AUSONIAN
MACARONI
ITALITE VESBITE

ITALY
CAPE: TESTA CIRCEO LICOSA
LINARO COLONNE FALCONE
PASSERO RIZZUTO SANVITO
TEULADA VATICANO
CAPITAL: ROMA ROME
CHEESE: ROMANO FONTINA
RICOTTA BELPAESE PARMESAN
TALEGGIO
COIN: LIRA LIRE TARI GRANO
PAOLI PAOLO SCUDO SOLDO
DANARO DENARO DUCATO
SEQUIN TESTONE ZECCHINO
FOOD: PASTA PIZZA SCAMPI
GNOCCHI LASAGNE POLENTA
RAVIOLI RISOTTO SPUMONI
TORTONI CAPONATA LINGUINE
MACARONI PEPERONI
FAMILY: ASTI ESTE AMATI CENCE
DORIA BORGIA MEDICI SFORZA
GULF: GAETA GENOA OROSEI
SALERNO TARANTO CAGLIARI
ORISTANO
ISLAND: ELBA LERO CAPRI LEROS
PONZA GIGLIO ISCHIA LINOSA
SALINA SICILY USTICA ALICUDI
ASINARA CAPRAIA GORGONA
LEVANZO PANAREA PIANOSA
SICILIA VULCANO FILICUDI
SARDINIA
ISLANDS: EGADI LIPARI TUSCAN
PELAGIE PONTINE TREMITI
LAKE: COMO ISEO NEMI GARDA
ALBANO LESINA LUGANO
VARANO BOLSENA PERUGIA

MAGGIORE BRACCIANO
MEASURE: PIE ORNA CANNA
PALMA PALMO PIEDE PUNTO
SALMA STAIO STERO BARILE
MIGLIE MIGLIO MOGGIO RUBBIO
TAVOLA TOMOLO BOCCALE
BRACCIO SECCHIO GIORNATA
POLONICK QUADRATO
MOUNTAIN: ROSA VISO AMARO
BLANC CORNO SOMMA CIMONE
BERNINA VESUVIUS
MOUNTAIN RANGE: ALPS ORTLES
APENNINES MARITIMES
NATIVE: ITALO LATIN OSCAN
ROMAN SABINE TIRANO TUSCAN
LOMBARD SIENESE LIGURIAN
VENETIAN
PASS: FREJUS BERNINA BRENNER
SPLUGEN
PORT: BARI POLA ZARA GENOA
TRANI ZADAR RIMINI TRIESTE
REGION: CARSO APULIA LATIUM
MARCHE MOLISE PUGLIA SICILY
UMBRIA ABRUZZI LIGURIA
TUSCANY VENETIA CALABRIA
CAMPANIA LOMBARDY
PIEMONTE SARDINIA
RESORT: LIDO SANREMO
TAORMINA
RIVER: PO ADDA AGRI ARNO LIRI
NERA RENO SELE TARO ADIGE
CRATI MANNU OGLIO PARMA
PIAVE SALSO STURA TIBER
TIRSO ANIENE BELICE MINCIO
OFANTO PANARO RAPIDO
SANGRO SIMETO TANARO
TEVERE TICINO BIFERNO
BRADANO CHIENTI METAURO
MONTONE OMBRONE PESCARA
RUBICON SECCHIA TREBBIA
VOLTURNO
SEA: IONIAN ADRIATIC LIGURIAN
STRAIT: MESSINA OTRANTO
BONIFACIO
TOWN: BRA RHO ACRI ALBA ASTI
BARI COMO DEGO ELEA ENNA
ESTE FANO GELA IESI LODI
NARO NOLA PISA POLA ROMA
ROME ACQUI ANZIO AOSTA
ASOLA AVOLA CAPUA CUNEO
EBOLI FIUME FORLI GENOA
IMOLA LECCE LUCCA MASSA
MILAN MONZA OSTIA PADUA
PARMA PAVIA TEANO TRENT
TURIN UDINE VELIA ALCAMO
AMALFI ANCONA ANDRIA
AREZZO CEFALU FAENZA
FOGGIA GENOVA MANTUA
MESTRE MILANO MODENA
NAPLES NAPOLI NOVARA RIVOLI
SPEZIA TRENTO VENICE VERONA
BERGAMO BOLOGNA BOLZANO
BRESCIA CARRARA CASERTA
CATANIA COSENZA CREMONA
FERRARA FIRENZE GORIZIA
IMPERIA LEGHORN LIVORNO
MARSALA MESSINA PALERMO

PERUGIA PISTOIA POMPEII
RAVENNA TARANTO TRIESTE
BRINDISI CAGLIARI FLORENCE
PIACENZA SORRENTO
SYRACUSE
VOLCANO: ETNA SOMMA VULCANO
VESUVIUS STROMBOLI
WATERFALL: TOCE
WEIGHT: CARAT LIBRA ONCIA
POUND CARATO DENARO
LIBBRA OTTAVA
WINE: SOAVE CHIANTI MARSALA
ORVIETO

ITALY AUSONIA HESPERIA SATURNIA
ITCH EWK EACH REEF RIFF YEUK
YEWK TICKLE ITCHING SCABIES
VANILLISM
ITCHING ITCHY YEUKY PRURIENT
PRURITIS URTICANT
ITEM ANA JOB TOT ENTRY POINT
THING DETAIL ARTICLE SEVERAL
(— **IN SERIES**) COURSE
(— **OF PROPERTY**) CHATTEL
(— **OF VALUE**) ASSET
(**APPENDED** —) ADDENDUM
(**COLLECTOR'S** —) SPOIL
(**DECORATIVE** —) CONCEIT
(**LUXURY** —) BOUTIQUE
(**NEWS** —) DISPATCH
(**UNPUBLISHED** —S) ANECDOTE
(**VALUELESS** —) BEAN
(**PL.**) CHECKAGE
ITEMIZE DETAIL
ITERATION PLEONASM
ITHURIEL'S-SPEAR GRASSNUT
ITINERANT ERRANT AMBULANT
ITINERARY DIET JOURNAL WAYBILL
(— **OF ROYAL PROGRESS**) GEST
ITINERATION EYRE
ITS HIS
ITSELF IT HERSELF
ITYS (**FATHER OF** —) TEREUS
(**MOTHER OF** —) PROCNE
ITZA PETEN
IULUS ASCANIUS
IVATAN BATAN
IVORY EBURE DENTINE ELEPHANT
(**DUST OF** —) EBURINE
(**WALRUS** —) RIBZUBA RIBAZUBA
IVORY BLACK ABAISER

IVORY COAST
CAPE: PALMAS
CAPITAL: ABIDJAN
DAM: BANDAMA
LANGUAGE: DIOULA
PEOPLE: ABE AKAN ATLE KOUA
KROU MANDE ABOURE LAGOON
MALINKE VOLTAIC
RIVER: KOMOE BANDAMA
CAVALLY SASSANDRA
TOWN: TABOU BOUAKE GAGNOA
SASSANDRA

IVORY GULL SNOWBIRD

IVORY NUT ANTA TAGUA JARINA
IVORY PALM TAGUA COROJO
  COROZO
IVORY TREE PALAY
IVY TOD GILL HOVE IVIN JILL PICRY

  ARALIA HEDERA HIBBIN ALEHOOF
  ARALIAD IVYWORT BINDWEED
  FOALFOOT
IWW WOBBLY

IXION (FATHER OF —) PHLEGYAS
  (SISTER OF —) CORONIS
  (WIFE OF —) DIA
IZMIR SMYRNA

J JAY JIG JULIETT
JAAL GOAT BEDEN JAELA
JAB GAG GIG JAG JOB POKE STAB
JABBER CHAT JAVER BURBLE
GABBER GABBLE JOBBER YABBER
CHATTER
JABIRU STORK CICONIID
JABOT RUFFLE
JACANA PARRA
JACARE CAIMAN CAYMAN
JACINTH LIGURE
JACK DIB FLAG JACA CRICK DICKY
KNAVE NANCA COLORS KATHAL
SCALET SETTER WENZEL MATADOR
BLOCKING JACKFISH POLIGNAL
SOURJACK TURNSPIT UPLIFTER
(— IN BOWLS) BABY MARK KITTY
MASTER MISTRESS
(— IN CARDS) PAM PUR TOM
BOWER CNAFE KITTY KNAPE KNAVE
MAKER KNIGHT VARLET WENZEL
VARLETTO
(— OF CLUBS) NODDY BRAGGER
MATADOR
(— OF SAME SUIT) NOB
(— OF TRUMPS) TOM JASS JASZ
BOWER HONOR PLAYBOY
(PIANO —) HOPPER STICKER
(SPINNING —) BEAT
JACKAL DIEB JACK KOLA THOS
CANID CANINE DRAGON SILVER
THOOID SIACALLE
JACKAROO RINGNECK
JACKASS JACK
JACKASS FISH MORWONG TERAKIHI
JACK BEAN OVERLOOK
JACK CREVALLE TORO
JACKDAW DAW KAE JACK SHELL
CADDOW CARDER CHOUGH KADDER
CADESSE DAWCOCK DAWPATE
GRACKLE
JACKER SLIPMAN TORCHER
JACKET SAC ETON JACK JUMP JUPE
SACK VEST ACTON COVER DICKY
JUPON POLKA SHRUG WAMUS
BIETLE BLAZER BOLERO CARACO
CORSET DOLMAN FECKET GANSEY
JERKIN JERSEY JUMPER RAILLY
REEFER SACQUE SADDLE SLEEVE
SLIVER SONTAG TABARD TEMIAK
WAMPUS WARMUS BEDGOWN
CANEZOU LOUNGER NORFOLK
PALETOT PALTOCK PEACOAT
RISTORI SPENCER SURCOAT
SWEATER CAMISOLE CARDIGAN
CHAQUETA HANSELIN JIRKINET
MACKINAW OVERSLOP PENELOPE
SEALSKIN
(— FOR TURKEY) APRON
(— LINED WITH STEEL) PLACCATE
(— OF INDIA) BANIAN BANIYA
(— UNDER ARMOR) ACTON TRUSS
(CROCHETED —) SONTAG
(HOODED —) GREGO ANORAK
GRIEKO
(MALAY —) BAJU BADJU
(UNDRESS MILITARY —) SHELL
(WORK —) BAWNEEN
JACKFRUIT JACA KATHAL
SOURJACK

JACKHAMMER SINKER PLUGGER
JACKKNIFE JACK PIKE BARLOW
JACKMAN SHELLMAN
JACK-OF-ALL-TRADES DOCTOR
TINKER GIMCRACK
JACKSCREW CRICK
JACKSMELT PEIXEREY
JACKSNIPE GID JED JACK PEERT
SCAPE SNIPE SNIGHT CHOROOK
CREAKER JUDCOCK SQUATTER
JACKSTAY JACK HORSE PARREL
JACKROD RAILWAY
JACKSTRAW SPILIKIN
JACK TREE NANGKA
JACOB ISRAEL
JACQUARD FACONNE
JADE YU DUN TIT HACK JAUD MINX
PLUG SLUT TIRE HUSSY QUEAN
TRASH BEJADE HARASS RANNEL
AXSTONE HILDING POUNAMU
(DIRTY —) SLAISTER
JADED FORGONE SHOPWORN
DISJASKIT
JAEGER LARI SKUA ALLAN BOSUN
LARID SHOOL BONXIE TEASER
TULIAC TRUMPIE DIRTBIRD
DUNGBIRD
JAG BUN JOG GIMP JAUG LOAD
SOSH TOOT SKATE TOOTH INDENT
JAGGED JAGGY HACKLY RAGGED
SCRAGGY SHAGGED SNAGGED
INDENTED SCRAGGLY TATTERED
JAGGERY GUR GOOR GOUR KHAUR
KHAJUR KITTUL
JAGUAR CAT OUNCE TIGER
PANTHER UTURUNCU
JAI ALAI PELOTA
(— COURT) FRONTON
JAIL CAN GIB JUG BOOB CAGE COOP
CRIB DUMP GAOL HELL HOLD HOLE
KEEP LAKE LOCK STIR WARD
CHOKY CLINK GRATE KITTY LIMBO
LODGE TENCH TRONK BUCKET
CARCEL COOLER ENJAIL JIGGER
LIMBUS LOCKUP TOLZEY FREEZER
FURNACE GEHENNA KIDCOTE
PINFOLD TOLLERY BASTILLE
CALABOZO HOOSEGOW IMPRISON
MILLDOLL TOLLHALL
(— TERM) JOLT
JAILBIRD LAG
JAILER ADAM GAOLER KEEPER
WARDEN TURNKEY INCLUDER
JAKE FINE HICK FELLOW
JAKES AJAX GONG
JALAP MECHOACAN
JALOPY CLUNKER
JAM DIP CRAM JAMB BLOCK CHOKE
CROWD STICK THRONG JACKPOT
JAMAICA (CAPITAL OF —) KINGSTON
(RIVER OF —) BLACK MINHO
JAMAICA COBNUT OUABE PIGNUT
JAMAICA DOGWOOD BABASCO
BARBASCO FISHWOOD
JAMAICAN RAINBIRD TOMFOOL
JAMAICA VERVAIN GERVAO
JAMB DURN ALETTE HAUNCH
REVEAL DOORPOST
JAMES JEM JIM JIMMY SEAMAS
SHAMUS

JANGLE CLAM SQUABBLE
JANGLING HARSH JANGLY AJANGLE
JANISSARY CREOLE RABIRUBIA
JANITOR DURWAN PORTER
JANIZARY SOLAK SOLACH
JANSENIST RIGORIST
JANUS IANUS BIFRONT
JAOB JOW

JAPAN

BAY: ISE MUTSU OTARU ARIAKE
ATSUMI SENDAI SURUGA
TOYAMA WAKASA UCHIURA
CAPE: TOI ESAN MINO NOMA SHIO
SOYA SUZU ERIMO KYOGA
RURUI MUROTO NOJIMA
TODOGA SHIRIYA ASHIZURI
SHAKOTAN
CAPITAL: TOKIO TOKYO
COIN: BU RIN SEN YEN OBAN
KOBAN OBANG TEMPO ICHEBU
ITZEBU KOBANG
ISLAND: IKI SADO BONIN HONDO
KURIL REBUN HONSHU KIUSHU
KURILE KYUSHU RYUKYU
CIPANGO LOOCHOO RISHIRI
SKIKOKU HOKKAIDO IKISHIMA
OKIGUNTO OKUSHIRI YAKUJIMA
LAKE: BIWA TOYA TOWADA
KUTCHAWA SHIKOTSU
MEASURE: BU JO SE BOO CHO
KEN TAN HIRO SHAKU TSUBO
MOUNTAIN: ZAO FUJI ASAHI
ASAMA YESSO ASOSAN ENASAN
HIUCHI KIUSIU YARIGA FUJISAN
HAKUSAN KUJUSAN TOKACHI
FUJIYAMA
SEA: SUO AMAKUSA
STRAIT: KII BUNGO OSUMI
NEMURO TANEGA TOKARA
TSUGARU TSUSHIMA
STREET: GINZA
TOWN: OME KOBE KURA MITO
NARA OITA UEDA AKITA ATAMI
FUKUI KIOTO KOCHI KYOTO
NIKKO OSAKA OTARU SAKAI
UJINA CHOSHI MATSUE NAGOYA
SASEBO SENDAI TAKADA
TOYAMA FUKUOKA NIIGATA
OKAYAMA OKAZAKI SAPPORO
HAKODATE KAMAKURA
KANAZAWA KAWASAKI
KUMAMOTO NAGASAKI
YOKOHAMA YOKOSUKA
VOLCANO: ASO ASAMA ASOSAN
HAKUSAN FUJIYAMA
WEIGHT: MO FUN KIN KON RIN SHI
KATI KWAN NIYO CARAT CATTY
MOMME PICUL KWAMME
HIYAKKIN

JAPAN NIPPON YAMATO CIPANGO
JAPAN CEDAR SUGI
JAPANESE JAP JAPONIC
JAPANESE APRICOT UME
JAPANESE CHERRY SAKURA
JAPANESE DEER SIKA
JAPANESE IRIS SHADOW

JAPANESE PERSIMMON KAKI
JAPANESE PLUM KELSEY
JAPANESE PORGIE TAI
JAPANESE QUINCE JAPONICA
JAPANESE VELVET BIRODO
JAPE GAUD JOKE
JAPONICA ASTILBE
JAR TUN CELL JANG JARG JOLT
  JURR OLLA BANGA CADUS CRUSE
  KADOS SHOCK DOLIUM HUSTLE
  HYDRIA IMPACT JUDDER KALPIS
  PANKIN PINATA PITHOS TINAJA
  CANOPUS CONCUSS PSYKTER
  STAMNOS TERRINE MARTABAN
  STINKPOT
  (2-HANDLED —) AMPHORA
  (BELL —) CLOCHE
  (BULGING —) OLLA
  (EARTHENWARE —) CAN NAN
  CROCK GAMLA PITHOS TERRINE
  (POROUS —) GURGLET
  (SQUAT —) KORO
  (STONE —) STEEN STONE CROPPA
  (WATER —) BANGA CHATTI CHATTY
  GUMLAH HYDRIA
JARGON CANT JIVE RANE SLUM
  ARGOT SLANG LINGUA LINSEY
  PATOIS PATTER PIDGIN SHELTA
  SIWASH CHINOOK CHOCTAW
  DIALECT JARGOON PALAVER
  BARRIKIN KEDGEREE POLYGLOT
  SCHMOOZE SHOPTALK
  (THIEVES' —) FLASH
JARRING JARG RUDE SOUR HARSH
  ROUGH DARING
JASMINE BELA MALATI PIKAKE
  JESSAMY WOODBINE
JASPER JASPIS MORLOP DIASPER
  CREOLITE
JAUNDICE AURIGO GULSACH
  ICTERUS JANDERS YELLOWS
  JAUNDERS GRASSERIE
JAUNDICED ICTERODE
JAUNT SALLY JAUNCE VAGARY
  JOURNEY
JAUNTILY AIRILY BOUNCILY
JAUNTING CAR SIDECAR OUTSIDER
JAUNTY PERK COCKY PERKY SASSY
  DAPPER JANTEE SHANTY FINICAL
  PERKING DEBONAIR

JAVA

ISLAND: BALI LOMBOK MADURA
MEASURE: PAAL
MOUNTAIN: GEDE MURJO RAOENG
  SLAMET SEMEROE SOEMBING
PORT: BATAVIA SURABAJA
TOWN: BOGOR DESSA KEDIRI
  MALANG BANDUNG BATAVIA
  JAKARTA SEMARANG SURABAJA
WEIGHT: POND TALI

JAVA ALMOND PILI CANARI KANARI
  TALISAY
JAVA COTTON KAPOK
JAVANESE KRAMA KROMO
JAVANESE SKUNK TELEDU
JAVA PLUM DUHAT JAMBUL
  LOMBOY JAMBOOL

JAVA SPARROW MUNIA PADDY
  RICEBIRD
JAVELIN COLP DART PILE ACLYS
  PILUM JAREED LANCET ASSAGAI
  HARPOON HURLBAT JAVELOT
  ACONTIUM GAVELOCK
JAW JIB BEAK CHAP CHAW CHOP
  JOWL WANG ANVIL CHAFT CHEEK
  CHOKE SCOLD CHAWLE FEELER
  JAWBONE MAXILLA MANDIBLE
  (— OF FORCEPS) BEAK
  (— OF SPIDER) FANG
  (— OF VISE) CHAP
  (—S OF BIRD) BILL
  (FALSE —) CLAMP
  (RECEDING NOSE AND UNDERSHOT
  —) LAYBACK
  (PL.) MAW BITS THROAT
JAWBONE JOWL WANG MAXfLLA
  CHAWBONE
JAWBREAKING CRACKJAW
JAY JAYPIET SIRGANG BLUECOAT
  MEATBIRD
JAYHAWKER KANSAN
JAZERANT GESSERON
JAZZ BOP JIVE HOTCHA
JEALOUS YELLOW EMULOUS
  ENVIOUS
JEALOUSY ENVY YELLOWS
  EMULATION
JEAN FROCKING
JEANPAULIA BAIERA
JEEP PEEP SEEP BANTAM
JEER BOB BOO MOB GECK GIBE
  GIRD JAPE JEST JIBE MOCK SKIT
  WIPE FLIRT FLOUT FLUTE FLYTE
  FRUMP GLAIK LAUGH SCOFF
  SCOMM SNEER TAUNT CHIACK
  DERIDE BARRACK RIDICULE
JEERING BIRD FLOUT DERISIVE
JEHOVAH JAH LORD JAHVE YAHWEH
  (— WITNESS) PIONEER
JEJUNE DRY ARID MEAGER INSIPID
JELL COME FIRM
JELLY GEAL JEEL JELL GELEE
  CULLIS JUJUBE ALCOGEL FISNOGA
  GELATIN JELLIFY FLUMMERY
  HYDROGEL QUIDDANY
  (CALF'S-FOOT —) SULZE
  (FRUIT —) ROB
  (MEAT —) ASPIC
JELLYFISH JELLY QUARL CARVEL
  MEDUSA ACALEPH AURELIA
  MEDUSAN SLOBBER SUNFISH
  SCYPHULA SEACROSS STROBILA
JELLYLIKE SLABBY
JENNY MULE JINNY
JEOPARDIZE EXPOSE HAZARD
  IMPERIL ENDANGER
JEOPARDY RISK PERIL DANGER
  HAZARD
JEQUIRITY BEAN EYEN RUTTEE
JERBOA GERBIL JUMPER
JEREED TZIRID
JEREMIAD TRAGEDY
JERK GAG JET NUD TIT BOUT CANT
  FIRK GIRD HIKE JERT JIRT JOLT
  JOUK KICK PECK SNAP SNIG YANK
  YERK BRAID CHUCK FLIRT HITCH

  SCHMO SNAKE SPANG SURGE
  TWEAK TWICK FILLIP JIGGER
  SWITCH TWITCH WRENCH FLOUNCE
  SPANGHEW
JERKED MEAT TASAJO
JERKILY HITCHILY
JERKIN JACKET
JERKY NERVY SHARP CHOPPY
  ELBOIC FLICKY FLINGY HITCHY
  JIGGETY CHOPPING PALMODIC
  RATCHETY SACCADIC
JEROBOAM REHOBOAM
JERSEY FROCK SHIRT GANSEY
  TRICOT ZEPHYR MAILLOT SINGLET
  CAMISOLE GUERNSEY
JERUSALEM ARIEL SOLYMA
  AHOLIBAH
JERUSALEM ARTICHOKE TUBER
  CANADA GIRASOL
JERUSALEM CHERRY SOLANUM
JERUSALEM OAK AMBROSIA
JERUSALEM SAGE PHLOMIS
  SAGELEAF
JERUSALEM THORN CASCOL
  RETAMA
JESSAMINE JASMINE WOODBINE
JEST BOG COG FUN JOE TAX BULL
  GAME GAUD GIRD JAPE JOKE JOSH
  PLAY QUIP QUIZ RAIL SKIT BOURD
  BREAK CHAFF CLOWN DROLL FLIRT
  GESTE GLEEK SPORT THING
  BANTER GLANCE JAPERY RAILLY
  TRIFLE DICTERY GAMMOCK JOLLITY
  WAGGERY DROLLERY RAILLERY
  (— SPITEFULLY) SLENT
JESTER FOOL MIME BUFFO CLOWN
  DROLL IDIOT JAPER JOKER PATCH
  WAMBA DISOUR MOTLEY YORICK
  BADCHAN BOURDER BUFFOON
  DIZZARD DROLLER JOCULAR
  JUGGLER PICADOR SCOFFER
  SCOGGIN TOMTRAM MERRYMAN
  OWLGLASS PLEASANT RAILLEUR
  TRINCULO
JESTING DROLL JAPERY WAGGISH
JESUIT PAULIST TERTIAN IGNATIAN
  LOYOLITE
JESUS GEE GIS IHC IHS JHS YHS
  JESU WISDOM
  (SAYINGS OF —) AGRAPHA
JET BOLT TAIL TANG BREAK DUMBY
  DUMMY JETTO SALLY SPOUT SPRAY
  SPURT DELUGE DOUCHE GAGATE
  SQUIRT FANTAIL JETTEAU SPATTER
  SPURTER FOUNTAIN SOFFIONE
  UPSPRING
  (— OF METAL) BREAK
  (— OF VOLCANIC STEAM) STUFA
  (SMALL —) SQUIB
JET-BLACK BUGLE
JETTING SALIENT
JETTISON DUMP JETSAM
JETTY JET DIKE GROIN JUTTY
  BRIDGE OVERHANG
JEW SAINT ESSENE JUDEAN LITVAK
  SEMITE SMOUCH TOBIAD BARABAS
  GRECIAN MARRANO SMOUSER
  APIKOROS CONVERSO GALICIAN
  JUDAHITE LANDSMAN SEPHARDI

(—S OUT OF ISRAEL) DIASPORA
(BALKAN —) LADINE
JEWEL GEM JOY DROP OUCH BIJOU
REGAL STONE BROOCH GEORGE
TRIFLE CRAPAUD GARLAND
POUNDER
(PL.) BULSE PERRIE
JEWELER GEMMARY LAPIDARY
JEWELRY ICE JUNK OUCH PARURE
COLLARET LAPIDARY
(MOCK —) LOGIE
(PIECE OF —) GAUD
JEWELWEED CEROLINE EARJEWEL
SNAPWEED
JEWFISH MERO GUASA WARSAW
PERCOID JUNEFISH MULLOWAY
SERRANID
JEWISH JUDAIC SEMITIC
(— BODY) VAAD
(— COMMUNITY) KEHILLAH
(— QUARTER) MELLAH
(— SCHOOL) ALJAMA
JEWRY GHETTO JUDAISM
JEW'S-HARP HARP TROMP TRUMP
GEWGAW FLAMFEW TRANGAM
GUIMBARD
JEW'S MALLOW DESI
JEZEBEL GILLIVER
JIB GIB DEMUR GIGUE GIBBET
SPITFIRE
JIBE (ALSO SEE GIBE) GEE KAY GAFF
GIBE JAPE JERK MOCK SKIT AGREE
FLIRD MARCH SNACK THRUST
JIFFY JIFF BRAID FLISK WHIFF
GLIFFY GLIFFING
JIG BUCK FRISK GIGUE SQUID
GARLIC JIGGER JIGGET JITTER
LOCATOR
(— FOR WASHING ORE) HUTCH
(FISHING —) PILK
JIGGER SHOT DANDY PIQUE
DOODAD GADGET JIGMAN VATMAN
CHIGGER
JIGGLE DIDDLE JUGGLE TEETER
JILT GUNK KICK SACK BEGOWK
BEGUNK MITTEN
JIMMY BETTY JAMES JEMMY
JIMSONWEED DATURA DEWTRY
JIMSON FIREWEED STRAMONY
JINGLE CHIME CLINK DINGLE RICKLE
TINKLE CHINKLE DINGDONG
JINGLING
(MEANINGLESS —) SPORT
JINGLING SMIT JANGLE RIGADIG
TINKLING
JINGO WARRIOR WARMONGER
JINKER WHIM
JINN DJIN JANN AFRIT GENIE AFREET
DJINNI SHAITAN
(PL.) JINNI
JINNI MARID AFREET ALUKAH
GENIUS YAKSHA YAKSHI JINNIVEH
JINRIKIMAN KURUMAYA
JINRIKISHA GOCART KURUMA
RICKSHAW
JINX HEX JONAH HOODOO
JIPIJAPA CHIDRA PALMILLA
TOQUILLA
JITTERBUG TRUCKING

JITTERY JUMPY SPOOKY AJITTER
JIVARO JIBARO SHUARA XIBARO
JOAN JUG JONE
(— OF ARC) PUCELLE
JOB LAY TUT CHAR FIST SHOP TURN
BERTH CHORE FIRST BILLET.
HUSTLE JOBSITE SWEATER
BUSINESS
(EASY —) BLUDGE
(SMALL —) CHORE JOBBLE
JOBBER BRAGER DEALER FLUNKY
BROGGER COURSER
JOB'S TEARS COIX ADLAI ADLAY
JOCKEY JOCK ROPER WASTER
CHANTER EQUISON TURFITE
SKIPJACK
(DISC —) DEEJAY
JOCOSE JOCO LEPID JOCULAR
JOCOTE MOMBIN
JOCOTE DE MICO BARBAS
JOCULAR GAY AIRY GLAD JOKY
DROLL FUNNY HAPPY JOLLY MERRY
WITTY BLITHE ELATED JAPISH
JOCOSE JOCUND JOKISH JOVIAL
JOYFUL JOYOUS LIVELY BUOYANT
COMICAL FESTIVE GLEEFUL
PLAYFUL WAGGISH ANIMATED
CHEERFUL DEBONAIR GLADSOME
HUMOROUS JOCATORY JOKESOME
LAUGHING MIRTHFUL
JOCULARITY FUN WAGGERY
JOCUND BUDGE JOCANT JOCULAR
JOE JO
(HALF —) JOANNES JOHANNES
JOE-PYE WEED EUPATORY
JOEWOOD JOEBUSH BARBASCO
IRONWOOD
JOG BOB HOD JAG JIG JOT MOG
KICK POKE SHOG SPUD STIR TROT
WHIG DUNCH HOTCH NUDGE TWEAK
DIDDLE JITTER JOGGLE JUNDIE
(— ALONG) FADGE FODGE
(— AWKWARDLY) DODGE
(— WITH ELBOW) DUNCH
JOGGER LAYBOY
JOGGLE HOTCH JUGGLE SHOGGLE
SHOOGLE
JOHANNES JOE PECA
JOHN IAN JEAN JOCK JONE JUAN
SEAN JOHANN SEAGHAN GIOVANNI
JOHNNYCAKE CORNCAKE
JOIN ADD COP FAY MIX PAN TAG TIE
UNY ALLY COPE FAIR FUSE GAIN
GLUE KNIT LINK MEET MELL SEAM
SOUD TAIL TEAM YOKE ANNEX
BLEND ENTER FRANK GRAFT
JOINT MERGE TENON UNITE WRING
ACCEDE ADJECT ADJOIN ASSIST
ATTACH CEMENT COCKET COMMIT
CONCUR ENGAGE INDENT JOGGLE
MARROW MINGLE PIECEN RELATE
RELIDE SPLICE STITCH STRIKE
COMBINE CONJOIN CONNECT
CONTACT INJOINT JOINING SHACKLE
ACCOUPLE COALESCE COMPOUND
COPULATE DOVETAIL JUNCTION
(— BATTLE) JOUST ENGAGE
(— BY SEWING) STITCH SUTURE
(— CLOSELY) FAY AFFY WELD
GRAFT

(— IN COMBAT) BUCKLE
(— IN MARRIAGE) WED TACK HITCH
COUPLE
(— THE PARTS OF) PIECE
(— TOGETHER) CLOSE COAPT
FRANK HITCH COUPLE ENGLUE
ENJOIN ASSEMBLE COAGMENT
COALESCE
JOINED JOINT ALLIED DIRECT
SEAMED ACCOLLE ADJUNCT
APPINED EMBOITE ADJUGATE
COMBINED CONJUNCT COPULATE
INTEGRAL
JOINER SNUG JOINTER
JOINING BAR JOIN SEAM BRIDE
CLOSE SPLICE BETWEEN JOINDER
ADDITION JUNCTION JUNCTIVE
JUNCTURE SYNECTIC
JOINT BED HAR HIP BUTT COXA FISH
HEAD HELL HOCK JOIN KNEE LITH
LOCK SEAL SEAM TUCK ANKLE
BRAZE BUILD CARDO CHASE ELBOW
MITER MITRE PLACE SCAPE SCARF
SPALD UNION UNITE WRIST BOXING
COMMON HAUNCH SCARPH SPLICE
STIFLE SUTURE TOGGLE UNITER
ARTHRON ARTICLE COGGING
DIGITAL FETLOCK FLEXURE ISCHIUM
JOINING KNUCKLE SCATTER
SHIPLAP SIAMESE CONJOINT
CONJUNCT COUPLING DIACLASE
DOVETAIL FLASHING JOINTURE
JUNCTURE SUBJOINT SUFFRAGO
TROCHOID VARIATOR
(— ABOVE HOCK) STIFLE
(— OF BIRD'S WING) FLEXURE
(— OF FLAIL) CAPEL
(— OF MEAT) BARON
(— OF SHIP) CHASE
(— OF STEM) NODE
(ANKLE —) COOT
(ELBOW —) NOOP
(FLEXIBLE —) HINGE
(GROOVED —) RABBET
(HIP —) COXA THURL
(MASONRY —) JOGGLE
(MINING —) CLEAT SLINE
(SCARF —) BOXING
(UNIVERSAL —) CARDAN
(VERTICAL —) BUILD
(WHEEL-LIKE —) TROCHITE
JOINTED ARTHROUS
JOINTED CHARLOCK KRAUT
RUNCH
JOINTER JOINER SKIMMER
JOINT FIR EPHEDRA
JOINT GRASS PASPALUM
JOIST GEEST LEDGE BRIDGE RAGLIN
SLEEPER CARRIAGE
(PL.) PIGGIN JOISTING
JOJOBA PIGNUT SHEEPNUT
JOKE BAR DOR FUN GAB GAG GIG
JOE KID ROT WIT FOOL GAFF GAME
GAUD GEGG JAPE JEST JOSH LICE
NOTE QUIP QUIZ TYPE BREAK
CRACK FLIRT GLEEK GRIND LAUGH
PRANK RALLY SPORT BANTER
JAPERY PLISKY WHEEZE JOKELET
WAGGERY CHESTNUT

(PRACTICAL —) BAR FUN GAG RIG
HOAX REAK SHAVIE HOTFOOT
(STALE —) CHESTNUT
(PL.) JAPERY
JOKER BUG DOR WAG CLOWN GRIND
SLAVE FARCER FOOLER GAGGER
JOKIST FARCEUR GIMMICK
FUNNYMAN HUMORIST JOKESTER
JOKING JOSH BANTER JOCOSE
(PRACTICAL —) GAME
JOLLIFICATION RAG RANT JOLLY
JOLLITY MIRTH GAIETY HILARITY
JOLLITRY
JOLLY GAY KID BUXOM GAWSY
WALLY CROUSE JOVIAL STRING
JOCULAR DISPOSED
JOLLY BOAT YAWL DANDY
JOLT JET JIG JOG JOT JUT BELT
BUMP DIRD DIRL HIKE JOWL JUMP
KICK SHOG JAUNT HOTTER IMPACT
JOGGLE JOSTLE JOUNCE JUMBLE
JOLTING JERKY BUMPITY HOTTERY
JONAH JINX JONAS HOODOO
JONQUIL JONK LILY DAFFODIL

JORDAN

CAPITAL: AMMAN
COIN: DINAR
MOUNTAIN: BUKKA DABAB ATAIBA
MUBRAK
REGION: PEREA BASHAN PERAEA
RIVER: JORDAN YARMUK
TOWN: AQABA ARIHA IRBID KARAK
ZARQA ZERKE NABLUS

JOSEPH JOSEY GIUSEPPE
JOSEPHINE BLUSH PHENY
JOSH GUY KID RIB JOKE CHAFF
STRING
JOSHI JOTI JOTISARU
JOSHUA JESUS
JOSTLE JOG JOLT JOSS PUSH SHOG
CROWD ELBOW HUNCH JUNDY
SHOVE HURTLE HUSTLE JOGGLE
JUNDIE JUSTLE SHOULDER
JOSTLING SCRAMBLE
JOT ACE DOT ATOM IOTA MITE TARE
WHIT GRAIN MINIM POINT TWINT
WIGHT TITTLE SCRUPLE SYLLABLE
(— DOWN) NICK
JOTTING TOT
JOTUNN GEIRROTH
JOUNCE HIKE JOLT JAUNT
JOURNAL TOE BOOK DIARY PAPER
BLAZER SERIAL DAYBOOK DIURNAL
GAZETTE GUDGEON JOURNEY
CASHBOOK NOCTUARY TRUNNION
(SEA —) LOGBOOK
JOURNAL BEARING RHODING
JOURNALIST SCRIBE WRITER
BYLINER DIARIAN
JOURNEY BE GO JOG RUN WAY
DIET EYRE FARE FORE GAIT GANG
GATE HIKE JUMP RACE RIDE ROAD
STEP TOUR TREK TRIP TURN WENT
BROAD COVER DRIVE JAUNT REISE
SITHE TRAIK TRAIL TURUS WEENT
ERRAND FLIGHT HEGIRA JUNKET
TRAVEL VAGARY COMMINO

EMBASSY ENTRADA EXCURSE
JORNADA JOURNAL MEANDER
PASSAGE STRETCH TRAVAIL
TROUNCE WALKING WAYFARE
GODSPEED PROGRESS
(— BY SEA) VOYAGE
(— DOWNSTREAM) DESCEND
(DAY'S —) DIET
(DESERT —) JORNADA
(FATIGUING —) TRAIK
(LONG —) TREK
(TEDIOUS —) TRANCE
JOURNEYING CRUISE
JOURNEYMAN YEOMAN
JOUST PLAY TILT JOSTLE JUSTLE
TOURNEY
JOUSTER TILTER
JOVIAL GAY BOON JOVY BULLY
JOLLY MERRY GENIAL HEARTY
MELLOW BACCHIC HOLIDAY
JOCULAR
JOVIALITY JOLLITY ROLLICK
HILARITY
JOWL CHOW CHAULE
(PL.) CHOPS
JOY JO WIN GLEE LIST PLAY BLISS
DREAM EXULT MIRTH REVEL GAIETY
HEYDAY DELIGHT ECSTASY ELATION
JOYANCE RAPTURE REVELRY
FELICITY GLADNESS HILARITY
PLEASURE
JOYFUL GAY GLAD BEAMY JOLLY
BLITHE FESTUS JOCUND JOVIAL
JOYANT JOYOUS GAUDFUL GLADFUL
GLEEFUL JOCULAR GLADSOME
JOYFULLY FAIN FAINLY GLADLY
JOYOUSLY
JOYLESS DESOLATE LUSTLESS
UNBLITHE
JOYOUS GAY GLAD JOLLY MERRY
YOUSE BLITHE JOVIAL FESTIVE
GIOJOSO GLEEFUL JOCULAR
FROHLICH SUNSHINY
JOYOUSNESS HILARITY
JUBILANT ELATED JOYFUL
EXULTANT
JUBILATION JOY JOYANCE JUBILEE
JUDAHITE JEW
JUDAISM JEWISM HEBRAISM
JUDAS TREE CERCIS
JUDEA JEWRY
JUDEO-SPANISH LADINO
JUDGE DAN JUS SEE WIG CAID CAZY
DEEM DOOM HOLD IMAM JUEZ JURY
KAZI SCAN AWARD COUNT COURT
DAYAN GAUGE HAKIM INFER JUDEX
MINOS OPINE PUNEE TRIER WEIGH
CENSOR CRITIC DANIEL DEEMER
DICAST DOOMER INTEND JUDGER
JURIST OPINER PUISNE SAMSON
SAMUEL SETTLE SQUIRE ACCOUNT
ADJUDGE ARBITER BENCHER
BRIDOYE CENSURE FLAGMAN
FOUJDAR HELIAST JURYMAN
JUSTICE MUNSIFF PODESTA
REFEREE SCABINE SHAMGAR
SUPPOSE APPRAISE CENTENAR
CONCLUDE CONSIDER DEEMSTER
DEMPSTER DIRECTOR DOOMSMAN

DOOMSTER ESTIMATE FOREDEEM
JEPHTHAH JUDGMENT JUDICATE
LINESMAN MINISTER MITTIMUS
ORDINARY QUAESTOR RECORDER
REGICIDE SCABINUS STRADICO
JUDGMENT ACT EYE BOOK DEEM
DOME DOOM REDE VIEW ARRET
AWARD FANCY JUISE SENSE SIGHT
SKILL TASTE ADVICE ASSIZE
DECREE ESTEEM JUWISE STEVEN
ACCOUNT CENSURE CONCEIT
HOLDING OPINION VERDICT WITTING
ESTIMATE JUDICIAL JUDICIUM
SAGACITY SENTENCE THINKING
JUDICATORY SYNOD
JUDICIOUS WISE CRITICAL JUDICIAL
MODERATE SENSEFUL SENSIBLE
WISELIKE
JUDO (— EXERCISES) KATA
(— PRACTICE) RANDORI
JUG CAN EWER JACK JUST ASCUS
ASKOS BUIRE GAMLA GOTCH
JORUM JUBBE STEAN BOGGLE
CROUKE GOGLET GOMLAH HYDRIA
CREAMER PITCHER CRUISKEN
LECYTHUS LEKYTHOS OENOCHOE
PROCHOOS
(— WITH SPOUT) BUIRE DOLLIN
(ALE —) TOBY
(BULGING —) GOTCH
(LEATHER —) JACK BOMBARD
(ONE-HANDLED —) URCEUS
(SPOUTLESS —) OLPE
JUGATED BAJOIRE
JUGGLE TRICK BAFFLE FUMBLE
CONJURE SHUFFLE
JUGGLER HARLOT CONJURER
JONGLEUR
JUGLONE NUCIN
JUGULARES DERIPIA
JUGUM FIBULA JUGULUM
JUICE JUS SEW BREE BROO FOND
OOZE SUCK ANIMA BLOND BLOOD
GRAVY HUMOR MOBBY PERRY
CASIRI CREMOR JIPPER SUCCUS
CAMBIUM AGUAMIEL HYPOCIST
VERJUICE
(— OF COCONUT) MILK
(— OF TREE) SAP LYCIUM
JELUTONG
(— OF UNRIPE FRUIT) OMPHACY
(APPLE —) CIDER
(CANE —) SLING
(CONCENTRATED —) SIRUP SYRUP
(DRIED —) ALOE KINO
(FERMENTED —) SURA GRAPE
(FRUIT —) ROB ROHOB
(GRAPE —) MUST SAPA STUM
(INTOXICATING —) SOMA
(LETTUCE —) THRIDACE
(MEAT —) BLOND
(POPPY —) CHICK
(TOBACCO —) AMBEER AMBIER
(PL.) ESSENCE HUMIDITY
JUICY FAT FRIM FRUM NAISH SAPPY
FRUITY SUCCOSE WATERISH
JUJUBE BER ELB TSAO LOTEBUSH
LOTEWOOD ZIZYPHUS
JUKEBOX PICCOLO

JUMBLE PIE ROG HASH MESS MUSS
RAFF BOTCH BOLLIX BUMBLE
FUDDLE GARBLE HUDDLE JUMPER
JUNGLE MEDLEY MOMBLE MUDDLE
PALTER RAFFLE WELTER WUZZLE
CLUTTER CONFUSE EMBROIL
GOULASH SHUFFLE DISORDER
MISHMASH RHAPSODY SMACHRIE
(— **OF SOUNDS**) LURRY
JUMBLED CRAZY HASHY JUMBLY
HUDDLING
JUMP HOP LEP NIP DART JETE LEAP
LUTZ SKIP SKIT STEN STOT TUMB
BOUND CAPER FENCE HALMA
SALTO SAULT SPANG SPEND START
STOIT VAULT DOUBLE FOOTER
HURDLE INSULT LAUNCH SPRING
SPRUNT STARRE WALLOP CISEAUX
CROWHOP SALTATE SKYLARK
BALLONNE
(— **ABOUT**) SKIT CAPER
(— **FROM AIRCRAFT**) BAIL BALE
(— **IN FENCING**) BALESTRA
(— **ON HORSEBACK**) LARK
(— **ON SKATES**) AXEL SALCHOW
(PL.) ALLEGRO
JUMPER LAMMY SWAGE BARKER
LEPPER HANDYMAN
JUMPING SALIENT SALTANT
JUMPY ITCHY
JUNCO SNOWBIRD
JUNCTION HIP FROG JOIN CLOSE
CROWN UNION FILLET INFALL
CONTACT JOINING MEETING UNITION
JUNCTURE
(— **OF EARTH AND SKY**) HORIZON
(— **OF STREAMS**) GRAINS
(— **OF THREADS**) FELL STOP
(— **ON TOOTH**) CERVIX
JUNCTURE PASS PINCH CRISIS
STRAIT ARTICLE BRACKET JOINING
OPHRYON EXIGENCY JOINTAGE
JOINTURE OCCASION QUANDARY

JUNEBERRY SHADBLOW SHADBUSH
JUNE BUG BUZZARD DUMCLOCK
JUNGLE BUSH RUKH SHOLA
BOONDOCK
JUNGLE BENDY WEENONG
JUNIOR PUNY CADET YOUNG PUISNE
YOUNGER
JUNIPER CADE EZEL GORSE GORST
SAVIN SABINE
JUNK CRAM GEAR GOOK TOPE
DRECK REFUSE SCULCH DISCARD
PLUNDER TONGKANG
(**WORTHLESS** —) SLUM
JUNKET TRIP KNACK JINKET SAFARI
JUNKMAN TATTER SCRAPMAN
SCAVENGER
JUNO MONETA PRONUBA
JUPITER JOVE STATOR FORTUNE
MUSHTARI TERMINUS
JUPITER'S BEARD JOUBARB
JUR LWO LUOH
JUREL RUNNER CREVALLE HARDTAIL
JURISDICTION SOC BAIL SOKE
FUERO HONOR REALM ABBACY
BANDON BEYLIK DANGER DIWANI
RIDING SPHERE DEANERY DEWANEE
DROSTDY EMIRATE KHANATE
BAILIERY FOUJDARY LIGEANCE
PASHALIC PROVINCE
(— **OF BISHOP**) SEE
(**COERCIVE** —) SWORD
(**MORMON** —) KEYS
JURISPRUDENCE LAW REPORTS
JURIST JUDGE MUFTI BREHON
LAWYER DOTTORE
JUROR JURAT ASSIZER JURYMAN
CENTUMVIR
JURY ARRAY PANEL QUEST ASSIZE
JURATA COUNTRY EMPANEL
INQUEST
(— **COUNTY**) VISNE
JURYMAN DICAST JURIST ASSIZER

JURY-RIGGED HAYWIRE
JUST ALL DUE EVEN FAIR FLOP LEAL
TRUE EQUAL FIRST LEVEL NOBUT
ROUND VALID ZADOC CANDID
GIUSTO HONEST JUSTIN JUSTUS
MERELY SQUARE EQUABLE
LEESOME UPRIGHT LIEFSOME
RIGHTFUL SKILLFUL UNBIASED
(— **AS**) AFTER
(— **HOVE CLEAR**) ATRIP
(— **IN TIME**) SONICA
(**ONLY** —) HARDLY SCARCELY
JUSTAUCORPS JUSTICO
JUSTICE LAW DOOM RIGHT SKILL
DHARMA EQUITY REASON HONESTY
SHALLOW SILENCE DEEMSTER
JUDGMENT JUSTITIA JUSTNESS
RECORDER
(— **OF PEACE**) BEAK SQUIRE
JUSTIFIABLY FAIRLY
JUSTIFICATION CALL COLOR
EXCUSE APOLOGY DEFENCE
WARRANT APOLOGIA
JUSTIFIED FAIR JUST
JUSTIFY AVOW CLEAR PROVE SALVE
DEFEND EXCUSE HONEST EXPLAIN
RECTIFY SUPPORT WARRANT
MAINTAIN SANCTION UNDERPIN
JUSTLY WELL TRULY EVENLY FAIRLY
EQUALLY HANDILY SQUARELY
JUSTNESS SQUARE FITNESS
JUSTICE ACCURACY
JUSTUS JESUS
JUT HANG BULGE JETTY JUTTY
BEETLE EXTEND IMPEND EXTRUDE
JUTE PAT DESI PAUT DAISEE
ARAMINA CHINGMA
JUTTING HANGING
JUVENILE YOUNG JEJUNE PUERILE
YOUTHFUL
JUXTAPOSED ADJACENT
JUXTAPOSITION BALANCE
CONTACT CONTRAST NEARNESS

K KA KAY KILO KING
KAABA CAABA ALCAABA
KABAYA BADJU CABIE
KABELJOU KOB
KABISTAN KUBA
KABOB KEBOB SHASLIK
KABUKALLI CUPIUBA
KACHARI BODO
KACHIN SINGFO SINGPO CHINGPAW
KADAGA COORG
KAFFIR KATI XOSA FINGO TEMBU
CAFFRE INFIDEL TAMBUKI WAIGULI
(— BOY) UMFAAN
KAGU GRUIFORM
KAIKAWAKA CEDAR
KAINGIN SWIDDEN
KAKI TRIUMPH
KALAPOOIAN LAKMIUT
KALE COLE KAIL COLLARD SPROUTS
BORECOLE
KALMUCK ELEUT UIRAD KHOSHOT
KALUMPIT ANAGEP
KAMAHI BIRCH TOWAI
KAMALA WURRUS ROTTLERA
KAMICHI SCREAMER
KANA IROFA IROHA
KANGAROO ROO EURO BILBI FLIER
FLYER TUNGO BOOMER FOSTER
WOILIE DIDELPH POTOROO
WALLABY BETTONGA BOONGARY
FILANDER FORESTER WALLAROO
(FEMALE —) DOE GIN
(YOUNG —) JOEY
KANGAROO APPLE GUNYANG
POROPORO
KANGAROO RAT JERBOA
KANHOBAL CONOB
KANKANAI IGOROT
KANS KUSA GLAGA KUSHA GLAGAH

KANSAS

CAPITAL: TOPEKA
COLLEGE: BAKER TABOR
BETHANY STERLING WASHBURN
COUNTY: ELK GOVE NESS RENO
TREGO NEMAHA ATCHISON
FORT: RILEY SCOTT
INDIAN: KANSA KIOWA PAWNEE
WICHITA COMANCHE
LAKE: CHENEY KIRWIN NEOSHO
MILFORD
MOUNTAIN: SUNFLOWER
NATIVE: JAYHAWK
NICKNAME: SUNFLOWER
PRESIDENT: EISENHOWER
RIVER: ARKANSAS MISSOURI
STATE BIRD: MEADOWLARK
STATE FLOWER: SUNFLOWER
STATE TREE: COTTONWOOD
TOWN: HAYS IOLA COLBY DODGE
SALINA CHANUTE LIBERAL
WICHITA

KANSAN JAYHAWK
KAOLIANG SORGHUM
KAPOK CEIBO FLOSS
KARAISM ANANISM
KARAKA KOPI
KARA KIRGHIZ BURUT BOUROUT

KARATAS PITA
KAREN SGAU SGAW
KARENNI PADAUNG
KARMA (BAD —) DEMERIT
KASKA NAHANE
KAT KHAT QUAT CAFTA
KATE KAI
KAUNAS KOVNO
KAURI COWRIE BERAIROU
KAVA AVA AWA YAQONA KAVAKAVA
YANGGONA
KAW AKHA
KAZOO BAZOO GAZOO ZARAH
HEWGAG MIRLITON
KEEL FIN BACK SEEL BARGE CARINA
CRISTA SERRULA
(— OF BIRD'S MANDIBLE) GONYS
(AFTERPART OF —) SKAG SKEG
KEEN DRY FLY GAY SHY YAP ACID
DEAR FINE GAIR GLEG HIGH PERT
TART TEEN WAIL WARM WILD
ACUTE BREME BRIEF BRISK EAGER
QUICK SHARP SMART SNELL SPICY
VIVID ASTUTE BITTER CAOINE
GREEDY LIVELY SEVERE SHREWD
SHRILL CUNNING HAWKING
MORDANT PARLISH PARLOUS
PUNGENT SERIOUS THIRSTY
KEENER HOWLER
KEENLY KEEN FELLY DEARLY
ACUTELY
KEENNESS EDGE ACUITY ACUMEN
PUNGENCY
(— OF SIGHT) ACIES
KEEN-SCENTED NOSEWISE
KEEN-SIGHTED EAGLE
KEEP HUG HAVE HOLD SALT SAVE
WAIT WITE BLESS ROCCA WITIE
COFFER DETAIN CONFINE CONTAIN
DEFORCE HUSBAND KEEPING
RESERVE CONSERVE MAINTAIN
PRESERVE RESTRAIN WITHHOLD
(— A COURSE) CAPE
(— A SMALL SHOP) CRAME
(— A WOUND OPEN) TENT
(— ABREAST) FOLLOW
(— AFLOAT) BUOY
(— AN EYE ON) STAG
(— APART) DOTTLE ISOLATE
SEPARATE
(— AT A DISTANCE) ESTRANGE
(— AWAY FROM) ABHOR AVOID
(— AWAY) ABSENT
(— BACK) HAP ROB STAY ARREAR
DETAIN RETARD RESERVE
(— COMPANY WITH) GANG MOOP
CONSORT
(— FREE) ESCHEW
(— FROM BOILING OVER) KEEL
(— FROM BURNING) REDD
(— HIDDEN) HOARD SECRETE
(— IN CIRCULATION) WIND
(— IN EXCITEMENT) ALARM ALARUM
(— IN MIND) RETAIN
(— IN ORDER) TARGE
(— IN STOCK) CARRY
(— IN THE TRACK) GATHER
(— IN) CAGE
(— OFF) FEND WEAR SHIELD

(— OUT) BAR EXPEL
(— POSSESSION) HARBOR
(— SCORELESS) BLANK
(— SECRET) HUSH WHIST
(— STRAIGHT) DIRECT
(— TABS ON) FINGER
(— TIME) GO
(— TO ONESELF) BOSOM
(— UNTIL YEAR OLD) HOG
(— UP) SUBSIST SUSTAIN CONTINUE
(— WAITING) DELAY
(— WARM) STIVE STOVE FOSTER
(— WATCH) TOUT WAIT BEWAKE
KEEPER NAB KEEP SCREW TUTOR
YEMER CUSTOS GAOLER JAILER
LIFTER LOOKER PARKER PASTOR
RAHDAR RANGER WARDEN BAILIFF
CURATOR GEARMAN PIKEMAN
PROVOST BEARWARD DEERHERD
DOLLYMAN ELDERMAN FEWTERER
GUARDANT GUARDIAN HOUNDMAN
TRAITEUR WARRENER
(— OF CATTLE) HAYWARD
(— OF DOGS) FEWTERER
(— OF ELEPHANT) MAHOUT
(— OF PRISON) GAOLER JAILER
WARDEN ALCAIDE
(DOOR —) DURWAN
KEEPING CARE WARD CHARGE
CUSTODY DETAINER
KEEPSAKE DRURY TOKEN GIFTBOOK
SOUVENIR
KEEVE TUB KIEVE
KEG CAG PIN TUB CADE CASK KNAG
WOOD ANKER BARRICO COSTREL
KELP KILP LEAG VAREC WRACK
GIRDLE SEAWEED BELLWARE
KELPIE BARB
KELT SLAT
KENAF DA GOMBO MESTA AMBARI
KANAFF PAPOULA STOKROOS
KENNEL STALL VENERY VENISON
DOGHOUSE
KENO HOUSE
KENTISH (— UNIT) YOKE

KENTUCKY

CAPITAL: FRANKFORT
COLLEGE: BEREA ASBURY
CENTRE BRESCIA URSULINE
COUNTY: ADAIR ESTIL TRIGG
FAYETTE MENIFEE MAGOFFIN
INDIAN: SHAWNEE CHEROKEE
IROQUOIS
LAKE: CUMBERLAND
RIVER: DIX OHIO SALT BARREN
STATE BIRD: CARDINAL
STATE FLOWER: GOLDENROD
STATE TREE: TULIP
TOWN: BEREA CORBIN HAZARD
GLASGOW PADUCAH DANVILLE
COVINGTON LEXINGTON

KENYA

BAY: FORMOSA
CAPITAL: NAIROBI
COIN: SHILLING

LAKE: MAGADI RUDOLF NAIVASHA VICTORIA
LANGUAGE: LUO KIKUYU SWAHILI
MEASURE: WARI
MOUNTAIN: KENYA KULAL NYIRU MATIAN LOGONOT
PEOPLE: LUO MERU BANTU KAMBA KISII LUHYA MASAI NANDI KIKUYU OGADEN BALUYHA HAMITIC HILOTIC TURKANA KIPSIGIS
RIVER: LAK ATHI TANA TURKWELL
TOWN: MERU KITUI NAROK KIPINI KISUMU MOYALE NAKURU NAYUKI ELDORET MALINDI MOMBASA

KERCHIEF CURCH ROMAL RUMAL ANALAV CYPRUS MADRAS NAPKIN PEPLUM CYPRESS KERCHER PANUELO THERESE BABUSHKA BANDANNA HEADRAIL KAFFIYEH KINGSMAN
KERF CARF SKAFF GROOVE UNDERCUT
KERI QRI KERE
KERMANSHAH COCONUT
KERMES GRAIN
KERNEL NUT BUNT CORE KERN MEAT PITH BERRY GOODY GROAT ACINUS ALMOND CARNEL PICKLE NUCLEUS
(**CORN —S)** HOMINY
(**UNHUSKED —S)** CAPES
(**PL.)** NIXTAMAL
KEROGEN SAPROPEL
KEROSINE PARAFFIN
KERSENNEH ERS ERVIL
KERSEY WASHER ORDINARY
KESTREL FANNER KEELIE STANNEL STANCHEL WINDHOVER
KETCH SAIC
KETONE IRONE ACETOL ARMONE CARONE CARVOL COTOIN HEXONE IONONE QUINOL ACETOIN ACETONE ACYLOIN BAEKEOL BENZOIN CAMPHOR CARVONE DYPNONE FLAVONE JASMONE MUSCONE PHORONE SHOGAOL THUJONE ACRIDONE ANTHRONE BUTANONE BUTYRONE CHALCONE CHALKONE CHROMONE DEGUELIN EXALIONE FENCHONE MENTHONE PROPIONE PULEGONE ROTENONE STEARONE TAGETONE THIENONE VALERONE XANTHONE
KETTLE LEAD STEW DIXIE BOILER CANNER FESSEL MARMIT MASLIN TRIPOD VESSEL CALDRON SKILLET STEWPOT CALABASH FLAMBEAU
KETTLEDRUM NAKER ATABAL KETTLE TIMBAL TYMBAL TIMBALE TYMPANY
KEVEL CAVEL KNAPPER
KEY CAY KAY CLEW CLUE CRIB FLAT JACK KING NOTE PLUG PONY DITAL SCREW TASTO WREST BUTTON CHIAVE CIPHER CLAVIS COTTER

SAMARA SPLINE WINDER DIGITAL LANGUET PASSKEY SPEAKER LATCHKEY
(**— FOR TUNING HARP)** WREST
(**— OF KEYBOARD INSTRUMENT)** MANUAL
(**— OF LIFE)** ANKH
(**— OF ORGAN)** TASTO DIGITAL
(**— OF PIANO)** IVORY NATURAL
(**— OF SPINET)** CHIP
(**— ON WOODWIND INSTRUMENT)** LANGUET SPEAKER
(**— UP)** STRING
(**—S OF CARILLON)** CLAVECIN
(**ARITHMETICAL —)** ADDITIVE
(**ASH —)** PIGEON
(**FALSE —)** GLUT
(**FEATHER —)** FIN STOP SPLINE FEATHER
(**SKELETON —)** GILT TWIRLER
(**TELEGRAPH —)** BUG TAPPER
KEYBOARD CLAVIER PEDALIER
KEYHOLE KEY LOCKHOLE
KEYNOTE A B D E KEY TONIC FINALIS
KEYSTONE KEY QUOIN VERTEX SAGITTA VOUSSOIR
(**— STATE)** PENNSYLVANIA
KEYWAY SPLINE KEYSLOT
KEX KECKSY
KHA KA KHMU KACHE LAMET
KHALAT SEERPAW
KHAN CAN CHAM HAWN TACON KHAKAN
KHAS-KURA NEPALI PAHARI PARBATI GORKHALI
KHATTISH HATTIC
KHEDIVE QUITEVE
KHELLIN VISAMMIN
KHOTANA KOYUKON
KHUSKHUS CUSCUS VETIVER
KIANG CHIGETAI HEMIONUS
KIBBLE GIG KETTLE
KIBBLER CRACKER
KICK BOOT FICK FLEG FLIG FOOT FUNK HEEL HOOF LASH PORR POTE PUNT SHIN TURF YERK ANGLE BUNCH FLING KEVEL PAUSE PUNCH SKELP SPANG SPURN CHARGE CORNER FITTER KICKER KICKUP SPIRAL VOLLEY DROPOUT FOUETTE KICKOFF DROPKICK
(**— ABOUT)** SPARTLE
(**— AS A HORSE)** FLING WINCE
(**— HEELS UP)** SPURN
(**— ON SHINS)** HACK SHINNER
(**BALLET —)** BRUSH
(**SOCCER —)** CORNER
KICKER TEDDER WINCER
KID COD FUN POD TUB FAWN FOOL JIVE JOKE CHILD FAGOT HORSE JOLLY KIDDY SPOOF KIDLET SQUIRT DECEIVE EANLING FATLING TICCHEN YOUNGER CHEVEREL YEANLING
KIDDING JOKE SPOOFERY
KIDNAP STEAL PANYAR SPIRIT
KIDNAPER SPIRIT PLAGIARY SNATCHER SPIRITER
KIDNAPING SNATCH PLAGIUM PLAGIARY

KIDNEY NEAR NEER REIN NEPHRON
(**PL.)** REINS ROGNONS
KIDNEY BEAN FRIJOLE
(**PL.)** FASELS
KIER KEEVE PUFFER
KIESELGUHR DOPE GUHR
KILL DO BAG END GET OUT PIP BANE BOLO COOK COOL DOWN FELL MORT NECK SLAY TAME WING BLAST BRAIN CROAK CULLE FETCH FORDO GANCH MISDO NAPOO QUELL SABER SCRAG SHOOT SMITE SNUFF SPEED SPEND SPILL SPOIL STALL STICK SWELT SWORD CORPSE DEADEN DIDDLE FAMISH FINISH HANDLE IMPALE MARTYR MURDER POISON STARVE UNLIVE ACHIEVE BUTCHER DESTROY EXECUTE FLATTEN HATCHET KILLING MORTIFY SMOTHER STONKER SUICIDE DEATHIFY DISPATCH DISSOLVE IMMOLATE JUGULATE STILETTO
(**— ANIMALS)** CONTROL
(**— BY STONING)** LAPIDATE
(**— BY SUBMERSION)** STIFLE
(**— CALF AFTER BIRTH)** DEACON
(**— CATTLE)** PITH
(**— EVERY TENTH)** DECIMATE
(**— GAME)** SATCHEL
(**— OFF)** ENECATE
(**— SMALL GAME)** BARK
(**— TIME)** GOOF
KILLDEER KILLDEE DEERKILL
KILLED KILT WINGED SKITTLED
(**FRESHLY —)** GREEN
KILLER GUN GUNMAN SLAYER TORPEDO MURDERER THRESHER
KILLER WHALE ORCA DOLPHIN GRAMPUS
KILLIFISH KELLY KILLY MINNOW COBBLER GUDGEON MAYFISH MUDFISH PANCHAX FUNDULUS ROCKFISH SACALAIT STUDFISH SWAMPINE
KILLING FELL KILL MORT QUELL TUANT MURDER CLEANUP HANGING CLEANING DISPATCH FELICIDE HOMICIDE
KILLJOY NARK GLOOM LEMON SOURPUSS
KILN BING KEEL LEHR OAST CULLE DRIER GLAZE STOVE TILER COCKLE CUPOLA TILERY FURNACE CALCINER LIMEKILN
KILOMETER LI
KILT QUELT PIUPIU FILIBEG PHILIBEG PETTICOAT
KILTER SKEET
KIN SIB KATI KITH CUNNE FLESH FAMILY AFFINITY RELATION
KIND ILK KIN LOT BOON CAST FAIR FORM GOOD HAIR HEND LIKE MAKE MEEK MILD MODE MOLD NICE RATE SELY SOFT SORT SUIT TYPE WING BREED CLASS GENRE GENUS GESTE ORDER SPICE STAMP BENIGN BLITHE FACILE GENDER GENTLE GOODLY HUMANE KIDNEY KINDLY

MANNER MISTER NATURE SPEECE
STRAIN STRIPE TENDER EDITION
FASHION FEATHER FLESHLY
LENIENT QUALITY REGIMEN SPECIAL
SPECIES SPECKLE FRIENDLY
GENEROUS MANSUETE OBLIGING
INDULGENT
(— OF PEOPLE) FOLK
(— OF) A
(DIFFERENT IN —) DIVERS
(DISTINCTIVE —) BRAND
(OF EVERY —) ALKIN
KINDLE BEET FIRE LUNT MOVE TAKE
TEND TIND FLAME LIGHT QUICK
SPUNK ALIGHT DECOCT ENFIRE
EXCITE IGNITE ILLUME EMBLAZE
ESPRISE INCENSE INFLAME SOLICIT
KINDLING
KINDLINESS CANDOR
KINDLING FIRE BAVIN FAGOT
TINDER IGNITION
KINDLY FAIR GAIN KIND NESH
AGREE COUTH HENDE NAISH
BENIGN BLITHE COUTHY GENIAL
HOMELY INNERLY FAVOROUS
GENEROUS GRACIOUS QUEMEFUL
TOWARDLY
KINDNESS LOVE ALOHA FAVOR
BOUNTY CANDOR LENITY SERVICE
CLEMENCY EASINESS GOODNESS
HUMANITY LENITUDE MILDNESS
KINDRED KIN SIB KIND KITH BLOOD
FLESH FAMILY KOBONG NATION
STRIND COGNATE KINFOLK KINSMEN
SIBSHIP AFFINITY
KINE KYE COWS
KINETIC ACTUAL
(— POTENTIAL) L
KING RI SO BAN DAM LOT LUD PUL
REX REY RIG ROY AGAG BALI BELI
BIJA BORS BRAN BRES CRAL CZAR
JEHU KRAL LEIR MARK NUDD NUMA
OMRI OTTO PHUL RAJA RIAL TSAR
TZAR WANG YIMA ARDRI BALOR
BELUS CONOR CREON DAGDA
DAHAK EGLON ETZEL GYGES HIRAM
HOGNI HOSEA IPHIS IXION JOASH
LAIUS LLUDD LYCUS MESHA MIDAS
MINOS NADAB NEGUS NORSE
NUADA PEKAH PRIAM RAJAH SAMMY
SWAMI ZIMRI ZOHAK AEOLUS
AGENOR AILILL ALBOIN ALONSO
ALOROS ARIOCH BLADUD CODRUS
DIOMED DUNCAN ELATHA FINGAL
FRODHI FROTHI GOEMOT INKOSI
KABAKA LEMUEL LYCAON MEMNON
MINYAS NESTOR NODONS OENEUS
OGYGES PELEUS PELIAS SAUGHT
SHESHA SVAMIN TEUCER URIENS
UZZIAH VASUKI AHAZIAH AMAIMON
AMYCLAS ANGEVIN ARTEGAL
ATHAMAS BAGINDA BELINUS
BUSIRIS CACIQUE CEPHEUS
CROESUS ELIBURE EPAPHUS
EPOPEUS ETHBAAL EURYTUS
GUNTHER HYGELAC INACHUS
JAMSHID JEHOASH JEHORAM
KINGLET LAERTES LATINUS
LEONTES MENAHEM MONARCH

PANDION PHINEUS POLYBUS
REGULUS ROMULUS ROYALET
SMERDIS SOLOMON VOLSUNG
ACRISIUS ADRASTUS AEGYPTUS
ALBERICH AMRAPHEL ASNAPPER
BAHMANID BRENNIUS CLAUDIUS
COPHETUA ELDORADO ETEOCLES
GILGAMES GOEMAGOT GOGMAGOG
GORBODUC HEZEKIAH HROTHGAR
JEHOAHAZ JEROBOAM KINGLING
LAOMEDON LISUARTE MANASSEH
MELIADUS MENELAUS ODYSSEUS
ORCHAMUS OSNAPPAR OVERKING
PADISHAH PEKAHIAH PENTHEUS
RAMESSID REHOBOAM RODERICK
RODOMONT ROITELET SARPEDON
SHEPHERD SISYPHUS TANTALUS
(— AND QUEEN OF TRUMPS) BELLA
(— CHANGED TO WOLF) LYCAON
(— OF ARMS) GARTER NORROY
(— OF BEASTS) LION
(— OF DWARFS) ALBERICH
(— OF FAIRIES) OBERON
(— OF TRUMPS) HONOR
(IRISH —) RI RIG ARDRI ARDRIGH
(POLYNESIAN —) ALII ARII ARIKI
KINGBIRD PIPIRI PETCHARY
KINGBOLT KING KINGPIN MAINPIN
KING CRAB LIMULID LIMULUS
PANFISH
KINGDOM WEI REALM REIGN WORLD
ESTATE MONERA MORVEN REGION
SAXONY MITANNI
KINGFISH BARB CERO HAKE HAKU
MINK TOMCOD CHENFISH SCIAENID
TOMMYCOD
KINGFISHER HALCYON PODITTI
TOROTORO
KINGLET REGULI
KINGLY REGAL ROYAL BASILIC
IMPERIAL MAJESTIC PRINCELY
KING PARAKEET WELLAT
KINGSHIP STOOL KINGDOM
ROYALTY DEVARAJA KINGHOOD
KING'S PEACE GRITH
KING'S SCHOLAR TUG
KING VULTURE PAP PAPA
KINK NIB SNICK BUCKLE DOGLEG
KINKLE
(— IN ROPE) GRIND
KINKAJOU POTTO HEYRAT
APOROSO
KINKING FLUTING
KINKY ENCOMIC KINKLED
KINO BIJA BIJASAL
KINSHIP SIB BLOOD NASAB STOOL
ENATION KINDRED SIBNESS SIBSHIP
AFFINITY AGNATION RELATION
KINSMAN KIN SIB ALLY BLOOD
AFFINE AGNATE COUSIN FRIEND
BROTHER GOTRAJA KINDRED
WINEMAY BANDHAVA RELATION
RELATIVE
KINSWOMAN SISTER KINDRED
RELATIVE
KIP SKIP GRASSER KIPSKIN UPSTART
KIRGHIZ QYRGHYZ
KIRN MELL
KISS BA LIP NEB BASS BUSS PECK

PREE MOUTH POGUE SLAKE SMACK
BEKISS CARESS SLAVER SMOOCH
SMOUCH OSCULATE
(— OF PEACE) PAX
(— WETLY) SLOBBER
(STOLEN —) SMOORICH
KISSING LIPWORK
KIT CHIT DUFFEL KITTEN POCHETTE
(LUMBERMAN'S —) TURKEY
(MESS —) CANTEEN
KITCHEN BUT GALLEY CUISINE
KITCHIE COOKROOM
KITE LAP CHIL CYTE HAWK GLEDE
CHILLA DRACHE DRAGON ELANET
FALCON PREYER SENTRY MILVINE
PUDDOCK PUTTOCK FORKTAIL
HELLKITE
KITTEN KIT KITTY KITTLE CATLING
KITLING
KITTIWAKE GULL WAEG ANNET
KITTY PICKUP TARROCK TIRRLIE
KITTY CAT BADRANS BAUDRONS
KIVA ESTUFA
KIWI APTERYX
KLAMATH WEED AMBER
GOATWEED
KLANG PHONE
KLIPSPRINGER KAINSI KLIPBOK
KLONDIKE CANFIELD SOLITAIRE
KNACK ART FEAT FEEL GATE GIFT
HANG CATCH QUIRK TRICK SLEIGHT
WRINKLE INSTINCT
KNACKER CLAPPER
(PL.) BONES
KNAPSACK WALLET MOCHILA
MUSETTE SNAPBAG SNAPSACK
KNAPWEED SWEEP BLUETOP
FLATTOP BALLWEED BELLWEED
BOLEWEED BULLWEED BUNDWEED
CENTAURY CLUBWEED CROPWEED
HARDHEAD IRONHEAD IRONWEED
KNOTWEED MATFELON
KNAVE BOY ELF LAD NOB PAM PUR
TOM JACK BOWER CHEAT MAKER
NODDY ROGUE TIGER COQUIN
HARLOT KNIGHT PICARO RASCAL
VARLET WENZEL CAMOOCH
CUSTREL PEASANT VILLAIN
SWINDLER VARLETTO
KNAVERY CATZERIE PATCHERY
KNAVISH ROGUISH SCAMPISH
KNAWEL KNOTWEED KNOTWORT
KNEAD ELT TEW MOLD POST STOCK
PETRIE MASSAGE
(— HIDES) STOCK
KNEADING (— MACHINE) BRAKE
KNEE GENU HOCK CROOK KNAPPER
SLEEPER SUFFRAGO
(— HOLLOW) HAM
(— OF COMPOSING STICK) SLIDE
KNEECAP CAP PATELLA
KNEEL SIT KNEE COUCH SHIKO
KOWTOW
KNEELER SPRINGER
KNEELING SHIKO BENDED
KNEEPAN ROTULA PATELLA
KNELL BELL RING TOLL KNOLL
STROKE
KNICKKNACK TOY KNACK TRICK

GEWGAW NOTION PRETTY GIMCRACK

KNIFE DAH DIE PIN SAX ULU BOLO BUCK MOON SAEX SHIM SHIV SPUD TANG BOWIE BURIN CHIVE FACON GULLY KNIVE KUKRI PANGA SHANK SHAVE SKEAN SLICE BARLOW BARONG CAMPIT CARVER COLTER COUTEL CUTTLE DAGGER DOCTOR JIGGER PANADE PARANG PAVADE PORKER PULLER RIMMER SICKLE SLICER TREVET TRIVAT WORKER BREAKER CATLING CHOPPER COUTEAU FIPENNY KIOTOME MACHETE PALETTE SCALPEL SEVERER SKINNER SLASHER SNICKER STICKER SUNDANG TICKLER WHITTLE BELDUQUE BILLHOOK CALABOZO JOCTELEG SERPETTE THWITTLE YATAGHAN
(— FOR BREAKING FLAX) BEATER
(— FOR LEATHER) PIN
(— FOR RUBBER DOUGH) DOCTOR
(BURMESE —) DAH DAO DOW
(CURRIER'S —) CLEANER
(ESKIMO —) ULU
(MORO —) BARONG
(SHOEMAKER'S —) BUTT
(SURGICAL —) CATLING SCALPEL BISTOURY EXSECTOR
(TANNER'S —) GRAINER
KNIFE-PLEATED KILTED
KNIGHT N ELF SIR ADUB GANO TULK EQUES EQUIS HORSE LANCE RIDER THANE TOLKE CABALL ERRANT PENCEL RITTER ROGERO GENILON PALADIN YOUNKER ALMANZOR BACHELOR BANNERET CAVALIER COLVILLE GANELONE IRONCLAD ISENBRAS PALMERIN RUGGIERO
(— IN CHESS) HORSE
(— OF ROUND TABLE) GAN BORS OWEN GARETH GAWAIN MODRED CARADOC CRADOCK GALAHAD GANELON EGLAMORE LANCELOT PALMERIN PERCIVAL TRISTRAM
(CARPET —) DAMMERET
KNIGHTHOOD CAVALRY
KNIPHOFIA TRITOMA
KNIT SET BIND KNOT PLAIT PURSE UNITE WEAVE COMPACT CONNECT WRINKLE CONTRACT
(— STOCKINGS) SHANK
KNITTED FLAT WOVEN
KNITTING LOOP STEEK
KNITTING NEEDLE WIRE
KNOB BOB BUR NOB NUB BEAD BOSS BURR CLUB DENT HEAD HEEL KNOP KNOT KNUB LIFT NODE PULL SNUG STUD TORE BERRY BULLA FORTE GEMMA KNURL NATCH ONION PLOOK PLUKE BUTTON CROCHE EMBOSS NOBBLE NUBBLE PIMPLE PISTON POMMEL FERRULE HORNTIP KNOBBLE BELLPULL DOORKNOB DRAWSTOP OMPHALOS
(— OF HAIR) TOORIE
(— OF ROCK) BUHR BURR KNUCKLE
(— ON BILL OF SWAN) BERRY

(— ON BUTT OF CANNON) GRAPE
(— ON CHAIR) POMMEL
(— ON DEER'S ANTLER) OFFER CROCHE
(— ON ROPE) MOUSE
KNOBBED NODOSE TOROSE TUBEROUS TYLOTATE
KNOBBY GOUTY KNOTTY GOUTISH KNOBBLY
KNOCK CON DAD HIT JOW JUT POP PUN RAP WAP BANG BASH BEAT BUMP CALL CHAP CHOP DASH DAUD DING DUMP DUNT HACK JOLT JOWL KNAP NOCK NOIT PLUG POLT POSS PUSH ROUT SLAM SLAY SNOP TANK TIRL WHAP WHOP CLUMP KNOIT POUND SMITE SNOCK STAVE STRAM THUMP BOUNCE DUNTLE KNATCH KNETCH STOTER CANVASS PINKING
(— ABOUT) RUMBLE
(— DOWN) DROP DUMP FELL FLOOR GRASS LEVEL SMITE SOUSE HURTLE RAFFLE UNPILE
(— OFF) SECURE
(— ON HEAD) MAZER MAZARD
(— OUT) OUT SAP CONK COOL KAYO FLATTEN STIFFEN
(— UNCONSCIOUS) COLDCOCK
(— WITH THE HORNS) DISH
KNOCKER CROW RISP HAMMER WHACKER
(DOOR —) CROW HAMMER RAPPER
KNOCK-KNEED VARUS VALGUS
KNOCKOUT KO KAYO CRUSHER NOBBLER
(PRETENDED —) DIVE
KNOLL NOB HIGH KNAP KNOB KNOW TOFT HEAVE HURST HYRST MOUND SHOAL COPPLE BOUROCK HUMMOCK
KNOP NOB KNOB KNOSP KNAPPE
KNOT BOB BOW BUN FAG NIB NOB NUB PIN TIE BEND BURR CHOU CLOD CLOT CLUB HARL KILL KNAG KNAR KNOB NODE NOIL NURL SLUG SNUB TRUE WAFT WALL CROWN DUNNE GNARL GNARR HALCH HALSH HATCH HITCH KNURL MOUSE NODUS NOEUD SNARL SNICK SWIRL TWIST WARRE BUTTON CLINCH CROCHE FINIAL GRANNY MASCLE SORTIE TANGLE BOWKNOT BOWLINE CHIGNON COCKADE GORDIAN MAYBIRD CICISBEO DRAWKNOT GRAYBACK KNITTING SLIPKNOT TRUELOVE
(— IN CLOTH) FAG BURL
(— IN COTTON FIBERS) NEP
(— IN SIGNAL FLAG) WAFT WEFT WHEFT
(— IN WOOD) PIN BURL BURR KNAG KNAR SNUB GNARL KNAUR KNURL
(— IN YARN) SLUG SNICK
(— OF HAIR) BUN COB PUG CLUB KNURL CHIGNON
(LOVE —) AMORET
(ORNAMENTAL —) BOW
(SHOULDER —) WING

(WALL —) WALE
KNOTGRASS LIGNUM HOGWEED PIGWEED BINDWEED BIRDWEED DOORWEED KNOTWEED KNOTWORT PINKWEED POLYGONY WIREWEED
KNOTTED KNIT NOUE TIED NOWED NODOSE SWIRLY CRABBED NODATED SCRAGGY
KNOTTY HARD CRAMP GOUTY COMMON CRAGGY GNARLY KNAGGY KNOBBY KNURRY NODOSE NODOUS COMPLEX GNARLED GOUTISH JOINTED KNARRED KNOTTED SCABROUS
KNOTWEED LIGNUM ALLSEED HOGWEED JUMPSEED POLYGONY
KNOW CAN CON KEN WIS WIT WOT CITE HAVE SABE WEET WIST WOTH SAVVY SKILL COGNIZE
(— NOT) NOOT
(—S NOT) NOTE
(DID NOT —) KENDNA
(DO NOT —) KENNA
KNOWABLE SENSABLE
KNOW-HOW SAVVY SKILL
KNOWING FLY HEP HIP FOXY GASH SPRY WISE AWARE CANNY DOWNY JERRY LEERY SPACK WITTY EXPERT SCIENT SCIOUS SHREWD WITFUL WITTER GNOSTIC SAPIENT
(— SUPERFICIALLY) SCIOLOUS
KNOWINGLY CANNILY SCIENTER SHREWDLY WITTERLY
KNOWLEDGE CAN WIT BOOK KITH KNOW LAIR LEAR LORE INWIT JNANA SKILL VIDYA ADVICE AVIDYA CLERGY GNOSIS NOESIS NOTICE WISDOM CUNNING DIANOIA HEARING KNOWING MEANING SCIENCE WITTING·DAYLIGHT DOCTRINE EPISTEME LEARNING LETTRURE NOTITION PRUDENCE SAPIENCE SCIENTIA
(— OF SPIRITUAL TRUTH) GNOSIS
(FAMILIAR —) HANG
(LATER —) AFTERWIT
(MYSTERIOUS —) ARCANUM
(PIECEMEAL —) SMATTER
(PRIVATE —) PRIVITY
(PUBLIC —) LIGHT
(SLICK —) ANGLE
(SLIGHT —) INKLING
(SUPERFICIAL —) SCIOLISM
(SUPREME —) PRAJNA
(SYSTEMATIZED —) SCIENCE
KNOWLEDGEABLE KNOWING SKILLED STUDIED
KNOWN EVER COUTH COMMON
(ACTUALLY —) SPECIOUS
(LITTLE —) FAMELESS
(NOT —) DARK SILENT
(OTHERWISE — AS) ALIAS
(PUBLICLY —) EXOTERIC
(UNMISTAKABLY —) STATED
(WIDELY —) COMMON
KNOW-NOTHING SAM
KNUCKLE KNUCK JARRET
KNUCKLEBONE DIB DOLOS TALUS COCKAL SHACKLE

KNURL MILL NULL DWARF SNARL
KNURLING NULLING REEDING
  KNULLING
KOALA BEAR BAALU BALOO SLOTH
  KOOLAH WOMBAT CARBORA
  PHALANGER
KOBOLD NIS NISSE HODEKEN
  HUTCHEN
KOEL KOIL KOKIL RAINBIRD
KOHL COHOL ALCOHOL
KOHLRABI BROMATIUM
KOKAN LAMPATIA
KOKO LEBBEK
KOKUM GARCINIA
KOKUMIN BAN
KOLA COLA BICHY GOORANUT
KOMBU KOBU KAMBOU CHAKOBU
KOMMETJE WALLOW COMITJE
KONAK YALI
KOOKABURRA KOOKA JACKASS
KOPECK KAPEIKA
KORAKAN RAGI RAGGI RAGGY
KORAN KITAB QURAN ALCORAN
  (SECTION OF —) SURA SURAH

KORE DESPOINA
KOREA (SEE NORTH KOREA OR
  SOUTH KOREA)
KOREC MIRA
KORINA LIMBA
KOS COAN
KOSIN KOUSSIN TAENNIN BRAYERIN
KOSO PANAMINT
KOULAN GOUR
KOWHAI GOAI PELU LOCUST
  SOPHORA
KOWTOW KNEEL SHIKO
KOYUKON TENA KHOTANA
KRAAL CRAW MANYATTA ZIMBABWE
KRAIT ADDER KORAIT BUNGARUM
KRATER KELEBE
KRAUNHIA WISTARIA
KREIS CIRCLE
KRIS CREASE CREESE DAGGER
KRISHNA VASUDEVA
KRONE CROWN CORONA
KRU KROOBOY KROOMAN
KRUMMHORN CREMONA CROMORNE
KSHATRIYA THAKUR

KUA MAKUA MAKWA
KUBA BUSHONGO KABISTAN
KUDZU VINE KOHEMP
KUI KHONDI
KU KLUXER KLUXER KLUCKER
  KLANSMAN
KUKURUKU IKPERE
KULANAPAN POMO
KUMAN POLOUTZY
KUMBUK ARJAN ARJUN
KUMMEL ALLASCH
KUMQUAT NAGAMI
KURRAJONG CALOOL LACEBARK
KURUKH ORAON
KUSA DARBHA
KUSIMANSEL MANGUE
KUTCHIN LOUCHEUX
KUWAIT (TOWN OF —) AHMADI
  HAWALLI ABDULLAH FAHAHEEL
KVASS QUASH
KWENI GURO
KYPHOSIS HUMPBACK
KYURINISH LESGHIN LEZGHIAN

L EL LIMA FIFTY
LAAGER LEEGTE LEAGUER
LABDACUS (FATHER OF —)
POLYDORUS
(MOTHER OF —) NYCTEIS
(SON OF —) LAIUS
LABDANUM MYRRH
LABEL TAG BILL FILE FICHE STAMP
TALLY TITLE DIRECT DOCKET
TICKET ENDSEAL LAMBEAU STICKER
(— ON SUIT OF CLOTHES) ETIQUET
LABELLUM LIP LABEL
(PART OF —) HYPOCHIL
LABIAL ROUND
LABIATE HOREHOUND
LABIUM LIP LABRUM
LABOR FAG TUG WIN CARK MOIL
TASK TAVE TILL TOIL WORK BEGAR
DELVE GRAFT GRIND HEAVE PAINS
SWEAT SWINK TEAVE TREAD WHILE
YAKKA CORVEE DRUDGE EFFORT
HAMMER STRIVE BULLOCK FATIGUE
MANUARY OPIFICE PROCURE
SERVICE SLAVERY TRAVAIL
TROUBLE TURMOIL BUSINESS
DRUDGERY EXERTION GROANING
INDUSTRY LABORAGE STRUGGLE
(— ARDUOUSLY) BILDER
(— HARD) THRASH THRIPPLE
(— UNDER) SUFFER
(DAY'S —) DARG JOURNEY
(DIFFICULT —) DYSTOCIA
(EXCESSIVE —) STRAIN
(FORCED —) BEGAR
(HARD —) HARD BULLWORK
(HIRED —) TOGT
(IMPOSED —) TASKAGE
(MENTAL —) HEADWORK
(SEVERE —) AGON
(UNPAID —) CORVEE
LABORATORY LAB SHOP KITCHEN
OFFICINA WORKSHOP
LABORED HEAVY FORCED SWEATY
STRAINED
LABORER (ALSO SEE WORKER AND
WORKMAN) BOY BHAR ESNE HIND
JACK JOEY MOZO PEON TOTY
BAGDI GUASO HUNKY NAVVY PALLI
PINER STIFF BALAHI BEGARI
BOHUNK COALER COOLIE DAYMAN
DILKER DOCKER FELLAH FLUNKY
FOGGER HEAVER HOLEYA JIBARO
LUMPER RAFTER TASKER WAYMAN
WORKER BRACERO BYWONER
CREWMAN DAYSMAN DIGGORY
DIRGLER DRAINER DVORNIK
HOBBLER MANUARY MAZDOOR
PICKMAN PIONEER PIPEMAN
PLOWMAN SANDHOG SCOURER
SHIPPER SMASHER SOUGHER
SPALLER STOCKER SWINKER
TOTYMAN WORKMAN BIJWONER
CHAINMAN COTTAGER DOLLYMAN
FARMHAND FLOORMAN GANGSMAN
HOLDSMAN SPADEMAN SPALPEEN
STRAPPER TIDESMAN
(INEXPERIENCED —) GREENER
LABORIOUS HARD HEAVY STIFF
SWEATY UPHILL ARDUOUS

OPEROSE SLAVISH TOILFUL
DILIGENT LABOROUS TOILSOME
LABRADOR TEA LEDUM GOWIDDIE
LABURNUM AWBER
LABYRINTH MAZE CIRCUIT MEANDER
LABYRINTHINE TORTUOUS
LAC LACCA LACQUER
LACE BEAT BEST FOND GOTA LASH
PEAK FILET LACIS LIVEN ORRIS
POINT SCREW SPRIG WEAVE
BLONDE CORDON DEFEAT EDGING
GRILLE LACING LASHER THRASH
TUCKER VENISE ALENCON ALLOVER
BULLION CURRAGH CUTWORK
FOOTING GALLOON GUIPURE
HONITON LATCHET MACRAME
MALINES MECHLIN MELANGE
NANDUTI TAMBOUR TATTING
TORCHON TROLLEY ARGENTAN
BOBBINET BONEWORK BOOTLACE
BRUSSELS DENTELLE ILLUSION
LACEWORK LIMERICK PEARLING
STAYLACE
(— EDGING) PUNTILLA
(— IN PLACE OF COLLAR) RUCHE
(— MAKER) TWISTHAND
(— PATTERN) TOILE
(KNOTTED —) TATTING
LACEBARK LAGETTO DAGUILLA
LACEWOOD
LACE BUG TINGITID
LACERATE REND TEAR ENBORE
HARROW MANGLE SCARIFY
FRACTURE
LACERATION RIP TEAR WOUND
LACEWOOD SYCAMORE
LACEWORK DENTELLE
LACHRYMOSE SAD TEARY WEEPY
MAUDLIN
LACINARIA LIATRIS
LACING LACET LINGEL ECHELLE
LANGUET
LACK FAIL LANK LIKE LOSS MAIM
MISS NEED VOID WANE WANT
FAULT MINUS DEARTH DEFECT
INLAIK ABSENCE BLEMISH DEFAULT
FAILURE PAUCITY VACANCY
SCARCITY SOLITUDE WANTROKE
(— CONFIDENCE) DOUBT
(— FAITH) DIFFIDE
(— HARMONY) DISAGREE
(— OF APPETITE) ANOREXIA
(— OF CLARITY) DARKNESS
(— OF COORDINATION) ASYNERGY
DYSERGIA
(— OF DEVELOPMENT) AGENESIS
(— OF EARNESTNESS) ITEMING
(— OF EFFUSIVENESS) RESERVE
(— OF EMOTION) APATHY
(— OF ENERGY) ATONY ANERGY
ATONIA
(— OF FLAVOR) SILENCE
(— OF FORESIGHT) MYOPIA
(— OF HARMONY) DISCORD
DISUNITY
(— OF INTENTION) ACCIDENT
(— OF INVOLVEMENT) DISTANCE
(— OF ORDER) ATAXY ATAXIA
DISARRAY

(— OF PATRIOTISM) INCIVISM
(— OF REFINEMENT) CRUDITY
(— OF SENSE OF SMELL) ANOSMIA
(— OF SENSE) FOLLY
(— OF STEADINESS) LEVITY
(— OF SYMPATHY) DYSPATHY
(— OF VIGOR) LANGUOR
(— OF VITALITY) ANEMIA ADYNAMIA
(— OF WIND) CALM
(— OF WORTH) IMMERIT
(— STRENGTH) DROOP
LACKADAISICAL LANGUID LISTLESS
LACKEY SKIP SLAVE LACQUEY
STAFFIER
LACKING BUT SHY BARE FREE
WANT ALACK GNEDE MINUS SHORT
ABSENT BARREN DEVOID WITHIN
WANTING DESOLATE INDIGENT
LACKLUSTER DULL FISHY CLOUDY
GLASSY
LACONIC CURT SHORT CONCISE
POINTED SPARTAN SUCCINCT
LA CORUNA GROIN
LACQUER LAC DOPE DUCO JAPAN
CHATON LACKER URUSHI VARNISH
LACTATION (— PERIOD) NOTE
LACTONE CUMARIN LIMONIN
MECONIN DIKETENE
LACTOSCOPE PIOSCOPE
LACUNA GAP BREAK
LACUSTRINE LAKISH
LAD BOY BUB MAN BOYO CARL CHAP
DICK HIND JOCK LOON SNAP BILLY
BUCKO CADDY CHIEL GROOM
YOUTH BURSCH CADDIE CALLAN
FELLOW LADDIE LADKIN MANNIE
NIPPER SHAVER CALLANT
MUCHACHO SPRINGER STRIPLING
(AWKWARD —) GROMET GRUMMET
(MISCHIEVOUS —) GAMIN
(MY —) AVICK
(SERVING —) GILLIE GOSSOON
LADDER STY STEE JACOB SCALE
AERIAL BANGOR ESCAPE PULEYN
GANGWAY POLEYNE POMPIER
(FIREMAN'S —) STICK
(FISH —) FISHWAY
(JACOB'S —) CHARITY
LADDIE JOCKEY LATHIE LADDOCK
LADDIKIE
LADE BAIL LAVE LADEN TRUSS
BURDEN FRAUGHT
(— INTO COOLER) STRIKE
LADEN HEAVY BELAST LOADED
FRAUGHT FREIGHT GESTANT
LADING LOAD CARGO FREIGHT
LADINO SPANIOL
LADLE DIP JET GAWN SKEP CLATH
CYATH KEACH STOOP DIPPER
LADING CUVETTE CYATHUS
KYATHOS POTSTICK
(— OUT SOUP) SLEECH
(— WITH HANDLES) CYATH SHANK
CYATHUS KYATHOS SKIPPET
(BRINE —) LOOT
(LARGE —) SCOOP
LADRONE TULISAN LATHERIN
LADY BIBI BURD DAME RANI DONNA
HANUM BEEBEE DOMINO FEMALE

KADINE RAWNIE SAHIBA SENORA
LADYKIN MADONNA SENHORA
SINEBADA
(— OF HIGH RANK) BEGUM
(— OF HOUSE) GOODWIFE
(BEAUTIFUL —) CLEAR
(TURKISH —) KHANUM
(PL.) LADYHOOD
LADYBUG VEDALIA
LADYFISH WRASSE PUDIANO
BONEFISH BONYFISH DONCELLA
LADYLIKE FEMALE
LADYLOVE LADY DELIA MINION
MISTRESS
LADY'S-COMB NEEDLES
LADY'S-MANTLE DEWCUP PADELION
LADY'S-SLIPPER DUCK YELLOW
NERVINE YELLOWS UMBILROOT
LAERTES (FATHER OF —) ARCESIUS
(MOTHER OF —) CHALCOMEDUSA
(SON OF —) ULYSSES
(WIFE OF —) ANTICLEA
LAG DRAG DRAW SLOG DELAY TRAIL
HOCKER LAGGER LINGER LOITER
STRING DRIDDLE LAGGING
(— IN PRODUCTION) SLIPPAGE
LAGGARD SLOW TARDY LAGGER
TORTOISE
LAGGING TARDY JACKET DEADING
LAGGARD CLEADING DRAWLING
FOREPOLE
LAGNIAPPE TIP GIFT BONUS PILON
PRESENT
LAGOMORPH PIKA RABBIT
LAGOON HAFF POOL BAYOU LIMAN
LAGUNA
LAID (— ACROSS WALL) INBOND
(— DOWN) THETIC THETICAL
(— WASTE) BARE
LAIR DEN LAY FORM HOLD SHED
EARTH HAUNT LODGE MEUSE
SQUAT HARBOR KENNEL SPELUNK
(— OF FOX) KENNEL
(— OF OTTER) HOLT HOVER
(— OF WILD BOAR) SOUNDER
LAISSE TIRADE
LAITY FOLK LAYMEN PEOPLE
LAIUS (FATHER OF —) LABDACUS
(SON OF —) OEDIPUS
(WIFE OF —) JOCASTA
LAKE LAY SEA VLY BAHR JAIL JHIL
LAGO LLYN LOCH MERE MOAT
SHOR TANK TARN VLEI VLEY BAYOU
CHOTT JHEEL LERNA LIMAN LOUGH
SPARK TUBIG LAGOON NYANZA
STROND ANCYLUS CARMINE
LAKELET TURLOUGH
(CASHEW —) AUBURN
(FENNY —) BROAD
(MOUNTAIN —) TARN
(RELATING TO —S) LIMNAL
(SALT —) SHOT CHOTT SHOTT
SALINA SALINE
(SMALL —) GURGES
(TEMPORARY —) PINAG
LAKE CARP DRUM LAKER
LAKE HERRING KIYI CISCO
GRAYBACK
LAKE TROUT POGY TOGUE
LAKE WHITEFISH POLLAN

LAKSHMI SRI SHREE
LAMA ELK AUCHENIA
LAMB BUM PET PUR CADE DEAR
DUPE LOME SOCK YEAN AGNUS
PESAH PODDY AGNEAU COSSET
HIEDER LAMBIE LAMKIN PESACH
SUCKER WASTER WEANER CHILVER
EANLING FATLING HOGLING
PASCHAL PERSIAN RUFFIAN
TWAGGER BAAHLING LAMBLING
PASSOVER YEANLING
(— AND WHEAT) KIBBE
(SCYTHIAN —) BAROMETZ
LAMBASTE CREAM SQUABASH
LAMBENT BRIGHT RADIANT
LAMBREQUIN MANTLING
LAMBSKIN LAMB BAGDAD BAGHDAD
SALZFELLE
LAMB'S QUARTERS MUCKWEED
LAMB'S WOOL WASSAIL
LAME BUM GAME HALT LAHN GAMMY
GIMPY GRAVEL TINSEL CRIPPLE
CRIPPLY HALTING HIPHALT
GORGERIN SPAVINED
(— A HORSE) STUB
LAMELLA PLICA FOLIUM FORNIX
LAMENESS HALT
LAMENT CRY WEY CARE DOLE HONE
HOWL KEEN MEAN MOAN PINE SIGH
TEAR WAIL WALY WEEP CROON
DUMKA GREET KINAH MOURN PLAIN
QINAH BEHOWL BEMOAN BEWAIL
BEWEEP COMMOS KOMMOS PLAINT
REPINE SORROW SQUAWK THREAP
YAMMER BEMOURN CONDOLE
DEPLORE EJULATE ELEGIZE
GRIZZLE REGRATE THRENOS
WAYMENT COMPLAIN MOURNING
THRENODY ULLAGONE WELLAWAY
LAMENTABLE YEMER RUEFUL
DOLEFUL PITIFUL PITIABLE
PLAINFUL YAMMERLY
LAMENTATION KEEN MOAN WAIL
DOLOR LINOS RUING TANGI LAMENT
PLAINT REGRET SORROW THRENE
PLANGOR TRAGEDY WILLAWA
CORONACH MOURNING PATHETIC
WAILMENT WELLAWAY LAMENTING
LAMINA FILM LAME LAMP LEAF
OBEX BLADE FLAKE LAMIN PLATE
SCALE SHELL TABLE CAPSULE
LAMINATE LEAFY FLAGGY
LAMINATED BUILT FOLIATE
TABULAR
LAMINATION SLABBING
LAMINITIS FOUNDER
LAMMAS DAY GULE TERM
LAMMERGEIER AREND
LAMP ARC EYE SEE DAVY GLIM INKY
JACK SLUT ALDIS ARGAND ASTRAL
BULLET HELION LAMPAD TARGET
ILLUMER LAMPION LAMPLET
LANTERN LUCERNE LUCIGEN
SUNLAMP SUNSPOT AEOLIGHT
CIRCLINE GASLIGHT SIDELAMP
TORCHERE
(— FOR FIREPLACE) KYLE
(4-CORNERED —) CHILL
(CHIMNEYLESS —) TORCH

(IRON —) CRUSIE
(MAKESHIFT —) BITCH
(SAFETY —) DAVY GEORDIE
(PL.) CLUSTER
LAMPBLACK LINK
LAMPETIA (FATHER OF —) APOLLO
(MOTHER OF —) NEAERA
LAMP HOLDER HUSK
LAMPOON PIPE GESTE LIBEL SQUIB
IAMBIC BERHYME PASQUIN
COCKALAN RIDICULE SATIRIZE
LAMPOONER PASQUIL PASQUIN
LAMPREY PRIDE LAMPER MYZONT
RAMPER SAYNAY SUCKER LAMPERN
LAMP RING CRIC
LAMPSHADE GLOBE
LAMPWICK MATCH
LANATE WOOLY LANOSE WOOLLY
LANCE PIC CANE DART SHAFT
SPEAR STAFF BROACH ELANCE
GLAIVE GLEAVE LANCET ROCKET
LANCELET SPICULUM
(KING ARTHUR'S —) RON
LANCE GUARD VAMPLATE
LANCE HEAD MORNE SOCKET
LANCER LANCE SOWAR UHLAN
LANCE REST QUEUE FEWTER
LANCET FLEAM FLEEM LANCELET
LANCEWOOD YAYA CIGUA CANELA
YARIYARI
LAND ERD ERF NOD RIB AGER DIRT
FOLD GALE GISH GORE JODO MARK
SITE SOIL EARTH EJIDO ETHEL
FIELD GLEBE JUGER PLANT SHORE
SOLUM ALIGHT ASSART FUNDUS
GROUND COMMONS COUNTRY
DEMESNE ELLASAR HOLDING
LANDING LIBRATE QUILLET
TERRENE ALLODIAL BOOKLAND
COMMONTY FARMLAND FLEYLAND
FOLKLAND POMERIUM PRAEDIUM
(— A PLANE) GREASE
(— BETWEEN FURROWS) SELION
(— BETWEEN RIVERS) DOAB
(— CLEARING) KAINGIN
(— CONVERTED TO TILLAGE)
TWAITE THWAITE
(— HAVING VALUE OF POUND PER
YEAR) LIBRATE
(— IN CONACRE) MOCK
(— IN GRASS) LAYER
(— LEFT FALLOW) ARDER
(— MEASURE) RIG
(— OF BLISS) GOKURAKU
(— OF GIANTS) UTGARTHAR
(— OF MANSION) DEMESNE
(— OF OPPORTUNITY) ARKANSAS
(— OF PLENTY) GOSHEN
(— OF REGION) MOLD MOULD
(— PLOWED IN A DAY) JORNADA
(— RECOVERED FROM SEA) INTAKE
INNINGS
(— REGULARLY FLOODED) SALTING
(— SURROUNDED BY WASTE) HOPE
(— UNIT) URE KIPUKA MECATE
MORGEN MANZANA VIRGATE
(ALLUVIAL —) BATTURE
(ANCESTRAL —) ETHEL
(ARABLE —) LEA LEY LAINE

(ARID —) DESERT STEPPE
(BOTTOM —) SLASH CALLOW
STRATH
(CHURCH —) GLEBE TERMON
(CHURCH —S) CROSS
(CLEARED —) ASSART
(COMMON —) EJIDO EXIDO STRAY
(CONTINENTAL —) MAIN
(CULTIVATED —) FARM ARADA
TILTH CULTURE FEERING WAINAGE
LABORAGE METAIRIE
(ENCLOSED —) CLOSE INTAKE
(FREEHOLD —) MULK
(GRAVELLY —) GEEST GRAVES
(GRAZING —) GRASS HIRSEL HIRSLE
FEEDING
(HEATHY —) ROSLAND
(HERITABLE —) ODAL UDAL
(IMAGINARY —) FAERIE COCKAYNE
LILLIPUT
(LEASED —) TACK
(LONG STRIP OF —) SLANG SPONG
(LOW —) BOG FEN GALL INKS
CARSE BOTTOM
(LOW RICH —) CARSE
(NATIVE —) BLIGHTY BIRTHDOM
HOMELAND
(OBDURATE —) TILL
(PARCEL OF —) FEU LOT MOCK
(PASTURE —) HA ALP FEED HOGA
WALK GRASS VELDT LEASON
(PLATEAU —) HIGHVELD
(PLOWED —) ARADA FALLOW
FURROW BREAKING
(PRIVATE —) SEVERAL
(PROMISED —) CANAAN
(PURE —) JODO SUKHAVATI
(RESOWN —) HOOKLAND
(ROUGH —) BRAKE
(SAVANNAH —S) LALANG
(SCRUBBY —) SCROG SCROGS
(SMALL PARCEL OF —) SUERTE
(SWAMPY —) WOODSERE
(TIMBER —S) STICKS
(WASTE —) HEATH
(WESTERN —) HESPERIA
(WET —) SOAK SWAMP SWANG
(WOODED —S) STICKS
(PL.) ACRES SUCKEN LAENDER
NOVALIA
LANDBOOK TERRIER
LANDED PRAEDIAL
LANDFORM CUSP CUESTA
LANDHOLDER LAIRD COSCET
TALUKDAR
LANDHOLDING BARONY
LANDING BANK YARD STAITH
LANDAGE ARRIVAGE FOOTPACE
HALFPACE LANDFALL
(SMOOTH —) GREASER
LANDING PLACE GHAT HARD
SCALE PALACE ARRIVAGE
LANDING STAGE MEAR STAGE
STAIR STAITH STELLING
LANDLADY WIFE DUENA PADRONA
GOODWIFE
LANDLORD HOST GOODMAN
PADRONE ZAMINDAR
LANDSMAL MAL

LANDMARK COPA DOLE DOOL MARK
MERE BAKEN BOUND CAIRN MARCH
MEITH SENAL CIPPUS SEAMARK
LANDMASS BULGE
LANDOWNER THANE BONDER
SQUIRE CACIQUE EFFENDI FREEMAN
BHUMIDAR FRANKLIN ZAMINDAR
(PL.) GAMORI GEOMOROI
LANDSCAPE BOCAGE PAYSAGE
SCENERY LANDSKIP
LANDSLIDE SLUMP LANDFALL
LANDSLIP
LAND SPRING LAVANT
LANDVOGT BAILIFF
LANE WAY GANG LOAN LOKE PASS
RACE VEIN WIND ALLEY CHASE
DRANG DRONG ENTRY BOREEN
VENNEL LANEWAY LOANING
TWITTEN DRIFTWAY
(AIR TRAFFIC —) CORRIDOR
(NARROW —) CHAR CHARE TEWER
BOREEN
(OCEAN —) SEAWAY
LANGUAGE (ALSO SEE DIALECT) LIP
CHIB CODE LEED RUNE LEDEN
LINGO SLANG LANGUS LINGUA
SPEECH TONGUE YABBER CABLESE
DIALECT IDIOLECT LEGALESE
(SPECIFIC —) GA GE HO MO VU AIS
AKA ATA EDO EFE EPE EVE EWE
FAN FON FOX FUL GEG HET ICA IJO
ILA KAI KAU KOL KOT KRU KUI LAB
LAI LAZ MON MRU SIA TWI UDI YAO
ZIA AFAR AGAO AGAU AGNI AHOM
AINU AKAN AKIM ALUR AMBO ANDI
ANTA ARUA AVAR BARI BEJA BIAK
BODO BONI BORA BUBE BUGI BULU
CARA CHAM CHIN CHOL CHUJ COOS
CORA COTO CREE CROW CUNA
DENE DOBU DYAK EFIK EKOI ERIE
EYAK FANG FIJI FULA FUNG GARO
GHEG GOLA GOLD HARE HEHE HOPI
HOVA HULA HUPA IBAN IDJO IJAW
IXIL KADU KAFA KAMI KAVI KAWI
KELE KOCH KOMI KONO KOTA KUKI
KURI LAHU LAKH LAPP LASI LATI
LAZI LESU LETT LUBA MANX MAYA
MOLE MORO NAGA NAMA NIAS NIUE
NUBA NUPE OGOR PALA PEGU PEUL
PUME RAMA SAHO SERB SERI SGAW
SHAN SIUS SORB SULU SUMO SUMU
SUSU TAAL TIAM TIBU TINO TODA
TSHI TUPI TUPY VEPS VOTE XOSA
ZULU ALEUT ALSEA ARAUA AUETO
AZTEC BAJAU BALTI BASSA BATAK
BATTA BAURE BEMBA BHILI BICOL
BILIN BONNY CAMPA CATIB CAYUA
CHANE CHIMU CHOCO CHOPE
COFAN COIBA COMAN CUEVA
CUMAN CUNZA CZECH DAFLA
DAYAK DIERI DINKA DUALA DUTCH
DYULA EMPEO FANTI FINGO FUNJI
GAFAT GALLA GANDA GETAN GETIC
GOLDI GONDI GREBO GREEK
GUAMO GUATO GURMA GYPSY
HABAB HAIDA HAIKH HATSA HAUSA
HINDI HUABI HUARI HURON HUSKY
HYLAM IGALA ILOKO IRAYA IRISH
JAKUN JATKI JUANG JUTIC KABYL

KAMBA KAMIA KANDH KAREN
KAROK KHASI KHMER KHOND KHUZI
KIOWA KISSI KIWAI KOINE KOLIS
KONDE KONGO KORKU KORWA
KOTAR KUMUK KUMYK KUSAN
KWOMA LAMBA LAMUT LANGO
LATIN LENCA LENDU LHOKE LHOTA
LIMBA LIMBU LUIAN LUNDA MAGHI
MAHRA MAHRI MALAY MALTO
MAORI MAZUR MBUBA MEDIC MENDI
MIKIR MODOA MOSSI MUONG MURMI
MURUT NAHUA NOGAI NORSE
NYORO ORAON ORIYA OROMO
OSCAN PALAU PAMIR PELEW PEUHL
PLATT PUNIC RONGA SAKAI SAMAL
SANTO SAXON SCOTS SERER SHILH
SHINA SHONA SICEL SIKEL SLAVE
SOTHO SOYOT SUOMI SWAZI TAINO
TAMIL TELEI TONGA TURKI UDISH
UIGUR URIYA UZBEK VOGUL WAYAO
WELSH WOLOF YAKUT YUNCA
ZERMA ABIPON ABKHAS ACAWAI
ACHOLI ADIGHE ADZHAR AFGHAN
AHTENA ALTAIC ANDAKI ANDHRA
ANDOKE ANGAMI APACHE APANTO
APIACA ARABIC ARANDA ARAONA
ARAWAK ARUNTA ATAROI AVANTI
AYMARA BAGOBO BAITSI BAKELE
BANIVA BASQUE BEAVER BHOTIA
BHUMIJ BIHARI BILAAN BILOXI
BONTOC BORORO BRAHUI BRETON
BRIBRI BUKAUA BULGAR BURIAT
CAGABA CANITA CARAJA CARIAN
CARIRI CAUQUI CAVINA CAYAPA
CAYUGA CAYUSE CEBUAN CHAGGA
CHAIMA CHANGO CHOCHO CHOKWE
COCAMA CONIBO COPTIC CREOLE
DAKOTA DANISH DOGRIB DYERMA
ESKIMO EUDEVE FRENCH FULANI
FULNIO FUTUNA GADDAN GALCHA
GALIBI GATHIC GENTOO GERMAN
GILAKI GILIAK GILYAK GOTHIC
GUAIMI GUETAR GUINAU GULLAH
GURIAN HAINAN HANTIK HARARI
HATTIC HEBREW HERERO HIBITO
IBANAG IBIBIO IFUGAO IGNERI
IGOROT INDIAN INDOIS INNUIT
INUPIK ISINAI ISLETA IVATAN
KABARD KACHIN KAFFIR KAIBAL
KALMUK KAMASS KANAKA KANURI
KEKCHI KHALKA KHAMTI KHARIA
KHOWAR KIKUYU KILIWA KODAGA
KODAGU KOIARI KOIBAL KOLAMI
KOREAN KORYAK KOTIAK KPEELE
KUNAMA KURNAI KURUKH KYURIN
LADINO LAGUNA LAHNDA LAHULI
LENAPE LEPCHA LIBYAN LIUKIU
LIVIAN LUSHAI LUVIAN LYCIAN
LYDIAN MAGAHI MAGYAR MANCHU
MANOBO MBONDO MBUNDA MEDIAN
MEGREL MINOAN MISHMI MISIMA
MOHAWK MONTES MUYSCA MYSIAN
NEWARI NINGPO NUBIAN NYANJA
OORIVA OSTIAK OVAMPO PAHARI
PALAIC PAPUAN PASHTO PAZAND
POLISH PUSHTO PUSHTU QUECHA
RASHTI REJANG ROMANY SAFINE
SAKIAN SALISH SAMOAN SANGIL
SANGIR SARCEE SASSAK SAVARA

SEDANG SEKANI SELKUP SELUNG
SEMANG SENECA SENUFO SESUTO
SHARRA SHASTA SILETZ SINDHI
SLOVAK SOMALI SONRAI SUBIYA
SURHAI SUSIAN TARTAR TAVGHI
TELEGU TELEUT TETTUM THONGA
TIPURA TUNGUS VANNIC VOTYAK
YANKEE YARURA YORUBA ZAREMA
ABENAKI ACHAGUA AEQUIAN
AKWAALA AKWAPIM ALABAMA
ALTRIAN AMANAYE AMHARIC
AMORITE AMUESHA APINAYE
ARAMAIC ARAPAHO ARAUCAN
ARECUNA ARGOBBA ARICARA
ARMORIC ASHANTI ASURINI
ATACAMA ATAKAPA AUSTRAL
AVESTAN AXUMITE BAGHELI
BAGIRMI BAINING BAKONGO
BALANTE BALUCHI BAMBARA
BANGALA BANNACK BASHKIR
BENGALI BEOTHUK BERBERI
BHOTIYA BHUTANI BOSNIAN BRITISH
BULANDA BUNDELI BUNYORO
BURMESE BUSHMAN CALIANA
CALINGA CARRIER CASHIBO
CATALAN CATAWBA CAWAHIB
CHACOBO CHARRUA CHATINO
CHEBERO CHECHEN CHIBCHA
CHIMILA CHINOOK CHIRINO
CHIWERE CHONTAL CHOROTI
CHUKCHI CHUMASH CHUROYA
CHUVASH CIBONEY CLALLAM
COCHIMI CORNISH COTONAM
COWLITZ CYMRAEG DAGBANE
DAGOMBA DANAKIL DANKALI
DARGHIN DEUTSCH DHEGIHA
DRAVIDA ENGLISH ESCUARA
ESSELEN EUSKERA FINNISH FLEMISH
FOOCHOW FRIESIC FRISIAN GAULISH
GOAJIRO GUAHIBO GUARANI
GUAYAKI GURUNSI GYARUNG
HAITIAN HANUNOC HIDATSA HITTITE
HUASTEC HUCHNOM HUICHOL
HURRIAN IBERIAN ILOKANO
ILONGOT INGALIK IPURINA ITALIAN
ITELMES ITONAMA JACUNDA
JAGATAI KAKHYEN KALINGA
KAMASIN KANAUJI KANNADA
KASHUBE KASSITE KIKONGO
KIPCHAK KIRANTI KIRGHIZ KIRUNDI
KLAMATH KOASATI KONKANI
KOYUKON KUBACHI KULAMAN
KURDISH KUTCHIN KUTENAI
LAMPONG LATVIAN LESGHIN
LOATUKO LUGANDA MAGADHI
MALTESE MAPUCHE MARATHI
MASKOKI MERCIAN MEXICAN
MINAEAN MINGREL MITANNI
MOABITE MOCHICA MONUMBO
MORATTY MORISCO NAHUATL
NICOBAR OSMANLI OSSETIC
PAHLAVI PALAUNG PANJABI
PARBATE PERMIAK PERMIAN
PERSIAN PICTISH PUNJABI PUQUINA
QUERCHI SABAEAN SALINAN
SAMBALI SAMNANI SAMNITE
SAMOYED SANDAWE SANTALI
SANTANA SEMITIC SERBIAN
SHAWANO SHAWNEE SHILLUH

SHIPIBO SHUSWAP SIAMESE
SIRIONO SIUSLAW SOGDIAN
SONGHAI SONGISH SORBIAN
SPANIOL SPANISH STIKINE SUBANUN
SVANISH SWAHILI SWEDISH
TAGALOG TIBETAN TUAMOTU
TURKISH UMBRIAN UMBUNDU
VISAYAN WALLOON WENDISH
YENISEI YIDDISH ZABERMA
ZONGORA ABANEEME ACHINESE
ACHUMAWI AKKADIAN AKSUMITE
ALACALUF ALBANIAN ALFURESE
AMAHUACA AMERICAN AMMONITE
ANGOLESE ANNAMESE ANZANIAN
APALACHI ARMENIAN ASSAMESE
ASSYRIAN ATJINESE AWISHIRA
BACTRIAN BALINESE BARBACOA
BECHUANA BHOJPURI BISCAYAN
BOSNISCH BOTOCUDO CAHUILLA
CAINGANG CANARESE CANOEIRO
CAQUETIO CARELIAN CARIJONA
CAYUBABA CHALDEAN CHAMORRO
CHEHALIS CHEMAKUM CHEYENNE
CHINGPAW CHIQUITO CHITRALI
COCONUCA COLUMBIA COMANCHE
CORAVECA CROATIAN CUSTENAU
DELAWARE DIEGUENO EGYPTIAN
ELAMITIC ETHIOPIC ETRUSCAN
FALISBAN FORMOSAN FRANKISH
FULFULDE GALICIAN GALLEGAN
GEORGIAN GERMANIC GORKHALI
GUAICURU GUJARATI HADENDOA
HAWAIIAN HITCHITI ILLINOIS
ILLYRIAN IROQUOIS JAPANESE
JAVANESE KANARESE KANAWARI
KANKANAI KASHMIRI KASUBIAN
KERMANJI KIMBUNDU KOLARIAN
LANDSMAL LANUVIAN LIGURIAN
LIHYANIC LILLOOET LIVONIAN
LUSATIAN MADURESE MAHRATTI
MAKASSAR MALAGASY MANDINGO
MARSHALL MASOVIAN MAYATHAN
MAZOVIAN MONGOLIC MUSKOGEE
NUMIDIAN NYAMWEZI OSSETIAN
PAMPANGO PHRYGIAN POLABIAN
PORTUGAL PRUSSIAN RABBINIC
ROMANIAN SABELLIC SANSKRIT
SAWAIORI SCOTTISH SCYTHIAN
SEBUNDOY SEECHELT SHAMBALA
SHIRIANA SHOSHONE SICILIAN
SLAVONIC SOUTHRON SQUAMISH
SUBARIAN SUBTIABA SUMATRAN
SUMERIAN TAHITIAN TALMUDIC
TAMASHEK THRACIAN TURCOMAN
VENETIAN VOLSCIAN WOGULIAN
YUGOSLAV YUKAGHIR CANAANITE
(— THAT CONDEMNS) ABUSE
(ARTIFICIAL —) RO IDO ARULO
NOVIAL VOLAPUK ESPERANTO
(FIGURATIVE —) IMAGERY
(FLORID —) SILLABUB
(FOOLISH —) STUFF FLUMMERY
(FOUL —) SMUT ORDURE
(GYPSY —) CALO
(INCOMPREHENSIBLE —) CHOCTAW
(INTERNATIONAL —) ANGLIC
(LATIN —) GRAMMAR HUMANITY
(NONSENSICAL —) BANTER
(OBSCENE —) BAWDY BAWDRY

(ORDINARY —) PROSE
(OVERPRETENTIOUS —) BOMBAST
(PERT —) SAUCE
(PIDGIN —) SABIR CAVITENO
FANAKALO
(PLAIN —) CLEAR
(SECRET —) ARGOT
(SHOWY —) FLUBDUB
(UNCLEAN —) SEWERAGE
(UNIVERSAL —) PASILALY
(WELSH —) CYMRAEG
(PL.) BALTIC FINNIC MAHORI SEMITIC
SUDANIC ILLYRIAN
LANGUE D'OC LEMOSI LIMOSI
LANGUET LANGUID LANGUAGE
LANGUID WAN LANK DOWIE FAINT
DREAMY FEEBLE SICKLY SUPINE
TORPID CARELESS FLAGGING
HEEDLESS INDOLENT LISTLESS
SLUGGISH
LANGUISH DIE FADE FALL FLAG
PINE WILT DROOP DWINE FAINT
SWOON SICKEN WITHER DECLINE
LANGUISHING FADE SICK LANGUID
LANGUOR KEF KIF ENNUI DEBILITY
LANGUR DOUC MAHA LOTONG
LUTONG SIMPAI WANDEROO
LANK LEAN THIN GAUNT LANKY
SLANK MEAGER MEAGRE SLUNKEN
LANKY LEAN RENKY SLINK GANGLY
GANGLING
LANOLIN LANUM DEGRAS
LANSEH DUKU LANSA LANZON
LANTANA OREGANO
LANTERN (ALSO SEE LAMP) BUAT
BOUET BOWET DARKY LIGHT
CUPOLA LOUVER PHAROS SCONCE
THOLUS CIMBORIC LANTHORN
(— ON ROOF) FEMEREIL
(DARK —) DARKY ABSCONSA
ABSCONCE
(ELEVATED —) PHAROS
(OPTICAL —) EPISCOPE
LANTERN FISH INIOME
LANTERN FLOUNDER MEGRIM
LANTERN FLY FULGORID
LANTERN PINION RUNDLE
TRUNDLE
LANYARD WAPP GILGUY LANIARD
BACKROPE
LAODAMIA (FATHER OF —) ACASTUS
(HUSBAND OF —) PROTESILAUS
(MOTHER OF —) HIPPOLYTE
LAODICE (FATHER OF —) PRIAM
(HUSBAND OF —) HELICAON
(MOTHER OF —) HECUBA
LAOIGHIS LEIX
LAOMEDON (SON OF —) PRIAM

LAOS
CAPITAL: VIENTIANE
COIN: KIP
MEASURE: BAK
MOUNTAIN: BIA LAI LOI SAN COPI
KHAT ATWAT KHOUNG TIUBIA
PEOPLE: LU KHA LAO MEO YAO
THAI

RIVER: NOI DONE KHONG MEKONG SEBANG
TOWN: NAPE PAKSE XIENG PAKLAY THAKHEK

LAP LEP LIP BARM FOLD GORE LICK SLAP SLOD SOSS SUCK WASH WELT LAPPER LAPPET SHOVEL INTERLAP
(— **IN STEEL**) SPILL
(— **OF STRAKES**) LAND
LAPACHOL TECOMIN
LAPBOARD PANEL
LAPDOG MESSAN MESSET SHOUGH
LAPEL LAPPET REVERE REVERS
LAPIDARY STONER GEMMARY LAPIDIST
LAPILLUS RAPILLO
(PL.) CINDER
LAPIS LAZULI AZURE
LAP-JOINTED CLINCH
LAPP LAPPISH LAPPONIC
LAPPED FOLIATED
LAPPET LAP PAN BARBE FANON LABEL CORNET INFULA PINNER
LAPSE DROP FADE FALL HALT SLIP ERROR FAULT FOLLY SPACE TRACT EFFLUX HIATUS LAPSUS DELAPSE ESCHEAT FAILURE PROCESS RELAPSE RESOLVE SLIDING ABEYANCE CADUCITY
(— **OF MEMORY**) BLACKOUT
(PL.) LACHES
LAPSED CADUCOUS
LAPSTRAKE CLINCH
LAPWING WEEP WYPE PEEWEE PLOVER TIRWIT HORNPIE PEEWEEP PIEWIPE TEUCHIT FLOPWING PEESWEEP TEEWHAAP TERUTERU
LARBOARD PORT BABURD
LARCENY THEFT FELONY ROBBERY BURGLARY STEALAGE
LARCH LARICK JUNIPER EPINETTE TAMARACK
LARD MORT SAIM ADEPS DAUBE ENARM FLARE FLECK FLICK AXUNGE ENLARD INLARD NEUTRAL SAINDOUX
LARDED PIQUE CADUCE CADUCOUS
LARDER CAVE PANTRY SPENCE BUTTERY LARDINER
LARGE BIG BULL FEAT GOOD LONG MAIN ROOM TALL AMPLE BULKY BURLY GRAND GREAT GROSS HUSKY JOLLY LARGY MACRO MAXIM RENKY ROUND SMART SPACY WALLY GAWSIE GOODLY HEROIC MAXIMA STRONG TRABAL BOWERLY CAPITAL COPIOUS FAIRISH FEARFUL HEALTHY HULKING LASKING LIBERAL MASSIVE SIZABLE CHOPPING PLUMPING SENSIBLE SWACKING
(— **AND HOLLOW**) CAVAL
(— **AND ROUND**) SIDE
(— **IN DIAMETER**) STOUT
(**APPALLINGLY** —) HIDEOUS
(**EXTREMELY** —) GIANT DECUMAN GIGANTIC

(**FAIRLY** —) SMART
(**INDEFINITELY** —) NTH INFINITE
(**MODERATELY** —) FAIR
(**UNUSUALLY** —) HEAVY SKELPIN SKELPING
(**VERY** —) HUGE ROYAL BOXCAR INGENT NATION GOLIATH INTENSE BEHEMOTH SLAPPING SWINGING WHACKING
LARGE-FOOTED MEGAPOD
LARGE-FRAMED ROOMY
LARGE-LETTERED UNCIAL
LARGELY BIG HARD BIGLY
LARGENESS MICKLE BREADTH FREEDOM GIANTISM LARGEOUR
LARGEST BEST MAXIMUS
LARIA BRUCHUS
LARIAT ROPE LASSO RIATA CABESTRO
LARK GAME FROLIC PEEWEE SCHEME LAVROCK LAYROCK SKYLARK CALANDER LAVEROCK
LARKA KOLS HO
LARKSPUR LOCOWEED
LARNITE BELITE
LARRIKIN NUT ROWDY HOODLUM
LARVA BOT BLOW BOTT CRAB GRUB HUHU SLUG TURK WOLF WORM ALIMA ASCON BARDY BRUKE ERUCA LEECH OTTER REDIA SYCON CORBIE COSSID DRAGON EPHYRA GRUGRU HOPPER LEPTUS LEUCON LOOPER MAGGOT MEASLE NIGGER PEDLAR TORCEL WABBLE WORMIL WOUBIT ATROCHA BUDWORM CADELLE CREEPER DIPORPA FIGWORM FLYBLOW GORDIAN HYPOPUS PEDDLER PLANULA PLUTEUS PREPUPA WIGGLER ACTINULA ANTIZOEA ARMYWORM BOLLWORM BOMBYCID BOOKWORM CASEWORM CERCARIA COENURUS CYRTOPIA DEUTOVUM DROPWORM EPHYRULA FIREWORM FURCILIA GEOMETER GILTTAIL GLOWWORM GNATWORM LEAFTIER LEAFWORM MUCKWORM NAUPLIUS PILIDIUM ROOTWORM SCYPHULA SEMIPUPA SILKWORM SKINWORM SPANWORM SPRAWLER STAGWORM SUBIMAGO TORNARIA VERMICLE WASPLING WIREWORM WOODGRUB WOODWORM
LARVACEA ATREMATA COPELATA
LARVAL NEPIONIC
LARYNGITIS CROUP
LASCIVIOUS LEWD NICE SALT HORNY LUBRIC WANTON BLISSOM FLESHLY GOATISH
LASCIVIOUSNESS LECHERY ASELGEIA LUXURITY
LASERWORT SILPHIUM
LASH CUT BEAT FIRK FLOG JERK LACE WELT WHIP WIRE YERK LEASE LEASH SCORE SKEEG SLASH THONG WHALE CANVAS LAINER LAUNCH STRIPE SWINGE SWITCH FLYFLAP KURBASH SCOURGE
(— **TOGETHER**) RACK
LASHER THONGMAN

LASHING YARK YERK GAMMON LISTING MOUSING SEIZING SLATING FRAPPING
(PL.) OODLES OODLINS SLITHERS
LASS TIB GILL PRIM TRULL DAMSEL KUMMER LASSIE DAMOZEL LASSIKY TENDREL MUCHACHA
LASSITUDE LANGUOR LETHARGY
LASSO LASH LAZO ROPE RIATA LARIAT CABESTRO
LAST ABY LAG DURE HOLD KEEP RIDE SAVE ABIDE FINAL SERVE ABEGGE ENDURE LATEST LATTER REMAIN ULTIMA UTMOST DARREIN DERNIER EXTREME PERDURE SUPREME CONTINUE EVENTUAL HINDMOST LATEMOST REARMOST TERMINAL ULTIMATE
(— **BUT ONE**) PENULT
(— **OUT**) SPIN STAY
(**AT** —) FINALLY
(**THE** —) OMEGA
LASTING FIXED LASTY DURANT DURING STABLE ABIDING DURABLE DUREFUL CONSTANT ENDURING LIVELONG REMANENT STANDING
(— **FOR LONG PERIOD**) AEONIC AEONIAL
(— **FOR ONE DAY**) DIARY DIURNAL
LASTINGNESS STAY DURATION
LAST SUPPER CENA COENA MAUNDY
LAT STAMBHA
LATCH FLY PIN HASP RISP CATCH CHAIR CLICK CLINK SNECK SNICK KEEPER CLICKET
LATCHET DAG TAB SANDAL LANGUET
LATCHING LASKET
LATCHKEY CLICKET PASSKEY
LATE LAG NEW DEEP RIPE SLOW TARDY TARDIVE UMWHILE ADVANCED LATEWARD SOMETIME UMQUHILE
LATELY LATE ALATE NEWLY
LA TENE MARNEAN
LATENT HIDDEN ABEYANT DORMANT LATITANT
LATER POI SIN ANON POST SYNE AFTER ELDER BEHIND FUTURE LATTER PUISNE ANOTHER INFERIOR UMQUHILE
LATERAL SIDE
LATERALLY SIDELONG
LATERITE CABOOK
LATEST LAST LATTER FARTHEST FURTHEST
LATEX GUTTA SORVA
LATH SLAT SPAIL SPALE SPELL SWALE REEPER SPLENT SPLINT STOOTH LATHING FOREPOLE LATHWORK
LATHE LAY SLEY TURN LAITH THROW BEATER WISKET
(— **FOR CYLINDERS**) BROAD
(— **OF LOOM**) LAY
(**TURNING** —) THROW
(**WATCHMAKER'S** —) TURN TURNS MANDREL

LATHER FOAM SUDS FROTH FREATH
SAPPLES
LATHERED SOAPY
LATIN ROMAN HISPERIC LATINITY
(— COMPOSITION) VULGUS
LATIN-AMERICAN LATIN LADINO
LATINO HISPANIC
LATINUS (DAUGHTER OF —) LAVINIA
(FATHER OF —) FAUNUS
(SON-IN-LAW OF —) AENEAS
(WIFE OF —) AMATA
LATITUDE SCOPE WIDTH EXTENT
HEIGHT
(HELIOCENTRIC —) LIMIT
LATONA (DAUGHTER OF —) DIANA
(FATHER OF —) COEUS
(MOTHER OF —) PHOEBE
(SON OF —) APOLLO
LATRIA ADORATION
LATRINE PRIVY TOILET BOGGARD
LATTER LAST FINAL RECENT
SECOND PRESENT
(— PORTION) AUTUMN
LATTICE GRATE HERSE TWINE
PINJRA UMBREL GRATING CANCELLI
(— OF POINTS) SATIN
(MOVING —) APRON
LATTICE PLANT LACELEAF
LATTICEWORK ARBOR GRATE
GRATING TUKUTUKU

LATVIA
CAPITAL: RIGA
COIN: LAT RUBLIS KAPEIKA
SANTIMAS
MEASURE: STOF KANNE STOFF
STOOF VERST ARSHIN KULMET
SAGENE VERCHOC KROUCHKA
POURVETE
PEOPLE: LETT
RIVER: AA OGRE GAUJA SALACA
LIELUPE
TOWN: CESIS LIBAU DVINSK
LIBAVA TUKUMS JELGAVA
REZEKNE DUNABURG VALMIERA
WEIGHT: LIESPFUND

LAUAN KALUNTI
LAUD EXTOL PRAISE ADVANCE
APPLAUD COMMEND GLORIFY
MAGNIFY EMBLAZON EULOGIZE
MACARIZE
LAUDATION EULOGY PRAISE
LAUDATORY SNEER EPENETIC
PRAISING
LAUGH GAFF CHUCK FLEER LEUGH
RISUS ARRIDE NICKER TITTER
CHORTLE GRIZZLE SNICKER
SNIGGER SNIRTLE TWITTER
LAUGHTER
(— CONTEMPTUOUSLY) SNORT
DERIDE
(— GLEEFULLY) CHECKLE
(— HYSTERICALLY) CHECKLE
(— IN AFFECTED MANNER) GIGGLE
(— IN COARSE MANNER) FLEER
GUFFAW
(— LIKE HEN) CACKLE
(— LOUDLY) GAFF GUFFAW

(— QUIETLY) GULE SMUDGE
CHUCKLE SNIRTLE
(BELLY —) BOFF BOFFOLA
(LOUD —) GAUSTER
LAUGHABLE ODD RICH COMIC
DROLL FUNNY MERRY QUEER WITTY
AMUSING COMICAL RISIBLE
STRANGE WAGGISH FARCICAL
HUMOROUS LAUGHING PLEASANT
SPORTIVE
LAUGHING RIANT RIDENT IRRISION
(— MATTER) MOWS
LAUGHING GULL PEWIT
LAUGHING OWL WEKAU WHEKAU
LAUGHINGSTOCK GUY BUTT JEST
JOKE SONG SPORT DERISION
RIDICULE
LAUGHTER JOKE MIRTH RISUS
SNIRT CACKLE LAWTER SPLEEN
HILARITY
LAUNCE LANT LANCE SMELT
AMMODYTE SANDLING
LAUNCH PUT BURST DRIVE LANCE
ELANCE STRIKE BAPTIZE PINNACE
STEAMER VIBRATE CATAPULT
(— HOSTILELY) DIRECT
LAUNCHER (ROCKET —) BAZOOKA
LAUNDER TYE WASH TRUNK SLUICE
STRAKE LAUNDRY
LAUNDRESS TRILBY LAVENDER
LAUNDRY WASH LAVATORY
LAUREL BAY IVY LAURY UNITE
WICKY DAPHNE KALMIA MALLET
MYRTLE CAJEPUT IVYWOOD
WOEVINE BREWSTER CALFKILL
(GROUND —) ARBUTUS
LAUREL OAK ACAJOU
LAURIC PICHURIC
LAURUSTINE VIBURNUM
LAUSUS (FATHER OF —) NUMITOR
MEZENTIUS
(SISTER OF —) ILIA
(SLAYER OF —) AMULIUS
LAUTVERSCHIEBUNG SHIFT
LAVA AA ASHES SPINE COULEE
LATITE SCORIA VERITE FAVILLA
LAPILLO MALPAIS ASPERITE
ORENDITE PAHOEHOE
(SCORIACEOUS —) AA SLAG
(SLAGGY —) SCORIA
LAVABO LAVATORY
LAVAGE LAVATION LAVEMENT
LAVALAVA SULU
LAVAN KALUNTI
LAVATORY BASIN LAVETTE
WASHROOM
LAVE LIP WASH BATHE SPLASH
LAVENDER BEHN ASPIC BEHEN
SPICK SPIKE INKROOT LAVANDIN
STICHADO
LAVER SION SLAKE SLOKE LOUTER
PHIALE AMANORI CISTERN
LAVINIA (FATHER OF —) LATINUS
(HUSBAND OF —) AENEAS
(MOTHER OF —) AMATA
LAVISH FREE LASH LUSH FLUSH
LARGE SPEND SPORT WASTE
COSTLY WANTON COPIOUS
OPULENT PROFUSE GENEROUS

LUCULLAN PRODIGAL SQUANDER
WASTEFUL
LAVISHNESS WASTE FINERY LAVISH
LAW ACT FAS IUS JUS LAY LEX ADAT
DOOM JURE RULE CANON DROIT
NOMOS TORAH BYELAW BYRLAW
DECREE DHARMA EQUITY DANELAW
DERECHO HALACHA HALAKAH
JUSTICE PRECEPT SETNESS
STATUTE JUDGMENT JUDICIAL
ROGATION STATEWAY TANISTRY
(—S OF MANU) SUTRA SUTTA
(BEDOUIN —) THAR
(DIETARY —S) KASHRUTH
(ISLAMIC —) ADA BAI ADAT SHERI
SHARIA SHERIAT
(MARRIAGE —) LEVIRATE
(OPPOSING —) ANTINOMY
(PROPOSED —) BILL
(UNIVERSAL —) HEAVEN
(PL.) LORS
LAW-ABIDING LAWFUL
LAWBREAKER FELON HOUGHER
LAWFUL DUE LEAL TRUE VERY
LEGAL LICIT LOYAL VALID KINDLY
LEEFUL ENNOMIC LEESOME
INNOCENT LIEFSOME RIGHTFUL
LAWGIVER MINOS MOSES SOLON
LAWYER LAWMAKER
LAWLESS LEWD UNRULY ILLEGAL
MOBBISH ANARCHIC
LAWLESSNESS ANOMY ANOMIE
LAWMAKER LEGIFER
LAWN ARBOR GRASS LINON SWARD
UMPLE CYPRUS BATISTE QUINTIN
TIFFANY
LAWSUIT LIS CASE SAKE SECTA
BRABBLE
LAWYER JET PEAT AVOUE PATCH
SHARK BREHON JURIST LAWMAN
LEGIST SQUIRE WRITER COUNSEL
TEMPLAR DEFENDER LEGISTER
TRAMPLER BARRISTER
LAX DULL FREE LASH LAZY LINK
SLOW SWAG WIDE LARGE LOOSE
RELAX SLACK TARDY REMISS
BACKWARD INACTIVE DISSOLUTE
LAXATIVE LAX LASK APERIENT
HYDROMEL LAPACTIC RELAXANT
SOLUTIVE
LAXITY LASCHETY LATITUDE
LAY LIE SET CLAP LAIC LEWD SLEY
SONG WAGE BIGHT COUCH DITTY
LATHE LEDGE QUIET STAKE STILL
COMMON HAZARD IMPOSE IMPUTE
APPEASE ASCRIBE LAYDOWN
POPULAR SECULAR
(— ASIDE) DOFF DOWN DUMP
SHUCK DEPOSE DIVEST DEPOSIT
(— AWAY) STORE
(— BARE) BARE NAKE TIRL TIRVE
DENUDE DETECT OPPOSE UNCOVER
DENUDATE
(— CLAIM) ASSERT BESPEAK
ARROGATE
(— CROSSWISE) COB
(— DOWN) ABDICATE
(— EGGS) BLOW WARP LEDGE
OVIPOSIT

(— **FLAT**) SQUAT ADPRESS
(— **HOLD OF**) FANG GRIP HENT
TAKE GRIPE LATCH ATHOLD
ATTACH COLLAR COMPRISE
(— **IN BIGHTS**) JAG
(— **IN COIL**) FLEMISH
(— **IN PLEATS**) FOLD
(— **LOW**) STREW STRIKE
(— **OF LOOM**) BEATER
(— **ON**) APPLY INFLICT
(— **OPEN**) BREAK CHINE EXPOSE
UNMASK
(— **OUT**) FRAY PLAT RANGE SPELD
SPEND BEWARE DESIGN EXTEND
SPREAD STREAK STREEK CHECKER
DEVELOP STRETCH CONTRIVE
(— **PRONE**) LEVEL
(— **RUBBLEWORK**) SNECK
(— **SIEGE**) INVEST
(— **SMOOTH**) EVEN
(— **SNARE FOR RABBITS**) HAY
(— **STONE**) PAVE
(— **STRAIGHT**) COMB
(— **TYPE**) CASE
(— **UP**) HEAP HIVE ADDLE HOARD
HUTCH STOCK TREASURE
(— **WASTE**) PEEL WEST HARRY
HAVOC HARASS RAVAGE DESTROY
DESOLATE FORWASTE
LAYBOY JOGGER
LAYDOWN LAYOUT SPREAD
LAYER BED LAY BARK CAKE COAT
DASS FACE FILM FLAP FOLD LAIR
SEAM SKIN WEFT ZONA CHESS
COUCH COVER CRUST CUTIS FLAKE
FLASH LEDGE SCALE CARPET
COURSE FASCIA FILLER FOLIUM
INTINE LAMINA LISSOM STREAK
BLANKET COATING CUTICLE
EPICARP FEATHER FLAVEDO
GANGMAN INLAYER LAMELLA
PACKING PHELLEM PROPAGO
PROVINE STRATUM SUBCOAT
SUPPORT ECTOCYST ECTOSARC
ENDOCYST ENDODERM EPIBLAST
EPIBLEMA EPISPORE EPITHECA
INTERBED MOLLISOL PERIOPLE
SUBCRUST
(— **IN FUNGI**) HYMENIUM
(— **OF BLOOD VESSEL**) EXTIMA
EXTERNA
(— **OF CELLS**) EXINE CORTEX
EXTINE CAMBIUM
(— **OF CLAY**) GLEY SELVAGE
SELVEDGE
(— **OF EARTH**) SPIT
(— **OF FAT**) LEAF FINISH
(— **OF FELT**) BAT BATT
(— **OF FIBER**) LAP
(— **OF FINE MATERIAL**) CUSHION
(— **OF FOREST GROWTH**)
SUBSTORY
(— **OF FUEL**) FIREBED
(— **OF GLASS**) CASING
(— **OF IRIS**) UVEA
(— **OF MEAT**) SPINE
(— **OF NERVE FIBERS**) ALVEUS
(— **OF ORGANIC MATTER**) FLOOR
(— **OF PLASMA**) BUFFCOAT

(— **OF ROCK**) CAP SHELF SHELL
SLATE FOLIUM SEPTUM BLISTER
SKULLCAP
(— **OF ROOTS**) SOLE
(— **OF SEDIMENT**) WARP
(— **OF SHALE**) BONE
(— **OF SHEEPSKIN**) FLESHER
(— **OF SHOE HEEL**) LIFT
(— **OF SILT**) VARVE
(— **OF SKIN**) DERM DERMA EPIDERM
(— **OF SOIL**) SOLUM CALLOW
CASING HARDPAN HORIZON
(— **OF STONES**) DASS DESS
(— **OF TANBARK**) HAT
(— **OF TISSUE**) BED DARTOS FASCIA
SEROSA ELASTICA EPIBLEMA
(— **OF TOBACCO LEAVES**) HANGER
(— **OF TURF**) FLAW
(— **OF WHITE MATTER**) CAPSULE
(— **OF WOOD**) CORE
(**BONY** —) LAMELLA CEMENTUM
(**BOTTOM** —) BEDDING
(**FLAT** —) BED FLAP FLAKE
(**GERM** —) MESODERM
(**IMPERVIOUS** —) LINING
(**OUTER** —) HUSK
LAYERING LAP GOOTEE STOOLING
LAYMAN LAIC CLERK IDIOT DEACON
SECULAR DEFENSOR EXHORTER
EXOTERIC FAMILIAR STRANGER
WORLDMAN
LAYOFF FURLOUGH
LAYOUT MISE DUMMY SETOUT
(— **OF CARDS**) TABLEAU
LAZARETTO SPITAL SPITTLE
LAZINESS LAZE SLOTH SLOUCH
OISIVITY
LAZULITE SIDERITE
LAZY ARGH IDLE LASS DOXIE DRONY
FAINT INERT LINGY LUSKY RESTY
SLOAN SLOTH CLUMSY LIMPSY
LURDAN LUTHER ORNERY SWEERT
TRAILY CLUMPST LUSKISH PEAKISH
SLIVING DROGHLIN FAINEANT
FECKLESS INDOLENT LITHERLY
OSCITANT SLOTHFUL SLUGGARD
THOWLESS TRIFLING
LEA LAY GRASS LAYER LAYLAND
LEALAND
LEACH TAP LETCH SOFTEN
LEAD GO TEE VAN WIN BEAR DADE
GIVE GROW HAVE HEAD HERD LEED
SLIP TAKE TEEM WORK BLAZE
BOUND BRING CARRY GREBE GUIDE
MAYNE PILOT PRESA SOUND START
TRAIN TREAT CONVEY DEDUCE
DIRECT ESCORT INDUCE INDUCT
LEADER SATURN BEGUILE CAPTAIN
CONDUCE CONDUCT LEADING
MARSHAL PIGTAIL PIONEER
PLUMBUM PLUMMET LEADSMAN
MANUDUCE MANUDUCT SQUIRREL
(— **A BAND**) BATON
(— **AND SUPPORT**) DADE
(— **ASIDE**) CHAR SINGLE
(— **ASTRAY**) ERR MANG TURN WARP
BEFOOL BETRAY ENTICE WANDER
WILDER DEBAUCH MISLEAD
MISWEND PERVERT SOLICIT

TRADUCE BEWILDER INVEIGLE
MISGUIDE
(— **AWAY**) CHAR ABDUCT DIVERGE
(— **BACK**) REDUCT
(— **FORCIBLY**) ESCORT
(— **IN CARD GAME**) SNEAK
(— **IN RACE**) LAP
(— **IN SINGING**) PRECENT
(— **INTO ERROR**) ABUSE DELUDE
(— **MONOXIDE**) MASSICOT
(— **ON**) TRAIL
(— **PASSIVE EXISTENCE**) VEGETATE
(— **POISONING**) PLUMBISM
(**BLACK** —) WAD WADD GRAPHITE
(**COLOR** —) PLOMB
(**DEEP-SEA** —) DIPSY DIPSEY
(**OVERLAPPING** —) DRIP
(**PLUMBING** —) BLUEY
(**SYMBOL FOR** —) PB
(**WHITE** —) KREMS CERUSE
LEAD-COLORED WAN BLAE
LEADEN HEAVY PLUMBEAN
LEADER BO BOH COB DUX HOB MIR
CAST COCK DUCE DUKE HEAD
HOBB JEFE NAIG NAIK OMDA SOUL
TYEE CHIEF DOYEN ELDER FIRST
MAHDI MOSES OMDEH PILOT SEYID
TRACE ARCHON CALIPH DESPOT
HEADER RECTOR SAYYID TYCOON
ACREMAN ADVISER CAPTAIN
CONDUCT DEMAGOG DRUNGAR
FOREMAN FUEHRER INDUCER
ACCENTOR CAUDILLO DIRECTOR
FUGLEMAN HEADSMAN HERETOGA
LODESMAN PANDARUS STRATEGE
(— **OF DACOITS**) BOH
(— **OF MUTINEERS**) ELECTO
(— **OF REVOLT**) ANARCH
(**BAND** —) BATONEER
(**CHOIR** —) CANTOR
(**CHORUS** —) CHORAGUS
(**COSSACK** —) HETMAN
(**FASCIST** —) RAS
(**INTELLECTUAL** —) BRAIN
(**MOB** —) MOBOCRAT
(**POLITICAL** —) SACHEM
(**PRAYER** —) IMAM
(**RELIGIOUS** —) AGA AGHA SHEIKH
(**SCOUT** —) AKELA SIXER
(**SPIRITUAL** —) GURU SADDIK
GUARDIAN
LEADERSHIP LEAD AEGIS MANRED
CONDUCT IMAMATE LEADING
MANRENT CHIEFDOM GUIDANCE
HEADSHIP HEGEMONY
LEADING BIG BEST COCK DUCT
HEAD LEAD MAIN CHIEF FIRST
PREMIER STELLAR GUIDANCE
(— **OUTWARD**) EMISSARY
(— **TO NOTHING**) IDLE
LEADSMAN SOUNDER
LEADWORK PLUMBAGE PLUMBING
LEADWORT CROWTOE PLUMBAGO
LEAF PAD BACK BARB BUYO FLAG
FLAP FOIL FOLD GEAR PAGE PALM
STUB BLADE BLANK FLIER FLYER
FOLIO FROND GRASS GUARD LEAVE
SCALE SEPAL SIGHT SPILL TEPAL
BONNET CADJAN COUPON FOLIUM

FRAISE FULZIE NEEDLE PEPPER
DAMIANA FOLDOUT HARNESS
LEAFLET TREFOIL WITNESS
PHYLLADE PHYLLOME
(— FAT) FLICK
(— FROM AXIL) BRACT
(— OF BOOK) PAGE FOLIO INSET
PLATE FLYLEAF
(— OF CALYX) BARB
(— OF CORN) HUSK
(— OF COROLLA) PETAL
(— OF DOOR) VALVE
(— OF HEDDLES) GEAR
(— OF PALM) FAN OLA CHIP OLLA
FROND LATANIER
(— OF SPRING) BACK
(BETEL —) PAN
(BIBLE —) COSTMARY
(DEAD —) FLAG
(HOLLOW —) PHYLLODE
(SPRING —) WRAPPER
(STRAWBERRY —) FRAISE
(THIN —) LAMELLA
(TOBACCO —) STRIP CUTTER
WRAPPER
(WASTE GOLD —) SKEWING
LEAFAGE FOLIAGE
LEAFHOPPER HOPPER JASSID
THRIPS HOMOPTER
LEAFLET PINNA TRACT MAILER
FOLIOLE STUFFER
(PAIR OF —S) JUGUM
(PL.) SENNA CATOBA
LEAFLIKE PHYLLINE
LEAFMOLD KOLINSKY
LEAFY GREEN LEAVY FOLIATE
FOLIOSE FRONDOSE
LEAGUE BOND BUND BANDY BOARD
GUEUX HANSA PARTY UNION WHEEL
CIRCUIT ALLIANCE SYSTASIS
(— OF NATIONS) GENEVA
(BUSH —S) STICKS
LEAGUED FEDERATE
LEAK BLOW SEEP WEEP GEYZE
SPUNK INLEAK SIGGER SPRING
ZIGGER LEAKAGE MELTERS
SCREEVE
(— IN ELECTRIC CIRCUIT) FAULT
LEAKAGE ESCAPE SEEPAGE
(— OF ELECTRICITY) CREEPAGE
(— OF GAS) SLIP
(— OF WIND) RUNNING
LEAKING ALEAK DRIBBLE NAILSICK
LEAKY LEAK UNTIGHT GIZZENED
LEAL FAITHFUL
LEAN BEND BONY HANG HEEL LANK
PEND POOR PRIN RACY RELY REST
STAY SWAY THIN TOOM EMPTY
GAUNT HIELD LANKY LEANY SLANK
SOUND SPARE STOOP HOLLOW
MEAGER RECUMB SKINNY SPRING
UPLEAN ANGULAR FATLESS INCLINE
SCRAGGY SCRAWNY SLUNKEN
STRINGY MACILENT SCRAGGED
SCRANNEL
(— FOR SUPPORT) ABUT
(— FORWARD) PROCLINE
(— OVER) WHAUVE
LEANER HOBBER

LEANING DRIFT FLAIR PENCHE
HANGING ACCLINAL ENCLITIC
FROMWARD
(— BACKWARD) SUPINE
(STRONG —) GENIUS PENCHANT
LEANNESS LANK POVERTY
SPARENESS
LEAN-TO SHED LINTER OUTSHOT
SKILLION
LEAP FLY HOP POP BEND DART DIVE
FALL GIVE JUMP LOPE LOUP RAMP
RISE SKIT WIND BOUND BREAK
CAPER DANCE EXULT FLIER FLYER
FRISK LUNGE PRIME SALTO SAULT
SCOPE SCOUP SPANG STEND VAULT
BOUNCE BREACH CURVET INSULT
LAUNCH SPRENT SPRING SPRUNT
WALLOP REBOUND SALTARY
SALTATE SUBSULT BUCKJUMP
LEAPFROG SPANGHEW UPSPRING
(— BACK) RESULT SPRUNT
(— FOR JOY) EXULT
(— IN DANCING) STOT
(— LIGHTLY) SKIP
(— OF HORSE) CURVET BALOTADE
CAPRIOLE
(— OF WHALE) BREACH
(— OUT) SALLY
(— OVER) FREE OVER SKIP CLEAR
HURDLE
(— UPON) ASSAIL
(BALLET —) JETE CABRIOLE
(FROLICSOME —) CAPER
(SUICIDAL —) BRODIE
(PL.) ALLEGRO
LEAPING GAMBOL SPRING SALIENT
SALTANT
LEARCHUS (BROTHER OF —)
MELICERTA
(FATHER OF —) ATHAMAS
(MOTHER OF —) INO
LEARN DO GET SEE WIT ARAL FIND
HAVE HEAR LEAR LERE EDIFY
GLEAN STUDY RECORD REALIZE
RECEIVE DISCOVER
(— FROM EXPERIENCE) ASSAY
LEARNED BLUE SEEN LERED LORED
DUCTUS BOOKISH CLERKLY
CUNNING ERUDITE STUDIED TUITIVE
ACADEMIC CLERGIAL LETTERED
OVERSEEN POLYMATH SCIENCED
(— MAN) OLLAV
(AFFECTEDLY —) INKHORN
(SOMETHING TO BE —) LIRIPIPE
LEARNEDLY CLERKLY
LEARNER PUPIL NOVICE TRAINEE
PRENTICE
(LATE —) OPSIMATH
LEARNING ART WIT BOOK LEIR
LERE LORE CLERGY WISDOM
APPRISE CUNNING GRAMMAR
INSIGHT LETTERS WISTING
BOOKLEAR BOOKLORE DOCTRINE
HUMANISM LETTRURE MATHESIS
PEDANTRY
LEASE FEU FEW LET SET FARM HIRE
RENT TACK COWLE DIMIT FIRMA
LISSE DEMISE POTTAH RENTAL
ASSEDAT CHARTER SETTING

BACKTACK SUBLEASE
LEASEHOLDER LIVIER
LEASH LEAD LYME SLIP LEASE
COUPLE STRING SWINGE
(— OF HOUNDS) HARL
(DOG —) SLIP TRASH TIRRET
(HAWK'S —) LOYN LUNE TIRRET
CREANCE
LEASING LOCATIO
LEAST LEST MINIMAL MINIMUM
MINIMUS
(AT —) HURE
LEAST FLYCATCHER CHEBEC
LEAST SANDPIPER PEEP OXEYE
STINT
LEATHER ELK KID BEND BOCK BUFF
CALF CAPE HIDE NAPA SEAL ADUST
ALUTA BALAT FLANK NIGER RETAN
SUEDE BULGAR CASTOR CHROME
LIZARD ORIOLE OXHIDE PEBBLE
RUSSET SKIVER TURKEY BELTING
BUFFING CANEPIN CHAMOIS
COWHIDE COWSKIN DEGRAIN
DOGSKIN DONGOLA HEADCAP
HOGSKIN KIDSKIN MURRAIN
PANCAKE PECCARY PERSIAN
SAFFIAN ANTELOPE BUCKSKIN
BULLNECK CABRETTA CALFSKIN
CAPESKIN CHEVEREL COLTSKIN
CORDOBAN CORDWAIN DEERSKIN
GOATSKIN KANGAROO LAMBSKIN
SHAGREEN
(— FOR DRESSING FLAX) RIBSKIN
(— SHREDS) MOSLINGS
(— STRIP) RAND
(ARABIAN —) MOCHA
(ARTIFICIAL —) KERATOL
(BOARDED —) BOX
(CORDOVAN —) CORDOBAN
CORDWAIN
(MOROCCO —) LEVANT MAROQUIN
(PATCH OF —) CLOUT
(PRUSSIAN —) SPRUCE
(RUSSIAN —) YUFT BULGAR RUSSIA
JUCHTEN
(SHEEPSKIN —) BOCK BUCK
(SOFT —) ALUTA
(SUPERIOR —) BUFF
(WASH —) LOSH LOSHE
LEATHERBACK LUTH
LEATHERFISH LIJA FOOLFISH
LEATHERJACKET FILEFISH
ZAPATERO
LEATHERLEAF CASSANDRA
LEATHERWOOD DIRCA WICOPY
BURNWOOD FIREWOOD IRONWOOD
LEADWOOD ROPEBARK
LEATHERWORKER TAWER BEDDER
CHAMAR MADIGA FLUFFER
CHUCKLER
LEAVE GO GET LET BUNK DROP
FADE FLEE HOOK LEAF PART QUIT
VADE VOID WALK AVOID FAVOR
FORGO GRACE SHOVE WAIVE
BUGGER DEPART DESERT DEVOID
FORLET PERMIT RETIRE SECEDE
STRAND VACATE FORLEIT FORLESE
FORSAKE LARGESS LIBERTY
LICENSE FAREWELL PATIENCE
UNTENANT

(— **ALONE**) FORBEAR DESOLATE
(— **BEHIND**) LET PLANT DISTANCE
(— **BRIGHT TRAIL**) STREAM
(— **BY WILL**) BEQUEATH
(— **COVER**) BREAK
(— **HASTILY**) SCUR SKIRR
(— **HURRIEDLY**) CUT BLOW FLEE
JUMP SCAT SKIP
(— **IN ISOLATION**) MAROON
(— **IN SAFEKEEPING**) CHECK
(— **NOTHING TO BE DESIRED**)
SATISFY
(— **OF ABSENCE**) ABSIT LIBERTY
FURLOUGH
(— **OFF**) CEASE DEVAL PETER
BILEVE CHEESE DESIST SURCEASE
(— **OUT**) BATE OMIT SKIP SLIP
ELIDE
(— **PORT**) CLEAR
(— **QUICKLY**) SCREW
(— **SECRETLY**) STEAL
(— **SUDDENLY**) KITE
LEAVEN ZYM ZYMO RAISE YEAST
INFUSE RAISING SOURING
LEAVENING EMPTINGS
LEAVES PATRIN FOLIAGE LEAFAGE
LEAFERY
(— **OF BAOBAB TREE**) LALO
(— **OF ORCHID**) FAHAM
(— **OF TOBACCO**) LEAF FLYINGS
SECONDS
(— **ON STEM AFTER WITHERING**)
INDUVIAE
(— **USED AS STYPTIC**) MATICO
(**BOILED** — **OF POTHERB**) CHARD
(**DRIED** —) LAUHALA
(**MEDICINAL** —) COCA FILE BUCCO
BUCKU FARFARA FUMARIA
(**PALM** —) ATAP ATTAP CADJAN
CAJANG
(**TEA** —) SOUCHONG
(**WITHERED** —) PININGS
LEAVE-TAKING VALE ADIEU
CONGEE PARTING WAYGANG
FAREWELL WAYGOING
LEAVING BIT
(PL.) RAFF SNUFF REFUSE RESIDUE
RESIDUUM

LEBANON
CAPITAL: BEIRUT BEYROUTH
COIN: LIVRE PIASTRE
MOUNTAIN: ARUBA HERMON
SANNINE KENISSEH
PLAIN: ELBIKA
RIVER: LYCOS DAMOUR LITANI
HASBANI LEONTES KASEMIEH
SEAPORT: TYRE SAIDA SIDON
BEIRUT
TOWN: SUR TYRE SAIDA SIDON
ZAHLE ZAHLHA TRIPOLI
MERJUYUN
VALLEY: BEQAA

LEBBEK KOKO KOKKO SIRIS
LEBKUCHEN LEKACH
LECHER GOAT LUXUR PALLIARD
LECHEROUS LEWD PRIME WANTON

BOARISH CODDING GOATISH
LUSTFUL LIKEROUS SCABROUS
SPORTIVE
LECHERY LUXURY
LECTERN DESK EAGLE LUTRIN
LATERAN LATTERIN
LECTION GOSPEL EPISTLE READING
PROPHECY
LECTIONARY LEGEND
LECTOR LISTER READER
LECTURE JOBE CREED FORUM
HOMILY LECTOR LESSON SERMON
ADDRESS EARBASH HEARING
PRELECT READING JOBATION
ORDINARY
LECTURER DOCENT LECTOR
READER DRYASDUST
LEDA (DAUGHTER OF —) HELEN
CLYTEMNESTRA
(**FATHER OF** —) THESTIUS
(**HUSBAND OF** —) TYNDAREUS
(**SON OF** —) CASTOR POLLUX
LEDGE BEAD BERM DESS LINE STEP
ALTAR BENCH CLINT SHELF SNOUT
BEARER OFFSET SETTLE STANCE
CHANNEL LEDGING RETABLE
LEDGEMAN BREAKER
LEDGER BOOK SLAB LIEGER
JOURNAL OVERLIER
LEDGER BOARD RIBBON
LEE LEW LEEWARD
LEECH GILL HARPY LEACH APODAN
BDELLOID HELMINTH
LEEK ALLIUM PORRET SCALLION
(— **COLORED**) PRASINE
LEER LEAR LOOK OGLE FLEER
LEERY SKIME SMIRK TWIRE
LEERFISH GARRICK
LEES LAGS ADDLE DRAFF DREGS
DROSS GROUT AMURCA BOTTOM
DUNDER MOTHER ULLAGE
GROUNDS EMPTINGS SEDIMENT
WINEDRAF
LEEWAN SOFA DIVAN
LEEWARD DOWNWIND
LEEWAY DRIFT
LEFT G CAR KAY GAWK NEAR OTHER
TOWARD DESERTED
(— **EYE**) OL OS
LEFT-HAND GAUCHE
LEFT HAND MG MS SM SIN
(— **PAGE**) VERSO
LEFTHANDED CAR GAUCHE
AWKWARD DUBIOUS OBLIQUE
KITHOGUE SOUTHPAW
LEFT-HANDER SOUTHPAW
LEFTOVER END REMNANT
(**TOBACCO** —) TOPPER
(PL.) SCRAN ANALECTS
LEG ARM GAM PEG PIN CRUS GAMB
JAMB LIMB TRAM BOUGH GAMBE
JAMBE REACH SHANK STICK STUMP
BENDER GAMBON GAMMON LEGLET
MOGGAN OVIGER PESTLE PLANTA
PROLEG WALKER FORELEG
TRESTLE FORELIMB
(— **OF HAWK**) ARM
(— **OF LAMB**) GIGOT WABBLER
WOBBLER

(— **OF TABLE**) BALUSTER
(— **OF WHEELBARROW**) STILT
(— **USED FOR FOOD**) PESTLE
(—**S OF ARTIFICAL FLY**) HACKLE
(**FURNITURE** —) CABRIOLE
(**MILK** —) WEED
(**TROUSER** —) SLOP
(**WIRE** —**S**) SLING
(**WOODEN** —) PEG STUMP TIMBER
(PL.) PROPS TONGS STAMPS STICKS
LEGACY ENTAIL LEGATE BEQUEST
HERITAGE WINDFALL
LEGAL LEAL LICIT SOUND VALID
LAWFUL SQUARE JURIDIC RIGHTFUL
LEGALISM NOMISM SCRIBISM
LEGALISTIC COURT
LEGATE ENVOY DEPUTY LEGATUS
CONSULAR LEGATARY PANDOLPH
LEGATION MISSION
LEGATO SMOOTH
LEGEND EDDA MYTH POSY SAGA
TALE FABLE STORY TITLE THREAP
CUTLINE HAGGADA
(**MAP** —) KEY
LEGENDARY FABLED FICTIOUS
LEGERDEMAINIST JUGGLER
LEGGING SPAT COCKER BOTTINE
GAMBADO BALATONG BOOTIKIN
CHIVARRA
(**LEATHER** —) STRAD
(PL.) CHAPS SHANKS BROGUES
COGGERS GAMASHES LEATHERS
OVERALLS
LEGIBLE FAIR READABLE
LEGION HOST TERZO TERZIO
LEGIONARY ANT DRIVER FORAGER
LEGISLATION DYSNOMY
LAWMAKING
LEGISLATOR SOLON LAWGIVER
LAWMAKER
LEGISLATURE DIET COURT THING
LAGTING RIKSDAG LANDRATH
RIGSRAAD
LEGITIMATE JUST TRUE VERY
LEGAL LEGIT LOYAL HONEST
KINDLY KOSHER LAWFUL REABLE
SQUARE LEGITIME
LEGITIMATELY FAIRLY MULIERLY
LEGPIECE JAMBEAU
LEGUME POD GUAR PULSE LOMENT
PODDER COCHLEA LEGUMEN
PODWARE SOYBEAN STROMBUS
LEIPOA LOWAN MEGAPOD PHEASANT
LEISHMANIASIS UTA ESPUNDIA
LEISTER SPEAR WASTER
LEISURE TIME TOOM VOID OTIUM
RESPITE VACANCY VACATION
LEISURELY SLOW SOODLY TIMELY
TOOMLY GRADUAL PICKTOOTH
LEMAN UNDERPUT
LEMMING CRICETID
LEMMUS MYODES
LEMNISCUS FILET FILLET LAQUEUS
LEMON DOG DUD CEDRA CHLOR
LEMONY CEDRATE FAILURE
KUMQUAT
LEMONADE COOLER
LEMON GRASS TANGLAD
LEMON SOLE MARYSOLE

LEMON VERBENA ALOYSIA
LEMUR MAKI VARI AVAHI INDRI
  KOKAM LORIS POTTO SIFAC ADAPID
  COBEGO COLUGO GALAGO KUBONG
  MACACO MAHOLI MONKEY SIFAKA
  NATTOCK PRIMATE SEMIAPE
  TARSIER AMPONGUE BABAKOTO
  MONGOOSE PRIMATAL TARSIOID
LEND OCKER PREST SECOND
  IMPREST
  (— AT INTEREST) GAVEL
  (— ITSELF) ALLOY
LENDING (— AGENCY) MOUNT
LENGTH LUG DREE TOWT PITCH
  SCOPE SIDTH COURSE EXTENT
  TOWGHT FOOTAGE DISTANCE
  LEGITUDE SIDENESS
  (— ATHWARTSHIP) ABURTON
  (— OF BRIDGE) BAY
  (— OF CABLE) SCOPE SHACKLE
  (— OF CHAIN) SHOT
  (— OF CLOTH) CUT
  (— OF FIBER) STAPLE
  (— OF FISHING LINE) CAST
  (— OF GEAR TOOTH) FACE
  (— OF HAIR IN FISHING LINE) IMP
  (— OF HAIR) KNOT
  (— OF LINE) LOYN
  (— OF METAL) SHAPE
  (— OF MOUTH) GAPE
  (— OF NET) LEAD
  (— OF ROPE) DRIFT SPOKE BRIDLE
  COURSE STOPPER
  (— OF SERVICE) STANDING
  (— OF SHOEMAKER'S THREAD) END
  (— OF THREAD) STITCH
  (— OF TILE) GAUGE
  (— OF TIMBER) BALK FLITCH
  (— OF TRIP) GATE
  (— OF WINDMILL ARM) WHIP
  (— OF YARN) KNOT TAPE CHASE
  SKEIN
  (AT FULL —) ALONG
  (CONTINUOUS —) STRETCH
  (FOCAL —) FOCUS
  (UNIT OF —) PIC PIK ROD FOOT
  INCH KILO PIKE REED VARA WRAP
  YARD METER SHAKU POLLEX
  FURLONG PLETHRON
  (UTMOST —) EXTREME
LENGTHEN EKE LONG DILATE
  EXPAND EXTEND LENGTH AMPLIFY
  DISTEND PRODUCE PROLONG
  STRETCH ELONGATE INCREASE
  PROTRACT
  (— BY INTERPOLATION) FARSE
LENGTHENING HOLD ECTASIS
  DIASTOLE
LENGTHWISE ALONG ALENGTH
  ENDLONG ENDWAYS ENDWISE
LENGTHY LONG LARGE PROLIX
  LONGFUL EXTENDED
LENIENCY FAVOR MERCY LENITY
  LENIENCE
LENIENT LAX EASY KIND MILD SOFT
  FACILE GENTLE HUMANE LENITIVE
LENITIVE MILD MITIGANT SEDATIVE
LENITY MERCY HUMANITY KINDNESS
  LENITUDE

LENO GAUZE
LENS EYE CROWN GLASS OPTIC
  FLASER READER APLANAT BIFOCAL
  CONCAVE CONTACT DOUBLET
  ACHROMAT EYEGLASS EYEPIECE
  HYPERGON LENTICLE LUNETTES
  MENISCUS
  (WITHOUT —) APHAKIA
LENT CAREME IMPREST
LENTICULAR PHACOID
LENTIGO FRECKLE
LENTIL LENS LINT TILL LENTILE
  LENTICLE
LEONTOCEBUS MIDAS
LEOPARD PARD TIGER PARDAL
  WAGATI LIBBARD PAINTER PANTHER
  PARDALE
  (SNOW —) IRBIS OUNCE
LEPCHA RONG RONGPA
LEPER LAZAR MESEL LAZARUS
LEPIDOMELANE ANNITE
LEPIDOPTERA GLOSSATA
LEPIDOSIS SCALING
LEPRECHAUN ELF LURACAN
LEPROSY LEPRA MESEL ALPHOS
  LAZARY MESELRY
LEPROUS MESELY MESELED
LEPTON MITE
LEPTOSPIROSIS JAUNDICE
LERP LAAP
LESBIAN EROTIC TRIBADE SAPPHIST
LESION PIT GALL HIVE SORE
  CRATER ESCHAR LEPRID ANTHRAX
  CHANCRE FISSURE LEPROMA
  BEESTING ERUPTION LEUKEMID
  TERTIARY

LESOTHO

CAPITAL: MASERU
FORMER NAME: BASUTOLAND
LANGUAGE: SOTHO SESOTHO
PEOPLE: BASOTHO
RIVER: ORANGE CALEDON
TOWN: LERIBE QUTHING
  MAFETENG

LESPEDEZA SERICEA
LESS FEW MIN MENO FEWER MINOR
  LESSER SMALLER WANTING
  (— BY A COMMA) MINOR
LESSEE FARMER TERMOR HUURDER
  TACKSMAN
LESSEN EBB BATE DOCK EASE FAIK
  FRET KILL LESS SINK WANE ABATE
  BREAK LOWER MINCE SMALL
  BUFFER DEJECT IMPAIR INLESS
  MINIFY MINISH NARROW REBATE
  REDUCE WEAKEN AMENUSE
  ASSUAGE CURTAIL DEPLETE
  DEPRESS ELEVATE LIGHTEN
  RELIEVE SHORTEN CONTRACT
  DECREASE DEROGATE DIMINISH
  DISCOUNT EMBEZZLE MITIGATE
  MODERATE PALLIATE
  (— FORCE) GELD
  (— IN VALUE) SHRINK CHEAPEN
  (— SENSITIVITY) DULL
  (— STRENGTH) WEAR

  (— TENSION) RELAX
  (— VELOCITY) DEADEN
LESSENING LETUP
LESSER MINUTE SMALLER INFERIOR
LESSER CELANDINE PILEWORT
LESSON TAX LEAR TASK STUDY
  EXAMPLE LECTURE PRECEPT
  READING DOCUMENT LIRIPOOP
  (DIFFICULT —) SOAK
  (TORAH —) PARASHAH
LESSOR SETTER
LEST UNLESS ANANTER ANAUNTERS
LET LAT SET HIRE ALLOW LEASE
  LEAVE LETTEN PERMIT SUFFER
  TENANT
  (— BAIT BOB) DIB
  (— BECOME KNOWN) SPILL
  (— BURN) BISHOP
  (— CONTINUE) DRILL
  (— DOWN) DEMIT DIMIT LOWER
  STOOP STRIKE SUBMIT
  (— FALL) DROP VAIL AVALE AWALE
  DEPOSE
  (— FLY) PEG BOLT FIRE WING
  (— GO) DROP FAIK QUIT DEMIT
  BILEVE DEMISE DISMIT UNHAND
  DISCARD UNSEIZE
  (— HIM TAKE) SUM
  (— IN) IMMIT INLET IMMISS ADHIBIT
  (— IT BE REPEATED) REPET
  (— IT STAND) STET
  (— KNOW) ACQUAINT
  (— LAND) GAVEL
  (— LOOSE) FREE SLIP LIBERATE
  (— OUT) TEAM WAGE BREAK SPILL
  ARRENT
  (— SLIP) CHECK FOREGO
LETDOWN HANGOVER
LETHAL FATAL DEADLY MORTAL
LETHARGIC INERT DROWSY SLEEPY
  DORMANT COMATOSE COMATOUS
  SLUGGISH SLUMBROUS
LETHARGY STUPOR TORPOR
  SLUMBER HEBETUDE INACTION
LETO LATONA
LETT BALT
LETTER EF EL EM EN EX HE AIN AYN
  BEE CEE CHI DEE EDH ESS ETA ETH
  GEE HET JAY KAY LIL PEE SIN TEE
  VEE YOD YOK ZED ZEE ALEF ALIF
  AYIN BETA BETH BILL BULL CHIT
  DEAD HETH IOTA KAPH SHIN SORT
  YODH YOGH AITCH ALEPH BLIND
  BREVE DELTA DEMIT FAVOR GAMMA
  GIMEL GRAPH KAPPA KNOWN
  KOPPA SIGMA STAVE STIFF ZAYIN
  ACCENT ADVICE ANSWER BILLET
  CADJAN CARTEL CHARTA COCKUP
  DALETH FAVVER ITALIC LAMBDA
  LAMEDH MEDIAL SCRIPT SIGLUM
  SUNNUD SYMBOL VERSAL CODICIL
  COLLINS CONTROL DIGAMMA
  DIPLOMA EPISTLE EPSILON
  KAREETA MISSIVE SPECIAL
  AEROGRAM ASCENDER ENCYCLIC
  MONITORY NUNDINAL PASTORAL
  (— OF DEFIANCE) CARTEL
  (— OF PERMISSION) EXEAT
  (—S DIMISSORY) APOSTOLI

(—S OF MARQUE) MART
(ANGLO-SAXON —) EDH ETH THORN
(AUTHORIZING —) BREVE
(BEGGING —) SCREEVE
(BLACK —) GOTHIC
(BREAD AND BUTTER —) COLLINS
(CAPITAL —) CAP UNCIAL CAPITAL
FACTOTUM
(FRIENDLY —) SCREED
(LOVE —) POULET
(OFFICIAL —) BRIEF
(PAPAL —) BULL TOME ENCYCLIC
(PRIVATE —) BOOK
(SHORT —) CHIT LINE NOTE BILLET
LETTERET
(SILENT —) MUTE
(SMUGGLED —) KITE
(SUBSCRIPT —) SUBFIX
(WORD —) LOGOGRAM
(PL.) MAIL APOSTOLI
LETTER BOX APARTADO
LETTER CARRIER CORREO
MAILMAN POSTMAN
LETTERER SKETCHER
LETTERING FAC WRITE INCUSE
LETTERPRESS TEXT CAPTION
LETTING FIRMA LOCATIO
LETTING-OUT DROPPING
LETTUCE COS GRASS SALAD
KARPAS SALLET ICEBERG ROMAINE
FIREWEED MILKWEED
LEUCIPPUS (DAUGHTER OF —)
PHOEBE HILAIRA
(FATHER OF —) OENOMAUS
(WIFE OF —) PHILODICE
LEUCITE LENAD
LEUCITITE ITALITE SPERONE
ALBANITE CECILITE
LEUCOCYTE NEOCYTE HEMAMEBA
MONOCYTE OXYPHILE
LEUCOMA WALLEYE
LEUCORRHEA WHITES
LEUKEMIA CHLOROMA LEUKOSIS
LEVANT EASTERN WORMSEED
LEVEE DIKE DYKE WALL WEIR
DURBAR STOPBANK
LEVEL BONE EVEN FAIR FLAT GLAD
LUTE PLAT RAZE SHIM EQUAL
FLUSH GRADE PLAIN PLANE POINT
SLICK SOLID CHARGE DOUBLE
EVENLY FIELDY NIVEAU SLIGHT
SMOOTH STRIKE TUNNEL FLATTEN
GALLERY GANGWAY DEMOLISH
LEVELLER SUBGRADE
(— A RAFTER) EDGE
(— AFTER PLOWING) BUSH
(— AND SCATTER) GELD
(— OF SOCIETY) STRATUM
(— OF STAGE) STUDY
(— OFF) HAMMER BULLDOZE
(— PLACE) PLANILLA
(COMMON —) PAR
(ENERGY —) SINGLET
(EYE —) EYELINE
(HIGHER —S) BRASS
(HIGHEST —) SUMMIT
(LOWEST —) FLOOR BOTTOM
HARDPAN
(MINING —) HEAD GALLERY

GANGWAY
(STRATIGRAPHIC —) HORIZON
(TOP —) HIGH CEILING
LEVELED BENT
LEVELER DIGGER
LEVELING EGALITE EGALITY
LEVER KEY PRY BEAM GAUL HOOK
HORN JACK SWAY TREE FLAIL FLIRT
HELVE PEDAL PINCH PLUTO PRIZE
SPOON STANG STANK SWIPE
THROW BINDER CLUTCH COUPER
DETENT FEELER GAFFLE HAMMER
HEAVER HOPPER LOWDER PORTER
ROCKER TAPPET TILLER BALANCE
BOOTLEG POINTER RAMHEAD
SHIPPER SWINGLE TREADLE
TRIGGER TUMBLER BACKFALL
GAVELOCK SELECTOR THROTTLE
(— ARM) NIGGER
(— FOR CROSSBOW) GAFFLE
GARROT
(— FOR TURNING RUDDER) HELM
TILLER
(— IN KNITTING MACHINE) JACK
(— LIKE CANTHOOK) PEAVY PEAVIE
(— OF GIN) START
(GEARSHIFT —) STICK
(SPINNING —) BOOTLEG
(SPOKELIKE —) SWINGLE
(THROTTLE —) GUN
(WEAVING —) LAM LAMM SWELL
BINDER TIPPLER
LEVERAGE PRY PRIZE
LEVIGATE DUST
LEVITY FOLLY HUMOR GAIETY
LEVOROTATORY LAEVO LEVOGYRE
NEGATIVE
LEVY CUT TAX CESS MISE REAR
LEVEL RAISE ASSESS EXTEND
EXTENT IMPOSE IMPOST UPTAKE
IMPRESS TRIBUTE DISTRAIN
DISTRESS SHIPPAGE
(— A TAX) GELD GELT TAIL STENT
(— DISTRESS) DRIVE
(IRISH —) MART
LEVYING EXACTION
LEWD NICE BAWDY FOLLY PRIME
RANDY HARLOT IMPURE LACHES
LUBRIC RAKISH WANTON HIRCINE
LEERING LUSTFUL OBSCENE
RAMMISH SCARLET SENSUAL
WHORISH PRURIENT SLUTTISH
UNCHASTE
LEWDNESS FOLLY RAKERY
LECHERY HARLOTRY PUTANISM
LEXICON CALEPIN WORDBOOK
LIABILITY DEBT DEBIT CHARGE
TRIBUTE
LIABLE APT ABLE OPEN GUILTY
EXPOSED OBVIOUS SUBJECT
AMENABLE INCIDENT
LIAISON BOND AFFAIR LINKING
INTIMACY INTRIGUE
LIANA CIPO BEJUCO BUSHROPE
LIANG TAEL
LIAR LEAR ANANIAS BOUNCER
CRACKER CRAMMER PROCTOR
WARLOCK WERNARD FABULIST
LIBATION AMBROSIA

LIBEL DEFAME MALIGN VILIFY
SLANDER
LIBELOUS FAMOUS
LIBERAL FAIR FREE GOOD OPEN
WHIG BROAD FRANK LARGE NOBLE
SOLUTE JANNOCK PROFUSE
ADVANCED GENEROUS HANDSOME
LARGEOUS PRODIGAL SEPARATE
(CANADIAN —) GRIT
(NOT —) CHARY SPARE
LIBERAL ARTS MUSES
LIBERALITY LARGE BOUNTY
BREADTH CHARITY FREEDOM
HONESTY LARGESS
LIBERALLY LARGE BROADLY
LIBERATE FREE QUIT FRITH REMIT
UNGYVE UNWRAP DELIVER MANUMIT
RELEASE UNSLAVE UNFETTER
UNTHRALL
LIBERATION FREEDOM RELEASE
DELIVERY KAIVALYA DISCHARGE

LIBERIA

CAPITAL: MONROVIA
CUSTOM: SANDE
HILLS: BOMI
MEASURE: KUBA
MOUNTAIN: UNI NIETE NIMBA
PEOPLE: GI KRU KWA VAI VEI
GOLA KROO KROU TOMA BASSA
GIBBI GISSI GREBO KPELLE
KROOBY KRUMAN KROOBOY
MANDINGO
RIVER: CESS LOFA MANNA MORRO
DOUOBE STJOHN CAVALLA
SANPEDRO
TOWN: GRIBO REBBO HARPER
NANAKRU BUCHANAN MARSHALL

LIBERTINE PUNKER PANURGE
STRIKER LOTHARIO STRINGER
LIBERTY MAY SOC EASE LARGE
LEAVE SCOPE ACCESS STREET
FREEDOM LARGESS LICENSE
WITHGANG
(— OF ACTION) PLAY SWING
(— OF ENTRANCE) INGRESS
(— OF GOING OUT) ISH
(— OF TURNING PIGS INTO FIELDS)
SHACK
(— TO BUY AND SELL) TOLL
(— TO HUNT) CHASE
(PARTIAL — OF HAWK) HACK
(SEXUAL —) INTIMACY
(UNDUE —) HEAD
LIBERTY CAP PILLEUS
LIBIDINIZATION EGOISM
LIBIDINOUS FLESHY FLESHLY
LIBRA AS PONDUS
LIBRARY AMBRY BIBLE MUSEUM
BHANDAR BOOKERY ATHENEUM
LIBRETTO BOOK WORD TESTO
TEXTBOOK

LIBYA

ALPHABET: TIFINAGH
CAPITAL: BENGASI BENGAZI
TRIPOLI

GULF: SIDRA SIRTE
MEASURE: SAA BOZZE DONUM
  JABIA TEMAN BARILE MISURA
  MATTARO
MOUNTAIN: BETTE
OASIS: KUFRA SEBHA TAZERBO
SEAPORT: HOMS DERNA SIDRI
  TOBRUK BENGAZI
TOWN: HOMS SEBHA SIDRI ZAWIA
  ELMARJ GARIAN MURZUQ
  MISURATA
WEIGHT: KELE UCKIA GORRAF
  TERMINO KHAROUBA

LICE CREEPERS
  (FISH —) EPIZOA
LICENSE CHOP GALE HEAD EXEAT
  LEAVE SLANG SWING BANDON
  CAROON FIRMAN INDULT PATENT
  PERMIT READER CAROOME CERTIFY
  CROTTLE FACULTY FREEDOM
  INDULTO LIBERTY LICENCE
  PLACARD WARRANT ESCAMBIO
  IMMUNITY MORTMAIN PASSPORT
  TEZKIRAH
  (— FOR CART) CAROOME
  (— PLATE) NUMBER
  (PEDDLER'S —) SLANG
LICENTIOUS GAY LAX FREE LEWD
  WILD FRANK LARGE LOOSE FILTHY
  UNRULY WANTON CYPRIAN FLESHLY
  IMMORAL LAWLESS LIBERAL
  UNYOKED
LICENTIOUSNESS DIRT LICENSE
LICHEN RAG MANNA USNEA ORCHIL
  CROTTAL CROTTLE CUDBEAR
  EVERNIA OAKMOSS PARELLA
  ARCHILLA CAREWEED LECANORA
  LUNGWORT PARMELIA ROCKHAIR
  TREEHAIR WARTWORT
LICIT LEGAL LAWFUL LEEFUL
LICK LAP LIKE SUCK MOUTH SLAKE
  CONQUER
LICKER-IN TUMBLE
LICKING GRUELING
LICORICE POMFRET SWEETROOT
LICORICE PILL CACHOU
LICYMNIUS (FATHER OF —)
  ELECTRYON
  (SISTER OF —) ALCMENA
  (SLAYER OF —) TLEPOLEMUS
LID DIP BRED DECK TYMP COVER
  BRIDLE EYELID POTLID CLAPPER
  CLICKET CLOSURE SCUTTLE
  SHUTTER COVERCLE
LIE FIB GAB LAY LIG LIN SIT YED
  CRAM FALL FLAW LIGG REST RIDE
  WHID DEVIL DWELL FABLE FEIGN
  LEASE STAND STORY FITTEN
  RAPPER RESIDE SPRAWL VANITY
  BOUNCER CONSIST CRACKER
  CRAMMER CRUMPER FALSITY
  GRABBLE LEASING PLUMPER
  TWISTER UNTRUTH WHACKER
  WHISKER WHOPPER
  (— ALONGSIDE) ACCOST
  (— AROUND) COMPASS
  (— AT ANCHOR) HOVE

(— AT FULL LENGTH) STRETCH
(— CONCEALED) DARKLE
(— CONTIGUOUS) CONFINE
(— DETECTOR) POLYGRAPH
(— DORMANT) SLEEP
(— DOWN) LEAN COUCH CHARGE
(— FLAT ON BELLY) GROVEL
(— HEAD TO WIND) TRY
(— HIDDEN) LURK MICHE TAPPISH
(— IN AMBUSH) HUGGER
(— IN BED) KIP THOKE
(— IN WAIT) AWAIT LOWER AMBUSH
FORELAY
(— IN WATER) DOUSE DROWN
(— NEXT TO) ADJOIN
(— OPPOSITE TO) SUBTEND
(— OVER) COVER
(— PRONE) GROVEL GRABBLE
(— PROSTRATE) STREEK
(— QUIET) SNUDGE
(— SNUG) CUDDLE
(— UNEVENLY) SAG
(— WITH SAILS FURLED) HULL
(IMPUDENT —) BOUNCE
(MONSTROUS —) STRAMMER

LIECHTENSTEIN
CAPITAL: VADUZ
CASTLE: VADUZ GUTEMBURG
MOUNTAIN: RHATIKON
RIVER: RHINE
ROMAN NAME: RHAETIA
TOWN: HAAG BALZER SCHAAN
  NENDELN
TRIBE: ALAMANNI

LIED BALLAD
LIEF DEAR LEAVE LEEVE LIEVE
  FREELY GLADLY BELOVED
LIEUTENANT LUFF ZANY LOUEY
  JAYGEE KEHAYA CAIMAKAM
  QAIMAQAM TENIENTE WOODVILE
LIFE IT VIE ZOE HIDE JIVA PUFF
  SNAP TUCK VALE ANIMA BEING
  BLOOD DEMON HEART LIFER QUICK
  SWEAT BIOSIS BREATH CANDLE
  COURSE ENERGY SPIRIT SPRITE
  LIFELET LIFEWAY VITALITY VIVACITY
  (— AFTER DEATH) FUTURITY
  (— IN HEAVEN) GLORY
  (— IN SOCIETY) SAMSARA SANSARA
  (— OF FURNACE LINING) CAMPAIGN
  (— OF THE SEA) HALIBIOS
  (ACADEMIC —) ACADEMIA
  (ANIMAL —) FLESH
  (ANIMAL AND PLANT —) BIOS BIOTA
  BIOLOGY EDAPHON
  (CLOISTERED —) VEIL
  (INTELLECTUAL —) JIVATMA
  (MONASTIC —) CLOISTER
  (MORAL —) DAENA
  (MOSS —) BRYOLOGY
  (PLANT —) FLORA BOTANY
  (ROBUST —) JUICE
  (SINGLE —) CELIBACY
  (TERRESTRIAL —) GEOBIOS
  (WITHOUT —) AZOIC
LIFE BELT SAFETY
LIFEBLOOD BLOOD SWEAT

LIFELESS ARID DEAD DULL FLAT
  AMORT HEAVY INERT VAPID ANEMIC
  TORPID SAPLESS DESOLATE
  GRIPLESS INACTIVE
LIFELESSLY DEADLY INERTLY
LIFELESSNESS ANEMIA
LIFELIKE VIVE QUICK EIDETIC
  ANIMATED SPEAKING
LIFE PRESERVER FLOAT NEDDY
LIFETIME AGE DAY WORLD LIVING
  LIFEDAY DURATION LIFELONG
LIFT WIN BOOM BUOY CAST COCK
  HEFT JACK REAR TOSS WEVE
  BOOST BREAK ELATE HEAVE HITCH
  HOICK HOIST HOOSH MOUNT PRESS
  RAISE SPOUT STEAL WEIGH BUCKET
  CLEECH SNATCH ELEVATE ENHANCE
  HEELTAP NAUNTLE BOOKLIFT
  CHAIRWAY ELEVATOR LEVITATE
  (— HAT) DOFF
  (— IN VEHICLE) SETDOWN
  (— OF WAVE) SCEND
  (— ONESELF) SOAR
  (— QUICKLY) PERK
  (— UP) HOVE CRANE ERECT EXALT
  EXTOL HORSE WEIGH ADVANCE
  ELEVATE NAUNTLE
  (— WITH BLOCK AND TACKLE)
  BOUSE
LIFTED ARRECT SUBLIME
LIFTER GAGGER SERVER HOISTER
  HOISTMAN
LIFTING HIKE UPTAKE
LIFT VALVE POPPET
LIGAMENT BAND BOND ARTERY
  PAXWAX STRING ZONULE ARMILLA
  LIGATURE
LIGAMENTOUS DESMOID
LIGATE BAR
LIGATURE CLAM PLICA DIGRAM
  PNEUMA STIGMA DIGRAPH
  LIGAMENT LIGATION
LIGGER TRIMMER
LIGHT BUG DAY GAY HAP LAW SHY
  SUN AIRY EASY FAIR FALL FINE
  FIRE FLUX GLIM LAMP LEET LUNT
  MILD SLUT SOFT BAVIN BLAZE
  CORKY FANAL FILMY FLAME FLEET
  FUFFY LEGER LOUGH MERRY PITCH
  QUICK SHEER SPILL WHITE BEACON
  BRIGHT CHAFFY FLOATY FLOSSY
  FLUFFY FROTHY GENTLE HAPPEN
  ILLUME KINDLE LANCET LUSTER
  LUSTRE MARKER PASTEL PHAROS
  SIGNAL SLUSHY STINGY STRIKE
  SUTTLE VOLAGE BENGOLA
  BUOYANT CRESSET FRAGILE
  GLITTER LAMBENT SFOGATO
  SMITHER SUMMERY TORTAYS
  TRIVIAL UNGRAVE BACKFIRE
  DAYLIGHT DELICATE DIAPHANE
  ELECTRIC EXPEDITE FEATHERY
  GASLIGHT GOSSAMER LEGGIERO
  LUMINARY PALOUSER SUNLIGHT
  SUNSHINE
  (— AND BRILLIANT) LAMBENT
  (— AND FIRE ON HORSE'S MANE)
  HAG
  (— AND FREE) FLYAWAY

(— **AND QUICK**) VOLANT
(— **CANDLES**) TOLLY
(— **FROM NIGHT SKY**) AIRGLOW
(— **IN WINDOW**) LANCET
(— **OF MORNING**) AURORA
(— **ON TV SCREEN**) SNOW
(— **UP**) FLASH GLOZE ILLUME
RELUME GLORIFY
(— **UPON**) STRIKE
(**BRIGHT** —) GLARE GLEAM
(**BURST OF** —) FLASH
(**CIRCLE OF** —) HALO NIMBUS
(**FAINT** —) GLIMMER SCARROW
(**FEEBLE** —) GLIMMER
(**FITFUL** —) SHIMMER
(**HARBOR** —) BUG
(**INNER** —) SEED
(**NEW** —) SEPARATE
(**NIGHT** —) MORTAR
(**PARKING** —S) DIMMERS
(**PERSIAN GOD OF** —) MITHRAS
(**REFLECTED** —) SKYME
(**SHIP'S** —) FANAL
(**SMALL** —) TAPER
(**TRAFFIC** —) BLINKER
(**WAVERING** —) FLICKER
LIGHT-COLORED BLONDE
LIGHTEN CLEAR LEVIN LIGHT RAISE
ALLEGE BLEACH ENCLEAR FOULDRE
MOLLIFY SWEETEN THUNDER
LEVIGATE
LIGHTENING BREAK
LIGHTER SCOW ACCON CASCO
WHERRY DROGHER GABBARD
PONTOON CHOPBOAT
LIGHTERMAN KEELER KEELMAN
LIGHT-HEADED IDLE LIGHT LIVELY
CARRIED GLAIKET
LIGHT-HEARTED GAY GLAD GIDDY
WINSOME CAREFREE DEBONAIR
VOLATILE
LIGHTHEARTEDNESS BUOYANCY
LIGHTHOUSE FANAL LIGHT BEACON
PHAROS LANTERN
LIGHTLESS APHOTIC
LIGHTLY LIGHT AIRILY FAIRILY
HOVERLY LEGGIERO SLIGHTLY
LIGHT-MINDED BLITHE
LIGHTNESS CHEER VALUE GAIETY
LEVITY AIRINESS BUOYANCY
LEGERETE LEGERITY
(— **OF MOVEMENT**) BALLON
LIGHTNING BOLT FIRE LAIT LEVIN
FULMEN METEOR FOULDRE
SULPHUR THUNDER FIREBALL
FIREBOLT WILDFIRE
LIGHT-O'-LOVE LEVERET
LIGHT-TEXTURED FOZY
LIGHTWOOD FATWOOD
LIGIA LIGYDA
LIGNEOUS WOODY XYLOID
LIGNIN LIGNOSE XYLOGEN
LIGNUM VITAE GUAYACAN
POCKWOOD
LIGROIN BENZINE CANADOL
LIGULA LANGUET
LIGULE STRAP LIGULA
LIKE AS DIG DOTE LIST LOVE ALIKE
ENJOY EQUAL FANCY SAVOR TASTE

ADMIRE AFFECT BELIKE LIKELY
MATTER PLEASE SEMBLE SIMILE
CONCEIT SIMILAR SEMBLANT
SUITABLE
(— **A GLAND**) ADEMOSE ADENOUS
(— **BETTER**) PREFER
(— **HAIR**) CRINITE
(**VERY** —) SIAMESE
LIKELIHOOD APTNESS
LIKELY APT FAIR LIKE READY LIABLE
PROOFY SEEMLY GRADELY SMITTLE
APPARENT FEASIBLE POSSIBLE
PROBABLE
(**MOST** —) BELIKE
LIKEN EVEN LIKE REMENE SEMBLE
COMPARE SMILIZE ASSEMBLE
RESEMBLE
LIKENESS DAP BLEE ICON IDOL
MAKE SECT BLUSH DUMMY GLIFF
IMAGE MORAL SHAPE EFFIGY
FIGURE STATUE KINSHIP PATTERN
PICTURE RETRAIT EQUALITY
HOMOLOGY PARALLEL PORTRAIT
(**PERFECT** —) SPIT
LIKEWISE EKE TOO ALSO ITEM
EITHER EQUALLY LIKEWAYS
(— **NOT**) NOR
LIKING GOO GRA PAY GOUT GUST
LIKE LUST FANCY FLAIR GUSTO
HEART SHINE SKILL SMACK TASTE
THEAT SWALLOW AFFINITY
APPETITE FONDNESS
(**ECCENTRIC** —) FOIBLE
LILAC LILAS MAUVE LAYLOCK
LILACIN SYRINGIN
LILY IXIA KELP SEGO AZTEC CALLA
CLOTE AUGUST LILIUM VALLEY
COCUISA MONOCOT LILYWORT
MARTAGON NENUPHAR
(**CLIMBING** —) GLORIOSA
(**PALM** —) TI
(**SEA** —) CRINOID
(**WATER** —) CANDOCK CAMALOTE
LILY OF THE VALLEY LILIUM
MUGGET MUGUEL MUGWET
LILYWORT SHINLEAF
LIMA BEAN HABA LIMA
LIMB ARM LEG CLAW FOOT KNOT
LITH TRAM WING ARTUS BOUGH
SPALD SPAUL SWAMP BRANCH
MEMBER PODITE FEATURE FLIPPER
FORCEPS NECTOPOD
LIMBA AFARA FRAKE
LIMBER BAIN FLIP LIMP LUSH LINGY
LITHE LISSOM SEMMIT SUPPLE
SWANKY BRUSHER BRUTTER
KNOTTER LIMMOCK PLIABLE
FLEXIBLE FLIPPANT
LIME CALX LIMA CEDRA CEDRAT
CHUNAM CITRON FUSTIC
(— **IN BRICK**) BOND
(**WILD** —) COLIMA
LIMESTONE HUM CAUK LIAS LYAS
MALM POROS CLUNCH KUNKUR
PISOLITE
(— **REGION**) KARST
LIME TREE LIME TEIL LINDEN
LIMIT END FIX BIND BUTT FINE HOLD
LINE LIST MARK MERE TAIL BLOCK

BOUND GAUGE HEDGE STENT STINT
VERGE BORDER BOURNE DEFINE
EFFLUX EXTENT FINISH FINITE
HAMPER LENGTH MODIFY NARROW
PALING SCRIMP TROPIC UPSHOT
ASTRICT CLOSURE COMPASS
CONFINE CONTENT HORIZON
MAXIMUM MEASURE BOUNDARY
CONTRACT DEADLINE IMPRISON
LIMITARY LIMITATE OUTGOING
RESTRAIN RESTRICT SOLSTICE
TERMINUS
(— **EFFECT**) ALLAY
(— **IN A FOREST**) BAIL
(— **MOTION**) HOLD
(— **OF VISION AT SEA**) KENNING
(**EXTREME** —) HEIGHT
(**LOWER** —) FLOOR
(**UPPER** —) CEILING
(**UTTER** —) EXTREME
(PL.) AMBIT CANCELS ENVIRONS
LIMITATION TAIL FRAME STINT
DENIAL CLOTURE RESERVE
(PL.) SWADDLE
LIMITED TAIL BORNE BRIEF SHORT
SMALL FINITE NARROW STINTY
STRAIT BOUNDED SPECIAL
CONFINED DEFINITE LIMITARY
(— **IN APPEAL**) CHICHI
LIMITING DEFINITE ADJECTIVE
EXCLUSIVE
LIMMA DIESIS
LIMMU EPONYM
LIMONENE CINENE CARVENE
CITRENE
LIMONIUM STATICE
LIMOUSINE BERLIN SUBURBAN
LIMP HIP HOP CLOP GIMP HALT HIMP
HOIT SOFT THIN HENCH HILCH
HITCH LINGY LOOSE LOPPY SLAMP
STILT FLABBY FLIMSY HAMBLE
HIMPLE HIRPLE HOBBLE LENNOW
LIMBER LIMPSY FLACCID LIMMOCK
SHAFFLE UNSMART DRAGGLED
DROOPING
LIMPET CHINK OPIHI SHELL ACMAEA
LIMPIN FLIDDER
LIMPID PURE CLEAR LUCID BRIGHT
CRYSTAL PELLUCID
LIMPING LAME GIMPY LIMPY ZOPPA
HALTING
LIMPLY LANKLY
LINAGE SPACE
LINALOOL LICAREOL
LINCHPIN FORELOCK
LINCTUS LOOCH LOHOCH LOHOCK
LINDEN LIN LIME LYNE TEIL TILIA
TILLET LINWOOD BASSWOOD
DADDYNUT WOODLIND
LINE BAR BOX FIX RAY ROW TAW
BOFF CASE CEIL COLA CRIB DASH
FACE FILE GAME GAPE LACE LARD
LATH LEAD LING MAIN MARK RACE
RANK RULE STOP TAUM WHIP
AGONE FAINT FEINT FLEET HATCH
LIGNE LINEA METER RANGE SCORE
STRIA TOUCH TRACE TRAIL TRAIN
TWIST BINDER CABURN CEVIAN
CREASE DEGREE DOUBLE EARING

GASKET ISOBAR ISOHEL ISOPAG
ISOTAC METIER NETTLE SECANT
SECOND SPRING STRING STRIPE
AZIMUTH BABBITT CATLINE
CONTOUR CREANCE ENVELOP
GUNLINE HIPLINE ISOCHOR
ISOGRAM ISOHYET ISONEPH
ISORITH ISOSTER ISOTOME KNITTLE
MARLINE NACARAT SCRATCH
WINDROW BALKLINE BISECTOR
BOUNDARY BUSINESS CHAMPAIN
DATELINE DEADLINE DIAGONAL
DIAMETER DRAGLINE DRUMLINE
FISHBACK GANTLINE GEODESIC
GIRTLINE HAIRLINE HANDLINE
HEXAPODY ISOGLOSS ISOGONIC
ISOPHANE ISOPHENE ISOPLERE
ISOTHERE ISOTHERM LANDWIRE
LIFELINE MARTINET SLIPBAND
STRINGER SUBCLONE SUBSTILE
SUBSTYLE UPSTROKE
(— AROUND STAMP) FRAME
(— AS CENTER FOR REVOLVING)
AXIS
(— HEARTH) FIX FETTLE
(— IN GLASS) STRING
(— IN HAT) HEADLINE
(— MINESHAFT) TUB
(— OF ACTION) LAY
(— OF BATTLE) FRONT
(— OF BUSINESS) WAY
(— OF CELLS) ANNULUS
(— OF CLIFFS) SCARP BREAKS
(— OF COLOR) SLASH STREAK
(— OF DANCERS) CHAIN
(— OF DESCENT) SIDE STEM STIRP
STOCK STRAIN ANCESTRY
(— OF DETERMINANT) COLUMN
(— OF DEVELOPMENT) STREET
(— OF DEVOLUTION) ENTAIL
(— OF FIBERS) CHRYSAL
(— OF FIRE HOSE) LEAD
(— OF FLOTATION) BEARINGS
(— OF FORTIFICATION) LIMES
ENCEINTE
(— OF HAY) WAKE WALLOW
(— OF HEALTH) HEPATICA
(— OF HIGH TIDE) LANDWASH
(— OF HOUSES) BLOCK
(— OF INTERSECTION) GROIN
BUTTOCK
(— OF JUNCTION) MEET SEAM
(— OF MERCURY) HEPATICA
(— OF PERSONS) QUEUE CORDON
STICKLE
(— OF PORES) HATCHING
(— OF SOLDIERS) RAY FILE RANK
WAVE CORDON
(— OF STITCHING) BASTING
(— OF TIMBERS) BOOM STOCKADE
(— OF TREES) SCREEN
(— OF TYPE) SLUG KICKER
(— OF UNION) SUTURE
(— ON A LETTER) SERIF
(— ON BOOK COVER) BAND
(— ON COAT) GORGE
(— ON DOLPHIN) STOP
(— ON HIGHWAY) BARRIER
(— THAT CUTS ANOTHER) SECANT

(— TO BIND CABLES) CABURN
(— TO FASTEN SAIL) EARING
GASKET
(— TO RAISE FLAG) LANIARD
LANYARD
(— TO START RACE) TRIG
(— TOUCHING ARC) TANGENT
(— UP) LAY
(— WITH BRICKS) GINGE
(— WITH PANELLING) WAINSCOT
(— WITH STONES) STEEN STEYN
(— WITH TIMBER) CRIB
(42 —S) LENGTH
(ANCHOR —) RODING
(BEARING —) CUT
(BOUNDARY —) MERE FENCE
BORDER ISOGLOSS
(BOUNDING —) SIDE BOUNDARY
(BRIEF —) ITEM
(COASTAL —) SEAMARK
(CONNECTING —) LIGATURE
(CONTINUOUS —) STRETCH
(CURVED —) ARC SLUR SWEEP
(DEMARCATION —) BOMBLINE
(DIAGONAL —) BIAS
(DIVIDING —) EDGE MIDRIB DIVISION
FRONTIER
(ELECTRIC —) HIGHLINE
(FACIAL —) TRAIT
(FINISHING —) TAPE WIRE
(FISHING —) TOME TROT FLEET
SNELL SNOOD LEADER LEDGER
NORSEL BACKING BOULTER SPILLER
SPILLET TRIMMER BLOWLINE
CORKLINE FISHLINE SNAGLINE
TROTLINE
(HORIZONTAL —) LEVEL
(IMAGINARY —) AGONE HINGE
GROOVE ISOBAR ISOGAM ISOHEL
ISOPAG HORIZON ISOBASE ISOBATH
ISOGRIV ISOHYET ISOLINE ISOTACH
ISOBRONT ISOCHASM ISOCHEIM
ISOCHLOR ISOCHORE ISOCRYME
ISOPHOTE ISOPLETH ISOSTERE
ISOTHERM
(INCLINED —) CANT
(LONGITUDINAL —) MERIDIAN
(MEDIAN —) RAPHE
(METRICAL —) EIGHT STAFF STICH
DIMETER SAPPHIC STICHOS
(MUSICAL —) ACCOLADE
(NAUTICAL —) EARING LACING
GESWARP MARLINE RATLINE
DOWNHAUL
(ONE-TENTH OF —) GRY
(PLOTTED —) ADIABAT
(RADIATING —) BEAM
(RAILROAD —) STEM STUB
(RAISED —) RIDGE
(SPECTRUM —) GHOST DOUBLET
SINGLET TRIPLET
(STARTING —) SCRATCH
(STRAIGHT —) CHORD BEELINE
STRAIGHT
(SUPPLY —) AIRLIFT
(SURVEYING —) WAD BASE CHAIN
(THEATRICAL —S) FAT
(TOW —) CORDELLE
(TRANSPORTATION —) FEEDER
CARRIER

(WAVY —) SQUIGGLE
LINEAGE GET KIN KIND RACE TEAM
BIRTH BLOOD SPACE STIRP STOCK
FAMILY HAVAGE NATION PARAGE
SOURCE SPRING STRAIN DESCENT
KINDRED PROGENY SUCCESS
ANCESTRY PEDIGREE
LINEAL DIRECT
LINEAMENT LINE TRACT TRAIT
FEATURE
LINEAR RUNNING
LINECUT ZINCO
LINED MASONED
LINEMAN FORWARD WIREMAN
CHAINMAN
LINEN LIN LAWN IRISH TOILE
BARRAS DAMASK DIAPER RAINES
SENDAL HOLLAND LOCKRAM
TABLING BARANDOS OSNABURG
PLATILLA
(— CLOSET) LOCKER
(— FOR SHIRTS) SARKING
(CHINESE —) KOMPOW
(COARSE —) HARN BARRAS
(FINE —) LAKE LAWN DAMASK
DIAPER RAINES
(HOUSEHOLD —) NAPERY TABLING
(SCRAPED —) LINT
(SPANISH —) CREA
LINER SHIP BASKET SCRIBER
STEAMER
LINEUP SHOWUP
LING BURBOT DRIZZLE STOKVIS
LINGA DILDO
LINGCOD CULTUS
LINGER LAG HANG HOVE LING STAY
CLING DALLY DELAY DEMUR DWELL
HAUNT HOVER PAUSE TARRY
DRETCH HANKER LOITER TARROW
DRINGLE
LINGERER LUNGIS LAGGARD
LINGERIE FRILLIES PRETTIES
LINGERING SLOW DELAY MOROSE
TARDANT DRAGGING
LINGO BAT CANT LINGUA PATTER
DIALECT
LINGUA GLOSSA TONGUE
LINGUAL GLOSSAL
LINGUISTIC GLOTTIC
LINGUISTICS GRAMMAR PHILOLOGY
LINIMENT EIK EMBROCHE
OPODELDOC
LININ PLASTIN
LINING FUR BACK COAT BAIZE
BRASS FACING PANNEL BABBITT
BUSHING CEILING FURRING
FURRURE THIMBLE TINNING
TUBBING CLEADING DOUBLING
DOUBLURE FIREBACK SHEETING
UNDERLAY WAINSCOT
(— FOR WELL) STEENING STEYNING
(— OF BEARING) JEWEL
(— OF FURNACE) BASQUE
FIREBACK
(— OF HAT) TIP
LINK JAR TIE TOW JOIN KNIT LUNT
SHUT YOKE NEXUS COPULA COUPLE
FASTEN FETTER TOUGHT CODETTA
CONNECT COUPLER ENCHAIN

INVOLVE LIAISON SHACKLE
CATENATE IDENTIFY VINCULUM
(— **ARMS**) CLEEK
(— **IN NETWORK**) LEG
(**COMPOUND** —) SWIVEL
(**WOODEN** —) LAG
LINKAGE BOND CELL COUPLING
LINKWORK
LINKED CONNEX INTEGRAL
LINKING HOOKUP ANNECTANT
(— **DEVICE**) LINCHPIN
LINKMAN LINKBOY LIGHTMAN
LINNET FINCH TWITE LENARD LINTIE
REDPOLL REDFINCH
LINSANG CIVET ZINSANG
LINSEED LINGET
LINSEY-WOOLSEY WINCEY
LINT FLY FLUE FLICK CADDIS
CADDICE CHARPIE CARBASUS
(**SCRAPED** —) XYSTUS
LINTEL CAP CLAVY HANCE CLAVEL
DARNER SUMMER SQUINCH
TRANSOM
LION CAT LLEW MORNE SHEDU
SIMBA LIONEL LIONET LEOPARD
(**MOUNTAIN** —) PUMA COUGAR
LION MONKEY LEONCITO
LION-TAILED MONKEY MACACO
MACAQUE WANDEROO
LIP BLOB MASK PUSS APRON CHOPS
GROIN MOUTH SPOUT TUTEL
LABIUM LABRUM ROUTER CHILOMA
LABELLUM UNDERLIP
(— **DISEASE**) PERLECHE
(— **OF BELL**) SKIRT
(— **OF COROLLA**) GALEA
(— **OF ORCHID**) SLIPPER
(— **OF PITCHER**) BEAK
(—**S OF MOOSE**) MUFFLE
(**FLAT** —) APRON
(**LOWER** —) JIB FIPPLE
(**PL.**) LABRAS CUSHION
LIPASE PIALYN
LIPIDE CERIDE ADIPOID STERIDE
TETHELIN
LIPOCHROME LUTEIN
LIPOMA STEATOMA
LIPPED LABIATE
LIPPIA WRIGHT ALOYSIA
LIP PLUG LABRET TEMETA
LIPPY STIMPART
LIQUEFIED FUSILE POTATE REMISS
RESOLVED
LIQUEFY RUN FUSE MELT RELENT
LIQUATE DISSOLVE ELIQUATE
LIQUEUR EAU OUZO RAKI AURUM
CREME NOYAU CHASSE GENEPI
KUMMEL PERNOD STREGA ANESONE
CORDIAL CURACAO PERSICO
RATAFIA RATIFIA ABSINTHE
ALKERMES ANGELICA ANISETTE
MANDARIN PRUNELLE VESPETRO
(**PL.**) EAUX
LIQUID AQUA BLASH DRINK FLUID
LEACH MOIST ACETAL FLUENT
FURANE AEROSOL BUCKING
CINEOLE EYEWASH FLOWAGE
VINASSE BLACKING EFFLUENT
EFFUSION EXCITANT FURFURAN

LEACHATE LIBATION SOLUTION
(— **IN CELL**) EXCITANT
(— **UNIT**) TUN CHENG SHENG SHING
POTTLE MUTCHKIN PUNCHEON
(**ACID-RESISTANT** —) GROUND
(**COLORING** —) HENNA
(**COOKING** —) BREE BROO BROTH
STOCK
(**DISTILLED** —) SPIRIT
(**FILTHY** —) ADDLE
(**INSULATING** —) ASKAREL
(**OILY** —) ANILINE CHLORAL
PICAMAR CARDANOL CREOSOTE
(**PERFUMED** —) COLLEN COLOGNE
(**REFUSE** —) SCOURAGE
(**REFUSE** —**S**) SEWAGE
(**SIZING** —) GLAIK
(**STERILIZED** —) JOHNIN
(**SYRUPY** —) HONEY
(**TANNING** —) LIME
(**THICK** —) DOPE SIRUP SYRUP
(**VISCOUS** —) TAR SCHRADAN
(**VOLATILE** —) ETHER ALCOHOL
DILUENT LIGROIN
(**WEAK** —) BLASH SLIPSLOP
LIQUIDATE SINK SETTLE
LIQUIDATION CLEANUP
LIQUOR ALE BUB DEW GAS LAP OKE
PAD POT RUM SUP TAP WET BEER
BREE FIRE FIZZ GEAR GROG LUSH
PURL SUCK SWIG TAPE TIFF BOGUS
BUDGE CEBUR DRINK GLASS
HOOCH KEFIR MOBBY NAPPY PERRY
PISCO SAUCE SHRAB SHRUB SICER
SKINK STICK BOTTLE CASSIS
CHICHA DIDDLE DOCTOR FOGRAM
FUDDLE GATTER GENEVA GUZZLE
HYDROL KIRSCH MASTIC MESCAL
POTTLE ROTGUT SAMSHU STRUNT
TIPPLE WHISKY BITTERN BRACKET
BRAGGET GROCERY PHLEGMA
SPUNKIE SUCTION TAPLASH
TEQUILA WAIPIRO WHISKEY
ABSINTHE BRAGWORT EYEWATER
HYDROMEL MEDICINE OKOLEHAO
POTATION RUMBOOZE FIREWATER
(— **CABINET**) TANTALUS
(— **CASE**) GARDEVIN
(— **FROM MUST**) ARROPE
(— **FROM PEARS**) PERRY PERRIE
(— **FROM WOOL-SCOURING**) SUD
SUDS
(— **MIXED WITH WINE**) DOCTOR
(— **SALE**) ABKARI
(— **TAKEN IN SODA WATER**) CINDER
(**ACID** —) VERJUICE
(**ALCOHOLIC** —) GIN ARAK HOOCH
ARRACK BRANDY SAMSHU AQUAVIT
BITTERS SNOOTFUL
(**ALCOHOLIC** —**S**) ARDENT
(**BITTER** —) TIRE
(**CHEAP** —) SMOKE
(**COLORLESS** —) GLYCID GLYCOL
GLYCIDOL GUAIACOL
(**CRAB APPLE** —) WHERRY
(**DISTILLED** —) DEW SOTOL GRAPPA
PHLEGM SCHNAPPS
(**DRUGGED** —) HOCUS
(**HARD** —) BOOZE

(**INTOXICATING** —) GROG LOAD
LUSH TAPE BUDGE GUZZLE KUMISS
HASHISH
(**MALT** —) ALE BUB BEER STOUT
ENTIRE PORTER
(**MOTHER** —) HYDROL BITTERN
(**RICE** —) SAMSHU
(**SPIRITUOUS** —) DEW GROG MOBBY
STRUNT WAIPIRO KAOLIANG
(**STRAIGHT** —) SHORT
(**STRONG** —) RUG TUBA VINO
HOGAN RUMBO STINGO
(**TAN** —) OOZE
(**TANNING** —) LAYAWAY TAILING
(**WEAK** —) SLIPSLOP
LIRA LIRE ZWANZIGER
(**ONE-TWENTIETH** —) SOLDO
LIRIPIPE TIPPET
LISSOME LITHE LIMBER NIMBLE
SUPPLE FLEXIBLE
LIST TIP BILL FILE HEEL LEET NOTE
POLL ROLL ROTA SWAG BRIEF
CANON GISTS INDEX PANEL SCORE
SCRIP SCROW SLATE AGENDA
CENSUS COLUMN DETAIL DOCKET
ERRATA HUDDLE LEGEND PURREL
RAGGER RAGMAN ROSTER SCREED
SCROLL SERIES CATALOG CITATOR
COMPILE DIPTYCH ITEMIZE LISTING
NOTITIA WAYBILL CALENDAR
CINCTURE HANDLIST PLATBAND
REGISTER SCHEDULE SYNONYMY
TITULARY
(— **OF BOOKS**) CANON
(— **OF CANDIDATES**) LEET SLATE
TERNA
(— **OF CONTESTANTS**) DRAW
SEEDING
(— **OF JURORS**) TALES
(— **OF MAP SYMBOLS**) LEGEND
(— **OF PASSERS WITHOUT HONORS**)
GULF
(— **OF RATES**) TARIFF
(— **OF THEATRICAL PARTS**) CAST
(**GENEALOGICAL** —) BEGATS
(**IMPRESSIVE** —) ARRAY
(**LEGAL** —) TABLEAU
(**PRAYER** —) BEADROLL
(**WINE** —) CARD
(**PL.**) CAREER
LISTEL QUADRA
LISTEN HARK HEAR LIST TEND
TENEZ ATTEND HARKEN INTEND
WHISPER
(— **TO**) DIG EAR HARK HEAR CATCH
ATTEND
LISTENER AUDITOR OTACUST
LISTENING PRICK AUDIENT HEARING
LISTER SULKY RIDGER
LISTERA OPHRYS
LISTING ITEM FRAME PARADE
LASHING
(— **OF JURORS**) ARRAY
LISTLESS DOPY DULL DOWFF FAINT
DONSIE SUPINE LANGUID UNLISTY
UNLUSTY CARELESS INDOLENT
UNHEARTY
LISTLESSLY DAVIELY
LISTLESSNESS APATHY UNLUST

LITANY AITESIS ROGATION
LITERAL VERBAL
LITERALLY SIMPLY
LITERARY BLUE BOOKISH LITERATE
   (— MATERIAL) KITSCH
LITERATE LETTERED
LITERATI CLERISY
LITERATURE FICTION LETTERS
   CLAPTRAP
   (SACRED —) VEDA SRUTI
   (WISDOM —) CHOKMAH HOKHMAH
LITHE BAIN SWACK CLEVER LIMBER
   SILKEN SUPPLE SVELTE WANDLE
   LISSOME FLEXIBLE

LITHUANIA
CAPITAL: KOVNO KAUNAS
COIN: LIT LITAS MARKA CENTAS
   FENNIG OSTMARK AUKSINAS
   SKATIKAS
NAME: LITVA LIETUVA
PEOPLE: BALT LETT ZHMUD
   LITVAK YATVYAG
RIVER: NERIS RUSNE DUBYSA
   NEMUNAS PREGOLYA
TOWN: MEMEL VILNA JELGAVA
   VILNIUS KAPSUKAS KLAIPEDA
   SIAULIAI

LITHUANIAN BALT ZHMUD
LITIGANT SUITOR
LITIGATE LAW PLEAD CONTEST
LITIGATION LAW LIS MOOT SUIT
   LAWING PLEADING PLEASHIP
LITMUS LAKMUS TURNSOLE
LITOTES MEIOSIS
LITTER DIG PIG BIER RAFF REDD
   BREED CABIN CLECK DOOLY DRECK
   HAULM MULCH SEDAN DOOLIE
   FARROW GOCART KINDLE KITTEN
   MAHMAL REFUSE CLUTTER LETTIGA
   LOUSTER MAMMOCK NORIMON
   RUMMAGE SCAMBLE BRANCARD
   CARRIAGE KINDLING MUNCHEEL
   PAVILION STRETCHER
   (— FOR LIVESTOCK) BEDDING
   (— OF PIGS) FAR FARE FARROW
   (— ON PACK ANIMAL) CACOLET
   (FOREST —) DUFF
LITTERED FOUL
LITTLE FEW LIL WEE LITE TINY VEEN
   CHOTA CRUMB SMALL TASTE
   WHONE BITTIE DAPPER LEETLE
   MINUTE PETITE PICKLE PUSILL
   KENNING MODICUM THOUGHT
   FRACTION SNIPPING
   (— BY LITTLE) EDGINGLY INCHMEAL
   (— LESS THAN) ABOUT
   (— MUSICALLY) POCO
   (— ONE) BUTCHA POPPET
   (A —) SOMEWHAT
   (INDEFINITELY —) NTH
LITTLENESS ATOMITY
LITTORAL COAST
LITURGY FORM RITE ABODAH
   MAARIB MINHAG NEILAH MINCHAH
   MYSTERY HIERURGY SHAHARIT
LIVE BE USE WIN KEEP LEAD STAY

ALERT ALIVE DWELL EXIST GREEN
HABIT LEEVE QUICK SHACK VITAL
HARBOR LIVELY LIVING REMAIN
RESIDE BREATHE INHABIT SUBSIST
CONTINUE CONVERSE VIGOROUS
   (— AT ANOTHER'S EXPENSE)
   COSHER
   (— BY BEGGING) CADGE SKELDER
   (— BY STRATAGEMS) SHARK
   (— FROM DAY TO DAY) EKE
   (— IN CONTINENCE) CONTAIN
   (— IN LUXURY) STATE
   (— IN PEACE) COEXIST
   (— IN SAME PLACE) STALL
   (— ON) SURVIVE
   (— RIOTOUSLY) JET
   (— TEMPORARILY) CAMP
   (— THROUGH) PASS TIDE
   (— TOGETHER) AGREE COHABIT
LIVE-BOX CAR
LIVE-FOREVER LULANG ORPINE
LIVELIHOOD BEING BREAD LIVING
   LIFEHOOD
LIVELINESS PEP FIRE FIZZ LIFE
   SPUNK BOUNCE GAIETY SPIRIT
   SPARKLE ACTIVITY VITALITY
   VIVACITY
LIVELONG LEELANG ENDURING
LIVELY GAY TID AIRY BRAG CANT
   FAST FESS GLEG KECK LIVE PERT
   RACY TAIT TRIG VITE VIVE WARM
   YARE AGILE ALERT ALIVE BONNY
   BRISK BUXOM CANTY CHIRK COBBY
   CORKY CRISP DESTO FRESH FRISK
   KEDGE KINKY MERRY PAWKY PEART
   PEPPY POKEY RUDDY SMART VIVID
   WHICK ACTIVE BLITHE BOUNCY
   CHEERY CHIRPY COCKET CROOSE
   CROUSE DAPPER FIERCE FRISCH
   GINGER JOCUND KIPPER LIVING
   NIMBLE QUIVER SEMMIT SPARKY
   SPRACK TROTTY VEGETE WHISKY
   WIMBLE ALLEGRO ANIMATE
   ANIMOSE BUCKISH BUOYANT
   GIGGISH GIOCOSO JOCULAR
   KINETIC LEBHAFT POINTED SPIRITY
   SPRINGY TITTUMY WINCING
   ANIMATED BOUNCING CHIRRUPY
   FRISKFUL FRISKING GALLIARD
   SKITTISH SMACKING SPANKING
   SPIRITED SPORTIVE STEERING
   STIRRING TRIPSOME VEGETOUS
   VOLATILE SPARKLING
LIVEN LACE CHEER ANIMATE
LIVE OAK ENCINA
LIVER MAW FOIE HEPAR VISCUS
   PUDDING
   (— ATROPHY) LUPINOSIS
   (— OF LOBSTER) TOMALLEY
LIVERWORT HEPATICA MOSSWORT
LIVERY SUIT CLOTH LIVRE UNIFORM
   CLOTHING
LIVESTOCK FEE WARE STOCK
   STORE STUFF CHATTEL BESTIALS
   FATSTOCK
LIVE WIRE HUSTLER
LIVID HAW WAN BLAE BLUE
LIVING KEEP ALIVE BEING BREAD
   GOING QUICK VITAL WHICK AROUND

LIVELY VIABLE ZOETIC ANIMATE
SUPPORT ANIMATED
   (— IN THE WORLD) SECULAR
   (— IN WAVES) LOTIC
   (— NEAR THE GROUND) EPIGEAN
   (— ON BANKS OF STREAMS) RIPAL
   RIPARIAN
   (— THING) QUICK
   (BARE —) CRUST
   (ECCLESIASTICAL —) BENEFICE
LIVRE FRANC
LIXIVIATE LEACH
LIXIVIUM LYE
LIZARD DAB EFT GOH UMA UTA
   DABB GILA IBIT SEPS TEGU TEJU
   URAN AGAMA ANOLE BLUEY DRACO
   GECKO GUANO SKINK SNAKE SWIFT
   TEIID TOKAY TWEEG VARAN AMEIVA
   ANGUID ARBALO DRAGON GOANNA
   HARDIM IGUANA LACERT LEGUAN
   MOLOCH TEIOID WORRAL ZONURE
   BUMMAJO CAUDATE CHEECHA
   DIAPSID MONITOR REPTILE SAURIAN
   SCINCID TUATARA TUCKTOO
   BASILISK KAKARIKI MOKAMOKA
   SCORPION SLOWWORM TEGUEXIN
   WHIPTAIL ZONUROID CHAMELEON
LIZARD FISH ULAE INIOME
   SOAPFISH SPEARING
LLAMA ALPACA VICUNA GUANACO
LLUDD NUDD
LO SEE ECCE
LOACH DOJO BEARDIE MUDFISH
LOAD LUG BUCK CARK CRAM DECK
   DRAW FILL HAUL LADE LAST LUMP
   PACK RAKE SEAM STEM STOW
   TOTE TURN BARTH CARGO DRAFT
   PITCH STACK TRUSS TURSE
   BURDEN CHARGE COMBLE DEMAND
   FODDER FOTHER HAMPER LADING
   LOADEN THRACK WEIGHT BALLAST
   CARLOAD DERRICK DRAUGHT
   ONERATE OPPRESS BACKPACK
   CARRIAGE ENCUMBER HEADLOAD
   SHIPLOAD
   (— A DIE FOR CHEATING) COG
   (— FABRICS) WEIGHT
   (— OF COAL) KEEL
   (— OF HAY OR CORN) HURRY
   (— OF LAMBS) DECK
   (— OF LOGS) PEAKER BUNKLOAD
   (— OF WOOL) TOD
   (— ON BACK) ENDORSE INDORSE
   (— SHIP) STEM
   (— TO CAPACITY) SATURATE
   (— TO EXCESS) ENCUMBER
   (ELECTRIC —) DEMAND
   (HORSE —) SEAM SUMAGE
   (LAST — OF GRAIN) WINTER
   (SMALL —) JAG JAGG JOBBLE
   (PL.) BUSHEL
LOADER CHARGER
LOADING LADING MARGIN
   ARRASTRE
LOADSTONE MAGNET SIDERITE
   LODESTONE
LOAF BAP BUM COB HACK HAKE
   HULL LAKE MIKE SLIM SORN BANGE

BREAD DRING MOUCH SHOOL SLIVE
SLOSH BROGUE CADDLE DIDDLE
GEORGE HALLAH RODNEY SLINGE
WASTEL HOOSIER MANCHET
SHACKLE SLOUNGE SOLDIER
OBLATION QUARTERN SHAMMOCK
(— AROUND) HULL HOWFF SLOSH
RODNEY
(— OF BREAD) COB BATON FADGE
MICHE TOMMY HALLAH TAMMIE
(BROWN —) GEORGE
(ROUND —) BUN
(SMALL —) BAP COB
(SUGAR —) TITLER
LOAFER BUM BEAT GRUB STIFF
BUMBLE KEELIE SLOUCH SLOVEN
BLUDGER COASTER FAITOUR
HOODLUM SLINKER SOLDIER
COBERGER HOOLIGAN LARRIKIN
SEASONER
LOAFING IDLE MIKE
LOAM RAB LAME SLIP LOESS REGUR
CLEDGE
LOAMY MELLOW
LOAN DHAN LEND LENT PREST
CREDIT DONATE MUTUUM FIXTURE
IMPREST
LOANBLEND HYBRID
LOATH LOTH LAITH LEATH SWEER
DAINTY BACKWARD
LOATHE HATE SHUN ABHOR LAITH
WLATE AGRISE DETEST DESPISE
SCUNDER SCUNNER NAUSEATE
LOATHING NAUSEA REVOLT
DISGUST
LOATHLY LAIDLY
LOATHSOME FOUL UGLY VILE
POCKY LAIDLY UNLIEF HATEFUL
LOATHLY OBSCENE TETROUS
WLATFUL DEFORMED NAUSEOUS
WLATSOME
LOBBY HALL FOYER NARTHEX
TAMBOUR ANTEROOM COULISSE
LOBBYIST PROMOTER
LOBE ALA FIN LAP AXIS LIST MALA
ALULA EXITE FIBER FIBRE FLUKE
GALEA LOBUS TOOTH UVULA
EARLAP FILLET FOLIUM GLOSSA
LAPPET LIGULE LOBING MANTLE
VANNUS VERMIS AROLIUM AURICLE
HEMAPOD LOBULUS EPICHILE
GLABELLA LABELLUM PALPIFER
PHYLLOID SQUAMULE
LOBED CUT LOMATINE
LOBSTER CRAY HOMARD DECAPOD
SHEDDER CRAWFISH CRAYFISH
LANGUSTA MACRURAN
(— ENCLOSURE) CRAWL
(— LESS THAN 10 INCHES LONG)
JOE
(FEMALE —) HEN
(SMALL —) PAWK NANCY
(UNDERSIZED —) SHORT
LOBSTER POT COY CRAIL CREEL
TRUNK FISHPOT
LOBULARIA KONIGA
LOCAL HOME NATIVE LIMITED
VICINAL REGIONAL EPICHORIC
LOCALE SITE LOCAL PLACE SCENE

LOCALITY SPA HAND PLAT SPOT
LOCUS PLACE POINT SITIO SITUS
STEAD HABITAT LATITUDE POSITURE
(BARREN —) GALL
(GUARDED —) POST
LOCALIZE SITUATE POSITION
LOCATE SITE SPOT PITCH PLACE
BESTOW BILLET SETTLE SITUATE
(— AT INTERVALS) SPOT
(— WATER) DIVINE
LOCATED SET FIXED SEATED
SITUATED
(— OFF THE HIGHWAY) DEVIOUS
LOCATING SYSTEM SOFAR
LOCATION FALL HOME PLOT SEAT
PLACE SITUS WHERE UBIETY
AMENITY STATION HOMESITE
STANDING
(ESSENTIAL —) EYE
(FOREST —) CHANCE
(GEOGRAPHIC —) SEAT
(MINING —) MYNPACHT
(NATURAL —) HABITAT
LOCH LOUGH LOCHAN
LOCK COT KEY FEAK FRIB HOLD
TRIM YALE CLASP SASSE DUBBEH
ENLOCK LUCKEN DAGLOCK
EARLOCK KEYLOCK PINLOCK
SPANNER DEADLOCK FORELOCK
(— IMPROPERLY) BIND
(— IN RIVER) SASSE
(— OF HAIR) COT TAG TUZ COTT
CURL FEAK TATE FLAKE FLOCK
FLUKE TRESS TANGLE COWLICK
EARLOCK FRIZZLE SERPENT
WIMPLER FORELOCK SIDELOCK
(— OF WOOL) TAG COTT FRIB
FLOCK STAPLE HASLOCK
(— UP) JAIL STOW CABINET
(CANAL —) CHAMBER
(DIRTY —) FRIB
(MATTED —) COT COTT DAGLOCK
(MUSKET —) ROWET
(PART OF —) STRIKE
(WHEEL —) REWET
LOCKED FAST LUCKEN
LOCKER HUTCH ASCHAM
LOCKERMAN NIBBLER SCOTCHER
SNIBBLER
LOCKJAW TETANUS TRISMUS
LOCKNUT JAMNUT KEEPER
LOCKOUT SHUTOUT
LOCKSMITH LOCKYER
LOCKUP JUG GAOL JAIL LOCK LOGS
CHOKY CLINK TRONK COOLER
HOOSEGOW
LOCOMOTION FLYING LATION
LOCOMOTIVE HOG PIG BOGY GOAT
HOGG MULE SHAG TANK BOGIE
DINKY DUMMY MOGUL PILOT DIESEL
DOCTOR DOLLIE DONKEY ENGINE
LOADER PUSHER SMOKER YARDER
BOBTAIL BOOSTER SHUNTER
STEAMER CALLIOPE CHOOCHOO
COMPOUND DOLLBEER
(— WITHOUT CARS) WILDCAT
(EXTRA —) HELPER
LOCOMOTOR ATAXIA TABES
LOCOWEED LOCO LEGUME PEAVINE

LOCUS PLACE EVOLUTE SURFACE
SYNAPSE CONCHOID ENVELOPE
HOROPTER
LOCUST WETA BRUKE HONEY
ACACIA CICADA QUAKER SKIPPER
TETRIGID
LOCUST TREE CAROB ACACIA
LOCUST ROBINIA ALGAROBA
LODE LEAD REEF VEIN LEDGE
COURSE FEEDER QUARRY COUNTER
LODESTONE MAGNET
LODGE DIG HUT INN LIE BEAT CAMP
HOST KEEP ROOM STAY STOW
TENT BOWER CABIN COUCH COURT
GROVE GUEST HOGAN HOTEL
HOUSE HOWFF LAYER LOGIS STICK
TARRY ALIGHT BESTOW BILLET
BURROW COSHER GESTEN GRANGE
HOSTEL RESIDE SETTLE BARRACK
LODGING QUARTER SOJOURN
EMBOLIZE HARBINGE
(— AND EAT) COSHER
(— FOR SAFEKEEPING) DEPOSIT
(— IN COURT) BOX
(LOCAL —) COURT
(SPORTSMAN'S —) SHEAL
LODGEPOLE PINE TAMARACK
LODGER INMATE ROOMER TENANT
LODGING BED CRIB GIST HAFT
HOST NEST GEAST LOGIS HARBOR
HOSTEL LIVERY HOSPICE HOUSING
COUCHANT GUESTING
(— FOR SOLDIERS) CASERN
(— OF MARABOUT) KOUBA
(PL.) DIGS DIGGINGS
LODGINGHOUSE INN KIP GITE STOP
HOTEL LOGIA LOCANDA PENSION
HOSTELRY
LODICULE SQUAMULA SQUAMULE
LOESS LIMON
LOFT BALK FLAT GOLF LAFT ATTIC
SOLAR GARRET SOLLAR HAYLOFT
COCKLOFT SCAFFOLD TRAVERSE
(HAY —) TALLET TALLIT
LOFTIEST SUPREME
LOFTINESS PRIDE HEIGHT DIGNITY
MAJESTY EMINENCE GRANDEUR
HIGHNESS
LOFTSMAN LINESMAN
LOFTY AIRY HIGH LOFT TALL ELATE
GRAND GREAT NOBLE PROUD
SKYEY STEEP WINGY AERIAL
ANDEAN HAUGHT TOPFUL TOWERY
UPWARD WINGED ANDESIC
ARDUOUS EMINENT EXCELSE
HAUGHTY SUBLIME ARROGANT
ELEVATED GENEROUS MAJESTIC
OLYMPIAN TOWERING
LOG NOG BUNK CLOG DRAG SKID
CHUCK CHUNK PIECE STICK STOCK
BATTEN BILLET PEAKER PEELER
SADDLE SAWLOG BACKLOG
DAYBOOK DEADMAN DEGRADE
JOURNAL LOGBOOK DEADHEAD
(— AS ANCHOR) DEADMAN
(— AS RAFTER) VIGA
(— BINDING A RAFT) SWIFTER
(— CAR) BUNK
(— FASTENED TO TRAP) DRAG

(— SUPPORTING MINE ROOF) NOG
(— WITH SPIKES IN END) DEADENER
(— WITHOUT BARK) BUCKSKIN
(ENCLOSED —S) BOOM
(FLOATING —S) DRIVE
(LOAD OF —S) PEAKER
(PILE OF —S) DECK ROLLWAY
(SAWED —) BOULE
(SLABBED —) CANT
(SMALL —) LOGGET
(SPLIT —) PUNCHEON
(STRIPPED —) BATTEN
(SUNKEN —) DEADHEAD
LOGANIN MELIATIN
LOGARITHM DENSITY
(— SYMBOL) PF PH PK RH
(NEGATIVE —) PH
LOGBOOK LOG JOURNAL
LOGE BOX BOOTH LODGE STALL
LOGGER RIDER BOWMAN DECKER
FALLER GOPHER HOOKER LIMBER
MARKER SCORER CHOPPER
FROGGER GRABBER SPOTTER
CATTYMAN
LOGGIA LODGE BALCONY MIRADOR
LOGIC NYAYA LOGICS CANONIC
WITCRAFT
(— OF DISCOVERY) HEURETIC
LOGICAL SANE RAISONNE RATIONAL
LOGMAN CHASER CHOPPER
LOGOGRAM IDEOGRAM
LOGOS WORD
LOGOTYPE SIG
LOG PERCH DARTER HOGFISH
ROCKFISH
LOGROLLING BIRLING
(— TOURNAMENT) ROLEO
LOGWOOD BRAZIL ADMIRAL
DYEWOOD BLUEWOOD HYPERNIC
LOGY DROWSY GROGGY
LOHAN RAKAN
LOIN LEER LISK ALOYAU LUNYIE
(2 UNCUT —S) BARON
(PORK —) GRISKIN
(PL.) REINS FILLET SADDLE
LOINCLOTH IZAR MALO MARO
DHOTI LUNGI PAGNE PAREU
MOOCHA PANUNG DHOOTIE
LOITER LAG CLUG FOOL HAKE HANG
HAWM HAZE HOVE LOUT MIKE
MUCK SLUG COOSE DELAY DRAWL
KNOCK MOUCH SHOOL SIDLE
TARRY COOTER DAWDLE LAGGER
LINGER MUCKER STRAKE TAIGLE
PROJECT SHAFFLE LALLYGAG
LOLLYGAG SCOWBANK SLAMMOCK
SLUMMOCK
LOITERER DRONE IDLER LAGGER
LAGGARD LURCHER
LOITERING SLIMSY LAGGARD
LOKAPALA MAHARAJA
LOKI (DAUGHTER OF —) HEL
(MOTHER OF —) ANGRBODHA
(WIFE OF —) SIGYN
LOLL FUG LOUT FROWST LOLLUP
LOUNGE SOZZLE SPRAWL RECLINE
SCAMBLE SCOWBANK
LOLLIPOP LOLLY SUCKER
SUCKABOB

LOLO NOSU
LONDON SMOKE COCKAGNE
(BRIDGE IN —) TOWER ALBERT
PUTNEY CHELSEA WATERLOO
(DISTRICT OF —) SOHO ACTON
ADELPHI ALSATIA BRIXTON
CHELSEA MAYFAIR
(MONUMENT IN —) GOG MAGOG
NELSON CENOTAPH VICTORIA
(RIVER OF —) THAMES
(STREET OF —) BOND FLEET
CANNON SAVILE DOWNING
WARDOUR HAYMARKET
(SUBURB OF —) KEW FINCHLEY
LONDONER FLATCAP
LONE LANE SOLE ALONE APART
SINGLE SOLITARY
(— STAR STATE) TEXAS
LONELINESS ONENESS VACANCY
SOLITUDE
LONELY ONLY SOLE VAST ALONE
UNKET UNKID WISHT ALANGE
DEAFLY SULLEN DEAVELY FORLORN
LONEFUL SOLEYNE DESOLATE
SECLUDED SOLITARY
LONESOME ALONE DOLEY LONELY
LANESOME SOLITARY
LONG HO DIE FAR FIT YEN ACHE
DREE HANK HONE ITCH LANG SIDE
TALL WILN WISH YAWN CRAVE
DREAM GREEN LATHY LONGA
MOURN STARK WEARY YEARN
ARIGUE ASPIRE DESIRE DREICH
HANKER HUNGER LINGER LONGUS
PROLIX STOUND THIRST LENGTHY
TEDIOUS WEILANG GEMINATE
INFINITE
(— AGO) FERN LANGSYNE
(— AND SLENDER) REEDY SQUINNY
(— AND UNIFORM IN WIDTH) LINEAR
(— FOR) CARE HONE COVET CRAVE
TASTE ASPIRE DESIRE SUSPIRE
(— RESTLESSLY) ITCH
(— SINCE) YORE
LONG-BILLED CURLEW SMOKER
LONGBOAT SLOOP
LONG-BODIED RACY RANGY
LONGERON SPAR
LONGEVITY VIVACITY
(— CHARACTER) SHOU
LONGING YEN ENVY ITCH LUST PINE
WISH BRAME YEARN DESIRE
HANKER TALENT THIRST ATHIRST
CRAVING THIRSTY WILLING WISHFUL
APPETENT APPETITE CUPIDITY
HOMESICK PRURIENT
LONGITUDINALLY ENDLONG
LONG-LASTING CHRONIC
LONGLEGS STILT
LONGLINE BULTOW
LONG-LIVED LONGEVE MACROBIAN
LONGSHOREMAN DOCKER
HOBBLER WHARFIE DOCKHAND
LONG-STANDING OLD
LONG-SUFFERING MEEK PATIENT
ENDURING PATIENCE
LONG-TAILED WHIDAH REDBILL
LONG TOM SKIPPER
LONG-WINDED PROLIX PROSAIC

LOOK LA LO AIR EYE KEN SEE SPY
CAST GAWK GAZE GIVE GLOM HEED
KEEK LATE LUCK MARK POKE SEEM
SWAP VIEW WAIT ACIES BLUSH
DEKKO FAVOR FLASH GLEAM GLEER
GLIFF GLINT SCREW SIGHT SQUIZ
VIZZY WLITE APPEAR ASPECT
EYEFUL GANDER GLANCE REGARD
REWARD VISION EYESHOT EYEWINK
INSIGHT SEEMING DISCOVER
LANGUISH OEILLADE
(— ABOUT) BELOOK SPECTATE
(— AFTER) TENT ATTEND FATHER
FETTLE PROCURE
(— ASKANCE) GLIM LEER SKEW
BAGGE GLENT GLEDGE SKLENT
(— AT) DIG SEE GLOM LAMP VIEW
GLISK ADVISE BEHOLD REGARD
REWARD CONSIDER SPECTATE
(— CLOSELY) PRY ESPY SCAN
(— CROSS-EYED) SHEYLE
(— DOWN UPON) SNOB DESPISE
(— DULLY) BLEAR
(— FIXEDLY) GAZE KYKE GLORE
STARE
(— FOR) SPY FOND SEEK GROPE
EXPECT PROPOSE RESPECT
(— FORWARD) EXPECT FORESEE
ENVISAGE ENVISION
(— GLANCINGLY) BLINK
(— IN SNEAKING MANNER) SNOOP
(— INTENTLY) GLOSE VISIE GLOWER
EYEBALL
(— INTO) SOUND SEARCH
(— OBLIQUELY) GLIME GOGGLE
SQUINT
(— OF DERISION) FLEER
(— OF PLANETS) ASPECTS
(— OUT) FEND MIND CHEESE
JIGGERS OUTLOOK
(— OVER) SCAN TOISE BROWSE
SURVEY EXAMINE
(— SEARCHINGLY) PEER PORE
TOOT
(— SLYLY) PEEP GLINK
(— SOUR) GLUNCH
(— STEADFASTLY) GLOAT
(— SULKY) LUMP
(— SULLEN) LOUR LOWER
(— UPON AS) ACCOUNT
(— WILDLY) GLOP WAUL WHAWL
(— WITH FAVOR) SMILE
(AMOROUS —) SMICKER
(BRIEF —) GLIM GLINT GLIMPSE
(LOVING —) BELGARD
(QUICK —) SCRY GLENT
(SEARCHING —) SCRUTINY
(SEVERE —) FROWN
(SIDELONG —) GLEE GLIME
(SLY —) GLEG GLIME TWIRE
(SULLEN —) GLOOM GLOUT
GLUNCH
(TENDER —) LANGUISH
(WANTON —) LEER
(PL.) DAPS
LOOKER BEAUTY HERDSMAN
SEARCHER
LOOKER-ON BEHOLDER
LOOKOUT TOUT SCOUT WATCH

BANTAY CONNER TOOTER FUNERAL OUTLOOK ATALAYAN BANTAYAN BARTIZAN COCKATOO PROSPECT TOWERMAN WATCHOUT

LOOM BEAM BULK HULK LEEM DOBBY FRAME GLOOM BEETLE DOBBIE DRAWLOOM HANDLOOM JACQUARD OVERPICK
(**— ATTACHMENT)** LAPPET

LOOM AXLE ROCKTREE

LOOM BAR EASER DAGGER

LOOMFIXER TACKLER

LOOM HARNESS LEAF HEADLE SIMBLOT MOUNTING

LOON DIVER IMBER WABBY COBBLE DUCKER GUNNER WHABBY PYGOPOD

LOOP BOW EYE LUG NOB TAB TAG ANSA BEND COIL FAKE HANK KINK KNOB KNOP LEAF LINK LOUP PURL BIGHT BRIDE CHAPE COQUE GUIDE LACET LATCH NOOSE PEARL PICOT SHANK STRAP TERRY WITHY BECKET BILLET BUCKLE FOLIUM HANGER HOLDER KEEPER KINKLE PARRAL SPIRAL STAPLE STITCH TWITCH COCKEYE COUPURE CRINGLE CRUPPER GROMMET KNUCKLE LATCHET SEGMENT ANTINODE COURONNE
(**— AND THIMBLES)** CLEW CLUE
(**— BY ICESKATER)** SPOON
(**— IN KNITTING)** STEEK
(**— IN MINER'S ROPE)** SLUG
(**— IN NEEDLEWORK)** BRIDE
(**— OF INTESTINES)** KNUCKLE
(**— OF IRON)** OOLLY
(**— OF ROPE)** FAKE BIGHT FLAKE KINCH NOOSE ANCHOR BECKET PARRAL SNORTER SNOTTER
(**— OF SCABBARD)** FROG
(**— OF TUBING)** SCROLL
(**— ON ARMOR)** VERVELLE
(**— ON SPINNING FRAME)** BAND
(**— ON SWORD BELT)** HANGER
(**HANGING —)** FESTOON
(**HEDDLE —)** DOUP
(**ORNAMENTAL —)** PICOT
(**SHOULDER —)** EPAULET
(**SURGICAL —)** CURET CURETTE
(**TIGHT —)** KINK KINKLE

LOOPER INCHWORM SPANWORM

LOOPHOLE LOOP CHINK MEUSE EYELET OILLET WICKET PORTHOLE

LOOSE GAY LAX EMIT FREE GLAD LASH LIMP OPEN SOFT UNDO WIDE WILD BAGGY CRANK FRANK LARGE LIGHT RELAX SLACK VAGUE WASHY ADRIFT FLUFFY LIMBER SLOPPY SOLUTE SPORTY SUBURB UNBIND UNGIRT UNLASH WOBBLY CHESSOM FLYAWAY IMMORAL MOVABLE RELAXED SHOGGLY STRINGY UNBOUND UNHITCH UNTIGHT DISCINCT FLOATING INSECURE LAXATIVE SHATTERY UNSTABLE
(**— ARROW)** BOLT
(**MORALLY —)** FRANK

LOOSE-JOINTED LANKY SHACKLY

LOOSELY SLACK LARGELY SLACKLY

LOOSEN LAX BREAK SLACK UNTIE LAXATE LIMBER UNBEND RESOLVE SLACKEN UNGRIPE UNLOOSE UNSCREW DISHEVEL UNSTRING
(**— ANCHOR)** TRIP
(**— ROCK)** GAD

LOOSENESS SLACK LAXITY LATITUDE

LOOSENING START SOLUTIVE SOLUTORY

LOOSESTRIFE KILLWEED PEATWEED PEATWOOD PRIMWORT

LOOT SACK SWAG BOOTY HARRY SPOIL STEAL THEFT HERSHIP PILLAGE PLUNDER SNAFFLE

LOOTING SACK

LOP DOD LAP CLIP DODD OCHE SNED SNIG TRIM SHRAG SHRED SHRUB STUMP TRASH TWINE SHROUD SNATHE TRASHIFY TRUNCATE
(**— OFF)** COW DOD CROP DODD HEAD SNAG SNEP PRUNE SHRED TRUNK DEFALK AMPUTATE

LOPE SHAG

LOPPER CLABBER

LOQUACIOUS GABBY FUTILE

LOQUACITY PRATE PRATTLE FUTILITY

LOQUAT BIWA NISPERO

LORAL FRENAL

LORD BEL DAM DEN DON GOD HER LOR MAR SID SIR DION DOMN EROS HERR LAUK LOSH SIRE TUAN ANGUS ARAWN BARON LAFEU LIEGE LUDDY NIGEL OMRAH RABBI SAHIB SWAMI DOMINE DUMAIN KYRIOS PRABHU SAYYID SIGNOR TANIST THAKUR CAMILLO CERIMON JACQUES JEHOVAH MARCHER OGTIERN VAVASOR BHAGAVAT DESPOTES DRIGHTEN GRANDPRE LORDLING MARGRAVE OVERLORD PALATINE SEIGNEUR SEIGNIOR SUPERIOR SUZERAIN THALIARD
(**— OF DARKNESS)** HYLE
(**— OF WORLD)** LOKINDRA
(**FEUDAL —)** DAUPHIN VAVASOR SUZERAIN

LORD CHANCELLOR WOOLPACK

LORDLINESS PRIDE

LORDLY PROUD SUPERB ARROGANT DESPOTIC

LORDOSIS SWAYBACK

LORDSHIP NAVY DYNASTY ERECTION SEIGNORY SIGNORIA

LORE LEAR LORUM MASTAX LEARNING

LORGNETTE STARER

LORICA LORIC SHEATH SHIELD

LORIKEET PARROT WARRIN CORELLA WEROOLE

LORIS KOKAM LEMUR SLOTH LEMUROID

LORN ALONE

LORRY RULLY ROLLEY

LORY LOORY CORELLA LORIKEET

LOSE LET TIN AMIT DROP TINE WANT

FORGO LAPSE LEASE TRAIL GAMBLE MISLAY FORBEAR FORFEIT FORLESE SLATTER
(**— AT CARDS)** BUST
(**— BET)** WRONG
(**— BRILLIANCE)** FAINT
(**— BY DEATH)** BURY
(**— BY GAMING)** GAME
(**— BY STUPIDITY)** BLUNDER
(**— CONTROL)** BLOW CRACK
(**— COURAGE)** DREEP TAINT
(**— FLAVOR)** FOZE APPAL APPALL
(**— FORCE)** COLLAPSE
(**— FRESHNESS)** FADE WILT WITHER
(**— HEART)** JADE FAINT QUAIL
(**— HOPE)** DESPAIR DESPOND
(**— LUSTER)** TARNISH
(**— MOISTURE)** GUTTATE
(**— NERVE)** CHICKEN
(**— OFFICE)** FALL
(**— ONE'S BREATH)** CHINK
(**— ONE'S WAY)** STRAY
(**— POWER)** FAIL DISSOLVE
(**— SELF-POSSESSION)** ABASH
(**— SPIRIT)** JADE
(**— STRENGTH)** GO FADE FAIL WEAKEN LANGUISH
(**— VISION)** DAZZLE
(**— WARMTH)** COOL CONGEAL
(**— WEIGHT)** ENSEAM

LOSS ACE COST HARM LEAK LOST MISS LAPSE QUALM WASTE BURIAL DAMAGE DAMNUM DEFEAT INJURY TINSEL AVERAGE DEBACLE DEFICIT EXPENSE JACTURE LEAKAGE LEESING MISTURE REPRISE AMISSION BREAKAGE CLEANING MISSMENT
(**— BY SIFTING)** ULLAGE
(**— IN WORKING)** SLIPPAGE
(**— OF ABILITIES)** COLLAPSE
(**— OF ACTIVITY)** AKINESIA
(**— OF APPETITE)** ANOREXIA
(**— OF CONSCIOUSNESS)** SWOON ABSENCE APOPLEXY BLACKOUT FAINTING
(**— OF ELASTICITY)** SET
(**— OF ELECTRICITY)** EFFLUVE
(**— OF EXPRESSION)** AMIMIA
(**— OF HAIR)** DEFLUX ALOPECIA PTILOSIS
(**— OF HOPE)** DESPAIR
(**— OF MEMORY)** AMNESIA
(**— OF PRESTIGE)** DISHONOR
(**— OF SCENT)** CHECK
(**— OF SENSE OF SMELL)** ANOSMIA
(**— OF SIZE)** WANE
(**— OF SOUND)** APOCOPE SYNCOPE APHERESIS
(**— OF SPEECH)** ALALIA APHASIA APHONIA
(**— OF VOICE)** ANAUDIA APHONIA
(**— OF VOWEL)** APHESIS
(**— OF WILL POWER)** ABULIA
(**CONTRACT —)** LESION

LOST GONE LORN TINT WASTE ASTRAY BUSHED HIDDEN NAUGHT FORFEIT FORLORN MISSING CONFUSED OBSCURED

LOT CUT HAP PEW CHOP CROP DEAL DOLE DOOM DRAW FALL FATE HEAP PACK PART PILE REDE SLEW SLUE SORS SORT BATCH BLOCK BREAK CAVEL FIELD GRACE GRIST GROSS LINES SHARE SHOOT SIGHT SITHE STAND TEEMS TROOP WEIRD AMOUNT BARREL BUNDLE CHANCE DICKER FARDEL OODLES TICHEL BOILING DESTINY FEEDLOT FORTUNE PORTION SANDLOT BACKYARD CABOODLE MOUTHFUL RIMPTION WOODLAND
(— OF 60 PIECES) SHOCK
(— OF PERSONS) BOODLE
(— OF TEA) BREAK
(BUILDING —) ERF
(BURIAL —) LAIR
(GREAT —) SWAG
(VACANT —) COMMON COMMONS
LOTION WASH EYEWASH EYEWATER LAVATORY
LOTS HEAPS TEEMS BUSHEL HODFUL
LOTTERY AMBO LOTTO TERNO RAFFLE TOMBOLA
LOTTO KENO BINGO TOMBOLA
(— GAME) HOUSE
LOTUS LOTE LOTOS WANKAPIN
LOTUS TREE SADR ZYZYPHUS
LOUCHEUX KUTCHIN
LOUD HARD HIGH MAIN CRUDE FORTE GAUDY GREAT HEAVY SHOWY STARK STOUR WIGHT BRASSY BRAZEN COARSE CRIANT FLASHY HOARSE VULGAR BLATANT CLAMANT HAUTAIN VIOLENT BIGMOUTH FRENZIED SLAMBANG STREPENT STRIDENT VEHEMENT
LOUDLY BOST ALOUD FORTE STARK
LOUDNESS STRESS SONORITY
(— UNIT) PHON SONE
LOUDSPEAKER WOOFER SPEAKER TWEETER BULLHORN SQUAWKER
LOUD-SPOKEN RANDY
LOUIS LUIGI LODOWIC

LOUISIANIAN CAJUN ACADIAN
LOUNGE HAWM LOLL SORN SOSS BANGE TRAIK FROUST FROWST GLIDER LOLLUP LOPPET RIZZLE SLINGE SOZZLE LAMMOCK SAUNTER SLOUNGE
LOUNGER IDLER SLOUNGER
LOUSE BOB BUG SOW CRAB CRUMB BOOGER BRAULA COOTIE GISLER PALMER SISTEN VERMIN MORPION PUCERON GRAYBACK
(FISH —) GISLER ARGULUS
(PLANT —) APHID APHIS
(WOOD —) SOW SLATER
(YOUNG —) NIT
LOUSEWORT RATTLE SNAFFLES
LOUSY SEEDY CRAPPY
LOUT HOB LOB LUG BOOR CHUB COOF GAUM GAWK LOON NOWT SWAB SWAD CHUMP CUDDY GNOFF LOURD ROBIN THRUM WHAUP YAHOO BOHUNK CLUNCH GOBBIN HOBLOB LOURDY LUBBER LUNGIS SLOUCH TRIPAL GROBIAN HAWBUCK LOBCOCK LOBLOLLY
(COUNTRY —) KERN BUMPKIN
LOUTISH SWAB HULKY SLOOMY BOORISH HULKING VILLAIN BOEOTIAN
LOUVER SLAT LOUVRE LUFFER DIFFUSER FEMERELL
(PL.) SHUTTER
LOVABLE AMABEL CUDDLY AMIABLE ADORABLE DOVELIKE LOVESOME
LOVABLENESS DEARNESS
LOVAGE SMELLAGE
LOVE GRA LOO AMOR EROS KAMA LIKE ALOHA AMOUR CUPID DRURY FANCY HEART MINNE TENDRE CHARITY EMBRACE FEELING DEVOTION KINDNESS LOVEHOOD PARAMOUR
(— IN RETURN) REDAME
(— OF MARVELOUS) TERATISM
(— TO EXCESS) IDOLIZE
(— TOWARD DEITY) BHAKTI
(CHRISTIAN —) CHARITY
(INTENSE —) FIRE
(NATURAL —) STORGE
(SELF-GIVING —) AGAPE
(UNLAWFUL —) LEMANRY
LOVED DEAR BELOVED
(MUCH —) SWEET
LOVE FEAST AGAPE
LOVE KNOT AMORET
LOVELINESS BEAUTY
LOVELOCK EARLOCK
LOVELY LOVING TENDER AMIABLE AMOROUS ADORABLE LOVESOME
LOVEMAKING AMOUR
LOVER GRA MAN BEAU CHAP AMANT AMOUR DRURY LEMAN ROMEO SPARK SWAIN AMADIS AMANTE MARROW MINION SQUIRE ADMIRER AMORIST AMOROSO CELADON GALLANT PATRIOT SPARKER SPECIAL SPRUNNY BELAMOUR CASANOVA CICISBEO PARAMOUR STREPHON

(MODEL —) LEILAH
(SILLY —) SPOON
LOVE SEAT CAUSEUSE
LOVING DEAR FOND TENDER AMATORY AMOROUS
LOW BAS BOO LAW MOO BASE KEEN MEAN ORRA ROUT SLOW VILE WEAK BLORE DIRTY GROSS LAICH PUTID SHORT SMALL SNIDE THIRD CALLOW EARTHY FILTHY GENTLE GRUBBY HARLOT HUMBLE LIMMER MENIAL RASCAL RIBALD SECRET SILKEN TURPID VULGAR BESTIAL IGNOBLE RAFFISH REPTILE SLAVISH SUBMISS SOUTERLY
(— AS OF A VOWEL) OPEN
(— DOWN) SIDE
(— IN LIGHTNESS) DULL
(— IN PERCEPTION) CRUDE
(— IN PITCH) GRAVE
(— IN QUALITY) HEDGE
(— IN SATURATION) GRAYISH
(— IN SPIRITS) BLUE DOWN GLOOMY DOWNCAST
(— IN TONE) SOFT SUBMISS
(— IN WATER) RACE
(— NUMBERS) MANQUE
(— POINT) TROUGH
(IMMEASURABLY —) ABYSMAL
LOWBORN WAFF
LOWBRED BASTARD PLEBEIAN
LOW-DOWN BUCKASS
LOWER CUT DIP LOW BASE BATE DOWN DROP DUCK FELL SINK ABASE ABATE ALLOY AVALE BELOW BLAME COUCH COWER DECRY DEMIT DOUSE FROWN GLOOM LEVEL SCOWL STOOP BEMEAN DEBASE DEJECT DEMEAN EMBASE GLOWER HUMBLE JUNIOR LESSEN MODIFY NETHER REDUCE SETTLE STRIKE SUBDUE SUBMIT BENEATH DECLASS DEGRADE DEPRESS SHORTEN DIMINISH DOWNWARD INFERIOR MODERATE
(— BANNER) VAIL
(— BY HALF STEP) FLAT
(— IN ESTEEM) CHEAPEN DEROGATE
(— IN PITCH) FLAT SHADE
(— ONESELF) SINK BEMEAN DESCEND
(— PRICES) BEAR
(— SAIL) AMAIN
(— THE HEAD) STOOP
LOWERING DIP DUCK DOWLY HEAVY LAPSE BEETLE SULLEN
(— OF BODY) FONDU
(— OF LAND) ABLATION
LOWEST LAST LEAST EXTREME LOWMOST
(— CLASS) LAG
(— POSSIBLE) KNOWDOWN
LOWING MUGIENT
LOWLAND LAICH POLDER LALLAND DOWNLAND
(— BESIDE RIVER) INKS
(BARREN —) LANDES

LOWLANDER SAXON ZHMUD SASSENACH

LOWLIER LESS

LOWLY LOW BASE SILLY HUMBLE BASEBORN

LOW-LYING CALLOW LALLAN INFERIAL SUBJECTED

LOW-MINDED BASE MEAN

LOWNESS LOWTH

  (— OF SPIRITS) GLOOM SPLEEN MEGRIMS

LOW-PITCHED GRUFF

LOW-SPIRITED HIPPED DEJECTED

LOY SLICK

LOYAL FAST FEAL FIRM HOLD LEAL REAL TRUE LIEGE PIOUS SOUND ARDENT HEARTY LAWFUL SECRET STANCH FAITHFUL YEOMANLY

LOYALIST TORY

LOYALLY SURELY

LOYALTY ARDOR FAITH FEALTY HOMAGE LEALTY REALTY SPIRIT REALITY DEVOTION FIDELITY

LOZENGE TAB JUBE COIGN QUOIN JUJUBE MASCLE QUARRY ROTULA RUSTRE TABLET TABULE TROCHE CREMULE DIAMOND TABELLA PASTILLE ROSEDROP

  (— OF CEMENT) WAFER

LOZI ROZI BAROTSE

LUBBER SWAB LOOBY SLOUCH LOBCOCK LILBURNE

LUBBERLY AWKWARD

LUBRICANT DOPE GREASE AQUADAG UNGUENT

LUBRICATE OIL DOPE GLIB GREASE LUBRIFY

LUBRICATOR OILER OILCAN

LUCARNE LUCOMBE

LUCENT BRIGHT LUCIBLE

LUCERNE LEGUME ALFALFA

LUCID SANE CLEAR AERIAL BRIGHT LIMPID CRYSTAL DILUCID LITERATE LUCULENT LUMINOUS

LUCIDITY SANITY

LUCIFER DEVIL PHOSPHOR

LUCK HAP CESS EURE SONS SPIN GRACE ISSUE CHANCE THRIFT FORTUNE HANDSEL SUCCESS VENTURE HAMINGJA

  (BAD — TO YOU) YLAHAYLL

  (BAD —) ACE DOLE DEUCE HOODOO UNLUCK AMBSACE

  (GOOD —) HAP FORTUNE THEEDOM

  (ILL —) UNHAP DIRDUM DISGRACE

  (RELATING TO —) ALEATORY

  (UNEXPECTED —) BUNCE

LUCKILY HAPPILY

LUCKY HOT CANNY HAPPY SONSY CHANCY LUCKLY LUCKFUL GRACIOUS

LUCRATIVE FAT GOOD GAINFUL

LUCRE SWAG

LUDICROUS AWFUL COMIC DROLL ABSURD FOOLISH HIDEOUS FARCICAL

LUDO UCKERS

LUFFA LOOFAH SPONGE

LUG EAR HUG TUG WAG SNUG SPUD

ZULU PATCH WALTZ

LUGGAGE SWAG TRAPS HATBOX BAGGAGE TRUSSERY

LUGGAGE CASE IMPERIAL

LUGGAR JAGGAR JUGGER LAGGAR

LUGGER CAT TOUP ZULU FIFIE

LUGUBRIOUS DOLEFUL DOLOROUS

LUGWORM LOB LUG LOBWORM SANDWORM

LUIGINO TEMIN

LUKEWARM LEW LUKE TEPID WLACH

LULL CALM DRUG FODE HUSH ROCK CROON HUSHO SLACK STILL SOPITE HUSHABY HUSHEEN

LULLABY LULL BALOO BALOW LULLAY HUSHABY HUSHEEN ROCKABY

LULLING DROWSY CIRCEAN

LUMBER BURR DEAL RAFF NANMU STOCK STRIP FINISH FLITCH REFUSE SAMCHU SHORTS TIMBER DEGRADE DUNNAGE GUMWOOD TRUNDLE STEPPING

  (INFERIOR —) SAPS SCOOT

LUMBERING AWKWARD LUMBERLY LUMBROUS

LUMBERJACK JACK TOPPER TIMBERER

LUMBERMAN PINER DOGGER SCORER CHOPPER GIRDLER TIMBERER

LUMINANCE HELIOS

LUMINARY LIGHT CANDLE PLANET

LUMINESCENCE FLAME

LUMINOSITY FIRE GLOW LIGHT VALUE

LUMINOUS LIGHT LUCID SHINY BRIGHT LUMINANT

LUMMOX LOBSTER

LUMP BAT BOB COB CUB DAB DAD FID GOB JOB NIB NOB NUB WAD BLOB BURL CLAG CLAM CLOT COOL COWL DUNT JUNK KNOB KNOT PONE SWAD TOKE BLOOM CHUCK CHUNK CLAUT CLUMP CLUNK GLEBE HUNCH KNOLL KNURL MOUSE SLUMP STONE WEDGE WODGE CLUNCH DOLLOP GOBBET HUBBLE HUDDLE LUMPET NUBBLE NUGGET CLUMPER CLUNTER PUMPKNOT

  (— IN CLOTH) BURL

  (— IN GLASS) YOLK

  (— OF BLACK LEAD) SOP

  (— OF BLOOD) CLOD

  (— OF COAL) NUBBLING

  (— OF DOUGH) DIP

  (— OF FAT) KEECH

  (— OF GLASS) BLOOM

  (— OF IRON) OOLLY

  (— OF LAVA) BOMB

  (— OF LINT) SLUG

  (— OF METAL) MASS SLUG

  (— OF ORE) ROCK HARDHEAD

  (— OF RUBBER) THIMBLE

  (— OF SALT) SALTCAT

  (— OF YEAST) BEE

  (LARGE —) DOLL HUNK

  (LITTLE —) NODULE KNOBBLE

  (ROUNDED —) CLOT

LUMPFISH GROSS PADDLE SUCKER

LUMPISH STODGY CHUCKLE

LUMPY GOBBY CHUNKY CLUNCH COBBLY

LUNACY MOON FOLLY MADNESS DELIRIUM INSANITY

LUNARIA SATINPOD

LUNARY VOLVELLE

LUNATIC GELT LOONY BEDLAM MADMAN MANIAC FANATIC FRANTIC CRACKPOT MOONLING MOONSICK

LUNCH CUT BAIT CRIB TIFF BEVER PIECE SNACK BRUNCH NACKET TIFFIN UNDERN BAGGING ELEVENS DEJEUNER DRINKING ELEVENER LUNCHEON

  (DAIRY —) CREMERIE

  (MINER'S —) SNAP

LUNCHEON CRIB LUNCH STULL TIFFIN DINETTE NOONMEAT

LUNCHROOM EATERY

LUNETTE OUTWORK

LUNG DRAGON LONGUE

LUNGE FOIN PASS SPAR POINT VENUE CHARGE ALLONGE

LUNGFISH CYCLOID DIPNOAN MUDFISH SIRENOID

LUNGS LIGHTS VISCUS BELLOWS

  (PERTAINING TO —) PULMONIC

LUNKHEAD DOLT JUGHEAD

LUNULE ALBEDO

LUO DHOLUO

LUPINE SUNDIAL

LURCH JOLL STOT SWAG STOIT CAREEN STOITER STUMBLE SWAGGER

LURCHING DRUNKEN ROLLING

LURE CON JAY BAIT HOOK ROPE TOLL WISE DECOY DRILL FEINT SLOCK SNARE SPOON SQUID STALE TEMPT TROLL ALLURE CAPPER CLARET ENTICE ENTRAP SEDUCE TREPAN VELURE GUDGEON INVEIGH PHANTOM PITFALL WOBBLER BUCKTAIL INVEIGLE LUREMENT

  (— INTO GAMBLING) HUSTLE

  (— OF CARRION) TRAIN

  (— WILDFOWL) STOOL

LURI ALUR

LURID RED PURPLE SULTRY CRIMSON GHASTLY

LURK DARE LOUT COUCH LOWER SKULK SLINK SNEAK AMBUSH DARKLE

LURKING LURKY GRASSANT

LUSCIOUS FOND RICH SWEET CREAMY DULCET DELICATE

LUSH GREEN LUSTY MOIST SAVORY FERTILE OPULENT THRIVING

LUST HELL KAMA BLOOD PRIDE DESIRE LIBIDO LIKING LUXURY NICETY PASSION COVETISE CUPIDITY

LUSTER NAIF GLASS GLINT GLOSS SHEEN SHINE WATER LUSTRE POLISH REFLET BURNISH GLIMPSE GLISTER LUSTRUM NITENCY

FULGENCE LUSTRATE RADIANCY
SPLENDOR
(— OF FIBER) BLOOM
(BRONZE-LIKE —) SCHILLER
LUSTERLESS WAN DEAD DULL
FISHY STARY
LUSTFUL HOT GAMY GOLE LEWD
RANK SALT CADGY LUSTY PRIME
RANDY RUTTY WANTON BEASTLY
CODDING FLESHLY FULSOME
JEALOUS RAMMISH RUTTISH
LIKEROUS
LUSTFULNESS SATYRISM
LUSTILY CRANK HOTLY
LUSTING ITCHY
LUSTRATION ABHISEKA
LUSTROUS CLEAR DOGGY NITID
BRIGHT GLOSSY ORIENT SHEENY
SILKEN SILVER SHINING SPLENDID
LUSTY BRAG CANT CRANK FLUSH
FRACK FRANK FRECK GUTSY HARDY
JUICY STIFF STOUT GAWSIE
ROBUST STURDY LUSTFUL LUSTICK
BOUNCING PHYSICAL SPORTIVE
VIGOROUS
LUTE TAR BIWA LAUD DOMRA NABIA
NABLE REBAB REBEC SAROD
CITOLE ENLUTE LORICA LUTING
SCREED ANGELOT BANDORE
DICHORD DYPHONE MANDOLA
MANDORE MINIKIN PANDORE
THEORBO VIHUELA ANGELICA
ARCHLUTE PENORCAN TAMBOURA
TEMPLATE TRICHORD
LUTER DAUBER PASTER
LUTJANID JEWFISH

LUXEMBOURG
CAPITAL: LUXEMBOURG
HIGHEST POINT: BURGPLATZ

LOWLAND: BONPAYS GUTLAND
MEASURE: FUDER
MOUNTAIN RANGE: ARDENNES
PLATEAU: ARDENNES
RIVER: OUR SURE SAUER ALZETTE
MOSELLE
TOWN: ROODT WILTZ PETANGE
VIANDEN DIEKIRCH

LUXURIANT GOLE LUSH RANK RICH
FRANK PROUD LAVISH WANTON
OPULENT PROFUSE TEEMING
PAMPERED PRODIGAL
LUXURIANTLY FATLY
LUXURIATE BASK WALLOW WANTON
LUXURIOUS HIGH LUSH NICE POSH
RANK SOFT GAUDY SWANK CAPUAN
DELUXE GILDED SILKEN SWANKY
WANTON ELEGANT LUCULLAN
PRODIGAL REGALADO SENSUOUS
TRYPHENA TRYPHOSA
LUXURIOUSLY HIGH DELUXE
LUXURY FRILL FINERY OUTRAGE
DELICACY ELEGANCE PLEASURE
RICHNESS
LUXURY-LOVING DELICATE
LYCANTHROPE WEREWOLF
LYCAON (DAUGHTER OF —)
CALLISTO
(FATHER OF —) PALASGUS
LYCEUM PLATFORM
LYCHNIS FIREBALL NONESUCH
LYCIUM RUSOT
LYCOPODIUM MOSS FOXTAIL
CROWFOOT STAGHORN
LYDIA MAEONIA
LYE LEY BOUK BUCK STRAKE
LESSIVE LIXIVIUM SOAPLEES
LYING FLAT FALSE LEASE CRETISM

LEASING MENTERY
(— APART) DISSITE
(— AT BASE OF MOUNTAINS)
PIEDMONT
(— CLOSE) QUAT
(— DOWN) DOWN LODGED
DORMANT COUCHANT
(— HID) LATITANT
(— IDLE) INACTIVE
(— ON BACK) SUPINE
(— ON FACE) PRONE
(— OVER) JACENT
(— UNDER GRASS) LEA
LYING-IN INLYING CHILDBED
GROANING
LYMPH CHYLE VIRUS
LYMPHAD GALLEY
LYMPHANGITIS WEED FILLING
LYMPHOGRANULOMA BUBO
LYMPHOMATOSIS FISHEYE
LYNCEUS (BROTHER OF —) IDAS
(FATHER OF —) AEGYPTUS
APHAREUS
(WIFE OF —) HYPERMNESTRA
LYNCH HANG DEWITT
LYNX LOSSE PISHU BOBCAT GORKUN
LUCERN CARACAL LUCIVEE
WILDCAT CARCAJOU
LYRE ASOR HARP LYRA SHELL
CHELYS KINNOR KISSAR TRIGON
CITHARA PHORMIX TESTUDO
BARBITON TRICHORD TRIGONON
LYREBIRD LYRETAIL PHEASANT
LYRIC LAY LIED HOKKU MELIC
GHAZEL TENSON CANCION
CHANSON DESCORT MADRIGAL
(LOVE —) ALBA
(PL.) SONG
LYTTA WORM

M EM EMMA MIKE METRO
(**WRONG USE OF —**) MYTACISM
M-1 GARAND
MA'AM MARM MISTRESS
MAARIB ARBIT ARBITH
MACA ENIMAGA
MACABRE SICK HORRIBLE
MACACA PITHECUS
MACADAMIZE METAL
MACAO (CHINESE NAME OF —)
AOMEN
(**ISLAND OF —**) TAIPA COLOANE
MACAQUE KRA BROH BRUH MACAC
MACHIN RHESUS
MACARIA (FATHER OF —) HERCULES
(**MOTHER OF —**) DEIANIRA
MACARONI DITALI
MACARONIC SKEW
MACAW ARA ARARA PARROT
MARACAN ARACANGA COCKATOO
MACE CROC MALL MAUL VERGE
MALLET SPARTH CATTAIL
(**REED —**) DOD DODD
(**ROYAL —**) SCEPTER SCEPTRE
MACE-BEARER BEADLE VERGER
MACEMAN
MACERATE SOUR STEEP
MACHAON (BROTHER OF —)
PODALIRIUS
(**FATHER OF —**) AESCULAPIUS
(**MOTHER OF —**) CORONIS
MACHETE GULOC PARANG CURTAXE
CUTLASH CUTLASS
MACHIAVELLIAN CRAFTY CUNNING
GUILEFUL
MACHINATION ARTIFICE INTRIGUE
SCHEMERY
MACHINE (ALSO SEE DEVICE AND
ENGINE) GIN HOG JIG SAW AGER
COMB GEAR JACK LIFT MULE PUMP
RASP TRAY WHIM WINK ADDER
AWNER BALER BENCH BILLY BOARD
BRAKE BREAK COPER CRANE DEVIL
EDGER FRAME FUDGE FUGAL JENNY
JERRY JOLLY LATHE LAYER METER
MIXER MOWER NAVVY RAKER
RESAW ROVER SCREW SETUP
SHEEN SIZER STAMP SULKY TRONE
VINER WILLY BARKER BEADER
BEAMER BEATER BEETLE BENDER
BILLER BINDER BOLTER BUCKLE
BUMPER BUTTER CANTER CAPPER
CARDER CONCHE COOLER CREWER
DECKER DOFFER DONKEY DRAPER
DREDGE DUSTER ENGINE FLAKER
FOLDER FOOTER FORMER GADDER
GAPPER GLAZER GRADER GRATER
GUMMER HEADER HEMMER HOBBER
HOGGER HOOPER HULLER HUSKER
IRONER JIGGER JORDAN KICKER
LEGGER LIFTER LINTER LOGGER
MAILER MANGLE MILLER MITRER
NAPPER NETTER NIBBER NIPPER
PACKER PEGGER PINNER PLATER
PUMPER RIPPER ROSSER ROTARY
ROUTER SANDER SCUTCH SEALER
SEAMER SHAKER SHAPER SHAVER
SINGER SKIVER SLICER SORTER
SPACER STOCKS STOKER TEDDER

TENTER TWINER VANNER WASHER
WELDER WILLOW ABRADER
AUTOMAT AVIATOR BACKHOE
BATCHER BELLOWS BLENDER
BOTTLER BRANNER BREAKER
CANDROY CAPSTAN CHIPPER
COMBINE CRUSHER DIBBLER
DRESSER EMULSOR ENCODER
ENROBER ERECTOR EXOSTRA
FLANGER FLOSSER FREEZER
GARNETT GLASSER GRAINER
GRINDER GROOVER GROUTER
HUMIDOR IRONMAN JOINTER
KNITTER KNOTTER MACHINA
MANGLER MATCHER MITERER
PLODDER PLUCKER POTCHER
PRINTER QUILLER REPRESS
RIVETER ROASTER SAMMIER
SCALPER SHEARER SHEETER
SIROCCO SLABBER SLASHER
SLITTER SLOTTER SLUBBER
SLUGGER SMASHER SPALLER
SPEEDER SPINNER SPONGER
SPOOLER SPRAYER STACKER
STAMPER STAPLER STEAMER
STEMMER STICKER TENONER
TEREBRA TOOTHER TRAMPER
TREATER TRIMMER TRUSSER
TWILLER TWISTER TYPOBAR
WHIPPER WHIZZER AERIFIER
AIRCRAFT BROACHER CALENDER
CANCELER CARTONER CLINCHER
COLLATOR COMPRESS DUNGBECK
ELEPHANT EXPLODER EXTRUDER
FINISHER FLYWINCH FORKLIFT
GATHERER HARDENER HAYMAKER
HERCULES HUMMELER IMPACTER
KILLIFER MORTISER MOULINET
ODOGRAPH OROGRAPH PROFILER
PULSATOR SCHIFFLI SCUTCHER
SHREDDER SOFTENER SPLITTER
SPREADER SPRIGGER SQUEEZER
STITCHER STRANDER STRIPPER
SURFACER TEMPERER THREADER
THRESHER THROSTLE TRAVELER
TRISPAST TUNNELER UPSETTER
WINNOWER ADDRESSER
MACHINE GUN STINGER CHAUCHAT
MACHINERY MINT TOPCAP SUCCULA
APPARATUS
MACHINE SHOP TURNERY
MACHINIST FRILLER THINNER
MACHINER
MACKEREL CHAD PETO TINK BLINK
OPELU SNOEK TUNNY BONITO
SAUREL TINKER BLINKER BLOATER
TASSARD HARDHEAD SCOMBRID
SEERFISH
(**— ABOUT 8 OR 9 INCHES**) TINK
TINKER
(**PICKLED —**) SCALPEEN
(**POOR BONY —**) SLINK SLINKER
(**YOUNG —**) SPIKE
MACKLE SLUR SHAKE MACULA
MACROSCOPIC GROSS
MACROSPECIES LINNEON
MAD FEY AWAY GITE GYTE HYTE
WOOD YOND ANGRY BRAIN CRAZY
DIPPY FOLLE RABID BEDLAM

FRENZY INSANE MANIAC WOODEN
BERSERK FANATIC FRANTIC
FURIOUS LUNATIC MADDING
MADDOCK MANKIND REDWOOD
WITLESS DELIRANT DEMENTED
DISTRACT INFORMAL MANIACAL
MINDLESS RAVENING
MADAGASCAR (SEE MALAGASY
REPUBLIC)
MADAM MEM MUM BAWD MAAM PANI
DONNA MADAME SENORA SENHORA
SIGNORA GOODWIFE MISTRESS
SINEBADA
MADAR YERCUM
MADDEN ENRAGE INCENSE INFLAME
DISTRACT
MADDENED ENRAGED FRENZIED
MADDER GAMENE LIZARY ALIZARI
GARANCE MUNJEET TANAGRA
GARANCIN SPURWORT WOODRUFF
MAD-DOG SKULLCAP MADWEED
HOODWORT
MADE SET BUILT COMPACT
PREPARED TIMBERED
(**— FLUID BY HEAT**) FUSILE
(**— OF DISSIMILAR PARTS**) MIXED
(**— OF FLAX**) LINEN
(**— OF GRAIN**) OATEN CEREAL
(**— OF IVORY**) EBURNEAN
(**— OF SILVER**) ARGENT
(**— OF STONE**) STONEN
(**— OF TWIGS**) VIRGAL
(**— SHORT**) CURTAL
(**— TART**) EUCHRED
(**— TO ORDER**) BESPOKEN
(**— TRANSLUCENT**) AJOURE
(**— UP**) ACCRETE
(**— WITH CEDAR**) CEDARN
MADE-BEAVER SKIN CASTOR
MADEIRA ISLANDS (ISLAND OF —)
GRANDE DEZERTE
(**TOWN OF —**) FUNCHAL
(**WINE OF —**) BUAL TINTA MALMSEY
SERCIAL VERDELHO
MADELON POLIXENE
MADHOUSE ASYLUM BEDLAM
MADHUCA BASSIA ILLIPE
MADLY WOOD CRAZY
MADMAN BEDLAM MANIAC FURIOSO
LUNATIC WOODMAN
MADNESS MAD FURY MOON WOOD
FOLLY FUROR MANIA BEDLAM
FRENZY LUNACY DEWANEE
ECSTASY MOONERY WIDDRIM
DELIRIUM DEMENTIA PIBLOKTO
WILLNESS WOODNESS WOODSHIP
MADONNA LADY VIRGIN
MADREPORE FUNGID
MADRIGAL ENSALADA
MADRONA LAUREL MANZANITA
MADTOM TADPOLE
MADWORT BUGLOSS
MAENAD FROW BASSARID
BACCHANTE
(**PL.**) BACCHAE
MAFIC FEMIC
MAFURA ROKA ELCAJA
MAGANI BAGANI
MAGAZINE BOOK DRUM FLAT IGLOO

SLICK STORE RETORT ALMACEN
JOURNAL CASSETTE
(BLACKWOOD'S —) MAGA
MAGDALEN MAUDLIN
MAGGOT MAD GRUB MAWK WORM
METHE GENTLE WARBLE WORMIL
MADDOCK SKIPPER MUCKWORM
MAGIC JUJU MAYA RUNE CRAFT
FAIRY GOETY SPELL TURGY GOETIC
TREGET VOODOO ALCHEMY
CANTRIP CONJURY DEVILRY
GLAMOUR GRAMARY MAGICAL
SORCERY BRUJERIA HECATEAN
WIZARDRY
(BLACK —) GOETY GOETIC
MALEFICE
(WHITE —) TURGY
MAGICAL WIZARD WONDER
HERMETIC NUMINOUS THEURGIC
MAGICIAN MAGE BOKOR MAGUS
UTHER CUNJAH GOETIC GOOFER
GUFFER MAGIAN MERLIN WABENO
WIZARD CHARMER GWYDION
KOSCHEI WIELARE WISEMAN
CONJURER FETISHER SORCERER
THEURGIC TROLLMAN
MAGISTERIAL LOFTY PROUD
AUGUST LORDLY HAUGHTY
STATELY ARROGANT DOGMATIC
MAGISTERY MASTERY
MAGISTRACY AMT PRYTANY
MAGISTRATE BEAK FOUD EPHOR
JUDGE JURAT MAYOR PRIOR REEVE
AMTMAN ARCHON AVOYER BAILIE
CENSOR CONSUL FISCAL KOTWAL
SYNDIC BAILIFF BURGESS DUUMVIR
ECHEVIN EPHORUS JUSTICE
NOMARCH PODESTA PRAETOR
PREFECT PROVOST STEWARD
SUFFETE TRIBUNE ALABARCH
ALDERMAN CAPITOUL DEFENSOR
DEMIURGE DICTATOR GOVERNOR
MITTIMUS PHYLARCH PRYTANIS
RECORDER STRADICO STRATEGE
HUNDREDER
(— IN CHANNEL ISLANDS) JURAT
(— OF ANCIENT ROME) EDILE
(— OF VENICE AND GENOA) DOGE
(MOHAMMEDAN —) CADI CADY
(SCOTCH —) STEWARD
MAGMA ICHOR
MAGMATIC JUVENILE
MAGNANIMITY HEIGHT FREEDOM
MAGNANIMOUS BIG FREE GREAT
LARGE LOFTY NOBLE HEROIC
EXALTED GENEROUS
MAGNATE MOGUL BASHAW TYCOON
MAGNESIA PULVIL
MAGNET FIELD ADAMAS MAGNES
ADAMANT SOLENOID TERRELLA
MAGNETISM IT DEVIL
MAGNETITE LOADSTONE
LODESTONE
MAGNETIZE TOUCH SATURATE
MAGNETOMETER DOODLEBUG
MAGNIFICENCE GITE POMP FLARE
GLORY STATE PARADE JOLLITY
ROYALTY GRANDEUR SPLENDOR
MAGNIFICENT RIAL GRAND NOBLE

ROYAL AUGUST LAVISH IMMENSE
STATELY SUBLIME GLORIOUS
GORGEOUS MAGNIFIC PALATIAL
PRINCELY SPLENDID
MAGNIFY LAUD ERECT EXALT
PRAISE ADVANCE DISTEND ENLARGE
GLORIFY GREATEN INCREASE
MAXIMIZE MULTIPLY
MAGNIFYING GLASS LOUPE
READER
MAGNILOQUENT TURGID BOMBAST
MAGNITUDE BULK MASS SIZE
DATUM LEVEL SOLID EXTENT
FIGURE PERIOD EXTREME
CONSTANT FUNCTION INFINITE
MAGNOLIA YULAN BIGBLOOM
CUCUMBER MAURICIO
(— STATE) MISSISSIPPI
MAGPIE MAG PIE PIET PYAT CISSA
KOTRI MADGE NINUT MARGET
NANPIE PIANET PIEMAG SIRGANG
HAGISTER MARGARET PHEASANT
PIENANNY
MAGPIE LARK PEEWEE GRALLINA
MAGPIE ROBIN DAYAL DHYAL
MAGUEY MESCAL CANTALA
MAGYAR SZEKEL SZEKLER
MAHATMA ARHAT
MAH-JONGG WOO
MAHOE EMAJAGUA
MAHOGANY SIPO ALMON CAOBA
CEDAR ACAJOU AGUANO SAPELE
THITKA ALBARCO AVODIRE
BAYWOOD GUNNUNG MADEIRA
RATTEEN TABASCO BANGALAY
HARDTACK TANGUILE
(INDIAN —) TOON
(PHILIPPINE —) BAGTIKAN
MAHONIA ASHBERRY ODOSTEMON
MAHOUND MACON
MAHUA FULWA MOWHA MOWRA
MADHUCA PHULWARA
MAHUANG EPHEDRA
MAIA (FATHER OF —) ATLAS
(MOTHER OF —) PLEIONE
(SON OF —) MERCURY
MAID AYAH GIRL MEDE SLUT CHINA
WENCH WOMAN MAIDEN SLAVEY
TWEENY VIRGIN ANCILLA GENERAL
MAIDKIN PHYLLIS PUCELLE
WENCHEL BRANGANE HANDMAID
SUIVANTE TIREMAID
(— IN WAITING) DAMSEL DAMOZEL
(— OF HONOR) MARIE
(— OF-ALL-WORK) SLAVEY GENERAL
(KITCHEN —) SCOGIE
(LADY'S —) AYAH TIREMAID
(NURSE —) BONNE
(OLD —) TABBY SPINSTER
(WAITING —) ABIGAIL SUIVANTE
MAIDEN MAY BIRD DAME GIRL MAID
DALAGA DAMSEL FROKIN MEISJE
COLLEEN CYDIPPE DAMOZEL
MADCHEN DAUGHTER
(— WITH BASKET ON HEAD)
CANEPHOR
MAIDENHAIR GINGKO ADIANTUM
MAIDENLY VIRGIN GIRLISH VIRGINAL
MAIDEN PINK SPINK DIANTHUS

MAIDSERVANT LASS BIDDY BONNE
ANCILLA LISETTE
MAIEUTIC HEBAMIC
MAIGRE BAR SCIAENID WEAKFISH
MAIL BAG DAK HOOD POST MATTER
AIRMAIL JACKPOT MAILBAG
ORDINAR POSTAGE POSTBAG
SEAPOST TAPPALL ORDINARY
(IMPROPERLY ADDRESSED —) NIX
NIXY
MAIN LINE MOST SHEER MIGHTY
MAILBAG BAG POUCH POSTBAG
MAILBOX POST PILLAR POSTBOX
MAILLECHORT ARGENTON
MAILLOT SWIMSUIT
MAILMAN POSTMAN BREVIGER
MAIM LAME BREAK TRUNK HAMBLE
MANGLE MAYHEM CRIPPLE
MUTILATE
(— AN ANIMAL) LAW MANK
MAIMED SPAVINED
MAIN HIGH CHIEF GRAND GREAT
PRIME CAPITAL LEADING FOREMOST

MAINE
CAPITAL: AUGUSTA
COLLEGE: BATES COLBY
BOWDOIN
COUNTY: KNOX WALDO KENNEBEC
AROOSTOOK
INDIAN: ABNAKI
LAKE: SEBEC SEBAGO RANGELEY
SCHOODIC MOOSEHEAD
MOUNTAIN: BIGELOW CADILLAC
KATAHDIN
NATIVE: MANIAC
RIVER: SACO KENNEBEC
AROOSTOOK KENNEBAGO
PENOBSCOT
STATE BIRD: CHICKADEE
STATE FLOWER: PINECONE
STATE NICKNAME: PINETREE
STATE TREE: PINE
TOWN: ORONO BANGOR KITTERY
BOOTHBAY OGUNQUIT
PORTLAND

MAINLY BROADLY CHIEFLY
MAINSTAY KEY ATLAS SINEW STOOP
PILLAR BACKBONE RELIANCE
MAINTAIN BEAR FEND FIND HOLD
KEEP LAST SAVE ADOPT ARGUE
CARRY CLAIM ESCOT SALVE
ADHERE ALLEGE ASSERT AVOUCH
DEFEND INTEND RETAIN THREAP
UPHOLD UPKEEP CONFIRM
CONTEND DECLARE DISPUTE
JUSTIFY NOURISH SUBSIST
SUPPORT SUSTAIN CONTINUE
PRESERVE
(— AS TRUE) AVOUCH SOOTHE
(— POSITION) STALL
(— WITHOUT REASON) ARROGATE
MAINTAINER FOUNDER RETAINER
MAINTENANCE KEEP LIVING
UPKEEP ALIMONY CUSTODY FINDING
KEEPING PREBEND SERVICE
(— OF POPULATION) BALANCE

MAITHILI TIRHUTIA
MAIZE CORN GRAIN CEREAL INDIAN
JAGONG STAPLE MEALIES
DJAGOONG
(— **CRUSHED WITH PESTLE**) STAMP
MAJAGUA HAU BARU BOLA MAHO
MOJO BURAO GUANA MAHOE
PURAU BALIBAGO CORKWOOD
EMAJAGUA
MAJESTIC HIGH GRAND LOFTY
REGAL ROYAL AUGUST KINGLY
SUPERB STATELY SUBLIME
ELEVATED IMPERIAL MAESTOSO
SPLENDID
MAJESTY DIGNITY AUGUSTUS
GRANDEUR KINGSHIP
MAJOON BANG BHANG
MAJOR DUR DURUM SHARP CAPITAL
GREATER MAGGIORE
MAJORITY BODY BULK FECK
CORPSE SUBSTANCE
(**ABSOLUTE —**) QUORUM
MAKARAKA IDDIO
MAKARI KOTOKO
MAKE DO CUT GAR LET MAY FORM
GIVE LEVY BRAND BUILD CAUSE
COVER FETCH FORGE FRAME SEIZE
SHAPE STAMP AUTHOR COBBLE
CREATE GRAITH INDUCE RENDER
CONFECT FASHION IMAGERY
IWURCHE PERFORM PRODUCE
CONTRIVE GENERATE
(— **A DIFFERENCE**) SKILL
(— **A MESS OF**) PIE
(— **A RUG**) HOOK
(— **A VISIT**) COSHER
(— **ACKNOWLEDGMENT**) CONFESS
(— **ACTIVE**) ENERGIZE
(— **AMENDS**) ABYE ATONE ABEGGE
ANSWER REDEEM EXPIATE REDRESS
(— **ANGRY**) GRAMY WRATH
(— **ATTRACTIVE**) GILD
(— **AWAY WITH**) ABOLISH EMBEZZLE
(— **BARE**) STRIP DENUDE
(— **BELIEVE**) LET PRETEND
(— **BETTER**) AMEND HEIGHTEN
(— **BLUE**) HIP
(— **BRIGHT**) ENGILD ILLUME
CLARIFY
(— **BRISK**) PERK
(— **BROWN**) TAN
(— **BY STAMPING**) MINT
(— **CANDLE**) DIP DRAW
(— **CERTAIN**) ASSURE ENSURE
(— **CHANNEL IN**) THROAT
(— **CHEERFUL**) SOLACE
(— **CHOICE**) OPT CHOOSE SELECT
(— **CLAMMY**) ENGLEIM
(— **CLEAR**) DECLARE DEVELOP
DISCUSS EXHIBIT EXPOUND LIGHTEN
DESCRIBE
(— **COLD**) REFREID
(— **COMPLETE**) SPHERE
(— **CONSPICUOUS**) ENNOBLE
(— **CONTENT**) SATISFY
(— **CULTIVABLE**) EMPOLDER
(— **CUT PRIOR TO LAYERING**)
TONGUE
(— **DESTITUTE**) BEREAVE

(— **DIFFERENT**) ALTER CHANGE
(— **DIRTY**) MOIL GRIME
(— **DISPLAY OF**) AFFECT DISCOVER
(— **DRUNK**) FOX SOUSE FUDDLE
SOZZLE
(— **DRY**) HAZLE HAZZLE
(— **EARLIER**) ADVANCE
(— **EFFERVESCENT**) AERATE
(— **EFFIGY**) GUY
(— **END OF**) SNIB FETCH
(— **ENDURING**) ANNEAL
(— **EQUAL**) WEIGH EQUATE
(— **EVEN**) GLAZE LEVEL WEIGH
SQUARE
(— **FACES**) GIMBLE MURGEON
(— **FALSE PRETENSES**) SHAM
(— **FAST**) FIX BAIL FAST GIRD KNIT
MAKE STOP BELAY HITCH BUCKLE
FASTEN SECURE
(— **FAT**) BATTEN
(— **FIRM**) FIX BRACE FASTEN
(— **FIT**) APTATE STRIKE
(— **FOOL OF**) DOR BORE DOLT
DORRE BEGOWK DOODLE
(— **FOOLISH**) DAFF GREEN NUGIFY
STULTIFY
(— **FOOTSORE**) SURBATE
(— **FROTHY**) MILL
(— **FULL**) FARCE FULFILL
(— **FUN OF**) GUY KID GAFF JEST
JOSH DROLL GLAIK SCOUT SMOKE
(— **FUSS OVER NOTHING**) FAFF
(— **GLAD**) FAIN
(— **GLASS**) FOUND
(— **GLOSSY**) SLEEK
(— **GLOW**) FURNACE
(— **GOLDEN**) ENDORE
(— **GRINDING NOISE**) GRINCH
(— **GURGLING SOUND**) CROOL
(— **HAPPY**) BLESS ENJOY REFORM
BEATIFY SATISFY FELICIFY
(— **HARD**) TAW STEEL ENDURE
HORNIFY
(— **HARDY**) FASTEN
(— **HEADWAY**) STEM WALK
ENFORCE
(— **HELPLESS**) STAGGER
(— **HOLY**) BLESS SACRE HALLOW
SANCTIFY
(— **HORSE SEEM YOUNGER**) BISHOP
(— **ILL**) MORBIFY
(— **IMMOBILE**) FREEZE
(— **IMPACT**) ASSAIL
(— **INCURSION**) HARRY
(— **INSIGNIFICANT**) MICRIFY
(— **INTO BUNDLE**) FARDEL
(— **INTO LAW**) ENACT
(— **INVALID**) DAMASK
(— **JOINT**) SYPHER
(— **KNOWN**) BID OUT GIVE WISE
AREAD BEKEN BREAK KITHE SOUND
SPEAK BEWRAY BROACH COUTHE
DENOTE DESCRY EXPOSE INFORM
REVEAL SPREAD CONFESS DECLARE
DELIVER DIVULGE PUBLISH SIGNIFY
UNCOVER ANNOUNCE DECIPHER
DISCLOSE DISCOVER INDICATE
PROCLAIM PROMULGE
(— **LESS DENSE**) THIN RAREFY

(— **LESS SEVERE**) MITIGATE
(— **LIABLE**) DANGER
(— **LOVE**) WOO COURT SPOON
GALLANT
(— **LUKEWARM**) WLECCHE
(— **LUSTERLESS**) FLATTEN
(— **MANIFEST**) EVINCE EXPLAIN
(— **MELANCHOLY**) HYP
(— **MELODIOUS**) ATTUNE
(— **MELODY**) DREAM
(— **MENTION**) SPEAK
(— **MERRY**) JET GAUD CHEER
SPORT FROLIC SHROVE DISPORT
REHAYTE
(— **METALLIC SOUND**) CHINK
(— **MISTAKE**) ERR BOOB GOOF
(— **MONOTONOUS NOISE**) DRONE
(— **MORAL**) ETHICIZE
(— **MUCH OF**) DAWT DANDLE
(— **MURMURING NOISE**) BUM
(— **NEAT**) FEAT SMUG TIDY GROOM
(— **NEST**) TIMBER
(— **NONMAGNETIC**) DEGAUSS
(— **NUMB**) DAZE ETHERIZE
(— **OFF**) BAG BOLT HOOK ANNEX
HEIST SPIRIT SCARPER
(— **ONE'S WAY**) AIRT BORE TRADE
(— **ONE**) UNE
(— **OPEN**) AIR PATEFY
(— **OUT**) FARE FILL GLEAN SKILL
DISCERN DECIPHER
(— **OVER**) TURN ALIEN CHANGE
RECOCT DELIVER REFORGE
(— **PALE**) CHALK
(— **PLEASANT**) SWEETEN
(— **POIGNANT**) SAUCE
(— **PREGNANT**) ENWOMB
(— **PROGRESS**) GAIN STEM GATHER
(— **PROUD**) WLENCH
(— **PUBLIC**) BLOW BLAZE BREAK
BLAZON DELATE DIVULGE FANFARE
PUBLISH BULLETIN
(— **QUIET**) ALLAY QUIET APPEASE
(— **RATTLING NOISE**) TIRL
(— **READY**) DO BUN GET BOWN
BUSK YARK BELAY DRESS PREST
PRIME FETTLE GRAITH ADDRESS
APPAREL DISPOSE PREPARE
(— **RECORD OF**) REFER
(— **REFERENCE**) MENTION
(— **RESISTANCE**) REBEL
(— **RESOLUTE**) STEEL
(— **RETURN FOR**) REQUITE
(— **RICH**) FREIGHT IMBURSE
(— **ROSY**) FLUSH
(— **RUSTLING SOUND**) FISSLE
FISTLE
(— **RUTTING CRY**) FREAM
(— **SCANTY LIVING**) EKE
(— **SERIES OF NOTES**) TINKLE
(— **SHIFT**) SCAMBLE
(— **SIGN OF CROSS**) BLESS
(— **SMALL**) MICRIFY BELITTLE
(— **SMALLER**) MINIFY COMPRESS
(— **SMOOTH**) SLAB GLAZE SLEEK
GENTLE HAMMER SCRAPE LEVIGATE
(— **SOFT**) NESH GENTLE
(— **SOGGY**) SOP
(— **SOUR**) FOX WIND

(— **SPIRITLESS**) MOPE
(— **SPORT OF**) LARK
(— **SPRUCE**) PERK SMARTEN
(— **STRAIGHT**) ADDRESS
(— **STRONG**) STEEL FASTEN
FORTIFY
(— **STUPID**) MOIDER STULTIFY
(— **SUITABLE**) ADAPT
(— **SURE**) SEE INSURE
(— **TIPSY**) FLUSTER
(— **TRANSITION TO**) MODULATE
(— **UP ACCOUNTS**) BREVE
(— **UP**) UP COOK FORM SPELL
INDITE SETTLE ANALYZE COMPACT
COMPOSE COMPUTE CONCOCT
CONFECT FASHION COMPOUND
COMPRISE DISPENSE
(— **USE OF**) FEE BUSK APPLY AVAIL
BROOK SERVE SPEND EMPLOY
EXECUTE IMPROVE UTILIZE
(— **VIBRANT SOUND**) CHIRR
(— **VOID**) ABATE ANNUL
(— **WAR**) WARRAY
(— **WET**) DRAGGLE
(— **WHISTLING NOISE**) WHEW
(— **WHITE**) BLANCH BLEACH
CANDIFY
(— **WORSE**) IMPAIR PEJORATE
MAKE-BELIEVE BORAK DUMMY
ASSUMED
MAKER DOER JACK KNAVE SMITH
FACTOR FORGER FORMER WORKER
CREATOR DECLARER OPERATOR
(— **OF ARROWS**) FLETCHER
(— **OF BARRELS**) COOPER
(— **OF POTS**) POTTER
(— **OF SADDLETREES**) FUSTER
(— **OF SONGS**) BULBUL
(— **OF TALLOW**) CHANDLER
MAKESHIFT JURY RUDE JERRY
TOUSY BEWITH KUTCHA APOLOGY
JACKLEG STOPGAP
MAKEUP FACE BUILD GETUP HABIT
SETUP SHAPE FACIES FORMAT
ANATOMY CONSIST FEATURE
TRAVESTY
MAKING FACT
MALABAR BAY
MALABAR ALMOND KAMANI
ALMENDRO
MALACEAE POMACEAE PYRACEAE
MALADJUSTMENT SCAR
MALADROIT ILL AWKWARD
UNHANDY BUNGLING
MALADY AMOK EVIL MORB CAUSE
GRIEF ONCOME AILMENT DISEASE
ILLNESS DISORDER MISCHIEF
SICKNESS
MALAGASAY LEMURIAN

MALAGASY REPUBLIC
ALTERNATE NAME: MADAGASCAR
CAPITAL: TANANARIVE
ISLAND GROUP: ALDABRA
LAKE: ALAOTRA
MEASURE: GANTANG
NATIVE: HOVA SAKALAVA
PEOPLE: HOVA COTIER MARINA

RIVER: IKOPA MANIA SOFIA
MANGOKY MANGORO ONYLAHY
TOWN: TULEAR MAJANGA
NOSSIBE TAMATAVE ANTISIRABE

MALAPROPISM SLIPSLOP
MALAR JUGAL
MALARIA MIASMA SHAKES PALUDISM
(— **PARASITE**) VIVAX
MALARIAL PALUDOSE PALUDOUS

MALAWI
CAPITAL: ZOMBA
COIN: KWACHA
FORMER NAME: NYASALAND
HIGHLANDS: SHIRE
LAKE: NYASA
LANGUAGE: YAO CEWA NGONI
TONGA NYANJA TUMBUKA
MOUNTAIN: MLANJE
PEOPLE: YAO BANTU CHEWA
NGURU NYANJA
TOWN: MZUZU BLANTYRE
LILONGWE
VALLEY: RIFT

MALAY AMOK ASIL AMUCK BAJAU
ILOCO JAKUN MANOBO ILOKANO
MALAYAN (— **TREE**) TERAP
MALAY APPLE OHIA JAMBO KAVIKA

MALAYSIA
CAPITAL: KUALALUMPUR
COIN: TRA TRAH
ISLAND: ARU GOA KAI OBI OMA
ALOR BALI GAGA JAVA MUNA
MURU SUL0 AMBON BANDA
BOHOL BUTON CERAM LUZON
MISOL PANAY SANGI SUMBA
TIMOR WETAR BANGKA BOEFON
BOEROE BORNEO BUTUNG
FLORES LOMBOK MADURA
PELENG SANGIR TALAUR
WAIGEU AMBOINA CELEBES
JAMDENA MINDORO MOROTAI
PALAWAN SALAJAR SALWATI
SUMATRA SUMBAWA BELITONG
DJAILOLO TANIMBAR
ISTHMUS: KRA
LANGUAGE: TAGALOG
MOUNTAIN: BULU NIUT RAJA
MURJO NIAPA LEUSER SLAMET
BINAIJA RINDJANI
PEOPLE: ATA BAJAU SEMANG
BISAYAN TAGALOG VISAYAN
RIVER: KUTAI PERAK BARITO
PAHANG
TOWN: DAVAO ILOILO KUPANG
MANADO KUCHING MALACCA
SANDAKAN
WEIGHT: TAEL WANG TAMPANG

MALCONTENT FRONDEUR
MALE HE DOG HIM MAN BUCK BULL
COCK JACK ADULT MANLY SPEAR
JOHNNY MANFUL MASCLE VIRILE

LALAQUI MANKIND MANLIKE
MANNISH PURUSHA
(— **OF ANIMALS**) TOM BUCK BULL
JACK STUD STALLION
(**GELDED** —) GALT
(**YOUNG** —) GROOM
MALECITE ETCHEMIN
MALEDICTION BAN WISH CURSE
MALISON ANATHEMA
MALEFACTOR BADDY FELON
BADDIE CULPRIT CRIMINAL
EVILDOER
MALEFIC TAKING
MALEFICENT BALEFUL
MALEO MEGAPOD
MALE ORCHIS CUCKOO CROWTOE
CULLION PURPLES RAGWORT
CROWFOOT
MALEVOLENCE SPITE ENMITY
GRUDGE HATRED MALICE RANCOR
SPLEEN
MALEVOLENT ILL EVIL FELL MALIGN
HATEFUL HOSTILE SPITEFUL
MALFORMATION CURL ERROR
HEMITERY
(— **OF CARNATION**) TWITTER
(— **OF FRUIT**) CATFACE
MALFORMED SHAMBLE

MALI
ANCIENT CITY: TIMBUKTU
CAPITAL: BAMAKO
LAKE: DO DEBO GAROU KORAROU
LANGUAGE: DOGON DYULA
MANDE MARKA PEULH BAMBARA
MALINKE SENOUFO SONGHAI
MOUNTAIN: MINA MANDING
PEOPLE: MOOR PEUL TUAREG
BAMBARA MALINKE SONGHAI
SENOULFO
RIVER: BANI BAGOE BAKOY NIGER
BAOULE AZAOUAK SENEGAL
TOWN: GAO SAN KAYES MOPTI
SEGOU SIKASSO

MALICE DOLE ENVY HAIN PIQUE
SPITE VENOM VIRUS ENMITY
GRUDGE RANCOR SPLEEN DESPITE
AMBITION
MALICIOUS SHREW TEENY BITTER
DOGGED MALIGN WANTON HATEFUL
HEINOUS LEERING SPITOUS
CANKERED SINISTER SPITEFUL
VENOMOUS
MALIGN ILL FOUL ABUSE LIBEL
WRONG BEWRAY DEFAME VILIFY
ASPERSE DEPRAVE HURTFUL
SLANDER
MALIGNANCY FEROCITY
MALIGNANT EVIL ATTRY FELON
FERAL SWART ATTERY MALIGN
ENVIOUS HATEFUL HELLISH PEEVISH
REPTILE VICIOUS WARLOCK
SHREWISH SPITEFUL VENOMOUS
VIPEROUS VIRULENT WRATHFUL
MALIGNITY LIVER VENOM VIRUS
HATRED MALICE RANCOR DESPITE
MALINGER DODGE SKULK
MALINGERER SCONCER

MALL WALK ALLEE
MALLARD TWISTER
(FLOCK OF —S) SORD SUTE
PADDLING
MALLEABLE MILD SOFT DUCTILE
BATTABLE
MALLEIN MORVIN
MALLEMUCK MOLLIE MALMARSH
MALLET MALL MAUL MELL GAVEL
BEATER BEETLE DRIVER HAMMER
DRESSER FLOGGER STRIKER
PLOWMELL
(— FOR BREAKING CLODS) BILDER
(CURRIER'S —) MACE
(HATTER'S —) BEATER
(PAVER'S —) TUP
MALLEUS HAMMER OSSICLE
PLECTRUM
MALLOW MAW DOCK HOCK ALTEA
KOKIO MALVA MAUVE CHEESE
ESCOBA GEMAUVE ABUTILON
PIEPRINT
MALMSEY MALVASIA
MALNUTRITION CACHEXY CACHEXIA
MALODOROUS GAMY HIGH NOSY
FETID SMELLY VIROSE VIROUS
MALT WORT
(GROUND —) GRIST
(REMAINS OF —) DRAFF
MALTASE GLUCASE
MALTHA BREA
MALTHOUSE MALTING
MALTOSE AMYLON
MALTREAT ABUSE DIGHT DEFOUL
DEMEAN HESPIL HUSPEL MISUSE
THREAT BEDEVIL MISGUIDE
MALTREATMENT ABUSE
MALVA DOCK MALLOW
MAMAMU MU
MAMBA COBRA ELAPOID
MAMMA MA MOM MAMA WIFE
MOMMA WOMAN MOTHER
MAMMAL OX ASS BAT CAT COW
DOG FOX PIG YAK BEAR BOAR
COON DEER GOAT HARE LION LYNX
MINK MOLE PUMA SEAL ZEBU
BEAST BISON CAMEL COATI COYPU
GENET HORSE HYENA LEMUR
LLAMA MOOSE OKAPI OTTER PANDA
RATEL SABLE SHEEP SHREW SKUNK
SLOTH SWINE TAPIR TIGER WHALE
ZORIL ALPACA ANIMAL BADGER
COUGAR CULPEO DESMAN DUGONG
FISHER FOUSSA GOPHER GRISON
JAGUAR MARTEN MONKEY OCELOT
TENREC VICUNA WALRUS WOMBAT
BUFFALO CARIBOU DOLPHIN
ECHIDNA GIRAFFE GLUTTON
GUANACO HIPPOID HUANACO
MANATEE OPPOSUM PECCARY
POLECAT PRIMATE RACCOON
SUCKLER SURICAT TARSIER
TYLOPOD WILDCAT ANTELOPE
BANXRING CACOMIXL CREODONT
ELEPHANT FALANAKA HEDGEHOG
KINKAJOU MAMMIFER PANGOLIN
REINDEER SQUIRREL
MAMMALIA MASTOZOA
MAMMEE ABRICO ABRICOT

MAMMILLA PAP TEAT NIPPLE
MAMMOTH HUGE LARGE GIGANTIC
MAN BO HE BOY GEE GUY HIM LAD
TAO WAT WER BUCK CHAL CHAP
COVE DICK EARL GENT GOME
HOMO JACK JONG MALE RINK TULK
BERNE BIMBO BIPED BLOKE CHURL
COVEY FORCE FREKE GROOM
GUEST HEART HOMME HORSE
JOKER SEGGE SWAIN WIGHT
BIMANE FELLOW HOMBRE MANTZU
WEPMAN BIMANUS HOMONID
KINSMAN MANKIND
(— AFFECTING FOREIGN WAYS)
MACARONI
(— DRESSED AS WOMAN) MALINCHE
(— IN DEBT) DYVOUR
(— IN PRIVATE STATION) IDIOT
(— IN TUG-OF-WAR) ANCHOR
(— LEADING 12TH NIGHT) BEAN
(— OF ALL WORK) MOZO
(— OF AUTHORITY) AGHA SEIGNIOR
(— OF BEAUTY) APOLLO
(— OF BRASS) TALOS
(— OF GREAT WEALTH) NABOB
(— OF HIGH RANK) CHAM KHAN
THAKUR GRANDEE
(— OF SUBSTANCE) IDLEMAN
(— OF THE COMMON PEOPLE) JACK
(— OF VIGOR) WYE
(— OF VIOLENCE) RABIATOR
(— OF WAR) ANDREW CARAVEL
CRUISER
(— TO MAN) SINGLE
(ARTIFICIAL —) GOLEM
(BACKGAMMON —) BLOT BUILDER
(BALD —) PILGARLIC
(BEST —) BRIDEMAN
(BIG —) COB BRUISER MUGWUMP
(BRISK —) SPARK
(CASTRATED —) SPADO EUNUCH
(CHIEF —) FOREMAN OPTIMATE
(CHURLISH —) NABAL BODACH
(CLEANING —) BUSBOY
(COMMON —) CARL STREET
YEOMAN
(COVETOUS —) HUNKS
(CRAFTY —) FOX
(CRUEL —) OGRE BRUTE
(DISAGREEABLE —) GLEYDE
(DISLIKED —) CUT
(DISSOLUTE —) RAKE
(ECCENTRIC —) GEEZER
(EDUCATED —) EFFENDI
(EFFEMINATE —) DILDO FAIRY SISSY
COCKNEY MEACOCK MIDWIFE
MILKSOP ANDROGYN
(END —) BONES BRAKE
(ENLISTED —) GI SNIPE AIDMAN
AIRMAN KEEPER STORES ARMORER
STRIKER SONARMAN
(ENTIRE —) EGO
(EXTINCT —) TEPEXPAN
(FAITHFUL —) TRUEMAN
(FANCY —) PONCE
(FASHIONABLE —) TOUPET
ELEGANT FOPLING GALLANT
(FIRST —) ASK ADAM ASKR TIKI
FOREMAN

(FOPPISH —) BLOOD
(FREE —) LIBER
(GRAY-HAIRED —) GRIZZLE
(GREAT —) VAVASOR
(HARDHEARTED —) KNARK
(HOLDUP —) FOOTPAD
(HOLY —) SADHU SAINT SANNYASI
(HONORS —) WRANGLER
(IDEAL —) SUPERMAN
(IMMORAL —) REP
(INEFFECTUAL —) DUFFER
(INSANE —) FURIOSO
(LADY'S —) FOPLING DAMMARET
(LAME —) BACACH
(LEARNED —) ULEMA LAMDAN
OLLAMH PUNDIT SAVANT SOPHIST
(LECHEROUS —) SATYR
(LEWD —) BROTHEL
(LIAISON —) COURIER
(LITERARY —) GIGADIBS
(LITTLE —) MANNET SHRIMP
MANNIKIN
(LUSTFUL —) GOAT
(MAINTENANCE —) CAMPMAN
(MARRIED —) HUSBAND BENEDICT
(MEDICINE —) PEAI DOCTOR
SHAMAN ANGAKOK
(MEEK —) MOSES
(MIGHTY —) SAMSON
(ODD-JOB —) JOEY
(OLD —) HAG OLD BOOL CUFF GAFF
CRONE DOBBY UNCLE BODACH
DUFFER FATHER GAFFER NESTOR
GERONTE STARETS ECKEHART
VELYARDE
(OLD-CLOTHES —) POCO
(ONE-ARMED —) WINGY
(ONE-EYED —) ARIMASP
(OVERFASTIDIOUS —) DUDE
(PARTY —) SIDESMAN
(PRIMITIVE —) URMENSCH
(PRINCIPAL —) HERO TOPARCH
(RASH —) HOTSPUR
(RICH —) DIVES CROESUS
(RIGHT-HAND —) HENCHMAN
(RIGHTEOUS —) SADDIK
(SERVING —) GARCON
(SOUND-EFFECTS —) CRAWK
(STERN —) GRIMSIRE
(STRAIGHT —) STOOGE
(STRONG —) KWASIND
(STRONG-ARM —) HOOD GORILLA
(STUPID —) SUBMAN
(THICKSET —) GRUB KNAR SPUD
(TOUGH —) KNAR
(UNEMPLOYED —) BATLAN
(UTILITY —) JUMPER
(VICIOUS —) YAHOO
(WHITE — LIVING WITH ABORIGINE)
COMBO
(WHITE —) BOSTON BUCKRA
CACHILA
(WILD —) WOODMAN WOODWOSE
(WISE —) NAB HAKAM SABIO SOLON
SOPHY NESTOR WIZARD SOLOMON
TOHUNGA
(WIZENED —) GNOME
(WRETCHED —) CAITIFF
(YOUNG —) BOY LAD JONG YOUTH

BOCHUR DAMSEL EPHEBE KNIGHT
BOUCHAL BUCKEEN YOUNKER
SPRINGAL
MANABOZHO MICHABOU WINABOJO
MAN-ABOUT-TOWN FLANEUR
MANACLE BAND BOND DARBY
HAMPER TIRRET SHACKLE
HANDCUFF HANDLOCK
(PL.) IRONS CHAINS
MANAGE DO GET MAN RUN BEAR
CURB FEND HACK HOLD KEEP LEAD
MAKE RULE TEND TOOL WIND
WORK BROOK CARRY DIGHT FORTH
FRAME GUIDE MAYNE ORDER SHIFT
SPEND STEER SWING WIELD
CONVEY DEMEAN DEVISE DIRECT
FETTLE GOVERN HANDLE INTEND
MANURE TEMPER AGITATE
CONDUCT DISPOSE EXECUTE
FINAGLE HUSBAND MINSTER
OFFICER OPERATE SOLICIT
STEWARD CONTRIVE ENGINEER
(— AWKWARDLY) FOOZLE
(— CLUMSILY) KEVEL
(— TO BEAR) AFFORD
MANAGEABLE EASY YARE BANTAM
DOCILE WIELDY DUCTILE FLEXIBLE
YIELDING
MANAGEMENT CARE HEEL WORK
CHARGE CONDUCT CONTROL
ECONOMY GESTION RUNNING
CARRIAGE DEMEANOR ENGINERY
MANAGERY MANEUVER REGIMENT
STEERAGE STEERING
(DOMESTIC —) MENAGE
HUSBANDRY
(GOOD —) EUTAXY
(SKILLFUL —) PRACTICE PRACTISE
MANAGER BOSS DOER AGENT
DAROGA DEPUTY PURSER SYNDIC
CURATOR HUSBAND STEWARD
WIELDER AUMILDAR DIRECTOR
DISPOSER ENGINEER HERENACH
INSTITOR
(— OF FARM) HIND GRIEVE
(ASSISTANT —) CAPORAL
(MINE —) CAPTAIN
(POLITICAL —) FUGLEMAN
MANAKIN PIPRA
MAN-AT-ARMS KNIGHT
MANATEE COWFISH HOGFISH
MERMAID LAMANTIN MUTILATE
SIRENIAN
MANBARKLAK JARANA KAKARAL
MANCALA WARI
MANCHU SHERRY
MANDAEAN SABAEAN
MANDARIN TOWKAY CHINESE
MANDARIN ORANGE SATSUMA
MANDATE BREVE ORDER BEHEST
CHARGE DECREE FIRMAN BIDDING
COMMAND PRECEPT PROCESS
MANDAMUS MANDATUM WARRANTY
(— OF GOD) JUDGMENT
MANDIBLE JOWL SETA JAWBONE
GNATHITE
(— PART) MALA
MANDINGO MANDE WANGARA
MANDOLIN OUD MANDORA

MANDRAKE ALRAUN DUDAIM
MANDREL BALL STUD SLEEVE
CHEMISE SPINDLE TRIBLET
MANDRILL MAIMON MORMON
MANE JUBA MONE CREST PITRI
MAN-EATER REQUIN REQUIEM
MANEGE TRAIN
MANEUVER PLAY TURN WISE
GAMBIT JOCKEY MANURE PESADE
VRILLE FINAGLE FINESSE ARTIFICE
DEMARCHE ENGINEER EXERCISE
STRATEGY WINDLASS
(- GENTLY) EASE
(AERIAL —) LOOP SPIN FISHTAIL
WINGOVER
(ILLEGAL —) GAME
(ROCK-CLIMBING —) LAYBACK
(SKIING —) SNOWPLOW
(WRESTLING —) ESCAPE BUTTOCK
MANEUVERABLE YARE
MANEUVERING FINESSE FLANKING
MANGE ITCH REEF SCAB CANKER
DARTARS SCABIES
MANGER BIN BUNK CRIB HECK
STALL CRATCH
MANGLE MAR HACK MOUTH BRUISE
GARBLE HACKLE IRONER MAGGLE
MURDER MAMMOCK LACERATE
MUTILATE
MANGO DIKA AMHAR AMINI BAUNO
AMCHOOR CARABAO PAHUTAN
(POINT OF —) NAK
MANGOSTEEN SANTOL GARCINIA
MANGROVE BACAO GORAN MANGLE
MYRTAL BACAUAN CERIOPS
COURIDA HANGALAI LANGARAI
MANGUE CHOLUTECA CHOROTEGA
MANGY SCABBY ROINISH SCABETIC
MANHANDLE SCRAG
MANHOOD ADAMHOOD
MANIA RAGE CRAZE FUROR FRENZY
DELIRIUM HYSTERIA INSANITY
MANIAC KILLER MADMAN FANATIC
LUNATIC
MANIFEST HAVE NUDE OPEN RIFE
SENE SHOW APERT CLEAR FRANK
GROSS KITHE NAKED OVERT PLAIN
PROVE SPEAK SUTEL ATTEST
COUTHE EVINCE EXTANT GRAITH
LIQUID OSTEND PATENT PHANIC
APPROVE CONFESS DECLARE
EVIDENT EXHIBIT EXPRESS OBVIOUS
SIGNIFY VISIBLE APPARENT
DISCLOSE DISCOVER INDICATE
PALPABLE PROCLAIM
(NOT —) LATENT
MANIFESTATION ACT SON BEAM
COMA GLINT AVATAR COMING
EFFECT OSTENT ADVANCE DISPLAY
EXPRESS SHOWING EPIPHANY
MANIFEST
(BARELY PERCEPTIBLE —) SCINTIL
(BRIEF —) GLEAM
(DIVINE —) SPIRIT SHEKINAH
(HORRIBLE —) CHIMAERA
(MORAL —) SOUL
(VAGUE —) GLIMMER
MANIFESTLY WITTERLY
MANIFESTO PLACARD

MANIFOLD MANY TURRET VARIOUS
FELEFOLD MANYFOLD MULTIPLE
MANIKIN ECORCHE PANTINE
PHANTOM HOMUNCIO HOMUNCLE
MANNIKIN
MANIOC CATELLA
MANIPLE FANON SUDARIUM
MANIPULATE COAX COOK DIAL
FAKE HAND STIR TOOL CROOK
HUMOR KNEAD SHAPE TREAT WIELD
CHIVVY GOVERN HANDLE JOCKEY
MANAGE SHUFFLE
(— BY DECEPTIVE MEANS) RIG
MANIPULATION PASS JUGGLERY
MANAGERY
MANITO ORENDA POKUNT MANITOU
TAMANOAS
MANKIND MAN FLESH SHEEP
WORLD SPECIES HUMANITY
UNIVERSE
MANLIKE MALE MANLY MANNISH
HOMINOID
MANLINESS ARETE VIRTUS MANSHIP
MANLY BOLD MALE HARDY MANNY
DARING VIRILE MANLIKE
MAN-MADE CULTURAL SYNTHETIC
MANNER AIR BAT JET LAT WAY
FORM GAET GARB GATE KIND MAKE
MIEN MODE RATE SORT THEW TOUR
WISE WONE GUISE LATES STYLE
TENUE TRICK COURSE CUSTOM
METHOD ADDRESS AMENITY
FASHION QUALITY QUOMODO
CARAPACE DEMEANOR LANGUAGE
(— OF APPROACH) ABORD
(— OF DOING) ACTION
(— OF HANDLING) HAND
(— OF MAKING ANYTHING)
FACTURE
(— OF SITTING) ASANA
(— OF SPEAKING) SLUR SOUGH
ACCENT GRAMMAR
(— OF WALKING) STEP
(AFFECTED —) AIR
(AMUSING —) DROLLERY
(ARROGANT —) BRAG HAUTEUR
(FORBIDDING —) SHELL
(FORMAL —) STARCH
(HABITUAL —) SONG
(OUTWARD —) TOUR FRONT
(SMOOTH —) JAPAN
(SWAGGERING —) SIDE
(USUAL —) HABIT
(PL.) CORNERS HAVINGS BREEDING
MANNERED CUTE MORATE THEWED
MANNERISM TRICK IDIASM
(PL.) DAPS
MANNERLY CIVIL
MANNERS MORES HAVANCE
HAVINGS BEAUETRY BREEDING
MANNITOL MANNITE PUNICIN
MAN-OF-WAR CARAVEL
MAN-OF-WAR FISH PASTOR
MANOR HAM BURY HALL TOWN VILL
COMMOTE MANSION LORDSHIP
TOWNSHIP
MANPOWER BRAWN LABOR
MANROOT IPOMOEA
MANROPE LIMMER

MANSERVANT (ALSO SEE SERVANT)
LAD MOZO GROOM VALET ANDREW
BUTLER TEABOY
MANSION DOME HOTEL HOUSE
MANSE SIEGE TOWER CASTLE
HARBOR HOSTEL CHATEAU
(— OF THE MOON) ALNATH
MANSLAUGHTER BLOOD FELONY
HOMICIDE
MANTEL CLAVY CLAVEL
MANTELET MANTA MANTLE
MANTLET GALAPAGO
MANTELPIECE BRACE PAREL
CLAVEL MANTEL MANTLING
MANTICORE MONTEGRE
MANTIS CAGN RACER REARER
MANTOID PROPHET
MANTIS CRAB SQUILLA
MANTLE CAPA HOSE PALL ROBE
CLOAK CREAM FROCK JABUL
LAMBA PALLA TUNIC CAMAIL
CAPOTE KHIRKA SLAVIN TABARD
CHLAMYS CHRISOM CHUDDAR
FERIDJI MANTEAU PAENULA
PALLIUM SLEEVES WHITTLE
WRAPPER BARRACAN CHRYSOME
MANTELET REGOLITH RICINIUM
STOCKING
MANTLEROCK REGOLITH
MANTO (FATHER OF —) HERCULES
TIRESIAS
(SON OF —) MOPSUS
MANTRA DHARANI GAYATRI
MANTRAM SAVITRI
MANTUA MANTY SEMAR
MANTZU MIAOTZE
MANUAL VADY COACH GREAT
TUTOR PORTAS CAMBIST CEMBALO
DIDACHE MANUARY BOMBARDE
HANDBOOK KEYBOARD ORDINARY
PORTHORS SYNOPSIS
(MAGICIAN'S —) GRIMOIRE
(NAVIGATION —) BOWDITCH
MANUAO IAO
MANUBRIUM HYPOSTOME
MANUFACTURE COIN FAKE MAKE
FORGE PERFORM PRODUCE
WORKING BOOKWORK
(— OF LIQUOR OR DRUGS) ABKARI
(ILLEGAL —) COINING
MANUFACTURED STORE
MANUFACTURER BRAND MAKER
WRIGHT DISKERY SPINNER
SUPPLIER
MANUMIT FREE LIBERATE
MANURE HOT MIG DUNG LIME MUCK
SAUR SOIL TATH FECES MIXEN
FULZIE SEASON SLEECH COMPOST
FOLDING GOODING POUDRET
DRESSING WORTHING
MANURED BONED
MANUS HAND
MANUSCRIPT CODEX FLIMSY
MATTER SCRIPT UNCIAL CURSIVE
PANDECT PINTURA WITNESS
EXEMPLAR
MANX CAT RUMPY
MANX SHEARWATER CREW PUFFIN
SCRABE SCRABER

MANY TEN FELE MUCH SERE FORTY
GREAT MAINT MOULT TWENTY
ENDLESS JILLION SEVERAL VARIOUS
MANIFOLD COUNTLESS
(BEING —) NUMEROUS
(GOOD —) HANTLE
(GREAT —) MORT RAFF SWITH
MANYATTA KRAAL
MANY-HANDED BRIAREAN
MANYROOT RUELLIA
MANY-SIDED VARIOUS
MAORI (— IMAGE) TIKI
(— LAW) UTU
(— VILLAGE) PA PAH KAINGA
(NOT —) PAKEMA
MAP KEY CARD DICE PLAT PLOT
CARTE CENTO CHART DRAFT INSET
QUART STILL DRAUGHT GRAPHIC
CARTGRAM GATEFOLD PLATFORM
MAPAU MAPLE MATIPO TARATA
PIRIPIRI
MAPLE MAZER DOGWOOD
SYCAMORE WINGSEED
(GROVE OF —) SAPBUSH
MAR BLOT SCAR SNIP BLOOM BOTCH
SHEND SPILL SPOIL BLOTCH
DEFACE DEFEAT DEFORM IMPAIR
INJURE BLEMISH DISGRACE
MARABOU STORK ARGALA MORABIT
MARANAO LANAO
MARASMUS MARCOR ATHREPSIA
MARAUD RAID DACOIT PICKEER
PILLAGE
MARAUDER TORY BANDIT BUMMER
LOOTIE PIRATE CATERAN LADRONE
(PL.) BLACKS
MARAUDING BANDITRY OUTRIDING
MARBLE MIB MIG PEA POT TAW
ALLY BOOL BOWL DUCK MARL
AGATE AGGIE ALLEY BONCE COMMY
IMMIE IVORY LINER PUREY RANCE
DOGGLE MARMOR MARVEL PARIAN
PEEWEE STEELY CARRARA CIPOLIN
GLASSIE GRIOTTE KNICKER
PARAGON PITCHER SHOOTER
BROCATEL DOLOMITE KNUCKLER
(BLACK —) JET
(PL.) TAW BOWLS PLUMPS HUNDRED
MARBLED MIRLY
MARCH FILE HIKE LIDE MARK MUSH
SLOG ROUTE TRACE TRINE TROOP
WALTZ DEFILE DOUBLE PARADE
REVIEW DEBOUCH STRETCH
FOOTSLOG PROGRESS
(— BEHIND) COVER
(— IN FRONT OF) LEAD
(— OBLIQUELY) INCLINE
(PL.) FRONTIER
MARCHING (— UP) ANABASIS
MARCHIONESS MARCHESA
MARQUISE
MARCOT GOOTE
MARCOTTAGE GOOTEE
MARE SEA YAD YADE YAUD GILLIE
GILLOT GRASNI HUNTRESS
MARE'S-TAIL HIPPURID
MARGARET MEG META MARGET
MARGOT GRETCHEN
MARGATE PORGY

MARGAY TIGER
MARGIN HEM RIM VAT BANK BRIM
BROW CURB EDGE FOLD INCH LIMB
LIST RAND BRINK EAVES MARGE
VERGE BORDER FRINGE LABRUM
LACING CUSHION DRAUGHT
MARGENT SELVAGE HAIRLINE
(— OF CARAPACE) DOUBLURE
(— OF CIRCLE) LIMB
(— OF LIP) PROLABIUM
(— OF PAGE) BACK
(— OF SAFETY) LEEWAY
(— OF SHELL) LABRUM LIMBUS
(— OF SUPERIORITY) LEAD
(— OF WING) TERMEN
(—S OF HERD) SWING
(SEA —) COAST
MARGOSA NIM NEEM NEEMBA
MARGRAVE RUDIGER MARKGRAF
MARIANA SILYBUM
MARIGOLD GOLD GULL SAMH AZTEC
BOOTS GOLDE GOOLS HELIO
BACLIN BUDDLE GOLDCUP GOLDING
GOLLAND KINGCUP MARYBUD
TAGETES
MARIJUANA POT WEED MOOCAH
LOCOWEED
MARINE JOLLY GALOOT GULPIN
GYRENE TOPMAN MARINAL
HALIMOUS MARITIME NAUTICAL
MARINER MARINE SAILOR SEALER
SEAMAN BUSCARLE SEAFARER
WARRENER
(PL.) SEAFOLK
MARINHEIRO ACAJOU
MARIONETTE PUPPY POPPET
PUPPET
MARITAL INTIMATE HUSBANDLY
MARITIME MARINE HALIMOUS
NAUTICAL
MARK AIM END HOB HUB MOT POP
BELT BLOT BUOY BUTT CHOP CLIP
DELE DINT FAZE FIST GOAL KEEL
LINE MIND NOTE RIST SCAR SEAR
SIGN SMOT SMUT SPOT TEND TEXT
TICK VIRE WAND WIND BADGE
BOTTU BRAND BREVE CHANT
CHECK CLOUD DATUM DITTO DRAFT
FLECK FRANK GHOST GRADE HILUM
KNIFE LABEL MARCH MARCO MEITH
NOKTA PRINT PROOF ROVER SCART
SCOPE SCORE SCUFF SPOOR
STAMP SWIRL TOKEN TOUCH TRACE
TRACK TRACT WATCH WHITE
ACCENT ALPIEU BEACON BESPOT
BLOTCH BUTTON CARACT DAGGER
DAPPLE DENOTE DIRECT INDICE
LETTER MARKER NOTICE OBJECT
SMUTCH STREAK STRIKE STROKE
SUCKER SYMBOL TARGET UPSHOT
WICKER WITTER BETOKEN CHARBON
COCKSHY DEMERIT DIAMOND
DRAUGHT EROTEME EXCUDIT
FINMARK IMPRESS IMPRINT INSIGNE
KENMARK SCARIFY SERRATE
SIGNARY SPECKLE STRIATE
SYMPTOM VESTIGE WAYMARK
BRACELET CROWFOOT DATEMARK
DIASTOLE DISPUNCT EVIDENCE

FOOTMARK FOOTSTEP IDENTIFY
IDEOGRAM MONUMENT NOTATION
(— A BIRD) BAND
(— AFTER ASSAY) TOUCH
(— AS SPURIOUS) ATHETIZE
(— BY BURNING) CHAR
(— BY CUTTING) SCRIBE
(— BY PLOWING) STRIKE
(— CROSSWISE) CRANK
(— DENOTING CORRUPT PASSAGE)
OBELUS
(— DIRECTIONS) ADDRESS
(— IN ARCHERY) CLOUT HOYLE
ROVER WHITE
(— IN CANON) LEAD
(— IN CURLING) TEE COCK
(— IN QUOITS) MOT
(— INDICATING CONTRACTION)
CORONIS
(— INDICATING DIRECTION) ARROW
(— OF ACKNOWLEDGEMENT)
ACCOLADE
(— OF DISGRACE) STAIN STIGMA
(— OF DISTINCTION) BELT
(— OF ESTEEM) LAUREL GARLAND
(— OF OFFICE) SEAL
(— OF OWNERSHIP) SWANMARK
(— OF PURITY) HALLMARK
(— OF REFERENCE) OBELISK
(— OF SIGNATURE) CROSS
(— OF SUPERIORITY) BELL
(— OF WEAVER) KEEL
(— OFF LAND) FEER PHEER
(— OFF) SUBTEND
(— ON ANIMAL'S FACE) BLAZE
STRIPE
(— ON CHART) VIGIA
(— ON EXAM) PASS
(— ON FEATHER) BAR SPANGLE
(— ON FOREHEAD) KUMKUM
(— ON PENNSYLVANIA BARNS)
HEXAFOOS
(— ON SHEEP) SMIT
(— ON SHIP) SURMARK
(— ON SKIN) PLOT CREASE
(— ON STAMP) CONTROL
(— OUT) CANCEL DELINE AIRMARK
APPOINT COMPART DESCRIBE
(— OVER GERMAN VOWEL) UMLAUT
(— OVER LETTER N) TILDE
(— OVER LONG VOWELS) MACRON
(— SHEEP OR CATTLE) BASTE
BUIST DEWLAP
(— TIME) COUNT
(— TO BE ATTAINED) BOGEY BOGIE
(— TO GUIDE VESSELS) MYTH
(— TRANSVERSELY) LADDER
(— UNDER LETTER C) CEDILLA
(— WITH LINES) HATCH CAMLET
(— WITH POINTED ROLLER) GRILL
(— WITH RIDGES) RIB
(— WITH STRIPES) WALE STREAM
(— WITH TAR) BASTE
(ACCENT —) VERGE
(ANGULAR —) HOOK
(BALLOT —) SCRATCH
(BOUNDARY —) MEAR MERE TERM
WIKE MEITH STAKE LANDMARK
(CADENCY —) BRISURE

(CANCELLATION —) BUMPER KILLER
(DIACRITICAL —) TIL TILDE
(DIRTY —) SMIRCH
(DISTINCTIVE —) BADGE INDICIA
(DISTINGUISHING —) ITEM COCARDE
EARMARK INSIGNE
(DOUBLE-DAGGER —) DIESIS
(EASY —) YAP SMELT
(EIGHTH —) URE
(EXACT —) NICK
(EXCLAMATION —) SCREAMER
(IDENTIFICATION —) MOLE CREST
SPLIT SIGNET WATTLE EARMARK
KENMARK LUGMARK COLOPHON
(LOW-WATER —) DATUM
(MERIDIAN —) MIRE
(MUSICAL —) PRESA CORONA
(PARAGRAPH —) PILCROW
(PROOFREADER'S —) STET CARET
(PUNCTUATION —) DASH STOP
BRACE BREVE COLON COMMA
HYPHEN PERIOD BRACKET DIERESIS
ELLIPSIS DIACRITIC SEMICOLON
(SECTARIAN —) BOTTU TILAKA
(SKATE —) CUSP
(SMALL ROUND —) DOT
(TRAMP'S —) MONICA MONNIKER
(WHITE —) RACHE
(PL.) POINTING
MARKED FAR GREAT SCORED
SEVERE SPOTTY COLORED EMINENT
MARCATO POINTED SCARRED
SPECKED SPOTTED
(— BY COLORED RINGS) AREOLATE
(— BY FURROWS) RIVOSE
(— BY INTELLIGENCE) ABLE
(— BY PROSTRATION) ALGID
(— BY REFINEMENT) ELEGANT
(— BY RIDGES) SERRIED
(— BY SHREWDNESS) ADROIT
(— BY SIMILARITY) AKIN
(— BY SIMPLICITY) ATTIC
(— BY WAVY LINES) GYROSE
(— OUT) DISTINCT
(— UP) FOUL
(— WITH BANDS) ZONATE
(— WITH SMALLPOX) FRETTEN
(— WITH SPOTS OR LINES) NOTATE
(EXTREMELY —) INTENSE
MARKEDLY BYOUS
MARKER HOB HUB DOLE FLAG MARK
STUMP TYPER BUTTON GUIDON
HOBBLE HUBBLE TABBER DAYMARK
SCRIBER
MARKET CURB GUNJ MART PORT
SALE SOOK VEND VENT CHEAP
CROSS GUNGE HALLE PASAR PRICE
TRONE TRYST BAZAAR BOURSE
OUTLET PARIAN RIALTO POULTRY
CHEAPING DEBOUCHE EMPORIUM
EXCHANGE MACELLUM
(CATTLE —) TRISTE
(MEAT —) SHAMBLES
MARKETABLE SUK SUQ SOUK
STAPLE SALABLE VENDIBLE
MARKETPLACE SUK SUQ SOUK
AGORA CHAWK CHOWK HALLE
PLAZA BAZAAR EMPORIUM
MARKING EYE HOOD COLLAR

CLOUDING SCARRING SCRIBING
(— OF WOOD) CURL GRAIN
(— ON FEATHER) SPANGLE
(— ON MARS) CANAL
(—S ON STEEL) DAMASK
(ANIMAL —) SADDLE SHIELD
(CATTLE —) JINGLEBOB
(CRESCENT-SHAPED —) LUNULA
LUNULE
(DROP-SHAPED —) GUTTA
(POSTAL —) INDICIA
(RINGLIKE —) ANNULUS
(STRIPED —) STRAKE
MARKKA FINMARK
MARKSMAN SHOT MARKER PLUFFER
SHOOTER SHOTMAN SHOOTIST
MARL MALM MARLITE
MARLI MARIE
MARLIN AU AGUJA
MARLINESPIKE FID JAEGER
PRICKER STABBER
MARMALADE CHEESE SQUISH
CODINIAC
MARMALADE TREE CHICO MAMMIE
SAPOTE ZAPOTE
MARMOSET MICO TITI SAGOIN
JACCHUS QUIRCAL SAIMIRI TAMARIN
WISTITI ORABASSU
MARMOT BOBAC PAHMI GOPHER
SUSLIK SCIURID SIFFLEUR
WHISTLER
MARMOTA ARCTOMYS
MAROON AZTEC PICNIC CIMARRON
MARQUEE CANOPY MARQUISE
MARQUISE NAVETTE
MARQUISETTE LENO
MARRANOS ANUSIM
MARRED CUPPY SCABBY SPECKED
MARRIAGE MUTA DAIVA HYMEN
KARAO BRIDAL BUCKLE SPLICE
SPOUSE EXOGAMY NUPTIAL
PUNALUA SPOUSAL WEDDING
WEDLOCK CONUBIUM LEVIRATE
OPSIGAMY
(— AFTER DEATH OF FIRST
SPOUSE) DIGAMY
(— AT ADVANCED AGE) OPSIGAMY
(— BELOW POSITION) HYPOGAMY
(— CONTRACT) KETUBAH
(— OUTSIDE FAMILY) EXOGAMY
(— PORTION) TOCHER
(— WITHIN GROUP) ENDOGAMY
MARRIAGEABLE NUBILE
MARRIED COVERT WEDDED
ESPOUSED
MARROW KEEST MARIE MERCH
MERGH MEDULLA
MARRY TIE WED FAST WIFE WIVE
CLEEK MATCH BUCKLE CROTCH
ENSURE MARROW SPLICE HUSBAND
NUPTIAL WEDLOCK DESPOUSE
(— OFF) BESTOW
MARS ARES MAMERS MARMAR
MAVORS MASPITER TEUTATES
(FATHER OF —) JUPITER
(MOTHER OF —) JUNO
(SON OF —) REMUS ROMULUS
MARSH BOG FEN HAG CARR DANK
FELL FLAM FLAT HOPE JHIL MASH

MIRE OOZE SOIL SUDS TARN VLEI
VLEY WASH WHAM FLASH GLADE
JHEEL LIMAN SLACK SLASH SLUMP
SWAMP MORASS PALUDE PUDDLE
CIENAGA CORCASS POCOSIN
PONTINE QUAGMIRE STROTHER
TURLOUGH
(SALT —) SALT SALINA SALINE
MARSHAL ARRAY MUSTER PARADE
JERONIMO MERECHAL
(— FACTS) HASH
MARSH ELDER JACKO
MARSH FEVER HELODES
MARSH GAS METHANE
MARSH HARRIER PUDDOCK
PUTTOCK
MARSHMALLOW MALLOW WYMOTE
MARSH MARIGOLD BOOTS CAPER
CRAZY GOOLS DRAGON GAMOND
GOWLAN COWSLIP ELKSLIP
GOLDCUP KINGCOB KINGCUP
MARYBUD DRUNKARD
MARSH PENNYWORT PENNYROT
WATERCUP
MARSH PINK SABBATIA
MARSH TEA LEDUM
MARSH TREFOIL BUCKBEAN
MARSH WREN LONGBILL
MARSHY FOGGY MOORY MOSSY
PONDY SNAPY SPEWY CALLOW
PLASHY QUAGGY QUASHY SLUMPY
HELODES MOORISH QUEACHY
PALUDIAL PALUDINE WATERISH
MARSUPIAL KOALA CUSCUS
POSSUM WOMBAT DASYURE
OPOSSUM KANGAROO
MART STAPLE EMPORIUM
MARTEN FOIN SABLE SOBOL FISHER
MARTRIX MUSTELID MUSTELIN
(GROUP OF —S) RICHESSE
MARTENSITE SORBITE
MARTIAL BELLIC WARLIKE WARRIOR
BELLICAL MILITARY
MARTIN MARTLET SWALLOW
MARTINET
MARTINMAS TERM
MARTYR STEPHEN WITNESS
SUFFERER
MARTYRDOM MARTYRY PASSION
MARVEL MARL MUSE FERLY SELLY
ADMIRE WONDER MAGNALE
MIRACLE MONSTER PORTENT
PRODIGY SELCOUTH
MARVELOUS MIRIFIC STRANGE
FABULOUS WONDROUS
MARY MOLL POLL MAMIE MAURA
MOLLY MIRIAM MARILLA

MARYLAND
BATTLESITE: ANTIETAM
CAPITAL: ANNAPOLIS
COLLEGE: HOOD GOUCHER
STJOHNS
COUNTY: CECIL TALBOT
ALLEGANY SOMERSET
INDIAN: CONOY NANTICOKE
LAKE: PRETTYBOY
MOUNTAIN: BACKBONE

NATIVE: WESORT TERRAPIN
NICKNAME: OLDLINE
RIVER: CHESTER POTOMAC
CHOPTANK PATUXENT
STATE BIRD: ORIOLE
STATE TREE: OAK
TOWN: EASTON TOWSON
ABERDEEN BETHESDA
POCOMOKE BALTIMORE

MARYSOLE CARTER LEADER
CARTARE
MASAI WAKWAFI WAKWAVI
MASCOT BILLIKEN
MASCULINE MALE DOGGY VIRILE
LALAQUI MANLIKE
MASH BEER CHAP MASA MASK MESH
SLOP CHAMP CREEM SMASH SMUSH
MUDDLE STILLAGE
MASHED CHAPPED DAUPHINE
MASHER FLIRT BEETLE
MASJID MOSQUE
MASK FACE HIDE JEST LOUP SLUR
VEIL BLOCK BLOOP CLOAK COVER
GRILL GUISE LARVE POINT VIZOR
DOMINO GRILLE MUZZLE SCREEN
VEILER VIZARD BECLOUD CONCEAL
CURTAIN MASKOID ANTEMASK
DEFILADE DISGUISE MASCARON
(— OUT) CROP
(GAS —) CANARY
(HALF —) LOO LOUP DOMINO
(PL.) AREITO
MASKED LARVATED VIZARDED
MASKER GUISARD MASQUER
MASKING MUMMERY MUMMING
COLORING
MASLIN MESTLEN MASHLOCH
MUNGCORN MASSELGEM
MASON LAYER BUILDER MASONER
COMACINE KNOBBLER LAMMIKIN
SCUTCHER
MASONRY ASHLAR BACKING
BLOCAGE MOELLON NOGGING
ISODOMUM QUOINING ROCKWORK
MASQUE MASK COMUS DEVICE
ANTIMASK DISGUISE
MASQUER REX
MASQUERADE MASK GUISE DOMINO
MASQUE PARADE MASKERY
DISGUISE
MASQUERADER RAGSHAG
MASQUERADING CARNIVAL
MASS BAT BED GOB SOP WAD BODY
BULK GOUT HEAP HEFT KNOT LEAD
LUMP MOLE OBIT STOW SWAD
AMASS BATCH BLOOM CLAMP
CLASH CLUMP CROWD CRUST
DIRGE GLOBE GORGE GROSS
MATTE MISSA SLUMP SOLID SPIRE
STORE WODGE COMMON GOBBET
NUGGET PROPER VOLUME WEIGHT
BOUROCK CONGEST DENSITY
MASKINS MESKINS NYSTERY
REQUIEM SALOMON CALAPITE
CONGERIE ENDOSOME FLOCCULE
MOUNTAIN SOULMASS
(— IN THE WHITE NILE) SUDD

(— OF BACTERIA) SLIME SYMPLASM
(— OF BLOSSOMS) BLOW
(— OF BLUBBER) MELON
(— OF BRANCHES) SPRAY
(— OF BUBBLES) FOAM
(— OF BUSHES) SHAG
(— OF CARPELS) SOREMA
(— OF CELLS) COMB CANCER
CUMULUS STALACE
(— OF CLOUDS) BANK
(— OF COAL) JUD
(— OF COLORS) BLOB
(— OF COTTON) FUSSOCK
(— OF CURED RUBBER) LOAF
(— OF DEBRIS) SLIDE
(— OF DOUGH) DUMPLING
(— OF FIBERS) KAPOK
(— OF FILAMENTS) FLOCCUS
(— OF FILTH) GORE
(— OF FRAGMENTS) BRASH
(— OF HAIR) GLIB TOUPET
(— OF ICE) BERG CALF FLOE FLAKE
PATCH ICICLE STURIS GROWLER
ICEBERG FLOEBERG
(— OF INSECTS) CACHE
(— OF IRON) BALL BLOB CORE
BLOOM INDUCTOR
(— OF LAVA) BOMB SPINE
(— OF LEAVES) FOLIAGE
(— OF LIMESTONE) HUM
(— OF LOOSE BOULDERS) CLATTER
(— OF METAL) SOW INGOT BUTTON
(— OF MOLTEN GLASS) GOB
GATHER PARISON
(— OF MUD) CLASH
(— OF ORE) BACK SLUG BUNNY
SQUAT
(— OF PEOPLE) CROWD HORDE
(— OF POMACE) CHEESE
(— OF ROCK) DOME NECK HORSE
LEDGE NAPPE SCALP SNOUT INLIER
SARSEN BOULDER FOOTWALL
(— OF SAND) PAAR
(— OF SOAP) CURD
(— OF SPORES) SORUS
(— OF SUGAR CRYSTALS) STRIKE
(— OF SUGAR) FONDANT
(— OF TISSUE) COLLAR GANGLION
(— OF WATER) HEAD
(— OF YARN) COP BALLOON
(— OF YOLK) LATEBRA
(— OVERHANGING) CORNICE
(— TOGETHER) HUDDLE
(—S OF DRIFTWOOD) EMBARRAS
(AMORPHOUS —) JUMBLE
SYMPLASM
(BILLOWY —) CLOUD
(BUSHY —) SHOCK
(COMPACT —) BRIQUET
(CONFUSED —) COT JUMBLE
JUNGLE CLUTTER RUMMAGE
SHUFFLE
(DISORDERLY —) SCRAMBLE
(EGG —) BUNION CULTCH SPONGE
(FATTY —) BEAN HEADSKIN
(FECAL —) SCYBALUM
(FLATTISH —) DAB
(FLUID —) FLUOR
(GLASSY —) SLAG

(GLOBULAR —) MOORBALL
(INDISTINCT —) SMUDGE
(IRREGULAR —) CUB
(LIVING —) BLASTEMA
(MOIST —) PULP
(MOUNTAIN —) OROGEN
(NUCLEAR —) SHIELD
(OVERSPREADING —) PALL
(PEAR-SHAPED —) BOULE
(POROUS —) FILTER
(PROJECTING —) BOSS
(PULPY —) SQUELCH
(RECTANGULAR —) BRICK
(ROOT —) SOLE
(ROUNDED —) COB NOB KNOB
BOLUS KUGEL BULLET RONDLE
(SEDIMENTARY —) GOBI
(SHAPED —) PAT LOAF
(SHAPELESS —) JELLY
(SLIPPERY —) SIND SLUD SLUDDER
(SLUSHY —) POSH
(SOFT —) MASH MOXA MUMMY
(SWOLLEN —) CERE
(TANGLED — OF HAIR) MOP KNURL
(UNCTUOUS —) LANOLIN
(UPRIGHT —) COLUMN
(PL.) MEINY MEINIE TRENTAL

MASSACHUSETTS
CAPE: ANN COD
CAPITAL: BOSTON
COLLEGE: SMITH AMHERST
  SIMMONS WHEATON WILLIAMS
  RADCLIFFE WELLESLEY
COUNTY: DUKES BERKSHIRE
  NANTUCKET BARNSTABLE
INDIAN: NAUSET POCOMTUC
ISLAND: DUKES NANTUCKET
LAKE: ONOTA QUABBIN ROHUNTA
  WEBSTER
MOUNTAIN: BRODIE POTTER
  ALANDER EVERETT GREYLOCK
MOUNTAIN RANGE: BERKSHIRE
POND: WALDEN
RIVER: NASHUA CHARLES
  CONCORD QUABOAG TAUNTON
  CHICOPEE DEERFIELD
STATE BIRD: CHICKADEE
STATE FLOWER: MAYFLOWER
STATE NICKNAME: BAY
STATE TREE: ELM
TOWN: AYER LYNN OTIS ATHOL
  BARRE LENOX AGAWAM
  DEDHAM GROTON NAHANT
  NATICK REVERE SAUGUS
  WOBURN HOLYOKE IPSWICH
  PEABODY TAUNTON BROCKTON
  CHICOPEE COHASSET SCITUATE
  UXBRIDGE YARMOUTH
UNIVERSITY: CLARK TUFTS
  HARVARD BRANDEIS

MASSACRE SLAY POGROM
CARNAGE SCUPPER BUTCHERY
SLAUGHTER
MASSAGE WISP KNEAD FACIAL
PETRIE SHAMPOO TRIPSIS LOMILOMI
MASSAGER MASSEUR VIBRATOR

MASSECUITE GUR FILLMASS
MASSED DENSE
MASSENA QUAIL COPPY
MASSIVE BIG BEAMY BULKY GROSS
HEAVY LUSTY MASSY SOUND STERN
STRONG HEALTHY HULKING
VOLUMED TIMBERED
MAST BUCK MAIN POLE SPAR OVEST
STICK STING DRIVER JIGGER
MIZZEN ARTEMON ASHERAH
MASTAGE SPANKER FOREMAST
MAINMAST SHIPMAST
(FALLEN —) SHACK
(SIXTH —) DRIVER
MASTAX TROPHI
MASTER DON HER JOE MAS RAB
SAB SIR ARCH BAAS BEAK BOSS
COCK FACE HERR JOSS KING LORD
MIAN SIRE TUAN BWANA MARSE
MASSA RABBI SAHIB SWAMI SWAMY
SWELL BRIDLE BUCKRA CASTER
DEACON DOMINE HUMBLE MAITRE
PATRON RECTOR RHETOR SIRCAR
WAFTER CAPTAIN CONQUER
DOMINIE DOMINUS EFFENDI
MAESTRO NAKHODA OGTIERN
PADRONE RABBANI RABBONI
AMAISTER BARGEMAN BEMASTER
KINGFISH LANDLORD MAGISTER
OVERCOME SLOOPMAN SURMOUNT
VANQUISH
(— OF CEREMONIES) EMCEE
VERGER COMPERE CHAIRMAN
(— OF CRAFT) KAHUNA
(— OF HOUSEHOLD) BALABOS
GOODMAN
(— OF REVELS) ALYTARCH
(— OF WHALER) SPOUTER
(FENCING —) LANISTA
(INFERIOR —) KNIFER
MASTER-AT-ARMS JAUNTY JAUNTIE
MASTERFUL LORDLY VIRILE
HAUGHTY ARROGANT MAGERFUL
MASTERPIECE TOPPIECE
MASTERY GREE GRIP GRIPE
COMMAND MAISTRY OVERHAND
MASTHEAD FLAG HIGHTOP
MASTICATE GUM CHAW CHEW
MASTICATORY BUYO
MASTIC BULLY JOCUM JOCUMA
MASTIC TREE ACOMA AUSUBO
COCUYO COCULLO
MASTIFF ALAN MASTY BANDOG
TIEDOG
MASTIGONEME FLIMMER
MASTITIS CLAP WEED GARGET
MAST TREE ASAK
MASTURBATE ABUSE
MASTURBATION ONANISM
FROTTAGE
MASTWOOD POON KAMANI
MAT COT RUG TOD BASS FLAT FLET
FOOT HAIR MOSS NIPA PACE RAFT
SHAG TAUT DOILY KILIM TATTY
COTTER FELTER FOOTER PAUNCH
PETATE TARGET COASTER CUSHION
DOORMAT KAITAKA MATTING
FOOTPACE FROSTING MATTRESS
SPANDREL

(— BORDER) TANIKO
(BOWLING —) FOOTER
(FIBER —) IE BASS
(PALM-LEAF —) YAPA
(PICTURE-FRAME —) FLAT
(POLYNESIAN —) LAUHALA
(SCOURING —) BEAR
(TABLECLOTH —) GARDNAP
(PL.) DUNNAGE
MATACHIN BOUFFON
MATACO CORONADO
MATADOR MAT ESPADA CAPEADOR
(— MOVEMENT) PASE
MATCH GO CAP VIE BOUT COPE
EVEN FERE LUNT MAKE MATE MEET
MILL MOTE PAIR PEEL PEER SIDE
SUIT AMATE EQUAL FIRER FUSEE
FUZEE MOUSE PARTY SPUNK TALLY
VENUE VESTA ASSORT CANCEL
COMMIT FELLOW KIPPIN MARROW
QUADER RUBBER SAMPLE SWATCH
COMPEER EXAMPLE IGNITER
ILLUMER KINDLER KIPPEEN LIGHTER
LUCIFER PARAGON PAREGAL
PATTERN PENDANT SINGLES
APPROACH BONSPIEL BREATHER
EUPYRION FOURSOME INFLAMER
LOCOFOCO PORTFIRE REANSWER
VESUVIAN VESUVIUS SEMIFINAL
(— AT DICE) MAIN
(BOXING —) SPAR FIGHT SLUGFEST
(CURLING —) SPIEL BONSPIEL
(DISHONEST —) CROSS
(GOLF —) NASSAU FOURSOME
(SHOOTING —) TIR SHOOT
(SLOW —) LUNT SMIFT SQUIB
(PL.) LIGHTS
MATCHED ASSORTED
MATCHING MARROW SUITABLE
MATCHLESS ALONE UNIQUE
NONESUCH PEERLESS
MATCHMAKER SHADCHAN
MATE CAWK FERE METE PAIR PEER
BILLY BREED BUDDY BULLY CLASP
CULLY DICKY MATCH PARTY TALLY
YERBA BUNKIE FELLOW FUTURE
MARROW PAREIL BROTHER
COMPEER COMRADE CONSORT
HUSBAND PARAGON NEIGHBOR
PIRRAURA
(BOATSWAIN'S —) BUFFER
(GUNNER'S —) LADY
(SECOND —) DICKY
MATERIAL FINE MOLD GAUZE
GOUGE HYLIC METAL MOULD PASTE
PLASS STUFF THING TRADE
BORROW CYANUS FABRIC GRAITH
HOGGIN MATTER PAPREG THINGY
APPAREL FOOTING SUBJECT
TEXTILE UNIDEAL WEIGHTY
ADDITIVE CORPORAL ECONOMIC
EQUIPAGE SENSIBLE SNOODING
TANGIBLE THINGISH
(— ELIMINATED) CULLAGE
(— FOR FERMENTING) GUILE
(— FOR OYSTER BEDS) CULCH
CULTCH
(— IN GRAIN) DOCKAGE
(— IN MAKING CEMENT) ADDITION

(— IN NEEDLEWORK) INKLE
(— OF CORDED SILK) CRYSTAL
(— OF SCREENINGS) HOGGIN
HOGGING
(— REMOVED BY SAW CUT) KERF
(— USED IN WAXING) BALL
(— WEIGHED) DRAFT DRAUGHT
(—S FOR MAKING GLASS) FRIT
(ABSORBENT —) DOPE
(ALLUVIAL —) SHINGLE
(ANCIENT —) MURRA MURRHA
(ARTISTIC —) KITSCH
(BAGGING —) HOPSACK
(BITUMINOUS —) KEROGEN
(BONY —) COSMINE
(BUILDING —) LATH ADOBE BRICK
STAFF SWISH TABBY TAPIA SILLAR
CONCRETE
(BUILDING —S) TIGNUM
(CLAY —) TAPIA
(CLAYEY —) GOUGE
(COLORING —) TINCTION
(COMBUSTIBLE —) KINDLING
(CONSTRUCTION —) BREEZE
(CORE —) NIFE
(CUSHIONING —) AIRFOAM
(DEPOSITED —) FOOTS
(DIAMOND —) BORT
(DOWNY —) FLUE
(DRESS —) FOULE VOILE PEELING
COTILLON
(DYEING —) SUMAC SUMACH
(EMROIDERY —) ARRASENE
(EXCAVATED —) SPOIL
(FACING —) ENAMEL
(FISSIONABLE —) STUFF
(FOUNDATION —) UNDERLAY
(GLUTINOUS —) GELATIN
(GRANULAR —) BASIS
(HARD —) CARBIDE
(HEAT-RESISTANT —) ALSIFILM
(ILLUSTRATIVE —) ART
(INSECTICIDAL —) SCABRIN
(INSULATING —) KERITE PECITE
BLANKET LAGGING OKONITE
MEGOTALC
(LEFTOVER —S) ARISINGS
(LOOSE —) SAND GRAVEL DETRITUS
(MINING REFUSE —) ATTLE
(MINUTE —) SESTON
(NUTRITIVE —) FUEL
(ORGANIC —) EXINITE
(PAPER-THIN —) FOIL
(PATCHING —) BOTCH
(PETRIFIED —) GEMSTONE
(POLISHING —) RABAT
(POWDERED —) FINES
(RAW —) STOCK STAPLE
(REFRACTORY —) GROG BULLDOG
CASTABLE
(RESIDUAL —) CEMENT
(RESOURCE —) SWIPE
(REVERSIBLE —) DAMASK
(SEDIMENTARY —) SILT
(SILK —) HONAN PEKIN FOULARD
SARCENET
(SLIMY —) SWARF
(SMOKING —) KEF KIF
(STIFF —) CANVAS

(STIFFENING —) BOXING
(TANNING —) SYNTAN
(TILE-STRENGTHENING —) WEB
(TRASHY —) SLUSH
(TWEEDY —) HOMESPUN
(TYPE-HIGH —) BEARER
(UNPUBLISHED —) INEDITA
(VOLCANIC —) EJECTA
(WATERPROOF —) KERATOL
(WORTHLESS —) GARBLE
(WOVEN —) LAPPET
(PL.) STOCK STUFF
MATERIALISM HYLISM SOMATISM
(DIALECTICAL —) DIAMAT
MATH MUTH MONASTERY
MATERIALISTIC SENSATE SENSUAL
BANAUSIC
MATERIALIZE REIFY DESCEND
MATER LECTIONIS GRAPHY
MATERNITY WARD NATUARY
MATGRASS NARD MATWEED
MATHEMATICIAN ALGORIST
GEOMETER
MATHEMATICS METHESIS
MATING NICK COUPLE DIALLEL
BREEDING HOMOGAMY PANMIXIA
MATRASS BOLTHEAD CUCURBIT
MATRIMONIAL MARITAL NUPTIAL
SPOUSAL CONJUGAL
MATRIMONY WEDLOCK MARRIAGE
MATRIMONY VINE JASMINE
JESSAMY BOXTHORN
MATRIX BED MAT SORT PLASM
SHELL SLIDE DYADIC MASTER
MOTHER STRIKE STROMA CALYMMA
FORMULA MATRICE PATTERN
PROPLASM
MATRON DAME
MATTE SLURRY REGULUS
MATTED COTTY FELTY PINNY
FELTED TAGGED TAUTED WAUKIT
STRINGY FELTLIKE
MATTER RES BONE CASE GEAR
HYLE ITEM RECK WHAT AMPER
FORCE PARTY SKILL STUFF THEME
AFFAIR ARGUFY BEHALF DITTAY
IMPORT ARTICLE CONCERN
MATERIA SIGNIFY SUBJECT
BUSINESS COMETHER MATERIAL
(— ADDED TO BOOK) APPENDIX
(— AROUND THE TEETH) TOPHUS
(— CONSTITUTING PERFUME)
ESSENCE
(— IN DISPUTE) ISSUE
(— OF BUSINESS) SHAURI
(— OF CONCERN) FUNERAL
(— OF INTEREST) GRIST
(— TO) CONCERN
(ALLUVIAL —) GEEST
(BRAIN —) ALBA
(CARTILAGINOUS —) GRISTLE
(COLORING —) DYE COLOR CROCK
EOSIN MORIN PIURI ALNEIN BUTEIN
FUSTIC INDIGO PIOURY CARMINE
CASTORY CUDBEAR LIGULIN
OENOLIN PIGMENT PUNICIN XANTHIN
ALGOCYAN FUSTERIC LAPACHOL
SCOPARIN TINCTION
(CORRUPT —) PUS ATTER

(DECAYED ORGANIC —) DUFF
(ESSENTIAL —) POINT
(EXPLANATORY —) HAGGADA
(FATTY —) SEBUM
(FECAL —) SIEGE
(FILTHY —) GUNK
(FOREIGN —) SOIL DROSS
(FOUL —) FILTH SORDES
(FRONT —) FOREWORD
(GELATINOUS —) BREAK SPAWN
(GRAY —) GLIOSA CINEREA
(INANIMATE —) AJIVA
(INFECTIOUS —) MIASMA
(MINERAL —) FLOAT FLOATS
(POTENTIAL —) PRAKRITI
(PRIMARY —) PRADHANA
(PRINTED —) BOX DISPLAY
(PULVERIZED —) ATTRITUS
(READING —) BODY
(SLIMY —) GLAIR
(SMALL —) MINUTIA
(SOFT —) PASH
(SUBJECT —) SCOPE CONTENT
(SUPPURATIVE —) PUS
(TRIVIAL —) JOKE
(TYPESET —) CHASE
(WASTE —) DIRT DRAFF DROSS
RAMMEL SEWAGE EXCRETA
(WORTHLESS —) SLAG GARBAGE
(WRITTEN —) SCRIVE
(PL.) HARNESS SQUARES
MATTER-OF-FACT DRY LITERAL
MATTER-OF-FACTNESS PROSE
MATTING MAT TAT BEAR BUMP
SIRKI TATTY SAWALI TATAMI
COCOMAT RABANNA
MATTOCK MAT BILL HACK MATAX
PICKAX TUBBAL TWIBIL GRUBBER
MATTRESS BED MAT TICK DIVAN
QUILT RESAI REZAI PALLET
MATRACE
MATURATE MATTER
MATURE AGE OLD BOLD FULL GRAY
RIPE ADULT MANLY RIPEN SHOOT
ACCRUE AUTUMN DECOCT DIGEST
MELLOW SEASON SEEDED
CONCOCT DEVELOP FURNISH
PERFECT PROVECT MATURATE
MATURED ADULT GROWN FORMED
HEADED MELLOW SEEDED
HOMOGAMY
(SEXUALLY —) HIGH
MATURING (— EARLY) RATHRIPE
MATURITY AGE RIPENESS
MATZOTH MATZOS AFIKOMEN
MAUDLIN BEERY MOIST FUDDLED
MAUDLINISM BATHOS
MAUL FAN TUG MALL MELL GAVEL
GLAUM BEATER BEETLE BEMAUL
MUZZLE
MAUND MAO MEIN MAHAN
MAUNDER HAVER
MAUNDY NIPTER MANDATE
MAUSOLEUM MOLE TOMB TURBEH
BARADARI
MAUVE PURPLE MAUVINE
MAW MAA GORGE CROPPY THROAT
MAWKISH CUTE SAPPY SOUPY
WALSH DRIPPY SICKLY VANILLA

MAXILLA SETA GNATHITE CULTELLUS

MAXILLIPED JAWFOOT GNATHITE

MAXIM SAW SAY DICT ITEM NORM RULE TEXT WORD ADAGE AXIOM GNOME LARGE MOTTO DICTUM SAYING SYMBOL BROCARD DICTATE IMPRESA PRECEPT PROVERB APHORISM APOTHEGM DOCTRINE MORALISM PROTASIS SENTENCE (PL.) LOGIA

MAXIMUM FULL CREST EXTREME OUTSIDE SUMMARY ULTIMATE

MAXWELL LINE WEBER

MAY CAN MUN MOWE MUST PRIME SHALL HEYDAY HAWTHORN SYCAMORE (3D OF —) RUDMASDAY

MAYA PRAKRITI

MAYAN COCOM (— **CALENDAR PERIOD**) UAYEB UINAL (— **GOD**) CHAC CHAAC

MAYAPPLE MANDRAKE

MAYBE MEBBE HAPPEN PERHAPS POSSIBLY

MAY DAY BELTANE

MAYFISH ROCKFISH

MAYFLOWER ARBUTUS

MAYFLY DUN DOON DRAKE NAIAD DAYFLY SPINNER EPHEMERA

MAYHEM FELONY

MAYONNAISE GOULASH DRESSING

MAYOR MAIRE BAILIFF DEMARCH PODESTA PROVOST PALATINE (**BULGARIAN** —) KMET (**SPANISH** —) ALCALDE

MAYORSHIP CHAIR

MAYPOLE SHAFT

MAYPOP MAYCOCK MARACOCK

MAYWEED BALDER COTULA MATHER HOGWEED COMPOSIT DILLWEED

MAZE JUNGLE WARREN CONFUSE BEWILDER LABYRINTH

MCCOY QUILL

ME I MA US

MEAD MEATHE HYDROMEL

MEADOW LEA ABEL MEAD VEGA WISH WONG FIELD GRASS LEASE MARSH SWALE WARTH CALLOW PARAMO SAETER SMOOTH POTRERO THWAITE CHINAMPA (**ARTIFICIAL** —) CHINAMPA (**IRISH** —) BAAN (**LOW** —) ING INGE HAUGH CALLOW

MEADOW CROWFOOT FROGWORT

MEADOW GRASS POA

MEADOWLAND ALP MOWING MOWLAND

MEADOWLARK ACORN MEDLAR

MEADOW MOUSE VOLE

MEADOW PEA COWPEA

MEADOW PIPIT WEKEEN CHEEPER TIETICK TITLING LINGBIRD TWITLARK

MEADOW SAFFRON UPSTART

MEADOW SAXIFRAGE SESELI

MEADOWSWEET SPIREA MEADWORT

MEAGER BALD BARE LANK LEAN NICE POOR GAUNT NAKED SCANT SILLY SKIMP SOBER SPARE JEJUNE LEEPIT LENTEN MEAGRE NARROW PILLED SCANTY SLIGHT SPARSE STINGY SCRAGGY SCRANNY SCRIMPY SCRUBBY SLENDER SPARING STARVED STERILE SCRATCHY

MEAGERLY BARELY SPARELY SPARINGLY

MEAGERNESS ECONOMY EXILITY TENUITY SPARENESS

MEAL AMYL ATTA BAKE CHOW FARM FEED HASH KAIL MEAT MONG TUCK COENA FLOUR MANGE SCOFF BUFFET COMIDA DINNER FARINA MANGER POLLEN REPAST SPREAD SQUARE SUPPER UNDERN BLOWOUT COOKOUT CRIBBLE NAGMAAL NOONING SETDOWN ALMUERZO CORNMEAL EVENMETE MEALTIDE ORDINARY TRENCHER (— **FROM CASSAVA ROOT**) FARINE FARINHA (— **GROUND BY HAND**) GRADDAN (— **OF FELLOWSHIP**) AGAPE (— **STIRRED WITH MILK**) STUROCH (**COARSE** —) GRIT GROUT KIBBLE GURGEONS (**COLLEGE** —) HALL (**CORN** —) MASA ATOLE (**ELABORATE** —) FEAST BANQUET (**FIRST** —) ALMUERZO (**FULL** —) GORGE (**HASTY** —) SNAP (**HEARTY** —) AIT (**IMPROMPTU** —) BITE CHECK (**LIGHT** —) BAIT CHECK FOURS (**MIDDAY** —) NOON (**MORNING** —) BRUNCH (**PURIM** —) SEUDAH (**SCANTY** —) PICK (**SMALL** —) SNAP MORSEL (**SOLITARY** —) SULLEN (**UNSORTED** —) ATTA (PL.) TUCKER

MEALTIDE MELTITH

MEALTIME CHOW MELTETH

MEALY FLOURY FARINOSE PERONATE

MEALYBUG COCCID

MEAN LOW BASE CLAM HARD LEAN MIDS NICE POKY SLIM VILE AGENT ARGUE DINGY DUSTY FOOTY GRIMY KETTY MANGY MESNE MEZZO MIDST MINGY MOYEN MUCKY NASTY PETIT PETTY RATTY RUNTY SCALL SCALY SCRUB SEEDY SILLY SMALL SNIDE SNIVY SORRY SOUND SPELL ABJECT BEMEAN COMMON DENOTE DESIGN DIRTEN FEEBLE FROWZY FRUGAL GRUBBY HUMBLE HUNGRY IMPORT INTEND LEADEN LITTLE MEASLY MEDIAL MEDIUM MIDDLE NARROW PALTRY PEANUT PILLED POKING RASCAL SCABBY SCREWY SCUMMY SCURVY SHABBY SLIGHT SNIFTY SNIPPY SORDID SQUALL STRAIT

TEMPER YELLOW AVERAGE CAITIFF CHANNEL CHETIVE COMICAL CONNOTE HACKNEY HILDING IGNOBLE MESQUIN MISERLY MOTETUS OBSCURE PEAKING PELTING PIGGISH PITIFUL PORTEND REPTILE ROINISH SCABBED SHABBED SIGNIFY VICIOUS BEGGARLY CHURLISH DOGGEREL MEDIOCRE MIDDLING PICAYUNE PITIABLE RASCALLY RIFFRAFF SHAMEFUL SNEAKING TWOPENNY WRETCHED

MEANDER WIND STRAY TWINE CIRCLE WIMPLE WINDLE SERPENT WINDING STRAGGLE

MEANING WIT HANG DRIFT SENSE SOUND IMPORT INTENT SEMEME PURPORT PURPOSE CARRIAGE INNUENDO SENTENCE STRENGTH (**BASIC** —) EFFECT (**DOUBLE** —) WHIM EQUIVOKE (**ESSENTIAL** —) CORE CONTENT (**IMPLIED** —) EMPHASIS (**MANIFEST** —) FACE (**REAL** —) SPIRIT (**SECRET** —) HEART

MEANINGFULNESS BODY

MEANINGLESS FECKLESS (— **LETTER OR CODE**) NULL

MEANNESS BEGGARY

MEANS MIDS AGENT DRIVE MESNE MOYEN PURSE THEME AGENCY AVENUE ENGINE MATTER MIDDES POCKET STRING WRENCH BALANCE BENEFIT DEMESNE FACULTY FASHION QUOMODO COURTESY (— **OF COMMUNICATION**) CANAL COMMERCE (— **OF DEFENSE**) HORN HEDGE SHIELD BULWARK (— **OF ESCAPE**) CHINK SCAPE FLIGHT (— **OF LIVING**) ALIMONY (— **OF OFFENSE**) ARM (— **OF PROTECTION**) SAFETY (— **OF SUPPORT**) HOLD ALIMENT SUPPORT

MEANSPIRITED POOR SUPINE CURRISH RECREANT

MEANTIME MEAN WHILE WHILES INTERIM

MEANTONE TERTIAN

MEANWHILE WHILST INTERIM MEANTIME

MEASLES RUBEOLA MORBILLI (**BLACK** —) ESCA APOPLEXY

MEASURE (ALSO SEE UNIT AND WEIGHT) AR BU EM EN HO KO LI MO RI SE TU AAM ARE AUM CAB CHO DRA ELL FAT FEN FIT FOU FUN GAD GAZ GUZ HIN HOB IMI KAB KAN KIP KOR KOS LEA LOG LUG MAU MIL MOY PIK RIG RIN ROD SAA SHO TON TUN VAT VOG WEY ACRE ALMA AUNE BARN BATH BEKA BOLL BOUW BUTT CADE CENT CHIH COOM COSS DEPA DOSE DRAA DRAM DYNE EPHI FALL FANG FOOT

FULL GAGE GERA GILL GIRT GOAD
GRAM GREX HAND HATT HIDE HOOP
HOUR IMMI INCH KNOT KOKU LAST
MEAL METE MILE NAIL NOOK PACE
PINT PIPE POLL REAM RIME ROOD
ROPE ROTL SAAH SACK SALM SEAH
SEAM SIZE SKEP SPAN STEP TAKT
TAPE TIME TRAM TRUG TSUN VARA
WIST YARD ALMUD AMBER ANKER
ARDAB ARURA BEKAH BIGHA BLANK
BODGE BRASS CABAN CABLE
CABOT CANDY CARAT CARGA
CATTY CAVAN CHAIN CHANG CHING
CLOVE COOMB CRANS CUBIT
CUMAL CUNIT DENUM DEPOH DIGIT
DRAFT DUNAM DUNUM EPHAH
GAUGE GERAH GIRTH HOMER
HUTCH JUGER LABOR LAGEN LIANG
LIBRA LIGNE LITER LITRE MEITH
METER METRE MINIM MODEL OUNCE
PEISE PERCH PLANK POUND QUIRE
RASER RHYME SALMA SCALE
SCORE SHAKU SHENG SHING SIEVE
SLEEP STACK STERE STONE STOOP
STOUP THERM TOISE TOVET TRACE
VERST YOJAN APATAN ARCHIN
ARPENT ARSHIN ASSIZE BARREL
BATMAN BEMETE BOVATE BUNDLE
BUSHEL CANADA CANTAR CHOMER
CHOPIN COLLOP COUDEE COVIDO
CUERDA DAVACH DAVOCH DECARE
DEGREE DENIER DIPODY DIRHAM
DRACHM ENGLER EXTENT FANEGA
FATHOM FEDDAN FINGER FIRKIN
FIRLOT FLAGON FODDER FORPET
FOTHER GALLON GRAMME HALEBI
HIDAGE KISHEN LEAGUE MICRON
MODULE MOGGIO MORGEN NUMBER
OITAVA OUROUB OXHIDE QANTAR
REASON SETIER SQUARE STERAD
STRIKE SULUNG TERMIN THRAVE
WINDLE YOJANA ADOULIE ALQUIRE
AMPHORA ANAPEST ARSHINE
BATTUTA BRACCIO BREADTH
CADENCE CALIPER CALORIE
CENTARE CENTNER CENTRAD
CHITTAK COMPASS CONGIUS
CONTAIN DECIARE DIOPTER
DRACHMA DRAUGHT ENTROPY
FARSAKH FARSANG FRUNDEL
FURLONG HECTARE HEMINEE
KILIARE NOCKTAT QUARTAN
QUARTER SCHEPEL SCRUPLE
SECCHIO SKEPFUL SKIPPLE
SPANGLE SPINDLE STADION
STADIUM TERTIAN VIRGATE
CAPACITY CARUCATE CENTIARE
CHETVERT CRANNOCK DACTYLIC
DECAGRAM DECIGRAM DESIATIN
DIAPASON HOGSHEAD INNOCENT
LANDYARD METEWAND PLOWGANG
PLOWGATE SCHOONER SCHOPPEN
STANDARD
(— DEPTH) SOUND
(— FOR DRINKS) JIGGER
(— FOR FISH) COT VOG CRAN LAST
DRAFT HAMPER DRAUGHT
(— FOR SHELLFISH) WASH
(— OF BEER) HANDLE

(— OF BUTTER) SPAN
(— OF CHAFF) FAN
(— OF COAL) TEN CORF KEEL
CHALDER CHALDRON
(— OF DEVELOPMENT) AGE
(— OF DISCREPANCY) LEEWAY
(— OF EELS) BIND STICK
(— OF EFFICIENCY) DUTY
(— OF FURS) MANTLE
(— OF GRAIN) MOY COOP
(— OF LIQUOR) FIFTH
(— OF MERCURY) FLASK
(— OF MINING CLAIMS) MERE
(— OF PEAS) COP
(— OF RAISINS) FRAIL
(— OF ROTATION) ANGLE
(— OF SILK) DRAMMAGE
(— OF STRAW) KEMPLE
(— OF SUPERIORITY) LEAD
(— OF TIMBER) TON STANDARD
(— OF WAR) BLOCKADE
(— OF WATCHES) LIGNE
(— OF WATERCRESS) HAND
(— OF WEIGHT FOR ARROWS)
SHILLING
(— OF WOOD) CORD STACK
(— OF WOOL FINENESS) BLOOD
(— OF WORK) POOL
(— OF YARN) LEA CLEW HEER
THREAD SPANGLE SPINDLE
(— OUT) BATCH
(ANGULAR —) ARC
(COERCIVE —) SANCTION
(DANCE —) TRACE
(DUE —) MANNER
(FULL —) SATIETY
(ROAD —) SCHENE
(SANCTIONED —) STANDARD
MEASURED NUMEROUS
MEASURELESS ENDLESS INFINITE
MEASUREMENT GAGE DEPTH
GAUGE LEVEL MEITH METAGE
DIALING MEASURE SOUNDING
(— FOR TAXATION) HIDE HIDAGE
(— OF CLOTH) ALNAGE
(— OF FINENESS) SET SETT
(LUMBER —) LAST
MEASURER METER
MEAT BEEF FISH FOOD LAMB LEAN
LIFT PORK FLESH STEAK VIFDA
VIVDA BUCCAN CAGMAG FLEECE
MATTER NUTTON TARGET PECKAGE
(— AND FISH) LAULAU
(— DRIED IN SUN) JERKY CHARQUI
PEMMICAN
(— OF CONCH) SCUNGILI
(— OF KID) CAPRETTO
(— WITH VEGETABLES) STEW
MULLIGAN
(BOILED —) SOD SODDEN BOUILLI
(BROILED —) GRISKIN GRILLADE
(BUFFALO —) FLEECE
(CANNED —) SPAM
(CHOPPED —) BURGER
(COCONUT —) COPRA
(CURED —) HAM
(CUT OF —) ARM
(DRIED —) MUMMY
(FAT —) SPECK

(FROZEN —) FRIGO
(INFERIOR —) CAGMAG STICKING
(JERKED —) BILTONG CHARQUI
(LEAN —) MUSCLE
(MINCED —) CHUET JIGOTE
RISSOLE SANDERS
(POTTED —) RILLETT
(RABBIT —) LAPAN
(RAGOUT OF —) HARICOT
(ROAST —) BREDE CABOB
(ROLLED —) BIRD
(SALTED —) JUNK MART
(SIDE —) SOWBELLY
(SMOKED —) BUCCAN
MEAT CURER BATHMAN
MEAT HOOK GAMBREL
MEAT JELLY ASPIC
MEATLESS PARVE LENTEN PAREVE
MEAT PIE PASTY
MEATUS BUR BURR ALVEARY
MEATY PITHY
MECATE MCCARTY
MECHANIC JOINER WRIGHT ARTISAN
FELTMAN SHOPMAN WORKMAN
MECHANICAL FROZEN INHUMAN
METALLIC AUTOMATIC
(NOT —) HORMIC
MECHANICALLY BLINDLY
MECHANISM FAN BOND FEED GEAR
KITE LIFT MOTE APRON CATCH
CROWD FORCE ORGAN SHAKE
SLIDE SPARK STEER ACTION
BOTTOM CUTOFF INFEED MOTION
SICKLE STRIKE BUILDER CHANNEL
CONTROL EJECTOR GIGBACK
GRIPPER GUNLOCK HOLDOUT
SETTING TRIPPER ACTUATOR
ELEVATOR KINETICS RACKWORK
SELECTOR SETWORKS SIGNALER
STEERING STOPWORK THROWOUT
MECHANIZE DESKILL AUTOMATE
MECONIN OPIANYL
MEDAL STAR AWARD STAMP PLAQUE
MEDALET OSCELLA
MEDALLION CAMEO TONDO PADUAN
PATERA PANHAGIA
MEDDLE TIG FOOL MELL MESS MIRD
TOUCH DABBLE FIDDLE FINGER
HECKLE POTTER PUTTER TAMPER
TANGLE TINKER
MEDDLER SNOOP SNOOPER
BUSYBODY KIBITZER STICKLER
STIFFLER BUTTINSKY
MEDDLESOME FRESH NEBBY
MEDDLING BUSY
MEDEA (BROTHER OF —) ABSYRTUS
(FATHER OF —) AEETES
(HUSBAND OF —) JASON AEGEUS
(MOTHER OF —) IDYIA
(SISTER OF —) CHALCIOPE
MEDIA ELASTICA
MEDIAL MEDIAN MEDIUM MIDDLE
AVERAGE
MEDIAN MEDIAL MESIAL AVERAGE
(— STRIP) MALL TERRACE
MEDIANT THIRD
MEDIATE MEAN REFEREE
MEDIATING MIDDLE MIDWAY
MEDIATOR MEANS MEDIUM

DAYSMAN MIDDLER PLACATER STICKLER

MEDIC HOP NONESUCH

MEDICAL IATRIC PHYSIC IATRICAL PAEONIAN

(— **WORK**) ALMONING

MEDICAMENT SMEGMA FRONTAL

MEDICINAL IATRIC PHYSIC MEDICAL THERIAL PHYSICAL SALUTARY THERICAL

MEDICINE DRUG MUTI PEAI DROPS GRUEL STEEL STUFF TONIC TRADE AMULET ECLEGM ELIXIR MAGUAL PHYSIC POWDER REMEDY SIMPLE ANODYNE CORDIAL HEPATIC LUCHDOM MIXTURE PLACEBO POROTIC PYROTIC SPLENIC AROMATIC DIGESTER DRUGGERY EARDROPS EMULGENT LAXATIVE LEECHDOM LENITIVE LOBLOLLY PECTORAL PHARMACY PULMONIC RELAXANT SPECIFIC STOMATIC (**CHINESE** —) SENSO (**QUACK** —) NOSTRUM (**SYSTEM OF** —) AYURVEDA (**UNIVERSAL** —) PANACEA (PL.) GALIANES

MEDICINE MAN PEAI DOCTOR KAHUNA PIACHE POWWOW SHAMAN SINGER ANGEKOK TOHUNGA CONTRARY POWWOWER

MEDIEVAL OLD GOTHIC

MEDIOCRE HACK MEAN SUCH MEDIUM AVERAGE INFERIOR MIDDLING PASSABLE

MEDITATE CAST CHEW MUSE GLOAT STUDY WEIGH PONDER RECORD IMAGINE PREPEND REFLECT REVOLVE COGITATE CONSIDER PURPENSE RUMINATE

MEDITATION MOYEN STUDY THINK DHYANA MUSING HIGGAION

MEDITATIVE MUSING MUSEFUL PENSIVE RUMINANT

MEDITERRANEAN MIDLAND

MEDIUM BATH EVEN LENS MEAN ETHER JUICE MIDST MOYEN ORGAN BALIAN BISTER BISTRE DIGEST MIDDLE MIDWAY ORACLE SLUDGE TEMPER PSYCHIC VEHICLE MEDIOCRE SHOWCASE CONTINUUM (— **OF EXCHANGE**) CURRENCY (— **OF TRANSMISSION**) AIR AIRWAVE (**CULTURE** —) AGAR STAB BROTH HYRAX SLANT CULTURE (**ENVELOPING** —) SWATH

MEDLAR MESPIL LAZAROLE

MEDLEY OLIO BABEL REVUE JUMBLE CHIVARI CLANGOR FARRAGO GOULASH MELANGE MIXTURE BROUHAHA KEDGEREE MACARONI MISHMASH RHAPSODY SLAMPAMP VARIORUM

MEDOC WINE LAFITTE

MEDREGAL BONITO

MEDULLA PITH MARROW

MEDULLA OBLONGATA BULB

MEDUSA JELLY QUARL GORGON

BLUBBER GERYONID

(**FATHER OF** —) PHORCYS

(**MOTHER OF** —) CETO

(**SLAYER OF** —) PERSEUS

(PL.) BRACT

MEEK LOW DAFT MURE LOWLY GENTLE HUMBLE PACIFIC LAMBLIKE YIELDING

MEERSCHAUM PIPE GRAVEL KIEFEKIL SEPIOLITE

MEET FIT KEP SEE COPE FACE FILL HENT NOSE CLOSE CROSS FRONT GREET INCUR OCCUR PIECE TOUCH ANSWER BATTLE BEMEET COMBAT CONCUR FULFIL INVENT SEMBLE CONTACT CONVENE CONVENT COUNCIL FULFILL SATISFY ASSEMBLE CONFRONT CONVERGE GAINCOPE (— **A BET**) SEE (— **A NEED**) SUFFICE (— **AT END**) BUTT (— **FACE TO FACE**) AFFRONT (— **SQUARELY**) ENVISAGE (— **VIOLENTLY**) CHECK HURTLE (— **WITH**) GET SEE BUMP FIND STRIKE (**ATHLETIC** —) GALA GYMKHANA

MEETING MOD FEIS MOOT CLOSE FORUM SABHA SHINE STOUR SYNOD TRYST ACCESS AUMAGA CAUCUS CHAPEL CLINIC HUDDLE POWWOW SEANCE CABINET CHAPTER COLLEGE CONTACT CONVENT COUNCIL JOLLITY MOOTING OCCURSE REVIVAL SEMINAR SITTING SYNAXIS ASSEMBLY CONGRESS DELEGACY ECCLESIA EXERCISE JUNCTION OSCULANT TERTULIA WARDMOTE (— **OF NEIGHBORS**) HUSKING (— **OF SCHOLARS**) LEVY (— **OF WORSHIPERS**) SERVICE (**ANGLO-SAXON** —) GEMOTE (**GENERAL** —) PRIME (**POLITICAL** —) CAUCUS (**PRIVATE** —) CONCLAVE (**SECRET** —) CABAL CONSULT (**SOCIAL** —) CLUB JOLLY HOBNOB (**TOWN** —) TUNMOOT

MEETINGHOUSE MORADA

MEETING PLACE AMBALAM TINWALD

MEGAPHONE VAMPHORN

MEGAPODE MALEO LEIPOA

MEGARA (FATHER OF —) CREON (**HUSBAND OF** —) HERCULES

MEGILP GUMPTION

MEHTAR BUNGY BHUNGI

MELANCHOLIA ATHYMY ATHYMIA SADNESS

MELANCHOLIC HYPPISH

MELANCHOLY WO SAD WOE BLUE DRAM DULL DUMP MARE BLUES DEARN DOWIE DREAR DUSKY GLOOM SORRY WISHT GLOOMY SOMBER SOMBRE SORROW SPLEEN SULLEN YELLOW CHAGRIN DOLEFUL DUMPISH ELEGIAC SADNESS

SPLEENY THOUGHT ATRABILE LIVERISH TRISTFUL

MELANESIAN DOBUAN KANAGA KANAKA EFATESE

MELANGE GOMBO GUMBO

MELANISM PHAEISM

MELANTERITE INKSTONE

MELATOPE EYE

MELD SET SAMBA SPREAD BOLIVIA DECLARE

MELEAGER (FATHER OF —) OENEUS (**MOTHER OF** —) ALTHAEA

MELEE BRAWL MEDLEY DOGFIGHT PELLMELL

MELIORATE MITIGATE

MELISMA JUBILUS

MELL KIRN

MELLIFLUOUS SUGARED HYBLAEAN

MELLOW AGE OMY HAZE LUSH MALM PLUM RICH RIPE SOFT FRUSH FLUTED GOLDEN MATURE

MELLOWED BEERY

MELODIOUS SOFT SOOT TUNY SWEET TUNED ARIOSO DULCET MELODIC MUSICAL SIRENIC SONGFUL STRENIC TUNABLE TUNEFUL CANOROUS CHARMING NUMEROUS SOUNDFUL (**EXCESSIVELY** —) SIRUPY SYRUPY

MELODRAMA HAM TANK

MELODY AIR HUM LAY ARIA NOTE TUNE CANTO CHANT CHARM DREAD MELOS MIRTH NIGUN CANTUS CHORAL GHAZEL MONODY NIGGUN STROKE CANZONA CANZONE CHORALE DESCANT HARMONY MEASURE MELISMA PLANXTY ROSALIA CAVATINA DIAPASON VOCALISE (— **COMPASS**) AMBITUS (**MOURNFUL** —) DUMP (**SYNAGOGAL** —S) CHAZANUT HAZANUTH

MELON PEPO GOURD MANGO CASABA CITRON DUDAIM MAYCOCK CUCURBIT HONEYDEW PEPONIDA PEPONIUM

MELT FLY RIN RUN BLOW FADE FLOW FLUX FUSE THAW FOUND LEACH SMELT SWEAL SWELT TOUCH GUTTER RELENT SOFTEN DISTILL FORMELT RESOLVE DISCANDY DISSOLVE ELIQUATE (— **AWAY**) SWEAL (— **DOWN**) RENDER (— **IRREGULARLY**) DROZE

MELTED RUN FONDU FUSED FUSILE

MELTING SOFT FUSILE FUSION

MELTWATER OUTWASH

MEMBER LIMB LITH BRANCH FELLOW FILLET GIRDER SOCIUS AMANIST ERANIST FAIRING ALBRIGHT AULARIAN BRIDLING (— **OF ANSAR**) HELPER (— **OF BALLET**) FIGURANT (— **OF BAND**) SIDEMAN (— **OF BODYGUARD**) HUSCARL (— **OF BROTHERHOOD**) ESSENE SENUSSI

(— OF CLAN) CHILD CALEBITE
(— OF CLERGY) DEFENSOR
(— OF COAST GUARD) SPAR
(— OF COUNCIL) CONSUL
HEEMRAAD
(— OF COURT) DICAST EPHETE
(— OF CREW) HAND IDLER LAYER
DRIVER STROKE BOWSMAN
FORETOP BRAKEMAN SHAREMAN
(— OF CULT) ANGEL AMIDIST
(— OF FACULTY) COUNSEL
LECTURER
(— OF FAMILY) FETII
(— OF FRATERNAL ORDER) ELK
SHRINER FORESTER KIWANIAN
(— OF FRATERNITY) GREEK
(— OF FRENCH ACADEMY)
IMMORTAL
(— OF GANG) HENCHMAN
(— OF GENTRY) SEIGNEUR
(— OF GIRL SCOUTS) BROWNIE
(— OF GREEK ARMY) EVZONE
(— OF GUILD) COMACINE
(— OF HOUSEHOLD) FAMILIAR
(— OF HUNTING PARTY) STANDER
(— OF INN OF COURT) ANCIENT
BENCHER
(— OF ITALIAN ARMY) ALPINO
(— OF KNOW-NOTHING PARTY) SAM
(— OF LEGISLATURE) SOLON
DEPUTY DELEGATE
(— OF LITERARY GROUP) FELIBRE
(— OF MIDDLE CLASS) BURGHER
(— OF PARLIAMENT) CONTENT
THINGMAN
(— OF PRIMROSE LEAGUE) KNIGHT
(— OF RELIGIOUS ORDER) DAME
FRIAR EUDIST FRAILE FRATER
HERMIT JESUIT SISTER ALEXIAN
BRINSER DERVISH HUSSITE
SEPARTE SERVANT CENOBITE
EXORCIST HUMANIST SALESIAN
(— OF RETINUE) SEQUEL SEQUENT
(— OF RUSSIAN ARISTOCRACY)
BOYAR BOYARD
(— OF SAME GENUS) CONGENER
(— OF SECRET ORGANIZATION)
DEMOLAY
(— OF SECRET SOCIETY) BOXER
(— OF SECT) DRUSE HASID KHOJA
AUDIAN BRAHMO CATHAR DIPPER
DOPPER IBADHI JUMPER KHLYST
SMARTA AISSAWA AJIVIKA AUDAEAN
CAINITE CHASSID DREAMER EMPIRIC
EUCHITE IBADITE ISAWIYA ISMAILI
RAPPIST SEVENER AQUARIAN
CALIXTIN EBIONITE FAMILIST
GLASSITE LABADIST SADDUCEE
SEVERIAN SIMONIAN
(— OF STAFF) ATTACHE
(— OF STATE) CITIZEN
(— OF STOCK EXCHANGE)
BOARDMAN
(— OF TEAM) SPARE BOBBER
KICKER
(— OF TRIBE) LEVITE JUDAHITE
LAMANITE
(— OF UPPER CLASS) EFFENDI
(— OF VARNA) SUDRA SHUDRA

(— OF WHITE RACE) HAOLE
(— OF WINDOW) APRON
(—S OF CLASS) FRY
(—S OF PROFESSION) FACULTY
(—S OF SECT) SKOPTSY
(—S OF TRIBUNAL) ACUERDO
(ARCHITECTURAL —) FAN ARCH
FLAT SILL SPAN GABLE SOCLE
STILE STILT CORBEL FASCIA
CONSOLE CORNICE
(CHURCH —) GREEK LATIN DANITE
DUNKER KIRKER TUNKER BAPTIST
BEGHARD BROTHER DUNKARD
KIRKMAN SECEDER ARMENIAN
BRYANITE CATHOLIC DISCIPLE
DOWIEITE JACOBITE
(CHURCH —S) FAITHFUL
(EVERY —) ALL
(FEEBLEST —) WRIG
(FULL —) GREMIAL
(OLDEST —) FATHER
(OVERHANGING —) BRACKET
(POLITICAL —) CADET ENDEK SHIRT
GUELPH HUNKER LEADER APRISTA
LEFTIST LIBERAL BUCKTAIL
DEMOCRAT HERODIAN LABORITE
(PROJECTING —) TENON
(SENIOR —) DOYEN
(TENSION —) HANGER
(TERMINAL —) TOE
MEMBERSHIP SEAT GARTER
GUILDRY
MEMBRANE RIM WEB CAUL COAT
DURA FELL HEAD TELA GALEA
HYMEN VELUM AMNION AMNIOS
EXTINE INTINE MENINX MOTHER
MUCOSA PLEURA RETINA SEPTUM
SEROSA TIMBAL TUNICA TYMPAN
BLANKET CAPSULE CHORION
CUTICLE EPICYTE HYALOID
OOLEMMA PUTAMEN STRATUM
VELAMEN ECTODERM ENDOCYST
ENVELOPE EPENDYMA EPISPORE
EXOLEMMA INDUSIUM INTEXINE
LABELLUM PATAGIUM PELLICLE
STRIFFEN
(— OF ORANGE) ZEST
(NICTITATING —) HAW
(TYMPANIC —) TYMPAN MYRINGA
DRUMHEAD DRUMSKIN
(PL.) ADNEXA ANNEXA MENINGES
MEMBRANOUS HUSKY SKINNY
HYMENOID SCARIOSE SCARIOUS
MEMENTO RELIC TOKEN MEMORY
TROPHY KEEPSAKE REMINDER
SOUVENIR
MEMINNA PEESOREH
MEMNON (FATHER OF —) TITHONUS
(MOTHER OF —) AURORA
(SLAYER OF —) ACHILLES
MEMOIR ELOGE RECORD HISTORY
MEMORIAL
MEMORABLE GRAND SIGNAL
CLASSIC NOTABLE MEMORIAL
NAMEABLE
MEMORANDA (SET OF —) TICKLER
MEMORANDUM BILL CHIT NOTE
SLIP BRIEF JURAT CIPHER DOCKET
MEMOIR MINUTE TICKET JOTTING

MEMORIAL NOTANDUM PROTOCOL
MEMORIAL AHU AGALMA CAHIER
FACTUM MEMOIR MEMORY RECORD
TROPHY DENKMAL MEMENTO
MENTION EBENEZER MONUMENT
MEMORIZE LEARN MANDATE
REMEMBER
MEMORY MIND HEART IMAGE STORE
RECALL RECORD MEMENTO
STORAGE MEMORIAL SOUVENIR
(OF POOR —) FLUFFY
(PAINFUL —) SCAR
MEN THEY ORANG INNUIT MANHEAD
MANHOOD MANKIND MENFOLK
HUMANITY
MENACE BOAST IMPEND THREAT
BOGEYMAN MINATORY THREATEN
MENACING STOUT SURLY FIERCE
TOWARD MINATORY
MEN-AT-ARMS CHIVALRY
MEND DO FIX BEET DARN HEAL
HELP STOP TINK AMEND CLOUT
EMEND GRAFT MOISE PALCH
COBBLE DOCTOR FETTLE RANTER
REFORM REPAIR SOLDER SPETCH
TINKLE IMPROVE INWEAVE REDRESS
RIGHTLE
(— BY ADDING FEATHERS) IMP
(— CLUMSILY) BOTCH
(— MEN'S CLOTHES) BUSHEL
MENDACIOUS FALSE DISHONEST
MENDACITY LYING DECEIT FALSITY
UNTRUTH
MENDER TINKER KETTLER
BEATSTER
MENDICANCY BEGGARY
MENDICANT NAGA DANDI FAKIR
FRIAR UDASI BEGGAR BHIKKU
FAKEER FRATER GOSAIN AJIVIKA
BAIRAGI EUCHITE VAIRAGI
PANDARAM SANNYASI
MENDING COBBLE
MENEL NELL
MENELAUS (BROTHER OF —)
AGAMEMNON
(FATHER OF —) PLISTHENES
(WIFE OF —) HELEN
MENHADEN POGY PORGY BUNKER
CHEBOG SHINER ALEWIFE BUGFISH
BUGHEAD CLUPEID ELLFISH
FATBACK OLDWIFE SAVELHA
SHADINE WHITING BONYFISH
HARDHEAD
MENHIR BOUTA GORSEDD PEULVAN
CATSTONE HAGIOLITH
MENIAL FAG BASE LOON PAGE
KNAVE DRIVEL HARLOT POTBOY
VARLET SERVILE SLAVISH BANAUSIC
SCULLION SERVITOR
MENISCOID CRESCENT
MENNONITE HOOKER AMISHMAN
AMMANITE HUTERITE
MENOETIUS (BROTHER OF —)
ATLAS PROMETHEUS
(FATHER OF —) ACTOR
(MOTHER OF —) AEGINA
(SON OF —) PATROCLUS
MENOPAUSE CLIMAX
MENSTRUATE FLOW

MENSTRUATING SICK
MENSTRUATION FLOW CURSE
FLUOR CRAMPS PERIOD COURSES
MENSTRUUM SOLVENT
MENTAL IDEAL GENIAL INWARD
MINDLY PHRENIC PSYCHIC
CEREBRAL
MENTALITY MIND SENSE ACUMEN
REASON SPIRIT PSYCHISM
MENTHA LABIATE
MENTHANE TERPANE
MENTHOL CAMPHOR
MENTION CALL CITE HINT MIND
MING MINT NAME CHEEP CLEPE
SPEAK TOUCH MEMBER NOTICE
SPEECH MEANING SPECIFY
SUGGEST CITATION INSTANCE
MEMORATE REHEARSE REMEMBER
(— BY NAME) NEMN NEMME
NEMPNE
(— CASUALLY) DROP
(HONORABLE —) ACCESSIT
MENTOR TEACHER CICERONE
MENTUM PERULA
MENU CARD CARTE
MEPERIDINE DEMEROL
MEPHISTOPHELIAN SATANIC
MERCAPTAN THIOL
MERCEDARIAN NOLASCAN
RANSOMER
MERCENARY HACK VENAL JACKAL
HESSIAN PINDARI HIRELING
WAGELING
MERCER SILKMAN
MERCERIZE SCHREINER
MERCHANDISE CARGO CHEAP
GOODS STUFF WARES ARTWARE
CHAFFER SHIPPER TRAFFIC
CHAFFERY SALEWARE
(CHEAP SHODDY —) BORAX
(RETURNED —) COMEBACK
MERCHANT ARAB SETH SETT TELI
WALLA BADGER FACTOR KITELY
NEPMAN RETAIL TAIPAN TRADER
ANTONIO CHAPMAN GOLADAR
HANSARD HOWADJI CHANDLER
HUCKSTER MARCHAND POVINDAH
SOUDAGUR
(GRAIN —) LAMBADI
(GREAT —) TAIPAN
(WINE —) VINTNER
MERCIFUL KIND MILD HUMANE
RUEFUL TENDER CLEMENT LENIENT
MILDFUL PITIFUL SPARING
GRACIOUS QUEMEFUL
MERCILESS GRIM CRUEL SHARP
BLOODY FIERCE SAVAGE WANTON
PITILESS
MERCURY HG AZOCH AZOTH
DRAGON HERMES SPIRIT CHIBRIT
MARKERY TEUTATES
(FATHER OF —) JUPITER
(MOTHER OF —) MAIA
MERCY LAW ORE HORE PITY RUTH
GRACE GRITH BLITHE LENITY
CHARITY CLEMENCY LENIENCY
MERE BARE NUDE ONLY PURE PUTE
SOLE VERY NAKED SHEER SINGLE
MEREL PIN

MERELY BUT JUST ONLY BARELY
PURELY SIMPLY SINGLY SOLELY
ALONELY UTTERLY ENTIRELY
SCARCELY
MERETRICIOUS CHEAP GAUDY
GILDED PUNKISH
MERGANSER SMEE SMEW HARLE
SNOWL SPIKE HERALD SAWNEB
WEASER BRACKET GARBILL
JACKSAW RANTOCK SAWBILL
TADPOLE TOWHEAD TWEEZER
WHEEZER EARLDUCK MOSSHEAD
MERGE FUSE JOIN BLEND ENTER
GLIDE UNIFY MINGLE COMMERGE
CONFLATE
MERGING BLEND FUSION
MERICARP COCCUS
**MERIDIAN (THOSE LIVING UNDER
SAME —)** ANTOECI
MERINGUE KISS
MERINO DELAINE
MERISTEM PERIBLEM
MERIT DUE EARN MEED PUNY
BROOK THANK WORTH DESERT
VIRTUE WRIHTE DEMERIT DESERVE
PUDDING
(— CONSIDERATION) COUNT
(POSSESSING —) WORTHY
MERITED JUST
(NOT —) INDIGN
MERITORIOUS CAPITAL MERITORY
THANKFUL VALOROUS
MERL BLACKIE
MERLON COP
MERMAID NIXIE SIREN MERROW
MERWOMAN
MERMAN SEAMAN MANFISH
MEROPE (BROTHER OF —)
PHAETHON
(FATHER OF —) CRESPHONTES
(HUSBAND OF —) SISYPHUS
(MOTHER OF —) CYPSELUS
MEROPODITE FEMUR MEROS
MEROZOITE AGAMETE
MERRILY GAILY GAMELY LUSTICK
JOYOUSLY
MERRIMENT FUN JOY GALE GLEE
JEST UTAS DERAY MIRTH FROLIC
SPLEEN DAFFERY DAFFING FESTIVE
JOLLITY WAGGERY HILARITY
MERRY GAY BOON CANT GLAD GOLE
BONNY CADGY CRANK DROLL
JOLLY LIGHT LUSTY MURRY SUNNY
VOGIE VOKIE BLITHE COCKET
FROLIC JOCANT JOCUND JOVIAL
JOYOUS LIVELY FEASTLY GLEEFUL
HOLIDAY JOCULAR LUSTICK
RAFFING WINSOME CHIRPING
DISPOSED FESTIVAL GAMESOME
GLEESOME LAUGHING PLEASANT
SPANKING SPORTFUL SPORTIVE
MERRY-ANDREW AIRY ZANY ANTIC
DROLL JESTER BUFFOON
MERRY-GO-ROUND CAROUSEL
TURNABOUT
MERRYMAKING ALE MAY RAG KIRN
PLOY REVEL GAIETY RACKET
SPLORE CARNIVAL
MERRYTHOUGHT WISHBONE

MERUS PALM
MESA MESILLA CARTOUCH
MESADENIA CACALIA
MESCAL PEYOTE WOKOWI MEXICAL
CHALLOTE
MESCALERO FARAON
MESENTERY CROW RUFFLE
MESH MASK MOKE CHAIN PITCH
SHALE ACCRUE ENGAGE MASCLE
SCREEN SCREENING
(— IMPROPERLY) BUTT
(IN —) DIRECT
MESHED ENGAGED
MESOCARP FLESH
MESOMORPHIC SOMAL SOMATIC
ATHLETIC
MESOPODIUM PETIOLE
MESOPOTAMIA (TREE OF —) HOMA
MESOTONIC TERTIAN MEANTONE
MESQUITE HONEY KEAWE PACAY
CASHAW ALGAROBA HONEYPOD
IRONWOOD MOSQUITO
MESS JAG JAM MIX MUX PIE SOP
CLAT FIST HASH JAMB MUCK MULL
MUSS SLUB SOSS STEW SUSS
BOTCH CAUCH JAKES STREW SWILL
BOLLIX BUNGLE CADDLE CLATCH
JUMBLE MUCKER PICKLE PUDDLE
SOZZLE TUMBLE MAMMOCK
MULLOCK SCAMBLE SLOTTER
COUSCOUS DISORDER LOBLOLLY
SHAMBLES SLAISTER
(— AROUND) JUKE
(— OF FOOD) SAND
(GREASY —) GAUM
(SLOPPY —) SLOBBER SLAISTER
MESSAGE CHIT MODE SAND SEND
WIRE WORD RUMOR BREVET
CIPHER ERRAND GOSPEL LETTER
SCROLL BLINKER BODWORD
DEPECHE EMBASSY MISSION
SENDING TIDINGS AEROGRAM
CREDENCE DISPATCH
(— BY FLAGS) HOIST
(— FROM GOD) ANGEL
(CHRISTIAN —) EVANGEL
(CIPHER —) SCYTALE
(COMPLIMENTARY —) RECADO
MESSALIAN EUCHITE
MESSENE (FATHER OF —) TRIOPAS
(HUSBAND OF —) POLYCAON
MESSENGER BODE PEON POST
SAND SEND TOTY VAUX ANGEL
ENVOY MUMMU VISOR BEADLE
BROKER BUNENE CHIAUS HERALD
LEGATE NUNCIO PIGEON RUNNER
APOSTLE CARRIER CASHBOY
CONTACT COURANT COURIER
EXPRESS FORAGER FORAYER
MALACHI MERCURY MESSAGE
MISSIVE NAMTARU PATAMAR
TOTYMAN TROTTER TRUMPET
EMISSARY FOREGOER HIRCARRA
LOBBYGOW NUNCIATE ORDINARY
PORTATOR
(— OF APSU AND TIAMAT) MUMMU
(— OF GOD) ANGEL
(— OF SHAMASH) BUNENE

(— OF THE GODS) HERMES MERCURY
(MOUNTED —) COSSID ESTAFET
(RELIGIOUS —) APOSTLE
(UNDERWORLD —) NAMTARU
MESSIAH CHRIST WOVOKA
MESSMATE YUBA
MESSUAGE HAW TOFT MEESE MIDSTEAD
MESSY GOOEY SLOPPY SOZZLY STICKY
MESTIZO CHOLO LADINO CURIBOCA MAMELUCO
METAL ORE TIN BODY DIET GOLD IRON LEAD ZINC BARIUM CESIUM CHROME COBALT COPPER INDIUM LATTIN NICKEL OSMIUM RADIUM SILVER SODIUM BISMUTH CADMIUM CALCIUM HAFNIUM IRIDIUM LITHIUM MERCURY RHENIUM RHODIUM THORIUM URANIUM YTTRIUM ALUMINUM ANTIMONY CHROMIUM DEADHEAD PLATINUM RUBIDIUM SCANDIUM TANTALUM TINCTURE TITANIUM TUNGSTEN VANADIUM
(— IN MASS) BULLION
(— IN SHEETS) LEAF PLATE
(BABBITT —) LINING
(GROUND —) BRONZING
(HEAVIEST —) OSMIUM
(IMPURE MASS OF —) REGULUS
(LIGHTEST —) LITHIUM
(LIQUID —) MERCURY
(MASS OF —) INGOT
(MOLTEN —) TAP SQUIRT
(OLD POT —) POTIN
(PERFORATED —) STENCIL
(PIECE OF CRUDE —) SLUG
(POINTED —) NAIL
(POROUS —) SPONGE
(SEMIFINISHED —) SEMIS
(SHEET —) DOUBLES KALAMEIN
(WASTE —) GATE
METALLIC HARD TINNY
METALLOPHONE SARON
METALWARE LORMERY GRAYWARE PONTYPOOL
METALWORK ZOGAN
METALWORKER BARMAN FOONER FORKMAN FOUNDER SUDSMAN
METAMERE SOMITE SEGMENT MEROSOME
METAMORPHOSE TURN SHAPE INDENIZE TRANSMEW
METAMORPHOSIS METABOLE PETALODY PHYLLODY SEPALODY
METANIRA (HUSBAND OF —) CELEUS
(SON OF —) DEMOPHON TRIPTOLEMUS
METAPHOR IMAGE TROPE FIGURE
METAPHORICAL FIGURAL FIGURATE TROPICAL
METASTOMA LABIUM
METATE QUERL
METE DEAL GIVE AWARD SERVE
METEMPSYCHOSIS SAMSARA
METEOR STAR ARGID CETID COMID DRAKE LUPID LYRID URSID ANTLID

AUGUST BOLIDE BOOTID CORVID CYGNID DRAGON HYDRID LIBRID LYNCID LYRAID PHASMA PISCID TAURID AQUARID AQUILID ARIETID AURIGID CAMELID CANCRID CEPHEID CORONID GEMINID MEATURE ORIONID PEGASID PERSEID POLARID PRODIGY COLUMBID CRATERID DRACONID ERIDANID FIREBALL FORNAXID HERCULID LACERTID SAGITTID SCORPIID SHOTSTAR TOUCANID VIRGINID
METEORITE BAETYL BOLIDE ANDRITE ATAXITE EUCRITE AEROLITE AEROLITH BAETULUS BAETYLUS IREOLITE SIDERITE SKYSTONE
METEOROLOGY AEROLOGY
METER IONIC METRE SEVEN ALCAIC RHYTHM CADENCE GAYATRI MEASURE SUBMETER VIAMETER YAWMETER
(10,000 —S) GREX
(CUBIC —) STERE
(MILLIONTH OF —) MICRON
(NETHERLANDS —) ELL
(SQUARE —) CENTIARE
(VEDIC —) GAYATRI
METHADONE AMIDONE
METHANE FORMENE
METHANOL WOODINE CARBINOL
METHEGLIN MEAD
METHOD ART WAY DART FORM GARB GATE KINK LINE MIDS MODE REDE RULE SORT ORDER STYLE TRACK USAGE COURSE ENGINE MANNER STEREO SYSTEM FASHION PROCESS TACTICS WRINKLE ADJUVANT STANDARD
(— OF ANGLING) HARLING
(— OF APPEALING) DHARNA DHURNA
(— OF COLORING TEA) FACING
(— OF CONSTRUCTION) JACAL
(— OF CULTIVATION) JUM JOOM STUMPING
(— OF DIETING) BANTING
(— OF DISTILLATION) DESCENT
(— OF ELECTION) SCRUTINY
(— OF FATTENING POULTRY) GAVAGE
(— OF INDUCTION) CANON
(— OF MILKING) NIEVLING
(— OF MURAL DECORATION) KHASI
(— OF PROCEDURE) GAME
(— OF TRACKING) DOVAP
(— OF TREATMENT) SCOPE
(CLEVER —) KINK KINKLE
(FIXED —) FORMULA
(MEDICAL —) CUSHION
(OUTMODED —) ARCHAISM
(PAINTING —) GOUACHE
(PRINTING —) AQUATONE
(SCIENTIFIC —) BACONISM
(SURVEYING —) STADIA
(USUAL —) COURSE PRACTICE
METHODICAL TRIG EXACT FORMAL ORDERLY REGULAR ORDINARY ORDINATE

METHODIST JUMPER WESLEYAN SWADDLING
METHODIZE REGULATE
METHYLAL FORMAL
METICULOUS FUSSY STICKY CAREFUL FINICAL FINICKY
METONYM SYNONYM
METRICAL MEASURED
(— QUANTITY) MATRA
METROPOLIS CITY SEAT CAPITAL
METROPOLITAN EPARCH
METTLE SAUL PRIDE SPUNK GINGER SPIRIT COURAGE
METTLESOME FIERY PROUD SKEIGH SPUNKY STUFFY FLIGHTY GINGERY SPIRITED
MEW WOW MEWL MIAOU MIAOW INTERMEW SEEDBIRD
MEWER WRAWLER
MEWL WRAWL
MEXICAN CHOLO LEPERO WETBACK
MEXICAN-AMERICAN PACHUCO
MEXICAN ELM MEZCAL
MEXICAN ONYX TECALI
MEXICAN PERSIMMON CHAPOTE
MEXICAN POPPY ARGEMONE
MEXICAN TEA BASOTE APASOTE FISHWEED WORMSEED

MEXICO
COIN: PESO TLAC ADOBE CLACO TLACO AZTECA CENTAVO PIASTER
LAKE: CHAPALA
MEASURE: PIE VARA ALMUD BARIL JARRA LABOR LEGUA LINEA SITIO FANEGA PULGADA
MOUNTAIN: BUFA BLANCO CUPULA PEROTE ORIZABA
PENINSULA: BAJA YUCATAN
PEOPLE: MAM CORA MAYA SERI XOVA AZTEC NAHUA OPATA OTOMI ZOQUE EUDEVE MIXTEC TOLTEC NAYARIT TEPANEC TOTONAC ZACATEC ZAPOTEC TEZCUCAN TOTONACO ZACATECO
RIVER: BRAVO LERMA BALSAS GRANDE PANUCO TABASCO GRIJALVA SANTIAGO
STATE: LEON NUEVO COLIMA OAXACA SONORA CHIAPAS DURANGO HIDALGO NAYARIT SINALOA TABASCO YUCATAN CAMPECHE QUINTANA VERACRUZ
TOWN: LEON TEPIC ARIZPE COLIMA JALAPA JUAREZ MERIDA OAXACA PARRAL POTOSI PUEBLA CANANEA DURANGO GUAYMAS MORELIA ORIZABA PACHUCA TAMPICO TORREON CULIACAN MAZATLAN MONCLOVA SALTILLO VERACRUZ
VOLCANO: COLIMA TOLUCA JORULLO PARICUTIN
WEIGHT: BAG ONZA CARGA LIBRA

MARCO ADARME ARROBA
OCHAVA TERCIO QUINTAL

MEZZANINE ENTRESOL
MIASMA MALARIA MAREMMA
MIB MIGGLE
MICA DAZE TALC GLIST SLUDE
BIOTITE GLIMMER ALURGITE
FUCHSITE
MICE (BREEDING PLACE FOR —)
MURARIUM
MICHAEL MIKE MICKY MICHEL
MIGUEL

MICHIGAN
BAY: SAGINAW THUNDER
KEWEENAW STURGEON
CAPITAL: LANSING
COLLEGE: ALMA WAYNE ADRIAN
ALBION CALVIN OLIVET OWOSSO
OAKLAND
COUNTY: IONIA IOSCO ALCONA
GOGEBIC OSCEOLA TUSCOLA
KALKASKA
INDIAN: OTTAWA
LAKE: BURT TORCH HOUGHTON
NATIVE: WOLVERINE
NICKNAME: WOLVERINE
RIVER: CASS HURON SAGINAW
ESCANABA
STATE BIRD: ROBIN
STATE FLOWER: APPLEBLOSSOM
STRAIT: MACKINAW
TOWN: ALMA CARO FLINT ADRIAN
ALPENA BADAXE OWOSSO
DETROIT LANSING SAGINAW
ANNARBOR CADILLAC
ESCANABA MANISTEE MUNISING
MUSKEGON CHEBOYGAN
KALAMAZOO

MICONIA TAMONEA
MICROBE GERM
MICROMETER BIFILAR
(— **CALIPER)** MIKE
MICRON MU
MICRONESIAN KANAGA NAURUAN
(— **ISLAND)** NUI GUAM ROTA TRUK
MAKIN NAURU WOTHO MAJURO
MICROORGANISM BUG GERM
AZOFIER BUTYRIC BACILLUS
MICROPHONE BUG MIKE PARABOLA
MICROPYLE FORAMEN
MICROSECOND (HUNDREDTH OF —)
SHAKE
MICROSCOPE GLASS SCOPE
MICROSCOPIC SMALL MINUTE
MICROSPECIES JORDANON
MICROSPOROPHYLL STAMEN
MICROTONE SRUTI SHRUTI
MICROTUS ARVICOLA
MIDDAY NOON UNDERN MIDNOON
NOONDAY MERIDIAN NOONTIME
MIDDEN BASURAL SAMBAQUI
MIDDLE MEDIO MESNE NAVEL
CENTER MEDIAL MEDIAN CENTRAL
MEDIATE MEDILLE

(— **OF SAIL)** BUNT
(— **OF SHIP)** WAIST
(— **OF WINTER)** HOLL HOWE
MIDDLE-AGED MIDDLING
MIDDLE EAST (— NATIVE) WOG
MIDDLEMAN BUTTY BROKER
DEALER FOGGER JOBBER LUMPER
BUMAREE BUTTYMAN HUCKSTER
REGRATER
MIDDLER PLATEMAN
MIDDLETONE HALFTONE
MIDDLING FAIR MEAN SOSO
NEUTRAL MEDIOCRE MEETERLY
(PL.) DUNST FARINA SHARPS
SIZINGS SEMOLINA WEATINGS
MIDGE GNAT SMUT MIDGET MINGIE
PUNKIE WEEVIL
MIDNIGHT NOON NOONTIDE
MIDPOINT BASION PORION STOMION
GNATHION
MIDRIB COSTA SHAFT MIDVEIN
(— **OF LEAF)** PEN
MIDRIFF APRON SKIRT
MIDSHIPMAN WART MIDDY PLEBE
REEFER SNOTTY OLDSTER
MIDST DEPTH CENTER MIDDLE
MIDWARD
MIDSUMMER DAY JOHNSMAS
MIDWAY MEDIO GAYWAY HALFWAY
MIDWIFE BABA DHAI GAMP
HOWDY LUCKY COMMER CUMMER
GRANNY HOWDIE KIMMER LUCINA
LUCKIE GRANNIE HEBAMME
MIEN AIR BROW VULT ASPECT
DEMEAN MANNER OSTENT BEARING
DEMEANOR
MIG MIB DUCK
MIGHT ARM BULK MOTE FORCE
MOUND POWER SHOULD STRENGTH
MIGHTILY HEFTILY
MIGHTINESS (HIGH —) HOGEN
MIGHTY FELL HIGH KEEN MAIN
MUCH RANK RICH VAST FELON
GREAT HEFTY STERN STOOR
POTENT STRONG VIOLENT
ENORMOUS FORCEFUL POWERFUL
PUISSANT SAMSONIC
MIGNONETTE WOLD RESEDA
LUTEOLA
MIGRAINE MEGRIM
MIGRANT MOVER
MIGRATE RUN FLIT TREK DRIFT
FLIGHT COLONIZE
MIGRATION TREK EXODUS FLIGHT
EELFARE EMOTION PASSAGE
DIASPORA
MIKADO DAIRI
MIKIR ARLENG
MILD LEW MOY CALM COLD EASY
FAIR LENT MEEK NESH PLUM SOFT
TAME WARM BALMY BUXOM GREEN
LIGHT LITHE MELCH MELSH MILKY
NAISH QUIET BENIGN FACILE GENIAL
GENTLE HUMBLE KINDLY REMISS
SMOOTH AMIABLE CLEMENT
LENIENT VELVETY BENEDICT
DOVELIKE FAVONIAN LENITIVE
MERCIFUL SOOTHING TRANQUIL
MILDEW OIDIUM

MILDLY FEEBLY GENTLY
MILDNESS MILD LENITY SUAVITY
CLEMENCY HUMILITY KINDNESS
MILE (3 —S) HOUR LEAGUE
(NAUTICAL —) KNOT KAIRI
(ONE-EIGHTH —) FURLONG
(SEA —) NAUT
MILESTONE LEAGUE
MILFOIL AHARTALAV
MILIEU CLIMATE TERRAIN AMBIENCE
MILITANT WARRISH FIGHTING
MILITARY MARTIAL WARLIKE
MILITANT SOLDIERY
(— **POST)** THANA
(— **SCIENCE)** LOGISTICS
MILITIA FYRD ARRAY MILICE
MILITIAMAN CHOCO UHLAN LUMPER
TRAINER SHIRTMAN
MILK COW LAC FUZZ LAIT PAIL SKIM
BLEED JUICE MILCH MULCT BOTTLE
ELICIT RAMMEL STROKE SUCKLE
EXPLOIT
(— **DRY)** STRIP
(— **OUT)** EMULGE
(— **PAN)** LEAD
(— **PRODUCT)** KHOA
(— **SICKNESS)** TIRES
(BREAST —) SUCK DIDDY
(COW'S —) MESS
(CURDLED —) SKYR TYRE TAYER
LOPPER CLABBER TATMJOLK
(FERMENTED —) KUMISS MATZOON
(NEW —) RAMMEL
(SOUR —) SKYR WHIG BONNY
BLEEZE BLINKY CLABBER JOCOQUE
(WATERY —) BLASH
MILK CART KIT PRAM BUNGEY
MILKFISH AWA BANGOS SABALO
SAVOLA BANDENG SABALOTE
MILKING (— PARLOR) BAIL
(— **TIME)** MEAL
MILKLESS PARVE PAREVE
MILKMAN KITTER CHALKER
MILK PAIL TRUG LEGLEN
MILK SHAKE FRAPPE
MILK SNAKE ADDER
MILKSOP SOP MOLLY COCKNEY
MILKWOOD MELKHOUT
MILKWORT SENECA CENTAURY
GAYWINGS
MILKY MILCHY LACTARY LACTEAL
OPALOID LACTEOUS
MILL FULL MILN STAR BREAK FLOUR
KNURL QUERN CHERRY FANNER
STAMPS BLOOMER MOLINET
PUGMILL SMUTTER ARRASTRA
BUHRMILL SPINNERY TRAPICHE
WALKMILL
(CHOCOLATE —) MOLINET
(FULLING —) STOCKS
(SHINGLING —) FORGE
(SUGAR —) CENTRAL TRAPICHE
MILLBOARD TARBOARD
MILLDAM WARREN WARRANT
MILLED GRAINED
MILLENARIAN CHILIAST
MILLENIUM CHILIAD
MILLER MILLMAN STOCKER
MULTURER NILLWARD

MILLER'S-THUMB BLOB CULL
CABOT CHABOT COTTOID MUDDLER
BULLHEAD
MILLET BUDA KODA KOUS MOHA
ARZUN BAJRA CHENA CUMBU
DUKHN DURRA GRAIN HIRSE KODRA
MILLY PANIC PROSO TENAI WHISK
BAJREE DHURRA HUREEK JONDLA
JOWARI MILIUM DAGASSA PANICLE
ZABURRO BIRDSEED KADIKANE
MILLHAND CROPMAN
MILLILITER MIL
MILLIMETER LI
  (THOUSANDTH OF —) MICRON
MILLINER ARTISTE MODISTE
MILLING GRAINING
MILLION CONTO QUENT
  (10 —) CRORE
MILLIPEDE JULID POLYPOD
DIPLOPOD PILLWORM RINGWORM
WIREWORM
MILLISECOND SIGMA
MILLPOND DAM MILLDAM BINNACLE
MILLPOOL
MILLRACE LADE LEAD LEAT
FOREBAY TAILRACE
MILLRYND INK
MILLSTONE RYND STONE BEDDER
LEDGER RUNNER
  (PL.) RUN
MILLSTREAM FLEAM
MILLWORKER DOGGER
MILO SORGHUM
MILPA LADANG
MILT MILK SEED SPLEEN
MILTONIST DIVORCER
MIMAS (FATHER OF —) THEANO
  (MOTHER OF —) AMYCUS
  (SLAYER OF —) MEZENTIUS
MIME ACTOR MIMER MIMIC
  (PL.) MIMIAMBI
MIMEOGRAPH RONEO
MIMIC APE HIT COPY MIME MINT
MOCK MOCKER MONKEY COPYCAT
IMITATE PAGEANT
MIMICRY APERY MIMESIS MOCKAGE
MOCKERY
MIMOSA AROMA CASSIE ALBIZZIA
HUISACHE TURMERIC
MINCE CHOP SHEAR FINICK
MINCED HACHE
MINCEMEAT GIGOT MINCE
MINCING NIMINY FINICAL MINIKIN
MIGNIARD SKIPJACK
MINCINGLY FINE GINGERLY
MIND CIT CHIT HEAD HEED MOOD
NOTE NOUS RECK SOUL BESEE
BRAIN SENSE SKULL WATCH
ANIMUS MATTER NOTICE PSYCHE
REGARD COURAGE SENSORY
SUBJECT THINKER THOUGHT
  (CONSCIOUS —) SENTIENT
  (INFINITE —) GOD
  (RIGHT FRAME OF —) TUNE
  (YEAR'S —) MINNING
MINDFUL HEEDY MINDLY HEEDFUL
MINE BAL PIT DELF HOLE HUEL
MEUM BARGH DELFT DELPH METAL
STOPE WHEAL COYOTE GOPHER

GROOVE RESCUE BONANZA
BORASCA COALPIT MINERAL
OPENCUT TORPEDO GOLCONDA
MYNPACHT PROSPECT
  (— BY BLASTING) SHOOT
  (— IRREGULARLY) GOPHER
  (— PASSAGE) SLUM
  (COAL —) ROB COALPIT COLLIERY
  (MILITARY —) FOUGADE FOUGASSE
  (OLD —) GWAG
  (RICH —) GOLCONDA
  (TIN —) STANNARY
  (UNPRODUCTIVE —) SHICER
  BORASCA
MINER PECK PICK PYKE BARER
DOGGY ARTIST BUCKER CUTTER
DAMMER DELVER DIGGER GANGER
GETTER HAGGER JUMPER MATTER
PELTER REEFER SNIPER STOPER
TINNER TOPMAN VANNER COLLIER
CRUTTER DIRGLER FEIGHER
GEORDIE GROOVER HITCHER
HUTCHER LEADMAN PICKMAN
PIKEMAN PIONEER PLUGMAN
ROCKMAN SNUBBER ENTRYMAN
HEADSMAN STRIPPER WINZEMAN
  (— WHO WORKS ALONE) HATTER
MINERAL JET GEET HOST MINE
SPAR BERYL BLOOM EARTH FLUOR
GLEBE GUEST LENAD SQUAT TRONA
ACMITE ALAITE AUGITE BARITE
BARYTE BLENDE CASTOR CERITE
COCKLE CURITE DAVYNE EGERAN
EHLITE ERRITE GALENA GARNET
GYPSUM HALITE HAUYNE HELVIN
HUMITE ILLITE IOLITE LABITE MIXITE
NATRON NOSEAN NOSITE PINITE
RUTILE SALITE SILICA SPHENE
SPINEL ADAMINE ADAMITE ADELITE
ALTAITE ALUMITE ALUNITE AMOSITE
APATITE ATOPITE AXINITE AZORITE
AZULITE AZURITE BAUXITE BAZZITE
BELLITE BISMITE BITYITE BOHMITE
BOLEITE BORNITE BRUCITE CALCITE
CELSIAN CYANITE DIAMOND DICKITE
DUFTITE EDENITE EPIDOTE ERIKITE
ERINITE EUCLASE FLOKITE GAGEITE
GAHNITE GEDRITE GLADITE GOTHITE
GUMMITE HELVINE HESSITE HOPEITE
HOWLITE HULSITE IHLEITE ILVAITE
INESITE INYOITE ISERITE JADEITE
JARLITE JOSEITE KEMPITE KERNITE
KOPPITE KOTOITE LANGITE LARNITE
LAURITE LAUTITE LEHIITE LEIFITE
LEONITE LEPTITE LEUCITE LOWEITE
MARTITE MELLITE OKENITE PALAITE
PENNINE PETZITE PYRITES RATHITE
REALGAR RETZIAN RHAGITE RINKITE
ROMEITE ROSSITE SENAITE SODDITE
SVABITE SYLVITE THORITE TURGITE
ULEXITE UTAHITE UVANITE VAUXITE
VOGLITE VRBAITE WARBITE WIIKITE
ZEOLITE ZINCITE ZOISITE ZORGITE
ZUNYITE AIKINITE ALLANITE
ALLUVIAL ALUNOGEN AMBONITE
ANAUXITE ANCYCITE ANDORITE
ANKERITE ARIEGITE ARMENITE
ARTINITE ASBOLITE AUGELITE
AUTUNITE AWARUITE BADENITE

BAKERITE BARARITE BARYLITE
BAVENITE BETAFITE BEYERITE
BILINITE BIXBYITE BLAKEITE
BLOEDITE BOOTHITE BORACITE
BOWENITE BRAGGITE BRAUNITE
BRAVOITE BROMLITE BRONZITE
BROOKITE BRUSHITE CALCSPAR
CARBOCER CEROLITE CHIOLITE
CHLORITE CHROMITE CIMOLITE
CINNABAR COHENITE COLUSITE
COOKEITE COSALITE CREEDITE
CROCOITE CRYOLITE DANALITE
DAPHNITE DATOLITE DELTAITE
DENDRITE DIASPORE DIGENITE
DIOPSIDE DIOPTASE DIXENITE
DOLOMITE DYSODILE EGUEIITE
ELIASITE ELPIDITE EMBOLITE
ENARGITE EPSOMITE ERIONITE
EUCOLITE EULYTINE EULYTITE
EUXENITE EVANSITE FASSAITE
FAYALITE FELDSPAR FERSMITE
FIBROITE FLINKITE FLUORITE
FOOTEITE FUCHSITE FUSINITE
GEMSTONE GENTHITE GIBBSITE
GINORITE GOETHITE GOYAZITE
GRIPHITE GROTHINE GROUTITE
GYROLITE HANKSITE HANUSITE
HARTTITE HATCHITE HAUERITE
HAUYNITE HEMATITE HOMILITE
HUGELITE IDOCRASE INDERITE
IODYRITE JALPAITE JAROSITE
JEZEKITE KALINITE KAMACITE
KASOLITE KEHOEITE KLEINITE
KOKTAITE KOLSKITE KRAUSITE
LAGONITE LAVENITE LAZULITE
LAZURITE LEVYNITE LEWISITE
LIMONITE LINARITE LOMONITE
LOWIGITE MARSHITE MEIONITE
MELILITE MELONITE MESITITE
MESOLITE MIERSITE MIMETITE
MISENITE MOLYSITE MONAZITE
MONETITE MORAVITE MOSESITE
NADORITE NASONITE NEPOUITE
NOCERITE NOSELITE OXAMMITE
PEGANITE PETALITE PIMELITE
PINNOITE PISANITE PODOLITE
PORODINE PRICEITE PRIORITE
RINNEITE ROSELITE SAGENITE
SALEEITE SALESITE SAPONITE
SASSOLIN SCAWTITE SHANDITE
SHARPITE SHORTITE SIDERITE
SMALTITE SMITHITE SODALITE
SPADAITE SPURRITE STANNITE
STIBNITE STILBITE STOLZITE
STRUVITE STURTITE SZMIKITE
TAGILITE TANGEITE TEALLITE
TENORITE TILASITE TITANITE
TRIPLITE TROILITE TYROLITE
TYSONITE URANOTIL VEGASITE
VOLTAITE VOLTZITE WEHRLITE
WEISSITE WELLSITE WILKEITE
WURTZITE XENOLITE XENOTIME
YENTNITE ZARATITE WILLEMITE
  (BLACK —) JET GEET CERINE
YENITE KNOPITE NIOBITE ALLANITE
GRAPHITE HIELMITE ILMENITE
ONOFRITE
  (BRIGHT —) BLENDE
  (BROWN —) CERINE EGERAN

GUILDITE JAROSITE
(FIBROUS —) ASBESTOS
(GRAY-WHITE —) TRONA HOPEITE
(GREEN —) AMESITE GAHNITE
ILESITE PRASINE PREHNITE
SMECTITE
(ORANGE —) SANDIX
(RADIATED —) ASTROITE
(RADIOACTIVE —) CURITE
(RARE —) CYMRITE EUCLASE
TYCHITE BARYLITE
(RED —) GARNET
(SOFT —) TALC KERMES
(TRANSPARENT —) MICA POLLUX
SODALITE
(WHITE —) BARITE HOWLITE
STILBITE
(YELLOW —) TOPAZ PYRITES
(YELLOWISH-GREEN —) EPIDOTE
ECDEMITE
MINERAL TAR MALTHA
MINERAL WATER SELTZER
MINERVA MENFRA
MINESWEEPER ALGERINE
MINGLE MIX FUSE JOIN MELL MOLD
MONG MOOL ADMIX BLEND MERGE
TWINE COMMIX FELTER HUDDLE
JUMBLE MEDDLE MEDLEY COMBINE
COALESCE CONFOUND
MINGLED FUSED MEDLEY CONFUSED
MINIATURE SMALL LITTLE POCKET
MINIKIN
MINIMAL BASAL LIMINAL
MINIMIZE DECRY MINCE LESSEN
SMOOTH SCISSOR BELITTLE
DISCOUNT
MINIMUM BARE BEDROCK
MINING WORK MINERY SPATTER
GROOVING
MINION PEAT SATAN MIGNON
DARLING MINIKIN CREATURE
MINIONETTE EMERALD
MINISTER PRIG CLERK DEWAN
ELDER ENVOY HAMAN PADRE VIZIR
ATABEG DEACON DIVINE GALLAH
PANDER PARSON PASTOR PESHWA
PRIEST VIZIER BROTHER DOMINIE
OFFICER PESHKAR PREFECT
PALATINE PREACHER
(— OF FINANCE) DEWAN
(— TO) TEND SERVE INTEND
(— WITHOUT SETTLEMENT)
STIBBLER
(PRIME —) PADRONE
MINISTRANT(PL.) SELLI SELLOI
MINISTRATION SERVICE TENDANCE
MINISTRY SERVICE
MINIUM SANDIX
MINIVER LASSET
MINK FAG HURON NORSE VISON
JACKASH KOLINSKY MUSTELIN
PLATINUM

MINNESOTA
CAPITAL: STPAUL
COLLEGE: BETHEL STOLAF
WINONA BEMIDJI HAMLINE
AUGSBURG CARLETON

COUNTY: ANOKA ISANTI ROSEAU
WASECA WABASHA HENNEPIN
INDIAN: SIOUX OJIBWA CHIPPEWA
LAKE: LEECH ITASCA BEMIDJI
SUPERIOR
MOUNTAIN: EAGLE MISQUAH
MOUNTAIN RANGE: CUYUNA
MESABI MISQUAH
NICKNAME: GOPHER NORTHSTAR
RIVER: RAINY STCROIX
STATE BIRD: LOON
STATE TREE: REDPINE
TOWN: ADA ELY MORA AUSTIN
DULUTH NEWULM WINONA
BEMIDJI FOSSTON HIBBING
MANKATO BRAINERD

MINNESOTAN GOPHER
MINNOW PINK GUPPY HITCH MINIM
MINNY BAGGIE MENNON DOGFISH
FATHEAD GULARIS PHANTOM
PINHEAD PINKEEN BONYTAIL
CYPRINID FLATHEAD GAMBUSIA
MOONFISH SATINFIN
(PL.) MENISE
MINOR FLAT LESS MOLL WARD
PETIT PETTY INFANT LESSER
SLIGHT
MINORESS CLARE CLARISSE
MINORITY FEW NONAGE INFANCY
MINOS (FATHER OF —) JUPITER
(MOTHER OF —) EUROPA
(SLAYER OF —) COCALUS
(WIFE OF —) PASIPHAE
MINSTER CHADBAND
MINSTREL BARD BADHAN HARPER
JOCKEY BADCHAN GLEEMAN
JOCULAR PARDHAN PIERROT
SONGMAN JONGLEUR
MINSTRELSY GLEE DREAM
MINT COIN NANA SAGE AJUGA BASIL
ORGAN THYME HYSSOP SAVORY
STRIKE ALLHEAL BALLOTA CAPMINT
LABIATE OLITORY OREGANO
PERILLA PHLOMIS POTHERB
STACHYS BERGAMOT CALAMINT
IRONWORT LAMPWICK LAVENDER
MARJORAM SAGELEAF SELFHEAL
MINTER MONEYER
MINUET MINAWAY
MINUS LESS WANTING
MINUTE FINE NICE TINY CLOSE
MINIM PRIME SMALL ATOMIC
MOMENT INSTANT SCRUPLE
DETAILED
(24 —S) GHURRY
MINX JADE PEAT SLUT SNIP HUSSY
HUZZY LIMMER SNICKET
MIRACLE SIGN ANOMY MARVEL
WONDER PRODIGY THEURGY
MIRACLE PLAY GUARY
MIRAGE SERAB CHIMERA FLYAWAY
LOOMING ILLUSION TOWERING
MIRE BOG DUB CLAY GLAR LAIR
MOIL SLOB SLUB SLUE SLUR ADDLE
CLART EMBOG FANGO GLAUR
SEUGH SLAKE SLUSH SQUAD STALL
SLOUGH SLUDGE SLUTCH CLABBER

GUTTERS SLUBBER WORTHING
MIRITI PALM MORICHE
MIRLITON KAZOO
MIRO TOMTIT
MIRROR FLAT BERYL GLASS IMAGE
STEEL STONE PEEPER PSYCHE
REFLEX SHINER SHOWER CONCAVE
HORIZON REFLECT DIAGONAL
SPECULUM
MIRTH GLEE CHEER DREAM SPORT
GAIETY BAUDERY DISPORT JOLLITY
HILARITY
(CONTEMPTUOUS —) SPORT
(VIOLENT —) SPLEEN
MIRTHFUL CADGY MERRY FESTIVE
GLEEFUL JOCULAR DISPOSED
LAUGHFUL
MIRY OOZY PUXY LAIRY MUCKY
SLAKY CLAGGY CLASHY LUTOSE
MIRISH SLABBY GUTTERY SLOUGHY
MISADVENTURE GRIEF ACCIDENT
CALAMITY CASUALTY DISASTER
MISANTHROPE CYNIC TIMON
MISANTHROPIC CYNICAL
MISANTHROPY TIMONISM
MISAPPLIED ABUSIVE
MISAPPLY ABUSE CROOK WREST
DISUSE MISUSE
MISAPPREHEND MISTAKE
MISAPPREHENSION ILLUSION
MISBECOME MISSIT MISSEEM
MISBEHAVE MISUSE MISBEAR
MISFARE MISHAVE MISLEAD
MISGUIDE
MISBELIEF MISCREED
MISCALCULATE DUTCH MISCAST
MISCOUNT
MISCALL BECALL MISNAME
MISCARRIAGE FAIL MISHAP FAILURE
ABORTION
MISCARRY FAIL MISGO FOUNDER
MISFARE MISGIVE BACKFIRE
MISCARRYING ABORTIVE
MISCELLANEOUS CHOW ORRA
SUNDRY ASSORTED CHOWCHOW
MISCELLANY CHOW VARIA MEDLEY
WHATNOT CHOWCHOW GIFTBOOK
MISCHANCE CALAMITY CASUALTY
DISASTER
MISCHIEF HOB ILL BANE EVIL HARM
HURT JEEL WRACK INJURY MURCHY
SORROW WONDER DEVILRY
KNAVERY SCADDLE DEVILTRY
MISCHIEF-MAKING URCHIN
MISCHIEVOUS BAD SLY ARCH IDLE
ROYT ELFIN HEMPY ROYET ELFISH
ELVISH GALLUS HEMPIE IMPISH
NOYANT SHREWD SULLEN WICKED
GALLOWS HARMFUL KNAVISH
LARKISH MOCKING NAUGHTY
PARLISH PLISKIE PUCKISH ROGUISH
SCADDLE UNHAPPY UNLUCKY
WAGGISH LITHERLY LUNGEOUS
SPORTIVE SPRITISH VENOMOUS
WANSONSY
MISCHIEVOUSNESS ROGUERY
MISCONCEPTION DELUSION
ILLUSION
MISCONDUCT CULPA DOLUS

OFFENCE OFFENSE DISORDER
MISCONSTRUCTION STRAIN
MISCONSTRUE MISJUDGE
MISCREANT KNAVE
MISDEED ILL MISS SLIP AMISS
UNWORK DEFAULT FORFEIT
OFFENCE OFFENSE DISORDER
MISDEMEANOR SIN CRIME FAULT
OFFENCE OFFENSE DISORDER
MISDIRECT MISGUIDE
MISER CUFF SKIN CHUFF CHURL
FLINT GRIPE HAYNE HUNKS NABAL
SCRAT SCRIB CODGER HUDDLE
NIPPER PELTER SCRIMP SNUDGE
WRETCH DRYFIST GOBSECK
NIGGARD SCRAPER CHINCHER
GATHERER HAPTERON HARPAGON
HOLDFAST MUCKERER MUCKWORM
PINCHGUT
MISERABLE WOE EVIL GRAY PUNK
SOUR DAWNY DEENY DUSTY MISER
WOFUL YEMER ABJECT CHETIF
CRUMBY CRUMMY ELENGE FEEBLE
PRETTY UNSELY WOEFUL FORLORN
SCRUFFY UNHAPPY WANSOME
FORSAKEN PITIABLE UNTHENDE
WRETCHED
MISERERE SUBSELLA
MISERLINESS MISERISM SNUDGERY
TENACITY
MISERLY WOE MEAN GRIPPY KNIVEY
STINGY CHINCHE WANSITH
SCRAPING SNUDGERY
MISERY WO WOE RUTH GNEDE .
GRAME WREAK THREAT ANGUISH
MISEASE TRAGEDY CALAMITY
DISTRESS WANDRETH WOWENING
MISFIRE SKIP SNAP
MISFORTUNE ILL BLOW DOLE DREE
EVIL HARM TEEN CURSE HYDRA
SCATH TRAIK DAMAGE DIRDUM
MISERY MISHAP RUBBER SCATHE
SORROW UNHEAL UNLUCK WANHAP
MALHEUR MISCARE MISFALL
MISFATE MISLUCK REVERSE
TRAGEDY TROUBLE UNSELTH
UNSPEED CALAMITY DISASTER
DISGRACE DISTRESS MISCHIEF
MISGIVING DOUBT QUALM
MISGOVERN MISRULE
MISGUIDED WET
MISHANDLE BUNGLE
MISHAP SLIP GRIEF SITHE UNHAP
WANHAP FORTUNE MISTIDE
ACCIDENT CASUALTY MISCHIEF
MISHEARING OTOSIS
MISHIT DUFF
MISHMASH BOTCH GOULASH
MISINFORM MIZZLE
MISINTERPRET WARP WRITHE
MISREAD MISCOUNT
MISJUDGE MISDEEM MISWERN
MISLAY LOSE DISPLACE MISPLACE
MISLEAD COG ERR BUNK DUPE
GULL HOAX BLUFF CHEAT FALSE
BETRAY DELUDE SEDUCE WILDER
CONFUSE DEBAUCH DECEIVE
MISLEAR INVEIGLE MISGUIDE

MISLEADING BLIND FALSE CIRCEAN
TORTIOUS
MISMANAGE BLUNK BLUNDER
MISLEAD MISRULE ILLGUIDE
MISGUIDE
MISOGYNIC CYNICAL
MISPLACE MISLAY MISPUT MISSET
DISPLACE
MISPLACED MALPOSED
MISPLAY BLOW DUFF ERROR FLUFF
FUMBLE
MISPRONOUNCE MISCALL STUMBLE
MISQUOTE GIVE
MISREPRESENT SKEW ABUSE BELIE
COLOR MISUSE FALSIFY SLANDER
MISCOLOR
MISREPRESENTATION FRAUD
CALUMNY DAUBERY GARBLING
MISS ERR HIP FAIL LACK LOSE SKIP
SLIP SNAB FORGO HANUM MISSY
PANNA SKIRT DESIRE FRAULEIN
MISTRESS SENORITA
MISSEL BIRD MAVIS SHIRL DRAINE
JAYPIE MISTLE SHRITE SYCOCK
CHERCOCK
MISSHAPE DEFORM
MISSHAPEN UGLY BLOWN DEFORM
THRAWN DEFORMED UNSHAPED
MISSILE GUN BALL BIRD BOLT DART
SHOT PLUMB SHAFT STONE BULLET
SEEKER BOMBARD GRENADE
MISSIVE OUTCAST PROJECT
(DEFECTIVE —) DUD
(PL.) MITRAILLE
MISSING LACK WANT ABSENT
WANTING
(— OF CUE) FLUFF
MISSION SAND CHARGE ERRAND
SORTIE VISITA MESSAGE BUSINESS
DEVOTION LEGATION
MISSIONARY APOSTLE COLPORTER

MISSISSIPPI
CAPITAL: JACKSON
COLLEGE: RUST ALCORN
BELHAVEN MILLSAPS TOUGALOO
COUNTY: HINDS YAZOO ATTALA
PANOLA TIPPAH NESHOBA
NOXUBEE ITAWAMBA
INDIAN: BILOXI TUNICA CHOCTAW
NATCHEZ CHICKSAW
LAKE: ENID SARDIS BARNETT
GRENADA OKATIBBEE
MOUNTAIN: WOODALL
NATIVE: MUDCAT TADPOLE
NICKNAME: MAGNOLIA
RIVER: LEAF PEARL YAZOO
BIGBLACK
STATE BIRD: MOCKINGBIRD
STATE FLOWER: MAGNOLIA
STATE TREE: MAGNOLIA
TOWN: BILOXI HELENA LAUREL
TUPELO WINONA BELZONI
CORINTH GRENADA NATCHEZ
BOGALUSA MERIDIAN
KOSCIUSKO

MISSIVE NOTE BILLET LETTER
EPISTLE MESSAGE MISSILE

MISSOURI
CAPITAL: JEFFERSONCITY
COLLEGE: AVILA DRURY TARKIO
LINCOLN WEBSTER STEPHENS
COUNTY: RAY IRON MACON
TANEY PETTIS DAVIESS
INDIAN: OSAGE
LAKE: OZARKS TABLEROCK
MOUNTAIN: TAUMSAUK
NATIVE: PUKE PIKER
NICKNAME: SHOWME
PLATEAU: OZARK
PRESIDENT: TRUMAN
RIVER: OSAGE
STATE BIRD: BLUEBIRD
STATE FLOWER: HAWTHORN
STATE TREE: DOGWOOD
TOWN: ELDON HAYTI LAMAR
MACON ROLLA BUTLER
BETHANY BOLIVAR CAMERON
LEBANON MOBERLY SEDALIA
STLOUIS HANNIBAL SIKESTON

MISSTATEMENT ERRATUM
MISSTEP TRIP
MIST DAG FOG MUG URE DAMP DRIP
DROW FILM HAAR HAZE MOKE
RACK ROKE SCUD SMUR BRUME
CLOUD DRISK GAUZE STEAM
MIZZLE NEBULE SEREIN SERENE
SMEETH
(COLD —) DROW BERBER
(DRIZZLING —) SMUR DRISK SMIRR
SMURR
(SMOKY —) SMOG
(WHITE —) HAG
(PL.) SMOKES
MISTAKE ERR BALK GAFF GOOF
MISS SLIP TRIP ERROR FAULT
GAFFE LAPSE BARNEY BOBBLE
ESCAPE MISCUE SLIPUP STUMER
BLUNDER CONFUSE DEFAULT
JEOFAIL STUMOUR WRONGER
CONFOUND MISPRINT MISPRISE
(STUPID —) BUBU BONER
MISTAKEN WRONG ASTRAY
OVERSEEN OVERSHOT TORTIOUS
MISTER DON REB HERR SENOR
SENHOR SIGNOR GOODMAN
SIGNIOR GOVERNOR
MISTFLOWER EUPATORY
MISTILY FOGGILY
MISTLETOE ALLHEAL GADBUSH
MISTREAT BANG VIOLATE
MISTRESS MRS PUG TOY AMIE BIBI
DAME DOLL DOXY LADY MISS PURE
AMIGA AMOUR DOLLY DONNA
DUENA FANCY LEMAN LUCKY
MADAM NANCY WOMAN BEEBEE
MINION MISSIS NEAERA PARNEL
SAHIBA SENORA TACKLE WAHINE
BEDMATE DELILAH HERSELF
HETAERA KITTOCK LEVERET
METREZA PADRONA SENHORA
SIGNORA SULTANA CAMPASPE
DESPOINA DULCINEA FARMWIFE
GOODWIFE GUDEWIFE HAUSFRAU
LADYLOVE LANDLADY MIGNIARD

PARAMOUR PECULIAR SINEBARA TIMANDRA
(— OF CEREMONIES) FEMCEE
MISTRUST MISTROW SURMISE DISTRUST JEALOUSE JEALOUSY MISDOUBT
MISTY HAZY MOKY DAGGY FILMY FOGGY MISKY MOCHY MOOTH RAWKY ROKEY BLURRY CLOUDY GREASY SMURRY STEAMY BRUMOUS OBSCURE NEBULOUS NUBILOUS VAPOROUS
MISUNDERSTAND MISKNOW MISTAKE
MISUSE ABUSE ABUSION PERVERT MALTREAT
MITE BIT ATOM CENT DITE DRAM ATOMY BICHO SPECK ACARID ACARUS CHIGOE LEPTUS MINUTE SMIDGE ACARIAN BDELLID CHIGGER DEMODEX SMIDGEN ARACHNID DIBRANCH FARTHING HANDWORM ORIBATID SANDMITE
MITER MITRE TIMBER TIMBRE
MITERWORT COOLWORT
MITIGATE BALM COOL EASE ALLAY DELAY MEASE RELAX REMIT SLAKE LENIFY LESSEN MODIFY PACIFY SOFTEN SOOTHE SUCCOR TEMPER ASSUAGE CUSHION ELEVATE QUALIFY RELEASE RELIEVE SWEETEN PALLIATE
(— PAIN) PLASTER
MITIGATING LENITIVE
MITTEN BOOT CUFF MITT MUFF LOOFIE MUFFLE NIPPER MUFFLER
MIX BOX BEAT CARD DASH FUSE JOIN KNIT MELL MENG STIR ADMIX ALLOY BLEND BRAID IMMIX KNEAD MISCE TWINE BLUNGE COMMIX CRUTCH GARBLE JUMBLE MEDDLE MEDLEY MINGLE MUDDLE PERMIX STODGE TEMPER WUZZLE BLUNDER SHUFFLE SWIZZLE CONFOUND LEVIGATE SCRAMBLE
(— AND STIR WHEN WET) PUG
(— CONFUSEDLY) BROIL
(— FLOCKS) BOX
(— LIQUORS) BREW
(— PLASTER) GAGE GAUGE
(— TEA) BULK
(— WINE) PART
(— WITH YEAST) BARM
(— WOOL OF DIFFERENT COLORS) TUM
(CONCRETE —) SOUP
MIXABLE MISCIBLE
MIXED CHOW IMPURE MEDLEY MOTLEY PIEBALD STREAKY CHOWCHOW
(— BLOOD) MESTIZO
(— CHALICE) KRASIS
(— UP) HAYWIRE
(NOT —) SINCERE
MIXER HOG BANBURY MUDDLER PICKLER
(CEMENT —) BOXMAN
(CONCRETE —) PAVER
MIXTURE AIR MIX BODY BREW DASH

FEED HASH MANG MULL OLIO PUER SOUP STEW ALGIN ALLOY BLEND BROMO DOUGH GUMBO SALAD STUFF FOURRE GARBLE GUNITE LIGNIN MASLIN MEDLEY MELLAY MINGLE MOTLEY TEMPER AMALGAM COMPOST CUSTARD FARRAGO FILICIN FORMULA GOULASH HEADING KOGASIN MELANGE MISTION MIXTION OLLAPOD RECEIPT TIMBALE ALKYLATE BLENDURE DRAMMOCK EMULSION POSSODIE POWSOWDY SOLUTION
(— ADDED TO WINE) DOSAGE
(— ATTRACTIVE TO PIGEONS) SALTCAT
(— FOR CAKE) BATTER
(— FOR DRESSING LEATHER) DUBBIN DUBBING
(— OF ALE AND OATMEAL) STOORY
(— OF ALKALOIDS) ADONIDIN JABORINE
(— OF BARKS) TONGA
(— OF CEMENT AND STONE) BUMICKY
(— OF CLAY AND ROCK) BODY
(— OF CLAY AND SAND) LOAM
(— OF DRUGS) SPECIES
(— OF ELEMENTS) DIDYMIUM
(— OF FEEDS) MASH
(— OF IMPURE ARSENIDES) SPEISS
(— OF OATS AND BARLEY) DREDGE
(— OF PRINCIPLES) EUONYMIN
(— OF PROTEINS) CROTIN
(— OF SALTS) SOYATE
(— OF SAND AND STONES) CHAD
(— OF SHALE AND SANDSTONE) HAZLE
(— OF SLAG AND ORE) BROWSE
(— OF VITAMINS) BIOS
(— OF WHITE AND BLACK) GRIZZLE
(— OF WINE, HONEY AND SPICES) CLARY
(— TO ADULTERATE LIQUORS) FLASH
(— TO WHITEN BREAD) HARDS
(— USED AS A FERMENT) BUB
(— USED AT SEDER) HAROSET CHAROSES
(ACUTE —) ACUTA
(AERIFORM —) GAS
(CARVER'S —) COMPO
(CAULKING —) BLARE
(CLAY —) COB SLIP
(COATING —) COLOR
(CONFUSED —) MESS CHAOS FUDDLE SOZZLE
(CRUMBLY —) STREUSEL
(EXPLOSIVE —) FIREDAMP
(FOOD —) FILLING
(FREEZING —) CRYOGEN
(GILDING —) ASSIETTE
(HYDROCARBON —) ABIETENE
(ITALIAN CONDIMENT —) TAMARA
(JUMBLED —) BOTCH
(MECHANICS' —) PUTTY
(PLASTIC CEMENT —) CLOY
(PRESERVATIVE —) STUFF
(SEASONED —) STUFFING

(SMOKING —) CHARAS CHURRUS
(TANNING —) PURE
(THICKENING —) ROUX
(UNPALATABLE —) DRAMMOCK
(WATERY —) SLURRY
(WELDING —) THERMIT
MIZZEN DANDY
MIZZONITE DIPYRE
MKS UNIT JOULE
MNEMONIC MEMORIAL
MOAN HONE MOON REEM WAIL CROON GROAN MOURN MUNGE QUIRK SOUGH MUNGER
MOANING SOUGH DIRGEFUL
MOAT FOSS DITCH FOSSE GRAFF RUNDEL
MOB CREW HERD ROUT COHUE CROWD HURRY PLEBE PLEBS MOBILE RABBLE TUMULT VOULGE DOGGERY CANAILLE RIFFRAFF VARLETRY
MOBILE FLUID MOVEABLE
MOBSTER HOODLUM
MOCCASIN PAC CONGO TEGUA SHOEPACK
(— WITH LEGS) LARRIGAN
(PL.) SHANKS
MOCCASIN FLOWER NERVINE
MOCHA BARK
MOCHICA YUNCA
MOCHILA MACHEER KNAPSACK
MOCK BOB DOR GAB MOW COPY DEFY GECK GIBE GIRD JAPE JEER JEST JIBE PLAY QUIZ BOURD DORRE ELUDE FLEER FLIRT FLOUT FRUMP HOKER KNACK MIMIC RALLY SCOFF SCORN SCOUT SLEER SPORT TAUNT BEMOCK DELUDE DERIDE ILLUDE NIGGLE IMITATE MURGEON RIDICULE
MOCKER MOWER GIRDER BOURDER FLOUTER SCORNER RAILLEUR
MOCKERNUT BULLNUT
MOCKERY DOR MOW GLEE JEER BOURD DORRE FARCE FLOUT GLAIK SCOFF SPORT BISMER HETHING LUDIBRY MOCKADO MOCKAGE DERISION ILLUSION RIDICULE SCOFFERY
MOCKING GAB ACID SPORT TRUMPERY
MOCKINGBIRD MIMUS MOWER MOCKER
MOCK ORANGE SYRINGA
MOCOA COCHE
MODE CUT JET TON WAY FORM GATE MOOD RAGA TONE TWIG WISE FERIO FINAL GENUS MODUS STATE STYLE ACTING BAROCO CESARE COURSE DATISI FAKOFO FANGLE FESAPO MANNER METHOD BAMALIP CALEMES CAMENES DABITIS DARAPTI DIBATIS DIMARIS DIMATIS DISAMIS FAPESMO FASHION FERISON FESTINO CELARENT DOKMAROK FELAPTON FRESISON
(— OF BEHAVIOR) THEW HABITUDE
(— OF BEING) CATEGORY
(— OF CONDUCT) LAW

(— **OF DRESS**) HABIT TENUE
(— **OF DRESSING HAIR**) MADONNA
(— **OF EXPRESSION**) IRONY
(— **OF MORAL ACTION**) CONDUCT
(— **OF PARTITIONING**) CANT
(— **OF PROCEDURE**) ORDER
SYSTEM
(— **OF RULE**) REGIME
(— **OF SPEECH**) LATINISM
(— **OF STANDING**) STANCE
(— **OF STRUCTURE**) BUILD
(**PREVAILING** —) GARB
(**TEMPORARY** —) VOGUE
MODEL WAX COPY FORM MOLD
NORM CANON DUMMY IDEAL LIGHT
MOULD NORMA SHAPE DESIGN
FUGLER GABARI MODULE PRAXIS
SOURCE DIORAMA EXAMPLE
GABARIT MODULET PARAGON
PATTERN PICTURE SAMPLER
CALENDAR ENSAMPLE EXEMPLAR
EXEMPLUM FORMULAR FUGLEMAN
MAQUETTE MODELLER MODULIZE
PARADIGM PROPLASM SPECIMEN
TYPORAMA
(— **OF HUMAN BODY**) FORM
MANIKIN
(— **OF STATUE**) ESQUISSE
(**INFERIOR** —) JALOPPY
(**MATHEMATICAL** —) SPACE
(**PRELIMINARY** —) MAQUETTE
PROPLASM
MODERATE BATE COOL CURB EASE
EASY EVEN MEEK SOFT ABATE
ALLAY ALLOY LIGHT LOWER MEZZO
MODER REMIT SLACK SLAKE SOBER
SWEET ARREST BRIDLE DECENT
GENTLE LESSEN MEANLY MIDWAY
MODEST MODIFY REMISS SEASON
SOFTEN SUBMIT TEMPER CENTRAL
CONTROL SLACKEN ATTEMPER
CENTRIST MEETERLY MIDDLING
MITIGATE MODERATO ORDINATE
PALLIATE PASSABLE
(— **IN BURNING**) SOFT
(— **OF THE WIND**) LOOM
MODERATELY GEY FAIR MEAN
MEETLY PRETTY MIDWISE
MEETERLY MIDDLING
MODERATENESS CLEMENCY
MODICITY
MODERATION MEAN STAY MINCE
SPARE MANNER MEDIUM REASON
COMPASS MEDIETY MODESTY
SOBRIETY IMMODESTY
MODERATO MASSIG
MODERN NEW LATE RECENT
NEOTERIC
MODEST SHY DEFT MURE NICE
SNUG DOUCE LOWLY QUIET SMALL
CHASTE DEMURE HUMBLE PUDENT
SIMPLE VIRGIN CLERKLY PUDICAL
DISCREET MAIDENLY PUDIBUND
RESERVED RETIRING SHAMEFUL
VERECUND VIRTUOUS
MODESTY PUDOR NICETY DECENCY
PUDENCY SHYNESS CHASTITY
FOREHEAD HUMILITY PUDICITY

MODICUM DROP BREAK SPICE
PENNORTH
MODIFICATION BOB ECAD FORM
SALT CHANGE ENGRAM FACIES
SANDHI SINGLE UMLAUT ENGRAMMA
(— **OF A REMEDY**) TINCTION
(**GLOTTAL** —) STOP
MODIFIED VARIANT
MODIFY EDIT VARY ALTER AMEND
HEDGE TOUCH BUFFER CHANGE
DOCTOR MASTER TEMPER ARABIZE
COMPARE FASHION QUALIFY
ATTEMPER DENATURE GRADUATE
MODERATE FAUCALIZE
(— **ARTICULATION**) COLOR
(— **COLOR**) TONE
MODILLION ANCON MODEL TRUSS
CARTOUCH
MODISH CHIC MODY SOIGNE TIMISH
TONISH STYLISH
MODISHNESS CHIC
MODULATE SINK INFLECT QUALIFY
MODULATION ACCENT CHANGE
CADENCE BUNCHING PASSAGIO
MOGUL PADISHAH
MOHAIR MOIRE
MOHAMMED MAHOMET MAHOUND
MUDEJAR PROPHET
MOHAMMEDAN MOSLEM PAYNIM
MAHOMET
MOHAMMEDANISM TURBAN
TURKERY MAUMETRY
MOHR MHORR GAZELLE
MOHUR MOOR AHMEDI
MOIETY MEDIETY
MOIST WET DAMP DANK DEWY NESH
UVID DABBY GIVEY GREEN HUMID
JUICY MADID MOCHY SAMMY SAPPY
SLACK SOAKY SOCKY SPEWY
SWACK WEEPY CLAMMY MOISTY
STICKY WETTISH HUMOROUS
MUCULENT
MOISTEN DIP WET DAMP MOIL
BASTE BATHE BEDEW JUICE LATCH
LEACH STEEP WOKIE DABBLE
DAMPEN HUMECT IMBRUE MADEFY
SPARGE TEMPER HUMIDIFY
IRRIGATE IRRORATE
(— **LEATHER**) SAM SAMMY
MOISTURE DEW WET BREE DAMP
DANK ROKE HUMOR MOIST WATER
PHLEGM AQUOSITY HUMIDITY
(— **DEFICIENT**) XERIC
(— **IN STONE**) SAP
(— **ON BEARD**) BARBER
(**CONDENSED** —) BREATH
MOJARRA SHAD PATAO
MOKI MOGUEY MOKIHI
MOKSHA MUKTI
MOLAR WANG FORMAL MOLARY
GRINDER
MOLASSES DIP LICK CLAGGUM
THERIAC TREACLE LONGLICK
MOLD DIE FEN PIG PLY SOW CALM
CAST CURB FORM MULL MUST SOIL
TRAP BLOCK CHAPE CHILL FRAME
INGOT MODEL MOULD MUCOR
PLASM PRINT SHAPE SHARE STENT
STINT VALVE COFFIN GABARI

INFORM LINGET MATRIX SQUARE
BASTARD FASHION FESTOON
MATRICE RILLETT SANDBOX SKILLET
TEMPLET COQUILLE FUMAGINE
HOODMOLD PROPLASM TEMPLATE
WHISKERS
(— **FOR METAL**) SOW SKILLET
(— **OF ASPIC**) DARIOLE
(— **OF SHIP**) SWEEP
(— **THAT ATTACKS HOPS**) FEN
MOLDAVITE TEKTITE
MOLDBOARD REEST
(— **SURFACE**) WREST
MOLDED FICTILE
MOLDER MURL CAPPER MANGLE
MOSKER FIGURER PLASTER PLASTIC
MOLDINESS FINEW MUCOR VINEW
MOLDING BEAD COVE CYMA DADO
GULA KEEL LIST OGEE OVAL CABLE
FILET GORGE LABEL LEDGE ROVER
STAFF BANDLE BASTON CASING
COLLAR CONGEE COVING FILLET
LISTEL MULLER REGLET SQUARE
ZIGZAG ANNULET BEADING
CHAPLET DOUCINE ECHINUS
EYEBROW FINGENT HIPMOLD
LOZENGE MOULAGE NECKING
SURBASE TONDINO TRINGLE
BAGUETTE BANDELET CASEMATE
CASEMENT CYMATION CYMATIUM
DANCETTE FUSAROLE HOODMOLD
KNURLING MOULDING NAILHEAD
NECKMOLD
(**CONCAVE** —) GORGE CONGEE
SCOTIA CAVETTO
(**CONVEX** —) REED CABLE OVOLO
THUMB TORUS BASTON REEDING
ASTRAGAL FUSAROLE
(**OGEE** —) TALON
(**OUTSIDE** —) BACKBAND
(**PL.**) LEDGMENT
MOLDY FUSTY HOARY MUCID
MUGGY MUSTY VINNY FOISTY
MOULDY FOUGHTY
MOLE COB UNT COBB MAIL OONT
PIER PILE TAPE WANT JUTTY
MOODY NEVUS TALPA TAUPE
ANICUT MOUDIE HYDATID TALPOID
MOLDWARP MOONCALF SORICOID
STARNOSE UROPSILE ZANDMOLE
MOLE CRICKET CHANGA
MOLECULE ACID ATOM BASE
AMMINE DIPOLE HYDROL LIGAND
HYDRONE SPECIES
MOLEHILL TUMP HOYLE WANTHILL
MOLE RAT SEMNI ZEMMI ZOKOR
SLEPEZ SPALACID ZANDMOLE
MOLEST GALL HAUNT TEASE
BOTHER HARASS HECKLE INFEST
PESTER MISLEST TROUBLE
MOLLIFY HUSH RELAX ADULCE
GENTLE PACIFY RELENT SOFTEN
SOOTHE TEMPER ASSUAGE DULCIFY
SWEETEN ATTEMPER MITIGATE
UNRUFFLE
MOLLIFYING MILD SUPPLING
MOLLUSK ARK CLAM CONE PIPI
SPAT BORER CHAMA CHANK CHINK
CLAMP CONCH COWRY DORIS DRILL

MUREX PINNA SNAIL VENUS AEOLID
BAILER BUBBLE CERION CHITON
COCKLE COURIE DOLIUM JINGLE
LEPTON LIMPET MUSSEL NERITA
OYSTER PECTEN PHOLAD PURPLE
SEMELE STROMB ABALONE
ASTARTE BIVALVE CARDITA
DECAPOD JUNONIA MOLLUSC
PIDDOCK SCALLOP TOHEROA
TREPANG TROPHON DUCKFOOT
FIGSHELL HALIOTIS NAUTILUS
PTEROPOD SAXICAVA STROMBUS
UNIVALVE VERMETUS
(— TRIBE) NAIADES
(LARVAL —) VELIGER
(YOUNG —) SPAT
MOLLYCODDLE MOLLY WANTON
INDULGE MILKSOP
MOLOSSUS (FATHER OF —)
PYRRHUS
(MOTHER OF —) ANDROMACHE
MOLT MEW CAST MUTE SHED MOULT
DISCARD EXUVIATE INTERMEW
MOLTEN FUSED
MOLTING BROKEN ECDYSIS
MOLYBDENUM (EXCESS OF —)
TEART
MOMBIN JOCOTE
MOMENT MO GIRD HINT SAND TICK
AVAIL BLINK BRAID CLINK CRACK
GLIFF GLISK JIFFY SHAKE SNIFT
SPURT STOUN TRICE VALUE FILLIP
GLIFFY MINUTE PERIOD SECOND
STOUND WEIGHT YAWING ARTICLE
INSTANT INSTANCE MOMENTUM
TWINKLING
(— FOR LEGERDEMAIN ACTION)
TEMPS
(— OF STRESS) CRISE
(CRITICAL —) BIT INCH CORNER
(DECISIVE —) CRISIS
(EXACT —) BIT POINT
(OPPORTUNE —) KAIROS
(SCHEDULED —) TIME
MOMENTARY MOMENTAL
TRANSIENT
MOMENTOUS FELL GRAVE EPOCHAL
FATEFUL WEIGHTY EVENTFUL
MOMENTOUSNESS GRAVITY
MOMENTUM WAY FORCE SPEED
IMPETUS
MON PEGUAN TALAING

MONACO
DYNASTY: GRIMALDI
LANGUAGE: FRENCH
PEOPLE: MONEGASQUES
PRINCE: LOUIS ALBERT HONORE
ANTOINE CHARLES RAINIER
FLORESTAN
RIVER: VESUBIE
SECTION: MONTECARLO
LACONDAMINE MONACOVILLE

MONAD JIVA HENAD MONAS
MONADNOCK BARABOO
MONARCH KING QUEEN DANAID

DIADEM PRINCE DANAINE EMPEROR
AUTOCRAT
MONARCHIAN PRAXEAN
MONARCHICAL KINGLY
MONARCHY KINGDOM
MONASTERY WAT ABBEY BADIA
LAURA RIBAT TEKKE TEKYA FRIARY
MANDRA VIHARA BONZERY
CERTOSA CONVENT KHANKAH
MINSTER CLOISTER LAMASERY
(ALGERIAN —) RIBAT
(BUDDHIST —) TERA KYAUNG
BONZERY LAMASERY
(CARTHUSIAN —) CERTOSA
(HINDU —) MATH
(MOSLEM —) TEKKE TEKYA
KHANKAH
MONASTIC MONKLY MONKISH
CENOBIAN MONACHAL
MONASTICISM MONKERY MONKISM
MONETARY EXPLICIT
MONEY (ALSO SEE COIN) AES BOX
DIB FEE FEI GET OOF ORO SAP TIN
WAD CASH COAT COIN COLE CRAP
CUSH DUBS DUST FUND GATE GELT
GILT GOLD HOOT JACK JAKE KALE
LOUR MINT MOSS MUCK PELF ROLL
SALT SAND SHAG SOAP SWAG
BEANS BLUNT BRASH BRASS BREAD
BUNCE BUNTS CHINK CHIPS CLINK
DARBY DIMES DOUGH DUMPS
FUNDS GREEN GRIGS IMPUT LUCRE
MOPUS OCHER PURSE RHINO
ROCKS ROWDY SCADS SHINY
SMASH SPUDS STIFF STUFF SUGAR
ARGENT BARATO BARREL BOODLE
CHANGE CUNYIE DANARO DINERO
FARLEU FARLEY FEUAGE FLIMSY
FUMAGE GRAITH HANSEL KELTER
MAZUMA POCKET SHEKEL SILVER
SPENSE SPLOSH STAMPS STEVEN
STUMPY TALENT WISSEL ADVANCE
CHATTEL CHINKER COUNTER
CRACKER CRUSADE DEPOSIT
FALDAGE GUNNAGE OOFTISH
SCRATCH SPANKER SPECIES
STOCKER CRIMPAGE CURRENCY
DEMIMARK INCOMING INTEREST
SPENDING STERLING STOCKING
XERAPHIN
(— BET) COMEBACK
(— DUE) DEVOIRS
(— FOR LIQUOR) WHIP
(— LENT) LUMBER
(— OF ACCOUNT) ORA
(— PAID TO BIND BARGAIN) ARLES
(— TAKEN IN) DRAWING
(ADDITIONAL —) BONUS
(AVAILABLE —) CAPITAL
(BAR —) BONK TANG
(BASE —) SHICE
(BRIBE —) SOAP BOODLE
(COUNTERFEIT —) BOGUS QUEER
BOODLE DUFFER SHOWFUL SLITHER
(EARNEST —) ARLES ARRHA
DEPOSIT HANDSEL HANDGELD
HANDSALE
(EXPENSE —) DIET
(FERRY —) NAULUM

(HARD —) SPECIE
(HAT —) TAMPANG
(HAVING NO —) FLYBLOWN
(INVESTED —) STOCK
(PAPER —) GREEN CABBAGE
CURRENCY FROGSKIN
(PASSAGE —) SHIPHIRE
(PRIZE —) PEWTER
(PROTECTION —) ICE
(PUSH —) SPIFF
(READY —) CASH DARBY READY
STUFF STUMPY
(REFUNDED —) DRAWBACK
(SHELL —) PEAG HAWOK WAKIKI
WAMPUM
(SILVER —) SYCEE
(SMALL SUM OF —) SPILL
(STANDARD BANK —) BANCO
(SUBSISTENCE —) BATTA
(TRAVELLING —) VIATICUM
(WIRE —) LARI LARIN LARREE
MONEYBAG FOLLIS
MONEY BELT ZONE
MONEY BOX TILL CHEST PIRLIE
MONEY-CHANGER SARAF SHROFF
ARGENTER
MONEY DRAWER TILL SHUTTLE
MONEYED RICH WEALTHY
MONEYLENDER BANYA CHETTY
USURER LOMBARD MAHAJAN
MARWARI SHYLOCK
MONEYMAKING BANAUSIC
MONEYWORT MANG MYRTLE
PRIMWORT
MONGOL HUN KALKA BALKAR
BURIAT DAGHUR SHARRA BERBERI
KALMUCK KHALKHA SILINGAL
(PL.) HU
MONGOOSE MUNG URVA CIVET
MUNGO MONGOE MEERKAT VANSIRE
MONGREL CUR DOG FICE FIST
CROSS FEIST LIMER SCRUB
BASTARD CURRISH PIEBALD
DOGGEREL
MONILIALES HYPHO
MONISM HENISM ONEISM
MONITION TUITION
MONITOR MARKER MENTOR
LANTERN PREFECT
MONITOR LIZARD IBID IBIT URAN
VARAN WARAL GOANNA WORRAL
MONITOR
MONK BO FRA COWL LAMA MARO
ARHAT BONZE CLERK FRATE FRIAR
PADRE YAHAN BHIKKU CULDEE
GALLAH GETSUL GOSAIN MONACH
VOTARY ARAHANT CALOYER
CLUNIAC GALLACH STARETS
STUDITE ATHONITE MARABOUT
MONASTIC SANNYASI TALAPOIN
TRAPPIST
(PL.) AGAPETI ACOEMETI
MONKEY APE CAY ORA PUG SAI TUP
BEGA BROH BRUH DOUC KAHA
MONA MONK MONO SAKI SIME TITI
TOTA WAAG ZATI ARABA CEBID
DIANA JACKO JOCKO KAHAU
MUNGA OATAS PATAS PUGGY
SAJOU TOQUE UNGKA BANDAR

COAITA COUXIA GRISON GRIVET
GUENON HOWLER LANGUR MACACO
MARTEN MIRIKI MONACH NISNAS
OUBARI PINCHE RILAWA SAMIRI
SIMIAN SIMPAI TEETEE VERVET
WARINE WEEPER WISTIT BHUNDAR
COLOBIN GUARIBA GUERZA
HANUMAN KALASIE LUNGOOR
MACAQUE MEERKAT MOUSTOC
OUAKARI PRIMATE ROLOWAY
SAIMIRI SAPAJOU STENTOR
TAMARIN ARAGUATO CAIARARA
CAPUCHIN DURUKULI ENTELLUS
LEONCITO MALBROUK MANGABEY
MARMOSET MARTINET MUSTACHE
ORABASSU PRIMATAL TALAPOIN
TCHINCOU WANDEROO
(LIKE A —) PUGGISH
MONKEY BREAD BAOBAB
MONKEY FLOWER MIMULUS
MONKEYPOT LECYTH KAKARALI
LECYTHIS SAPUCAIA
MONKEY PUZZLE PINON PINION
MONKEYSHINE SINGERIE
(PL.) HORSE
MONKFISH MONK SQUATINA
MONKISH CENOBIAN MONASTIC
MONK PARROT LORO
MONKSHOOD ATIS ACONITE
ACONITUM NAPELLUS MOUSEBANE
MONO MONACHI
MONOACETATE ACETIN
MONOCARPELLARY SIMPLE
MONOCHORD MAGAS MAGADIS
UNICHORD
MONOCHROME CAMAIEU MONOTINT
MONOCLE QUIZ EYEGLASS
MONOCLINOUS PERFECT
MONOECISM SYNOECY SYNOEKY
MONOGRAM IHS JHS YHS CIPHER
HERALD CHRISMON
MONOGRAPH STUDY BULLETIN
DISCOURSE
MONOLITH MENHIR PILLAR
(CIRCLE OF —S) CROMLECH
MONOLITHIC GLOBAL
MONOLOGIST DISEUSE
MONOLOGUE MONOLOGY
SOLILOQUY
MONOPHTHONGAL PURE
MONOPHTHONGIZE SMOOTH
MONOPHYSITE AGNOETE AGNOITE
JACOBITE
(PL.) ACEPHALI
MONOPLANE TAUBE PARASOL
MONOPODE SKIAPOD
MONOPOLIZE LURCH ABSORB
CONSUME ENGROSS
MONOPOLY REGIE TRUST CARTEL
APPALTO
MONOSACCHARIDE OSE DIOSE
HEXOSE MONOSE GLYCOSE
HEPTOSE
MONOTONOUS ARID DEAD DULL
FLAT WASTE DREARY SAMELY
SODDEN ADENOID HUMDRUM
INSIPID IRKSOME TEDIOUS
BORESOME DRUDGING SAMESOME
UNVARIED VEGETABLE

MONOTONY DRAB DRYNESS
DULLNESS SAMENESS
MONOXENOUS DIRECT
MONSOON VARSHA
MONSTER OGRE BILCH LARVA
MORMO RAHAB TERAS UNMAN
ELLOPS GERYON MAKARA SHRIMP
TYPHON BICORNE CHIMERA
CYCLOPS DIDYMUS DIPYGUS
ECHIDNA GRENDEL GRIFFIN
GRIFFON SLAPPER UNBEAST
WARLOCK JANICEPS LINDWORM
MOONCALF TARASQUE TYPHOEUS
UROMELUS LEVIATHAN
(— WITH 100 EYES) ARGUS
(— WITH 100 HANDS) BRIAREUS
(9-HEADED —) HYDRA
(FABULOUS —) KRAKEN TANIWHA
(FEMALE —) HARPY LAMIA SCYLLA
(HALF-BULL HALF-MAN —)
MINOTAUR
(MAN-DEVOURING —) OGRE LAMIA
(MYTHICAL —) HARPY SCYLLA
SPHINX CHIMERA WARLOCK
MINOTAUR
(SEA —) BELUE KRAKEN PISTRIX
(SUPERNATURAL —) LARVA
(TWO-BODIED —) DISOMUS
(WATER —) NICKER
MONSTRANCE SUN
MONSTROSITY FREAK DIPYGUS
MONSTER ABORTION IMMANITY
MOONCALF TERATISM
MONSTROUS VAST ENORM GIANT
FIENDLY FLAMING HIDEOUS TITANIC
BEHEMOTH COLOSSAL DEFORMED
ENORMOUS FLAGRANT GIGANTIC
PYTHONIC SLAPPING
MONTAGNARD SEKANI

MONTANA

CAPITAL: HELENA
COLLEGE: CARROLL
COUNTY: HILL TETON FERGUS
WIBAUX PONDERA MISSOULA
INDIAN: CROW ATSINA SALISH
ARAPAHO KUTENAI SIKSIKA
SHOSHONE
LAKE: HEBGEN FLATHEAD
FORTPECK MEDICINE
MOUNTAIN: AJAX BALDY COWAN
SPHINX TORREY GRANITE
HILGARD TRAPPER GALLATIN
PENTAGON SNOWSHOE
MOUNTAIN RANGE: CRAZY LEWIS
POCKY BIGBELT
NICKNAME: BIGSKY TREASURE
RIVER: MILK TONGUE KOOTENAI
MISSOURI
STATE BIRD: MEADOWLARK
STATE FLOWER: BITTERROOT
TOWN: BUTTE HAURE MALTA
HARDIN HELENA BOZEMAN
CHINOOK CHOTEAU FORSYTH
GLASGOW ROUNDUP BILLINGS
MISSOULA

MONTANIST PHRYGIAN

MONTENEGRO

COIN: PARA FLORIN PERPERA
LAKE: SCUTARI SHKODER
MOUNTAIN: DURMITOR
NAME: ZETA ILLYRIA CRNAGORA
PORT: BAR ULCINJ ANTIVARI
DULCIGNO
RIVER: ZETA MORACA
TOWN: NIKSIC CETINJE TITOGRAD
PODGORICA

MONTH AB AV BUL MAY PUS SOL
ZIF ZIW ABIB ADAR AHET APAP ASIN
ELUL IYAR JETH JULY JUNE KUAR
MAGH MOON TYBI AGHAN APRIL
ASARH CHAIT IYYAR MAIUS MARCH
NISAN PAYNI RABIA RAJAB SAFAR
SAWAN SEBAT SHVAT SIVAN SIWAN
TEBET THOTH TIZRI UINAL AUGUST
BHADON CHOIAK JUMADA JUNIUS
KARTIK KISLEV KISLEW KISLEY
MECHIR MESORE NISSAN NIVOSE
PAOPHI PHAGUN SAPHAR SHABAN
SHABAT TAMMUZ TISHRI VEADAR
ABAGHAN APRILIS BAISAKH BYSACKI
CHAITRA CHISLEV ETHANIM
FLOREAL HESHVAN JANUARY
MARTIUS OCTOBER PACHONS
PHALGUN RAMADAN SARAWAN
SHAABAN SHAWWAL THAMMUZ
VENTOSE BRUMAIRE DECEMBER
DULKAADA FEBRUARY FERVIDOR
FRIMAIRE GAMELION GERMINAL
MESSIDOR MUHARRAM NOVEMBER
PLUVIOSE POSEIDON PRAIRIAL
SEXTILIS ZULKADAH SEPTEMBER
(IN NEXT —) PROXIMO
(IN PRECEDING —) ULTIMO
(PRESENT —) INSTANT
(SIX —S) SEMESTER
MONTHLY MENSAL
MONUMENT VAT WAT LECH TOMB
CROSS STONE TABUT TITLE BILITH
DOLMEN HEARSE MEMORY RECORD
TROPHY CHAITYA CHHATRI
CHORTEN DENKMAL FUNERAL
TRILITH BILITHON CENOTAPH
MEMORIAL MONOLITH TROPAION
(— OF HEAPED STONES) CAIRN
(PILLARLIKE —) SHAFT STELA
STELE
MOO LOW
MOOCH BUM CADGE SPONGE
MOOCHER MIKER CADGER GRAFTER
MOOD CUE FIT TID MIND TIFF TIFT
TONE TUNE VEIN WHIM DEVIL
FRAME FREAK HEART HUMOR SPITE
PLIGHT SPIRIT SPLEEN SPRITE
STRAIN TALENT TEMPER CAPRICE
FANTASY FEATHER JUSSIVE
ATTITUDE
(— IN LOGIC) BARBARA
(— OF BAD TEMPER) DORTS
(— OF DEPRESSION) LETDOWN
(CROSS —) FRUMPS
(FRIVOLOUS —) JEST
(GROUCHY —) DODS
(IRRITABLE —) GRIZZLE

(SULKY —) PET
(SULLEN —) STRUNT SULLENS
MOODY SAD GLUM SULKY BROODY
GLOOMY MOROSE SULLEN MOODISH
PENSIVE
MOON BUAT LAMP LUNA MAHI DIANA
LUNET LUCINA PHOEBE CHANDRA
CYNTHIA LEWANNA LUNETTE
MOONLET FOGEATER MENISCUS
SATELLES
(FULL —) PLENILUNE
(NEW —) PRIME
(PART OF COURSE OF —) MANSION
(WANING —) WANIAND
MOONBLIND LUNATIC
MOONEYE HIODONT
MOONEYE CISCO BLOATER
MOON-EYED LUNATIC
MOONFISH SUNFISH JOROBADA
MOONFLOWER ACHETE
MOONLIGHT FLESH MOONGLOW
MOONRAT GYMNURE
MOONSET MOONDOWN MOONFALL
MOONSHINE MOON SHINE SHINNY
BOOTLEG BLOCKADE
MOONSTRUCK LUNATIC
MOONWORT LUNARY HONESTY
MOOR FEN BENT FELL POST BEACH
BERTH HOVEL TURCO COMMOTY
COMONTE MARRANO MOGRABI
MOORMAN MORESCO MORISCO
(INFERTILE —) LANDE
MOOR COCK GORCOCK MUIRCOCK
MOORING DOCK MOORAGE
MOORLAND OUTFIELD
MOOSE BELL ELAND CERVID
ORIGNAL
MOOSEWOOD DIRCA
MOOT MUTE STIR PORTMOOT
MOP BOB SOP SWAB MALKIN MERKIN
MOPPET SCOVEL
(— FOR CLEANING CANNON)
MERKIN
(— OF HAIR) TOUSLE
(BAKER'S —) MALKIN MAWKIN
MOPANE IRONWOOD
MOPCAP MOB
MOPE MUMP POUT SULK BROOD
GLOOM
MOPING FUSTY DUMPISH
MORA LOVE TIME LIMMA SEMEION
MORAL TAG PURE CIVIL ETHIC
EPIMYTH ETHICAL UPRIGHT
HONORARY
(PL.) THEW
MORALISTIC DIDACTIC
MORALITY MORALS VIRTUE
MORALIZING PI
MORASS BOG FLOW MOSS ROSS
SUMP FLUSH MARSH SLACK
SLOUGH QUAGMIRE
MORAY PUSI ELGIN HAMLET
MURAENA
MORBID SICK MORBOSE PECCANT
MORDANT HANDLE SPIRIT CAUSTIC
STRIKER SCATHING
MORE MO MAE PIU HELDER
(— OR LESS) HALFWAY
(— THAN ADEQUATE) AMPLE

(— THAN ENOUGH) TOO
(— THAN HALF) BETTER
(— THAN ONE OR TWO) SUNDRY
(— THAN ONE) SEVERAL
(— THAN SUFFICIENT) ABUNDANT
(— THAN THIS) YEA
(— THAN) BUT OVER ABOVE RISING
PLUSQUAM
(LITTLE —) ADVANTAGE
MOREEN TABBY
MOREL HELVELLA MORIGLIO
MORELLO MOREL GRIOTTE
MULBERRY
MOREOVER EKE TOO ALSO MORE
AGAIN EITHER BESIDES FARTHER
FURTHER THERETO LIKEWISE
OVERMORE
MOREPORK PEHO RURU MOPOKE
MOPEHAWK
MORGUE LIBRARY MORTUARY
MORION CABASSET
MORMON COHAB SAINT DANITE
(— STATE) UTAH
MORNING GAY MORN MATIN
MORROW UNDERN COCKCROW
MORNTIME
(IN THE —) MANE
MORNING GLORY NIL KOALI
TWINER GAYBINE IPOMOEA
MANROOT PILIKAI BINDWEED
SCAMMONY
(— GROWING AMONG GRAIN) BEAR
MORNING STAR VENUS DAYSTAR
LUCIFER MERCURY BARTONIA
MORO LUTAO SAMAL YAKAN ILLANO
DOLOANO MARANAO
MOROCCO MAROQUIN

MOROCCO

CAPE: NUN NOUN
CAPITAL: RABAT
COIN: OKIA RIAL OKIEH DIRHAM
MOUZOUNA
DISTRICT: ERRIF
MEASURE: KALA SAAH FANEGA
IZENBI TOMINI
MOUNTAIN: TOUBKAL
MOUNTAIN RANGE: RIF ATLAS
PEOPLE: MOOR BERBER KABYLE
MOSLEM MUSLIM
PORT: SAFI CEUTA RABAT SAFFI
AGADIR TETUAN LARACHE
MAZAGAN MELILLA MOGADOR
TANGIER
PROVINCE: CEUTA MELILLA
RIVER: DRA MOULOUYA
TOWN: FES FEZ SAFI RABAT
AGADIR MEKNES TANGIER
MARRAKECH
WEIGHT: ROTL ARTAL ARTEL
GERBE RATEL KINTAR QUINTAL

MORON FOOL AMENT IMBECILE
MORONITY MOROSIS
MOROSE GLUM GRUM SOUR MOODY
RUSTY SURLY CRUSTY GLOOMY
STINGY SULLEN CRABBED CROOKED
PEEVISH STROUNGE

MOROSENESS ASPERITY
MORPHEME BASE ETYMON
COGNATE
MORPHOLOGICAL FORMAL
MORRIS MILL MERELS
MORSEL BIT NIG ORT TIT BITE GNAP
SNAP SCRAN BUCKONE MORCEAU
NOISETTE PARTICLE SKERRICK
(— OF CHEESE) TRIP
(— OF CHOCOLATE) BUD
(— OF SEASONED MEAT) GOBBET
(CHOICE —) TIDBIT TITBIT
MORTAL BEING DYING FATAL HUMAN
VITAL DEADLY FINITE LETHAL
BRITTLE DEATHLY DEATHFUL
MORTALITY FLESH MURRAIN
MORTALLY DEADLY FATALLY
MORTAR DAB COMPO DAGGA
GROUT LARRY ROYAL SORKI SWISH
CANNON CEMENT HOLMOS MINNIE
POTGUN BEDDING COEHORN
DAUBING PERRIER POUNDER
PUGGING SOORKEE
(— AND PESTLE) DOLLY DOLLIE
(— EXTRUDED BETWEEN LATHS)
KEY
(— FOR ROCKETS) TROMBE
(— FOR SALUTES) CHAMBER
(— MADE WITH STRAW) BAUGE
(INFERIOR —) SLIME
(SMALL —) HOBIT ROYAL TINKER
(THIN —) LARRY
MORTARBOARD CATERCAP
TRENCHER
MORTAR BOAT PALANDER
MORTGAGE DIP LAY BOND LIEN
ENGAGE MONKEY OBLIGE WADSET
WEDDEED THIRLAGE
MORTGAGOR REVERSER
MORTIFICATION ENVY SHAME
SPITE CHAGRIN GANGRENE
NECROSIS VEXATION
MORTIFIED ASHAMED
MORTIFY ABASE ABASH SHAME
SPITE HUMBLE CHAGRIN CRUCIFY
MACERATE
MORTISE GAIN COCKET
(SIDE OF —) CHEEK
MORTUARY MORGUE FUNERARY
SAWLSHOT
MORWONG TARAKIHI
MOSAIC AUCUBA EMBLEM MUSIVE
SCREEN FRISOLEE INTARSIA
TERRAZZO
(POTATO —) CRINKLE
MOSLEM MOOR HADJI HAFIZ HANIF
ISLAM MALAY SALAR TURBAN
ISLAMIC MOORMAN SANGGIL
SARACEN ISLAMITE SANGUILE
MOSQUE JAMI MOSCH DURGAH
MASJID MESKED
MOSQUITO GNAT CULICID GAMBIAE
SKEETER ANOPHELE DIPTERAN
MOSS FOG MNIUM USNEA HYPNUM
MUSKEG FOXFEET GULAMAN
HAIRCAP PILIGAN TORTULA
CROWFOOT MOSSWORT SPHAGNUM
STAGHORN
(— HANGING FROM TREE) WEEPER

MOSSBUNKER MENHADEN
MOSSI MOLE MORE
MOSSI-GURUNSI GUR
MOSS PINK PHLOX
MOSSTROOPER RIDER
MOSSY FOGGY HOARY MUSCOSE
MOST BEST MOSTLY FARTHEST
MOSTLY MOST FECKLY CHIEFLY
MOSTDEAL
MOT JEST
MOTE ATOM ATOMY FESCUE
MOATHILL
MOTEL COURT
MOTH GEM NUN PUG HAWK MOTE
PAGE APPLE ATLAS EGGAR EGGER
FLAME GAMMA IMAGO PISKY PLUME
SAMIA SWIFT THORN USHER WITCH
ANTLER BAGONG BURNET COSSID
DAGGER DATANA HERALD HUMMER
JUGATE LACKEY LAPPET MILLER
MOODER PLUSIA QUAKER RUSTIC
SPHINX THISBE TINEID TISSUE
TUSSUR ARCTIAN ARCTIID
BAGWORM BUDWORM CRAMBID
CRININE DELTOID DRINKER
EMERALD EMPEROR EUCLEID
FESTOON FIGWORM FOOTMAN
FRENATE HOOKTIP NOCTUID
PEGASUS PSYCHID PYRALIS
SLICKER STINGER SYLINID TINEOLA
TORTRIX TUSSOCK URANIID
VAPORER ZYGENID AEGERIID
ARMYWORM BOMBYCID CATOCALA
CECROPIA CINNABAR COCHYLIS
FISHTAIL FORESTER GEOMETER
GOLDTAIL GRISETTE HAWKMOTH
HEPIALID KNOTHORN MOTHWORM
PHYCITID PLUTELLA SPHINGID
SPRAWLER WAINSCOT
(— BREEDER) AURELIAN
(VERY SMALL —) MICRO
MOTH BALL REPELLER
MOTHER INA MOM DAME MAMA
MADRE MAMMA MAMMY MATER
MINNY MODUR MITHER MULIER
VENTER GENETRIX
(— OF THE GODS) RHEA
(DIVINE —) MATRIGAN
(GREAT —) AGDISTIS
(NOURISHING — OF MAN) CYBELE
(SEVEN —S) MATRIS
(SIDE OF —) ENATE
MOTHERLAND COUNTRY
MOTHERLY MATERNAL MATRONAL
MOTHER-OF-PEARL NACRE PEARL
MOTIF SPRIG DESIGN DEVICE MOTIVE
SCALLOP APPLIQUE
MOTILE ZO ZOO
MOTION WAY FARD FEED GIRD
MOVE SIGN WHID HURRY PAVIE
APPORT MOMENT MOTIVE TRAVEL
UNREST IMPULSE ACTIVITY
MOVEMENT OVERTURE
(— OF AIR) AIRFLOW
(— OF HORSE) AIR
(— TO) ALLATIVE
(ABRUPT —) CHOP
(CAM —) COULIER
(CIRCULAR —) GYRE COMPASS

(CONFUSED —) GURGE
(DANCE —) CAPER
(DIZZY —) SWIMBEL
(EXPRESSIVE —) GESTURE
(FORWARD —) HEADWAY
(GLIDING —) SWIM SKITTER
(HEAVING —) ESTUS AESTUS
(HURRIED —) HUSTLE
(ILLEGAL —) BALK BAULK
(IRREGULAR —) SWAG
(JERKING —) BOB LIPE JIGGLE
(LATERAL —) DRIFT
(QUIVERING —) TREMOR
(RAPID —) SCOUR
(REARING —) PESADE
(RECIPROCATING —) SEESAW
(ROTARY —) SWAY BACKSPIN
SIDESPIN
(SHOWY —) FANFARE
(SIDEWAYS —) CRAB
(SLOW —) CRAWL
(SPINNING —) ENGLISH
(SWIMMING —) FLUTTER
(UPWARD —) HEAVE
(VIGOROUS —) SKELP
(VIOLENT —) JERK RAPT BENSEL
(WAVERING —) SHAKE
(WAVING —) WAFF
(WHIRLING —) SWIRL
MOTIONLESS DEAD ASLEEP
IMMOBILE STAGNANT STIRLESS
MOTION PICTURE CINE FILM FLICK
MOVIE BIOPIC CINEMA TALKIE
CHEAPIE SMELLIE FLICKERS
(PL.) SILENTS
MOTIVATE ANIMATE INSPIRE
MOTIVATED COVERT
MOTIVE GOAD SAKE SPUR CAUSE
MOTIF SCORE ACTUAL DESIRE
OBJECT SPRING ATTACCO IMPULSE
PATTERN RESPECT RINCEAU
SUBJECT INSTANCE STIMULUS
(ALLEGED —) PRETEXT
MOTLEY MIXED MEDLEY RAGTAG
MOTTLED PIEBALD
MOTMOT HOUTOU SAWBILL
PICARIAN
MOTOR AUTO TOOT MOVER ENGINE
ROTATOR TURBINE EFFERENT
MOTORBOAT LAUNCH AUTOBOAT
RUNABOUT
MOTORCAR MOTOR DOODLEBUG
MOTORCYCLE CYCLE MOTOR
STEED TRICAR AUTOETTE TRICYCLE
MOTORIST AUTOIST
MOTORMAN CARMAN WATTMAN
TROLLYMAN
MOTORTRUCK DRAY LORRY
CAMION BOBTAIL FLATBED
MOTTLE CHECK TABBY SPONGE
MOTTLED JAZZ PINTO MOTLEY
RUMINATE SPLASHED
MOTTO MOT WORD AXIOM CACHET
DEVICE EUREKA LEGEND REASON
IMPRESA EPIGRAPH
(— IN A RING) POSY
(— OF CALIFORNIA) EUREKA
(— OF MAINE) DIRIGO
MOUE FACE

MOUFLON MUSIMON
MOULIN CHIMNEY
MOUND AHU COP HOW LAW LOW
BALK BANK BOSS BUND BUTT GOAL
HILL HUMP KNOW MOLE POME TELL
TEPE TERP TUFT TUMP AGGER
BERRY DHERI ESKAR ESKER KNOLL
MONDE MOTTE MOUNT PINGO RAISE
STUPA TOMAN BARROW CAUSEY
MEILER RIDEAU ANTHILL BOUROCK
HILLOCK MAMELON BACKSTOP
BARBETTE SNOWBANK TEOCALLI
(— ABOUT A PLANT) TUMP
(— FOR MEMORIAL) CAIRN
(— IN BUILDING MATERIAL) DIMPLE
(— OF DETRITUS) WASH
(— OF ICE) DOME
(— OF WOOD TO BE CHARRED)
MEILER
(BURIAL —) LAW LOW TOR TOLA
BERRY GUACA HUACA BARROW
KURGAN TUMULUS
(FORTIFIED —) DUN
(GLACIAL —) KAME
(MILITARY —) BARBETTE
(PALISADED —) MOTTE
(VOLCANIC —) HORNITO
MOUNT BEN STY BACK HEAD RIDE
RISE SCAN ARISE BIPOD BOARD
CLIMB HEAVE HINGE SPEEL SPIRE
SWARM ASCEND ASPIRE MORIAH
CHARGER COLLINE HAIRPIN
HARNESS BESTRIDE MOUNTAIN
MOUNTING MOUNTURE SURMOUNT
(— A HORSE) FORK LIGHT WORTH
(— BY STEPS) SCAN
(— ON PIN) STICK
(— ON WINGS) SOAR
(STEREOTYPE —) CORE
MOUNTAIN BEN KOP BERG CIMA
DAGH FELL KLIP KNOB MONS MONT
NEBO PICO PIKE JEBEL MOUNT
RANGE BARROW BUNDOC GILEAD
GUNONG HEIGHT PISGAH HELICON
MONTURE NUNATAK BUNDUCKS
(— INHABITED BY SPIRIT) GUACA
HUACA
(— MASS) OROGEN
(— PASS) GHAT GHAUT
(— STATE) MONTANA
(— TRACT) DUAR
(AT BASE OF —) PIEDMONT
(FABLED —) KAF MERU
(GREEK —) OSSA PELION HELICON
OLYMPUS MAENALUS
(HIGH —) ALP
(ROUND —) REEK
(SMALL —) NOB KNOB BUTTE
(SNOW —) JOKUL
(SUBMARINE —) GUYOT SEAMOUNT
MOUNTAIN ASH SORB SORBUS
DOGBERRY MOZEMIZE ROUNTREE
WINETREE
MOUNTAIN BEAVER SEWELLEL
MOUNTAIN BINDWEED SOLDANEL
MOUNTAIN CAP SCALP
MOUNTAIN CLIMBER CRAGSMAN
MOUNTAIN CRANBERRY
FOXBERRY

MOUNTAINEER WASIR WAZIR
HEIDUC HAYDUCK HILLMAN
ORESTES MONTESCO TIERSMAN
(PL.) GUTI GUTIANS
MOUNTAIN GOAT IBEX MAZAME
MOUNTAIN LAUREL IVY HEATH
ERICAD KALMIS LAUREL IVYWOOD
CALFKILL
(THICKET OF —) SLICK
MOUNTAIN LINNET TWITE
MOUNTAIN LION PUMA COUGAR
MOUNTAIN MAHOE EMAJAGUA
MOUNTAIN MISERY TARWEED
MOUNTAINOUS RANGY VICIOUS
MOUNTAIN PARSLEY FLUELLEN
MOUNTAIN RANGE KAF QAF TIER
SIERRA SAWBACK DINDYMUS
MOUNTAIN SICKNESS VETA
MOUNTAINSIDE FELLSIDE
MOUNTAINTOP MAN DOME
MOUNTAIN WOOD ROCKWOOD
MOUNTEBANK IMPOSTOR
OPERATOR
MOUNTED CARDED SADDLE
EASELED EQUITANT
MOUNT ETNA MONGIBEL
MOUNTING MOUNT SCAPE ASCENT
FLIGHT MONTANT SOAKING
INCABLOC MOUNTURE
(— OF GEM) CHASE
(STYLE OF —) SETTING
MOURN DOLE KEEN SIGH WAIL
PLAIN GRIEVE LAMENT SORROW
GRIZZLE
MOURNER WAILER WEEPER
(HIRED —) SAULIE
(PROFESSIONAL —) BLACK KEENER
MOURNFUL SAD BLACK SORRY
WEEPY RUEFUL DERNFUL SIGHFUL
WAILFUL DEJECTED DIRGEFUL
ELEGIOUS FUNEREAL MAESTIVE
MESTFULL YEARNFUL PLAINTIVE
MOURNING DOLOR SHIVA DISMAL
WIDOWED
(— CLOTH) RADZIMIR
MOUSE MURINE MYGALE RODENT
VERMIN ARVICOLE CRICETID
MYOMORPH
(LIKE A —) MURIFORM
(MEADOW —) VOLE
(STRIPED —) KUSU
MOUSEBIRD COLY
MOUSE DEER PLANDOK
MOUSETRAP TIPE
MOUSING KEEPER
MOUTH OS GAB GAM GOB JIB MUG
MUN NEB ORF ROW YAP BEAK BEAL
BOCA HEAD MUSS PUSS SHOP TRAP
YAWN BAZOO BOCCA BRACE CHOPS
CODON STOMA TUTEL GEBBIE
KISSER MUZZLE RABBLE RICTUS
SUCKER THROAT CLAPPER
FLUMMER OSTIOLE STOMACH
LORRIKER PAVILLON
(— AND THROAT) COPPER WHISTLE
(— OF CANYON) ABRA
(— OF GLASS FURNACE) BOCCA
(— OF HARBOR) BOCA
(— OF PERITHECIUM) OSTIOLE

(— OF RIVER) BEAL BOCA LADE
ENTRY INFLUX ESTUARY OSTIARY
(— OF SHAFT) BRACE
(— OF TRUMPET) BELL CODON
PAVILLON
(— PARTS OF ARTHROPOD) TROPHI
(KILN —) KILNEYE KILNHOLE
(SORE — OF SHEEP) ECTHYMA
(WRY —) MURGEON
(PL.) ORA
MOUTHFUL GAG GOB SUP GNAP
GOLEE GOBBET
MOUTHPART BILL
MOUTHPIECE BAR BEAK BOCAL
MOUTH FIPPLE SYRINX PROPHET
(— OF BAGPIPE) MUSE
(— OF PIPE) STEM
MOUTHWASH GARGLE
MOUTH-WATERING SALIVANT
MOVABLE FREE LOOSE MOBILE
PORTABLE REMUABLE
(PL.) MEUBLES
MOVE GO ACT FIG GEE GET WAG
BOOM BORE BUCK BUMP CALL
DRAW FIRK FLIT GOAD HEAT KNEE
MAKE PIRL ROLL SILE SPUR STEP
STIR SWAY WORK ANKLE BLITZ
BUDGE CARRY CAUSE CROWD
DRAFT HEAVE IMPEL LIGHT MARCH
MUDGE QUECH REMUE ROUSE
SHAKE SHIFT GAMBIT HANDLE
HUSTLE INCITE INDUCE KINDLE
MOTION PROMPT QUITCH REMBLE
SASHAY STRAKE ACTUATE AGITATE
ANIMATE DISTURB DRAUGHT
FLUTTER INSPIRE MIGRATE
PROVOKE AMBULATE BULLDOZE
CATAPULT DEMARCHE DISLODGE
DISPLACE MOTIVATE
(— A RESOLUTION) FIRST
(— ABOUT) WEND DISPACE
SHUFFLE CONVERSE LOCOMOTE
(— ACROSS) THWART
(— ACTIVELY) YANK
(— AIMLESSLY) BOGUE
(— ALONG) SHOG
(— APART) SPREAD
(— AS IN STUPOR) DAVER
(— ASIDE) SKEW
(— ASUNDER) SINGLE
(— AT TOP SPEED) LICK
(— AWAY) CUT MOG DECAMP
RECEDE
(— AWKWARDLY) HODGE HIRSEL
LARRUP SHAMBLE
(— BACK) FADE ARSLE RECUR
RECEDE RETIRE RETREAT
(— BACKWARD AND FORWARD) GIG
SWAY DARTLE DIDDLE SHUFFLE
SHUTTLE
(— BOOM OR SAIL) JIB
(— BRISKLY) FAN HALE STIR FRICK
FRIKE FRISK KNOCK SQUIRT
TRANCE TRAVEL WHIPPET
(— BY FITS AND STARTS) JIFFLE
(— BY JERKS) HITCH JIGGET JIGGLE
JINKLE
(— BY SMALL SHOCKS) JOG
(— BY WHEELS) ROLL TRUNDLE

(— CHESS PIECE) DEVELOP
(— CLUMSILY) HOIT JOLL PAUT
BARGE KEVEL HIRSEL LUMBER
TOLTER GALUMPH STUMBLE
(— DIAGONALLY) CATER
(— DOWN) SILE STOOP DECLINE
DESCEND
(— FORCIBLY) SHOVE
(— FORWARD) BREAK ADVANCE
PROGREDE
(— FURTIVELY) LEER GLIDE SLINK
SLIVE SNEAK STEAL
(— GRADUALLY) EDGE
(— HAPHAZARDLY) BUCKET
(— HASTILY) SCUR SKIRR
(— HAUGHTILY) SWOOP
(— HEAVILY) LUG LUMP FLUMP
LUMBER
(— IN AGITATION) SEETHE
(— IN CIRCLES) MILL PURL
(— IN MARBLES) FULK
(— IN RIPPLES) CURL
(— IN SHUFFLING MANNER) MOSEY
(— IN SMALL DEGREES) INCH
(— IN WATER) SQUELCH
(— IN WAVES) LAP CRINKLE
(— INWARDLY) ENMOVE
(— JERKILY) JAG BUCK FLIP KICK
FLIRT BUCKET TWITCH
(— LANGUIDLY) MAUNDER
(— LAZILY) HULK
(— LEISURELY) AMBLE
(— LIGHTLY) BRUSH FLUFF
(— LOOSELY) SLOP
(— NERVOUSLY) DITHER
(— NIMBLY) KILT WHIP DANCE
(— OFF) FIRK RYNT MORRIS
(— ON) MOG VAMP SUCCEED
WHIGFARE
(— OUT OF SIGHT) SINK
(— OUT) BLOW
(— QUICKLY) BOB FIG DUCK FIRK
FLAX FLIT GIRD JINK KITE WHAP
WHEW YANK FLASH GLENT SKEET
SKITE SPANK SQUIB STAVE STOUR
THROW NIDDLE STRIKE WALLOP
SKIMMER
(— QUIETLY) SLIP
(— RAPIDLY) BANG BOLT BUZZ
HEEL HURL THUD CHASE GLINT
SCOUR CAREER GIGGIT HURTLE
AGITATE CLATTER HIGHTAIL
(— RESTLESSLY) FIG FIKE ITCH
SQUIB JIFFLE KELTER
(— SHAKILY) HOTTER
(— SIDEWISE) CRAB EDGE SIDLE
SLENT
(— SLOWLY) LAG MOG INCH PANT
PAUT SLUG BOGUE CRAWL CREEP
DRAWL FUDGE SLOOM SNAIL
HAGGLE LINGER TRINTLE
(— SMOOTHLY) SLIP DRIFT FLOAT
GLIDE SLEEK GLISSADE
(— SPIRALLY) GYRATE
(— STEADILY) FORGE
(— STEALTHILY) GLIDE SLINK
SMOOT SNAKE
(— STIFFLY) CRAMBLE CRAMMEL
(— SUDDENLY) BOLT LASH YERK

GLENT START FLOUNCE STARTLE
(— SWIFTLY) CUT FLY BOOM LEAP RAKE SCUD SPIN BREEZE COURSE SWIFTEN
(— THROUGH AIR) FLY
(— TO AND FRO) FAN FLOP DODGE SHAKE WIGWAG AGITATE
(— TO ANOTHER PLACE) ADJOURN
(— TO LEEWARD) DRIVE
(— UNEASILY) FIDGET
(— UNSTEADILY) BICKER BUMBLE FALTER HOBBLE WABBLE WAMBLE WELTER WOBBLE BLUNDER STAGGER STUMBLE
(— UP AND DOWN) BOB HOWD SEESAW TEETER
(— UPWARD) ARISE ASCEND GRADUATE
(— VESSEL) KEDGE
(— VIGOROUSLY) FLOG STRAY
(— VIOLENTLY) DASH FLOG HURL LASH LEAP SWASH AGITATE COMMOVE
(— WAVERINGLY) FLEET
(— WEAKLY) FLAG
(— WITH BEATING MOTION) FLAP
(— WITH EFFORT) ACHE
(— WITH LEAPS) SKIP SPRING
(— WITH NOISY ACTIVITY) BUSTLE
(— WITH SHORT TURNS) ZIGZAG
(CHESS —) KEY COOK NECK PLOY GAMBIT KEYMOVE
(SUCCESSFUL —) SCORE
(SUDDEN —) GAMBADE
MOVED MOSSO ANIMATE FRANTIC
(— BY LOVE) AMOROUS
(EASILY —) FLESHLY SKINLESS
MOVEMENT EDDY MOTO PLAY STIR CARRY CAUSE FLICK FLISK FLOAT FRONT GESTE MUDGE TREND UKIYO ACTION CURSUS ENTREE MOMENT MOTION PIAFFE SPRAWL STROKE CURRENT FURIANT GAMBADO GESTURE KINESIS PIAFFER UKIYÖYE BUSINESS FEMINISM FUTURISM HASKALAH STIRRING
(— BY ORGANISMS) TAXIS
(— FOR POLITICAL UNION) ENOSIS
(— FROM POINT TO POINT) PASSAGE
(— IN BULLFIGHT) SUERTE
(— OF AIR) SPIRIT
(— OF CHORUS) STROPHE
(— OF CLOUDS) CARRY
(— OF HORSE) LEVADE
(— OF LOOM) MOUSING
(— OF PROTOPLASM) CYCLOSIS
(— OF ROPE) SURGE
(— OF SHIP) STERNWAY
(— OF TIDE) LAKIE
(— OF TROOPS) LIFT
(— TOWARD GOAL) STRIDE
(AGITATED —) WORKING
(ART —) CUBISM
(BACKWARD —) BACKUP BACKLASH BACKWASH
(BALLET —) FRAPPE FOUETTE FLICFLAC
(BOBBING —) BOBBLE

(BODILY —) ACTION
(BOWEL —) LAXATION
(BOXING —) SPAR
(BRISK —) SNAP
(CIRCULAR —) CYCLING
(CLEVER —) PAW
(DANCE —) BRISE CLOSE GIGUE GLIDE SPIRAL BATTERIE
(DARTING —) FLIRT
(DOWNWARD —) DECLINE
(DROLL —) GAMBADE GAMBADO
(ENLIGHTENMENT —) HASKALAH
(EXPANSION —) BOOM
(FENCING —) VOLT
(FLAPPING —) FLAFF
(FORWARD —) SWEEP ADVANCE PROGRESS INCESSION
(FROLICKING —) FRISK GAMBOL
(GRADUAL —) CREEPISM
(GYMNASTIC —) KIP SWING DISMOUNT
(HUMOROUS —) BURLA
(INDEPENDENCE —) SWADESHI
(INVOLUNTARY —) REFLEX
(JERKING —S) BALLISM
(JERKY —) SNATCH
(LATERAL —) LEEWAY
(MASS —) STAMPEDE
(MILITARY —) BOUND MANEUVRE
(MUSICAL —) AIR DUET BURLA DUMKA LARGO ENTREE FINALE SARABAND SYMPHONY
(OSCILLATING —) HUNT
(PAINTING —) FAUVISM
(POETRY —) IMAGISM
(POLITICAL —) LEFTISM GAULLISM
(QUICK —) PAW DART WHIP YERK GLENT SHAKE GLANCE
(RATIONALISTIC —) DEISM
(REELING —) STAGGER
(RELIGIOUS —) JOCISM STUNDISM
(RETROGRADE —) SLIP CREEP
(RETURN —) BACKHAUL
(RHYTHMIC —) DANCE
(ROCKING —) HOWD
(ROWING —) HOICK
(SKILLED —) SUERTE
(SPASMODIC —) JUMP HICCUP SPRUNT HICCOUGH
(SPRINGY —) LILT
(STEALTHY —) SLINK
(SUDDEN —) HITCH SPANG START FLICKER
(SWAYING —) SWAG
(SWIFT —) SWOOSH
(THEOLOGICAL —) ARIANISM
(TUMULTUOUS —) HORROR EMOTION
(TURNING —) CARACOLE
(UP AND DOWN —) SEESAW
(UPWARD — OF VESSEL) SCEND
(UPWARD —) BULGE SCEND
(WALKING —) AMBLE
(WATCH —) EBAUCHE BAGUETTE
(ZIGZAG —) TACK
MOVER MOTIVE
MOVIE (ALSO SEE MOTION PICTURE) FLICK FLICKS SLEEPER
MOVING WAY HIGH ASTIR GOING

QUICK AFLOAT MOVENT ANIMATE CURRENT AMBULANT FLITTING POIGNANT TOUCHING
(— ABOUT) AROUND AMBULANT
(— AIMLESSLY) ERRANT
(— BACKWARDS) CRAB
(— DOWN LINE) ACTIVE
(— FORWARD) ADVANCE
(— HAPHAZARDLY) AFLOAT
(— IN MANY DIRECTIONS) DIFFUSE
(— RAPIDLY) STICKLE SKELPING
(— SLOWLY) SOFT GLACIAL
(— TO AND FRO) AGITATED
(NOT —) STICKY STABILE
MOVINGLY PATETICO
MOW CUT BARB GOAF SKIM CRADLE SCYTHE SICKLE DESECATE
(— BEANS) THROAT
(— FOR STORING GRAIN) TOSS
(— OF CORN) CANSH
(HAY —) TASS
MOWER MEADER
(FOREMOST —) LORD
MOWING MATH MOWTH SHEAR
MOZAMBIQUE (LAKE OF —) CHUALI NHAVARRE
(RIVER OF —) SAVE MSALU LUGENDA ZAMBEZI
(TOWN OF —) TETE BEIRA ZUMBO CHEMBA PAFURI
MOZZETTA CAMAIL
MR HERR SIGNOR SIGNIOR SIGNORE
MRS FRAU MISS PANI HANOUM SENORA SENHORA SIGNORA GOODWIFE
MUCH FAR FELE MICH REAL WELL GREAT HEAPS MOLTO MOULT SIZES MICKLE MUCHLY ABUNDANT MUCHWHAT
(— CALLED FOR) LEEFTAIL
(PRETTY —) GAILY GAYLY
(SO —) ALL SUCH TANTO INSOMUCH
(TOO —) TROP TROPPO
(VERY —) ALL BADLY GREAT HEAPS LOADS SWITHE SWYTHE APLENTY GEYLIES GREATLY
MUCILAGE GUM MUCUS MUCAGO
MUCILAGINOUS MALACOID
MUCK CACK SOIL
MUCOID BLENNOID
MUCUS SNOT MUCOR BUBBLE MUCAGO PHLEGM SNIVEL PITUITE
MUD DAB FEN CLAY DIRT FANC GLAR LAIR MIRE MOIL SAUR SIND SLAB SLEW SLOB SLOP SLUB SLUD SLUE SLUR SUMP CLART FANGO GLAUR GUMBO SLAKE SLIME SLOSH SLUSH SPOSH SQUAD WAISE PELOID SLOUGH SLUDGE CLABBER GUTTERS MURGEON SLOBBER SLODDER SLUDDER SLUTHER SULLAGE
(LACUSTRINE —) GYTTJA
MUDAR AK AKUND ASHUR MADOR YERCUM AKMUDDAR
MUDCAP ADOBE
MUD CAT FLATHEAD
MUDCAT STATE MISSISSIPPI

MUDDLE MIX BALL DOZE HASH
MASH MESS MULL MUZZ SOSS
ADDLE SNAFU BEMUSE BURBLE
FOITER FUDDLE HUDDLE JUMBLE
MAFFLE MIZZLE MOFFLE MUCKER
POTHER PUDDLE TANGLE BECLOUD
BEDEVIL BLUNDER FLUSTER
POOTHER STUPEFY BEFUDDLE
BEWILDER CONFOUND DISORDER
FLIUNDER
MUDDLED ADDLE BEERY FOGGY
FUZZY MUSED MUZZY DRUMLY
GROGGY BESOTTED CONFUSED
MUDDY DEEP FOUL GLET OOZY SICK
DIRTY DROVY DUBBY GUMLY SLAKY
CLAGGY CLARTY CLASHY DREGGY
DROUMY DRUMLY LIMOUS PUDDLY
SALLOW SLABBY SLOBBY SLOPPY
SLUBBY SLUDGY TURBID CLATCHY
GUTTERY MUDDIFY MUDDISH
SLOUGHY CLABBERY LUTULENT
SLOBBERY
(— BY STIRRING) STUDDLE
MUDFISH BOWFIN KOMTOK
MUDFLOW LAHAR MUDSPATE
MUDGUARD WING CUTTOO
SPLASHER
MUDHOLE PULK SLOUGH LOBLOLLY
MUD MINNOW DOGFISH MUDFISH
MUD PUPPY DOGFISH
MUERMO ULMO
MUFF BLOW BOBBLE MUFFLE
SNUFFKIN
MUFFIN COB GEM SINK COBBE
HAZEL SINKER MANCHET
MUFFLE MOB MOP PAD DAMP DULL
MUTE NOSE WRAP BUMBLE DEADEN
MUZZLE SHROUD STIFLE ENVELOP
(— A BELL) CLAM
(— THE HEAD) MOBLE
MUFFLED DEAD DEAF DULL CLOSE
THICK HOLLOW INWARD WRAPPED
MUFFLER SCARF MUFFLE SILENCER
MUG TOT CANN FACE STEIN NOGGIN
PEWTER SEIDEL CANETTE GODDARD
BLACKPOT SCHOPPEN
(ALE —) TOBY
(LIQUOR —) CAN GUN
MUGGER GOA
MUGGING YOKING
MUGGINS SNIFF
MUGGY FOZY MUNGY PUGGY
STICKY MUGGISH PUTHERY
MUGWORT BULWAND MUGWEED
MUISCA CHIBCHA
MUISHOND ZORIL ZORILLE
MULATTO PARDO GRIFFE GRIQUA
GRIFFIN TERCERON
MULBERRY AL AAL ACH AUTE KOZO
MORE WAUKE ALROOT MURREY
MORELLO SOURBUSH SYCAMINE
MULBERRY FIG SYCAMORE
MULCT FINE CHECK AMERCE
SCONCE FORFEIT PENALTY
MULE BUCKER HYBRID ACEMILA
IRONMAN JARHEAD JUGHEAD
RATTAIL SUMPTER CENCERRO
HARDTAIL QUADROON QUATERON
(DROVE OF —S) ATAJO MULADA

MULE ARMADILLO MULITA
MULE DRIVER SKINNER
MULE SHOE PLANCHE
MULETEER ASSMAN ARRIERO
MULISH STUPID STUBBORN
MULL CHAW BOSOM FETTLE MULMUL
STEATIN
MULLEIN TORCH AGLEAF ICELEAF
DOVEWEED FELTWORT FOXGLOVE
HAGTAPER LUNGWORT VERBASCO
MULLER DAMPENER
MULLET BOBO LISA LIZA BOURI
GARAU KANAE MOLET HARDER
MULLOID GOATFISH MUGILOID
SPRINGER
(UNPIERCED —) STAR
MULLOWAY JEWFISH KINGFISH
SCIAENID
MULTICOLORED CALICO
MULTIFARIOUS MANIFOLD
MULTIFARIOUSNESS VARIETY
MULTIFORM DIVERSE
MULTILINGUAL POLYGLOT
MULTIPLE DECUPLE SEPTUPLE
MULTIPLICAND FACIEND
MULTIPLICATION INCREASE
DUPLATION
MULTIPLICITY MULTEITY
MULTIPLIER FACIENT COFACTOR
MULTIPLY VIE BREED LAYER
DOUBLE INVOLVE ENGENDER
INCREASE MANIFOLD
MULTITUDE ARMY CRAM HEAP HIVE
HOST ROUT RUCK CLOUD CROWD
FLOTE POWER SHOAL SWARM
HIRSEL HOTTER LEGION MAMPUS
MEINIE NATION THRONG SMOTHER
(PL.) FLOCKS
MULTITUDINOUS MYRIAD MANIFOLD
NUMEROUS
MULTIVALENT POLYAD
MULTURE THIRL THIRLAGE
MUM CLUM DARK MUMMER
MUMBLE CHEW MUMP BROCK
CHELE MOUTH CHAVEL FAFFLE
FUMBLE HOTTER HUMMER MAFFLE
MOFFLE PALTER DRUMBLE
FLUMMER GRUMBLE
MUMBLER MAFFLER
MUMBLETY-PEG KNIFE
MUMMER ACTOR GUISER GUISARD
MUMMERY MORRIS HODENING
PUPPETRY
MUMMICHOG MUDFISH
MUMMY CONGO MUMMIA SKELET
MUMMY BROWN BAY SNUFF
TAMARACK
MUMMY CASE SLEDGE
MUMPS BRANKS
MUNCH CHEW CHUMP MANGE
MUNGE
MUND GRITH
MUNDANE WORLD EARTHLY
FLESHLY SECULAR TERRENE
SUBSOLAR
MUNG BEAN MUG GRAM MONGOE
BALATONG
MUNIA MAYA PADDA
MUNICIPAL TOWN

MUNICIPALITY CITY TOWN CABILDO
MUNIFICENCE BOUNTY ROYALTY
MUNIFICENT ROYAL LIBERAL
MUNIFIC PROFUSE MAGNIFIC
PRINCELY
MUNJ MOONJA MANJEET
(CULMS OF —) SIRKI SIRKY
MUNTIACUS CERVULUS
MUNTJAC KAKAR RATWA KIDANG
MURAL TOPIA FRESCO
MURCIA (RIVER OF —) SEGURA
(TOWN OF —) MULA LORCA TOTANA
MURDER BANE KILL SLAY BLOOD
BURKE DEATH SCRAG FELONY
MURDUM KILLING MURTHER
THUGGEE HOMICIDE MASSACRE
THUGGERY THUGGISM
MURDERER BANE CAIN KILLER
ASSASSIN
MURDEROUS FELL GORY CRUEL
FELON BLOODY SAVAGE DEATHFUL
MURKINESS GLOOM
MURKY DARK BLACK DIRTY MIRKY
MUDDY CLOUDY PUDDLY
MURMUR HUM BRUM BURR CLUM
HUZZ MUSE BROOL GRANK INKLE
MOURN RUMOR SOUCH SOUGH
BABBLE GRUDGE GRUTCH HUMMER
MUTTER PIPPLE RUMBLE MURGEON
WHIMPER WHISPER WHITTER
COMPLAIN
(— AGREEABLY) CHIRM
(CONFUSED —) BABBLE
(DEEP —) BROOL
MURMURING BUZZ BRABBLE
MURGEON RUMOROUS
MURRAH SURTI
MURRAL DALAG
MURRE TINK ARRIE LUNGIE STRANY
TINKER ROCKBIRD
MURREY SANGUINE
MUSA SABA
MUSANG POWCAT POLECAT
MUSCA FLY
MUSCADINE BULLACE
MUSCAT (SEE OMAN)
MUSCLE EYE LIRE THEW FLESH
MOUSE SINEW BENDER BICEPS
CORACO FLEXOR LACERT PENNON
RECTUS SOLEUS TENSOR AGONIST
AMBIENS CANINUS DELTOID
DILATOR ERECTOR EVERTOR
FLECTOR GLUTEUS ILIACUS
LEVATOR MUSCULE NASALIS
OBLIQUE ROTATOR SCALLOP
TRICEPS VAGINAL ABDUCTOR
ADDUCTOR ADJUSTER ANCONEUS
ARRECTOR BIVENTER DIDUCTOR
EXTENSOR GEMELLUS GRACILIS
INVERTOR MASSETER MENTALIS
OBLIQUUS OMOHYOID OPPONENS
PALMARIS PATHETIC PECTORAL
PERONEUS PROCERUS PRONATOR
RETENTOR SCALENUS SERRATUS
SPINALIS SPLENIUS TEMPORAL
TIBIALIS
(HAVING LUMPY —S) LOADED
(PL.) BRAWN THEWS
MUSCLE SUGAR INOSITE INOSITOL

MUSCOVY DUCK PATO SCOVY
MUSCULAR ROPY HUSKY THEWY
BRAWNY ROBUST STRONG TOROSE
ATHLETIC
MUSCULATURE DETRUSOR
MUSE CLIO DUMP REVE AMUSE
DREAM ERATO STUDY THINK THALIA
URANIA EUTERPE REFLECT
CALLIOPE COGITATE CONSIDER
MEDITATE POLYMNIA RUMINATE
(PL.) PIERIDES
MUSEUM MUSEE
MUSH KASHA SLUSH MUSHER
SEPAWN SOFKEE POLENTA
SAGAMITE SCRAPPLE
MUSHROOM FAT CEPE FLAT DEATH
MITRA AGARIC BEAVER BUTTON
FUNGUS BLEWITS BOLETUS
BROILER LEPIOTA MUSHRUMP
WHITECAP
MUSHY SOPPY
MUSIC RAG DRAG GLEE JAZZ NOME
CANOR CHIME GIMEL GYMEL MURKY
NOISE SWING DREHER MUSICA
DESCANT FORLANA LANCERS
LANDLER MUSICAL MUSICRY
FALSETTO FANDANGO GUARACHA
(CALYPSO —) GOOMBAY
(CONCERTED —) ENSEMBLE
(EVENING —) DREAM SERENA
(IDENTIFYING —) SIG
(LIVELY —) GALOP FURLANA
(MORNING —) AUBADE
(RESOUNDING —) HIGGAION
(SAD —) MESTO
(SENTIMENTAL —) SCHMALZ
SCHMALTZ
(STACCATO —) SECCO
MUSICAL LYRIC SWEET LIQUID
LYRICAL TUNEFUL HARMONIC
NUMEROUS
MUSICAL INSTRUMENT GLY GUE
KIN TAR UKE ZEL ALTO ASOR BELL
CRUT DRUM GLEE GLEW GORA
HARP HORN LIRA LUTE LYRE OBOE
SANG SAWM TAAR TUBA VINA VIOL
ANVIL AULOS BANJO BLOCK BUGLE
CELLO CHENG CRWTH CUICA
DOMRA FLUTE GORAH GOURA
GUDOK GUIRO GUSLA GUSLE
KAZOO NABLA ORGAN REBAB
REBEC ROCTA RUANA SAROD
SHAWM SHENG TARAU TELYN
TRUMP VIOLA ZANZE ZINKE BALAFO
BONANG CABASA CITOLE CORNET
CROUTH CYMBAL DOUCET FIDDLE
GENDER GLARIN GUITAR GUSLEE
JARANA RAPPEL REBECK RIBIBE
SABECA SANTIR SPINET TABRET
TREBLE TYMPAN URHEEN VIOLET
VIOLIN ZITHER ALTHORN ANGELOT
ANKLONG ARGHOOL BAGPIPE
BANDORE BANDURA BASSOON
BAZOOKA CELESTA CHEKKER
CITHARA CLARINA CLAVIER CLAVIOL
DICHORD DOLCIAN DOLCINO
DULCIAN FISTULA FLUTINA GAMELIN
GITTERN HELICON KANTELE
MAGADIS OCARINA PANDURA

PIBCORN RACKETT SAMISEN
SARANGI SARINDA SAXHORN
SERPENT SISTRUM THEORBO
TRUMPET UKULELE URANION
ADIAPHON AKALIMBA AUTOHARP
AUTOPHON BARBITON CALLIOPE
CASTANET CLARINET CORNPIPE
CRESCENT DULCIMER DYOPHONE
EUPHONON FIDICULA FLAUTINO
HORNPIPE HUMSTRUM KRUMHORN
LAPIDEON MELODION NEGILOTH
NEHILOTH PENORCON PHONIKON
PSALTERY SCHWEGEL SERINGHI
SOURDINE SYMPHONY TAMBOURA
TAROGATO TRICHORD TROMBONE
VIRGINAL ZAMBOMBA
(PL.) BRASS FAMILY STRINGS
MUSICALITY HARMONY
MUSIC HALL GAFF MELODEON
MUSICIAN BARD WAIT ASAPH LINOS
VIOLA BOPPER MUSICO VIOLER
VIOLIN BANDMAN BOPSTER CELLIST
GAMBIST ORPHEUS TWANGER
VIOLIST KORAHITE MARIACHI
MINSTREL MUSICKER THRUMMER
TWANGLER
(PL.) ENSEMBLE WAITSMEN
MUSING PENSIVE MUSARDRY
MUSK MOOST CATTAIL AMBRETTE
FIXATIVE
MUSK DEER CERVID KASTURA
MUSKELLUNGE LONGE MUSKIE
MUSKET FUSIL FUZIL MATCH
DRAGON JINGAL ENFIELD GINGALL
BANDHOOK BISCAYEN CULVERIN
ESCOPETA SNAPHAAN TOPHAIKE
MUSKET BALL GOLI
MUSKETEER FUSILEER STRELITZ
MUSKET FORK GAFFLE
MUSKMELON MANGO ATAMON
WUNGEE SPANSPEK
MUSKOGEE CREEK SEMINOLE
MUSK OX OVIBOS
MUSKRAT SQUASH ONDATRA
MUSQUASH
MUSK SHREW SONDELI
MUSK TURTLE STINKER STINKPOT
MUSKWOOD CAOBA
MUSKY MOSCHATE
MUSLIM LAZ ALIM SIDI SWAT TURK
ARAIN HAFIZ IBADHI KAZAKH
TURBAN ABBADID AYYUBID BAGIRMI
BASHKIR IBADITE KHAKSAR
MUDEJAR SUNNITE ALAOUITE
ISLAMIST ISLAMITE QADARITE
SIFATITE
(— BEADS) TASBIH
(— BROTHERHOOD) TARIQA
(— CHIEF) RAIS REIS
(— DOCTRINE) TAWHID
(— FOUNDATION) WAKF WAQF
(— JUDGE) CAID QAID
(— MYSTIC) SUFI
(— PLAY) TAZIA
(— PRACTICE) PURDAH
(— PRINCIPLE) TAQIYA
(— SCHOLARS) ULAMA ULEMA
(— SECT) WAHHABI MURJIITE
(— TOMB) TABUT

(— TREE) TUBA
(PL.) SHIA SHIAH SUNNI
MUSLIN BAN MULL DORIA SWISS
GURRAH MULMUL SHALEE SHILLA
TANJIB BETEELA FACTORY JAMDANI
ORGANDY STENTER SEERHAND
TARLATAN
(PL.) COSSAS
MUSS FUFFLE RUMPLE GLOMMOX
UNDRESS
MUSSEL CLAM UNIO NAIAD ANODON
JINGLE LACERT MUCKET PALOUR
BIVALVE GLOCHID MYTILID UNIONID
BULLHEAD DEERHORN
MUSSELCRACKER BISKOP
MUST BIT BUD BUT MAN MAY MUN
BOOD MAUN SAPA STUM DULCE
SHALL
(— BE TAKEN) SUM
(— NOT) MAUNNA
MUSTACHE WALRUS VALANCE
WHISKER
MUSTACHE MONKEY MOUSTOC
MUSTANG PONY BRONCO SPHINX
MUSTARD CRESS SENVY SINEWY
AWLWORT CADLOCK KEDLOCK
SINAPIS AUBRIETA CHADLOCK
CHARLOCK FLIXWEED
MUSTARD GAS YPERITE
MUSTELUS GALEUS
MUSTER LEVY RAISE SPUNK GATHER
HOSTING MARSHAL RECRUIT
MUSTINESS FUST MUST
MUSTY HOAR FUNKY FUSTY HOARY
MOLDY MUCID RAFTY VINNY FOISTY
FROWZY FOUGHTY FROWSTY
COBWEBBY
MUTABLE FICKLE MUTATORY
VARIABLE
MUTATE SPORT
MUTATION SHIFT SPORT CHANGE
MUANCE SILKIE ANAGRAM
(VOWEL —) UMLAUT
MUTE PAD DUMB ECHO LENE SURD
BLACK MEDIA WHIST DAMPER
MUFFLE SILENT STIFLE TENUIS
SORDINE SOURDINE
(— FOR TRUMPET) DERBY
MUTED DULL SORDO STILL
DISCREET SOURDINE
MUTENESS SILENCE DUMBNESS
MUTILATE MAR HACK MAIM BREAK
GARBLE INJURE MANGLE MARTYR
MITTLE CONCISE CASTRATE
EMBEZZLE
(— AN ANIMAL) LAW
MUTILATION STRIP
MUTINEER PANDY MUTINADO
MUTINOUS UNRULY
MUTINY REVOLT STRIFE
MUTISM ALALIA
MUTTER CROOL MOTRE HOTTER
HUMMER MUMBLE MURMUR PATTER
THROAT CHANNER CHUNNER
CHUNTER GRUMBLE MAUNDER
TOOTMOOT
MUTTERING GROWL
MUTTON BRAXY VIFDA VIVDA
MOUTON BRAXIES

(LEG OF —) CABOB WABBLER WOBBLER
MUTTONBIRD OII
MUTTONFISH SAMA ABALONE EELPOUT MOJARRA
MUTUAL COMMON
MUZZLE NOSE MOUTH SNOUT FOREFACE
 (— FOR FERRET) COPE
 (— OF CANNON) CHOPS
MUZZLE-LOADER CAPLOCK MUZZLER
MYALL YARRAN WARRIGAL
MYCELIUM SPAWN MYCELE TAPESIUM
MYCTERIA TANTALUS
MY DEAR MACHREE
MYIASIS STRIKE

MYNA MINA MYNAH GRACKLE
MYOCOMMA FLAKE
MYRIAD HOST COUNTLESS
MYRIAPOD JULID POLYPOD PAUROPOD MILLIPEDE
MYRRH STACTE
MYRTLE MYRT LILAC BALTIC JAROOL ARRAYAN JAPONICA RAMARAMA
MYSELF SELF MYSEN HERSELF
MYSID SHRIMP
MYSOST PRIMOST
MYSTERIOUS DIM DARK DEEP EERY SELI EERIE SABLE WAKON ARCANE EXOTIC MYSTIC OCCULT SECRET CRYPTIC PUCKISH UNCANNY UNCOUTH ABSTRUSE ESOTERIC NUMINOUS SIBYLLIC

MYSTERIOUSLY DARKLY EERILY HEIMLICH
MYSTERY MIST RUNE CABALA ENIGMA SECRET ARCANUM SECRECY
MYSTIC SUFI OCCULT ORPHIC SECRET EPOPTIC ESOTERIC
MYSTICAL MISTY MYSTIC ANAGOGIC TELESTIC
MYSTICALLY GHOSTLY
MYSTICISM SUFIISM
MYSTIFY BEAT BEFOG BOTHER MUDDLE PUZZLE BECLOUD CONFUSE BEWILDER
MYTH SAGA FABLE LEGEND MYTHOS ALLEGORY
MYTHICAL FABLED FABULOUS FICTIOUS

N EN NU NAN
NAASSENE OPHITE
NAB HAT NIB GRAB HEAD KNAB
CATCH SEIZE ARREST CLUTCH
COLLAR NIBBLE NOBBLE SNATCH
CAPTURE APPREHEND
NABAL (WIFE OF —) ABIGAIL
NABALOI IBALOI IGOROT
NABK NUBK NABAK NEBUK NABBUK
NEBACK NEBBUK NEBBUCK
NABOB DIVES NAWAB NOBOB
DEPUTY VICEROY GOVERNOR
PLUTOCRAT
(— DEPUTY) NAWAB
(PL.) NABOBRY
NACELLE CAR BOAT BASKET
CHASSIS COCKPIT SHELTER
NACHSCHLAG SPRINGER
AFTERNOTE
NACKET BOY CAKE LUNCH NOCKET
NACRE PEARL SHELLFISH
NADIR BATHOS BEDROCK
(OPPOSED TO —) ZENITH
NAG CUT TIT BAIT FRAB FRET FUSS
GNAW JADE PLUG PONY PROD
SNAG TWIT ANNOY COBRA HOBBY
HORSE SCOLD SKATE SNAKE STEED
TEASE BADGER BERATE BOTHER
DOBBIN GARRAN GLEYDE HAGGLE
HARASS HECKLE HECTOR KEFFEL
PADNAG PESTER PLAGUE WANTON
HACKNEY HENPECK TORMENT
DINGDONG HARANGUE IRRITATE
PARAMOUR
(AMBLING —) HOBBY
NAGA SEMA COBRA KABUI LHOTA
SNAKE
NAGKASSAR SURIGA
NAGOR TOHI ANTELOPE REEDBUCK
NAHANE KASKA
NAHOOR SHA SNA SHEEP URIAL
BHARAL OORIAL
NAHUATL AZTEC CAZCAN MEXICA
NAHUM ELKOSHITE
NAIAD NAIS NYMPH MUSSEL
HYDRIAD
NAIL CUT FIX HOB PIN TEN BOSS
BRAD BRAG BROD CLAW CLOY
DUMP HOOF PILE SLUG SPAD STUB
STUD TACK TRAP AFFIX CATCH
CLOUT DRIVE GROPE PLATE SCALE
SEIZE SPEED SPIKE SPRIG TALON
BULLEN CLENCH CLINCH COOLER
CORKER DETAIN FASTEN GARRON
HAMMER SECURE SINKER TACKET
TENTER TINGLE UNGUIS UNGULA
CAPTURE FASTENER HOLDFAST
ROSEHEAD SPARABLE SPIKELET
TENPENNY TRICOUNI
(— BITING) ONYCHOPHAGIA
(— GROWTH) ONYCHAUXIS
(HEADLESS —) SPRIG
(HOOKED —) TENTER TENTERHOOK
(INGROWN —) ONYXIS ACRONYX
(MARKING —) SPAD SPEED
(OLD HORSESHOE —) STUB
(SHOEMAKER'S —) SPARABLE
(TOED —) TOSHNAIL
NAILROD STICKWEED

NAIVE OPEN RACY FRANK GREEN
CANDID SIMPLE ARTLESS NATURAL
CHILDISH INNOCENT UNTAUGHT
CHILDLIKE GUILELESS INGENUOUS
UNTUTORED UNWORLDLY
(— GIRL) INGENUE
NAIVETE GREENNESS SIMPLICITY
NAKED BALD BARE MERE NUDE
OPEN CLEAR EXACT PLAIN STARK
BARREN CUERPO SCUDDY SIMPLE
EXPOSED LITERAL OBVIOUS
MANIFEST STRIPPED SMOCKLESS
UNADORNED UNCLOTHED
UNCOVERED
NAKED OAT PILLAS PILCORN
PILKINS
NAKEDWOOD MABI SNAKEWOOD
NAKHI MOSO MOSSO
NAMAYCUSH CREE FISH LAKER
LONGE LUNGE TOGUE TROUT
LONGUE SISCOWET
NAMBY-PAMBY INANE SILLY VAPID
CODDLE INSIPID KEEPSAKE
NAME DUB FIX NOM SET CALL CITE
FAME NAIL NOMB NOUN TERM
ALIAS CLAIM CLEPE COUNT ETHIC
NEVEN NOMEN POINT QUOTE STYLE
TITLE ADDUCE APPEAL GOSSIP
MONICA REPUTE SELECT ALLONYM
APPOINT BEHIGHT DECLARE
ENTITLE EPITHET MENTION MONIKER
SPECIFY VOCABLE CATEGORY
CHRISTEN COGNOMEN IDENTIFY
IDENTITY INDICATE ENUMERATE
(— TABLET) FACIA
(— WRITTEN BACKWARDS) ANANYM
(ADDED —) AGNAME AGNOMEN
(ALTERNATIVE —) BUNCH
(ANCESTOR'S —) EPONYM
(ANOTHER —) ALIAS
(ASSUMED —) PEN ALIAS
ONOMASTIC PSEUDONYM
SOBRIQUET
(BAD —) CACONYM
(DAY —) AHAU
(DERIVATION OF —) EPONYMY
(FIRST —) FORENAME PRAENOMEN
(GOOD —) HONOR CREDIT
(REGISTERED —) AFFIX
(TECHNICAL —) ONYM
(WELL-SUITED —) EUONYM
NAMED CITED HIGHT DUBBED
YCLEPT ONYMOUS YCLEPED
NAMELESS BAS
NAMELY FOR VIZ SCIL NOTED TOWIT
FAMOUS SCILICET
NAMEPLATE MASTHEAD
NAMESAKE EPONYM JUNIOR
HOMONYM
NANDI BANANDE MUNANDI KIPSIKIS
NANDU RHEA
NANISM DWARFISM
NANNAR SIN
NANNY GOAT NURSE
NANTICOKE TOAG
NAOMI MARA
(DAUGHTER-IN-LAW OF —) RUTH
NAOS CELLA SHRINE TEMPLE
NAP GIG NOD RAS CALK CAMP

DOWN DOZE FUZZ LINT PILE RUFF
SHAG WINK COVER DOVER FLUFF
GRASP SEIZE SLEEK SLEEP STEAL
CATNAP DROWSE SIESTA SNOOZE
EMERIZE SLUMBER
(TO RAISE —) TEASE
NAPE NOD CUFF NECK NUKE POLL
NUCHA NUQUE SCRAG SCURF
NODDLE SCRUFF TURMP NIDDICK
NAPERY LINEN DOILIES NAPKINS
NAPHTALITE ENAN AHIRA
NAPHTHA NEFTE PETROLEUM
NAPKIN CLOTH DOILY TOWEL
DIAPER NAPERY KERCHIEF
SUDATORY HANDCLOTH SERVIETTE
NAPLES BISCUIT LADYFINGER
NAPLESS HARD
NAPOLEON (— III) LOUIS
BOUSTRAPA
(BATTLE OF —) ULM ACRE JENA
WATERLOO
(BIRTHPLACE OF —) CORSICA
(BROTHER-IN-LAW OF —) MURAT
(GAME LIKE —) PAM
(ISLAND OF —) ELBA HELENA
CORSICA
(MARSHALL OF —) NEY
(MOTHER OF —) HORTENSE
(PLACE OF VICTORY FOR —) LODI
LIGNY
NAPPE DECKE
NAPPY ALE DISH DOWNY HEADY
WOOLY LIQUOR SHAGGY STRONG
WOOLLY COTTONY FOAMING
VILLOUS
NARCISSUS LILY PLANT CRINUM
EGOIST FLOWER LILIUM JONQUIL
(LOVED BY —) ECHO
(TRUMPET —) DAFFODIL
NARCOTIC KAT BANG DOPE DRUG
HEMP JUNK BHANG DAGGA ETHER
OPIUM HEROIN OPIATE ANODYNE
COCAINE CODEINE HASHISH
NARCEIN HYPNOTIC MORPHINE
TAKROURI DIACODION MARIJUANA
SOPORIFIC
(— AGENT) GAZER
(— DOSE) LOCUS
(— PLANT) DUTRA MANDRAKE
(SMALL AMOUNT OF —) SNIFTER
(PL.) JUNK STUFF
NARCOTINE OPIANE
NARD SPICE ANOINT RHIZOME
MUSKROOT SPIKENARD
NARDOO ARDOO NARDU CLOVER
NARGIL COCONUT
NARGILEH PIPE HOOKA HOOKAH
NARGHILE
NARK SPY VEX NOTE ANNOY TEASE
OBSERVE INFORMER IRRITATE
NARRA NAGA ASANA APALIT
NARRATE SPIN TELL BRUIT STATE
STORY DEPICT DETAIL DEVISE
RECITE RELATE REPORT DISCUSS
RECOUNT STORIFY DESCRIBE
REHEARSE
NARRATION TALE FABLE STORY
DETAIL ACCOUNT HAGGADA
SYNAXAR DELIVERY HAGGADAH

NARRATIVE EPIC JOKE MYTH SAGA
TALE CONTE DRAMA FABLE PROSE
STORY COMEDY JATAKA LEGEND
ACCOUNT EPISODE HISTORY
MEMOIRS MIDRASH NOVELLA
PARABLE RECITAL ALLEGORY
ANECDOTE APOLOGUE ARETALOGY
HAGIOLOGY
(— **POEM**) EPIC EPOS SAGA
(**BRIEF** —) ANECDOTE
(PL.) ACTA EXEMPLA
NARRATOR TESTO TELLER RELATOR
SAGAMAN TALESMAN RACONTEUR
NARROW JERK LEAN MEAN NEAR
POKY SLIT TRUE BORNE CLOSE
RIGID SCANT SHARP SMALL SOUND
TAPER ANGUST BIASED LINEAR
LITTLE MEAGER STRAIT STRICT
TWITCH BIGOTED ERICOID LIMITED
PRIMARY SLENDER THRIFTY
CONDENSE CONTRACT PAROCHIAL
(— **DOWN STAVES**) BUCK
(— **DOWN**) CONFINE
(— **INLET**) RIA
(**NOT** —) CATHOLIC
(**VERY** —) HAIRBREADTH
NARROWED LISTED INSWEPT
CONTRACT
NARROWING CAP CHOKE INTAKE
STENOSIS
NARROWLY WIDE STRAITLY
NARROW-MINDED BORNE
NARROWNESS BIAS BIGOTRY
NARSINGA TRUMPET
NARTHECIUM ABAMA
NARTHEX HALL STOA ENTRY FOYER
LOBBY PORCH PORTICO PRONAOS
VESTIBULE
NASAB NUSUB KINSHIP
NASAL NOSY NARINE RHINAL
TWANGY ADENOID STRINGY
NASCENCY BIRTH ORIGIN GENESIS
BEGINNING
NASEBERRY SAPODILLA
NASHGAB OAF GOSSIP
NASI OFFICER PATRIARCH
NASICORN RHINOCEROS
NASTIKA ATHEIST
NASTURTIUM CAPUCINE NOSEWORT
RADICULA STURSHUM STURTION
NASTY BAD PAH FOUL MEAN UGLY
DIRTY FILTHY HORRID ODIOUS
RIBALD BAGGAGE DEFILED
HARMFUL OBSCENE SQUALID
UNCLEAN INDECENT NAUSEOUS
DANGEROUS MALICIOUS OFFENSIVE
NAT NOT DEMON SPIRIT
NATAL INBORN INNATE NATIVE
GLUTEAL CONGENIAL
NATAL PLUM AMATUNGULA
NATANT AFLOAT FLOATING
SWIMMING
NATATORIUM BATH POOL
NATCHEZ STINKER STINKARD
NATION BENI FOLK GEAT HOST
LAND LEDE RACE VOLK AEDUI
CASTE CLASS FANTI REALM
STATE TRIBE FANTEE GEATAS
PEOPLE WAGOGO ARVERNI

COUNTRY SOCIETY LANGUAGE
COMMUNITY MULTITUDE
(— **SYMBOL**) FLAG CREST
(**HEBREW** —) JACOB
(**LARGE** —) COLOSSUS
NATIONAL CITIZEN FEDERAL
GENTILE GENTILIC
(— **DEMOCRACY**) ENDEX
NATIONALISM JINGOISM PHYLETISM
NATIONALITY FLAG
NATIVE ITE RAW SON TAO BORN
FREE GOOK HOME KIND LIVE NEIF
WILD INNER NATAL PUNTI EPIROT
GENIAL INBORN INNATE KINDLY
NORMAL SIMPLE VIRGIN CITIZEN
DENIZEN DZUNGAR ENDEMIC
GENUINE NATURAL PAISANO
POLISTA DOMESTIC GRASSCUT
HABITUAL HOMEBORN HOMEMADE
INHERENT LANDSMAN ORIGINAL
PRIMEVAL PRISTINE RESIDENT
YAMMADJI ABORIGINE CONGENIAL
INGRAINED INHERITED INTRINSIC
ORIGINARY TAWNYMOOR
(— **BEAR**) KOALA
(— **BEECH**) FLINDOSA
(— **MINERAL**) LIVE
(— **OF BENGAL**) KOL
(— **OF CHINA**) CELESTIAL
(— **OF FENS**) SLODGER
(— **OF FLORIDA KEYS**) CONK
CONCH
(— **OF ILLINOIS**) SUCKER
(— **OF IRELAND**) BOGTROTTER
(— **OF LONDON**) COCKNEY
(— **OF LOW CLASS**) TAO
(— **OF MADAGASCAR**) HOVA
(— **OF MALAYA**) INFIEL
(— **OF MARITIME PROVINCES**)
BLUENOSE
(— **OF N. CAROLINA**) TARHEEL
(— **OF NEW GUINEA**) BOONG
(— **OF NEW SOUTH WALES**)
CORNSTALK
(— **OF PHILIPPINES**) GUGU
(— **OF SCOTLAND**) GEORDIE
(— **OF SOUTHERN ILLINOIS**)
EGYPTIAN
(— **OF W. AUSTRALIA**) GROPER
(— **PLANT**) INDIGINE
(— **WHO TEACHES**) CATECHIST
(**BORN AND BRED AS A** —) CREOLE
(**FREE** —) TIMAWA
(**UNCIVILIZED** —) MYALL
NATIVITY BIRTH GENESIS GENITURE
HOROSCOPE
NATTERJACK NEWT TOAD
NATTY CHIC NEAT POSH TIDY TRIG
TRIM NIFTY SMART SPICY DAPPER
JAUNTY SPRUCE FOPPISH
NATURAL RAW BORN EASY FOOL
HOME KIND OPEN RACY REAL WILD
NAIVE USUAL CANCEL CASUAL
COMMON CONJON CRETIN DIRECT
HOMELY INBORN INBRED INNATE
KINDLY NATIVE NORMAL PHYSIC
ARTLESS GENUINE QUADRUM
REGULAR INHERENT LIFELIKE
ORDINARY PHYSICAL UNCOINED

PRIMITIVE REALISTIC UNASSUMED
UNFEIGNED
(— **LOGARITHM**) LN
(— **TALENT**) DOWER FLAIR
(**NOT** —) AFFECTED
NATURALIZE ADAPT ADOPT
ACCUSTOM ACCLIMATE ENDENIZEN
HABITUATE
NATURALLY SN KINDLY GENIALLY
NATURALNESS EASE NAIVETE
NATURE ILK BENT BIOS CAST CLAY
FORM HAIR KIND MAKE MOOD RACE
SORT TYPE COLOR OUSIA SHAPE
STATE TENOR ANIMAL DHARMA
FIGURE HEAVEN KIDNEY PHYSIS
STRIPE ESSENCE FEATHER QUALITY
SPECIES PRAKRITI UNIVERSE
CHARACTER
(— **DIVINITY**) NYMPH
(— **GOD**) PAN
(— **GODDESS**) CYBELE ARTEMIS
(— **OF GOD**) DIVINITY
(— **PRINT**) PHYTOGRAPH
(— **SPIRIT**) NAT
(— **WORSHIP**) PHYSIOLATRY
(**APPARENT** —) STUDY
(**CONCEALED** —) LATENCY
(**DIVINE** —) DEITY
(**EMOTIONAL** —) HEART
(**ESSENTIAL** —) ESSE FORM GENIUS
(**HUMAN** —) FLESH MANHEAD
MANKIND
(**INHERENT** —) GENIUS
(**INTRINSIC** —) BOTTOM
(**MORAL** —) ETHNOS
(**OF THE SAME** —) HOMOGENEOUS
(**ORGANIC** —) BIOS
(**PERT. TO** —) COSMO
(**ROUGH** —) SPINOSITY
(**SPECIAL** —) IDIOM
(**SPIRITUAL** —) INTERNAL
(**ULTIMATE** —) ESSENCE
NAUGHT NIL EVIL ZERO AUGHT
NAGHT OUGHT CIPHER NOUGHT
WICKED NOTHING USELESS
WORTHLESS
NAUGHTY BAD PAW SAD EVIL
WRONG PAWPAW SHREWD WICKED
OBSCENE WAYWARD IMPROPER
NAUPATHIA SEASICKNESS
NAUSEA PALL QUALM DISGUST
NAUSITY LOATHING SICKNESS
ANTIPATHY DIZZINESS
NAUSEATE TURN TWIST WLATE
REVOLT SICKEN DISGUST STOMACH
DISTASTE
NAUSEATED ILL SICKISH QUALMISH
SQUEAMISH
NAUSEATING NASTY WAUGH
QUEASY BILIOUS FULSOME
BRACKISH STAWSOME LOATHSOME
REVOLTING SICKENING
NAUTICAL (ALSO SEE NAVIGATION)
NAVAL MARINE MAUTIC MARINAL
OCEANIC TARRISH MARITIME
NAVIGABLE
(— **FLAG**) CORNET PENNON
NAUTILUS MOLLUSK ARGONAUT
ARGONAUTA

(— **COMMANDER**) NEMO
NAVAHO DINE NAVAJO LONGHAIR
(— **GROUP**) OUTFIT
(— **RITE**) WAY
NAVAL SEA MARINE NAUTICAL
NAVIGABLE
(— **DEPOT**) BASE
(— **FORCE**) NAVY FLEET ARMADA
SQUADRON
(— **JAIL**) BRIG
NAVE HOB HUB NEF APSE BODY FIST
PACE AISLE NATHE NIEVE CENTER
NAVEL NOMBRIL OMPHALOS
UMBILICUS
NAVIGABLE BOATABLE PORTABLE
NAVIGATE KEEL SAIL DRIVE GUIDE
SKIFF STEER AVIATE COURSE
CRUISE DIRECT MANAGE TRAVEL
CONDUCT CONTROL JOURNEY
OPERATE TRAVERSE ASTROGATE
NAVIGATION HOMING VOYAGE
NAUTICS PASSAGE SAILING TRAFFIC
CABOTAGE SHIPPING
(— **MEASURE**) TON KNOT SEAM
FATHOM
(— **SYSTEM**) LORAN
NAVIGATOR FLYER NAVVY PILOT
AIRMAN AVIATOR COPILOT LABORER
AERONAUT SEAFARER SPACEMAN
NEPTUNIAN NEPTUNIST
NAVITE BASALT
NAVVY HAND WORKER LABORER
NAVIGATOR
NAVY FLEET SHIPFERD
(— **BOARD**) ADMIRALTY
(— **OFFICER**) CPO AIDE MATE
BOSUN CHIEF ENSIGN ADMIRAL
ARMORER CAPTAIN COMMANDER
COMMODORE
(— **RADIO OPERATOR**) SPARKS
(— **VESSEL**) PT SUB CARRIER
CRUISER FLATTOP DESTROYER
SUBMARINE TRANSPORT
NAWOB NABOB NUWAB RULER
VICEROY
NAY NO NAI NEI NOT DENY EVEN
NYET FLUTE NEVER DENIAL REFUSE
REFUSAL NEGATIVE
NAZARD STOP NASAT
NAZE NASE HEADLAND
NAZI BROWN HITLERITE
(— **SYMBOL**) FYLFOT SWASTIKA
NAZIM VICEROY GOVERNOR
NEANDERTHAL CAVEMAN
NEANIC IMMATURE YOUTHFUL
NEAR AD AT BY IN GIN KIN NAR AKIN
BAIN DEAR FAST GAIN HARD HEND
INBY NEXT NIGH ABOUT ANEAR
ANENT ASIDE CLOSE FORBY HANDY
HENDE JUXTA MATCH NUDGE
ROUND SHORT TOUCH ALMOST
AROUND BESIDE CLIMAX HEREBY
NARROW STINGY TOWARD WITHIN
ADVANCE AGAINST FORTHBY
SIMILAR THRIFTY VICINAL ADJACENT
APPROACH IMMINENT INTIMATE
(— **AKIN**) GERMANE
(— **POINT**) PP

(— **THE BEGINNING**) EARLY
FORMER
(— **THE EQUATOR**) LOW
(— **THE MOUTH**) ADORAL
(— **THE SURFACE**) EBB FLEET
(— **THE WIND**) HIGH AHOLD
(**CONVENIENTLY** —) HANDSOME
NEARBY AROUND GAINLY LOCALLY
ADJACENT
NEARER HITHER
(— **FRANCE**) CISALPINE
(— **ROME**) CISALPINE
(— **THE REAR**) AFTER
NEAREST NEXT EWEST CLOSEST
NEARMOST PROCHAIN IMMEDIATE
PROXIMATE
(— **THE STERN**) AFTERMOST
NEARLY GAIN JUST LIKE MOST
MUCH ABOUT ALMOST FECKLY
NEARSIGHTED MYOPIC PURBLIND
NEAT GIM NET COSH COWS DEFT
DINK FEEL FEIL GENT JIMP MACK
NICE OXEN PRIM PURE SMUG SNOD
SNUG TIDY TOSH TRIG TRIM BULLS
CLEAN CLEAR COMPT CRISP DINKY
DONCY DONSY DOUCE EXACT
FEATY FETIS JEMMY NATTY PREST
QUEME SMART SMIRK TERSE TIGHT
ADROIT BOVINE CATTLE CLEVER
DAINTY DAPPER DIMBER DONSIE
HEPPEN MINION POLITE QUAINT
SPANDY SPRUCE BANDBOX
CONCISE ORDERLY PERJINK
PRECISE REFINED SHAPELY
UNMIXED MENSEFUL SKILLFUL
STRAIGHT TASTEFUL DEXTEROUS
SHIPSHAPE UNDILUTED WHOLESOME
NEATLY SNUG DEFTLY FAIRLY
FEATLY SMARTLY SPRUCELY
NEATNESS MENSE DEFTNESS
ELEGANCE SPRUCERY
NEB EAR NIB TIP BEAK BILL NOSE
POINT SNOUT

NEBRASKA

CAPITAL: LINCOLN
COLLEGE: DANA DOANE
  DUCHESNE HASTINGS
COUNTY: LOUP OTOE DEUEL
  SARPY COLFAX NEMAHA
INDIAN: OTO OMAHA PONCA
  PAWNEE
RIVER: LOGAN DISMAL PLATTE
  ELKHORN NIOGRARA
STATE BIRD: MEADOWLARK
STATE FLOWER: GOLDENROD
STATE NICKNAME: CORNHUSKER
STATE TREE: ELM
TOWN: COZAD OMAHA GERING
UNIVERSITY: CREIGHTON

NEBRIS FAWNSKIN
NEBULA SKY CRAB SPOT VAPOR
BALAXY SPIRAL PLANETARY
NEBULIZE ATOMIZE
NEBULOUS DIM DARK HAZY FOGGY
MISTY MUDDY VAGUE CLOUDY
MYSTIC TURBID CLOUDED EVASIVE
SHADOWY UNCLEAR DREAMLIKE

NEBULA SKY CRAB SPOT VAPOR
GALAXY SPIRAL PLANETARY
NEBULIZE ATOMIZE
NEBULOUS DIM DARK HAZY FOGGY
MISTY MUDDY CLOUDY MYSTIC
TURBID CLOUDED SHADOWY
UNCLEAR
NECESSARILY NEEDS NEEDLY
PERFORCE
NECESSARY NEEDY PRIVY VITAL
FRIEND TOILET KINSMAN NEEDFUL
FORCIBLE INTEGRAL ESSENTIAL
INTRINSIC
(PL.) ALIMENT MISTERS
NECESSITATE FORCE IMPEL
COMPEL DEMAND ENTAIL OBLIGE
REQUIRE CONSTRAIN
NECESSITY USE CALL DUTY FATE
FOOD LACK MUST NEED TASK
WANT DRINK ANANKE BESOIN
MISTER MUSCLE NEEDBE URGENCY
PERFORCE
(— **OF MOVING**) ZUGZWANG
(**BY** —) PRESENTLY
(PL.) BREAD
NECK COL NUB PET CAPE CRAG
CROP HALS KISS WAKE BEARD
CHOKE CRAIG HALSE SCRAG SPOON
SWIRE TRAIL BEHEAD CARESS
CERVIX COLLET COLLUM FONDLE
STRAIT CHANNEL EMBRACE
ISTHMUS SQUEEZE TUBULUS
LALLYGAG
(— **ARTERY**) CAROTID
(— **MUSCLE**) SCALENUS
(— **OF BOTTLE**) THROTTLE
(— **OF LAMB**) TARGET
(— **OF VOLCANO**) CORE
(**BACK OF** —) NOD NAPE NUCH
NUQUE SCRUFF NIDDICK
(**PERT. TO** —) JUGULAR CERVICAL
(**RED** —) ROOINEK
NECK AND NECK TIE EVEN CLOSE
NECKBAND BAND COLLAR COLLET
SHIRTBAND
NECKCLOTH BOA TIE RUFF AMICE
CHOKE SCARF STOLE CHOKER
CRAVAT BURDASH NECKTIE
PANUELO STARCHER BARCELONA
SOLITAIRE STEINKIRK
NECKERCHIEF GIMP RAIL FOGLE
BELCHER FOULARD NECKLET
KERCHIEF NECKATEE NECKCLOTH
NECKENGER
NECKING COLLAR GORGERIN
NECKLACE BEE LEI TORC BEADS
CHAIN NOOSE CARCAN CHOKER
COLLAR GORGET SANKHA TAWDRY
TORQUE BALDRIC CHAPLET RIVIERE
SAUTOIR LAVALIER NEGLIGEE
ESCLAVAGE
NECKLINE COWL SCOOP
NECK RUFF FRAISE QUELLIO
NECKTIE BOW TIE ASCOT SCARF
CHOKER CRAVAT GRAVAT OVERLAY
(— **PARTY**) HANGING LYNCHING
NECROMANCER GOETIC MAGICIAN
NECROMANCY GOETY MAGIC

GRAMARY SORCERY WIZARDRY EGROMANCY
NECROPOLIS CEMETERY
NECROPSY AUTOPSY
NECTAR N HONEY AMBROSIA
NECTAR BIRD EATER HONEY SUNBIRD
NECTARINE NECTRON NECTARIN
NECTARY SPUR GLAND NECTARIUM
NEDDER ADDER
NEDDY HORSE DONKEY
NEE BORN
NEED ASK NUD LACK TAKE THAR WANT CRAVE DRIVE THARF BEHOVE BESOIN DEMAND DESIRE MISTER STRAIT BEHOOVE NEEDHAM POVERTY REQUIRE URGENCY DISTRESS EXIGENCY MISCHIEF EMERGENCE EXTREMITY NECESSITY
NEEDFIRE WILDFIRE
NEEDFUL VITAL INTEGRAL ESSENTIAL NECESSARY REQUISITE
NEEDLE SEW VEX YEN ACUS DARN GOAD TIER WIRE ANNOY BLUNT POINT SHARP SPIKE STRAW STYLE BODKIN DARNER STYLUS OBELISK PRICKER PROVOKE SPICULE TUMBLER
 (— HOLE) EYE
 (— SORTER) HANDER
 (COMB. FORM) ACU
 (PINE —) SPILL
 (PINE —S) PININGS
 (PL.) TWINKLES
NEEDLE BUG NEPID RANATRA
NEEDLEBUSH URY PINBUSH
NEEDLEFISH GAR SNOOK AGUJON BELONID LONGJAW
NEEDLE GUN RIFLE DREYSE
NEEDLELIKE ACUATE ACERATE ACEROSE ACEROUS ACIFORM ACICULAR BELONOID SPLINTERY
NEEDLEMAN TAILOR
NEEDLESS AMOK
NEEDLEWORK SEWING SAMPLER SEAMING TATTING KNITTING WOOLWORK HEMSTITCH INSERTION
NEEDY BARE POOR INDIGENT NEEDSOME HUNGARIAN PENNILESS
NEEP NEPE TURNIP
NE'ER-DO-WELL BUM PELF LOSEL SCHLEMIEL SHIFTLESS WORTHLESS
NEFANDOUS IMPIOUS EXECRABLE
NEFARIOUS WICKED HEINOUS IMPIOUS FLAGRANT HORRIBLE INFAMOUS ATROCIOUS
NEGATE DENY SUBLATE
NEGATION NAY NOT EMPTY DENIAL REFUSAL ANNULMENT NONENTITY
NEGATIVE NA NE NO CON NAE NAY NIT NIX NON NOR NOT NUL DENY FILM VETO NEVER NAYWARD STAMPER APOPHATIC PRIVATIVE
 (— PREFIX) IL IM IN IR UN DIS NON
 (— PRINCIPLE) YIN
NEGLECT DEBT FAIL HANG OMIT SLIP FAULT FORGO SHIRK SLOTH WAIVE BYPASS CESSER FOREGO FORGET IGNORE LACHES LOITER

PERMIT SLIGHT DEFAULT DISOBEY FAILURE OVERSEE RESPECT FORSLACK OMISSION OVERLOOK OVERSLIP RECKLESS DISREGARD MISLIPPEN OVERSIGHT PRETERMIT
NEGLECTED TACKY SHABBY UNDONE DORMANT OBSOLETE
NEGLECTFUL LAX REMISS CARELESS DERELICT HEEDLESS RECKLESS DISSOLUTE
NEGLIGEE ROBE MANTEAU MATINEE UNDRESS PEIGNOIR DISHABILE NIGHTGOWN
NEGLIGENCE CULPA LACHES DEFAULT LASCHETY DISREGARD OVERSIGHT
NEGLIGENT LAX LASH SOFT SLACK OVERLY REMISS CARELESS DISCINCT SLOVENLY YEMELESS DISSOLUTE
NEGLIGIBLE FAT
NEGOTIATE DEAL SELL BROKE FLOAT TREAT TROKE TRUCK TRYST ADVISE ASSIGN CONFER DICKER DIRECT MANAGE PARLEY SETTLE ARRANGE BARGAIN CHAFFER CONDUCT CONSULT DISCUSS ENTREAT CONCLUDE ENTREATY TRANSACT TRANSFER TEMPORIZE
NEGOTIATION DEAL DICKER PARLEY TREATY PASSAGE ENTREATY PRACTICE
NEGRITO ATA ATI ITA AETA AKKA BATWA BLACK KARON SEMANG TAPIRO ABENLEN BAMBUTE
NEGRO FON JUR LUO LWO SUK AKIM ALUR BENI BINI BONI BUCK CROW EGBA FONG IRON MADI MOKE NUBA NUPE SIDI BENIN BLACK BONGO CUFFY DARKY DINKA DJUKA FULUP FUZZY HATSA MUNGO SAMBO SEPIA SEREC SMOKE TEMNE GULLAH HUBSHI AKWAPIM DAHOMAN GEECHEE QUASHIE SANDAWE SHILLUK SWELLUH BECHUANA ETHIOPIAN MANGBATTU
 (— BLOOD) TARBRUSH
 (GOLD COAST —) GA FANTI
 (LIBERIAN —) KRU VAI VEI GREBO ICROO KRUMAN KROOBOY
 (MALE —) BUCK
 (OLD —) UNCLE
NEIGH NIE NVE WHI HINNY NICKER WHINNY WIGHER WHICKER
NEIGHBOR BOR ADJOIN BORDER FELLOW NEIPER ACCOLENT BORDERER CONFINER UCALEGON
 (PL.) KITH CONFINES
NEIGHBORHOOD WAY AREA HAND VENUE BARRIO LOCALE REGION PURLIEU SECTION DISTRICT ENVIRONS PROCINCT VICINAGE VICINITY BAILIWICK COMMUNITY PROXIMITY TERRITORY
NEIGHBORING NIGH NEARBY CONFINE VICINAL ACCOLENT ADJACENT
NEIGHBORLY FOLKSY FOLKSEY AMICABLE

NEITHER NOT NATHER NITHER NOWDER
 (— RIGHT NOR WRONG) ADIAPHOROUS
NELEUS (BROTHER OF —) PELIAS
 (DAUGHTER OF —) PERO
 (FATHER OF —) NEPTUNE
 (MOTHER OF —) TYRO
 (SON OF —) NESTOR
 (WIFE OF —) CHLORIS
NELLORE ONGOLE
NEMA EELWORM FILAMENT NEMATODE ROUNDWORM
NEMATOCYST CNIDA DESMONEME PENETRANT
NEMESIS BANE FATE UPIS AGENT AVENGER PENALTY
NENTSI SAMOYED SAMOYEDE
NEOPHYTE TYRO EPOPT NOVICE AMATEUR CONVERT BEGINNER PROSELYTE YOUNGLING
NEOPLASM TUMOR GROWTH TUMOUR SARCOMA NEWGROWTH
NEOTERIC NEW LATE FRESH NOVEL MODERN RECENT
NEP KNOT CATNIP CATMINT CLUSTER

NEPAL

CAPITAL: KATMANDU
COIN: MOHAR RUPEE
MOUNTAIN: EVEREST
NATIVE: AOUL LIMBU MURMI NEWAR GURKHA GORKHALI
RIVER: KALI KOSI MUGU SETI BABAI BHERI RAPTI SARDA GANDAK KARNALI NARAYANI
TOWN: PATAN BIRGUNJ BHADGAON LALITPUR BHAKTAPUR

NEPENTHE DRUG PLANT POTION ANODYNE
NEPHELINE LENAD MINERAL SOMMITE ELEOLITE
NEPHEW OY OYE NEVE VASU NEFFY NEVOY NIECE NEPOTE BENVOLIO
NEPHRITE JADE POUNAM AXSTONE POUNAMU TREMOLITE
NEPTUNE LER PAN SEA GREEN OCEAN PLATE SEAGOD
 (BROTHER OF —) PLUTO JUPITER
 (CONSORT OF —) SALACIA
 (DISCOVERER OF —) GALLE
 (EMBLEM OF —) TRIDENT
 (FATHER OF —) SATURN
 (MOTHER OF —) RHEA
 (SISTER OF —) JUNO
NEREID NYMPH NEREIS THALIA THETIS CYMODOCE
NEREIDES (FATHER OF —) NEREUS
 (MOTHER OF —) DORIS
NERO TYRANT FIDDLER
 (MOTHER OF —) AGRIPPINA
 (SUCCESSOR TO —) GALBA
 (VICTIM OF —) LUCAN SENECA
 (WIFE OF —) OCTAVIA
NERVE RIB CORD GALL GRIT GUTS LINE SAND VEIN CHEEK CHORD

CRUST PLUCK PUDIC SINEW SPUNK STEEL TENON VAGUS VIGOR APLOMB COSTAL DARING DENTAL ENERGY FACIAL LUMBAR RADIAL SACRAL STRING AXILLAR COELIAC COURAGE SAPHENA SCIATIC SPINDLE ABDUCENS AUDACITY BOLDNESS CERVICAL COOLNESS EFFERENT EMBOLDEN STRENGTH TEMERITY AUTONOMIC ENCOURAGE EYESTRING
(— **CELL**) ANAXON NEURON DIAXONE DENDRAXON
(— **CENTER**) BRAIN CORTEX PLEXUS
(— **FIBERS**) PONS
(— **NETWORK**) RETIA PLEXUS
(— **SLEEP**) NEURO HYPNOTISM
(PL.) HORRORS JITTERS

NERVELESS DEAD WEAK BRAVE INERT UNNERVED FOOLHARDY POWERLESS

NERVOUS EDGY TOEY FUSSY GOOSY JUMPY TENSE TIMID WINDY FIDGET SINEWY SPOOKY TOUCHY UNEASY FEARFUL FRETFUL JITTERY RESTIVE SCADDLE NEUROTIC TIMOROUS EXCITABLE SENSITIVE TREMULOUS TWITTERLY
(— **MALADY**) APHASIA NEURITIS
(— **SEIZURE**) TIC ANEURIA

NERVURE RIB NERVE NEURON CUBITAL

NERVY BOLD RASH JERKY PUSHY BRAZEN SINEWY STRONG FORWARD JITTERY IMPUDENT INTREPID VIGOROUS EXCITABLE

NESS RAS CAPE SUFFIX HEADLAND

NEST BED DEN EST JUG WEB AERY BIKE BINK DRAY DREY EYRY HOME LAIR NIDE REDD SHED TRAP ABODE AERIE BROOD EYRIE HAUNT HOUSE NIDUS SWARM CLUTCH COLONY CUDDLE HOTBED RESORT WURLEY CABINET LODGING RETREAT VESPIARY WITHYPOT LARVARIUM PENDULINE RESIDENCE TERMITARY
(— **OF ANIMALS**) BED
(— **OF ANT**) FORMICARY
(— **OF BOXES**) INRO
(— **OF EGGS**) CLUTCH

NESTLE JUG LAP LIE PET NEST SNUG NICHE SPOON BURROW CUDDLE FIDGET NUZZLE PETTLE SETTLE SNUDGE CHERISH SHELTER SNUGGLE SNUZZLE

NESTLING BABY BIRD EYAS NEST POULT SQUAB CUDDLE RETREAT BIRDLING NIDULATE FLEDGLING

NESTOR SAGE SOLON LEADER ADVISER ADVISOR COUNSELOR PATRIARCH

NET BAG GIN HAY LAM POT WEB CAUL FIKE FLAN FLEW FLUE FYKE GAIN HAAF KELL LACE LAUN LAWN LEAD MESH MOKE NEAT PURE RETE SALE TOIL TRAP TRIM WEIR BRAIL CATCH CLEAN CLEAR DRIFT GAUZE LACIS PITCH POUND SCOOP SEIZE SNARE SNOOD TRAWL TRINK TULLE

YIELD BAGNET BASKET BRIGHT COBWEB ENTRAP FABRIC GROUND LEADER MALINE MASILE PANTER PROFIT RAFFLE SAGENE SAPIAO TOWNET TUNNEL DRAGNET ENSNARE FLYTAIL LAMPARA MALINES NETWORK PROTECT RETICLE RINSING SCRINGE SHELTER SPILLER STALKER TRAINEL TRAMMEL MESHWORK SALAMBAO BUCKSTALL RETICULUM

NETHER DOWN BELOW LOWER UNDER NEDDER DOWNWARD INFERIOR INFERNAL

NETHERLANDS
CANAL: ORANJE JULIANA DRENTSCH
CAPITAL: AMSTERDAM
CHEESE: EDAM GOUDA LEYDEN
COIN: CENT DOIT RYDER FLORIN GULDEN STIVER DUCATON ESCALIN GUILDER STOOTER
ISLAND: TEXEL AMELAND VLIELAND
MEASURE: EL AAM AHM AUM ELL KAN MUD VAT ZAK DUIM LOOD MIJL ROOD ROPE VOET ANKER CARAT ROEDE STOOP WISSE BUNDER KOPPEN LEGGER MAATJE MUDDLE MUTSJE STREEP SCHEPEL MIMGELEN OKSHOOFD STEEKKAN
NAME: HOLLAND
NATIVE: DUTCH DUTCHMAN
PROVINCE: DRENTHE LIMBURG UTRECHT ZEELAND FRIESLAND GRONINGEN GELDERLAND OVERIJSSEL
RIVER: EEM LECK MAAS WAAL YSEL DONGE HUNSE MEUSE YSSEL DINTEL DOMMEL KROMME SCHELDT
TOWN: EDE ASTEN BREDA HAGUE AALTEN ARNHEM LEIDEN HAARLEM TILBURG UTRECHT AALSMEER ENSCHEDE NIJMEGEN AMSTERDAM EINDHOVEN GRONINGEN ROTTERDAM
WEIGHT: ONS LAST LOOD POND BAHAR GREIN KORREL WICHTJE ESTERLIN

NETHERWORLD HADES SHADES
NETLIKE MESHY NETTY RETIARY RETICULAR
NETTING BAR CAUL LING MESH SCREEN DEEPING FISHNET FOOTING BOBBINET WIREWORK
NETTLE VEX FRET LINE ANNOY CNIDA ETTLE PEEVE PIQUE STING HENBIT ORTIGA RUFFLE SPLICE URTICA AFFRONT BLUBBER BLUETOP KNITTLE PROVOKE STINGER IRRITATE CLOWNHEAL GLIDEWORT SMARTWEED
(— **RASH**) HIVES UREDO URTICARIA

(— **TREE**) LOTUS GYMPIE
(**WHITE DEAD** —) ARCHANGEL
NETWORK WEB CAUL FRET MAZE MESH MOKE RETE CHAIN LACIS BRIDGE COBWEB CRADLE PLEXUS RESEAU SAGENE SYSTEM DRAGNET DIPLEXER GRIDIRON KNITTING WATTLING RETICULUM
(— **OF CRACKS**) CRACKLE
(— **ON MAP**) GRATICULE
NEUME PES VIRGA CLIVIS PNEUMA PODATUS PUNCTUM VIRGULA CLIMACUS QUILISMA SEQUENCE TORCULUS SCANDICUS
NEURAL DORSAL NERVAL NEURIC
NEURALGIA SCIATICA COSTALGIA
NEURITE AXON AXONE
NEUROTIC DRUG NERVOUS
(— **CONDITION**) LATAH
NEUTRAL GRAY INERT SWEET AMORAL MIDDLING NEGATIVE UNBIASED COLORLESS IMPARTIAL
(— **IN COLOR**) SOBER
(**OPTICALLY** —) INACTIVE
NEUTRALIZE KILL ANNUL BLUNT ERASE CANCEL ABOLISH BALANCE CORRECT DESTROY NULLIFY VITIATE NEGATIVE SATURATE FRUSTRATE
NEUTRINO LEPTON

NEVADA
CAPITAL: CARSONCITY
COUNTY: NYE ELKO STOREY WASHOE
INDIAN: WASHO PAIUTE
LAKE: MEAD RUBY TAHOE WALKER PYRAMID
RIVER: REESE TRUCKEE HUMBOLDT
STATE BIRD: BLUEBIRD
STATE FLOWER: SAGEBRUSH
STATE NICKNAME: SILVER
STATE TREE: PINON
TOWN: ELY ENKO RENO FALLON NELLIS SPARKS LASVEGAS

NEVE ICE FIRN SNOW NEPHEW GLACIER
NEVER NAY NIE NOT NARY NARRA NIVER NOWHEN
NEVER-NEVER DREAMLAND
NEVERTHELESS BUT YET STILL ALWISE ALGATES HOWBEIT HOWEVER WHETHER
NEVUS MOLE SPOT TUMOR NAEVUS SPIDER SPILUS FRECKLE LENTIGO SPILOMA BIRTHMARK
NEW NEO NEU RAW LATE NOVA FRESH GREEN MOIST NOVEL YOUNG MODERN RECENT UNUSED VIRGIN ANOTHER FOREIGN STRANGE UNTRIED UPSTART INITIATE NEOTERIC ORIGINAL YOUTHFUL BEGINNING
(— **BUT YET OLD**) NOVANTIQUE
(**BRAND** —) SPICK
(**COMB. FORM**) NEO

NEWBORN YEANLING
NEW CALEDONIA (— BIRD) KAGU
  (CAPITAL OF —) NOUMEA
  (ISLAND OF —) HUON BELEP DEPINS
  LOYALTY WALPOLE
  (SEAPORT OF —) NOUMEA
NEWCASTLE GOTHAM
NEWCOMER SETTLER COMELING
  FRESHMAN MALIHINI RINGNECK
  GREENHORN IMMIGRANT KIMBERLIN
NEW DEAL (— AGENCY) CCC NRA
  NYA TVA
NEWEL POST SPINDLE
NEW ENGLAND (— INHABITANT)
  YANK YANKEE JONATHAN
  (— SETTLER) PILGRIM PURITAN
NEWFOUNDLAND (— CAPE) RACE
  (— HOUSE) TILT
  (— INHABITANT) OUTPORTER

NEW GUINEA
BAY: ORO MILNE
GULF: HUON PAPUA
ISLAND: BUKA MANUS MUSSAU
ISLAND GROUP: CRETIN NINIGO
  SAINSON SOLOMON
MOUNTAIN: ALBERT VICTORIA
NATIVE: KARON PAPUAN
PORT: LAE DARU WEWAK MADANG
RIVER: FLY HAMU SEPIK AMBERNO
TOWN: LAE WAU DARU SORON
  AITAPE KIKORI RABAUL

NEW HAMPSHIRE
CAPITAL: CONCORD
COLLEGE: DARTMOUTH
COUNTY: COOS BELKNAP
LAKE: SQUAM OSSIPEE SUNAPEE
  UMBAGOG WINNIPESAUKEE
MOUNTAIN: MORIAH PAUGUS
  WAUMBEK CHOCORUA
  MONADNOCK
MOUNTAIN RANGE: WHITE
NOTCH: CRAWFORD FRANCONIA
PRESIDENT: PIERCE
RIVER: SACO ISRAEL BELLAMY
  SOUHEGAN MERRIMACK
STATE BIRD: FINCH
STATE FLOWER: LILAC
STATE TREE: BIRCH
TOWN: KEENE EXETER NASHUA
  HANOVER LACONIA

NEW HEBRIDES (CAPITAL OF —)
  VILA
  (ISLAND OF —) EPI TANA EFATE
  MAEWO MABRIM MALEKULA

NEW JERSEY
CAPITAL: TRENTON
COLLEGE: UPSALA
COUNTY: ESSEX UNION BERGEN
  CAMDEN MORRIS PASSAIC
  MONMOUTH
INDIAN: DELAWARE
PRESIDENT: CLEVELAND

RIVER: DENNIS HAYNES MANTUA
  RAMAPO MULLICA PASSAIC
  RARITAN COHANSEY TUCKAHOE
STATE BIRD: GOLDFINCH
STATE FLOWER: VIOLET
STATE NICKNAME: GARDEN
STATE TREE: REDOAK
TOWN: LODI CAMDEN NEWARK
  NUTLEY RAHWAY TOTOWA
  BAYONNE HOBOKEN HOHOKUS
  MATAWAN NETCONG ORADELL
  PARAMUS PASSAIC TEANECK
  TENAFLY WYCKOFF CARTERET
  FREEHOLD METUCHEN
  SECAUCUS WATCHUNG
UNIVERSITY: RUTGERS PRINCETON

NEWLY ANEW AGAIN AFRESH
  LATELY FRESHLY NEWLINS
  RECENTLY
NEWMARKET MICHIGAN SARATOGA
  GRABOUCHE

NEW MEXICO
CAPITAL: SANTAFE
COUNTY: LUNA MORA QUAY TAOS
  OTERO CATRON CHAVES
  HIDALGO
CULTURE: MIMBRES
INDIAN: TEWA TIWA ZUNI JEMEZ
  PECOS APACHE NAVAHO
  NAVAJO PUEBLO
RIVER: UTE GILA PECOS SANJOSE
STATE BIRD: ROADRUNNER
STATE FLOWER: YUCCA
STATE TREE: PINON PINYON
TOWN: JAL BELEN RATON CLOVIS
  DEMING GALLUP GRANTS
  ARTESIA SOCORRO

NEWS BUZZ DOPE UNCA UNKO
  WORD CLASH FERLY ADVICE
  CRACKS FERLIE GOSPEL NOTICE
  REPORT EVANGEL KHUBBER
  TIDINGS WITTING NOUVELLE
  KNOWLEDGE SPEERINGS
  (— AGENCY) AP UP DNB INS UPI
  TASS ANETA DOMEI REUTERS
  (— BEAT) SCOOP
NEWSBOY NEWSY CAMELOT
  CARRIER
NEWSMONGER GOSSIP TATTLER
  NOVELANT NOVELIST QUIDNUNC
  REPORTER
NEWSPAPER RAG NEWS DAILY
  ORGAN PAPER PRESS SHEET TIMES
  ARRIBA HERALD SERIAL SUNDAY
  COURANT DIURNAL GAZETTE
  JOURNAL MERCURY TABLOID
  TRIBUNE NEWSPRINT
  (— USED BY PICKPOCKET) STIFF
  (PL.) PRESS
NEWSPAPERMAN PRESSMAN
NEWSSTAND BOOTH KIOSK STALL
  STAND BOOKSTALL
NEWT ASK EFT ESK EVET EBBET
  EFFET LIZARD TRITON AXOLOTL

CRAWLER CREEPER REPTILE
MANKEEPER
NEW YEAR'S DAY NAURUZ
  NOROOSE NOWROZE
NEW YEAR'S EVE HAGMENA
  HOGMANAY

NEW YORK
AVENUE: PARK FIFTH MADISON
  FLATBUSH
BAY: JAMAICA PECONIC MORICHES
BOROUGH: BRONX KINGS QUEENS
  BROOKLYN MANHATTAN
BUILDING: RCA PANAM CHRYSLER
  FLATIRON
CANAL: ERIE GOWANUS
CAPITAL: ALBANY
COLLEGE: BARD CCNY IONA PACE
  FINCH UNION HUNTER VASSAR
  WAGNER ADELPHI BARNARD
  CANISIUS HAMILTON SKIDMORE
COUNTY: ERIE KINGS TIOGA
  YATES BROOME CAYUGA
  NASSAU ONEIDA OSWEGO
  OTSEGO PUTNAM QUEENS
  SENECA ULSTER CHEMUNG
  GENESEE NIAGARA STEUBEN
  SUFFOLK CHENANGO DUTCHESS
  HERKIMER ONONDAGA
  RICHMOND ROCKLAND
  SARATOGA SCHUYLER
INDIAN: CAYUGA MOHAWK ONEIDA
  SENECA MOHICAN MONTAUK
  IROQUOIS ONONDAGA
ISLAND: FIRE LONG ELLIS STATEN
  FISHERS LIBERTY SHELTER
  GOVERNORS MANHATTAN
LAKE: ERIE CAYUGA GEORGE
  ONEIDA OTISCO OTSEGO
  OWASCO PLACID SENECA
  CONESUS HONEOYE ONTARIO
  SARANAC SCHROON SUCCESS
  SARATOGA
MOUNTAIN: BEAR MARCY
MOUNTAINS: TACONIC CATSKILL
  ADIRONDACK
NICKNAME: EMPIRE GOTHAM
PRESIDENT: FILLMORE VANBUREN
  ROOSEVELT
PRISON: TOMBS ATTICA SINGSING
RIVER: TIOGA HARLEM HOOSIC
  HUDSON MOHAWK OSWEGO
  GENESEE NIAGARA
SQUARE: TIMES UNION HERALD
  MADISON
STATE BIRD: BLUEBIRD
STATE FLOWER: ROSE
STATE NICKNAME: EMPIRE
STATE TREE: SUGARMAPLE
STREET: WALL BOWERY
  BROADWAY
SUBWAY: BMT IND IRT LEX
TOWN: RYE ROME ILION ISLIP
  NYACK OLEAN OWEGO UTICA
  ATTICA AUBURN COHOES
  ELMIRA GOSHEN ITHACA ONEIDA
  OSWEGO TAPPAN ARDSLEY
  BABYLON BATAVIA BUFFALO
  CONGERS ENDWELL GENESEO

HEWLETT MAHOPAC MASSENA
MERRICK MINEOLA MONTAUK
ONEONTA PENNYAN POTSDAM
SUFFERN SYOSSET WANTAGH
YAPHANK YONKERS BETHPAGE
CATSKILL HERKIMER KINGSTON
OSSINING SYRACUSE TUCKAHOE
ROCHESTER
UNIVERSITY: LIU NYU ADELPHI
COLGATE CORNELL FORDHAM
HOFSTRA YESHIVA COLUMBIA
WATERFALL: NIAGARA

NEW ZEALAND
BAY: OHUA HAWKE LYALL
AWARUA CLOUDY GOLDEN
FITZROY PEGASUS POVERTY
RANGAUNU
CAPE: EGMONT FAREWELL
PALLISER
CAPITAL: WELLINGTON
GULF: HAURAKI
ISLAND: OTEA STEWART
PUKETUTU
LAKE: OHAU HAWEA TAUPO
PUKAKI PUPUKE TEKAPO
WANAKA BRUNNER ROTORUA
WAKATIPU
MOUNTAIN: COOK FLAT OWEN
CHOPE LYALL MITRE OTARI
STOKES AORANGI PIHANGA
TUTAMOE TYNDALL ASPIRING
EARNSLAW
NATIVE: ATI ARAWA MAORI
RINGATU
PENINSULA: MAHIA OTAGO
RIVER: MOKAU WAIPA CLUTHA
TAMAKI WAIHOU WAIROA
WAIKATO MANAWATU
STRAIT: COOK FOVEAUX
TOWN: LEUIN ORETI OTAKI TAUPO
CLUTHA FOXTON NAPIER
OAMARU PICTON TIMARU
DUNEDIN RAETIHI ROTORUA
AUCKLAND KAWAKAWA
VOLCANO: RUAPEHU NGAURUHOE
TONGARIRO

NEXT POI NEAR SYNE THEN UNTO
WISE AFTER EWEST FIRST LATER
NEIST RIGHT BESIDE COMING
SECOND TIDDER TOTHER CLOSEST
NEAREST DIRECTLY PROCHAIN
PROCHEIN ADJOINING IMMEDIATE
(— AFTER) THEN FOLLOWING
(— IN ORDER) EKA
(— MONTH) PROXIMO
(— OF KIN) GOEL
(— TO LAST) PENULT
NEXUS TIE BOND LINK CHAIN
NGAIO KIO KAIO NAIO TREE
NHANG GIAI
NIAM-NIAM ZANDE AZANDE AZANDI
ZANDEH AZANDEH BABUNGERA
NIB NEB PEN BEAK BILL KINK TEAT
POINT PRONG SCORER

NIBBLE EAT NAB NIB NIP BITE GNAW
KNAB KNAP MOOP MOUP PECK PICK
CHAMP GNARL MOUSE PIECE SHEAR
ARRODE BROWSE CHAVEL NATTLE
PICKLE PILFER CHIMBLE GNABBLE
GNATTER KNABBLE SNAGGLE

NICARAGUA
CAPITAL: MANAGUA
COIN: PESO CENTAVO CORDOBA
ISLAND: OMETEPE
LAKE: MANAGUA
MEASURE: VARA CAHIZ MILLA
SUERTE TERCIA CAJUELA
ESTADAL MANZANA
MOUNTAIN: MADERA MOGOTON
PORT: CORINTO
RIVER: COCO TUMA WANKS
GRANDE ESCONDIDO
TOWN: LEON MASAYA GRANADA
MANAGUA JINOTEGA
MATAGALPA
WEIGHT: BAG CAJA TONELADA

NICCOLITE ARITE KUPFERNICKEL
NICE APT FIT FEAT FINE GOOD JUMP
KIND NEAT NYCE PURE CANNY
EXACT FUSSY NIECE SWEET BONITA
BONITO DAINTY GENTIL MINUTE
PEACHY QUAINT QUEASY SPICED
STRICT SUBTLE TICKLE CORRECT
ELEGANT FINICAL GENTEEL MINCING
PERJINK PICKING PRECISE PRUDISH
REFINED DECOROUS DELICATE
EXACTING PLEASANT PLEASING
TICKLISH
(TOO —) SUPERFINE
NICELY JUMP
NICETY HAIR DELICACY JUSTNESS
CRITICISM CURIOSITY PRECISION
(PL.) PERJINKITIES
NICHE BAY WRO APSE CANT COVE
NOOK SLOT HERNE HOVEL NIECE
NITCH ALCOVE ANCONA COVERT
CRANNY GROOVE MIHRAB RECESS
RINCON EDICULE HOUSING RETREAT
ROUNDEL AEDICULA CREDENCE
TOKONOMA HABITACLE
NICK CUT JAG MAR NAG NOB CHIP
DENT DINT HACK NACK SLAP SLIT
CHEAT CHICK GOUGE NITCH NOTCH
PRICK SCORE SLACK SNICK TALLY
TRICK ARREST RECORD DEFRAUD
(— OF TIME) GODSPEED
NICKEL JIT COIN JITNEY NIMBUS
(ALLOY OF —) INVAR KONEL MONEL
(CONTAINING —) NICCOLIC
(SYMBOL OF —) NI
NICKELODEON JUKEBOX
NICKER NEIGHER
NICKNAME DUB DOEG NICK ALIAS
AGNAME BYWORD HANDLE MONICA
TONAME CRACKER EKENAME
MISNAME MONIKER NICKERY
COGNOMEN MONARCHO MONICKER
TARTUFFE SOBRIQUET
NICKNAMING PROSONOMASIA
NICTATE WINK BLINK CLOSE TWINK
TWINKLE NICTITATE

NIDDICK NAPE
NIDE NID NEST BROOD LITTER
NIDGE NIG SHAKE QUIVER
NIDGET HOE FOOL IDIOT
NIDOR ODOR AROMA SAVOR SCENT
SMELL
NIECE OY OYE NEPHEW
NIELLO TULA
NIEPA NIOTA KARINGHOTA
NIEVE FIST HAND NEIF SERF NATIVE
NIFTY FINE GOOD KEEN SMART
STYLISH
NIGER JOLIBA KWORRA RAMTIL
(CAPITAL OF —) NIAMEY
(MOUTH OF —) NUN
(NATIVE OF —) PEUL HAUSA
DJERMA FULANI SONGHA TOUBOU
TUAREG
(OASIS IN —) KAOUAR
(RIVER OF —) DILLIA
(TOWN OF —) MARADI TAHOUA
ZINDER

NIGERIA
CAPITAL: LAGOS
NATIVE: ARO EBO EDO IBO IJO
VAI BENI EBOE EFIK EJAM EKOI
NUPE BENIN HAUSA FULANI
YORUBA
PORT: LAGOS CALABAR
PROVINCE: ISA OYO KANO NUPE
ONDO IJEBU OGOJA WARRI
OWERRI ADAMAWA
RIVER: OLI GANA YOBE BENUE
NIGER KADANU SOKOTO
GONGOLA KOMADUGU
TOWN: ABA ADO EDE ISA IWO JOS
BIDI BUEA KANO OFFA YOLA
LAGOS ZARIA IBADAN ILESHA
ILORIN KADUNA MUSHIN
TAKOBA CALABAR ONITSHA
OSHOGBO ABEOKUTA
TREE: AFARA

NIGGARD CHURL CLOSE MISER
NIGON PIKER SCART TIGHT NIGGER
SCRIMP SCRUNT STINGY CHINCHE
DRYFIST NITHING PUCKFIST
SCRIMPER EARTHWORM PINCHBECK
PINCHFIST PUCKFOIST SKINFLINT
NIGGARDLY MEAN CLOSE STINT
NARROW NIGHLY SCANTY SCREWY
SKIMPY SORDID STINGY STRAIT
CHINCHE MISERLY
NIGGERFISH CONY HIND CONEY
GROUPER GUATIVERE
NIGH AT NEAR ANEAR ANIGH CLOSE
ALMOST NEARLY ADJACENT
NIGHT PM EVE DARK NUIT DARKY
DEATH NACHT NOCHE SLEEP
DARKMANS DARKNESS
(— AND DAY) NYCHTHEMERON
(COMB. FORM) NYCTI
(DEPTH OF —) HOLL
(GODDESS OF —) NOX NYX
(LAST —) YESTREEN
(NORSE —) NATT NOTT
(PERT. TO —) NOCTURNAL

(STAY OUT ALL —) PERNOCTATE
NIGHT APE DURUKULI
NIGHT BLINDNESS NYCTALOPIA
NIGHTCAP HOW COWL DOWD
HOUVE PIRNY BIGGIN PIRNIE
DOREMEUSE SUNDOWNER
NIGHTCLUB CAFE CLUB SPOT BOITE
BISTRO CABARET DANCERY
NIGHTERY
NIGHTDRESS SLOP WILYCOAT
WYLIECOAT
NIGHTFALL EEN EVE DUSK EVEN
SHUTTING TWILIGHT
(OCCURRING AT —) ACRONICAL
NIGHTGOWN TOOSH BEDGOWN
NIGHTIE WYLIECOAT
NIGHTHAWK PISK CUIEJO BULLBAT
NIGHTINGALE JUG BULBUL
FLORENCE PHILOMEL
(— SOUND) JUG
(SWEDISH —) LIND JENNY
(PL.) WATCH
NIGHTJAR POTOO EVEJAR
DERHAWK SPINNER WHEELER
MOREPORK
NIGHT LAMP VEILLEUSE
NIGHTMARE ALP HAG MARA MESS
DREAM FANCY FIEND VISION
INCUBUS CACODEMON CAUCHEMAR
EPHIALTES
(— CAUSER) MARE
NIGHTSHADE HERB DWALE MOREL
HENBANE MORELLE SANDBUR
SOLANUM TROMPILLO
NIHIL NIL NICHIL NOTHING
NIHILIST ANARCHIST SOCIALIST
NIL ZERO NILGAI IPOMOEA NOTHING

NILE

AS GOD: HAPI
BIRD: IBIS WRYNECK
BOAT: BARIS CANGIA NUGGAR
DAHABEAH
CAPTAIN: RAIS REIS
DAM: ASWAN
FALLS: RIPON
FISH: BAGRE SAIDE BICHIB
DOCMAC MORMYRID
MORMYROID
ISLAND: RODA PHILAE
NATIVE: MADI NILOT
NEGRO: JUR LUO LWO SUK
PLANT: SUDD LOTUS
REGION: NUBIA
SOURCE: TSANA
TOWN: QUS ABRI ARGO IDFU ISNA
QINA ASYUT CAIRO REJAF SAITE
ROSETTA
TRIBUTARY: ATBARA KAGERA
VALLEY DEPRESSION: KORE

NILGAI NIL NYLGAU ANTELOPE
NEELGHAW
NIMBLE FLY DEFT FLIP FLIT GLEG
LISH SPRY SWAK YARE AGILE BRISK
FLEET LIGHT QUICK SWACK TRICK
WIGHT ACTIVE CLEVER FEIRIE
LIMBER LISSOM LIVELY PROMPT
QUIVER SPRACK SUPPLE VOLANT

DELIVER LISSOME SWIPPER
FLIPPANT TRIPPING SENSITIVE
SPRIGHTLY
NIMBLENESS HASTE SLEIGHT
LEGERITY DEXTERITY LIGHTNESS
NIMBLE-WITTED VOLABLE
NIMBUS AURA HALO NIMB CLOUD
GLORY SHINE VAPOR GLORIA
AUREOLA AUREOLE
NIMIETY EXCESS
NINCOMPOOP ASS DOLT FOOL
POOP NINNY NINCOM WITLING
BLOCKHEAD SIMPLETON
NINE IX NIE NYE TEAM COMET
POTHOOK
(— A.M.) UNDERN MIDMORN
(— ANGLED FIGURE) NONAGON
(— DAYS DEVOTION) NOVENA
(— FOLD) NONUPLE
(— HEADED MONSTER) HYDRA
(— HUNDRED) SAN
(— INCHES) SPAN
(— OF CLUBS OR DIAMONDS)
COMET
(— OF DIAMONDS) BRAGGER
(— OF TRUMPS) DIX MENEL
SANCHO
(— YEAR CYCLE) JUGLAR
(GROUP OF —) ENNEAD
(MUSIC FOR —) NONET
NINEBARK ROSACEAN SEVENBARK
NINEHOLES BUMBLEPUPPY
NINEPIN SQUAIL SKITTLE SKITTLES
(PL.) KEELS KAYLES NINEPEGS
NINETEENTH LARIGOT
NINETIETH NONAGESIMAL
NINETY KOPPA
NINEVEH (FOUNDER OF —) NINUS
NINE WORLDS HEL ASGARD
ALFHEIM MIDGARD NIFLHEIM
VANAHEIM JOTUNNHEIM
MUSPELLSHEIM SVARTALFAHEIM
NINNI ISHTAR
NINNY DOLT FOOL LOUT DUNCE
IDIOT NONNY PATCH SAMMY SPOON
FONDLE NOODLE FONDLING
BLOCKHEAD NIDDICOCK
PEAKGOOSE SIMPLETON
NINON SHEER
NINTH (EVERY —) NONAN ENNEATIC
NIOBATE TODDITE SIPYLITE
COLUMBATE
NIOBE HERB HOSTA FUNKIA
(BROTHER OF —) PELOPS
(FATHER OF —) TANTALUS
(HUSBAND OF —) AMPHION
(SISTER-IN-LAW OF —) AEDON
NIOBIUM COLUMBIUM
NIP CUT SIP VEX BITE BUMP CLIP
DRAM GIVE KNIP NIPE PECK SNUB
TANG TAUT TUCK BLAST CHEAT
CHECK CHILL CLAMP DRAFT FROST
PINCH SEIZE SEVER SNAPE SNEAP
THIEF BENUMB BLIGHT CATNIP
TIPPLE TWITCH WITHER SARCASM
SQUEEZE WETTING COMPRESS
FROSTBITE VELLICATE
NIPA PALM ATAP ATTAP DRINK
NIPPER BOY LAD CLAW CRAB GRAB

HAND BITER CHELA MISER THIEF
CUNNER URCHIN GRIPPER INCISOR
BRAKEMAN
NIPPERS DOG NIP BITS NIPS TONGS
GRATER PLIERS TURKIS FORCEPS
PINCERS OSTEOTOME
NIPPLE BUD DUG PAP TIT BEAN
TEAT DIDDY DUMMY SPEAN NIBBLE
PILLAR MAMILLA PAPILLA THELIUM
(— POINT) THELION
NIPPLEWORT BALLOGAN
WARTWEED WARTWORT
NIPPY BOLD
NIRVANA EMPTINESS
NIS NIX NISSE GOBLIN KOBOLD
BROWNIE
NISUS POWER EFFORT IMPULSE
ENDEAVOR
(DAUGHTER OF —) SCYLLA
NITER NITRE PETER PETRE POTASH
SALTPETER
NITHER BLAST DEBASE SHIVER
TREMBLE
NITID GAY BRIGHT GLOSSY SPRUCE
SHINING LUSTROUS NITIDOUS
NITO AGSAM
NITON RADON
NITRATE SALT ESTER COTTON
AZOTATE
NITRIC AZOTIC
NITRIDE BORAZON
NITRITE AZOTITE
NITROGEN GAS AZOTE ALKALIGEN
NITROGLYCERIN TNT SOUP SIRUP
SYRUP GLONOIN GLONOINE
NITWIT DAW DOPE DIZZARD
SIMPLETON
NIX NO HARD NECK NICKER NOBODY
SPIRIT SPRITE UNDINE NOTHING
NJAVE ADJAB DIAVE
NO NA NE NAE NAH NAW NAY NIT
NIX NUL BAAL BAIL BALE NONE
NYET NAPOO NAPOOH NOGAKU
(— ONE) NIX NEMO
(— POINTS IN TENNIS) LOVE
NOAH NOE
(DOVE OF —) COLUMBA
(FATHER OF —) LAMECH
(GRANDSON OF —) ARAM
(GREAT-GRANDSON OF —) HUL
(MEXICAN —) COXCOX
(RAVEN OF —) CORVUS
(SON OF —) HAM SEM SHEM
JAPHETH
(WINE CUP OF —) CRATER
NOB NAB BLOW HEAD NAVE KNAVE
SWELL HANDLE TIPTOPPER
NOBILITY RANK ELITE GRACE
GENTRY STATUS DIGNITY KWAZOKU
PEERAGE QUALITY STATION
BARONAGE SZLACHTA ELEVATION
(MEMBER OF TATAR —) MURZA
(ROMAN —) RAMNES
NOBLE DON ALII DOGE DUKE EARL
EDEL EPIC FAME FREE GENT GOOD
GRAF HIGH JARL JUST KAMI KUGE
LORD PEER PURE RIAL ARIKI ATHEL
BARON BROAD BURLY COUNT
DUCAL ERECT ETHEL FURST GRAND

GREAT HIRAM KHASS LOFTY MANLY
MORAL MURZA PROUD ROYAL
STATE AUGUST COUSIN EPICAL
FLAITH GENTLE GESITH HAUGHT
HEROIC JUNKER KINGLY LORDLY
LUCUMO MANFUL SIRDAR SUPERB
THAKUR WORTHY YONKER
ACERBAS CACIQUE GALLANT
GLAUCUS GLORIED GRANDEE
HIDALGO LIBERAL MAGNATE
MARQUIS PATRICK STAROST
STATELY STEWARD SUBLIME
VOLPONE PANGLIMA

NOBLEMAN DUKE EARL EMIR LORD
PEER BARON COUNT ORLOV PARIS
THANE COUSIN MILORD ORLOFF
THAKUR HIDALGO MILORD ORLOFF
HIDALGO MAGNATE MARQUIS
STAROST VOLPONE YOUNKER
ADELIGER ALMAVIVA BELARIUS
MARCHESE MARQUESS LANDGRAVE

NOBLENESS HONOR DIGNITY
(— OF BIRTH) EUGENY

NOBLEWOMAN LADY MILADY
DUCHESS PEERESS BARONESS
COUNTESS

NOBODY NIX NEMO NONE NADIE
NOMAN SCRUB SCARAB NOTHING
JACKSTRAW

NOCENT GUILTY HARMFUL HURTFUL
NOXIOUS CRIMINAL

NOCTURNAL NIGHT NOXIAL
NIGHTLY NIGHTISH MOONSHINE
(— ANIMAL) COON POSSUM
OPOSSUM
(— BIRD) OWL
(— CARNIVORE) RATEL
(— MAMMAL) BAT LEMUR
(— SIGNS) ZODIAC

NOCTURNE LULLABY UHTSONG
PAINTING SERENADE

NOD BOB BOW ERR NAP NID NIP
BECK BEND DOZE NAPE SIGN SLIP
SWAY WINK DROOP LAPSE ASSENT
BECKON DODDLE DROWSE NODDLE
NUTATE SALUTE SIGNIFY

NODDING DROWSY NUTANT
ANNUENT CERNUOUS DROOPING
NUTATION

NODDY AUK FOOL JACK NOIO TERN
KNAVE NINNY DROWSY FULMAR
NOODLE SLEEPY HACKNEY
TOMNODDY SIMPLETON

NODE BOW BUMP KNOB KNOT LUMP
PLOT JOINT NODUS POINT TUMOR
BULBIL NODULE DILEMMA GRANULE
KNUCKLE FOLLICLE PHYTOMER
SWELLING TUBERCLE
(— OF GRASS) KNOT
(— OF POEM) PLOT
(— OF STEM) JOINT

NODULE BOB AUGE BUMP KNOT
LUMP MASS NODE YOLK FLINT
GEODE PHYMA MILIUM BLISTER
CATHEAD GRANULE LEPROMA
NABLOCK SARCOID AMYGDALE
AMYGDOLE TUBERCLE WHITEHEAD
(— OF FLINT) CORE
(PL.) BEADING

NOEL XMAS CAROL NOWEL NATALIS
CHRISTMAS

NOGGIN ALE CUP MUG NOG PEG PIN
GILL HEAD PAIL PATE DRINK
GOGGAN NAGGIN NOODLE

NOIL FIBER PINION

NOISE (ALSO SEE SOUND) ADO AIR
BUM DIN GIG HUM POP ROW BANG
BOOM BRAY BUMP BURR HOOT
KLOP MUSH PEAL RALE RASH REEL
RERD ROTE ROUT SLAM ZING
ALARM BABEL BLARE BLAST BLOOP
BRAWL BRUIT BURLE CHANG CHIRM
CLICK DREAM GRASS JERRY KNOCK
LARRY LEDEN PLASH QUONK REERE
RERDE RUMOR SLORP SNORE
SOUND STEER SWISH CACKLE
CLAMOR DUNDER GOBBLE GOSSIP
HUBBUB NORATE OUTCRY RACKET
RANTAN RATTLE REPORT SPLASH
SQUAWK STEVEN STRIFE TUMULT
UPROAR BLUSTER BRATTLE
CLITTER CRACKLE ORATION
SCANDAL SPATTER STREPOR
STRIDOR FLICFLAC QUONKING
TINTAMAR CONFUSION
(ELECTRIC —) GRASS

NOISELESS QUIET STILL SWEET
TACIT SILENT APHONIC CATLIKE

NOISEMAKER BELL HORN GRAGER
RATTLE CLAPPER SQUEAKER

NOISETTE HAZEL HAZELNUT

NOISOME FOUL RANK FETID NASTY
PUTRID RANCID HARMFUL HURTFUL
NOXIOUS NUISOME STINKING
OFFENSIVE

NOISY LOUD CLASHY CREAKY
BLATANT DINSOME FRANTIC
MOILING RACKETY RIOTOUS
ROUTOUS BRAWLING CLATTERY
SONOROUS STREPENT HILARIOUS
RATTLEBAG

NOLL HEAD NODDLE NOODLE

NOMA CANKER

NOMAD ARAB BEJA LURI MOOR
SAKA SHUA ALANI GYPSY IGDYR
JAREG ROVER SHUWA NOMADE
ROAMER ROVING SEMITE SLUBBI
TUAREG BAZIGAR BEDOUIN
SARACEN SCENITE SHORTZY
SHUKRIA SOLUBBI TOUAREG
KABABISH SCYTHIAN SHINWARI
AMALEKITE MIGRATORY
(— PEOPLE) ALANI
(PL.) AKHLAME

NOMADIC ERRATIC VAGRANT
VAGABOND FOOTLOOSE ITINERANT

NOM DE PLUME PENNAME
TELONISM PSEUDONYM

NOME ELIS NOMOS MELODY
NOMARCHY PROVINCE

NOMENCLATURE LIST NAME TERM
ONYMY NAMING GLOSSARY
REGISTER CATALOGUE

NOMINAL PAR BASIC PAPER
FORMAL SLIGHT UNREAL TITULAR
TRIVIAL PLATONIC TRIFLING
(— RECOGNIZANCE) DOE

NOMINATE CALL LEET NAME ELECT

NEVEN SLATE SELECT APPOINT
ENTITLE PRESENT PROPOSE
SPECIFY DESIGNATE POSTULATE

NOMINY SPEECH RIGMAROLE

NONAGE NEANT INFANCY MINORITY
PUPILAGE

NONAGREEMENT DISSENT

NON-ALCOHOLIC SMALL

NON-ARAB SHANGALLA

NONASPIRATE LENE

NONBELIEVER PAGAN ATHEIST
AGNOSTIC

NONCE NANES NONES NOANCE
PRESENT PURPOSE OCCASION

NONCHALANT COOL GLIB ALOOF
CASUAL JAUNTY CARELESS
DEBONAIR

NON-CHRISTIAN INFIDEL

NONCITIZEN TENSOR PEREGRINUS

NONCLERIC LAY LAIC

NONCOMBUSTIBLE APYROUS

NONCOMMITTAL NEUTRAL

NONCONFORMIST REBEL NONCON
BEATNIK FANATIC HERETIC
SECTARY BOHEMIAN RECUSANT
DISSENTER
(— IN ART) FAUVE

NONCONFORMITY HERESY
ADHARMA DISSENT NEGLECT
REFUSAL RECUSANCE RECUSANCY

NONCONTINUOUS DISCRETE

NONDISCLOSURE FRAUD

NONDO LOVAGE ANGELICO

NONDUALISM ADVAITA

NONE NO UN NAE NIN NANE NARY
NEEN NONES

NONEGO NOTSELF

NONELASTIC BROAD

NONENTITY ZERO AUGHT CIPHER
NOBODY NOUGHT NOTHING NULLITY

NONESSENTIAL CASUAL FRILLY
UNNEEDED EXTRINSIC
(— IN RELIGION) ADIAPHORON

NONESUCH APPLE MODEL PARAGON
PATTERN PARADIGM MATCHLESS
NONPAREIL UNRIVALED

NONEXISTENT NULL NAPOOH
NOUGHT NONBEING
(PRACTICALLY —) FAT

NONFEASANCE BREACH

NON GRATA UNWELCOME

NONGYPSY GAJO

NONINJURY AHIMSA

NON-JEW GOI GOY

NONJUROR USAGER

NON-LATIN SAXON

NONLEGATO DETACHE DETACHED

NON-MOSLEM GENTILE

NONPAREIL BEST POPE TYPE
PARAGON PERFECT SUPREME
UNEQUAL NONESUCH PEERLESS
UNRIVALED

NONPAYMENT DISHONOR

NONPLUS SET FAZE POSE STOP
BLANK FLOOR POSER STICK STUMP
TRUMP BAFFLE GRAVEL PUZZLE
RATTLE CONFUSE MYSTIFY
PERPLEX STAGGER QUANDARY
DULCARNON EMBARRASS

NONPLUSSED FOOLISH
NONPOISONOUS EDIBLE
NONPROFESSIONAL BUM LAY LAIC
AMATEUR
NONSENSE BAH GAS GUP PAH ROT
BILK BLAA BLAH BOSH BUFF BUNK
COCK CRAP FLAM FLUM GOOK
JUNK PISH POOH PUNK TOSH BALLS
BLASH DROOL FOLLY FUDGE HAVER
HOOEY SPOOF STITE STUFF TRASH
TRIPE WAHOO BABBLE BUNKUM
DRIVEL FADDLE FOLDER KIBOSH
LINSEY NAVERS RUBBLE SQUISH
TRIVIA BLARNEY BLATHER
BUNCOME EYEWASH FARRAGO
INANITY LOCKRAM TOSHERY
TRIFLES TWADDLE CLAPTRAP
DISHWASH FALDEROL FLIMFLAM
FLUMMERY GALBANUM MACARONI
MOROLOGY PISHTOSH SKITTLES
SPLUTTER TRUMPERY ABSURDITY
FRIVOLITY MOONSHINE POPPYCOCK
SILLINESS
(— **CREATURE**) GOOP SHOO SNARK
SHIMOO
NOODLE BEAN FOOL HEAD NIZY
NOLL PATE NINNY NIZEY NODDY
PASTA PASTE BOODLE NODDLE
NOGGIN LOKSHEN NOGHEAD
NOUILLE BLOCKHEAD SIMPLETON
(— **DISH**) PANSIT RAVIOLI
KREPLACH
(PL.) MEIN FARFEL FERFEL LASAGNA
LASAGNE LOKSHEN FETTUCINI
NOOK IN BAY OUT WRO CANT COVE
GLEN HERN HOLE NALK NUCK NUIK
ANGLE HALKE HERNE NEUCK NICHE
ALCOVE CANTLE CORNER CRANNY
RECESS CREVICE NOOKERY
RETREAT
NOON M APEX DINE NOWN SEXT
DINNER MIDDAY UNDERN MIDNOON
MERIDIAN
NOONDAY (— **REST**) NAP SIESTA
MERIDIAN
NOOSE TIE TOW BOND DULL GIRN
HEMP LACE LOOP ROPE TRAP
BIGHT CATCH GRANE HITCH HONDA
KINCH LASSO LATCH LEASH SNARE
SNARL WIDDY CAUDLE CHOKER
CLINCH ENTRAP HALTER LARIAT
SPRING TETHER TIPPET TWITCH
CHOCKER ENSNARE EXECUTE
LANIARD LANYARD SPRINGE
NECKLACE SQUEEZER TWITCHEL
(— **FOR HAULING LOG**) CHOKER
CHOCKER
(— **FOR SNARING FISH**) DULL
(— **IN A CORD**) KINCH
(HANGMAN'S —) SQUEEZER
NOOTKA AHT AHOUSAHT MOATCAHT
MOOACHAHT
NORATE NOISE RUMOR GOSSIP
NORDIC ARIAN ARYAN
NORI AMANORI
NORITE GABBRO OLIGOSITE
NORM PAR RULE TYPE CANON
GAUGE MODEL NORMA DHARMA
MEDIAN AVERAGE MODULUS

PATTERN STANDARD TEMPLATE
NORMA MOLD RULE GAUGE MODEL
SQUARE PATTERN TEMPLET
STANDARD TEMPLATE
NORMAL PAR FULL HOME JUST
MEAN SANE CLEAR ERECT USUAL
FORMAL NATIVE SCHOOL AVERAGE
NATURAL NEUTRAL REGULAR
TYPICAL ORDINARY STANDARD
CUSTOMARY
NORMANDY (**BEACH IN** —) OMAHA
(**CAPITAL OF** —) ROUEN
(**RIVER IN** —) EURE ORNE SEINE
NORN FATE URTH WURD WYRD
NORNA SKULD URDHR URTHR
VERDHANDI VERTHANDI
NORSEL BAND LINE ORSEL FILLET
NOSSEL ORSELLER
NORTH SEPTENTRION

NORTH CAROLINA
CAPE: FEAR LOOKOUT HATTERAS
CAPITAL: RALEIGH
COLLEGE: ELON CATAWBA
DAVIDSON
COUNTY: ASHE DARE HOKE WAKE
BERTIE BLADEN ONSLOW
YADKIN YANCEY CATAWBA
PAMLICO
INDIAN: ENO COREE CHERAW
MORATOK PAMLICO CHOWANOC
HATTERAS
MOUNTAIN: HARRIS MITCHELL
PRESIDENT: POLK JOHNSON
RIVER: HAW TAR NEUSE CHOWAN
LUMBER PEEDEE YADKIN
ROANOKE
SOUND: BOGUE CROATAN
PAMLICO
STATE BIRD: CARDINAL
STATE FLOWER: DOGWOOD
STATE NICKNAME: TARHEEL
STATE TREE: PINE
TOWN: DURHAM LENOIR SHELBY
EDENTON HICKORY ROXBORO
TARBORO GASTONIA
CHARLOTTE
UNIVERSITY: DUKE

NORTH DAKOTA
CAPITAL: BISMARCK
COLLEGE: JAMESTOWN
COUNTY: EDDY TRAILL PEMBINA
INDIAN: MANDAN ARIKARA
HIDATSA
RIVER: RUSH CEDAR HEART
JAMES SOURIS DESLACS
SHEYENNE WILDRICE
STATE BIRD: MEADOWLARK
STATE FLOWER: PRAIRIEROSE
STATE NICKNAME: SIOUX
FLICKERTAIL
STATE TREE: ELM
TOWN: FARGO MINOT

NORTHERN PIKE ARCTIC BOREAL
NORTHEN

(— **BEAR**) POLAR RUSSIA
(— **CONSTELLATION**) URSA
ANDROMEDA

NORTH KOREA
CAPITAL: PYONGYANG
COIN: WON HWAN
RIVER: NAM YALU IMJIN TUMEN
TAEDONG
TOWN: HAEJU HEIJO KEIJO
ANDONG ANTUNG JUSHIN
POCHON WONSAN HAMHUNG
HUICHON HUNGNAM KAESONG
SINUIJU CHONGJIN

NORTH STAR STATE MINNESOTA

NORTH VIETNAM
CAPITAL: HANOI
COIN: DONG
COMMUNIST PARTY: VIETCONG
GULF: TONKIN TONKING
MOUNTAIN: FANSIPAN
NATIVE: HOA MAN MEO TAY KINH
NUNG THAI MUONG
NEWSPAPER: NHANDAN
PORT: BENTHUY HONGGAI
HAIPHONG
REGION: ANNAM TONKIN
RIVER: BO CA DA LO MA CHU
GAM KOI CHAY NHIHA
TOWN: BACNINH CAOBANG
DONGHOI NAMDINH VIETTRI
THANHHOA HAIPHOANG

NORWAY
CAPE: NORDKAPP
CAPITAL: OSLO
COIN: ORE KRONE
COUNTY: AMT OSLO FYLKE
TROMS BERGEN OPLAND
TROMSO FINMARK HEDMARK
OSTFOLD NORDLAND ROGALAND
TELEMARK VESTFOLD
DANCE: GANGAR HALLING
SPRINGAR SPRINGLEIK
INLET: IS KOB RAN ALST ANDS
BOKN NORD OFOT SALT SUNN
TYRI VEST FIORD FJORD FOLDA
LAKSE SOGNE BJORNA HADSEL
HORTENS TRONDHEIM
ISLAND: VEGA BOMLO DONNA
FROYA HITRA HOPEN SENJA
SMOLA ALSTEN AVEROY
BOUVET HINNOY KARMOY
SOLUND VANNOY GURSKOY
LOFOTEN MAGEROY SEILAND
JANMAYEN SVALBARD
LAKE: ALTE ISTER MJOSA SNASA
FEMUND ROSTAVN TUNNSJO
MEASURE: FOT MAL POT ALEN
MAAL KANDE FATHOM SKIEPPE
MOUNTAIN: SOGNE KJOLEN
NUMEDAL BLODFJEL SNOHETTA
TELEMARK USTETIND

PARLIAMENT: LAGTING STORTING ODELSTING
PLATEAU: DOURE FJELD HARDANGER
RIVER: OI ENA ALTA OTRA RANA TANA BARDU BEGNA LAGEN ORKLA OTTER RAUMA REISA GLOMMA LOUGEN NAMSEN PASVIK
TOWN: GOL NES BODO MOSS ODDA OSLO VOSS BJORT FLORO HAMAR MOLDE SKEIN SKJAK BERGEN HORTEN LARVIK NARVIK ALESUND ARENDAL DRAMMEN SANDNES STAVANGER
WEIGHT: LOD MARK PUND SKAALPUND BISMERPUND

NOSE CAP NEB NIZ PRY PUG SPY BEAK BOKO CONK NASE GROIN LORUM NASUS SCENT SMELL SNIFF SNOOP SNOUT TRUNK BEEZER CYRANO DETECT GNOMON MUFFLE MUZZLE NOZZLE PECKER SEARCH SNITCH SOCKET ADVANCE PERFUME SMELLER DISCOVER INFORMER OLFACTOR PERCEIVE PROBOSCIS SCHNOZZLE
(— A LOG) SNIPE
(— BAG) MORRAL
(— CARTILAGE) SEPTUM
(— DISEASE) OZENA OZOENA
(— DIVE) VRILLE
(— FLUTE) PUNGI POOGYE
(— INFLAMMATION) CORYZA RHINITIS
(— MEDICINE) ERRHINE
(— OF ANIMAL) GROIN
(— OPENING) NARE
(— PARTITION) VOMER
(— PIECE) NASAL
(— RING) PIRN
(BLUNT —) SNUB
(FLAT —) PUG SNUB
NOSEBAND BOSAL MUSROL CAVESSON
NOSEBLEED EPISTAXIS RHINORRHAGIA
NOSEGAY BOB ODOR POSY POESY SCENT TUTTY BOUQUET CORSAGE PERFUME
NOSINESS CURIOSITY
NOSING CURB
NOSTALGIA LONGING YEARNING
NOSTALGIC ELEGIAC ELEGIACAL
NOSTOLOGY GERIATRICS
NOSTRADAMUS SEER PROPHET PHYSICIAN
NOSTRIL ALA NARE THIRL THRILL BLOWHOLE
(PERT. TO —) NARIAL NARINE
(PL.) NARES NARIS SNUFFERS
NOSU LOLO
NOSY BEAKY PRYING CURIOUS FRAGRANT INTRUSIVE
NOT NA NE NAE NAY NOR PAS BAAL BAIL BALE NICHT SHORN SORRA

NOUGHT POLLED SHAVEN NEITHER HORNLESS NEGATIVE
(— ANY) NO NUL NANE NARY NONE NAIRY NOKIN STEAD
(— AT ALL) NEVER LITTLE NOWAYS NOWHIT NOWISE
(— FINAL) NISI
(— THE SAME) OTHER ANOTHER DIFFERENT
(— TO BE REPEATED) NR
(— WANTED) DETROP SUPERFLUOUS
(ALMOST —) SCARCELY
(COULD —) NOTE
(PREFIX MEANING —) IL IM IN IR UN NON
NOTABLE VIP FINE FABLED FAMOUS GIFTED NOTARY SIGNAL UNIQUE EMINENT STORIED SUBLIME DISTINCT ESPECIAL EVENTFUL HISTORIC MEMORABLE NOTORIOUS
NOTARY NOTAR GRAFFER NOTEBOOK OBSERVER OFFICIAL SCRIVENER
NOTARY PUBLIC TABELLION
NOTATION HOLD MEMO NOTE ENTRY SYSTEM MARKING
(PHONETIC —) ROMIC
NOTATOR NOTER RECORDER
NOTCH CUT DAG DAP GAP HAG JAG JOG PEG COPE DENT DINT GAIN GIMP KERF MUSH NICK NOCK SLAP SLOT SNIP STEP WARD CRENA GABEL GRADE HILUM SCORE SHARD SHERD TALLY CROTCH DEFILE DEGREE HOLLOW INDENT JOGGLE RECORD SCOTCH CRENATE GUDGEON SERRATE INCISION UNDERCUT
(— BETWEEN HILLS) SLAP
(— ON VERTEBRAE) HYPANTRUM
(— TO FELL TREE) UNDERCUT
NOTCHED EROSE JAGGY RAGULE RAGULY SERRATE CRENATED
NOTE BON DOG IOU JOT KEY SEE TEN UNE BILL CARD CENT CHIT ESPY FAME FLAT GOOD HEED MARK MEMO NAME NOIT SIGN SOLE SONG TONE TUNE VIEW CHECK FIVER GLOZE LABEL PRICK SHORT SIXTH SOUND STIFF TENTH TOKEN TRAIT TWANG ATTEND BILLET DEGREE EXCUSE FIGURA FLIMSY LETTER MELODY MINUTE NOTICE POLICY RECORD REGARD REMARK RENOWN REPORT SECOND STRAIN TENNER BETOKEN COMMENT DISCORD MESSAGE MISSIVE NATURAL OBSERVE PUNCTUS REDBACK ANNOTATE BLUEBACK BRADBURY BREVIATE DISPATCH EMINENCE MARGINAL PERCEIVE POSTFACE TREASURY GREENBACK
(— FROM TRAIN) BUTTERFLY
(— OF ASSAULT) WARISON
(— OF HUMOR) TRAIT
(— OF SCALE) DO FA LA MI RE SI SO TI UT ARE SOL
(— OF SNIPE) SCAPE

(— OF WARNING) WATCHWORD
(— ON SHOPHAR) TEKIAH
(— TO RECALL DOG) FORLOIN
(—S ON HUNTING HORN) SEEK
(100-POUND —) CENTURY
(ALTERED —) ACCIDENTAL
(BANK —S) CABBAGE
(BASS —) DRONE
(BIRD'S —) JUG CHIRP
(EIGHTH —) UNCA QUAVER
(ESCAPE —) ECHAPPEE
(EXPLANATORY —) SCHOLIUM ANNOTATION
(GRACE —) NACHSCHLAG
(HALF —) MINIM
(HARSH —) BLOB
(HIGH-PITCHED —) BEEP
(HIGHEST —) ELA
(LONG —) LARGE
(LOVE —) POULET
(LOWEST —) KEY GAMUT
(MARGINAL —) TOT QUOTE POSTIL APOSTIL
(MUSICAL —) ALT MESE MIND BREVE GAMUT SHARP ALAMIRE MEDIANT PUNCTUS PARAMESE
(NONHARMONIC —) CAMBIATA
(POUND —) BRADBURY
(PROMISSORY —) DOG GOOD HUNDI
(QUARTER —) CROTCHET SEMIMINIM
(SIXTEENTH —) DEMIQUAVER SEMIQUAVER
(SIXTY-FOURTH —) HEMIDEMISEMIQUAVER
(THIRTY-SECOND —) SUBSEMIFUSA DEMISEMIQUAVER
(TWO —S) DUPLET
(WHOLE —) SEMIBREVE
(PL.) ANA GAMUT STRAIN NUMBERS TIRALEE
NOTEBOOK LOG DIARY NOTARY RECORD STREET JOURNAL
NOTECASE WALLET POCKETBOOK
NOTED COUTH FAMED GREAT NAMELY EMINENT INSIGNE RENOWNED DISTINGUE
NOTEWORTHY BIG SOLEMN EMINENT NOTABLE SPECIAL BODACIOUS
NOTHING NIL NIX FREE LUKE NILL WIND ZERO AUGHT BLANK NIHIL CIPHER NAUGHT NOBODY NOUGHT TRIFLE NULLITY SCRATCH USELESS BAGATELLE
(— BUT) ALL
(— DOING) NAPOO NAPOOH
(— MORE THAN) MERE
(— OTHER THAN) ONLY
NOTHINGNESS NOT NADA ZERO NOUGHT VACUITY NIHILITY
NOTICE AD BAN SEE SPY CALL ESPY GOME HEED IDEA KEEP MARK MIND NEWS NOTE PIPE RIDE SIGN SPOT TWIG ALARM AWAIT COUNT EDICT FLOAT NOTAM ORDER QUOTE ADVICE ALLUDE BILLET ESPIAL NOTION PERMIT READER REGARD REMARK REWARD AFFICHE ARTICLE DISCERN MENTION OBSERVE

PLACARD PROGRAM WARNING BULLETIN MONITION PERCEIVE WITTERING
(— UNEXPECTEDLY) CATCH
(ADVANCE —) HERALDRY
(COMMENDATORY —) BLURB
(DEATH —) OBIT OBITUARY
(FAVORABLE —) RAVE
(LEGAL —) CAVEAT
(MARRIAGE —) BANS BANNS
(OFFICIAL —) EDICT SUMMONS BULLETIN CITATION
(PUBLIC —) BAN EDICT BULLETIN SPOTLIGHT

NOTICEABLE CRUDE GROSS FLASHY SIGNAL EVIDENT NOTABLE POINTED SALIENT HANDSOME PALPABLE STRIKING PROMINENT
(UNDESIRABLY —) CONSPICUOUS

NOTIFICATION DRUM NOTE NOTICE SUMMONS
(PUBLIC —) SIGN

NOTIFY ALL BID CRY JOG CITE PAGE TELL WARN INFORM NOTICE SIGNAL APPRISE DECLARE FRUTIFY PUBLISH ACQUAINT INTIMATE

NOTION BEE GEE BUZZ IDEA IDEE KINK MAZE OMEN VIEW WHIM FANCY FREIT IMAGE SENSE THING WARES BELIEF CEMENT DESIRE DONNEE GADGET NAGGOT NOTICE THEORY VAGARY BROMIDE CONCEIT CONCEPT FANTASY INKLING MAROTTE OPINION THOUGHT WRINKLE CATEGORY FOLKLORE PHANTASY SUPPOSAL WHIMWHAM INTENTION SENTIMENT WHIRLIGIG
(FALSE —) IDOL
(FIXED —) TICK
(FOOLISH —) VAPOR VAPOUR
(PUERILE —) BOYISM
(SUPERSTITIOUS —) FREET FREIT
(PL.) SMALLS SMALLWARE

NOTORIETY FAME ECLAT GLORY HONOR RUMOR RENOWN REPUTE PUBLICITY

NOTORIOUS BIG KNOWN ARRANT COMMON CRYING FAMOUS NOTARY STRONG EVIDENT NOTABLE NOTOIRE APPARENT FLAGRANT INFAMOUS MANIFEST EGREGIOUS

NOTORNIS TAKAHE

NOTWITHSTANDING BUT FOR THO YET EVEN WITH ALGATE MAUGER MAUGRE AGAINST ALGATES DESPITE HOWBEIT HOWEVER ALTHOUGH NATHLESS WHATRECK

NOUGAT NUT CANDY NUTSHELL

NOUGHT BAD NIL NOT NOWT ZERO NOCHT WRONG NOTHING USELESS WORTHLESS

NOUMENAL ONTAL ONTIC

NOUN MANE WORD THING SUPINE NOMINAL CONSTRUCT INCREASER
(INDEFINABLE —) APTOTE
(KIND OF —) COMMON PROPER DIPTOTE REGULAR TRIPTOTE MONOPTOTE
(QUOTATION —) HYPOSTASIS

(VERBAL —) GERUND

NOURISH AID FEED FOOD GROW BREED NORSH NURSE TRAIN BATTLE BREAST FOISON FOSTER NORICE REFETE SUCCOR SUCKLE SUPPLY CHERISH DEVELOP EDUCATE NURTURE NUTRIFY PROVIDE SUPPORT SUSTAIN MAINTAIN CULTIVATE STIMULATE

NOURISHING ALMA RICH ALIBLE BATTLE HEARTY STRONG NUTRIENT ALIMENTAL HEALTHFUL NUTRITIVE WHOLESOME

NOURISHMENT DIET FETE FOOD KEEP MEAT MANNA FOISON FOSTER ALIMENT PABULUM PASTURE NUTRIMENT REFECTION

NOUS MIND REASON ALERTNESS INTELLECT

NOUVEAU RICHE PARVENU UPSTART

NOVEL HOT NEW BOOK EPIC RARE FRESH PROSE RECIT ROMAN STORY DARING RECENT SERIAL THRILL FICTION ROMANCE STRANGE UNUSUAL NEOTERIC ORIGINAL THRILLER UNCOMMON NARRATIVE PAPERBACK
(BRIEF —) CONTE

NOVELTY FAD NEWEL RENEW CHANGE NEWNESS PRIMEUR WRINKLE FRESHNESS

NOVEMBER 1 SAMUIN SAMHAIN

NOVICE DUB HAM BOOT COLT PUNK PUNY TIRO TYRO CHELA GOYIN PUPIL ROOKY YOUTH DRONGO RABBIT ROOKIE TYRONE AMATEUR CONVERT LEARNER STARTER STUDENT YOUNKER BACHELOR BEGINNER FRESHMAN INEXPERT NEOPHYTE ARCHARIOS GREENHORN

NOVITIATE FUCHS NOVICERY PROBATION

NOW NOO YET ARAH HERE ARRAH NONCE SINCE TODAY EVENOO EXTANT ANYMORE CURRENT INSTANT PRESENT FORTHWITH
(— AND THEN) SOMETIMES STOUNDMEAL
(BUT —) ERSTWHILE
(JUST —) ENOW FRESH

NOWADAYS ANYMORE

NOWEL DRAG

NOX NYX
(BROTHER OF —) EREBUS
(FATHER OF —) CHAOS

NOXIOUS ILL EVIL FETID DEADLY NOCENT NOYOUS PUTRID BANEFUL DAMPISH HARMFUL HURTFUL NOCUOUS NOISOME SCADDLE TEDIOUS VICIOUS INFAMOUS VIRULENT INJURIOUS MIASMATIC OFFENSIVE PESTILENT POISONOUS
(— AIR) MALARIA
(MORALLY —) UNWHOLESOME

NOZZLE BIB JET TIP BEAK BIBB NOSE ROSE VENT GIANT SNOUT SPOUT TWEER GROVEL OUTLET MONITOR NIAGARA ORIFICE

SHUTOFF ADJUTAGE ROSEHEAD VERMOREL NOSEPIECE
(BLAST FURNACE —) TUYERE
(MINING —) GIANT

NUANCE SHADE NICETY FINESSE GRADATION VARIATION

NUB EAR HUB JAB JAG KEY NOB CORE CRUX GIST HANG KNOB KNOT KNUB LUMP NECK PITH SNAG HEART NUDGE POINT KERNEL NUBBIN EXECUTE

NUBBIN EAR STUB STUMP

NUBIA WRAP CLOUD SCARF

NUBIAN NUBA BARABRA HADENDOA
(— MUSICAL INST.) SISTRUM

NUBILOUS FOGGY MISTY VAGUE CLOUDY OBSCURE

NUCHA NAPE NECK NUKE NUCHE

NUCLEAR ELEMENTARY

NUCLEATE SEED

NUCLEOSIDE VICINE INOSINE CYTIDINE ADENOSINE

NUCLEUS HUB CELL CORE GERM KERN PITH ROOT SEED CADRE FOCUS HEART MIDST SPERM UMBRA CENTER COLONY DEUTON KARYON KERNEL MIDDLE ISOTOPE NIDULUS MEROCYTE HABENDULA MESOPLAST
(— OF CELL) KARYON
(— OF STARCH GRAIN) HILUM
(— OF SUNSPOT) UMBRA
(ATOMIC —) SPECIES
(CELL —) SYNCARYON HEMIKARYON

NUDE BARE LOOSE MODEL NAKED SEASAN STATUE UNCLAD DENUDED EXPOSED PICTURE PAINTING STRIPPED UNDRESSED
(FRENCH —) ALESAN
(NOT —) DECENT
(RUN —) STREAK

NUDGE JOG NOG NUB WAG GOAD JOLT KNUB LUMP POKE POTE PROD PUSH BLOCK CHUCK DUNCH ELBOW

NUDISM NATURISM GYMNOSOPHY

NUDIST ADAMITE NUDIFIER GYMNOSOPH

NUGATORY IDLE NULL VAIN EMPTY PETTY FUTILE HOLLOW INVALID TRIVIAL USELESS TRIFLING FRUSTRATE WORTHLESS

NUGGET EYE LOB GOLD HUNK LUMP MASS SLUG PRILL YELLOW

NUISANCE BANE BORE EVIL HARM HURT PAIN PEST STING INJURY PLAGUE TERROR VEXATION ANNOYANCE

NULL NIL VOID EMPTY INEPT IRRITE INVALID NULLIFY USELESS VACUOUS NUGATORY FRUSTRATE

NULLAH GORGE GULLY NULLA NALLAH RAVINE

NULLIFY BEAT FLAW LAME NULL UNDO VETO VOID ABATE ANNUL ELIDE ERASE LAPSE CANCEL DEFEAT NEGATE OFFSET REPEAL REVOKE ABOLISH COUNTER DESTROY ABROGATE EVACUATE STULTIFY FRUSTRATE

NUMB DEAD DRUG DULL DAZED

FUNNY STONY ASLEEP BENUMB
CLUMSY DEADEN STUPID TORPID
STUPEFY ENFEEBLE HEBETATE
HELPLESS RIGESCENT TABETLESS
NUMBER SUM BAND BODY COPY
CURN DRAW HERD HOST LOTS MAIN
MANY MESS MORT SLEW SURD
TALE TELL COUNT DATUM DIGIT
FOLIE GRIST GROUP INDEX ISSUE
SCADS SCORE STAND TOTAL
WHOLE ADDEND AMOUNT BUNDLE
CIPHER ENCORE FACTOR FIGURE
FILLER HIRSEL MYRIAD POLICY
RECKON SCALAR TICHEL CHIFFER
COMPUTE DECIMAL DIVISOR
FOLIATE SEVERAL CARDINAL
FRACTION NUMERATE QUANTITY
CALCULATE MULTITUDE
(— OF ARROWS) END
(— OF ATOMS) CHAIN
(— OF BEASTS) HERD
(— OF BOMBS) STICK
(— OF BRICKS) CLAMP
(— OF CATTLE) SOUM
(— OF FUR SKINS) TIMBER
(— OF HANKS OF YARN TO POUND)
COUNT
(— OF HAWKS) CAST
(— OF HONEYBEES) CLUSTER
(— OF NEEDLES) GAGE GAUGE
(— OF POEMS) EPOS
(— OF SHEARERS) BOARD
(— OF TEA CHESTS) BREAK
(— OF TRICKS) BOOK
(— OF WORDS) FOLIO
(—S GAME) BUG
(BALLET —) ENTREE
(CARDINAL —) ONE TWO ALEF
ALEPH THREE
(COMPLEX —) IMAGINARY
(CONSIDERABLE —) WHEEN HATFUL
FISTFUL
(DESCRIBABLE —) SCALAR
(EXCESS —) ADVANTAGE
(EXCESSIVE —) SPATE
(EXTRA —) ENCORE
(GOLDEN —) PRIME
(GREAT —) LAC HEAP HOST LAKH
MORT BREAK HIRST MEINY POWER
SHOAL SIGHT SWARM LEGION
MYRIAD INFINITE INFINITY
THOUSAND MULTITUDE
(GREAT —S) FLOCKS
(GREATER —) MO
(INDEFINITE —) LAC STEEN SUNDRY
THARVE JILLION SEVERAL THREAVE
UMPTEEN
(IRRATIONAL —) SURD
(LARGE —) ARMY FECK HERD HOST
LUMP PECK SLEW ARRAY CROWD
FORCE SCADS SHEAF SPATE STACK
STORE WORLD GALLON HIRSEL
HIRSLE LEGION MELDER BILLION
JILLION
(LARGE —S) STRENGTH
(LEAF —) FOLIO
(LEAST WHOLE —) UNIT
(ODD —S) IMPAIR
(OPPOSITE —) COUSIN

(ORDINAL —) FIRST THIRD SECOND
(PUT ON SERIAL —) FOLIO
(SMALL —) FEW CURN CURRAN
HANDFUL PAUCITY SPATTER
(TOTAL —) AMOUNT
(VAST —) HORDE
(WHOLE —) ALL DIGIT INTEGER
NUMBERED MENE
NUMBERING TALE COUNT
FOLIATION
NUMBFISH TORPEDO
NUMBING WARELESS
NUMBLES UMBLES INNARDS
NOMBLES VISCERA ENTRAILS
NUMBNESS STUPOR STUPIDITY
NUMEN DEITY GENIUS SPIRIT
VESTAL DIVINITY
NUMERAL (ALSO SEE NUMBER) SUM
WORD DIGIT CIPHER FIGURE LETTER
CHAPTER
(— STYLE) ROMAN ARABIC
(CLOCK —) CHAPTER
NUMERATIVE PEN SEGREGATIVE
NUMEROUS BIG LOTS MAIN MANY
RANK RIFE GREAT LARGE STOUR
DIVERS GALORE LEGION MYRIAD
SUNDRY UNRIDE COPIOUS
CROWDED ENDLESS FEARFUL
FERTILE PROFUSE SEVERAL
TEEMING UMPTEEN ABUNDANT
FREQUENT MANIFOLD MULTIPLE
POPULOUS THRONGED EXTENSIVE
MULTIFOLD NUMBERFUL PLENTIFUL
(— AND POWERFUL) MAIN
(MODERATELY —) FAIR
(VERY —) EXCESSIVE
NUMIDIA (BIRD OF —) DEMOISELLE
(CITY OF —) HIPPO
(KING OF —) JUGURTHA
NUMSKULL NUM DAFF DOLT FLAT
DUNCE LACKWIT BONEHEAD
BLOCKHEAD
NUN BIRD SMEW CLARE CLERK
MONIAL PIGEON SISTER TERESA
VESTAL VOWESS CONFINE DEANESS
DEVOTEE EXTERNE MINCHEN
MONKESS RECLUSE TEATINE
THEATIN CHAPLAIN CLARISSE
PRIORESS TITMOUSE URBANIST
URSULINE VISITANT VOTARESS
ANGELICAL LORETTINE PRIESTESS
RELIGEUSE
(— BIRD) MONASE TITMOUSE
(— HEADDRESS) WIMPLE
(— HOOD) FAILLE
(— MOTH) TUSSOCK
(— ORDER) MARIST TRAPPIST
LORETTINE OOMINICAN
(CHIEF —) ABBA ABBESS MOTHER
(LATIN —) VESTA
(SON OF —) JOSHUA
NUNCIATE NUNCIO ANNOUNCER
MESSENGER
NUNCIO ENVOY NUNCE LEGATE
NUNTIUS DELEGATE MESSENGER
NUNCUPATE DECLARE DEDICATE
INSCRIBE PROCLAIM DESIGNATE
PRONOUNCE

NUNCUPATIVE ORAL SPOKEN
UNWRITTEN
NUNNERY ABBEY NUNRY CONVENT
CLOISTER MINCHERY
(HEAD OF —) ABBESS
NUPSON FOOL SIMPLETON
NUPTIAL BRIDAL GENIAL THORAL
MARITAL WEDDING ESPOUSAL
HYMENEAL MARRIAGE
(PL.) SPOUSAL ESPOUSAL
HYMENEALS WIFETHING
NUQUE NAPE NECK
NURSE AMAH AYAH BABA CARE DHAI
FEED NANA NUSS REAR SUCK TEND
BONNE MAMMY NANNY NORSH
ATTEND BAYMAN CRADLE FOMENT
FOSTER GRANNY KEEPER NANNIE
NORICE NUZZLE SISTER SITTER
SUCKLE UMFAAN CHERISH FURTHER
NOURISH NURTURE PROMOTE
CULTIVATE ENCOURAGE NURSEMAID
(— A GRIEVANCE) SULK
(— OF HIAWATHA) NOKOMIS
(— OF ULYSSES) EURYCLEA
(— OF ZEUS) AMALTHEA CYNOSURA
(— SHARK) GATA
(GULLIVER'S —) GLUMDALCLITCH
(WET —) DHAI DHOLL
NURSERY RACE CRECHE BROODER
FOSTERAGE
NURSLING BABY NORRY NURRY
FOSTER FOUNDLING
NURTURE CARE DIET FEED FOOD
REAR TEND BREED NURSE TRAIN
COCKER FOSTER NUZZLE CHERISH
EDUCATE SUPPORT BREEDING
NORTELRY TRAINING EDUCATION
ESTABLISH NUTRIMENT
NUSAIRI ANSARIE
NUT ACA BEN BUR COB GUY JOU NIT
TAP ANTA BURR COLA CORE DOLT
FOOL FROG HEAD KOLA LORE MAST
NITE PILI PITH SEED TASK ACORN
BETEL BONGA BUNGA CRANK FRUIT
GLANS HAZEL HICAN JUVIA PECAN
TRYMA ALMOND BONDUC BRAZIL
CASHEW FELLOW HICCAN ILLIPE
KERNEL PEANUT PIGNON PINION
PYRENE CASTANA FILBERT HICKORY
PROBLEM APPLENUT BEECHNUT
BREADNUT CHESTNUT GOORANUT
LARRIKIN CAPOTASTO CHINKAPIN
ECCENTRIC MACADAMIA PHILOPENA
(— COAL) ANTHRACITE
(— GRASS) SEDGE
(— OF VIOLIN BOW) FROG
(— PINE) PIGNON PINOON PIGNOLIA
(CASHEW —) SEDGE
(CONSORT OF —) GEB KEB
(DAUGHTER OF —) ISIS NEPHYTHYS
(FALLEN —S) SHACK
(PALM —) BETEL LICHI COCOANUT
(PERT. TO —) NUCAL
(RIPE —) LEAMER
(RUSH —) CHUFA
(SON OF —) RA
(PL.) MASTAGE
NUT-BEARING NUCIFEROUS
NUTCRACKER XENOPS CRACKER

PILLORY MEATBIRD NUTCRACK
NUTHATCH NUTPECKER
NUTHATCH SITTA TOMTIT XENOPS
JARBIRD SITTINE TITMOUSE
NUTJOBBER
NUTHOOK BEADLE CONSTABLE
NUTLET NUCULE PYRENA PYRENE
GYROLITH
NUTMEG SEED TREE SPICE BEAVER
CALABASH NOTEMIGGE NOTEMUGGE
(— COVERING) MACE
(— STATE) CONNECTICUT
NUTRIA FUR COYPU GREGE NEUTRIA
RAGONDIN
NUTRIENT STARTER
(PL.) FOOD HEMOTROPHE
NUTRIMENT DIET FOOD KEEP
VIANDS ALIMENT PABULUM
SUPPORT
NUTRITION EUTROPHY TROPHISM
(IMPERFECT —) DYSTROPHY
DYSTROPHIA
NUTRITIOUS BATTLE BAITTLE
TROPHIC
NUT-SHAPED NUCIFORM
NUTSHELL SHELL INCLUDER
NUTTY GAGA NUTS RACY ZANY
BUGGY QUEER SPICY FRUITY

LOVING SPRUCE AMOROUS FOOLISH
PIQUANT ZESTFUL DEMENTED
PLEASANT ECCENTRIC FLAVORFUL
NUX VOMICA SNAKEWOOD
NUZZLE DIG PET ROOT NURSE
SNUFF BURROW CARESS FONDLE
FOSTER NESTLE NUDDLE NURTURE
SNOOZLE SNUGGLE SNUZZLE
NYE EYAS NEST NIDE BROOD FLOCK
NYMPH FLY GIRL MAIA MITE MUSE
PINK PIXY PUPA TICK AEGLE DRYAD
HOURI LARVA NAIAD NIXIE OREAD
SIREN SYLPH BYBLIS CYRENE
DAMSEL DAPHNE HELICE HESTIA
KELPIE MAIDEN NEREID SPRITE
SYRINX UNDINE CORYCIA ERYTHEA
HESPERA LIRIOPE OCEANID
CALLISTO CYNOSURA EURYDICE
MARPESSA PROSOPON BUTTERFLY
HAMADRYAD
(— BELOVED BY PAN) SYRINX
(— BELOVED OF NARCISSUS) ECHO
(— OF FOUNTAIN) EGERIA
SALMACIS
(— OF HILLS) OREAD
(— OF MEADOWS) LIMONIAD
(— OF MESSINA STRAIT) SCYLLA

(— OF MT. IDA) OENONE
(CITY —) POLIAD
(LAKE —) NAIAD LIMNIAD
(OCEAN —) SIREN GALATEA
OCEANID
(QUEEN OF —S) MAB
(RIVER —) NAIS NAIAD
(SEA —) MERROW NEREID CALYPSO
GALATEA MERMAID
(WATER —) NAIS EGERIA LURLEI
UNDINE APSARAS HYDRIAD
JUTURNA EPHYDRIAD
(WOOD —) DRYAD NAPEA
ARETHUSA
(PL.) HYADS THRIAI CAMENAE
NYMPHAEA CASTALY CASTALIA
NYMPHOMANIAC (BOVINE —)
BULLER
NYROCA AYTHYA
NYSSA TUPELO
NYSTAGMUS TIC WINK
NYX NOX NIGHT
(— PERSONIFIED) NIGHT
(BROTHER OF —) EREBUS
(DAUGHTER OF —) DAY ERIS LIGHT
(HUSBAND OF —) CHAOS
(SON OF —) CHARON

O HO OH OCH ZERO CIPHER OMICRON

OAF AUF BOOR DOLT FOOL LOUT CLOWN DUNCE IDIOT OUPHE YOKEL MUCKER NASHGAB PALOOKA POMPION BLOCKHEAD FOUNDLING SCHLEMIEL SIMPLETON

OAHU (— BIRD) JIBI

OAK CLUB CORK HOLM ILEX BRAVE BRIAR EMORY HOLLY ROBLE ROBUR ACAJOU BAREEN CERRIS ENCINA KERMES STRONG TOUMEY VALOMA AMBROSE BELLOTA BELLOTE DURMAST EGILOPS KELLOGG PALAYAN TURTOSA BEEFWOOD BLUEJACK CHAMPION CHAPARRO FLITTERN WAINSCOT BLACKJACK CHINKAPIN
(— BARK) CRUT
(— FRUIT) MAST ACORN CAMATA BELLOTE
(JERUSALEM —) AMBROSE
(WHITE —) ROBLE
(YOUNG —) FLITTERN

OAKUM OCCAM

OAKWOOD MESA

OAR AIR BOW PLY ROW PALM PEEL POLE ALOOF BLADE ROWER SCULL SPOON SWAPE SWEEP YULOH PADDLE PALLET PROPEL OARSMAN PROPELLER
(— BLADE) PALM PEEL WASH
(— FULCRUM) LOCK THOLE OARLOCK ROWLOCK
(BOW —) GOUGER
(HANDLE OF —) GRASP
(INBOARD PORTION OF —) LOOM
(STERN —) SCULL SKULL

OARLOCK LOCK THOLE ROWLOCK

OARSMAN OAR REMEX ROWER BOWMAN STROKE BENCHER SCULLER WATERMAN

OASIS BAR OJO SPA MERV SIWA WADI WADY SPRING

OAST HOST KILN OVEN COCKLE OASTHOUSE

OAT AIT WOT FEED FOOD PIPE POEM SKEG SONG AUCHT CHEAT GRAIN HAVER PEARL ANGORA EGILOPS
(— HUSK) SHOOD FLIGHT
(— RENT) AVENAGE
(EDIBLE PORTION OF —) GROATS
(FALSE WILD —S) FATUOID
(HUSKED —) SHEALING
(NAKED —) PILLAS PILCORN
(UNTHRASHED —) OATHAY
(WILD —S) HAVERGRASS
(PL.) CORN GRAIN HAVER GROUTS PROVENDER WHITECORN

OATCAKE CAPER HAVERCAKE SOURBREAD

OATEN AITEN

OATH OD ADS BAN DAD DOD GAD GAR GOL GOR GUM ODD SAM VOW BOND CRUM CUSS DARN DRAT ECOD EGAD EGOD GEEZ GOSH HECK JEEZ JING NIGS SANG SLID SLUD WORD BEDAD BEGAD BEGOB BLIMY CURSE DAMME DEUCE GOLLY HOKEY MORDU PARDY SACRE SFOOT SLIFE SNIGS SWEAR YERRA ADSBUD APPEAL CRACKY CRIKEY CRIPES CRUMBS FEALTY JABERS JERNIE NEAKES PARDIE PLEDGE RAPPER SBLOOD SLIGHT STRUTH ZOUNDS BEGORRA BEGORRY BEJESUS BYRLADY CORBLEU GADSLID GEEWHIZ GEEWIZZ JEEPERS JIMMINY MORBLEU ODSFISH ODZOOKS PROMISE THUNDER ANATHEMA BEJABERS BODYKINS CRICKETY GADZOOKS JURAMENT PITIKINS SANCTION SEREMENT SNIGGERS SPLUTTER AFFIDAVIT BEJABBERS BLASPHEMY DODGASTED EXPLETIVE PROFANITY SACRAMENT SLIDIKINS SWEARWORD

OATMEAL OATS STODGE YELLOW POTTAGE DRAMMOCK PORRIDGE
(— BREAD) ANACK JANNACK
(— CAKE) PONE SCONE

OBCLUDE HIDE OCCLUDE

OBDURATE FIRM HARD BALKY HARSH INERT ROCKY ROUGH STARK STONY DOGGED INURED MULISH RUGGED SEVERE STURDY SULLEN ADAMANT CALLOUS HARDENED PERVERSE STUBBORN IMPASSIVE UNBENDING

OBEAH OBI OBIA CHARM FETISH VOODOO

OBECHE ARERE AYOUS SAMBA

OBEDIENCE ORDER FEALTY CONTROL SERVICE DOCILITY OBEISANCE

OBEDIENT RULY TALL TAME BUXOM DOCILE PLIANT DEVOTED DUTEOUS DUTIFUL HEEDFUL MINDFUL ORDERLY SUBJECT AMENABLE BIDDABLE YIELDING ATTENTIVE OBSERVING SERVIABLE TRACTABLE
(— TO THE HELM) HANDY

OBEDIENTARY PRIOR

OBEDIENT PLANT DRAGONHEAD

OBEISANCE BOW LEG JOUK BINGE CONGE HONOR SALAM CONGEE CURTSY FEALTY HOMAGE SALAAM CURTSEY DEFERENCE HUMBLESSO REFERENCE

OBELISK MARK PYLON SHAFT DAGGER GUGLIA GUGLIO NEEDLE OBELUS PILLAR AGUGLIA MONUMENT HAGIOLITH

OBERON KING POEM FAIRY OPERA SATELLITE
(WIFE OF —) TITANIA

OBESE FAT FOZY PLUMP PUDGY PUFFY PURSY STOUT FLESHY PORTLY PYKNIC ROTUND TURGID ADIPOSE PURSIVE BLUBBERY LIPAROUS CORPULENT

OBESITY FAT FATNESS LIPOSIS ADIPOSIS FOZINESS ADIPOSITY

OBEY EAR HEAR HEED MIND DEFER YIELD COMPLY FOLLOW OBEISH SUBMIT EXECUTE OBSERVE OBTEMPER
(— HELM) STEER

OBFUSCATE DIM CLOUD DARKEN MUDDLE OBFUSK CONFUSE MYSTIFY OBSCURE PERPLEX STUPEFY BEWILDER

OBI OBE SASH CHARM OBEAH FETICH FETISH GIRDLE

OBIT MASS REST DEATH NOTICE OBITAL DECEASE RELEASE SERVICE OBITUARY NECROLOGY OBSEQUIES

OBJECT AIM END TAP BALK BEEF CARE CARP FINE GOAL IDEA ITEM KICK MAIN MIND PASS WHAT ARGUE CAVIL DEMUR GRIPE PINCH POINT SCOPE SIGHT TELOS THING AFFAIR DESIGN EMBLEM ENTITY FIGURE GADGET INTENT MATTER MOTIVE OPPOSE TARGET ARTICLE DINGBAT DISLIKE DISSENT MEANING PROTEST PURPOSE QUARREL REALITY RECLAIM NOUMENON TENDENCY CHALLENGE INTENTION SPECTACLE
(— HAVING FLAWS) SPOIL
(— OF AMBITION) MAIN
(— OF ART) VASE CURIO VIRTU ANTIQUE BIBELOT FIGURINE
(— OF CRITICISM) BUTT
(— OF DEVOTION) IDOL TOTEM FETISH
(— OF DISGUST) UG
(— OF DREAD) BOGY BOGEY BOGIE BOGGIE BUGBEAR
(— OF KNOWLEDGE) SCIBILE
(— OF PILGRIMAGE) CAABA KAABAH
(— OF PURSUIT) SHADOW
(— OF RELIANCE) STAY
(— OF RIDICULE) FUN GAME
(— OF SCORN) GECK SCOFF BYWORD HISSING DERISION
(— OF THOUGHT) CONSTRUCT
(— OF WONDER) ADMIRATION
(— TO BE TILTED AT) QUINTAIN
(BELOVED —) MINION DARLING MISTRESS
(BULKY —) WODGE
(CONICAL —) ACORN
(CONSPICUOUS —) LANDMARK
(CONTAMINATED —S) FOMITES
(CURVED —) BELLY
(CYLINDRICAL —) BOLE
(DECORATIVE —) BIBELOT
(DESIRABLE —) GRAIL
(FACTORY-MADE —S) ARTWORK
(MINUTE —) ATOM MITE
(ROUND —) RONDEL TRINDLE TRUNDLE
(SACRED —) URIM ZOGO GUACA HUACA SHRINE CHURINGA
(SILLY —) INANITY
(SMALL —) PIRLIE
(TRANSCENDENTAL —) ENTITY
(ULTIMATE —) TELOS
(VILE —S) SCUM
(WORTHLESS —) SPLINTER

OBJECTION OB BAR BUT BEEF CRAB FUSS KICK CAVIL DEMUR DOUBT CHESON QUARREL QUIBBLE SCRUPLE QUESTION CHALLENGE CRITICISM EXCEPTION

OBJECTIONABLE VILE AWFUL

HORRID GHASTLY UNLUSTY
UNLIKELY FRIGHTFUL OBNOXIOUS
OFFENSIVE
OBJECTIVE AIM END FAIR GAME
GOAL HOME REAL SAKE OUTER
ACTUAL AMORAL ANIMUS DESIGN
MOTIVE TARGET PURPOSE
DETACHED TANGIBLE UNBIASED
DIRECTION INTENTION POSITIVAL
QUAESITUM ULTIMATUM
OBJURGATE BAN JAW DAMN ABUSE
CHIDE CURSE DECRY BERATE
REBUKE REPROVE UPBRAID
VITUPER EXECRATE CASTIGATE
OBLATE MONK OFFER DEDICATE
MONASTIC
OBLATION CORBAN OFLETE SACRED
CHARITY ANAPHORA DEVOTION
OFFERING SACRIFICE
OBLIGATE COMMIT STRICT
OBLIGATED LIABLE
OBLIGATION DUE IOU TIE VOW BAIL
BAND BOND CALL DEBT DUTY KNOT
LOAD LOAN MUST NOTE OATH
ONUS SEAL CHECK OUGHT SCORE
ARREAR BURDEN CHARGE CONSOL
CUSTOM FEALTY PLEDGE ANNUITY
BONDAGE PROMISE TRIBUTE
CONTRACT HYPOTHEC SECURITY
WARRANTY AGREEMENT LIABILITY
(— NOT TO MARRY) CELIBACY
(— TO RENDER RENT) CUSTOM
(MORAL —) BOND DUTY
(PL.) STRINGS
OBLIGATORY BINDING BOUNDEN
FORCIBLE IMPOSING LIGATORY
INCUMBENT MANDATORY
OBLIGE PUT HOLD PAWN DRIVE
FAVOR FORCE COMPEL ENGAGE
PLEASE GRATIFY REQUIRE
CONCLUDE MORTGAGE CONSTRAIN
OBLIGED FAIN BOUND DEBTED
BOUNDEN DEBTFUL FAVORED
PLEASED PLEDGED BEHOLDEN
GRATEFUL OBSTRICT BEHOLDING
OBLIGATED
OBLIGING KIND BUXOM CIVIL
CLEVER TOWARD AMIABLE
FAVOROUS AGREEABLE COURTEOUS
FAVORABLE OFFICIOUS
OBLIQUE AWRY BIAS SIDE SKEW
ASKEW BEVEL CROSS SLANT
ASLANT ASWASH LOUCHE SQUINT
THWART ASKANCE CROOKED
EMBELIF EVASIVE SCALENE SIDLING
SLOPING DIAGONAL INCLINED
INDIRECT SIDELONG SIDEWAYS
SIDEWISE SLANTING TORTUOUS
INDICULAR UNDERHAND
(— IN MINING) CLINIC
(— STROKE) SLASH SOLIDUS
(— WORK) SWASHWORK
OBLIQUELY AGEE AWRY BIAS
AGLEE ASIDE ASKEW AWASH SLANT
SLOPE ASLANT ASWASH ASKANCE
EMBELIF BIASWISE SIDELONG
SIDEWAYS SIDEWISE
OBLIQUITY DIRT SWEEP DIRTINESS
OBLITERATE INK BLOT DELE RASE

RAZE WIPE ANNUL BLACK COVER
ERASE SMEAR CANCEL DELETE
EFFACE SPONGE ABOLISH DESTROY
EXPUNGE OUTRAZE SCRATCH
OVERSCORE
OBLITERATION BLOT RASURE
ERASURE NEGATION SYNIZESIS
OBLIVION LETHE LIMBO PARDON
AMNESTY NIRVANA SILENCE
OUBLIANCE
OBLIVIOUS AMORT BLISSFUL
HEEDLESS OBLIVIAL FORGETFUL
OBLONG CHITON EVELONG
AVELONGE EVENLONG ELONGATED
(ROUNDED —) ELLIPSE
OBLOQUY ABUSE BLAME ODIUM
INFAMY CALUMNY CENSURE
REPROOF CONTEMPT DISGRACE
DISHONOR OBLICQUE
OBNOXIOUS FOUL PERT VILE CURST
CURSED FAULTY HORRID LIABLE
ODIOUS RANCID SEPTIC HATEFUL
INVIDIOUS OFFENSIVE REPUGNANT
VERMINOUS
OBOE PIPE REED WAIT AULOS
SHAWM SURNAI SURNAY HAUTBOY
MUSETTE PIFFERO CHIRIMIA
HAUTBOIS SCHALMEY SZOPELKA
CHALUMEAU
(— DI CACCIA) TENOROON
FAGOTTINO
(BASS —) RACKETT
OBOLE MAIL MAILLE
OBSCENE PAW FOUL LEWD NAST
BAWDY GROSS NASTY ROCKY
COARSE FILTHY IMPURE RIBALD
SMUTTY VULGAR KNAVISH PROFANE
IMMODEST INDECENT LOATHSOME
OFFENSIVE REPULSIVE SALACIOUS
(— CULT) AISCHROLATREIA
OBSCURATION COVER ECLIPSE
OBSCURE DIM FOG BLOT BLUR
DARK DEEP HARD HART HAZY HIDE
PALE SLUR BEDIM BEFOG BLANK
BLIND CLOUD COVER DUSKY FAINT
FOGGY GLOOM INNER LOWLY
MIRKY MISTY MUDDY MURKY SHADE
SMEAR STAIN VAGUE BEMIST
CLOUDY DARKEN DARKLE DEADEN
DELUDE GLOOMY HUMBLE MYSTIC
OCCULT OPAQUE REMOTE SHADOW
SOMBER SUBTLE BECLOUD BENIGHT
CLOUDED CONCEAL CONFUSE
CRABBED CRYPTIC ECLIPSE
ENCRUST ENVELOP OBLIQUE
OVERLAY OVERTOP SHADOWY
SLUBBER TARNISH UNCLEAR
UNKNOWN UNNOTED ABSTRUSE
DARKLING DISGUISE DOUBTFUL
FAMELESS MYSTICAL NAMELESS
OBSTRUSE OVERSILE
(MAKE —) BECLOUD
OBSCURED HAZY HIDDEN BLINDED
CLOUDED DUSKISH DARKSOME
DISGUISED INFUSCATE
OBSCURITY FOG MIST CLOUD
GLOOM SHADE CALIGO SHADOW
DIMNESS OPACITY PRIVACY SILENCE

DARKNESS TENEBRES BLINDNESS
SECLUSION
(PL.) MURLEMEWES
OBSECRATE BEG PRAY BESEECH
ENTREAT PETITION
OBSEQUIES MASS OBIT PYRE WAKE
RITES SERVICE FUNERALS
OBSEQUIOUS SLICK MENIAL SUPPLE
COURTLY DEVOTED DUTEOUS
DUTIFUL FAWNING SERVILE SLAVISH
VERNILE CRINGING OBEDIENT
OBEISANT TOADYING ASSIDUOUS
ATTENTIVE COMPLIANT
(— PERSON) LIMBERHAM
OBSEQUY RITE EXEQUY RITUAL
FUNERAL CEREMONY
OBSERVANCE ACT FORM RITE RULE
FREET HONOR CUSTOM REGARD
KEEPING CEREMONY PRACTICE
ADHERENCE ATTENTION DEFERENCE
INDICTION SOLEMNITY
(— OF PROPRIETIES) DECORUM
BREEDING ETIQUETTE
(RELIGIOUS —) NOVENA
SACRAMENT
(SUPERSTITIOUS —) FREET FREIT
(PL.) FUNERAL CEREMONY
OBSERVANT ALERT EYEFUL
CAREFUL HEEDFUL MINDFUL
DILIGENT VIGILANT WATCHFUL
OBSERVATION EYE SPY HEED IDEA
NOTE RAOB VIEW SIGHT ESPIAL
LOGION NOTICE REGARD REMARK
AUSPICE AUTOPSY COMMENT
CONTACT DESCANT OPINION
EYESIGHT GAZEMENT SCHOLION
SCHOLIUM ASSERTION ATTENTION
ESPIONAGE
(ECOLOGICAL —S) ANNUATION
(PRELIMINARY —) PROEM
OBSERVATIONISM SCHAULUST
OBSERVATORY LICK TOWER
LOOKOUT PALOMAR
OBSERVE LO EYE SEE SPY ESPY
HEED HOLD KEEP LOOK MAKE
MARK MIND NARK NOTA NOTE OBEY
SPOT TENT TOUT TWIG WAIT YEME
ABIDE QUOTE SMOKE STUDY UTTER
WATCH ADHERE ADVERT ATHOLD
BEHOLD DETECT DEVISE FOLLOW
NOTICE NOTIFY REGARD REMARK
SURVEY COMMENT DISCERN
EXPRESS MENTION PROFESS
RESPECT WITNESS PERCEIVE
PRESERVE SPECTATE ADVERTISE
CELEBRATE SOLEMNIZE
(— CLOSELY) SMOKE
(— DULLY) BLEAR
OBSERVER O BIRDER CORNER
WATCHER AUDIENCE INFORMER
ONLOOKER BYSTANDER SCRUTATOR
SPECTATOR
OBSESS RIDE BESET HAUNT HARASS
INVEST OBSEDE BESIEGE HAGRIDE
POSSESS PREOCCUPY
OBSESSED CRAZY DOTTY HAPPY
HIPPED BESOTTED
OBSESSION TIC CRAZE MANIA
SIEGE MAGGOT ECSTASY FIXATION

OBSIDIAN CORE LAVA IZTLE IZTLI LAPIS

OBSOLETE OLD DEAD PAST DATED PASSE BYGONE EFFETE ABOLETE ANCIENT ARCHAIC CLASSIC DISUSED EFFACED EXTINCT OUTWORN OUTDATED OUTMODED OVERWORN DISCARDED

OBSTACLE BAR DAM LET BOYG BUMP DRAG JUMP OBEX SNAG STAY STOP BLOCK CHECK CLAMP CRIMP FENCE HITCH HYDRA SPOKE STICK STILE ABATIS BUNKER FRAISE HOCKET HURDLE OBJECT RETARD ANSTOSS BARRIER CHICANE FIVEBAR STOPPER BLOCKADE MOLEHILL BARRICADE CONDITION HINDRANCE ROADBLOCK TURNAGAIN
(— TO VIRTUE) SLANDER
(GOLF —) HAZARD
(INSURMOUNTABLE —) IMPASSE

OBSTETRICIAN ACCOUCHEUR

OBSTETRICS MAIEUTICS MIDWIFERY

OBSTINATE SET SOT DOUR FIRM SULY BALKY FIXED ROWDY RUSTY STIFF STOUT TOUGH ASSISH CUSSED DOGGED KNOBBY MULISH STEEVE STUFFY STUPID STURDY SULLEN UNRULY ASININE BULLISH CRABBED FROWARD PEEVISH RESTIVE WILLFUL CROTCHED OBDURATE PERVERSE PREFRACT RENITENT STOMACHY STUBBORN FORERIGHT PIGHEADED STONEWALL TENACIOUS
(NOT —) SUPPLE

OBSTREPEROUS LOUD WILD NOISY UNRULY CLAMOROUS

OBSTRUCT BAR DAM DIT GAG JAM CLOG COOP DITT FILL FOUL JAMB STOP TRIP BESET BLANK BLOCK CHAIN CHECK CHOKE CROSS DELAY HEDGE THROW ARREST CUMBER FORBAR HAMPER HOBBLE IMPEDE OPPOSE PESTER RETARD STIFLE THWART WAYLAY WINDER BARRIER FORELAY OCCLUDE BLOCKADE EMBOLIZE ENCUMBER FLOUNDER OPPILATE BARRICADE EMBARRASS INCOMMODE

OBSTRUCTION BAR DAM GAG LET RUB BOOM BUMP SLUG SNAG STAY STOP BLOCK CHOKE GORCE HITCH SPOKE HAMPER TAPPEN THWART BARRACE BARRAGE BARRIER BLINDER CHOKAGE EMBOLISM OBSTACLE STOPPAGE EMPHRAXIS
(— IN OILWELL) BRIDGE
(— IN RIVER) GORGE
(— IN TEAT) SPIDER
(— IN VALVE) GAG
(— OF BLOOD VESSEL) EMBOLISM
(— OF PINE LEAVES) TAPPEN
(INNER —) LOAD

OBTAIN BEG BUM BUY EKE GET WIN EARN FANG FIND GAIN HENT REAP ANNEX CADGE CATCH ETTLE REACH AREACH ARECHE ARRIVE ATTAIN BORROW DERIVE EXPEDE SECURE SPONGE ACHIEVE ACQUIRE CAPTURE CHEVISE COMPASS DEMERIT EXTRACT POSSESS PREVAIL PROCURE RECEIVE SUCCEED PURCHASE SCROUNGE
(— BY CHANCE) DRAW
(— BY HEAT) EXCOCT
(— BY REQUEST) IMPETRATE
(— BY THREAT) EXTORT
(— CONTROL) ENGROSS
(— DISHONESTLY) CROOK SHARP FLEECE NOBBLE SKELDER
(— MONEY FROM) BLEED
(— PERMISSION) CLEAR

OBTAINABLE GOING GETTABLE AVAILABLE DERIVABLE SECURABLE

OBTAINED (— AT SCENE OF CRIME) LATENT

OBTRUDE JET SORN EJECT EXPEL GLARE FLAUNT IMPOSE MEDDLE THRUST INTRUDE INTERFERE

OBTRUSIVE FRESH PUSHY GARISH BLATANT FORWARD PUSHING BUMPTIOUS INTRUSIVE

OBTUND DULL BLUNT QUELL DEADEN

OBTURATOR MUSHROOM

OBTUSE DIM DULL BLINK BLUNT CRASS DENSE THICK OPAQUE STUPID BOEOTIAN HEBETATE PURBLIND
(NOT —) ACUTE

OBVERSE FACE FRONT CONVERSE
(— OF COIN) MAN HEAD

OBVIATE PREVENT PRECLUDE FORESTALL

OBVIOUS LOUD OPEN BROAD CLEAR CRUDE FRANK GROSS NAKED OVERT PLAIN SLICK STARK LIABLE PATENT BLATANT EVIDENT EXPOSED GLARING SHALLOW SUBJECT VISIBLE APPARENT DISTINCT MANIFEST PALPABLE BAREFACED PROMINENT
(NOT —) DEEP INNER ARCANE HIDDEN MASKED OCCULT SECRET SUBTLE DELICATE DOUBTFUL PROFOUND INEVIDENT

OBVOLUTE CONTORTED OVERLAPPING

OCA OKA TUBER OXALIS SORREL SOURSOP

OCARINA CAMOTE

OCCASION SEL BOUT CALL GIVE HINT NEED SELE SITH TIDE TIME TURN BREAK CASUS CAUSE CHARE EVENT INFER NONCE RAISE SITHE SLANT STOUR WHILE YIELD AFFAIR AUTHOR CHANCE COURSE EXCUSE PERIOD REASON STOUND CHASOUN INSPIRE PRETEXT QUARREL CEREMONY ENGENDER EXIGENCY FUNCTION INCIDENT INSTANCE CONDITION ENCHEASON HAPPENING
(— GRIEF) GRIEVE
(— OF EXCITEMENT) ALARM ALARUM
(DEFINITE —) TIDE

(FAVORABLE —) ADVANTAGE
(FESTIVE —) UTAS BEANO HOLIDAY SHINDIG BEANFEST
(HAPPY —) SIMHAH SIMCHAH
(SOCIAL —) COFFEE
(SPECIAL —) CEREMONY

OCCASIONAL ODD ORRA STRAY ANTRIN CASUAL DAIMEN SCARCE POPPING EPISODIC FUGITIVE SPORADIC IRREGULAR

OCCASIONALLY EVERY BETIMES SOMETIME SOMETIMES

OCCASIVE SETTING WESTWARD

OCCIDENTAL WEST PONENT WESTERN HESPERIAN WESTERNER

OCCLUDE SORB CLOSE ABSORB OBSTRUCT

OCCLUSAL MORSAL

OCCLUSION CORONARY ARTICULATION

OCCULT MAGIC ARCANE HIDDEN LATENT MYSTIC SECRET VOODOO ALCHEMY CRYPTIC ECLIPSE UNKNOWN ESOTERIC MYSTICAL SIBYLLIC CONCEALED RECONDITE SIBYLLINE
(— SCIENCE) ESOTERICS

OCCULTATION ECLIPSE

OCCULTISM MAGIC CABALA MYSTERY

OCCUPANT HOLDER INMATE RENTER TENANT CITIZEN DWELLER RESIDENT INCUMBENT
(— OF THEATER GALLERY) GOD

OCCUPATION ART JOB LAY USE CALL GAME LINE NOTE TOIL WORK BERTH CRAFT GRAFT TRADE CAREER EMPLOY METIER RACKET SPHERE TENURE THRIFT CALLING CONCERN CONTROL MYSTERY PURSUIT QUALITY SERVICE ACTIVITY BUSINESS FUNCTION INDUSTRY INVASION VOCATION
(— OF MIND) ABSORPTION
(SUBORDINATE —) HOBBY AVOCATION

OCCUPIED BUSY FULL HELD KEPT RAPT TOOK ACTIVE INTENT ENGAGED ABSORBED CAPTURED
(FULLY —) ENGROSSED

OCCUPY LIE SIT USE BUSY FILL HAVE HOLD KEEP TAKE WARM AMUSE BELAY BESET DWELL ABSORB BETAKE EMPLOY ENGAGE EXPEND FULFIL OBTAIN TENANT COHABIT CONCERN CONTAIN ENGROSS ENTREAT IMPROVE INHABIT INVOLVE OVERSIT PERVADE POSSESS SWALLOW DISSOLVE GARRISON INTEREST POURPRISE
(— ILLEGALLY) JUMP
(— QUARTERS) CAMP

OCCUR BE GO COME COOK FALL GIVE MAKE MEET PASS RISE SORT ARISE BREAK CLASH EXIST INCUR LIGHT APPEAR ARRIVE BEFALL BETIDE CHANCE HAPPEN PROCEED TRANSPIRE
(— AGAIN) RECUR REPEAT

(— BY CHANCE) LIGHT
(— TO) CROSS ENTER STRIKE
OCCURRENCE GO HAP CASE FACT
ITEM NOTE REDE EVENT WEIRD
EPISODE PASSAGE INCIDENT
JUNCTURE OCCASION ENCOUNTER
FREQUENCE HAPPENING
(CHANCE —) ADVENTURE
CONTINGENT
(COMMON —) USE FREQUENCY
(FREQUENT —) COMMUNITY
(SIMULTANEOUS —) COINCIDENCE
(SUPERNATURAL —) MIRACLE
(UNEXPECTED —) SUDDEN
BLIZZARD BOMBSHELL
(UNFORTUNATE —) CASUALTY
(UNUSUAL —) ODDITY
OCCURRING (— AT NIGHTFALL)
ACRONICAL
(— AT REGULAR INTERVALS) HORAL
(— AT TWILIGHT) CREPUSCULAR
(— BY TURN) ALTERNATE
(— EVERY EIGHT DAYS) OCTAN
(— EVERY FOURTH YEAR)
PENTETERIC
(— FREQUENTLY) COMMON
(— IN USUAL PLACE) ENTOPIC
OCEAN SEA BLUE BRIM DEEP MAIN
POND BRINE DRINK ARCTIC INDIAN
EXPANSE NEPTUNE PACIFIC
ATLANTIC ANTARCTIC
(— FLOATING MATTER) ALGAE
LAGAN FLOTSAM
(— ROUTE) LANE
(— SPRAY) IRONWOOD CREAMCUPS
(— SWELL) SEA
(ON THE —) ASEA
OCEANIA MALAYA AUSTRALIA
MELANESIA POLYNESIA
(SACRED OBJECT OF —) ZOGO
OCEANIC NAVAL MARINE PELAGIC
NAUTICAL AEQUOREAL
OCEANUS TITAN
(DAUGHTER OF —) DORIS OCEANID
EURYNOME
(FATHER OF —) URANUS OURANOS
(MOTHER OF —) GAEA GAIA
(SISTER OF —) TETHYS
(SON OF —) NEREUS
(WIFE OF —) TETHYS
OCELLUS EYE EYELET STEMMA
EYESPOT
OCELOT CAT TOGER LEOPARD
WILDCAT
OCHER RUD SIL KEEL OAKER OCHRE
TIVER ABRAUM RADDLE ALMAGRA
TANGIER
(BLACK —) WAD WADD
(RED —) RUD KEEL TIVER ABRAUM
REDDLE RUBRIC RUDDLE KOKOWAI
(YELLOW —) SIL SPRUCE
OCOTILLO COACHWHIP
CANDLEWOOD
OCREA OCHREA SHEATH
OCTAHEDROID HYPERCUBE
TESSERACT
OCTAVE UTAS UTIS EIGHT EIGHTH
OTTAVA HUITAIN DIAPASON
SHEMINITH

(— FLUTE) FLAUTINO
(— OF THE SEVENTH) FOURTEENTH
(— SINGING) MAGADIZE
(DIMINISHED —) SEMIDIAPASON
(TRIPLE —) TRIDIAPASON
OCTAVO EIGHTS
OCTET OCTAVE OCTUOR HUITAIN
OTTETTO
OCTAVIA (BROTHER OF —)
AUGUSTUS
(HUSBAND OF —) ANTONY
OCTOPUS HEE POLYP POULP PREKE
SQUID CUTTLE CATFISH POLYPOD
POLYPUS SCUTTLE DIBRANCH
OCTOPEAN DEVILFISH
(— ARM) TENTACLE
(SECRETION OF —) INK
OCTOROON METIS MESTEE MUSTEE
MESTIZO METISSE OCTAROON
OCTROI TAX GRANT PRIVILEGE
OCTUPLE EIGHTFOLD
OCUBY RUM
OCULAR OPTIC VISUAL OCULARY
OPTICAL ORBITAL EYEPIECE
ODD AUK AWK OUT RUM FELL LEFT
LONE ORRA RARE CRAZY DIPPY
DROLL EXTRA FUNNY IMPAR OUTRE
QUEER UNKET UNKID WEIRD IMPAIR
QUAINT SINGLE UNEVEN UNIQUE
AZYGOUS BIZARRE COMICAL
CURIOUS ERRATIC STRANGE
UNEQUAL UNUSUAL FANCIFUL
FREAKISH PECULIAR SINGULAR
UNPAIRED BURLESQUE ECCENTRIC
FANTASTIC GROTESQUE LAUGHABLE
SQUIRRELY UNMATCHED WHIMSICAL
(— JOBMAN) JOEY
ODDBALL SPOOK
ODDITY GIG QUIP RUMNESS
QUIZZITY
(PL.) PURLICUES
ODDMAN UMPIRE ARBITER FLOATER
REFEREE
ODDS BISK EDGE CHALK PRICE
BISQUE DISCORD DISPUTE QUARREL
HANDICAP VARIANCE ADVANTAGE
DISPARITY
(— AND ENDS) ORTS BROTT
REFUSE SCRAPS GIBLETS SECONDS
FEWTRILS REMNANTS SHAKINGS
ETCETERAS FRAGMENTS
(AT —) ACROSS
(EXTRAVAGANT —) POUNDAGE
ODE HYMN POEM SONG LYRIC
PAEAN PSALM MONODY ODELET
CANZONA CANZONE EPICEDE
CANTICLE PALINODE PINDARIC
SERENATA STASIMON EPICEDIUM
EPINICION PARABASIS
ODEON HALL ODEUM GALLERY
THEATER
ODIN OTHIN WODAN WODEN WOTAN
(BROTHER OF —) VE VILI
(CREATED BY —) ASK EMBLA
(DAUGHTER-IN-LAW OF —) NANNA
(DESCENDANT OF —) SCYLD
(FATHER OF —) BOR BORR
(HALL OF —) VALHALLA
(HORSE OF —) SLEIPNER

(MOTHER OF —) BESTLA
(PALACE OF —) SYN
(SON OF —) TYR THOR VALI BALDR
BALDER
(SWORD OF —) GRAM
(WIFE OF —) FRIA RIND FRIGG
RINDR FRIGGA
ODIOUS FOUL LOTH UGLY VILE
LOATH INFAND ODIBLE HATABLE
HATEFUL HEINOUS HIDEOUS
DAMNABLE FLAGRANT INFAMOUS
ABHORRENT INVIDIOUS OBNOXIOUS
OFFENSIVE REPUGNANT
ODIUM HATRED STIGMA DISLIKE
AVERSION DISFAVOR DISGRACE
DISHONOR ANTIPATHY
(PUBLIC —) ENVY
ODOMETER ODOGRAPH VIAMETER
WAYWISER HODOMETER
PEDOMETER
ODONTALGIA TOOTHACHE
ODOR AIR FUME FUNK NOSE OLID
TANG WAFF WAFT AROMA EWDER
FETOR FLAIR FUMET NIDOR SCENT
SMACK SMELL SNUFF SPICE STINK
BREATH FLAVOR FOETOR HODURE
REPUTE STENCH BOUQUET
ESSENCE FUMETTE NOSEGAY
PERFUME VERDURE PUNGENCE
EFFLUVIUM EMPYREUMA
FRAGRANCE REDOLENCE
(— FROM FLOWERS) FUME
(— OF GAME) FUMET
(— OF HAY) NOSE
(BAD —) EWDER FROWST STENCH
(DISGUSTING —) STINK
(FOUL —) FIST
(FRESH —) YMUR
(PUNGENT —) SPICE
(SPICY —) BALM
(STUDY OF —S) OSMICS
ODORIFEROUS BALMY OLENT
ODOROUS FRAGRANT
ODOROUS FOUL BALMY OLENT
SMELLY ODORANT AROMATIC
FRAGRANT NIDOROSE NIDOROUS
PERFUMED REDOLENT SCENTFUL
SMELLFUL
ODYSSEUS ULYSSES
(DOG OF —) ARGOS
(FATHER OF —) LAERTES SISYPHUS
(FRIEND OF —) MENTOR
(ISLAND OF —) ITHACA
(SON OF —) TELEGONUS
TELEMACHUS
(WIFE OF —) PENELOPE
OECIST OEKIST COLONIZER
OEDIPUS OEDIPAL
(BROTHER-IN-LAW OF —) CREON
(DAUGHTER OF —) ISMENE ANTIGONE
(FATHER OF —) LAIUS
(FOSTER MOTHER OF —) PERIBOEA
(MOTHER OF —) JOCASTA
(SON OF —) ETEOCLES POLYNICES
(WIFE OF —) JOCASTA
OEIL-DE-BOEUF OCULUS
OEILLADE OGLE ELIAD EYLIAD
GLANCE ILLIAD
OENOCHOE OLPE PROCHOOS

OENOMETER VINOMETER
OESTRID FLY
(— **LARVA**) BOT
OESTRUS RUT FURY HEAT STING
DESIRE ESTRUS FRENZY IMPULSE
STIMULUS
OEUVRE OPUS WORK
OF A O BY DE OFF VAN VON FROM
HAVE TILL WITH ABOUT
(— **AGE**) AE
(— **ALL**) AVA ALDER ALLER
(— **DEATH**) M
(— **EACH**) ANA PER SING
(— **THIS DAY**) HODIERNAL
(— **THIS MONTH**) HM
OFF BY AFF FAR ODD WET AFAR
AGEE AWAY DOFF DOWN GONE
ALONG ASIDE RIGHT WONKY
WRONG ABSENT CUCKOO DEPART
REMOTE DISTANT FURTHER
REMOVED SEAWARD TAINTED
ABNORMAL OPPOSITE
(— **GUARD**) TARDY
(— **THE PATH**) ASTRAY
(— **THE SUBJECT**) AFIELD
(— **THE WIND**) ROOM ROOMWARD
(**FAR** —) DISTANT
OFFAL GURRY WASTE REFUSE
CARRION DOGMEAT GARBAGE
LEAVING RUBBISH GRALLOCH
(— **OF FISH**) GURRY STOSH
(**MILLING** —**S**) GRIT
OFFBREAK GOOGLY
OFF-CENTER ECCENTRIC
EXCENTRIC
OFF-COLOR BLUE SUGGESTIVE
OFFEND CAG ERR PET SIN VEX GALL
HARM HUFF HURT MIFF RASP RASS
ABUSE ANGER ANNOY GRATE GRILL
PIQUE SHOCK SPITE TOUCH WRONG
AGUILT ATTACK GRIEVE INJURE
INSULT NETTLE REVOLT AFFRONT
DEFAULT DISDAIN MORTIFY
OUTRAGE PROVOKE REGRATE
STOMACH UMBRAGE VIOLATE
CONFRONT DISTASTE IRRITATE
TRESPASS DISOBLIGE DISPLEASE
OFFENDED HUFF MIFF SORE
AVERTED FROISSE INJURED
INSULTED
OFFENDER SINNER CULPRIT
MISDOER PECCANT HABITUAL
OFFENDANT
(**FIRST** —) STAR
OFFENSE PET SIN HUFF LACK SLIP
WITE ABUSE CRIME ERROR FAULT
GRIEF GUILT MALUM PIQUE SNUFF
ATTACK BIGAMY DELICT FELONY
PIACLE PRITCH REATUS STRUNT
AFFRONT DEFAULT DEMERIT
DUDGEON LARCENY MISDEED
OUTRAGE SCANDAL UMBRAGE
PECCANCY TRESPASS EXTORTION
INDECORUM INDIGNITY THEFTBOTE
(— **AGAINST LAW**) MALUM DELICT
DELICTUM
(— **AGAINST MORALITY**) EVIL CRIME
OFFENSIVE BAD ACID EVIL FOUL
HARD UGLY BILGY CRUDE DIRTY

FETID GROSS NASTY SLIMY COARSE
FROWZY GARISH HORRID RANCID
RIBALD ROTTEN ABUSIVE BEASTLY
FULSOME HATEFUL HIDEOUS
NOISOME RASPING SCARLET
DREADFUL INVADING MEPHITIC
SHOCKING STINKING UNSAVORY
LOATHSOME OBNOXIOUS
REPUGNANT REVOLTING
OFFER GO BID PUT BODE GIVE HAND
LEND PLEA SHOW TAKE TEND
DEFER HEAVE PARTY SHORE START
ADDUCE AFFORD ALLEGE DELATE
INJECT OBLATE OPPOSE PREFER
SUBMIT SUPPLY TENDER ADVANCE
BIDDING COMMEND EXHIBIT
PRESENT PROFFER PROPINE
PROPOSE SUGGEST OVERTURE
VOLUNTEER
(— **EXCUSE**) ALIBI
(— **FOR SALE**) HAWK EXPOSE
(— **IN SACRIFICE**) IMMOLATE
(— **PROOF**) APPROVE
(— **PUBLICLY**) JACTITATE
(— **TO VERIFY**) AVER
(**LAST** —) ULTIMATUM
(**SOLEMN** —) PLEDGE
(**UNACCEPTED** —) POLLICITATION
OFFERING BID ALMS BALI DALI DEAL
GIFT HOST SOMA DOLLY ENTRY
CORBAN NUZZER OFLETE PIACLE
PRESENT RETABLO TRIBUTE
ANATHEMA DEVOTION DONATION
LIBATION OBLATION PESHKASH
PIACULUM SACRIFICE
(— **TO GOD**) CORBAN DEODATE
(— **TO HOUSEHOLD DEITIES**) BALI
(**PEACE** —**S**) PACIFICS
(**RELIGIOUS** —) OBLATION
(**SACRIFICIAL** —) HOLOCAUST
(**THEATRICAL** —) FLUFF
(PL.) HIERA ALTARAGE INFERIAE
OFF-GLIDE EXIT VOCULE DETENTE
OFFHAND CURT GLIB SOON ADLIB
BLUSH HASTY ABRUPT BREEZY
CASUAL BRUSQUE READILY
CARELESS CAVALIER GLANCING
INFORMAL EXTEMPORE IMPROMPTU
UNSTUDIED
OFFICE HAT JOB SEE BOMA DUTY
NONE PART POST ROLE ROOM
SHOP TASK TOGA WIKE WORK
PLACE STINT TRUST WIKEN YAMEN
ABBACY AGENCY BUREAU CHARGE
DAFTAR DIWANI DUFTER METIER
MISTER BULLPEN CAMARIN
CENTRAL DEWANEE DROSTDY
EDILITY PYSTERY SERVICE STATION
SURGERY AEDILITY CAPACITY
CUTCHERY ENSIGNCY FUNCTION
KINGSHIP MINISTRY POSITION
PROVINCE WOOLPACK BAILIWICK
BANKSHALL SITUATION
(— **BOY**) CHOKRA
(— **CHIEF**) BOSS MANAGER
(— **OF BISHOP**) LAWN
(— **OF JUDGE**) BENCH ERMINE
(— **OF PROFESSOR**) CHAIR

(— **OF ROMAN CURIA**) DATARY
DATARIA
(— **OF RULER**) REGENCY
(— **OF THE DEAD**) DIRGE
(— **WORKER**) CLERK STENO TYPIST
SECRETARY
(**BRANCH** —) WING
(**CASHIER'S** —) CAISSE
(**CLERICAL** —) CASSOCK
(**DIVINE** —) AKOLUTHIA
(**ECCLESIASTICAL** —) FROCK
BENEFICE EXORCIST
(**HIGH** —) DIGNITY
(**LITURGICAL** —) SEXT SERVICE
(**MORNING** —) ORTHRON ORTHROS
(**NAVAL** —**S**) BEACH
(**PRIESTLY** —) SACERDOCY
(**PRINTING** —) CHAPEL IMPRIMERY
(**RECORD** —) CHANCERY
(**RESIGN AN** —) DEMIT
(**TIMEKEEPER'S** —) PENNYHOLE
OFFICEHOLDER IN WINNER
OFFICIAL PLACEMAN
OFFICER (ALSO SEE OFFICIAL) COP
TAB AIDE EXEC EXON FLAG HOLD
NASI SWAB VOGT AGENT CHIEF
CRIER DEWAN DIWAN GRAND
GRAVE GROOM JURAT SEWER
TAXOR USHER ALCADE BEADLE
BEAGLE BUTLER CENSOR DEPUTY
DIRECT ENSIGN GAILLI GEREFA
HERALD KOTWAL LAWMAN LICTOR
MANAGE ORATOR PARNAS REDTAB
SYNDIC TINDAL ALNAGER ASSIZER
BAILIFF COMMAND CONDUCT
CORONER DUUMVIR EPAULET
FEDERAL FEODARY GAVELER
GENERAL JEMADAR KLEAGLE
LOBSTER MUSTANG NAPERER
PANTLER PATROON REGIDOR
SANCTUM SCHEPEN SHERIFF
SPEAKER STEWARD WHIPPER
WOODMAN ADJUTANT ALDERMAN
ALGUACIL ANDREEVE BANNERET
CHAFFWAX COFFERER CURSITOR
DOORWARD FORESTER GOVERNOR
GRASSMAN MERESMAN MINISTER
QUESTEUR REPORTER TIPSTAFF
VISCOUNT WOODWARD CONSTABLE
DIKEGRAVE FINANCIER INTENDANT
SCHOOLMAN TAHSILDAR
(— **OF CHURCH**) ABBOT ELDER
DEACON SEXTON ANTISTES
DEFENSOR LAMPADARY SACRISTAN
(— **OF COURT**) MACER BAILIFF
FEODARY FILACER CURSITOR
DEMPSTER EXAMINER SERGEANT
ASSOCIATE BYRLAWMAN
SURROGATE
(— **OF FORESTS**) AGISTER AGISTOR
(— **OF KING'S STABLES**) AVENER
(**BARDIC** —) DRUID
(**CHIEF** —) NASI DEWAN DAROGA
PARNAS
(**CUSTOMS** —) GAGER SHARK
GAUGER JERQUER DOUANIER
SEARCHER SURVEYOR TIDESMAN
(**GREEK** —) STRATEGOS STRATEGUS
(**JAPANESE** —) SHIKKEN

(MASONIC —) EAST KING DEACON STEWARD
(MILITARY —) NAIG NAIK COMES MAJOR SUBAH ENSIGN NAIQUE RANKER SARDAR SIRDAR CAPTAIN COLONEL GENERAL JEMADAR MARSHAL SUBADAR WARRANT COMMANDER RABSHAKEH SHAVETAIL
(MINOR —) CHINOVNIK
(NAVAL —) CPO EXON MATE SWAB BOSUN ENSIGN PURSER YEOMAN ADMIRAL CAPTAIN MUSTANG SPOTTER YOUNKER SUNDOWNER
(POLICE —) PIG RURAL EXEMPT JAVERT KOTWAL RUNNER SBIRRO ALYTARCH SEARCHER THANADAR DETECTIVE
(PUBLIC —) JUDGE FISCAL NOTARY PODESTA
(ROMAN —) LICTOR
(SHERIFF'S —) FANG BEAGLE BAILIFF BULLDOG HUISSIER
(STAFF —) TAB AIDE REDTAB ADJUTANT
(TURKISH —) AGA AGHA MUTE VIZIR VIZIER BINBASHI
(PL.) BRAID BRASS STAFF

OFFICIAL (ALSO SEE OFFICER) AGA BEG DEY VIP AMIN BOSS KUAN KWAN TRUE AGENT AHONG AMALA AMBAN AMEEN AMLAH CLERK EDILE EPHOR GYANI HAJIB HOMER JURAT LIMMU LINER MAYOR NAZIR REEVE SAHIB AEDILE ARCHON ATABEG BASHAW CENSOR CONSUL EPARCH EPONYM FISCAL FORMAL GABBAI GRIEVE HAZZAN HERALD LAWMAN MASTER NOTARY PANDIT PREVOT RABMAG SATRAP SCRIBE SEALER SINGER TAOTAI TAOYIN TRONER VERGER WARDEN WEDANA ALMONER APOSTLE ASIARCH BURGESS CERTAIN JEMADAR LANDRAT MARSHAL MOORMAN PRISTAW REFEREE STALLAR STARTER SUBASHI APPROVED CARDINAL CELLARER CUSTOMER DOGBERRY GOVERNOR LINESMAN MANDARIN PRYTANIS VESTIARY EXECUTIVE MAJORDOMO
(— APPROVAL) VISA VISE
(— DECREE) WRIT UKASE
(BLUNDERING —) DOGBERRY
(POMPOUS —) BUMBLE
(PL.) KEYS PHAR OMLAH

OFFICIATE ACT FILL SERVE SUPPLY PERFORM CELEBRATE
OFFICIATOR DEICIDE
OFFICIOUS BUSY COOL PERT SAUCY FORMAL FORTHY PUSHING ARROGANT IMPUDENT INFORMAL MEDDLING OFFICIAL INBEARING
OFFING OFF FUTURE PICTURE
OFFISH CLAMMY UPSTAGE
OFFSCOURINGS MUD SCURF
OFF-SEASON LAYOFF
OFFSET SLAB STEP ALTAR CRIMP ERASE POISE CANCEL CONTRA

JOGGLE REDEEM SETOFF BALANCE COUNTER LATERAL RETREAT SETBACK PROPAGULE
(— ON BULB) SPLIT
OFFSHOOT GET PUP ROD SON LIMB SPUR BOUGH ISSUE SCION SHOOT SPRIG BRANCH FILIAL GROWTH MEMBER SPROUT ADJUNCT APOPHYSIS FILIATION OUTGROWTH
(— OF LAKE) BAYOU
OFFSHORE DEEPWATER
OFFSPRING BOY FRY IMP KID KIN SON BRAT CHIT HEIR SEED SLIP BIRTH BREED BROOD CHILD FRUIT ISSUE SCION SPAWN BEGATS DUSTEE EMBRYO FOSTER GRIQUA JUMART PROLES RESULT STRAIN STRIND MORISCO NISHADA OUTCOME PRODUCE PRODUCT PROGENY YOUNGER CHILDREN DAUGHTER DEMISANG GENITURE INCREASE KINDLING BAIRNTEAM MUSTAFINA
(— OF FAIRIES) CHANGELING
(— OF NEGRO AND MULATTO) GRIFFE
(— OF WITCH) HAGSEED HOLDIKEN
(MYTHICAL —) JUMART
(PREMATURE —) CASTLING
OFICINA WORKS OFFICE FACTORY
OFLETE WAFER OBLATION OFFERING
OFTEN OFT AFTEN OFTLY COMMON EFTSOONS FREQUENT REPEATED
(VERY —) CONTINUALLY
OGDOAD EIGHT OCTOAD OGDOAS OCTONARY
OGEE (ALSO SEE MOLDING) CYMA GULA TALON MOLDING
OGIVAL HEATER
OGLE EYE GAZE LEER LOOK MASH STARE GLANCE EXAMINE MARLOCK SMICKER OEILLADE
OGRE ORC BRUTE DEMON GHOUL GIANT HUGON TYRANT YAKSHA BUGABOO BUGBEAR MONSTER WINDIGO
OGRESS PELLET GUNSTONE
OGTIERN LORD MASTER
OGYGIAN ANCIENT PRIMEVAL
OH OU OW ACH OUCH

OHIO
CAPITAL: COLUMBUS
COLLEGE: KENT HIRAM KENYON XAVIER ANTIOCH OBERLIN DEFIANCE
COUNTY: ERIE ROSS MIAMI STARK SUMMIT CUYAHOGA HAMILTON
INDIAN TRIBE: ERIE WYANDOT
NATIVE: BUCKEYE
NICKNAME: BUCKEYE
PRESIDENT: TAFT GRANT HAYES HARDING GARFIELD HARRISON MCKINLEY
RIVER: MIAMI MAUMEE SCIOTO CUYAHOGA MUSKINGUM
STATE BIRD: CARDINAL
STATE FLOWER: CARNATION
STATE TREE: BUCKEYE

TOWN: ADA LIMA AKRON BEREA NILES XENIA CANTON DAYTON LORAIN TOLEDO COLUMBUS SANDUSKY CLEVELAND

OIL BEN FAT ILE ULE BALM CHIA DIKA FUEL ZEST BRIBE CRUDE JUICE OLEUM SMEAR STOCK TRAIN ULYIE ULZIE ACEITE ANOINT BINDER BUTTER CARDOL CHRISM EUPION GREASE LIQUOR SAFROL SMOOTH ZACHUN CEDRIUM ESSENCE LANOLIN MYRRHOL PHLOROL RETINOL VETIVER BERGAMOT COUMARAN ERIGERON GINGEROL PHTHALAN SDRAVETS TETRALIN CARVACROL LUBRICATE PETROLEUM
(— BEETLE) MELOE MELOID
(— CAKE) SEEDCAKE
(— CAN) OILER
(— CASK) RIER
(— LAMP) LUCIGEN
(— OF TURPENTINE) CAMPHENE CAMPHINE
(— PALM) OILBERRY
(— PAN) SUMP
(— PLANT) SESAME
(— ROCK) SHALE LIMESTONE
(— TREE) EBOE POON TUNG MAHWA
(— VESSEL) DRUM OLPE CRUET CRUSE TANKER CRESSET
(— WELL) DUSTER GASSER GUSHER WILDCAT
(BUTTER —) GHEE
(COAL —) PHOTOGEN
(CONSECRATED —) CHRISM
(FISH —) GURRY
(FIXED —) COCUM KOKAM KOKUM
(FLOWER —) ABSOLUTE
(FRAGRANT —) ATAR OTTO ATTAR OTTAR CAFFEOL CAFFEONE GERANIOL
(INFERIOR —) MIDDLING
(LINSEED —) CARRON LINOLEUM
(MINERAL —) NAPHTHA KEROSENE
(PINE —) FROTHER
(SOLID —) KIKUEL
(VEGETABLE —) MACASSAR
(VULCANIZED —) FACTICE
(WHALE —) SPERM
OILBIRD FATBIRD GUACHARO
OILFISH ESCOLAR
OILSEED TIL TEEL SESAME LINSEED RAPESEED
OILSKIN OIL OILER SQUAM OILCASE OILCOAT SLICKER
OILSTONE HONE SHALE WHETSTONE
OILY FAT GLIB BLAND FATTY LOEIC SOAPY SUAVE GREASY OILISH OLEOSE OLEOUS SMARMY SMOOTH SUPPLE PINGUID SERVILE SLIPPERY UNCTUOUS COMPLIANT PLAUSIBLE
OINTMENT BALM MULL NARD SALVE BALSAM CERATE CEROMA UNGUENT SPIKENARD
OILBIRD FATBIRD GUACHARO

OILFISH ESCOLAR
OILSEED TIL TEEL SESAME LINSEED RAPESEED
OILSKIN OIL OILER SQUAM OILCASE OILCOAT SLICKER
OILSTONE HONE SHALE WHETSTONE
OILY FAT GLIB BLAND FATTY OLEIC SOAPY SUAVE GREASY OILISH OLEOSE OLEOUS SMARMY SMOOTH SUPPLE PINGUID SERVILE SLIPPERY UNCTUOUS COMPLIANT PLAUSIBLE
OINTMENT UNG BALM MULL NARD PASTE SALVE SMEAR BALSAM CERATE CEROMA CHARGE CHRISM GREASE POMADE REMEDY UNGUENT EYESALVE POPULEON REMOLADE SPIKENARD WHITFIELD
(— OF GODS) AMBROSIA
OJIBWAY CHIPPEWA SAULTEUR CHIPPEWAY
OKA OCHA OQUE OQUI OCQUE
OKAPI GIRAFFINE
OKAY OK YES HUNK OKEH HUNKY APPROVE CORRECT SANCTION AUTHORIZE
OKIA OKET OUNCE
OKINAWA (CAPITAL OF —) NAHA

OKLAHOMA
CAPITAL: OKLAHOMACITY
COLLEGE: CAMERON LANGSTON PHILLIPS
COUNTY: KAY ATOKA CADDO ALFALFA OKFUSKEE OKMULGEE
INDIAN TRIBE: WACO WICHITA TAWAKONI
LAKE: EUFAULA OOLOGAH
MOUNTAINS: OZARK OUACHITA
NATIVE: OKIE SOONER
RIVER: RED GRAND WASHITA ARKANSAS CANADIAN CIMARRON
STATE BIRD: FLYCATCHER
STATE FLOWER: MISTLETOE
STATE TREE: REDBUD
TOWN: ADA ALVA ENID HUGO ALTUS MIAMI PONCA TULSA ELRENO GUYMON IDABEL LAWTON SAPULPA SHAWNEE ANADARKO FORTSILL MUSKOGEE

OKRA GOBO OKRO BAMIA BENDY GOBBO GOMBO GUBBO GUMBO OCHRA BENDEE MALLOW BANDAKA BANDICOY BANDIKAI
OLD AGY ELD AGED AULD COLD WOLD YALD ANILE HOARY STALE WOULD FORMER FOROLD INFIRM MATURE SENILE SHABBY VETUST AGEABLE ANCIENT ANTIQUE ARCHAIC ELDERLY FORWORN UMWHILE DECREPIT MEDIEVAL OBSOLETE DODDERING HACKNEYED SENESCENT VENERABLE
(— AND MELLOW) CRUSTY
(— BAILEY) GAOL JAIL PRISON
(— CLOTHESMAN) POCO

(— FAITHFUL) GEYSER
(— HAND) LONGTIMER
(— MAID) SPINSTER THORNBACK
(— MAN) ANTIQUITY WHITEBEARD
(— SOD) EIRE ERIN IRELAND
(— SQUAW) DIVER HOUND MOMMY CALLOO CALLOW COWEEN DUCKER QUANDY OLDWIFE SCOLDER COCKAWEE LONGTAIL SHARPTAIL SOUTHERLY
(— WOMAN) HAG CRONE GAMMER
(GROWING —) SENESCENT
(OF —) WHILOM ERSTWHILE
OLD BAY STATE MASSACHUSETTS
OLD DOMINION STATE VIRGINIA
OLDER MORE ALDER ELDER SENIOR ANCESTOR
OLD-FASHIONED CORNY DOWDY FUSTY PASSE FOGRAM FOGRUM QUAINT STODGY ANCIENT ANTIQUE ARCHAIC ELDERLY VINTAGE FRUMPISH OBSOLETE CRINOLINE PRIMITIVE
OLD FRANKLIN STATE TENNESSEE
OLD LINE STATE MARYLAND
OLD-WOMANISH ANILE
OLEANDER LAUREL DOGBANE ROSEBAY
OLEFIN ALKENE
OLEIC RAPIC RAPINIC
OLEORESIN GUM ANIME APIOL ELEMI TOLUS BALSAM GURJUN IRIDIN COPAIBA GALIPOT LABDANUM TACAMAHAC
OLFACTION SMELL OSMESIS SMELLING ESPHRESIS
OLIGARCHY KREMLIN
OLIGARCHIC FEUDAL
OLIGOCLASE SUNSTONE
OLIO STEW MEDLEY MELANGE MIXTURE MISHMASH PASTICCIO POTPOURRI
OLIPHANT HORN ELEPHANT
OLIPRANCE ROMP SHOW FROLIC JOLLITY
OLIVE OLEA MORON BRUNET LIERRE OLIVER OXHORN PIMOLA RESEDA BAROUNI CITRINE MISSION MORILLON OLEASTER
(— FLY) DACUS
(AMERICAN —) DEVILWOOD
(OVERRIPE —) DRUPE
OLIVER NOLL HAMMER HOLLIPER
OLIVET PEARL
OLLA JAR JUG OLE POT OLAY PUCHERA PUCHERO
OLLA PODRIDA HASH OLIO MEDLEY POTPOURRI
OLM PROTEUS SALAMANDER
OLOGY ISM SCIENCE
OLYMPIAN CELESTIAL
OLYNTHUS ASCULA
OMAGUA CAMBEVA
OMAN (CAPITAL OF —) MASQAT MUSCAT
(LANGUAGE OF —) ARABIC BALUCHI
(MOUNTAIN OF —) SHAM HAFIT HARIM NAKHL TAYIN AKHDAR

(NATIVE OF —) ADNAN QAHTAN BALUCHI
(TOWN IN —) SUR NIGWA MASQAT MATRAH SALALAH
OMASUM BOOK BOUK BIBLE FARDEL MANYPLIES
OMBER SOLO UMBRE HOMBRE MEDIATOR QUADRILLE
OMEGA END LAST
OMELET AMLET AMELET FOOYUNG FOOYOUNG FRITTATA
OMEN BODE LUCK SIGN ABODE AUGUR BODER FREET FREIT GUEST TOKEN WEIRD WHATE AUGURY HANDEL HANSEL AUSPICE PORTENT PRESAGE PRODIGY WARNING CEREMONY FOREBODE SOOTHSAY HARBINGER
OMENTUM WEB CAUL ZIRBUS EPIPLOON
OMINOUS DIRE DOUR GRIM FATAL BODING DISMAL SHREWD AUGURAI BALEFUL BANEFUL BODEFUL DIREFUL DOOMFUL FATEFUL MENACING SINISTER THUNDERY PROPHETIC
OMISSION OUT CHASM SALTUS DEFAULT FAILURE MISPICK NEGLECT SILENCE PASSOVER OVERSIGHT
(— OF A LETTER) APOCOPE
(— OF SYLLABLES) SYNCOPE
(TACIT —) SILENCE
OMIT CUT LET BALK BATE DROP EDIT KILL MISS PASS SKIP SLIP ABATE ELIDE OBMIT SPARE BELEVE CANCEL DELETE EXCEPT FORGET IGNORE DISCARD EXPUNGE NEGLECT DISCOUNT OVERLOOK OVERSKIP OVERSLIP DISREGARD
OMITTED VIDE
OMMATIDIUM FACET FACETTE
OMNIBUS BUS BUSS BARGE HERDIC JOGGER PIRATE AUTOBUS MOTORBUS KITTEREEN
OMNIPOTENT GOD ABLE DEITY GREAT ARRANT MIGHTY ALMIGHTY POWERFUL UNEQUALED UNLIMITED
OMNISCIENT WISE LEARNED POWERFUL PANSOPHIC
OMOPLATE SCAPULA
OMPHALOS HUB BOSS KNOB NAVEL CENTER UMBILICUS
ON O AN IN TO ONE SUR ATOP AWAY OVER UPON ABOUT ABOVE AHEAD ALONG ANENT WITHIN FORWARD
(— A HATCH) ABROAD
(— ACCOUNT OF) IN FOR
(— ALL SIDES) ABOUT AROUND
(— AND ON) EVER FOREVER TEDIOUS
(— EARTH) BELOW
(— END) TOGETHER
(— FOOT) UP AFOOT TOWARD FOOTBACK
(— HAND) ALONG
(— HIGH) ALOFT
(— THE CONTRARY) BUT RATHER

(— THE MOVE) AFOOT
(— THE OTHER HAND) BUT AGAIN
HOWEVER ALTHOUGH
(— THE OTHER SIDE) OVER ACROSS
(— THE WAY) AWAY AGATE
(— TIME) PROMPT
(— TOP OF) ATOP ABOVE ALOFT
(— WHAT ACCOUNT) WHY
ONAGER ASS GOUR KULAN KOULAN
ONAGRA ALACRAN CATAPULT
SCORPION
ONCE ANE EEN ERST AINCE ONCET
WHILE YANCE FORMER WHILOM
QUONDAM UMWHILE FORMERLY
SOMETIME UMQUHILE WHENEVER
ERSTWHILE
(— MORE) YET AGAIN ENCORE
ITERUM
ONDRATA FIBER
ONE J AE AN HE UN AIN ANE ANY
EIN MAN OON TAE UNA UNE WON
YAE YAN YEN YIN YOU SAME SOLE
SOME TANE TEAN THIS TONE TOON
UNAL UNIT WHON WONE ALONE
ALPHA UNITY WOONE FELLOW
PERSON SINGLE UNIQUE UNITED
NUMERAL PRONOUN SIMPLUM
UNBROKEN SINGLETON UNDIVIDED
UNMARRIED
(— AFTER ANOTHER) ABOUT
TANDEM SERIALLY SERIATIM
(— BORN A SERF) NEIF NEIFE
(— BY ONE) APIECE SINGLY
OVERHEAD
(— CONDEMNED WRONGFULLY)
CALAS
(— CURIOUS TO KNOW ALL)
QUIDNUNC
(— DETESTED) WARLING
(— DEVOTED TO PARTICULAR ART)
IST
(— EASILY TRICKED) CULLY
(— ENGAGED IN MARAUDING)
LOOTIE
(— ENROLLED IN ARMY) DRAFTEE
(— GIVEN TO DEVILTRY) HELLION
(— INSTRUCTED IN SECRET
SYSTEM) EPOPT
(— LATE) SERO
(— NOT A REGULAR MASON)
COWAN
(— OF PAIR) FELLOW DOUBLET
(— OVERZEALOUS) HYPER
(— SENT FORTH) APOSTLE
(— TENTH) TITHE
(— THAT UNDERGOES CHANGE)
MUTANT
(— THOUSAND) MIL
(— TWENTY-FOURTH) CARAT
(— UNKNOWN) QUIDAM
(— VERSED IN LITERATURE) SAVANT
(— WHO BRINGS MEAT TO TABLE)
DAPIFER
(— WHO DISPLAYS
FASTIDIOUSNESS) EPICURE
(— WHO DOCTORS SOMETHING)
COOK
(— WHO EXCELS) ACE
(— WHO FABRICATES) SMITH

(— WHO FOLLOWS ARMY) SUTLER
(— WHO FORSAKES FAITH)
APOSTATE
(— WHO FRUSTRATES PLAN)
MARPLOT
(— WHO HAS ATTAINED
PERFECTION) SIDDHA
(— WHO IS AWAY) ABSENTEE
(— WHO LOADS SHIP) BUNKER
(— WHO MAKES LIVING BY
TRICKERY) CADGER
(— WHO MANAGES) GERENT
(— WHO REGULATES GUN) TRAINER
(— WHO REMOVES NUISANCE)
ABATOR
(— WHO REPRESENTS NEWEST) NEO
(— WHO TESTS) CONNER
(— WHOSE MIND IS IMPAIRED BY
AGE) DOTARD
(— WITH FIRST-HAND INFORMATION)
INSIDER
(BLESSED —) BHAGAVAT
(EVIL —) WOND SHAITAN SHEITAN
(EXTRAORDINARY —) DOOZY
DOOZER
(LITTLE —) BUTCHA PICKANINNY
(LOVED —) MINION
(SWEET —) HONEYCOMB
(TIMELESS —) AKAL
ONEGITE AMETHYST GEMSTONE
ONENESS UNION UNITY CONCORD
ONEHOOD UNICITY UNITUDE
IDENTITY SAMENESS AGREEMENT
ONE-NIGHT STAND GIG
ONEROUS HARD HEAVY ARDUOUS
ONEROSE WEIGHTY EXACTING
GRIEVOUS LABORIOUS
ONE-SIDED ECCENTRIC UNILATERAL
ONETIME FORMER FORMERLY
ERSTWHILE
ONFALL ONSET ATTACK ASSAULT
ON-GLIDE TENSION ENTRANCE
ONION BOLL CEPA LEEK LILY CIBOL
PEARL ALLIUM LILIUM PORRET
BERMUDA HOLLEKE PICKLER
SHALLOT AYEGREEN RARERIPE
SCALLION VALENCIA
(ROPE OF —S) REEVE
(SEASONED WITH —S) LYONNAISE
(STRING OF —S) TRACE
ONKOS TOPKNOT
ONLOOKER BOOK GAZER WITNESS
AUDIENCE BEHOLDER OVERSEER
BYSTANDER SPECTATOR
ONLY ALL BUT JUST LONE MERE
ONCE SAVE SOLE AFALD ALONE
ARRAH FIRST MERED NOBUT OLEPY
ANERLY BARELY MERELY NOBBUT
SIMPLE SINGLE SINGLY SOLELY
ALLENARLY EXCEPTING
(— THIS) MERE
(BEING —) SIMPLE
ONMUN HANGUL HANKUL
ONOMATOPOEIC ECHOIC IMSONIC
MIMETIC IMITATIVE
ONRUSH BIRR SHAKE ATTACK
TIDEWAY
ONSET DASH DINT FALL FARD RESE
RUSH BRAID BRUNT FAIRD FRUSH

START STORM STOUR VENUE
ACCESS AFFRET ATTACK CHARGE
COURGE IMPACT INSULT ONFALL
POWDER THRUST ASSAULT
BRATTLE BEGINNING ENCOUNTER
ONSLAUGHT
ONSETTER CAGER HITCHER
ONSLAUGHT LASH BLAST ONSET
ATTACK ASSAULT DESCENT
SISERARA SALIAUNCE
ONSTEAD ONSET FARMHOUSE
HOMESTEAD
ONTARIO (CANAL IN —) TRENT
RIDEAU
(CAPITAL OF —) TORONTO
(LAKE IN —) SIMCOE
(TOWN IN —) GALT LONDON
OTTAWA WINDSOR HAMILTON
KINGSTON KITCHENER
ONTO ATOP ABOARD
ONTOGENY DEVELOPMENT
ONUS DUTY LOAD BLAME BURDEN
CHARGE WEIGHT INCUBUS
ONWARD AWAY AHEAD ALONG
FORTH UPWARD FORTHON
FORWARD TOWARDS FORERIGHT
ONYX ONIX NICOLO TECALI ONYCHIN
JASPONYX SARDONYX
(MEXICAN —) ALABASTER
OOCYTE PROGAMETE GAMETOCYTE
OODLES HEAP LOTS MANY SCADS
LASHINGS SLITHERS ABUNDANCE
OOGONIUM NUCULE OOCYST
OOGONE
OOLAK WOLLOCK
OOLONG TEA
OOMPH PEP VIGOR ENERGY
OOPAK TEA
OORALI CURARE
OORIAL SHA SHEEP URIAL
OOTHECA OVISAC
OOZE OZ BOG MUD SOP DRIP EMIT
LEAK MIRE SEEP SLEW SLOB SLUE
WEEP EXUDE GLEET MARSH SLIME
SWEAT WEEZE EXHALE SICKER
SLEECH SLOUGH SLUDGE SQUASH
SQUDGE STRAIN SCREEVE TEICHER
PERCOLATE
(— OUT) SEW SPEW SPUE
OOZING WEEPY SQUDGY SEEPAGE
SPEWING WEEPING
OOZY OASY SEEPY WASHY SLEECHY
ULIGINOUS
OPAH CRAVO SUNFISH KINGFISH
MARIPOSA MOONFISH
OPAL GEM NOBLE RESIN FIORITE
GIRASOL HYALITE ISOPYRE
JASPOPAL MENILITE SEMIOPAL
CACHOLONG GEYSERITE
OPALESCENT OPALED OPALINE
IRISATED
OPALEYE GREENFISH
OPAQUE DIM DARK DULL DENSE
MUDDY SHADY THICK VAGUE
OBTUSE STUPID CLOUDED OBSCURE
ABSTRUSE EYESHADE
OPEN GO DUP LAX OPE AIRY AJAR
BARE FAIR FLUE FREE GIVE PERT
UNDO VIDE AGAPE APERT BEGIN

BLOWN BREAK BROAD BURST CHINK CLEAR CRACK FLARE FRANK FRESH LANCE LOOSE MUSHY NAKED OVERT PLAIN RELAX SPALD SPLAT SPLAY START UNBAR UNPEG UNTIE APPERT CANDID DIRECT ENTAME EXPAND EXPOSE FACIAL FORTHY GAPING HONEST LIABLE OUVERT PATENT PUBLIC SINGLE SPREAD UNBOLT UNFOLD UNFURL UNGLUE UNLOCK UNROLL UNSEAL UNSHUT UNSPAR UNSTOP UNTINE UNWINK VACANT ARTLESS BLOSSOM DISPART FIELDEN OBVIOUS OUTLINE SINCERE UNCLOSE UNHINGE APPARENT COMMENCE DISCLOSE EXPLICIT EXTENDED INITIATE MANIFEST PERVIOUS RESERATE UNFASTEN

(— A VEIN) BROACH
(— AIR) ALFRESCO
(— AND CLEANSE) WILLOW
(— CLOTH) SCUTCH
(— COUNTRY) VELDT WEALD
(— EYES OR LIPS) SEVER
(— THE WAY) INVITE PIONEER
(— TO PURSUIT) FAIR
(— UP) START DEVELOP DISPART DISCLOSE
(— VIOLENTLY) SPORT
(— WIDE) YAWN EXPAND STRETCH
(— WIDELY) GAPE
(FULLY —) WIDE AGAPE YAWNING
(HALF —) MID AJAR
(TOO —) OVERBARISH
OPENBILL OPENBEAK
OPENED APPAUME ECHAPPE
OPENER KEY KNOB LATCH SESAME APERIENT
(— IN POKER) PAIR JACKS
(FURROW —) SHOE STUBRUNNER
(OYSTER —) HUSKER
OPENHANDED FREE LIBERAL GENEROUS RECEPTIVE
OPENING OS CUT EYE GAP YAT ANUS BORE DAWN DOOR DROP FENT FLUE GATE HOLE LOOP PASS PORE PORT PYLA RIFT RIMA SLAP SLIT SLOT SPAN VENT VOID YAWN YEAT BLEED BRACK BREAK CHASM CHINK CLEFT CROSS DEBUT GRILL HILUM INLET LIGHT MOUTH SCOOT SINUS START THIRL WIDTH ADITUS AVENUE BREACH CASING CHANCE GRILLE HIATUS INTAKE LACUNA MEATUS OILLET OUTLET PORTAL SLUICE SPREAD CREVASS CREVICE DISPLAY FISSURE ORIFICE OUTCAST SWALLET APERTURE BUNGHOLE CREVASSE ENTRANCE OVERTURE PLUGHOLE SCISSURE TEASEHOLE
(— IN EARTH) GROTTO CHIMNEY SWALLOW
(— BELOW PENTHOUSE) GALLERY
(— FOR ESCAPE) MUSE MEUSE
(— FROM SEA) INDRAFT
(— IN ANTHER) STOMIUM
(— IN DECK) SCUTTLE

(— IN FLOOR OR ROOF) HATCH SKYLIGHT
(— IN GARMENT) FENT ARMHOLE
(— IN LOCK TUMBLER) GATING
(— IN MINE) EYE ADIT RAISE SHAFT WINZE WINNING
(— IN MOLD) POUR
(— IN PICTURE FRAME) SIGHT
(— IN PILLAR OF COAL) JENKIN JUNKING
(— IN ROCK) GRIKE
(— IN SALMON TRAP) SLAP
(— IN SEA CAVE) GLOUP
(— IN SKIRT) PLACKET
(— IN SPONGE) APOPYLE
(— IN STAGE) DIP
(— IN TENNIS COURTS) GRILLE HAZARD GALLERY
(— IN TROUSERS) SPARE
(— IN VAULT) LUNET LUNETTE
(— IN WALL) BOLE DREAMHOLE
(— OF EAR) BUR BURR
(— OF ESOPHAGUS) CARDIA
(— OF GEYSER) CRATER
(— OF PRAIRIE) BAY
(— OF SHELL) GAPE
(— THROUGH BULWARKS) GANGWAY GUNPORT SCUPPER
(— TO ASH PIT) GLUT
(— WIDE) DEHISCENT
(— WITH LID) SCUTTLE
(— WITHOUT TREES) BLANK
(ARCHED —) ALCOVE ARCADE
(CHECKERS —) ALMA DYKE FIFE CROSS CENTER SOUTER BRISTOL GLASGOW PAISLEY WHILTER DEFIANCE SWITCHER
(CHESS —) DEBUT GAMBIT DEFENCE DEFENSE
(EROSIONAL —) FENSTER
(FUNNELLIKE —) CHOANA
(GRILL —) GUICHET
(JAR —) PITHOIGIA
(MOUTHLIKE —) STOMA OSTIUM
(SMALL —) PORE SLOT CHINK STOMA CRANNY EYELET LACUNA CATHOLE CREVICE DOGHOLE FORAMEN PINHOLE QUARREL FENESTRA
(WINDOWLIKE —) SPLITE FENESTRA
OPENLY FREELY BROADLY FRANKLY PUBLICE ROUNDLY STRAIGHT
OPEN-MINDED LIBERAL
OPENMOUTHED GAPING GREEDY RAVENOUS CLAMOROUS
OPENNESS FREEDOM PATENCY DAYLIGHT FRANKNESS ROUNDNESS
OPENWORK LATTICE TRACERY CAGEWORK FILIGREE FRETTING FRETWORK
OPEN-WORKED AJOURISE
OPERA AIDA FAUST LAKME MANON NORMA THAIS TOSCA BOHEME CARMEN DAPHNE ERNANI LOUISE MIGNON OTELLO RIENZI SALOME ELEKTRA FIDELIO BURLETTA FALSTAFF IOLANTHE LOKACOLO PARSIFAL TRAVIATA WALKYRIE LOHENGRIN PAGLIACCI RHEINGOLD

RIGOLETTO SIEGFRIED TROVATORE
(— DIVISION) SCENA
(— GLASS) GLASS JUMELLE LORGNET LORGNETTE
(— HAT) GIBUS CLAQUE
(— SONG) ARIA
(— STAR) DIVA
(16TH CENTURY —) PASTORALE
(COMIC —) BUFFA
(HORSE —) WESTERN
(SPANISH —) ZARZUELA
(TV OR RADIO —) SOAP
OPERANT EFFICIENT OPERATIVE
OPERATE GO ACT CUT MAN RUN PUSH TAKE WORK DRIVE MULES AFFECT EFFECT MANAGE CONDUCT PROCEED FUNCTION
(— BY HAND) MANIPULATE
(— GUNS) SERVE
(— MINE) FLUSH
(— RADIO) BLOOP
OPERATIC LYRIC
OPERATING GOING
(FULLY —) AFLOAT
OPERATION DEED PLAY BLAST AGENCY EFFECT VIRTUE PROCESS CREATION EXERCISE FUNCTION PRACTICE EXECUTION INFLUENCE PROCESSUS
OPERATIVE EYE HAND ARTIST LIVING ARTISAN MECHANIC DETECTIVE EFFECTIVE
OPERATOR DEL DOER AGENT BAKER DEWER NABLA PILOT QUACK BEAMER BILLER BOLTER BUMPER BUSMAN CAPPER DEALER DEGGER DRIVER DUNGER DYADIC GAGGER JOCKEY KICKER RAGGER TRADER AVIATOR BREAKER CENTRAL CHEESER DENTIST FACIENT GLASSER JOGGLER MANAGER OPERANT SURGEON IDENTITY CONDUCTOR
(INFERIOR —) PLUG
(RADIO —) HAM SPARKS SPARKER
(TRUCK —) GIPSY GYPSY
OPERCULUM LID FLAP ONYCHA OPERCLE APTYCHUS COVERING EYESTONE MANDIBLE
OPERETTA ZARZUELA
OPEROSE BUSY IRKSOME DILIGENT LABORIOUS
OPHIDIAN ASP EEL SNAKE CONGER REPTILE SERPENT
OPHITE CAINIAN CAINITE
OPIATE DOPE DRUG HEMP DWALE OPIUM DEADEN ANODINE HYPNOTIC NARCOTIC SEDATIVE DORMITARY PAREGORIC SOPORIFIC
OPIFICER OPIFEX WORKMAN ARTIFICER
OPINE DEEM JUDGE THINK PONDER BELIEVE SUPPOSE OPINIATE
OPINION CRY EYE MOT BOOK DOXY FAME IDEA MIND VIEW WEEN DOGMA FANCY FUTWA GUESS HEART SENSE SIGHT TENET THINK VARDI VARDY VOICE ADVICE ASSENT BELIEF DEVICE DICTUM

ESTEEM GROUND NOTION REPUTE
SCHISM CENSURE CONCEIT
CONCEPT CONSENT COUNSEL
DIANOIA FEELING HOLDING
MEASURE SEEMING THINKSO
THOUGHT TROWING VERDICT
DECISION DOCTRINE JUDGMENT
SUFFRAGE SENTIMENT
(COLLECTION OF —S) SYMPOSIUM
(EXAGGERATED —) BIGHEAD
(EXPRESSION OF —) VOTE
(FAVORABLE —) BROO ESTEEM
(MOHAMMEDAN —) FUTWA
(SET OF PROFESSED —S) CREDO
(UNORTHODOX —) HERESY
OPINIONATED DOGMATIC
CONCEITED OBSTINATE PRAGMATIC
OPIUM HOP MUD DRUG OPIE POST
CHANDU CHANDOO MECONIUM
TOXICANT
(— ALKALOID) CODEIN CODEINE
MORPHINE NARCOTIN NARCOTINE
PAPAVERIN
(— POPPY) NEPENTHE
OPIUMISM THEBAISM
OPOSSUM QUICA YAPOK POSSUM
YAPOCK OYAPOCK SARIGUE
VULPINE MARSUPIAL PHILANDER
TACUACINE
(— SHRIMP) MYSID MYSOID
OPPONENT FOE ANTI ENEMY PARTY
RIVAL ALOGIAN OPPOSER ASSILANT
ADVERSARY
(— OF GOV CLINTON) BUCKTAIL
(BOORISH —) BOEOTIAN
(IMAGINARY —) WINDMILL
OPPORTUNE FIT PAT HAPPY LUCKY
READY TIMELY APROPOS FITTING
TIMEFUL SUITABLE FAVORABLE
OPPORTUNELY TIMELY APROPOS
HAPPILY
OPPORTUNIST CREEPER
OPPORTUNISTIC SHUFFLING
OPPORTUNITY GO MAY OPE SEL
EASE HENT MEAN MINT ROOM SELE
SHOT TIDE TIME SIGHT SLANT
SPACE CHANCE SEASON SQUEAK
LEISURE OPENING RESPITE
VANTAGE APPROACH FACILITY
OCCASION ADVANTAGE
(— TO PROCEED) WAY
(FAVORABLE —) SHOW TIME
OPPOSE PIT VIE WAR BUCK COPE
DEFY FACE HEAD MEET NOSE STEM
WARN WEAR ARGUE BLOCK CHECK
CLASH CROSS FIGHT FRONT OCCUR
REBEL REBUT REPEL BATTLE
BREAST COMBAT DEFEND NAYSAY
OBJECT OBTEND OPPUGN REPUGN
RESIST THWART WITHER CONTEST
COUNTER GAINSAY OBVIATE
REVERSE WITHSET CONFLICT
CONFRONT CONTRAST FRONTIER
OBSTRUCT ENCOUNTER WITHSTAND
(— BY ARGUMENT) REBUT
(— ONE IN AUTHORITY) REBEL
DEFORCE
OPPOSED ANTI ALIEN AVERSE
ADVERSE AGAINST COUNTER

HOSTILE CONTRARY ANTARCTIC
REPUGNANT
(PERSISTENTLY —) RENITENT
OPPOSITE TO ANENT POLAR
ACROSS ANENST AVERSE FACING
WITHER ADVERSE COUNTER
FORNENT INVERSE OBVIOUS
REVERSE ANTIPODE CONTRARY
CONTRAST CONVERSE ANTIPODAL
REPUGNANT
(— MIDDLE OF SHIP'S SIDE) ABEAM
(— OF TRUTH) DEVIL
(— THE ALTAR) WEST
(— THE SUN) ANTISOLAR
OPPOSITION CON ATILT STOUR
THWART DISCORD CONTRAST
OBSTACLE ANIMOSITY COLLISION
HOSTILITY RENITENCY
(ELECTRICAL —) IMPEDANCE
OPPRESS SIT HOLD LADE LOAD PEIS
RACK RAPE RIDE SWAY THEW
CROWD CRUSH GRIND GRIPE HEAVY
PEISE POISE PRESS WEIGH WRONG
BETOIL BURDEN DEFOIL DEFOUL
EXTORT HARASS HARROW NIDDER
NITHER RAVISH SUBDUE THREAT
AFFLICT DEPRESS INGRATE
OVERLAY REPRESS SQUEEZE
TRAMPLE CONFRONT DISTRESS
ENCUMBER PRESSURE SUPPRESS
OVERPOWER OVERTHROW
OVERWHELM
(— WITH DREAD) HAGRIDE
(— WITH HEAT) SWELTER
OPPRESSED SERVILE
OPPRESSION GRIPE PRESS THRALL
MIZRAIM DULLNESS PRESSURE
EXTORTION GRIEVANCE LASSITUDE
OPPRESSIVE HOT DIRE DOWY HARD
CLOSE DOWIE FAINT HARSH HEAVY
BITTER LEADEN SCREWY SEVERE
SMUDGY SULTRY TORRID URGENT
WEIGHT ONEROUS SLAVISH
GRIEVOUS GRINDING RIGOROUS
OPPRESSIVELY STRAIT
OPPRESSOR CSAR CZAR NERO
TSAR TZAR EGLON TYRANT
INCUBUS
OPPROBRIUM ENVY ABUSE ODIUM
SCORN SHAME INFAMY INSULT
CALUMNY DISDAIN OFFENSE
SCANDAL DISGRACE DISHONOR
REPROACH CONTUMELY
OPS (ASSOCIATE OF —) CONSUS
(CONSORT OF —) SATURN
(DAUGHTER OF —) CERES
(FESTIVAL OF —) OPALIA
(PERSONIFICATION OF —) FAUNA
TERRA TELLUS
OPT CULL PICK WISH ELECT CHOOSE
DECIDE OPTATE SELECT
OPTIC EYE OCULAR VISUAL
OPTICAL (— APPARATUS) LENS
GLASS ALIDAD ALIDADE
OPTOMETER PERISCOPE TELESCOPE
OPTIMIST UTOPIANIST
OPTIMISTIC GLAD ROSY SUNNY
JOYOUS BULLISH HOPEFUL

ROSEATE EUPEPTIC SANGUINE
EXPECTANT
OPTION UP CALL DOWN CHOICE
SPREAD REFUSAL STRADDLE
PRIVILEGE
OPTIONAL ELECTIVE VOLUNTARY
OPULENT FAT LUSH RICH WELI
AMPLE FLUSH PLUSH SHOWY
LAVISH MONEYED PROFUSE
WEALTHY ABUNDANT AFFLUENT
LUXURIANT PLENTIFUL SUMPTUOUS
OPUS WORK ETUDE STUDY
(OVERLABORED —) LUCUBRATION
OQUASSA QUASKY
OR NE ARE AUT ERE ORE GOLD
OTHER TOPAZ EITHER YELLOW
ORACHE SALTBUSH GREASEWOOD
ORACLE SEER TRIP SIBYL TRIPOD
TRIPOS DIVINER AUTOPHONE
ORACULAR OTIC VATIC ORPHIC
DELPHIC VATICAL DELPHIAN
PYTHONIC PROPHETIC
ORAL ALOUD PAROL VOCAL BUCCAL
PAROLE SONANT SPOKEN VERBAL
UTTERED UNWRITTEN
ORALE FANON
ORANGE KING MOCK CERES CHILE
CHILI CHINO FLAME GENIP HEDGE
NAVEL OSAGE TENNE AURORA
BODOCK BRAZIL COPPER MIKADO
NAVAHO SUNTAN TEMPLE TITIAN
UVALHA COWSLIP FLORIDA
LEATHER MACLURA PAPRIKA
PONCEAU PUMPKIN RANGPUR
SEVILLE TANGELO TANGIER
BERGAMOT BIGARADE CHINOTTI
CLAYBANK FLAMINGO HONEYDEW
JACINTHE MANDARIN MARATHON
MOROCCAN POMANDER SUNBURST
VALENCIA BUCCANEER CARNELIAN
PERSIMMON TANGERINE
(— GRASS) KNITWEED PINEWEED
(— HAWKWEED) FIREWEED
HIERACIUM
(— MEMBRANE) ZEST
(— MILKWORT) CANDYWEED
(— PIECE) LITH SEGMENT
(— ROCKFISH) FLIOMA
(— SEED) PIP
(BROWNISH —) SPICE
(LARGE —) KING
(MOCK —) SERINGA
(OSAGE —) HEDGE BODOCK
(SOUR —) CURACAO BIGARADE
CHINOTTO
(SWEET —) CHINA CHINO
ORANGEBIRD TANAGER
ORANGELEAF KARAMU
ORANGEMAN MARKSMAN
ORANGEWOOD OSAGE
ORANG LAUT BAJAU
ORANGUTAN APE MIAS ORANG
PONGO SATYR SATIRE SATURY
PRIMATE SALTIER WOODMAN
WOODSMAN
ORAON KURUKH
ORATE PLEAD SPEAK SPIEL SPOUT
ADDRESS DECLAIM LECTURE
BLOVIATE HARANGUE DISCOURSE
SPEECHIFY

ORATION EULOGY HESPED SERMON ADDRESS CONCION HARANGUE SUASORIA OLYNTHIAC PANEGYRIC PHILIPPIC
(— OF CICERO) PHILIPPIC
(FUNERAL —) ELOGE ELOGY MONODY ELOGIUM ENCOMIUM
ORATOR RHETOR DEMAGOG SPEAKER STUMPER CICERONE BOANERGES DEMAGOGUE PLAINTIFF SPOKESMAN
ORATORIO ELIJAH RORATORIO
ORATORICAL ELOQUENT RHETORICAL
ORATORY CHAPEL SACRARY ORACULUM SPEAKING ELOCUTION ELOQUENCE PROSEUCHE
ORB EYE SUN BALL MOON STAR EARTH GLOBE MOUND ORBIT CIRCLE PLANET SPHERE CIRCUIT ENCLOSE ENCIRCLE SURROUND FIRMAMENT
ORBED LUNAR ROUND GLOBATE
ORBIT AUGE PATH APSIS CYCLE TRACK CIRCLE SOCKET SPHERE CIRCUIT ELLIPSE EYEHOLE ECCENTRIC
(POINT IN —) APSIS APOGEE EPIGEE SYZYGY PERIGEE
ORC OGRE ORCA GIANT WHALE GRAMPUS
ORCHARD TOPE ARBOR GROVE ARBOUR GARDEN HUERTA OLIVET VERGER ARBUSTUM FRUITERY PEACHERY POMARIUM SUGARBUSH
(— GRASS) DOGFOOT COCKSFOOT
ORCHESTRA BAND GROUP CHAPEL CAPELLE GAMELAN KAPELLE ENSEMBLE GAMELANG SYMPHONY
(— BELLS) GLOCKENSPIEL
(— CIRCLE) PARQUET PARTERRE
(SECTION OF —) BRASS WINDS WOODS STRINGS WOODWINDS PERCUSSION
ORCHESTRATE SCORE ARRANGE COMPOSE
ORCHESTRION HARMONICON APOLLONICON
ORCHID FAAM FAHAM PETAL VANDA CYMBID DUFOIL LAELIA PURPLE AERIDES ANGULOA BOATLIP CALYPSO CULLION FLYWORT LYCASTE POGONIA VANILLA ARETHUSA CALANTHE DENDROBE GYNANDER LABELLUM RAMSHEAD SATYRION CORALROOT HABENARIA TWAYBLADE
ORCHIS CROWTOE CROWFOOT CRAKEFEET
ORDAIN LAW PUT DEEM DOOM LOOK MAKE SEND WILL WITE ALLOT ENACT JAPAN ORDER SHAPE WIELD WRITE DECREE PRIEST ADJUDGE APPOINT ARRANGE BEHIGHT COMMAND DESTINE DICTATE FORTUNE INSTALL PREPARE
ORDEAL FIRE GAFF TEST TRIAL CALVARY GAUNTLET
(— TREE) AKAZGA TANGHIN TANGUIN

ORDER BAN BID RAY SAY TAX BOON CALL CASE CHIT FIAT FORM ORDO RANK RULE SAND SECT STOP SUIT TELL TIFF TRIM WILL WORD ALIGN ARRAY CHIME CLASS DIGHT EDICT GENUS GRADE GUIDE HAVOC PRESS QUIET RANGE SHIFT STATE TAXIS WHACK ASSIGN AVAUNT BILLET CEDULA CHARGE COSMOS CURFEW DECREE DEGREE DEMAND DIRECT ENJOIN FIRMAN FOLLOW GRAITH HOOKUM INDENT KILTER MANAGE METHOD NATURE ORDAIN POLICE POTENT SERIES SETTLE SYNTAX SYSTEM ADJUDGE ARRANGE BESPEAK BIDDING BOOKING COMMAND COMPOSE DISPOSE EMBARGO FLOATER MANDATE PRECEPT PROCESS SOCIETY KODASHIM
(— OF ANGELS) CHOIR QUIRE MIGHTS THRONES DOMINIONS
(— OF BELLS) CHANGE
(— OF COURT) SIST VACATUR
(— OF HOLY BEINGS) HIERARCHY
(— OF WORSHIP) AGODUM
(— OFF) TURN
(— TOBACCO LEAF) CASE
(CIVIL —) EUNOMY
(COSMIC —) TAO RITA
(GOOD —) EUTAXY
(KNIGHTHOOD —) DANNEBROG
(LACKING —) AMISS MESSY MUSSY ROUGH CHAOTIC UNKEMPT CONFUSED
(LEGAL —) SIST STET WRIT DAYWRIT SUMMONS SENTENCE SUBPOENA
(LOWER — OF MAN) ALALUS
(MINOR CHURCH —) BENET
(MONASTIC —) SAMGHA SANGHA
(TRAIN —) FLIMSY
(UNIVERSAL —) KIND
(WRITTEN —) CHECK DRAFT BILLET DRAUGHT
ORDERED BANDBOX BESPOKE REGULAR SCRAPED COHERENT
(WELL —) TRIM
ORDERLINESS METHOD SYSTEM CLARITY DECORUM
ORDERLY AIDE DULY NEAT RULY SNOD TIDY TRIM CRISP SOWAR SUWAR BATMAN BURSCH COSMIC FORMAL MODEST ORDENE GRADELY REGULAR SHAPELY DECOROUS GALLOPER GRAITHLY OBEDIENT PEACEABLE SHIPSHAPE
ORDINANCE LAW DOOM FIAT RITE BYLAW EDICT ASSIZE DECREE RECESS CONTROL MANDATE SETNESS STATUTE WORKING DECRETUM JUDICIAL REGIMENT TAKKANAH DIRECTION
ORDINANT DIHELY DIHELIOS DIHELIUM
ORDINARY LAY LOW SOS FESS LALA MEAN PALL RUCK BANAL CROSS NOMIC PLAIN PROSE USUAL COMMON FILLET MODERN NORMAL

PAIRLE SIMPLE VULGAR AVERAGE NATURAL PROSAIC SALTIRE SAUTIER TRIVIAL VULGATE EVERYDAY FAMILIAR HABITUAL MEDIOCRE MIDDLING PLEBEIAN RUMTYTOO WORKADAY QUOTIDIAN SHAKEFORK
ORDINATE ORDER ORDAIN APPOINT ORDERLY REGULAR MODERATE TEMPERATE
ORDNANCE LAW GUNS ARMOR ORGUE FALCON MINION PETARD PEDRERO RABINET SERPENT WEAPONS BASILISK PETERERO ARTILLERY
ORDO ORDER ALMANAC DIRECTORY
ORE (ALSO SEE MINERAL) TIN CHAT DISH DRAG FELL GOLD IRON LEAD MINE POST PULP ROCK CRAZE CRUDE FAVOR GLORY GRACE HONOR MANTO MERCY METAL PRILL COPPER CUPRITE FLOATER RESPECT SEAWEED SMEDDUM CLEMENCY KNOCKING CARBONATE REVERENCE
(— CRUSHER) DOLLY
(— DEPOSIT) LODE SCRIN BONANZA
(— LAYER) SEAM STOPE
(— LOADING PLATFORM) PLAT
(— MASS) SQUAT
(— NOT DRESSED) WORK
(— WITH STONE ADHERING) CHAT CHATS
(BROKEN —) DIRT
(CRUDE —) HEADS
(CUBE —) SIDERITE
(EARTHY-LOOKING —) PACO
(HORSEFLESH —) BORNITE
(IMPURE —) SPEISS HALVANS
(IRON —) OCHER OCHRE MINION IRONMAN LIMNITE MINETTE OLIGIST TURGITE HEMATITE JACUTINGA
(LEAD —) BOOZE GALENA
(LUMP OF —) HARDHEAD
(MERCURY —) GRANZA CINNABAR
(SOLID —) RIB
(TIN —) ROWS CRAZE SCOVE WHITS FLORAN TINSTUFF
(WORTHLESS —) SLAG DROSS MATTE
OREAD PERI NYMPH

OREGON

MOUNTAIN RANGE: BLUE COAST CASCADE
RIVER: ROGUE IMNAHA OWYHEE POWDER UMPQUA BLITZEN KLAMATH SILVIES COLUMBIA DESCHUTES
STATE BIRD: MEADOWLARK
STATE FLOWER: GRAPE
STATE NICKNAME: BEAVER
STATE TREE: FIR
TOWN: NYSSA EUGENE ASTORIA PORTLAND CORVALLIS

ORE-PRODUCING QUICK
ORESTES (FATHER OF —) AGAMEMNON
(FRIEND OF —) PYLADES
(MOTHER OF —) CLYTEMNESTRA
(SISTER OF —) ELECTRA IPHIGENIA
(WIFE OF —) HERMIONE
ORGAN CUP GILL LIMB PART CHELA FLOAT GREAT HEART MEANS PAPER REGAL SERRA ELATER FEEDER FEELER HAPTOR MEDIUM SPLEEN SUCKER CONSOLE JOURNAL ARMATURE EFFECTOR ISOGRAFT MAGAZINE MELODICA MYCETOME EQUIPMENT HARMONIUM NEWSPAPER PORTATIVE
(— GALLERY) LOFT
(— OF HEARING) EAR
(— OF SENSE) SENSE SENSORY
(— OF SILKWORM) FILATOR
(— OF TOUCH) TACTOR TACTUS
(— PIPE) REED FLUTE SCHWEGEL
(— STOP) ECHO HARP OBOE SEXT TUBA VIOL ACUTA DOLCE FLUTE ORAGE QUINT TENTH VIOLA BIDARA CURTAL CYMBAL DECIMA DULCET FUGARA GEDACT NASARD OCTAVE SCHARF TIERCE TROMBA BASSOON BOMBARD BOURDON CELESTE CLARION CREMONA DOLCIAN DOUBLET DULCIAN FAGOTTO GEDECKT PICCOLO POSAUNE SERPENT TERTIAN TRUMPET TWELFTH VIOLINA BOMBARDE CARILLON CLARINET DIAPASON DULCIANA GEMSHORN REGISTER TENOROON TROMBONE WALDHORN DOUBLETTE HARMONICA PRINCIPAL SAXOPHONE
(— VIBRATO) TREMOLO
(BRISTLELIKE —) SETA
(CHINESE —) CHENG
(HAND —) SERINETTE
(OLFACTORY —) NOSE
(RESPIRATORY —) LUNG
(SMALL —) REGAL
(VOCAL — OF BIRDS) SYRINX
(WASTE —) KIDNEY
ORGANIC VITAL INBORN NATURAL INHERENT
ORGANISM WOG BODY ECAD GERM GUEST PLANT AEROBE ANIMAL EMBRYO SYSTEM DIPLONT DISEASE MACHINE PLANONT SUSCEPT

HEMAMEBA PATHOGEN PLANKTER MESOPHILE
(— CHARACTERISTIC) MIXIS
(COMPOUND —) STOCK
(MINUTE —) AMEBA MONAD SPORE
(MODIFIED —) ECAD
(PELAGIC —S) NEKTON
(POLITICAL —) LEVIATHAN
(SIMPLE —) MONAD
(PL.) BENTHON BENTHOS HAYSEED NEUSTON
ORGANIZATION ART BIG ITO CLUB FIRM KLAN CADRE FIDAC FORUM HOUSE MAFIA SETUP AUMAGA CHURCH OUTFIT SURVEY SYSTEM CHARITY COMPANY CONCERN DEMOLAY ECONOMY GIDEONS MENORAH SOCIETY CONGRESS PATRONAGE STRUCTURE
(— OF ACTORS) COMPANY
(— OF DEALERS) AUCTION
(— OF EXPERIENCE) SCHEMA
(— WITH MANY BRANCHES) OCTOPUS
(ARMY —) LANDSTORM
(AUXILIARY —) AID SYNODICAL
(COLLEGE —) FRAT ALUMNA ALUMNI ALUMNUS SORORITY
(JEWISH —) ITO MENORAH
(MUSICAL —) BAND COMBO CAPELLE KAPELLE ENSEMBLE ORCHESTRA
(POLICE —) GESTAPO
(POLITICAL —) PARTY VEREIN HETAERIA HETAIRIA APPARATUS
(SAMOAN —) AUMAGA
(SECRET —) WOW BPOE ELKS MOOSE MASONS MIDEWIN
(SOCIAL —) POLICE
(WAR VETERANS —) AVC DAV GAR SAR VFW FIDAC AMVETS
(WOMEN'S —) DAR WAF WRC WCTU SORORITY
ORGANIZE FORM EDIFY FOUND MODEL RALLY DESIGN EMBODY ARRANGE MODULIZE REGIMENT UNIONIZE BLUEPRINT INSTITUTE INTEGRATE STRUCTURE
ORGANIZED FORMED ORGANIC
(BADLY —) INCONDITE
ORGIASTIC SATURNALIAN
ORGY LARK RITE ROMP BINGE REVEL SPREE FROLIC SHINDY REVELRY WASSAIL CAROUSAL CEREMONY
(PL.) ORGIACS DEBAUCHERIES
ORIANA (FATHER OF —) LISUARTE
(LOVER OF —) AMADIS
ORIBI OUREBI ANTELOPE BLEEKBOK PALEBUCK
ORIEL BAY CHAPEL DORMER RECESS WINDOW BALCONY GALLERY MIRADOR PORTICO CORRIDOR
ORIENT DAWN EAST ADAPT BUILD PEARL PLACE SHEEN ADJUST LEVANT LOCATE LUSTER RISING GLOWING INCLINE RADIANT SUNRISE LUSTROUS SPARKLING
ORIENTAL ASIAN PEARL BRIGHT

INDIAN ORTIVE RISING EASTERN SHINING INDOGEAN LUSTROUS PELLUCID PRECIOUS BRILLIANT LEVANTINE
ORIENTATION ASPECT PHORIA STRIKE COLORING LOCALITY
ORIFICE BUNG HOLE PORE VENT INLET MOUTH STOMA BLOWER CAVITY OUTLET RICTUS SIPHON THROAT CHIMNEY EARHOLE FORAMEN OPENING OSCULUM OSTIOLE APERTURE FUMAROLE INTROITUS
(— IN VOLCANIC REGION) FUMAROLE
(— OF INFUNDIBULUM) LURA
(BREATHING —) SPIRACLE
(VOLCANIC —) BLOWER
ORIGANUM ORGANY MARJORAM ORGAMENT
ORIGIN NEE GERM KIND RISE ROOT SEED BIRTH CAUSE START STOCK FATHER GROWTH NATURE PARENT SOURCE SPRING EDITION GENESIS LINEAGE UPSTART NASCENCE UPSPRING BEGINNING INCEPTION OFFSPRING PARENTAGE
(— ON EARTH) EPIGENE
(FOREIGN —) ECDEMIC
ORIGINAL NEW HOME SEED FIRST FRESH NOVEL PRIME STOCK FONTAL NATIVE PRIMAL PRIMER SAMPLE PRIMARY RADICAL SEMINAL NASCENCY PRISTINE AUTHENTIC AUTOGRAPH BEGINNING INVENTIVE OFFSPRING PRIMITIVE
(NOT —) DERIVED
ORIGINALITY INGENUITY
ORIGINATE COIN COME DATE GROW HEAD MAKE MOVE OPEN REAR RISE SIRE ARISE BEGIN BIRTH BREED CAUSE ENDOW FOUND HATCH RAISE START AUTHOR CREATE DERIVE DESIGN DEVISE FATHER INVENT SPRING CAUSATE DESCEND EMANATE PROCEED PRODUCE COMMENCE CONCEIVE CONTRIVE DISCOVER GENERATE INITIATE INSTITUTE
ORIGINATION DESCENT GENESIS BREEDING ORIGINAL COSMOGONY ETYMOLOGY
ORIGINATOR AUTHOR FATHER CREATOR INVENTOR GENERATOR
ORIOLE PIROL BUNYAH LARIOT LORIOT CACIQUE FIGBIRD PEABIRD FIREBIRD GOLDBIRD HANGBIRD HANGNEST TROUPIAL
ORION RIGEL ALGEBAR
(BELT OF —) ELLWAND
(HOUND OF —) ARATUS
(SLAYER OF —) ARTEMIS
ORKNEY ISLANDS (CAPITAL OF —) KIRKWALL
(ISLAND OF —) HOY POMONA ROUSAY SANDAY STRONSAY
ORLE ORLET BORDER FILLET WREATH BEARING CHAPLET TRESSURE

ORLOP DECK ARLOUP
ORMER ABALONE
ORMOLU GILT GOLD ALLOY BRASS
VARNISH
ORNAMENT BOB DUB FLY FOB GAY
JOY PIN POT TAG TEE TOY URN
BALL BOSS CURL DICE ETCH FALL
FRET FROG GAUD GEAR HUSK
KNOP LEAF NULL OUCH RULE STAR
TOOL TRIM WALY WING ADORN
BRAID BULLA CHASE CROSS CROWN
DECOR EXORN FUSEE GRACE
GUTTA HELIX HONOR INLAY LUNET
MENSK MENSO OVOID PATCH
POPPY PRUNT SPANG SPRAY SPRIG
STALK TRAIL TRICK WALLY AMULET
ANKLET ATTIRE BEDAUB BEDECK
BILLET BRANCH BROOCH BUTTON
CIMIER COLLAR DIAPER DOODAD
EDGING EMBOSS ENRICH FINERY
FLORET FLOWER GORGET INSERT
LABRET LUNULA NIELLO OFFSET
PAMPRE PARURE PATERA ROCOCO
ROSACE RUNTEE SETOFF TABLET
TAHALI TEMPLE TIRADE AGREMEN
AKROTER AMALAKA BIBELOT
BUCRANE CIRCLET COCARDE
CORBEIL CROCKET EARPLUG
ECHINUS ENGRAVE ENHANCE
FURNISH GADROON GARNISH
NETSUKE RINCEAU SEXFOIL STRIGIL
TREFOIL TRINKET APPLIQUE
DECORATE FLOURISH GIMCRACK
LAVALIER SWASTIKA
(— FOR HEAD) MIND TARGET
(— ON SHIP) BADGE
(CHILD'S —) GAY
(CLAW-LIKE —) GRIFFE
(DRESS —) FROG LACE JABOT
SEQUIN SPANGLE
(HEAD —) TIARA TEMPLE
(HORSE COLLAR —) HOUNCE
(MUSICAL —) TURN
(PENDANT —) BOB BULLA ANADEM
BANGLE TASSEL EARRING LAVALIER
(SHOULDER —) EPAULET
(TAWDRY —) GINGERBREAD
(PL.) FIGGERY KNAVERY AGREMENS
ORNAMENTAL FANCY CHICHI FRILLY
LILYTURN BLUEBEARD
ORNAMENTATION BOSS FOIL
ACORN DECOR ADORNO BABERY
CHICHI CILERY DICING CUSPING
ECHELLE LACWORK STYLING
FROUFROU HEADWORK PURFLING
ROCAILLE STAFFAGE TRESSURE
(CHEAP —) TINSEL
(EXTRAVAGANT —) ROCOCO
(MUSICAL —) GRUPPO GRUPPETTO
ORNAMENTED FIGURY FOILED
ORNATE TAWDRY ADORNED
FLOUNCY FROSTED TREFLEE
WROUGHT GOFFERED SINNOWED
ELABORATE STELLATED
ORNATE GAY FINE FANCY FUSSY
GIDDY SHOWY DRESSY FLORID
FLOSSY PURPLE SUPERB AUREATE
BAROQUE FLOWERY TAFFETA
MANDARIN OVERRIPE SPLENDID

ELABORATE UNNATURAL
(EXTREMELY —) GIDDY
ORNERY CONTRARY
ORNITHOLOGIST AUDUBON
BIRDMAN
OROTUND FULL CLEAR SHOWY
MELLOW STRONG POMPOUS
RESONANT SONOROUS BOMBASTIC
ORP FRET WEEP
ORPHAN PIP WARD FOUNDLING
STEPCHILD
ORPHANED ORBATE
ORPHEUS (BIRTHPLACE OF —)
PIERIA
(FATHER OF —) APOLLO OEAGRUS
(MOTHER OF —) CALLIOPE
(WIFE OF —) EURYDICE
ORPHREY BAND BORDER
ORPIMENT ORPIN HARTAL SPIRIT
ARSENIC HARTAIL
ORPINE SEDUM LIVELONG
BAGLEAVES EVERGREEN
ORRA ODD IDLE ORROW WORTHLESS
ORRIS GIMP IRIS LACE BRAID
ORRICE GALLOON
ORT BIT END CRUMB SCRAP MORSEL
REFUSE TRIFLE LEAVING REMNANT
FRAGMENT LEFTOVER
ORTHODOX GOOD GREEK SOUND
USUAL PROPER CANONIC CORRECT
ACCEPTED STANDARD CUSTOMARY
ORTHODOXY TRUTH SOUNDNESS
ORTHOGRAPHY WRITING
ORTHOPTERON WALKER
ORTOLAN BIRD RAIL SORA BUNTING
BOBOLINK WHEATEAR
ORTSTEIN HARDPAN
ORYX BEISA PASANG PASENG
GAZELLE GEMSBOK ANTELOPE
LEUCORYX
OS BONE ESKAR ESKER MOUTH
OPENING ORIFICE
OSAGE ORANGE HEDGE OSAGE
BODOCK BOWWOOD
OSCILLATE LOG WAG HUNT ROCK
SWAY VARY SQUEG SWING WAVER
WEAVE SHIMMY FEATHER VIBRATE
FLUCTUATE
OSCILLATION HOWL WAVE SHOCK
SEICHE SHIMMY SQUEAL FLUTTER
LIBRATION VIBRATION
OSCULATE BUSS KISS
OSCULATORY PAX
OSIER ROD WAND EDDER SALIX
SKEIN SPLIT WITHY BASKET
SALLOW WICKER WILLOW
DOGWOOD WILGERS REDBRUSH
(— CAGE) TUMBREL
(— WILLOW) TWIGWITHY
OSIRIS HERSHEF UNNEFER
(BROTHER OF —) SET SETH
(CROWN OF —) ATEF
(FATHER OF —) GEB KEB SEB
(MOTHER OF —) NUT
(SISTER OF —) ISIS
(SON OF —) HORUS ANUBIS
(WIFE OF —) ISIS
OSMANLI TURK TURKISH
OSPREY GLED HAWK OSSI GLEDE

BALBUSARD OSSIFRAGE
OSSATURE SKELETON OSSEMENTS
OSSE DARE ATTEMPT PRESAGE
PROMISE VENTURE PROPHESY
RECOMMEND UTTERANCE
OSSEOUS BONE BONY SPINY LITHIC
OSTEAL
OSSICLE BONE INCUS ADORAL
STAPES ALVEOLE BONELET
MALLEUS SCUTELLA
OSSIFICATION OSTOSIS UROSTEON
METOSTEON SIDEBONES
OSSUARY URN TOMB GRAVE VAULT
OSSARIUM
OSTEND SHOW REVEAL EXHIBIT
MANIFEST
OSTENSIBLE SEEMING APPARENT
SPECIOUS
OSTENT AIR MIEN SIGN TOKEN
DISPLAY PORTENT
OSTENTATION POMP SHOW CLASS
ECLAT FLARE PRIDE STRUT SWANK
VAUNT PARADE DISPLAY FLUTTER
PAGEANT PORTENT PRESAGE
FLOURISH FRIPPERY PRETENSE
SHOWINESS SPECTACLE
OSTENTATIOUS ARTY LOUD GAUDY
SHOWY SWANK FLASHY SPORTY
SWANKY TURGID FLAUNTY GLARING
OBVIOUS POMPOUS SPLASHY
FASTUOUS ELABORATE
OSTERIA INN TAVERN
OSTIOLE PORE MOUTH STOMA
OPENING ORIFICE APERTURE
OSTRACIZE BAN BAR CUT SNUB
EXILE BANISH PUNISH REJECT
ABOLISH CENSURE EXCLUDE
BLACKBALL PROSCRIBE
OSTRACON SHELL FRAGMENT
POTSHERD
OSTRICH EMU RHEA NANDU
BREVIPEN STRUCION
(— FEATHER) BOO
(JERKED —) BILTONG
OSTYAK KHANTY
OSWEGO TEA BALM
OTAHEITE TAHITI
(— APPLE) HEVI MACUPI
OTALGIA EARACHE
OTHELLO MOOR
(FRIEND OF —) IAGO
(WIFE OF —) DESDEMONA
OTHER HE MO ELSE MORE ALTER
FORMER NOTHER SECOND TIDDER
TOTHER ALTERUM FURTHER
DISTINCT DIFFERENT
(COMB. FORM) HETERO
(PL.) LAVE REST LUTRA
OTHERNESS ALTERITY
OTHERWISE OR NOT ELSE ENSE
ALIAS SECUS ALITER EXCEPT
BESIDES ELSEHOW ELSEWAY
OTIC AURAL AUDITORY ORACULAR
AURICULAR
OTIOSE IDLE LAZY VAIN ALOOF
FUTILE OTIANT REMOTE STERILE
USELESS INACTIVE INDOLENT
REPOSING

OTOLITH SAGITTA LAPILLUS
OTOSTEON
OTOLOGIST AURIST
OTTAVINO PICCOLO
OTTER DOG FUR PUP FISH NAIR
PELT BITCH HURON LOUTRE
SIMUNG TACKLE ANNATTO PERIQUE
MAMPALON MUSTELIN PARAVANE
(— TAIL) POLE
(DEN OF — S) HOLT
(SEA —) KALAN
OTTOMAN (ALSO SEE TURKEY)
POUF SEAT TURK COUCH DIVAN
SQUAB STOOL FABRIC OTHMAN
POUFFE SULTANE FOOTSTOOL
(— COURT) PORTE
(— GOVERNOR) PASHA
(— LEADER) OSMAN
(— PROVINCE) VILAYET
(— STANDARD) ALEM
(— SUBJECT) RAIA RAYAH
OUABE HOGNUT
OUAKARI ACARI UKARI MONKEY
UAKARI
OUCH OH OW ADORN BEZEL CLASP
JEWEL NOUCH BROOCH FIBULA
NOUCHE BRACELET NECKLACE
ORNAMENT
OUGHT BIT BUD BUT MOW BOOD
BOOT MOTE MUST ZERO SHALL
BELONG CIPHER NAUGHT NOUGHT
SHOULD BEHOOVE
OUNCE URE OKET OKIA ONCA ONCE
ONZA OKIEH UNCIA CHEETAH
LEOPARD WILDCAT
(EIGHT —S) CUPFUL
(ONE-16TH OF —) DRAM
(ONE-20TH OF —) EASTERLING
(ONE-8TH OF —) DRAM
OUPHE ELF OOF OUF GOBLIN
OUR UR ORE URE WER WIR HORE
NOTRE UNSER
(— LORD) NS
(— SAVIOR) NSIC
OURICURY LICURI LICURY
CABECUDO
OURSELVES USSELF USSELS
USSELVEN
OUSIA NATURE ESSENCE
SUBSTANCE
OUST BAR BUMP FIRE SACK CHUCK
EJECT EVICT EXPEL BANISH
DEBOUT REMOVE CASHIER DISCARD
DISMISS SUSPEND DISSEIZE
FORJUDGE ELIMINATE
OUSTING AMOTION
OUT EX AWAY DOWN HORS FORTH
ABSENT BEGONE ISSUED OOTWITH
OUTWARD EXTERNAL PUBLISHED
(— LOUD) BOST
(— OF BREATH) BLOWN
(— OF COMMISSION) BUNG
(— OF DATE) OLD DOWDY PASSE
OUTWORN TIMEWORN OVERDATED
(— OF DOORS) FOREIGN THEREOUT
(— OF EXISTENCE) AWAY
(— OF KILTER) ALOP AWRY CRANK
BROKEN

(— OF ONE'S MIND) FEY DAFT
DELEERIT
(— OF ORDER) AMISS KAPUT
FAULTY DEFICIENT
(— OF PLACE) AMISS INEPT
(— OF PLAY) DEAD FOUL
(— OF SIGHT) DOGGO INVISIBLE
(— OF SORTS) CROOK CROSS
HUMPY NOHOW COMICAL PEEVISH
(— OF THE WAY) BY BYE ASIDE
BLIND CLEAR CLOSE AFIELD
REMOTE
(— OF THIS LIFE) HYNE
(— OF TUNE) FALSE SCORDATO
(— OF) EX FROM DEHORS OUTWITH
(FARTHER —) UTTER
OUTAGE VENT ULLAGE HEADSPACE
OUT-AND-OUT GROSS SHEER
SWORN UTTER ARRANT DIRECT
WHOLLY ABSOLUTE COMPLETE
CRASHING
OUTBREAK FIT ROW RASH RIOT
BURST SALLY EMEUTE PLAGUE
REVOLT RUCKUS TUMULT UPROAR
BOUTADE OUTCROP RUCTION
BLIZZARD ERUPTION OUTBURST
EXPLOSION
(— OF EMOTIONALISM) HYSTERIA
(— OF TEMPER) MOORBURN
(SUDDEN —) SPURT
OUTBUILDING BARN SHED LODGE
PRIVY BARTON GARAGE HEMMEL
OUTHOUSE SKEELING SKILLING
BACKHOUSE
OUTBURST BOUT CROW FLAW FUME
GALE GUST RAGE TIFF AGONY
BLAST BLAZE BREAK BRUNT BURST
FLARE FLASH GEARE SALLY SPATE
START STORM ACCESS BLOWER
BLOWUP ESCAPE FANTAD FANTOD
GOLLER TIRADE TUMULT BLOWOUT
OUTCROP PASSION TANTRUM
TORRENT ERUPTION EXPLOSION
(— OF ANGER) FIT GERE GEARE
TATTER
(— OF ORATORY) SQUIRT
(— OF SPEECH) STRAIN
(— OF TEMPER) FUFF TIFF
BLOWOUT
(SPACE —) SUPERNOVA
OUTCAST EXILE LEPER RONIN
SHREW ABJECT PARIAH AOUTLET
ISHMAEL MISSILE OUTWALE
CASTAWAY CHANDALA REJECTED
VAGABOND DIALONIAN
(HOMELESS —) ARAB
(JAPANESE —) ETA RONIN
OUTCOME END OUT FATE TERM
CLOSE EDUCT EVENT HATCH ISSUE
LOOSE PROOF UPSET BROWST
EFFECT EXITUS OUTLET PERIOD
RESULT SEQUEL UPSHOT EMANATE
PROGENY SUCCESS FATALITY
AFTERMATH
OUTCROP CROP LEDGE BASSET
BLOSSOM BLOWOUT OUTBREAK
OUTBURST
OUTCROPPING BULT SCABROCK
OUTCRY CAW CRY HUE YIP BAWL

BRAY DITE GAFF HOWL REAM ROAR
SCRY UTAS YARM YELL ALARM
BOAST DITTY NOISE OUTAS SHOUT
STINK WHAUP BELLOW CLAMOR
HOLLER RACKET SCREAM SHRIEK
STEVEN TUMULT CALLING EXCLAIM
PROTEST SCREECH SHILLOO
COMPLAINT PHILLILEW
(PUBLIC —) STINK
OUTDATED CRINOLINE
OUTDISTANCE DROP SKIN OUTGO
SURPASS OUTSTRIP
OUTDO CAP COB COP COW POT TOP
BANG BEAT BEST FLOG EXCEL
OUTGO TRUMP WORSE DEFEAT
EXCEED OUTACT NONPLUS
SURPASS OVERCOME
OUTDOORS FORTH OUTBY OUTBYE
OUTSIDE
OUTER BUT ALIEN ECTAD ECTAL
UPPER UTTER FOREIGN OUTSIDE
OUTWARD EXTERIOR EXTERNAL
FORINSEC
OUTERMOST FINAL UTTER UTMOST
EVEREST EXTREME OUTWARD
FARTHEST REMOTEST
OUTFACE DEFY RESIST SUBDUE
CONFRONT OVERCOME
OUTFIELDER GARDENER OUTSCOUT
OUTFIT KIT RIG GANG GARB REAR
REEK SUIT TEAM UNIT DRESS EQUIP
GETUP HABIT TROUP ATTIRE
CONREY DUFFEL FITOUT LAYOUT
CLOTHES FURNISH SHEBANG
EQUIPAGE FURNITURE GRUBSTAKE
(INFANT'S —) LAYETTE
(SPARE —) CHANGE
OUTFLANK OUTWING OVERWING
OUTFLOW FLUX DRAIN ISSUE
OUTGO EFFLUX ESCAPE OUTPOUR
OUTGO EXIT EXCEL ISSUE OUTDO
EFFLUX EGRESS EXCEED OUTLAY
OUTLET OUTRUN OUTCOME
PRODUCT SURPASS OUTSTRIP
OUTGROWTH BUD JAG FOOT HAIR
LEAF MOSS SPUR CLAMP FRUIT
HILUM HYPHA SCALE SPINE ACULEA
COCKLE CUPULE FIBRIL ENATION
FEATHER ISIDIUM APPENDIX
EPIDERMA HAPTERON INDUSIUM
OFFSHOOT CARBUNCLE
EMERGENCE
OUTHOUSE SHED SKEO BIFFY
LODGE PRIVY BIGGIN LINHAY
OUTHUT LATRINE SKEELING
SKILLION
OUTING OUT SKIP STAY TRIP
JUNKET PICNIC COOKOUT HOLIDAY
CLAMBAKE VACATION WAYGOOSE
EXCURSION WAYZGOOSE
OUTLANDER PARDESI
OUTLANDISH ALIEN EXOTIC REMOTE
BIZARRE FOREIGN STRANGE
UNCOUTH PECULIAR BARBAROUS
FANTASTIC GROTESQUE UNEARTHLY
OUTLAST ELAPSE SURVIVE
OVERBIDE
OUTLAW BAN BAR CACO HORN
TORY EXILE EXLEX FLEME RONIN

ARRANT BADMAN BANDIT BANISH BRUMBY COWBOY DACOIT UNLEDE BANDIDO ISHMAEL FUGITATE FUGITIVE PROHIBIT PROSCRIBE PROSCRIPT
(IRISH —) WOODKERN
(JAPANESE —) RONIN
(PL.) MANZAS
OUTLAWED ILLEGAL ILLICIT LAWLESS
OUTLAWRY EXILE UTLAGARY
OUTLAY COST OUTGO EXPENSE PENSION
OUTLET BORE DRIP EXIT VENT ISSUE EGRESS ESCAPE EXITUS FUNNEL OUTAGE OPENING FUMEDUCT OVERFLOW SINKHOLE AVOIDANCE
(— FOR COASTAL SWAMP) BAYOU
(— OF CARBURETOR) BARREL
(— OF SPRING) EYE
(AIR —) GRILL GRILLE
OUTLIER KLIP KLIPPE
OUTLINE MAP BOSH ETCH FLOW FORM LINE PLAN PLAT BRIEF CHALK CHART DRAFT FRAME MODEL SHAPE TRACE AGENDA APERCU DESIGN DOODLE FIGURE FILLET LAYOUT SCHEMA SCHEME SCROLL SKETCH SURVEY CAPSULE CONTOUR DRAUGHT ELEMENT EXTRACT FEATURE GABARIT ISOTYPE PROFILE SUMMARY DESCRIBE SKELETON SYLLABUS SYNOPSIS GUIDELINE TREATMENT
(— HASTILY) SPLASH
(— OF A SCIENCE) GRUNDRISS
(— OF ANIMAL'S BODY) UNDERLINE
(— OF PLAY) SCENARIO
(— SHARPLY) ITALICIZE
(CURVING —) SWING
(DOUBLE —) FRINGE
(SHADOWY —) GHOST
OUTLIVE OUTLAST OUTWEAR SURVIVE OVERBIDE
OUTLOOK MIND VIEW FRONK FRONT VISTA ASPECT CLIMATE LOOKOUT PURVIEW FRONTAGE OUTSIGHT PROSPECT
(BRASH —) FACE
(MEDICAL —) PROGNOSIS
(SELF-CONFIDENT —) SWAGGER
OUTMANEUVER HAVE OUTPLAY
OUTMODED COLD DATED KARUT PASSE RUSTY BYGONE EFFETE ANTIQUE ELDERLY OBSOLETE
OUTPLAY HAVE
OUTPOST STATION FOREPOST OUTGUARD
OUTPOURING FLOW GALE GUSH FLOOD RIVER EARFUL LAVISH STREAM OUTFLOW FUSILLADE
OUTPUT CUT GET CROP MAKE EXPEL GRIST POWER YIELD ENERGY UPCOME TURNOUT
OUTRAGE RAPE ABUSE INSULT OFFEND RAVISH ABUSION AFFRONT OFFENSE VIOLATE VIOLENCE INDIGNITY

OUTRAGEOUS ENORM DAMNED HEINOUS OBSCENE UNGODLY FLAGRANT INFERNAL SHAMEFUL SHOCKING ATROCIOUS DESPERATE MONSTROUS
OUTRANK CAMP PREFER SURPASS
OUTRE ODD BIZARRE STRANGE ECCENTRIC
OUTREACH CHEAT EXCEED EXTEND OUTWIT SEARCH DECEIVE SURPASS OVERREACH
OUTRIDER HAYDUK HEIDUK HEYDUCK
(PL.) SWING
OUTRIGGER BOOM PROA BUMKIN RIGGER SPIDER
OUTRIGHT RUN BALD CLEAN TOTAL WHOLE DIRECT ENTIRE OPENLY WHOLLY ABSOLUTE COMPLETE DIRECTLY ENTIRELY
OUTRIVAL WIN EXCEL OUTDO DEFEAT ECLIPSE SURPASS
OUTRUN BEAT COTE NICK PASS OUTGO EXCEED ATRENNE FORERUN OUTFOOT PREVENT
OUTRUSH GUST
OUTSET START SETOUT BEGINNING THRESHOLD
OUTSHINE BLIND EXCEL OUTDO STAIN DAZZLE DEFACE DISTAIN SURPASS OVERSHINE
OUTSIDE BUT OUT BOUT FREE OUTBY UTTER AFIELD OUTFACE SURFACE EXTERIOR EXTERNAL
(— BOUNDS) ALOGICAL
(— OF) BESIDE
(COMB. FORM) ECTO
OUTSIDER ALIEN OUTMAN BOUNDER ISHMAEL EXOTERIC STRANGER EXTRANEAN FOREIGNER PHILISTER
OUTSKIRTS SIDE SKIRTS OUTSHIFTS
OUTSMART SLICK
OUTSPOKEN BOLD FREE LOUD APERT BLUFF BLUNT BROAD FRANK NAKED PLAIN ROUND CANDID DIRECT ARTLESS EXPRESS EXPLICIT
OUTSTANDING ACE BIG ARCH RARE AMONG FAMED NOTED SMASH BANNER FAMOUS GIFTED HEROIC MARKED SIGNAL SNAZZY UNPAID EMINENT PALMARY STELLAR SUBLIME SUPREME FABULOUS INSPIRED SEASONED SKELPING SLAMBANG SMACKING STANDOUT BEAUTIFUL PRINCIPAL PROMINENT UNSETTLED
OUTSTAY TARRY
OUTSTRETCHED STENT EXPANDED EXTENDED
OUTSTRIP CAP TOP WIN BEST COTE LEAD LOSE PASS EXCEL OUTDO STRIP EXCEED OUTRUN DEVANCE SURPASS DISTANCE OVERCOME TRANSCEND
OUTVIE SURPASS OUTSTRIP
OUTWARD ECTAD OUTER OVERT DERMAD EXODIC EXTERN FORMAL EXTREME VISIBLE APPARENT EXTERIOR EXTERNAL OBSOLETE

OUTFORTH EXTRINSIC
OUTWEIGH WEIGH OUTPOISE OVERBEAR
OUTWIT FOX POT BALK BEST FOIL HAVE BLOCK CHECK CROSS BAFFLE EUCHRE FICKLE JOCKEY OVERGO THWART STONKER OUTSHARP CROSSBITE OVERREACH
OUTWORK BRAY JETTY FLECHE TENAIL HORNWORK HORSEHOE TENAILLE
OUTWORN WAPPENED
OUZEL PIET AMSEL COLLY OUSEL OWZEL DIPPER THRUSH WHISTLER
OVAL O ELLIPSE STADIUM VESICAL VULVATE AVELONGE NUMMULAR VULVIFORM
OVARY CORAL GONAD GERMEN OARIUM OOPHORON
OVATION HAND APPLAUSE
OVEN OON UMU KILN LEAR LEER LEHR OAST BAKER BENCH GLAZE GLOOM HANGI KOHUA TANUR TILER CALCAR MUFFLE CABOOSE FURNACE KITCHEN
(— FORK) FRUGGAN FRUGGIN
(— MOP) SCOVEL
OVENBIRD BAKER FURNER HORNERO TEACHER ACCENTOR
OVER BY BYE OER TOO ALSO ANEW ATOP BACK DEAD DONE GONE UPON ABOVE AGAIN ALOFT ATOUR ATURN CLEAR ENDED EXTRA VAULT ABROAD ACROSS AROUND BEYOND DESSUS EXCESS UPWARD SURPLUS THROUGH FINISHED
(— AGAINST) FORNENT
(— AND ABOVE) ATOP ATOUR BESIDES
(ALL —) NAPOO NAPOOH SURTOUT
(PREFIX) SUR SUPER SUPRA
OVERABUNDANCE WASTE EXCESS SURPLUS PLETHORA
OVERACT HAM EMOTE OUTDO BURLESQUE
OVERALLS SLIP CHAPS JEANS TONGS DENIMS
OVERAWE COW ABASH DAUNT BUFFALO BROWBEAT
OVERBEARING HIGH PROUD LORDLY OVERLY HAUGHTY ARROGANT BULLYING INSOLENT SNOBBISH IMPERIOUS MASTERFUL
OVERBURDEN COVER HOIST PESTER CONGEST OVERLAY ENCUMBER STRIPPING SURCHARGE
OVERBUSY FUSSY PRAGMATIC
OVERCAST DIM SEW BIND DARK DULL GLUM CLOUD HEAVY SERGE CLOUDY DARKEN GLOOMY LOWERY CLOUDED
OVERCHARGE GYP SOAK CROWD GOUGE STICK STING BURDEN EXCISE OPPRESS EXTORTION
OVERCOAT MINO BENNY GREGO SHUBA BANGUP CAPOTE RAGLAN SLIPON TOPPER ULSTER PALETOT SPENCER SURTOUT TOPCOAT BENJAMIN COONSKIN TAGLIONI

COTHAMORE GREATCOAT
INVERNESS
OVERCOATING DUFFEL DUFFLE
OVERCOME DO AWE GET WAR WIN
BEAT BEST DING LICK LOCK MATE
POOP SACK SUNK TAME WAUR
CHARM CRUCH DAUNT DROUK
DROWN FORDO STILL STOOP
THROW APPALL BEATEN BUSHED
CRAVEN DEFEAT EXCEED FOREDO
HURDLE MASTER OUTRAY PLUNGE
SUBDUE VICTOR CONFUTE
CONQUER DEPRESS ENFORCE
RECOVER SMOTHER CONVINCE
OUTSTRIP SUPERATE SURMOUNT
SURPRISE
(— **DIFFICULTIES**) SWIM
(— **WITH FATIGUE**) FORDO FOREDO
(— **WITH WEARINESS**) HEAVY
(**BE** — **BY HEAT**) SWELTER
OVERCONFIDENT SECURE POSITIVE
OVERCROWD CONGEST
SURCHARGE
OVERDECORATED GARISH
OVERDEVELOPED GAUDY
OVERDO EXCEED EXHAUST FATIGUE
PERCOCT OVERCOOK OVERWORK
BURLESQUE
OVERDONE FUSTIAN EXUBERANT
OVERDOSE SICKENER
OVERDRESS SAC SACK DIZEN
SAQUE POLONAISE
OVERDRIED SLEEPY
OVERDUE BACK LATE TARDY
UNPAID ARREARS BELATED
DELAYED EXCESSIVE
OVEREAGER FEVERISH FEVEROUS
OVEREAT GORGE SLOFF SATIATE
GOURMAND
OVERELABORATE NIGGLE
OVEREXERT TORLE TORFEL
OVERPLY
OVERFED RANK FULSOME
OVERFLOW REE COME FLUX SLOP
SWIM TEEM VENT BRIME FLOAT
FLOOD SPATE SPILL ABOUND
DEBORD OUTLET OVERRUN
REDOUND BOILOVER EXUNDATE
INUNDATE OUTSWELL SUBMERGE
(— **FROM MOLD**) SPEW SPUE
OVERFLOWING FLOW AWASH
FLOAT DELAVY DELUGE ALLUVIO
COPIOUS FRESHET PROFUSE
INUNDANT EXUBERANT LANDFLOOD
SUPERFLUX
OVERGARMENT SMOCK BLOUSE
DUSTER
OVERGROWN FOZY RANK GAWKY
BRANCHY FULSOME SPRATTY
SPRITTY
OVERHAND WHIP
OVERHANG JUT BEND EAVE RAKE
BULGE JETTY BEETLE SHELVE
TOPPLE FANTAIL OVERLAP PROJECT
SUSPEND
OVERHANGING BEETLE SHELVY
HANGING PENDENT IMMINENT
OBUMBRANT PENTHOUSE
OVERHAUL EXAMINE OVERHAIL

RENOVATE FOREREACH
OVERHEAD COST ABOVE ALOFT
BURDEN ONCOST UPKEEP EXPENSE
OVERTOP
OVERHEAT PARBOIL
OVERLAP LAP RIDE SYPHER
SHINGLE IMBRICATE INTERSECT
OVERLAPPING JUGATE RIDING
EQUITANT OBVOLUTE IMBRICATE
(— **IN FUGUE**) STRETTA STRETTO
OVERLAY CAP LAP CEIL COAT
APPLY COUCH COVER GLAZE
PATCH PLATE CEMENT CRAVAT
SPREAD STUCCO VENEER ENCRUST
OPPRESS OVERLIE SMOTHER
APPLIQUE TEMPLATE
(— **WITH GOLD**) BEAT GILD
OVERLOAD GLUT CHARGE
ENCUMBER SURCHARGE
OVERLOADED PLETHORIC
PLETHOROUS
OVERLOOK BALK MISS OMIT PASS
SKIP SLIP WINK FORGO ACQUIT
EXCUSE FOREGO FORGET IGNORE
MANAGE OVERGO ABSOLVE
COMMAND CONDONE FORGIVE
INSPECT MISKNOW NEGLECT
CONFOUND DOMINATE DISREGARD
DISSEMBLE
OVERLOOKER GAITER
OVERLORD LIEGE DESPOT ISWARA
SATRAP TYRANT ISHVARA SUZERAIN
TYRANNIZE
OVERLY CAP TOO
OVERLYING BROCHANT INCUMBENT
OVERMAN CHIEF LEADER ARBITER
FOREMAN REFEREE OVERSEER
SUPERMAN
OVERMANTLE (— **TREATMENT**)
TRUMEAU
OVERMASTER GET
OVERMATCH BEST DEFEAT EXCEED
SURPASS VANQUISH
OVERMODEST PRIM PRUDISH
OVERMUCH TOO EXCESS SURPLUS
EXCESSIVE
OVERNICE FEAT FUSS SAUCY
DAINTY QUAINT SPRUCE FINICKY
PRECISE DENTICAL PRECIOUS
SQUEAMISH
OVERPLAY HAM
OVERPOWER AWE BEAT ROUT
RUSH CRUSH DROWN QUELL
SWAMP WHELM COMPEL DEFEAT
DELUGE ENGULF MASTER OVERGO
SUBDUE WRIXLE CONQUER
CONTROL OPPRESS REPRESS
CONVINCE OUTSCOUT SCUMFISH
SURPRISE
(— **WITH HEAT**) SWELT
(— **WITH LIGHT**) DAZZLE
OVERPOWERING DIRE FIERCE
KILLING DAZZLING STUNNING
DESPERATE MONSTROUS
OVERPRECISE FINICKY CLERKISH
PRECIEUSE
OVERREACH DO POT DUPE GRAB
CHEAT COZEN CHOILE GREASE
NOBBLE OUTWIT OVERGO DECEIVE

OVERREADY FORWARD
OVERREFINED QUAINT PRECIOUS
OVERRIPE FRACID SQUSHY
SQUUSHY
OVERRIPENESS SEED
OVERRULE VETO GOVERN
ABROGATE OVERCOME
OVERRULING GREAT PREDOMINANT
OVERRUN TEEM BESET CRUSH
SWARM DELUGE EXCEED INFEST
INVADE OVERGO RAVAGE SPREAD
DESTROY
OVERSEE TEND WATCH DIRECT
HANDLE MANAGE SURVEY EXAMINE
INSPECT NEGLECT DISREGARD
SUPERVISE
OVERSEER BOSS CORK JOSS
EPHOR GRAVE REEVE BISHOP
CENSOR DRIVER GAFFER GRIEVE
KEEKER MIRDHA TINDAL WARDEN
BAILIFF CAPATAZ CAPORAL
CURATOR FOREMAN HEADMAN
KANGANI MANAGER MANDOER
MAYORAL OVERMAN PRISTAW
TAPSMAN BANKSMAN CHAPRASI
DECURION MARTINET SURVEYOR
VILLICUS
(— **OF MACHINERY**) TENTOR
(**SPIRITUAL** —) PASTOR PRIEST
OVERSENSITIVE TICKLISH
OVERSENTIMENTAL SLOPPY
OVERSHADOW DIM CLOUD COVER
DWARF SHADE TOWER DARKEN
EFFACE ECLIPSE OBSCURE
UMBRAGE DOMINATE OVERCAST
OVERSHOE GUM BOOT GUME
ARCTIC GAITER GALOSH GOLOSH
PATTEN RUBBER SANDAL FLAPPER
EXCLUDER FOOTHOLD PANTOFLE
OVERSIGHT EYE CARE HOLE SLIP
ERROR FAULT GAFFE LAPSE WATCH
CHARGE BLUNDER CONTROL
JEOFAIL MISTAKE OMISSION
TUTELAGE DIRECTION
(**LEGAL** —) JEOFAIL
OVERSKIRT PEPLUM PANNIER
OVERSOFT QUASHY
OVERSPREAD FOG CAST CLOT
DECK PALL BATHE BREDE CLOUD
COVER SMEAR STREW CLOTHE
DELUGE DOODLE INDUCE SCATTER
SUFFUSE BESPREAD
OVERSTATE MAGNIFY EXAGGERATE
OVERSTEP PASS EXCEED SURPASS
OVERSUPPLIED RANK
OVERT OPEN PATENT PUBLIC
OBVIOUS APPARENT MANIFEST
OVERTAKE PASS ATAKE CATCH
ATTAIN DETECT ENSNARE OVERHIE
FOREHENT OVERHAUL
(— **BY DARKNESS**) BENIGHT
OVERTASK DRIVE
OVERTAX HOIST EXCEED STRAIN
STRESS
OVERTHROW TIP CAST DASH DOWN
FALL FELL FOIL FOLD HURL RAZE
ROUT RUIN RUSH WALT WEND
ALLAY EVERT FLING LEVEL QUASH
UPSET WORST WRACK WRECK

DEFEAT DEJECT REPUTE SLIGHT
TOPPLE TUMBLE UNSEAT WRITHE
AFFLICT CONQUER CONVELL
DESTROY DISMISS RUINATE
SUBVERT UNDOING UNHORSE
CONFOUND DEMOLISH OVERCOME
REVERSAL SUPPLANT VANQUISH
CHECKMATE CONFUSION
(— BY TRIPPING) CHIP
OVERTONE PARTIAL HARMONIC
OVERTOP COW OVERREACH
OVERTURE OFFER PROEM ADVANCE
OPENING PRELUDE APERTURE
PROPOSAL SINFONIA VORSPIEL
(INDECENT —) ASSAULT
OVERTURN TIP CAVE COUP KEEL
TILT WALT WELT TERVE THROW
UPSET WELME WHALM WHELM
SLIGHT TIPPLE TOPPLE WELTER
CAPSIZE DESTROY PERVERT
REVERSE SUBVERT
OVERWEIGHT OUTGANG
OVERWHELM BOWL BURY SINK
SLAY AMAZE COVER CRUSH DROOK
DROUK DROWN FLOOD SEIZE SPATE
SWAMP CUMBER DEFEAT DELUGE
ENGULF OBRUTE PLUNGE QUELME
QUENCH ASTOUND CONFUTE
CONQUER ENGROSS FLATTEN
IMMERSE INFLOOD OPPRESS
ASTONISH DISTRESS INUNDATE
SUBMERGE AVALANCHE
OVERWORK HOIN TIRE TOIL SWEAT
SURMENAGE
OVINE OVIN OVILE SHEEP SHEEPLIKE
OVOID OVATE OBOVOID
OVOLO OVAL THUMB BOLTEL
OVULE EGG NIT GERM SEED
EMBRYO OVULUM GEMMULE
SEEDLET
OVUM EGG OVAL SEED SPORE
OOSPHERE
OWAIA TREE BOBO
OWE DUE OWN REST AUGHT OUGHT
SHALL POSSESS ATTRIBUTE
OWER DEBTOR
OWL ULE BUBO LULU MOMO RURU

SURN TYTO UTUM JENNY MADGE
NINOX PADGE SCOPS STRIX TAWNY
WEKAU AZIOLA HOOTER HOWLET
KETUPA MUCARO RAPTOR STRICH
VERMIN WHEKAU BOOBOOK
HARFANG KATOGLE WAPACUT
WOOLERT BILLYWIX MOREPORK
(— CALL) HOOT
(LIKE AN —) STRIGINE
(YOUNG —) UTUM OWLET
OWN AIN OWE AVOW FESS HAVE
HOLD HOWE MEET NAIN SELF ADMIT
AUGHT OUGHT MASTER CONCEDE
CONFESS POSSESS
OWNER BEL MALIK WALLA HOLDER
DOMINUS HERITOR ODALLER
(— OF ESTATE) ALIRD
(— OF FISHING PLANT) PLANTER
(— OF YACHT) AFTERGUARD
(PLANTATION —) COLON
(SHEEP —) NABAL
OWNERSHIP ODAL UDAL AUGHT
TITLE CORNER SEIZIN SEIZURE
SEVERAL TENANCY DOMINIUM
PROPERTY COMMUNITY
OX YAK ANOA AVER BEEF BUFF BULL
GAUR MUSK NAWT NEAT NEWT
NOWT OWSE REEM RUNT STOT
URUS ZEBU AIVER BISON BUGLE
GAYAL SANGA STEER TOLLY TSINE
BOVINE MITHAN BANTENG BUFFALO
KOUPREY TWINTER SELADANG
TALLOWER
(CAMBODIAN —) KOUPREY
KOUPROH
(HORNLESS —) MOIL
(SMALL —) RUNT
(TAME —) COACH
(WILD —) URE ANOA BUFF GAUR
REEM URUS BISON BUGLE BANTIN
BANTENG BUFFALO SELADANG
(YEARLING —) STIRK
(YOUNG —) STOT
OXBLOOD KAZAK COPTIC KAZAKH
OXEN NOWT OWSEN CATTLE
OXEYE BOCE GOLD ASTER CLOUD

DAISY GOLDE DUNLIN PLOVER
TARPON
OXFORD DOWN SHOE CLOTH
OXONIAN SLIPPER
OXGANG OSKEN BOVATE OXGATE
OXLAND PLOWGANG
OXIDATION RUST
OXIDE EARTH FLOSS CADMIA MOILES
ZAFFER CALCINE LIMONITE
DJALMAITE
(— OF CALCIUM) LIME
(— OF IRON) RUST COLCOTHAR
MAGNETITE
OXLIP PAGLE PAIGLE PRIMULA
MILKMAID PRIMROSE PRIMWORT
OXSHOE CUE
OXYGEN GAS OZONE OXYGENIUM
OXYGENATE AERATE VENTILATE
OYSTER COPIS COUNT PINNA PLANT
SHELL COTUIT HUITRE NATIVE
REEFER BIVALVE MOLLUSK
RATTLER SHARPER BLUEPOINT
GREENGILL LYNNHAVEN
(— BED) PARK STEW LAYER SCALP
CLAIRE SCALFE OYSTERAGE
(— CATCHER) OLIVE PYNOT TIRMA
KROCKET PIANNET REDBILL
SCOLDER SHELDER PILWILLET
SKELDRAKE
(— CRAB) PINNOTERE
(— FOSSIL) OSTRACITE
(— MEASURE) WASH
(— PLANT) SALSIFY
(— SHELL) HUSK TEST SHUCK
(— SMALLER THAN QUARTER)
BLISTER
(— SOLD BY POUND) COUNT
(2,3, OR 4 —S) WARP
(IRISH —) POWLDOODY
(ROCK —) CHAMA
(VEGETABLE —) SALSIFY
(YOUNG —) SET SPAT
OYSTERFISH TAUTOG TOADFISH
OZARK STATE MISSOURI
OZOCERITE MALTHA NEFTGIL
OZONE AIR

P PAPA PETER
PA DAD PAW FORT PAPA DADDY
FATHER VILLAGE STOCKADE
PABULUM FOOD FUEL PROG CEREAL
ALIMENT SUPPORT NUTRIMENT
PAC BOOT SHOE MOCCASIN
PACA CAPA CAVY LAVA LABBA
AGOUTI RODENT
PACE FIG PAD RIP WAY BEMA CLIP
GAIT LOPE PASS PELT RACK RATE
STEP TEAR TROT WALK AMBLE
BRAWL CANTO SLINK SPACE SPEED
STEEK SWING TEMPO TRACE TREAD
CANTER GALLOP STRAIT STRIDE
CHANNEL CHAPTER DOGTROT
MEASURE PASSAGE SCUTTLE
(FAST —) ROMP
(RAPID —) CRACKER
(SLOW —) JOG CREEP
(PL.) MANAGE
PACER HORSE AMBLER SPANKER
TRIPPLER
PACHISI LUDO UCKERS PARCHESI
PACHYDERM HIPPO RHINO
ELEPHANT
PACIFIC CALM MEEK MILD IRENE
IRENIC PLACID SERENE PEACEFUL
TRANQUIL PEACEABLE
(— ISLAND PINE) IE KOU IEIE LEHUA
PACIFIER DUMMY COMFORTER
PACIFIST BOLO
PACIFY PAY CALM EASE LULL STAY
ABATE ALLAY AMESE MEASE PEASE
QUELL QUIET STILL PECIFY SERENE
SETTLE SOFTEN SOOTHE APPEASE
ASSUAGE MOLLIFY PLACATE
QUALIFY STIEKLE MITIGATE
ALLEVIATE RECONCILE
PACK JAM PUN WAD BALE CADE
CRAM DECK FILL GANG JAMB LADE
LOAD PAIR STOW SWAG TAMP TUCK
COUCH CRAME CROWD DRESS
FLOCK HORDE SKULK SOMER STEVE
STORE STUFF TRUSS BARREL
BODDLE BUDGET BUNDLE CARTON
DUFFLE EMBALE ENCASE FARDEL
HAMPER IMPACT THWACK TURKEY
WALLET PANNIER PORTAGE
RUMMAGE SUMPTER KNAPSACK
(— ANIMAL) ASS MULE BURRO
CAMEL HORSE LLAMA DONKEY
PACKER
(— BUILDER) GOBBER
(— JURY) WATER
(— LOOSELY) HOVER
(— OF BEARS) SLOTH
(— OF CARDS) STOCK
(— OF DOGS) CRY KENNEL
(— OF FOXES) GROUP SKULK
(— OF HOUNDS) CRY HUNT MUTE
(— OFF) WAG SHANK TURSE
(— ROAD) PACKWAY
(— TIGHTLY) STIVE
PACKAGE PAD BALE BOLT PAIR
DUMMY TRUSS BINDLE BUNDLE
PACKET PARCEL SAMPLE SEROON
DORLACH
(— OF CIGARETTES) DECK

(— OF GOLDBEATER'S SKINS)
SHODER
(— OF LEAF) BOOK
(— OF PEPPERS) ROBBIN
(— OF STAMPS) KILOWARE
(— OF VELLUM) KUTCH
(— OF VENEER) FLITCH
(— OF WOOL) BAG PAD BUTT
FADGE
(YARN —) CONE CHEESE
PACKER BALER LINER ROPER
CANNER
PACKET BOAT BOOK DECK ROLL
SCREW BUNDLE PARCEL SACHET
(— OF VELLUM) CUTCH KUTCH
PACKHORSE SOMER JAGGER
PACKER SUMPTER
PACKING CUP RAGS GAUZE PAPER
STRAW WASTE GASKET GROMMET
STOWAGE STOPPING
(— MATERIAL) BALINE GASKET
(CLAY —) LUTE
PACKINGHOUSE MEATWORKS
PACKMAN HAWKER
PACKSACK KYACK
PACKSADDLE BAT BARDEL
APAREJO
PACT CARTEL PACTUM TREATY
BARGAIN COMPACT LOCARNO
ALLIANCE CONTRACT COVENANT
AGREEMENT
PAD MAT WAD WAY BLAD BOSS
FROG LURE MUTE PATH PUFF ROAD
ROLL SHOE WALK WASE BLOCK
INKER PERCH PILCH QUILT STENT
STINT STUFF TABBY TRAMP BASKET
BUFFER BUSTLE DAUBER HOLDER
JOCKEY NUMNAH PADDLE PADNAG
PANNEL PILLOW SPONGE TABLET
TRUDGE VELURE WREATH BOLSTER
BOMBAST CUSHION FOOTPAD
PILLION SASHOON
(— IN CRIB) BUMPER
(— OF STRAW) SUNK WASE
(— ON HORSE'S FOOT) FROG
(ETCHER'S —) DABBER
(HAIR —) RAT MOUSE TOQUE
(INKING —) INKER TOMPION
(PERFUMED —) SACHET
(SADDLE —) PANEL PILLOW PILLION
PADAUK CORAIL
PADDER MANGLE
PADDING TABBY CADDIS BOLSTER
BOMBAST BUSHING CADDICE
FILLING PACKING ROBBERY
WADDING MAHOITRE STUFFING
PADDLE OAR ROW SPUD WADE
ALOOF CANOE SLICE SPANK
BUCKET DABBLE PETTLE PUNISH
STRIKE TODDLE SPANKER SPURTLE
LUMPFISH
(— BOX) WHEELHOUSE
(— FOR FLOUR) SLICK
(TAILOR'S —) BEATER
PADDLEFISH GANOID DUCKBILL
STURGEON POLYODONT SPADEFISH
SPOONBILL
PADDOCK LOT FROG PARK CLOSE
FIELD SLEDGE GARSTON LOANING

BIRDCAGE
PADDYMELON QUOKKA PADMELON
PADISHAH SULTAN PADASHA
POTSHAW
PADLOCK LOCK FASTEN SECURE
CLOSING FASTENER HORSELOCK
(— LINK) SHACKLE
PADRE MONK CLERIC FATHER
PRIEST CHAPLAIN
PADRONA LANDLADY MISTRESS
PADRONE BOSS CHIEF MASTER
PATRON LANDLORD INNKEEPER
PAEAN ODE HYMN SONG PRAISE
OUTBURST TRIUMPHAL
PAGAN ATA BUID BATAK BUKID
APAYAO BAGOBO BANGON BILAAN
BONTOC ETHNIC PAYNIM SABIAN
ALANGAN DUMAGAT GENTILE
HEATHEN INFIDEL SARACEN
SUBANUN UNGODLY IDOLATOR
PAGANDOM PAYNIM
PAGE BOY CALL LEAF MOTH SIDE
CHILD FACER FOLIO GROOM SHEET
DONZEL ERRATA SUMMON VARLET
BUTTONS CALLBOY FUNNIES
PAVISER SERVANT HENCHMAN
ICHOGLAN
(— BOTTOM) TAIL
(BLANK —S) CANCEL
(FACING —) SPREAD
(LADY'S —) ESCUDERO
(LAST FEW —S) BACK
(LEFTHAND —) VERSO
(RIGHTHAND —) RECTO OUTPAGE
(TITLE —) TITLE UNWAN RUBRIC
(PL.) ODDMENTS
PAGEANT JEST POMP SHOW ANTIC
PARADE RIDING TABLEAU TAMASHA
TRIUMPH AQUACADE CAVALCADE
SPECTACLE WATERWORK
PAGEANTRY POMP PARADE
HERALDRY SPLENDOR
PAGODA PON TAA HOON WATT
TEMPLE VARELLA
PAHOUIN FAN FANG
PAHUTAN PAHO
PAID EVEN RESOLUTE
(— IN COIN) DRY
(— IN FULL) SATISFIED
PAIL CAN COG PAN SOA SOE BEAT
BOWK GAWN MEAL STOP TRUG
BOWIE COGUE CRUCK DANDY ESHIN
SKEEL STOOP BLICKY BUCKET
COGGIE HARASS KETTLE LEGLEN
NOGGIN PIGGIN SITULA THRASH
COLLOCK
(MILK —) KIT SOE TRUG ESHIN
LEGLEN
(ON WHEELS) DANDY
(POTTERY —) SEAL
(SMALL —) KIT BLICKY BLICKIE
(WOODEN —) COG COGUE LUGGIE
PIGGIN
PAIN ACHE AGRA BALE CARE CARK
FRET GRUE HARM HURT PANG SITE
SORE TEEN TINE WARK AGONY
BEANS CRAMP DOLOR GRIEF GRIPE
PINCH PINSE SCALD SMART STING

STOUN THRAW THROE WOUND
BARRAT GRIEVE MISERY SHOWER
STITCH TWINGE AFFLICH ALGESIS
ANGUISH EARACHE HURTING
MYALGIA OFFENCE PENALTY
TORTURE TRAVAIL TROUBLE
DISTRESS FLEABITE
(— IN BACK) NOTALGIA SCIATICA
(— IN HAND) CHIRAGRA
(— IN SIDE) STEEK
(— OF MIND) AGONY
(— RELIEVER) OPIATE ANODYNE
ASPIRIN
(FILL WITH —) YEARN
(SHARP —) WRING
(STOMACH —) GRIPES GNAWING
(WRENCHING —) TORSION
(PL.) LABOR WHILE EFFORT
TROUBLE

PAINFUL BAD ILL DIRE EVIL FELL
SORE SOUR TART ANGRY CRUEL
SHARP SORRY BITTER STICKY
GRIPING HURTFUL IRKSOME
PENIBLE PUNGENT EXACTING
TERRIBLE TORTUOUS DIFFICULT
HARROWING

PAINSTAKING BUSY LOVING
CAREFUL PENIBLE DILIGENT
EXACTING ASSIDUOUS ELABORATE

PAINT BLOT COAT DAUB DRAW FARD
GAUD LIMN PENT PICT SOIL COLOR
FEIGN FUCUS GRAIN ROUGE STAIN
BEDAUB DAZZLE DEPICT ENAMEL
FRESCO OPAQUE SHADOW SKETCH
BESMEAR PORTRAY PRETEND
SCUMBLE AIRBRUSH DECORATE
DESCRIBE DISGUISE URFIRNIS
CALCIMINE
(— A PIPE) SOIL
(— FACE OR BODY) FUCUS PARGET
(— HASTILY) SQUIGGLE
(— SKETCHILY) SPLASH
(— THROUGH PATTERN) STENCIL
(— WITH COSMETICS) POP POT
FARD

PAINTBRUSH WICKAWEE
NOSEBLEED

PAINTED PINTO FUCATE PASTOSE
GOFFERED
(— BEAUTY) VANESSA
(— BUNTING) POP NONPAREIL
(— CUP) WICKAWEE PAINTBRUSH
(— WAKE-ROBIN) SARA

PAINTER FAUVE ARTIST DAUBER
PICTOR PANTHER SIGNIST SIGNMAN
WORKMAN BRUSHMAN LUMINIST
MURALIST NAZARENE STIPPLER
DECORATOR TACTILIST
(PL.) ECLECTICS

PAINTING ART OIL PAT PATA DRAFT
MURAL PIECE TABLE WATER
CANVAS CROUTE FRESCO MINERY
TITIAN BODEGON CAMAIEU
CARTOON DAUBING GRADINO
GRAPHIC HISTORY FROTTAGE
PREDELLA SEAPIECE SYMPHONY
(— EQUIPMENT) OIL BRUSH EASEL
PAINT CANVAS PALLET

(— IN COLLOIDAL MEDIUM)
TEMPERA
(— OF EVERYDAY LIFE) GENRE
(— OF FOLIAGE) BOSCAGE
(— ON PLASTER) SECCO FRESCO
(— WITH OPAQUE COLORS)
GOUACHE
(CIRCULAR —) TONDO
(RELIGIOUS —) PIETA TANKA
(SCENIC —) SCAPE
(SMALL —) TABLET
(THREE PANEL —) TRIPTYCH
(PL.) GENRE

PAIR DUO TWO ZYG CASE DIAD
DUAD DUAL MATE SIDE SPAN TEAM
TWIN YOKE BRACE MARRY MATCH
TWAIN UNITE COUPLE GEMINI
COUPLET DOUBLET JUMELLE
TWOSOME
(— OF FILMS) BIPACK
(— OF MILLSTONES) RUN
(— OF SHOTS) BRACKET
(— OF TONGS) GRAMPUS GRAPPLE
(— OF WINGS) SHEARS
(— ROYAL) PARIAL
(ONE OF —) IMPAIR NEIGHBOR
(PL.) GEMELS

PAIRED GEMEL JUGATE ZYGOUS
JUMELLE

PAISLEY PRINT SHAWL DESIGN
FABRIC

PAIUTE DIGGER

PAJAMAS SHALWAR SLEEPER

PAKISTAN
BAY: SOYMIANI
CANAL: NARA ROHRI
CAPE: FASTA JADDI JIWANI
CAPITAL: ISLAMABAD
COIN: ANNA RUPEE
DAM: TARBELA
LANGUAGE: URDU PUSHTU SINDHI
BALUCHI BENGALI PUNJABI
MOUNTAIN: TIRICHMIR
MOUNTAIN RANGE: MAKRAN
KIRTHAR HIMALAYA SULAIMAN
NATIVE: BENGAL PATHAN SINDHI
BALUCHI PUNJABI
PORT: CHALNA KARACHI
RIVER: NAL BADO RAVI ZHOB
DASHT INDUS CHENAB GANGES
JHELUM KUNDAR PORALI
JAMUNNA
STATE: DIR SWAT KALAT KHARAN
CHITRAL KHAIRPUR
TOWN: DACCA CHALNA KHULNA
LAHORE MULTAN QUETTA
KARACHI SIALKOT LYALLPUR
PESHAWAR SARGODHA
WEIGHT: SEER TOLA MAUND

PAKTONG TUTENAG

PAL ALLY CHUM JACK PARD BILLY
BUDDY CHINA CRONY LOUKE
COBBER COPAIN DIGGER FRIEND
COMRADE PARTNER COMPANION

PALACE SALE CHIGI COURT SERAI
STEAD CASTLE ELYSEE LOUVRE
PALAIS ALCAZAR EDIFICE LATERAN
MANSION PALAZZO TRIANON
VATICAN ZWINGER SERAGLIO
WHITEHALL
(— OF SATAN) PANDEMONIUM
(FAIRY —) SHEE SIDHE

PALADIN HERO PEER ANSEIS
ASTOLF KNIGHT CHAMPION
DOUZEPER

PALAMON (RIVAL OF —) ARCITE
(WIFE OF —) EMELYE

PALANQUIN JAUN JUAN KAGE KAGO
DANDI DOOLI DOOLY PALKI SEDAN
DOOLIE LITTER PALKEE TONJON

PALATABLE SAPID SPICY TASTY
DAINTY SAVORY MOREISH DELICATE
LUSCIOUS PLEASING SAPOROUS
AGREEABLE DELICIOUS TOOTHSOME

PALATAL SOFT FRONT VELAR
GUTTURAL

PALATE TASTE VELUM RELISH
GOURMET URANISCUS

PALATIAL LARGE ORNATE STATELY
SPLENDID

PALATINE CAPE OFFICER PALADIN
PALATIAL

PALAVER GASH SLUM TALK CAJOLE
DEBATE GLAVER JARGON PARLEY
CHATTER FLATTER WHEEDLE
CAJOLERY FLATTERY

PALE DIM WAN ASHY BLOC FADE
GREY GULL LILY PALL SICK WHEY
ASHEN BLAKE BLATE BLEAK CLOSE
FAINT FENCE GREEN LIGHT LINEN
LIVID LURID MEALY STAKE STICK
WHITE ANEMIC BLANCH CHALKY
CHANGE DOUGHY FALLOW FEEBLE
PALLID PASTEL PICKET REGION
REMISS SICKLY SILVER WATERY
WHITEN DEFENSE GHASTLY
HAGGARD INSIPID OBSCURE
WATERISH
(IN —) HAURIENT

PALEA PALET SQUAMELLA

PALENESS WAN PALLOR ACHROMA

PALESTINE (SEE ISRAEL)

PALETOT COAT JACKET OVERCOAT
GREATCOAT

PALFREY HORSE PALFRY

PALIMPSET TABLET PARCHMENT

PALING PALE FENCE FLAKE LIMIT
PALIS STAKE PICKET FENCING
BLENCHING

PALISADE HAY BOMA PALE PEEL
CLIFF FENCE RIMER STAKE HURDIS
PICKET BARRIER ENCLOSE FORTIFY
HURDIES STACKET TAMBOUR
ESPALIER
(MILITARY —) CIPPUS
(PL.) BAIL BARRIER

PALL FOG BORE CLOY PALE SATE
CLOAK CLOTH FAINT QUALM STALE
WEARY MANTLE NAUSEA SHROUD
DISGUST SATIATE ANIMETTA
MORTCLOTH

PALLET BED COT PAD COUCH QUILT
BLANKET MATTRESS PLANCHER
PALLIARD BEGGAR LECHER RASCAL
VAGABOND
PALLIATE EASE HIDE MASK VEIL
ABATE CLOAK COLOR COVER
GLOSS GLOZE LITHE BLANCH
LESSEN REDUCE SMOOTH SOFTEN
SOOTHE CONCEAL CUSHION
SHELTER DISGUISE MITIGATE
PALLID WAN ASHY PALE PALY
BLEAK WASHY WAXEN WHITE
SALLOW GHASTLY BLOODLESS
COLORLESS INNOCUOUS
PALL-MALL MAIL
PALLOR ASH WAN PALE ASHES
PALENESS
PALM DOM ATAP BRAB BURI BUSU
COCO DATE DOUM FLAT HIDE JARA
KOKO LOOF NIOG NIPA PAWN SAGO
SLIP TARA ARCHA ARECA ARENG
ASSAI BONGA BUNGA CARRY
COCOA COYOL CURUA DATIL FOIST
HOWEA INAJA JAGUA LOULU MERUS
NIKAU RATAN SABAL SALAK TECUM
TUCUM UNAMO YAGUA YARAY
ANAHAO ASSAHY BACABA BURITI
CHONTA COHUNE CONTAR COROJO
GEBANG GOMUTI GRUGRU JAMBEE
JUPATI KENTIA KITTUL LAWYER
NIBONG PACAYA RAFFIA ROTANG
THENAR TOOROO TROPHY APRICOT
BABASSU CARANDA CONCEAL
COQUITO ERYTHEA GEONOMA
MORICHE PUPUNHA SAGWIRE
TALIPOT URUCURI JACITARA
LATANIER
(— **FERN**) PONJA
(— **FOOD**) NUT COCO DATE NIPA
SAGO SURA ASSAI TAREE TODDY
COCONUT
(— **JUICE**) SURA
(— **LEAF**) OLA OLLA CAJAN FROND
(— **LILY**) TI
(— **OF HAND**) FLAT LOOF VOLA
TABLE THENAR
(— **OFF**) COG FOB TOP SHAB FOIST
TRUMP
(— **OUT**) APPAUME
(**BETEL** —) ARECA BONGA PUGUA
PINANG
(**CLIMBING** —) RATTAN
(**FEATHER** —) HOWEA GOMUTI
URUCURI
(**SPINY** —) PEACH GRIGRI GRUGRU
PALMARY CHIEF PALMAR SUPERIOR
PALMATE FLAT BROAD LOBED
WEBBED
PALMER LOUSE FERULE STROLL
TRAVEL VOTARY WANDER FOISTER
PILGRIM
PALMETTO CABBAGE PALMITO
BIGTHATCH
(— **STATE**) SOUTHCAROLINA
PALMODIC JERKY
PALMYRA BRAB TALA LONTAR
RONIER TADMOR BASSINE
(**QUEEN OF** —) ZENOBIA

PALP FEEL TOUCH CAJOLE FEELER
HANDLE PALPUS FLATTER
TENTACLE
PALPABLE BALD RANK PLAIN
PATENT AUDIBLE EVIDENT OBVIOUS
TACTILE APPARENT DISTINCT
MANIFEST TANGIBLE CORPOREAL
PALPATION THROB WALLOP DIPPING
PITAPAT
PALPEBRA EYELID
PALPITATE PANT QUAP THROB
FLACKER FLICKER FLUTTER
PULSATE
PALPITATION BEAT DUNT PANT
FLICKER FLUTTER PULSATION
THROBBING
(— **OF HEART**) THUMB
PALSIED SHAKY SHAKING
PARALYZED TOTTERING TREMBLING
TREMULOUS
PALSY PARLESIE PARALYSIS
PALTER FIB LIE BABBLE HAGGLE
MUMBLE PARLEY TRIFLE BARGAIN
CHAFFER CHATTER QUIBBLE
SHAFFLE
PALTRY BALD BARE BASE MEAN
ORRA PUNY SCAB VILE WAFF
FOOTY MINOR PETTY SCALL SCRUB
SILLY TRASH CHETIF FLIMSY
SHABBY SLIGHT TRASHY WOEFUL
HILDING PELTING PIMPING PITIFUL
RUBBISH SCABBED SCRUBBY
TRIVIAL PICAYUNE PICKLING
PIDDLING TRIFLING
PALUDAL MARSHY
PAMPA PLAIN PRAIRIE
PAMPAS (— **CAT**) KODKOD PAJERO
(— **DEER**) MAZAME
PAMPER PET BABY CRAM DELT
GLUT POMP HUMOR SPOIL TUTOR
WALLY CARESS COCKER CODDLE
COSHER COSSET CUDDLE DANDLE
FONDLE MAUNGE POSSET TIDDLE
CHERISH COCKNEY FORWEAN
GRATIFY INDULGE SATIATE
SMOODGE SAGINATE
PAMPHLET JACK LEAD QUIRE SHEET
TRACT FOLDER BOOKLET CATALOG
LEAFLET NOVELET BROCHURE
CHAPBOOK WORKBOOK CATALOGUE
PAN FIT TAB VLY MELL PART PRIG
VLEI WASH AGREE BASIN BATEA
COVER GRAND SHEET UNITE
FRACHE LAPPET PANKIN PATINA
SPIDER VESSEL CRANIUM CREAMER
HARDPAN PORTION ROASTER
SKILLET SUBSOIL RIDICULE
(— **FOR COALS**) BRAZIER
(— **OF BALANCE**) BOWL BASIN
SCALEPAN
(— **WITH 3 FEET**) POSNET
(**EVAPORATING** —) ROOM COVER
TACHE SALTPAN
(**GOD** —) FAUNUS
(**IRON** —) YET FRACHE
(**LONG-HANDLED** —) PINGLE
(**MILK** —) LEAD
(**OIL** —) SUMP

PANACEA CURE ELIXIR REMEDY
SOLACE CUREALL HEALALL
NEPENTHE

PANAMA
CAPITAL: PANAMA
COIN: BALBOA
CROP: ABACA CACAO
GULF: DARIEN CHIRIQUI
LAKE: GATUN
MEASURE: CELEMIN
MOUNTAIN: CHICO GANDI
COLUMAN SANTIAGO
MOUNTAIN RANGE: VERAGUA
PORT: CRISTOBAL
PROVINCE: COCLE COLON
CHIRIQUI VERAGUAS
RIVER: CHEPO SAMBU TUIRA
BAYANO PANUGO CHAGRES
TOWN: COLON DAVID AZUERO
BALBOA PANAMA PENONOME
SANTIAGO
TREE: YAYA MARIA QUIRA ALFAJE
CATIVO

PANAMA HAT JIPIJAPA
PANAMINT KOSO
PANCAKE FLAM AREPA CREPE
FADGE FLAWN KISRA LEFSE TOURT
BLINTZ FRAISE FROISE CRUMPET
FLAPPER FLIPPER FRITTER
HOTCAKE PIKELET CORNCAKE
FLAPJACK FLIPJACK
(**PL.**) LEFSEN
PANCREAS BUR NUT
PAND PAWN DRAPERY
PANDA WA WAH BEARCAT
PANDAVA BHIMA
PANDECT COMPENDIUM
PANDEMONIUM DIN HELL CHAOS
NOISE TUMULT UPROAR DISORDER
CONFUSION
PANDER BAWD PIMP BULLY CATER
MICHER PURVEY RUFFIAN WHISKIN
PROCURER BAWDSTROT
PANDORA BANDORE
(**BROTHER OF** —) PROMETHEUS
(**HUSBAND OF** —) EPIMETHEUS
PANE GLASS GLAZE LOZEN PANEL
QUIRK SHEET SHOCK SLASH
QUARRY SECTION PORTLIGHT
PANEGYRIC ELOGE ELOGY EULOGY
PRAISE ORATION TRIBUTE
ENCOMIUM LAUDATION
PANEL FIN PAN JURY SKIN BOARD
GROUP LABEL TABLE ABACUS
ASSIZE COFFER HURDLE MIRROR
PADDLE PILLOW ROSACE TABLET
TYMPAN CAISSON CONSOLE
FLIPPER LACUNAR DECORATE
MANDORLA
(— **IN FENCE**) LOOP
(— **IN GARMENT**) LAP STEAK
(**3-PART** —) TRIPTYCH

(CIRCULAR —) ROUNDEL
(GAUZE —) SCRIM
(GLAZED —) LAYLIGHT
(LEGAL —) ARRAY
(RECESSED —) ORB COFFER LACUNAR
(SUNKEN —) CAISSON CASSOON
PANFISH SCUP
PANG ACHE CRAM FILL GIRD PAIN STAB TANG AGONY PINCH PRONG SPASM STANG STOUN STUFF THROE SHOWER STOUND TWINGE ANGUISH TRAVAIL
(PL.) GNAWINGS
PANGOLIN MANID MANIS ANTEATER EDENTATE TANGILIN
PANGWE FAN FANG
PANHANDLE BEG CADGE SKELB SKILDER
(— STATE) WV WVA
PANIC FEAR FRAY FUNK WILD ALARM AMAZE CHAOS SCARE FRIGHT SCHRIK TERROR SWITHER
PANICKY FUNKY
PANICLE JUBA WHISK ANTHELA
PANNIER BAG PED SERON BASKET CAJAVA CURAGH DORSEL DORSER DOSSAL DOSSER PANTRY CORBEIL CURRACK KAJAWAH KEDJAVE
PANOPLY POMP ARMOR UNIFORM
PANORAMA VIEW RANGE SCENE SWEEP VISTA NEORAMA PICTURE SCENERY CYCLORAMA POLYORAMA
PANPIPE SICU SIKU QUILL ANTARA SYRINX ZAMPOGNA
PANSY FANCY PENSE VIOLA KISSES PENSEE VIOLET TRINITY FANTASQUE HEARTEASE
PANT FAB ACHE BEAT BLOW FUFF GAPE GASP HECH LONG PANK PECH PEGH PINE PIPE PUFF TIFT HEAVE QUIRK STECH SUGGE THROB YEARN ANHELE ASPIRE FRIESE PANTLE PULSATE
PANTAGRUEL (COMPANION OF —) PANURGE
(FATHER OF —) GARGANTUA
(MOTHER OF —) BADEBEC
PANTALOONS PANTS TROUSERS
PANTHEIST AMALRICIAN
PANTHEON TEMPLE ROTUNDA VALHALL VALHALLA
PANTHER CAT PARD PUMA COUGAR JAGUAR LEOPARD PAINTER PANTILE
PANTIES SCANTIES
PANTILE TILE IMBREX BISCUIT HARDTACK
PANTING ANHELOSE ANHELOUS
PANTOGRAPH EIDOGRAPH POLYGRAPH
PANTOMIME PLAY PANTO
PANTRY CAVE STUE AMBRY COVEY CUDDY CLOSET LARDER SPENCE BUTLERY BUTTERY PANNIER PANTLER SERVERY SPICERY CUPBOARD
PANTS JEANS LEVIS BRIEFS SLACKS DRAWERS JODHPUR BREECHES

BRITCHES KICKSIES KNICKERS SNUGGIES TROUSERS
(LEATHER —) CHAPS LEDERHOSEN
PANUELO COLLAR RUFFLE KERCHIEF NECKCLOTH
PANZER TANK
PAP DUG TIT POBS TEAT NIPPLE EMULSION FLUMMERY
PAPA PA DAD PAP PAW POP SIN BABA EVIL DADDY LOVER PAPPY BABOON FATHER POTATO PRIEST HUSBAND VULTURE
PAPAL (ALSO SEE POPE) POPAL PAPANE POPELY APOSTOLIC
PAPAW PAPA ASIMEN PAPAIO ASIMINA CORAZON JASMINE
PAPAYA PAPAW LECHOSA
PAPER LIL WEB BILL BOND BLANK BROKE ESSAY STUDY THEME ASTHMA BINDLE CARTEL PAPIER REPORT RETREE VESSEL CHEVIOT EXHIBIT JOURNAL WRITING YOSHINO DOCUMENT MONOGRAPH VALENTINE
(— FOLDER) STROKER
(— MAKER) WASHERMAN
(— NAUTILUS) ARGONAUT
(— PULP) WATERLEAF
(— QUANTITY) PAGE REAM QUIRE SHEET BUNDLE
(ABSORBENT —) BLOTTER TOWELLING
(BUILDING —) FELT
(BUNDLE OF —S) DUFTER DOSSIER
(CHINESE —) INDIA
(DAMAGED —) BROKE CASSE SALLE RETREE
(FOLDED —) SADDLE AIRPLANE
(GLOSS —) GILL
(HARD —) PELURE
(HEAVY —) FELT
(LINING —S) SKIPS
(NEGOTIABLE —) STIFF
(OFFICIAL —) TARGE HOOKUM DOCUMENT
(PARCHMENT —) VELLUM PERGAMYN
(PHOTOGRAPHIC —) SEPIA
(SIZE OF —) CAP COPY DEMI NOTE POST POTT TOWN ATLAS CROWN FOLIO LARGE LEGAL ROYAL SIXMO ALBERT BILLET CASING LETTER MEDIUM THIRDS BASTARD CABINET EMPEROR THEOREM ELEPHANT FOOLSCAP IMPERIAL
(STRIP OF —) TAPE
(THIN —) FLIMSY PELURE TISSUE ONIONSKIN
(TOILET —) BUMF
(UNCUT —) BOLT
(WALL —) TENTURE
(WATERMARKED —) BATONNE
(WRAPPING —) SKIP KRAFT SEALING SCREENING
(WRITING —) FLAT LINEN WEDDING
PAPERBARK CAJEPUT MILKWOOD
PAPERBOARD BENDER VENEER CARDBOARD CHIPBOARD PULPBOARD

PAPILLA CERAS DEIRID NIPPLE PAPULA MAMMULA THELIUM
(PL.) CERATA
PAPILLOMA ANGLEBERRY
PAPIO MORMON
PAPIST TORY PAPANE CATHOLIC POPELING
PAPPUS DOWN THISTLEDOWN
PAPPY PA DAD PAW PAPA SOFT MUSHY PULPY FATHER SUCCULENT
PAPRIKA PIMENTO PIMIENTO
PAPUA (BAY OF —) DYKE MILNE ACLAND HOLNICOTE
(RIVER OF —) FLY KIKORI PURARI
(TOWN OF —) BUNA DARU KIKORI SAMARAI
PAPUAN ARAU BIAK HULA KATE BUANG EKARI KIWAI KWOMA SIVAI SULKA BAITSI BANARO IATMUL KEREWA KOIARI ARAPESH BAINING
PAPULE WHELK PIMPLE
PAPYRUS REED PAPER SEDGE BIBLOS GLUMAL SCROLL BULRUSH
(— STRIP) ORIHON
PAR BY NORM EQUAL NORMAL AVERAGE EQUALITY
(ONE OVER —) BOGIE
(ONE UNDER —) BIRDIE
(TWO UNDER —) EAGLE
PARA FODDA PERAU PARRAH
PARABLE MYTH TALE FABLE STORY APOLOG BYWORD MASHAL SAMPLE BYSPELL PROVERB ALLEGORY FORBYSEN LIKENESS
PARABOLA ARC CURVE ANTENNA
PARACHUTE SILK CHUTE BROLLY DROGUE STREAMER
PARACHUTIST PATHFINDER
(PL.) STICK
PARACLETE AIDER HELPER PLEADER ADVOCATE CONSOLER COMFORTER
PARADE JET TOP POMP SHOW WALK MARCH STRUT FLAUNT MUSTER REVIEW STROLL CORTEGE DISPLAY EXHIBIT MARSHAL CEREMONY EXERCISE FLOURISH GRANDEUR SPLENDOR PAGEANTRY
(— GROUND) MAIDAN
(UNSUBSTANTIAL —) PAGEANT
PARADED AFFICHE
PARADISE EDEN JODO BLISS JENNA AIDENN GOLOKA HEAVEN ELYSIUM NIRVANA
(— OF INDRA) SVARGA SWARGA
(— TREE) ACEITUNA STAVEWOOD
PARADOX KOAN ANTINOMY
PARADOXURE MUSANG
PARAFFIN ALKANE
PARAGON GEM PINK TYPE IDEAL MODEL APERSEE PATTERN PEROPUS PHOENIX NONESUCH NONPARIEL
PARAGRAPH ITEM SIGN CAPUT PAUSE CLAUSE NOTICE RUBRIC ARTICLE INITIAL PILCROW SECTION MATERIAL PEELCROW PERSONAL SUBLEADER
(— MARK) PILCROW

PARAGUAY
CAPITAL: ASUNCION
COIN: GUARANI
DEPARTMENT: GUAIRA ITAPUA
  OLIMPO CAAZAPA BOQUERON
LAKE: VERA YPOA YPACARAI
LANGUAGE: GUARANI
MEASURE: PIE LINE LINO VARA
  LEGUA LINEA CORDEL CUADRA
  CUARTA FANEGA
PLAIN: CHACO
RIVER: YPANE ACARAY PARANA
  CONFUSO
TOWN: LUQUE PILAR CAACUPE
  CAAZAPA TRINIDAD
  CONCEPCION VILLARRICA
WEIGHT: QUINTAL

PARAKEET CONURE PARROT
  WELLAT ARATINGA KAKARIKI
  POPINJAY ROSEHILL GREENLEEK
PARALLEL EVEN LIKE ALONG EQUAL
  MATCH SECOND EXAMPLE FRONTAL
  PARAGON ANALOGUE LIKENESS
  MULTIPLE QUANTITY
PARALLELOGRAM RHOMB OBLONG
  SQUARE RHOMBUS RHOMBOID
  RECTANGLE
PARALYSIS CRAMP PALSY SHOCK
  PARESIS DIPLEGIA
PARALYZE DARE DAZE STUN PALSY
  SCRAM ASTONY CONGEAL IMPALSY
  TORPEDO
PARALYZED NUMB PALSIED
  CRIPPLED
PARAMOUNT ABOVE CHIEF RULER
  SOVRAN CAPITAL SUPREME
  DOMINANT SUPERIOR SUZERAIN
  SOVEREIGN
PARAMOUR DOLL PRIM PURE
  LEMAN LOVER WOMAN WOOER
  AMORET FRIEND MASTER MINION
  FRANION GALLANT HETAERA
  RUFFIAN SERVANT SPECIAL
  SULTANA STALLION BOYFRIEND
PARAPET BUTT WALL BAHUT REDAN
  BARBET BONNET TRENCH BULWARK
  PLUTEUS RAILING RAMPART
  ENVELOPE TRAVERSE
PARAPH RUBRIC
PARAPHERNALIA GEAR EQUIPAGE
  APPARATUS EQUIPMENT TRAPPINGS
PARAPHRASE FARSE REWORD
  TARGET TARGUM PREFACE
  THARGUM VERSION TRANSLATE
PARASITE BUG BUR FLY BURR
  MOSS SPIV TRYP CHARK DRONE
  LEECH SHARK TOADY VIRUS
  FEEDER FUNGUS GNATHO SHADOW
  SPONGE SUCKER BLEEDER
  SPONGER TAGTAIL DICYEMID
  ENTOZOON HANGERON SLAVERER
  INFESTANT POTHUNTER SACCULINA
  SPARGANUM TOADEATER
  TUBHUNTER

(— ON TROUT) SUG
(PL.) ECTOZOA ENTOZOA
  DRIFTWOOD
PARASITIC CYTOZOIC TRENCHER
  BIOPHILOUS
(— JAEGER) SHOOI DIRTBIRD
PARASOL SHADE AOGIRI SHADOW
  ROUNDEL TIRESOL KITTYSOL
  SUNSHADE UMBRELLA
(— MUSHROOM) LEPIOTA
PARAVANE OTTER
PARBOILED LEEPIT
PARCEL LOT DEAD DEAL DOLE METE
  PACK PART WISP BULSE BUNCH
  GROUP PIECE BUNDLE DIVIDE
  FARDEL PACKET PASSEL CONACRE
  PACKAGE PORTION COMMODITY
(— OF DIAMONDS) SERIES
(— OF GROUND) LOT PICK CLOSE
  SOLUM SUERTE CONACRE PENDICLE
(— OF HEMP FIBER) PIG
(— OF JEWELS) BULSE
(— OUT) ALLOT
PARCH DRY FRY BURN COOK SEAR
  ROAST TOAST PEARCH RIZZER
  SCORCH BRISTLE BRUSTLE
  GRADDAN SHRIVEL TORREFY
  TORRIFY
PARCHED ARID HUSK SERE ADUST
  FIERY GIZZEN TORRID THIRSTY
  SCORCHED
PARCHING URENT
PARCHMENT LARK FOREL CHARTA
  MEZUZAH PAPYRIN SCYTALE
  DRUMHEAD PALIMPSEST
(— PAPER) DOCKET PERGAMYN
(FINE —) VEL VELLUM
(PIECE OF —) MEMBRANE
(ROLL OF —) PELL SCROLL
PARD PAL CHUM TIGER FRIEND
  LEOPARD PANTHER PARTNER
  COMPANION
PARDON FREE CLEAR COVER GRACE
  MERCY REMIT SPARE ACQUIT
  ASSOIL EXCUSE SHRIVE ABSOLVE
  AMNESTY CONDONE FORGIVE
  REPRIEVE TOLERATE EXCULPATE
PARDONABLE VENIAL VENIABLE
  EXCUSABLE
PARDONER QUESTOR QUAESTOR
PARE CUP CHIP COPE FLAY PEEL
  SKIN FRIZZ SHAVE SKELP SLIPE
  SPADE CHISEL REDUCE REMOVE
  RESECT CURTAIL WHITTLE
(— LEATHER) SKIVE
(— SOD) BURNBEAT
(— STAVES) BUCK
(— STONE) BOAST
PAREGORIC ANODYNE MITIGATING
PAREL PARELL APPAREL CLOTHING
  ORNAMENT
PARENCHYMA AMYLOM MESOPHYL
PARENT DAD DAM MAMA PAPA SIRE
  DADDY ELDER MATER PATER
  AUTHOR FATHER MOTHER ORIGIN
  FORBEAR GENITOR ANCESTOR
  BEGETTER FILICIDE GUARDIAN

PARENTAGE KIND BIRTH BROOD
  FAMILY ORIGIN PROGENY
  ENGENDURE
PARENTHESIS HOOK ASIDE PAREN
  BRACKET TOENAIL INNUENDO
  INTERVAL INTERLUDE
(PL.) HOOKS CURVES
PAREVE NEUTRAL
PARGET COAT GYPSUM PARIET
  PLASTER DECORATE WHITEWASH
PARGO MUTTONFISH
PARHELION DOG SUN SUNDOG
PARIAH PAREA ISHMAEL OUTCAST
PARIAN CHINA MARBLE PORCELAIN
PARIETAL SOMAL SOMATIC
PARI-MUTUEL TOTE TOTALIZER
PARING CHIP FOIL SHRED SPECK
  GUBBIN PARURE PEELING
(FISH —S) GUBBINS
(PL.) BOXING
PARIS ALEXANDER
(— AIRPORT) ORLY
(FATHER OF —) PRIAM
(MOTHER OF —) HECUBA
(PALACE IN —) ELYSEE LOUVRE
  TUILERIES
(RIVER OF —) SEINE
(STOCK EXCHANGE IN —) BOURSE
(SUBWAY IN —) METRO
(WIFE OF —) OENONE
PARISH CURE HOUSE TITLE CHARGE
  SOCIETY PECULIAR OUTPARISH
(— HEAD) PASTOR PRIEST MINISTER
(— MEETING) VESTRY
PARISON BLOW GATHERING
PARITY ANALOGY EQUALITY
  LIKENESS GRAVIDITY
PARK HAY PEN HOLE STOP WAIT
  GREEN LEAVE CIRCLE DAPHNE
  GARDEN PRATER COMMONS
  DIAMOND PADDOCK TERRACE
  PARADISE TETRAGON
PARKA PARCA ANORAK
PARLANCE TALK IDIOM SPEECH
  DICTION DISCOURSE
PARLAY DOUBLE
PARLEY DODGE PARLE SPEAK
  TREAT UTTER CONFER INDABA
  PALTER PAROLI DISCUSS PALAVER
  PARLING DISCOURSE TEMPORIZE
PARLIAMENT DIET RUMP TING
  COURT SENAT CORTES FANTAN
  MAJLIS SAEIMA COUNCIL ESTATES
  LAGTING RIKSDAG CONGRESS
  CONVERSE STORTING VOLKSRAAD
(SCAND. —) THING
PARLIAMENTARIAN APRONEER
PARLOR BEN BOOR HALL
  FOREROOM LOCUTORY SNUGGERY
  SOLARIUM
(COUNTRY —) SPENCE
(MILKING —) BAIL
PARLORMAID MATRON
PARLOUS KEEN RISKY CLEVER
  SHREWD CUNNING CRITICAL
  PERILOUS DANGEROUS HAZARDOUS
PARMESAN GRANA

PAROCHIAL PETTY NARROW
PAROCHIAN SECTARIAN
PARODIST SPOOFER
PARODY RIB SKIT SPOOF SATIRE
TRAVESTY BURLESQUE IMITATION
PAROLE FAITH PLEDGE LICENSE
PROMISE
PARONOMASIA PUN AGNOMINATION
PARONYCHIA FELON PANARIS
NAILWORT
PAROTITIS MUMPS
PAROXYSM FIT KINK PANG AGONY
COLIC QUIRK SPASM STORM STOUR
THROE ACCESS ATTACK FRENZY
ORGASM RAPTUS SHOWER
RAPTURE EPITASIS AGITATION
PARR PAR SAMLET SCEGGER
SKEGGER BRANDLIN BRANDLING
PARROT ARA HIA KEA COPY ECHO
JAKO KAKA LORO LORY POLL VAZA
ARARA CAGIT MACAW MIMIC POLLY
AMAZON CAIQUE CONURE KAKAPO
REPEAT TIRIBA CORELLA GRASSIE
LORILET COCKATOO LORIKEET
LOVEBIRD PARAKEET PICARIAN
POPINJAY BROADTAIL COCKATEEL
PARROT FISH LORO SCAR LANIA
LAUIA SCAUR VIEJA COTORO
SCARUS LABROID MUDFISH
OLDWIFE BLUEFISH
PARRY FEND STOP WARD AVOID
BLOCK DODGE EVADE FENCE PRIME
QUART SIXTE OCTAVE PARADE
QUINTE SECOND THWART TIERCE
COUNTER DEFLECT EVASION
PARSE PACE PEARCE ANALYZE
DIAGRAM DISSECT CONSTRUE
ANATOMIZE
PARSI ZOROASTRIAN
(— HOLY BOOK) AVESTA
(— PRIEST) MOBED DASTUR
PARSIMONIOUS GARE MEAN NEAR
NIGH CLOSE SCANT SPARE TIGHT
FRUGAL NARROW SCARCE SCOTCH
SKIMPY SORDID STINGY STRAIT
MISERLY SCRIMPY SPARING
COVETOUS GRASPING GRUDGING
SCREWING WRETCHED MERCENARY
NIGGARDLY PENURIOUS RETENTIVE
PARSLEY ACHE CUMIN UMBEL
CICELY CONIUM ELTROT KARPAS
CHERVIL HOGWEED FLUELLIN
PARSLEY CAMPHOR APIOL APIOLE
PARSNIP TANK WYPE UMBEL
CONIUM MADNEP CADWEED
HOGWEED BUNDWEED QUEENWEED
PARSON RECTOR CROAKER PATRICO
PERSONA MINISTER PREACHER
GUIDEPOST
(— COUNTRY —) RUM
(PL.) PARSONRY
PARSONAGE GLEBE MANSE
RECTORY PASTORATE PASTORIUM
PARSON BIRD POE TUI KOKO TUWI
POEBIRD POYBIRD
PART DEL END LOT PAN DEAL DOLE
FECK GRIN HAET HALF HAND PANE
ROLE ROVE SECT SHED SIDE SOME

TWIN PARTY PIECE QUOTA SEVER
SHARE SHODE SNACK SPLIT TWAIN
BEHALF CANTON CLEAVE DEPART
DETAIL DIVIDE FEEDER FINGER
MEMBER MINUTE MOIETY PARCEL
PORTIO QUORUM SECTOR SINGLE
SUNDER UNYOKE DISJOIN ELEMENT
FEATURE FRUSTUM PORTION
SECTION SEGMENT SEVERAL
ALIENATE DISSEVER DIVISION
ELIQUATE FRACTION LIRIPIPE
(— HAIR) SHADE
(— OF ANIMAL'S TAIL) DOCK
(— OF BEEF) CHUCK SKINK
(— OF BLAST FURNACE) BOSH
BELLY
(— OF BOW) PEAK
(— OF CAM WHEEL) LOBE
(— OF CANNON) CHASE
(— OF CHAIR) SPLAT
(— OF COMPASS) FLY
(— OF CONCERTO) CEMBALO
(— OF CROSSBOW) LATH
(— OF DIAMOND) BEZEL
(— OF FLEECE) LEECH
(— OF FOWL'S COMB) BLADE
(— OF GUN SHIELD) APRON
(— OF HARBOR) FAIRWAY
(— OF HAWK'S BEAK) CLAP
(— OF HIDE) RANGE
(— OF HOOKAH) CHILLUM
(— OF POETIC FOOT) ARSIS
(— OF PORK LOIN) GRISKIN
(— OF RIVER) FRESH
(— OF SADDLE TREE) FORK
(— OF STAIR TREAD) NOSING
(— OF STAMEN) ANTHER
(— OF SWORD BLADE) FOIBLE
(— OF SWORD) FORTE
(— OF TEMPLE) CELLA
(— OF TONGUE) DORSUM
(— OF TURTLE) CALIPEE
(— OF VIOLIN BOW) BAGUET
(— OF WHEEL) SPEECH
(— THAT REVOLVES) ROTOR
(— WITH) GIVE LOSE SELL LEAVE
DONATE ABANDON
(24TH —) CARAT
(360TH —) DEGREE
(ACCOMPANYING —) BURDEN
OBBLIGATO
(ASSUMED —) FIGURE
(BAGLIKE —) SAC
(BEST —) FAT YOLK CREAM
FLOWER MARROW
(BRISTLELIKE —) SETA
(BROADEST — OF PLANK) TOUCH
(CENTRAL —) HUB BODY CORE
HEART KERNEL
(CHOICE —) ELITE
(CLEAR — OF LIQUID) SWIM
(CLOSING —) HEEL
(COARSE — OF FLAX) HURDS
(CONICAL —) BULLET
(CURVED —) START
(DEPRESSED —) HOLLOW
(DISTANT —S) FARNESS
(DUPLICATE —) SPARE

(EDIBLE — OF CLAM) CHEEK
(ESSENTIAL —) PITH
(ESSENTIAL —S) STAMINA
(FIFTH —) QUINTUS
(FINAL —) LAST SHANK EPILOG
(FIRST —) FRONT PRIME INITIAL
BEGINNING
(FOURTH —) FARDEL FERLING
(FRONT —) VAUNT BREAST
FORESIDE
(GREATER —) HEFT SUBSTANCE
(HARDEST —) BRUNT
(HIGHEST —) CROP CROWN HEIGHT
(HUNDREDTH —) CENTESM
(IMPAIRING —) ALLOY
(IN —) HALVES
(INNERMOST —) FUND
(INSTRUMENTAL —) HAND
CONTINUO
(INTERLACED —) TWINE
(LARGE —) FORCE
(LATERAL — OF HEAD) CHEEK
(LATTER —) HEEL
(LEAST —) STITCH
(LOWER — OF ROBE) BASES
(LOWER —) SECONDO
(LOWEST —) FOOT BOTTOM
GROUND DESCENT
(MAIN —) BODY BULK SUBSTANCE
(MATERIAL —) GIST
(MIDDLE — OF NIGHT) HOWE
(MIDDLE —) DEEP CENTER
(MINOR —) BIT COG
(MINUTE —) PRICK TITTLE
(MISSING —) LACUNA
(MOST IMPORTANT —) EYE
FOREHAND
(MOST SERIOUS —) DICKENS
(OF HORSE'S THIGH) GASKIN
(OVERDUE —) ARREAR
(PRINCIPAL —) BODY MAIN GROSS
(PRIVATE —) THING MEMBER
(PROJECTING —) ARM JAG JET JOG
APSE LOBE SPURN
(PROTUBERANT —) BOSS BULGE
(REJECTED —S) CHANKINGS
(REMAINING —) BUTT DREG HEEL
(REMOTEST —) EXTREMITY
(RINGLIKE —) ANNULUS
(ROOTLIKE —) RADICLE
(ROUNDED —) BULB
(SAWLIKE —) SERRA
(SECRET —) RECESS
(SLENDER —) NECK
(SMALL —) BIT ATOM FLOW TITHE
DETAIL MINUTE SNIPPET
(SMALLEST —) ATOM WHIT MINIM
(SOFT — OF BREAD) CRUMB
(SOFT — OF VEIN) LEATH
(SOLO —) CALL
(STILL — OF WATER) KELD
(SWINGING —) FLAIL
(TELLING —) POINT
(TENTH —) TITHE
(THIN — OF WALL) ALLEGE
(THIRD —) THIRDENDEAL
(TOP —) HEADPIECE
(TWELFTH —) INCIA POINT UNCIAL

(UPPER —) CHIEF RIDGE OVERPARTY
(UPPERMOST —) TOP PEAK CHIEF UPSIDE TOPSIDE
(VAUDEVILLE —) OLIO
(VITAL —) HEART
(WINGLIKE —) ALA
(WORST —) DEPTH
(WORTHLESS —) DREGS
PARTAKE BITE PART SHARE DIVIDE PARTEN
(— OF) USE HAVE SHARE TASTE TOUCH IMPART
PARTAN CRAB
PARTED PARTITE
PARTHAON (FATHER OF —) AGENOR
(MOTHER OF —) EPICASTE
(SON OF —) OENEUS
(WIFE OF —) EURYTE
PARTIAL HALF PART SEMI BIASED UNFAIR COLORED HALFWAY UNEQUAL HARMONIC INCLINED PARTISAN PROPENSE SKELETON FAVORABLE
PARTIALITY FAVOR RESPECT AFFECTION SPECIALTY
PARTIALLY HALF HALFWAY HALFWISE
PARTICIPANT BOOK ACTOR PARTY MEMBER PARTNER DUETTIST PARTABLE PARTISAN
(SUBORDINATE —) STOOGE
(PL.) FIELD
PARTICIPATE JOIN SIDE ENTER SHARE ENGAGE ENLIST IMPART COMPETE PARTAKE
(— IN) GO HAVE JOIN STAY STAND TASTE COMMON STICKLE
PARTICIPATION HAND PLOT SOCIETY INTEREST
(COMMON —) COMMUNITY
PARTICIPLE VERBID
PARTICLE ACE BIT DOT FIG GRU JOT RAY ATOM BETA CORN CROT DUST GRUE HAET IOTA KNIT MITE MOTE SNIP SPOT STIM WHIT ALPHA BOSON FLAKE FLECK GHOST GRAIN MESON POINT SHRED SPECK STARN STIME THRUM TWINT FILING GEIGER LEPTON MOMENT PANGEN RIZZOM SMIDGE SMITCH TITTLE AMICRON FERMION GEMMULE GRANULE NUCLEUS PSYCHON SMIDGIN ACCEPTER SMIDGEON POSITRINO SCINTILLA
(— IN BLOOD) EMBOLUS
(— IN INTERNAL EAR) OTOCONIUM
(— OF FIRE) SPARK
(— OF GOLD) COLOR
(— OF SOOT) ISEL IZLE SMUT AIZLE
(—S IN BEER) FLOATERS
(—S OF GRAIN) CHOP
(ATOMIC —) ION ELECTRON
(ELECTRIFIED —) ION ANION PROTON THERMION
(FINE ICY —S) SLEET
(JAGGED —) SPLINTER
(LEAST POSSIBLE —) MINIM

(LINGUISTIC —) SERVILE
(MINUTE —) JOT ORT RAY ATOM GRAIN SPECK RAMENT GRANULE MOLECULE RAMENTUM
(NEGATIVE —) NOR NOT
(NUCLEAR —S) FALLOUT
(POSITIVELY-CHARGED —) CATION KATION
(SMALL —) NIP BLEB CORN MOTE GRAIN SPECK AMICRON GRANULE SPRINKLE SUBMICRON
(TINY —) ATOMY
(ULTIMATE —) PSYCHON
(PL.) DUST FINES SWARF SIZINGS CUTTINGS FURFURES
PARTI-COLORED PIED FANCY MOTLEY PARTED PIEBALD BUTTERFLY HARLEQUIN
PARTICULAR AND ATOM FIXY ITEM NICE SELF FUSSY PARTY POINT THING CHOOSY DAINTY DETAIL MINUTE MOROSE REGARD SINGLE STICKY ARTICLE CAREFUL CERTAIN CORRECT FINICKY PRECISE PRIVATE RESPECT SEVERAL SPECIAL UNUSUAL CLERKISH CONCRETE ESPECIAL PECULIAR PICKSOME PRECIOUS SINGULAR SUBALTERN
(NOT —) INCURIOUS
PARTICULARLY ONLY EXTRA SINGLY SPECIAL EXPRESSLY SPECIALLY
PARTING DEATH GOODBYE FAREWELL
(— AS OF HAIR) SHED
PARTISAN PIKE SIDER STAFF BIASED FACTOR FAUTOR MARIAN ZEALOT CALOTIN DEVOTEE GUISARD PARTNER ADHERENT CRISTINO ESPOUSER FAVORITE FENNOMAN FOLLOWER JACOBITE MOSSBACK SIDESMAN STALWART URBANIST HIGHFLIER MAZZINIST OCHLOCRAT OLIVERIAN SECTARIAN TERRORIST
(NOT —) CATHOLIC
(PL.) FOLLOWING
PARTITION BAR CUT DAM FIN FLAG SEPT WALL SHOJI SPEER STAGE WITHE BAFFLE DIVIDE PARPAL SCONCE SCREEN SEPTUM BARRIER ENCLOSE GRATING PINFOLD PORTION SCANTLE BRATTICE BULKHEAD CLEAVAGE DIVISION STOPPING TRAVERSE DASHBOARD DAYABHAGA ICONOSTAS STOOTHING
(— BETWEEN STALLS) TRAVIS TREVIS TRAVISS
(— IN CHIMNEY) WITH WITHE
(— IN COTTAGE) SPEER HALLAN
(— IN LOUDSPEAKER) BAFFLE
(— IN WATERWHEEL) WREST
(— OF ESTATE) BOEDELSCHEIDING
(— OF LATH AND PLASTER) STOOTHING
(HORIZONTAL —) STAGE
(MINING —) SOLLAR STOPPING
(PL.) CANCELLI

PARTLET HEN WOMAN PERTELOT
PARTLY WHAT PARCEL PARTIM HALFLINGS
PARTNER BOY PAL ALLY HALF MATE PARD WIFE BUDDY BUTTY PARTY FELLOW MARROW SHARER COMRADE CONSORT HUSBAND CAMARADA COPEMATE SIDEKICK YOKEMATE
(— OF DUMMY) VIVANT
(DANCING —) GIGOLO CAVALIER
PARTNERSHIP HUI AXIS FIRM HOUSE FUSION CAHOOTS COMPANY SOCIETY SOCIETEIT
PARTRIDGE HUN BIRD KYAH YUTU LERWA RUDGE TITAR CHUKAR REDLEG SEESEE CHEEPER PATRICK SHRIMPI TINAMOU BOBWHITE FRANCOLIN FRENCHMAN TETRAONID
(— NOISE) JUCK
(SAND —) TEHOO
(YOUNG —) CHEEPER SQUEALER
PARTRIDGEBERRY BOXBERRY COWBERRY EYEBERRY ONEBERRY SNOWBERRY TWINBERRY
PART-TIME PARCEL
PARTURITION EUTOCIA TRAVAIL CHILDBED DELIVERY DYSTOCIA
PARTY DO BAL BEE CRY TEA CLAN DRUM GALA SECT SIDE BINGE BRAWL CABAL CRUSH GROUP LEVEE COMITE FIESTA FROLIC FRONDE GERMAN INFARE JUNKET PERSON SETOUT SHINDY SHOWER BLOWOUT CANTICO COMPANY FACTION GREGORY PATARIA SHINDIG DRINKING FENNOMAN POTLATCH POUNDING SOCIABLE SQUANTUM TERTULIA CONCISION INCLINING
(— GIVEN AT HOME) HUDDLE
(AFTERNOON —) TEA RECEPTION
(BEACH —) CLAMBAKE
(BRIDAL —) SEND SHOWER
(DANCING —) HOP GERMAN CANTICO HOEDOWN FANDANGO
(DRINKING —) KNEIPE POTATION SYMPOSIUM
(DRUNKEN —) BLIND
(EVENING —) BALL SOIREE GREGORY TERTULIA
(FISHING —) HUKILAU
(HUNTING —) FAID
(INFORMAL —) SOCIABLE TERTULIA
(IRISH —) HOOLEY
(MASQUERADE —) GUISE
(MEN'S —) STAG SMOKER
(POLITICAL —) SAM SIDE WAFD HOOKS LABOR CAUCUS FRONDE SWARAJ ZENTRUM MINSEITO KENSEIKAI SQUADRONE
(POPULAR —) HOOKS
(SCOUTING —) ESPIAL
(SUPPLY —) BRIGADE
(TEA —) DRUM TEMPEST
(THIRD —) STRANGER
PARULIS GUMBOIL
PARVENU SNOB ARRIVE UPSTART

ARRIVIST MUSHROOM ARRIVISTE
PASCH PACE PAQUE EASTER
PASSOVER
PASCHAL LAMB CANDLE SUPPER
PASSOVER
PAS DE DEUX DUET
PASE FAROL NATURAL VERONICA
PASEAR WALK AIRING EXCURSION
PROMENADE
PASHA DEY EMIR PASAHAW
PASHTO AFGHAN
PASIPHAE (CHILD OF —) ARIADNE
PHAEDRA
(HUSBAND OF —) MINOS
PASQUEFLOWER BADGER GOSLING
APRILFOOL
PASQUINADE PIPE SQUIB SATIRE
LAMPOON PASQUIL
PASS BY GO COL DIE END FIG GAP
SAG USE ABRA BEAL CEDE CHIT
COMP COVE DREE DROP FALL FARE
FLIT FOIN GATE GHAT GULF HAND
HAVE LANE LEAD PACE RIDE ROLL
SEEK SILE SLAP SLIP STEP WADE
WALK WEAR WEND WIND CANTO
DREIE ENACT FLEET GHAUT GORGE
HALSE HURRY KOTAL LAPSE LITHE
LUNGE NOTCH OCCUR ORDER
PAPER PUNTA REACH RELAY SHAKE
SHOOT SMITE SPEND STRIP TRADE
UTTER WASTE WHELM YODEL
BILLET CONVEY DEFILE DEMISE
ELAPSE EXCEED HAPPEN PASSUS
PERMIT SPIRAL TICKET TRAVEL
TWOFER ABSOLVE ALLONGE
APPROVE BREATHE DESCEND
DEVOLVE DIFFUSE LATERAL
OVERGET PASSAGE UNDERGO
JUNCTURE REBOLERA PURWANNAH
(— A BALL) FEED HEEL
(— ABRUPTLY) LEAP
(— ALONG) DERIVE
(— AWAY) DIE SET FLEE WING
DEPART EXPIRE PERISH FORFARE
FORTHGO OVERDRIVE
(— BACK AND FORTH) FIG
CRISSCROSS
(— BAD COIN) SMASH
(— BETWEEN HILLS) BEAL SLAP
SLACK
(— BY) COTE OMIT SKIP VADE
WEND APASS CLEAR FORGO
FOREGO IGNORE OVERGO INTERMIT
OVERHEAVE
(— GRADUALLY) FADE
(— IN BULLFIGHT) SUERTE
(— IN POKER) BREATHE
(— INTO USE) ENURE INURE
(— JUDGMENT ON) DEEM
SENTENCE
(— LIGHTLY) BRUSH SKATE SKITTER
(— OFF) SHAM FOIST
(— ON) LEAK PACE
(— ONE'S LIFE) TRADE
(— OUT) CONK DEBOUCH EXHAUST
(— OVER LIGHTLY) SKIM SWEEP
OVERSKIP
(— OVER QUICKLY) SCUD FLEET

(— OVER) DO HIP BALK FREE SKIM
SKIP SLIP COVER CROSS ELIDE
FLEET SCOUR SWEEP TRANCE
OVERHIP INTERMIT OVERLOOK
OVERPOST PROGRESS TRAVERSE
(— QUICKLY) FLIT SPIN SPEED
STRIKE
(— THROUGH A BLOCK) REEVE
(— THROUGH NARROW WAY) THRID
THREAD
(— THROUGH) CROSS REEVE TRACE
DIVIDE OVERGO PIERCE SUFFER
EXCURSE PERVADE OVERPASS
OVERRIDE PERMEATE PROGRESS
PENETRATE
(— TIME) DRIVE SPEND TRADE
(— UNHAPPILY) DREE
(— UP) REJECT DECLINE
DISREGARD
(— WITH DIFFICULTY) WADE
(— WITH VIOLENCE) RAKE
(CUSTOMS —) CARNET
(FENCING —) FOIN LUNGE PUNTA
(FORWARD —) AERIAL
(HOCKEY —) CENTER
(MOUNTAIN —) COL GAP SAG GATE
GHAT SLIP CLOVE GHAUT KLOOT
KOTAL POORT SWIRE SWIRL
BEALACH
(NARROW —) ABRA GULF SLYPE
DEFILE
(SUDDEN —) LUNGE
PASSABLE FIT FAIR SOSO TOLLOL
GENUINE ADEQUATE MEDIOCRE
MODERATE POSSIBLE TRAVELED
PERMEABLE TOLERABLE
PASSABLENESS INDIFFERENCE
PASSABLY SEEMLY
PASSAGE CUT GAT GUT ROW VIA
WAY WRO ADIT BELT BORD DOOR
EXIT FARE FLUE FORD GANG GATE
HALL ITER LANE PACE PASS PAWN
RACE RAMP SLIP SLUM VENT WELL
AISLE ALLEY ALURE BAYOU BEARD
BOGUE CANAL CHOPS CHUTE
CLOSE CREEK CRUSH DRAFT DRIFT
DRIVE ENTRY FLYBY FORTE GLADE
GOING GORGE INLET JETTY MEUSE
PATCH PORCH SHUNT SLYPE
SOUND ACCESS ADITUS APORIA
ARCADE ATRIUM AVENUE BRIDGE
BURROW BYPASS CAREER COURSE
DEFILE DROMOS EGRESS ELAPSE
FAUCES HIATUS MEATUS PARODE
RELIEF SCREEN SLUICE STRAIT
TRAJET TRANCE TRAVEL TUNNEL
VOYAGE ARCHWAY BALTEUS
CHANNEL CHAPTER CONDUIT
COULOIR DIAZOMA DOGTROT
DRAUGHT ESTUARY EXCERPT
FISTULA FRAUGHT GALLERY
GANGWAY GATEWAY ISTHMUS
JOURNEY MANHOLE OFFTAKE
OUTTAKE PARADOS PROCESS
TRANSIT APPROACH AQUEDUCT
CLOISTER COMMERCE DEBOUCHE
DELETION PARADIGM SENTENCE
SHIPPING SINUSOID SPILLWAY

(— IN BOOK) WHERE EXCERPT
(— OF THREAD) FLOAT
(— TO STOMACH) SWALLOW
(— TO TOMB) DROMOS SYRINX
(—S OF LITERATURE) BEAUTIES
(AIR —) FLUE THIRL WINDWAY
THIRLING VENTIDUCT
(CENSORED —) CAVIAR
(CONTINUOUS —) LAPSE
(COVERED —) OPE PAWN PEND
(DIFFICULT —) APORIA
(LITERARY —) TEXT QUOTE
EXCERPT SNIPPET QUOTATION
(MINE —) RUN ADIT HEAD ROOF
SLUM DRIVE LEVEL SHAFT THIRL
AIRWAY STENTON UNDERCAST
(MUSICAL —) CUE CODA LINK
BREAK FORTE STAVE ARIOSO
FUGATO LEGATO REPEAT CADENZA
CODETTA FANFARE STRETTO
FLOURISH SPICCATO STACCATO
SYMPHONY VOCALISE
(NARROW —) GUT HASS ALLEY
GORGE JETTY NOTCH SLYPE
SMOOT DEFILE NARROW STRAIT
(SECURE — OF) CARRY
(SUBTERRANEAN —) POSTERN
(SWIFT —) FLIGHT
(WATER —) TICKLE TICKLER
PASSAGE HAWK TARTARET
PASSENGER
PASSAGEWAY (ALSO SEE PASSAGE)
BORD FLUE GANG HALL LANE PACE
PASS PEND PORT RACE SHED SLIP
WENT YAWN AISLE ALLEY ALURE
CHUTE DRIFT DRONG ENTRY GOING
LUMEN RAISE SHOOT SMOOT
STULM ACCESS AIRWAY AVENUE
COURSE DINGLE FUNNEL GUTTER
INTAKE MANWAY RUNWAY TRANCE
ZAGUAN DOORWAY GALLERY
SLIPWAY TWITTEN WALKWAY
WAYGATE CALLEJON CORRIDOR
HATCHWAY
(CLEARED — IN CROWD) HALL
(COVERED —) ARCADE CLOISTER
(MINE —) BORD BOARD DRIFT
SLANT STULM WINZE
(NARROW —) SLIP AISLE SMOOT
(SLOPING —) RAMP
PASSANT PAST CURRENT CURSORY
PASSING EPHEMERAL
PASSE AGED PAST WORN FADED
BELATED OBSOLETE OUTMODED
PASSENGER FARE INSIDE
FERRYMAN TRAVELER WAYFARER
(— WHO AVOIDS PAYING FARE) NIP
STOWAWAY
(— WITHOUT TICKET) HARE
(AIRPLANE —) BIRDMAN
(UNBOOKED —) CAD
(PL.) WAYBILL
PASSEPARTOUT SPANDREL
PASSERBY PASSER PASSANT
BYPASSER SAUNTERER
PASSERINE PERCHER
PASSIFLORA TACSO
PASSING DEATH DYING ELAPSE

CURSORY PASSADO RUNNING
SLIDING ELAPSING FLEETING
ENACTMENT EPHEMERAL
WAYFARING
(— BETWEEN) INTERCURRENT
(— BY) COTE
(— INTO EACH OTHER) FONDU
(— OF HOURS) TIME
(— OF TIME) EFFLUX
(SLOWLY —) LAG
PASSION IRE FIRE FURY HEAT LOVE
LUST RAGA RAGE TEAR TIDE WILL
ZEAL ANGER ARDOR BLOOD BRAME
CHAFE DEVIL ERROR FLAME LETCH
MANIA RAJAS SPUNK WRATH
AFFECT CHOLER DESIRE FERVOR
MOTHER PELTER SATTVA SPLEEN
TALENT WARMTH EARNEST
EMOTION EROTISM FEELING
OUTRAGE VULTURE APPETITE
DISTRESS VIOLENCE PADDYWACK
(— FOR DOING GREAT THINGS)
MEGALOMANIA
(— FOR MUSIC) MELOMANIA
(ANGRY —) FUNK
(ANIMAL —) KAMA
PASSIONATE HOT FOND WARM
FIERY GUTSY QUICK WHITE ARDENT
FERVID FIERCE FUMOUS IREFUL
STORMY SULTRY TORRID AMOROUS
FLAMING PEPPERY THERMAL
CHOLERIC FRENETIC VASCULAR
VEHEMENT WRATHFUL DIONYSIAN
IRASCIBLE
PASSIONATELY HASTILY FERVIDLY
PASSIONFLOWER MAYPOP
BULLHOOF
PASSIONLESS COLD FREDDO
PASSIVE INERT STOIC PATHIC
STOLID PATIENT FEMININE INACTIVE
SIGNLESS YIELDING APATHETIC
PASSIVENESS QUIETISM
PASSOVER PESAH PHASE PASQUE
PESACH
(— FESTIVAL) SEDER
(JEWISH —) EASTER
PASSPORT CHOP PASS CONGE
CONGEE DUSTUK DUSTUCK
FURLOUGH TESCARIA TEZKIRAH
SAFEGUARD
PASSUS PACE PART PASS STEP
CANTO DIVISION
PASSWORD WORD TOKEN DUSTUK
TESSERA WATCHWORD
PAST BY AGO WAS GONE YOND
YORE AFTER AGONE APAST ASIDE
ENDED SINCE BEHIND BYGONE
FOREBY PRETER ANOTHER
FOREGONE PRETERIT COMPLETED
(LONG —) HIGH
(TIME NOT LONG —) YESTERDAY
PASTE HIT PAP BEAT BLOW DIKA
DUFF GLUE MISO PACK PATE
CREAM DOUGH FALSE GESSO
HENNA PUNCH STICK ATTACH
BATTER FASTEN GROUND PANADA
RASTIK STRASS BUCKETY CLOBBER
COLOGNE DRAWOUT FILLING

GORACCO GUARANA STICKUM
BADIGEON BARBOTINE
(— FOR CAULKING) BLARE
(— FOR LINING HEARTHS) BRASQUE
(— FOR SHOES BOOTS) CLOBBER
BLACKING
(— OF CLAY) BATTER
(— TO FILL HOLES IN WOOD AND
STONE) BADIGEON
(ALIMENTARY —) FEDELINI
SCUNGILLI SPAGHETTI
(AROMATIC —) PASTILE
(COLORING —) HENNA
(DRIED —) GUARANA
(EARTHY —) ENGOBE
(FISH —) BAGOONG
(MEDICATED —) ELECTUARY
(PORCELAIN —) PATE
(POTTER'S —) BARBOTINE
(TOBACCO —) GORACCO
(WEAVER'S —) SOWENS BUCKETY
PASTEBOARD CARD SHAM FLIMSY
TICKET MATBOARD
PASTEDOWN LINING
PASTEL WOAD LIGHT CRAYON
PICTURE DELICATE
PASTEN HOBBLE TETHER PASTOUR
SHACKLE
PASTILLE CACHOU CANDLE
LOZENGE
PASTIME GAY TOY GAME PLOY
HOBBY SPORT GOSSIP OLEARY
SAILING AMUSEMENT DIVERSION
PASTOR HERD ANGEL RABBI
CURATE KEEPER PRIEST RECTOR
DOMINIE VICAIRE GUARDIAN
MINISTER SHEPHERD
PASTORAL POEM DRAMA RURAL
RUSTIC BUCOLIC CROSIER IDYLLIC
ROMANCE ARCADIAN
PASTORALIST SQUATTER
PASTRY PIE FLAN HUFF PUFF SOCK
TART TUCK CORNET DANISH ECLAIR
ABAISSE CARCAKE STRUDEL
NAPOLEON TALMOUSE TURNOVER
APPLEJACK
(— COOK) PASTLER
(— SHELL) BOUCHEE DARIOLE
TIMBALE TALMOUSE
(— STRIPS) LATTICE
(— WHEEL) JAGGER
(SWEET —) DOUCET
PASTURAGE FEED GANG GATE
STRAY COLLOP EATAGE FORAGE
HERBAGE SHEEPGATE
PASTURE ALP FOG HAG HAM ING
LEA PEN TYE BENT FEED GAET
GANG GATE GISE GIST HAFT HALF
HEAF HOGA INGE KEEP PARK AGIST
DRIFT EJIDO GRASS GRAZE LAYER
LEASE RANGE VELDT INTAKE
MEADOW OUTRUN SAETER
COWGATE FOGGAGE GRAZING
HERBAGE LEALAND POTRERO
VACCARY VICTUAL HERDWICK
OUTFIELD SHEEPWALK
(— GRASS) TORE GRAMA
(— IN STUBBLE) SHACK

(— LAND) RAKE TACK LEASOW
(HILL —) HOGA
(MOUNTAIN —) SETER SAETER
SHIELING
(SHEEP —) HEAF EWELEASE
(SHETLAND I. —) SETER
(SUMMER —) AGOSTADERO
(WET —) SLINK
PASTURELAND BENT SOUM
PASTURING RELIEF PANNAGE
PASTY PIE PATE PATTY DOUGHY
FRACID SAMBOUSE
PAT APT DAB DIB TAP TIG BLOW
CLAP GLIB JUMP PALP TICK CHUCK
FITLY FIXED IMPEL THROW CARESS
DABBLE SMOOGE SOOTHE STRIKE
STROKE TIMELY APROPOS CHERISH
FITTING PATAPAT READILY
SUITABLE PERTINENT
PATAGIUM TEGULA TIPPET SCAPULA
PARACHUTE PTERYGODE
PATAGONIA (DEITY OF —) SETEBOS
(RODENT OF —) CAVY MARA
(TREE OF —) MANIU ALERCE
ALERSE
PATAMAR COURIER PATTAMAR
MESSENGER
PATAYAN YUMAN
PATCH BIT EKE FLY BOUT LAND
MEND SKIP SPOT SWAB SWOB
VAMP BLAZE BODGE CLOUT CLUMP
COVER FRIAR FUDGE PIECE SAVER
SCRAP SPECK SPLAT BLOTCH
COBBLE DOLLOP GORGET MOUCHE
PARCEL REVAMP SOLDER SPETCH
SWATCH TINKLE CLAMPER CLOBBER
INWEAVE PELIOMA REMNANT
(— AS ORNAMENT) MOUCHE
(— CLUMSILY) BOTCH CLOUT
CLAMPER
(— OF COLOR) CLOUP DAPPLE
SPLASH SPECULUM
(— OF DARK HAIR) SMUT
(— OF DIRT) MIRE
(— OF FEATHERS) BIB CAP
(— OF ICE) RONE
(— OF LAND) RODHAM
(— OF LEATHER) SPECK
(— OF LIGHT) GLADE
(— OF PRINT) FUDGE
(— OF RUFFLED WATER) ACKER
(— OF SALIVA) SIXPENCE
(— OF TIRE) BOOT
(— ON BOAT) TINGLE
(— ON PRINTED PAGE) FRIAR
(— ON THROAT) GORGET
(— TOGETHER) CONSARCINATE
(— UP) HEAL MEND
(BALD —) AREA
(LIVID —) PELIOMA
(OOZY —) SPEW SPUE
(OPEN — IN FOREST) CAMPO
(SHOULDER —) FLASH
PATCHOULI PACCIOLI PATCHLEAF
PATCHWORD WASTEWORD
PATCHWORK BOTCH CENTO
CENTON JUMBLE SCRAPS
PATCHERY FRAGMENTS PASTICCIO

PATE PIE TOP HEAD BROWN PASTE
PASTY PATTY BADGER NOGGIN
NOODLE COSTARD COXCOMB
PATELLA CAP PAN DISH VASE
ROTULA KNEECAP KNEEPAN
WHIRLBONE
PATEN ARCA DISC DISH DISK PLATE
PATINA PLATEN VESSEL
PATENT ARCA BALD OPEN BERAT
BROAD OVERT PLAIN SUNNUD
EVIDENT LICENSE OBVIOUS
APPARENT ARCHIVES MANIFEST
PALPABLE PRIVILEGE
PATER FATHER PRIEST
PATERFAMILIAS MASTER
PATERNAL FATHERLY
PATERNITY FATHER ORIGIN
PATESI ISHSHAKKU
PATH ARC PAD RUN RUT TAN WAY
BERM FARE GATE LANE LEAD LINE
LODE RACE RACK ROAD TRIG TROD
WALK ALLEY BYWAY GOING JETTY
PISTE ROUTE SPACE TRACK TRACT
TRADE TRAIL BOSTAL BYPASS
CAMINO CASAUN CIRCLE COMINO
COURSE GROOVE SLEUTH SPHERE
SWATHE TRENCH CHANNEL
ERGODIC FAIRWAY FOOTWAY
HIGHWAY LANDWAY MEANDER
PASSAGE RODDING SIDEWAY
TARIQAT TOWPATH TRAFFIC
TRUNDLE WAYGATE BORSTALL
CENTRODE CROSSCUT DRIFTWAY
TRAILWAY TWITCHEL CROSSWALK
(— BETWEEN HEDGES) TWITCHEL
(— CUT IN MOWING) SWATH
SWATHE
(— FOLLOWED BY ENERGY)
ERGODIC
(— MADE BY ANIMAL) PIST PISTE
(— OF CELESTIAL BODY) ORBIT
(— OF CLOUDS) RACK
(— OF MOVING POINT) CURVE
LOCUS
(— OF RACE) STRIP
(— UP STEEP HILL) BOSTAL
BORSTAL BORSTALL
(BRIDLE —) SPURWAY
(CLOSED —) CIRCUIT
(NARROW —) BERM RACK TRIG
RODDIN TROCHA RODDING
(P. I. FOOT —) SENDA
(STONE-PAVED —) STEEN
(SUFI —) TARIQAT
(WINDING —S) AMBAGES
PATHAN TURI AFRIDI SIVATI BAJOURI
BANGASH PAYTHAN DANGARIK
PATHETIC SAD SILLY TEARY
TENDER FORLORN PITIFUL
DOLOROSO PATETICO STIRRING
TOUCHING AFFECTING
PATHIC MORBID VICTIM PASSIVE
CATAMITE DISEASED SUFFERER
SUFFERING
PATHOGEN VIRUS
PATHOS BATHOS SNIVEL
PATHWAY (ALSO SEE PATH) RUN
LANE PATH RACK COURSE RAMBLA
RAMBLE RODDIN BORSTAL RODDING

PATIENCE CALM THILD BEARANCE
STOICISM COMPOSURE ENDURANCE
FORTITUDE
PATIENT CASE CURE MEEK SOBER
BOVINE PASSIVE ENDURING
THOLEMOD SUFFERANT
(— OF ASYLUM) BEDLAM
(BE —) BEAR
(HYDROPATHIC —) WATERER
(MEDICAL —) CURE
PATIO COURT COURTYARD
PATOIS CANT GOMBO GUMBO
CREOLE JARGON DIALECT
PATRIARCH JOB ABBA ENOS LEVI
NASI NOAH PAPA POPE ALDER
ELDER JACOB PITRI DESPOT
JOSEPH NESTOR ABRAHAM ANCIENT
VETERAN VENERABLE
PATRICIAN NOBLE EMPEROR
PATRICK NOBLEMAN GENTLEMAN
PATRIMONY PORTION ANCESTRY
HERITAGE LONGACRE
PATRIOT LOVER AMATEUR
PATRIOTIC PUBLIC ENVELOPE
NATIONAL
PATROL GUARD SCOUT WATCH
STOOGE PATROLE PROTECT
PATROLMAN COP GUARD FLATFOOT
INSPECTOR
PATRON BUYER GUEST STOOP
AVOWRY CLIENT FATHER FAUTOR
JAJMAN ACCOUNT PADRONE
PATROON PROCTOR SPONSOR
ADVOCATE CHAMPION CUSTOMER
DEFENDER GUARDIAN MAECENAS
(PL.) FOLLOWING
PATRONAGE AEGIS FAVOR AVOWRY
CUSTOM FAVOUR ACCOUNT
AUSPICE FOMENTO HEARING
BUSINESS PADROADO
(— AND CARE) AUSPICE
PATRONAL TITULAR
PATRONIZE USE DEIGN FAVOR
DEFEND FATHER PROMOTE
PROTECT EMPATRON FREQUENT
PATROON TRACT CAPTAIN
SUPPORTER
PATTEE FORMY FORMEE
PATTEN BASE CLOG FOOT SHOE
SKATE STAND STILT CHOPIN
GALOSH RACKET SANDAL CREEPER
RACQUET SUPPORT CIOPPINO
SNOWSHOE
PATTER CANT TALK TIRL LINGO
HAPPER JARGON BLATHER BLATTER
CHATTER DIALECT
PATTERING PITAPAT
PATTERN CUT FUR SET BASE CAST
COMB COPY FORM GIMP IDEA LAUE
MOLD NORM PLAN SEME STAR
WAVE BISON BYSEN CHECK DECOR
DISME DRAFT EPURE GUIDE IDEAL
INLAY MODEL MOIRE MOULD NOTAN
PLAID SEMEE WATER BASKET
BURELE CANVAS CHECKS DESIGN
DIAPER ENTAIL ETOILE FABRIC
FIGURE FLORAL FORMAT FORMER
LACERY MAGPIE MATRIX MIRROR
MODULE MUSTER ONDULE PATRON

POUNCE RANDOM RECIPE SAMPLE
SQUARE STRIPE SYSTEM ALLOVER
CHEVRON EXAMPLE FACONNE
FILLING FOLKWAY GESTALT
GRIZZLE HOBNAIL MEANDER
MEANING MULLION PARAGON
PROJECT SAMPLER SLEIGHT
STENCIL TEMPLET CALENDAR
DYNAMICS FILIGREE HATCHING
ILLUSION PARADIGM PLATFORM
STRICKLE PROTOTYPE
(— IN BRAIN) GYRATION
(— OF BEHAVIOR) HABIT DISPLAY
(— OF CADENCE) CURSUS
(— OF LARGE SQUARES) DAMIER
(— OF SCARS) KELOID
(— OF SEPARATE OBJECTS) SEME
(— OF STRESS) SUPERFIX
(— OF TARTAN) SET SEET SETT
SETTE
(— ON PAPER) BURELAGE
(— ON STAMP) GRILL GRILLE
(— USED BY SILVERSMITHS) WORK
BOROON
(CROSS-BARRED —) PLAID
(FACIAL —) BLAZE
(GARMENT —) SLOPER
(HAT —) BLOCK
(KNITTING —) ARGYLE
(PORCELAIN —) FITZHUGH
(RUG —) AINALEH
(SHOE —) FORME
(SKATING —) EDGE
(SOCIAL —) FAMILISM
(SPEECH —) IDIOLECT
(STRIPED —) BARRE
(TAILOR'S —) PROTRACTOR
(TATTOO —) MOKO
(TREE —) HOM HOMA
(WEAVING —) DRAW
PATTERNED GOFFERED
PATTY TABLET BOUCHEE PRALINE
PATTYPAN VOLAUVENT
(— SHELL) DARIOLE TALMOUSE
CROUSTADE
PATULOUS OPEN SPREAD
DISTENDED
PAUCITY LACK DEARTH FEWNESS
EXIGUITY SCARCITY
PAUL PAOLO
(ASSOCIATE OF —) DEMAS SILAS
TITUS ARTEMAS BARNABAS
PAULDRON POLLET EPAULET
PALERON POLDRON POLLETTE
PAULOPOST DEUTERIC
PAULOWNIA KIRI
PAUNCH TUN BELLY PENCH RUMEN
ABDOMEN STOMACH GUNDYGUT
POTBELLY
PAUNCHY BLOATED
PAUPER BEGGAR INDIGENT
ROUNDSMAN
PAUPERISM BEGGARY
PAUSE HO HEM HALT HANG HOLD
LULL REST RUFE STAY STOP WAIT
ABIDE BREAK CEASE CHECK COMMA
DELAY DEMUR DEVAL DWELL
HOVER LIMMA POISE SELAH TARRY
TENOR BREACH BREATH CORONA

CUTOFF FALTER HANKER HIATUS
PERIOD STANCE CAESURA FERMATA
RESPITE VIRGULE BREATHER
INTERVAL
(— **BEFORE HURDLE)** DWELL
(SUDDEN —) CHECK
(PL.) LIMMATA CAESURAE
PAUT PAW POKE POWT STAMP
FINGER
PAVANE DANCE PADUAN
PAVE LAY PATH STUD TILE COVER
FLOOR CAUSEY COBBLE QUARRY
SMOOTH OVERLAY PREPARE
RUDERATE
(— **WITH STONES)** STEEN CAUSEY
PAVED COBBLED
PAVEMENT SLAB HEARTH PAEPAE
TELFORD ASAROTUM FLAGGING
FLOORING PATHMENT PEDIMENT
PITCHING SIDEWALK TROTTOIR
WASHBOARD
PAVER CUBER PAVIOR
PAVID TIMID AFRAID FEARFUL
PAVILION BASE FLAG TELD TENT
FOLLY KIOSK PINNA ROYAL CANOPY
ENSIGN HOWDAH LITTER PANDAL
PALLION COVERING GLORIETTE
PAVILLON CHINOIS CRESCENT
PAVING FLAG SETT BLOCK BRICK
DALLE PAVER STEAN STEEN STONE
COBBLE TARMAC ASPHALT
TELFORD PITCHING FLAGSTONE
(SQUARE —) MITCHEL
PAVIS COVER PAVADE PAVOIS
SHIELD PROTECT
PAW PAT PUD TOE CLAW FOOT
GAUM GRAB HAND MAUL PATY
PAUT PORT FLAIL PATTE TRICK
CLUTCH FUMBLE HANDLE PATTEE
CRUBEEN FLIPPER FORELEG
FOREFOOT
PAWKY SLY ARCH BOLD CANNY
SAUCY CRAFTY LIVELY SHREWD
CUNNING FORWARD SQUEAMISH
PAWL COG DOG BOLT HAND SEAR
STOP TENT TRIP CATCH CLICK
DETENT FINGER PALLET TONGUE
CLAWKER RATCHET
PAWN DIP POP WED FINE GAGE
HOCK SOAK VAMP WAGE SPOUT
SWEAT ENGAGE LUMBER OBLIGE
PIGNUS PLEDGE WADSET COUNTER
HOSTAGE PEACOCK CHESSMAN
MOSKENEER
(PL.) PHALANX
PAWNBROKER MOUNT UNCLE
BROKER LUMBERER
PAWNEE PANEE SKIDI WATER
ALMOND BISCUIT PLEDGEE
PAWNIE PAWN PEACOCK
PAWNSHOP PAWN SPOUT LOMBARD
POPSHOP
PAX BOARD PEACE TRUCE FRIEND
TABLET
PAY DO BUY FEE TIP ANTE FOOT
FORK GIVE MEET RENT SOLD WAGE
BATTA CLEAR COUGH DOUSE
PLANK SCREW SHEPE SOUND
WAGES YIELD ANSWER BETALL

DEFRAY IMPEND REWARD SALARY
SETTLE COMMUTE DEADRAY
HALVANS IMBURSE REQUITE
SATISFY SOULDIE STIPEND TRIBUTE
(— **ATTENTION)** DIG SEE COME
GAUM HARK HEED TENT ADVERT
REGARD
(— **COURT TO)** NUT SUE GALLANT
(— **DOWN)** DOUSE
(— **FLIRTATIOUS ADVANCES)** QUEEN
(— **FOR LIQUOR)** BIRL
(— **FOR)** ABY BUY BYE COUP ABIDE
COVER STAND ABEGGE
(— **HEAVY PENALTY)** SMART
EXPIATE
(— **HOMAGE)** CHEFE CHEVE CHIVE
SALAAM ADULATE
(— **IN ADVANCE)** IMPRESS
(— **MONEY)** PINGLE
(— **OF SOLDIER)** SAWDEE
(— **OFF)** LIFT SINK ACQUIT
(— **OUT)** BLEED SPEND STUMP
EXPEND DISBURSE
(— **TAXES)** GILD
(— **UP)** ANTE QUIT SETTLE
LIQUIDATE
(— **WITH IOU)** VOWEL
(ADVANCE —) IMPREST
(DAILY —) DIET
(EXTRA —) BATTA BONUS KICKBACK
(SMALL —) SCREW
PAYABLE DUE C4RTAL
PAYEE HOLDER ENDORSER
PAYMASTER BAKSHI BUKSHI
PURSER BUKSHEE PAGADOR
PAYMENT CRO DUE FEE TAX BILL
CENS DOES DOLE DUTY ERIC FEAL
FINE GALE GILD HIRE LEVY MAIL
TACK TOLL BONUS CANON CLAIM
GAVEL MAILL MENSE PREST PRICE
YIELD ANGILD BOUNTY CHARGE
LINAGE PAYOLA PLEDGE REBATE
RETURN REWARD TARIFF ADVANCE
ALIMONY ANNUITY BENEFIT
CUSTOMS DEPOSIT FOOTAGE
GARNISH PANNAGE PENSION
PRIMAGE SOLUTIO STIPEND
SUBSIDY SUBSIST TREWAGE
TUITION CASUALTY FOREGIFT
GRATUITY KICKBACK MALIKANA
MARITAGE MONEYAGE TREASURY
WOODGELD HEADPENNY
MALGUZARI
(— **FOR INJURY)** UTU
(— **FOR LABOR)** MEED
(— **FOR OFFENSE)** ENACH
(— **FOR RELEASE)** LOOSING
(— **OF FEE)** FEAL
(— **OF MINERS)** FOOTAGE YARDAGE
(— **ON DELIVERY)** COD
(DEMAND —) DUN BILL
(EVADE —) BILK DEFAULT
(HOMICIDE'S —) KELCHIN
(PERIODICAL —) GALE GAVEL
PAYNIM PAGAN PANIME HEATHEN
INFIDEL PAGANDOM
PAYOFF FIX BRIBE CLIMAX PROFIT
REWARD DECISIVE RECKONING
PEA DAL TUR DHAL GRAM LANG

SEED ARHAR CHICK CICER GANDUL
LEGUME PIGEON PODDER CARMELE
CATJANG KHESARI POWDARE
TANGIER GARVANRO
(— **DOVE)** ZENAIDA
(— **HARVESTER)** VINER
(— **PETAL)** KEEL
(EARLY —S) HASTINGS
(PARCHED —S) CARLS CARLINS
(PL.) POIS GRAIN
PEABIRD ORIOLE WRYNECK
PEACE PAX CALM EASE FINE LIOS
LISS REST AMITY FRITH GRITH
LISSE QUIET TRUCE REPOSE
SAUGHT SHALOM CONCORD
HARMONY REQUIEM
(GODDESS OF —) IRENE
(SYMBOL OF —) DOVE TOGA OLIVE
PEACEABLE FAIR SOME CIVIL QUIET
STILL GENTLE SILVER ORDERLY
PACIFIC SOLOMON AMICABLE
SACKLESS
PEACEFUL CALM SOME SOBER
STILL IRENIC PLACID SILVER
HALCYON PACIFIC
PEACE PIPE CALUMET
PEACH BLAB PAVY CLING PAVIE
SNEAK SPLIT TRUMP ACCUSE
BETRAY CARMAN CROSBY FOSTER
INDICT INFORM OREJON PEENTO
SALWEY ELBERTA PERSIAN PIENTAO
WHITTLE CRAWFORD ISABELLA
ROSEWORT
(— **STATE)** GEORGIA
(— **STONE)** PUTAMEN
PEACHBLOW FAKIR
PEACHBLOW FAKIR
PEACOCK MAO PAON PAVO PAWN
POSE PEKOK STRUT PAJOCK
PAVONE POWNIE PEAFOWL
PHASIANID
(— **TAIL)** TRAIN
(CONGO —) AFROPAVO
PEACOCK BITTERN SUN
PEACOCK BUTTERFLY IO
PEACOCK FISH WRASSE
PEACOCK FLOWER FLAMBEAU
POINCIANA
PEA CRAB PINNOTERE
PEAG TAX TOLL BEADS PAAGE
PEACK PEAGE PEDAGE WAMPUM
PEAI PIAY PIACHE
PEA JACKET PEACOAT
PEAK BEN NAB NOB PAP PIC TOP
TOR ACME APEX BEAK CIMA CUSP
DENT DOLT DOME KNOB KNOT PICO
PIKE TOLT BLOOM CREST CROWN
PIQUE PITCH PITON POINT SLINK
SNEAK STEAL STUMP CLIMAX
CUPULA SHASTA SHRINK SUMMIT
ZENITH EPITOME MAXIMUM
CENTROID
(— **OF ANCHOR)** PEE
(— **OF CAP)** SCOOP
(ICE —) SERAC
(ISOLATED —) TOLT
(SHARP —) HORN
(SNOW-CAPPED —) DOME CALOTTE
PEAKED WAN PALE THIN DRAWN
PIKED SHARP COPPED SICKLY

SLIMSY POINTED SLIMPSY
PEAKEDNESS KURTOSIS
PEAL CLAP RING TOLL CHIME CRACK
GRILSE SHOVEL MINNING RESOUND
SUMMONS THUNDER CARILLON
(— OF THUNDER) CLAP REEL
PEANUT BUR FLAX MANI MEAN
PETTY PINDA GOOBER PINDAL
ARACHIS BEENNUT ARACHIDE
EARTHPEA GRASSNUT KATCHUNG
VALENCIA MONKEYNUT
(— DISEASE) TIKKA
PEA POD COB PYSE QUASH PESCOD
(POORLY FILLED —) POP
(UNRIPE —) SQUASH
PEAR BOSC DIEGO MELON SABRA
BEURRE BURREL PANINI SECKEL
WARDEN WINTER KIEFFER PRICKLY
AMBRETTE BERGAMOT TASAJILLO
(PRICKLY —) TUNA NOPAL OPUNTIA
PEAR HAW THORN
PEARL GEM MABE TERN GRAIN
NACRE ONION PICOT UNION
BOUTON OLIVET ORIENT BAROQUE
BDELIUM BLISTER CATARACT
MOONBEAM MARGARITE
(— WEIGHT) TANK
(IMITATION —) OLIVET
(IRREGULAR —) SLUG
(PIERCED —) WIDOW
(SEED —) ALIOFAR
(SMOKED —) MITRAILLE
PEARL BLUSH ROSETAN
PEARL MILLET KOUS CUMBU
DUCHN DUKHN KOUSE JONDLA
DAGASSA
PEARLSIDES ARGENTIN
PEARLWEED SAGINA POVERTY
SEALWORT
PEARLY NACRY NACROUS PRECIOUS
PEARLY EVERLASTING LIVELONG
MOONSHINE
PEAR-SHAPED FULL MELLOW
ROUNDED PYRIFORM
PEASANT TAO BOND BOOR HERA
HIND KERN KONO KOPI PEON RAYA
RYOT SERF BAIRU BOWER CHURL
KNAVE KULAK RAYAH SWAIN
COTMAN COTTAR FARMER FELLAH
RASCAL RUSTIC BONDMAN
LABORER PAISANO VILLAIN
CHOPSTICK
(— CLASS) JACQUERIE
(— OF INDIA) RYOT KISAN RAIYAT
(ARABIC —) FELLAH
(IRISH —) KERN KERNE
(RUSSIAN —) KULAK MUZHIK
MUZJIK
PEASE CROW TERN
PEASHOOTER TRUNK BLOWER
PISTOL BLOWGUN
PEAT GOR PET SOD VAG COOM FUEL
MOOR MUCK MULL TURF COOMB
LAWYER MINION YARPHA DARLING
FAVORITE
(— BOG) CESS YARPHA
(— CUTTER) PINER
(— SPADE) SLADE TUSKAR TWISCAR
(DRIED — FOR FUEL) VAG
(LAYER OF —) FLAW

PEA TREE KATURAI
PEATY KETTY
PEBA PEVA ARMADILLO
PEBBLE DIB FLAX JACK PLUM
CHUCK SCREE STONE BANTAM
GIBBER GRAVEL QUARTZ SHILLA
SYCITE CHUCKIE CRYSTAL STANNER
JACKSTONE
(PL.) BEACH DREIKANTER
PECAN NOGAL PACANE
PECCADILLO FAULT OFFENSE
MISCHIEF
PECCANT FAULTY MORBID CORRUPT
SINNING DISEASED
PECCARY JAVALI WARREE TAGASSU
TAYASSU JAVELINA TAYASSUID
PECK DAB DOT JOB NIP BEAK BILL
CARP FOOD GRUB HOLE JERK KISS
PYKE PITCH PRICK STOCK THROW
HATFUL NIBBLE PEGGLE PICKLE
PIERCE STROKE CHIMBLE
(1-4TH OF —) LIPPY FORPET FORPIT
LIPPIE
PECKER BILL NOSE COURAGE
SPIRITS
PECTEN COMB MARSUPIUM
PECTORAL SANDPIPER JACK PERT
PEERT BROWNY BROWNIE
CHOROOK CREAKER FATBIRD
HAYBIRD KRIEKER SQUATTER
TRIDDLER JACKSNIPE
PECULATE STEAL MISUSE
EMBEZZLE
PECULIAR ODD VERY QUEER
PROPER QUAINT UNIQUE CURIOUS
PRIVATE SEVERAL SPECIAL
STRANGE UNUSUAL SEPARATE
SINGULAR SPECIFIC
PECULIARITY KINK IDIOM QUIRK
TRAIT TRICK TWIST IDIASM ODDITY
AEOLISM FEATURE IRISHRY
CROTCHET HEADMARK
(— IN BOWL) BIAS
(— OF SPEECH) IDIOLOGISM
(CROTCHETY —) FIKE
PECUNIARY POCKET MONETARY
FINANCIAL
PED BASKET HAMPER PANIER
PEDAGOGUE TUTOR PEDANT
DOMINIE SQUEERS TEACHER
THWACKUM
PEDAGOGY SCHOOL DIDACTICS
EDUCATION
PEDAL LEVER SWELL TREADLE
FOOTFEED PEDALIAN THROTTLE
(— COUPLER) TIRASSE
(PIANO —) CELESTE
PEDANT PRIG DUNCE TUTOR
DORBEL PURIST TASSEL ACADEME
PEDAGOG GAMALIEL DRYASDUST
OLOFERNES
PEDANTIC STODGY BOOKISH
DONNISH ERUDITE INKHORN
TEACHING
PEDDLE HAWK SELL CADGE SHOVE
TRANT TRUCK HIGGLE MEDDLE
PIDDLE RETAIL COLPORT
PEDDLER ARAB SMOUS BADGER
CRAMER JAGGER JOWTER MUGGER

STROLL WALKER NIGGLER
ROADMAN SANDBOY SWADDER
TROGGER TRUCKER HUCKSTER
BOXWALLAH DUSTYFOOT
(— OF DOPE) FIXER
(— OF DRESS PIECES) DUDDER
(— OF FISH) RIPIER RIPPER
(ITINERANT —) SMOUS SMOUSE
SMOUSER STROLLER
(MOHAM. —) BORA
(STREET —) CAMELOT
(WARES OF —) TROGGAN
PEDESTAL ANTA BASE BASIS BLOCK
STAND PILLAR PODIUM ROCKER
AKROTER SUPPORT PADMASANA
PEDESTRIAN PED DULL FOOT SLOW
HIKER FOOTER HOOFER WALKER
FOOTMAN PROSAIC PLODDING
WINGLESS
PEDICEL RAY STEM SCAPE STALK
PEDUNCLE FOOTSTALK
PEDIGREE STEMMA DESCENT
LINEAGE ANCESTRY PETEGREU
PUREBRED
PEDIMENT FRONTAL FRONTON
FASTIGIUM
PEDIPALP(PL.) LABIUM
PEDOMETER ODOGRAPH WAYWISER
PEDRERO PERRIER PETRARY
PEDUNCLE STEM SCAPE STALK
STIPES PEDICEL EYESTALK
HYPOCARP
(PL.) CRURA
PEEK PEEP PIKE GLANCE GLIMPSE
PEEKABOO PEEP BOPEEP PEEPEYE
PEEL BARK HARL HULL HUSK PARE
RIND SKIN FLAKE FLIPE SCALE
SLIPE STAKE STRIP CORTEX
SHOVEL SPITTLE UNDRESS
BARKPEEL ORANGEADO
(— OFF) HARL CRAZE FLAKE SHUCK
(BAKER'S —) PALE SPITTLE
(ORANGE OR LEMON —) ZEST
ORANGEAT
PEELER CRAB BOBBY CORER
HUSTLER SHEDDER SPUDDER
PILLAGER
PEELING RIND SKIN PARING PARURE
PEEN PIN PYNE RIVET
PEEP PRY SPY JEEP PEEK PEER
PULE SKEG STEP TOOT TOTE TOUT
CHEEP CHIRP DEKKO GLINT PIPIT
SNOOP TWEET DEGREE GLANCE
SQUEAK SQUINNY PEEKABOO
(— SHOW) RAREE
PEEPER EYE TOM FROG KEEK
VOYEUR
PEEPHOLE PEEP JUDAS EYELET
CREVICE
PEEPING NOSY PRYING
PEER PRY DUKE EARL FEAR GAZE
LOOK LORD MATE PEEP TOUT
BARON EQUAL GLINT GLOZE MATCH
NOBLE RIVAL STARE STIME THANE
TWIRE APPEAR FELLOW OLIVER
PINKER COMPERE
PEERAGE RANK DIGNITY BARONAGE
NOBILITY TENEMENT
PEERING SQUINNY

PEERLESS SUPREME MATCHLESS NONPAREIL UNRIVALED

PEESWEEP FINCH PEWIT LAPWING PEEWEEP

PEEVE IRK ANNOY GRUDGE NETTLE IRRITATE

PEEVISH SOUR CROSS DORTY PENSY SNACK TECHY TEENY TESTY TETTY THRAW TIFFY WEMOD CRUSTY GIRNIE HIPPED SNARLY SNUFFY SULLEN TATTER TOUCHY TWARLY TWAZZY TWITTY UPPISH UPPITY VAPORY CRABBED FRATCHY FRECKET FRETFUL FROWARD GROUCHY PETTISH SPLEENY TEDIOUS TIFFISH WASPISH PHRAMPEL PINDLING SANSHACH TWANKING

PEEWEE BOOT RUNT TINY PEWEE MARBLE LAPWING

PEG FIX HOB HUB NOB NOG PIN HOBB KING KNAG PLUG SCOB SHAG STEP CLEAT DOWEL DRINK NOTCH PERCH PITON PRONG SPELL SPILE SPILL STAKE THOLE THROW TOOTH WADDY DEGREE DOWELL FAUCET MARKER NORMAN PICKET REASON SPIGOT TAPOUN TIPCAT PINNING PRETEXT SCOLLOP SPERKET SUPPORT TRENAIL
(— **FOR PLAYING GAME**) CAT SPILIKIN
(— **FOR SADDLES**) SPERKET
(— **OF STRINGED INSTRUMENT**) CHEVILLE
(— **OUT**) DIE FAIL
(**IRON** —) PITON
(**THATCH** —) SCOB

PEGA REMORA

PEGALL BASKET PACKALL

PEGASUS QUAVIVER HYPOSTOME

PEG TOP PIRY PEERY PEERIE

PEIGNOIR GOWN DRESS KIMONO NEGLIGEE

PEISE BLOW FORCE PASSE POISE POIZE IMPACT WEIGHT BALANCE POISURE

PEKAN WEJACK

PELAGE FUR HAIR PILAGE

PELAGIC MARINE AQUATIC OCEANIC PELAGIAN

PELEUS (BROTHER OF —) TELAMON
(**FATHER OF** —) AEACUS
(**HALF-BROTHER OF** —) PHOCUS
(**SON OF** —) PELIDES ACHILLES
(**WIFE OF** —) THETIS ANTIGONE

PELF GAIN BOOTY LUCRE MONEY SPOIL TRASH PILFER PILFRE REFUSE RICHES WEALTH COMPOST

PELICAN DOVE ALCATRAS ONOCROTAL
(— **STATE**) LOUISIANA

PELISSE POSTIN POSTEEN

PELL BEAT PELE PELT HURRY PEELE HASTEN

PELLAGRA MAIDISM PELAGRA

PELLET BB WAD BALL CAST PILL SHOT BOLUS PRILL STONE BEEBEE BULLET FECULA OGRESS PILULE

CASTING GRANULE PALLION TRATTLE BUCKSHOT GUNSTONE HAILSTONE
(**SNOW** —**S**) GRAUPEL
(**PL.**) SHOT

PELLICLE FILM SCUM SKIN CRUST CUTICLE EPISTASIS

PELLITORY BERTRAM BERTRUM WALLWORT

PELL-MELL RUSH MELPELL DISORDER HEADLONG

PELLOCK PALACH PORPOISE

PELLUCID CLEAR BRIGHT LIMPID ORIENT CRYSTAL

PELMA TRACK

PELMET CORNICE VALANCE PALMETTE

PELOPONNESUS (CITY OF —) SPARTA
(**PEOPLE OF** —) MOREOTE
(**RIVER GOD OF** —) ALPHEUS

PELOPS (FATHER OF —) TANTALUS
(**SON OF** —) ATREUS TROEZEN PITTHEUS THYESTES
(**WIFE OF** —) HIPPODAMIA

PELORIA EPANODY

PELT FUR KIT BEAR BEAT BLOW CAPE CAST COON DASH FELL HIDE HURL KITT PELL PUSH RACK SKIN BESET CHUNK FITCH HURRY SABLE SLASH SPEED STONE WHACK BADGER BEAVER FISHER PELTER SERVAL SPRING BETHUMP COONSKIN
(— **OF SEAL, WITH BLUBBER**) SCULP
(— **WITH MISSILES**) BUM SQUAIL
(— **WITH STONES**) LAPIDATE
(**BEAVER** —) BLANKET

PELTAST SOLDIER

PELTATE SCUTATE

PELTER SKEET

PELTING SLASHING

PELTRY FURS SKINS

PELUDO POYOU ARMADILLO

PEN COT CUB GET HOK MEW PAR PIN STY BOLT CAGE COOP CROO CROW FAUD FOLD JAIL STUB WALK YARD BUGHT CRAWL CREEP CUBBY HUTCH KRAAL POINT QUILL STYLE WRITE BOUGHT CORRAL CRUIVE FASTEN FLIGHT HURDLE INDITE RECORD STYLUS ZAREBA CONFINE WARKLOOM
(— **CATTLE**) STANCE
(— **FOR CATTLE**) CUB LOT CREW CRUE LAIR REEVE
(— **FOR ELEPHANTS**) KRAAL
(— **FOR HOGS OR SLAVES**) CRAWL
(— **OF CUTTLEFISH**) GLADIUS
(— **POINT**) NEB NIB STUB
(— **UP**) FRANK STIVE
(**AUTHOR'S** —) STYLE STYLUS
(**FOUNTAIN** —) STICK
(**REED** —) CALAMUS

PENALIZE CHECK

PENALTY BETE CAIN DOOM FINE LOSS PAIN BEAST JUISE MULCT AMENDE AMERCE SOLACE FORFEIT NEMESIS SURSIZE BLOODWIT

HARDSHIP SCAFFOLD

PENANCE TAP SORE SHRIFT SORROW REMORSE SUFFERING

PEN CASE PENNER POPPET

PENCEL FLAG PENNON STREAMER PENNONCEL

PENCHANT BENT TASTE GENIUS LIKING LEANING FONDNESS

PENCIL PEN RED WAD BLUE LEAD WADD LINER SHEAF SKETCH STYLUS POINTEL CHARCOAL KEELIVINE
(**SLATE** —) SKAILLIE
(**PL.**) STATIONERY

PENCILWOOD MORDORE

PENDANT BOB JAG DROP FLAG JAGG PEND TAIL AGLET BULLA GUTTA POINT AIGLET LUSTER PALAOA PLAYER TABARD TARGET TASSEL EARDROP LANGUET SUPPORT LAVALIER

PENDENT LOP BAGGED ICICLE HANGING PROMISS

PENDULOUS LOP SLOUCH HANGING CERNUOUS DROOPING

PENDULUM SWING PENDLE SWINGEL SWINGLE VIBRATILE
(**INVERTED** —) NODDY

PENELOPE (FATHER OF —) ICARIUS
(**FATHER-IN-LAW OF** —) LAERTES
(**HUSBAND OF** —) ULYSSES ODYSSEUS
(**SUITOR OF** —) AGELAUS

PENEPLAIN STRATH ENDRUMPF

PENETRATE CUT DIG DIP SEE BITE BORE DIVE GORE PASS PINK SINK STAB WADE BREAK DRILL DRIVE ENTER IMBUE PROBE SEIZE THIRL CLEAVE FATHOM FICCHE GIMLET INVADE PIERCE RIDDLE SEARCH STRIKE THRILL WIMBLE DISCERN PERVADE
(— **MENTALLY**) ENTER
(— **ONE'S MIND**) SOAK

PENETRATED (EASILY —) MELLOW

PENETRATING ACID KEEN ACUTE LEVEL SHARP ASTUTE DEADLY SHREWD SHRILL SUBTLE GIMLETY INGOING INTRANT KNOWING PUNGENT PERCEANT REACHING TRENCHANT

PENETRATION DEPTH ACUMEN FATHOM INROAD INGOING INSIGHT SEEPAGE INCISION INVASION SAGACITY

PENGUIN AUK DIVER GENTU ARCTIC DIPPER GENTOO JOHNNY PINWING BREVIPED MACARONI
(**PL.**) IMPENNES

PENINSULA CAPE MULL NECK INDIA BILAND BYLAND ISLAND PENILE

PENITENCE RUE REGRET SORROW PENANCE PENANCY REMORSE

PENITENT RUER SORRY HUMBLE WEEPER STANDER CONTRITE
(— **OF 3RD STAGE**) KNEELER

PENITENTIARY JUG PEN JAIL STIR TENCH PRISON PENITENT

PENMAN CLERK AUTHOR SCRIBE
WRITER
PENMANSHIP HAND SCRIPT
PENSHIP WRITING
PENNANT FANE FLAG WHIP COLOR
ROGER BANNER CORNET PENCIL
PENNON PENSIL PINION PINNET
MEATBALL REPEATER STREAMER
PENNILESS POOR BROKE NEEDY
BANKRUPT INDIGENT STRAPPED
PLACKLESS
PENNON FLAG VANE WING ANVIL
BANNER PENCIL PENOUN PINION
FEATHER
PENNON SPAR PEGGYMAST

PENNSYLVANIA
CAPITAL: HARRISBURG
COLLEGE: JUNIATA URSINUS
LYCOMING
COUNTY: BERKS BUCKS TIOGA
CAMBRIA JUNIATA VENANGO
WYOMING LYCOMING
MOUNTAIN RANGE: POCONO
ALLEGHENY
NATIVE: AMISH DUTCH
PRESIDENT: BUCHANAN
RIVER: LEHIGH CLARION JUNIATA
LICKING TOWANDA CALDWELL
DELAWARE SCHRADER
ALLEGHENY SCHUYLKILL
MONONGAHELA SUSQUEHANNA
STATE BIRD: GROUSE
STATE FLOWER: LAUREL
STATE NICKNAME: KEYSTONE
STATE TREE: HEMLOCK
TOWN: ERIE ETNA PLUM YORK
AVOCA EASTON EMMAUS
SHARON ALTOONA EPHRATA
HERSHEY READING BRYNMAWR
SCRANTON SHAMOKIN
BETHLEHEM CHARLEROI
GETTYSBURG PITTSBURGH
UNIVERSITY: PITT DREXEL LEHIGH
TEMPLE BUCKNELL DUQUESNE
VILLANOVA

PENNY DY AES MEG RED SOU GILL
BROON BROWN OULAP PENCE
COPPER FOLLIS SALTEE STIVER
BROWNIE STERLING
(— DREADFUL) HORRIBLE
(DUTCH —) STIVER
(HALF —) HALFLIN
(OLD SCOTCH —) TURNER
(PL.) PENCE FOLLES
PENNYCRESS FANWEED STINKWEED
PENNY-PINCHING STINGY
PENNYROYAL PULIOL HEDEOMA
HILLWORT TICKWEED SQUAWWEED
PENNYWEIGHT DWT PENNY WEIGHT
STERLING
PENSION WAGE PAYMENT STIPEND
SUBSIDY TRIBUTE GRATUITY
MALIKANA
PENSIVE MESTO MOODY PENSY
SOBER DREAMY MUSING PENCEY
WISTFUL THOUGHTY

PENT CAGED PENNED CONFINED
ENCLOSED RESERVOIR
PENTACLE STAR HEXAGRAM
PENTAGRAM
PENTAD QUINTAD
PENTASTICH POEM UNIT STANZA
STROPHE
PENTECOST SHABUOTH
WHITSUNDAY
PENTHEUS (GRANDFATHER OF —)
CADMUS
(MOTHER OF —) AGAVE
PENTHOUSE PENT ROOF SHED
AERIE ANNEX HANGAR LOOKUM
SHADOW PLUTEUS BULKHEAD
SKEELING SKILLION
PENTOSAN ARABAN
PENTOSE APIOSE RIBOSE
PENTYL AMYL
PENURIOUS MEAN POOR BARREN
SCANTY STINGY MISERLY WANTING
INDIGENT HIDEBOUND NIGGARDLY
PENURY WANT BEGGARY BORASCO
POVERTY SCARCITY INDIGENCE
PRIVATION
PEON HAND PAWN SERF SLAVE
PELADO THRALL FOOTMAN
LABORER PEASANT SOLDIER
CONSTABLE
PEONY PINY MOUTAN
PEOPLE ARO LOG MEN PUL TAT VAI
YAO AKRA ASHA BENI BUGI CHIN
CHUD EMIM FOLK GENS HERD HIMA
HUMA IRON LAND LEDE LUBA LURI
PHUD PHUL PHUT RACE RAIS REMI
SAFI SARA SEBA SERE TEMA THEY
TOMA TULU USUN VITI VOLK WARE
AFIFI AVARS BENIN BONGO CATTI
CHAGA COURS DEMOS DUALA
EDONI ELYMI FOLKS GENTE GOMER
HAUSA JACKS LAITY LANAO LENDU
LUREM MARSI MASAI NOGAI ORANG
PUNAN QUADI RAMBO ROTSE
SACAE SALAR SAURA SHAKA STOCK
TAURI VOLTA WARUA WORLD
ABABUA ACHUAS AFSHAR AISSOR
ANGAMI ANGLES ARUNTA AVIKOM
BAHIMA BAKELE BAKUBA BALUBA
BELTIR BOSHAS BULLOM CIMBRI
COMMON DAIONE GENTRY GILAKI
GILEKI HAUSSA HERERO HERULI
KANWAR KPUESI KRUMAN MANTZU
MINYAE MOSCHI NATION OVAMPO
PAMIRI PUBLIC RAMUSI RUTULI
SAFINI SAMBAL SATRAE SEMANG
SHARRA TADJIK TAGAUR TELUGU
TUNGUZ TURSHA VENETI VOLCAE
WACAGO WAHIMA YNDOYS YUECHI
ZAMBAL ACHANGO ASTOMOI
BAGANDA BAGARRA BAKALAI
BANGALA BANGASH BAROTSE
BUNYORO DARDANI DENIZEN
DURZADA FALISCI GAETULI
GENERAL GEPIDAE GUHAYNA
INHABIT IRISHRY ISSEDOI ITALICI
KINDRED KURANKO MAKONDE
MESHECH MITANNI NABALOI
PICENES PICTAVI PUKHTUN ROHILLA
SAMBURU SENONES SILURES

SUKKIIM TIRURAI VESTINI WABUNGA
WACHAGA WAKAMBA WANGONI
(— HAVING DISTINCT LANGUAGE)
TONGUE
(— OF FASHION) FLOSS
(— OF GOOD BREEDING) GENTRY
GENTILITY
(ABORIGINAL —) JAKUN KHMER
KODAGU SEKHWAN
(ANCIENT —) CARA CHAM JUNG
ELYMI GETAE HURRI ICENI SACAE
SERES SICULI DARDANI FALISCI
FIRBOLG KIPCHAK SEQUANI SILURES
(CAVE-DWELLING —) HORITE
(COMMON —) DEMOS PLEBE
VULGAR VULGUS TILIKUM
SNOBBERY
(EXTINCT —) KOT CHONO COFAN
COREE CHANGO CHATOT GUINAU
HIBITO SAPONI SHIRINO
(FOREST —) SAKAI SAORA SAURA
(HONORABLE —) HONESTY
(LOWEST CLASS OF —) CANAILLE
(MARITIME —) LAMUT
(MOUNTAIN —) HUZUL HUTZUL
(NOMADIC —) SHUA HORDE IGDYR
IHLAT SHUWA HABIRU SHAGIA
SARACEN SHAMMAR SHORTZY
SHUKRIA
(OLD —) ANCIENTRY
(ORDINARY —) LAYFOLK
(PAGAN —) IRAYA HANUNOO
SUBANUN
(PRIMITIVE —) DAFLA IRULA KADIR
KURUKH CHENCHU
(WHITE —) ALBICULI
(PL.) MAKHZAN
PEOPLED ABAD SETTLED POPULATE
PEORIA MASCOUTEN
PEP GO VIM DASH VERVE VIGOR
ENERGY GINGER ANIMATE QUICKEN
ACTIVITY
PEPLUM GOWN SKIRT TUNIC PEPLOS
OVERSKIRT
PEPO GOURD MELON SQUASH
PUMPKIN PEPONIDA PEPONIUM
PEPPER CAVA IKMO ITMO KAVA SIRI
BETEL CHILI MANGO PIPER SIRIH
MATICO TOPEPO CAYENNE PAPRIKA
PIMENTA RELIENO JALAPENO
KAVAKAVA
(JAVA —) CUBEB
(RED —) LADYFINGER
PEPPER-AND-SALT JASPER
PEPPERGRASS CRESS CANARY
ANOUNOU COCKWEED
PEPPERMINT MENTHE LABIATE
PEPPER TREE MOLLE HOROPITO
PIMIENTO
PEPPERWORT DITTANDER
PEPPERY HOT FIERY SAUCY SPICY
TOUCHY PIQUANT PUNGENT
SPIRITED STINGING
PEPPY GINGERY
PEPTONE ASCARON
PER BY THE EACH THROUGH
PERADVENTURE HAP DOUBT
MAYBE CHANCE MAPPEN MAYHAP
HAPPILY PERHAPS POSSIBLY

PERAMBULATE WALK RAMBLE
STROLL PERAMBLE TRAVERSE
PERAMBULATION WEND
PERAMBULATOR BUGGY WAGON
BASSINET VIAMETER WAYWISER
PEDOMETER
PERATE OPHITE
PERCEIVE SEE ESPY FEEL FIND
GAUM HEAR KNOW LOOK MIND
NOTE SCAN TWIG SCENT SENSE
SMELL TASTE TOUCH BEHOLD
COTTON DESCRY DIVINE FIGURE
NOTICE REMARK SURVEY COGNIZE
DISCERN OBSERVE REALIZE
SENSATE COMPRISE DESCRIBE
UNDERNIM
PERCENTAGE CUT AGIO PART
SHARE PROFIT PORTION SCALAGE
DEFLATOR
(MINING —) LEY
PERCEPT IDEA
PERCEPTIBLE NOTABLE TACTILE
VISIBLE APPARENT PALPABLE
SENSIBLE TANGIBLE TRACTABLE
(FAINTLY —) SHADOWY
(HARDLY —) FAINT
PERCEPTION RAY BUMP GAUM
TACT SAVOR SCENT SENSE SIGHT
ACUMEN VISION CLOSURE FEELING
GLIMMER NOSTRIL BEARINGS
DELICACY OUTSIGHT COGNITION
SENSATION SENTIMENT
(DIM —) GLIMMER
(MENTAL —) TACT TOUCH
SENSATION
PERCEPTIVE QUICK SHARP SUBTLE
KNOWING SENSITIVE
PERCH BAR BAS LUG PEG ROD SIT
BASS JOUK MADO OKOW PERK PIKE
POLE POPE SEAT BARSE BEGTI
BEKTI BLOCK LIGHT REACH ROOST
RUFFE STAFF ALIGHT BUGARA
CALLOP PERCID SAUGER SETTLE
ZANDER ZINGEL ALFIONE HOGFISH
STATION ROCKFISH MARTENIKO
TRUMPETER
(2-YEAR OLD —) EGLING
PERCHANCE HAPLY MAYBE
AUNTERS FORTUNE PERHAPS
POSSIBLY
PERCHER STAKER
PERCHTA BERTHA
PERCOLATE MELT OOZE PERK SEEP
SIFT SILT SIPE SOAK WEEP DRILL
EXUDE LEACH EXHALE FILTER
STRAIN
PERCOLATION SIPING SEEPAGE
LEACHING
PERCOLATOR SIPER BIGGIN
CAFETIERE DISPLACER
PERCUSSION BLOW IMPACT
STROKE PNEUMATIC
PERDITION HELL LOSS RUIN
BOWWOWS BALLYWACK DAMNATION
PEREGRINATE TOUR WALK TRAVEL
WANDER JOURNEY SOJOURN
TRAVERSE
PEREGRINE ALIEN EXOTIC ROVING
PILGRIM STRANGE IMPORTED

PEREGRINE FALCON SAKER
GENTLE TASSEL TERCEL
PEREMPT QUASH DEFEAT DESTROY
PEREMPTORY FLAT FINAL UTTER
EXPRESS HAUGHTY ABSOLUTE
DECISIVE DOGMATIC POSITIVE
ESSENTIAL
PERENNIAL HERB CAREX LIANA
PEONY SEDUM BANANA CENTRO
BLUEWEED CONSTANT ENDURING
KNAPWEED TOADFLAX CONTINUAL
EVERGREEN PERPETUAL
RECURRENT
PERFECT ALL BACK CURE FILL FINE
FULL HOLY PURE SURE EXACT
FINAL FULLY IDEAL PLAIN RIGHT
RIPEN SHEER SOUND TOTAL UTTER
WHOLE ENTIRE EXPERT FINISH
REFINE SPHERE CERTAIN CONCOCT
CONTENT CORRECT CROWNED
DEVELOP GEMLIKE IMPROVE
PLENARY PRECISE SINLESS
SPHERAL TYPICAL COMPLETE
FLAWLESS INFINITE INTEGRAL
(— IN RIGHTEOUSNESS) HOLY
(— SCORE) MAX
PERFECTED EXACT SUMMED
FINISHED PERQUEIR
PERFECTION ACME PINK BLOOM
IDEAL BEAUTY FINISH PLENTY
FULNESS PARAGON FINALITY
FINENESS MATURITY RIPENESS
ERUDITION
(TYPE OF —) PARAGON
PERFECTIVE TELIC
PERFECTLY SPAN QUITE IDEALLY
PERQUEIR
PERFIDIOUS FALSE SNAKY DISLEAL
SNAKISH DISLOYAL SPITEFUL
FAITHLESS
PERFIDY DECEIT TREASON
FALSEHOOD FALSENESS
TREACHERY
PERFORATE EAT DOCK HOLE DRILL
PRICK PUNCH SIEVE THIRL PIERCE
POUNCE RIDDLE THRILL PINHOLE
PUNCTURE PENETRATE TEREBRATE
(— A STAMP) CENTER
PERFORATED OPEN CRIBROSE
PERFORATION BORE HOLE THIRL
TORET BROACH EYELET STIGMA
TRESIS FORAMEN PINHOLE SEPTULA
STENCIL DIABROSIS
PERFORM DO ACT CUT KIP CHAR
FILL FULL HAVE KEEP LAST MAKE
PLAY SHOW STEP CHARE DIGHT
ENACT EXERT FETCH ACQUIT
COMMIT EFFECT FULFIL RENDER
ACHIEVE EXECUTE EXHIBIT EXPLOIT
FUNGIFY FURNISH IWURCHE
PRESENT PRESTATE
(— AWKWARDLY) BOGGLE
(— BADLY) BOLLIX
(— BRILLIANTLY) STAR SPARKLE
(— CLUMSILY) THUMB BUNGLE
(— FULLY) END
(— HASTILY) SKIMP SCAMP
(— HURRIEDLY) SLUR
(— IN DANCING) FIGURE

PERFORMANCE ACT JOB DEED
FEAT HAND SHOW TEST WORK
CAPER SLANG SPORT STUNT
ACTING ACTION BALLET EFFECT
HORARY MASQUE ACCOUNT
ACROAMA BENEFIT BOOKING
CONCERT EXPLOIT MATINEE
MUMMERY SHOWING FAREWELL
FUNCTION PRACTICE STERACLE
(— FOR ONE) SOLO
(— OF DUTY) FEASANCE
(— OF OBLIGATION) SOLUTIO
(— VARIATIONS) COUNTER
(— WITH SENTIMENTALITY) DROOL
(ARAB —) FANTASIA
(CHRISTMAS EVE —) GOMBAY
(CLUMSY —) BUNGLE
(DRAMATIC —) TOPENG
(FIRST —) PREMIERE
(NO —) RELACHE
(PAST —) FORM
(TRIAL —) AUDITION
(VULGAR —) BLOWOFF
PERFORMER ACT DOER GEEK MOKE
STAR ACTOR SHINE ARTIST DANCER
KINKER LEADER PLAYER WORKER
ACROAMA ARTISTE GAMBIST
HORNIST HOTSHOT SOLOIST
EXECUTOR SPARKLER HAMFATTER
HEADLINER
(— ON SEVERAL INSTRUMENTS)
MOKE
(— WITH NEGRO DIALECT)
HAMBONE
(BURLESQUE —) GRINDER
(CIRCUS —) LEAPER
(INFERIOR —) HAM SHINE
PERFUME ATAR BALM FUME MUSK
NOSE OTTO AROMA ATTAR CENSE
CIVET MYRRH SCENT SMELL SPICE
CARVOL CHYPRE EMBALM FLAVOR
IONONE CARVONE DIAPASM
ESSENCE INCENSE JASMINE
NOSEGAY ODORIZE SWEETEN
BERGAMOT MARECHAL ORANGERY
PATCHOULI
(— BASE) MUSK CIVET NEROL
NEROLI
(POWDERY —) PULVIL
PERFUNCTORY CURSORY
CARELESS APATHETIC
PERGOLA ARBOR BOWER RAMADA
BALCONY TRELLIS
PERHAPS HAPS MAYBE ABLINS
BELIKE HAPPEN MAPPEN MAYHAP
ABLINGS LIGHTLY PERCASE
POSSIBLY
PERI ELF FAIRY SPRITE
PERIAPT CHARM AMULET
PERICARP BUR BOLL BURR
BLADDER
PERICRANIUM HEAD BRAIN
PERIDOTITE PICRITE EULYSITE
JOSEFITE SAXONITE WEHRLITE
PERIGEE EPIGEUM
PERIGYNIUM UTRICLE
PERIL RISK WERE WATHE CRISIS
DANGER HAZARD MENACE SCYLLA
THREAT THRONG TRANCE

JEOPARDY CHARYBDIS
PERILOUS KITTLE DOUBTFUL
DREADFUL INFAMOUS DANGEROUS
HAZARDOUS
PERIMETER RIM OUTLINE
BOUNDARY PERIPHERY
PERIOD GO AGE DOT END EON ERA
AEON DATE LIFE RACE SPAN STOP
TERM TIDE TIME YEAR AVAIL CLOSE
CYCLE EPACT EPOCH LABOR LAPSE
PATCH POINT SPACE SPELL STAGE
CUTOFF GHURRY HEMERA MOMENT
PARODY PICTUN SEASON STOUND
ACCOUNT DICOLON FLORUIT
PASTIME SESSION STADIUM
STRETCH DURATION INDUCIAE
INSTANCE LIFETIME SENTENCE
(— ENDING FROST) FRESH
(— FOR WHICH ENJOYED) TENURE
(— IN DEVELOPMENT) STAGE
(— OF 10 YEARS) DECADE
(— OF 100 YEARS) AGE CENTURY
(— OF 1000 YEARS) CHILIAD.
MILLIAD
(— OF 14 MINUTES, 24 SECONDS)
CENTIDAY
(— OF 2 MONTHS) DIMESTER
(— OF 2 YEARS) BIENNIUM
(— OF 20 TUNS) KATUN
(— OF 20 YEARS) KATUN
(— OF 260 DAYS) TONALMATL
(— OF 5 DAYS) PENTAD LUSTRUM
(— OF 50 YEARS) JUBILE JUBILEE
(— OF 7 DAYS) HEBDOMAD
(— OF 7 YEARS) SEPTENARY
(— OF ACTION) GO BOUT
(— OF DECLINE) SUNSET EVENING
(— OF DRYNESS) DROUTH
DROUGHT
(— OF FESTIVITY) WAKES
(— OF GLOOM) DEAD
(— OF GRACE) DAY
(— OF HEAT) CALLING
(— OF HUMID WEATHER) SIZZARD
(— OF IMMATURITY) SWADDLE
(— OF INSTRUCTION) LESSON
(— OF LIFE) AGE ELD SPAN
(— OF MILITARY SERVICE) HITCH
(— OF MOTILITY) SWARMING
(— OF MOURNING) SHIVA SHIBAH
(— OF PERFORMING) STANZA
(— OF PLAY) HALF CHUKKER
QUARTER
(— OF RECREATION) HOLIDAY
VACATION
(— OF REMISSION) JUBILEE
(— OF REST) SMOKO BREATHER
(— OF REVOLUTION OF HEAVENLY
BODY) ORB
(— OF TIME) DAY HOUR WEEK
YEAR MONTH DECADE MINUTE
SECOND
(— OF WORK) SHIFT SPELL STINT
(— PRECEDING IMPORTANT EVENT)
EVE
(CLASS —) HOUR
(CULTURAL —) HORIZON
(DEFINITE —) MOMENT
(DISTINCTIVE —) EPOCH

(DULL —) SLACK
(EVOLUTIONAL —) HEMERA
(GEOLOGICAL —) JURA KAROO
EOCENE ALGOMAN HORIZON
CAMBRIAN DEVONIAN JURASSIC
SILURIAN TERTIARY TRANSVAAL
(HAPPY —) MILLENIUM
(HYPOTHETICAL —) ACME
(LONG —) EON AEON CYCLE
(MEETING —) SESSION
(MENSTRUAL —) TERMS
(OCCASIONAL —) SNATCH
(PENITENTIAL —) LENT
(RECURRING —) EMBER
(SHORT —) BIT FIT BLINK SHAKE
SPELL SPURT SNATCH
PERIODIC ERAL ANNUAL CYCLIC
ETESIAN REGULAR FREQUENT
SEASONAL
(NOT —) LOOSE
PERIODICAL DAILY PAPER SHEET
ANNUAL DIGEST REVIEW ETESIAN
FANZINE JOURNAL TABLOID
DREADFUL EXCHANGE MAGAZINE
EPHEMERIS
PERIODICALLY TERMLY
PERIPATETIC ROVING RAMBLING
ITINERANT
PERIPHERAL DEEP OUTER DISTAL
DISTANT EXTERNAL MARGINAL
PERIPHERY LIP RIM BRIM DOME
EDGE AMBIT LIMIT SKIRT AREOLA
BORDER BOUNDS FRINGE AMBITUS
CONTOUR SUBURBS SURFACE
CONFINES PERIMETER
PERISCOPE ALTISCOPE HYPOSCOPE
OMNISCOPE
PERISH DIE FADE FALL RUIN TINE
TYNE QUAIL SPILL SWELT WASTE
DEPART EXPIRE STARVE DESTROY
FORFARE MISCARRY
(— GRADUALLY) FADE
PERISHABLE SOFT DYING CADUKE
BRITTLE FUGITIVE
PERISHED MUSHY
PERISTOME FRINGE
PERITE SKILLED
PERITHECIUM ALVEOLA
PERITONEUM RIM SIPHAC
PERIWIG FLASH GALERA PERUKE
TOUPEE GALERUM PERWICK
PERIWINKLE PERY PIRE WINK
PERRY SNAIL MYRTLE WINKLE
DOGBANE PINPATCH SENGREEN
BLUEBUTTON
PERJINK NEAT TRIM PRECISE
PERJURE FORSWEAR
PERJURED MANSWORN
PERK BRISK PERCH PREEN PRINK
FRESHEN SMARTEN
PERKY AIRY PERT COCKY JAUNTY
CHIPPER
PERMANENCE STAY STABILITY
PERMANENT FIXED STABLE ABIDING
DURABLE LASTING STATIVE
CONSTANT ENDURING REMANENT
STANDING INDELIBLE
PERMANENTLY KEEPS
PERMEABLE POROUS

PERMEATE FILL SEEP SOAK BATHE
IMBUE DRENCH INFORM INVADE
ANIMATE PERVADE DOMINATE
SATURATE PENETRATE
PERMEATED SHOT
PERMIAN DYAS DYASSIC
PERMISSIBLE FREE POSSIBLE
CONGEABLE
(NOT —) NEFAS
PERMISSION MAY FIAT LIEF CONGE
DARST FAVOR GRACE GRANT LEAVE
ACCESS ACCORD CONSENT LIBERTY
LICENSE SANCTION
PERMISSIVE TOLERANT
CONCESSORY
PERMIT LET CHOP GIVE LEVE PASS
ADMIT ALLOW CONGE EXEAT FAVOR
GRACE GRANT LEAVE SERVE
ACCORD BETEEM CEDULA DUSTUK
ENDURE ENTREE SUFFER CONCEDE
CONSENT DUSTUCK FACULTY
LICENSE PLACARD POMPANO
WARRANT DISPENSE
(— NEGATIVELY) TOLERATE
(— TO TAKE) SOAK
PERMITTED FREE LOOT LICIT
ALLOWED INNOCENT SUPPOSED
(— BY LAW) LEGAL
PERMUTATION BARTER CHANGE
EXCHANGE
PERNICIOUS BAD ILL EVIL FATAL
QUICK SWIFT DEADLY MALIGN
WICKED BALEFUL BANEFUL
HARMFUL HURTFUL NOISOME
NOXIOUS RUINOUS
PERNIO CHILBLAIN
PEROPUS PARAGON
PERORATION EPILOG PERIOD
CLOSING PURLICUE
PERPEND JUMPER PARPEN PONDER
REFLECT THROUGH
PERPENDICULAR SINE ERECT
PLUMB SHEER ABRUPT NORMAL
APOTHEM UPRIGHT BINORMAL
CATHETUS EVENDOWN VERTICAL
PERPENDICULARLY BOLT SHEER
SHEERLY
PERPENDICULARITY APLOMB
PERPETRATE DO COMMIT EFFECT
PERFORM
PERPETUAL ETERN ENDLESS
ETERNAL CONSTANT INFINITO
UNENDING CONTINUAL PERENNIAL
PERPETUALLY EVER ALWAYS
FOREVER
PERPETUATE CONTINUE ETERNIZE
MAINTAIN
PERPLEX CAP MAR SET VEX BEAT
CLOG DOIT DOZE FIKE MAZE STUN
AMAZE BESET BLAIK STUMP TWIST
BAFFLE BOGGLE BOTHER CUMBER
DARKEN FICKLE GRAVEL HAMPER
HARASS HOBBLE KITTLE MAMMER
MITHER MOIDER MUDDLE PLAGUE
POTHER POTTER PUTTER PUZZLE
RAFFLE RIDDLE TWITCH WILDER
WRIXLE BEDEVIL BUMBAZE
CONFUSE DIFFUSE EMBROIL
MYSTIFY NONPLUS PLUNDER

STAGGER STUMBLE TORMENT
BEWILDER SURPRISE WINDLASS
PERPLEXED MAZY ANXIOUS
NONPLUS PUZZLED CONFUSED
TROUBLED INTRICATE
PERPLEXING HARD MAZY CRABBY
KNOBBY KNOTTY CARKING
COMPLEX CRABBED QUISCOS
BAFFLING
PERPLEXITY FOG KNOT WERE
BRAKE FOITER HOBBLE PUCKER
TANGLE ANXIETY STICKLE TROUBLE
POSEMENT SURPRISE CONFUSION
LABYRINTH
(**MENTAL** —) STUDY
(**RELIEVE OF** —) CLEAR
PERQUISITE FEE TIP PERK VAIL
GOUPIN GOWPEN INCOME ADJUNCT
APANAGE VANTAGE CONQUEST
GRATUITY
(**PL.**) PICKING
PERRINIST LIBERTINE
PERRIER PEDRERO
PERSE BLUE
PERSECUTE VEX BAIT ANNOY
CHASE HARRY HOUND WRACK
WRONG HARASS PESTER PURSUE
AFFLICT CRUCIFY DRAGOON
OPPRESS TORMENT TORTURE
PERSECUTED JOB REFUGEE
PERSECUTOR TORQUEMADA
PERSEPHONE KORE DESPOINA
PRAXIDIKE
(**DAUGHTER OF** —) CORA KORE
(**FATHER OF** —) ZEUS JUPITER
(**HUSBAND OF** —) HADES PLUTO
(**MOTHER OF** —) CERES DEMETER
PERSEUS RESCUER CHAMPION
(**FATHER OF** —) ZEUS JUPITER
(**GRANDFATHER OF** —) ACRISIUS
(**MOTHER OF** —) DANAE
(**STAR OF** —) ATIK ALGOL
(**VICTIM OF** —) MEDUSA
(**WIFE OF** —) ANDROMEDA
PERSEVERANCE GRIT STAMINA
INDUSTRY PATIENCE TENACITY
CONSTANCY
PERSEVERE CANK KEEP TORE
ABIDE STICK INSIST REMAIN
PERSIST CONTINUE
PERSEVERING BUSY HARD STILL
RESOLUTE ASSIDUOUS INSISTENT
PERSIA (SEE IRAN)
PERSIAN PERSE GILAKI HAJEMI
IRANIC DURZADA HADJEMI IRANIAN
MEMNONIAN
(**— RED DEER**) MARAL
PERSICARY REDLEG REDLEGS
REDSHANK HEARTEASE HEARTWEED
PEACHWORT
PERSIFLAGE BANTER RAILLERY
PERSIMMON KAKI SIMON SIMMON
ZAPOTE CHAPOTE HYAKUME
TRIUMPH
(**— TREE**) GAB GAUB LOTUS
PERSIST HOLD KEEP LAST URGE
ADHERE ENDURE INSIST REMAIN
SUBSIST CONTINUE PERSEVERE
PERSISTENCE GUTS

PERSISTENCY TENACITY
PERSISTENT SET DREE FIRM HARD
GREAT STOUT DOGGED DREECH
GRITTY HECTIC SLEUTH DURABLE
RESTANT RESTIVE CONSTANT
ENDURING HOLDFAST OBDURATE
RESOLUTE SEDULOUS STUBBORN
ASSIDUOUS OBSTINATE PRIMITIVE
PERSON CAT EGG EGO GUY MAN
ONE BABY BODY CHAL CHAP DUCK
FISH FOOD FORM GINK HOOK LEDE
LIFE NABS SELF SOUL BEING
BOSOM CHILD COOKY GHOST
HEART HUMAN PARTI PARTY PIECE
STICK THING WATCH WIGHT ANIMAL
BUGGER ENTITY FELLOW GALOOT
GAZABO JOHNNY KIPPER NUMBER
SINNER SISTER SPIRIT SPRITE
ARTICLE BLISTER WAGTAIL
SPECIMEN TILLICUM
(**— ACTING FOR ANOTHER**) PROXY
(**— ASSOCIATED WITH WORK**)
WALLAH
(**— BEARING HEAVY BURDEN**)
CAMEL
(**— BEHIND THE TIMES**) FOGY
FOGEY
(**— BRINGING GOOD LUCK**) MASCOT
(**— FROM WHOM FAMILY IS
DESCENDED**) STIRPS
(**— NAMED**) NOMINEE
(**— NOT OF NOBLE BIRTH**)
ROTURIER
(**— OF AGE**) COOT FALDWORTH
(**— OF CONSEQUENCE**) BIGGIE
BIGWIG TALLBOY
(**— OF COURAGE**) SPARTAN
(**— OF INFLUENCE**) CAPTAIN
HEAVYWEIGHT
(**— OF MEAN BIRTH**) GUTTERBLOOD
(**— OF RANK**) STATE MAGNATE
EMINENCE
(**— RESEMBLING ANOTHER**) SOSIA
(**— TO SERVE WRIT**) ELISOR
(**— TOO STRONG FOR ASSAILANT**)
TARTAR
(**— WITH MENTAL TWIST**) CRANK
(**— WITH NERVOUS DISORDERS**)
NEUROTIC
(**— WITH QUEER IDEAS**) ROZUM
(**— WITHOUT STAMINA**) JELLYFISH
(**—S IN AMBASSADOR'S SUITE**)
COMES
(**ABJECT** —) SLAVE
(**ABSENT-MINDED** —) MUSARD
(**AFFECTED** —) GIMCRACK
(**AGGRESSIVE** —) SHOVER HOTSHOT
(**ANNOYING** —) FIEND
(**ARABIZED** —) MOZARAB
(**ARROGANT** —) HUFF TENGU
(**ATTRACTIVE** —) CUTEY CUTIE
KNOCKOUT
(**AVARICIOUS** —) YISSER
(**AWKWARD** —) PUT GAWP HICK
RUBE SLAM STAG STEG STIFF
GUFFIN TUMFIE HOOSIER KITHOGE
LOBSTER SLOMMACK SPELDRIN
(**BAD** —) UNSEL

(**BALD** —) BALLARD BALDHEAD
SKINHEAD
(**BANISHED** —) WRETCH
(**BAPTIZED** —) MEMBER ILLUMINATO
(**BASE** —) CUT RASCAL CAITIFF
HILDING PUTTOCK
(**BELOVED** —) FLAME HEARTROOT
(**BIG-BELLIED** —) GORBELLY
(**BLACK** —) BLECK
(**BOASTFUL** —) BLOWER GASCON
(**BOORISH** —) GOOP
(**CALLOW** —) GORLIN SMARTY
GOSLING
(**CANONIZED** —) SAINT
(**CARELESS** —) HASH TASSEL
(**CHICKENHEARTED** —) HEN
(**CHILDISH** —) BAUBLE WHIMLING
(**CHUNKY** —) JUNT
(**CHURLISH** —) TIKE TYKE
(**CIRCLE OF** —S) COTERIE
(**CLEVER** —) BIRD WHIZ WHIZZ
MERCURY
(**CLOWNISH** —) BUFFOON HOBNAIL
VILLAIN
(**CLUMSY** —) DUB BOOB GAWK
SLOB TIKE TYKE JUMBO STAUP
STIFF DUFFER KEFFEL LUMMOX
HODMADOD
(**COARSE** —) COW STIRK BABOON
MUCKER
(**COMBATIVE** —) DRAGON
GAMECOCK
(**COMMONPLACE** —) MUT MUTT
BROMIDE
(**CONCEITED** —) IT HUFF COXCOMB
PRAGMATIC
(**CONFUSED** —) FOOSTERER
(**CONTEMPTIBLE** —) YAP HEEL PUKE
SCAB SKIN SWAB CATSO SHRUB
SKITE SKUNK SNIPE INSECT SHICER
STINKER BLIGHTER PETTITOES
(**COWARDLY** —) FUGIE SISSY SLINK
SQUIB
(**CRAFTY** —) TOD FILE SHARK
JESUIT
(**CRAZED** —) PSYCOPATH
(**CRINGING** —) SNAKE SNOOL
FLUNKY SPANIEL
(**CRUEL** —) LAMB FIEND MALISON
(**CUNNING** —) PIE
(**DAINTY** —) MIMMOCK
(**DEAD** —) DEFUNCT DECEASED
DECEDENT
(**DECREPIT** —) WITHERLING
(**DEFORMED** —) CRILE CALIBAN
HODMADOD
(**DENSE** —) DUFFER
(**DEPRAVED** —) SKATE
(**DESPICABLE** —) HOUND SLAVE
CAITIFF
(**DESTITUTE** —) PAUPER
(**DIMINUTIVE** —) BANTY MIDGE
BANTAM MIDGET
(**DIRTY** —) DRIVEL HOWLET
(**DISABLED** —) DUCK CRIPPLE
INVALID
(**DISAGREEABLE** —) GOOP PILL
QUAT SKITE RATBAG
(**DISGRUNTLED** —) SOREHEAD

(DISHONEST —) ROGUE ROTTER BEZONIAN
(DISLIKED —) WARLING
(DISSOLUTE —) RIBALD STRIKER
(DOLTISH —) BLOCK SWINE
(DRUNKEN —) LUSH TUMBREL TUMBRIL
(DULL —) LOB BORE DODO GOON GOOP GRUB LUMP MOME MOPE SLOB CLUNK DROUD STICK STOCK LACKWIT LOBCOCK OPACITY
(DULL-WITTED —) DOPE GUMP DUNCE
(DWARFISH —) CROWL SHURF
(DYING —) MORIBUND
(ECCENTRIC —) COON GINK TIKE TYKE GAZABO GAZEBO FANTAST
(EFFEMINATE —) SOFTY SQUAW SOFTIE BADLING SOFTLING SMOCKFACE
(ELDERLY —) SENIOR SOAKER GRAYHEAD
(EMACIATED —) FRAME WASTREL SKELETON
(EMPTY-HEADED —) NITWIT
(ENROLLED —) MEMBER
(ENTERTAINING —) COMEDIAN
(EVIL —) QUED SCUM QUEDE SHREW
(EXPERIENCED —) EXPERT SOAKER STAGER
(EXTORTIONATE —) SCREW
(EXTRAORDINARY —) ONER BUSTER
(FADED —) SHARGAR SHARGER
(FAMOUS —) DON NOTORIETY
(FANTASTIC —) KICKSHAW
(FASHIONABLE —) GIMCRACK
(FASTIDIOUS —) MIMMOCK DELICATE
(FAT —) GURK BLIMP FATSO QUILT SQUAB STOUT
(FAWNING —) COGGER SPANIEL
(FEEBLEMINDED —) FEEB IDIOT MORON IMBECILE
(FEROCIOUS —) LAMB
(FICKLE —) ROVER MOONCALF
(FINE —) WHIPPA
(FLABBY —) HUDDERON
(FLASHY —) KID FLASHER
(FOOLISH —) FOP GUMP HOIT JERK BOOBY SOFTY BAUBLE DOODLE DOTARD DRIVEL HOWLET GOSLING GUBBINS
(FRANK —) TELLTRUTH
(FUSSY —) FAD FADDLE GRANNY SPOFFY GRANNIE
(GAY —) GRIG HUZZA
(GOOD-FOR-NOTHING —) KET PELF TASSEL WASTER WANHOPE WASTREL
(GOSSIPING —) SHULER SHUILER
(GOSSIPY —) BIGMOUTH NEWSMONGER
(GRAVE —) SOBERSIDES
(GREEDY —) GORB GRASPER PUTTOCK
(GROTESQUE —) GUY GOLLIWOGG
(GRUMPY —) SOURBELLY
(GULLIBLE —) JAY BOOB GULPIN

LOBSTER FLATHEAD SHLEMIEL WOODCOCK
(GYPSY —) CHI CHAI
(HARD —) MALISON
(HATEFUL —) TOAD
(HEAVY —) STODGER
(HEAVY-SET —) LUMP
(HOT-TEMPERED —) SPARK
(HUMPBACKED —) LORD
(HUNGRY —) HUNGARIAN
(IDLE —) RAGABASH SLUGGARD
(IGNORANT —) BABE BOOB PORK IDIOT
(ILL-BRED —) BOOR CHURL CLOWN
(ILL-MANNERED —) GRUB SKUNK
(ILL-NATURED —) CRAB HUNKS
(ILL-TEMPERED —) CRAB ETTERCAP TAISTREL
(IMMATURE —) BUD SQUAB GORLIN
(IMMORAL —) PERDU IMPURITAN
(IMPERTINENT —) PAUK PAWK SNIP
(IMPORTANT —) HONOR MUGWUMP
(IMPOTENT —) SPADO
(IMPUDENT —) SAUCE SQUIRT SAUCEBOX
(INANE —) SHAUP
(INEXPERIENCED —) BABE INGENUE BEGINNER
(INFERIOR —) BATA SHRUB SHABBLE
(INSIGNIFICANT —) DAB MUT MUTT BILSH CREEP JOKER SHURF SPRAT SQUIB ABLACH PEANUT PINKEEN WHIFFET GNATLING GRILDRIG PIGWIGEON
(INTRACTABLE —) BUCKIE TARTAR HAGGARD HARDCASE
(IRASCIBLE —) TOUCHWOOD
(LAME —) VULCAN
(LANK —) TANGLE GANGEREL
(LARGE —) CHUNK WHIPPA SKELPER STODGER STRAPPER
(LASCIVIOUS —) SUCCUBUS
(LAST — IN CONTEST) MELL
(LAZY —) BUM DAW HOIT POKE IDLER TRAIL LORDAN LURDAN BLELLUM LAZYLEGS SLUGGARD
(LEAN —) RIBE SHARGER THINGUT
(LEARNED —) CLERK ERUDIT ACHARYA SCHOLAR LITERATO WISEACRE LITERATUS
(LIGHTHEADED —) BEEHEAD
(LITERATE —) SCHOLAR
(LITTLE —) SMOLT SMOUT
(LIVELY —) GRIG BIRKIE HEMPIE WHISKER
(LOUD-VOICED —) STENTOR
(LOW —) PACK SCUM RASCAL BEASTMAN
(LOW SOCIETY —) MUDSILL
(LUBBERLY —) OAF
(LUMBERING —) PUMPKIN TUMBREL TUMBRIL
(LUMPISH —) DROUD
(LUSTY —) BILCH BILSH
(MAD —) MADLING
(MARRIED —) WIFE SPOUSE HUSBAND MATRIMONY
(MEAN —) RIP SCAB CHURL HOUND

MISER SKATE SNEAK SHICER BASTARD DOGBOLT BEZONIAN HUCKSTER STINKARD EARTHWORM
(MEDDLESOME —) BREVIT HESSIAN
(MISCHIEVOUS —) IMP LIMB PEST TOOL HEMPIE HELLION WHIPSTER
(MISERABLE —) SNAKE SWELP WRETCH
(MISERLY —) SKATE SCROOGE PINCHGUT PINCHBACK
(MONSTROUS —) WAMPUS
(NAIVE —) JERK CLUCK GUNSEL INGENUE INNOCENT
(NEGLECTED —) TACKY TACKEY
(NIMBLE —) MERCURY
(NOISY —) YAP HOWLET
(OBJECTIONABLE —) CUR COYOTE FOUTER
(OBSTINATE —) DONKEY STIFFNECK
(ODD —) GIG CURE QUIZZY RATBAG
(OFFENSIVE —) TICK SKITE STINKER
(OLD-FASHIONED —) FRUMP
(PALTRY —) PELTER
(PECULIAR —) BIRD CASE
(PEEVISH —) GRIZZLER SPLENETIC
(PERT —) PIE FLIRT
(POMPOUS —) PUFFIN POMPIST
(POT-BELLIED —) GORREL
(PRIVATE —) JUDEX
(PROSAIC —) PHILISTINE
(PRYING —) POKER PEEPER SMELLER
(PUGNOSED —) CAMUS CAMUSE
(PUNY —) SCART SHILP SHRIMP TITMAN
(PURITANICAL —) WOWSER
(QUEER-LOOKING —) JIGGER
(QUERULOUS —) GRUMP JACKDAW
(QUICK-TEMPERED —) SPUNKIE WILDCAT SPITFIRE
(RAGGED —) ROTO SHAGRAG TATTERWAG
(RAPACIOUS —) SHARK CATERER
(RECKLESS —) MADCAP RAMSTAM
(RED-HAIRED —) BRIQUE
(RESTLESS —) RAMPLER RAMPLOR RANTIPOLE
(RETICENT —) CLAM
(RICH —) MONEYBAGS
(RIDICULOUS —) GOOF HARE MONIMENT MONUMENT
(RIOTOUS —) ROARER
(ROUGH —) TOWSER
(ROUGH-LOOKING —) RULLION
(RUDE —) HICK PORK RULE CHURL CLOWN GROBIAN
(RUSTIC —) COON KERN KERNE HAYSEED HOMESPUN
(SAINTLY —) SADDIK
(SAUCY —) PIET
(SCRAWNY —) SCART SCRAG
(SELF-CENTERED —) HEEL DEVIL FLANEUR
(SELF-RIGHTEOUS —) PHARISEE
(SENSUAL —) SWING CARNALIST
(SHAMEFUL —) BISMER
(SHORT —) CRILE FADGE KNURL STUMP

(SHOWY —) FLASH FLASHER HOTSHOT
(SHREWD —) FILE YEPE HARDHEAD
(SICK —) SICK MALADE PATIENT AEGROTANT
(SILENT —) MUM MUMCHANCE
(SILLY —) FOP CAKE GUMP SOFT DOBBY GOOSE SOFTY SPOON CUCKOO NIMSHI SOFTIE GOOSECAP LIRIPIPE LIRIPOOP SOFTHEAD
(SIMPLE —) DRIP LAMB IDIOT PIGWIGEON
(SKINNY —) SCRAE SCARECROW
(SLATTERNLY —) SLATE
(SLIM —) SWABBLE
(SLOTHFUL —) SLOWBELLY
(SLOVENLY —) HASH SLOB SLORP TRAIL STREEL SLOMMACK STREELER
(SLUGGISH —) LUMP DOLDRUM DRUMBLE LOBCOCK
(SLY —) COON SLYBOOTS SNECKDRAW SNICKDRAW
(SMALL —) GRIG AGATE DWARF SPRAT INSECT MORSEL POPPET SACKET GNATLING
(SOPHISTICATED —) WELTKIND
(SPIRITLESS —) MOPE STICK
(SPITEFUL —) HELLCAT ETTERCAP
(SPRUCE —) SPRUSADO
(STINGY —) CHURL HAYNE STINGY
(STOCKY —) STUMP
(STOLID —) CLAM THICKSKIN
(STRANGE —) WAMPUS
(STRAY —) WAIF
(STUBBORN —) STOUT
(STUNTED —) URF SCRUNT SHARGAR
(STUPID —) ASS DUB JAY MUT BETE BOOB DODO DOLT DOPE DRIP GAUM GAWP GOOF GUMP HASH HOIT JERK MOKE MUTT BLOCK BUCCA CLUCK CLUNK DUNCE HOBBY JUKES LOACH MORON SHEEP STIRK STOCK STUPE SUMPH SWINE THICK WAMUS BOODLE DAWKIN DIMWIT DODUNK DONKEY DUFFER GANDER GILLIE GRANNY GUNSEL LUMMOX LURDAN NITWIT NOODLE SACKET STUPEX TUMFIE TUMPHY BLUNTIE DULLARD FATHEAD FUSSOCK HOWFING JACKASS JUGHEAD MUDHEAD SAPHEAD SCHNOOK BONEHEAD BULLHEAD DOTTEREL DUMBBELL FLATHEAD GAMPHREL IRONHEAD MOLDWARP MUMPHEAD STUNPOLL THICKWIT HODMANDOD MUMCHANCE THICKHEAD
(STURDY —) LUMP CHUNK STALWART
(SULKY —) GLUMP GRUMP SUMPH GROUCH
(SURLY —) CRUST HUNKS
(TACITURN —) OYSTER
(TALKATIVE —) GASSER BLELLUM BIGMOUTH
(TALL, AWKWARD —) GAMMERSTANG

(TENDER —) LAMBKIN
(THICKSET —) NUGGET
(THIRD —) GOOSEBERRY
(THOUGHTLESS —) AIRLING SKIPPER BIRDBRAIN
(TINY —) KEEROGUE
(TIRESOME —) BROMIDE PILLBORE
(TREACHEROUS —) JUDAS SNAKE VIPER GUNSEL SERPENT
(TROUBLESOME —) COW PEST HELLION HESSIAN
(TRUSTWORTHY —) TRAIST STANDBY
(UNATTRACTIVE —) GOON GRUB SCUG CREEP
(UNBENDING —) STIFF
(UNCHASTE —) SHORTHEELS
(UNCIVILIZED —) VISIGOTH
(UNCOUTH —) APE PUT STIFF BABOON SLOMMACK
(UNDERSIZED —) DURGAN SPARROW
(UNFAITHFUL —) INFIDEL
(UNHANDY —) FOUTER
(UNHAPPY —) UNSEL
(UNIQUE —) ONER
(UNKNOWN —) INCONNU STRANGER
(UNMARRIED —) MAIDEN AGAMIST BACHELOR CELIBATE SPINSTER
(UNREASONABLE —) DUFFER
(UNSCRUPULOUS —) CATSO KNAVE
(UNSOPHISTICATED —) JAY HICK NYAS HAYSEED CORNBALL INNOCENT
(UNTHANKFUL —) INGRATE
(UNTIDY —) STREEL
(UNWIELDY —) FUSTILUGS
(USELESS —) POOP SWAB UNSEL
(VALOROUS —) HERO
(VENOMOUS —) SPITPOISON
(VIGOROUS —) SNEEZER
(VIOLENT —) DRAGON SPITFIRE
(VORACIOUS —) HUNGARIAN
(VULGAR —) MUCKER
(WANTON —) FLIRT WHIPSTER
(WEAK —) SHILP SOFTY WHIMLING
(WEAK-MINDED —) SAPHEAD TOTTYHEAD
(WELL-BORN —) FREE
(WHITE —) FAY OFAY GRIFFIN EUROPEAN PALEFACE
(WICKED —) DEVIL SATAN SHREW UNLEAD UNLEDE SATANIST
(WILD —) HELLICAT RANTIPOLE
(WILY —) PIE
(WITHERED —) RUNT
(WITLESS —) WITHAM WITTOME SLABBERER
(WITTY —) WITSHIP SPARKLER
(WORNOUT —) HUSHEL
(WORTHLESS —) YAP FILE GEAR HOIT JADE LOON SCUM TOOT CRUMB LOREL LOSEL SCOUT SHAND BAUBLE BUGGER FELLOW FOUTRA SHICER BUDMASH GULLION BLIGHTER VAGABOND PHARMAKOS
(WRETCHED —) MISER MISERY
(YOUNG —) CUB KID COLT LAMB CHILD HEMPY SMOLT SMOUT SPRIG

YONKE GUNSEL HEMPIE JUNIOR CHICKEN CHOOKIE GRISTLE LAMBKIN JUVENILE STRIPLING (PL.) FRY
PERSONABLE COMELY SHAPELY HANDSOME
PERSONAGE DON DUSE NIBS BLOKE FIGURE SHOGUN TYCOON
(GREAT —) SOPHI SOPHY SUFFEE
PERSONAL SELF PRIVY DIRECT PRIVATE CHATTELS CORPORAL INTIMATE
(— EFFECTS) DUNNAGE
PERSONALITY EGO DRAW SELF SOUL BEING ETHOS HEART EGOITY FIGURE CONTROL FACULTY DEMIURGE PRESENCE SELFHOOD SELFNESS
PERSONATE ACT FEIGN MIMIC MASKED PERSON TYPIFY PRESENT
PERSONATION (SHAM —) IDOL
PERSONIFICATION SOUL GENIUS
(— OF DIVINE VIRTUE) EON
(— OF JUSTICE) THEMIS
PERSONIFY EMBODY INCARNATE PERSONIZE
PERSONNEL BLOOD STAFF KITCHEN PHYSIQUE
PERSPECTIVE OPTICS DISTANCE TELESCOPE
PERSPICACIOUS KEEN ACUTE SHREWD
(MAKE —) CLEAR
PERSPICACITY WIT ACUMEN
PERSPICUOUS CLEAR LUCID PLAIN PRECISE VISIBLE MANIFEST LIGHTSOME
PERSPIRATION DEW SUDOR SUINT SWEAT HIDROSIS OLIGIDRIA SUDORESIS
PERSPIRE PUG MELT BREAN SWEAT SWELTER TRANSPIRE
PERSUADE CON GET WIN COAX GAIN RULE SNOW TICE URGE WISE ARGUE BRING EDUCE SUADE SWADE WEISE ADVISE ARGUFY ASSURE CAJOLE ENGAGE ENTICE INDUCE REMOVE SUBORN CONVERT DISPUTE ENTREAT IMPRESS PREVAIL SATISFY CANOODLE INFLUENCE
PERSUADED PLIABLE GULLIBLE RESOLVED SENSIBLE
PERSUASION KIND SORT BELIEF SUASION JUDGMENT
PERSUASIVE COGENT INDUCTIVE PROTEPTIC
PERT BOLD CHIC FESS FLIP KECK SPRY TRIM ALERT ALIVE BARDY BRISK COCKY DONSY KISKY PEART PIERT QUICK SASSY SAUCY SMART TAUNT CLEVER COCKET COMELY DAPPER FRISKY SWASHY THWART PAUGHTY INSOLENT PETULANT
(— TALK) CHELP
PERTAIN BE LIE BEAR COME LONG BELIE TOUCH AFFEIR BEFALL BELIMP BELONG RELATE RETAIN

CONCERN
(— TO) RINE

PERTAINING (— TO A BISHOP)
LAWN
(— TO AIR) AURAL PNEUMATIC
(— TO ALL NATURE) PAMPHYSIC
(— TO ANIMALS) ZOIC
(— TO ANKLE) TARSAL
(— TO APOLLO) PYTHIAN PAEONIAN
(— TO APOSTLE) PETRINE
(— TO ARMPIT) AXILLAR
(— TO ARMY) MARTIAL STRATONIC
(— TO ARROW) SAGITTAL
(— TO ATHENA) PALLADIAN
(— TO BACK) DORSAL TERGAL
(— TO BATH) BALNEAL
(— TO BEAM) TRAGAL
(— TO BEARD) BARBAL
(— TO BED) THORAL
(— TO BEES) APIAN APIARIAN
(— TO BELLY) ALVIN ALVINE
VENTRAL VENTRIC
(— TO BIBLICAL LAW) LEVITIC
(— TO BIRDS) AVIAN AVINE
ORNITHIC VOLUCRINE
(— TO BIRTH) NATAL
(— TO BODIES AT REST) STATIC
(— TO BODY) SOMAL SOMATIC
(— TO BONE) OSSAL OSTEAL
(— TO BOSOM) GREMIAL
(— TO BRACELET) ARMILLARY
(— TO BRANCHES) RAMOUS
(— TO BREADMAKING) PANARY
(— TO BREAKFAST) ENTACULAR
(— TO BREAST) PECTORAL
(— TO BREASTBONE) STERNAL
(— TO BRISTLES) SETAL
(— TO BROTHEL) STEWISH
(— TO BUNCH) COMAL
(— TO CALF OF LEG) SURAL
(— TO CALF) VITULINE
(— TO CART) PLAUSTRAL
(— TO CARTHAGINIANS) PUNIC
(— TO CARVING) GLYPHIC
(— TO CAVE) SPELEAN SPELUNCAR
(— TO CHAIN) CATENARY
(— TO CHAMBER) CAMERAL
(— TO CHARIOTEER) AURIGAL
(— TO CHEEK) MALAR
(— TO CHESS) SCACCHIC
(— TO CHINA) SINIAN SINISIAN
(— TO CITY) CIVIC URBAN
(— TO CLAN) SEPTAL
(— TO CLAY) BOLAR
(— TO CLOTHES) VESTIARY
VESTURAL
(— TO COINS) NUMMARY
NUMISMATIC
(— TO COLOR) CHROMATIC
(— TO COMB) PECTINAL
(— TO CONSTRUCTION) TECTONIC
(— TO CORK) SUBERIC SUBEROUS
(— TO COUGH) TUSSAL TUSSIVE
(— TO COURT) AULIC JUDICIAL
JUDICIARY
(— TO CROCKERY) PIG
(— TO CROWN) CORONAL
(— TO DANCING) SALTATORY
TRIPUDIAL

(— TO DAUGHTER OR SON) FILIAL
(— TO DAWN) EOAN
(— TO DEFENSE) PHYLACTIC
(— TO DESERTS) EREMIC
(— TO DIAPHRAGM) PHRENIC
(— TO DINNER) CENATORY
(— TO DOVE) COLUMBINE
(— TO DREAMS) ONEIRIC ONIROTIC
(— TO DRINKING) BIBITORY
(— TO EARTH) GEAL TELLURIC
TERRANEAN
(— TO EARTHQUAKE) SEISMAL
SEISMIC
(— TO EAST) EOAN
(— TO ESSENCE) BASIC
(— TO EUNUCH) SPADONIC
(— TO EVENING) VESPER
(— TO EYELIDS) BLEPHARAL
(— TO FACE) PROSOPIC
(— TO FAIR) NUNDINAL
(— TO FAITH) PISTIC
(— TO FEET) PEDAL PEDARY
(— TO FERMENTATION) ZYMIC
ZYMOTIC
(— TO FIELDS) AGRARIAN
(— TO FINGERS) DIGITAL
(— TO FISHING) HALIEUTIC
(— TO FLEAS) PULICENE PULICOSE
(— TO FLESH) SARCOUS
(— TO FLOCK) GREGAL
(— TO FLOOD) DILUVIAL DILUVIAN
(— TO FLOWERS) FLORAL ANTHINE
(— TO FOREARM) CUBITAL
(— TO FOREHEAD) METOPIC
(— TO FORM) MORPHIC
(— TO FOX) VULPINE
(— TO FRESH WATER) LIMNETIC
(— TO FROGS) ANURAN RANINE
(— TO FRUIT) POMONAL POMONIC
(— TO FUNERALS) EXEQUIAL
(— TO FUNGUS) MYCETOID
(— TO FURNACE) FORNACIC
(— TO GARDEN) HORTULAN
(— TO GARRISON) PRESIDIAL
(— TO GENTILES) ETHNIC
(— TO GLASS) VITREOUS
(— TO GOVERNMENT) ARCHICAL
POLITICAL
(— TO GRANDPARENTS) AVAL
(— TO GRINDING) MOLINARY
(— TO GROUND) SOLARY
(— TO GROVE) NEMORAL
(— TO GUMS) ULETIC GINGIVAL
(— TO HAIR) PILAR CRINAL PILARY
(— TO HAND) CHIRAL MANUAL
(— TO HEAD) CEPHALIC
(— TO HEAP) ACERVAL
(— TO HEART) CARDIAC
(— TO HEAT) CALORIC THERMAL
THERMIC
(— TO HIPS) SCIATIC
(— TO HOLIDAY) FERIAL
(— TO HORIZON) MUNDANE
(— TO HORSE) EQUINE HIPPIC
CABALLINE
(— TO HOSPITALITY) XENIAL XENIAN
(— TO HOUSE) DOMAL
(— TO HUNGER) FAMELIC
(— TO HUNTING) VENATIC VENERIAL

(— TO INTELLECT) NOETIC
(— TO INTESTINES) ALVIN ALVINE
(— TO JAW) MALAR GNATHAL
GNATHIC
(— TO JOURNEY) VIATIC
(— TO KIDNEY) RENAL NEPHRIC
(— TO KNOWLEDGE) GNOSTIC
(— TO LAP) GREMIAL
(— TO LAUGHING) GELASTIC
(— TO LAUGHTER) RISORIAL
(— TO LEARNING) PALLADIAN
(— TO LEG) CRURAL
(— TO LIFE) VITAL ZOETIC
(— TO LINE) FILAR
(— TO LIPS) LABIAL
(— TO LIVER) HEPATIC JECORAL
(— TO LOINS) LUMBAR
(— TO LOVE) EROTIC AMATORY
(— TO LUCK) ALEATORY
(— TO LUNGS) PULMONIC
PNEUMONIC PULMONARY
(— TO MANKIND) COMMON
ANTHROPIC
(— TO MARBLE) MARMORIC
(— TO MARKET) NUNDINAL
(— TO MARRIAGE) MARITAL
HYMENEAL
(— TO MARS) AREAN MAMERTINE
MAVORTIAL
(— TO MASS) MOLAR
(— TO MASTER) HERILE
(— TO MEADOWS) PRATAL
(— TO MECCA) MECCAWEE
(— TO MEMORY) MNESTIC
MNEMONIC
(— TO MIDDAY) MERIDIAN
(— TO MILK) LACTARY LACTEAL
(— TO MILL) MOLINARY
(— TO MIRROR) SPECULAR
(— TO MOISTURE) HYGRIC
(— TO MOON) LUNAR SELENIC
SELENIAN
(— TO MORNING) MATIN MATINAL
(— TO MOTION) GESTIC KINETIC
(— TO MOUNTAINS) MONTANE
(— TO MOUTH) ORAL OSCULAR
STOMATIC
(— TO MUSCLE) SARCOUS
(— TO MUSIC) HARMONIC
(— TO NAVEL) OMPHALIC
(— TO NECK) JUGULAR
(— TO NEPHEW) NEPOTAL
(— TO NIGHT) NOCTURNAL
(— TO NOSE) NASAL RHINAL
(— TO NUT) NUCAL
(— TO NUTRITION) TROPHIC
(— TO OAK) QUERCINE ROBOREOUS
(— TO OCEAN) PELAGIC OCEANOUS
THALASSIC
(— TO OLD AGE) SENILE GERATIC
GERONTIC
(— TO OPEN SKY) SUBDIAL
(— TO PARLOR) BEN BOOR
(— TO PASTURES) PASCUAL
(— TO PAWNBROKER) AVUNCULAR
(— TO PEACOCK) PAVONINE
(— TO PERSPIRATION) SUDORIC
(— TO PICTURE) ICONIC
(— TO PIGS) PORCINE

(— **TO PINE**) WARRYN
(— **TO PLAGUE**) LOIMIC
(— **TO PLEASURE**) HEDONIC
(— **TO POETRY**) MUSAL IAMBIC
(— **TO POISON**) TOXIC
(— **TO POTTERY**) CERAMIC
(— **TO PRIESTS**) SACERDOTAL
(— **TO PRISON**) CARCERAL
(— **TO PULSE**) SPHYGMIC
(— **TO PUNISHMENT**) PENAL
PUNITIVE
(— **TO QUEEN**) REGINAL
(— **TO RAIN**) HYETAL PLUVIAL
(— **TO RAINBOW**) IRIDAL
(— **TO REMOTE PLACE**) FORANE
(— **TO RESONANCE**) SYNTONIC
(— **TO RING**) ARMILLARY
(— **TO RISING**) ORTIVE
(— **TO RIVER BANK**) RIPARIAN
(— **TO RIVER**) AMNIC POTAMIC
RIVERINE FLUMINOSE
(— **TO ROAD**) VIATIC
(— **TO ROCK**) PETREAN SAXATILE
(— **TO ROD**) BACULINE
(— **TO SABLES**) ZIBELINE
(— **TO SAIL**) VELIC
(— **TO SALVATION**) SOTERIAL
(— **TO SANDARAC**) THYINE
(— **TO SATURDAY**) SABBATINE
(— **TO SEAL**) SIGILLARY
SPHRAGISTIC
(— **TO SEAM**) SUTURAL
(— **TO SEASHORE**) LITTORAL
(— **TO SEAWEED**) ALGOUS
(— **TO SENSE OF TASTE**)
GUSTATIVE
(— **TO SHEEP**) VERVECINE
(— **TO SHEPHERDS**) PASTORAL
(— **TO SHERIFF**) VICONTIEL
(— **TO SHIN**) CNEMIAL
(— **TO SHIP**) NAVICULAR
(— **TO SHOPMAN**) APOTHECAL
(— **TO SHOULDER**) ALAR SCAPULAR
(— **TO SIGNS**) SEMIC SEMANTIC
(— **TO SILVER**) ARGENTAL
(— **TO SISTER**) SORORAL
(— **TO SKIN**) DERIC DERMAL
CUTICULAR
(— **TO SLEEP**) SOMNIAL MORPHETIC
(— **TO SNAKE**) ANGUINE
(— **TO SOFT PALATE**) VELAR
(— **TO SONG**) MELIC
(— **TO SPECTACLE**) THEORIC
(— **TO SPEECH**) PHEMIC
(— **TO SPINAL CORD**) MYELIC
(— **TO SPRING**) VERNAL
(— **TO STARS**) ASTRAL STELLAR
SIDEREAL
(— **TO STATE AFFAIRS**) PRAGMATIC
(— **TO STEPMOTHER**) NOVERCAL
(— **TO STOMACH**) GASTRIC
(— **TO STORKS**) PELARGIC
(— **TO SULPHUR**) THIONIC
(— **TO SUMMER**) ESTIVAL AESTIVAL
(— **TO SUN**) SOLAR HELIAC
(— **TO SUNDAY**) DOMINICAL
(— **TO SUNDIAL**) SCIATHERIC
(— **TO SUPPER**) CENATORY
(— **TO SURFACE OF ANYTHING**)
FACIAL

(— **TO SWALLOWS**) HIRUNDINE
(— **TO SWEAT**) SUDORIC
(— **TO SWIMMING**) NATATORY
(— **TO SWINEHERD**) SYBOTIC
(— **TO TAIL**) CAUDAL
(— **TO TAILOR**) SARTORIAL
(— **TO TEARS**) LACRIMAL
LACHRYMAL
(— **TO TEMPO**) AGOGIC
(— **TO THE BEAUTIFUL**) ESTHETIC
AESTHETIC
(— **TO THIEVING**) KLEPTISTIC
(— **TO THIGH**) CRURAL
(— **TO THREAD**) FILAR
(— **TO THROAT**) GULAR JUGULAR
(— **TO TILE**) TEGULAR
(— **TO TIN**) STANNIC
(— **TO TITHES**) DECIMAL
(— **TO TITMICE**) PARINE
(— **TO TOMB**) TOMBAL
(— **TO TONGUE**) GLOSSAL LINGUAL
(— **TO TORTOISES**) CHELONIAN
(— **TO TOUCH**) TACTILE
(— **TO TOWER**) TURRICAL
(— **TO TREES**) DENDRAL ARBOREAL
(— **TO TWENTY**) VICENARY
(— **TO UNCLE**) AVUNCULAR
(— **TO VESSEL**) VASAL
(— **TO VIRGIN**) PARTHENIAN
(— **TO VOW**) VOTAL
(— **TO WAGON**) PLAUSTRAL
(— **TO WALLS**) MURAL PARIETAL
(— **TO WAR**) POLEMICAL
(— **TO WASPS**) VESPAL VESPINE
(— **TO WAX**) CERAL
(— **TO WEAVING**) TEXTORIAL
(— **TO WEIGHT**) BARIC PONDERAL
PONDERARY
(— **TO WELL**) PHREATIC
(— **TO WHALES**) CETIC
(— **TO WHEAT**) VULGARE
(— **TO WHEELS**) ROTAL
(— **TO WIFE**) UXORIAL
(— **TO WIND**) EOLIAN ONEUMATIC
(— **TO WINE**) VINIC VINOUS
(— **TO WINE-MAKING**) OENOPOETIC
(— **TO WINGS**) ALAR PTERIC
EXRUPEAL PTEROTIC
(— **TO WINTER**) HIEMAL
(— **TO WISDOM**) PALLADIAN
(— **TO WOMANKIND**) MULIEBRAL
(— **TO WOODPECKERS**) PICINE
(— **TO WOODS**) SYLVAN NEMORAL
(— **TO WORMS**) VERMICULAR
(— **TO WOUNDS**) VULNERAL
(— **TO WRIST**) CARPAL
(— **TO YESTERDAY**) PRIDIAN
(— **TO YEW**) TAXINE
PERTINACIOUS FIRM STIFF DOGGED
ADHERING STUBBORN OBSTINATE
PERTINENCY FORCE
PERTINENT APT FIT PAT HAPPY
COGENT PROPER TIMELY ADAPTED
APROPOS GERMANE POINTED
TELLING INCIDENT MATERIAL
RELATIVE RELEVANT
PERTURB BITE GRATE UPSET
WORRY DISMAY AGITATE CONFUSE

CONTURB DERANGE DISTURB
TROUBLE
PERTURBATION DISMAY FLIGHT
POTHER POOTHER STICKLE
TROUBLE TURMOIL EVECTION
AGITATION
PERTURBED UNEASY
PERTUSSIS COUGH CHINCOF
CHINCOUGH

PERU

CAPITAL: LIMA
COIN: SOL LIBRA DINERO
CENTAVO
DEPARTMENT: ICA LIMA PUNO
CUSCO CUZCO JUNIN PIURA
TACNA ANCASH LORETO
TUMBES
ISLAND: CHINCHA
LAKE: TITICACA
LANGUAGE: AYMARA QUECHUA
MEASURE: TOPO VARA GALON
CELEMIN FANEGADA
MOUNTAIN: HUAMINA COROPUNA
HUASCARAN
PERIOD: RECUAY
RIVER: NAPU RIMAC SANTA TIGRE
YAGUAS YAVARI CURARAY
MARANON PASTAZA UCAYALI
AMAZONAS APURIMAC
HUALLAGA URUBAMBA
TOWN: ICA LIMA PUNO CUZCO
PAITA PISCO CALLAO IQUITOS
AREQUIPA TRUJILLO
VOLCANO: MISTI YUCAMANI
WEIGHT: LIBRA QUINTAL

PERUKE WIG FLASH GALERA
TOUPEE GALERUM PERIWIG
WIGGERY
PERUSAL SIGHT LECTURE SCRUTINY
PERUSE CON READ SCAN STUDY
HANDLE SEARCH SURVEY EXAMINE
INSPECT
PERVADE FILL BATHE IMBUE
DRENCH INSTIL OCCUPY INSTILL
PERMEATE TRAVERSE
PERVADED STIFF
PERVERSE AUK AWK CAM CAR
AWRY WOGH WRAW CROSS DONSY
GAMMY THRAW WROTH CUSSED
DIVERS LOUCHE THRAWN THWART
WICKED WILFUL WRAIST AWKWARD
DIVERSE FORWARD FROWARD
OBLIQUE WAYWARD CAMSHACH
CRANKISH STUBBORN
PERVERSELY AUK AWK ATHWART
OVERWART
PERVERSION WREST ABUSION
(— **OF TASTE**) MALACIA
PERVERT WRY DRAW RACK RUIN
SKEW TURN WARP ABUSE CROOK
GLOSS TWIST UPSET DEBASE
DETORT DIVERT GARBLE INVERT
MISUSE POISON WRENCH WRITHE
CONTORT CORRUPT DEGRADE
DEPRAVE DEVIATE DISTORT
MISTURN SUBVERT TRADUCE

VITIATE MISWREST

PERVERTED BAD WICKED ABUSIVE CORRUPT TWISTED VICIOUS

PERVERTER WRESTER

PERVIOUS LEACHY PERVIAL PERVADING

PES NEUME TENOR PODATUS

PESKY VERY PLAGUY ANNOYING DEVILING EXTREMELY

PESO DURO CONANT DOLLAR CAROLUS PATACAO

PESSIMISM WELTSCHMERZ MISERABILISM

PESSIMIST ALARMIST JEREMIAH WORRYWART

PESSIMISTIC GLOOMY ALARMED BEARISH CYNICAL DOWNBEAT

PEST BANE TICK WEED MOUSE MYZUS TRAIK INSECT PLAGUE SCHELM SORROW VERMIN NUDNICK SANDMITE BUTTINSKY

PESTER DUN HOX NAG RIB TIG HAKE ANNOY DEVIL TEASE WORRY BADGER BOTHER HARASS INFEST MOLEST BEDEVIL TORMENT TROUBLE OBSTRUCT

PESTHOUSE LAZARET LAZARETTO

PESTICIDE BIOCIDE FUMIGANT

PESTILENCE PEST DEATH QUALM PLAGUE MURRAIN EPIDEMIC MORTALITY

PESTILENT FATAL DEADLY VEXING NOXIOUS

PESTLE MIX BRAY GRIND PESTL PILUM STAMP BEETLE BRAYER MULLER PISTIL CHAPPER POUNDER STAMPER

PET TOY CADE COAX DAUT DEAR DUCK HUFF LAMB NECK PEAT SOCK SULK TIFF DRUNT DUCKY HUMOR QUIET SPOIL SPOON TETCH CARESS CODDLE COSHER COSSET CUDDLE DANDLE DAUTIE DAWTIE FADDLE FANTAD FANTOD FONDLE GENTLE PAMPER PETKIN SMOOCH SQUALL STROKE WANTON CHERISH DARLING INDULGE PINKENY TANTRUM TIDLING UMBRAGE WHITHER CANOODLE FAVORITE TIDDLING PADDYWACK

PETAL ALA HELM HOOD LEAF WING BANNER
(— IN PEA FLOWER) VEXILLUM
(— OF IRIS) STANDARD
(UPPER —) HOOD BANNER
(PL.) COROLLA

PETALIA NYCTERIS

PETARD PITTARD FIREWORK

PETATE BANIG

PETECHIA STIGMA

PETER P FADE FAIL PEAK SAFE WANE CEASE PEDRO PIERS PIERRE SIGNAL DWINDLE
(— OUT) FIZZLE

PETIOLE STEM SPINE STALK STIPE PODEON PEDUNCLE PHYLLODE

PETITE SMALL LITTLE MIGNON MIGNONNE

PETITION ASK BEG SUE BILL BOON

PLEA PRAY SUIT VOTE WISH APPLY ORATE PLEAD APPEAL DESIRE INVOKE MOTION PLACIT PRAYER STEVEN ADDRESS BESEECH ENTREAT IMPLORE ORATION SOLICIT ROGATION SUFFRAGE
(MAKE —) SUE
(PL.) PRECES

PETITIONER BEGGAR ORATOR SUITOR BEADSMAN ENTREATER PLAINTIFF

PETO WAHOO

PETREL BILL TITI CAHOW MITTY NELLY PRION WITCH SPENCY TEETEE ASSILAG GLUTTON KAEDING SEABIRD SEAFOWL STINKER ALLAMOTH FORKTAIL STINKPOT ALLAMOTTI NIGHTHAWK

PETRIFY DAZE DEADEN STONIFY STUPEFY LAPIDIFY FOSSILIZE GORGONIZE

PETRIFYING STONY GORGON

PETROL GAS GASOLINE

PETROLATUM VASELINE

PETROLEUM OIL CRUDE PETROL NAPHTHA
(— INDUSTRY) OILDOM

PE-TSAI PECHAY

PETTED CADE DANDILY

PETTICOAT BAJO GORE KILT SLIP SOUS DICKY GREEN JUPON PAGNE SOUSE KIRTLE LUHINGA PLACKET WHITTLE BALMORAL BASQUINE WILYCOAT
(— OF TARGET) GREEN

PETTIFOG FOG CAVIL BICKER

PETTIFOGGER FOGGER SHYSTER LEGULEIAN

PETTINESS NAGGLE PARVINIMITY

PETTING COLLING

PETTISH HUFFY FRETFUL PEEVISH PLAINTIVE

PETTY TIN BASE JERK MEAN ORRA PUNY VAIN GRIMY MINOR PETIT PUNEE SMALL MEASLY MINUTE PALTRY PEANUT POKING PUISNE PUSILL SNIFTY KITLING PIMPING TRIVIAL TWATTLE CHILDISH FIDDLING INFERIOR NIGGLING NUGATORY PICAYUNE SNIPPETY TRIFLING PAROCHIAL

PETULANT PERT CROSS SAUCY SHORT TESTY TIFFY FEISTY SULLEN WANTON WILFUL CRABBED FRETFUL FROWARD HUFFISH PEEVISH WASPISH PERVERSE SNAPPISH

PEUMUS BOLDU

PEW PUE BOUT DESK PFUI PUGH SEAT SLIP BENCH BUGHT STALL BOUGHT

PEWEE PEWIT PEEWEE

PEWTER CUP BIDRI BIDRY MONEY PUDER BIDERY TRIFLE PEAUDER SADWARE TUTENAG
(— MARK) TOUCHMARK

PEYOTE HIKULI

PFENNIG PENNING

PHAEDRA (FATHER OF —) MINOS
(HUSBAND OF —) THESEUS

PHAETON DUKE FAETON SPIDER STANHOPE

PHAETON BUTTERFLY BALTIMORE

PHALANGER ARIEL TAPOA CUSCUS OPOSSUM PENTAIL SQUIRREL

PHALAROPE LOBIPED COOTFOOT LOBEFOOT WHALEBIRD

PHALERA BEAD BOSS DISK STUD CAMEO

PHANTASM DREAM FANCY GHOST VAPOR FIGURE SHADOW SPIRIT FANTASY PHANTOM SPECIES SPECTER SPECTRE

PHANTASMAL UNREAL SPECTRAL

PHANTASY FANCY FANTASY PHANTASIA

PHANTOM IDOL BOGEY BOGLE DUMMY GHOST IMAGE PHASM SHADE SHAPE UMBRA BOGGLE DOUBLE FANTOM IDOLON IDOLUM SHADOW SPIRIT BUGBEAR EIDOLON ELUSIVE FANTASY SPECIES SPECTER ILLUSORY ADAMASTOR

PHARAOH ALE FARO PHARO TYRANT BUSIRIS

PHARAOH'S HEN VULTURE

PHARISEE MUGWUMP NICODEMUS

PHARMACIST DRUGGIST DISPENSER

PHARMACY FERMACY DRUGSTORE

PHAROS CLOAK LIGHT TORCH BEACON LANTERN

PHARYNGEAL FAUCAL

PHARYNX MASTAX PROBOSCIS

PHASE EFT END LEG FAZE SIDE ANGLE FACET GRADE STAGE ASPECT AVATAR BACKLASH PASSOVER DICHOTOMY
(INITIAL —) BUD
(LOWEST —) BATHOS
(TRANSITORY —) STREAK

PHASM FANTOM METEOR PHASMA PHANTOM

PHEASANT CHIR GUAN ARGUS CHEER KALIJ MINAL MONAL GROUSE LEIPOA MAGPIE MONAUL MOONAL PUKRAS KALLEGE FIREBACK ITHAGINE RINGNECK TRAGOPAN MACARTNEY
(BREEDING PLACE FOR —S) STEW
(BROOD OF —S) NID NYE NIDE
(YOUNG —) POULT

PHEASANT CUCKOO COUCAL

PHEASANT DUCK PINTAIL MERGANSER

PHEASANT FINCH WAXBILL

PHEASANT'S-EYE ROSARUBY

PHELLEM CORK SUBER

PHENOBARBITOL LUMINAL

PHENOCRYST INSET

PHENOL LACCOL THYMOL ALOESOL CREOSOL DURENOL EUGENOL ORCINOL CHAVICOL RESORCIN

PHENOMENON FIRE ANOMY COLOR EVENT IMAGE ARTHUS EFFECT METEOR MIRAGE SHADOW ISOTOPY MIRACLE PARADOX PROCESS SYMPTOM ASTERISM PRAKRITI SIDERISM SUNQUAKE LANDSPOUT

PHENYLSALICYLATE SALOL

PHIAL CUP FIAL VIAL BOTTLE
VESSEL
PHILABEG KILT FILIBEG
PHILANDER FOOL WOLF DALLY
FLIRT SMOCK
PHILANTHROPIC HUMANE
PHILANTHROPIST ALTRUIST
HUMANITARIAN
PHILANTHROPY CHARITY
ALMSGIVING
PHILIP PIP PHILP SPARROW
PHILIPPIC SCREED TIRADE ABUSIVE
DIATRIBE

PHILIPPINES
ARCHIPELAGO: SULU
CAPITAL: BAGUIO MANILA
QUEZONCITY
COIN: PESO PESETA CENTAVO
FIBER: ERUC ABACA BUNTAL
ISLAND: CEBU BOHOL LEYTE
LUZON PANAY SAMAR NEGROS
MASBATE MINDORO PALAWAN
MINDANAO
LAKE: TAAL LANAO
LANGUAGE: MORO BICOL IBANAG
ILOCANO TAGALOG VISAYAN
MEASURE: LOAN BRAZA CABAN
CAUAN CHUPA GANTA APATAN
BALITA QUINON
MOUNTAIN: APO IBA MAYON
PULOG BANAHAO
NATIVE: ATA ATI ITA TAO AETA
ATTA ETAS MORO SULU BICOL
TAGAL VICOL IGOROT TIMAUA
BISAYAN TAGALOG FILIPINO
PROVINCE: ABRA ALBAY CAPIZ
DAVAO LANAO RIZAL CAVITE
ILOILO TARLAC SURIGAO
RIVER: ABRA AGNO MAGAT PASIG
AGUSAN LAOANG CAGAYAN
MINDANAO PAMPANGA
TOWN: AGOA CEBU ALBAY DAVAO
LAOAG PASAY VIGAN APARRI
BAGUIO CAVITE ILAGAN ILOILO
MANILA BACALOD BASILAN
DAGUPAN CALOOCAN
TREE: DAO IBA TUA TUI ACLE
ANAM ATES BOGO DITA IPIL
GUIJO LAUAN LIGAS ALUPAG
ANAHAU ARANGA ANONANG
APITONG TINDALO ALMACIGA
AMPALAYA
VOLCANO: APO MAYO CANLAON
WEIGHT: CATTY FARDO PICUL
PUNTO LACHSA QUILATE
CHINANTA

PHILISTINE BOOB GIGMAN MUCKER
BABBITT GITTITE BOEOTIAN
BARBARIAN BOURGEOIS HYPOCRITE
(PL.) PULESATI PURASATI
CAPHTORIM
PHILOLOGIST LAVENGRO LINGUIST
PHILOLOGY SEMITICS
PHILOMACHUS MACHETES
PHILOMELA STOP FILOMEL
(FATHER OF —) PANDION
(RAVISHER OF —) TEREUS

(SISTER OF —) PROCNE
(SLAIN BY —) ITYS
PHILOSOPHER WIT SAGE CYNIC
STOIC ARTIST IONIAN LEGIST
DOTTORE ELEATIC ERISTIC
SCHOLAR SOPHIST SUMMIST
THINKER ZETETIC ACADEMIC
EPOCHIST MAGICIAN VIRTUOSO
ACADEMIST ALCHEMIST DIALECTIC
PHYSICIAN SCHOOLMAN
PHILOSOPHER'S STONE ADROP
MICROCOSM
PHILOSOPHIC SAGE
PHILOSOPHY ETHICS GOSPEL
SYSTEM TAOISM APRISMO COSMISM
DUALISM INQUIRY MIMAMSA
SCEPSIS HINDUISM HUMANISM
IDENTISM IDEOLOGY LEGALISM
OCCAMISM STOICISM NOUMENISM
SOCRATISM VEDANTISM
(— OF LIFE) LIGHTS
PHILTER DRUG CHARM WANGA
FILTER POTION AMATORY
PHLEBOTOMIZE BLEED VENESECT
PHLEBOTOMUS TATUKIRA
PHLEGM FLEM GLEET MUCUS
WATER FLEUME PITUITE MOUSEWEB
PHLEGMATIC CALM COOL DULL
SLOW INERT MUCOID SLEEPY
WATERY VISCOUS COMPOSED
SLUGGISH APATHETIC IMPASSIVE
PHLOEM BAST LEPTOME
PHLOGISTIC FIERY HEATED
BURNING FLAMING
PHLOMIS SAGELEAF
PHLOX CYME FLOX ALBION BEACON
COBAEA
PHOEBE FEBE FIVE MOON DIANA
PEWEE ARTEMIS
(DAUGHTER OF —) LETO
(MOTHER OF —) GAEA
PHOEBUS SUN APOLLO PHOIBUS
PHOENICIA (COLONY OF —)
CARTHAGE
(GODDESS OF —) TANIT BALTIS
TANITH ASTARTE
(KING OF —) AGENOR
(TOWN OF —) ACRE TYRE SIDON
SAREPTA
PHONEME MORPH TONEME
LARYNGAL
PHONEMIC BROAD
PHONOGRAM LOGOGRAM
SINOGRAM
PHONOGRAPH VIC PHONO
VICTROLA
(— RECORD) DISK PLATTER
PHONY FAKE SHAM BOGUS FAKER
FALSE BRUMMY BUNYIP PHONEY
IMPOSTOR SPURIOUS
PHOSPHATE EHLITE FLOATS
APATITE CABOCLE CACOXENE
GRIPHITE
PHOSPHORESCENCE BRIMING
MARFIRE
PHOSPHORESCENT PHOSPHOR
NOCTILUCOUS
PHOTISM SYNOPSY
PHOTOENGRAVER ZINCOGRAPHER

PHOTOENGRAVING HALFTONE
HELIOGRAPH
PHOTOGRAPH MUG FILM LENS
SNAP CARTE IMAGE PHOTO SHOOT
STILL CANDID GLOSSY MOSAIC
RETAKE SCENIC STEREO AIRVIEW
PICTURE TINTYPE LIKENESS
PORTRAIT SNAPSHOT TABLETOP
CYCLOGRAM
(— SIZE) PANEL
(X-RAY —) SKIAGRAM
PHOTOGRAPHER LENSMAN
CAMERIST CAMERAMAN
PHOTOGRAPHY STEREO
PHOTOGENY
PHOTOMETER LUCIMETER
PHOTOMONTAGE COLLAGE
PHOTON BOSON TROLAND
PHRASE CRY HIT MOT SET CRIB
FUSS HAVE IDEA TERM WORD
COMMA COUCH IDIOM LABEL
LEMMA POINT STATE STYLE TOPIC
TROPE BYWORD CLAUSE CLICHE
DITTON DORISM GRUPPO HOBNOB
NOTION PNEUMA PRAISE SAVING
SLOGAN ATTACCO DICTION EPITHET
PASSAGE CONCEIVE DIVISION
DORICISM FLATTERY IDEOGRAM
IRISHISM LATINISM LEITMOTIV
(— DIFFERENTLY) TURN
(— UNCTUOUSLY) DROOL
(MUSICAL —) ATTACCO SUBJECT
(PET —) SHIBBOLETH
(REDUNDANT —) CHEVILLE
(STOCK —) CANT
(TRITE —) CLICHE
(WELL-TURNED —) STROKE
PHRASEOLOGY CANT STYLE
DIALECT DICTION WORDING
LOCUTION PARLANCE
PHRATRY CLAN
PHRENETIC PYTHIAN FRENETIC
PHRENIC MENTAL
(PL.) PSYCHOLOGY
PHRIXOS (FATHER OF —) ATHAMUS
(MOTHER OF —) NEPHELE
(SISTER OF —) HELLE
PHRYGIA (GOD OF —) ATYS ATTIS
SABAZIOS
(KING OF —) MIDAS
PHRYNIN BUFIDIN
PHTHISIS DECAY
PHYLACTERY FILACTERY
(PL.) TEFILLIN TEPHILLIN
PHYLE TRIBE
PHYLUM HOKA CLASS HOKAN
NADENE BRYOZOA ANNELATA
ANNELIDA CHORDATA DIVISION
LIGNOSAE
PHYMA TUMOR
PHYSALIS POP POPPER TOMATILLO
PHYSETER CATODON
PHYSIC CURE HEAL FISIC PURGE
TRADE REMEDY MEDICAL NATURAL
RELIEVE DRUGGERY
PHYSICAL ILL LUSTY SOMAL BODILY
CARNAL DISTAL NATURAL SOMATIC
CORPORAL CURATIVE EXTERNAL
MATERIAL CORPOREAL

(PURELY —) BRUTE

PHYSICIAN ASA DOC PILL CURER GALEN HAKIM LEECH MEDIC QUACK ARTIST BAIDYA DOCTOR FELLOW HEALER INTERN MEDICO DOTTORE EMPIRIC SURGEON ALIENIST RESIDENT SAWBONES SUNDOWNER

PHYSICIST HYLOZOIST

PHYSIC NUT TUBA CURCAS PIGNON TARTAGO

PHYSIOCRAT ECONOMIST

PHYSIOGNOMY MUG FACE PHIZ PHIZZ VIZNOMY PORTRAIT VISENOMY

PHYSIOLOGY BIONOMY ZOONOMY

PHYSIQUE BODY BUILD COOST HABIT FIGURE STRENGTH

PHYSOCARPUS NEILLIA OPULASTER

PHYSOSTIGMINE ESERE ESERINE

PHYTOMER PHYTON PODIUM

PI JUMBLE CONFUSE PREACHY CONFUSION

PIA PI GABI GABGAB MARMOT

PIACLE SIN CRIME GUILT OFFENSE

PIAN YAWS FRAMBESIA

PIANETTE PYNOT PIANINO

PIANIST CEMBALIST CLAVIERIST

PIANO SOFT FLOOR GRAND GRANT STORY FLUGEL GENTLY SOFTLY SPINET SQUARE CLAVIAL CLAVIER GIRAFFE PIANOLA QUIETLY UPRIGHT MELOTROPE

PIASSAVA IYO JARA BAHIA PIACABA

PIASTER KURUS

PIATTI CYMBALS

PIAZZA PORCH SQUARE BALCONY GALLERY PORTICO VERANDA PIAZZETTA

PIC PEAK LANCE PIQUE PICADOR

PICA M EM LINE

PICARD PYKAR

PICARO KNAVE ROGUE TRAMP BOHEMIAN VAGABOND

PICAROON ROGUE PICARO PIRATE CORSAIR WRECKER

PICAYUNE PIC PETTY MEASLY PALTRY PISTAREEN

PICCADILL RABATA REBATE REBATO

PICCOLO BUSBOY JUKEBOX FLAUTINO OTTAVINO

PICHICIAGO ARMADILLO CHLAMYPHORE

PICK NIB BILL CULL GAFF HACK LIFT PIKE PILK SHOT WALE ADORN BEELE BREAK CAVIL ELECT FLANG LEASE PILCH PLUCK PRIDE CHOICE CHOOSE GATHER PICKAX PUDDLE TWITCH BARGAIN CASCROM DIAMOND DRESSER MANDREL

(— APART) TOW

(— OUT) CULL SPOT TAKE WELE CRONE GLEAN GARBLE SELECT

(— POCKETS) FIG FILE FOIST TOUCH

(— TOBACCO) STRIP

(FILLING —) ABB

PICKAX PIX BEDE BILL PIKE GURLET TUBBER TWIBIL TWIBILL

PICKED PICK TRIM PIKED CHOSEN

DAINTY PEAKED SELECT ADORNED POINTED

PICKER COD HOPPER

(BERRY —) HURTER

(PEA —) VINER

PICKEREL JACK SNAKE DUNLIN SAUGER SLINKER WALLEYE

PICKERELWEED TULE WAMPEE

PICKER-UP FINDER

PICKET PEG PALE POST TERN FENCE STAKE FASTEN PALING TETHER ENCLOSE FORTIFY PICQUET PALISADE OUTPICKET

PICKLE BOX ALEC DILL MESS PECK ACHAR BRINE GRAIN MANGO SAUCE SOUSE ATSARA CAPERS DAWDLE HIGDON KERNEL KIMCHI MUDDLE NIBBLE PIDDLE PILFER PLIGHT TRIFLE CONDITE CONFECT TROUBLE VITRIOL MARINADE

(FISH —) ALEC

PICKLED DRUNK MURIATED POWDERED MARINATED

PICKLOCK LOCK PICKER

PICK-ME-UP SCREW PICKUP

PICKPOCKET DIP FIG GUN NIP BUNG FILE WIRE DIVER FILER FOIST BUZZER CANNON DIPPER FIGBOY HOOKER RATERO FOISTER MOBSMAN CLYFAKER CUTPURSE KNUCKLER BUZZGLOAK

(HELPER OF —) STALL BULKER

PICKUP BRUSH TRUCK ARREST BRACER ANACRUSIS

PICNIC FRY BALL GIPSY GYPSY BURGOO FROLIC MAROON OUTING SHOULDER SQUANTUM SUMMERING

PICOT LOOP PEARL PERLE

PICOTAH SWEEP PACOTA

PICTOGRAPH GLYPH PICTOGRAM

PICTORIAL GRAPHIC

PICTURE GAY MAP OIL COPY DAUB ICON IKON LIMN SIGN VIEW DECAL FRAME IMAGE LINER PAINT PHOTO PIECE PINAX PRINT SCENE SHAPE STAMP STORY TABLE CACHET CANVAS CHROMO CUTOUT DEPICT EMBLEM MARINE PASTEL SEMBLE SHADOW STEREO TABLET CUTAWAY DIORAMA DIPTYCH EMBLEMA ETCHING EXHIBIT FASHION FEATURE GOUACHE GRAPHIC HISTORY MIZRACH PAYSAGE PORTRAY PORTURE RETRAIT SCENERY TABLEAU VANDYKE AIRSCAPE AUTOTYPE DESCRIBE DROLLERY ENVISION IDEOGRAM KAKEMONO LANDSKIP LIKENESS MAKIMONO MONOTINT OVERDOOR PAINTING PORTRAIT PROSPECT RITRATTO SEASCAPE SINGERIE SKYSCAPE TRIPTYCH VIGNETTE ENCAUSTIC

(— IN 3 COMPARTMENTS) TRIPTYCH

(— IN BOOK) GAY

(— MAT) SPANDREL

(— OF MONKEYS) SINGERIE

(— ON ROLLER) KAKEMONO MAKIMONO

(— PUZZLE) REBUS JIGSAW

(—S IN BOOKS) BABY

(COMIC —) DROLLERY

(RELIGIOUS —) TANKA

(STEREOSCOPIC —) ANAGLYPH

PICTURESQUE VIVID EXOTIC QUAINT SCENIC GRAPHIC IDYLLIC ROMANTIC PICTORIAL

PICUL TAN PICO PIKOL

PIDDLE PICK PLAY DAWDLE PICKLE PUTTER TRIFLE

PIDDLING JERK PALTRY TRIVIAL USELESS FOOTLING TRIFLING JERKWATER

PIDDOCK DACTYL PHOLAD PHOLAS

PIDGIN LANGUAGE SABIR

PIE PAI FLAM FLAN HEAP MESS PATE PILE TART DOWDY FLAWN PASTY PATTY TORTA TOURT AFFAIR BRIDLE CHEWET MAGPIE PASTRY TOURTE COBBLER SMASHER STRUDEL BAKEMEAT CRUSTADE FLAPJACK PANDOWDY SURPRISE TURNOVER SMASHOVER

PIEBALD PIE PIED PIET MIXED PIETY PINTO CALICO MOTLEY SKEWBALD

PIECE BAT BIT COB CUT DAM FIG JOB LAB LOG MAN TUT GIRL MIND PART PISE PLAY DAGON DRAMA DWANG FLOOR PEZZO SCRAP SHARD SHERD SHRED SLICE SNODE STEEK STUCK THROW COLLOP FARDEL FUGATO GOBBET PARCEL STITCH CANTLET EXAMPLE FLINDER FLITTER MORCEAU OPINION PICTURE PORTION SEGMENT DUOLOGUE EMBOLIUM FANDANGO PAINTING

(— AT END) HEELPIECE

(— FOR TWO) DUET DUOLOGUE

(— IN CHECKERS) DAM

(— IN ORGAN) THUMPER

(— OF ARMOR) JAMB JAMBE

(— OF BAD LUCK) DIRDUM

(— OF BLANKET) DAGON

(— OF BLUBBER) BIBLE

(— OF DECEPTION) BEGUNK

(— OF DECORATED METAL) NIELLO

(— OF FALSE HAIR) JANE

(— OF FIBER) NOIL

(— OF FIRED CLAY) TILE

(— OF GROUND SURROUNDED BY WASTE) HOPE

(— OF HARD WOOD) MOOT

(— OF LAND) HAM LOT BUTT GORE LEASE SPONG SQUAT HUERTA RINCON SECTION SOLIDATE

(— OF LIGHT ORDNANCE) ASPIC

(— OF LINEN) AMIT AMICE

(— OF LOG) SLAB

(— OF MAST) TONGUE

(— OF MATZOTH) AFIKOMEN

(— OF MEAT) EYE HEEL RAND COLLOP EPIGRAM

(— OF METAL) JAG COIN JAGG SPRAG

(— OF MONEY) COG SOU SHINER

(— OF NEEDLEWORK) SAMPLER

(— OF NONSENSE) FUDGE TRIMTRAM

(— OF ORE) CHAT
(— OF SAIL) HULLOCK
(— OF SEPARATED LAND) BUTT
(— OF SKIN FOR GLOVE) TRANK
(— OF SKIN) BLYPE
(— OF SLATE) SLAT
(— OF SOAP) BALL
(— OF SOMETHING EDIBLE) STULL
(— OF TIMBER) FISH COULISSE
FOREHOOK
(— OF TOAST) SLINGER
(— OF TOBACCO) FIG
(— OF TRACK) LEAD RUNBY
(— OF TRICKERY) CROOK
(— OF TURF) FLAG DIVOT SCRAW
SHIRREL
(— OF WOOD) KIP LATH APRON
BOARD CHUMP CHUNK PLANK
SPOON WADDY BILLET COMMON
STOWER TIMBER LIPPING
(— OF WORK) JOB CHAR TURN
(— OF WRITING) SCREED SCREEVE
(— OUT) EKE
(— SPLIT OFF) SPLINT
(— TO PREVENT SLIPPING) CLEAT
(—S OF MACARONI) DITALI DITALINI
(100-REAL GOLD —) ISABELLA
(25-CENT —) CUTER
(4-DOLLAR GOLD —) STELLA
(ARTILLERY —) DRAKE SAKER
LANTACA
(BACKGAMMON —) STONE
(BROAD —) SHEET
(BROKEN —) BRACK FRACTION
(BUTTING —) SHEET
(CHESS —) PIN KING PAWN ROOK
QUEEN BISHOP CASTLE KNIGHT
OFFICER
(END — OF BUCKET) CANT
(FLAT —) FLAP FLAKE
(FUR —) PALATINE
(GOLD —) SLUG TALI
(IN —S) LIMBMEAL
(IRREGULAR —) SNAG
(LARDED — OF MEAT) DAUB
(LARGE —) HUNK MOLE STULL
DOLLOP
(LITERARY —) CAMEO
(LITTLE —) STNEKI
(LONG —) STRIP
(MOVABLE — IN VIOLIN BOW) NUT
(MUSICAL —) ITEM CHORO DANCE
ETUDE CHASER LESSON ALLEGRO
ANDANTE CONCERTO DUOLOGUE
ENTRACTE INVENTION
(NARROW —) LABEL STAVE STRIP
(ODD — OF CARPENTRY)
DUTCHMAN
(ROTATING —) CAM ROTOR
SPINDLE
(SAMPLE —) SWATCH
(SHAPELESS —) DUMP MAMMOCK
(SIDE —) RIB JAMB JAMBE
(SINGLE —) LENGTH
(SLENDER —) SPILL SLIVER
(SMALL — OF FLESH) GIGOT
(SMALL — OF WOOD) KIP
(SMALL —) BIT BOB NOB PEA CHIP
SNIP TATE CRUMB PATCH PRILL

SCRAP SPECK MORSEL SIPPET
DRIBLET FLITTER PALLION SPLINTER
(SMALL —S) MATCHWOOD
(STRENGTHENING —) DWANG
HURTER
(TAPERING —) GORE GUSSET
(THICK —) JUNK HUNCH
(THIN —) SHIM FLAKE SHIVE SLICE
(WEDGESHAPED — OF WOOD) GLUT
SHIM
(PL.) MATERIAL NOBLEMEN
PIECEWORK SETWORK TUTWORK
TASKWORK
PIECEWORKER JOBBER
PIECRUST BREAD COFFIN ABAISSE
PIED PINTO SHELD MAGPIED PIEBALD
PIED ANTELOPE BONTEBOK
PIEDFORT PATAGON
PIED WAGTAIL COB COBB PEER
PILE PILLAR WAGGIE WASHER
WATERIE SEEDBIRD WASHDISH
WASHTAIL
PIEPLANT RHUBARB RHAPONTIC
PIER COB ANTA BELT COBB DOCK
MOLE PILE QUAY TILT GROIN JETTY
JOWEL JUTTY LEVEE STILT WHARF
BRIDGE BUNDER MULLION STAGION
PIEDROIT STELLING
(— CAP) SUMMER
(HALF —) RESPONSE
PIERCE CUT DAB DAG DEG DIG JAB
RIT BARB BEAR BITE BORE BROB
BROD CLOY DART DIRL GORE HOLE
HOOK LACE LACK PASS PINK PROB
RIVE ROVE STAB STOB TAME TANG
WHIP BREAK DRILL ENTER GOUGE
GRIDE LANCE PERCH PITCH POACH
PREEN PROBE PRONG SHEAR SNICK
SPEAR SPIKE STEEK STICK STING
THIRL ATTAME BROACH CLEAVE
DAGGER EMPALE FICCHE GIMLET
IMPALE LAUNCH PRITCH RIDDLE
SEARCH SKEWER STITCH STRIKE
THRILL THRING THRUST WIMBLE
ASSAGAI JAVELIN ENTHRILL
LACERATE PUNCTURE
PIERCED AJOURE CRIBRAL PERTUSE
CRIBROSE PERFORATE
PIERCING SHY FELL HIGH KEEN
LOUD TART CLEAR EAGLE SHARP
SNELL ARROWY BITTER BORING
SHREWD SHRILL SNITHE SNITHY
CUTTING GIMLETY POINTED
PUNGENT DRILLING INCISIVE
PERCEANT POIGNANT POUNCING
STABBING STICKING
PIERHEAD MOLEHEAD
PIET PYOT DIPPER MAGPIE
PIETIST LABADIST
PIETISTIC DEVOUT
PIETY HONOR LOYALTY PIETISM
DEVOTION SANCTION GODLINESS
PIFFLE FOLDEROL
PIG (ALSO SEE HOG, SWINE) COW
FAR HAM HOG SLIP BACON BONAV
BROCK CHEAT CHUCK GRICE INGOT
PIGGY SHOAT APEREA BONHAM
COCHON FARROW GUSSIE HOGGIE
PORKET PORKIN SUCKER TITMAN

WEANER BONNIVE GLUTTON
GRUMPHY HOGLING PIGLING
ROOKLER GRUNTLING
(BROOD OF —S) TEAM
(EIGHT —S) FODDER
(SMALLEST — OF LITTER) TITMAN
ANTHONY DILLING TANTANY
TANTONY
(SUCKLING —) ROASTER
(UNDERSIZED —) RUNT TITMAN
TEATMAN
(YOUNG —) ELT FAR SLIP GRICE
GURRY BONEEN BONHAM
SQUEAKER
PIG DEER BABIRUSA
PIGEON DOO NUN OWL TOY BARB
CLAY DOVE JACK KING KITE LUPE
RUFF RUNT SPOT BALDY DOWVE
FRILL HOMER KOKLA PIPER SQUAB
WONGA CULTER CULVER CUSHAT
DODLET DRAGON FEEDER HELMET
JEWING MAGPIE MANUMA MAUMET
MODENA POUTER PRIEST ROCKER
SHAKER TRERON TURBIT TURNER
WATTLE ANTWERP CARNEAU
CARRIER CROPPER FANTAIL FINIKIN
JACOBIN MALTESE PINTADO
SWALLOW TIPPLER TUMBLER
BALDHEAD CAPUCHIN FINIKING
HORSEMAN MANUTAGI RINGDOVE
SQUABBER SQUEAKER SQUEALER
FRILLBACK TOOTHBILL
(CLAY —) BIRD GYROPIGEON
(STOOL —) PIG NARK
PIGEON BLOOD GARNET
PIGEON HAWK MERLIN
PIGEONHOLE BOX SLOT LABEL
SHELVE ANALYZE CELLULE
CLASSIFY CUBBYHOLE
(PL.) STOCK
PIGEON HOUSE COT DOOKET
DOVECOT COLUMBARY
PIGEON PEA DAL TUR TARE ARHAR
DAHIL GANDUL TURNER TURNOR
CATJANG
PIGEON WOODPECKER FLICKER
PIGGERY PIGS PIGSTY HOGGERY
POTTERY SWINERY CROCKERY
PIGGIN HANDY PIPKIN
PIGHEADED WILLFUL PERVERSE
STUBBORN OBSTINATE
PIGHTLE PIKLE PICKLE PIDDLE
PIGTAIL
PIG IRON GRUNDY
PIGLET PORKLING
PIGLIKE SUIFORM SUILINE
PIGMENT (ALSO SEE DYE, COLOR)
BLUE HEME BROWN COLOR EARTH
GREEN HUMIN MORIN PAINT STAIN
TONER BRONZE CEROID CERUSE
IDAEIN LITHOL MALVIN ORANGE
PURPLE SIENNA VIOLET GOUACHE
PAINTRY PUCCOON STAINER
TURACIN ALTHAEIN COLORANT
EXTENDER GOSSYPOL PAINTURE
TINCTURE UROPHEIN
(— FOR WOODWORK) KOKOWAI
(BLACK —) ABAISER MELANIN
(BLUE —) BICE SMALT CYANIN

ALTHEIN CERULEUM MARENNIN
(BLUE-GREEN —) LEUCOCYAN
(BROWN —) MUMMY SEPIA UMBER
BISTER FUSCIN ASTERIN
(BROWNISH-YELLOW —} SIENNA
(GREEN —) VERDITER
(MADDER-ROOT —) RUBIATE
(ORANGE-RED —) REALGAR
(RED —) HAEM LAKE ARUMIN
PATISE SANDYX AMATITO KOKOWAI
PUCCOON SCARLET SINOPIA
CAPSUMIN URORUBIN URRHODIN
VERMILION
(RED-VIOLET —) TURACIN
(WHITE —) CERUSE ANATASE
LITHOPONE
(YELLOW —) FLAVIN ETIOLIN
FISETIN GAMBOGE PUCCOON
DIATOMIN GALANGIN GENTISIN
ORPIMENT UROBILIN
PIGMENTATION COLOR LENTIL
LENTIGO JAUNDICE NIGRITIES
PIGNUS PAWN PLEDGE
PIGNUT HOGNUT
PIGS' FEET CRUBEEN PETTITOES
PIGSKIN SADDLE FOOTBALL
PIGSNEY EYE DARLING
PIGSTY FRANK HOGCOTE HOGGERY
PIGGERY SWINESTY
PIGTAIL PLAIT QUEUE COLETA
PIGWASH SWILL
PIGWEED QUINOA BEETROOT
CARELESS GOOSEFOOT
PIK DRA PICKI PICKL ENDAZE
ENDASEH
PIKA CONY HAIR HARE LEPORID
LAGOMORPH
PIKE GED DORE DORY GADE GEDD
JACK LUCE TANG TOUG TUCK
HAKED LUCET SNAKE SNOOK STING
VOUGE SALMON SAUGER JAVELIN
WALLEYE BLOWFISH GLASSEYE
JACKFISH NORTHERN PARTISAN
PICKEREL POULAINE TURNPIKE
PIKELET CRUMPET
PIKEMAN PIKE WATTLEBOY
PIKE PERCH PERCID SANDER
SAUGER ZANDER
PIKER TRAMP VAGRANT TELLTALE
TIGHTWAD VAGABOND
PILASTER ANTA PIER RIDGE ALETTE
RESPOND TELAMON
PILCHARD FUMADO ALEWIFE
SARDINE MENHADEN
PILE COP FUR LOT NAP PIE TIP BALE
BANK BING BULK BUNG BURR COCK
DASS DECK DESS DOWN HACK HAIR
HEAP LEET LOAD PEEL PIER POLE
POOK PYRE REEK RUCK SESS SHAG
SPUD AMASS CANCH CLAMP
CROWD FAGOT POINT SPILE SPIRE
STACK STILT TOWER CASTLE
FAGGOT FENDER FILLER GALGAL
PILLAR RICKLE RUCKLE FORTUNE
JAVELIN PYRAMID REACTOR
SPINDLE CROWBILL INCREASE
SANDPILE
(— CROSSWISE) COB
(— CURD) CHEDDAR

(— OF BRICKS) HACK
(— OF CLOTH) LAY
(— OF HAY) RICK SHOCK DOODLE
HAYCOCK HAYRICK
(— OF ICE) HUMMOCK
(— OF LOGS) DECK
(— OF PLATES) BUNG
(— OF REFUSE) DUSTHEAP
(— OF SALT FISH) BULK
(— OF SEALSKINS) PAN
(— OF SHEAVES) SESS
(— OF SHEETS) LIFT
(— OF STONES) ISLAND STONAGE
WARLOCK
(— OF TOBACCO) BULK
(— OF WOOD) STRAND
(— TO BE BURNT) PYRE
(— UP) CORD RICK COMPILE
(— WHEAT SHOCKS) STITCH
(IRON —) SPINDLE
(LITTLE —) HOT HOTT
(LOOSE —) RICKLE
(ROCK —) HOODOO
(SMALL —) COCK CANCH
(PL.) FIG DRIFT
PILEA ADICEA
PILEATED WOODPECKER
LOGCOCK WOODCOCK
PILE DRIVER TUP FISTUCA
HERCULES IMPACTER
(— DOLLY) FOLLOWER
(— WEIGHT) RAM TUP MONKEY
PILEUS CAP MITRA PILEOLUS
PILEWORT CRAIN CRANE FICARY
FIGWORT CELANDINE
PILFER ROB CRIB HOOK PELF PICK
PILK PRIG SMUG SNIG FILCH
MOOCH PILCH PROWL SHARP
SLOCK STEAL SWIPE FINGER
MAGPIE MOOTCH NIBBLE PICKLE
SMOUCH SNITCH CABBAGE
MANAVEL PLUNDER PURLOIN
SNAFFLE UNHITCH PETTIFOG
SCROUNGE
PILFERER PRIG TAKER SLOCKER
FINGERER SLOCKSTER
PILFERING MICHING PICKING
THIEVISH
PILGRIM HAJI HADJI HAJJI PALMER
PELERIN PEREGRIN WAYFARER
PILGRIMAGE TRIP TURUS VOYAGE
JOURNEY
(— TO MECCA) HADJ
PILING SPILING STOCKADE
(PL.) STOCKADE
PILL PIL ROB BALL BARK GOLI PEEL
POOL CREEK CACHOU EXTORT
UNHAIR DESPOIL DIURNAL GLOBULE
GRANULE PARVULE PILLULE
PREFORM BASEBALL GOOFBALL
BLACKBALL CIGARETTE
(AROMATIC —) CACHOU
(LARGE —) BALL BOLUS
(LITTLE —) PILULA PILULE
PILLAGE LOOT PEEL PILL PREY
SACK BOOTY FORAY HARRY REAVE
RIFLE SPOIL HARROW MARAUD
PICORY RAPINE RAVAGE DESPOIL
PICKEER PLUNDER RANSACK

ROBBERY BOOTHALE EXPILATE
PURCHASE SPOLIATE DEVASTATE
PILLAGER PEELER PILLER ROBBER
SACKER SPOILER SNAPHANCE
PILLAGING EXECUTION PREDATORY
PILLAR COG HERM JAMB PACK PIER
PILE POST PROP STUD TERM JAMBE
NEWEL SHAFT STELA STELE STOCK
STONE STOOP STUMP CIPPUS
COLUMN HERMES PILLER STAPLE
BEDPOST DEADMAN TRESTLE
TRUMEAU BOUNDARY MASSEBAH
PEDESTAL RESPONSE STANCHION
(— CAPPED WITH SLAB) BILITH
(— IN LARGE DOORWAY) TRUMEAU
(— IN MINE) STOOK STUMP
(— OF COAL) SPURN STOOK STOOP
(— SUPPORTING ARCH) RESPONSE
(— SURMOUNTED BY HEAD)
HERMES
(—S OF HERCULES) ABILA CALPE
(4-SIDED —) OBELISK
(BUDDHIST —) LAT
(CHANGED TO —) OLENUS
(EARTH —) HOODOO
(SACRED —) ASHERAH
(SEMITE —) MASSEBAH
(STONE —) CIPPUS
(TEMPORARY —) DEADMAN
(PL.) CRURA
PILLARIST STYLITE
PILLAS PILCORN PILKINS
PILLBOX SCATULA
PILLBUG ISOPOD KEESLIP MILLEPED
PILLWORM CHEESELIP
PILLED BALD SHAVEN TONSURED
PILLION PAD PILLOW SADDLE
CUSHION
PILLORY THEW JOUGS TRONE
CRUCIFY HALSFANG
PILLOW COD BOTT DAWN PEEL PILE
REST FLOAT WANGER BOLSTER
CUSHION FUSTIAN HEADING
OREILLER
PILLOWCASE BEAR PILL SHAM
PILLIVER
PILM DUST
PILON BONUS LAGNIAPPE
PILOSE HAIRY PILEOUS
PILOT ACE SPY KIWI COACH GUARD
GUIDE STEER AIRMAN ESCORT
MANAGE THAMUS AVIATOR CAPTAIN
CONDUCT HOBBLER LODEMAN
SHIPMAN WINGMAN AIREDALE
GOVERNOR HELMSMAN PALINURUS
WHEELSMAN
PILOT BIRD PLOVER
PILOT FISH ROMERO JACKFISH
AMBERFISH
PILOTHOUSE TEXAS CHARTHOUSE
PILUM PESTLE JAVELIN
PIMENTA MYRTAL
PIMENTO PIMINTA ALLSPICE
PIMIENTO
PIMP MACK BULLY CADET FAGOT
PONCE SNEAK MACRIO PANDER
RUFFIAN INFORMER PROCUROR
PURVEYOR SCOUNDREL
PIMPERNEL BURNET WAYWORT

EYEBRIGHT MARGELINE WINCOPIPE
PIMPLE GUM NOB PAP BURL KNOB
PUSH QUAT SPOT HICKY PLOOK
PLOUK PLUKE PAPULA PAPULE
TETTER BUBUKLE PUSTULE
PIMGENET WHEYWORM
PIN FID FIX HOB HUB LAG LEG NOG
PEG PEN ACUS APEX AXLE BANK
BOLT MOOD PEEN POST PRIN PROP
PYNE RUNG STUD DRIFT HUMOR
KAYLE POINT PREEN SPILL THOLE
BOBBIN BROACH BROOCH CALIGO
COTTER CURLER FASTEN HATPIN
NORMAN PINNET SKEWER SPIGOT
TEMPER TENPIN TOGGEL TONGUE
TRIFLE BAYONET CONFINE ENCLOSE
GUDGEON IMPOUND LOCKPIN
PAIRPIN PUSHPIN SPINDLE TAMPION
TANGENT TUMBLER FORELOCK
PINNACLE
(— FOR FITTING PLANKS) SETBOLT
(— IN AXLETREE) LINCHPIN
(— IN RIFLE) TIGE
(— OF DIAL) STYLE GNOMON
(— OF LANTERN PINION) RUNDLE
(— OF WATCH) DART
(— ON CLAVICHORD KEY) TANGENT
(— TO HOLD BEDCLOTHES)
BEDSTAFF
(— USED AS TARGET) HOB
(BELAYING —) CAVIL
(BOWLING —) DUCKPIN HEADPIN
KINGPIN SLEEPER
(BOWLING —S) DEADWOOD
(CARPENTRY —) DOWEL
(COUPLING —) DRAWBOLT
(ENGAGING —) BAYONET
(HAIR —) BARRETTE
(HEADED —) RIVET
(JEWELED —) PROP
(OAR —) THOLE
(ORNAMENTAL —) AGLET AIGLET
(PIVOT —) PINTLE
(SMALL —) LILL MINIKIN MICROPIN
(SPLIT —) COTTER FORELOCK
(SURVEYOR'S —) ARROW
(TAPERED —) DRIFT
(TIRLING —) RISP
(WOODEN —) SPILE TRENAIL
(PL.) LEGS KAILS DEADWOOD
PINACOID BASE HEMIDOME
PINAFORE SLIP TIDE TIDY TIER
TYER DAIDLY SAVEALL SLIPPER
GABERDINE
PINBALL MACHINE PACHINKO
PINCASE POPPET
PINCE-NEZ NIPPER LORGNON
NOSEPINCH
PINCERS TEU TEW CLAM CHELA
TUARN PLIERS TURKIS WYNRIS
FORCEPS MULLETS NIPPERS
PINCHER PINSONS TWEEZERS
PINCH NIP TOP VEX WRY BITE CLAM
HURT PUSH STOP TUCK CRIMP
GRIPE HINCH PUGIL SNUFF SQUAT
STEAL STINT TAPER THEFT TWEAK
WRING ARREST CLUTCH EXTORT
HARASS NARROW SNITCH STRAIT
STRESS TWINCH TWITCH SCRINCH

SQUEEZE JUNCTURE PRESSURE
SHORTAGE STRAITEN VELLICATE
(— OF SNUFF) SNEESH SNEESHIN
(— WITH HUNGER) CLAM CLEM
PINCHBECK SHAM CHEAP SPURIOUS
PRETENDED
PINCHED CHITTY WASTED HAGGARD
PUNGLED SQUINCH
PINCHPENNY CARL MISER NIGGARD
NIGGARDLY
PINDARIC ODE WILD
PINE IE ARA LIM CHIL CHIR FADE
FLAG HALA HONE IEIE KAIL WANT
AGGAG DROOP DWAIN GRIEF KAURI
MATAI MATSU MOURN OCOTE PINON
WANZE WEARY WRIST YEARN
APACHE AROLLA DUSTER FAMINE
GRIEVE HUNGER LAMENT PANDAN
SHRINK SORROW STARVE TOATOA
TORFEL WITHER CYPRESS DAISING
DWINDLE FORPINE FOXTAIL
JEFFREY LAUHALA TARWOOD
TORMENT TORTURE AKAMATSU
AUSTRIAN GALAGALA LANGUISH
LOBLOLLY LONGLEAF PINASTER
STAGHORN TANEKAHA VANQUISH
(— AWAY) DROOP DWINE SNURP
WANZE WINDER FORPINE
MACERATE
(AUSTRALIAN —) BEEFWOOD
(GROUND —) FOXTAIL
(PITCH —) THYME
PINEAPPLE BOMB NANA PINA PINO
PITA ANANA ANANAS ABACAXI
GRENADE
PINE FINCH SISKIN
PINE MARTEN SABLE
PINE NEEDLE SHAT SPILL PINING
ALFILARIA
(PL.) TWINKLES
PINE TREE STATE MAINE
PINFEATHER PEN STUMP STIPULE
PINFISH CHUB SPOT JIMMY PORGY
SARGO
PINFOLD POUND
PING KNOCK
PINGUIN MAYA ANANAS AGUAMAS
PINUELA HUIPILLA
PINGUITUDE FATNESS OBESITY
OILINESS
PINION NOIL WING PINON QUILL
PENNON SECURE LANTERN PINACLE
SHACKLE TRUNDLE FLIGHTER
WALLOWER
PINION WHEEL MOBILE
PINITOL SENNITE MATEZITE
PINK JAG PIP CYME DAWN DECK
FADE MICE PING STAB WINK ADORN
BLINK CORAL ELITE MOVED SWELL
WOUND AURORE BISQUE CHERUB
FIESTA HEIGHT MINNOW POUNCE
SHRIMP SILENE TATTOO ZEPHYR
ANNATTO ARBUTUS BEGONIA
BERMUDA BLOSSOM EXTREME
PARAGON REVEREE SANDUST
TUSSORE CONFETTI COQUETTE
DECORATE DIANTHUS GILLIVER
LIMEWORT RADIANCE RECAMIER
PINKED JAGGED

PINKIE PIRLIE
PINKROOT REDROOT WORMWEED
STARBLOOM
PINNA EARFLAP PINNULE APHLEBIA
AURICULA PAVILION
PINNACE BARK CROWN WOMAN
BARQUE PINNAGE MISTRESS
PINNACLE IT PIN TOP ACME APEX
CREST CROWN SERAC SPIRE
THUMB FINIAL HEIGHT SUMMIT
GENDARME
(ICE —) SERAC
(ROCKY —) TOR HOODOO AIGUILLE
GENDARME
PINNATE WINGED
PINNER PINDER FLANDAN STICKER
PINOCHLE BINOCLE GOULASH
AIRPLANE
(— SCORE) MELD
PINPILLOW PIMPLO
PINPOINT ISOLATE
(— OF LIGHT) GLEAM
PINT O GULL PINNET SWIGGER
OCTARIUS
(9-10THS —) MUTCHKIN
(FOURTH —) GILL JACK
(HALF —) CUP NIP GILL JACK
CUPFUL NIPPERKIN
PINTADO CERO PIED SIER SEARER
SIERRA SPOTTED KINGFISH
PINTAIL DUCK SMEE SPIKE SPRIG
GROUSE SMETHE CRACKER
LADYBIRD LONGNECK PIKETAIL
PINTANO PILOT COCKEYE CHIRIVITA
PINTID EMPEINE
PINTO BEAN ROSILLO
PINWEED(PL.) LECHEA
PINWHEEL WINDMILL
PINWORM NEMA OXYURID
PIN WRENCH SPANULE
PIONEER BLAZE GUIDE MINER
GROPER HALUTZ SETTLE CHALUTZ
EXPLORE EARLIEST EMIGRANT
ORIGINAL RAWHIDER
PIOUS PI HOLY FROOM GODLY
MORAL SEELY DEVOUT DIVINE
INWARD PIETIC CANTING DUTIFUL
GODDARD PITEOUS SAINTED
SAINTLY FAITHFUL RELIGIOUS
PIP DIE CHIP ECHO KILL PAIP PEEP
SPOT SPECK DEFEAT PIPPIN
BLACKBALL
PIPAL BO FIG
PIPE TD BIN GUN HUB TAP TEE CALL
CANE DALE DRIP DUCT FLUE HOSE
LINE MAIN MUTE PULE REED TILE
TUBE WEEP WORM BLAST BRAIL
BRIAR CANAL CANEL CINCH CRANE
CROSS CUTTY HOOKA PROBE PUNGI
QUILL RIDER RISER SPOUT STAND
STRAW TEWEL TRUMP TRUNK VOICE
BRANCH BURROW CALEAN CASING
DUCTUS FAUCET FILLER GEWGAW
HEWGAG HOGGER KINURA NIPPLE
NOTICE NOZZLE OFFLET OFFSET
POOGYE RANKET SLEEVE SLOUCH
SLUICE SUCKER TROWEL TUBULE
TUNNEL UPTAKE WEEPER CHANNEL
CHANTER CHIBOUK CONDUIT

DUCTURE FISTULA HYDRANT
SERVICE SPARGER SPINDLE
SUCTION TALLBOY TWEEDLE
WHISTLE CALIDUCT DOWNTAKE
GALOUBET LAMPHOLE MIRLITON
NARGHILE NARGILEH PENSTOCK
SEMIDOLE SUSPIRAL TELLTALE
THRIBBLE
(— AS NAVIGATION AID) SPINDLE
(— BENDER) HICKEY
(— BOWL) STUMMEL
(— FOR CONDUCTING WATER)
LEADER
(— JOINT) TURNOUT
(— OF ORE) BUNNY
(— OF PAN) SYRINX
(— OF QUEEN BEE) TEET
(— ON BAGPIPE) DRONE CHANTER
(— SUPPORT) CRADLE
(— TAB) TACK
(— TO MUFFLE TRUMPET) SORDINE
(— USED IN WELL) STRING
(— WITH SOCKET ENDS) HUB
(4 LENGTHS OF —) FOURBLE
(CEREMONIAL —) CALUMET
(CLAMMING —) BRAIL
(CONNECTING —) HOGGER
(FLUE —) LABIAL
(HEATING —) CALIDUCT
(MUSICAL —) BODY GEWGAW
FISTULA SORDINE HORNPIPE
SCHWEGEL
(OATEN —) OAT
(ORGAN —) FLUE KINURA LABIAL
ERZAHLER SCHWEGEL TREMOLANT
(PEACE —) CALUMET
(SEWER —) SLANT
(SHEPHERD'S —) REED LARIGOT
(SNAKE-CHARMER'S —) PUNGI
(TOBACCO —) GUN CLAY BRIAR
BRIER CUTTY HOOKA STRAW
CALEAN DUDEEN HOOKAH BULLDOG
CHIBOUK CHILLUM CORNCOB
BILLIARD CALABASH
(TOY —) HEWGAG
(VERTICAL —) STACK LAMPHOLE
(WATER — FOR ENGINE) SLOUCH
PIPED DRUNK JETTED
PIPEFISH EARL LONGJAW
PIPELAYER YARNER
PIPESTEM STOPPEL STOPPLE
PIPETTE PIPET TASTER
PIPEWORT HATPIN WOOLWEED
PIPING HOSE SOFT VERY CRYING
ROULEAU WAILING WEEPING
TRANQUIL
PIPING CROW CASSICAN FLUTEBIRD
PIPIRI PITIRRI
PIPISTRELLE BAT NOCTULE
PIPIT PEEP TEETAN WEKEEN
CHEEPER SKYLARK TIETICK TITLARK
TITLING WAGTAIL LINGBIRD
TWITLARK
PIPPIN PIP APPLE PEPPIN RIBSTON
PIPSISSEWA EVERGREEN
WINTERGREEN
PIQUANCY SALT ZEST FLAVOR
GINGER TARTNESS
PIQUANT BOLD RACY JUICY NUTTY

SALTY SHARP SPICY TASTY ZESTY
LIVELY SEVERE CUTTING PEPPERY
PUNGENT STINGING
PIQUE FRET GOAD PEAK PICK PIKE
PYKE TICK ANNOY PRISE SNUFF
SPITE STING HARASS MALICE
NETTLE PRITCH STRUNT CHIGGER
OFFENSE PROVOKE UMBRAGE
IRRITATE MARCELLA
PIRACY CAPTURE PIRATISM
PIRAGUA CANOE DUGOUT PIROGUE
PETTIAGUA
PIRANHA PIRAI CARIBE PIRAYA
PIRARUCU PAICHE ARAPAIMA
PIRATE CAPER ROVER ROBBER
VIKING CATERAN CORSAIR PICKEER
SCUMMER ALGERINE MAROONER
PICAROON BUCCANEER SALLEEMAN
(— FLAG) ROGER BLACKJACK
PIRIPIRI BIRK BIRCH MAPAN
PIRL SPIN TWINE TWIST REVOLVE
PIRN QUILL BOBBIN PIRNIE SPINDLE
PIROGUE CANOE PERIOQUE
PIROPLASM BABESIA
PIROSHKI PIROGEN
PISCINA POOL TANK BASIN
SACRARY LAVATORY SACRARIUM
PISE CAJON PISAY
PISHOGUE CHARM SPELL SORCERY
WITCHERY
PISMIRE ANT EMMET
PISOLITE PEASTONE
PISTACHIO FISTIC PISTICK
PISTIL CHIVE CARPEL UMBONE
POINTEL
(PL.) GYNECIUM
PISTILLATE FEMALE
PISTOL DAG GAT GUN POP ROD
BULL DAGG IRON TACK FLUTE
RIFLE STICK BARKER BUFFER
BULDER BULLER CANNON DRAGON
HEATER POTGUN RIFFLE BULLDOG
DUNGEON SHOOTER TICKLER
DERINGER REPORTER REVOLVER
(TOY —) SPARKLER
PISTON BUCKET FORCER PALLET
SUCKER EMBOLUS PLUNGER
(— HUB) SPIDER
PIT PET POT PUT BURY CIST DELF
DELL DISC DISK FOSS HELL HOLE
KIST LAKE MINE PLAY PUTT SILO
SINK SUMP SWAG TURN WEEM
WELL ABYSM ABYSS CRYPT DELFT
DITCH FOSSA FOVEA FROST GRAVE
LEACH MATCH PITCH PORUS SLACK
SLUIG TREAD AREOLE BORROW
BUNKER KERNEL OPPOSE RADDLE
WALLOW ABADDON ALVEOLA
AMPULLA BOTHROS CHARPIT
FOSSULA FOXHOLE HANDLER
LATRINE MEGARON PINHOLE
VARIOLE WINNING CYPHELLA
DOWNFALL FAVEOLUS FENESTRA
POCKMARK PUNCTULE WELLHOLE
(— FOR BAKING) IMU UMU
(— FOR OFFERINGS) BOTHROS
(— OF STOMACH) MARK WIND
(— OF THEATER) GROUND

(— ON COCKROACH HEAD)
FENESTRA
(— ON LICHENS) LACUNA CYPHELLA
(— SACRED TO DEMETER)
MEGARON
(BITTER —) STIPPEN
(BOTTOMLESS —) ABYSS ABADDON
BARATHRUM
(COAL —) HEUCH HEUGH
(FODDER —) SILO
(MAORI —) RUA
(MIRY —) SLUIG
(RIFLE —) SANGAR
(ROOFED —) CIST KIST
(SALT —) VAT PEZOGRAPH
(SAND —) BUNKER
(SMALL —) AREOLE LACUNA
STAPLE
(TANNING —) LIME LAYER LEACH
HANDLER LAYAWAY SUSPENDER
PITA PITO YUCCA ARGHAN
PITCH DIP FIT KEY LAB MEL PIC
BUCK CANT CHAT CODE COOK DING
FALL FORK HURL PECK PICK PLUG
RAKE TELL TONE TOSS ABODE
BOOST BUNCH FLING LABOR LURCH
PLANT SLENT SLOPE SPIEL THROW
TWIRL BINDER DIRECT ENCAMP
FILLER LENGTH MALTHA MANJAK
PLUNGE SQUARE TOTTER TUMBLE
VOLLEY WICKET CURRENT NARRATE
ALKITRAN OVERHANG
(— AT A MARK) LAG
(— FROM FIR TREES) ALKITRAN
(— OF HELIX) JAW
(— TENT) TELD
(ABOVE —) SHARP
(AUCTION —) SETBACK
(BASEBALL —) CURVE STRIKE
CRIPPLE SPITTER FADEAWAY
KNUCKLER SPITBALL
(BELOW —) FLAT
(COBBLER'S —) CODE
(FULL —) VOLLEY
(GLANCE —) MANJAK MANJACK
(HIGH —) BLOOPER
(HIGHEST —) PRIDE
(IDENTITY IN —) UNISON
(MINERAL —) BITUMEN
PITCH APPLE COPEI CUPAY
PITCHED SET
PITCHER JUG JACK OLLA PILL PRIG
BUIRE CRUET GALON GORGE
GOTCH AFTABA CROUKE GALLON
HURLER POURIE STRAIN URCEUS
CANETTE CHUCKER FLINGER
GROWLER STARTER STOPPER
TWIRLER URCEOLE AIGUIERE
ASCIDIUM OENOCHOE SOUTHPAW
MOUNDSMAN
(— AND CATCHER) BATTERY
(— FOR BEER) GROWLER
(— SHAPED LIKE MAN) TOBY
(— WITH ONE HANDLE) URCEUS
(BULGING —) GOTCH
(EARTHEN —) GEORG GORGE
(RELIEF —) FIREMAN
(RELIEF —S) BULLPEN
(WIDEMOUTHED —) EWER

PITCHER PLANT BISCUIT FLYTRAP
FEVERCUP FOXGLOVE WATERCUP
NEPENTHES SKUNKWEED
PITCHFORK EVIL PICK PIKE PICKEL
SHEPPECK PITCHPIKE
(THATCHER'S —) GROOM
(PL.) HARD
PITCHHOLE CAHOT
PITCHMAN VENDER SALESMAN
PITCH PIPE TUNER EPITONION
PITEOUS MEAN PALTRY PITIFUL
MERCIFUL MOURNFUL PIERCING
PITFALL PIT FALL TRAP SNARE
DANGER TRAPFALL
PITH JET PUT SAP CORE GIST MEAT
PULP PUTT HEART VIGOR ENERGY
KERNEL MARROW ESSENCE
EXTRACT MEDULLA NUCLEUS
PAPYRUS STRENGTH
PITH HELMET TOPI TOPEE
PITH TREE AMBATCH
PITHY CRISP MEATY SAPPY TERSE
STRONG CONCISE LACONIC
MARROWY
PITIABLE SAD SEELY WOFUL
RUEFUL WOEFUL FORLORN PITIFUL
PITIFUL MEAN MEEK RUTH SILLY
SORRY PALTRY RUEFUL TENDER
HANGDOG RUESOME RUTHFUL
MERCIFUL PATHETIC
PITILESS GRIM CRUEL STERN STONY
SAVAGE RUTHLESS UNPITIED
MERCILESS
PITTANCE BIT ALMS DOLE GIFT MITE
SONG TRIFLE BEQUEST
PITTED FOVEATE OPPOSED
ALVEOLATE
PITTER STONER
PITURI BEDGERY PITCHERY
PITY RUE MEAN MOAN PETE PITE
RUTH MERCY PIETY REIVE SCATH
PATHOS MERCIFY REMORSE
WAESUCK CLEMENCY SYMPATHY
PIVOT TOE CRUX SLEW TURN HEART
CENTER SLOUGH WORDLE
GUDGEON TRAVERSE TRUNNION
PIVOTAL POLAR CENTRAL
(— POINT) KNUCKLE
PIVOTING DISHRAG
PIVOT STAND PEDESTAL
PIXY ELF FAIRY PYGMY ROGUE
IMPISH RASCAL SPRITE PUCKISH
ROGUISH
PIXILATED DAFFY DOTTY DRUNK
PIXIE BEMUSED PUCKISH TOUCHED
CONFUSED
PIZE OATH PISE CURSE
PLACABLE WEAK QUIET PACABLE
PEACEFUL YIELDING FORGIVING
PLACARD BILL POST TITLE POSTER
TICKET AFFICHE REDLINE
STOMACHER
PLACATE CALM GENTLE PACIFY
PLEASE SOOTHE APPEASE FORGIVE
PLACE L DO BIT FIX PUT SET AREA
HOLE LIEU PLAT PLOT POSE POST
RANK ROOM SEAT SITE SITU SPOT
STEP STOW TEXT VICE YARK BEING
ESTER ESTRE HOUSE JOINT LOCUS

PLAZA POSIT SCENE SITUS STALL
STATE STEAD STELL STOUR WHERE
BESTOW CHARGE GROUND IMPOSE
INVEST LAYOUT LOCALE LOCATE
OFFICE POSSIE ROOMTH ALLODGE
ARRANGE DEPOSIT KITCHEN
STATION ABDITORY DIGGINGS
EMPORIUM LOCATION POSITION
(— ALONE) ISOLATE
(— ALTERNATELY) STAGGER
(— APART) ENISLE
(— BEFORE) APPOSE PREFIX
(— BY FORCE) PILT
(— CROSSWISE) THWART
(— FISH IN SALTING BIN) KENCH
(— FOR CATTLE) CAMP
(— FOR DUMPING RUBBISH) SHOOT
(— FOR MORTAR AND BRICK) FROG
(— FOR PHEASANTS) STEW
(— FOR PRAYERS) IDGAH
(— FOR RABBITS) WARREN
(— FOR RECEPTION) RECEIPT
(— FOR RUBBISH DEPOSITS)
LAYSTALL
(— FOR SEETHING) STEW
(— FOR SLEEPING) BED BUNK DOSS
FLOP LAIR LIBKIN
(— FOR TRAINING HORSES) LONGE
(— FROM WHICH JURY IS TAKEN)
VENUE
(— IN COMPACT MASS) STOW
(— IN ORDER) ARRAY ENRANK
(— IN WATERFALL) LEAP
(— IN) INNEST
(— OF AMUSEMENT) GAFF
(— OF ASSEMBLY) AGORA CURIA
SYNAGOG
(— OF BURIAL) AHU KIL KILL LAIR
GRAVE LAYSTOW CATACOMB
CEMETERY GOLGOTHA LAYSTALL
(— OF BUSINESS) BANK AGENCY
KNACKERY
(— OF CONCEALMENT) DEN BOMA
BLIND STALE HIDING HIDEOUT
HIDEAWAY
(— OF CONFINEMENT) BRIG CAGE
COOP LIMBO PRISON BULLPEN
(— OF CONFUSION) BABEL
TROYTOWN
(— OF DESTRUCTION) ABADDON
(— OF DWELLING) WANE
(— OF ENTERTAINMENT) INN JOINT
DANCERY HANGOUT HOSTELRY
(— OF EXERTION) ARENA
(— OF EXILE) PATMOS
(— OF MISERY) HELL
(— OF NETHER DARKNESS) EREBUS
(— OF NOISE) BABEL
(— OF PROTECTION) PORT SCUG
(— OF REFUGE) ARK BAST HOLD
ASYLUM ADULLAM HIDEOUT
(— OF RESIDENCE) SOIL DOMICILE
(— OF RESORT) PURLIEU
(— OF RESTRAINT) LIMBO
(— OF SACRIFICE) ALTAR
(— OF SAFETY) GRITH HAVEN
WARRANT
(— OF SECURITY) GRITH ASYLUM
CORRAL HARBOR GARRISON

(— OF SHELTER) LEW HOLD JOUK
COVER
(— OF SUBMISSION) CANOSSA
(— OF TORMENT) GOLGOTHA
(— OF WORSHIP) HEIAU BETHEL
CHAPEL CHURCH DESERT SHRINE
TEMPLE GURDWARA SYNAGOGUE
(— WHERE 4 OR MORE WAYS MEET)
CARFAX
(— WHERE FOOD IS KEPT) LARDER
(— WHERE MEAT IS SMOKED)
BUCAN BUCCAN
(— WHERE OUTCASTS GATHER)
HELL
(— WHERE ROADS CROSS) LEET
(— WHERE STREAM IS RAPID)
SHARP
**(— WHERE TROOPS HALT
OVERNIGHT)** ETAPE
(BOGGY —) SLUMP
(BREEDING —) NIDUS LOOMERY
PELICANRY
(CHIEF —) HEADSHIP
(CIRCULAR —) ORBELL
(CONSECRATED —) HIERON
(DRINKING —) BOOZER MUMHOUSE
(DRY —) SEARING
(DWELLING —) BY BYE DEN SEE
HAFT HIVE HOME BEING HOUSE
HOWFF SOJOURN HABITACLE
(EATING —) CAFE GRUBBERY
(EMPTY —) BLANK SPACE
(ENCLOSED —) BIN HAY WORTH
SEVERAL
(ESSENTIAL —) EYE
(FAMILIAR —) KITH
(FAULTY — IN THREAD) TRAP
(FILTHY —) STY
(FIRST —) BLUE LEAD STRAIGHT
(FORTIFIED —) LIS LISS CASTLE
FASTNESS
(GATHERING —) SHOP AGORA
FOYER JOINT LESCHE
(HALTING —) MARAH
(HIDING —) MEW CACHE HIDEL
HOARD STASH COVERT HIDDELS
RETREAT STOWAWAY
(HIGH —) EMINENCE
(HOLLOW —) GULF HOLE HOLL
SCOOP CAVITY ALBERCA SINKHOLE
(INHABITED —) ABADI
(LANDING —) GHAT HARD LEVEE
SCALE PALACE HELIPORT
(LEVEL —) PLANILLA
(LODGING —) CAMP LOGIS BIDING
BILLET LIBKEN
(LURKING —) HOLD HOLE HOARD
HULSTER
(MARKET —) AGORA TRONE
MARKET RIALTO
(MARSHY —) SLEW SLOO SLUE
SLUMP SLOUGH
(MEETING —) CLUB COURT FORUM
GUILD TRYST TOLSEL TOLZEY
AMBALAM KLAVERN TINWALD
(MUDDY —) SOIL
(NESTING —) JUG NIDARY
(OPEN —) ENAJIM
(OTHERWORLDLY —) EMPYREAN

(RAVELED —) FRAY
(REMOTE —) JERICHO
(RESTING —) LAY CAMP FORM GIST
LAIR PARAO CRADLE
(ROCKY —) ROCHER
(SACRED —) HAREM HIERON
CHAITYA SANCTUM
(SALTING —) SALADERO
(SECRET —) LAIR CORNER CRANNY
(SHADY —) GLOOM SWALE
FRESCADE UMBRACLE
(SHELTERED —) NOOK SCUG
SUCCOR
(STOPPING —) HALT MANZIL
(STORAGE —) DEPOT HOARD
LODGE SPICERY STORAGE
STOWAGE DOCKYARD
(SWAMPY —) FLUSH SOUGH
(THIRD —) SHOW
(TIGHT —) JAM JAMB
(WATCH —) TOOTHILL
(WRETCHED —) DEN MISERY
(PL.) LOCI
PLACEBO TOADY VESPERS
PARASITE
PLACED FIXED BESTEAD
(— ON ITS SIDE) LAZY
PLACEHOLDER VARIABLE
PLACE-NAME TOPONYM
PLACENTA MAZA
PLACENTAL MAZIC
PLACID CALM COOL EVEN MEEK
MILD SOFT DOWNY QUIET SUANT
SUENT GENTLE SEDATE SERENE
SMOOTH PACIFIC TRANQUIL
THROBLESS
PLACKET FENT SPARE WOMAN
CLOSING PETTICOAT
PLAGIARISM CRIB PLAGIUM
PLAGIARIST TAKER COPYIST
PLAGIARIZE CRIB LIFT STEAL
PLAGUE DUN IMP VEX FRAB FRET
GNAW PEST TWIT BESET CURSE
DEATH DEUCE HARRY QUALM
TEASE TRAIK WEARY WORRY
WOUND BURDEN HAMPER HARASS
INFEST PESTER PESTIS SORROW
WANION DESTROY MURRAIN
PERPLEX SCOURGE TORMENT
TORTURE TROUBLE HANDICAP
OUTBREAK
PLAGUY VERY PESKY VEXING
MURRAIN PESTFUL INFERNAL
PLAICE FLUKE FLATFISH FLOUNDER
PLAID CALM FAKE MAUD PLOD
TARTAN BRACKEN BRECHAN
PLAIN DRY LOW BALD BARE CHOL
EASY EVEN FLAT OPEN PLAT RIFE
VEGA WALD WOLD BLAIR BLUNT
BROAD CAMPO CORAH FIELD FRANK
GREEN GROSS LAUND LEVEL LLANO
MOURN NAKED PAMPA PROSE
ROUND SEBKA SILLY SMALL TALAO
UNORN BEMOAN BEWAIL CHASTE
CUESTA GRAITH HOMELY HONEST
HUMBLE LENTEN MACHAR PUSZTA
RUSTIC SABANA SEVERE SIMPLE
SINGLE SMOOTH ARTLESS EVIDENT
GENUINE IDAVOLL INARTED LEGIBLE

OBVIOUS POPULAR TERRACE
APPARENT CAMPAIGN DISTINCT
EVERYDAY EXPLICIT FAMILIAR
HOMEMADE HOMESPUN ITHAVOLL
PALPABLE PIEDMONT SEMPLICE
STRAIGHT
(— AMONG TREES) LAUND
(— OF ARGENTINA) PAMPA
(— OF RUSSIA) STEPPE
(ALKALI —S) USAR
(ALLUVIAL —) APRON HAUGH
(ARCTIC —) TUNDRA
(DESOLATE —) CHOL
(LOW-LYING —) MACHAR MACHAIR
(MARSHY —) BLAIR
(SALINE —) SEBKA SEBKHA
(SALT —) SALADA
(SLOPING —) HOPE CUESTA
CONOPLAIN
(SMALL GRASSY —) CAMAS CAMASS
QUAMASH
(TREELESS —) BLED TUNDRA
SAVANNA SAVANNAH
(UNOCCUPIED —) DESERT
(PL.) VIZCACHA
PLAIN CHANT CF
PLAINCLOTHESMAN SPLIT
PLAINLY FAIR BARELY FAIRLY
FLATLY SIMPLY BROADLY FRANKLY
DIRECTLY
PLAINNESS PROSE INNOCENCE
PLAINSMAN LLANERO
PLAINSONG GROUND
PLAINT WAIL PLANT LAMENT
COMPLAINT
PLAINTEXT CLEAR
PLAINTIFF SUER ACTOR ORATOR
PURSUER QUERENT
PLAINTIVE SAD CROSS PINING
DOLENTE ELEGIAC FRETFUL
MOANFUL PEEVISH PETTISH
DOLOROSO MANGENDO PETULANT
WAILSOME SORROWFUL
PLAIT CUE PLY KNIT PAIR PLAT RUFF
TURN WALE WAND BRAID BREAD
CRIMP FETCH FITCH PEDAL PINCH
QUEUE QUILL QUIRK TRACE TRESS
WEAVE BOHDER DOUBLE GATHER
GOFFER PLEACH PLIGHT RUMPLE
TUSCAN WIMPLE WRITHE FROUNCE
PIGTAIL SCALLOM COMPLECT
(— FOR HAT) DUNSTABLE
(— OF STRAW) MILAN TRACE
(SERIES OF —S) KILTING
PLAITED PLISSE DEVIOUS PLICATE
PLAITING PLISSE LEGHORN
PLAN AIM ART LAY WAY CARD CAST
COUP DART FOOT GAME HANG IDEA
MIND MOOD PLAT PLOT REDE WENT
ALLOW BRIEF CHART DARTY DRAFT
DRIFT ETTLE FRAME HOBBY MODEL
REACH SHAPE TRACE ADVICE
AGENDA BEREDE BUDGET CIPHER
DECOCT DESIGN DEVISE ENGINE
FIGURE INTEND LAYOUT METHOD
MODULE ORDAIN PROJET SCHEMA
SCHEME SURVEY THEORY ARRANGE
CONCERT COUNSEL DRAWING
FORELAY NOSTRUM PATTERN

PROJECT PURPOSE COGITATE
CONSPIRE CONTRIVE ENGINEER
FORECAST FOREGAME LANDSKIP
MEDITATE PLATFORM PRACTICE
SCHEDULE SKELETON STRATEGY
(— AHEAD) FORECAST
(— OF FUTURE PROCEDURE)
PROGRAM
(— ON A FLOOR) EPURE
(— TOGETHER) CONCERT
(5-YEAR —) PIATILETKA
(GROUND —) TRACE GRUNDRISS
PLANARIAN PLATODE TRICLAD
FLATWORM
PLANE AXCI BEAD DADO FACE FLAT
HOLL MILL AXIAL CHUTE CROZE
FACET GLIDE HOULE HOWEL LEVEL
MESON SHOOT STICK TABLE WHISK
AEQUOR BEADER HOLLOW REEDER
ROUTER SMOKER SNIBEL COURIER
INSHAVE JOINTER SURFACE
WITCHET BULLNOSE DECLINER
LEEBOARD MERIDIAN RECLINER
SYCAMORE TRAVERSE
(— HANDLE) TOAT TOTE
(— OF CLEAVAGE) BACK
(— OF EARTH'S ORBIT) ECLIPTIC
(— OF ROCK) BED
(—S OF GUNNERY FIRE) SHEAF
(ENEMY —) BANDIT
(INCLINED —) RAMP SLIP
(MOLDING —) HOLL HOULE HOLLOW
(PERSPECTIVE —) TABLE
(RABBET —) PLOW RABAT PLOUGH
REBATE FILLETER
(SLOPING —) CUESTA
PLANER JOINTER SURFACER
PLANER TREE HORNBEAM
SYCAMORE
PLANET SUN BODY IRIS JOVE MARS
MOON STAR EARTH GLOBE HYLEG
PLUTO SHREW VENUS WORLD
SATURN SPHERE URANUS VULCAN
ALMUTEN ANARETA BENEFIC
FORTUNE JUPITER MERCURY
NEPTUNE PRIMARY CHASUBLE
LUMINARY RECEPTOR TERRELLA
WANDERER
(— IN A NATIVITY) ALMUTEN
(BENEVOLENT —) FORTUNE
(CONTROLLING —) LORD
(HYPOTHETICAL —) VULCAN
(MALEFICENT —) SHREW
(RULING —) DOMINATOR
(SMALL —) IRIS ASTEROID
TERRELLA
PLANETARIUM ORRERY
PLANETOID UNDINE ASTEROID
PLANE TREE CHINAR PLATAN
COTONIER PLANTAIN SYCAMORE
PLANET-STRICKEN SIDERATED
PLANISPHERE ASTROLABE
METEOROSCOPE
PLANK CLAM HOOD PATA PLAT RAIL
SOLE WAIR BOARD CLAMP PATTA
SHIDE SWALE THEAL DAGGER
FLITCH ROOFER CLAPPER CROSSER
DEPOSIT MADRIER RIBBAND

STEALER FOREPOLE GARBOARD STRINGER
(— 6 FT. X 1 FT.) WARE
(— AS PROTECTION) SHOLE
(— OVER BROOK) CLAM
(—S IN BRIDGE) CHESS
(—S LESS THAN 6 FT.) DEAL
(CURVED —) SNYING
(ROUGHHEWN —) SLAB
PLANK DRAG RUBBER
PLANK END STUB
PLANKING GORE RACK HATCH
SWALE CEILING LAGGING BERTHING
BRATTICE GARBOARD WATERWAY
PLANKSHEER WATERWAY
PLANKTON KRILL
PLANOMILLER SLABBER
PLANT AJI BED SET SOW ACHE ALGA
ARUM BURY CROP FAST HERB HIDE
MORE RAPE SALT SEED SLIP TREE
WORT ABACA AGAVE ARGEL CAROA
CHIVE CLOTE CLOVE EARLY FANCY
GRAFT HEATH INTER INULA JALAP
KEIKI PITCH SHRUB YERBA ACACIA
AKELEY ALASAS ANNUAL BEDDER
CACOON CALALU CARROT COKERY
COTTON ESCAPE FICOID FORCER
GALAXY GROWTH KARREE LENTIL
LIGGER MANUKA MEDICK MESCAL
PEPINO SETTLE SPRING ULLUCU
YARROW ABANDON ALKANET
ALYSSUM BREWERY CONCEAL
CUTTING DAGGERS ENCELIA
HAEMONY IMPLANT JIKUNGU
LETTUCE PICKERY RAMBONG
SAWMILL ABUTILON AGERATUM
AGRIMONY ANGLEPOD BIENNIAL
BLUEBELL CONSOUND DRAWLING
DYEHOUSE EMERGENT ENGINERY
FUMEROOT GASWORKS GROMWELL
HAWKWEED HONEWORT KNAPWEED
LARKSPUR
(— 2ND CROP) ETCH
(— BY SPADING) SPIT
(— DEEPLY) HEEL
(— FIRMLY) BRACE
(— GROWING IN WATER) BILDERS
HYDROPHYTE
(— IN ROWS) DRILL
(— OF MEADOWS) POOPHYTE
(— ROOTED IN GROUND) LIANA
LIANE
(— SUPPORTING PARASITES)
SUSCEPT
(— TREE) MOTCH
(— WITH NO DISTINCT MEMBERS)
THALLUS
(— WITH THREE PISTILS) TRIGYN
(— WITH THREE STAMENS)
TRIANDER
(AIR —) FLOPPERS
(ANCIENT —) CYCAD
(AQUATIC —) ALISMA NUPHAR
SUGAMO TAWKEE AMBULIA
AWLWORT FROGBIT DUCKWEED
(AROMATIC —) MINT NARD BASIL
CUMIN TANSY THYME AMOMUM
CUMMIN DITTANY ALBAHACA
LAVENDER SPIKENARD

(AUSTRALIAN —) LILAC STYLO
LIGNUM LANCEPOD
(BULBOUS —) GALTONIA
(CLIMBING —) VETCH LAWYER
ULLUCE CORALITA
(COMPOSITE —) SUCCORY
HAWKWEED
(CONSECRATED —) HAOMA
(CREATED —) BARAMIN
(CREEPING —) IPECAC KAREAO
KAREAU
(CROSSBRED —) HYBRID
(CRUSHING —) BREAKER
(DWARF —) CUMIN STUNT
(DYE —) WAD ANIL WOAD WOLD
WOALD MADDER
(E. INDIAN —) JATI
(ETIOLATED —) ALBINO
(FIBER —) ALOE FLAX HEMP PITA
CAJUN RAMIE SISAL
(FLOWERING —) HOP ROSE DAISY
HOLLY POPPY ORCHID VIOLET
HAWTHORN LARKSPUR POLYGALA
PRIMROSE SNOWDROP
(FORAGE —) RAPE ALFALFA
DAINCHA
(GERMINATING —) SPIRE
(GRAIN —) TEFF
(HEDGE —) ESPINO
(HEMP —) FIMBLE
(IMMATURE —) KEIKI
(LEAFLESS —) ULEX DODDER
RESTIAD TRIURID
(MALE —) MAS MACRANDER
(MARSH —) FERN JUNCUS CATTAIL
(MEDICINAL —) ALOE HERB ERICA
ARNICA CATNEP CATNIP IPECAC
SIMPLE ACONITE BONESET GENTIAN
LOBELIA CAMOMILE
(NON-FLOWERING —) FERN
(NURSERY —) SEEDLING
(PEPPER —) ARA
(PISTILLATE —) FEMALE
(POISONOUS —) COWBANE DEATHIN
(POTTED —) BONSAI
(POWER —) HYDRO
(PRICKLY —) BRIAR BRIER CACTUS
CARDON NETTLE TEASEL TEAZEL
PRICKFOOT
(PUNGENT —) PEPPER
(RAPIDLY-GROWING —) FILLER
(REEDY —) SPRIT
(RENDERING —) KNACKERY
(SENSITIVE —) MIMOSA
(SIBERIAN —) BADAN
(SPINOUS —) KANTIARA
(STAMINATE —) HUSBAND
(SUBMERGED —) ENALID
(SUCCULENT —) ALOE HERB
GASTERIA HAWORTHIA LOUSELEEK
(SWORD-LEAVED —) LEVERS
(THALLOPHYTIC —) LICHEN
(TRAILING —) ARBUTUS
(TUFTED —) DRYAS
(TWINING —) SMILAX CLIMBER
BINDWEED SCAMMONY
(UNIDENTIFIED —) HORDOCK
(WATER —) LIMU LOTUS AQUATILE
STARFRUIT

(WEEDY —) DOCK KNAWEL
(YOUNG —) SET SPRINGER
(PL.) FLORA
PLANTAGENET ANGEVIN
PLANTAIN COCK PALA ALISMA
FINGER PISANG WABRON BENTING
NETLEAF PANTANO RIBWORT
SITFAST BALISIER BUCKHORN
FIREWEED FLEAWORT ISPAGHUL
RATSBANE ROADWEED WAYBREAD
PLANTAIN EATER TOURACO
SPLITBEAK
PLANTAIN LILY FUNKIA
PLANTATION PEN HOLT WALK
FINCA GROVE BOSKET BOWERY
COLONY ESTATE SHAMBA SPRING
YERBAL CAFETAL FAZENDA
NOPALRY PINETUM THICKET
ARBUSTUM HACIENDA TRAPICHE
VINEYARD
(HEMP —) LATE
PLANTED LISTED
PLANTER SNAG COLON SOWER
FARMER SETTLER PLANTATOR
PLANTING GROVE SATION
PLANTING STICK DIBBLE
PLANT LOUSE APHID PSYLLID
PUCERON HOMOPTER
PLAQUE CHIP PINAX PLATE PLATEAU
SARCOID NAMEPLATE STOMACHER
PLASH LIP DASH BLASH PLOSH
PLOUT PLEACH PUDDLE SPLASH
SPATTER SPECKLE
PLASMA LATEX PLASM
PLASTER CAST DAUB HARL LEEP
LOCK TEER CLEAM GATCH PARGE
SLICK SMALM STAFF TOPIC TREAT
CHARGE CHUNAM GAGING MORTAR
PARGET SPARGE STOOTH STUCCO
BLISTER MALAGMA DIACULUM
DIAPALMA SINAPISM VESICANT
(— WITH COW DUNG) LEEP
(— BETWEEN LATHS) CAT
(— OF PARIS) GESSO GYPSUM
(2 COATS OF —) RENDERSET
(COARSE —) GROUT
(MEDICAL —) TOPIC TREAT CHARGE
SPARADRAP
(MUSTARD —) SINAPISM
PLASTERBOARD GYPSUM
PLASTERED DRUNK SOUSED
SWACKED
PLASTERER DAUBER DAUBSTER
PARGETER SPREADER
PLASTERING KEY SETWORK
ROUGHCAST
PLASTIC FOAM RICH SIRUP LABILE
PLIANT ACETATE CATALIN CRYSTAL
DUCTILE ORGANIC CREATIVE
FLEXIBLE LAMINATE MELAMINE
TECTONIC UNCTUOUS FORMATIVE
PLASTICIZER CAMPHOR
PLASTRON DICKEY CALIPEE
PLAT BED FLAT FOOD PLAN PLOT
SLAP BRAID LEVEL PLACE PLAIN
PLAIT BUFFET WATTLE ARRANGE
FLATTEN PLATEAU QUADRAT
PLATANIST SUSU

PLATANUS PLANE COTONIER
SYCAMORE
PLATBAND IMPOST LINTEL EPISTYLE
PLATE BAT CAP CUT DIP DOD EAR
FIN GIB WEB ANAL BACK BRIN CASE
CAST CURB DIAL DISK DROP FISH
GILL GONG GULA HOME HOOF LAME
LEAF MOLD NAIL ORAL RETE ROSE
SHOE SHUT SLAB SOLE STUD TACE
TRAY AMPYX ANODE BASAL BELLY
BLADE CHAIR CLAMP CLEAT CLOUT
FACIA FENCE FLOOR FLUKE FORCE
GLAND GUARD GULAR LAMEL
PATEN PYGAL SCALE SCUTE SHEET
SHOLE SLICE STAMP STAVE STRAP
TABLE TASSE TERNE TRAMP UNCUS
WATER ADORAL BAFFLE BRIDGE
BUCKLE CASTER CIRCLE CLICHE
COLLAR COPPER COSTAL CRUSTA
DAMPER DASHER EPIGNE FASCIA
FILLER FOLIUM FRIZEL GENIAL
GNOMON GORGET GUSSET LABIAL
LAMINA LOREAL MASCLE MATRIX
MENTAL MENTUM MOTHER PALLET
PATTEN PLATEN RADIAL SCREEN
SCUTUM SEPTUM SERVER SHEATH
SHROUD SPLINT STAPLE TARSUS
TEGMEN TURTLE TYMPAN VESSEL
BESAGNE BOLSTER BRACKET
BRACTEA BUCCULA BUCKLER
CHARGER CLYPEUS COASTER
CORNULE CORONET CRYSTAL
DOUBLER ETCHING FRIZZLE
FRONTAL GRAVURE HUMERAL
INKBLOT MORDANT MYOTOME
NEPTUNE PETALON PRIMARY
ROSTRAL ROUNDEL SPANGLE
STEALER STEELER TERGITE
TESSERA VENTRAL ASSIETTE
BEDPLATE BIQUARTZ BRACHIAL
CELLOCUT DIASCOPE DRAWBACK
ELECTRUM EPIGYNUM EPIPROCT
EPISTOME FIREBACK FLOUNDER
SKEWBACK STAPLING STRINGER
SUBPLATE SURPRINT
(— COVERING KEYHOLE) DROP
(— COVERING MIDDLE EAR)
TEGMEN
(— IN AIRPLANE WING) SPOILER
(— IN BATTERY) GRID
(— IN ORGAN PIPE) LANGUET
(— IN STEAM BOILER) SPUT
DASHER
(— OF BALEEN) BLADE
(— OF CTENOPHORE) COMB
(— OF GELATIN) BAT
(— OF GLASS) SLIDE
(— OF JAW) AURICLE
(— OF PRECIOUS METAL) BRACTEA
(— OF SOAP FRAME) SESS
(— OF SUNDIAL) GNOMON
(— ON LANCE SHAFT) VAMPLATE
(— ON SADDLE) SIDEBAR
(— ON SATCHEL STRAP) OLIVE
(— ON THROAT OF FISH) GULAR
(— ON WATERWHEEL) SHROUD
(—S OF CARDING MACHINE) ARCH
(—S OF GUN CARRIAGE) FLASK
(ARMOR —) SPLINT AILETTE

(COMMUNION —) PATEN
(DEEP —) MAZARINE
(DORSAL —) ALINOTUM
(EARTHEN —) MUFFIN
(FASHION —) SWELL
(FIREPLACE —) IRONBACK
(FLAT —) APRON
(GOLD — ON FOREHEAD) PATA
PATTA
(GROOVED TRAM —) GULLY GULLEY
(GUARD —) SHELL
(HINGED —) SHUT
(HOME —) DISH
(HOT —) GRILL GRILLE
(IRON —) STAVE LATTEN MARVER
LAPSTONE SKEWBACK MOLDBOARD
TURNPLATE TURNSHEET
(LARGE —) DOUBLER
(LOCK —) SELVEDGE
(NAME —) FACIA
(PERFORATED —) DOD GRID
PINNULE
(PITCHER'S —) SLAB MOUND
(RIMLESS —) COUPE
(SIEVE —) LATTICE
(THIN —) LAME LAMP LAMINA
LAMELLA
(THIN TIN —) TAIN TAGGERS
(WALL —) PAN RASEN
(WOODEN —) TRENCHER
PLATEAU PLAT FJELD KAROO KARST
TABLE CAUSSE HAMADA MESETA
NIVEAU PARAMO SABANA UPLAND
ANASAZI PLATFORM
PLATEHOLDER CASSETTE
PLATER VATMAN CLAIMER
COLLARMAN
PLATFORM TOP BANK BEMA DAIS
DECK DRIP DROP DUCK FLAT GHAT
KITE PACE PLAT STEP WING APRON
BENCH BLIND BLOCK CHAIN DUKAN
FLAKE FLOAT HEIAU SOLEA STAGE
STAND STOEP STOOL STOOP STULL
STUMP TOLDO ARBOUR AZOTEA
BRIDGE DESIGN GANTRY HURDLE
ISLAND MACHAN PAEPAE PALLET
PERRON PILLAR PODIUM PULPIT
RUNWAY SETTLE SLEDGE ALMEMAR
BALCONY BATTERY CATWALK
ESTRADE FORETOP GALLERY
LANDING LOGEION PADDOCK
PATTERN ROLLWAY ROSTRUM
SKIDWAY SOAPBOX TRIBUNE
FOOTPACE HUSTINGS SCAFFOLD
STALLAGE
(— FOR ACTORS) LOGEION
THEOLOGIUM
(— FOR ALTAR) PREDELLA
(— FOR DRYING FISH) FLAKE
(— FOR PUBLIC SPEAKING) BEMA
PODIUM TRIBUNE
(— FOR STORING FOOD) WHATA
(— IN CHURCH) SOLEA
(— IN SYNAGOGUE) ALMEMAR
(— IN TEMPLE) DUKAN
(— IN TREE) MACHAN
(— OF GALLOWS) DROP
(— ON RUNNERS) SLEDGE
(— ON TOP OF HOUSE) AZOTEA

(— ON WHEELS) SKID DOLLY FLOAT
(— TO SUPPORT MINERS) STULL
(GUN —) BARBET SPONSON
BARBETTE
(LEADSMAN'S —) CHAIN
(MINE —) STULL SOLLAR SOLLER
(MOHAMMEDAN STONE —)
MASTABA
(MOUNTED —) SKID
(NAUTICAL —) FORETOP MAINTOP
ROUNDTOP
(ORE —) BUDDLE
(RAILROAD —) DOCK DOCKEN
TRAINWAY
(RAISED —) DAIS PYAL STAND
STOEP STOOL STOOP LISSOM
PANTALAN
(ROCK —) STANCE
(SLEEPING —) KANG
(STAIRCASE —) HALFPACE
HATHPACE
(WOOD —) PLANCHER
PLATING ARMOR SKIRT
PLATINUM COSTLY PLATINA
PLATITUDE TRUISM BROMIDE
DULLNESS STALENESS TRITENESS
PLATONIST IDEIST
PLATOON SQUAD VOLLEY PELOTON
PLOTTON
PLATTER DISH DISK LANX ASHET
GRAIL PLATE RECORD CHARGER
TRENCHER
PLATY MOON MOONFISH
PLATYPUS DUCKBILL DUCKMOLE
MALLANGONG
PLAUDIT APPLAUD APPROVAL
ENCOMIUM
(PL.) PRAISE APPLAUSE
PLAUSIBILITY COLOR
PLAUSIBLE FAIR OILY SNOD GLOSSY
AFFABLE POPULAR CREDIBLE
PROBABLE PROVABLE SPECIOUS
SUITABLE
PLAY FUN JEU JIG RUN RUX TOY
AUTO BEAR COME DAFF DEAL DICE
DRAW FAIR GAME JEST LAKE MOVE
MUCK PLEE PUNT ROMP SPIN TUNE
WAKE CARRY CHARM DALLY DRAMA
ENACT FLIRT FROST HORSE SHOOT
SOTIE SOUND SPIEL SPORT STUCK
WREAK YEDDE ACTION COMEDY
COQUET DANDLE DIVIDE FILLER
FROLIC GAMBLE GAMBOL GAMING
GHOSTS MUSERY NUMBER PIDDLE
ROLLIX TRIFLE CONSORT CUTBACK
DISPORT EXECUTE EXPLOIT
GUIGNOL HISTORY HOLIDAY
MIRACLE PAGEANT PASSION
PRELUDE STAGERY VENTURE
BURLETTA MORALITY SKITTLES
(— A DOMINO) SET POSE
(— A PART) DO ACT ENTER
GAMMON GUIZARD
(— A PIPE) CHARM
(— ABOUT) SPANIEL
(— AGAINST) BUCK
(— AN INSTRUMENT) BOW BLOW
SWAY FINGER TWEEDLE
(— AT COURTSHIP) FLIRT

(— BAGPIPE) SKIRL DOODLE DOUDLE
(— BY STROKES) STRIKE
(— FANFARE) FLOURISH
(— FAST AND LOOSE) PALTER
(— FIRST CARD) LEAD
(— FLORIDLY) DIVIDE
(— FOR TIME) STALL
(— GOLF BALL) DRIVE
(— IMPOSTER) MUMP
(— IN MUD) MUDLARK
(— IN POOL) BURST
(— IN STREAKS) FORK
(— IN TRIGGER) CREEP
(— JAZZ) BLOW
(— LEGATO) SUSTAIN
(— LOOSELY) WAVE
(— LOUT) SWAB SLUBBER
(— MEAN TRICKS) SHAB
(— NERVOUSLY) FIDGET
(— OF COLORS) IRIS
(— OF FOAM) HOOD
(— OF LIGHT) GLORY
(— ON WORDS) PUN CLENCH CLINCH
(— THE BUFFOON) DROLL
(— THE BULLY) BLUSTER
(— THE FOOL) HOIT
(— THE HYPOCRITE) FACE
(— THE TOADY) SUPE
(— TRICKS) JAPE JINK
(— TRUANT) WAG JOUK MICHE MOOCH MOUCH PLUNK TRONE MOOTCH
(— UNSKILLFULLY) STRUM FOOZLE
(— WITH) DANDLE
(AMOROUS —) GAME
(BOISTEROUS —) ROMP
(BRIDGE —) COUP ECHO SIGNAL SQUEEZE
(END —) SHAKE
(FARCICAL —) SOTIE
(FOOTBALL —) DOWN KEEP SAFETY CUTBACK SPINNER
(IN —) ALIVE
(MASKED —) GUISE
(MIRACLE —) AUTO GUARY MIRACLE
(RAPID CHESS —) SKITTLES
(USED IN —) LUSORY
(PL.) THEATER VANGELI
PLAYA BEACH SEBKA SALINA SEBKHA
PLAY-BY-PLAY DETAILED
PLAYER IT CAP END BACK DUCK SIDE ACTOR BLACK COLOR GUARD BANKER BUSKER FEEDER STAGER STROLL TENTER ALTOIST FIELDER FORWARD GAMBLER STRIKER TRIFLER TURQUET BUDGETER GAMESTER HORNSMAN STROLLER
(— IN CHESS) BLACK WHITE
(— IN CHOUETTE) CAPTAIN
(— OF JAZZ) CAT
(— WHO CUTS CARDS) PONE
(— WHO IS IT) HE
(— WHO SCORES ZERO) DUCK
(— WITH LOWEST SCORE) BOOBY
(BACKGAMMON —) TABLER

(BASEBALL —) SHORT SACKER CATCHER FIELDER LEADOFF PITCHER BACKSTOP
(BASKETBALL —) CAGEMAN HOOPMAN HOOPSTER
(BOWLING —) LEAD
(CARD —) EAST HAND PONE WEST BLIND DUMMY NORTH SOUTH JUNIOR SENIOR BRAGGER DECLARER
(CRICKET —) LEG BOWLER INNING
(CROQUET —) MALLET
(DICE —) SHOOTER
(FLUTE —) AULETE
(FOOTBALL —) END GUARD SLANT BUCKER CENTER TACKLE BLOCKER FLANKER GRIDDER SNAPPER FULLBACK HALFBACK SCATBACK
(LACROSSE —) HOME COVER ATTACK STICKMAN
(LEAPFROG —) BACK
(POKER —) AGE
(RUGBY —) SCRUM HOOKER
(SOCCER —) CAP INNER BOOTER
(STUPID —) HAM
(TENNIS —) SMASHER
(UNSKILLFUL —) DUB
(VOLLEYBALL —) SPIKER
(WEAK —) RABBIT
PLAYFUL ELFIN MERRY FRISKY GAMBOL JOCOSE LUSORY TOYISH WANTON COLTISH GIOCOSO JIGGISH JOCULAR TOYSOME GAMESOME HUMOROUS LARKSOME SPORTFUL SPORTIVE KITTENISH
PLAYFULNESS FUN BANTER GAMMICK GAMMOCK
PLAYGROUND OVAL CLOSE PLAYSTOW PLAYSTEAD
PLAYHOUSE HOUSE MOVIE CINEMA THEATER
PLAYING FROLIC LAKING
(— CARD) ACE JACK KING TREY DEUCE QUEEN TAROT
(— CARDS) DECK
(— LIGHTLY) LAMBENT
PLAYTHING DIE TOY HOOP KNACK PLAIK SPORT BAUBLE LAKING SUCKER TRIFLE PLAYOCK
PLAYWRIGHT AUTHOR DRAMATIST PLAYMAKER
PLAZA PLEIN SQUARE ZOCALO
(— DE TOROS) BULLRING
PLEA BAR BID PLY MOOT NOLO SUIT ALIBI CLAIM PLEAD ABATER APPEAL EXCUSE REFUGE APOLOGY CONTEND DEFENCE LAWSUIT PRETEXT QUARREL DILATORY ENTREATY PRETENSE
PLEACH PLAIT PLASH INTERLACE
PLEAD BEG SUE MOOT PLEA PRAY PRIG SHOW URGE COUNT ORATE ALLEGE APPEAL ASSERT PLAYTE PURSUE ENTREAT IMPLORE SOLICIT WRANGLE ADVOCATE LITIGATE
(— FOR) SOLICIT PETITION
PLEADER ACTOR VAKIL PATRON SUITOR VAKEEL COUNTOR ADVOCATE

PLEADING PLEA PAROL ANSWER PAROLE ADVOCACY COGNOVIT DEMURRER INTENDIT MEMORIAL
PLEASANT FUN GAY BEEN BIEN BRAW FAIR FINE GLAD GOOD HEND JOLI NEAT TRIM WEME BIGLY BONNY CANNY COUTH CUSHY DOUCE DRUNK DUCKY GREEN HAPPY HENDE HODDY JOLLY LEPID LISTY MERRY NUTTY QUEME SMIRK SUAVE SWEET TIPSY WALLY WETHE COMELY DAINTY DULCET GENIAL KINDLY SAVORY SMOOTH AFFABLE ELEGANT FARRAND JANNOCK LEESOME WINSOME DELICATE GLORIOUS GRATEFUL HEAVENLY LIEFSOME LIKESOME LOVESOME THANKFUL TOWARDLY
PLEASANTLY FAIR WINLY FAIRLY AFFABLY SWEETLY GENIALLY LIKINGLY
PLEASANTNESS GAIETY NAAMAN AMENITY SUAVITY JOCUNDITY
PLEASANTRY WIT JEST JOKE SPORT BANTER JESTING JOLLITY WAGGERY
PLEASE PAY GAME LIKE LIST LUST SUIT WANT WISH AGREE AMUSE BITTE CHARM ELATE FANCY HUMOR QUEME SAVOR TASTE ARRIDE KITTLE OBLIGE REGALE SOOTHE TICKLE CONTENT DELIGHT GLADDEN GRATIFY PLACATE REJOICE SATISFY APPLEASE
(— FORWARD) FS
PLEASED FAIN FOND GLAD APAID HAPPY PROUD BUCKED CONTENT GLADSOME
(BE —) GAME
PLEASING AMEN GLAD GOOD LIEF NICE SOFT AMENE DICTY SOOTH SWEET CLEVER DREAMY FACILE FLASHY GAINLY LIKING LUSTLY AMIABLE BLESSED CORKING DARLING LIKEFUL TUNABLE WELCOME CHARMING DELICATE FAVOROUS FETCHING GRACEFUL GRACIOUS GRATEFUL HEAVENLY INVITING LIKESOME PLACABLE PLAUSIVE SPECIOUS
(— TO EAR) HARMONIC
(— TO EYE) EESOME
(— TO HEAR) FAIR
(VERY —) SNAZZY
PLEASURABLE GOOD JOLLY ANIMAL MIRTHFUL
PLEASURE JO EST FUN JOY BANG BOOT EASE ESTE GREE KAMA LIST LUST PLAY WILL KICKS MIRTH SAVOR SOOTH TASTE DAINTY DEDUIT GAIETY GAYETY LIKING LUXURY NICETY VOLUPT COMFORT DELIGHT GRATIFY JOLLITY JOYANCE VOLUPTY DELICACY FRUITION GLADNESS HILARITY VOLUPTAS
(SELFISH —) LECHERY
(STOLEN —) STOUTH STOWTH
(PL.) DELICIAE
PLEASURE SEEKER FRANION

PLEAT SET FOLD POKE FLUTE FRILL PINCH PLAIT PRANK GUSSET SUNRAY

PLEATED SUNBURST

PLEBE PLEBS FRESHMAN

PLEBEIAN LOW BASE PLEB SNOB COMMON HOMELY VULGAR IGNOBLE LOWBORN POPULAR BASEBORN EVERYDAY HOMESPUN INFERIOR MECHANIC ORDINARY RUPTUARY

PLEBISCITE VOTE DECREE

PLECTRUM PICK SPUR QUILL UVULA MALLEUS POINTEL PLECTRON
(— **OF HARP**) FESCUE

PLEDGE LAY VAS VOW WAD WED BAND CLAP EARL GAGE HAND HEST HOCK PASS PAWN WAGE WOID WORD FAITH SIKER SPOUT STAKE SWEAR SWEAT TOKEN TROTH TRUTH WAGER ARREST BORROW COMMIT ENGAGE IMPAWN IMPONE LUMBER PIGNUS PLEVIN PLIGHT SICCAR SICKER VADIUM WADSET BARGAIN BETROTH CAUTION EARNEST HOSTAGE PROMISE BOTTOMRY MORTGAGE SECURITY SPONSION VADIMONY
(— **IN DRINKING**) PROPINE

PLEDGED HIGHT SWORN ASSURED ENGAGED PIGNORATE
(— **TO MARRY**) SURE

PLEDGET DOSSIL

PLEIADES MAIA MEROPE ALCYONE CELAENO ELECTRA STEROPE TAYGETA

PLEIN-AIRIST LUMINIST

PLEISTHENES (**FATHER OF** —) ATREUS
(**MOTHER OF** —) AEROPE
(**SON OF** —) MENELAUS AGAMEMNON

PLENARY FULL ENTIRE PLENAL PERFECT ABSOLUTE COMPLETE

PLENITUDE PLENITY PLEROMA FULLNESS PLETHORA ABUNDANCE

PLENTEOUS RICH COPIOUS FERTILE AFFLUENT FRUITFUL GENEROUS ABOUNDING EXUBERANT

PLENTIFUL OLD FULL RANK RICH RIFE AMPLE HEFTY LARGE ROUTH SONSY STORE ENOUGH GALORE LAVISH SONSIE COPIOUS FERTILE LIBERAL OPULENT PROFUSE UBEROUS ABUNDANT FRUITFUL NUMEROUS EXUBERANT

PLENTIFULLY RIFE FREELY GALORE APLENTY

PLENTY WON BAIT COPY MANY RAFF SONS AMPLE CHEAP COPIA FOUTH PRICE ROUTH SONSE TEEMS FOISON SCOUTH UBERTY LASHINGS
(**GREAT** —) LASHINGS

PLEON TELSON ABDOMEN

PLEONASM ITERATION MACROLOGY TAUTOLOGY

PLETHORA EXCESS PLURISY FULLNESS PLEURISY POLYEMIA PROFUSION REPLETION

PLETHORIC TUMID TURGID SWOLLEN INFLATED

PLEURISY EMPYEMA

PLEURON SCAPULA

PLEXUS RETE GLOMUS NETWORK PROPLEX GENIPLEX

PLIABLE WAXY WEAK LITHY WAXEN DOCILE LIMBER PLIANT SEMMIT SUPPLE BOWABLE FICTILE FINGENT FLEXILE PLASTIC WINDING CUSHIONY FLEXIBLE COMPLIANT

PLIANCY FLEXURE FACILITY

PLIANT APT FLIP SWAK BUXOM LITHE SWACK YOUNG DOCILE LIMBER SUPPLE DUCTILE FLEXILE PLIABLE SLIPPER WILLOWY APPLIANT FLEXIBLE SUITABLE WORKABLE

PLICA FOLD TRICHOMA

PLICATE FOLD PLEAT FOLDED FANLIKE PLAITED

PLIERS BENDER FLEXOR GRATER FLECTOR PINCERS

PLIGHT PLY FOLD ARRAY BRAID DRESS PLAIT POINT STATE WOVEN ATTIRE ENGAGE PICKLE PLEDGE PLISKY TAKING BETROTH MISCHIEF

PLIGHTED ASSURATE

PLIM PLUM STOUT SWELL INFLATE PLIABLE

PLINTH ORLE ORLO BLOCK ABACUS PATAND QUADRA SUBBASE FOOTSTALL SCAMILLUS

PLOD JOG GRUB PLOT SLOG STOG TORE TROG VAMP POACH TRAMP TRASH DRUDGE SLOUCH TRUDGE PLUNTHER
(— **ALONG**) PEG TORE
(— **THROUGH MUD**) SLOUGH

PLODDER GRUB DIGGER SLOGGER

PLOIARIA EMESA

PLOP FLUMP PLUMP HEAVILY

PLOT BREW CAST PACK PLAN PLAT CABAL DRIFT FRAUD GLEBE GRAPH GREEN HATCH MODEL PLECK SCALD STORY STUDY WATCH ACTION BRIGUE CLIQUE DESIGN DEVISE GARDEN MALIGN MYTHOS SCHEME SHAMBA TAMPER AGITATE COLLUDE COMPACT COMPASS CONJECT CONNIVE CONTOUR DRAUGHT FEEDLOT LAZYBED MACHINE PRETEND QUADRAT QUARTER SWIDDEN ARGUMENT COGITATE CONSPIRE CONTRIVE INTRIGUE PRACTICE PROTRACT SEMINARY
(— **OF 1-2 ACRE**) ERF
(— **OF GRASS**) SONK
(— **OF LAND**) ERF LOT PLAT SHOT FORTY MILPA PATCH PLECK SPLAT COMMON SCHERM SHAMBA HAGGARD LAZYBED SEVERAL
(**GARDEN** —) BED ERF QUINTA QUARTER
(**UNPRODUCTIVE** —) HIRST

PLOTTER PACKER HATCHER JACOBIN SCHEMER DESIGNER ENGINEER

PLOUK KNOB PIMPLE

PLOVER DROME KOLEA OXEYE PILOT SANDY STILT KILDEE QUAILY TURNIX COLLIER COURSER DOTTREL LAPWING MAYCOCK OWLHEAD PAPABOT WRYBILL BULLHEAD DULWILLY HILLBIRD KILLDEER RINGNECK SPURWING SQUEALER TOADHEAD WHISTLER WIREBIRD

PLOW EAR ERE BOUT DISK FOIL HINT MOLE PLOD RIVE ROVE SLUG STIR SULK SULL TILL BREAK FLUNK SPLIT SULKY THROW ARAIRE BUSTER DIGGER FALLOW FURROW GOPHER JUMPER LISTER PLOUGH RAFTER ROOTER RUTTER SULLOW BACKSET BREAKER HUSBAND SCOOTER SULCATE TWISTER FIREPLOW FURROWER GANGPLOW SNOWPLOW TURNPLOW
(— **CROSSWISE**) THORTER
(— **HANDLE**) STILT
(— **LIGHTLY**) SKIM RIFFLE
(— **PART**) PINHEAD
(**PL.**) OUTSIGHT

PLOWBOY YOKEL

PLOWING ARDER EARTH ARDURE ARATION CARUAGE STIRRING

PLOWLAND CARUE CARVE TILTH CARUCATE TEAMLAND

PLOWMAN PLOWER TILLER ACREMAN

PLOWSHARE LAY SLIP SOCK LAVER REEST SHARE JUMPER
(— **BONE**) VOMER PYGOSTYLE

PLOY BENT BOWED SPORT RAMBLE TACTIC PURSUIT ACTIVITY ESCAPADE

PLUCK GO PUG ROB TUG BOUT CROP CULL DRAG GAME GRAB PELT PICK PILL POOK PULL RACE RASE RASH SAND TUCK ARBER ARBOR BREAK DRAFT HANGE NERVE PILCH PLOAT PLUME RANCH SMITE SPUNK STEAL STRIP AVULSE DECERP EVULSE FLEECE GATHER PIGEON PLITCH PLOUGH QUARRY SNATCH SPIRIT TWINGE TWITCH COURAGE DEPLUME PLUNDER BOLDNESS DECISION DEMOLISH GAMENESS
(— **AS A STRING**) TIRL PINCH
(— **FEATHERS**) STUB
(— **LEAVES**) BLADE
(— **OF SHEEP OR CALF**) RACE GATHER
(— **UP COURAGE**) CHEER
(— **WOOL BY HAND**) ROO

PLUCKED PLUMED PIZZICATO

PLUCKY GAMY SANDY GRITTY SPUNKY FIGHTING

PLUG BUG FID PEG PIN TAP TOP WAD BLOW BONE BOTT BUNG FILL JADE ROOT SHOT SLOG STOP SWAT SWOT BOOST DOWEL DUMMY PILOT PUNCH SHACK SKATE SPILE STUFF SWEAT BOXING BULLET COMEDO DOSSIL DOTTLE FIDDLE SPIGOT BOUCHON BUSHING CHAMBER CHUGGER FERRULE STOPPER

STOPPLE DRIVECAP FUSEPLUG
PELELITH STOPCOCK
(— FOR CANNON) TAMPION
(— IN GRENADE) BOUCHON
(— IN ORGAN PIPE) STOPPLE
TAMPION
(— OF CLAY) BOTT
(— OF OAKUM) FID
(— OF VOLCANO) CORE
(— UP) CLAM STOP ESTOP
RAMFORCE
(FISHING —) BUG
(NOSE —) TEMBETA TEMBETARA
(WASTE —) WASHER
(WATER —) HYDRANT
PLUG-IN JACK
PLUG-UGLY THUG ROWDY TOUGH
RUFFIAN ROUGHNECK
PLUM GAGE JOBO RISE ISLAY JAMAN
PRUNE SWELL BEAUTY CHENEY
DAMSEL DAMSON KELSEY SAPOTE
APRICOT BULLACE BURBANK
FORTUNE ORLEANS PRUNELLO
ROSACEAN ROSEWORT VICTORIA
WINDFALL
(COCO —) ICACO
(JAVA —) DUHAT JAMBUL JAMBOOL
JAMBOLAN
(WILD —) SKEG SLOE ISLAY
PLUMAGE ROBE FLUFF HACKLE
SHROUD FEATHER FLOCCUS
JUVENAL PENNAGE FEATHERS
PARADISE PTILOSIS
PLUMB BUNG BOTTOM SINKER
EXACTLY PLUMMET UTTERLY
ABSOLUTE COMPLETE DIRECTLY
ENTIRELY VERTICAL
PLUMBAGO LUSTER LUSTRE
GRAPHITE LEADWORT
PLUMB BOB PLUMMET
PLUMB LINE MERKHET
PLUM CURCULIO TURK WEEVIL
PLUME PEN TIP TUFT CREST EGRET
PRIDE PRUNE DEPRIVE DESPOIL
FEATHER PANACHE AIGRETTE
(— ON HELMET) CREST PANACHE
(— ON HORSE) PLUMADE
(— ON TURBAN) CULGEE
(EGRET —) OSPREY
(MILITARY —) PANACHE
PLUME NUTMEG SASSAFRAS
PLUMMET LEAD FLOAT PLUMB
WEIGHT
PLUMMING BRONZING
PLUMP FAT BOLD FAIR FLOP FULL
PLOP SLAP SOSS TIDY BLUNT
BONNY CLUMP FLUMP FUBBY
FUBSY GROUP JOLLY PLUNK SAPPY
SLEEK SMACK SQUAB STOUT THICK
BONNIE CHUBBY CRUMBY CRUMMY
DIRECT FATTEN FLATLY FLESHY
FODGEL GAWSIE PLUNGE PUBBLE
ROTUND BLUNTLY BUNTING
CLUSTER DISTEND FULSOME
RIBLESS THRODDY FLESHFUL
(— AND ROSY) BUXOM
(— AND ROUND) CHUBBY
PLUM POCKET FOOL
PLUMULE FEATHER GEMMULA
GEMMULE GEOBLAST ACROSPIRE

PLUNDER GUT ROB BOOT FANG
JUNK LOOT PILL POLL PREY RAPE
REIF RIPE RUMP SACK SWAG
BOOTY CHEAT GAINS HARRY PLUCK
PREDE RAVEN RENNE RIFLE SCOFF
SHAVE SPOIL STRIP BEZZLE
BOODLE CREACH DACOIT FLEECE
FORAGE HARROW MARAUD PANYAR
PROFIT RAPINE RAVAGE DESPOIL
ESCHEAT FREIGHT PILFERY PILLAGE
SACKAGE SPULZIE BOOTHALE
FREEBOOT
PLUNDERER THIEF BANDIT BUMMER
POLLER RAPTOR ROBBER VANDAL
ROUTIER SPOILER MARAUDER
RAPPAREE
PLUNDERING PREY SACK MARAUD
RAPINE ESCHEAT PURCHASE
SPECHERY SPOILFUL SPOILING
PREDATORY
PLUNGE BET DIG DIP CAVE DIVE
DOOK DUCK DUMP JUMP PURL
PUSH RAKE RISK SINK SOSS BURST
DOUSE FLING PITCH PLUMP SOUSE
SWOOP FOOTER GAMBLE HEADER
LAUNCH SPLASH THRUST WALLOP
BRAINGE IMMERSE PLOUNCE
SUBMERGE
(— INTO WATER) ENEW
(— INTO) CLAP ENGULF IMMERGE
PLUNGER RAM SWAB FORCE
DUCKER POMMEL BLUNGER
STRIKER
PLUNGING FLING
PLUNK DIVE PLONK PLUCK PLUMP
DOLLAR SUPPORT SUDDENLY
PLUNTHER PLOD FLOUNDER
PLURALIST TOTQUOT
PLURALITY MAJORITY MORENESS
TRIALITY
PLUS GAIN WITH EXTRA SURPLUS
ADDITION INCREASE POSITIVE
PLUSH EASY BEAVER VELOUR
SUPERIOR
PLUSHY SWANK SWANKY
PLUTEUS WAGON PARAPET
PLUTO DIS HADES ORCUS
(BROTHER OF —) JUPITER NEPTUNE
(FATHER OF —) SATURN
(WIFE OF —) PROSERPINE
PLUTOCRAT NABOB RICHARD
PLUTONIC HYPOGENE INTRUSIVE
VULCANIAN
PLUTUS (ASSOCIATE OF —) TYCHE
EIRENE
(FATHER OF —) IASION
(MOTHER OF —) DEMETER
PLY RUN BEAT BEND BIAS CORD
CORE DRAM FOLD MOLD SAIL URGE
ADAPT APPLY EXERT LAYER STEER
TWIST WIELD YIELD COMPLY
DOUBLE HANDLE TRAVEL EXERCISE
(— WITH DRINK) BIRL ROSIN
(— WITH DRUGS) HOCUS
(OF ONE —) SINGLE
PNEUMA NEUM SOUL NEUME
BREATH SPIRIT
PNEUMATIC HAMMER GUN
PNEUMATOCYST FLOAT

PNEUMONIA PULMONITIS
POACH PUG ROB COOK DROP POKE
PUSH SINK BLACK DRIVE FORCE
POTCH STEAL BLEACH PLUNGE
INTRUDE
POACHED EGGS MOONSHINE
POACHER BLACK POGGE SPOACH
LURCHER STALKER WIDGEON
BALDPATE BULLHEAD
(SALMON —) REBECCA REBEKAH
(PL.) BLACKS
POALES GLUMALES
POCHARD DUCK SMEE DIVER POKER
SCAUP DUNAIR DUNKER DUNBIRD
REDHEAD WHINGER GOLDHEAD
WHINYARD
POCHETTE KIT VIOLIN HANDBAG
POCKET BOX CLY FOB PIT CLAY
KICK POKE PRAT BASIN BURSE
MEANS POUCH PURSE STEAL
ACCEPT BECKET CASING CANTINA
PLACKET SWALLOW TROUSER
ENVELOPE ISOLATED MONETARY
PROFONDE SUPPRESS CONDENSED
MINIATURE
(— A WRONG) PURSE
(BILLIARD —) POT HOLE HAZARD
(MAGICIAN'S —) PROFONDE
(NOODLE —S) KREPLACH
(ORE —) CHURN BONANZA
(SMALL —) FOB
(TROUSER —) FOB PRAT BECKET
(WATER —) TINAJA ALBERCA
(PL.) KREPLACH
POCKETBOOK BAG KICK SKIN
PURSE INCOME READER WALLET
HANDBAG LEATHER BILLFOLD
NOTECASE
POCKET GOPHER TUZA QUACHIL
POCKETING COUP
POCKETKNIFE PIGSTICKER
POCKMARK PITHOLE
POD BAG COD GAM KID POP SAC
BALL BEAN BOLL HUSK POKE SWAD
BURSE CAROB FLOCK POUCH
QUASH SHAUP SHELL SHUCK SNAIL
WHAUP LEGUME PESCOD SCHOOL
HARICOT PEASCOD PEASECOD
PODOCARP POTBELLY SEEDCASE
TAMARIND
(— FORMING) KID
(— OF LEGUME) KID
(— OF MESQUITE) HONEYPOD
(EXPLOSIVE —) SANDBOX
(SUBTERRANEAN —) EARTHNUT
(UNRIPE —) SQUASH
(PL.) SUNT GARAD BABLAH GARRAT
GONAKIE ALGAROBA
PODIUM DAIS FOOT WALL LECTERN
PODOCARP YACCA
PODWARE PODDER
POEM GEM LAI LAY ODE DUAN EPIC
JOSE MELE POSY RUNE SONG
DIRGE DITTY HAIKU IWEIN METER
STAFF VERSE AMHRAN AUBADE
BALLAD CACCIA CARMEN CYCLIC
DIXAIN EPOPEE EROTIC ESTRIF
HEROID MELODY MONODY PIYYUT
SESTET SONNET TENSON TERCET

BUCOLIC CANTARE CANTATA
CANZONE DESCORT DIZAINE
ECLOGUE ELEGIAC FLITING
GEORGIC SOTADIC TRIOLET VIRELAI
VIRELAY VOLUSPA ACROSTIC
AMOEBEUM BRINDISI CANTICLE
DINGDONG DOGGEREL INVICTUS
LIMERICK MADRIGAL TELESTIC
THEOGONY TRISTICH TROCHAIC
VERSICLE
(— ABOUT DEBATE) ESTRIF
(— ABOUT SHEPHERDS) ECLOGUE
(— GREETING DAWN) AUBADE
(— OF 10 LINES) DIZAINE
(— OF 14 LINES) SONNET
(— OF LAMENTATION) ELEGY
(AMATORY —) EROTIC SONNET
(EPIC —) EPOS EPOPEE LUSIAD
THEBAID
(HOMELY —) DIT
(IRISH —) AMHRAN
(JAPANESE —) HAIKU
(LITURGICAL —) VIDDUI VIDDUY
SELIHOTH
(LOVE —) AMORETTO
(LYRIC —) LAI LAY ODE ALBA
EPODE GHAZEL RONDEL CANZONA
PARTIMEN
(PART OF —) PASSUS
(PASTORAL —) IDYL IDYLL BUCOLIC
(PERSIAN —) GHAZAL
(RELIGIOUS —) HYMN
(RURAL —) GEORGIC
(SACRED —) PSALM YIGDAL
(SATIRICAL —) IAMBIC KASIDA
(SHORT —) DIT DITTY EPILOG
SONNET EPIGRAM EPILOGUE
EPYLLION
(TONE —) BALLADE
(WELSH —) CYWYDD
(PL.) AZAHROT MAKINGS
POET OG RSI BARD FILE FILI FIRI
LARK MUSE SCOP SWAN ARION
LAKER LINOS LINUS LYRIC MAKAR
MAKER ODIST RISHI SAYER SCALD
SKALD FINDER GNOMIC IBYCUS
LAKIST LYRIST SHAPER SINGER
DICHTER ELEGIAC EPICIST IDYLIST
IMAGIST MUSAEUS ORPHEUS
PROPHET FERAMORZ GEORGIAN
LAUREATE LUTANIST MINSTREL
SONGSTER TROUVERE
(IRISH —) FILI
(MEDIOCRE —) RIMER RHYMER
(MINOR —) BARDIE
POETASTER BARDET BAVIAN BAVIUS
POETITO BARDLING VERSEMAN
POETIC ODIC LYRIC STILTED
PEGASEAN POEMATIC
POETRY SONG BLANK MELIC POEMS
VERSE EPOPEE POESIS SONIOU
DOGGREL KALEVALA
(FINNISH —) RUNES
(GOD OF —) BRAGI
(MUSE OF —) ERATO THALIA
EUTERPE CALLIOPE
POGROM RIOT PILLAGE MASSACRE
POGY POGIE MENHADEN
POIGNANT APT HOME KEEN ACUTE

SHARP SMART BITING BITTER
MOVING SEVERE URGENT CUTTING
POINTED PUNGENT SATIRIC INCISIVE
PIERCING PRESSING STINGING
STRIKING TOUCHING AMAREVOLE
POINCIANA DELONIX FLAMBEAU
GULMOHAR FLAMBOYER
POINSETTIA BANNER FIREFLOWER
POINT AIM DOT JOT NAK NEB NIB
NUB PEG PIN RES WAY APEX BACK
BOKE CHAT CUSP FORK GAFF GAME
GOOD HEAD HOLD ITEM KNOT LACE
LOOK NAIL PEAK PICK PILE PINT
SPOT STOP WHET BEARD CHALK
DIGIT FOCUS INDEX LEVEL MUCRO
PITCH PRICK PUNCH PUNCT PUNTA
PUNTO REFER STAND TEACH THING
TOOTH ALLUDE BROACH CRAYON
CUSPIS CUTOFF DEGREE DIRECT
FLECHE JUGALE MATTER NOSING
PERIOD THESIS TITTLE VERTEX
ZYGION APICULA ARTICLE BENEFIT
CRUNODE ESSENCE GATEWAY
PUSHPIN SHARPEN TANJONG
TRAGION ANNOUNCE PUNCTULE
STRIPPER
(— AT ISSUE) BEEF CRUX
(— AT WHICH LEAF SPRINGS) AXIL
(— BEHIND EAR) ASTERION
(— FOR PHONOGRAPH RECORD)
STYLE
(— IN CAPSTAN) STRIPPER
(— IN CONSONANT) DAGHESH
(— IN DEBATE) ISSUE
(— IN ORBIT OF PLANET) AUGE
APSIS APOGEE SYZYGY APOJOVE
PERIGEE APASTRON APHELION
(— IN QUESTION) ISSUE
(— IN SEVEN-UP) GIFT
(— IN SOME GAMES) PUNT
(— NEAREST EARTH) PERIGEE
(— OF A BORDER) VANDYKE
(— OF ANCHOR) BILL
(— OF ANTLER) PRONG
(— OF ANVIL) HORN
(— OF CELESTIAL SPHERE)
ANTAPEX
(— OF CHIN) BUTTON
(— OF CONTACT) EPHAPSE
(— OF CRESCENT MOON) CUSP
(— OF DECLINE) EBB
(— OF DIVERGENCE) AXIL
(— OF ECLIPTIC) LAGNA SOLSTICE
(— OF EPIGRAM) STING
(— OF HONOR) PUNDONOR
(— OF INTEREST) CLOU
(— OF INTERSECTION) FOOT
STAURION
(— OF JAVELIN) SAGAIE
(— OF JUNCTION) MEET BREGMA
LAMBDA
(— OF LABEL) LAMBEAU
(— OF LAND) ODD CAPE SPIT
MORRO HEADLAND
(— OF LEAF) MUCRO
(— OF LIFE) HYLEG
(— OF LIGHT) GLINT SPANGLE
(— OF LIGHTNING ROD) AIGRETTE
(— OF LIPS) CHEILION

(— OF MANGO) NAK
(— OF ONSET) BRINK
(— OF ORIGIN) HIVE SOURCE
FOUNTAIN
(— OF PEN) NEB NIB
(— OF PETAL) LACINULA
(— OF REFERENCE) STYLION
(— OF STAG'S HORN) START
(— OF STORY) KNOT
(— OF STYLUS) CUTTER
(— OF SUPPORT) BEARING
(— OF TEMPERATURE) SOLIDUS
(— OF TIME) DATE INSTANT
JUNCTURE
(— OF TOOTH) CUSP
(— OF UMBRELLA) FERRULE
(— OF VIEW) EYE ANGLE FRONT
SLANT COLORS CORNER GROUND
RESPECT FUTURISM
(— OF VIOLIN BOW) HEAD
(— OF WEAPON) BARB
(— ON AUGER OR BIT) SPUR
(— ON BACKGAMMON BOARD)
FLECHE
(— ON CURVE) TACNODE
(— ON JAW) GONION
(— ON STAG'S HORN) BROACH
(— ON SUNDIAL) NODE
(— OUT) SHOW DIGIT INFER ASSIGN
DIRECT ENSIGN FINGER MUSTER
NOTIFY REMARK PRESAGE INDICATE
(ASTROLOGICAL —) INGRESS
(BARBED —) FORK
(BLUNT —) MORNETTE
(CARBON —) CRAYON
(CARDINAL —) EAST WEST HINGE
NORTH SOUTH
(CARDINAL —S) CARDINES
(CHRONOLOGICAL —) ERA EPOCH
(COMPASS —) E N S W NE NW SE
SW ENE ESE NNE NNW SSE SSW
WNW WSW AIRT AIRTH RHUMB
COURSE
(CRITICAL —) JUMP
(CROWNING —) CAPSHEAF
CAPSTONE
(CRUCIAL —) CRUX
(CULMINATING —) HEAD COMBLE
(DOUBLE — OF CURVE) ACNODE
CRUNODE
(ESSENTIAL —) MAIN
(EXACT —) TEE
(EXCESS —S) LAP
(EXCLAMATION —) BANG
SCREAMER
(EXTREME —) END
(FARTHEST —) APOGEE SOLSTICE
(FINAL —) UPCOME
(FIXED —) ABUTMENT
(GLAZIER'S —) SPRIG
(HALFWAY — IN CRIBBAGE)
CORNER
(HIGHEST —) TIP ACME APEX AUGE
NOON PEAK CREST FLOOD APOGEE
CLIMAX HEIGHT PERIOD SUMMIT
VERTEX ZENITH EVEREST MAXIMUM
MERIDIAN SOLSTICE
(LAST —) END
(LATERAL —) ALARE

(LOWEST — OF HULL) BILGE
(LOWEST —) NADIR BOTTOM
BEDROCK
(MAIN —) JET SUM GIST
(MEDIAN —) HORMION
(NO —S) LOVE
(ONE'S STRONG —) FORTE
(PEDAL —) DRONE
(PIVOTAL —) KNUCKLE
(PRECISE —) NICK
(PROJECTING —) CRAG PEAK
BEARD
(SHARP —) PRICK PRICKLE
(SINGLE —) ACE
(SKULL —) TYLION
(STATIONARY —) SPINODE
(STRIKING —) SALIENCE
(STRONG —) FORTE
(TAPERING —) ACUMEN
(TENNIS —) LET CHASE BISQUE
(TENTH OF —) MOMENT
(TERMINAL —) GOAL BOURN BREAK
AIRPORT
(TO THE —) COGENT
(TOP —) TUFT
(TURNING —) CARDO EPOCH CRISIS
(UNIPLANAR —) UNODE
(UTMOST —) EXTREME SUBLIME
(VANTAGE —) TOWER
(VOWEL —) SERE
(WEAK —) BLOT
POINT-BLANK BLUNT PLAIN POINT
DIRECT WHOLLY EXPRESS DIRECTLY
POINTED SET HOME ACUTE EXACT
FIXED PEAKY PIKED TANGY TERSE
FITCHE LIVELY OXEOTE PEAKED
PECKED PICKED SPIRED ANGULAR
FITCHEE LACONIC PRECISE SPICATE
ZESTFUL ACICULAR ACULEATE
CULTRATE DIACTINE PUNCTUAL
STELLATE
POINTER TIP YAD COCK HAND
WAND DUBHE INDEX POINT FESCUE
FINGER GUNDOG INDICE SILKER
STYLUS FLUSHER INDICANT
SIGNITOR
(— IN GREAT BEAR) DUBHE DUBBHE
(— ON ASTROLABE) ALMURY
(— ON GAUGE) ARM
(TEACHER'S —) FESCUE
(PL.) MEN GUARDS YADAYIM
POINTLESS DRY ILL DULL FLAT
INANE SILLY VAPID FRIGID STUPID
INSIPID WITLESS
POINTSMAN TRAPPER LATCHMAN
SWITCHMAN
POISE PEE CALM HEAD REST SWAY
TACT BRACE PEIZE APLOMB OFFSET
PONDER BALANCE BEARING DIGNITY
OPPRESS POISURE DELIVERY
EASINESS SERENITY
(— RECIPROCAL) RHE
POISED SET FACILE HOVERING
(BE —) LIBRATE
POISER HALTER
POISON FIG GAS BANE BIKH DRAB
DRUG GALL TUBA VERY ATTER
TAINT TOXIN VENOM VIRUS ANTIAR
DERRIS INFECT RANKLE TOXIFY

TOXOID BABASCO CORRUPT
ENVENOM FLYBANE PERVERT
PHALLIN TANGHIN VITIATE
ACQUETTA DELETERY RATSBANE
VENENATE
(— IN DEATH CUP) PHALLIN
(ARROW —) HAYA INEE URALI
ANTIAR ANTJAR CURARE CURARI
DERRIS
(FISH —) AKIA CUBE DERRIS HAIARI
BABASCO BARBASCO
(RAT —) ANTU
(VIRULENT —) BIKH TANGHIN
POISONED BUCKEYED TOXICATE
VENENATE VENOMOUS
POISONER SEPSIN CANIDIA VENEFIC
VENOMER
POISON HEMLOCK BUNK CICUTA
POISONING PYEMIA GASSING
JIMMIES BOTULISM MYCETISM
PLUMBISM ICHTHYISM LATHYRISM
POISON IVY CLIMATH MARKERY
MERCURY MARKWEED
POISON OAK YEARA
POISONOUS ATTRY TOXIC ATTERY
VENENE VIROSE VIROUS NOISOME
NOXIOUS DELETERY MEPHITIC
TOXICANT VENENATE VENOMOUS
VIRULENT MALIGNANT
POISON SUMAC BURTREE
DOGWOOD
POISON TOBACCO HENBANE
POISONWOOD BUMWOOD
POITREL ARMOR PECTRON
POKE BAG DAB DIG DUB HIT JAB
JOG PUG PUR TIG WAD BROD PAUT
PORR PROD PROG RAUK RUCK
SACK SOCK STAB STIR NIDGE
POACH PROKE PROTE PUNCH
ROUSE STEER STOKE COWBOY
DAWDLE INCITE PIERCE POCKET
POUNCE POUTER PUGGLE PUTTER
WALLET PRODDLE
(— ABOUT) ROKE
(— AROUND) ROOT SCROUNGE
(— LIGHTLY) POTTER PUTTER
(— WITH FOOT) SCUFF
(— WITH NOSE) SNUZZLE
POKE-IN STRANDER
POKELOKEN BOGAN LOGAN
POKER DART DRAW FLIP POIT PORR
POTE STUD BLUFF BOGIE CURATE
GOBLIN STOKER ACEPOTS
FRUGGAN LOWBALL PASSOUT
POCHARD SHOTGUN BASEBALL
COALRAKE JACKPOTS MISTIGRI
SHOWDOWN
(— CHIP) JETON JETTON
(— HAND) RUNT FLUSH SKEET
KILTER PELTER STRAIGHT
(FORM OF —) DRAW STUD
POKEWEED PAN POCAN SCOKE
COAKUM GARGET FOXGLOVE
INKBERRY REDBERRY
POKY DEAD DULL JAIL SLOW DOWDY
POKEY POKING SHABBY STODGY
STUFFY STUPID CRAMPED TEDIOUS

POLAK BALSA POLLACK
POLAR ARCTIC EMANANT PIVOTAL
DIRECTRIX
POLARIS ALRUCABA
POLE BAR LAT LEG LUG POL POY
ROD SKY XAT BEAM BIND BROG
COPE FALL HOOK KENT MAST NEAP
PALO PERK PIKE PROP SKID SPAR
TREE UFER CABER FOCUS MASUR
MAZUR PERCH QUANT REACH
SHAFT SPEAR SPOKE STAFF STANG
STILT STING STODE SWAPE SWIPE
BEACON BORITY CROTCH FLOWER
IMPOSE JUFFER KILHIG RICKER
RISSLE RYPECK SPONGE STOWER
TONGUE BARLING HEAVENS
TOWMAST ALESTAKE FLAGPOLE
FOOTPICK POLANDER STANDARD
(— AS EMBLEM OF SOVEREIGNTY)
KAHILI
(— AS HOLDFAST FOR BOATS)
RYPECK
(— FOR BEARING COFFIN) SPOKE
(— FOR PROPELLING BOAT) POY
(— FOR TOSSING) CABER KEBAR
(— HOLDING SAIL) BOOM MAST
SPRIT
(— OF TIMBER WAGON) NIB JANKER

(— OF VEHICLE) NEAP
(— ON TWO WHEELS) JANKER
(— USED AS SIGN) ALEPOLE
ALESTAKE
(— WITH BIRD DECOY) STOOL
(BOAT —) SPRIT
(CARRIAGE —) BEAM
(COUPLING —) REACH
(FIR —) UFER UPHER JUFFER
(FISHING —) WAND
(FORKED —) CROTCH
(LOGGING —) JANKER KILHIG KILLIG
(LONG —) PEW
(MANGROVE —) BORITY
(MINE —S) LAGGING
(NEGATIVE —) CATHODE
(PUNT —) QUANT STOWER
(RANGE —) FLAG
(SACRED —) ASHERAH
(SHEPHERD'S —) KENT
(SPRINGY —) BINDER
(STABLE —) BAIL
(STOUT —) KILHIG RICKER
(WATER-RAISING —) SWEEP
POLEAX STAFF POLEARM
POLECAT FITCH SKUNK ZORIL
FERRET FICHAT WEASEL FOUMART
FOULMART PERWITSKY SARMATIER
(— PELT) FITCH
POLE FLOUNDER SOLE
POLEHEAD TADPOLE
POLESTAR STAR GUIDE POLARIS
LODESTAR
POLICE GUARD WATCH GOVERN
CONTROL JEMADAR OCHRANA
POLIZEI PROTECT TOXOTAE
OPRICHNIC
(SECRET —) CHEKA
POLICEMAN COP JOE KID NAB PIG
BULL FLIC FUZZ GRAB JACK JOHN
PEON SLOP TRAP ZARP BOBBY
BULKY BURLY GAZER PEACE RURAL
SCREW SEPOY ASKARI BADGER
BOBBIE COPPER FISCAL FLATTY
HARMAN JOHNNY PEELER REDCAP
RUNNER SHAMUS CRUSHER
FOOTMAN GHAFFIR GUMSHOE
JEMADAR OFFICER SHOOFLY
TROOPER ZAPTIAH BARGELLO
BLUECOAT DOGBERRY FLATFOOT
GENDARME MINISTER
(CLUB OF —) BILLY STAFF
SPONTOON TRUNCHEON
(PL.) FINEST
POLICE STATION THANA BARGELLO
KOTWALEE
POLICY WIT DEAL FRONT ORDER
GOVERN NUMBER TICKET WISDOM
AUTARKY COUNSEL CUNNING
FLOATER LEFTISM LOTTERY
TONTINE VOUCHER ARTIFICE
SAGACITY STATEWAY
(CHOSEN —) COURSE
(PL.) APRISMO
POLISH BOB LAP MOP RUB RUD
BUFF DUCO FILE POLE CLEAN
FRUSH GLAZE GLOSS GRACE RABAT
ROUND SHINE SLICK STONE AFFILE
BARREL LUSTER PUNISH REFINE

RUMBLE SHAMMY SLIGHT SMOOTH
STREAK BEESWAX BURNISH
CHAMOIS FURBISH LACQUER
PERFECT VARNISH ELEGANCE
LEVIGATE SIMONIZE URBANIZE
POLISHED FINE COMPT ROUND
SHINY SLICK TERSE BUFFED FACETE
GLOSSY ELEGANT GALLANT
GENTEEL POLITIC REFINED
CULTURED
(NOT —) BLIND
POLISHER BUFFER GLAZER
WAGWAG WIGWAG DOLLIER
GLOSSER LAPIDARY SMOOTHER
POLISHING SANDING FROTTAGE
LIMATION
(— MATERIAL) RABAT
POLITE NEAT TIDY TRIM CIVIL SUAVE
GENTLE SMOOTH URBANE COURTLY
GALLANT GENTEEL DISCREET
LUSTROUS COURTEOUS
POLITENESS FINISH TASHRIF
COURTESY ELEGANCE URBANITY
POLITES (FATHER OF —) PRIAM
(MOTHER OF —) HECUBA
POLITIC WARY WISE SUAVE AROFUL
CRAFTY CUNNING TACTFUL
DISCREET PROVIDENT
POLITICAL (— ASSN.) VEREIN
(— PARTY) GOP TORY WHIG LABOR
POLITICIAN BOSS STATIST
WARWICK PIPELAYER STATESMAN
POLITY SERFISM
POLL COW DOD NOT POW ROB CHUB
COLL DODD HEAD NAPE NOTT PASH
CROWN SKULL STRIP CENSUS
FLEECE PARROT CANVASS DESPOIL
PILLAGE PLUNDER POLLARD
POLLACK LOB GADE LAIT GADID
LYTHE BILLET LAITHE BADDOCK
SILLOCK WALLEYE BLUEFISH
COALFISH GRAYFISH LORICATE
MOULRUSH
POLLARD CHU COW BRAN POLL
STAG SHEEP CHEVAN DODDLE
DOTARD BOLLING LOPPARD
WOOSERE
POLLARD TREE DOTARD RUNNEL
POLLED NOT NOTT POLEY
HORNLESS
POLLEN DUST MEAL FLOUR FARINA
POWDER BEEBREAD
(— BRUSH) SCOPA
(— TUBE) SPERMARY
POLLER VOTER BARBER POLLSTER
POLLEX THUMB
POLLINATE SELF FECUNDATE
FECUNDIZE FERTILIZE
POLLINATING SIBBING
POLLIWOG TADPOLE
POLLOCK PODLER
POLLUTE FOIL FOUL SOIL BLEND
DIRTY SMEAR TAINT BEFOUL DEFILE
INFECT MUDDLE RAVISH ADULTER
DEBAUCH PROFANE VIOLATE
POLLUTED FOUL DRUNK TURBID
CORRUPT
POLLUTING FILTHY
POLLUTION STAIN SULLAGE

FOULNESS IMPURITY
POLLUX POL HERCULES
(BROTHER OF —) CASTOR
(MOTHER OF —) LEDA
POLO (PERIOD IN —) CHUKKER
POLONAISE POLACCA FACKELTANZ
POLONIUS CORAMBIS
(DAUGHTER OF —) OPHELIA
(SON OF —) LAERTES
POLT BLOW THUMP STROKE
POLTERGEIST GHOST SPIRIT
POLTROON IDLER COWARD CRAVEN
WRETCH DASTARD COWARDLY
SLUGGARD
POLYANDRIUM CEMETERY
POLYGALA GAYWINGS
POLYGON DECAGON HEXAGON
NONAGON HEPTAGON PENTAGON
CHILIAGON MULTANGLE
POLYGRAPH KEELER
POLYHEDRON BEAD
POLYMER DIMER HYDROL HEXAMER
(— UNIT) MER

POLYNESIA
CHESTNUT: RATA
IMAGE: TIKI
ISLAND: COOK LINE SAMOA
TONGA EASTER ELLICE PHOENIX
ISLE: MOTU
KING: ALII ARII ARIKI
LANGUAGE: UVEA TAGALOG
MOUND: AHU
NATIVE: ATI MAORI KANAKA
NIVEAN TONGAN NESOGAEAN
PRINCIPLE: TIKI
WOMAN: VAHINE

POLYNESIAN MAORI KANAKA
TONGAN FUTUNAN
POLYNICES (BROTHER OF —)
ETEOCLES
(FATHER OF —) OEDIPUS
(MOTHER OF —) JOCASTA
(WIFE OF —) ARGIA
POLYNOMIAL CUBIC
POLYP CORAL HYDRA TUMOR ZOOID
ISOPOD HYDRULA OCTOPOD
POLYPARY ZOARIUM
POLYPHONY FABURDEN
COUNTERPOINT
POLYPIDOM CORMUS
POLYSACCHARIDE LEVAN GELOSE
GLYCAN INULIN IRISIN MANNAN
AMYLOSE DEXTRAN FUCOSAN
HEXOSAN POLYOSE GALACTAN
GLYCOGEN LICHENIN SECALOSE
SINISTRIN
POLYZOAN POLYP CESTODE
RADIATE
POMACE MUST RAPE POMMY STOCK
STOSH CHEESE
POMADE CIDER POMATUM LIPSTICK
OINTMENT
POMANDER POUNCET
POMATO TOPATO
POME BALL APPLE GLOBE
JUNEBERRY

POMEGRANATE GRENAT GRENADE
BALAUSTA
POMELO SHADDOCK GRAPEFRUIT
POMERANIA (CAPITAL OF —)
STETTIN
(CITY IN —) THORN TORUN ANKLAM
(ISLAND IN —) RUGEN USEDOM
(PROVINCE IN —) POMORZE
POMFRET BULLY HENFISH
POMME DE TERRE POTATO
POMMEL BOB FIB NOB BEAT HORN
KNOB PAIK PAKE TORE NEVEL
BRUISE BUFFET CRUTCH FINIAL
PLUMMET
POMP BRAG FARE WEAL BOAST
PRIDE STATE ESTATE PAMPER
PARADE RIALTY SCHEME SPRUNK
BOBANCE DISPLAY PAGEANT
PANOPLY SPLURGE CEREMONY
EQUIPAGE GRANDEUR SEMBLANT
SPLENDOR
POMPANO DART JUREL ALLICE
CARANX PERMIT ALEWIFE COBBLER
OLDWIFE CARANGID MACKEREL
(— CLAM) COQUINA
POMPOSITY TUMOR TUMOUR
BIGHEAD BIGNESS
POMPOUS BIG BUG BUDGE JELLY
LARGE SHOWY TUMID WIGGY
AUGUST TURGID BLOATED
BOMBAST FUSTIAN OROTUND
STILTED SWOLLEN TURGENT
BEWIGGED INFLATED SWELLING
IMPORTANT
PONCEAU GRANAT
PONCHO MANGA RUANA
POND (ALSO SEE POOL) LAY LUM
DELF DIKE MOAT PULK SLEW STEW
TANK VLEI VLEY CANAL DECOY
DELFT LACHE LETCH STANK WAYER
CLAIRE LAGOON LOCHAN PUDDLE
SALINA SLOUGH SPLASH STAGNE
MULLETRY
(— FOR OYSTERS) CLAIRE
(— MAN) JACKER
(ARTIFICIAL —) AQUARIUM
(DIRTY —) SOAL
(FISH —) GURGES
(FISH STORING —) STEW
(SMALL —) KHAL
(STAGNANT —) DUB
PONDER CON CAST CHAW MUSE
PORE ROLL TURN BROOD STUDY
WEIGH ADVISE EXPEND REASON
RECORD REMORD BALANCE
COMPASS EXAMINE IMAGINE
PERPEND REFLECT REVERIE
REVOLVE APPRAISE COGITATE
CONSIDER MEDITATE
PONDERABILITY WEIGHT GRAVITY
PONDEROUS DULL SLOW BULKY
GRAVE HEAVY SOGGY AWKWARD
WEIGHTY UNWIELDY IMPORTANT
PONDEROUSNESS HEFT
POND HEN COOT
PONDMAN JACKER
PONDOKKIE HUT HOVEL
PONE CAKE LUMP WRIT PAUNE
PUDDING SWELLING

PONGEE PAUNCHE SHANTUNG
PONIARD STAB BODKIN DAGGER
STYLET POINADO
PONT FERRY FLOAT BRIDGE
FERRYBOAT
PONTIC DUMMY
PONTICELLO BREAK MAGAS
PONTIFF POPE BISHOP PRIEST
PONTIFEX
PONTOON FLOAT RHINO BRIDGE
PONY CAB RAW TAT CAVY YABU
DALES GRIFF PAINT PINTO POWNY
TACKY TRICK WELCH WELSH
BASUTO BHUTIA BRONCO CAYUSE
EXMOOR GARRAN SHELTY TANGUN
TATTOO ENGLISH HACKNEY
MANIPUR MUSTANG SHELTIE
FORESTER GALLOWAY SHETLAND
(STUDENT'S —) CRIB TROT BICYCLE
(PL.) DALES
POODLE SHOCK BARBET
POOK HEAP PICK PULL PLUCK
STACK
POOKA PUCK GOBLIN SPECTER
POOL (ALSO SEE POND) CAR DIB
DUB LAY LUM PIT POL POT POW
BOOK CARR DIKE FARM JHIL LAKE
LIDO LINN LLYN LUMB MERE PANT
PEEL PLUD POLK POND PULE PULK
RING SINK SLEW SOIL SWAG TANK
TARN WEEL BAYOU BOWLY DECOY
FLASH FLUSH FRESH JHEEL KITTY
LETCH LOUGH MEARE PLASH
PLUMB SLACK STANK STELL STILL
THERM TRUNK CARTEL CHARCO
FLODGE LAGOON LASHER PLUNGE
PUDDLE SILOAM SPLASH STABLE
CARLINE CATHOLE CUSHION
JACKPOT PLASHET SNOOKER
STAGNUM INTERLOT QUINIELA
(— AT JERUSALEM) BETHESDA
(— BELOW WATERFALL) LIN LINN
LLYN
(— WITH SALMON NETS) STELL
(— WITHOUT OUTLET) STAGNUM
(ARTIFICIAL —) CUSHION
(AUCTION —) CALCUTTA
(DIRTY —) SUMP
(FISH —) TRUNK STEWPOND
(MOUNTAIN —) TARN
(MUDDY —) LETCH
(SWIMMING —) BATH LIDO
NATATORY
POON DILO PEON PUNA DOMBA
KEENA TAMANU SIRPOON
MASTWOOD
POONGHIE RAHAN PRIEST PUNGYI
PHONGHI TALAPOIN
POOP DOCK FIRE GULP TOOT CHEAT
COZEN STERN BEFOOL ISLAND
DECEIVE EXHAUST HINDDECK
OVERCOME
POOR BAD SAD BASE EVIL FOUL
LEAN LEWD PUNK SICK SOUR THIN
DINKY EXILE FOOTY GROSS JERRY
KETTY SCALY SEELY SILLY SOBER
SORRY UNORN FEEBLE HUMBLE
HUNGRY LEADEN MEAGER MEAGRE
MEASLY PILLED PORAIL PRETTY

SCANTY SHABBY STREET CODFISH
HAPLESS NAUGHTY SCRAWNY
SCRUBBY SQUALID TRIVIAL
UNLUCKY INDIGENT PRECIOUS
SCRANNEL SNEAKING UNTHENDE
(— BOY) HERO
POORHOUSE MEASONDUE
POORLY ILL BADLY SADLY BARELY
FEEBLY SIMPLY SLIGHT SHABBILY
POOR SOLDIER FRIARBIRD
POORTITH POVERTY
POP GO DOT GUN HIT TRY BLOW
DART HOCK JUMP PAWN SODA
BREAK CRACK KNOCK SHOOT
ATTACK EFFORT FATHER POPPER
STROKE THRUSH ASSAULT ATTEMPT
CONCERT EXPLODE INSTANT
REDWING BACKFIRE SUDDENLY
POPDOCK FOXGLOVE
POPE PAPA PAPE RUFF BISHOP
PUFFIN SHRIKE PONTIFEX
FISHERMAN
POPERY POPEISM PAPISTRY
POPE'S-EYE NUT NOIX
POPGUN SCOOT PENGUN POTGUN
PLUFFER
POPINJAY PARROT PAPINGO
POPLAR ABBEY ABELE ALAMO
ASPEN BAHAN LIARD BALSAM
POPPLE BAUMIER ABELTREE
WHITEBARK
POPLIN TABINET
POPOLOCA CHOCHO
POPPY HEAD BLAVER CANKER
COPROSE EARACHE PONCEAU
REDWEED ARGEMONE BALEWORT
BOCCONIA HEADACHE DANNEBROG
SQUATMORE
(CORN —S) SOLDIERS
POPPYCOCK BOSH FOLLY STUFF
HAVERS
POPPYFISH POMPANO
POPPY SEED MAW MOHNSEED
POPULACE MOB MASS CROWD
DEMOS PLEBS MASSES MOBILE
PEOPLE COUNTRY
POPULAR LAY POP COMMON
GOLDEN SIMPLE VULGAR CROWDED
DEMOTIC VULGATE APPROVED
FAVORITE PEOPLISH PLEBEIAN
POPULARITY VOGUE CLAPTRAP
POPULATE MAN BREED PLANT
WORLD PEOPLE INHABIT
POPULATION DEME COLONY
FLOTSAM KINDRED TOPODEME
UNIVERSE
POPULUS SALIX
PORBEAGLE LAMNA SHARK LAMNID
LAMNOID
PORCELAIN JU KO CHINA MURRA
SPODE MURRHA NANKIN BISCUIT
CELADON DRESDEN NANKEEN
MANDARIN STEATITE
(VARIETY OF —) CAEN KUAN ARITA
HIZEN IMARI KYOTO AMSTEL
SEVRES BUDWEIS DRESDEN
LIMOGES MEISSEN SWANSEA
HAVILAND KAKIEMON CHANTILLY
PORCH HOOD STOA LANAI STOEP

STOOP INGANG PARVIS PIAZZA
PORTAL RAMADA BALCONY GALILEE
NARTHEX PASSAGE POIKILE
PORTICO PRONAOS VERANDA
ANTENAVE GALLERIE SOLARIUM
TRANSEPT VESTIBLE
(FRONT —) ANTICUM
PORCUPINE QUILL URSON
CAWQUAW COENDOU ERECTER
ERICIUS PORKPEN HEDGEHOG
HEDGEPIG
PORCUPINE ANTEATER ECHIDNA
PORCUPINE FISH ERIZO ATINGA
BURFISH DIODONT
PORCUPINE GRASS SPINIFEX
PORE GAZE GLOSE GLOZE STARE
STUDY TRYPA PONDER ALVEOLA
CINCLIS OSTIOLE TUBULUS
BAJONADO JOLTHEAD LENTICEL
PORGY TAI SCUP PARGO PLUMA
POGGY BESUGO MAMAMU PAGRUS
SPARID MARGATE MENHADEN
SPADEFISH
PORK HAM HOG PIG LARD BACON
BRAWN MONEY SWINE BALDRIB
LARDOON MIDDLING
(CHOP) BALDRIB GRISKIN
(— AND SALMON) LAULAU
(— SHOULDER) HAND
(SALT —) BACON SPECK SOWBELLY
PORKFISH SISI CATALINETA
PORKY FAT GREASY
PORNOGRAPHIC LEWD CURIOUS
OBSCENE
PORNOGRAPHY CURIOSA
ESOTERICA
POROUS OPEN LIGHT LEACHY
CELLULAR
PORPHYRY ELVAN EURITE ELVANITE
GRORUDITE
PORPOISE WHALE PALACH PUFFER
COWFISH DOLPHIN HOGFISH
PELLOCK PULLOCK SNUFFER
CETACEAN GAIRFISH
PORRECT EXTEND TENDER PRESENT
PORRET LEEK ONION PORETT
SCALLION
PORRIDGE KHIR POBS ATOLE
BROSE GROUT GRUEL BURGOO
CROWDY SKILLY SOWENS TARTAN
BROCHAN BURGOUT OATMEAL
POBBIES POLENTA POTTAGE
FLUMMERY SAGAMITE
PORRINGER TASTER TRINKET
PORT GATE GOAL LEFT MIEN WICK
WINE CARRY CREEK HAVEN HITHE
SALLY SCALE STATE APPORT
HARBOR INPORT REFUGE AIRPORT
BEARING DIGNITY LIBERTY
OUTPORT ANTEPORT DEMEANOR
LARBOARD MALTOLTE PORTHOLE
PRESENCE
PORTABLE MOBILE MOVABLE
BEARABLE
PORTAGE PACK CARGO CARRY
TARBET FREIGHT TONNAGE
HAULOVER
PORTAL DOOR GATE PORCH
DOORWAY ENTRANCE
PORTAMENTO DRAG GLIDE SCOOP

SLIDE PORTATO GLISSADE
PORTCULLIS BAR SHUT HERSE
ORGUE CATARACT
PORTE-MONNAIE PURSE
PORTE GATE
PORTEND BODE AUGUR DIVINE
EXTEND BESPEAK BETOKEN
PREDICT PRESAGE DENOUNCE
FOREBODE FORECAST FORETELL
PORTENT AYAH LUCK SIGN SOUND
TOKEN AUGURY MARVEL OSTENT
WONDER AUSPICE PREDICT
PRESAGE PRODIGY CEREMONY
DISASTER SOOTHSAY
PORTENTOUS AWFUL GRAVID
BODEFUL DOOMFUL FATEFUL
OMINOUS POMPOUS DOOMLIKE
DREADFUL INFLATED SINISTER
PORTER BEER MOZO HAMAL STOUT
TAMEN BADGER BEARER COOLIE
DARWAN DURWAN ENTIRE KHAMAL
REDCAP SUISSE DROGHER
HUMMAUL JANITOR PITCHER
REMOVER BADGEMAN CARGADOR
CHAPRASI LODGEMAN PORTITOR
RECEIVER
(— AND STOUT) COOPER
(JAPANESE —) AKABO
(MEAT —) PITCHER
(MEXICAN —) TAMEN
PORTFOLIO BLAD
PORTIA (HUSBAND OF —) BRUTUS
(LOVER OF —) BASSANIO
(MAID OF —) NERISSA
PORTIA TREE MAHO BENDY MAHOE
PORTICO STOA WALK XYST ORIEL
PORCH XYSTA ZAYAT PARVIS
PIAZZA SCHOOL XYSTUS BALCONY
GALLERY NARTHEX PRONAOS
TERRACE VERANDA PORTICUS
POSTICUM VERANDAH
PORTION BIT CUP CUT DAB JAG LAB
LOT PAN BLAD DALE DEAL DOLE
DOSE FATE FECK JAGG PART SIZE
WHAT DOWER PIECE RATIO SHARE
SLICE SNACK WHACK CANTLE
CANTON COLLOP DETAIL GOBBET
MATTER PARCEL RASHER EXCERPT
PARTAGE SECTION SEGMENT
TODDICK TRANCHE FRACTION
FRAGMENT PITTANCE QUANTITY
SCANTLET FODDERING
(— DRUNK) DRAFT DRAUGHT
(— OF ACTOR'S PART) LENGTH
(— OF ARROW) BREAST
(— OF BIRD SONG) TOUR
(— OF BREAD OR BEER) CUE
(— OF CITRUS RIND) ALBEDA
(— OF ESTATE) LEGITIM
(— OF FARMLAND) BEREWICK
(— OF FLOODPLAIN) BANCO
(— OF FODDER) JAG
(— OF FOOD) HELP GOBBET
HELPING
(— OF HIDE) HEAD
(— OF LAND) BLOCK PATTI INTAKE
DIVISION DONATION
(— OF LIQUOR) STICK DIVIDEND
(— OF LITURGY) ANAPHORA

(— OF MAST) HOUSING HOUNDING
(— OF PASTURE) BREAK
(— OF POEM) STRAIN
(— OF RUG) GRIN
(— OF SERPENT'S BODY) TRAIN
(— OF STEM) BOON
(— OF STORY) SNATCH
(— OF STREAM) LAVADERO
(— OF TEA) DRAWING
(— OF TIME) SPAN DISTANCE
(— OF TOBACCO) CUD
(— OF TONGUE) BLADE
(ADDITIONAL —) RASHER
(ALLOTTED —) MOIRA SCANTLING
(BRIDE'S —) DOWRY
(CLOTTED — OF, BLOOD) CRUOR
(COARSER —) BOLTINGS
(EARLY —) SPRING
(INHABITED — OF EARTH) ECUMENE
(LATTER —) AUTUMN EVENING
(MAIN —) CORPSE
(MARRIAGE —) DOT DOTE TOCHER
(MINUTE —) GRAIN
(MOST VALUABLE —) CHIEF
(PERCEPTIBLE —) KENNING
(REPRESENTATIVE —) SAMPLE
(SIGNIFICANT —) CHAPTER
(SIZABLE —) DUNT
(SMALL — OF LIQUOR) DOLLOP
HEELTAP
(SMALL —) BIT DAB DOT DRAM
DROP SOSH CHACK SPICE SPUNK
SHADOW MODICUM REMNANT
SCANTLE SMIDGEN SOUPCON
SCANTLET
(TRIFLING —) SMACK
PORTLY FAT FULL AMPLE STOUT
GOODLY STATELY SWELLING
PORTMANTEAU BAG HOOK VALISE
POCKMANKY
PORTRAIT BUST ICON IKON IMAGE
IMAGO MODEL PIECE STATUE
VISAGE PORTRAY RETRAIT
LIKENESS RITRATTO VERONICA
(— ON COIN) EFFIGY
PORTRAY GIVE LIMN LINE BLAZE
ENACT IMAGE PAINT CIPHER
CLOTHE DEPICT FIGURE SHADOW
FEATURE IMITATE PICTURE
DECIPHER DESCRIBE RESEMBLE

PORTUGAL
BAY: SETUBAL
CAPITAL: LISBON
CAPE: MONDEGO ESPICHEL
COIN: JOE REI PECA REAL CONTO
COROA DOBRA INDIO ESCUDO
MACUTA PATACA TESTAO
VINTEM CENTAVO CRUSADO
MOIDORE EQUIPAGA
COLONY: MACAO TIMOR ANGOLA
GUINEA PRINCIPE
ISLAND: TIMOR
ISLANDS: MADEIRA
MEASURE: PE ALMA BOTA MEIO
MOIO PIPA VARA ALMUD BRACA
FANGA GEIRA LEGOA LINHA
MILHA PALMO ALMUDE CANADA

COVADO QUARTO ALQUIER
ESTADIO FERRADO SELAMIN
ALQUEIRE TONELADA
MOUNTAIN: ACOR GEREZ MARAO
MOUSA PENEDA ESTRELA
MONCHIQUE
RIVER: SOR TUA LIMA MINO MIRA
SADO SEDA TAGO TEJO DOURO
MINHO SABAR TAGUS VOUGA
ZATAS CAVADO CHANCA
TAMEGA ZEZERE MONDEGO
GUADIANA
TOWN: FARO OVAR BRAGA EVORA
PORTO GUARDA OPORTO
COIMBRA FUNCHAL SETUBAL
BRAGANCA
UNIVERSITY: COIMBRA
WEIGHT: GRAO ONCA LIBRA
MARCO ARROBA OITAVA
ARRATEL QUINTAL
WINE: PORT

PORTULACA MOSS PURSLANE
PORWIGLE TADPOLE
POSAUNE TROMBONE
POSE SET SIT HOARD MODEL OFFER
PLANT STICK BAFFLE NONPLUS
PEACOCK POSTURE PRESENT
POSITION PRETENSE PROPOUND
QUESTION
POSEIDON NEPTUNE EARTHSHAKER
(BROTHER OF —) ZEUS
(FATHER OF —) KRONOS
(MOTHER OF —) RHEA
(WIFE OF —) AMPHITRITE
POSER FACER POSEUR PUZZLE
STAYER STICKER STUMPER
TWISTER EXAMINER STICKLER
BANDARLOG
POSH SWAGGER
POSING OPPOSAL
(— TECHNIQUE) PLASTIQUE
POSIT FIX PUT SET PLACE AFFIRM
ASSUME
POSITING PONENT
POSITION LAY LIE HANG LINE POSE
RANK SITE CENSE COIGN PLANT
POSTE SITUS STAND STATE STEAD
ASSIZE FIGURE HEIGHT OCTAVE
OFFICE STANCE UBIETY VALGUS
POSTURE STATION ATTITUDE
CAPACITY DOCTRINE VOCATION
(— OF AFFAIRS) STATUS
(— OF FEAR) GAZE
(— OF HEAVENLY BODY) HARBOR
(— OF VESSEL) GAUGE HEIGHT
(— WITH NO ESCAPE) IMPASSE
(— WITH NO RESPONSIBILITY)
SINECURE
(DISTINGUISHED —) HONOR
(EMBARRASSING —) FIX HOLE
(FENCING —) CARTE SIXTE SIXTH
QUARTE TIERCE SACCOON
SECONDE SEPTIME
(FOREMOST —) HEAD LEAD STEM
(INITIAL —) ANLAUT
(MEDIAL —) INLAUT
(RELATIVE —) RANK TERMS

BEARING FOOTING STANDING
(SOCIAL —) CASTE STATE VALOUR
(SYMBOLIC —) HASTA
POSITIONAL SITUAL
POSITIVE POS POZ COOL DOWN
FLAT PLUS SURE BASIC SHEER
UTTER ACTIVE DIRECT THETIC
GENUINE HEALTHY ABSOLUTE
CONCRETE DEFINITE DOGMATIC
EXPLICIT INHERENT RESOLUTE
SIGNLESS THETICAL
(THREE —S) KROMOGRAM
POSITIVELY BUT POS FLAT PLUS
QUITE FAIRLY INDEED STRICTLY
POSITIVISM COMTISM CERTAINTY
DOGMATISM
POSITRON LEPTON
POSSESS GET OWE OWN HAVE
HOLD WALD BOAST BROOK OUGHT
REACH WIELD MASTER OBTAIN
OCCUPY BEDEVIL ENVELOP FURNISH
INHABIT INHERIT INSTALL INSTATE
SMITTLE ACQUAINT DOMINATE
INSTRUCT
POSSESSED MAD CALM COOL
OUGHT CRAZED JERUSHA
ENTHEATE
(— BY EVIL SPIRIT) DEMONIAC
POSSESSION AVER HAND HOLD
YHTE AUGHT GRASP STATE CLUTCH
CORNER HAVIOR SASINE SEISIN
SEIZIN WEALTH CONTROL COUNTER
DEMESNE DEWANEE FINGERS
KEEPING MASTERY SEIZURE
CONQUEST DEFIANCE PROPERTY
(— OF COMMON FEATURES)
AFFINITY
(— OF KNOWLEDGE) SCIENCE
(— WITH QUIET ENJOYMENT) SEISIN
SEIZIN
(BURDENSOME —) ELEPHANT
(RELIGIOUS —) POWER
(TEMPORAL —S) WORLD
(TEMPORARY —) LEND
(PL.) ALLS STORE STUFF WRACK
DOMAIN ESTATE GRAITH PROPER
CAPITAL FORTUNE HAVINGS LIVINGS
POSSET CURDLE PAMPER
POWSOWDY BALDUCTUM
MERRYBUSH
POSSIBILITY MAY MAYBE POSSE
CHANCE
POSSIBLE ABLE RIFE MAYBE LIKELY
EARTHLY ELIGIBLE FEASIBLE
PROBABLY POTENTIAL
POSSIBLY MAPPEN LIGHTLY
PERHAPS PERCHANCE
POSSUM TAIT FEIGN PRETEND
POST DAK SET TIE BITT BOMA CAMP
DAWK DOLE FAST FORT MAIL META
POLE ROOM SPOT SPUD STOB STUD
TREE BERTH CHEEK CLOSH CRANE
NEWEL PLACE SPILE SPRAG STAKE
STAND STILT STING STOCK STODE
STOOP STULP STUMP BILLET
CIPPUS COLUMN CROTCH FENDER
GIBBET INFORM OFFICE PICKET
PILLAR SAMSON SCREEN STAPLE
STOOTH STOWER TRUNCH ASHERAH

BOLLARD COURIER GARETTA
PLACARD POSTAGE POSTBOX
QUARTER STATION STUDDLE
UPRIGHT BANISTER DEADHEAD
LEGPIECE MAKEFAST PRESIDIO
PUNCHEON QUINTAIN STRADDLE
(— AS RACE MARKER) META
(— ON PIER) FAST BOLLARD
DEADHEAD
(BOUNDARY —) TÉRM STOOP
TERMINUS
(CHIMNEY —) SPEER
(CUSTOMS —) CHOKEY
(DOOR OR GATE —) DURN
(ECCLESIASTIC —) BENEFICE
(FENCE —) DROPPER
(HANGING —) GIBBET
(INDIAN MILITARY —) TANA TANNA
THANA
(MILITARY —) FORT GARRISON
(MOORING —) DOLPHIN
(OBSERVATORY —) CUPOLA
(SACRED —) ASHERAH
(SIGN —) PARSON
POSTAGE POST STAMPAGE
POSTAGE-FREE FRANCO
POSTAGE STAMP DUE HEAD
STICKER
POSTBOY YAMSHIK YEMSCHIK
POSTILION
POST CHAISE JACK POCHAY
POSCHAY
POSTER BILL CLAP SNIPE CLAPPE
AFFICHE PLACARD SHOWING
STICKER STREAMER
POSTERIOR BACK REAR CAUDAL
DORSAL POSTIC RETRAL ADAXIAL
BUTTOCKS
(PL.) WHEERIKINS
POSTERIORLY RETRAD
POSTERITY SEQUEL KINDRED
FUTURITY
POSTERN SIDE CLOCKET KLICKET
PRIVATE POSTICUM
POSTHOUSE YAM MUTATION
POSTICHE WIG SHAM SWITCH
TOUPEE PRETENSE SPURIOUS
POSTIL HOMILY COMMENT
POSTILION COURIER POSTBOY
YAMSHIK
POSTLUDE SORTIE SORTITA
EPILOGUE
POSTMAN MAIL CORREO MAILBAG
MAILMAN
POST OFFICE BOMA CORREO
POSTHOUSE
POSTPONE OFF STAY WAIT DEFER
DELAY FRIST REFER REMIT WAIVE
FUTURE LINGER RELONG RETARD
ADJOURN DEGRADE OVERSET
PROLONG RESPECT SUSPEND
CONTINUE PROROGUE REPRIEVE
WITHHOLD
POSTPONED DEFERRED
POSTPONEMENT MORA STAY
DELAY RESPECT RESPITE
POSTRIDE COURIER POSTILION
POSTSCRIPT EKE ENVOY
POST SUPPORT CROWFOOT

POSTULANT NOVICE
POSTULATE AXIOM CLAIM ASSERT ASSUME DEMAND THESIS PERHAPS PETITION PRINCIPLE
POSTURE SET POSE SEAT SITE ASANA FRONT HEART PLACE SHAPE SQUAT STATE LOUNGE SLOUCH STANCE BEARING CROWHOP STATION STATURE ATTITUDE CARRIAGE POSITION
  (— OF DEFENSE) GUARD
  (DANCE —) HOLD
  (KNEELING —) SHIKO
POSY POESY TUTTY FLOWER BOUQUET NOSEGAY ANTHOLOGY
POT BAG CAN COOP FOOL JUST LEAD OLLA PINT POOL RUIN CREWE CROCK CRUSE DIXIE KITTY SHANT SHOOT ALUDEL CHATTY CHYTRA JORDAN JORDEN KETTLE MARMIT MASLIN MONKEY OUTWIT PINGLE PIPKIN POCKET POSNET CHAMBER CUVETTE DECEIVE POTSHOT SEETHER SKILLET YETLING FAVORITE JACKSHEA PRESERVE MARIJUANA
  (— FOR CATCHING FISH) COOP
  (— OF BRASS) MASLIN
  (— OF DRINK) SHANT
  (— WITH 3 FEET) POSNET
  (12-GALLON —) DIXY DIXIE
  (BULGING —) OLLA
  (BUSHMAN'S —) JACKSHAY JACKSHEA
  (CHAMBER —) JERRY JORDAN JORDEN COMMODE JEROBOAM
  (CHIMNEY —) CAN TUN
  (EARTHEN —) OLLA CROCK CHATTY PIPKIN
  (LEATHER —) GISPIN
  (LOBSTER —) COY TRUNK
  (LONG-HANDLED —) PINGLE
  (MELTING —) CRUCIBLE
  (PEAR-SHAPED —) ALUDEL
  (SMALL ROUND —) LOTAH
  (TEA —) TRACK
POTABLE DRINK BEVERAGE POTATORY
POTAGE SOUP BROTH
POTAMOGETON PONDWEED PONDGRASS
POTASH KALI SALINE PEARLASH POLVERINE
  (— FACTORY) ASHERY
POTASSIUM K KALIUM POTASS
  (— DICHROMATE) CHROME
POTASSIUM NITRATE GROUGH
POTATION POT DRAM DRAFT DRINK LIBATION
POTATO PAP YAM CHAT PAPA SPUD YAMP IDAHO RURAL TATER TUBER BATATA CAMOTE KUMARA LUMPER MURPHY PRATEY SKERRY BURBANK EPICURE SOLANUM BLUENOSE
  (— BALL) NOISETTE
  (— MASHER) RICER CHAPPER
  (— SLICES) LATTICE
  (— STATE) IDAHO MAINE
  (—S AND CABBAGE) COLCANNON

  (FRENCH FRIED —) CHIP
  (FRENCH FRIED —S) GAUFRETTES
  (JAPANESE —) IMO
  (STEWED —S) STOVIES
  (WITH —S) PARMENTIER
  (PL.) WARE CHUNO
POT BEARER POTIFER
POTBELLIED PODDY STOMACHY
POTBELLY PAUNCH TUNBELLY
POTBOY GANYMEDE
POTE KICK MOPE POIT POKE PUSH NUDGE PLATE POKER SHOVE THRUST
POTEEN POTHEEN WHISKEY POTWHISKY
POTENCE STUD CROSS GIBBET
POTENCY FORCE POWER VIGOR ORENDA VIRTUE EFFICACY STRENGTH VITALITY
POTENT ABLE MAIN RICH STAY STIFF CAUSAL COGENT CRUTCH MIGHTY STRONG DYNAMIC SUPPORT WARRANT FORCIBLE POWERFUL PUISSANT VIGOROUS VIRTUOUS VIRULENT
POTENTATE KING RULER POTENT PRINCE DICTATOR DOMINION SOVEREIGN
POTENTIAL EH LATENT VIRTUAL IMPLICIT INCHOATE POSSIBLE PREGNANT
  (— ENERGY) ERGAL
POTENTIALITY POSSE POWER DUNAMIS DYNAMIS CAPACITY PREGNANCY
POTGUN PISTOL POPGUN BRAGGART
POTHER ADO VEX FUSS STEW STIR WORRY BOTHER BUSTLE HARASS POTTER PUTTER PUZZLE PERPLEX TURMOIL
POTHERB WORT WERTE GREENS OLITORY POTWORT QUELITE SPINACH TAMPALA
POTHOLE POT KETTLE TINAJA
POTHOOK HAIK HAKE CROOK HANGLE RACKAN SLOWRIE TRAMMEL COTTEREL
POTHOUSE TAVERN ALEHOUSE MUGHOUSE
POTION DOSE DRUG DRAFT DRINK DWALE STUFF DRENCH POISON AMATORY MIXTURE PHILTER PHILTRE NEPENTHE
POTLATCH GIFT FEAST PARTY POTLACH FESTIVAL
POT MARIGOLD GOLD GOLDE SUNFLOWER
POTPOURRI OLIO STEW MASLIN MEDLEY POTPIE RAGOUT FANTASIA PASTICHE JAMBALAYA
POTRO COLT
POTSHERD BIT TEST CROCK SHARD SHERD FRAGMENT OSTRACON PANSHARD
POTTAGE SEW SOUP SOWL STEW BROTH BRUET BREWIS BROWET POTAGE OATMEAL PULMENT
POTTED DRUNK CANNED
  (— MEAT) RILLETT

POTTER FAD FUSS MUCK POKE ANNOY DAKER TRUCK BOTHER DABBLE DACKER DIDDLE DISHER DODDER FIDDLE FOOTLE FOTTER JOTTER KUMHAR MUDDLE NANTLE NIGGLE PETTLE POUTER TIDDLE TIFFIE TIFFLE TRIFLE CLOAMER CROCKER DISTURB FIGURER FOSSICK HANDLER NAUNTLE PERPLEX PLOWTER PRODDLE THROWER TROUBLE CERAMIST TERRAPIN
  (— OFFICIOUSLY) TEW
  (MACHINE OF —) JOLLY
POTTERER TWIRLER
POTTERY POT BANK CHUN DELF GROG WARE BIZEN CROCK DELFT GLOST ROUEN SPODE BASALT FICTIL KASHAN MIMPEI ASTBURY BELLEEK BOCCARO BRISTOL DIPWARE FIGMENT JETWARE KAMARES POTBANK POTWARE POTWORK REDWARE SATSUMA TICKNEY TZUCHOU BUCCHERO CERAMICS FIGULINE GRAYWARE SLIPWARE
  (— CIVILIZATION) MINYAN
  (— CULTURE) PUCARA
  (— DECOR) MISHIMA
  (— DECORATED WITH SCRATCHING) GRAFFITO
  (ANCIENT —) KAMARES GRAYWARE
  (BLACK —) BASALT
  (CHINESE —) KUAN
  (CRUSHED —) GROG
  (HINDU —) UDA
  (RICHLY COLORED —) MAJOLICA
POTTERY TREE CARAIPE
POTTINGER COOK POTYCARY
POTTO LEMUR APOSORO KINKAJOU
POTTY CRAZY FOOLISH TRIVIAL SNOBBISH
POUCH BAG COD JAG POD SAC BELL CYST POKE BULGE BURSA POKKE PURSE BUDGET CAECUM CRUMEN GIPSER PACKET POCKET PURSET SACHET ALFARGA ALFORJA CANTINA CRUMENA GIPSIRE MOCHILA OVICYST SCROTUM SPORRAN SWALLOW BURSICLE PROTRUDE SPEUCHAN
  (— OF FLY) AEROSTAT
  (— ON DEER'S NECK) BELL
  (TOBACCO —) DOSS
POUF PUFF OTTOMAN
POULAINE PIKE CRAKOW
POULPE POULP CUTTLE OCTOPUS
POULTICE QUILT STUPA STUPE MALAGMA EPITHEME SINAPISM
POULTRY FOWL HENS DUCKS GEESE PULLEN PEAFOWL PIGEONS PULLERY TURKEYS CHICKENS PULLAILE VOLAILLE
POUNAMU JADE PUNAMU NEPHRITE
POUNCE NAB CHOP CLAP JUMP POKE SWAP SWOP FLECK PRICK PUNCH SOUSE SWOOP TALON EMBOSS PIERCE TATTOO BOBCOAT DESCEND SPRINKLE

(— **UPON**) TIRE STOOP

POUND L LB BUM DAD LIB PIN PUN
SOV BEAT CHAP DRUB FRAM PELT
PIND POON POSS PUND QUID SKIT
THUD TRAP TUND CRUSH FRAME
KNOCK LABOR LIVRE STAMP THUMP
TRAMP WEIGH BATTER HAMMER
LUMBER NICKER POUNCE PRISON
THRASH CONTUND CONTUSE
PINFOLD THUNDER LAMBASTE
RESTRAIN
(— **FINE**) BRAY
(**1-8TH OF** —) HANDFUL
(**100** —**S**) CENTAL CENTURY
(**12** —**S OF BUTTER**) GAUN
(**25** —**S**) PONY PONEY
(**32, 56, OR 75** —**S OF RAISINS**)
FRAIL
(**500** —**S**) MONKEY
(**FISH** —) KEEP MADRAGUE
(**ISRAELI** —**S**) LIROTH
POUNDMASTER PINDER PINNER
PONDER

POUR JAW RUN TUN YET BIRL BREW
DROP EMIT FILL FLOW GOSH GUSH
HELD LASH LAVE RAIN TEEM TOOM
VENT FLOOD FLUSH HEELD HIELD
POWER SLIDE SOUSE SPILL SPOUT
STREAM CASCADE CHANNEL
DIFFUSE SUFFUSE
(— **AWAY**) STAVE
(— **BACK**) REFUND
(— **BEER OR WINE**) BIRL
(— **CLUMSILY**) SLOSH
(— **COPIOUSLY**) HALE
(— **DOWN**) RASH SILE SHOWER
DESCEND DISPUNGE
(— **FORTH**) SHED TIDE VENT WELL
DISTILL OVERFLOW
(— **FREELY**) SWILL
(— **FROM ONE VESSEL TO
ANOTHER**) DECANT JIRBLE
TRANSFUSE
(— **IN DROP BY DROP**) INSTIL
INSTILL
(— **IN**) INFUSE INFOUND INHELDE
(— **LIKE RAIN OR TEARS**) LASH
(— **MELTED WAX**) BASTE
(— **MOLTEN LEAD**) YOTE
(— **OFF**) SLUICE
(— **OIL UPON**) ANOINT
(— **OUT**) FILL SEND SHED SKINK
STOUR UTTER EFFUSE LIBATE
DIFFUND DIFFUSE
(— **UPON**) AFFUSE
POURBOIRE TIP GRATUITY
TRINKGELD
POURER TEEMER INFUSER
POURPOINT GIPON JUPON QUILT
DOUBLET
POUT BIB MOP MAID MOUE PUSS
SULK BOODY GROIN CATFISH
EELPOUT BULLHEAD PROTRUDE
POUTERIA LUCUMA
POUTING BOUDERIE
POVERTY LACK NEED WANE WANT
DEARTH PENURY BEGGARY
DEFAULT TENUITY DISTRESS

PUIRTITH SCARCITY WANDRETH
POVERTY PLANT HEATH HEATHER
LINGWORT
POVERTY-STRICKEN POOR NAKED
NEEDY SQUALID SHIRTLESS
POWDER DUST KISH MILL MULL
SAND CHALK CURRY ERBIA FLOUR
GRIND HEMOL KOSIN PICRA STOUR
CEMENT CHARGE CHINOL DECAMP
DERMOL EMPASM ESCAPE FARINA
FILITE GERATE KAMALA KERMES
KUMKUM MELLON PEYTON PINOLE
POUNCE RACHEL SMEETH YTTRIA
ALCOHOL BESTREW BROCADE
LUPULIN SCATTER SMEDDUM
SPACKLE SPODIUM ALGAROTH
CATAPASM DYNAMITE FLUMERIN
PALEGOLD
(— **A SHIELD**) GERATE
(— **FOR BRONZING**) BROCADE
(— **OBTAINED BY SUBLIMATION**)
FLOWERS
(— **TO MASK SWEAT ODOR**)
EMPASM EMPASMA
(— **USED IN CHOCOLATE**) PINOLE
(**ABRASIVE** —) EMERY
(**ANTHELMINTIC** —) KOSIN
(**ANTIMONY** —) KOHL
(**ASTRINGENT** —) BORAL
(**BLEACHING** —) CHEMIC
(**BROWNISH** —) LIGNIN
(**CATHARTIC** —) KAMALA
(**COLORING** —) HENNA
(**FINE** —) DUST POUNCE ALCOHOL
(**FLUORESCENT** —) FLUMERIN
(**GOA** —) ARAROBA
(**GOLD** —) VENTURINE
(**GRAPHITIC** —) KISH
(**GRAY** —) ANTU
(**HAIR** —) MUST
(**MALT** —) SMEDDUM
(**PERFUMED** —) ABIR SACHET
(**PINK** —) CALAMINE
(**POISONOUS** —) ROBIN
(**REDDISH** —) ABIR KUMKUM
SIMMON
(**ROSE-COLORED** —) ERBIA
(**SACHET** —) PULVIL
(**SILICEOUS** —**S**) SILEX
(**SMOKELESS** —) FILITE PEYTON
CORDITE AMBERITE INDURITE
SOLENITE
(**WHITE** —) CHINOL YTTRIA HYPORIT
SCANDIA HALAZONE LANTHANA
PARAFORM
(**YELLOW** —) KOSIN DERMOL
MELLON LUPULIN MALARIN SAMARIA
TANNIGEN
POWDERED SEME SPICED PICKLED
SEASONED
POWDER PUFF PLUFF
POWER ARM ART JUS ROD SAY SUN
VIS BEEF BULK DINT GIFT GRIP
HAND HANK HEAP HORN IRON KAMI
MAIN MANA MAYA SOUP SWAY
WALD WILL AGENT CROWN DEMON
DEVIL FORCE GRACE HUACA HYDRO
INPUT LURCH MIGHT SINEW SKILL
STEAM VALUE VIGOR WAKON WIELD

YARAK APPEAL BREATH CLUTCH
CREDIT DANGER DEGREE DOUGHT
EFFORT ENERGY FOISON IMPACT
MOLOCH SHAKTI STROIL STROKE
SWINGE TALENT VIRTUE WEIGHT
BALANCE BOSSDOM COMMAND
CONTROL DEMESNE DESTINY
DUNAMIS DYNAMIS ENTHEOS
FACULTY POTENCY VALENCY
VOLTAGE WAKONDA ACTIVITY
AUTONOMY CAPACITY COERCION
DELEGACY DEMIURGE DISPOSAL
DOMINION INTEREST LEVERAGE
LORDSHIP SEIGNORY STRENGTH
(— **OF ACID**) BASICITY
(— **OF ATTRACTION**) ALLURE
(— **OF CHOICE**) LIBERTY
(— **OF DIVORCE**) TAFWIZ
(— **OF ENTRY**) INGRESS
(— **OF GIVING**) PROPINE
(— **OF HEARING**) AUDITION
(— **OF KNOWING**) JNANASHAKTI
(— **OF MANIFESTATION**) MAYA
(— **OF MOVING AT SEA**) YARAGE
(— **OF PERFORMING**) ART
(— **OF RESISTANCE**) STAMINA
(— **OF TRANSMUTATION**) ALCHEMY
(— **OF VISION**) KEN
(— **OF WINE**) SEVE
(— **TO CONVINCE**) FORCE
(—**S OF EVIL**) HELL
(**CIVIL** —) CAESAR
(**COERCIVE** —) SWORD
(**DIVINE** —) MOIRA
(**ELEVATING** —) LIFT
(**EMOTIONAL** —) STOMACH
(**EXTRAPHYSICAL** —) MANA
(**FIFTH** —) SURSOLID
(**FOCAL** —) DIOPTRY
(**GROWTH** —) BATHMISM
(**HYPOTHETICAL** —) FORTUNE
(**IMPERSONAL** —) WAKAN WAKON
WAKANDA
(**INTELLECTUAL** —) WIT
(**LEGAL** —) JUS
(**MAGIC** —) ORENDA
(**MAGNETIC** —) MAGNES
(**MENTAL** —) HABITUS
(**MORMON** —) KEYS
(**NATURAL** —) OD
(**OCCULT** —) MAGIC
(**PERSUASIVE** —) RHETORIC
(**PERUVIAN** —) HUACA
(**POLITICAL** —) DOMINIUM
(**RATIONAL** —) EYE
(**REFLECTIVE** —) ALBEDO
(**ROYAL** —) RIAL
(**SACRED** —) KAMI
(**SECOND** —) SQUARE
(**SOVEREIGN** —) SWAY THRONE
(**SPIRITUAL** —) NGAI
(**STAYING** —) STAMINA
(**SUPERNATURAL** —) CHARISMA
(**SUPREME** —) EMPIRE HEAVEN
IMPERIUM
(**THIRD** —) CUBE
(**VITAL** —) SPIRITS
POWERBOAT SEDAN SKIFF GLIDER
CRUISER STINKPOT GASOLINER

POWERFUL BIG FAT ABLE DEEP
HIGH MAIN RANK RICH VERY FORTE
HEFTY HUSKY LUSTY STARK STOUT
VALID VIVID WIGHT WILDE COGENT
HEROIC MIGHTY POTENT SEVERE
STRONG CAPABLE FECKFUL
INTENSE POLLENT RICHARD
SKOOKUM STAVING VALIANT
FORCIBLE PUISSANT VIGOROUS
POWERLESS WEAK FEEBLE UNABLE
HELPLESS IMPOTENT
POWWOW PAWAW CONFAB FROLIC
COUNCIL MEETING SESSION
CONJURER
POX ROUP CANKER PLAGUE VARIOLA
(FOWL —) SOREHEAD
(SHEEP —) OVINIA
POYOU PELUDO ARMADILLO
PRABHU LORD CHIEF WRITER
PRACTICABLE AGIBLE DOABLE
USABLE FEASIBLE POSSIBLE
PRACTICAL HARD UTILE ACTUAL
THINGY USEFUL OPERARY VIRTUAL
WORKING BANAUSIC HOMESPUN
PRACTIVE THINGISH
(— JOKE) WAGGERY
(NOT —) PROFESSORY
PRACTICALLY ALMOST NEARLY
REALLY VIRTUALLY
PRACTICE ACT ISM LAW SUE TRY
URE USE KEEP LIVE PLAN PLOT
ADOPT APPLY ASSAY DRILL FOUND
GUISE HABIT HAUNT TRADE TRAIN
TREAD USAGE CUSTOM EMPLOY
FOLLOW GROOVE OCCUPY PRAXIS
RECORD BRUSHUP ENHAUNT
KNOCKUP OPERATE PROCEED
PROFESS RANDORI USAUNCE
ACTIVISM ALARMISM EXERCISE
FREQUENT GALENISM
(— CHEATING) FOIST
(— DECEPTION) DEACON
(— DILIGENTLY) PLY
(— FRAUD) SHARK
(— HYPOCRISY) CANT
(— OF AN ART) PRAXIS
(— OF MEDICINE) GALENISM
(— ROWING) TUB
(— WITCHCRAFT) HEX
(BINDING —) LAW
(CEREMONIAL —) RITE
(COMMUNAL —) SUNNA SCHEME
SUNNAH INTRIGUE
(CORRUPT —) ABUSE WHORE
(DIPLOMATIC —) ALTERNAT
(DISHONEST —S) CROSS
(HORTICULTURAL —) CUTTAGE
(MEDICAL —) ALLERGY
(RELIGIOUS —) CULT CULTUS
(SUPERSTITIOUS —) FREET
(UNDERHAND —) JUGGLING
(VICIOUS —) MOLOCH
PRACTICED EXPERT VERSED
PRACTIC SKILLED VETERAN
HACKNEYED
PRACTICING EXERCENT
PRACTITIONER DOCTOR HEALER
LAWYER NOVICE LEARNER
EXERCENT FELDSHER HUMANIST

HERBALIST HOMEOPATH
PRAD HORSE
PRAENOMEN AULUS CAIUS GAIUS
TITUS GNAEUS LUCIUS MANIUS
MARCUS SEXTUS SERVIUS SPURIUS
MAMERCUS NUMERIUS TIBERIUS
PRAESEPE CRIB CRATCH MANGER
BEEHIVE
PRAGMATIC BUSY BUSYBODY
DOGMATIC MEDDLING OFFICIOUS
PRACTICAL
PRAIRIE BAY BLED CAMAS CAMASS
MEADOW PLATEAU QUAMASH
(— STATE) ILLINOIS
PRAIRIE BERRY TROMPILLO
PRAIRIE CHICKEN GROUSE
PRAIRIE DOG GOPHER MARMOT
PRAIRIE WOLF COYOTE
PRAISE CRY LOF FUME HERY LAUD
LOSE LOVE PRES ADORE ALLOW
ALOSE BLESS CAROL CHANT CRACK
DEIFY EXTOL GLORY HERSE HONOR
KUDOS PLAUD PRIZE ROOSE SALVE
VALUE WURTH ANTHEM BELAUD
EULOGY FRAISE HILLEL KUDIZE
LOANGE LOVING ORCHID SALUTE
TONGUE ACCLAIM ADULATE
APPLAUD COMMEND FLATTER
GLORIFY MAGNIFY NOSEGAY
PLAUDIT PUFFING TRIBUTE
WORSHIP APPLAUSE BLESSING
DOXOLOGY ENCOMIUM EULOGIZE
(— BE TO GOD) LD
(— IN THANKSGIVING) JOY
(— INORDINATELY) FUME
(— OF ANOTHER'S FELICITY)
MACARISM
(— TO GOD ALWAYS) LDS
(EFFUSIVE —) FUSS
(EXCESSIVE —) FLATTERY
ADULATION
(INSINCERE —) CLART DAUBING
(PUBLIC —) PRECONY
(SING FALSE —S) CHANT
PRAISED JUDAH JUDITH LAURELED
(UNDULY —) BEPUFFED
PRAISEWORTHY WORTHY AMIABLE
GLORIOUS LAUDABLE SPLENDID
EXEMPLARY
PRAJAPATI KA PITRI
PRAKRIT PALI MAGADHI
PRAM CARRIAGE HANDCART
PUSHCART STROLLER
PRANCE STIR BRANK CAPER DANCE
JAUNT PRANK CAREER CAVORT
CURVET GAMBOL JAUNCE TITTUP
TRANCE PRANKLE SWAGGER
CAKEWALK
PRANCER HORSE DANCER CAPERER
PRANK JIG RAG RIG DECK DIDO
FOLD GAME JEST LARK PRAT REAK
ADORN CAPER FREAK SHINE SKITE
TRICK VAGUE BROGUE CURVET
FEGARY FIGARY FROLIC GAMBOL
SHAVIE VAGARY MARLOCK SPANGLE
ESCAPADE PRANCOME RIGWIDDIE
(PL.) REX GAMES JINKS
PRANKISH TRICKSY
PRASINE LEEK

PRAT PUSH NUDGE TRICK
PRATE GAB BUCK BUKH BUKK CARO
CHAT CLAP CLAT TALK BLATE
BOAST CLASH SCOLD BABBLE
CACKLE CLAVER JANGLE SQUIRT
TONGUE BLATHER BLATTER
CHATTER CLATTER PRATTLE
TWATTLE
PRATING GAFF CHATTER
PRATIQUE CUSTOM PRODUCT
PRATTLE CHAT CLACK BABBLE
BURBLE JANNER JAUNER YATTER
BLATTER CHATTER CLATTER
JAUNDER PRITTLE TRATTLE
TWADDLE BAVARDAGE
PRATTLING CHAVISH
PRAWN CARID NIPPER PENEID
SHRIMP SQUILLA CARIDEAN
CARIDOID CREVETTE MACRURAN
PRAWN KILLER SQUILLA
PRAXIS HABIT ACTION CUSTOM
PRACTICE
PRAY ASK BEG BID BLESS CRAVE
DAVEN SOUGH VOUCH INVITE
ENTREAT IMPLORE REQUEST
WRESTLE INVOCATE
(— FOR) BOON
PRAYA BUND BEACH STRAND
PRAYER ACT AHA AVE VOW BEAD
BENE BOON PLEA SUIT VOTE
AGNUS ALENU NAMAZ SALAT
ABODAH APPEAL ECTENE ERRAND
LITANY MANTRA MATINS ORISON
STEVEN VESPER YIZKOR BIDDING
COMPLIN FATIHAH GAYATRI
GEULLAH KADDISH MEMENTO
ORATION PRECULE PREFACE
TAHANUN ANAPHORA APOLYSIS
CATHISMA DEVOTION KEDUSHAH
MISERERE PETITION SUFFRAGE
TEHINNAH
(— BEADS) ROSARY
(— BOOK) MAHZOR MISSAL
SERVICE
(— LEADER) IMAM
(— OF DISMISSAL) APOLYSIS
(— RUG) NAMAZLIK
(— SHAWL) TALLITH
(— STICK) BAHO PAHO
(— TOWER) MINARET
(CANONICAL —S) BREVIARY
(CHIEF MOHAMMEDAN —) NAMAZ
(HINDU —) GAYATRI
(INWARD —) ACT
(JEWISH —) ALENU ABODAH
GEULLAH HOSHANA KADDISH
(LAST — OF DAY) COMPLIN
(LONG —) CATHISMA
(MUSLIM —) SALAH SALAT
(OPENING —) COLLECT
(SHORT —) GRACE COLLECT
(SILENT —) SECRET
(PL.) HOURS NORITO TIKKUN
CHAPLET
PRAYING ORISON IMPRECANT
PREACH EDIFY SOUGH TEACH
EXHORT GOSPEL SERMON DELIVER
HOMILIZE
PREACHER KHATIB MAGGID PARSON

TUBMAN DARSHAN LOLLARD
MARTEXT PROPHET ROUNDER
TEACHER TUBBIST TUBSTER
EXHORTER KOHELETH MINISTER
PARDONER PULPITER QOHELETH
SERMONER SPINTEXT SWADDLER
VARTABED
(PL.) PULPIT
PREACHING SPELL PULPIT SERMON
HEARING KERUGMA KERYGMA
PROPHECY PULPITRY SPELLING
PREACHY DIDACTIC
PREAMBLE PREFACE WHEREAS
PREARRANGED SET
PREBEND CANONRY
PREBENDARY PROVEND
PRE-CAMBRIAN MOINE EOZOIC
ARCHEAN
PRECARIOUS DICKY RISKY SHAKY
CASUAL INFIRM UNSURE DUBIOUS
CATCHING DELICATE INSECURE
PERILOUS UNSTABLE DANGEROUS
UNCERTAIN
PRECAUTION CARE GUARD CAUTEL
PRECEDE LEAD FOREGO HERALD
FORERUN PREFACE PREVENT
ANTECEDE PREAMBLE
PRECEDENCE LEAD PRIMACY
HERALDRY PRIORITY
(RIGHT OF —) PAS
(SOCIAL —) LEVEL
PRECEDENT LEAD SIGN MODEL
TOKEN USAGE INSTANCE ORIGINAL
SPECIMEN STANDARD AUTHORITY
PRECEDING OLD FORE WEST
BEFORE FORMER LEADING
ADJACENT PREVIOUS
(— ALL OTHERS) FIRST
PRECENTOR CANTOR PSALMIST
LETTERGAE
PRECEPT LAW HEST LINE RULE
TORA WRIT ADAGE AXIOM BREVE
MAXIM ORDER SUTRA SUTTA TORAH
BEHEST DICTATE MANDATE
WARRANT DOCTRINE DOCUMENT
LANDMARK
PRECEPTIVE DIDACTIC MANDATORY
PRECEPTOR TUTOR MASTER
PRECINCT BEAT AMBIT BOUND
CLOSE DOMAIN HIERON COLLEGE
LENAEUM SOCIETY TEMENOS
DISTRICT ENVIRONS
(PL.) AMBIT
PRECIOUS DEAR FINE LIEF RARE
VERY CHARY CHERE GREAT HONEY
CHOICE COSTLY DAINTY GOLDEN
POSING SILVER TENDER PRECISE
AFFECTED ORIENTAL OVERNICE
VALUABLE WORTHFUL
PRECIOUSNESS PRICE
PRECIPICE LIN KHUD LINN LLYN
PALI CLIFF KRANS SCREE SHEER
STEEP KRANTZ CLOGWYN
DOWNFALL HEADWALL
PRECIPITATE GEL CURD HURL
RASH HASTY HURRY SHOOT SPEED
STEEP ABRUPT COAGEL HASTEN
SLUDGE SUDDEN TUMBLE UNWARY
DISTILL LYCOPIN SUBSIDE

CATALYZE HEADLONG PROCLIVE
SETTLING
(— DYE) STRIKE
PRECIPITATELY HEADLING
HEADLONG SLAPDASH
PRECIPITATION HAIL MIST RAIN
SNOW HASTE SLEET VIRGA
PRECIPITOUS FULL RASH BRANT
BRENT HASTY STEEP ABRUPT
CHICHI STEEPY SUDDEN PRERUPT
HEADLONG
PRECIS JUNONIA SUMMARY
ABSTRACT
PRECISE SET FLAT HARD JUMP JUST
TIDY TRIG TRUE VERY CLEAN
CLOSE EXACT PRESS RIGID SOUND
FORMAL STARCH STRICT BUCKRAM
CAREFUL CERTAIN CLERKLY
CORRECT EXPRESS PERFECT
PERJINK STARCHY ABSOLUTE
ACCURATE DEFINITE EXPLICIT
HAIRLINE PUNCTUAL
PRECISELY BUT EVEN JUST CLEAN
SHARP FINELY JUSTLY STRAIT
EXACTLY
PRECISENESS RIGOR RIGOUR
PRIMNESS
PRECISIAN PRIG PURITAN
PRECISION NICETY CLARITY
ACCURACY DELICACY ELEGANCE
JUSTNESS
PRECISIONIST PEDANT
PRECLUDE BAR DENY STOP CLOSE
CROSS DEBAR ESTOP FORBID
HINDER IMPEDE OBVIATE PREVENT
SILENCE CONCLUDE INTERPEL
PRECOCIOUS PRECOX UNRIPE
FORWARD PREMATURE RATHERIPE
PRECONCEIVE IDEATE
PRECONDITION PRIUS
PRECURSOR USHER HERALD INITIAL
ANCESTOR PRODROME WAYMAKER
HARBINGER HEMIAUXIN
PREDACITY RAVEN RAVIN
PREDATOR COACTOR
PREDATORY HUNGRY HARMFUL
RAVENOUS
PREDECESSOR ANCESTOR
FOREGOER
(PL.) OLDERS
PREDELLA FOOTPACE
PREDESTINATION FATE DESTINY
ELECTION
PREDESTINE DOOM SLATE
FOREDOOM FOREPOINT
PREDETERMINE DESTINE FORECAST
PREDICAMENT FIX JAM SOUP SPOT
CLASS STATE STEAD PICKLE PLIGHT
SCRAPE DILEMMA IMPASSE
CATEGORY JUNCTURE QUANDARY
PREDICANT FRIAR PREACHER
DOMINICAN
PREDICATE BASE FOUND AFFIRM
ASSERT PRAISE PREACH COMMEND
DECLARE EXTREME PREDICT
PROCLAIM
PREDICT LAY BODE CALL DOPE
READ REDE AUGUR WEIRD HALSEN
FORESAY PRESAGE FOREBODE

FORECAST FORETELL PROPHESY
SOOTHSAY
(— EVIL) CROAK
PREDICTION DOPE WEIRD AUGURY
BODING BODWORD PORTENT
PRESAGE BODEWORD FORECAST
PROPHECY VATICINE
PREDILECTION BIAS HANG FANCY
FAVOR LIKING RELISH FONDNESS
PREDISPOSE BEND INCLINE
SUBJECT
PREDISPOSED PRONE PARTIAL
TENDING INCLINED
PREDISPOSITION ITCH DIATHESIS
PREDOMINANT GREAT RULING
CAPITAL REIGNING SUPERIOR
CULMINANT HEGEMONIC
PREDOMINATE RULE DOMINE
EXCEED GOVERN PREVAIL
PREE KISS PRIE TEST TASTE TRIAL
PRYING SAMPLE PROVING TASTING
PREEMINENT BIG TOP HIGH STAR
FIRST GRAND GREAT PALMARY
PASSING STELLAR SUPREME
FOREMOST PRECLARE SPLENDID
SUPERIOR PARAMOUNT
PREEMPT COLLAR
PREEN PIN PERK PICK TRIM DRESS
GLOAT PLUME PRINK PRUNE SWELL
TRICK BROOCH GODWIT SMOOTH
REPLUME
(— WINGS) WHET
PREFACE FRONT PROEM USHER
HERALD PRESAY PRECEDE
PREPOSE EXORDIUM FORETALK
FOREWORD PREAMBLE PROLOGUE
PREFATORY PROEMIAL
PREFECT WALI EPARC EPARCH
MONITOR PROVOST GOVERNOR
PRESIDENT
PREFECTURE EPARCHY
(CHINESE —) FU
(JAPANESE —) KEN
(TIBETAN —) JONG
PREFER LAY LIKE LOVE BRING
ELECT EXALT FAVOR OFFER
CHOOSE PROFER SELECT OUTRANK
PREFECT PRESENT PROMOTE
PROPOSE SURPASS
PREFERABLE LIEF RIGHT RATHER
ELIGIBLE
PREFERENCE GOO LIKE FAVOR
DESIRE LIKING RATHER DRUTHERS
FAVORITE PRIVILEGE PROMOTION
PREFIGURE TYPE IDEATE SHADOW
TYPIFY FORERUN FORESEE PREDICT
FORESHOW
PREFIX DUN DOON PREPOSE
PREGNANCY CYESIS TROUBLE
ACCYESIS FETATION OOCYESIS
GESTATION
PREGNANT BIG GONE OPEN GREAT
HEAVY QUICK READY BAGGED
CAUGHT COGENT GRAVID PAROUS
ENCEINT FERTILE GESTANT
TEEMING WEIGHTY CHILDING
FORCIBLE GERMINAL PRESSING
PREHALLUX CALCAR
PREHEND SEIZE

PREHISTORIC IMMEMORIAL
PREINDICATE PRESAGE FORESHOW
PREJUDICE BIAS DOWN HARM HURT
KINK TURN DERRY DAMAGE IMPAIR
INJURY SCUNDER SCUNNER
JAUNDICE PREJUDGE
PREJUDICED BIGOTED INSULAR
PARTIAL
PREJUDICIAL BIASED HURTFUL
CONTRARY DAMAGING INIMICAL
SINISTER
PRELATE CHIEF LEADER PRIEST
HIERARCH ORDINARY SUPERIOR
PRELIMINARY PRIOR PRELIM
PREFACE PRELUDE LIMINARY
PREAMBLE PREVIOUS
PRELUDE PROEM VERSET DESCANT
FORERUN INTRADA PREFACE
ANTELUDE BORSPIEL OVERTURE
RITORNEL VERSETTE VORSPIEL
PREMATURE UNRIPE IMMATURE
PREVIOUS TIMELESS UNTIMELY
PREMEDITATE FORNCAST
PURPENSE
PREMEDITATED SET STUDIED
PREPENSE
PREMIER CHIEF FIRST OLDEST
LEADING EARLIEST
PREMISE LEMMA MAJOR ASSUME
GROUND REASON SUMPTION
PREMIXED INSTANT
PREMIUM USE AGIO BACK AWARD
BONUS FANCY PRIZE SHAVE USURY
BOUNTY DEPORT REWARD
CONTANGO DONATIVE FOREGIFT
GIVEAWAY
PREMONITION OMEN HUNCH
NOTICE BODWORD PRESAGE
WARNING BODEWORD FORESCENT
PREMUNE SALTED
PREOCCUPATION HEART INSIGHT
FIXATION
PREOCCUPIED DEEP LOST RAPT
CRAZY ABSENT FILLED INTENT
CRACKED ABSORBED ENGROSSED
PREPARATION DIA FIG BALM DIBS
DOPE PREP CREAM FLASH GLAZE
JELLY READY ACETUM BLEACH
BLUING DERRIS FACIAL LOTION
MEGILP NEBULA PEPSIN SIMPLE
APPREST CLEANER DIPPING
EMANIUM ESSENCE ETHIOPS
EXTRACT FITNESS FONDANT
LINCTUS MELLITE PLACEBO
TRYPSIN VARNISH ABSTRACT
CONSERVE COSMETIC FIXATURE
GELOSINE INHALANT LAUDANUM
MEDICINE RACAHOUT TRAINING
MAKEREADY
(— **CONTAINING HONEY**) MELLITE
(— **FOR COLORING LIQUORS**) FLASH
(— **OF GRAPEJUICE**) DIBS
(**AROMATIC** —) ELIXIR
(**CHEESE** —) FONDU
(**CHEESELIKE** —) YOGURT YOGHURT
(**COSMETIC** —) HENNA
(**ENZYME** —) KOJI
(**EYELID** —) KOHL
(**IMPURE RADIOACTIVE** —) EMANIUM

(**INTOXICATING** —) BOZA
(**MEDICAL** —) STUFF
(**OPIUM** —) LAUDANUM
(**SALINE** —) LICK
(**SLOPPY** —) SLIBBERSAUCE
(**SWEET** —) DULCE
(**UNCTUOUS** —) CERATE
PREPARATORY PIONEER
PREPARE DO FIT FIX GET LAY ABLE
BUSK COOK GIRD MAKE PARE PLOT
PREP TILL YARK ATTLE BLEND
BRACE DIGHT DRAFT DRESS EQUIP
FRAME ORDER PREDY READY TRAIN
ADJUST DESIGN GRAITH ORDAIN
ADDRESS AFFAITE APPAREL
APPOINT CONCOCT CONFECT
DISPOSE EDUCATE PRODUCE
PROVIDE QUALIFY INSTRUCT
(— **BANQUET**) COVER
(— **BY BOILING**) BREW DECOCT
(— **BY HEAT**) FRIT
(— **CAPON**) SAUCE
(— **FISH**) CALVER
(— **FOOD**) DO COOK
(— **FOR BUILDING**) FRAME
(— **FOR BURIAL**) EMBALM
(— **FOR DISPLAY**) DRESS
(— **FOR PUBLICATION**) EDIT
(— **HASTILY**) RASH
(— **HEMP**) TAW
(— **LAND**) CURE
(— **ONESELF**) ADDRESS
(— **TEASEL HEADS**) CARP
PREPARED UP APT BUN FIT SET
BAAN BOON BOUN BOWN GIRT RIPE
YARE ALERT BOUND PREST READY
GRAITH CURRIED EQUIPPED
(**QUICKLY** —) RUNNING
PREPENSE DESIGN FORETHOUGHT
PREPONDERANCE MAJORITY
DOMINANCE
PREPONDERATE EXCEED INCLINE
SURPASS DOMINATE OUTWEIGH
PERSUADE
PREPOSSESS BIAS PREVENT
PREPOSSESSION BENT BIAS FETICH
FANTASY PREJUDICE
PREPOSTEROUS RICH INEPT
ABSURD FOOLISH LAPUTAN
GROTESQUE
PREROGATIVE GRACE HONOR
RIGHT ESNECY REGALE FACULTY
PECULIAR PRIVILEGE
PRESA LEAD
PRESAGE BODE HINT OMEN OSSE
SIGN ABODE AUGUR TOKEN
AUGURY BETIDE BETOKEN FORESEE
OMINATE PORTEND PREDICT
FOREBODE FORECAST FOREDOOM
FORETELL INDICATE PREAMBLE
PROPHESY
PRESBYTER ELDER PRIEST PRESTER
ANTISTES MINISTER
PRESBYTERIAN WHIG
PRESBYTERY SENIORY EXERCISE
PARSONAGE
PRESCIENCE PRESAGE FORESIGHT
PREVISION
PRESCIND SEVER DETACH

PRESCRIBE SET TAX ALLOT GUIDE
LIMIT ORDER ASSIGN DEFINE
DIRECT ENJOIN INDITE ORDAIN
APPOINT CONFINE CONTROL
DICTATE RESTRAIN
PRESCRIBED SET BASIC THETIC
THETICAL FORMULARY
PRESCRIPT LAW COMMAND
MANDATE PRECEPT
PRESCRIPTION RX BILL FORM
CIPHER RECIPE DICTATE FORMULA
PRESENCE EYE FACE SELF BEING
ASPECT BEARING COMPANY
ASSEMBLY INSTANCE
(**DIRECT** —) IMMEDIACY
PRESENT AIM BOX NOW BILL BOON
GIFT GIVE HAND HERE NEAR NIGH
SAND SHOW BEING CUDDY DOLLY
ENTER FEOFF GRANT NONCE OFFER
PLACE RAISE READY STAGE THERE
ACCUSE ACTUAL ADDUCE ALLEGE
AROUND BESTOW BOUNTY BROACH
CLOTHE CUMSHA DONATE DURANT
HANSEL KHILAT LATTER MODERN
NEARBY PREFER REGALE REGALO
XENIUM COMMEND CUMSHAW
DISPLAY DOUCEUR ETRENNE
EXHIBIT EXPOUND FAIRING FURNISH
HANDSEL INSTANT LARGESS
PERFORM PORRECT PRETEND
PROPINE RESIANT TASHRIF
BLESSING CONGIARY DONATION
GRATUITY INSTANCE LAGNAPPE
OFFERING PESHKASH RESIDENT
SOULCAKE SPORTULA
(— **AS GIFT**) DASH
(— **FOR ACCEPTANCE**) TENDER
(— **FROM PUPIL TO TEACHER**)
MINERVAL
(— **IN DETAIL**) DISCUSS
(— **IN MIND**) DEAR
(— **ONESELF**) APPEAR
(— **TO SOLDIERS**) CONGIARY
(— **TO STRANGER**) XENIUM
(— **TO VIEW**) YIELD
(— **WITHOUT WARRANT**) OBTRUDE
(**ALWAYS** —) CHRONIC
(**BRIDEGROOM'S** —) HANDSEL
(**CEREMONIAL** —) KHILAT
PRESENTATION BILL GALA GIFT
SHOW DROLL IMAGE DHARMA
MUSTER SCHEMA BILLING DISPLAY
EPITOME HOOKUPU PRESENT
SPECIES ANALYSIS BESTOWAL
DELIVERY DONATION EXPOSURE
CANDLEMAS
PRESENTIMENT FEELING PRESAGE
BODEMENT FOREFEEL PRENOTION
PRESENTLY NOW ANON ENOW
SOON SHORTLY DIRECTLY
PRESERVATION FILING SAVING
KEEPING SERVATION
PRESERVATIVE SALT BORAX SPICE
SUGAR CONSERVE TREATMENT
PRESERVE CAN JAR CORN HAIN
HOLD KEEP SAVE BLESS GUARD
SERVE SPARE SWEET WITIE ATHOLD
BOTTLE COMFIT DEFEND EMBALM
FREEZE GOGGLE POWDER RETAIN

SECURE SHIELD UPHOLD CONDITE
FORFEND KYANIZE PROTECT
RAISINE RESERVE SUCCADE
SUSTAIN CHOWCHOW CONSERVE
ENSHRINE MAINTAIN MOTHBALL
PARADISE WITHSAVE
(— **BY BOILING WITH SUGAR)**
CANDY
(— **BY SALTING)** CORN CURE SALT
(— **OF GRAPES)** RAISINE
(— **WOOD)** KYANIZE
(**GAME** —) MOOR SHIKARGAH
(**HUNTING** —) WALK
(PL.) KONFYT
PRESERVED WET CONFECT
BRANDIED POWDERED
PRESIDE RULE GUIDE DIRECT
MODERATE
(— **OVER)** KEEP
PRESIDENCY MADRAS PRYTANY
PRESIDENT MIR FOUD PREX PROXY
REEVE DEACON RECTOR PRAESES
PREFECT
(— **OF SUPREME COURT)** LAWMAN
(— **OF TRADE)** DEACON
PRESIGNIFY PRESAGE FORETOKEN
PRESS FLY HUG JAM SIT BEAR BEND
CRAM DOME DROP DRUK HORN
HUSH IRON JAMB KISS PLOT SERR
THEW TUCK URGE VICE YERK
ARGUE BESET BRIZZ CHAFE CHIRT
CROWD CRUSH DRIVE EXACT
FORCE KNEAD MIDST PRIZE SCREW
SHREW SMASH STAMP STUFF TWIST
WEIGH WRING ASSAIL CHISEL
CLOSET COARCT CRUNCH GOFFER
HARASS JOBBER MANGLE NUDDLE
PREACE SQUASH STRAIN STRESS
THRAST THREAP THREAT THREEP
THRIMP THRING THRONG THRUST
AFFLICT ATTEMPT BESEECH
BESIEGE CONCISE CRUMPLE
EMBRACE ENVIRON FLATBED
IMPRESS MACHINE OPPRESS
SCROOGE SCRUNGE SQUEEZE
THRUTCH CALENDER COMPRESS
PRESSURE SCROUNGE SQUEEGEE
SURROUND
(— **AGAINST)** CONTACT
(— **CLOSE)** NUDDLE
(— **CLOSELY AND PAINFULLY)** MASH
(— **DOWN)** QUAT
(— **FOR WINE)** TORCULAR
(— **FORWARD)** DRIVE BREAST
(— **HARSHLY)** GRIND
(— **IN CHEESE VAT)** CHISEL
CHIZZEL
(— **INTO)** THRIMBLE THRUMBLE
(— **ON ANVIL)** HORN
(— **ONWARD)** STRETCH
(— **OUT)** EXTRUDE
(— **PAPER)** COUCH
(— **TOGETHER)** SERRY
(— **UPON)** ELBOW DOWNBEAR
(— **WITH HEAD OR HORNS)** BOX
(— **WITH VIOLENCE)** DRIVE
PRESS AGENT FLACK
PRESSED SERRIED
(— **WITH BUSINESS)** THRONG

(— **WITH LEFTHAND FOREFINGER)**
BARRED
PRESSING RASH CRYING URGENT
CLAMANT EARNEST EXIGENT
INSTANT SQUEEZE CRITICAL
PREGNANT
PRESSMAN PIG MINDER PROVER
PRINTER
PRESSURE JAM HEAD HEAT PEND
PUSH SWAY DRIVE FORCE IMAGE
PINCH STAMP DURESS STRESS
THRONG WEIGHT BEARING
MERCURY PUSHING SQUEEZE
TENSION URGENCY EXACTION
EXIGENCY FUGACITY PRESSION
(— **GROUP)** LOBBY
(— **OF 1 DYNE)** BARAD
(— **ON INSTRUMENT STRING)** STOP
(— **UNIT)** TORR MICRON
(**LIQUID** —) HEAD
(**MANUAL** —) TAXIS
(**VAPOR** —) FUGACITY
PRESSURE COOKER STEAMER
AUTOCLAVE
PRESSWORK BACKUP
PRESTIDIGITATOR PALMER
JUGGLER PYTHONIC
PRESTIGE FACE MANA CASTE IKBAL
IZZAT KUDOS CACHET STATUS
STATURE ILLUSION INFLUENCE
PRESTO QUICKLY SPEEDILY
PRESUME BEAR DARE GROW IMPLY
INFER ASSUME EXPECT DARESAY
SUPPOSE
PRESUMING ARROGANT FAMILIAR
PRESUMPTION JOLLITY OUTRAGE
PRESUME AUDACITY SUCCUDRY
SURQUIDY
PRESUMPTUOUS BOLD PERT FRESH
PROUD WICKED WILFUL FORWARD
HAUGHTY ARROGANT ASSUMING
FAMILIAR INSOLENT FOOLHARDY
PRESUPPOSE IMPLY POSIT ASSUME
EXPECT PREMISE FORETAKE
PRETA PETA
PRETEND ACT LET FAKE MAKE
MOCK SHAM CLAIM FEIGN AFFECT
ASPIRE ASSERT ASSUME GAMMON
INTEND OBTEND POSSUM RECKON
SEMBLE ATTEMPT PORTEND
PRESUME PROFESS SUPPOSE
VENTURE SIMULATE
(— **IGNORANCE)** CONNIVE
(— **TO)** FA
PRETENDED FAKE SHAM BOGUS
FALSE IRONIC UNREAL ALLEGED
ASSUMED COLORED FEIGNED
SEEMING AFFECTED IRONICAL
SIMULATE
PRETENDER FOP FAKE IDOL CHEAT
COWAN FAKER FRAUD QUACK
PSEUDO SEEMER AEOLIST
CLAIMANT IMPOSTOR INTENDER
TARTUFFE
(— **TO LEARNING)** SCIOLIST
PRETENDING FICTION
PRETENSE ACT AIR FACE GRIM
MIEN PLEA RUSE SCUG SHAM SHOW
SIGN WILE CLOAK COLOR COVER

FEINT GLOSS GLOZE STUDY
EXCUSE HUMBUG CHARADE FAITERY
FASHION FICTION GRIMACE
PRETEXT PURPOSE UMBRAGE
ARTIFICE DISGUISE POSTICHE
POSTIQUE SEMBLANT
PRETENSION PARADE VANITY
PRETEXT
PRETENTIOUS BIG BRAG HIGH SIDY
FLASH GAUDY PUFFY SHOWY
BRAGGY GEWGAW GLOSSY PUFFED
ROCOCO SHODDY TINSEL BOMBAST
POMPOUS TOPPING BRAGGART
PRETENTIOUSNESS SIDE SWANK
PRETERMIT OMIT NEGLACT
SUSPEND INTERRUPT
PRETERNATURAL GOUSTY GOUSTIE
STRANGE ABNORMAL UNCOMMON
UNEARTHLY
(— **BEING)** MARE
PRETEXT PEG FLAM MASK PLEA
CLOAK COLOR COVER GLOSS
SALVO STALL EXCUSE REFUGE
SCONCE APOLOGY UMBRAGE
OCCASION PRETENCE
PRETTIFY EYEWASH
PRETTY APT GEY PAT ABLE BRAW
CUTE DEFT FAIR FEAT FINE GAIN
GENT GOOD JOLI MILD POOR TRIM
BONNY DINKY JOLIE POOTY PURTY
QUITE SWEET BONITA DIMBER
FINELY INCONY MINION PRATTY
RATHER TRETIS CLEMENT CUNNING
DOLLISH GENTEEL BUDGEREE
PRECIOUS
(— **WELL)** GAILY GAYLY
PRETTY-PRETTY KEEPSAKE
PREVAIL WIN BEAR BEAT REIGN
WIELD INDUCE OBTAIN CONQUER
PERSIST SUCCEED TRIUMPH
DOMINATE
(— **BECAUSE BEYOND CONTROL)**
RAGE
(— **OVER)** SURMOUNT
(— **UPON)** GET FOLD LEAD ARGUFY
ENTICE INDUCE OBTAIN ENTREAT
OVERSWAY
PREVAILING RIFE GOING USUAL
CURRENT DOMINANT
PREVALENCE RUN
PREVALENT UP RIFE BRIEF
COMMON POTENT CURRENT
GENERAL POPULAR REGNANT
CATHOLIC EPIDEMIC POWERFUL
PREVARICATE LIE EVADE STRAY
WANDER QUIBBLE SHUFFLE
PREVENT BAR LET HELP KEEP NILL
SHUN STAY STOP TENT WARN
AVERT CHECK DEBAR DETER ESTOP
ARREST DEFEND FORBID FORLET
HINDER OUTRUN RETAIN REVOKE
SECURE FORFEND FORLEIT
IMPEACH INHIBIT PRECEDE RETRACT
ANTEVERT INTERPEL PRECLUDE
WITHHOLD
(— **OPPONENT FROM SCORING)**
CHICAGO
PREVENTION PREFACE ESTOPPEL
OBSTACLE PREJUDICE

PREVIEW SNEAK FUTURAMA
PREVIOUS HASTY PRIOR BEFORE FORMER RATHER EARLIER LEADING FOREGONE
PREVIOUSLY ERE YET ERST FORE SUPRA BEFORE ALREADY HASTILY PRIORLY FORMERLY HITHERTO
PREVISION FORESEE FORECAST FORESIGHT
PREY ROB FEED GAME SOYL TIRE BOOTY PREDE RAVEN RAVIN SPOIL QUARRY RAVAGE RAVINE VICTIM CAPTURE PILLAGE PLUNDER ROBBERY SPREATH VULTURE
(— UPON) DEVOUR PICAROON DEPREDATE
PREYER KITE
PRIAM (DAUGHTER OF —) CREUSA POLYXENA CASSANDRA
(SLAYER OF —) PYRRHUS
(SON OF —) PARIS HECTOR TROILUS
(WIFE OF —) HECUBA
PRIAPISM TENTIGO
PRICE LAY ANTE COST FARE FEER FIAR FIER FOOT ODDS PRYS RATE BRIBE CHEAP CLOSE VALUE WORTH CHARGE FIGURE HANSEL TARIFF AVERAGE CATALOG CRANAGE EXPENSE FURNACE HANDSEL PRETIUM STORAGE CARRIAGE FERRIAGE INTEREST
(— FOR KEEPING GOODS) STORAGE
(LOW —) WANWORTH
(PROPER —) VALUE
(REDUCED —) SALE BARGAIN
(RISING —S) BOOM INFLATION
PRICELESS RARE COSTLY UNIQUE UNSALABLE
PRICK DOT JAG BROD DROB FOIN GOAD JAGG PECK PING PROG SPUR STAB TANG URGE DRESS ERECT POINT PREEN PUNCH STEEK BROACH GALLOP INTENT LAUNCH POUNCE PRITCH SKEWER STITCH TARGET THRUST TWINGE POINTED BULLSEYE
(— OUT) SPOT
(— PAINFULLY) STING
(— WITH NAIL) CLY CLOY
PRICKED PIQUE
PRICKER PROD NEEDLE STABBER
PRICKET DAG SNUFFER SPITTER
PRICKING SMART PUNGENT RETRACT POIGNANT POINTURE PUNCTION
PRICKLE PIKE SETA SPEAR THORN BASKET ACANTHA ACULEUS PRINKLE SPICULA
PRICKLY BURRY JAGGY SHARP SPINY URCHIN SPINOSE SPINOUS STICKLY THISTLY ECHINATE MURICATE SCABROUS SCRATCHY SPICULAR STICKERY STINGING VEXATIOUS
PRICKLY ASH RUEWORT
PRICKLY PEAR TUN TUNA NOPAL SABRA OPUNTIA PINPILLOW
PRICKLY-POINTED PUNGENT

PRICKLY POPPY COCKSCOMB
PRIDE HEAT HORN LUST POMP RUFF ADORN CREST GLORY ORGUL PLUME PRIME WLANK EXCESS HUBRIS METTLE NOSISM VANITY COMPANY CONCEIT DISDAIN EGOTISM GLORIFY HAUTEUR STOMACH SURQUIDY WLONKHEDE
(— ONESELF) PIQUE
(EXCESSIVE —) SWELLING
PRIDEFUL FASTUOUS
PRIEST EN CURA CURE DEAN EZRA IMAM MAGA COHEN EPULO IMAUM ISIAC MOBED PADRE PATER SABIO SARIP VICAR ZADOK ABACES AMAUTA BHIKKU BISHOP DASTUR DIVINE FALMEN FATHER FLAMEN GALLAH GALLUS GELONG GETSUL GOSAIN JETHRO KAHUNA LEVITE POWWOW SHAMAN ANANIAS ARBACES CALCHAS CASSOCK CHANTER DESTOUR DUSTOOR GALLACH LAOCOON PANDITA PAPALOI PATENER PATRICO PHINEAS POONGEE PRESTER STOLIST TEACHER TOHUNGA BABAYLAN BEROSSOS CHRYSEIS HANANIAH KASHYAPA MINISTER PANDARAM PENANCER PONTIFEX POONGHIE SACERDOS SEMINARY SOGGARTH SYRIARCH TALISMAN VARDAPET ZADOKITE
(— OF APOLLO) CALCHAS CHRYSEIS
(— OF CYBELE) CORYBANT
(— OF RAMA) KASHYAPA
(— OF RHEA) CURETE
(BABYLONIAN —) BEROSSOS
(BUDDHIST —) LAMA BHIKKU GELONG POONGEE POONGHIE
(CHIEF — OF SHRINE) EN
(CHIEF —) SYRIARCH
(EGYPTIAN —) ARBACES CHOACHYTE
(EUNUCH —) GALLUS
(FRENCH —) PERE SULPICIAN
(GYPSY —) PATRICO
(HIGH —) ELI SARIP DASTUR KAHUNA DESTOUR PHINEAS PONTIFF PRELATE CAIAPHAS HIERARCH JEHOIADA PONTIFEX
(HINDU —) PANDARAM
(INCA —) AMAUTA
(LAMAIST —) GETSUL
(MAORI —) TOHUNGA
(MORO —) SARIP PANDITA
(MOSLEM —) TALISMAN
(PAGAN —) BABAYLAN
(PARISH —) CURA CURE PAPA POPE PARSON PERSON SECULAR
(ROMAN —) EPULO FLAMEN
(TIBETAN —) LAMA
(VAISHNAVA —) GOSAIN
(PL.) LUPERCI
PRIEST-DOCTOR SHAMAN WABENO
PRIESTESS NUN ENTUM HORSE MAMBO MAMBU BACBUC PYTHIA DIOTIMA MAMALOI PHOIBAD PHITONES
(— OF APOLLO) PYTHIA PHOEBAD

(— OF THE BOTTLE) BACBUC
(BABYLONIAN —) ENTUM
(VOODOO —) HORSE
PRIESTFISH CHERNA ROCKFISH
PRIESTHOOD SALII SACERDOCY
PRIEST-KING PATESI
PRIESTLY LEVITIC SACERDOTAL
PRIG BEG FOP BRAD BUCK NAIL SMUG DANDY FILCH PLEAD STEAL THIEF FELLOW HAGGLE PERSON PILFER TINKER ENTREAT PURITAN QUIBBLE
PRIGGER THIEF
PRIM MIM NEAT TRIG TRIM MIMZY DEMURE FORMAL MIMSEY PRIVET PROPER STUFFY MISSISH PRECISE PRIMSIE
PRIMACY CHIEFTY PRIMITY HEADSHIP
PRIMA DONNA DIVA STAR
PRIMARY CYAN BASIC CHIEF FIRST PRIME CAUCUS DIRECT FONTAL MANUAL MAGENTA RADICAL ARCHICAL CARDINAL HYPOGENE ORIGINAL PRIMEVAL
PRIMATE BISHOP GALAGO LEADER PREMAN PRINCIPAL
PRIME MAY FANG FILL LOAD MAIN CHIEF COACH FIRST PRIDE TONIC YOUTH CHOICE FLOWER SPRING CENTRAL LEADING LUSTFUL PREPARE DOMINEER ORIGINAL YOUTHFUL PRINCIPAL
PRIME MINISTER ATABEG PREMIER
PRIMER ABC CAP WAFER CORDERY HORNBOOK
PRIMEVAL OLD NATIVE ANCIENT OGYGIAN PRIMARY PRISTINE PRIMITIVE
PRIMING MORSING TWOPENNY CLEARCOLE
PRIMING IRON DRIFT
PRIMING WIRE PICKER
PRIMITIVE DARK CRUDE EARLY FIRST GROSS NAIVE PLAIN PRIME FANTEE GOTHIC PRIMAL SAVAGE SIMPLE ANCIENT ARCHAIC PRIMARY PRISCAN BARBARIC EARLIEST IGNORANT ORIGINAL PRISTINE
PRIMNESS PRUDERY
PRIMORDIAL CRUDE FIRST PRIMARY ARCHICAL EARLIEST PRIMEVAL
PRIMORDIUM BUD
PRIMP PRIM ADORN PREEN PRINK
PRIMROSE GAY OXLIP SPINK FLOWER SUNCUP COWSLIP FLOWERY SCABISH AURICULA PLUMROCK SCURVISH AFTERGLOW PIMPERNEL
PRIMULA OXLIP COWSLIP PRIMWORT
PRINCE MIN RAS DUKE EARL EMIR IMAM KHAN KING KNEZ LORD NASI RAJA RANA RIAL SAID WANG ALDER EBLIS EMEER FURST GEBIR PWYLL RAJAH SAYID ARJUNA DESPOT DYNAST SHERIF SOLDAN BHARATA ELECTOR GLAUCUS HELENUS MONARCH TANCRED TOPARCH ZERBINO ARCHDUKE CARDINAL

MAMILIUS OROONOKO PLORIZEL RASSELAS SARPEDON
(— OF ABYSSINIA) RAS RASSELAS
(— OF APOSTATE ANGELS) DEVIL EBLIS
(— OF ARGO) DIOMED DIOMEDES
(— OF BOHEMIA) FLORIZEL
(— OF DARKNESS) DEVIL SATAN
(— OF DEMONS) BEELZEBUB
(— OF DYFED) PWYLL
(— OF SALERNO) TANCRED
(— OF SCOTLAND) ZERBINO
(— SOLD INTO SLAVERY) OROONOKO
(— WITH CHARLEMAGNE) ASTOLF ASTOLFO
(ANGLO-SAXON —) ADELING ATHELING
(ARAB —) SHERIF
(CHINESE —) WANG
(GERMAN —) FURST ELECTOR
(INDIAN —) RAJA RANA RAJAH BHARATA AHLUWALIA
(LYCIAN —) GLAUCUS SARPEDON
(MOHAMMEDAN —) SOLDAN
(MOSLEM —) IMAM SAID SAYID SAYYID SHEIKH SOLDAN
(PETTY —) SATRAP VERGOBRET
(SERVIAN —) CRAL
(SLAVIC —) KNEZ
(TROJAN —) HELENUS
PRINCELY NOBLE ROYAL KINGLY STATELY SOVEREIGN
PRINCE'S FEATHER LILAC PILEWORT
PRINCESS AIDA ELSA RANI DANAE PALLA RANEE SARAH CREUSA GLAUKE ILDICO MADAME PSYCHE ANTIOPE CORONIS PHYLLIS DRAUPADI MAHARANI
(— CHANGED INTO CROW) CORONIS
(— MOTHER OF ZEUS) ANTIOPA ANTIOPE
(— OF ARGOS) DANAE
(— OF CORINTH) CREUSA GLAUKE
(— WHO SLEW ATTILA) ILDICO
(MOHAMMEDAN —) BEGUM
(THRACIAN —) PHYLLIS
(TYRIAN —) DIDO
PRINCEWOOD CYP BARIA CYPRE CERILLO CANALETE SALMWOOD
PRINCIPAL ARCH BOSS HEAD HIGH MAIN STAR CHIEF FIRST GRAND GREAT PRIME STOCK AUCTOR CORPUS MASTER STAPLE CAPITAL CAPTAIN CENTRAL CHATTEL DOMINUS PREMIER PRIMARY SALIENT STELLAR FOREMOST OFFICIAL PRESTANT PRINCELY
(— OF SCHOOL) PRECEPTOR HEADMASTER
PRINCIPALITY ZUPA ARZAVA ARZAWA ORANGE SATRAPY APPANAGE DESPUTAT
PRINCIPLE JUS LAW RTA TAO BASE FATE RITA RULE SEED YANG AGENT AXIOM BASIS CANON CAUSE DATUM PRANA SPARK STUFF TENET

ANIMUS CNICIN COGITO CORTIN ELIXIR EMBRYO FAGINE GOSPEL ARCHEUS BROCARD BUFAGIN CLYSSUS ELEMENT FORMULA GENERAL PRECEPT QUASSIN RADICAL THEOREM URGRUND DOCTRINE GOSSYPOL INTIMISM LANDMARK NICOTINE SANCTION SPECIFIC TINCTURE
(— ACCEPTED AS TRUE) CANON
(— FROM TOAD) BUFAGIN
(— IN BEECHNUTS) FAGINE
(— OF BLESSED THISTLE) CNICIN
(— OF COTTONSEED) GOSSYPOL
(— OF EXISTENCE) TATTVA
(— OF INDIVIDUATION) AHANKARA
(— OF KEY IN MUSIC) TONALITY
(— OF REST) ADHARMA
(COSMIC —) HEAVEN URGRUND PRAJAPATI
(DOGMATIC —) DICTUM
(ELEMENTARY —) BROCARD
(FEMALE —) YIN
(FIRST —) ABC SEED ARCHE
(FUNDAMENTAL —) GROUNDSEL
(GERMINAL —) STAMEN
(GOVERNING —) HINGE
(GUIDING —) SQUARE
(LIFE —) SOUL GHOST PRANA
(MALE —) YANG PURUSHA
(MOHAMMEDAN THEOLOGICAL —) IJMA
(MORAL —) SCRUPLE
(NARCOTIC —) FAGINE
(ONTOLOGICAL —) DHARMA
(PRIMAL —) APEIRON
(PROMINENT —) KEY
(RHYTHMICAL —) ACCENT
(SPIRITUAL —) SOUL
(SUMMARY OF —S) CREED
(VITAL —) JIVA SPIRIT STAMEN ARCHAEUS
PRINK PERK PRIG WINK ADORN PRICK PRIMP PRUNE BEDECK SMUDGE
PRINT CUT GAY GUM DRUK MARK TYPE FUDGE PORTY PRESS SEPIA STAMP BANNER BORDER CARBON CARBRO ENFACE LETTER STRIKE BROMOIL DROPOUT DUOTYPE ENGRAVE GRAPHIC GRAVURE IMPRESS PUBLISH TRACING VANDYKE VESTIGE WOODCUT AQUATONE CALOTYPE CHLORIDE DRYPOINT HALFTONE INSCRIBE LEIMTYPE MONOTYPE POSITIVE URUSHIYE
(— OTHER SIDE) BACK
(— TO RIGHT) ADSCRIPT
PRINTED FONTED
PRINTER TYPO TWICER PRESSMAN IMPRIMENT
(AID TO —) DEVIL
(PL.) TYPOTHETAE
PRINTER'S DEVIL FLY
PRINTING TIRAGE EDITION VIGOREUX CHARACTER IMPRIMERY
(LAST —) THIRTY
PRION PETREL

PRIONID BEETLE
PRIONODON LINSANG
PRIOR ERE OLD FORE PAST EIGNE ELDER FORMER RATHER ALREADY EARLIER FARTHER ANTERIOR FOREHAND HITHERTO PREVIOUS
PRIORITY PRIVILEGE PRECEDENCE
PRIORY ABBEY NUNNERY CLOISTER PRIORATE
PRISM BLOCK NICOL CYLINDER SPECTRUM WERNICKE
PRISMATIC SHOWY BRILLIANT
PRISON GIB JUG BRIG COOP GAOL HELL HOCK HOLD HOLE JAIL KEEP LAKE QUAD QUOD SHOP STIR WARD BAGNE CLINK FLEET GRATE KITTY LODGE POUND RATEL TENCH TRONK VAULT BAGNIO BAILEY BUCKET CARCEL CARCER COOLER JIGGER RATTLE BASTILE BOCARDO BULLPEN COLLEGE COMPTER CONFINE COUNTER DUNGEON FREEZER GEHENNA KIDCOTE LUDGATE NEWGATE DARTMOOR HOOSEGOW TOLBOOTH TRIBUNAL
(— CAMP) OFLAG
(— IN ROME) TULLIANUM
(AUSTRALIAN —) TENCH
(UNIVERSITY —) CARCER
PRISONER CON POW MUTE LIFER DETENU INMATE REMAND CAITIFF CAPTIVE CONVICT GAOLBIRD JAILBIRD LONGTIMER
PRISONER'S BASE CHEVY CHIVY
PRISSY PRIM FUSSY DAINTY FINICKY PRUDISH PRIGGISH SISSIFIED
PRISTINE NEW PURE FIRST FRESH ANCIENT PRIMARY ORIGINAL PRIMEVAL PRIMITIVE UNSPOILED
PRIVACY RECESS SECRET PRIVITY RETREAT SECRECY DARKNESS INTIMACY INTIMITY SOLITUDE SECLUSION
(IN —) ASIDE
(PL.) VERENDA
PRIVATE SNUG ALONE GUIDE KHASS PRIVY SHARE CLOSET COVERT INWARD POCKET SECRET STANCH POSTERN SECRECY SEVERAL SOLDIER CIVILIAN ESOTERIC HOMEFELT INTERNAL INTIMATE PERSONAL SINGULAR UMBRATILE
PRIVATEER CAPER PIRATE ALABAMA CORSAIR DUNKIRK PICKEER
PRIVATELY ASIDE INWARDLY SECRETLY
PRIVATION LOSS WANT PENURY PERISH ABSENCE POVERTY HARDSHIP
PRIVET PRIM HEDGE SKEDGE IBOLIUM PRIMWORT PRIMPRINT
PRIVILEGE UP PUT SOC DOWN HAND STAR TEAM CLAIM ENTRY FAVOR FRANK GRACE HONOR REGAL RIGHT THEAM EXCUSE INDULT MUNITY OCTROI OPTION PATENT WARREN CHARTER FALDAGE FREEDOM LIBERTY MITZVAH PASSAGE GRANDEZA STANDAGE

(— **TO USE THINGS**) BOTE
(**ACQUIRED** —) EASEMENT
(**POKER** —) EDGE
(**POOL** —) STAR
PRIVILEGED CURULE EXEMPT
LICENSED
(— **PLACE**) WARREN
PRIVY WC GONG BIFFY DRAFT ISSUE
JAKES PETTY QUIET SIEGE CLOSET
OFFICE SECRET DRAUGHT FOREIGN
LATRINE PRIVATE DONICKER
FAMILIAR INTIMATE OUTHOUSE
PERSONAL STEALTHY WARDROBE
PRIZE CUP FEE GEM PRY BELL BEND
GAME GREE PALM PREY PRIX RATE
RISK AWARD BACON BOOTY LEVER
PLATE PLUME PRICE PURSE STAKE
VALUE WAGER ESTEEM GLAIVE
PRAISE PREMIO TROPHY BENEFIT
CAPTURE GARLAND PREMIUM
ESTIMATE LEVERAGE PURCHASE
REPRISAL TREASURE
(— **FOR LAST**) MELL
(**FIRST** —) BLUE
(**LOTTERY** —) LOT TERN
PRIZE CUP PEWTER
PRIZED DEAR CHARY
PRIZEFIGHT GO BOUT MILL MATCH
SCRAP
PRIZEFIGHTER BOXER BLEEDER
FIGHTER SLUGGER PUGILIST
PRIZE MONEY GUNNAGE
PRO TO FOR FAVORING
PROA PARO PRAU PROW PAROO
PRAHU CARACOA
PROBABILITY ODDS SHOW CHANCE
PROBABLE MAYBE LIKELY PROBAL
TOPICAL APPARENT FEASIBLE
POSSIBLE
PROBABLY BELIKE LIKELY
PROBATION TEST PROOF TRIAL
PAROLE EVIDENCE
PROBATIONER STIBBLER
PROBE SEEK SIFT STOG TENT ENTER
GROPE SOUND FATHOM SEARCH
SEEKER STYLET THRUST ACCOUNT
EXAMINE INQUIRY SOUNDER
GYROMELE
PROBITY HONESTY INTEGRITY
RECTITUDE
PROBLEM NUT SUM WHY BOYG
CRUX DUAL ISSE KNOT BLAIK
HYDRA POSER APORIA ENIGMA
BUGBEAR DILEMMA FUNERAL
GORDIAN GRUELER TICHLER
EXERCISE HEADACHE JEOPARDY
QUESTION STICKLER
(**CHESS** —) DUAL MOVER SUIMATE
MINIATURE
PROBLEMATICAL DUBIOUS
DOUBTFUL PUZZLING UNCERTAIN
UNDECIDED
PROBOSCIS NOSE SNOUT TRUMP
TRUNK ANTLIA LINGUA SIPHON
SYPHON TONGUE ROSTRUM
PROBOSCIS MONKEY KAHA KAHUA
PROCAVIA HYRAX
PROCEDURE BIAS FORM HAVE VEIN
DRAFT ORDER TENOR TRACK

AFFAIR COURSE METHOD POLITY
SYSTEM DRAUGHT PROCESS
PRODUCT ACTIVITY PROTOCOL
(**PRESCRIBED** —S) CEREMONY
(**ROUNDABOUT** —) CIRCUITY
(**SECRET** —) STEALTH
(**UNWISE** —) FOLLY
PROCEED DO GO BANG BEAR FAND
FARE FLOW FOND HAVE MAKE
MARK MOVE PASS ROAM ROLL
SEEK STEP TAKE TOOL TOUR WEAR
WEND WIND YEDE AMBLE ARISE
DRESS FOUND FRAME ISSUE MARCH
REACH BREEZE INTEND PURSUE
RESULT SPRING STRAKE STRIKE
ADVANCE AGGRESS DEVOLVE
EMANATE FORTHGO PRETEND
STRETCH CONTINUE PROGRESS
(— **AIMLESSLY**) CIRCLE
(— **ALONE**) SINGLE
(— **CLUMSILY**) FLOUNDER
(— **OBLIQUELY**) CUT
(— **RAGGEDLY**) HALT
(— **RAPIDLY**) STRETCH
(— **UNSTEADILY**) DRIDDLE
(— **WITH DIFFICULTY**) STRUGGLE
(PL.) TAKE VAIL AVAILS INCOME
PROFITS PROVENT RETURNS
PREVENUE
PROCEEDING ACT DEED FARE PLOY
STEP AFFAIR AMPARO COURSE
DOMENT ISSUANT MEASURE
ONGOING PASSANT QUIETUS
TEMANET WARRANT CONCURSO
INSTANCE PLACITUM PRACTICE
(— **BY THREES**) TERNARY
(— **FROM GOD**) DIVINE
(— **FROM THE EARTH**) TELLURIC
(**COURT** —S) TRIAL
(**INDIRECT** —S) AMBAGES
(**PARLIAMENTARY** —S) HUSTINGS
(**RECORDED** —S) ACTA
PROCERITY HEIGHT TALLNESS
PROCESS RUN FANG FOOT TINA
WRIT CREST FURCA HAMUS MUCRO
SPINA CALCAR CAPIAS CILIUM
COURSE FEELER HABEAS INTEND
METHOD REPORT ACCOUNT
FURCULA GOBBING HAMULUS
ISOLATE LAMELLA MANDATE
SPATULA SUMMONS ACTIVITY
APPENDIX FILAMENT FRENULUM
GRAINING INSTANCE
(— **OF BONE**) HORN
(— **OF CHANGE**) ACTION
(— **OF CREATING VACUUM**)
EXHAUST
(— **OF DYEING**) BATIK HANKING
(— **OF METALPLATING**) ACIERAGE
(— **OF PACKING**) GOBBING
(— **OF REASONING**) ALGEBRA
(— **OF SUPPLYING WANTAGE**)
ULLING
(— **ON FISH'S HEAD**) LACINIA
(— **PAPER**) CONVERT
(— **TO RECOVER LAND**) DADENHUDD
(**ABRUPT** —) MUCRO
(**ALCHEMICAL** —) DIPLOSIS
(**ARTISTIC** —) FROTTAGE

(**CALENDERING** —) SWISSING
(**CARBON** —) AUTOTYPE
(**CERAMIC** —) FIRING
(**COATING** —) BLOOMING
(**CURVED** —) HAMUS
(**DEVELOPMENTAL** —) ANCESTRY
(**EARLIKE** —) AURICLE
(**FALCONRY** —) IMPING
(**FINISHING** —) BRUSHING CRABBING
(**FORKED** —) FURCA FURCULA
(**HELMETLIKE** —) CASQUE
(**HOOKLIKE** —) HAMULUS
(**HORNSHAPED** —) CORNICLE
(**INTELLECTUAL** —S) COGITO
(**KNOBLIKE** —) BOSS
(**LEGAL** —) BAIL SUIT CAUSE
ATTAINT INSTANCE
(**MATHEMATICAL** —) ADDITION
DIVISION
(**MENTAL** —) COMPOUND
(**MINING** —) STOPING
(**MOVIE-MAKING** —) SLATING
(**NERVELIKE** —) AXON AXONE
(**PHOTOGRAPHIC** —) CARBRO
(**POINTED** —) AWN SPINE STYLUS
LANGUET
(**PRINTING** —) GRAVURE STENCIL
INTAGLIO
(**REORGANIZATION** —) HEMIXIS
(**SMALL POINTED** —) AWN
(**SPINNING** —) JACKING
(**TEXTILE** —) DECATING
(**WEAVING** —) HATCHING
(**WINGLIKE** —) ALA FIN
PROCESSED DOWN FINISHED
PROCESSION POMP WALK CORSO
DRIVE TRACE TRAIN BRIDAL
EXEQUY LITANY PARADE STREAM
CORTEGE FUNERAL THIASOS
TRIONFO TRIUMPH ENTRANCE
PROGRESS
(**BOISTEROUS** —) SKIMMITY
(**IRISH CIVIC** —) FRINGES
PROCLAIM BID CRY BAWL DEEM
HORN OYES OYEZ SCRY SING TOOT
TOUT BLARE BOAST CLAIM GREDE
KNELL SOUND SPEAK BLAZON
BOUNCE DEFAME HERALD INDICT
OUTCRY CLARION DECLARE
DIVULGE PROTEST PUBLISH
TRUMPET ANNOUNCE DENOUNCE
RENOUNCE
(— **ALOUD**) ROAR
(— **PUBLICLY**) PRECONIZE
(— **WITH BIG TALK**) BOUNCE
PROCLAMATION CRY HUE BANS
FIAT RERD BANDO BANNS BLAZE
EDICT UKASE PLACARD PROGRAM
PROCLIVITY BENT ANLAGE APETITE
APTNESS LEANING TENDENCY
PROCNE (**FATHER OF** —) PANDION
(**HUSBAND OF** —) TEREUS
(**SISTER OF** —) PHILOMENA
(**SON OF** —) ITYS
PROCONSUL GALLIO PROVOST
PROCRASTINATE LAG TIME DEFER
DELAY LINGER ADJOURN POSTPONE
PROROGUE TEMPORIZE
PROCRASTINATION DELAY
CUNCTATION

PROCREANT FRUITFUL
PROCREATE WIN SIRE BEGET
ENGENDER GENERATE OCCASION
PROCREATION INCREASE
PROCREATOR AUTHOR
PROCTOR LIAR PROG ACTOR AGENT
PROXY BEGGAR RECTOR MONITOR
PROCUTOR
PROCUMBENT HUMIFUSE
PROSTRATE
PROCURABLE PARABLE
PROCURATOR PROXY PILATE
PROCTOR
PROCURE GET WIN FANG FIND GAIN
GIVE HALE BRING INFER TOUCH
EFFECT INDUCE OBTAIN ACHIEVE
ACQUIRE COMPARE CONQUER
CONTRIVE PURCHASE
PROCURER PIMP PROXENET
PURVEYOR
PROCURESS HACK LENA PANDER
COMMODE PINNACE
PROD DAB EGG GIG JAB JOG BROD
BROG GOAD HEEL POKE PROG
HURRY NUDGE PROBE INCITE
JOSTLE THRUST IRRITATE
PRODIGAL PROD FLUSH LARGE
COSTLY LAVISH WANTON WASTER
PROFUSE SPENDER WASTRIE
WASTRIFE
PRODIGALITY WASTE WASTRY
WASTRIFE PROFUSION
PRODIGIOUS HUGE VAST GIANT
AMAZING IMMENSE STRANGE
ABNORMAL ENORMOUS GIGANTIC
MONSTROUS
PRODIGY OMEN SIGN MARVEL
OSTENT WIZARD WONDER MONSTER
PORTENT CEREMONY
PRODITION TREASON BETRAYAL
PRODUCE DO GO ANTE BEAR FORM
GIVE GROW MAKE REAR SHOW
TEEM WAGE BEGET BIRTH BREED
BRING BROOD BUILD CARRY CAUSE
DRIVE FORGE FRAME HATCH ISSUE
RAISE SPAWN THROW TRADE YIELD
APPORT CREATE EFFECT GROWTH
INCOME INVENT INWORK SECURE
ADVANCE ANIMATE COMPOSE
DEPROME GIGNATE INSPIRE
OUTWORK PRODUCT PROLONG
PROVENT CONCEIVE CONFLATE
ENGENDER GENERATE INCREASE
LENGTHEN OFFSPRING
(— A COPY OF) TYPE
(— AN EFFECT) ACT AFFECT
(— AUDIBLE EFFECT) SOUND
(— CROPS) CARRY
(— DULL APPEARANCE) CHILL
(— FRUIT) TEEM
(— HEAT) ENRAGE
(— PAID FOR RENT) CAIN
(— SHARP NOISE) CRINK
(AGRICULTURAL —) PODWARE
(FARM —) HUSBANDRY
(MINING —) LEY
PRODUCER GASMAN BEARING
SHOWMAN DIRECTOR GAZOGENE
OUTPUTTER

PRODUCING IN PROCREANT
PRODUCT HEIR ITEM BRAND CHILD
FRUIT GROSS OUTGO SPAWN
ALCLAD EFFORT FABRIC GROWTH
RESULT UPCOME OUTTURN
PRODUCE PROGENY TURNOUT
OUTBIRTH
(— OF ROCK DECAY) LATERITE
(—S OF LAND) ESPLEES
(—S OF ORCHARD) BIKKURIM
(ADDITION —) ADDUCT
(CHEESE AND MILK —S) GERVAIS
(CHOICE —) CAVIAR
(COMPLETED —) TURNOFF
(LEGISLATIVE —) ACT
(MATHEMATICAL —) SQUARE
(MINERAL —) HUTCH
(OXIDATION —) SUBSCALE
(RESIDUAL —) LATERITE
(SECONDARY —) CONGENER
(SURPLUS —S) ARISINGS
(TRANSFORMATION —) BAINITE
(WASTE —) RESIDUENT
(WORTHLESS —) CHAFF
PRODUCTION WORK FORGE FRUIT
GROSS PIECE YIELD GROWTH
EDITION GUIGNOL PRODUCE
ARTIFICE INDUCTION OPERATION
(— OF MEDIUM) APPORT
(— OF YOUNG) INCREASE
(BEST —S) FAT
(SUCCESSFUL —) HIT
PRODUCTIVE FAT RICH LOOSE
QUICK ACTIVE BATTLE PAROUD
STRONG CAUSING FERTILE GAINFUL
HEALTHY TEEMFUL TEEMING
CHILDING CREATIVE FRUITFUL
GERMINAL
PROEM PREFACE PRELUDE PROHEIM
FOREWORD OVERTURE PREAMBLE
PROETUS (BROTHER OF —)
ACRISIUS
(FATHER OF —) ABAS
(MOTHER OF —) OCALEA
(WIFE OF —) ANTEA
PROFANATION VIOLENCE
SACRILEGE
PROFANE LAY NOA BLUE FOUL
ABUSE COARSE DEBASE DEFILE
DEFOIL DEFOUL UNHOLY VULGAR
WICKED GODLESS IMPIOUS
POLLUTE SECULAR UNGODLY
VIOLATE WORLDLY TEMPORAL
UNHALLOW
PROFANITY OATH CURSE
LANGUAGE BLASPHEMY
PROFESS OWN AVOW ADMIT CLAIM
AFFECT AFFIRM ALLEGE ASSERT
ASSUME FOLLOW PRESUME
PRETEND PURPORT PRACTICE
PROFESSION ART BAR LAW COAT
FEAT GAME WALK CRAFT FAITH
FORTE TRADE CAREER CHURCH
EMPLOY METIER CALLING FACULTY
QUALITY SERVICE ADVOCACY
BUSINESS COACHING FUNCTION
SOLDIERY VOCATION
PROFESSIONAL PRO COLT PAID
HIRED EXPERT SKILLED TRAINED
FINISHED

PROFESSOR DON PROF HANIF
LAWYER REGENT ADJOINT
ACADEMIC EMERITUS
PROFESSORSHIP CHAIR FAUTEUIL
PROFFER BID CAP GIVE TEND TENT
DEFER DODGE ESSAY OFFER
EXTEND OPPOSE PREFER PROFRE
TENDER ATTEMPT PRESENT
HESITATE
PROFICIENCY SIGHT SKILL ABILITY
APTNESS MAITRISE
PROFICIENT ADEPT EXPERT SALTED
VERSED SKILLED SKILLFUL
PROFILE FORM FLANK SKETCH
CONTOUR OUTLINE SECTION
PROFIT AID GET NET WIN BOOT
GAIN MEND NOTE SKIN VAIL AVAIL
EDIFY FRAME LUCRE SCALP SPEED
BEHOOF INCOME MAKING RETURN
ACCOUNT ADVANCE BENEFIT
CLEANUP FURTHER GETTING
IMPROVE MILEAGE PLUNDER
REVENUE VANTAGE WINNING
CLEANING INCREASE INTEREST
(— BY) BROOK
(UNDERCOVER —) SQUEEZE
(PL.) GRAVY ISSUE AVAILS JALKAR
ESPLEES
PROFITABLE FAT GOOD UTILE
GOLDEN GAINFUL HELPFUL
PAYABLE BEHOVELY ECONOMIC
PROVABLE REPAYING VAILABLE
REWARDING
PROFLIGATE DEFEAT CORRUPT
IMMORAL RIOTOUS SPENDER
VICIOUS WASTREL DEPRAVED
FLAGRANT OVERCOME RAKEHELL
WASTEFUL
PROFOUND DEEP HARD WISE ABYSS
DEPTH HEAVY OCEAN SOUND THICK
PITCHY STRONG ABYSMAL INTENSE
ABSTRUSE COMPLETE REACHING
THOROUGH
PROFUNDITY ABYSS DEPTH FATHOM
DEEPNESS
PROFUSE FREE LUSH SLAB FRANK
GALORE LAVISH COPIOUS LIBERAL
ABUNDANT GENEROUS PRODIGAL
SQUANDER WASTEFUL
PROFUSELY HEARTILY
PROFUSION WASTE EXCESS LAVISH
FLUENCY OPULENCE
PROG FOOD GOAD POKE PROD
PROWL TRAMP BEGGAR FORAGE
PROCTOR
PROGENITOR BURI MANU ROOT
SIRE PITRI STOCK PARENT
ANCESTOR
PROGENY BED GET IMP KIN CLAN
KIND SEED TEAM BROOD CHILD
FRUIT ISSUE STRAIN STRIND
INCROSS KINDRED LINEAGE
OUTCOME PRODUCT CHILDREN
FRUITAGE INCREASE OUTBIRTH
OUTCROSS OFFSPRING
(— OF WATER-BUFFALO AND YAK)
DZO
(— OF WITCH AND DEMON) HOLD
(INSECT —) SOCIETY

PROGNOSIS FORECAST PROPHASIS
PROGNOSTIC OMEN SIGN TOKEN
PRESAGE PROPHECY
PROGNOSTICATE BODE AUGUR
SPELL BETOKEN CONJECT PREDICT
PRENOTE FOREBODE FORESHOW
FORETELL PROPHESY
PROGNOSTICATION RACE
PRESAGE FOREBODE FORECAST
PROGRESS PROPHECY
PROGNOSTICATOR SEER DOOMER
PROPHET HARUSPEX
PROGRAM CARD SHOW FORUM
AGENDA DESIGN SCHEME AGENDUM
PREFACE CLAMBAKE FESTIVAL
GIVEAWAY GUIDANCE JAMBOREE
PLAYBILL SCHEDULE SEQUENCE
SYLLABUS
PROGRAMMA EDICT DECREE
PREFACE PROGRAM
PROGRESS WAY BIRL DENT FARE
GAIN GROW MOVE RACE RISE STEM
STEP TOUR WEAR WEND WENT
BUILD DRIFT FORGE GOING MARCH
SWING WEENT ASCENT BUFFET
COURSE GROWTH STREEK ADVANCE
DEVELOP FOOTING HEADWAY
IMPROVE JOURNEY ONGOING
PASSAGE PROCESS
(— **CLUMSILY**) SCRAMBLE
(— **ERRATICALLY**) FLAIL
(— **FEEBLY**) DODDER
(— **INTELLIGENTLY PLANNED**)
TELESIA TELESIS
(— **NOISILY**) CHORTLE
(— **SLOWLY**) CRAWL
(**SINGLE** —) THROUGH
PROGRESSED FAR
PROGRESSION WAY SWING COURSE
GALLOP ADVANCE PASSAGE
PROGRESS SEQUENCE
(— **OF CHORDS**) SWIPE
(**MUSICAL** —) SKIP
(**SMOOTH** —) SLIDE
PROGRESSIVE ACTIVE ONWARD
FORWARD GRADUAL LIBERAL
PROGRESSIVELY STILL
PROHIBIT BAN BAR STOP VETO
BLOCK DEBAR ESTOP DEFEND
ENJOIN FORBID HINDER OUTLAW
FORFEND FORWARN INHIBIT
PREVENT DISALLOW PRECLUDE
SUPPRESS
PROHIBITED HOT TABU TABOO
ILLEGAL ILLICIT UNLAWFUL
VERBOTEN
PROHIBITION BAN NAY NON VETO
ORDER BARRIER DEFENCE DEFENSE
EMBARGO FORBODE ESTOPPEL
PROHIBITING VETITIVE
PROHIBITIONIST DRY PUSSYFOOT
PROJECT GAB GAG JET JUT LAP
TUT BEAM CAST GAME IDEA PLAN
POKE SWIM BULGE CHART DRAFT
DRIVE IMAGE JETTY JUTTY SETUP
SHOOT STICK THROW BEETLE
DESIGN DEVICE ESTATE EXTEND
FILLIP OUTJUT PROPEL SCHEME
SCREEN SHELVE EXTRUDE GOSPLAN

IMAGINE KNUCKLE PATTERN
BUSINESS CONTRIVE OUTREACH
OUTSHOOT PROPOSAL PROTRUDE
SPANGHEW
(**UNETHICAL** —) SCHEME
(**VISIONARY** —) BABEL
PROJECTILE BALL BOLT CASE SHOT
SHAFT TRACER OUTCAST POUNDER
SHRAPNEL
(— **DESIGNED TO SET FIRE TO
HOUSES**) CARCASS
(**EXPLOSIVE** —) BOMB SHELL
(**SUBMARINE** —) TORPEDO
(PL.) LEAD SHOT SALVO STUFF
PROJECTING BEETLE SHELVY
EMINENT JUTTING OUTSHOT
SALIENT SNAGGLED
PROJECTION ARM CAM COG DOG
EAR FIN GIB JET JOG JUT NAG NUT
TOE BEAK BOSS BROW BUHR COAK
COCK CROC CUSP HEEL HORN KEEL
KICK KINK KNAG KNOB KNOP LOBE
RIDE SNUG SPUD SPUR TEAT WING
BULGE CLEAT EJECT ELBOW FENCE
FURCA JUTTY SHANK SHOOT SPIKE
TOOTH BRANCH CORBEL CROSET
FUSULA HEARTH ICICLE MENTUM
PALATE RELISH TAPPET BREAKER
DRAWING EPAULET EYEBROW
FETLOCK KNUCKLE LANGUET
ORILLON PRICKER PRICKLE
RESSAUT AJUTMENT CASCABEL
DENTICLE EMINENCE FOOTLOCK
OVERHANG SALIENCE SHOULDER
SPROCKET STERIOMA OUTTHRUST
(— **CONNECTING TIMBER**) COAK
(— **EXTENDING BACKWARD**) BARB
(— **FROM CASTING**) SPRUE
(— **FROM SHIP'S KEEL**) SPONSON
(— **IN CLOCK**) SQUARE
(— **IN ORCHIDS**) MENTUM
(— **OF FOREHEAD**) ANTINION
(— **OF JAW**) GNATHISM
(— **OF PEAT**) HAG
(— **OF RAFTER**) SALLY
(— **ON CANNON**) CASCABEL
(— **ON GUN**) CROC LUMP
(— **ON HARNESS**) HAME
(— **ON HORSE'S LEG**) FETLOCK
(— **ON HORSESHOE**) STICKER
(— **ON LOCK**) FENCE STUMP
(— **ON MAST**) STOP
(— **ON OVARY**) STIGMA
(— **ON POCKETKNIFE**) KICK
(— **ON SALMON JAW**) GIB
(— **ON WHEEL**) GUB GROUSER
GROUTER
(— **OVER AIR PORT**) EYEBROW
(**FIREPLACE** —) HOB
(**JAGGED** —) SNUG
(**SHARP** —) BARB FANG
(**SUBMERGED** —) KNOLL
(PL.) GRAIN BARLEY
PROJECTOR KINO LANTERN
PLANNER SCHEMER BIOSCOPE
EPISCOPE VITASCOPE
PROLAMIN ZEIN SEINE GLIADIN
HORDEIN KAFIRIN SECALIN

PROLAPSE PTOSIS BLOWOUT
FALLING
PROLETARIAN POPULAR
PROLETARIAT MASSES
PROLIFIC BIRTHY BREEDY BROODY
FECUND FERTILE PROFUSE TEEMING
ABUNDANT FRUITFUL SPAWNING
(**BE** —) INCREASE
PROLIX LARGE WORDY DIFFUSE
LENGTHY PROSAIC TEDIOUS
VERBOSE TIRESOME WEARISOME
PROLOGUE BANS BANNS INDEX
PREFACE
PROLONG DREE LENG LONG SPIN
DEFER DELAY DRIVE ELONG TWINE
DILATE EXTEND LINGER SPREAD
DISPACE PRODUCE RESPITE
SUSTAIN CONTINUE ETERNIZE
LENGTHEN POSTPONE PROROGUE
PROTRACT
PROLONGATION BEAK AORTA
CONUS STIPE STYLE FERMATA
ACROSOME GYNOBASE LABELLUM
PROLONGED GREAT PROLIX
DELAYED EXTENDED SOSTENUTO
PROMENADE MAIL MALL PIER PROM
WALK CORSO FRONT PASEO PRADO
MARINA PARADE PASEAR ALAMEDA
GALLERY FRESCADE
(**CARRIAGE** —) TOUR
PROMETHEUS (**FATHER OF** —)
IAPETUS
(**MOTHER OF** —) CLYMENE
PROMINENCE BUR NOB BURR KNOB
NOOP UMBO AGGER BULLA CREST
GRAIN OLIVA SWELL TYLUS ACCENT
CALCAR NODULE TRAGUS BILLING
BUTTOCK CONDYLE FASHION
HAMULUS KNUCKLE LINGULA
AMYGDALA EMINENCY EMPHASIS
GLABELLA PULVINAR SALIENCE
TUBERCLE
PROMINENT BIG BOLD BEADY
BRENT GREAT STEEP BEETLE
MARKED SIGNAL BLATANT BOLTING
CAPITAL EMINENT JUTTING LEADING
NOTABLE OBVIOUS SALIENT
AQUILINE MANIFEST STRIKING
(**SOCIALLY** —) SWELL
PROMISCUOUS LIGHT CASUAL
RANDOM CARELESS
PROMISCUOUSLY TAGRAG
PROMISE VOW AVOW BAND HEST
HETE HOPE HOTE OSSE PASS PLEA
SURE WORD FAITH GRANT HIGHT
TRUTH ASSURE BEHEST ENGAGE
FIANCE HALSEN INSURE PAROLE
PLEDGE PLIGHT PROMIT BEHIGHT
BETROTH WARRANT CONTRACT
COVENANT GUARANTY BETROTHAL
(— **IN MARRIAGE**) BETROTH
ESPOUSE AFFIANCE
(— **TO PAY**) NOTE
(— **TO TAKE IN MARRIAGE**) AFFY
PROMISED VOTARY
(— **IN MARRIAGE**) SURE HIGHT
ENGAGED
PROMISING APT FAIR BRIGHT
LIKELY PROOFY TOWARD GRADELY
TOWARDLY

PROMISSORY NOTE IOU HUNDI HOONDI TICKET

PROMONTORY HOE NAB BEAK BILL HEAD MULL NAZE NESS NOOK NOUP PEAK SCAW SKAW TOOT ELBOW POINT REACH SNOUT SALIENT FORELAND HEADLAND

PROMOTE AID HELP LOFT AVAIL BOOST EXALT NURSE RAISE SERVE SPEED ASSIST EXCITE FOMENT FOSTER LAUNCH PREFER ADVANCE DIGNIFY ELEVATE FORWARD FURTHER IMPROVE PREFECT PRODUCE PROMOVE SUCCEED SUPPORT INCREASE SUBSERVE

PROMOTER AGENT FRIEND ABETTOR BOOSTER BUBBLER BROACHER HUMANIST

PROMOTION LIFT REMOVE ADVANCE PROMOVAL

PROMPT APT CUE MOVE URGE YARE ALERT PREST QUICK READY SERVE SWIFT WILLY YEDER EXCITE INDITE MATURE NIMBLE SPEEDY SUDDEN ANIMATE FORWARD PROVOKE SUGGEST PUNCTUAL REMINDER
(— TO EVIL) SUGGEST

PROMPTER CUER CALLER MEMORIST ORDINARY SOUFFLEUR

PROMPTING CALL BEHEST BEHIND MOTIVE
(SPIRITUAL —) LEADING

PROMPTLY UP PAT TID TIT SOON TITE PRONTO YARELY PRESTLY QUICKLY DIRECTLY SPEEDILY

PROMPTNESS ALACRITY CELERITY DISPATCH

PROMULGATE SPREAD DECLARE PUBLISH PROCLAIM

PRONAOS ANTICUM

PRONE APT BENT EASY FLAT FREE GRUF BUXOM GIVEN GROOF JACENT LIABLE SUPINE BEASTLY BESTIAL DORMANT SUBJECT ADDICTED COUCHANT DISPOSED DOWNWARD PROPENSE
(— TO TAKE UP FADS) ISMY
(NATURALLY —) PROLIVE

PRONG NEB NIB PEG PEW BILL FANG FORK HOOK PUGH SPUR TANG TENG TINE TING GRAIN SPADE SPEAN SPRONG FOURCHE TICKLER GRAINING
(— FOR EXTRACTING BUNG) TICKLER
(— FOR FISH) PEW PUGH
(— OF ANTLER) KNAG TIND TINE
(— OF FORK) SPEAN

PRONGHORN CABREE CABRIT MAZAME BERENDO BERRENDO

PRONOUN HE IT ME MY WE YE ANY HER HIM HIS ONE OUR SHE THY WHO YOU OURS THAT THEM THEY THOU WHAT WHOM YOUR THINE WHICH WHOSE ITSELF MYSELF HERSELF HIMSELF OURSELF WHOEVER YOURSELF OURSELVES
(GENDERLESS —) THON

PRONOUNCE SAY PASS ACUTE
SPEAK UTTER PREACH RECITE TONGUE ADJUDGE BEHIGHT CENSURE MOUILLE
(— FREE) ABSOLVE
(— GUILTY) CONDEMN
(— HOLY) BLESS

PRONOUNCED HIGH MARKED DECIDED HOWLING INTENSE MOVABLE
(— AS FRICATIVE) GRASSEYE
(NOT —) SOFT

PRONOUNCEMENT FIAT CURSE DICTUM DICTAMEN

PRONTO QUICK QUICKLY PROMPTLY

PRONUNCIATION BROGUE DICTION ETACISM LIAISON DELIVERY ENCLISIS ORTHOEPY
(BAD —) CACOEPY LABDACISM
(BROAD —) PLATEASM
(CORRECT —) ORTHOEPY
(ROUGH —) BUR BURR

PROOF MARK SLIP TEST ESSAY PREWE TOKEN TOUCH TRIAL GALLEY ORDEAL REASON RESULT REVISE ATTEMPT OUTCOME PROBATE SHOWING UTTERLY VOUCHER WARRANT ANALYSIS CACOLOGY DOCUMENT EVICTION EVIDENCE GOODNESS MONUMENT
(— SPIRIT OF WINE) SVT
(— OF WRONGDOING) GOODS
(PL.) STRING WARRANTY

PROOFREADER MARK CAP DELE STET CARET

PROP LEG BROB POST REST SPUR STAY STUD TRIG APPUI BRACE PERCH PUNCH RANCE SCOTE SHORE SHOVE SOUSE SPRAG SPURN STAFF STELL STOOP STULL COLUMN CROTCH CRUTCH SCOTCH SHORER STAYER UPHOLD FULCRUM PINNING STUDDLE SUPPORT SUSTAIN BUTTRESS CROTCHET DUTCHMAN UNDERLAY UNDERSET
(— AS TRAP) TEEL
(— FOR ROOF OF MINE) GIB
(— UP) CUSHION

PROPAGANDA BOLOISM AGITPROP

PROPAGATE BREED HATCH LAYER EXTEND SPREAD STRIKE DIFFUSE GEMMATE PRODUCE PUBLISH ENGENDER GENERATE INCREASE POPULATE TRANSMIT

PROPAGATION BREED BREEDING DIVISION INCREASE LAYERAGE OFFSPRING

PROPEL ROW CALL CAST FIRE FLIP KENT POLE PUSH SEND URGE DRIVE FLICK IMPEL KNOCK PRICK RANGE SPANK THROW HURTLE LAUNCH PROJECT
(— BALL) STROKE
(— BOAT WITH FEET) LEG
(— BOAT) OAR ROW SET KENT POLE SCULL BUSHWACK
(— ONESELF) HAUL
(— PUCK) CARRY

PROPELLER FAN SCREW AIRSCREW WINDMILL

PROPENSITY YEN BENT ITCH LURCH APTNESS IMPULSE LEANING PRONITY APPETITE FONDNESS INTEREST TENDENCY

PROPER FIT OWN GOOD JUST MEET TRUE WELL PREST RIGHT UTTER COMELY DECENT HONEST LAWFUL MODEST SEEMLY CAPITAL CORRECT FITTING GRADELY SEEMING SKILFUL THRIFTY ABSOLUTE BECOMING CONGREVE DECOROUS FORMULAR IDONEOUS PECULIAR RIGHTFUL SORTABLE SUITABLE VIRTUOUS
(APPARENTLY —) SPECIOUS
(BE — TO) BESEEM

PROPERLY DULY WELL FITLY TRULY FAIRLY FEATLY GLADLY MEETLY RIGHTLY

PROPERTY AVER BONA DHAN TOOL WAIF ASSET AUGHT GOODS GRANT MOYEN STATE STOCK THING WORTH APPEAL DEVISE ESTATE HAVIOR KELTER LIVING MUSHAA REALTY TALENT USINGS WEALTH ACQUEST APANAGE CHATTEL DEMESNE ESCHEAT ESSENCE FACULTY FITNESS HARNESS HAVINGS QUALITY WARISON ALLODIAL CATALLUM HOLDINGS PECULIUM
(— BELONGING TO WOMAN) STRIDHAN
(— FROM WIFE TO HUSBAND) DOS
(— GIVEN BY WILL) DEVISE
(— OF MATTER AT REST) INERTIA
(— SECURED DISHONESTLY) HARL
(— SEIZED BY FORCE) SPOIL
(ABSOLUTE —) ALODIUM
(ENEMY —) HEREM
(LANDED —) DOMAIN ESTATE DEMESNE PRAEDIUM
(MOVABLE —) GEAR CHATTEL EFFECTS CATALLUM
(PERSONAL —) FEE BONA GOODS STUFF INSIGHT PLUNDER
(PRIVATE —) SEVERAL
(RURAL —) FINCA
(STOLEN —) PELF STEALTH
(THEATRICAL —S) PROPS
(WITHOUT —) LACKLAND

PROPHECY SPAE WEIRD EXHORT PREACH PREDICT BODEMENT FORECAST FORESHOW SOOTHSAY VATICINE SIBYLLISM

PROPHESY OSSE SPAE AREAD AUGUR DIVINE EXHORT PREACH OMINATE PORTEND PREDICT ARIOLATE FORETELL

PROPHET GAD AMOS JOEL SEER ANGEL AUGUR DRUID ELIAS HOSEA JONAH MICAH MOSES NAHUM SILAS SYRUS ARIOLE BALAAM DANIEL ELIJAH HAGGAI ISAIAH MERLIN MORONI NATHAN PYTHON SAMUEL EZEKIEL MALACHI SPAEMAN HABAKKUK JEREMIAH
(PL.) VATES NEBIIM

PROPHETESS ANNA ANNE HULDA SIBYL PYTHIA DEBORAH PHOIBAD

SEERESS VOLUSPA DRUIDESS
SPAEWIFE CASSANDRA PYTHONESS
PROPHETIC FATAL MANTIC FATEFUL
FATIDIC DELPHIAN SIBYLLIC
VATICINAL
PROPINE TIP GIFT EXPOSE PLEDGE
PROFFER
PROPINQUITY KINSHIP AFFINITY
NEARNESS VICINITY PROXIMITY
PROPITIATE MILD ATONE PACIFY
APPEASE RECONCILE
PROPITIATORY HILASMIC
PROPITIOUS FAIR KIND HAPPY
LUCKY BENIGN DEXTER KINDLY
HELPFUL PRESENT FRIENDLY
GRACIOUS MERCIFUL FAVORABLE
PROMISING
PROPONENT BACKER ADVOCATE
SUPPORTER
PROPORTION END LOT DOSE SIZE
CHIME FRAME QUOTA RATIO SCALE
SHARE ACCORD DEGREE EXTENT
FORMAT QUOTUM ANALOGY
BALANCE COMPASS CONTENT
MEASURE EURYTHMY QUANTITY
SYMMETRY
(— **OF CATTLE TO GIVEN AREA**)
SOUM
(— **OF MALT IN BREWING**) STRAIK
(**ALLOTTED** —) STENT STINT
(**EXACT** —) SQUARE
(**SMALL** —) TITHE
PROPORTIONATENESS CONTOUR
PROPOSAL BID KITE MOVE PLAN
PLEA VOEU GRACE OFFER PARTY
DEMAND FEELER MOTION MOTIVE
PROJECT PROPOSE PURPOSE
OVERTURE SCHEDULE SENTENCE
(**TENTATIVE** —) SNIFF
PROPOSE FACE MOVE PLAN POSE
SHOW WISH OFFER ALLEGE DESIGN
INJECT INTEND MOTION ADVANCE
EXHIBIT IMAGINE PROPINE PURPOSE
SUPPOSE CONFRONT CONVERSE
PROPOUND
(— **FOR DISCUSSION**) MOOT
(— **RESOLUTION**) FIRST
(— **TENTATIVELY**) SUGGEST
PROPOSITION R FACT AXIOM
MODAL OFFER THEME AFFAIR
CONNEX MEMBER PORISM GENERAL
INVERSE PREMISS PROBLEM
THEOREM TYCHISM BUSINESS
CONTRARY EMPIREMA IDENTITY
IRENICON JUDGMENT NEGATION
OVERTURE PROPOSAL PROTASIS
SENTENCE SINGULAR SUPPOSAL
(— **IN LOGIC**) TERMAL
(— **LEADING TO CONCLUSION**)
PREMISE
(**PARTICULAR NEGATIVE** —) O
(**PRELIMINARY** —) LEMMA
(**UNIVERSAL NEGATIVE** —) E
PROPOUND POSE OFFER POSIT
START STATE INVOKE PROPOSE
PURPOSE
PROPOUNDER HYLICIST
PROPRIETOR LORD LAIRD MALIK
OWNER MASTER PATRON TANIST

YEOMAN ESQUIRE PATROON
ABSENTEE BONIFACE SQUARSON
TALUKDAR YEOWOMAN
PROPRIETY GRACE IDIOM MENSE
ESTATE NATURE REASON DECENCY
DECORUM ESSENCE FITNESS
HOLDING CIVILITY PROPERTY
ETIQUETTE
PROPROCTOR RECTOR
PROPULSION DRIFT EJECTION
PROPULSIVE ELASTIC
PRORATE ALLOT ASSESS DIVIDE
APPORTION
PROROGUE DEFER ADJOURN
PROLONG POSTPONE PROTRACT
PROSAIC DRAB DULL FLAT FOOT
PROSE PROSY PROLIX STODGY
STOLID STUPID FACTUAL HUMDRUM
INSIPID LITERAL TEDIOUS TIRESOME
WORKADAY
PROSCENIUM FRAME STAGE
PROSCRIBE BAN TABU EXILE TABOO
FORBID OUTLAW REJECT PROHIBIT
PROSCRIPTION EXILE OUTLAWRY
PROSE CHAT PROSY GOSSIP
PROSAIC TEDIOUS SEQUENCE
ELOQUENCE
PROSECUTE LAW SUE HOLD URGE
CARRY ENSUE ACCUSE CHARGE
DEDUCE FOLLOW INDICT INTEND
PURSUE IMPLEAD
PROSECUTOR DA FISCAL PURSUER
SAKEBER PROMOTER QUAESTOR
(**PUBLIC** —) ACTOR
PROSELYTE CONVERT NICOLAS
NEOPHYTE PURSUANT
(**JEWISH** —) GER
PROSER HAVERER GRATIANO
PROSODY METER METRICS
PROSPECT HOPE VIEW SCENE
SPECK VISTA CHANCE CHIEVE
FUTURE REGARD SEARCH SURVEY
COMMAND EXPLORE FOSSICK
HORIZON LOOKOUT OUTLOOK
PROJECT RESPECT LANDSKIP
OFFSCAPE
(— **FOR GOLD**) SPECK
(— **WITHOUT SYSTEM**) GOPHER
(**FORBIDDING** —) DESERT
PROSPECTING LOAMING
PROSPECTIVE VIEW WATCH
LOOKOUT EXPECTED
PROSPECTOR SNIPER FOSSICKER
SOURDOUGH
(**LONE** —) HATTER
PROSPECTUS PROGRAM
PROSPER DO DOW FAY HIE LIKE
RISE THEE CHEVE CHIVE EDIFY
FRAME LIGHT SPEED BATTEN
THRIVE BLOSSOM SUCCEED
WELFARE FLOURISH
PROSPERITY HAP GLEE GOOD SEEL
SONS WEAL IKBAL SONSE HEALTH
THRIFT FORTUNE SUCCESS
THEEDOM WELFARE FLOURISH
(**GOD OF** —) FREY
PROSPERO (**DAUGHTER OF** —)
MIRANDA
(**SERVANT OF** —) ARIEL

PROSPEROUS UP FAT BEEN BEIN
BIEN BOON GOOD FELIX FLUSH
HAPPY LUCKY PALMY SONSY
EUROUS GILDED SONSIE WELSOM
HALCYON HEALTHY THRIVEN
WEIRDLY SUNSHINE THRIVING
WEALSOME
PROSTITUTE BAG BAT CAT COW
DOG MOB AUNT BAWD DOXY DRAB
HACK MAUX MISS MUFF PUNK SLUT
STEW TRUG BROAD CRACK MAWKS
PAGAN STALE WHORE BULKER
CALLET CHIPPY DEBASE GIRLIE
HARLOT HOOKER LIMMER MUTTON
RANNEL TOMATO TRADER VIZARD
BAGGAGE BROTHEL CRUISER
CYPRIAN HACKNEY HETAERA
HUSTLER PAPHIAN PINNACE
POLECAT PUCELLE SELLARY
BERDACHE COMMONER CUSTOMER
HACKSTER MAGDALEN MERETRIX
OCCUPANT RUMBELOW SLATTERN
STRUMPET VENTURER
PROSTITUTION BORDEL SACKING
BORDELLO HARLOTRY PUTANISM
PROSTRATE LOW FELL FLAT GRUF
RASE RAZE FLING GROOF PRONE
STOOP THROW ATTERR CUMBER
FALLEN REPENT WEAKEN FLATTEN
DEJECTED HELPLESS OVERCOME
PROSTERN DEPRESSED
(— **ONESELF**) HURKLE
(**BECOME** —) FALL
PROSTRATION SHOCK KOWTOW
COLLAPSE
PROSY DRY DULL JEJUNE HUMDRUM
INSIPID PROSAIC PROSISH TEDIOUS
TIRESOME
PROTAGONIST HERO ACTOR
LEADER PALADIN ADVOCATE
CHAMPION
PROTAMINE SALMINE STURINE
CLUPEINE
PROTEAN EDESTAN VARIABLE
PROTECT CAP BANK BIEL BIND DIKE
FEND FORT HILL KEEP REDE SAVE
WARD WEAR BLESS CHAIN CLOUT
COURE COVER FENCE GANGE
GRATE GUARD HEDGE PAVIS SHADE
SHEND UMBER ASSERT BORROW
CHIELD DEFEND SCREEN SHADOW
WARISH BULWARK CHERISH
CUSHION FASCINE FORFEND
SECLUDE SHELTER SUPPORT
WARRANT BESTRIDE CHAMPION
DEFILADE PRESERVE
(— **AGAINST RAIN**) FLASH
(— **BY COVERING**) HILL
(— **BY WINDING WITH WIRE**) GANGE
(— **FROM INTRUSION**) TILE TYLE
(— **IRON OR STEEL**) BARFF
PROTECTED SHADY IMMUNE
CLOUTED GUARDED SHEATHED
SHIELDED
PROTECTING TUTELAR TUTELARY
SECUREFUL
PROTECTION LEE EGIS HOLD WARD
AEGIS ARMOR BIELD COVER GRITH
GUARD SHADE TARGE TOWER

AMULET ASYLUM AVOWRY ESCORT
FENDER REFUGE SAFETY SCONCE
SCREEN SHADOW SHROUD AUSPICE
CUSTODY DEFENCE HOUSING
MANTLET SHELTER TUITION
UMBRAGE WARRANT BLINDAGE
COVERAGE DEFILADE PASSPORT
SECURITY TUTAMENT TUTELAGE
(— **FOR SAILOR**) HORSE
(— **FROM LOSS**) INDEMNITY
(— **FROM RAIN**) OMBRIFUGE
(— **FROM SUN**) HAVELOCK
(— **FROM WEATHER**) LEWTH
(— **RIGHT**) MUND
(**VALUABLE** —) EDMUND
(**WISE** —) RAYMOND
PROTECTIVE (— **SURFACE**) LAGGING
PROTECTOR BIB GUARD BRACER
FAUTOR KEEPER PATRON REGENT
WARRANT DEFENDER GUARDIAN
PECTORAL PRESIDENT
(— **OF PROSTITUTE**) BULLY
(— **OF VINEYARDS**) PRIAPUS
PROTEGE WARD PUPIL SMIKE
PROTEIN ABRIN ACTIN RICIN SOZIN
AVIDIN CASEIN FIBRIN GLOBIN
MYOGEN ALBUMIN AMANDIN
ELASTIN GELATIN GLIADIN HISTONE
HORDEIN KERATIN LIVETIN MUCEDIN
SERICIN ALEURONE COLLOGEN
FERRITIN GLOBULIN GLUTELIN
GORGONIN IPOMOEIN PROLAMIN
(**RICH IN** —**S**) NARROW
PROTEOSE ALBUMOSE ELASTOSE
GELATOSE
PROTEST AVER BEEF FUSS HOWL
KICK BROCK CROAK DEMUR AFFIRM
ASSERT BOWWOW EXCEPT HOLLER
OBJECT OBTEST PLAINT SQUAWK
SQUEAL CONTEST INVEIGH PUBLISH
RECLAIM RHUBARB SCRUPLE
TESTIFY HARRUMPH PROCLAIM
(— **AGAINST INJUSTICE**) HARO
PROTESTANT ALASCAN GENEVAN
GOSPELER HELVETIC HUGUENOT
SWADDLER
PROTEUS OLM AMOEBA
PROTHESIS CREDENCE PARABEMA
PROTHORAX COLLAR CORSELET
MANITRUNK
PROTOPINE FUMARINE
PROTOPLASM PLASMA PLASSON
SARCODE OVOPLASM PERIPLAST
SOLEPLATE
PROTOPLAST CELL ENERGID
PROTOTYPE IDEAL MODEL FATHER
EXAMPLE PATTERN ANTITYPE
EXEMPLAR
PROTOZOAN AMEBA FORAM MONAD
MONER AGAMETE ARCELLA BABESIA
BODONID CILIATE PROTIST RADIATE
STENTOR DIDINIUM HYPOZOAN
(**PL.**) MICROZOA
PROTRACT DRAG DRAW DREE PLOT
SPIN DEFER DELAY DRIVE TRACT
TRAIL TRAIN DILATE EXTEND
LINGER SPREAD DETRACT PROLONG
CONTINUE LENGTHEN
PROTRACTED DREE LONG DREICH

PROLIX LENGTHY DRAGGING
EXTENDED
PROTRUDE BUG JUT LILL LOLL
POUT BLEAR BULGE BUNCH POUCH
SHOOT START STICK STRUT SWELL
EXSERT EXTEND EXTRUDE KNUCKLE
PROJECT HERNIATE OUTPOINT
OUTREACH OUTSHOOT
PROTRUDING STEEP BUNCHY
GOGGLE BLABBER EMINENT
JUTTING
PROTRUSION LAP NOB BURR KNOB
POUT HERNIA SALIENCE SHOULDER
TYLOSOID
PROTUBERANCE BUD HUB JAG
NOB NUB WEN BEAN BOLL BOSS
BULB BUMP HEEL HUMP JAGG KNOB
KNOP KNOT LUMP NODE PUFF SCAB
SNAG STUB UMBO WART BULGE
BUNCH CAPUT GLAND GNARL
HUNCH KNURL SWELL TORUS
TUBER TUMOR CALLUS HUBBLE
PIMPLE POMMEL EXTANCY PAPILLA
EMINENCE FLANKARD NODOSITY
SWELLING
(— **AT BASE OF BIRD'S BILL**) CERE
SNOOD
(— **BEARING SPINE**) UMBO
(— **FROM SWELLING**) PUFF
(— **IN SIDE OF DEER**) FLANKARD
(— **ON A CASTING**) SCAB
(— **ON BONE**) EMINENCE
(— **ON HORSE'S HOOF**) BUTTRESS
(— **ON MANDIBLE OF GEESE**) BEAN
(— **ON SADDLEBOW**) POMMEL
(— **ON SALAMANDER**) BALANCER
(— **ON TONGUE**) PAPILLA
(**KNOBLIKE** —) CAPUT
(**OCCIPITAL** —) INION
(**RAGGED** —) JAG JAGG
(**ROUGH** —) HUB
(**SKIN** —) WEN MOLE WART PIMPLE
PROTUBERANT BULGY BUMPY
PROUD STRUT TUMID BUCKED
EXTANT GOGGLE BOTTLED BULGING
EMINENT GIBBOUS SALIENT
SWOLLEN
(**REGULARLY** —) CONVEX
PROUD FESS GLAD HIGH IKEY LOFT
PERK RANK SIDE VAIN BRANT
CHUFF GELLY GREAT JELLY LOFTY
NOBLE ORGUL PRIDY SAUCY STEEP
STIFF STOUT VOGIE WINDY WLONK
COPPED ELATED FIERCE LORDLY
ORGUIL PENCEY QUAINT SKEIGH
SKEIGH UPPISH UPPITY VAUNTY
HAUGHTY SUBLIME SWOLLEN
TOPPING ARROGANT EXULTANT
GLORIOUS IMPOSING INSOLENT
ORGULOUS SPLENDID STOMACHY
PROUDLY HIGH
PROVE TRY FAND FOND PREE SHOW
TEST ARGUE ASSAY EVICT TAINT
TASTE TEMPT ARGUFY EVINCE
SUFFER VERIFY BALANCE CONFESS
CONFIRM CONVICT DERAIGN
IMPROVE JUSTIFY CONCLUDE
CONVINCE EVIDENCE INDICATE
INSTRUCT MANIFEST

(— **FALSE**) BELIE BETRAY FALSIFY
(— **GUILTY**) ATTAINT
(— **OUT**) SERVE
(— **TITLE**) DEDUCE
(— **VALID**) DEFEND
PROVED TRIED EXPERT PROBATE
PROVENCAL LANGUEDOC
ROMANESQUE
PROVENDER HAY CORN FEED FOOD
OATS STRAW PROVAND PROVIANT
PROVERB SAW SAY REDE WORD
ADAGE AXIOM CREED GNOME
SOOTH BALLAD BYWORD DITTON
DIVERB MASHAL SAYING SPEECH
SYMBOL WHEEZE BYSPELL IMPRESA
NAYWORD PARABLE APHORISM
FORBYSEN PAROEMIA SCHOLION
SCHOLIUM SENTENCE SOOTHSAY
PROVIDE DO FIT SEE FEND FILL
FIND GIRD LEND LOOK BLOCK
CATER ENDOW ENDUE EQUIP SPEED
STOCK STORE AFFORD FOISON
PURVEY SUBORN SUPPLY EXHIBIT
FORESEE FURNISH INSTORE
PREPARE ACCOUTER APPANAGE
DISPENSE PURCHASE
(— **AHEAD OF TIME**) ADVANCE
(— **AMUSEMENT**) DISTRACT
(— **FOOD**) GRUB CATER SCAFF
(— **FOR**) FEND SERVE CHEVEYS
CHEVISE PROVANT
(— **STINGILY**) SKINCH
(— **SUPPORT**) ESCOT
(— **WITH DOWRY**) DOT
(— **WITH HIP-ROOF**) COOT
(— **WITH**) BESEE
PROVIDED IF BODEN FIXED READY
SOBEIT PROVISO INSTRUCT
PREPARED
PROVIDENCE THRIFT ECONOMY
PRUDENCE
PROVIDENT WARY WISE FRUGAL
SAVING CAREFUL PRUDENT THRIFTY
PROVINCE LAN AREA NOME WALK
AIMAK BANAT FIELD MOUTH NATAL
NOMOS REALM SHENG SHIRE
SUBAH BANNAT EMPIRE EYALET
MALAGA MONTON REGION SIRCAR
SPHERE SYSSEL YAMATO DEMESNE
DONGOLA EPARCHY MUDIRIA
PURVIEW RECTORY VILAYET
APPANAGE DISTRICT FUNCTION
MUDIRIEH NOMARCHY
(**SUBDIVISION OF EGYPTIAN** —)
KISM
(**PL.**) OUTLAND
PROVINCIAL HICK BORNE CRUDE
NARROW RUSTIC STUFFY INSULAR
SUBURBAN
PROVISION BOARD CHECK GRIST
FODDER MATTER PURVEY STOVER
UNLESS WRAITH APPREST CAUTION
CODICIL DOWNSET KEEPING
SLEEPER VICTUAL WARNISH
WARNISON
(**BOUGHT** —**S**) ACATERY
(**SUBORDINATE** —) ITEM
(**PL.**) CHOW FOOD JOCK KEEP LOAN
BOUGE CATES SCRAN STORE

TERMS TOMMY ANNONA VIANDS VIVRES COMMONS WARNAGE WAYFARE VICTUALS

PROVISO SALVO CAVEAT CLAUSE CAUTION CONDITION

PROVOCATION APPEAL INCENTIVE

PROVOCATIVE GUTTY SALTY AGACANT PIQUANT IRRITANT APPEALING

PROVOKE BOG EGG GIG IRE TAR VEX BEAR DARE HUFF MOVE PICK STIR TARR TEEN URGE WORK ANGER ANGRY ANNOY EAGER EVOKE FRUMP PIQUE TAUNT TEMPT APPEAL ELICIT EVINCE EXCITE GRIEVE HARASS INCITE KINDLE NETTLE PROMPT SUMMON TICKLE AFFRONT ILLICIT INCENSE INFLAME INSPIRE VROTHER CATALYZE IRRITATE

PROVOST JUDGE PRIOR REEVE KEEPER WARDEN STEWARD

PROW BOW BEAK SPUR STEM PRORE SNOUT SPERON STEVEN DIVIDER GALLANT VALIANT

(— **OF GONDOLA**) FERRO

PROWESS FEAT PROW VALOR NOBLEY BRAVERY COURAGE

PROWL OWL PROG ROAM LURCH MOOCH MOUSE RAVEN BREVIT RAMBLE

PROWLER WALKER SLASHER TENEBRION

PROWLIKE PROREAN

PROWLING GRASSANT

PROXIMATE NEXT CLOSE DIRECT CLOSEST NEAREST PROXIME IMMINENT PROXIMAL

PROXIMITY SHADOW NEARNESS PRESENCE VICINITY

PROXY VICE AGENT VICAR BALLOT MANDAT PROCTOR

(PL.) ELECTION

PRUDE COMSTOCK

PRUDENCE CARE ADVICE CAUTEL WISDOM CAUTION COUNSEL SLEIGHT FORECAST FORELOOK

PRUDENT FIT SAGE WARE WARY WISE CANNY DOOSE DOUCE SOLID SYKER VERTY FRUGAL QUAINT SEKERE SICCAR POLITIC THRIVEN CAUTIOUS DISCREET

PRUDISH NICE PRIM MIMZY MIMSEY PRIGGISH RUDIBUND VICTORIA

PRUDISHNESS NICETY PUDENCY

PRUNE COW LOP TOP CLIP COLL COUL GELD PLUM SNED SPUR TAME TRIM CLEAN DRESS KNIFE PLUMB PREEN PRIME PURGE SHEAR SHRED SHRUB TWIST DEHORN REFORM SHRIDE SNATHE SWITCH AMPUTATE CASTRATE RETRENCH

(— **SEVERELY**) DEHORN

(**IMPERFECTLY RIPENED** —) FROG

PRUNING HOOK SARPE CALABOZO

PRUNING KNIFE CALABOZO SERPETTE

PRUNING SHEARS SECATEUR

PRURIENT ITCHY

PRURITIS ITCH

PRUSSIAN PRUTENIC

PRY GAG NOSE NOTE PEEK PEEP PEER TEET JIMMY LEVER PRIZE SNOOP BREVIT FERRET PIGGLE POTTER PUTTER CROWBAR GUMSHOE LEVERAGE

(— **ABOUT**) OWL MOUSE SNOOK SCROUNGE

(— **INTO AND REPEAT**) RAVE

(— **INTO**) BREVIT

PRYING NOSY NOSEY CURIOUS PEEPING

PSALM ODE HYMN SONG DIRGE GATHA ANTHEM CANTATE CHORALE INTROIT MISERERE

(100TH —) JUBILATE

(95TH —) VENITE

(98TH —) CANTATE

PSALMS HALLEL

(**BOOK OF** —) PSALTER

PSALTERIUM BOOK LYRA OMASUM PSALTER PSALTERY

PSALTERY GUSLA SAUTREE

PSEUDO FAKE MOCK SHAM BOGUS FALSE FEIGNED SPURIOUS

PSEUDOCARP HIP

PSEUDONYM ALIAS ANONYM JUNIUS

PSHAW SHA POOH SUGAR SHUCKS

PSORIASIS ALPHOS

PSYCHE MIND SELF SOUL

PSYCHIATRIST ALIENIST

PSYCHOANALYST FREUDIAN

PSYCHOLOGY HORMISM HEDONICS ANIMASTIC FORMALISM

PSYCHOPATH MATTOID

PSYCHOSIS INSANITY SENILITY

PSYCHOTIC MAD CRAZY INSANE

PSYLLA DIMERAN

PSYLLIUM FLEAWORT

PTAH (— **EMBODIED**) APIS

(**ASSOCIATED WITH** —) SEKHET

PTARMIGAN RYPE GROUSE LAGOPODE

PTEROCARPUS LINGOUM

PTEROSAUR DIAPSID

PTERYGIUM WEBEYE

PTERYGOID EXTERNUM

PTERYLA TRACT

PTISAN TEA TISANE

PTOLEMY SOTER

(**WIFE OF** —) CLEOPATRA

PTOMAINE NEURIN SEPSIN SAPRINE GADININE

PUB BAR INN BOOZER LOUNGE SHANTY TAVERN

PUBBLE FAT FULL PLUMP

PUB-CRAWL BARHOP

PUBESCENCE DOWN SCURF YOUTH TOMENT

PUBESCENT HIRSUTE VILLOUS

PUBLIC KUNG OPEN TOWN CIVIC OVERT WORLD COMMON SOCIAL VULGAR GENERAL OMNIBUS POPULAR EXTERNAL MATERIAL NATIONAL

(**GENERAL** —) GALLERY

PUBLICAN FARMER KEEPER ZACCHEUS CATCHPOLL

PUBLICATION BOOK ORDO BIBLE FOLIO ISSUE SHEET ANNUAL BLAZON DIGLOT SERIAL WEEKLY ALMANAC BOOKLET ELZEVIR JOURNAL MONTHLY WRITING BIWEEKLY BULLETIN DOCUMENT EMISSION EXCHANGE PRODROME EPHEMERIS

PUBLIC HOUSE BAR INN PUB BOOZER PUBLIC SALOON HOSTELRY POTHOUSE

PUBLICIST AGENT SOLON WRITER

PUBLICITY AIR ECLAT BUILDUP PUFFERY RECLAME BALLYHOO BROUHAHA DAYLIGHT HERALDRY PROMOTION

PUBLICIZE CRY BLURB BREAK BRUIT HERALD BALLYHOO HEADLINE

PUBLIC SQUARE PLAZA PLEIN ZOCALO

PUBLISH ASH BLOW CALL EDIT EMIT VEND VENT CARRY ISSUE PRINT SPEAK UTTER BLAZON BROACH DEFAME EVULGE EXPOSE SPREAD CENSURE DECLARE DIFFUSE DIVULGE GAZETTE PROTEST DENOUNCE DISCLOSE EVULGATE PROCLAIM PROMULGE

(— **BANNS OF MARRIAGE**) CRY SPUR OUTASK

(— **IN CHURCH**) ASK

(— **WITHOUT AUTHORIZATION**) PIRATE

PUBLISHER CRIER EDITOR PRINTER STATIONER

PUCCOON GROMYL ALKANET GROMWELL BLOODROOT

PUCE FLEA

PUCK ELF LOB PUG BLOW BUTT DISK POKE POOK DEMON DEVIL FAIRY PEWKE SPORT RUBBER SPRITE STRIKE PUCKREL HOBGOBLIN

PUCKER DRAW FULL RUCK PURSE REEVE TIZZY COCKLE COTTER FURROW LUCKEN WRINKLE CONTRACT AGITATION CONSTRICT

PUCKERED BULLATE COCKLED WRINKLED BULLIFORM

PUCKFIST BRAGGART PUFFBALL

PUCKISH PUXY ELFIN IMPISH WHIMSICAL

PUDDING DICK DUFF LINK SAGO DOWDY KUGEL MERIT BURGOO FENDER HACKIN HAGGIS HAUPIA JAUDIE SPONGE TANSEY TARTAN DESSERT ADEQUACY BLOODING HEDGEHOG LIVERING PANDOWDY WHITEPOT CHARLOTTE

(— **CONTAINING KALE**) TARTAN

(— **OF FLOUR**) DUFF

(**BOILED** —) HOY

(**FRUIT** —) HEDGEHOG

(**HASTY** —) MUSH SEPON SUPAWN

(**HAWAIIAN** —) HAUPIA

(**MEAT** —) ISING HACKIN HACKING

(**SUET** —) KUGEL

PUDDINGWIFE PUDIANO DONCELLA GLUEFISH

PUDDLE DUB PANT PLUD POOL PULK ROIL SLAB SLOP SOSS SUMP PLANT PLASH PUDGE CHARCO FLODGE MUDDLE PUDDER SPLASH TAMPER CONFUSE PLASHET SLODDER SPUDDLE BEFUDDLE
(MUD —) DUB SLOP LOBLOLLY
PUDDLER'S RABBLE STRIKE
PUDENCY MODESTY DELICACY
PUDGY MIRY BULKY MUDDY SQUAT CHUBBY SPUDDY
PUDU VENADA
PUEBLO ANASAZI
PUELCHE PAMPA TEHUELET
PUERILE WEAK SILLY BOYISH JEJUNE TRIVIAL CHILDISH IMMATURE YOUTHFUL

PUERTO RICO
BAY: SUCIA RINCON BOQUERON AQUADILLA
CAPITAL: SANJUAN
ISLAND: MONA CULEBRA VIEQUES
LAKE: LOIZA CARITE CAONILLAS
MEASURE: CUERDA CABALLERIA
RIVER: CAMUY CANAS YAUCO ANASCO TANAMA FAJARDO
TOWN: CAYEY COAMO PONCE DORADO MANATI ARECIBO FAJARDO GUAYAMA HUMACAO MAYAGUEZ

PUFF GUF POP BLOW BRAG DRAG FLAM FLAN GUFF GUST HUFF PANT SHOW WAFF WAFT ELATE ERUPT EXTOL FLUFF GLURB QUIFF STECH SWELL WHIFF CAPFUL EXPAND FLATUS BLUSTER EXPLODE GRATIFY INFLATE WHIFFET BRAGGART OVERRATE WINDGALL BOUILLONE
(— FROM SHELL BLAST) BURST
(— OF WIND) FLAM TIFT SCART FLATUS HUFFLE
(— OUT SMOKE) EFFUME
(— OUT) BELL BLUB VENT BLUBBER EFFLATE INFLATE
(— UP) BLOW HUFF RISE BLOAT HEAVE BLADDER
(— VIOLENTLY) BLAST
(CREAM —) DUCHESSE
(SUDDEN —) FLAN FLAW GUST
PUFFBALL FIST FUZZ PUFF SMOKE FUNGUS PUFFIN BULLFICE BULLFIST PUCKFIST SNUFFBOX
PUFFBIRD BARBET MONASE NUNLET DREAMER NUNBIRD BARBACOU
PUFFED BLUB BOLLEN BLOATED SOUFFLE SWOLLEN ARROGANT INFLATED
(— OUT) BAGGY BOUFFANT
(— UP) RANK POBBY ASTRUT BLOATED SWOLLEN TURGENT
(BE — UP) BELL
PUFFER ATINGA BALLER BLOWER SLIMER TAMBOR BURFISH EGGFISH BLOWFISH TOADFISH
PUFFIN LOOM PAPE POPE MARROT MULLET MARROCK WILLOCK

COCKANDY PARAKEET TOMNODDY TOMNORRY
(HAWAIIAN —) AO
PUFFY SOFT BLOAT FAFFY GUMMY GUSTY PURSY CHUBBY FLUFFY PURFLY PERSIVE SWOLLEN BLADDERY BOUFFANT DROPSICAL
PUG FOX IMP PET BOXER CHAFF GOUGE SPOOR TRACK TRAIL CAMOIS CAMUSE GOBLIN MONKEY MISTRESS PUGILIST FOOTPRINT
PUGILIST PUG MILLER BRUISER SLOGGER
PUG-NOSED CAMUS CAMUSE
PUISNE PUNY LATER PETTY JUNIOR YOUNGER INFERIOR
PUISSANCE ARMY FORCE POWER CONTROL POTENCY PROWESS DOMINION STRENGTH
PUJUNAN MAIDU
PUKKA GOOD REAL GENUINE LASTING COMPLETE SUPERIOR AUTHENTIC
PUKRAS PHEASANT KOKLAS
PULCHRITUDE GRACE BEAUTY
PULE CRY PEEP CHIRP COWRY WHINE SNIVEL WHIMPER
PULING PULY SPINDLY WHINING
PULL IN PU EAR LUG POO POU ROG RUG TIT TOW CHUG CLAW DRAG DRAW DUCT HALE HARL HAUL HOOK RUGG SWIG TIRE TREK TUSH TWIG YANK BOUSE BREAK BUNCH DRAFT HEAVE HITCH IMPEL PLUCK POLLE PROOF TRICE TWEAK ASSUME COMMIT GATHER OBTAIN PLITCH RUGGLE SECURE TWITCH UPROOT WRENCH ATTRACT EXTRACT
(— A BELL) SET
(— ABOUT) TEW SOOL TOSE TOZE MOUSLE
(— APART) RAVE REND TEAR DIVULSE
(— AWAY) AVEL AVELL WREST REVULSE
(— BY EARS) SOLE SOWL
(— DOWN) UNPILE DESTROY DEMOLISH
(— HERE AND THERE) TOOZLE TOUSLE
(— NOSE) SNITE
(— OF DRUM) EAR
(— OFF) CROP DRAW STRIP AVULSE
(— ON FISHING ROD) STRIKE
(— OUT) RAX EXTRACT OUTBRAID
(— QUICKLY) YANK
(— ROUGHLY) WAP TOWSE WOUSE
(— SUDDENLY) TRICE
(— THE LEG) STRING
(— TOGETHER) KNOT ATTRACT
(— TRIGGER) SQUEEZE
(— UP BY THE ROOTS) ARACE
(— UP) LOUK
(— WITH JERK) HOICK SWITCH
(ZIPPER —) SLIDER
PULLDEVIL SCROUGER SCRODGILL
PULLER KNOCKER
PULLER-IN CLICKER

PULLET HEN EAROCK EEROCK EIRACK MABYER POULARD POULAINE
PULLEY RIM CONE DRUM BLOCK FUSEE FUZEE IDLER WHEEL DRIVEN IDLEBY JOCKEY POLYVE RIGGER SHEAVE SHIVER WHARVE CAPSTAN FERRULE TIGHTER TRUCKLE WHARROW PULLISEE PURCHASE TROCHLEA
(PL.) TRISPAST JACKANAPES
PULLOVER JERSEY SWEATER
PULLULATE BUD TEEM SWARM MULTIPLY
PULMONATE LUNGED
PULP PAP PUG CHUM BROKE JELLY NERVE SLUSH STOCK STUFF MARROW SQUEEZE SQUELCH
PULPIT PEW TUB AMBO BEMA DESK WOOD CHAIR PREACH ROSTRUM TRIBUNE
(— BOARD) TYPE
(— FOR CHOIR BOOKS) ANALOGION
(MOSLEM —) MIMBAR MINBAR
(OPEN-AIR —) TENT
PULPY SOFT SPEWY FLABBY FLESHY SIDDER SIDDOW BACCATE SQUELCHY
PULSATE BEAT BRIM FLAP PANT PUMP THROB COURSE STRIKE PALPITATE
PULSATION BEAT HEARTBEAT LIFEBLOOD VIBRATION
(— OF ARTERY) ICTUS
PULSE DAL BEAT DOHL TAKT URAD WAVE POUCE STUFF THROB BATTUTA IMPULSE PULSIDGE SPHYGMUS VITALITY
PULVERIZE BUCK DRAG FINE MEAL MULL STUB CRUSH FLOUR GRIND POUND POWDER ATOMIZE DEMOLISH VANQUISH COMMINUTE
PULVERIZED FINE POWDERED
PULVERIZER MULLER
PULVERULENT DUSTY CRUMBLY POWDERY
PUMA COUGAR PAINTER PANTHER
PUME YARURA
PUMICE PUMEX PUMIE
PUMMEL FIB BEAT DRUB PAIK SLAT POUND SLATE THUMP POUNCE
PUMP GIN GUN FORK JACK COURT FORCE HEART PLUMB SLUSH DOCTOR DORSAY FORCER SINKER VOLUTE BOOSTER DOWNTON EJECTOR EVACTOR PITWORK SLUDGER SYRINGE TOEPLER BEERPULL ELEVATOR INFLATER INJECTOR PULSATOR
(— ON SHIPS) DOWNTON
(GAS —) BOWSER
(HAND —) GUN
(MINE —S) SET
(SET OF —S) LIFT
PUMP DOCTOR GRATHER
PUMPER RACKER
PUMPERNICKEL BOMBERNICKEL
PUMPKIN PEPO CHUMP GOURD PEPON QUASH CITRUL CUCURB

CUSHAW SQUASH QUASHEY
CUCURBIT PEPONIDA

PUMPKINSEED RUFF SUNNY
FLATFISH FLOUNDER REDBELLY

PUN NICK WHIM ALLUDE CLINCH
QUIBBLE EQUIVOKE PARAGRAM
CALEMBOUR

PUNCH DAB DIG HUB JAB SET BASH
BLOW BOFF BUST DING PLUG POKE
SETT SOAK SOCK TIFF DOUSE
DRIFT FORCE GLOGG PASTE PENCH
SHORT SLOSH CANCEL INCUSE
PATRIX PAUNCH SHAPER STRIKE
TRACER MATTOIR PERLOIR
STARTER EMBOSSER GROUNDER
PRITCHEL PUNCTURE SWATCHEL
THICKSET

(**CHASING** —) TRACER

(**ETCHER'S** —) MATTOIR

(**HORSESHOE** —) PRITCHEL

(**OVAL** —) PLAISHER

PUNCHBOARD PUSHCARD

PUNCH BOWL SNEAKER

PUNCHED PERTUSE

PUNCHEON CASK PULE SNAP
PUNCH

PUNCHER COWBOY SOCKER

PUNCHINELLO CLOWN BUFFOON
PUGENELLO

PUNCH PRESS BEAR DROP

PUNCHY POUNCY FORCEFUL

PUNCTILIOUS NICE EXACT STIFF
FORMAL CAREFUL POINTED
PRECISE PUNCTUAL

PUNCTUAL DUE EXACT PROMPT
CAREFUL PRECISE ACCURATE
DEFINITE DETAILED EXPLICIT

PUNCTUATE MARK STOP
EMPHASIZE

PUNCTUATION MARK DOT DASH
STOP BRACE COLON COMMA PRICK
SLASH HYPHEN PERIOD STIGME
BRACKET VIRGULE ELLIPSIS
SEMICOLON

PUNCTURE HOLE PICK PINK PROD
STAB DRILL POINT PRICK PUNCH
STICK NEEDLE PIERCE PIQURE
DEFLATE DESTROY PUNCTUM
CENTESIS

PUNDIT SVAMI SWAMI CRITIC PANDIT
TEACHER

PUNGENCY HEAT SALT SNAP
ACRIMONY KEENNESS PIQUANCY
SALTNESS

PUNGENT HOT TEZ BOLD FELL
KEEN RACY SALT TART ACRID
ACUTE BRISK QUICK SHARP SMART
SNELL SPICY BITING BITTER SHRILL
SNAPPY CAUSTIC MORDANT
PEPPERY PIQUANT POINTED
TELLING CAYENNED PIERCING
POIGNANT STABBING STINGING

PUNGI BIN

PUNIC PUNICAL FAITHLESS

PUNISH FIT FIX PAY BUCK CANE
COLT COOK CUCK FINE FLOG GATE
SORT WIPE ABUSE BIRCH CURSE
ORDER SCOUR SHEND SLATE SPILL
STOCK STRAP TWINK WREAK

AMERCE AVENGE CAMPUS FERULE
FOLLOW IMMURE LESSON REFORM
SCHOOL STRIKE CHASTEN
CONSUME CORRECT CORRIGE
DEPLETE PENANCE REQUITE
SCOURGE CARTWHIP CHASTISE
DISTRAIN

(— **BY COMPENSATION**) FINE
AMERCE

(— **BY CONFINEMENT**) GATE

(— **BY FINE**) MULCT

(— **BY LASHING WRISTS**) BUCK

PUNISHING HARD GRUELING

PUNISHMENT GIG FINE LASH PAIN
PINE RACK SACK WITE YARD BEANS
GRUEL LIBEL PANDY PEINE SMART
WRACK WREAK DESERT DIRDUM
FERULE LESSON PICKET EXAMPLE
GALLOWS GANTLET JANKERS
PAYMENT PENALTY PENANCE
PENANCY REVENGE SCOURGE
HERISSON JUDGMENT PUNITION
STOCKING SUPPLICE EXECUTION

(**CAPITAL** —) SCAFFOLD

(**MILITARY** —) JANKERS

PUNITIVE PENAL PUNITORY

PUNK BAD BOY FUNK JERK MONK
POOR PUNG CONCH SPONK SPUNK
AMADOU BUNKUM NOVICE
HOODLUM RUFFIAN BEGINNER
GANGSTER INFERIOR NONSENSE
STRUMPET TERRIBLE TOUCHWOOD

PUNKIE MIDGE MIDGET

PUNNING ALLUSIVE BIVERBAL

PUNSCH ARRACK

PUNSTER SPEED

PUNT BET HIT POY KENT KICK
QUANT GAMBLE GARVEY SKERRY

PUNTER BIDDER GAMBLER SCALPER
SERVITOR

PUNY WEAK DAWNY DEENY DWARF
FRAIL PETTY SCRAM WEARY JUNIOR
MAUGER NOVICE PUISNE RECENT
SICKLY SPROTY MANIKIN PIMPING
QUEECHY SHILPIT YOUNGER
DROGHLIN INFERIOR PINDLING

(— **PERSON**) TITMAN

PUP PUPPY WHELP

PUPA EGG NYMPH PUPPET TUMBLER
WIGGLER FLAXSEED WRIGGLER
CHRYSALIS

PUPIL BOY GYTE TYRO WARD BLACK
CADET CHILD ELEVE NORRY NURRY
RAPIN TUTEE ALUMNA GRADER
INFANT JUNIOR SENIOR LEARNER
PAULINE SCHOLAR SOJOURN
STUDENT ABSENTEE DISCIPLE
RUGBEIAN SCHOOLER

(— **AT HEAD OF CLASS**) DUX

(— **IN STUDIO**) RAPIN

(— **OF EYE**) BLACK PEARL SIGHT

(**ANGLO-INDIAN** —) CHELA

(**BOARDED** —) SOJOURN

PUPILAGE (**WARDSHIP PEDANTISM**

PUPPET BABY DOLL DUPE IDOL
MOTE BABBY DROLL DUMMY
MAUMET MOTION POPPIN STOOGE
WAJANG WAYANG GUIGNOL
DROLLERY MARIONET

(— **PLAY**) WAJANG

(— **SHOW**) VERTEP

PUPPIS STERN

PUPPY FOP PUP DOLL DOUGH
WHELP PUPPET

(**FEMALE** —) GYP

(**GREYHOUND** —) SAPLING

PURBLIND BISME BISSON

PURCHASABLE VENAL CORRUPT

PURCHASE BUY WIN EARN FISH
GAIN KOOP WHIP BOOTY HEDGE
PRIZE DUPLEX EFFECT EMPTIO
TACKLE ACQUIRE BARGAIN EMPTION
PILLAGE PROCURE BARRATRY

(— **AND FATTEN CATTLE**) HIGGLE

PURCHASER BUYER EMPTOR
VENDEE CHAPMAN POULTER
SHOPPER CUSTOMER

PURE NET CAST EVEN FAIR FINE
FREE FULL GOOD HOLY MERE NEAT
PUTE TRUE CLEAN CLEAR FRESH
MORAL NAKED SHEER STARK
SYCEE UTTER WHITE WHOLE
CANDID CHASTE ENTIRE IMMIXT
LIMPID PISTIC SIMPLE VESTAL
VIRGIN CATHARI GENUINE PERFECT
SINCERE ABSOLUTE ABSTRACT
COMPLETE DOVELIKE INNOCENT
SERAPHIC SPOTLESS VIRGINAL
VIRTUOUS

PUREE SOUP CREAM

PURGATIVE PURGE SENNA DIASENE
DRASTIC TURPETH ALOEDARY
CLEANSER EVACUANT CATHARTIC

PURGATORY PAIN SWAMP

PURGE LAX RID FIRE FLUX SOIL
CLEAR SCOUR DRENCH PHYSIC
REMOVE SEETHE SHRIVE SPURGE
CHISTKA CLEANSE DETERGE
ABSTERGE

PURIFICATION BAPTISM ELUTION
LUSTRUM VASTATION

PURIFY TRY BOLT FINE PURE WASH
CLEAN PURGE SNUFF BLEACH
DISTIL FILTER REFINE SETTLE
SPURGE WINNOW BAPTIZE CHASTEN
CLEANSE EPURATE EXPIATE
LAUNDER SUBLIME SWEETEN
DEPURATE EXORCISE FILTRATE
LUSTRATE SANCTIFY SCAVENGE
SPRINKLE

(— **ORE**) DILVE

PURIFYING SMECTIC DEPURANT

PURIRI TEAK BULREEDY IRONWOOD

PURITAN PRIG SAINT CANTER
CROPPY BLUENOSE CATHARAN
GOSPELER ROUNDHEAD

PURITANICAL BLUE STRICT
GENTEEL PRECISE

PURITY PURE ASSAY HONOR WHITE
CANDOR SATTVA VIRTUE FINESSE
CHASTITY FINENESS PURENESS

PURL RIB EDDY KNIT PEARL UPSET
RIPPLE TOTTLE CAPSIZE OVERTURN

PURLIEU HAUNT
(PL.) BOUNDS CONFINES ENVIRONS

PURLOIN CAB CRIB WEED BRIBE
FILCH STEAL SWIPE FINGER PILFER
PIRATE CABBAGE SURREPT
ABSTRACT

PURPLE GAY VIOL REGAL SHOWY
BLATTA BLOODY CROCUS EVEQUE
MIGNON ARDOISE FUCHSIA FUCHSIN
HEATHEN LOGWOOD PETUNIA
PONTIFF AMARANTH BURGUNDY
CAMERIER CYCLAMEN EGGPLANT
EMINENCE IMPERIAL MAUVETTE
WISTARIA
  (DELICATE —) MAUVE
  (VISIBLE —) RHODOPSIN
PURPLE FISH MUREX
PURPLE GALLINULE SULTAN
  SULTANA HYACINTH
PURPLE LOOSESTRIFE KILLWEED
PURPLE RAGWORT JACOBY
PURPLE SANDPIPER REDLEG
  REDLEGS ROCKBIRD
PURPORT FECK GIST PORT DRIFT
SENSE TENOR DESIGN EFFECT
IMPART IMPORT INTEND INTENT
BEARING MEANING PROFESS
PURPOSE COVERING DISGUISE
STRENGTH
PURPOSE GO AIM END GOAL IDEA
MAIN MEAN MIND MINT PLAN SAKE
TALK TEND WEEN WILL ARTHA
CAUSE ETTLE HEART LEVEL SCOPE
STUDY THINK DESIGN DEVICE
EFFECT INTEND INTENT OBTENT
PREFIX SCHEME COMPASS COUNSEL
DESTINE EARNEST IMAGINE
MEANING PROPOSE DEVOTION
FUNCTION PLEASURE PROPOUND
DISCOURSE
  (FIXED —) HEART
  (MORAL —) ETHOS
PURPOSEFUL AIMFUL POINTED
PURPOSIVE TELIC HORMIC
PURPOSELESS WASTE AIMLESS
  FECKLESS
PURPURA MUREX PURPLES PELIOSIS
PURPURE GOLP GOLPE PURPLE
  MERCURY
PURR MURR THRUM WHURL DUNLIN
PURSE BAG CLY JAN BUNG CLAY
CLOY KNIT POKE PUSS SKIN BULSE
BURSE DUMMY FUNDS MEANS
POUCH SPUNG COMMON FOLLIS
GIPSER POCKET PUCKER READER
SHAMMY ALMONER GIPSIRE
LEATHER SPORRAN BUCKSKIN
BURSICLE CRUMENAL
PURSE CRAB PAGURID
PURSER CLERK BURSAR BOUCHER
  PINCHGUT NIPCHEESE
PURSING MIMP
  (— OF MOUTH) PRIM
PURSLANE PUSSLY PIGWEED
PURSLANE TREE SPEKBOOM
PURSUANCE SUING SEQUENCE
PURSUE BAY RUN SUE HUNT SEEK
CHASE CHEVY CHIVY ENSUE HOUND
QUEST SLATE STALK TRADE
COURSE FOLLOW GALLOP TRAVEL
BEDEVIL HOTFOOT CONTINUE
PRACTICE
  (— ZIGZAG COURSE) TACK
PURSUER FOLLOWER PLAINTIFF
  QUESTRIST

PURSUIT FAD HUNT SUIT CAPER
CAUSE CHASE CRAFT HOBBY
COURSE SEARCH ASSAULT ACTIVITY
ENTREATY
PURSUIVANT BUTE MARCH FALCON
ORMOND ATHLONE CARRICK
ANTELOPE DINGWALL FOLLOWER
PURSY FAT OBESE PUFFY
  ASTHMATIC
PURULENT PYIC ATTRY ATTERY
PURVEY PANDER SUPPLY FORESEE
  PROVIDE
PURVEYOR CATER TAKER ACHUAS
PROWER CATERER ACHATOUR
MANCIPLE
PUS WARE AMPER FESTER MATTER
  WORSUM QUITTER
PUSH CA DUB JAM JOG JUR PUT
BANG BIRR BOIL BOOM BORE BUNT
DING DUSH FLOG KENT PICK PILT
PING PORR POSS POTE STOP BLITZ
BOOST BRUSH BUNCH CROWD
CRUSH DRIVE DUNCH ELBOW
HUNCH NUDGE PINCH POACH
POUSE SCAUT SHOVE SKELP STICK
STOVE EXTEND HURTLE HUSTLE
JOGGLE JOSTLE POTTER PROPEL
THRING THRONG THRUST ASSAULT
IMPETUS IMPULSE OPERATE
PERPLEX SHUFFLE THRUTCH
CONTRUDE INCREASE SHOULDER
STRAITEN DISMISSAL
  (— ALONG) TUSH
  (— APART) SPREAD
  (— ASIDE) SHOG
  (— BY STICK) KENT POLE
  (— FORWARD) ADVANCE
  (— GENTLY) NUDGE
  (— INTO) INVADE
  (— MONEY) SPIFF
  (— ON) BEAR YERK
  (— OUT) DEBOUT LAUNCH
  (— RUDELY) HORSE HUSTLE
  (— TO FULL STRIDE) EXTEND
  (— TOGETHER) CONTRUDE
  (— UP) BOOST
  (— WITH ELBOW) ELBOW HUNCH
  (— WITH FEET) DIG SCAUT
  (— WITH HEAD) BUNT BUTT
  (STRONG —) BEVEL
PUSH BUTTON PUSH PRESSEL
PUSHCART BARROW TROLLEY
PUSHER PLUNGER TRAILER
  TRAMMER WHEELER
PUSHY FORWARD AGGRESSIVE
PUSILLANIMOUS WEAK TIMID
  FEEBLE COWARDLY TIMOROUS
PUSS CAT FACE HARE CHEET CHILD
  MOUTH RABBIT BAUDRONS
PUSTULE NOB BEAL BURL KNOB
POCK PUSH QUAT WART ACHOR
AMPER BLAIN WHEAL WHELK
BLOTCH FESTER PIMPLE TETTER
ANTHRAX BLISTER ERUPTION
WHEYWORM
PUT DO BET LAY PIT SET BANG BUTT
FILL GIVE GROW PILT REST URGE
ADAPT APPLY DIGHT DRIVE FOCUS
PLACE STALL STATE STEAD STEEK

STELL WAGER ASSIGN BESTOW
DECAMP IMPOSE INVEST PHRASE
REPOSE SPROUT THRUST DEPOSIT
EMPLACE EXPRESS INFLICT
SUBJECT
  (— AN END TO) DATE SNIB ABATE
NAPOO SNUFF SPIKE STASH STILL
STINT SOPITE STANCH ASSUAGE
EXPIATE SATISFY ABROGATE
DEMOLISH SURCEASE
  (— ANOTHER IN PLACE OF) RELIEVE
  (— APART) DISPART
  (— ASIDE) BLOW HAIN SAVE SHUNT
SHUFFLE
  (— AT REST) HUSH
  (— AWAY) STOW COVER ELONG
HUTCH SHIFT RECOND DIVORCE
  (— BACK INTO USE) RESTORE
  (— BACK) REMIT REMISE
  (— BEFORE) PROFER ANTEPONE
  (— DOWN) LAY DEMIT QUELL
DEPOSE SQUASH DEPRESS
OPPRESS REPRESS SILENCE
DIMINISH SUPPRESS
  (— EDGE ON) TED
  (— FLAX UPON A DISTAFF) DIZEN
  (— FORTH BLOSSOMS) GEM
  (— FORTH) GEM CAST GIVE PUSH
EXERT LANCE PROFER STRETCH
  (— GRAIN IN BARN) END
  (— IN AGONY) THROE
  (— IN CHARGE) COMMIT
  (— IN COMPETITION) PIT
  (— IN DANGER) SCUPPER
  (— IN DREAD) ADRAD
  (— IN MOTION) AROUSE
  (— IN OPERATION) LAUNCH
  (— IN ORDER) DO SET REDD SIDE
SORT TRIM DIGHT MENSE SHIFT
TRICK ADJUST DAIKER GRAITH
ORDAIN SETTLE ARRANGE CLARIFY
DISPOSE REDRESS INSTRUCT
  (— IN PLACE) POSE
  (— IN POSSESSION) SEISE
  (— IN PRISON) WARD
  (— IN) ENTER INSERT INTROMIT
  (— INFORMATION INTO) ADDRESS
  (— INTO BARN) END
  (— INTO CASE) SHEATHE
  (— INTO CIRCULATION) EMIT
SPRING
  (— INTO ECSTASY) ENTRANCE
  (— INTO EFFECT) EXECUTE
SANCTION
  (— INTO IRONS) BOLT
  (— INTO RHYTHM) METER METRE
  (— LIQUOR INTO CASK) TUN
  (— OFF) DOFF HAFT DEFER DELAY
DEMUR FOIST PARRY REMIT REPRY
SHIFT TARRY THROW LINGER
RETARD SHELVE ADJOURN
FORSLOW PROLONG RESPITE
POSTPONE
  (— ON AIRS) PROSS FINICK REVEST
  (— ON ALERT) ALARM
  (— ON COVER) HACKLE
  (— ON GUARD) ALERT CAUTION
  (— ON HAT) COVER
  (— ON PRETENSE) AFFECT

(— **ON SALE**) SHOP
(— **ON SHORT ALLOWANCE**) SCRIMP
(— **ON STRING**) ENFILE
(— **ON**) DON APPLY CRACK DRAPE
ENDUE MOUNT STAGE ASSUME
INVEST ADDRESS
(— **OUT BATSMAN**) SKITTLE
(— **OUT OF ACTION**) HAMPER
(— **OUT**) GET OUT DOUT OUST
DOWSE EVICT EXERT OUTED SLAKE
SLOCK RETIRE DISMISS EXCLUDE
EXTINCT FORJUDGE
(— **RIGHT**) AMEND
(— **ROAD METAL ON**) STEEN
(— **THROUGH A STRAINER**) TAMMY
(— **TO FLIGHT**) AFLEY FEAZE GALLY
(— **TO RIGHTS**) SORT DIGHT
(— **TO SHAME**) DASH ABASH SHEND
UPBRAID
(— **TO SLEEP**) OPIATE SOPITE
SOPORATE
(— **TO USE**) STOW APPLY BESTOW
(— **TO WORK**) HARNESS
(— **TOGETHER**) ADD JOIN BUILD
COMPILE COMPOSE CONCOCT
CONFECT ASSEMBLE COMPOUND
(— **UP HAY**) BOTTLE
(— **UP WITH**) GO BEAR BIDE HACK
BROOK ENDURE SUFFER COMPORT
STOMACH SWALLOW TOLERATE
(— **UP**) ANTE ERECT FLUSH
DISPENSE
(— **UPON**) GAMMON
(— **WITH ANOTHER**) APPOSE
PUTCHER PUTLOG PUTCHEN
PUTLOCK
PUTREFACTION ROT DECAY
PUTREFACTIVE SEPTIC
PUTREFY ROT DECAY SWEAT
FESTER POLLUTE PUTRESCE
PUTRESCENT PUTRID ROTTEN
PUTRID FOUL SOUR VILE LOUSY

ROTTEN CORRUPT DECAYED
FRIABLE VICIOUS DEPRAVED
PUTT CLOWN BORROW GOBBLE
PUTTEE PAT PATA GAITER BANDAGE
LEGGING
PUTTER FUSS MESS MUCK TRUCK
CADDLE DAWDLE MUCKER MUCKLE
PIDDLE TINKER FRIGGLE
PUTTY BEDDING
PUTTYROOT CRAWFOOT
PUTZ CRECHE
PUXY SWAMPY QUAGMIRE
PUZZLE CAP GET SET BEAT CRUX
DEAD LICK POSE BEFOG GRIPH
POSER QUEER REBUS STICK BAFFLE
BOTHER ENIGMA FICKLE FOITER
GLAIKS JIGSAW KITTLE RIDDLE
CONFUSE MYSTERY MYSTIFY
NONPLUS PERPLEX STICKER
TAISSLE TANGRAM TRANGAM
ACROSTIC BEFUDDLE BEWILDER
CONFOUND DISTRACT DUMFOUND
ENTANGLE INTRIGUE REMBLERE
CROSSWORD
PUZZLED ASEA
PUZZLING KNOTTY KNOTTED
RIDDLING DIFFICULT
PYCNANTHEMUM KOELLIA
PYCNOGONID SPIDER
PYGARG ADDAX OSPREY
PYGIDIUM PODEX
PYGMALION (**FATHER OF** —) BELUS
MUTGO AGENOR
(**MURDERED BY** —) SICHAEUS
(**SISTER OF** —) DIDO
(**STATUE FASHIONED BY** —)
GALATEA
PYGMY ELF AKKA AMBA DOKO
ACHUA AFIFI ATOMY BATWA DWARF
GNOME PIXIE PIGMEW WOCHUA
ACHANGO ASHANGO MANIKIN
DWARFISH NEGRILLO VAALPENS
DANDIPRAT

PYGMY GOOSE GOSLET
PYGMY RATTLESNAKE
MASSASAUGA
PYGOSTYLE VOMER
PYKNIC SQUAT STOCKY STHENIC
MUSCULAR
PYRAMID BENBEN HOPPER
TEOCALLI
(— **OF CRAYFISH**) BUISSON
(**DOUBLE** —) TWIN ZIRCONOID
(**INVERTED** —) HOPPER
PYRAMIDAL HUGE ENORMOUS
IMPOSING
PYRAMIDICAL TAPER
PYRAZINE ALDINE PIAZIN DIAZINE
PYRE BALE TOPHET BONFIRE
BALEFIRE
PYRITE BALE MUNDIC
(PL.) BRAZIL STANNITE FIRESTONE
MAGISTRAL MARCASITE
PYROLA LIMONIUM SHINLEAF
PYROMANIAC FIREBUG ARSONIST
PYRONE CUMALIN
PYROPHYLLITE PENCIL
PYROTECHNICS FIREWORKS
PYROXENE AUGITE SALITE SAHLITE
DIALLAGE DIOPSIDE
PYROXENITE ARIEGITE MARCHITE
OSTRAITE NIKLESITE
PYRRHIC DIBRACH
PYRRHULOXIA GROSBEAK
BULLFINCH
PYRROLE AZOLE
PYTHON ADJIGER PEROPOD
ANACONDA
PYTHONESS WITCH PHITONES
PYTHONIC HUGE INSPIRED
ORACULAR MONSTROUS PROPHETIC
PYX BOX CAPSA CASKET VESSEL
BINNACLE CIBORIUM
PYXIDIUM CAPSULE

Q KU CUE KUE QUEEN QUEUE
QUEBEC
QUA HERON QUABIRD
QUACK PUFF WHACK SALVER
SUBTLE EMPIRIC IMPOSTOR
OPERATOR SANGRADO CHARLATAN
QUACKERY HUMBUG
QUADRAGESIMA LENT
QUADRANGLE QUAD CLOSE COURT
TETRAGON
QUADRANT BOW RADIAL SQUARE
QUARTER TETRANT ALTIMETER
QUADRATE SUIT AGREE IDEAL
QUADER SQUARE PERFECT
BALANCED
QUADRIC CONICOID
QUADRILATERAL TRAPEZIA
TETRAGRAM
(PL.) TESSARA
QUADRILLE CONTREDANSE
(PL.) LANCERS
QUADROON QUATERON TERCERON
QUADRUPED BABIRUSA
QUADRUPLE FOURBLE FOURFOLD
QUADRUPLET FOURLING QUARTOLE
QUAFF QUAX TOOT DRINK QUASS
WAUCHT CAROUSE TRILLIL
QUAG BOG MARSH SHAKE QUIVER
QUAGMIRE BOG FEN GOG HAG QUA
SOG LAIR PUXY QUAW MARSH
MIZZY SWAMP MORASS PUDDLE
BOGMIRE PUCKSEY
QUAHOG CLAM COHOG VENUS
BULLNOSE
QUAIL COW LOWA WEET COLIN
DAUNT QUAKE SPOIL WASTE
BLENCH CURDLE FLINCH SHRINK
TURNIX WITHER DECLINE HEMIPOD
TREMBLE ROBWHITE
(YOUNG —) SQUEALER
QUAINT DRY ODD NAIVE STRANGE
FANCIFUL HANDSOME
QUAKE JAR QUOG RESE CHILL
QUAIL SHAKE QUIVER SHIVER
FLUTTER SHUDDER TREMBLE
QUAKER ASPEN HERON FRIEND
OBADIAH WHACKER HICKSITE
TREMBLER BEACONITE BROADBRIM
SHADBELLY
(— STATE) PENNA PENNSYLVANIA
QUAKER GRAY ACIER
QUAKING ASPEN QUAKY TREPID
SHAKING TREMBLING
QUAKING GRASS COWQUAKE
WAGWANTS
QUALIFICATION NATURE RESERVE
SHADING CAPACITY
QUALIFIED FIT ABLE MEET FITTED
FITTEN LIKELY CAPABLE ELIGIBLE
SUITABLE AUTHENTIC
(NOT —) INAPT INHABILE
QUALIFIER MODIFIER
QUALIFY FIT DASH ADAPT ALLAY
EQUIP HEDGE ENABLE MODIFY
SOFTEN TEMPER ABSOLVE CERTIFY
ENTITLE LICENSE PREPARE
GRADUATE MODERATE RESTRAIN
RESTRICT
QUALITY Y BRAN BUMP CHOP COST

FEEL GUNA LEAD SORT COLOR
GRACE STATE TRAIT ASSIZE
BARREL FABRIC STRAIN THREAD
TIMBER ADJUNCT CALIBER KINSHIP
STATURE ACCIDENT MOVEMENT
PROPERTY
(— OF PERSONAL EMOTIONS)
PATHOS
(— OF PHOTOGRAPH) CONTRAST
(— OF TONE) TIMBRE
(— OF VOWELS) LENGTH
(— PECULIAR TO ONESELF) SEITY
(AESTHETIC —) TASTE
(ARTISTIC —) VIRTU
(ATTRACTIVE —) TAKE
(BASIC —) GRAIN
(BASIC —S) STUFF
(COLOR —) TONE
(ESSENTIAL —) ALLOY SPECIES
SUCHNESS
(GOOD —) THEW
(HEREDITARY —) STRAIN
(IMPECCABLE —) FINISH
(INCISIVE —) BITE
(INNATE —) LARGESS
(INTELLECTUAL —) BROW
(NATURAL —) TARAGE
(OBJECTIONABLE —) ANILITY
(OF HIGH —) FRANK
(PERVASIVE —) AROMA
(PHYSICAL —S) BOTTOM
(PRIMAL —) GUNA
(PUNGENT —) SNAP
(RELATIVE —) RATE
(SPRINGY —) SPINE
(STRUCTURAL —) TEXTURE
(SUBDUED —) SHADE
(SUBTLE —) BOUQUET
(SUPERIOR —) SUPER FINENESS
(TRIED —) TOUCH
(UNUSUAL —) SURD
(WAVY — OF HAIR) FLIX
QUALM CALM DROW PALL NAUSEA
SQUEAM SCRUPLE
QUALMISH TEWLY SICKISH
SQUEAMISH
QUAMOCLIT MOONFLOWER
QUANDARY FIX PUXY TANGLE
DILEMMA NONPLUS SWITHER
DOLDRUMS JUNCTURE
QUANDONG PEACH
QUANTIC NONIC OCTIC SEPTIC
SEXTIC QUADRIC QUINTIC
QUANTIFIER PREFIX
QUANTITY JAG SUM SUP BODY
DEAL DISH DOSE FECK JAGG LIFT
MASK SOME SOUD WARE BATCH
BREAK CLASH GRIST KITTY SIEGE
TROOP WHEEN ACTION ADDEND
AMOUNT BAGFUL BOTTLE BUDGET
DICKER EFFECT HANTLE NUMBER
SPINOR THRAVE CONTENT FOOTAGE
PORTION QUANTUM GLASSFUL
KNIFEFUL LADLEFUL
(— OF ARROWS) SHEAF
(— OF BUTTER) CHURNING
(— OF CLOTHES) BUCKING
(— OF COTTONSEED) CRUSH
(— OF CUT TREES) FALL

(— OF DRINK) HOOP DRAFT
DRAUGHT
(— OF ELECTRICITY) FARADAY
(— OF EXPLOSIVE) CHARGE
(— OF FISH OR GAME) TAKE CATCH
DRAFT DRAUGHT
(— OF GRAIN) GAVEL
(— OF HAY) TRUSS
(— OF IRRIGATION WATER) DUTY
(— OF LIQUID) DROP JAUP SLASH
GOBBET
(— OF LIQUOR) HEELTAP
(— OF LUMBER) RUN
(— OF METAL) BLOW
(— OF MUD) CLASH
(— OF NARCOTICS) BINDLE
(— OF PAPER) TOKEN
(— OF PRODUCE) BURY
(— OF RAISINS) FRAIL
(— OF THREAD) LEASE
(— OF WOOD) HAG FATHOM
(ESTIMATED —) WEY
(EXCESSIVE —) GLUT SPATE
(FIXED —) CONSTANT
(GREAT —) HOST MORT MUCH
HIRST SIGHT STORE BARREL
FOREST SLATHER TUMMELS
(LARGE —) ACRE BOLT DEAL FECK
HEAP MASS PECK SCAD SLEW
FLOOD FORCE GRIST JORUM
POWER SCADS SHEAF STACK
STORE BUCKET BUSHEL DICKER
DOLLOP GALLON MATTER MELDER
CLUTHER SKINFUL HECATOMB
MOUNTAIN
(LEAST —) BEDROCK
(MINUTE —) DRAM DROP SHADE
SCRUPLE
(NOTEWORTHY —) CHUNK
(RELATIVE —) DEGREE
(SETTLED —) SIZE
(SIZABLE —) SCUMP
(SMALL —) ACE BIT SUP DASH
DUST HAET HAIR HARL IOTA PEAK
SOSH SPOT CANCH PRILL SMACK
SPICE SQUIB TOUCH JOBBLE
MORSEL PICKLE SAMPLE SONGLE
STIVER CAPSULE CURTSEY DRIBBLE
DRIBLET EPSILON HANDFUL
MODICUM SMICKET SPATTER
TODDICK FARTHING MOUTHFUL
PENNORTH SCANTLET
(UNDIRECTED —) SCALAR
(VARYING —) SKID
QUANTUM PHONON PHOTON
QUAPAW KWAPA ARKANSAS
QUARANTINE DETAIN ISOLATE
SANCTION
QUARENTENE ROOD FURLONG
QUARREL JAR YED BEEF CHIP DEAL
FEUD FRAY FUSS JARL JOWL MIFF
NIFF ODDS PICK PLEA SPAT BRACK
BRAWL BRIGE BROIL FLITE FLUSK
GRUFF HURRY JOWER NOISE PIQUE
SCOLD SCRAP SHINE STOUR UPSET
WRALL AFFRAY BARNEY BREACH
BREEZE BRIGUE DEBATE DIFFER
DUSTUP FRACAS FRATCH GARROT
JANGLE MATTER QUARRY RIPPET

SQUARE SQUEAL STRIFE THREAP THREEP THWART BRABBLE DISGUST DISPUTE FACTION OUTCAST PRABBLE RUCTION SIMULTY STASHIE SWAGGER TUILZIE WRANGLE DISAGREE MOORBURN SPLUTTER SQUABBLE TRAVERSE
(— IN WORDS) JANGLE
(NOISY —) ROW FRACAS KICKUP
(PETTY —) MIFF SPAT TIFF
QUARRELING BICKER CONTEK CHIDING CONTECK
QUARRELSOME RIXY UGLY ROWTY FEISTY SCRAPPY DRAWLING FRAMPOLD FRATCHED PETULANT PHRAMPEL FRACTIOUS
(NOT —) AMICABLE
QUARRELSOMENESS SQUARING WARIANCE
QUARRIED (NOT —) LIVE
QUARRIER FACEMAN QUARION
QUARRY DELF GAME LODE MEAT CHASE DELFT DELPH PLUCK LATOMY REWARD LATOMIA LOZENGE
(HAWK'S —) MARK
QUARRYMAN SCABBLER SCAPPLER
QUART SHANT WHART
(1-8TH —) GILL
(2 —S) FLAGON
(4 —S) GALLON
(METRIC —) LITER
(ONE-HALF —) PINT
QUARTE FOURTH
QUARTER PART STUD EAVER GRITH TRACT BARRIO BEHALF BESTOW CANTON COLONY FARDEL HARBOR SECTOR CONTRADA FAUBOURG FIERDING STANDARD POBLACION
(— IN BATTLE) GRITH
(— OF A POUND) TRIPPET
(— OF BEEF OR MUTTON) BOUT
(— OF CITY) BLOCK GHETTO
(— OF COMPASS) PLAGE
(— OF FLAG) CANTON
(— OF HOUR) POINT
(— OF HUNDRED) FIERDING
(— OF YEAR) RAITH
(— ONESELF) SORN
(— UPON) LAY
(JEWISH —) ALJAME
QUARTERING LASKING CHUMMAGE
QUARTER NOTE CROTCHET
QUARTER REST SOSPIRO
QUARTERS BOTHY BILLET BOTHIE LIVERY MENAGE FARDELS CHUMMERY DIGGINGS LODGMENT
(— FOR IMMIGRANTS) HOSTEL
(— OF SALVATION ARMY) BARRACKS
(HIGH —) AERY EYRY AERIE EYRIE
(JUNIOR OFFICERS' —) GUNROOM
(MEN'S —) SELAMLIK
(MONASTERY —) FRATRY
QUARTET FOURSOME
QUARTILE SQUARE TETRAGON
QUARTO FOURS
QUARTZ IRIS ONYX SARD AGATE FLINT PRASE TARSO TOPAZ JASPER

MORION PEBBLE PLASMA SILICA ALENCON CITRINE CRYSTAL RUBASSE SINOPLE AMETHYST BASANITE SARDONYX SIDERITE YENTNITE
QUARTZITE GANISTER SILCRETE
QUASH CASS CRUSH QUELL SPIKE SQUAT SOPITE CASSARE PEREMPT SUPPRESS
QUAT FOUR GLUT SQUASH SATIATE UPSTART
QUATERNION TETRAD QUADRATE
QUATREFOIL TRESSURE
(DOUBLE —) EIGHTFOIL
QUAVER QUAP CROMA SHAKE TRILL WAVER CHROMA FALTER QUIVER WABBLE WOBBLE WRIBLE FREDDON VIBRATE
QUAVERY WARBLY UNSTEADY
QUAY KEY POW QUAI LEVEE BUNDER STRAND
QUEACH BOG FEN MARSH THICKET
QUEASINESS KECK SICKNESS
QUEASY NICE SICK SQUEEZY DELICATE NAUSEATED SQUEAMISH
QUEBRACHO BREAKAX AXMASTER IRONWOOD AXBREAKER
QUEBRADA BROOK GULLY RAVINE FISSURE
QUECHUA INCAN KICHUA
QUEEN REG DAME FERS LADY MEDB RANI AEDON BEGUM FIERS RANEE ATOSSA REGINA ROXANA TAILTE TAMARA ARGANTE ATHALIA CANDACE JOCASTE OMPHALE PHEARSE STATIRA TITANIA BRUNHILD GERTRUDE GLORIANA GUINEVER MAHARANI
(— AND KING OF TRUMPS) BELLA
(— CITY) CINCINNATI
(— IN CHESS) FERS LADY FIERS
(— OF CLUBS) SPADILLA
(— OF DENMARK) GERTRUDE
(— OF ETHIOPIA) CANDACE
(— OF FAIRY LAND) MEDB GLORIANA
(— OF GEORGIA) TAMARA
(— OF GOTHS) TAMORA
(— OF HEARTS) ELIZABETH
(— OF HEAVEN) HERA
(— OF JUDAH) ATHALIA
(— OF LYDIA) OMPHALE
(— OF SHEBA) BALKIS BILKIS
(— OF SPADES) BASTA LIZZY
(— OF THE ADRIATIC) VENICE
(— OF THE ANTILLES) CUBA
(— OF THE EAST) ZENOBIA
(— OF THEBES) JOCASTA
(— OF TRUMPS) HONOR
(FAIRY —) MAB ARGANTE TITANIA
(INDIAN —) RANI SUNK MAHARANI
(MOHAMMEDAN —) BEGUM
QUEEN ANNE'S LACE UMBEL
QUEEN BEE KING
QUEEN ELIZABETH DIANA ORIANA CYNTHIA
QUEENFISH WAHOO CROAKER DRUMFISH
QUEENLY HAUGHTY REGINAL MAJESTIC

QUEENROOT YAWSHRUB
QUEEN'S-DELIGHT YAWSHRUB
QUEENSLAND HEMP SIDA JELLYLEAF
QUEER HEX ODD RUM HARM DICKY DIPPY DROLL FAINT FUNNY GIDDY NUTTY RUMMY COCKLE HIPPED QUEASY QUISBY UNIQUE AMUSING COMICAL CURIOUS DISRUPT ERRATIC STRANGE TOUCHED WHIMSIC FANCIFUL OBSESSED PECULIAR
(— THING) QUOZ
QUEERNESS ODDITY
QUEEST RINGDOVE
QUELL DIE CALM FLOW HUSH KILL QUAY SLAY ABATE ALLAY CRUSH QUASH QUIET YIELD PACIFY PERISH REDUCE SOOTHE SPRING STANCH STIFLE KILLING REPRESS SQUELCH SUPPRESS
QUEME QUIM HANDY WHEAM COMELY PLEASE GRATIFY PLEASANT
QUENCH COOL DAMP SIND ALLAY CHECK CRUSH SLAKE SLOCK STILL STANCH STIFLE ASSUAGE SLOCKEN AUSTEMPER
QUENCHED EXTINCT
QUENCHER STANCH
QUENCHING FRITTING
QUERECHO VAQUERO
QUERELA AUDITA
QUERENT INQUIRER PLAINTIFF
QUERN KERN MILL METATE MILLSTONE
QUERULOUS WHINY FRETFUL PEEVISH NATTERED PETULANT IRRITABLE
QUERY ASK DOUBT DEMAND INQUIRE INQUIRY QUESTION
QUEST ASK BAY GAPE SEEK DEMAND EXAMINE PURSUIT SEEKING VENTURE
QUESTING OUTREACH
QUESTION ASK HOW SPY POSE QUIZ TALK ARGUE DOUBT DREAD QUERY ACCUSE CHANCE CHARGE DEMAND LEADER MATTER PONDER REASON SHRIVE EXAMINE INQUIRE INQUIRY PROBLEM SCRUPLE OVERTURE RELEVANT RESEARCH STICKLER
(— AMBIGUOUSLY WORDED) RIDDLE
(— FRETFULLY) RAME
(BAFFLING —) POSER
(PERPLEXING —) STUMPER
(UNSOLVED —) CRUX
QUESTIONABLE (NOT —) DECENT
QUESTIONER APPOSER INQUIRER
QUESTIONING DUBIOUS
QUESTIONABLE FISHY QUEER SHAKY UNSAFE CLOUDED DUBIOUS DOUBTFUL
QUESTION MARK QUERY QUAERE EROTEME
QUESTIONNAIRE POLL INVENTORY
QUETCH STIR TWITCH
QUETZAL QUESAL TROGON

QUEUE CUE COLA LINE BRAID PIGTAIL CROCODILE

QUEY KOY WHY WHEY HEIFER

QUIBBLE COG PUN BALK CARP QUIB QUIP CAVIL DODGE EVADE QUIRK SALVO AMBAGE BAFFLE BICKER HAFFLE BRABBLE CAPTION CHICANE QUIBLET QUIDDIT QUILLET SHUFFLE QUILLITY CONUNDRUM

QUICA OPOSSUM SARIGUE

QUICK APT RAD YAP FAST FLIT GLEG KECK KEEN LISH LIST PERT RATH RIFE SNAP SOON WHAT WHIT WICK AGILE ALIVE APACE BRISK CHEAP FLEET HASTY MERRY PREST RAPID READY SHARP SHORT SNACK SNELL SWIFT SWITH TOSTO TRICK VISTO YARRY ACTIVE CLEVER FACILE KITTLE NIMBLE PROMPT PRONTO SNAPPY SPEEDY SUDDEN DARTING SCHNELL SHUTTLE DEXTROUS TRIPPING
(— AND NEAT) DEFT
(— AS A FLASH) WHIP
(— IN PERCEPTION) ACID
(— IN RESPONSE) GNIB
(— TO DETECT) SMOKY
(— TO FLARE UP) GASSY
(— TO LEARN) APT
(— TO MOVE) YARE
(LIGHT AND —) VOLANT

QUICKEN PEP MEND STIR WHET HURRY SPEED ACUATE AROUSE HASTEN INCITE KINDLE REVIVE VIVIFY ANIMATE ENLIVEN REFRESH SHARPEN EXPEDITE INSPIRIT

QUICKENING FLICKER REVIVAL STIRRING

QUICKLY TID TIT CITO FAST RIFE SOON TIVY WHIP YARE NEWLY RADLY RATHE SHARP SKELP SNACK SNELL SWITH TIGHT WIGHT YEPLY ASTITE BELIVE HOURLY PRESTO PRONTO RASHLY EFTSOON PRESTLY READILY SPEEDILY WIKIWIKI
(— AND WITH FORCE) SWAP
(MORE —) TIDDER TITTER STRETTO

QUICKNESS HASTE SPEED AGILITY ACTIVITY CELERITY DISPATCH KEENNESS SAGACITY
(MENTAL —) NOUS SLEIGHT LEGERITY

QUICKSAND FLOW SYRT SYRTIS SWALLOW

QUICK-SELLING LEEFTAIL

QUICKSILVER OREMIX MERCURY TIERRAS HEAUTARIT

QUICK-SPEAKING PROMPT

QUICK-TEMPERED DONCY DONSY IRASCIBLE

QUICK-WITTED APT SHARP SMART NIMBLE KNOWING

QUID FID CHEW SOVEREIGN
(— OF TOBACCO) CUD FID

QUIDDANY JELLY SYRUP CODINIAC

QUIDDITY QUIBBLE WHATNESS

QUIDNUNC GOSSIP BUSYBODY

QUIESCENCE STASIS DORMANCY

QUIESCENT QUIET LATENT STATIC RESTING INACTIVE

QUIET QT ST COY LAY CALM COSH DEAD DUMB EASE EASY HUSH LOUN LOWN LULL REST ROCK SNUG SOFT WEME ACCOY CANNY CIVIL DOWNY LEVEL PEACE PEASE QUATE QUELL QUEME RESTY SALVE SHADY SILKY SLEEP SOBER SQUAT STILL SUANT WHIST DREAMY GENTLE PACIFY PLACID RETIRE SAUGHT SEDATE SERENE SETTLE SILENT SMOOTH SOFTLY SOOTHE SOPITE STEADY STILLY HUSHFUL ORDERLY REQUIEM RESTFUL SILENCE DECOROUS PEACEFUL TRANQUIL UNRUFFLE
(— DOWN) DILL
(MAKE —) ALLAY
(STEALTHILY —) SLINKY

QUIETISM MOLINISM

QUIETLY FAIR CANNY STILL WINLY EVENLY GENTLY SOFTLY TIPTOE

QUIETNESS REST REPOSE SERENITY

QUIETUDE CALM INERTION

QUIETUS REST DEATH RELEASE

QUILL COP PEN RIB PIRN FLOAT STALK BOBBIN FESCUE PINION SLEEVE CALAMOS PRIMARY TRUNDLE
(— FOR WINDING THREAD) COP
(PORCUPINE —) PEN

QUILLBACK SAILFISH SKIMBACK

QUILLWORT ISOETES FERNWORT

QUILT BEAT GULP WALT WELT WHIP DUVET REZAI CADDOW CHALON PALLET THRASH SWALLOW MATTRESS POULTICE COMFORTER

QUILTING MARCELLA

QUIMPER NICE

QUINCE COYNE ANGERS SQUINCH JAPONICA
(BENGAL —) BEL BAEL

QUINCE SEED CYDONIUM

QUININE KINA SPECIFIC

QUINK BRANT

QUINONE EMBELIN

QUINTAIN FAN

QUINTE FIFTH

QUINTESSENCE CREAM ELIXIR CLYSSUS OSMAZOME

QUINTUPLE QUINARY FIVEFOLD QUINIBLE

QUIP GIBE JEST JOKE CRACK QUIRK SALLY SCOFF TAUNT CONCEIT QUIBBLE

QUIRA CAOBA ROBLE HORMIGO VENCOLA MACAWOOD

QUIRE CHOR SEXTERN
(20 —S) REAM
(PL.) INSIDES

QUIRK BEND KINK QUIP TURN CLOCK CROOK TWIST CONCEIT QUIBBLE FLOURISH PAROXYSM MANNERISM

QUIRQUINCHO PICHI PELUDO

QUIRT WHIP ROMAL

QUIS WOODCOCK

QUIT GO DROP NASH PART QUAT AVOID BELAY CEASE DOUSE LEAVE SHIFT SHOOT STASH WHITE BEHAVE CIVITE DESERT DESIST FOREGO RESIGN SECEDE VACATE ABANDON FORSAKE RELEASE UNTENANT

QUITCH COUCH QUICK SCUTCH TWITCH

QUITCLAIM ACQUIT RELEASE DISCHARGE

QUITE SO ALL BUT GEY BRAW EVEN FAIR FREE FULL JUST PLAT WELL CLEAR CLOSE FULLY SHEER STARK CLEVER DAMNED ENOUGH JUSTLY MERELY TOTALLY
(NOT —) HARDLY

QUITRENT CANON

QUITS EVEN EVENS UPSIDES

QUITTER PUS SLAG PIKER COWARD JUMPER SHIRKER TURNBACK

QUIVER DIRL QUAG QUOG BEVER NIDGE QUAKE SHAKE TRILL WAVER WIVER BICKER COCKER DIDDER DINDLE SHEATH SHIMMY SHIVER TREMOR WAMBLE DORLACH FLUTTER FRISSON SHUDDER TREMBLE TWIDDLE TWITTER VIBRATE FLICHTER WERSLETE

QUIVERING ASPEN AGUISH DIDDER DITHER QUAGGLE QUAKING AGITATED ATREMBLE

QUIVER TREE KOKERBOOM

QUIXOTIC IMAGINARY VISIONARY

QUIZ ASK GUY HOAX MOCK CHAFF EXAMINE QUESTION RIDICULE

QUIZZICAL ODD QUEER QUIZZY CURIOUS WHIMSICAL

QUO KA

QUOD JAIL QUAD PRISON

QUOIN COIN ANGLE GOIGN CORNER LOZENGE KEYSTONE VOUSSOIR

QUOIT CIST DISC DISH DISK LINER DISCUS HOBBER CROMLECH

QUOMODO HOW WAY MEANS MANNER

QUONDAM OLD ONCE WHILE FORMER ONETIME SOMETIME

QUORATEAN KAROK

QUORUM CORAM HOUSE MINYAN MAJORITY

QUOTA PART BOGEY SHARE QUOTIENT

QUOTATION PRICE QUOTE EXTRACT SNIPPET EPIGRAPH
(— DEVELOPED INTO ESSAY) CHRIA

QUOTATION MARK GUILLEMET

QUOTE CITE COAT COTE MARK NAME NOTE ADDUCE ALLEGE RECITE REPEAT EXCERPT EXTRACT OBSERVE REHEARSE
(— SARCASTICALLY) FLOUT

QUOTH CO KO CUTH QUAD QUOD SAID SPOKE UTTERED

QUOTIDIAN DAILY TRIVIAL ORDINARY

QUOTIENT QUOTE FRACTION

QUTB POLE

R AR ROGER ROMEO
(**UVULAR —**) BURR
RA RE RAE SHU TEM ATMU BACIS
HORUS MENTU KHEPERA SOKARIS
RABBAN MASTER TEACHER
RABBET CHECK GROOVE BACKJOINT
FILLISTER
RABBI TANA AMORA CACAM HAKAM
TANNA MASTER SABORA KHAKHAM
TEACHER GAMALIEL SABORAIM
(**PL.**) AMORAIM TANNAIM
RABBIT BUN REX TAN BUNT CONY
JACK POLE RACK BUNNY CAPON
CREAM CUNNY DUTCH FRIER LAPIN
ANGORA ASTREX CONEEN HAVANA
OARLOP PARKER POLISH SILVER
TAPETI WOOLER BEVEREN
CONYNGE FLEMISH LEPORID
SNOWSHOE WARRENER
(**— BURROW**) CLAPPER
(**— FUR**) CONY SCUT CONEY FLICK
LAPIN FLITCH
(**— MEAT**) LAPAN
(**— SKIN**) RACK
(**— TAIL**) SCUT
(**— WARREN**) CONYGER
(**CASTRATED —**) CAPON
(**FEMALE —**) DOE
(**MALE —**) BUCK
(**YOUNG —**) KITTEN
(**PL.**) FLICK WARREN
RABBITFISH SPINY
RABBLE MOB TAG GING HERD ROUT
SCUM FRAPE SCAFF SCUFF TRASH
MEINIE RADDLE RAFFLE RAGTAG
RASCAL TAGRAG DOGGERY
PUDDLER RABBLER RANGALE
TRAFFIC BRAGGERY CANAILLE
RAGABASH RIFFRAFF VARLETRY
(**DISORDERLY —**) HERD
RABBLE-ROUSER DEMAGOG
RABID MAD RAGING FRANTIC
FURIOUS RABIOUS RABITIC
FRENZIED RAVENING VIRULENT
RABIES LYSSA MADNESS PIBLOKTO
RAVENING
RACCOON COON COATI GUARA
TEJON AGUARA MAPACH WASHER
AGOUARA ARCTOID RATTOON
CRABEATER
RACE CAP CUP LOG ROD RUN BENT
CONE DASH DRAG GEST HUMP KIND
LINE NAME RAIS RAZE RINK TEAM
TRAM BLOOD BREED BRUSH CASTE
CHEVY CORSO DERBY FLESH
HOUSE ISSUE PLATE PURSE RATCH
REACH ROUTE SPEED STAKE
STAMM STIRP STOCK BROOSE
CHEVVY COURSE FAMILY NATION
PEOPLE PHYLON RUNOFF SPRING
STIRPS STRAIN STRIND BIOTYPE
CENTURY CLAIMER CLASSIC
HACKNEY HUNDRED KINDRED
LINEAGE MATINEE NURSERY
PROGENY PROSAPY RACEWAY
REGATTA STADIUM FUTURITY
HANDICAP MARATHON WALKOVER
OFFSPRING
(**— A HORSE**) CAMPAIGN

(**— AT WEDDING**) BROOSE BROUZE
(**— FOR BALL-BEARINGS**) CONE
(**— OF BARLEY**) BENT
(**— OF GODS**) VANIR
(**— OF PEOPLE**) VANS AMALS VANIR
HAZARA YADAVA BAMBUTE FIRBOLG
GIANTRY NISHADA RASENNA
REPHAIM AMALINGS
(**— OF UNDERGROUND ELVES**)
DROW
(**— OF WINDMILL**) CURB
(**HORSE —**) DERBY PLATE SPRINT
MATINEE FUTURITY WALKOVER
(**HUMAN —**) MAN MANKIND SPECIES
(**IMPROMPTU —**) BRUSH
(**JUMPING —**) SCURRY
(**LENTEN —S**) TORPIDS
(**MILL —**) LADE
(**PRELIMINARY —**) HEAT
(**ROWING —**) SCULLS REGATTA
(**RUNNING —**) MILE RELAY SPRINT
HUNDRED HURDLES
(**SHORT —**) BICKER
(**SHORT-DISTANCE —**) DASH
SCURRY SPRINT
(**SKI —**) SLALOM DAUERLAUF
(**PL.**) FOURS
RACECOURSE LIST OVAL PIST RING
TURF EPSOM CAREER CIRCUS
STADIE STRETCH GYMKHANA
SPEEDWAY
RACEHORSE DOG PACER RACER
SLEEPER TROTTER BANGTAIL
(**— THAT HAS NEVER WON**) MAIDEN
(**2-YEAR OLD —**) JUVENILE
(**INFERIOR —**) PLATER HAYBURNER
(**PL.**) RUCK
RACEME STRIG
RACER CRACK SNAKE RUNNER
BICYCLIST CINDERMAN
RACETRACK DROMOS FURLONG
RACEWAY CANAL TRACK GROOVE
CHANNEL FISHWAY
RACHEL POWDER
(**HUSBAND OF —**) JACOB
(**SON OF —**) JOSEPH BENJAMIN
RACHIS SPINE SPINDLE
(**— OF HOP STROBILE**) STRIG
RACHITIS RICKETS
RACIAL GENTILE GENTILIC PHYLETIC
RACIST COLOR
RACK GIN RAK RAT TUB BINK BUCK
CASE HACK HECK SHOG TACK
AMBLE BRAKE DRIER DRYER FLAKE
FRAME POKER THROW TOUSE
TRAIN WRACK WRECK WRING
CIRCLE CRATCH CUDGEL ENGINE
NIPPER PULLEY TREBLE WRENCH
AFFLICT AGONIZE PENRACK
POTTARO TORMENT TORTURE
BARBECUE EQUULEUS PINEBANK
SAWHORSE
(**— ATTACHED TO WAGON**)
SHELVING OUTRIGGER
(**— FOR BARRELS**) JIB
(**— FOR CHINAWARE**) FIDDLE
(**— FOR DISHES**) BINK
(**— FOR FEEDING**) HACK HAYRACK
(**— FOR FODDER**) HECK CRATCH

(**— FOR PLATES**) CREEL
(**— FOR STORAGE**) FLAKE
(**— IN THRESHER**) SHAKER
(**DRYING —**) CRIB TREBLE
(**WOODEN —**) BUCAN
RACKED WRUNG TORTURED
RACKET BAT DIN GAME BANDY
MUSIC RAZOO CLAMOR CROSSE
DRIVER HUBBUB HUSTLE RAQUET
RATTLE BUSINESS REVELING
STRAMASH
(**TENNIS —**) SCUFE
RACKETEER HOOD HUSTLER
GANGSTER
RACKETT CERVALET CERVELAT
RACKING FIERCE
RACKMAN TOPMAN
RACON BEACON
RACONTEUR STORYTELLER
RACQUET GAZELLE
RACY GAMY LEAN SEXY JUICY
SALTY SMART SPICY LIVELY RISQUE
PIQUANT PUNGENT ZESTFUL
SPIRITED
RAD EAGER QUICK READY AFRAID
ELATED
RADAR (**— NAVIGATION SYSTEM**)
LANAC
(**— SYSTEM**) OBOE
RADARSCOPE PPI HSCOPE
RADDLE PIT BEAT SCAR RAVEL
RUDDLE THRASH SEPARATOR
RADIAL RAY QUADRANT
RADIANCE RAY GLOW LEAM GLARE
GLEAM GLINT GLORY LIGHT SHINE
LUSTER AUREOLA GLITTER
SPLENDOR
RADIANT BEAMY SHEEN SHINY
ABLAZE BRIGHT GOLDEN LUCENT
SHEENY AURORAL BEAMFUL
BEAMING FULGENT LAMBENT
GLORIOUS LUSTROUS RELUCENT
SPLENDID
(**— INTENSITY**) J
RADIATE RAY BEAM POUR SHED
SHINE EFFUSE SPREAD EFFULGE
EMANATE
RADIATED PENCILED STELLATE
RADIATION AURA LIGHT INFRARED
(**— DOSAGE**) REM REP
(**— UNIT**) LANGLEY
RADIATOR HEATER EMANATOR
(**SET OF —S**) STACK
RADICAL KEY SURD BASAL GROUP
RADIX ROUGE ULTRA CAPRYL
HEROIC CAPITAL CAPROYL DRASTIC
EXTREME FORWARD HERETIC
JACOBIN LEFTIST LEVELER LIBERAL
PRIMARY CARDINAL LOCOFOCO
(**CHEMICAL —**) AMYL CARYL CETYL
GROUP ACETYL CAPRYL PHENYL
PHYTYL HALOGEN LINALYL
CARBAMYL QINNAMAL
RADICALISM EXTREMISM
JACOBINISM
RADICEL ROOTLET
RADICLE (**— THAT DEVELOPS IN
GRAIN**) COME
RADIENT ORIENT

RADIO AIR SET WIRELESS
(**— OPERATOR**) HAM SPARKS
(**— SYSTEM**) TBS
RADIOGRAM FLIMSY
RADIOGRAPH EXOGRAPH SKIAGRAM
RADISH RUNCH DAEKON DAIKON
RIFART CADLOCK CRADLOCK
CRUCIFER CROSSWEED
RADIUS RAYON SPOKE SWEEP
THROW ADRADIUS
RADIX BASE ROOT ETYMON RADICLE
RADON NITON THORON ACTINON
EXRADIO
RADULA RIBBON TONGUE
RAFF LOW IDLE SCUM SWEEP TRASH
COMMON JUMBLE LUMBER RABBLE
RAFFLE RAGTAG SNATCH RUBBISH
RAFFISH RAKISH TAWDRY UNKEMPT
RAFFLE MOVE RAFF JUMBLE RABBLE
REFUSE RUBBISH
RAFT COW CRIB MOKI BALSA BATCH
FLOAT TABLE DINGEY DINGHY
JANGAR MOKIHI PIPERY RADEAU
JANGADA ZATTARE CATAMARAN
(**— OF INVERTED POTS**) GHARNAO
(**— OF LOGS**) BOOM CRIB
(**— WITH CABIN**) COW
(**BAMBOO —**) RAKIT
(**FIRE —**) CATAMARAN
(**LUMBER —**) BATCH
RAFT DOG RAKER
RAFTER HIP BALK BLAD FIRM SILE
SOIL SPAR SPUR VIGA BLADE
CABER RIDGE BOUGAR CARLINE
RAFFMAN SLEEPER
(**— OF TURKEYS**) FLOCK
RAFTY RAW DAMP FUSTY MUSTY
RANCID
RAG JAG TAT HOAX JAGG SAIL
ANNOY CLOUT PRANK SCOLD
SCRAP SHRED WIPER GIBBOL
LIBBET RAGGLE TAGRAG TATTER
FLITTER REMNANT TORMENT
RAGSTONE STRAGGLE NEWSPAPER
(**— GATHERER**) TATTER
(**PL.**) DUDS CADDIS FITTERS
RAGGERY FLITTERS
RAGAMUFFIN MUFFLIN BEGGARLY
SHABROON TITMOUSE
RAGE GO AWE FAD RAG WAX BAIT
BEEF FARE FOAM FRET FUFF FUME
FUNK FUNX FURY GLOW GRIM HEAT
PELT RAMP RASE RESE TAVE TEAR
WOOD ANGER BRETH CHAFE CRAZE
FUROR PADDY STORM TEAVE TEVEL
VOGUE WRATH FRENZY FURORE
PELTER TYAUVE BLUSTER FASHION
FUFFIAN MADNESS PASSION
TEMPEST INSANITY WOODNESS
PADDYWACK
(**BE IN A —**) RANT
RAGFISH ICOSTEID
RAGGED DUDDY HARSH FRAYED
JAGGED SCOURY UNEVEN SHAGRAG
SHREDDY TATTERY SCRAGGLY
SCRATCHY TATTERED
RAGGED ROBIN ROBIN CUCKOO
RAGGEE MAND RAGI MARUA
MANDUA KORAKAN ELEUSINE

RAGGLE-TAGGLE MOTLEY
RAGING HOT GRIM WILD YOND
RABID FIERCE FURIAL FERVENT
PELTING VIOLENT FLAGRANT
FURIBUND WRATHFUL
RAGOUT GOULASH HARICOT
TERRINE SALPICON CHIPOLATA
PULPATONE
(**— OF GAME**) SALMI SALMIS
RAGPICKER BUNTER RAGMAN
TATTER
RAGWEED HAYWEED HOGWEED
AMBROSIA IRONWEED KINGHEAD
KINGWEED RICHWEED FRANSERIA
RAGWORT CUSHAG JACOBY
BENWEED CAMMOCK SEGGROM
LIFEROOT
RAID RADE ROAD TALA FORAY
HARRY PINCH REISE REIVE CREACH
FORAGE HARASS INROAD MOLEST
PANYAR RAZZIA BODRAGE
BORDRAG CHAPPOW DESCENT
JAYHAWK OUTFALL OUTRAKE
OUTRIDE OUTROAD SPREATH
COMMANDO SPOILING
(**AIR —**) BLITZ
(**CATTLE —**) SPREAGH SPREATH
(**WARLIKE —**) HERSHIP
RAIDER REDLEG BUSHWACK
RAIL BAR BULL COOT GIRD JEST
KOKO LIST MOHO RANT RAVE SKID
SORA TRAM WEKA WING CRAKE
EASER FENCE GUARD PLATE RAVEL
REILE SCOFF SCOLD SLENT STANG
STANK STEEL SWEAR BANTER
BEDWAY CALLET FENDER RUNNER
SKITTY TIKLIN BIDCOCK BILCOCK
COURLAN INVEIGH OARCOCK
RACKWAY TOPRAIL BULLHEAD
CANCELLI CORNBIRD PORTLAST
TOADBACK VIGNOLES
(**— AT**) JEST CURSE SCOFF RATTLE
REVILE
(**— OF BED**) STOCK
(**— OF RAILWAY SWITCH**) TONGUE
(**— ON GUN PLATFORM**) TRINGLE
(**— ON HAY VEHICLE**) THRIPPLE
(**— ON SHIP**) FIFE
(**ALTAR —**) SEPTUM
(**ARCHED —**) HOOPSTICK
(**CHAIR —**) LEDGE
(**FENCE —**) RIDER
(**PL.**) RAILING CANCELLI RAILROAD
RAIL CHAIR CARRIAGE
RAILING BAR SEPT GRATE RAVEL
FENDER FIDDLE GITTER VEDIKA
BARRIER GALLERY PARAPET
CANCELLI ESPALIER HANDRAIL
PARCLOSE TRAVERSE
RAILLERY GAFF HASH JEST JOKE
RAGE CHAFF RALLY SPORT BANTER
BLAGUE HOORAY HURRAH SATIRE
TRIFLE MOCKERY BADINAGE
DICACITY RABULOUS RIDICULE
RAILROAD EL ROAD YARD STEEL
COALER FEEDER GRANGER
TRAMWAY CEINTURE ELEVATED
(**— CAR**) IDLER
RAILROAD CHAIR SADDLE

RAILSPLITTER MAULER
RAILWAY ROAD TUBE COGWAY
SUBWAY COGROAD INCLINE
TRANVIA WIREWAY ASCENSOR
PLATEWAY TRAMROAD FUNICULAR
RAIMENT RAY GARB CLOTH
APPAREL CLOTHES VESTURE
CLOTHING DRESSING
(**SPLENDID —**) SHEEN
RAIN WET ISLE MIST SMUR ULAN
WEET STORM DELUGE MIZZLE
SERENE SHOWER SOAKER DRIZZLE
DOWNPOUR SPRINKLE
(**— AND SNOW**) SLEET
(**— HEAVILY**) TEEM
(**— LIGHTLY**) SMUR SPIT SPRINKLE
(**— OF SPARKS**) SHOWER
(**DRIZZLING —**) DAG
(**FINE —**) MIST SEREIN SERENE
(**GOD OF —**) PARJANYA
(**HEAVY —**) PASH SPOUT
(**LIGHT —**) WEATHER HEATDROPS
(**SHORT —**) SHOWER
(**SUDDEN —**) SKEW
(**WHIRLING —**) SKIRL
(**WIND-DRIVEN —**) SCAT
(**PL.**) VARSHA
RAINBIRD KOEL TOMFOOL
STORMBIRD
(**— OF JAMAICA**) HUNTER
RAINBOW ARC BOW ARCH IRIS
GAMUT METEOR SUNBOW ILLUSION
(**BROKEN —**) WINDDOG WINDGALL
RAINBOW FISH GUPPY MAORI
RAINBOW RUNNER SKIPJACK
SHOEMAKER
RAINBRINGER KACHINA
RAINCOAT MAC MACK PONCHO
BURSATI OILSKIN SLICKER
GOSSAMER
RAINFALL PLOUT SKIFF SKIFT
ONDING STEMPLOW
RAIN GAGE UDOMETER
RAINSPOUT RONE
RAINSTORM WET SPATE
RAIN TREE SAMAN ZAMAN GUANGO
ZAMANG ALGAROBA GENISARO
MONKEYPOD
RAINY WET KICK FRESH JUICY
RAYNE SAPPY WEETY BLASHY
DRIPPY PLUNGY SPONGY PLUVIAL
PLUVINE SHOWERY WEEPING
CLUTTERY PLUVIOUS SLATTERY
(**— SEASON**) VARSHA
RAISE END SET WIN BUMP BUOY
GROW HAIN HEFT HIGH HIKE HOVE
JACK KICK LEVY LIFT MAKE OVER
REAR ROOF STIR TELD TOSS AREAR
BLOCK BOOST BREED BUILD CAIRN
CHOCK CRANE DIGHT ELATE ENSKY
ERECT EXALT FORCE GREET HANCE
HEAVE HEEZE HEVEN HOISE HOIST
HORSE LEAVE MOUND MOUNT
PRICK RISER ROUSE VOICE ASSIST
BETTER CREATE DOUBLE EMBOSS
EXHALE GATHER LEAVEN MUSTER
NANTLE PREFER REMOVE RISING
UPHOLD UPLIFT ADDRESS ADVANCE
COLLECT ELEVATE ENHANCE

LIGHTEN NOURISH PRESENT
PROMOTE RECRUIT UPSHOOT
ANGELIZE HEIGHTEN INSPIRIT
RELEVATE
(— A BUMP) CLOUR
(— A NAP) TEASE TEASEL TEAZLE
(— ALOFT) SPHERE
(— BY ASSESSMENT) LEVY
(— BY HAND) NOB
(— CLAMOR) BRAWL
(— IN PITCH) SHARP
(— OBJECTIONS) CAVIL BOGGLE
(— ONESELF) CHIN
(— TO 3RD POWER) CUBE
(— TO HIGH DEGREE) STRAIN
(— UP) BUOY AREAR ELATE EXALT
EXTOL ELEVATE CIVILIZE
RAISED HIGH UPSET ARRECT
HOGGED EXALTED ELEVATED
MOUNTANT UPLIFTED UPRAUGHT
RAISIN FIG PASA PLUM LEXIA ZIBEB
REYSON CURRANT SULTANA
MUSCATEL
(PL.) SPICE
RAJ RULE REIGN
RAJA KING CHIEF RULER PRINCE
PANGLIMA
RAJMAHAL CREEPER JITI CHITI
JETEE JEETEE
RAJPUT SAMMA SUMRA GAHRWAL
RAZBOOCH
RAKE GO HOE RIP WAY COMB PATH
RACK RAFF RAVE REAP ROAM ROUE
ROVE RUCK BLOOD CLAUT PITCH
SCOOP SCOUR SULKY TIGER
PLUNGE RABBLE ROLLER SEARCH
RANSACK SCRATCH LOTHARIO
SCRAPPLE
(— GRAIN) GAVEL
(— UP IN ROWS) HACK
(— WITH GUNFIRE) SCOUR STRAFE
ENFILADE
(— WITHOUT TEETH) LUTE
(BUCK —) SWEEP
(CRANBERRY —) SCOOP
(HORSE-DRAWN —) GLEANER
(OYSTER —) GLEANER
RAKEHELL RASCAL IMMORAL
LIBERTINE
RAKER GUMMER ROOKER
RAKISH SLANG JAUNTY SPORTY
WANTON DASHING CARELESS
DEVILISH RANTEPOLE
RALE RATTLE SIFFLE SIBILUS
RALLENTANDO DRAG RITARD
RALLY KID DRAG JOKE MOCK RELY
STIR BULLY JOLLY QUEER BANTER
DERIDE REVIVE COLLECT CLAMBAKE
RIDICULE SPEAKING
RAM PUN TIP TUP BUCK CRAM PACK
RAME STEM TEAP TOOP ARIES
CHOKE CRASH POACH ROGER SLIDE
BEETLE CHASER RANCID ROSTRUM
BULLDOZER WETHERHOG
WETHERTEG
(— OF WAR VESSEL) SPUR
(CASTRATED —) WETHER
RAMA MELCHORA
(WIFE OF —) SITA

RAMADA ARBOR PORCH
RAMAGE WILD RAMMISH UNTAMED
RAMAGE HAWK BRANCHER
RAMBLE RAKE ROAM ROVE WALK
JAUNT PROWL RANGE TRACE
TROLL RUMBLE STROLL VAGARY
WAMBLE WANDER ENRANGE
EXCURSE SPROGUE TROUNCE
FLAGARIE SCRAMBLE SPATIATE
(— AIMLESSLY) HAZE
RAMBLING GAD CURSORY DEVIOUS
WINDING DESULTORY SCATTERED
RAMBUNCTIOUS RUDE WILD
ROUGH UNRULY UNTAMED VIOLENT
RAMBUTAN SOAPWORT
RAMENTUM PALEA PALET SCALE
SHAVING
RAMIE ORTIGA
RAMIFICATION ARM RAMUS
BRANCH OFFSHOOT OUTGROWTH
RAMIFY BRANCH SPRANGLE
RAMMAN ADAD ADDA ADDU
RAMMED EARTH PISE
RAMMEL TRASH RUMMLE RUBBISH
RAMMER HEAD BOSER PUNNER
WORMER
RAMOSE CLADOSE BRANCHED
RAMP RUN BANK EXIT RAGE RANK
SLIP STORM EASING FROLIC
FOOTPAD SLIPWAY GRADIENT
RAMPAGE RAGE ROMP BINGE
SPRAY SPREE STORM RANDAN
RAMPAGEOUS UNRULY GLARING
RAMPANT VIOLENT
RAMPANT RANK PROFUSE SALIANT
SALIENT SEGREANT
RAMPART BRAY LINE WALL AGGER
ARGIN VALLUM BULWARK DEFENSE
PARAPET RAMPIER BARBICAN
MUNITION BARRICADE
RAMPER LAMPREY
RAMPIKE SNAG RAUNPICK
ROUNSPIK
RAMROD FORMAL GUNSTICK
RAMSHACKLE RUDE UNRULY
RICKETY SHACKLY UNSTEADY
RAMSON RAMP GARLIC BUCKRAM
(PL.) RAMS
RAMSTAM RASH HEADLONG
RECKLESS
RAN ARN
RANCEL SEARCH RANSACK
RANCH RUN FARM TEAR FINCA
CHACRA OUTFIT SPREAD WRENCH
STATION ESTANCIA HACIENDA
RANCHE NATURAL
RANCHER COWMAN GRAZIER
SHEEPMAN CATTLEMAN
RANCID RAM RANK SOUR FROWY
RAFTY RASTY REEST RESTY
FROWZY ODIOUS ROTTEN
RANCOR GALL HATE SPITE ENMITY
GRUDGE HATRED MALICE
ACRIMONY
RANCOROUS ACRID VENOMOUS
MALIGNANT
(NOT —) GOOD
RAND EDGE ROON RUND BORDER
HIGHLAND

RANDAN SPREE RANTAN UPROAR
RAMPAGE
RANDOM BANK FORCE LOOSE
STRAY CASUAL CHANCE CHANCY
AIMLESS RANDALL RENDOUN
SHOTGUN UNAIMED VAGRANT
(AT —) HOBNOB
(SOMEWHAT —) LONG
RANDY LEWD RUDE SPREE BEGGAR
VIRAGO LUSTFUL RIOTOUS
CAROUSAL
RANGE KEN ROW ALLY AREA BEAT
GATE GAUT GHAT LINE RANK ROAM
ROVE SCUM SHOT TOUR WALK
ALIGN BLANK CARRY FIELD GAMUT
HILLS ORBIT REACH SCOPE SHOOT
SPACE STAND START SWEEP SWING
VERGE COURSE DANGER EXTEND
EXTENT LENGTH RADIUS RAMBLE
SCOUTH SPHERE STROLL WANDER
BOWSHOT COMPASS DEMESNE
EARSHOT GUNSHOT HABITAT
HORIZON PURVIEW CLASSIFY
DIAPASON EARREACH EYEREACH
LATITUDE PANORAMA
(— OF ARROW) FLIGHT
(— OF BRICK) COURSE
(— OF FOOD) FARE
(— OF FREQUENCIES) SPECTRUM
(— OF GOVERNANCE) DOMAIN
(— OF GUN) CARRY RANDOM
GUNSHOT
(— OF HILLS) GAUT GHAT HUMP
TIER CHAIN GHAUT RIDGE SIERRA
SAWBACK BACKBONE
(— OF ORGANISM) BIOZONE
(— OF PASTURE) GANG
(— OF PLANKS) STRING
(— OF PRINTING TYPES) SERIES
(— OF SIGHT) KEN SCAN EYESHOT
KENNING
(— OF TONES) KEY SCALE
GRADATION
(— OF VISION) EYE SIGHT KENNING
(— OF WAVELENGTH) BAND
(— OVER) SWEEP
(ARCHERY —) BUTTS GREEN
(COOKING —) KITCHENER
(SHOOTING —) MES GALLERY
(TEMPERATURE —) CONE
RANGE FINDER STADIA
MEKOMETER
RANGE POLE PICKET
RANGER ROVER ROBBER MONTERO
FIREWARD
RANGOON SHERRY
RANGY OPEN ROOMY SPACIOUS
RANK RAY ROW SEE DANK FOOT
FORM FOXY GOLE GREE LINE RAMP
RATE ROOM SEED SOUR STEP TIER
CENSE CHOIR CLASS FETID FRANK
FUSTY GRADE GROSS HONOR
LEVEL MARCH ORDER QUIRE RANGE
ROWTY SIEGE SPACE STALL STAND
STATE TCHIN TRAIN AFFAIR AGREGE
DEGREE ERMINE ESTEEM FIGURE
LAVISH PARAGE RATING SPHERE
STATUS STRONG CALIBER CALLING
DIGNITY DUKEDOM EARLDOM

FOOTING GLARING RAMMISH RAMPANT STATION WORSHIP ABSOLUTE EARLSHIP ENSIGNCY EQUIPAGE FLAGRANT GENTRICE LADYSHIP PALPABLE STINKING
(— AND FILE) RANGALE
(— OF GENTLEMEN) GENTRY GENTILITY
(— OF SERGEANT-AT-LAW) COIF COIFFE
(ACADEMIC —) AGREGE
(BOTTOMMOST —) CELLAR
(HIGH —) DIGNITY EMINENCE
(LOWEST —) SCOURING
(MILITARY —) GRADE AIRMAN CORNET CHAOUSH
(NOBLE —) ADELAIDE
(SAME —) KIND
(SOCIAL —) CLASS ESTATE HERALDRY POSITION

RANKLE FRET CHAFE FESTER INJURE RANCOR DESTROY INFLAME

RANSACK RIG DRAG RAKE RIPE SACK SEEK RIFLE DACKER RANCEL SEARCH PLUNDER RUMMAGE

RANSOM FINE RAME REDEEM RESCUE RESGAT EXPIATE

RANSTEAD TOADFLAX

RANT CAVE HUFF RAIL RAND MOUTH REVEL ROUSE SCOLD SPOUT STEVEN BOMBAST CAROUSE DECLAIM FROTHING
(— AND RAVE) FAUNCH

RANTING RANTISM TEARCAT

RANTIPOLE WILD CARROT RAKISH SEESAW ROMPING

RANULA CYST FROGTONGUE

RANUNCULUS MOSS GOLLAND CROWFOOT HEDGEHOG BUTTERCUP

RAOULIA HAASTIA

RAP BOB CON CHAP GRAB KNAP TIRL TUNK WRAP CLICK CLINK KNOCK STEAL TOUCH BARTER HANDLE

RAPACIOUS CRUEL GREEDY TAKING RAVENING RAVENOUS

RAPACITY RAVEN RAVIN CUPIDITY EXTORTION

RAPE COLE ABUSE COLZA FORCE NAVET NAVEW TOUCH ATTACK FELONY RAPEYE TURNIP ASSAULT DESPOIL NAVETTE OPPRESS PLUNDER RAPTURE STUPRUM COLESEED COLEWORT DISHONOR STUPRATE SUPPRESS

RAPESEED COLZA RAVISON

RAPHUS DIDUS

RAPID GAY FAST CHUTE HASTY MOSSO QUICK ROUND SAULT SHARP SHUTE TOSTO WINGY RIFFLE SPEEDY WINGED SCHNELL SKELPIN STICKLE TANTIVY SLAPPING SPEEDFUL
(—S IN RIVER) SAULT DALLES RIFFLE STICKLE CATARACT
(MORE —) STRETTO

RAPIDITY HASTE SPEED RADEUR CELERITY VELOCITY

RAPIDLY APACE CHEAP FLEETLY

HASTILY SPEEDILY QUICKFOOT

RAPIER TUCK TUKE BILBO ESTOC SHARP STOCK VERDUN TOASTER

RAPINE FORCE RAVIN PILLAGE PLUNDER VIOLENCE

RAPPAREE ROBBER CREAGHT VAGABOND

RAPPORT ACCORD HARMONY RELATION AGREEMENT

RAPSCALLION ROGUE RASCAL VILLAIN HOSEBIRD VAGABOND

RAPT LOST WRAP TENSE INTENT RAVISH TRANCE CARRIED ENGAGED RAPTURE ABDUCTED ABSORBED ECSTATIC

RAPTORES RAPACES

RAPTURE JOY BLISS DELIGHT ECSTASY PAROXYSM RHAPSODY

RARA AVIS PHENIX RARITY WONDER PHOENIX

RARE FINE REAL SELD THIN ALONE EARLY GREAT ANTRIN CHOICE GEASON INCONY SCARCE SEENIL SELDOM SINDLE SUBTLE SULLEN UNIQUE ANTERIN CURIOUS TENUOUS UNUSUAL CRITICAL SELDSEEN SINGULAR UNCOMMON

RAREFACTION POROSIS

RAREFIED HIGH THIN SUBTILE ABSTRUSE AETHERED ESOTERIC

RAREFY THIN DILUTE EXTENUATE

RARELY SELDEN SELDOM

RARENESS RARITY TENUITY SCARCITY

RARITY SWAN CURIO RELIC RARIETY TENUITY RARENESS
(PL.) CURIOSA

RASCAL BOY CAD DOG IMP LOW RAP BASE DUCK FILE KITE LOON MEAN SHAG SMAK CATSO FILTH GANEF GIPSY KNAVE ROGUE SCAMP SHELM SLAVE SMAIK THIEF ABLACH BRIBER BUDZAT BUGGER COQUIN HARLOT LIMMER RABBLE RAGGIL RIBALD SCHELM SORROW TINKER BLEEDER CAMOOCH GLUTTON HESSIAN NEBULON PEASANT RAPTRIL SHELLUM SKEEZIX SKELLUM VILLAIN HOSEBIRD LIDDERON PALLIARD PICAROON RAKEWELL RUBIATOR SKALAWAG SPALPEEN TAISTREL VAGABOND WIDDIFOW

RASCALITY FOIST RABBLE KNAVERY ROGUING RASCALRY

RASCALLY BASE MEAN ROOKY GALLUS LIMMER GALLOWS KNAVISH RAGGILY SHAGRAG WIDDIFOW

RASE PULL RAIS RAZE ERASE PLUCK INCISE SNATCH

RASH ID CUT BRASH HARDY HASTY HEADY SLASH SLICE DARING SUDDEN UNWARY URGENT BULRUSH HOTSPUR RABBISH BLIZZARD CARELESS ERUPTION EXANTHEM HEADLONG HEEDLESS MADBRAIN OVERSEEN PRESSING RECKLESS TEMEROUS

RASHER SLICE COLLOP TRIFLE COLOPPE

RASHLY HEADILY HEADLONG

RASHNESS RAGE RESE ACRISY TEMERITY HEADINESS

RASKOLNIK POPOVETS

RASP RUB FILE RAPE ERUCT GRATE TOOTH RAPEYE RUBBER RIFFLER DENTICLE
(SHOEMAKER'S —) FLOAT

RASPBERRY AKPEK BAZOO MOLKA AVARIN RASPIS PLUMBOG ARNBERRY BLACKCAP BOGBERRY CUTHBERT MULBERRY RESPASSE ROSACEAN

RASPING HARSH ROUGH STOOR STOUR HOARSE RASION RAZZLY GRATING RAUCOUS GUTTERAL
(PL.) SCOBS

RASPY HARSH GRATING SCREAKY SCRABBLY

RASSE CIVET WEASEL

RAT BUCK DAMN DRAT HEEL NOKI ROTN SCAB VOLE KIORE LOUSE METAD RATON SELVA ZEMMI ZEMNI CRABER MURINE RODENT ROTTAN SLEPEZ VERMIN YUNGAS CUSHION CONFOUND INFORMER MYOMORPH
(INDIAN —) KOK

RATAPLAN RATTAN RATTLE

RATCH RASH REND ROCH SPOT NOTCH STREAK RATCHET STRETCH

RATCHET DOG PAWL CLICK DETENT ROCHET

RAT CHINCHILLA ABROCOME

RATE LAY RAG SET CESS CHOP GAIT GIVE HAND KIND RANK RATA ABUSE CULET CURVE PRIZE RATIO REBUT SCOLD STENT STYLE VALUE ZAKAT ASSIZE GALLOP ACCOUNT CARTAGE DESERVE FASHION MILLAGE REPROVE CLASSIFY ESTIMATE QUANTIFY
(— HIGHLY) PRICE
(— OF ASCENT) GRADE
(— OF DRAINAGE) FREENESS
(— OF EXCHANGE) BATTA
(— OF INTEREST) DISCOUNT
(— OF MOTION) BAT SPEED
(— OF MOVEMENT) PACE TEMPO
(— OF RECKONING) FOOT
(— OF SPEED) BAT AGOGE
(— OF TRANSFER) FLUX
(— OF TUITION) CULET
(— SCHEDULE) TARIFF
(AT ANY —) HURE
(BIRTH —) NATALITY

RATE BOOK STREET

RATEL BADGER BURIER

RATH CAR HILL REUT RUTH EARLY MOUND QUICK REUTE SWIFT BETIMES CHARIOT YOUTHFUL

RATHER Y BUT GEY LIKE SOON LOURD QUITE ASTITE BEFORE FAIRLY HELDER KINDLY PRETTY RUTHER SEEMLY TIDDER TITTER EARLIER INSTEAD MIDDLING SOMEWHAT
(— THAN) ERE BEFORE

RATIFICATION AMEN RATE SANCTION

RATIFY AMEN PASS SEAL SIGN VISA ENSEAL FASTEN OBSIGN APPROVE CONFIRM SCEPTER CANONIZE ROBORATE SANCTION

RATING E RANK CENSE CLASS GRADE WRITER STANDING

RATIO Q PI GAIN RATE SINE SLIP INDEX RESON SETUP SHEAR ASPECT CAMBER DECADE QUOTUM REASON REYSON SECANT AVERAGE PORTION CONTRAST SOLIDITY

RATIOCINATION LOGIC THOUGHT REASONING

RATION DOLE RATIO ALLOCATE
(— OF BREAD) TOMMY
(ANIMAL —) CHOW
(EXTRA —S) BUCKSHEE
(HOG —) SWILL
(PL.) FOOD BOUCH COMMON

RATIONAL SANE SOBER LOGICAL REASONAL SENSIBLE THINKING

RATIONALIZE THOB EXPLAIN

RATITE EMU MOA KIWI RHEA OSTRICH STRUTHIAN

RAT KANGAROO TUNGO POTOROO SQUEAKER

RATOON SHOOT SPROUT SUCKER

RATTAIL MULE ARREST GRENADIER

RATTAN CANE SEGA ROTAN BEJUCO ROTANG SWITCH RATTOON

RATTLE DIN BIRL BURL RICK TIRL CLACK CROTAL GRAGER HENPEN MARACA RACKLE RICKLE RIFFLE ROTTLE RUCKLE RUTTLE CHACKLE CLACKER CLAPPER CLATTER CLICKET CREAKER GNATTER GROGGER SHATTER SISTRUM SKELLAT CAIXINHA CHOCALHO COWWHEAT
(CRIER'S —) CLAPPER
(IRON —) SKELLAT SKILLET

RATTLER LIE ROMBLE RUMBLER

RATTLESNAKE BELLTAIL CASCABEL CASCAVEL
(— PLANTAIN) NETLEAF RATSBANE

RATTLESNAKE ROOT BUGBANE JOYLEAF

RATTLETRAP GEWGAW TRIFLE RICKETY

RATTLING BRISK HUSKY SLAPPING SPLENDID CREPITANT

RATTY NASTY SHABBY UNKEMPT WORTHLESS

RATWA MUNTJAC

RAUCOUS LOUD HARSH COARSE HOARSE SQUAWKY STRIDENT

RAUN ROE ROWN SPAWN

RAUPO CATTAIL

RAVAGE EAT PREY RIOT RUIN SACK FORAY HARRY HAVOC SPOIL WASTE FORAGE DESPOIL DESTROY OVERRUN PILLAGE PLUNDER DEFLOWER DESOLATE POPULATE SPOLIATE

RAVE MAD RAGE RAND WOOD AWEDE BLURB CRUSH RATHE ROUSE STORM DELIRE WANDER

RAVEL FAG RUN FRAY FRET REYLE SNARL EVENER LADDER RADDLE RUNNER SLOUGH TANGLE CONFUSE INVOLVE PERPLEX RAILING UNWEAVE

RAVELIN RABLIN OUTWORK DEMILUNE

RAVEN RALPH CORBEL CORBIE CORBIN FORAGE RAVINE WAYBIRD
(BRIGHT —) BERTRAM

RAVENING CRUEL RABIES

RAVENOUS GREEDY LUPINE TOOTHY WOLFISH RAPACIOUS VORACIOUS

RAVINE DEN GAP GUT LIN DELL DRAW GILL GULL KHOR KHUD LINN LLYN SIKE WADI BREAK BUNNY CHASM CHINE CLOVE DONGA FLUME GHYLL GLACK GORGE GOYAL GOYLE GRIFF GRIKE GULCH GULLY HEUCH KLOOF SLADE SLAKE STRID ARROYO CLEUCH CLOUGH COULEE DIMBLE DINGLE DUMBLE GULLEY HOLLOW NULLAH RAMBLA SHEUGH STRAIT BARRANCA QUEBRADA

RAVING RAVERY DELIRANT FRENZIED DELIRIOUS

RAVISH ROB RAPE ABUSE CHARM FORCE HARRY SPOIL ABDUCT ATTACK DEFILE AFFORCE CORRUPT DELIGHT ENFORCE OPPRESS OUTRAGE OVERJOY PLUNDER POLLUTE VIOLATE DEFLOWER ENTRANCE STUPRATE SUPPRESS UNMAIDEN

RAVISHER RAPTER RAVENER

RAVISHMENT ECSTASY RAPTURE TRANSPORT

RAW RA ROW BRUT LASH RUDE BLEAK CHILL CRUDE FRESH GREEN HARSH NAKED RAFTY SHARP BITTER COARSE CUTCHA KUTCHA UNRIPE VULGAR WAIRSH NATURAL NOUVEAU UNBOUND VERDANT WEARISH WEERISH IMMATURE RAWBONED UNCOOKED UNEDITED VISCERAL
(— AND COLD) CRIMPY

RAWBONED RAW BONY LEAN GAUNT LANKY SCRAG SCRAWNY

RAWHIDE WHIP WHANG COWHIDE COWSKIN GREENHIDE PARFLECHE

RAWNESS CRUDITY

RAY BEAM BETA DORN SOIL WIRE ALPHA BRAND DRESS EQUIP FLAIR FLAKE FLATH GLEAM GLEED ORDER RAYON ROKER SKATE BATOID CHUCHO OBISPO RADIAL RADIUS RAIOID SEPHEN STREAM TRYGON VISUAL BATFISH COWFISH DEWBEAM DRILVIS FIDDLER HOMELYN PLACOID RAIMENT TORPEDO WAIREPO BRACHIUM MOONBEAM NUMBFISH PLOWFISH PYLSTERT STINGRAY
(— OF LIGHT) GLINT SPEAR GLANCE SUNRAY SUNBEAM
(— OF STARFISH) ARM
(FEMALE —) MAID
(FIN —) SPINE

RAYON BEAM RADIUS DUCHESS

RAZE CUT FLAT RUIN ARASE ERASE LEVEL STREW ARRACE EFFACE SCRAPE SLIGHT UNPILE DESTROY SCRATCH SUBVERT UNBUILD DEMOLISH

RAZOR SHIV TUSK MUSSEL RASOIR SHAVER RATTLER SLASHER CUTTHROAT

RAZORBACK STATE ARKANSAS

RAZOR-BILLED AUK FALK TINK MURRE NODDY SCOOT SCOUT SKOOT TINKER SKIMMER WILLOCK ROCKBIRD

RAZOR CLAM PIROT RASOR SOLEN SPOUT RASOIR

RAZZ CHIACK RIDICULE RASPBERRY

RAZZIA RAID FORAY INCURSION

RAZZING RAZOO

RE RAY ANENT ACTION MATTER REGARDING

REACH GO GET HIT RAX RUN WIN BEAT COME FIND GAIN HAWK HENT MAKE REEK REIK RYKE SHOT SORT SPAN SPIT TEND BRACE CROSS FETCH GRASP PERCH RANGE RETCH TOUCH ADVENE ARRIVE ATTAIN DANGER EXTEND FATHOM LENGTH OBTAIN SNATCH STREEK STRIKE ACHIEVE COMPASS CONTACT GUNSHOT OVERGET POSSESS RECOVER STRETCH
(— ACROSS) SPAN OVERSTRIDE
(— AN END) STAY
(— BY EFFORT) ATTAIN
(— BY FIGURING) STRIKE
(— FORTH) EXTEND
(— GOAL) HAIL
(— OUT) UTTER SPREAD STRETCH
(— TO) LINE
(— TOTAL) AMOUNT
(— UNDERSTANDING) AGREE
(— WITH END) ABUT
(EXTREME —) PITCH STRETCH
(TRY TO —) ASPIRE

REACHER INGIVER

REACT ACT BUCK BEHAVE RETROACT

REACTION BELT BUZZ KAHN WOHL START WIDAL FAVISM RECOIL BLOWOFF EMOTION FEELING SETBACK BACKLASH EXCHANGE GUARDING KICKBACK
(— TIME) LATENCY
(VIOLENT —) SONG

REACTIONARY WHITE BOURBON BACKWARD

REACTIVATED AWAKE ACTIVE

REACTIVATOR ACTIFIER

REACTOR CHOKER FURNACE INDUCTOR

READ GO CON KRI QRI SEE CALL KERE QERI TURN CHOKE JUDGE SOLVE WRITE PERUSE RELATE FORESEE LEARNED LECTION PREDICT ABOMASUM DECIPHER FORETELL INDICATE OVERLOOK
(— ALOUD) LINE DEACON
(— HERE AND THERE) BROWSE

(— **MECHANICALLY**) RETINIZE
(— **OF**) SEE
(— **OFF**) DICTATE
(— **PROOF**) HORSE
(— **RAPIDLY**) DIP SKIM GOBBLE
(— **SLOWLY**) SPELL
(— **SYSTEMATICALLY**) FREQUENT
(— **WITH PROFOUND ATTENTION**)
PORE STUDY
READER PURSE DIPPER LECTOR
LISTER MAFTIR GRANTHI PISTLER
DEVOURER
(**CHILD'S** —) TENPENNY
(**CHURCH** —) LECTOR ANAGNOST
(PL.) FOLLOWING
READILY PAT YERN APTLY PREST
YERNE EASILY GAINLY PROBABLY
SPEEDILY
READINESS ART EASE GIFT PRESS
SKILL BELIEF GRAITH ADDRESS
FLUENCY FREEDOM ALACRITY
FACILITY GOODWILL
(**IN** —) APOISE AGAINST
READING KRI QRE QRI KERE KERI
QERI KTHIB KETHIB LESSON
LECTION LECTURE PERUSAL
SETTING
(PL.) PROCINCT
READING DESK AMBO LECTERN
READJUST MEND ADVANCE
READY UP APT BUN FIT RAD YAP
BAAN BAIN BOON BOUN BOWN FREE
GIRT GLIB GNIB RIFE RIPE TALL
YARE APERT EAGER FRACK HANDY
HAPPY PREDY PREST PRIME QUICK
SWIFT THERE TIGHT ADROIT
APPERT FACILE GRAITH HEARTY
PROMPT PRESENT RENABLE
WILLING CHEERFUL DEXTROUS
HANDSOME PREGNANT PREPARED
PROVIDED SKILLFUL
(— **FOR ACTION**) ARM EXPEDITE
(— **WITH WORDS**) FLUENT
(**NOT** —) SET BOUND GROOM
FORWARD DISPOSED IMPROMPT
INCLINED
READY-MADE SALE STORE BOUGHT
REAGENT ETCHANT REACTOR
ALTERANT REACTIVE
REAL BODY FAIR GOOD LEAL LEVY
PURE RIAL TRUE VERY VRAI PAKKA
PUCKA PUKKA RIGHT ROYAL SOLID
SOOTH ACTUAL ENTIRE HONEST
THINGY CORDIAL GENUINE GRADELY
SINCERE THINGAL CONCRETE
DEFINITE EXISTENT GRAITHLY
POSITIVE THINGISH
(**1-8TH** —) TLAC TLACO
(**EXTERNALLY** —) TANGIBLE
REALGAR ARSENIC ROSAKER
SANDARAC
REALISM REALITY LITERALISM
REALISTIC HARD SOBER VIVID
EARTHLY LIFELIKE PROBABLE
REALITY FEAT TRUE BEING SOOTH
THING TRUTH ACTUAL DASEIN
EFFECT VERITY SUBJECT IDENTITY
OVERSOUL REALNESS TRUENESS
(**LIMITED** —) SOMEWHAT

(**ULTIMATE** —) GOD SOURCE
DIVINITY SUBSTANCE
(PL.) REALIA
REALIZATION SENSE CRUSHER
FRUITION AWAKENING
REALIZE GAIN KNOW FETCH LEARN
SENSE EFFECT FULFIL ACQUIRE
CONCEIVE
REALIZED BODILY
(**FULLY** —) COMPLETE
REALLY ARU WIS ARAH HALF JUST
ARRAH TRULY WISHA FINELY
INDEED SIMPLY SURELY ACTUALLY
(**NOT** —) ILL ALMOST
REALM LAND SOIL BOURN CLIME
RANGE REIGN REWME RICHE
CIRCLE DEMAIN EMPIRE HEAVEN
REALTY REGION SPHERE DEMESNE
GAELDOM KINGDOM NOTALIA
ROYALME TERRENE CLUBLAND
DEVILDOM DOMINION ELDORADO
GHOSTDOM GIPSYDOM NOTOGAEA
(— **OF DARKNESS**) PO
(— **OF FABULOUS RICHNESS**)
ELDORADO
(— **OF THOR**) THRUTHHEIM
THRUTHVANG
(**MARINE** —) NOTALIA TROPICALIA
(**VISIONARY** —) CLOUDLAND
REALTY FEALTY REAUTE ROYALTY
REAM FOAM RIME SEED SKIM CHEAT
CREAM FROTH FRAISE RHYMER
STRETCH
(PL.) INSIDES OUTSIDES
REAMER BUR BURR SPUD DRIFT
RIMER BROACH CHERRY FRAISE
RANCER RHYMER RIMMER WIDENER
REANIMATE WAKE RENEW REVIVE
RECREATE
REANIMATED AWAKE
REAP BAG CUT REP CROP RIPE
GLEAN SHEAR GARNER GATHER
SICKLE HARVEST
REAPER LORD COCKER TASKER
WINNER CRADLER SICKLER
(**GRIM** —) DEATH
REAPING HOOK SICKLE TWIBIL
CROTCHET
REAPPEARANCE RENTREE
EMERSION
REAR AFT BACK HIND HINT JUMP
LIFT STEN TOSS BREED BUILD
CARVE ERECT JUNCH STEND
ACHTER AROUSE CRADLE FOSTER
NURSLE SUCKLE APPREAR ARRIERE
EDUCATE ELEVATE NOURISH
NURTURE UPBRING BUTTOCKS
HINDMOST REARWARD
(— **CAREFULLY**) TIDDLE
(**NEARER THE** —) AFTER
(**TO THE** — **OF**) ABAFT
(**TO THE** —) BACK BEHIND
REARED (— **BY HAND**) CADE
(**DELICATELY** —) SOYLED
REARHORSE MANTIS
REARING FRESNE PESADE FORCENE
RAMPANT
(— **UP**) STEND
REARRANGE DO ADJUST JIGGER

REORDER READJUST
REARRANGEMENT WAGNER
DIAGENESIS
REARWARD AFT BACKWARD
REASON PEG WAY HOTI NOUS REDE
SAKE TALK ARGUE CAUSE COUNT
LOGOS PROOF RATIO SCORE SENSE
SKILL THING THINK TOPIC EXCUSE
GROUND MANNER MATTER MOTION
NOESIS ACCOUNT PREMISE
QUARREL SUBJECT TUITION
ARGUMENT ENCHESON LOGICIZE
VERNUNFT
(— **FOR PRIDE**) BOAST
(**LACKING** —) INEPT
REASONABLE FAIR JUST SOBER
SKILFUL FEASIBLE MODERATE
RATIONAL SENSIBLE
REASONABLENESS EPIKY EPIKIKA
FITNESS FAIRNESS SOBRIETY
REASONABLY SOON
REASONER (**FALLACIOUS** —)
SOPHIST
REASONING LOGIC ERGOTISM
RATIONAL
(**CLUMSY** —) ARGAL
(**FALLACIOUS** —) CIRCLE SOPHISTRY
REASSEMBLE RELY
REASSUME REVOKE REPRISE
REAVE ROB REFE SEIZE SPLIT
REMOVE DESPOIL PILLAGE PLUNDER
UNRAVEL
REB RABBI REBEL MISTER
REBAB GUSLE
REBATE BLUNT CHECK LESSEN
RIBBET DIMINISH DISCOUNT
DRAWBACK KICKBACK
REBEC LYRE SAROD RIBIBE RUBIBLE
REBEKAH (**HUSBAND OF** —) ISAAC
(**SON OF** —) ESAU JACOB
REBEL REB KICK RISE TURN BRAND
FAUVE ANARCH CROPPY MUTINE
REVOLT FRONDEUR
(— **IN ART**) FAUVE
(PL.) REBELDOM
REBELLION MUTINY PUTSCH
REVOLT MISRULE UPRISING
REBELLIOUS RUSTY ANARCHIC
MUTINOUS AUDACIOUS INSURGENT
REBIRTH REVIVAL
REBOUND DAP HOP HANG KISS
STOT CANON CAROM STITE BOUNCE
CARROM RECOIL RESULT BRICOLE
REDOUND RICOCHET SNAPBACK
(— **ERRATICALLY**) KICK
REBOUND CLIP RETAINER
REBUFF SLAP SNIB SNUB CHECK
FLING REPEL DEFEAT DENIAL
REBUKE REBUTE REPULSE
REBUKE NIP WIG BAWL RATE REDD
SNEB SNIB SNUB TRIM BARGE
BLAME CHECK CHIDE DRESS SAUCE
SCOLD SNAPE SNEAP TOUCH
DIRDUM GANSEL LESSON RATING
RATTLE REHETE REMORD CHIDING
CORRECT HOTFOOT LECTURE
REPROOF REPROVE SARCASM
BLESSING BUSINESS CHASTISE
KEELHAUL REPROACH SCORCHER

THREAPEN UNDERNIM

REBUS BADGE ENIGMA PUZZLE
RIDDLE

REBUT REPEL RECOIL REFUTE
REPULSE RETREAT DISPROVE

RECALCITRANT UNRULY RENITENT
OBSTINATE RESISTANT

RECALL CITE BRING UNSAY REMAND
REMIND RETURN REVOKE UNLOOK
RECLAIM RETRACE RETRACT
REVIVAL UNSHOUT REMEMBER
WITHCALL WITHDRAW
(— FONDLY) CHERISH

RECANT UNSAY ABJURE REVOKE
UNSING DISAVOW RETRACT
SWALLOW PALINODE RENOUNCE

RECAPITULATE SUM UNITE RECITE
REPEAT RECOUNT REHEARSE
REITERATE SUMMARIZE

RECAPTURE RETAKE RECOVER

RECEDE DIE EBB BACK FADE STEP
VARY RECUR DEPART DIFFER
RETIRE SHRINK DECLINE DIGRESS
RETREAT CONTRACT DIMINISH
ELONGATE WITHDRAW

RECEIPT CHIT RECU RESET APOCHA
BINDER RECIPE WARRANT
(PL.) GATE TAKE SALES INCOME
ENTRADA

RECEIVE GET BEAR FALL GAIN HAVE
HOLD TAKE ADMIT AFONG CATCH
GREET GUEST LATCH RESET
ACCEPT ASSUME BORROW DERIVE
GATHER HARBOR RECULE BELIEVE
CONTAIN EMBRACE INHERIT
SUSTAIN UNDERFO PERCEIVE
(— A CRIMINAL) RESET
(— AS GUEST) FANG HOST VANG
GREET
(— AS MEMBER) INCEPT
(— AS REWARD) REAP
(— FROM LOTTERY) DRAW
(— SHEETS) FLY
(— WITH PLEASURE) GRATIFY

RECEIVER FENCE PHONE PERNOR
SINDICO CYMAPHEN DONATARY
REHEATER
(— IN BANKRUPTCY) SINDICO
(— OF INCOME) PERNOR
(— OF STOLEN GOODS) LOCK
FENCE
(TELEGRAPH —) INKER INKWRITER
(TELEPHONE —) PHONE CYMAPHEN

RECENSION REVIEW SURVEY
CENSURE CRITIQUE

RECENT HOT NEW LATE PUNY
ENDER FRESH GREEN HOURLY
LATELY LATTER MODERN CURRENT
HOLOCENE NEOTERIC
(MOST —) LAST

RECENTLY ANEW JUST LATE NEWLY
LASTLY LATELY FRESHLY LATTERLY

RECENTNESS YOUTH

RECEPTACLE ARK BIN BOX CAN
CUP DIP FAT PAN TIN TUB URN VAT
BATH BOAT BOWL CASE CELL CIST
DOVE DROP FACK FONT HELL HOLD
LOOM RACK RECU SAFE SINK TIDY
TOUR ARBOR CARRY CREEL KIOSK
KITTY RESET SCOOP STEAN STEEN
TABLE TORUS BASKET BUCKET
BUTLER CARTON CUPULE DIPPER
DRAWER HAMPER HOPPER MORTAR
PITCHI POCKET RECEIT SHRINE
TABLET TROUGH ASHTRAY CAPSULE
CARRIER CORBULA DUSTBIN
ENVELOP HEADBOX LATRINE
OMNIBUS OSSUARY PARISON
SANDBOX SETTLER SOAPBOX
STOWAGE TRAVOIS BURSICLE
CANISTER CESSPOOL FOREBOOT
GYNOBASE HONEYPOT LOCKFAST
OSSARIUM OVERFLOW PERFUMER
SPITTOON STOCKPOT SEPULCHER
(— FOR ABANDONED INFANTS)
TOUR
(— FOR BONES) OSSUARY
OSSARIUM
(— FOR BROKEN TYPE) HELL
(— FOR BUTTER) RUSKIN
(— FOR COAL) BUNKER
(— FOR CONVEYING) APRON
(— FOR DRY ARTICLES) FAT
(— FOR FOUL THINGS) SINK
(— FOR GLASS BATCH) ARBOR
(— FOR HOLY WATER) FONT
(— FOR ORE-CRUSHING) MORTAR
(— FOR POKER CHIPS) KITTY
(— FOR SACRED RELICS) TABLE
SHRINE TABLET SEPULCHRE
(— FOR SAVINGS) SOCK
(— FOR SEWING MATERIALS) TIDY
(— FOR TREASURE) HANAPER
(— FOR TYPE CASES) RACK
(— FOR VOTES) SITULA
(— IN BOTTLE-MAKING MACHINE)
PARISON
(— OF CLAY OR STONE) STEAN
STEEN
(— ON WEIGHING SCALES) PAN
(— OVER ALTAR) DOVE
(CLAY —) BOOT
(DILATED —) GYNOBASE
(ELECTRICAL —) BASEPLUG
(INCENSE —) ACERRA
(OPEN —) TRAY
(PURSELIKE —) BURSICLE
(TAILOR'S —) HELL
(WOODEN —) SEBILLA

RECEPTION TEA ROUT COURT
CRUSH DIFFA LEVEE SALON TREAT
ACCOIL DURBAR RUELLE SOIREE
SQUASH ACCUEIL COUCHEE
MATINEE OVATION PASSAGE
RECEIPT RECUEIL TEMPEST
FUNCTION GREETING PERNANCY
REACTION SOCIABLE
(— AT BEDTIME) COUCHEE
(— OF NATIVE PRINCES) DURBAR
(— OF SOUND) AUDIO
(ARABIC —) DIFFA
(CORDIAL —) WELCOME
(CROWDED —) SQUASH
(FASHIONABLE —) LEVEE SALON
(WEDDING —) INFARE

RECEPTIVE SENSORY OPENHANDED

RECEPTOR STOCK RECEIVER
DOMINATOR

RECERCELEE SARCELLY

RECESS ALA ARK BAY BOX COD
CUP PAN BOLE COVE DEEP HOLE
NOOK TRAP AMBRY BOSOM CANAL
CAVUM CLEFT CREEK HAVEN HITCH
INLET NICHE ORIEL PRESS SINUS
ALCOVE ANCONA CAVERN CENTER
CHAPEL CIRQUE CLOSET COFFER
CRANNY GROTTO INDENT LOCULE
RABBET REBATE BEDSITE CONCAVE
CREVICE LOCULUS MANHOLE
RETREAT SINKING INTERVAL
LOCKHOLE OVERTURE TABLINUM
TOKONOMA TRAVERSE VACATION
(— BETWEEN CAPES) BAY
(— FOR FAMILY RECORDS)
TABLINUM
(— FOR HINGE LEAF) PAN
(— FOR PIECE OF SCULPTURE)
ANCONA
(— IN CHURCH WALL) AMBRY
(— IN COLON) HAUSTRUM
(— IN JAPANESE HOUSE)
TOKONOMA
(— IN MOUNTAIN) CIRQUE
(— IN ROCK) HITCH
(— IN SIDE OF HILL) CORRIE
(— IN SIDE OF ROOM) ALA
(— IN WALL) BOLE NICHE ALCOVE
(— ON STAGE) CANOPY
(INMOST —) BOSOM
(PL.) FLASH

RECESSED SUNK SUNKEN

RECESSION BUST RETREAT

RECESSIVE BACKWARD RECEDING
RETIRING WITHDRAWN

RECHERCHE RARE CHOICE EXOTIC
CURIOUS PRECIOUS UNCOMMON
EXQUISITE

RECIDIVIST REPEATER

RECIPE RX FORM RULE FORMULA
RECEIPT

RECIPIENT HEIR DONEE ALMSMAN
DONATEE LAUREATE

RECIPROCAL CROSS COMMON
MUTUAL SECANT SEESAW
(— OF A POISE) RHE
(— OF VISCOSITY) FLUIDITY

RECIPROCATE REPAY RETURN
REQUITE RETROACT

RECIPROCITY SHU ISOPOLITY
MUTUALITY

RECITAL TALE ASHRE CITAL RECIT
STORY EXPOSE LITANY PARADE
REPEAT TIKKUN READING RELATION
(— OF PRAYER) GEULAH HAMOTZI
KEDUSHAH
(UNTRUE —) TALE

RECITATION DHIKR READING
RECITAL RHAPSODY

RECITATIVE SCENA CHANSON

RECITE SAY CARP TELL STATE
INTONE RECKON RELATE RENDER
REPEAT DECLAIM DECLINE DICTATE
NARRATE RECOUNT REHEARSE
(— AS ELOCUTION EXERCISE)
DECLAIM
(— IN MONOTONE) INTONE
(— METRICALLY) SCAN

(— MONOTONOUSLY) CHANT CHAUNT
(— NUMBERS) COUNT
(— PRAYERS) BENSH DAVEN
(— TIRESOMELY) THRUM
(— WITH GREAT EASE) RUSH
RECITER SCALD SKALD ANTERI DISEUR CONTEUR DISEUSE HOMERIST ILIADIST RHAPSODE
RECITING CHARM
RECK RAK CARE DEEM PASS MATTER REGARD CONCERN CONSIDER ESTIMATE
RECKLESS RASH WILD FOLLE PERDU MADCAP RACKLE SAVAGE GALLOWS RAMSTAM CARELESS HEADLONG HEEDLESS BLINDFOLD
RECKLESSLY FAST BLIND RAMSTAM HEADLONG HEADFIRST
RECKON RET ARET CAST DATE ITEM RATE RECK RELY TALE TELL TOTE ALLOT AUDIT CLAIM CLASS COUNT JUDGE PLACE RETTE SCORE TALLY THINK ASSIGN FIGURE IMPUTE NUMBER REPUTE TOTTLE ACCOUNT ASCRIBE COMPUTE INCLUDE PRETEND RECOUNT SUPPOSE SUPPUTE CONSIDER ESTIMATE
(— IN) INCLUDE
RECKONING TAB BILL NICK POST SHOT TAIL TALE COUNT SCORE TALLY COMPOT LAWING REASON TAILYE TOTTLE ACCOUNT DAYTALE TAILZEE COMPUTUS
RECLAIM IN TAME OBJECT RECALL REDEEM REFORM RESCUE SUBDUE PROTEST RECOVER RESTORE
(— FROM SAVAGE STATE) CIVILIZE
RECLAIMANT GOEL
RECLINE LIE LIG LEAN LOLL REST COUCH ACCUMB RECUMB UPLEAN DISCUMB
(— LANGUIDLY) GAULSH
RECLUSE NUN MONK CULDEE HERMIT REMOTE ASCETIC EREMITE INCLUSA INCLUSE ANCHORET INCLUSUS SECLUDED SOLITARY
(PL.) SECLUSE
RECOGNITION FAME SPUR HONOR SENSE CREDIT STATUS FEELING KENNING KNOWING AGNITION SANCTION
(— OF ACHIEVEMENT) LAUREL
RECOGNIZE KEN SEE ESPY FACE KNOW SPOT TELL ADMIT ALLOW BLINK CROWN HONOR KEETH KITHE KYTHE ACCEPT ACKNOW AGNIZE BEKNOW COUTHE REVISE CORRECT DISCERN REALIZE ACCREDIT
(— IN ANY CAPACITY) AGNIZE
RECOGNIZED GOOD CLEAR KNOWN CLASSIC FAMILIAR
RECOIL SHY BALK KICK TURN REBUT SHRUG SHUCK START STRAM BLENCH BOUNCE FLINCH RECULE RESILE RESULT RETORT SHRINK REBOUND REDOUND REVERSE BACKLASH REJOUNCE
(WITHOUT —) DEADBEAT

RECOLLECT RECALL RECORD RETAIN COMPOSE RECOVER RECOLETO REMEMBER
RECOLLECTION MIND MEMORY RECALL RECORD MINDING THOUGHT MEMORIAL SOUVENIR
RECOMMENCE RENEW REOPEN RESUME REPRISE
RECOMMEND MOVE OSSE PLUG TOUT WISH ADVISE COMMIT PRAISE PREFER COMMEND CONSIGN COUNSEL ENTRUST ADVOCATE RECOMMIT
RECOMMENDATION CHIT VOEU ADVISE COUNSEL TESTIMONY
(PARTY —) COUPON
(SERVANT'S —) CHIT
RECOMPENSE PAY MEED MEND MENSE QUITS REPAY YIELD AMENDS BOUNTY HADBOT REWARD SALARY GUERDON IMBURSE PAYMENT PREMIUM REQUITE RESTORE SATISFY SERVICE
RECONCILE GREE WEAN ADAPT AGREE ATONE ACCORD ADJUST SETTLE SHRIVE REUNITE HARMONIZE
RECONCILED FAIN VAIN SAUGHT
RECONCILIATION ATONE ACCORD SAUGHT REUNION IRENICON
RECONDITE DARK DEEP HIGH HIDDEN MYSTIC OCCULT SECRET CRYPTIC CURIOUS OBSCURE RETIRED ABSTRACT ABSTRUSE ESOTERIC
RECONNAISSANCE RECCE RECCO RECCY SURVEY
RECONNOITER SCOUT RECALL SURVEY EXAMINE PICKEER DISCOVER REMEMBER
RECONSIDER REVIEW FORTHINK
RECONSTRUCT REPAIR REEVOKE REMODEL RESTORE
RECORD CAN CUT BOOK CARD DATE DISC ITER NICK PAGE ROLL SING SLIP WICK ALBUM CHART DIARY ENACT ENTER ENTRY FASTI GRAPH JUMBO PRICK QUIPO QUIPU SIJIL SLATE STYLE TITLE ANNALS CHARGE DOCKET LEGEND MEMOIR SCROLL SPREAD WARBLE ACCOUNT CALENDS CITATOR DUBBING KALENDS LEXICON MENTION MYOGRAM SHOWING TICKLER TRACING ANAGRAPH ARCHIVES CYLINDER ENTRANCE ERGOGRAM HERDBOOK INSCROLL JUDGMENT KYMOGRAM LAUEGRAM MARIGRAM MELOGRAM MEMORIAL MONUMENT ONDOGRAM PANCHART PRESSING REGISTER REMEMBER SCHEDULE STUDBOOK
(— BY NOTCHES) SCORE
(— OF CAR MOVEMENTS) JUMBO
(— OF DOCUMENT) PROTOCOL
(— OF EVENTS) FASTI
(— OF HUMANITY'S FATE) SIJIL SIJILL

(— OF JOURNEY) JOURNAL ITINERARY
(— OF LOAN) CHARGE
(— OF MUHAMMAD'S SAYINGS) HADIT
(— OF MUSCULAR WORK) ERGOGRAM
(— OF PROCEEDINGS) ACTA ITER JOURNAL MINUTES
(COURT —) EYRE
(DAILY —) DIARY
(FORMAL —) ACT
(HISTORICAL —) STORY
(PHONOGRAPH —) DISC DISK SINGLE BISCUIT SHELLAC
(SHIP'S —) LOG
(PL.) LIBER ANNALS ARCHIVE
RECORDER FLUTE BOOKER FLAUTO NOTATOR GREFFIER REGISTER
RECORDING ALBUM ALIVE LABEL CUTTING
RECOUNT MING TELL COUNT DEVISE RECITE REGARD RELATE REPEAT SPREAD EXPRESS HISTORY NARRATE CONSIDER DESCRIBE REHEARSE
RECOUP DEDUCT REGAIN RECOVER INDEMNIFY
RECOUPLING HOOKUP
RECOURSE SUIT ACCESS REFUGE RESORT STRING REGRESS RESTAUR RISORSE
(HAVE —) RECUR
RECOVER DOW COUR COWR CURE FIRM HEAL KERE COVER REACH UPSET BOUNCE RECURE REGAIN RESCUE RESUME RETAKE RETIRE REVERT REVOKE WARISH DELIVER OVERGET OVERPUT OVERSET READEPT RECLAIM RECRUIT REPAREL REPRISE RESTORE RETRIEVE
RECOVERER DIGESTER
RECOVERY CURE RECOUR RECURE REMEDY RETURN SALVAGE COMEBACK SNAPBACK
RECREANT FALSE CRAVEN YELLOW APOSTATE COWARDLY DESERTER RECRAYED
RECREATE AMUSE EVOKE REVIVE
RECREATION PLAY SPORT SOLACE RENEWAL ACTIVITY DIVERSION PALINGENY
(PERIOD OF —) HOLIDAY VACATION
RECREATIVE PLAYING
RECREMENT SLAG DROSS SCORIA
RECRUIT BLEU BOOT FRESH RAISE GATHER INTAKE MUSTER RECREW REPAIR REVIVE RECOVER REFRESH RESTORE ASSEMBLE BEZONIAN CONSCRIPT
(RAW —) ROOKY ROOKIE
RECTANGLE BOX SQUARE CHECKER
(COTTON —) HUIPIL
(CURVILINEAR —) TESSERA
(WOVEN —) SINKER
RECTANGULAR SQUARE BOXLIKE EMERALD
RECTIFICATION LIMATION

RECTIFIER DIODE COLUMN DETECTOR EXCITRON
RECTIFY AMEND EMEND RIGHT ADJUST BETTER DETECT REFORM REMEDY CORRECT IMPROVE REDRESS EMENDATE REGULATE
RECTITUDE DOOM EQUITY JUSTICE PROBITY
RECTOR RULER LEADER PARSON PERSONA INCUMBENT
RECTUM SIEGE TEWEL
RECUMBENT IDLE JACENT CUMBENT LEANING RESTING INACTIVE REPOSING
RECUPERATE RALLY REFETE REGAIN RECOVER RECRUIT RETRIEVE
RECUR CYCLE REFER REPEAT RESORT RETURN REOCCUR REVOLVE REAPPEAR
(— **CONSTANTLY**) HAUNT
RECURRENCE RESORT RETURN ATAVISM REPRISE ITERANCE ITERANCY RECOURSE
(— **OF SOUND**) CADENCE
RECURRENT CYCLIC FREQUENT
RECURRING ROLLING CONTINUAL
(— **ANNUALLY**) ETESIAN
(— **EVERY THIRD DAY**) TERTIAN
(— **ON NINTH DAY**) NONAN NONANE
(— **ON SEVENTH DAY**) SEPTAN
(**CONSTANTLY** —) ETERNAL
(**CONTINUALLY** —) CONSTANT
RECURVED ERICOID
RECUTTING FRESHING
RED (ALSO SEE COLOR) GOYA GULY PINK PUCE ROJO ROSY RUBY ANGRY CANNA CORAL FIERY JUDAS ROUGE RUDDY RUFUS ARCHIL AZALEA BLOODY CERISE FLORID FULGID GARNET HECTIC NECTAR ORCHIL ORIENT RAISIN RUBRIC TITIAN TRYPAN VERMIL WANTON CARMINE GLOWING NACARAT PIMENTO RADICAL RUBELLE RUBIOUS STAMMEL VERMILY ARMENIAN AUBUSSON BORDEAUX CARDINAL CHOLERIC COLORADO FLAGRANT MANDARIN MOROCAIN RUBICUND SANGUINE ARTILLERY
(— **AND INFLAMED**) BLOODSHOT
(— **PLANET**) MARS
(**ANTIQUE** —) CANNA
(**BRIGHT** —) TULY CHERRY PUNICIAL VERMILION
(**DARK** —) CLARET
(**EUREKA** —) PUCE
(**FIERY** —) MINIUM
(**GRAYISH** —) AZALEA
(**HERALDIC** —) GULES
(**IRON OXIDE** —) AGATE TARRAGONA
(**PURPLISH** —) LAKE MAGENTA
(**WAX** —) COPPER
(**YELLOWISH** —) MAROON
RED ADMIRAL VANESSA
RED-BACKED SHRIKE POPE
RED BANEBERRY REDBERRY TOADROOT

RED BAY PERSEA
RED-BELLIED (— **TERRAPIN**) SLIDER SKILPOT
(— **WOODPECKER**) CHAB
RED-BREASTED BREAM FLATFISH FLOUNDER
RED-BREASTED KNOT GRAYBACK GREYBACK
REDBUD CERCIS JUNEBUD
RED CAMPION ROBIN SOLDIER
RED CEDAR SAVIN SABINA JUNIPER
RED CLOVER SAPLING TREFOIL TRIFOLY
RED CURRANT GOYA RIZZLE TIZZAR
REDD RID COMB OPEN LITTER NEATEN REFUSE RESCUE SETTLE ARRANGE DELIVER SMARTEN UNBLOCK UNRAVEL
RED DEER OLEN STAG
(**FEMALE** —) HIND
(**MALE** —) HART STAG
REDDEN RUD FIRE RUBY BLUSH FLUSH LIGHT ROUGE RUDDY BLOODY RUBIFY RUBRIC RUDDLE EMPURPLE
REDDISH REDDY RUDDY RUFUS FLUSHY RUFOUS COLORADO PYRRHOUS
RED DRUM SPOT REDFISH
REDEEM BUY WIN SAVE ALESE CLEAR REPRY BORROW OFFSET RANSOM DELIVER FULFILL JUSTIFY RECLAIM WITHBEG AGAINBUY LIBERATE
REDEEMER GOEL SAVIOR
REDEMPTION RANSOM REFORM SAFETY SALVATION
REDEYE BASS RUDD VIREO WHISKY SUNFISH
RED-EYE CATSUP CICADA WHISKY
RED-EYED VIREO REDEYE GRASSET PREACHER
RED-FACED FLUSHED SCARLET
REDFIN DACE SHINER REDHORSE YELLOWFIN
REDFISH SALMON FATHEAD ROSEFISH
RED GOOSEFOOT PIGWEED SOWBANE
RED GROUPER MERO NEGRE REDBELLY
RED GROUSE GORHEN GORCOCK LAGOPODE MOORBIRD MUIRFOWL
RED GUM JARRAH EUCALYPT
RED GURNARD CUR ELLECK ROCHET SOLDIER
REDHAIRED RUFUS
REDHEAD DIVER FINCH POCHARD KIZILBASH
RED HIND GRAYSBY GROUPER CABRILLA
REDHORSE REDFIN SUCKER
REDIA SPOROSAC
REDIRECT DISPLACE READDRESS
REDISTILL COHOBATE
REDISTRIBUTE FRESHEN REASSIGN
RED LAVER SLOKE
REDNESS RED RUD GLOW HEAT

RUDD RUBOR ERYTHEMA RUBEDITY
(— **OF SKY**) AURORA
REDO REDACT RESTYLE
(— **UNSKILLFULLY**) BOTCH
RED OCHER TIVER ABRAUM RUDDLE
REDOLENCE BALM AROMA SCENT
REDOLENT RICH ODOROUS SCENTED AROMATIC FRAGRANT SMELLING
RED OSIER WILLOW REDBRUSH
REDOUBT FEAR MASK DREAD SCHANZ SCONCE
REDOUBLE REECHO INTENSIFY
REDOUND TURN ACCRUE BILLOW CONDUCE REFLECT OVERFLOW
RED RASPBERRY CUTHBERT
REDRESS HEAL DRESS REDUB AVENGE OFFSET REFORM RELIEF REMEDE REMEDY REPAIR ADDRESS CORRECT RECTIFY REFOUND RELIEVE
RED ROCKFISH TAMBOR
RED SAGE LANTANA
RED SANDALWOOD CHANDAM
REDSHANK CLEE TEUK SHAKE GAMBET REDLEG YELPER PELLILE TATTLER
REDSKIN RED ROJO TAWNY INDIAN
REDSTART YELPER BRANTAIL FIRETAIL WHITECAP FIREFLIRT
RED STOPPER EUGENIA IRONWOOD
RED-TAILED (— **HAWK**) REDTAIL
(— **TROPIC BIRD**) KOAE
RED-TAPISM BEADLEDOM
RED-THROATED LOON WABBY
REDTOP COUCH FIORIN FINETOP FINEBENT FURZETOP BLUEJOINT
REDUCE CUT BATE DOCK DROP EASE PARE PULL THIN ABASE ABATE ALLAY APPAL BREAK DRAFT ELIDE LOWER QUELL SCANT SHAVE SLAKE SLASH SMELT DEDUCE DEFALK DEJECT DELETE DEPOSE DILUTE HUMBLE LESSEN REBATE REDUCT SHRINK SUBACT SUBDUE WEAKEN ABANDON ABRIDGE ASSUAGE ATOMIZE CHANCER CONQUER CURTAIL DEFLATE DEGRADE DEPLETE DWINDLE ECLIPSE FRITTER INHIBIT RESOLVE RETREAT SCISSOR SHORTEN SUBJECT ATTEMPER CONDENSE DECREASE DIMINISH MINIMIZE
(— **ACCORDING TO FIXED RATIO**) SCALE
(— **ANGLE**) CHAMFER
(— **BULK**) BLEND
(— **LUMBER**) SIZE
(— **PROFITS**) SQUEEZE
(— **PURITY**) ALLOY
(— **STONE BLOCKS**) SPALL SPAWL
(— **THE VALUE**) DECRY BEGGAR DEPRAVE
(— **TO A MEAN**) AVERAGE
(— **TO ASHES**) CREMATE
(— **TO CARBON**) CHAR
(— **TO FINE PARTICLES**) ATOMIZE
(— **TO FLAT SURFACE**) LEVEL
(— **TO INSIGNIFICANCE**) DROWN

(— **TO LOWER GRADE**) BREAK DEMOTE DEGRADE
(— **TO NIL**) CLOSE
(— **TO NOTHING**) ANNUL
(— **TO PASSIVITY**) CHINAFY
(— **TO POWDER**) GRIND PULVERIZE
REDUCED SUNK TAIL BROKEN DWARFED DEGRADED WEAKENED VESTIGIAL
REDUCTION BUST LETUP SLASH CUTBACK CUTDOWN DOCKAGE SHAVING ANALYSIS DILUTION DISCOUNT SHRINKAGE
(— **IN FORCE**) RIF
(— **IN PITCH**) DROP
(— **IN PRICE**) SAVING CONCESSION
REDUNDANCY EXCESS NIMIETY SURPLUS PLEONASM PLETHORA VERBIAGE TAUTOLOGY
REDUNDANT WORDY LAVISH PROFUSE SURPLUS VERBOSE SWELLING EXCESSIVE
REDWING POP THRUSH WINDLE GADWALL WINNARD
REDWOOD MAD AMBOYNA BARWOOD FURIOUS SEQUOIA MAHOGANY
RE-ECHO REWORD REBOUND RESOUND REDOUBLE
REED NAL RIE RIX SAG BENT JUNK PIPE PIRN RODE SLEY TULE ARROW DONAX SPEAR TWILL BENNEL RADDLE SAGGON CALAMUS FISTULA WHISTLE WINDING
(— **FOR WARPING**) WRAITHE
(— **FOR WINDING THREAD**) PIRN SPOOL
(— **IN ORGAN**) VIBRATOR
(— **OF LOOM**) COMB
(**FOXTAIL** —) DOD
(**GIANT** —) DONAX
(**MUSICAL** —) OAT
(**WEAVER'S** —) SLAY SLEY RADDLE SLEIGH
(PL.) SPEAR
REED BENT CARRIZO
REEDBIRD BOBOLINK
REEDBUCK BOHOR NAGOR REITBOK
REED BUNTING RINGBIRD
REED CANARY GRASS SPIRE DAGGERS
REED END TONGUE
REEDING GADROON MILLING STRIGIL GRAINING
REED MACE RAUPO CATTAIL MATREED
REED ORGAN MELODEON HARMONIUM
REED PIPE MIRLITON
REED WARBLER PITBIRD
REEDY THIN WEAK FRAIL TWILLED
REEF CAY KAY KEY CAYO LODE RYFT VEIN ATOLL LEDGE SHELF STICK BOILER REEFER SADDLE SKERRY BAGREEF BALANCE BIOHERM MAKATEA TOMBOLO
REEFER CAR COAT STICK JACKET MUGGLES
REEK FOG FUG EMIT FUME HEAP

MIST PILE RICK RISE VENT EQUIP EXUDE ISSUE NIDOR SMEEK SMOKE STEAM VAPOR EXHALE OUTFIT EMANATE
(— **WITH CORRUPTION**) FESTER
REEL PIRN ROCK SPIN SWAB SWIM TURN GIDDY SPOOL SWIFT TRULL WAVER WHEEL WHIRL WINCE BOBBIN RECOIL SWERVE TUMULT WAGGLE WALTER WELTER WINDER WINDLE WINNLE WINTLE BALLOON STAGGER SWABBLE TITUBATE
(— **FOR DRAWING SILK**) FILATURE
(— **FOR WARP DRYING**) BALLOON
(— **FOR WINDING YARN**) PIRN SWIFT
(— **OFF A STORY**) SCRIEVE
(— **USED FOR YARN**) CRIB
(**DYEING** —) WINCE
(**FISHING** —) TROW TROLL TRULL WINCH
(PL.) REVELS
REELER TWINER
REELING TURN AREEL STAGGERY WAMBLING
REEM MOAN URUS UNICORN
REEVE REE REFE THREAD BAILIFF PROVOST STEWARD OVERSEER
REFECTION MEAL RELIEF REPAST
REFECTORY FRATER FRATRY
REFER DEFER LEAVE POINT ADVERT ALLUDE APPEAL ASSIGN CHARGE COMMIT DELATE DIRECT IMPUTE PREFER RELATE SUBMIT ASCRIBE REJOURN RELEGATE
(— **TO SOMETHING REPEATEDLY**) HARP
(— **TO**) SEE CITE INTEND CONCERN CONSULT MENTION INTIMATE
REFEREE BREHON UMPIRE ARBITER AUDITOR
REFERENCE TAB FOLIO REMIT SIGIL APPEAL REGARD RENVOI MEANING RESPECT ALLUSION HANDBOOK INNUENDO RELATION
(**SATIRICAL** —) GLANCE
REFERENDUM POLL MANDATE
REFINE RUN TRY BOLT EDIT FILE FINE PURE CUPEL EXALT PLAIN SLICK SMELT AFFINE DECOCT EXCOCT FILTER GARBLE SMOOTH CONCOCT ELEVATE SUBLIME SWEETEN HUMANIZE URBANIZE
(— **AS GOLD**) TEST CARAT
(— **PULP**) JORDAN
(— **SUGAR**) CLAY
(— **WINE**) FORCE
REFINED FINE GENT NEAT NICE TRIE EXACT PURED TERSE CHASTE EXCOCT INLAND NIMINY POLITE QUAINT SUBTLE CLEANLY COURTLY ELEGANT GENTEEL PRECISE SCRAPED DELICATE ELEVATED HIGHBRED PRECIEUX SERAPHIC
(**NOT** —) CRUDE
(**TOO** —) FINESPUN
REFINEMENT GRACE POLISH CULTURE FINESSE DELICACY ELEGANCE POLITURE SUBTLETY URBANITY

REFINER TRIER JORDAN PURIFIER
REFINING HUMAN FINING CULTURE AFFINAGE
REFINISH ANTIQUE
REFLECT COW MUSE PORE SHOW BLAZE FLASH GLASS GLINT IMAGE SHINE STUDY THINK DAZZLE DEBATE MIRROR PONDER RECORD REFLEX RELUCE RETORT RETURN REVISE STEVEN EXPRESS REDOUND REFRACT SHIMMER COGITATE CONSIDER MEDITATE REDOUBLE RUMINATE
(— **IRREGULARLY**) SCATTER
(— **UPON**) SPECULATE
REFLECTED DERIVED MIRRORED SPECULAR
REFLECTION ECHO FOLD IDEA SKIT BLAME GHOST GLARE GNOME DEBATE MUSING PONDER REFLEX RETURN SHADOW CENSURE COUNSEL SPECIES THOUGHT EYESHINE MOONPATH THINKING
(— **OF SELF IN ANOTHER'S EYES**) BABY
REFLECTIVE PENSIVE THOUGHTFUL
(— **POWER**) ALBEDO
REFLECTOR FLAT CRITIC HASTER SHINER HORIZON DIFFUSER HASTENER SPECULUM
REFLEX COPY IMAGE TROPISM ALLUSION
(**NOT** —) IDEOMOTOR
REFLUX EBB EBBING REFLOW
REFOREST REBOISE
REFORM MEND AMEND EMEND PRUNE BETTER REBUKE REPAIR CENSURE CORRECT DISBAND RECLAIM RECTIFY REDRESS
REFORMATORY COLLEGE MAGDALEN
REFORMER APOSTLE UTOPIAN UTOPIAST JANSENIST
REFRACT DIVIDE REFLECT REFRINGE
REFRACTION REBATE REBOUND DIACLASIS
REFRACTORY SULLEN UNRULY WANTON ALUNDUM FROWARD RESTIVE VICIOUS WAYWARD MUTINOUS PERVERSE STUBBORN CAMSTEERY
REFRAIN BOB TAG CURB DOWN KEEP SHUN AVOID FORGO SPARE WONDE BURDEN CHORUS DESIST FOREGO LUDDEN RETAIN THRAIN ABSTAIN FORBEAR LULLABY REFREIT TORNADA FALDERAL OVERCOME OVERWORD REPETEND RESTRAIN WITHDRAW
(— **FROM INDULGENCE**) ABSTAIN
(— **FROM TELLING**) LAYNE
(— **FROM USING**) BOYCOTT
(— **FROM**) CAN HELP AVOID SPARE WAIVE FOREGO RESIGN
(— **OF SONG**) BOB TAG DOWN FOOT WHEEL BURDEN CHORUS FALDEROL
(**MEANINGLESS** —) DERRY
REFRESH FAN COOL REST CHEER

FRESH SLAKE CAUDLE REFECT
REFETE REHETE REPOSE REVIVE
UNTIRE COMFORT FORTIFY
FRESHEN QUICKEN RECRUIT
IRRIGATE RECREATE
REFRESHING DEWY BALMY FRESH
TONIC CALLER LIVING COOLING
REFRESHMENT BAIT LUNCH
CHARITY NUNCHEON REFRESCO
COLLATION
(PL.) FOURS
REFRIGERANT ICE COOLER
AMMONIA COOLING CRYOGEN
REFRIGERATE CHILL
REFRIGERATOR FRIG FRIDGE
ICEBOX FREEZER CONDENSER
(— **CAR**) REEFER
REFUGE ARK HOME PORT ROCK
SOIL BIELD GRITH HAVEN RESET
ASYLUM BILBIE COVERT HARBOR
REFUTE RESORT SPITAL SUCCOR
ALSATIA CRANNOG RESERVE
RETREAT SHELTER UMBRAGE
WARRANT CRANNOGE FORTRESS
HIDEAWAY MAGDALEN RESOURCE
SAFEHOLD
REFUGEE REFFO COWBOY FUIDHIR
FUGITIVE
REFULGENT BRIGHT SHINING
RELUCENT BRILLIANT
REFUND REPAY UPSET REFOUND
RESTORE DRAWBACK KICKBACK
REFURBISH DUST RENEW REVAMP
FRESHEN BRIGHTEN RENOVATE
REFUSAL NAY VEE WARN WONT
DENIAL MITTEN NAYSAY REPULSE
ACCISMUS DECLINAL NEGATION
(— **TO SPEAK**) APHRASIA
REFUSE NAY NIL SUD BALK COOM
DENY DUST JUNK KEMP NAIT NILL
NITE PELF PELT REDD SCUM SKIM
SOIL SUDS WARN BAVIN COOMB
CRAWN DEADS DRAST DROSS
EXPEL FLOCK NITTE OFFAL RENAY
REPEL SCRAN STENT STUFF SWASH
SWILL TRADE TRASH WAIVE WASTE
COLDER DANDER DEBRIS FORBID
LITTER LUMBER MIDDEN NAYSAY
PALTRY PELTRY RAFFLE RECUSE
REFUGE REJECT SCRUFF SCULCH
SHORTS SORDES SORDOR SPILTH
BACKING BAGGAGE BROCKLE
DECLINE DETRACT DETRECT
DISAVOW DISOBEY FORSAKE
GARBAGE GUBBINS MULLOCK
OFFSCUM OUTCAST PRUNING
SOILAGE SULLAGE WITHNAY
WITHSAY CRASSIER DENEGATE
DISALLOW DISCLAIM GARBLING
LEAVINGS RIFFRAFF SWEEPAGE
WITHHOLD
(— **ADMISSION**) CLOSE
(— **FROM CHARCOAL OR COKE**)
BREEZE
(— **FROM COFFEE BERRIES**)
TAILINGS
(— **FROM CUTTING UP WHALE**)
GURRY
(— **FROM MELTING METALS**) SLAG
DROSS SCORIA

(— **FROM SIFTING COFFEE-BEANS**)
TRIAGE
(— **FROM THRESHING**) HUSK
COLDER
(— **GREASE**) COOM COOMB
(— **OF MINE**) DEAD
(— **OF CROP**) STOVER
(— **OF FLAX**) PAB POB HARDS
HURDS
(— **OF FRUITS**) MUST
(— **OF GRAIN**) PUG
(— **OF GRAPES**) MARC
(— **OF INSECT**) FRASS
(— **OF OIL MILLS**) SHODE
(— **OF SILK**) STRASS
(— **OF SPICES**) GARBLE
(— **OF WHALE**) GURRY TWITTER
(— **OF WOOL**) BACKINGS
(— **TO APPROVE**) VETO
(— **TO GO**) JIB BALK
(— **TO RECOGNIZE**) CUT
(— **TO SUPPORT**) BOLT
(— **TO TALK**) DUMMY
(**BREWERY** —) DRAFF
(**FISH** —) CHUM GUBBINS
(**FOOD** —) SWILL
(**LEATHER** —) SPETCHES
(**PLANT** —) SCROFF
(**STREET** —) FULLAGE
REFUTATION DISPROOF ELENCHUS
HYPOBOLE
REFUTE DENY AVOID REBUT REFEL
ASSOIL CONFUTE CONVELL
CONVICT REPROVE REVINCE
CONFOUND DISPROVE INFRINGE
REDARGUE
REGAIN READEPT RECOVER
RETRIEVE
(— **SOMETHING LOST**) RECOUP
REGAL REAL ROYAL KINGLY PURPLE
RIGGAL RIGOLE STATELY IMPERIAL
MAJESTIC PRINCELY REGALIAN
SPLENDID
REGALE FETE FEAST TREAT PLEASE
DELIGHT REFRESH
REGALIA KIT ROYALTY
REGALO GIFT BONUS TREAT
REGARD CON CARE DEEM FIND
GAZE GIVE HEED HOLD LIKE LOOK
MARK MIND RATE RECK TELL YEME
ADORE COUNT FAVOR HONOR
TREAT WEIGH ADMIRE ASPECT
BEHOLD ESTEEM FIGURE GLANCE
HOMAGE IMPUTE INTEND LIKING
MOTIVE NOTICE RECKON REMARK
REWARD SURVEY ACCOUNT
ADJUDGE OBSERVE RESPECT
RESPITE CONSIDER ENVISAGE
ESTIMATE
(— **AS HOPELESS**) DEPLORE
(— **AS OBJECT OF GREAT
INTEREST**) LIONIZE
(— **AS PROPER**) ACCEPT
(— **AS**) SEE
(— **HIGHLY**) ADMIRE CONSIDER
(— **WITH PROFOUND RESPECT**)
REVERE VENERATE
(— **WITH REPUGNANCE**) ABHOR
(**ATTENTIVE** —) EYE

(**MENTAL** —) EYE
(PL.) COMPLIMENTS
REGARDED (— **WITH AFFECTION**)
DEAR AFFECTED
REGARDING ABOUT ANENT
APROPOS
REGARDLESS DEAF CARELESS
HEEDLESS RECKLESS
(— **OF THAT**) BUT
REGATTA HENLEY LIBERTY
REGENCY RULE DOMINION
REGENERATE RENEW REFORM
REVIVE RECLAIM GRACIOUS
RENOVATE
(**NOT** —) CIVIL
REGENT RULER RULING WARDEN
SHIKKEN GOVERNOR PANGERANG
(— **DIAMOND**) PITT
(— **OF NORTH**) KUBERA KUVERA
REGIME FASCISM CAFETERIA
REGIMEN CURE DIET KEEP RULE
REGIMENT
REGIMENT BUFF RULE COLOR
TERCIO GUIDANCE INFANTRY
SLASHERS
(**28TH** —) SLASHERS
(**BRITISH** —) GRAYS GREYS
(**COSSACK** —) PULK
(**FRAMEWORK OF** —) CADRE
(**INDIA** —) PULTON PULTUN
(**SPANISH** —) TERCIO
(**TURKISH** —) ALAI
REGION DO ERD EYE GAU WON
AREA BELT KITH KNOT PART SOIL
WONE WOON ZONE CLIME COAST
EARTH EXURB INDIA MARCH PAGUS
PLACE PLAGE REALM SHIRE TRACT
TROAD ALKALI BORDER CENTER
DESERT DOMAIN EXTENT GILEAD
GROUND GUIANA TATARY CLIMATE
CONFINE COUNTRY DEMESNE
ENCLAVE IMAMATE KINGDOM
MALABAR STATION TARTARY
CHIEFDOM CLUBLAND DEMERARA
DISTRICT ENVIRONS EPISTOME
FLATLAND FORTRESS FRONTIER
KRATOGEN LAKELAND LATITUDE
NAPHTALI PROVINCE REGIMENT
SERICANA STANNARY
(— **ABOVE MOUTH**) EPISTOMA
EPISTOME
(— **ADJACENT TO BOUNDARY**)
MARCH
(— **BEYOND ATMOSPHERE**) SPACE
(— **BEYOND DEATH**) CANAAN
(— **BORDERING ON HELL**) LIMBO
(— **FAR AWAY**) STRAND
(— **NEAR EQUATOR**) DOLDRUMS
(— **NOTED FOR MANY CONFLICTS**)
COCKPIT
(— **OF AMPLITUDE**) ANTINODE
(— **OF COLD AND DARKNESS**)
NIFLHEL NIFLHEIM
(— **OF DEAD**) AMENTI UTGARTHAR
(— **OF JAPAN**) DO
(— **OF MARS**) LIBYA
(— **OF OCEAN**) COUNTRY
(— **OF ORIGIN**) CRADLE
(— **OF PHOTOSPHERE**) FACULA

(— **OF SHIFTING SAND**) ERG
(— **OF SIMPLE PLEASURE**) ARCADY
ARCADIA
(— **OF SOURCE OF GOLD**) OPHIR
(— **OF TISSUE**) FIELD
(— **WITHOUT LAW**) ALSATIA
(— **WITHOUT WOODS**) WOLD WEALD
(**CELESTIAL** —**S**) LANGI
(**COASTAL** —) LITTORAL
(**CULTIVATED** —) GARDEN
(**DARKISH** —**S ON MARS**) MARE
(**DESERT** —) ERG HAMADA
(**DESERTED** —) WASTE
(**DESOLATE** —) PUNA
(**DISTANT** —) THULE
(**E. INDIAN** —) DESH
(**ELEVATED** —) ALTITUDE
(**FOREST** —) TAIGA
(**FORESTED** —) MONTANA
(**GEOGRAPHICAL** —) BOWL SIDE
(**HEAVENLY** —) SPHERE
(**IDEAL** —) JINNESTAN
(**INFERNAL** —**S**) ABYSS TARTAR
TARTARUS
(**LARGE** —) COMPAGE
(**LIMESTONE** —) KARST
(**MOUNTAINOUS** —) SIERRA
(**OPEN** —) SAVANNAH
(**ORIENTAL** —) INDOGAEA
(**STAGNANT** —) EDDY
(**SUPERIOR** —) HIGH
(**TREELESS** —) HIGHMOOR
(**UPPER** —) HIGH LOFT
(**UPPER** —**S**) ETHER
(**WOODED** —) FOREST
(**PL.**) DIGGINGS
REGIONAL LOCAL SECTIONAL
REGISTER PIE BEAR BOOK FREE
LIST PILE POLL READ ROLL STOP
ALBUM DIARY ENROL ENTER FASTI
GRILL SIJIL SLATE ANNALS BEHAVE
LEDGER MUSTER RECORD REGEST
ASCRIBE CALENDS CATALOG
COUCHER INDORSE KALENDS
NOTITIA ROTULET ARCHIVES
CADASTER CALENDAR GREFFIER
INDICATE INSCRIBE MENOLOGY
PEDIGREE POLLBOOK TOLLBOOK
STROHBASS
(— **OF JUDGMENTS**) DOCKET
(**LOWEST** —) CHALUMEAU
(**MIDDLE** —) CLARINO
(**OFFICIAL** —) TABLEAU CADASTER
REGISTRAR GUARD ACTUARY
PATWARI PUTWARI GREFFIER
RESIDENT
REGISTRY FLAG STUDBOOK
REGLET FILET BATTEN FILLET
RIGLET
REGRATER HUCKSTER
REGRESS EGRESS RETURN
ANALYSIS RECOURSE
REGRET REW RUE RUTH GRIEF
DESIRE RELENT REPENT SORROW
DEPLORE REGRATE REMORSE
FORTHINK REPINING
REGRETFUL BAD SORRY REPINING
REGRETTABLE DIRTY DOLOROUS
REGULAR DUE SET EVEN FULL JUST

WEAK SOBER SUANT SUENT USUAL
FORMAL NORMAL SQUARE STATED
STEADY CORRECT NATURAL
ORDERED ORDERLY ORDINAL
PERFECT TYPICAL UNIFORM
COMPLETE CONSTANT DECOROUS
FORMULAR HABITUAL ORDINARY
ORDINATE TESSERAL
REGULARITY METHOD SQUARE
SYSTEM EVENNESS SYNAPHEA
(— **OF NATURE**) LAW
REGULARLY DULY EVEN ORDERLY
PROPERLY STATEDLY
REGULATE SET RULE WIND BOOST
FRAME GUIDE ORDER RIGHT SHAPE
ADJUST ASSIZE BEHAVE DIRECT
GOVERN MASTER RADDLE SETTLE
SQUARE TEMPER ARRANGE
CONTROL DISPOSE MEASURE
QUALIFY RECTIFY ATTEMPER
MODERATE MODULIZE
(— **FOOD**) DIET
(— **PITCH**) KEY STOP
REGULATED ORDENE ORDERED
REGULATING BEHIND
REGULATION LAW RULE BYLAW
ORDER REGLE USUAL CURFEW
ZABETA CONTROL PRECEPT
STATUTE VOICING DISPOSAL
STEERAGE
(— **OF PRICE**) ASSIZE
REGULATOR GUIDE DISPOSER
GOVERNOR
REGULUS MATTE SLURRY KINGLET
REHABILITATE REABLE RESTORE
REINSTATE
REHASH RECHAUFFE
REHEARSAL CALL HEARSAL
HERSALL PREVIEW CLAMBAKE
NARRATION
REHEARSE TELL TRAIN DETAIL
RECITE RELATE DECLINE NARRATE
RECOUNT DESCRIBE PRACTICE
REHEAT FLASH
REHOBOAM ROBOAM
(**FATHER OF** —) SOLOMON
REICHSTAG DIET
REIF PLUNDER ROBBERY
REIGN RING RULE REALM RICHE
EMPIRE GOVERN KINGDOM PREVAIL
REGIMENT
(— **IN INDIA**) RAJ
REIMBURSE PAY REPAY DEFRAY
RECOUP REFUND REBURSE
INDEMNIFY
REIN CURB STOP CHECK SWING
THONG GOVERN BABICHE LEATHER
PLOWLINE RESTRAIN
(**PL.**) LINES RIBBONS
REINDEER REIN CERVID TARAND
CARIBOU CERVINE CERVOID
REINDEER MOSS SWARD
REINFORCE BAR GUY BACK FACE
STAY BRACE FORCE INLAY STUFF
SUPER CRADLE DOUBLE GUSSET
HARDEN MUSCLE SUPPLY AFFORCE
BOLSTER BULWARK ENFORCE
GROMMET NERVATE STIFFEN
SUPPORT

(— **ROAD**) SKID
REINFORCED KEYED SPLICED
REINFORCEMENT CREW FUEL STAY
BRACE HURTER CUNETTE SPLICING
STRAINER
(**PL.**) SUCCOR SUPPLY
REINVIGORATE QUICK REVIVE
RECRUIT RENERVE
REITERATE BACK REITER REPEAT
RESUME ITERATE REHEARSE
REJECT BEG ORT CAST DICE JILT
NILL SPIN ABHOR BANDY BELIE
BRUSH EJECT SCOUT ABJECT
ABJURE DELETE DESERT IGNORE
RECUSE RESPUE CASHIER DISCARD
FORSAKE REPULSE ATHETIZE
DISCLAIM DEFY FAIL KICK CHECK
REFEL REPEL SPURN WAIVE REFUSE
RETORT ABANDON CONTEMN
DECLINE DISCARD DISMISS
FORSAKE PROJECT REPROVE
REPULSE ABNEGATE DISALLOW
FORSWEAR RENOUNCE THROWOUT
(— **A STUDENT**) PLUCK PLOUGH
(— **COPY**) SPIKE
REJECTED OFFCAST OUTCAST
CASTAWAY
REJECTION SACK BRUSH SPURN
DENIAL MITTEN REBUFF REFUSAL
REPULSE DEFIANCE TURNDOWN
(— **OF DOCTRINE**) HERESY
REJOICE JOY FAIN GAME CHEER
ENJOY EXULT GLORY BLITHE
PLEASE DELIGHT GLADDEN
JUBILATE
REJOICING GLEE MIRTH FESTIVITY
REJOIN TAUNT ANSWER REUNITE
REJOINDER REPLY ANSWER
COUNTER RESPONSE
REJUVENATE UNOLD
REKINDLE RELUME REVIVE
RELAPSE SINK WEED LAPSE RECIDE
RETURN BACKSET SUBSIDE
BACKCAST WITHDRAW
RELATE SAY ALLY BEAR JOIN READ
TELL PITCH REFER SPELL STATE
TOUCH ALLUDE ASSERT DELATE
DETAIL DEVISE RECITE REPORT
REPUTE COGNATE CONCERN
DECLARE INVOLVE NARRATE
PERTAIN RECOUNT CALABASH
DESCRIBE REHEARSE
(— **TO**) TOUCH
RELATED KIN SIB AKIN ALLIED
(— **BY FATHER'S SIDE**) AGNATE
(— **ON MOTHER'S SIDE**) ENATE
ENATIC COGNATE
RELATING (**ALSO SEE PERTAINING**)
(— **TO A RECENT PAST**) ERST
(— **TO**) AGAINST
RELATION KIN SIB TALE BLOOD
FETII AFFINE DATIVE REGARD
ACCOUNT BEARING HISTORY
KINSHIP KINSMAN RAPPORT
RESPECT SCHESIS TELLING
AFFINITY HABITUDE RELATIVE
TENDENCY REHEARSAL RISHTADAR
(— **BETWEEN SPECIES**) AFFINITY
(— **OF LIKENESS**) ANALOGY

(BLOOD —) KIN SIB
(FIXED —) RATIO
(FRIENDLY —S) AMITY
(SYNTACTIC —) FUNCTION
(WORKING —) GEAR
RELATIONSHIP KIN BLOOD ACTION
AGENCY AMENITY AMITATE
ANGULUS BEARING CONTACT
KINDRED KINSHIP LIAISON RESPECT
SIBNESS SIBREDE SOCIETY AFFINITY
AGNATION CONTRAST GOSSIPRY
RELATIVE SYMPATHY COGNATION
FILIATION
(BUSINESS —) ACCOUNT
(CLOSE —) BOSOM AFFIANCE
INTIMACY BELONGING
(INHARMONIOUS —) OUTS
(MARITAL —) BED
(MUTUAL —) TERMS SYMMETRY
(SEXUAL —) AFFAIR
(SOCIAL —) FOOTING
RELATIVE KIN ALLY BLOOD AFFINE
AGNATE ALLIED COUSIN GERMAN
KINDRED KINSMAN APPOSITE
COGNATUS RELATION RELEVANT
PERTINENT
(PL.) KIN SIB FOLK KINDRED
KINFOLK KINNERY KINSFOLK
RELAX LAX GIVE REST ABATE BREAK
LOOSE REMIT SLACK DIVERT
LAXATE SOFTEN UNBEND UNGIVE
UNKNIT DEBLOCK RELEASE
RESOLVE SLACKEN UNPURSE
MITIGATE UNBUCKLE UNCLENCH
RELAXATION EASE LAZE REST
CREEP LETUP RELAX SOLACE
DETENTE LETDOWN BREATHER
DIVERSION
RELAXED LAX LASH LOOSE SLACK
SONSY REMISS SONSIE INFORMAL
RESOLVED UNBENDED UNBRACED
RELAXING ANIMAL ANODYNE
DETENTE
(— POINT) SEAR
RELAY SPELL RELIEF REMUDA
AVANTLAY REPEATER
(— OF DOGS) VAUNTLAY
(— OF PALANQUIN BEARERS) DAK
RELEASE LES LET BAIL DROP EMIT
FREE LESE LIOS LISS SHED SLIP
TRIP UNDO ERUPT LEISS LOOSE
MUKTI REMIT SLAKE ASSOIL DEMISE
EXCUSE EXEMPT LAUNCH MOKSHA
REMISE SPRING UNBEND UNTACK
UNWORK ABSOLVE APATHIA
DELIVER DETENTE DISBAND
FREEDOM QUIETUS SOLUTIO
UNSTICK DELIVERY DISPENSE
DISSOLVE LIBERATE DISCHARGE
(— AS DOGS) UNLEASH
(— DANCING PARTNER) BREAK
(— EMOTION) ABREAST
(— FROM CONFINEMENT) UNMEW
UNPEN SPRING STREET
(— FROM DEBT) FREITH
(— FROM MILITARY) INVALID
(— FROM SLAVERY) MANUMIT
(— ON ONE'S WORD) PAROLE
(PRESS —) HANDOUT

RELEASED OFF FREE EXEMPT
RELEGATE DOOM EXILE BANISH
COMMIT DEMOTE REJECT DEGRADE
(— TO OBSCURITY) DOWN
RELENT COME MELT ABATE YIELD
REGRET REPENT LIQUEFY MOLLIFY
SLACKEN
RELENTLESS GRIM HARD HARSH
STERN STONY BITTER SAVAGE
STRICT AUSTERE PITILESS
RIGOROUS
RELEVANT APT VALID GERMAN
APROPOS GERMANE APPOSITE
MATERIAL PERTINENT
RELIABILITY STEEL CREDENCE
RELIABLE GOOD HARD SURE TRUE
SOLID SOUND THERE TRIED TRUST
DINKUM STEADY TRUSTY CERTAIN
FAITHFUL SOOTHFUL STRAIGHT
RELIANCE HOPE TRUST CREDIT
AFFIANCE MAINSTAY
(— ON FAITH) FIDEISM
RELIC HUACO REMAIN ANTIQUE
HALIDOM LEAVING MEMENTO
RELIQUE VESTIGE SOUVENIR
SURVIVAL
(PL.) CORPSE HALIDOM REMAINS
RELICT WIDOW REMANIE RESIDUAL
SURVIVOR EPIBIOTIC
RELIEF AID LAX SOB BOOT BOTE
EASE HELP RELAY SCRUB SPELL
SWING ESCAPE REMEDY SUCCOR
COMFORT FEEDING REDRESS
RILIEVO EASEMENT REPOUSSE
(TEMPORARY —) HITCH
RELIEVE ROB BEET EASE FREE HELP
LIOS LISS ALLAY LIGHT LISSE LITHE
RIGHT SLAKE SPARE SPELL ASSIST
LESSEN PHYSIC REMEDY REMOVE
RESCUE SOOTHE SUCCOR UNMAZE
ASSUAGE COMFORT DELIVER
DEPRIVE FRESHEN LIGHTEN
REDRESS REFRESH SUCCEED
SUPPORT SUSTAIN SWEETEN
ALIGHTEN DIMINISH MITIGATE
RELEVATE
(— A SAIL) SPILL
(— OF OFFICE) AX AXE
(— OF SIN) CONFESS
RELIGIEUSE NUN CLERGESS
RELIGION BON DIN LAW SECT
BONBO CREED DAENA FAITH OBEAH
PIETY SOPHY DHARMA SHINTO
SYSTEM TAOISM ELOHISM JAINISM
JUDAISM ORPHISM PERSISM RELIGIO
SIKHISM SYNAGOG BUDDHISM
CAODAISM HINDUISM MAZDAISM
PEYOTISM
(— OF ABRAHAM) HANIFIYA
(— OF TIBET) BON
(CHRISTIAN —) WAY
(UNORTHODOX —) CULT
RELIGIOUS HOLY EXACT GODLY
PIOUS RIGID DEVOUT DIVINE
SACRED FERVENT GHOSTLY
ZEALOUS
(— HOUSE) KELLION
RELINQUISH LAY LET CEDE DROP
QUIT DEMIT FORGO GRANT LEAVE

WAIVE YIELD CANCEL DESERT
RESIGN ABANDON FORSAKE
RELEASE ABDICATE ABNEGATE
LINQUISH RENOUNCE
RELIQUARY ARCA CASKET CHASSE
COFFER MEMORY SHRINE STEEPA
TABLET CHORTEN HALIDOM
MEMORIA FERETORY
RELISH CHOW DASH EDGE GOUT
GUST LIKE SOUL SOWL TANG ZEST
ACHAR ENJOY GUSTO RELES
SAVOR SOWLE SPICE TASTE TRACE
ATSARA DEGUST FLAVOR LIKING
SAVOUR BOTARGO OUTWORK
STOMACH APPETITE FONDNESS
(— FOR FOOD) CHAW
(INTELLECTUAL —) TASTE
(MENTAL —) PALATE
(ROMAN —) GARUM
(SALT OR ACID —) ACHAR
RELUCENT RADIANT SHINING
GLEAMING
RELUCTANCE GRUDGE AVERSION
ANTIPATHY RENITENCE
(— UNIT) REL
RELUCTANT SET SHY CAGY LOTH
NICE CHARY LOATH SWEER THRAW
AFRAID AVERSE DAINTY FORCED
SWEERT UNFAIN ASHAMED HALTING
BACKWARD GRUDGING LOATHFUL
THRAWART
RELY AFFY BANK BASE LEAN LITE
REST STAY COUNT RALLY TRUST
DEPEND GROUND RECKON REPOSE
CONFIDE
(— ON) LIPPEN VENTURE
REMAIN LIE SIT BIDE REST STAY
STOP ABIDE CLING DWELL LEAVE
STAND TARRY THOLE BELIVE
ENDURE MANENT RESIDE SUBSIST
SURVIVE CONTINUE
(— AWAKE) VIGILATE
(— IN DEADLOCK) HANG
(— MOTIONLESS) STAGNATE
(— UNDER HEAT TREATMENT) SOAK
**(— UNDISTURBED AFTER HEAT
TREATMENT)** AGE
(— UNUSED) LIE
(— UPRIGHT) STAND
(—S IN MASH TUN) GRAINS
(—S IN PIPEBOWL) TOPPER
(—S OF CANE) BEGASS BAGASSE
(—S OF FIRE) EMBER EMBERS
(—S ON STAGE) MANET
(ANIMAL —S) SPOILS
(FOUL —S) SCURF
(PL.) CHAR DUST ASHES DECAY
DRAFF GHOST SHARD SHERD
BURIAL DEBRIS FOSSIL RELIEF
CARCASS REMNANT RESIDUE
REMAINDER HEEL LAVE REST
PLUGS ARREAR EXCESS RELIEF
BALANCE REMNANT RESIDUE
SURPLUS LEAVINGS LEFTOVER
RESIDUAL RESIDUUM
(— OF ATOM) CORE
(PL.) GARBLINGS LEFTMENTS
REMAINING BIDING REMNANT
LEFTOVER REMANENT RESIDUAL

REMARK DIG SAY SEE GIRD HEED
NOTE WORD GLOSS STATE TOKEN
EARFUL GAMBIT NOTICE REGARD
COMMENT DESCANT DISCANT
OBSERVE PERCEIVE
(**— BRIEFLY**) GLANCE
(**AMIABLE —**) DOUCEUR
(**AMUSING —**) GAG
(**BITING —**) BARB
(**CONCLUDING —S**) ENVOI
(**CUTTING —**) DIG SPINOSITY
(**EMBARRASSING —**) BREAK
(**EXPLANATORY —**) SCHOLION
SCHOLIUM
(**FOOLISH —**) INANITY
(**INSULTING —**) SLUR
(**JEERING —**) JEST SKIT
(**LAUGH-PROVOKING —**) GAG
(**SARCASTIC —**) HIT GIRD SLANT
(**SATIRICAL —**) JEST SKIT SGAFT
(**SHARP —**) GANSEL STINGER
(**SILLY —**) FADAISE
(**STALE —S**) BILGE
(**UNCOMPLIMENTARY —**) BRICKBAT
(**WITTY —**) JEST CRACK
REMARKABLE FORBY GREAT
SIGNAL STRONG NOTABLE STRANGE
UNUSUAL FABULOUS MARKABLE
SINGULAR SPANKING STRIKING
UNCOMMON BODACIOUS
(**NOT —**) INCURIOUS
REMARKABLY UNCO UNKO JOLLY
UNCOW DEUCED UNCOLY SIGNALLY
REMEDIAL RELEVANT SALUTARY
REMEDILESS BOOTLESS
REMEDY AID BOT BOOT BOTE CURE
GAIN HALE HEAL HELP REDE AZOTH
MANDS REDUB SHERE TOPIC
PHYSIC RECOUR RECURE RELIEF
REPAIR RESIDY URETIC ANTACID
CORRECT DRASTIC ICTERIC
OTALGIC PLASTER RECTIFY
REDRESS RELIEVE ANTIDOTE
MEDICINE PHARMACY RECOVERY
REMEDIAL SPECIFIC
(**— COUNTERACTING POISON**)
TREACLE ANTIDOTE
(**— FOR ALL DISEASES**) PANACEA
CATHOLICON
(**— FOR JAUNDICE**) ICTERIC
(**— TO REDUCE FEVER**) FEBRIFUGE
(**CHINESE —**) SENSO
(**EXTERNAL —**) TOPIC
(**FAVORITE —**) NOSTRUM
(**SECRET —**) ARCANUM
(**TAPEWORM —**) EMBELIA
(**UNIVERSAL —**) AZOTH
(**WITHOUT —**) BOOTLESS
REMEMBER MEM MIN MEAN MIND
MINE MING IDEATE MEMBER RECALL
RECORD REMIND RETAIN REWARD
BETHINK MENTION
(**— REMORSEFULLY**) REMORD
REMEMBRANCE MIN MIND MEMORY
RECORD MEANING MINDING MINNING
MEMORIAL REMINDER SOUVENIR
REMIND JOG MIN MIND MINE MING
IMMIND PROMPT REMEMBER
REMINDER MEMO PROD TWIT

TOUCH PROMPT MINDING MONITOR
SOUVENIR
REMINISCENCE MEMORY RECALL
ANAMNESIS
REMISE RETURN RELEASE REPLACE
CARRIAGE
REMISS LAX LAZY MILD PALE FAINT
SLACK TARDY BEHIND DILUTED
LANGUID CARELESS DERELICT
DILATORY HEEDLESS
REMISSION CURE LIOS LISS
PARDON REMISE LOOSING
REMITTAL
REMISSNESS LACHES LASHNESS
REMIT SEND COVER LOOSE RELAX
CANCEL EXCUSE PARDON REMAND
REMISS RESIGN ABSOLVE FORGIVE
RELEASE SUSPEND ABROGATE
MITIGATE MODERATE
REMNANT END TAG DREG FENT
REST RUMP RUND RELIC STUMP
TRACE REMAIN LEAVING REMAINS
SURVIVOR
(**— OF CLOTH**) FENT
(**— OF FOOD**) CRUST
(**— OF ROCK MASS**) KLIP KLIPPE
(**— OF VEIL**) ANNULUS
(**—S OF FILLETS**) SCISSEL
(**—S OF VEIL**) CORTINA
(**VESTIGIAL —**) SHADOW
(**PL.**) EPIPLASM
REMODEL MEND RECAST CONVERT
REMONSTRANCE PROOF ADVICE
COUNSEL PROTEST REPROOF
EVIDENCE
REMONSTRANT ARMINIAN
REMONSTRATE ARGUE PROTEST
REPROVE COMPLAIN
REMORA CLOG DRAG PEGA SUCKER
GUAICAN PEGADOR ECHENEID
LOOTSMAN STAYSHIP STOPSHIP
SUCKFISH
REMORSE HELL PITY RUTH PRICK
REGRET REMORD
(**— OF CONSCIENCE**) GRUDGE
REMORSEFUL BAD PITIFUL
CONTRITE GUILTSICK
REMOTE FAR OFF DEEP FERN HIGH
LONG ALOOF HOARY UTTER
ALENGE DISTAL ELENGE EXEMPT
OTIOSE SECRET DEVIOUS DISSITE
DISTANT EXTREME FAILING
FARAWAY FOREIGN OBSCURE
OUTSIDE ABDITIVE ARMCHAIR
INTERIOR OUTLYING OUTWORLD
SECLUDED
(**— FROM LIFE**) SCHOOLISH
(**MOST —**) ULTIMA EXTREME
HINDMOST ULTIMATE
REMOTELY CLEAN DISTANTLY
REMOTENESS AWAYNESS DISTANCE
REMOTER FARTHER ULTERIOR
REMOVABLE DATIVE REMOTIVE
REMOVAL AX AXE EXILE AMOTION
CLEANUP ERASION ABLATION
EXCISION EXERESIS OFFGOING
REMOTION
(**— OF COAL**) GETTING

(**— OF ICE FROM GLACIER**)
ATTRITION
REMOVE GET PUT RID BATE COMB
DELE DRAW FILE FLIT FREE LIFT
MOVE PARE QUIT RAZE VOID WEED
APART AUFER AVOID BLAST BRUSH
CLEAR EMITY ERASE EVOID HEAVE
HOIST LIGHT PLANE RAISE REPEL
SHIFT SHUCK SLASH SLIPE STRIP
SWEEP WAIVE BANISH CANCEL
CHANGE CONVEY DEDUCT DEGREE
DEPART DEPOSE EFFACE ELOIGN
EXEMPT EXPORT MINISH RELEVE
SPIRIT AMOLISH DEPRIVE DESCENT
DISMISS DISPOST DIVORCE
EXCERPT RESCIND RETRACT
REVERSE STRANGE SUBDUCT
SUBLATE ABSTRACT ASPIRATE
DISPLACE DISPLANT ESTRANGE
EVACUATE RETRENCH SUPPLANT
TRANSFER WITHDRAW
(**— A STITCH**) DECREASE
(**— BARK FROM LOG**) ROSS
(**— BIT BY BIT**) SCAMBLE
(**— BY CUTTING**) ABLATE
(**— BY DEATH**) SNATCH
(**— CLOTHING**) DOFF STRIP
(**— COLOR**) BLEACH
(**— COVER**) UNCAP
(**— DEFECTS**) SCARF
(**— DIRT**) BLADE GARBLE
(**— EXCESS METAL**) CUT
(**— FROM CHECKER BOARD**) HUFF
(**— FROM OFFICE**) DEPOSE RECALL
DISMISS
(**— FROM REMEMBRANCE**) COVER
(**— GILLS**) BEARD
(**— HAIR**) DEPILATE
(**— HUSKS AND CHAFF**) GELD
(**— INSIDES OF FISH**) GIB GIP
(**— JUDGE**) ADDRESS
(**— LOWER BRANCHES**) BRASH
(**— MAST**) UNSTEP
(**— ORE**) EXTRACT
(**— PARTICLES OF GOLD LEAF**)
SKEW
(**— POTATOES**) GRABBLE
(**— QUEEN BEE**) DEMAREE
(**— ROOTS**) GRUB
(**— SEED FROM FLAX**) RIBBLE
(**— SEEDS**) STONE
(**— SKIN**) HULL HUSK
(**— SPROUTS FROM**) CHIT
(**— STALK FROM**) STRIG
(**— STAMENS**) CASTRATE
(**— TABLECLOTH**) DRAW
(**— THE TOP OF**) COP
(**— TROUSERS**) DEBAG
(**— WASTE TO FIBER**) GARNETT
(**— WOOL**) BELLY
(**— WORKS OF STOLEN WATCH**)
CHURCH
REMOVED UP OFF AWAY ALIEN
ALOOF APART REMOTE DISTANT
SEMOTED ABSTRACT
REMOVER MOVER CROPMAN
KNOTTER
REMUDA CAVY CAVAYARD
CAVYYARD

REMUNERATE PAY REPAY REWARD
GRATIFY SATISFY CONSIDER
REIMBURSE
REMUNERATION PAY REWARD
SALARY PAYMENT
REMUNERATIVE GAINFUL
REWARDING
REMUS (BROTHER OF —) ROMULUS
RENAISSANCE NARA REBIRTH
REVIVAL
RENAL NEPHRIC
RENCOUNTER CLASH FIGHT
DEBATE CONTEST CONFLICT
REND PULL RENT RIVE TEAR TOIL
BREAK BURST DIVEL RATCH ROWEL
SEVER SPLIT WREST CLEAVE
SCREED WRENCH DIVULSE
RUPTURE WREATHE DISPIECE
DISTRAIN FRACTURE LACERATE
SPLINTER
(— AND DEVOUR) TIRE
RENDER DO PAY PUT TRY BEAR
DRAW ECHO EMIT MAKE RENT RIND
DEFER PRICK REPAY YIELD RECITE
REPEAT RETURN DELIVER PRECARY
REFLECT REQUITE RESTORE
SERVICE TALLAGE TRANSMIT
(— ACID) PRICK
(— AGREEABLE) DULCIFY
(— AS LARD) TRY
(— ASSISTANCE TO SHIP) FOY
(— CAPABLE) ACTIVATE
(— CLEAR) OPEN
(— FIT) ADAPT
(— GODLIKE) DEIFY
(— HEAVY WITH FOOD) STODGE
(— HOMAGE) ATTORN
(— IMMUNE) FRANK VASTATE
(— INEFFECTIVE) VITIATE
(— KNOTTY) GNARL
(— OBLIQUE) SPLAY
(— OBSCURE) DARKLE
(— OF BOON WORK) PRECARY
(— QUIET) ACCOY
(— SENSELESS) STUN ASTONISH
(— TURBID) ROIL
(— UNFIT) DENATURE
(— UNSTABLE) UNHINGE
(— VERDICT) PASS
(— VOID) CASS DEFEAT
RENDERED RENDU TRIED
RENDERING RENDU ENGLISH
VERSION RENDITION
(— OF SCENE) STUDY
RENDEZVOUS DATE HAUNT TRYST
REFUGE HANGOUT MEETING
RETREAT
(— FOR SHIPS) DOWN
RENDITION ACCOUNT CONDUCT
DELIVERY
RENEGADE DORAX PERVERT
TRAITOR APOSTATE RENEGADO
RUNAGADO RUNAGATE TURNCOAT
RENEGE BEG NIG DENY RENIG
DESERT REVOKE RETRACT
FAINAIGUE
RENEW NEW REST FRESH RECALL
REFORM RENOVE REPEAT RESUME
REVIVE INSTORE REBUILD REFRESH

REPLACE RESTORE
(— WINE) STUM
RENEWAL RENEW REVIVAL
NOVATION
RENNET LAB RUEN VELL STEEP
RENNIN RUNNET EARNING
ABOMASUM YEARNING CHEESELIP
RENOUNCE PUT CEDE DEFY DENY
QUIT DEVOW FORGO RENAY WAIVE
ABJURE DISOWN FORLET FORSAY
RECANT REFUSE REJECT RENEGE
RESIGN REVOKE ABANDON
DECLARE FORLEIT FORSAKE
RETRACT WITHSAY ABDICATE
ABNEGATE DISCLAIM FORSPEAK
FORSWEAR MANSWEAR PROCLAIM
RENOVATE DUST RENEW REVIVE
FURBISH REFRESH RESTORE
RENOVIZE
(— HAT) MOLOKER MOLOCKER
RENOWN BAY BRAG FAME ECLAT
GLORY KUDOS PRICE RUMOR
ESTEEM LUSTER RENONE REPORT
EMPRISE SWAGGER WORSHIP
PRESTIGE NOTORIETY
RENOWNED FAMED NOBLE NOTED
FAMOUS EMINENT RENOMME
GLORIOUS MAGNIFIC RENOMMEE
RENT LET SET TAX FARM GALE
GAPE HIRE MAIL RACK RIME RIVE
SLIT TEAR TOLL WAGE BREAK
CANON CENSO CUDDY ENDOW
GANCH GAVEL SPLIT BLANCH
BREACH BROKEN CENSUS CHASMA
CUSTOM GAUNCH INCOME SCHISM
SCREED STRENT CHARTER CHIEFRY
FISSURE MAILING MOLLAND
ONSTAND RENTAGE REVENUE
RUPTURE TRIBUTE CHAMPART
CHIEFERY HEADRENT STALLAGE
VECTIGAL WAYLEAVE LANDGAFOL
(— BY BOAR'S TUSK) GANCH
GAUNCH
(— IN LIEU OF SUPPER) CUDDY
(— OF LAND PAID IN KIND) CAIN
(ANNUAL —) CANON
(EARTHQUAKE —) SCARLET
(GROUND —) CENSO CENSUS
(OATS IN LIEU OF —) AVENAGE
RENTAL PORT TONNAGE TRIBUTE
TUNNAGE
RENTED LETTEN
RENTER FARMER RANTER CHIPPER
BOXHOLDER
RENUNCIATION DENIAL APOSTASY
DEFIANCE DISAVOWAL REJECTION
SACRIFICE
REP CANNELE DROGUET POPELINE
REPAIR DO EIK EKE FIX IMP HEAL
HELP MEND TINE AMEND BOTCH
DIGHT EMEND HAUNT RALLY REDUB
RENEW STORE TRADE UPSET
ASTORE BUSHEL COBBLE COGGLE
DOCTOR FETTLE RECURE REFORM
REMEDY REPASS RESORT RETURN
UPKEEP CORRECT INFAINT REDRESS
REPAREL RESTORE SERVICE
FLOCKING RETRIEVE REVIVIFY
(— BOAT) CAREEN

(— CLUMSILY) BOTCH
(— FENCE) MOUND
(— ROAD) SKID
(— SHOE) FOX TAP
REPAIRED VAMPED
REPAIRER DOCTOR COBBLER
WOFFLER CEMENTER
(SHOE —) JACKMAN BENCHMAN
(TEXTILE —) SMASHER
REPAIRMAN FETTLER
REPARATION BOTE AMENDS
REMEDY REWARD DAMAGES
REDRESS REPAIRS REQUITAL
REPARTEE WIT KNACK REPLY
RETORT RIPOST RIPOSTE
BACKCHAT BADINAGE COMEBACK
GIFFGAFF
REPAST BAIT FEED FOOD MEAL
BEVER FEAST TREAT DRINKING
(— BETWEEN MEALS) BEVER
BRUNCH BANQUET
(HASTY —) SNACK
(LIGHT —) BAIT VOID VOIDEE
COLLATION
REPAY MEED QUIT APPAY TALLY
YIELD ACQUIT ANSWER REFUND
RETORT RETURN REWARD REQUITE
RESTORE
REPEAL ANNUL CANCEL RECALL
REVOKE ABANDON ABOLISH
RESCIND REVERSE ABROGATE
DEROGATE DISENACT RENOUNCE
REPEAT SAY ECHO GAIT RAME RANE
SHOW TELL DITTO QUOTE RECUR
RENEW RESAY REVIE THRUM
ANSWER RENDER RESUME RETAIL
SECOND DECLINE DIVULGE ITERATE
PRESENT REPLICA DINGDONG
REDOUBLE REHEARSE
(— BY ROTE) PARROT
(— MONOTONOUSLY) CUCKOO
DINGDONG
(— OF PATTERN) GAIT
(— TIRESOMELY) DIN
REPEATED OFTEN CONSTANT
FREQUENT
REPEATEDLY OFT EVERY THRICE
REPEATER GUN RIFLE WATCH
PISTOL FLOATER HOLDOVER
REPEL FEND TURN WARD FENCE
REBUT DEFEND REBEAT REBUFF
REFUSE REJECT REPUGN RESIST
REVOLT DISGUST PELLATE REPULSE
PROPULSE
REPELLENT DOPE GRIM HARSH
CAMPHOR HATEFUL SQUALID
REPELLING HARD SICKLY
REPENT REW RUE MOURN GRIEVE
REGRET REPTANT CREEPING
FORTHINK
REPENTANCE REW RUE PITY RUTH
RUING REGRET SORROW PENANCE
REMORSE
REPERCUSSION ECHO TENOR
RECOIL REPULSE BACKWASH
REPERTORY REP BOOK LIST INDEX
ARSENAL CATALOG
REPETITION BIS REP COPY ECHO
PLOCE REVIE TROLL DILOGY

REPEAT MENTION RECITAL REPRISE
IDENTITY ITERANCE ITERANCY
NEMBUTSU PALILOGY PARROTRY
RECOVERY REDOUBLE REHEARSAL
(— **IN REVERSE ORDER**) EPANODOS
(— **OF HOMOLOGOUS PARTS**)
MERISM
(— **OF SPEECH FORMS**) ROTE
(— **OF WORD**) ANAPHORA
(**UNINSPIRED** —) STENCIL
REPHAIM EMIM
REPINE FRET PINE WEAKEN
COMPLAIN
REPINING MURMUR REGRET
PLAINTIVE
REPLACE SWAP SWOP RENEW
REPAY SHIFT STEAD CHANGE
FOLLOW REFUND REMISE REPONE
SUPPLY FRESHEN RESTORE
SUCCEED DISPLACE SUPPLANT
REPLACEMENT CUT ERSATZ
(— **FOR HAND**) HOOK
(— **OF CONSONANT**) LENITION
REPLENISH CHUNK REFIT RENEW
SUPPLY NOURISH PERFECT PLENISH
REPLETE RESTORE SUFFICE
REPLETE FAT FULL RIFE SATED
STOUT STUFF FILLED GORGED
IMPLETE COMPLETE HONEYPOT
REPLETION FULTH FULNESS
SURFEIT FULLNESS PLETHORA
SATURITY
REPLICA BIS PUP COPY IDEA CHARM
IMAGE REVIE FACSIMILE
REPLICATION ECHO REPLY ANSWER
REJOINDER
REPLY CAP JAWAB KNACK RESAY
ANSWER REJOIN RETORT RETURN
REPLIAL RESOUND RESPOND
REPARTEE REPLIQUE RESPONSE
SIMILITER
REPORT CRY POP FAME ITEM NOTE
TELL VENT VOTE WORD AUDIT
BRUIT COVER CRACK NOISE REFER
ROUND RUMOR SCALE STATE
STORY VOICE BREEZE CAHIER
CREDIT DELATE DETAIL FINGER
GOSSIP RAPORT RECITE RELATE
RENOWN REPUTE RETURN RUMBLE
SPEECH STEVEN SURVEY THREAP
ACCOUNT HANSARD HEARING
HEARSAY INKLING KHUBBER
NARRATE OPINION PROCESS
RECITAL ADVISORY DECISION
DESCRIBE HEMOGRAM VERBATIM
GRAPEVINE
(— **NEWS**) COVER
(— **OF GUN**) CLAP
(— **OF INFRACTION**) GIG
(— **OF PROCEEDINGS**) CAHIER
(— **OF TIMBER SURVEYOR**) CRUISE
(**ABSURD** —) CANARD
(**BELIEVED** —) CREDIT
(**CASUAL** —) FABLE
(**COMMON** —) CRY FAME SPEECH
(**FALSE** —) SHAVE CANARD FURPHY
SLANDER
(**FLYING** —) SOUGH
(**HONORABLE** —) TONGUE

(**LAW** —) CASE
(**MILITARY** —) STATE SITREP
(**NEWS** —) FLASH SCOOP
(**NOISY** —) RUMBLE
(**OFFICIAL** —) HANSARD
(**POPULAR** —) RUMOR RUMOUR
(**PUBLIC** —) FAME
(**UNFAVORABLE** —) SKIN
(**UNVERIFIED** —) VOICE GRAPEVINE
(**VAGUE** —) BREEZE
REPORTER LEGMAN PISTOL
CREEPER PRESSMAN STRINGER
(**YOUNG** —) CUB
REPORTING BEAT COVERAGE
REPOSE RO BED LIE CALM EASE
RELY REST PEACE PLACE POISE
QUIET SLEEP REPAST RECLINE
EASINESS QUIETUDE SERENITY
(— **LAZILY**) FROWST
REPOSITORY ARK AMBRY CAPSA
DEPOT HOARD VAULT ARMORY
CASKET MUSEUM VESTRY ARCHIVE
CABINET CAPSULE GENIZAH
GRANARY HANAPER SPICERY
MAGAZINE TREASURY SEPULCHER
REPOSOIR REPOSE
REPOSSESS PULL RECOVER
REPREHEND WARN BLAME CHIDE
REBUKE CENSURE REPRISE
REPROVE CRITICIZE
REPREHENSIBLE ILL AMISS
BLAMABLE CRIMINAL CULPABLE
SCABROUS
REPREHENSION BLAME REBUKE
CENSURE OBLOQUY REPROOF
REPRESENT GIVE LIKE LIMN SHOW
TYPE SHADE DEPICT SEMBLE
TYPIFY DISPLAY EXHIBIT FASHION
PICTURE PORTRAY PROTEST
TRADUCE DEFIGURE DESCRIBE
RESEMBLE
(— **CONCRETELY**) THING
(— **IN LANGUAGE**) ACT BODY DRAW
ENACT IMAGE SPEAK BLAZON
CLOTHE EMBODY FIGURE SAMPLE
BETOKEN EXPRESS DECIPHER
(— **ON STAGE**) ACT
REPRESENTATION SUN BUST FORM
ICON IDEA IDOL IKON SHOW SWAG
ANGLE DRAFT FANCY IMAGE INSET
LABEL MEDAL TABUT AVOWAL
BUDDHA EFFIGY FIGURE FLEECE
MODULE OBJECT SCHEMA SCHEME
SKETCH SUNRAY WAYANG
ANATOMY DIORAMA DRAUGHT
DRAWING EPITOME EXPRESS
EXTRACT FOLIAGE MAJESTY
SCENERY TABLEAU BESTIARY
BLAZONRY CREATION EPIPHANY
EXTERIOR IDIOGRAM LIKENESS
TYPORAMA
(— **OF SERPENT**) BASIL DRAGON
BASILISK
(— **OF SHRINE OF HUSAIN**) TABUT
(— **OF VISION**) AISLING
(**DIPLOMATIC** —) DEMARCHE
(**FACSIMILE** —) TYPORAMA
(**FAINT** —) SHADOW
(**FUNERAL** —) CADAVER

(**GRAPHIC** —) CHART BISECT
(**HERALDIC** —) LEOPARD LIONCEL
(**MENTAL** —) FANCY IMAGE
(**MINIATURE** —) MODEL
(**SYMBOLIC** —) ALLEGORY
REPRESENTATIVE REP FAIR TYPE
AGENT ENVOY VAKIL ASSIGN
COMMON DEPUTY EMBLEM LEDGER
SAMPLE VAKEEL BURGESS GRIEVER
TRIBUNE TYPICAL DECURION
DELEGATE EMISSARY EXPONENT
FIELDMAN GASTALDO INTIMATE
OBSERVER SALESMAN SPECIMEN
(— **OF ATMOSPHERE**) AERIAL
(**MANUFACTURER'S** —) BLOCKMAN
(**PL.**) COMMONS
REPRESS CURB HUSH BLUNT BRIDE
CHAIN CHECK CHOKE CRUSH DAUNT
DROWN QUELL SQUAT COERCE
DEADEN REBUKE STIFLE CONTROL
DEPRESS INHIBIT REPRIME SILENCE
SWALLOW COMPRESS RESTRAIN
RESTRICT RETRENCH REVOCATE
STRANGLE SUPPRESS WITHHOLD
REPRESSED SULLEN STIFLED
REPRIEVE DELAY GRACE ESCAPE
REPRISE RESPITE SUSPEND
POSTPONE
REPRIMAND WIG BAWL CALL CHEW
JACK SKIN SLAP SLON SNEB SNIB
TASK CHECK CREED SLATE SLOAN
SPANK TARGE CARPET EARFUL
REBUKE CENSURE CHAPTER
LECTURE REPROOF REPROVE
DRESSING
REPRINT COPY DEPRINT OFFPRINT
REIMPOSE TAUCHNITZ
REPRISAL PRIZE REPRISE REQUITAL
RECAPTION
REPROACH ILL TAX BLOT GIBE JIBE
LACK NOSE NOTE SLUR SPOT TEEN
TWIT WITE ABUSE BLAME BRAID
CHIDE SCOLD SHEND TAUNT WHITE
BISMER INFAMY REBUKE REVILE
UPCAST VILIFY CENSURE CONDEMN
REPROOF REPROVE SLANDER
UMBRAID UPBRAID WITHNIM
DISHONOR REDARGUE REVILING
REPROACHFUL BITTER ABUSIVE
SHAMEFUL
REPROBATE HARD LOST SCAMP
DISOWN RASCAL REJECT SINNER
ABANDON CENSURE CORRUPT
EXCLUDE REPROVE DEPRAVED
DISALLOW HARDENED SCALAWAG
SKALAWAG
REPRODUCE BUD HIT COPY BREED
SPORE RECITE REPEAT PORTRAY
MULTIPLY REFIGURE REMEMBER
REPRODUCTION CAST COPY REVI
IMAGE ECTYPE RECALL STEREO
EDITION ELECTRO EXOGAMY
FISSION REPLICA REVIVAL APOMIXIS
BLOCKOUT GAMOGAMY HOMOGAMY
LIKENESS
(— **OF SOUND**) AUDIO
REPROOF PROD RATE BLAME
CHECK LESSON REBUKE CHIDING
LECTURE SETDOWN JOBATION

REPROACH REPROVAL SCOLDING TAXATION JAWBATION

REPROVE TAP BAWL FLAY FRIE JOBE RATE SNIB TRIM BLAME CHECK CHIDE CRAWL SCOLD SHEND SHENT SNEAP BERATE CHASTE REBUKE REFORM SCHOOL THREAT CENSURE CONDEMN CORRECT IMPROVE LECTURE UPBRAID WITHNIM ADMONISH CHASTISE REDARGUE REPROACH UNDERNIM WITHTAKE

REPTILE LOW MEAN WORM GUANA SNAKE GAVIAL LIZARD MOLOCH TURTLE CRAWLER CREEPER DIAPSID GHARIAL PROTEUS SAURIAN SERPENT TUATARA BASILISK CREEPING CYNODONT DINOSAUR GALESAUR MESOSAUR MOSASAUR PLIOSAUR STEGOMUS SYNAPSID TORTOISE ALLIGATOR CROCODILE

REPTILIAN HERPETIC

REPUBLIC STATE SOVIET POBLACHT
(FRENCH —) MARIANNE
(IDEAL —) ICARIA
(IMAGINARY —) OCEANA

REPUBLICAN RED QUID STALWART SANSCULOT

REPUDIATE DEFY ABJURE DISOWN RECANT REJECT DECLINE DISAVOW DISCARD DIVORCE RETRACT DISCLAIM DISVOUCH RENOUNCE

REPUDIATING NAKIR

REPUGNANCE ENMITY HATRED HORROR DISGUST DISLIKE DISTASTE LOATHING

REPUGNANT ALIEN DIRTY ADVERSE HATEFUL OPPOSED INIMICAL OPPOSITE REPULSIVE

REPULSE FOIL ROUT RUSH CHECK FLING REBUT REFEL REPEL SMEAR DEFEAT DENIAL REBUFF REBUTE REFUSE REJECT

REPULSIVE COLD DAIN EVIL LOTH UGLY VILE LOATH GREASY LAIDLY FULSOME HATEFUL LOATHLY SQUALID SCABROUS UNHONEST

REPULSION UG DISLIKE AVERSION

REPUTABLE GOOD HONEST WORTHY CREDIBLE ESTIMABLE

REPUTATION REP FAME LOSE NAME NOTE PASS GLORY HONOR IZZAT NOISE RUMOR SAVOR VOICE CREDIT ESTEEM RECORD RENOWN SHADOW LAURELS OPINION RESPECT WORSHIP STANDING
(EVIL —) INFAMY
(GOOD —) STANDING

REPUTE FAME ODOR RANK WORD NOISE SAVOR THINK RECKON REGARD STATUS OPINION RESPECT WORSHIP ESTIMATE JUDGMENT POSITION
(ILL —) SLANDER

REPUTED DIT PUTATIVE

REQUEST ASK BEG CALL PLEA PRAY SEEK SUIT TELL WISH CLAIM LIBEL QUEST YEARN APPEAL BEHEST DEMAND DESIRE DIRECT ENCORE INVITE MOTION BESPEAK COMMAND ENTREAT INQUIRY REQUIRE SOLICIT ENTREATY INSTANCE PETITION ROGATION
(— FOR HELP) SOS
(STRONG —) DUN DEMAND

REQUIEM HYMN MASS REST DIRGE PEACE QUIET REPOSE REQUIN

REQUIN SHARK TOMMY

REQUIRE ASK HAVE LACK NEED TAKE WANT CLAIM CRAVE EXACT FORCE GAVEL COMPEL DEMAND DEPEND DESIRE ENJOIN ENTAIL EXPECT GOVERN MISTER OBLIGE BEHOOVE DICTATE INVOLVE SOLICIT

REQUIRED DUE SET SUPPOSED

REQUIREMENT CALL NEED LEGAL ORDER BEHEST DEMAND NECESSITY
(PL.) EXIGENCE EXIGENCY

REQUISITE DUE NEED NEEDY VITAL NEEDFUL ESSENTIAL NECESSARY

REQUISITION ORDER DEMAND INDENT EMBARGO REQUEST

REQUITAL WAR APPAY MERIT REPAY SERVE TALLY YIELD ACQUIT DEFRAY REWARD GRATIFY PAYMENT REVENGE CONSIDER FORYIELD REPRISAL

RERAILER DIAMOND

REREAD DOUBLE

RERECORD DUB

REREDOS SCREEN BRAZIER DRAPERY RETABLO FIREBACK REARDOSS

REREMOUSE BAT

RES POINT THING MATTER SUBJECT

RESCIND LIFT ANNUL CANCEL REMOVE REPEAL REVOKE ABOLISH RETRACT RETREAT ABROGATE

RESCRIPT EDICT ORDER DECREE LETTER EPISTLE

RESCUE RID FREE HELP REDD SAVE BORROW RANSOM REDEEM RESKEW SUCCOR WARISH DELIVER RECLAIM RECOVER RELEASE SALVAGE DELIVERY LIBERATE RECOURSE

RESEARCH ARBEIT SEARCH ENQUIRY INQUIRY

RESECT EXCISE

RESEDA LEEK MENNUET

RESEMBLANCE SWAP SIMILE ANALOGY AFFINITY LIKENESS PARALLEL VICINITY
(DIM HAZY —) BLY
(SLIGHT —) BLUSH

RESEMBLE AGREE BRAID FAVOR IMAGE LIKEN APPEAR DEPICT FIGURE SEMBLE COMPARE IMITATE PORTRAY ASSEMBLE SIMULATE

RESEMBLING LIKE SAME SEMBLE SIMILAR SEMBLANT
(— AN EGG) OVULARIAN
(— COMB) PECTINAL
(— GOOSE) ANSERINE
(— HORSE) EQUOID
(— IVORY) EBURNEAN EBURNOUS EBURNEOID
(— SALT) HALOID

(— STAR) STELLATE
(— WALL) MURAL

RESENT HATE MEAN INDIGN MALIGN STOMACH SUGGEST

RESENTFUL HARD HURT BITTER ENVIOUS JEALOUS STOMACHY

RESENTMENT HURT DEPIT PIQUE SNUFF SPITE CHOLER ENMITY GRUDGE HATRED MALICE RANCOR DISDAIN DUDGEON OFFENCE OFFENSE STOMACH UMBRAGE JEALOUSY HEARTBURN

RESERVATION DIBS SALVO SPACE SAVING UNLESS BOOKING CAUTION KEEPING PROVISO RESERVE FORPRISE RESERVAL
(MENTAL —) SALVO SCRUPLE

RESERVE BOOK CAVE FUND HOJU HOLD KEEP SALT SAVE SPARE BACKUP NICETY SEPONE SEPOSE TRIARY BACKLOG CAUTION CONTROL DIGNITY SEPOSIT SHYNESS TENENUE COLDNESS DISTANCE FALLBACK FORPRISE IMMODEST WITHHOLD STOCKPILE
(HOME —S) LANDSTURM
(MILITARY —) HOJU YOBI TRIARY TRIARII
(MONETARY —) CUSHION
(PL.) FAT KOKUMIN STRENGTH

RESERVED COY DRY SHY COLD UNCO ALOOF CHARY SAVED BOOKED DEMURE MODEST SILENT STANCH COSTIVE DISTANT RETIRED STRANGE RETICENT RETIRING STANDOFF WITHHELD
(— FOR ROYAL USE) KHASS
(NOT —) COMMON

RESERVOIR DAM BOSS FONT KEEP LAKE PENT SUMP TANK BASIN FOUNT STANK STORE CENOTE SIPHON SOURCE SYPHON CISTERN CLEARER FAVISSA FOREBAY IMPOUND PISCINA RECEIPT AFTERBAY DEPOSITO FOUNTAIN MAGAZINE STANDAGE
(— OF WEATHERGLASS) STAGNUM

RESET HELP ABODE ALTER RECEPT RESORT SUCCOR RECEIPT REPLANT SHARPEN WELCOME

RESIDE BIG WIN BIGG HOME LIVE STAY TELD WONT ABIDE DWELL LODGE REMAIN CONSIST SOJOURN HABITATE
(— TEMPORARILY) LIE STOP

RESIDENCE DUN WON DOON HALL HOME SEAT SEMI STAY WENE WONE ABODE COURT DAIRI DEMUR HOUSE MAHAL MANSE YAMUN BIDING DUKERY ELYSEE HOSTEL MANOIR TENSER DEANERY DROSTDY EMBASSY SOJOURN CURATAGE DOMICILE DWELLING LEGATION RESIANCE RESIANCY RESIDUUM SEDIMENT SETTLING
(— FOR STUDENTS) INN
(— OF ARCHBISHOP) PALACE
(— OF CHIEF OF VILLAGE) TATA
(— OF ECCLESIASTIC) MANSE DEANERY CURATAGE

(— OF FRENCH PRESIDENTS)
ELYSEE
(— OF MANDARIN) YAMEN YAMUN
(— OF MIKADO) DAIRI
(— OF PRIEST) CONVENTO
(— OF SOVEREIGN) PALACE
(— OF SULTAN) SERAGLIO
(FORTIFIED —) DUN
(HILL —) RATH
(OFFICIAL TURKISH —) KONAK
(RURAL —) SEAT FARMSTEAD
(SUMMER —) MAHAL
(TEMPORARY —) STAY
RESIDENT GER FIXED LEGER LIVER
INMATE LEDGER STABLE CITIZEN
DENIZEN DWELLER PRESENT
RESIANT RESIDER RESTING
HABITANT INHERENT KAMAAINA
MINISTER
(— AT A UNIVERSITY) GREMIALE
(— OF HAWAII) KAMAAINA
(— OF WEST. AUSTRALIA) GROPER
(ALIEN —) GER METIC
(CHINESE — OF TIBET) AMBAN
(FOREIGN-BORN —) ALIEN
(OLD —) STANDARD
RESIDUAL RELICT REMANIE
REMANENT
RESIDUE ASH DREG FOOT GUNK
HEEL LAFE LAVE LEES REST SILT
SLAG UNIT MAZUT SHARD SHERD
BEGASS BORING BOTTOM GRUFFS
RELICS BAGASSE CINDERS REMAINS
HARDHEAD LEAVINGS LEFTOVER
REMANENT RESIDUUM SEMICOKE
TAILINGS
(— FROM FAT) CRAP
(— FROM OLIVES) SANZA
(— FROM REFINING TIN) HARDHEAD
(— IN STILL) BOTTOM BOTTOMS
(— OF COAL) COKE SEMICOKE
(— OF COKE) BREEZE
(— OF COMBUSTION) ASH
(— OF HONEYCOMB) SLUMGUM
(— OF PETROLEUM) MAZUT
(— OF SHINGLES) SPALT
(FRIABLE —) CALX
(INSOLUBLE —) MARC
(PL.) TANKAGE
RESIDUUM TAIL BOTTOM DEPOSIT
RESIDUE SEDIMENT
RESIGN QUIT DEMIT FORGO REMIT
YIELD PERMIT SUBMIT ABANDON
COMMEND DELIVER FORGIVE
ABDICATE RENOUNCE
RESIGNATION PATIENCE DEMISSION
SURRENDER
RESILIENCE GIVE LIFE BOUNCE
RECOIL SPRING REBOUND
BUOYANCY
RESILIENT BOUNCY SUPPLE WHIPPY
ELASTIC SPRINGY FLEXIBLE
RESIN ALK LAC BALM BATU BREA
ALKYD AMBER ANIME COPAL
CUMAR ELEMI EPOXY GUGAL
GUGUL KAURI PITCH ROSEL ROSET
SIRUP SYRUP ANTIAR BINDER
CHARAS DAMMAR GOOGUL GUACIN
HARTIN MASTIC STORAX TAMANU

ACOUCHI ACRYLIC AMBRITE
BENZOIN BISABOL DERRIDE FLUAVIL
GAMBOGE SAGAPEN SHELLAC
ALKITRAN ALMACIGA BAKELITE
BDELLIUM CACHIBOU CANNABIN
COLOPHAN EUOSMITE FORMVAIL
GALAGALA GALLIPOT GEDANITE
GUAIACUM MALAPAHO MELAMINE
OPOPANAX SANDARAC SCAMMONY
(— DRAWN FROM TREES) CHIP
(— FROM HEMP) CHARAS
(— FROM NORWAY SPRUCE) THUS
(— OF FIR TREE) BLOB
(FOSSIL —) AMBER AMBRITE
HARTITE GEDANITE GLESSITE
RETINITE
(GRADE OF —) SORTS
(GUM —) GUGUL LASER MYRRH
ANTIAR BISABOL GAMBOGE
BDELLIUM
(NARCOTIC —) CHARAS CHURUS
(TURPENTINE —) ALK GALIPOT
RESINOID ALNUIN HELONIN LOBELIN
ASCLEPIN CERASEIN CHELONIN
TRILLIIN
RESINOUS ROSETY ROSETTY
RESIST BUCK FACE STAY REPEL
STAND DEFEND IMPUGN OPPOSE
REPUGN WITHER CONTEST DISPUTE
GAINSAY KNUCKLE RESERVE
WITHSET OUTSTAND
(— AUTHORITY) REBEL DEFORCE
(— SEPARATION) ATTRACT
RESISTANCE DRAG LOAD OHMAGE
REBUFF WITHER BALLAST ANTITYPY
BLOCKAGE FASTNESS FRICTION
HARDNESS OBSTACLE SEDITION
(— OF COTTON FIBERS) DRAG
(— OF KEYS) ACTION
**(— THAT EXPLOSIVE MUST
OVERCOME)** BURDEN BURTHEN
(— TO ATTACK) DEFENCE DEFENSE
(— TO CHANGE) INERTIA
(— TO COLOR CHANGE) FASTNESS
(— TO SLIPPING) BOND
RESISTANT HARD STOUT STABILE
STUBBORN
(— TO CHANGE) FAST STICKY
RESISTING OBSTANT RELUCTANT
RESISTOR BLEEDER REOSTAT
DIVERTOR RHEOSTAT
RESOLUTE BOLD FIRM GRIM BRAVE
FIXED HARDY MANLY STERN STIFF
STOUT GRITTY MANFUL PLUCKY
STANCH STEADY STUFFY STURDY
ANIMOSE ANIMOUS DECIDED
CONSTANT FAITHFUL INTREPID
POSITIVE STALWART STUBBORN
UNSHAKEN
RESOLUTELY TALLY FIRMLY
STOUTLY
RESOLUTION VOW SAND THEW
NERVE PARTY PLUCK POINT
STARCH ACUERDO BESLUIT
CENSURE COURAGE MANHEAD
MANHOOD PURPOSE RESOLVE
ANALYSIS DECISION DIERESIS
ENACTURE STRENGTH

RESOLVE ACT BEND MELT SOIL
UNDO LAPSE RELAX SALVE SOLVE
SOYLE UNTIE VOUCH ADJUST
ADVICE ASSOIL DECIDE DECREE
FACTOR INCIDE REDUCE SETTLE
STEVEN ABSOLVE ANALYZE
APPOINT BETHINK CONSULT
PURPOSE CONCLUDE DISSOLVE
UNRIDDLE UNTANGLE
(— GRAMMATICALLY) PARSE
(— INTO ELEMENTS) ANALYSE
ANALYZE
RESOLVED BENT BOUND INTENT
INTENSE RESOLUTE
(HALF —) GOOD
RESONANCE BODY EMPATHY
RAPPORT RESOUND SYNTONY
TYMPANY SONORITY VIBRANCY
RESONANT BIG BRASS RINGY
OROTUND RINGING SILVERY
VIBRANT PLANGENT SONORANT
SONOROUS SOUNDFUL SOUNDING
RESORT GO RUN SPA BEAT DOME
HOWF LIDO SEEK TEEM TOUR TURN
CAUSE FRAME HAUNT HOWFF JOINT
RECUR RESET VISIT ESCORT FINISH
REPAIR RETURN REVERT THRONG
COMPANY PIMLICO RECOURSE
RESOURCE TEETOTUM
(— TO DEVIOUS METHODS) FINAGLE
(— TO) SEEK
(DISREPUTABLE —) KEN DIVE
(LOW —) KEN DIVE STEW SPITAL
(MEANS OF —) REFUGE
(WORKINGMEN'S —) TEETOTUM
RESOUND DIN DUN ECHO PEAL RING
SOUND REECHO EXPLODE REBOUND
RESPEAK
RESOUNDING BRASS REVERB
EMPHATIC FORCEFUL RESONANT
RUMOROUS
(— WITH TALK) ABUZZ
RESOURCE WON BOOT FUND WONE
MEANS SHIFT REFUGE RESORT
STOPGAP PURCHASE
(PL.) EASE FOND GAIN FUNDS
MEANS SINEW FACULTY FOISONS
PURCHASE STRENGTH
RESOURCEFUL APT FENDY SHARP
SMART CLEVER FACILE SHIFTY
PLANFUL
RESOURCEFULNESS SENSE SHIFT
AGILITY
RESPECT ORE WAY DUTY FACE
HEED HORE LOOK MARK DEFER
DULIA FRONT HONOR IZZAT PARTY
VALUE ASPECT BEHALF DETAIL
ESTEEM HALLOW HOMAGE NOTICE
REGARD CONCERN OBSERVE
RESPITE SUSPECT TASHRIF
WORSHIP CONSIDER HABITUDE
RELATION VENERATE
(PL.) DEVOIR
RESPECTABLE GOOD SMUG DOUCE
DECENT PROPER FRUSANT
CULOTTIC
RESPECTFUL AWFUL CIVIL CAREFUL
DUTEOUS DUTIFUL HEEDFUL
REVERENT

RESPIRATION SIGH EUPNEA
ANAPNEA DYSPNEA EUPNOEA
ROARING GRUNTING
RESPIRATOR MUZZLE CUIRASS
RESPIRE BLOW LIVE REST EXHALE
REVIVE BREATHE SNUFFLE SUSPIRE
RESPITE SOB REST STAY TRUE
DELAY PAUSE BARLEY BREATH
LAYOFF REGARD REMISE LEISURE
RESPECT INTERVAL REPRIEVE
SURCEASE
RESPLENDENCE GLORY FULGENCE
FULGENCY SPLENDOR
RESPLENDENT LUCID SHEEN
BRIGHT GILDED ORIENT SILVER
AUREATE SHINING GLORIOUS
GORGEOUS LUSTROUS SPLENDID
SUNSHINY
RESPOND REACT REPLY ANSWER
RETURN TRISAGION
(— TO LURE) STOOL
RESPONDENT ANSWERER APPELLEE
RESPONSE AMEN ECHO CHORD
REPLY SNAFF ANSWER EARFUL
VOLLEY INTROIT RESPOND
ANTIPHON BEHAVIOR INSTINCT
REACTION REANSWER
(— OF KEYS) ACTION
(— OF SHIP) STEERING
RESPONSIBILITY BALL CARE DUTY
ONUS WITE BLAME GUILT CHARGE
RESPONSIBLE GOOD SOLID DIRECT
LIABLE AMENABLE
RESPONSION REPLY ANSWER
(PL.) SMALLS
RESPONSIVE OPEN SOFT WARM
GUILTY MUTUAL SUPPLE TENDER
MEETING AMENABLE SENSIBLE
(— TO BEAUTY) ESTHETIC
(NOT —) IMMUNE
RESPONSIVENESS TOUCH FEELING
RESPONSORY ANTHEM LIBERA
GRADUAL RESPOND
REST BED LAY LIE SET SIT SOB
BASE BLOW CALM CAMP EASE
HANG HEEL LAIR LAVE LEAN LIOS
LISS PROP RELY RIDE RUST STAY
STOP COUCH FOUND LEATH PAUSE
PEACE POISE QUIET RENEW ROOST
SLEEP SPELL STAND TRUST WREST
ANCHOR BOTTOM FAUCRE FEWTER
GROUND INSIST REMAIN REPOSE
SETTLE SIESTA STEADY UNTIRE
ADHARMA BALANCE BREATHE
CAESURA CLARION COMFORT
GALLOWS NOONING RECLINE
REFRESH REMNANT REQUIEM
RESIDUE RESPITE SILENCE
SLUMBER SOJOURN SUFFLUE
SUPPORT SURPLUS AKINESIS
INTERVAL QUIETUDE STANDOFF
VACATION
(— FOR SPEAR OR LANCE) QUEUE
FAUCRE FEWTER
(— FOR SUPPORT) ABUT
(— FOR TYMPAN) GALLOWS
(— HORSE) WIND
(— IDLY) SLUG
(— LAZILY) FROWST

(— ON PLANER) SIDEHEAD
(— ON SUPPORT) BOTTOM
(— UPRIGHT) STAND
(HALF —) MINIM SOSPIRO
(LATHE —) STEADY
(LEG —ON SADDLE) CRUTCH
(MUSKET —) GAFFLE
(NOONDAY —) NAP SIESTA
(QUARTER —) SOSPIRO
RESTATE REHASH
RESTATEMENT HASH SUMMARY
RESTAURANT CAFE DINER GRILL
HOUSE PLACE BISTRO BUFFET
EATERY AUTOMAT BEANERY
CABARET CANTEEN OSTERIA
TEAROOM HIDEAWAY BRASSERIE
CHOPHOUSE TRATTORIA
(— KEEPER) BISTRO TRAITEUR
RESTFUL COOL SOFT QUIET PLACID
EASEFUL RELAXED SOOTHFUL
TRANQUIL
RESTHARROW WHIN CAMMOCK
SITFAST LANDWHIN
RESTHOUSE KHAN SERAI AMBALAM
CHHATRI KHANKAH
RESTING DORMANT
RESTING PLACE (ALSO SEE
RESTHOUSE) FORM GIST GITE
STAGE CHHATRI DHARMSALA
RESTITUTION AMENDS RETURN
RECOVERY
RESTIVE BALKY FUDGY ITCHY
RESTY RUSTY FIDGETY UNRESTY
UNWAYED CONTRARY INACTIVE
RESTLESS SKITTISH SLUGGISH
STUBBORN UNWIELDY
RESTLESS ANTSY FIKIE FUDGY
ITCHY FITFUL HAUNTY HECTIC
ROVING UNEASY AGITATO ERETHIC
FIDGETY FLIGHTY FRETFUL INQUIET
RAMPLER RAMPLOR RESTIVE
TEWSOME TOSSING UNQUIET
UNRESTY VARIANT WAKEFUL
FEVERISH FEVEROUS STEERING
(— FLYCATCHER) GRINDER
RESTLESSNESS STIR FIDGET
UNREST DISQUIET JACTATION
RESTORATION REPAIR RETURN
RENEWAL RESTORE REVIVAL
EXCHANGE RECOVERY REMITTER
RESTORAL
RESTORATIVE ACOPON BALSAMIC
SALUTARY SANATIVE ANALEPTIC
RESTORE FIX CURE HEAL AMEND
BLOCK COVER REDUB REFER
RENEW REPAY STORE YIELD
ASTORE DOCTOR RECALL REDEEM
REFORM REFUND RELATE RENDER
REVERT REVIVE CONVERT ENSTORE
INPAINT REBUILD RECLAIM
RECOVER RECRUIT REFOUND
REFRESH REPLACE REVOLVE
DECOHERE REANSWER RESTITUE
RETRIEVE
(— CONFIDENCE) REASSURE
(— TO CIVIL RIGHTS) INLAW
(— TO HEALTH) CURE HEAL MEND
(— TO ORDER) STILL
RESTRAIN DAM BATE BIND BOLT

BUCK COOP CRIB CURB DAMP GRAB
GYVE HEAD HEFT KEEP REIN SHUT
SINK SNEB SNIB SNUB STAY STEM
STOP STOW CHAIN CHECK COART
CRAMP DETER GUARD LEASH MINCE
REPEL SHUNT SOBER STILL STINT
TRASH ARREST BOTTLE BRIDLE
CHASTE COERCE DETAIN ENJOIN
FETTER FORBID GOVERN HALTER
HAMPER HINDER KENNEL OBLIGE
REBUKE RETAIN RETIRE REVOKE
STIFLE STRAIN TEMPER ABRIDGE
CHASTEN COHIBIT CONFINE
CONTAIN CONTROL ENCHAIN
EXCLUDE INHIBIT INJUNCT QUALIFY
RECLAIM REFRAIN REPRESS
RETRACT SHACKLE SNAFFLE
SWADDLE BULLDOZE COMPESCE
COMPRESS HANDCUFF IMPRISON
RESTRICT SIDELINE WITHDRAW
WITHHOLD
(— BY FEAR) OVERAWE
(— HAWK'S WING) BRAIL
(— MOTION) SNUB
RESTRAINED SOBER CHASTE
SEVERE ASHAMED DISCREET
RESERVED
RESTRAINT BIT BEND CLOG CURB
HEFT STAY STOP CHECK CRAMP
FORCE LEASH SPARE STENT STINT
ARREST BRIDLE DURESS FETTER
STAYER AWEBAND BONDAGE
CONTROL DURANCE EMBARGO
MANACLE RESERVE SNAFFLE
TRAMMEL SOBRIETY
(— OF GOODS) HOCK
RESTRICT TIE CURB HOLD BOUND
CHAIN COART FENCE HEDGE STINT
THIRL COARCT COERCE CORRAL
CORSET ENTAIL HAMPER NARROW
ASTRICT COHIBIT QUALIFY REPRESS
SCANTLE SWADDLE CONTRACT
DEROGATE DIMINISH RESTRAIN
STRAITEN
(— MEANING) MODIFY
RESTRICTED CLOSE LOCAL CLOSED
FINITE NARROW STRAIT STRICT
OBLIGATE
RESTRICTION STENT STINT BURDEN
DENIAL BARRIER CONFINE RESERVE
BLACKOUT CABOTAGE
(PL.) BARS SWADDLE
RESTRICTIVE SEVERE BINDING
STYPTIC COACTIVE LIMITARY
LIMITING CONFINING
RESTY LAZY RESTIVE INACTIVE
INDOLENT SLUGGISH
RESULT GO END OUT ECHO FALL
FAVE GROW RISE TAKE BACON
BRING CHILD ENSUE EVENT FRUIT
FUDGE ISSUE PROOF EFFECT
EFFORT ENDING FINISH FOLLOW
GROWTH RECOIL REVERT SEQUEL
SPRING UPCOME UPSHOT ENTRAIN
FINDING OUTCOME PROCEED
REBOUND REDOUND SUCCEED
SUCCESS FRUITAGE SEQUENCE
(— FAVORABLY) SUCCEED
(— FROM) SUE

(ALGEBRAIC —) DUAL EXPANSION
(AS A —) AGAIN
(INCONCLUSIVE —) DOGFALL
(INEVITABLE —) NEMESIS
(PATHOLOGICAL —S) ALCOHOLISM
(REWARDING —) HAY
(SECONDARY —) SEQUELA
(PL.) AFTERINGS
RESULTANT CONCEPT OUTCOME
PROGENY
RESUME RENEW REOPEN RECOVER
SUMMARY CONTINUE PURLICUE
REASSUME RENOVATE REOCCUPY
(PL.) EXCERPTA
RESURRECTION RISE RIST UPRIST
REBIRTH REVIVAL
RESURRECTION PLANT FERNWORT
RESUSCITATE REVIVE QUICKEN
SUSCITE REVIVIFY
RESUSCITATION KATSU RENEWAL
REVIVAL
RET RAIT RATE SOAK DEWROT
RETAIL REGRATE HUCKSTER
(— STORE) WAREHOUSE
RETAILER DEALER CLOTHIER
HUCKSTER
RETAIN HAVE HOLD KEEP SAVE
CATCH ATHOLD CONTAIN RESERVE
CONTINUE MAINTAIN PRESERVE
(— MOMENTUM) DRIFT
RETAINER FOOL HEWE LACKEY
MENIAL RIBALD SEQUEL YEOMAN
HOBBLER HUSCARL JACKMAN
LACQUEY PANDOUR SERVANT
TRAVERS EMPLOYEE FOLLOWER
HENCHMAN MYRMIDON BURKUNDAZ
(JAPANESE —) SAMURAI
(PL.) FOLK
RETALIATE REPAY AVENGE RETORT
REQUITE
RETALIATION QUITS MARQUE
TALION REPRISAL REQUITAL
(MAKE —) TURN
(VINDICTIVE —) REVENGE
RETALIATORY COUNTER
RETARD LAG CHOP DAMP DRAG
SLOW STEM BRAKE DEFER DELAY
ELONG TARDY TARRY THROW
TRASH BACKEN BELATE DEADEN
DETAIN HINDER INHIBIT SLACKEN
ENCUMBER OBSTRUCT PROTRACT
RESTRAIN
RETARDANT (FIRE —) BORAX
RETARDATION LAG DRAG DELAY
RETARDED DARK BEHIND LAGGED
SIMPLE OVERAGE
RETARDING LENTANDO
RETCH GAG BOKE KECK HEAVE
REACH VOMIT KECKLE RECCHE
STRAIN
RETEM JUNIPER
RETENTION MEMORY RETAIN
HOLDING KEEPING RETINUE
RETIARIUS RETIARY GLADIATOR
RETICENCE RESERVE SECRECY
RESTRAINT
RETICENT DARK SNUG SECRET
SILENT MIMMOUD SPARING
RETICENTLY HEIMLICH

RETICULATE MESHED NETTED
RETICULE BAG CABAS SACHET
WORKBAG CARRYALL RIDICULE
RETICULUM NET MITOME NETWORK
MATTULLA
RETINOL CODOL
RETINOPHORE VITRELLA
RETINUE CREW GING PORT ROUT
SUIT TAIL MEINY SUITE TIRED TRAIN
FAMILY REPAIR RETAIN COMPANY
CORTEGE SOWARRY EQUIPAGE
TENDANCE BODYGUARD
(— OF CAVALRY) SOWARRY
(VILLAINOUS —) BLACKGUARD
RETIRE GO GET DRAW GIVE AVOID
LEAVE MICHE REBUT DEPART
LOCATE RECALL RECEDE RECESS
RECOIL SHRINK SURVEY PENSION
REGRADE RETRACT RETREAT
WITHDRAW
(— IGNOMINIOUSLY) SLINK
RETIRED QUIET SECRET DEVIOUS
OBSCURE OUTGONE PRIVATE
SECLUSE SHADOWY ABSTRUSE
EMERITUS
(— FROM PLAY) DOWN
RETIREMENT SHADE RECESS
SECESS PRIVACY PRIVATE RETREAT
FIRESIDE SOLITUDE
RETIRING SHY NESH TIMID DEMURE
MODEST FUGIENT RESERVED
UMBRATIC
(— ROOM) RECAMERA
RETORT MOT QUIP RISE SNAP VENY
QUIRK REPAY REPLY ANSWER
REGEST RETURN RIPOST BOMBOLA
CORNUTE CRUSHER PELICAN
REFLECT SQUELCH BACKWORD
BLIZZARD COMEBACK MAGAZINE
RECEIVER REPARTEE
(CURT —) SNAPHANCE
(GROUP OF —S) SETTING
(WITTY —) KNACK
RETRACE RECALL FLYBACK
RETREAT UNTREAD BACKTRACK
RETRACT BACK UNSAY ABJURE
DISOWN RECALL RECANT RECEDE
REVOKE SHRINK UNLOOK RESCIND
RETREAT SWALLOW PALINODE
RENOUNCE WITHDRAW
RETRACTED INNER
RETRACTION PALINODE PALINODY
RETREAT DEN DOME DROP FADE
GIVE NEST ROUT ARBOR AVOID
BOWER NICHE QUAIL QUIET SHADE
START ASHRAM ASYLUM BACKUP
CASTLE RECEDE RECESS REFUGE
RETIRE REVOLT CABINET DESCEND
PRIVACY RETIRAL RETRACT
SHELTER ANABASIS CRAWFISH
DISMARCH FALLBACK FASTNESS
NESTLING RECOURSE RECULADE
SOLITUDE STAMPEDE WITHDRAW
CREEPHOLE KATABASIS
(— FOR FISH) HOD
(RELIGIOUS —) ASRAM ASHRAM
(SECURE —) STRENGTH
RETRENCH OMIT EXCISE LESSEN

REDUCE ABRIDGE CURTAIL
SHORTEN
RETRENCHMENT CUT RAMPART
EXCISION RETIRADE LESSENING
RETRIBUTION PAY RETURN
REWARD WISSEL MANNAIA PENALTY
REVENGE REQUITAL
RETRIEVE SHACK RECALL RECURE
REGAIN REPAIR RESCUE REVIVE
CORRECT RECOVER RESTORE
SALVAGE
RETRIEVER FINDER GUNDOG
LABRADOR WATERRUG
RETROFLEX DEMAL CORONAL
CEREBRAL INVERTED REFLEXED
RETROGRADE RECEDE RETRAL
DECLINE INVERSE OPPOSED
REGREDE RETREAT BACKWARD
DECADENT REARWARD WITHDRAW
RETROGRESS SINK REGRESS
BACKSLIDE
RETROGRESSION SINK REGRESS
RETREAT FALLBACK
RETUND DULL TURN BLUNT REFUTE
RETURN EBB GET COME TURN VAIL
RECUR REFER REPAY REPLY VISIT
YIELD AIRWAY ANSWER HOMING
REMISE RENDER REPAIR REPASS
REPORT RESORT RETIRE RETORT
RETOUR REVERT CLEANUP
PAYMENT REBOUND REDOUND
REFLECT REPRISE REQUITE
RESTORE REVENUE ATTOURNE
DIVIDEND ELECTION EPANODOS
FEEDBACK REACCESS REANSWER
RECOURSE RECOVERY REDITION
(— FROM DEATH) ARISE
(— OF MERCHANDISE) COMEBACK
(— TO ZERO) FLYBACK
(GROUNDED —) BOND
(TENNIS —) GET BOAST
RETURNING REDIENT REMEANT
REDITION
REUNION COLLEGE HERENIGING
(— WITH BRAHMA) NIRVANA
REUNITE RALLY REUNE REJOIN
RECONCILE
REVEAL BID BARE BLAB HINT JAMB
KNOW OPEN SHOW TELL WRAY
BREAK EXERT SPEAK SPLIT UNRIP
UNTOP UTTER YIELD ACCUSE
APPEAR BETRAY BEWRAY DESCRY
DETECT EVINCE IMPART OSTEND
PATEFY SPRING UNHELE UNLOCK
UNMASK UNVEIL UNWRAP BESPEAK
CLARIFY CONFESS DEVELOP
DISPLAY DIVULGE UNCLOAK
UNCOVER UNSHALE UNTRUSS
DECIPHER DISCLOSE DISCOVER
INDICATE MANIFEST UNBURDEN
UNSHADOW UNSHROUD
(— BY SIGNS) EXHIBIT
(— SECRETS) BABBLE
(— UNINTENTIONALLY) BETRAY
REVEILLE LEVET ROUSE SIGNAL
TRAVALLY
REVEL JOY MASK RANT RIOT BIZLE
FEAST GLOAT GLORY WATCH
BEZZLE FROLIC GAVALL SPLORE

TRESCA WALLOW WANTON
CAROUSE DELIGHT ROISTER
TRESCHE CAROUSAL DOMINEER
FESTIVAL WITHDRAW
(PL.) REVELRY
REVELATION TORA TORAH EXPOSE
ORACLE REVEAL BATHKOL
BATHQOL SHOWING GIVEAWAY
OVERTURE
(— OF GOD'S WILL) LAW
(SUDDEN —) KICK
REVELER GREEK RANTER RIOTER
FRANION PIERROT ROISTER
BACCHANT CAROUSER
REVELRY JOY ORGY RIOT RIOTISE
WASSAIL CARNIVAL CAROUSAL
FESTIVAL
REVENANT GHOST WRAITH SPECTER
REVENGE HELL WREAK WROIK
AVENGE ULTION REQUITE REQUITAL
REVANCHE
REVENGED EVEN
REVENUE RENT JAGIR MANSE YIELD
INCOME ENTRADA FINANCE PROFITS
HACIENDA INCOMING
(— FROM WATER RIGHTS) JALKAR
(— REVENUE PAID TO POPE) ANNAT
(STATE —) HACIENDA
REVERBERATE DIRL ECHO RING
REPEL RETORT REVERB REBOUND
REDOUND REFLECT RESOUND
REVERBERATING REBOANT
RESONANT SOUNDING
REVERBERATION ECHO REDOUND
REBOATION
REVERE ADORE HONOR ADMIRE
ESTEEM HALLOW RESPECT
WORSHIP VENERATE
REVERENCE AWE ORE CULT FEAR
DREAD HONOR MENSK PIETY
WURTH HOMAGE REGARD WORSHIP
DEVOTION VENERANT VENERATE
WORTHING
(— FOR ANIMALS) ZOISM
(IRRATIONAL —) FETICH FETISH
REVEREND SRI SHRI SHREE SVAMI
SWAMI POTENT STRONG
REVERENT DEVOUT STRONG
AWESOME DUTIFUL
REVERENTIAL PIOUS SOLEMN
REVERIE DUMP DWAM DREAM
DWALM STUDY PONDER MEMENTO
MOONING DAYDREAM TRAUMEREI
REVERSAL KNOCK CHANGE DOUBLE
SWITCH BACKCAST BACKFLIP
OVERTURN THROWBACK
TURNABOUT
REVERSE BACK DOWN FACE FLOP
JOLT ANNUL CHECK UPSET VERSO
CHANGE DEFEAT INVERT REPEAL
RETURN REVERT REVOKE BACKSET
COUNTER INVERSE PUTBACK
RETREAT REVERSO SETBACK
SNIFTER SUBVERT BACKCAST
CONTRARY CONVERSE OPPOSITE
OVERTURN RAMVERSE TRAVERSE
WATERLOO
(— OARS) SHEAVE
(— OF COIN) PILE TAIL WOMAN

(— OF NOTE) BACK
(— PAGE OF BOOK) VERSO
REVERSO
REVERSED INVERSE REVERTED
ROVESCIO
(NOT —) DIRECT
REVERSI QUINOLAS
REVERSION SCRAPS ATAVISM
ESCHEAT REMNANT FEEDBACK
REVERTAL REVERTER THROWBACK
REVERT ANNUL ADVERT RESORT
RESULT RETOUR RETURN REVOKE
ESCHEAT RESTORE RECOURSE
BACKSLIDE
(— TO A SUPERIOR) FALL
REVETMENT SODWORK
REVIEW HASH VIEW REVIE NOTICE
REVISE SURVEY BRUSHUP RECENSE
REJUDGE CRITIQUE REVIEWAL
REVISION
REVILE CALL RAIL ABUSE BLEIR
BRAWL REBUT SCOLD SHEND
SHENT MISUSE VILIFY MISCALL
MISNAME BACKBITE DISGRACE
EXECRATE REPROACH
REVILING ABUSION BLASPHEMY
REVISE EDIT ALTER REDACT
REFORM REVIEW CORRECT
RECENSE REFLECT REVISIT
REVISER REDACTOR REFORMER
REVIEWER
REVISION REVIEW SURVEY REVISAL
REVIEWAL EPANAGOGE
REVITALIZER BRACER
REVIVAL IMAGE REBIRTH WAKENING
REVIVE DAW EBB WAKE FETCH
QUICK RALLY RENEW ROUSE
EXHUME GINGER RECALL RELIVE
REVERT REVOKE EKPHORE ENLIVEN
FRESHEN FURBISH QUICKEN
REFRESH RESPIRE RESTORE
REDIVIVE REKINDLE RENOVATE
RETRIEVE
(— FIRE) CHUNK
REVOCATION REPEAL REVERSAL
ADEMPTION
REVOICE ECHO
REVOKE LIFT ADEEM ANNUL RENIG
CANCEL RECALL RECANT RENEGE
REPEAL REVERT ABOLISH COMMUTE
FINAGLE RECLAIM RESCIND
RETREAT REVERSE ABROGATE
REVOCATE
(— A LEGACY) ADEEM
REVOLT REBEL REPEL START
MUTINY OFFEND RELUCT UPROAR
MUTATION SEDITION UPRISING
JACQUERIE
REVOLTING GARISH HORRID
BILIOUS FEARFUL HATEFUL
HIDEOUS DREADFUL
REVOLUTION GYRE RIOT TOUR
TURN CYCLE WHEEL CHANGE
ANARCHY CIRCUIT REVOLVE
GYRATION MUTATION NOVATION
ROTATION SEDITION
REVOLUTIONARY RED RADICAL
ROTATING BOLSHEVIK
REVOLUTIONIST REDSHIRT

REVOLVE BIRL GYRE PIRL ROLL
SPIN TIRL TURN WELT PIVOT
THROW TREND TROLL TWINE VERSE
WHEEL WHIRL CENTER CIRCLE
GYRATE PONDER ROTATE SPHERE
SWINGE WAMBLE AGITATE VERSATE
CONSIDER OVERTURN REVOLUTE
(CAUSE TO —) TRUNDLE
REVOLVER GAT GUN ROD RIFLE
STICK CANNON CUTTER HOGLEG
PISTOL RIFFLE BULLDOG DUNGEON
REVOLVING ORBY VOLUBLE
GYRATORY VOLUTION
REVUE SHOW REVIEW FOLLIES
REVULSION FEAR REACTION
REWARD FEE PAY UTU GREE MEED
RENT SPUR WAGE AMEED BOOTY
BRIBE CROWN LOWER MERIT PLUME
SHEPE YIELD BOUNTY DESERT
GERSUM SALARY TROPHY WEDFEE
AUREOLE GUERDON PREMIUM
RENTAGE STIPEND WARISON
DIVIDEND EXACTION REMEMBER
REQUITAL
(— FOR INFORMATION ON CATTLE
THIEVES) TASCAL
(— OF VICTORY) CROWN
(— TO HOUNDS) HALLOW
(ILLUSORY —) CARROT
(UNEXPECTED —) JACKPOT
REWARDED APAID BOUNTIED
REWARDING FAT PREMIANT
(FINANCIALLY —) JUICY
REWRITTEN PALIMPSEST
REZAI ROSEI COVERLET MATTRESS
RHABDUS SCOPULA
RHADAMANTHUS (FATHER OF —)
JUPITER
(MOTHER OF —) EUROPA
RHAPSODIC CONFUSED EFFUSIVE
RAPTUROUS
RHAPSODY JUMBLE MEDLEY
BOMBAST ECSTASY RAPTURE
(— SECTION) LASSU
RHATANY LEGUME
RHEA EMU EMEU NANDU NANDOW
RATITE OSTRICH AGDISTIS
AVESTRUZ
(DAUGHTER OF —) JUNO CERES
VESTA
(FATHER OF —) URANUS
(HUSBAND OF —) SATURN
(MOTHER OF —) GAEA
(SON OF —) PLUTO NEPTUNE
RHEBOK PEELE REHBOC
RHENIUM BOHEMIUM
RHEOMETER STROMUHR
RHEOSTAT DIMMER
RHESUS BANDAR BUNDAR MONKEY
BHUNDER MACAQUE
RHETORIC SPEECH BOMBAST
PROSAIC ELOQUENCE
RHETORICAL FLORID FORENSIC
SWELLING
RHETORICIAN ORATOR RHETOR
RHEUM GORE TEARS CHOLER
SPLEEN
RHINARIUM MUFFLE
RHINE DITCH RUNNEL

RHINESTONE DEWDROP
  (PL.) GLITTER
RHINO CASH MONEY PONTOON
RHINOCEROS FOW ABADA BADAK
  RHINO BORELE KEITLOA UNICORN
  UPEYGAN NASICORN
RHINOCEROS BEETLE UANG
  SCARABAEID
RHINOCEROS HORNBILL TOPAU
RHIPIDION FLABELLUM
RHIZOID RHIZINA ROOTLET
RHIZOME KAVA NARD ARUKE CAAPI
  STOCK ARALIA ARNICA ASARUM
  GINGER IPECAC STOLON BERBERY
  CALAMUS CULVERS GENTIAN
  SCOPOLA ZEDOARY ASPIDIUM
  BARBERRY BERBERIS HELONIAS
  KAVAKAVA TRILLIUM TRITICUM
  VERATRUM
  (PL.) INULA GERANIUM

RHODE ISLAND
CAPITAL: PROVIDENCE
COLLEGE: BROWN BRYANT
INDIAN: NIANTIC
MOTTO: HOPE
NATIVE: GUNFLINT
RIVER: PAWTUXET
STATE FLOWER: VIOLET
STATE TREE: MAPLE
TOWN: BRISTOL NEWPORT
  CRANSTON KINGSTON

RHODE ISLAND BENT FURZETOP
RHODE ISLANDER GUNFLINT

RHODESIA
CAPITAL: SALISBURY
LANGUAGE: ILA BANTU
PEOPLE: BANTU MASHOMA
  MATABELE BALOKWAKWA
RIVER: SABI LIMPOPO ZAMBEZI
RUINS: ZIMBABWE
TOWN: GWELO UMTALI BULAWAYO

RHODODENDRON ROSEBAY
  SPOONHUTCH
  (THICKET OF —) SLICK
RHOMB LOZEN WHEEL CIRCLE
  LOZENGE
RHOMBUS DIAMOND LOZENGE
RHUBARB ROW HASSEL CITRINE
  DISPUTE YAWWEED PIEPLANT
RHYME CHIME CLINK VERSE
  CRAMBO POETRY RHYTHM TINKLE
  MEASURE
  (— ROYAL) TROILUS
  (PL.) RIMUR
RHYTHM BEAT STOT TIME CHIME
  METER PULSE SWING CADENCE
  RAGTIME MOVEMENT SEQUENCE
RHYTHMICAL CADENCED MEASURED
  NUMEROUS
RIA CREEK INLET
RIAL COIN RYEL ROYAL KINGLY
  SPLENDID
RIALTO MART BRIDGE EXCHANGE

RIANT GAY RIDENT LAUGHING
  MIRTHFUL
RIATA LASSO LARIAT
RIB FIN KID BULB CORD DIKE JOKE
  PURL SLAT WALE WIFE CORSE
  COSTA GROIN NERVE OGIVE PEARL
  RIDGE VARIX VITTA WHELP BRANCH
  LIERNE PARODY RIPPLE SCROLL
  TIMBER TONGUE BRISTLE FEATHER
  NERVURE PLEURAL STRATUM
  FORMERET SIDEBONE
  (— IN GROINED ROOF) SPRINGER
  (— OF INSECT WING) VEIN
  (— OF SHIP) WRONG
  (— OF VIOLIN) BOUT
  (—S OF UMBRELLA) FRAME
  (SHORT —S) CROP
  (STRENGTHENING —) FEATHER
  (PL.) SLATS
RIBALD ROGUE COARSE RASCAL
  VULGAR
RIBALDRY HASH HARLOTRY
RIBAND RIBBON SCROLL
RIBBED RIBBY CORDED
RIBBING SPOOFERY
RIBBON BAR BOW FOB PAN BEND
  COST PADS BRAID CORSE FILET
  LABEL PADOU PIECE RUBAN SHRED
  TASTE BENDEL CADDIS CORDON
  FERRET FILLET LISERE RADULA
  RECORD RIBAND SHOWER STRING
  TAWDRY TISSUE TONGUE BANDING
  SAUTOIR TORSADE BANDEROL
  BOOKMARK FRAGMENT TRESSURE
  (— AS BADGE OF HONOR) CORDON
  (— AS HEADDRESS) TRESSOUR
  TRESSURE
  (— FOR BORDER) LISERE
  (— HANGING FROM CROWN) JESS
  (— USED FOR GARTERS) CADDIS
  CADDICE
  (COLORED —S) DIVISA
  (END OF —S) FATTRELS
  (FLOATING —) PAN
  (KNOT OF —S) SORTIE
  (LINGUAL —) TONGUE
  (SILK —) CORSE PADOU TASTE
  (WATERED —) PADS
  (PL.) REINS
RIBBON FERN PTERIS
RIBBONFISH GARFISH GUAPENA
  AGUAVINA BANDFISH DEALFISH
RIBBONLIKE TAENFORM TAENIATE
  TAENIOID
RIBBON TREE AKAROA HOIHERE
  HOUHERE LACEBARK
RIBGRASS WINDLES BUCKHORN
  HARDHEAD PLANTAIN
RIBWORT KLOPS HEADMAN RATTAIL
  SOLDIER WINDLES HARDHEAD
  HEADSMAN PLANTAGO
RICE AUS AMAN BORO PADI PAGA
  RISE SELA TWIG ARROZ BATTY
  BIGAS CANIN CHITS GRAIN MACAN
  PADDY PALAY PATNA BRANCH
  CEREAL CONGEE SIDDHA ANGKHAK
  MANOMIN RISOTTO
  (— BOILED WITH MEAT) PILAF PILAU
  PILAW

  (— COOKED WITH MEAT) RISOTTO
  JAMBALAYA
  (— FIELD) SAWAH
  (— IN HUSK) PALAY
  (— OF 2ND OR 3RD GRADE) CHITS
  (— POLISHINGS) DARAC
  (BOILED —) CANIN KANIN
  (HUSKED —) CHAL
  (INFERIOR —) PAGA
  (LONG-STEMMED —) AMAN
  (MOUNTAIN —) SMILO
  (SHORT-STEMMED —) AUS
  (SPRING —) BORO
  (UNCOOKED —) BIGAS
  (UNMILLED —) PADI PADDY
  (WILD —) MANOMIN
RICEBIRD BUNTING CACIQUE
  SPARROW BOBOLINK
RICE FLOWER PIMELEA
RICEGRASS BARIT SACATE ZACATE
RICH FAT ABLE DEEP FAIR HIGH
  LUSH OOFY WARM GLEBY OPIME
  PLUMP ROUND TINNY VIVID BATFUL
  COSTLY DAEDAL FRUITY HEARTY
  PLUMMY PLUSHY PODDED SUPERB
  ULRICA AMUSING BAITTLE COPIOUS
  FERTILE MONEYED OPULENT
  PINGUID PLASTIC WEALTHY
  ABUNDANT AFFLUENT GENEROUS
  HUMOROUS
  (— IN FAME) RODERICK
  (— IN GIFTS) PREMIOUS
  (— IN INTEREST) JUICY
  (— IN MALT) HEAVY
  (— IN SILICA) ACID
  (— IN TIMBRE) GOLDEN
  (— MAN) DIVES
  (— OF SOIL) PINGUID
RICHARD DICCON
RICHES GOLD PELF WEAL LUCRE
  WORTH MAMMON TALENT WEALTH
  FORTUNE OPULENCE RICHESSE
  TREASURE
RICHLY HIGH AMPLY FATLY FULLY
  DEARLY
RICHNESS BODY SUMEN LUXURY
  ELEGANCE FECUNDITY
RICHWEED RAGWEED COOLWEED
RICK GOAF GOFE REKE CANCH
  RICKLE SPRAIN WRENCH CORNRICK
RICKETY SHAKY SHACKY SHACKLY
  UNSOUND RACHITIC SHATTERY
  UNSTABLE TOTTERING
RICKMATIC CONCERN BUSINESS
RICOCHET SKIP SKITE GLANCE
  REBOUND
RICTUS GRIN GRIMACE
RID FREE QUIT SHED SHUT CLEAR
  EGEST REDDE SCOUR SHIFT ACQUIT
  REMOVE DELIVER
  (— OF INSECTS) BUG
  (— OF WEEDS) CLEAN
  (— ONESELF OF) DOFF DEPOSIT
  DISPATCH
RIDDANCE SHUT RELIEF DISPATCH
RIDDER SIFT SIEVE RIDDLE
RIDDLE SIFT BLAIK GRIPH REBUS
  DEBASE ENIGMA FOITER PUZZLE
  RUDDLE SCREEN CORRUPT EXPLAIN

GRIDDLE GRIPHUS MYSTIFY PERPLEX PROBLEM CRATEMAN PERMEATE

(**— AS GRAIN**) REE
(PL.) MURLEMEWES

RIDDLER CRATEMAN

RIDE GO RIB BAIT DOSA HACK HURL LAST LIFT PRIG SAIL TOOL CROSS DRIVE TEASE BANTER CANTER DEPEND DODGEM GALLOP JUMBLE NOTICE SADDLE HAYRIDE JOYRIDE OVERLAP SURVIVE TANTIVY BESTRIDE

(**— FAST**) PRICK POWDER
(**— HARD**) POUND BUCKET
(**— IN HIRED VEHICLE**) JOB
(**— ON HORSE**) BOOT LARK BURST JOCKEY SCHOOL
(**— TO HOUNDS**) GO
(**AMUSEMENT PARK —**) SWING

RIDER TACK ANNEX CROSS HAZER LABEL COWBOY JOCKEY SITTER ALLONGE CODICIL NAGSMAN PRICKER CAVALIER DESULTOR HORSEMAN

(**DUKEY —**) BRAKEMAN
(**DUMMY —**) CROSS

RIDGE AAS ARM FIN RIB RIG RYG BALK BAND BANK BARB BROW BULT BURR BUTT COMB DRUM FRET FULL HACK HILL KEEL LINK LIST PAHA PUFF RAIN REAN ROLL SHIN SPUR WAVE WELT BARGH CHINE COSTA CREST EARTH EAVES GONYS GYRUS JUGUM KNURL LEDGE RINGE RUDGE SCOUT SHANK SPINE TORUS VARIX WHELP BRIDGE CARINA COLLOP CREASE CRISTA CUESTA CULMEN DIVIDE DORSUM FRENUM RAFTER RIDEAU SADDLE SELION SUMMIT ANNULET APODEMA BREAKER BUCCULA COLLINE COSTULA EYEBROW EYELINE HOGBACK HUMMOCK INTHROW PROPONS RIGGING SOWBACK WINDROW WITHERS WRINKLE YARDANG CATOCTIN CINGULUM FOREDUNE HEADLAND RESTBALK SHOULDER

(**— BETWEEN FURROWS**) STITCH RESTBALK
(**— IN BREASTPLATE**) TAPUL
(**— IN COAL SEAM**) HORSEBACK
(**— IN HORSE'S MOUTH**) EAR
(**— MADE BY PLOWING**) HACK SELION
(**— MADE BY TOOL**) BUR BARB BURR
(**— OF BIRD'S BILL**) CULM CULMEN
(**— OF BRAIN CORAL**) COLLINE
(**— OF BREASTBONE**) KEEL
(**— OF CLAY**) DOWLE
(**— OF EARTH**) BALK
(**— OF FLESH**) COLLOP
(**— OF HORSE'S NECK**) CREST
(**— OF LAND**) BULT RAIN SELION STITCH HOGBACK
(**— OF SAND IN WATER**) REEF SANDBAR

(**— OF SCAPULA**) SPINE
(**— OF SNOW**) SASTRUGA ZASTRUGA
(**— OF UNPLOWED LAND**) LINCH LINCHET
(**— OF WAVE**) CREST
(**— ON BOOK**) HUB
(**— ON CLOTH**) WALE
(**— ON CROWN OF TOOTH**) CINGULUM
(**— ON FINGERBOARD OF GUITAR**) FRET
(**— ON FISH SCALE**) CIRCULUS
(**— ON FRUITS OF CARROT FAMILY**) JUGUM
(**— ON GLUMES**) CARINA
(**— ON MOLLUSK SHELL**) COSTULA
(**— ON SEA FLOOR**) SWELL
(**— ON SEASHORE**) STANNER
(**— ON SHEET METAL**) BEAD
(**— ON SIDE OF SADDLE**) PUFF
(**— ON SKIN**) WALE
(**— ON VIOLIN**) NUT
(**— PROTECTING CAMP**) RIDEAU
(**— WITH SHARP SUMMIT**) HOGBACK
(**—S ON ROCK**) LAPIES
(**ANATOMICAL —**) CARINA
(**BEACH —**) FULL
(**CHEWING —**) ENDITE
(**CONNECTING —**) HAUSE
(**CONVOLUTED —**) GYRUS
(**DRAINAGE —**) BREAKER
(**GLACIAL —**) OS KAME PAHA ESKAR ESKER ESCHAR
(**HAIRLIKE —**) LIRA
(**ICE —**) SERAC
(**ISOLATED —**) BARGH
(**LONG STONY —**) RAND
(**MOUNTAIN —**) COMB SIERRA BACKBONE
(**NARROW —**) DRUM RAZORBACK
(**PROJECTING —**) SCOUT
(**RESIDUAL —**) CATOCTIN
(**SAND —**) DUNE WAVEMARK
(**SHARP-CRESTED —**) ARETE
(**SLIGHT —**) PROPONS
(**UNPLOWED —**) BALK BAULK
(**WOODED —**) CHENIER
(PL.) KNURLING

RIDGED RIDGY SHARP CARINATE

RIDGELING RIG REGALD RIDGIL RIGGOT RIGINAL

RIDGEPOLE ROOFTREE

RIDICULE FUN GUY MOB PAN RIG TAX GAME GIBE JEER JEST JIBE JOEY MOCK PLAY QUIZ RAZZ SKIT TROT TWIT BORAK CHAFF CLOWN HORSE IRONY MIMIC MOMUS QUEER RALLY SCOFF SMOKE SNEER TAUNT BANTER DERIDE EXPOSE RAILLY SATIRE BUFFOON LAMPOON MOCKERY SARCASM DERISION RAILLERY SATIRIZE SPOOFERY

RIDICULOUS DOTTY DROLL FUNNY SILLY ABSURD INSANE COMICAL FOOLISH MOCKING DERISIVE DERISORY FARCICAL INDECENT

RIDING AWHEEL LIVELY OVERLAP PRICKANT SHIVAREE TRITHING CHEVACHIE

(**— ACADEMY**) MANAGE MANEGE
(**— CROP**) ROD
(**— WHIP**) CROP QUIRT

RIDOTTO BALL REDOUTE

RIEM RHEIM RIMPI STRAP THONG

RIFE EASY FULL RANK QUICK READY ACTIVE FILLED NIMBLE STRONG CURRENT REPLETE ABUNDANT INCLINED MANIFEST NUMEROUS

RIFFLE RIFF WAVE RAPID RIPPLE SHUFFLE WATERFALL

RIFFRAFF MOB RAFF SCAFF TRASH RABBLE REFUSE RUBBISH CANAILLE POPULACE RAGABASH

RIFLE RIG ROB KRAG RIPE PIECE YAGER CARBIN JEZAIL JUZAIL RIFFLE SNIDER ARISAKA BULLPUP BUNDOCK BUNDOOK CARABIN CARBINE DESPOIL ENFIELD ESCOPET MARTINI PILLAGE PLUNDER RANSACK SPORTER BANDHOOK BUNDHOOK REPEATER SPLITTER STRICKLE TAKEDOWN CHASSEPOT

(**— BALL CASING**) THIMBLE
(**— PIN**) TIGE

RIFLEMAN JAGER JAEGER
(PL.) RIFLERY

RIFT RIVE BELCH CHASM CRACK SPLIT CLEAVE DIVIDE BLEMISH FISSURE CREVASSE
(**— IN TIMBER**) LAG

RIG RI FIG REG HOAX JEST JOKE REEK WIND DRESS EQUIP GETUP PRANK RIDGE SPORT STORM TRICK BANTER CLOTHE GUNTER ROTARY SADDLE SCHEME MARCONI SPUDDER SWINDLE BACKSTAY RIDICULE
(**TRUCKING —**) SEMI

RIGADOON DANCE RIGODON

RIGEL REGEL ALGEBAR

RIGGED (FULLY —) ATAUNT

RIGGER CLIMBER SLINGER SCAFFOLD

RIGGING NET GEAR ROOF RIDGE TACKLE CLOTHING JACKSTAY TACKLING

RIGHT DUE FEE FIT IUS OFF REE SAY SOC BANG DUTY FAIR FLOP GALE GOOD HAND ITER JUST LIEN REAL RECT REET SANE SLAP SOKE TEAM TRUE WELL CLAIM DRESS DROIT ENTRY EXACT FAVOR FERRY LEGAL RICHT SOUND STRAY TECHT TITLE ACTION ACTUAL BALLOT DEMAND DEXTER EATAGE EQUITY PROPER PUTURE ANNUITY APANAGE AUBAINE CORRECT DERECHO DESIRED FACULTY FALDAGE FITTING FOLDAGE FREEDOM GENUINE HAYBOTE LIBERTY LICENSE PRENDER RECTIFY RELIEVE SLAPDAB UPRIGHT WARRANT BANALITY BLOODWIT FIREBOOT FORESTRY HEIRSHIP INTEREST LIFERENT SEIGNORY SLAPDASH STALLAGE STRAIGHT SUFFRAGE SUITABLE THIRLAGE

(— AND LEFT) HAY HEY
(— AS COMMAND TO HORSES) REE
(— EYE) OD
(— HAND) MD OPENBAND
(— IN A THING) INTEREST
(— IN WIFE'S INHERITED PROPERTY)
CURTESY
(— OF CHOICE) OPTION
(— OF EXIT) ISH
(— OF FREE QUARTERS) CORODY
(— OF HOLDING COURT) TEAM
(— OF INQUIRY) SOKEN
(— OF OWNERSHIP) TITLE
COMMONTY
(— OF PASTURAGE) FEED STINT
EATAGE COWGATE COMMONAGE
HORSEGATE
(— OF PRECEDENCE) PAS
(— OF PROTECTION) MUND
(— OF USING ANOTHER'S
PROPERTY) EASEMENT
(— OF USING GRASSLAND) EATAGE
(— SIDE) OFFSIDE
(— TIME) TID
(— TO COLLECT REVENUE) DIWANI
DEWANEE DEWANNY
(— TO COMMAND) IMPERIUM
(— TO CUT WOOD) VERT
GREENHEW
(— TO DRAW WATER) HAUSTUS
(— TO DRIVE BEAST) ACTUS
(— TO PASS OVER LAND) ITER
(— TO SEIZE PROPERTY) ANGARY
(— TO SHOOT FIRST) CAST
(— TO WORK IN MINE) BEN
(ALL —) HUNK JAKE HUNKY
(FEUDAL —) THIRL THIRLAGE
(INDIAN LEGAL —) HAK HAKH
(LEGAL —) IUS JUS JURE DROIT
ACCESS APPEAL COMMON FISHERY
HYPOTHEC
(LEGAL —S) JURA
(MINING —) GALE
(NOT —) ACUTE
(PROPERTY —) DOMINIUM
(WIDOW'S —) TERCE TIERCE
(PL.) DIBS JURA
RIGHT ANGLE RECTANGLE
(HUNDREDTH OF —) GRAD GRADE
RIGHTEOUS GOOD JUST GODLY
MORAL ZADOC ZADOK DEVOUT
FITTING PERFECT SKILFUL UPRIGHT
INNOCENT VIRTUOUS
RIGHTEOUSNESS DOOM DHARMA
EQUITY JUSTICE HOLINESS
JUDGMENT JUSTNESS MORALITY
RECTITUDE
RIGHTFUL DUE JUST TRUE LEGAL
KINDLY LAWFUL PROPER FITTING
RIGHTFULNESS JUSTICE
RIGHT-HANDED DEXTRAL SKILLED
DEXTROUS CLOCKWISE
RIGHT-HANDWISE DEASIL DESSIL
DEISEAL CLOCKWISE
RIGHTLY RITE FITLY ARIGHT FAIRLY
JUSTLY HANDILY PERQUEER
SUITABLY
RIGHT WHALE BOWHEAD BALAENID
MYSTICETE NORDCAPER

RIGID SET ACID CARK FIRM HARD
HIGH FIXED SOLID STARK STERN
STIFF STONY STOUT TENSE TOUGH
FORMAL FROZEN MARBLY SEVERE
STARCH STICKY STRICT AUSTERE
IRONCLAD RIGOROUS STRAIGHT
INELASTIC STRINGENT
(— IN SELF-DENIAL) ASCETIC
RIGIDITY FROST RIGOR RIGOUR
BUCKRAM SETNESS HARDNESS
STIFFNESS
RIGMAREE COIN TRIFLE
RIGMAROLE RANE NOMINY RABBLE
SLAMPAMP SLAMPANT AMPHIGORY
RIGOR TYRANNY ASPERITY
HARDNESS SEVERITY
RIGOROUS FIRM HARD CLOSE
CRUEL EXACT HARSH HEFTY RIGID
STERN STIFF BITTER FLINTY SEVERE
STRICT STRONG AUSTERE DRASTIC
PRECISE DISTRICT DRACONIC
EXACTING IRONCLAD STRAIGHT
(MORALLY —) PURITANIC
(NOT —) INEXACT
(UNDULY —) HARSH
RILE VEX ROIL ANGER IRRITATE
RILL PURL SIKE CLEFT DRILL PRILL
GROOVE RILLOCK RIVULET
BROOKLET RIVELING TRICKLET
ARROYUELO WATERSHUT
RILLSTONE VENTIFACT
RIM HEM LIP BEAD BRIM CURB EDGE
SHOE BEZEL BRINK CHIME EAVES
FELLY FRAME HELIX SKIRT BORDER
CALKER CHOANA FILLET FLANGE
MARGIN EXCIPLE
(— HOLDING WATCH CRYSTAL)
BEZEL BEZIL
(— OF BASKET) HOOP
(— OF COROLLA) ANNULUS
(— OF CRATER) SOMMA
(— OF EAR) HELIX
(— OF HORSESHOE) WEB
(— OF INSECT'S WING) TERMEN
(— OF SANIO) CRASSULA
(— OF TIN) LIST
(— OF WHEEL) FELLY FELLOE
(— ON CASK) CHIMB CHIME CHINE
(— ON CLOG) CALKER
(— SURROUNDING FLAGELLUM)
CHOANA
(EXTERNAL —) FLANGE
(PROTECTIVE —) BANK
(RAISED —) BOSS
RIMA CHINK CLEFT RIMULA FISSURE
RIME RIM HOAR RIND RUNG CRACK
CRUST FROST ROUND CRANREUCH
RIMPLE FOLD RIPPLE WRINKLE
RIND BARK PEEL PILL RYND SKIN
CRUST FROST SWARD CITRON
SWARTH
(— OF HAM) SKIN
(— OF MEAT) SPINE
(— OF POMEGRANATE) GRANATUM
(— OF ROASTED PORK) CRACKLING
RING GO BEE BOW BUR CUP DEE DIE
EKE FAM JOW ORB PIT RIM AMBO
BAIL BAND BELL BONG BURR CRIC
CURB DING DIRL ECHO GYRE HOOP

JING LOOP MAIL PASS PEAL RACE
RINK RUSH SHUT SING TANG TOLL
VIRL WISP AMBON ANLET ARENA
BAGUE CAROL CHIME CLANG CYCLE
GRAIN GROUP GUARD GUIDE JEWEL
KNELL LUNET PISTE RIGOL ROUND
ROWEL TORUS VERGE WAFER
WITHE BECKET BROUGH BUTTON
CIRCLE CIRCUS CLIQUE COLLAR
COLLET DINDLE EYELET FAMBLE
GIMMER GIRDLE HARROW KEEPER
LARIGO LEGLET RINGLE RUNDLE
RUNNER SIGNET TORQUE TURRET
VIROLE WASHER ANNULUS ARMILLA
CIRCUIT CLAPPER COMPASS
COUPLER CRINGLE DIAMOND
FAMELEN FERRULE GALLERY
GARLAND GROMMET GUDGEON
MANILLA NUCLEUS PACKING
RESOUND ROWLOCK SHACKLE
STIRRUP THIMBLE BRACELET
BULLRING CINCTURE CORONULE
DINGDONG DRAUPNIR DUSTBAND
ENCIRCLE FAIRLEAD PACIFIER
SONORITY SURROUND TRAVELER
(— A TREE) FRILL
(— AROUND ARTICULAR CAVITY)
AMBON
(— AROUND MOON) BROCH
(— AROUND NIPPLE) AREOLA
(— AT EACH END OF CINCH)
LARIGO
(— ATTACHED TO JIB) HANK
(— BELLS) FIRE
(— FOR CARRYING SHOT) LADLE
(— FOR SECURING BIRD) VERVEL
(— FOR TRAINING HORSES) LONGE
(— FORMING HANDLE OF KEY) BOW
(— OF ANNULATED COLUMN)
BAGUE
(— OF BOILER) STRAKE
(— OF COLOR) STOCKING
(— OF DOTS AROUND EDGE OF
COIN) GRAINING
(— OF LIGHT) GLORY
(— OF ODIN) DRAUPNIR
(— OF RIDING SCHOOL) PISTE
(— OF ROPE) HANK BECKET
GARLAND GROMMET SNORTER
SNOTTER
(— OF SPINES) CORONULE
(— OF STANDING STONES) CAROL
(— OF TWO HOOPS) GEMEL
GEMMEL
(— ON BATTLEAX) BUR BURR
(— ON BIRD'S TIBIA) ARMILLA
(— ON DECK) CRANCE
(— ON GUN CARRIAGE) LUNET
LUNETTE
(— ON HINGE) GUDGEON
(— ON LAMP) CRIC
(— ON LANCE) BURR
(— ON UMBRELLA ROD) RUNNER
(— SUPPORTING LAMPSHADE)
GALLERY
(— SURROUNDING BUGLE) VIROLE
(— SUSPENDING COMPASS) GIMBAL
(— TO ENCLOSE DEER) TINCHEL
TINCHILL

(— **UNDER BEEHIVE**) EKE
(— **USED AS MONEY**) MANILLA
(— **USED AS VALVE**) WAFER
(— **WITH GROOVED OUTER EDGE**) THIMBLE
(— **WITH VIBRATION**) DIRL
(**BRIGHT** —) HALATION
(**CERVICAL** —) TORQUE
(**CURTAIN** —) EYE
(**FINGER** —) HOOP
(**FLESHY** —) ANNULUS
(**HARNESS** —) DEE BUTTON LARIGO TERRET TORRET TURRET
(**INTERLINKED METAL** —S) MAIL
(**JOINED** —) GIMMER GIMMOR
(**LITTLE** —) ANNULET
(**LUMINOUS** —) BROUGH
(**NOSE** —) PIRN
(**OIL** —) WIPER
(**PACKING** —) LUTE
(**PLAITED** —) RUSH WISP
(**SURGICAL** —) CURETTE
(**TAPERING SHANK** —) BELCHER
(**TARGET** —) SOUS SOUSE
(**TOOTHED IRON** —) HARROW
(**TOP OF** —) BEZEL BEZIL
RINGDOVE QUIST CUSHAT CUSHIE QUEEST TOOZOO ZOOZOO COWSHOT COWSHUT
RINGED GYRATE ZONATE ANNULAR
RINGED SNAKE COLUBRID
RINGER CHEER YOUTH COWBOY CROWBAR STOCKMAN
RINGHALS COBRA
RINGING BELL BRIGHT FERVID JANGLE CLANGOR OROTUND SINGING DECISIVE RESONANT SONORANT SONOROUS TINNIENT
(**CHANGE** —) CINQUES SINGLES
RINGLET CURL LOCK TENDRIL
(— **ON FOREHEAD**) FAVORITE
RING-NECKED TORQUATE
RING-NECKED DUCK DOGY SCAUP MOONBILL RINGBILL BLACKJACK
RING OUZEL AMSEL THRUSH WHISTLER
RING PLOVER SANDY COLLIER DULWILLY RINGNECK
RING-SHAPED ANNULAR ANNULARY ANNULATE CIRCULAR
RINGWORM TINEA KERION TETTER SERPIGO
RINGWORM BUSH SENNA
RINK GLACIARIUM
RINSE NET SIND WASH RANGE RENCH RENSH RINGE SCIND SWILL BLUING DOUCHE CLEANSE
RINSING NET SIND FLUSH RESIDUE
RIOT DIN HURL BRAWL REVEL WORRY ATTACK CLAMOR EXCESS JUMBLE MEDLEY RANTAN SPLORE TUMULT ANARCHY CONFUSE DESPOIL REVELRY BLOODWIT CAROUSAL
RIOTOUS ROID ROYD ROYD WILD NOISY RANDY RANTY HEMPIE RANDIE STORMY WANTON BACCHIC PROFUSE ROARING ABUNDANT BACCHIAN

RIP RIT COOP REAT TEAR BREAK SHARK SHRED SLITE UNSEW BASKET RIPPLE UNSEAM
RIPE FIT BOLD LATE DRUNK READY MATURE MELLOW SIDDER SIDDOW DIGESTED FINISHED SEASHORE SUITABLE
(**EARLY** —) HASTY RARERIPE
RIPEN AGE ADDLE AUGUST DIGEST MELLOW CONCOCT CRIMSON DEVELOP PERFECT COMPLETE MATURATE
RIPENESS MATURITY
RIPOSTE REPLY RETORT THRUST REPARTEE
RIPPER RIPSAW BOBSLED HUMDINGER
RIPPET FUSS TUMULT UPROAR DISPUTE QUARREL
RIPPING FINE GRAND SWELL CAPITAL TIPPING SPLENDID
RIPPLE FRET RIFF SEED WAVE ACKER CRISP TWINE COCKLE DIMPLE JABBLE LIPPER RIMPLE RUFFLE RUMBLE WIMPLE CRINKLE WAVELET WRINKLE
(— **ALONG**) DADE
RIPPLING BREAK BULGE JABBLE ARIPPLE
(— **ON SURFACE**) HORROR
RIPSAW RIPPER SPLITSAW
RIPSNORTER SNIFTER HUMDINGER
RISE COME DRAW FLOW GROW HEAD HIGH HIKE HOLT HOVE LIFT PLUM SOAR ARISE BEGIN CANCH CHEER CLIMB ERECT HEAVE HOIST MOUNT OCCUR PITCH PLUFF RAISE ROUSE SCEND SOURD STAND START SURGE SWELL TOWER YEAST ASCEND ASCENT ASPIRE AURORA BILLOW EMERGE GROWTH HAPPEN HEIGHT ORIGIN RESULT RETORT SOURCE SPRING THRIVE UPDIVE UPREAR ADVANCE APPLAUD HUMMOCK REDOUND UPHEAVE UPSHOOT EMINENCE FLOURISH HEIGHTEN INCREASE LEVITATE SCENSION UPSPRING
(— **ABOVE**) SURMOUNT
(— **ABRUPTLY**) SKYROCKET
(— **AGAIN**) RESURGE
(— **AND FALL**) LOOM HEAVE WELTER
(— **AS PRICE**) MEND
(— **GRADUALLY**) LOOM
(— **IN BLISTERS**) YAW
(— **IN CLOUDS**) STOOR
(— **IN MINE FLOOR**) HOGBACK
(— **IN PRICES**) BULGE
(— **IN VALUE**) IMPROVE
(— **OF CURVE**) CAMBER
(— **OF HAWK AFTER PREY**) MOUNTY
(— **OF SHIP'S LINES**) FLIGHT
(— **OF WATER**) FLOOD
(— **PRECIPITOUSLY**) SKY
(— **RAPIDLY**) KITE
(— **SHARPLY**) BREAK
(— **SUDDENLY**) BOOM SPRING
(— **SWIFTLY**) BOIL

(— **TO BAIT**) TAKE
(— **TO GREAT HEIGHT**) TOWER
(— **TO PEAK**) SWELL
(— **UP**) FUME REAR ASCEND INSURRECT
(**SHARP** —) HOGBACK
RISER HEAD RAISE FEEDHEAD INSURGENT
RISHI RSI POET SAGE SAINT DEVARSHI KASHYAPA MAHARSHI
RISIBLE FUNNY GELASTIC LAUGHABLE
RISING BOIL BULL RIST ARISE ARIST ORIENT SOURCE STRAKE UPREST UPWITH MONTANT PUSTULE SURGENT EMERGENT INCREASE MOUNTANT EXCEEDING
(— **ABRUPTLY**) BOLD
(— **AND FALLING**) TIDAL
(— **AS OF HAWK**) SOURCE
(— **BY DEGREES**) GRADIENT
(— **GRADUALLY**) SOFT
(— **HIGH**) AERIAL
(— **SHARPLY**) ABRUPT
(— **STEEPLY**) BLUFF
RISK GO RUN SET GAGE JUMP LUCK PAWN PERIL RISCO STAKE STAND THROW WAGER WATHE CHANCE DANGER GAMBLE HAZARD PLIGHT THREAT BALANCE IMPERIL VENTURE ENDANGER EXPOSURE
RISKY BOLD CHANCY DARING KITTLE RISQUE PARLISH PARLOUS TECHOUS TICKLISH
RISP BUSH RASP STEM TWIG STALK BRANCH SCRATCH
RISQUE BLUE RACY BROAD DARING SCABROUS
RISS-WURM NEUDECKIAN
RIT CUT RIP RUT REND SLIT TEAR SCRATCH
RITE KEX ASAL BORA BRIS FORM HAKO SOMA BRITH HONOR RIGHT SRADH ABDEST AUGURY EXEQUY FETISH OFFICE PANSIL PIACLE POOJAH RITUAL BAPTISM FUNERAL KATCINA LITURGY MYSTERY OBSEQUY SRADDHA TASHLIK CEREMONY HIERURGY HUSKANAW MORTUARY PIACULUM
(**PL.**) CULT SACRA SERVICE
RITUAL FORM RITE SOLEMN AGENDUM HAGGADA LITURGY OBSEQUY SERVICE CEREMONY VISPARAD VISPERED
RITZY HAUGHTY SNOBBISH
RIVAGE BANK RIVE COAST SHORE
RIVAL VIE EVEN PEER SIDE MATCH COMPETE CORRIVE EMULATE CORRIVAL EMULATOR OPPONENT
RIVALRY VIE GAME PARAGON JEALOUSY STRIVING EMULATION
RIVE RIP PLOW REND STAB TEAR CRACK REAVE SEVER SPLIT WEDGE CLEAVE SUNDER THRUST SHATTER FRACTURE
RIVER EA LE LEE REE RIO TJI ALPH BAHR GEON ILOG KILL WADI WADY BAYOU FLOOD GANGA GIHON GJOLL

GLIDE HABOR INLET KIANG TCHAI
BARCOO GUTTER KHUBUR NYANZA
STRAIT STREAM CHANNEL COCYTUS
ESTUARY FROEMAN ILISSUS
PHARPAR RUBICON SENEGAL
AFFLUENT ERIDANUS PACTOLUS
STAIRCASE
(— CHANNEL) ALVEUS
(— NEAR GATE OF HEL'S ABODE)
GJOLL
(— OF ATTICA) ILISSUS
(— OF DAMASCUS) PHARPAR
(— OF LYDIA) PACTOLUS
(— OF PARADISE) GEON GIHON
(— OF QUEENSLAND) BARCOO
(— OF UNDERWORLD) STYX LETHE
ACHERON COCYTUS FLEGETON
(AFRICAN —) NYANZA SENEGAL
(CHINESE —) HO KIANG
(EGYPTIAN —) BAHR NILE
(FULL —) BANKER
(JAVANESE —) TJI
(MINOR —) BAYOU
(SACRED —) ALPH GANGA
(SMALL —) BACHE TCHAI
RIVERBANK RIPA RIPE
RIVERBED LAAGTE BATTURE
(DRY —) WADI WADY
RIVERBOAT COG BARGE FOIST
PULWAR
RIVER DUCK TEAL MALLARD
WIDGEON GREENWING
RIVERINE (— FISH) HUCHO
RIVERWEED WATERWEED
RIVET STUD ROOVE PANHEAD
FLATHEAD
(— ATTENTION) GRIP
(— HEAD) CUPHEAD
RIVULET RUN BURN GILL LAKE
MOTH RILL BACHE BATCH BAYOU
BOURN BROOK GHYLL RITHE
RINDLE RUNLET RUNNEL STREAM
STRIPE STRYPE CHANNEL RIVERET
BROOKLET
RIXY TERN
RIZZAR DRY PARCH RASOUR
RAZOUR CURRANT HADDOCK
RIZZOM BIT EAR RISOM STALK
STRAW RISSOM
ROACH HOG BUTT ROCK SPOT
BRAISE BLATTID SUNFISH
ROAD LEG PAD TAO WAY BELT
BORD CASH DRAG DRUN FARE
GAET GANG GATE LINE LODE LOKE
PASS PATH PAVE PIKE RADE RAID
RIDE RODE ROTE ROUT SLAB SPUR
WENT BARGH BLAZE BYWAY CLOSE
DRIFT DRIVE DROVE FORAY GAITE
GOING METAL PRAYA ROUTE TRACE
TRACK BYROAD CAMINO CAREER
CAUSEY CHEMIN COURSE DUGWAY
FEEDER RIDING ROUGHT RUNWAY
SLOUGH STREET TARMAC TRAJET
CALZADA CARTWAY ESTRADA
GANGWAY HIGHWAY LANDWAY
OUTGANG PACKWAY PASSAGE
RAILWAY RAMPIRE ROADWAY
ROLLWAY SKIDWAY TELFORD
AUTOBAHN BEALLACH BLACKTOP

BROADWAY CHAUSSEE CORDUROY
FOOTRILL HORSEWAY OVERPASS
RIDGEWAY SPEEDWAY TRACKWAY
TRAMROAD TRAVERSE TURNPIKE
WAGONWAY
(— BORDERING SHORE) PRAYA
(— FOR LOGGING) SKIDWAY
CROSSHAUL
(— IN COAL MINE) BORD BOARD
FOOTRILL
(— ON CLIFF) CORNICHE
(— SCRAPER) HARL HARLE
(— SURFACE) TELFORD
(CEMENT OR CONCRETE —) SLAB
(COUNTRY —) BOREEN DRIFTWAY
(DESCENDING —) BAHADA BAJADA
(IMPASSABLE —) SLOUGH IMPASSE
(IMPROVISED —) CASH
(MILITARY OR PUBLIC —) AGGER
(NARROW —) DRANG DRUNG
RODDIN
(PAVED —) CALZADA CHAUSSEE
(PRINCIPAL —) ARTERY
(PRIVATE —) LOKE DRIVE DRIVEWAY
(RAISED —) AGGER RAMPIRE
CAUSEWAY
(ROMAN —) ITER CAUSEY
(SIDE —) BRANCH SHUNPIKE
(STEEP —) BRAE PATH BARGH
SPRUNT
(TEMPORARY —) SHOOFLY
(UNIMPROVED —) DROVE
(ZIGZAG —) SWITCHBACK
ROADBED BALLAST BITUMEN
ROADBOOK MAP ITINERARY
ROAD DONKEY ROADER
ROADMAN PEDDLER SALESMAN
CANVASSER
ROADMASTER OVERSEER
ROAD RUNNER CUCKOO PAISANO
ROADSIDE HEDGE
ROADSTEAD RAID DOWNS
ROADSTER BUGGY TRAMP DRIVER
BICYCLE RUNABOUT RACEABOUT
SPEEDSTER
ROADWAY DECK EXIT STREET
MACADAM SLIPWAY TRUCKWAY
ROAM GO ERR RUN WAG RAKE
RAME RAVE ROIL ROLL ROVE WALK
GIPSY GYPSY KNOCK RANGE SCAMP
SPACE STRAY TAVER VAGUE
WAVER BANGLE RAMBLE STROLL
SWERVE TAIVER VAGARY WANDER
GALLANT PROCEED SQUANDER
VAGABOND
(— FURTIVELY) PROWL
ROAMING ERROR ROAMAGE
FUGITIVE
ROAN HORSE GRIZZLE
ROANOKE WAMPUM
ROAR CRY BAWL BEAL BELL BERE
BOOM BRAY HOWL HURL RAIR
RARE RERD ROIN ROME ROUT YELL
BROOL CRACK RERDE ROUST
SHOUT SNORE BELLOW BULDER
BULLER CLAMOR GOLLAR GOLLER
RUMMES SCREAM SHRIEK STEVEN
BLUSTER RUMMISH ULULATE

(— AS BOAR) FREAM
(— LIKE WIND) HURL
(— OF SURF) ROTE
(LOW —) BROOL
ROARING RUT LOUD AROAR BRISK
ROUST BELLOW BOOMING RIOTOUS
THRIVING
ROARING BOY TWIBIL TWIBILL
ROARING GAME CURLING
ROARING MEG CANNON
ROAST RAZZ ROTI SOAK BREDE
PARCH ASSATE CODDLE REMOVE
TORREFY TORRIFY BARBECUE
RIDICULE
(STUFFED —) FARCI
ROASTED ASADO
(NOT —) GREEN
ROASTER BURNER SCORCHER
ROASTING ASSATION
ROASTING JACK TURNSPIT
ROB COP EASE FAKE FLAP NICK
PEEL PELF PICK PILL POLL PREY
PULL RAMP RIPE ROLL TOBY BENIM
BRIBE FLIMP HARRY HEAVE HEIST
LURCH PINCH PLUCK PLUME PROWL
REAVE RIFLE ROIST SHAKE SPOIL
SPUNG STEAL STRUB TOUCH
HARROW HIJACK HUSTLE PILFER
RAVISH STRIKE THIEVE DEPRIVE
DESPOIL PLUNDER RUMPADE
SNAFFLE UNPURSE DEFLOWER
SPOLIATE
(— HOUSE) MILL
(— OF CHASTITY) DEFILE
(— OF FORCE) COOL
(— OF JOY) DESOLATE
(— OF VIGOR) ETIOLATE
(— WITH VIOLENCE) RAMP
ROBALO SNOOK SNOWK SERGEANT
ROBBED RUBATO
(NOT —) UNPILLED
ROBBER PAD FOMOR LARON THIEF
BANDIT BRIBER DACOIT FORMOR
HOLDUP LATRON RIFLER BRIGAND
FOOTPAD HEISTER LADRONE
MOONMAN PRANCER RAVENER
ROUTIER SPOILER TOBYMAN
BARRABAS FOMORIAN PILLAGER
RABIATOR
(— ON HIGH SEAS) PIRATE
(— WHO USES VIOLENCE)
RABIATOR
(GRAVE —) GOUL GHOUL
(HIGHWAY —) PAD FOOTPAD
TOBYMAN
(INDIAN MURDEROUS —) DACOIT
(IRISH —) WOODKERN
(MOUNTAIN —) CHOAR
(NIGHT —) MOONMAN
(SEA —) FOMOR FORMOR
FOMORIAN
(WANDERING —) ROUTIER
ROBBERY JOB JUMP REIF RIFE
HEIST SCREW STALE FELONY
HOLDUP STOWTH BRIBERY DACOITY
LARCENY PILLAGE PLUNDER
REAVERY STICKUP THUGGEE
PURCHASE
(— ON HIGH SEAS) PIRACY

(HIGHWAY —) TOBY
ROBE GOWN VEST KANZU STOLA CHIMER KIMONO KITTEL MANTLE REVEST ARISAID BUFFALO GALABIA SURCOAT VESTURE WOLFSKIN
(— FOR THE DEAD) HABIT
(— OF MONARCH) PLUVIAL
(— PRESENTED BY DIGNITARY) KHALAT KHILAT
(— REACHING TO ANKLES) TALAR
(ACTOR'S —) SYRMA
(BAPTISMAL —) CHRISOM
(BISHOP'S —) CHIMER CHIMERE
(CIRCULAR —) CYCLAS
(CORONATION —) COLOBIUM DALMATIC
(DERVISH'S —) KHIRKA KHIRKAH
(EMPEROR'S —) PURPLE
(FUNERAL —) SABLE
(JEWISH —) KITTEL
(KING'S —) DALMATIC
(LOOSE) MANT CAMIS CAMUS CYMAR SIMAR SYMAR MANTUA MANTEAU
(MASQUERADE —) VENETIAN
(MEXICAN —) MANGA
(MONK'S —) HAPLOMA
(OUTER —) JAMA
(TARTAN —) ARISAID
(TURKISH —) DOLMAN
(WHITE —) CHRISOM
ROBERT DOB POP RAB DOBBIN POPKIN
ROBERT OF LINCOLN BOBOLINK
ROBIN PINFISH REDDOCK RUDDOCK TOOTLER WINGFISH REDBREAST
ROBIN GOODFELLOW ELF PUCK FAIRY SPRITE HOBGOBLIN
ROBINIA LOCUST
ROBIN SANDPIPER KNOT DOWITCHER
ROBORANT TONIC
ROBOT GELEM GOLEM AUTOMAT TELEVOX
ROBUST ABLE FIRM HAIL HALE HARD IRON RUDE HARDY HUSKY LUSTY RENKY SOUND STARK STIFF STOUR STOUT TOUGH VALID WALLY HEARTY RUGGED SINEWY STRONG STURDY HEALTHY VALIANT MUSCULAR PITHSOME SWACKING VIGOROUS STRAPPING
(NOT —) SLENDER
ROBUSTNESS VALIDITY
ROC BIRD BOMB RUKH ROQUE SIMURG SIMURGH
ROCHET CLOAK SMOCK CAMISIA
ROCK CAP JOW LOG PAY RAG DAZE HOST KLIP REEL RUKH SIAL SIMA SWAY SWIG TOSS BRACK CLIFF FLOOR GREET GRUSS HORSE LEDGE ROACH ROQUE SHAKE SHOWD SKARN STONE TRILL FACIES GROUND TOTTER COUNTRY FOLIATE
(— AROUND DRILL HOLE) COLLAR
(— CHUNK) KNUCKLE
(— IN ANOTHER ROCK) XENOLITH
(— IN MINE) CAPPING
(— IN SEA) STACK

(— SURFACE) KARREN
(— VIOLENTLY) STAGGER
(ARTIFICIAL —) GRANOLITH
(BANDED —) BAR
(BARE —) SCARTH
(CAP —) COVER
(COMPACT —) BASEMENT
(COUNTRY —) RIDER
(CRUSHED —) GREET
(CRYSTALLINE —) SCHIST DIORITE GREISEN
(DECAY OF —S) GEEST LATERITE
(DECOMPOSED —) GOSSAN GOZZAN
(DENSE —) ADINOLE
(EXTRUSIVE —) DACITE SPILITE ANDESITE CIMINITE
(FISSILE —) SHALE SHAUL
(FLUID —) LAVA
(FRAGMENTAL —) PSEPHITE
(GRANULAR —) GABBRO OOLITE DIORITE IJOLITE KOSWITE
(GRANULATED —) GRUSS
(HARD —) WHIN
(HIGH —) SCOUT
(IGNEOUS —) BOSS SIAL SIMA TRAP BASALT DUNITE GABBRO URTITE FELSITE GRANITE MINETTE SYENITE ESSEXITE TONALITE
(IMPURE —) CHERT
(INSULAR —) SKERRY
(INSULATED —) SKERRY
(INTRUSIVE —) HORTITE MAENAITE
(IRON-BEARING —) GAL
(ISOLATED —) SCAR SCARR SCAUR
(JUTTING POINT OF —) KIP
(METAMORPHIC —) SKARN GNEISS SCHIST BUCHITE GONDITE LEPTITE ECLOGITE HORNFELS LIMURITE
(MICA-BEARING —) DOMITE
(MOLTEN —) MAGMA
(PLUTONIC —) TAWITE HOLLAITE TURJAITE
(POROUS —) TUFA TUFF ARSOITE
(PROJECTING —) CLINT
(PULVERIZED —) FLOUR
(RARE —) ALNOITE
(ROUGH —) CRAG KNAR SCARTH
(ROUNDED —) ROGNON SHEEPBACK
(SEDIMENTARY —) CRAG IRONSTONE SANDSTONE
(SLATY —) PLATE SCHALSTEIN
(SOLID —) GIBBER
(STUDY OF —S) LITHOLOGY
(SUBMERGED —) SHELF
(UNDERLYING —) FLOOR
(VOLCANIC —) TUFA TUFF BASALT DOMITE LATITE TAXITE ASHSTONE RHYOLITE TEPHRITE TRACHYTE
(WORTHLESS —) GANG GANGUE
(PL.) ROCHER
ROCKAWAY CARRIAGE
ROCK BADGER CONY HYRAX
ROCK BASS REDEYE CABRILLA
ROCKBRUSH ROSILLA
ROCK CEDAR SABINO
ROCK CRESS SICKLEPOD
ROCK DEBRIS TALUS
ROCK DOVE SOD
ROCKER CRADLE SHOOFLY

ROCKET DRAKE REBUKE STREAK YELLOW CONGREVE SKYLIGHT STARSHIP FIREDRAKE
(DYER'S —) WELD WOLD WOALD WOULD
ROCKET SALAD ROQUETTE
ROCKFISH JACK RENA REINA VIUVA FLIOMA GOPHER RASHER TAMBOR CORSAIR GARRUPA GROUPER BOCACCIO CHINAFISH GREENLING
ROCK HARE KLIPHAAS
ROCK HIND MERO AGAUJI
ROCK HOPPER MACARONI
ROCKLING BAUD GADE ROKER SORGHE WHISTLER
ROCK NATIVE SNAPPER
ROCK PIPIT TIETICK
ROCK RABBIT PIKA HYRAX HYRACOID
ROCKROSE CISTUS HUDSONIA ROCKCIST SAGEROSE DAYFLOWER SUNFLOWER
ROCK SALT EMOL AMOLE HALITE
(BLOCK OF —) PIG
ROCK SANDWORT CYME
ROCKSHAFT SHAFT ROCKER WEIGHBAR
ROCK TROUT BOREGAT GREENLING
ROCKWEED TANG FUCUS FUCOID SEATANG SEAWEED
ROCK WHITING KELPFISH STRANGER
ROCKY DAFT HARD STONY CLINTY OBSCENE PETREAN PETROUS UNCOUTH OBDURATE UNSTABLE DIFFICULT RUPELLARY
ROCKY MOUNTAIN (— GOAT) MAZAME
ROCOCO ORNATE QUAINT BAROCCO BAROQUE OUTMODED
ROD BAR BOW CUE GAD GUY LUG PIN TIE BOLT CALM CAME CANE CORE FALL FORK GOAD GONG LINK MACE POLE RAVE SCOB SNAP STEM STUD WAND WHIP YARD ARBOR BIRCH CATCH DOWEL LYTTA OSIER PERCH POWER PUNCH REACH ROUND SETUP SHOOT SPELK SPILL SPOKE SPRAG STAFF STEEL STICK STING TEYNE TOMMY TRACE VERGE WIPER BALEYS BROACH CANARY CARBON CENTER CRUTCH ETALON FERULA FINGER GLOWER HANGER PISTOL PITMAN PODGER RADDLE RAMMER SKEWER SPRING STADIA SWITCH TOGGLE WATTLE WICKER BACULUS CROPPIE DRAWROD ELLWAND FEATHER FESTUCA PLUNGER POINTER POTHOOK PRICKER PROBANG PROLONG SCALLOM SCEPTER SPINDLE STADIUM STICKER TYRANNY VIRGULA WHISKER WINDING AXOSTYLE BACKSTAY BILBERRY BODSTICK BOWSTAVE DIPSTICK JACKSTAY KINGBOLT REVOLVER STRAINER TRAVELER WEEDHOOK
(— AS SYMBOL OF OFFICE) VERGE
(— BEARING TRAFFIC SIGNAL) STANCHION

(— **FOR ALIGNING HOLES)** PODGER
(— **FOR CARRYING GLASS)** FORK
(— **FOR DISCIPLINE)** YARD FERULA
FERULE
(— **FOR FASTENING THATCH)** SPELK
SPRINGLE
(— **FOR FIREARM BORE)** WIPER
(— **FOR GLASS-MAKING)** PUNTY
FASCET PONTEE PONTIL CROPPIE
(— **FOR HOLDING MEAT)** SPIT
(— **FOR TRANSMITTING MOTION)**
TRACE
(— **IN ARC LAMP)** CARBON
(— **IN CRICKET)** STUMP
(— **IN INTERFEROMETER)** ETALON
(— **IN MINE PUMP)** SPEAR
(— **IN NERNST LAMP)** GLOWER
(— **IN SPINNING WHEEL)** SPINDLE
(— **OF FOUNDRY MOLD)** LANCE
(— **OF LOOM)** SHAFT
(— **OF WOOD)** SCOB
(— **ON LOGGING TRUCK)** RAVE
(— **POINTED AT BOTH ENDS)**
SKEWER
(— **SYMBOLIZING AUTHORITY)**
BACULUS
(— **TO BIND A CONTRACT)** FESTUCA
(— **TO FASTEN SAILS)** JACKSTAY
(— **TO IMMERSE SHEEP)** CRUTCH
(— **TO URGE BEAST)** GOAD PROD
(— **UPSET AT ONE END)** SETUP
(— **USED AS KEY)** TOMMY
(— **WITH ENDS AT RIGHT ANGLES)**
STRAINER
(— **WITH SPONGE ON END)**
PROBANG
(— **WITH T-HEAD)** TOGGLE
(**AXIAL** —) VIRGULA AXOSTYLE
(**BASKETRY** —) OSIER
(**BUNDLE OF** —**S)** DRIVER
(**CARTILAGINOUS** —) LYTTA
COLUMELLA
(**CLAMMING** —) BRAIL
(**CONNECTING** —) PITMAN
(**CURTAIN** —) TRINGLE
(**DANCER'S** —) CROTALUM
(**DIVINING** —) TWIG DOWSER
(**FISHING** —) GAD CALCUTTA
(**FLEXIBLE** —) RADDLE WATTLE
(**FORKED** —) CRUTCH
(**GEM-CUTTING** —) SETTER
(**GRADUATED** —) STADIA STADIUM
(**IRON** —) SNAP
(**KNITTING** —) NEEDLE
(**LEAD** —) CAME
(**LOGGING** —) CANARY
(**MEASURING** —) JUDGE SPILE
STADIA ELLWAND METEWAND
METEYARD
(**PLIABLE** —) WINDING
(**SMALL** —) LANCE
(**STRENGTHENING** —) RIB
(**SUPPLE** —) SWABBLE
(**TETHERING** —) STAKE
(**THIN** —) TEYNE SCALLOM
(**TIE** —) ANCHOR
(**UMBRELLA** —) STRETCHER
(**WITHE** —) BILBERRY
RODENT RAT CONY DEGU HARE

MARA MOCO MOLE PACA PIKA UTIA
VOLE CONEY COYPU GUNDI HUTIA
JUTIA LEROT MOUSE TUCAN ZOKOR
AGOUTI BEAVER BITING CURURO
GERBIL GLIRID GNAWER GOPHER
JERBOA MARMOT MURINE MUROID
RABBIT SOKHER BLESMOL CHINCHA
DIPODID GEOMYID GNAWING
HAMSTER LEMMING LEVERET
MUSKRAT ABROCOME CAPIBARA
DORMOUSE LEPORIDE OCTODONT
SEWELLEL SPALACID SQUIRREL
TUCOTUCO VISCACHA VIZCACHA
RODEO ROUNDUP
RODLIKE VIRGATE
RODMAN CLASHY CLASHEE
　CHAINMAN
RODOMONTADE BRAG RANT BOAST
　BLUSTER BOMBAST BRAGGART
ROD-SHAPED RHABDOID VIRGULATE
ROE RA DOE FRY PEA RAA RAE HIND
　KELK RAUN ROUN ROWN CORAL
　TRUBU CAVIAR
ROEBUCK GIRL CHEVREUIL
ROGER RAM HODGE ROGUE
ROGUE BOY GUE IMP NYM KEMP
　KITE ROAG CATSO CRACK CRANK
　GIPSY GREEK GYPSY HEMPY KNAVE
　SCAMP SHELM BEGGAR BORGER
　BUGGER CANTER COQUIN CURTAL
　HARLOT LIMMER PICARA PICARO
　RASCAL SORROW TINKER BLEEDER
　ERRATIC FOISTER HALLION
　LADRONE PANURGE SHARPER
　SKELLUM SWINGER VILLAIN
　COMROGUE HEMPSEED PICAROON
　SWINDLER WHIPJACK
ROGUERY ROPERY KNAVERY
　LOONERY WAGGERY PATCHERY
　PRIGGISM TRICKERY TRUANTRY
ROGUISH SLY ARCH ROGUY WICKED
　KNAVISH TRICKSY VAGRANT
　WAGGISH ESPIEGLE SCAMPISH
　DISHONEST
ROGUISHNESS KNAVERY ARCHNESS
ROIL VEX FOUL RILE ANNOY
　BLUNDER DISTURB STUDDLE
　BEWILDER DISORDER IRRITATE
ROILED TURBID
ROISTER REVEL ROIST SCOUR
　CAROUSE GALRAVAGE
ROISTERER MUN GREEK HUZZA
　HECTOR RIOTER SCOURER TWIBILL
　EPHESIAN
ROISTERING HOYDEN
ROKE FOG DAMP MIST REEK ROWK
　STIR FOGGY SMOKE STEAM VAPOR
ROKELAY ROCOLO
ROLE BIT JOB LEAD PART ROTE
　HEAVY FIGURE CLOTHES BUSINESS
　FUNCTION LIRIPIPE
ROLL BAP BUN ROW WEB BOLT COIL
　CURL FILE FLOW FURL LIST MILL
　PASS REEL ROAM ROTA SWAG
　WELT WIND WRAP BAGEL BREAD
　BUILD DANDY DICKY ENROL FLUTE
　ROYLE SPLIT TRILL TROLL WHELM
　BILLOW BUNDLE CIRCLE ELAPSE
　ENFOLD GOGGLE GROVEL KIPFEL

LEGEND MUSTER PONDER ROSTER
ROTATE SCROLL UPWIND VOLUME
WAMBLE WANDER WHELVE WINTLE
WREATH BISCUIT BRIOCHE
CROCKET ENVELOP MANCHET
REVOLVE ROTULET ROTULUS
STRETCH TERRIER TRUNDLE
TWISTER BROTCHEN CANNELON
CONSIDER CRESCENT JACKROLL
LAMINATE PORTEOUS REGISTER
SEDERUNT SPREADER VOLUTATE
(— **A BALL)** BOWL
(— **ABOUT)** WALTER SCAMBLE
(— **AS A SHIP)** SEEL LURCH
(— **AS STONE)** REEL
(— **BY)** WALK
(— **CLOSELY)** FURL
(— **EYES)** WALL WAUL WHAWL
GOGGLE
(— **GLASS)** MARVER
(— **INTO A BALL)** CLEW CLUE
(— **OF BREAD)** BAP SEMMEL
TAMMIE
(— **OF CLOTH)** BOLT WREATH
(— **OF COINS)** ROULEAU
(— **OF DOUGH)** TWIST
(— **OF DRIED BARK)** QUILL
(— **OF DRUM)** HURRY
(— **OF DUST)** KITTEN
(— **OF HAIR)** ROACH ROWEL
CROCKET
(— **OF HAY)** WAKE
(— **OF LINT OR LINEN)** TENT DOSSIL
(— **OF LUGGAGE)** SWAG
(— **OF MINCED MEAT)** RISSOLE
(— **OF OFFENDERS)** PORTEOUS
(— **OF PAPER)** SPILL STOMP STUMP
(— **OF PARCHMENT)** BOOK PELL
(— **OF ROULETTE WHEEL)** COUP
(— **OF SPUN YARN)** PRICK
(— **OF TOBACCO)** CAROT CIGAR
PRICK SEGAR CAROTTE
(— **OF WALLPAPER)** BOLT
(— **OF WHEAT BREAD)** MANCHET
(— **OF WOOL)** ROVE ROVING
CARDING
(— **ON LITTLE WHEELS)** TRUNDLE
(— **ONWARD)** DEVOLVE
(— **OVER)** COMB JOLL WELTER
(— **TO RUB DOWN DRAWING)**
STUMP
(— **TOGETHER)** CONVOLVE
(— **UP SLEEVES)** REEVE
(— **UP)** FURL STOW COLLAR
(**BLANKET** —) BINDLE SHIRALEE
(**DANDY** —) DANCER
(**HOLLOW** —) CANNELON
(**LONG** —) FLUTE
(**PADDED** —) BURLET
(**PENNY** —) TOMMY
(**TWISTED** — **OF WOOL)** SLUB
(**WHIP** —) BACKREST
ROLLED (— **IN SUGAR)** SANDED
ROLLER FLY BOWL BRAY DRUM
　JACK LEAD MILL PUCK RUBY BREAK
　DANDY FINER GODET INKER RIDER
　SHELL WAVER WINCH BRAYER
　BREAST DOFFER DUCTOR FASCIA
　MANGLE ROWLET RUNNER CARRIER

CLEARER MOIETER TRUCKLE
HEDGEHOG SQUEEGEE STRIPPER
TROUPAND
(— **FOR MASSAGER**) ROULETTE
(— **IN HORSE'S BIT**) CRICKET
(— **IN ORGAN**) TRUNDLE
(— **IN STEELWORKS**) COGGER
(— **TO CLEAR FABRIC**) MOIETER
(**CARDING** —) BREAST WORKER
SQUIRREL STRIPPER
(**CHINESE** —) SIRGANG
(**DREDGING** —) HEDGEHOG
(**DROP** —) DUCTOR
(**GRINDING** —) BREAK
(**INKING** —) BRAYER
(**PRINTING** —) DANDY SHELL
BRAYER DAMPENER
(**STONE** —) MAMMY TOTER
(**SURGICAL** —) FASCIA
(**TOOTHED** —) PRICK PRICKER
ROLLER COASTER SWITCHBACK
ROLLERMAN BRAKER JACKMAN
LEVERMAN
ROLLER SKATE PEDOMOTOR
ROLLICK PLAY ROMP FROLIC ROLLIX
ROLLICKING GAY WILD MERRY
JOVIAL LIVELY
ROLLING CURL GOGGLE WHEELY
SWAYING TRILLED LURCHING
VOLUTION
(— **OF SCROLL**) GELILAH
(— **OF SHIP**) LABOR
ROLLTOP TAMBOUR
ROLY-POLY ROTUND PUDDING
TUMBLER SALTWORT
ROM RO GYPSY ROMANY
ROMAN BRAVE LATIN NOBLE PAPAL
ANTIQUA UPRIGHT GOWNSMAN
(— **COLLAR**) RABAT
ROMAN CATHOLIC ROME ROMAN
PAPIST ROMIST BABYLONIC
ROMANCE WOO GEST ANTAR FANCY
FEIGN GESTE KATHA NOVEL STORY
ANTARA UTOPIA FANTASY FICTION
ROMANZA
(— **LANGUAGE**) FRENCH ITALIAN
SPANISH
ROMAN-FLEUVE SAGA

ROMANIA

CANAL: BEGA
CAPITAL: BUCHAREST
COIN: BAN LEI LEU LEY
DISTRICT: ALBA BANAT BIHOR
DOBRUJA DOBROGEA
MARAMURES
LAKE: SINOE
MOUNTAIN: BIHOR NEGOI CODRUL
RODNEI CALIMAN PIETROSU
OLD NAME: DACIA
PASS: ROSUL
PROVINCE: ARDEAL MOLDAVIA
WALACHIA
RIVER: ALT JIU OLT PRUT ALUTA
ARGES BUZDU MOROS MURES
OLTUL SCHYL SIRET VEDEA
CRASNA DANUBE ARGESUL
BISTRITA IALOMITA

RIVER PORT: BRAILA GALATI
GALATZ
TOWN: ARAD CLUJ IASI BACAV
CERNA JASSY NEAMT SIBIU
TURNU BRAILA BRASOV GALATI
GALATZ LVPENI CRAIOVA
FOCSANI PLOESTI SEVERIN
CERNAVTI KISHENEF KOLSOVAR
TEMESVAR

ROMANIST MISSARY
ROMANIZATION LATINXUA
ROMANSH LADIN
ROMANTIC AIRY WILD IDEAL
ADRENT DREAMY GOTHIC POETIC
UNREAL FERVENT FABULOUS
FANCIFUL
ROMANY RO ROM GIPSY GYPSY
ROMAN
ROME (CHAPEL IN —) SISTINE
(**FOUNDER OF** —) ROMULUS
(**HILL IN** —) CAELIAN VIMINAL
AVENTINE PALATINE QUIRINAL
(**RIVER IN** —) TIBER
ROMP REG RIG LARK PLAY ROIL
FRISK SHIRL SPORT TRAIN FROLIC
GAMBOL HOORAY HOYDEN HURRAH
RIPPET COURANT GAMMOCK
RAMMACK RUNAWAY
ROMPERS JUMPER JUMPERS
ROMPING ROYT ROYET
RONCADOR GRUNT CROAKER
SCIAENID
RONE BUSH BRAKE GUTTER THICKET
RONG LEPCHA
RONGA THONGA
RONSDORFER ZIONITE ELLERIAN
ROOD RUD REED ROPE CROSS
SPAWN STANG CRUCIFIX
ROODLES RANGDOODLES
ROOF TOP ATAP BACK DECK DOME
FLAT ATTAP COVER HOUSE RAISE
RISER SHELL THACK AZOTEA
BONNET CUPOLA SUMMIT TECTUM
CHOPPER CRICKET GAMBREL
MANSARD RIGGING TECTURE
BULKHEAD HOUSETOP SAWTOOTH
SEMIDOME
(— **MEMBER**) PURLIN
(— **OF CARRIAGE**) IMPERIAL
(— **OF CAVERN**) DOME
(— **OF MINING CAGE**) BONNET
(— **OF MOUTH**) PALATE
(— **OF NASOPHARYNX**) VAULT
(— **OF RAILWAY CAR**) DECK
(— **OVER STAGE**) SHADOW
(— **PORTION**) MONITOR
(**CLOTH** —) CHUTT
(**FALSE** —) CRICKET
(**FLAT** —) LEADS AZOTEA TERRACE
(**STEEPLY TAPERING** —) SPIRE
(**THATCHED** —) ATAP ATTAP
CHOPPER
(**VAULTED** —) DOME
ROOFING HEALING SHINDLE
PANTILING
ROOK ROC CROW DUPE RUKH
CHEAT CRAKE JUDGE TOWER

BLACKY CASTLE DEFRAUD
CASTILLO SWINDLER
ROOKERY ROOST RUMPUS BUILDING
ROOKIE COLT DRONGO NOVICE
RECRUIT BEGINNER
ROOM WON AULA CAFE CRIB FARM
HALL KILN LIEU PLAY SALA SEAT
SLUM WAME WENE WONE ATTIC
BERTH CUDDY DIVAN EWERY HOUSE
LODGE OECUS PLACE SALLE SCOPE
SHACK SOLAR SPACE STALL STOVE
STUDY BELFRY BREAST CAMERA
CASINO CHAPEL ESTUFA EXEDRA
HAMMAM LEEWAY MARGIN PARVIS
SCOUTH SINGLE SMOKER SOLLAR
STANCE STANZA STUDIO CABINET
CAMARIN CHALMER CHAMBER
EPINAOS FREEZER GALLERY
HOLDING HYPOGEE KITCHEN
LAUNDRY LIBRARY SEMINAR
SERVERY SMOKERY SURGERY
AEDICULA ASSEMBLY BASEMENT
DRYHOUSE HOTHOUSE HYPOGEUM
LAVATORY NYMPHEUM SCULLERY
SWEATBOX TABLINUM THALAMUS
(— **BEHIND FACADE**) ATTIC
(— **BETWEEN KITCHEN AND DINING
ROOM**) SERVERY
(— **CONTAINING FOUNTAIN**)
NYMPHEUM
(— **DUG IN CLIFF**) HYPOGEE
HYPOGEUM
(— **FOR ACTION**) LEEWAY
(— **FOR BATHING**) HAMMAM
(— **FOR CONVERSATION**) EXEDRA
(— **FOR FAMILY RECORDS**)
TABLINUM
(— **FOR KEEPING FOOD**) LARDER
PANTRY
(— **FOR PAINTINGS**) GALLERY
(— **FOR PRIVATE DEVOTIONS**)
ORATORY
(— **FOR PUBLIC AMUSEMENTS**)
CASINO THEATER
(— **FOR STOWAGE**) LASTAGE
(— **FOR TABLE LINEN**) EWERY
(— **IN COAL MINE**) BREAST
(— **IN HAREM**) ODA
(— **IN KEEP**) DUNGEON
(— **IN PREHISTORIC BUILDING**) CELL
(— **IN REAR OF TEMPLE**) EPINAOS
(— **IN SIDE OF LARGER ROOM**) ALA
(— **IN TOWER**) BELFRY
(— **OF STUDENTS' SOCIETY**) HALL
(— **ON SHIP**) CABIN STOKEHOLD
(— **OVER CHURCH PORCH**) PARVIS
(— **OVER STAGE**) SHADOW
(— **TOGETHER**) CHUM
(— **UNDER BUILDING**) CELLAR
(**CHILDREN'S** —) NURSERY
(**DINING** —) CENACLE DINETTE
REFECTORY
(**DRAWING** —) SALON SALOON
(**DRESSING** —) SHIFT BOUDOIR
CAMARIN VESTUARY WARDROBE
TIREHOUSE
(**ESKIMO ASSEMBLY** —) KASHGA
(**EXHIBITION** —) THEATER
(**GRINDING** —) HULL

(HEATED —) STEW
(HIGH —) AERY EYRY AERIE EYRIE
(INNER —) BEN INBY INBYE SPENCE
(INSULATED —) FREEZER
(LIVING —) HOUSE LANAI SALON
SERDAB SOLARIUM VOORHUIS
(MONASTERY —) CELL LAVABO
(NARROW —) CRIB
(OCTAGONAL —) TRIBUNA
(PRIVATE —) SNUG SCHOLA
(PUEBLO ASSEMBLY —) ESTUFA
(READING —) ATHENEUM
(RECEPTION —) DIVAN PARLOR
MANDARAH
(REFRIGERATED —) COOLER
(RETIRING —) RECAMERA
(ROMAN —) ATRIUM AEDICULA
FUMARIUM
(ROUND —) ROTUNDA
(SEA —) BERTH
(SECLUDED —) DEN
(SERIES OF —S) SWEEP
(SITTING —) SITTER BOUDOIR
(SLEEPING —) DORMER BEDROOM
DORMITORY
(SMALL —) ALA CELL SNUG STEW
CUBBY CUDDY LOBBY CLOSET
CUBICLE SNUGGERY
(SMOKING —) DIVAN DIWAN
TABAGIE
(SORTING —) SALLE
(STEAM —) STOVE
(STORAGE —) CAMARIN MAGAZINE
THALAMUS
(SWEATING —) SUDARIUM
SUDATORY LACONICUM
(THRONE —) AIWAN
(TOP —) GARRET IMPERIAL
(UPPER —) SOLAR
ROOMMATE CHUM ROOMY ROOMIE
ROOMY WIDE LARGE RANGY SPACY
ROOMSOME SPACIOUS
ROOSE RUSE EXTOL PRAISE
FLATTER BOASTING BRAGGING
ROOST EVE SIT BAUK JOUK TIDE
PERCH GARRET HARBOR LODGING
ROOKERY SHELTER
ROOSTER COCK GAME GALLO
MANOC GAMECOCK
ROOT DIG PRY ROI TAP BASE BULB
CHAY CHOY GRUB MOOR MOOT
MORE RACE SPUR TAIL CHEER
FIBER FRUIT GROOT GROUT HEART
IREOS LAPPA RADIX STOCK ALRAUN
BOTTOM CARROT CATGUT GROUND
MUZZLE ORIGIN SENEGA SETTLE
SUMBAL SUMBUL ACONITE ALKANET
AZAFRAN BIACURU BONIATA
CALUMBA CHICORY COLUMBO
CRAMPON GINSENG IMPLANT
IPOMOEA NUNNARI PARIERA
RADICAL RUMMAGE TURPETH
DEDENDUM EARTHNUT
(— BRANCH) TAPOUN
(— CONTAINING STARCH) KOONTI
(— DEEPLY) SCREW
(— OF GINGER) RACE
(— OF ORCHID) CULLIONS
(— OF TOOTH) FANG

(— OF TREE) TANG SPURN
(— OF WORD) THEME
(— OUT) GRUB STUB STOCK
EVULSE DISPLANT SUPPLANT
(— TUBERCLE) CLOG
(— WORD) ETYMON
(— YIELDING RED DYE) CHAY CHOY
CHAYA
(—S FOR SEWING CANOES) WATAP
WATAPEH
(—S OF ACONITE) BIKH NABEE
(CANDIED —) ERYNGO
(DRIED —) JALAP ALTHEA SENECA
BRYONIA KRAMERIA LICORICE
SCAMMONY
(DRIED —S) INULA IPECAC
KRAMERIA VERATRUM
(EDIBLE —) YAM BEET EDDO
RADISH TURNIP WASABI PARSNIP
RUTABAGA TUBERCLE
(FERN —) ROI
(FINE —) STRING
(FRAGRANT —S) VETIVER
(MASS OF FIBROUS —S) SPONGE
(MEDICINAL —) JALAP LAPPA
GINSENG
(PROJECTING —) SPUR
(ROASTED BEET —) BONKA
(STUMP AND —) MOCK
(PL.) CULVERS
ROOTCAP CALYPTRA SPONGIOLE
ROOTED FIXED CHRONIC
(DEEPLY —) BESETTING
ROOTER FAN PLUGGER
ROOTLET CRAMPON RADICEL
RADICLE
(PL.) COME CULMS
ROOTSTOCK PIP ROI TARO ORRIS
CASAVA DANNUM GINGER ORIGIN
PANNUM STOLON BISCUIT
TURMERIC
ROPE GAD GUY TIE TOW TUG CEEL
COLT CORD FALL FAST GUSS HEMP
JEFF JUNK LIFT LINE ROOD SEAL
SOAM SPAN STAY TACK TAIL TAUM
TOME VANG WARP BRACE BRAIL
CABLE CABUL CHECK CHORD
LASSO LONGE SHANK STRAP STROP
SWEEP TRACE TWIST WANTY WIDDY
WITHE CABLET HALTER INHAUL
LARIAT LISSOM LIZARD MECATE
PINION RAPEYE RUNNER SHROUD
SLATCH STRAND STRING TETHER
WARROK AWEBAND BEDCORD
BOBSTAY CATFALL CRINGLE
ENTRAIL HALYARD LASHING
LEEFANG OUTHAUL PAINTER
PAZAREE PENDANT PIGTAIL
SEAMING SERPENT SERVICE
STIRRUP SWIFTER BACKBONE
BACKSTAY BUNTLINE CABESTRO
CORDELLE DOWNHAUL DRAGLINE
FOREFOOT FORETACK HALLIARD
HAULYARD INHAULER JACKSTAY
LIFELINE NECKLACE PASSAREE
PROLONGE ROUNDING SEQUENCE
THRAMMLE BREECHING
(— A STEER) HEEL
(— COLLAR) PARRAL PARREL

(— COVERING) QUILTING
(— FOR FASTENING GATE) CRINGLE
(— FOR FISH) STRINGER
(— FOR TRAINING HORSE) LONGE
(— FOR TYING CATTLE) CEEL SEAL
AWEBAND
(— HANDLE) FETTLE SHACKLE
(— HOLDING RAFT TOGETHER)
BRAIL
(— JOINT) TUCK
(— OF 10 OR MORE INCHES) CABLE
(— OF HAIR) CABESTRO
(— OF ONIONS) REEVE
(— OF STRAW) GAD SIME VINE
SIMON SUGAN FETTLE SIMMON
SOOGAN
(— ON DERRICK) TELEGRAF
(— ON FISHING NET) PINION
SEAMING
(— ORNAMENTATION) TORSADE
(— PASSING AROUND DEADEYE)
STRAP STROP
(— STOLEN FROM DOCKYARD)
RUMBO
(— WITH HOOK AND TOGGLE)
PROLONGE
(— WITH SWIVEL AND LOOP)
TOGGEL TOGGLE
(— WOUND AROUND CABLE)
KECKLING
(—S IN RIGGING) CORDAGE
(ANCHOR —) RODE VIOL VOYAL
(BELL —) TYALL HANGER
(CIRCUS —) JEFF
(DRAFT —) SOAM
(DRAG —) GUSS
(FLAG-RAISING —) HALYARD
(FOOT —) HORSE
(GRASS —) SOGA
(GUIDE —) DRAGLINE
(HANDLE —) FETTLE
(HANGMAN'S —) HEMP TIPPET
(HARNESS —) TRACE HALTER
(HARPOON —) FOREGOER
(NAUTICAL —) TIE TYE COLT FANG
LIFT STAY VANG BRACE BRAIL
SHEET SLING STRAP STROP GILGUY
HAWSER INHAUL LACING RATLIN
SHROUD BOBSTAY BOWLINE
CATFALL GESWARP LANYARD
LEEFANG OUTHAUL PAINTER
PAZAREE PENDANT PENNANT
PIGTAIL RATLINE SNORTER
SNOTTER STIRRUP STOPPER
SWIFTER BACKBONE BACKSTAY
BUNTLINE DOWNHAUL FORETACK
JACKSTAY PASSAREE ROUNDING
SELVAGEE WOOLDING
(PART OF —) SLATCH
(SHORT —) SHANK
(SHORT CART —) WANTY
(SMALL HANDMADE —) FOX
(SMUGGLER'S —) LINGTOW
(TALLOWED —) GASKET
(TOW —) CORDELLE
(WIRE —) HAULBACK JACKSTAY
(WORN OR POOR —) JUNK
(PL.) CORDAGE
ROPEBAND RABAND

ROPEMAKER FOLLOWER RATLINER
ROPEWALKER FUNAMBULO
ROPEWAY TRAMWAY WIREWAY
CABLEWAY
ROPY SINEWY STRINGY VISCOUS
MUSCULAR GLUTINOUS
ROQUE CROQUET
ROQUELAURE CLOAK ROCOLO
ROCKLAY
RORIPA RADICULA
RORQUAL SEI FINBACK
ROSARY BEADS CORONA TASBIH
BEADING BEADROLL
(— BEAD) GAUD GAUDY
(MOHAMMEDAN —) COMBOLOIO
ROSE ASH GUL KNOT MOSS ROIS
BRIAR BRIDE BUCKY FLUSH RHODA
CANKER POMPON BOURBON
BURBANK GLAIEUL HUGONIS
LOZENGE MANETTI MONTHLY
OPHELIA RAMBLER AGRIMONY
COLUMBIA DOGBERRY LOKELANI
PEDELION
(COTTON —) CUDWEED
ROSE ACACIA ROBINIA
ROSE APPLE JAMBO JAMBOS
JAMBOSA
ROSEATE SPOONBILL AJAJA
ROSE-BREASTED (— COCKATOO)
GALAH
ROSEBUSH ROSER BALWARRA
ROSE CAMPION LYCHNIS
ROSE-COLORED OPTIMISTIC
(— STARLING) PASTOR TILYER
ROSEFISH BRIM BREAM BERGYLT
REDFISH
(YOUNG —) SNAPPER
ROSE HIP CHOOP CHOUP
ROSELLE SORREL SABDARIFFA
ROSEMARY COSTMARY MOORWORT
ROSMARINE
ROSE MOSS PURSLANE PORTULACA
ROSET BRAZIL
ROSETTE CHOU KNOT COCKADE
ROSEWOOD BUBINGA MOLOMPI
JACARANDA
ROSIN FLUX COLOPHONY
(— SPIRIT) PINOLIN
ROSS SCALP
ROSSER BARKER PEELER SCALPER
SLIPPER
ROSTER LIST ROTA SCROLL
REGISTER
ROSTRATE BEAKED
ROSTRUM PEW AMBE BEAK GUARD
SNOUT PULPIT ACROTER TRIBUNE
ROSY ROSEN BLUSHY AURORAL
HEALTHY AUROREAN BLOOMING
BLUSHFUL
ROT COE RET DOTE DOZE DROP
FOUL JOKE LEAK POKE SOUR WROX
DECAY SPOIL TEASE BLUING
FESTER ROTTEN CORRUPT
HOOFRUT PUTREFY NONSENSE
STAGNATE
(— BY EXPOSURE) RET
(— OF GRAPES) SLIPSKIN
(APPLE —) FROGEYE
(FOOT —) FOUL

(FRUIT —) LEAK
(LIVER —) COE
ROTA LIST ROLL ROSTER ROTULA
ROTARY CIRCLE GYRATORY
ROTATE RUN BIRL GYRE ROLL SPIN
TURN PIVOT SCREW WHEEL GYRATE
REVOLVE TRUNDLE ROTIFORM
ALTERNATE
(— HIPS) GRIND
ROTATING VOLUBLE
ROTATION SPIN TURN ROUND TWIRL
GYRATION SPINNING WHIRLING
(— ON BALL) STUFF
ROTCHE BULL RATCH ROTGE
DOVEKEY DOVEKIE BULLBIRD
ROTE CRWTH HEART ROTTA REPEAT
ROTIFER POLYP LIPOPOD LORICATE
PLOIMATE
ROTL RATTEL WEIGHT ROTTOLO
(PL.) ARTAL ARTEL
ROTOGRAVURE ROTO COLOROTO
ROTOR IMPELLER
ROTTED PECKY
ROTTEN BAD FOUL ROXY SOUR
ADDLE DAZED MOSEY PUTID
AMPERY FRACID MOOSEY PUTRID
DECAYED SPOILED DEPRAVED
UNSTABLE
(HALF —) DOTED DOATED
(PARTIALLY —) DRUXY
ROTTING SLEEPY CARIOUS
ROTTLERA KAMALA
ROTULA ROUND TROCHE KNEEPAN
PATELLA
ROTUND FAT PLUMP ROUND STOUT
CHUBBY SUBROUND
ROTURIER PEASANT PLEBEIAN
RUPTUARY
ROUE RAKE DEBAUCHEE
ROUGE RED FARD BLUSH PAINT
FUCATE REDDEN RUDDLE CLINKER
SCRIMMAGE
(ANIMAL —) CARMINE
ROUGH RU ROW RUF BEAT FOUL
GURL HARD HASK LAMB ROID ROYD
RUDE THUG WILD ACRID BLUFF
BLUNT BRUTE CHURL CRUDE DIRTY
GOBBY GROFF GURLY HAIRY HARSH
HEFTY JAGGY LUMPY REWCH
ROUCH ROWDY RUGGY RUVID
STARK STEER STERN STOUR TOUGH
TOUSY WIGHT BORREL BROKEN
BRUSHY BURRED CHOPPY COARSE
COBBLY CRABBY CRAGGY ELBOIC
ENEVEN HACKLY HISPID HOARSE
HOBBLY HORRID HUBBLY INCULT
JAGGED KNAGGY KNOTTY NOGGEN
RAGGED RAMAGE RASPED ROBUST
RUFFLE RUGGED RUMBLY RUSTIS
SEVERE SHAGGY SKETCH TOOSIE
TRYING UNFEEL UNFELE UNFINE
UNKIND UNMILD UNRIDE ABUSIVE
AUSTERE BOORISH CRABBED
HIRSUTE INEQUAL INEXACT JARRING
RABBISH RAMMAGE RAPLOCH
RUFFLED SCABRID STICKLE STICKLY
UNCOUTH UNKEMPT VICIOUS
ASPERATE CHURLISH DEPOLISH
IMPOLITE LARRIKIN OBDURATE

SCABROUS SCRAGGED STUBBORN
UNGENTLE UNTENDER MANHANDLE
(— EDGES) FASH
(— IT) SIWASH
(— UP ARROW FEATHERS)
SPRANGLE
(MAKE —) SHAG
ROUGHAGE FODDER AVERAGE
BALLAST CELLULOSE
ROUGH-AND-READY BURLY TOWSY
TOWZIE MAKESHIFT
ROUGHCAST PARGET SPARGE
ROUGHHEW SLAPDASH
ROUGHEN FRET GAIG HACK EMERY
FEAZE FLOCK FROST TOOTH
ABRADE CRISLE STIVER CRIZZLE
ENGRAIL SCRATCH UNSMOOTH
(— BRICK WALL) STAB
ROUGHER BULLDOGGER
(PONY —) STRANDER
ROUGH-HOB GASH
ROUGH-MILL GASH
ROUGHNECK ROWDY TOUGH
MUCKER UNCOUTH BANGSTER
ROUGHNESS GAFF GRAIN SCUFF
TOOTH RUFFLE CRIZZLE CRUDITY
ACRIMONY ASPERITY
(— OF SEA) LIPPER
(— OF SKIN) GOOSESKIN
GOOSEFLESH
(— OF WALL) KEY
ROUGHOMETER VIAGRAPH
ROULADE VOLATA ARPEGGIO
ROULETTE FILET FILLET TROCHOID
(1-18 IN —) MANQUE
(13-24 IN —) MILIEU
(HIGH — NUMBERS) PASSE
ROUNCEVAL GIANT LARGE
MONSTER GIGANTIC
ROUND BALL BEAT BEND BOLD
BOUT FAST FULL GIRO HEAD RICH
ROON ROTA TOUR TRIM WALK
ABOUT AMPLE BEADY BRISK CATCH
DANCE GLOBE HAMBO HARSH
LARGE MOONY ORBED PLAIN
ROMAN RONDO SPOKE TROLL
TUBBY CIRCLE COURSE ENTIRE
MELLOW NEARLY ROTUND ROUNDY
RUBBER RUNDLE SPHERY SPIRAL
STOWER STREAK ZODIAC ANNULAR
CIRCUIT SHAPELY CIRCULAR
COMPLETE CROSSBAR ENCIRCLE
GLOBULAR SONOROUS LABIALIZE
(— EDGES OF TIMBER) BEARD
(— END OF LOG) SNIPE
(— FREQUENTLY GONE OVER) BEAT
(— IN BOWLING) FRAME
(— IN CARDS) GRAND
(— OF ACTIVITIES) SWING
(— OF APPLAUSE) HAND JOLLY
PLAUDIT
(— OF CHAIR) BALUSTER
(— OF KNITTING) BOUT
(— OF LADDER) STAVE
(— OF PLAY) LAP
(— OFF) TOP CROWN FILLET
(— OUT) ORB BELLY INTEGRATE
(— UP) CORRAL WRANGLE
SCROUNGE

(PLUMP AND —) CHUBBY
(SWEDISH —) HAMBO
ROUNDABOUT PLUMP DETOUR
ROTARY CURVING DEVIOUS
CIRCULAR INDIRECT TORTUOUS
(— MOVEMENT) WINDLASS
ROUNDED FULL BOMBE BOWLY
CONVEX MELLOW ROTUND TERETE
ARRONDI BUNTING CONCAVE
GIBBOUS SHAPELY COMPLETE
FINISHED HOOPLIKE SONOROUS
(— OUT) PLUM
ROUNDEL HEURT PLATE POMME
PELLET FOUNTAIN
(— AZURE) HURT
(— GULES) TORTEAU TORTEAUX
(— OR) BEZANT BYZANT
(— PURPURE) GOLP GOLPE
(— SABLE) GUNSTONE
(— SANGUINE) GUZE
(— VERT) POMEY
ROUNDER SOAKER WASTREL
INFORMER
ROUNDERS TUT PATBALL TUTBALL
ROUNDHEAD SWEDE CROPPY
WEAKFISH
ROUND HERRING SHADINE
STRADINE
ROUNDHOUSE BARN POOP LOCKUP
ROUNDNESS ROTUND SPHERICITY
(— OF RIBS) SPRING
ROUND POMPANO PERMIT
PALOMETA
ROUND ROBIN ANGLER SERIES
PANCAKE SEQUENCE
ROUNDSMAN VANMAN SWINGMAN
WATCHMAN
ROUNDUP RODEO CAMBER GATHER
ROUNDWORM NEMA ASCARID
EELWORM GORDIAN HELMINTH
NEMATODE STRONGYL
ROUP ROLP ROOP CROAK CLAMOR
AUCTION SHOUTING
ROUSE DAW GIG HOP JOG BAIT
CALL DRAW FIRK GOAD MOVE RANT
RAVE STIR WAKE WHET AMOVE
ERECT MOUNT RAISE START STEER
UPSET WAKEN AROUSE BESTIR
EXCITE FOMENT KINDLE NETTLE
RATTLE REVIVE RUFFLE WECCHE
AGITATE ANIMATE DISTURB
EKPHORE ENLIVEN HEARTEN
INFLAME STARTLE INSPIRIT
IRRITATE
(— TO ACTION) HIE ALARM ALARUM
BESTIR ALACRIFY
ROUSTABOUT FLOORMAN
RAZORBACK
ROUT MOB DRUM FUSS HERD BRANT
CHASE COHUE CROWD EJECT
FLOCK LURCH SMEAR SNORE
CLAMOR DEFEAT FLIGHT NUMBER
RABBLE SOIREE THRONG UPROAR
CONFUSE CONQUER DEBACLE
SCATTER SPARPLE TEMPEST
ASSEMBLY CONFOUND DISTRESS
VANQUISH
ROUTE WAY BELT GATE GEST LINE
PASS PATH SEND TRACE TRACK

AIRWAY CAREER COURSE CUTOFF
SKYWAY TRAJET CHANNEL CIRCUIT
LANDWAY SHUTTLE CORRIDOR
DISTANCE LIFELINE SHORTCUT
TRAVERSE
(— MARKED OUT) ITER
(— TO DEFEAT) SKIDS
(CIRCUITOUS —) DETOUR
(MIGRATION —) FLYWAY
(OCEAN —) LANE
ROUTH PLENTY ABUNDANT
ROUTINE RUT GRIND ROUTE TROLL
GROOVE HARNESS EVERYDAY
(DOMESTIC —) HOMELIFE
(WEARISOME —) TREADMILL
ROVE RUN RAKE RAVE ROAM GUESS
KNOCK RANGE ROWAN SPACE
STRAY FORAGE MARAUD RAMBLE
STROLL WANDER SPATIATE
STRAGGLE TRANSCUR
(— ON THE WING) FLIT
ROVER FLIRT HOYLE STAKE STRAY
MASHER RANGER VIKING GANGREL
SCUMMER MARAUDER SLIVERER
TRAVELER WANDERER COLORADAN
ROVING END SLUB NOMAD ARRANT
ERRANT DEVIOUS NOMADIC
RAMPLER VAGRANT GADABOUT
RAMBLING RESTLESS SLUBBING
**(— IN SEARCH OF KNIGHTLY
ADVENTURE)** ERRANTRY
ROW LAY OAR RIG SET DUST FILE
LINE MUSS PULL RULE TIER ALLEY
BRAWL CHESS FIGHT MOUTH NOISE
ORDER RANGE RINGE SCOLD
SWATH TRAIN BARNEY BERATE
COURSE DUSTUP GARRAY KICKUP
LISSOM PADDLE POTHER RACKET
RUCKUS SHINDY STREET STROKE
BOBBERY BRULYIE QUARREL
SHINDIG CATEGORY OUTBURST
REMIGATE SQUABBLE
(— BACKWARD) STERN
(— OF BENCHES) STACK
(— OF CASKS) LONGER
(— OF CORN, BARLEY, ETC.) RIG
(— OF DRY HAY) STADDLE
(— OF GRAIN) SWATH SWATHE
(— OF GRASS) HACK SWATH
(— OF GUNS) TIRE
(— OF HOUSES) CRESCENT
(— OF SEATS) BARRERA
(— OF SEED) DRILL
(— OF VEGETABLES) RINGE
(PL.) EPEIRA
ROWAN RAN RODDIN
ROWAN TREE CARE SORB WICKY
WITCH RODDEN RODDIN WICKEN
WIGGEN QUICKEN RANTREE
WHITTEN WITCHEN ROUNTREE
ROWBOAT GIG OAR BARK OARS
PLAT BARIS COBLE DINGY FUNNY
KOBIL SCULL SKIFF BARQUE CAIQUE
DINGHY LURKER WHERRY SCULLER
(— SEAT) TAFT
(CLINKER-BUILT —) FUNNY
(FLAT-BOTTOMED —) DORY
(SMALL —) COG
ROWDY TOU BHOY CASH MONEY

ROUGH TOUGH TOMBOY UNRULY
VULGAR HOODLUM RAFFISH
BARRATER LARRIKIN STUBBORN
ROWDYISM YAHOOISM
ROWEN EDGROW RAWING
AFTERMATH ROUGHINGS
ROWER URGER GALIOT STROKE
OARSMAN STERNMAN CAIQUEJEE
(— ON UPPER SEATS) THRANITE
(OUTERMOST —) THALAMITE
(SECOND LEVEL —) ZYGITE
ROWING CREW
ROWLOCK LOCK CRUTCH OARLOCK
RULLOCK
ROYAL EASY REAL RIAL ELITE
REGAL SMALT AUGUST KINGLY
REGIUS SOVRAN SUPERB BASILIC
GLORIOUS IMPERIAL IMPOSING
MAJESTIC PAVILION
(— MACE) SCEPTER SCEPTRE
ROYAL ANTELOPE MADOQUA
KLEENEBOC
ROYAL FERN OSMOND OSMUND
ROYALIST TORY ULTRA REGIAN
TANTIVY CAVALIER MUSCADIN
ROYALLY PURPLEY
ROYAL PALM COYAL
ROYALTY LOT ALII GALE BONUS
REGAL REALTY MAJESTY PENALTY
LORDSHIP NOBILITY REGALITY
ROYET WILD HARSH UNRULY
ROMPING
RUB DUB BARK BILL FILE FRAY FRET
FRIG FROT RISP WIPE CHAFE DIGHT
FEEZE FRUSH GRATE GRAZE GRIDE
LABOR SCOUR SCRUB SMEAR
STONE FRIDGE RUBBER STREAK
BEESWAX FRICACE FURBISH
MASSAGE
(— AS A ROPE) SNUG
(— AS ANIMALS) SHAB
(— AWAY) ERODE ABRADE
(— BOOT) BONE
(— DOWN) WIPE STRAP
(— ELBOWS) JOSTLE JUSTLE
(— GENTLY) STRIKE STROKE
(— HARD) SCOUR SCRUB
(— HARSHLY) GRIND
(— LIGHTLY) GRAZE
(— OFF) CROCK ABRADE ABRASE
(— OUT) ERASE EFFACE EXPUNGE
(— ROUGHLY) GRATE
(— SNUFF) DIP
(— THE SKIN OFF) SHAW
(— TOGETHER) FIDDLE
(— VELVET FROM ANTLERS)
BURNISH
(— WITH GREASE) DUB
(— WITH OIL) ANOINT
RUBBED TERSE
RUBBER BUNA FOAM PARA BUTYL
CREPE RASER ALASKA BISUIT
CAUCHO DAPICO ERASER NIGGER
RUNNER BURUCHA EBONITE
ELASTIC GUAYULE RAMBONG
BORRACHA FRICTION NEOPRENE
SERNAMBY SERWAMBY SOVPRENE
(— CITY) AKRON
(HARD —) EBONITE

(RECLAIMED —) SHODDY
(PL.) SHAB
RUBBERIZE FRICTION
RUBBER TREE ULE MILKER
RAMBONG
RUBBING CHAFE CARESS ABRASION
FRICTION FROTTAGE FRICATION
RUBBISH KET CRAB FLAM FLUM
GEAR GWAG MULL PELF PELT RAFF
ROSS TRAG BRASH CRAWM CULCH
OFFAL SCOWL SLUSH STENT STUFF
TRADE TRASH TRUCK WASTE
COLDER DEBRIS GARBLE KELTER
LITTER PALTRY RAFFLE REFUSE
RUBBLE SCULCH SHRUFF SPILTH
BAGGAGE BEGGARY MULLOCK
RUMMAGE SLITHER TAFFIKE
TRAFFIC FIRETRAP NONSENSE
RIFFRAFF TRASHERY TRUMPERY
(VEGETABLE —) WRACK
RUBBISHY POUCY PALTRY TRASHY
BAGGAGE RUMMAGY
RUBBLE BRASH STENT TALUS
BACKING SLITHER
RUBE JAY BOOR HICK JAKE JASPER
BUMPKIN BUSHMAN HAYSEED
CORNBALL
RUBELLA ROTELN
RUBICUND RED ROSY RUDDY
FLORID FLUSHED
RUBIGINOUS RUSTY
RUBLE RO RUBLIS
(ONE-HALF —) POLTINIK
RUBRIC RED NAME CANON CLASS
TITLE CONCEPT CATEGORY
RUBRICATE MINIATE
RUBY AGATE RUBIN PYROPE
ANTHRAX SPARKLE VERMEIL
RUBY SPINEL BALAS ALMANDINE
RUCHING COQUILLE
RUCK RUT HEAP PILE RICK CROWD
SQUAT STACK TRASH CREASE
FURROW HUDDLE PUCKER RUBBISH
WRINKLE
RUCKUS ADO ROW FIGHT FRACAS
ROOKUS
RUCTION HURRY RUCKUS QUARREL
RUPTION FRACTION
RUDD REDEYE
RUDDER HELM STEER STERN TIMON
HELLIM RUTHER STEERER
STEERAGE GOVERNAIL
(— BACK) TALON
(— EDGE) BEARDING
(— OF WINDMILL) TAIL
(DIVING —) HYDROVANE
(PART OF —) STOCK
RUDDERFISH CHOPA OPALEYE
RUDDINESS RUBEDITY
RUDDLE RED BOLE KEEL SMIT
ROUGE
RUDDY RED RODE RUDE FRESH
VIVID BLOWSY BLOWZY FLORID
LIVELY GLOWING RUDDISH
BLUSHFUL RUBICUND SANGUINE
RUDDY DUCK ROOK BOOBY NODDY
PADDY SPRIG BOBBER DUNBIRD
GREASER PINTAIL SLEEPER
SPATTER BLUEBILL BULLNECK

HARDHEAD WIRETAIL
RUDE ILL RAW BOLD IRON LEWD
WILD BLUFF BLUNT GREEN GROSS
PLUMP ROUGH STOUR SURLY
UNORN ABRUPT BITTER BORREL
CALLOW CLUMSY COARSE DUDGEN
GOTHIC HOMELY HOYDEN INCULT
RIBALD ROBUST RUGGED RUSTIC
SAVAGE SHAGGY SIMPLE STORMY
UNFEEL UPLAND VULGAR ARTLESS
BOORISH CARLAGE CARLISH INCIVIL
LOUTISH LOWBRED NATURAL
UNCOUTH UNHENDE CHURLISH
CLUBBISH HOMESPUN IMPOLITE
INSOLENT MECHANIC PORTERLY
STUBBORN SYLVATIC UNGENTLE
UNPOLITE YOKELISH
(— AND BOLD) HOIDEN HOYDEN
RUDENESS GAFF
RUDIMENT GERM ANLAGE VESTIGE
BEGINNING
(PL.) ABC ALPHABET ELEMENTS
GRAMMATES
RUDIMENTARY BASIC GERMING
ABORTIVE ABECEDARY ELEMENTAL
EMBRYONIC
(MOST —) FIRST
RUE RU REWE MOURN CATGUT
REGRET REPENT SORROW BORONIA
TENTWORT
RUEFUL SAD RUELY WOEFUL
DOLEFUL PITIABLE
RUFF SET APEX FURY PAPE POPE
CREST PRIDE REEVE TEASE TEAZE
TRUMP COLLAR RABATO RUFFLE
TIPPET ZENITH ELATION PASSION
QUELLIO REBATER ROTONDE
PICKADILL
RUFFED BUSTARD HOUBARA
RUFFED LEMUR VARI
RUFFIAN MUN LAMB PIMP THUG
TORY BULLY DEVIL ROUGH ROWDY
TIGER APACHE BRUTAL COARSE
CUTTER CUTTLE MOHAWK MOHOCK
PANDER TOWSER HOODLUM
SWEATER TUMBLER HACKSTER
HOOLIGAN
RUFFLE VEX BAIT FRET HOOP ROOL
RUFF BULLY FRILL GRAZE JABOT
PLEAT ROUSE SHIRR ABRADE
ATTACK GATHER NETTLE RIPPLE
BLUSTER BRISTLE DERANGE
FLOUNCE FLUTTER PANUELO
STIFFEN SWAGGER TROUBLE
DISHEVEL DISORDER DISTRACT
FURBELOW IRRITATE QUILLING
SKIRMISH
(— THE TEMPER) ROIL
RUFFLED ROUGH UNKEMPT
**RUFFLING (— ON THE SURFACE OF
WATER)** HORROR
RUG TUG BAKU COZY HAUL MAUD
PULL SNUG TEAR WRAP BIJAR
HERAT HEREZ JURUK KAZAK KHILA
KONIA KULAH KUMEH LADIK MECCA
MELAS MOSUL NAMDA SENNA
TEKKE TUZLA USHAK YURUK ZOFRA
AFSHAR BALUCH KANARA KAROSS
KASHAN KIRMAN MOGHAN NAMMAD

PERGAM RUNNER SHIRAZ SMYRNA
TABRIZ TILPAH TOUPEE WILTON
BALUCHI BERGAMA BOKHARA
BUFFALO DERBEND DRUGGET
FERAHAN GIORDES GOREVAN
HAMADAN ISPAHAN SHEERAZ
SHIRVAN YARKAND AUBUSSON
DOMESTIC FOOTPACE PANDERMA
SARABAND SEDJADEH SERABEND
WOLFSKIN
(— OF SKINS) KAROSS WOLFSKIN
(PLAID —) MAUD
(PRAYER —) GHIORDES NAMAZLIK
(REVERSIBLE —) KILIM
RUGA FOLD CREASE WRINKLE
RUGBY FOOTER RUGGER FOOTBALL
(— PLAY) SCRUM
RUGGED RUDE WILD HAIRY HARDY
ROUGH STIFF COARSE CRAGGY
HORRID JAGGED KNAGGY KNOTTY
ROBUST SAVAGE STRONG STURDY
UNEVEN CRABBED GNARLED
OBDURATE SCRAGGED VIGOROUS
RUIN DO MAR POT BANE BANG
COOK CRAB DAMN DASH DOOM
FALL FATE FELL HELL JACK KILL
LOSS RASE RAZE SINK TALA BLAST
BOTCH BREAK CRUSH DECAY EXILE
GUBAT HUACA LEESE LEISS SHEND
SHOOT SMASH SPEED SPILL SPLIT
SPOIL SWAMP WRACK WRAKE
WRECK BEDASH BLIGHT CANCEL
COOPER DAMAGE DEFACE DEFEAT
DIDDLE DISMAY FOREDO INJURY
RAVAGE UNMAKE BOWWOWS
CORRUPT DESTROY FLATTEN
FORLESE FORWORK LEESING
PERVERT SHATTER SUBVERT
TORPEDO UNDOING BANKRUPT
COLLAPSE DEMOLISH DESOLATE
DISASTER DOWNFALL
(— AT GAMBLING) SHRUB
(SPIRITUAL —) FALL
(PL.) ASHES DEBRIS RELICS RUDERA
ZIMBABWE
RUINATION DOGS
RUINED FLAT GONE LORN KAPUT
BROKEN FALLEN NAUGHT NOUGHT
FORLORN BANKRUPT DESOLATE
RUINER MARPLOT
RUINOUS DEADLY BANEFUL
DECAYED SHENDFUL WASTEFUL
CUTTHROAT
RULE LAW MAN RAJ WIN DASH KING
NORM SWAY WALD WARD YARD
AXIOM CANON GUIDE JUDGE MAXIM
NORMA ORDER REGLE REIGN RICHE
RIGHT RULER SPILE STAFF SUTRA
SUTTA WIELD ALIDAD CUTOFF
DECIDE DECREE DITION DOMINE
EMPIRE ENTAIL GNOMON GOVERN
MANAGE MASTER METHOD REGNUM
SQUARE VASSAL BROCARD
COMMAND CONTROL COUNSEL
DICTATE DIETARY FORMULA
PLUMMET PRECEPT PRESIDE
REGENCY REGIMEN THEOREM
DICTAMEN DOCTRINE DOMINATE
FUNCTION LEGALISM MODERATE

ORDINARY OVERLEAD PERSUADE
REGIMENT REGNANCY STANDARD
TYRANNIS
(— OUT) EXCLUDE
(— TYRANNICALLY) HORSE
(—S OF CONDUCT) ETIQUETTE
(—S OF DUELING) DUELLO
(ABSOLUTE —) AUTARCHY
(OPPOSING —) ANTINOMY
RULER DEY GOG JAM MIN OBA AMIR
CZAR DAME DUKE EMIR INCA KING
LORD OBBA RULE TSAR TZAR
ALDER AMEER DECAN EMEER HAKIM
MPRET MWAMI NAGID NAWAB
SCALE SOPHI STEER SUBAH ZUPAN
APHETA ARCHON AUTHOR CAESAR
DESPOT DUARCH DYNAST EPARCH
FERULE HERSIR ISWARA KABAKA
KAISER MASTER NIMROD PATESI
PENLOP RECTOR REGENT SAWBWA
SHERIF SOLDAN SUFFEE SULTAN
TYRANT ADMIRAL ALIDADE
BOURBON DEMARCH FAIPULE
ISHVARA KHEDIVE MONARCH
MORMAER PTOLEMY RECTRIX
REGULUS REIGNER TOPARCH
TRIARCH WIELDER AUGUSTUS
BASILEUS DRIGHTEN EXILARCH
GOVERNOR HEPTARCH INTERREX
OLIGARCH PADISHAH PENTARCH
PHYLARCH REGINALD TARAFDAR
WHIPKING
(— IN A NATIVITY) APHETA
(— OF ENCLOSURE) HENRY
(CURVED —) SWEEP
(ELF —) AUBREY
(INCA —) CURACA
(JEWISH —) EXILARCH
(MONGOLIAN —) HUTUKTU
(MOSLEM —) SOLDAN
(STRONG —) REGINALD
(TATAR OR MOGUL —) CHAM
RULING CALL CHIEF REGENT
SOVRAN CURRENT HOLDING
REGITIVE HEGEMONIC
RUM ODD ROME OCUBY QUEER
RUMBO TAFIA TAFFIA BACARDI
CACHACA JAMAICA PECULIAR
SWITCHEL EXCELLENT
RUMBLE CROWL DICKY GROWL
RUMOR SNORE BUMBLE HOTTER
HUMBLE LUMBER WAMBLE
GRUMBLE QUARREL
RUMBO RUM GROG LIQUOR
RUMEN CUD PAUNCH STOMACH
RUMINANT OX COW YAK BULL DEER
GOAT CAMEL LLAMA MOOSE SHEEP
STEER TAKIN ALPACA MAZAME
VICUNA GIRAFFE QUIDDER
ANTELOPE TUBICORN
RUMINATE CHAW CHEW MULL MUSE
CONCOCT REFLECT SAUNTER
CONSIDER
RUMINATION MERYCISM
RUMKIN RUMMER
RUMMAGE GRUB ROUT SEEK
BUSTLE FORAGE TOUSLE UPROAR
FOSSICK RANSACK ROMMACK
DISORDER SKIRMISH UPHEAVAL

(— ABOUT FOR A PROFIT) FOSSICK
(— SALE) JUMBLE
RUMMY GIN RUM TUNK QUEER
CANASTA COONCAN DRUNKARD
OKLAHOMA
RUMOR CRY SAW BUZZ FAMA FAME
TALK WORD BRUIT MUDGE NOISE
SOUGH SOUND STORY VOGUE
VOICE BREEZE FURPHY GOSSIP
MURMUR POTGUN RENOWN REPORT
RUMBLE CLATTER HEARING
HEARSAY INKLING OPINION
WHISPER NORATION GRAPEVINE
RUMORED AFLOAT
RUMP ASS FUD ARSE BEAM CULE
DOCK DOUP CROUP NATCH PODEX
STERN BOTTOM CURPIN CROUPON
CRUPPER HURDIES PLUNDER
BANKRUPT BUTTOCKS DERRIERE
RUMPF CORE
RUMPLE FOLD MUSS WISP TOUSE
TOWSE MOUSLE ROMBLE CRUMPLE
SCRUNCH WRINKLE
RUMPUS RAG ROW BRAWL SHINE
CLAMOR FRACAS HUBBUB RUCKUS
TOWROW UPROAR ROOKERY
ROWDYDOW
RUMSHOP BAR SALOON TAVERN
BARROOM TAPROOM DRUNKERY
RUN GO BYE ERN FLY FOG GAD HOP
JOG LAM LEG PLY RIN RUB URN
BUNK CALL FLEE FLOW FUSE HARE
HEAT HEEL HUNT IRNE KITE LEAD
LEAP MELT PASS PLAY RACE RAKE
RINN ROAM ROVE TEND TRIG TRIP
TROT TURN WALK WEEP WORK
ASSAY BLEND BREAK CHASE COAST
EXTRA GOING HURRY NOTCH POINT
SCOUP SPEED SPEND STAND TABLE
TRACE BICKER CAREER COURSE
ELAPSE ESCAPE EXTEND GALLOP
HASTEN LADDER MANAGE RESORT
ROTATE SPRENT SPRINT STREAM
TUMBLE VOLATA ACCURRE
CONDUCT CONTAIN FLUTTER
LIQUEFY OPERATE PASSAGE
RETREAT SKELTER STRETCH
FUNCTION TRANSCUR
(— ABOUT) TIG FISK DISCURRE
(— ACROSS) STRIKE
(— AGAINST) JOSTLE
(— AGROUND) BEACH GRAVEL
HURTLE STRAND STRIKE
(— ALONG EDGE OF) SKIRT
(— AS STOCKING) LADDER
(— AT HIGH SPEED) SCORCH
(— AT THE NOSE) SNIVEL
(— AT TOP SPEED) SPRINT
(— AWAY FROM DEBTS) LEVANT
(— AWAY IN PANIC) STAMPEDE
(— AWAY) FLY GUY FLEE HIKE JINK
JUMP SMUG ELOPE SCRAM SMOKE
DECAMP SCAMPER SCARPER
FUGITATE SKEDADDLE
(— BEFORE A GALE) SCUD
(— BEFORE A JUMP) FEAZE FEEZE
(— BETWEEN) INTERCUR
(— BLINDLY) SKITTLE
(— CLUMSILY) LOPPET TUMBLE

(— COUNTER) BELY BELIE CROSS
(— DOWN) SLUR OVERRUN
(— HARD) DIG
(— HIGH) FLOOD
(— IN CRICKET) BYE WIDE EXTRA
NOTCH
(— IN DROPS) WEEP
(— INTO) INCUR
(— ITS COURSE) LAPSE
(— OBLIQUELY) SQUINT
(— OF CLAPBOARDING) STRAKE
(— OF MULE CARRIAGE) DRAW
(— OF SHAD) SPURT
(— OF STAIRS) GOING
(— OFF) BOLT SCADDLE
(— ON SKIS) SCHUSS
(— OUT) EXCUR ISSUE PETER
(— OVER) HEAT TRAMP OVERFLOW
(— RAPIDLY) KITE RAKE SCUR
SCOUR SKIRR SPLIT CAREER
(— SOAP) FRAME
(— SPEEDILY) CHASE CAREER
(— SWIFTLY) HARE LEAP SCUD
CHEVY CHIVY
(— THROUGH) PIERCE DISCURRE
(— TO EXERCISE HORSE) HEAT
(— TO) ACCURRE
(— TOGETHER) HERD MUDDY
CLUTTER
(— TRAINS) BLOCK
(— WILD) GAD ESCAPE STARTLE
(— WILDLY) STARTLE
(— WITH AFFECTED PRECIPITATION)
SCUTTLE
(— WITH SKIPS) SCOUP
(— WITH VELOCITY) DART
(BRIEF —) STREAK FLUTTER
(END —) SWEEP
(GLASS FURNACE —) BLAST
(OBSTACLE —) GYMKHANA
(RAPID MUSICAL —) TIRADE VOLATA
(SAILING —) STRETCH
(SHEEP —) SLAIT STATION
(SHORT —) FAIL BICKER SCURRY
FLUTTER RAMRACE SCUTTLE
RUNAGATE APOSTATE FUGITIVE
RENEGADE RUNABOUT VAGABOND
WANDERER
RUNAWAY ROMP RUNNER DECISIVE
DESERTER FUGITIVE RUNAGATE
RUNDI HUTU
RUNDLE DRUM RUNG ORBIT CIRCLE
SPHERE WINDLASS
RUNDLET KEG BARREL
RUN-DOWN BAD SHODDY SQUALID
DERELICT
RUNE WEN WYN WYNN CHARM
OGHAM SPELL SECRET MYSTERY
RUNG RIM GREE RIME STEP ROUND
SCALE SPELL SPOKE STAFF STAIR
STALE STAVE STEAL TREAD WRUNG
DEGREE RUNDLE STOWER STREAK
CROSSBAR TRAVERSE
(— OF CHAIR) SPELL
(— OF LADDER) RIME STEP RANGE
SPOKE STALE RONDLE STREAK
(— OF ROPE WALK) STAKE
(PL.) STILE

RUNIC ALPHABET FUTHARK
FUTHORC
RUNIC LETTER THORN
RUNLET RUSH RINDLE RUNNEL
STREAM RIVELING
RUNNEL RILL BROOK RHINE RINDLE
RUNLET POLLARD RIVULET
STREAMLET
RUNNER SOW GOER POST SCUD
SHOE SKID BLADE COBIA FLOAT
RACER SCARF SKATE SLIDE SPRAY
TEDGE CURSOR HEELER KANARA
RENNER STOLON TOUTER CHANNEL
COURIER HARRIER SARMENT
CURSITOR SKIPJACK TRAILING
(— FOR GRINDING STONE) MARTIN
(BLUE —) HARDTAIL
(FLUME —) HERDER
(PAIR OF —S) SLOOP
(RACE —) SCUTTLER
(SLED —S) BOB
(SLEDGE —S) SLIPES
RUNNING RUN CARE EASY RACE
FLUID QUICK COURSE LIVING
COURANT CURRENT CURSIVE
FLOWING HOTFOOT SCUTTER
SLIDING FUGITIVE
(— ABOUT) COURANT CURSORY
(— ACROSS) DIAGONAL
(— OF SHIPS TOGETHER) ALLISION
(— TOWARD) APPULSE
(— VERTICALLY) DOWN
(FIRST —S) HEAD
(NOT —) DEAD
RUNNING GEAR MOBILE
RUNT BOOR SCRUB SLINK STEER
STUMP STUNT HEIFER PEEWEE
SCRUMP TITMAN URLING BULLOCK
SHARGAR SHARGER SLINKER
RECKLING
RUNTY MEAN SURLY SCRUBBY
SCRUNTY STUNTED DWARFISH
RUNWAY RUN TIP DUCT TRAIL
TARMAC SLIPWAY AIRSTRIP
DOLLYWAY
(— OF HARE) FILE
RUPEE DIB CHIP SICCA ROUPIE
(100,000 —S) LAC LAKH
(ONE-SIXTEENTH —) ANNA
(TENS OF —S) RX
RUPERT'S DROP TEAR
RUPIA RUPEE ERUPTION
(HALF —) PARDO PARDAO
RUPTURE BLOW REND RENT BREAK
BURST CRACK SPLIT BREACH
HERNIA RHEXIS DISRUPT RUPTION
FRACTION FRACTURE HERNIATE
RUPTURED BROKEN
RURAL RUSTIC BUCOLIC COUNTRY
AGRESTIC ARCADIAN LANDWARD
PASTORAL VILLATIC
RUSE HOAX ROSE SHIFT STALL
TRICK WREST ARTIFICE TRICKERY
RUSH FLY FOG RIP RIX RUB SAG
BANG BENT CLAP DASH DUSH FALL
GIRD HURL HUSH JUNK LASH LEAP
LUSH PASH RACE RACK RASH RESE
RISH ROUT SCUD SHOT SLUR SPUR
SWIP TEAR TILT WHIP WIND ADRUE

CARRY CHASE CHUTE DRASH DRIVE
FEEZE FLASH FLUSH FRAIL FRUSH
HURRY ONSET PIPES PREEL SCOUR
SEAVE SHOOT SPART SPATE SPRAT
SPRIT SPROT START STAVE STORM
WHIRL CHARGE DELUGE FESCUE
HURTLE JUNCUS POWDER RAMACK
RANDOM RAVINE STREAK THRESH
ASSAULT BRATTLE BULRUSH
DAILIES DEBACLE JUNCITE RAMMISH
RAMRACE SKELTER SMOTHER
SWITHER TANTIVY TORNADO
WHITHER CATARACT DEERHAIR
SALTWEED SPLATTER VANQUISH
(— ABROAD) FLUSH
(— AGAINST) CHARGE
(— AWAY) BOLT FLEE
(— DOWN) TRACE
(— FOR WEAVING) FRAIL
(— HEADLONG) BOIL RUIN SPURN
STAMPEDE
(— OF LIQUID) HEAD FLUSH
(— OF WATER) FRESH SHOOT
SPOUT SWASH
(— OF WORDS) SPATE
(— OUT) SALLY
(CLUMP OF —S) RASHBUSS
(COMMON —) FLOSS
(DOWNWARD —) HURL
(FLAT —) SHALDER
(FORCEFUL —) JET
(NOISY —) SCUTTER
(ONWARD —) BIRR SURGE
(PL.) REXEN
RUSHING HURL SCUD FURIOUS
HUDDLING IMPETUOUS
(— OF WIND) GUST
RUSHLIGHT SEAVE
RUSH NUT CHUFA
RUSK ZWIEBACK
RUSSELL'S VIPER DABOIA DABOYA
JESSUR KATUKA

RUSSIA	
CAPITAL: MOSCOW	
COIN: KOPEK RUBLE GRIVNA	
KOPECK	
COLLECTIVE FARM: KOLHOZ	
KOLKHOZ	
DISTRICT: KARELIA	
FORTRESS: KREMLIN	
LAKE: ARAL NEVA SEGO CHANY	
ELTON ILMEN ONEGA BAYKAL	
SELETY TAYMYR TENGIZ	
ZAYSAN BALKHASH	
MEASURE: FUT LOF DUIM FASS	
LOOF STOF FOUTE KOREC	
LIGNE OSMIN PAJAK STOFF	
VEDRO VERST ARSHIN CHARKA	
LINIYA PALETZ SAGENE TCHAST	
BOTCHKA CHKALIK GARNETZ	
VERCHOC BOUTYLKA CHETVERT	
KROUSHKA	
MOUNTAIN: POBEDY BELUKHA	
MOUNTAIN RANGE: ALAI URAL	
CAUCASUS	
NAME: USSR SOVIET MUSCOVY	

PENINSULA: KOLA CRIMEA
KARELIA KAMCHATKA
PORT: EISK ANAPA ODESSA
RIVER: IK OB DON ILI KET NER
OKA ROS TAZ TYM USA AMGA
AMUR KARA LENA NEVA OREL
SURA SVIR URAL LOVAT MEZEN
NADYM ONEGA TEREK TOBOL
VOLGA ABAKAN DONETS IRTYSH
DNIEPER PECHORA
SEA: ARAL AZOV KARA BLACK
BAIKAL OKHOTSK
TOWN: KIEV OMSK OREL PERM
GOMEL KASAN KAZAN KYZYL
MINSK PENSA PSKOV TOMSK
IGARKA KERTCH KURGAN NIZHNI
ODESSA ROSTOV SARTOV
URALSK ALMAATA BATAISK
DONETSK IRKUTSK IVANOVO
KALININ RYBINSK KOSTROMA
ORENBURG SMOLENSK
TAGANROG TASHKENT VLADIMIR
VORONEZH YAROSLAV

RUSSIAN IVAN RUSS SLAV VELIKA
(— BRAID) SOUTACHE
(— HEMP) RINE
(— POOL) CARLINE
(LITTLE —) RUSSENE RUTHENE
UKRAINIAN
RUSSIAN BANK CRAPETTE
RUSSIAN CALF FUDGE
RUSSIAN THISTLE SALTWORT
TUMBLEWEED
RUSSIAN TURNIP RUTABAGA
RUSSIAN WOLFHOUND BORZOI
RUST CLOWN DROSS ROOST ROUST
UREDO AERUGO CANKER CORRODE
FERRUGO OXIDIZE
(— OF PLANTS) HEMIFORM
LEPTOFORM
(KNOT OF —) TUBERCULE
RUSTIC HOB JAY PUT BOOR CARL
CHAW HICK HIND JAKE JOCK RUDE
BACON BUSHY CARLE CHUFF
CHURL COLIN DAMON DORIC HODGE
ROUGH RURAL RURIC SILLY YOKEL
AGREST BUMKIN COARSE FARMER
GAFFER HONEST JOBSON RUSSET
SAVAGE SCOLOC SCOLOG STURDY
SYLVAN UPLAND ARTLESS BOORISH
BUCOLIC BUMPKIN BUSHMAN
COUNTRY DAPHNIS FIELDEN
GEORGIC HAYSEED HOBNAIL
HOOSIER LANDMAN PAISANO
PEASANT PLOWMAN THYRSIS
WAYBACK AGRESTIC DAMOETAS
GEOPONIC LANDWARD MOSSBACK
CHAWBACON
(NOT —) CIVIL
(UNCOUTH —) JAKE
(YOUTHFUL —) SWAIN
(PL.) COUNTRYFOLK
RUSTLE FISLE STEAL FISSLE FISTLE
HIRSEL REESLE BRUSSEL BRUSTLE
CRINKLE REESTLE SKITTER WHISTLE
(— OF SILK) SCROOP
(— UP) SNAVVLE

RUSTLER THIEF WADDY DUFFER WADDIE HUSTLER

RUSTLING ARUSTLE CRINKLY FROUFROU SOUGHING FRICATION SUSURROUS

RUSTY HOARY MOROSE ROOSTY SULLEN CANKERY OUTMODED

RUT RAT BRIM RACK RAIK RUCK TRACK TREAD CREASE FURROW GROOVE STRAKE UPROAR CHANNEL OESTRUS WRINKLE

(— IN PATH) GAY

RUTABAGA BAGA SWEDE TURNIP

RUTH PITY MERCY MISERY REGRET SORROW CRUELTY REMORSE SADNESS SYMPATHY

(HUSBAND OF —) BOAZ

(MOTHER-IN-LAW OF —) NAOMI

(SON OF —) OBED JESSE

RUTHENIAN RUSSENE RUSSNIAK UKRAINIAN

RUTHLESS GRIM CRUEL BRUTAL PITILESS CUTTHROAT

RUTILE NIGRINE SAGENITE

RUTTER PLOW DRAGOON GALLANT TROOPER

RUTTISH RANK LUSTFUL

RWANDA
CAPITAL: KIGALI
LAKE: KIVU
LANGUAGE: KIRUNDI SWAHILI
MOUNTAIN: KARISIMBI

MOUNTAIN RANGE: MITUMBA
PEOPLE: TWA HUTU TUTSI
RIVER: KAGERA AKANYARU LUVIRONZA
TRIBE: BATWA BAHUTU WATUSI BATUTSI

RYE RAY RIE ERAY REYE SPELT WHISKY GENTLEMAN

RYEGRASS RAY EAVER DARNEL

RYMANDRA KNIGHTIA

RYND BAIL RHIND MILRIND

RYOT RAYAT FARMER RAIYAT TENANT TILLER PEASANT

S ESS SUGAR SIERRA
SABBATH SUNDAY SABAOTH
  SHABBAT SHABBOS
SABER KUKRI SABRE BANCAL
  BASKET TULWAR TUWAUR ATAGHAN
  CIMETER YATAGAN ACINACES
  SCIMITAR
SABICU JIQUE JIQUI
SABLE DWALE SAPLE OGRESS
  SATURN DIAMOND ZIBELINE
  (ROUNDEL —) PELLET
SABLEFISH SKIL BESHOW COALFISH
  SKILFISH
SABOTAGE MASTIC DESTROY
SAC BAG GUT POD CYST SACK
  ASCUS BURSA FLOAT POUCH THECA
  VOLVA ACINUS AMNION SACCUS
  AMPULLA BLADDER CAPSULE
  CISTERN HYGROMA UTRICLE
  VESICLE BROODSAC FOLLICLE
  SACCULUS SPERMARY
SACCHARIN SWEET STICKY SUGARY
  GLUCOSE GLUSIDE
SACCHAROSE SUCROSE
SACERDOTAL HIERATIC PRIESTLY
SACHEM SAGAMORE
SACK BAG BED MAT SAC LOOT
  POCK POKE BAYON GOOSE HARRY
  POUCH SPOIL BUDGET POCKET
  RAVAGE SACKET SACQUE DISMISS
  PILLAGE PLUNDER RANSACK
  SACKAGE SACKBAG DESOLATE
  PACKSACK PEIGNOIR
  (— OF PALM LEAVES) BAYONG
  (MAIL —) BUM
  (PACK —) KYACK
  (SAD —) BOLO
SACKBUT SAMBUKE TROMBONE
SACKING SACK GUNNY CROCUS
  SACKEN HESSIAN POLDAVY
  SOUTAGE
SACRAMENT BAPTISM MYSTERY
  PENANCE
SACRED HOLY TABU HUACA SACRE
  SAINT SANCT SANTO TABOO DIVINE
  SACRAL HALLOWED HEAVENLY
  NUMINOUS REVEREND
SACRED FIG PIPAL
SACRED FISH KANNUME
SACREDNESS CHURINGA SANCTITY
  TJURUNGA
SACRIFICE GIVE HOST LOSS OFFER
  SPEND YAJNA CORBAN FOREGO
  VICTIM EXPENSE CHILIOMB
  IMMOLATE KAPPARAH LITATION
  OBLATION OFFERING PASSOVER
  SPHAGION
  (— OF 100 OXEN) HECATOMB
  (— OF 1000 OXEN) CHILIOMB
  (— OF CARGO) JETTISON
  (PL.) HAGIGAH CHAGIGAH
SACRIFICIAL PIACULAR
SACRILEGIOUS IMPIOUS
SACRISTAN SEXTON SACRIST
SACRISTY SEXTRY SACRARY
  VERGERY PARATORY
SACROSANCT SACRED
SAD WAN DARK DOWY DRAM BLACK
  DREAR DUSKY MESTO MOODY

SABLE SOBER SORRY WEARY
YEMER DREARY SOLEMN SULLEN
TRISTE WOEFUL DOLEFUL DUMPISH
FORLORN FUNEBRE LUCTUAL
MOANFUL SOBERLY UNHAPPY
DEJECTED GROANFUL MOURNFUL
MOURNING PITIABLE SUBTRIST
TRISTIVE UNBLITHE
SADDEN SAD DUMP GLOOM GRIEVE
  ATTRIST CONTRIST DISTRESS
SADDENED BROKEN
SADDENING LUCTUAL
SADDLE PAD RIG SAG TAG LOAD
  SUNK CHINE PANEL PILCH SELLE
  STICK BURDEN HEADER RECADO
  PIGSKIN PILLION
  (— COVER) MOCHILA
  (— FOR ONE-LEGGED RIDER)
  SOMERSET
  (— STUFFED WITH STRAW) SODS
  (— WITH) STICK
  (— WORKER) LORIMER
  (LIGHT —) PILCH PILLION
  (MOTORCYCLE —) PILLION
  (PACK —) BAT
  (STRAW —) SUNK SUGGAN
  (WITHOUT A —) ASELLATE
SADDLEBACK JACK JACKBIRD
SADDLEBAG ALFORJA CANTINA
  SUMPTER TEETSOOK
  (PL.) JAGS JAGGS
SADDLE BLANKET CORONA
SADDLEBOW BOW ARSON
SADDLECLOTH HOUSE NAMDA
  HOUSING PADCLOTH SHABRACK
SADDLEMAKER FUSTER KNACKER
SADDLE MAT FLET
SADDLEPAD PANEL PILLOW
SADDLER CODDER KNACKER
  LORIMER WHITTAW
SADISTIC SICK CRUEL SADIC
SADLY SAD UNWINLY
SADNESS DUMP RUTH DREAR
  DUMPS GLOOM GRIEF UNWIN
  SORROW
SAD SACK BOLO
SAFAWID SUFI
SAFE RUG CRIB PETE SURE WELL
  SALVA SIKER SOUND SECURE
  SICCAR HEALTHY SYKERLY
  COCKSURE SILVENDY
  (— FOR MEAT) KEEP
  (— TO DEAL WITH) CANNY
SAFEBLOWER PETEMAN
SAFEBREAKER YEGG YEGGMAN
SAFE-CONDUCT COWLE GRITH
  CONDUCT PASSPORT
SAFECRACKER BOXMAN PETEMAN
  PETERMAN TORCHMAN
SAFEGUARD SAVE WARD GUARD
  HEDGE SALVE DEFEND SAFETY
  SECURE BASTION BULWARK
  WARRANT FREEWARD
SAFEKEEPING CUSTODY STORAGE
SAFELY SAFE SICCAR SICKER
  SURELY SECURELY
SAFETY SALUTE SURETY WARRANT
  SECURITY

SAFETY ZONE ISLET ISLAND
  REFUGE
SAFFLOWER KUSUM ALAZOR
  SAFFRON
SAFFRON CROCUS AZAFRAN
  CROCEUS
SAFROLE SHIKIMOL
SAG BAG DIP TIE SWAG CREEP
  DROOP PLANK SLUMP SAGGON
  CURTAIN DEFLATE
SAGA EDDA EPIC MYTH TALE RIMUR
  LEGEND NJALSAGA
SAGACIOUS DEEP CANNY SHARP
  ARGUTE SHREWD CORDATE
  SAPIENT
SAGACITY POLICY WISDOM
  YEPHEDE SAPIENCE
SAGE RSI WARE WISE WITE CLARY
  IMLAC KATHA RISHI SABIO SOLON
  SOPHY ABARIS DHARMA SALVIA
  SAULGE SHREWD WIZARD EYESEED
  MAHATMA SAPIENT SOPHIST
  TOHUNGA WISEMAN DEVARSHI
  MAHARSHI WISEACRE
SAGEBRUSH SAGE HYSSOP
  SAGEWOOD
SAGENESS SAPIENCE
SAGGER COFFIN SETTER CASSETTE
SAGGING DRAG SWAG PTOSIS
SAGITTA ARROW
SAGITTARIUS ARCHER
SAGO PALM CYCAD
SAGRADA CASCARA
SAGUARO SUAHARO SUWARRO
  PITAHAYA
SAHIDIC THEBAIC
SAIBLING TORGOCH
SAID DIT QUOTH STATED RELATED
SAIL JIB LUG RAG BEAT GALE HAUL
  MAIN SCUN SLAT SWAN SWIM WING
  DANDY FLEET FLIER FLOAT FLYER
  JUMBO RAFFE SCALE SHEET
  ACCOST CANVAS COURSE CRUISE
  DRIVER JIGGER LATEEN MIZZEN
  MUSLIN SINGLE ARTEMON LUGSAIL
  SKYSAIL SPANKER SPENCER
  TRYSAIL BACKWIND FORESAIL
  GAFFSAIL HEADSAIL MAINSAIL
  MOONSAIL NAVIGATE RINGSAIL
  STAYSAIL STUNSAIL
  (— ALONG COAST) COAST ACCOST
  (— AROUND) TURN DOUBLE
  (— BRISKLY) SPANK
  (— BY THE WIND) STRETCH
  (— CLOSE TO WIND) PINCH
  (— DOWN) AVALE AWALE
  (— FASTER) FOOT
  (— IN SPECIFIED DIRECTION) STAND
  (— OF WINDMILL) ARM AWE EIE
  FAN VAN EIGHE FLIER FLYER
  SWEEP SWIFT
  (— ON COURSE) HAUL WORK
  (— QUIETLY) GHOST
  (— RAPIDLY) SCUR SKIRR
  (— SWIFTLY) RAMP
  (— TO WINDWARD) THRASH
  (— WITH WIND ABEAM) LASK
  (3-CORNERED —) JIB TRINKET
  (FRAGMENT OF —) HULLOCK

(LIGHT —) SHADOW
(LOWEST —) COURSE
(PART OF —) SLAB
(SMALL —) ROYAL
(TRIANGULAR —) RAFFE LATEEN
BENTINCK
(WIND —) BADGIR
(PL.) VELA KITES LINENS SAILAGE
CLOTHING
SAILBOAT SAIL SCOW BULLY DANDY
NABBY SAPIT SCOUT SHARP SKIFF
SLOOP SNIPE CANGIA DINGHY
QUODDY SAILER SATTIE CATBOAT
SCOOTER SHALLOP SHARPIE
KEELBOAT SAILSHIP SKIPJACK
(WITCH'S —) SIEVE
SAILFISH BOHO WOOHOO GUEBUCU
LONGJAW VOILIER VOLADOR
BILLFISH
SAILOR GOB TAR JACK TOTY GUARD
KLOSH LAKER LIMEY CALASH
CLASHY DAYMAN DECKIE HEARTY
MARINE MATLOW SEAMAN TARPOT
TIERER TOPMAN MARINAL MARINER
MATELOT SHIPMAN SWABBER
WARRIOR YARDMAN CANOTIER
COXSWAIN DECKHAND FLATFOOT
GALIONJI GUNLAYER LANDSMAN
LITHSMAN MASTHEAD SHIPMATE
WATERDOG WATERMAN WATERRUG
YARDSMAN
(EAST INDIAN —) LASCAR
(OLD —) SALT
(SCANDINAVIAN —) KLOSH
SAILORLIKE TARRISH
SAILOR'S-CHOICE BREAM PIGFISH
PINFISH WHITING
SAIL YARD RAE
SAINFOIN ESPARCET
SAINT PIR RSI DADU HOLY QUTB
WALI ALVAR ARHAT RISHI SANTO
BHAGAT HALLOW PATRON SANTON
CANONIZE MARABOUT
(CHINESE —) IMMORTAL
(PATRON —) AVOWRY
(PILLAR —) STYLITE
(PL.) SS
SAINT ELMO'S FIRE HERMO
CASTOR FUROLE HELENA
ST-JOHN'S-BREAD CAROB
ST-JOHN'S-WORT AMBER TUTSAN
CAMMOCK
SAINTLINESS HOLINESS SANCTITY
SAINTLY DEVOUT ANGELIC SAINTED
BEATIFIC SAINTISH
(— PERSON) ZADDIK
ST REGIS RANERE
SAJ SAIN
SAKE SAKI SCORE
SAKI BISA MONK COUXIA MONKEY
YARKEE
SALABLE VENAL SELLING SELLABLE
VENDIBLE
SALACIOUS LEWD SALT RUTTISH
SCARLET SCABROUS
SALAD SALLET COLESLAW
(CORN —) FETTICUS
SALADA SALINA
SALAL SHALLON

SALAMANDER OLM SOW BEAR
NEWT TWEEG GOPHER LIZARD
TRITON AXOLOTL CRAWLER
CREEPER DOGFISH MECODONT
SALAMICH SHADRACH
SAL AMMONIAC SPIRIT SALMIAC
SALARY PAY HIRE SCREW WAGES
INCOME PACKET PENSION STIPEND
SALE FAIR VENT BREAK HEDGE
TOUCH BOURSE VENDUE AUCTION
MOHATRA SELLING HANDSALE
KNOCKOUT PORTSALE
(— BY AUCTION) CANT BLOCK
(— BY OUTCRY) ROUP ROWP
HAMMER
(— OF OFFICE) BARRATRY
(— OF TOBACCO) BREAK
(PUBLIC —) AUCTION
(RUMMAGE —) JUMBLE
SALESMAN CLERK BAGMAN RUNNER
SELLER BOOKMAN DRUMMER
OUTRIDER
SALESMANSHIP SELLING
SALESPERSON CLERK
SALESWOMAN WINSTER SHOPGIRL
VENDEUSE
SALIENT SPUR BULGE CHIEF ARGINE
BASTION SALTANT
SALIENTIA ANURA ANOURA
ECAUDATA
SALINA SHOR SALINE
SALINE SALT SALAR SALTY MARINAL
SALIVA SPIT DROOL WATER DRIVEL
SLAVER SPUTUM SPITTLE
(— FLOW) PTYALISM
SALIVARY SIALIC
SALIVATION PTYALISM SLOBBERS
SALLET SALADE
SALLOW WAN SICK ADUST LURID
MUDDY SALIX SAUCH SAUGH PALLID
YELLOW
SALLY GRIP JERK PASS QUIP SAIL
QUICK START ESCAPE GAMBIT
SORTIE GAMBADE OUTFALL
OUTLEAP DEMARCHE
SALMON DOG LAX LOX SAM KETA
MASU PINK AMOUT COHOE COUNT
HADDO HOLIA SMOLT SMOOT
SPROD TECON ALEVIN BAGGIT
KIPPER LAUREL MYKISS SAMLET
SAUQUI SILVER TAIMEN ANADROM
ANNATTO BLUECAP BOTCHER
CHINOOK DOGFISH GILLING
KAHAWAI KOKANEE NEWFISH
REDFISH RUNFISH SAWMONT
SHEDDER SOCKEYE BLUEBACK
BRANDLIN GOLDFISH HUMPBACK
LASPRING SALMONID SPRINGER
(— AFTER SPAWNING) KELT
SHEDDER
(— BEFORE SPAWNING) GILLING
GIRLING
(— ENCLOSURE) YAIR
(— IN 2ND OR 3D YEAR) SMOLT
(— IN 2ND YEAR) SPROD HEPPER
GILLING
(— IN 3D YEAR) PUG MORT
(— ON FIRST RETURN FROM SEA)
GRILSE

(BLUEBACK —) NERKA SAUQUI
SOCKEYE
(CURED —) KIPPER
(DOG —) CHUM KETA
(FEMALE —) RAUN BAGGIT
(HUMPBACK —) HADDO HOLIA
(MALE —) GIB BUCK COCK
(MILTER —) EKE
(NEWLY HATCHED —) PINK ALEVIN
(SMALL —) PEAL SKIRLING
(SPENT —) JUDY SLAT RUNFISH
(YOUNG —) FOG PARR PEAL GRILSE
HEPPER JERKIN SAMLET BOTCHER
ESSLING SKEGGER LASPRING
SALMONELLOSIS KEEL
SALON HALL SALOON GALLERY
SALOON CAFE CUDDY DIVAN SALON
SHADE BARROOM CANTINA
RUMSHOP SCATTER DEADFALL
DRINKERY DRUNKERY EXCHANGE
SALPA SALP THALIA
SALSIFY GOATBEARD
SALT SAL CORN KERN SAWT BRINY
ZIRAM AMIDOL AURATE GAMMON
HALITE MALATE OLEATE OSMATE
POWDER SALINE URANIN KAINITE
LACTATE MALEATE NIOBATE
PHYTATE TROPATE ABIETATE
BRACKISH HALINOUS PIMELATE
PLUMBITE
(— OUT) CUT GRAIN
(DOUBLE —) ALUM
(HAIR —) ALUNOGEN
(LUMP OF —) SALTCAT
(METAL —) SILICATE
(MIXTURE OF —S) REH
(ROCK —) PIG HALITE
SALTATE JUMP
SALT BOILER WELLER
SALTBUSH BLUEBUSH
SALTCELLAR SALT CELLAR SELLER
SHAKER SALTFAT SALTFOOT
SALTED SALEE
SALTICID ATTID
SALT PAN PLAYA
SALTPETER NITER NITRE PETER
ANATRON PRUNELLA
SALT PIT VAT WICH WYCH
SALT PORK SOWBELLY
SALTWORKS SALINA SALTERN
SALTERY SALTPANS
SALTWORT KALI BARILLA SALSOLA
KELPWORT
SALTY SALT BRINY SALINE HALINOUS
SALUBRIOUS HEALTHY SALUTARY
SALUTARY GOOD BENIGN HEALTHY
HELPFUL BENEDICT
SALUTATION AVE HAIL ALOHA
SALUS MIZPAH SALAAM SALUTE
REGREET SLAINTE WELCOME
DIEUGARD GREETING HAEREMAI
(DRINKING —) SKOAL PROSIT
PROFACE
SALUTE CAP HAIL HEIL KISS MOVE
YULE CHEER DRINK GREET HALCH
HONOR SALUE SALVO COLORS
EMBRACE CONGREET
SALVADOR BAHIA

SALVAGE SAVE SALVE RECOVERY
SCROUNGE
SALVAGER SALVOR
SALVATION BODAI MOKSHA SAFETY
NIRVANA KAIVALYA SAVEMENT
SOULHEAL
(— **APPROACH**) MARGA
SALVE SAW TAR SALVO SAUVE
NERVAL SUPPLE PLASTER UNGUENT
OINTMENT
SALVER TRAY SERVER WAITER
PLATEAU
SALVIA CHIA SAGE CLARY
MEJORANA MINTWEED
SALVO SALUTE SPREAD PROVISO
TRIBUTE STRADDLE
(PL.) LADDER
SAMARA KEY CHAT
SAMARIA AHOLAH
SAMARITAN CUTHEAN CUTHITE
SAMBA CARIOCA
SAMBAR ELK MAHA RUSA
SAME A ID EAD ILK ONE IDEM LIKE
SELF VERY DITTO EQUAL SAMEN
IDENTIC SELFSAME
(— **AS**) IQ
(— **PLACE**) IB
(**THAT** —) THILK THICKE
SAMENESS ONENESS EQUALITY
IDENTITY MONOTONY
SAMNITES SABELLI
SAMOA (CAPITAL OF —) APIA
PAGOPAGO
(**COIN OF** —) TALA
(**ISLAND OF** —) OFU TAU ROSE
MANUA UPOLU SAVAII OLOSEGA
TUTUILA
(**MOUNTAIN OF** —) FITO SAVAII
MATAFAO
SAMOGITIAN ZHMUD
SAMOYED TUBA KOIBA YURAK
BELTIR KAIBAL NENTSI KAMASSIN
SAMPHIRE SALTWEED
SAMPLE DIP CAST PREE CHECK
ESSAY TASTE TRIAL CHANCE
COUPON FLOWER MUSTER SWATCH
TASTER EXAMPLE EXCERPT
PATTERN SAMPLER TASTING
INSTANCE PULLDOWN SPECIMEN
(— **OF METAL**) DIET
SAMPLING SOUNDING
SAMURAI BUSHI RONIN
SAN SAMPI
SANAD SUNNUD
SANBENITO SAMARRA
SAN BLAS TULE
SAN CARLOS ARIVAIPA
SANCTIFICATION HOLINESS
SANCTIFY SACRE SACRI DEDICATE
SANCTIMONIOUS DEVOUT
SANCTION AMEN FIAT ALLOW PIETY
ASSENT BISHOP RATIFY APPROVE
ENDORSE JUSTIFY PASSAGE
SUPPORT ACCREDIT APPROVAL
CANONIZE COURTESY SUFFRAGE
SANCTIONED CANONICAL
SANCTITY SANTY HALIDOME
HOLINESS
SANCTUARY ADYT BAST BEMA FANE

HOLY SOIL ABBEY ALTAR BAMAH
GIRTH GRITH SECOS SEKOS TOWER
ADYTON ADYTUM ASYLUM CHAPEL
HAIKAL REFUGE SENTRY SHRINE
SACRARY SHELTER CABIRION
DELUBRUM HALIDOME HOLINESS
(— **FOR LAWBREAKERS**) ALSATIA
SANCTUM ADYT ADYTON ADYTUM
SAND DIRT GRIT ARENA GRAIL
SONDE GRAVEL ISERINE ISERITE
PARTING ASBESTIC BLINDING
(— **FOR STREWING ON FLOORS**)
BREEZE
(— **HILL**) DENE DUNE
(— **IN KIDNEYS**) ARENA
(— **MIXED WITH GRAVEL**) GARD
DOBBIN
(— **ON SEA BOTTOM**) PAAR
(**BRAIN** —) SABULUM ACERVULUS
(**COLORED** —) SMALT
(**DEAUVILLE** —) STUCCO
SANDAL TIP BAXA FLAT SOCK
TEGUA CALIGA CHARUK PATTEN
TATBEB RULLION SCUFFER
FOOTHOLD GUARACHE HUARACHO
SANDAL TREE SANTOL
SANDALWOOD NAIO ALGUM ALMUG
MAIRE CHANDAM SAUNDERS
SANDALWOOD TREE ILIAHI
SANDARAC TREE ARAR LIGNUM
SANDBAG SANDCLUB
SAND BANK AIR CHAR MEAL SAND
BATCH HURST HYRST KNOCK SHELF
SHOAL
SANDBAR BALK LOOP SAND BARRA
SHOAL TOWHEAD
SANDBLASTER FROSTER BLASTMAN
SAND BORER SMELT
SANDBOX TREE ASSACU
SAND COLIC SABURRA
SAND DARTER SPECK
SAND DUNE TOWAN BARCHAN
SAND EEL GRIG SANDFISH
SANDEMANIAN GLASSITE
SANDERLING OXBIRD
SAND FLEA SCREW SCROW
SANDBOY
SAND-FLY BUSH TURMERIC
SAND GROUSE GANGA ROCKER
ATTAGEN PINTAIL
SAND HOLE BUNKER
SANDIVER NATRON
SAND LAUNCE LANT SMELT
WRIGGLE AMMODYTE SANDLING
SCRIGGLE
SAND LILY SOAPROOT
SANDMAN DUSTMAN
SANDPAPER TREE CHAPARRO
SANDPIPER JACK KNOT PEEP RUFF
STIB WEET OXEYE SNIPE STINT
TEREK TIPUP WADER DUNLIN
GAMBET OXBIRD PLOVER REDLEG
TEETER TILTER TILTUP TRINGA
BROWNIE CHOROOK CREEKER
FATBIRD FIDDLER HAYBIRD KRIEKER
MONGLER MONGREL REDBACK
TATTLER TIPTAIL GRAYBACK
LEADBACK PEETWEET ROCKBIRD
SANDPEEP SHADBIRD SQUATTER

SWEESWEE TELLTALE TRIDDLER
(**FEMALE** —) REEVE
(**FLOCK OF** —S) FLING
SAND PIT BUNKER
SAND ROCKET FLIXWEED
SAND SHARK BONEDOG
SANDSTONE FAKE FLAG GRES GRIT
SAND GAIZE HAZEL ARCOSE
ARKOSE ARENITE CARSTONE
COCONINO GANISTER PSAMMITE
RUBSTONE SANDROCK
(**BLOCK OF** —) SARSEN
SANDSTORM BURAN HABOOB
TEBBAD
SANDUST VANITY
SANDWICH BURGER GRINDER
WESTERN
SANDWORT LONGROOT SANDWEED
SANDY DEEP GRISTY SANDED
ARENOSE PSAMMOUS SABULINE
SABULOUS
SANE SAFE WISE LUCID RIGHT
FORMAL HEALTHY RATIONAL
SENSIBLE
SANGA-SANGA ESSANG
SANGUINARY GORY CRUEL BLOODY
CRIMSON SANGUINE
SANGUINE FOND GUZE MURREY
HEMATIC HOPEFUL SARDONYX
SANHEDRIN GEROUSIA
SANICLE ALLHEAL SELFHEAL
SANIOUS ICHOROUS
SANITARY HYGIENIC
SANITY SENSE REASON BALANCE
LUCIDITY SANENESS
SAN MARINO (CHURCH OF —) PIEVE
(**DISTRICTS OF** —) CASTELLI
(**MOUNTAIN OF** —) TITANO
(**SUBURB IN** —) BORGO
SANNUP SQUAW
SANSKRIT HINDU
(— **SOUND OR SIGN**) VISARGA
(— **WORK**) VEDANGA
SANS SERIF DORIC GOTHIC
SANTA MARIA TREE BIRMA GALBA
CALABA
SANTONICA WORMSEED
SAP GOON MINE OOZE RASA SEVE
HUMBO KEEST LYMPH SAPPER
WEAKEN ALVELOZ FLUXURE
SAPHEAD
(— **COURAGE**) DAUNT
(**PALM** —) TODY TODDY
(**POISONOUS** —) UPAS
(**SUGAR MAPLE** —) HUMBO
SAPAJOU SAJOU WARINE
SAPANWOOD BOKOM SIBUCAO
SAPEK DONG
SAPID SIPID FLAVORY
SAPIENT WISE SHREWD KNOWING
SAPLING SCOB PLANT SAPLE SPIRE
RUNNEL SPRING TILLER STADDLE
ASHPLANT SEEDLING SHILLALA
SPRINGER
(— **AMONG FELLED TREES**) WAVER
SAPODILLA GUM CHICA CHICO
DILLY ACHRAS MAMMEE SAPOTA
SAPOTE ZAPOTE NISPERO
NISBERRY

SAPONIFYING KILLING
SAPONIN GITONIN SENEGIN CYCLAMIN STRUTHIN
SAPONITE PIOTINE
SAPOTA MATASANO
SAPPHIRE SAFIR TOPAZ ADAMAS ASTRION HYACINTH
SAPPHIRINE GURNARD TUB
SAPPY FRIM FRUM SAPFUL
SAPSAP PEPEREK
SAPUCAIA COCO COCOA KAKARAL
SAPWOOD SAP BLEA SPLENT SPLINT GUAYABI LISTING ALBURNUM
SARA (— WOMAN) UBANGI
SARABAITES REMOBOTH
SARACEN CORSAIR
SARAH ATOSSA
SARAKOLLE WAKORE
SARASVATI VAC VACH BENTEN
SARCASM RUB GIBE WIPE FLING IRONY TAUNT RUBBER SATIRE BROCARD RIDICULE SCORCHER
SARCASTIC ACID WITTY BITING IRONIC ACERBIC CUTTING MORDANT INCISIVE SARDONIC SATIRICAL
SARCASTICALLY DRILY DRYLY ACIDLY
SARCOCARP FLESH
SARCOPHAGUS TOMB COFFIN
SARCOPSYLLA TUNGA
SARDINE BANG LOUR SARD SILD CLUPEID PILCHARD SARDELLE

SARDINIA
CHEESE: ROMANO PECORINO
COIN: CARLINE
GREEK COLONY: OLBIA
GULF: OROSEI ASINARA CAGLIARI ORISTANO
MOUNTAIN: RASU FERRY LINAS GALLURA LIMBARA SERPEDDI VITTORIA
NAME: SARDEGNA
PROVINCE: NUORO SASSARI CAGLIARI
RIVER: MANNU TIRSO LASCIA COGHINAS
TOWN: NUORO SASSARI THATARI CAGLIARI IGLESIAS

SARGASSUM GULFWEED
SARGO ZEBRA
SARI PATOLA TAMEIN
SARONG PAU KAIN COMBOY KIKEPA
SARSAPARILLA NUNNARI SHOTBUSH
SASH BAR BELT BENN FAJA GATE TOBE SCARF TAPIS TOWEL FASCIA GIRDLE BURDASH CHASSIS TUBBECK CASEMENT CORSELET
(JAPANESE —) OBI
(WINDOW —) CHESS
SASHAY CHASSE
SASH BAR MUNTIN ASTRAGAL
SASSABY TSESSEBE
SASSAFRAS FILE SALOP SALOOP SAXIFRAX
SASSY KICKY
SATAN ANGEL DEVIL EBLIS FIEND

SHREW BELIAL LUCIFER SATANAS DIABOLUS SATANAEL
SATANIC SABLE INFERNAL
SATCHEL HANDBAG KEESTER
SATE GLUT SATIATE SATISFY SATURATE
SATED SAD BLASE
SATEEN VENETIAN
SATELLITE MOON ARIEL LUNET DEIMOS MOONET OBERON PHOBOS ACOLYTE ACOLYTH LUNETTE ORBITER SPUTNIK TRABANT UMBRIEL COURTIER FOLLOWER
(— OF JUPITER) IO EUROPA CALLISTO GANYMEDE
(— OF SATURN) RHEA DIONE MIMAS TITAN PHOEBE TETHYS IAPETUS JAPETUS HYPERION
SATIATE CLOY FILL GLUT PALL QUAT SADE SATE FLESH GORGE SERVE STALL ENGLUT STODGE RASSASY SATISFY SURFEIT SATURATE
SATIATED SICK JADED SATED
SATIATING STODGY FULSOME
SATIETY FULNESS SURFEIT CLOYMENT
SATIN SAY ATLAS CYPRUS MUSHRU COOTHAY CYPRESS SATINET
(SILK —) DUCHESS
SATINFLOWER SAFFRON
SATINPOD HONESTY LUNARIA
SATINWOOD HAREWOOD
SATIRE WIT GRIND IRONY IAMBIC LAMPOON SARCASM SOTADIC RIDICULE
SATIRIC BITTER IRONIC ABUSIVE CAUSTIC CUTTING POIGNANT SLASHING
SATIRIST GRIND SATIRE JUVENAL PASQUIN
SATIRIZE SKIN SKIT GRIND EXPOSE IAMBIZE LAMPOON PASQUIN
SATISFACTION CRO FIN PAY UTU EASE GREE BELLY ENACH TREAT AMENDS ASSETH REASON COMFORT CONTENT DELIGHT GLADNESS PLEASURE
SATISFACTORILY SPROWSY CLEVERLY
SATISFACTORY FAIR GOOD WELL DUCKY HUNKY CLEVER DECENT ADEQUATE LAUDABLE
SATISFIED SAD FAIN FULL GLAD PAID VAIN APAID CHUFF PROUD ASSURED CONTENT GRUNTLED SENSIBLE WILCWEME
SATISFY PAY EVEN FEED FILL MEET SAIR SATE SUIT ADEEM APPAY QUEME SERVE SLAKE SPEED ANSWER DEFRAY PLEASE STODGE SUPPLY ASSUAGE CONTENT EXPLETE FULFILL GRATIFY GRUNTLE RESPOND SATIATE STAUNCH SUFFICE SATURATE
(— APPETITE) STAY
(— BY PROOF) CONVINCE
(— NEEDS) DO ADJUST
SATISFYING DUE AMPLE SQUARE PERFECT

SATURATE SOG GLUT SATE SOAK DRAWK IMBUE SOUSE STEEP DRENCH IMBIBE SEETHE SODDEN DRUNKEN INGRAIN SATIATE SLOCKEN
(— WITH SYRUP) CANDY
SATURATED SOBBY SOGGY SOPPY SODDEN SPONGY DRUNKEN
SATURATION CHROMA PURITY SATURITY
SATURN: (FATHER OF —) URANUS
(MOTHER OF —) GAEA
(SATELLITE OF —) RHEA DIONE MIMAS TITAN TETHYS JAPETUS HYPERION ENCELADUS
(SON OF —) JUPITER
SATURNINE SULLEN SATANIC
SATYAGRAHA GANDHISM
SATYR FAUN SAUMON SALTIER WOODMAN WOODWOSE
SATYRIASIS TENTIGO
SAUCE MOLE SASS SOWL BERCY CHILE CHILI CREAM CREME CURRY GRAVY PESTO CATSUP GANSEL MORNAY ROBERT KETCHUP MARENGO SOUBISE SUPREME TABASCO VELOUTE BECHAMEL CHAWDRON DRESSING DUXELLES MATELOTE POIVRADE RAVIGOTE REMOLADE
(CURRY —) SAMBAL
(FISH —) ALEC BAGOONG
(SALAD —) DRESSING
(SAVORY —) DIP
(THICK —) LEAR
SAUCEDISH SAUCER BIRDBATH
SAUCEPAN GOBLET POSNET SKILLET STEWPAN
SAUCER BIRD PATERA PHIALE CAPSULE
SAUCINESS SAUCE DICACITY
SAUCY BOG ARCH BOLD COXY BRASH DONSY DORTY FRESH LIPPY PAWKY POKEY SASSY SMART BANTAM COCKET COPPED CROUSE THWART FORWARD PAUGHTY MALAPERT PETULANT SANSHACH
SAUDI ARABIA: (CAPITAL OF —) JIDDAH RIYADH
(COIN OF —) RIYAL
(DESERT REGION OF —) NEFUD DAHANA ALNAFUD
(PLATEAU OF —) NEJD
(TOWN OF —) HAIL MECCA MEDINA ALHOFUF
(WEIGHT OF —) OKE
SAUNTER IDLE ROAM ROVE TOIT AMBLE RANGE SHOOL SIDLE STRAY TRAIK BUMMEL DACKER DANDER FAFFLE LINGER LOITER LOUNGE POTTER PUTTER RAMBLE SOODLE STREEL STROLL TODDLE WANDER SNAFFLE STAIVER STRAVAGE
SAURA MAGA
SAUREL SCAD XUREL GASCON BLUEFISH SKIPJACK
SAURY LONGJAW SKIPPER BILLFISH GOWDNOOK SKIPJACK
SAUSAGE POT LINK COPPA GIGOT

BOUDIN POLONY SALAMI BOLOGNA
BOLONEY CHORIZO PUDDING
SAVELOY BLACKPOT CERVELAT
DRISHEEN KIELBASA LIVERING
ROLLICHE
(KIND OF —) METT
SAUTE PANFRY
SAUTERNE YQUEM
SAVAGE ILL FELL GRIM RUDE WILD
BRUTE CRUEL EAGER FELON FERAL
STERN FIERCE GOTHIC BRUTISH
FERVENT HOWLING INHUMAN
MANKEEN MANKIND ROPABLE
UNCIVIL VIOLENT WILROUN
CANNIBAL PITILESS THEREOID
WARRAGAL
SAVAGELY FELLY UNMANLY
SAVAGERY FURY FEROCITY
SAVANNA CAMPO SABANA
(— LANDS) LALANG
SAVANT ARTIST VIRTUOSO
SAVE BAR WIN HAIN HELP KEEP
SAFE STOP SALVE SPARE SPELL
DEFEND EXCEPT RESCUE SAVING
SCRIMP DELIVER HUSBAND
SALVAGE WARRANT CONSERVE
PRESERVE
SAVIN HEATH SABINE JUNIPER
SAVING FRUGAL THRIFT ECONOMY
SPARING THRIFTY
SAVINGS FAT ADDLINGS
(— CLUB) MENAGE
SAVIOR LORD SAVER SOTER
REDEEMER
SAVOR EDGE SALT SAPOR SMACK
TASTE DEGUST FLAVOR RELISH
RESENT SAVOUR SEASON TASTEN
SAPIDITY
SAVORLESS FOND INSIPID
SAVORY GUSTY MERRY SAPID
TASTY DAINTY SMERVY GUSTFUL
GUSTABLE TASTEFUL
SAVVY SABE
SAW SAG SEY WEB BUCK REDE
ADAGE FREIT GNOME SCEAR SPOKE
JIGSAW PITSAW RIPSAW SAYING
SCRIBE BACKSAW BUCKSAW
CONVERT DRAGSAW FRETSAW
HACKSAW HANDSAW HEADRIG
HEADSAW PROVERB SLABBER
WHIPSAW CROSSCUT SENTENCE
(— INTO LOGS) BUCK
(— LENGTHWISE OF GRAIN) RIP
(— OF SAWFISH) SERRA
(— WITH TWO BLADES) STADDA
(CIRCULAR —) BUR BURR EDGER
DAPPER TRIMMER
(CROSSCUT —) BRIAR
(CYLINDER —) CROWN TREPAN
TREPHINE
SAWAN SRABAN SHRAVAN
SAWDUST COOM COOMB SAWINGS
SAW FERN DYGAL BUNGWALL
HARDFERN
SAWFISH RAY BATOID COMBFISH
SAWFLY CEPHID
SAW GATE FRAME
SAWHORSE BUCK JACK SETTER
SAWBUCK TRESTLE

SAW KERF SKAFF
SAWMILL RASPER
(— DEVICE) KICKER
(— WORKER) PONDMAN LEVERMAN
SAWYER WETA SAWER PITMAN
TOPMAN KNOTTER
SAXHORN ALTO TUBA ALTHORN
SAXTUBA BARITONE BARYTONE
SAXIFRAGE BAUERA BENNET SESELI
ASTILBE ROCKFOIL SELFHEAL
SENGREEN
SAXONIAN MINDEL
SAXOPHONE SAX ALTO TENOR
SOPRANINO
SAY DEED MEAN MOVE TAKE TELL
SPEAK SPELL AUTHOR QUETHE
RELATE REMARK SAYING REHEARSE
(— A BLESSING) BENSH
(— FOOLISHLY) BLABBER
(— FURTHER) ADD
(— GLIBLY) SCREED
(— NO TO) NAIT NICK
(— OVER AGAIN) REPEAT
(— SPITEFUL THINGS) BACKBITE
(— TOO MUCH) OVERSAY
(— UNDER OATH) DEPOSE
SAYING DIT SAW SAY DICT ITEM
REDE TEXT WORD ADAGE AXIOM
CHRIA DITTY FREIT MAXIM SPEAK
BALLAD BYWORD DICTUM DIVERB
LOGION DICTION PROVERB
APOTHEGM SENTENCE SPEAKING
(— LITTLE) DUMB
(—S OF JESUS) AGRAPHA
(—S OF RELIGIOUS TEACHER)
LOGIA
(CLEVER —) QUIP
(CURRENT —) DICTUM
(OBSCURE —) ENIGMA
(QUICK —) JERK
(TERSE —) EPIGRAM
(TRUE —) SOOTHSAW
(WISE —) SCHOLIUM
(WITTY —) MOT SALLY DICTERY
WITNESS
(WITTY —S) FACETIAE
SCAB RAT ROIN SHAB SNOB CRUST
CANKER ESCHAR RATTER GREENER
RUBBERS BLACKLEG BLACKNEB
SCABBARD CHAPE SHEATH PILCHER
SCABBARD FISH HIKU
SCABBLE SCAB SCALP
SCABBY MANGY SCALD ROINISH
SCABIOUS
SCABIES ITCH SCAB PSORA
SCABIOSA KNAUTIA
SCABIOUS SCABIA BLUECAP
BUNDWEED PREMORSE
SCABROUS SULTRY ASPEROUS
SCAD AKULE XUREL GOGGLER
QUIAQUIA
SCAFFOLD CAGE PEGMA STAGE
BRIDGE CATASTA HAYLOFT
STAGING HOARDING
SCAFFOLDING DOCK STAGING
SCALD BURN LEEP PLOT SCAD
BLAST PLOUT SCAUD BLANCH
SCALDER
SCALE LEAF PELA STEP TAPE CLIMB

FLAKE GAMUT GENUS GULAR PALEA
PELOG PELOK PELTA POISE SCUTE
SHALE SHARD SHELL SHERD SHIVE
TRUNK ASCEND CAUDAL CINDER
COCCID FORNIX GUNTER IMBREX
KELVIN LABIAL LADDER LAMINA
LIGULE LOREAL MENTAL OCULAR
PERULE RAMENT RONDLE RUSTRE
SHIELD SQUAMA STRIGA BALANCE
CLINKER ELYTRON FRONTAL
FULCRUM HUMERAL LATERAL
NUCHALE REAUMUR ROSTRUM
VENTRAL VERNIER ANALEMMA
BRACHIAL LECANIUM LODICULE
MEALYBUG ODOPHONE RAMENTUM
SCRAMBLE SQUAMULE TEMPORAL
UROSTEGE
(— DOWN) DEGRADE
(— OF 7 TONES) SEPTAVE
(— OF CORNSTALK) SHIVE
(— USED BY TAILORS) LOG
(GRADUATED —) RETE
(GREAT —) GAMUT
(SHAD —) CENIZO
(PL.) CHAFF DANDER
SCALEBOARD SCABBARD
SCALEPAN BASIN
SCALER CULLER SOOTER
SCALES TRON TRONE BALANCE
SCALETAIL SQUIRREL
SCALLION PORRET
SCALLOP CRENA QUEEN SQUIN
PECTEN COQUILLE DOUGHBOY
ESCALLOP PECTINID
SCALLOPED INVECTED
SCALP SCAUP SKELP ATTIRE
SCALPER PUNTER
SCALY SCABBY SQUAMY LEPROSE
PALEATE LEPIDOTE SCABROUS
SQUAMOSE
SCAMP LAD RIP LIMB SLIM ROGUE
SKEMP SKIMP THIEF BOOGER
BUGGER NICKUM SINNER SORREL
SORROW HALLION HESSIAN
PEASANT RAMMACK SCUBBER
SKELLUM SNOOZER SCALAWAG
SLYBOOTS SPALPEEN VAGABOND
WIDDIFOW
SCAMPER CHEVY SCOUP CHIVVY
BRATTLE SKITHER SKITTER
SCAN PIPE GLASS METER DEVISE
SURVEY EXAMINE
SCANDAL GUP CLASH CRACK ECLAT
SHAME CALUMNY SCANMAG
SLANDER
SCANDALIZE SHOCK
SCANDALMONGER CLAT
SCANDALOUS UNHOLY SHAMEFUL
SCANDINAVIAN DANE LAPP NORSE
SWEDE VIKING LOCHLIN NORSEMAN
NORTHMAN SCANDIAN VARANGIAN
(PL.) OSTMEN
SCANT SHY JIMP LEAN MEET POOR
SCAMP SHORT SKIMP SPLAY
BARISH GEASON LITTLE SCANTY
SKINNY STINGY STINTY SLENDER
SCRATCHY
SCANTILY BARELY FEEBLY SMALLY
SCANTLY SPARSELY

SCANTINESS PENURY PARCITY
EXIGUITY SPARSITY
SCANTLING STUD FILET JOIST
FILLET BOLSTER RIBBAND
STUDDING
SCANTY BARE JIMP LANK LEAN
POOR SLIM EXILE GNEDE SCANT
SHORT SILLY SKIMP SPARE FRUGAL
MEAGER SCRIMP SKIMPY SLIGHT
SPARSE SCRANNY SCRIMPY
SLENDER SPARING EXIGUOUS
SCAPOLITE DIPYRE
SCAPULA BLADE OMOPLATE
SCAPULAR CUCULLA
SCAR ARR EYE WEM SEAM SEAR
CHALK FESTER KELOID RADDLE
STIGMA TRENCH CHELOID SCARIFY
CICATRIX SMALLPOX CICATRICE
(— **ON SAWED STONE**) STUN
(— **ON SEED**) HILUM
(— **ON TREE**) CATFACE
SCARAB ATEUCHES
SCARCE DEAR RARE THIN SLACK
DAINTY GEASON CLASSIC
UNCOMMON
SCARCELY ILL VIX JIMP SCANT
BARELY HARDLY MERELY ONETHE
SCARCE SCRIMP WENETH SCANTLY
UNEATHS UNNETHE
SCARCITY LACK WANT FAULT
SCANT DEARTH FAMINE RARITY
PAUCITY
SCARE COW BOOF BREE FAZE FEAR
FLEG FLIG FRAY GAST HUSH SHOO
ALARM GLIFF GLOFF SPOOK
AFFRAY FRIGHT GASTER SCARIFY
STARTLE TERRIFY AFFRIGHT
FRIGHTEN
(— **BIRDS**) KEEP
SCARECROW BOGLE BUCCA MOGGY
BOGGLE DUDMAN MALKIN MAUMET
MAWKIN SCARER SHEWEL BOGGART
BUGABOO DEADMAN HODMADOD
SHAWFOWL
SCARED SCART SCARY AFRAID
GOOSEY STREAKED
SCAREMONGER ALARMIST
SCARF BARB HOOD SASH ABNET
ASCOT BARBE CLOUD CYMAR FICHU
LUNGI NUBIA SHADE STOCK STOLE
TABLE THROW CRAVAT REBOZO
SCREEN SQUARE TAPALO TIPPET
UPARNA BURDASH DOPATTA
FOULARD MUFFLER NECKTIE
OVERLAY PUGGREE SAUTOIR
TALLITH CLAUDENT COINTISE
LIRIPIPE LIRIPOOP MANTILLA
MUFFETEE SLENDANG
(— **ON KNIGHT'S HELMET**) COINTISE
(**ARABIAN** —) CABAAN
(**FEATHER** —) BOA
(**PRAYER** —) TALLIS TALLITH
SCARFING GRAFTING
SCARIFY LIFT
SCARLET LAC RED PINK TULY GRAIN
KERMES
SCARLET HAW HAWTHORN
SCARLET IBIS GUARA
SCARLET LYCHNIS FIREBALL
NONESUCH

SCARLET TANAGER REDBIRD
FIREBIRD
SCARLIKE ULOID
SCARP CLIFF SCARF ESCARP
SCARPLET
SCATHING MORDANT SCALDING
SCATHINGLY ROUNDLY
SCATOLOGICAL BARNYARD
SCATTER DAD SOW TED FLEE SALT
SCAT SEED SHED SPEW VOID FLING
SCALE SCHAL SEVER SHAKE SPRAY
STREW STROW DISPEL SHOWER
SKIVER SPARSE SPREAD SPRENG
WINNOW DIFFUSE DISBAND DISJECT
FRITTER RESOLVE SCAMBLE
SHATTER SKINKLE SKITTER
SLATTER SPARKLE SPARPLE
SPATTER SWATTER DISPERSE
INTERSOW SEPARATE SPLUTTER
SPRINKLE SQUANDER SQUATTER
(— **BAIT FOR FISH**) TOLE TOLL
(— **OVER**) BESTREW
(— **WATER**) SPLASH
SCATTERED LAX OPEN STRAY
DAIMEN SPARSE DIFFUSE SPOTTED
FUGITIVE SPARSILE
SCATTERING SOWING DIASPORA
SCATTERY
SCAUP DUCK DOGS DIVER DUCKER
DUNBIRD POCHARD BLUEBILL
GRAYBACK SHUFFLER
SCAVAGE SCEWING
SCAVENGE CLEANSE GARBAGE
SCAVENGER BUNGY BHANGI
BHUNGI MEHTAR REMOVER SCAFFIE
CORYDORA HALALCOR
SCAZON CHOLIAMB
SCEAT SKEAT STYCA
SCENE JOG SET CODA CYKE FLAT
SITE VIEW ARENA STAGE BRIDGE
VISION EPISODE PAGEANT COULISSE
EXTERIOR INTERIOR PROSPECT
TABLETOP
(— **IN OPERA**) SCENA
(— **OF ACTION**) STAGE
(— **OF ACTIVITY**) BEEHIVE
(— **OF CONFUSION**) BABEL BEDLAM
(**CLOSING** —) FINALE
(**FINAL** —) CURTAIN EPILOGUE
SCENERY DROP FLAT DECOR
CUTOUT IMAGERY PROFILE
(**PIECE OF** —) MASKING
SCENESHIFTER GRIP
SCENT AIR DRAG NOSE ODOR VENT
WIND CIVET FAULT FLAIR RELES
SAVOR SMACK SMELL SNIFF SNUFF
SPOOR TASTE ESSENCE INCENSE
NOSEGAY ODORIZE VERDURE
FUMIGATE MARECHAL PASTILLE
(— **OF ANIMAL FOLLOWED BY
HOUNDS**) FEUTE
(— **OF COOKING**) NIDOR
(— **OF FOX**) DRAG
(**FALSE** —) RIOT
(**LOST** —) FAULT
SCENTED OLENT ODORATE
PERFUMY ESSENCED
SCEPTER ROD WAND VERGE
BAUBLE CEPTER FERULA WARDER

SCHEDULE BOOK CARD HOLD LIST
SKED TIME PANEL SCRIP SCROW
SETUP SLATE TABLE SCROLL
CATALOG TABLEAU CALENDAR
REGISTER
(— **OF DUTIES**) TARIFF
(— **OF GAMES**) SEASON
SCHEDULED DUE
SCHEELITE TUNGSTEN
SCHEMA FORM
SCHEME AIM GIN LAY WAY WEB
CAST DART GAME PLAN PLAT PLOT
REDE SWIM ANGLE BABEL CADRE
DODGE DRAFT DRIFT KNACK PINAX
REACH SCALE SETUP SHIFT TABLE
THINK TRAIN BRIGUE BUBBLE
CIPHER DESIGN DEVICE DEVISE
FIGURE HOOKUP POLICY SCHEMA
SYSTEM TAMPER THEORY UTOPIA
COUNSEL DRAUGHT GIMMICK
IMAGINE KNAVERY NOSTRUM
PROJECT PURPOSE CONTRIVE
FORECAST GIMCRACK IDEOLOGY
INTRIGUE MANEUVER PLATFORM
PRACTICE TRIPOTER WINDMILL
(— **OF RANK**) LADDER
(**BETTING** —) SYSTEM
(**DECEITFUL** —) SHIFT
(**DELUSIVE** —) BUBBLE
(**DIAGRAMMATIC** —) PINAX
(**FANCIFUL** —) WINDMILL
(**FAVORITE** —) NOSTRUM
(**VISIONARY** —) BABEL
SCHEMER ARTIST DESIGNER
ENGINEER SCHEMIST SLEEVEEN
SCHEMING SCHEMY PLANFUL
SPIDERY FETCHING PRACTICE
SCHISM RENT SCISSION SCISSURE
SCHISMATIC HERETIC
SCHIST RAG AMPELITE MICACITE
MYLONITE OLLENITE PHYLLITE
SCHIZONT MONONT AGAMONT
SCHIZOPHRENIA CATATONY
SCHNAPPER WOLLOMAI
SCHOLAR TUG DEMY GAON IMAM
CLERK PUPIL DIVINE DOCTOR
FELLOW JURIST LAMDEN MASTER
PANDIT SABORA SAVANT SCOLOG
SHEIKH BIBLIST BOOKMAN DANTIST
LATINER LEARNER MAULANA
STUDENT DISCIPLE HEBRAEAN
HUMANIST ISLAMIST MASORITE
TABERDAR THAUMASTE
SCHOLARLY CLERKLY ACADEMIC
SCHOLARSHIP ART BOOK BURSE
BURSARY DEMYSHIP LEARNING
SCHOOL GAM TOL EDDY PREP
AGGIE BOOKS ECOLE HEDER MYAYA
SAKHA TEACH TRADE TRAIN TUTOR
ALJAMA CAMPUS CHEDER CHURCH
KUTTAB KYAUNG MADHAB MALIKI
RABFAK SCHOLA SCHULE SQUEEL
TRIPOS ACADEME ACADEMY
CRAMMER MADRASA PENSION
STUDIUM YESHIVA AUDITORY
DOCUMENT EXERCISE EXTERNAT
PEDAGOGY SEMINARY
(— **FOR SINGERS**) MAITRISE
(— **OF BLACKFISH**) GRIND

(— OF BUDDHISM) CHAN DHYANA SANRON
(— OF FISH) HERD SCALE
(— OF HINDU PHILOSOPHY) NYAYA
(— OF PAINTING) GENRE
(— OF PHILOSOPHY) SECT ACADEMY AUDITORY
(— OF VEDA) SAKHA SHAKHA
(— OF WHALES) GAM POD
(ART —) LUMINISM
(AZTEC —) CALMECAC
(COMPARATIVE —) FOLKLORE
(DAY —) EXTERNAT
(ELEMENTARY —) GRADES
(HIGH —) HIGH ACADEMY COLLEGE
(MOSLEM —) HANAFI KUTTAB SHAFII HANBALI
(REFORM —) BORSTAL
(RELIGIOUS —) ALJAMA YESHIVA
(RIDING —) MANEGE
(SANSKRIT —) TOL
(SCOTCH —) SQUEEL
(SECONDARY —) LYCEE LYCEUM COLEGIO
(WRESTLING —) PALESTRA
SCHOOLBOOK COCKER
SCHOOLBOY SCUG PETTY CLERGION
SCHOOLHOUSE PORTABLE
SCHOOLING LEARNING
SCHOOLMASTER CAJI CAXI AKHUN KHOJA KHODJA MASTER PEDANT AKHOOND DOMINIE PEDAGOG ORBILIUS
SCHOOLROOM HOMEROOM
SCHOOL SHARK TOPE TOPER
SCHOOLWORK BOOKWORK
SCHOONER JACK TERN QUART QUINT WUINT PUNGEY BALLAHOO
SCHORL COCKLE
SCHRADAN OMPA
SCHROTHER SHREDDER
SCHUYT SHOE SCOUT EELBOAT
SCIATICA BONESHAW
SCIENCE ART OLOGY SOPHY MATHESIS SCIENTIA
(— OF ALGAE) ALGOLOGY
(— OF ANIMALS) ZOOLOGY
(— OF AQUEOUS VAPOR) ATMOLOGY
(— OF ATOMS) ATOMICS
(— OF BEING OR REALITY) ONTOLOGY
(— OF BIOLOGICAL STATISTICS) BIOMETRY
(— OF BREEDING) GENETICS
(— OF CAUSES) ETIOLOGY
(— OF CHARACTER) ETHOLOGY
(— OF CLASSIFICATION OF DISEASES) NOSOLOGY
(— OF DOSES) DOSOLOGY POSOLOGY
(— OF EARTH'S FORMATION) GEOGONY
(— OF EXCHANGE) CAMBISTRY
(— OF FERMENTATION) ZYMOLOGY
(— OF FORMS OF SPEECH) GRAMMAR
(— OF FRUIT GROWING) POMOLOGY

(— OF FUNDS MANAGEMENT) FINANCE
(— OF GEMS) GEMMARY GEMOLOGY
(— OF GOD) DIVINITY
(— OF GOVERNMENT) POLITICS
(— OF HEALTH MAINTENANCE) HYGIENE
(— OF HEAT) PYROLOGY
(— OF HISTORY OF EARTH) GEOLOGY
(— OF IDEAS) IDEOLOGY
(— OF LAW) NOMOLOGY
(— OF LIFE INFLUENCES) EUGENICS
(— OF LIFE OF TREES) SILVICS
(— OF LIFE) BIOLOGY
(— OF LIGHT) OPTICS
(— OF MEASURING TIME) HOROLOGY
(— OF MEDIEVAL CHEMISTRY) ALCHEMY
(— OF MIDWIFERY) TOKOLOGY
(— OF MORAL DUTY) ETHICS
(— OF MOSSES) BRYOLOGY
(— OF MOUNTAINS) OROLOGY
(— OF MUSCLES) MYOLOGY
(— OF NUMBERS COMBINATIONS) ALGEBRA
(— OF PERSUADING A GOD) THEURGY
(— OF PLANTS) BOTANY
(— OF RACIAL IMPROVEMENT) EUGENICS
(— OF REASONING) LOGIC
(— OF RECORDING GENEALOGIES) HERALDRY
(— OF REFRIGERATION) CRYOLOGY
(— OF REMEDIES) ACOLOGY
(— OF SERUMS) SEROLOGY
(— OF SOUND) PHONICS ACOUSTICS
(— OF SPATIAL MAGNITUDES) GEOMETRY
(— OF STRUCTURE OF ANIMALS) ANATOMY
(— OF THE EAR) OTOLOGY
(— OF TIDES) TIDOLOGY
(— OF VERSIFICATION) PROSODY
(— OF VIRTUE) ARETAICS
(— OF WEIGHT OR GRAVITY) BAROLOGY
(— OF WINES) ENOLOGY OENOLOGY
(LEGAL —) LAW
(MILITARY —) STRATEGY
(NATURAL —) STINKS PHYSICS
(RELIGIOUS —) THEOLOGY
SCIMITAR SAX SEAX TURK KHEPESH TULWAUR
SCINDAPSUS POTHOS
SCINTILLATE SNAP FLASH GLEAM GLANCE GLITTER SPARKLE TWINKLE
SCINTILLATION SPARKLE SPARKLET
SCION IMP ROD CION CYON ROOT SLIP GRAFT SPRIG BRANCH SPROUT SARMENT SETLING
SCISSORS SHEARS CLIPPER SECATEUR
SCLERITE TORMA LABIUM PLANTA PLAGULA AXILLARY EPIMERON

SCLERODERMA MORPHEA
SCLEROPROTEIN SPONGIN
SCLEROTIUM ERGOT SCLEROTE TUCKAHOE
SCOFF DOR GAB GALL GIBE GIRD JEER JIBE MOCK RAIL CURSE FLEER FLOUT GLEEK SCORN SCOUT SNEER TAUNT DERIDE REPROVE RIDICULE
SCOFFER MOCKER ABDERITE
SCOLD JAW MAG MOB NAG RAG ROW WIG YAP BAWL CALL CAMP CANT DING FRAB FUSS HAZE JACK JOBE JOWL JUMP RAIL RANT RATE REDD RICK SHAW SNAG SNUB TUCK YAFF ABUSE BARGE BASTE BOAST CHIDE DRESS FLIRT FLITE PRATE SCALD SCORE SHORE SHREW SLANG TARGE VIXEN BERATE BOUNCE CALLET CAMPLE CARPET HAMMER HOORAY HURRAH MAGPIE RATTLE REHETE REVILE TATTER THREAP TONGUE YAFFLE CHANNER REPROVE TRIMMER TROUNCE BALLYRAG BERATTLE CHASTISE CIDESTER DINGDONG LIPBRAID RIXATRIX
SCOLDING JAW HURL JESSE SCOLD DIRDUM JAWING RAKING RATTLE SISERA FLITING HEARING LECTURE RAGGING WIGGING BLESSING CARRITCH JOBATION
SCOLEX HEAD
SCOLYTUS IPS
SCONCE SWAPE APPLIQUE
SCONE FARL FARLE
SCOOP BAIL DRAG ROUT DIDLE GOUGE KEACH SHAUL SKEET BUCKET DIPPER DISHER SHOVEL WIMBLE SCRAPER SKIMMER SKIPPET SCOOPFUL
(— FOR CANNON) LADLE
(— FOR DAMPENING CANVAS) SKEET
(— FOR GRAIN) WECHT
(— UP) LAP LAVE GATHER
(CHEESE —) PALE
(JAI ALAI —) CHISTERA
(LONG-HANDLED —) DIDLE
(SURGICAL —) CURET CURETTE
SCOOT SCOUT SKEET SKYHOOT
SCOPE AREA AMBIT RANGE REACH SCOOP SWEEP VERGE SCOUTH SPHERE TETHER BREADTH CIRCUIT OPERAND PURVIEW CONFINES DIAPASON LATITUDE
(— OF VISION) COMMAND
(FREE —) SWING
SCOPOLINE OSCIN OSCINE
SCORCH BURN CHAR PLOT SCAM SEAR ADURE ADUST PARCH PLAUT REESE SCALD SCAUM SINGE SWEAL SWELT BIRSLE BISHOP DEGREE SMITCH SOTTER SPARCH SWINGE SWITHE BLISTER BRISTLE FRIZZLE SCORKLE SCOWDER SWITHEN SWITHER TORRIFY FIREFANG SCOWTHER
SCORCHED ADUST LEEPIT
SCORCHER SIZZLER

SCORCHING BAKING FIRING ADURENT SCALDING

SCORE ACE CUT RUN CARD DROP GAME GOAL HOLE MAKE MARK NICK POST RIDE SLOG CHASE CORGE COUNT EXTRA NOTCH OPERA TALLY COOREE FURROW SAFETY SCOTCH SCRIVE SPADES STRING TARGET TICKET TWENTY CONVERT SCORING SCRATCH SQUEEZE GAMEBALL PARTITUR

(— FOR ALE) ALESHOT

(— IN BRIDGE) BOARD BONUS SWING

(— IN CRIBBAGE) GO PEG FIFTEEN

(— IN CRICKET) BLOB CENTURY

(— OF NOTHING) DUCK

(APTITUDE —) STANINE

(BASKETBALL —) HOOP

(BOWLING —) PINFALL

(GOLF —) DEUCE EAGLE BIRDIE BUZZARD

(PINOCHLE —) LAST

(TENNIS —) CALL FIVE LOVE DEUCE FORTY FIFTEEN

(TIE —) HALVE DEADLOCK

(PL.) MUSIC

SCORED SULCATE SULCATED

SCOREKEEPER SCORER TALLIER TALLYMAN

SCORER NIB MARKER NOTCHER

SCORIA SCUM SLAG CINDER SULLAGE

SCORIFIER CAPSULE

SCORIFY SMELT

SCORN GECK LOUT HOKER SCARN SPURN BISMER SLIGHT CONTEMN DESPISE DESPITE DISDAIN CONTEMPT DERISION MISPRIZE

SCORNFUL SAUCY SCORNY SNIFFY SNIFTY HAUGHTY FRUMPISH INSOLENT

SCORNFULLY ASKEW ASWASH

SCORPION NEPA ALACRAN STINGER UROPYGI ARACHNID PEDIPALP WHIPTAIL

SCORPION FISH LAPON SERRAN HOGFISH SCULPIN LORICATE RASCACIO

SCORPION FLY PANORPID

SCOT (ALSO SEE SCOTSMAN) CELT JOCK KELT SAXON SCOTTY BLUECAP SCOTSMAN

(PL.) SAWNY SAWNEY LALLANS

SCOTCH TRIG SCOTS SCOTTISH

SCOTCHMAN MAC GAUL SANDY TARTAN SCOTCHY SCOTTIE SCOTSMAN

SCOTER COOT FILK DIVER SCOUT WHILK BASQUE DUCKER SURFER PISHAUG SCOOTER SKUNKTOP

SCOTIA MOUTH

SCOTIST DUNCE

SCOTLAND
BAY: SCAPA
CAPITAL: EDINBURGH

COIN: DEMY BODLE GROAT PLACK RIDER BAWBEE

COUNTY: AYR BUTE FIFE ROSS ANGUS BANFF MORAY NAIRN PERTH ARGYLL LANARK ORKNEY BERWICK KINROSS PEEBLES RENFREW SELKIRK WIGTOWN ABERDEEN AYRSHIRE CROMARTY DUMFRIES ROXBURGH SHETLAND STERLING

FIRTH: LORN CLYDE FORTH MORAY SOLWAY PENTLAND

ISLAND: JURA LONA MULL RHUM SKYE ARRAN BARRA ISLAY LEWIS HARRIS ORKNEY SHETLAND

ISLANDS: ORKNEY HEBRIDES SHETLAND

LAKE: TAY NESS MORAR LAGGAN LINNHE LOMOND KATRINE RANNOCH

LANGUAGE: ERSE LALLAN LALLAND

MEASURE: COP BOLL CRAN FALL MILE PECK PINT ROOD ROPE SPAN, CRANE LIPPY FIRLOT AUCHLET CHALDER CHOPPIN MUTCHKIN STIMPART

MOUNTAIN: HOPE ATTOW DEARG NEVIS TINTO WYVIS CHEVIOT MACDHUI

NATIVE: GAEL PICT SCOT

ORDER: THISTLE

RESORT: OBAN

RIVER: AYR DEE DON ESK TAY DOON GLEN NITH NORN SPEY AFTON ANNAN FORTH GARRY TWEED YTHAN AFFRIC TEVIOT TUMMEL DEVERON FINDHORN

SEAPORT: ALLOA LEITH DUNDEE ABERDEEN

TOWN: AYR DUNS OBAN ALLOA BRORA CUPAR ELLON LEITH PERTH SALEN TROON DUNDEE GIRVAN HAWICK DUNKELD GLASGOW PAISLEY ABERDEEN DUMFRIES GREENOCK KIRKWALL STIRLING

WEIGHT: BOLL DROP TRONE BUSHEL

SCOTLAND ALBANY ALBION SCOTIA ALBAINN ALBANIA

(NORTHERN —) PICTLAND

SCOTSMAN SANDY SAWNY

SCOTTISH SCOTCH SCOTLAND

SCOTTISH TERRIER DIEHARD SCOTTIE VERMINER

SCOUNDREL RAP PIMP SCAB VILE WARY BLECK FILTH KNAVE SHREW SMAIK SWEEP THIEF WHAUP BRIBER LIMMER SLOVEN VARLET CATAIAN GLUTTON HALLION NITHING SCROYLE SKELLUM VILIACO VILLAIN WARLOCK BEZONIAN LIDDERON MASCHANT

SCOUNDRELLY VILLAIN

SCOUR ASH BEAT RAKE SCUM SEEK SCOOR SCRUB SKIRR SWEEP DRENCH SCURRY SLUICE DEGRADE FURBISH BACKWASH STONEFILE

(PL.) SKIT

SCOURER BLOOMER DOLLIER PICKLER

SCOURGE EEL TAW LASH CURSE FLAIL KNOUT SLASH SWING BALEYS PLAGUE SWINGE SCORPION

SCOURGER WHIPSTER

SCOURING BEAT SCOUR HUSHING SCRUBBING

SCOUT SPY BEAR LION SKIP ROVER SPIAL VISOR ESPIAL GAYCAT DESPISE MARINER PICKEER PIONEER SCOURER WATCHER EMISSARY OUTRIDER OUTSCOUT SCURRIER SKIRMISH

(BOY —) CUB BOBCAT SCOUTER WEBELOS EXPLORER

SCOW ACCON FLOAT GARVEY

SCOWL LOUR FROWN GLARE GLOOM GLOUT LOWER SKIME GLOWER VENNER GLOOMING

SCOWLING FROWNY GLARING

SCRAGGY WEEDY

SCRAM HOP LAM BUNK BUGGER

SCRAMBLE MUSS SPURL SCRAWM SPRAWL CLAMBER LOUSTER SCRABBLE SCRAFFLE SCRATTLE SPRACHLE

SCRAP BIT END JAG PIP CRAP ITEM JAGG JUNK PICK SNAP BRAWL GRAIN PATCH SCRAN SHRED THRUM WASTE DISCARD MAMMOCK REMNANT FRACTION SCRAPPET SKERRICK SNATTOCK

(— FOR PATCHING) SPETCH

(— OF PAPER) SCRIP

(— OF SONG) CATCH

(— OF WRITING) SCRAPE

(LITERARY —S) ANA

(RAGGED —) SCART

(PL.) ORTS SCRAN RELICS SCROFF GARBAGE GUBBINGS

SCRAPE LEG RUB CLAW COMB RAZE CLAUT CURET ERADE ERODE GRATE GRAZE GRIDE SCALP SCART SCUFF SHAVE ABRADE RUGINE SCREED SCROOP CORRADE CURETTE JACKPOT SCRATCH SCRABBLE

(— ALONG) HARL HARLE SHOOL

(— GOLF CLUB ON GROUND) SCLAFF

(— OFF) SPUD

(— OUT) ERASE HOLLOW

(— SKINS) MOON SCUD FLESH HARASS

(— TOGETHER) RAKE GLEAN MUCKER SCAMBLE

(— WITH FEET) SCAUT

SCRAPED BRIGHT

SCRAPER PAN HARL SLIP CURET GLOVE HARLE QUIRL RASER SPOON DOCTOR FRESNO GRADER GRATER CURETTE FLANGER LEVELER SLUSHER STRIGIL GRATTOIR SCRAPPLE TERRACER UNHAIRER

SCRAPING GRIDE RASURE
(CRACKER —S) CUSH
(METAL —S) DIET
(PL.) RAMENTA
SCRAPMAN CHIPMAN
SCRAPPER BREAKER FIGHTER
SCRAPPLE PANHAS PONHAWS
SCRAPPY BITTY
SCRATCH RAT RIT CLAW CRAB
RACE RAIN RAKE RAPE RASE RAUK
RAZE RISP RIST SLUG STUN CHALK
CLAUT CLAWK FRUSH GRAZE
RANCH SCART SCLUM SCORE
SCRAB SCRAT SCROB SCRUB
SHRUB SKELP TEASE TOUCH
BRUISE CANCEL CRATCH RASURE
RIPPLE SCORCH SCOTCH SCRAPE
SCRAWK SCRAWL SCRAWM SCRAZE
SCRIVE TORACE DECLARE EMERIZE
EXPUNGE SCARIFY SCRABBLE
SCRATTLE SCRIBBLE
SCRATCHER RASER
SCRAWL SCRAWM SPRAWL
SCRATCH SCRABBLE SCRIBBLE
SQUIGGLE
SCRAWNY BONY LEAN SLINK
SCRANK SCRAGGY SCRANKY
SCRANNY SCRAGGED
(— PERSON OR ANIMAL) RIBE
SCREAM CRY YAW REME WEAK
YARM YAUP YAWL YAWP YOWT
SKIRL SHRAME SHRIEK SHRILL
SQUALL SQUAWL YAMMER
SCREECH YELLOCH SKELLOCH
SCREAMER CHAJA ANHIMA
SCREECH QUAWK QUOCK SCREAM
SCREEK SCRITCH SKREIGH
SKELLOCH
SCREECH OWL STRICH
SCREED TIRADE
SCREEN TRY CAGE GOBO HARP
HIDE LAWN MASK PICK REJA SCUG
SEPT SIFT TENT ARRAS BLIND
CHEEK CHICK CLOAK CLOSE COVER
FIGHT GAUZE GRATE HOARD SHADE
SHOJI SIEVE SPEER SPIER TATTY
BAFFLE BASKET CANVAS DEFEND
ESCORT MEDIUM PURDAH RESEAU
SCHERM SCONCE SHAKER SHIELD
SHROUD THREAD VOIDER CEILING
CONCEAL CURTAIN FLYWIRE
GOGGLES GRIZZLY REREDOS
SECLUDE SHELTER SHUTTER
TESTUDO TROMMEL BACKSTOP
BESCREEN BLINDAGE COVERING
DIFFUSER ECLIPSER EXCLUDER
HOARDING OCCULTER PARAVENT
PARCLOSE PAVISADE SCREENER
SPLASHER STRAINER TRAVERSE
UMBRELLA
(— ALONGSIDE SHIP) PAVISADE
(— BEHIND ALTAR) REREDOS
(— FOR BATTING PRACTICE) CAGE
(— FOR SHIP'S COMBATANTS)
FIGHT
(— FOR SIZING ORE) GRATE
TROMMEL
(— FOR THEATER LIGHT) JELLY
MEDIUM

(— OF BAMBOO SLIPS) CHEEK
CHICK
(— OF BRUSHWOOD) SCHERM
(— OF FIRE) BARRAGE
(— OF SHIELDS FOR TROOPS)
TESTUDO
(— OF TAPESTRY) ARRAS CEILING
(— ON AUTOMOBILE) GRILL GRILLE
(— TO PROTECT LOOKOUTS)
DODGER
(— USED BY ARCHERS) PANNIER
(BULLETPROOF —) MANTA MANTEL
MANTELET
(CHANCEL —) JUBE
(FIRE —) FENDER
(MECHANICALLY ACTUATED —)
GRIZZLY
(PAPER —) SHOJI
(PL.) CANCELLI
SCREENED BLIND SECLUDED
SCREENINGS CULM SLACK SLECK
SCREENPLAY SCENARIO
SCREW HOB VISE WORM CRICK
FEEZE SCROW TEMPER TOGGLE
COCHLEA AIRSCREW FLATHEAD
SETSCREW THUMBKIN WINDMILL
(KIND OF —) ALLEN MEANTIME
SCREW BEAN MESQUITE
SCREWPOD TORNILLA
SCREWED SQUINCH
SCREWER WORMER
SCREWMAN JACKMAN
SCREW PINE IE ARA HALA IEIE
AGGAG PALMA VACOA VACONA
LAUHALA PANDANUS
SCREW TREE TWISTY
SCRIBBLE SQUIB DOODLE SCRAWL
SCRATCH SCRABBLE SQUIGGLE
SCRIBE EZRA CLERK THOTH
BOOKER SCRIVE SOPHER WRITER
GRAFFER MASORET SCRIVAN
NOVERINT PENCLERK SCRIPTOR
SCRIVANO
(PL.) SOPHERIM
SCRIMMAGE BULLY ROUGE BICKER
SPLORE SKIRMISH
SCRIMP HINCH SCREW SKIMP
SCRIPT BOOK NEUM RONDE SERTA
SERTO NASKHI NESKHI SCRITE
SOOLOOS THULUTH BASTARDA
GURMUKHI HIRAGANA KANARESE
MAGHRIBI MAITHILI MEROITIC
NASTALIQ SCENARIO
SCRIPTURE WRIT AGAMA CHING
SUTRA SUTTA
(PL.) BIBLE GRANTH GRUNTH
TANACH TENACH SHASTRA
SCRIVENER PENMAN WRITER
GRAFFER SCRIVER NOVERINT
SCROFULA EVIL CRUELS
SCROLL BEND ROLL LABEL SCRIT
AMULET ESCROL LEGEND SCRAWL
STEMMA VOLUME VOLUTE EVOLUTE
PAPYRUS RINCEAU BANDEROL
CARTOUCH
SCROLL-LIKE TURBINAL
SCROPHULARIA FIGWORT
SCROTUM BAG COD PURSE

SCRUB FILE SCROG COPPET
SCODGY CLEANSE SCRUBBER
YANNIGAN
SCRUBBY SHRUBBY
SCRUBLAND GARIGUE GARRIGUE
SCRUFF CUFF SCUFF SCROFF
SCRUPLE PASS DEMUR DOUBT
FORCE POINT QUALM STAND STICK
BOGGLE SCOTCH STRAIN STICKLE
STUMBLE
SCRUPULOUS NICE SPICED TENDER
CAREFUL FINICKY PRECISE
DELICATE
SCRUTINIZE PRY SEE SPY SCAN
AUDIT PROBE SIGHT SOUND VISIT
SURVEY EXAMINE INSPECT
ENSEARCH
SCRUTINIZING NARROW SCANNING
SCRUTINY EYE SEARCH CANVASS
EXAMINE HAWKEYE PERUSAL
SCRYER SEER
SCUD RACK RAMP SKID SKIM SCOOT
SCUDO FILIPPO
SCUFF SLARE SLIDE SCLAFF
SCUFFER SCUFFLE SHUFFLE
SCUFFLE CUFF BUSTLE CLINCH
TUSSLE WISTER BRULYIE SHAMBLE
SHUFFLE SCRUFFLE
SCULL FUNNY SKULL
SCULLERY SINKROOM
SCULLION GIPPO SCULL SLUSH
GALOPIN SWILLER CUSTROON
QUISTRON
SCULPIN COTTID GRUBBY JOHNNY
BIGHEAD DRUMMER BULLHEAD
BULLPOUT CABEZONE HARDHEAD
LORICATE SCALAWAG
SCULPTOR GRAVER IMAGER
MARBLER PLASTIC
SCULPTURE CAMEO DRAFT GRAVE
SCULP BRONZE ENTAIL GISANT
SCULPT CARVING DRAUGHT
ENGRAVE GRADINO IMAGERY
INSCULP STABILE MORTORIO
NATIVITY PORTRAIT PREDELLA
SCULLION
SCULPTURED GRAVEN GLYPHIC
SCUM BRAT FOAM GALL HEAD REAM
SCUD SILT SKIM SKIN DROSS FROTH
SCURF SLOAK SLOKE SPUME
FLURRY REFUSE RIDDAM SCRUFF
BLANKET CACHAZA OFFSCUM
LAITANCE SANDIVER SCOURING
SCUMMING
SCUP BREAM PORGY SPARID
SCUPPAUG
SCURF SCALD DANDER FURFUR
SCRUFF DANDRUFF
SCURFY SCALD SCURVY LEPROSE
SCRUFFY SCABROUS
SCURRILITY ABUSE REPROACH
SCURRILOUS LOW FOUL VILE DIRTY
GROSS RIBALD VULGAR ABUSIVE
SCURRIL INDECENT
SCURRY BELT CRAB SKIN CURRY
HURRY SKICE SKURRY SCUFFLE
SCUTTER SCUTTLE SKELTER
SKITTER
SCURRYING SKITTER

SCURVY SCALD SCUMMY SHABBY ROYNOUS SCORBUCH SCORBUTE UNLIKING
SCUTAGE ESCUAGE
SCUTATE CLYPEATE
SCUTCH SCOTCH SWINGLE
SCUTE PLATE SCUTUM SCUTELLA
SCUTELLATION SCALING
SCUTIFORM PELTATE
SCUTTLE HOD CRAB SKEP BEETLE MANHOLE SCUDDLE SCUTTER
SCYLLA (FATHER OF —) NISUS TYPHON
SCYLLITOL INOSITOL
SCYPHUS PYXIS
SCYTHE SY LEA HOOK MEAK CRADLE
SCYTHIAN LAMB BAROMETZ
SEA ZEE BAHR BLUE BRIM FOAM FRET GULF HOLM LAVE MAIN RACE TIDE WAVE BRINE BRINY FLOAT FLOOD LOUGH OCEAN AEQUOR PONTUS SEALET STRAND TETHYS CHANNEL HYALINE NEPTUNE BOSPORUS DEEPNESS SEAFLOOD THALASSA
(— DIVINITY) TRITON
(— GOD) PROTEUS
(— LETTER) PASSPORT
(HEAVY —) POPPLE
(MODERATE —) SEAWAY
SEA ANEMONE POLYP DAHLIA OPELET ACTINIA VESTLET ACTINIAN ZOANTHID
SEA BASS HANAHILL HUMPBACK SERRANID TALLYWAG
SEA BEAR OTARIOID
SEABIRD HAGDON
SEA BISCUIT BREAD GALETTE PANTILE
SEABOARD COAST
SEA BREAD HARDTACK
SEA BREAM CARP CHAD PORGY ROMAN BRAISE SARGUS SPARID TARWHINE
SEACOAST BANK SEABOARD SEASHORE
SEA COW SIREN DUGONG RHYTINA SIRENIAN
SEA CUCUMBER BALATE TREPANG CUCUMBER SYNAPTID TEATFISH
SEADOG FOGBOW
SEA DRAGON PEGASID QUAVIVER
SEA DUCK DIVER EIDER DIPPER DUCKER SCOTER
SEA EAGLE ERN ERNE PYGARG PYGARGUS
SEAFARER SEAGOER
SEA FOX THRASHER
SEA GIRDLE CUVY CUTWEED
SEA GULL COB GOR MEW COBB ANNET COBBE POPELER
SEA-GYPSY SELUNG
SEA HOLLY ERYNGO ERYNGIUM
SEA KALE COLE
SEAL CAN FIX FOB GUM BULL CHOP CORK HARP HOOD JARK LUTE BLANK BULLA CLOSE EAGLE PHOCA SIGIL STAMP SWILE THONG UGRUG

URSUK WAFER ASSEAL BEATER CACHET COCKET DOTARD ENSEAL ENSIGN FASTEN GASKET MAKLUK MATKAH OBSIGN PHOCID RANGER SEALCH SECURE SIGNET CONFIRM CONSIGN COWROID ENGLUTE HOODCAP IMPRESS QUITTER SADDLER SEALING SEALKIE SIGNARY WEDDELL ADHESIVE BACHELOR BEDLAMER BRELOQUE CYLINDER MANDORLA PINNIPED SECRETUM SEECATCH SIGILLUM SIGNACLE TANGFISH VALIDATE
(— FOR WATCH CHAIN) ONION BRELOQUE
(— OFF) CAP
(— OVER CORK) CAPSULE
(3-YEAR OLD —) TURNER
(BEARDED —) URSUK MAKLUK
(EARED —) OTARY
(FEMALE —) MATKA
(GOLD —) BEZEL
(HARBOR —) DOTARD RANGER TANGFISH
(HERD OF —S) PATCH
(IMMATURE —) BEDLAMER
(MALE —) WIG SADDLER BACHELOR SEECATCH
(NEWFOUNDLAND —) SWILE RANGER
(PAPAL —) BULL BULLA
(SHETLAND —) SILKIE
(YEARLING —) HOPPER
(YOUNG —) PUP BEATER JACKET BLUEBACK
SEA LACE WHIPLASH
SEA LAVENDER INKROOT STATICE
SEALED CLOSE
SEALER CAPPER GASKET
SEA LETTUCE LAVER SLAKE SLOKE SEAWEED
SEALSKIN SKIN SCULP MATARA
SEALSKIN COAT NETCHA
SEALYHAM TERRIER
SEAM DRY BAND DART FASH FELL PURL REND DEVIL PEARL SPILL FAGGOT INSEAM STREAK SUTURE SEAMLET JUNCTURE OVERSEAM
(— IN INGOT) SPILL
(— IN SHIP'S HULL) DEVIL
(— OF COAL) RIDER SPLIT STREAK
(IRREGULAR —) FASH
SEAMAN SALT JACKY ARTIST CALASH LUBBER SAILOR MARINER MASTMAN SHIPMAN SHIPPER SMASHER WAISTER YOUNKER DESERTER SEASONER
SEAMARK MEITH
SEAMED SEAMY RUGGED
SEA MILE NAUT
SEAMOUNT GUYOT
SEAMSTER TAILOR SEMPSTER
SEAMSTRESS SEAMER SEWSTER
SEANCE SITTING
SEA NETTLE BLUBBER
SEA ONION SCILLA
SEA OTTER KID KALAN
SEA OXEYE SALTWEED SAMPHIRE
SEA PINK THRIFT SABBATIA

SEAPLANE HYDRO AIRBOAT AEROBOAT
SEA PLANTAIN GIBBALS
SEA POACHER BULLHEAD
SEAPORT PARA PORT GROIN NATAL HARBOR MACASSAR
SEA PUSS OFFSET
SEAR BURN FIRE SERE FLAME FRIZZ ENSEAR SCORCH SIZZLE FRIZZLE
SEA RAVEN SCULPIN
SEARCH FAN SPY BEAT COMB DRAG DRAW FAND FOND GAPE HUNT LAIT RAKE RIPE ROUT SEEK SIFT WAIT FRISK PROBE QUEST SNOOP VISIT DACKER DREDGE FERRET FUMBLE RANCEL SLEUTH ENQUIRE EXPLORE FOSSICK INQUEST INQUIRE INSPECT RANSACK SCRINGE ZETETIC FINECOMB OUTREACH SCRABBLE SCROUNGE
(— ABOUT) GRUB PROG GROPE
(— BY FEELING) GROPE
(— DEEPLY) TENT
(— EVERYWHERE) BUSK
(— FOR FOX'S TRAIL) CIPHER
(— FOR GAME) DRAW GHOOM QUEST
(— FOR GOLD) FOSSICK
(— FOR KNOWLEDGE) OUTREACH
(— FOR PROVISIONS) FORAGE
(— FOR SMUGGLED GOODS) DACKER JERQUE
(— FOR WEAPONS) FRISK
(— FOR) FORK HUNT LAIT REQUIRE
(— GROPINGLY) GLAMP
(— INTO) EXQUIRE INDAGATE
(— OUT) FERRET INVENT EXQUIRE
(— SHIP) RUMMAGE
(— SYSTEMATICALLY) COMB
(— THROUGH) TURN
(— UNDERWATER) FISH
(SYSTEMATIC —) SWEEP
SEARCHER FINDER
SEARCHING HARD SHREWD CURIOUS GROPING
SEARED ADUST
SEARING CAUTERY
SEA ROBIN GURNARD WINGFISH
SEA ROVER VIKING SCUMMER
SEASAN NUDE
SEASCAPE SEAPIECE
SEA SCORPION COBBLER
SEA SERPENT ELOPS
SEASHELL PROP
SEASHORE SEA RIPE CLEVE COAST MARINE SEASIDE SEABEACH SEABOARD SEACOAST
SEASICKNESS HILO NAUPATHIA
SEA SNAIL LIPARIAN
SEA SNAKE CHITAL KERRIL
SEASON BEEK CORN DASH FALL PERT SALT SEEL TIDE TIME GRASS SAUCE SAVOR SHEMU SPICE AUTUMN EASTER FLOWER HARDEN HAYING MASTER SPRING STEVEN STOUND SUMMER WINTER BUDTIME FLYTIME HARVEST KITCHEN OATSEED SEEDTIME
(— FOR HERRING FISHING) DRAVE

(— HIGHLY) DEVIL
(— IN THE SUN) HAZE
(— OF JOY) JUBILEE
(— OF MERRYMAKING) CARNIVAL
(CLOSED —) SHUTOFF
(DULL —) SLACK
(EGYPTIAN —) AHET PERT SHEMU
(HAYING —) HAYING HAYSEL
(LENTEN —) CAREME
(RAINLESS —) DRY
(RAINY —) KHARIF VARSHA
(REGULARLY RECURRING —) EMBER
(SPRING —) WARE APRIL GRASS
(THE RIGHT —) TID
SEASONABLE PAT TIDY TIMELY
TIDEFUL TIMEFUL VETERAN
TOWARDLY
SEASONABLY TIMELY APROPOS
BETIMES
SEASONED SAGY SALT SALTED
INDIENNE POWDERED
(MILDLY —) 3WEET
SEASONER SURFACER
SEASONING SALT SPICE SEASON
SPICING
SEA SQUIRT ASCIDIAN
SEA SWALLOW TERN
SEAT BOX CAN SEE SET BANK BOSS
COSY DAIS FLOP FORM FROG ROOM
SILL SLIP SUNK TOIT ASANA BENCH
CELLE CHAIR DICKY SELLA SELLE
SETTE SIEGE SLIDE STALL STOOL
BOUGHT DODONA EXEDRA HUMPTY
INSIDE RUMBLE SADDLE SEATER
SEGGIO SETTEE SETTLE THWART
BUTTOCK CUSHION GRADINE
GRADINO INSTALL OTTOMAN
SEATING TABORET TRANSOM
BLEACHER ENTHRONE PULVINAR
SEGGIOLA SUBSELLA WOOLPACK
(— AT PUBLIC SPECTACLE)
PULVINAR
(— FOR CLERGY) SEDILE
(— FOR GRINDER) HORSING
(— FOR PLANE IRON) FROG
(— OF BIRTH) SIDE
(— OF EMOTIONS) CHEST SPLEEN
(— OF FEELINGS) STOMACH
(— OF HARE) FORM
(— OF INTELLECT) HEAD
(— OF KNOWLEDGE) RUACH
(— OF ORACLE) DODONA
(— OF PITY) BOWEL
(— OF POWER) SEE
(— OF REAL LIFE) SOUL
(— OF RESPONSIBILITY) SHOULDER
(— OF RULE) OGDOAD
(— OF TURF) SUNK
(— OF UNDERSTANDING) SKULL
(— ON ELEPHANT'S BACK) TOWER
CASTLE HOWDAH
(— ONESELF) LEAN PITCH
(— SLUNG ON POLES) HORSE
(— WITH BRAZIER BELOW)
TENDOUR
(— WITHIN WINDOW OPENING)
CAROL
(AIRPLANE —) DORMETTE
(BACKLESS —) STOOL HASSOCK

(BISHOP'S —) APSE BISHOPRIC
(CANOPIED —) COSY COZY
(CARRIAGE —) DICKY
(CHIMNEY —) SCONCE
(CHURCH —) PEW DESK STALL
SEDILE
(COACH —) BOOT POOP
(COUNTRY —) TOWER GRANGE
QUINTA
(DRAPED —) MUSNUD
(DRIVER'S —) BOX DICKY FORETOP
(ELEVATED —) PERCH
(FIXED —) DAIS
(KEY —) KEYWAY
(LONG —) BANK FORM BENCH
(NIPPLE —) LUMP
(OARSMAN'S —) TAFT
(PORCH —) GLIDER
(RECLINING —) DORMEUSE
(ROWER'S —) THWART
(ROYAL —) SIEGE STEAD THRONE
(STAGECOACH — S) BASKET
(STRAW —) BOSS
(TIER OF —S) TENDIDO
(UNRESERVED —S) BLUES
SEA TANGLE FURBELOW
SEA TROUT SEWEN SMELT KIPPER
HERLING HIRLING BODIERON
(— AFTER SPAWNING) KELT
(YOUNG —) PEAL
SEA TURTLE CHELONID
SEA URCHIN WANA REPKIE ARBACIA
CIDARID ECHINID ECHINUS RADIATE
(FOSSIL —) ECHINITE
SEAWALL BULWARK
SEAWARD OFF MAKAI
SEAWEED ORE AGAR ALGA KELP
LIMU MOSS NORI OOZE REEK REIT
TANG WARE DRIFT DULSE KOMBU
LAVER SLAKE SLOKE VAREC VRAIC
WRACK DELISK FUCOID FUNORI
TANGLE HAITSAI OARWEED
OREWEED OREWOOD REDWARE
SEATANG SEAWARE CARAGEEN
CORALINE GULFWEED HEMPWEED
ROCKWEED SARGASSO SEABEARD
WHIPCORD WHIPLASH
(PL.) LUMUT
SEBESTEN MYXA
SECANT SEC CHORD
SECCO FRESCO
SECEDE SPLINTER
SECESSIONIST SECESH SEPARATE
SECLUDE TACKLE ENCLOSE ISOLATE
RECLUSE CLOISTER
SECLUDED COY SHY DEEP CLOSE
QUIET HIDDEN REMOTE SECRET
PRIVATE RETIRED SECLUSE
HIDEAWAY MONASTIC SEPARATE
UMBRATIC
SECLUSION RECESS SHADOW
PRIVACY PRIVITY RETREAT
SECRECY SEQUEST SOLITUDE
SECOND AID SEC ABET BACK BETA
TICK OTHER VOUCH ASSIST LATTER
MOMENT TARTAN TIDDER TOTHER
ANOTHER INSTANT SUPPORT
SUSTAIN STICKLER
(— BASE) KEYSTONE

(— IN COMMAND) DEPUTY
(— PERSON USE) TUISM
(1000TH OF A —) SIGMA
(60TH OF A —) THIRD
SECONDARY BY BYE SUB SLACK
DONKEY SECOND CUBITAL DERIVED
INFERIOR
(PL.) FLAGS
SECONDHAND USED
SECOND-RATE COMMON INFERIOR
SECOND-RATER PIKER
SECRECY DERN HUSH HIDING
SECRET PRIVACY PRIVITY SILENCE
DARKNESS SCUGGERY VELATION
SECRET SLY DARK DERN BLIND
CABAL CLOSE PRIVY QUIET ARCANE
CLOSET COVERT HIDDEN INWARD
POCKET STOLEN ARCANUM
COUNSEL CRYPTIC EPOPTIC
FURTIVE MYSTERY PRIVACY
PRIVATE PRIVITY RECLUSE RESERVE
RETIRED SECRETA UNKNOWN
ESOTERIC HIDLINGS MYSTICAL
SNEAKING STEALTHY
SECRETARY CLERK COPPY BARUCH
MUNSHI RAPTOR SCRIBE FAMULUS
MUNSHEE MOONSHEE
SECRETE HIDE NICHE RESET
SECERN SECRET CONCEAL
SECLUDE SALIVATE SEPARATE
(— MILK) LACTATE
(— ONESELF) HIVE
(— SALIVA) DROOL
SECRETION INK LAC GOWL LAAP
LERP MILT SPIT WOOL HUMOR
LAARP MUCUS SEPIA SLIME SPADE
CEMENT SALIVA SMEGMA CERUMEN
CHALONE FLOCOON HORMONE
SPITTLE ENDOCRIN
(THICKENED —) GUM
(WAXY —) LERP LAARP
SECRETIVE SLY DARK SNUG
COVERT SECRET SILENT INVOLVED
SECRETIVENESS SECRECY
SLYNESS
SECRETLY CLOSE DARKLY DERNLY
SECRET CLOSELY HIDLINGS
INWARDLY
SECT SET ZEN BABI CULT JODO
KIND SHIN ALOGI BHORA ISAWA
PANTH BOHORA DONMEH HERESY
SCHISM SCHOOL DHUNDIA DOCETAE
HASIDIM ISAWIYA KHALSAH
RINGATU SECTARY SEQUELA
SHAIKHI SHINGON SIVAISM SUBSECT
AGNOETAE AHMADIYA AISSAOUA
MURJIITE NAASSENE SECTUARY
SHAKTISM
(MEMBER OF —) KHLYST OPHITE
YEZIDI MOLOKAN NUSAIRI LINGAYAT
SECTARIAN CULTIST HERETIC
MAZHABI SECTARY SECTIST
SECTARY JESUIT HERETIC SECTIST
SECTUARY SEPARATE
SECTION CUT END AREA PACE PART
SECT UNIT CAPUT FRUST SHARE
TMEMA BILLET BRANCH BRIDGE
CANTON LENGTH MEMBER SECTOR
ARTICLE CUTTING HEADING

SEGMENT TRANCHE ADDENDUM
DIVISION FRACTION
(— AROUND HOP KILN) CURB
(— OF A BODY) LAMINA
(— OF AVICENNA'S WORK) FEN
(— OF BLOOM) STAMP
(— OF BUILDING) ENTRY
(— OF FENCE) FLAKE
(— OF FILM) EXPOSURE
(— OF FILTER) LEAF
(— OF FISHING TACKLE) TRACE
(— OF GARMENT) GORE
(— OF GLASS) SHAWL
(— OF HIGH GROUND) DIVIDE
(— OF KORAN) SURA
(— OF LADDER) FLY
(— OF LOG) BOLT FLITCH
(— OF LOOM) LAY
(— OF NET) DEEPING
(— OF NEWSPAPER) LEAD
(— OF PARLIAMENT) LAGTHING
(— OF PSALTER) CATHISMA
(— OF RHAPSODY) LASSU
(— OF ROOF) SEVERY
(— OF ROOTSTOCK) BIT
(— OF SHIP) STEERAGE
(— OF SONG) STOLLEN
(— OF THREE SHEETS) TERNION
(— OF TRENCH) BAY
(— OF VIOLIN) BOUT
(— OF WOOD) HAG
(— OF YARN) SLUB
(—S OF SCENERY) BOOK
(4-PAGE —) OUTSERT
(CONCLUDING —) ABGESANG
(CONIC —) PARABOLA
(DULL —) LONGUEUR
(LOWEST —) BOTTOM
(MINE —) BORASQUE BORRASCA
(MUSICAL —) CODA EPILOG FINALE
(NARROW —) STRIPE
(NATIVE —) KASBA CASBAH
(ONE-SIXTEENTH OF —) FORTY
(PERCUSSION —) BATTERY
SECTIONALISM LOCALISM
SECTOR AREA HOUSE
SECULAR LAIC COMMON EARTHLY
PROFANE WORLDLY TEMPORAL
SECURE FID GET GIB KEY POT SEW
WIN BAIL BOLT BOND CAUK COCK
COLD EASY FAST FIND FIRM FRAP
GAIN GIRD HOOK LAND MOOR NAIL
SAFE SEAL SHOT SNUG STAY SURE
WARM BELAY BLOCK CINCH CLEAT
SLOUR SOUND STRAP TRUST
ANCHOR ASSURE BECKET BUTTON
CLINCH DEFEND ENSURE FASTEN
OBTAIN PLEDGE SETTLE SICCAR
SICKER STABLE STAPLE TRAIST
BULWARK CONFINE DUNNAGE
FORFEND FORTIFY RAMPIRE
WARRANT GARRISON PRESERVE
(— A SAIL) TRICE
(— AGAINST INTRUSION) TILE
(— AID OF) ENLIST
(— BAIT) EBB
(— FROM LEAKING) COFFER
(— WITH BARS) GRATE
SECURED BOUND SETTLED

SECURELY FAST SAFE SICCAR
SICKER STRAIT SURELY SOLIDLY
SOUNDLY
SECURITY PUP BAIL BAND EASE
GAGE SEAL WAGE FRITH GRITH
GUARD QUIET STOCK BORROW
CEDULA EQUITY PLEDGE SAFETY
SCREEN SEVERE SURETY VADIUM
CAUTION DEFENSE DEPOSIT
FLOATER HOSTAGE SHELTER
SLEEPER WARRANT COLONIAL
COVENANT FASTNESS GUARANTY
HYPOTHEC STRENGTH VADIMONY
(PL.) PERCENTS
SEDAN SEDIA JAMPAN SALOON
TONJON TOMJOHN BROUGHAM
SEDATE CALM COOL DOUCE QUIET
SOBER STAID SERENE EARNEST
SERIOUS SETTLED DECOROUS
SEDATENESS SOBRIETY
SEDATIVE AMYTAL CALMANT
LENITIVE QUIETIVE SOOTHING
SEDENTARY STILL SESSILE
INACTIVE
SEDGE SAG LING RAIT REIT STAR
CAREX CHUFA TIKUG BHABAR
EHUAWA GLUMAL THATCH TOETOE
TOITOI BULRUSH MONOCOT
PAPYRUS SNIDDLE TUSSOCK
GALANGAL JIMSEDGE
SEDGE FLY GRANAM GRANNOM
SEDGE WARBLER WREN MOCKBIRD
REEDBIRD
SEDGY SAGGY SEGGY TWILLED
SEDIMENT CARR DREG FAEX FOOT
GOBI LEES MULM SILT WARP DRAST
DREGS FECES FOOTS MAGMA
BOTTOM SIMMON SLUDGE DREWITE
GROUNDS GRUMMEL SAPROPEL
SETTLING
(— OF BEER OR ALE) CRAP
(IRON —) CAR CARR
(REDDISH —) SIMMON
SEDITION REVOLT TREASON
SEDITIOUS RIOTOUS FACTIOUS
MUTINOUS
SEDUCE DRAW JAPE LOCK DECOY
TEMPT WRONG ALLURE BETRAY
ENTICE DEBAUCH ENSNARE
MISLEAD SUGGEST TRADUCE
INVEIGLE
(— WITH THE EYE) LEER
SEDUCER UNDOER LOTHARIO
SEDUCTION LURE BRIBE CHARM
SEDULOUS BUSY INTENT STUDIED
DILIGENT UNTIRING
SEDULOUSNESS INDUSTRY
SEDUM MOSS ORPINE SENGREEN
SEE LO EYE KEN SPY VID ESPY
LOOK MIND NOTE PIPE SEAT SEGE
SPOT VIDE VIEW BESEE CATCH
CHAIR SIEGE SIGHT STOOL TENEZ
WATCH ATTEND BEHOLD DESCRY
NOTICE QUAERE REMARK SURVEY
ARCHSEE DISCERN GLIMPSE
OBSERVE WITNESS CATHEDRA
CONCEIVE PERCEIVE
(— ABOVE) VS
(— BELOW) VI

(— FIT) CHOOSE
(— INTO) INSEE
(— TO) FIX
(— VISIONS) SCRY
SEED BEN MAW NIB PIP BEAN BOIL
CHAT CORN DIKA GERM KOLA LIMA
MOTE SETH TARE BEHEN BERRY
CACAO CARAT GRAIN SEMEN
SPAWN SPERM STONE ABILLA
ACHENE ACINUS CARNEL FENNEL
KERNEL LEGUME LENTIL NICKER
NUTLET PIGNON PIPPIN TILLEY
ACHIOTE ACHUETE ALPISTE
ANISEED BUCKEYE CALINUT FRIJOLE
HARICOT HAYSEED SEEDKIN
SEEDLET SEMINAL AMBRETTE
COKERNUT CYDONIUM DILLSEED
FLAXSEED FLEASEED HEMPSEED
PIGNOLIA PRINCIPE SEEDLING
SEEDNESS
(AROMATIC —S) ANISE
(EDIBLE —) PEA BEAN
(FENUGREEK —) HELBEH
(GRAPE —) ACINUS
(IMMATURE —) OVULE
(MUSTARD —) SENVY SINEWY
(NUTLIKE —) PEANUT
(OILY —) ABILLA
(PALM —) COROZO
(POPPY —) MAW MOHNSEED
(SESAME —) JINJILI GINGELLY
(PL.) ANISE COFFEE SESAME ZERAIM
IGNATIA LARKSPUR
SEEDCAKE WIG WIGG
SEEDCASE TEST TESTA THECA
SEED COAT TESTA SPIRICLE
SEEDED ARABLE
SEEDER SEEDMAN
SEEDLING FREE LINER
SEEDY MANGY SCUFFY
SEEING SIGHT SIGHTED
(— THAT) SITH SINCE
SEEK ASK BEG SIC WOO FAND FEEL
FISH FOND FORK HUNT LAIT LOOK
SICK SIFT COURT DELVE ESSAY
FETCH SCOUR APPETE BOTTOM
FERRET FOLLOW FRAIST PURSUE
SEARCH FORSEEK INQUIRE
RANSACK REQUIRE RUMMAGE
SOLICIT ENDEAVOR
(— AFTER) SUE SUIT ENSUE
EXPLORE
(— AIMLESSLY) PROG
(— FAVOR) WISH
(— FOR) APPETE EXPLORE
(— IN MARRIAGE) WOO PRETEND
(— OUT) COMB ENSEARCH
(— TO ATTAIN) ASPIRE
SEEKER TRACER PETITOR ZETETIC
SEARCHER
(— AFTER FACTS) GRADGRIND
(— OF KNOWLEDGE) PHILONIST
(JOB —) CHANCER
(PLEASURE —) FRANION
SEEKING SOKE SOKEN ZETETIC
SEEM BID EYE SEE FARE LOOK PEER
SOUND APPEAR BESEEM REGARD
(— TO BE) LIKE
(IT —S) SEMBLE

SEEMING GUISE QUASI LIKELY
SEEMLY APPARENT SEMBLANT
SEEMINGLY QUASI SEEMLY
SEEMING
SEEMLINESS GRACE DECENCY
DECORUM
SEEMLY FIT TALL CIVIL COMELY
DECENT LIKELY MODEST BECOMING
DECOROUS GRACEFUL
SEEP LEAK OOZE SIPE EXUDE
SEEPAGE SEEP SIPAGE SPRING
SEEPY WEEPY
SEER SIR SWAMI MOPSUS SCRYER
PROPHET CHALDEAN MELAMPUS
SEERBAND TURBAN
SEERESS SAGA SIBYL VOLVA
ALRUNE ALBRUNA PHOIBAD
SEESAW PUMP TILT DANDLE TEETER
TIDDLE TILTER TITTER TOTTER
SEETHE FRY JUG BOIL CREE ITCH
STEW WALL WALM BULLER HOTTER
SIMMER BLUBBER ELIXATE
FERMENT
SEETHING ASEETHE BOILING
HUMMING ITCHING SCALDING
SEGMENT CUT LAP FALL HAND LITH
MERE PART BLANK CHORD ELITE
FEMUR FURCA SHARE SLICE TMEMA
CANTLE GLOSSA LENGTH SAMPLE
SYZYGY ARTICLE DIGITUS EXERGUE
FESTOON ISOMERE MYOMERE
MYOTOME SECTION SETIGER
ANTIMERE BRACHIUM COLUMNAL
DACTYLUS DIVISION GONOTOME
HYPOMERE INTERVAL MESOMERE
METAMERE MYOCOMMA NARICORN
(— OF CASK) CANT
(— OF CAULIFLOWER) FLOWERET
(— OF CIRCLE) SECTION
(— OF COMMUNITY) FACIES
(— OF EARTH'S CRUST) GRABEN
(— OF FIBER) BAND
(— OF IRIS) FALL
(— OF LEAF) LACINIA
(— OF MAXILLA) STIPES SUBGALEA
(— OF RATTLESNAKE'S RATTLE)
BUTTON
(— OF SPEECH) DOMAIN
(HERALDIC —) FLANCH FLANCHE
(INSTRUCTIONAL —) LESSON
(MERE —) SNAPSHOT
(PEASANT —) HERA
SEGMENTATION CLEAVAGE
SEGMENTED INSECTED
SEGNO SIGN
SEGREGATE SHED SEVER INTERN
ISOLATE CLASSIFY INSULATE
SEPARATE
SEIGNORAGE ROYALTY
SEIGNORY LORDSHIP
SEINE NET FARE TUCK TRAIN
POCKET SAGENE SPILLER
MADRAGUE
SEISIN VESTURE
SEIZE BAG CAP CLY GET HAP NAB
NAP BEAK BONE CLAW CLUM FANG
GALL GLOM GRAB GRIP GRUP HAND
HENT HOOK JUMP KEEP LEVY NAIL
RAMP SMUG SNAP SPAN TAKE TIRE

YOKE CATCH CESSE CLASP CLEEK
CLICK DRIVE GRASP GRIPE LATCH
PINCH RAVEN RAVIN REACH REAVE
SNACK ARREST ASSUME ATTACH
CLUTCH COLLAR EXTEND FASTEN
FREEZE GOBBLE NOBBLE QUARRY
SECURE SNATCH ASSEIZE CAPTURE
ENCLASP ENCLOSE GRABBLE
GRAPPLE IMPOUND POSSESS
PREHEND SCAMBLE SWALLOW
ARROGATE COMPRISE DISTRAIN
SPUILZIE SURPRISE UNDERNIM
(— AND HOLD FIRMLY) TRUSS
(— BAIT) STRIKE
(— BY NECK) SCRAG COLLAR
SCRUFF
(— PREY) CHOP
(— SUDDENLY) NAB NIP SWOOP
SNATCH
(— UPON) ATTACK INFECT
(— WITH CLAWS) STRAIN
(— WITH TEETH) BITE
(— WITH WHOLE HAND) GLAUM
(— WITHOUT RIGHT) USURP
SEIZIN SASINE VESTURE
SEIZING FANG GRIP MARQUE
CAPTION SEIZURE
SEIZURE PIT BITE HOLD GRIPE
ICTUS SPELL ARREST EXTENT
PRISAL RAPTUS TAKING ANGARIA
CAPTION CONCEIT TELLACH
DISTRESS STOPPAGE
SELDOM RARE SELD RARELY
UNOFTEN
SELDOM-SEEN ANTRIN ANTERIN
SELECT ORT TAP TRY CULL PICK
SIFT SORT TAKE WALE DRAFT
ELECT ELITE PITCH TRIED ASSIGN
BALLOT CHOICE CHOOSE CLUBBY
DECIDE DESUME EXEMPT PREFER
SINGLE WINNOW DRAUGHT
EXCERPT EXTRACT OUTLOOK
EXIMIOUS HANDPICK SELECTED
(— BY LOT) DRAW
(— BY PATTERN) SWATCH
(— JURY) STRIKE
SELECTED DRAFT ELECT FANCY
DRAUGHT
SELECTING DRAFT GARBLING
SELECTION BLAD CHAP CULL ITEM
PICK CHOICE CHOOSE EXCERPT
EXTRACT ELECTION HAFTARAH
PERICOPE
(— OF PSALMS) HALLEL
(VERSE —) SINGSONG
SELECTIVE CHOOSY ECLECTIC
SELF EGO SEL SEN JIVA SELL SOUL
DAENA NATURE PERSON PSYCHE
(INNER —) ANIMA
(OWN —) AINSELL NAINSEL
(SUPREME UNIVERSAL —) ATMAN
SELF-ACCUSATION GUILT
SELF-AGGRANDIZING IMPERIAL
SELF-ASSERTIVE BRASH PERKY
CHESTY BLUSTERY
SELF-ASSURANCE CHEEK APLOMB
COOLNESS
SELF-ASSURED CALM CONFIDENT
SELF-CENTERED SELFISH

SELF-CENTEREDNESS EGOTISM
SELFHOOD
SELF-COMMAND NERVE
SELF-CONCEIT NOSISM
SELF-CONCEITED COXY PENSY
COCKSY PENCEY
SELF-CONFIDENCE CREST HUBRIS
JOLLITY OPINION
SELF-CONFIDENT FLUSH CHESTY
SELF-CONSCIOUS GAWKY BASHFUL
SELF-CONTAINED ABSOLUTE
SELF-CONTAINMENT CLOSURE
SELF-CONTRADICTORY ABSURD
SELF-CONTROL STAY WILL
ENCRATY MODESTY RETENUE
PATIENCE
SELF-DECEPTION FLATTERY
SELF-DENIAL DENIAL
SELF-DENYING ASCETIC
SELF-DESTRUCTION SUICIDE
SELF-DESTRUCTIVE SUICIDAL
SELF-DETERMINATION FREEDOM
AUTONOMY
SELF-DISCIPLINE ASCESIS
SELF-ENRICHMENT GROWTH
SELF-ESTEEM EGO PRIDE CONCEIT
SELFNESS
SELF-EVIDENT MANIFEST
SELF-EXALTATION NOSISM ELATION
SELF-EXISTENT BEER INCREATE
UNCAUSED
SELF-FERTILIZATION AUTOGAMY
SELF-FULFILLMENT FREEDOM
SAMADHI
SELF-GENERATION AUTOGENY
SELF-GLORIFICATION VANITY
SELF-GOVERNMENT SWARAJ
SELF-HEAL ALLHEAL HOOKHEAL
HOOKWEED
SELFHOOD SEITY EGOITY IPSEITY
OWNHOOD PROPRIUM SELFNESS
SELF-IDENTITY IPSEITY
SELF-IMPORTANT PURDY CHESTY
BIGGETY POMPOUS
SELF-INDULGENCE NICETY
PLEASURE
SELFISH PIGGISH SELFFUL
DISSOCIAL
SELFISHNESS EGO SELF EGOTISM
SUICISM PHILAUTY SELFHOOD
SELFNESS
SELF-LOVE CONCEIT PHILAUTY
SELF-POLLUTION ONANISM
SELF-POSSESSED COOL ASSURED
COMPOSED
SELF-POSSESSION APLOMB
COOLNESS
SELF-REALIZATION FREEDOM
ENERGISM
SELF-RELIANT BOLD FREE
SELF-REPROACH GUILT REGRET
SELF-RESTRAINT HO HOO ASCESIS
CONTROL RESERVE RETENUE
HAVLAGAH
SELF-RIGHTEOUS STUFFY
SELF-SACRIFICING HEROIC
GALLANT
SELFSAME SAME SELFSAID
IDENTICAL

SELFSAMENESS IDENTITY
SELF-SATISFIED SMUG STODGY
ASSURED
SELF-SUFFICIENCY ASEITY ASEITAS
AUTARCHY
SELF-SUFFICIENT ABSOLUTE
SELF-WILLED SET SENSUAL
WAYWARD CONTRARY
SELION BUTT
SELL DO GIVE VEND CHEAP PITCH
SHAVE TRADE UTTER AFFORD
BARTER MARKET AUCTION BARGAIN
(— **AT LOW PRICE**) DUMP
(— **BELOW COST**) FOOTBALL
(— **BY AUCTION**) CANT ROUP
(— **FOR**) BRING FETCH
(— **IN SMALL QUANTITIES**) RETAIL
(**BUY AND** —) CHOP
SELLER BOOMER BUSKER CADGER
VENDOR CHANTER FLESHER
CHANDLER
(**WINE** —) ABKAR
SELLING (SPECULATIVE —)
AGIOTAGE
SELSYN SYNCHRO
SELVAGE LIST GOUGE FORREL
LISTING STICKING
SEMANTEME RHEME
SEMANTICS SEMOLOGY
SEMAPHORE FISHTAIL
SEMBLANCE FACE SHOW SIGN
COLOR GHOST GLOSS GUISE IMAGE
SCHEME VISAGE PRETEXT SEEMING
UMBRAGE LIKENESS SEMBLANT
SKERRICK
(— **OF DIGNITY**) FACE
(— **OF REALITY**) DREAM
(**FALSE** —) COLORING
SEME SEMY GUTTY HURTY FLEURY
GOUTTE GUTTEE BEZANTE
SEME-DE-LIS FLORETTY
SEMELE (BROTHER OF —)
POLYDORUS
(**FATHER OF** —) CADMUS
(**MOTHER OF** —) HARMONIA
(**SISTER OF** —) INO AGAVE
AUTONOE
(**SON OF** —) BACCHUS
SEMEN SEED SPERM
SEMESTER HALF
SEMIDARKNESS DUSK
SEMIDIAMETER RADIUS
SEMIDOME CONCHA
SEMIFLUID SOFT HUMOR
SEMIGLOSS EGGSHELL
SEMINARY YESHIVA JUVENATE
SEMIOPAQUE HORNY
SEMIPORCELAIN GOMBROON
SEMIRAMIS (HUSBAND OF —) NINUS
(**MOTHER OF** —) DERCETO
SEMITE JEW ARAB HARARI SYRIAN
SEMITIC SHEMITE ARAMAEAN
ASSYRIAN CHALDEAN
SEMITIC JEWISH
(— **LANGUAGE**) GAFAT
SEMITONE FEINT LIMMA DEMITONE
HEMITONE
SEMOLINA SUJI SEMOLA
SENATE BOULE SENATO COUNCIL

SENATUS GEROUSIA SENATORY
(— **AND PEOPLE OF ROME**) SPQR
(— **DIVISION**) PRYTANY
SENATOR SOLON CONSUL FATHER
LAWMAKER
SENATORSHIP TOGA
SEND MIT FAST PACK SHIP ENVOY
SCEND THROW ADDRESS CHANNEL
COMMAND CONSIGN DELIVER
FORWARD DISPATCH TRANSMIT
(— **ABOUT**) TROLL
(— **ALOFT**) CROSS
(— **AWAY**) MAND SHIP AMAND
BANISH DISBAND DISMISS RELEGATE
(— **BACK**) ECHO TURN WISE REMIT
REMAND REMISE RENVOY RESEND
RETURN REFRACT
(— **BY MAIL**) DROP
(— **DOWN**) DEMIT DIMIT STRIKE
(— **FOR**) SUMMON
(— **FORTH IN RAYS**) RADIATE
(— **FORTH**) BEAR CAST EMIT MAND
DIMIT FLING EFFUSE OUTSEND
(— **IN**) IMMIT IMMISS INTROMIT
(— **MESSAGE**) BLINKER
(— **OFF UNCEREMONIOUSLY**) SHANK
(— **OFF**) WING
(— **OFFICIALLY**) ISSUE
(— **OUT**) BEAM EMIT AMAND SHOOT
SPEED DEDUCE DEPORT LAUNCH
DIFFUSE EXPEDITE
(— **TO JAIL**) LAG MITTIMUS
(— **TO PERDITION**) CONFOUND
SENDING SAND
(— **OUT**) EMISSIVE

SENEGAL
CAPITAL: DAKAR
MOUNTAIN: GOUNOU
NATIVE: PEUL SOCE DIOLA FOULA
LAOBE SERER WOLOF FULANI
SERERE BAMBARA MALINKE
TUKULER MANDINGO
RIVER: FALEME GAMBIA SALOUM
SENEGAL
TOWN: THIES KAOLACK RUFISQUE

SENILE DOLD DOTARD
SENILITY DOTAGE CADUCITY
PROGERIA
SENIOR AINE DEAN SIRE DOYEN
ELDER ANCIENT SUPERIOR
SENIORITY AGE ANCIENTY
SIGNEURY
SENNET SPET SIGNET
SENOR DON
SENORITA MISS SRTA SRITA
SENSATION FEEL ITCH SOUR SENSE
TABET TASTE TIBBIT VEDANA
FEELING ESTHESIS
(— **OF COLD**) RHIGOSIS
(— **OF FRIGHT**) FRISSON
(— **OF HEAT**) HOTNESS
(**ANTICIPATORY** —) FOREFEEL
(**BURNING** —) ARDOR
(**DARTING** —) SHOOT
(**STRONG** —) CREEP
(**SUBJECTIVE** —) AURA

(**TASTE** —) GUST BITTER
(**TINGLING** —) DIRL
(**VIBRATING** —) FREMITUS
(**VISUAL** —) PHOSE PHOTOMA
SENSATIONAL GORY YELLOW
SAFFRON SPLASHY THRILLY
STUNNING
SENSATIONALISM BLARE SENSISM
SENSE WIT FEEL SALT SMELL
LETTER MATTER REASON SCONCE
WISDOM FEELING HEARING
MARBLES MEANING SMEDDUM
CARRIAGE GUMPTION JUDGMENT
(— **OF APPREHENSION**) ANXIETY
(— **OF HEARING**) EAR
(— **OF HUMOR**) MUSIC
(— **OF ONENESS**) KINSHIP
(— **OF OUTRAGE**) SHOCK
(— **OF PANIC**) JITTERS
(— **OF RIGHT**) GRACE
(— **OF SIGHT**) VISION
(— **OF SMELL**) SCENT
(— **OF SUPERIORITY**) EGOTISM
(— **OF TOUCH**) FEEL TASTE
(— **ON ONE'S WORTH**) PRIDE
(**COMMON** —) SALT BALANCE
GUMPTION
(**DISCRIMINATING** —) FLAIR
(**LACKING** —) INEPT
(**PLAIN** —) ENGLISH
(**SOUND** —) MATTER
SENSE-DATUM SENSUM
SENSELESS MAD COLD DUMB
FRIGID STUPID UNWISE FOOLISH
IDIOTIC PEEVISH SOTTISH UNIDEAED
SENSIBILITY HEART SENSE FEELING
DELICACY ESTHESIA JUDGMENT
(**PL.**) FEELINGS
SENSIBLE SANE WISE AWARE PRIVY
ACTUAL FEELABLE MATERIAL
PASSIBLE RATIONAL SENSICAL
SENTIENT WISELIKE
SENSITIVE FINE KEEN SORE ALIVE
QUICK LIABLE NIMBLE TENDER
TETCHY FEELING NERVOUS PRICKLY
ALLERGIC DELICATE EROGENIC
SENSIBLE SENTIENT SKINLESS
TOUCHOUS
(— **TO PAIN**) TART
(**NERVOUSLY** —) TOUCHY
SENSITIVENESS SENSE TOUCH
ALGESIA DELICACY
SENSITIVE PEA HONEYCUP
SENSITIVE PLANT MIMOSA
SENSITIVITY FLESH DELICACY
FINENESS
SENSORY SENSUAL AFFERENT
SENSUAL LEWD BRUTE MUDDY
CARNAL FLESHY SULTRY WANTON
BESTIAL BRUTISH FLESHLY LESBIAN
SWINISH PANDEMIC SENSUOUS
SENSUALITY FLESH LIKING LUXURY
SENSUOUS SOFT SATINY SENSAL
FLESHLY SENSUAL LUSCIOUS
SENSIBLE
SENTENCE DIT RAP SAW DAMN
DOOM TIME AWARD FUTWA JUISE
TENER TROPE ARREST COMMIT
DECREE DEPORT JUWISE REASON

ADJUDGE CENSURE CONDEMN
FLOATER IMPRESA LAGGING
FOREDOOM JUDGMENT VERSICLE
(— **INDICATING CHARACTER)**
MOTTO
(**CONCISE —S)** LACONICS
(**IMPRISONMENT —)** LAG RAP LIFE
LAGGING STRETCH
(**MUSICAL —)** PERIOD
(**SHORT —)** CLAUSE
(**WITTY —)** ATTICISM
SENTENTIOUS CONCISE LACONIC
SENTIENCE SENSE
SENTIENT FEELING SENSILE
SENSIVE SENSEFUL SENSIBLE
SENTIMENT MIND POSY ETHNOS
GENIUS HOBNOB PLEDGE FEELING
(**SLOPPY —)** DRIP
SENTIMENTAL SLAB SOFT CORNY
GOOEY GUSHY MUSHY SAPPY
SOBBY SOPPY SOUPY FRUITY
SLUSHY SPOONY SUGARY SYRUPY
INSIPID MAUDLIN MAWKISH
ROMANTIC SCHMALZY SNIVELLY
SENTIMENTALISM BATHOS
SCHMALZ SCHMALTZ
SENTIMENTALIST SOFTHEAD
SENTIMENTALITY GOO HAM MUSH
SIRUP SYRUP BATHOS
SENTINEL WAIT DEINO GUARD
WATCH BANTAY PICKET SENTRY
PICQUET COCKATOO PEPHEDRO
WATCHMAN
(**MOUNTED —)** VEDET VEDETTE
(PL.) GRAEAE GRAIAE
SENTINEL BOX STATION
SENTRY KITE WATCH SENTINEL
SEPAL LEAF HELMET LEAFLET
SEPARATE CUT TOM COMB CULL
CURD DEAL FALL FRAY FREE HAZE
PART REDD SERE SIFT SORT TWIN
BLEED BREAK CALVE ELONG FENCE
FLAKE HEDGE PARTY SCALE SEVER
SIEVE SKILL SPLIT TWAIN TWIST
ABDUCT ABRUPT ASSORT AVULSE
BISECT CLEAVE DECIDE DEPART
DETACH DIGEST DIVIDE DIVISI
PROPER REMOTE SCREEN SECERN
SECRET SEJOIN SETTLE SINGLE
SOLUTE SPREAD SUNDER SUNDRY
SWATCH UNLUTE WINNOW ABSCISE
ABSCISS BRACKET CONCERN
DIALYZE DISJOIN DISLINK DISPAIR
DISPART DIVERSE EXPANSE FISSION
ISOLATE SCATTER SECTION
SEJUNCT SEVERAL SWINGLE
ABSTRACT BULKHEAD DETACHED
DIFFRACT DISCRETE DISJOINT
DISSEVER DISSOLVE DISTINCT
DISTRACT DISUNITE DIVIDANT
DIVIDUAL FRACTION LAMINATE
LEVIGATE LIBERATE PECULIAR
SEVERATE SPORADIC UNMINGLE
UNSOLDER UNSTRING
(— **BY BEATING)** SCUTCH
(— **BY CROSSWALL)** ABJOINT
(— **BY PICKING)** LEASE LEAZE
(— **COINS)** JOURNEY
(— **COMBATANTS)** STICKLE

(— **FIBERS)** HACKLE
(— **FROM HERD)** IMPRIME
(— **GRAIN FROM CHAFF)** FAN CAVE
WINNOW
(— **HAIR)** BLOCK
(— **INTO COMPONENTS)** STRIP
(— **INTO FLOCKS)** DRAFT DRAUGHT
(— **INTO SHREDS)** TEASE
(— **ONESELF)** ABDICATE
(— **ORE)** JIG SMELT DILLUE
(— **SHEEP)** DRAW
(— **THREADS)** SLEY SLEAVE
SEPARATED FREE ALONE BROKEN
DISTANT DIVIDED ABSTRACT
ISOLATED RESOLVED
(— **BY INTERVAL)** OPEN
SEPARATELY APART SINGLY
SUNDRY SEVERAL SUNDERLY
SEPARATING BETWEEN
SEPARATION GAP GULF PART SHED
CHASM SPLIT SCHISM BARRIER
DIVORCE ELUTION PARTING
ANALYSIS AUTOTOMY AVULSION
CREAMING DECISION DIALYSIS
DISTANCE DISUNION DIVISION
INCISION SHEDDING TWINNING
(— **OF LEAF)** CHORISIS
(— **OF MAN AND WIFE)** ZIHAR
DIVORCE
(— **OF METALS)** DEPART
(— **OF PIGMENT)** FLOATING
(— **OF WORD PARTS)** TMESIS
(— **OF YEAST IN BEER)** BREAK
SEPARATIST ZOARITE BIMMELER
SEPARATOR RAVEL PARTER
CREAMER SETTLER SEVERER
SUBSIDER
SEPARATRIX SLASH DIAGONAL
SEPIA COCONUT SEPIARY
SEPOY TELINGA
SEPT KIN
SEPTET SEPTUOR
SEPTIVALENT HEPTAD
SEPTUAGINT LXX
SEPTUM VITTA TABULA MYOTOME
PHRAGMA MYOCOMMA
SEPULCHER BIER GRAVE TITLE
MONUMENT MORTUARY
SEPULCHRAL HOLLOW CHARNEL
TUMULARY
SEQUEL SUITE EFFECT SEQUENT
BACKWASH SEQUENCE
SEQUENCE ROPE SUIT TRACT TRAIN
DOCKET ENTAIL SEQUEL SERIES
STRING CADENCE CORONET
SEQUENT SUCCESS SPECTRUM
STRAIGHT
(— **OF BEHAVIOR)** ACT
(— **OF BILLIARD SHOTS)** BREAK
(— **OF CARDS)** STRINGER
(— **OF CHESS MOVES)** DEFENCE
DEFENSE
(— **OF EVENTS)** CYCLE
(— **OF MELODRAMA)** CHASE
(— **OF ROCK UNITS)** SECTION
(— **OF SOUNDS)** AFFIX
(**ACTING —)** EXTERIOR
(**CUSTOMARY —)** COURSE
(**FILM —)** INTERCUT

(**LITURGICAL —)** CANON
SEQUENT ENSUANT SEQUITUR
SEQUESTER SINGLE ISOLATE
RECLUDE
SEQUESTERED LONELY PRIVATE
RECLUSE RETIRED SECLUDED
SOLITARY
SEQUIN CHICK SPANG VENTIN
ZEQUIN CHEQUIN CHEQUEEN
VENETIAN ZECCHINO
(PL.) GLITTER
SERAGLIO HAREM SERAI ZENANA
SERAPHIC BEATIFIC
SERBOCROATIAN ILLYRIAN
SERE SEAR SERULE UNGREEN
HALOSERE
SERENADE AUBADE HORNING
ALBORADA NOCTURNE SERENATA
(**MOCK —)** SHIVAREE
SERENADER WAIT
SERENE CALM EVEN CLEAR LITHE
SEDATE SMOOTH HALCYON
DECOROUS
SERENITY CALM PEACE REPOSE
SERF BOND THEW CHURL HELOT
SLAVE THEOW PENEST SERVUS
THRALL BONDMAN COLONUS
PEASANT ADSCRIPT PRAEDIAL
YANACONA
SERFDOM BONDAGE HELOTRY
SERFAGE SERVAGE HELOTISM
SERFHOOD SERFSHIP
SERGE SAGATHY
SERGEANT TOP SARGE CHIAUS
DESKMAN SERVANT TOPKICK
SERIAUNT
SERGEANT-AT-LAW COUNTOR
COUNTOUR
SERGEANT FISH LING CABIO COBIA
SNOOK BONITO CUBBYYEW
SERGEANT MAJOR PINTANO
SERIALLY SERIATIM
SERIEMA CARIAMA GRUIFORM
SCREAMER
SERIES RUN SET ECCA RANK SUIT
TIRE CHAIN DRIFT DWYKA ORDER
SUITE TALLY TRACE COURSE
EOCENE SEQUEL STRING SYSTEM
BATTERY CASCADE CATALOG
BEADROLL SEQUENCE
(— **GATHERED TOGETHER)** SORITES
(— **OF ABSTRACTS)** SYLLABUS
(— **OF ARCHES)** ARCADE
(— **OF BALLET TURNS)** CHAINE
(— **OF BOAT RACES)** REGATTA
(— **OF CELLS)** FILAMENT
(— **OF CHARACTERS)** CLINE
(— **OF CHESS MOVES)** COOK
(— **OF CLASHES)** CLATTER
(— **OF COMMUNITIES)** SERE
(— **OF DANCE MOVEMENTS)** ADAGIO
(— **OF DRAIN TILES)** FIELD
(— **OF EVENTS)** EPOS ACTION
(— **OF EXTRACTS)** CATENA
(— **OF FORTIFICATIONS)** CEINTURE
(— **OF IMAGES)** DREAM
(— **OF LEGENDS)** SAGA
(— **OF LIPS)** GILL
(— **OF MEETINGS)** SESSION

(— **OF METAL DISKS)** PILE
(— **OF MILITARY OPERATIONS)**
CAMPAIGN
(— **OF MOVEMENTS)** DANCE
(— **OF NEIGHBORING LOTS)** COTE
(— **OF NOTES)** GAMUT GLISSADE
(— **OF PASSES)** FAENA
(— **OF PILES)** DRIFT
(— **OF POEMS)** DIVAN DIWAN
(— **OF PRAYERS)** COURSE SYNAPTE
(— **OF RACES)** CIRCUIT
(— **OF REASONS)** ARGUMENT
(— **OF RINGS)** COIL GIMMAL
(— **OF ROOMS)** SWEEP
(— **OF SHOTS)** BURST
(— **OF SIMILAR STRUCTURES)**
STROBILA
(— **OF SLALOM GATES)** FLUSH
(— **OF SLIPS)** DOCK
(— **OF SOILS)** CECIL
(— **OF STAIRS)** FLIGHT
(— **OF STAMPS)** SET
(— **OF STITCHES)** STAY
(— **OF STRAPS)** LADDER
(— **OF TANKS)** SOAPER
(— **OF THREADS)** BINDER STUFFER
(— **OF TONES)** SCALE
(— **OF TRAVELS)** ODYSSEY
(— **OF VERSES)** ANTIPHON
(— **OF WORDS)** ACROSTIC
ALPHABET
(**CARD** —) CORONET
(**CONNECTED** —) CATENA
(**CONSECUTIVE** —) STREAK
(**DANCE** —) DOUBLE
(**GEOLOGICAL** —) ECCA DWYKA
KENAI EOCENE KEEWATIN
(**IMPRESSIVE** —) ARRAY
(**RADIOACTIVE** —) FAMILY
SERIOUS RUM SAD DEEP HIGH
ACUTE GRAVE HEAVY SOBER SOLID
STAID DEMURE SEDATE SEVERE
SOLEMN SOMBER SOMBRE SULLEN
AUSTERE CAPITAL EARNEST
SERIOSO WEIGHTY GRIEVOUS
SERIOUSLY BAD ILL DOWN SADLY
DEEPLY GRAVELY SOLIDLY
SERIOUSNESS EARNEST GRAVITY
SADNESS
SERMON SPELL HOMILY ADDRESS
FUNERAL SEREMENT SERMONET
SERMONIZING MORALITY
SEROPURULENT SANIOUS
SEROUS ICHOROUS
SEROW JAGLA SERAU
SERPENT (ALSO SEE SNAKE) AHI
SEPS WORM ABOMA ADDER APEPI
ATHER OPHIS SIREN SNAKE TRAIN
CHITAL DIPSAS DRAGON GERARD
HYDRUS PYTHON APOPHIS PRESTER
SCYTALE JARARACA
(— **WORSHIPER)** NAASSENE
(**FEATHERED** —) GUCUMATZ
KUKULKAN
(**NORSE** —) GOIN
(**SACRED** —) AVANYU AWANYU
(**SKY** —) AHI
SERPENTINE SNAKY SPIRY OPHITE
SNAKISH BOWENITE METAXITE
SCROLLED

SERPENT STAR OPHIURAN
SERRANO PERCOID GITANEMUK
SERRATE SAWED ARGUTE RAFFLE
NOTCHED SERRIED
SERRATION SERRA DENTILE
SERUM WHEY FLUID BIOLOGIC
SERVANT BOY FAG KID MAN PUG
TAG AMAH BATA COOK DASI DAVY
HELP HIND JACK LUCE MATY MOZO
ALILA BAGOT BOOTS BOULT DAVUS
GILLY GROOM HAMAL MAMMY
SEWER SLAVE SOSIA SPEED USHER
ABDIEL ANDREW BATMAN BEARER
BILDAR BUTLER CHAKAR CLASHY
DORINE EWERER FEEDER FERASH
FLUNKY GILLIE GRUMIO HAIDUK
HARLOT KHAMAL MENIAL PAMELA
SIRCAR SLAVEY TEABOY TEAGUE
TRANIO VARLET VASSAL VOIDER
ANCILLA BOOTBOY BOUCHAL
COURIER DUFTERY FAMULUS
FEODARY FERRASH FLUNKEY
FOOTMAN GENERAL GHILLIE
MALCHUS PANDOUR PANTLER
PAPELON PIQUEUR PISANIO
WASHPOT ASSIGNEE CHAPRASI
CROMWELL DOMESTIC FOLLOWER
GRASSCUT HENCHMAN HOUSEBOY
MANCIPLE MINISTER OUTRIDER
PANTHINO PHILOTUS PINDARUS
SERGEANT SERVITOR STANDARD
TRENCHER VADELECT WARDMAID
KITCHENER
(— **IN CHARGE OF BREAD)** PANTLER
(— **IN CHARGE OF DAIRY)** DEY
(— **IN OFFICE)** DUFTERY
(— **OF SCHOLAR OR MAGICIAN)**
FAMULUS
(— **WHO CARVES)** TRENCHER
(— **WHO CLEARS TABLE)** VOIDER
(— **WHO RUNS BEFORE CARRIAGE)**
PIQUEUR
(— **WHO SERVES TABLE)** SEWER
(**ARMED** —) PANDOUR
(**ARMY** —) BATMAN LASCAR
(**BENGAL** —) MEHTAR SIRCAR
(**BODY** —) VALET SIRDAR
(**BOY** —) BOY KNAVE CHOKRA
BOUCHAL
(**CAMP** —) BILDAR
(**CLOWNISH** —) SPEED LAUNCE
(**COLLEGE** —) GYP SKIP SCOUT
(**FEMALE** —) AMA NAN AMAH DASI
GIRL LASS MAID MAMMY NURSE
WENCH PAMELA SKIVVY ANCILLA
HANDMAID MUCHACHA WARDMAID
(**GENERAL** —) FACTOTUM
(**HEAD** —) BUTLER TINDAL
(**HIGH PRIEST'S** —) MALCHUS
(**HINDU** —) DAS DASI
(**HOUSE** —) COOK HEWE SEWER
DOMESTIC MATRANEE SCULLION
(**KITCHEN** —) COOK WASHPOT
(**LORD OR KING'S** —) THANE
(**LYING** —) FAG
(**MAID** —) NAN BONNE
(**MAN** —) BOY JACK MOZO SWAIN
VALET ANDREW GILLIE KNIGHT

GHILLIE KHANSAMA MUCHACHO
SERVITOR
(**MISCHIEVOUS** —) TEAGUE
(**PETULANT** —) DORINE
(**PHILIPPINE** —) BATA ALILA
(**SCOTTISH** —) JURR
(**SOLDIER'S** —) PAGE
(**TRUSTY** —) TROUT
(**PL.**) FOLK VOLK STAFF FAMILIA
NETHINIM
SERVE DO KA ACT AID HOP GIVE
HELP LEAP SHEW SLAP STAY TEND
TOSS WAIT COVER FRAME HORSE
SARRA STAND ANSWER ASSIST
FRIEND INTEND SAIRVE SARROW
SETTLE SPREAD SUCCOR ADVANCE
ASSERVE BESTEAD CONVENT
FORWARD FURTHER SERVICE
FUNCTION
(— **A DISH)** MESS
(— **AS ESCORT)** SQUIRE
(— **AS HOST)** GIVE
(— **AS SUBSTITUTE)** PASS
(— **AS WELL AS)** AVAIL
(— **DRINK)** SKINK
(— **FOOD)** HASH KITCHEN
(— **FOR PASTURE)** GRAZE
(— **OBSEQUIOUSLY)** LACKEY
LACQUEY
SERVER SALVER ACOLYTE MINISTER
SERVICE AID FEE CENS DUTY HELP
RITE TIDE YOKE FAVOR MUSAF
STEAD DEVOIR EMPLOY ERRAND
FACTOR OFFICE YIZKOR BENEFIT
BONDAGE CHAKARI CORNAGE
FUNERAL LITURGY OBSEQUY
RETINUE SERVAGE SERVING
BREEDING EQUIPAGE FUNCTION
HEADWARD KINDNESS MINISTRY
ROUNDING SERVITUM TENDANCE
(**ASSIGNED** —) MYSTERY
(**BODYGUARD** —) INWARD
(**BREAKFAST** —) DEJEUNER
(**CHORAL** —) MATIN
(**CHURCH** —) LAUDS CHAPEL
CHURCH HEARING STATION SYNAXIS
EVENSONG
(**COFFEE** —) CABARET
(**COMPULSORY** —) ANGARIA
(**DOMESTIC** —) CHAKARI
(**FEUDAL** —) BOON AVERA SEAWARD
HEADWARD
(**MILITARY** —) ARMS CAMP DUTY
ESCUAGE
(**MILITIA** —) COMMANDO
(**RELIGIOUS** —) AHA SEDER
COMMON
(**SECRET** —) OGPU
(**TENNIS** —) ACE LET
SERVICEABLE USEFUL DURABLE
THRIFTY FRIENDLY VAILABLE
SERVICE TREE SORB SORBUS
CHECKER
SERVILE BASE BOND ABJECT
MENIAL SUPINE VASSAL CAITIFF
SLAVISH VERNILE COISTREL
CRAWLING CRINGING SERVIENT
THEWLIKE
SERVILITY CRINGE

SERVING OBED SMACK DISHFUL HELPING SERVIENT WHIPPING

SERVITOR FAG GROOM PUNTER SERVANT PUNTSMAN

SERVITUDE USE VIA YOKE BONDAGE SERVICE SLAVERY SERVITUS THEOWDOM THIRLAGE

SERVOMECHANISM SERVO BOOSTER

SERVOMOTOR RELAY SERVO

SESAME TIL TEEL BENNE BENNI SEMSEM VANGLO OILSEED WANGALA AJONJOLI BENISEED SERGELIM

SESBANIA AGATI

SESQUITERPENE CEDROL CLOVENE COPAENE HUMULENE

SESSION DAY BOUT DIET HOUR SEAT COURT CLINIC SCHOOL SEANCE ACUERDO HEARING SEMINAR SITTING CONGRESS SEDERUNT SEMESTER
(JAM —) CLAMBAKE
(PL.) ASSIZES

SESTERTIUS BRONZE

SESTINA SEXTAIN

SET DO DIP FIX GEL KIT LAY MOB PUT SIC SIT SOT CASE CREW CUBE GAGE GANG GIVE JELL KNIT KNOT NEST PAIR PICK PILT POSE REST SETT SORT STEP STOW BATCH CLASS CLOCK CROWD FIXED GAUGE GLADE GROUP INFIX PAVER PLACE POSIT STACK STAID STAND STEAD STEEK STICK SUITE ADJUST CIRCLE DEFINE FASTEN FINALE FORMAL GLAZED GROUND HARDEN IMPOSE SERIES SETTLE SPREAD SQUARE STATED BATTERY COMPANY COMPOSE CONFIRM COTERIE DEPOSIT DISPOSE ENCHASE FACTION IMPLANT INSTATE PLATOON SERVICE STATION STIFFEN STRATUM EQUIPAGE PANTALON SEQUENCE SOLIDIFY STANDARD
(— A PERIOD) DATE
(— A PRICE) ASK
(— ABOUT) FALL FANG GANG BEGIN ADDRESS
(— AFLOAT) LAUNCH
(— APART) SHED DESIGN DEVOTE EXEMPT SACRED SEPONE SEPOSE APPOINT ISOLATE RESERVE ALLOCATE DEDICATE INSULATE SEPARATE
(— ARROWS IN ORDER) FRUSH
(— AS ONE'S SHARE) ALLOT
(— ASIDE) BAR DISH DROP HAIN SIDE SINK SLIP BURKE KAPUT SEPOSE BRACKET EARMARK PURLOIN RESERVE SUSPEND ABROGATE DISPENSE OVERRIDE OVERRULE REVERSED
(— AT DEFIANCE) BEARD
(— AT LIBERTY) FREE RELEASE LIBERATE
(— BACK TO BACK) ADDORSED ADDOSSED

(— CLOSE TOGETHER) PAVEED
(— DOG ON) SIC SLATE
(— DOWN UNDER NAME) TITLE
(— DOWN) JOT LAY GIVE LAND SCORE EXPONE DEPOSIT
(— EDGEWISE) SURBED
(— ERECT) COCK
(— FIRMLY) FIRM STEM PLANT POSIT
(— FORTH) DRAW ETCH SHOW GIVEN STATE DEPART EXPOSE SPREAD ARTICLE DISPLAY ENOUNCE EXHIBIT EXPOUND PRESENT PROPONE PROPOSE PURPOSE PROPOUND
(— FORWARD) PREFER ADVANCE
(— FREE) BAIL EASE REMIT SKILL SOLVE ACQUIT ASSOIL ABSOLVE DELIVER ENLARGE UNLOOSE WINFREE DISPLACE DISSOLVE EXPEDITE UNVASSAL
(— GOING) INITIATE
(— IN EARTH) STRIKE
(— IN FROM MARGINS) INDENT
(— IN MOTION) SOW
(— IN OPERATION) DRIVE
(— IN OPPOSITION) PIT
(— IN ORDER) ARRAY FRUSH ADIGHT DAIKER FETTLE INFORM ADDRESS
(— INTO A GROOVE) DADO
(— INTO) INLAY
(— LIMITS TO) SPAN BOUND
(— OF 3 ANIMALS) LEASH
(— OF ACTORS) CAST
(— OF ARMS) CONVEYER
(— OF BARS) CONCAVE
(— OF BELLS) RING CHIME CARILLON
(— OF BOOKS) PLENARY
(— OF CARS) DRAG
(— OF CHIMES) DOORBELL
(— OF CIRCUMSTANCES) CASE EGIS FRAME
(— OF CORDS) SIMPLE
(— OF DISHES) GARNISH SERVICE CUPBOARD
(— OF EIGHT) OGDOAD
(— OF EXERCISES) KATA
(— OF FACTS) BOOK
(— OF FISH NETS) DRIFT
(— OF FOLDED SHEETS) QUIRE
(— OF FOUR) WARP
(— OF FURNITURE) SUITE DINETTE
(— OF GARMENTS) SUIT
(— OF GEARS) GEARSET
(— OF HIDES) KIP
(— OF HOUNDS) VANLAY VAUNTLAY
(— OF IDEAS) SYSTEM
(— OF JEWELLED ORNAMENTS) PARURE
(— OF LEAVES) COROLLA
(— OF LETTERS) ALPHABET
(— OF MUSICAL INSTRUMENTS) CONSORT
(— OF OPINIONS) CREDO
(— OF ORGAN PIPES) STOP
(— OF PINS) KAILS KNOCKOUT
(— OF POINTS) INTERVAL

(— OF PUMPS) LIFT
(— OF QUADRILLES) LANCERS
(— OF RADIATORS) STACK
(— OF ROOMS) STORY
(— OF RULES) CODE EQUITY DECALOG
(— OF SAILS) CANVAS
(— OF SHELVES) STAGE BUFFET DRESSER WHATNOT
(— OF SKI FASTENINGS) BINDING
(— OF STAVES) SHOOK
(— OF STEPS) LADDER
(— OF SYMBOLS) KATAKANA
(— OF TABLES) COMPUTUS
(— OF TEETH) DENTURE
(— OF TEN) DECADE
(— OF THREE) BALE
(— OF TOOLS) STRING
(— OF TRAMS) JOURNEY
(— OF TYPEFACES) FAMILY
(— OF VALUES) CURRENCY
(— OF VATS) SOLERA
(— OF VERSES) STAVE
(— OF VOWELS) SERIES
(— OF WARP THREADS) LEA
(— OFF TO ADVANTAGE) ADORN COMMEND
(— OFF) FOIL SEVER SHOOT ACCENT BUNDLE BALANCE EMBLAZE CONTRAST DECORATE EMBLAZON
(— ON END) UPEND
(— ON FIRE) SPIT TIND LIGHT ACCEND IGNIFY IGNITE KINDLE ENFLAME INFLAME ENKINDLE
(— ONESELF) GO
(— OUT) FOUND SALLY START INTEND STARTLE
(— OVER) COUCH
(— RIGHT) REDD ADJUST SCHOOL SQUARE CORRECT REDRESS
(— SNARE) TAIL TILL
(— SOLIDLY) EMBED
(— STRAIGHT) DRESS
(— THICKLY) STUD
(— TO MUSIC) AIR DITTY
(— TRAP) TELD
(— TYPE) KEYBOARD
(— UP IN COLUMNS) TABULAR
(— UP) AREAR ERECT RAISE INSTALL UPDRESS ACTIVATE
(— UPON) BESET ATTACK AGGRESS BROWDEN
(— UPRIGHT) ERECT STAND
(— VALUE) APPRAISE
(— WITH BRISTLES) STRIGOSE
(— WITH GEMS) CHASE
(ANTIGEN —) SEROTYPE
(BECOME —) STRIKE
(CHESS —) MEINY MEINIE
(CHROMOSOME —) GENOME COMPLEX
(COMPLETE —) STAND
(INFINITE —) FAMILY
(MINIATURE —) DIORAMA
(RADIO —) BLOOPER
(SMART —) TON
(STAGE —) SCENE

(UNALTERABLY —) STOUT
(PL.) DECOR
SETA STALK WHISK CHAETA SETULA
SETULE CROTCHET PODETIUM
SETBACK DASH JOLT KNOCK LURCH
BACKSET LICKING PUTBACK
BUSINESS COMEDOWN HAYMAKER
SETLINE GEAR TRAWL BULTOW
OUTLINE TROTLINE
SETTEE SETTLE WINDSOR
SETTER SOFA GUNDOG DROPPER
FLUSHER SETTLER
SETTERWORT PIGROOTS
SETTING SET FALL PAVE CHASE
MIDST SETUP CHATON MILIEU
FERMAIL MONTURE SITTING
INTERIOR MARQUISE MOUNTING
SHOWCASE
(— APART) BETWEEN
(— FREE) SOLUTION
(— OF GEM) FOIL OUCH CHASE
GALLERY
(— OF REED) CAAMING
(— OF WHEELS) CAMBER
(CAMERA —) BULB
(FAMILIAR —) HOME
(MUSICAL —) CREDO BALLAD
BALLADE
(SHUTTER —) TIME
(STAGE —) SCENE
SETTLE BED FIT FIX PAY SAG SET
SIT TAX BANK BIND CALM DAIS
DEAS FAST FIRM HAFT LEND NEST
REST ROOT SEAT SINK SNUG TOIT
AGREE CLEAR COUCH ISSUE LIGHT
LODGE ORDER PITCH PLACE PLANT
QUIET SQUAT STATE STILL ADJUST
ASSIGN CLINCH DECIDE DECREE
ENCAMP LOCATE NESTLE PURIFY
RESIDE SCREEN SECURE SOOTHE
SOPITE SQUARE ACCOUNT APPEASE
APPOINT ARRANGE BALANCE
CLARIFY COMPONE COMPOSE
CONCERT CONFIRM DEPOSIT
DERAIGN INHABIT RESOLVE SUBSIDE
COLONIZE REGULATE SQUATTLE
(— AMICABLY) COMPOUND
(— DOWN) CAMP SLUMP STEADY
DESCEND
(— ITSELF) INVEST
(— LANDS ON A PERSON) ENTAIL
(— ON) POINT
(— UPON) AFFIX AGREE TIGHT
(— VERTICALLY) SQUASH
SETTLED SAD SET FIRM FIXED QUIET
STAID FORMED RANGED SEATED
SEDATE SQUARE STAPLE STATED
CERTAIN DECIDED EMPIGHT
STATARY DECOROUS RESOLVED
STANDING
(NOT —) FARROW
SETTLEMENT AUL DEAL FINE FORK
POST BARRIO COLONY DIKTAT
MOSHAV WINDUP ACCOUNT
BIVOUAC FINANCE MAABARA
OUTPOST STATION CLERUCHY
DECISION DISPATCH JOINTURE
KEVUTZAH PRESIDIO SETTLING
SHOWDOWN TOWNSHIP

(— OF MONKS) SCETE SKETE
(COLLECTIVE —) KVUTZA KIBBUTZ
(MARRIAGE —) MAHR ARRAS
DOWNSET
(NEW ZEALAND —) PA PAH
(RAPID —) BOOM
SETTLER METIC SAHIB LIVYER
NESTER GRUELER PEOPLER
PILGRIM PIONEER TRIMMER
FINISHER GACHUPIN HABITANT
SHAGROON SIBERSKI SIBERYAK
(— IN AUSTRALIA) GROPER
SETTLING SIT
(— OF ESTATE) ENTAIL
(PL.) LEES SEDIMENT
SET-TO BOUT TURN PLUCK FETTLE
TURNUP BRANGLE
SETUP SET SITTER
SEVEN SEPT ZETA ZAYIN HEPTAD
SEPTET HEBDOMAD SEPTETTE
(— OF DIAMONDS) POPE
(— OF TRUMPS) MANILLA
(GROUP OF —) PLEIAD
SEVENFOLD SEPTUPLE
SEVEN-UP SLEDGE
SEVER AX AXE CUT BITE DEAL HACK
REND SLIT TWIN SHEAR SHRED
CLEAVE DEPART DETACH DIVIDE
SUNDER DISALLY DISCERP DISCIDE
DISJOIN OUTRIVE DISSEVER
PRESCIND SEPARATE SEVERIZE
SEVERAL ODD TEN SERE WHEEN
DIVERS SUNDRY DIVERSE VARIOUS
DISTINCT MULTIPLE
SEVERALLY APIECE SEVERAL
SEVERANCE SUNDER SOLUTION
(— OF RELATIONSHIPS) AIR
SEVERE BAD DRY ACID BLUE DEAR
DOUR DURE FIRM HARD IRON KEEN
ROID RUDE SALT SIDE SORE TART
TAUT ACUTE BREME CRUEL EAGER
GRUFF HARSH RETHE RIGID ROUGH
SHARP SMART SNELL SOBER
SOUND STARK STEER STERN STIFF
STOUR BITING BITTER BRUTAL
CHASTE COARSE FROSTY HETTER
SIMPLE SOLEMN STRICT TORVID
UNKIND UNMILD ACERBIC ASCETIC
AUSTERE CHRONIC CONDIGN
CRUCIAL CUTTING DRASTIC
SERIOUS SPARTAN TORVOUS
UNCANNY VIOLENT WEIGHTY
ACULEATE EXACTING GRIEVOUS
GRINDING HORRIBLE IRONCLAD
IRONHARD RIGOROUS SCATHING
STALWART STRAIGHT
(MOST —) EXTREME
SEVERELY BAD HARD BADLY STARK
STIFF HARDLY SORELY STRONG
HEAVILY ROUGHLY SMARTLY
SOUNDLY STITHLY SHREWDLY
SEVERIAN AGNOETE AGNOITE
SEVERITY FROST RIGOR CRUELTY
TORVITY TYRANNY ACRIMONY
ASPERITY FERVENCY HARDNESS
RIGIDITY SORENESS VIOLENCE
SEW SUE FELL SEAM SLIP PREEN
STEEK NEEDLE STITCH OVERSEW
THIMBLE OVERHAND

(— A CORPSE) SOCK
(— LOOSELY) BASTE
(— TO REINFORCE) BAR
(— WAVED PATTERN) DICE
SEWAGE SOIL WASTE SOILAGE
SULLAGE AFFLUENT DRAINAGE
SEWERAGE
SEWELLEL BEAVER BOOMER
SEWER SINK SIRE DRAFT DRAIN
FLEET ISSUE MAKER SHORE
CLOACA KILTER TACKER VENNEL
BELTMAN COPYIST CULVERT
DRAUGHT GULLION JAWHOLE
SHIRRER PIQUIERE
SEWING TACK SUTURE SEMPSTRY
SEX KIND SECT GENDER
(FEMALE —) SMOCK
(MALE —) WEPMANKIN
SEXLESS NEUTER EPICENE
SEXT MIDDAY
SEXTET SESTET SEXTUOR SESTETTO
SEXTON SAXON SHAMUS WARDEN
SACRIST SHAMASH VESTURER
SEXTUPLE SENARY
SEXTUPLET SESTOLE SEXTOLE
SESTOLET SEXTOLET
SEXUAL GAMIC INTIMATE
SEXY FREUDIAN
SHA YASHIRO
SHAB RUBBERS
SHABBINESS WAFFNESS
SHABBY BASE MEAN POKY WORN
DINGY DOWDY MANGY RATTY
SCALD SEEDY TACKY CHEESY
FROWZY GRUBBY SCABBY SCOFFY
SCOURY SCURVY SHODDY SHROVY
SLEAZY TAGRAG BUNTING MESQUIN
SCALLED SCRUBBY SCRUFFY
SCUFFED SHABBED SQUALID
PALTERLY SLIPSHOD WAFFLIKE
SHACK COE HUT CRIB SHAG HUMPY
HUTCH SHANTY
SHACKLE COP TIE BAND BIND BOLT
BOND GYVE LOCK STAY BASIL
BILBO CLAMP COPSE CRAMP CRANK
HUMPY TRASH TRAVE FETTER
GARTER HAMPER PINION SHANGY
STAYER SWATHE COTTAGE
COUPLER FETLOCK MANACLE
PASTERN SNACKLE TRAMMEL
RESTRAIN
(PL.) IRONS
SHACKLER SLOTTER
SHAD BUCK CHAD ALLIS ALOSE
TRABU ALLICE TWAITE ALEWIFE
ANADROM CLUPEID FLATFISH
SAWBELLY
SHADBUSH DOGWOOD SERVICE
SHADDOCK LUCBAN POMELO
POMPION
SHADE EYE CAST DULL SCUG SHED
TONE VEIL BLEND COLOR ENNUE
GHOST GLIDE GLOOM GRAIN SCAUM
SWALE SWILL TASTE TINCT TINGE
TRACE UMBER UMBRA DEGREE
FRESCO SHADOW SHIELD SHROUD
SPRITE STRAIN STRIPE TONING
CURTAIN ECLIPSE GRADATE
HACHURE PROTECT SECTION

SHADING UMBRAGE HALFTONE
UMBRELLA
(— OF COLOR) EYE TONE
(— OF DIFFERENCE) NUANCE
(— OFF) GRADUATE
(EYE —) UGLY
(OVERHANGING —) CANOPY
(WINDOW —) STORE
SHADED OMBRE SHADY DRUMLY
SOMBER SOMBRE DARKLING
SHADINESS GLOOM
SHADING FLUTING LAYERING
SHADOW FOX BLOT SCUG TAIL
CLOUD SHADE UMBER UMBRA
CLEEKS DARKEN FINGER SHROUD
TAILER ISOGYRE PHANTOM
SCARROW SUGGEST UMBRAGE
UMBRATE PENUMBRA PHANTASM
SHEPHERD
SHADOWED DARKLING
SHADOWINESS GLOOM
SHADOWLESS ASCIAN WHITEOUT
SHADOWY MISTY VAGUE GLOOMY
GHOSTLY OBSCURE
SHADRACH ANANIAS HANANIAH
SHADY DARK CLOUDY SHADOW
SHADOWY UMBROSE ADUMBRAL
SHAFT BAR NIB ROD BALK BOLT
DART FUST HOLE PILE POLE TRAM
WELL ARBOR HEUGH QUILL REACH
SCAPE SHANK SHOOT SNEAD
SPRAG STAFF STALE STAVE STEAL
STILT STING THILL TRUNK BOLTEL
CANNON COLUMN GNOMON SCAPUS
STAPLE TILLER UPRISE VAGINA
BOWTELL CHIMNEY INCLINE
MANDREL SPINDLE CAMSHAFT
DOWNCAST ESCONSON HOISTWAY
LAMPHOLE SHAFTWAY STANDARD
WEIGHBAR WELLHOLE
(— CONNECTING WHEELS) AXLE
(— IN GLACIER) MOULIN
(— IN WATCH) STEM
(— OF CANDLESTICK) BALUSTER
(— OF CARRIAGE) FILL SILL THILL
(— OF CART) ROD TRAM SHARP
STANG
(— OF CAVERN) DOME
(— OF CHARIOT) BEAM
(— OF CLUSTERED PIER) BOLTEL
(— OF COLUMN) FUST TIGE SCAPE
(— OF FEATHER) SCAPE SCAPUS
(— OF MINE) PIT WORK GRUFF
HEUCH HEUGH SLOPE GROOVE
STAPLE INCLINE WINNING
(— OF PADDLE) ROUND
(— OF SPEAR OR LANCE) TREE
STALE
(— OF WAGON) STAVE THILL
LIMBER
(HARNESS —) HEALD
(HOLLOW —) CANNON
(MAIN —) ARBOR
(ORNAMENTAL —) VERGE
(SCYTHE —) SNEAD
(STAIRWAY —) VICE
(TWISTED —) TORSO
(VENTILATION —) UPCAST UPTAKE
WINDHOLE

SHAG PILE
SHAGGY SHAG SWAG HARSH NAPPY
ROUGH SHOCK TATTY TOUSY
BRUSHY COMATE RAGGED TOOSIE
HIRSUTE SHAGRAG SQUALID
SWAGGED THRUMMY VILLOUS
TATTERED
SHAGREEN GALUCHAT
SHAGROON PILGRIM
SHAKE BOB DAD JAR JOG ROG WAG
JOLT JOWL PLUM QUAG RESE ROCK
SHOG STIR SWAY TOZE WEVE
WHAP WHOP HOTCH JAUNT KNOCK
NIDGE QUASH SHOCK SWING TRILL
DIDDER DITHER DODDER DODDLE
EXCUSS GOGGLE HOTTER HUSTLE
JOGGLE JOUNCE JUMBLE QUATCH
QUAVER QUITCH QUIVER ROGGLE
RUFFLE SHIMMY SHIVER TOTTER
WAMBLE WANGLE WARBLE WEAKEN
WOBBLE AGITATE BRANDLE
CHOUNCE CONCUSS SHUDDER
STAGGER SUCCUSS TREMBLE
TWITTER WHIFFLE WHITHER
BRANDISH CONVULSE ENFEEBLE
(— HERRING) SCUD
(— LIGHTLY) LIFT
(— OFF) ARISE EXCUSS
(— TO SEPARATE) HOTCH
(— UP) JABBLE JUMBLE RATTLE
(WIND —) ANEMOSIS
SHAKER DUSTER SIFTER DREDGER
JUMBLER POUNCET SANDBOX
SHAKING ASHAKE TREMOR JARRING
AGITATED
(— OF AIRPLANE) BUFFET
SHAKTI TARA PRAKRITI
SHAKTIS MATRIS
SHAKY CRANK DICKY QUAKY ROCKY
TOTTY WONKY WOOZY AGUISH
CRANKY GROGGY INFIRM WAMBLY
CASALTY DWAIBLE DWEEBLE
PALSIED RICKETY SHOGGLY
TITTUPY TOTTERY COGGLEDY
INSECURE
SHALE BAT BASS BONE CLOD FLAG
KOLM METAL PLATE XALLE KILLAS
SHILLET MUDSTONE SLIGGEEN
SHALL SE MAY MUN MUST SALL
(— NOT) SANNA SHANT SHANNA
SHALLOON CUBICA
SHALLOT CIBOL ALLIUM ESCHALOT
SCALLION
SHALLOW EBB BANK FLAN FLAT
FLUE GLIB FLEET INANE SHOAL
SILLY SMALL FLIMSY FROTHY
LITTLE RIFFLE SLIGHT UNDEEP
CRIPPLE CURSORY TRIVIAL
MAGAZINY
(PL.) FORD
SHALLOWNESS INANITY
SHAM BAM FOB FOX GIG FAKE HOAX
MOCK PUFF BLUFF BOGUS CHEAT
DUMMY FALSE FEIGN FRAUD LETON
QUEER ASSUME BRUMMY BUNYIP
CHOUSE DECEIT DUFFER HUMBUG
PSEUDO STUMER FALSITY FORGERY
GRIMACE MOCKISH PLASTER

PRETEND STUMOUR PRETENSE
SPURIOUS
SHAMAN PEAI CURER MACHI
KAHUNA WABENO ANGEKOK
TOHUNGA CONTRARY WITCHMAN
SHAMBLE SHALE SHOOL SCAMBLE
SHACHLE SHACKLE SKEMMEL
ABATTOIR SHAMMOCK
(PL.) BUTCHERY
SHAMBLING SHACKLY
SHAME SISS ABASH AIDOS SPITE
ASHAME BISMER REBUKE MORTIFY
SCANDAL SLANDER CONTEMPT
DISGRACE DISHONOR REPROACH
SHENDING VERGOYNE VITUPERY
(— BY CENSURE) TOUCH
SHAMEFACED SHY
SHAMEFACEDNESS PUDENCY
SHAMEFUL BASE FOUL MEAN
GROSS HONTOUS IGNOBLE
FLAGRANT IMPROPER INFAMOUS
SHAMELESS HARD BRASH ARRANT
BRAZEN BASHLESS BROWLESS
IMMODEST IMPUDENT
SHAMELESSNESS BRASS
SHAMPOO TRIPSIS
SHAMROCK SEAMROG SHAMROOT
SHANK BODY CRUS GAMB JAMB
TANG FENUR GAMBE CANNON
NIBBLE TARSUS KNUCKLE
(THREAD —) STEM
SHANNY BULLY
SHANTY BOIST HUMPY HUTCH
SHACK CHANTIER DOGHOUSE
SHAPE AX ADZ AXE CUT DIE HUE
ADZE BEAT BEND CAST COLE COPE
DRAW FACE FAIR FORM HACK MOLD
NICK BEVEL BLOCK BOAST BUILT
COLOR DRAPE DRESS FEIGN FORGE
FRAME GUISE HORSE JOLLY LATHE
MODEL MOULD SWAGE BROACH
CHISEL CUTOUT EFFORM FIGURE
FORMER FRAISE HAMMER JIGGER
SQUARE CHANNEL CONFORM
CONTOUR FASHION GESTALT
INCLINE PATTERN TONNEAU
CONTRIVE LIKENESS
(— BY HAMMERING) SMITH
(— DIAMOND) BRUTE
(— GARMENTS) BOARD
(— METAL) SWAGE EXTRUDE
(— OF BUST) TAILLE
(— OF ENVELOPE FLAP) KNIFE
(— ON POTTER'S WHEEL) THROW
(— ONE'S COURSE) ETTLE
(— RIGHTLY) FIT
(— ROUGHLY WITH CHISEL) BOAST
(— ROUGHLY) BOAST SCABBLE
SCAPPLE
(— STONE) BROACH SCABBLE
(CLAY —) FLOATER
(CONICAL —) BEEHIVE
(GEM —) BAGUET BAGUETTE
(GLOVE —) TRANK
(SPIRALLING —) SWIRL
(SURFACE —) GEOMETRY
(UNBLOCKED —) HOOD
SHAPED BUILT FITTED BLOCKED
FEATURED

(— LIKE BEAN) FABIFORM
(— LIKE BOAT) SCAPHOID
(— LIKE BUCKLER) SCUTATE
(— LIKE CLUB) CLAVATE CLUBBED
(— LIKE CONE) CONIFORM
(— LIKE CUP) SCYPHATE
(— LIKE DOME) DOMAL
(— LIKE EAR) AURIFORM
(— LIKE HALBERD) HASTATE
(— LIKE HEART) CORDATE
(— LIKE HOOK) ANKYROID
(— LIKE KEEL) CARINATE
(— LIKE LEAF) FOLIATE
(— LIKE LENS) LENTOID
(— LIKE NEEDLE) ACUATE
(— LIKE RING) ANNULAR
(— LIKE ROD) BACILLAR
(— LIKE S) SIGMATE
(— LIKE SHIELD) ASPIDATE
CLYPEATE
(— LIKE SICKLE) FALCULAR
(— LIKE SPINDLE) FUSOID
FUSIFORM
(— LIKE SPUR) CALCARINE
(— LIKE STAR) ASTROID
(— LIKE STRAP) LIGULATE
(— LIKE SWORD) GLADIATE
(— LIKE THREAD) FILIFORM
(— LIKE WEDGE) CUNEAL CUNEATE
(— LIKE X) SALTIRE
(— WITH AX) HEWN
SHAPELESS DUMPY DEFORM
DUMPTY INFORM FORMLESS
UNSHAPED
SHAPELINESS DELICACY
SHAPELY GENT TRIM CLEAN TIGHT
DECENT FORMAL GAINLY FORMFUL
SHAPABLE
SHAPING DESCENT
SHARD SCAUR SHERD SHRED
(PL.) PITCHER
SHARE CUT END LOT CANT DALE
DEAL DOLE HAND PART PLOT RENT
SCOT SNIP DIVVY ENTER PARTY
QUOTA RATIO SHEAR SHIFT SLICE
SNACK SNICK SNUCK SPLIT WHACK
COMMON COPART DEPART DIVIDE
FINGER IMPART RATION SHOVEL
PARTAGE PARTAKE PORTION
DIVIDEND DIVISION INTEREST
PURPARTY
(— A BED) BUNK
(— EQUALLY) HALVE
(— OF EXPENSES) LAW CLUB
(— OF LAND) DAIL DALE FREEDOM
(— OF PROFIT) LAY
(— OF STOCK) STOCK ACTION
(— QUARTERS) CHUM
(— SECRETS) CONFIDE
(ALLOTED —) DOLE
(ANCESTRAL —) PATTI
(FULL —) SKINFUL
(GREATER —) FECK
(LEGAL —) HAK
(ONE'S —) AFFERE
(PROPORTIONAL —) QUOTA
SHARECROPPER BYWONER
CROPPER
SHARED JOINT BETWEEN

SHARING (— OF EXPENSE) CLUB
(— VICARIOUSLY) ARMCHAIR
SHARK FOX GATA HAYE KULP MAKO
MANO TOPE GUMMY HOMER HOUND
LAMIA TIGER TOPER DAGGAR
GALEID PALOMA REQUIN WHALER
ACRODUS BONEDOG DOGFISH
FOXFISH HUNFYSH PLACOID
REQUIEM SLEEPER SOUPFIN
SQUALID SUNFISH TIBERON
TIGRONE TUBARON BULLHEAD
HYBODONT ROUSETTE SAILFISH
SEAHOUND SKAAMOOG SPEAREYE
SQUATINA THRASHER
(YOUNG —) CUB SHARKLET
SHARP DRY SHY ACID ACRE CUTE
EDGY FELL FINE GAIR GASH GLEG
GNIB HARD HIGH KEEN PERT SALT
TART ACERB ACRID ACUTE ALERT
BRASH BREME BRISK CRISP DOWNY
EAGER EDGED FALSE HARSH NEBBY
PEERY QUICK SMART SNELL SQUAB
STEEP STIFF VIVID YAULD ARGUTE
ASTUTE BITING BITTER BRIGHT
CRISPY DIESIS GLASSY JAGGED
PLUCKY SEVERE SHREWD SHRILL
SNELLY SNITHE STINGY TOOTHY
TWEAKY UNRIDE ANGULAR
AUSTERE BRITTLE CAUSTIC
CUTTING GINGERY PIQUANT
POINTED PUNGENT SHARPEN
SLICING SPINOUS VARMINT VIOLENT
HATCHETY INCISIVE POIGNANT
SHARP-EDGED CULTRATE
SHARPEN EDGE FILE FINE HONE
KEEN WHET BRISK FROST GRIND
POINT RAISE SHARP SLYPE STONE
STROP ACCENT AFFILE STROKE
ENHANCE QUICKEN SMARTEN
EXACUATE HEIGHTEN
SHARPENED ACUATE
SHARPENER SHARPER STROPPER
(SCYTHE —) RIP RIFLE
SHARPER GUE GYP BITE KITE ROOK
SKIN SNAP BITER CHEAT CROOK
GREEK ROGUE SHARK SHARP
BESTER COGGER NICKUM PICARO
ROOKER SHARPY BARNARD
CATATAN GAMBLER SHARKER
SPIELER BLACKLEG DECEIVER
PIGEONER SWINDLER
SHARPLY DAB SHARP SNACK ACIDLY
ROUNDLY SHEERLY SMARTLY
STEEPLY
SHARPNESS WIT EDGE SALT WHET
PLUCK ACRITY ACUITY ACIDITY
ACERBITY ACRIDITY ACRIMONY
EDGINESS PUNGENCY
SHARP-POINTED ACUATE
ACULEATE
SHARPSHOOTER VOLTIGEUR
SHARP-SIGHTED SIGHTY LYNCEAN
SHARP-TAILED GROUSE PINTAIL
SHARP-WITTED CANNY SNELL
SHREWD
SHASTRA PURANA SASTRA
(— CLASS) SRUTI
SHATTER BLOW DASH DICE BLAST
BREAK BURST CRASH CRAZE

CREEM FRUSH SMASH SMOKE SPLIT
WRECK SHIVER SPIDER BEGUILE
CHATTER CONVEIL EXPLODE
SMATTER TORPEDO DEMOLISH
DYNAMITE SPLINTER
(— CLAY TARGET) KILL
SHATTERED BROKEN BROOZLED
DODDERED
SHAVE BARB BITE DRAW PARE RAZE
GLACE GRAZE SKIVE SCHAWE
SCRAPE FLATTEN UPRIGHT
SHAVED POLLED SHAVEN
SHAVEN NOT NOTT PILLED
TONSURED
SHAVING SHAVE SHRED SPALE
SPELL RAMENT RAMENTUM
(PL.) COOM COOMB SCOBS
MOSLINGS
SHAWL MAUD LAMBA MANTA MANTO
NUBIA PATTU TOZIE AFGHAN
ANGORA KAMBAL PEPLOS PEPLUM
PEPLUS PUTTOO SERAPE TAPALO
TOILET ZEPHYR AMLIKAR PAISLEY
WHITTLE WRAPPER CASHMERE
EPIBLEMA SLENDANG TURNOVER
(COARSE —) KAMBAL
(COTTON —) FARDA
(PLAID —) MAUD
(TASSELED —) TALLITH
SHAWM WAIT SHALM BOMBARD
SCHALMEI
SHE A HE HEO HER SHU HAEC SCHO
SHEAF TIE BEAT BUNG GAIT GERB
OMER FLASH GAVEL GERBE GLEAN
BATTEN THRAVE HATTOCK
CAPSHEAF CORNBOLE
(— LEVIED AS TAX) CORNBOLE
(— OF ARROWS) FLASH
(— OF FLAX OR HEMP) BEAT BEET
GLEAN
(— OF GRAIN) GAIT GARB HOSE
GARBACE
(LAST — OF CORN) NECK
(LAST — OF HARVEST) KIRN
(PROTECTING —) HATTOCK
(UNBOUND —) REAP GAVEL
SHEAR COW CUT DOD LIP NOT CLIP
CROP NOTT TRIM BREAK FORCE
SHARE SHEER SHIRL SLIDE STRIP
FLEECE STRESS
SHEARABLE TONSILE
SHEARER SNAGGER
SHEARLING SHEARHOG
(PL.) ALPACA
SHEARS LEWIS SNIPS FORFEX
SHEARER SNOUTER SECATEUR
SHEARWATER HAG CREW COHOW
HAGDON HAGLET PETREL PUFFIN
SCRABE PIMLICO SCRABER SEABIRD
HACKBOLT
SHEATFISH WELS DORAD WALLER
CATFISH SILURID
SHEATH COT HOT BOOT CASE CYST
HOSE HOTT ARMOR CHAPE FOREL
GAINE SHADE SHEAF SPILL THECA
CONDOM FORREL MYELIN OCHREA
QUIVER SLOUGH VAGINA AXILEMMA
EPILEMMA SCABBARD STANDARD
VAGINULA

(— **FOR BOOK**) FOREL FORRIL
(— **FOR FINGER**) STALL
(— **FOR GAMECOCK'S SPUR**) HOT
HOTT
(— **OF CIGARETTE**) SPILL
(— **OF PLOW**) STANDARD
(**MEDULLARY** —) CORONA
SHEATHBILL PADDY
SHEATHE CLAD COPPER MUZZLE
IMPLATE
SHEATHING SKIN ARMOR COPPER
FACING SHEATH INLAYER SHIPLAP
SLITWORK
SHEA TREE KARITE KARITI
SHEAVE SHEAF SHIVER HATTOCK
TRUCKLE
(**24 —S OF GRAIN**) THRAVE
THREAVE
SHED BOX CUB SOW ABRI CAST
COTE DROP HELM HULL KILN MOLT
POUR SHUD SKEO SLIP HIELD
HOVEL MOULT SCALE SHADE SPILL
THROW VINEA ZAYAT BELFRY
BROACH DINGLE EFFUSE GARAGE
HANGAR HEMMEL INFUSE LINHAY
MISTAL PANDAL SLOUGH COTTAGE
DIFFUSE DISCARD MUSCULE
RADIATE SKIPPER EXUVIATE
SKEELING SKILLION WOODSHED
(— **BLOOD**) BROACH
(— **DROPS**) DRIZZLE
(— **FEATHERS OR HORNS**) MEW
(— **FOR LIVESTOCK**) SHIPPEN
(— **FOR SHEEP**) SHEALING
(— **OVER MINE SHAFT**) COE
(— **TEARS**) GIVE
(— **TO PROTECT SOLDIERS**)
TESTUDO
(**CATTLE** —) CUB HELM LAIR
BELFRY
(**MOVABLE** —) SOW BAIL MUSCULE
(**TEMPORARY** —) PANDAL
(**WEATHER** —) DINGLE
SHEDDING FALL SPILTH ECDYSIS
APOLYSIS
SHE-DEMON LAMIA
SHEEN GLAZE SHINE LUSTER
LUSTRE SHIMMER
SHEEP SNA TEG DOWN LAMB LONK
MUGS SHIP SOAY URIN ZENU
ANCON BOVID DUMBA HEDER HUNIA
MUGGS OVINE SAIGA SHORN TAGGE
AOUDAD ARGALI BARHAL BHARAL
BIDENT CHURRO DECCAN DORPER
DORSET EXMOOR HIRSEL MARKER
MASHAM MERINO MUTTON NAYAUR
OXFORD PANAMA PAULER ROMNEY
WETHER WOOLIE WOOLLY BIGHORN
BLEATER BRAXIES CHEVIOT
CRIOLLA DELAINE DISHLEY FREEZER
FRONTER JUMBUCK KARAKUL
LINCOLN POLLARD SUFFOLK
TARGHEE TWINTER VERMONT
BIKANERI COMEBACK COTSWOLD
DARTMOOR HERDWICK LONGWOOL
LUGHDOAN RUMINANT SHEARHOG
SHEARING TALLOWER THRINTER
(— **DIFFICULT TO HANDLE**)
COBBLER

(— **IN 2ND YEAR**) HOB TAG TEG
TAGGE TWINTER
(— **THAT HAS SHED PORTION OF
WOOL**) ROSELLA
(— **TO BE SHEARED**) BOARD
(**3-YEAR-OLD** —) THRINTER
(**DEAD** —) BRAXY
(**FEMALE** —) EWE GIMMER SHEDER
(**HORNLESS** —) NOT NOTT
(**LOST** —) WAIF
(**MALE** —) RAM TUP BUCK HEDER
(**MOUNTAIN** —) IBEX
(**OLD** —) GUMMER
(**THICK-WOOLED** —) MUG
(**UNSHORN** —) HOG TEG
(**WILD** —) SHA ARGAL RASSE URIAL
AOUDAD ARGALI BHARAL SHAPOO
BURRHEL MOUFLON
(**YOUNG** —) HOG HOGG HOGGEREL
SHEEPBERRY ALISIER VIBURNUM
SHEEPCOTE SHEPPEY
SHEEPDOG KELPIE SHELTY BOBTAIL
MALINOIS SHETLAND
SHEEP FLY FAG
SHEEPFOLD REE FANK KRAAL
REEVE STELL BOUGHT BARKARY
SHEPPEY SHEEPCOT
SHEEPHERDER SNOOZER
STOCKMAN
SHEEPISH SHY
SHEEP LAUREL IVY HEATH WICKY
KALMIA LAUREL CALFKILL LAMBKILL
SHEEPLIKE OVINE
SHEEPMAN HOBBER
SHEEP PLANT RAOULIA
SHEEP ROT CAW
SHEEP RUN STATION
SHEEPSHEAD JAMES JEMMY JIMMY
PARGO PORGY TAUTOG FATHEAD
PERCOID SPAROID
SHEEPSHEARER GUN
SHEEPSKIN ROAN SLAT MOUTON
SOLDIER CAPESKIN LAMBSKIN
WOOLFELL WOOLSKIN
(— **TANNED WITH BARK**) BASAN
BASIL
(— **THAT SWEATS UNEVENLY**)
SOLDIER
(— **WITHOUT WOOL**) SLAT
(**ROUGH-TANNED** —) CRUST
SHEEP SORREL SOURWEED
SHEEP TICK FAG KEB KED KADE
SHEEPWALK SLAIT
SHEER BOLD FINE MAIN MERE PURE
BLANK BRANT CRUDE FRANK STARK
STEEP SIMPLE CLOTTED GAZETTE
EVENDOWN
(**MADE OF — FABRIC**) PEEKABOO
SHEET FIN CARD FILM FINE FLAT
FOIL LEAF SILL BLANK FLONG
FOLIO NAPPE CANVAS CIRCLE
DOUBLE FASCIA FENDER FLIMSY
SHROUD SINDON BLANKET
CHUDDER FLOGGER FRISKET
LEAFLET PALLIUM PAPYRUS
WRAPPER AIRSHEET EIGHTEEN
FOLLOWER HANDBILL INTERLAY
SHEETLET
(— **ADDED TO DEED**) FOLLOWER

(— **ATTACHED TO INVOICE**) APRON
(— **FOR BRIDGE SCORES**) FLOGGER
(— **OF CELLULOID**) CEL CELL
(— **OF CLOUDS**) PALLIUM
(— **OF DOUGH**) STRUDEL
(— **OF FIBER**) BAT LAP BATT
(— **OF ICE**) GLARE GLAZE
(— **OF IRON**) CRAMPET CRAMPIT
(— **OF LAVA**) COULEE
(— **OF LEAD**) SOAKER
(— **OF LEATHER**) BUFFING
(— **OF MICA**) FILM
(— **OF PAPER**) FLAT FOLIO FRISKET
LEAFLET HANDBILL
(— **OF PARCHMENT**) SKIN
FOLLOWER
(— **OF RUBBER**) DAM
(— **OF STRAW**) YELM
(— **OF SUGAR**) SLAB
(— **OF TISSUE**) FASCIA
(— **OF TOBACCO**) BINDER
(— **OF WATER**) NAPPE
(— **USED FOR MATRIX**) FLONG
(**HEATED** —) CAUL
(**METAL** —**S**) LATTENS
(**NEWS** —) GAZETTE
(**ORGANIZATION** —) BILL
(**PERFORATED** —) SIEVE
(**PROTECTIVE** —) CURTAIN
(**THEATRICAL** —) SIDE
(**THIN** —**S OF IRON**) DOUBLES
(**TRANSPARENT** —) GELATINE
(**WINDING** —) SINDON SUDARY
SHEETING DOMESTIC AMERIKANI
SHEKINAH GLORY
SHELDRAKE SHELDER BARGOOSE
SHELF BANK BERM BINK DECK DESS
STEP TACK BENCH LEDGE SKELF
STAGE STOOL MANTEL SCONCE
SETTLE SHELVE BACKBAR BRACKET
COUNTER PLATEAU CREDENCE
CUPBOARD
(— **BEFORE STOVE**) HEARTH
(— **BEHIND ALTAR**) GRADINE
GRADINO RETABLE
(— **IN MINE**) BUNNING
(— **OF ROCK**) CAR LENCH
LENCHEON
(**ALTAR** —) BUTSUDAN
(**CONTINENTAL** —) PLATFORM
(**FIREWORKS** —) BALLOON
(**RAISED** —) SETTLE
SHELL ARD HUD PEN POD BAND
CASK CHOU CONE HARD HOOF
HULL HUSK MAIL OBUS PELL PILL
PIPI PUPA SKIN SWAD UMBO UNIO
BALAT CHANK CHINK CONCH COPIS
CRUMP CRUST DRILL FRITZ GOURD
MITER MITRA MUREX ORMER SCAUP
SHALE SHARD SHEAL SHERD SHOCK
SHUCK TESTA TIARA TROCA TURBO
VALVE VENUS ANOMIA BUCKIE
BULLET BURGAU CERION COCKLE
CONKER COWRIE CRUSTA DENTAL
DOLIUM ECLAIR JINGLE LORICA
MAROON NOUGAT NUCULA PULLET
PURPLE SANKHA SINGLE SLOUGH
STROMB TERBRA TRITON TURBAN
VANNET VENTER VOLUTE WINKLE

BALLOON CARACOL CARCASS
COCONUT DARIOLE DISCINA
GLADIUS LIMACEL MARINER
PAPBOAT PHILINE PROJECT
SCALLOP SPICULE SPINDLE
SPONDYL THIMBLE TOHEROA
TORPEDO TOXIFER TROCHID
TRUMPET UNICORN BACULITE
BACULOID CARAPACE CONCHITE
COQUILLE CYLINDER DUCKFOOT
EGGSHELL ENVELOPE ESCALLOP
FIGSHELL FOCALOID FRUSTULE
HELICINA MERINGUE OLIVELLA
PUPARIUM SEASHELL SOLARIUM
STROMBUS UNIVALVE VELUTINA
VERMETID VERMETUS WARRENER
WHIZBANG WOODCOCK
(— CONTAINING MEDICINE)
CAPSULE
(— OF DIATOM) FRUSTULE
(— OF OYSTER) HUSK SHUCK
(— OF SHIP) HULK SKIN
(— OF SLUG) LIMACEL
(— SYSTEMATICALLY) COMB
(—S FROM GUN) STUFF
(ANTIAIRCRAFT —) FLAK
(CARTRIDGE —S) BRASS
(CAST —S) EXUVIAE
(CUSTARD-FILLED —) ECLAIR
DARIOLE
(FOSSIL —) DOLITE AMMONITE
BACULITE BALANITE CONCHITE
(HOWITZER —) OBUS
(MATHEMATICAL —) HOMEOID
(OYSTER —S) CULCH CULTCH
(PASTRY —) CORNET DARIOLE
TIMBALE TALMOUSE
(SNAIL —) CONKER HODMADOD
(SPIRAL —) CHANK
(TORTOISE —) HOOF
(VEGETABLE —) DOLMA
SHELLED VINED
SHELLFISH COCK NACRE PIROT
LIMPET WIGGLE MOLLUSK PERIWIG
SHELLING RATTLES
SHELL-LESS OON
SHELL MONEY UHLLO WAKIKI
SHELTER CAB HUT LEE LOO ABRI
BURY EAVE GIDE GITE HERD HIDE
HIVE JOKE JOUK ROOF SCOG SCUG
BARTH BENAB BERRY BIELD BOIST
BOTHY BOWER CABIN CLEAD CLOAK
COVER EMBAY HAVEN HOARD
HOUSE HOVEL HOVER HOWFF
HUTCH LEWTH LITHE RESET SHADE
SHEAL ASYLUM AWNING BELFRY
BILBIE BOOLEY BOUGHT BURROW
COVERT CRADLE DEFEND DUGOUT
GABION GUNYAH HANGAR HARBOR
HOSTEL PANDAL REFUGE SCONCE
SCREEN SHADOW SHIELD SHROUD
SUKKAH BOROUGH CABINET
CARPORT CHAMBER DEFENSE
EMBOSOM EMBOWER HOUSING
NACELLE QUARTER RETREAT
ROOFING TABERNA UMBRAGE
WANIGAN WICKIUP BESCREEN
DOGHOUSE ENSCONCE LODGMENT
PALLIATE SECURITY SNOWSHED
WAYHOUSE

(— FOR CATTLE) HELM BOOLY
STELL HEMMEL
(— FOR CROP WATCHERS) KISI
(— FOR DANCES) ENRAMADA
(— FOR SENTRY) GUERITE
(— FROM WEATHER) LEWTH
(— OVER BEEHIVE) HOOD
(BULLETPROOF —) MANTLET
MANTELET
(CONCRETE-AND-STEEL —) PILLBOX
(CRAMPED —) HUTCH
(FISH —) CROY
(LEAFY —) LEVESEL
(MINING —) TALPA
(PORTABLE —) MANTA CABANA
(ROCK —) KRAPINA
(ROUGH —) JACAL
(TEEPEELIKE —) CHUM
(TEMPORARY —) HALE HOLD CABIN
BIVOUAC
SHELTERED LEE LEW LOWN BIELD
LITHE SHADY COVERT
(— SPACE) KILLOGIE
SHELTERING BIELDY SHADING
SHELTERLESS HOMELESS
ROOFLESS
SHELVE DISH BURKE SHELF
SHELVES STAGE ETAGERE
SHENG SANG CHENG SHING
(ONE-HUNDREDTH —) CHAO
SHEOL HELL
SHEPHERD HERD SHEP COLIN
CORIN GADDI GYGES SWAIN FEEDER
PASTOR TARBOX CORYDON
DAPHNIS DRAFTER GADARIA
KURUMBA THYRSIS TITYRIS
MELIBEUS MENALCAS PASTORAL
SHEEPMAN STREPHON
(GERMAN —) ALSATIAN
SHEPHERDESS DELIA MOPSA PHEBE
DORCAS BERGERE GALATEA
PASTORA PERDITA
SHEPHERD'S-PURSE TOYWORT
CASEWEED COCOWORT
SHERBET ICE GLACE SORBET
GRANITA SOUFFLE
SHERD SCARTH
SHERIFF FOUD FOWD SCULT XERIF
DEPUTY GRIEVE SCHOUT SHIRRA
BAILIFF SHREEVE SHRIEVE
ALGUACIL HUISSIER SHIREMAN
VISCOUNT
SHERRY FINO CLOVE JEREZ XERES
DOCTOR MANCHU SOLERA
OLOROSO RANGOON SHERRIS
MONTILLA
SHEVRI SESBAN
SHICER DUFFER
SHIELD ECU EGIS HIDE PELT AEGIS
APRON BIELD BOARD CLOAK COVER
FENCE GUARD GULAR MULGA
PATCH PAVIS PELTA PYGAL SCUTE
SHEND TARGE YELDE ANCILE
ANGARA BLAZON CASQUE DEFEND
FENDER GUNTUB GYROMA LINDEN
MENTAL OCULAR PAUNCH RONDEL
SCREEN SCUTUM SECURE TARGET
BUCKLER CLIPEUS CONCEAL
PANNIER PAVISSE PRIDWIN

PROTECT ROSTRAL ROTELLA
ROUNDEL SHELTER SUPPORT
TESTUDO CARTOUCH CUCULLUS
HIELAMEN INSULATE MARGINAL
PRESERVE RONDACHE STERNITE
SUNSHADE BREASTING
(— BELOW A DAM) APRON
(— FOR ARCHERS) PANNIER
(— FOR HORSE) BIB
(— FOR LAMP) BONNET CHIMNEY
(— OF A STIRRUP) HOOD
(— OF ABORIGINES) MULGA
HIELAMEN
(— OF CONTINENT) CORE
(— OF HIDE) SKILDFEL
(— OF SOMITE) STERNITE
(— OF TRILOBITE) CEPHALON
(— ON MAST) PAUNCH
(— ON THROAT OF FISH) GULAR
(— OVER BASE OF FAN) CANOPY
(BONY —) CARAPACE
(BULLETPROOF —) MANTA MANTLET
MANTELET
(HERALDIC —) BLAZON
(KING ARTHUR'S —) PRIWEN
PRIDWIN
(LEATHER —) CHAFE
(SACRED —) ANCILE
(SIBERIAN —) ANGARA
(WICKERWORK —) SCIATH
SHIELDBEARER SQUIRE ESQUIRE
PELTAST ESCUDERO SCUTIFER
SHIELD BUG STINKBUG
SHIELD FERN FERNGALE
SHIELDMAKER TYCHIOS
SHIELD-SHAPED PELTATE SCUTATE
THYROID
SHIFT JIB BACK CHOP FEND FLIT
HAUL MOVE RUSE SHIP TACK TOUR
TURN VARY VEER WEND BREAK
BUDGE CREEP CYMAR DRIFT HOTCH
QUIRK SHIRK SHUNT SIMAR SKIFT
SLIDE SMOCK SPELL TRICK BAFFLE
CHANGE DENIAL DEVICE DOUBLE
PALTER SKYFTE SWERVE SWITCH
CUTBACK EVASION FRESHEN
SHUFFLE SLEIGHT WHIFFLE
ARTIFICE DISLODGE DISPLACE
DOGWATCH DOUBLING MUTATION
REVIRADO TRANSFER TRAVERSE
TURNOVER WINDLASS
(— ABOUT AS THE WIND) LARGE
(— ABRUPTLY) JUMP
(— IN DANCING) BALANCE
(— IN TACKING) JIB
(— ORDER OF BELLS) HUNT
(— RAILROAD EQUIPMENT) DRILL
(— SUDDENLY) FLY CHOP GYBE
JIBE
(— WEIGHT) WING
(MINING —) CORE
SHIFTING FLUID QUICK CHOPPING
DRIFTING FLOATING SLIPPAGE
VARIABLE VEERABLE
SHIFTLESS DRIFTY SOZZLY
DRIFTING FECKLESS HAVELESS
SHIFTLESSNESS SLOUCH
SHIFTY GREASY DEVIOUS EVASIVE
HANGDOG SLIDING SLIPPERY

SHIITE SHIAH SECTARY SHAIKHI TWELVER

SHILHA SHLU CHLEUH

SHILL STICK BONNET CAPPER BOOSTER

SHILLING BOB HOG CHIP HOGG LEVY DEENER HARPER TESTON TEVISS THIRTEEN
(20 —S) POUND
(21 —S) GUINEA
(5 —S) CROWN DECUS

SHILLY-SHALLY BACK BOGGLE

SHIM GLUT LINER SHIMMER

SHIMMER FLASH GLIMMER SHIMPER SKIMMER

SHIN SHANK SKINK SWARM CNEMIS SHINNY

SHINDIG SHINDY SHIVOO

SHINE RAY SUN BEAM BUFF GLOW LAMP LEAM LINK STAR BLARE BLICK BLINK BLOOM EXCEL GLAIK GLARE GLEAM GLEIT GLENT GLINT GLISS GLORE GLORY GLOSS GLOZE SHEEN SKYRE STARE BEACON DAZZLE GLANCE LUSTER LUSTRE SCANCE EFFULGE GLIMMER GLISTEN GLITTER RADIATE REFLECT SHIMMER SPARKLE RUTILATE
(— BRIGHTLY) BEEK FLAME LIGHT
(— FAINTLY) SCARROW
(— UPON) SUN SMITE

SHINER CHUB DACE BREAM REDFIN CYPRINID WINDFISH

SHINER-UP PATCHER

SHINGLE SHIM BEACH SHAKE SLATE CHESIL KNOBBLE STARTER

SHINGLER NOBBLER

SHINGLES ZONA ZOSTER

SHININESS GLARE GLAZE GLOSS

SHINING GLAD NEAT CLEAR GLARY LIGHT LUCID SHEER WHITE ARDENT ARGENT ASHINE BRIGHT FULGID GLOSSY GOLDEN LUCENT NITENT ORIENT SERENE SHEENY SPUNKY STARRY ADAZZLE BURNING FULGENT GLARING GLIMMER LAMPING FLASHING GLEAMING LUCULENT LUSTRANT LUSTROUS NITIDOUS RELUCENT RUTILANT SPLENDID STARLIKE SUNBEAMY SUNSHINY

SHINLEAF PYROLA

SHINNY PEG SHINTY

SHINTO (— SECT) RYOBU

SHIP (ALSO SEE BOAT AND VESSEL) ARK CAT COG HOY NAO BARK BOAT BOOM GRAB HAND HULK KEEL LADE NAVY PAHI PINE PINK SAIL SEND SNOW TREE WOOD ZULU CHECK LAKER OILER PINTA PRORE RAZEE SCOUT SCREW SKIFF WHELP ANDREW ARGOSY BARKEY BARQUE BOTTOM CARTEL CASTLE CHASER COALER CODMAN DECKER DIESEL GALIOT GALLEY HOLCAD HOPPER LANCHA LATEEN LORCHA MASTER MISTIC MOTHER PACKET PUFFER RUNNER SAILER SALVOR SEALER SMOKER TONNER TRAVEL VESSEL

ADMIRAL CARRACK CLIPPER COLLIER FACTORY FELUCCA FOREIGN FRIGATE FRUITER GABBARD GALLEON GUNBOAT INVOICE MACHINE MULETTA ONERARY PATAMAR PINNACE POLACRE SHALLOP SHIPLET SPITKIT STEAMER BALANDRA BALINGER BILANDER CAPITANA DRUMBLER FLAGSHIP GALLEASS GAYDIANG INDIAMAN JAPANNER LANCHARA MAGAZINE PESSONER PIPPINER REPEATER SAILSHIP SCHOONER SMUGGLER SPANIARD
(— BUILT FROM NAILS OF DEAD) NAGLFAR
(— OF ARGONAUTS) ARGO
(— OF NORSEMEN) KEEL
(CLUMSY —) HULK
(DEPOT —) TENDER
(ESCORT —) CORVETTE
(FLEET OF —S) ARMADA
(JAPANESE —) MARU
(MALAY —) COUGNAR
(NOVA SCOTIAN —) BLUENOSE
(OBJECT SHAPED LIKE A —) NEF
(PIRATE —) GALLIVAT
(PRIZE —) CAPTURE
(QUARANTINE —) LAZARET
(RECEIVING —) GUARDO
(REMOTE-CONTROLLED —) DRONE
(SLOW —) BUCKET
(STORE —) FLUTER
(SUPPLY —) COPER COOPER
(UNTRIM —) BALLAHOO
(VIKING —) DRAKE
(PL.) NAVY MARINE SEACRAFT SHIPPING

SHIPFITTER FITTER ERECTOR

SHIPMENT CARLOT RAILING DISPATCH SHIPPAGE

SHIPSHAPE NEAT TIDY TRIM CIVIL ATAUNT ORDERLY

SHIP SWEEPER TOPASS TOPIWALA

SHIPWAY BERTH

SHIPWORM ARTER BORER COBRA TEREDO PILEWORM WOODWORM

SHIPWRECK WRACK NAUFRAGE

SHIPWRIGHT WAYMAN BUILDER

SHIRE DERBY SHEER COUNTY

SHIRK FUNK GOOF MIKE BLINK BUDGE DODGE FEIGN FUDGE SKULK SLACK RODNEY FINAGLE SHACKLE SHAFFLE SOLDIER SHAMMOCK

SHIRKER FUNK PIKER FUNKER ROTTER BLUDGER SLACKER SLINKER SUGARER COBERGER EMBUSQUE SCOWBANK

SHIRR SMOCK

SHIRT TOB JUPE SARK TOBE BLUEY HAIRE JUPON KAMIS SHIFT BANIAN BANIYA CAMISA CAMISE PALAKA UNDERGO VAREUSE KAMLEIKA
(HAIR —) HAIRE CILICE
(SLEEVELESS —) FECKET
(WORKMAN'S —) FROCK
(WORNOUT —) DICKY

SHIRTING CHEVIOT HARVARD HOLLAND SARKING

SHIRTWAIST BLOUSE GARIBALDI

SHITTIMWOOD BOXWOOD

SHIVAREE BELLING CHIVARI HORNING SERENADE

SHIVER JAR GIRL GRUE BEVER BREAK CHILL CREEM CREEP FRILL GROWS QUAKE SHRUG SLICE CHIVER DITHER DUDDER GROOSE HOTTER NIDDER NITHER QUIVER SHRIMP SPLINT CHITTER FLICKER FRISSON SHATTER SHITHER SHUDDER TREMBLE KAMLEIKA SPLINTER

SHIVERING CHILL OURIE TREMOR ASHIVER

SHOAL BAJO BANK FLAT REEF SPIT BARRA DRAVE FLOTE SCULL SHELF SCHOOL SHALLOW TOWHEAD

SHOAT GURRY SHOOT SHOTT

SHOCK COP JAR BLOW BUMP DINT JOLT RACK SHOG STUN TURN APPAL BRUNT GAVEL GLIFF GLOFF SHAKE STOOK STOUR DISMAY FRIGHT IMPACT JOSTLE JUMBLE REJOLT RICKLE ROLLER STRIKE ASTOUND CANVASS DISGUST HATTOCK HORRIFY STAGGER STARTLE STUPEFY TERRIFY DISEDIFY GLIFFING SURPRISE
(— OF CORN) STOOK STOUT STITCH
(MENTAL —) TRAUMA

SHOCK ABSORBER SHOCK BUFFER DASHPOT SNUBBER

SHOCKED AGHAST

SHOCKER RICKER STOOKER

SHOCKING GRIM AWFUL HORRID UNHOLY BURNING FEARFUL FEARING GHASTLY HIDEOUS DREADFUL ENORMOUS HORRIBLE

SHOD CALCED

SHODDY SOFT CHEAP FOOTY SOFTS SLEAZY

SHOE BAL CUE PAN BOOT BROG CLOG DRAG FLAT HALF SKID SOCK TURN BLAKE DERBY KLOMP MOYLE ROMEO SABOT SCRAE SLING SPIKE STOGA STOGY STRAP ANKLET BEAKER BROGAN BROGUE BUSKIN CALIGA CALIGO CHOPIN COBCAB COCKER CRAKOW CREOLE DORSAY GAITER GALOSH KILTIE MULLER PATTEN PINSON POLISH SADDLE SANDAL SECQUE BAUCHLE BLUCHER CALCEUS CHOPINE COWHIDE FLIPPER RULLION SHOEPAC SLIPPER SNEAKER BALMORAL BRODEKIN COLONIAL PLIMSOLL SABOTINE SANDSHOE SKEWBACK SLIPSLOP SOLLERET
(— FOR GRINDING) MULLER
(— FOR MULE) PLANCHE
(— IN TRUSS OR FRAME) SKEWBACK
(— NOT FASTENED ON) PUMP
(— OF A SLEDGE) HOB
(— OF AN OX) CUE
(— OF COMIC ACTOR) BAXA
(— OF SUBWAY CAR) PAN
(— REPAIRER) JACKMAN

(— TO CHECK WHEEL) DRAG SKID
(— USED AS BRAKE) SKATE
(— WORN ON EITHER FOOT)
STRAIGHT
(—S AND STOCKINGS) FEET
(BABY'S —) CACK
(HOBNAILED —) TACKET
(LARGE —S) GUNBOATS
(LOW-CUT —) SOCK GILLY ANKLET
BUSKIN SLIPPER COLONIAL
(MILITARY —) CALIGA
(OLD —) BAUCHLE
(PIKED —) BEAKER
(RAWHIDE —) HIMMING
(SPORTS —S) GILLIES
(STEEL —) SOLLERET
(THIN —) PINSON SCLAFF
(WINGED —S) TALARIA
(WOODEN —) KLOMP SABOT
PATTEN RACKET RACQUET
(WORN —) SCRAE
(PL.) SHEEN SHOON SHUNE SCHONE
FOOTGEAR
SHOEMAKER SNOB FOXER SOLER
ARCHER CHAMAR CODGER COZIER
FUDGER GOUGER SOOTER SOUTER
VAMPER COBBLER CRISPIN
CROWNER SHOEMAN SNOBBER
UPPERER CORVISER SNOBSCAT
SHOEMAKING SNOBBING
SHOGUN TYCOON
SHOO HOOSH DISPEL
SHOOK PACK BLANK SHAKE
SHOOT DAG GUN IMP PAY POT PUT
ROD BANG BOLT BROD CANE CHIT
CION DRAW LEAF PLUG SLIP WEFT
BLAST BLAZE BROWN DRILL DRIVE
EXPEL FLUSH FROND GEMMA
GLEAM LANCE LAYER PLUFF SCION
SHEET SOBOL SPEAR SPRAY SPRIG
SPRIT SPURT SQUIB STICK STOOL
TUBER TURIO VIMEN BRANCH
FLIGHT FLOWER GERMEN GROWTH
HEADER HURTLE LAUNCH LEADER
OFFSET RATOON SALLOW SOBOLE
SPRING SPROUT STOLON STOVEN
STRIKE SUCKER TILLER TURION
BUDLING CHIMNEY DROPPER
SCOURGE SPIRING TENDRIL
TENDRON THALLUS ANAPHYTE
APOBLAST CATAPULT TRAILING
(— A MARBLE) LAG TAW KNUCKLE
(— A WHALE) STRIKE
(— ASIDE FROM MARK) DRIB
(— AT LONG RANGE) SNIPE
(— DOWN) SPLASH
(— DUCKS) SKAG
(— FORTH) JET GLEAM SPIRE
(— FROM DEER'S ANTLER) SPELLER
(— INDISCRIMINATELY) BROWN
(— MOOSE OR DEER) YARD
(— OF A TREE) STOW WHIP LANCE
BRANCH
(— OUT) JUT CHIT DART
(— SEAL) SWATCH
(— UP) SPIRE SPURT
(—S USED AS FODDER) BROWSE
(FIRST —S) BRAIRD
(FLEXIBLE —) BINE

(LATERAL —) ARM
(ORE —) BONANZA
(PAWNBROKER'S —) SPOUT
(SUGARCANE —) LALO
(TENDER —) FLUSH
(WILLOW —) SALLOW
SHOOTER SCOOT BLASTER
GUNSTER PLUFFER SHOTMAN
SKEETER
SHOOTING COCKING GUNNING
GUNPLAY HUNTING POTTING
SHOOTING STAR METEOR COWSLIP
SHOOTER PRIMWORT
SHOP CRIB TOKO BURSE STORE
KOSHER SHOPPE TIENDA WINKEL
ALMACEN APOTHEC BOTTEGA
CABARET MERCERY SPICERY
TABERNA TURNERY BOUTIQUE
COOKSHOP CREMERIE EMPORIUM
ESPRESSO EXCHANGE MAGAZINE
SHOWSHOP SLOPSHOP TENDEJON
WAREROOM
(BARBER —) BARBERY
(BLACKSMITH —) SMITHY
(LIQUOR —) SALOON
(OLD CLOTHES —) FLIPPERY
(PAWNBROKER'S —) LUMBER
SPROUT
(REPAIR —) GARAGE
(SUTLER'S —) CANTEEN
SHOPKEEPER CIT ARAB BAKAL
CHETTY SOUDAGUR
SHOPLIFT BOOST
SHOPLIFTER BOOSTER
SHORE GIB TOM BANK RIPE RIVE
SAND SIDE BEACH BENCH CLIFF
COAST RAKER RANCE SHOAR
WARTH RIVAGE STRAND BUTTRESS
DOCKSIDE LANDFALL LANDSIDE
SEACOAST
SHOREBIRD TATTLER WRYBILL
SURFBIRD
SHORE CRAB OCHIDORE
SHOREFISH OPALEYE
SHORER BRACER CRIBBER
SHORN NOT NOTT POLLED
TONSURED
SHORT AIM LAG LOW SHY BAIN
CURT NEAR NIGH SOON BLUFF
BRIEF BUNTY CLOSE CRISP CUTTY
FUBBY FUBSY PUNCH SQUAB
UNDER CRISPY SCARCE STUGGY
STUNTY SUDDEN ULLAGE BOBTAIL
BRUSQUE CURTATE LACONIC
SQUIDGY STUBBED SUMMARY
SNAPPISH SUCCINCT
(— AND FLAT) CAMUS
(— AND THICK) CHUNKY STOCKY
STUBBY STUMPY TRUNCH
TRUNCHED
(— AND THICKSET) NUGGETY
(— AS OF WOOL) FRIBBY
(— PERSON OR ANIMAL) PUNCH
(STOUT AND —) BUNTY CHUFFY
PLUGGY THICKSET
(PL.) BERMUDAS
SHORTAGE FAMINE DROUGHT
WANTAGE UNDERAGE
SHORTCHANGE FLUFF SHORT

SHORTCOMING SIN DEFECT FOIBLE
SHORT-COUPLED CHUFFY
SHORTCUT CUTOFF
SHORT-EARED OWL MOMO
SHORTEN CUT CLIP STAG ELIDE
SLASH REDUCE ABRIDGE CURTAIL
EXCERPT CONTRACT DIMINISH
RETRENCH
(— AND THICKEN IRON) JUMP
(— GRIP) CHOKE
SHORTENED CURTED BOBTAIL
CURTATE ABRIDGED
SHORTENING (— OF SYLLABLE)
SYSTOLE
SHORTEST LEAST
SHORTHORN DURHAM
SHORT-LIVED FRAGILE
SHORTLY DUMPILY DIRECTLY
SHORT-NAPPED RAS
SHORTNESS BREVITY CURTNESS
UNLENGTH
SHORT-RANGE TACTICAL
SHORT-SIGHTED SANDED PURBLIND
SHORTSIGHTEDNESS MYOPIA
SHORT-TEMPERED SNIPPY SNUFFY
SHORT-TERM FLOATING
SHORT-WINDED PURSY PURFLY
PURFLED PURSIVE
SHOT POP SET BLUE CASE JOLT
OVER SETT SLUG BLANK FLIER
FLING FLUFF FLYER OUTER PLUFF
SHOOT TOWEL WHITE CARTON
CENTER CENTRE FOLLOW MUDCAP
REBOTE ALIIPOE BOMBARD
CUTAWAY DEADEYE GUNSHOT
LANGREL PELICAN SIGHTER
BLIZZARD BUCKSHOT HAILSHOT
LANGRAGE MARKSHOT SCORCHER
(— BEYOND TARGET) OVER
(— FOR CULVERIN) PELICAN
(— IN FIFTH CIRCLE) WHITE
(— IN FOURTH CIRCLE) BLACK
(— IN THIRD CIRCLE) BLUE
(— OF NARCOTIC) FIX
(— STRIKING BULL'S-EYE) CARTON
(ARCHERY —) GREEN
(BADMINTON —) CLEAR
(BILLIARD —) DRAG STAB CAROM
MASSE SCREW FOLLOW SAFETY
SPREAD BRICOLE SCRATCH
(BOW —) DRAFT
(CAMERA —) INTERCUT
(CROQUET —) SPLIT FOLLOW
(CURLING —) INWICK OUTWICK
(FINAL —) UPSHOT
(GOOD —) SCREAMER
(PISTOL —) BARK
(POOL —) BREAK
(SIZE OF —) F T BB FF TT BBB
DUST BUCKSHOT
(TENNIS —) ACE LOB DINK SERVE
SMASH
(VOLLEY OF —S) BLIZZARD
SHOTGUN DOUBLE TUPARA
PEPPERER
SHOULD MOW SUD WANT OUGHT
(— NOT) SHUDNA SHOULDNA
SHOULDNT
SHOULDER DOD AXLE CLOD DODD

GAIN HUMP SHIP STEP SULD BOUGH
PITCH SPALL SPULE VERGE AXILLA
EPAULE RELISH SPAULD KNUCKLE
RIMBASE SHOUTHER
(— AROUND TENON) RELISH
(— OF BOLT) NAB
(— OF FIREARM STOCK) RIMBASE
(— OF FLY) CHEEK
(— OF PORK) HAND PICNIC
CUSHION
(— OF RABBIT OR HARE) WING
(— OF ROAD) BERM BERME
HAUNCH QUARTER
(— PAIN) OMODYNIA
(BEVELED —) GAIN
(PL.) FOREBOWS
SHOULDER BLADE SPALD SPEAL
SCAPULA
SHOUT BAY BOO CRY HOY HUE
BAWL CALL CROW GAPE HAIL HOCH
HOOP HOOT REME ROOT ROUP
ROUT SCRY TOOT YELL BRAWL
CHEER CLAIM CLEPE CRACK GREDE
HAVOC HOLLO HUZZA REERE
WHEWT WHOOP ABRAID BOOHOO
CLAMOR GOLLAR GOLLER HALLOO
HOLLER HURRAH STEVEN YAMMER
ACCLAIM SHILLOO GARDYLOO
LULLILOO SCRONACH
(— AS CHILDREN) BELDER
(— DERISIVELY) BARRACK
(— OF APPROVAL) BRAVO
(— OF ENCOURAGEMENT) HARK
(— OF JOY) IO
(HUNTING —) CHEVY
SHOUTING HUE GLAM ROUP ROUT
HOLLO CLAMOR HOLLOA JUBILEE
SHOVE JUT PUT BUNT DUSH FEND
MUCK PICK POTE PUSH SHOG SHUN
BOOST CROWD DUNCH ELBOW
HUNCH SHIVE SHUNT HUSTLE
JOSTLE JUSTLE MUSCLE THRUST
SCAMBLE
(— IN MARBLES) FULK
SHOVEL FAN VAN CAST PEEL SPUD
SCOOP SHOOL SPADE SPOON
SCOPPIT SCUPPIT SLUDGER
DUCKBILL DUCKFOOT STROCKLE
(— FOR COIN) MAIN
(— FOR DRESSING ORE) VAN
(BRICKMAKING —) CUCKHOLD
(CASTING —) SCUTTLE
(CHARCOAL BURNER'S —) RABBLE
(FIRE —) PEEL SLICE
(GRATED —) HARP
(MINER'S —) BANJO
(PERFORATED —) SKIMMER
SHOVELER SCOOPER WHINGER
BLUEWING SHOULERD WHINYARD
SHOW DO SAY SEE WIS BOSH CALL
DASH HAVE ITEM LEAD MARK MIEN
SCAW SEEM SHEW TENT VIEW
WEAR WISE ARGUE ASSAY EXERT
FLASH GLOSS GLOZE KITHE PRIDE
PROVE SHINE SIGHT SLANG SPORT
TEACH ACCUSE ASSIGN BETRAY
BLAZON CHICHI COUTHE DENOTE
DETECT DEVICE DIRECT ENSIGN
ESCORT EVINCE EXPOSE FIGURE

FLAUNT GAIETY GAYETY LAYOUT
MUSTER OBJECT PARADE REVEAL
SCHEME SPREAD SPRUNK ADVANCE
ANALYZE BALLOON BESPEAK
BETOKEN BRAVURA BREATHE
DECLARE DISPLAY DIVULGE EXHIBIT
EXPRESS FASHION MONSTER
PRESAGE PRODUCE PROPOSE
SELLOUT SHOWING SIGNIFY
TRIUMPH COLORING CONCLUDE
EVIDENCE FLOURISH FORESHOW
INDICATE MANIFEST PRETENCE
SEMBLANT SIDESHOW
(— APPROVAL) CLAP APPLAUD
(— CONTEMPT) SCOFF
(— DISCONTENT) GROUCH
(— DISPLEASURE) POUT
(— ENTHUSIASM) DROOL
(— FORTH) BLAZE CIPHER
(— IN PUBLIC CELEBRATION)
PAGEANT
(— ITSELF) APPEAR
(— MERCY) SPARE
(— OF LEARNING) SCIOLISM
(— OF LIGHT) BLINK
(— OF REASON) COLOR
(— OF VANITY) AIR
(— OFF) FLASH SPORT SWANK
PARADE
(— ONESELF) BE
(— POSITION OF) MEITH
(— PROMISE) FRAME SHAPE
(— RESPECT FOR) REGARD
(— REVERSE TREND) REACT
(— SIGNS OF GIVING WAY) WAVER
(— SIGNS OF ILLNESS) GRUDGE
(— THE BOTTOM) KEEL
(— THE SIGHTS) LIONIZE
(— THE TEETH) GIRN GRIN
(— THE WAY) LEAD CONDUCT
(— TO BE FALSE) BELIE DISPROVE
(— UNKINDNESS) WAIT
(— WITHOUT SUBSTANCE) FORM
(ARTFUL —) GRIMACE
(FALSE —) FUCUS BUBBLE TINSEL
ILLUSION
(FLOOR —) CABARET
(GAUDY —) HOOPLA BRAVERY
(MERE —) PHANTOM
(MOMENTARY —) FLASH
(ORNATE —) FLUBDUB
(OSTENTATIOUS —) SPRUNK
DISPLAY
(OUTSIDE —) VARNISH
(OUTWARD —) FUCUS VISAGE
(PUPPET —) DROLL MOTION
WAJANG WAYANG GUIGNOL
(RIDICULOUS —) FARCE
(RUDIMENTARY —) SATURA
(SPECIOUS —) GLOZE
(SUPERFICIAL —) GLOSS VENEER
(TRAVELLING —) SLANG
SHOWCASE ISLAND VITRINE
SHOWER WET HAIL RAIN SCAT SUMP
AUGER BLASH SKITE SOUSE
FLURRY PELTER SHEWER DRIBBLE
SHATTER WEATHER COMMORTH
SCOUTHER
(CONCENTRATED —) BARRAGE

(HEAVY —) SUMP
(RAIN —) RASH
(SUDDEN —) SCUD SKIT BRASH
PLUMP
SHOWERY BRASHY CLASHY SCATTY
SHOWILY GAILY BRAVELY GAUDILY
SHOWINESS DASH GLARE GLITTER
FLOURISH GEWGAWRY SPLENDOR
SHOWING SPRANK SPARKLE
(— SAME NATURE) AKIN
(SUPERFICIAL —) FACE
SHOW-ME STATE MISSOURI
SHOW-OFF CUTUP
SHOWY GAY FINE LOUD NICE RORY
DASHY FLARY FLASH FRESH GAUDY
GIDDY GRAND SPICY TOPPY VAUDY
VIEWY BRANKY BRAZEN BRUMMY
CHICHI DRESSY FLASHY FLOSSY
GARISH GEWGAW GLOSSY JAUNTY
PURPLE SHANTY SPANKY SPORTY
TAWDRY DASHING FLAUNTY
GALLANT GAUDFUL HOTSHOT
POMPOUS SHOWFUL SHOWISH
SPLASHY CLAPTRAP FASTUOUS
GIMCRACK GORGEOUS ORGULOUS
SPARKISH SPECIOUS SPLENDID
TRUMPERY
(NOT —) CIVIL LENTEN DISCREET
SHRED DAG HOG JAG RAG ROND
ROON SNIP WISP BLYPE CLOUT
SHRAG SHRIP CULPON SCREED
SLIVER TARGET FRITTER SHATTER
FILAMENT
(— FISH) SCROD
(— OF CLOTHES) TACK
(— OF FLESH) TAG
(— OF HAIR) TAIT
(PL.) TAVERS CADDICE TAIVERS
SHREDDED CUT
SHREDDER DEVIL
SHREW JES TANA PRESS RANNY
SOREX VIXEN CALLET JUMPER
MIGALE TARGER TARTAR TUPAIA
VIRAGO BLARINA HELLCAT
MUSKRAT PENTAIL SCYTALE
TUPAIID SINSRING SORICINE
SORICOID UROPSILE
(TREE —) BANXRING
SHREWD DRY SLY ACID CUTE FELL
GASH SAGE TIDY WARE WISE
ACUTE CAGEY CANNY HEADY
PAWKY POKEY SHARP SMART
SWACK ARGUTE ARTFUL ASTUTE
CLEVER CRAFTY SPRACK SUBTLE
CUNNING GNOSTIC KNOWING
PARLISH PARLOUS PRACTIC
SAPIENT
(— PERSON) FILE
SHREWDLY SLILY CANNILY
ASTUTELY
SHREWDNESS SAVVY ACUMEN
POLICY SLYNESS GUMPTION
SAGACITY CALLIDITY
SHREWISH CURST CURSED SHREWD
VIXENISH
SHREWMOUSE MYGALE SCYTALE
SHRIEK CRY YIP YARM YELL CHIRK
SKIRL SCREAM SCRIKE SHRIKE
SKRIKE SPRAICH

SHRIKE POPE BATARA BOUBOU BRUBRU FISCAL FLASHER FLUSHER LOGHEAD MIGRANT MINIVET TRILLER BELLBIRD FALCONET PUFFBACK WOODCHAT

SHRILL HIGH KEEN ACUTE PIPEY SHARP SHILL SHIRL ARGUTE BRASSY GLASSY PIPING SQUEAK TREBLE HAUTAIN MINIKIN SCREAKY STRIDENT

(MAKE — NOISE) POTRACK

SHRIMP GRIT APANG CARID MYSID PARVA PRAWN NIPPER PANDLE ARTEMIA BROWNIE CAMARON DECAPOD POLYPOD REDTAIL SPECTER SPECTRE CARIDEAN CRAWFISH CREVETTE MACRURAN

SHRINE ADYT NAOS GUACA HUACA ISEUM MAZAR STUPA ZIARA ADYTON ADYTUM CHASSE DAGABA DAGOBA DURGAH HALLOW HIERON MEMORY SAMADH ZIARAT CHAITYA CHORTEN EDICULE FANACLE MARTYRY MEMORIA SACRARY TEMENOS THESEUM AEDICULA DELUBRUM FERETORY FERETRUM GURDWARA LARARIUM MARABOUT PANTHEON VALHALLA

(— STUDY) NAOLOGY

SHRINK COY SHY DUCK FULL FUNK GIVE PEAK ABHOR ARGHE CLING COWER CRINE QUAIL RELAX RIVEL SHRAM SHRUG SHUCK START WINCE BLANCH BLENCH BOGGLE COTTER CRINGE FLINCH LESSEN RECOIL SCRUMP SETTLE SHRIMP WEAZEN CRIMPLE DWINDLE SCUNNER SHRIVEL COLLAPSE CONTRACT

(— FROM DRYNESS) GIZZEN

SHRINKAGE SETTLE SHRINK SINKAGE

(— OF TYPE) SQUEEZE

SHRINKING COY SHY TIMID BLETHE DASTARD FULLING LOATHFUL TIMOROUS

SHRIVE SHRIFT CONFESS SHRIEVE

SHRIVEL SEAR BLAST CLING CRINE PARCH RIVEL SHRAM SNERP WIZEN COTTER GIZZEN SCORCH SCRUMP SHRINK WEAZEN WITHER CROZZLE

SHRIVELED WEDE CLUNG CORKY THIRL GIZZEN STARKY PUNGLED SHIRPIT WIZENED WRITHEN SHRAMMED WRIZZLED

SHROPSHIRE SALOP

SHROUD HIDE SARK CLOAK CRAPE DRAPE HABIT SHEET SWIFT EMBOSK HEARSE KITTEL MUFFLE SCREEN SHADOW SINDON SUDARY BENIGHT CONCEAL CURTAIN INVOLVE SWIFTER CEREMENT

(PL.) PUTTOCK

SHROVETIDE SHROVE GUTTIDE CARNIVAL

SHROVE TUESDAY FASTENS GUTTIDE

SHRUB TI BAY HAW KAT MAY QAT TOD AKIA ALEM BUSH COCA HOYA

INGA ITEA KARO KEUR KHAT MUSK ULEX AKALA AKELA ALDER ALISO ARUSA BOCCA BROOM CEIBO CUMAY ELDER GOOMA GOUMI HAZEL HENNA IXORA LEDUM LEMON LILAC MAQUI MARIA MUDAR RETEM SALAL SHROG SUMAC TOYON ZILLA ABELIA AGRITO AKONGE AMULLA ANAGUA ANILAO ARALIA ARUSHA AUCUBA AUPAKA AZALEA BLOLLY CENIZO CHEKAN CHERRY CISTUS CORREA DAPHNE DHAURI DRIMYS FEIJOA FRUTEX JACATE JOJOBA KARAMU KOWHAI LABRUM LARREA LAUREL MATICO MYRTLE NARRAS PENAEA PITURI RAETEM SAVINE STORAX STYRAX AFERNAN AGARITA AMORPHA ARBORET ARRAYAN ARRIMBY AZAROLE BANKSIA BORONIA BUCKEYE CANTUTA CHACATE CHAMISE CHANCHE DEUTZIA EHRETIA ENCELIA EPACRID EPHEDRA FUCHSIA GUMWOOD GUTWORT HOPBUSH HOPSAGE JASMINE JETBEAD JEWBUSH JOEWOOD KUMQUAT LANTANA MAHONIA NUNNARI PAVONIA PEABUSH PIMELEA RHODORA SPIRAEA TARBUSH THEEZAN ABELMOSK ALLTHORN BARBERRY CAMELLIA CARAGANA COMEBACK COPALCHE DRACAENA GOATBUSH GOWIDDIE GRAVILEA HARDHACK HARDTACK HAWTHORN HIBISCUS IRONWOOD KEURBOOM KOROMIKO MOORWORT NINEBARK OCOTILLO OLEASTER OSOBERRY PIPEWOOD PONDBUSH ROSEMARY SANDSTAY SANDWOOD SASANQUA SHRUBLET SNOWBALL SNOWBELL SNOWBUSH SOAPBARK STANDARD

(AROMATIC —) THYME CLUSIA BORONIA HOGBUSH ALLSPICE

(AUSTRALIAN —) GOOMA BUDDAH DRIMYS GEEBUNG MILKBUSH SANDSTAY

(CHINESE —) KERRIA

(CLIMBING —) CATCLAWS SOLANDRA

(DESERT —) AFERNAN

(EVERGREEN —) BOX BAGO ILEX TITI BOLDO ERICA FURZE HEATH HOLLY KOSAM PYXIE SALAL SAVIN TOYON BAUERA DAHOON KALMIA LAUREL PEPINO RUSCUS SAKAKI ARDISIA BARETTA JASMINE JUNIPER MADRONA CALFKILL CARAUNDA EVONYMUS OLEANDER SASANQUA

(FRAGRANT —) JASMINE HUISACHE MEJORANA MEZEREON ROSEMARY

(HAWAIIAN —) AKALA AKELA ILIMA KOKIO OLONA

(LOW —) AYAPANA

(MEXICAN —) BLUEBUSH

(NEW ZEALAND —) KARO KAWA TUTU KARAMU KIEKIE KAWAKAWA KOROMIKO

(PASTURE —) COWBERRY

(PHILIPPINE —) IPILIPIL

(POISONOUS —) GIF CUBE LITHI SUMAC GIFBLAAR LABURNUM

(PRICKLY —) CAPER COLIMA BRAMBLE CATCLAWS

(SPINY —) ULEX AROMA GORSE JUNCO ESPINO BUMELIA CARISSA CYTISUS GENISTA GOATBUSH GRANJENO GUAJILLO HUAJILLO

(STRONG-SMELLING —) SALTWORT

(STUNTED —) SCRAB SCROG SCRUB

(THORNY —) CHANAR HAWTHORN

(TREELIKE —) ARBUSCLE

(TROPICAL —) INGA MAJO HENNA CAMARA DERRIS MOMBIN OLACAD PERSEA HAMELIA JEWBUSH LANTANA SOAPBARK

(WEST INDIAN —) ANIL RATWOOD MILKWOOD

(XEROPHYTIC —) SAXAUL

SHRUBBERY MOGOTE ARBORET

SHRUG SHUG HURKLE SHRINK

SHRUNKEN LANK CLUNG PUNGLED SLUNKEN WIZENED CONTRACT

(— HEAD) TSANTSA

SHUCK HULL SHACK SHELL SHOCK

SHUDDER GRUE CREEP HIRCH QUAKE SHRUG AGRISE GROOSE HIRTCH HOTTER HURKLE SHIVER FRISSON TREMBLE

SHUDDERING RIGOR

SHUFFLE JANK MAKE MILK SLUR SCUFF SHALE SHIFT SHOOL JUGGLE RIFFLE RUFFLE SCLAFF SHOVEL DRAGGLE QUIBBLE SHACKLE SHAFFLE SHAMBLE SLIPPER SLUTHER

SHUN FIN SHY BALK FLEE TABU VOID WARE AVOID EVADE EVITE SHUNT TABOO ASTART DEVOID ESCAPE ESCHEW REFUSE SHRINK DECLINE FORBEAR FORSAKE

SHUNT AYRTON BRIDGE BYPASS SWITCH

SHUSH HUSH WHISH SUPPRESS

SHUSWAP ATNAH

SHUT FAST HASP MAKE SEAL SHOT SLAM SLOT SPAR TAKE TEEN TINE CLOSE LATCH STEEK STICK CLOSED CABINET OCCLUSE UPCLOSE

(— EYES) WINK

(— IN) BAR LAP CAGE COPSE EMBAR EMBAY FORBAR PENTIT TACKLE BELOUKE ENCLAVE

(— OFF) SCREEN SECLUDE

(— OUT) BAR DEBAR REPEL SKUNK HINDER DEPRIVE EXCLUDE OCCLUDE OUTSHUT PRECLUDE

(— TOGETHER) CLASP

(— UP) BAR CUB MEW PENT STOP CHOKE FRANK STIVE STOVE CLOSET EMBOSS ENJAIL IMMURE IMPARK CONDEMN CONFINE DUNGEON ENCLOSE IMPOUND INCLUDE OCCLUDE OPPRESS PARROCK RECLUSE SECLUDE CONCLUDE PRECLUDE

(HALF —) PINK

SHUTDOWN LAYOFF

SHUTOUT SKUNK

SHUTTER LID DROP SHUT BLIND SHADE CUTOFF DOUSER AUTOMAT BUCKLER SHUTTLE JALOUSIE
(— **IN ORGAN**) SHADE
(— **OF TRIPTYCH**) VOLET
SHUTTING CLAUDENT
SHUTTLE FLY FLUTE SHUNT BROCHE LOOPER SWIVEL SHITTLE
SHUTTLECOCK BIRD PETECA VOLANT
SHY COY JIB MIM SCAR SHAN SHUN SKIT UNKO WILD BLATE CAGEY CHARY DEMUR FLING SCARE SHUNT SQUAB TIMID UNCOW BOGGLE BOOGER DEMURE MODEST SHANNY SKIEGH TARTLE BASHFUL GAWKISH RABBITY STRANGE TREMBLY UPSTAGE BACKWARD DAPHNEAN FAROUCHE RETIRING SHEEPISH SKITTISH SWAIMOUS WILLYARD
SHYNESS COYNESS MODESTY RESERVE TIMIDITY
SIALAGOGUE SALIVANT
SIAM (SEE THAILAND)
SIAMANG UNGKA GIBBON
SIB SEPT AYLLU SIBLING SIBSHIP CALPULLI
SIBERIA (GULF IN —) OB
(**MOUNTAIN RANGE IN —**) URAL ALTAI
(**NATIVE IN —**) YAKU SAGAI TATAR KIRGIZ TARTAR KIRGHIZ YUKAGIR
(**RIVER IN —**) OB ILI KET PUR TAZ TYM AMGA AMUR LENA MAYA ONON UCUR ALDAN ISHIM NADYM SOBOL TOBOL ANGARA IRTYSH OLEKMA VILYUY
(**TOWN IN —**) OMSK CHITA KYZYL TOMSK IGARKA KURGAN BARNAUL IRKUTSK LENINSK YAKUTSK
SIBERIAN SQUILL SCILLA
SIBYL SYBIL SIBYLLA VOLUSPA AMALTHEA
SIC SOOL

SICILY
CAPE: BOEO FARO PASSARO
CAPITAL: PALERMO
CATHEDRAL: MONREALE
COIN: LITRA UNCIA
GULF: NOTO CATANIA
ISLAND: EGADI LIPARI USTICA
MEASURE: SALMA CAFFISO
MOUNTAIN: EREI ETNA MORO SORI IBREI NEBRODI
NATIVE: ELYMI SICEL SICANI SICULI
OLD NAME: TRINACRIA TRIQUETRA
PROVINCE: ENNA RAGUSA CATANIA MESSINA PALERMO TRAPANI SIRACUSA
RIVER: SALSO TORTO BELICE SIMETO PLATANI
SEAPORT: ACI CATANIA MARSALA MESSINA PALERMO TRAPANI
TOWN: ENNA NOTO RAGUSA CATANIA MARSALA MESSINA

TRAPANI SYRACUSE
VOLCANO: ETNA AETNA

SICK BAD ILL BADLY CRONK CROOK MORBID MAWKISH SEASICK UNWHOLE CROPSICK MALADIVE PHYSICAL STREAKED
SICKEN TIRE TURN WEARY SUNDER SUNNER WEAKEN DISGUST SURFEIT NAUSEATE
SICKENING FELL SICKLY FULSOME SICKISH NAUSEOUS
SICKISH DAUNCY
SICKLE HOOK CROOK
SICKLY WAN FLUE FOND PALE PUKY SICK DAWNY DONCY FAINT GREEN PEAKY SILLY TEWLY WEARY WISHT AMPERY CLAMMY CRANKY FEEBLE INFIRM PUKISH PULING WANKLY WEAKLY INVALID LANGUID MAWKISH PEAKING PEAKISH PIMPING QUEECHY SICKISH WEARISH WEERISH DELICATE DISEASED MALADIVE PINDLING
SICKNESS (ALSO SEE DISEASE) SICK SORE TAKING AILMENT DISEASE ILLNESS SURFEIT DISORDER
(**MILK —**) SLOWS TIRES
(**MOTION —**) KINETOSIS
(**MOUNTAIN —**) SOROCHE
SIDA ILIMA ESCOBA
SIDE COST EDGE FACE HALF HAND KANT LEAF PART BOARD CHEEK FLANK LATUS PARTY SITHE BEHALF PTERON ENGLISH PENDANT FORESIDE SIDELONG
(— **BY SIDE**) ACCOLE ACCOSTED PARALLEL
(— **OF ATTIC**) SKEELING SKILLING SKILLION
(— **OF BOOM JAW**) HORN
(— **OF BOW**) BELLY
(— **OF CAVITY**) WALL
(— **OF DECK**) GANGWAY
(— **OF DITCH**) SCARP
(— **OF DIVIDERS**) LEG
(— **OF FACE**) CHEEK
(— **OF GATE**) FOLD
(— **OF GEM**) BEZEL
(— **OF HEARTH**) BREAST
(— **OF HILL**) SCUG
(— **OF HOG**) FLITCH
(— **OF HORSESHOE**) BRANCH
(— **OF LACE**) FOOTING
(— **OF LOG**) RIDE
(— **OF NAVE**) AISLE
(— **OF OPENING**) JAW JAMB
(— **OF PIG**) BACON
(— **OF QUADRANGLE**) PANE
(— **OF RABBET**) LEDGE
(— **OF RACECOURSE**) STRETCH
(— **OF RECTANGLE**) SQUARE
(— **OF ROOF**) CATSLIDE
(— **OF SHIP**) BEAM WALE BOARD BULWARK LARBOARD SEABOARD
(— **OF TENNIS RACKET**) ROUGH SMOOTH
(— **OF TRIANGLE**) LEG

(— **OF TYPE**) BACK
(— **OF VALLEY**) COTEAU
(— **PIECE**) RAVE
(— **SHELTERED FROM WIND**) LEE LEW LEEWARD
(— **WITH**) SUFFRAGE
(—**S OF GALLERY**) SLIPS
(**BACK —**) REAR BEHIND BACKSIDE
(**DRESSED —**) FACE
(**FOR EACH —**) ALL
(**MOUNTAIN —**) PUNA VETA SOROCHE
(**OUTER — OF SKIN**) GRAIN
(**RIGHT — OF SWORD**) INSIDE
(**RIGHT —**) FACE
(**UNDERNEATH —**) BOTTOM
SIDEBAR HOUND
SIDEBOARD ABACUS BUFFET SERVER DRESSER CELLARET CREDENCE CREDENZA
SIDE DISH OUTWORK
SIDEPIECE BAR BOW JAMB WING CHEEK GUSSET EARPIECE LANDSIDE
SIDESLIP SKID SLIP DRIFT DRILL
SIDESMAN HOGGLER QUESTMAN
SIDESTEP BEG AVOID DODGE
SIDEWALK WALKWAY TROTTOIR
SIDEWISE ASIDE ASIDEN
SIDING CURB SPUR GARAGE
SIDLE EDGE SLIVE SAUNTER
SIDRA PARASHAH
SIEGE BOUT SEDGE ASSIEGE JOURNEY LEAGUER
(— **ENGINE**) WARWOLF
SIERRA CERO SERRA SAWBACK KINGFISH

SIERRA LEONE
CAPITAL: FREETOWN
COIN: LEONE
LANGUAGE: KRIO MENDE TEMNE
MEASURE: LOAD KETTLE
MOUNTAIN: LOMA
NATIVE: VAI KONO LOKO SUSU KISSI LIMBA MENDE TEMNE FULANI GALLINA SHERBRO MANDINGO
RIVER: MOA JONG SEWA ROKKEL SCARCY
SEAPORT: HEPEL BONTHE SULIMA
TOWN: BO KISSI KENEMA

SIESTA NAP MERIDIAN
SIEVE FRY TRY BOLT BUNT DRUM HARP LAWN PREE SCRY SHOE SIFT SILE SIZE TEMS GRATE RANGE SCALP TAMIS TAMMY TEMSE BOLTER RANGER RIDDER RIDDLE SEARCE SEARCH SEMMET SIFTER WEIGHT BOULTEL CHAFFER CRIBBLE DILLUER PRICKLE TIFFANY SEARCHER STRAINER
SIFT REE TRY BOLT DUST SCRY RANGE SCALP SIEVE TEMSE DREDGE GARBLE RIDDER RIDDLE SCREEN SEARCE WINNOW CANVASS CRIBBLE DRIBBLE SIFTAGE CRIBRATE

(— FLOUR) DRESS
(— IN MINING) LUE
(— IN) INFILTER
(— MEAL) BUNT
(— SHOT) TABLE
(— WHEAT) SCALP
SIFTER SIEVE BOLTER CASTER
SIEVER
SIFTING DRIFT GARBLING
(PL.) BOLTING FANNINGS SIEVINGS
SIGH SOB PECH SIFE SOCK WIND
MOURN SIGHT SITHE SOUGH TWANK
BEMOAN BEWAIL SORROW SUTHER
DEPLORE SINGULT SUSPIRE
SIGHT EYE KEN RAY BONE ESPY
FACE GAZE PEEP SEET VIEW FERLY
RAISE SCENE SCOPE SICHT TRACK
VISIE VIZZY BEHOLD DESCRY
OBJECT TICKET VISION DISCERN
DISPLAY EYESHOT GLIMPSE
MONSTER CONSPECT DISCOVER
EYESIGHT GUNSIGHT
(— FOR GUN) LEAF PEEP SCOPE
VISIE VIZZY HAUSSE GUNSIGHT
(— OF COMPASS) VANE
(— ON SURVEYOR'S STAFF) TARGET
(— TO SEE IF LEVEL) BONE
(—S OF CITY) LIONS
(AMAZING —) STOUND
(IMAGINARY —) VISION
(PITIFUL —) RUTH
(SORRY —) BYSEN
(STRANGE —) FERLY FERLIE
SIGHTER ALINER ALIGNER
SIGHTING LANDFALL
(— DEVICE) ALIDADE
SIGHTLY VIEWLY EYEABLE
SIGLOS DARIC
SIGN INK AYAH DASH FIRM HINT
HIRE MARK NOTE OMEN TYPE
BADGE COLON FRANK GHOST
GUIDA HAMZA INDEX SIGIL SINGE
SPOOR STAMP TOKEN TRACE
ASSIGN AUGURY CARACT EFFECT
EMBLEM ENGAGE ENSIGN FUGLER
INDICE MOTION NOTICE PARAPH
REMARK SIGLUM SIGNAL SIGNET
SIGNUM SYMBOL TITTLE WITTER
ALEBUSH AUSPICE CHECKER
CHEQUER CONSIGN EARMARK
ENDORSE INDICIA INSIGNE KNOWING
PORTENT PRESAGE PRODIGY
PROFFER SHINGLE SHOWING
SIGNARY SURMISE SYMPTOM
VESTIGE WARNING CEREMONY
INDICANT INSTANCE MONUMENT
PROCLAIM SIGNACLE SYLLABIC
TELLTALE
(— DOCUMENT) FIRM
(— FOR KEYNOTE) ISON
(— OF ALEHOUSE) LATTICE
(— OF AN IDEA) EMBLEM
(— OF APPROVAL) CACHET
(— OF CONTEMPT) FIG
(— OF DANGER) SEAMARK
(— OF GLOTTAL STOP) HAMZA
HAMZAH
(— OF MULTIPLICATION) DOT
(— OF ZODIAC) LEO RAM BULL

CRAB GOAT LION ARIES HOUSE
LIBRA TWINS VIRGO ARCHER
CANCER FISHES GEMINI PISCES
TAURUS VIRGIN BALANCE SCORPIO
AQUARIUS SCORPION
(— ON MAP) ICON
(ASTROLOGICAL —) CIPHER
(MATHEMATICAL —) NAME
FUNCTOR
(MUSICAL —) GUIDA SEGNO SWELL
SIMILE FERMATA
(OUTWARD —) EVIDENCE
(SANSKRIT —) ANUSVARA
(SLIGHT —) SURMISE
(SUBSCRIPT —) SUBFIX
(SUPERSTITIOUS —) GUEST
(TAVERN —) BUSH ALEBUSH
ALEPOLE CHECKER CHEQUER
ALESTAKE
(TRAMP'S —) MONICA MONIKER
(VOWEL —) SEGOL SEGHOL
(PL.) INDICIA INSIGNIA
SIGNAL OS CUE GUN PST WAG BALK
BECK BELL BUZZ CALL COND FLAG
GATE HASH SIGN WAFT WAVE WINK
ALARM ALERT BLINK FLARE FUSEE
FUZEE LIGHT SHAPE SHORT SPEAK
TOKEN WHIFF ALARUM BANNER
BEACON BECKON BUZZER ENSIGN
HERALD MARKER OFFICE RECALL
SIGNET TARGET WAVING WIGWAG
BLINKER CHAMADE EMINENT
NOTABLE RETREAT TURNOUT
CRANTARA DIAPHONE FLAGFALL
LOGOGRAM STANDARD STRIKING
(— FISHERMEN) BALK
(— FOR A PARLEY) CHAMADE
(— FOR WHALERS) WAIF
(— IN WHIST) ECHO PETER
(— OF DISTRESS) SOS
(— ON HORN) SEEK BLAST STRAKE
(— TO ATTACK) CHARGE
(— TO BEGIN ACTION) CUE
(— WITH FLAGS) WIGWAG
(AUDIO —) HUM
(BOAT'S —) WAFF WAFT
(DEATH —) KNELL
(FOG —) FOGHORN TORPEDO
DIAPHONE
(HUNTER'S —) SEEK PRIZE GIBBET
STRAKE
(MILITARY —) FLARE TURNOUT
ASSEMBLY
(NAVAL —) SECURE
(RADIO —) BEAM
(RAILROAD —) BANJO BOARD
FUSEE FUZEE TARGET HIGHBALL
(WARNING —) ALARM KLAXON
TOCSIN
SIGNALLING TICKTACK
SIGNALMAN FLAGS BELLBOY
BELLMAN
SIGNATE SENNET
SIGNATORY SIGNEE SIGNER
SIGNATURE BOLT FIRM HAND VISA
FRANK SHEET SIGIL THEME SIGNUM
TUGHRA SECTION HANDWRIT
SIGNATOR
SIGNBOARD SIGN SHINGLE

SIGNET SIGIL
SIGNIFICANCE WIT BODY SOUND
AMOUNT IMPORT INTENT LETTER
STRESS WEIGHT BEARING CONTENT
GRAVITY MEANING SENTENCE
STRENGTH
(DEVOID OF —) JEJUNE
(HIDDEN —) HYPONOIA
(LACKING —) INANE
SIGNIFICANT REAL GREAT
AUGURAL EPOCHAL OMINOUS
POINTED SERIOUS SENSEFUL
SPEAKING
SIGNIFICANTLY SENSIBLY
SIGNIFICATION SENSE VALOR
VALUE ETYMON IMPORT MOMENT
NOTION MEANING CARRIAGE
SIGNIFIE
SIGNIFICS SENSIFICS
SIGNIFY BE SAY BEAR GIVE MAKE
MEAN NOTE SIGN WAVE AUGUR
IMPLY SKILL SOUND SPEAK SPELL
TOKEN UTTER AMOUNT ARGUFY
ASSERT BEMEAN DENOTE EMPLOY
IMPORT INTEND MATTER SIGNAL
BESPEAK BETOKEN CONNOTE
DECLARE EXPRESS PORTEND
PRETEND DESCRIBE INDICATE
INTIMATE MANIFEST
SIGNPOST GUIDE MERCURY
WAYMARK HANDPOST
SIGURD (HORSE OF —) GRANI
(SLAIN BY —) FAFNIR
(SLAYER OF —) HOGNI
(WIFE OF —) GUDRUN
SIKH AKALI SINGH UDASI MAZHABI
SIKKIM (CAPITAL OF —) GANGTOK
(NATIVE OF —) RONG BHOTIA
LEPCHA
(RIVER OF —) TISTA
SIKSIKA SIHASAPA
SILENCE GAG MUM CALK CLUM
HUSH REST CHOKE FLOOR QUIET
SHUSH SQUAT STILL CLAMOR
MUFFLE SETTLE STIFLE WHISHT
CONFUTE SQUELCH DUMBNESS
PRECLUDE SUPPRESS
SILENCED STILL
SILENCER SOURDINE
SILENT MUM CLUM HUSH HUST
MUET MUTE SNUG CLOSE STILL
TACIT WHIST MUETTE SULLEN
TIPTOE WHISHT APHONIC UNWORDY
ASPIRATE RESERVED RETICENT
TACITURN
SILHOUETTE SHADE ISOTYPE
SILICA FLINT SILEX TRIPOLI
SILICATE MICA ALVITE CERITE
EUCLASE ILVAITE LOTRITE ZEOLITE
CALAMINE ERIONITE WELLSITE
SILICEOUS SHELLY
SILICLE POUCH SILICULE
SILICOSIS CON
SILK SAY SOY CRIN ERIA LOVE
MUGA FLOSS GREGE HONAN JAPAN
TABBY BLATTA CRACKS CULGEE
DUCAPE FRISON MANTUA RADIUM
SENDAL SHALEE SHILLA SOUPLE
TUSSAH ALAMODE CHIFFON

HABUTAI PERSIAN SQUEEZE
TSATLEE TUSSORE YAMAMAI
ARMOZEEN ARMOZINE LUSTRINE
MILANESE
(— FOR LININGS) SARSNET
SARCENET
(HEAVY —) CRIN ARMOZINE
(RAW —) GREIGE MARABOU
TAYSAAM TSATLEE MARABOUT
(REFUSE —) BUR BURR
(TWILLED —) SURAH TOBINE
FOULARD LOUSINE
(UNDYED —) CORAH
(UNTWISTED —) SLEAVE
(UPHOLSTERY —) TABARET
(WASTE —) KNUB NOIL FRISON
SILK COTTON KAPOK
SILK-COTTON TREE BULAK SEMUL
SIMAL YAXCHE BENTANG MUNGUBA
POCHOTE
SILKEN SILL SERIC SILKY SUAVE
SEREAN
SILK GRASS KARATAS
SILK GUM SERICIN
SILK OAK LACEWOOD
SILKSMAN SCALPER
SILK TREE SIRIS
SILKWORM ERI ERIA SINA TUSSAH
TUSSORE YAMAMAI BOMBYCID
SILKY GLOSSY SILKEN
SILKY CORNEL REDBRUSH
SILKY TAMARIN MARIKINA
SILL GIRD SOLE PLATE PATAND
PATTEN SADDLE MUDSILL DOORSILL
SILLINESS BOSH FOLLY BETISE
GOOSERY INANITY SIMPLES
IDLENESS NONSENSE
SILLY TID BETE DAFT FOND FOOL
NICE VAIN APISH BALMY BUGGY
CAKEY DENSE DILLY DIZZY GOOFY
INANE SAPPY SEELY BLASHY
CRANKY CUCKOO DAWISH DOTARD
DOTTLE FOOTLE FRUITY GUCKED
PAULIE SAWNEY SHANNY SIMPLE
SINGLE SKIVIE SLIGHT SPOONY
VACANT ASININE FATUOUS FOOLISH
FOPPISH FRIBBLE GLAIKET PEEVISH
SCRANNY SHALLOW UNWITTY
ANSERINE FEATLESS FOOTLING
FOPPERLY
(BE —) DRIVEL
SILOXANE SILICON
SILT DREGS SLEECH DEPOSIT
RESIDUE SULLAGE BULLDUST
SILVER LUNA MOON PINA DIANA
PLATE SYCEE WEDGE WHITE
ALBATA ARGENT SILLER BULLION
VERMEIL ARGENTUM STERLING
ARGENTINE
(— STATE) NEVADA
(DEBASED —) VELLON
(GILDED —) VERMEIL
SILVER BELL HALESIA BELLWOOD
COWLICKS
SILVERFISH SHINER SLICKER
FISHTAIL WOODFISH
SILVERING BACKING
SILVERSIDES IAO BRIT TINK BRITT
FRIAR SMELT TAILOR TINKER

GRUNION ATHERINE PEIXEREY
PEJERREY SKIPJACK
SILVERSMITH SONAR
SILVER TREE IRONWOOD
SILVER TREE FERN PITAU
SILVERVINE CATVINE
SILVERWEED TANSY
SILVERWING CINDER
SILVERY WHITE ARGENT SILVER
SILVERN
SILYBUM MARIANA
SIMAR CYMAR SYMAR ZIMARRA
SIMILAR LIKE SUCH ALIKE EVENLY
LIKELY SIMILE COGNATE KINDRED
SEEMABLE SELFLIKE SUCHLIKE
SUITABLE
SIMILARITY SIMILE ANALOGY
HOMOLOGY HOMOTAXY LIKENESS
PARALLEL SAMENESS
SIMILARLY EQUALLY LIKEWISE
SIMILE ICON IKON IMAGE FIGURE
SUIVEZ COMPARE
SIMILITUDE IMAGE FIGURE
ANALOGY PARABLE PORTRAIT
SIMMER FRY CREE SILE STEW
SIMPER SOTTER TOTTLE
SIMON ZELOTES
SIMONY BARRATRY
SIMOOM SAMUM SAMIEL
SIMPER MINCE SMIRK BRIDLE
SIMPLE LOW BALD BARE EASY FOND
MERE NICE ONLY PURE RUDE SNAP
VERY WEAK AFALD BLEAK DIZZY
GREEN NAIVE NAKED PLAIN SEELY
SILLY SMALL SOBER CHASTE
GLOBAL HOMELY HONEST HUMBLE
NATIVE OAFISH RUSTIC SEMPLE
SEVERE SINGLE STUPID VIRGIN
ARTLESS ASININE AUSTERE
BABYISH FATUOUS FOOLISH
ONEFOLD POPULAR SIMPLEX
SPECIES EXPLICIT HOMEMADE
INNOCENT SACKLESS SEMPLICE
SOLITARY
SIMPLE-MINDED SEELY SILLY
INNOCENT
SIMPLETON AUF AWF COX DAW
FON NUP OAF SAP SOT BOOB CAKE
COOT CULL FLAT FOOL GABY GAUP
GAWP GOFF GOUK GOWK GOWP
GUFF PEAK SIMP SOFT TONY TOOT
ZANY COKES GALAH GOOSE IDIOT
IKONA JACOB LOACH NINNY NODDY
PRUNE SAMMY SMELT SPOON
TOMMY BADAUD DAUKIN FONDLE
GANDER GAUPUS GAWNEY GOTHAM
GREENY GULPIN JOSSER NINCUM
NOODLE NUPSON SAWNEY SIMKIN
SIMPLE DAWPATE GOMERAL
GUBBINS JUGGINS MAFFLIN
MUGGINS WIDGEON ABDERITE
FLATHEAD FONDLING INNOCENT
JEANJEAN JOCRISSE KNOTHEAD
MOONCALF MOONLING OMADHAUN
PEAGOOSE SILLYTON SOFTHEAD
WISEACRE WOODCOCK
SIMPLICITY NICETY PURITY
MODESTY NAIVETE ELEGANCE
SIMPLIFY CLARIFY EXPOUND

SIMPLY JUST ALONE FONDLY
MERELY PLATLY CRUDELY QUIETLY
NATIVELY
SIMULATE ACT FAKE MOCK FEIGN
MIMIC AFFECT ASSUME SEMBLE
SIMULE SKETCH
SIMULATED FAINT FAKED ERSATZ
FICTIOUS
SIMULATION ACTING ANALOGUE
PRETENSE
SIMULTANEOUS CONJOINT
CONJUGATE
SIMULTANEOUSLY ONCE
TOGETHER
SIN ERR CULP DEBT ENZU EVIL HELL
PAPA VICE BLAME CRIME ERROR
FAULT FOLLY GUILT SLOTH WATHE
WRONG AGUILT COMMIT FELONY
NANNAR OFFEND PIACLE PLIGHT
VENIAL FRAILTY OFFENSE
HAMARTIA INIQUITY PECCANCY
QUEDSHIP TRESPASS
(DEADLY —) ACEDIA
(ORIGINAL —) ADAM
SINCALINE CHOLINE
SINCE AS AGO FOR FRO NOW GONE
SETH SITH SYNE BEING WHERE
FORWHY BECAUSE SITHENS
WHEREAS INASMUCH SITHENCE
SINCERE GOOD REAL TRUE AFALD
FRANK DEVOUT ENTIRE HEARTY
HONEST SIMPLE SINGLE CORDIAL
EARNEST GENUINE ONEFOLD
UPRIGHT FAITHFUL
SINCERELY TRULY SIMPLY SINGLY
DEVOUTLY ENTIRELY HEARTILY
SINCERITY FAITH HEART HONESTY
REALITY
SINDON CORPORAL
SINEW THEW FIBER FIBRE NERVE
LEADER SINNER TENDON
SINEWY WIRY NERVY THEWY
ROBUST FIBROSE FIBROUS STRINGY
TENDINAL
SINFONIA SYMPHONY
SINFUL BAD EVIL VILE NEFAS
WRONG WICKED UNGODLY VICIOUS
PIACULAR
SING HUM JIG LIP CANT CARP GALE
HYMN LILT TUNE CAROL CARRY
CHANT CHIRL CROON DIRGE DITTY
DRING FEIGN LYRIC RAISE TOUCH
YEDDE CHAUNT CHORUS DIVIDE
INTONE MELODY RECORD RELISH
STRAIN WARBLE CHORTLE
COUNTER DESCANT GRIDDLE
SINGING TWEEDLE CHERUBIM
FALDERAL MODULATE SINGSONG
VOCALIZE
(— ABOUT) BESING
(— ABOVE TRUE PITCH) SHARP
(— AS A BEGGAR) GRIDDLE
(— BRISKLY) KNACK
(— CHEERFULLY) LILT
(— FLORIDLY) DIVIDE
(— HARSHLY) SCREAM
(— IN A CRACKED VOICE) CRAKE
(— IN CHORUS) CHOIR
(— IN LOW VOICE) CROON

(— **IN SWISS MANNER**) YODEL
(— **LOUDLY**) BELT TROLL TROLLOL
(— **PRAISES**) LAUD
(— **ROMANCES**) GEST GESTE
(— **SECOND PART**) SURCENT
(— **SOFTLY**) SOWF SOWTH
(— **WITH FLOURISHES**) ROULADE
SINGAPORE (**RIVER IN** —) SUNGEI
  SELETAR
  (**STRAIT OF** —) JOHORE SEMBILAN
SINGE GAS BURN SWEAL GENAPP
  SCORCH SWINGE SCOWDER
  SWITHEN FIREFANG
SINGER ALTO BARD LARK SWAN
  BASSO BUFFA BUFFO SKALD VOICE
  BULBUL BUSKER CANARY CANTOR
  LYRIST SONGER BASSIST CHANTER
  CROONER PRIMOMO SOLOIST
  SONGMAN SOPRANO TROLLER
  WARBLER BAYADERE CANTADOR
  CASTRATO CHANTEUR FALSETTO
  GRIDDLER MELODIST MONODIST
  THAMYRIS VOCALIST
  (— **OF FOLK SONGS**) CANTADOR
  (— **OF THE GODS**) GANDHARVA
  (**FEMALE** —) SONGBIRD
  (**MENDICANT** —) BUSKER
  (**PRINCIPAL** —) PRIMOMO
  (**PROVENCAL** —) MUSAR
SINGING CANT SCAT CHANT LYRIC
  HYMNODY JONGLERY
  (— **CAROLS**) PLYGAIN HODENING
  (**CANTORIAL** —) HAZANUTH
  HAZZANUT
  (**SIMULTANEOUS** —) CHORUS
SINGLE ODD ONE LAST ONLY SOLE
  UNAL AFALD SIMPLE SOLEIN
  SULLEN UNIQUE VERSAL ALONELY
  AZYGOUS ONEFOLD SEVERAL
  SIMPLEX TWOSOME PECULIAR
  SEPARATE SINGULAR SOLITARY
  SPORADIC
  (— **OUT**) CUT SPOT ISOLATE
  SEPARATE
SINGLE-FOOT RACK
SINGLEHANDEDLY SINGLY
SINGLENESS UNITY ONENESS
SINGLETON (— **LEAD**) SNEAK
SINGLY SINGLE SOLELY SLONELY
SINGPHO CHINGPAW
SINGSONG SOUGH CHANTING
SINGULAR ODD RARE QUEER SEENIL
  SINGLE STRANGE PECULIAR
SINGULARISM HENISM
SINGULARITY DOUBLET ONENESS
  ONLINESS
SINISTER AWK CAR KAY DARK DIRE
  FELL GRIM DISMAL LOUCHE
  OBLIQUE OMINOUS
SINISTRAL REVERSED
SINK DIP DOP EBB LUM SAG SET
  SYE BORE DRAU DRAW DROP FADE
  FAIL FALL GOWT HELD KILL LUMB
  SILE SWAG AVALE DRAFT DRAIN
  DROOP DROWN HIELD LAPSE
  LOWER MERGE POACH SQUAT
  STOOP SWAMP VERGE DOLINA
  DOLINE DRENCH GUTTER PLUNGE
  PUDDLE RESIDE SETTLE COMMODE

DECLINE DESCEND DRAUGHT
FOUNDER GULLION IMMERSE
RELAPSE SCUTTLE SUBSIDE
SWALLOW DECREASE SINKHOLE
SOAKAWAY
(— **A WELL**) DRILL
(— **AND FALL**) TWINE
(— **AS IN MUD**) LAIR
(— **DOWN**) BOG AVALE STOOP
DECLINE
(— **FANGS INTO**) STRIKE
(— **INTO OOZE**) WASEL
(— **NAILHEAD**) SET
(— **SUDDENLY**) SLUMP
(— **UNDER TRIAL**) QUAIL
SINKBOX BOX SINK BATTERY
SINKER BUR BURR SINK DIPSY
  PLUMB BULLET
SINKHOLE SINK PONOR UVALA
  CENOTE COLLECT
SINKING GONE SINKAGE
  (— **DOWN**) FONDU
SINKIUSE COLUMBIA
SINLESS INNOCENT
SINLESSNESS HOLINESS
SINNER DEBTOR PECCANT
SINNING PECCANT
SINUATE GYROSE
SINUOSITY WRIGGLE
SINUOUS WAVY SNAKEY SINUATE
  SNAKISH TORTILE WINDING
  INDENTED SWANLIKE
SINUS BOSOM RECESS LOCULUS
  TEARPIT
SINUSITIS ROUP
SIOUAN ABANIC DAKOTA SANTEE
  SAPONI CATAWBA DACOTAH
SIOUX (— **FORCE**) WAKAN WAKON
SIP BIB NIP SUP BLEB SEEP SLUP
  SUCK TIFF KEACH SNACK WHIFF
  TIPPLE TICKLER DELIBATE
SIPHON CRANE THIEF VALINCH
  FLINCHER
SIPPING LIBANT
SIPUNCULOIDEA ACHAETA INERMIA
SIR PO DAN DEN DON PAN AZAM
  HERR MIAN STIR TUAN SAHIB
  SENOR SEYID SIEUR MESSER
  SAYYID SIGNOR SIRREE DOMINUS
  EFFENDI MESSIRE SIGNIOR SIGNORE
  GOSPODIN GOVERNOR
  (**PL.**) LORDINGS
SIRCAR BANIAN
SIRE BEGET THROW FATHER GETTER
SIREN HOOTER LIGEIA LIGYDA
  LORELEI MERMAID SIRENIAN
SIRENIAN COWFISH MUTILATE
SIRENOMELUS SYMPUS SYMMELUS
SIRICID UROCERID
SIRIS KOKO LEBBEK
SIRIUS SOTHIS TISHIVA CANICULA
SIRLOIN SEY BACKSEY
SIRMUELLERA BANKSIA
SIRUP WAX LICK GOLDY SYRUP
  GOWDIE GREENS LIQUER ORGEAT
  RUNOFF CLAIRCE ECLEGMA
  MOLASSES QUIDDANY
SIRWASH SIDELINE
SISAL CABUYA SISALANA

SISKIN TARIN
SISSIFIED PRISSY
SISSOO TALI SHISHAM
SISSY SIS CISSIE SISTER CHICKEN
SISTER NUN SIB SIS GIRL NURSE
  SISSY TITTY WOMAN EXTERN
  PERSON
  (**YOUNGER** —) CADETTE
  (**PL.**) SISTERN SISTREN
SISTERHOOD SORORITY
SISTERLY SORORAL
SISYPHUS (**FATHER OF** —) AEOLUS
  (**WIFE OF** —) MEROPE
SIT SET LEAN SEAT BENCH PRESS
  ROOST SQUAT WEIGH BESTRIDE
  (— **ABRUPTLY**) CLAP
  (— **ASTRIDE**) CROSS HORSE
  STRADDLE
  (— **ERECT LIKE A DOG**) BEG
  (— **FORCIBLY**) DOSS
  (— **IN JUDGMENT**) DEEM
  (— **ON**) BROOD COVER
  (— **OVER EGGS**) RUCK BROOD
SITATUNGA NAKONG
SITE AREA PLOT SEAT SITU SOLE
  SPOT TOFT FIELD PLACE SITUS
  STAND STANCE BIVOUAC DAMSITE
  HABITAT STEADING
  (— **OF BIRD SEXUAL DISPLAY**) LEK
  (— **OF HUNT**) DRIVE
  (— **OF SMELTER**) BOLE
  (**EXCAVATION** —) DIG
  (**THRESHING** —) SETTING
SITTER DOLLY DOLLIE INSESSOR
SITTING DIET SEAT ASSIS SEANCE
  SEDENT SEJANT SESSION
  CONGRESS SEDERUNT
SITUATE PLACE POSITION
SITUATED SET SEATED STATURED
  (— **OPPOSITE**) COUNTER
SITUATION JOB LIE CASE PASS
  PLOT POST SEAT SITE SPOT BERTH
  SIEGE SITUS STATE STEAD ASSIZE
  CHANCE ESTATE OFFICE PLIGHT
  STATUS EPISODE PICTURE PORTENT
  POSTURE STATION INCIDENT
  INSTANCE POSITURE STANDING
  UBIQUITY
  (— **BESET BY DIFFICULTIES**)
  SCRAPE
  (— **IN CRIBBAGE**) GO
  (— **IN FARO**) CATHOP
  (— **OF PERPLEXITY**) HOBBLE STRAIT
  (**AMUSING** —) BAR
  (**AWKWARD** —) SCRAPE
  (**CRITICAL** —) CLUTCH
  (**DIFFICULT** —) BOX PUXY BOGGLE
  NINEHOLES
  (**DISTRESSING** —) STYMIE
  (**EXECRABLE** —) ATROCITY
  (**FAVORABLE** —) BREAK
  (**FINAL** — **OF ACT**) CURTAIN
  (**HOPELESSLY DOOMED** —)
  RATTRAP
  (**NECESSITOUS** —) BREACH
  (**PAINFUL** —) DISTRESS
  (**RELATIVE** —) BEARING
  (**UNSATISFACTORY** —) DILEMMA
  (**VEXATIOUS** —) HEADACHE

(VILE —) DUNGHILL
(ZODIACAL —) HAYZ
SITZ BATH SITZBAD SEMICUPE
SITZMARK BATHTUB
SIVA RUDRA SHIVA ISVARA SHAMBU
BHAIRAVA MAHADEVA NATARAJA
SIX VAU WAW SICE SISE HEXAD
HEXADE SENARY SEXTET STIGMA
DIGAMMA SIXSOME
SIXFOLD SEXTUPLE
SIX-FOOTED HEXAPOD
SIXMO SEXTO
SIXPENCE HOG PIG BEND KICK
SIMON SPRAT TIZZY BENDER
FIDDLE TANNER TESTON CRIPPLE
FIDDLER TESTRIL
SIXTEENTH ANA ANNA
SIXTIETH (— PART OF DAY) GHURRY
SIXTY SAMECH SAMEKH
SIZABLE SNUG LARGE HANDSOME
SIZE WAX AREA BIND BULK MARK
MASS DRESS GIRTH MOUND PLANK
SCALE EXTENT FORMAT GROWTH
MICKLE MOISON PICNIC SIZING
BIGNESS CONTENT CORSAGE
FITTING THIRTEEN TWELVEMO
(— OF BOOK) FOLIO
(— OF CARDS) TOWN LADIES
(— OF HOLE) BORE
(— OF HOSIERY) POPE
(— OF PAPERBOARD) LARGE
(— OF PARTICLE) GRIND
(— OF ROPE) GRIST
(— OF TYPE) GEM PICA RUBY
AGATE CANON ELITE PEARL MINION
PRIMER BREVIER DIAMOND
EMERALD ENGLISH PARAGON
(— YARN) SLASH
(CLOTHING —) LONG SHORT STOUT
JUNIOR PETITE
(EXTRA LARGE —) SUPER
(RELATIVE —) SCALE
(UNUSUAL —) OUTSIZE
SIZING DRESSING SLASHING
(— LIQUID) GLAIR
SIZZLE FRIZZ
SKAT CAT NULL TOURNEE
SKATE BOB RAY TUB RAJA RINK
SKIT TINK TUBE FLAIR SCULL
BATOID DOCTOR FLATHE PATENT
PATTEN ROCKER ROLLER RUNNER
SKETCH TINKER CHOPINE FLAPPER
PLACOID SKETCHER
(— MARK) CUSP
(FEMALE —) MAID
SKATER PATTENER SKETCHER
SKEDADDLE BUNK
SKEET KELTER KILTER PELTER
SKEIN RAP HANK HASP SCAN
BOTTOM SLEAVE SELVAGE
SKEINER RANDER SLIPPER
SKELETIN SPONGIN
SKELETON CUP CAGE MORT RAME
ATOMY BONES FRAME LOOFAH
SICULA SKELET ANATOMY CARCASS
RAWBONE ARMATURE CORALLUM
MANDIBLE OSSATURE
SKELETON KEY GILT SCREW
TWIRLER

SKEPTIC DOUBTER INFIDEL ZETETIC
APIKOROS APORETIC
SKEPTICAL APOREIC DOUBTFUL
SKEPTICISM HUMISM UNBELIEF
SKETCH BIT DASH DRAW LIMN PLAN
VIEW VITA DRAFT ENTER PAINT
TRACE APERCU DESIGN DOODLE
SCHEME SPLASH CROQUIS
DRAUGHT DRAWING ETCHING
OUTLINE SCHIZZO MONOGRAM
PROSPECT VIGNETTE
(— BEFOREHAND) INDICATE
(AUTOBIOGRAPHICAL —) VITA
(BIOGRAPHICAL —) ELOGY ELOGIUM
(FIRST —) ESQUISSE
(HERALDIC —) TRICK
(OUTDOORS —) LANDSKIP
(PRELIMINARY —) DRAFT ABBOZZO
MAQUETTE
(ROUGH —) NOTE POCHADE
ESQUISSE
(SATIRICAL —) SKIT
SKEW ASKEW GAUCHE
SKEWBACK SPRINGER
SKEWER PROD PROG SPIT PRICK
TRUSS SKIVER TASTER
SKEWERER TUBER
SKI SKEE SNOWSHOE
(— DOWN SLOPE) SCHUSS
(— METHOD) PASSGANG
(— MOVEMENT) RUADE
(— POSITION) VORLAGE
(— RACING) LANGLAUF
(— TURN) TELEMARK
(PL.) BOARDS
SKID DOG DRAG SLEW SLUE TRIG
DRIFT DRILL SLOUGH SKIDPAN
SLIPPER TRIGGER SIDESLIP
(— LOGS) SNAKE TWICH TRAVOY
TWITCH
(— ON RAIL) SKATE
(FENDER —) GLANCER
SKIDDER SNAKER
SKIDI LOUP
SKIDWAY PIT
SKIER KANONE SNOWBIRD
SKIFF SKIFT CAIQUE DINGHY
SAMPAN CURRANE SKIPPET
SKIING TOURING
SKIL BESHOW SKILFISH
SKILL ART CAN WIT FEAT FEEL HAND
PATE TACT CRAFT DRAFT HAUNT
KNACK TRICK ENGINE TECHNE
ABILITY ADDRESS APTNESS
CUNNING FINESSE MASTERY
MYSTERY SCIENCE SLEIGHT
ARTIFICE CAPACITY CHIVALRY
DEFTNESS FACILITY INDUSTRY
LEARNING
(LACK OF —) INERTIA
(NAVIGATION —) SEACRAFT
SKILLED OLD WISE ADEPT ASTUTE
PERITE SCIENT SKILLY VERSED
HOTSHOT PRACTIC EDUCATED
SKILLFUL
SKILLET PRIG SPIDER
SKILLFUL APT SLY ABLE DEFT FEAT
FILE FINE GOOD PERT TIDY WISE
ADEPT CANNY FITTY HANDY HENDE

READY SLICK SWEET ADROIT
ARTFUL CLEVER CRAFTY DAEDAL
EXPERT HABILE SCIENT SKILLY
SOLERT SUBTLE CUNNING SKILLED
DEXTROUS PRACTIVE SLEIGHTY
TACTICAL
SKILLFULLY DEFTLY CRAFTILY
SKILLFULNESS CRAFT
SKIM TOP RIFF SCUD SCUM SCUN
SCUR SILE SKIP FLEET GRAZE
SCALE SKIFF SKIRR SKIVE BROWSE
RABBLE SAMPLE DESPUME SKITTER
(— ON WATER) SCHOON
SKIMMED FLAT FLET
SKIMMER FALK LARI SKEP SCOOP
LINGEL SCUMMER CUTWATER
SKIMMINGS SCRUFF
SKIMP JIMP SLUR SCAMP SKINCH
SKIMPY JIMP CHARY SPARE SCANTY
STINGY
SKIN KIP KIT BACK BARK CASE CAST
DERM FELL FLAY FLEA HIDE HILD
KITT MORT PEAU PEEL PELT RIND
BALAT BLYPE BRAWN FLOAT GENET
SLUFF STRIP SWARD PELTRY
SWARTH UNCASE CUTICLE DOESKIN
ENDERON KIDSKIN LEATHER
PELLAGE SKIMMER BUCKSKIN
DRUMHEAD LAMBSKIN PARADERM
PELLICLE SEALSKIN TEGUMENT
VITILIGO WOOLFELL
(— FOR BOOKBINDING) BASAN
(— OF BACON) SWARD
(— OF BOARDS) CARPET
(— OF FRUIT) PEEL
(— OF GOOSE) APRON
(— OF INSECT) CAST
(— OF POTATO) JACKET
(— OF POULTRY NECK) HELZEL
(— OF RABBIT) RACK CONEY
(— OF SEAL) SCULP
(— OF THE HEAD) SCALP
(— OF WALNUT) ZEST
(— OF YOUNG CALF) SLINK DEACON
(— WITH WOOL REMAINING ON IT)
WOOLFELL
(60 —S) TURN
(BARE —) BUFF
(BEAVER —) PLEW
(BOAR'S —) SHIELD
(CAST —) SPOIL SLOUGH EXUVIAE
(CHAFED OR SORE —) IRE
(CHAMOIS —) FURWA
(DEEP LAYER OF THE —) CUTIS
(FAWN —) NEBRIS
(INNER PART OF THE —) DERMA
(LAMB — PREPARED LIKE FUR)
BUDGE
(OUTER —) HUSK
(PENDULOUS FOLD OF —) DEWLAP
(ROUGHTANNED —) CRUST
(SHARK —) SHAGREEN
(SHEEP —) BASIL
(SQUIRREL —) VAIR
(THICKENED —) BRAWN
(THIN —) FILM PELLICLE STRIFFEN
SKINFLINT SKIN FLINT SCREW
HUDDLE PELTER SCRAPER SKEEZIX
SKINK ADDA SCINCID SCORPION

SKINNY BONY LEAN THIN SLINK
SKIP DAP HIP BALK BOUT FOOT
JUMP LEAP SLIP TRIP BOUND
CAPER DANCE FRISK SALTO SCOON
SCOPE SCOUP SKITE SMOKE VAULT
GAMBOL GLANCE LAUNCH SPRING
GUNBOAT SKIPPER SKITTER
TRIPPLE PORPOISE
(— SCHOOL) TIB
SKIPJACK SKIP BONITO SKIPPER
SKIPPER IHI SKIP LAODAH LOWDAH
SERANG SHIPPER
SKIRMISH FRAY BRUSH CLASH
MELEE SKIRM BICKER HASSLE
PICKEER RUNNING
SKIRMISHER HUSSAR
SKIRMISHING SPARRING
SKIRT CUT LAP BANK BASE COAT
ENGI JUPE SAYA TUBE COAST
JUPON LABIE PAREU PASIN STRIP
TREND TWIST BASQUE DIRNDL
HOBBLE JUMPER KIRTLE PEPLUM
SARONG TAMEIN QUARTER
BASQUINE PULLBACK SKIRTING
(ARMOR —) TASSES LAMBOYS
(DIVIDED —) CULOTTE
(HOOPED —) TUBTAIL
(TARTAN —) KILT ARISAID
(PL.) DOCK DOCKEN
SKIRTING SKIRT PLINTH
(PL.) BROKES
SKIT BLACKOUT
SKITTAGETAN HAIDA
SKITTISH SHY CORKY GOOSY WINDY
FLISKY KITTLE SKEIGH SPOOKY
FLIGHTY SCADDLE SKADDLE
STARTLY BOGGLISH SKITTERY
STARTFUL
SKITTLES KAYLES KITTLES SQUAILS
SKUA BONXIE JAEGER TEASER
TULIAC STINKPOT WHIPTAIL
SKULDUGGERY JOUKERY PAWKERY
SKULK DERN JOUK LURK LUSK
MOOCH SCOUT
SKULL BEAN POLL CRANY MOOCH
SCALP SCAUP VAULT COBBRA
PALLET SCONCE CRANIUM HARNPAN
HEADMOLD PANNICLE
(— BONE) VOMER
(— POINT) TYLION
(BACK OF —) OCCIPUT
(INCOMPLETE —) CALVARIA
(UPPER HALF OF —) SINCIPUT
SKULLCAP COIF PIXY PIXIE SKULL
VAULT BEANIE COIFFE CALOTTE
CAPELINE HOODWORT
(ARABIAN —) CHECHIA
(JEWISH —) YAMILKE YARMULKE
(STEEL —) SECRET
SKUNK ANNA PUSS HURON SKINK
SNIPE ZORIL CHINCHA POLECAT
SEECAWK SMELLER CONEPATE
CONEPATL MUSTELID PHOBYCAT
ZORRILLO
(JAVANESE —) TELEDU
SKUNK CABBAGE COLLARD
POCKWEED
SKY BLUE HIGH LIFT LOFT POLE TIEN
AZURE CARRY DYAUS ETHER LANGI

VAULT CAELUS CANOPY HEAVEN
REGION WELKIN ELEMENT HEAVENS
OLYMPUS TENGERE WEATHER
(ICE —) ICEBLINK
SKYLARK LARK YERK
SLAB BAT CANT CLAM LECH PARE
SLAT BLADE DALLE LINER PANEL
PLANK SLATE STELA STELE TABLE
WADGE ABACUS FLITCH MARVER
MIHRAB PAVIOR RUNNER FLAPPET
PLANCHE PORPHYRY PUNCHEON
SLABWOOD
(— OF CLAY) BAT
(— OF COAL) SKIP SLIP
(— OF LIMESTONE) BALATTE
(— OF MARBLE) DALLE
(— OF PEAT) SCAD
(— OF SANDSTONE) COMAL
(— OVER BROOK) CLAM
(MEMORIAL —) LEDGER
(PAINTER'S —) SLANT
(STONE —) PLANK STELA STELE
INKSTONE
SLACK DRY LAX CULM DUFF NESH
SLOW SOFT CHECK FLOWN LOOSE
SLAKE TARDY ABATED FLABBY
FLAPPY REMISS UNGIRT BACKING
MAKINGS RELAXED SLACKEN
SMEDDUM CARELESS DILATORY
INACTIVE SLOBBERY
(— IN TRIGGER) CREEP
(— SHEET OF SAIL) FLOW
(COAL —) COOM COOMB
(PL.) BAGS
SLACKEN LAG PAY EASE FLAG
SLOW DELAY DOWSE LOOSE RELAX
SLACK SLAKE START SURGE
EXOLVE RELENT UNBEND
(— SPEED) HANG
SLACKENING HANG LETUP DETENTE
LETDOWN SLACKAGE
SLACKER SPIV ROTTER COUCHER
SLINKER EMBUSQUE
SLACKNESS LACHES LASHNESS
SLADE SOLE
SLAG SCAR DROSS CINDER DANDER
SCORIA SLAKIN THOMAS QUITTER
SLACKEN
SLAIN FALLEN
SLAKE ABATE SLACK LESSEN
QUENCH REFRESH SATISFY
SLAKING FAT
SLAM CLAP DASH FLUB SLOG SLOT
VOLE CLASH GRAND PLANK SLOSH
STRAM CHELEM FLOUNCE
SLANDER CANT BELIE LIBEL NOISE
BEFOUL DEFAME INJURE MALIGN
MISSAY ASPERSE CALUMNY
OBTRECT SCANDAL TRUMPET
BACKBITE DEROGATE STRUMPET
SLANDERER JUROR
SLANDEROUS FAMOUS VILIPEND
SLANG CANT ARGOT FLASH DIALECT
SLANT TIP CANT FLUE SKEW TILT
BEVEL DRAFT SLOPE SPLAY STOOP
FLANCH SKLENT DRAUGHT
COLORING DIAGONAL
SLANTED CANTED COLORED
COCKEYED

SLANTING BIAS CANT SKEW SLOPE
ASLANT ASLOPE SKLENT SQUINT
LOXOTIC OBLIQUE SLOPING
AVELONGE COLORING OVERWART
SIDELONG
SLANTINGLY AHOO ASWASH
SLANTLY
SLANT LINE VIRGULA VIRGULE
SLAP BOX DAB BLIP BLOW CLAP
CUFF FLAP LICK PLAT SCUD SLAT
SNUB SPAT TACK BLIBE CLINK
CRACK POTCH SKEEG SKELP
SMACK SPANK TWANG TWANK
BLEEZE BUFFET SCLAFF SLIGHT
STRIKE TINGLER WHERRET
BACKSLAP
(— HARD) BLAD
(RANDOM —) FLAY
SLAPDASH BUCKEYE
SLASH CAG CUT JAG COUP GASH
HASH PANE RACE RASH SLIT TOPS
KNIFE MINCE SCORE SKICE SLISH
RAMMEL SCORCH STREAK SLITTER
DIAGONAL SLASHING
SLASHED JAGGED DECOPED
TATTERED
SLASHING ABATIS
SLAT BOW LAG FLAT PALE SLOT
WAND BLADE SCLAT STAVE SPLINE
EUPHROE BEDSTAFF
SLATE RAG SLAT FRAME KILLAS
TABLET TICKET SHALDER SHINDLE
SLATING
(— IN SMALL IRREGULAR PIECES)
SCANTLE
(BLUE —) SHIVER SKAILLIE
(EXPOSED PART OF ROOFING —)
BARI
(SURFACE —) BONE
SLATER HELER HELLIER SLATTER
SKIMMITY
(TOOL OF —) STAKE
SLATTERN DAB DAW MAB FROW
MAUX SLUT TRUB DOLLY FAGOT
MAWKS MOGGY MOPSY BLOUSE
CLATCH DOLLOP MALKIN STREEL
TRAPES LADRONE TROLLOP
HUCKMUCK SLUMMOCK
SLATTERNLY DOWDY BLOWSY
DAWISH FROWZY SORDID TRAPISH
SLATTERN SLOVENLY
SLAUGHTER WAL FELL KILL SLAM
SLAY BUTCH HALAL QUELL BATTUE
MURDER STRAGE BUTCHER
CARNAGE KILLING SHAMBLE
BUTCHERY MASSACRE OCCISION
SHECHITA
(— ACCORDING TO MOSLEM LAW)
HALAL
(— OF LARGE NUMBER) HECATOMB
(WHOLESALE —) QUELL
SLAUGHTERER KILLER SHOHET
SHOCHET
SLAUGHTERHOUSE ABATTOIR
BUTCHERY MATADERO SHAMBLES
(— WORKER) LIMEMAN
SLAUGHTERING SHEHITA SHECHITA
SLAV VEND WEND CZECH HUNKS

HUNKY SLAVE USKOK CROATIAN MORAVIAN

SLAVE DAS ARDU BOND DASI DUPE ESNE SERF DAVUS HELOT SWINK THEOW ALIPIN ALLTUD CUMHAL FORSAR GUINEA HIEROS MAMLUK SLAVEY THRALL VASSAL BONDMAN CAPTIVE CHATTEL FORSADO HACKNEY PEDAGOG SERVANT SLAVISH BONDMAID LORARIUS MAMELUKE MANCIPLE MORGIANA PRAEDIAL SLAVELET THEOWMAN
(— IN TEMPLE) HIEROS
(— WHO WHIPS OTHERS) LORARIUS
(DEFORMED —) CALIBAN
(FREED —) CLIENT
(FUGITIVE —) MAROON CIMMARON
(GALLEY —) FORSAR FORSADO SFORZATO
(HAREM —) ODALISK
(HINDU —) DAS DASI
(PL.) CHIURM COFFLE HELOTRY TOXOTAE

SLAVER DROOL FROTH DRIVEL DRIBBLE SLABBER SLOBBER SALIVATE

SLAVERY YOKE THRALL BONDAGE HELOTRY MIZRAIM THRALDOM

SLAVEY DRUDGE

SLAVISH MEAN MENIAL

SLAVONIC (— BEING) VILA

SLAY KILL SMITE SPILL MURDER STRIKE BUTCHER EXECUTE STRANGLE

SLAYER BANE HOGNI KILLER MURDERER

SLEAZY FLIMSY

SLED LUGE TODE JUMBO SCOOT SLIDE SLIPE SLOOP HURDLE JUMPER SLEDGE SLEIGH BOBSLED CLIPPER COASTER DOGBOAT DOGSLED MONOSKI POINTER SLIPPER TRAILER TRAVOIS HANDSLED SKELETON TOBOGGAN

SLEDGE DAN DRAG DRAY PULK SLED GURRY PULKA SLIDE SLIPE TRAIL TRAIN TROLL TRUNK SLEIGH KOMATIK PADDOCK TROLLEY TRAINEAU
(— FOR CRIMINALS) HURDLE
(— FOR STRAIGHTENING RAILS) GAG
(LOG —) SLOOP TIEBOY
(MINER'S —) MALLET

SLEDGEHAMMER SMASHER

SLEEK SNOD CLOSE JOLLY SILKY SLICK TRICK SILKEN SLEEKY SLIGHT SMARMY SMOOTH SVELTE SLEEKIT SOIGNEE SLIPPERY

SLEEKNESS GLOSS

SLEEP BED KIP LIB LIE NAP CALK CAMP DORM DOSS DOZE HALE REST WINK BALMY DORSE ROOST SWOON DROWSE SIESTA SNOOZE SOMNUS SWEVEN SLUMBER WINKING
(— BROKEN BY SNORING) GRUFF
(— ON A PERCH) JOUK
(DEEP —) SWOON

(LIGHT —) SLOOM
(PRETENDED —) DOGSLEEP
(PROFOUND —) SOPOR
(SHORT —) NAP SIESTA SNOOZE

SLEEPER TIE FENDER DORMANT DORMEUSE ELEOTRID STRINGER

SLEEPING BED ASLEEP DORMANT

SLEEPLESS LIDLESS WAKEFUL RESTLESS WATCHFUL

SLEEPLESSNESS WATCH INSOMNIA

SLEEPY DOZY HEAVY NODDY PEEPY DROWSY GROGGY MORPHIC SLEEPISH SLUMBERY SOMNIFIC

SLEET STORM

SLEEVE ARM BAND POKE ARMLET MANCHE MOGGAN BUSHING CATHEAD CUBITAL HOUSING THIMBLE
(— ON A SHAFT) CANNON
(— ON GUN) BAND
(HANGING —) TAB
(LEG-OF-MUTTON —) GIGOT
(LONG —) POKE
(TAPERED —) SKEIN

SLEIGH SLO PUNG SLED BOOBY SLIPE TRAIN BERLIN CUTTER SLEDGE CARIOLE TRAINEAU

SLEIGHT ARTIFICE

SLENDER FINE HAIR JIMP LANK LEAN PRIN SLIM THIN DELIE EXILE FAINT LATHY REEDY SLANK SLEEK SMALL SPIRY SWAMP WISPY FILATE SEMMIT SLIGHT SPINNY SPIRED STALKY SVELTE TENDER GRACILE LISSOME SLIVERY SPIRLIE SQUINNY TENUOUS THREADY WASPISH ACICULAR ETHEREAL HAIRLIKE SPINDLED

SLENDERNESS EXILITY TENUITY

SLEW LOT RAFT SLUE STROKE

SLICE CUT BITE CHOP FLAG FLAP JERK SHED STOW CANCH CAPER GIGOT LEACH SHARE SHAVE SHIVE SKELB SLIPE SLIVE CANTLE COLLOP CORNET CULPON SHIVER SLIVER TARGET THIBLE TRENCH SECTION SHAVING TRANCHE COSSETTE TURNOVER
(— CUT IN PLOWING) FLAG
(— OF BACON) BARD BARDE LARDON RASHER
(— OF BREAD) BUTTY WHANG CROUTE TRENCHER
(— OF CHEESE) KEBBOC
(— OF COAL) SKIP
(— OF FISH) COBBIN
(— OF MEAT) STEAK COLLOP CUTLET SCALLOP TAILZIE
(— OF SMOKED SALMON) CORNET
(— REMOVED FROM ROADWAY) CANCH
(— WITH MOTIONS) SAW
(—S OF APPLES) CHOPS
(LARGE —) BLAD DODGE
(THICK —) SLAB
(THIN —) CHIP SECTION

SLICED CUT

SLICK LOY GLIB SNUG SLEEK

CLASSY GLOSSY SMOOTHY SLIDDERY

SLICKER FLOAT SLICK SMOOTH SLEEKER SMOOTHER

SLIDE SCLY SKID SLEW SLIP SLUR BALOP CHUTE COAST COULE CREEP GLIDE HURRY MOUNT SCOOT SHIRL SLADE FINDER SLOUGH SLIDDER SLITHER SLUTHER FADEAWAY GLISSADE SLIDEWAY
(— A DIE) SLUR
(— CARDS) SKIN
(— DOWN) RUSE SLUMP
(— FOR LOWERING CASKS) POLEYNE
(— ON DRUMHEAD) BRACE
(— SIDEWISE) SKID
(TENT —) EUPHROE

SLIDER REGISTER

SLIDEWAY PULLEY

SLIDING COULE

SLIGHT CUT OFF EASY FINE HURT POOR SLAP SLIM SLUR SNUB THIN WEAK FILMY GAUZY LIGHT MINOR SCANT SMALL SOBER FLIMSY FORGET LACHES LITTLE MINUTE REMOTE TWIGGY FRAGILE GRACILE NEGLECT NOMINAL SHALLOW SKETCHY SLENDER SLIGHTY THREADY VILLAIN DELICATE MISPRIZE OVERLOOK SCRANNEL VILIPEND

SLIGHTER LESS

SLIGHTEST FIRST LEAST

SLIGHTINGLY LIGHTLY

SLIGHTLY FAINTLY SOMEWHAT

SLIGHTNESS DELICACY GRACILITY

SLIM THIN GAUNT WANDY SLIGHT SLENDER TENUOUS

SLIME GLIT GORE OOZE SLAB SLIP SLUM GLEET SLAKE SLOAK SLOKE SLEECH SLUDGE SCHLICH SLUBBER SLUTHER

SLIMY OOZY SLAB MUCID GLAIRY GLEETY GLETTY LIMOUS MUCOUS SNOTTY SLEECHY MUCULENT

SLINE JOINT

SLING DUST LOOP FLING HONDA SLUNG BRIDGE BRIDLE HALTER SLACKIE
(— FOR HAULING GAME) TUMPLINE
(— OF BRAIDED FIBERS) MA

SLINGER FUNDITOR

SLINGSHOT SLING SLAPPY TWEAKER CATAPULT SHANGHAI

SLINK SLY CAST HINT LEER LOOP LURK PEAK SHIRK SLING SLUNK SNEAK SLINKY
(— AWAY) SHAG SLOKE FLINCH MIZZLE SHRINK

SLIP DIP IMP NOD SLY BALK CARD CHIT DOCK FALL JINK LOOP RUSE SKEW SKID SLEW SLUR SPEW BEWET BEWIT BONER CHECK DAGGE ERROR FLIER FLYER GLIDE LABEL LAPSE SCAPE SHIFT SHIRL SKATE SKITE SLICK SLIDE SLIPE SLIVE SLUMP STALK SURGE COUPON ENGOBE LAPSUS MISCUE

SLOUGH SLURRY TICKET UNSLIP
DELAPSE FOUNDER ILLAPSE
MISSTEP MORTISE SLIDDER
SLUTHER SNAPPER STUMBLE
BOOKMARK GERTRUDE GLISSADE
HEADBAND QUICKSET SCHEDULE
SIDESLIP SLIPPAGE SLIPPING
(— AWAY) GO BILK SKIN WISE
EVADE ELAPSE
(— BY) ELAPSE
(— FROM A PLANT) STALLON
(— OF FISH) RAND
(— OF PAPER) ALLONGE
(— OF WOOD) SPILL
(— OFF COURSE) SLEW SLOUGH
(— ON CARELESSLY) SLIVE
(— OUT) TIB
(— SECRETLY) CREEM
(— SMOOTHLY) SWIM
(CERAMICS —) SLOP ENGOBE
(INFANT'S —) GERTRUDE
(PILLOW —) BIER
SLIPCASE CASE FOREL FORREL
SLIPKNOT BOW SNITTLE DRAWKNOT
SLIPMAN JACKER
SLIPOVER OVERSLIP
SLIPPER FLAT MULE NEAP PUMP
SOCK TURN GLAVE MOYLE ROMEO
SCUFF BALLET BOOTEE DORSAY
JULIET PANTON PINSON SANDAL
SCLAFF SCLIFF BAUCHLE CHINELA
CRAKOWE EVERETT SCUFFER
BABOUCHE FEWTERER PANTOFLE
SCLAFFER SLIPSHOE
SLIPPERINESS SLIDDER
SLIPPERY GLEG GLIB SLID GLARY
GLINT SLAPE SLEEK SLICK SOAPY
SWACK CRAFTY GLINSE GREASY
LUBRIC SHIFTY SLIPPY ELUSIVE
EVASIVE GLIDDER SHUTTLE SLIDDRY
SLIDING SLITHER GLIBBERY
SLABBERY SLICKERY SLIDDERY
SLITHERY
SLIPPERY DICK DONCELLA
SLIPSHOD JERRY SLOPPY UNKEMPT
SLAPDASH SLOVENLY
SLIPSTREAM RACE
SLIT CUT EYE JAG KIN NAG RIT FENT
GATE PORT RACE RENT SCAR SLOT
VENT CRACK SPARE BOUCHE
CRANNY OSTIUM STRENT FISSURE
PLACKET SLITTED SLOTTEN
WINDWAY APERTURE BOTHRIUM
(— HIND LEG) HARL
(— IN EDGE OF SHIELD) BOUCHE
(— IN STONE) GRIKE
(— MADE BY CUT) KERF
(ORNAMENTAL —) SLASH
SLITHER SLIDE HIRSEL SLIDDER
SLUTHER
SLIVER TOP SHAVE SKELF SLICE
SPELK SPELL SHIVER DELIVERY
SPLINTER
(— OF WOOL) ROLL ROVE
(SPINNING —) END RIBBON
DELIVERY
SLOB JOKER SLUDGE SLOBBER
SLOMMACK
SLOBBER SLOP SLUP SMALM

SMARM SLAVER SLABBER SLATHER
SLIVVER BESLAVER
SLOBBERY SLOBBY SMARMY
SLAVERY
SLOE SLA SNAG SLONE
SLOG SLOSH STRIKE
SLOGAN CRY CACHET PHRASE
CATCHCRY SLUGHORN WARDWORD
SLOOP STAR BOYER COMET SMACK
SCHUIT HOOGAARS
SLOP SLAP SOSS SQUAB SWILL
SOSSLE SOZZLE HOGWASH
SLATTER
(— AROUND) SLAISTER
(PL.) SLIVERS SLIPSLOP SLOPPAGE
SLOPE UP DIP LIE BAND BANK BENT
BRAE CANT CAST CURB DROP FALL
HANG HILL LEAN PALI RAKE RAMP
RISE SIDE SINK TILT BEVEL CLIFF
COAST GAMMA HIELD PINCH SCARP
SLANT SLENT SLOOP SPLAY STEEP
TALUS VERGE YUNGA ASCENT
BAJADA BATTER BROACH GLACIS
HADING SHELVE TUMBLE UPBROW
UPRISE CUTBANK DESCENT
DOWNSET FORESET HANDING
INCLINE LEANING PENDANT
UPGRADE VERSANT WEATHER
BANKSIDE DRIPPING GLISSADE
GRADIENT SHOULDER SIDELING
SNOWBANK
(— BACK) BATTER
(— DOWN) SHED
(— OF CUESTA) INFACE
(— OF ROOF) CURB
(— OF STERNPOST) RAKE
(— UPWARD) CLIMB ASCEND
BATTER
(DOWNWARD —) HANG DEVALL
DECLINE DESCENT HANGING
DOWNHILL
(GENTLE —) GLACIS
(MARGINAL —) CESS
(MOUNTAIN —) ADRET
(STEEP —) BROW HEADWALL
SLOPING CANT DEVEX SLANT SLOPE
SLOPY ASLOPE SHELVY DECLIVE
DOWNHILL SIDELING
(— ABRUPTLY) BOLD
(— BACKWARD) SUPINE
SLOPPY JUICY SOPPY SLABBY
SOZZLY SPLOSHY SLABBERY
SLAPDASH SLATTERN SLATTERY
SLIPSHOD WATERISH
SLOSH DOWSE SLASH SLUSH SOUSE
SQUDGE SPLODGE
SLOT COVE DROP SCROLL SPLINE
KEYHOLE GUIDEWAY
SLOTH AI UNAU TARDO ACEDIA
IGNAVY ACCIDIE IGNAVIA BRADYPOD
EDENTATE PIGRITIA SLUGGING
SLOTH BEAR BHALU ASWAIL
SLOTHFUL FAT ARGH IDLE LAZY
INERT LITHER THOKISH UNLUSTY
DELICATE INDOLENT SLUGGISH
SLOUCH LOUCH LARRUP LOLLOP
LOUNGE SLIDDER TROLLOP
SHAMMOCK SLOUCHER
SLOUCH HAT SMASHER

SLOUGH CORE SHED SLEW SLUE
BAYOU RAVEL SHUCK SLONK SLUFF
SPOIL SWAMP ESCHAR DISCARD
LAMMOCK
SLOVEN BESOM CLART SLUSH
TROLLY HALLION TRACHLE
HUDDROUN
SLOVENLY DOWDY GAUMY MESSY
BLOWZY CLATTY FROWZY GRUBBY
SHABBY SLOPPY SLOVEN TRAILY
UNTIDY BUNTING SLIVING SLOUCHY
UNSONCY CARELESS HUDDROUN
SLIPSHOD SLOBBERY SLUBBERY
SLUTTISH TROLLOPY
SLOW BOG LAG LAX LEK WET ARGH
DREE DULL LATE LAZY LENT SKID
SLUG SULK BLUNT DUNCH DUNNY
HEAVY HOOLY INERT POKEY SLACK
SLOTH SWEER TARDE TARDO
TARDY UNAPT ARREST BEHIND
DRIECH DUMMEL HINDER RETARD
SLOOMY SOODLY TRAILY COSTIVE
DRONISH HALTING LAGGARD
LANGUID SLACKEN SOAKING
STRANGE TARDANT TEDIOUS
UNREADY DILATORY INACTIVE
LATESOME SLUGGISH
(— DOWN) SEIZE
(— IN BURNING) SOFT
(— IN MOVEMENT) GRAVE INERT
SULKY
(— OF MIND) STUPID
(— TO LEARN) BACKWARD
(— TO RESPOND) GROSS
(— UP) SLACK SLACKEN
(MODERATELY —) ANDANTE
(MUSICALLY —) LENTO
(PLEASANTLY —) SOFT
(VERY —) LARGO
SLOW-BURNING PUNKY
SLOWED STIFF
SLOWER LATTER
SLOW LORIS KOKAN
SLOWLY SLOW DULLY GRAVE
HOOLY LENTO ADAGIO GENTLY
HEAVILY
SLOW-MOVING SLEEPY DORMANT
DRAWLING SLUGGISH
SLOWNESS LAG SLOTH LENTOR
TARDITY LATENESS
SLOW-WITTED FAT DENSE STUPID
SLOWWORM HAGWORM
SLUDGE GUNK SLOB
SLUE SLEW SWAMP SLOUGH
SLUG BUST LINE MILL PLOW SHOT
SNAG STEW ARION CLUMP LIMAX
SNAIL RATTLE STRIKE SNIFTER
TREPANG GEEPOUND
SLUGGARD DAW SLOW SLUG
DRONE CAYNARD LUGGARD
SWINGER SLOWBACK SLUGABED
SLUGGISH LAG DOZY DULL FOUL
LATE LAZY SLOW BROSY DOPEY
DRONY FAINT HEAVY INERT LOURD
RESTY SULKY BOVINE DRAGGY
DROWSY LEADEN SLEEPY SLOOMY
SLUGGY SUPINE TORPID COSTIVE
DORMANT DRONISH LAGGARD
LANGUID LENTOUS LUMPISH

RESTIVE DILATORY INACTIVE INDOLENT LOURDISH SLOTHFUL SLOTTERY SLUGGARD

SLUGGISHNESS LEAD SLOTH APATHY LENTOR PHLEGM INERTIA LANGUOR

SLUICE CLOW GOOL GOTE GOUT SASSE SLUSH TRUNK CLOUGH FENDER LAUNDER PENSTOCK WASTWEIR

SLUICEWAY FLASH

SLUM BUSTI BUSTEE WARREN

SLUMBER DORM DOVE DOZE JOUK REST ROUT SLEEP SLOOM DROWSE

SLUMP FALL FLOP SOSS SLOUCH LETDOWN TROLLOP

SLUR BIND SLIM COULE GLIDE SLIME SCRUFF SLIGHT SLUBBER LIGATURE **(— IN PRINTING)** SHAKE

SLURRY SLIP

SLUSH MIRE POSH SIND SLOP FLUSH SLOSH SPOSH STUFF SWASH SWOSH LOPPER SLUTCH SLOBBER SLODDER

SLUSHY SLASHY SLOPPY SLOSHY SLUDGY STICKY SPLASHY SLOBBERY

SLUT MAUX BITCH FILTH QUEAN DOLLOP DRAZIL DROSSEL SLATTERN

SLUTTISH SLUTTY SORDID

SLY ARCH FOXY SLEE SLID SLIM CANNY COONY LOOPY PAWKY POKEY SLOAN SNAKY ARTFUL CRAFTY FELINE SUBTLE SUPPLE CUNNING EVASIVE FURTIVE LEERING SUBTILE UNFRANK GUILEFUL SLEIGHTY SNEAKING STEALTHY THIEVISH

SLYNESS CUNNING PAWKERY STEALTH ARCHNESS

SMACK BANG BARK BUSS KISS SALT SCAT SLAP TANG TROW VEIN BAWLY GOUFF SAVOR SNACK TASTE BARQUE FLAVOR SMATCH SMACKEE SPANKER BRAGOZZO SLAPDASH TINCTURE **(— OF)** RELISH

SMACKING SKELPING

SMALL BIT SMA WEE BABY MEAN PINK SEED SLIM TINY WEAK BIJOU BITTY DAWNY DEENY DINKY ELFIN PETIT PETTY PINKY POKEY TEENY WEENY BANTAM FRIBBY GRUBBY LITTLE MINUTE NARROW PEANUT PETITE SLIGHT SMALLY CAPSULE NAGGISH NANITIC PICCOLO QUEECHY SCRIMPY SLENDER THRIFTY PILULOUS SNIPPETY **(— AND NUMEROUS)** MILIARY **(— AND THICK)** DUMPY DUMPTY **(— BUT TANGIBLE)** CERTAIN **(— PORTION)** MODICUM **(DAINTILY —)** MIGNON **(EXCESSIVELY —)** BOXY **(NOT —)** GOOD **(VERY —)** WEE FINE TINY DWARF PUSIL PYGMY TEENY MINUTE MINIKIN TIDDLEY DWARFISH

SMALLAGE MARCH

SMALLCLOTHES SHORTS SMALLS

SMALL CRANBERRY FENBERRY

SMALLER LESS MINOR LESSER

SMALLEST FIRST LEAST MINIM TITMAN MINIMUS

SMALLHOLDER TOFTMAN

SMALL-MINDED PETTY

SMALLNESS EXILITY FEWNESS PAUCITY EXIGUITY SCARCITY

SMALLPOX POX VARIOLA ALASTRIM

SMALT ROYAL ESCHEL SMALTZ ZAFFER ASMALTE

SMART YEP BRAW FESS FLIP FOXY GNIB NICE PINK RACY SNAP SPRY TRIG ACUTE BRISK CLEAN DINKY FLASH HEADY JIMMY KIPPY NIFTY NOBBY NUTTY PEERT PRANK PRIDY SASSY SAUCY SHARP SLEEK SLICK SMIRK SMOKE SMUSH SPICY SPRIG STING SWANK SWISH TIGHT TIPPY TOFFY TRICK AKAMAI BRAWLY CHEESY CLEVER DAPPER GIGOLO JAUNTY KITTLE PERTLY SHREWD SPANKY SPIFFY SPRINK SPRUCE STOUND SWANKY SWIDGE TIDDLY KNOWING PUNGENT SWAGGER TOFFISH VOGUISH BRUSHING **(— IN APPEARANCE)** POSH **(— IN DRESS)** GALLANT

SMART ALECK FLIP SMARTY

SMARTEN FINE PUSS SMUG SLICK TITIVATE

SMARTLY SMART SNACK YEPLY TIDELY

SMARTNESS TON SNAP SMART SWISH

SMARTWEED CULERAGE REDKNEES

SMASH BASH BUMP CAVE DASH PASH RUSH SCAT TRAP BREAK CRACK CRASH CRAZE SOCKO STAVE WRECK CRACKER SHATTER SMASHUP DEBRUISE DEMOLISH OVERHEAD STRAMASH **(— A GAP)** BREACH

SMASHED BUNG STOVEN BROOZLED

SMASHING CRACKING

SMASHUP STRAMASH

SMATTERING SMACK SMATCH SMATTER

SMEAR RUB BLOT BLUR CLAM DAUB DOPE GAUM GLOB GORM MOIL CLEAM DITCH GLAIR SLAKE SLARE SMALM SMARM SULLY BEDAUB BESLAB DEFILE PLATCH SLAVER SLURRY SMIRCH SMOOCH SMUDGE SPREAD STREAK STRIKE BEPAINT BESMEAR PLASTER POLLUTE SPLOTCH SLAISTER **(— OVER)** ENGLUTE **(— WITH BLOOD)** GILD **(— WITH EGG WHITE)** GLAIR **(— WITH MUD)** CLART SLIME **(— WITH SOMETHING STICKY)** GAUM GORM LIME **(— WITH TAR)** PAY **(— WITH WAX)** CERE

SMEAR DAB FLATFISH MARYSOLE

SMEARED FOUL BROSY MUSSY

SCOVY BLOODY SMUDGY BLURRED BEGUMMED

SMEARY DAUBY GAUMY

SMEDDUM SMITHUM

SMELL FUNK FUST GUSH NOSE ODOR VENT AROMA FETOR FLAIR SAVOR SCENT SMACK SNIFF SNOOK SNUFF STIFE TASTE OLFACT RESENT SMEECH BREATHE PERFUME REFLAIR VERDURE **(— AFTER PREY)** BREVIT **(— OFFENSIVELY)** REEK **(DAMP FUSTY —)** RAFT **(DISAGREEABLE —)** GOO STENCH **(HAVING PLEASANT —)** SNIFTY **(MUSTY —)** FUST **(OFFENSIVE —)** FUNK FETOR STINK MEPHITIS **(STRONG —)** HOGO **(SWEET —)** SWEET

SMELLY FUGGY WHIFFY SMELLFUL

SMELT DECOCT INANGA EPERLAN ICEFISH ELIQUATE SALMONID SPARLING SPERLING **(FRY OF —)** PRIM

SMEW NUN PIED SMEE DIVER SMETHE

SMILAX LILY SARSA LILIUM

SMILE BEAM GRIN FLASH FLEER SMEER ARRIDE SMUDGE SMIRKLE **(— AMOROUSLY)** SMICKER **(AFFECTED —)** SMIRK **(SELF-CONSCIOUS —)** SIMPER

SMILING GOOD RIANT SMILY SMIRKY TWINKLY SMILEFUL

SMIRCH SMIT SOIL SMEAR SULLY SLURRY SOILURE TARNISH

SMIRCHED DINGY

SMIRK DRAD YIRN SIMPER SMICKER SMIRKLE SMURTLE

SMITE DUNT FRAP GIRD SLAY FLING SKITE STRIKE **(— WITH LIGHTNING)** LEVEN

SMITH MIMIR REGIN BOSSER FORGER SMITHY FARRIER GLUTTER SMITHER STEELER WAYLAND FLOORMAN FORGEMAN PANSMITH

SMITHSONITE CALAMINE

SMITHY FORGE SMIDDY STITHY STUDDIE FARRIERY

SMITTEN EPRISE STRICKEN

SMOCK BRAT SLOP KAMIS SMOKE JIBBAH JUMPER CHEMISE SMICKET

SMOKE PEW USE FLAN FOGO FUFF FUME FUNK HAVE LUNT NAVE PIPE REEK ROKE TOVE DRINK REECH SMEEK SMORE SMUSH STIVE VAPOR WHIFF BREATH BUCCAN POTHER SMEECH SMUDGE INCENSE SMOLDER SMOTHER BACONIZE **(— MARIJUANA)** BLAST **(FROST —)** BARBER **(OFFENSIVE —)** FUNK **(TOBACCO —)** BLAST

SMOKEHOUSE FUMATORY

SMOKEJACK STACKMAN

SMOKER FUNKER

SMOKESTACK STACK FUNNEL TUNNEL CHIMNEY

SMOKE TREE ZANTE FUSTET FUSTIC SCOTINO

SMOKING ROOM DIVAN TABAGIE

SMOKY HAZY ROKY DINGY FUMID FUMISH FUMOSE SMUDGY SMUISTY

SMOLDER SMUSH SMOTHER

SMOLDERING PUNKY

SMOLT SMELT SMOUT SPROD

SMOOCH LALLYGAG LOLLYGAG

SMOOTH DUB FAT LAP NOT BOSS COMB DRAG EASE EASY EVEN FACE FAIR FLAT FLAT GLAD GLEG GLIB HONE IRON LENE NOTT REET SLID SNOD SOFT BLAND BRENT CLEAR COUTH DARBY DIGHT DOLCE DRESS EMERY FLOAT FRAZE GLARE GOOSE HOWEL LEVEL LITHE PLAIN PLANE PRESS QUIET SCARF SILKY SLAPE SLEEK SLICK SMOLT SNUFF SOAPY SUANT SUAVE SUENT TERSE ABRASE BUFFED CREAMY EQUATE EVENLY FETTLE FLUENT GLOSSY GREASE GREASY LEGATO LIMBER MANGLE POLITE SCREED SILKEN SLIGHT STREAK STRIKE STROKE SVELTE UNFRET BOULDER ERUGATE FLATTEN SLEEKIT EXPLICIT GLABRATE GLABROUS GLIBBERY GRAZIOSO LEVIGATE SARSENET SLIDDERY SQUEEGEE STRICKLE UNRUFFLE
(**— BY BREAKING LUMPS)** BILDER
(**— MARBLE)** GRIT
(**— ONESELF UP)** PREEN
(**— OVER)** GLOZE PLASTER
(**— TYPE)** KERN
(**HYPOCRITICALLY —)** SLEEK
(**PHONETICALLY —)** LENE LENIS

SMOOTHER GLAZER

SMOOTHLY SLICK EASILY EVENLY GLIBLY SMOOTH SPROWSY SWEETLY POLITELY

SMOOTHNESS EASE FLUENCY

SMOOTH-RUNNING SWEET

SMOOTH WINTERBERRY CANHOOP

SMOTHER BURKE CHOKE SMEAR SMOKE SMORE MOIDER QUEZEN SMUDGE STIFLE FLASKER OPPRESS QUEASON SMOLDER SMUDDER

SMOTHERED ETOUFFE STIFLED

SMUDGE GAUM SLUR SMUT SOIL SOOT CROCK SMEAR SMOKE SMOOCH SMUTCH SMOLDER SMOTHER SOILURE

SMUDGED SMUTCHY

SMUG SMUSH SUAVE SMUDGE

SMUGGLE RUN STEAL BOOTLEG SHUFFLE

SMUGGLER OWLER RUNNER SPOTSMAN

SMUGGLING OWLING

SMUGLY FATLY

SMUT BUNT COOM BLACK BLECK COLLY COOMB CROCK GRIME SMOOT SMITCH SMUTCH SMATTER COLBRAND

SMUTCH BLOT SMIRCH SMITCH SMOUCH SMUDGE

SMUT GRASS TUSSOCK

SMUTTY BAWDY DIRTY SOOTY SULTRY BARNYARD FREUDIAN

SMYRNA USHAK

SNACK BIT CUT BAIT BITE SNAP TAPA CHACK CHECK SHARE SNICK TASTE GOUTER MUNGEY SNATCH NUNCHEON

SNAFFLE GAG

SNAG KNAG SNUG STUB POINT PLANTER SNAGGLE
(PL.) EMBARRAS

SNAIL HUA PILA SNAG CHINK DRILL HELIX OLIVA PHYSA SHELL THAIS TURBO WHELK CERION CONKER DODMAN NATICA PHYSID PURPLE TRITON WINKLE RISSOID UNICORN VERTIGO ZONITID CASSIDID ESCARGOT HODMADOD JANTHINA LYMNAEID MELANIAN NERITOID RAMSHORN SOLARIUM

SNAILFLOWER CARACOL

SNAKE (ALSO SEE SERPENT AND REPTILE) ASP BOA BOM NAG BOBA BOID BOMA JUBO NAGA NAJA SNIG ABOMA ASPIC COBRA CONGO CRIBO DRILL JIBOA KRAIT MAMBA PTYAS RACER SNECK TIGER VIPER BOIGID BONGAR CANTIL CHITAL DABOIA ELAPID GOPHER HISSER JESSUR KERRIL PYTHON ROLLER RUNNER TAIPAN WENONA ADJIGER ANILIID BOKADAM CAMOODI CRAWLER CREEPER CULEBRA DIAPSID HAGWORM LABARIA LANGAHA PRESTER RATTLER REGULUS REPTILE SERPENT SPITTER WALPAPI ANACONDA BONETAIL BUNGARUM CASCAVEL CERASTES CROTALID EGGEATER FLATHEAD HAIRWORM JARARACA KEELBACK MOCCASIN OPHIDIAN RINGHALS SNAKELET VIPERINE

SNAKEBARK IRONBARK

SNAKEBIRD DARTER PLOTUS ANHINGA DUCKLAR

SNAKEHEAD MURRAL

SNAKELIKE ANGUINE

SNAKEMOUTH POGONIA

SNAKEPIECE POINTER

SNAKEROOT STEVIA BABROOT BUGBANE SANGREL SANICLE SAWWORT POOLWORT RICHWEED WHITETOP

SNAKESKIN SPOIL HACKLE SLOUGH
(CASTOFF —S) EXUVIAE

SNAP SET ZIP BARK BITE CHOP GNAP HUFF JERK KNAP LIRP SETT BREAK CLACK FILIP FLICK GANCH KNACK KNICK SMACK SNACK BLUDGE SNAPPY SNATCH FASTENER PUSHOVER SNAPHEAD
(**— AT)** HANCH
(**— LIGHTLY)** KNICK
(**— OFF)** SNIP
(**— TOGETHER)** CRASH
(**— UP)** SNUP SNAFFLE
(**— WITH FINGER)** LIRP FILIP THRIP FILLIP

SNAPBACK PASSBACK

SNAPDRAGON BULL SNAPS BULLER BULLDOG DOGMOUTH

SNAPE FLINCH

SNAPPER UKU BRIM JOCU SESI BREAM PARGO VORAZ CUBERA HUSSAR JENOAR LAWYER NATIVE TAMURE ULAULA COCKNEY CRACKER BIAJAIBA CACHUCHO FLAMENCO GNATSNAP LUTIANID WILLOMAI SCHNAPPER

SNAPPING DOGGISH

SNAPPING BEETLE ELATER SKIPPER SNAPPER ELATERID SKIPJACK

SNAPPING TURTLE LOGHEAD SHAGTAIL

SNAPPISH CRUP EDGY PUXY CROSS SNACK TESTY WASPY CUTTED SNAGGY SNAPPY SNIPPY DOGGISH PEEVISH

SNAPPY CRISP JEMMY ZIPPY

SNARE GIN HAY NET PIT SET BUKE FANG GIRN GRIN HOOK LACE LIME TOIL TRAP WAIT WIRE BRAKE CATCH FRAUD GNARE LATCH LEASH SINEW SNARL SNIRL STALE SWEEK TRAIN COBWEB GILDER PANTER SNATCH SPRINT TREPAN TUNNEL ENSNARE OVERNET PITFALL SETTING SNICKLE SPRINGE BIRDLIME INVEIGLE LIMEBUSH SPRINGLE TENDICLE
(**— DEER)** WITHE
(**— FOR ELEPHANTS)** KEDDAH

SNARL ARR BITE CARL GIRN GNAR GURR HARL HURR NARR TWIT WAFF YARR GNARL GNARR GRILL KNURL RAVEL SNIRL TWINE BOWWOW BUMBLE GAUNCH MUCKER TANGLE VENNER GRIZZLE GRUMBLE

SNARLED SNAFU

SNARLER CYNIC

SNARLING LATRANT

SNATCH HAP NAB NIP GRAB HINT RACE RASE SNAP SNIP WHIP WRAP YERK YUCK BRAID CATCH CLAWK CLICK EREPT GANCH GRASP GRIPE PLUCK SNACK STRIP SWIPE SWOOP TWEAK WREST SNITCH STRIKE TWITCH WRENCH CLAUGHT GRABBLE SCAMBLE VULTURE

SNEAK GRUB LEER LOOP LOUT LURK PEAK PIMP SHUG SNIG LURCH MEECH SCOUT SHIRK SKULK SLIDE SLINK SLIPE SLIVE SLOKE SNEAP SNICK SNOOK BLIFIL MICHER WEASEL SLOUNGE SNIGGLE SNEAKSBY
(**— AWAY)** SLIPE
(**— OFF)** MAG SHAB
(**PRYING —)** SNOOP

SNEAKER CREEPER GUMSHOE

SNEAKING HANGDOG PEAKING SLIVING

SNEAKY FURTIVE MEECHING

SNEER SHY FLON GIBE GIRD GIRN GULE JEER JERK JIBE MOCK FLEER FLING FLOUT GLEEK JAUNT SCOFF SLARE SLEER SNIRT GIZZEN

SNEEST WRINKLE RIDICULE
SNEERING FRUMPERY
SNEEZE NEESE NEEZE ARREST
(— AT) CONDEMN DESPISE
SNEEZEWEED ALANT ROSILLA
HELENIUM
SNEEZEWOOD NIESHOUT
SNEEZEWORT HARDHEAD
PTARMICA
SNEEZING PTARMIC
SNELL SNOOD TIPPET GANGING
SNICK TIP SNECK
SNICKER TITTER SMIRKLE SNIGGER
SNIGGLE
SNIFF NOSE TIFT VENT WIND SMELL
SNAFF SNIFT SNUFF SNIVEL
SNAFFLE SNIFFLE SNOTTER
SNIFTER SLUG BALLOON INHALER
SNIGGER WHICKER
SNIGGLE BRAGGLE
SNIP CUT CLIP CROP SHRED SNICK
SNIPE JACK NICK WISP SCAPE SNITE
WADER WILLET BLEATER BLITTER
DOWITCH HUMILITY LONGBILL
SHADBIRD
SNIPER TEASER BUSHWACK
SNIVEL BUBBLE SNIFFLE SNIFTER
SNOTTER SNUFFLE
SNOB SNAB SNOOT FLUNKY
SHONEEN SNOBBER
SNOBBISH DICKTY SNOBBY SNOOTY
UPSTAGE
SNOOK SNOOT ROBALO
SNOOP PRY PEEK PEEP SNEAK
BREVIT PIROOT GUMSHOE
SNOOPER CREEP BUSYBODY
SNOOPY CURIOUS
SNOOZE SLEEP SNOOZLE
SNORE ROUT SNARK SNORK SNORT
SNOCKER SNOTTER
SNORING STERTOR RHONCHUS
SNORT BLOW ROUT SNUR TOOT
VENT FNESE SNARK SNEER SNORE
SNORK WHOOF EXCLAIM SNIFTER
SNOCKER SNORKEL SNORTLE
SNOTTER
SNOUT NEB SAW BILL NOSE WROT
GROIN SNOOT MUFFLE MUZZLE
NOZZLE GRUNTLE ROSTRUM
SNOUT BEETLE CURCULIO
SNOUT MITE BDELLID
SNOW CORN DRIP GRUE COVER
SPOSH STORM SUGAR WHITE
POWDER COCAINE GRAUPEL
RAMPART WEATHER SCOUTHER
WINDSLAB
(— PELLETS) GRAUPEL
(— SLIGHTLY) SPIT
(DISSOLVING —) FLUSH
(DRIFTED —) WINDLE
(GLACIER —) FIRN NEVE BLIZZ
(HEAVY FALL OF —) PASH
(MUSHY —) SLOB
(NEW-FALLEN —) MANNA
(PARTLY MELTED —) SLUSH
(WHIRLING —) SKIRL
SNOWBERRY MOXA WAXBERRY
SNOWBIRD JUNCO
SNOW BUNTING OATFOWL

SNOWBIRD SNOWFOWL
SNOW COCK JERMONAL
SNOWDRIFT YOWDEN
SNOWDROP TREE BELLWOOD
COWLICKS TISSWOOD
SNOWFALL PASH SKIFF SKIFT
FLURRY ONDING
SNOWFLAKE FLAG FLAUCHT
SNOW FLEA PODURAN PODURID
SNOW GOOSE WAVY
SNOWINESS NIVOSITY
SNOW LEOPARD IRBIS
SNOWLESS GREEN
SNOWMAN YETI
SNOW MOUNTAIN JOKUL
SNOWSHOE WEB PATIN PATTEN
RACKET RACQUET
SNOWSTORM PURGA DRIFTER
BLIZZARD
SNOWY NIVAL WHITE NIVEOUS
SNUB AIR RITZ SLAP SNIB FRUMP
SNEAP SWANK REBUFF REBUTE
SIMOUS SLIGHT SNOUCH SNUBBY
SETDOWN
SNUBBING MAIL
SNUBBY PUGGISH
SNUB-NOSED SIMOUS
SNUFF TOP VENT MUSTY SNIFF
SNUSH TABAC COHOBA PULVIL
RAPPEE SNEESH STIFLE SNUFFLE
BERGAMOT MACCABOY ORANGERY
SMUTCHIN
SNUFFBOX MILL
SNUFFBOX BEAN CACOON
SNUFFER PRICK DOUTER TOPPER
PRICKER
SNUFFLE SNIVEL SNAFFLE SNIFFLE
SNIFTER
SNUG LEW RUG BIEN COSH COZY
NEAT TAUT TEAT TOSH TOSY
CANNY CLOSE COUTH POVIE QUEME
TIGHT PENTIT COUTHIE SNUGGERY
SNUGGISH
SNUGGLE SNUG BURROW CUDDLE
SNUDGE CROODLE SNUZZLE
SNUGLY SHORT COSILY
SO SAE SUCH THAT THIS THUS
THISSEN INSOMUCH SUCHWISE
THUSWISE
(— AM I) LIKEWISE
(— BE IT) AMEN
(— FAR AS) QUOAD
(— TO SPEAK) FAIRLY
(NOT —) SECUS
(QUITE —) EXACTLY
SOAK RET SOB SOD SOG SOP WET
BOWK BUCK SIPE BINGE DROUK
DROWN SOUSE STEEP TOAST
DRENCH EMBAIN IMBIBE IMBRUE
SEETHE SODDEN SPONGE INSTEEP
MICKERY SWELTER SATURATE
(— A CASK) GROG
(— FLAX) RET RATE
(— IN) SOP FEATHER
SOAKED SOGGY SOPPY SOBBED
SODDEN WATERY DRUNKEN
SOBBING DRAGGLED
SOAKING BATH SUING SOGGING
INFUSION

SOAP SAPO SUDS CHIPS STOCK
NIGGER CASTILE TALLATE WINDSOR
SANDSOAP
(CAKE OF —) TABLET TABULATE
(LIQUID —) FIT
SOAPBARK QUILLAI SOAPWOOD
SOAPFISH JABON
SOAP PLANT AMOLE PALMILLO
SOAPROOT SOAPWEED
SOAPSTONE ALBERENE STEATITE
SOAPSTONER TALCER
SOAPWORT BORITH COWHERB
SAPONARY SOAPROOT SOAPWEED
SOAR FLY STY KITE FLOAT MOUNT
PLANE SPIRE TOWER ASPIRE
AIRPLANE
SOARING FLIGHT ICARIAN SPIRING
ESSORANT
SOB YEX SIKE SNOB SNUB SOUGH
BLUBBER SINGULT
SOBBING GREET
SOBER SAD CALM COOL SAGE CIVIL
FRESH GRAVE QUIET STAID DOULCE
SEDATE SEVERE SOLEMN SOMBER
STEADY EARNEST PENSIVE
REGULAR SERIOUS UNFOXED
DECOROUS MODERATE
SOBRIETY DRYNESS GRAVITY
SOBRIQUET BYNAME HAWKEYE
SO-CALLED ALLEGED
SOCCER FOOTER FOOTBALL
SOCIABLE COSY CHUMMY CLUBBY
FOLKSY SOCIAL AFFABLE AMIABLE
INNERLY CLUBABLE FAMILIAR
FELLOWLY INFORMAL
SOCIAL DISTAL SUPPER SOCIABLE
SOCIETAL
(— WORKER) ALMONER
SOCIALISM ETATISM MARXISM
GUESDISM
SOCIALIST FABIAN NIHILIST
SOCIALIZE CIVILIZE
SOCIETY BUND HALL HERD SANG
GUILD MONDE SABHA SAMAJ SANGH
SOKOL MENAGE NANIGO PARISH
SYSTEM VEREIN ACADEMY COLLEGE
COLORUM COMPANY COUNCIL
KINGDOM SOCIETE THIASOS
EXCHANGE HETAERIA PRECINCT
SOCIETAS SODALITY SORORITY
(— OF RELIGIOUS FANATICS)
COLORUM
(CHORAL —) CHOIR
(CLOWN —) KOSHARE KOYEMSHI
(CRAFT —) ARTEL
(DEBATING —) POP
(GYMNASTIC —) SOKOL
(HIGH —) SWELLDOM
(LITERARY —) HALL
(RELIGIOUS —) CHURCH
(SECRET —) HUI EGBO HOEY PORO
TONG LODGE OGBONI PURRAH
(UTOPIAN —) ANARCHY
SOCINIAN RACOVIAN
SOCIOLOGY DEMOTICS
SOCK BOP ONE BIFF BUST HOSE
VAMP ANKLET ARGYLE VAMPEY
STOCKING
(— OF GOAT'S HAIR) UDO

(INFANT'S —) BOOTEE BOOTIE
(JAPANESE —) TABI
SOCKET BOX CUP PAD POD BUSH
CELL HOSE LEAD NOSE SHOE CHAIR
POINT SHANK BUCKET BUDGET
COLLET EYEPIT NOZZLE POCKET
SAUCER SCONCE ALVEOLE
COCKEYE FERRULE FUTCHEL
GUDGEON THIMBLE TORULUS
ALVEOLUS DRAWHEAD
(— **FOR LANCE**) PORT
(— **FOR LENS**) CELL
(— **FOR MOUTHPIECE**) BIRN
(— **IN GOLF CLUB HEAD**) HOSE
HOSEL
(— **OF BONE**) POT
(— **OF HINGE**) PAN
(— **OF MILLSTONE**) INK COCKEYE
(— **OF WATER PIPE**) BELL
(BIT —) POD
SOCLE ZOCCO
SOCRATES (— **METHOD**) MAIEUTIC
SOD HUB BEAT DELF FAIL FLAG
SCAD SONK TURF DELPH GAZON
GLEBE SCRAW SWARD CLOWER
TERRON SODDING
SODA BARILLA
SODA POP TONIC
SODDEN SAMMY SAPPY SOGGY
POACHY DRAGGLED
SODIUM NA SODA NATRIUM
SODIUM BICARBONATE SODA
BICARB
SODIUM BORATE BORAX
SODIUM CARBONATE SODA TRONA
ANATRON BARILLA SALSODA
SODIUM CHLORIDE SALT HALITE
SODIUM THIOSULFATE HYPO
SODOMITE DOG BUGGER SPINTRY
BOUGERON
SOEVER SOME
SOFA BOIST COUCH DIVAN SQUAB
CANAPE LOUNGE SETTEE
CAUSEUSE SOCIABLE
SOFFIT GATHER PLANCIER
SOFT COY TID FEIL LASH LIMP LUSH
MILD MURE NASH PLUM SART TOSY
WAXY WEAK BALMY BLAND CUSHY
DABBY DOLCE DOWNY FAINT GIVEY
HOOLY LENIS LIGHT MALMY MELCH
MUSHY PADDY PAPPY PIANO PLIFF
SILKY SLACK SMALL SOAPY SOOTH
SWASH SWEET WAXEN WETHE
YAPPY CASHIE CREAMY EFFETE
FLAGGY FLOSSY FLUFFY GENTLE
LYDIAN MELLOW PIPING PLACID
SAMMEL SIDDER SILKEN SLOPPY
SOFTLY SPONGY SPOONY TENDER
UNDURE CLEMENT COTTONY
DUCTILE FLESHLY LENIENT
SQUASHY CUSHIONY FEMININE
FLEXIBLE HOTHOUSE LADYLIKE
SARCENET SQUELCHY TRANQUIL
(— **AND FLEXIBLE**) FLOPPY
(— **AND LIFELESS**) DOUGHY
(— **IN TEXTURE**) SUPPLE
(VERY —) SQUASHY
SOFT-COVER PAPERBACK
SOFTEN CUT CREE MELT SOAK

SOFT TAME ALLAY BATCH BREAK
FRIZZ LITHE MALAX TOUCH WOKIE
DIGEST GENTLE LENIFY PACIFY
RELENT SOOTHE SUBDUE SUBMIT
TEMPER WEAKEN APPEASE
ASSUAGE CUSHION LENIATE
MOLLIFY QUALIFY SWEETEN
UNSTEEL AMOLLISH ATTEMPER
ENFEEBLE HUMANIZE MITIGATE
MODULATE PALLIATE PRETTIFY
(— **BY BOILING**) CREE
(— **BY KNEADING**) MALAX
(— **BY STEEPING**) MACERATE
(— **COLOR**) CUT SCUMBLE
(— **FIBERS**) BREAK
(— **GRADUALLY**) SQUAT
(— **JUTE**) BATCH
(— **LEATHER**) BREY FRIZ FRIZZ
(— **METAL**) ALLAY
(— **TONE**) SURD
SOFTENED ROXY ANODYNE
FLEXUOUS
SOFTENING LENIENT MALACIA
BLETTING
SOFTER MANCANDO
SOFTHEARTED TENDER
SOFTLY BAJO SOFT FAIRLY GENTLY
SWEETLY CREAMILY TENDERLY
SOFTNESS SOFT MOLLITIES
(— **IN COAL SEAM**) LUM LUMB
SOFT-SHELLED TURTLE FLAPPER
FLIPPER FLAPJACK
SOFT-SOAP CON
SOFT-SPOKEN MEALY
SOGGY SAD DUNCH SOBBY SODDEN
SPONGY WATERY
SOIL DAG DUB MUD RAY SOD BLOT
BLUR CLAY CLOD DAUB DIRT DUST
FOIL FOUL GRIT LAND MIRK MOOL
MOSS MUCK MURK MUSS SAUR SILE
SLUR SMUT SOOT TASH BULLI
CROCK EARTH GLEBE GRIME
GUMBO LAYER MUCKY ROSEL
SLUSH SMEAR SOLUM SOULE
SPARK STAIN SULLY BARING
BEDAUB BEMIRE BEMOIL GROUND
PODZOL SLURRY SMIRCH SMOOCH
SMUDGE SPLASH SUDDLE BEGRIME
BENASTY BESMEAR BESMOKE
BETHUMB FEWMAND POLLUTE
REGOSOL SEEDBED TARNISH
TRACHLE AGROTYPE ALLUVIAL
BEDABBLE BESMIRCH BUCKSHOT
FLYSPECK LATERITE RENDZINA
WOODCOCK
(— **ABOVE CLAY**) KELLY
(— **DEPOSITED BY WIND**) ELUVIUM
(— **FORMED BY DECAY**) GEEST
(— **INTERMEDIATE BETWEEN SAND AND CLAY**) ROSEL
(— **PREPARED FOR SOWING**) TILTH
(— **REMOVED FROM ORE**) BARING
(— **WITH GREASE**) LARD
(AGGREGATE —) PED
(ALKALINE —) SOLONETZ
(ASHLIKE —) PODSOL PODZOL
(CLAYEY —) GALT MALM MAUM
ADOBE SOLOD SOLOTH
(DRY —) GROOT

(FRIABLE —) CRUMB
(GRAVELLY —) ROACH GROWAN
(HARD —) RAMMEL
(INFERTILE —) GALL
(LEACHED —S) LATOSOL
(PLUMBER'S —) SMUDGE
(POROUS —) SPONGE
(POTTING —) COMPOST
(PRAIRIE —) BRUNIZEM
(SILTY —) GUMBO
(SPRINGY —) WOODSERE
(ZONAL —) SEROZEM SIEROZEM
SOILAGE SOIL SMUDGE SOILING
SOILED FOUL BLACK DINGY DIRTY
MUSSY SOOTY TARRY SMUDGY
SMUTTY SNUFFY THUMBED
DRAGGLED SHOPWORN
SOIL-EXPOSING EROSIVE
SOIREE EVENING
SOJOURN LIE BIDE STAY STOP
ABIDE ABODE TARRY RESIDE
ALLODGE MANSION STATION
SOJOURNER PILGRIM
SOKOL FALCON
SOL SOH SOU ALCOSOL EMULSOID
HYDROSOL SOLUTION
SOLA SHOLA PAUKPAN
SOLACE CHEER CHEERER COMFORT
SWEETEN SOLATION
SOLAR SOLLER SOLARIUM
(— **SYSTEM APPARATUS**) ORRERY
SOLAR DISK ATEN ATON
(CENTER OF —) CAZIMI
SOLD SELT BOOKED
(ILLICITLY —) BOOTLEG
SOLDER PALE BRAZE FLOAT
SOWDER SPELTER
SOLDERER BROGUER
SOLDERING IRON COPPER DOCTOR
SOLDIER SON TAP BLEU BOLO
GOUM GUGÚ KERN LEVY SHOT
SWAD TULK WART BERNE CROAT
FRITZ GUARD GUFFY KHAKI LANCE
LIMEY LINER MINER NIZAM PERDU
PIKER PIVOT POILU SAMMY SWEAT
TOLKE TOMMY TOPAS ASKARI
BONAGH BUMMER DARTER DIGGER
EXPERT GALOOT GUNNER GURKHA
HAIDUK HEINIE HOSTER LANCER
MARKER PIETON REITER SENTRY
SKIEUR SOLDAT SWADDY THRASO
WEAPON ZOUAVE BILLJIM BLIGHTY
BRIGAND CARABIN CATERAN
CORSLET DARTMAN DOGFACE
DRAGOON FEDERAL FEEDMAN
FIGHTER GENETOR GOUMIER
HOBBLER INVALID MATROSS
ORDERLY PALIKAR PANDOUR
PAVISOR PIKEMAN POLTAST
PRIVATE REDCOAT REGULAR
REISTER SCARLET SLINGER
SOLDADO STRIKER TROOPER
VETERAN WARRIOR ARQUEBUS
BEZONIAN BLUECOAT BUCKSKIN
BUFFCOAT CAMELEER CAVALIER
DESERTER FENCIBLE FUGLEMAN
FUSILIER GALLOPER GENDARME
GRAYBACK GRAYCOAT IRONSIDE
JANIZARY KHANDAIT LANCEMAN

LINESMAN MILITANT MIQUELET MUSTACHE PIOUPIOU RAPPAREE SENTINEL SERVITOR SILLADAR SPEARMAN SWORDMAN TOLPATCH TRANSFER TRIARIAN WARFARER WHIFFLER YARDBIRD
(— OF MUSCOVITE GUARD) STRELITZ
(— WITH SIDE WHISKERS) BADGER
(ALBANIAN —) PALIKAR
(ALGERIAN —) ARBI
(ANT —) MAXIM
(AUSTRALIAN —) ANZAC DIGGER BILLJIM
(BOMBAY —S) DUCKS
(BRITISH —) LIMEY TOMMY BLIGHTY LOBSTER REDCOAT
(BRUTAL —) PANDOUR
(COWARDLY —) CAPITANO
(FILE OF 6 —S) ROT
(FILIPINO —) GUGU
(FOOT —) KERN PAGE PEON PIETON FOOTMAN TOLPATCH
(GERMAN —) HUN FRITZ HEINE KRAUT HEINIE
(GREEK —) EVZONE HOPLITE
(INCOMPETENT —) BOLL
(INDIAN —) SEPOY GURKHA
(INVALID —) FOGY FOGEY
(IRREGULAR —) CATERAN JAYHAWK MIQUELET SILLADAR
(MOROCCAN —) ASKARI
(MOUNTED —) LANCER DRAGOON GENETOR LOBSTER TROOPER VEDETTE CAVALIER
(OLD —) GROGNARD
(PROFESSIONAL —) SAMURAI
(REVOLUTIONARY —) REDCOAT BUCKSKIN
(ROMAN —S OF THIRD LINE) TRIARY TRIARII
(RUSSIAN —) IVAN
(SCOTTISH —) JOCK
(TURKISH —) NIZAM REDIF
(PL.) FOOT ELITE TERZO TROOP TERTIA CATERVA ENOMOTY MILITIA VELITES FORAGERS INFANTRY SOLDIERY
SOLDIERLY WARLIKE
SOLDIERY HORSE MILITIA SEBUNDY MILITARY SIBBENDY
SOLE CORK FACE GADE MERE ONLY SLIP SOCK SPUR AFALD ALONE CLUMP OLEPI PELMA WHOLE GADOID INSOLE ONLEPY PLANTA SINGLE SOLEYN SULLEN THENAR TONGUE UNIQUE ANACANTH FLATFISH HOGCHOKE MARYSOLE SINGULAR SOLITARY
(— A SHOE) SPECK
(— FOR WALKING OVER SAND) BACKSTER
(— OF BIRD'S FOOT) PTERNA
(— OF FOOT) PLAT VOLA PELMA PLANT
(— OF PLANE) FACE
(— OF PLOW) SLADE
(HALF —) SHOULDER
(TOWARD THE —) PLANTAD

SOLELY SOLE ALONE SIMPLY SINGLY WHOLLY SHEERLY ENTIRELY
SOLEMN DEEP SAGE BUDGE SOBER DEVOUT FORMAL RITUAL EARNEST SERIOUS WEIGHTY FUNEREAL
SOLEMNITY OBIT RITE SACRE GRAVITY SEVERITY
SOLEMNIZE KEEP SEAL
SOLEMNLY GRAVE HIGHLY
SOLENODONT AGOUTA ALMIQUE
SOLEPIECE SOLE GIRDER
SOL-FA SOLMIZATE
SOLICIT ASK BEG SUE WOO DRUM MOVE SEEK TOUT URGE APPLY COURT CRAVE TREAT ACCOST HUSTLE INVITE INVOKE BESEECH CANVASS ENTREAT IMPLORE INSTANT PROCURE REQUEST APPROACH PETITION
SOLICITATION SUIT QUEST CANVASS INSTANT SOLICIT ENTREATY INSTANCE
SOLICITOR LAWYER WRITER ADVOCATE TRAMPLER
SOLICITOUS URGENT CAREFUL CURIOUS JEALOUS DESIROUS CONCERNED
SOLICITUDE CARE FEAR HEED PAIN YEME HEART WORRY ANXIETY CONCERN BUSINESS JEALOUSY
SOLID DRY SAD CONE CUBE FAST FIRM FULL HARD CHAMP LEVEL MASSY MEATY SOUND STIFF STOUT THICK TIGHT SECURE STABLE STRONG STURDY COMPACT CUPRENE UNIFORM CONSTANT GROUNDLY MATERIAL STERLING
(GEOMETRICAL —) CONE CUBE PRISM CONOID CUPROID FRUSTUM
(PL.) POCHE
SOLIDARITY CIVILITY
SOLIDIFIED SOLID HARDENED
SOLIDIFY DRY SET JELL SHOOT HARDEN COMPACT STIFFEN CONCRETE
SOLIDITY SADNESS FASTNESS FIRMNESS HARDNESS
SOLIDLY FIRMLY SQUARE STOUTLY GROUNDLY
SOLIDUS BEZANT NOMISMA DIAGONAL HYPERPER
(HALF —) SEMIS
SOLIPSISM EGOISM
SOLITAIRE CLARINO CANFIELD KLONDIKE NAPOLEON PATIENCE SOLITARY
SOLITARY ODD WAF LONE SOLE ALONE ELYNG LONELY ONLEPY SAVAGE SINGLE SOLEYN SULLEN EREMITE PRIVATE RECLUSE UNCOUTH WIDOWED DESOLATE EREMITIC ISOLATED LONESOME SECLUDED SEPARATE
SOLITUDE PRIVACY RETREAT SOLITARY
SOLLERET SABBATON
SOLO ARIA CALL ARIOSO CAVATINA SPADILLA

SOLOMON ISLANDS (CAPITAL OF —) HONIARA
(ISLAND OF —) BUKA TULAGI MALAITA CHOISEUL
SOLOMON'S SEAL LILY SEALWORT
SOLOMON SAM KOHELETH
SOLON SAGE GNOMIC GNOMIST SENATOR LAWMAKER
SOLSTICE SUNSTAY SUNSTEAD
SOLUBLE FRIM FRUM FIXED SOLUTE SOLVABLE
SOLUTION IT LYE AQUA EUSOL STAIN TINCT ACETUM ANSWER ASSOIL DOCTOR ERASER SALINE EXTRACT EYEWASH LACQUER RESOLVE SOLUTIO WORKING ANALYSIS LEACHATE TINCTURE
(— ADDED FOR GOOD MEASURE) INCAST
(— OF CHESS PROBLEM) COOK
(— OF FERMENTED BRAN) DRENCH
(— OF GUM TRAGACANTH) BED
(ALCOHOLIC —) ESSENCE
(PICKLING —) SOUSE
(PRESERVING —) BOLIN
(SALINE —) BRINE
(SOAP —) NIGRE
(STERILE —) JOHNIN
(VISCOUS —) GLUE
(WATERY —) EAU SAF
SOLVE DO FIX READ UNDO WORK BREAK CRACK LOOSE SALVE ANSWER ASSOIL CIPHER FIGURE REDUCE RIDDLE SOLUTE RESOLVE UNRAVEL DECIPHER DISSOLVE
SOLVENT ETHER ELUENT SPIRIT ACETONE ALCOHOL BENZINE COUPLER DILUENT REMOVER SPOTTER CARBITOL SOLVABLE STRIPPER TETRALIN
(UNIVERSAL —) ALKAHEST
SOMALI SOMAL SHUHALI
(PL.) ASHA
SOMALIA (COIN OF —) BESA
(DIVISION OF —) HAWIYA
(MEASURE OF —) TOP CABA CHELA DARAT TABLA CUBITO
(MOUNTAIN RANGE OF —) GUBAN
(NATIVE OF —) GALLA HAWIYA ISBAAK SOMALI DANAKIL
(RIVER OF —) JUBA NOGAL SCEBELI
(TOWN OF —) MERCA BERBERA HARGEISA KISIMAYU
(WEIGHT OF —) PARSALAH
SOMATIC SOMAL BODILY
SOMBER SAD DERN DULL GRAVE SOBER GLOOMY LENTEN SOLEMN SOMBRE SULLEN AUSTERE SERIOUS DARKSOME SOMBROUS
SOME ANY ODD THIS CERTAIN
SOMEBODY QUIDAM SOMEONE
SOMEDAY ONCE
SOMEHOW HOW ONEHOW SOMEWAY SOMEGATE
SOMEONE SUCH
SOMERSAULT FLIP TOPPLE FLIFFUS SPOTTER TWISTER BACKFLIP SOMERSET
SOMETHING WHAT ALIQUID

WHATNOT SOMEWHAT
(— **ABNORMAL**) FREAK
(— **ADDED**) IMP EXTRA DOCTOR
(— **ATTRACTIVE**) DUCK
(— **BELIEVED**) CREDIT
(— **BIG**) BOUNCER
(— **BRIGHT RED**) CORAL
(— **CHERISHED**) APPLE
(— **COMMONPLACE**) DROSS
(— **CONSECRATED**) SACRUM
(— **CONTRARY TO LOGIC**) ALOGISM
(— **CORRUPT**) CARRION
(— **COUNTERFEIT**) DUFFER
(— **DIFFICULT**) STINKER
(— **DISLIKED**) DOGMEAT
(— **DONE**) GERENDUM
(— **ELABORATE**) DEVICE
(— **ELUSIVE**) FUGITIVE
(— **EXCELLENT**) DANDY
(— **EXCESSIVE**) LUXUS
(— **EXTRAORDINARY**) SNORTER
(— **FALSE**) HOOEY
(— **FAMILIAR**) KNOWN
(— **FIRST-RATE**) CHEESE
(— **FLAWED**) CRIPPLE
(— **FOOLISH**) IDIOCY FATUITY
(— **FORGOTTEN**) CORPSE
(— **FORKED**) CORNUTE
(— **FRAUDULENT**) CROSS
(— **HORRIFYING**) SHOCKER
(— **IDENTICAL**) ISOMORPH
(— **ILL-DEFINED**) BLOB
(— **IN ADDITION TO ORDINARY**)
BONUS
(— **INCOMPLETE**) END
(— **INFERIOR**) DOG CULL LESS
CAGMAG
(— **INJURIOUS**) ENEMY
(— **INSIGNIFICANT**) STRAW
FEATHER SNICKET FRAGMENT
(— **INTRICATE**) KNOT
(— **LARGE**) GIANT SMASHER
(— **MADE UP**) FIGMENT
(— **NOT ESSENTIAL**) FRILL
(— **NOT EXPLAINED**) MYSTERY
(— **NOTABLE**) DEUCE
(— **OF GREAT VALUE**) EYETOOTH
(— **OF LITTLE VALUE**) SHUCK
FOUTER FOUTRA
(— **OF NO VALUE**) HAW DAMN
BAUBEE DOCKEN
(— **OFFERED FOR LOAN**) PREMIUM
(— **OR OTHER**) ANYTHING
(— **OUTSTANDING**) BROTH DOYEN
GASSER STANDOUT
(— **PAINFUL**) GAFF
(— **PATCHED UP**) VAMP
(— **POOR**) FLUMMERY
(— **PRECIOUS**) DUMPLING
(— **PREJUDICIAL**) FOE
(— **PROVOKING**) DEVIL
(— **REPELLENT**) SPINACH
(— **RISKED**) HAZARD
(— **SHAPELESS**) DUMP
(— **SHOWY**) FLOSS
(— **SHRIVELED**) SCRUMP
(— **SMALL**) DOT SNIP
(— **SPECTACULAR**) DILLY
(— **STICKY**) CAB

(— **STOLEN**) CRIB
(— **STRANGE**) FANTASIA
(— **SUPERLATIVE**) DARB
(— **TAUGHT**) DOCUMENT
(— **THAT IS LIGHT**) SKIFF SKIFT
(— **THAT WHIRLS**) GIG
(— **TO BIND BARGAIN**) EARNEST
(— **TRIVIAL**) CHIP FLUFF
(— **UNDECIDED**) ACRISY
(— **UNINTELLIGIBLE**) GREEK
(— **UNPLEASANT**) GUCK SOUR
(— **UNSPECIFIED**) ITEM
(— **UNSUBSTANTIAL**) FROTH
(— **UNTRUE**) HOKUM
(— **USELESS**) CRAP BLANK
(— **VILE**) DUNG
(— **WORTHLESS**) BOTH DUST
HOKUM DUFFER AMBSACE
(— **WRITTEN**) SCRIPT
SOMETIME FORMER SOMDEL
WHILOM ANCIENT QUONDAM
SOMEDEAL SOMEPART SOMEWHEN
SOMETIMES NOW TOO WHILE
WHILES UMQUHILE
SOMEWHAT BIT SOME RATHER
SLIGHT SUMMAT ALIQUID
SOMEDEAL
SOMEWHERE SOMERS SOMEGATE
SOMITE ZONITE SEGMENT TERGITE
GONOTOME MEROSOME MESOMERE
SOMATOME
SOMNIFEROUS OPIATE SOMNIFIC
SOMNUS HYPNUS
SON BEN BOY LAD ANAC FILS FITZ
ZONE CHILD KIBEI MOPSY FILIUS
JUNIOR REUBEN EPAPHUS
EPIGONUS MONSIEUR
(— **OF CHIEF**) OGTIERN
(— **OF KING OF FRANCE**) DAUPHIN
(— **OF NISEI**) SANSEI
(— **OF PEER**) MASTER
(— **OF SUDRA**) CHANDALA
(**DAVID'S FAVORITE** —) ABSALOM
(**FOURTH** —) MARTLET
(**ILLEGITIMATE** —) NEPHEW
(**YOUNG** —) MOPSY
(**YOUNGER** —) CADET
SONAR ASDIC
SONCHUS DINDLE
SONG AIR DIT JIG LAY UTA CANT
DUAN FOLK GATO GLEE LEED MELE
NOTE RANT RUNE SANG TUNE
BLUES CANSO CAROL CHANT
CROON DILDO DITTY MELOS MOLPE
VOCAL BALLAD BRANLE BUBBLE
CANTIC CANZON CARMEN CHANTY
CHORUS HIMENE JINGLE MELODY
ORPHIC SHANTY STRAIN VINATA
WAIATA WARBLE BACCHIC BALLATA
CANCION CHANSON COMIQUE
DESCANT MELISMA MELODIA
REQUIEM REVERDI ROMANCE
SCOLION SONGLET THRENOS
BIRDSONG BRINDISI CANTICLE
CANZONET COONJINE FLAMENCO
JUBILATE PALINODE RHAPSODY
SERVENTE SINGSONG ZORTZICO
(— **ACCOMPANYING TOAST**)
BRINDISI

(— **FOR TWO VOICES**) GYMEL
(— **OF BASQUES**) ZORTZICO
(— **OF BIRD**) LAY KOLLER
(— **OF JOY**) CAROL PAEAN
JUBILATE
(— **OF MINSTREL**) YEDDING
(— **OF OCEANIA**) HIMENE
(— **OF PRAISE**) HYMN CAROL
ANTHEM CHORALE
(— **UNACCOMPANIED**) GLEE
(— **WITH MONOTONOUS RHYME**)
VIRELAI VIRELAY
(—**S OF BIRDS**) RAMAGE
(**ANDALUSIAN** —) SAETA
(**ART** —) LIED
(**BOAT** —) JORRAM
(**CEREMONIAL** —**S**) AREITO
(**CRADLE** —) HUSHO
(**CUBAN** —) GUAJIRA COMPARSA
(**DANCE** —) BALLAD BAMBUCO
(**DRINKING** —) BACCHIC WASSAIL
(**EVENING** —) SERENA EVENSONG
SERENATA
(**FOLK** —) SON FADO FOLK BLUES
DOINA BYLINA CANTIGA JUBILEE
(**FUNERAL** —) DIRGE MONODY
EPICEDE THRENODY
(**FUNEREAL** —) ELEGY
(**GAY** —) LILT
(**GERMAN** —) LIED
(**HAWAIIAN** —) MELE
(**HEBREW** —) HATIKVAH
(**IMPROMPTU** —) SCOLION
(**JAPANESE** —) UTA
(**LOVE** —) CANSO CANZO FANCY
AMORET AUBADE SERENA
SERENATA
(**MELISMATIC** —) DIVISION
(**MOCKING** —) JIG
(**MORNING** —) MATIN AUBADE
(**MOURNFUL** —) DUMP PLAINT
ENDECHA
(**NEW ZEALAND** —) WAIATA
(**NIGHT** —) COMPLIN
(**NO** —**S**) UTAI
(**NUPTIAL** —) HYMEN
(**PART** —) CHACE TROLL CACCIA
CANZONET FROTTOLA MADRIGAL
(**PASTORAL** —) OAT
(**PLAIN** —) GROUND
(**PORTUGUESE** —) FADO
(**RELIGIOUS** —) HYMN CAROL
PSALM SHOUT ANTHEM POLYMNY
SIRVENT
(**SAILOR'S** —) CHANTY SHANTY
(**SANSKRIT** —) GITA
(**STUPID** —) STROWD
(**VINTAGE** —) VINATA
(**WORK** —) HOLLER
(**PL.**) ZEMMI AREITO
SONGBIRD CHAT IORA LARK WREN
MAVIS ROBIN SABIA SIREN VEERY
VIREO BULBUL CANARY LINNET
MOCKER ORIOLE SINGER THRUSH
CATBIRD GRASSET WARBLER
BENGALEE BLUEBIRD BOBOLINK
CARDINAL SONGSTER
SONGSTER SINGER WARBLER
SONG THRUSH MAVIE MAVIS

SON-IN-LAW GENER MAUGH
SONOROUS SHILL TONOUS
OROTUND VIBRANT RESONANT
SOUNDFUL SOUNDING
SONOROUSLY DEEPLY
SONSHIP FILIETY
SOOLOOS THULUTH
SOON ERE ANON CITO TITE EARLY
NEWLY RADLY RATHE BELIVE
SUDDEN TIMELY BETIMES ERELONG
PRESTLY SHORTLY DIRECTLY
SPEEDILY
SOONER ERE ERER ERST FIRST
BEFORE TITTER
(— STATE) OKLAHOMA
(— THAN) OR ERE
SOONEST ERST RATHEST
SOOT COOM IZLE SMUT STUP SUMI
BLECK BROOK COLLY COOMB
CROCK GRIME SOTIK FULIGO
SMOUCH SMUTCH SPODIUM
(— ON GRATE BAR) STRANGER
SOOTHE COY DEW BALM CALM DILL
EASE HUSH LULL ACCOY ALLAY
CHARM DULCE HUMOR QUELL
SALVE STILL BECALM PACIFY
SETTLE SMOOTH SOLACE STROKE
SUPPLE ADDULCE ASSUAGE
COMPOSE CONSOLE DEMULCE
FLATTER GRUNTLE LULLABY
PLASTER QUALIFY ATTEMPER
MITIGATE UNRUFFLE
SOOTHER ANODYNE
SOOTHING MILD BALMY BLAND
DOWNY DULCE STILL SWEET
ANIMAL DREAMY DULCET GENTLE
SMOOTH ANODYNE BALSAMIC
SEDATIVE
SOOTHSAY SORT
SOOTHSAYER SEER AUGUR WEIRD
ARIOLE DIVINE ARUSPEX DIVINER
CHALDEAN HARUSPEX TIRESIAS
SOOTY COLLY SMUTTY BROOKIE
COLLIED
SOOTY ALBATROSS NELLIE
QUAKER STINKER BLUEBIRD
STINKPOT
SOOTY SHEARWATER TITI
SOP SPONGE SUGARSOP SWEETSOP
SOPHER SCRIBE
SOPHISM FETCH ELENCH FALLACY
SOPHEME
SOPHIST SOPH DUNCE
SOPHISTICATE GARBLE MONDAINE
SOPHISTICATED WISE BLASE CIVIL
SALTY SVELTE WORLDLY
SOPHISTICATION CHIC
SOPHISTRY DECEIT FALLACY
SOPHISM
SOPORIFIC DWALE DROWSY OPIATE
SLEEPY HYPNOTIC NARCOTIC
SOMNIFIC
SOPPY JUICY SOAKY
SOPRANO CANARY TREBLE
DESCANT CASTRATO
SORB LUSATIAN
SORBIAN WENDISH
SORBOSE ACROSE
SORCERER MAGE BOYLA BRUJO

WITCH BOOLYA NAGUAL VOODOO
WIZARD KORADJI WARLOCK
WIELARE FETISHER MAGICIAN
WITCHMAN
(PL.) GOETAE
SORCERESS BRUJA CIRCE LAMIA
WITCH ARMIDA HECATE BABAJAGA
KORRIGAN WALKYRIE
SORCERY OBI MAGIC SPELL
MAKUTU PISHOGUE PRESTIGE
SORTIARY WIGELING WITCHERY
WITCHING
(VOODOO —) WANGA OUANGA
SORDES SABURRA
SORDID RAW BASE GAMY MEAN VILE
DIRTY DUSTY MUCKY CHETIF
GRUBBY SODDEN MESQUIN SQUALID
CHURLISH
SORE BUM FOX PET BUBA CHAP
DEAR GALL KIBE KYLE OUCH BLAIN
BOTCH GAMMY AGNAIL BITTER
BOUBAS CANKER FESTER MELLIT
MORMAL RANKLE TAKING CATHAIR
CHANCRE SORANCE SCALDING
(— ON HORSE'S FOOT) MELLIT
(ARTIFICIAL —) FOX
(SUMMER —S) CALORIS LEECHES
SORENESS FROG
SORGHUM CANE CUSH MILO BATAD
DARSO DURRA SORGO CHOLAM
HEGARI IMPHEE KAFFIR SHALLU
FETERITA KAOLIANG
SOROCHE PUNA
SORREL OCA OKA SORE CUCKOO
HEARTS OXALIS RUBICAN SOUROCK
ALLELUIA STABWORT
SORREL TREE TITI ELKWOOD
SOURWOOD
SORROW WO RUE WOE BALE CARE
DOLE HARM MOAN RUTH SORE
TEEN DOLOR GRAME GRIEF MOURN
RUING SARRA UNWIN GRIEVE
LAMENT MISERY REGRET STOUND
UNLUST ANGUISH CONDOLE
DEPLORE PENANCE REGRATE
REMORSE THOUGHT TROUBLE
WOEFARE CALAMITY DISTRESS
DOLEANCE DREARING EGRIMONY
MOURNING
SORROWFUL BAD SAD WAN CHARY
DREAR TRIST WOFUL DISMAL
DOLENT DREARY RUEFUL DOLEFUL
LUCTUAL RUESOME UNHAPPY
WAILFUL CONTRITE DESOLATE
DOLESOME DOLOROSO GRIEFFUL
MOURNFUL PITIABLE
SORROWFULLY SADLY WRATH
HEAVILY
SORRY BAD SAD WOE HURT VEXED
UNFAIN PITIFUL CONTRITE
WRETCHED
SORT KIN LOT BRAN COMB GERE
HUMP KIND RANK SUIT WING WORK
BRACK BREED GENUS GRADE
SAVOR SPICE ASSORT BARREL
DILLUE GARBLE GENDER KIDNEY
MANNER MISTER NATURE STRAIN
STRIPE FASHION SPECIES SPECKLE
VARIETY CLASSIFY SEPARATE

(— COTTON BY STAPLE) STAPLE
(— MAIL) CASE
(— MERCHANDISE) BRACK
(— OF PERSON) LIKE
SORTER SHALEMAN
SORTIE ISSUE SALLY ATTACK
OUTFALL
SORTILEGE LOT
SORTING GARBLING
(— ROOM) SALLE
SORVA BORRACHA
SOT LUSH SOAK DRUNK LOURD
TOPER LOURDY BLOTTER DASTARD
TOSSPOT DRUNKARD
SOTHO SUTO SESUTO
SOTIK SOOT
SOUFFLE FONDU FONDUE
SOUGHT QUESITED
SOUL BA EGO ALMA ANIMA ATMAN
GHOST HEART SHADE BUDDHI
DIBBUK NATURE PNEUMA PSYCHE
SPIRIT SPRITE NEPHESH PURUSHA
INTERNAL
(—S OF THE DEAD) LEMURES
(ANIMAL — IN MAN) NEPHESH
(DISEMBODIED —) KER
(EGYPTIAN IMMORTAL —) BA
(INDIVIDUAL —) JIVA
(LIBERATED —) KEVALIN
(UNIVERSAL —) HANSA
(WANDERING —) DIBBUK DYBBUK
SOULFULLY GEISTLICH
SOULLESS TURNIPY
SOU MARQUE STAMPEE
SOUND GO CRY FIT BLOW DING
DRIP FAST FERE FIRM FLOG GLUG
GOOD HAIL HALE KYLE NOTE RING
SAFE SANE TEST TONE TRIG WISE
AFFIX BLAST BUGLE CHEEP FLICK
FRESH GLIFF GLUCK GRIND GROPE
HODDY NOISE PLANG PLUMB PROBE
RIGHT SLUSH SOLID SPANG SPANK
SPEAK SWASH VALID WHOLE
BICKER BIRDIE DORSAL ENDING
ENTIRE FATHOM FAUCAL HEARTY
INTACT LAGOON ROBUST SIGNAL
SINGLE SONANT SPLASH STABLE
STURDY HEALTHY HEARING
HURLING PERFECT PHONEME
PLUMMET SCRATCH SONANCE
VOCABLE FLAWLESS FOOTFALL
GRINDING GROUNDLY LAUGHTER
RELIABLE SEARCHER SYLLABIC
WAKELESS
(— A BAGPIPE) DOODLE
(— BELL) PEAL RING KNELL KNOLL
(— DRUM OR TRUMPET) TUCK
(— FORTH) BOOM
(— IN GREEK AND LATIN) AGMA
(— IN MIND) FORMAL
**(— INDEPENDENTLY OF THE
PLAYER)** CIPHER
(— LESS LOUD) FALL
(— LIKE THUNDER) BRONTIDE
(— LOUDLY) TANG LARUM
(— MELODIOUSLY) CHARM
(— OF BAGPIPE) DRONE
(— OF BEATING) RATAPLAN
(— OF BELL) DING PEAL RING

KNELL STROKE DINGDONG
TINGTANG
(— OF BIRD) JUG
(— OF BULLET) ZIP
(— OF CONTEMPT) HUMPH
(— OF CORK) CLOOP CLUNK
(— OF DISAPPROVAL) BOO HOOT
BAZOO
(— OF DOG) BOOK
(— OF DYING PERSON'S VOICE)
TAISCH
(— OF ENGINE) CHUG
(— OF EXPLOSION) BOUNCE
(— OF F) DIGAMMA
(— OF FLUTE) TOOTLE
(— OF GLOTTAL STOP) HAMZA
HAMZAH
(— OF HEN) CLUCK
(— OF HOG) GRUNT
(— OF HOOF) CLOP
(— OF HORN) BEEP TOOT
(— OF HORSE) BLOWING
(— OF PLUCKED STRING) TUM
(— OF POURING LIQUID) GLUG
GLUGGLUG
(— OF RAIN) SPAT
(— OF RENDING) SCAT
(— OF SHEEP) BAA BLEAT
(— OF STEAM ENGINE) CHUFF
(— OF STRAW OR LEAVES) RUSTLE
(— OF TRUMPET) CLARION
(— OF WIND IN TREES) WOOSH
(— OUT) FEEL
(—S HAVING RHYTHM) MUSIC
(ABNORMAL —) BRUIT
(ADVENTITIOUS —) RALE
(BLOWING —) SOUFFLE
(BRAWLING —) CHIDE
(BUBBLING —) BLATHER
(BUZZING —) Z WHIR WHIRR
(CLICKING —) SNECK
(CONSONANT —) ALVEOLAR
(COOING —) CHIRR TURTUR
(CRACKLING —) RISK
(CRISP —) BLIP
(CRUNCHING —) CRUMP SCRUNCH
(DELICATE —) TINK TINKLE
(DISCORDANT —) JAR BRAY JANGLE
(DISTINCTIVE —) SONG
(DULL —) CLONK FLUMP SQUELCH
(EXPLOSIVE —) POP BARK CHUG
PUFF SNORT REPORT
(FAINT —) PEEP GLIFF WHISHT
INKLING
(FINAL —) AUSLAUT
(GULPING —) GLUCK
(GUTTURAL —) GROWL
(HARSH —) JAR BRAY BLARE CLASH
CRANK TWANG SCROOP DISCORD
STRIDOR
(HEAVY —) DUMP
(HIGH-PITCHED —) TING
(HISSING —) FIZZ SIZZ SWISH
SIZZLE
(HOLLOW —) CHOCK THUNGE
(HUMMING —) HUM BURR SUUM
DRONE SINGING
(INDISTINCT —) BLUR SURD
(INITIAL — OF WORDS) ANLAUT

(JINGLING —) SMIT
(LAPPING —) SLOOSH
(LIGHT REPEATED —) PITAPAT
(LOUD —) PEAL BLARE CLANG
CRASH CLANGOR
(LOW-PITCHED —) BASS
(MEANINGLESS —S) GABBLE
(MEDIAL —) INLAUT
(MENTALLY —) SANE WISE
(MOANING —) SUUM SOUGH
(MOURNFUL —) GROAN
(MUSICAL —) CHIME
(NASAL —) ANUSVARA
(NON-SIGNIFICANT —) GLIDE
(NONVIBRATORY —) FRICTION
(PLEASING —) EUPHONY EUPHONIA
(RASPING —) BUZZ SKIRR SCROOP
(REPEATED —) ECHO
(RESONANT —) BONG
(REVERBERATING —) PLANG
(RINGING —) CLANG CLANK CLING
TWANG RINGLE DINGDONG
(ROARING —) BEAL
(RUSHING —) SWOOSH HURLING
(RUSTLING —) FISSLE FISTLE
(SCRAPING —) GRIDE
(SHARP —) POP PING SNAP CHINK
CRAKE KNACK SPANG SQUIRK
(SHRILL —) CHEEP KNACK SKIRL
SCREED SQUEAK STRIDOR
(SHUFFLING —) SCUFFLE
(SIBILANT —) HISS SHISH SHUSH
(SLIGHT —) SWISH
(SNORING —) SNORK
(SOBBING —) YOOP
(SPEECH —) SURD DOMAL TENUE
VOWEL APICAL PHONEME
CEREBRAL
(SPLASHING —) LAP CHUNK FLURR
SPLAT SWASH
(SPOKEN —) BREATH
(SQUEAKY —) CREAK
(SQUELCHING —) SQUASH
(STRANGLED —) GLUB GLUG
(SWISHING —) SCHLOOP
(TELEPHONE —) SIDETONE
(TRAMPING —) STUMP
(TRILLING —) CHIRR CHIZZ
HIRRIENT
(TUNEFUL —) HARMONY
(UNPLEASANT —) BLOOP
(WARNING —) ALARM SIREN
ALARUM TOCSIN
(WHIRRING —) BIRR FLURR SKIRR
(WHISPERING —) SUSURRUS
(WHISTLING —) STRIDOR
SOUND-ABSORBENT ACOUSTIC
SOUNDBOARD BELLY
SOUNDER TICKER LEADMAN
SOUNDING RAWIN SONANT INKLING
SONDAGE SONATION
(— HARSH) BRAZEN
(— OF BELL) CURFEW
(— OF ORGAN PIPE) CIPHER
(— WITH REVERBERATIONS)
PLANGENT
SOUNDLY FAST TIGHT FIRMLY
SOUNDNESS SANITY FITNESS
SOBRIETY STRENGTH

SOUP BREE KAIL KALE BROTH
GUMBO POSOL BISQUE BORSCH
BURGOO JOUTES POZOLE BORSCHT
GARBURE MARMITE CONSOMME
GAZPACHO MINESTRA MORTREUX
(— UP) SUPE
(BARLEY —) SMIGGINS
(BEEFSKIN —) SKINK
(CABBAGE —) SHCHI STCHI
(CLEAR —) CONSOMME JULIENNE
(JELLIED —) GAZPACHO
(LARGE QUANTITY OF —) SLASH
(THICK —) BISK GUMBO HOOSH
PUREE BISQUE BURGOO CHOWDER
GARBURE POTTAGE HOTCHPOT
MORTREWES
(THIN —) BROTH
SOUR AWA DRY YAR ACID ASIM
CRAB DOUR FOXY GRIM GRUM
HARD TART TURN ACERB ACRID
AIGRE EAGER GOURY GRUFF MUSTY
TEART BITTER CRUETY CURDLE
PONTIC RUGGED SULLEN TORVID
ACETOSE ACIDIFY AUSTERE
SUBACID ACERBATE VINEGARY
(SLIGHTLY —) BLINK BLINKY
ACESCENT
SOURCE FONS FONT HAND HEAD
HIVE MINE RISE RIST ROOT SEED
FOUNT SPAWN SURGE AUCTOR
AUTHOR BOTTOM CENTER FATHER
FONTAL ORIGIN PARENT RESORT
STAPLE EDITION FOUNTAIN
WELLHEAD
(— OF AID) RECOURSE
(— OF ANCESTRAL LINE) STOCK
(— OF ANNOYANCE) BOGY BOGIE
HARROW BUGBEAR
(— OF ASSURANCE) FORTRESS
(— OF CONCERN) BUGABOO
(— OF CONFIDENCE) ANCHOR
(— OF DISPLEASURE) DISGUST
(— OF ENERGY) TAPAS
(— OF HAPPINESS) SUNSHINE
(— OF HARM) CURSE
(— OF HONOR) CREDIT
(— OF INCOME) TITLE REVENUE
(— OF INFORMATION) CHECK
(— OF INSPIRATION) CASTALIA
CASTALIE
(— OF LAUGHTER) SPLEEN
(— OF LIGHT) LAMP
(— OF NOURISHMENT) BREAST
(— OF POWER) STRENGTH
(— OF REGRET) SCATH SCATHE
(— OF STREAM OR RIVER) FILL
(— OF STRENGTH) HORN
(— OF SUPPLY) SHOP FEEDER
ARSENAL
(— OF TROUBLE) HEADACHE
(— OF WATER) BRON SPRING
(— OF WEALTH) GOLCONDA
KLONDIKE
(ENCLOSED —) FLOW
(FROM ANOTHER —) ALIUNDE
(MALIGNANT —) CANCER
(PHYSICAL —) MOTHER
(PRIMARY —) RADIX
SOURDOUGH LEAVEN

SOURED FOXY QUARRED
SOURNESS ACIDITY ACERBITY
ACRIMONY ASPERITY TARTNESS
VERJUICE
SOURSOP CORRESOL GUANABANA
SOURWOOD TITI ELKWOOD
SOUSE DIP DUCK TOSH STOOP
PLUNGE SOZZLE
SOUTANE SIMAR ZIMARRA
SOUTH MIDI AUSTER MIDDAY
MERIDIAN
(FARTHER —) BELOW

SOUTH AFRICA
BAY: ALGOA FALSE
CAPE: AGULHAS
CAPITAL: CAPETOWN PRETORIA
COIN: CENT RAND POUND FLORIN
LANGUAGE: BANTU HINDI TAMIL
TELUGU BUJARATI
MOUNTAIN: AUX KOP KATHKIN
INJASUTI
NATIVE: YOSA BANTU NAMAS
PONDO DAMARA SWAHILI
BECHUANA HOTTENTOT
PROVINCE: TRANSVAAL
RIVER: MODDER MOLOPO ORANGE
KURUMAM LIMPOPO OLIFANTS
TOWN: AUS MARA STAD BENONI
DURBAN SEVERN UMTATA
KOKSTAD MAFEKING

SOUTH CAROLINA
CAPITAL: COLUMBIA
COLLEGE: COKER FURMAN
LANDER CITADEL CLAFLIN
CLEMSON ERSKINE WOFFORD
COUNTY: AIKEN HORRY DILLON
JASPER OCONEE SALUDA
FORT: SUMTER
INDIAN: PEDEE SEWEE CUSABO
SANTEE WAXHAW CATAWBA
SUGEREE WATEREE CONGAREE
LAKE: MARION MURRAY CATAWBA
WATEREE HARTWELL MOULTRIE
MOUNTAIN: SASSAFRAS
NATIVE: WEASEL PALMETTO
PLATEAU: PIEDMONT
PRESIDENT: JACKSON
RIVER: BROAD EDISTO PEEDEE
SALUDA SANTEE ASHEPOO
SAVANNAH
STATE BIRD: WREN
STATE FLOWER: JESSAMINE
STATE TREE: PALMETTO
TOWN: AIKEN GREER UNION
BELTON CAMDEN CHERAW
CONWAY DILLON SENECA
SUMTER BAMBERG LAURENS
MANNING BEAUFORT FLORENCE
NEWBERRY WALHALLA

SOUTH CAROLINIAN WEASEL
PALMETTO

SOUTH DAKOTA
BUTTE: MUD CROW SULLY FINGER
SADDLE THUNDER DEERSEARS

CAPITAL: PIERRE
COLLEGE: HURON YANKTON
COUNTY: DAY BRULE MOODY
SPINK CUSTER JERAULD
YANKTON MELLETTE
INDIAN: BRULE SIOUX DAKOTA
CHEYENNE
LAKE: OAHE BIGSTONE TRAVERSE
MONUMENT: RUSHMORE
MOUNTAIN: BEAR SHEEP TABLE
CROOKS HARNEY MOREAU
NICKNAME: COYOTE
RIVER: JAMES MOREAU CHEYENNE
MISSOURI
STATE BIRD: PHEASANT
STATE FLOWER: PASQUE
STATE TREE: SPRUCE
TOWN: LEAD HURON CUSTER
EUREKA LEMMON MILLER
WINNER STURGIS WEBSTER
YANKTON ABERDEEN
DEADWOOD SISSETON

SOUTHERLY AUSTRINE
SOUTHERN SUDIC AUSTRAL
MERIDIAN SOUTHRON
SOUTHERN CROSS CRUX CROSS
CROSIER
SOUTHERNER CAVALIER SOUTHRON
SOUTHERN FRANCE MIDI
SOUTHERN ILLINOIS EGYPT
SOUTHERN INDIA DRAVIDA

SOUTH KOREA
BAY: KANGHWA
CAPITAL: SEOUL
COIN: WON HWAN
MOUNTAIN: CHIRI
RIVER: HAN KUM PUKHAN SOMJIN
NAKTONG YONGSAN
TOWN: MASAN MOKPO PUSAN
SUWON TAEGU CHINJU CHONJU
INCHON KUNSAN TAEJON
KWANGJU CHUNCHON

SOUTHLAND AUSTER
SOUTH SEA ISLANDER KANAKA

SOUTH VIETNAM
CAPITAL: SAIGON
LANGUAGE: CHAM KHMER RHADE
MEASURE: GANG PHAN THON
MOUNTAIN: BADINH NINHHOA
KNONTRAN NGOKLINH
TCHEPONE
NATIVE: CHAM MALAY
PORT: DANANG SAIGON QUINHON
NHATRANG
REGION: ANNAM COCHIN
RIVER: BA MEKONG DONGNAI
TOWN: HUE HOIAN ANNHON
DANANG QUINHON SONGCAN
TAYNINH PHANRANG QUANGTRI
VINHLOI
WEIGHT: CAN YET UYEN

SOUTHWESTER SQUAM

SOUVENIR RELIC TOKEN FAIRING
NICKNACK
SOVEREIGN BEY SIR SOV BEAN
CHAM CHIP FREE KHAN QUID SHAH
SKIV JAMES NEGUS NIZAM QUEED
CHAGAN COUTER GUINEA KAISER
KINGLY MASTER PRINCE SAMORY
SHINER SOLDAN SOVRAN SULTAN
CROWNED MONARCH ZAMORIN
DOMINANT IMPERIAL SUFFRAIN
SUZERAIN
(DIVINELY —) THEARCHIC
(FELLOW —) COUSIN
(HEAVENLY —) TENNO HEAVEN
(MOSLEM —) SOLDAN
SOVEREIGNTY SWAY CROWN REIGN
DIADEM EMPERY EMPIRE THRONE
DEMESNE DYNASTY KINGDOM
MAJESTY SCEPTER SCEPTRE
AUTARCHY DOMINION IMPERIUM
MONARCHY REGALITY REGNANCY
SOVRANTY
(— OF REASON) AUTONOMY
(JOINT —) SYNARCHY
SOVIET (ALSO SEE RUSSIA) VOLOST
COUNCIL GUBERNIA
SOW HOG GILT SEED SHED YILT
DRILL PLANT PLUMP STREW
CHANNEL GRUMPHY IMPLANT
OVERSOW SCATTER ENGENDER
INTERSOW SEMINATE
SOW BUG ISOPOD SLATER
ISOPODAN
SOWENS SONS SWEENS FLUMMERY
WASHBREW
SOWER SEEDER SEEDMAN
SEEDSTER SEMINARY
SOWING SATION SEMENCE
SEEDNESS
SOWN SEME SATIVE SEEDED
SEMEED
SOW THISTLE DINDLE GUTWEED
HOGWEED MILKWEED
SOY SHOYA SHOYU
SOYBEAN SOJA SOYA
SPA BATH CURE HYDRO
SPACE AREA BLUE CORD COSO
DENT FACE LUNG PALE RANK ROOM
SIDE VOID ABYSS BLOCK CHINK
CLEFT FIELD PLACE RANGE HIATUS
INDENT MATTER ROOMTH ARRANGE
FOREIGN GUNNIES LEGROOM
ROOMAGE SPACING SPATIUM
DIASTEMA DISTANCE EXOCOELE
INTERVAL
(— ABOVE EARTH) AIRSPACE
(— AMONG MUSCLES) SINUS
(— AROUND HOUSE) AMBIT
(— AT WHARF) BERTHAGE
(— BEHIND ALTAR) FERETORY
(— BETWEEN BED AND WALL)
RUELLE
(— BETWEEN BRIDGE PIERS) LOCK
(— BETWEEN CONCENTRIC
CIRCLES) ANNULUS
(— BETWEEN DECKS) LAZARET
(— BETWEEN EYE AND BILL) LORE
(— BETWEEN FEATHERS) APTERYLA

(— **BETWEEN FLUTINGS**) FILET FILLET GORGERIN
(— **BETWEEN FURROWS**) RIG
(— **BETWEEN PAGES**) GUTTER
(— **BETWEEN RAILROAD TIES**) CRIB
(— **BETWEEN SAW TEETH**) GULLET
(— **BETWEEN SHIP'S BOWS AND ANCHOR**) HAWSE
(— **BETWEEN STRANDS**) CANTLINE
(— **BETWEEN TEETH**) DIASTEMA
(— **BETWEEN THUMB AND LITTLE FINGER**) SPAN
(— **BETWEEN TIMBERS**) SPIRKET
(— **BETWEEN TWO WIRES**) DENT
(— **BETWEEN VEINS OF LEAVES**) AREOLA
(— **DEVOID OF MATTER**) VACUUM VACUITY
(— **FOR SECRETION**) BAG
(— **IN CHURCH**) KNEELING
(— **IN COIL OF CABLE**) TIER
(— **IN FOREST**) GLADE
(— **IN MINE**) GOB
(— **IN THEATER**) BOX
(— **IN TYPE**) CORE
(— **OCCUPIED**) VOLUME
(— **OF TIME**) DAY PULL STEAD GHURRY STITCH INTERVAL
(— **ON BILLIARD TABLE**) BALK BAULK
(— **ON COIN**) EXERGUE
(— **OVER STAGE**) FLIES
(— **OVERHEAD**) HIGH
(— **UNDER STAGE**) DOCK
(— **USED AS LIVING-ROOM**) LANAI
(— **WITHIN LIMITS**) CONTENT
(**AIR** —) CENTRUM
(**ARCHITECTURAL** —) METOPE PEDIMENT SACELLUM
(**BARE — ON BIRD**) APTERIUM
(**BLANK** —) ALLEY LACUNA
(**BOUNDLESS** —) INFINITE
(**CLEAR** —) FAIRWAY HEADWAY DAYLIGHT
(**COUNTER** —) BACKBAR
(**CRAMPED** —) CUBBY
(**EMPTY** —) AIR BLANK CAPACITY
(**ENCLOSED** —) AREA BOWL HATCH VERGE CHAMBER CIRCUIT CLOSURE COMPASS PTEROMA CLOISTER CONFINES
(**EUCLIDEAN** —) FLAT
(**FLAT** —) HOMALOID
(**LEVEL** —) PLATEA PARTERRE
(**NARROW** —) SLOT STRAIT
(**OPEN — OF WATER**) WAKE
(**OPEN** —) OUT LAWN ALLEY COURT LAUND TAHUA MAIDAN AREAWAY FAIRWAY LOANING APERTURE DAYLIGHT KNEEHOLE
(**OVERHANGING** —) DOME
(**POPLITEAL** —) HAM HOCK
(**ROOF** —) CELL
(**SEATING** —) CAVEA
(**SHELTERED** —) KILLOGIE
(**STORAGE** —) ATTIC
(**TRIANGULAR** —) SPANDREL
(**UNFILLED** —) GAP GAPE CAVITY HOLLOW BREAKAGE

(**VAULTED** —) ALCOVE
(**VERTICAL** —) HEADROOM
(**WORKING** —) COUNTER
SPACED MEATIC
SPACIOUS ROOM SIDE WIDE AMPLE BROAD RANGY ROOMY GOLDEN BARONIAL SCOPIOUS
SPADE DIG LOY FECK LILY PEEL PICK SPIT SPUD DELVE DIDLE GRAFF SLADE SLANE TRAMP DIGGER PADDLE SERVER SHOVEL TUSKAR GRAFTER SCAFFLE SCUPPIT SPADDLE SPITTER TWISCAR
(**LONG NARROW** —) LOY
(**PEAT** —) SLADE SLANE TUSKAR
(**PLASTERER'S** —) SERVER
(**TRIANGULAR** —) DIDLE
SPADEFISH POGY PORGY MOONFISH
SPADEFUL SPIT SPITFUL
SPAGHETTI PASTA SLEEVING
SPAGNUOLO LADINO

SPAIN

CAPE: AJO NAO GATA CREUS MORAS PALOS PENAS PRIOR DARTUCH ORTEGAL SALINAS TORTOSA ESPICHEL MARROQUI SACRATIF
CAPITAL: MADRID
COIN: COB DURO PESO REAL DOBLA CUARTO DINERO DOBLON ESCUDO PESETA ALFONSO CENTIMO PISTOLE REALDOR DOUBLOON
DIALECT: BASQUE CATALAN GALICIAN
ISLAND: IBIZA PALMA GOMERA HIERRO ALBORAN MAJORCA MINORCA MALLORCA TAGOMAGO TENERIFE
ISLANDS: CANARY BALEARIC
MEASURE: PIE CODO COPA DEDO MOYO PASO VARA BRAZA CAFIZ CAHIZ CARGA LEGUA LINEA MEDIO MILLA PALMO SESMA ARROBA CORDEL CUARTA ESTADO FANEGA RACION YUGADA AZUMBRE CANTARA CELEMIN ESTADEL PULGADA ARANZADA FANEGADA
MOUNTAIN: GATA ANETO ROUCH TEIDE ESTATS NETHOU TELENO BANUELO CERREDO PERDIDO ALMANZOR MONTSENY MULHACEN PENALARA
MOUNTAIN RANGE: CUENCA GREDOS MORENA TOLEDO ALCARAZ DEMANDA MONCAYO MALADETA MONEGROS PYRENEES
NAME: ESPANA IBERIA HISPANIA
NATIVE: CATALAN IBERIAN
PORT: ADRA NOYA VIGO CADIZ GADES GADIR GIJON PALOS ABDERA CORUNA MALAGA ALMERIA ALICANTE BARCELONA
PROVINCE: JAEN LEON LUBO ALAVA AVILA CADIZ SORIA

BURGOS CORUNA CUENCA GERONA HUELVA HUESCA LERIDA MADRID MALAGA MURCIA ORENSE OVIEDO TERUEL TOLEDO ZAMORA ALMERIA BADAJOZ CACERES CORDOBA GRANADA LOGRONO NAVARRA SEGOVIA SEVILLA VIZCAYA ALBACETE ALICANTE BALEARES PALENCIA VALENCIA ZARAGOZA
REGION: LEON ARAGON BASQUE MURCIA CASTILE GALICIA NAVARRE ASTURIAS CASTILLA VALENCIA
RIVER: SIL TER CEGA EBRO ESLA LIMA MINO TAJO ULLA ADAJA CINCA DOURO DUERO GENIL JALON JUCAR NAVIA ODIEL RIAZA SEGRE TAGUS TINTO TURIA ALAGON ARAGON ERESMA HUERVA JARAMA ORBIGO SEGURA TOROTE ALMERIA ALMONTE ARLANZA BARBATE CABRIEL DURATON GALLEGO HENARES MIJARES PERALES GUADIANA
TOWN: ASPE BAZA ELDA HARO IRUN JAEN LEON LUGO OLOT REUS ROTA SAMA VIGO BAENA BEJAR CADIZ CIEZA CUETA ECIJA EIBAR ELCHE GIJON IBIZA JEREZ JODAR LORCA OLIVA PALMA RONDA SIERO UBEDA XERES YECLA ZAFRA AVILES AZUAGA BILBAO BURGOS DUENCA GANDIA GERONA GETAFE GUADIX HELLIN HUELVA HUESCA JATIVA LERIDA LUCENA MADRID MALAGA MATARO MERIDA MURCIA ORENSE OVIEDO TERMEL TOLEDO UTRERA ZAMORA BADAJOS CORDOBA DAIMIEL GRANADA JUMILLA LINARES LOGRONO MANRESA SEGOVIA SEVILLA TARRASA VITORIA BADALONA FIGUERAS PAMPLONA SABADELL SANTIAGO TORRENTE VALENCIA ZARAGOZA
WEIGHT: ONZA FRAIL GRANO LIBRA MARCO TOMIN ADARME ARROBA DINERO DRACMA OCHAVA ARIENZO QUILATE QUINTAL CARACTER TONELADA
WINE: RIOJA SHERRY

SPALL SCALE SPAWL GALLET
SPAN ARCH BEAM PAIR CHORD SPANG SWING BRIDGE EXTEND SPREAD OPENING QUARTER BESTRIDE
(— **WITH FINGERS**) SPEND
(**UNSUPPORTED** —) BEARING
SPANDREL GROIN ALLEGE SPANDLE
SPANGLE AGLET PRANK SPANG SEQUIN CHEQUEEN SPANGLET ZECCHINO

SPANGLED POWDERED SPANKLED
SPANIARD DON DIEGO MULADI
SPANIEL TRASY COCKER SUSSEX
PAPILLON SPRINGER WATERRUG
SPANISH ALJAMIA
SPANISH-AMERICAN CHINO
SPANISH BAYONET IZOTE YUCCA
SPANISH HOGFISH LADYFISH
SPANISH JACINTH SCILLA
SPANISH JASMINE MALATI
SPANISH MACKEREL SIERRA
SPANISH PLUM SIRUELAS
SPANISH STOPPER IRONWOOD
SPANK PRAT SCUD SKELP SLIPPER
SPANKER DRIVER
SPANKING SMACKING
SPANNER KEY WRENCH
SPANNING ASTRIDE
SPAR BEAM BOOM CAUK CLUB GAFF
MAST RAFT SPUR YARD CABER
SPAAD SPATH SPELK SPRIT STODE
BOUGAR STEEVE BASTITE DERRICK
DOLPHIN JIBBOOM RIBBAND
BOWSPRIT LAZULITE
(BITTER —) DOLOMITE
(HEAVY —) CAUK BARITE BARYTE
SPARE BONY FAIK HAIN LEAN NICE
SAVE SLIM THIN FAVOR LANKY
SPELL LENTEN SKIMPY RESERVE
SLENDER PRESERVE
SPARGE PIPE WEEPER
SPARING CHARY GNEDE SCANT
SPARE DAINTY FRUGAL STINGY
ENVIOUS ECONOMIC SPAREFUL
(— OF WORDS) CURT
(NOT —) HANDSOME
SPARINGNESS PARCITY SCARCITY
SPARK FUNK IZLE AIZLE GRAIN
LIGHT PURSE SPERK SPUNK
FLANKER SPARKLE SPUNKIE
SPARKLET
(VITAL —) GHOST LIGHT
SPARKER IGNITER
SPARKLE FUNK SNAP WINK BLINK
FLASH GLENT GLINT SHINE SPARK
GLANCE KINDLE SIMPER CRACKLE
FLANKER GLIMMER GLISTEN
GLISTER GLITTER RADIATE SHIMMER
SKINKLE SPANGLE TWINKLE
SPRINKLE
SPARKLER TWINKLER
SPARKLING DEWY CRISP QUICK
SUNNY SPUNKY STARRY CREMANT
DIAMOND SHINING TWINKLY
MOUSSEUX SMIRKING SPERLING
(MAKE —) AERATE
SPARLING SMELT
SPARROW SPUG DICKY DONEY
FINCH HEMPY ISAAC PADDA PADDY
SPRIG SPRUG CHIPPY PHILIP
SPRONG TOWHEE CHANTER CHIPPIE
DUNNOCK FIELDIE HAYSUCK
PINNOCK SPADGER SPURDIE
TITLENE TITLING TITTLIN ACCENTOR
FIRETAIL HAIRBIRD WHITECAP
SPARROW HAWK MUSKET
SPARHAWK
SPARSE BALD THIN MEAGER SCANTY
THRIFTY

SPARTAN LACONIC
SPASM QUALM TONUS ENTASIA
FLUTTER RAPTURE SPASMUS
MYOTONIA PAROXYSM
(— OF PAIN) GRIP
(—S OF WHALE) FLURRY
(TONIC —) HOLOTONY
SPASMODIC FITFUL SNATCHY
SPASMIC SPASTIC SPURTIVE
SPAT SEED BROOD JOWER GAITER
LEGGING BOOTHOSE BOOTIKIN
SPATE SLUICE
SPATHE CYMBA SHEATH
SPATHIC SPARRY SPATHOSE
SPATIAL STERIC
SPATTER DASH JAUP BERAY SKIRP
SLART SPARK SPURT DABBLE
SPLASH SQUIRT BESPAWL BESPETE
SHATTER SMATTER SPATTLE
SPIRTLE SPLATTER SPRINKLE
(— WITH FOAM) EMBOSS
(— WITH MUD) JAP BEMUD SPARK
SPATTERDASH SPAT BONNET
GAITER CUTIKIN LEGGING
BOOTHOSE BOOTIKIN
SPATTERDOCK DUCK CLOTE TUCKY
WOKAS NUPHAR BONNETS
CANDOCK
SPATULA SPAT SLICE THIBLE THIVEL
CESTRUM SPATTLE SPLATTER
SPAVIN JACK SPAVIE VARISSE
SPAWN RUD RAUN REDD RUDD SILE
SPORE TODDER
SPAWNEATER SHINER
SPAWNING SICK MILKY SEEDING
SPAY FIX GELD ALTER DESEX SPADE
CHANGE SPEAVE CASTRATE
SPEAK ASK CUT SAY CANT CARP
MEAN MOOT MOVE TALE TALK TELL
WORD BREAK MOUTH NEVEN ORATE
PARLE SOUND SPELL SPIEL UTTER
ACCENT PARLEY PATTER QUETHE
SERMON SPEECH SQUEAK TONGUE
ADDRESS BESPEAK DECLAIM
DELIVER EXCLAIM PARRALL
CONVERSE REHEARSE
(— ABUSIVELY) JAW
(— AFFECTEDLY) MIMP KNACK
(— AGAINST) ACCUSE GAINSAY
FORSPEAK
(— ANGRILY) ROUSE CAMPLE
(— AT LENGTH) DISSERT ENLARGE
(— BROKENLY) FALTER
(— CAJOLINGLY) COLLOGUE
(— CONFUSEDLY) HATTER CLUTTER
SPLATHER
(— CONTEMPTUOUSLY) SCOFF
(— CRITICALLY) LAUNCH
(— CURTLY) BIRK SNAP
(— EVIL) BLACKEN
(— FALSELY) ABUSE
(— FAMILIARLY) HOBNOB
(— FIRST TO) ACCOST
(— FOOLISHLY) PRATE GIBBER
(— HALTINGLY) HACK HAMMER
STAMMER
(— HOARSELY) CROAK CROUP
(— ILL OF) KNOCK DEPRAVE
DETRACT

(— IMPERFECTLY) LISP
(— IMPUDENTLY) CHEEK
(— IMPULSIVELY) BLURT
(— IN DRAWL) DRANT DRAUNT
(— IN JEST) FOOL
(— IN ONE'S EAR) HARK
(— IN POINTLESS MANNER) DROOL
(— IN STUMBLING WAY) STUTTER
(— IN UNDERTONE) WHISPER
(— IN WHINING VOICE) CANT
(— INDISTINCTLY) FUMBLE JABBER
MUFFLE MAUNDER SPLUTTER
(— INEPTLY) BUMBLE
(— INSOLENTLY) SNASH
(— LOUDLY) TANG
(— MINCINGLY) NAB MIMP
(— MONOTONOUSLY) DROLL
(— OF) CALL NEVEN MENTION
(— OUT) LEVEL SHOOT
(— PLAYFULLY) BANTER
(— POMPOUSLY) CRACK
(— PROFUSELY) PALAVER
(— QUERULOUSLY) CREAK
(— RAPIDLY) TROLL GIBBER JABBER
SQUIRT CHATTER
(— RESENTFULLY) HUFF
(— RHETORICALLY) DECLAIM
(— SARCASTICALLY) GIRD
(— SHORTLY) JERK
(— SLIGHTINGLY OF) BELITTLE
(— SLOWLY) DRAWL
(— THROUGH THE NOSE) SNAFFLE
(— TRUTH) SOOTHSAY
(— WITH EMPHASIS) DWELL
(— WITH LIPS CLOSED) MUMBLE
SPEAKEASY SHEBEEN
SPEAKER VOICE BRYTHON LOCUTOR
MOUTHER STYLIST EPILOGUE
SPEECHER
(ORATORICAL —) SPOUTER
(PUBLIC —) ORATOR STUMPER
SPEAKING STEVEN LOQUENT
SPELLING
(— ARTICULATELY) MEROP
MEROPIC
(— MANY LANGUAGES) POLYGLOT
(EVIL —) PRATING
SPEAR GAD DART FRAM GAFF PIKE
GRAIN LANCE REJON SHAFT STAFF
VALET AMGARN BORDUN BROACH
FIZGIG FRAMEA GIDJEE GLAIVE
WASTER ASSEGAI BOURDON
HARPOON IMPALER JAVELIN
TRIDENT VERUTUM EELSPEAR
GAVELOCK LANCEGAY STANDARD
WALSPERE
(EEL —) ELGER PILGER
(FISH —) GIG GAFF TREN POACH
FIZGIG GRAINS FISHGIG LEISTER
SNIGGER
(SALMON —) WASTER
SPEARFISH AGUJA GOGGLE MARLIN
BILLFISH LONGJAWS
SPEAR GRASS SPANIARD
SPEARHEAD BUNT GAFF SPUD
CORONAL
SPEARMINT MENTHE LABIATE
SPEAR-SHAPED HASTATE
SPEAR THROWER ATLATL

WOMMALA WOOMERAH
SPEARWORT BANEWORT
SPECIAL VERY EXTRA KHASS
CONCRETE ESPECIAL PECULIAR
SPECIFIC
SPECIALIST SWELL EXPERT HERALD
LEGIST ALTAIST ARABIST FAUNIST
FEUDIST GRECIAN OLOGIST
SURGEON AQUINIST ARBORIST
BANTUIST BOTANIST ETHICIST
GEMARIST GEOGNOST GEOMETER
HEBRAIST HOMERIST LATINIST
URBANIST
SPECIES FOLK FORM KIND SORT
BROOD CLASS EIDOS GENRE
ESPECE MANNER MISTER APOMICT
FEATHER SPECIAL ANALOGUE
GENOTYPE INDIGENE
(ATOMIC —) DAUGHTER
SPECIFIC EXPRESS SPECIAL TRIVIAL
CONCRETE ESPECIAL
SPECIFICALLY NAMELY
SPECIFICATION MENTION
SPECIFICITY HECCEITY
SPECIFIED SET GIVEN
SPECIFY DESIGN DETAIL ARTICLE
EXPRESS MENTION INDICATE
NOMINATE
SPECIMEN CAST TEST ESSAY
FACER MODEL SPICE CHANCE
SAMPLE SWATCH EXAMPLE ICOTYPE
ISOTYPE PATTERN SAMPLER
ALLOTYPE EXEMPLAR HOLOTYPE
HYPOTYPE IDEOTYPE INSTANCE
(ADDITIONAL —) COTYPE
(EXTRAORDINARY —) BENDER
(FEMALE —) GYNETYPE
(FINEST —) PEARL
(LARGE —) ELEPHANT
(SMALL —) SPRIG
SPECIOUS GAY FAIR FALSE WHITE
FACILE GLOSSY HOLLOW TINSEL
PAGEANT PLAUSIVE PROBABLE
SPURIOUS
SPECIOUSNESS DISGUISE
SPECK DOT PIN PIP MOTE SPOT
TICK WHIT BLACK GLEBE PLECK
APHTHA SPECKLE FLYSPECK
NUBECULA
(— IN LINEN) SPRIT
(— ON FINGERNAIL) GIFT
(BLACK —) DARTROSE
SPECKLE FLECK GARLE SPECK
MIZZLE PECKLE STIPPLE
SPECKLED SHELD FIGGED MAILED
MENALD SANDED BLOBBED
BRACKET PECKLED SPECKED
SPECKLY FRECKLED IRONSHOT
IRRORATE JASPERED STIPPLED
SPECTACLE POMP SHOW SPEC
BYSEN SIGHT CIRCUS DEVICE
OBJECT EYEMARK PAGEANT
SPECIES TAMASHA MONUMENT
NAUMACHY STERACLE
(ODD —) TRACK
(SORRY —) BIZEN BYSEN
(WATER —) AQUACADE
SPECTACLES PAIR SPECS BRILLS
LUNETS PEEPER SIGHTS GLASSES

GOGGLES WINKERS CHEATERS
SPECTACULAR VIEWY PAGEANT
SPECTATOR FAN VIEWER WITNESS
BEHOLDER OBSERVER OVERSEER
RAILBIRD VIEWSTER
(PL.) DEDANS
SPECTER BUG BOGY MARE BOGIE
BOGLE GHOST LARVA POOKA
SPOOK TAIPO BOGGLE EMPUSA
PHOOKA REDCAP SHADOW SPIRIT
SPOORN WRAITH BOGGART
BUGBEAR PHANTOM RAWHEAD
REDCOWL SPECTRE GUYTRASH
PHANTASM PRESENCE REVENANT
SPECTRUM
SPECTRAL SPOOKY GHOSTLY
SHADOWY
SPECULATE JOB STAG GAMBLE
PONDER CONSIDER RUMINATE
THEORIZE
SPECULATION THEORY THEORIC
VENTURE GAMBLING IDEOLOGY
(DISHONEST —) BUBBLE
SPECULATIVE ACADEMIC
SPECULATOR PIKER GAMBLER
PLUNGER SCALPER BUMMAREE
OPERATOR
SPECULUM METAL MIRROR DILATER
DIOPTER DIOPTRIC
SPEECH GOB LIP SAW SAY TAT TOY
COAX LEED REDE RUNE TALE
DUALA FRUMP GLOZE LEDEN LINGO
SERMO SPEAK SPELL SPOKE SQUIB
VOICE BREATH DILOGY EPILOG
GAELIC GASCON GILAKI JARGON
LEMOSI ORISON REASON SALUTE
STEVEN TONGUE ADDRESS
BROCARD EASTERN MEITHEI
ORATION VULGATE EPILOGUE
GALICIAN HARANGUE LANGUAGE
LOCUTION LOQUENCE MORAVIAN
QUESTION SONORITY SPEAKING
(— FORM) LEXEME
(— IN GREEK DRAMA) RHESIS
(— IN PLAY) SIDE
(— REDUCER) VOCODER
(AFFECTED —) CANT
(BITTER —) DIATRIBE
(BOASTFUL —) BLUSTER
(BOMBASTIC —) SQUIRT HARANGUE
(COARSE —) HARLOTRY
(CONFUSED —) SPUTTER
(CONTEMPTUOUS —) FRUMP
(IRRITABLE —) SNAP
(JAVANESE —) KRAMA
(LONG —) MONOLOG
(LONG-DRAWN —) TIRADE
(MOCKING —) TRIFLE
(OBSCURE —) ENIGMA
(OFFENSIVE —) INJURY
(PRETENTIOUS —) FUSTIAN
(ROUNDABOUT —) CIRCUIT
(SANCTIMONIOUS —) SNUFFLE
(SINGSONG —) CANT
(SLANDEROUS —) EVIL
(VAPID —) WASH
SPEECHIFIER SPOUTER
SPEECHLESS DUMB MUTE SILENT
SPEECHMAKING SPOUTING

(— TO GAIN APPLAUSE) BUNKUM
BUNCOMBE
SPEED BAT HIE RIP RUN FLEE FOOT
GAIT HIGH PACE PELT PIRR POST
TILT BLAST HASTE HURRY SMOKE
WHIRL ASSIST CAREER FOURTH
HASTEN STREAK QUICKEN WHIZZLE
AIRSPEED CELERITY DISPATCH
EXPEDITE FASTNESS MOMENTUM
RAPIDITY VELOCITY
(— OF NAUTICAL MILE) KNOT
(— OF PITCH) STUFF
(— UP) HASTEN CATALYZE
EXPEDITE
(AT FULL —) AMAIN
(AUTOMOTIVE —) LOW HIGH DRIVE
FIRST THIRD FOURTH SECOND
REVERSE
(DRIVING —) SWING
(GOOD —) BONALLY
SPEEDILY CITO SOON APACE RATHE
BELIVE BETIMES HYINGLY QUICKLY
TANTIVY
SPEEDING HURTLING
SPEEDWELL CATEYE HENBIT
FLUELLEN NECKWEED NICKWELL
SPEEDY FAST SOON HASTY QUICK
RATHE SWIFT RAKING SUDDEN
POSTING TANTIVY EXPEDITE
SPEEDFUL SPINNING
SPELEOLOGIST CAVEMAN
SPELL GO FIT HEX JAG HACK JINX
MOJO PULL RUNE TACK TAKE TIFF
TIME TOUR TURN BRIEF CHARM
CRAFT CRASH MAGIC PATCH SPACE
WANGA WEIRD WHEEL ACCESS
GLAMOR GOOFER GRIGRI GUFFER
MAKUTU MANTRA PERIOD SNATCH
STREAK CANTRIP SORCERY
SPELDER CANTRAIP EXORCISM
GREEGREE MALEFICE PISHOGUE
(— OF ACTIVITY) BOUT
(— OF EXERCISE) BREATHER
(— OF LISTLESSNESS) DOLDRUMS
(— OF SHIVERING) AGUE
(— OF WEATHER) SNAP SLANT
SEASON
(BREATHING —) BLOW
(BRIEF —) SNATCH
(DRINKING —) FUDDLE
(EVIL —) JINX
(FAINTING —) DROW DWALM
(NIPPING —) SNAPE
(STORMY —) FLAW
(VOODOOISTIC —) WANGA
SPELLBIND ENCHANT
SPELLBINDING BASILISK
SPELLING GRAPH WRITING
SPELT FAR EMMER FITCH SPELTZ
SPELTZ EMMER
SPEND COST DREE DROP LEAD
PASS STOW WARE WEAR DALLY
DREIE SERVE SHOOT TRADE
BESTOW BEWARE EXPEND LAVISH
OUTRUN CONSUME DISPEND
EXHAUST UNPURSE CONFOUND
CONTRIVE DISBURSE
(— FRUITLESSLY) DAWDLE
(— IN IDLENESS) DRONE

(— LAVISHLY) BLUE SPORT DEBAUCH
(— MONEY) MELT
(— RECKLESSLY) BLOW LASH
(— SUMMER) ESTIVATE
(— TIME TEDIOUSLY) DRANT
(— TIME) DREE FOOL DREIE
(— WASTEFULLY) SPILL SQUANDER
SPENDTHRIFT WASTER PANURGE ROUNDER SPENDER WASTREL PRODIGAL
SPENSER IMMERITO
SPENT DONE WEARY EFFETE OVERWORN
SPERM SEED SEMINIUM
SPERMACETI SPERM CETACEUM
SPERMOGONIUM PYCNIUM
SPERMOPHILE MARMOT SUSLIK
SPERM WHALE CACHALOT
SPET SIGNET SINNET
SPEW PUKE SPUE VOMIT
SPHAERIUM CYCLAS
SPHAGION HIERA
SPHAGNUM MUSKEG
SPHALERITE JACK BLENDE
SPHENODON HATTERIA
SPHERE ORB AREA BALL BOWL LOKA SHOT FIELD GLOBE RANGE SCOPE CIRCLE CROTAL DOMAIN HEAVEN REGION RUNDLE COUNTRY ELEMENT GLOBOID KINGDOM ORBICLE EARTHKIN EMPYREAL EMPYREAN MOVEABLE PROVINCE
(— OF ACTION) AMBIT ARENA WORLD DOMAIN
(— OF ACTIVITY) FIELD FRONT
(— OF AUTHORITY) DIOCESE
(— OF INFLUENCE) DOMAIN SATRAPY
(— OF LIFE) EARTH WORLD STATION
(— OF OPERATION) THEATER THEATRE
(— OF WORK) TITLE
(CELESTIAL —) CYCLE ELEMENT
(ENCOMPASSING —) AMBIENT
(MAGNETIZED —) EARTHKIN TERRELLA
(METAL —) HAMMER
(SMALL —) ORBICLE SPHERULE
(TINKLING —) CROTAL
SPHERICAL ORBIC GLOBAL ROTUND GLOBATE GLOBOSE ORBICAL SPHERIC GLOBULAR
SPHERULE GLOBULE VARIOLE
SPHINX MUSTANG COLOSSUS HAWKMOTH
SPICA AZIMECH
SPICCATO PIQUE
SPICE MACE VEIN AROMA CLOVE EPICE TASTE GINGER NUTMEG PEPPER SEASON STACTE SPICERY SPICING ALLSPICE CINNAMON SEASONER
SPICEBUSH BENZOIN SNAPWOOD
SPICED SPICY POWDERED
SPICKNEL MEW SCLERE BEARWORT
SPICULE OXEA TOXA ASTER CHELA CYMBA DESMA DIACT SIGMA SPINE

STYLE ACTINE ANCHOR MONACT SCLERE STYLUS TRIACT TRIPOD TYLOTE CALTROP DIACTIN EUASTER HEXAXON MONAXON PINULUS SPERULA SPICKLE TETRACT TORNOTE TRIAENE TRIAXON TYLOTUS HEXASTER ISOCHELA OXYASTER POLYAXON SCLERITE SPHERULA SPICULUM STRONGYL TETRAXON TRICHITE TYLASTER
SPICY RACY SEXY GAMEY NUTTY SWEET SPICED GINGERY FRAGRANT SPICEFUL
SPIDER BUG COB ARAIN ATTID COBBE COPPE LOPPE NANCY TAINT ANANSI ARRAND EPEIRA HUNTER KATIPO WEAVER ARANEID CREEPER DRASSID JAYHAWK KNOPPIE POKOMOO RETIARY SERPENT SKILLET SOLDIER SPINNER ARACHNID ATTERCOP CTENIZID DICTYNID ETTERCAP KARAKURT ORBITELE PHALANGY PHOLCOID SALTICID SOLPUGID TELARIAN ULOBORID VENANTES WANDERER TARANTULA
SPIDER CRAB MAIAN MAIID
SPIDERFLOWER QUARESMA
SPIDER MONKEY SAJOU COAITA SAPAJOU
SPIDERWORT TRINITY
SPIELER BARKER
SPIGOT TAP SPILE DOSSIL DOZZLE STOPCOCK
SPIKE GAD BROB PICK PIKE PILE SPUR TINE PITON ROUGH SPEAR MOOTER PRITCH SPADIX SPIKER TENTER ALICOLE GADLING PRICKER PRICKET TRENAIL TURNPIN SPIKELET STROBILE WHEATEAR
(— OF CEREAL) EAR
(BRACTED —) AMENT
(DRIED —S) CANNABIS
SPIKED SPICATE SPINDLED
SPIKELET CHAT ALICOLE LOCUSTA SPICULE
SPIKENARD PHU NARD ARALIA SUMBUL ARALIAD IVYWORT SPIGNET SPIGNUT
SPILE TAP SPILL FOREPOLE
SPILL LET DRIP SHED SLOP FLOSH SCALE SPILE SQUAB STAVE JIRBLE PURLER SLATTER SLOBBER TURNOVER
(— FOR LIGHTING PIPES) FIDIBUS
SPIN CUT BIRL DRAW GYRE HURL PIRL PURL SCREW SPONE TWIST WEAVE WHIRL FOLLOW GYRATE VRILLE WAMBLE TWIZZLE TEETOTUM
(— AND MAKE HUM) BUM
(— AROUND) SWING
(— ON BASEBALL) STUFF
(— ON BILLIARD BALL) SIDE
(— OUT) SHOOT
(— SILK) THROW
(— SMOOTHLY) SLEEP
(— UNEVENLY) TWITTER
SPINACH SAVOY EPINARD OLITORY POTHERB

SPINAL CORD AXION NUCHA MYELON
(WHITE MATTER OF —) ALBA NUKE
SPINDLE PIN AXLE HASP SPIT STEM STUD ARBOR FLOAT QUILL SPIKE SPILL VERGE BOBBIN BROACH CANNON FUSEAU BOLSTER MANDREL SPINNEL TRENDLE WHARROW
(AXLE —) ARM
(FOURTH OF —) HASP
(ONE 24TH OF —) HEER
SPINDLE TREE GAITER DOGWOOD PEGWOOD EUONYMUS
SPINDLING SPEARY SPINDLY SPIRLIE
SPINDLY LEGGY PULING
SPINE HORN PIKE PILE SETA SPUR CHINE PRICK QUILL SPEAR SPIKE SPINA THORN ACUMEN CHAETA RACHIS ACANTHA ACICULA FULCRUM GLOCHIS PAXILLA PRICKER PRICKLE ROSTRUM SPINULE ACICULUM BACKBONE ILLICIUM PAXILLUS PELELITH SPICULUM SPINELET
(— OF SURGEON FISH) TUCK
(CURVATURE OF —) LORDOSIS
SPINEL BALAS CANDITE ESPINEL VERMEIL PICOTITE SPINELLE
SPINELESS SLAVISH
SPINET ESPINET GIRAFFE OCTAVINA SOURDINE VIRGINAL
SPINNERET GALEA MAMMULA SPINNER
SPINNING LANIFICE
(— WEB) TELARIAN
SPINNING JENNY MULE JENNY
SPINNING MULE IRONMAN
SPINNING WHEEL TURN CHARKHA CHURRUCK
SPINSTER TABBY VIRGIN
SPINULE(PL.) CTENII
SPINY PICKED THORNY
SPINY OYSTER SPONDYLE
SPINY RAT OCTODONT
SPIRACLE STOMA STIGMA BLOWHOLE
SPIRAEA MAY ROSACEAN
SPIRAL COIL CURL GYRE SPIN SCREW SNARE SPIRE BUTTON GURGES LITUUS SCREWY SCROLL SPIRED TWIRLY VOLUTE HELICAL ROLLING SPIROID STROPHE WINDING WREATHY GYROIDAL HELICINE HELICOID
SPIRANT VAU WAW HISS OPEN DURATIVE
SPIRANTHES IBIDIUM
SPIRE SHAFT SIKAR SPEAR TAPER TOLLY BROACH FLECHE PRICKET SHIKARA SIKHARA SPIRALE SPIRELET
SPIRE-BEARER SPIRIFER
SPIREME SKEAN SKEIN
SPIRIT GO FLY NAG VIM AITU AKUA ALMA ATUA BRIO DASH DOOK ELAN FIRE GALL GIMP HYLE JINN LIFE MARC MARE MIND MOOD SOUL

TONE ZEMI ZING AGIEL ARDOR
ARIEL ASURA AZOTH CHEER DEMON
DHOUL DJINN DOBBY ETHOS FLING
GEIST GHOST GORIC GUACA HAUNT
HEART HOLDA HUACA JINNI LARVA
NUMEN PLUCK POWER PRETA
RALPH SAINT SHADE SHRAB SPOOK
SPUNK VERVE ASTRAL ASUANG
BOTTOM BREATH CHULPA CCURIL
DAEMON ESPRIT FAINTS FYLGJA
GENIUS GINGER INWARD KOBOLD
LESHEY METTLE MORALE ORISHA
PNEUMA PYTHON SPRAWL SPRITE
TAFFIA WRAITH ALCOHOL BRAVERY
CONTROL CORDIAL COURAGE
ENTRAIN EUDEMON KNOCKER
MANITOU PISACHI PURUSHA
RAPPIST SMEDDUM STOMACH
CALVADOS ERDGEIST FAMILIAR
FOLLETTO PHANTASM SPIRACLE
SPIRITUS
(— DWELLING IN JEWEL) AZOTH
(— DWELLING IN MINES) KNOCKER
(— HAUNTING PRINTING HOUSES)
RALPH
(— OF DEAD) CHINDI CHINDEE
(— OF DEATH) CHULPA
(— OF DECEASED) AKH
(— OF FERTILITY) YAKSA YAKSHA
YAKSHI
(— OF HOSTILITY) ANIMUS
(— OF LOYALTY) PIETAS
(— OF MAN) AKH
**(— OF ONE WHO HAS MET VIOLENT
DEATH)** PISACHI
(— OF PHYSICAL HEART) AB
(— OF TRAGEDY) COTHURN
(— OF UNBAPTIZED BABE) TARAN
(— WHICH ACTUATES CUSTOMS)
ETHOS
(—S OF LOWER WORLD) INFERI
(—S OF THE DEAD) MANES
(ANCESTRAL —) ANITO KATCHINA
(ARDENT —) RAK RACK ARRACK
(ASTRAL —) AGIEL ASTRAL JOPHIEL
UUCHATON
(AVENGING —) FURY ALECTO
ALASTOR MEGAERA
(COMBATIVE —) SWORD
(DISEMBODIED —) KUEI KWEI SOUL
GHOST LARVA SHADE ASUANG
SPECTER SPECTRE
(DIVINE —) ISVARA ISHVARA
(EARTH —) ERDGEIST
(EFFULGENT —S) ARDORS
(EMANCIPATED —) MUKTATMA
(EVIL —) DEV HAG IMP OKI BAKA
BENG BOKO BOLL DEVA DUSE
MARA OKEE ASURA BUGAN DAEVA
DEMON DEVIL JUMBY OTKON
DAITYA DIBBUK DYBBUK LILITH
AHRIMAN BUGGANE CASZIEL
INCUBUS KANAIMA SHAITAN
SHEITAN SKOOKUM WINDIGO
ASMODEUS BAALPEOR BEELPEOR
HOBOMOCO
(FAMILIAR —) FLY GENIUS HARPIER
(FEMALE —) DUFFY DUPPY DUSIO
HOLDA UNDINE BANSHEE ATAENSIC

BABAJAGA BELFAGOR BELFAZOR
(FIGHTING —) DEVIL
(FOREST —) MIMING
(FULL OF —) CRANK
(FULL OF —S) BRAG
(GOOD —) EUDEMON
(GOVERNING —) ANIMUS
(GUARDIAN —) ANGEL TOTEM
FYLGJA NAGUAL
(HIGH —) GINGER COURAGE
(HIGH —S) CREST GAIETY HEYDAY
ELATION
(HOSTILE —S) LEMURES
(HOUSEHOLD —S) LARES PENATES
(HUMAN —) JIVATMA
(IMPISH —) PO
(IMPURE —) FAINTS
(IN VIGOROUS —S) FIERCE
(LOW —S) DUMP BLUES DISMALS
(MALEVOLENT —) BHUT GORIC
LARVA
(MALICIOUS —) DOBBY
(MALIGNANT —) IMP KER GYRE
DEMON
(MANLY —) SPLEEN
(MISCHIEVOUS —) KOBOLD
TIKOLOSH
(MOUNTAIN —) RUBEZAHL
(MOVING —) SOUL
(MUSICAL —) BRIO
(NATURE —) NAT
(PARTY —) FACTION
(REFINED —) ELIXIR
(RESOLUTE —) SPRAWL
(SEA —) TANGIE
(SOOTHSAYING —) PYTHON
(SUPERNATURAL —) FAMILIAR
(SYLVAN —) LESHY SYLVAN
(TRICKSY —) ARIEL
(TUTELARY —S) DIS LARES
(VITAL —) TUCK
(VOLATILE —) ESSENCE
(WATER —) ARIEL KELPY UNDINE
(WICKED —) IMP THURSE
(PL.) IGIGI DAUBER
SPIRITED BRAG FELL RACY TALL
BEANY BIRKY CRANK EAGER FIERY
FLUSH KEDGE KINKY LIFEY SASSY
SEEDY SMART SPICY VIVID AUDACE
FIERCE GINGER LIVELY METTLE
PLUCKY SKEIGH SPRUCE SPUNKY
VIVACE ANIMATO DASHING
FORWARD HUMMING NERVOUS
PEPPERY SPIRITY DESIROUS
FRAMPOLD GENEROUS PHRAMPEL
SLASHING STOMACHY VASCULAR
SPIRITEDLY GAMELY
SPIRITLESS DEAD MEAN MEEK TAME
AMORT FAINT MILKY MUSTY SEEDY
SOGGY VAPID DREEPY FLASHY
LEADEN SODDEN SOFTLY WOODEN
INSIPID LANGUID FECKLESS
FLAGGING LISTLESS THEWLESS
SPIRITLESSLY DAVIELY
SPIRITLIKE ETHEREAL
SPIRITS LACE RAKI HOOCH MANES
FETTLE PECKER FEATHER LEMURES
WAIPIRO
SPIRITUAL ABOVE DEVOUT INWARD

MISTLY GHOSTLY CHURCHLY
INTERNAL NUMINOUS SUPERIOR
(— LEADER) ZADDIK
SPIRITUALISM SPOOKISM
SPIRITUALITY HEAVEN
SPIRITUALIZE REFINE
SPIRITUOUS HARD
SPIROCHETE BORRELIA
SPIT FUFF RACK FROTH REACH
SPAWL BROACH SPITTLE SANDSPIT
SPITTING
SPITE ENVY ONDE DEPIT LIVOR
PIQUE VENOM MALICE MAUGRE
RANCOR SPLEEN DESPITE AMBITION
SPITEFUL CATTY NEBBY SNAKY
ELVISH SULLEN WANTON CATTISH
ENVIOUS PEEVISH SNAKISH VICIOUS
WASPISH CANKERED KNAPPISH
VENOMOUS
SPITFIRE PEPPERBOX
SPITTING SNAKE RINGHALS
SPITTLE SPIT SPAWL SPUTUM
SLOBBER
SPITTOON GABOON PIGDAN
SPITBOX CRACHOIR CUSPIDOR
SPLANCHNIC VISCERAL
SPLASH JAW LAP DASH GLOB GOUT
JAUP LOSH LUSH SKIT SOSS SPAT
WASH BLASH FLASH FLICK FLOOD
FLOSH PLASH PLOUT QUASH SKIRP
SLART SLASH SLOSH SLUSH SQUAT
SWILK BEDASH DABBLE DOLLOP
JABBLE LABBER PLATCH SLUNGE
SOZZLE SPLOSH SPRENT SQUIRT
SPATTER SPIRTLE SPLODGE
SPLURGE SWATTER SPLAIRGE
SPLATHER SPLATTER SPLOTHER
SPLUTHER SPLUTTER
(— OF COLOR) GOUT
(SLIGHT —) GILP
SPLASHBOARD FENDER SPLASHER
SPLASHING SWASH FLASHY JABBLE
DASHING SPATTER SPLUTTER
SWASHING
SPLASHY BLASHY SLOPPY SPRAWLY
SPLATTER DASH BLASH SPLAIRGE
SPLAY FLAN
SPLAYFOOT FLATFOOT
SPLEEN BILE LIEN MELT MILT
STOMACH
SPLEENY PEEVISH
SPLENDID GAY BRAW FINE RIAL
BRAVE GRAND JOLLY NOBLE
PROUD REGAL ROYAL SHEEN
SHOWY STOUT WALLY WLONK
CANDID COSTLY SIGHTY SOLEMN
SPIFFY SUPERB ELEGANT GALLANT
SHINING SUBLIME TEARING
BARONIAL CHAMPION CLINKING
GLORIOUS GORGEOUS MAJESTIC
ORGULOUS RATTLING SLASHING
STUNNING
(CHEAPLY —) TINNY
SPLENDIDLY FINE FINELY SPROWSY
SPLENDOR SUN UMA GITE LUXE
POMP BLAZE GLARE GLEAM GLORY
SHEEN SHINE FULGOR LUSTER
LUSTRE PARADE RUFFLE CLARITY
DISPLAY JOLLITY GRANDEUR

RADIANCE SUMPTURE

SPLENETIC SULLEN VAPORY PEEVISH

SPLENIC LIENAL

SPLICE FOOT JOIN SCAB PIECE SCARE SKELB CROTCH PIECEN SPLICING

SPLICER STRAPPER

SPLINE FIN FEATHER

SPLINT SCOB FANON MATCH SPELK SPELL TASSE SPLENT THOMAS CALIPER SPLINTER
(— FOR FRACTURE) JUNK

SPLINTER BROOM BURST PURSE SHAKE SHIDE SHIVE SKELB SLICE SPAIL SPALE SPALT SPEEL SPELK SPELL SPILE SPILL SPLIT SPOON SLIVER SPLEET SPLINT FLINDER SHATTER SLITHER SPLITTER

SPLINTERY SKELVY

SPLINTWOOD ALBURNUM

SPLIT AX AXE CUT RIT BUCK CHAP CONE DUNT GAIG MALL MAUL REND RENT RIFT RIVE SKAG SLAT TEAR BREAK CHECK CHINE SHAKE SHEAR SLENT SLIVE SMASH SPALD SPLAT CLEAVE CLOVEN CREASE DIVIDE FLAGGY FLERRY SCHISM SPRING SUNDER BIVALVE SHATTER SLITHER CREVASSE SCISSION SCISSURE SPLINTER
(— FISH) SCROD
(— IN BOWLING) BEDPOSTS
(— OFF) SPALL SPAWL SCREEVED
(— TICKET) SCRATCH

SPLITTERMAN BOLTER

SPLITTING FLAGGY FISSION SCISSION
(PL.) FILMS

SPLOTCH DAB BLOB DASH HALO SPOT FLICK SMUDGE SPECKLE SPLATCH SPLURGE

SPLURGE BINGE SPRAY SPREE SPLASH

SPLUTTER FUFF GLUTTER SPATTER SPUTTER SPLOTHER

SPODOPTERA LAPHYGMA

SPODUMENE KUNZITE TRIPHANE

SPOIL MAR ROT BLOT BOOT COOK DAZE FANG FOIL FRAB GAIN KILL MANK PELF PREY ADDLE BITCH BLEND BOOTY BOTCH CROSS DECAY QUAIL QUEER SHEND SPILL STAIN STRIP TOUCH WALLY COOPER CORPSE CURDLE DEFACE DEFORM FORAGE INJURE MANGLE RAVAGE TIDDLE BEDEVIL BLEMISH CONNACH CORRUMP CORRUPT ESTREPE INDULGE MULLOCK PILLAGE PLUNDER SPOLIUM TARNISH VIOLATE BANKRUPT CONFOUND DISGRACE MISGUIDE SPOLIATE

SPOILED BAD BLOWN DAZED MUSTY CADISH STICKIT BRATTISH
(EASILY —) GINGER

SPOILER HARROWER

SPOILFIVE MAW

SPOILS BAG LOOT SKIN SWAG

BOOTY FORAY SPOLIA PILLAGE PLUNDER

SPOILSPORT NARK LETGAME

SPOILT MARDY

SPOKE RUNG QUOTH SPACK SPAKE LOWDER SPONDIL SPONDYL

SPOKEN ORAL SAID VERBAL

SPOKESMAN MOUTH HERALD PROPHET SPEAKER TRUMPET

SPOLIATION SPOIL RAPINE PILLAGE PLUNDER SPOILING

SPONGE BOT FORM MUMP POLE SILK SORN SWAB ASCON CADGE GRASS LUFFA SCAFF SHARK SHIRK SYCON ASCULA COSHER LEUCON LOOFAH MALKIN MOPPET RHAGON ROLLER YELLOW BADIAGA BLEEDER GELFOAM RADIATE SCOURER SCRUNGE SYCONID ZIMOCCA DEADBEAT HARDHEAD HEDGEHOG MANDRUKA OLYNTHUS REDBEARD SILICEAN SPHERIDA SUBERITE ZOOPHYTE
(YOUNG —) SEEDLING

SPONGER BOT TRAMP SPONGE SCAMBLER SMOOTHER

SPONGINESS FOZINESS

SPONGING TRENCHER

SPONGY FOZY FUZZY QUAGGY

SPONSOR COACH GOSSIP SURETY WITNESS
(— AT BAPTISM) HEAVE

SPONSORSHIP EGIS AEGIS

SPONTANEOUS FREE CARELESS FREEWILL UNTAUGHT

SPONTANEOUSLY KINDLY SELFLY

SPOOK GYRE GHOST HAUNT SCARE

SPOOL COB COP REEL QUILL SPILL SPULE TWEEL TWILL BOBBIN BROACH CHEESE COPPIN CARRIER
(— FOR NETS) GURDY

SPOON HORN CUTTY LABIS SHELL COCHLEA JUMBLER MUDDLER SKIMMER SPINNER STIRRER BARSPOON COCHLEAR GOBSTICK
(EUCHARISTIC —) LABIS
(FISHING —) TROLL
(LONG-HANDLED —) LADLE
(SKIMMING —) LINGEL SKIMMER
(SNUFF —) PEN

SPOONBILL AJAJA SPOONY POPELER CICONIID

SPOON-SHAPED COCHLEAR SPATULAR

SPOOR SIGN SPUR PISTE

SPORADIC POPPING ISOLATED

SPORANGIUM THECA OOTHECA

SPORE CYST SEED SPORID AGAMETE AKINETE BISPORE ISOLATE SPORULE SWARMER CONIDIUM GONIDIUM

SPOROCYST ZOOCYST SPOROSAC

SPORT FUN GIG KID MUM RIE RUX SEE TOY ALSO GAME GAUD GLEE JEST JOKE LAKE LARK PLAY PLOY RAGE TAIT BREAK DALLY DROLL FREAK MIRTH FROLIC LAUGHS POPJOY RACING SHIKAR SKIING BOATING CAMOGIE DISPORT

DUCKING FOWLING MARLOCK PASTIME ROLLICK ROUNDER SAILING SPANIEL FALCONRY PLEASURE
(— OF HAWKING) RIVER
(BOISTEROUS —) HIJINKS
(JAPANESE —) KENDO
(ROUGH —) ROMP
(WATER —S) NAUTICS AQUATICS

SPORTING VARMINT SPORTIVE

SPORTIVE GAY TAIT LARKY MERRY FRISKY JOCUND LIVELY LUSORY TOYFUL TOYING WANTON COLTISH FESTIVE GAMEFUL JESTING JOCULAR PLAYFUL TOYSOME TRICKSY WAGGISH FROLICKY GAMESOME PLAYSOME PLEASANT SPORTFUL

SPORTIVENESS HELL KNAVERY

SPORTSMAN SPORT ATHLETE SHIKARI

SPORTSMANLIKE CLEAN SPORTY

SPORTY FLASH RORTY FLASHY RAKISH

SPORULE GRANULE

SPOT BIT DAB PIP WEM BLOT CHUB DIRT DRAB FLAW GALL MOIL MOLE PLOT SCAM SITE SKIP SLUR SMUT SOIL SPAT TICK AMPER BLACK CLOUD FLECK GARLE GOODY GUTTA HATCH JIMMY MACLE PATCH PLACE PLECK POINT ROACH SMEAR SPLAT STAIN SULLY TACHE TAINT WHERE BLANCH BLOTCH DAPPLE FOGDOG GERATE MACULE MAZUCA MOTTLE SMUDGE SMUTCH SPLECK STIGMA BLEMISH CHARBON CHECKER FLECKER FRECKLE GUTTULA MASOOKA OCELLUS OLDWIFE SMATTER SMITTER SPATTER SPECKLE SPLOTCH SPOTTLE STATION STIPPLE TERRAIN FENESTRA LOCALITY MACULATE PUNCTULE SPARKLET SPRINKLE
(— A SHIELD) GERATE
(— IN CLOTH) YAW
(— IN MINERAL) MACLE
(— IN PAPER) SHINER
(— IN SAW BLADE) BLOB
(— IN STEEL) STAR
(— IN WOOD) WEM
(— IN YARN) MOTE
(— OF INK) MONK
(— OF PAINT) DAUB
(— OF QUICKSAND) SUCKHOLE
(— ON CAT'S FACE) LAVALIER
(— ON CAT) BUTTON
(— ON EGG) EYE
(— ON FINGERNAIL) GIFT
(— ON FOREHEAD) TILAK TILAKA
(— ON HAWK) GOUT
(— ON HORSE) RACE SNIP STAR RACHE
(— ON HORSES'S TOOTH) CHARBON
(— ON INSECT WINGS) BULLA
(— ON MOTH'S WINGS) FENESTRA
(— ON PLAYING CARD) PIP
(— ON SUN) FACULA GRANULE SUNSPOT

(**—S IN BOOKS**) FOXING
(**BARREN —**) GALL
(**BLIND —**) SCOTOMA SCOTISIS
(**BROWN —**) SPRAIN SPRAING
(**CRUSTY —**) SCAB
(**ESSENTIAL —**) EYE
(**FERTILE —**) OASIS
(**FIRM — IN BOG**) HAG
(**GREEN — IN VALLEY**) HAW
(**INFLAMED —**) AMPER
(**LEAF —**) TIKKA BLACKARM
(**LIVER —S**) CHLOASMA
(**LIVID —**) TOKEN
(**LOW —**) DIP SWAMP HOLLOW
(**RED —**) FLEABITE
(**RETIRED —**) SHADE
(**ROUGH — IN WOVEN GOODS**) FAG
(**SCABBY —**) SCALD
(**SKIN —**) MOLE BLISTER FRECKLE
LENTIGO
(**SMALL —**) DOT PLECK STIGMA
LUNULET SPARKLET
(**SOILED —**) SLOP
(**SORE —**) BUBU BOTCH
(**SWAMPY —**) FLAM
(**TIGHT —**) JAM JACKPOT
(**WEAK —**) GALL HOLE CHINK NERVE
(**WORN —**) FRAY FRET
(**PL.**) MOONING
SPOTLESS FAIR PURE WEMLESS
INNOCENT
SPOTLIGHT ARC SPOT DEUCE
SPOTTED MARLY SCOVY SHELD
CALICO FIGGED HAWKED MACLED
MAILED MARLED MIRLED SPOTTY
TICKED BRACKET BROOKED
FINCHED MOTTLED PARDINE
SPARKED SPECKED SPECKLY
TIGROID FRECKLED LITURATE
MACULOSE SPECKLED STIPPLED
SPOTTED EAGLE RAY MILLER
OBISPO
SPOTTED FLYCATCHER COBWEB
RAFTER WALLBIRD
SPOTTED GUM EUCALYPT
SPOTTED JEWFISH GUASA
SPOTTED SANDPIPER TIPUP
TILTUP CREEKER TIPTAIL
SPOTTED SPURGE DOVEWEED
SPOTTED WINTERGREEN
RATSBANE
SPOTTED WOODPECKER WITWALL
SPOTTER DOTTER
SPOTTY MEALY PATCHY PLATTY
SCABBY SPOTTED
SPOUSE EX MAKE WIFE BRIDE
MATCH PARTY FELLOW MARROW
CONSORT ESPOUSE HUSBAND
SPOUT JET LIP BEAK DALE GEAT
GUSH NOSE SHOE SPILE SPUME
SPURT NOZZLE RIGGOT SPLOIT
SPROUT STRONE STROUP BUBBLER
FOUNTAIN GARGOYLE
(**RAIN —**) RONE
SPOUTER VAPORER
SPOUTING BLOW SALIENT
SPRAG TRAILER
SPRAGGER SCOTCHER
SPRAIN RICK CHINK STAVE THRAW

THROW WRAMP WREST WRICK
STRAIN WRENCH STREMMA
SPRAT SMY SPRET SPRIT GARVIE
ALFIONE GARVOCK
(**—S CAUGHT EARLY IN SEASON**)
DROVE
SPRAWL LOLL TAVE SPURL SCRAWL
GRABBLE SCAMBLE SPARTLE
SPELDER SCRAMBLE SPRADDLE
SPRANGLE STRADDLE
SPRAWLING SPRANGLY
SPRAY FOG HOSE SCUD SPRY STEW
SPREE STOUR SWISH TRAIL TWIST
SHOWER SPARGE SPLASH SPRANG
SPRITZ CURTAIN SPAIRGE SYRINGE
INHALANT SPRANGLE
(**— FROM SMALL WAVES**) LIPPER
(**— MASH**) SPARGE
(**— OF GEMS**) AIGRETTE
(**REDUCE TO —**) NEBULIZE
SPREAD BED FAN LAY RUN COAT
DRAW FLUE SPAN TELD TUCK VEIN
WALK APPLY CLEAM CREEP FLARE
KILIM PASTE SCALE SLICE SPEND
SPLAT SPLAY STALK STREW WIDEN
BUTTER EXTEND FLANGE LARDER
LAYOUT MANTLE SETOUT THRUST
UNFOLD UNFURL BROADEN
CANVASS DIFFUSE DISPLAY DISTEND
EXPANSE EXPLAIN FEATHER
OPENING SCATTER STRETCH
DIASPORA DISPENSE DISPERSE
HUMIFUSE INCREASE MULTIPLY
SPLATHER STRAGGLE
(**— ABROAD**) TOOT DELATE SPRING
DIVULGE EMANATE
(**— APART**) GAPE
(**— AS GOSSIP**) BUZZ
(**— BY REPORT**) BLOW NOISE
NORATE
(**— DEFAMATION**) LIBEL
(**— FOR DRYING**) TED
(**— INTO**) INVADE
(**— LIKE GRAIN**) FLOOR
(**— NEWS**) HORN
(**— ON THICK**) COUCH SLATHER
(**— OUT**) FAN FLOW OPEN SPAN
ASPAR BREDE SPLAT SPLAY SPRAY
EXPAND FLANGE FRINGE MANTLE
OUTLAY SPRAWL UNLOCK DIFFUSE
DISPAND DISTENT EXPLAIN FEATHER
DIFFUSED SPRADDLE SPRANGLE
STRAGGLY
(**— OUTWARD**) FLARE
(**— OVER**) LAP DASH COVER
SUFFUSE
(**— PAINT**) KNIFE
(**— THINLY**) BRAY DRIVE TOUCH
SCANTY
(**— TO THE WIND**) SET
(**— TO**) CATCH
(**EVENLY —**) SUANT
(**TAPESTRY-WOVEN —**) KILIM
SPREADER PLOW PLOUGH SANDER
SPREADING FLAN BUSHY FLANGE
PATENT ASPREAD DIFFUSE FLARING
SPRAYEY PATULENT PATULOUS
SPRANGLY
(**— OF LIGHT**) HALATION

(**— RAPIDLY**) RUNNING
(**NOT —**) ERECT
(**SLOW —**) CREEPAGE
SPREE BAT BUM JAG BLOW BUST
GELL RANT SOAK TEAR TIME TOOT
BEANO BINGE BOOZE BURST DRINK
DRUNK SOUSE SPRAY BENDER
BUSTER HOORAY HURRAH RANDAN
RANTAN BLOWOFF JAMBOREE
WINGDING
SPRIG POINT
(**—S FOR MOURNING**) CYPRESS
SPRIGGER STRIPPER
SPRIGHTLINESS GAIETY AIRINESS
ALACRITY BUOYANCY VIVACITY
SPRIGHTLY GAY TID AIRY GNIB
PERT WARM ALIVE BRISK CANTY
CRISP DESTO MERRY QUICK
ALEGER JAUNTY LIVELY SPANKY
WIMBLE CHIPPER DELIVER JOCULAR
SPARKLY LIFESOME PLEASANT
SPRING EN AIN BUG EYE FLY HOP
JET OJO URN VER WAX BATH BOLT
BOUT BUCK DART FLOW FONT
GEON HAIR HEAD JUMP KELD LEAP
PERT RISE SEEP SKIP SOAK STEM
URNA WALM WARE WELL WIND
ARISE BOUND DANCE FLIRT FOUNT
FRESH GIHON GLENT GRASS ISSUE
LYMPH PRIME QUELL SALLY SOURD
SPEND SPOUT START STEND SURGE
THROW VAULT BOUNCE CHARCO
DERIVE GAMBOL GEYSER JUMPER
LOCKET ORIGIN PIRENE RESORT
RESULT SILOAM SOURCE SPRINT
VENERO BUDTIME EMANATE
ESTUARY FLOUNCE GAMBADO
PROCEED REBOUND WRAPPER
BACKSTAY BANDUSIA CASTALIA
FOUNTAIN SPANGHEW
(**— AWKWARDLY**) KEVEL
(**— BACK**) RECOIL RESULT RETORT
REBOUND
(**— DOWN**) ALIGHT
(**— FORWARD**) LAUNCH
(**— FROM**) DESCEND
(**— OF THE YEAR**) VER VOAR
(**— ON SHEARS**) BACKSTAY
(**— SEASON**) APRIL GRASS BUDTIME
(**— SUDDENLY**) FLY BOUNCE
(**— TO FASTEN NECKLACE**) LOCKET
(**— UP**) ARISE SHOOT SPROUT
BURGEON UPSPRING
(**BOILING —**) TUBIG
(**CARRIAGE —**) ROBBIN
(**ERUPTIVE —**) WALM GEYSER
(**GUSHING —**) CHARCO
(**HOT —**) SPRUDEL
(**INTERMITTENT —S**) GIPSIES
GYPSIES
(**LAND —**) LAVANT
(**MECHANICAL —**) RESORT RESSORT
(**MINERAL —**) SPA
(**SALT —**) LICK SALINE
(**WARM —S**) THERMAE
(**WATCH —**) SLEEVE
SPRING BEAUTY LETTUCE
SPRINGBOARD BATULE TREMPLIN
SPRINGBOK GAZELLE SPRINGER

SPRING CHAPLET JAMMER
SPRINGILY BOUNCILY SPONGILY
SPRINGINESS GIVE LIFE
SPRINGING LAUNCH SALIENT
(— **BACK**) RESULT ELASTIC
(— **FROM STEPS**) GRADY
SPRINGLIKE VERNAL
SPRING ORANGE STYRAX
SPRINGTAIL PODURA FURCULA
PODURID SKIPTAIL
SPRINGTIME VER GERMINAL
SPRINGY WHIPPY ELASTIC FLEXIBLE
SPRINKLE ASH DAG DEG BLOW
DAMP SHED SPIT FLASH SHAKE
SPURT WATER BEDROP DABBLE
POUNCE SPARGE SPRENT SPRINK
SQUIRT ARROUSE ASPERGE
ASPERSE DRIZZLE RANTIZE
SCATTER SKINKLE SKITTER SPAIRGE
SPARKLE SPARPLE SPATTER
SPATTLE SPERPLE SPURTLE
DISPUNGE INTERSOW SPITTING
SPRINGLE STRINKLE
(— **IN BAPTISM**) RANTIZE
(— **OF RAIN**) SPIT
(— **SEED**) SPRAIN
(— **TOBACCO**) BLOW
(— **WITH FLOUR**) DREDGE
(— **WITH POWDER**) DUST
(— **WITH SALT**) CORN
(— **WITH SAND**) SAND
SPRINKLED SEEDED SPRENT
(— **OVER**) BESPRENT
SPRINKLER SPARGER SPRAYER
WATERER DAMPENER STRINKLE
SPRINKLING SEME LACING SPARGE
STRANK RANTISM STIPPLE
STOURING
(— **OF PEOPLE**) SALT
SPRINT BICKER SPRENT SPRUNT
SPRITE AND ELF HOB PUG SEE ALSO
PIXY PUCK BUCCA DOBBY FAIRY
HOLDA PIXIE GOBLIN PILWIZ SPIRIT
SPOORN UMBRIEL COLTPIXY
GLAISTIG WATERMAN
(**WATER** —) NIX NECK NIXIE NICKER
SPRITELY WIMBLE
SPROCKET WHELP
SPROUT BUD PUT BROD CHIT CHUN
CION DRAW TOOT CATCH CHICK
SCUTE SHOOT SPEAR SPIRE SPRIT
SPURT BRAIRD GERMEN RATOON
SIRING STOVEN TELLER TILLER
BURGEON COPPICE SPURTER
TENDRON
(— **OF BARLEY**) TAIL
(**FIRST** —**S**) BREER BRAIRD BREIRD
(**STUMP** —) TILLER
SPRUCE GIM DEFT JIMP NEAT POSH
SMUG SPRY TRIG TRIM BRISK
COMPT CRISP DINKY FRESH JEMMY
JIMMY NATTY SLICK SMART SMIRK
SPIFF SPRIG DAPPER PICKED
SPONGE SPRUNT SPRUSH FINICAL
FOPPISH SMARTEN SMICKER
SPRUNNY EPINETTE TITIVATE
SPRUE RUNNER PSILOSIS
SPRUER GATER
SPRY AGILE BRISK QUICK NIMBLE

SPUD BARKER PADDLE SPUDDER
SPUME EST BEES FOAM FROTH
YEAST
SPUNK GETUP SPRAWL SMEDDUM
SPUR ARM GAD GIG EDGE GAFF
GOAD KNAG MOVE STUD TANG
DRIVE PRICK PRONG ROWEL SPURN
BROACH CALCAR DIGGER EXCITE
FOMENT GAFFLE GRIFFE INCITE
MOTIVE OFFSET RIPPON SICKLE
SPERON WEAPON BICYCLE
GABLOCK INCITER LORMERY
SCRATCH COCKSPUR GAVELOCK
(— **OF COCK**) HEEL
(— **ON HORSESHOE**) CALK
(—**S OF COCK**) WEAPON
SPURGE BALSAM INTISY SUNWEED
CATEPUCE DOVEWEED FLUXWEED
MILKBUSH MILKWEED TITHYMAL
WARTWEED WARTWORT
SPURIOUS DOG FAKE SHAM BOGUS
FUNNY QUEER SHICE SNIDE NOTHAL
PSEUDO BASTARD NOTHOUS
SYNDIETIC
SPURN FOOT TACK SCORN REJECT
CONSPUE CONTEMN DECLINE
DESPISE DISDAIN
SPURRY YARR FRANK COWQUAKE
SANDWEED
SPURT JET GILP GIRD GOUT JAUP
SPAR SPIN BURST CHIRT FLASH
PULSE SALLY SPOUT GEYSER
RANDOM SPLURT SPRING SPROUT
SQUIRT SPATTER
SPUTTER SPIT FIZZLE SOTTER
SPATTER SPLUTTER
SPUTUM SPIT
SPY FLY PRY ESPY NARK NOSE STAG
TOOT TOUT WAIT WORM LOWER
PERDU PLANT SCOUT SNEAP SPIAL
SPION WATCH BEAGLE BEHOLD
DESCRY GAYCAT MOUTON PEEPER
PERDUE SEARCH SHADOW SPIRAL
TOUTER WAITER EXAMINE LURCHER
OTACUST SMELLER SPOTTER
WATCHER DISCOVER EMISSARY
HIRCARRA MOUCHARD
(— **ON RACEHORSES**) TOUT
(— **UPON**) LAY
(**PLANTED** —) STOOGE
(**POLICE** —) SETTER
SPYBOAT VEDET VEDETTE
SQUAB PIPER SQUABBY SQUEAKER
SQUEALER SQUILGEE
SQUABBLE MUSS BRAWL SCRAP
BICKER JANGLE SQUALL BOBBERY
BRABBLE BRANGLE CONTEND
PRABBLE QUARREL SWABBLE
SQUAD CREW DECURY TWENTY
PLATOON
(— **OF DETECTIVES**) HOMICIDE
SQUADRON SOTNIA SQUADER
SQUALID DINGY DIRTY MANGY
SEEDY FILTHY FROWZY SCABROUS
SQUALL DROW FRET GUST MEWL
WAUL BARAT FRESH PERRY SKELP
BAYAMO FLURRY SQUAWK
BORASCA SUMATRA TORNADO
BORASQUE CHUBASCO

SQUALOR DIRT
SQUAMA ALULA TEGULA
SQUANDER SOT BLOW BLUE BURN
GAME LASH WARE SPEND SPILL
SPORT WASTE LAVISH MAFFLE
MUDDLE PADDLE PALTER PERISH
TIPPLE CONSUME DEBAUCH
DEBOISE DISPEND PROFUSE
SCATTER SKITTLE SLATHER
SWATTER EMBEZZLE MISSPEND
SQUATTER
SQUANDERER PRODIGAL
SQUANDERING WASTEFUL
SQUARE FIX EDGE EVEN FOUR FULL
POST QUAD SUIT AGREE CHECK
CROSS FRAME HUNKY PLACE PLAIN
PLAZA SUPER BLOCKY DINKUM
ISAGON PIAZZA QUARRY ZENZIC
ZOCALO CARREAU CHECKER
COMMONS EMERALD UPRIGHT
QUADRANT QUADRATE SQUADRON
TETRAGON
(— **A STONE**) PITCH
(— **FOR BOWLING SCORE**) FRAME
(— **OF CANVAS**) SKATE
(— **OF CLOTH**) PANE
(— **OF DOUGH**) KNISH
(— **OF FRAMING**) PAN
(— **OF GLASS**) QUARREL
(— **OF TURF**) DIVOT QUADREL
(— **OFF**) BUTT
(— **ON BILLIARD TABLE**) CROTCH
(— **ON CHESSBOARD**) HOUSE POINT
(**BUILDINGS FORMING** —) INSULA
(**CARPENTER'S** —) NORMA
(**LINEN** —) SUDARIUM
(**PATTERN OF** —**S**) DAMIER
(**WOVEN** —) SINKER
SQUARED HEWN QUARTO SQUARE
SQUARE DANCE TUCKER
SQUARE-DEALING WHITE
SQUARELY BUNG FAIR FULL FLUSH
SPANG FAIRLY DIRECTLY
(— **AND SHARPLY**) SMACK
SQUARISH BOXY
SQUASH PEPO QUAT GOURD SQUAB
CASHAW CUCURB CUSHAW
MARROW SIMNEL SQUISH SQUUSH
TURBAN HUBBARD PUMPKIN
CUCURBIT CYMBLING PEPONIUM
ZUCCHINI
SQUASH BUG STINKBUG
SQUASHY SWASHY SQUUSHY
SQUAT QUAT RUCK STUB SWAT
SWOT COWER DUMPY FUBSY
HUNCH PUDGY SQUAB FODGEL
HUNKER HURKLE QUATCH STOCKY
STUBBY SQUATTY TAPPISH
SQUATTLE THICKSET
SQUATINA RHINA
SQUATTER NESTER BYWONER
SQUAW JACK WEBB HOUND WENCH
MAHALA SQUARK
SQUAWBUSH SHOVAL
SQUAWFISH CHUB BOXHEAD
BIGMOUTH CHAPPAUL
SQUAWK SCRAWK SQUALL SQUARK
SQUAWL COMPLAIN
SQUAWROOT CLAPWORT ELOTILLO

SQUEAK GIKE PEEP WEAK CHEEP QUEAK SCRAWK SCROOP SQUEAL

SQUEAKY CREAKY

SQUEAL PIP FINK HOWL SWEEL SCREAK WHISTLE

SQUEALER FINK CANARY

SQUEAMISH HELO NICE NAISH PAWKY PENSY DAINTY DAUNCH PENCEY QUAINT QUEASY SPICED TICKLE WAIRCH WAMBLY FINICAL MAWKISH WEARISH NAUSEOUS OVERNICE

SQUEAMISHNESS NICETY DISGUST DELICACY

SQUEEZE EKE HUG JAM NIP CLAM MULL MURE VISE ZEST BUNCH CHIRT CREEM CROWD CRUSH PRESS SQUAB SQUAT WRING GRUDGE QUEASE SCRUMP SCRUZE SQUASH STRAIN THRIMP THRING THRONG TWEEZE TWITCH SCRINGE SCROOGE SCROUGE SCRUNCH SCRUNGE SQUEEGE SQUINCH COMPRESS CONTRACT PRESSURE SHOEHORN THRIMBLE THRUMBLE

(— FROM) SPONGE

(— IN) FUDGE

(— INTO) THRIMBLE

(— OUT) PINCH STRAIN

SQUEEZED STRETTA STRETTO

SQUEEZER REAMER ALLIGATOR

SQUELCH QUELCH SQUASH SQUISH SQUIDGE

SQUELCHER BLIZZARD

SQUETEAGUE DRUM DRUMMER SQUETEE BLUEFISH CHICKWIT WEAKFISH

SQUIB MOTE FILLER EXPLODER

SQUID PLUG

SQUIGGLE SCRIGGLE

SQUILL SCILLA SLANGKOP

SQUINT GLEE GLEG SKEN SKEW BAGGE GLENT GLEDGE GOGGLE SHEYLE SKELLY SQUINCH SQUINNY

SQUINT-EYED GLEE GLEED

SQUINTING LOUCHE

SQUIRE SWAIN DONZEL TIMIAS ARMIGER ESQUIRE SQUIRET YOUNKER HENCHMAN SCUTIGER SERVITOR SQUIREEN

SQUIRM CURL WIND TWINE WRING WRITHE WRESTLE WRIGGLE SCRIGGLE SQUIGGLE

SQUIRREL BUN CON BUNT LEAD SCUG BUNNY XERUS BOOMER CHIPPY GOPHER RODENT TAGUAN ARDILLA SCHILLU SCIURID CHIPMUNK EGGEATER GRAYBACK JELERANG RATATOSK

(— SKIN) VAIR

(FLYING —) ASAPAN

SQUIRRELFISH ALAIKI MARIAN MOJARRA SERRANO SOLDIER SANDFISH WELSHMAN

SQUIRREL SHREW TANA TUPAIA PENTAIL

SQUIRT CHIRT SCOOT SKITE SLIRT SPIRT SPOUT SPURT SQUIB SQUIT SPLOIT SPRENT SPRITZ SCOOTER SQUITTER

STAB DAB DAG JAB JAG JOB DIRK GORE PINK PROB SHIV STOB STOG STUG YERK CHIVE KNIFE POACH PRICK PRONG STICK STOKE BROACH DAGGER PIERCE POUNCE SLIVER STITCH THRUST BAYONET STAGGER PRICKADO STILETTO STOCCADO STOCCATA

(— IN MIDBREAST) SLOT

STABBING THORNY JABBING PUNGENT STICKING

STABILITY POISE BALANCE SADNESS FIRMNESS SECURITY

STABILIZE FIX SET EVEN TRIM POISE SCHOOL STEADY BALANCE BALLAST STIFFEN

STABILIZER ACARDITE

STABLE BYRE FAST FIRM SURE HARAS HEMEL SOLID SOUND STALL STIFF STOUT TAMBO LINTER LIVERY SECURE SICKER STATIC STEADY STRONG STURDY DURABLE EQUERRY LASTING OXHOUSE SETTLED SHIPPEN STABILE IMMOBILE RESIDENT STANDING

(ROYAL —S) MEWS

STABLEBOY LAD JACKBOY

STABLEMAN OSTLER HOSTLER

STACCATO TUT SECCO DETACHE SALTATO RICOCHET SALTANDO

(NOT —) TENUTO

STACK COB MOW SOW BIKE DESS LEET PACK PILE POKE RICK CANCH CLAMP GOAVE POAKE SCROO SHOCK STAKE STALK STOCK COLUMN FUNNEL RICKLE CALENDER STACKAGE

(— BRICKS) SCINTLE

(— IN KILN) BOX

(— LUMBER) STICK

(— OF ARMS) PILE

(— OF BRICK) LIFT

(— OF CERAMICS) BUNG

(— OF CORN) SHOCK

(— OF FISH) BULK

(— OF GRAIN) RICK

(— OF HIDES) BED

(— OF PANS) SWEATER

(— OF SHEETS) BOOK

(HAY OR CORN —) HOVEL

(SMALL —) COB CANCH RICKLE

(TILE —) WELL

STACKER CROWDER PITCHER STACKMAN

STACKYARD MOWIE MOWHAY HAGGARD

STADIUM BOWL STADE STAGE FURLONG STADION COLISEUM

STAFF PIN ROD TAU TAW CANE CLUB KENT LIMB MACE MALL MAUL PIKE POLE RUNG TREE VARE YARD BATON CROOK CROSS KEVEL NIBBY PEDUM PERCH STAVE STICK SUITE VERGE BASTON CADUCE CEPTER CLEEKY CROCHE CRUTCH FAMILY FERULE GROUND LITUUS MULETA POTENT PRITCH RADIUS RISSLE TAIAHA THYRSE WARDER BACULUS BOURDON CAMBUCA CROSIER

CRUMMIE DISTAFF FESTUCA PALSTER SCEPTER SCEPTRE STADDLE THYRSUS CADUCEUS CRUMMOCK PARTISAN PASTORAL PLOWFOOT TIPSTAFF

(— AT END OF NET) BRAIL

(— OF AUTHORITY) VARE VERGE

(— WITH CROSSPIECE) POTENT

(BISHOP'S —) BAGLE BACULUS CROSIER CROZIER PASTORAL

(FIELD MARSHAL'S —) BATON

(FORKED —) LINSTOCK

(GRADUATED —) LIMB

(HOTTENTOT —) KIRVI

(MAGICIAN'S —) RHABDOS

(NEWSPAPER —) DAYSIDE

(NUBIAN —) KUERR

(PLASTERER'S —) BEATER

(SHEPHERD'S —) KENT CROOK

(TEACHING —) FACULTY

(THIEVES' —) FILCH

STAG HART ROYAL SPADE STAIG WAPITI BULLOCK KNOBBER POINTER KNOBBLER

(— OF 8 YEARS OR MORE) ROYAL

(— OF THE 3D YEAR) SPIRE

(— THAT HAS CAST HIS ANTLERS) POLLARD

(3-YEAR OLD —) SPADE

(DEAD —) MORT

(HORNLESS —) HUMMEL

(TURNED TO —) ACTAEON

STAG BEETLE LUCANID

STAGE LEG BANK GEST POST STEP TREK DUMMY ETAGE FLAKE GRADE PEGME PHASE POINT SCENE STAIR STATE BOARDS DEGREE HEMMEL PERIOD STRIDE CATASTA MANSION ROSTRUM STADIUM INSTANCE PLATFORM SCAFFOLD

(— FOR DRYING FISH) FLAKE

(— FOR HAY) HEMMEL

(— IN DELIRIUM) TILMUS

(— IN FEVER) FLUSH

(— IN PORCELAIN FURNACE) HOWELL

(— IN TRAVELING) GEST

(— MANAGER) REGISSEUR

(— OF CUPOLA) LANTERN

(— OF DEVELOPMENT) ERA BLOSSOM

(— OF GLACIATION) ACHEN MINDEL

(— OF INSECT) INSTAR

(— OF LIFE) AGE ASRAMA ASHRAMA

(— OF PERSONALITY) LATENCY

(— OF ROCKET) BOOSTER

(— OF THEATER) SCAENA THEATRON

(— WHERE SLAVES WERE SOLD) CATASTA

(BOTTOMMOST —) CELLAR

(COMIC —) SOCK

(FINAL —) CLOSE FINISH STRETCH

(FIRST —) YOUTH SPRING

(FLOATING —) DUMMY

(FLOOD —) CREST

(GEOLOGICAL —) GUNZ GLACIAL

(INITIAL —) INFANCY

(LANDING —) STAIR BRIDGE STAITH
STELLING
(MOVING —) PEGMA PEGME
(RADIO —) STEP
(THIRD —) AUTUMN
STAGECOACH DILLY STAGE
STAGEHAND DAYMAN
STAGER SOAKER
STAGGER REEL ROLL STOT DAVER
DODGE HODGE STITE STOIT
DACKER FALTER GOGGLE STIVER
SWAVER WALTER WAMBLE WELTER
WIGGLE WINTLE MEGRIMS STACHER
STACKER STAMMER STOITER
STOTTER STUMBLE SWAGGER
VANDYKE WAUCHLE TITUBATE
STAGGERBUSH LAMBKILL
STAGGERED STURTAN STURTIN
STAGGERS DUNT GOGGLES
STAVERS VERTIGO
STAGHEAD SPIKETOP
STAGING STAGE CRIPPLE DERRICK
HURRIES
STAGNANCY STASIS
STAGNANT DEAD DULL INERT STILL
STATIC COBWEBBY SLUGGISH
STAGNATE STANDING
STAGNATION STASIS TORPOR
LANGUOR
STAID SET CIVIL GRAVE SOBER
DEMURE STEADY EARNEST SERIOUS
DECOROUS
STAIN DYE LIT WEM BLOT BLUR
BUFF DIRT DRAB FILE FOIL HURT
MEAL MOLE RUST SCAM SLUR
SMAD SMIT SMUT SOIL SPOT TASH
BLACK BLEND CLOUD DIRTY HATCH
PAINT PLECK SMEAR SPECK SULLY
TACHE TAINT TINGE WEMMY
BREATH GIEMSA IMBRUE INFAMY
INFECT MACULA SMIRCH SMUDGE
SMUTCH SPLASH STIGMA SUDDLE
ATTAINT BESTAIN BLEMISH DEPAINT
DISTAIN SLUBBER SOILURE
SPATTER SPLOTCH STADDLE
TARNISH BESMIRCH CARMALUM
DISCOLOR DISGRACE DISHONOR
FLYSPECK MACULATE TAINTURE
(— BLACK) EBONIZE
(— IN LINEN) MELL
(— ON BRICK) SCUMMING
(— WITH BLOOD) ENGORE
STAINED FOXY RUSTY SMUDGY
SMUTCHY
(— BY DECAY) DOATY
(— WITH BLOOD) BLOODY IMBRUED
STAINED GLASS VITRAIL
STAINER TRACER
STAINLESS CHASTE INNOCENT
STAIR STY GREE RUNG STEP
DEGREE COCHLEA ESCALIER
(MINING —) LOB
(PL.) PAIR PITCH FLIGHT DANCERS
ESCALIER
STAIRCASE SCALE ESCALIER
(SPIRAL —) SPIRAL CARACOLE
STAIRWAY STOOP GREESE PERRON
DESCENT ESCALIER
(— ON RIVER BANK) GHAT

(CURVED —) SWEEP
(SHIP'S —) LADDER
(WINDING —) VICE TURNPIKE
STAKE BET HOB LAY SET TAW VIE
WAD WED ANTE BENT GAGE MAIN
PALE PAWN PEEL POOL RISK STAB
STOB TREE WAGE PITCH SPILE
SPOKE SPRAG STOCK STOOP
STOUR WAGER BAIKIE CAULIS
CHANCE CORNER CROTCH ENGAGE
GAMBLE HAZARD IMPONE LOGGAT
LOGGET PALING STOWER TRUNCH
WEDFEE STOATER STUCKEN
VENTURE INTEREST PALISADE
PEASTICK STUCKING
(CART —) RUNG
(COMPULSORY — IN POKER) BLIND
(POINTED —) SOULE SOWEL PICKET
(SURVEYORS' —) HUB
(TETHERING —) PUTTO
(TINSMITH'S —) TEEST
STAKE-SHAPED SUDIFORM
STALACE COLUMELLA
STALE OLD COLD HOAR PALL SICK
WORN BLOWN DUSTY FROWY
HOARY MOLDY MUSTY RAFTY
SANDY TRITE FROWZY MOULDY
STUFFY EXOLETE FROUGHY INSIPID
OVERWORN STAGNANT
(DAMP AND —) WAUGH
STALEMATE PATT STALE
STALK BUN RAY CORN MOTE POLE
RISP STAM STEG STEM TIGE QUILL
SCAPE SHANK SPEAR SPIRE STAKE
STALE STEAL STIPE STUMP WRIDE
COULIS RATOON STIPES CASTOCK
PEDICEL PETIOLE SPINDLE
FILAMENT PEDUNCLE PODETIUM
STALKLET STERIGMA
(— OF BUCKWHEAT) STRAW
(— OF CRINOID) COLUMN
(— OF GRAIN) RESSOM RIZZOM
(— OF GRASS) BENT SPEAR
(— OF HAY) RISP
(— OF PLANT) SPINDLE TENACLE
(— OF SPOROGONIUM) SETA
(— OF STAMEN) FILAMENT
(— OF SUGAR CANE) RATOON
(— OF UMBEL) RAY
(—S OF GRAIN) KARBI STRAW
(CABBAGE —) CASTOCK
(CROSSBOW —) TILLER
(DRY —) KEX KECK
(FLOWER —) SCAPE
(HOLLOW —) BUN KEX
(PL.) HAULM STRAW WRIDE IWAIWA
STALL BIN BOX CUB PEW BULK CRIB
SPAR STAW BOOSE BOOSY BOOTH
CRAME PITCH STAND STASH
CARCER CARREL TRAVIS WICKET
BALAGAN CABINET SHAMBLE
BUTCHERY STANDING TRAVERSE
(— FOR TIME) HAVER STRETCH
(— IN CLOISTER) CAROL
(— IN COAL MINE) BREAST WICKET
(— IN MUD) STOG
(— IN ROMAN CIRCUS) CARCER
(CHURCH —) PEW
(THEATER —) LOGE FAUTEUIL

STALLED STOODED
STALLION SIRE STAG STUD ENTRE
HORSE COOSER ENTIRE STALLAND
STALWART RUDE STARK STIFF
WIGHT STRONG STURDY BUIRDLY
VALIANT
STAMEN TAMIN STAMMEL
STAMINA GUTS SAND BOTTOM
STAMMER FAM HACK MANT STOT
STUT GANCH WLAFF FAFFLE
FALTER FAMBLE HACKER HAFFLE
HAMMER HOCKER HOTTER MAFFLE
MAMMER YAMMER FRIBBLE
STUMBLE STUTTER HESITATE
SPLUTTER TITUBATE
STAMMERING HACK TRAULISM
STAMP CHOP COIL DRUB FAKE
MARK NIXY PAUT POSS RUFF SEAL
SNAP TYPE APPEL BLOCK DOLLY
ERROR FRANK LABEL LOCAL NIXIE
PRINT PUNCH STOCK STOMP STUNT
TENOR TOUCH WRITE ACCENT
CACHET CLICHE DOCKER FULLER
INCUSE INCUTE INDENT LOCKUP
PASTER POUNCE SCRIBE SHAPER
SIGNET STRAMP STRIKE CARRIER
CHARACT EDITION IMPRESS IMPRINT
MINTAGE POUNDER REPRINT
SEEBECK SPECIAL SQUELCH
STICKER TAXPAID WRAPPER
HALLMARK ORIGINAL PRESSURE
PUNCHEON
(— AFTER ASSAY) TOUCH
(— BOOK COVER) BLIND
(— FOR CUTTING DOUGH) DOCKER
(— HERRING BARREL) DUNT
(— HIDES) STOCK
(— HOLES) STOACH
(— OUT) SCOTCH
(— WITH DIE) DINK
(BOOKBINDING —) BLOCK FILLET
(CANCELLING —) KILLER
(HALF OF —) BISECT
(HAND —) CANCELER
(OFFICIAL —) CHOP
(POSTAGE —) AIR DUE CAPE FAKE
HEAD ERROR LABEL LOCAL BUREAU
INVERT AIRMAIL BICOLOR CHARITY
CLASSIC REPRINT STICKER
ADHESIVE COLONIAL ORIGINAL
SPECIMEN
(REVENUE —) FISCAL TAXPAID
(SMART —) APPEL
(PL.) MIXTURE KILOWARE
STAMPEDE RUSH BLITZ CHUTE
DEBACLE STAMPEDO
STAMPER FANCIER STOMPER
STAMPING TITLING
STANCE STATION STANDING
(— OF GOLFER) ADDRESS
(— OF HORSE) GATHER
STANCH FIRM STEM STIFF STOUT
HEARTY TRUSTY STAUNCH
FAITHFUL RESOLUTE
STANCHION BAIL PITON CROTCH
CRUTCH STENCIL STANCHEL
STANCHER
STAND GO JIB SET BANK BEAR BIER
DESK HALT RACK RANK REST STAY

ZARF BLOCK ERECT FRAME FRONT
KIOSK NIPOD STALL STICK STONE
STOOL CASTER COLORS ENDURE
HASTER INSIST PATTEN PILLAR
SMOKER STANZA STOUND STRIKE
TEAPOY TRIPOD TRIVET CONSIST
DIOPTER EPERGNE FOURBLE
LECTERN STATION TABORET
TRESTLE TROLLEY ATTITUDE
BLEACHER COATRACK CROWFOOT
FRIPPERY GUERIDON HASTENER
INKSTAND POSITION SCAFFOLD
STALLAGE STANDING STANDISH
STILLAGE STILLING STILLION
(— **AS SPONSOR**) FANG HEAVE
CHRISTEN
(— **AT AN ANGLE**) CATER
(— **AT ATTENTION**) BACK
(— **BACK**) BACCARE BACKARE
(— **BEFORE A FIRE**) FOOTMAN
(— **BEHIND**) COVER
(— **BY**) SERVE
(— **CLOSE**) CROWD ENVIRON
(— **FASTENED TO MESS TABLE**)
CROWFOOT
(— **FIRM**) STAY
(— **FOR AUCTIONING**) BLOCK
(— **FOR BARRELS**) JIB THRALL
(— **FOR COFFIN**) BIER
(— **FOR COMPASS**) BINNACLE
(— **FOR CONFINING HEAT**) HASTER
HASTENER
(— **FOR DRESSES**) FRIPPERY
(— **FOR DRILL PIPE**) FOURBLE
(— **FOR FINJAN**) ZARF
(— **FOR TILES**) CRISS
(— **FOR WRITING MATERIALS**)
STANDISH
(— **FOR**) DENOTE
(— **GUARD**) COVER
(— **IN AWE**) FEAR
(— **OF FOREST**) GROWTH
(— **OF PLANTS**) STOOL
(— **OFF**) AROINT
(— **ON AND OFF SHORE**) BUSK
(— **ON END**) STARE UPEND
(— **ON TWO FEET**) BIPOD DUOPOD
(— **OUT**) CUT TOOT FLAUNT
(— **READY**) ABIDE
(— **STILL**) HO HOO HALT STAY
(— **TO SHOOT**) ADDRESS
(— **TREAT**) MUG SHOUT
(— **UNSTEADILY**) STAGGER
(— **UP STIFF**) STIVER
(— **UP TO**) CONFRONT
(— **WITH LEGS APART**) STRIDE
(**CONCESSION** —) JOINT
(**FIRECLAY** —) CRANK
(**ONE-NIGHT** —) GIG
(**PRINTER'S** —) BANK FRAME
(**PULPIT-LIKE** —) AMBO
(**RAISED** —) PERGOLA
(**SCULPTOR'S** —) CHASSIS
(**SHOOTING** —) BUTT
(**THREE-LEGGED** —) TRIVET
STANDARD ALEM DICK FIAR FLAG
GAGE IDEA MARK NORM SIGN TEST
TOUG ALLOY BOGEY CANON CHECK
DOLLY DRAKE EAGLE GAUGE IDEAL

JEDGE MODEL NORMA SCALE
STAND STOOL AQUILA ASSIZE
BANNER CORNET DOLLIE FILLER
SOCKET SQUARE STAPLE TIPONI
TRIPOD VIOLLE ANCIENT CLASSIC
DECORUM DRAPEAU LABARUM
MODULUS STANDER BRATTACH
GONFALON MOUNTING ORIFLAMB
ORTHODOX VEXILLUM
(— **IN GATE**) STRIKE
(— **OF CONDUCT**) LINE GNOMON
(— **OF PERFECTION**) IDEAL
(— **OF PERFORMANCE**) BOGY
BOGEY BOGIE
(— **OF PITCH**) DIAPASON
(— **OF QUALITY**) GRADE
(—**S OF BEHAVIOR**) ETHICS
(**LIGHT** —) CARCEL
(**TURKISH** —) ALEM TOUG
(**PL.**) LIGHTS HOLSTERS
STANDARD-BEARER ENSIGN
ALFEREZ ANCIENT STALLER
SIGNIFER STANDARD
STANDARDIZE FORDIZE MACHINE
CALIBRATE
STANDEL STORER
STANDING BEING ERECT STATE
CREDIT ESTEEM RESPECT
STAGNANT
(— **ALONE**) SEPARATE
(— **BY ITSELF**) ABSOLUTE
DETACHED
(— **ERECT**) HORRENT
(— **INCOORDINATION**) ASTASIA
(— **ON STEPS**) DEGRADED
(— **OUT CLEARLY**) EMINENT
(— **OUT**) BOLD EXTANT SALIENT
(— **POSITION**) OFFHAND
(**MODE OF** —) STANCE
(**SOCIAL** —) LEVEL ESTATE FASHION
STATION
STANDPATTISM TORYISM
STANDPOINT STANCE
STANDSTILL JIB SET HALT REST
STAY STAND STANCE
STANZA CALL RANN ENVOI ENVOY
STAFF STAND STAVE VERSE
BASTON DIXAIN DIZAIN OCTAVE
SEPTET SESTET SEXTET SIXAIN
STANCE STANZO HUITAIN SEXTAIN
STROPHE TRIOLET TROILUS
CINQUAIN OCTONARY QUATRAIN
QUINTAIN RISPETTO SETTAINE
TRISTICH
STAPES STIRRUP
STAPLE LOOP FLOSS STITCH
STEEPLE VERVELLE
STAR COR SUN BEID FIRE LAMP
ASTER COMES DWARF GIANT
MOLET RISHI SHINE STARN ALNATH
ASTRAL BINARY COUPLE DOUBLE
ETOILE LUCIDA MULLET NITHAM
SHINER SPHERE STELLA BENEFIC
DINGBAT ESTOILE GEMINID STARLET
STARNIE ASTERISK ASTEROID
HEXAGRAM MALEFICE PENTACLE
SUBDWARF SUBGIANT VARIABLE
(**7** —**S OF GREAT BEAR**) CAR
(**COMPANION** —) COMES

(**DOG** —) SEPT SOPT SEPTI SIRIUS
(**EVENING** —) VENUS HESPER
VESPER EVESTAR HESPERUS
(**FEATHER** —) COMATULA
(**GUIDING** —) LOADSTAR LODESTAR
(**MORNING** —) VENUS DAYSTAR
PHOSPHOR
(**NEW** —) NOVA
(**OFFICER'S** —) PIP
(**PULSATING** —) CEPHEID
(**SHOOTING** —) METEOR SHOOTER
(**SPECIFIC** —) YED ADIB ALYA ATIK
CAPH ENIF ENIR IZAR KIED MAIA
NAOS PHAD SADR VEGA WEGA
ACRAB ACRUX AGENA ALCOR
ALGOL ALKES ANCHA ARNEB
CHARA DABIH DELTA DENEB DUBHE
GIEDI GUIAM GUYAM HAMAL HAMUL
JUGUM MERAK MIZAR NIBAL NIHAI
PHAET PHARD RIGEL SAIPH SPICA
TEJAT WASAT WEZEN ZOZMA
ADHARA ALHENA ALIOTH ALKAID
ALMACH ALTAIR ALUDRA APOLLO
ARIDED CASTOR CELENO CHELEB
DIPHDA ELNATH ETAMIN GIENAH
HYADES KOCHAB LESUTH MAASYM
MARKAB MARKEB MARSIC MEGREZ
MENKAB MENKAR MERACH MEROPE
MIRFAK MIRZAM NEKKAR PHECDA
POLLUX PROPUS RANICH SCHEAT
SHEDIR SIRIUS THABIT THUBAN
ACUBENS ALBIREO ALCHIBA
ALCYONE ALGENIB ALGIEBA
ALGORAH ALMAACK ALNILAM
ALNITAH ALPHARD ALPHIRK
ALSHAIN ANTARES AZIMECH
BUNGULA CANOPUS CAPELLA
ELECTRA GIANSAR GOMELZA
GRUMIUM MEBUSTA MELUCTA
MENCHIB MINTAKA MUFRIDE
POLARIS PROCYON REGULUS
ROTANIM RUCHBAR SCHEDAR
SEGINUS SHELLAK STEROPE
TARAZED TAYGETA TEGMINE
THEENIM ACHERNAR ALPHECCA
ARCTURUS ASTERION DENEBOLA
GRAFFIAS HERCULES MULIPHEN
PRAESEPE SCALOOIN SCHEMALI
SHERATAN
(**THREE** —**S**) KIDS ELLWAND
TRIANGLE
STAR APPLE CAIMITO
STARCH AMYL ARUM SAGO STIFF
TIKOR AMYDON AMYLUM FARINA
FECULA CASSAVA CURCUMA
FAECULA MARANTA TALIPOT
AMIDULIN DRESSING FIXATURE
GLUCOSAN
(**ANIMAL** —) GLYCOGEN
STARCHED FORMAL
STARE EYE BORE DARE GAPE GAUM
GAUP GAWK GAWP GAZE GOVE
GYPE KIKE LOOK PORE GLARE
GLORE GLOWER GOGGLE EYEBALL
(— **IDLY**) GOVE GOAVE
(— **VACANTLY**) GOWK
(**COLD** —) FISHEYE
STARFISH PAD STAR RADIATE
ASTEROID OPHIURAN

STARING STEEP ASTARE GOGGLE
GOOGLY HAGGARD
STAR JELLY STARSHOT
STARK BUCK CARK FAIR HARD
CRUDE HARSH STIFF STARCH
DESOLATE METALLIC
STARLIKE ASTRAL SPHERY
STARLING SALI STARE BEAVER
PASTOR TILYER SPREEUW STARNEL
STAYNIL CHEPSTER CUTWATER
SHEPSTER
STARRED LIZARD HARDIM
STARRING FEATURED
STARRY ASTRAL STARNY STELLED
SIDEREAL
STAR SAPPHIRE ASTERIA ASTRION
ASTROITE
STAR-SHAPED ASTROID
START DIG SET BOLT BOUN DART
DASH HEAD JERK JUMP OPEN TURN
WHIP BEGIN BIRTH BRAID BREAK
BUDGE ENTER FLIRT GLENT ONSET
RAISE ROUSE THROW BOGGLE
BROACH FLINCH INTEND OFFSET
SETOFF SETOUT STRIKE TWITCH
GETAWAY OPENING STARTLE
SUNRISE COMMENCE CONCEIVE
INCHOATE OUTSTART
(— A HORSE) WINCE
(— ASIDE) SHY SKIT DODGE
(— BURNING) SPIT KINDLE
(— FERMENTATION) PITCH
(— OF BIRD'S FLIGHT) SOUSE
(— OUT) FRAME INTEND
(— UP) JUMP ASTART ASTERT
(SUDDEN —) SHY SQUIRT
STARTER KOJI
(BUNG —) FLOGGER
STAR THISTLE CALTROP CALTHROP
STARTING INCOMING
STARTLE SOHO ALARM SCARE
SHOCK START STURT AFFRAY
BOGGLE BOOGER FRIGHT FRIGHTEN
SURPRISE
STARTLING ALARMING SHOCKING
STARVATION LACK FAMINE
STARVE CLEM FAST FAMINE FAMISH
AFFAMISH
STARVED MEAGER MEAGRE
STARVEN
STARVED-LOOKING SLINK
STARVELING SHARGAR SHARGER
STARVING CLUNG
STARWORT ASTROFEL
STATE WU LAY PUT SAY CASE MODE
NAME POMP PORT TERM TIFF COVIN
ESTER ESTRE POLIS SPEAK STADE
TERMS TUATH WHACK AFFIRM
AGENCY ASSERT ASSURE CAESAR
EFFEIR EMPIRE ESTATE IMPORT
NATION PLIGHT POLICY POLITY
RENDER RIALTY SOVIET STATUS
STEVEN CIVITAS DECLARE DESERET
DUKEDOM ENOUNCE EXPOUND
EXPRESS KINSHIP PROPOSE
SPECIFY STATION TERMINE
DEVACHAN DOMINION FRANKLIN
HEGEMONY INDICATE KINGSHIP
REPUBLIC STATELET

(— EXPLICITLY) DEFINE
(— FORMALLY) ENOUNCE
(— IN NORTH CAROLINA) FRANKLIN
(— OF AFFAIRS) CASE ARRAY
STATUS
(— OF ALARM) GAST FEEZE SCARE
(— OF AMAZEMENT) STOUND
(— OF ANGER) FUME
(— OF APATHY) STUPOR
(— OF BEING CUT) SCISSION
(— OF BEING DRAWN) TRACTION
(— OF BEING OVERFULL) PLETHORA
(— OF BEING POISONOUS) TOXICITY
(— OF BEING WORSE) PEJORITY
(— OF CONCENTRATION) DHARANA
DHAYANA SAMADHI
(— OF CONFUSION) FOG FLAP HACK
MUSS CHAOS SWIRL HASSLE
HUBBUB FLUMMOX TROYTOWN
(— OF CONSECRATION) IHRAM
(— OF COOPERATION) HOOKUP
(— OF DISASTER) SMASH
(— OF DISORDER) HELL MUSS
FANTAD ANARCHY
(— OF DISSENSION) SCISSION
(— OF DISTURBANCE) GARBOIL
(— OF DOUBT) MIST
(— OF EAGERNESS) HURRY
(— OF ECSTASY) SWOON
(— OF ENCHANTMENT) SPELL
(— OF ENLIGHTENMENT) BODHI
(— OF EXALTATION) FURY ECSTASY
(— OF EXCITATION) FOMENT
(— OF EXCITEMENT) FRY FLAP
GALE HIGH SNIT STEW FEEZE
HOIGH DITHER DOODAH HUBBUB
FANTEEG FLUSTER KIPPAGE
SWELTER FANTIGUE
(— OF EXHAUSTION) GONENESS
(— OF FEAR) FUNK JELLY SCARE
(— OF HAPPINESS) ELYSIUM
PARADISE
(— OF HEALTH) EUCRASIA
(— OF HUMILIATION) DUST
(— OF IDEAL PERFECTION) UTOPIA
(— OF IMPERFECTION) SCARCITY
(— OF INACTION) DEADLOCK
(— OF INCIPIENCE) EMBRYO
(— OF INTENSITY) BUILD
(— OF IRRITABILITY) FUME GALL
FANTAD
(— OF JOY) JUBILEE
(— OF MELANCHOLY) GLOOM
(— OF MENTAL INACTIVITY)
TORPOR
(— OF MENTAL READINESS)
ATTITUDE
(— OF MIND) CUE HIP CASE MOOD
HUMOR FETTLE CARAPACE
(— OF MISERY) HELL GEHENNA
(— OF NEGLECT) LIMBO
(— OF OPPOSITION) DEFIANCE
(— OF OSTRACISM) COVENTRY
(— OF PERTURBATION) CRISE
(— OF PREOCCUPATION) CARE
(— OF READINESS) GUARD
(— OF REALITY) ACT
(— OF REJECTION) GATE
(— OF REPOSE) CALM

(— OF RETIREMENT) GRASS
(— OF REVERIE) DUMP
(— OF SENSITIVITY) NERVES
(— OF SLUGGISHNESS) COMA
(— OF SUSPENSE) TRANCE
(— OF TENSION) FANTEEG STRETCH
FANTIGUE
(— OF THE SOUL) BARDO
(— OF THINGS) FARE PASS
(— OF TRANQUILLITY) KEF KIF
PEACE
(— OF UNCERTAINTY) FOG FLUX
(— OF UNREST) FERMENT
(— OF WEATHER) FREEZE
(— OF WORRY) TEW SWEAT FANTAD
(— POSITIVELY) AFFIRM
(— UNDER OATH) ALLEGE
(AGITATED —) FUSS SNIT STIR
CHURN STORM LATHER SWIVET
(BUFFER —) GLACIS
(CHINESE —) WU SHU WEI
(DAZED —) DAMP
(DEPRESSED —) GLOOM WALLOW
(DISTURBED —) STIR STORM
UNREST
(DOMINANT —) SUZERAIN
(DROWSY —) DOVER
(EMOTIONAL —) FEVER FEELING
(FEUDAL —) WEI
(FICTITIOUS —) FABLE
(FILTHY —) DIRT
(FREE —) SAORSTAT
(GLOOMY —) DUMP
(HIGHEST —) SUPREME
(HORIZONTAL —) LEVEL
(INDONESIAN —) NEGARA
(IRISH —) TUATH
(LIQUID —) FLUOR FLUIDITY
(MARRIED —) SPOUSAL
(MENTAL —) EARNEST DELUSION
(MORBID —) HIP IODISM
(MORMON —) DESERET
(NEUTRAL —) BUFFER
(PECUNIARY —) FACULTY
(PERTURBED —) DEVIL
(PROFOUND —) DEPTH
(SWISS —) CANTON
(ULTIMATE —) END
(UNFAVORABLE —) FOULNESS
(VERIFIED —) FACT
STATED GIVEN CERTAIN
(DIRECTLY —) EXPRESS
STATEHOUSE CAPITOL
STATELINESS STATE DIGNITY
MAJESTY GRANDEUR
STATELY DATE BURLY GRAND
LARGO LOFTY NOBLE REGAL STATE
STOUT AUGUST COUPON PORTLY
SOLEMN SUPERB TOGATE GALLANT
BARONIAL IMPOSING MAESTOSO
MAJESTIC STATEFUL
STATEMENT SAY BILL VOTE WORD
AXIOM BRIEF COUNT DIXIT LIBEL
STATE STORY BELIEF DICTUM
DOCKET EXPOSE FACTUM RETURN
SAYING SPEECH ACCOUNT ADDRESS
ANALOGY DISSENT EPITAPH
EPITOME FORMULA INVOICE
MENTION SHOWING ABSTRACT

ANTINOMY ARGUMENT AVERMENT
BULLETIN DELIVERY EQUATION
EXPLICIT JUDGMENT PROPOSAL
SCHEDULE SENTENCE SPEAKING
SYNGRAPH SYNOPSIS
(— **AS PRECEDENT**) AUTHORITY
(— **OF OPINION**) CHANT
(— **OF RELATIONS**) THEOREM
(— **ON DRUG LABEL**) LEGEND
(**AUTHORITATIVE** —) DICTUM
(**CASUAL** —) REMARK
(**CONCISE** —) SCHEME APHORISM
(**CONDENSED** —) RESUME SYNOPSIS
(**DEFAMATORY** —) LIBEL
(**EXAGGERATED** —) STRETCH
(**FABRICATED** —) CANARD
(**FINAL — OF ACCOUNT**) AUDIT
(**FINANCIAL** —) BUDGET
(**FOOLISH** —) INANITY
(**FORMAL** —) CITATION
(**IRRATIONAL** —) ALOGISM
(**OBSCURE** —) ENIGMA
(**PLAINTIFF'S** —) BODY
(**POMPOUS** —) BRAG
(**SELF-CONTRADICTORY** —)
PARADOX
(**SOOTHING** —) SALVE
(**UNTRUE** —) LIE
STATER COLT TURTLE PEGASUS
CYZICENE
STATEROOM BIBBY CABIN
STATESMAN GENRO SOLON FATHER
STATIST WARWICK JACOBEAN
WEALSMAN
STATICE ARMERIA LIMONIUM
STATION BY BYE FIX ORB RUN SET
GARE POST RANK ROOM STOP
BEING CHOKY DEPOT PLACE POSTE
SIEGE STAGE STALL STAND STATE
DEGREE LOCATE STANCE CONTROL
CUARTEL DIGNITY HABITAT
OUTPOST GARRISON PILTDOWN
POSITION STANDING TERMINAL
TERMINUS TRANSFER
(— **IN BASEBALL**) BASE
(— **IN LIFE**) BEING CALLING
(— **OF HERON**) SEDGE SIEGE
(**CONCEALED** —) AMBUSH
(**CUSTOMS** —) CHOKEY
(**EXALTED** —) PURPLE
(**POLICE** —) TANA TANNA THANAH
KOTWALEE
(**POST** —) DAK
(**RADIO** —S) CHAIN NETWORK
(**RAILWAY** —) GARE CABIN
(**SIGNALLING** —) BANTAY BEACON
(**SURVEYING** —) STADIA
(**TRADING** —) FACTORY
(**WAY** —) TAMBO
STATIONARY SET FAST FIXED STILL
LEDGER STATIC DORMANT SITFAST
STABILE STATARY IMMOBILE
STATISTICIAN ANALYST STATIST
STATOBLAST SPORE
STATUARY IMAGERY
STATUE HERM ICON IDOL IKON
TERM BUSTO HERMA IMAGE MOSES
AGALMA BRONZE HERMES MEMNON
STATUA WEEPER XOANON ILISSUS

PASQUIN PICTURE STATURE
STATUTE ACROLITH CARYATID
MARFORIO MONUMENT PANTHEUM
PORTRAIT VICTORIA
(— **ENDOWED WITH LIFE**) GALATEA
(— **OF GIGANTIC SIZE**) COLOSSUS
(**COLOSSAL** —) GOG MAGOG
STATUETTE WAX EMMY OSCAR
WINNIE TANAGRA FIGULINE
FIGURINE SIGILLUM
STATURE PITCH GROWTH HEIGHT
INCHES WASTME CAPACITY
STATUS RANK SEAT PLACE STATE
ASPECT FOOTING STATURE
STANDING
(— **OF YOUNGER SON**) CADENCY
(**HIGH** —) CACHET
(**LEGAL** —) CAPUT
(**SECONDARY** —) BACKSEAT
STATUTE ACT LAW LEX DOOM EDICT
ASSIZE DECREE SETNESS SITTING
STATUTUM TANZIMAT
(— **FAIR**) MOP
STATUTORY LEGAL
STAUNCH FAST STOUT FAITHFUL
STAVE LAG SLAT STAP SHAKE STAFF
STOVE VERSE BASTON STANZA
WATTLE
(— **IN**) BILGE BULGE
(**SET OF** —S) SHOOK
(**PL.**) LAGGEN LAGGIN STICKS
STAVING
STAY DAY GET LIE BASE HOLD LEND
PROP REST SIST STOP WAIT ABIDE
ABODE APPUI DEFER DELAY DEMUR
DWELL LEAVE STINT TARRY THOLE
ARREST ATTEND BIDING DETAIN
EXPECT GUSSET POTENT REMAIN
TIMBER UPHOLD EMBASSY JIBSTAY
LAYOVER MANSION SOJOURN
SUSPEND BACKSTAY CONTINUE
FORESTAY HORNSTAY MAINSTAY
(— **AWAY**) SKIP
(— **BEHIND**) LAG
(— **CLEAR**) AVOID
(— **FOR**) AWAIT
(— **THE NIGHT**) BUNK HOSTLE
(— **WITH**) STICK
(**PRIEST'S** —) STATION
(**TAILORING** —) BRIDLE
(**PL.**) JUMPS JUPES BODICE
STAY-AT-HOME HOMEBODY
HOMESTER
STAYER BONER
STAYLACE AGLET AIGLET
STAYSAIL JUMBO
STEAD LIEU ROOM VICE PLACE
BEHALF
STEADFAST SAD FAST FIRM SURE
TRUE ROCKY STAID STEER STABLE
STANCH STEADY CERTAIN EXPRESS
SETTLED STAUNCH VALIANT
CONSTANT FAITHFUL RESOLUTE
STEADFASTLY FIRM FIRMLY
INTENTLY
STEADILY SAD FAST STEADY
STEADINESS NERVE BALANCE
STEADING ONSET ONSTEAD
STEADY GUY SAD BEAU EVEN FIRM

SURE TRIG TRUE CANNY FRANK
LEVEL SOBER STUDY SUANT TIGHT
STABLE STANCH BALLAST EQUABLE
STABILE STATARY STAUNCH
CONSTANT DECOROUS DILIGENT
FAITHFUL RESOLUTE TRANQUIL
UNSHAKEN
(— **AT ANCHOR**) HOLSOM
STEAK BROIL SHELL FLITCH TUCKET
GRISKIN
STEAL BAG CAB CLY COP FOX GYP
LAG NAP NIM NIP RAP RIG BONE
CHOR COON CRIB FAKE GLOM
HOOK LIFT LURK MAGG MAKE MILL
NAIL NICK PEAK PICK PRIG SLIP
SMUG ANNEX BOOST BRIBE CLOUT
CREEP FETCH FILCH FLIMP FRISK
GLIDE HARRY HEIST HOIST LURCH
MOOCH MOUCH PINCH PLUCK
POACH SCOFF SHAKE SHARP SHAVE
SLIDE SNAKE SNARE SNEAK STALK
SWIPE TOUCH TRUFF COLLAR
CONVEY FINGER HIJACK MOOTCH
NOBBLE PILFER SNITCH STRIKE
THIEVE BESTEAL CABBAGE
PLUNDER PURLOIN SCHLEPP
SKYUGLE SNABBLE SNAFFLE
SURREPT ABSTRACT CRIBBAGE
EMBEZZLE LIBERATE MANARVEL
PECULATE SCROUNGE SHOPLIFT
(— **A GLANCE**) GLIME
(— **A WATCH**) FLIMP
(— **ALONG**) SLIME SLINK
(— **AWAY**) LOOP SLINK
(— **BY ALTERING BRANDS**) DUFF
(— **CALVES**) NUGGET
(— **CATTLE**) DUFF RUSTLE
(— **COPPER FROM VESSEL'S**
BOTTOM) TOSH
(— **OFF**) RUN
(— **SLYLY**) SCROUNGE
STEALER (CATTLE —) DUFFER
ABACTOR
STEALTHILY SIDLINS THIEFLY
SIDELINS
STEALTHY CATTY PRIVY ARTFUL
FELINE TIPTOE CATLIKE FURTIVE
SNEAKING THIEVISH
STEAM OAM ROKE STEM BLAST
SMOKE SWEAT VAPOR BREATH
POTHER CUSHION
STEAMBOAT KICKUP STEAMER
STEAMER CLAM LINER TENDER
STEAMER CUNARDER
STEAMER DUCK RACER LOGHEAD
STEAMSHIP SCREW STEAM
STEAMER SEATRAIN SHOWBOAT
STEAM SHOVEL NAVVY NAVVIE
STEATIN MULL
STEATITE LARDITE POTSTONE
SOAPROCK
STEATOPYGOUS RUMPY
STEED ROIL STEAD PEGASUS
SLEIPNER
STEEL RAIL BLOOM BRACE FUSIL
TERNE WEAPON WHITTLE FLEERISH
(— **FOR STRIKING FIRE**) ESLABON
(— **FOR USE WITH FLINT**) FUSIL
FURISON FLEERISH

(— INLAID WITH GOLD) KOFT KOFTGARI
(DAMASCUS —) DAMASK
(INDIAN —) WOOTZ
(MOLTEN —) HEAT
STEELER BONER
STEELING ACIERAGE
STEELWORKER HOOKER STICKMAN STRANDER STRANNER
STEELYARD BISMER DESEMER DOTCHIN STATERA
STEENBRAS BISKOP
STEEP SOP BATE BOLD BOWK BUCK DRAW DUNG ELVA LIME MASH SOAK STAY STEW STEY BRANT BRENT HATCH HEAVY HILLY QUICK SHARP SHEER SOUSE STIFF ABRUPT BLUFFY CLIFFY CLIFTY DECOCT IMBIBE INFUSE SPRUNT STEEPY ARDUOUS BRASQUE CLIVOSE INSTEEP PRERUPT STICKLE HEADLONG MACETATE SATURATE SIDELING STIFFISH STRAIGHT
STEEPED SODDEN
STEEPING SOUSE INFUSION
STEEPLE SPEAR SPIRE
STEEPLECHASE CHASE GRIND
STEER COX PLY BEEF BULL HELM LEAD STEM STOT GUIDE SPADE SPADO STERN TOLLY CANNER RUDDER BULLOCK STOCKER COWBRUTE MOSSHORN NAVIGATE
(— VEHICLE) DRIVE
(FAT —) BEAST
(HORNLESS —) NOT NOTT
(VICIOUS —) LADINO
(WILD —) YAW YEW COWBRUTE
(YOUNG —) STOT STOTT
STEERAGE STERN
STEERER CAPPER
STEERSMAN PILOT WHEEL PATRON SLEWER CANOPUS SHIPMAN STEERER COXSWAIN HELMSMAN SEACUNNY STERNMAN WHEELMAN
STEIN SHANT
STELE SHAFT EUSTELE
STELLAR STARRY
STELLATE STARRY ASTROSE
STEM BUN BASE BEAM BINE BIRN CANE CULM NOSE PIPE PROW RISP ROOT RUNT STUD DTRAW FILUM HAULM SCAPE SCREW SHAFT SHANK SHOOT STALE STALK STEAL STICK STIPE STOCK THEME TRUNK TUBER BRANCH CAUDEX CAULIS DERIVE SCAPUS SPRING CAULOME CONTAIN FULCRUM HOPBINE HOPVINE PEDICEL PETIOLE PLASHER SPINDLE STEMLET TIGELLA CAULICLE ENGENDER FORESTEM PEDUNCLE PIPESTEM TIGELLUM
(— OF ARROW) SHAFT
(— OF BANANAS) COUNT
(— OF GLASS) BALUSTER
(— OF GRAPES) RAPE
(— OF HOOKAH) SNAKE
(— OF MATCH) SHAFT
(— OF MUSHROOM) STIPE
(— OF MUSICAL NOTE) TAIL FILUM VIRGULA

(— OF PIPE) STAPPLE
(— OF PLANT) AXIS RUNT CAULIS
(— OF SHIP) PROW STEMPOST
(— OF TREE) BOLE
(—S OF CULTIVATED PLANTS) HAULM
(BULBLIKE —) CORM
(DRY WITHERED —) BIRN
(EDIBLE —) EDDO
(GRIEF —) KELLY
(MAIN — OF DEER'S ANTLERS) BEAM
(ORNAMENTAL —) STAVE
(PITHY JOINTED —) CANE
(THORNY —) LAWYER
(TWINING —) BINE
STEMLESS ACAULINE
STEMMA OCELLUS OCELLANA PEDIGREE
STEMMER STRIPPER
STENCH FOGO HOGO FETOR SMELL STINK WHIFF FOETOR MEPHITIS
STENCIL (— PROCESS) POCHOIR
STENCILED GOFFERED
STENOSIS SMALLING
STEP CUT FIT JOG PEG PIP BEMA DESS FOOT GREE LINK PACE PEEP RUNG STAP BRASS CORTE DODGE FLIER FLYER GRECE NOTCH POINT STAGE STAIR TOOTH TRACE TREAD DEGREE GRADIN RUNDLE STRIDE WINDER CURTAIL DESCENT FOOTING GRADINE GRADING COONJINE DEMARCHE DOORSTEP FOOTPACE FOOTSTEP FORESTEP PREDELLA STRATLIN
(— ASIDE) DIGRESS
(— BACKWARD) DODGE
(— BY STEP) GRADATIM
(— DOWNWARD) DESCENT
(— FOR GEM MOUNTING) KITE
(— FORWARD) ADVANCE
(— IN A BEARING) BRASS
(— IN BELL RINGING) DODGE
(— IN DOCK) ALTAR
(— IN SELF-ESTEEM) PEG
(— IN SOCIAL SCALE) CUT
(— LIVELY) SKELP
(— OF LADDER) RIME RUNG ROUND RUNDLE
(— OF TUSK) TOOTH
(— SUPPORTING MILLSTONE) TRAMPOT
(—S OF BOWLER) APPROACH
(ALTAR —S) GRADUAL
(BALLET —) SISSONE SISSONNE
(BALLET —S) ALLEGRO
(BOUNDING —) SKIP
(CLUMSY —) STAUP
(DANCE —) DIP PAS SET BUZZ DRAG DRAW FLAT SHAG SKIP BRAWL CHASS COULE GLIDE IRISH STOMP BRANLE CANTER CHASSE DOUBLE INTURN STRIDE BRANSLE BUFFALO FISHTAIL GLISSADE
(FALSE —) HOB SLIP SPHALM SNAPPER SPHALMA STUMBLE
(FIRST —) STARTER RUDIMENT
(FLIGHT OF —S) GRECE GRICE

PERRON GEMONIES
(HALF —) HALFTONE SEMITONE
(MINING —) LOB STEMPEL STEMPLE
(POMPOUS —) STRUT
(PRIM —) MINCE
(SET OF —S) STILE
(STATELY —) STALK
(PL.) STY STILE LADDER
STEPFATHER FATHER STEPSIRE
STEPLADDER TRAP STEPS
STEPMOTHER MOTHER HANGNAIL STEPDAME
(RELATING TO —) NOVERCAL
STEPPE PUSZTA
STEPPED STOPEN
STEREOISOMER ANOMER EPIMER
STEREOTYPE CAST CLICHE STEREO
STEREOTYPED CHAIN STAGE TRITE USUAL STEREO
STERILE DRY DEAD DEAF GELD POOR AXENIC BARREN GALLED MEAGER MULISH OTIOSE ASEPTIC ACARPOUS BANKRUPT IMPOTENT
STERILITY ATOCIA APHORIA
STERILIZE INSULATE
STERILIZING BURNING
STERLING SOUND
(100,000 POUNDS —) PLUM
STERN GRIL GRIM HARD POOP ASPER CRUEL GRUFF HARSH RIGID ROUGH ROUND STARK STOUR FLINTY GLOOMY GRIMLY SHREWD STRICT SULLEN TORVID UNKIND WICKED AUSTERE TORVOUS STEERAGE STERNFUL STRAIGHT
(— OF SHIP) DOCK APLUSTRE
STERNFAST PROVISO
STERNNESS RIGOR TORVITY SEVERITY
STERNPOST POST STEM MAINPOST
STERNUTATIVE ERRHINE PTARMIC
STERNUTATOR ERRHINE
STEROL AMYRIN STERIN AMBRAIN
STEVEDORE STOWER TRIMMER WHARFIE CARGADOR DOCKHAND
STEVENSON, R.L. TUSITALA
STEW JUG FRET ITCH SLUM SNIT BREDI CIVET CURRY DAUBE STIVE STOVE SWEAT BURGOO HODDLE MUDDLE PAELLA SEETHE SIMMER BROTHEL CALDERA GOULASH HARICOT NAVARIN PUCHERO STOVIES FRIJOADA HOTCHPOT MORTREUX MULLIGAN STEWPOND STUFFATA
(— A HARE) JUG
(— IN A SAUCE) DAUBE
(— MADE IN FORECASTLE) HODDLE
(— OF TRAMPS) MULLIGAN
(FISH —) STODGE CHOWDER
(IRISH —) STOVIES
(MUTTON —) NAVARIN
STEWARD HIND VOGT DEWAN DIWAN GRAFF GRAVE FACTOR FARMER GRIEVE LOOKER SIRCAR SIRDAR CURATOR DAPIFER FLUNKEY GRANGER HUSBAND MAORMOR MORMAOR PESHKAR PROCTOR PROVOST SPENCER SPENDER

VILLCUS APPROVER BHANDARI
CELLARER CONSUMAH GASTALDO
HERENACH KHANSAMA LARDINER
MALVOLIO MANCIPLE PROVISOR
STEADMAN
(JOCKEY CLUB —) STIPE
STEWED SODDEN
STEWING ITCHING
STEWPAN STEW COCOTTE SKILLET
STHENELUS (FATHER OF —)
PERSEUS CAPANEUS ANDROGEOS
(MOTHER OF —) EVADNE
ANDROMEDA
(SON OF —) EURYSTHEUS
(WIFE OF —) NICIPPE
STHENOBOEA (FATHER OF —)
IOBATES
(HUSBAND OF —) PROETUS
STIBNITE SURMA STIBIUM ANTIMONY
STIBOPHEN FUADIN
STICHIC SERIAL
STICK CAT CLA DIP GAD HEW WAN
BROG BUFF CHOP CLAG CLAM CLUB
CRAB GLUE HANG HURL PALO PICK
POLE POTE RICE RUNG STAY TREE
YARD BATON BRAIL CAMAN CLAME
CLAVE CLEAM CLING CROME
DEMUR HURLY PRICK SPELK STAFF
STAKE STANG STAVE STEND STING
STOCK STOKE VALET VERGE
WADDY ADHERE ATLATL BALLOW
BATLER BATLET BATTLE BILLET
BROACH BULGER CEMENT CLEAVE
CLEEKY COHERE CUDGEL FESCUE
HOCKEY INHERE KIPPIN LIBBET
MALLET RADDLE RAMMER RISSLE
STRIKE STRING THIVEL TWITCH
BACKSET BATLING CAMMOCK
CUMMOCK GAMBREL HURLBAT
KILNRIB KIPPEEN MOLINET NOBBLER
SHANGAN SPURTLE WOOLDER
ASHPLANT BLUDGEON BRINGSEL
BRINSELL CATPIECE CATSTICK
DIPSTICK DUTCHMAN GIBSTAFF
GOBSTICK KILNTREE POTSTICK
SPREADER
(— AS ARCHERY MARK) WAND
(— FAST) JAM JAMB SEIZE FITCHER
(— FASTENED TO DOG'S TAIL)
SHANGAN
(— FOR ADMITTING TENANTS)
VERGE
(— FOR KILLING FISH) NOBBLER
(— FOR MAKING FENCE) RADDLE
(— FOR MIXING CHOCOLATE)
MOLINET
(— FOR SNUFF) DIP
(— FOR THATCHING) SPAR GROOM
SPELK SPRINGLE
(— IN MUD) STODGE
(— IN OPERATION) FREEZE
(— IT OUT) LAST
(— OF A FAN) BRIN
(— OF CANDY) GIBBY
(— OF CHALK) CRAYON
(— OF ORCHESTRA LEADER) BATON
(— OUT) BUG POKE BULGE SHOOT
EXTEND EXXERT EXTRUDE
(— REGULATING SLUICEWAY)
CATPIECE

(— SEPARATING LUMBER PILES)
STICKER
(— TO BEAT CLOTHES) BATLER
BATLET
(— TO DISTEND CARCASS) STEND
BACKSET
(— TO HOLD BOW) TILLER
(— TO HOLD LOG LOAD) DUTCHMAN
(— TO KEEP ANIMAL QUIET)
TWITCH
(— TO MARK CROSSING) BROG
(— TO POKE WITH) POTE
(— TO REMOVE HOOK FROM FISH)
GOBSTICK
(— TO STRETCH NET) BRAIL
(— TO STUFF DOLLS) RAMMER
(— TO THROW AT BIRDS) SQUAIL
(— TO TIGHTEN KNOT) WOOLDER
(— TOGETHER) CLOT BLOCK CLING
BALTER CEMENT COHERE
COAGMENT
(— UP) COCK
(— USED AS POINTER) FESCUE
(BAMBOO —) LATHI LATHEE
(BASKETRY —) LEAGUE
(BENT —) RIFLE
(FIELD HOCKEY —) BULGER
CAMMOCK
(FISHING —) GAD
(FORKED —) GROM GROOM
(HOCKEY —) CAMAN HURLY
HOCKEY HURLEY SHINNY CAMMOCK
CUMMOCK DODDART
(IRON-POINTED —) VALET
(KNOBBED —) BILLET
(LACROSSE —) CROSSE
(LARGE —) MOCK
(MARKING —) LEAD
(ODD —) JAY
(POLISHING —) BUFF
(PRAYER —) PAHO
(PRINTER'S —) SHOOTER
(RANGE-FINDING —) STADIA
(ROUND —) DOWEL SPINDLE
(STIRRING —) MUNDLE POOLER
SPURTLE POTSTICK SWIZZLER
(STOUT —) BAT LOWDER
(TALLY —) TAIL
(THROWING —) ATLATL HORNERAH
(TOBACCO —) LATH
(WALKING —) CANE KEBBY WADDY
JAMBEE JOCKEY KEBBIE WHANGEE
ASHPLANT GIBSTAFF
STICKER HINGE LABEL STRIP WAFER
HOPPER PASTER BLEEDER
CROSSER MOPSTICK STICKLER
STICK-IN STRANDER
STICKINESS TACK
STICKING ADHERENT ADHESION
COHESION COHESIVE
STICKLE DEMUR BOGGLE HAGGLE
HIGGLE
STICKLEBACK BAGGIE BANDIE
HACKLE GHOSTER PINFISH
STICKLER (— FOR FORMALITY)
TAPIST
STICKMAN DEALER
STICKY CAB CLAM CLIT ICKY DABBY
FATTY GAUMY GLUEY GOOEY

GUMMY JAMMY MALMY PUGGY
SHORT TACKY TOUGH CLAGGY
CLAMMY CLARTY CLOGGY PLUCKY
VISCID VISCOUS ADHESIVE
STIFF BUM SAD CARK HARD NASH
TRIG BUDGE CLUNG RIGID SOLID
STARK STEER STITH STOUR THARF
TOUGH BOARDY CLEDGY CLUMSY
CLUNCH FORMAL FROZEN PLUGGY
STARKY STEEVE STICKY STILTY
STOCKY STURDY UNEASY WOODEN
ANGULAR COSTIVE STARCHY
STILTED RAMRODDY RIGOROUS
STAFFISH
(SOMEWHAT —) CARKLED
STIFFEN GUM SET SIZE BRACE
STARK STIFF STRUT TRUSS HARDEN
STARCH STOVER STARKEN
(— PRICE) HARDEN
STIFFENED FUSED CARKLED
STIFFENER KNEE COUNTER
STIFFENING PUFF DRESS
STIFFNESS KINK RIGOR STARCH
BUCKRAM PRIMNESS RIGIDITY
SEVERITY
STIFLE DAMP SLAY CHOKE CRUSH
STIVE STUFF MUFFLE QUENCH
FLASKER QUERKEN SMOTHER
STRANGLE SUPPRESS THROTTLE
STIFLED DEAF ETOUFFE
STIFLING STUVY SMUDGY POTHERY
SMOTHERY
STIGMA BLOT FOIL NOTE SLUR
SPOT BRAND ODIUM STAIN TAINT
BLOTCH BLEMISH
STIGMATIZE BLOT BRAND
DENOUNCE
STILBITE DESMINE
STILE STY STICK TIMBER
STILETTO BODKIN STYLET PIERCER
POINTEL
STILL BUT COY LAY YET BODY CALM
COSH HUSH LOWN LULL WORM
CHECK QUIET WHIST HOWEER
HUSHED PACIFY QUENCH SETTLE
SILENT SOOTHE SUBDUE WITHAL
ALEMBIC CORNUTE HOWEVER
PELICAN SILENCE CUCURBIT
RECEIVER RESTRAIN STAGNANT
STILLERY SUPPRESS
(— PART) KELD
STILLAGE SLOP STILLING STILLION
STILL-HUNT STALK
STILLNESS CALM HUSH REST PEACE
SILENCE STATION
STILT KAKI POGO TILT LAWYER
PATTEN SCATCH YEGUITA
LONGLEGS STILTIFY TRIANGLE
STILTED LOFTY STIFF FORMAL
POETIC STILTY POMPOUS
STIMULANT STIM INULA BRACER
FILLIP GINGER HARMAL PHYTIN
CAMPHOR REVIVER ADONIDIN
AMMONIAC EXCITANT STIMULUS
STIMULATE FAN HOP PEP FUEL
GOAD HYPO MOVE SEED SPUR STIR
URGE WHET FILIP IMPEL ROUSE
SPARK STING AROUSE EXCITE
FILLIP INCITE SPIRIT TICKLE UPSTIR

ANIMATE ENLIVEN INNERVE INSPIRE
QUICKEN ACTIVATE FARADIZE
IRRITATE MOTIVATE
STIMULATING SEXY BRISK
PUNGENT EROGENIC EXCITING
GENEROUS INCITANT STIRRING
(— **ANGER**) ADRENAL
STIMULATION IMPETUS
(**MENTAL** —) SPRITE
STIMULUS CUE AURA BROD EDGE
GOAD HYPO SPUR STIM STING
FILLIP MOTIVE SOURCE BAHNUNG
IMPETUS OESTRUS
STING NIP BITE BURN FOIN GOAD
TANG ATTER DEVIL PIQUE PRICK
STANG TOUCH NETTLE ACULEUS
BUGBITE PIERCER IRRITATE
STIMULUS
STINGILY STRAIT SCARCELY
STINGING KEEN SMART PEPPERY
PIQUANT POINTED PRICKLY
PUNGENT ACULEATE NETTLING
SCALDING URTICANT
STINGING ANT KELEP
STINGRAY ANGLER OBISPO TRYGON
BATFISH LOPHIID STEPHEN STINGER
WAIREPO
STINGY DRY DREE GAIN GAIR HARD
MEAN NEAR NIGH CLOSE MINGY
SCALY TIGHT DRIECH GRIPPY
HUNGRY NARROW SCABBY SCARCE
SCRIMY SKIMPY SKINNY SNIPPY
STRAIT CHINCHY CHINTZY MISERLY
NIGGARD
STINK FOGO GOAD STEW SMELL
SMEECH STENCH
STINKBIRD HOACIN HOATZIN
STINKING FOUL HIGH FETID PUTID
STINKY
STINKWOOD DOGWOOD
STINT TASK GRIST PINCH SCANT
SNAPE SKINCH STINGY TANTUM
SCANTLE
(**SHORT** —) SNATCH
(**WITHOUT** —) FREELY
STIPE STEM STALK
STIPEND ANN HIRE ANNAT WAGES
SALARY PENSION PREBEND
PROVEND COMMENDA
STIPENDIARY BEAK
STIPPLE SPONGE
STIPPLED DOTTED
STIPULATE ARTICLE PROTEST
COVENANT
STIPULATION IF ANNEX CLAUSE
ARTICLE PREMISE PROVISO
COVENANT
(PL.) TERMS
STIPULE SPINE SHEATH STIPEL
STIPULA TENDRIL
STIR DO ADO FAN GOG PUG WAG
BEET BUZZ CARD FUSS MOVE PEAL
RAUK ROKE WAKE AMOVE BUDGE
CHURN CREEP ERECT FUROR
HURRY MUDGE POACH RAISE
ROUST SLICE SPARK STING STOOR
STURT TEASE TOUCH AROUSE
AWAKEN BUBBLE BUSTLE CRUTCH
EXCITE FLURRY GINGER HUBBUB

JUMBLE KIAUGH MUDDLE POUTER
QUINCH QUITCH REMBLE REMOVE
ROUNCE STODGE SUMMON TATTER
ACTUATE ANIMATE BLATHER
FLUTTER PROVOKE STARKLE
SWIZZLE TROUBLE
(— **ABOUT**) KNOCK
(— **CALICO COLORS**) TEER
(— **DRINK**) MUDDLE SWIZZLE
(— **LIQUID**) ROG
(— **SOIL**) CHISEL
(— **UP WITH YEAST**) BARM
(— **UP**) FAN MIX BUZZ DRUM FUSS
MOVE PROG ROIL TOSS AMOVE
AREAR AWAKE ERECT QUICK ROUSE
SNURL SPOOK STOKE TARRY
BESTIR BOTHER CHOUSE EXCITE
INCITE JOSTLE KINDLE PUDDLE
RUMBLE TICKLE UPSTIR AGITATE
ANIMATE COMMOVE DISTURB
PRODDLE PROVOKE STUDDLE
TORMENT UNQUEME DISTRACT
STIRRER HOG DOLLY ROUSER
RUMMAGER
STIRRING RACY ASTIR DEEDFUL
THRILLY EXCITING PATHETIC
STIRRUP IRON CHAPELET STEELBOW
STITCH BAR RUN SEW KNIT LOOP
PURL WHIP CABLE CLOSE POINT
PREEN PUNTO STEEK ACCRUE
FESTON SUTURE TRICOT CROCHET
POPCORN FAGOTING
(— **OF CLOTHES**) TACK
(PL.) JOURS FILLING
STITCHBIRD IHI
STITCHDOWN SEWROUND
STITCHER WHIPPER
STITCHING SERGING FAGOTING
STOATING WHIPPING
STITCHWORT PAIGLE ALLBONE
SNAPPER HEADACHE SNAPJACK
SNAPWORT
STITHY STUDY SMITHY STIDDY
STUDDY
STOAT VAIR ERMINE WEASEL
CLUBSTER FUTTERET WHITRACK
STOCK COP DOG KIN ROD CANT
CROP FILL FOND FUND SEED SELL
STEM TRIP BLOND BLOOD BROTH
CASTE CREAM FLESH HOARD ISSUE
STALE STIRP STORE STUFF TALON
BUDGET CHOKER COMMON FUTURE
KAFFIR SHARES STOVEN STRAIN
SUPPLY CAPITAL DESCENT PILLORY
PROSAPY PROVIDE REPLETE
RESERVE BONEYARD CROSSBAR
DIESTOCK GILLIVER GUNSTOCK
MAGAZINE MERCHANT ORDINARY
SECURITY
(— **OF ANCHOR**) CROSS
(— **OF BREEDING MARES**) STRUDE
(— **OF FOOD**) FARE
(— **OF GRAIN**) COP
(— **OF MORPHEMES**) LEXICON
(— **OF WEAPONS**) ARSENAL
(— **OF WHIP**) CROP
(— **OF WINE**) CELLAR
(— **SOLD SHORT**) BEAR
(**FARM** —) BOW

(**LANGUAGE** —) SALISH SIOUAN
BOROTUKE
(**MEAT** —) BLOND BOUILLON
(**PLASTIC** —) BISCUIT
(**RAILROAD** —) GRANGER
(PL.) FOODS CIPPUS HARMAN
TIMBER CATASTA KAFFIRS
STOCKADE BOMA PEEL ETAPE
ZAREBA BARRIER TAMBOUR
STOCKADO
STOCK EXCHANGE BOURSE
COULISSE
STOCKFISH STOCK LUTFISK TITLING
SPELDING SPELDRON
STOCKING HOSE SOCK SHANK
STOCK CALIGA MOGGAN SCOGGER
SHINNER
(**FOOTLESS** —) HOGGER HUSHION
(**SOLELESS** —) TRAHEEN
(PL.) HOSE BUSKINS BOOTHOSE
STOCKJOBBING AGIOTAGE
STOCKWORK CARBONA
STOCKY FAT COBBY DUMPY GROSS
SQUAT STOUT CHUMPY CHUNKY
DUMPTY STUBBY STUGGY STUNTY
BUNTING COMPACT HEAVYSET
STOCKISH THICKSET
STODGY STUFFY STUGGY
STOIC IMPASSIVE
STOKEHOLD FIREROOM
STOKER FIREMAN BLOCKMAN
STOLE STAW ARMIL ORARY ARMILLA
ORARION
STOLEN HOT INOME STOUN FURTIVE
(— **GOODS**) MAINOUR
STOLID BEEFY CLUMSE STUPID
WOODEN CLUMPST DEADPAN
PASSIVE
STOLIDITY MORGUE
STOLON WIRE SOBOL SOBOLE
SOLENIUM
STOMACH MAW CROP GUTS KYTE
MARY POKE READ TANK WAME
WOMB BINGY BROOK GORGE
GROUF HEART TUMMY BINGEE
BINGEY BONNET CROPPY GEBBIE
PECHAN CONCOCT CRAPPIN
GIZZARD ABOMASUM
(— **OF ANIMAL**) CRAW
(— **OF CALF**) VELL
(— **OF RUMINANT**) READ RUMEN
BONNET OMASUM PAUNCH
ABOMASUM MANIFOLD RODDIKIN
(**PIG'S** —) JAUDIE
STOMACHACHE FANTAD GULLION
STOMACHER GIMP TRUSS ECHELLE
PLACARD POITREL FOREPART
STOMACHIC COTO CORNUS
GENTIAN ANTHEMIS
STONE DAM GEM BOND DUCK FLAG
HERD KLIP KNAR MARK ROCK STEN
TRIG BAUTA CAPEL DRAKE GUARD
LAPIS PAVER PITCH SCRAE SCREE
SNECK STANE ASHLAR BEDDER
BENBEN CEPHAS CHATON CLOSER
COBBLE GAMAHE GIBBER HEADER
JUMPER LEDGER MARVER METATE
MULLER NUTLET PEEVER PINNER
RUNNER SUMMER TORSEL ANGRITE

CALLAIS DINGBAT DONNOCK
DORNICK GLIDDER KNEELER
KNICKER PERPEND PITCHER
PUTAMEN RATCHEL STANNER
SURFACE THROUGH BAETULUS
CABOCHON DENDRITE EBENEZER
HAGSTONE LAPIDATE LAPILLUS
LAPSTONE MACEHEAD MONOLITH
NAKHLITE SKEWBACK TOPSTONE
(— ADHERING TO LEAD ORE) KEVEL
(— AS AMULET) HAGSTONE
(— AS IT COMES FROM QUARRY)
RUBBLE
(— AS ROAD MARKER) LEAGUE
(— AT DOOR) RYBAT
(— BLOCK) ASSIZE
(— FOR GLASS-ROLLING) MARVER
(— FORMING CAP OF PIER)
SUMMER CUSHION
(— HARD TO MOVE) SITFAST
(— HEAP) MAN
(— IN BLAST FURNACE) DAM
(— IN MEMORY OF DEAD)
MONUMENT
(— IN SMALL FRAGMENTS)
RATCHEL
(— OF FRUIT) COB PIT PAIP COBBE
NUTLET PYRENE PUTAMEN
(— OF PYRAMID SHAPE) BENBEN
(— PROVIDING CHANGE OF
DIRECTION) KNEELER
(— SET IN RING) CHATON
(— SHOT FROM STONE-BOW) JALET
(— TO DEATH) LAPIDATE
(— USED AS MONUMENT) MEGALITH
(— USED IN GAME) DUCK DRAKE
(— WITH INTERNAL CAVITY) GEODE
(—S FROM CRUSHER) TAILINGS
(—S IN WATER) STANNERS
(ARTIFICIAL —) ALBOLITE
(BINDING —) PERPEND THROUGH
PIERPONT
(BOND —) GIRDER KEYSTONE
(BOUNDARY —) TERM TERMINUS
(BROKEN — USED FOR ROADS)
BALLAST MACADAM
(BUILDING —) SUMMER MITCHEL
SPERONE
(CARVED —) CAMEO CUVETTE
(CASTING —) TYMP
(CHINA —) PETUNSE
(CLAY —) LECH
(COPING —) SKEW TABLET TABLING
CAPSTONE
(CURLING —) HOG HERD GUARD
LOOFIE POTLID
(DESERT —) GIBBER
(DRUID —) SARSEN
(DRYING —) STILLAGE
(EDGING —) SETTER
(FLAT —) PLAT DRAKE LEDGER
(FOUNDATION —) BEDDER
(GLITTERING —) DAZE
(GRAVE —) BAUTA STELE
(GREEN —) CALLAIS
(GRINDING —) METATE MULLER
(HOLY —) BEAR
(HOPSCOTCH —) PEEVER PALLALL
(IMAGINARY —) ADAMANT

(KIDNEY —) NEPHRITE
(LAST — IN COURSE) CLOSER
(LOOSE —) GLIDDER
(MEMORIAL —) BAUTA EBENEZER
(METEORIC —) ANGRITE NAKHLITE
(MIDDLE —) HONEY
(MONUMENTAL —) LECH
(PAVING —) PAVER PITCHER
(PHILOSOPHER'S —) ADROP
(PRECIOUS —) GEM OPAL RUBY
EWAGE JEWEL TOPAZ ADAMAS
LIGURE SHAMIR ASTERIA ASTRION
CRAPAUD CUVETTE DIAMOND
DIONISE EMERALD GELATIA JACINTH
OLIVINE SARDIUS AMETHYST
ASTROITE HYACINTH PANTARBE
SAPPHIRE YDRIADES
(PRECIOUS —S) PERRIE
(REFUSE —) ROACH
(SACRED —) BAETYL BAETULUS
(SEMIPRECIOUS —) ONYX SARD
MURRA GARNET CITRINE TIGEREYE
(SHARPENING —) HONE WHET
(SHOEMAKER'S —) LAPSTONE
(SMALL ROUND —) JACK
(SOFTENED —) SAP
(STEPPING —) GOAT
(STRATIFIED —) FLAG SLAB
(TALISMANIC —) GAMAHE
(UNSQUARED —) BACKING
(UPRIGHT —) BAUTA MENHIR
MASSEBAH
(PL.) LAPIDES LAPILLI
STONEBASS BAFARO WHAPUKU
STONEBOAT DRAY
STONEBOW RODD
STONECHAT CHAT SMICH
WHEATEAR
STONECROP SEDUM ORPINE
PRICKET WALLWORT
STONE CURLEW BUSTARD
STONECUTTER JADDER LAPICIDE
SCABBLER SCAPPLER SQUAREMAN
STONEFLY NAIAD
STONEHAND LOCKUP
STONELIKE LITHOID
STONEMAN IMPOSER
STONE MARTEN FOIN
STONEMASON DORBIE
STONE PARSLEY HONEWORT
STONE PINE PINON
STONE ROLLER MAMMY MOMMY
TOTER
STONE TOTER CUTLIPS
STONEWALLER STICKER
STONEWARE GRES BASALT JASPER
BASALTES CANEWARE
STONINESS LAPIDITY PETREITY
STONY RIGID COBBLY PETROUS
LAPIDOSE PETROSAL
STOOL FORM MORA SEAT STAB
COPPY CROCK HORSE STOLE
TREST BUFFET CREEPY CURRIE
TRIPOD TUFFET COMMODE CREEPIE
KNEELER SHAMBLE TABORET
TRESTLE TUMBREL BARSTOOL
STILLAGE
(3-LEGGED —) THRESTLE
(CLOSE —) TOM

(CUCKING —) THEW
(LOW —) COPPY SUNKIE CREEPIE
STOOLBALL TUTBALL
STOOL PIGEON NARK SNITCH
STOOGE STOOLIE
STOOP BOW BEND LEAN LOUT SINK
COUCH DEIGN STOPE STULP
COORIE CROUCH HUCKLE BALCONY
DECLINE DESCEND RUCKSEY
SUCCUMB
(— OF HAWK) SOUSE
STOOPING DUCK ASTOOP DESCENT
STOP HO BAS COG CUT DAM DIE
DOG END HOO LIN MAR SET BALK
BODE BUNG CALK CALL COOL DROP
EASE HALT HELP HOLD HOOK KILL
QUIT REED REST SIST SNUB STAP
STAY STEM STOW TEAT TENT TOHO
TRIG VIOL WEAR WHOA ABIDE
AVAST BASTA BELAY BLOCK BRAKE
BREAK CAULK CEASE CHECK
CHOKE CLAMP CLOSE DELAY
EMBAR HITCH LEAVE MEDIA PEACE
POINT QUINT SCOTE SLAKE SPARE
SPRAG STAND STASH STEEK STICK
STINT VIOLA AEOLIN ANCHOR
ARREST ASTINT BIFARA BOGGLE
BORROW CHEESE CLAMOR COLLAR
DESIST DETAIN GRAVEL INSTOP
MONTRE NASARD PERIOD SCOTCH
SQUASH STANCE STANCH STIFLE
TENUIS TROMBA BASSOON
CAESURA MELODIA MUSETTE
OPPRESS SOJOURN STATION
TERTIAN TWELFTH ASPIRATA
BACKSTOP BOMBARDE PRECLUDE
RECORDER STOPOVER STOPPAGE
SUPPRESS SURCEASE TENOROON
WALDHORN WITHSPAR
(— AS IF FRIGHTENED) BOGGLE
(— BLAST) DAMP
(— FLOW) BAFFLE STANCH
(— FOR FOOD) BAIT
(— FOR HORSE) BLOW
(— FROM FERMENTING) STUM
(— GROWTH) BLAST
(— GUN BREECH) OBTURATE
(— IN EARLY STAGES) ABORT
(— IN SPEAKING) HAW
(— LEAK) CALK CAULK FOTHER
(— ROWING) EASY
(— SHORT) JIB
(— SWINGING) SET
(— UNDESIREDLY) STALL
(— UP) DAM CALK CLOG CLOY FILL
PLUG CHINK ESTOP STUFF STANCH
STAUNCH OPPILATE
(— USING) SINK
(— WITH CLAY) PUG
(— WORK) SECURE
(BRIEF —) CALL
(GLOTTAL —) STOD CATCH STOSS
STOSSTON
(HARPSICHORD —) LUTE
(ROUGH —) ASPIRATA
(SUCTION —) CLICK
(TEMPORARY —) PAUSE SUSPEND
(VOICELESS —) TENUIS
(PL.) REEDWORK

STOPCOCK BIB BIBB BIBCOCK
TURNCOCK
STOPLIGHT IMPEDER
STOPOVER LAYOVER
STOPPAGE JAM ALLAY CHECK
HITCH LEATH STICK STINT ARREST
DEVALL STASIS EMBARGO GASLOCK
REFUSAL SHUTOFF STOPPLE
SHUTDOWN STOPWORK
(— OF DEVELOPMENT) ATROPHY
(WORK —) LOWSIN STRIKE
STOPPED PILEATA
(— WITH HAND) BOUCHE
STOPPER WAD BUNG CORK STOP
VICE CHECK FIPPLE STANCH
BOUCHON CLOSURE SHUTOFF
STOPGAP STOPPLE TAMPION
STOPCOCK
STOPPING STAY HOLDUP STOPPAGE
STORAGE STORE STOWAGE
BESTOWAL
STORAX COPALM STACTE STYRAX
LORDWOOD
STORE CAVE CRIB DECK FOND FUND
HOLD KEEP MASS SAVE SHOP
STOW TOKO CACHE DEPOT HOUSE
HUTCH STASH STOCK UPLAY
BAZAAR GARNER GIRNEL RECOND
STEEVE SUPPLY TIENDA WINKEL
ARSENAL BHANDAR BOOTERY
GROCERY HARVEST HUSBAND
IMBURSE REPOSIT RESTORE
BOUTIQUE EMPORIUM EXCHANGE
GARRISON MAGAZINE TENDEJON
WAREROOM WARNISON
(— BEER) AGE LAGER
(— CROP) BARN
(— FODDER) ENSILE
(— IN A MOW) GOVE
(— IN LUMBER CAMP) VAN
(— KEPT BY CHINESE) TOKO
(— OF FOOD) LARDER
(— OF WEALTH) FORTUNE
(— UP) FUND POWDER IMBURSE
SQUIRREL
(ABUNDANT —) MINE
(HIDDEN —) BIKE
(LARGE —) RAFF
(LIQUOR —) GROGGERY
(RESERVE —) SLUICE
(RICH —) ARGOSY
(SMALL —S) SLOPS
(PL.) SAMAN SUPPLY
STOREHOUSE BIKE GOLA CACHE
DEPOT ETAPE STORE ARGOSY
ARMORY BODEGA GODOWN PALACE
PANARY STAPLE VINTRY ARSENAL
BHANDAR CAMALIG CAMARIN
GRANARY STORAGE MAGAZINE
SADDLERY TREASURE
(— FOR BREAD) PANARY
(RAISED —) WHATA FUTTAH PATAKA
(UNDERGROUND —) PALACE
STOREKEEPER MERCHANT
STOREMAN
STOREROOM CAVE GOLA WARD
GOLAH BODEGA CELLAR DINGLE
BOXROOM BUTTERY GENIZAH
LAZARET POULTRY THALAMUS

(PAWNBROKER'S —) LUMBER
STORESHIP FLUTE
STORK WADER ARGALA JABIRU
SIMBIL HURGILA MAGUARI MARABOU
ADJUTANT CICONIID MARABOUT
OPENBEAK OPENBILL
STORKLIKE PELARGIC
STORKSBILL ERODIUM
STORM RIG WAP BLOW HAIL HUFF
RAGE RAMP RAND RAVE WIND
BLIZZ BLOUT BRASH DEVIL DRIFT
FORCE ORAGE STOUR ATTACK
BARBER EASTER EXPUGN WESTER
BLUSTER BRAVADO CYCLONE
DUSTING EQUINOX GAUSTER
PISACHI SHAITAN SNIFTER TEMPEST
TORMENT WEATHER BLOWDOWN
CALAMITY ERUPTION UPHEAVAL
WILLIWAW
(— OF BLOWS) STOUR
(DUST —) DEVIL DUSTER HABOOB
KHAMSIN PEESASH SHAITAN
(FURIOUS —) TEMPEST
(HAWAIIAN —) KONA
(SEVERE —) PEELER SNIFTER
(VIOLENT —) FLAW TUFAN CYCLONE
SNORTER
STORM DOOR DINGLE
STORMY FOUL GURL RUDE WILD
DIRTY DUSTY GURLY GUSTY STARK
WINDY COARSE RUGGED UNFINE
WINTRY FURIOUS NIMBOSE RIOTOUS
SQUALLY TROUBLE VIOLENT
AGITATED BLUSTERY CLUTTERY
ORAGIOUS TEMPESTY
STORMY PETREL MITTY WITCH
SPENCY
STORY GAG SAW DECK DIDO FLAT
LORE REDE TALE TEXT YARN ATTIC
CRACK ETAGE FABLE FLOOR KATHA
PITCH PROSE RECIT SOLAR SPELL
SPIEL STAGE STORE CUFFER
FABULA FLIGHT PISTLE SCREED
SOLLAR ADVANCE HAGGADA
HISTORY MANSARD MARCHEN
PROCESS RECITAL ANECDOTE
DREADFUL ENTRESOL
(— FROM THE PAST) LEGEND
(— OF BEEHIVE) SUPER
(— OF BUILDING) DECK FLAT ATTIC
CHESS ETAGE FLOOR PIANO SOLAR
STAGE FLIGHT SOLLAR MANSARD
ENTRESOL
(— OF HEROES) SAGA
(ABSURD —) CANARD
(ADVENTURE —) YARN
(AMUSING —) DROLLERY
(BIRTH —) JATAKA
(DOLEFUL —) JEREMIAD
(EERIE —) CHILLER
(FAKE —) STRING
(FALSE —) SHAVE CANARD
WHOPPER
(MADE-UP —) FUDGE
(MONSTROUS —) BANGER
(MORBIDLY SENSATIONAL —)
DREADFUL
(MYSTERY —) WHODUNIT
(NEWS —) SIDEBAR

(NEWSPAPER —) LEAD FEATURE
(OLD —) DIDO
(POMPOUS —) BRAG
(PREPOSTEROUS —) CUFFER
(RIBALD —) HARLOTRY
(SATIRICAL —) SKIT
(SHORT —) CONTE NOVELLA
(STALE —) CHESTNUT
(UPPER —) ATTIC GARRET
HYPEROON
(PL.) LEGENDA
STORY BOOK TALEBOOK
STORYTELLER CONTEUR DISCOUR
DISSOUR
STOUP STOOP BENITIER
STOUT FAT SAD FIRM STUT TRIM
BROSY BULKY BUNTY BURLY
COBBY FRACK FRECK GREAT
HARDY KEDGE OBESE PLUMP
PODDY PUNCH STARK STERN
FLESHY PORTER PORTLY PRETTY
PYKNIC ROTUND SQUARE STRONG
STUFFY STURDY BOWERLY REPLETE
FORCIBLE POWERFUL ROBOREAN
STALWART THICKSET
(— PERSON) GURK
STOUTHEARTED GOOD VALIANT
STOUTLY FAST HARDILY
STOUTNESS STRENGTH
STOVE HOD STOW BOGEY CHULA
PEACH PLATE CHULHA COCKLE
COOKER HEATER PRIMUS BRASERO
CHAUFFER FRANKLIN POTBELLY
(— FOR DRYING GUNPOWDER)
GLOOM
(— ON SHIP) GALLEY
(RUSSIAN —) PEACH
(WARMING —) KANGRI
STOVER OVENSMAN
STOW BIN BOX SET CRAM LADE
MASS CROWD DOUSE STORE
BESTOW COOPER STEEVE DUNNAGE
RUMMAGE
STOWAGE BURTON
STOWED IN
STOWER TOPPER
STOWING BINNING GOBBING
STRABISMUS CAST CROSS SQUINT
TROPIA ANOPSIA COCKEYE
WALLEYE
STRADDLE SADDLE SPREAD STRIDE
BESTRIDE SPRADDLE STRIDDLE
STRAGGLE ROVE RANGLE SPRAWL
STREEL TAGGLE WANDER DRAGGLE
MEANDER SCRAMBLE SPRANGLE
STRAGGLER STRAY
STRAGGLING RAGGED RAGGLED
SPRAYEY SCRATCHY VAGULOUS
STRAIGHT BOLT FAIR FULL GAIN
BRANT CLEAN DOGGY FLUSH RIGHT
SHORT SPANG ARIGHT DIRECT
HONEST STRAIT STRICT BOBTAIL
UPRIGHT DIRECTLY SEQUENCE
(— AHEAD) ANON PLUMP OUTRIGHT
(— UP AND DOWN) SHEER CLEVER
EVENDOWN
(NOT —) CRAZY
STRAIGHTEDGE RULER STRICKLE
STRAIGHTEN GAG ORDER STENT

EXTEND SQUARE UNKINK COMPOSE
RECTIFY STRETCH
(— BY HEATING) SET
(— NEEDLE) RUB
(— RAILS) GAG
STRAIGHT-FIBERED BROAD
STRAIGHTFORWARD EVEN PLAT
APERT FRANK LEVEL NAKED ROUND
CANDID DEXTER DIRECT HONEST
SIMPLE SQUARE JANNOCK SINCERE
EVENDOWN HOMESPUN OUTRIGHT
STRAIGHT
(NOT —) CROOKED PLAITED
STRAIGHTFORWARDLY SINGLY
SQUARE STRAIGHT
STRAIGHT-THINKING CLEAR
STRAIGHTWAY ANON AWAY RIGHT
ARIGHT BEDEEN BEDENE DIRECTLY
STRAIN FIT LAG RAX SIE TAX TRY
TUG ACHE BEND CALL DASH DRAG
HEAT HEFT LAWN NOTE PULL RANN
SILE SINE SOLO SONG VEIN WORK
BRUNT CHAFE DEMUR DRAIN FORCE
HEAVE PRESS RETCH SHADE SHEAR
STOCK SURGE TAMMY TOUCH
WREST WRICK CLENCH EFFORT
EXTEND EXTORT FILTER INTEND
SPRAIN SPRING STREAK STRESS
STRIND THRONG DESCANT DISCANT
EUPLOID FATIGUE STRAINT
STRETCH STROPHE TENSION
TORMENT DIAPASON DIATRIBE
DIHYBRID SUBBREED
(— MILK) SIE SYE
(— OF AN ARCH) THRUST
(— OF CHICKENS) ANCOBAR
(— OF RAILING LANGUAGE)
DIATRIBE
(— ON BUGLE) MOT
(— ON HORN) MOT RECHASE
RECHEAT
(— THROUGH COLANDER) COIL
(CONCLUDING —) CADENCE
(MUSICAL —) FIT SOLO POINT
(MUSICAL —S) TOUCH
(MUTANT —) SALTANT
STRAINED PENT TENSE INTENSE
LABORED INTENDED
STRAINER CAGE ROSE SILE RENGE
SIEVE STRUM TAMIS TAMMY THEAD
SEARCE SEARCH CRIBBLE
COLATORY COLATURE SEARCHER
(— OF TWIGS) HUCKMUCK
(COFFEE —) GRECQUE
(MILK —) SAY MILSEY MILSIE
(WICKER —) THEAD THEDE
STRAINING CUTE COILED ASTRAIN
INTENSE COLATURE
STRAIT CUT GUT BAND BELT FRET
KYLE NECK PACE BRAKE CANAL
PHARE PINCH SHARD ANGUST
FRETUM NARROW PLUNGE CHANNEL
EURIPUS BOSPORUS JUNCTURE
(IN —S) SET
(NEWFOUNDLAND —) TICKLER
(PL.) CHOPS PRESS EXTREMES
STRAITEN PINCH SCANT STRAIT
STRAITENED CRIMP NARROW
CRIMPED

STRAITJACKET CAMISOLE
STRAITLACED STIFF BLUENOSED
STRAKE SHEER COURSE RISING
STREAK COAMING SAXBOARD
(PL.) TIRE
STRAMONIUM DEWTRY
STRAND PLY TOP BANK CORE FLAT
TOWT BEACH BRAID CLIFF PRAYA
READY SHORE LISSOM SINGLE
SLIVER STRAIN STRIKE SUTURE
HAIRLINE
(— OF HAIR) LICK SWITCH
(— OF PROTOPLASM) BRIDGE
STRANDED ISOLATED
STRANDER EDGER
STRANGE ODD EERY FELL FREM
NICE RARE UNCO ALIEN EERIE
FREMT FUNNY NOVEL QUEER UNKET
UNKID WOOZY ALANGE FERLIE
QUAINT UNIQUE UNKENT UNKIND
CURIOUS ERRATIC HEATHEN
UNHEARD UNKNOWN UNUSUAL
FANCIFUL INSOLENT INSOLITE
PECULIAR SELCOUTH SINGULAR
UNCOLIKE UNCOMMON UNKENNED
UNKINDLY
STRANGER COME UNCO UNKO
ALIEN GUEST FRENNE GANGER
INCOME INMATE FUIDHIR INCOMER
UNCOUTH MALIHINI OUTCOMER
PEREGRIN
STRANGLE CHOKE GRAIN GRANE
SNARL WORRY STIFLE GARROTE
QUACKLE GARROTTE JUGULATE
THROTTLE
STRANGLEHOLD CHANCERY
STRANGUL
STRAP BAR TUG BAND CLIP CURB
GIRD HASP RIDE RIEM BRACE
CHEEK GIRTH GUIGE PATTE RIDER
RISER SABOT SLING STROP THONG
TRACE ANKLET BACKER RILLET
COLLAR ENARME GARTER HALTER
HANGER LAINER LATIGO SANDAL
TOGGLE WARROK BABICHE
BOWYANG CRIBBER DOLPHIN
LANYARD LATCHET LEATHER
RIEMPIE STIRRUP TICKLER WEBBING
BACKSTAY BRETELLE SQUILGEE
TURNBACK WRISTLET
(— AROUND HORSE'S THROAT)
CRIBBER
(— AROUND MAST) DOLPHIN
(— FOR SHIELD) GUIGE ENARME
BRETELLE
(— IN FLAIL) TAPLING
(— OF BRIDLE) REIN
(— OF SENNIT) BACKER
(— ON HAWK'S LEAD) JESS JESSE
SENDAL
(— WITH SLIT END) TAWS TAWSE
(ANKLE —) BRACELET
(DOOR —) HASP
(MINER'S —) BYARD
(SHOE —) BAR
(STIRRUP —S) CHAPELET
(TIE —) SHANK
(U-SHAPED —) STIRRUP
(PL.) LADDER

STRAP FERN LONGLEAF
STRAPHANGER COMMUTER
STRAPPER SPLICER
STRAPPING SWANK CHOPPING
SLAPPING SWANKING
STRAP-SHAPED LORATE LIGULAR
LIGULATE
STRATA TERRANE UNDERAIR
(— OF COAL) MEASURES
STRATAGEM JIG COUP LOCK RUSE
TRAM TURN WILE ANGLE DRAFT
FETCH FRAUD GUILE JOKER KNACK
TRAIN TRICK WREST BLENCH
DECEIT DEVICE HUMBUG POLICY
TRAPAN TREPAN WOIDRE WRENCH
FINESSE SLEIGHT ARTIFICE
CONTOISE FARFETCH INTRIGUE
LIRIPIPE LIRIPOOP PRACTICE
PRACTISE QUENTISE STRATEGY
STRATEGY GAME FINESSE
STRATIFICATION BEDDING
STRATIFIED BEDDED VARVED
STRATUM BED CAP CUT LAY RIB
FAST LAIN SEAM COUCH ELITE
FLOOR LAYER LEDGE SHELF TABLE
COUCHE GIRDLE GRAVEL LAYING
LISSOM PINNEL AQUAFER AQUIFER
ENTIRIS FISHBED SUBSOIL UPRIGHT
AQUIFUGE FAHLBAND SUBGRADE
(— OF COAL) BENCH
(— OF FIRECLAY) THILL
(— OF PALE COLOR) FAHLBAND
(— OF SANDSTONE) PINNEL
(— OF SOIL) SOD
(— OF STONE) GIRDLE
(SOCIAL —) CUT
(THIN —) SEAM LENTIL
STRAW BAKU GLOY MOTE REED
RUSH TOYO WASE HAULM PEDAL
SHILF STALK STREW YEDDA FESCUE
FETTLE PANAMA RIZZOM SIPPER
TUSCAN BANGKOK SABUTAN
STUBBLE WINDLIN STRAMMEL
(— CUT FINE) CHAFF
(— FOR MAKING HATS) SENNIT
BANGKOK LEGHORN SABUTAN
(— FOR THATCHING) YELM
(— MEASURE) KEMPLE
(— TO PROTECT PLANTS) MULCH
(BROKEN —) BHUSA BHOOSA
(COOKERY —S) PAILLES
(PLAITED —) SENNIT
(WAXED —) STRASS
STRAWBERRY BERRY DUNLAP
FRAISE RUNNER HAUTBOY FRUTILLA
HAUTBOIS KLONDIKE ROSACEAN
STRAWBERRY BUSH WAHOO
EUONYMUS EVONYMUS FISHWOOD
STRAWBERRY FINCH AMADAVAT
AVADAVAT
STRAWBERRY SHRUB BUBBY
COWBERRY
STRAWBERRY TOMATO PHYSALIS
STRAY ERR ODD FALL RAVE ROVE
WAFF WAIF WALK DRIFT RANGE
TRAIK VAGUE WAVER ESTRAY
RANGLE SWERVE VAGARY WANDER
WILDER DEVIATE FORLORN

STRAYER DIVAGATE MAVERICK STRAGGLE

STRAYING ASTRAY ERRANT ABERRANT VAGATION

STREAK PAY RAY BAND SEAM VEIN WALE FLAKE FLECK FLICK FREAK GARLE GLADE SLASH FACULA SMUDGE STRAIN STRAKE STREAM STRIPE FLECKER SPRAING STIPPLE DISCOLOR TRAVERSE
(— IN FABRIC) CRACK SHINER
(— IN GLASS) SKIM
(— IN HAIR) BLAZE
(— IN SKY) ICEBLINK
(— IN WOOD) ROE
(— OF BLUBBER) BLANKET
(— OF LIGHT) STREAM
(— ON SURFACE OF SUN) FACULA
(— WITH FINE STRIPES) LACE
(—S FROM PLANE) CONTRAIL
(BACTERIOLOGICAL —) STROKE
(LOSING —) SLUMP
(THEATRICAL —) HAM
(WHITE —) SHIM

STREAKED ROWY LACED BRINDLE BROCKED BROOKED FINCHED SPARKED STRIPED WHIPPED BRINDLED IRONSHOT PINROWED

STREAKY ROWY SCOVY STREAKED

STREAM EA PUP RIO RUN BECK BURN FLOW FLUX FORD GILL GOTE KHAL KILL LAKE PUIT PURL RILL SICK SIKE SILE SPIN TIDE BACHE BATCH BAYOU BOGUE BROOK CREEK DRILL DRINK FLARE FLASH FLEAM FLOOD FLOSS FLUOR FRESH GHYLL NYMPH PRILL RITHE RIVER SWAMP TCHAI TRAIN ARROYO BANKER BOURNE BRANCH BURNIE CANADA COULEE FILLER FLUENT GUZZLE OUTLET PIRATE RANDOM RUNDLE RUNNEL SLUICE SPRUIT STRAND STRONE CHANNEL CURRENT DRIBBLE FLUENCE FRESHET RIVULET TRICKLE AFFLUENT INFLUENT
(— ALONG) SLIDE
(— FULL TO TOP) BANKER
(— OF AIR OR SMOKE) PEW
(— OF ELECTRODES) BEAM
(— OF LAVA) COULEE
(— OF SIRUP) THREAD
(— OF SPEECH) STRAIN
(— OUT) BREAK
(FLOWING —) NYMPH
(HIGH-SPEED —) JET
(MYTHOLOGICAL —S) ELIVAGAR
(SLOW —) OOZE
(SLUGGISH —) LANE
(SMALL —) BECK LAKE SIKE DRAFT RITHE COULEE SICKET SQUIRT STRIPE DRAUGHT GRINDLE
(THIN —) TRICKLE TRICKLET
(TIDAL —) COVE SEAPOOSE
(TRANSIENT —) RILL
(TRICKLING —) DRILL
(TURBID —) DRUVE
(UNDERGROUND —) AAR SWALLET
(VIOLENT —) TORRENT

(WEAK —) DRIP

STREAMER FLAG VANE GARTER GUIDON LAPPET PENCEL PENNON SCROLL SIMPLE WIMPLE BANDEROL FILAMENT
(— OF MOSS) WEEPER
(PAPER —S) CONFETTI

STREAMING SLUICY ASTREAM CYCLOSIS DOWNPOUR

STREAMLET RILL RILLET RUNDLE RUNLET RUNNEL RIVULET

STREAMLINE SIMPLIFY
(— FLOW) LAMINAR

STREAMLINED CLEAN SLEEK

STREET ROW RUE WAY CHAR DRUM GATE PAVE STEM TOBY BLOCK BORGO CALLE CANON CHAWK CORSO DRIVE AVENUE BOWERY CANYON CAUSEY RAMBLA CHAUSEE POULTRY TERRACE THROUGH ARTERIAL BROADWAY BYSTREET CONTRADA PROSPECT
(— IN BARCELONA) RAMBLA
(— IN FLORENCE) BORGO
(MAIN —) CHAWK CHOWK TOWNGATE
(NARROW —) CHAR ALLEY CHARE
(PRINCIPAL —) ARTERY
(SIDE —) HUTUNG

STREETCAR TRAMCAR ELECTRIC

STREET CLEANER ORDERLY CLEANSER

STREET CLEANING SLOPPING

STREETWALKER CRUISER

STRENGTH EL ARM VIR BEEF DRAW GRIP GUTS HEAD HORN IRON MAIN THEW BRAWN CRAFT ETHAN FIBER FIBRE FORCE HEART JUICE MIGHT NERVE POWER SINEW VIGOR ENERGY FOISON MAUGHT STARCH VIRTUE COURAGE STAMINA STHENIA CAPACITY FIRMNESS VALIDITY
(— OF ACID OR BASE) AVIDITY
(— OF ALE) STRIKE
(— OF CARD HAND) BODY
(— OF CHARACTER) GRISTLE
(— OF CURRENT) AMPERAGE
(— OF SOLUTION) TITER TITRE
(— OF SPIRITS) PROOF
(— OF TEA) DRAW
(— OF WILL) BACKBONE
(— OF WINE) SEVE

STRENGTHEN IMP ABLE BACK BIND FIRM FRAP HELP PROP SOUD STAY BRACE CLEAT FORCE SINEW STEEL THRAP TONIC TRUSS ANNEAL ASSURE DEEPEN ENDURE ENFIRM ENFORT GABION HARDEN INTEND MUNIFY MUNITE NEEDLE SETTLE STRING STRONG AFFORCE BUCKRAM COMFORT CONFIRM ENFORCE FASCINE FORTIFY NERVATE QUICKEN RAMPIRE SUPPORT THICKEN BUTTRESS ENERGIZE ENTRENCH HEIGHTEN ROBORATE

STRENGTHENED BULLED

STRENGTHENING ROBORANT

STRENGTHLESS DOWLESS

STRENUOUS HARD EAGER ARDUOUS WILLING VIGOROUS

STREPSIPTERON STYLOPS

STRESS HIT BRUNT ICTUS PINCH SHEAR ACCENT STRAIN THRONG CENTROID DOWNBEAT EMPHASIS
(— OF SOUND) LENGTH

STRESSED TONIC STRONG

STRETCH EKE LAG LIE RAX RUN BEAT DRAW LAST MAIN PASS RACK REAM ROLL SPAN TEND BOARD BURST FETCH RATCH RETCH SIGHT SPELL SWAGE VERGE EXTEND LENGTH SMOOTH STRAIN STRAKE STREEK DISPLAY DISTEND EXPANSE SPELDER ELONGATE STRAIGHT LENGHTEN
(— CLOTH) TENTER
(— INJURIOUSLY) SPRAIN
(— IRREGULARLY) TRAIL
(— LEATHER) DRAFT STAKE DRAUGHT
(— METAL) FORM
(— OF ARMS) FATHOM
(— OF GROUND) BRECK
(— OF INTERVAL) CARSE
(— OF LAND) SWALE COMMON GALLOP COMMONS
(— OF ROAD) SIGHT
(— OF SEA) CHOP
(— OF TIME) TIFF
(— OF WALL) CURTAIN
(— OF WATER) GLIDE LEVEL LOGIN FAIRWAY
(— OUT) GROW SPIN REACH STENT STRUT TWINE INTEND OUTLIE SPRAWL SPREAD SPRING DISTEND OUTSPAN PORTEND ELONGATE
(— THE NECK) CRANE
(GRASSY —) DRINN
(LEVEL —) LAWN

STRETCHED (— OUT) PORRECT PROJECT PROLATE ELONGATE EXTENDED
(TENSELY —) TAUT TORT STIFF

STRETCHER COT GURNEY LITTER ANGAREP TROLLEY ANGAREEB STRAINER

STREW BED SOW CLOT DUST LARD SPEW BESET STRAW STRAY STROW LITTER SPREAD BESTREW SCATTER SKINKLE SPARKLE
(— WITH BULLETS) SPRAY

STREWING SEME

STREWN DOTTED BESPRENT

STRIA CORD STRIOLA DRAGLINE STRIOLET

STRIATE VEIN

STRIATION STREAK STRIGA

STRICKEN STREAKED

STRICKER TIPPLER

STRICKLE SWEEP STRIKER

STRICT HARD TAUT TRUE CLOSE EXACT HARSH RIGID STARK STERN GIUSTO SEVERE STRAIT STRONG ASCETIC AUSTERE PRECISE DISTRICT RESTRICT RIGOROUS
(NOT —) LAX SCIOLTO

STRICTLY NARROW STRAIT CLOSELY
PROPERLY
STRICTNESS RIGOR RIGIDITY
RIGORISM SEVERITY
STRIDE SAIL STEP FLOAT SKELP
SPANG STEND STRUT LAMPER
STROAM STROKE STROME
BESTRIDE POINTING STRIDDLE
(— **LOFTILY**) STALK
(— **PURPOSEFULLY**) SLING
STRIDENT HARD HARSH BRASSY
GLASSY SHRILL RAUCOUS YELLING
GRINDING
STRIDULATE PITTER
STRIFE TUG WAR WIN BATE FEUD
HOLD PLEA BRIGE CHEST FLITE
JEHAD JIHAD NOISE STOUR STROW
STRUT STURT BARRAT DEBATE
ESTRIF MUTINY STRIVE CONTEST
DISCORD DISPUTE HURLING
QUARREL CONFLICT CONTRAST
DISPEACE STRUGGLE
(**CIVIL** —) STASIS
STRIGIL COMB SCRAPER
STRIKE GO BAT BOB BOP BOX BUM
COB CUE DAD DUB GET HAB HIT
JOB JOW LAM LAY PUG RAP ABRE
BAFF BEAK BEAT BELT BILL BLAD
BLIP BUFF BUMP CHAP CLUB COIN
COPE COSH CUFF DING DINT DONG
DUNT FALL FANG FIRK FLAP FLOG
FRAP GIRD GOWF HACK HURT JOWL
KILL KNEE LASH LILT LUSH MARK
NAIL PAIK PLAT PUCK ROUT SLAM
SLAP SLAT SLAY SLOG SLUG SOCK
SPAR SPAT SWAP SWAT SWIP TAKE
WHOP WIPE ANGLE BATON CATCH
CHECK CHIME CHINK CLOUT CLUNK
CRACK CRUNT DEVEL DOUSE
DOWSE DRIVE DUNCH FETCH FILCH
FILIP FLAIL KNOCK PANDY PASTE
POKER POTCH SABER SKELP SKITE
SLOSH SMACK SMITE SNICK SOUND
SPANK SQUAP STAMP STEEK
SWACK SWEEP SWIPE SWISH
THROW WHALE WHANG ACOUPE
AFFECT AFFRAP ATTAIN BATTER
BOUNCE BUFFET COURSE DUNDER
FETTLE FILLIP HAMMER INCUSE
INCUTE KEEPER SLOUGH STOUSH
STRICK STRIPE SWITCH THRASH
WALLOP BEARING FLYFLAP IMPINGE
KNUCKLE PERCUSS STRIKER
TURNOUT WHAMPLE WILDCAT
STOPPAGE STOPWORK STRICKLE
(— **A WICKET**) BREAK
(— **ABOUT**) FLOP
(— **AGAINST**) RAM BANG STUMP
ASSAULT COLLIDE
(— **AND REBOUND**) CAROM
(— **CRICKET BALL**) EDGE
(— **DOWN**) LAY FALL SLAY WEND
FLASH FLOOR AFFLICT SIDERATE
(— **DUMB**) DUMFOUND
(— **FEET TOGETHER**) HITCH
(— **FORCIBLY**) GET CLOUT DEVEL
SLASH
(— **GENTLY**) PAT
(— **GOLF BALL**) HOOK DRIVE
SCLAFF

(— **HEAVILY**) BASH DUNT FLOP
SLUG CLUMP SLOUGH
(— **IN CURLING**) WICK
(— **LIGHTLY**) BOB DAB SPAT FLICK
(— **OF LOCK**) KEEPER STRIKER
(— **ON HEAD**) COP NOBBLE
(— **OUT**) FAN TAKE CROSS ELIDE
CANCEL EXPUNGE OUTLASH
EXCUDATE
(— **REPEATEDLY**) DRUM LICK
(— **SHARPLY**) CUT SNICK
(— **SMARTLY**) NAP RAP KNAP
(— **TEETH TOGETHER**) GNASH
(— **TOGETHER**) CLASH KNACK
(— **UP**) LILT YERK RAISE
(— **VIOLENTLY**) RIP BASH DING
SOUSE BENSEL
(— **WITH AMAZEMENT**) CONFOUND
(— **WITH BAT**) DRIVE
(— **WITH FEAR**) ALARM ASTONISH
(— **WITH FIST**) PLUG NODDLE
(— **WITH FOOT**) KICK BUNCH SPURN
STAMP
(— **WITH HAMMER**) CHAP JOWL
MELL
(— **WITH HORNS**) BUNT BUTT HOOK
(— **WITH SPEAR**) STICK
(— **WITH STICK**) SQUAIL
(— **WITH WHIP**) JERK LASH QUIRK
(— **WITH WONDER**) SURPRISE
(**BOWLING** —**S**) DOUBLE
(**HUNGER** —) ENDURA
(**LABOR** —) STEEK STICK TURNOUT
WALKOUT
(**MINING** —) TREND
(**THREE** —**S**) TURKEY
STRIKEBREAKER FINK BLACKLEG
STRIKER BATMAN DRUMMER
TURNOUT PULSATOR
STRIKER-OUT SETTER
STRIKING FITTY FRESH SHOWY
VIVID DARING SIGNAL STRONG
SALIENT SKELPIN COLORFUL
CONFLICT DRAMATIC KNOCKOUT
SENSIBLE SPEAKING
STRING LAG BAND CORD FILE LACE
MEAN PAIR SLIP TAPE TAUM BRAID
BRIDE CHORD POINT SINEW SNEAD
STRAP CORDON STRAND TREBLE
MINIKIN LIGATURE RHAPSODY
(— **OF BEADS**) ROSARY CHAPLET
NECKLACE
(— **OF CASH**) QUAN TIAO
(— **OF DRUM**) SNARE
(— **OF FIDDLE**) THARM
(— **OF FLAGS**) HOIST
(— **OF LOCK**) KEEPER
(— **OF LYRE**) TRITE
(— **OF MUSICAL INSTRUMENT**) WIRE
CHORD DRONE CATLING MINIKIN
(— **OF ONIONS**) REEVE TRACE
(— **OF RAILWAY CARS**) SET
(— **OF SUGAR CRYSTALS**) COB
(— **OF VEGETABLES**) STRAP
(— **OF VIOL**) MEAN
(— **TOBACCO**) SEW
(**BONNET** —) BRIDE
(**E** —) QUINT
(**LEADING** —) BAND

(**ORNAMENTAL** —) CORDON
(**SURGICAL** —) LIGATURE
(**VIOLIN** —) THAIRM VIBRATOR
(**WEAVING** —) LEASH
STRING BEAN SNAP HARICOT
SNAPPER
STRINGCOURSE LEDGE TABLE
CORDON STRING
STRINGENT HARD RIGID SEVERE
STRICT EXTREME
STRINGER BALK BAULK
STRINGHALTED CRAMPY
STRINGY ROPY WOOLY SINEWY
THONGY WOOLLY GARGETY
SINEWED
STRIP BAR LAG TAG BAND BARE
BEAD BELT BEND BUSK DRIP FUSE
GAGE GAIR HILD HUSK LIST MALL
NAKE NUDE PEEL RAND ROLL SACK
SHIM SKIN TIRR WELT CLEAN DRIVE
EXUTE FILET FLAKE GAUGE GLEAN
GUARD HARRY LABEL LINER LYNCH
PANEL PLUME REEVE SHEAR SHRED
SKELP SLIPE SPEEL SPOIL STRAP
STROP STRUB SWATH UNGUM
UNRIG BORDER BOXING BRIDGE
COLLAR CULPON DENUDE DEVEST
DIVEST FEELER FILLET FLEECE
LIBBET MATRIX PANUNG SCROLL
SPLINE STREAK STRIPE TARGET
UNBARE UNBARK UNCASE BANDAGE
BEREAVE CHANNEL DEPLUME
DEPRIVE DESPOIL DISROBE
FEATHER FLOUNCE LAMBEAU
LANGUET NAILROD PINRAIL
PLUNDER UNCLOAK UNCOVER
UNDRESS BOOKMARK COSSETTE
DISARRAY DISENDOW DISTRUSS
FOOTBAND SEPARATE
(— **A PLANT**) SPRIG
(— **BARK**) PILL
(— **BINDING STALKS TO WALL**)
TACK
(— **BLUBBER FROM WHALE**) FLENSE
(— **EAR OF CORN**) SILK
(— **FOR DRAWING CURVED LINES**)
SPLINE
(— **FOR GUIDING PLASTER**) BEAD
(— **FOR MAKING TUBE**) SKELP
(— **HANGING AROUND SKIRT**)
FLOUNCE
(— **IN BASKETMAKING**) INSIDES
(— **IN BEEHIVE**) STARTER
(— **IN CANING**) SPLENT SPLINT
(— **IN TYPEWRITER**) DRAWBAND
(— **OF CANVAS**) FOOTBAND
(— **OF CLOTH**) LIST PATA RIND
GUARD BANNER DUTCHMAN
(— **OF CORK**) SPREADER
(— **OF FABRIC**) FLIPPER
(— **OF FAT**) FATBACK LARDOON
(— **OF FIELD HOCKEY AREA**) ALLEY
(— **OF FUR**) GROTZEN
(— **OF GRASS**) VERGE
(— **OF HIDE**) SPECK DEWLAP
(— **OF LAND**) BUTT LAND RAIK RAIN
RAKE TANG BREAK CREEK SLANG
SLIPE SPONG SCREED SELION
STRAKE STRIPE FURLONG ISTHMUS

CORRIDOR SIDELING
(— OF LEATHER) LAY RAND WELT
APRON RANGE THONG BACKSTAY
(— OF LEAVES) TWIST
(— OF LINEN) SETON
(— OF MASONRY) ARCHBAND
(— OF OFFICE) BREAK
(— OF OSIER) SKEIN
(— OF PALM LEAF) CADJAN CAJANG
(— OF PASTRY) STRAW
(— OF PLANKING) APRON
(— OF PRAIRIE) COVE
(— OF PROVISIONS) FORAGE
(— OF RANK) DEGRADE
(— OF ROADWAY) LANE
(— OF RUBBER) CUSHION
(— OF TURF) PARKING
(— OF UNPLOWED LAND) GAIR
HADE HEADLAND
(— OF WATER) INLET
(— OF WOOD) LAG LAT LATH LIST
SHAW SLAT WELT CHINK CLEAT
STAVE BATTEN INWALE REEPER
REGLET FOOTING FURRING STICKER
TRACKER FOOTLING
(— OFF SKIN) CASE FLAY
(— OFF) TIRL FLIPE FLYPE SLIPE
(— ON FOLDING DOORS) ASTRAGAL
(— ON PRINTER'S GALLEY) LEDGE
(— ON SQUASH COURT) TELLTALE
(— ON TIRE) CHAFER
(— SEPARATING LINES OF TYPE)
LEAD REGLET
(CAMOUFLAGING —) GARLAND
(COMIC —) FUNNY
(CONSTRUCTION —S) LAGGING
(CORSET —) BUSK
(DEPENDENT —) LAMBEAU
(DIVIDING —) CLOISON
(HORSESHOE-SHAPED —) BAIL BALE
(IRON IN —S) NAILROD
(NARROW —) SEAM SLAT SLIP TAPE
REEVE STRAKE
(PAPER —) ORIHON
(PROJECTING —) FEATHER
(RAISED —) RIDGE
(STRENGTHENING —) BEND
(THATCHING —) LEDGER
STRIPE BAR RAY BAND BEND LIST
PALE SLAT WALE WEAL WELT ZONE
FLECK PLAGA STRIA STRIP SWATH
VITTA WHEAL BORDER CLAVUS
COTICE FRENUM LADDER RIBBON
STRAKE STREAK STREAM COTTISE
SPRAING MUSTACHE TRAVERSE
(— OF CHEVRON) ARC
(— OF COLOR ON CHEEK) FRENUM
FRAENUM
(— ON ANIMAL'S FACE) SNIP BLAZE
(— ON FABRIC) CROSSBAR
(— ON MILITARY SLEEVE) SLASH
(ENCIRCLING —) ZONE
(PURPLE —) CLAVUS
(SET OF —S) BAR
STRIPED BANDY PALED PIRNY
RAWED RAYED ROWED WALED
ZONED BARRED CORDED LISTED
PIRNED BROCKED TIGROID VITTATE
FASCIATE STRIPPED

STRIPED BASS ROCKFISH SERRANID
STRIPED MAPLE DOGWOOD
STRIPING HAIRLINE
STRIPLIGHT BORDER
STRIPLING LAD SLIP STIRRA
YONKER SPAUGHT YOUNKER
SKIPJACK SPRINGAL
STRIPPED BARE NUDE NAKED
HUSKED PICKED PLUMED UNPEELED
STRIPPER STEMMER SPRIGGER
STRIPPING STROKINGS
(PL.) JIBBINGS
STRIPTEASER STRIPPER ECDYSIAST
STRIVE AIM HIE TEW TRY TUG DEAL
FEND PAIN TOIL WORK BANDY
DRIVE EXERT FIGHT FORCE LABOR
PRESS BUCKLE BUFFET DEBATE
INTEND PINGLE STRAIN STRIKE
AGONIZE CONTEND CONTEST
DISPUTE ENFORCE SCUFFLE
CONTRAST ENDEAVOR PURCHASE
STRUGGLE
(— AFTER) SEEK FOLLOW CANVASS
(— FOR SUPERIORITY) VIE
(— IN OPPOSITION) RIVAL CONTEND
(— TO EQUAL) EMULATE
(— TO OVERTAKE) ENSUE
STRIVING NISUS HORMIC STRIFT
CONATUS CONATION
STRIX SYRNIUM
STROBILE BUR BELL BURR CHAT
CONE BRUSH
STROKE BAT COY CUT DAB FIT JOW
ODD PAT PET POP RUB BAFF BEAT
BLOW CHAP CHOP CLAP COUP
DASH DENT DING DINT DIRD DRAW
DUNT EDGE FIRK FLAP FLEG FLIP
FLOP FUNG GOWF HURT JERK JOWL
KERF LASH LICK NACK PAIK PEAL
PECK SHOT SMIT SWAP TILT TIRE
TUCK WELT WHAP WIPE BRUSH
CHASE DOUSE DOWSE DRAFT
FLACK FLICK FORCE HATCH ICTUS
MINIM PANDY PULSE SHOCK SLASH
SLING SLIVE SLOSH STRIP SWEEP
SWING SWIPE THROW TRAIT TRICE
WHACK CARESS CENTER FONDLE
FOOZLE GENTLE GLANCE PLAGUE
PLUNGE SMOOTH STRAIK STRAKE
STRIKE STRIPE DRAUGHT OUTLASH
SOLIDUS VIRGULE APOPLEXY
DRUMBEAT FOREHAND INSTROKE
SCORCHER
(— IN PAINTING) HAND
(— IN PENMANSHIP) MINIM
(— IN TENNIS) LET LOB BOAST
CHASE SMASH BRICOLE BACKHAND
FOREHAND
(— OF A LETTER) DUCT STEM SERIF
CROSSBAR
(— OF BAD FORTUNE) CLAP
(— OF BELL) JOW BELL JOWL
KNELL TELLER
(— OF FORTUNE) CAST BREAK
FELICITY
(— OF LUCK) HIT FLUKE STRIKE
TURNUP CAPTION
(— OF SCYTHE) SWATH SWATHE
(— OF SHEARS) SNIP

(— OF WIT) FLIRT
(— OF WORK) BAT CHAR
(— ON THE PALM) LOOFIE
(BILLIARDS —) SPOT STUN FLUKE
FORCE MASSE HAZARD
(CONNECTING —) LIGATURE
(CRICKET —) CUT GLANCE
(CUTTING —) GIRD
(DOUBLE SPINNING —) DRAW
(DRUM —) DRAG
(GOLF —) ODD BAFF BISK HOOK
LIKE SLICE BISQUE FOOZLE SCLAFF
APPROACH
(HOCKEY —) JOB SCOOP
(JERKY —) STAB
(LIGHTNING —) BOLT
(MEDICAL —) ICTUS APOPLEXY
(ORNAMENTAL —) FLOURISH
(QUICK —) FLIP
(SKATING —) EDGE MOHAWK
CHOCTAW
(SMART —) FIRK
(SOOTHING —) COY
(SWIMMING —) CRAWL
(SWINGING —) HEW
(SWORD —) MONTANTO
STROLL JET IDLE ROAM ROVE
ANTER JAUNT RANGE STRAY TRAIK
BUMMEL DACKER DANDER GANDER
LOUNGE PALMER RAMBLE SOODLE
STROAM STROME WANDER
SAUNTER TURNOUT SPATIATE
STRAVAGE
STROLLER SULKY TRAMP SHULER
SHUILER VAGRANT BOHEMIAN
STROLLING FLANERIE FUGITIVE
STROMA ECOID OECOID
STRONG FAT FIT HOT FELL FERE
FIRM FORT HALE HANG HARD HIGH
IRON KEEN RANK SURE TRIG TRIM
ACRID BONNY FORCY FRECK FRESH
HARDY HEAVY HOGEN HUSKY JOLLY
LUSTY NAPPY NERVY ORPED PITHY
SHARP SMART SOLID SOUND STARK
STEER STERN STIFF STOUR STOUT
SWITH THEWY VALID VIVID WIGHT
YAULD ARDENT BRAWNY BUCKRA
BUNKUM FEIRIE FIERCE MIGHTY
POTENT PRETTY ROBUST RUGGED
SECURE SEVERE SINEWY STABLE
STANCH STARCH STURDY WIELDY
BOARDLY BUIRDLY DOUGHTY
DURABLE EXALTED FECKFUL
HUFFCAP HUMMING INTENSE
LUSTFUL NERVOUS SKOOKUM
STHENIC ATHLETIC BIDDABLE
MUSCULAR REVERENT ROBOREAN
SPANKING STALWART STIFFISH
VIGOROUS
STRONGBOX PETE COFFER
DEEDBOX
STRONGEST EXTREME
STRONGHOLD HOLD KEEP PIECE
PLACE TOWER CASTLE WARDER
CITADEL KREMLIN FASTHOLD
FASTNESS FORTRESS FRONTIER
STRENGTH
STRONGLY BUT SAD BADLY SWITH
FIRMLY STRONG DURABLY FRESHLY

HEFTILY SOLIDLY STITHLY STOUTLY
HEARTILY
STRONG-SCENTED HIGH RANK
STRONG-SMELLING FOXY
STROP RIP STRAP
STROPHE ALCAIC LAISSE STANZA
SAPPHIC
STROPHIUS (FATHER OF —)
CRISSUS
(SON OF —) PYLADES
STRUCK (— SHARPLY) SMITTEN
(— WITH AMAZEMENT) AGHAST
STRUCTURAL ANATOMIC TECTONIC
(— UNIT) IDANT
STRUCTURE CAGE FALX FORM
MAKE ANNEX BOOTH CABIN FLOAT
FRAME GETUP HOUSE KIOSK PEGMA
SETUP SHAPE STOCK BRIDGE
CAGEOT FABRIC GANTRY GIRDER
ISOGEN KELSON TIMBER COTTAGE
EDIFICE FAIRING FEATURE GATEWAY
GESTALT KEELSON MANSION
NURAGHE OUTCAST PAGEANT
STADIUM TURNOUT ZEUGITE
AEDICULA AIRCRAFT AIRFRAME
BUILDING BUTTRESS CRIBWORK
DOMATIUM ENDOCONE ESCORIAL
HEADWORK MOUNTURE NEOMORPH
SKELETON STANDARD
(— BUILT IN WATER) PIER
(— CONTAINING KILN) HOVEL
(— EXTENDED INTO SEA) JETTY
(— FOR PIGEONS) COTE
(— FRAMING SHIP) KEELSON
(— OF CARTRIDGE) ANVIL
(— OF PRETENSION) PERRON
(— ON ROOF) CUPOLA FEMERELL
(— ON SHIP) BLISTER
(— ON STEAMER) TEXAS
(— PRODUCING SMOOTH OUTLINE)
FAIRING
(— SHELTERING INSECTS)
DOMATIUM
**(— SUPPORTING AIRSHIP
PROPELLER)** PYLON
(— WITHIN SHELL) ENDOCONE
(ANATOMICAL —) BUD APRON
CARINA CRESCENT
(ANTICLINAL —) SWELL
(ARCHED —) FORNIX
(BODILY —) FRAME PHYSIQUE
(BRICK —) KANG HOVEL
(BRISTLELIKE —) ARISTA
(BRONZE AGE —) HENGE
(CABINLIKE —) CABANA
(CLIMBING —) LADDER
(COMPLEX —) EMBOLUS
(CONELIKE —) PYRAMID
(CONICAL —) BULLET
(CROWNLIKE —) CORONA
(CYLINDRICAL —) SILO
(DEADENING —) BAFFLE
(DEFENSIVE —) CAT
(FORTIFIED —) CAVALIER
(GENERAL —) GETUP
(GEOLOGICAL —) CAMBER
(HIGH —) TOWER
(HOLLOW —) SHELL
(KNEE-LIKE —) GENU

(LENS-SHAPED —) LENTOID
(LOFTY —) BABEL STEEPLE
(LOGICAL —) EIDOS
(ORGANIZED —) BULK
(ORIENTAL STORIED —) PAGODA
(ORNAMENTAL —) KIOSK
(PLANT —) DISC DISK
(POINTED —) BEAK
(PUEBLO —) KIVA
(RAISED —) CIMBORIO
(RAMSHACKLE —) COOP
(RINGLIKE —) ANNULUS
(RUDE STONE —S) SPECCHIE
(SACRIFICIAL —) ALTAR
(SENTENCE —) SYNTAX
(SHELTERING —) COT
(SICKLE-SHAPED —) FALX
(SLENDER —) HAIR
(STONE —) TAULA
(TEMPORARY —) HUT
(THEATER —) SKENE
(UNDERLYING —) BOTTOM
(UNSTABLE —) COBHOUSE
(WATERTIGHT —) CAMEL
(WHITE —) ALBEDO
STRUGGLE IT TEW TUG VIE WIN
AGON COPE DEAL FEND FICK FRAB
GAME PULL TAVE TOIL FIGHT FLING
HEAVE LABOR STRAY SWORD
TEAVE TWEIL WORRY WRELE
BATTLE BUCKLE BUFFET BUSTLE
COMBAT EFFORT HASSLE JOSTLE
JUSTLE PINGLE RELUCT SEESAW
SPRAWL SPRUNT STIVER STRIFE
STRIVE TERVEE TUSSLE WARSLE
WIDDLE AGONIZE CLAMBER
CONTEND CONTEST DISPUTE
FLOUNCE GRAPPLE SCUFFLE
TUILYIE WARFARE WAUCHLE
WRESTLE CONFLICT ENDEAVOR
FLOUNDER SCRAFFLE SCRAMBLE
SLUGFEST SPRANGLE SPRATTLE
(— ALONG) HOBBLE
(— CONVULSIVELY) SPRAWL
(— FOR LARGESS) SCAMBLE
(— FORTH) ELUCTATE
(— TO GAIN FOOTING) SCRABBLE
SPROTTLE
(AGONIZED —) THROE
(CONFUSED —) MUSS
(DEATH —) AGONY
(HAND-TO-HAND —) GRAPPLE
(HAPHAZARD —) SCUFFLE
(SPIRITUAL —) PENIEL
(UNCEREMONIOUS —) SCRAMBLE
STRUGGLER LAOCOON
STRUM THRUM
STRUMA GOITER GOITRE
STRUMPET BRIM PUNK TRULL
WENCH WHORE BLOWEN BULKER
STIVER TOMBOY TOMRIG COCOTTE
SUCCUBA DOLLYMOP PUNKLING
SUCCUBUS VENTURER
(WORN-OUT —) HARRIDAN
STRUT JET BRAG COCK POMP SPUR
CORSO MAJOR PRINK SWANK
SASHAY STROKE STROOT STRUNT
NAUNTLE PEACOCK STEMPLE
SWAGGER TRANSOM

STRUTTER HAM
STRUTTING COCKING
STUB BUTT SNAG SPUD STOB STUD
CHECK ERGOT GUARD HINGE
STUMP SPRUNT
STUBBLE BUN ETCH MANE SHACK
ARRISH EDDISH STOVER STUMPS
EEGRASS GRATTEN STIBBLE
STUBBORN SOT ROWDY RUSTY
STIFF STOUT STUNT THRAW TOUGH
MULISH STURDY THWART BULLDOG
PEEVISH PIGGISH RESTIVE
WAYWARD WILLFUL OBDURATE
PERVERSE STUNKARD THRAWART
STUBBORNNESS STOMACH
ADAMANCY
STUBBY STUB CUTTY SQUAT
STOCKY STUMPY STUBBED
STUCCO ALBARIUM
STUCK FAST MASHED STICKIT
STOODED
STUCK-UP BUG FROSTED
STUD SET BOLT BOSS KNOB KNOP
KNOT NAIL RACE SLUG SPOT BESET
BULLA CLOUT HARAS JOIST WRIST
ASHLAR ENSTAR INSTAR STOOTH
STRING CONTACT POTENCE
QUARTER STUDDLE PUNCHEON
STANDARD STUDDERY
(— FARM) HARAS
(— IN BOOT SOLE) SLUG
(— IN WATCH) POTENCE
(— SHOES) HOBNAIL
(— WITH NAILS) CLOUT
(INTERMEDIATE —) PUNCHEON
(ORNAMENTED —) AGLET AIGLET
STUDDED BOSSY BILLETY STELLED
BILLETTE
STUDDLE POST ROIL
STUDENT BOY DIG WIT COED PLUG
PREP SMUG SOPH AGGIE BAHUR
FUCHS GRIND MEDIC PUPIL SIZAR
SPOON BOCHER BURSAR BURSCH
INTERN JUNIOR JURIST MEDICO
OPTIME PRIMAR PRIMER PUISNE
SCOLOG SENIOR ADVISEE CLASSIC
DANTEAN EDUCAND ETONIAN
FAILURE GOLIARD GRECIAN
INTERNE INTRANT LEARNER
MOOTMAN OPPIDAN PASSMAN
PHARMIC PLUGGER SCHOLAR
STUDIER TEMPLAR THEOLOG
BOTANIST CABALIST COLLEGER
DEMOTIST DISCIPLE EDUCATOR
FEMINIST HOMERIST HOSTELER
ISLAMIST PREMEDIC REPEATER
SECONDAR SUBSIZAR TRANSFER
(— IN TALMUDIC ACADEMY) BAHUR
(— LAST IN CLASS) SPOON
(— OF LOW RANK) TERNAR TERNER
(— WHO LIVES IN TOWN) OPPIDAN
(1ST-YEAR —) FUCHS
(3RD-YEAR —) JUNIOR TERTIAN
(ABNORMALLY ABSORBED —) SAP
(DAY —) EXTERN EXTERNE
(DIVINITY —) STIBBLER
(DRUDGING —) PLUG
(ENGLISH SCHOOL —) BLUE SWOT
ETONIAN SWOTTER

(GRADUATE —) FELLOW
(LAW —) PUNEE JURIST LEGIST
PUISNE TEMPLAR STAGIARY
(MILITARY —) CADET
(NON-COLLEGIATE —) TOSHER
(PLODDING —) DIG SMUG
(WANDERING —) GOLIARD
(PL.) GOWN CLASS HOUSE SEMINAR
STUDIED COOL STUDIOUS
STUDIO LOT SHOT ATELIER
BOTTEGA GALLERY
STUDIOUS BOOKY BOOKISH
CLERKLY DILIGENT SEDULOUS
STUDY CON BEAT BONE BOOK CASE
MUZZ SIFT STUD GRIND ESTUDY
EXAMEN LESSON MUSEUM SCOLEY
SURVEY ABBOZZO ACCOUNT
ANALYZE CANVASS CROQUIS
POCHADE REVOLVE SANCTUM
ANALYSIS BOOKWORK CONSIDER
EXERCISE MEDITATE SCRUTINY
TYPOLOGY
(— HARD) DIG MUG BONE SMUG
STEW SWOT
(— OF PUNISHMENT) PENOLOGY
(— OF SACRED EDIFICES) NAOLOGY
(— OF SNOW AND ICE) CRYOLOGY
(— UNDER PRESSURE) CRAM
(ART —) ABBOZZO CROQUIS
POCHADE
(CLAY —) BOZZETTO
(MUSICAL —) ETUDE
(PRELIMINARY —) SKETCH
(UNINTERESTING —) GRIND
STUFF PAD RAM WAD CRAM GAUM
GEAR PANG STOP TACK TUCK
WHAT CROWD DUROY FARCE
FORCE KEDGE METAL PASTE SQUAB
TRADE FABRIC GRAITH KIBOSH
MATTER PAUNCH STEEVE STODGE
TACKLE TIMBER BOMBARD
BOMBAST DRUGGET ELEMENT
ENFARCE DIAPHANE MARINATE
MATERIAL SPLUTTER WHIPPING
(— AND NONSENSE) HAVERS
PICKLE PIFFLE
(— FILLET OF VEAL) BOMBARD
(≈ FULL) STODGE
(— OF POOR QUALITY SILK) RASH
(— ONESELF) MAST
(— POULTRY) FARCE MARINATE
(— WITH DRESSING) QUILT
(COTTON —) CALICO
(HOUSEHOLD —) GEAR
(INFERIOR —) MOCKADO
(SILKEN —) TARS TARSE DIAPHANE
(STICKY —) GOOK
(THIN —) CRAPE
(THIN SILK —) LOVE
(WISHY-WASHY —) BLASH
(WOOLEN —) DUROY TWILLY
DRUGGET
(WORTHLESS —) GEAR HOGWASH
STUFFED PANG TRIG BLOAT FARCI
STODGY BLOATED BOMBAST
STUFFING PAD TAR FARCE STECH
STUFF BOMBAST FARCING SAWDUST
STUFFAGE
(— FOR MATTRESS) PULU

STUFFY CLOSE FUBBY FUBSY FUGGY
STIVY WOOLY WOOLLY FROUSTY
STULTIFY SOT PUPPIFY
STUMBLE CHIP FALL HAMP PECK
STOT TRIP HAMEL LURCH SPURN
STOIT STUMP BUMBLE CHANCE
FALTER HALPER HAMBLE HAPPEN
LUMPER OFFEND STEVEL TUMBLE
WAGGER BLUNDER FOUNDER
SCAMBLE SNAPPER STAMMER
STAMPLE STOITER STOTTER
STUMMER FLOUNDER THRUMBLE
STUMBLING HACK HURTING
OFFENCE OFFENSE
STUMP CAG JOB SET BUTT DOCK
GRUB LUMP MORE RUNT SNAG
STAB STAM STOB STUB STUD
CHUNK SCRAB STICK STOCK STOMP
STOOL STOOP STOWL DOTARD
NUBBIN SCRUNT SPRONG STOVEN
WICKET DODDARD RAMPICK
RAMPIKE SLEEPER STUMMEL
BALDHEAD HUSTINGS STUBBLES
(— AND ROOT) MOCK
(— OF TAIL) STRUNT
(CIGAR —) TOPPER
(CRICKET —) STICKS
(DEAD —) RUNT
(TREE —) MOCK STOW STOCK
STOOP ZUCHE DOTARD NUBBIN
STOVEN DODDARD
(WALNUT —) BUTT
STUMPY SNUB BUNTY SNUBBED
STUN DIN BOWL DAZE DAUNT DAVER
DEAVE DOVER DOZEN DROWN
STONY ASTONY BEDAZE BENUMB
DEADEN DEAFEN NOBBLE STOUND
WITHER ASTOUND DAMMISH
SANDBAG SILENCE STUPEFY
STUPEND ASTONISH
(— BY A SHOT) CREASE
STUNNED SILLY STUPENT ASTONIED
STUNNER KNOCKER THUMPER
TRIMMER
STUNNING CRASHING SHOCKING
STUNT GAG KIP BLAST CANOE
CROWL DWARF STINT STOCK
BARANI BARONI CRADDY DOLPHIN
BACKBEND CATALINA CRUCIFIX
PORPOISE SUPPRESS
(SWIMMING —) SHARK SPIRAL
STUNTED URLED GRUBBY RUNTISH
SCROGGY SCRUBBY SCRUFFY
SCRUNTY
STUPA TOPE CHORTEN
STUPEFACTION STOUND STUPOR
STUPEFIED MAD DAMP DAZED
MAZED SILLY BEMAZED DONNERT
DOZENED DOZZLED STUPENT
BESOTTED DATELESS MINDLESS
STUPEFIER OPIUM
STUPEFY FOX BAZE DAMP DAZE
DOZE DRUG DULL GOOF MAZE
STUN BESOT DAUNT DAVER DEAVE
DIZZY DOZEN SHEND SMOKE STONY
ASTONE ASWEVE BENUMB DUDDLE
FUDDLE MUDDLE STOUND ASTOUND
CONFUSE FORDULL SLUMBER
SMNIATE STUPEND ASTONISH

BEFUDDLE BEWILDER CONFOUND
MORPHINE SOPORATE
STUPEFYING STONY
STUPENDOUS GREAT IMMENSE
ENORMOUS
STUPID FAT BETE DOWF DULL DUMB
DUNT FOOL HAZY LEWD NICE NUMB
SLOW BLUNT BRUTE CRASS DENSE
DUNNY GLAKY GOOSY GROSS
HEAVY INERT MOSSY MUZZY SILLY
THICK ASSISH BARREN CUCKOO
DAWKIN DOITED DROWSY DUMMEL
HEBETE LOGGER OBTUSE OPAQUE
SIMPLE STOLID STULTY STURDY
SUMPHY URLUCH WOODEN ASININE
BRUTISH CHUCKLE DOLTISH
DOWFART DUFFING DUMPISH
FATUOUS FOOLISH FOPPISH
GAWKISH GLAIKIT GULLISH INSULSE
LUMPISH LURDANE PEAKISH
PINHEAD PROSAIC SOTTISH TAIVERT
TOMFOOL VACUOUS WITLESS
ANSERINE BAYARDLY BESOTTED
BLOCKISH BOEOTIAN CLODDISH
DONNERED DUNCICAL FOOTLESS
GAUMLESS HEADLESS IMBECILE
STOCKISH
(— PERSON) HOIT JUKES SUMPH
LUMMOX TUMFIE KALLIKAK
STUPIDITY BETISE BOBBERY
DENSITY DUNCERY FATUITY
DULLNESS DUMBNESS HEBETUDE
STUPOR FOG SOG DAMP DOTE
SOPOR SWARF STOUND TRANCE
NARCOMA LETHARGY NARCOSIS
STURDILY BUFF TOUGH
STURDY GID BUFF DUNT RUDE TALL
THRO BURLY CRANK FELON HARDY
HUSKY LUSTY SOLID SOUND STARK
STERN STIFF STOUT VAUDY WALLY
FEERIE PLUGGY ROBUST RUGGED
RUSTIC SQUARE STABLE STEADY
STEEVE STOCKY STRONG STUGGY
VIRILE FECKFUL UPRIGHT VALIANT
STALWART STUBBORN VIGOROUS
YEOMANLY
STURGEON HUSO ELOPS BELUGA
GANOID MAMMOSE STERLET
STUTTER FAM BUFF HACK MANT
STOT STUT GANCH FAMBLE HABBER
HABBLE STAMMER
STUTTERER RATTLER
STUTTERING TRAULISM
STY PEN QUAT STYE WEST FRANK
PIGPEN STITHE HORDEOLUM
STYLE AIR CUT DUB PEN SAY TON
WAY CHIC FACE FORM GARB KIND
MODE MOLD NAME PILE RATE TWIG
VEIN GENRE GETUP GUISE SHAPE
STATE SWANK TASTE FESCUE
FORMAT GNOMON GOTHIC PHRASE
STEELE STYLUS UMBONE COSTUME
DIALECT DICTION FASHION INSTYLE
QUALITY EQUIPAGE LANGUAGE
MARINISM NARRANTE PULLBACK
(— OF ARCHITECTURE) ORDER
DRAVIDA GEORGIAN
(— OF COOKING) CUISINE
(— OF DRESS) GUISE

(— **OF GEM SETTING**) BOX
(— **OF HANDWRITING**) CHANCERY
SCRIPTION
(— **OF HAT**) BLOCK
(— **OF MOUNTING**) SETTING
(— **OF MUSIC**) BOOGIE
(— **OF PAINTING**) GENRE
(— **OF PENMANSHIP**) HAND
(— **OF SPEAKING**) ADDRESS
(**AFFECTED** —) EUPHUISM
(**ARTISTIC** —) GUSTO GOTHIC
ARTIFICE DANDYISM
(**BOOKBINDING** —) ALDINE MAIOLI
MAJOLI FANFARE GROLIER
ETRUSCAN HARLEIAN ROXBURGH
(**CUSTOMARY** —) GATE
(**DISTINCTIVE** —) CLOTHES
(**FAVORED** —) GROOVE
(**HAIR** —) CROP TETE
(**INFLATED** —) FUSTIAN
(**LATEST** —) KICK
(**PRETENTIOUS** —) BOMBAST
(**PROPER** —) WEAR
(**THEATRICAL** —) LYCEUM
STYLET SPEAR STILET STYLUS
TROCAR MANDRIN STILETTE
STYLIDIUM CANDOLEA
STYLISH CHIC DOSS DOGGY NIFTY
NOBBY SASSY SHARP SMART
SWELL TIPPY TOPPY CHEESY
CLASSY DAPPER FLOSSY JAUNTY
SWANKY TONISH DASHING DOGGISH
GENTEEL KNOWING SWAGGER
TOFFISH
STYLOID BELONOID
STYLUS GAD PEN STYLE CUTTER
GREFFE TRACER HARPAGO POINTEL
PYROPEN
STYPTIC ALUM AMADOU MATICO
BAROMETZ STANCHER
STYRENE STYROL CINNAMOL
STYX (**FATHER OF** —) OCEANUS
(**HUSBAND OF** —) PALLAS
(**MOTHER OF** —) TETHYS
SUAEDA DONDIA
SUAN PAN SOROBAN
SUAVE OILY SMUG SOFT BLAND
SOAPY SVELT GLOSSY SILKEN
SMOOTH FULSOME UNCTUOUS
SUAVELY CREAMILY
SUAVITY URBANITY
SUB GRASS
SUBALTERN WART
SUBBASE PLINTH
SUBCINCTORIUM BALTEUS
BALTHEUS
SUBCLASS GENDER BRYALES
CESTODA CYCLIAE DIGENEA
SPECIES AMOEBAEA ANAPSIDA
CESTODES COPEPODA GANOIDEI
SELACHII
SUBCUTANEOUS DEEP
SUBDEACON MINISTER
SUBDIVIDE CARVE MINCE
SUBDIVISION DEN OBE SEX BEAT
CAZA DHER HAPU ITEM TASU
BUNDA CORPS CURIA DEKAN DHERI
FERAE FORTY HSIEN IOWAN NAHIE
OKRUG PHYLE SITIO STAGE TALUK

TARAF TURMA UINTA ALBIAN
ARENIG BANNER BUREAU CERCLE
CIRCLE COHORT COLUMN DAKOTA
DANIAN DOGGER FACIES GUELPH
HEMERA IMBREX LENGTH LUDLOW
MARKAZ NAHIYE OBLAST ONEIDA
SANJAK SECTOR SERIAL SHIRAZ
STRAIN SUBAGE TAHSIL TASSOO
TEHSIL BUKEYEI CENTURY
CHEMUNG CHIRIPA COCHITI
COMARCA ECOTYPE ELEMENT
EPARCHY EPISODE GENESEE
MONTANA PHRATRY RONDOUT
SASTEAN SECTION SEEDBED
SUBAREA SUBLINE SUBPLAT
SUBPLOT SUBRACE SUBZONE
SUPPORT TRENTON TRINITY
WASATCH WASHITA WENLOCK
WICHITA BANOVINA DISTRICT
DIVISION DJAGATAY ENDBRAIN
FLOTILLA GUBERNIA LOCATION
MONTEREY NAUCRARY PRECINCT
STOCKTON SUBCASTE SUBORDER
SUBSTAGE SUBTRIBE TOWNSHIP
(— **OF SCOUTS**) CREW
(**EGYPTIAN** —) KISM
SUBDOMINANT FOURTH
SUBDUE ADAW BEAT BEND QUAY
TAME ACCOY ALLAY AMATE CHARM
CRUSH DAUNT DOMPT QUAIL
QUASH QUELL SOBER STILL
ADAUNT BRIDLE CHASTE DEBELL
DISMAY EVINCE GENTLE MASTER
QUENCH REDUCE SUBACT SUBMIT
UNWILD ABANDON AFFAITE
CAPTURE CHASTEN CONQUER
REPRESS REPRIME SUCCUMB
CONVINCE OVERCOME SUPPEDIT
SUPPRESS SURMOUNT VANQUISH
SUBDUED MAK SOFT TAME SOBER
STILL UNDER BROKEN CHASTE
GENTLE ASHAMED SUBMISS
SOURDINE
SUBFAMILY KHOISAN CUSHITIC
ACRAEINAE
SUBGROUP BAND FAMILY
SUBHEAD BOXHEAD SIDEHEAD
SUBIMAGO DUN
SUBINDEX SUFFIX
SUBIRRIGATE SUB SUBWATER
SUBIRRIGATION SUBBING
SUBJECT DUX PUT ABLE ALLY BODY
BONE ITEM TEXT HOBBY PLACE
STOOP STUDY TESTO THEMA
THEME TOPIC GROUND IMPOSE
LIABLE PATHIC REDUCE SACOPE
SUBDIT SUBMIT THRALL VASSAL
CITIZEN FEODARY FEUDARY
OBVIOUS SERVILE ELECTIVE
INCIDENT INFERIOR OBEDIENT
OCCASION SENTENCE SUBJUGAL
(— **OF DISCOURSE**) NOUN
(— **OF FUGUE**) GUIDA
(— **OF PROPOSITION**) EXTREME
(— **TO ABUSE**) REVILE
(— **TO ARGUMENT**) MOOT
(— **TO BAD TEMPER**) MOODY
(— **TO CHANGE**) MUTABLE FUGITIVE
(— **TO CRITICISM**) SCOURGE

(— **TO FATE**) FIE
(— **TO PERCOLATION**) DISPLACE
(— **TO SOME ACTION**) TREAT
(**CONTROVERTED** —) ISSUE
(**LOYAL** —) LIEGE
(**PL.**) FOLK
SUBJECTION SLAVERY SERVITUS
THIRLING
SUBJECTIVE IMMANENT INSEEING
INTERNAL PECTORAL EPISTEMIC
SUBJUGATION BONDAGE
SERVITUDE
SUBKINGDOM PHYLUM ANNULOSA
CHORDATA
SUBLEADER HEADMAN
SUBLEASE FARMOUT SUBTACK
SUBLET JOB SUBSET CONACRE
SUBLEASE
SUBLIME FUME GRAND LOFTY
NOBLE REFINE SOLEMN WINGED
ELEVATO EXALTED EMPYREAL
EMPYREAN MAGNIFIC MAJESTIC
SERAPHIC SPLENDID
(— **IN STYLE**) MILTONIC
SUBLIMITY GRANDEUR
SUBLUNARY EARTHLY
SUBMARINE SUB BOAT DIVER FRITZ
GUPPY SUBSEA PIGBOAT TIDDLER
SUBMEDIANT SIXTH
SUBMERGE BOG DIP BURY DIVE
DUNK HIDE SINK SOAK TAKE
DROWN SOUSE SWAMP WHELM
DELUGE DRENCH ENGULF DEMERGE
IMPLUNGE INUNDATE SUBMERSE
SURROUND
SUBMERGENCE ONLAP
SUBMISSION VAIL PATIENCE
SUBMISSIVE MEEK BUXOM DEMISS
DOCILE DUTIFUL PASSIVE SERVILE
SLAVISH SUBJECT SUBMISS
UNERECT OBEDIENT RESIGNED
YIELDING
(— **TO WIFE**) UXORIOUS
SUBMISSIVENESS SLAVERY
SUBMIT BOW EAT ABOW BEND CAVE
LEAN OBEY TAKE VAIL AVALE
DEFER HIELD STAND STOOP YIELD
ASSENT DELATE RESIGN CONSIGN
KNUCKLE SUBJECT SUBMUSE
SUCCUMB TRUCKLE
(— **FOR CONSIDERATION**) REMIT
(— **TAMELY**) EAT
(— **TO**) ABIDE STAND SUFFER
SUBNORMAL SICK ABNORMAL
SUBORDER LARI ALCAE APODA
APODI GALLI GRUES ARDEAE
COHORT CUCULI SAURIA AGLOSSA
ANSERES ARCACEA ASCONES
CORACII COSTATA SARCURA
SYCONES ACRASIDA ADEPHAGA
BATOIDEI COLUMBAE CORACIAE
CURSORIA ENOPLINA EUSUCHIA
FALCONES FREGATAE SELACHII
SUBORDINARY ENDORSE ROUNDEL
SUBORDINATE SUB SINK PETTY
SCRUB UNDER EXEMPT MINION
PUISNE SECOND YEOMAN SERVANT
SERVILE SUBJECT HENCHMAN
INFERIOR MYRMIDON PARERGAL

POSTPONE SERVIENT
SUBORN HAVE BRIBE
SUBOVAL PETALOID
SUBPHYLUM EUCHORDA
SUBPOENA SUMMONS
SUBRACE STOCK
SUBSCRIBE SIGN ASSENT ASCRIBE
CONSIGN SUBSIGN
SUBSCRIBER RAILBIRD
SUBSCRIPT INFERIOR
SUBSEQUENT AFTER LATER
FUTURE PUISNE ENSUING POSTNATE
SUBSEQUENTLY SO LATER SINCE
SUBSERVIENT OILY VASSAL
DUTEOUS SERVILE SLAVISH
OFFICIAL
SUBSHRUB STOCK GUAYULE
COLUMNEA
SUBSIDE DIE EBB LAY LIE CALM
FALL LULL SILE SINK VAIL ABATE
ALLAY LAPSE RESIDE SETTLE
ASSUAGE RELAPSE UNSWELL
WITHDRAW
SUBSIDENCE FALL SETTLING
SUBSIDIARY CHILD DONKEY
SUBSIDY
SUBSIDIZE BONUS
SUBSIDY AID BONUS BOUNTY
POUNDAGE
SUBSILICIC BASIC
SUBSIST BE LIVE RELY
SUBSISTENCE BEING LIVING
SUBSISTENT ENTITY
SUBSOIL PAN LECK SOLE SHRAVE
RATCHEL
SUBSTAGE CARY GUNZ IOWAN
MANKATO STADIAL TAZEWELL
SUBSTANCE FAT SUM BODY CORE
GIST GITE TACK WHAT ADROP
AGENT ALLOY ARCHE FOMES
GREAT KEEST METAL MOYEN OUSIA
PROOF SENSE STUFF THING
BOTTOM GADUIN GETTER IMPORT
MATTER STAPLE WEALTH AEROSOL
AGAROID ANTIGEN COLICIN
COLLOID CONTENT ELEIDIN
EMANIUM ERGUSIA ESSENCE
HYALINE MEANING PURPORT
REAGENT SUBJECT SUPTION
ACCEPTOR ADDITIVE ADHESIVE
ALLERGEN AMBEROID ANTIFOAM
BASSORIN HARDNESS MATERIAL
(— CAPABLE OF EXPANSION)
DILATANT
(— FORMED IN VINEGAR) MOTHER
(— FROM CRUSHED APPLES)
POMACE
(— IN BLOOD) ALEXINE ABLASTIN
(— IN LIGHT BULBS) GETTER
(— IN WOODY TISSUE) LIGNIN
(— OF DENTINE) IVORY
(— OF EXTREME HARDNESS)
ADAMANT DIAMOND
(— PRODUCING POISONOUS
ATMOSPHERE) GAS
(— SURROUNDED BY FOREIGN
TISSUE) ENCLAVE
(— TO ADD STABILITY) BALLAST
(— TRANSPORTING GERMS) FOMES

(— USED AS HYPNOTIC) URAL
(— USED IN DETECTING OTHERS)
REAGENT
(— WITH MOLDY ODOR) CHARACIN
(ADHESIVE —) GLUE GLOEA PASTE
CEMENT STICKER
(AMORPHOUS —) GLASS RESIN
LIGNIN PECTIN FERRITE SAPONIN
(AROMATIC —) BALSAM
(ASTRINGENT —) ALUM CATECHU
(BITTER —) ALOIN LININ ILICIN
(BLACK —) SOOT BLECK
(CLEANSING —) LYE
(COLLOIDAL —) ALGIN EXPANDER
(COMBUSTIBLE —) COAL
(CORROSIVE —) CAUSTIC
(CRYSTALLINE —) LAURIN ALANINE
HELENIN ELATERIN
(DARK —) ATRAMENT
(DISSOLVED —) SOLUTE
(ETERNAL —) DHARMA ADHARMA
(FATLIKE —) DEGRAS LIPOID
ERGUSIA
(FATTY —) SMEAR SUBERIN
(FERMENTATION —) LEAVEN
(FIBROUS —) COTTON
(FILAMENTOUS —) HARL
(FILMY —) GOSSAMER
(FIRST —) YLEM
(GRINDING —) ABRASIVE
(GUMMY —) GUM GURRY AMYLOID
GLACTAN
(HARD ANIMAL —) BONE ENAMEL
(HORNY —) BALEEN CHITIN
CHONDRIN
(HYPOTHETICAL —) FLUID INOGEN
PROTYL
(IDEAL —) CONTINUUM
(INFLAMMABLE —) BITUMEN
(INSOLUBLE —) CARRIER HYALOGEN
(LIVERLIKE —) HEPAR
(NARCOTIC —) DRUG
(NITROGENOUS —) LACTENIN
(POISONOUS —) ARSENIC PHRYNIN
EXOTOXIN
(POWDER OF ANY —) FLOUR
(POWDERY —) STOUR
(PREDOMINATING —) BASE
(RESINOUS —) LAC COPAL
COPALINE COPALITE
(SELF-DEFENSIVE —) ACRAEIN
(SEMISOLID —) GEL
(SOUR —) ACID
(STICKY —) GOO GOOP SIZE STICK
GLUTEN BIRDLIME
(SUBTLE —) SPIRIT
(SWEET —) SUGAR
(SYNTHETIC —) HORMONE
(TRANSLUCENT —) HYALINE
(UNBREAKABLE —) ADAMANT
(UNCREATED —) ADHARMA
(VISCOUS —) GLAIR GREASE
SLUBBER
(VITAL —) KEEST
(WAXY —) CERIN PARAFFIN
SUBERINE
SUBSTANDARD BAD BAUCH
SUBSTANTIAL FAT FIRM MEATY
PUKKA STOUT ACTUAL BODILY

HEARTY SQUARE STABLE STANCH
STUFFY STURDY MASSIVE MATERIAL
SUBSTANT TANGIBLE
SUBSTANTIATE BACK CONFIRM
SUPPORT VALIDATE
SUBSTANTIVE DIRECT
SUBSTITUTE SUB VICE AKORI
EXTRA PROXY VICAR BEWITH
CHANGE DEPUTY DOUBLE ERSATZ
COMMUTE REPLACE RESERVE
STANDBY STOPGAP SUBDEAN
SUFFECT SUPPOSE DISPLACE
EMERGENT
(— FOR TEA) TIA FAHAM
(NOT —) FULL
(POOR —) APOLOGY
SUBSTITUTION SHIFT CHANGE
ERSATZ ENALLAGE EXCHANGE
NOVATION
(— OF SOUNDS) LALLATION
SUBSTRATUM SUB GROUND
SUBBING SUBJECT
SUBSTREAM MATTER
SUBSTRUCTURE PODIUM FOOTING
SUBSUME COVER EXPLAIN INCLUDE
SUBSUMING GENERIC
SUBTENANT VAVASOUR
SUBTERFUGE MASK BLIND CROOK
QUIRK SHIFT TRICK WRINK CHICANE
ARTIFICE PRETENCE TRAVERSE
VOIDANCE
SUBTILE SUBTLE TENUOUS
SUBTITLE TITLE LEADER CAPTION
SUBTLE SLY FINE NICE WILY WISE
ACUTE ARGUTE CRAFTY FRAGILE
SUBTILE CLERGIAL
(TOO —) FINESPUN
SUBTLETY FRAUD DECEIT EXILITY
FINESSE DELICACY FINENESS
QUIDDITY QUOLIBET
SUBTLY FINE SLILY SLYLY
SUBTRACT BATE PULL TAKE SHAVE
DEDUCE DEDUCT DETRACT
SUBDUCE SUBDUCT SUBTRAY
DIMINISH
SUBTRIBE HAPU SENAAH SEMNONES
SUBURB ANNEX BORGO BARRIO
PETTAH BANLIEU ENDSHIP
FAUBOURG
(PL.) SKIRTS ENVIRONS OUTPARTS
SUBURBIA
SUBURBIA VILLADOM
SUBVERSION FALL SABOTAGE
SUBVERSIVE RUINOUS
SUBVERT SAP KILL RAZE RUIN
EVERT UPSET GAINSAY OVERSET
REVERSE RUINATE OVERTURN
SUBVERTED LOST
SUBWAY DIVE METRO
SUCCEED GO FAY HIT FARE RISE
WORK CLICK ENSUE FADGE PROVE
SPEED COTTON FOLLOW SECOND
THRIVE ACHIEVE PROSPER
THROUGH FLOURISH SUPPLANT
(— TO THRONE) ACCEDE ASCEND
SUCCEEDING VICE AFTER CHANGE
ULTERIOR
SUCCESS DO GO HIT MAX WIN WOW
BANG CESS LUCK SMASH SPEED

THRIFT EXPLOIT FORTUNE FURTHER THEEDOM FELICITY GODSPEED
(— IN A MATCH) GAME
(BRILLIANT —) ECLAT
(SUDDEN —) KILLING
(UNEXPECTED —) JACKPOT
(WORLDLY —) ARTHA
SUCCESSFUL HOT SOCK LUCKY SPEEDFUL THRIVING
SUCCESSFULLY GREAT HAPPILY PROUDLY
SUCCESSION RUN SUIT ROUND SUITE TRACK ASSISE COURSE SEQUEL SERIES STREAM STRING HEIRDOM SUCCESS ANCESTRY DIADOCHE MUTATION SEQUENCE
(— OF CHANGES) FLUX
(— OF CHORDS) CADENCE
(— OF CRUSTS) CALICHE
(— OF STAGES) CASCADE
(— OF WAVES) CRIMP
(— RULERS) DYNASTY
SUCCESSIVELY AROW
SUCCESSOR HEIR CALIF HERES CALIPH HAERES EPIGONUS
(— OF CHIEFTAIN) TANIST
(— OF MUHAMMAD) CALIF CALIPH
(PL.) DIADOCHI
SUCCINCT BRIEF SHORT TERSE CONCISE LACONIC SUMMARY
SUCCINIC DIACETIC
SUCCOR AID HELP RESET SERVE SPEED ASSIST RELIEF RESCUE SUPPLY UPTAKE COMFORT DELIVER PRESIDY RELIEVE SECOURS SUSTAIN BEFRIEND
SUCCULENT FRIM FRUM LUSH JUICY LUSHY PAPPY PULPY SAPPY YOUNG CASHIE FLESHY TENDER WATERISH
SUCCUMB BREAK QUAIL STOOP TRAIK YIELD
SUCH SIC SICK THAT SWICH
SUCHNESS TATHATA
SUCK SOUK SWIG SWOOP SUCKLE
(— DRY) SOAK
(— UP) DRINK ABSORB TIPPLE
SUCKEN THIRL
SUCKER CHUB FISH GULL SOBOL THIEF CHUPON CUPULE MULLET RATOON REDFIN SOBOLE SPROUT SQUARE SUPPER TILLER CUTLIPS GONOTYL LOCULUS OSCULUM SCOURGE BOTHRIUM HUMPBACK PUSHOVER REDHORSE SURCULUS
SUCKLE FEED MILK SUCK LACTATE NOURISH
SUCKLING SUCKER LACTANT SUCKLER TEATLING
SUCTION INTAKE
SUCTORIA ACINETAE

SUDAN
CAPITAL: KHARTOUM
DESERT: NUBIAN
LANGUAGE: GA EWE IBO KRU EFIK
　MOLE TSHI YORUBA MANDINGO
MEASURE: UD

MOUNTAIN: KINYETI
NATIVE: DAZA GOLO NUER SERE
　DINKA FULAH HAUSA MOSSI
　NUBIYIN
REGION: DARFUR KASSALA
　KORDOFAN
RIVER: NILE
TOWN: KOSTI MEROE ATBARA
　ALUBAYD MALAKAL OMDURMAN
WEIGHT: HABBA

SUDANESE FULA FULAH
SUDAN GRASS GARAVA GARAWI
SUDDEN FERLY HASTY ICTIC SWIFT ABRUPT FIERCE SNAPPY SPEEDY PRERUPT HEADLONG SPURTIVE SUBITANY SUBITOUS
SUDDENLY BOB POP BOLT FLOP SLAP AMAIN SHORT SKELP SOUSE ASTART BOUNCE PRESTO SUBITO ASUDDEN UNAWARES
SUDDENNESS ATTACK SUDDENTY
SUDORIFIC SWEAT SWEATER HIDROTIC SUDATORY
SUDRA VELLALA
SUDS BUCK FOAM SAPPLES SOAPSUDS
SUE LAW WOO SUIT IMPLEAD TROUNCE
SUET TALLOW
SUFFER BYE GET LET BEAR DREE FIND GAIN HURT PAIN PINE ALLOW DREIE LABOR PROVE SMART SMOKE STAND THOLE ABEGGE ENDURE PERMIT AGONIZE SUPPORT SUSTAIN UNDERGO TOLERATE
(— AGONY) THROE
(— AT STAKE) SMOKE
(— DEFEAT) BOW
(— FOR) ABY ABYE ABIDE
(— FROM TIME) AGE
(— GREAT AFFLICTION) GROAN
(— HUNGER) CLEM STARVE AFFAMISH
(— LOSS OF) GIVE
(— PAIN) STOUND ANGUISH
(— PENALTY) SWEAT
(— REMORSE) RUE
(— RUIN) WRECK
(— SYNCOPE) FAINT
(— THROUGH) PASS
(— TO ENTER) ADMIT
SUFFERABLE PATIBLE
SUFFERANCE PAIN MISERY PATIENCE THOLANCE
SUFFERER MARTYR AMNESIC DOORMAT PATIENT
SUFFERING BALE COST DREE HURT PAIN PINE RACK DOLOR GRIEF SMART WRAKE PATHIC PATHOS THRALL INVALID LANGUOR PASSION PASSIVE TRAVAIL DISTRESS HARDSHIP
(— FROM HANGOVER) CHIPPY
(— FROM ILL HEALTH) DOWN
(— OF MIND) CARE
(—S OF CHRIST) AGONY

SUFFICE DO LAST REACH SERVE SATISFY
SUFFICIENCY ENOUGH ADEQUACY
SUFFICIENT DUE FAIR GOOD AMPLE DECENT ENOUGH BASTANT ADEQUATE RELEVANT COMPETENT
(BARELY —) SCANT SKIMP SCRIMPY
(BE — FOR) COVER
SUFFICIENTLY DULY WELL ENOUGH
SUFFIX POSTFIX
SUFFOCATE CHOKE DROWN SMOOR STIVE STUFF SWELT SLOKEN STIFLE OVERLIE QUACKLE SMOLDER SMOTHER SCUMFISH STRANGLE THROTTLE
SUFFRAGE VOTE VOICE TONGUE VERSICLE
SUFFUSE FILL BATHE EMBAY INFUSE
SUFFUSION COLOR
SUGAR CANDY DIOSE IDOSE MELIS PIECE SUCRE THIRD ACROSE ALDOSE ALLOSE FUCOSE GULOSE HEXOSE INVERT KETOSE LYXOSE OCTOSE PANELA TALOSE TRIOSE XYLOSE AGAVOSE ALTROSE BASTARD CHITOSE GLUCOSE GLUTOSE GLYCOSE LACTOSE MALTOSE PAPELON PENOCHI PENTOSE PENUCHE SORBOSE SUCROSE SWEETEN TETROSE THREOSE BROWNING CONCRETE CYMAROSE DEXTROSE FRUCTOSE FURANOSE LEVULOSE PYRANOSE RHAMNOSE RHODEOSE SECALOSE TURANOSE
(BROWN —) CARAIBE JAGGARY JAGGHERY
(COARSE —) RAAB
(CRUDE —) GUR HEAD MELADA CONCRETE
(INFERIOR —) BASTARD
SUGARCANE CANE GRAIN GLUMAL RATOON MATTRESS
(— SAP) LIQUOR
SUGARHOUSE (PART OF —) PURGERY
SUGARLESS DRY
SUGARPLUM KISS
SUGARY FAT SUGAR SWEET OVERRIPE
SUGGEST JOG BEAR GIVE HINT MINT IMPLY OFFER SPEAK ALLUDE INDITE INFUSE MOTION PROMPT RESENT SUBMIT CONNOTE DICTATE INSPIRE INDICATE INTIMATE
(— DRINKING) PROPOSE
(— INSIDIOUSLY) INFUSE
(— STRONGLY) ARGUE
SUGGESTIBLE SOFT
SUGGESTION CUE CAST HINT TANG GLIFF ADVICE BREATH MOTION SMATCH INKLING LEADING PROFFER REMNANT SOUPCON WRINKLE INNUENDO INSTANCE PROPOSAL
SUGGESTIVE ANICONIC PREGNANT
(— OF MELODY) CANOROUS
SUICIDAL KAMIKAZE
SUIT DO GO APT DOW FIT GEE HIT SET SIT ACTO LIKE LIST PAIR SORT

ADAPT AGREE APPLY BEFIT BESIT
CLUBS COLOR DRAPE DRESS
FADGE FANCY FRAME HABIT LEVEL
MATCH PLEAD QUEME SAVOR
SERVE SHAPE STAND SUING TALLY
AFFEIR ANSWER BECOME COHERE
COMPLY DITTOS HEARTS PRAYER
SPADES SPEECH SQUARE BEHOOVE
COMPORT COSTUME COULEUR
PURSUIT REQUEST SEERPAW
DIAMONDS INSTANCE QUADRATE
SKELETON STANDARD TAILLEUR
TROPICAL
(— AT LAW) ACTO CASE LAWSUIT
(SWIMMING —) BATHER BIKINI

SUITABILITY (MUTUAL —) DECENCY
IDONEITY SYMPATHY

SUITABLE APT FIT PAT ABLE FEAT
GAIN GOOD JUMP JUST MEET TALL
WELL WEME DIGNE EQUAL FITTY
QUEME RIGHT SUITY COMELY
FITTEN GAINLY GIUSTO HABILE
HONEST LIABLE LIKELY PROPER
SUITLY AVENANT COMMODE
CONDIGN CONGRUE FITTING
IDONEAL PLIABLE SEEMING
BECOMING ELIGIBLE FEASIBLE
HANDSOME IDONEOUS SORTABLE
(— FOR STAGE PERFORMANCE)
ACTING

SUITABLENESS APTNESS HONESTY
APTITUDE PROPERTY

SUITABLY FITLY MEETLY TIDELY
APROPOS GRADELY

SUITCASE BAG CAP GRIP CAPCASE
DORLACH KEESTER

SUITE SET SUIT SWEEP SWEET
SERIES PARTITA RETINUE
ENSEMBLE EQUIPAGE
(— OF MOLDINGS) LEDGMENT
(— OF ROOMS) FLAT CHAMBER

SUITED FIT ADAPT SEEMLY ADAPTED
ASSORTED
(POORLY —) CROOK

SUITING COVERT CHEVIOT

SUITOR MAN SUER SWAIN WOOER
GALLANT SERVANT

SUKU WASUKUMA

SULFIDE GLANCE CUBANITE
SULFURET

SULFUR BRIMSTONE

SULK DOD PET CHAW CRAB DORT
GLUM SULL BOODY FRUMP GLUMP
GROUT GRUMP GROUCH SNUDGE
THURMUS
(PL.) GEE HUMP MUMPS FRUMPS
SULLENS BOUDERIE

SULKER MUMPER

SULKINESS DORT GRUMP

SULKY CART CHUFF DODDY DORTY
GOURY HUFFY HUMPY CHUFFY
GLUMPY GROUTY JINKER SNUFFY
STUFFY SULLEN SUMPHY DOGGISH
HUFFISH MUMPISH
(NOT —) GOOD

SULLEN DOUR FOUL GLUM GRIM
SOUR BLACK CHUFF CROSS DUMPY
FELON GRUFF HARSH MOODY
RUSTY STERN SULKY SURLY

WEMOD CRUSTY DOGGED GLOOMY
GLUMMY GLUMPY GLUNCH GROUTY
MOROSE MULISH SOMBER SOMBRE
STUFFY AUSTERE CRABBED
CYNICAL FRETFUL LOURING
MUMPISH PEEVISH CHUMPISH
CHURLISH LOWERING PETULANT
SPITEFUL STUNKARD

SULLENNESS GEE DORT GLUM
MUMPS STOMACH

SULLIED DIRTY SPOTTED

SULLY BLOT BLUR DASH FOUL SLUR
SMIT SMUT SOIL CLOUD DIRTY
GRIME SMEAR SMOKE STAIN TAINT
DARKEN DEFILE SMIRCH SMUTCH
ATTAINT BEGRIME BESMEAR
BLEMISH CORRUPT DISTAIN ECLIPSE
POLLUTE SLUBBER TARNISH
BESMIRCH

SULPHATE ALUM BARITE ILESITE
LOWEITE SULFATE VITRIOL
KRAUSITE

SULPHIDE HEPAR GLANCE ZARNEC
SULFIDE ZARNICH CUBANITE
(PL.) MATTE

SULPHUR ORE SPIRIT SULFUR
YELLOW QUEBRITH BRIMSTONE

SULPHURIC ACID VITRIOL

SULTAN SOLDAN

SULTANATE SULTANY ZANZIBAR

SULTANESS SOWDONES

SULTRY CLOSE FLUSH FAINTY
SMUDGY POTHERY PUTHERY
SWELTRY FEVERISH

SUM ALL GOB CASH DRAB DUMP
FARM FINE FOOT FUND MASS TALE
DEDIT GROSS KITTY SUMMA TOTAL
WHOLE AMOUNT DEMAND DYADIC
FIGURE NUMBER DECUPLE INGOING
MANBOTE SUBSIDY SUMMARY
SUMMATE ENTIRETY OCTONION
QUANTITY MOUNTANCE
(— AND SUBSTANCE) TOUR SHORT
UPSHOT
(— AS COMPENSATION FOR
KILLING) MANBOTE
(— FOR REENLISTMENT) GRATUITY
(— FOR SCHOLARSHIP) BURSARY
(— IN BASSET) SEPTLEVA
(— OF 25 POUNDS) PONY PONEY
(— OF 3 FARTHINGS) GILL
(— OF 500 POUNDS) MONKEY
(— OF DETERMINANTS) STIRP
(— OF EXPONENTS) DEGREE
(— OF FACTORS) COMPLEX
(— OF GOOD QUALITIES) ARETE
(— OF MONEY) POT BANK COVER
STOCK BUNDLE ACCOUNT STIPEND
(— OF) SIGMA
(— PAYABLE AT FIXED INTERVALS)
FARM
(— RISKED) STAKE
(— UP) ADD TOT FOOT RECKON
SUBSUME SUMMATE COMPRISE
CONCLUDE PERORATE
(ENTIRE —) SOLIDUM
(EXCESS —) BONUS
(FORFEITED —) DEDIT
(GREAT —) PLUNK SIGHT MICKLE

(LARGE —) GOB SCREAMER
(PETTY —) CENT DIME DRAB
(SMALL — OF MONEY) SPILL
DRIBBLE DRIBLET
(TRIFLING —) HAY
(UNEXPENDED —S) SAVINGS
(VECTOR —) GRADIENT

SUMAC KAREE SUMACH ANACARD
BURTREE SCOTINO SHOEMAKE

SUMATRA (LANGUAGE IN —) NIAS
(MEASURE OF —) PAAL
(MOUNTAIN IN —) LEUSER KERINTJI
(RIVER IN —) HARI MUSI ROKAN
DJAMBI
(TOWN IN —) ACHIN KUALA MEDAN
NATAL SOLOK DJAMBI LANGSA
PADANG RENGAT BONKULIN

SUMBUL SAMBUL MUSKROOT

SUMERIAN ACCADIAN AKKADIAN

SUMMARIZE PRECIS RESUME
ABSTRACT

SUMMARY SUM LEAD BRIEF CHART
SCORE SHORT SUMMA TOTAL
PRECIS RESUME SUMMAR CHAPTER
CONCISE EPITOME EXTRACT
MEDULLA VIDIMUS ABSTRACT
ARGUMENT BREVIARY BREVIATE
DRUMHEAD HEADNOTE SUCCINCT
SYNOPSIS
(— OF FAITH) SYMBOL
(— OF PRINCIPLES) CREED

SUMMATION SUM DIGEST SUMMARY

SUMMER SHEMU SOMER AESTAS
SIMMER DORMANT
(OF —) ESTIVAL

SUMMER CYPRESS KOCHIA

SUMMER FLOUNDER PLAICE

SUMMERHOUSE FOLLY KIOSK
MAHAL TUPEK ALCOVE CASINO
GAZEBO PAGODA CABINET

SUMMER HYACINTH GALTONIA

SUMMER TANAGER REDBIRD

SUMMERWOOD LATEWOOD

SUMMIT DOD SUM TIP TOP VAN
ACME APEX BALD CRAP DODD
HELM KNAP KNOT PEAK ROOF
CREST CROWN SPIRE COMBLE
HEIGHT VERTEX ZENITH CALOTTE
SUMMARY SUMMITY PINNACLE
(— OF TUBE) MOUTH
(— WITHOUT FOREST) BALD
(ROCKY —) KNOT
(ROUND —) DOD DODD
(SNOW-CAPPED —) CALOTTE

SUMMON BAN CRY BUZZ CALL CITE
DRUM HAIL SIST BUGLE CHARM
CLEPE EVOKE HIGHT KNELL SOUND
VOUCH ACCITE ADVOKE BECALL
COMPEL DEMAND SOMPNE VOCATE
ACCERSE COMMAND CONJURE
CONVENE CONVENT CONVOKE
PROVOKE SUMMONS WHISTLE
ASSUMMON EXORCISE
(— FOR HIRING) YARD
(— INTO COURT) DEMAND
(— TOGETHER) BAND MUSTER
ASSEMBLE
(— UP) FIND GATHER COLLECT

SUMMONER SUMNER LOCKMAN

SOMPNER OUTRIDER
SUMMONING CALL ARRAY
(**— OF KING'S VASSALS**) BAN
SUMMONS BAN CRY CALL BIDDING
CALLING STICKER WARNING
WARRANT CITATION VOCATION
(**FALCONER'S —**) WO
SUMP SINK STANDAGE
SUMPTUOUS RICH GRAND SHOWY
WLONK COSTLY DELUXE SOLEMN
SUPERB COSTLEW ELEGANT
SPLENDID
SUMPTUOUSNESS DAINTY
SUMPTURE
SUN SOL ATEN ATON INTI LAMP
STAR SENGE SURYA TITAN SUNLET
DAYSTAR IOSKEHA PHOEBUS
SAVITAR JOUSKEHA
(**— MOON AND STARS**) HOST
(**RISING —**) HERAKHTI
SUNAPEE TROUT SAIBLING
SUNBEAM BANANA
SUN BEAR BRUANG
SUNBIRD MAMO CADET
SUN BITTERN CARLE CAURALE
SUNBIRD
SUN BLIND UMRELLA
SUNBONNET TILT UGLY CRESIE
KAPPIE SHAKER
SUNBURN GREENING HELIOSIS
SUNBURNT ADUST TANNED
SUNBURST SUNRAY SUNBREAK
SUNSHINE
SUNDAE GEDUNK
SUNDAY EXAUDI JUDICA GAUDETE
TRINITY
(**THIRD — AFTER EASTER**) JUBILATE
SUNDER PART TWIN BREAK SEVER
TWAIN TWINE DEPART DIVIDE
SINDER ASUNDER DISALLY DISJOIN
DIVORCE DISSEVER SEJUGATE
SEPARATE UNSOLDER
SUNDEW DROSERA EYEBRIGHT
SUNDIAL DIAL GHURRY HOROLOGE
SCAPHION SOLARIUM
SUN DISK ATEN ATON CAKRA
CHAKRA
SUNDOG WINDGALL
SUNDOWNER WHALER TUSSOCKER
SUN-DRIED TILED
SUNDROPS SCABISH
SUNDRY DIVERS DIVERSE SEVERAL
SUNFISH SUN HURO MOLA RUFF
BREAM FLIER FLYER ROACH SUNNY
KIVVER MOLOID REDEAR REDEYE
CRAPPIE CROPPIE PERCOID
BLUEGILL FLATFISH FLOUNDER
HEADFISH MOONFISH PONDFISH
WARMOUTH
SUNFLOWER GOLD HELIO CANADA
GOLDEN SUNFOIL GIRASOLE
TURNSOLE
(**— STATE**) KANSAS
SUN-GREBE FINFOOT SUNBIRD
GRUIFORM
SUNK SUNKEN
(**— TO LOW STATE**) ABJECT
SUNKEN SUNK HOLLOW
SUNLESS BLAE

SUNLIGHT GLARE
SUNN SAN SANN DAGGA SANAI
JANAPA MADRAS JANAPAN
SANNHEMP
SUNNITE IHLAT SUNNI SUNNIAH
SUNNY GOOD SUNSHINE
SUN PARLOR SOLARIUM
SUNRISE ARIST SUNUP ORIENT
SUNSET SUNFALL
(**— STATE**) OREGON ARIZONA
SUNSHADE PARASOL ROUNDEL
TIRESOL SOMBRERO
SUNSHINE SUN SHINE SUNLIGHT
(**— STATE**) FLORIDA
SUNSPOT SPOT FACULA MACULA
SUNSPURGE SUNWEED TURNSOLE
WARTWEED WARTWORT
SUNSTROKE HELIOSIS SIRIASIS
SUNTAN MERIDA
SUN TREE HINOKI
SUNWISE DEASIL DESSIL
SUNYATA VOID
SUP EAT DINE SOWP FEAST
CONSUME SWALLOW
SUPAWN MUSH
SUPERABOUND OVERFLOW
SUPERABUNDANCE FLOOD EXCESS
CATARACT PLETHORA PLEURISY
SUPERABUNDANT RANK LAVISH
PROFUSE
SUPERALTAR PREDELLA
SUPERANNUATE OVERYEAR
SUPERB GRAND GOLDEN GORGEOUS
SPLENDID
SUPERCARGO MERCHANT
SUPERCILIOUS GRAND POTTY
PROUD OVERLY SNIFFY SNIPPY
SNOOTY SNOTTY SNUFFY HAUGHTY
ARROGANT CAVALIER SNIFFISH
SUPERIOR
SUPERCLASS AGNATHA
SUPERCONSCIOUSNESS SAMADHI
SUPERCOOL SUBCOOL SURFUSE
SUPERFAMILY APINA APOIDEA
BOVOIDEA
SUPERFICIAL GLIB ECTAL SUPER
FACIAL FACILE FLIMSY FORMAL
FROTHY GLASSY OVERLY SLIGHT
OUTSIDE OUTWARD SHALLOW
SKETCHY SLIGHTY SURFACE
SURFACY EXTERNAL MAGAZINY
SMATTERY DEPTHLESS
SUPERFICIALLY FLEET
SUPERFICIES TERM EXTENT
SUPERFLUITY FAT FRILL LUXUS
EXCESS OVERSET SURFEIT
(**CONFUSING —**) FLUTHER
SUPERFLUOUS SPARE USELESS
NEEDLESS
SUPERFRONTAL FRONTLET
SUPERHEATED GASEOUS
SUPERHUMAN DEMON DAEMON
DIVINE INHUMAN UNHUMAN
SUPERIMPOSE LAY OVERLAY
SURPRINT
SUPERIMPOSING DISSOLVE
SUPERINTEND CON CONN GUIDE
OVERSEE PRESIDE
SUPERINTENDENCE CARE

CONTROL EPISCOPY GUIDANCE
SUPERINTENDENCY EDILITY
AEDILITY
SUPERINTENDENT BOSS SUPE
EPHOR SUPER EDITOR VENEUR
VIEWER CAPTAIN EPHORUS
MANAGER DIRECTOR OVERSEER
SURVEYOR SWINGMAN
SUPERIOR JOE AYNE COOL FINE
MORE OVER TRIE ABBOT ABOVE
CHIEF CREAM EIGNE ELDER ELITE
EXTRA FANCY FRANK GREAT LIEGE
PRIOR UPPER ABBESS BETTER
COCKUP CUSTOS DOMINA FATHER
FORBYE MAHANT SELECT SENIOR
STRONG FORTHBY PALMARY
RANKING ABNORMAL DOMINANT
GUARDIAN SINGULAR SPLENDID
SUPERIAL
(**— OF CONVENT**) HEGUMEN
(**— TO**) BEFORE
SUPERIORITY DROP GREE PRICE
HEIGHT MASTERY PROWESS
EMINENCE PRIORITY
(**MENTAL —**) GENIUS
SUPERLATIVE RAVING CURIOUS
CRASHING OLYMPIAN PEERLESS
SWINGING
(**ABSOLUTE —**) ELATIVE
SUPERLATIVELY CRACKING
SWINGING
SUPERMAN OVERMAN
SUPERNATURAL DIVINE NUMINOUS
SUPERIOR
(**— FORCE**) WAKANDA
SUPERSTITION FREIT IDOLATRY
SUPERORDER GLIRES
SUPERPOSE APPLY
SUPERSCRIBE DIRECT
SUPERSCRIPT SUPERIOR
SUPERSEDE REPLACE OVERRIDE
SUPPLANT
SUPERSTITIOUS FREITY
SUPERTONIC SECOND
SUPERVENE FOLLOW
SUPERVISE GUIDE DIRECT GOVERN
HANDLE SURVEY FOREMAN
OVERSEE ENGINEER OVERLOOK
CHAPERONE
SUPERVISION EYE CARE DUTY
HAND CHECK CHARGE
SUPERVISOR BULL EPHOR GUIDE
SUPER CENSOR GASMAN RUNMAN
SOURER WARDEN DESKMAN
ALYTARCH CHAIRMAN FLOORMAN
FOREHAND KNIFEMAN LEACHMAN
MASHGIAH OVERSEER
SUPINE INERT DROWSY LANGUID
SERVILE UPRIGHT CARELESS
INACTIVE INDOLENT LISTLESS
SLUGGISH
SUPPER MEAL CUDDY HOCKEY
PASCHAL
(**HARVEST-HOME —**) HOCKEY
(**LAST —**) MAUNDY
SUPPING CENATION
SUPPLANT FOLLOW REMOVE
REPLACE DISPLACE DISPLANT
SUPPLE BAIN FLIP OILY SOFT LINGY

LITHE SLAMP SWACK AJOINT
LIMBER LITHER LUTHER SUMPLE
SWANKY WANDLE LISSOME PLIABLE
SPRINGE FLEXIBLE
SUPPLEJACK SOAPWORT
SUPPLEMENT ARM EKE MEND TACK
ANNEX SUPPLY BOLSTER CODICIL
ADDENDUM APPENDIX BOUNTITH
(PL.) FIXINGS
SUPPLEMENTAL SPECIAL
SUPPLEMENTARY ADDED RIPIENO
REMANENT
SUPPLENESS WHIP
SUPPLIANT ASKER PLEADING
SUPPLICATE BEG PRAY CRAVE
PLEAD INVOKE OBTEST SUPPLY
BESEECH ENTREAT IMPLORE
REQUEST SOLICIT PETITION
SUPPLICATION CRY VOW BEAD BILL
LIBEL VENIE LITANY PRAYER
CRAVING SYNAPTE ENTREATY
PETITION PLEADING ROGATION
ROGATIVE SUFFRAGE
SUPPLICATORY EUCTICAL
SUPPLIED (— WITH FOOD) THORN
(AMPLY —) ABUNDANT
(SCANTILY —) BARE
SUPPLIER SOURCE
SUPPLIES STOCK STUFF DUFFEL
STORES VICTUAL ESTOVERS
ORDNANCE
SUPPLY FEED FILL FIND FRET FUND
GIVE HEEL LEND LINE ARRAY
CATER ENDUE EQUIP INDUE OFFER
SERVE STOCK STORE STUFF YIELD
BUDGET DONATE EMPLOY FOISON
LAYOUT POCKET SUBMIT ADVANCE
FORTIFY FRAUGHT FURNISH
LISSOME PROVIDE
(— ABUNDANTLY) SWILL
(— ARRANGED BEFOREHAND)
RELAY
(— FOR AN OCCASION) GRIST
(— OF MONEY) BANKROLL
(— OF POTENTIAL JURORS) TALES
(— OF TIN) SERVING
(— PROVISIONS) PURVEY
(— THE NEED) FOR
(— WITH CLOTHES) INFIT
(— WITH FUEL) STOKE
(— WITH MONEY) GILD
(— WITH OXYGEN) AERATE
(— WITH WATER) FANG
(CACHED —) CAVE
(CONSTANT —) STREAM
(EXTRA —) RESERVE
(FRESH —) RECRUIT
(HIDDEN —) HOARD
(INADEQUATE —) DEARTH
(OVERABUNDANT —) SURFEIT
(PLENTIFUL —) CHOICE
(RESERVE —) CUSHION
(RICH —) ARGOSY
(SCANTY —) SCANT
SUPPORT AID ARM BAY BED BOW
KAI LEG PEG RIB TIE TOM ABET
ABUT AXIS BACK BASE BEAM BEAR
BUOY CRIB DADE FEND FIND FIRM
FORK FUEL HAVE HELP HOLD KEEP

KILP LIFT POST PROP RACK REST
ROCK SALT SIDE STAY STEM STUD
TRIG ADOPT ANGEL APPUI ATLAS
BIPOD BLOCK BRACE CARRY CHAIR
CHEER CHOCK CLEAT CRANK
FAVOR FLOAT FRAME OXTER PLUNK
RANCE SALVE SHORE SPURN STAFF
STAKE STEAD STELL STIPE STOCK
STRUT STULL TOWER VOUCH WEIGH
ANCHOR ASSERT ASSIST BARROW
BEHALF CHEVAL COLUMN CORSET
CRADLE CRUTCH DEFEND DONKEY
DUOPOD GARTER PATTEN PILLAR
POTENT PULPIT PUTLOG SADDLE
SECOND SHIELD SOCKET SPLINT
STAYER STEADY SUFFER TASSEL
TIMBER TINGLE TORSEL UPHAND
UPHOLD UPKEEP UPTAKE WHIMSY
ARMREST BACKING BOLSTER
COMFORT CONFIRM CRIPPLE
DEADMAN ENDORSE FINDING
FULCRUM GROMMET HOUSING
JACKLEG JUSTIFY KEEPING
KNUCKLE NOURISH NURTURE
PABULUM PROTECT RADICAL
SPIRALE SQUINCH STADDLE
STANDER STIFFEN STIRRUP SUBSIST
SUSTAIN THICKEN TRESTLE
ADJUMENT ADVOCATE BALUSTER
BEFRIEND BESTRIDE BOOKREST
BUTTRESS CAPSHORE FAIRLEAD
FOOTREST FORESTAY FORTRESS
HANDREST HOLDFAST JACKSTAY
KEYSTONE MAINSTAY MAINTAIN
MOUNTING NEEDLING OVERCAST
PEDESTAL PEDIMENT STANDARD
STILLAGE STOCKING STRENGTH
SYMPATHY UNDERLIE UNDERPIN
UNDERSET
(— FOR ANVIL) STOCK
(— FOR BELL CLAPPER) BALDRIC
(— FOR CATALYST) CARRIER
(— FOR HEAVY MACHINERY)
BUNTING
(— FOR LEVER) BAIT
(— FOR LIFE-CAR) BAIL
(— FOR MILL) LOWDER
(— FOR MINE PASSAGE) OVERCAST
(— FOR PLATFORM) STEMPEL
STEMPLE
(— IN A LATHE) DOCTOR
(— IN PAPERMAKING TUB) DONKEY
(— OF COPING) KNEELER
(— OF MOLD CORE) ARBOR
ARBOUR
(— OF RAIL) CHAIR BALUSTER
(— THROUGH BIT AND BRIDLE)
APPUI
(CRUTCHLIKE —) DEADMAN
(ELBOW-SHAPED —) CRANK
(EMBEDDED —) SPURN
(FIREPLACE —) ANDIRON
(GIVE —) FEED
(INCLINED —) RIDER
(MINING —) CAP FRAME
(PORTABLE —) STOOL
(PRINCIPAL —) BACKBONE
(TEMPORARY —) NEEDLING
(UPRIGHT —) POPPET BANISTER

(WHEELED —) CARRIAGE
(PL.) SHIPWAY
SUPPORTED BASED BLOCKED
ACCOSTED SUCCINCT
(— BY EVIDENCE) PROBABLE
SUPPORTER ALLY JOCK ATLAS
STOOP COHORT DRAGON SATRAP
BOOSTER DEVOTEE FAVORER
FOUNDER LAUDIAN PATROON
PROPPER SUPPORT ADHERENT
ASSERTER ERASTIAN ESPOUSER
FAVORITE HENCHMAN UPHOLDER
CHURCHITE
(ATHLETIC —) CUP JOCK
(CHIEF —) STOOP
(PL.) SECOND
SUPPORTING BEHIND BEARING
SUPPOSE SAY SEE SET WIS WIT
DEEM POSE READ TAKE TROW
WEEN ALLOW COUNT ETTLE FANCY
GUESS JUDGE OPINE SEPAD THINK
ASSUME DEVISE DIVINE EXPECT
RECKON BELIEVE CONCEIT
DARESAY IMAGINE PRESUME
PROPOSE SUPPONE SURMISE
CONCEIVE CONCLUDE CONSIDER
OPINIATE
SUPPOSED ALLEGED ASSUMED
PUTATIVE
SUPPOSING IF
SUPPOSITION IF IDEA FICTION
SURMISE WEENING
SUPPOSITORY BOUGIE CANDLE
PESSARY
SUPPRESS LAY DOWN GULP HIDE
HUSH SINK SLAY SNUB STOP BLACK
BURKE CHOKE CRUSH ELIDE QUASH
QUELL SHUSH SMORE SPIKE STILL
QUENCH SQUASH STIFLE CONTAIN
CUSHION INHIBIT OPPRESS
REPRESS SILENCE SMOLDER
SMOTHER SQUELCH RESTRAIN
STRANGLE SUPPRIME VANQUISH
SUPPRESSED BLIND CENSORED
SUPPRESSION ABEYANCE AMEIOSIS
BLACKOUT
(— OF VOWEL) ELISION
(— OF WORD SOUNDS) SYNCOPE
ECLIPSIS
SUPPURATE RUN BEAL WHEAL
DIGEST MATTER QUITTER
MATURATE
SUPPURATION PYOSIS BEALING
COCTION
SUPPURATIVE DIGERENT
SUPRACLAVICLE SCAPULA
SUPREMACY PALM PRIMACY
DOMINION OVERRULE
SUPREME HIGH LAST CHIEF VITAL
SUBLIME SUMMARY TOPLESS
FOREMOST GREATEST PEERLESS
SURA FATIHA FATIHAH
SURCHARGE PACK
SURCINGLE WANTY ROLLER
SURCOAT JUPON CYCLAS KABAYA
SURD SHARP ATONIC FLATED
SURE COLD BOUND SECURE SICKER
STEADY WITTER ASSURED CERTAIN

PERFECT COCKSURE POSITIVE UNERRING

SURELY WIS FINE SURE PARDY REDLY ATWEEL PARDIE

SURENESS SURETY SECURITY

SURETY VAS ANDI BAIL BAND BORROW CAUTION ENGAGER SOVERTY SPONSOR BAILSMAN SECURITY

SURETYSHIP SPONSION

SURF BREACH KALEMA (— **NOISE**) RUT ROTE

SURFACE DAY AREA FACE ORLO PLAT RYME SIDE BOSOM FLOOR STONE SWARF CHROME FINISH GROUND SCRUFF ASPHALT BLANKET COUNTER ENVELOP OUTFACE OUTSIDE STRETCH ADHEREND CONCRETE EXTERIOR PLATFORM
(— **BETWEEN FLUTES OF SHAFT**) ORLO
(— **BETWEEN TRIGLYPH CHANNELS**) MEROS
(— **IN BEATER**) BACKFALL
(— **OF BEAM**) BACK
(— **OF BODY**) FLESH HABIT
(— **OF COAL**) BUTT
(— **OF CRICKET FIELD**) CARPET
(— **OF DIAMOND**) SPREAD
(— **OF EARTH**) DUST GROUND TERRENE
(— **OF ESCUTCHEON**) FIELD
(— **OF GROUND OVER MINE**) DAY
(— **OF PARACHUTE**) CANOPY
(— **OF RIFLE BARREL**) LAND
(— **OF SAWED LUMBER**) FUR
(— **OF TOOTH**) TRITOR
(— **OF VAULT**) GROIN
(— **OF WATER**) RYME SCRUFF
(— **WITHIN EARTH**) GEOID
(**CONCAVE** —) LAP
(**CURVED** —) BELLY
(**DULL** —) MAT MATTING
(**FLAT** —) BED FLAT AEQUOR PAGINA
(**FLOOR** —) BOWL
(**GEOMETRIC** —) TORE CONOID SPHERE CONICOID CYLINDER HELICOID
(**GLOSSY** —) GLAZE
(**GROOVED** —) DROVE
(**HAIRY** —) NAP
(**HORIZONTAL** —) LEVEL
(**INCLINED** —) CANT DESCENT
(**MINERAL** —) DRUSE
(**PAVED** —) FOOTWALK
(**PILE** —) FRIEZE
(**PLANE** —) AREA FACET
(**PRINCIPAL** —) FACE
(**PRINTING** —) CUT
(**PROTECTIVE** —) LAGGING
(**ROAD** —) MACADAM CORDUROY
(**ROUGH** —) KEY CRIZZLE STUBBLE
(**ROUGHENED** —) MAT FOOTGRIP
(**SLIPPERY** —) GLARE
(**SLOPING** —) SHELVING
(**STRIKING** —) BLADE
(**UNDER — OF SKI**) PALM

(**UNGLOSSY PAINT** —) FLAT
(**UPPER** —) NOTAEUM
(**UPRIGHT** —) JAMB

SURFACER SEASONER

SURF DUCK COOT SCOTER

SURFEIT CLOY FILL GLUT SATE STAW STALL STUFF AGROTE ENGLUT SICKEN SATIATE SATIETY SURCLOY SATURATE

SURFEITED SAD SICK BLASE JADED WEARY REPLETE SATIATED

SURF FISH PERCH ALFIONA

SURF SCOTER COOT SCOTER SURFER PISHAUG SKUNKTOP

SURF SHINER SPARADA

SURGE GUST TIDE WASH DRIVE GURGE LUNGE SPURT SWELL BILLOW BREACH COURSE WALLOW WALTER ESTUATE REDOUND AESTUATE UNDULATE
(**SHOREWARD** —) SUFF

SURGEON (ALSO SEE PHYSICIAN AND DOCTOR) LEECH ARTIST INTERN MEDICO OPERATOR SAWBONES
(**TREE** —) TREEMAN

SURGEONFISH TANG TANGE DOCTOR MEDICO BARBERO SURGEON SAWBONES

SURGERY KNIFE

SURGING WALE ESTURE ESTUOUS

SURICATE ZENICK MEERKAT

SURINAM TOAD PIPA PIPAL

SURINAMINE ANDIRINE ANGELINE

SURLINESS MOROSITY

SURLY BAD ILL GRUM LUNT BLUFF CHUFF GRUFF GURLY PURDY ROUGH RUNTY RUSTY CHUFFY CRUSTY GRUFFY GRUMPY MOROSE RUGGED SNARLY SULLEN CHURLISH

SURMISE DEEM REDE GUESS INFER TWANG SURMIT JALOUSE SUSPECT WEENING MISTRUST

SURMOUNT TOP BEAT TIDE CROWN ENSIGN HURDLE MASTER OUTTOP OVERGO SUBDUE CONQUER SURPASS OVERCOME SUPERATE
(— **DIFFICULTIES**) SWIM

SURMOUNTING BROCHANT

SURNAME BYNAME SURNOUN COGNOMEN OVERNAME SURSTYLE

SURPASS CAP COB TOP WAR BANG BEAT CAMP COTE DING FLOG FOIL HEAD PASS SHED WHAP EXCEL OUTDO OUTGO ATREDE BETTER EXCEED OUTRAY OUTVIE OUTWIT OVERDO PRECEL ECLIPSE FORPASS OUTPEER OVERTOP PARAGON PRECEDE ANTECEDE DISTANCE DOMINATE OUTCLASS OUTMATCH OUTRANGE OUTREACH OUTSTRIP OUTWRITE SURMOUNT

SURPASSING BEST FINE ABOVE PASSANT PASSING DOMINANT TOWERING

SURPLICE COTTA EPHOD CHRISOM (PL.) WHITES

SURPLUS OVER PLUS REST EXCESS LUMBER VELVET OVERAGE

OVERRUN OVERSUM ARISINGS LEFTOVER OVERCOME OVERMUCH OVERPLUS

SURPRISE CAP SHED SWAN YACH AMAZE SHOCK SNEAK FERLIE WAYLAY WONDER ASTOUND GLOPPEN PERPLEX STARTLE ASTONISH BEWILDER CONFOUND DUMFOUND
(**BY** —) ABACK
(**EXCLAMATION OF** —) QUOTHA
(**EXPRESS** —) MIRATE
(**SUDDEN** —) KICK

SURPRISING FERLIE STRIKING

SURRA MBORI

SURREJOINDER TRIPLY

SURRENDER HEM LET PUT CEDE CESS DING FALL QUIT TAKE REMIT YIELD ADDICT REMISE RENDER RESIGN SUBMIT ABANDON CONCEDE DELIVER FORSAKE KAMERAD ABDICATE ABNEGATE DEDITION DELIVERY RENOUNCE UNDERLIE
(— **BY DEED**) REMISE

SURREPTITIOUS SECRET BOOTLEG FURTIVE SNEAKING

SURROUND HEM LAP ORB BELT DIKE DYKE FOLD GIRD GIRT HOOP WRAP BESET BRACE CLASP EMBAY EMBED FENCE HEDGE IMBED INARM ROUND BECLIP BEGIRD BEGIRT CIRCLE COLLET CORRAL ENFOLD ENWRAP FORSET GIRDLE IMPALE INCASE INVEST SPHERE SWATHE ARROUND BESEIGE BESTAND COMPASS EMBOSOM ENCLAVE ENCLOSE ENROUND ENVELOP ENVIRON INVOLVE WREATHE CLOISTER ENCIRCLE ENTRENCH STOCKADE
(— **WITH BOOM**) CRIB
(— **WITH CORD**) GIRT
(— **WITH MORTAR**) GROUT

SURROUNDED AMID AMONG AMIDST AMONGST BETWEEN

SURROUNDING MIDST ROUND CIRCUM AMBIENT
(PL.) SCENE HARNESS ENVIRONS

SURVEILLANCE SCRUTINY STAKEOUT

SURVEY SEE DIAL SCAN VIEW AVIEW STOCK STUDY PERUSE REGARD REVIEW SEARCH CANVASS CAPSULE OVERSEE SURVIEW THEORIC EPISCOPY LUSTRATE OVERLOOK OVERVIEW PROSPECT SURVEYAL TRAVERSE
(— **RAPIDLY**) GLANCE
(— **TIMBER**) SKYLOOK
(**BRIEF** —) APERCU

SURVEYING GEODESY GROMATICS
(**MINE** —) LATCHING

SURVEYOR BOLO ARTIST DIALER DIALLER NOTEMAN CHAINMAN GROMATIC LEVELMAN

SURVIVAL ECHO RELIC RELICT
(**ANACHRONISTIC** —) LEFTOVER
(**USELESS** —) SNUFF

SURVIVE LAST BILEVE OUTLAST
OUTLIVE
SURVIVOR RELICT
SUSCEPTIBILITY CAVIL SENSE
EMOTION FEELING FRAILTY
(**— TO ILL-HEALTH**) DELICACY
SUSCEPTIBLE EASY SOFT LIABLE
FEELING PATIENT SENSIBLE
TOLERANT
(**— TO CHANGE**) CASALTY
SUSIAN ELAMITE
SUSLIK SISEL ZIZEL MARMOT
SUSPECT FEAR DOUBT FANCY
GUESS SMOKE THINK BELIEVE
ENDOUTE JALOUSE MISDEEM
SUPPOSE DISTRUST JEALOUSE
MISDOUBT MISTRUST
(**NOT —**) COLD
SUSPECTED SPOTTED SUSPECT
SUSPEND CALL HALT HANG OUST
SHUT SIST STAY BREAK CLOSE
DEBAR DEFER DEMUR EXPEL POISE
REMIT SLING SWING APPEND
DANGLE ADJOURN EXCLUDE
FLUIDIZE INTERMIT OVERHANG
REPRIEVE SCAFFOLD SUSPENSE
(**— ANCHOR**) COCKBILL
SUSPENDED SWING AFLOAT LATENT
HANGING PENDANT PENDENT
PENSILE HOVERING SUSPENSE
SUSPENDER GALLUS GARTER
BRETELLE
(**PL.**) BRACES GALLOWS GALLUSES
SUSPENSE DEMUR POISE
SUSPENSION FOG BREI FUME SIST
STAY STOP DELAY DOUBT MAGMA
SMOKE BREACH CUTOFF SLURRY
AEROSOL FAILURE RESPITE
ABEYANCE BACTERIN EMULSION
INFUSION SHUTDOWN SUSPENSE
WISHBONE
(**— OF JUDGMENT**) EPOCHE
(**— OF NOISE**) HUSH
(**— OF RESPIRATION**) SYNCOPE
SUSPENSIVENESS DRIVE
SUSPENSORY SUPPORT
SUSPICION HINT DOUBT SOUPCON
SURMISE SUSPECT UMBRAGE
DISTRUST JEALOUSY MISDOUBT
MISTRUST TINCTURE
SUSPICIOUS SHY FISHY LEERY
PEERY QUEER SMOKY JEALOUS
SUSPECT DOUBTFUL WAFFLIKE
SUSPICIOUSLY ASKANCE
SUSQUEHANNA CONESTOGA
SUSTAIN ABET BACK BEAR BUOY
DURE HELP HOLD LAST PROP STAY
ABIDE CARRY FAVOR SPRAG STAND
ASSIST CONVEY ENDURE FOSTER
SECOND SUCCOR SUFFER UPHOLD
UPSTAY CONTAIN NOURISH
OUTBEAR PROLONG SUPPORT
UNDERFO BEFRIEND BUTTRESS
CONTINUE MAINTAIN PRESERVE
SUSTAINED SOUTENU
SUSTENANCE GEAR SALT BREAD
FOISON LIVING RELIEF ALIMENT
PABULUM TABLING
SUSU GERIP SOOSOO DOLPHIN

SUSURRUS WHISPER
SUTLER PROVANT VIVANDIE
SUTTEE SATI
SUTURE SEAM RAPHE SETON
HARMONY PTERION
SVANTOVIT TRIGLAV
SWAB GOB MOP SWOB PATCH
DOSSIL SPONGE EPAULET SWABBER
SQUILGEE
SWADDLE SWEEL SWATHE
SWAG DRUM GAME LOOT BOOTY
LUCRE MONEY BOODLE FESTOON
MATILDA
SWAGE BOSS MOUTH UPSET FULLER
JUMPER SHAPER SWAGER SWEDGE
FLATTER
(**PL.**) OLIVER
SWAGGER JET ROY BRAG COCK
FACE ROLL BOAST BRAVE NUTTY
STRUT SWANK SWASH BOUNCE
GOSTER HECTOR PARADO PRANCE
RENOWN RUFFLE SPROSE BLUSTER
BRAVADO GAUSTER PANACHE
ROISTER SOLDIER DOMINEER
TIGERISM
SWAGGERER HUFF SWAG FACER
TIGER CUTTLE JETTER PISTOL
BRAVADO HUFFCAP RUFFLER
FANFARON
SWAGGERING HUFFY FACING
GASCON HUFFCAP TEARCAT
BLUSTERY TIGERISH
SWAGMAN WHALER DRUMMER
TRAVELER
SWAIN COLIN CUDDY STREPHON
SWAINSONA INDIGO
SWALE SLASH
SWALLOW OFF SUP BOLT DOWN
GAUP GAWP GLUT GULP SINK TAKE
CLUNK DRINK GORGE GURGE
POUCH QUILT SLOCK SWOOP
ABSORB ENGLUT ENGULF GLUTCH
GOBBET GOBBLE GODOWN GUZZLE
IMBIBE INGEST MARTIN POCKET
PROGNE SWELLY CONSUME
ENGORGE ARUNDELL WITCHUCK
(**— GREEDILY**) BEND SLUP GORGE
GULCH SWILL WORRY INHALE
(**— HASTILY**) SWAP SWOP GLOUP
(**— IN AGAIN**) RESORB
(**— UP**) GULF SWAMP ABSORB
DEVOUR
(**— WITH GREEDINESS**) ENGORGE
(**LOSS OF ABILITY TO —**) APHAGIA
(**NOISY —**) SLURP
(**WOMAN TURNED INTO —**) PROCNE
SWALLOWTAIL TROILUS
SWAMP BOG FEN FLAT FLOW MIRE
MOSS SLEW SLUE SOAK SUMP VLEI
VLEY WHAM WHIN FLUSH LERNA
LETCH MARSH SWALE SWANG
URMAN DELUGE DISMAL ENGULF
MORASS SLOUGH CIENAGA
POCOSIN GREENING INUNDATE
QUAGMIRE
SWAMP COTTONWOOD LIAR
SWAMPER BUSHER GOPHER
SWAMPHEN COOT

SWAMP LOOSESTRIFE PEATWEED
PEATWOOD
SWAMP MAHOGANY GUNNUNG
SWAMP MILKWEED DAGGA
SWAMPY PUXY BOGGY POOLY
CALLOW POACHY QUASHY QUEASY
SLUMPY MOORISH
SWAMPY CREE MASKEGON
SWAN COB ELK PEN OLOR CYGNET
HOOPER SWANNET WHOOPER
(**FLOCK OF —S**) GAME MARK
SWANFLOWER SWANWORT
SWANK CHIC
SWANKY SWASH
SWAP CHOP SWOP TRADE TRUCK
DICKER EXCHANGE
SWARD SOD TURF SPINE SWARF
SWATH SWARTH
SWARM FRY SNY BIKE CAST FARE
HOST KNIT NEST SORT SWIM
CLOUD CROWD FLOCK FLUSH
FRACK HORDE SNARL FLIGHT
HOTTER RABBLE SWARVE THRONG
SUBCAST
(**— IN**) FILL
(**— OF BEES**) BIKE HIVE
(**— OF INSECTS**) BAND FLIGHT
(**— OF PEOPLE**) BIKE DRIFT
(**THIRD — OF BEES**) COLT
SWARMING ALIVE ASWARM SWARMY
SWARTBACK SWARBIE
SWARTHY DUN DARK BLACK DUSKY
GRIMY MOORY SWART MORIAN
SWARTH BISTRED BISTERED
SWASH SWIG SWILL SWATCH
SWABBLE SWASHWAY
SWASHBUCKLER SWASH GASCON
SLASHER SWASHER
SWASTIKA FYLFOT GAMMADION
SWAT SWOT DEHGAN STRIKE
SWATH SWIPE STADDLE
SWATHE LAP BIND WRAP SWARF
SWADDLE WINDROW
SWATTER FLYSWAT
SWAY NOD WAG BEAR BIAS FLAP
HIKE LILT ROCK ROLL RULE SWAB
SWAG SWIG TILT TOSS WALD WAVE
CARRY CHARM LURCH POWER
REIGN SHAKE SWALE SWING WAVER
WHEEL AFFECT ALLURE CAREEN
DIRECT EMPIRE WAGGLE COMMAND
SHOGGIE STAGGER SWABBLE
SWIGGLE
SWAYBACK WARFA LORDOSIS
RENGUERA
SWAYING ASWAY ROLLING
SWAZILAND (**CAPITAL OF —**)
MBABANE
(**LANGUAGE OF —**) SISWATI
(**RIVER IN —**) USUTU KOMATI
MHLATUZE UMBULUZI
(**TOWN IN —**) MANZINI
SWEAR VOW VUM DAMN SINK SNUM
SWAN SWOW TAKE CURSE ADJURE
AFFIRM BEDAMN DEPONE DEPOSE
OBJURE CONJURE DEJERATE
EXECRATE FORSWEAR
(**— FALSELY**) RAP MOUNT
FORSWEAR MONSWEAR

SWEARING JURATION
(FALSE —) PERJURY
SWEARWORD CUSS
SWEAT DEW WET STEW WASH
BREAN MADOR SUDOR SUDATE
LAUNDER PARBOIL SWELTER
SWIVVET TRANSUDE
(— SKINS) STALE
(DYNAMITE —) LEAK
SWEATBOX HOTBOX
SWEATER FROCK GANSEY JUMPER
WOOLLY CARDIGAN SLIPOVER
SWEATHOUSE TEMESCAL
SWEATING TUB ASWEAT SWELTRY
SUDATION SUDATORY
SWEATY PUGGY ASWEAT PERSPIRY
SUDOROUS SWEATFUL

SWEDEN

CAPITAL: STOCKHOLM
COIN: ORE KRONA SKILLING
DIVISION: AMT LAEN SKANE
OREBRO UPPSALA GOTALAND
JAMTLAND SWEALAND
GULF: BOTHNIA
ISLAND: OLAND GOTALAND
LAKE: SILJAN VANERN MALAREN
VATTERN DALALVEN HJALMREN
STORAVAN
MEASURE: AM ALN FOT MIL REF
TUM FAMN STOP FODER KANNA
KAPPE LINJE NYMIL SPANN
STANG TUNNA FATHOM JUMFRU
KOLLAST OXHUVUD TUNLAND
FJARDING KAPPLAND KOLTUNNA
MOUNTAIN: SARV AMMAR OVIKS
HELAGS SARJEK
PROVINCE: KALMAR OREBRO
GOTLAND HALLAND UPPSALA
ALVSBORG BLEKINGE ELFSBORG
JAMTLAND MALMOHUS
WERMLAND
RIVER: DAL UME GOTA KLAR LULE
KALIX PITEA RANEA LAINIO
LJUSNE TORNEA WINDEL
ANGERMAN
TOWN: UMEA BODEN BORAS
EDANE FALUN GAVLE LULEA
MALMO PITEA VISBY YSTAD
ARVIKA OREBRO LUDVIKA
UPPSALA GOTEBORG NYKOPING
VASTERAS
WEIGHT: ASS LOD ORT MARK
PUND STEN UNTZ NYLAST
LISPUND SKEPPUND

SWEEP BUCK DUST RAFF SOOP
SWAY TILT BESOM BROOM DIGHT
DRIFT FETCH SCOPE SKIRL SWIPE
SWOOP BREADTH CLEANSE
PICOTAH SHADOOF STRICKLE
(— A NET) BEAT
(— MAJESTICALLY) SWAN
(— OF SCYTHE) SWATH SWATHE
(— OFF) SLIPE
(— ON CULTIVATOR) SKIN
(CHIMNEY —) CHUMMY SWEEPY
RAMONEUR

(HAY —) BUCK
SWEEPBOARD STRICKLE
SWEEPER BUNGY SWEEP TOPAZ
BHANGI BHUNGI MEHTAR PRYLER
ROADER SOOPER TOPASS
BROOMER TUBEMAN BHUNGINI
MATRANEE SCRUBBER
SWEEPING SURGE RASANT SWEEPY
(— FOR FISH) DRAFT DRAUGHT
(PL.) DUST FULVIE FULZIE RIFFRAFF
SWEET DOUX DUMP FOOL SOOT
SUCK CREAM DILIS DOUCE DULCE
FRESH HONEY MERRY SOOTH SPICY
SPLIT DULCET FRUITY GENTLE
SILKEN SILVER SIRUPY SUGARY
DARLING FAIRING HONEYED INSIPID
MUSICAL PANDROP SUGARED
SWEETLY WINNING WINSOME
AROMATIC ENGAGING FLUMMERY
LIEBLICH LUSCIOUS NECTARED
PLEASANT
(SLIGHTLY —) SEC
SWEET BAY BREWSTER MAGNOLIA
SWEETBREAD BUR BURR
(— OF DEER) INCHPIN
SWEETBRIER BEDEGUAR EGLANTINE
SWEET CALABASH KURUBA
SWEET CASSAVA AIPI AIPIM
SWEET CICELY MYRRH
SWEET CLOVER LOTUS MELILOT
SWEET COLTSFOOT LAGWORT
SWEETEN CANDY HONEY SUGAR
SWEET PURIFY ADDULCE CLEANSE
DULCIFY FRESHEN MOLLIFY
PERFUME MITIGATE
SWEET FENNEL FINOCHIO
FLORENCE
SWEET FERN FERNGALE
SWEETFISH AYU
SWEET FLAG SEDGE BEEWORT
CALAMUS
SWEET GALE GOLD GAGEL
BAYBUSH FLEAWOOD GALEWORT
GALLBUSH
SWEET GUM AMBER COPALM
STORAX BILSTED
SWEETHEART JO BOY GRA HON
JOE LAD PUG SIS AGRA BABY BEAU
DEAR DOLL DOXY FAIR GILL GIRL
JILL LADY LASS LIEF LOVE MASH
MORT POUT AGRAH BULLY BUSSY
CHERI COOKY DOLLY DONAH
DONEY DRURY FLAME LEMAN
LOVER PUGGY SPARK SWEET
COOKIE EMILIA FELLOW FRIEND
MOPSEY PIGEON STEADY WAHINE
AMOROSA BELOVED PHYLLIS
PIGSNEY QUERIDA SPRUNNY
SWEETIE TOOTSIE DOWSABEL
DULCINEA FOLLOWER LADYBIRD
LADYLOVE LIEBCHEN LOVELASS
MISTRESS SWEETING TRUELOVE
SWEETLEAF DYELEAVES
SYMPLOCOS
SWEET MARJORAM OREGANO
SWEETMEAT DUMP KISS DULCE
GOODY PLATE SPICE TOFFY
BUCAYO COMFIT DRAGEE DREDGE
JUNKET BANQUET CARAWAY

CLAGGUM LOUKOUM PENUCHE
SUCCADE CONSERVE HARDBAKE
MARZIPAN
(PL.) BALUSHAI CONFETTI
SWEETNESS DULCE HONEY SIRUP
SYRUP DULCOR DOUCEUR DULCITY
SUAVITY FLORIMEL WORDNESS
SWEET ORANGE CHINA CHINO
SWEET PEA CATGUT LATHYRUS
SWEET PEPPERBUSH CLETHRA
SOAPBUSH
SWEET POTATO YAM SWEET
BATATA CAMOTE KUMARA
SWEET RUSH SQUINANT
SWEET-SMELLING AROMATIC
SWEETSOP ANON ATES ATIS ATTA
CORAZON SWEETING
SWEET-SOUNDING MERRY
SWEET VIOLET FINELEAF
SWEET WILLIAM DIANTHUS
SWELL BAG NIB NOB BEAL BELL
BLAB BLOW BLUB BOLL BULB BULK
BUMP BUOY DOME FILL GROW
HOVE HUFF HUSH PINK PLIM RISE
TOFF TONY WAVE BELLY BLOAT
BULGE BUNCH FLASH PLUFF SMART
STOCK STRUT SURGE TULIP BILLOW
BOWDEN DILATE EXPAND GROWTH
LOVELY SPRING STROUT TUMEFY
UPRISE AUGMENT BLUBBER
BURGEON DISTEND INFLATE
SWAGGER OVERBLOW TURGESCE
(— OF GUN MUZZLE) TULIP
(— OF WATER) HUSH SURF FLOOD
SURGE
(— OUT) BAG POD BUNT DRAW
POUT BOSOM BILLOW SPONGE
BALLOON BLADDER
(HEAVY —) RUN SEA
SWELLDOODLE EGGFISH
SWELLED BIAS
SWELLFISH BLOWER PUFFER
TAMBOR
SWELLING BIG BUR NOB PAP PIN
BLAB BUBO BUMP BURR CLAP
COWL CURB FROG FULL GALL KNOB
KNOT NODE POKE PONE AMPER
BLAIN BOTCH BOUGE BULGE BUNCH
BUNNY EDEMA JETTY MOUSE
SURGE SWELL TUMOR ANCOME
ASWELL BOSOMY BUNCHY CALLUS
FLATUS GIBBER GROWTH KERNEL
PIMPLE STRUMA SWELTH WARBLE
AMPULLA BOSSING CAPELET
CHAGOMA CUSHION GOUNDOU
HAPTERE PUSTULE SURGENT
TURGENT UREDEMA UROCELE
APOSTEME BULLNECK CHEMOSIS
DACRYOMA FURUNCLE GLANDULE
GOURDING HAPTERON HEMATOMA
MUCOCELE NODOSITY PUMPKNOT
QUELLUNG STYLOPOD VESSICON
(— IN HORSE'S CHEST) ANTICOR
(— OF PLANT TISSUE) GALL
(— OF THE CHEEK) HONE
(— ON ANIMAL'S JOINTS) BUNNY
(— ON HEAD) COWL
(EYE —) STY STYE
SWELTER STEW SWELT

SWELTERING STEWY SULTRY SWELTRY

SWERVE BOW CUT LUG BIAS FADE JOUK SKEW VARY WARP SHEER STRAY DEPART DEVIATE DIGRESS DIVERGE

SWIDDEN CAINGIN KAINGIN

SWIFT CRAN FAST FLIT MAIN VITE FLEET HASTY LIGHT QUICK RAPID SNELL SWITH WIGHT WINDY ARROWY MARLET NIMBLE RAKING SOUPLE SPEEDY STRICT SUDDEN SWIFTY TOTTER WINGED COLLIER DEVELIN FLIGHTY POSTING SWALLOW TANTIVY DEVELING HEPIALID PEGASEAN SCREAMER SCUTTLER SQUEALER SWIFTLET

SWIFTLY FAST SWAP APACE SNELL SNELLY LIGHTLY STEEPLY TANTIVY

SWIFTNESS FOOT HASTE SPEED CELERITY FASTNESS VELOCITY

SWIG SCOUR SWILL SWING SWIGGLE

SWILL SOSS SLOSH SLUICE HOGWASH PIGWASH SWILLING

SWIM COWD SAIL SOOM SPAN TEEM BATHE CRAWL FLEET FLOAT GLIDE SWARM OVERFLOW
(— IN NEW DIRECTION) MILL
(— TOGETHER) SCHOOL

SWIMMER BATHER NATATOR

SWIMMING ASWIM NATANT FLOTANT NATATION
(— STUNT) MARLIN WALKOVER

SWIMMING POOL POOL THERM PLUNGE THERME PISCINA NATATORY

SWINDLE DO CON GIP GYP JOB RIG BILK FLAP HAVE MACE PULL RAMP ROOK ROPE SWIZ BUNCO BUNKO CHEAT FLING FOIST GOUGE LURCH PLANT ROGUE SHARK SHARP SHAVE SLANG SPOOF SWIZZ UNCLE BOODLE BUCKET DIDDLE FIDDLE HUSTLE INTAKE NOBBLE SUCKER TREPAN FINAGLE THIMBLE VERNEUK FLIMFLAM

SWINDLER DO FOB GYP LEG BILK FYNK HAWK SKIN CHEAT CROOK FAKER GREEK HARPY KNAVE MACER ROGUE CHIAUS GOUGER INTAKE RINGER ROOKER SALTER SHAVER VERSER MACEMAN MAGSMAN NOBBLER SHARPER SLICKER SPIELER BARNACLE BLACKLEG FINAGLER GILENYER LUMBERER PIGEONER SHELLMAN TRAMPOSO
(DECOY —) BARNARD

SWINDLING MACE BUNCO BUNKO ROOKY SHARK GYPPERY JOUKERY CHEATERY JOOKERIE

SWINE HOG OIC PIG SOW BOAR GALT GILT PORK SUID YILT DUROC ESSEX SWIPE WHITE GUSSIE POLAND PORKER PORKET BUSHPIG PECCARY SUFFOLK SUIDIAN CHESHIRE HYOTHERE LANDRACE TAMWORTH
(— AND FOOD) PANNAGE

(— AND MAN) OMNIVORA

SWINEHERD GURTH HOGMAN EUMAEUS HOGHERD HOGWARD

SWINE-LIKE GADARENE

SWING GO HIKE JUMP LILT SCUP STOT SWAY SWEE TURN SHAKE SHOWD SLING SWALE TREND DANGLE GYRATE HANDLE SWINGE SWITCH SWIVEL TOTTER JUMPING SHOGGIE SWINGEL WAMPISH BRANDISH FLOURISH
(— A SHIP) SPRING
(— AROUND) JIB SLEW SLUE SLOUGH
(— BY BATTER) CUT
(— FROM POSITION) CANT
(— FROM SIDE TO SIDE) JOW
(— FROM THE TIDE) TEND
(— OF PENDULUM) BEAT
(— OF SAIL) GYBE JIBE
(— OF SWORD) MOULINET
(— OUT OF LINE) SWAG
(— THE FOREFEET) DISH
(RHYTHMICAL —) LILT
(WILD —) HAYMAKER

SWINGING BANK ASWING SWINGY

SWINGLE SWORD SCUTCH SWIPPLE

SWING SEAT TRANSOM

SWINISH SOWISH HOGGISH PORCINE

SWIPE COP CHOP GLOM WIPE SNAKE STEAL VULTURE

SWIRL BOIL GULF HURL PURL WALM GURGE SWALE SWEEL SWORL SWOOSH WREATHE
(— OF SALMON) BULGE

SWIRLING VORTICAL

SWISH HISH WHIP SMART SWILL WHISH

SWISS MUFF SWISSER
(— PINE) MUGHO

SWITCH GAD TAN TWIG WAND AZOTE BIRCH BREAK SHUNT SWISH CHANGE CUTOUT DERAIL DIPPER FERULA FERULE LARRUP RATTAN SCUTCH SILENT SPRING HICKORY KIPPEEN SCOURGE SQUITCH HAIRWORK POSTICHE
(— FOCUS) FADE
(ELECTRIC —) KEY
(RAILROAD —) GATE POINT

SWITCH ENGINE GOAT

SWITCHMAN SHUNTER SWITCHER

SWITZERLAND

BAY: URI

CANTON: URI ZUG BERN VAUD BASEL AARGAU GENEVA GLARUS LUZERN SCHWYZ TICINO VALAIS ZURICH GRISONS THURGAU FRIBOURG OBWALDEN

CAPITAL: BERN BERNE

COIN: FRANC RAPPE RAPPEN ANGSTER DUPLONE BLAFFERT

LAKE: URI ZUG THON AGERI LEMAN MORAT BIENNE BRIENZ GENEVA LUGANO SARNEN WALLEN ZURICH HALLWIL LUCERNE LUNGERN VIERWALD

MEASURE: POT AUNE ELLE FUSS IMMI MUID PIED SAUM ZOLL LIEVE LIGNE LINIE MAASS MOULE POUCE SCHUH STAAB TOISE PERCHE SETIER STRICH JUCHART KLAFTER VIERTEL

MOUNTAIN: JURA RIGI ROSA BLANC CENIS KARPF LINARD PIZELA BERNINA BEVERIN GRIMSEL PILATUS ROTONDO BALMHORN JUNGFRAU MATTERHORN

MOUNTAIN PASS: CENIS FURKA ALBERG MALOJA BRENNER GRIMSEL SIMPLON SPLUGEN LOTSCHEN

NAME: HELVETIA

RIVER: AAR INN AARE THUR BROYE DOUBS LINTH REUSS RHINE RHONE MAGGIA SARINE TICINO PRATIGAU

TOWN: BALE BERN BIEL BRIG CHUR SION BASEL VEVEY GENEVA GLARUS LUZERN SCHWYZ ZURICH FYZABAD HERISAU LUCERNE LAUSANNE MONTREUX

VALLEY: AAR ZERMATT ENGADINE

WEIGHT: PFUND CENTNER QUINTAL

SWIVEL LOPER SWAPE SWIPE CASTER FIDDLE TIRRET TOGGLE TONGUE TRAVERSE TRUNNION

SWOLLEN BLUB FULL PLIM RANK BLOWN CHUFF GOUTY GREAT GUMMY POBBY PROUD TUMID BOLLEN BRAWNY BULLED GOURDY TURGID BESTRUT BLOATED BLUBBER BULBOUS GIBBOSE GIBBOUS GOURDED GOUTISH TURGENT BEPUFFED BLADDERY TUMOROUS

SWOON KEEL SWEB SWIM DROWN DWALM FAINT SLOOM SOUND SWARF SWELT STOUND SWOUND TRANCE ECSTASY SWITHER SYNCOPE SWOONING

SWOONING ASWOON SYNCOPE

SWOOP CHOP JOUK SWAP SWOP SOUSE STOOP SWOPE POUNCE SOURCE DESCEND

SWOOPING SOUSE

SWORD FOX SAX BILL DIRK FALX GRAM IRON PATA SAEX SPIT TOOL TURK BILBO BLADE BRAND DEGEN DIEGO ESTOC GULLY KNIFE KUKRI PRICK RIPON SABER SABRE SHARP STEEL ANDREW BARONG BILBOA CATTAN DAMASK DUSACK FLORET GLAIVE HANGER KHANDA KUKERI MIMING PARANG PINKER PORKER RAPIER SMITER SPATHA TILTER TIZONA TOLEDO WAFTER BALMUNG BRANDON CURTANA CUTLASH CUTLASS ESPADON ESTOQUE FERRARA FLEURET IMPALER JOYEUSE MALCHUS MORGLAY

SHABBLE SLASHER SNICKER
SPURTLE TOASTER WHIFFLE
WHINGER ACINACES BASELARD
CAMPILAN CLAYMORE DAMASCUS
DURENDAL FALCHION FLAMBERG
SCHLAGER SPADROON SPITFROG
WACADASH WHINYARD
(— OF CHARLEMAGNE) JOYEUSE
(— OF CID) TIZONA
(— OF HERMES) HARPE
(— OF LANCELOT) ARONDIGHT
(— OF ROLAND) DURENDAL
(— OF SIEGFRIED) GRAM BALMUNG
(— OF SIR BEVIS) MORGLAY
(— OF ST. GEORGE) ASCALON
ASKELON
(— USED BY ST. PETER) MALCHUS
(BLUNT —) WAFTER SCHLAGER
(CELTIC —) SAX SAEX
(DOUBLE-EDGED —) KEN PATA
KHANDA SPATHA
(DUELLING —) EPEE SHARP
(DYAK —) PARANG
(FENCING —) EPEE FOIL SABER
SABRE RAPIER
(HALF OF —) FORTE
(JAPANESE —) CATAN CATTAN
KATANA WACADASH
(LONG —) SPATHA WHIFFLE
(MATADOR'S —) ESTOQUE
(MORO —) BARONG CAMPILAN
(NARROW —) TUCK
(NORMAN —) SPATHA
(PERSIAN —) ACINACES
(POINTLESS —) CURTANA
(RUSTY —) SHABBLE
(SHORT —) DIRK ESTOC KUKRI
SKEAN WHINGER WHINYARD
(THRUSTING —) ESTOC STOCK
(TWO-HANDED —) ESPADON
CLAYMORE
(WOODEN —) WASTER STRICKLE
SWORD-BEARER VERGER SELICTAR
PORTGLAVE
(PL.) ENSIFERI
SWORD DANCER MATACHIN
SWORDFISH AU ESPADA ESPADON
XIPHIAS ALBACORA BILLFISH
BOATBILL FORKTAIL XIPHIOID
SCOMBROID
SWORDPLAY SPADROON
SWORD-SHAPED ENSATE ENSIFORM
GLADIATE
SWORDSMAN BLADE BLADER
FENCER SLASHER SWORDER
THRUSTER
SWORDTAIL HELLERI
SWORN AVOWED
SYAGUSH SHARGOSS
SYBARITE EPICURE
SYBARITIC SENSUOUS
SYCAMORE MAY DAROO COTONIER
LACEWOOD PLANTAIN
SYCEE SHOE
SYCOPHANCY FAWNERY
SYCOPHANT TOADY COGGER
FAWNER GNATHO HANGBY TAGTAIL
CLAWBACK PARASITE
SYCOPHANTIC FAWNING SERVILE

SLAVISH OBEDIENT TRENCHER
SYCOSIS MENTAGRA
SYENITE APPINITE TRACHYTE
SYLLABARY KANA IROFA IROHA
SYLLABIC SONANT CENTROID
SONANTIC
SYLLABLE ARSIS BREVE GROUP
SHORT DISEME SYLLAB THESIS
TRISEME ASSONANT
(— DENOTING ASSENT) OM
(BOBIZATION —) BO CE DI GA GE
LO MA NI
(LAST — BUT ONE) PENULT
(LAST —) ULTIMA
(LONG —) LONG
(MUSICAL —) DI DO FA FI LA LE LI
ME MI RA RE RI SE SI SO TA TE TI
TO UT SOL
(REFRAIN —) DILDO
(SHORT —) MORA SHORT
(STRONG —) STRESS
(UNACCENTED —S) THESIS
SYLLABUS PROGRAM VIDIMUS
HEADNOTE SYNOPSIS
SYLLOGISM BARBARA ABDUCTION
ENTHYMEME
(SERIES OF —S) SORITES
SYLPH ARIEL SYLPHID
SYLVAN WOODY FOREST SILVAN
WOODEN WOODISH SYLVATIC
SYLVITE HARDSALT
SYMBIOSIS LICHENISM MUTUALISM
NUTRICISM
SYMBOL KEY CODE FISH FOUR ICON
IDOL IKON MARK NEUM SEAL SIGN
TYPE CREST CROSS EAGLE IMAGE
INDEX CARACT CIPHER EMBLEM
ENSIGN FIGURE LETTER PNEUME
SHADOW SIGNAL FACIEND MANDALA
PALATAL CEREMONY CONSTANT
DIRECTOR EXPONENT GUTTURAL
IDEOGRAM LOGOGRAM OPERATOR
SWASTIKA SYMBOLUM TRISKELE
(— FOR WAVELENGTH) LAMBDA
(— OF DISTINCTION) BELT HONOR
(— OF FAITHFUL DEAD) ORANT
(— OF FRANCE) LILY
(— OF MONK) COWL
(— OF PHYSICIAN) CADUCEUS
(— OF RAILROAD) HERALD
(— OF SPRING) KARPAS
(— OF STRENGTH) HORN
(— OF SUN) DISC DISK
(— ON UNCHANGEABLENESS)
LEOPARD
(— REPRESENTING THE ABSOLUTE)
TAIKIH
(ALGEBRAIC —) EXPONENT
(CRICKET —) ASHES
(CRUSADERS' —) CROSS
(CURVED —) HOOK
(KOREAN —) TAHGOOK
(MAGIC —) CARACT
(MATHEMATICAL —) KNOWN
FACTOR FACIEND OPERAND
(PHALLIC —) LINGA LINGAM
(PICTOGRAPHIC —) ISOTYPE
(PRINTING —) DIAGONAL
(PRONUNCIATION —) ENG

(RELIGIOUS —) LABRYS
(PL.) KATAKANA
SYMBOLIC GRAPHIC SHADOWY
ANICONIC
SYMBOLICAL ALLUSIVE MYSTICAL
SYMBOLISM CONOLOGY
SYMBOLIZE BODY SIGN TOKEN
FIGURE SAMPLE SHADOW SYMBOL
TYPIFY EXPRESS PORTEND SIGNIFY
RESEMBLE
SYMMETRICAL FORMAL DIMERIC
REGULAR SHAPELY SPHERAL
BALANCED
(NOT —) SKEW
SYMMETRY MEASURE
SYMPATHETIC AKIN FERE SOFT
WARM HUMAN FELLOW KINDLY
TENDER PIETOSO SIMPATICO
SYMPATHIZER FABIAN BLACKNEB
SHAYSITE
SYMPATHY PITY RUTH FLESH PHILIA
CONSENT EMPATHY AFFINITY
KINDNESS
SYMPHONY SINFONIA
SYMPOSIUM POTATION
SYMPTOM MARK NOTE SIGN
SHOWER STIGMA INSTANCE
PRODROME
SYNAGOGUE SHUL SCHUL ALJAMA
PROSEUCHA
SYNAPSIS PAIRING
SYNAPTE ECTENE EKTENE
SYNARTHROSIS SUTURE
SYNCHRO SELSYN
SYNCHRONIZER SPEEDGUN
SYNCLINE DOWNFOLD ISOCLINE
SYNCOPATED ZOPPA ABRIDGED
SYNCOPE SWOON COTYPE FAINTING
SYNDICATE HUI GROUP
SYNDICATED CANNED
SYNECDOCHE MERISM
SYNERGIST BOOSTER SESAMIN
SYNOD SOBOR
SYNODAL SENAGE
SYNONYM ANTONYM HOMONYM
EUPHONYM POLYONYM
SYNOPSIS BRIEF TABLE EPITOME
SUMMARY ABSTRACT SCENARIO
SYLLABUS
SYNSACRUM SACRARY
SYNTACTICAL FORMAL
SYNTHESIS SUMMA FUSION
SYSTASIS
SYNTHETIC ERSATZ SYSTATIC
SYPHILIS POX LUES SYPH CRINKUM
GRINCOME

SYRIA

CAPITAL: DAMASCUS
COIN: POUND TALENT PIASTER
DISTRICT: ALEPPO HAURAN
LAKE: DJEBOID TIBERIAS
MEASURE: MAKUK GARAVA
MOUNTAIN: HERMON LIBANUS
NAME: ARAM
NATIVE: DRUSE ANSARIE
   SARACEN ANSARIEH
RIVER: ASI BARADA JORDAN

KNABUR ORONTES EUPHRATES
TOWN: ALEP HAMA HOMS NAWA
BUSRA CALNO DERRA HALAB
HAMAH IDLIB JERUD RAQQA
ALEPPO BALBEL LATAKIA
SELEUCIA
WEIGHT: COLA ROTL ARTAL
ARTEL RATEL TALENT

SYRINGE GUN HYPO ENEMA SCOOT
DOUCHE FILLER SQUIRT SCOOTER
SERRING
SYRINGIN LILACIN
SYRNIUM STRIX
SYRYENIAN SYRYAN ZYRIAN
(PL.) KAMI KOMI
SYRUP DIBS LICK SIRUP ORGEAT
ANTIQUE ECLEGMA FALERNUM
QUIDDANY
(STARCH —) GLUCOSE
SYRUPY FRUITY
SYSTEM ISM AREA CREDO FRAME
ORDER CIRCLE METHOD SCHEME
STEREO SYNTAX COMPLEX DUALISM
ECONOMY FAGGERY NAVARHO
REGIMEN ENSEMBLE GALENISM
RELIGION UNIVERSE
(— OF BARS) LATTICE
(— OF BELIEFS) FAITH
(— OF BELL CHANGES) CATERS
QUATERS STEDMAN
(— OF CORDS) BRIDLE
(— OF CROSSING THREADS) LEASE
(— OF ETHICS) SELFISM

(— OF EXCHANGE) KULA
(— OF FAITH) CREED
(— OF GEARS) COMPOUND
(— OF JOINTS) CLEAT
(— OF LANGUAGE SIGNS) SIGNARY
(— OF LAW) EQUITY
(— OF LINES IN EYEPIECE) RETICLE
RETICULE
(— OF MANUAL TRAINING) SLOJD
SLOYD
(— OF MEANING) SEMANTIC
(— OF MEDICINE) AYURVEDA
(— OF NUMERALS) ALGORISM
(— OF OCCULT THEOSOPHY)
CABALA
(— OF PHILOSOPHY) HUMISM
HOBBISM SAMKHYA SANKHYA
STOICISM
(— OF PHONETIC NOTATION) ROMIC
(— OF PRINCIPLES) CODE
(— OF RAYS) ASTER
(— OF ROCKS) CENOZOIC
DEVONIAN SILURIAN
(— OF RULE) REGIME
(— OF RULES) ART
(— OF SOLMIZATION) FASOLA
(— OF SPACES) LACUNOME
(— OF SYMBOLS) CODE
(— OF TENANCY) CROFTING
(— OF TRANSPORTATION) AIRLINE
AIRMAIL
(— OF TRUSSING) CABANE
(— OF VALUES) ETHOS
(— OF WEIGHTS) TROY

(— OF WIRES) HARNESS
(— OF WORSHIP) CULT CULTUS
(— OF WRITING) KANJI BRAILLE
ALPHABET
(ACOUSTICAL —) SODAR
(AGRICULTURAL —) KOLKOZ
KOLKHOS
(ALARM —) BUG
(BETTING —) ALEMBERT
(COLLOIDAL —) SOL
(COMMUNICATION —) BLOWER
CIRCUIT
(CULTURAL —) ISLAM
(DEFENSE —) SAGE
(DISPERSE —) GEL
(ELECTRICAL —) SELSYN
(GEOLOGICAL —) KEEWATIN
TERTIARY
(HAULING —) DILLY
(IRRIGATION —) KAREZ
(LANGUAGE —) LATINXUA
(NAVIGATION —) GEE LANAC
SHORAN
(RELIGIOUS —) LAW CULT CULTUS
SHIISM SUNNISM DRUIDISM
(RHYTHMIC —) STROPHE GLYCONIC
(SOCIAL —) CASTE
(STAR —) GALAXY
(TECHNOLOGICAL —) FORDISM
(TELEVISION —) SCOPHONY
(TRUCK —) TOMMY
SYSTEMATIC ORDERLY REGULAR
METHODIC
SYSTEMATIZE CODIFY ORGANIZE

T TEE TARE TANGO
TAAL AFRIKAANS
TAB JAG PAN TAG BILL COST CHECK
FLASH PRICE TALLY WATCH EARTAB
EARTAG SIGNAL TOEPLATE
TABANID GADFLY
TABERNACLE PIX PYX HOVEL
SACRARY
TABES WASTING
TABETIC MARCID
TABLATURE LYRAWAY PICTURE
PAINTING
TABLE KEY PIE PYE RUN BANK BUCK
DAIS DESK FORM MESS BELLY
BENCH BOARD CANON CHART PINAX
PLANK SCALE STALL STAND STONE
WAGON COMMON SCHEME TABLET
TABULA TARIFF TRIPOD VANNER
CABARET CAMBIST CONSOLE
COUNTER DIAGRAM DIPTYCH
DRESSER PROJECT SHAMBLE
TABLEAU TESSERA TROLLEY
WHIRLER CALENDAR CREDENCE
GUERIDON PEDIGREE PEMBROKE
REGIMENT SPECULUM STILLAGE
TOILETTE VANITORY
(— FOR BOWING HAT-BODY) HURL
(— FOR GLAZING LEATHER) BANK
(— FOR ORNAMENT) CARTOUCH
(— FOR PHOTOGRAPHIC PLATES)
WHIRLER
(— FURNISHED WITH MEAL) SPREAD
(— IN STORE) COUNTER
(— OF ANCESTORS) PEDIGREE
(— OF CONTENTS) INDEX METHOD
(— OF DECLINATIONS) REGIMENT
(— TOP) AMOEBA
(— USED IN FELTING A HAT) BASON
(— WITH BRAZIER BENEATH)
TENDOOR TENDOUR
(ARITHMETIC —) TARIFF
(ASTROLOGICAL —) SPECULUM
(BOTANIC —) KEY
(CIRCULAR —) ROUNDEL
(COMMUNION —) ALTAR
(DINING —) MAHOGANY
(DRESSING —) TOILET VANITY
TOILETTE
(FOLDING —) SERVETTE
(INNER —) HOME
(MASSAGE —) PLINTH
(MUSICAL —) DIAGRAM
(NIGHT —) SOMNO
(PRINCIPAL —) DAIS
(PROFUSELY ORNAMENTED —)
PEMBROKE
(SERVING —) WAGON
(SHAKING —) SLIMER
(SMALL —) KURSI STAND TABORET
TABOURET
(TEA —) TEAPOY
(WRITING —) DESK
TABLEAU LAYOUT PAGEANT
TABLECLOTH CLOTH COVER
TABLE D'HOTE DINNER
TABLELAND PLAT PUNA PUNO
KAROO TABLE KARROO PLATEAU
BALAGHAT
TABLET PAX BRED ALBUM FACIA

PIECE PINAX SLATE TABLE TABULA
TABULE TROCHE ASPIRIN CODICIL
DIPTYCH PALETTE PREFORM
TABLING CARTOUCH CHURINGA
TABULATE TRIPTYCH
(— BEARING SYMBOL OF CHRIST)
PAX
(— FOR PUBLISHING LAWS)
PARAPEGM
(— OVER SHOP FRONT) FACIA
FASCIA
(MEDICATED —) ASPIRIN JELLOID
TABELLA
(MEDICINAL —) DISC DISK TROCHE
(MEMORIAL —) BRASS TABUT
(PAINTER'S —) PALETTE
(SQUARE —) ABACK
(UPRIGHT —) STELA STELE
(VOTIVE —) PINAX
(WRITING —) CODICIL TRIPTYCH
TABLEWARE CHINA FLATWARE
HAVILAND
TABOO KAPU TABU TAPU
FORBIDDEN INEFFABLE
TABOR ATABAL TABRET TIMBRE
TABORIN TIMBREL
TABULATION SCALE SCHEME
TABLING
TABUT TAZIA TAZEEA
TACHOMETER CUTMETER
TACHYGLOSSUS ECHIDNA
TACIT SILENT IMPLICIT
TACITURN DUMB STILL SILENT
RESERVED
TACK LAY BEAT CAST STAY BASTE
BOARD FETCH ENTAIL LAVEER
TACKET TINGLE SADDLERY
(GLAZIERS' —) BRAD
TACKER GUN SPREADER
TACKLE CAT RIG TAW SWIG TACK
YOKE ANGLE FALLS ATTACK
BURTON COLLAR GARNET JIGGER
LEDGER RUNNER STEEVE TAGLIA
TEAGLE DERRICK HALYARD
HARNESS RIGGING FISHFALL
PURCHASE TACKLING
(— FOR RAISING BOAT) FALLS
(— TO HOIST ANCHOR) CAT
(COMBINATION OF —S) JEER JEERS
(FISHING —) TEW LEGER OTTER
LEDGER
TACT TOUCH ADDRESS CONDUCT
DELICACY
TACTFUL DISCREET GRACEFUL
TACTFULLY HAPPILY
TACTLESS BRASH
TACTIC GAME
TADPOLE POWHEAD BULLHEAD
POLEHEAD POLLIWOG PORWIGLE
TAEL LIANG
TAENNIN KOSIN KOUSIN
TAFFETA TABBY FLORENCE
TAFFY GUNDY TOFFY TOFFEE
CLAGGUM
TAG HE EAR TAB TIG TAIL TICK
AGLET DAGGE LABEL TALLY TOUCH
AIGLET EARTAB EARTAG FOLLOW
SWATCH TAGGLE TAGRAG TICKET
TIGTAG HANGTAG

(— OF A LACE) AGLET AIGLET
(ANGLING —) TOUCH
(ORNAMENTED —S) FANCY
TAGALOG PULAHAN
TAGESTES MARIGOLD
TAGRAG SHAGRAG
TAHITI (CAPITAL OF —) PAPEETE
(FORMER NAME OF —) OTAHEITE
(MOUNTAIN IN —) OROHENA
TAHR KRAS JHARAL
TAHSILDAR TALUKDAR
TAI LI AHOM SHAM THAI PORGY
KHAMTI
TAIGA URMAN
TAIL BOB BUN CUE BUNT BUSH CLUB
FLAG POLE SCUT BRUSH CAUDA
SNAKE START STERN TRAIN TWIST
FLIGHT FOLLOW RUMPLE SWITCH
TAILET TAILLE FANTAIL FOXTAIL
RATTAIL
(— OF ARTIFICIAL FLY) TOPPING
(— OF BELL CLAPPER) FLIGHT
(— OF BIRD OR ANIMAL) CUE POLE
START
(— OF BIRD) FAN
(— OF BOAR) WREATH
(— OF CART) ARSE
(— OF COAT) DOCK
(— OF COMET) BEARD STREAM
STREAMER
(— OF DEER) FLAG SINGLE SHINGLE
(— OF DOG) FLAG STERN
(— OF FISH) UROSOME
(— OF FLY) WHISK
(— OF FOX) BUSH BRUSH FOXTAIL
(— OF HARE OR RABBIT) BUN FUD
BUNT SCUT
(— OF HORSE) BOB
(— OF MAN'S TIED HAIR) CLUB
(— OF METEOR) TRAIN
(— OF MUSICAL NOTE) QUEUE
(— OF PUG DOG) TWIST
(— OF SQUIRREL) BUN
(— OF STANZA) CODA
(DRAGON'S —) KETU
(STUMP OF —) STRUNT
(TIP OF —) TAG
TAILBAND FOOTBAND
TAILBOARD ENDGATE ENDBOARD
ENDPIECE
TAILED CAUDATE CAUDATED
TAILING CHAT
(PL.) SAND TAIL GRUFFS
TAILLE TALLY
TAILLESS ACAUDAL ANUROUS
ACAUDATE ECAUDATE
TAILOR SLOP SNIP BUILD DARZI
GORER SHRED DARZEE FULLER
SARTOR SNYDER STITCH BOTCHER
CABBAGE SNIPPER TIREMAN
CLOTHIER SEAMSTER SEMPSTER
SHEPSTER
(ITINERANT —) CARDOOER
TAILORBIRD DARZEE
TAILPIECE QUEUE ANQUERA
TAILRACE AFTERBAY
TAILSPIN FLICKER
TAILSTOCK DEADHEAD
TAINO HAITIAN

(— BELIEFS) ZEMIISM

TAINT HAUL HOGO MOIL SMUT SPOT VICE CLOUD STAIN TOUCH DARKEN INFECT REMORD SMIRCH SMUTCH ATTAINT BLEMISH CORRUPT DEBAUCH ENVENOM FLYBLOW FORRUMP POLLUTE TARNISH VITIATE EMPOISON TAINTURE

TAINTED OFF GAMY HIGH BLOWN PINDY SAPPY TAINT WEMMY ROTTEN SINFUL SMUTTY CORRUPT FLYBLOWN

TAIWAN (CAPITAL OF —) TAIPEI **(ISLAND GROUP OF —)** MATSU PENGHU QUEMOY **(MOUNTAIN IN —)** TZUKAO YUSHAN HSINKAO **(OTHER NAME OF —)** FORMOSA **(RIVER IN —)** WUCHI TACHIA CHOSHUI HUALIEN TANSHUI **(TOWN IN —)** TAINAN TAIPEI KEELUNG TAICHUNG

TAJIN TOTONAC

TAJ MAHAL (SITE OF —) AGRA

TAKE COP HIT NIM NOB BEAR BONE DRAW FANG GLOM HAVE LEAD TACK TEEM TOLL ADOPT AFONG BRING CARRY CATCH CREEL FETCH GRASP GRIPE LATCH SEIZE SNAKE ACCEPT CLUTCH COTTON DERIVE EXTEND FERRET FINGER RECIPE SNATCH TAKING ATTRACT CABBAGE CAPTURE RECEIVE UNPURSE UNDERNIM

(— A BATH) TOSH

(— A CERTAIN POSITION) SIT

(— A DIRECTION) STEER

(— A DRINK) SMILE

(— A LITTLE) DELIBATE

(— A NAP) DOSS

(— A STAND) ASSERT

(— ACTION) ACT

(— ADVANTAGE) DO ABUSE BLUDGE CLUTCH EXPLOIT

(— AFTER) BRAID FOLLOW

(— AIM) BEAD

(— AS ONE'S OWN) ADOPT

(— AWAY) BATE EASE HENT LIFT TOLL WISP BENIM BLEED HEAVE REAVE STEAL CONVEY DEDUCE DEDUCT DEMISE DEPOSE DEVEST DIVEST ELOIGN EXEMPT REMOVE UNVEST ABJUDGE BEREAVE DEPRIVE DETRACT FORTAKE RETRACT SUBDUCE SUBLATE ABSTRACT DEROGATE DIMINISH SUBTRACT

(— BACK TO ONESELF) RESUME

(— BACK) RECALL RECANT REVOKE RETRACT

(— BY FRAUD) BOB

(— BY LEVY) ESTREAT

(— BY STEALTH) HOOK SNITCH

(— BY STORM) EXPUGN INVADE SURPRISE

(— CARE) FIX SEE GARE KEEP MIND TEND WARD YEME NURSE BEWARE GOVERN INTEND CUIDADO HUSBAND CHAPERON

(— CENSUS OF) MUSTER

(— CHANCE) DICE RISK

(— CHARGE OF) CURE SOLICIT

(— CHARGE) ATTEND

(— COVER) COOK

(— DAMAGE) BANGE

(— DINNER) DINE

(— DOWN) STOOP STRIKE

(— EXCEPTION) DEMUR STRAIN

(— FOOD) EAT DINE GRUB

(— FOR GRANTED) BEG ASSUME

(— FOR ONESELF) CAB

(— FOR RESALE) FLOG

(— FORM) FORM INFORM

(— FRAUDULENTLY) STEAL STRIKE

(— FRIGHT) BOOGER

(— FROM DEPOSIT) DRAW

(— FROM) DETRACT

(— GOLFING STANCE) ADDRESS

(— GREAT DELIGHT) REVEL

(— HEART) BRACE

(— HEED) RECK TENT

(— HOLD) GET BITE GRAB PINCH SEIZE ARREST BEGRIPE

(— HOLIDAY) LAKE

(— IN BY LEAKING) LADE

(— IN LIVESTOCK) AGIST

(— IN SAIL) BRAIL

(— IN) IN EAT SUP BITE HOAX KEEP DOWSE DRINK ABSORB DEVOUR ENFOLD GATHER HARBOR INCEPT INGEST INSORB INSUME INTAKE MUZZLE BEGRIPE EMBRACE INCLUDE

(— INTO HANDS) TOUCH EMBRACE

(— LEGALLY) ATTACH

(— LEVEL OF) BONE

(— LUNCH) TIFFIN

(— MEALS) BOARD

(— NOTE OF) NB COUNT SMOKE NOTICE WITNESS

(— OATH) ABJURE

(— OFF) OFF DOFF LIFT VAIL DOUSE SHUCK STRIP DEDUCT

(— OFFENSE) DORT HUFF

(— ON) MOUNT START

(— ONE'S LEAVE) CONGEE

(— ONESELF) BETAKE

(— OUT OF EARTH) EXTER

(— OUT) DELE KILL EXCERPT AIRBRUSH

(— PAINS) BOTHER

(— PART) LEAD FIGHT ENGAGE

(— PLACE) BE DO GO COME GIVE PASS ARISE BEFALL HAPPEN

(— PLEASURE IN) ENJOY ADMIRE

(— PORTION OF) PARTAKE

(— POSSESSION) GRIP ANNEX BESET SEIZE SPOIL EXTEND CONQUER INHERIT DISTRAIN

(— REFUGE) HIDE SOIL EVADE HAVEN WATCH

(— ROOT) MARE MORE ENROOT STRIKE

(— SHAPE) JELL

(— SHELTER) HOWF NESTLE SHROUD

(— SUPPER) SUP

(— THE PLACE OF) ENSUE SECOND

SUPPLY DISPLACE SUPPLANT

(— THOUGHT) ADVISE

(— TO BE TRUE WITHOUT PROOF) PRESUME

(— TO TASK) JACK CARPET

(— TO WING) FLUSH

(— UNAWARE) DECEIVE

(— UP AGAIN) RESUME

(— UP WITH) ALL

(— UP) ENTER MOUNT ADSORB ASSUME GATHER HANDLE STRIKE

(— WELL OR ILL) RESENT

(— WIND ON OPPOSITE QUARTER) JIBE

TAKEN TON TAIN

(— ABACK) BLANK

(— AWAY) ADEMPT

TAKEOFF SPOOF SCRAMBLE

TAKEOUT STACK

TAKER PERNOR

TAKING HOT TAKY ADOPTION PERNANCY

(— EVERYTHING INTO ACCOUNT) OVERALL

(— OF LIFE) BLOOD

(— PLACE) AGATE

TALAK AHSAN

TALARI PATACA PATACOON

TALAUS (FATHER OF —) BIAS **(MOTHER OF —)** PERO **(SON OF —)** ADRASTUS **(WIFE OF —)** LYSIMACHE

TALC SPAAD TALCUM AGALITE STEATITE

TALE SAW DIDO JEST LEED REDE TELL BOURD CRACK FABLE RECIT SPELL SPOKE STORY WINDY AITION FABULA LEGEND PISTLE PURANA FABLIAU FICTION HISTORY MARCHEN ROMANCE ANECDOTE FOLKTALE SPELLING

(— OF ACHIEVEMENTS) GEST GESTE

(— OF GOLD COAST NEGROS) NANCY

(COMIC COARSE —) FABLIAU

(DEVISED —) AITION

(EPIC —) TAIN

(FALSE —) VANITY SLANDER

(FATEFUL —) WEIRD

(FOLK —) NANCY THRENE

(HUMOROUS —S) FACETIAE

(MERRY —) BOURD

(POETIC NARRATIVE —) SAGA

(SHORT —) LAI CONTE

TALEBEARER BUZZER GOSSIP TATTLER TALEPYET TELLTALE

TALEBEARING TALEWISE

TALENT GIFT HEAD VEIN DOWER DOWRY VERVE CICHAR GENIUS ABILITY CHARISM FACULTY CAPACITY CHARISMA

TALENTED ABLE CLEVER GIFTED

TALER ORT THALER

TALIPES CLUBFOOT

TALISMAN ANGLE CHARM IMAGE SAFFI AMULET GRIGRI SAPHIE SCARAB TELESM ICHTHUS ICHTHYS GREEGREE

TALK GAB JAW JIB SAW SAY YAP
BUCK BUKH CANT CARP CHAT CHIN
GAFF GIVE GUFF KNAP MEAN TALE
TOVE WORD CRACK FABLE MOUTH
PARLE PITCH SPEAK SPELL SPIEL
SPOKE TUTEL COMMON GAMMON
INDABA KORERO PATTER SERMON
SPEECH STEVEN TOMGUE YABBER
ADDRESS DISCUSS LIPWORK
PALABRA PALAVER PARRALL
PURPOSE WINDJAM CAUSERIE
COLLOQUY CONVERSE LANGUAGE
PARLANCE QUESTION
(— ABOUT) HASH
(— BACK) SASS
(— BIG) BOUNCE
(— BOASTFULLY) GAS
(— BOMBASTICALLY) BEMOUTH
(— CASUALLY) DISH
(— CONFIDENTIALLY) CUTTER
(— CONFUSEDLY) HOTTER
(— DISMALLY) CROAK
(— EMPTILY) BLOW
(— FAMILIARLY) TOVE CONFAB
(— FATUOUSLY) BABBLE
(— FONDLY) COO
(— FOOLISHLY) BLAT FLAP HAVER
BABBLE DRIVEL FOOTER FOOTLE
GABBLE GIBBER SAWNEY TOOTLE
BLATHER BLETHER
(— GLIBLY) PATTER
(— GLIBLY) SCREED
(— IDLY) GAB BLAB CHIN GASH
FABLE GABBLE JANGLE TATTLE
CHATTER GNATTER PRATTLE
(— IMPUDENTLY) SASS
(— INACCURATELY) BLAGUE
(— INARTICULATELY) CHUNNER
CHUNTER
(— INCESSANTLY) YANK BURBLE
CHATTER
(— INCOHERENTLY) BABBLE
HOTTER MITHER MOIDER
(— INCONSIDERATELY) BLAT
(— INFORMALLY) HOBNOB
(— INSOLENTLY) SNASH
(— INTENDED TO DECEIVE)
GAMMON PALAVER
(— IRRATIONALLY) RAVE
(— MONOTONOUSLY) DRONE
(— NEEDLESSLY) PALAVER
(— NOISILY) CLAP BLATTER
BRABBLE
(— NONSENSE) GAS ROT DROOL
FUDGE
(— OFFICIOUSLY) BLEEZE
(— PERTLY) CHELP
(— PRIVATELY) COLLOGUE
(— RAPIDLY) GABBLE JABBER
GNATTER
(— SCANDAL) HORN
(— SNAPPISHLY) KNAP
(— SPORTIVELY) DAFF
(— SUPERFICIALLY) SMATTER
(— TEDIOUSLY) DINGDONG
(— THOUGHTLESSLY) BLAB
(— TOGETHER) DEVISE
(— VAGUELY) WOOZLE
(— VOLUBLY) CHIN PATTER

(— WEAKLY) DRIVEL
(— WITH) CONTACT
(— WITHOUT MEANING) GABBLE
(ABSURD —) BOSH
(ABUSIVE —) HOKER JAWING
(ARROGANT —) GUM BRAG
(BOASTFUL —) BULL GAFF
(BOMBASTIC —) FLASH
(COMMON —) FAME FABLE
HEARSAY
(DECEPTIVE —) GAMMON
(EMPTY —) GAS BOSH GASH FRASE
GLOZE FRAISE BLAFLUM GASSING
PRATTLE BALLYHOO GALBANUM
(ENTHUSIASTIC —) JAZZ
(FALSE —) BALLYHOO
(FAMILIAR —) CONFAB CHITCHAT
(FANTASTIC —) GUYVER
(FOOLISH —) GUP GAFF JIVE BLEAT
CLACK FABLE BLETHERS
(FORMAL —) ADDRESS
(GLIB —) JIVE
(IDLE —) GAB BLAB BUFF CHAT
GAFF GEST GUFF FABLE GESTE
BABBLE CLAVER GOSSIP JANGLE
CHATTER CLATTER PALAVER
TWATTLE BABBLING
(IMPUDENT —) PRATE SLACK
(INCOHERENT —) GABBER JABBER
(INFORMAL —) CAUSERIE
(INSINCERE —) BUNKUM
(JESTING —) CHAFF JAPERY
(LIGHT —) TRIFLING
(MEANINGLESS —) SLIPSLOP
(NONSENSICAL —) BLABBER
BLATHER FOLDEROL
(PIOUS OR SANCTIMONIOUS —) PI
(RAPID —) GABBLE JABBER
CHATTER CLATTER
(SCOLDING —) HARANGUE
(SILLY —) BUFF CLART FOOTLE
TWADDLE
(SMALL —) CHAT BACKCHAT
CHITCHAT
(SMOOTH —) GLOZE BLARNEY
(TRIFLING —) PRATTLE CHITCHAT
(USELESS —) WASTE
(VIOLENT —) BLUSTER
(WEAK —) SLIPSLOP
(WHINING —) BLEAT
TALKATIVE COSY GASH GLIB NAWY
BUZZY TALKY CHATTY CLASHY
CRACKY FLUENT FUTILE VOLUBLE
BIGMOUTH FLIPPANT TELLSOME
TALKATIVENESS FUTILITY
TALKER CAMPER POTGUN CAUSEUR
SPIELER
(IDLE —) WHIFFLER
(PROFESSIONAL —) JAWSMITH
(SENSELESS —) RATTLE
TALKING (LOUD —) NORATION
TALKING-TO EARFUL LECTURE
TALKY GABBY
TALL HIGH LANKY LOFTY STEEP
WANDY CRANEY PROCERE
(— AND FEEBLE) TANGLE
(VERY —) TAUNT
TALLAGE CUTTING
TALLER DOMINANT

TALLOW SUET SEVUM ARMING
TAULCH
TALLY TAB JUMP SUIT AGREE CHECK
COUNT SCORE STICK STOCK
CENSUS STRING SWATCH TAILYE
COMPORT TAILZIE
TALMUD GEMARA
TALON FANG SERE UNCE CLUTCH
POUNCE UNGUIS WEAPON
(— OF TOOTH) HEEL
TALONID HEEL
TALPA TESTUDO
TALTHIB GLAGA GLAGAH
TALUS SCREE RUBBLE ASTRAGAL
TAMANDUA ANTEATER
TAMARACK LARCH LARIX EPINETTE
TAMARIN PINCHE JACCHUS
LEONCITO MARIKINA MARMOSET
TAMARIND SAMPALOC
TAMARISK ATLE JHOW HEATH
TAMASHEK TUAREG
TAMBOURINE RIKK TAAR DAIRA
TAMBO TABOUR TIMBER TABORIN
TIMBREL
TAME MAN DEAD MEEK MILD PACK
ACCOY ATAME BREAK DAUNT MILKY
SPAKE CADISH ENTAME GENTLE
INWARD MEEKEN UNWIFE AFFAITE
CORRECT INSIPID SUBDUED
CICURATE DOMESTIC MANSUETE
(— FALCON) MAN RECLAIM
TAMED BROKE GENTLE
TAMIL VELLALA
TAMMY TAMIS STAMIN
TAMONEA MICONIA
TAM-O-SHANTER TAM TAMMY
TAMP PUG STEM
TAMPER FIX COOK FAKE FOOL GAFF
TOUCH DABBLE FIDDLE MEDDLE
MONKEY POTTER PUDDLE PUTTER
TEMPER FALSIFY TRINKLE
TAMPION TOMKIN TAMPOON
TAM-TAM GONG
TAN FAN ARAB BARK ADUST ASCOT
DRESS TANKA TAWNY ORIOLE
COCONUT EMBROWN LEATHER
SUNBURN
(BEACH —) SEDGE
(TROTTEUR —) BAY
TANACETYL THUJYL
TANAGER YENI LINDO REDBIRD
WARBIRD CARDINAL EUPHONIA
FIREBIRD ORGANIST
TANBARK BARK TAWN AVARAM
TURWAR ALGERIAN ALGERINE
TANDAN EELFISH
TANEKAHA TOATOA
TANG NIP TING VEIN SHANK STRAP
TASTE TWANG RELISH TANGLE
TONGUE SEATANG FAREWELL
TANGELO UGLI
TANGENCY CONTACT
TANGENT SLOPE
TANGERINE NAARTJE MANDARIN
TANGIBLE ACTUAL TACTILE
CONCRETE MATERIAL PALPABLE
TANGLE COT ELF TAT FANK FOUL
HARL SHAG TAUT HARLE KNURL
SNARL SNIRL THRUM TWINE WOPSE

BALTER ENTRAP HANGER JUNGLE
MOMBLE MUCKER RAFFLE SLEAVE
TAFFLE TARDLE TAUGHT TEIHTE
BRANGLE TAISSLE THICKET
FURBELOW SCROBBLE
(PL.) COBWEB
TANGLED AFOUL TOUSY MESHED
SNARLY TAUTED IMPLICIT INTORTED
INVOLVED
(— **UP**) HAYWIRE
TANGLEHEAD PILI
TANGY BRISK
TANHA TRISHNA
TANK DAM DIP TAL BOSH SUMP
BASIN MIXER STANK STEEP TRUNK
BLOWUP BOILER HOPPER PANZER
TROUGH BATTERY BLOWPIT
BREAKER CISTERN FLUSHER
PISCINA PLUNGER POACHER
SETTLER STEEPER BLEACHER
DIGESTOR LANDSHIP SUBSIDER
(— **FOR DYE OR SOAP**) BECK
(— **FOR FISH**) STEW TRUNK
AQUARIUM STEWPOND
(— **IN SHIP**) FOREPEAK
(**ARMORED** —) FLAIL WHIPPET
LANDSHIP
(**PAPER MANUFACTURING** —)
POACHER
(**PHOTOGRAPHIC** —) CUVETTE
(**POTTER'S** —) PLUNGER
(**RECTANGULAR** —) BOWLY
(**SALT MANUFACTURING** —)
GRAINER
(**STORAGE** —) CHEST
(**SUGAR REFINING** —) TIGER
BLOWUP
(**TANNING** —) FLOATER
(PL.) HEAVIES
TANKAGE AMMONATE
TANKARD GUN JACK FACER STOOP
STOUP PEWTER POTTLE TANKER
GODDARD
TANNED BROWN RUDDY TAWNY
BRONZED
(**NOT** —) RAW
TANNER EGGER SAMAR BARKER
STAKER PERCHER
TANNING PASTING
(— **SOLUTION**) PLUMPER
TANSY COSTMARY
TANSY MUSTARD FLIXWEED
FLUXWEED
TANSY RAGWORT RAGWEED
TANTALIZE GRIG JADE TEASE
HARASS
TANTALUS (DAUGHTER OF —) NIOBE
(**FATHER OF** —) JUPITER THYESTES
(**MOTHER OF** —) PLUTO
(**SON OF** —) PELOPS
(**WIFE OF** —) DIONE
TANTAMOUNT SAME
TANTRA AGAMA
TANTRUM HISSY TIRRIVEE WINGDING

TANZANIA
CAPITAL: DARESSALAM
LAKE: RUKWA

NATIVE: BANTU SUKUMA
   MAKONDE SWAHILI
RIVER: RUVU WAMI RUAHA
   KAGERA RUFIJI RUVUMA
   PANGANI MBENKURU
TOWN: WETE KILWA MOSHI TANGA
   ARUSHA DODOMA KIGOMA
   MWANZA TABORA MTAWARA
   MOROGORO
WEIGHT: FARSALAH

TAO MAN PEASANT
(— **PRACTICE**) WUWEI
TAP BOB DAB PAT TAT TIP TIT TOP
BEAT COCK DRUB FLIP JOWL PENK
TICK TIRL TUNK APPEL FLIRT QUILL
SNOCK START ALETAP BROACH
CANNEL DABBLE FAUCET NATTLE
TAPLET DRAWOFF HEELTAP
PERCUSS
(— **A CASK**) QUILL STRIKE
(— **A DRUM**) TUCK
(— **FOR A LOAN**) TIG
(— **ON SHOE**) CLUMP UNDERLAY
(— **ON THE SHOULDER**) FOB
(— **REPEATEDLY**) DRUM
(— **THE GROUND**) BEAT
(**FENCING** —) BEAT
(**MASTER** —) HOB HUB
(**SMART** — **OF THE FOOT**) APPEL
TAPA KAPA SIAPO KIKEPA
TAPACOLA TURCO
TAPE LEAR FERRET GARTER SCOTCH
TAPERY YNKELL BINDING MEASURE
TAPELINE TELETAPE
(**FISH** —) SNAKE
(**LAMP** —) WICK
(**LINEN** —) INKLE
(**METALLIC** —) GALLOON
(**NARROW** —) TASTE
(**RED** —) WIGGERY
TAPE GRASS EELGRASS
TAPEMAN CHAINMAN
TAPER DRAW RISE DRAFT GAUDY
SCARF SNAPE SWAGE CIERGE
DRAUGHT LIGHTER PRICKET
TRINDLE DIMINISH
(— **OF A SPRING**) DRAW
(— **OF PATTERN**) STRIP
(— **OFF**) CEASE TONGUE
TAPERED BARRELED BOATTAIL
GRADUATED
TAPERING SHARP SPIRAL SPIRED
TERETE SPIRING FUSIFORM
SUBULATE
TAPER ROD PODGER
TAPESTRY ARRAS TAPET TAPIS
COSTER DORSER DOSSER CEILING
GOBELIN HANGING SUSANEE
VERDURE AUBUSSON MORTLAKE
TAPEWORM TAPE LIGULA TAENIA
COENURE HYDATID PLATODE
BANDWORM COENURUS DAVAINEA
FLATWORM HELMINTH
(PL.) CYSTICA
TAPHOLE TAP FLOSS MOUTH
TAPIR ANTA KUDA DANTA TENNU
TAPIROID

TAPPED ABROACH
TAPPET WIPER
TAPROOM TAP SALOON BARROOM
BUVETTE TAPHOUSE
TAPSTER NICKPOT SKINKER
TAPUYAN GE GES GHES BUGRE
GESAN JUYAS CAYAPO GOYANA
CAMACAN CARAHOS COROADO
TIMBIRA APINAGES BOTOCUDO
CAINGANG CHAVANTE
TAR PAY BREA BINDER ALKITRAN
(**BIRCH** —) DAGGETT
(**MINERAL** —) MALTHA
TARA DOLMA
TARANTULA HUNTER JAYHAWK
MYGALID
TARBOOSH FEZ
TARDIGRADA ARCTISCA
TARDILY SLOWLY
TARDINESS SLOTH TARDITY
TARDY LAG LAX DREE LATE SLOW
SLACK DREIGH LAGGED REMISS
LAGGING DILATORY LATESOME
TARE VETCH LEAKAGE
(PL.) FILTH
TARES ZIZANY
TARGET AIM MOT BUTT MARK WAND
CLOUT LEVEL PRICK ROVER SCOOP
SCOPE TARGE WHITE BANNER
NIVEAU OBJECT SLEEVE COCKSHY
INCOMER OUTGOER SARACEN
POPINJAY
(— **OF KNEELING FIGURE**) SQUAW
(— **OF LEVELING STAFF**) VANE
(— **OF RIDICULE**) GAME
(— **RING**) SOUS
(**EASY** —) SITTER
(**PIECE OF** —) SCAB
(**RAILROAD SWITCH** —) BANNER
(**STRIKE A** —) KEYHOLE
(**THROWN** —) COCKSHY COCKSHUT
(**TOWED** —) DROGUE
(**UNIDENTIFIED** —) SKUNK
TARHEEL STATE NORTHCAROLINA
TARIFF AVERAGE TRIBUTE
TARNISH DIM BLOT SMIT SOIL
CLOUD DIRTY STAIN SULLY TACHE
BREATH DARKEN DEFILE INJURE
SMIRCH ASPERSE BEGRIME
BESMEAR OBSCURE BESMIRCH
DISCOLOR
TARO COCO DALO EDDO GABE KALO
MASI TALO COCCO KAROU TANIA
TANYA COCKER TARROW YAUTIA
DASHEEN MALANGA COCOROOT
EDDYROOT
TAROT NAIB TAROCCO
TARPON SABALO
TARRAGON TARCHON ESTRAGON
TARRY BIDE STAY STOP ABIDE
DALLY DEMUR PAUSE ARREST
LINGER REMAIN SOJOURN
TARSIER LEMUR
TARSOMETATARSUS SHANK
TARSUS HAND ANKLE DIGITAL
(**BIRD'S** —) SHANK
TART ACID FLAN SOUR BOWLA
CUPID EAGER SHARP SNIPPY
SUNKET PIQUANT POLYNEE

PUNGENT SUBACID TARTLET
TURNOVER
TARTAN PLAID
  (— PATTERN) SETT
TARTAR ARGAL ARGOL CALCULUS
TARTNESS ACRITY ACIDITY
  VERDURE ACERBITY ASPERITY
  VERJUICE
TASK FAG JOB TAX CHAR DARG TOIL
  CHARE CHORE GRIND KNACK
  LABOR NULLO STINT CHARGE
  DEVOIR NIYOGA PENSUM RAMSCH
  TOURNE FATIGUE SWEATER
  TRAVAIL BUSINESS EXERCISE
  TRAUCHLE
  (— AS PSYCHOLOGICAL TEST)
  AUFGABE
  (ASSIGNED —) STENT STINT DEVOIR
  (EASY —) PIPE SNAP SETUP
  (ONEROUS —) CORVEE
  (ROUTINE —) DRUDGE
TASKMASTER DRIVER TASKER
  RAWHIDER
TASMANIA (CAPITAL OF —) HOBART
  (LAKE IN —) ECHO SORELL
  (MOUNTAIN IN —) DROME NEVIS
  BARRON CRADLE LOMOND
  HUMBOLDT
  (RIVER IN —) ESK HUDN TAMAR
  GORDON JORDAN PIEMAN DERWENT
  (TOWN IN —) BURNIE HOBART
TASMANIAN DEVIL DASYURID
TASMANIAN WOLF HYENA
  THYLACINE
TASSEL TAG TUFT LABEL THRUM
  TARCEL TARGET TOORIE CORDELLE
  (PL.) ZIZITH
TASTABLE GUSTABLE
TASTE EAT GAB GOO LAP SIP CAST
  DASH GOUT GUST HINT PREE RASA
  SALT TANG TEST TINT WAFT ASSAY
  DRINK FANCY GUSTO HEART PROVE
  RELES SAVOR SHADE SKILL SMACK
  SNACK SPICE TOOTH TOUCH
  DEGUST FLAVOR GENIUS LIKING
  PALATE RELISH SAMPLE SMATCH
  ATTASTE PREGUST SOUPCON
  THOUGHT APPETITE JUDGMENT
  PENCHANT SAPIDITY
  (— COMBINED WITH APTITUDE)
  FLAIR
  (— IN MATTERS OF ART) FANCY
  (BAD —) GOTHISM
  (DECIDED —) PENCHANT
  (DELICATE —) BREED
  (DISCRIMINATING —) SKILL
  (GOOD —) DECORUM
  (STRONG —) GOO
  (PL.) MERIDIAN
TASTEFUL NEAT ELEGANT GUSTOSO
TASTELESS DEAF FLAT FLASH
  MALMY VAPID WERSH WALLON
  FATUOUS INSIPID INSULSE WEARISH
  UNSAVORY
TASTER TRIER
TASTING ASSAY
  (— OF MALT) CORNY
TASTY GUSTABLE TASTEFUL
TATAR KIN JUNG KITAN SOYOT

CHAZAR KHAZAR KHITAN KHOZAR
SHORTZY MELETSKI
(PL.) HU
TATOUAY CABASSOU
TATTER JAG RAG TAG SHRED
  FITTER LIBBET TAGRAG TARGET
  FLITTER TROLLOP
  (PL.) DUDS TAVERS FITTERS
  RIBBONS TAIVERS FLITTERS
TATTERED DUDDY BEATEN TAGGED
  FORWORN TATTERY TOTTERED
TATTLE BLAB GASH CHEEP CLASH
  CLYPE PEACH SNEAK TUTEL GOSSIP
  QUATCH SNITCH TATTER TITTLE
  CLATTER
TATTLER LAB CLASH SNIPE FABLER
  GAMBET GOSSIP TUTLER YELPER
  TITTLER TELLTALE
TATTLING LEAKY FUTILE
TATTOO TAT MOKO PINK POUNCE
TATTOOED PINKED
  (— MAN) YUN
TATTOOING MOKO
TAUGHT MAK TEACHED INSTRUCT
  (EASILY —) DOCIBLE
TAUNT BOB MOB CHIP GIBE JAPE
  JEER JEST MOCK PROG SKIT TWIT
  CHECK FRUMP GLAIK JAUNT SCOFF
  SCORN SLANT SLARE SLART DERIDE
  SNEEST UPCAST SARCASM TWITTER
  RIDICULE
TAUNTING RAIL
TAUPE MOLESKIN
TAUROTRAGUS OREAS ORIAS
TA-URT THOUERIS
TAUT SNUG TORT STIFF TIGHT
  CORDED
TAUTEN SNUB STIFFEN SWIFTER
  TENSION
TAUTOG CHUB MOLL LABROID
TAVERN INN BUSH HOWF VENT
  MITER MITRE TAMBO BISTRO
  CABACK BUVETTE CABARET
  OSTERIA TABERNA GASTHAUS
  ORDINÁRY POTHOUSE TAPHOUSE
TAW TER SCORE MARBLE GLASSIE
  SHOOTER
TAWDRY CHEAP GAUDY GILDED
  TINSEL
TAWNY FUSC BRUSK DUSKY FULVID
  TANNED FULVOUS JACINTH
TAW-SUG SULU
TAX LAY LOT CAST CESS DUTY GELD
  GELT GILD LEVY POLL RATE SCAT
  SCOT SESS TAIL TASK TOLL ABUSE
  AGIST DONUM FINTA HANSA HANSE
  LEKIN MAILL OBROK QUINT SCATT
  STENT TOUST VERGI WATCH ZAKAH
  ZAKAT ABKARI ASSESS AVANIA
  BURDEN CEDULA DEMAND EXCISE
  EXTENT HIDAGE IMPOST JEZIAH
  KHARAJ MURAGE OCTROI OCTROY
  PAVAGE PURVEY SENSUS STRAIN
  SURTAX VINAGE BOOMAGE
  BOSCAGE CHANCER CHEVAGE
  CHIVAGE CONDUCT FINANCE
  GABELLE LASTAGE PATENTE
  PENSION POLLAGE PONTAGE
  SCUTAGE STIPEND TAILAGE

TERRAGE TRIBUTE ALCABALA
AUXILIUM BONAUGHT CARUCAGE
CORNBOLE DANEGELD EXACTION
EXERCISE KERNETTY MALTOLTE
OBLATION PESHKASH ROMESCOT
ROMESHOT STACKAGE SUPERTAX
TAXATION WHEELAGE
(— AT HARVESTTIME) CORNBOLE
(— FOR STORING LOGS) BOOMAGE
(— OF ONE-FIFTH) QUINT
(— ON EVERY PLOW) CARUCAGE
(— ON HERRING CATCH) LASTAGE
(— ON LIQUOR) ABKARI
(— ON SALT) GABELLE
(— ON UNBELIEVERS) KHARAJ
(— ON WALLS) MURAGE
(— ON WOOD) BOSCAGE
(— ON WOOL) MALETOTE
MALTOLTE
(— TO PETTY PRINCES) KERNETTY
(— TO SYNAGOGUE) FINTA
(— TO TENTH AMOUNT) TITHE
(— UNDULY) STRAIN
(CAPITATION —) JIZYA JIZYAH
(CHINESE —) LEKIN LIKEN LIKIN
(EXTRAORDINARY —) AUXILIUM
(IRISH —) BONAGHT
(MOHAMMEDAN —) JEZIAH
(PARISH —) PURVEY
(PHILLIPINES —) CEDULA
(POLL —) TOLL CENSUS
(RUSSIAN —) OBROK
(SPANISH —) ALCABALA ALCAVALA
(TURKISH —) VERGI AVANIA
TAXABLE LISTABLE
TAX COLLECTOR TITHER GABELLER
TAXGATHERER POLLER TAXMAN
TAXI JIXIE CRAWLER
TAXICAB CAB HACK CRUISER
  MOTORCAB
TAXIDERMY NASSOLOGY
TAXING SEVERE GRUELING
TAXON MONERA
TAXONOMIST LUMPER SPLITTER
TAYASSU PECARI
TAYRA GALERA
TCHAMBULI CHAMBERI
TEA CHA CHIA TCHA THAM TSIA
  ASSAM CAPER CHAIS CONGO
  FAHAM HYSON MIANG PEKOE STEEP
  CONGOU KEEMUN OOLONG PTISAN
  SUNGLO REDROOT TWANKAY
  AUTUMNAL GOWIDDIE SOUCHONG
  WORMSEED
  (AFRICAN —) CAT KAT QAT KHAT
  QUAT
  (BLACK —) BOHEA CONGO OOPAK
  OOPACK SYCHEE
  (COARSE —) BANCHA
  (HIGH-GRADE —) GYOKURO
  (INFERIOR —) BOHEA
  (MEDICINAL —) TISANE
  (MEXICAN —) BASOTE APASOTE
  (POOR —) BLASH
TEA BOWL CHAWAN
TEACAKE LUNN SCONE
TEACH ARAL LEAR READ SHOW
  TECH TENT CARRY COACH EDIFY
  ENDUE LEARN SPELL TRAIN TUTOR

WISSE INFORM PREACH SCHOOL
BITECHE EDUCATE EXAMPLE
EXPOUND GRAMMAR AMAISTER
DISCIPLE DOCUMENT INSTRUCT
PUPILIZE
(— TO FIGHT) SPAR
TEACHABLE DOCILE DOCIBLE
TEACHABLENESS DOCITY DOSSETY
TEACHER RAB ALIM GURU AKHUN
BIDDY CADET GUIDE MOLLA RABBI
REBBE TUTOR USHER AKHUND
AMAUTA DOCENT DOCTOR DOZENT
FATHER MADRIH MAULVI MENTOR
MULLAH PANDIT PUNDIT RABBAN
READER REGENT RHETOR SUPPLY
ACHARYA ALFAQUI DOMINIE
MAESTRA MAESTRO MUNCHEE
MURSHID PEDAGOG SHASTRI
SOPHIST SPONSOR STARETS
TRAINER ALFAQUIN AYUDANTE
DIRECTOR EDUCATOR EXTENDER
GAMALIEL MAGISTER MELAMMED
MISTRESS MOONSHEE MUJTAHID
(— OF ELOQUENCE) RHETOR
(— OF EMINENCE) MAESTRO
(— OF HIGH LEARNING) SOPHIST
(— OF KORAN) ALFAKI ALFAQUIN
(— OF PAUL) GAMALIEL
(INCA —) AMAUTA
(MOHAMMEDAN —) COJA HODJA
KHOJA KHOJAH
TEACHING LAW DHARMA DOCENT
LESSON LORING ACROAMA TUITION
BUDDHISM DIDACTIC DOCTRINE
DOCUMENT TUTELAGE
(PL.) ACOUSMA BROWNISM
CACODOXY DIDACTICS
TEAK SAJ DJATI EBONY
TEAKETTLE SUKE SUKEY CHAFER
KETTLE POURIE CRESSET
TEAL CRICK BLUEWING GARGANEY
SARCELLE
TEAM SET FIVE PLOW SIDE SPAN
YOKE DRAFT SWING PLOUGH
SEXTET DRAUGHT CARTWARE
(— 2 ABREAST, 1 LEADING) SPIKE
UNICORN
**(— HARNESSED ONE BEFORE
ANOTHER)** TANDEM
(— OF 3 HORSES ABREAST) TROIKA
(— OF GLASSWORKERS) SHOP
CHAIR
(— THAT FINISHES LAST) DOORMAT
(2-HORSE —) PODANGER
(3-HORSE —) RANDOM
(ATHLETIC —) CLUB
(BASEBALL —) NINE
(BASKETBALL —) FIVE
(FOOTBALL —) ELEVEN
TEAMSTER CARTER TEAMEO
CARTMAN SKINNER TEAMMAN
TEAPOT TRACK TRACKPOT
TEAR RIP RIT RUG TUT CLAW PILL
PULL RACE RASE RAVE REND RIVE
RUGG SKAG SNAG STUN BREAK
CLAUT LARME PEARL SHARK SLENT
SPALT SPLIT TOUSE CLEAVE
HARROW RANCHE RIPPLE SCHISM
SCREED WRENCH CHATTER

CONVELL DISCIND EYEDROP
SCRATCH DISTRAIN FRACTURE
LACERATE LACHRYMA TEARDROP
(— APART) REND TEASE DISCERP
DIVULSE
(— ASUNDER) DIVEL
(— AWAY) AVULSE
(— DOWN) UNPILE DESTROY
DEMOLISH
(— IN NEGATIVE) SLUG
(— INTO PIECES) DRAW TOLE DEVIL
SHRED TEASE LANIATE
(— INTO SHREDS) HOG DEVIL
TATTER
(— INTO) LAMBAST LAMBASTE
(— OFF) STRIP ABRUPT DISCERP
(— OPEN) PROSCIND
(— UP BY THE ROOTS) ARACHE
(PL.) DEW BRINE RHEUM EYEWATER
TEARDROP EYEWATER
TEARFUL SOFT TEARY WEEPY
LIQUID WATERY WEEPLY FLEBILE
MAUDLIN SHOWERY SNIVELY
SNIVELLY
TEARING SCREED
(— AWAY) AVULSION
TEARPIT LARMIER
TEASE COD FUN ROT TAR TRY TUM
BAIT DRAG FASH FRET HARE HOCK
JADE JIVE JOSH LARK NARK RAZZ
TARR TOUT WORK CHAFF CHEEK
CHEVY DEVIL FEEZE TARIE TAUNT
TOOSE WRACK BANTER BOTHER
CADDLE CHIVVY HARASS HOORAY
HURRAH MOLEST MURDER PESTER
PLAGUE HATCHEL TERRIFY
TORMENT WHERRET
TEASEL KING TASSEL TEASLE
MANWEED
TEASELER GIGGER TEASER
TEASELING MOZING
TEASER TIZEUR
TEASING CHAFF MERRY BANTER
DEVILING QUIZZING
TEAT DUG PAP TIT DIDDY SPEAN
NIPPLE SUCKLE
TEA TREE TI MANUKA
TECHNICIAN SWITCHER
TECHNIQUE FEAT GATE WRINKLE
COQUILLE INDUSTRY SPICCATO
(BILLIARD —) FOLLOW
(DANCE —) HEELWORK
(DECORATION —) IKAT
(JUMPING —) SCISSORS
(WRESTLING —) GLIMA
(WRITING —) CUBISM
TECHNOLOGY FISHERY TECHNIC
CERAMICS
TECMESSA (FATHER OF —)
TELEUTAS
(HUSBAND OF —) AJAX
(SON OF —) EURYSACES
TECOMIN LAPACHOL
TECTRIX COVERT
TEDDER KICKER
TEDIOUS DEAD DREE DULL LATE
POKY PROSY ALENGE BORING
DREECH DREIGH ELENGE MORTAL
IRKSOME PREACHY PROSAIC

VERBOSE BORESOME DRAGGING
TIRESOME WEARIFUL
TEDIUM IRK YAWN ENNUI BOREDOM
TEE COCK TIGHT TOZEE WITTER
BULLHEAD
TEEM SNY FLOW SWIM SWARM
ABOUND BUSTLE SCRAWL
TEEMER SHOOTMAN
TEEMING BIG ALIVE TUMID FERTILE
GUSHING TEEMFUL BRAWLING
PREGNANT SWARMING
TEENY SMALL
TEESWATER MUGS MUGGS
TEETER ROCK WAVER JIGGLE
QUIVER SEESAW TREMBLE
TEETH CTENII CHOPPERS CRACKERS
GRINDERS
(HAVING —) IVORIED
(SET OF —) DENTURE
TEETHRIDGE ALVEOLE ALVEOLUS
TEETOTUM TOTUM WHIRLIGIG
TEGETICULA PRONUBA
TEGMENTUM ROOF
TEGULA SQUAMA EPAULET SCAPULA
PATAGIUM SQUAMULA
TEGUMENT COAT TEGMEN
TEHUELCHE PATAGON
TEJU TEIOID JACUARU TEGUEXIN
TELAMON ATLAS
(BROTHER OF —) PELEUS
(FATHER OF —) AEACUS
(MOTHER OF —) ENDEIS
(SON OF —) AJAX TEUCER
(WIFE OF —) GLAUCE HESIONE
TELAMONES ATLANTES
TELEDU BADGER STINKARD
TELEGONUS (FATHER OF —)
ULYSSES
(MOTHER OF —) CIRCE
(SON OF —) ITALUS
(WIFE OF —) PENELOPE
TELEGRAM TAR WIRE FLASH FLIMSY
TELEGRAPH WIRE CABLE BUZZER
TELEGRAM TELOTYPE
TELEMACHUS (FATHER OF —)
ULYSSES
(MOTHER OF —) PENELOPE
(SON OF —) LATINUS
TELENCEPHALON ENDBRAIN
TELEOLOGICAL TELIC FINALIST
TELEOLOGY FINALITY
TELEPHASSA (DAUGHTER OF —)
EUROPA
(HUSBAND OF —) AGENOR
(SON OF —) CADMUS PHOENIX
TELEPHONE PHONE HANDSET
TELEPHOTE DIAPHOTE
TELEPHUS (FATHER OF —)
HERCULES
(MOTHER OF —) AUGE
TELESCOPE TUBE COUDE GLASS
SCOPE TRUNK ALINER FINDER
ALIGNER BINOCLE TRANSIT
PROSPECT SPYGLASS
(SURVEYOR'S —) LEVEL
TELEVISION AIR
TELIOSPORE TELEUTO
TELL SAY DEEM MEAN MOOT READ
SHOW TALE AREAD AREED BREAK

BREVE COUNT NEVEN PITCH SPELL
STORY TEACH UTTER AUTHOR
DEVISE IMPART INFORM MUSTER
QUETHE RECITE RELATE REPEAT
REPORT REVEAL CONFESS DIVULGE
NARRATE PARTAKE RECOUNT
ACQUAINT REHEARSE
(— **CONFIDENTIALLY**) CONFIDE
(— **CONFUSEDLY**) SPLATHER
(— **EARNESTLY**) ASSURE
(— **IN ADVANCE**) FORESAY
(— **LIES**) BELY LIGE BELIE
(— **OFF**) JAR
(— **ROMANCES**) GEST GESTE
(— **SECRETS**) CHEEP CLYPE SPILL
(— **STRIKINGLY**) CRACK
(— **TALES**) CANT
TELLER SPINNER STORIER TALLIER
FABLEIST FABULIST SENACHIE
TELLING REDE PUNGENT POWERFUL
(— **OF SECRETS**) BLAB
TELLTALE BLAB CLASH TATTLER
TITTLER REGISTER
TELLURIDE ALTAITE
TELSON PLEON
TELUGU GENTU GENTOO TELINGA
TEM TUM ATMU ATUM
TEMERITY GALL CHEEK AUDACITY
RASHNESS
TEMPER CUE MAD BAIT BATE COOL
DASH DRAW MOOD MULL NEAL
PADD SCOT TONE ALLOY BIRSE
BLOOD CREST DELAY FRAME GRAIN
HUMOR IRISH SAUCE SOBER TRAMP
ADJUST ANIMUS ANNEAL DANDER
MASTER MONKEY SEASON SPLEEN
STRAIN SUBMIT CHASTEN CLIMATE
COURAGE HACKLES QUALIFY
STOMACH EBENEZER GRADUATE
MITIGATE MODERATE MOORBURN
(— **CLAY**) TAMPER
(— **METAL**) ALLAY
(— **OF MIND**) CUE SPIRIT
(**CAPRICIOUS** —) SPLEEN
TEMPERAMENT GEMUT HEART
HUMOR CRASIS KIDNEY TEMPER
STOMACH SANGUINE
TEMPERAMENTAL FITIFIED
TEMPERANCE MEDIETY SOBRIETY
TEMPERATE CALM COOL MILD SOFT
GREEN SOBER TEMPRE MODERATE
ORDINATE
TEMPERATURE SUN HEAT TEMP
HOTNESS
TEMPERED HARD SOBER SARCENET
TEMPEST GALE THUD WIND ORAGE
STORM TUMULT TORMENT TURMOIL
WEATHER
TEMPESTUOUS WILD GUSTY STERN
WINDY RUGGED STORMY VIOLENT
STALWART
TEMPLATE CURB NORMA TEMPLET
PADSTONE STRICKLE
TEMPLE VAT WAT DEUL FANE NAOS
RATH CANDI GUACA HUACA KIACK
KOVIL MARAE RATHA CHANDI
HAFFET HERION MANDIR SACRUM
SHRINE TEOPAN TJANDI VIHARA
HERAEUM HERAION TEMPLET

TEMPLUM VARELLA OLYMPIUM
PANTHEON RAMESEUM TEOCALLI
VALHALLA
(— **AREA**) MANDAPA
(**CAVE** —) SPEOS
(**FIJI** —) BURE
(**HAWAIIAN** —) HEIAU
(**PART OF** —) PRONAOS
(**SHINTO** —) SHA JINJA JINSHA
YASHIRO
(**STUDY OF** —S) NAOLOGY
(**TOWERLIKE** —) ZIGGURAT
TEMPLET FORMER
TEMPO TAKT TIME AGOGE
MOVEMENT
TEMPORAL CARNAL TIMELY
EARTHLY PROFANE SECULAR
TEMPORARY FLYING INTERIM
STOPGAP WHILEND EPISODAL
EPISODIC TEMPORAL
TEMPORIZER DRIFTER POLITIC
TEMPT EGG FAND FOND LURE TEMP
TENT COURT ALLURE ASSAIL
ENTICE INVITE SEDUCE ASSAULT
ATTEMPT SOLICIT SUGGEST
TEMPTATION TRIAL ATTEMPT
TESTING
TEMPTER DEVIL
TEMPTING ALLURING INVITING
TEMPTRESS SIREN DELILAH
TEN ICRE IOTA CHANG DIKER
CHEUNG DECADE DENARY DICKER
ARTICLE BRISQUE
(— **OF TRUMPS**) GAME
TEN'A KOYUKON
TENACE FORK
TENACIOUS FAST ROPEY TOUGH
CLEDGY DOGGED GRIPPY PLUGGY
STICKY STRONG GRIPPLE ADHESIVE
GRASPING HOLDFAST
TENACIOUSNESS TENACY
FASTNESS
TENACITY LENTOR COURAGE
TENACULUM CLASP
TENANCY CONACRE JOINTURE
TENANT KMET LEUD SAER BARON
CEILE DRENG LAIRD BORDAR
COTTAR COTTER DRENGH GENEAT
HOLDER INMATE LESSEE MOLMAN
RADMAN RENTER SOCMAN VASSAL
CHAKDAR COTTIER FEODARY
FEUDARY GAVELER HOMAGER
SOCAGER SOKEMAN VAVASOR
COLIBERT CUSTOMER SERGEANT
SUCKENER
(**LIFE** —) LIVIER LIVEYER
(**NEW** —) INCOME INCOMER
TENCH CYPRINID
TEN COMMANDMENTS DECALOG
TEND HOP NOD RUN SET WRY BABY
BEND DRAW GROW KEEP MAKE
MIND MOVE TENT DRESS GROOM
NURSE OFFER SOUND TREND
VERGE WATCH GOVERN INTEND
CHERISH CONDUCE DECLINE
INCLINE PROPEND
(— **A FIRE**) STOKE
(— **IN A CERTAIN DIRECTION**) LEAD
(— **TO ONE POINT**) CONVERGE

(— **TOWARD**) AFFECT
(— **WHILE AT PASTURE**) GRAZE
TENDENCY SET BENT BIAS HAND
TONE VEIN DRAFT DRIFT DRIVE
HABIT KNACK TENOR TREND TWIST
ANIMUS COURSE EONISM GENIUS
MOTION APTNESS CONATUS
DRAUGHT IMPULSE LEANING
NITENCY SAMKARA APTITUDE
INSTINCT STEERING VERGENCY
(— **IN NATURE**) KIND
(— **TO APPROACH**) ADIENCE
(— **TO STICK TOGETHER**) CLANSHIP
(— **TO WITHDRAW**) ABIENCE
(— **TO WRATH**) TIDE
TENDER TID BEAR COCK FINE FOND
FRIM FRUM KIND NESH SOFT SORE
TAKE TART TENT WARM CAGER
DEFER FRAIL GREEN OFFER PAPPY
DELATE DRIVER GENTLE GIMPER
GINGER HUMANE LOVELY RAISER
SILKEN ADVANCE AMABILE
AMOROUS CONCHER CRAMPER
FLESHLY MASHMAN OBLATIO
PATACHE PINNACE PITEOUS PITIFUL
PORRECT PROFFER RUTHFUL
STENTER CAMELEER COCKBOAT
EFFETMAN FEMININE HEATSMAN
HERDSMAN LADYLIKE MERCIFUL
MORTISER SPREADER
TENDERFOOT DUDE INNOCENT
TENDERHEARTED HUMAN PITIFUL
TENDERLOIN FILET FILLET
UNDERCUT
TENDERLY FONDLY GENTLY
AMOROSO
TENDERNESS CHERTE TENDER
DELICACY FONDNESS KINDNESS
SYMPATHY TENERITY YEARNING
(— **OF FEELING**) FLESH
TENDINOUS SINEWY
TENDON CORD TAIL CHORD NERVE
SINEW TENON LEADER STRING
TENDRIL CURL CLASP CROOK TWIST
CIRRUS WINDER CAPREOL CIRRHUS
TENTACLE
TENEMENT LAND RENT CHAWL
DECKER LIVING WARREN HOLDING
LETTING BUILDING PRAEDIUM
TENES (FATHER OF —) CYNCUS
(**MOTHER OF** —) PHILONOME
(**SLAYER OF** —) ACHILLES
TENET ADOXY CREDO CREED
DOGMA BELIEF GNOMON HOLDING
MISHNAH PARADOX DOCTRINE
(**PL.**) FAITH FAMILISM
TENFOLD DENARY DECUPLE
TENNE TAWNY ORANGE HYACINTH

TENNESSEE
CAPITAL: NASHVILLE
COLLEGE: FISK LANE SIENA
BETHEL BELMONT LAMBUTH
LEMOYNE MILLIGAN TUSCULUM
VANDERBILT
COUNTY: DYER KNOX RHEA
COCKE GILES MEIGS OBION
GRUNDY MCMINN SEVIER UNICOI

BLEDSOE FENTRESS
INDIAN: SHAWNEE CHEROKEE
CHICKASAW
LAKE: DOUGLAS CHEROKEE
REELFOOT WATTSBAR
MOUNTAIN: GUYOT LOOKOUT
MOUNTAIN RANGE: SMOKY
NATIONAL PARK: SHILOH
NATIVE: WHELP
NICKNAME: VOLUNTEER
PRESIDENT: POLK JACKSON
RIVER: ELK DUCK CANEY
HOLSTON HIWASSEE
CUMBERLAND
STATE BIRD: MOCKINGBIRD
STATE FLOWER: IRIS
STATE TREE: POPLAR
TOWN: ALCOA PARIS CAMDEN
SPARTA DICKSON MEMPHIS
PULASKI GALLATIN KNOXVILLE

TENNIS (— SHOT) LET LOB DINK
TENON COG PIN COAK STUB TUSK
LEWIS TOOTH TABLING DOVETAIL
LEWISSON
TENOR PES FECK TONE VEIN
COURSE EFFECT TAILLE TENURE
CURRENT PURPORT STRENGTH
TENDENCY TENORINO
TENOROON FAGOTTINO
TENOR VIOL VIOLET
TENOR VIOLIN ALTO
TENPINS NEWPORT
TENPOUNDER AWA CHIRO MACABI
BONEFISH BONYFISH LADYFISH
SKIPJACK SPRINGER
TENREC TANGUE CENTETES
CENTETID HEDGEHOG HEDGEPIG
TENSE EDGY RAPT TAUT STIFF
CORDED FLINCH FUTURE INTENT
NARROW STRAIT STRICT BRITTLE
INTENSE PRIMARY FRENETIC
PRETERIT SYNTONIC
TENSION BENT HEAT DRIVE STEAM
SATTVA SPRING STRAIN STRESS
TROPPO BALANCE STRAINT
TENSURE ISOTONIA
TENT AUL TOP HALE PAWL TAWN
TELD TILT CABIN CRAME LODGE
TOPEK TUPIK CANNAT CANVAS
DOSSIL SEARCH WIGWAM BALAGAN
CABINET KIBITKA MARQUEE
SPARVER TABERNA TENTLET
TENTORY ZDARSKY PAVILION
TENTICLE TENTWORK
(— WHERE GOODS ARE SOLD)
CRAME
(CIRCULAR —) YURT YOURT YURTA
KIBITKA
(INDIAN —) TEPEE WIGWAM
(SAMOYED —) CHUM
(SOUTH AMERICAN —) TOLDO
TENTACLE HORN SAIL PACLE
FEELER BRACHIUM
TENTATIVE GINGERLY
TENT CATERPILLAR WEBWORM
TENTERER RACKER RATCHER
TENTH DIME TITHE DECIMA

(— OF CENT) MILL
(— OF LINE) GRY
TENUITY EXILITY DELICACY
TENUOUS FILMY FOGGY FRAIL
TENDER FRAGILE GASEOUS
SLENDER SUBTILE ETHEREAL
GOSSAMER
(TOO —) FINESPUN
TENUOUSNESS FRAILTY
TENURE FEU TAKE TERM GAVEL
JAGIR BARONY CAPITE JAGHIR
SOCAGE ALMOIGN BONDAGE
BORDAGE BURGAGE CENSIVE
CURTESY FARMAGE JAGHEER
SOCCAGE SOREHON COPYHOLD
DRENGAGE FREEHOLD OVERLAND
SOCMANRY SUITHOLD VAVASORY
VENVILLE
TEPEE CHUM TENT TIPI LODGE
TEEPEE WICKIUP
TEPHROSIA CRACCA
TEPID LEW WARM WLACH WLECH
LUKEWARM
TEQUISLATEC CHONTAL
TERATOMA EMBRYOMA
TERCET TRISTICH
TEREBINTH TEIL
TEREDO WOODWORM
TERETE CENTRIC
TEREUS (FATHER OF —) MARS
(SON OF —) ITYS
(WIFE OF —) PROCNE
TERGITE TERGUM PYGIDIUM
TERGIVERSATION DECEIT
TERM HALF NAME NOME WORD
LEASE RHEMA SPEAK STYLE TRYST
ABBACY GNOMON NOTION PARODY
EPITHET EXTREME SESSION
SUBJECT SUMMAND TERMINE
VOCABLE EQUIVOKE HEADWORD
MAHALATH POCHISMO SEMESTER
TERMTIME
(— IN JAIL) JOLT
(— IN LOGIC) CONSTANT
(— OF ADDRESS) CUSSWORD
(— OF ADDRESS) SIRRAH MADONNA
(— OF CONTEMPT) SLIPE PILCHER
TITIVIL
(— OF DEFERENCE) AHUNG
(— OF ENDEARMENT) ASTOR
CHUCK COCKY HONEY ASTHORE
MACHREE STOREEN POSSODIE
POWSOWDY
(— OF IMPRISONMENT) LAG
LAGGING STRETCH
(— OF PUNISHMENT) JOB
(— OF RATIO) EXTREME
(— OF REPROACH) MINGO
(— OF SYLLOGISM) EXTREME
ARGUMENT
(ARITHMETICAL —) NOME GNOMON
(HYPHENED —) COMPOUND
(LITERAL —S) LETTER
(SOCIAL —S) FOOTING
(UNIVERSAL —) CONCEPT
(PL.) LAY MEANS
TERMAGANT JADE SHREW VIXEN
VIRAGO
TERMINABLE FINITE

TERMINAL JACK LAST POLE ANODE
DEPOT IMPUT INPUT MUCRO
CATHODE POTHEAD DESINENT
TERMINATE CUT END ABUT CALL
HALT KILL ABORT BLEED CEASE
CLOSE ISSUE LAPSE EXPIRE FINISH
FOREDO RESULT INCLUDE TERMINE
COMPLETE CONCLUDE DISSOLVE
TERMINATED EXPIATE
TERMINATING FINAL
(— ABRUPTLY) BLIND
(SUDDENLY —) ABRUPT
TERMINATION END ISH DATE TERM
CLOSE EVENT ISSUE ENDING EXITUS
EXPIRY FINALE PERIOD UPSHOT
TERMINUS
(— OF CHURCH CHOIR) CHEVET
(— OF FURNITURE LEGS) FOOT
(— OF RIGHT) LAPSE
TERMINATIVE FINITIVE
TERMINOLOGY JARGON
TERMINUS END FLAT
(— IN FINGERPRINT) DELTA
(— OF PERIOD) TIME
TERMITE ANAI ANAY KING NASUTE
WORKER POLILLA
TERMITOPHILE SYMPHILE
TERN KIP DARR INCA LARI NOIO PIRL
PIRR RIXY LARID NODDY PEARL
SCRAY SKEER SKIRR STERN CHIRRE
KERMEW PICKET GOELAND MEDRICK
PIRRMAW RITTOCK SEAFOWL
STRIKER TARRACK TERNLET
MANUSINA SPARLING TIRRACKE
TERPENE CARENE PINENE BORNANE
SANTENE THUJENE CAMPHENE
FENCHENE LIMONENE NOPINENE
TERRA GE GAEA TELLUS
(DAUGHTER OF —) RHEA THEA
PHOEBE TETHYS THEMIS
MNEMOSYNE
(HUSBAND OF —) URANUS
(SON OF —) OCEANUS
TERRACE POY DAIS PNYX STEP
XYST BENCH HEIAU LINCH OFFSET
LINCHET CHABUTRA
(LOUNGING —) LANAI
(NATURAL —) MESA
TERRA JAPONICA GAMBIR
GAMBIER
TERRAPENE CISTUDO
TERRAPIN EMYD COUNT COODLE
POTTER SLIDER TURPIN TURTLE
EMYDIAN FEUILLE SKILPOT
REDBELLY
(FEMALE —) HEIFER
(MALE —) BULL
TERRARIUM VIVARIUM
TERRELLA EARTHKIN
TERRENE EARTHLY
TERRESTRIAL EARTHY EARTHLY
TERRENE PLANETAL SUBLUNAR
SUBSOLAR
TERRET CRINGLE
TERRIBLE DIRE UGLY GHAST LURID
DEADLY TARBLE TRAGIC TURBLE
DIREFUL FEARFUL FERDFUL
GHASTLY HIDEOUS ALMIGHTY
BHAIRAVA FLEYSOME HORRIBLE

TERRIFIC TIMOROUS TRAGICAL
TERRIBLY FELLY FIERCE GRISLY
  CONSARN
TERRIER SKYE LHASA BOSTON
  DANDIE RATTER SCOTTY DIEHARD
  SCOTTIE ABERDEEN AIREDALE
  RATTONER SEALYHAM VERMINER
  WIREHAIR
TERRIFIC FINE SWEET GORGON
  FEARFUL GORGEOUS
TERRIFIED AFRAID AGHAST
  GHASTLY
TERRIFY AWE COW HAG BREE DARE
  FEAR FLAY FLEY DREAD GALLY
  SCARE ADREAD AFFRAY AGRISE
  AWHAPE DISMAY FLIGHT FREEZE
  FRIGHTEN
TERRIFYING GHASTLY HIDEOUS
  FLEYSOME TERRIBLE
TERRITORIALISM ITOISM
TERRITORY FEE GOA HAN SOC
  AREA MARK PALE SOKE BANAT
  DUCHY FIELD MARCH STATE TUATH
  BORDER COLONY DOMAIN EMPERY
  EMPIRE GROUND APANAGE CONFINE
  COUNTRY DEMESNE DUKEDOM
  EARLDOM ENCLAVE EPARCHY
  REGENCY SATRAPY APPANAGE
  CASTLERY CONFINES CONQUEST
  DISTRICT DOMINION IMPERIUM
  LIGEANCE LUCUMONY PARMESAN
  PASHALIK REGALITY SEIGNORY
TERROR AWE FEAR FRAY ALARM
  APPAL DREAD PANIC AFFRAY
  ALARUM APPALL FRIGHT HORROR
  DRIDDER DREDDOUR SURPRISE
TERRORISM NIHILISM
TERRORIST GOONDA ALARMIST
  SICARIUS
TERRORIZE FRIGHTEN
TERROR-STRICKEN AWFUL
TERSE CURT COMPACT CONCISE
  LACONIC POINTED SUMMARY
  UNWORDY SUCCINCT
TERSENESS BREVITY LACONISM
TERTIARY NEOZOIC PALAEIC
TESSELLATED MOSAIC
TESSELLATION AREOLE
TESSERA TILETTE ABACULUS
  TESSELLA
TEST CON SAY TRY FAND FEEL
  FOND TASK TENT ASSAY AVENA
  CANON CHECK ESSAY GROPE ISSUE
  PROBE PROOF PROVE SENSE
  SOUND TASTE TEMPT TESTA TOUCH
  TRIAL SAMPLE TIENTA APPROOF
  APPROVE AUSSAGE CONTROL
  EXAMINE GANTLET PLUMMET
  TESTATE BIOASSAY EXERCISE
  GAUNTLET SEROLOGY STANDARD
  (— EGGS) CANDLE
  (— FOR WEIGHT AND FINENESS)
  PYX
  (— GROUND) BOSE
  (— OF COURAGE) SCRATCH
  (— OF CRINOID) CALYX
  (— OF ORE) VAN
  (SEVERE —) CRUCIBLE
  (SYPHILIS —) KOLMER

TESTA TEST LORICA EPISPERM
TESTACEOUS SHELLY
TESTAMENT TEST QUETHE
  WITWORD
TESTAR TETARD
TESTATOR LEGATOR
TESTED FIRED TRIED WEIGHED
TESTER TRIER CONNER PROVER
  SPARVER DENIERER TESTIERE
  (BUTTER —) SEARCHER
TESTICLE STONE BALLOCK DIDYMUS
  GENITOR
TESTIFY SPEAK SWEAR AFFIRM
  DEPONE DEPOSE WITTEN WITNESS
  EVIDENCE
  (— FALSELY) MOUNT
  (— TO) BESPEAK
TESTIMONIAL SCROLL
TESTIMONY TEST ATTEST PROBATE
  TESTATE TESTIFY WITNESS
  EVIDENCE
TESTING ASSAY CRUCIAL
TESTIS BALL GONAD STONE
  BALLOCK CULLION KNOCKER
  SPERMARY
  (PL.) COBS CODS COJONES
  DOWSETS
TEST TUBE PROOF TESTER
  PROBATE
TESTUDINATA CHELONIA
TESTUDO SNAIL GALAPAGO
  TORTOISE
TESTY DONCY MUSTY TUTTY DONSIE
  PATCHY SPUNKY PEEVISH TETTISH
  TOUSTIE WASPISH SNAPPISH
TETANIC SPASTIC
TETANUS LOCKJAW HOLOTONY
TETE-A-TETE TWOSOME CAUSEUSE
TETHER BAND STAKE TEDDER
  TOGGLE PASTERN CABESTRO
  (— A HAWK) WEATHER
TETHYS APLYSIA
  (DAUGHTERS OF —) OCEANIDES
  (FATHER OF —) URANUS
  (HUSBAND OF —) OCEANUS
  (MOTHER OF —) TERRA
TETHYUM CYNTHIA
TETRACHORD GENUS HYPATON
  LICHANOS
TETRACTYS TETRAD
TETRAD FOURFOLD
TETRADRACHMA OWL
TETRAGONAL DIMETRIC
TETRAHEDRITE FAHLERZ FAHLORE
  PANABASE
TETRAHEXAHEDRON FLUOROID
TETRAHYDRIDE GERMANE
  STANNANE
TETRASACCHARIDE LUPEOSE
TETTER DARTRE
TETTIX ACRYDIUM
TEUCER (FATHER OF —) TELAMON
  SCAMANDER
  (MOTHER OF —) HESIONE
TEUTON GOTH LOMBARD
TEUTONIC GOTHIC GERMANIC
  GOTHONIC

TEXAS

CAPITAL: AUSTIN
COLLEGE: SMU TCU RICE WILEY
  BAYLOR
COUNTY: BEXAR ERATH GARZA
  FANNIN GOLIAD YOAKUM
  ZAPATA ZAVALA HIDALGO
  REFUGIO ATASCOSA
FORTRESS: ALAMO
INDIAN: LIPAN BILOXI KICHAI
  SHUMAN HASINAI COMANCHE
  TONKAWAN
LAKE: FALCON TEXOMA AMISTAD
NATIVE: TEJANO
NICKNAME: LONESTAR
PRESIDENT: JOHNSON
  EISENHOWER
RIVER: RED PECOS BRAZOS
  NUECES TRINITY
STATE BIRD: MOCKINGBIRD
STATE FLOWER: BLUEBONNET
STATE TREE: PECAN
TOWN: GAIL VEGA WACO BRYAN
  MARFA OZONA PAMPA TYLER
  BORGER DALLAS DENTON
  ELPASO KILEEN LAREDO
  ODESSA QUANAH SONORA
  ABILENE HOUSTON LUBBOCK
  AMARILLO BEAUMONT
  FLOYDADA GALVESTON

TEXAS BUCKTHORN LOTEBUSH
TEXAS FEVER TRISTEZA
TEXT BODY MIQRA PLACE SAKHA
  TESTO PURANA SCRIPT SHAKHA
  TEXTUS TEXTLET ANTETHEM
  PERICOPE VARIORUM
  (— OF ADVERTISEMENT) COPY
  (— OF OPERA) LIBRETTO
  (— SET TO MUSIC) ORATORIO
  (SHASTRA —) SRUTI SHRUTI
TEXTBOOK DUNCE TUTOR GENETICS
TEXTILE (ALSO SEE FABRIC) SABA
  STUFF GREIGE MOCKADO SAGURAN
  SINAMAY TEXTURE TIFFANY
  (— MACHINE) WILLOW
  (PL.) DRAPE
TEXTURE WEB BONE HAND KNIT
  WALE WOOF GRAIN COBWEB
  FABRIC WEFTAGE FRACTURE
  (— OF SOAP) FIT
THAI LAO SIAMESE

THAILAND

CAPITAL: BANKOK BANGKOK
COIN: AT ATT BAHT FUANG TICAL
  PYNUNG SALUNG SATANG
ISLAND: PHUKET
ISTHMUS: KRA
MEASURE: WA KEN NIV NMU RAI
  SAT SEN SOK WAH YOT KEUP
  NGAN TANG YOTE KWIEN LAANG
  SESTI TANAN KABIET KAMMEU
  CHAIMEU ROENENG CHANGAWN
MOUNTAIN: KHIEO MAELAMUN
NATIVE: LAO THAI

PLAIN: KHORAT
RIVER: CHI NAN PING MENAM
  MEKONG MEPING
TOWN: UBON PUKET RANONG
  AYUDHYA AYUTHIA BANGKOK
  LOPBURI RAHAENG SINGORA
  SONGKLA KHONKAEN KIANGMAI
  THONBURI
WEIGHT: HAP PAI SEN SOK BAHT
  HAPH KLAM KLOM CATTY
  CHANG COYAN PILUL FLUANG
  SALUNG SOMPAY TAMLUNG

THALER DALER
THALLOGEN AMPHIGEN
THALLOID FRONDOSE
THALLUS FROND THALAMUS
  THAMNIUM
THAMNOPHIS EUTAENIA
THAMYRAS (FATHER OF —)
  PHILAMMON
  (MOTHER OF —) ARGIOPE
THAN AS NA NE OR TO AND BUT
  NOR THEN TILL
THANE THEGN BANQUO GESITH
  ABTHAIN MACDUFF
THANK GRACE MERCY REGRACY
  REMERCY
THANKFUL GRATEFUL
THANKLESS INGRATE SLOWFUL
THANKS TA GRACE MERCI MERCY
  GRAMERCY
THANKSGIVING GLORY DOXOLOGY
THANK-YOU-MA'AM CAHOT
THAT AS AT SE BUT HOW THE THO
  WHO YAT LEST THAM THIK THON
  WHAT YOND THICK THILK THOUGH
  BECAUSE
  (— IS TO SAY) NAMELY
  (— ONE) ILLE
  (— WHICH HAS TO BE PROVED)
  IQED
  (— YONDER) THON
THATCH NIPA DATCH SIRKI SIRKY
  STING THRUM CADJAN
  (— OVER BEEHIVE) HOOD
THATCHED THACK REEDED
THATCHER HELER CROWDER
  HELLIER THACKER
THAUMAS (DAUGHTER OF —) IRIS
  HARPY
  (FATHER OF —) NEPTUNE
  (MOTHER OF —) TERRA
  (WIFE OF —) ELECTRA
THAUMATURGIST(PL.) GOETAE
THAUMATURGY MAGIC
THAW GIVE MELT FRESH UNTHAW
  DEFROST
THE LA LE SE TA THI THAM THEY
  YARE THERE
THEA CAMELLIA
  (FATHER OF —) URANUS
  (HUSBAND OF —) HYPERION
  (MOTHER OF —) TERRA
THEANO (FATHER OF —) CISSEUS
  (HUSBAND OF —) ANTENOR
  (SISTER OF —) HECUBA
THEATER CINE GAFF KINO CAVEA

HOUSE LEGIT ODEUM SCENE STAGE
CINEMA OZONER ADELPHI COCKPIT
GUIGNOL ORPHEUM THEATRE
BIOSCOPE COLISEUM PANTHEON
SHOWSHOP SPELLKEN STRAWHAT
THEATRON
THEATRICAL HAMMY STAGY
  DRAMATIC SCENICAL SINGSONG
THEATRICALITY HAM
THEBAN LAIUS NIOBE AMPHION
  CADMEAN JOCASTA OEDIPUS
  PENTHEUS
THECA CUP URN CELL VAGINA
  CAPSULE PYXIDIUM VAGINULE
THEELIN ESTRONE FEMININ OESTRIN
THEFT CRIB LIFT HEIST PINCH
  SCORE STEAL FURTUM STOUTH
  BRIBERY LARCENY MICHERY
  PICKING PILFERY ROBBERY
  STEALTH BURGLARY STEALAGE
  STEALING
  (LITERARY —) PIRACY
  (PETTY —) CRIB PICKERY
THEIR ARE HER ORE HORE YARE
THEIRS HERN THEIRN
THEM A EM HI UM HEM MUN HEMEN
THEME DUX BASE IDEA TEMA TEXT
  DITTY HOBBY MOTIF PLACE SCOPE
  TESTO THEMA TOPIC URLAR
  MATTER MYTHOS SUBJECT
  ANTETHEM
  (— OF FUGUE) DUX
  (HACKNEYED —) CLICHE
  (RECURRING —) BURDEN
THEMIS (DAUGHTER OF —) DICE
  IRENE EUNOMIA
  (FATHER OF —) URANUS
  (HUSBAND OF —) JUPITER
  (MOTHER OF —) TERRA
THEMSELVES HEM HEMSELF
THEN SO AND POI THO ANON SYNE
THENCE AWAY THEN THEREFRO
THEOCRACY KHALSA
THEODOLITE TAIPO TRANSIT
  TRANSEPT
THEOLOGIAN FAQIH ULEMA DIVINE
  MUJTAHID
THEOLOGY KALAM IRENICS DIVINITY
  POIMENIC POLEMICS
THEORBO ARCHLUTE
THEOREM DUAL LEMMA CONVERSE
THEORETIC PURE
THEORETICAL BOOK CLOSET
  THEORIC ABSTRACT ACADEMIC
  ARMCHAIR PLATONIC
THEORIST OPINATOR
THEORIZE SUGGEST
THEORIZING IDEOLOGY
THEORY ISM OVISM EROTIC ETHICS
  HOLISM LAXISM SYSTEM AGOGICS
  ATOMISM CAMBISM DUALISM
  FORMISM HOBBISM PEELISM
  PLENISM THEORIC TYCHISM
  ACOSMISM AXIOLOGY DITHEISM
  DYNAMISM ENERGISM ESTHETIC
  ETIOLOGY FEMINISM FINITISM
  GHOSTISM GOBINISM HEDONICS
  IDEALISM IDEOLOGY MOLINISM
  MONADISM PROGRESS SEMANTIC

SEMIOTIC SPERMISM
THEOW SERF THRALL THEWMAN
THERAPEUTICS ACEOLOGY
THERAVADA HINAYANA
THERE ERE YARE ALONG VOILA
  WHERE YONDER THEASUM THITHER
THEREABOUTS NEARBY
THEREAFTER UPON THENCE
THEREFORE SO ERGO THEN ARGAL
  HENCE FORTHY IGITUR THENCE
THEREON UPON
THEREUPON SO SINCE WITHAL
  THEREON THEREUP
THEREWITH MIT WITH
THERIACA GALENA
THERMOMETER GLASS HYDRA
  CELSIUS REAUMUR
THERMOPLASTIC SARAN
THERMOSTAT DETECTOR PYROSTAT
THERSANDER (FATHER OF —)
  POLYNICES
  (MOTHER OF —) ARGIA
  (SLAYER OF —) TELEPHUS
THESAURUS TREASURE
THESE THIR THIS THEASUM
THESEUS (FATHER OF —) AEGEUS
  (MOTHER OF —) AETHRA
  (SON OF —) HIPPOLYTUS
  (WIFE OF —) PHAEDRA
THESIS ACT THEMA DOWNBEAT
  LOGICISM THESICLE
THESTIUS (DAUGHTER OF —)
  ALTHAEA
  (FATHER OF —) PARTHAON
  (MOTHER OF —) EURYTE
  (SON OF —) TOXEUS PLEXIPPUS
THETIS (FATHER OF —) NEREUS
  (HUSBAND OF —) PELEUS
  (MOTHER OF —) DORIS
  (SON OF —) ACHILLES
THEY A HI THO THEI
  (— READ) LEG
THIAMINE ANEURIN
THICK FAT SAD HAZY SLAB BLIND
  BROAD BURLY BUSHY CLOSE
  CRASS DENSE FOGGY GREAT
  GROSS MURKY SOLID SQUAB STIFF
  STOUT CHUMPY COARSE GREASY
  LUBBER SLABBY SPISSY STOCKY
  STODGY BLUBBER GRUMOUS
  FAMILIAR LUTULENT MOTHERED
  (— WITH SMOKE) SMUDGY
  (11 POINTS —) HEAVY
  (SHORT AND —) SQUAT
THICKEN BODY CLOT FULL BREAK
  KEECH LITHE DEEPEN HARDEN
  ENGROSS STIFFEN
THICKENED BODIED BULLED
  FURRED CALLOUS CLUBBED
THICKENING FALX LEAR ROUX
  SWELL CALLUS CLAVATE LIAISON
  PLACODE CRASSULA PYCNOSIS
  EPHIPPIUM
  (— OF COAL SEAM) SWELLY
  (— OF LETTER STROKE) STRESS
THICKET COP RONE SHAG SHAW
  BLUFF BRAKE CLUMP COPSE DROKE
  HEDGE QUICK SHOLA SLICK THICK
  BOSKET BUSHET COVERT GREAVE

JUNGLE MALLEE QUEACH SPINNY
BOSCAGE BOSQUET BRUSHET
COPPICE CORYLET SPINNEY
WOODRIS CHAMISAL QUICKSET
SHINNERY THICKSET

THICKHEADED DULL DENSE

THICKHEADED FLY CONOPID

THICK-KNEE CURLEW DIKKOP
BUSTARD

THICKLY STEFLY

THICKNESS PLY BODY LAYER
DIAMETER
(**— OF CHIP**) CUT FEED
(**— OF CLOTH**) LAY
(**— OF METAL**) GRIP
(**— OF PAPER**) BULK CALLIPER
UNDERLAY
(**ONE — OVER ANOTHER**) LAYER
(**SECOND —**) DOUBLING

THICKSET STUB BEEFY PUNCH
SQUAT THICK CHUMPY HUMPTY
PLUGGY STOCKY STUBBY STUGGY
NUGGETY SQUATTY

THIEF GUN NIP CHOR GILT '.IFT MILL
PRIG BUDGE CREEP CROOK FAKER
GANEF PIKER SNEAK TAKER TILER
ANGLER CANNON CLOYER DISMAS
GONOPH HOOKER KALLAN LIFTER
MICHER NIMMER NIPPER PICKER
PIRATE RATERO ROBBER SNATCH
TOSHER WASTER BOOSTER
COLLERY FOOTMAN GORILLA
GRIFTER HARRIER HEISTER
LADRONE LURCHER MEECHER
MERCURY PRIGGER PRIGMAN
PROLLER PROWLER SNAPPER
SPOTTER STEALER THIEVER
CLYFAKER CONVEYER CUTPURSE
FINGERER HARROWER PETERMAN
PICAROON PICKLOCK PILFERER
PRIGSTER SNATCHER
(**— AT A MINE**) CAVER
(**CATTLE —**) BLOTTER PLANTER
RUSTLER
(**CLEVER —**) KID CANNON
(**CRUCIFIED —**) DISMAS
(**MOUNTAIN —**) CHOAR
(**NIGHT —**) SCOURER
(**PETTY —**) HOOKER SLOCKER
(**RIVER —**) ACKMAN LUMPER
(**VAGABOND —**) WASTER
(**WHARF —**) TOSHER

THIEVE NIM

THIEVING LAW SHARK PUGGING
PROGGERY STEALING

THIEVISH STEALY FURTIVE KLEPTIC
SCADDLE PRIGGISH

THIEVISHNESS PRIGGISM

THIGH HAM HOCK FEMUR FLANK
GAMMON
(**— PAIN**) MERALGIA

THILL FILL SILL BLADE SHAFT
LIMBER

THIMBLE SKEIN BUSHEL GOBLET
SLEEVE CRINGLE

THIMBLEBERRY MULBERRY

THIN HOE LEW FINE FLUE FUSE
LANK LEAN LIMP PRIN RARE SLIM
WEAK WHEY EXILE FRAIL GAUNT
GAUZY LATHY PEAKY SHEER SLINK
SMALL SPARE SWAMP THIRL WASHY
WIZEN AERIAL BLASHY DILUTE
FLUTED HOLLOW MAUGER MEAGER
MEAGRE PEAKED SCRANK SEROSE
SEROUS SHELLY SKINNY SLIGHT
SPINNY SUBTLE TENDER TWIGGY
WATERY WEAKEN COVERED
FOLIOUS FRAGILE GRACILE
HAGGARD SANIOUS SCRAGGY
SCRAILY SCRANKY SCRAWNY
SHALLOW SHILPIT SLENDER
SPINDLY TENUOUS THREADY
ARANEOUS CACHETIC EGGSHELL
HAIRLINE ICHOROUS MACILENT
SCRAGGED SCRANNEL SKINKING
VAPORISH WATERISH SPINDLING
(**— AND PINCHED**) CHITTY
(**— LEATHER**) DOLE
(**— OUT**) HOE CHOP DISBUD
FEATHER
(**— SEEDLINGS**) SINGLE
(**— THE WALLS**) IRON

THINE TUUM

THING JOB RES BABY ITEM SORT
WHAT CHEAT CHOSE ANIMAL
DINGUS FELLOW GILGUY MATTER
ARTICLE DINGBAT MINIKEN
SHEBANG WHATNOT THINGLET
(**— DONE**) FACT ACTUS
(**— FOUND**) TROVE
(**— OF LITTLE ACCOUNT**) GEWGAW
(**— OF LITTLE VALUE**) NIFLE TRIFLE
TRINKET
(**— OF LITTLE WORTH**) STIVER
(**— TO BE REGRETTED**) DAMAGE
(**— TO EXHIBIT**) BRAVERY
(**—S PROHIBITED**) VETANDA
(**ANOTHER —**) ALIUD
(**CONSECRATED —**) ANATHEMA
(**ENORMOUS —**) MONSTER
(**ENTIRE —**) INTEGRAL
(**EXTRAORDINARY —**) ONER
(**FAIR —**) POTATO
(**FIT —**) CHECKER
(**GOOD —**) WELFARE
(**HOLY —S**) HAGIA KODASHIM
(**IMPORTANT —**) ACE
(**INSIGNIFICANT —**) SCRAT
(**INSIGNIFICANT —S**) SMATTER
(**JEWISH —S**) JUDAICA
(**LITTLE —S**) FEWTRILS
(**LIVING —S**) BIOTA
(**MISSHAPEN —**) ABORTION
(**NEW —**) NEWEL
(**OUTMODED —**) SNUFF
(**PETTY —**) SHABBLE
(**PRECIOUS —**) JEWEL
(**PRECISE —**) POINT
(**RIDICULOUS —**) MONUMENT
(**RIGHT —**) POTATO
(**ROTTEN —**) ROTTOCK
(**SAD —**) RUTH
(**SILLY —**) TRIMTRAM
(**SINGLE —**) UNIT
(**SMALL —**) SNIPPET
(**STRAY —**) WAIF
(**STUNTED —**) SCRUNT SNEESHIN
(**SURE —**) CERT SNIP

(**TERRIFYING —**) BOGEYMAN
(**UNEXPECTED —**) GODSEND
(**UNIQUE —**) ONER UNICUM
(**UNREAL —**) NOMINAL
(**UNSUBSTANTIAL —**) PUFF
(**WORLDLY —S**) EARTH
(**WORNOUT —**) SNUFF HUSHEL
(**PL.**) GEAR REALIA SQUARES

THING-IN-ITSELF THINGY
NOUMENON

THINGUMBOB DODAD DOODAD
JIGGER THINGUM

THINK LET SEE WIS WIT DEEM FEEL
HOLD MAKE MEAN MINT MULL MUSE
READ TROW WEEN ALLOW FANCY
GUESS JUDGE LOUSE OPINE PANSE
SEPAD ESTEEM EXPECT FIGURE
IDEATE RECKON REPUTE BELIEVE
CONCEIT IMAGINE REFLECT
SUPPOSE COGITATE CONSIDER
ENVISAGE
(**— BEST**) SEEM
(**— HARD**) YERK
(**— OF AS**) ACCOUNT
(**— OF**) MIND PURPENSE
(**— OVER**) BETHINK
(**— UP**) INVENT
(**— UPON**) BROOD
(**— WELL OF**) APPROVE

THINKER SOPHIST
(**CHINESE —**) LEGALIST

THINKING CONCEIT THOUGHT
(**CLEVER —**) HEADWORK

THINLY AIRILY SPARSE SPARSELY

THINNESS RARITY EXILITY FINESSE
TENUITY EXIGUITY

THINNING BALK BAULK CLEANING

THIRD FACE GAMMA TERCE THREE
DITONE TERTIA TIERCE

THIRDLY TERTIO

THIRD-RATE C3 HEDGE

THIRD-RATER PIKER

THIRST DRY ADRY DRYTH APOSIA
DROUTH THRIST DROUGHT DIPSOSIS

THIRSTING SITIENT

THIRSTY DRY ADRY ATHIRST
DROUGHTY

THIS HE SO THIK THILK

THISTLE PUHA HOYLE CARDON
DASHEL DINDLE FISTLE TEASEL
CALTROP CARLINA GUTWEED
RAURIKI WARATAH BEDEGUAR
CALTHROP COMPOSIT ECHINOPS
MILKWEED

THITHER TO YON YOND THERE
YONDER ULTERIOR YONDWARD

THOAS (**DAUGHTER OF —**)
HYPSIPYLE
(**FATHER OF —**) BACCHUS
(**MOTHER OF —**) ARIADNE
(**WIFE OF —**) MYRINE

THOMIST AQUINIST

THOMSONITE MESOLE MESOTYPE
OZARKITE

THONG RIEM BRAIL GIRTH LASSO
LEASH ROMAL STRAP THUNK
WHANG WHANK LACING LINGEL
STRING TWITCH AMENTUM BABICHE

LANIARD LANYARD LATCHET RIEMPIE
(— ON JAVELIN) AMENTUM
(HAWK'S —) BRAIL
THOR THUNAR THUNOR
THORACIC DORSAL
THORAX CHEST TRUNK BREAST PEREION ALITRUNK CORSELET FOREBODY
THORITE ENALITE ORANGITE
THORN BROD BUSH GOAD PIKE STUG BRIAR BRIER DOORN PRICK SPIKE FUSTIC JAGGER PRICKER STICKER COCKSPUR THORNLET (PL.) SPEAR HAYBOTE
THORN APPLE HAW METEL STAMONY
THORNBACK RAY DORN ROKER
THORNBILL TOMTIT
THORNY HARD SPINY PRICKLY SCROGGY SPINOUS THISTLY THORNED
THORON RADON
THOROUGH RUN DEEP FIRM FULL SOUND ERRANT HOLLOW STRICT HOTSHOT INGOING REGULAR COMPLETE GROUNDLY INTIMATE
THOROUGHBRED HOTBLOOD
THOROUGHFARE BUND DRUM ROAD ALLEY AVENUE STREET HIGHWAY PARKWAY WHITEHALL
THOROUGHGOING PAKKA ARRANT ERRANT HEARTY PROPER PUREDEE RADICAL ABSOLUTE PROFOUND TRUEBRED
THOROUGHLY BUT FULL GOOD INLY CLEAN FULLY PROOF DEEPLY GAINLY KINDLY PROPER RICHLY RIPELY WHOLLY ROUNDLY SOAKING SOBBING SOGGING SOUNDLY DRIPPING GROUNDLY HEARTILY INWARDLY
THOROUGHWORT BONESET
THOSE THEM THEY YOND
THOTH DHOUTI
THOUGH AS AND SET YET ALTHO ALTHOUGH
THOUGHT CARE IDEA MOOD VIEW FANCY TASTE TRACE NOTION PENSEE CONCEIT CONCEPT COUNSEL OPINION SURMISE PEMMICAN RUMINATE
(— OUT) ADVISED
(CAREFUL —) ADVICE ACCOUNT
(HIGHEST —) IDEE
(REASONED —) STUDY
(UNCLEAN —) SEWERAGE
(WELL-EXPRESSED —) STROKE
THOUGHTFUL EARNEST PENSIVE SERIOUS STUDIED THOUGHTY
THOUGHTFULNESS GRACE COUNSEL
THOUGHTLESS RASH DIZZY GLAKY SUPINE GLAIKET RAMSTAM HEEDLESS RECKLESS
THOUSAND CHI MIL GRAND MILLE CHILIAD
(10 —) MYRIAD
(100 —) LAC LAKH

THOUSANDTH (— OF CUBIC CENTIMETER) LAMBDA
(— OF INCH) MIL
(HUNDRED —) SSU
THRACIAN GETE GETAN GETIC THRAX
THRALL SERF GURTH SLAVE CAPTIVE
THRALLDOM BONDAGE SLAVERY THIRLAGE
THRASH DAD LAM PAY TAN BANG BEAT BELT COMB DING DRUB DUST FLAX LACE LICK LOUK MILL PAIL SOLE SOWL SWAP SWOP TOSE WALK WHAP WHIP WHOP YERK BASTE BELAM BLESS CURRY DRASH FLAIL FRAIL LINCH LINGE NOINT SLATE SWACK SWING TABOR TARGE THUMP TOWEL TWINK WHALE WHANG ANOINT BUMFEG CUDGEL FETTLE JACKET MUZZLE RADDLE STOUSH SWINGE TANCEL THREAP THRESH THWACK WALLOP LAMBACK LEATHER SWADDLE TROLLOP TROUNCE BETHWACK BUMBASTE LAMBASTE LAMBSKIN RIBROAST
THRASHER THREAPER THRESHER
THRASHING TOCO BELTING LICKING WARMING WHALING DRUBBING
THRASYMEDES (FATHER OF —) NESTOR
(MOTHER OF —) ANAXIBIA
THREAD BAR END BAVE CHIP CLEW CLUE CORD DOUP FILE FILM GIMP GOLD LACE LINE POIL PURL SILK TRAM WIRE WORM BRIDE CHIVE FIBER FIBRE FLOAT FLOSS HYPHA INKLE REEVE SCREW SETON SHIVE SHOOT SHUTE STEEK TWEER TWIRE TWIST WATAP BOTTOM COBWEB COTTON ENFILE FIBRIL INFILE SINGLE STAMEN STITCH STRAIN STRAND STRING TISSUE BABICHE BASTING DOUPING SLUBBER SPIREME TWITTER WARPING ACONTIUM FILAMENT GOSSAMER LIGATURE PICKOVER RAVELING SPINNING SPIRICLE
(— AROUND BOWSTRING) SERVING
(— IN SEED COATING) SPIRICLE
(— LEGS OF RABBIT) HARL HARLE
(— OF SCREW) WORM
(— OF WAX) SWARF
(— USED FOR COCOON) BAVE
(—S THAT CROSS WARP) WEFT WOOF
(40 —S) BEER BIER
(BADLY TWINED —) SLUBBER
(BALL OF —) CLEW CLUE CLOWE GLOME
(BUTTONHOLE —S) BAR
(COARSE —) GIRD
(COARSEST — IN LACE) GIMP
(COILED —) COP
(FLOATING —) PICKOVER
(HARD —) LISLE
(LINEN —) LINE INCLE INKLE
(LOOSELY TWISTED —S) BUMP

(METAL —) LAME WIRE
(OAKUM —) PLEDGET
(PULLED —) SNAG
(REFUSE —S) BUR BURR
(SHOEMAKER'S —) END LINGEL LINGLE
(SILK —) TRAM TRAME DOUPIONI
(SOFT SHORT —) THRUM
(STRONG —) GOUNAU
(SURGICAL —) SETON
(WARP —) END STAMEN
(WAXED —) TACKER
(WEFT —) SHOT
(PL.) FLOSS
THREADBARE BARE SEAR SERE TRITE PILLED SHABBY NAPLESS
THREADFIN SEER SEIR SULEA BARBUDO KINGFISH SEERFISH
THREADFISH COBBLER SUNFISH
THREADING SCREW STRINGING
THREADLIKE FILATE FILOSE
THREAT ATTACK MENACE THUNDER (PL.) MINES
THREATEN BRAG FACE BOAST SHORE ATTACK IMPEND MENACE ENDANGER MINATORY
THREATENED FRAUGHT
THREATENING BIG GLUM UGLY ANGRY BOAST SABLE GREASY BANEFUL RAMPANT MINATORY MINITANT
(— TO RAIN) HEAVY
THREE TREY GIMEL LEASH TRIAS TERNARY TERNION
(— CENT PIECE) TRIME
(— IN ONE) TRIUNE
(— MILES) LEAGUE
(— OF A KIND) GLEEK BRELAN TRIPLET
(GROUP OF —) TRIO TRIAD TRIPLE
(SET OF —) PAIRIAL
THREE-DIMENSIONAL CUBIC CUBICAL
THREEFOLD TERN TRINE TERNAL TREBLE TRINAL TRIPLE TERNARY TRIFOLD TRIPLEX THRIBBLE
THREE-FORKED TRISULC
THREEPENCE JOEY TREY THRIP THRUM TICKEY TICKIE
THRENODY HEARSE THRENE
THRESH COB BEAT CAVE LUMP WHIP BERRY FLAIL FRAIL SPELT STAMP THRASH
THRESHEL DRASHEL
THRESHER TASKER
THRESHER SHARK FOX FOXFISH WHIPTAIL
THRESHOLD HEAD SILL SOLE DEARN LIMEN DRASHEL DOORSILL
THRIFT SAVING VIRTUE ECONOMY STATICE THEEDOM
THRIFTILY NEAR
THRIFTLESS WASTEFUL
THRIFTY CANNY FENDY PUIST FRUGAL SAVING CAREFUL SPARING
THRILL JAG BANG DIRL GIRL KICK FLUSH SHOOT THIRL DINDLE STOUND TICKLE TREMOR ENCHANT FRISSON VIBRATE FREMITUS

(SHARP —) ZING
THRILLING VIBRANT TINGLING
THRINTER FRONTER
THRIPID PHYSOPOD
THRIPS BLACKFLY PHYSOPOD
THRIVE DOW GROW LIKE RISE THEE
ADDLE FADGE MOISE PROVE THRAM
BATTEN BATTLE CATTER CHIEVE
PROSPER STORKEN SUCCEED
WELFARE FLOURISH THRODDEN
(— IN) LOVE
THRIVING BIEN GRUSHIE THRIFTY
BLOOMING TOWARDLY
THRIVINGLY GAILY GAYLY BRAVELY
THROAT MAW CRAG CROP GOWL
GULA HALS HASS LANE GORGE
HALSE SWIRE FAUCES GARGET
GULLET GUTTUR GUZZLE RICTUS
CHANNEL JUGULUM STOMACH
SWALLOW WEASAND THRAPPLE
THROPPLE THROTTLE
(— OF ANCHOR) CLUTCH
(— OF COROLLA) FAUCES
(— OF FROG) KNEE
(MOUTH AND —) WHISTLE
(SORE —) HOUSTY
THROATLATCH FIADOR
THROB ACHE BEAT BELK DRUM
DUNT LEAP PANT QUOP WARK
FLACK STANG WARCH STOUND
STRIKE STROKE WALLOP FLACKER
PULSATE VIBRATE FLICHTER
(— IN PAIN) SHOOT
(RAPID —S) FRIMITTS
THROBBING DUNT ATHROB THRILL
PITAPAT
THROE PANG PULL STOUR SHOWER
PAROXYSM
(—S OF DEATH) AGONY
THROMBIN PLASMASE
THROMBOPLASTIN COAGULIN
CYTOZYME
THROMBOSIS SHOCK CORONARY
THRONE GADI ASANA GADDI GADHI
SELLE SIEGE STALL STATE STEAD
STOOL SEGGIO SHINZA TRIBUNE
CATHEDRA SEGGIOLA SINHASAN
(BISHOP'S —) SEE APSE CATHEDRA
THRONE ROOM AIWAN
THRONG CREW HEAP HOST ROUT
CHIRT CROWD FLOCK FRACK POSSE
PRESS SHOAL SWARM RESORT
THRAVE THREAT THRIMP THRUST
COMPANY TEMPEST THRUTCH
SURROUND
(— OF SEAFOWL) SAVSSAT
(CONFUSED —) LURRY
THRONGED ALIVE FREQUENT
NUMEROUS
THROTTLE GUN CHOKE STIFLE
GARROTE STRANGLE THROPPLE
THROUGH BY PER DONE THRU WITH
ROUND AROUND
(RIGHT —) TILL
THROUGHOUT ABOUT ABROAD
BEDENE BIDENE DURING ENTIRE
PASSIM SEMPRE OVERALL THRUOUT
THROW GO DAB HIP HIT PAT PEG
PUT SHY ACES BIFF BUCK BUNG

CALE CAST CHIP COOK CUCK DART
DASH DROW HAIL HANK HIPE HULL
HURL HYPE JERK LACE MILL PECK
PICK SEND SKIM SLAT SOSS TOSS
TURF VANG WARP WURP YEND
CHUCK CHUNK DOUSE FLICK FLING
FLIRT FLURR HEAVE PITCH SLING
SPANG DEVEST ELANCE HAUNCH
HURTLE INJECT LAUNCH SLIGHT
THRILL BLUNDER BUTTOCK
COCKSHY MANGANA UPTHROW
VIBRATE CATAPULT JACULATE
(— ABOUT) BOUNCE
(— ASIDE) DEVEST
(— AWAY) DICE DOFF BANDY WAIVE
PROJECT JETTISON SQUANDER
(— BASEBALL) BURN
(— BY KICKING) WINCE
(— CARELESSLY) COB
(— DICE) JEFF
(— DOWN) EVEN PILE LODGE
DETURB THRING FLATTEN
(— FORTH) EJECT
(— FORWARD) LAUNCH
(— HEAVILY) LOB
(— HEEDLESSLY) SLIGHT
(— IN CRAPS) CRAP CRABS
BOXCARS
(— INTO CONFUSION) CLUB
FLUTTER CONFOUND CONVULSE
(— INTO DISORDER) ADDLE BOLLIX
DERANGE DISRANK DISRUPT
EMBROIL DISARRAY
(— INTO PERPLEXITY) FLUMMOX
(— INTO WASTE) BACK
(— JERKILY) FLIRT
(— LIGHT UPON) ILLUME
(— LIQUID) JAW
(— OF A STEER) DOGFALL
(— OF SHUTTLE) SHOT SHOOT
SHUTE
(— OF THREES) COCKEYES
(— OFF COURSE) EMIT SHED
DERAIL
(— OFF) CANT CAST SPILL SLOUGH
CONFUSE UNBURDEN
(— ONESELF) CLAP
(— OPEN) DISPARK
(— OUT) FIRE HOOF LADE BELCH
EJECT ERUPT SPOUT DETURB
IGNORE EXTRUDE
(— QUICKLY) LASH
(— SIDEWISE) SHY
(— SILK) THROWST
(— SMARTLY) SLAT
(— STEER) BUST
(— STICKS) SQUAIL
(— STONES) ROCK
(— TOGETHER) HUDDLE
(— UNDER) SUBJECT
(— UP) CAVE PICK VOMIT
(— VIOLENTLY) BUZZ DING PASH
SOCK SMASH HURTLE WHITHER
SPANGHEW
(— WITH A JERK) JET CANT SQUIRR
FLOUNCE
(— WITH GREAT FORCE) BUZZ
SWACK
(— WITHOUT VIOLENCE) HURL

(CHEATING — OF DICE) KNAP
(FREE —) FOUL
(LARIAT —) HOOLIAN
(LOWEST — AT DICE) AMBSACE
AMESACE
(WRESTLING —) HANK HIPE HYPE
BUTTOCK BACKHEEL
THROWAWAY DODGER
THROWBACK ATAVISM
THROWER TRAMMER THROWSTER
(SPEAR —) ATLATL
THROWING DARTING
THROWING-STICK ATLATL
WOMMERA WOOMERA HORNERAH
TROMBASH TRUMBASH
THROWN (— AWAY) CASTAWAY
(— DOWN) DEJECTED
THROWSTER TWISTER
THRUM FUM STRUM THUMB
THRUSH POP OMAO SOOR APTHA
BREVE FRUSH GRIVE MAVIS OUZEL
PITTA SABIA SHAMA SHIRL SPREW
UZZLE VEERY APHTHA DRAINE
JAYPIE KICKUP MISSEL OLOMAO
PULISH SHRITE JAYPIET REDWING
WAGTAIL BELLBIRD CHERCOCK
FORKTAIL PRUNELLA SHAGBARK
THRASHER THROSTLE THRUSHEL
THRUSTLE URTICATE WOODCHAT
THRUSHLIKE TURDOID
THRUST DAB DEG DIG DUB JAB JAG
JAM JOB POP PUG BANG BEAR BIRR
BOKE BORE BUCK BUTT CANT CHOP
CRAM DART DASH DUSH FOIN HURL
KICK LICK MURE PASS PICK PILT
POKE PORR POSS POTE PROD PUSH
SEND SINK SPAR STAB STOP TILT
VENY WHAP WHOP BREAK DRIFT
DRIVE EXERT HUNCH LUNGE POACH
POINT PROKE PUNCH SHOOT SPANK
STAVE STICK STOKE STUFF THROW
DARTLE PLUNGE POUNCE STITCH
STRAIN STRESS STRIKE STRIPE
BEARING IMPULSE SHOULDER
STOCCADO
(— A LANCE) AVENTRE
(— ASIDE) DAFF SHUFFLE
(— AWAY) DOFF SHOVE DETRUDE
ABSTRUDE
(— DOWN) THRING DEPULSE
DETRUDE
(— IN) INSERT STRIKE INTRUDE
(— OF ARCH) DRIFT
(— OF EXPLOSION) BLOWOUT
(— ONESELF) CHISEL
(— OUT) REACH STRUT EXSERT
DETRUDE EXTRUDE OBTRUDE
PROTRUDE
(— SUDDENLY) STRIKE
(— THROUGH) ENFILED
(— WITH ELBOW) HUNCH
(— WITH GREAT FORCE) BUZZ
(— WITH NOSE) NUDDLE
(— WITH WEAPON) FOIN SHOVE
(DAGGER —) DAG
(FENCING —) PASS VENY VENUE
REPOST TIMING PASSADO RIPOSTE
STOCCADO STOCCATA
(HOME —) HAI HAY

(MATADOR'S —) ESTOCADA
(SARCASTIC —) GIRD
THUD BAFF DUMP PHUT PLOD SWAG
DOYST FLUMP POUND SQUELCH
THUG GOON GOONDA RODMAN
GORILLA HOODLUM GANGSTER
THUJA BIOTA
THUJONE SALVIOL
THULUTH SOOLOOS
THUMB POLLEX THENAR THROOM
(BALL OF —) THENAR
THUMBSTALL POUCER POUSER
THUMP COB DAD DUB BANG BEAT
DING DIRD DRUB DUNT KNUB LUMP
PAKE POLT SOSS THUD TUNK YARK
YERK BLAFF BLIBE BUNCH CLOUR
CLUNK CRUMP KNOCK POUND
TABOR THACK WHELK BOUNCE
HAMMER PUMMEL THUNGE
THUMPING WHAPPING WHOPPING
THUNDER SULFUR FOULDRE
SULPHUR INTONATE
THUNDERBOLT BOLT FIRE VAJRA
FULMEN FOULDRE ARTIFACT
FIREBOLT
THUNDERSQUALL BAYAMO
VENDAVAL
THUNDERSTONE ARTIFACT
THUNDERSTORM HOUVARI
TEMPEST TORNADO
THURIBLE CENSER
THUS AS SIC DYCE THUSLY
THISWISE THUSGATE
THWACK DUNT CRUMP SOUSE
THWART BALK WART BENCH CROOK
CROSS SPITE THROW ZYGON
BAFFLE SCOTCH STYMIE SNOOKER
CONTRAIR CONTRARY TRAVERSE
THWARTING CROSS CROSSING
THYESTES (BROTHER OF —)
ATREUS
(FATHER OF —) PELOPS
(MOTHER OF —) HIPPODAMIA
THYLACINE YABBI
THYINE THUGA THUYA
THYME MARUM PELETRE HILLWORT
SERPOLET
TI KI TOI TITI
TIARA MITER CIDARIS TIARELLA
TIBBU DAZA TEDA

TIBET

CAPITAL: LASSA LHASA
COIN: TANGA
LAKE: ARU BAM BUM NAM MEMA
TOSU JAGOK TABIA DAGTSE
GARHUR KASHUN SELING
TANGRA YAMDOK KYARING
TERIMAN TSARING ZILLING
JIGGITAI
LANGUAGE: BODSKAD
MOUNTAIN: KAMET SAJUM KAILAS
BANDALA
MOUNTAIN RANGE: KAILAS
KUNLUN HIMALAYA
NATIVE: BHOTIA BHOTIYA
RIVER: NAK NAU SAK SONG INDUS
SUTLEJ MATSANG SALWEEN

TOWN: NOH KARAK LHASA
GARTOK TOTLING GYANGTSE
SHIGATSE

TIBETAN BALTI DRUPA BHOTIA
BHUTIA CHAMPA DROKPA KHAMBA
KHAMBU PANAKA SHERPA TANGUT
BHOTIYA BHUTANI GYARUNG
TIBIA SHIN SHANK CNEMIS SHINBONE
TIBOURBOU CORTEZ
TIC FIXATION
(ONE SUBJECT TO —) TIQUEUR
TICK FAG JAR KEB BEAT KADE NICK
PEAK PICK PIKE CHALK CHICK
CRIKE PIQUE STRAP IXODID PALLET
TALAJE TAMPAN ACARIAN ARGASID
BEDTICK IXODIAN PINOLIA
ARACHNID CARAPATO GARAPATA
GARAPATO TURICATA
TICKED MACKEREL
TICKET LOT TAG BLANK CHECK
DUCAT FICHE TOKEN BALLOT
BILLET COUPON DOCKET PIGEON
POLICY RETURN BENEFIT ETIQUET
CONTRACT DEADHEAD STOPOVER
TRANSFER
(COMMISSION —) SPIFF
(FREE —) PASS
(LOTTERY —) BLANK HORSE
BENEFIT
(SALES —) TRAVELER
(SEASON —) IVORY
(PL.) PAPER
TICKET WINDOW GUICHET
TICKING KISS TICK BEDTICK
TICKLE AMUSE TEASE EXCITE KITTLE
PLEASE THRILL TIDDLE CUITTLE
TICKLISH GOOSEY KITTLE KITTLY
QUEASY TENDER TOUCHY TRICKY
KITTLISH
TICKSEED COREOPSIS
TICK TREFOIL BEDSTRAW SAINFOIN
TICKSEED
TIDBIT SAYNETE BEATILLE
KICKSHAW
TIDDLEYWINK SQUAIL
TIDE FLOW NEAP WAVE AGGER
ROUST SPRING OVERTIDE
SEAFLOOD
(— MOVEMENT) LAKIE
TIDINGS NEWS WORD RUMOR
SOUND UNCOW ADVICE MESSAGE
(GLAD —) GOSPEL
TIDY RID COSH MACK NEAT SIDE
SMUG SNOD SNUG TAUT TOSH TRIG
WEME CHART DONCY DONSY
DOUCE NATTY QUEME TIGHT
DONSIE FETTLE POLITE SPOONY
ALLIGATE MACKLIKE MENSEFUL
TIE BOW LAP TYE BAND BIND BOND
CAST DRAW KILT KNOT LACE LOCK
ROOT WISP YOKE ASCOT BRACE
CADGE LEASH NEXUS POINT THRAP
THROW TRUSS ATTACH BUNDLE
CONNEX COUPLE FASTEN LIGATE
SECURE DOGFALL FOULARD
JAZZBOW NECKTIE SHACKLE
SLEEPER SPANCEL TABLEAU

CROSSTIE INTERTIE LIGATURE
STANDOFF STRINGER VINCULUM
(— BENEATH) SUBNECT
(— IN TENNIS) DEUCE
(— IN WRESTLING) DOGFALL
(— KNOT) CAST
(— LEGS) HOBBLE
(— ONIONS) TRACE
(— SCORE) PEELS
(— THE SCORE) EQUALIZE
(— TOGETHER) KNIT LEASH
HARNESS
(— UP SHORT) SNUB
(— UP) SNUB TRAMMEL LIGATURE
TWITCHEL
(LEATHER —) WANTY
(MADE-UP —) TECK
(NEEDLEWORK —) BRIDE
(PL.) GILLIES
TIED FAST KNIT SQUARE
TIEPIN SCARFPIN STICKPIN
TIE PLATE TURTLE
TIER ROW BANK DECK RANK CHESS
STORY WITHE DEGREE PINAFORE
(— OF CASKS) RIDER
(— OF SEATS) CIRCLE
(— OF SHELVES) STAGE
TIERCE LEASH THIRD
TIFF MIFF TIFT
TIFFIN CONDOR
TIGER SHER SHIR TIGRE TIGERKIN
TIGER CAT CHATI
TIGERFOOT IPOMOEA
TIGER SNAKE ELAPID ELAPOID
TIGHT WET FULL HARD SNUG TAUT
TIDY CLOSE DENSE DRUNK STENT
TENSE STINGY STRAIT STRICT
AIRTIGHT
TIGHTEN JAM CALK FIRM FRAP
CAULK CINCH CLOSE FEEZE SCREW
THRAP WRENCH STRAITEN
TIGHTFISTED STINGY
TIGHT-LIPPED SILENT
TIGHTLY FAST HARD SHORT STRAIT
CLOSELY
TIGHTS MAILLOT LEOTARDS
TIGHTWAD FIST PIKER STIFF
TILDE TIL WAVE TITTLE
(HAVING A —) CURLY
TILE LUMP FAVUS KASHI LATER
SLATE IMBREX LAPPET PAMENT
QUARRY SLATER TEGULA AZULEJO
CARREAU CONDUIT PANTILE
QUARREL STARTER MAINTILE
(— USED IN MOSAIC) ABACULUS
(HEXAGONAL —) FAVUS
(HOLLOW —) BACKING
(LARGE —) DALLE QUARL QUARLE
(MAH JONG —) HONOR SEASON
(ONE-HALF —) HEAD
(PERSIAN —) KASHI
(ROUNDED —) CREASE
(SMALL —) TILETTE
(SQUARE —) QUADREL QUARREL
TILER HELER HELLIER
TILL TO EAR FIT LOB CASH FARM
PLOW TEAL TOIL DRESS LABOR
UNTIL WHILE FURROW MANURE
PLOUGH TILLER WHILST HUSBAND

SHUTTLE DUCKFOOT OXHARROW
TILLABLE EARABLE
TILLAGE ARABLE GAINOR MANURE
ARATION CULTURE TILTURE
TILLED GEOM TOILED
TILLER HELM STERN STOOL
HUSBAND KILLIFER
TILLING EARTH FALLOW
TILT DIP TIP TOP BANK CANT CAVE
COCK HEEL LIST SWAG TRAP
BRASH HEELD HIELD JOUST STOOP
TIPUP CASTER TILTER TOPPLE
CURRENT TOURNEY COCKBILL
QUINTAIN
(— BRICK) HACK
(— IN WATER) DABBLE
(— OF BOWSPRIT) STAVE
(— OF NOSE) KIP KIPP
TILTED ACOCK ASTOOP
TILT HAMMER OLIVER
TILTING DIP JOUSTING
TIMBAL DRUM TYMBALON
TIMBER CAP LOG RIB BEAM BIBB
BUNK CLOG DRAM FELL FISH FROG
GIRT PUMP RAFF SKID SPAR SPUR
TREE WOOD CAHUY CAVEL CRUCK
FLOOR GRIPE JOIST KEVEL LEDGE
ORGUE PLATE RIDER SISSU SPALE
STICK BEARER BRIDGE BUMPER
CAMBER CORBEL DAGGER FENDER
FOREST KNIGHT LIZARD ROOFER
SISSOO SUMMER TIMMER BOLSTER
CARLING DEADMAN DIVIDER
FALLAGE FUTCHEL FUTTOCK
GROUSER PARTNER PITWOOD
RIBBAND TRANSOM CORDWOOD
COULISSE DOGSHORE FOREHOOK
STRINGER STUMPAGE TRIPSILL
WOODFALL
(— BETWEEN TRIMMERS) HEADER
(— CUT TO LENGTH) JUGGLE
(— IN MINE) COG STULL LIFTER
DIVIDER JUGGLER
(— KEPT DRY) BRIGHT
(— ON SLED) BUNK
(— PIECE) PUTLOG
(— SAWED AND SPLIT) LUMBER
(— SUPPORTING CAP) LEGPIECE
(— SUSTAINING YARDS) MAST
(— TO PROP COAL) BROB
(CONVEX —) CAMBER
(CURVED —) CRUCK
(CUT —) FELL
(FELLED —) HAG
(FLOOR —) JOIST SUMMER
(FLOORING —) BATTEN
(FRAMING —) PUNCHEON
(HORIZONTAL —) REASON
(NORWEGIAN —) DRAM
(PHILIPPINE —) LAUAN
(PRINCIPAL — OF VESSEL) KEEL
(ROOF —) LEVER RAFTER
(ROOFING —S) SILE
(SHIP'S —) KEEL KNEE RUNG SPUR
LEDGE WRONG DAGGER HARPIN
LACING SCROLL BRACKET FUTTOCK
STEMSON DOGSHORE STANDARD
(SHIPBUILDING —S) STOCKS
DEADWOOD HARPINGS

(SLABBED —) CANT
(SUPPORT —) SILL GIRDER LEDGER
STRINGER
(SYSTEM OF —S) BOND
(UNCUT —) STUMPAGE
(WEATHERBEATEN —) DRIKI
TIMBERLAND STICKS WOODLAND
TIMBERMAN BRACER
TIMBO CUBE AJARI
TIMBRE CLANG COLOR KLANG
COLORING
TIMBREL TABOR TABOUR
TIME DAY ELD BELL BOUT HINT
HOUR SELE TIDE WHET ABYSS
CHARE EPOCH FLASH FRIST KALPA
SITHE SPACE STOUN STOUR TEMPO
TEMPS VOLTA WHACK WHILE
COURSE KAIROS PERIOD SEASON
STOUND TEMPUS CADENCE
DEWFALL SESSION MOVEMENT
(— AFTER) POST
(— ALLOWED FOR PAYMENT)
USANCE
(— FOR PAYING) KIST
(— FOR PAYMENT) CREDIT
(— GRANTED) FRIST
(— IN SERVICE) AGE
(— INTERVENING) INTERIM
MEANTIME
(— LONG SINCE PAST) YORE
(— OF BEAUTY) BLOOM
(— OF CRISIS) EXIGENT
(— OF DYING) LAST
(— OF EXPIRY) ISH
(— OF EXUBERANCE) CARNIVAL
(— OF FEASTING) GUTTIDE
(— OF HIGHEST STRENGTH)
HEYDAY
(— OF LIGHT) DAY
(— OF MATURITY OR DECLINE)
AUTUMN
(— OF NEWS STORY) BREAK
(— OF OLD AGE) SUNSET
(— OF QUIET) DEAD
(— OF REST) BREATH SABBATH
(— OF WOE) WOSITH
(— TO COME) FUTURITY
(ANOTHER —) AGAIN
(AT ANOTHER —) ALIAS
(BRIEF —) TINE FLASH THROW
(BY THE —) AGAINST
(EACH —) ONCE
(EXTENDED —) TRAIN
(FIXED —) HOUR STEVEN
(GAY —) FRISK WHOOPEE
(GOOD —) BALL BASH BEANO
JOLLY BARNEY FROLIC HOLIDAY
(HARD —) GYP BUSINESS
(IMMEASURABLY LONG PERIOD OF
—) EON AEON
(INFINITE —) ABYSS
(LONG —) AGE
(OLD —S) ELD
(PAST —) FORETIME
(POINT OF —) MOMENT
(RIGHT —) TID
(SECOND —) YET EFTSOON
EFTSOONS
(SET —) TRYST

(SHORT —) TIFF SPACE START
MINUTE STOUND
(SPARE —) TOOM
(TRIPLE —) TRIPLA
(UNENGAGED —) LEISURE
(WORKING —) CORE
(PL.) SYSE
TIME CLOCK BUNDY TELLTALE
TIMELESS AGELESS ETERNAL
DATELESS
TIMELESSNESS ETERNITY
TIMELY PAT DULY TIDY COGENT
TIMEFUL TIMEOUS TOWARDLY
TIMEPIECE DIAL CLOCK TIMER
VERGE WATCH GHURRY PENDULE
HOROLOGE HOROLOGY
TIMETABLE SCHEDULE
TIMID SHY ARGH EERY NESH SELY
SHAN BAUCH BLATE EERIE FAINT
PAVID SCARE SCARY AFRAID
COWARD ASHAMED BASHFUL
FEARFUL FRIGHTY NERVOUS
RABBITY SCADDLE STRANGE
TREMBLY COWARDLY FEARSOME
GHASTFUL RETIRING TIMOROSO
TIMOROUS
TIMIDITY SHYNESS TIMERITY
FUNKINESS
TIMIDLY SMALL
TIMOR (CAPITAL OF —) DILI
(COIN OF —) AVO PATACA
(ISLAND OF —) MOA LETI LAKOR
(LANGUAGE OF —) TETUM
(TOWN IN —) KUPANG ATAMBUA
TIMOROUS FAINT MILKY TIMID
AFRAID COWISH TREPID FEARFUL
FERDFUL FEARSOME SHEEPISH
TEMEROUS TIMOROSO
TIN SN DIXY JOVE DIXIE KATIN
SWELL TINNY KHATIN JUPITER
PILLION STANNUM PRILLION
TINGLASS
(MESS —) DIXY DIXIE
(ROOFING —) TERNE
(SHEET —) LATTEN LATTIN
(TIE — CAN TO TAIL) TAILPIPE
TINAMOU YUTU MACUCA YNAMBU
TATAUPA MARTINET
TINCAL ALTINCAR
TINCTURE BUFO DRUG COLOR
IMBUE SMACK STAIN TAINT TENNE
TINCT ARGENT ARNICA ELIXIR
DIAMOND ARAMAIZE INFUSION
LAUDANUM TAINTURE
TINDER SPUNK AMADOU TENDRE
FIREBOX
TINE KNAG SNAG TANG GRAIN
OFFER POINT PRONG RIGHT TOOTH
GRAINING TINEWARE TINEWEED
(ANTLER'S —) RIGHT CROCKET
SURROYAL
TIN FOIL TAIN
TINGE DYE EYE HUE CAST DASH
TINT WOAD COLOR FLUSH IMBUE
PAINT SAVOR SHADE STAIN TAINT
TINCT SEASON SMUTCH BEPAINT
DISTAIN GLIMPSE DISCOLOR
TINCTION TINCTURE
TINGED FLORID GILDED

TINGGIAN ITNEG ITANEG
TINGLE SOO BURN DIRL GELL GIRL
THIRL DINDLE SWIDGE TINKLE
PRINGLE PRINKLE TRINKLE
TINKER PRIG TINK CAIRD FIDDLE
FIDGET MUGGER KETTLER PROJECT
TRAVELER
TINKLE TINK DINDLE DINGLE TINGLE
TRINKLE TWINKLE
TINNER TINKER
TINSEL GAUDY TINSY TINNET
TINT DYE EYE COLOR ENNUE GRAIN
TINCT TINGE SPRAING
(— IN HORSE'S COAT) BLOSSOM
(— WITH COSMETICS) SURFLE
(CLANG —) TIMBRE
TINTED TINCT
TINWORKS STANNARY
TINY TINE BITSY BITTY DEENY SMALL
TEENY TIDDY WEENY ATOMIC BITTIE
WEESHY MINIKIN ATOMICAL
TIP CAP DIP END FEE NEB TOP APEX
CANT CAVE COCK HEEL HELD HORN
KEEL LEAD LIST PALM PIKE PILE
SWAG TILT TYPE VAIL GRIFF HEELD
MUCRO POINT POUCH SPIRE SPURE
STEER CAREEN CENTER CENTRE
TICKLE TIPLET TIPPLE TOPPLE
WHEEZE APICULA CUMSHAW
DERTRUM DOUCEUR GRIFFIN
POINTER WRINKLE APICULUS
BONAMANO ENTOMION FOOTHOLD
GRATUITY
(— OF ANTENNA) ARISTA
(— OF BILLIARD CUE) LEATHER
(— OF BIRD'S BILL) DERTRUM
(— OF FOX'S BRUSH) CHAPE
(— OF SKI) SHOVEL
(— OF SPIDER) BULB
(— OF STAMP) SHOE
(— OF TOE) POINTE
(— OF TONGUE) CORONA
(— OF UMBO) BEAK
(— OF WHEAT KERNEL) BRUSH
(— OF WHIP) SNAPPER
(— ON ORGAN PIPE) TOE
(— OVER) TOP PURL
(— UP) CANT
(ABRUPT —) MUCRO
(BOW —) HORN
(INWARD —) BANK
(LARGE —S) LARGESS LARGESSE
TIPCART COUPE COCOPAN
TIPCAT CAT PIGGY PUSSY KITCAT
PIGGIE
TIPPED BANKED
(EASILY —) CRANK
TIPPER DUMPER THROWER TIPPLER
TIPPET FUR AMICE SCARF ALMUCE
SINDON LIRIPIPE LIRIPOOP
TIPPLE BIB NIP POT SOT DRAM GILL
BIBBER BIBBLE FUDDLE PUDDLE
SIPPLE TIPPLER TOOTHFUL
TIPPLER SOUSE TOAST WINER
BIBBER BOLLER BUBBER DRAMMER
PANURGE POTATOR TUMBLER
WHETTER ALESTAKE MALTWORM
TIPPLING POTTING BIBACITY
BIBATION

TIPSY CUT BOSKY DRUNK FRESH
MUSED TIGHT TOZIE BUMPSY
GROGGY SLEWED SPRUNG EBRIOSE
EBRIOUS EXALTED ELEVATED
MUCKIBUS OVERSEEN PLEASANT
TIP-TOP SWELL TIPPY TOPPING
TIRADE SCREED STOUSH JEREMIAD
TIRE DO FAG HAG LAG BORE CORD
FLAT FLOG JADE KILL MOIL SHOE
LABOR SPARE WEARY CASING
HAGGLE HARASS SICKEN TIRING
TUCKER BALLOON EXHAUST
FATIGUE FRAZZLE TRACHLE
CLINCHER FORSPEND
(— OUT) HAG FLOG THEAD BEJADE
HARASS
(WORN —) CARCASS
TIRED SAD TAM BEAT BOEG DEAD
TIRY BLOWN WEARY AWEARY
BLEARY BUSHED PLAYED TAVERT
FORWORN TAIVERT FATIGATE
FORWAKED
TIREDNESS FATIGUE
TIRESOME DRY DREE FAGGY
ALANGE BORING DREICH PROLIX
IRKSOME PROSAIC TEDIOUS
BORESOME BROMIDIC ENNUYANT
LONGSOME
TIRING DRUDGING
TIRL RISP
TIRTHANKARA JINA
TISAMENUS (FATHER OF —)
ORESTES THERSANDER
(MOTHER OF —) HERMIONE
TISANE PTISAN TILLEUL
TISSUE FAT WEB CORK FOIL PITH
TELA TEXT FACIA GLEBA GRAFT
SUBER TRAMA CALLUS DARTOS
DIPLOE FABRIC FASCIA LIGNUM
PANNUS PHLOEM SHEATH TEXTUS
ADENOID ALBUMEN BINDWEB
CAMBIUM CLYPEUS EPITELA
EXPLANT HYDROME KLEENEX
MESTOME NEURINE PHLOEUM
TEXTURE TWITTER ADHESION
BLASTEMA DESMOGEN ECTODERM
ENDODERM EPIPLOON HISTOGEN
HYPODERM ISOGRAFT MERISTEM
OSTEOGEN PERIDERM PERIDESM
STEREOME
(— OF FUNGUS) CENTRUM
(— SURROUNDING TEETH) GUM
(BLACK —) CLYPEUS
(CONNECTING —) STROMA TENDON
LIGAMENT
(CORK —) SUBER
(FATTY —) LARD GREASE
(HARD —) BONE
(HYPOTHETICAL —) COAGULIN
(LYMPHOID —) TONSIL
(NERVE —) GANGLION
(SOFT —) FLAB
(VEGETABLE —) ARMOR
(WOOD —) LIGNUM VITRAIN
(PL.) CHIRATA CHIRETTA MESODERM
TISWIN TESVINO TEXGUINO
TIT TID MESIA TITTY BLUECAP
COLETIT MUFFLIN
TITAN BANA LETO MAIA ASURA

ATLAS COEUS CREUS CRIOS DIONE
THEIA CRONOS CRONUS PALLAS
PHOEBE TETHYS THEMIS IAPETUS
OCEANUS HYPERION
TITANIC HUGE GREAT TITAN
IMMENSE COLOSSAL GIGANTIC
TITANITE SPHENE GROTHITE
LEDERITE LIGURITE
TITANIUM DIOXIDE ANATASE
TITA ROOT MISHMI MISHMEE
TITHE DIME TEIND TENTH DECIMA
PREBEND TITHING
TITHING BORGH BORROW DECIME
DENARY DECENARY
TITHINGMAN DEAN DECURION
TUTTIMAN
TITHONUS (FATHER OF —)
LAOMEDON
(MOTHER OF —) STRYMO
TITI ORA TEETEE WISTIT SAIMIRI
WISTITI IRONWOOD MARMOSET
ORABASSU OUISTITI
TITILLATE KITTLE TICKLE
TITILLATING GAMY GAMEY
TITLARK PIPIT TEETING
TITLE AGA AYA BAN BEG BEY DAN
DOM DUE FRA JAM LAR MIR PAN
SAG SIR ABBA ABBE AGHA AMIR
ANBA DAME DEVI EMIR FRAY GAON
GRAF HAJI HERR KHAN KNEZ LARS
NAME PANI SIDI SLUG ABGAR
ABUNA AMEER CCOYA CLAIM
CROWN EMEER FRATE GHAZI
GOODY GRACE HADJI HAJJI HAKAM
HANUM HONOR KNIAZ KNYAZ MIRZA
MPRET NAWAB NEGUS NIZAM
PANNA RABBI RIGHT SINGH SOPHI
SOPHY UNWAN BASHAW BEGANI
COUSIN DEGREE DEMAND DESPOT
DOMINE EXARCH HANDLE HUZOOR
LEGEND MADAME MASTER MEHTAR
MISTER PESHWA PREFIX SHERIF
SQUIRE SUFFEE TITULE VIDAME
ALFEREZ ALTESSE ALTEZZA
BAHADUR CANDACE CAPTION
CONVITO CRAWLER DIGNITY
EFFENDI EPITHET ESQUIRE FIDALGO
GAEKWAR GRAVITY HEADING
HIDALGO INFANTE KHEDIVE
MAHARAO MESSIRE RABBONI
SHAREEF TITULUS VOIVODE
BANNERET BASILEUS COMMENDA
CONVIVIO EMINENCE GOSPODIN
HIGHNESS HOLINESS HOSPODAR
INTEREST LOKINDRA MAGISTER
MAHARAJA MAHARANA MAHARSHI
MISTRESS MONSIEUR PADISHAH
PRINCIPE RAUGRAVE SUBTITLE
TAMBURAN TITULADO
(— ACQUISITION) USUCAPT
(— OF BOOK) QUARE
**(— OF MEMBER OF PRIMROSE
LEAGUE)** KNIGHT
(— OF RESPECT) SIR SRI COJA LIEF
MIAN SHRI SIDI BURRA HODJA
KHAJA KHOJA MADAM SAHIB
KHOJAH MADAME MILADY
(BENEDICTINE —) DOM
(MOCK —) IDLESHIP

TITMOUSE MAG NUN TIT MAGG
OXEYE PARUS SPICK FUFFIT HEFFEL
PUFFER TOMTIT VERDIN BLUECAP
BUSHTIT COLETIT COLMOSE
GOLDTIT GRIGNET HAGMALL
JACKSAW MUFFLIN PINCHEM
PINNOCK TINNOCK TITMALL
TOMNOUP CHICADEE HACKMALL
OVENBIRD REEDLING SHABROON
SHARPSAW
TITTER GIGGLE SNICKER TWITTER
TITTLE JOT TITLE MINUTE
TITULAR LEGAL HONORARY
TITYUS (FATHER OF —) TERRA
JUPITER
(MOTHER OF —) ELARA
TIU ER EAR TIW TYR ZIO ZIU TIWAZ
SAXNOT
TIV MUNCHI
TIZZY PUCKER SWIVET SWIVVET
TLAKLIUT ECHE LOOT WISHRAM
TLEPOLEMUS (FATHER OF —)
HERCULES
(MOTHER OF —) ASTYOCHIA
(SLAYER OF —) SARPEDON
TLINGIT SITKA KOLUSH SUMDUM
CHILCAT CHILKAT STIKINE
TMESIS DIACOPE
TNT TROTYL
TO A AD FOR INTO TILL UNTO UPON
(— A CONCLUSION) OUT
(— BE SURE) EVEN
(— BE) IBE
(— COME) BEHIND
(— COMPLETION) DOWN
(— IT) TOOT SESSA
(— PRESS) DOWN
(— SUCH DEGREE) EVEN
(— THAT TIME) UNTIL
(— THE END) AF
(— THE OPPOSITE SIDE) ACROSS
(— THE REAR) ABAFT ASTERN
(— THIS PLACE) HERE HITHER
(— THIS) HERETO
(— VICTORY) ABU ABOO
(— WHAT) WHERETO
(— WIT) NAMELY INNUENDO
SCILICET
TOAD PAD AGUA BUFO FROG HYLA
PIPA PODE HYLID PADDO PADDY
PIPAL PIPID TOADY ANURAN
CRAPON PEEPER BUFONID CHARLIE
CRAPAUD CRAWLER CREEPER
FROGLET GANGREL HOPTOAD
PADDOCK PODDOCK PUDDOCK
QUILKIN REPTILE SERPENT
GANGEREL
TOADFISH SAPO SARPO GRUBBY
SLIMER CABEZON FROGFISH
LORICATE SCORPION
TOADFLAX FLAX FLAXWEED
FLAXWORT FLUELLEN GALLWEED
GALLWORT RAMSTEAD
TOAD RUSH SALTWEED
TOADSTOOL CANKER FUNGUS
TOADY FAWN SUCK TOAD ZANY
COTTON EARWIG FAWNER FLUNKY
GREASE LACKEY FLUNKEY LACQUEY
PLACEBO SHONEEN TRUCKLE

BOOTLICK LICKSPIT PARASITE
TOADYING GNATHONIC
TOADYISM FLUNKISM
TOAST WET TOSS BREDE ROUSE
SKOAL TRINQ BIRSLE BUMPER
CHEERS HEALTH PLEDGE PROSIT
BRISTLE CAROUSE CHEERIO
FRIZZLE LEHAYIM PROFACE
PROPINE RESPECT SLAINTE
WASSAIL BRINDISI
(— AND ALE) SWIG
(— ONESELF) LEEP
(JACOBITE —) LIMP
TOBACCO CANE CAPA HAND LEAF
LUGS NAVY POAK POKE QUID ROLL
SHAG WEED BACCO BACCY BACKY
BROKE CUBAN DARKS FOGUS
PETUN REGIE SMOKE SNOUT TABAC
TWIST BACKER BRIGHT BURLEY
COLORY COWPEN FILLER HAVANA
RETURN TOMBAC TUMBAK CAPORAL
CRACCUS GAGROOT GORACCO
KNASTER LATAKIA NAILROD NICOTIA
ORONOKO PERIQUE PIGTAIL
SOTWEED UPPOWOC CANASTER
HONEYDEW MAKHORKA MARYLAND
NICOTIAN ORONOOKO SEEDLEAF
VIRGINIA
(— AND PAPER) MAKINGS
(— CAKED IN PIPE BOWL) DOTTEL
DOTTLE TOPPER
(— HAVING OFFENSIVE SMELL)
MUNDUNGO
(— IN ROPES) BOGIE
(— JUICE) AMBEER PRAISS
(— MOISTENED WITH MOLASSES)
HONEYDEW
(— MOSAIC) WALLOON
(— PASTE) GORACCO
(— ROOM) PRIZERY
(— WORKER) LOOPER LEAFBOY
LEAFGIRL
(CAKED —) HEEL
(COARSE —) SHAG SCRAP CAPORAL
(CUT —) PICADURA
(DRIED —) TABACUM
(HARD-PRESSED —) NAILROD
(INDIAN —) GAGROOT PUKEWEED
EYEBRIGHT
(INFERIOR —) LUGS
(LADIES' —) CUDWEED
(LOWER LEAVES OF —) FLYING
(PERSIAN —) SHIRAZ TUMBEK
TUMBEKI
(PERUVIAN —) SANA
(POOR QUALITY —) DOGLEG
(PULVERIZED —) SNUFF
(QUID OF —) CUD
(RAW —) LEAF
(ROLLED —) CARROT
(SMALL PIECE OF —) FIG
(VIRGINIA —) COWPEN VIRGINIA
TOBACCO WORM HORNWORM
TOBOGGAN CARIOLE CARRIOLE
TOCHARIAN A AGNEAN
TOCHARIAN B KUCHEAN
TODAY DAY NOW NOWADAYS
TODDLE TOT FADGE DADDLE DIDDLE
DODDLE PADDLE TOTTLE WADDLE

TODDLER TROT GANGREL TROTTIE
TODDY TOD TUBA TERRY SAGWIRE
TO-DO ADO FUSS STIR WORK STINK
DOMENT HOOPLA FLUSTER
FOOSTER FOOFARAW TRAVALLY
TODY ROBIN
TOE TER DIGIT DACTYL HALLUX
MINIMUS TOENAIL POULAINE
(— OF BIRD) HEEL
(LITTLE —) MINIMUS
(PL.) TUN TAIS TOON
TOEPLATE SHOD
TOFF NOB
TOGA GOWN ROBE TOGUE TRABEA
TOGETHER ONCE SAME YFERE
BEDENE INSAME JOINTLY ENSEMBLE
(— WITH) AND INTO
TOGGLE COTTAR COTTER TOGGEL
NETSUKE
TOGO (CAPITAL OF —) LOME
(LANGUAGE OF —) EWE TWI MINA
HAUSA KABRAIS LOTOCOLI
(NATIVE OF —) EWE MINA CABRAI
KABRAI OUATCHI
(RIVER IN —) OTI ANIE HAHO MONO
(TOWN IN —) ANECHO PALIME
SOKODE ATAKPAME
TOIL FAG TUG DARG GRUB HACK
MOIL MUCK PLOD TASK WORK
LABOR SCRAT SLAVE SWINK TWEIL
BILDER DRUDGE EFFORT HAMMER
MITHER MOIDER STRIVE UNRUFE
FATIGUE TRAVAIL TURMOIL
DRUDGERY INDUSTRY
TOILER SLAVE MOILER WORKER
TOILET CAN LOO HEAD JOHN BIFFY
CRAPPER BASEMENT BATHROOM
LAVATORY PLUMBING
TOILSOME HARD SWEATY ARDUOUS
TOILFUL MOILSOME SWEATFUL
TOJOLABAL CHANABAL
TOKAY TUCKTOO
TOKEN BUCK CENT HARP SIGN TYPE
BADGE CHECK INDEX SCRIP BEAVER
CASTOR COLLAR COPPER COUPON
DOLLAR EMBLEM JETTON MARKER
OSTENT REMARK SIGNAL TICKET
WITTER AUSPICE COUNTER
EARNEST INDICIA MEMENTO
PRESAGE SYMPTOM TESSERA
BUNGTOWN COINTISE EVIDENCE
FOOTSTEP FORBYSEN INSTANCE
KEEPSAKE MONUMENT SHILLING
SIGNACLE
(— OF LUCK) HANSEL HANDSEL
(— OF RESPECT) SALUTE
(— OF SUPERIORITY) PALM
(— OF VICTORY) LAUREL
(CANADIAN —) HARP
(LOVE —) DRURY AMORET
(PORCELAIN —S) PI
TOKHARI KUCHEAN
TOLERABLE GAY SOSO PRETTY
TARBLE PATIBLE BEARABLE
PASSABLE PORTABLE
TOLERABLY GAIN GEYAN FAIRLY
MEETLY MEETERLY
TOLERANCE MERCY SHERE LEEWAY
REMEDY

TOLERANT SOFT BENIGN

TOLERATE GO BEAR BIDE HACK
HAVE ABIDE ALLOW BROOK SPARE
STAND STICK ACCEPT ENDURE
PARDON PERMIT SUFFER COMPORT
SUPPORT SUSTAIN

TOLERATION WITHGANG

TOLL JOW TAX JOWL PIKE RENT
KNELL PEAGE CAPHAR EXCISE
PEDAGE PESAGE BOOMAGE
KEELAGE LASTAGE LOCKAGE
MULTURE PASSAGE PICCAGE
PONTAGE SCAVAGE SUMMAGE
TERRAGE TOLLAGE TRONAGE
BERTHAGE STALLAGE WEIGHAGE
WHEELAGE
(PL.) CUSTOMS RAHDARI RATTAREE

TOLLHOUSE TOLLERY

TOLLIKER DUMMY

TOLSEN FOOTSTEP

TOLUENE DILUENT

TOLYL CRESYL

TOMAHAWK HATCHET NEOLITH

TOMATO TOM BERRY BURBANK

TOMB PIR CIST MOLE GRAVE GUACA
HUACA MAZAR SPEOS TABUT
THOLE TURBE BURIAL CHULPA
DARGAH DURGAH GALGAL HEARSE
SAMADH SHRINE SYRINX THOLOS
TROUGH TURBEH CHULLPA
MASTABA OSSUARY TOMBLET
TRITAPH CENOTAPH CISTVAEN
CUBICULO HALLCIST KISTVAEN
MARABOUT MASTABAH MONUMENT
TREASURY
(— OF MOSLEM SAINT) ZIARA
ZIARAT
(CAVE —) SPEOS
(PREHISTORIC —) KURGAN

TOMBAC ORSEDE ORSEDUE

TOMBOY GAMINE HOYDEN TOMRIG

TOMBSTONE SLAT TITLE THROUGH

TOMCAT GIB TOMMY PODGER
THOMAS

TOMCOD GADE GADID SMELT
GADOID WHITING TOMMYCOD

TOMENTUM WOOL

TOMFOOLERY HELL HORSE

TOMMY FOOL PODGER REQUIN

TOMMYROT WAHOO

TOMMY TALKER KAZOO

TOMORROW MANANA MORROW
TOMORN

TOMTATE CAESAR

TON TUN TOUN STYLE

TONALAMATL TZOLKIN

TONALITY KEY

TONE A F DO FA LA MI RE SI SO TI
DOH KEY SOH SOL CALL FLAT NOTE
COLOR COUAC DRONE FIFTH FORTE
PRIME SHARP SIXTH SOUND STYLE
TONUS ACCENT DEGREE FOURTH
SECOND FORMANT MEDIANT
PARTIAL DEMITINT ELEVENTH
FORENOTE HARMONIC SONORITY
(— A DRAWING) STUMP
(— DOWN) DRAB TAME SOFTEN
SUBDUE
(BROKEN —) CRACK

(COMPLEX —) KLANG
(DEEP —) BASS
(DOMINANT —) ANIMUS
(DRAWLING —) DRANT DRAUNT
(KEY —) KEYNOTE
(LOUD —) FORTE
(LOW —) SEMISOUN
(MONOTONOUS —) DRONE
(SHARP NASAL —) TWANG
(SIGNIFICANT —) ACCENT
(SINGLE UNVARIED —) MONOTONE
(STRIDENT —) COUAC
(WHINING —) GIRN

TONGA (CAPITAL OF —) NUKUALOFA
(COIN OF —) PAANGA
(ISLAND OF —) ONO TOFUA VAVAU
HAAPAI
(TOWN OF —) NEIAFU

TONGS SNAPS SERVER FORCEPS
GRAMPUS TUEIRON SCISSORS

TONGUE COG GAB CHIB CLAP KALI
NEAP PAWL POLE REED CLACK
IDIOM VOICE GADABA GLOSSA
KABYLE KALIKA LANGUE LINGUA
SPEECH CLAPPER DIALECT FEATHER
ILOKANO LANGUET DOVETAIL
LANGUAGE LORRIKER PLECTRUM
(— IN FLOORING) SPLINE
(— OF BELL) CLAPPER
(— OF JEW'S-HARP) TANG
(— OF LAND) REACH LANGUE
LANGUET
(— OF OXCART) COPE
(— OF SHOE) FLAP KILTY KILTIE
(— OF VEHICLE) NEAP SHAFT
(BELLOWS —) GUSSET
(GIVE —) PRATE
(GOSSIPING —) CLACK CLACKER
(PIVOTED —) PAWL
(ROMANY —) ROMANES
(PL.) GAURA

TONGUEFISH SOLE

TONGUE-LASH SCOLD

TONGUE-LASHING RAT TOCO
BUSINESS

TONGUE-TIED SILENT

TONIC DO DOH ALOE KEEP PICJI
BRACER SAMBUL SONANT SUMBUL
BONESET CALAMUS CALOMBO
CHIRATA COLOMBA DAMIANA
FUMARIA GENTIAN KEYNOTE
NERVINE SALICIN TONICAL
ANTHEMIS BARBERRY BERBERRY
HELONIAS ROBORANT TRILLIUM

TONICITY MYOTONIA

TONKA BEAN GAIAC CUMARU
GUAIAC COUMAROU

TONNA DOLIUM

TONNAGE PORTAGE

TONSIL ALMOND KERNEL ADENOID
AMYGDAL AMYGDALA

TONSILITIS QUINSY

TONSURE CROWN SHAVE SHEAR
CORONA DIKSHA RASURE

TONSURED PEELED PILLED SHAVED

TOO SO ALSO OVER TROP LUCKY
OVERLY LIKEWISE

TOOL (ALSO SEE IMPLEMENT AND
INSTRUMENT) AX ADZ AWL AXE BIT

BUR DIE DIG GIN GUN HOB KEY LAP
LOY RIP SAW SAX TAP TIT VOL ZAX
ADZE BORE BRAY BURR CLAW
COMB DADO DISC DISK DUPE EDGE
FILE FLAY FROE FROG FROW GAGE
HACK HAWK HONE LEAF LOOM MILL
PICK ROLL SEAX SLED SNAP SPID
SPUD STOP TAMP TIER VISE AUGER
BLADE BORAL BORER BRAKE
BRAND BREAK BRUSH BURIN DARBY
DOLLY DRIFT DRILL DUMMY EDGER
FLAKE FLOAT FLUTE GAUGE GOUGE
GUIDE HARDY HOBBY HOWEL KNIFE
KNURL LEVEL MAKER MODEL PLANE
POINT PRUNT PUNCH QUIRK SABER
SABRE SCREW SHAVE SHELL SLICE
SLICK SNIPE SPADE SPEAR SPLIT
STAKE STAMP STING STOCK STRIG
STYLE SWAGE TEWEL TOYLE UPSET
VALET WAGON BEADER BEATER
BIFACE BLADER BODKIN BROACH
BUFFER CALKER CHASER CHISEL
CLEAVE COGGLE COLTER CRADLE
CRANNY CUTTER DEVICE DIBBLE
DIGGER DOCTOR DRIVER ENGINE
FASCET FERRET FILLET FLANGE
FLORET FLUTER FORMER FRAISE
FULLER GIMLET GLAZER GOFFER
GRAVER GUMMER HACKER HAMMER
HEMMER HOGGER HOLDER HULLER
JIGGER JUMPER LADKIN LASTER
LIFTER NIBBER PALLET PARTER
PICKAX PICKER PLIERS PROPER
PUPPET REAMER RIPPER ROCKER
RUNNER SAPPER SCRIBE SEATER
SHAPER SHAVER SHEARS SHOVEL
SKIVER SLATER SOCKET SQUARE
STYLET STYLUS SWIVEL TAGGER
TASTER TONGUE TREPAN TURNER
TURREL TWILLY VEINER WAGGON
WIGWAG WIMBLE WORDLE WORMER
YANKEE ABRADER BLOCKER
CALIPER CAULKER CHAMFER
CHIPPER CHOPPER CLEANER
CLEAVER COULTER CREASER
DIAMOND DOLABRA DRESSER
FISTUCA FLANGER FREEZER
FROTTON GRAINER GROOVER
GRUBBER GUDGEON JOINTER
KNOTTER LOGHEAD MITERER
POINTEL POINTER PROFILE RIVETER
ROUGHER ROUNDER SCAUPER
SCORPER SCRIBER SCRIVER
SCURFER SLASHER SLEEKER
SLICKER SPLAYER SPUDDER
STEMMER STRIKER STROKER
TICKLER TREBLET TWIBILL UPRIGHT
WRAITHE BIFACIAL BILLHOOK
BOOTJACK BURGOYNE CALLIPER
CREATURE CRIPPLER CROSSCUT
CROWFOOT DUCKFOOT ELEVATOR
EXPANDER FLOUNDER GRAVETTE
GRIFFAUN POLISHER PRITCHEL
PROPERTY PUNCHEON RAVEHOOK
RECAPPER SCRAPPLE SCULPTOR
SPLITTER STIPPLER STRICKLE
STRINGER SURFACER THWACKER
TOLLIKER WARKLOOM WORKLOOM
SCRATCHER

(— A BOOK) FINISH
(PL.) TEW FISH GEAR TRADE
CUTLERY GIBBLES PIONERY
ENGINERY
TOOLED GOFFERED
(— WITHOUT GILDING) BLIND
TOOLHOLDER TURRET MONITOR
TOOLSHED DOGHOUSE
TOON LIM CEDAR TOONWOOD
TOOT BLOW TOWT BLAST SOUND
TRUMPET
TOOTH BIT COG GAM JAG PEG DENS
DENT FANG LEAF RASP SNAG TIND
TINE TUSH TUSK IVORY MOLAR
PEARL PRONG RAKER TENON
BROACH CANINE CUSPID CUTTER
DENTAL INDENT JOGGLE TRIGON
TRITOR DENTILE DIVIDER GRINDER
INCISOR LATERAL SURDENT
UNCINUS ABUTMENT BICUSPID
BLEPHARA DENTICLE EYETOOTH
GAGTOOTH MARGINAL PREMOLAR
SAWTOOTH SPROCKET TOOTHLET
TRIGONID
(— OF A MOSS) BLEPHARA
(— OF HORSE) DIVIDER
(— OF MOLLUSC) MARGINAL
(— OF PINION) LEAF
(— OF RADULA) UNCINUS
(— ON ROTATING PIECE) WIPER
(ARTIFICIAL —) DUMMY PONTIL
(CANINE —) CUSPID HOLDER
LANIARY CYNODONT DOGTOOTH
EYETOOTH
(GEAR —) COG GUB DENT
ADDENDUM SPROCKET
(HARROW —) TINE
(MOLAR —) WANG
(UPPER SURFACE OF —) TABLE
TOOTHACHE WORM DENTAGRA
TOOTHED SERRATE VIRGATE
SERRATED
TOOTHLESS GUMMY
TOOTHPICK QUILL ARKANSAN
TOOTHWORT CROWTOE COOLWORT
TOP CAP COP GIG TAP TIP ACME
APEX BEAT COCK CULM HEAD HELM
ROOF SKIM STOP BLOOM CHIEF
COVER CREST CROWN FANCY
GIGGE RIDGE SPIRE STRIP TOTUM
TRUMP UPPER CALASH CAPOTE
CULMEN SUMMIT UPWARD VERTEX
SPINNER ROUNDTOP SURMOUNT
TEETOTUM
(— FOR CHIMNEY OR PIPE) COWL
HOOD
(— OF ALTAR) MENSA
(— OF AUTOMOBILE) HEAD HOOD
(— OF CAPSTAN) DRUMHEAD
(— OF FURNACE) ARCH
(— OF GLASS) PRETTY
(— OF HEAD) MOLD PATE MOULD
SCALP VERTEX
(— OF HELMET) SKULL
(— OF HILL) KNAG KNAP KNOLL
(— OF INGOT) CROPHEAD
(— OF MOUNTAIN) MAN
(— OF PLANT OR TREE) CROP
(— OF ROOF) DECK

(— OF SPINDLE) COCKHEAD
(— OF THUNDERCLOUD) INCUS
(— OF WOODEN STAND) CRISS
(—S OF CROP) SHAW
(BOOT —) RUFF
(BOX —) COUPON
(CARRIAGE —) CALASH
TOPAZ PYCNITE PYCNIUM
TOPCOAT OVERCOAT SIPHONIA
TOPE DHER DHERI STUPA SOUPFIN
TOPER BOUSER CUPMAN POTMAN
POTTER SIPPER SUPPER TROUGH
BOMBARD POTLING SWILLER
TOSSPOT BLACKPOT DRUNKARD
MALTWORM
TOPI TIANG
TOPIC HARE ITEM TEXT HOBBY
THEMA THEME BURDEN GAMBIT
GROUND MATTER SUBJECT
OCCASION
TOPKNOT ONKOS TOPPING
TOPMAN COB
TOPMINNOW GUPPY LIMIA GULARIS
HELLERI SAILFIN GAMBUSIA
TOPOGRAPHIC TERRAIN
TOPPLE TOP TILT LEVEL TOTTLE
TOPSAIL RAFFE RAFFEE
TOPSOIL KELLY
TOPSTONE CAPSTONE
TOPSWARM TOPCAST
TOPSY-TURVY COCKEYED
REELRALL
TOQUE ZATI MUNGA MACACO
RILAWA MACAQUE
TOQUILLA JIPIJAPA
TORCEL BURN BERNE BORNE
TORCH DUCK JACK LAMP LINK LUNT
PINE WASE WISP BLAZE BRAND
FLARE MATCH FOCKLE LAMPAD
MASHAL MUSSAL BRANDON
CRESSET GRIDDLE LUCIGEN
ROUGHIE TORCHET FLAMBEAU
TORCHBEARER KERYX LINKBOY
LINKMAN DADUCHUS TORCHMAN
TOREADOR TORERO CAPEADOR
TORIL CHIQUERO
TORMENT WO TAW TRY WOE BAIT
BALE FRET MOIL PAIN PANG PINE
RACK TUCK CHEVY CURSE DEVIL
GRILL HARRY SCALD TEASE TWIST
WRING CHIVVY HARASS HARROW
HECTOR INFEST PLAGUE TRAVEL
AFFLICT BEDEVIL CRUCIFY HAGRIDE
HATCHEL MALISON PERPLEX
PINDING TERRIFY TORTURE TRAVAIL
DISTRAIN LACERATE MACERATE
(EXTREME —) AGONY
TORMENTED CRUCIATE
TORMENTIL SEPTFOIL
TORMENTING PLAGUY
TORMINA TORSION
TORN RENT BROKEN BLASTED
TORNADO VORTEX CYCLONE
TRAVADO TWISTER
TORPEDO FISH SHELL SQUIB BATOID
TORPID FOUL NUMB BROSY INERT
SODDEN STUPID TOGGER LANGUID
TORPENT COMATOSE COMATOUS
SLUGGISH

TORPIFY DAZE ETHERIZE
TORPOR COMA SLEEP SWOON
ACEDIA SLUMBER LETHARGY
TORQUE BEE SARPE TWIST
TORRENT FLOW RUSH FLOOD SPATE
STREAM NIAGARA
TORREYA SAVIN TUMION
TORRID HOT SULTRY BOILING
TORSALO BERNE
TORSION STRESS DIDROMY
TORT LIBEL WRONG
TORTE DOBOS
TORT-FEASOR ACTOR
TORTICOLLIS WRYNECK
TORTILLA TOSTADO
TORTOISE EMYD BEKKO GAPER
COOTER GOPHER TURTLE EMYDIAN
HICATEE MUNGOFA TESTUDO
GALAPAGO KASHYAPA SHELLPAD
SHELLPOT TERRAPIN
TORTOISESHELL CAREY
TORTUOUS CRANKY SCREWY
SINUATE WRIGGLY SINUATED
TORTURE TAW BOOT CARD FIRE
PAIN PANG PINE RACK AGONY
SCREW TWIST ENGINE EXTORT
IMPALE MARTYR AFFLICT AGONIZE
BOOTING CRUCIFY PERPLEX
TORMENT
TORTURER BOURREAU
TORUS CORK TORE BASTON BOLTEL
BOUTELL BOWTELL THALAMUS
TORY BANDIT OUTLAW ROBBER
PEELITE TANTIVY LOYALIST
TOSS COB LAB SHY BUNG CANT
CAST CAVE DOSS FLAP FLIP HIKE
PASS SHAG SLAT TOUT CHAFE
CHUCK FLICK FLING FLIRT FLURR
HEAVE TEAVE THROW BETOSS
BOUNCE DANDLE TOTTER WALTER
WELTER WENTLE BLANKET TURMOIL
WAMPISH WHEMMEL
(— A COIN) SKY
(— A JACK) LAG
(— ABOUT) SWAB TAVE POPPLE
THRASH THRESH TORFLE WAMPISH
(— ASIDE) BANDY
(— AWAY) BLOW
(— HEAD) CAVE GECK
(— OF THE HEAD) HEEZE
(— OFF) SWAP SWOP
(— ON WAVES) SURGE
(— TO AND FRO) WALK
(— TOGETHER CONFUSEDLY)
SCRAMBLE
(— WITH THE HORNS) DOSS HIKE
TOSSING SURGING
(— OF BULLFIGHTER) COGIDA
TOSTAO TESTON
TOTAL SUM TOT DEAD MERE TALE
COUNT GROSS MOUNT SUMMA
UTTER WHOLE ENTIRE GLOBAL
OMNIUM SUMMED TOTTLE EMBRACE
FOOTING GENERAL PERFECT
ABSOLUTE COMPLETE ENTIRETY
SURMOUNT TEETOTAL
TOTALITY ALL BODY HEAP BEING
ALLNESS ECOLOGY ETERNITY

HUMANITY INTEGRAL INTERVAL
OMNITUDE
TOTALLY COLD GOOD QUITE
WHOLLY
TOTEM HUACA
TOTTER TOT ROCK TOIT WALT
SHAKE WAVER COGGLE DODDER
DOTTER FALTER JOGGLE STAVER
SWERVE TITTER TOTTLE WAMBLE
WANGLE WAPPER BRANDLE FRIBBLE
STAGGER TREMBLE WHITHER
TITUBATE
TOTTERING SHAKY GROGGY
CRAMBLY PALSIED RICKETY
TOTTERY TITUBANT WAMBLING
TOUCAN TOCO TUCANA ARACARI
TOUCH GET RAP TAG TIG TIP ABUT
BILL DASH FEEL HAND KISS KNEE
MEET PALP PEAL PLAY RAKE RINE
TACT TAKE GLISK GRAZE GROPE
SPICE TAINT TASTE TATTO TINGE
TRAIT TREAT AFFECT ATTAIN
CARESS FINGER GLANCE HANDLE
REGARD SCRUFF SMUTCH STRAIN
TACTUS TWITCH ATTAINT ATTINGE
CONTACT FEELING SOUPCON
TACTION FLOURISH TINCTURE
(— A KEY) STRIKE
(— BRIEFLY) GLANCE
(— CARESSINGLY) FLATTER
(— CLOSELY) IMPINGE
(— GENTLY) DAB TAT TICK BRUSH
(— LIGHTLY) GRAZE SCUFF SKIFF
(— OF BRUSH) HAND
(— OF COLOR) EYE
(— OF PAINT) GLOB
(— OF PLEASURE) GLISK
(— RIGHTLY) NICK
(DELICATE —) STROKE
(FINISHING —) HOODER COPESTONE
(SLIGHT —) SKIFF SMATCH
TOUCHDOWN ROUGE
TOUCHED FEY DOTTY
TOUCHING ABOUT LIBANT TENDER
AGAINST CONTACT TANGENT
ADJACENT POIGNANT
(— LIGHTLY) LAMBENT
TOUCHSTONE TEST TOUCH LYDITE
BASANITE STANDARD
TOUCHWOOD FUNK MONK PUNK
SPUNK PUNKWOOD
TOUCHY HUFFY MIFFY SNAKY
FEISTY KITTLE SNAKEY SNUFFY
SPUNKY TENDER TETCHY GROUCHY
NERVOUS PEEVISH TEMPERY
TICKLISH
TOUGH RUM BHOY HARD TAUT WIRY
CLUNG HARDY STIFF STOUT WITHY
KNOTTY SINEWY STARCH STRONG
HICKORY BULLYBOY LEATHERY
UNTENDER
TOUGHEN TAW ANNEAL ENDURE
HARDEN TEMPER
TOUGHENED CLUNG
TOUGHNESS TUCK FIBER FIBRE
STRENGTH TENACITY
TOUPEE RUG DOILY SCALP
POSTICHE TOPPIECE
TOUR GIRO TURN SWING TOWER

TURUS JUNKET SAFARI JOURNEY
INVASION PROGRESS TOURETTE
(— OF DUTY) HERD STATION
(CANARY —) GLUCK GLUCKE
TOURACO LORY LOURIE TURAKOO
TOURBILLON KARRUSEL
TOUR DE FORCE STUNT
TOURIST TOURER TRIPPER VISITANT
TOURMALINE SHORL SCHORL
DRAVITE ACHROITE SIBERITE
TOURNAMENT TILT JOUSTS
TOURNEY BONSPIEL CAROUSEL
TOURNEUR DEALER
TOURNEY PLAY
TOURNIQUET GARROT STANCH
TWISTER STANCHER TORCULAR
TOUSLE SOOL SOWL RUMPLE
TOOZLE
TOUSLED TOWZIE TUMBLED
UNKEMPT
TOUT SKIV BRUIT PLIER STEERER
TOW CRIB HAUL PULL HURDS STUPE
TRACK TRACT CODILLA CORDELLE
TOWAGE TRACKAGE
TOWAI BIRCH KAMAHI
TOWARD AD INTO TORT ANENT
ANENST AGAINST FORNENT
ADVERSUS GAINWARD
(— CENTER OF EARTH) DOWN
(— CENTER) CENTRAD
(— ONE SIDE) ASLANT
(— THE END) SF
(— THE HEAD) ANTERIOR
(— THE REAR) ABACK DORSAD
BACKWARD
(— THE RIGHT) DEXTRAD
(— THE SIDE) LATERAD
(— THE STERN) AFTER
TOWEL CLOUT WIPER DIAPER
LAVABO RUBBER
TOWER TOR PEEL PIKE REAR RISE
SOAR SPUR TOUR BABEL BROCH
HEAVE MINAR MOUNT PYLON SIKAR
SPIRE STUPA TEXAS ASCEND
ASPIRE BELFRY CASTLE CHULPA
DOKHMA DONJON GOPURA ROLLER
RONDÉL SPRING TURRET BASTIDE
CHULLPA DERRICK GIRALDA
LANTERN MIRADOR NURAGHE
SHIKARA SHIKHARA STEEPLE
TALAYOT TORREON TOURNEL
TRACKER TURRION BARBICAN
BASTILLE CLOGHEAD DOMINEER
RONDELLE SCRUBBER TOURELLE
TOWERLET
(— CONTAINING COKE) SCRUBBER
(— FOR SENTINEL) GUERITE
(— OF FORT) SPUR
(— OF MOSQUE) MINARET
(— OF SILENCE) DAKHMA
(— ON SUMMIT) PIKE
(— OVER) DROWN BESTRIDE
(ATTACHED —) DETAIL
(BELL —) CARILLON
(CONNING —) SAIL
(FRACTIONATING —) STILL
(PYRAMIDAL —) SIKAR VIMANA
SHIKARA SIKHARA
(SIGNAL —) BANTAYAN

(WIND —) BADGIR
TOWERING EMINENT SUPERNAL
AMBITIOUS
TOWERMAN LEVERMAN
TOWER MUSTARD CRUCIFER
TOWHEE JOREE CHEWINK CHEEWINK
TOWING TRACKAGE
TOWLINE CORDELLE
TOWN BY BYE HAM WON CAMP CITY
STAD WENE WICK BAYAN BOURH
BRUGH BURGH DERBY MACHI
PLACE PLECK SIEGE STAND STEAD
VILLE CIUDAD HAMMON ORANGE
PUEBLO STAPLE BASTIDE BOROUGH
CHESTER OPPIDUM QUIVIRA
TOWNLET BOOMTOWN BOURGADE
ENCEINTE HOMETOWN TOWNSHIP
(DESOLATED —) GUBAT
(FORTIFIED —) BURG BURGH
ENCEINTE
(MYTHICAL —) QUIVIRA
(SMALL —) SHTETL SHTETEL
(UNFORTIFIED —) BOURGADE
(WALLED —) CHESTER
(PL.) PARGANA
TOWN HALL HALL CABILDO
RATHAUS TOLBOOTH STADHOUSE
TOWNSHIP DEME DORP VILL BAYAN
TREEN BOROUGH
TOWNSMAN CAD CIT SNOB TOWNY
TOWNEE BURGHER CITIZEN
COCKNEY OPPIDAN
(PL.) BURGWARE
TOWROPE TOW GUNLINE TOWLINE
CORDELLE
TOXALBUMIN ROBIN PHALLIN
TOXEMIA BLACKLEG ECLAMPSIA
TOXIC VENOMOUS
TOXIN BOTULIN EXOTOXIN
TOY DIE GAY TOP COCK DOLL FOOL
MOVE PLAY BLOCK DALLY FLIRT
HAPPY KNACK LAKIN PLAID SPORT
TRICK WALLY BAUBLE DANDLE
DOODLE FADDLE FINGER FIZGIG
GEWGAW LAKING PRETTY PUPPET
RATTLE SUCKER BLOWOUT CRICKET
DREIDEL PLAYOCK TANGRAM
TRINKET TUMBLER WHIZZER
GIMCRACK KICKSHAW PINWHEEL
SQUAWKER SQUEAKER TEETOTUM
WINDMILL ZOETROPE
(— AMOROUSLY) MIRD
(— WITH) PADDLE
(FLYING —) PIGEON
TOYON TOLLON CHAMISO
TRACE RUN TUG WAD CAST ECHO
HINT LICK MARK RACK SHOW SIGN
STEP TANG TINT TROD BRING
GHOST GLEAM GLIFF GRAIN PRINT
SHADE SPOOR STAMP STEAD THEAT
TINGE TOUCH TRACK TRACT TRAIL
TRAIN TRESS DERIVE ENGRAM
HARBOR LACING RESENT SHADOW
SKETCH SMUTCH STRAIN STREAK
SWATHE COCKEYE GLIMPSE
MENTION REMNANT SOUPCON
SURMISE SYMPTOM THOUGHT
UMBRAGE VESTIGE WHISPER
DESCRIBE ENGRAMMA FOOTSTEP

SKERRICK TINCTURE WAINROPE
(— A BEE) COURSE
(— A CURVE) SWEEP
(— A DESIGN) CALK
(— MATHEMATICALLY) GENERATE
(— OF A HARE) FARE
(— ON CHART) PRICK
(— THE COURSE OF) DEDUCE
(HARNESS —) TUG THEAT TREAT
(MEMORY —) ENGRAM ENGRAMME
(SLIGHT —) GHOST STAIN SMATCH
SPARKLE
(SLIGHTEST —) SCINTIL
(PL.) FEUTE
TRACER SEEKER OUTLINER
SEARCHER
TRACERY FANWORK FROSTING
TRAILERY
TRACHEA ARTERY WINDPIPE
(— OF CRANE) TRUMP
TRACHEID HYDROID
TRACHYANDESITE ARSOITE
VULSINITE
TRACHYTE PIPERNO
TRACING BAROGRAM POLYGRAM
TRAILING
TRACK DOG PUG RAT RUT TAN WAD
WAY CLEW CLUE DRAW FARE FOIL
FOOT HUNT LANE MARK PAGE PATH
PIST RACE RACK RAIK RAIL ROAD
SHOE SLOT SPUR TROD VENT
BLOCK CHUTE DRIFT FEUTE HOUND
LODGE PISTE PLANE SLIDE SPACE
SPOOR STEAD SWATH TRACE
TRACT TRADE TRAIL TRAIN TREAD
BEARER COURSE GROOVE HARBOR
LADDER RETURN RUNWAY SIDING
SLEUTH STRAIN SWATHE CHANNEL
FOILING FOOTING PATHWAY
TANGENT TRAFFIC VESTIGE
BACKBONE FOOTSTEP GUIDEWAY
TRANSFER TRECKPOT TREKPATH
WAGONWAY
(— FOR ROPE) CHANNEL
(— GAME) DRAW
(— OF DEER) SLOT STRAIN
(— OF GAME IN GRASS) FOILING
(— OF HARE) FILE
(— OF WOUNDED BEAST) PERSUE
(— ON PRINTING PRESS) BANK
BEARER
(RAILROAD —) LEAD SPUR STUB
SIDING TANGENT APPROACH
BACKBONE
(RUNNING —) FLAT CINDERS
(SHORT BRANCH —) RETURN
(SIDE —) LIE HOLE
(SKATER'S —) FLAT
(TEMPORARY —) SHOOFLY
(WORM —) NEREITE
TRACKER PUGGI PUGGY TRAILER
TRAILMAN
TRACKLESS INVIOUS PATHLESS
TRACKMAN SPIKER
TRACT AREA BEAT DUAR FLAT ZONE
CAMPO COAST DRIVE ESSAY FIELD
GRABE HORST PATCH SWEEP
TRACK BARONY BUNDLE EXTENT
REGION ENCLAVE EURIPUS

QUARTER ROYALTY TERRAIN
TRACTUS BROCHURE CAMPAGNA
CAMPAIGN CINGULUM DISTRICT
FARMHOLD FORESTRY PAMPHLET
PROVINCE TOWNSITE TREATISE
(— KEPT IN NATURAL STATE) PARK
(— OF BARREN LAND) BARREN
DERELICT
(— OF GRASSLAND) PRAIRIE
(— OF LAND) CRU DOAB DUAB
DUAR GORE MARK BLOCK CHASE
CLAIM EJIDO FRITH GRANT LAINE
SCOPE SWELL EIGHTY ESTATE
FOREST GARDEN ISLAND POLDER
STRATH AIRPORT QUILLET RESERVE
TERRAIN BOUNDARY CLEARING
DERELICT FARMHOLD INTERVAL
SCABLAND SLASHING
(— OF MUDDY GROUND) SLOB
(— OF OPEN UPLAND) DOWN
DOWNS
(— OF UNCOVERED ICE) GLADE
(— OF WASTE LAND) HEATH
(BOGGY —) RUNN MORASS
(CLAYEY —) TAKYR
(CLEARED —) JUM JHUM JOOM
(DRY —) SEARING
(FORESTLESS —) STEPPE
(GENITAL —) BEARING
(IRREGULAR —) GORE
(OPEN —) VEGA SLASH
(SANDY —) DEN DENE
(SWAMPY —) FLOW BAYGALL
(UNOCCUPIED AND UNCULTIVATED
—) DESERT
(WATERLESS —) THIRST
TRACTABLE EASY SOFT BUXOM
TAWIE DOCILE GENTLE TOWARD
DUCTILE FLEXILE AMENABLE
FLEXIBLE GUIDABLE TOWARDLY
YIELDING
TRACTARIANISM PUSEYISM
TRACTION DRAFT DRAUGHT
TRACTOR CAT MULE DRAGON
BOBTAIL CRAWLER PEDRAIL
(TRAILER —) RIG
TRADE CHAP CHOP COUP DEAL SELL
SWAP CHEAP CRAFT GRAFT PRICE
TREAD TROKE TRUCK BAKERY
BARTER CHANGE EMPLOY HANDLE
MISTER NIFFER OCCUPY SCORCE
SCORSE BARGAIN CALLING
CHAFFER FACULTY MYSTERY
SCIENCE BUSINESS CABOTAGE
EXCHANGE
TRADEMARK CHOP MARK BRAND
COUPON
TRADER SART BANYA PLIER BALIJA
CHETTY DEALER MONGER NEPMAN
TROKER CHAPMAN MARWARI
SANGLEY TRUCKER ASTORIAN
CHANDLER KURVEYOR MERCHANT
OPERATOR
(HORSE —) JOCKEY
(INEXPERIENCED —) LAMB
TRADESMAN CIT BAKAL COOPER
EGGLER SELLER TENSOR FRUITER
GOLADAR OCCUPIER UPHOLDER
TRADESWOMAN WINSTER

TRADITION CABAL STORY SUNNA
CABALA SMRITT SUNNAH THREAP
HALACHA HALAKAH HEREDITY
HERITAGE TRANSFER
(PL.) LEGEND
TRADITIONAL CLASSIC
TRADUCE ILL SLUR ABUSE DEFAME
MALIGN VILIFY ASPERSE DETRACT
TRAFFIC COUP DEAL MANG MART
MONG BROKE TRADE BARTER
PALTER TRAVEL CHAFFER DEALING
BUSINESS CHAFFERY COMMERCE
EXCHANGE
(— IN SACRED THINGS) SIMONY
(— IN SLAVES) MAGONIZE
TRAFFICKER COUPER DEALER
TRAGEDY BUSKIN TRAGIC TROIADES
TRAGIC DIRE DREADFUL THESPIAN
TRAGICOMEDY DRAME
TRAGOPAN MONAL
TRAGUS EARLET
TRAIL PAD PUG DRAG FOIL HARL
HUNT NECK PATH PIST SLOT BLAZE
CRAWL DRAIL PISTE ROUTE SPOOR
STOCK SWEEP TRACE TRADE TRAIN
COMING DAGGLE FOLLOW RUNWAY
SHADOW SLEUTH STRAIN TAIGLE
TRAPES DRAGGLE TRAFFIC
OUTRAIL STRIGGLE TRAILERY
(— ALONG) STREEL TRAPES
(— OF A FISH) LOOM
(— OUT) STREAM
(— THROUGH MUD) DAGGLE
(DESCENDING —) BAHADA BAJADA
(MOUNTAIN —) CLIMB
(WAGON —) RUDLOFF
TRAILBLAZER HARBINGER
TRAILER SEMI COACH BOXCAR
CARAVAN FLATBED FROGGER
GONDOLA
TRAIN SET DRAG GAIT SECT TILL
TURN ZULU BEARD BREED COACH
DRESS DRILL ENTER FOCUS LOCAL
RANGE TRACE TRACT TRADE TRAIL
TRYNE DIRECT GENTLE GROUND
INFORM MANURE NUZZLE RAPIDE
REPAIR SCHOOL SEASON STRING
SUBWAY AFFAITE BRIGADE
CARAVAN EDUCATE FREIGHT
GEARING LIMITED PEDDLER
RATTLER RETINUE SHUTTLE
VARNISH CIVILIZE DISCIPLE
ELECTRIC EQUIPAGE EXERCISE
HIGHBALL INSTRUCT MANIFEST
REHEARSE
(— AN ANIMAL) BREAK
(— FINE) GAUNT
(— FOR FIGHTING) SPAR
(— OF ANIMALS) COFFLE
(— OF ATTENDANTS) CORTEGE
(— OF COMET) TAIL
(— OF EXPLOSIVE) FUSE
(— OF MINING CARS) JAG RUN TRIP
(FUNERAL —) CONVOY
(PACK —) CONDUCTA
(RAILROAD —) DRAG HOOK LOCAL
PICKUP EXPRESS FREIGHT LIMITED
RATTLER

TRAINED GOOD MADE ADEPT BROKE
BROKEN
TRAINEE BOOT CADET
TRAINER FEEDER JINETE LANISTA
TRAINING DRILL THEAT ASCESIS
ASKESIS CULTURE NURTURE
PAIDEIA BREEDING
(— IN HUMANITIES) CIVILITY
(— OF HORSE) DRESSAGE
(RELIGIOUS —) SADHANA
TRAIT ITEM LEAD MARK VEIN ANGLE
CHARM KNACK TRACT AMENITY
ELEMENT HALLMARK JAPANISM
(CULTURE —) SURVIVAL
(FOREIGN —) EXOTISM
(GOOD —) THEW
(UNDESIRABLE —) DEMON DAEMON
(WELL-DEFINED —) STREAK
(PL.) CORNERS
TRAITOR JUDAS RUSTY WARLOCK
ISCARIOT PRODITOR SQUEALER
TRADITOR TREACHER
TRAITOROUS FALSE FELON
TRAJECTORY SPORABOLA
TRA-LA-LA TRALIRA
TRAM TUB DRAM TRAMCAR
TRAMMEL TRANVIA
(SET OF —S) JOURNEY
TRAMCAR TRAM DUMMY PICKUP
TRAMMEL TRAM HAMPER STIFLE
COTTEREL
TRAMMER PUTTER
TRAMONTANE OVERBERG
TRAMP BO BUM PAD BOOM HAKE
HIKE HOBO HUMP PUNK SLOG
SWAG VAMP WALK YEGG BURLY
CAIRD CLAMP JAVEL PIKER SHACK
STIFF STRAG TRAIK TRAIL TRASH
TROMP TROUT BAGMAN GAYCAT
JOCKER PICARO STODGE STRAMP
STROLL TINKER TRANCE TRAPES
TRUANT TRUDGE DRUMMER
FLOATER RUFFLER SWAGGER
SWAGMAN TRAIPSE TRAMPLE
TROUNCE TROWANE YEGGMAN
FOOTSLOG GANGEREL STROLLER
TRAVELER VAGABOND SUNDOWNER
(— ABOUT) WAG
(LONG —) HUMP
(PL.) MONKERY
TRAMPING MONKERY
TRAMPLE HOX JAM PUG FARE FOIL
FULL HOOF CHAMP SCAUT SPURN
TRAMP TRASH TREAD DEFOIL
DEFOUL PADDLE SAVAGE STOACH
STRAMP WADDLE OPPRESS
OVERRUN SCAMBLE FORTREAD
OVERRIDE
TRANCE RAPTUS AMENTIA ECSTASY
SAMADHI
TRANQUIL CALM COOL EASY LOWN
MILD SOFT EQUAL QUIET STILL
GENTLE PACATE PIPING SERENE
CALMATO EQUABLE PACIFIC
RESTFUL PEACEFUL
TRANQUILIZE CALM LULL QUIET
STILL BECALM PACIFY SERENE
SETTLE SOFTEN SOOTHE APPEASE
COMPOSE

TRANQUILIZING SOOTHING
TRANQUILLITY KEF LEE EASE REST
PEACE SATTVA SERENE HARMONY
QUIETAGE QUIETUDE SERENITY
TRANS ANTI
TRANSACT DO PASS AGITATE
CONDUCT PERFORM
TRANSACTION DEAL GAGE GAGER
ACTION AFFAIR MARGIN SPREAD
BARGAIN MOHABAT PASSAGE
CONTRACT KNOCKOUT
(PL.) ACTA BUSINESS
TRANSCEND PASS SOAR EXCEED
OVERTOP SURPASS
TRANSCENDENTAL ACOSMIC
TRANSCENDING EXQUISITE
TRANSCRIBE COPY BRAILLE
DESCRIBE EXSCRIBE
TRANSCRIBED CANNED
TRANSCRIBER COPIER COPYIST
TRANSCRIPT COPY SCORE TENOR
DOUBLE APOGRAPH EXSCRIPT
TRANSCRIPTION(PL.) PAZAND
PAZEND
TRANSEPT PLAGE PORCH
TRANSFER CEDE DEED FLIT GIVE
SALE SELL TURN CABLE CARRY
CROSS DROGH REFER REMIT SHIFT
ASSIGN ATTORN CHANGE DECANT
DELATE DONATE REMOVE SWITCH
CESSION CONNECT CONSIGN
DELIVER DEVOLVE DISPONE
MIGRATE TRADUCE ALIENATE
ANTEDATE CROCKING DELEGATE
DELIVERY DONATION EXCHANGE
TRANSACT TRANSUME VIREMENT
(— DYE) EXHAUST
(— HEAT) CONVECT
(— HOMAGE) ATTORN
(— MOLTEN GLASS) LADE
(— OF ENERGY) FLOW
(— OF PROPERTY) DEED GIFT
GRANT DISPOSAL
(— PIGMENT) FLUSH
TRANSFERENCE DEMISE EMOTION
REMOVAL DELATION DISPOSAL
TRANSFER
TRANSFIGURE DEIFY CLARIFY
TRANSFIX FIX DART PITCH STAKE
STICK SKEWER THRILL
TRANSFORM TURN SHIFT TOUCH
CHANGE STRIKE CONVERT FASHION
PERMUTE CATALYZE DISGUISE
HETERIZE
(— ENERGY) ABSORB
TRANSFORMATION CHANGE
HAIRWORK
TRANSFORMER SET DIMMER
JIGGER TEASER VARIAC BALANCE
BOOSTER HEDGEHOG
TRANSFUSE ENDUE INDUE
TRANSGRESS ERR SIN BREAK
OFFEND OVERGO DIGRESS DISOBEY
VIOLATE INFRINGE OVERPASS
OVERSLIP OVERSTEP
TRANSGRESSION SIN SLIP CRIME
FAULT SCAPE BREACH DELICT
ESCAPE MISDEED OFFENSE
DELICTUM OVERLOUP TRESPASS

TRANSGRESSOR SINNER OFFENDER
TRANSIENCE FUGACITY
TRANSIENT FLIGHTY PASSING
FLEETING FUGITIVE
TRANSIENTLY HOVERLY
TRANSIT BINOCLE PASSAGE
TRANSEPT
TRANSITION CUT JUMP LEAP SEGUE
SHIFT FERMENT PASSAGE
TRANSITORINESS CADUCITY
TRANSITORY FLEET CADUCE FLYING
BRITTLE PASSANT PASSING SLIDING
VOLATIC WHILEND CADUCOUS
FLEETING FLITTING TEMPORAL
VOLATILE
TRANSLATE DRAW MAKE TURN
WEND RENDER CONVERT ENGLISH
EXPOUND TRADUCE CONSTRUE
INTERPRET
TRANSLATION CAB KEY CRIB PONY
STEP TROT GLOSS HORSE TARGUM
UNSEEN BICYCLE CABBAGE
ENGLISH THARGUM TRADUCT
VERSION SUBTITLE VERBATIM
(— OF THE CLASSICS) JACK
(LOAN —) CALQUE
TRANSLATOR TURNER
TRANSLUCENT CLEAR LUCID LIMPID
LUCENT HYALINE
TRANSMIGRATION SAMARA
SAMSARA SANSARA
TRANSMISSION ENTAIL DESCENT
GEARBOX SENDING TRANSFER
(— OF SOUND) AUDIO
(— TO OFFSPRING) HEREDITY
TRANSMIT AIR EMIT SEND CARRY
CONVEY DEMISE DERIVE ENTAIL
EXPORT IMPACT IMPART RENDER
CONDUCT FORWARD TRADUCE
TRADUCT TRAJECT BEQUEATH
DESCRIBE
TRANSMITTER TUBA SLAVE SPARK
BEACON JAMMER SENDER VEHICLE
RADIATOR
TRANSMITTING ALIVE
TRANSMUTE CHEMIC CHEMICK
ENNOBLE PERMUTE EXCHANGE
TRANSMUE TRANSUME
TRANSOM PATIBLE TRAVERSE
TRANSPARENCY SLIDE
TRANSPARENT THIN CLEAR FILMY
LUCID BRIGHT LIMPID LUCENT
CRYSTAL FRAGILE HYALINE
HYALOID DIOPTRIC LUCULENT
LUMINOUS LUSTROUS PELLUCID
TRANSPIRE HAPPEN
TRANSPLANT SPOT SHIFT DEPLANT
TRANSPORT DAK JOY ROB BEAR
BOAT BUSS DAWK DRAY HAUL
PORT RAPE RAPT RIDE SHIP CANOE
CARRY DROGH FERRY FLUTE GILLY
BANISH BARREL CONVEY DEPORT
GALLOP WAFTER ECSTASY EXPRESS
FRAUGHT ONERARY RAPTURE
TRADUCE TROOPER CABOTAGE
CARRIAGE DAYDREAM ENRAVISH
PALANDER
(— FOR CRIME) LAG
(— LOGS) BOB

(— **ORE**) SLUSH
TRANSPORTATION AIR DAK FARE
AIRLIFT BOATAGE FREIGHT TRAJECT
TRANSPORT
TRANSPORTED RAPT
(— **BY GLACIER**) ERRATIC
TRANSPOSE CONVERT REVERSE
TRANSPOSITION SHIFT ANSWER
ANAGRAM
TRANSUBSTANTIATION METUSIA
TRANSVAAL DAISY GERBERA
TRANSVAALER TAKHAAR
TRANSVERSE CROSS FACING
THWART OBLIQUE
TRANSVERSELY ATHWART
TRANSVESTISM EONISM
TRANSVESTITE BERDACHE
TRAP COY GET GIN PIT SET FALL
GIRN GRIN HOOK LACE LIME NAIL
PUTT TIPE TOIL WAIT WEEL BRAKE
BRIKE CATCH LEASH PLANT POUND
SNARE SPELL STALE SWICK SWIKE
TRAIN CRUIVE EELPOT ENGINE
KEDDAH POCKET QUILEZ SNATCH
STAYER WILLOW FLYTRAP PITFALL
PITFOLD PUTCHEN PUTCHER
RATTRAP SETTING SPRINGE
TRAMMEL BIRDLIME COALHOLE
DEADFALL DOWNFALL TRAPROCK
(— **FOR BIRDS**) SCRAPE
(— **FOR LARGE GAME**) HOPO
(— **FOR RABBITS, MICE, ETC**) TIPE
TYPE
(— **FOR RATS**) CLAM
(— **FOR SALMON**) PUTT
(— **FOR SMALL ANIMALS**) HATCH
(— **FOR THE FEET**) CALTROPS
(— **IN POKER**) SANDBAG
(— **INTO SERVICE**) CRIMP
(**FISH** —) FYKE KILL LEAP WEEL
WEIR CREEL WILLY CORRAL
WILLOW
(**SAND** —) BUNKER
TRAPDOOR DROP SLOT TRAP
SCRUTO VAMPIRE TRAPFALL
TRAPPED CORNERED
TRAPPER WIRER VOYAGEUR
TRAPPINGS GEAR JHOOL ARMORY
TOGGERY BARDINGS EQUIPAGE
HOUSINGS
TRAPSHOOTING SKEET
TRASH ROT BOSH GEAR GOOK JUNK
PELF RAFF TOSH TRAG CLART
DRECK DRUSH STUFF SWASH
THROW TRADE TROKE WASTE
WRACK BUSHWA CULTCH KELTER
PALTRY RAMMEL REFUSE RUBBLE
SCULCH TROUSE BAGGAGE
BEGGARY FULLAGE GARBAGE
PEDLARY RUBBISH TOSHERY
TRAFFIC BLATHERY CLAPTRAP
FLUMMERY MUCKMENT PEDDLERY
SKITTLES SMACHRIE TRASHERY
TRUMPERY
TRASHY CHEAP FLASH TOSHY TRIPY
PALTRY SLUSHY BAGGAGE RUBBISH
RIFFRAFF RUBBISHY SIXPENNY
TRUMPERY
TRAVAIL PAIN TASK TOIL AGONY

LABOR TORMENT
TRAVEL GO BAT BUS FLY GIG WAG
FARE GANG HIKE PASS PATH RIVE
TOTE TRIP VAMP WEND COVER
KNOCK SLOPE THROW TRACK
CRUISE TRANCE VOYAGE EXPRESS
JOURNEY TRAVAIL TRUNDLE
WAYFARE PROGRESS TRAVERSE
(— **ACROSS SNOW**) MUSH
(— **AIMLESSLY**) SAUNTER
(— **ALONG GROUND**) TAXI
(— **AROUND**) TURN COAST CIRCLE
GIRDLE COMPASS
(— **AT GOOD SPEED**) CRACK
(— **AT HIGH SPEED**) HELL BARREL
SCORCH
(— **AT RANDOM**) DRIFT
(— **AT SPEED OF**) DO
(— **BACK AND FORTH**) SHUNT
COMMUTE
(— **BY AIRCRAFT**) AIR FLY AIRPLANE
(— **BY OX WAGON**) TREK
(— **FAST**) STREAK
(— **IN A VEHICLE**) TOOL
(— **ON FOOT**) HIKE SHANK
KNAPSACK
(— **ON WATER**) SAIL
(— **OVER**) TRANCE TRAVERSE
(— **THROUGH WOODS**) BUSHWACK
(— **THROUGH**) GO
(— **WITHOUT EQUIPMENT**) SIWASH
(**DAY'S** —) JORNADA JOURNAL
JOURNEY
TRAVELER GOER CRAWL FARER
GUEST HORSE BAGMAN GANGER
KILROY POSTER SAILOR VIATOR
CRUISER DRUMMER FOOTMAN
HOWADJI LEEFANG PILGRIM
SWAGGIE TRAILER TREKKER
WAYGOER ARGONAUT EXPLORER
MAGELLAN OUTRIDER VOYAGEUR
WAYFARER
(**COMPANY OF** —**S**) CARAVAN
TRAVELER'S JOY HAGROPE
BINDWITH
TRAVELING ERRANT
TRAVELING SALESMAN RIDER
DRUMMER
TRAVERSE DO GO SEE BURN DENY
KNEE LIFT MAKE PASS SPAN WALK
COAST COVER CROSS SHEAR
SWEEP THIRL TRACE TRACK CIRCLE
COURSE DENIAL OVERGO PERCUR
TRAVEL WANDER CHANNEL
JOURNEY MEASURE OVERRUN
PARADOS PERVADE DESCRIBE
OVERPASS OVERWEND SCRAMBLE
UNTHREAD
TRAVERTINE TOPHUS
TRAVESTY EXODE PARODY SATIRE
EXODIUM TRAVEST
TRAVOIS DRAY TRAVOY ALLIGATOR
TRAWL SEINE BOULTER DRAGNET
STOWNET TRAWLNET
TRAWLER PAREJA BRAGOZZO
TRAY HOD CASE TILL TRUG BATEA
BOARD FLOAT SCALE SLICE SUSAN
GALLEY MONKEY SALVER SERVER
SERVET VOIDER WAITER BALANCE

CABARET COASTER CONSOLE
SHALLOW DEJEUNER
(— **FOR CRUMBS**) VOIDER
(— **FOR DRYING FISH**) FLAKE
(— **FOR MATCH SPLINTS**) CAUL
MONKEY
(— **FOR SHELLFISH**) FLOAT
(— **FOR TYPE**) GALLEY
(— **TO CATCH OVERFLOW**) SAFE
(**CIRCULAR** —) ROUNDEL
TREACHEROUS FOUL CATTY FALSE
PUNIC SNAKY SWACK FELINE
FICKLE HOLLOW YELLOW SNAKISH
FRAUDFUL IMPOSING PLOTTING
SLIDDERY
TREACHERY GUILE SWICK TRAIN
DECEIT FELONY PERFIDY TREASON
UNTRUTH DASTARDY DISTRUST
TRAHISON TRAITORY
TREACLE DIBS CLAGGUM THERIAC
TREAD FIT PAD BEAT FOOT PATH
POST RUNG STEP VOLT CLAMP
TRACK TRADE DEFOIL DEFOUL
PADDLE CRAWLER FEATHER
FOOTING RETREAD TREADER
FOOTSTEP
(— **CLUMSILY**) CLUMP BALTER
(— **DOWN SHOE HEEL**) CAM
(— **HEAVILY**) SPURN TRAMPLE
(— **OF FOWL'S EGG**) GRANDO
(— **ON**) FOIL
(— **TO MUSIC**) FOOT
(**TIRE** —) COVER
TREADLE PEDAL CHALAZA
TREASON SEDITION
TREASURE POSE ROON HOARD
PRIZE STORE TROVE VALUE
BURSAR COFFER FINDAL GERSUM
WEALTH ASTHORE FINANCE
THESAUR WARISON GARRISON
TREASURY
(— **STATE**) MONTANA
(**LITTLE** —) STOREEN
(**PL.**) CIMELIA
TREASURE BOX HANAPER
TREASURED DEAR CHARY
PRECIOUS
TREASURER BOWSER BURSAR
FISCAL GABBAI BOUCHER HOARDER
SPENDER BHANDARI COFFERER
HAZNADAR PROVISOR RECEIVER
TREASURY FISC FISK KIST CHEST
HOARD PURSE COFFER CORBAN
FISCAL FISCUS BOWSERY BURSARY
CHAMBER CHECKER CHEQUER
HORDARY AERARIUM THESAURY
TREASURE
TREAT RUN USE DEAL DOSE HOCK
LEAD PLAY BEANO BESEE COVER
DIGHT GUIDE LEECH SERVE SETUP
SHOUT TRACT TRAIT WRITE
DEMEAN DOCTOR GOVERN HANDLE
LIQUOR PADDLE REGALO CONDUCT
ENTREAT GARNISH ACTIVATE
AIRBRUSH
(— **A HIDE**) DRUM
(— **AS EQUAL**) EVEN
(— **BADLY**) ILLGUIDE
(— **CARELESSLY**) BANG BANDY

(— CLOUDS) SEED
(— CONFIDENTIALLY) HUSH
(— CRUELLY) CRUCIFY
(— DAINTILY) PAMPER
(— DIABOLICALLY) BEDEVIL
(— DISCOURTEOUSLY) DISGRACE
(— FIBERS) GILL
(— FLOUR) AGENIZE
(— FONDLY) DANDLE
(— FUR) CARROT
(— GENTLY) FAVOR
(— ILLNESS) POMSTER
(— IMPROPERLY) MISUSE
(— IMPUDENTLY) NOSE
(— LIGHTLY) SCRUFF
(— LOVINGLY) COAX
(— MALICIOUSLY) SPITE
(— MASH) LAUTER
(— OF DRINKS) SETUP
(— OF) DISCOURSE
(— ROUGHLY) BANG MUMBLE
GRABBLE MALTREAT
(— SILK TO RUSTLE) SCROOP
(— SLIGHTINGLY) LIGHTLY
(— STEEL) HARVEY
(— UNFAIRLY) DO
(— UNSKILLFULLY) FOOZLE
(— WITH ACID) SOUR
(— WITH CARE) CODDLE
(— WITH CONTEMPT) HUFF SNUB
BLURT FLIRT FLOCK FLOUT FLAUNT
BAUCHLE
(— WITH HEAT) FOMENT
(— WITH HONOR) RESPECT
(— WITH INATTENTION) FORGET
(— WITH INDULGENCE) FONDLE
(— WITH PARTIALITY) ACCEPT
(— WITH RESPECT) HONOR
(— WITH RIDICULE) SCOUT
(— WITH RUDENESS) FRUMP
(— WITH TAR) BLACK
(— WITH TENDERNESS) CODDLE
(NEW YEAR'S EVE —) HAGMENA
HOGMANAY
TREATISE AGAMA DONET FAUNA
FLORA LIBEL SILVA SUMMA SYLVA
TRACT TREAT BOTANY POETRY
POMONA SERTUM SYSTEM ALGEBRA
ANATOMY BIOLOGY COMMENT
DIETARY GEOLOGY GRAMMAR
HISTORY PANDECT PHYSICS
PINETUM POETICS ZOOLOGY
ALMAGEST BROCHURE CALCULUS
DIDACTIC ECTHESIS EXERCISE
GENETICS GEOMANCY GEOMETRY
GERMANIA HORNBOOK LAPIDARY
MONUMENT PANTHEON PASTORAL
PRACTICE SITOLOGY SPECULUM
TRACTATE
TREATMENT CURE WORK TREAT
USAGE ANIMUS DETAIL FACIAL
QUARTER BEHAVIOR DEMEANOR
ENTREATY
(— BY MASSAGE) SEANCE
(— FOR WOOLLENS) SPONGING
(BAD —) MISUSAGE
(COLD —) FREEZE
(COMPASSIONATE —) MERCY
(CONTEMPTUOUS —) SPURN

(CRUEL —) SEVERITY
(DIRE —) DOLE
(HARMFUL —) ABUSE
(INHUMAN —) CRUELTY
(LUXURIOUS —) DELICACY
(SEVERE —) ROUGH
TREATY MISE ACCORD CARTEL
CONCORD ENTENTE LOCARNO
ALLIANCE TREATISE
TREBLE TRIPLE DESCANT MINIKIN
SOPRANO TRIPLUM
TREBUCHET DONDINE DONDAINE
TREE TI ACH AMA ARN ASH BAY BEL
BEN BUR DAK DAR EBO ELM FIG FIR
GUM HAW KOA KOU LIN OAK SAJ
SAL TAL TUI ULE YEW ACLE AGBA
AKEE ANAM ANAN ANDA ARAR
ASAK ASOK ATIS ATLE AULU AUSU
BAKU BITO BOGO BREA BURI BURR
CADE COLA CRAB DATE DHAK DILO
DITA DOON EBOE IPIL JACK KINO
KOKO LIME MABI MORA OHIA PALA
PINE POLE POON SADR SORB SUPA
TALA TAWA TCHE TEAK TEIL TITI
TOON TREW TUNG TUNO UPAS
VERA WOOD YATE YAYA AALII
ABETO ABURA ACANA ACAPU
ACOMA AFARA AGATI AGOHO AKEKI
ALAMO ALANI ALDER ALGUM ALISO
ALMON ALMUG AMAGA AMAPA
AMBAK ANABO ANJAN APPLE
ARACA ARBOR ARECA ARJAN
ARJUN ARTAR ASOKA ASPEN ATLEE
BABUL BALAO BALSA BALTA BANAK
BEECH BEHEN BETIS BIRCH BONGO
BOREE BOSSE BUMBO CACAO
CARAP CAROB CEBIL CEDAR CEIBO
DADAP DHAVA DHAYA DILLY DURIO
ELDER GABUN GAIAC GENIP GINEP
GINKO HAZEL ICICA IXORA JAMBO
JIQUE JIQUI KAPOR KAPUR KEENA
KOKAN KOKIO KONGU KUSAM
LANSA LARCH LARIX LEHUA LEMON
LICCA LIMBA LINDE LINER LINGO
MAHOE MAHUA MAMIE MAPLE
NARRA NIEPA NURSE OADAL OSAGE
OSIER PACAY PAPAW PECAN PIPER
RAULI ROBLE ROHAN ROWAN SALAI
SAMAN SASSY SCRAG SIMAL SIRIS
SISSU STICK SUMAC TABOG TARFA
TENIO TERAP TIKUR TIMBO TINGI
TOONA TUART ULMUS UMIRI URUCA
URUCU UVITO WAHOO YACAL
YACCA YULAN ZAMAN AHKROT
AKEAKE ALAGAO ALERGE ALERSE
ALFAJE ALMOND ALUPAG AMAMAU
AMBASH AMUGIS AMUYON ANAGAO
ANAGUA ANAQUA ANGICO ANILAO
ARALIA ARANGA ARBUTE AUSUBO
AZALEA BABOEN BACURY BAHERA
BAKULA BALSAM BANABA BANAGO
BANANA BANCAL BANIAN BANYAN
BARBAS BATAAN BIRIBA BOMBAX
BONDUC BONETE BOTONG BRAUNA
BUCARE BUSTIC CALABA CAMARA
CANELA CANELO CAPUMO CARAPA
CASSIA CATIVO CAUCHO CEDRON
CHALTA CHERRY CHICHA CHINAR
CHOGAK CITRON COBOLA COCUYO

CUMBER DATURA DHAMAN DHAURA
DHAURI DRIMYS DURIAN ELCAJA
EMBLIC EMBUIA FEIJOA FILLER
FUSTIC GABOON GINGKO GUAIAC
GURJAN GURJUN IDESIA IDIGBO
ILIAHI ILLIPE ILLUPI JAGUEY JUJUBE
KAMALA KEMPAS KINDAL KITTUL
LANSAT LANSEH LAUREL LIGNUM
LINDEN LITCHI LOCUST LONGAN
MAFURA MALLET MAYTEN MEDLAR
MILKER ORANGE PANAMA PAWPAW
PIQUIA POPLAR RAMBEH ROHUNA
RUNNEL SABICU SABINO SANDAN
SANTOL SAPELE SAPOTA SAPOTE
SATINE SAWYER SERAYA SINTOC
SISSOO SOUARI STYRAX SUMACH
SUNDRI TALUTO TARATA TEETEE
TIKOOR TIMBER TINGUY TOATOA
TOTARA TUPELO URUCUM URUSHI
UVALHA WABAYO WAHAHE WALNUT
WAMARA WAMPEE WANDOO
WATTLE YACHAN YAGHAN YAMBAN
YOHIME ZAMANG ACHIOTE ACHUETE
AILANTO AKEPIRO AMBATCH
AMBOINA AMUGUIS AMUYONG
ANABONG ANNATTO ANONANG
APITONG APRICOT ARARIBA
ARAROBA ARBORET ARBUTUS
AROEIRA ASSAGAI AVOCADO
AVODIRE BANILAD BANKSIA
BECUIBA BENZOIN BILLIAN BOLLING
BUBINGA BUCKEYE BUISSON
CADAMBA CAJAPUT CANELLA
CARAIPE CASTANA CATALPA
CAUTIVO CERILLO CHAMPAC
CHECHEM CHECKER CHENGAL
COCULLO CONIFER COUMARU
CURUPAY CYPRESS DEADMAN
DESCENT DETERMA DHAMNOO
EPACRID FRUITER GONDANG
GRIBBLE GUMIHAN HICKORY
HOLLONG HOPBUSH HORMIGO
KAMASSI KAMBALA KICKXIA
KITTOOL KOKOONA KOOMBAR
KUMQUAT LOGWOOD MADRONA
MANJACK MARGOSA PARAIBA
PEREIRA PIMENTO PULASAN
PYRAMID RATWOOD REDWOOD
SERINGA SERVICE SHITTAH SPINDLE
STOPPER SUNDARI SURETTE
TANGELO TANGHIN TARAIRI
TARATAH TARWOOD TINDALO
TREELET TWISTER URUNDAY
VETERAN WALAHEE WALLABA
WEENONG WONGSHY WONGSKY
YAMANAI YOHIMBI ACEITUNA
ALGAROBA ALLSPICE ALMACIGA
ALMANDER ALMENDRO ALOEWOOD
AMARILLO ARAGUANE ARBOLOCO
ARBUSCLE AVELLANO BAKUPARI
BASSWOOD BAYBERRY BELLWOOD
BINDOREE BITANHOL BLACKBOX
BOARWOOD BORRACHA BREADNUT
CABREUVA CAMELLIA CAMUNING
CARAGANA CARAUNDA CHAMPACA
CHESTNUT CHINCONA CHINOTTO
COPALCHE CRABWOOD CUCUMBOL
DEADFALL DOMINANT DOTTEREL
DOVEWOOD DRACAENA DRUMWOOD

ETABALLI FIREFALL FORESTER
GAMDEBOO GEELHOUT GENISARO
GUACACOA GUAYROTO HALAPEPE
HARDTACK HARDWOOD HOLDOVER
HORNBEAM HOROPITO IRONWOOD
ISHPINGO ITCHWOOD JELOTONG
JELUTONG KAJUGARU KINGWOOD
KNOBWOOD LACEBARK LEADWOOD
LORDWOOD MAHOGANY MANDARIN
MILKWOOD MOKIHANA OLEASTER
ONEBERRY PEDIGREE PINKWOOD
RAMBUTAN RASAMALA SANDARAC
SANDWOOD SAPUCAIA SASSWOOD
SEBESTEN SHAGBARK SHAVINGS
SILKWOOD SLOGWOOD SOAPBARK
STANDARD SUCUPIRA SWEETSOP
SYCAMORE TAMARACK TAMARIND
TANEKAHA TREELING TURMERIC
ZAPATERO
(— CUT BACK) DOTARD POLLARD
(— FURNISHING SUPPORT TO VINE)
HUSBAND
(— IN STREAM) SAWYER
(— LEFT IN CUTTING) HOLDOVER
(— ON WALL) RIDER
(— OVER 2 FT. DIAMETER) VETERAN
(— SYMBOLIZING UNIVERSE)
YGDRASIL
(— WITH BRANCHES TRIMMED) LOP
LOPSTICK
(—S IN FOREST) STAND
(AROMATIC —) CLUSIA LABIATE
(AUSTRALIAN —) ASH GUM TOON
BELAH BELAR BOREE BUNDY BUNYA
GIDIA HAZEL KARRI NONDA PENDA
SALLY WILGA BAOBAB DRIMYS
GIDGEE GIMLET GYMPIE KOWHAI
MARARA PEROBA SALLEE
DOGWOOD GEEBUNG BEEFWOOD
CARABEEN COOLABAH FLINDOSA
GRAVILEA IRONBARK LACEBARK
QUANDONG ROSEBUSH SANDSTAY
SOAPWOOD TILESEED
(BIG —) SEQUOIA
(CEYLON —) HORA
(CITRUS —) SHADDOCK
(CLOTHES —) COSTUMER
(CLUMP OF —S) TOLL TUMP STELL
(CUBAN —) JIQUE JIQUI GUACACOA
(CURSED —) WARYTREE
(DEAD —) RUNT SNAG RAMPIKE
(DEAD —S) DRIKI
(DECAYED —) DOTTEREL
(DWARF —) SCRUB ARBUSCLE
(EVERGREEN —) FIR YEW PINE SUGI
TAWA ABIES ATHEL CAROB CEDAR
CLOVE HOLLY LARCH LEMON OLIVE
THUJA BALSAM BIBIRU COIGUE
COIHUE KANAGI KAPUKA LOQUAT
ORANGE SPRUCE ARDISIA BEBEERU
BILIMBI CONIFER HEMLOCK JUNIPER
MADRONA EUCALYPT EUONYMUS
(FAMILY —) STEMMA DESCENT
PEDIGREE
(GENEALOGICAL —) ARBOR JESSE
(GROWTH OF —S) SYLVAGE
(GUM —) KARI KINO BABUL BALTA
BUMBO ICICA KARRI KIKAR GIMLET
MALLET STORAX TEWART WANDOO

GOMMIER COOLIBAH
(HAWAIIAN —) KOA LEHUA ILIAHI
(INFERNAL —) ZAQQUM
(JAPANESE —) KAYA KIAKI KEYAKI
KADSURA KATSURA
(MANDARIN —) SATSUMA
(MEXICAN —) ULE AMAPA DRAGO
EBANO SERON CAPULI CATENA
CHILTE CAPULIN COPALCHE
(MYTHICAL —) TUBA
(NEW ZEALAND —) AKE KARO KAWA
MIRO PUKA RATA RIMU TAWA TORU
WHAU HINAU KAORI KAURI MAIRE
MANGI MAPAU MATAI TOWAI
AKEAKE KAMAHI KANUKA KAPUKA
KARAKA KARAMU KAWAKA KONINI
MANUKA PURIRI TARATA TITOKI
TOATOA TOTARA WAHAHE AKEPIRO
MANGEAO PUKATEA TARAIRI
TARWOOD KAWAKAWA KOHEKOHE
MAKOMAKO
(ORNAMENTAL —) LABURNUM
(PHILIPPINES —) DAO IBA TUA TUI
BOGO DITA IFIL IPIL AGOHO AGOJO
ALMON AMAGA ANABO BAYOG
BAYOK BETIS DANLI GUIJO LAUAN
LIGAS TABOG YACAL ALAGAO
ALUPAG AMUYON ANAGAP ANUBIN
ARANGA BANUYO BATAAN BATETE
BATINO BOTONG DUNGON KATMON
LANETE MABOLO MARANG MOLAVE
SAGING TALUTO AMUGUIS
AMUYONG ANABONG ANOBING
ANONANG APITONG BINUKAU
CAMAGON DANGLIN MANCONO
MAYAPIS TINDALO ALMACIGA
BITANHOL KALIPAYA KALUMPIT
LUMBAYAO MACAASIM MALAPAHO
TANGUILE
(POISONOUS —) GUAO UPAS LIGAS
TANGHIN TANQUEN
(POLYNESIAN —) MACUDA
(SHADE —) ELM DILLY GUAMA
HEVEA CATALPA HALESIA INKWOOD
JOEWOOD SYCAMORE
(SHOWY —) ASAK ASOK ASOKA
(SMALL —) AKE BOX TCHE ALDER
CUMAY DWARF HENNA NGAIO
SERON AKEAKE BLOLLY CHANAR
JOJOBA KOWHAI ARBORET
INKWOOD JOEWOOD KADAMBA
STADDLE TREELET EMAJAGUA
HARDTACK HUISACHE OLEASTER
SNOWBELL SOURWOOD TREELING
(SPINY —) LIME AROMA AROMO
HONEY BOOGUM BUCARE BUMELIA
CATECHU COLORIN LAVANGA
COCKSPUR
(STANDING —) FILLER
(STUNTED —) SCRAB SCRUB
SCRUNT
(THORNY —) BEL BAEL BREA
LEMON AMBACH SAMOHU AMBATCH
(TIMBER —) ASH DAR ENG FIR SAL
ACLE ANDA BAKU COCO CUYA EKKI
IPIL PELU PINE TALA TEAK ACAPU
ALMON AMAPA AMATE AMBAY
ANJAN ARACA BANAK BIRCH CAROB
CEDAR COCOA CULLA EBONY ERIZO

FOTUI HALDU ICICA IROKO KAURI
KHAYA KIAKI KOKAN MANIU MAPLE
NARRA ROBLE TIMBO ALERCE
ALUPAG BABOEN BACURY BANABA
BANCAL CARBON CHUPON CORTEZ
DAGAME DEGAME DUKUMA ESPAVE
FREIJO GAMARI GUMHAR IMBUIA
JACANA LEBBEK MUERMO SANDAN
SATINE AMUGUIS AROEIRA BECUIBA
BILLIAN CARAIPI CYPRESS ESPAVEL
GATEADO GOMAVEL GUARABU
GUAYABI HARPULA HOLLONG
KOOMBAR LAPACHO REDWOOD
AMARILLO BOARWOOD CABREUVA
CARACOLI COCOBOLO CRABWOOD
DONCELLA GUATAMBU GUAYACAN
MAHOGANY SLOGWOOD SUCUPIRA
(TRAINED —) ESPALIER
(TROPICAL —) AKEE AULU DALI
EBOE EKKI GUAO INGA MABA MAHO
MAJO PALM SHEA ACKEE BALSA
BONGO COUMA DALLI FOTUI GUAMA
GUARA ICICA ILAMA JIGUA MARIA
NEPAL NJAVE POOLI TARFA ANUBIN
BAKULA BALATA BANANA CASHEW
CEDRON CHUPON GENIPA HACKIA
ITAUBA LEBBEK LECYTH MAMMEE
PERSEA ANGELIN ANNATTO
CAULOTE COPAIBA DATTOCK
EHRETIA EUGENIA GATEADO
GUACIMO LAPACHO MAJAGUA
MOMBINI SANDBOX SOURSOP
SURETTE BEEFWOOD CALABASA
CAMUNING CORKWOOD FUNTUMIA
MUSKWOOD PATASHTE SWEETSOP
TAMARIND
(UNARMED —) ALBIZZIA
(VARNISH —) DOON THEETSEE
(XEROPHYTIC —) SAXAUL
(YOUNG —) RUNNEL SPRING TILLER
SAPLING SEEDLING SPRINGER
(PL.) BLUFF RINDS SILVA
TREE CREEPER TOMTIT
TREE CYPRESS GILIA
TREE DUCK FIDDLER YAGUAZI
TREE FROG FERREIRO
TREE MOSS USNEA
TREENAIL NOG GUTTA MOOTER
TRUNNEL
TREE PEONY MOUTAN
TREE TOAD HYLA HYLID ANURAN
TREETOP LAP LOP
TREFOIL CANCH LOTUS CLAVER
CROWTOE BEDSTRAW SAINFOIN
TICKSEED
TREHALOSE MYCOSE
TRELLIS TRAIL PERGOLA TARLIES
ESPALIER
TREMATODE FLUKE MARITA
STRIGEID
TREMBLE DARE DIRL RESE BEVER
QUAKE SHAKE SLOWS WIVER
AGRISE DIDDER DINGLE DITHER
DODDER FALTER HOTTLE NITHER
QUAVER QUIVER SHIMMY THRILL
TITTER TOTTER TREMOR TRYMIE
WABBLE WOBBLE FLICKER
SHUDDER STAGGER TWIDDLE
WHITHER THRIMBLE

(PL.) TIRE TIRES
TREMBLER BUZZER HAMMER
VIBRATOR
TREMBLING BEVER SHAKY DITHER
TREMOR TREPID AQUIVER DODDERY
QUAKING QUAVERY QUIVERY
TREMBLY TWITTER
TREMBLY WOOZY
TREMENDOUS BIG AWFUL GIANT
GREAT LARGE TEARING ENORMOUS
HORRIBLE TERRIBLE TERRIFIC
MONSTROUS
TREMOLO HURRY TRILLO
TREMOR RIGOR SHAKE DINDLE
QUIVER THRILL SHUDDER TREMBLE
TREMULOUS ASPEN QUAKY SHAKY
PALSIED SHIVERY TREMBLY
SKIMMERY TINGLING
TRENCH GAW SAP FOSS GRIP GURT
LINE MOAT SICK SIKE TAJO TRIG
BOYAU CHASE DITCH DRAIN DRILL
FLOAT FOSSE GRAFF GRAFT GRAVE
GROOP SEUCH TRINK COFFER
FURROW GUTTER SHEUGH ACEQUIA
CUNETTE OPENCUT SLIDDER
ENCROACH LOCKSPIT SPREADER
THOROUGH TRESPASS
(— **BELOW FOREST FIRE)** GUTTER
(— **FOR BURYING POTATOES)** CAMP
(— **FOR DRAIN TILES)** CHASE
(— **FORMED BY BANKING
VEGETABLES)** GRAVE
(**ARTIFICIAL** —) LEAT
(**IRRIGATION** —) FLOAT SUGSLOOT
TRENCHANT ACID EDGED SHARP
TUANT INCISIVE
TRENCHER PLATTER ROUNDEL
TREND BEND BIAS HAND TONE TURN
BULGE CURVE DRIFT SENSE SLANT
SWING TENOR SQUINT STRIKE
CURRENT DOWNSIDE MOVEMENT
TENDENCY
(**LOWERING PRICE** —) EASE
TREPANG BALATE SWALLO
SWALLOW TITFISH TEATFISH
TREPIDATION FEAR DISMAY
TRESPASS DEBT GILUT POACH
BREACH FURTUM INVADE INTRUDE
OFFENSE ENCROACH ENTRENCH
INFRINGE INTRENCH OVERLOUP
TRESS CURL LOCK TAIL BRAID
SWITCH RINGLET WIMPLER
TRES-TINE TRAY ROYAL
TRESTLE MARE HORSE INRUN
CHEVALET SAWHORSE
TREVALLY TURRUM
TREWS TROUSERS
TRIACETATE ACETIN EUROBIN
TRIAD TRIAS TRINE TRIUNE TERNARY
TERNION TRILOGY TRINARY TRINITY
TRIMURTI TRIRATNA
TRIAL SHY TRY BOUT DOOM FIRE
HACK OYER STAB TEST TURN
ASSAY CROSS ESSAY GRIEF ISSUE
POINT PROOF TASTE TOUCH WHACK
ASSIZE EFFORT EQUITY TRINAL
APPROOF ATTEMPT CALVARY
DISGUST HEARING PROVING
SCRATCH CRUCIBLE EXERCISE

JUDGMENT QUAESTIO TENTAMEN
(— **BY BATTLE)** WAGER
(— **BY ORDEAL)** ORDALIUM
(— **FOR HOUNDS)** DERBY
(— **OF SPEED)** DASH
(**EXPERIMENTAL** —) TENTAMEN
(**SEVERE** —) ORDEAL CRUCIBLE
TRIANGLE APEX CYMBAL OXYGON
TRIGON ISOCELE PYRAMID SCALENE
TRINITY TRIQUET DINGDONG
TRIANGULAR HEATER CUNEATE
HASTATE
(— **AREA)** QUIRK
(— **CLOTH)** GORE
(— **INSET)** GODET
TRIBAL GENTILE GENTLIC TRIBULAR
TRIBE AO GI ATI AUS BOH EVE EWE
GOG KHA KIN KRA ROD SUK YAO
ADAI AKAN AKHA AKIM AKKA BAYA
BONI CLAN DAGO GUHA PURU
QUNG RACE RAVI REKI SAHO SEID
SHIK SHOR SIOL SOGA SUKU SUSU
TOBA TURI TUSH UBII VEPS VILI
VIRA YANA AEQUI ANGKA APTAL
ARAWA BASSI BATAK BESSI CHANG
CINEL DADJO DEDAN DIERI FIRCA
GIBBI HORDE HOUSE ICENI KAJAR
KANDH KEDAR KHOND KIWAI
KONGO KOTAR KREPI LANGO MARSI
MBUBA MENDE MENDI MOSSI MUTER
NANDI PHYLE PONDO QUADI SERER
SOTIK STAMM SUEVI TAIPI TAULI
TCAWI TEKKE TELEI TUATH VEPSE
VOLOF WAKHI WARRI WASHO
WAYAO YOMUD ADIGHE AGAWAM
ANAMIM ANTEVA APAYAO ARAINS
BANYAI BASOGA BUDUMA BUSAOS
CHAMPA CHAWIA CHORAI DOROBO
FAMILY HERULI KARLUK KEREWA
KHAMTI KONYAK KORANA LOBALE
MANGAR MOLALA NATION NERVII
PAHARI PHYLON POKOMO RAMNES
SHAGIA SICULI SIMEON SUKUMA
TAINUI TAMOYO TCHIAM TELEUT
THUSHI TUSHIN TYPEES VENETI
WABENA WABUMA WAGOMA
WAGUHA WAHEHE WARORI WASOGA
WAVIRA ZARAMO ZEGUHA ZENAGA
ABABDEH ABANTES AIAWONG
AKWAPIM AMAKOSA ANOMURA
ANTAIVA ARVERNI BAGIRMI
BAKATAN BAKONGO BAKUNDA
BAMBARA BASONGO CABINDA
CHAOUIA CHAUWIA CHITALI
CHONTAL CHUKCHI COLLERY
DADAYAG DADSCHO ILLANUN
JAZYGES KABINDA KABONGA
KHOKANI KOLDAJI KONIAGA
KOREISH KUBACHI KURUMBA
LLANERO NAIADES PALAUNG PARISII
PIMENTO RAURACI SAMBALA
SAMBARA SEKHWAN SENONES
SEQUANI SHAMMAR SHERANI
SHUKRIA SILIPAN SUIONES SUKKIIM
TAKELMA TARKANI TURKANA
VIDDHAL WAGWENO WAICURI
WAMBUGU WAREGGA WASANGO
ZONGORA AMAFINGO ANDOROBO
ASHANGOS ASSHURIM AWABAKAL

BARKINJI BATETELA BOANBURA
CHERUSCI GEZRITES JICAQUES
KUKURUKU LANDUMAN NEBAIOTH
ORUNCHUN PALLIVAN PHASIRON
PUPULUCA PURUPURU RAHANWIN
SAKALAVA SHINWARI SINGSING
SINTSINK TCHUKCHI TENGGRIS
USTARANA WANGATTA WAPOGORO
WAPOKOMO
(— **OF ISRAEL)** DAN GAD ASHER
REUBEN EPHRAIM ISSACHAR
MANASSEH
(**CHINESE** —**S)** HU
(**PRIVILEGED** —) MAGHZEN
MAKHZAN
(**SEA GYPSY** —) SELUNG
TRIBROMOETHANOL AVERTIN
TRIBULATION AGONY MISERY
SORROW DISTRESS
TRIBUNAL BAR FEME ROTA VEHM
COURT FEHME FORUM JUNTA
VEHME MAJLIS ACUERDO ESGUARD
MEJLISS RIGSRET AREOPAGY
TRIBUNE BEMA VELUTUS
TRIBUTARY ARM BRANCH FEEDER
TYBURN
TRIBUTE AID FEE TAX GELT LEVY
PORT RENT SCAT CANON GAVEL
HANSE MAILL SALVO SCATT
CHAUTH HERIOT HIDAGE HOMAGE
IMPOST CARATCH CHEVAGE
CHIEFRY OVATION PENSION
SYNODAL TREWAGE AUXILIUM
BRENNAGE HEREGELD PESHKASH
ROMESCOT ROMESHOT
TRICE GIRD BLINK THROW INSTANT
TRICHECHUS MANATUS
TRICHINA NEMATODE
TRICHION CRINION
TRICHOME SCALE
TRICHOMONIASIS CANKER
ABORTION
TRICK DO BOB COG CON CUN DAP
DOR FOB FOX FUB FUN GIN GUM
JIG JOB PAW BILK BITE BORE CHAW
CHIP DIDO DIRT DUPE FAKE FIRK
FLAM FLUM FOOL GAFF GAME GAUD
GECK GULL HAVE HOAX JAPE JEST
JINK JOUK JUNT LOCK LURK PASS
PAWK PRAT PULL RORT RUSE SELL
SKIT SLUR TURN WILE WIPE WOOL
BLEAR BLINK CATCH CHEAT CONNU
CRAFT CREEK CROOK CULLY
CURVE DODGE DORRE ELUDE FEINT
FETCH FOURB FRAUD GLEEK GRIFT
GUILE KNACK PAVIE PLANT PRANK
SHIFT SHINE SKITE SLICK STUNT
TRAIN TRUFF TWIST WHEEL WREST
WRINK BAFFLE BANTER BEGUNK
BEJAPE BLENCH BROGUE CAUTEL
CHOUSE CRADDY DECEIT DELUDE
DOUBLE EUCHRE FOURBE HOCKET
HUMBUG JOCKEY JUGGLE MANNER
PLISKY POLICY SCONCE SHAVIE
SPRING TREPAN VAGARY WHEEZE
WINNER CANTRIP CHICANE CONCEIT
FICELLE FINESSE FORWARD
GUILERY KNAVERY MARLOCK
PAGEANT SHUFFLE SLEIGHT

WHIZZER ARTIFICE CHALDESE
CLAPTRAP CLOWNADE CONTOISE
CROTCHET DELUSION DOUBLING
FLAGARIE FLIMFLAM GILENYIE
INTRIGUE JEOPARDY PRACTICE
PRANCOME PRESTIGE QUENTISE
SLAMPAMP TRAVERSE TRICKING
(— OUT) FINIFY
(BEGUILING —) WILE
(CARD —) CLUB HEART SPADE
STICH DIAMOND WEAVING
(FRAUDULENT —) RIG TOP
(JUGGLING —) FOIST
(KNAVISH —) DOGTRICK
(LOVE —) AMORETTO
(MEAN —) TOUCH
(MONKEY —) SINGERIE
(OLD —) CONNU
(PETTY —S) CRANS
(SIX —S) BOOK
(SMART —) LIRIPIPE LIRIPOOP
(STUPID —) SHINE
(VEXING —) CHAW
(WRESTLING —) CHIP CLICK FAULX
FORWARD
(PL.) DAGS
TRICKER TRUMPER
TRICKERY DOLE GAFF SHAM TRAP
TRAY WILE COVIN FRAUD HOCUS
SHARK TRAIN CAUTEL COVINE
DECEIT JAPERY JUGGLE TREGET
DODGERY FALLACY GULLERY
JOUKERY KNAVERY PAWKERY
SLEIGHT ARTIFICE CHEATING
JOOKERIE JUGGLERY PRACTICE
TRICKING TRUMPERY
TRICKILY FOXILY
TRICKINESS PAWKERY
TRICKISH KNAVISH FRAUDFUL
TRICKLE DRIP DRILL STILL TRILL
DISTIL DRIVEL SICKER SIGGER
STRAIN ZIGGER DISTILL DRIBBLE
DRIZZLE TRINTLE
TRICKSTER GULL SHAM TRAPAN
SLICKER TRICKER SLEEVEEN
TRAMPOSO
TRICKSY ELFISH QUIRKSEY
TRICKY SLY DEEP BRAID DODGY
FIKIE GAUDY ROWDY SNIDE ARTFUL
CATCHY LUBRIC QUIRKY SHIFTY
SMARTY TWISTY DEVIOUS SLANTER
TRICKLE WINDING FLIMFLAM
JUGGLING LUBRICAL SHIFTFUL
SKITTISH SLIDDERY SLIPPERY
TORTUOUS TRICKING
TRICLINIC ANORTHIC
TRICOT JERSEY
TRICYCLE VELO CYCLE TRIKE
WHEEL TANDEM TRICAR RANTOON
ROADSTER SOCIABLE
TRIDENT VAJRA TRISUL TRISULA
TRIED TESTED PROBATE WEIGHED
RELIABLE
TRIFLE ACE BOB DAB HAW PIN SOU
TOY BEAN COOT DOIT FICO FOOL
HAIR HOOT JAUK MOCK MOTE PLAY
RUSE DALLY FLIRT FLUKE GLAIK
ITEMY NIFLE PLACK POINT SCRAT
SPORT TRICK TRUFF BAWBEE

BREATH DABBLE DANDLE DAWDLE
DELUDE DIBBLE DOODAD DOODLE
FADDLE FESCUE FIDDLE FOOTER
FOOTLE FRIVOL GEWGAW MONKEY
NIDDLE NIGNAY PADDLE PALTER
PETTLE PICKLE PIDDLE PIGGLE
PINGLE POTTER PUTTER TIFFLE
VANITY WANTON FEATHER FRIBBLE
NOTHING QUIDDLE THOUGHT
TRANEEN TRINKET TRIVIAL WHIFFLE
COQUETTE FALDERAL FLIMFLAM
FOLDEROL GIMCRACK KICKSHAW
MOLEHILL NIHILITY NUGAMENT
RIGMAREE TRANTLUM
(— WITH) JANK DANDLE DELUDE
NIGGLE
(ATTRACTIVE —) CONCEIT
(LITERARY —) TOY
(MERE —) SONG STRAW
(MEREST —) FIG
(PL.) NUGAE TRIVIA GIBLETS
FEWTRILS
TRIFLER DOODLE PLAYER FLANEUR
FOOTLER FRIBBLE NUGATOR
PINGLER TWIDDLER WHIFFLER
TRIFLING AIRY FOND IDLE FUNNY
INANE LIGHT PETTY POTTY SILLY
SMALL FLIMSY FUTILE LEVITY
LIMUTE LITTLE PALTRY SIMPLE
STRAWY TOYISH FOOLISH FRIBBLE
ITEMING TRIVIAL TWATTLE
COQUETRY FIDDLING FLIMFLAM
FRIPPERY IMMOMENT NUGATORY
PIDDLING SNIPPING
TRIFOLIUM CLOVER TREFOIL
TRIG TRIM CHIPPER
TRIGGER VERGE TRICKER
TRIGGERFISH COCUYO TURBOT
OLDWIFE BALISTID FILEFISH
OLDWENCH
TRIGON TRINE SABBEKA SACKBUT
SAMBUCA TRIGONON
TRIGONOMETRY SPHERICS
TRILL BURR FLAP ROLL SHAKE
QUAVER THRILL TRILLO WARBLE
TRILLET
TRILLIUM SARA TRUE SARAH TRUMP
BENJAMIN TRUELOVE
TRILOBITE EODISCID
TRIM AX AXE CUT DUB GIM LIP LOP
NET BARB BEAD BUTT CLIP CROP
DEFT DINK FEAT FUSS GASH GIMP
HACK JIMP LACE NEAT PICK SNAG
SNOD SNUG SPUR STOW TACK
TOSH TRIG BRAID BRUSH CLEAN
COPSE DRESS FITTY GENTY HEDGE
KEMPT KNIFE PREEN PRIME PRUNE
PURGE SAUCY SHAVE SHEAR
SHRAG SHRIP SLEEK SMART SMIRK
SPRIG STUMP TIGHT TRICK VERGE
BARBER DAPPER DONSIE DOUBLE
FETTLE PICKED REFORM SHROUD
SPRUCE SVELTE SWITCH TRIMLY
CHIPPER FEATHER FLOUNCE
SCISSOR MANICURE ORNAMENT
TRIMMING
(— A BOAT) SIT
(— ENDS OF HAIR) SHIRL
(— HEDGE) DUB

(— HIDES) ROUND
(— MEAT) CONDITION
(— SAIL) FILL
(— SEAMS) FETTLE
(— SHOE) FOX
(— TREES) PRIME SWAMP
(— WITH EMBROIDERY) GIMP PANEL
TRIMLY SMARTLY SPRUCELY
TRIMMED PEEKABOO
TRIMMER FINER BRIDLE TACKER
VOLANT ROUNDER SMOCKER
SCRATTER
TRIMMING COQ FUR GIMP LACE
BRAID CHAPE COQUE FRILL GUARD
INKLE JABOT RUCHE ERMINE
LACING OSPREY PURFLE ROBING
BEADING FALBALA FURRING
GALLOON MARABOU PUFFING
BRAIDING EAVESING FALDERAL
FOLDEROL FROSTING FROUFROU
FURBELOW JEWELING PAILETTE
PEARLING PICKADIL PLASTRON
SOUTACHE SPAGHETTI STRAPPING
(PL.) LOP FLOTS SHORTS FIXINGS
LOPPING BRAIDING FRILLIES
TRIMURTI TRINITY
TRINE TRENE TRIGON
TRINIDAD-TOBAGO (CAPITAL OF —)
PORTOFSPAIN
(POINT OF —) GALERA
(RIVER OF —) ORTOIRE
(TOWN OF —) ARIMA LABREA
SIPARIA
TRINITARIAN MATHURIN
TRINITY TRIAD TRIAS TRINE TRIUNE
GODHEAD TERNARY TRIMURTI
TRINUNITY
TRINKET TOY DIDO GAUD BIJOU
HEART KNACK TAHLI BAUBLE
DEVICE DOODAD GEWGAW BIBELOT
TRANGAM TRANKUM GIMCRACK
TRANTLUM TRINKLET WHIMWHAM
(PL.) TRINKUMS
TRINKETRY KNAVERY
TRINITROTOLUENE TOLITE TRITON
TRIO GLEEK TERZET TRIUNE
TERZETTO
TRIOLEFIN TRIENE
TRIONYX AMYDA
TRIOPAS (DAUGHTER OF —)
IPHIMEDIA
(FATHER OF —) NEPTUNE
(MOTHER OF —) CANACE
(SON OF —) ERYSICHTHON
TRIOPS APUS
TRIP HOP JAG JET JOG TIP BOUT
CHIP FOOT GAIT GATE RAKE SKIP
TOUR TROT TURN BROAD DANCE
DRIVE HITCH JAUNT SALLY CRUISE
ERRAND FLIGHT HEGIRA OFFEND
OUTING RAMBLE SAFARI SASHAY
VOYAGE JOURNEY SAILING
SETDOWN STUMBLE TRIPPER
CAMPAIGN PERIPLUS
(— ALONG) CHIP LINK
(— IN WRESTLING) CHIP CLICK
(— INTO COUNTRY) CAMPAIGN
(— UP) SUPPLANT
(HUNTING —) SHOOT

(PLEASURE —) JUNKET
TRIPE PAUNCH ROLPENS TRILLIBUB
TRIPLE TRINE TREBLE TERNARY
TRIFOLD TRIPLEX THRIBBLE
TRIPLET TRIN BRELAN PARIAL
TERCET TRIOLE TRIPLE TERZINA
TRIOLET HEMIOLIA TRILLING
TRIPLING TRISTICH
TRIPLETAIL SAMA CHOBIE FLASHER
GROUPER
TRIPLICITY TRIGON
TRIPOD CAT TRIP SPIDER TEAPOY
TRIPOS TRIVET TRESTLE
TRIPODY HEMIEPES
TRIPOLI SILEX TRIPEL
TRIPPER DECKMAN
TRIPTOLEMUS (FATHER OF —)
CELEUS
(MOTHER OF —) METANIRA
TRISMUS LOCKJAW TETANUS
TRITE FADE HACK WORN BANAL
CONNU CORNY HOARY MUSTY
STALE VAPID BEATEN COMMON
MODERN HACKNEY PERCOCT
TRIVIAL SHOPWORN
TRITENESS BATHOS
TRITERPENOID CERIN
TRITON NEWT TRUMPET
(FATHER OF —) NEPTUNE
(MOTHER OF —) AMPHITRITE
TRITURATE POUND POWDER
TRITURATION TRIPSIS
TRITURUS MOLGE
TRIUMPH WIN PALM INSULT PREVAIL
VICTORY CONQUEST
(— OVER) SCALP
TRIUMPHANT VICTOR JUBILANT
TRIUMPHING OVANT
TRIUNGULIN CRAWLER
TRIVET SPIDER TRIPOD TRESTLE
TRIPPER BRANDISE
TRIVIAL JERK NICE VAIN LEGER
LIGHT PETTY SILLY SMALL TIDDY
FIDFAD FOOTLE SLIGHT TOYISH
COMICAL PIPERLY PUERILE
SHALLOW TIDDLEY DOGGEREL
FEATHERY FOOTLING GIMCRACK
PIDDLING PILULOUS TRIFLING
TRINKETY
(NOT —) SOLID EARNEST
TRIVIALITY FOLLY NIGNAY TRIFLE
INANITY IDLENESS NONSENSE
NUGACITY
TROCHANTER SCAPULA
TROCHE ROTULA TABLET CACHUNDE
PASTILLE
TROCHEE CHOREE CHOREUS
TROCHEUS
TROCHLEA PULLEY
TROCTOLITE GABBRO
TRODDEN TRADED
(MUCH —) BEATEN
TROGLODYTIC SPELEAN
TROGON QUEZAL QUETZAL
TOCORORO
TROILUS (FATHER OF —) PRIAM
(MOTHER OF —) HECUBA
(SLAYER OF —) ACHILLES
TROJAN TROIC DARDAN ANTENOR

(PL.) TEUCRI
TROLL HARL SPIN TROW HARLE
MOOCH TRAWL TROLLOL
TROLLER MOOCHER
TROLLOP CUT DOXY BITCH DOXIE
TROLL TRULL DOLLOP
TROMBONE BONE TRAM BUSINE
POSAUNE SACKBUT SLIPHORN
TRONA URAO
TROOP FARE GING ROUT TURM
ROUTE SOLAK STAND TURMA
WERED CORNET RISALA ROUGHT
SCHOOL THREAT TICHEL TROUPE
COMPANY COMITIVA
(— OF ARMED MEN) CREW
(— OF FOXES) SKULK
(—S ATTACHED TO SOVEREIGN)
GUARDS
(—S IN BATTLE ARRAY) SHELTRON
(—S ON WING OF ARMY) ALARES
(ASSAULTING —S) WAVE
(BOMBAY —S) DUCKS
(CAVALRY —) CORNET
(GIRL SCOUT —) SHIP
(LIGHT-ARMED —S) PSILOI
(SCOTTISH —S) JOCKS
(PL.) PARADE
TROOPER BARGIR RUTTER BARGEER
TROPARION HIRMOS HEIRMOS
TROPARY KATABASIS
TROPE IMAGE EVOVAE
TROPHONEMA VILLUS
TROPHOZOITE CEPHALIN SPORADIN
TROPHY BAG PALM PRIZE SCALP
REWARD LAURELS
TROPIC SOLAR TROPHIC
TROPINE HYOSCINE
TROS (FATHER OF —) ERICTHONIUS
(MOTHER OF —) CALLIRRHOE
(SON OF —) ILUS GANYMEDE
ASSARACUS
TROT JOG SPUD TRIG FADGE HURRY
PIAFFE
TROTH CERTY TROGS TRUTH CERTIE
TROTTER DRIVER CRUBEEN
SPANKER
TROUBADOR MINSTREL SORDELLO
TROUBLE ADO AIL DIK HOE ILL IRK
MAR WOE BEAT BUSY CAIN CARK
EARN FASH FIKE JEEL MASH MOIL
PAIN PINE ROUT SORE STIR TEEN
TINE TRAY UNRO WORK ANNOY
BESET CROSS DROVE DUTCH GRIEF
HAUNT LABOR ROWEL SMITE SPITE
STEER STURT SUSSY THRIE TWEAK
WHILE WORRY BOTHER BURBLE
CADDLE CUMBER DITHER EFFORT
GRIEVE GRUDGE HARASS KIAUGH
MOLEST POTHER RATTLE RUBBER
SORROW TAKING THREAT UNEASE
UNRUFE WORRIT AFFLICT AGITATE
ANXIETY CHAGRIN DISEASE DISTURB
DRUBBLE EMBROIL FASHERY
INFLICT PERTURB PILIKIA SCRUPLE
SPUTTER THOUGHT TRACHLE
TRAVAIL TRIBBLE TURMOIL
BUSINESS DARKNESS DISORDER
DISQUIET DISTRESS NOISANCE
VEXATION WANDRETH

(— ONE'S SELF) PASS
(PL.) CHAGRINS
TROUBLED DRUBLY DRUMLY
GRUMLY QUEASY FRETFUL
HAUNTED HARASSED
TROUBLESOME DIK ILL HARD FIKIE
SHREWD STICKY HARMFUL
TEWSOME UNTOWARD
TROUBLED CAREFUL AGITATED
TROUBLESHOOTER FIXER
TROUBLESOME SAD PLAGUY
UNEASY PESTFUL ANNOYING
FASHIOUS SPITEFUL
TROUBLESOMENESS BOTHER
TROUBLING CHRONIC
TROU-DE-LOUP TRAPHOLE
TROUGH BOX CUP HOD RUN TOM
BACK BOSH BUNK COVE DAIL DALE
DISH DORR SHOE SINK TRAY TROW
BAKIE CHUTE DITCH LAVER SHOOT
SHUTE SLIDE SPOUT STRIP ALVEUS
BACKET BUDDLE GUTTER HARBOR
LAVABO MANGER RUNNER SALTER
SINKER SLUICE STRAKE TROGUE
VALLEY WALLOW CHENEAU
CONDUIT LAUNDER RIFFLER
TRENDLE TROFFER LAVATORY
(— FOR ASHES) BAKIE
(— FOR COOLING INGOTS) BOSH
(— FOR PAPER PULP) RIFFLER
(— FOR WASHING ORE) TOM HUTCH
STRIP BUDDLE STRAKE
(— IN MONASTERY) LAVABO
(— OF A WAVE) SULK
(— OF CIDER MILL) CHASE
(— OF ROCK) SYNCLINE
(— OF THE SEA) ALVEUS
(ANNULAR —) CUP
(EAVES —) CANAL CHENEAU
(GLACIAL —) DORR
(SHEEP-DIPPING —) DUP
(WOODEN —) TRUG BAKIE TROGUE
TROUNCE MOP FLOG TRAMP
WHOMP COURSE CUDGEL CANVASS
TROUNCING LACING WARMING
TROUPE SERVANTS CUADRILLA
TROUSER STROSSER
TROUSERING CASINET
TROUSERS BAGS CORDS DUCKS
JEANS KICKS PANTS SLOPS TONGS
TREWS BRAIES DENIMS SHORTS
SKILTS SLACKS WHITES BOTTOMS
BRACCAE BROGUES KERSEYS
NANKINS SHALWAR SLIVERS
STRIDES BLOOMERS BREECHES
FLANNELS KICKSEYS MOLESKIN
NANKEENS OVERALLS SHINTYAN
TROUT CHAR KELT PEAL POGY
BROOK BROWN CHARR LAKER
LUNGE SEWEN SHARD SQUET SQUIT
TRUFF FINNOC KIPPER MYKISS
QUASKY SALTER TAIMEN TRUCHA
TULADI BOREGAT BROOKIE
BROWNIE COASTER HERLING
OQUASSA POUNDER RAINBOW
SQUETEE AUREOLUS BODIERON
GILLAROO HARDHEAD KAMLOOPS
SAIBLING SALMONID SISCOWET
(SMALL —) SCURLING SKIRLING

(YOUNG —) WHITLING
TROUVERE BLONDEL
TROW DROW TRUE FAITH BELIEF
COVENANT
TROWEL HAWK LEAF PIPE DARBY
DERBY FLOAT TAPER TREWEL
(HEARTSHAPED —) HEART DOGTAIL
(MOLDER'S —) LEAF TAPER
(PLASTERER'S —) FLOAT
TRUANT HOOKY TRONE TROUT
MICHER MEECHER TRIVANT
VAGRANT
TRUCE PAX BARLEY TREAGUE
INDUCIAE
TRUCK DAN UTE BUNK CORF DRAB
DRAG DUCK DUMP GUNK RACK
WYNN BOGIE BUGGY DILLY DOLLY
GILLY LORRY BARTER BUMMER
CAMION DIESEL DROGUE DRUGGE
DUMPER JITNEY SLOVEN TIPPER
TURTLE CARAVAN FOURGON
GONDOLA SKIDDER SLEEPER
TROLLEY TRUCKLE TRUNDLE
DELIVERY HAULAWAY TRANSFER
(COAL —) DAN
(LOGGING —) BUNK BUMMER
(MINING —) CORF BARNEY
(TIMBER —) DRUG WYNN
TRUCKLE FAWN TOADY SLAVER
TRUCKLING SERVILE
TRUCULENCE BRAG
TRUCULENT MEAN CRUEL HARSH
FIERCE SAVAGE SCATHING
TRUDGE JOG PAD HAKE PLOD STOG
JAUNT TRACE TRAMP TRASH
STODGE TRAIPSE
TRUE SO GOOD JUST LEAL PURE
REAL VERY VRAI PLUMB RIGHT
SOOTH SOUND VERAY FIDELE
LAWFUL DEVOTED GENUINE
GERMANE PRECISE SINCERE
STAUNCH FAITHFUL RELIABLE
RIGHTFUL SOOTHFUL UNERRING
(— TO THE FACT) LITERAL
(QUESTIONABLY —) ALLEGED
TRUFFLE TRUB TRUFF EARTHNUT
TRUISM SOOTH
TRULL DELL BLOWZE CALLET
TRULY YEA AWAT EVEN IWIS JUST
QUITE SOOTH SYKER TIGHT ATWEEL
DINKUM INDEED SIMPLY VERILY
INSOOTH SOOTHLY VERAMENT
WITTERLY
TRUMP DIS DIX LOW PAM LILY RUFF
BASTA BASTO DEECE TROMBE
MANILLA MATADOR TRIUMPH
SPADILLE
(2ND HIGHEST —) MANILLE
TRUMPERY MOCKADO GIMCRACK
PEDDLERY
TRUMPET BEME LURE TUBA TRUMP
BOZINE BUCCIN CORNET KERANA
LITUUS TROMBA TULNIC ALCHEMY
BUCCINA CLARINO CLARION
KERRANA SALPINX NARSINGA
SLUGHORN SOURDINE WATERCUP
TRUMPET BELL CODON PAVILON
TRUMPET CALL DIAN DIANA
SENNET

TRUMPET CREEPER TECOMA
COWHAGE CREEPER FOXGLOVE
HELLVINE
TRUMPETER MOKI AGAMI TRUMP
TOOTER JACAMIN TUBICEN YAKAMIK
TRUMPETER FISH MOKI MOKIHI
TRUMPETER PERCH MADO
TRUMPETS WATERCUP
TRUMPETWOOD IMBAUBA
TRUNCATED STUBBED TRUNKED
TRUNCHEON BATON WARDER
SPONTON PARTISAN SPONTOON
TRUNDLE HURL RUNG TROLL
RUNDLE TRUCKLE WALLOWER
TRUNK BOX BODY BOLE BOOT BULK
KIST LICH RUNT STAM STEM STUD
CABER PETER SHAFT STICK STOCK
TORSO ARIGUE BARREL CAUDEX
COFFER LOCKER CARCASS
CORSAGE STOWAGE TRUNCUS
SARATOGA
(ARTERIAL —) AORTA
(ELEPHANT'S —) SNOUT
(FOSSIL —) CYCAD
(SMALL —) HATBOX
**(TREE — OVER 8 INCHES IN
DIAMETER)** MAST
(TREE —) BOLE BUTT STICK
(TRIMMED TREE —) LOG
(WORSHIPPED TREE —S) IRMINSUL
TRUNKFISH CHAPIN BOXFISH
COWFISH
TRUSS SPAN WARREN
(— OF STRAW) WAP
(— UP) KILT
TRUST AFFY HOPE LITE POOL RELY
REST TICK TREW TROW FAITH FRIST
GROUP TRUTH BELIEF CARTEL
CHARGE CORNER CREDIT DEPEND
FIANCE LIPPEN OFFICE TICKET
BELIEVE BETRUST CONFIDE
CREANCE CRIANCE JAWBONE
SECRECY VENTURE AFFIANCE
COMMENDA CREDENCE MONOPOLY
RELIANCE
TRUSTED FIDUCIAL
TRUSTEE FEOFEE SINDICO VISITOR
MUTWALLI
TRUSTWORTHINESS HONOR TRUST
HONESTY CREDENCE AXIOPISTY
TRUSTWORTHY SAFE SURE SOOTH
SOUND SYKER TRIED HONEST
SECRET SECURE SICKER STABLE
TRUSTY COCKSURE CREDIBLE
FIDUCIAL RELIABLE TRUSTFUL
TRUSTY TRIG FECKFUL STAUNCH
FAITHFUL RELIABLE
TRUTH TAO UNA SOOTH TROTH
WHITE SATTVA VERITY VERITAS
VERACITY VERIDITY VERIMENT
(— TABLE) MATRIX
(IDEAL —) CHRIST DHARMA
(IN —) CERTES
(RELATING TO —) ALETHIC
(ULTIMATE —) LIGHT SUNYATA
TRUTHFUL TRUE VERY SOOTH
HONEST VERIDIC
TRUTHFULLY GOSPELLY

TRUTHFULNESS HONESTY
VERACITY
TRY GO SHY BURL HACK PENK PREE
SEEK SLAP TEST TIRL TURN AFOND
ASSAY CRACK ESSAY ETTLE FLING
GROPE JUDGE OFFER PROVE SENSE
SOUND TASTE TEMPT TOUCH
WHACK WHIRL APPOSE ASSAIL
FRAIST GRIEVE STRIVE AFFLICT
AFFORCE APPROVE ATTEMPT
DISCUSS ESPROVE IMITATE
STAGGER ENDEAVOR STRUGGLE
(— DESPERATELY) AGONIZE
(— FOR GOAL) SHOT
(— HARD) STRIVE
(— OUT) SAMPLE AUDITION
(— TO ATTAIN) AFFECT
(CASUAL —) FLING
(QUICK —) SLAP
TRYING ARDUOUS CRUCIAL
GRUELING
TRYSAIL SPENCER
TSETSE FLY KIVU GANDI DIPTERAN
GLOSSINA
T-SHAPED TAU
TSILTADEN CHILION
TSUBO BU
TSWANA CHUANA SECHUANA
TUAREG IMOHAGH IMOSHAGH
TUATARA GUANA GUANO IGUANA
HATTERIA
TUB FAT HOD KID KIT SOE SOW TUN
VAT BACK BOWK COOL CORF COWL
GAWN KNOP MEAL TYND TYNE
BOWIE ESHIN KEEVE KIVER SKEEL
STAND BUCKET KEELER KILLER
KIMNEL TROUGH TURNEL BATHTUB
BREAKER SALTFAT TANKARD
TRUNDLE KOOLIMAN LAVATORY
(— FOR ALEWIVES) HOD
(— FOR AMALGAMATING ORES)
TINA
(— FOR BREAD) BARGE
(— OF BUTTER) COOL
(— OF HOGWASH) SWILLTUB
(— USED AS DIPPER) HANDY PIGGIN
(— WITH SLOPING SIDES) SHAUL
(BREWER'S —) BACK KEEVE
(LAUNDRY —) WASHTRAY
(MESS —) KID KIT
(MINING —) CORF
(TANNING —) LEACH
(WATER —) DAN JAILER
(WOODEN —) KIT SOE KIMNEL
TRINDLE
TUBA BASS HELICON BOMBARDON
TUBE TAG BEAK BODY BOOT CANE
CASE CAST CORE DRUM DUCT
HORN HOSE PIPE REED WORM
BATON CANAL CORER CROOK
CRYPT DRAIN GLAND HEART LINER
QUILL SIGHT SLIDE SPILE SPOUT
THECA THIEF TRUMP TUBAL VALVE
AUDION CALCAR CANNEL CANNON
COLUMN CORNET DEWCAP FILTER
GULLET HEADER NOZZLE OCTODE
SLEEVE SUCKER SYRINX THROAT
TRIODE TUBING TUBULE TUNNEL
UPTAKE VESSEL BLOWGUN

CHIMNEY CONDUIT CUVETTE
DROPPER FERRULE FISTULA
HOUSING OOBLAST OVIDUCT
QUILLET ROSTRUM SALPINX
SHALLOT SNORTER SNUFFER
SOXHLET STOPPLE THIMBLE
TUBULUS VENTURI ADJUTAGE
BOMBILLA CORNICLE DIATREME
DRAWTUBE FAIRLEAD GRADUATE
ORTHICON OVARIOLE PENSTOCK
PIPESTEM SAUCISSE SIPHONET
SLEEVING URCEOLUS ZOOECIUM
(— AT BASE OF PETAL) CALCAR
(— CARRYING BASSOON
MOUTHPIECE) CROOK
(— COVERING TRACE CHAIN) PIPING
(— FOR DEPOSITING CONCRETE)
TREMIE
(— FOR DRINKING MATE) BOMBILLA
(— FOR LINING WELL) WELLRING
(— FOR STIFFENING STRING) TAG
(— FOR TRANSFERRING LIQUID)
SIPHON SYPHON
(— FOR WINDING THREAD) COP
(— FROM SHIP'S PUMP) DALE
(— IN ENGINE CYLINDER) LINER
(— OF BALLOON) APPENDIX
(— OF GUN) BORE BARREL
(— OF RETORT) BEAK ROSTRUM
(— OF SPIRIT LEVEL) BUBBLE
(— OF TOBACCO) CIGARET
(— TO LINE A VENT) BOUCHE
(— TWISTED IN COILS) WORM
(— USED IN WHALING) LULL
(AMPLIFIER —) STAGE
(BONE —) SNUFFER
(DISTILLING —) TOWER
(ELECTRO —) BULB
(ELECTRODE —) AUDION
(ELECTRON —) DIODE DRIVER
KLYSTRON PLIOTRON
(FIREWORKS —) LEADER
(GLANDULAR —) CRYPT
(GLASS —) SIGHT MATRASS
(HONEY —) NECTARY SIPHONET
(KNITTED —) STOCKING
(PAPER —) LEADER PASTILLE
(PASTRY —) CORNET
(POLLEN —) SPERMARY
(RECTIFIER —) IGNITRON
(SILK — OF SPIDER) SPIGOT
(SPEAKING —) GOSPORT
(SUCKING —) STRAW
(SURGICAL —) CANNULA
(THERMOMETER —) STEM
(VACUUM —) DIODE KEYER HEXODE
HEPTODE DYNATRON
TUBELET CIRCLET
TUBER ANU SET ANYU BULB CLOG
ROOT SEED SETT YAMP SALEP
JICAMA PIGNUT POTATO WAPATA
WINDER YAUTIA EARTHNUT
MURRNONG
TUBERCLE PEARL NODULE STEMMA
CUSPULE VERRUCA
TUBERCULAR PHTHISIC
TUBERCULOSIS CON CLYERS
DECLINE SCROFULA
TUBING HOSE TUBAGE

TUBMAN DUCKER
TUBULAR PIPY PIPED TUBATE
CANNULAR
(NOT —) FARCTATE
TUBULE TRACHEA TUBULET
TUBULUS
TUCANO BETOYAN
TUCK TOKE STUFF TRUSS FLANGE
(— IN) TRUSS TROUSS
(— UP) FAKE KILT
TUCKER CORDER KILTER PLEATER
TUESDAY (SECOND — AFTER
EASTER) HOCKDAY HOKEDAY
TUFF TRASS PEPERINO PORODITE
SANTORIN
TUFT EAR FAG FOB NOB SOP TOP
COMA DOWN KNOB KNOP MOCK
TUFF TUSK BEARD BUNCH CREST
FLOCK STUPA THRUM WHISK
CIRRUS DOLLOP PAPPUS PENCIL
TASSEL TUFFET CIRRHUS FEATHER
FLOCCUS HOBNAIL PANACHE
SCOPULA TOPKNOT TOPPING
TUSSOCK FLOCCULE
(— OF BRISTLES) BIRSE
(— OF CLOTH) FAG
(— OF DOWN) FRIEZE
(— OF FEATHERS) EAR HORN HULU
EGRET
(— OF FILAMENTS) BYSSUS
(— OF GRASS) FAG SOP MOCK
HASSOCK TUSSOCK
(— OF HAIR ON HORSE'S HOOF)
FETLOCK
(— OF HAIR) TOP TUZZ BRUSH
SWITCH COWLICK FEATHER
FLOCCUS SCOPULA TOPKNOT
IMPERIAL KROBYLOS
(— OF HAY) SOP
(— OF MALE TURKEY) BEARD
(— OF WOOL) FOB TUSK TUZZ
FLOCK
(— ON BIRD'S HEAD) COP CUCK
EGRET
(— ON PINEAPPLE) CROWN
(— ON SEED PLANT) PAPPUS
(— ON SPIDER'S FEET) SCOPULA
(—S OF ROPE YARN) THRUM
(VASCULAR —) GLOMUS
TUFTED COMOSE TAPPET TAPPIT
TUG LUG RUG TIT TOG CHUG DRAG
HALE HAUL PULL TOIL TUCK CHUFF
HITCH PLUCK SHRUG TRACE
RUGGLE TOWBOAT TUGBOAT
TUGBOAT TOW TUG TOWBOAT
TRACKER
TUI POE TUA KOKO TUWI POEBIRD
TUITION CUSTODY
TULIP LILY LILIUM BIZARRE BREEDER
TURNSOLE
TULIP TREE POPLAR BASSWOOD
CUCUMBER
TULIPWOOD AUBURN
TULLE ILLUSION
TUMATAKURU IRISHMAN MATAGORY
TUMBLE TOP COUP WALT LATCH
SPILL THROW TIFLE TRACE COTTON
GROVEL PURLER TIFFLE TOPPLE

WALTER WAMBLE WELTER STUMBLE
WHEMMEL
(— OVER) TIPPLE WALLOP
TUMBLE-DOWN RUINOUS
TUMBLER NUT CLICK GLASS LEVER
WIPER ROLLER ACROBAT DRUMMER
TIPPLER TOPPLER
TUMID TURGID BLOATED BULGING
FUSTIAN TURGENT INFLATED
TUMOROUS
TUMOR PAP WEN BEAL PIAN WART
AMPER BOTCH MYOMA NEVUS
PHYMA SWELL AMBURY ANBURY
EPULIS GLIOMA GYROMA INCOME
KELOID LIPOMA MYXOMA NUROMA
RISING WARBLE ADENOMA ANGIOMA
CYSTOMA DERMOID DESMOID
FIBROID FIBROMA LUTEOMA
MYELOMA OSTEOMA OSTEOME
SARCOMA TESTUDO THYMOMA
ULONCUS ATHEROMA BLASTOMA
CHLOROMA CHORIOMA EMBRYOMA
GLANDULE HEMATOMA HEPATOMA
HOLDFAST LYMPHOMA MELANOMA
MELICERA ODONTOMA PHLEGMON
PLASMOMA PSAMMOMA SCIRRHUS
SEMINOMA TERATOID TERATOMA
WINDGALL
(— OF EYELID) GRANDO
(— ON HORSES'S LEGS) JARDE
(PUSTULAR —) BLAIN
(SKIN —) OUCH
(STUDY OF —S) ONCOLOGY
TUMULT DIN COIL FARE FLAW FRAY
FUSS HURL MUSS REEL RIOT ROUT
VISE BRAWL BROIL HURLY HURRY
LURRY NOISE ROUST STOOR STOUR
WHIRL BUSTLE CLAMOR DIRDUM
EMEUTE FRACAS HUBBUB MUTINY
RABBLE RIPPET RUFFLE STEERY
UPROAR UPSTIR BLUSTER BOBBERY
FACTION FERMENT GARBOIL
TEMPEST TURMOIL DISORDER
SEDITION STIRRING
TUMULTUOUS HIGH LOUD RUDE
NOISY ROUGH STORMY FURIOUS
HURRIED LAWLESS RIOTOUS
VIOLENT AGITATED CONFUSED
DRAWLING HURTLING
TUMULUS MOTE TUMP MOUND
BARROW BURIAN COTERELL
TUN CASK HAAB
(20 —S) KATUN
(ONE-THIRD —) TERTIAN
TUNA AHI ATUN TUNNY BLUEFIN
PELAMYD ALBACORE KAWAKAWA
TUNE AIR ARIA DUMP FADO LEED
NOTE PORT RANT SONG CHARM
CHORD DRANT POINT ATTUNE
GROUND MAGGOT STRAIN STRING
GUAJIRA HALLING MEASURE
MELISMA SONANCE ANGLAISE
FANDANGO GUARACHA HABANERA
(— A HARP) WREST
(— AN INSTRUMENT) STRING
(DANCE —) FURIANT ANGLAISE
GALLIARD
(FOLK —) FADO
(HILLBILLY —) HOEDOWN

(LIGHT —) TOY
(LITTLE —) CATCH
(LIVELY —) LILT SPRING HORNPIPE
(MELANCHOLY —) DUMP
(SACRED —) CHORAL CHORALE
(TRADITIONAL —) TONE
TUNEBO TAME GUACICO
TUNEFUL TUNY CHANTANT
TUNESOME
TUNEFULNESS MELODY
TUNGSTEN W WOLFRAM SCHEELIN
TUNGUS EVENK LAMUT
TUNIC COAT JAMA JUPE VEST
COTTE FROCK GIPPO JAMAH JUPON
PALLA ACHKAN BLIAUT CAMISE
CHITON CYCLAS FECKET HARDIE
KABAYA KIRTLE TABARD ARISARD
BLEAUNT CAMISIA PALTOCK
SURCOAT TUNICLE COLOBIUM
GANDOURA SUBTUNIC SUBUCULA
SUKKENYE
(— OF MAIL) HAUBERK
(HOODED FUR —) SOVIK
TUNICATE SALP SALPA SALPID
ASCIDIAN TUNICARY UROCHORD
TUNICLE SACCOS
TUNING ANESIS
TUNING FORK EVEL EVIL FORK
TUNER DIAPASE DIAPASON
MODULANT
TUNING HAMMER KEY

TUNISIA
CAPE: BON BLANC
CAPITAL: TUNIS
COIN: DINAR
GULF: GABES TUNIS HAMMAMET
ISLAND: DJERBA
LAKE: ACHKEL DJERID BIZERTE
MEASURE: SAA SAH SAAH CAFIZ
WHIBA METTAR
PORT: SFAX GABES TUNIS SOUSSE
BIZERTE
RIVER: MEDJERDA
TOWN: BEJA SFAX SUSA GABES
GAFSA MATEUR NABEUL
SOUSSE BIZERTE JENDOUBA
TEBOURBA ZAGHOUAN
WEIGHT: SAA ROTL ARTAL ARTEL
RATEL UCKIA KANTAR

TUNNEL ADIT BORE CAVE PUKA
SINK TUBE DRIFT DRIVE KAREZ
STALL BURROW PIERCE
(— INTO AN IGLOO) TOSSUT
TUNNY TUNA ALBACORE SCOMBRID
(YOUNG —) PELAMYD
TUP TIP TRIP MONKEY BLISSOM
TURBAN PAT MOAB PATA SASH
TUFT LUNGI MITER MITRE PATTI
TOWEL TUFFE MANDIL WRAPPER
KAFFIYEH PUGGAREE SEERBAND
TOLIPANE TULIPANT TURBANTO
TURBELLARIA APROCTA
TURBELLARIAN FLATWORM
TURBID FAT RILY DROVY GUMLY
MUDDY ROILY DRUMLY GRUMLY
QUALLY FECULENT LUTULENT

TURBIDITY RILE
TURBOT BRET BRILL WHIFF
FLATFISH
TURBULENCE FURY UPROAR
FERMENT RIOTING
TURBULENT GURL HIGH LOUD RUDE
WILD ROUGH WROTH RUGGED
STORMY UNRULY YEASTY FURIOUS
RABBISH RACKETY TROUBLE
VIOLENT MUTINOUS
TURDUS MERULA
TUREEN DISH TERRINE
TURF SOD VAG CESS DELF FAIL
FALE FEAL FLAG FLAT FLAW PONE
SUNK DELFT SCRAW SPINE SWARD
TRUFF FLAUGHT SHIRREL SODDING
(— CUT BY GOLF STROKE) DIVOT
(— FOR LINING PARAPET) GAZON
(DRIED — FOR FUEL) VAG
(PARED —) BEAT
(ROUGH —) GOR
(SMALL PIECE OF —) TAB
(THIN LAYER OF —) FLAW
TURF SPADE SLANE
TURGID TUMID INFLATED
TURGIDNESS TYMPANY
TURK TURCO TURKO SELJUK
CORSAIR OSMANLI OTTOMAN
TURQUET KONARIOT
TURKANA ELKUMA

TURKEY
CAPE: INCE BAFRA ANAMUR
HINZIR KARATAS KEREMPE
CAPITAL: ANKARA
COIN: PARA AKCHA ASPER ATTUN
REBIA AKCHEH SEQUIN ZEQUIN
ALTILIK BESHLIK PATAQUE
PIASTER MEDJIDIE ZECCHINO
DISTRICT: PERA BEYOGLU CILICIA
GULF: COS ANTALYA
LAKE: TUZ VAN EGRIDIR BEYSEHIR
MEASURE: DRA OKA OKE PIK
DRAA HATT KHAT KILE ZIRA
ALMUD BERRI DONUM KILEH
ZIRAI ARSHIN CHINIK DJERIB
FORTIN HALEBI PARMAK
NOCKTAT
MOUNTAIN: AK ALA KARA HASAN
HINIS HONAZ MURAT MURIT
ARARAT BINGOL BOLGAR
SUPHAN ERCIYAS KARACALI
PROVINCE: SERT SIIRT ANGORA
EYALET
RIVER: DICLE FIRAT GEDIZ HALYS
IRMAK KIZIL MESTA SARUS
SEIHUN SEYHAN SEYLAN TIGRIS
SAKARYA MAEANDER
SEAPORT: ENOS IZMIR MERSIN
SAMSUN TRABZON ISTANBUL
TOWN: URFA ADANA BURSA IZMIR
KONYA MARAS SIIRT SIVAS
AINTAB EDESSA EDIRNE ELAZIZ
MARASH SAMSUN ERZURUM
KAYSERI SCUTARI USKUDAR
ISTANBUL STAMBOUL
WEIGHT: OKA OKE DRAM KILE
ROTL ARTAL ARTEL CEQUI

CHEKE KERAT MAUND OBOLU
RATEL BATMAN DIRHEM KANTAR
MISKAL DRACHMA QUINTAL
YUSDRUM

TURKEY STAG STEG BUSTARD
ERECTER ERECTOR GOBBLER
ALDERMAN
(MALE —) TOM
(YOUNG —) POULT
TURKEY BUZZARD AURA
BROMVOEL BROMVOGEL GALLINAZO
TURKEY-COCK STAG
TURKEY OAK CERRIS
TURKI KAZAK QAZAQ KAZAKH
TURKISH TURK TURCIC OSMANLI
OTTOMAN
TURKISH DELIGHT LOUKOUM
TURKOMAN SEID ERSAR
TURK'S CAP LILY MARTAGON
TURMERIC REA ANGO HALDI OLENA
HULDEE AZAFRAN CURCUMA
TURMIT TURNIP
TURMOIL ADO DIN COIL DUST MOIL
TOIL TOSS BURLE HURLY HURRY
STROW TOUSE WHIRL HASSLE
JABBLE UPROAR WELTER CLUTTER
EMOTION FERMENT GARBOIL
HURLING MAKADOO RUMMAGE
TEMPEST DISPEACE DISQUIET
TURN GO BOW CUT GEE JAR RUN
TON WIN AIRT BEND BOUT BOWL
CALE CAST CHAR CHOP COCK EDDY
GIRO HACK HEAD HINT HURL JAMB
KINK PULL QUIP ROLL ROVE SLEW
TOUR VEER VERT VICE WAFT WELT
WIND AIRTH ANGLE BLANK CHARE
CRANK CRASH CREEK CRICK
CROOK ELBOW FEEZE GLINT PIVOT
PLUCK PRICK QUIRK SHIFT SPELL
SWING SWIRL TARVE TERVE TREND
TRILL TROLL TWINE TWIST VERSE
VOLTI WHEEL WREST ATTURN
BOUGHT CIRCLE COURSE DEPEND
DIRECT DOUBLE GRUPPO GYRATE
INDENT INTEND INTURN POSSET
QUEEVE RESORT RETURN ROTATE
SPIRAL STRAIN SWIVEL TOURNE
TURKEN VOLUME VOLUTE WIMPLE
CONVERT CRANKLE CRINKLE
DEFLECT DISTURB FLEXION
FLEXURE FLOUNCE INCLINE INFLECT
PASSADE REVERSE REVOLVE
SERPENT TWINGLE TWISTER
VERSATE WREATHE CLINAMEN
DOUBLING FLECTION TOURNURE
VOLUTION
(— ABOUT) SLEW SLUE SLOUGH
WINDLASS
(— AGAINST) CROSS
(— AROUND) GYRE WELT WEND
RATCH BEWEND SPHERE
(— ASIDE) ERR WRY DAFF SKEW
WARD ABHOR AVERT BLENK DETER
EVADE FENCE GLENT SHEER WAIVE
BLENCH DEPART DETURN DIVERT
SWERVE SWITCH CRINKLE DECLINE
DEFLECT DEVIATE DIGRESS

DIVERGE PERVERT SCRITHE
(— AT DRINKING) TIRL
(— ATTENTION) ADVERT ADDRESS
(— AWAY) DOFF AVERT CHARE
HIELD REPEL AVERSE DESERT
DETURN DIVERT REVOLT ABANDON
DECLINE REVERSE OVERTURN
WITHTURN
(— AWRY) CONTORT
(— BACK ON) RUMP
(— BACK) KEP ABORT FLIPE FLYPE
RETORT RETURN REVERT REFLECT
UNTWIST RENVERSE
(— BROWN) AUGUST
(— BY TOSSING) FLAP
(— CARD FACE UP) BURN
(— DOWN) DIP DENY
(— FOR BETTER) CRISIS
(— IN ARCHERY) END
(— IN CROQUET) BISK BISQUE
(— IN ROPE) NIP RIDER
(— INSIDE OUT) EVERT INVERT
(— INTO ICE) CONGEAL
(— INTO VINEGAR) ACETIFY
(— LEAVES OF BOOK) LEAF TOSS
(— OF AFFAIRS) GO JOB KICK
(— OF CABLE) BITTER
(— OF DUTY) TOUR SHIFT TRICK
(— OF EVENTS) WENT
(— OF FANCY) GUST
(— OF MIND) FREAK
(— OF TIDE) PINCH
(— OF WIT) FLIRT
(— OF YARN) MOUSING
(— OFF) SHUNT DIVERT
(— ON LATHE) THROW
(— ON) HIT
(— OUT TO BE) PROVE EXFLECT
(— OUT) GO USH BEAR FALL FARE
OUST SORT TAKE CHIVE FUDGE
OUTPUT SUCCEED
(— OUTWARD) EVERT SPLAY
(— OVER) CANT FLAP FLIP KEEL
VETTE VOLVE CLINCH DESIGN
AGITATE CAPSIZE
(— POINT OF) ABATE
(— RAPIDLY) SPIN TIRL GIDDY
(— RIGHT) HAP HUP
(— SAIL YARD) BRACE
(— SKIS) STEM
(— SOUR) FOX BLINK PRILL BLEEZE
CHANGE SOUREN
(— SUDDENLY) FLOP
(— TO NEAR SIDE) HAW
(— TO OFF SIDE) GEE
(— TO ONE SIDE) CORNER GOGGLE
(— TO THE LEFT) HAW PORT WIND
WYND
(— UP NOSE) FLIRT SNURL
(— UP) FACE HAPPEN
(— UPSIDE DOWN) CANT COUP
WHELM INVERT QUELME WHELVE
(— VESSEL IN CIRCLE) CHAPEL
(— WHEELS) CRAMP
(— YELLOW) FIRE
(COMPLETE —) LAP
(DOWNWARD —) SLIDE
(ECCENTRIC —) CRANKUM
(FORTUNATE —) BREAK

(HALF —) CARACOLE
(IN —) AROUND
(SHARP —) DOUBLE WRENCH
ZIGZAG HAIRPIN
(SKI —) SWING CHRISTIE TELEMARK
(SUDDEN —) CURL
(PL.) ALLEGRO
TURNBUCKLE TURNEL TURNBOUT
TURNCOAT APOSTATE RENEGADE
TURNED SOUR VERSED COCKEYED
INFLEXED
(— ABOUT) CONVERSE
(— BACK) EVOLUTE
(— DOWNWARD) ABASED DEFLEXED
(— EDGEWISE) BLIND
(— INWARD) VARUS
(— TOWARD ONE SIDE) AWRY
(— TOWARD) ANODIC
(— UP) ACOCK URVED
(— WRONG WAY) AWK
TURNER SLICE BODGER SLIDER
TWIRLER
TURNING HEAD TWIST VOLTA WRINK
DETOUR ROTARY FLEXION FLEXURE
VOLVENT FLECTION STREPSIS
WHEELERY
(— OF EYE) CAST
(— SOUR) ACESCENT
(— TO RIGHT) DEXTRO
(— TOWARD STEM) ADVERSE
(METAL —S) SWARF
(PL.) SCULL
TURNIP BAGA NAPE NEEP RAPE
NAVEW SWEDE RAPEYE TURMUT
CRUCIFER RUTABAGA
(PL.) KRAUT RAPPINI
TURNIP-SHAPED NAPIFORM
RAPACEUS
TURNIX QUAIL HEMIPOD ORTYGAN
HEMIPODE
TURNKEY SCREW LOCKSMAN
TURNOUT RIG SETOUT EQUIPAGE
TRANSFER
TURNOVER BRAMBLE EMPANADA
FLAPJACK
(PL.) PIROJKI PIROSHKI
TURNPIN TAMPION
TURNSOLE HELIO
TURNSPIT HASTLER
TURNSTILE TIRL STILE TURNGATE
TURNPIKE
TURNSTONE PLOVER REDLEG
CHICARIC CREDDOCK
TURNTABLE RACER ROTARY
NONSYNC PLAYBACK
TURNUS (FATHER OF —) DAUNUS
(MOTHER OF —) VENILIA
(SLAYER OF —) AENEAS
TURPENTINE THUS TURPS SCRAPE
THINNER
(BORDEAUX —) GALIPOT
TURPITUDE FEDITY
TURQUOISE TURKEY TURKIS
CALAITE CALLAIS
TURRET BELFRY CUPOLA GARRET
GAZEBO LOUVER TOURET GUERITE
MIRADOR MONITOR BARTIZAN
GUNHOUSE TURRICLE PEPPERBOX
TURTLE EMYD ARRAU CARET CAREY

TORUP COODLE COOTER JURARA
SLIDER THURGI TURKLE CRAWLER
CREEPER EMYDIAN JUNIATA
LOGHEAD SNAPPER TORTUGA
CHELONID FLAPJACK HAWKBILL
MATAMATA SHAGTAIL STINKPOT
TERRAPIN TORTOISE
(— HAVING COMMERCIAL SHELL)
CHICKEN
(OLD —) MOSSBACK
TURTLEHEAD BALMONY CHELONE
CODHEAD
TUSCANY COLCOTHAR
TUSK CUSK HORN IVORY TOOTH
ELEPHANT
(— OF WILD BOAR) RAZOR
(ELEPHANT'S —) SCRIVELLO
TUSSLE TUG BICKER TASSEL
TOUSLE WARSLE
TUXEDO TUX TUCK
TUSSOCK HASSOCK
TUT HOOT TOOT HOOTS
TUTELAGE TUTELE YEMSEL
NURTURE TEACHING
TUTELARY GENIUS
TUTOR DON TUTE COACH TRACH
DOCENT FEEDER GROUND MASTER
PEDANT SCHOOL GRINDER TEACHER
CRANSIER CREANCER GOVERNOR
PANGLOSS PUPILIZE
TUTTI RIPIENO
TUTU TOOT TUPAKIHI
TWADDLE ROT FUDGE HAVER
BABBLE DRIVEL FOOTLE PIFFLE
TOOTLE TWATTLE NONSENSE
SLIPSLOP
TWANA COLCINE
TWANG TANG PLUCK SNUFFLE
TWANGLE TWANKLE
TWAYBLADE DUFOIL TWIFOIL
(PL.) LISTERA
TWEAK FEAK TWIG
TWEED PATTU PATTOO
TWEEZERS TIT TWIRK TWINGE
TWITCH MULLETS PINCERS
PINCETTE VOLSELLA
TWELFTH TWALT DOZENTH
(— OF INCH) SECOND
(— OF LIGHT PERIOD) INCH
(— PART) UNCIA
TWELVE TWAL DOZEN DICKER
DODECADE
TWELVEMONTH TOWMONT
TWELVER IMAMI
TWELVE-TONE SERIAL
TWELVE-TONE-ROW SET
TWENTIETH VIGESIMAL VINGTIEME
TWENTY KAPH CORGE KAPPA
SCORE COOREE
TWENTY-FIVE QUARTERN
TWENTY-FOURTH CARAT
TWENTY-ONE VANJOHN BLACKJACK
TWICE BIS DOPPIO
(— A DAY) BID
TWIDDLE TWEEDLE TWITTER
TWIG COW CHAT RICE RISP SLIP
WAND YARD BIRCH BRIAR BRIER
SHRAG SHRED SPRAY SPRIG STICK
TWIST VIRGA WAVER WITHE BALEYS

FESCUE GREAVE SALLOW SPRING
SWITCH WATTLE WICKER SCOLLOP
TWIGLET ANAPHYTE
(— **FOR SNUFF**) DIP
(— **GROWING FROM STUMP**) WAVER
(— **IN BIRD SNARE**) SWEEK
(— **WORN AT SACRIFICES**)
INARCULUM
(—**S FOR BURNING**) CHATWOOD
(—**S FOR WATTLING**) FRITLES
(—**S MADE INTO BROOM**) BESOM
(**BARE** —) COW
(**DRIED** —) CHAD
(**LITTLE** —) SURCLE
(**THATCHING** —) SCOLLOP
(**WILLOW** —) SALLOW ANAPHYTE
TWIGGED VIRGATE
TWIGGY SPRAYEY
TWILIGHT DIMPS DUMPS GLOAM
TWALE DIMMET DIMMIT UGHTEN
DUCKISH COCKSHUT EVENGLOW
GLOAMING GRISPING CREPUSCLE
(— **OF THE GODS**) RAGNAROK
(**DARKER PART OF** —) DUSK
(**MORNING** —) DAWN
TWILL WALE CHINO CADDIS RUSSEL
CADDICE DUNGAREE
TWILLED CORDED
TWIN DUAL GEMEL SOSIE DIDYMUS
JUMELLE SIAMESE TWINDLE
DIDYMATE DIDYMOID DIDYMOUS
PARASITE TWINLING
(**PL.**) GEMEL COUPLET
TWINE MAT COIL DUNE LACE PIRL
WIND WRAP TWIRL TWIST INFOLD
INTORT ANAMITE ENTWINE
SKEENYIE
(**HANK OF** —) RAN
(**PITCHED** —) WHIPPING
TWINEBUSH PINBUSH
TWINFLOWER LINNAEA
TWINGE GIRD PANG PULL SHOOT
TOUCH TWANG STOUND
(— **OF CONSCIENCE**) SCRUPLE
(— **OF PAIN**) GLISK
TWINKLE WINK BLINK TWEER TWINK
TWIRE SIMPER WINKLE SPARKLE
TWINKLING MOMENT TWINKLY
TWINLEAF HELMETPOD
TWIRL SPIN TIRL DRILL QUERL TRILL
TWIRK TWIST WHIRL TRUNDLE
TWIDDLE TWIZZLE
(— **OF BAGPIPE**) WARBLER
TWIST BOB CUE MAT PLY WIN WIP
CAST COIL CURL DRAW HURL KICK
KINK PIRL RICK SKEW SLEW SLUB
SLUE TURN WARP WIND WISP WORK
CHINK CRANK CRICK CRINK CROOK
CURVE FEEZE GNARL KINCH PLAIT
QUIRK QUIRL REEVE SCREW SKELL
SNAKE SNIRL SNURL SPIRE SWIRL
THROW TWEAK TWIND TWINE TWIRE
TWIRL WINCE WITHE WREST
BOUGHT DETORT EXTORT HANKLE
INTORT QUEEVE SLOUGH SPRAIN
SQUIRL SQUIRM STRAND TWEEZE
WAMBLE WARPLE WASHIN WICKER
WIMBLE WRABBE WRITHE CHIGNON
CONTORT CRANKLE CROOKLE

CRUMPLE DISTORT ENTWINE
ENTWIST FLOUNCE GIMMICK
SQUINCH TORTURE TWISTER
TWISTLE TWIZZLE WREATHE
WRIGGLE CLINAMEN CONVOLVE
ENTANGLE FOREHARD FORETURN
SPRINKLE SQUIGGLE VOLUTION
(— **A ROPE**) DALLY
(— **AWAY**) WAIVE
(— **BACK**) RETORT
(— **FORCIBLY**) WRING
(— **IN A ROPE**) GRIND SQUIRM
(— **IN GRAIN OF A BOW**) BOUGHT
(— **IN ONE'S NATURE**) KINK
(— **OF FACE**) STITCH
(— **OF HAY**) HAYBRAND
(— **OF PAPER**) SPILL
(— **OF PEN IN WRITING**) QUIRK
(— **OF SPEECH**) CRANK
(— **OF THE MOUTH**) DRAD
(— **OF TOBACCO**) ROLL
(— **OF YARNS**) FORETURN
(— **OUT OF SHAPE**) CONTORT
(— **SHARPLY**) FEAK
(— **TOGETHER**) CABLE RADDLE
TWISTED CAM KAM WRY AWRY
TORT KINKY SCREW TORSE WRONG
ATWIST GAUCHE HURLED KNOTTY
SCREWY SKEWED SWIRLY THROWN
TURKEN TWISTY WARPED WRITHE
CRISPED CROOKED GNARLED
KNOTTED SCREWED TORQUED
TORTILE TORTIVE WHELKED
WREATHY COCKEYED IMPLICIT
INTORTED INVOLVED NONPLANE
THRAWART WREATHEN
TWISTING DALLY KNECK AJOINT
TWIRLY TWIDDLY SQUIGGLY
STREPSIS
TWIT TIT CHECK TAUNT ETWITE
TWITTER RIDICULE
TWITCH TIC TIT FEAK FIRK JERK
JUMP PIRN TWIG WINK YANK PLUCK
START THRIP TWEAK TWICK TWIRK
QUATCH QUETCH QUITCH TWINGE
TWITCHEL
TWITCHING TIC JERKS PALMUS
WORKING SACCADIC
TWITTER TWIT CHIRM GARRE TWINK
JARGON WARBLE CHIPPER CHITTER
QUITTER TWITTLE WHITTER
TWO TWA BOTH TWAY TWIN TWAIN
BINARY COUPLE DOUBLE
(— **LINES**) LONGWAYS
(— **OF A KIND**) BRACE
(**IN** —) ATWO
(**US** —) UNC
TWO-COLORED BICHROME
TWO-FACED JANUS JANIFORM
TWO-FIFTEEN PM TIME
TWOFOLD DUAL DUPLE BACKED
BIFOLD DOUBLE DUPLEX DIGONAL
DIPLOID TWIFOLD DIDYMATE
DIDYMOID DIDYMOUS DIPLASIC
TWEYFOLD
TWO-FOOTED BIPED
TWO-FORKED BIFURCAL
TWO-HANDED BIMANAL BIMANOUS
TWO-HORNED BICORN BICORNED

TWOPENCE TUPPENCE
TWOS POT DEUCE
TWO-UP SWY
TYCOON SHOGUN TAIKUN
TYDEUS (**FATHER OF** —) OENEUS
(**MOTHER OF** —) PERIBOEA
(**SON OF** —) DIOMEDES
TYMPANUM DRUM TYMPAN
EARDRUM EPIPHRAGM
TYNDAREUS (**FATHER OF** —)
OEBALUS
(**WIFE OF** —) LEDA
TYPE CUT ILK CAST KIND MAKE
MOLD NORM SORT TAKE BOGUS
IMAGE MOULD STAMP EMBLEM
KICKER LETTER NATURE SHADOW
STRIPE SYMBOL TAKING TIMBER
BATARDE FASHION PARABLE
ANTETYPE EXEMPLAR
(— **BLOCK**) QUAD
(— **OF EXCELLENCE**) PARAGON
(— **PLACED BOTTOM UP**) TURN
(— **SET UP**) MATTER
(**ASSORTMENT OF** —) FONT
(**DANCE** —) LASYA
(**DISARRANGED** —) PI PIE
(**GERMAN** —) FRAKTUR
(**HEAVY-FACED** —) IONIC
(**HIGHEST** —) PINK
(**IDEAL** —) CHRIST
(**OPPOSITE** —) ANTITYPE
(**PHYSICAL** —) HABIT
(**RACIAL** —) DEHWAR
(**REPRESENTATIVE** —) GENIUS
(**SET** —) STICK
(**STYLE OF** —) DORIC ELITE GOUDY
GREEK IONIC KABEL ROMAN
BODONI CASLON GOTHIC HEBREW
ITALIC JENSON MODERN BOOKMAN
CENTURY ELZEVIR EMERALD
FULLFACE GARAMOND
TYPEBAR(**PL.**) BASKET
TYPEFACE FACE BOLDFACE
SANSERIF
TYPEHOLDER PALLET
TYPESETTER MONO
TYPESETTING FAT PHAT
TYPEWRITER MILL TYPER TYPIST
PORTABLE
TYPHON (**FATHER OF** —) TARTARUS
(**MOTHER OF** —) TERRA
TYPHOON WIND CYCLONE TUFFOON
TYPICAL FAIR TYPAL TYPIC USUAL
AVERAGE CLASSIC PATTERN
PERFECT REGULAR
TYPIFY TYPE IMAGE SHADOW
EPITOMIZE REPRESENT SYMBOLIZE
TYPIFYING GENERIC
TYR ER EAR TIU TYRR
TYRANNICAL LORDLY SLAVISH
ABSOLUTE DESPOTIC
TYRANNIZE DOMINEER OVERLORD
TYRANNOUS ABSOLUTE
TYRANNY ROD DESPOTISM
TYRANT ANARCH DESPOT NIMROD
FUEHRER PHARAOH PHALARIS
TYRANT FLYCATCHER PEWEE
TYRO HAM COLT PUPIL NOVICE

RABBIT TYRONE BEGINNER
NEOPHYTE
(FATHER OF —) SALMONEUS

(HUSBAND OF —) CRETHEUS
(MOTHER OF —) ALCIDICE
(SON OF —) AESON NELEUS PELIAS

PHERES AMYTHAON
TYRRHENIAN ETRUSCAN
TYTO ALUCO STRIX

U UNCLE UNION
UDDER BAG DUG TID EWER ELDER
SUMEN VESSEL

UGANDA
CAPITAL: KAMPALA
COLLEGE: MAKERERE
FORMER CAPITAL: ENTEBBE
LAKE: KYOGA ALBERT EDWARD
GEORGE VICTORIA
LANGUAGE: ATESO GANDA
LUGANDA SWAHILI
MOUNTAIN: ELGON
NATIVE: ATESO BANTU LANGO
ACHOLI ANKOLE BAGISU BAKIGA
BASOGA BATORO BAGANDA
BUNYORO LUGBARA NILOTIC
SUDANIC
PLATEAU: ANKOLE
PROVINCE: BUGANDA
RIVER: ASWA KAFU PAGER
KATONGA
SEAPORT: MOMBASA
TOWN: JINJA MBALE ENTEBBE
MOMBASA

UGLY FOUL AWFUL OUGLE SNIVY
UNKED CRANKY DREEPY GORGON
HOMELY LAIDLY CRABBED GRIZZLY
HIDEOUS HOUGHLY VICIOUS
GRUESOME UGLISOME UNLOVELY
UGLY-TEMPERED SNARLISH
UGNI BLANC TREBBIANO
UIGHUR JAGATAI
UITOTAN KAIMO WITOTAN
UKE JARANA
UKULELE UKE TAROPATCH
ULCER FRET KYLE SORE WOLF
BOTCH ULCUS MORMAL TETTER
CHANCRE EGILOPS ENCAUMA
AEGILOPS FONTANEL FOSSETTE
ULCUSCLE
(ARTIFICIAL —) ISSUE
ULCERATING EXEDENT
ULCERATION CARIES BEDSORE
HELCOSIS
ULEX LING
ULEXITE TIZA
ULNA CUBIT CUBITAL CUBITUS
ULTIMATE IT DIRE LAST FINAL
ULTIME SUPREME ABSOLUTE
EVENTUAL FARTHEST ULTIMITY
ULTIMATELY FINALLY
ULTIMO PAST
ULTRA EXTREME FANATIC FORWARD
ULTRACONSERVATISM TORYISM
ULTRACONSERVATIVE WHITE
ULTRAFASHIONABLE RITZY SWELL
SWAGGER
ULTRAMONTANISM CURIALISM
ULUA PAPIO PAPIOPIO
ULYSSES (FATHER OF —) LAERTES
(MOTHER OF —) ANTICLEA
(SLAYER OF —) TELEGONUS
(SON OF —) TELEMACHUS
(WIFE OF —) PENELOPE
UMBEL RAY RADIUS SERTULE
UMBELLA SERTULUM UMBELLET

UMBELLIFERONE CUMARIN
COUMARIN
UMBER OMER OMBER PARTRIDGE
UMBILICUS NAVEL
UMBO BEAK UMBONULE
UMBONES NATES
UMBRA DOGFISH MUDFISH NUCLEUS
UMBRINE
UMBRAGE PIQUE SNUFF OFFENSE
UMBRELLA BELL GAMP MUSH
BROLLY CHATTA PAYONG PILEUS
CHATTAH GINGHAM ROUNDEL
FITTISOL KITTYSOL MUSHROOM
TYRASOLE
UMBRELLA BIRD COTINGA
COTINGID
UMBRELLA BUSH MILJEE
UMBRELLA PALM KENTIA
UMBRELLA PLANT SEDGE GLUMAL
UMBRELLA TREE WAHOO
ELKWOOD MAGNOLIA
UMBRETTE UMBRE HOMBRE
UMBRET CICONIID
UMBRIAN IGUVINE
UMBURANA ROBLE
UMLAUT MUTATION METAPHONY
UMPIRE UMP JUDGE TRIER ARBITER
DAYSMAN ODDSMAN STICKLER
UNABASHED BROWLESS
UNABBREVIATED FULL
UNABLE UNHABILE
UNACCENTED GRAVE LIGHT ATONIC
UNACCEPTABLE DREADFUL
UNACCOMPANIED BARE SOLO
ALONE SINGLE
UNACCOUNTABLE STRANGE
UNACCUSTOMED UNUSED
STRANGE INSOLITE WONTLESS
UNACQUAINTED STRANGE
UNCOUTH
UNADORNED DRY BALD STARK
RUSTIC SIMPLE AUSTERE INORNATE
UNADULTERATED NET FRANK
HONEST VIRGIN GENUINE SINCERE
UNADVANTAGEOUSLY ILL
UNAFFECTED EASY REAL PLAIN
HOMELY NATIVE RUSTIC SIMPLE
ARTLESS BUCOLIC SINCERE
SEMPLICE
UNAFRAID BOLD BRAVE DEFIANT
UNAGGRESSIVE AMIABLE
UNALERT SUPINE
UNALLOYED DEEP SOLID VIRGIN
GENUINE
UNALTERABLE IMMUTABLE
UNAMBIGUOUS EXPLICIT
UNANIMATED FLAT VAPID INSIPID
UNANIMITY ATTACK CONSENT
UNANIMOUS SOLID WHOLE
UNANIME UNIVOCAL
UNAPPROACHABLE STATELY
UNARMED BARE INERM UNBARBED
UNASSAILABLE SECURE
UNASSUMED NATURAL
UNASSUMING SHY HUMBLE MODEST
SIMPLE NATURAL RETIRING
UNATTACHED FREE LOOSE SINGLE
UNATTENDED SINGLE
UNATTRACTIVE BLAH UGLY WORSE

HOMELY FRUMPISH UNLIKELY
UNAVAILING VAIN FUTILE GAINLESS
UNAVOIDABLE SHUNLESS
UNAVOWED SECRET
UNAWARE UNWARE WITLESS
HEEDLESS INNOCENT UNBEWARE
WARELESS
UNAWARES ABACK SHORT
UNBALANCED HITE DOTTY NUTTY
FRUITY UNEVEN FANATIC
DERANGED LOPSIDED
UNBAR UNSLOT
UNBARRED UNSTOKEN
UNBECOMING RUDE INEPT INDIGN
UNMEET BENEATH IMPROPER
INDECENT UNSEEMLY UNWORTHY
UNBELIEF UNFAITH
UNBELIEVABLE HOT THIN
UNBELIEVER PAGAN GIAOUR
ATHEIST DOUBTER INFIDEL
SCOFFER SKEPTIC
UNBEND REST THAW FRESE RELAX
UNTIE EXTEND DISBEND UNCROOK
UNBENDING RIGID STARK STERN
STIFF THARF OBDURATE RAMRODDY
RESOLUTE
UNBIASED FAIR JUST DETACHED
UNBIND FREE UNDO UNTIE UNGIRD
UNDRESS
UNBLAMABLE INNOCENT
UNBLEACHED BLAE BLAY ECRU
BEIGE BROWN
UNBLEMISHED FAIR PURE SOUND
ENTIRE SPOTLESS
UNBLOCK REDD
UNBLOODY INCRUENT
UNBOLT OPEN UNBAR UNPIN
UNBOSOM OPEN
UNBOUGHT UNCOFT
UNBOUND FREE LOOSE
UNBOUNDED HUGE
UNBRANDED SLICK NATIVE
UNBROKEN DEAD FLAT FERAL
FLUSH SOLID SINGLE CERRERO
UNRACED STRAIGHT UNBACKED
WAKELESS
UNBUILD DESTROY
UNBUILT UNBIGGED
UNBURDEN EMPTY UNLOAD UNSHIP
UNBURNISHED WHITE MATTED
UNCANNY EERY UNCO EERIE SCARY
UNCOW UNKID WEIRD WISHT
CREEPY SPOOKY UNCOUTH
ELDRITCH POKERISH
UNCASTRATED INTACT
UNCAUGHT UNHENT
UNCEASING ENDLESS ETERNAL
EASELESS MINUTELY
UNCEREMONIOUS CURT BLUFF
BLUNT SHORT ABRUPT FAMILIAR
INFORMAL
UNCERTAIN WAW DARK HAZY WILD
FLUKY SHADY SHAKY WAUGH
CASUAL CLOUDY CRANKY FITFUL
FLUKEY GLEAMY QUEASY CASALTY
CHANCEY COMICAL DUBIOUS
TRICKSY VARIOUS WILSOME
CATCHING DELICATE FLICKERY
FUGITIVE HOVERING INSECURE

SLIPPERY TECHNOUS TICKLISH

UNCERTAINTY MIST WERE DEMUR DOUBT MAYBE BAFFLE BALANCE DUBIETY CASUALTY SUSPENSE UNSURETY

UNCHALLENGED ACCEPTED

UNCHANGEABLE FAST STABLE DURABLE ETERNAL

UNCHANGING STATIC ETERNAL UNIFORM STATICAL

UNCHASTE LEWD FRAIL LIGHT IMPURE WANTON FORLAIN HAGGARD SCARLET IMMODEST

UNCHASTITY BAWDRY STUPRUM ADULTERY

UNCHECKED LIBERAL RAMPANT

UNCIFORM HAMATUM

UNCINARIA NECATOR

UNCIVIL RUDE BLUFF ROUGH RUSTY CRUSTY RUGGED UNFEEL IMPOLITE

UNCIVILIZED RUDE WILD MYALL INCULT SAVAGE UNCIVIL IGNORANT SYLVATIC

UNCLAD LOOSE UNDRESSED

UNCLE EME OOM YEME BUNKS NUNKY NUNCLE

UNCLEAN FOUL TREF VILE BLACK TARRY TERFA TREFA COMMON FILTHY IMMUND IMPURE DEFILED

UNCLEANNESS DIRT FOULNESS

UNCLEAR DIM HAZY SHAGGY

UNCLEARLY DIMLY

UNCLENCH UNDOUBLE

UNCLOSE OPE OPEN UNHASP DISCLOSE

UNCLOTHE TIRL SPOIL UNRIG DEVEST DESPOIL

UNCLOUDED CLEAR

UNCOIL UNLINK

UNCOLORED FAIR

UNCOMBED UNKAMED UNTEWED

UNCOMBINED FREE FRANK

UNCOMELY INDECENT

UNCOMFORTABLE HOT EVIL POOR HARSH UNKET UNKID QUEASY STICKY UNFELE

UNCOMMON MUCH NICE RARE SELD UNCO BYOUS FORBY UNCOW VAUDY DAINTY FORBYE SCARCE SPECIAL STRANGE UNUSUAL SINGULAR UNWONTED

UNCOMMONLY UNCO BYOUS EXTRA UNCOW UNCOLY

UNCOMMONNESS SCARCITY

UNCOMMUNICATIVE DUMB SILENT PRIVATE RESERVED

UNCOMPLICATED RURAL HONEST SIMPLE

UNCOMPOUNDED SIMPLE SIMPLEX

UNCOMPROMISING ACID FIRM GRIM RIGID STERN STOUT ULTRA SEVERE STRICT STRONG EXTREME

UNCONCEALED BARE OPEN OUVERT APPARENT

UNCONCERN APATHY EASINESS

UNCONCERNED COOL EASY BLAND CASUAL CARELESS

UNCONCERNEDLY LIGHTLY

UNCONDITIONAL FREE FRANK

UTTER SIMPLE ABSOLUTE EXPLICIT TERMLESS

UNCONFINED LAX FREE LOOSE

UNCONGENIAL HATEFUL INGRATE KINDLESS

UNCONNECTED GAPPY DETACHED

UNCONQUERED INVICT INVICTED

UNCONSCIOUS OUT COLD BRUTE ASLEEP BLOTTO CUCKOO TORPID UNAWARE COMATOSE IGNORANT.

UNCONSTRAINED FREE UNNET SIMPLE FAMILIAR

UNCONTROLLABLE WILD

UNCONTROLLED FREE LIBERAL UNBITTED

UNCONVENTIONAL LOOSE CASUAL DEVIOUS BOHEMIAN INFORMAL

UNCONVINCING FALSE FISHY

UNCOOKED RAW

UNCOUNTABLE SUMLESS

UNCOUPLE CUT DISLINK

UNCOUTH RUDE CRUDE DORIC GURLY UNKED UNKIT GOTHIC JUNGLY QUAINT RENISH AWKWARD BOORISH CUBBISH HIRSUTE LOUTISH UNGAINLY YOKELISH (— PERSON) TUG

UNCOVER BARE DOFF HUNT ROUT TIRL TIRR BREAK STRIP TIRVE UNLAP UNLID UNWRY DETECT EXHUME SEARCH UNBARE UNCASE UNHALE UNVEIL UNDRAPE UNEARTH DISCLOSE DISCOVER UNMANTLE UNMUFFLE

UNCOVERED BARE OVERT

UNCTION CHRISM OINTMENT

UNCTUOUS FAT OILY SALVY SLEEK SOAPY SUAVE GREASY COURTLY PINGUID

UNCULTIVATED RAW BRUT FERAL DESERT FALLOW INCULT SAVAGE SLOVEN WILDERN

UNCULTURED RUDE INCULT ARTLESS

UNCUT RASPED

UNDAMAGED WHOLE

UNDARKENED CLEAR

UNDAUNTED BOLD BRAVE MANLY SPARTAN FEARLESS INTREPID

UNDE WAVY UNDEE

UNDECAYED GREEN

UNDECEIVE DISABUSE

UNDECIDED MOOT DUBIOUS PENDING DOUBTFUL WAVERING

UNDECIDEDLY HUMDRUM

UNDECLARED SECRET

UNDEFENDED UNKEPT

UNDEFILED PURE CHASTE INTACT VIRGIN

UNDEFINED OBSCURE

UNDELIVERABLE DEAD

UNDEMONSTRATIVE COLD ASEPTIC LACONIC RESERVED

UNDENIABLE BRUTAL

UNDENIABLY INDEED

UNDEPENDABLE CASUAL FLUFFY

UNDER SUB BAJO BELOW INFRA NEATH SOTTO ANEATH ANUNDER BENEATH

(— **ORDERS**) SUPPOSED

(— **THE WORD**) IV

(— **THE YEAR**) SA

(— **THIS TITLE**) HT

(— **THIS WORD**) SV SHV

(— **WAY**) AFOOT

UNDERBODICE JUMP BASQUINE

UNDERBRUSH FILTH COVERT GARSIL MAQUIS RAMMEL ABATURE

UNDERBURNED SOFT

UNDERBUTLER WASHPOT

UNDERCARRIAGE BOGY BOGEY BOGIE

UNDERCLAY WARRANT

UNDERCLOTHES LININGS

UNDERCOAT PILE ALPACA SURFACER

UNDERCOVER SECRET

UNDERCRUST ABAISSE

UNDERCURRENT UNDERLAY UNDERRUN UNDERSET

UNDERCUT JAD HOLE LAME POOL SUMP KIRVE NOTCH

UNDERDONE RARE

UNDERDRAWERS FLANNELS

UNDERESTIMATE DISPRIZE MINIMIZE

UNDERFRAME SOLE

UNDERGARMENT BAND SLIP CYMAR SIMAR SKIRT SMOCK TUNIC WAIST BODICE CAMISE CILICE CORSET GIRDLE STAMIN CHEMISE DOUBLET DRAWERS STAMMEL TALLITH KNICKERS (PL.) SMALLS FLANNELS FLIMSIES SNUGGIES

UNDERGO SERVE ENDURE SUFFER SUSTAIN

UNDERGRADUATE MAN TASSEL SERVITOR

UNDERGROWTH RUSH RAMMEL SPRING BUSHWOOD

UNDERHAND SLY DERN SHADY BYHAND SECRET OBLIQUE INVOLVED SINISTER SNEAKING

UNDERHANDED DERN FUNNY FILTHY SECRET SINISTER

UNDERIVED ORIGINAL

UNDERLAYER SLASHING

UNDERLIE SUBTEND

UNDERLING MENIAL SEQUEL UNDERER INFERIOR

UNDERLYING COVERT IMPLICIT

UNDERMINE SAP CAVE HOLE POOL ERODE KNIFE WEAKEN FOUNDER SUBVERT ENFEEBLE SUPPLANT

UNDERMINED ROTTEN

UNDERNEATH BELOW BENEATH UNNEATH

UNDERNSONG TIERCE

UNDERPANTS BRIEFS BLOOMERS KNICKERS

UNDERPART BELLY

UNDERPASS DIVE SUBWAY

UNDERRATE DECRY DISCOUNT

UNDERRUN BOTTOM

UNDERSACRISTAN CUSTOS

UNDERSHIRT VEST SHIFT SHIRT CAMISA JERSEY LINDER SEMMIT

SINGLET WRAPPER
UNDERSHRUB HEATH PINKEYE
  SEEPWEED SUBSHRUB
UNDERSIDE BOTTOM BREAST
  (— **OF CLOUD**) BASE
  (— **OF FINGER**) BALL
  (— **OF FLOOR**) CEILING
UNDERSIZED DEENY SCRUB STUNT
UNDERSKIRT QUILT CRINOLINE
UNDERSTAND CAN CON GET KEN
  SEE GAUM HAVE MAKE TAKE TWIG
  BRAIN ENTER GRASP REACH SAVVY
  SEIZE SENSE SKILL SPELL ACCEPT
  COTTON FIGURE FOLLOW INTAKE
  INTEND SUBAUD UPTAKE CONCEIT
  DISCERN COMPRISE CONCEIVE
  CONSTRUE CONTRIVE FORSTAND
  PERCEIVE PERSTAND UNDERNIM
UNDERSTANDING KEN WIT GAUM
  HEAD CLASP HEART INWIT SENSE
  SKILL ACCORD INTENT NOTION
  REASON TREATY UPTAKE COMPACT
  CONCEPT ENTENTE INSIGHT
  MEANING WITNESS DAYLIGHT
  (**IMPERFECT** —) DARKNESS
UNDERSTATEMENT LITOTES
UNDERSTOOD LUCID SUPPOSED
  (— **ONLY BY SPECIALLY INITIATED**)
  ESOTERIC
  (**EASILY** —) EASY CLEAR EXTANT
  (**NOT** —) DARKSOME
UNDERSTUDY DOUBLE
UNDERSURFACE SOLE
UNDERTAKE GO TRY DARE FANG
  FOND GRANT OFFER ASSUME
  INCEPT PLEDGE ATTEMPT EMBRACE
  EMPRISE PRETEND UNDERFO
  CONTRACT PRESTATE
  (— **RESPONSIBILITY**) ACCEPT
  ANSWER
UNDERTAKER UPHOLDER
UNDERTAKING JOB AVAL TASK
  CAUTIO EFFORT SCHEME VOYAGE
  ATTEMPT CALLING PROJECT
  VENTURE COVENANT
  (— **IN CARDS**) CONTRACT
  (**UNPROFITABLE** —) FOLLY
UNDERTEACHER USHER
UNDERTONE INKLING SUBTONE
UNDERTOW SEAPOOSE
UNDERVALUE DECRY DISPRIZE
  DISVALUE
UNDERWAIST CAMISOLE
UNDERWATER (— **DEVICE**) OTTER
  PARAVANE
UNDERWEAR BRIEFS SHORTS
  SKIVVY UNDIES DESSOUS HEAVIES
  LINGERIE PRETTIES
UNDERWING CATOCALA
UNDERWOOD FRITH BOSCAGE
  COPPICE
UNDERWORLD DUAT DEWAT HADES
  ORCUS SHEOL MICTLAN XIBALBA
  GANGLAND
UNDERWRITE SIGN INSURE
  ENDORSE
UNDERWRITER INSURER
UNDESERVED INDIGN
UNDETERMINED UNSET DUBIOUS

AORISTIC DOUBTFUL INFINITE
UNDEVELOPED CRUDE SLOVEN
  GERMING IMMATURE JUVENILE
UNDEVIATINGLY SMACK
UNDIFFERENCED ENTIRE
UNDIFFERENTIATED GLOBAL
  AMERISTIC
UNDIGESTED CRUDE
UNDIGNIFIED DOGGREL DOGGEREL
UNDILUTED MERE NEAT PURE
  NAKED SHEER SHORT STRAIGHT
UNDIMINISHED ENTIRE
UNDIMMED CLEAR
UNDINE NIX
UNDISCIPLINED WANTON COLTISH
UNDISCLOSED HIDDEN SEALED
UNDISCRIMINATING GROSS
UNDISGUISED BALD PLAIN
UNDISMAYED ONFLEMED
UNDISPUTED LIQUID
UNDISTINGUISHED GROSS
  COMMON UNNOBLE FAMELESS
  NOTELESS
UNDISTORTED CLEAR
UNDISTURBED SOUND VIRGIN
  TRANQUIL
UNDIVIDED WHOLE ENTIRE SINGLE
UNDO COOK SLIP FORDO SPEED
  UNPAY DEFEAT DIDDLE FOREDO
  UNBIND UNKNIT UNLOCK UNTUCK
  UNWORK DEFEISE DESTROY
  UNRAVEL UNRIVET UNTWIRL
  UNWEAVE UNWREST DECIPHER
  DISSOLVE DISTRUSS UNFASTEN
UNDOER ACHAN
UNDOGMATIC AGNOSTIC
UNDOING DEFEAT DOWNFALL
UNDOMESTICATED WILD FERAL
  FERINE
UNDOUBTEDLY SURELY FRANKLY
UNDRESS MOB DOFF FLAY TIRR
  STRIP UNRAY UNRIG DEVEST
  DIVEST UNBUSK UNCASE UNLACE
  UNRIND UNROBE UNTIRE DISCASE
  UNARRAY UNREADY UNSPOIL
  UNTRUSS NEGLIGEE UNATTIRE
UNDRESSED UNDIGHT
UNDUE EXTREME
UNDULATE WAVE WAVY FLOAT
  SWING BILLOW GYROSE KELTER
  UNDATE UNDOSE FLICKER UNDATED
UNDULATING SURGING FLEXUOUS
  INDENTED
UNDULATION FOLD ROLL WAVE
  CRIMP TEETER WAVING CRIMPING
UNDULATORY WAVY
UNDUTIFULNESS IMPIETY
UNDYED CORAH
UNDYING IMMORTAL
UNEARTH DIG MOOT EXPOSE
  UNCOVER DISCOVER
UNEARTHLY EERY EERIE WEIRD
  AWESOME UNCANNY UNGODLY
UNEASINESS ENVY GENE FIDGET
  NETTLE SORROW UNEASE AILMENT
  ANXIETY DISEASE MISEASE
  TROUBLE DISQUIET DISTASTE
UNEASY SICKLY FIDGETY INQUIET

RESTIVE UNQUIET WORRIED
  RESTLESS
UNEDUCATED SIMPLE IGNORANT
UNEMBELLISHED DRY PROSE
  AUSTERE
UNEMOTIONAL DRY COLD COOL
  STOIC STONY STOICAL
UNEMOTIONALLY EVENLY
UNEMPLOYED IDLE ORRA VOID
  OTIANT OTIOSE VACANT IDLESET
  LEISURE UNBUSIED
UNEMPLOYMENT IDLENESS
UNENCUMBERED VACANT
  EXPEDITE
UNENDING ABYSMAL AGELONG
  CHRONIC ENDLESS UNDYING
  TERMLESS TIMELESS
UNENJOYABLE JOYLESS
UNENLIGHTENED MISTY HEATHEN
  IGNORANT
UNENTHUSIASTIC COLD
UNEQUAL IMPAR DISPAR UNEGAL
  UNEVEN INEQUAL INFERIOR
  (— **TO STRAIN**) FEEBLE
UNEQUALED UNIQUE NONESUCH
UNEQUIVOCAL DIRECT SQUARE
  DEFINITE DISTINCT EXPLICIT
UNERRING DEAD TRUE DEADLY
  INERRANT
UNERRINGLY CLEAN
UNEVEN EROSE GOBBY HAGGY
  JAGGY MEALY ROUGH HOBBLY
  PLATTY RAGGED RUGGED SPOTTY
  TWITTY UNFAIR UNLIKE DIURNAL
  ERRATIC HOTTERY INEQUAL
  STREAKY UNEQUAL HUMMOCKY
  SCRATCHY SNAGGLED
  (— **IN COLOR**) CLOUDY
UNEVENNESS BUMP WAVE FRAZE
  ANOMALY ASPERITY
UNEVENTFUL STILL UNDATED
UNEXCITED LEVEL
UNEXCITING DEAD DULL TAME
  BORING PROSAIC
UNEXPECTED EERY EERIE ABRUPT
  SUDDEN UNWARY INOPINE
  UNLOOKED
UNEXPECTEDLY UNWARES
  UNAWARES
UNEXPIRED ALIVE
UNEXPLAINED HIDDEN
UNEXPOSED RAW
UNFADABLE FAST
UNFADED FRESH BRIGHT
UNFAILING SURE DEADLY INFALLID
  UNERRING
UNFAIR FOUL WRONG BIASED
  SHABBY UNEVEN UNJUST DEVIOUS
  PARTIAL SLANTER UNEQUAL
  UNSEEMLY WRONGFUL
UNFAIRLY HARDLY
UNFAIRNESS INEQUITY
UNFAITHFUL INFIDEL TRAITOR
  DISLOYAL RECREANT
UNFALTERING SURE TRUE STEADY
  UNERRING
UNFAMILIAR NEW FREMD HEATHER
  STRANGE UNKNOWN
UNFASTEN FREE OPEN UNDO

LOOSE UNPIN UNBIND UNHASP UNLIME UNLINK UNLOCK UNMAKE UNTINE UNDIGHT UNHITCH UNSTECK UNTRUSS

UNFATHOMABLE ABYSSAL PROFOUND

UNFATHOMED COSMIC

UNFAVORABLE BAD ILL FOUL HARD POOR SHREWD UNFAIR UNKIND ADVERSE AWKWARD FROWARD HOSTILE UNHAPPY BACKWARD CONTRARY INIMICAL SINISTER UNKINDLY

UNFAVORABLY BADLY CROSS

UNFEELING COLD DULL HARD CRASS CRUEL HARSH ROCKY STERN STONY BRUTAL LEADEN MARBLE STOLID CALLOUS OBDURATE

UNFEELINGLY HARSHLY

UNFEELINGNESS APATHY

UNFEIGNED OPEN TRUE HEARTY CORDIAL NATURAL SINCERE

UNFETTERED FREE UNGYVED

UNFILLED BLANK EMPTY VACANT VACUOUS

UNFINISHED RAW GRAY GREY KACHA KUTCHA RAGGED KACHCHA STICKIT IMMATURE

UNFIRED GREEN

UNFIRM UNFAST

UNFIT BAD SICK UNAPT WISHT WRONG COMMON FAULTY NOUGHT UNTIDY DISABLE UNFITTY IMPROPER UNFITTEN UNLIKELY UNLIKING

UNFITTING UNMEETLY

UNFLEDGED SQUAB CALLOW

UNFLINCHING LEVEL STAUNCH

UNFOLD OPEN BREAK BURST SOLVE UNLAP UNTIE DEPLOY EVOLVE EXPAND EXPLAT FLOWER SPREAD UNFURL UNPLAT UNROLL UNTUCK BLOSSOM DEVELOP DISPLAY DIVULGE EXPLAIN UNPLAIT UNRAVEL UNWEAVE UNDOUBLE UNPLIGHT

UNFOLDED EVOLUTE EXPANDED

UNFOLDING DISPLAY
(— OF EVENTS) ACTION
(— TO VIEW) BURST

UNFORCED EASY GLIB WILLING

UNFORESEEN SUDDEN IMPREVU UNAWARE

UNFORMED CALLOW INFORM

UNFORTUNATE ILL EVIL POOR DONCY WEARY SHREWD HAPLESS UNHAPPY UNLUCKY LUCKLESS UNTOWARD WANHAPPY

UNFREQUENTED EMPTY UNCOUTH SOLITARY

UNFRIENDLY ILL COLD FOUL CHILL BITTER CHILLY FIERCE FROSTY UNSOME HOSTILE INGRATE STRANGE INIMICAL

UNFROCK DEFROCK DEGRADE DISFROCK UNPRIEST

UNFRUITFUL BLUNT BARREN EFFETE WASTED STERILE USELESS INFECUND

UNFULFILLMENT BREACH

UNFURL SPREAD UNFOLD DEVELOP OUTROOL

UNFURNISHED BARE VACANT

UNGAINLY LANKY SPLAY WEEDY CLUMSY UNGAIN AWKWARD BOORISH NUNTING UNHEPPEN UNLICKED UNWIELDY

UNGENEROUS MEAN SHABBY STINGY GRUDGING

UNGIRDED DISCINCT

UNGODLINESS ATHEISM IMPIETY

UNGODLY SINFUL WICKED GODLESS IMPIOUS PROFANE

UNGOVERNABLE WILD UNRULY FROWARD IMPOTENT

UNGRACEFUL HARD CLUMSY ANGULAR AWKWARD HALTING UNTOWARD

UNGRACEFULLY HARSHLY

UNGRACIOUS GRUFF UNFEEL UNFELE SNAPPISH

UNGRATEFUL UNKIND INGRATE

UNGROOMED UNDRESSED

UNGUARDED STIFF

UNGUENT CEROMA CHRISM PIMENT POMADE POMATUM UNCTION OINTMENT

UNGULATE HOG PIG DEER HORSE TAPIR HOOFED AMBLYPOD ELEPHANT

UNGUMMED BRIGHT

UNHALLOWED IMPURE UNHOLY PROFANE

UNHAMPERED FREE DIRECT EXPEDITE

UNHAPPINESS MISERY SORROW ILLFARE SADNESS UNBLISS

UNHAPPY SAD DISMAL UNLUCKY UNLUSTY WANSOME DEJECTED DOWNBEAT DOWNGONE WOBEGONE WRETCHED

UNHARMED SAFE UNSHENT

UNHARNESS UNGEAR OUTSHUT UNHORSE UNTACKLE

UNHEALED GREEN

UNHEALTHY BAD MORBID QUEASY SICKLY UNHALE NAUGHTY PECCANT MALADIVE

UNHEATED COLD

UNHEEDED IGNORED UNTENTED

UNHEEDING DEAF CARELESS

UNHESITATING READY UNPOISED

UNHITCH OUTSPAN

UNHOLY IMPURE WICKED IMPIOUS PROFANE

UNHORSE PURL THROW UNCOLT DISMOUNT UNSADDLE

UNHURRIED EASY SLOW SOFT SOBER

UNHURT SAFE HARMLESS HURTLESS UNHARMED

UNIAT MALKITE MELCHITE

UNICORN LIN REEM KILIN LICORN LICORNE NARWHAL HOWITZER

UNICORN FISH LIJA UNIE

UNICORN PLANT MARTINOE

UNICUM UNION

UNIDENTIFIED FACELESS INCOGNITO

UNIFICATION SYSTEM ENSEMBLE

UNIFIED GLOBAL

UNIFIER UMBRELLA

UNIFORM KIT DEAD EVEN FLAT JUST LIKE SELF SUIT BLUES CLOTH KHAKI SOLID SUITY GLOBAL GREENS LIVERY SINGLE STEADY EQUABLE REGULAR SIMILAR SUNTANS CONSTANT EQUIFORM EQUIPAGE MEASURED STANDARD UNIVOCAL
(— IN HUE) FLAT
(LEATHER —) BUFF
(NOT —) SQUALLY
(PRISONER'S —) STRIPES

UNIFORMITY ONENESS EQUALITY EVENNESS MONOTONY SAMENESS

UNIFORMLY EVENLY EQUALLY

UNIFY MERGE UNITE CEMENT COMPACT UNITIZE COALESCE

UNILATERAL SECUND

UNIMAGINATIVE DULL SODDEN STUPID LIMITED LITERAL PROSAIC UNIDEAL PEDANTIC

UNIMPAIRED FRESH SOUND ENTIRE INTACT
(— BY) DEVOID

UNIMPASSIONED SOBER WHOLE STEADY

UNIMPEDED FREE EXPEDITE

UNIMPORTANT VAIN PETTY CASUAL SIMPLE TRIVIAL IMMOMENT TRINKETY

UNINFORMED GREEN UNTOLD IGNORANT

UNINHABITED WILD EMPTY DESERT VACANT DESOLATE WASTEFUL

UNINHIBITED LARGE

UNINJURED INTACT SINCERE

UNINSPIRED HACK STODGY DRYASDUST

UNINSTRUCTED IGNORANT

UNINTELLIGENT DUMB OBTUSE STUPID ASININE FOOLISH VACUOUS

UNINTELLIGIBLE BLIND MISTY OPAQUE MYSTICAL

UNINTENTIONAL UNMEANT

UNINTERESTING DRY ARID COLD DRAB DREE DULL FADE FLAT DREAR SANDY STALE BORING DREICH JEJUNE INSIPID BROMIDIC FRUMPISH

UNINTERMITTENT ITHAND

UNINTERRUPTED SMOOTH STEADY ENDLESS ETERNAL STRAIGHT

UNINTERRUPTEDLY AWAY

UNIO MUSSEL

UNION ZYG BLOC DUAD ALLOY GROUP JOINT NONOP UNITY ENOSIS FUSION GREMIO TAWHID CONCERT CONTACT MEETING ONENESS SOCIETY ADHESION ALLIANCE COHESION ESPOUSAL JOINTURE JUNCTION JUNCTURE SODALITY SYSTASIS TRIALISM VINCULUM
(MARITAL —) BED
(SEXUAL —) COPULA COUPLING

(TURKISH —) JETTRU
UNIONIST REFUGEE
UNIQUE ODD SOLE UNIC ALONE
UNION SINGLE SULLEN UNICUM
ALONELY SOLEYNE SPECIAL
STRANGE ISOLATED SINGULAR
UNIQUENESS SOLITUDE
UNISON FIRST HOMOPHONY
UNIT (ALSO SEE MEASURE) ONE
ATOM KLAN FLOOR HUMIT MONAD
NEPER ADDRESS DIOPTER ELEMENT
ENERGID KLAVERN
(— IN COUNTING FISH) MEASE
(— IN EARTHWORK) FLOAT FLOOR
(— OF 100 MEN) CENTURY
(— OF ABSORPTION) SABIN
(— OF ACCELERATION) GAL
(— OF ACTION) EPISODE
(— OF ANGULAR MEASURE)
CENTRAD
(— OF ARCHEOLOGICAL
CLASSIFICATION) ASPECT
(— OF BRIGHTNESS) STILB
LAMBERT
(— OF CAPACITANCE) JAR
(— OF CAPACITY) LAST ARDAB
ARDEB AMPHORA
(— OF COMIC STRIP) BOX
(— OF COUNTING) POINT
(— OF DESIGN) LARME
(— OF DISTANCE) DAY
(— OF ELASTANCE) DARAF
(— OF ELECTRIC CAPACITY) FARAD
(— OF ELECTRIC CONDUCTANCE)
MHO
(— OF ELECTRIC FORCE) VOLT
KILOVOLT STATVOLT
(— OF ELECTRIC INDUCTANCE)
HENRY
(— OF ELECTRIC INTENSITY)
AMPERE OERSTED
(— OF ELECTRIC RELUCTANCE) REL
STATOHM
(— OF ELECTRIC RESISTANCE) OHM
BEGOHM
(— OF ELECTRICITY) ES COULOMB
(— OF ENERGY) ERG JOULE
ATOMERG QUANTUM
(— OF FINENESS) CARAT KARAT
(— OF FLOW) CUSEC
(— OF FLUIDITY) RHE
(— OF FLUX DENSITY) GAUSS
(— OF FORCE) G DYNE STAPP
STHENE POUNDEL
(— OF FREQUENCY) HERTZ
FRESNEL
(— OF GOVERNMENT) DEME LAND
KREIS GEMEINDE
(— OF ILLUMINANCE) LUX
(— OF INTERSTELLAR SPACE)
PARSEC
(— OF LAND AREA) ARE SULUNG
(— OF LANGUAGE) SYLLABLE
(— OF LIGHT INTENSITY) PYR
(— OF LIGHT) LUMEN
(— OF LOUDNESS) SONE DECIBEL
(— OF MACHINERY) STAND
(— OF MAGNETIC FLUX) WEBER

(— OF MAGNETIC FORCE) KAPP
GILBERT
(— OF MAGNETIC INTENSITY)
GAMMA
(— OF MAGNIFICATION) DIAMETER
(— OF MASS) SLUG DALTON
AVOGRAM
(— OF MEMORY) BIT
(— OF METRICAL QUANTITY) MATRA
(— OF MOMENT) DEBYE
(— OF MOMENTUM) BOLE
(— OF NARCOTIC) JOLT
(— OF NYLON FINENESS) DENIER
(— OF ONE INCH) BUTTON
(— OF PAIN INTENSITY) DOL
(— OF PERMEABILITY) DARCY
(— OF PIPE) FOURBLE
(— OF POWER) WATT DYNAM
KILOWATT PONCELET
(— OF PRESSURE) BAR BARAD
BARIE BARYE GWELY CENTIBAR
(— OF PRESSWORK) TOKEN
(— OF RADIATION) LANGLEY
(— OF RADIOACTIVITY) CURIE
(— OF ROCKET) STAGE
(— OF SATURATION) SATRON
(— OF SOCIETY) CLAN HORDE
CHAPTER
(— OF SPEECH) WORD
(— OF SPEED) BAUD KNOT
(— OF THICKNESS) POINT
(— OF TIME) BEAT SVEDBERG
(— OF TRADING) CONTRACT
(— OF VELOCITY) VELO
(— OF VISCOSITY) POISE STOKE
SECONDS
(— OF WAVELENGTH) ANGSTROM
(— OF WEIGHT) SSU TON GRAM
CARAT GRAIN OUNCE POUND STEIN
ARROBA GRAMME
(— OF WIRE MEASUREMENT) MIL
(— OF WORK) ERG CROP HOUR
ERGON JOULE KILERG DINAMODE
(— OF YARN SIZE) CUT
(— OF ZO) CORGE
(ADMINISTRATIVE —) HSIEN AGENCY
BUREAU DISTRICT
(ARBITRARY —) OLFACTY
(ARCHERY —) END
(ARMY —) LEGION BRIGADE
COMPANY MAHALLA
(ARTILLERY —) BATTERY
(AVAILABLE AS —) MARRIED
(BOWLING —) ALLEY
(BOY SCOUT —) SHIP
(BUILDER'S —) SQUARE
(CIGAR-MANUFACTURING —)
BUCKEYE
(COLLECTIVE —) COMMUNE
(COMBAT —) ARMAMENT
(DISCRETE —) FRACTION
(EDUCATIONAL —) COURSE
(ELECTROMAGNETIC —) ABFARAD
ABHENRY MAXWELL ABAMPERE
(FUNDAMENTAL —) BASE
(GRAMMATICAL —) JUNCTION
(HARMONIC —) CELL
(HOUSING —) HUTMENT
(HYPOTHETICAL —) ID IDANT

(LIFE —) BIOPHORE
(LIVING —) BIONT BIOGEN
(LOGARITHMIC —) BEL
(LOGGING —) CHANCE
(MILITARY —) ARMY GOUM CORPS
GROUP LANCE SQUAD BRIGADE
PLATOON SECTION COMMANDO
DIVISION REGIMENT SQUADRON
(NAZI —) FEHME
(ORGANIZATIONAL —) CELL
ACTIVITY
(PHOTOMETRIC —) VIOLLE
(POLITICAL —) SOVIET
(RHYTHMIC —) BASIS COLON
(SELF-PERPETUATING —) BIOSOME
(SOCIAL —) SEPT GROUP KRAAL
SOCIUS
(STORAGE —) BUFFER
(TERRITORIAL —) STAKE STATE
COMMOT CANTRED CANTREF
KINGDOM
(THERMAL —) THERM CALORY
CALORIE
(TRIBAL —) TOWNSHIP
(VOTING —) CENTURY
UNITE ADD MIX ONE OOP PAN SAM
SEW UNE UNY ALLY BAND BIND
CLUB COAK FUSE HASP JOIN KNIT
KNOT LINK SAMM SEAM SOUD UNIT
BANDY CLOSE GRADE GRAFT INONE
JACOB JOINT MERGE NITCH UNIFY
WHOLE ATTACH CEMENT CONCUR
COUPLE EMBODY ENTIRE GATHER
LAUREL LEAGUE SOLDER SPLICE
STRIKE SUTURE ACCRETE AMALGAM
CLUSTER COALITE COMBINE
CONJOIN CONNECT CONSORT
JACOBUS SIAMESE ALLIGATE
ANCYLOSE ANKYLOSE ASSEMBLE
COALESCE COMPOUND CONCRETE
CONSPIRE COPULATE FEDERATE
LAMINATE COLLIGATE
(— BY INTERWEAVING) PLEACH
SPLICE
(— BY THREADS) SEW STITCH
(— CLOSELY) FAY YOT WELD
CEMENT COTTON
(— FOR INTRIGUE) CABAL
(— HOSE) COLLECT
(— IN MARRIAGE) WED SACRE
SACRI SPLICE SPOUSE
(— METALS) WELD SWEAT
UNITED ONE TIED ADDED FUSED
JOINT ALLIED CONNATE ENDLESS
UNIONED COMBINED CONCRETE
CONJOINT CONJUNCT FEDERATE
UNITING SUTURE
UNITY UNION SYSTEM ONENESS
UNITUDE IDENTITY SODALITY
SYMPATHY TOTALITY
(— OF SPIRIT AND NATURE)
ABSOLUTE
UNIVERSAL ALL LOCAL TOTAL
WHOLE WORLD COMMON GLOBAL
PUBLIC VERSAL GENERAL GENERIC
CATHOLIC ECUMENIC
(TRANSCENDENT —) IDEA
UNIVERSALITY ALLNESS OMNITUDE
UNIVERSE ALL LOKA MASS OLAM

WORLD COSMOS SYSTEM
CREATURE EXEMPLAR
(SIDEREAL —) SPACE
UNIVERSITY STUDY CAMPUS
SCHOOL ACADEMY COLLEGE
MADRASA STUDIUM VARSITY
MADRASAH
UNJUST HARD UNFAIR WICKED
UNEQUAL UNRICHT UNRIGHT
WRONGFUL
UNJUSTIFIED INVALID
UNJUSTLY UNDULY FALSELY
UNKEELED RATITE
UNKEMPT FROWZY RUGGED
SHAGGY INCOMPT RAFFISH
RUFFLED SHAGRAG TOUSLED
DRAGGLED SCRAGGLY SLIPSHOD
STRUBBLY UNCOMBED
UNKIND BAD ILL MEAN VILE CRUEL
HARSH STERN SEVERE UNMEEK
UNKINDNESS DISFAVOR
UNKNOWABLE SEALED
UNKNOWN IGN UNCO UNKET UNKID
IGNOTE MUNKAR SEALED SECRET
UNWARE UNWIST FARAWAY
OBSCURE UNCOUTH UNHEARD
IGNORANT UNAWARES UNKENNED
UNWITTING
UNLADEN LEAR LEER
UNLATCH UNSNECK
UNLAWFUL ILLEGAL ILLICIT
NONLICET UNLEEFUL UNLEISUM
UNLEARNED LEWD GROSS
BOOKLESS IGNORANT UNLEARED
UNLESS BUT NIF LESS NISI SAVE
BINNA NOBUT LESSEN ONLESS
WITHOUT
(— BEFORE) NIPR NIPRI
(— OTHERWISE NOTED) NAN
UNLETTERED LEWD BORREL
IGNORANT
UNLIGHTED BLIND LAMPLESS
UNLIKE DIFFORM DISLIKE DIVERSE
(MOST —) OTHEREST
UNLIKELY DUBIOUS
(MOST —) LAST
UNLIMITED VAST SOVRAN
UNTERMED
(— IN POWER) ALMIGHTY
UNLINED SINGLE
UNLOAD TIP DROP DUMP HOVEL
DECANT STRIKE UNLADE UNSHIP
UNSTOW DELIVER DEPLETE
DETRUCK DISLOAD UNTRUSS
DISCHARGE
UNLOCK UNMAKE RESERATE
UNLOUKEN
UNLOOSE OUTWIND UNRIVET
UNLUCKY FAY ILL EVIL FOUL DONSY
DISMAL DONSIE HOODOO HAPLESS
INFAUST UNHAPPY UNCHANCY
UNTOWARD
(— THING) AMBSACE
UNMAN UNDO CRUSH UNNERVE
UNMANAGEABLE ROID DONSY
RANDY RESTIVE CHURLISH
STAFFISH
UNMANLY SOFT MANLESS UNLUSTY
UNMANNERLY RUDE BOORISH

UNCIVIL IMPOLITE UNGENTLE
UNMARKED MAVERICK NOTELESS
UNMARRIED ONE LONE SOLE OLEPI
YOUNG ONLEPY SINGLE
UNMASK EXPOSE UNFACE DISMASK
UNCLOAK
UNMASKING EXPOSURE
UNMEASURED UNMEET MODELESS
UNMELODIOUS SCRANNEL
UNMERCHANTABLE SALABLE
SALEABLE
UNMERCIFUL CRUEL PITILESS
RUTHLESS
UNMETHODICAL CURSORY
UNMINDFUL SLOWFUL CARELESS
HEEDLESS MINDLESS
UNMISTAKABLE FLAT OPEN BROAD
CLEAR FRANK PLAIN PATENT
EXPRESS APPARENT DECISIVE
MANIFEST UNIVOCAL
UNMISTAKABLY SIGNALLY
UNMITIGATED GROSS ARRANT
DAMNED SOVRAN PERFECT
PUREDEE REGULAR ABSOLUTE
UNMIX EXSOLVE
UNMIXED DEEP MERE PURE SELF
SOLE BLANK SHEER UTTER IMMIXT
SIMPLE STRAIGHT
UNMODIFIED BRUTE STRAIGHT
UNMOLESTED SACKLESS
UNMOVED CALM COOL FIRM STONY
TIGHT IMMOTE SERENE ADAMANT
IMMOVED
UNMOVING INERT IMMOBILE
IMMOTIVE
UNMUSICAL NOTELESS SCABROUS
UNNATURAL EERY EERIE CLAMMY
CREEPY UNKIND STRANGE
UNCANNY VIOLENT ABNORMAL
FARCICAL KINDLESS UNKINDLY
UNNECESSARY USELESS NEEDLESS
UNNEEDED WASTE
UNNERVE UNMAN UNMAKE WEAKEN
ENERVATE PARALYZE
UNNERVED SHOOK
UNNOTICED SILENT
UNOBJECTIONABLE VENIAL
UNOBSERVANT HEEDLESS
UNOBSTRUCTED FAIR FREE OPEN
APPARENT
UNOBTRUSIVE SHY MODEST
SEDATE DISCREET RETIRING
UNOCCUPIED IDLE VOID BLANK
EMPTY WASTE VACANT LEISURE
UNSEATED WASTEFUL
UNORGANIZED ACOSMIC INCHOATE
UNORTHODOX HERETIC
UNOSTENTATIOUS SHY QUIET
LENTEN MODEST
UNPACK UNFARDLE
UNPAID DUE UNQUIT UNWAGED
HONORARY WAGELESS
UNPAIRED IMPAR
UNPALATABLE SOD HARD BITTER
BRACKISH
UNPARALLELED ALONE UNIQUE
EPOCHAL PEERLESS SINGULAR
UNPEERED
UNPERTURBED BLAND STILL

UNPLEASANT BAD ACID EVIL HARD
NICE SOUR UGLY AWFUL CRUDE
GRIMY GUMMY HAIRY HARSH
MUCKY ROUGH BRUTAL CRIMPY
RANCID STICKY THRAWN UNFELE
UNGAIN UNLIEF BEASTLY BILIOUS
GHASTLY INGRATE SPINOUS
UNLUSTY UNQUEME UNSONCY
CHISELLY DREADFUL HORRIBLE
INDECENT SCABROUS UNLOVELY
UNPLEASANTLY QUEER HARDLY
UNWINLY
UNPLEASANTNESS ILLNESS
UNPLOWED LEA
UNPOETICAL MUSELESS
UNPOLISHED ILL RUDE BLIND
CRUDE ROUGH COARSE INCULT
RUGGED RUSTIC SAVAGE SHAGGY
UPLAND INCOMPT UNKEMPT
AGRESTIC
UNPOPULARITY ENVY
UNPRACTICED RAW FRESH
UNTRADED
UNPREDICTABLE CHANCY CRANKY
ERRATIC
UNPREJUDICED FAIR
UNPREMEDITATED CASUAL
UNPREPARED TARDY
UNPREPOSSESSING SEEDY
UNPRETENDING LOWLY HOMELY
HUMBLE
UNPRETENTIOUS HOMY HOMEY
PLAIN SOBER COMMON HOMELY
HUMBLE MODEST SIMPLE DISCREET
HOMESPUN
UNPRINCIPLED LIMMER
UNPRODUCTIVE DRY SHY ARID
DEAD DEAF LEAN ADDLE DUSTY
WASTE BARREN GEASON SAPLESS
STERILE WOODSERE
UNPRODUCTIVENESS BORASCO
BORASQUE BORRASCA
UNPROFESSIONAL LAY LAICAL
UNPROFITABLE BAD DRY DEAD
SECK BARREN BOOTLESS GAINLESS
UNGAINLY
UNPROGRESSIVE SLOW DORMANT
BACKWARD
UNPROMISING BLUE DUBIOUS
UNPRONOUNCED MUTE
UNPROPITIOUS ILL EVIL FOUL
THRAW MALIGN SULLEN ADVERSE
AVERTED INFAUST OMINOUS
THRAWART
UNPROTECTED NAKED EXPOSED
HELPLESS
UNPUBLISHED INED INEDITED
UNQUALIFIED NET BARE FULL MERE
PURE BLACK PLUMP SHEER UNFIT
DIRECT ENTIRE UNABLE CLOTTED
PLENARY IMPLICIT INHABILE
UNQUESTIONABLE ASSURED
CERTAIN DECIDED ABSOLUTE
DECISIVE DISTINCT
UNQUESTIONED CLEAR
UNQUESTIONING IMPLICIT
UNRAVEL REDD UNDO BREAK
ENODE FEAZE RAVEL SOLVE TIFFLE

UNFOLD UNKNIT UNLACE ENODATE
RESOLVE
UNREAL GOTHIC CHEMICK FANCIED
SHADOWY AERIFORM CHIMERIC
FARCICAL ILLUSORY NOTIONAL
SCENICAL VISIONAL
UNREALISTIC CHIMERIC
UNREALIZED BEHIND
UNREASONABLE ABSURD FANATIC
ABSONANT
UNREASONABLENESS ALOGY
INSANITY
UNREASONABLY SINFULLY
UNREASONING BRUTE
UNRECOGNIZED UNSUNG CRYPTIC
UNWITTED
UNRECOVERABLE DEAD
UNRECTIFIED IMPURE
UNREDEEMED CHEAP
UNREFINED RAW DARK LOUD
BRUTE CRUDE DORIC GROSS
COARSE COMMON EARTHY JUNGLY
VULGAR BOORISH UNCOUTH
UNKEMPT DREADFUL SWAINISH
UNREFLECTING GLIB
UNREGENERACY ADAM
UNREGENERATELY MANLY
UNREHEARSED IMPROMPTU
UNRELATED FREMD STRAY UNAKIN
UNTOLD EXTREME FRAMMIT
POSITIVE
UNRELAXED UNSLAKED
UNRELENTING GRIM HARD IRON
CRUEL STERN SEVERE RIGOROUS
UNRELIABLE FISHY SHADY FICKLE
GREASY UNSAFE CASALTY STREAKY
WILDCAT FECKLESS GLIBBERY
SLIPPERY TICKLISH
UNRELIEVED DEAD BRUTE ABJECT
EXQUISITE
UNREMITTING BUSY FAST HARD
DOGGED
UNREMUNERATIVE HONORARY
UNRESERVED FREE CLEAN FRANK
ROUND COMMON UNCLOSE EXPLICIT
UNRESERVEDNESS FREEDOM
UNRESISTING BUXOM
UNRESPONSIVE DEAD DUMB
BARREN SILENT STUBBORN
UNREST MOTION AILMENT DISREST
WANREST DISQUIET CHEMISTRY
PSYCHOSIS
UNRESTRAINED LAX FREE WILD
BROAD FANTI FRANK LARGE LOOSE
FACILE FANTEE LAVISH UNTIED
WANTON FLYAWAY RAMPANT
RIOTOUS FAMILIAR FREEHAND
LAXATIVE PINDARIC
UNRESTRAINT LICENSE IMMUNITY
UNRESTRICTED FREE GLOBAL
SOVRAN UNZONED
UNRETURNED UNYOLDEN
UNREVEALED UNTOLD
UNRIG STRIP
UNRIGHTEOUSNESS ADHARMA
UNRIPE RAW CRUDE GREEN CALLOW
UNCURED IMMATURE
UNROBE DISROBE UNDRESS
DISARRAY

UNROLL EVOLVE UNCURL DEVELOP
OUTROLL TRINDLE UNTREND
UNROOF TIRL TIRR TIRVE DISROOF
UNRUFFLE SMOOTH SOOTHE
MOLLIFY
UNRUFFLED CALM COOL EASY EVEN
QUIET SOBER STILL ASLEEP PLACID
SEDATE SERENE SMOOTH
DECOROUS
UNRULY HIGH RAMP ROYT TOUGH
HAUNTY WANTON LAWLESS
RAMMAGE ROPABLE UNRULED
VICIOUS WANRULY WAYWARD
INDOCILE MUTINOUS
UNSADDLE UNPANEL
UNSAFE HOT EXPOSED INSECURE
PERILOUS
UNSATISFACTORY BAD ILL EVIL
CROOK SHREWD WRETCHED
UNSATISFYING DUSTY HOLLOW
UNSAVORY WERSH INSIPID WEARISH
UNSAY WITHDRAW
UNSCHOLARLY BOOKLESS
UNSCRUPULOUS SKIN BRAZEN
DEVIOUS DEXTROUS RASCALLY
UNSEASONABLE LAT UNRIPE
UNTIDY UNCHANCY UNTIMELY
UNSEASONED RAW GREEN
UNSEAT ADDRESS DISSEAT
UNSEEING BLIND GAZELESS
UNSEEMLY HOIDEN UNFAIR
IMPROPER INDECENT SEEMLESS
UNMEETLY UNWORTHY
UNSEEN SECRET UNEYED VIEWLESS
UNSERRIED LOOSE
UNSETTLE JAR TURN UNFIX UNSET
UPSET COMMOVE DERANGE
DISTURB STAGGER UNHINGE
UNQUEME DISORDER DISQUIET
DISTRACT
UNSETTLED MOOT LIGHT SHAKY
UNSAD VAGUE BROKEN FICKLE
QUEASY VAGOUS DUBIOUS SHUTTLE
UNSTAID RESTLESS UNSTABLE
UNSHAKABLE DOGGED ADAMANT
IRONCLAD
UNSHAKEN FIRM STEADY UNMOVED
UNSHOOK RESOLUTE
UNSHAPELY DEFORMED UNMACKLY
UNSHARED SOLE
UNSHEATH DISCASE
UNSHEATHED BARE
UNSHOD BAREFOOT DISCALCED
UNSHORN UNPOLLED
UNSIGHTLY UGLY MESSY HOMELY
INDECENT
UNSKILLED JAY PUNY GREEN
PUISNE UNGAIN UNSEEN STRANGE
FECKLESS
UNSKILLFUL ILL EVIL RUDE
ARTLESS UNFEATY BUNGLING
TINKERLY UNHEPPEN
UNSMILING GLUM AUSTERE
UNSOCIABLE SULLEN INSOCIAL
UNSOILED CLEAN
UNSOPHISTICATE SQUARE
UNSOPHISTICATED JAY NAIF PURE
FRANK GREEN NAIVE SILLY CALLOW
SIMPLE BUCOLIC VERDANT

HOMEBRED HOMESPUN INNOCENT
UNSOUND BAD ILL EVIL SICK ADDLE
CRAZY CRONK DICKY DOTTY DOZED
SANDY SHAKY ABSURD FAULTY
FLAWED HOLLOW INFIRM INSANE
ROTTEN UNHALE INVALID RICKETY
UNWHOLE
UNSOUNDNESS CRACK INSANITY
UNSPIRITUAL CARNAL
UNSPOILED RACY UNSHENT
UNSPOKEN TACIT SILENT
UNSPORTSMANLIKE DIRTY
UNSPOTTED CLEAR SPOTLESS
UNSTABLE FLUX BATTY LOOSE
SANDY BROTEL CHOPPY FICKLE
FITFUL FLITTY LABILE LUBRIC
ROTTEN SHIFTY TICKLE UNFIRM
WANKLE WANKLY DWAIBLE
DWAIBLY DWEEBLE RICKETY
SLIDDER SLIDDRY VOLUBLE
FEVERISH FIRMLESS FUGITIVE
INSECURE LUBRICAL REMUABLE
SKITTISH SLIPPERY TICKLISH
TOTTLISH VARIABLE
(MENTALLY —) BRAINISH
UNSTEADILY GROGGILY
UNSTEADINESS FALTER
UNSTEADY WALT CRANK CRONK
DOTTY FLUKY LIGHT NERVY SLACK
TIPPY TIPSY TOTTY UNSAD WALTY
WONKY COGGLY FICKLE FLICKY
FLUFFY GROGGY JIGGLY JOGGLY
SWIMMY TOTTIE WAFFLY WAGGLY
WAMBLY WANKLE WEEWAW
WEEWOW DODDERY GLAIKIT
JIGGETY QUAVERY TITTUPY
TOTTERY WAYWARD STAGGERY
TICKLISH TITUBANT UNSTABLE
VARIABLE
UNSTINTED LAVISH ENDLESS
UNSTRESS SLACK
UNSTRESSED SHORT
UNSTRING DISSOLVE
UNSTUDIED GLIB CASUAL CARELESS
GLANCING
UNSUBDUED VIRGIN UNBOWED
UNSUBSTANTIAL TOY LIMP THIN
WINDY AERIAL CHAFFY FLIMSY
SLEAZY SLEEZY SLIGHT UNREAL
FOLIOUS FRAGILE INSOLID
SHADOWY TENUOUS FILIGREE
FINESPUN FOOTLESS GIMCRACK
VAPOROUS
UNSUCCESSFUL BAD MANQUE
UNSPED STICKIT UNHAPPY
ABORTIVE
UNSUITABLE INEPT UNAPT UNDUE
UNFIT UNKIND UNMETE UNCOMELY
UNGAINLY UNLIKELY
UNSUITABLENESS IMPOLICY
UNSUITED BAD
UNSULLIED FAIR PURE CLEAR
VIRGIN INNOCENT SPOTLESS
VIRGINAL
UNSUPPLIED HELPLESS
UNSUPPORTED BLIND NAKED
BACKWARD STAYLESS
UNSURE TIMID INFIRM DOUBTFUL
INSECURE UNSICKER

UNSURPASSED CHAMPION
UNSUSPECTING INNOCENT
UNSWEET UNSOOT
UNSWERVING FIXED FLUSH LOYAL
DIRECT STEADY STRICT STURDY
STAUNCH
UNSWERVINGLY HEADLONG
UNSYMMETRICAL LOPSIDED
UNSYMPATHETIC HARD STONY
FROZEN GLASSY HOSTILE KINDLESS
UNTAINTED FREE GOOD PURE
INNOCENT
UNTAMED WILD FERAL RAMAGE
SAVAGE HAGGARD RAMMISH
WARRAGAL
UNTANGLE FREE SLEAVE UNLACE
UNTAUGHT WASTE UNLERED
IGNORANT
UNTHINKABLE PUERILE
UNTHINKING GLIB BRUTE CASUAL
FECKLESS HEEDLESS
UNTHINKINGLY STUPID
UNTIDINESS JAKES LITTER
UNTIDY DOWDY GAUMY MESSY
ROOKY BUNTING DRAGGLY LITTERY
RUMMAGY UNSIDED DRAGGLED
SLOVENLY STRUBBLY UNHEPPEN
UNTIE UNDO UNBIND UNLASH
UNLATCH UNTRUSS UNTWINE
UNFASTEN
UNTIL AD OR TO GIN HENT INTO
UNTO FORTO TWELL WHILE WHILES
WHILST PENDING
(— **THEN**) BEFORE
UNTILLED INCULT UNEARED
UNTIMELY UNTIDY IMMATURE
PREVIOUS TIMELESS
UNTIRING BUSY SEDULOUS
TIRELESS
UNTITLED (— **MEN**) AUMAGA
UNTOLD VAST UNQUOD
UNTOUCHABLE DOM HARIJAN
CHANDALA
(**PL.**) PANCHAMA
UNTOUCHED FREE INTACT
UNTOWARD ILL UNRULY FROWARD
WAYWARD
UNTRAINED RAW RUDE GREEN
HAGGARD
UNTRAMMELED FREE
UNTRIED MAIDEN UNSOUGHT
UNTRIMMED UNTEWED
UNTRODDEN PATHLESS UNFOOTED
UNTROUBLED CHEERY
UNTRUE FLAM FALSE LEASE WRONG
UNFAST DISLOYAL
UNTRUSTWORTHINESS FALSITY
UNTRUSTWORTHY SHAKY LIMBER
TRICKY UNSURE SLIDDERY
SLIPPERY
UNTRUTH LIE FABLE LEASE SKLENT
FALSITY UNTROTH
UNTRUTHFUL SLANTER
UNTUTORED IGNORANT
UNTWILLED PLAIN
UNTWINE FRESE UNTWIST
UNTWIST FAG FEAZE UNLAY UNSPIN
UNTWIRL
UNTWISTED SLEIDED

UNUSABLE WASTE INUTILE
UNUSED IDLE FRESH WASTE INURED
MAIDEN DERELICT INITIATE
UNWONTED
UNUSUAL ODD EERY RARE SELD
TALL CRAZY EERIE FORBY NOVEL
UTTER WEIRD EXEMPT FORBYE
SCREWY SINGLE UNIQUE STRANGE
ABNORMAL DISTINCT ESPECIAL
INSOLENT KNOCKOUT SELCOUTH
SINGULAR SPANKING UNCOMMON
UNTRADED UNWONTED
UNUSUALLY EXTRA
UNVARIED SAMELY
UNVARNISHED EVERYDAY
UNVARYING FLAT FRANK LEVEL
STABLE UNIFORM
UNVEIL REVEAL UNCOVER UNCROWN
UNDRAPE UNSCREEN UNWIMPLE
UNVERSED STRANGE
UNWANTED STRAY TRAMP FAULTY
UNWARRANTED UNDUE
UNWARY RASH UNAWARE CARELESS
HEEDLESS WARELESS
UNWASHED SOAPLESS
UNWASTEFUL FRUGAL
UNWAVERING FIRM CLEAN LEVEL
SOLID GLASSY STABLE EXPRESS
STAUNCH
UNWAVERINGLY FAST
UNWEAKENED CLEAR
UNWELL ILL EVIL SICK BADLY
CROOK AILING CHIPPY WICKED
COMICAL
UNWHOLESOME ILL EVIL SICK
CAGMAG IMPURE MORBID SICKLY
CORRUPT NOISOME NOXIOUS
UNCLEAN DISEASED
UNWIELDY BULKY CLUMSY UNRIDE
AWKWARD HULKING CUMBROUS
UNGAINLY
UNWILLING CHARY LOATH SWEER
WERSE AVERSE ESCHEW
BACKWARD GRUDGING
UNWILLINGLY MAUGER MAUGRE
UNWILLINGNESS GRUDGE NOLITION
UNWIND UNCLEW UNREEL UNREAVE
UNTWINE
UNWISE FALSE INANE SIMPLE
FOOLISH WITLESS
UNWITTING UNWIST WEETLESS
UNWOMANLY MANKIND
UNWORLDLY WEIRD ASTRAL
UNWORTHY BASE INDIGN BENEATH
UNDIGNE WANWORDY
UNWOUNDED COLD
UNWREATHE UNPLAT
UNWRINKLED BRANT BRENT
UNWROUGHT RAW LIVE
UNYIELDING SET ACID DOUR FAST
FIRM GRIM HARD RIGID STARK
STIFF STITH STONY TOUGH FLINTY
FROZEN GLASSY KNOBBY STEELY
STURDY ADAMANT AUSTERE
COSTIVE FROWARD CHURLISH
OBDURATE OBEDIENT STUBBORN
UNYOKE UNTEAM OUTSHUT
OUTSPAN
UP ON ONE OOP ABOUT ASTIR

DORMY DORMIE
(— **AND ABOUT**) AFOOT
(— **TO THE TIME**) UNTIL
(— **TO**) INTO
(— **YONDER**) UPBY UPBYE
(**FARTHER** —) ABOVE
(**HIGH** —) ALOFT
UPANISHAD ISHA KATHA
UPAS DITA CHETTIK
UPBEAT ARSIS AUFTAKT ANACRUSIS
UP-BOW POUSSE
UPBRAID CHEW RAIL SNUB TUCK
TWIT ABUSE ROUSE SCOLD TAUNT
UPBRAY EMBRAID REPROVE
DISGRACE OUTBRAID
UPCARD STARTER
UPFOLD SADDLE ANTICLINE
UPHEAVAL BOIL UPLIFT RUMMAGE
UPTHROW
UPHILL UPBANK UPWITH
UPHOLD AID TOM ABET BACK FAVOR
AFFIRM ASSERT DEFEND SOOTHE
BOLSTER SUPPORT SUSTAIN
CHAMPION MAINTAIN PRESERVE
UPHOLDER DEFENDER ERASTIAN
FEUDALIST
UPHOLDING BEHIND
UPHOLSTER SQUAB
UPHOLSTERER TAPISER UPHOLDER
UPLAND DOWN DOWNS MAUKA
COTEAU FASTLAND
(**PL.**) BRAES DOWNS
UPLAND PLOVER QUAILY HILLBIRD
PAPABOTE
UPLIFT TOSS BOOST TOWER
UPTHRUST
UPLIFTED ERECT EXALTEE
UPON ON PON SUR INTO OVER
ABOVE AGAINST
(— **THAT**) THEREAT
UPPER VAMP SKIVE VAMPEY
SUPERIOR
(**PL.**) FINISH
UPPERCUT BOLO
UPPER HURONIAN LAWSON
UPPERMOST UMEST UPMOST
OVEREST BUNEMOST OVERMOST
UPPER VOLTA (**CAPITAL OF** —)
OUAGADOUGOU
(**LANGUAGE OF** —) BOBO LOBI
SAMO MANDE MOSSI
(**MOUNTAIN IN** —) TEMA
(**NATIVE OF** —) BOBO LOBI SAMO
BISSA HAUSA MANDE MARKA MOSSI
PUEHL TUAREG SENOUFO VOLTAIC
YATENGA MANDINGO
(**RIVER IN** —) VOLTA SOUROU
UPRAISED SUBLIME
UPRIGHT FAIR GOOD HARR JUST
PROP STUD TIDY TRUE ANEND
CHEEK ERECT GUIDE JELLY MORAL
RIGHT ROMAN SETUP STALE STALK
STILE DIRECT ENTIRE HONEST
SQUARE FRIZZEN HOUSING
JANNOCK PITPROP SINCERE
INNOCENT RIGHTFUL STANDARD
STANDING STRAIGHT VERTICAL
VIRTUOUS
(**NOT** —) BEVEL

(PL.) STUDDING

UPRIGHTNESS HONOR TRUTH
EQUITY HONESTY PROBITY
JUSTNESS

UPRISING RIOT EMEUTE MUTINY
PUTSCH REVOLT TUMULT UPRISE
UPRISAL

UPROAR DIN RUT CAIN GILD MOIL
RIOT ROUT BURLE CHANG FUROR
HURLY RUMOR STOUN STOUR
CLAMOR DIRDUM FRACAS HABBLE
HUBBLE HUBBUB RANDAN RATTLE
RIPPET RUCKUS RUMBLE SHINDY
STEVEN STOUND TUMULT CATOUSE
FERMENT GAUSTER ORATION
OUTROAR RUCTION STASHIE
TURMOIL BROUHAHA SCOUTHER
STIRRING TINTAMAR

UPROARIOUS FURIOUS ROUTOUS

UPROOT HACK LOUK MORE UNROUT
UNPLANT DISPLANT ROOTWALT
SUPPLANT

UPROOTED LUMPEN

UPSET ILL TIP TOP TUP CAVE COUP
COWP FUSS JUMP PURL TILT TURN
WELT EVERT KNOCK ROUSE SHAKE
SKELL WHELM BOTHER DISMAY
QUELME TIPPLE TOPPLE UPCAST
WALTER CAPSIZE DERANGE
DISTURB FRAZZLE HAYWIRE
OVERSET PERVERT REVERSE
SLATTER SUBVERT TEMPEST
TURMOIL CAPSIZAL DISTRAIT
OVERTILT OVERTURN STREAKED
SUPPLANT TURNOVER
(EASILY —) FUSSY

UPSHOT ISSUE SHORT UPSET
EFFECT SEQUEL UPPING OUTCOME
UPSHOOT UPSTROKE

UPSIDE-DOWN CRAZY OVERHAND
UPSEDOUN

UPSTAIRS ABOVE

UPSTANDING GRADELY

UPSTART KIP QUAT SNIP SQUIRT
UPSKIP DALTEEN PARVENU
ARRIVIST MUSHROOM SKIPJACK
UPSPRING

UP-TO-DATE ABREAST TODAYISH

UPWARD ALOFT UPLONG UPWAYS
UPWITH SKYWARD UPALONG
UPWARDS

UPWARD-MOVING ANABATIC

URAEUS ASP

URAMIL MUREXAN

URANUS OURANOS HERSCHEL
(WIFE OF —) GAEA

URAO TRONA

URARTAEAN KHALDIAN

URARTU VAN

URATE LITHATE

URBAN TOWN URBIC URBANE
BURGHAL

URBANE CIVIL SUAVE POLITE
SVELTE AMIABLE GRACIOUS

URBANITY SUAVITY ELEGANCE

URCHIN IMP ELFIN GAMIN KEELIE
NIPPER HURCHEON

URD MUNGO

URDEE MATELEY

URDU REKHTA REKHTI MOORISH

URGE ART DUN EGG HIE PLY PUT
SIC SUE TAR YEN BROD COAX
CRAM EDGE FIRK GOAD MOVE PING
SICK SPUR WHIP CROWD DRIVE
FILIP FORCE HOOSH IMPEL LABOR
PRICK SPANK TREAT COMPEL
DEHORT DESIRE ENGAGE EXCITE
FILLIP HARDEN HOICKS HUSTLE
INCITE INDUCE INVITE MOTION
PROPEL STRAIN THREAP THREAT
ANIMATE COMMOVE ENFORCE
INSTANT OPPRESS PERSIST SOLICIT
SUGGEST URGENCY INSTANCE
PERSUADE
(— IMPORTUNATELY) DUN PRESS
(— ON A HORSE) HUP CRAM CHUCK
(— ON) EGG ERT HAG SOOL ALARM
CHIRK CROWD DRIVE FILIP HASTE
HURRY IMPEL YOICK ALARUM FILLIP
HARDEN HASTEN INCITE
(— STRONGLY) EXHORT SOLICIT
(— WITH VEHEMENCE) DING

URGENCY NEED PRESS STRESS
URGENCE EXIGENCY INSTANCE
INSTANCY

URGENT HOT DIRE RASH ACUTE
HASTY STRONG BURNING CLAMANT
EXIGENT INSTANT URGEFUL
CRITICAL PRESSING PRESSIVE

URGING QUEST

URIAL SHA OORIAL

URINAL DUCK SANITARY

URINATE WET LEAK EMPTY STALE
PIDDLE EVACUATE

URINATION MICTION NOCTURIA

URINE MIG SIG LAGE LANT WASH
STALE WATER NETTING EMICTION
(— USED AS COSMETIC) LOTIUM

URN JAR EWER KIST URNA VASE
CAPANNA
(— FOR MAKING TEA) KITCHEN
SAMOVAR
(— IN KENO) GOOSE
(BURIAL —) OSSUARY
(CINERARY —) DINOS DEINOS
(STONE —) STEEN

URN-SHAPED URCEOLAR

UROCHORDA ASCIDIA TUNICATA

UROSTYLE COCCYX

URSA MAJOR OKNARI CHARIOT
WAGONER WAGGONER

URSINE ARCTOID

URTICARIA HIVES UREDO CNIDOSIS

URTICASTRUM LAPORTEA

URUGUAY

CAPITAL: MONTEVIDEO
DEPARTMENT: ROCHA SALTO
FLORES ARTIGAS SORIANO
ESTUARY: PLATA
LAKE: MERIN MIRIM DIFUNTOS
MEASURE: VARA LEGUA CUADRA
SUERTE
RIVER: MALO MIRIM NEGRO
ULIMAR CUAREIM QUEGUAY
YAGUARON CEBOLLATI
TOWN: MELO MINAS ROCHA
SALTO RIVERA DURAZNO
FLORIDA PAYSANDU
WEIGHT: QUINTAL

URUGUAYAN ORIENTAL

URUS TUR URE AUROCHS

US S HIS HIZ HUZ

USABLE FIT UTIBLE SERVABLE

USAGE USE ASAL FORM WONE
HABIT HAUNT SUNNA USURE
CUSTOM MANNER FASHION
HALACHA HALAKAH USATION
PRACTICE
(BAD —) ABUSAGE
(HARD —) GRIEF
(RELIGIOUS —) RITUS
(PL.) CEREMONY

USE URE BOOT CALL DUTY HAVE
NAIT NOTE USUS WISE APPLY AVAIL
GUIDE HABIT SPEND TREAT USAGE
WASTE BEHOOF EMPLOY FINISH
HANDLE OCCUPY USANCE ACCOUNT
ADHIBIT ENTREAT IMPROVE SERVICE
UTILITY ACCUSTOM EXERCISE
FUNCTION PRACTICE
(— AS WONTED) ADOPT
(— EXPERIMENTALLY) TRY
(— FIGURE OF SPEECH) TROPE
(— IMPROPERLY) ABUSE
(— INDISCRIMINATELY) HACK
(— OF MORE WORDS THAN
NECESSARY) PLEONASM
(— OF NEW WORD) NEOLOGY
(— OF SUBTERFUGE) CHICANE
(— UP) EAT TIRE WEAR SHOOT
ABSORB DEVOUR EXPEND GUZZLE
PERUSE CONSUME EXHAUST
OVERWEAR
(— WASTEFULLY) SPILL
(— WITH FULL COMMAND) WIELD
(EXCESSIVE — OF FACE AND
HANDS) ABHINAYA
(FOR TEMPORARY —) JURY
(FRUGAL —) SPARE
(GENERAL —) CURRENCY
(LITURGICAL —) RITE
(MUCH IN —) GREAT
(UNRESTRICTED —) FREEDOM

USED WONT
(— CONTINUOUSLY) HOT
(— IN FLIGHT) VOLAR
(— UP) ALL BEAT SHOT SPENT
FOREWORN
(MUCH —) GREAT HACKNEY

USEFUL GAIN GOOD UTILE UTIBLE
HELPFUL THRIFTY BEHOVELY
UTENSILE
(— FOR LONG TIME) HARD

USEFULNESS USE AVAIL VALUE
WORTH PROFIT MILEAGE UTILITY

USELESS IDLE LEWD VAIN VOID
WIDE EMPTY DOLESS NOUGHT
OTIOSE SCREWY TRASHY INUTILE
STERILE VAINFUL BOOTLESS
FOOTLESS FOOTLING WASTEFUL

USELESSNESS FUTILITY IDLENESS

USER USUS

USHABTI SHAWABTI

USHER BOW USH SHOW HERALD ISCHAR SEATER CHOBDAR HUISHER JANITOR MARSHAL STEWARD

USSR (SEE RUSSIA)

USUAL RIFE COMMON FAMOUS NORMAL SOLEMN VULGAR WONTED AVERAGE GENERAL NATURAL REGULAR TYPICAL USITATE EVERYDAY FREQUENT HABITUAL ORDINARY ORTHODOX

USURER SHARK GAVELER HARPAGON

USURP ASSUME INVADE PRESUME ACCROACH ARROGATE

USURY GAVEL OCKER USURE USANCE GOMBEEN

UTAH

CAPITAL: SALTLAKECITY
COLLEGE: WEBER
COUNTY: JUAB CACHE PIUTE SEVIER TOOELE UINTAH SANPETE
INDIAN: UTE
LAKE: SALT SWAN SEVIER
MOTTO: INDUSTRY
MOUNTAIN: LENA LION WAAS KINGS PEALE TRAIL FRISCO NAVAJO SWASEY GRANITE GRIFFIN HAWKINS PENNELL LINNAEUS
MOUNTAIN RANGE: CEDAR HENRY HOGUP UINTA WAHWAH TERRACE CONFUSION
NATIONAL PARK: ZION
NICKNAME: MORMON BEEHIVE
RIVER: WEBER JORDAN SEVIER
STATE BIRD: SEAGULL
STATE FLOWER: SEGOLILY
STATE TREE: SPRUCE
TOWN: MOAB OREM DELTA HEBER KANAB LOGAN MAGNA MANTI NEPHI OGDEN PRICE PROVO KEARNS TOOELE VERNAL

UTENSIL (ALSO SEE IMPLEMENT AND TOOL) HOD BOAT IRON MOLD PECK STEW BAKER FRIER FRYER GRILL KNIFE MOULD RICER SCOOP SHEET SHELL SIEVE SLICE ULLER BEATER BREWER COOKER DABBER FUNNEL GRATER GRILLE KETTLE LINGEL MASKER POPPER PUSHER SHAKER SIFTER BRAZIER BROILER DUSTPAN FLIPPER GLUEPOT MUDDLER SCUMMER SKIMMER STEAMER STIRRER TOASTER CALABASH GRIDIRON SAUCEPAN SAUCEPOT SHREDDER SPOUCHER STRAINER (— FOR COVERING FIRE) CURFEW (LITURGICAL —) ASTERISK (PL.) BATTERY COOKWARE IRONWARE

UTERUS WOMB BELLY METRA MATRIX BEARING

UTILITARIAN USEFUL ECONOMIC

UTILITY USE AVAIL USAGE PROFIT BENEFIT SERVICE

UTILIZE USE EMPLOY ENLIST CONSUME EXPLOIT HARNESS HUSBAND

UTMOST END BEST LAST MOST FINAL EXTREME OUTMOST SUPREME DAMNDEST POSSIBLE UTTEREST

UTOPIA ZION

UTOPIAN IDEAL

UTOPIANISM FUTURISM

UTRAQUIST CALIXTIN

UTRICULUS ALVEUS

UTTER ASK OUT SAY BARK BLOW BOOM DRIB FAIR GASP GIVE HURL MAIN MOOT MOVE PASS PURE RANK SEND VENT VERY BLACK COUGH CRUDE FETCH FRAME FRANK GROSS ISSUE MOUTH RAISE SHEER SOUND SPEAK SPELL STARK THICK TOTAL VOICE ACCENT BROACH DAMNED DIRECT INTONE PARLEY PROFER TONGUE BLUSTER BREATHE DELIVER ENOUNCE EXCLAIM EXPRESS OUTMOST OUTTELL PERFECT PROLATE UPBRAID ABSOLUTE BLINKING COMPLETE CRASHING INTONATE (— ABRUPTLY) BLURT (— AFFECTEDLY) KNAP MINCE (— ARGUMENTS) BLAZE (— CASUALLY) DROP (— EXPLOSIVELY) BOLT (— FALSEHOODS) FABLE (— FOOLISHLY) BLABBER (— HALTINGLY) BLUBBER (— HURRIEDLY) CHOP (— IN HARSH VOICE) GRIT GRATE (— INADVERTENTLY) SLIP (— INDISTINCTLY) CHEW (— LOUD CRY) BRAY BLARE (— LOUDLY) CRY BLAT CALL HALLO HALLOO HULLOO PRABBLE (— LOW SOUNDS) MURMUR WHISPER (— MEANINGLESS SOUNDS) BABBLE (— RAPIDLY) FIRE CHATTER (— RAUCOUSLY) BLAT (— REPETITIVELY) CHIME (— RHETORICALLY) DECLAIM (— SOLEMNLY) SWEAR (— STUPIDLY) BLUNDER (— SUDDENLY) CRACK (— UNCTUOUSLY) DROOL (— VIGOROUSLY) FLING (— WITH EFFORT) HEAVE

UTTERANCE CRY GAB CALL OSSE DITTY PAROL VOICE ACCENT ACTION BREATH CHORUS DRIVEL GIBBER ORACLE PAROLE EXPRESS INKLING LALLING STATUTE DELIVERY FOOTNOTE HOMESPUN JUDGMENT LOCUTION SYLLABIC (— FROM A DIVINITY) ORACLE (— OF VOCAL SOUNDS) PHONESIS (CONDEMNATORY —) INFAMY (DEFECTIVE —) STAMMER (FAINT —) INKLING (FOOLISH —) DRIVEL (FOOLISH —S) GUFF (GUSHING —) EFFUSION (IMPULSIVE —) BLURT (MALICIOUS —) SLANDER (OFFENSIVE —) AFFRONT (PROPHETIC —) OSSE (PUBLIC —) AIR (SHORT —) DITTY (SOLEMN —) EFFATE EFFATUM (VAPID —) CUCKOO (PL.) BYRONICS

UTTERED SPOKEN

UTTERLY DOG BONE DEAD BLACK OUTLY PROOF HOLLOW MERELY BLANKLY OUTERLY SHEERLY PROPERLY

UVULA CION UVULE PLECTRUM STAPHYLE

UVULARIA OAKESIA

UZBEK JAGATAI

V VEE FIVE VICTOR
(INVERTED —) CARET
VACANCY HOLE WANT VACUIT
VACUITY VACATION
VACANT IDLE VOID BLANK EMPTY
FISHY INANE WASTE DEVOID
HOLLOW DORMANT UNFILLED
(BECOME —) FALL
VACATE QUIT TOLL VOID AVOID
EMPTY WAIVE VACANT ABANDON
RESCIND ABROGATE EVACUATE
VACATION OUT REST LEAVE OUTING
RECESS HOLIDAY NONTERM
VACANCY
(SUMMER —) LONG
VACCINE BACTERIN BIOLOGIC
VACCINIA COWPOX
VACILLATE SWAG WAVE DACKER
DITHER HALPER WABBLE WOBBLE
SHAFFLE STICKLE WHIFFLE
HESITATE
VACILLATING INFIRM HALTING
VACILLATION WAVERING
VACUITY BLOW VACANCY FONTANEL
VACUOUS DULL BLANK EMPTY SILLY
VACANT
VACUUM GAPE VOID VACANCY
VACUITY VACATION
VAGABOND BUM VAG HOBO KERN
JAVEL ROGUE SHACK STIFF BRIBER
CANTER HARLOT JOCKEY PICARA
PICARO RODNEY RUNNER TAGRAG
TRUANT WAFFIE ERRATIC FAITOUR
GADLING GANGREL OUTCAST
SCOURER SWAGMAN SWINGER
TINKLER TRUCKER VAGRANT
VAURIEN WASTREL BOHEMIAN
BRODYAGA CURSITOR CUSTROUN
FUGITIVE GLASSMAN PALLIARD
RAPPAREE RUNABOUT RUNAGATE
WHIPJACK
VAGARY WHIM FANCY FREAK VAGUE
CAPRICE CONCEIT CRANKUM
FLAGARIE VAGRANCY
(PL.) HUMORS
VAGINATE SHEATHED
VAGRANCY MOPERY ROGUING
VAGRANT BUM WAFF WAIF CAIRD
PIKER PIKEY ROGUE SKELB STRAG
TRAMP ARRANT CASUAL SHAKER
SHULER TINKER TRUANT VAGROM
VAGUER WAFFIE DEVIOUS DRIFTER
ERRATIC FLOATER GANGREL
ROGUISH SKILDER SWAGMAN
TINKLER TRAMPER TROGGER
BRODYAGA PLANETIC STROLLER
VAGABOND SHACKLING
VAGUE LAX DARK HAZY FOGGY
FUZZY GROSS LOOSE MISTY
CLOUDY DREAMY MYSTIC SHAGGY
BLURRED EVASIVE OBSCURE
SHADOWY UNFIXED CONFUSED
INFINITE NUBILOUS
VAGUELY DIMLY DARKLY DUMBLY
DREAMILY
VAIN MAD IDLE NULL PUFF VOID
WANE EMPTY FLORY PROUD SAUCY
VOGIE WASTE FLIMSY FUTILE
HOLLOW VAUNTY BIGGITY CARRIED

TRIVIAL VAINFUL CONCEITY
NUGATORY PEACOCKY VAPOROUS
WASTEFUL
(NOT —) SOLID
VAINGLORY RUFF GLORY VANITY
ELATION
VAINLY IDLY TOOMLY
VAIR POTENT
VAISRAVANA BISHAMON
VAISYA BAIS BICE
VAJRA DORJE
VALANCE PELMET FRONTLET
PALMETTE
VALE DALE DEAN DELL BACHE
BATCH ENNIS
VALEDICTORY FAREWELL
VALENCE ADICITY ATOMISM
VALERIAN HELIO BENNET SUMBUL
ALLHEAL CUTHEAL SETWALL
CETEWALL
VALERIC PENTOIC
VALET MAN ANDREW SIRDAR
TARTAR WALLIE CRISPIN TIREMAN
VALIANT SAD BRAG PREU PROW
WILD BRAVE LUSTY ORPED PROUD
STOUT WIGHT FIERCE HEROIC
DOUGHTY GAILLARD GALLIARD
INTREPID STALWART VIRTUOUS
VALID FAIR GOOD JUST LEGAL
SOUND COGENT LAWFUL BINDING
ETERNAL WEIGHTY FORCIBLE
VAILABLE VALIDOUS VALUABLE
VALIDATE FIRM SEAL VALID AFFIRM
CONFIRM
VALIDITY FORCE VIGOR STRENGTH
VALISE BAG GRIP MAIL DORLACH
SATCHEL VALLIES SUITCASE
VALKYRIE SHIELDMAY
VALLECULA VALLEY
VALLEY DIB GUT COMB COOM COVE
DALE DELL DENE GILL HOLE HOPE
HOWE HOYA PARK VALE WADI
WADY ATRIO BACHE BREAK CHASM
COMBE COOMB DHOON GHYLL
GLACK GOYAL GOYLE SLACK SLADE
SWALE TEMPE YUNGA BOLSON
BOTTOM CANADA CLOUGH COULEE
DINGLE HOLLOW LAAGTE LEEGTE
RINCON STRATH AIJALON BLOWOUT
GEHENNA VAALITE
(— BETWEEN CONES OF VOLCANO)
ATRIO
(— IN THESSALY) TEMPE
(— ON MOON'S SURFACE) RILL
CLEFT RILLE
(— ON MT BLANC) NANT
(CIRCULAR —) RINCON
(DEEP —) CANON CANYON
(FLAT-FLOORED DESERT —)
BOLSON
(GRASSY MOUNTAIN —) HOLE
(LOWEST PART OF —) SOLE
(MINIATURE —) GULLY GULLEY
(NARROW —) DEAN DENE GLEN
GLACK GOYLE KLOOF CLOUGH
(SECLUDED —) GLEN DINGLE
(TRENCHLIKE —) COULEE
VALOR ARETE MERIT VALUE BOUNTY
VALOUR BRAVERY COURAGE

PROWESS STOMACH CHIVALRY
VALIANCY
VALOROUS BRAVE VIRTUOUS
VALUABLE DEAR COSTLY PRIZED
WORTHY EMINENT WEALTHY
PRECIOUS PRIZABLE SINGULAR
VALUATION PRIZE VALOR VALUE
ESTEEM EXTENT ESTIMATE
TAXATION
VALUE SET COST FECK FOOT HOLD
RATE TELL AVAIL CARAT CHEAP
COUNT FORCE PRICE PRIZE STAMP
STENT STOCK VALOR WORTH
ASSESS ASSIZE EQUITY ESTEEM
EXTENT FIGURE HIDAGE MATTER
MOMENT PRAISE REGARD VALURE
VALUTA VIRTUE ACCOUNT ADVANCE
APPRIZE CAPITAL CHERISH
COMPUTE PRETIUM RESPECT
VALENCY WERGILD ESTIMATE
EVALUATE GOODWILL SPLENDOR
TREASURE VALIDITY VALLIDOM
(— HIGHLY) PRIZE ENDEAR
(— OF ANGLE) EPOCH
(— OF COW) SET
(— OF TIMBER) STUMPAGE
(ABSOLUTE —) MODULUS
(AESTHETIC —) AMENITY
(ESTABLISHED —) PAR
(GOOD —) SNIP
(MATHEMATICAL —) EXTREMUM
(NEGATIVE —) DISVALUE
(STUDY OF —) AXIOLOGY
(TESTED —) ASSAY
VALUED DEAR
VALUELESS BAFF STRAWY
NAUGHTY
VALVE TAP COCK DISC DISK GATE
ORAL STOP CHOKE CLACK MIXER
VALVA WAFER CUTOUT DAMPER
KICKER PALLET POPPET POTLID
SCUTUM SLUICE SUCKER VENTIL
WASHER CLICKET DRAWOFF
PETCOCK REDUCER SCALLOP
SCOLLOP SHUTOFF VALVULA
VALVULE DRAWGATE EPITHECA
EPIVALVE STOPCOCK THROTTLE
(— OF BARNACLE) SCUTUM
(— OF MUSICAL INSTRUMENT)
PISTON VENTIL
(— OF PUMP BOX) FANG
(THIN —) WAFER
(TRIPLE —) KICKER
VAMBRACE BRACELET
VAMOOSE SCRAM CHEESE DECAMP
SKIDDOO
VAMPIRE LAMIA ALUKAH
VAN WAN FORE LEAD SAIL FRONT
TRUCK VAUNT WAGON VAWARD
CARAVAN FOURGON FOREWARD
KHALDIAN
VANADATE UVANITE TURANITE
VANDAL HUN HUNLIKE SARACEN
HOOLIGAN
VANE FAN TEE WEB COCK TAIL WING
FAINE BUCKET TARGET DOGVANE
FLIGHTER VEXILLUM
(— OF ARROW) FEATHER
(— OF CONVEYOR BELT) FLIGHT

(— OF FEATHER) WEB FLUE
VEXILLUM
(— OF SURVEYING STAFF)
TRANSOM
(— OF WINDMILL) FAN FANE TAIL
FAINE
(COOLING — IN BREWING)
FLIGHTER
VANESSA PYRAMEIS
VANGUARD FORLORN
VANISH DIE FLY DROP FADE FLEE
MELT PASS SANT WEDE WEND
CLEAR FLEET SAUNT SLIDE EXHALE
EVANISH SCATTER CONQUEST
DISSOLVE EVANESCE
(— BY DEGREES) DRILL
VANISHED LAPSED EXTINCT
VANITY ABEL POMP VAIN FOLLY
PRIDE EGOISM FEATHER FOPPERY
INANITY SANDUST IDLENESS
IDLESHIP
VANNER SLIMER
VANNIC KHALDIAN
VANQUISH GET WIN BEAT LICK MILL
UTTER EXPUGN MASTER OUTRAY
SUBDUE THRASH CONQUER
OVERWIN SMOTHER CONQUEST
OVERCOME SURMOUNT VENKISEN
VANQUISHED CRAVEN
VAPID DRY DULL FADE FLAT STALE
TRITE JEJUNE INSIPID WATERISH
VAPOR FOG FUME REEK ROKE STEW
BOAST BRUME EWDER HUMOR
SMOKE STEAM STIFE BREATH
VAPOUR EXHAUST HALITUS
(HOT —) LUNT
(NOXIOUS —) DAMP
(PL.) BRUME
VAPORIZATION BURNUP
VAPORIZE DRIVE FLASH STEAM
AERATE AERIFY VAPORATE
VAPOROUS FUMY FUMID HUMID
FUMISH FUMOSE STEAMY VOLATILE
VARANGIAN VARIAG WARING
(PL.) ROS
VARIABILITY HETERISM
VARIABLE FLUX FREE CHOPPY
FICKLE FITFUL KITTLE WRAIST
CEPHEID FACIENT FLUXILE MUTABLE
ROLLING STREAKY UNEQUAL
VARIANT VARIOUS ARGUMENT
FLOATING FLUXIBLE SHIFTING
SKITTISH UNSTABLE VEERABLE
(EXCEEDINGLY —) PROTEAN
VARIANCE ODDS DISCORD DISPUTE
VARIANT STATE
(— IN WHEAT) SPELTOID
(PL.) DIAPHONE
VARIATION REX TURN ERROR
ROGUE SHADE CHANGE DOUBLE
JITTER SWITCH CYCLING DESCANT
EXTREME SHADING VARIETY
WINDING DIVISION DYNAMICS
HETERISM MUTATION
(— IN AIR PRESSURE) ROBBING
(— IN CURRENT) SURGE
(— IN FREQUENCY) SWINGING
(— IN SPEED) HUNTING
(— OF COLOR) ABRASH

(— OF PUPIL OF EYE) HIPPUS
(— OF SHOE) SPRING
(— OF VOWELS) ABLAUT
(ALLOWABLE —) LEEWAY
(BALLET —) ATTITUDE
(TOPOGRAPHICAL —) BREAK
(PL.) PIBROCH
VARICOCELE RAMEX
VARIED SORTY DAEDAL SEVERAL
VARIANT VARIOUS MANIFOLD
VARIED BUNTING PRUSIANO
VARIEGATE DROP FRET FLECK
FREAK SHOOT DAPPLE STRIPE
VARIFY CHECKER
VARIEGATED FAW PIED SHOT JASPE
LYART SHELD DAEDAL MARLED
MENALD MOSAIC SKEWED CHECKED
DAPPLED FREAKED FRETTED
PECKLED SPARKED VARIOUS
DISCOLOR FRECKLED OVERSHOT
PANACHED SKEWBALD
VARIEGATION COLOR
VARIETY FORM KIND MODE SORT
BRAND BREED CLASS SPICE
CHANGE STIRPS STRAIN STRIPE
SPECIES VARIENS
VARIOLA HORSEPOX
VARIOUS MANY SERE DIVERS
SUNDER SUNDRY VARIED DIVERSE
SEVERAL VARIANT MANIFOLD
VARISCITE UTAHITE
VARLET BOY LAD GIPPO JIPPO
PAVISER COISTREL VARLETTO
VARNISH DOPE JAPAN LACKER
MEDIUM PUNDUM FIXATIF LACQUER
VEHICLE VERMEIL FIXATIVE
OVERGILD THEETSEE
VARY HUNT ALTER BREAK DRIFT
SHIFT SPORT CHANGE DIFFER
RECEDE VARIFY CHECKER DEVIATE
DISSENT DIVERGE VARIATE
DISAGREE
VARYING CURRENT
VASE PYX URN OLLA VASA VASO
ASKOS CYLIX DINOS DIOTA KYLIX
PYXIS BASKET BOWPOT COTULA
COTYLA CRATER DEINOS DOLIUM
FILLER HYDRIA KALPIS KOTYLE
KRATER LEKANE SITULA AMPHORA
AMPULLA CANOPUS PATELLA
POTICHE PSYKTER SCYPHUS
SKYPHOS STAMNOS URCEOLE
BOUGHPOT LECYTHUS LEKYTHOS
MURRHINE PROCHOOS
(— FOR PERFUME) CONCH
(— ON PEDESTAL) TAZZA
(—S UNDER THEATER SEATS)
SCHEA
VASODILATOR KELLIN KHELLIN
VASSAL MAN WER BOND LEUD CEILE
LIEGE SLAVE CLIENT GENEAT
SACOPE BONDMAN FEEDMAN
FEODARY HOMAGER RUDIGER
SAMURAI SERVANT SUBJECT
PALATINE
(PL.) MANRED
VASSALAGE MANRED MANRENT
VAST HUGE BROAD ENORM GREAT
LARGE STOUR VASTY COSMIC

IMMANE MIGHTY UNTOLD IMMENSE
VASTITY ENORMOUS INFINITE
MOUNTAIN SPACIOUS
VASTNESS IMMANE GRANDEUR
WIDENESS
VAT ARK BAC DIP FAT PIT TAP TUN
BACK BECK COOM FATE GAAL GAIL
GYLE KEEL KIER TINE APRON
COOMB FETTE FLOAT KEEVE KIEVE
ROUND STAND STEEP KIMNEL
MOTHER BLUNGER DRAINER
GRAINER KEELVAT STEEPER
PRESSFAT
(— USED IN MEASURING SLIPS) ARK
(BREWER'S —) BACK FLOAT KEEVE
UNION CUMMING
(CHEESE —) CHESSEL CHESSET
CHESSART
(COOLING —) KELDER
(DYER'S —) JIG LEAD DYEBECK
(EVAPORATING —) APRON GRAINER
(FERMENTING —) TUN COMB COOM
GYLE KEEL COOMB FLOAT
(TANNER'S —) TAP HANGER
SPENDER
(TEXTILE —) KIER
(WINE —) LAKE
VAUDEVILLE ZARZUELA
VAULT BOUT COPE JUMP LEAP PEND
SKIP TOMB VOLT WOWT AZURE
CROFT CRYPT EMBOW VOLTO
CUPOLA FORNIX SHROUD DUNGEON
TESTUDO VALTAGE CATACOMB
LEAPFROG MONUMENT
(— IN CEILING) LACUNAR
(— OF HEAVEN) WELKIN
(— OF SKY) CONVEX ZENITH
CONCAVE
VAULTED CONCAVE CRYPTED
EMBOWED
VAULTING POMADA POMMADO
VAUNT GAB BRAG BOAST ROOSE
VOUST AVAUNT INSULT GLORIFY
FLOURISH
(— ONESELF) WIND
VAUNTMURE MANURE
VEAL VEAU SLINK FRICANDO
(LIKE —) VITULINE
VECTOR I K PHASOR GRADIENT
VEDDOID PANYAN
VEDIC (— PRINCIPLE) RTA RITA
VEER CUT DIP FLY CAST CHOP SLEW
SLUE SWAY WYRE FETCH SHIFT
SWOOP BROACH CHANGE SLOUGH
SWERVE TUMBLE DEVIATE WHIFFLE
VEERING DRIFT CHOPPY
VEGETABLE PEA YAM BEAN BEET
CORN KALE LEEK OKRA CHARD
GRASS ONION SABZI SALAD
CARROT CELERY LEGUME LENTIL
POTATO RADISH SQUASH TOMATO
TOPEPO TURNIP BLOATER CABBAGE
CELTUCE LETTUCE PARSNIP
PEASCOD RHUBARB SPINACH
VEGETAL BROCCOLI EGGPLANT
RUTABAGA
(— MATTER) SUDD
(—S FOR MARKET) TRUCK
(EARLY —) PRIMEUR

(EARLY —S) HASTINGS
(GARDEN —S) SASS SAUCE
(HYBRID —) GARLION
VEGETATION HERB COVER GREEN
SCRUB GROWTH HERBAGE
COVERAGE PLANTAGE PLEUSTON
SMELLAGE
(DECOMPOSED —) STAPLE
(SCRUB —) BRUSH
(UNWANTED —) FILTH
VEGETATIVE PLANTAL
VEHEMENCE FURY GLOW HEAT
RAGE WARMTH STRENGTH
VIOLENCE
VEHEMENT HOT HIGH KEEN LOUD
ANGRY EAGER FIERY HEFTY YEDER
ARDENT BITTER FERVID FIERCE
FLASHY HEARTY HEATED RAGING
STRONG ANIMOSE ANIMOUS
FURIOSO INTENSE JEALOUS
VIOLENT
VEHEMENTLY PELLMELL
VEHICLE BUS CAB CAR FLY VAN
ARBA AUTO CART DUKE FLAT GOER
JEEP SLED TAXI TEAM WAIN ARABA
BRAKE BREAK BUGGY CARRY DILLY
FLAIL GUIDE HANSA NODDY STAGE
WAGON BLADER CHARET CISIUM
DIESEL HEARSE JITNEY MEDIUM
PEDRAL RANDEM SLEDGE SLEIGH
SURREY TRISHA TROIKA CARRIER
CHARIOT CRUISER HOTSHOT
ICEBOAT KIBITKA MACHINE MINIBUS
OMNIBUS PEDICAB PEDRAIL
SHUTTLE SPEEDER SPRAYER
STEAMER STEERER TARTANA
TAXICAB TRAVOIS TURNOUT UTILITY
AUTORAIL AUTOSLED CARRIAGE
CHARETTE CYCLECAR DEADHEAD
DELIVERY ELECTRIC FILMOGEN
SHOWCASE SOCIABLE UNICYCLE
(— DRAWN BY BULLOCK) EKKA
(— FOR COLORS) MEGILP
(— FOR HAULING) TRACTOR
(— ON RUNNERS) SLED CARRO
SLEDGE SLEIGH ICEBOAT AUTOSLED
(— PULLED BY MAN) BROUETTE
RICKSHAW
(— RUNNING ON RAILS) LORRY
TRAIN
(— WITH 3 HORSES ABREAST)
TROIKA
**(— WITH 3 HORSES BEHIND EACH
OTHER)** RANDEM
(2-WHEELED —) GIG CART SULKY
TONGA CISIUM JINGLE LIMBER
BICYCLE CALECHE CROYDON
RICKSHAW
(AMMUNITION —) CAISSON
(AMPHIBIOUS —) BUFFALO
(AWKWARD —) ARK
(CHILD'S —) PRAM WALKER
SCOOTER STROLLER
(COVERED —) SEDAN LANDAU
CARAVAN KIBITKA
(EARTH-MOVING —) SCOOP
(LITTLE —) HINAYANA
(LUMBERING —) TUG TODE
(OBSOLETE —) CRATE

(POOR-QUALITY —) DOG
(RUDE —) KIBITKA
(SLEDGE-LIKE —) GAMBO
(WHEELLESS —) DRAY
(PL.) PARK
VEIL WRY FALL FILM HIDE MASK
WRAP COVER GLOSS SHADE VELUM
VIMPA VOLET WREIL BUMBLE FAILLE
SHADOW SHROUD VEILER WEEPER
WIMPLE CORTINA CURTAIN
ENDOTYS PARANJA VEILING
ENDOTHYS HEADRAIL MAHARMAH
MANTILLA TELEBLEM
(— IN CHURCH) AER ENDOTYS
ENDOTHYS
(— ON FUNGI) CORTINA
(DOUBLE —) YASHMAK
(HUMERAL —) SUDARY
(WIDOW'S —) WEEPER
VEILED COVERT VELATED
SHROUDED
VEILING PURDAH GOSSAMER
VEIN BAR LOB RIB CAVA LODE MOOD
RAKE REEF VENA AMPER CLOUD
COMES COSTA LEDGE MEDIA NERVE
RIDER SCRIN VARIX LEADER MEDIAL
STRAIN STREAK VENULA VENULE
AXILLAR AZYGOUS CUBITAL
DROPPER JUGULAR NERVURE
PRECAVA PRESTER SAPHENA
VEINLET AXILLARY EMULGENT
PREMEDIA PROFUNDA SUBCOSTA
(— OF LEAF) RIB COSTA MIDRIB
(— OF MINERAL) STREAK STRINGER
(— OF ORE) LODE ROKE LEDGE
RIDER SCRIN LEADER STRING
DROPPER UNDERSET
(— OF WING) CUBIT CUBITAL
CUBITUS SUBCOSTA SUBCOSTAL
(GRANITIC —) ELVAN
(QUARTZ —) SADDLE
(VARICOSE —) AMPER
VEINED MARBLED NERVOSE
VELA SAILS
VELAR GUTTURAL
VELD BUSHVELD SOURVELD
VELELLA SALLYMAN
VELLEITY WOULDING
VELLINCH FLINCHER
VELLUM ORIHON
VELOCIPEDE HOBBY STEED TRICAR
BICYCLE DICYCLE RANTOON
SPEEDER DRAISINE TRICYCLE
VELOCITY DRIFT CELERITY RAPIDITY
STRENGTH
(— OF 1 FOOT PER SECOND) VELO
(— OF FLOW) CURRENT
VELOUR SOLEIL
VELOUTE POULETTE
VELUM VEIL VELAMEN VELARIUM
VELVET PILE YUZEN BIRODO VELURE
FRAYING VELLUTE
VELVETEEN TRIPE
VELVET GRASS FOG
VELVETLEAF DAGGA PAREIRA
VENAL CORRUPT SALABLE HIRELING
SALEABLE VENDIBLE
VEND HAWK SELL UTTER MARKET
PEDDLE

VENDIBLE VENAL SALABLE
SALEABLE
VENDOR FAKER SELLER VENDER
BUTCHER HUSTLER PITCHER
PURLMAN VIANDER PITCHMAN
SAUCEMAN VENDITOR
VENEER BURL BURR JAPAN SHOOK
SKILLET
VENEERER DUSTER
VENERABLE OLD HOAR SAGE
HOARY AUGUST SACRED VETUST
ANCIENT VENERAL VINTAGE
VENERATE FEAR DREAD HALLOW
REVERE VENERE RESPECT WORSHIP
VENERATED HOLY SACRED
HALLOWED
VENERATION AWE CULT DULIA
CULTISM RESPECT DEVOTION
VENETIAN RED SIENA SIERRA
VENETIAN SUMAC SCOTINO

VENEZUELA

CAPITAL: CARACAS
COIN: REAL MEDIO FUERTE
BOLIVAR CENTIMO MOROCOTA
GULF: PARIA
MEASURE: GALON MILLA FANEGA
ESTADEL
MOUNTAIN: PAVA YAVI DUIDA
ICUTU CONCHA CUNEVA PARIMA
IMUTACA MASAITI RORAIMA
NATIVE: CARIB TIMOTE TIMOTEX
GUARAUNO
RIVER: META APURE CAURA
ARAUCA CARONI CUYUNI
GUANARE ORINOCO ORITUEO
PARAGUA SUAPURE VICHADA
GUAVIARE VENTUARI
STATE: LARA APURE SUCRE ZULIA
ARAGUA FALCON MERIDA
BOLIVAR COJEDES GUARICO
MONAGAS TACHIRA YARACUY
CARABOBO TRUJILLO
TOWN: AROA CORO ATURES
CUMANA MERIDA BARINAS
CABELLO GUAWARE MARACAY
MATURIN CARUPANO TACUPITA
VALENCIA
WEIGHT: BAG LIBRA

VENGEANCE WREAK WRECK
AVENGE ULTION WANION ALASTOR
REVENGE VINDICT REQUITAL
VINDICTA
VENILIA (HUSBAND OF —) DAUNUS
(SISTER OF —) AMATA
(SON OF —) TURNUS
VENISON BILTONG
VENOM GALL ATTER VIRUS POISON
SWELTER CROTALIN CROTALUS
VENOMOUS TOXIC ATTERN DEADLY
SNAKEY VENOMY BANEFUL NOXIOUS
SMITTLE SNAKISH POISONED
VIPERINE VIRULENT
VENT EMIT HOLE REEK BELCH DRAIN
FROTH ISSUE TEWEL OUTAGE
OUTLET CHIMNEY EXPRESS
OPENING ORIFICE OUTCAST

OUTFALL OUTTAKE RELEASE
VENTAGE APERTURE BREATHER
DIATREME FONTANEL MOFFETTE
SESPERAL SPIRACLE SUSPIRAL
VENTHOLE VOMITORY
(— IN EARTH'S CRUST) VOLCANO
(VOLCANIC —) BOCCA DIATREME
SOLFATARA
VENTILATE AIR WIND AERATE
EXPRESS
VENTILATION AERAGE AIRING
VENTILATOR BADGIR LOUVER
FEMERELL
VENTING GUST
VENTRAL HEMAL STERNAL
ANTERIOR INFERIOR
VENTRICLE HEART TRICORN
DIACOELE
VENTURE HAB RUN SET CAST DARE
JUMP KITE LUCK MINT REST RISK
WAGE ETTLE FLIER FLYER FROST
RISCO SALLY STAKE TEMPT WAGER
CHANCE DANGER HAZARD SASHAY
FLUTTER IMPERIL JEOPARD
PRESUME ENDANGER GETPENNY
(— AT DICE) THROW
(— TO SAY) DARESAY
VENTURESOME BOLD RASH RISKY
DARING TEMEROUS
VENTURESOMELY CHANCILY
VENUS LOVE VESPER LUCIFER
HESPERUS PHOSPHOR
(FATHER OF —) JUPITER
(HUSBAND OF —) VULCAN
(MOTHER OF —) DIONE
(SON OF —) CUPID AENEAS
VENUSEAN VENEREAN
VERACIOUS TRUE VERY TRUTHY
SINCERE VERIDIC FAITHFUL
TRUTHFUL
VERACITY HSIN TROTH TRUTH
VERITY FIDELITY
VERANDA PYAL LANAI PORCH
STOOP PIAZZA BALCONY GALERIE
GALLERY
VERB RHEMA ACTIVE NOMINAL
DEPONENT
(AUXILIARY —) BE DO CAN MAY
HAVE MUST WILL SHALL
VERBAL ORAL WORDY
VERBATIM DIRECT VERBAL
DIRECTLY
VERBENA ALOYSIA VERVAIN
VERBENALIN CORNIN
VERBIAGE TALK
VERBOSE WINDY WORDY PROLIX
VERBAL DIFFUSE WORDISH
(NOT —) LEAN
VERDANT BOSKY GREEN VIRID
VERDICT WORD VARDI ASSIZE
FINDING OPINION DECISION
JUDGMENT VEREDICT
VERDIGRIS AERUGO CANKER
VERDET
VERDIN GOLDTIT
VERDURE GREENTH GREENERY
VIRIDITY
VERGE TOP EDGE WAND YARD
TOUCH BORDER TRENCH TRIGGER

VERGER WANDSMAN
VERGILIAN MARONIAN MARONIST
VERIFICATION AUDIT AVERRAL
CHECKUP AVERMENT
VERIFY AVER TRUE AUDIT CHECK
PROVE ATTEST RATIFY COLLATE
CONFIRM CONTROL JUSTIFY
SUPPORT
VERILY AMEN FAITH PARDY CERTES
INDEED PARDIE FAITHLY
VERITABLE REAL TRUE VERY
ACTUAL HONEST PROPER GENUINE
VERIMENT
VERITY TROTH TRUTH VERIDITY
VERJUICE VARGE
VERMICULE VAALITE
VERMICULITE KERRITE MACONITE
VERMIFUGE KOSIN HARMAL HARMEL
KAMALA KAMELA KOOSIN HELONIAS
VERMILION RED GOYA MINIUM
PAPRIKA PIMENTO VERMEIL
ZINOBER CARMETTA CINNABAR
TOREADOR
VERMIN FILTH CARRION VARMINT
VERMIS WORM

VERMONT

CAPITAL: MONTPELIER
COLLEGE: BENNINGTON
MIDDLEBURY
COUNTY: ESSEX ORANGE
ORLEANS LAMOILLE
LAKE: CASPIAN DUNMORE
SEYMOUR CHAMPLAIN
MOUNTAIN: BROMLEY HOGBACK
PROSPECT MANSFIELD
MOUNTAIN RANGE: GREEN
TACONIC
PRESIDENT: ARTHUR COOLIDGE
RIVER: SAXTONS NULHEGAN
WINOOSKI
STATE BIRD: THRUSH
STATE FLOWER: CLOVER
STATE TREE: MAPLE
TOWN: BARRE STOWE GRAFTON
NEWFANE RUTLAND
UNIVERSITY: NORWICH

VERMOUTH CINZANO CHAMBERY
VERNACULAR LINGO COMMON
JARGON PATOIS ROMAIC VULGAR
CHALDEE DIALECT SCOTTISH
VERNALIZE IAROVIZE JAROVIZE
YAROVIZE
VERONICA HEBE SUDARIUM
VERNICLE
VERRUCOSE WARTY WARTED
VERSATILE HANDY FICKLE MOBILE
FLEXILE
VERSE FIT EPIC LINE POSE RANN
RICH RIME SONG BLANK IONIC
METER METRE RHYME STAVE STICH
TANKA ADONIC ALCAIC BURDEN
CHIAVE CYWYDD DIPODY HEROIC
JINGLE PANTUN SCAZON STANZA
VERSET ANAPEST DICOLON
DOGGREL ELEGIAC PAEONIC
PENNILL SAPPHIC SAVITRI SOTADIC

STICHOS TRIPODY TROILUS
CHOLIAMB DACTYLIC DINGDONG
DOGGEREL GLYCONIC LEONINES
PRIAPEAN RESPONSE SENTENCE
SINGSONG TERETISM TRIMETER
VERSICLE
(— FORM) VIRELAY KYRIELLE
(— OF 14 LINES) SONNET
(— OF 2 FEET) DIPODY DIMETER
(— OF 6 FEET) CHOLIAMB SENARIAN
SENARIUS
(— WITH LIMPING MOVEMENT)
SCAZON
(DEVOTIONAL —) ANTIPHON
(HINDU —) SLOKA
(JAPANESE —) HAIKAI
(UNMELODIOUS —) TERETISM
(PL.) TRIPOS PINDARICS
VERSED SEEN WITTY BESEEN
TRADED STUDIED FREQUENT
OVERSEEN SCIENCED
(WELL —) SKILLFUL
VERSICLE VERSE VERSET STICHOS
SUFFRAGE
VERSIFIER BARD POET RHYMER
VERSER METERER
VERSIFY METER
VERSION DRAM DRAUGHT EDITION
READING TURNING
(SHORT —) BRIEF
(SIMPLIFIED —) KEY
(TRANSLATED —) CONSTRUE
VERSO REVERSE
VERT VERD POMME VENUS PRASINE
SINOPLE GREENHEW
VERTEBRA AXIS ATLAS DORSAL
LUMBAR SACRAL ACANTHA
CENTRUM CERVICAL METAMERE
PROATLAS RACKBONE SPONDYLE
VERTEBRATA CRANIATA CRANIOTA
VERTEBRATE CRANIATE SAUROPSID
VERTEX APEX COPE POLE CROWN
PITCH SUMMIT VERTICAL
VERTICAL ERECT PLUMB SHEER
WHIRL ORTHAL UPRIGHT COLUMNAR
SHEERING STRAIGHT
VERTICALLY PLUMP ENDLONG
SHEERLY DIRECTLY PALEWISE
VERTICIL WHORL
VERTIGINOUS DIZZY
VERTIGO DINUS TIEGO MEGRIM
MIRLIGO SWIMMING WHIRLING
VERUMONTANUM COLLICLE
VERVAIN GERVAO FROGFOOT
IRONWEED
VERVE DARE DASH BOUNCE ENERGY
PANACHE VITALITY VIVACITY
VERY SO ALL BIG DOG GAY GEY
MUY BRAW DEAD FELL FULL JUST
MAIN MUCH PURE RARE REAL SAME
SELF SUCH TRES UNCO WELL ASSAI
AWFUL BLAME BULLY CRAZY
DOOMS JOLLY MOLTO PESKY RIGHT
SOWAN SUPER SWITH UNCOW
VERRA BITTER BLAMED DAMNED
DEUCED FREELY GAINLY LIVING
MAINLY MASTER MIGHTY NATION
POISON PROPER STRONG VERRAY
WONDER AWFULLY BOILING

GALLOWS GREATLY PASSING
SOPPING STRANGE DEUCEDLY
DREADFUL ENORMOUS FAMOUSLY
POWERFUL PRECIOUS SPANKING
SWINGING WHACKING
VESICANT LEWISITE
VESICA PISCIS MANDORLA
VESICATORY BLISTER
VESICLE BLEB CYST APTHA BULLA
BURSE FLOAT APHTHA AMPULLA
BLADDER HYDATID POMPHUS
UTRICLE VACUOLE AEROCYST
MIDBRAIN VESICULA
VESICULAR BULLOSE BULLOUS
VESPERAL TOWEL
VESPERS LYCHNIC PLACEBO
EVENSONG
VESSEL (ALSO SEE BOAT AND SHIP)
GO CAN CAT COG CUP FAT GUM
HOY NEF PIG POT TUB VAS VAT VIA
BARK BOAT BODY BOMB BOOT
BOSS BOWL BRIG BUSH BUSS CASK
CELL COWL DISH DRIP DUCT GAWN
GRAB HORN HULK JACK JUNK LOTA
PINK PINT POST PROW SAIL SHIP
SNOW TING YAWL AMULA BAKIE
BARGE BASIN BIDET BIKIE BOCAL
BOYER CADUS CANNE CHURN
COGUE CRACK CRAER CRAFT
CRARE CRUET CRUSE DIOTA DUBBA
FLASK GLOBE GUIDE JUBBE KETCH
LADLE LAKER LAVER LINER PIECE
PYKAR SCOOP SMACK STEAM STILL
XEBEC YANKY ZABRA BANKER
BARQUE BARREL BILALO BOILER
BOTTLE BOUTRE BUCKET BURNER
CAIQUE CANNER CAPPIE CHARGE
CODMAN COFFIN CONCHA COOLER
COPPER CRATER CRAYER CRUISE
CUTTER DECKER DEINOS DOGGER
DUBBAH ELUTOR FESSEL FIRKIN
FLAGON HOLCAD HOOKER JAGGER
KERNOS KETTLE KRATER LANCHA
LATEEN LEKANE LORCHA MASLIN
MONKEY MULLER PACKET PANKIN
PATERA PICARD PITHOS POURIE
ROLLER SALTER SATTIE SEALER
SERVER SETTEE SHIBAR SITULA
SMOKER TARTAN TENDER TOPMAN
VESICA WHALER BAGGALA BALLOEN
BALLOON BLICKEY BLICKIE
BUGGALO CARAVEL CARRIER
CISTERN CLIPPER CORSAIR
COUGNAR CRAGGAN CRESSET
CRISSET CRUISER CUVETTE
DRIFTER DRINKER DROGHER
FELUCCA FLYBOAT FRIGATE
GABBARD GABBART GAIASSA
GALASSA GUNBOAT ORANGER
PATAMAR PINNACE POACHER
POLACRE PSYKTER REDUCER
SALTFAT SCALDER SEEDLIP
SETTLER SPARGER SPOUTER
STEAMER STEEPER TRACHEA
TRENDLE UTENSIL BELANDER
BENITIER BILANDER BILLYBOY
BIRDBATH BLEACHER CORVETTE
CRUCIBLE CRUISKEN CUCURBIT
DECANTER DIGESTER DUTCHMAN

EFFERENT EMISSARY FIREBOAT
FLESHPOT GALLIPOT GALLIVAT
GAROOKUH GAYDIANG HELLSHIP
HONEYPOT INKSTAND INRIGGER
IRONCLAD IRONSIDE KEELBOAT
LATEENER LAVATORY NITRATOR
PICAROON SCHOONER SMUGGLER
SPITTOON WATERPOT
(— FOR COAL) GEORDIE
(— FOR DYE) TOBY
(— FOR HEATING LIQUIDS) ETNA
(— FOR HOLY WATER) FAT FONT
STOCK STOOP STOUP
(— FOR HYPODERMIC USE) AMPUL
AMPULE AMPOULE
(— FOR LIQUID WASTE) DRIP
(— FOR MEASURING ORE) HOPPET
(— FOR MOLTEN METAL) LADLE
(— FOR ORE WASHINGS) LOOL
(— FOR PERFUMES) CENSER
(— FOR SOLDIER'S FOOD) MESSTIN
(— FOR WINE SAMPLING) TASTER
(— HOLDING CONDIMENTS) CRUET
CASTER
(— IN MINE) CORB
(— MADE OF HOLLOW LOG) GUM
(— OF BARK) COOLAMAN
COOLAMON COOLIMAN
(— OF HORN) BUGLE
(— ON TRIPOD) HOLMOS
(— ROWED BY OARS) CATUR
GALLEY
**(— STATIONED IN ENGLISH
CHANNEL)** GROPER
(— USED IN MAKING GLAZE) HILLER
(ABANDONED —) DERELICT
(ARMORED —) CRUISER IRONCLAD
IRONSIDE
(BAPTISMAL —) FONT
(BARGELIKE —) PANGARA
(BLOOD —) AORTA ARTERY
BLEEDER EFFERENT
(BREWER'S —) ROUND
(CANDLEMAKING —) JACK
(CHEMIST'S —) BATH FLASK STILL
BEAKER RETORT
(CHINESE —) JUNK SAMPAN
(CIRCULAR —) KIT
(CLUMSY —) CRAY CRARE
HAGBOAT
(COASTING —) DHOW DONI GRAB
PONTIN SHEBAR SHIBAR TRADER
COASTER GRIBANE
(CODFISHING —) BANKER CODMAN
(DECORATIVE —) AIGUIERE
(DISTILLING —) BODY STILL RETORT
CUCURBIT
(DRINKING —) CAP CUP TIN BOOT
PECE FOUNT GLASS GOURD JORUM
SCALE BICKER CAPPIE CHOPIN
COOPER COOTIE DIPPER DUBBER
FIRLOT GOBLET KITTIE QUAICH
QUAIGH RABBIT RUMKIN BIBERON
CANAKIN CANIKIN GALLIOT
SCYPHUS SKINKER SKYPHOS
TANKARD CANNIKIN CYLINDER
(DUTCH —) KOFF YANKY HOOKER
SCHUIT SCHUYT
(EARTHEN —) PIG BAYAN PANKIN

TINAGE CRAGGAN
(ELECTROPLATING —) TROUGH
(EUCHARISTIC —) AMA PYX AMULA
PYXIS FLAGON COLUMBA CHRISMAL
CIBORIUM
(GLASS —) VERRE UNDINE BALLOON
(HERRING-FISHING —) BUSS
(HOLLOW METALLIC —) BELL
(INVERTED —) BELL
(LADLING —) GAUN
(LARGE-NECKED —) JORDAN
(LATEEN-RIGGED —) DHOW LATEEN
LATEENER
(LEATHER —) BOOT JACK OLPE
GIRBA DUBBER
(LEVANTINE —) JERM SAIC
(LONG-NECKED —) GOGLET GUGLET
(LYMPHATIC —) LACTEAL
(MALAYAN —) PROA COUGNAR
(MELTING —) GRISSET
(OPEN —) LOOM
(PERFORATED —) LEACH
(PINECONE-SHAPED —) THYRSE
(PORTUGUESE —) MULET
(RARE —) SNOW
(SEED —) POD BUTTON
(SERVING —) ARGYLE ARGYLL
SERVER
(SHALLOW —) KIVER SKEEL BEDPAN
PANCHION
(SMALL —) CAG HOY VIAL PHIAL
VEDET JIGGER LIEPOT PICARD
TINLET YETLIN FLIVVER VEDETTE
YETLING GALLIPOT
(TOP-HEAVY —) CRANK
(TURKISH —) MAHONE
(WHALING —) WHALER SPOUTER
(WICKER —) POT
(WINE —) AMA AMULA TINAGE
(WOODEN —) COG KIT BOSS BAKIE
KIVER BICKER CAPPIE COOTIE
DUDDIE FIRKIN STOUND
(PL.) CRAFT WAFTAGE
VEST GARB GOWN ROBE GILET
ACCRUE ATTACH FECKET INVEST
JACKET JELICK LINDER WESKIT
ENFEOFF CLOTHING
(— IN) STATE
VESTA WAX
(FATHER OF —) SATURN
(MOTHER OF —) RHEA
(SISTER OF —) JUNO CERES
VESTED BESTEAD DONATIVE
VESTIBULE HALL ENTRY FOYER
PORCH ATRIUM EPINAOS NARTHEX
PASSAGE ANTEROOM VESTIARY
VESTIGE TAG DREG MARK RACK
SIGN PRINT RELIC SPARK TRACE
TRACK TRACT UMBRA SHADOW
MENTION LEFTOVER TINCTURE
VESTIGIAL REDUCED
VESTING ADITIO
VESTITURE TIRE RAIMENT TUNICLE
VESTMENT ALB CAP ALBE COPE
PALL VEST AMICE COTTA EPHOD
FANON RABAT RASON STOLE
RHASON ROCHET SACCOS SAKKOS
VAKASS MANIPLE ORARION PALLIUM
PILLION PLUVIAL TUNICLE VESTURE

CHASUBLE DALMATIC PHRYGIUM
RATIONAL SCAPULAR SURPLICE
VESTIARY
(PL.) GARB GEAR DRESS CLOTHING
VESTRY SACRISTY VESTIARY
VESUVIANITE EGERAN CYPRINE
IDOCRASE VESUVIAN XANTHITE
VETCH DAL ERS AKRA LUCK TARE
TINE ERVIL FITCH AXSEED FECCHE
THETCH ARVEJON TINETARE
TINEWEED
VETERAN VET CHAUVIN EMERITUS
HARDENED SEASONED
VETERINARIAN VET LEECH FARRIER
VETERINARY VET FARRIERY
VETIVER BEN KHUS CUSCUS KUSKUS
KHASGHAS KHUSKHUS
VETO KILL DISALLOW NEGATIVE
VEUGLAIRE FOWLER
VEX FRY TEW CARK CHAW FASH
FAZE FRET FYKE GALL HALE ITCH
RILE ROIL RUCK TEEN TOUT YOKE
ANGER ANNOY CHAFE FRUMP
GRAME GRILL GRIND GRIPE HARRY
SCALD SPITE STURT TARRY TEASE
WORRY WRACK WRATH YEARN
BOTHER BURDEN CORSIE COTTER
CUMBER GRIEVE GRUDGE HARASS
HARROW INFEST NETTLE OFFEND
PLAGUE POTHER RUFFLE THREAT
WORRIT BEDEVIL CHAGRIN DESPITE
PERPLEX PROVOKE TORMENT
BULLYRAG EXERCISE IRRITATE
MACERATE
VEXATION VEX CHAW FASH MOIL
TEEN TRAY CHAFE CROSS ERROR
GRIEF HARRY PIQUE SPITE STEAM
WORRY BOTHER REPINE CHAGRIN
DISGUST NOISANCE SORENESS
VEXATIOUS SORE TEEN PESKY
ACHING FIERCE SHREWD VEXFUL
IRKSOME PRICKLY TARSOME
ANNOYING CUMBROUS FRAMPOLD
PHRAMPEL UNTOWARD VEXATORY
WEARIFUL
VEXED DIK MAD RILY SORE TEEN
WAXY WILD WRAW ANGRY NARKY
RAGGY ROILY MIFFED MUFFED
SHIRTY SNUFFY FRABOUS GRIEVED
IRKSOME OUTDONE
(EASILY —) CROSS
VEXILLUM WEB VEXIL BANNER
STANDARD
VEXING CHRONIC TECHING
WAYWARD ANNOYING NETTLING
TEACHING
V-GOUGE VEINER
VIABLE VITAL HEALTHY
VIAL AMPUL CRUET PHIAL AMPULE
CASTER CASTOR AMPOULE
VIANDS CATE DIET FOOD CHEER
VIANDRY VICTUALS
VIBRANT RINGY BRAWLING
RESONANT SONOROUS VIGOROUS
VIBRATE JAR WAG BEAT CAST DIRL
PLAY ROCK TIRL WHIR PULSE
QUAKE SWING THIRL THROB TRILL
WAVER DINDLE JUDDER QUAVER
QUIVER SHIVER THRILL WARBLE

CHATTER FLUTTER LIBRATE
STAGGER TREMBLE TWIDDLE
EVIBRATE FLICHTER RESONATE
(— ABNORMALLY) SHIMMY
VIBRATING (— OF AIRPLANE)
BUFFET
VIBRATION BUZZ DIRL FLIP TIRL
SWING DINDLE QUAVER QUIVER
THRILL TREMOR DANCING FLUTTER
TEMBLOR DIADROME FREMITUS
VIBRANCY
(— OF SAW) CUPPING
(RATTLING —) JAR
VIBRATO TRILL WHINE
VIBRATOR TREMBLER
VIBRISSA FEELER SMELLER
VIBURNUM MAE MAY SNOWBALL
VICAR PROXY DEPUTY STALLAR
ALTARIST STALLARY
VICE SIN EVIL CRIME FAULT TAINT
ULCER DEFECT DEPUTY INIQUITY
VICE-GERENT EPHOR
VICE-PRESIDENT (— OF
SANHEDRIN) ABBETDIN
VICEREGENT VICAR SUBPRIOR
VICEROY EARL VALI NABOB NAWAB
NAZIM SUBAH EXARCH KEHAYA
PROREX PROVES SATRAP WARDEN
PROVOST TSUNGTU SUBAHDAR
VICIA FABA
VICINITY HERE SHADOW ENVIRONS
(— OF MINE SHAFT) COLLAR
(NEAR —) SUBURBS
VICIOUS BAD ILL EVIL LAZY LEWD
MEAN UGLY VILE ROWDY TOUGH
SINFUL STRONG VITIAL WICKED
CORRUPT IMMORAL SKAITHY
DEPRAVED DEVILISH FRATCHED
INFAMOUS THEWLESS
VICIOUSNESS VICE
VICISSITUDE CHANGE MUTATION
(— OF FORTUNE) WEATHER
VICTIM BUTT DUPE GOAT GULL
PREY PATHIC CASUALTY
(— FOR SHARPERS) JAY
(INTENDED —) CHUMP
(SACRIFICIAL —) HOST MERIAH
(UNFORTUNATE —) BASTARD
VICTIMIZATION RIDE
VICTIMIZE HOAX BUNCO BUNKO
COZEN
VICTOR COCK CAPTOR MASTER
WINNER BANGSTER
VICTORFISH AKU
VICTORIA (FATHER OF —) PALLAS
(MOTHER OF —) STYX
VICTORIAN GENTEEL
VICTORIOUS VICTOR WINNING
VICTORY WIN PALM PRICE BETTER
SUBDUE VICTOR SACKING TRIUMPH
WINNING CONQUEST DECISION
WALKOVER
(EASY —) BREEZE
(OVERWHELMING —) SWEEP
VICTUAL BIT VITE VITTLE
(BROKEN —S) SCRAN
(PL.) KAI BITE CHOW FOOD GRUB
PROG SAND VIVERS
VICTUALER PURVEYOR

VIDELICET NAMELY SILICET
VIE ENVY JOSTLE STRIVE COMPETE
CONTEND CONTEST EMULATE
VIETNAM (SEE NORTH VIETNAM AND
SOUTH VIETNAM)
VIETNAMESE ANNAMESE
VIEW EYE KEN FACE GLOM MAKE
VISE AVIEW BLUSH CATCH MOUTH
SCAPE SCENE SIGHT VISTA VIZZY
ADVICE ADVISE ASPECT DEVICE
GLANCE REGARD SURVEY ALOGISM
CONCEIT FEELING GLIMPSE
KENNING LOOKOUT OFFLOOK
OPINION RESPECT SCENERY
SURVIEW THOUGHT AIRSCAPE
CONSPECT EYESIGHT OFFSCAPE
SEASCAPE SENTENCE
(— ATTENTIVELY) GAZE
(— CLOSELY) INSPECT
(— FROM AFAR) DESCRY
(— FROM ANGLE) SLANT
(— OF MAN) DUALISM
(— WITH SURPRISE) ADMIRE
(BRIEF —) SNAPSHOT
(COMPREHENSIVE —) PANORAMA
(GENERAL —) LANDSKIP
(OPEN —) LIGHT
(PHYSICAL —) INSIGHT
(SATISFYING —) EYEFUL
VIEWPOINT SIGHT LAXISM
VIGIL WAKE WATCH WAKING
AGRYPNIA
VIGILANCE WATCH JEALOUSY
VIGILANT AGOG WARE WARY ALERT
AWAKE AWARE CHARY SHARP
JEALOUS WAKEFUL CAUTIOUS
WATCHFUL
VIGOR GO SAP VIM VIR VIS BIRR
DASH EDGE ELAN LUST PITH SEVE
SNAP TUCK ARDOR DRIVE FLUSH
FORCE GREEN JUICE NERVE POWER
ENERGY ESPRIT FOISON GINGER
SPRAWL SPRING STARCH VIGOUR
VIRTUS FREEDOM SMEDDUM
STAMINA STHENIA FLOURISH
STRENGTH TONICITY VITALITY
(FULL OF —) LIFESOME
(MENTAL —) DOCITY SPIRIT
(RENEWED —) REST
VIGOROUS YEP ABLE CANT FRIM
HALE LIVE RUDE SPRY YEPE CRANK
EAGER FRACK FRANK JUICY LUSTY
NIPPY PITHY SASSY SOLID STARK
STIFF STOUT TOUGH VIVID FLORID
GOLDEN HEARTY LIVELY POTENT
ROBUST RUGGED SINEWY SQUARE
STRONG BUCKISH CHIPPER CORDIAL
DRASTIC FECKFUL FURIOUS
HEALTHY NERVOSE NERVOUS
VALIANT VIBRANT ZEALOUS
ATHLETIC BOUNCING CHOPPING
FORCEFUL MUSCULAR SLAMBANG
SLASHING STUBBORN VEHEMENT
VIGOROSO YOUTHFUL
(NOT —) GENTEEL
VIGOROUSLY DOWN FELL HARD
VERN CRANK SNELL TIGHT VERNE
HARDLY SNELLY FRESHLY SMARTLY
STOUTLY WIGHTLY HEARTILY

VIGOROUSNESS ENERGY FREEDOM
VIKING DANE WIKING NORSEMAN
VIKRAMADITYA BIKRAM
VILE BAD BASE CLAM FOUL CHEAP
MUCKY POCKY RUSTY SLIMY WILLE
ABJECT CRUSTY DRAFTY DRASTY
FILTHY LECHER NOUGHT PALTRY
SORDID TURPID UNKIND BENEATH
CAITIFF CORRUPT DEBASED
HATEFUL IGNOBLE SLAVISH VICIOUS
BASEBORN DEPRAVED UNKINDLY
VILENESS FEDITY VILITY
VILIFICATION REPROACH
VILIFY ILL VILE ABUSE LIBEL STAIN
DEFAME MALIGN REVILE SLIGHT
ASPERSE BLACKEN DEBAUCH
DETRACT TRADUCE REPROACH
STRUMPET
VILIPEND BELITTLE
VILL HAM TOWN TOWNSHIP
VILLA ALDEA DACHA DATCHA
QUINTA TRIANON
VILLAGE BY AUL BYE GAV HAM KOM
PAH REW BURG DORP HOME MURA
TOWN VILL WICK ALDEA BOURG
CASAL PLACE THORP VICUS ALDEIA
BARRIO BUSTEE CASTLE GOTHAM
HAMLET HAMMON MOUZAH PETTAH
PUEBLO AMBALAM BOROUGH
CAMPODY CASERIO ENDSHIP
MAABARA MISSION OUTPOST
BEREWICK BOURGADE CAMPOODY
CRANFORD TOLDERIA VILLACHE
VILLAGET VILLAKIN
(— IN WHICH BARLEY IS GROWN)
BEREWICK
(— OUTSIDE OF FORT) PETTAH
(AFRICAN —) STAD KRAAL
(ARABIAN —) DOUAR
(ARGENTINE —) TOLDERIA
(FRENCH —) BASTIDE
(IMAGINARY —) CRANFORD
(INDIAN —) CASTLE PUEBLO
CAMPODY CAMPOODY
(JAPANESE —) MURA BUSTI BUSTEE
(JAVANESE —) DESSA
(MALAY —) CAMPONG KAMPONG
(MAORI —) KAIK KAIKA KAINGA
(MEXICAN —) EJIDO
(NEW ZEALAND FORTIFIED —) PA
PAH
(RUSSIAN —) MIR STANITSA
STANITZA
VILLAIN IAGO LOUT SERF BADDY
BRAVO CHURL DEMON DEVIL FAGIN
FELON HEAVY KNAVE ROGUE
SCAMP SHREW BADDIE VILIACO
SCELERAT
VILLAINOUS BAD EVIL GALLUS
GALLOWS KNAVISH VILEYNS
FLAGRANT RASCALLY
VILLAINY CRIME KNAVERY
VILLEIN SERF CHURL COTTER
VILLAR BONDMAN TOWNMAN
VILLAIN COTARIUS
VILLI (HAVING —) ZONARY
VILLOUS SHAGGY
VIM ZIP GIMP ZING FORCE VIGOR

ENERGY GINGER SPIRIT STARCH
VINEGAR
VINA BEN BIN BINA
VINCENTIAN LAZARIST
VINDICATE FREE CLEAR RIGHT
WREAK ACQUIT ASSERT AVENGE
EXCUSE UPHOLD ABSOLVE DERAIGN
JUSTIFY PROPUGN REVENGE
SUSTAIN
VINDICATION APOLOGY THEODICY
VINDICATOR VINDEX ASSERTER
DEFENDER
VINDICTIVE HOSTILE PUNITIVE
SPITEFUL VENGEFUL
VINE AKA FIG HOP IVY IYO BINE
CARO GOGO ODAL SOMA TINE
AKEBI BUAZE BWAZI CAAPI CACUR
GUACO KAIWI KUDZU LIANA PALAY
PRIVY TACSO TIMBO TRAIL TWINE
WITHE WONGA BEJUCO CISSUS
COBAEA COWAGE DERRIS DODDER
ECANDA GERKIN IPOMEA JICAMA
LABLAB RUNNER TURURI TWINER
ULLUCO WINDER APRICOT BIGROOT
BONESET BRAMBLE CALAMUS
CATVINE CERIMAN CLIMBER
COWHAGE COWITCH CUPSEED
EPACRID GHERKIN IPOMOEA
LAVANGA PAREIRA PUMPKIN
TRAILER VINELET YANGTAO
ATRAGENE BINDWEED BOXTHORN
CLEMATIS COMEBACK CUCUMBER
CUCURBIT DECUMARY DOLICHOS
EARDROPS EARTHPEA EVONYMUS
GULANCHA HEARTPEA HEMPWEED
MUSCATEL REDWITHE TINETARE
TINEWEED TRAILERY TRAILING
TREEBINE VINIFERA WINETREE
WISTARIA WISTERIA
VINEGAR EISEL ESILL ACETUM
ALEGAR ASCILL SOURING
BEEREGAR VINAIGRE
VINEGAR EEL EELWORM
VINEGARY ACETOSE ACETOUS
VINEGROWER VINITOR
VINEYARD CRU CLOS COTE VINER
VINERY WINEYARD
VINGT-ET-UN MACAO MACCO
VINOUS WINY
VINTAGE OLD VINT WINE CUVEE
ARCHAIC CLASSIC VENDAGE
OUTMODED
VIOL GUE GIGA LIRA TURR GIGUE
GUDOK TARAU VOYAL VOYOL
CHELYS FIDDLE VIELLE VIOLET
MINIKIN QUINTON SARINDA SULTANA
VIHUELA VIOLONE BARBITON
BASSETTE SERINGHI VIOLETTE
VIOLA ALTO QUINT TENOR TENORE
VIOLET
VIOLA BASTARDA BARITONE
BARYTONE
VIOLA DA BRACCIO QUINT
VIOLA D'AMORE VIOLET
VIOLA DA GAMBA GAMBA
VIOLATE ERR SIN FLAW ABUSE
BREAK CRACK FORCE HARRY
LOOSE VIOLE WRONG BREACH
BROACH DEFILE INVADE OFFEND

RAVISH DEBAUCH DISOBEY FALSIFY
INFRACT OUTRAGE POLLUTE
DEFLOWER DISHONOR FORSWEAR
FRACTURE INFRINGE MISTREAT
STUPRATE SURPRISE TEMERATE
TRESPASS VIOLENCE
VIOLATED FRACTED INFRACT
VIOLATION SIN DEBT ABUSE CRIME
ERROR FAULT SALLY BREACH
INJURY
(HOCKEY —) STICKS
VIOLATOR WRONGER
VIOLENCE FURY NEED RAGE RUFF
BRUNT FORCE RIGOR STORM
BENSIL ESTURE HUBRIS RANDOM
RAPINE STOUSH BENSAIL BENSALL
OUTRAGE FEROCITY SEVERITY
SORENESS
(LETHAL —) DEATH
VIOLENT BIG HOT TEZ DERF HARD
HIGH MAIN RANK RUDE WILD WOOD
ACUTE FIERY HEADY HEAVY HEFTY
RABID SHARP SMART STARK STERN
STIFF STOOR STOUR STOUT WROTH
BROTHE FIERCE HEARTY MANIAC
MIGHTY SAVAGE SEVERE STORMY
STRONG STURDY SUDDEN CRIMSON
FURIOUS HOTSPUR RAMMISH
RAPEFUL RUFFIAN TEARING
VIOLOUS WILSOME CHURLISH
DIABOLIC FLAGRANT FORCEFUL
IMPOTENT MANIACAL RIGOROUS
SEETHING SLAMBANG STALWART
VEHEMENT
VIOLENTLY HARD AMAIN HOTLY
HARDLY SORELY HOPPING SOUNDLY
VIOLET CANON GRAPE MAUVE VIOLA
BLAVER CANYON DAHLIA DAMSON
EVEQUE JOHNNY HOOKERS LOBELIA
OPHELIA PRELATE PRIMULA
PUREAYN CLEMATIS DAMEWORT
FINELEAF IANTHINE ROOSTERS
WISTERIA
VIOLIN GUE KIT ALTO GIGA AMATI
CROWD GEIGE GIGUE REBAB REBEC
STRAD TARAU VIOLA CATGUT
CHORUS CROUTH FIDDLE FITHEL
REBECK TAILLE VIOLON CATLING
CHROTTA CREMONA THEYAOU
VIOLAND VIOLINO GUARNERI
KEMANCHA VIOLOTTA
VIPER ASP HABU ADDER ASPIC
ATHER URUTU WYVER ASPIDE
DABOIA DABOYA JESSUR KATUKA
KUPPER HAGWORM MAMUSHI
VIPERID AMMODYTE CERASTES
JARARACA VIPERINE
VIRAGO RANDY AMAZON BELDAM
CALLET BELDAME TRIMMER VIRAGIN
RIXATRIX
VIREO REDEYE GRASSET TEACHER
GREENLET PREACHER
VIRGATE YOKE VERGE YARDLAND
(HALF —) MANTAL
VIRGIN NEW LIVE MAID PURE FRESH
CHASTE MAIDEN VESTAL INITIAL
PUCELLE DOROTHEA PARAMOUR
(— OF PARADISE) HURI HOURI

VIRGINAL CHERRY INTACT
SYMPHONY TRIANGLE

VIRGINIA

CAPITAL: RICHMOND
COLLEGE: AVERETT HOLLINS
MADISON RADFORD LONGWOOD
COUNTY: BATH PAGE BLAND
FLOYD SMYTH SURRY WYTHE
AMELIA LOUISA ACCOMAC
HENRICO PULASKI ROANOKE
CULPEPER FLUVANNA
TAZEWELL
INDIAN: SAPONI TUTELO
MONACAN MANAHOAC
MEHERRIN NOTTAWAY
POWHATAN
LAKE: KERR SMITH
MOUNTAIN: CEDAR ELLIOT
ROGERS BALDKNOB
MOUNTAIN RANGE: CLINCH
ALLEGHENY BLUERIDGE
PRESIDENT: TYLER MONROE
TAYLOR WILSON MADISON
HARRISON JEFFERSON
WASHINGTON
RIVER: DAN JAMES POTOMAC
RAPIDAN
STATE BIRD: CARDINAL
STATE FLOWER: DOGWOOD
STATE TREE: DOGWOOD
TOWN: GALAX LURAY SALEM
MARION BEDFORD BRISTOL
EMPORIA NORFOLK PULASKI
ROANOKE DANVILLE HOPEWELL
MANASSAS STAUNTON
TAZEWELL

VIRGINIA COWSLIP LUNGWORT
VIRGINIA CREEPER CREEPER
WOODBIND WOODBINE
VIRGINIA KNOTWEED JUMPSEED
VIRGINIAN BEAGLE COOHEE
CAVALIER TUCKAHOE
VIRGINIA SNAKEROOT SANGREL
SNAGREL
VIRGINIA STICKSEED SOLDIERS
VIRGINIA WATERLEAF SHAWNY
VIRGINIA WILLOW ITEA
VIRGINITY HONOR PUCELAGE
VIRGIN MARY DESPOINA
THEOTOCOS
VIRGIN'S-BOWER LOVE HONESTY
MOONWORT
VIRGULE VIRGULA DIAGONAL
VIRIDIAN EMERAUDE
VIRILE MALE MANLY
VIRILITY LUST GREEN MANHEAD
MANHOOD
VIRTUAL IMPLICIT
VIRTUALLY BUT NEARLY MORALLY
VIRTUE JEN HSIN THEW ARETE
FAITH GRACE POWER VALOR VERTU
WORTH BOUNTY DHARMA CHARISM
CHARITY JUSTICE PROBITY QUALITY
CHARISMA CHASTITY EFFICACY
GOODNESS MORALITY PARAMITA
(CONFUCIAN —) LI
(PL.) CIVISM

VIRTUOSO EXPERT SAVANT
ESTHETE LAPIDARY
VIRTUOUS GOOD PURE BRAVE CIVIL
MORAL CHASTE HONEST MODEST
GODDARD SAINTED SINCERE
UPRIGHT VIRTUAL STRAIGHT
VIRULENCE VIRUS
VIRULENT ACRID RABID DEADLY
MALIGN VIROSE NOXIOUS VIRIFIC
VENOMOUS
(LESS THAN —) MITIS
VIRUS VENOM POISON PATHOGEN
SPECIFIC
VIS PEIKTHA
VISAGE FACE CHEER IMAGE VISOR
ASPECT FASHION
VISCERA GUTS HASLET INSIDE
UMBLES GARBAGE GIBLETS
HASSLET INMEATS INNARDS INSIDES
NUMBLES ENTRAILS
VISCID SLAB WAXY GOOEY GLAIRY
STICKY LENTOUS STRINGY VISCOUS
MOTHERED
VISCIDITY LENTOR
VISCOSITY BODY
(— UNIT) POISE
VISCOUS LIMY ROPY SIZY SLAB
GOBBY GUMMY ROPEY SLIMY STIFF
TARRY SIRUPY SLABBY SMEARY
SNOTTY STICKY THONGY VISCID
LENTOUS SQUISHY VISCOSE
MUCULENT
VISE GEE CHAP JACK SHOP VICE
CHEEK CLAMP CRAMP WINCH
VISHNU RAMA VASU KALKI KRISHNA
BALARAMA BHAGAVAT
VISIBLE OUT FAIR SEEN CLEAR
GROSS EXTANT SIGHTY EVIDENT
GLARING OBVIOUS SIGHTLY
APPARENT DIOPTRIC EXPLICIT
EXTERNAL MANIFEST PROSPECT
(BARELY —) DARK
(SCARCELY —) DIM
VISION EYE RAY DREAM FANCY
SIGHT FANTAD SEEING SWEVEN
AISLING SHOWING SPECTER
SPECTRE EYESIGHT PHOTOPIA
(— IN DIM LIGHT) SCOTOPIA
(BLURRED —) SWIMMING
(DEFECTIVE —) ANOPIA
(IMAGINARY —) SHADOW
(IMPERFECT —) DARKNESS
(MULTIPLE —) POLYOPIA
VISIONARY FEY AERY AIRY WILD
IDEAL VIEWY ASTRAL INSANE
SHANDY UNREAL DREAMER
FANTAST LAPUTAN UTOPIAN
ACADEMIC DELUSIVE FANCIFUL
FINESPUN IDEALIST NOTIONAL
PHANTAST QUIXOTIC ROMANTIC
UTOPIAST VISIONER
VISIT DO GAM SEE VIS CALL CHAT
STAY APPLY HAUNT TRYST VIZZY
COSHER RESORT RETURN CEILIDH
CEILIDHE FREQUENT INVASION
(— BETWEEN WHALERS) GAM
(— PERSISTENTLY) INFEST
(— PROFESSIONALLY) ATTEND
(— RELATIVES) COUSIN

(— WRETCHED NEIGHBORHOODS)
SLUM
(CEREMONIAL —) SELAMLIK
VISITATION SENE VISIT SENDING
VISITING ACTIVE SOCIAL
VISITOR GUEST LAKER CALLER
VISITANT
(MEALTIME —) SCAMBLER
(PL.) COMPANY
VISOR BILL SIGHT UMBER UMBRE
VIZOR BEAVER MESAIL UMBRIL
VIZARD EYESHADE
VISTA VIEW SCENE OUTLOOK
VISUAL OPTIC OCULAR SCOPIC
VISORY VISIBLE
VISUALIZE SEE FANCY IDEATE
SYMBOL IMAGINE PICTURE
CONCEIVE ENVISAGE
VITAL LIVE BASIC CHIEF FRESH
SAPPY LIVELY MOVING VIABLE
ZOETIC ANIMATE CAPITAL CORDIAL
EXIGENT NEEDFUL ESSENTIAL
VITALITY SAP VIM LIFE COLOR
GUSTO JUICE BIOSIS BREATH
ENERGY FOISON HEALTH STARCH
VIVENCY STRENGTH
(DEFICIENT —) ASTHENIA
(LACKING —) STUFFY TURNIPY
VITALIZE ACTIVATE ENERGIZE
VITAMIN BIOTIN CITRIN NIACIN
ADERMIN ANEURIN CHOLINE
THIAMIN TORULIN ADVITANT
INOSITOL NUTRAMIN ORYZANIN
VITAMINE
VITIATE BEAT SPOIL TAINT CANCEL
DEBASE POISON CORRUPT DEPRAVE
VITIATED PICAL CORRUPT
VITICULTURIST VIGNERON
VITREOUS GLASSY GLAIZIE VITREAN
VITROUS
VITRIFY GLAZE
VITRIOL BLUEJACK COPPERAS
(PL.) SORY
VITRIOLIC SHARP BITING BITTER
CAUSTIC MORDANT SCATHING
VITUPERATE RAIL ABUSE CURSE
SCOLD BERATE REVILE
VITUPERATION ABUSE VITUPER
VITUPERATIVE ABUSIVE REVILING
SHAMEFUL
VIVACE VIVO LEBHAFT
VIVACIOUS GAY AIRY BRISK CRISP
MERRY SUNNY ACTIVE LIVELY
LIVING SPARKY VIVACE ANIMATE
JOCULAR ANIMATED SPIRITED
SPORTIVE
VIVACITY BRIO FIRE LIFE ZEAL
ARDOR VERVE VIGOR ESPRIT
GAIETY GAYETY SPIRIT SPRAWL
SPARKLE
VIVARIUM STEW VIVARY STEWPOND
VIVAT HOCH
VIVERRINE CIVET GENET FOUSSA
MUSANG LINSANG FALANAKA
MONGOOSE SURICATE
VIVID DEEP HARD KEEN LIVE RICH
VIVE BRISK FRESH GREEN LURID
QUICK RUDDY SHARP GARISH
LIVELY LIVING STRONG VISUAL

EIDETIC FLAMING FREAKED GLARING GLOWING GRAPHIC INTENSE VIOLENT COLORFUL DISTINCT DRAMATIC SLASHING STRIKING VIGOROUS

VIVIDNESS COLOR EMPHASIS

VIVIFY LIFE FOMENT ANIMATE QUICKEN SPARKLE

VIVIPARUS PALUDINA

VIXEN BARD FURY SCOLD SHREW VIRAGO TAGSTER TRIMMER

VIZIER WAZIR ATABEG ATABEK VISIER

VLACH WALLACH

V-MAIL AIRGRAPH

VOCABULARY CANT SLANG JARGON DICTION LEXICON POCHISMO WORDBOOK
(UNDERWORLD —) ARGOT

VOCAL GLIB ORAL VOWEL FLUENT TONGUED VOCULAR ELOQUENT

VOCALIST BOPPER SINGER BOPPIST BOPSTER SONGSTER VOCALLER

VOCATION CALL HOBBY METIER CALLING SCIENCE

VOCATIONAL BANAUSIC

VOCIFERATION CLAMOR OUTCRY

VOCIFEROUS LOUD NOISY BAWLING BLATANT BRAWLING STRIDENT

VODKA SAMOGON SAMOGONKA

VOGUE CUT TON CHIC MODE TURN STYLE CUSTOM FASHION RECLAME PRACTICE

VOGUL MANSI

VOICE SAY VOX EMIT GIVE HARP PIPE TONE TURN WISH FROTH LEDEN RAISE RUMOR SOUND UTTER ACTIVE CHOICE STEVEN TAISCH THROAT TONGUE EXPRESS OPINION SONORIZE DIATHESIS
(— PRAISE) SLAVER
(ARTIFICIAL —) FALSETTO
(FIFTH —) QUINTUS
(HOARSE —) FOGHORN
(LOWEST —) BASS BASSO
(MIDDLE —) MOTETUS
(PRINCIPAL —) CANTUS
(PUBLIC —) CRY
(SINGING —) ALTO BASS TENOR BREAST SOPRANO BARITONE FALSETTO
(TENOR —) TAILLE
(UPPER —) DESCANT DISCANT

VOICED SOFT WEAK TONIC MEDIAL SONANT PHTHONGAL

VOICELESS MUM DUMB HARD MUTE SURD SHARP ATONIC FLATED SILENT ANAUDIA APHONIC SPIRATE APHONOUS BREATHED NOTELESS

VOID NO BAD FREE KORE LEAR LEER MUTE NULL PASS ABYSS AVOID BLANK EGEST EJECT EMPTY INEPT LAPSE PURGE SLICE SPACE WASTE DEVOID HOLLOW VACANT VACUUM CONCAVE INVALID VACANCY VACUITY EVACUATE INDIGENT NONBEING
(— OF FEELING) BLATE
(— OF SENSE) INANE
(— OF SUBSTANCE) JEJUNE

VOIDED FALSE CLECHE CLECHY CLECHEE

VOILE NINON

VOLATILE LIGHT FIGENT LIVELY VOLAGE BUOYANT DARTING ELASTIC FLIGHTY FLYAWAY GASEOUS FUGITIVE SKITTISH VAPOROSE VAPOROUS FUGACIOUS

VOLATILITY LEVITY

VOLCANO APO DOME ETNA ASKJA PELEE SHASTA VULCAN FURNACE VULCANO FUMAROLE KRAKATOA SPITFIRE VESUVIUS
(MUD —) SALSE SALINELLE

VOLE CRABER CRICETID

VOLITATION FLIGHT VOLATION

VOLITION WILL CHOICE INTENT VOLENCY

VOLLEY CROWD DRIFT VOLEE FLIGHT BARRAGE PLATOON BLIZZARD

VOLPLANE GLIDE

VOLSUNG WAELS

VOLT VOLTA REPOLON
(— AMPERE UNIT) VAR

VOLTAGE KICKBACK

VOLTAIC GUR GALVANIC

VOLTE-FACE BACKFLIP

VOLUBILITY FLUENCY

VOLUBLE GLIB WORDY FLUENT

VOLUME MO PEN BAND BOOK BULK SIZE TOME SPACE CUBAGE CONTENT DIURNAL MENAION VOLUMEN CAPACITY CUBATURE SOLIDITY STRENGTH
(— OF SOUND) STRESS
(— OF WORT) LENGTH
(PATTERN —) DUMMY

VOLUMINOUS FULL AMPLE BULKY LARGE BOUFFANT

VOLUNTARILY WILLES WILLICHE

VOLUNTARY FREE WILLY SORTIE WILFUL PRELUDE SORTITA WILLFUL WILLING ELECTIVE FREEWILL HONORARY OPTIONAL POSTLUDE UNFORCED

VOLUNTEER OFFER ENLIST PROFFER STRANGER
(— STATE) TENNESSEE

VOLUPTUARY SYBARITE

VOLUPTUOUS ADIN LUXIVE LYDIAN SULTRY WANTON SENSUAL DELICATE LUSCIOUS SENSUOUS

VOLUPTUOUSNESS DELICE LUXURY

VOLUTE TURN HELIX SCROLL VOLUTA CILLERY VOLUTION

VOLUTION COIL TWIST WHORL

VOLVA CUP WRAPPER

VOMIT CAT PUT BALK BOCK BOKE CACK CAST PICK PUKE SICK SPEW SPUE VOME WOOM BRAKE EVOME HEAVE REACH RETCH SHOOT POSSET REJECT VOMITO CASCADE CASTING REGORGE DISGORGE PARBREAK SICKNESS VOMITING

VOMITING BOKE EMESIS PYEMESIS

VOMITUS SPEW SPUE

VOODOO HEX OBI CHARM OBEAH HOODOO SORCERER
(— DESIGN) VERVER
(— SPELL) MOJO

VOODOOISM VODUN WANGA

VORACIOUS GORB GREEDY BULIMIC ESURINE GLUTTON THROATY EDACIOUS ESURIENT RAVENING RAVENOUS

VORACITY EDACITY

VORTEX APEX EDDY GYRE SWIRL WHIRL

VOTARESS NUN

VOTARY PALMER ZEALOT DEVOTEE SECTARY ADHERENT DEVOTARY FOLLOWER

VOTE AYE CON NAY PRO ELECT FAGOT GRACE VOICE BALLOT DIVIDE FAGGOT TONGUE APPROVE PLUMPER SUFFRAGE
(— AGAINST) NAY KNIFE
(— APPROVAL) CONFIRM
(— FOR) AY AYE PRO SUPPORT
(— OF ASSENT) PLACET

VOTER BOLTER POLLER CHOOSER ELECTOR FLOATER ASSENTOR

VOTIVE VOWED

VOTYAK UDMURT

VOUCH ABLE ASSURE ATTEST AVOUCH ENDORSE ACCREDIT

VOUCHER CHIT CHALAN POLICY TICKET WARRANT

VOUCHSAFE GIVE SEND DEIGN GRANT VOUCH BETEEM PLEASE WITSAFE

VOUSSOIR QUOIN WEDGE KEYSTONE SPRINGER

VOW LAY VUM AVOW OATH SNUM VOTE SWEAR VOUCH BEHEST PLEDGE BEHIGHT PROMISE PROTEST

VOWEL SHWA WIDE GLIDE SCHWA VOCOID AUGMENT GEMINATE
(— POINT) SERE
(CHANGE OF —) UMLAUT
(GROUP OF 2 —S) BROAD DIGRAM DIGRAPH
(PREFIXED —) AUGMENT
(SHORT —) MATRA

VOYAGE SAIL TRIP VIAGE CRUISE FLIGHT TRAVEL CARAVAN JOURNEY PASSAGE SAILING STEAMER PERIPLUS SHIPPING

VOYAGING SEA NAVIGANT

VULCANITE EBONITE

VULCANIZATION BURNING

VULCANIZE BURN CURE METALIZE

VULCANIZER CEMENTER

VULGAR LOW LEWD LOUD RUDE FLASH GROSS SLANG SLIMY COARSE COMMON PORTER RABBLE VULGUS WOOLEN BOORISH GENERAL KNAVISH LOWBRED MOBBISH OBSCENE POPULAR SECULAR TABLOID VILLAIN WOOLLEN CHURLISH MECHANIC PANDEMIC PLEBEIAN PORTERLY POTHOUSE SOUTERLY

VULGARIAN SLOB RAFFISH

VULGARITY SHODDY FOULNESS
  HARLOTRY
VULGARIZE PLEBIFY PROFANE
VULGARIZED DEGRADED
VULGARLY CHEAPLY
VULNERABILITY GAP EXPOSURE

VULNERABLE LIABLE EXPOSED
VULPINE FOXY ALOPECOID
VULTURE AURA GEIR PAPA AREND
  GRAAP GRAPE GRIPE SWIPE URUBU
  CONDOR CORBIE FALCON GRIPHE
  RAPTOR SNATCH TORGOS GRIFFIN

  GRIFFON GRYPHON NEKHEBT
  AASVOGEL DIRTBIRD GEREAGLE
  NEKHEBET ZOPILOTE GALLINAZO
VULVA DOCK PUDENDUM
VUM SNUM

W WAW WHISKEY WILLIAM
WA VU KAWA LAWA
WABBLE COCKLE COGGLE HOBBLE
WAGGLE WARBLE WAUBLE WOBBLE
WABBLY COGGLE WAGGLY WOBBLY
WABBY LOON WHABBY
WABRON WAYBERRY
WACKY CRAZY INSANE MENTAL
ERRATIC
WAD BAT BET BOB PAD COLF LINE
POKE SWAB SWOB WISP WAGER
PLEDGE SCOURER GRAPHITE
WADDLE WAG HODDLE PODDLE
TODDLE WALLOP WIDDLE WAUCHLE
WADDY PEG STICK COWBOY
RUSTLER WHADDIE
WADE FORD WYDE SLOSH PLODGE
PLOUTER PLUTTER
(— **IN MUD**) LAIR
WADI OUED WASH GULLY RAVINE
WADSET PAWN PLEDGE MORTGAGE
WAFER HOST ABRET OBLEY CACHET
GAUFRE LAVASH MATZOH OFLETE
POPADAM FLATBROD
WAFF WAG FLAP GUST ODOR PUFF
WAVE WHIFF PALTRY FLUTTER
GLIMPSE LOWBORN
WAFFIE VAGRANT VAGABOND
WAFFLE GOFER WAFER GAUFRE
BLATHER
WAFT PUFF WHEFT WHIFF BECKON
WAG LUG NOD WIG WIT WOG CARD
CHAP FLAG WAFF WALK DROLL
JOKER SHAKE TROLL FARCER
JESTER NICKUM WADDLE WAGGLE
WAGWIT WIGWAG HUMORIST
SLYBOOTS
WAGE FEE PAY WAR HIRE LEVY
FIGHT WADGE WEDGE EMPLOY
ENGAGE PACKET
(— **BATTLE**) STRIKE
WAGER GO BET LAY SET VIE WED
GAGE HOLD PAWN TOSS WOID
BOUND PRIZE RAISE REVIE SPORT
STAKE STOOP WADGE DEPONE
GAMBLE IMPONE LEVANT WEDFEE
STOATER QUINELLA
WAGES FEE PAY UTU GAGE HIRE
MEED GAGES TUNCA REWARD
SALARY PENSION SERVICE STIPEND
GRATUITY LABORAGE PAYCHECK
REQUITAL
WAGGISH DROLL JOKEY JOCOSE
JESTING JOCULAR ROGUISH
WAGSOME HUMOROUS SPORTIVE
WAGGLE WAG WIGGLE WOBBLE
WOGGLE
WAGON CAR FLY VAN CART CHAR
DRAY PLOW RACK TEAM TRAM
WAIN WANE BUGGY DILLY JERKY
RULLY TRUCK CAMION ROLLEY
SPIDER TELEGA CAISSON CHARIOT
COASTER FOURGON TUMBREL
TUMBRIL DEMOCRAT LANDSHIP
RUNABOUT WHITETOP
(— **WITHOUT SPRINGS**) JERKY
TELEGA
(**BAGGAGE** —) FOURGON
(**COVERED** —) VAN CARAVAN

LANDSHIP CONESTOGA
(**LUMBER** —) GILLY
(**MINING** —) TRAM RULLY ROLLEY
(**ROUNDUP** —) HOODLUM
(**RUSSIAN** —) TELEGA
(**STATION** —) SUBURBAN
(**TEA** —) SERVER
WAGONER AURIGA TREKKER
WAINMAN
WAGONLOAD FODDER FOTHER
WAGONMAN FOOTMAN
WAGTAIL MOLLY OATEAR WAGGIE
WASHER WATERIE SEEDBIRD
WASHDISH WASHTAIL
WAHINE WIFE WOMAN FEMALE
VAHINE FEMININE MISTRESS
WAHOO ONO PETO BASSWOOD
EUONYMUS GUARAPUCU
WAIF WEFT STRAY FEEBLE PALTRY
STRAFE CURRENT IGNOBLE
WASTREL
WAIL CRY WOW BAWL GURL HOWL
KEEN MOAN RAME YARM CROON
MOURN ULULU LAMENT YAMMER
EJULATE PLANGOR ULULATE
ULLAGONE
WAILING WO WOE LAMENT ULULANT
WAIN CART WAGON WEYNE CHARIOT
WAINSCOT CEIL
WAINSCOTING CEILING PANELING
WAIST JOSIE BASQUE BLOUSE
BODICE HALTER MIDDLE TAILLE
CORSAGE PIERROT
WAISTCOAT VEST BENJY GILET
FECKET JERKIN VESKIT WESKIT
SINGLET CAMISOLE
WAISTER TROUNCER
WAIT BIDE HOLD KEEP LITE PARK
STAY TEND WHET ABIDE DEFER
HOVER TARRY WATCH ATTEND
DEPEND EXPECT HARKEN LAYOUT
LINGER
(— **A WHILE**) TAIHOA
(— **FOR**) KEEP ABIDE AWAIT
ATTEND EXPECT
(— **ON**) HOP SEE SERVE INTEND
LACKEY
(— **TABLE**) HASH SERVE
WAITER MOZO CARHOP DRAWER
FLUNKY GARCON HASHER KIDNEY
SALVER TENDER THOMAS DAPIFER
FLUNKEY KELLNER PANNIER
PICCOLO SERVITOR KITMUDGAR
WAITING DORMANT
WAITRESS HASHER PHYLLIS
WAIVE ABEY DEFER EVADE FORGO
ABANDON DECLINE FORSAKE
POSTPONE RENOUNCE
WAKA CANOE
WAKE WAK CROW NECK PLAY STIR
ALERT REVEL ROUSE TANGI TRAIL
VIGIL WATCH AROUSE AWAKEN
EXCITE FEATHER
WAKEFUL ALERT WACKER
RESTLESS VIGILANT WAKERIPE
WALKRIFE WATCHFUL
WAKEFULNESS VIGIL WATCH
INSOMNIA
WAKE-ROBIN SARA SARAH TRILLIUM

WAKF WAQF VAKUF VACOUF
WALACHIAN RUMAN VLACH
ROMANESE
WALAHEE ALAHEE
WALAPAI HUALPAI
WALDENSIAN LEONIST PATARIN
SABOTIER
WALE RIB PICK WEAL WELT RIDGE
WHELP CHOICE HARPIN STROKE
(**PL.**) BEND HARPINS
WALES CYMRU CAMBRIA

WALES

BAY: SWANSEA CARDIGAN
TREMADOC
COUNTY: FLINT RADNOR DENBIGH
ANGLESEY CARDIGAN
MONMOUTH PEMBROKE
HILLS: MALVERN
LAKE: VYRNWY
LANGUAGE: CYMRAEG
MEASURE: COVER CANTRED
CANTREF LESTRAD LISTRED
CRANNOCK
MOUNTAIN: SNOWDEN
MOUNTAIN RANGE: BERWYN
CAMBRIAN
PEOPLE: CYMRY KYMRY WELSH
PORT: CARDIFF
RIVER: DEE USK WYE TAFF TEME
TOWY TEIFI SEVERN VYRNWY
TOWN: RHYL ROSS FLINT TOWYN
AMLWCH BANGOR BRECON
CARDIFF NEWPORT SWANSEA
HEREFORD HOLYHEAD
PEMBROKE

WALK GO JET MOG FOOT GAIT
GANG HIKE HOOF LAMP PACE PAUT
REEL STEP TROD ALLEE ALLEY
ARBOR LEAVE MARCH PORCH
SHANK SLOPE SPACE STALK TRACE
TRACK TRADE TRAMP TREAD
TROOP ATTEND AVENUE BEHAVE
BOUNCE BRIDGE BROGUE DANDER
PASEAR SASHAY STROKE TODDLE
TRAVEL TRUDGE BERCEAU
CRAMBLE FOOTING GALLERY
SHUFFLE STRETCH TRACHLE
TRAIPSE TURNOUT AMBULATE
ARBORWAY FLAGGING FRESCADE
NAVIGATE TRAVERSE
(— **ABOUT**) SLOSH
(— **AFFECTEDLY**) PRINK
(— **AIMLESSLY**) PAUP POAP
(— **AWKWARDLY**) STAUP SHAMBLE
(— **BEFORE**) PREAMBLE
(— **BRISKLY**) LEG SKELP
(— **CAUTIOUSLY**) STALK
(— **CLUMSILY**) JOLL STUMP LOPPET
(— **FOR CATTLE**) GANG
(— **FOR EXAMINING ENGINE**)
GALLERY
(— **FOR EXERCISE**) HIKE GRIND
(— **HEAVILY**) PLOD STUMP TRAMP
LAMPER PLODGE
(— **IDLY**) DANDER POTTER SAUNTER
(— **IN AFFECTED MANNER**) MINCE

(— LAME) LIMP HIRPLE HOBBLE CRIPPLE
(— LEISURELY) AMBLE DANDER STROLL
(— ON) BEAT TREAD
(— OUT) FLOUNCE
(— RAPIDLY) LAMP STAVE
(— SHAKILY) DOTTER
(— SLOWLY) JET LAG
(— SMARTLY) LINK
(— STEADILY) SNOVE SNOOVE
(— UNSTEADILY) REEL FALTER STAVER STAGGER STUMBLE
(— WAVERINGLY) SHEVEL WARPLE
(— WITH DIFFICULTY) CRAMBLE CRAMMEL LOUTHER
(— WITH JERK) HIRCH
(— WITH LOFTY GAIT) JET
(— WITH OSTENTATION) PRANCE
(— WITH SHUFFLE) COONJINE
(— WITH STRIDES) STAG
(— WITH TREES) XYST XYSTUS ALAMEDA
(— WITHOUT LIFTING FEET) SCUFF
(BACKSTAGE —) BRIDGE
(COOL —) FRESCADE
(COVERED —) CLOISTER
(COVERED —) PORCH
(FOLIAGE-COVERED —) BERCEAU
(HARD —) STRAM SWINGE
(LIMPING —) GIMP
(LONG —) STRAM
(POMPOUS —) STRUT
(PUBLIC —) XYST XYSTUS ALAMEDA
(RAISED —) GALLERY
(SHADED —) MALL ARBOR
(TEDIOUS —) TRAIL
WALKER GOER FOOTER FULLER GANGER FOOTMAN TODDLER (PL.) FEET
WALKING HOTFOOT PASSANT AMBULANT GRADIENT TRIPPING
WALKING STICK BAT CANE GIBBY KEBBY STICK WADDY KEBBIE SPECTER ASHPLANT GIBSTAFF WOODHORSE
WALKOUT STRIKE
WALKWAY CATWALK SIDEWALK
WALL WA DAM FIN MUR WAW BAIL BELT CELL CORE CRIB CURB DICK DIKE DRUM DYKE FACE HEAD MURE PACK SKIN SPUR WING WOGE ATTIC BOARD CHEEK CRUST DIGUE EMURE FENCE HEDGE MEURE MURAL PIRCA SHOJI WOGHE WOUGH BAFFLE BAILEY BATTER CUTOFF DOKHMA IMMURE LEADER PARIES PRETIL REBOTE RIPRAP SCREEN SEPTUM SHIELD VALLUM CHEMISE CURTAIN ENCLOSE MIZRACH PARAPET PERPEND PLUTEUS REREDOS TAMBOUR FIREBACK SPANDREL TRAVERSE
(— ABOVE FACADE) ATTIC
(— AROUND) IMMURE
(— BEHIND ALTAR) REREDOS
(— BETWEEN TWO OPENINGS) PIER
(— CARRYING CUPOLA) DRUM
(— CARRYING ROOF) BAHUT

(— CROSSING RAMPART) SPUR
(— IN ROMAN ARENA) SPINA
(— IN TRUCK) HEADER
(— OF BLAST FURNACE) DAM INWALL FIREBACK
(— OF CLAY) COTTLE
(— OF HOOF) CRUST
(— OF MINE) FACE
(— OF MOUTH) CHEEK
(— OF TENT) KANAT CANAUT
(BODY —) MANTLE
(CIRCULAR —) CASHEL
(CORE —) HEARTING
(CURVED —) SWEEP
(DIVIDING —) SEPTUM
(END — OF BUILDING) GABLE
(FISH —) LEADER
(HIGHEST PART OF —) CRAPWA
(INNER SLOPE OF —) BATTER
(LOG —) CRIB
(LOW —) BAHUT PODIUM PLUTEUS
(LOWER PART OF —) DADO
(OUTER — OF CASTLE) BAIL BAILEY
(PEAT —) COP
(PUDDLE —) HEARTING
(RETAINING —) CRIB BULKHEAD
(SCARPED —) GHAT
(SECONDARY —) CHEMISE
(SUSTAINING —) RIPRAP
(THINNED PART OF —) ALLEGE
(VENTRAL —) STERNUM
(WING —) AILERON
(PL.) PERICARP
WALLABA APA
WALLABY WURRUP TOOLACH WURRUNG BOONGARY KANGAROO PADMELON WHIPTAIL
WALLACHIAN RUMAN
WALLAROO EURO
WALLBOARD GOBO
WALLET JAG JAGG MAIL POKE BOGET BOUGE BULCH BULGE SCRIP BUDGET READER SACKET ALFARGA ALFORJA LEATHER BILLFOLD NOTECASE
WALLEYE WHALL SAUGER LEUCOMA WATCHEYE EXOTROPIA
WALLEYED PIKE DORE DORY JACK PERCID SALMON WALLEYE PICKEREL
WALLFLOWER CUBA CHEIR GILLY JACKS KEIRI GELOFER WARRIOR GILLIVER
WALL HAWKWEED LUNGWORT
WALLOP BEAT BEER FLOP SLUG SOCK PASTE POUND VALOP GALLOP IMPACT WALLOW FLUTTER TROUNCE FLOUNDER LAMBASTE
WALLOW FADE LAIR ROLL SOIL SLOSH WALWE GROVEL MUDDLE WALTER WELTER WITHER SLUDDER SWELTER FLOUNDER KOMMETJE VOLUTATE
WALLOWISH FLAT WELSH INSIPID
WALLPAPER GROUND SCENIC HANGING TENTURE TAPESTRY
WALL PEPPER SEDUM STONECROP
WALL PLATE PAN RASEN
WALL RUE TENTWORT

WALLY TOY FINE SPOIL PAMPER ROBUST STRONG STURDY SPLENDID VIGOROUS
WALNUT ACAPU NOGAL TRYMA AKHROT BANNUT HEARTNUT **(BRAZILIAN —)** EMBOYA IMBUIA (PL.) JUGLANS
WALNUT SHELL BOLSTER
WALPI HUALPI
WALRUS MORSE WALTRON PELAGIAN PINNIPED ROSMARINE
WALT CRANK UNSTEADY
WALTZ LUG CARRY MARCH VALSE BOSTON BREEZE FLOUNCE
WAMARA CLUBWOOD IRONWOOD PANOCOCO
WAMBLE ROLL SPIN WAMEL NAUSEA REVOLVE
WAMBLY FAINT SHAKY
WAME WEM WAMB WYME BELLY
WAMPUM PEAG FADME HAWOK MONEY PAAGE SEWAN FATHOM SEAWAN ROANOKE
WAMUS JACKET WAMPUS WARMUS
WAN DIM HAW FADE PALE PALY SICK BLAKE FAINT WHITE FEEBLE PALLID SALLOW GHASTLY LANGUID
WANAPUM SOKULK
WAND ROD VARE YARD BATON STAFF STICK VERGE VIRGA FERULA THYRSE WATTLE RHABDOS THYRSUS CADUCEUS
WANDER BAT BUM ERR GAD WAG HAAK HAIK HAKE MAZE MUCK RAVE ROAM ROIL ROLL ROVE WALK WILL WORE DAVER DRIFT GLAIK KNOCK RANGE ROGUE SHACK SLOSH STRAY TAVER TRAIK VAGUE WAIVE WAVER CANDER DANDER DAUNER FORAGE LOITER MITHER MOIDER MUCKER PALMER PERUSE RAMBLE RANGLE STRAKE STROLL SWERVE WILDER MEANDER TRAFFIC TRAIPSE VAGRATE VANDYKE CUTICULA SQUANDER STRAGGLE STRAVAGE
(— ABOUT) DIVAGATE
(— ABSTRACTEDLY) MOON
(— AIMLESSLY) SWAN SLOSH TRACE MEANDER
(— AS A VAGABOND) SHACK
(— AS A VAGRANT) LOITER
(— AT RANDOM) SQUANDER
(— ERRATICALLY) SWASH
(— FROM DIRECT COURSE) STRAGGLE
(— FROM PLACE TO PLACE) WAG
(— IDLY) HAKE LOUT MAUNDER SHACKLE
(— IN DELIRIUM) DWALE DWALL
(— IN MIND) DAVER DANDER DELIRE
(— LEISURELY) BUMMEL
(— RESTLESSLY) FEEK
WANDERER WAIF ROVER VAGUE RANGER PILGRIM RAMBLER FUGITIVE RUNAGATE TRAVELER VAGABOND
WANDERING GAD ROAM ERROR STRAY VAGUE ARRANT ASTRAY

ERRANT MOBILE ROVING VAGANT
VAGOUS DEVIOUS NOMADIC
ODYSSEY VAGANCY WINDING
ABERRANT FLOATING FUGITIVE
PELASGIC PLANETAL PLANETIC
RAMBLING RESTLESS TRAILING
VAGABOND WINDRING

WANDFLOWER GALAX SPARAXIS

WANDOROBO WAASI

WAND-SHAPED VIRGATE

WANE GO EBB SET WELK WILK
DECAY UNWAX WANZE REPINE
DECLINE DWINDLE DECREASE
(— OF MOON) WADDLE

WANGA CHARM SPELL OUANGA
WONGAH SORCERY

WANGLE FAKE SHAKE WIGGLE
FINAGLE

WANIGAN ARK CHEST COFFER
WANGUN

WANT HURT LACK LIKE MISS NEED
OONT PINE VOID WANE WONT
CRAVE FAULT FORGO BESOIN
CHOOSE DEARTH DEFECT DESIRE
MISTER PENURY PLIGHT ABSENCE
BEGGARY BLEMISH BORASCA
DEFAULT MISEASE NEEDHAM
POVERTY REQUIRE VACANCY
MISCHIEF WANTROKE
(— EXCEEDINGLY) DIE
(— OF ENERGY) ATONY
(— OF GOOD SENSE) FOLLY
(— OF REST) UNRO
(— OF SUCCESS) FAILURE
(— OF VIGOR) DELICACY

WANTAGE ULLAGE

WANTING LACK VOID WANE ALACK
MINUS ABSENT LACKING MISSING
INDIGENT
(— ORIGINALITY) BANAL

WANTON JAY NAG DAFT GOLE IDLE
LEWD NICE RAGE SKIT CADGY
DALLY LIGHT SAUCY GIGLET
GIGLOT HARLOT HAUNTY LACHES
LUBRIC RAKISH RIGSBY TICKLE
TOYING TOYISH UNRULY COLTISH
FULSOME GIGGISH HAGGARD
IMMORAL KITTOCK LUSTFUL
PAPHIAN RIGGISH RIOTOUS
SMICKER WAYWARD FLAGRANT
LUSCIOUS MISTRESS PETULANT
PLAYSOME RUMBELOW SLIPPERY
SPITEFUL SPORTIVE UNCHASTE

WANTONNESS FOLLY PRIDE SPORT
RAGERY SUCCUDRY SURQUIDY

WAP BIND BLOW WHOP WRAP BLAST
FIGHT KNOCK STORM TRUSS
BUNDLE STRIKE

WAPITI ELK ALCE DEER LOSH LUSH
STAG MARAL MOOSE CERVID
WAMPOOSE

WAR WIN CAMP FEUD MART FIGHT
SWORD WORSE WORST BATTLE
CONTEND CRUSADE CONFLICT
GUERILLA OVERCOME
(RELIGIOUS —) JEHAD JIHAD

WARBLE SING CAROL CHANT CHIRL
CHIRM SHAKE TRILL YODEL JARGON
RALISH WARNEL WORMIL DESCANT

VIBRATE WOURNIL

WARBLE FLY OXFLY BOTFLY
GADFLY OESTRID OESTRIAN

WARBLER CUT KIT CHAT SMEU
WREN FITTE CANARY EYSOGE
SMEUTH SYLVIA TITIEN CREEPER
CROMBEC FANTAIL HAYBIRD
HAYSUCK PITBIRD REDPOLL SYLVIID
TROCHIL BEAMBIRD BLACKCAP
FAUVETTE MALURINE MOCKBIRD
OVENBIRD PINCPINC REDSTART
REEDBIRD RIRORIRO

WAR CLUB MAR MER MERE MERAI
MARREE

WAR CRY ALALA SLOGAN

WARD CARE GUARD MAHAL VICUS
WAIRD WATCH ALUMNA BARRIO
CALPUL DEFEND ROWENA KEEPING
NATUARY CALPOLLI CONTRADA
(— OFF) FEND WEAR WERE AVERT
AWARD FENCE PARRY REPEL
SHIELD BUCKLER EXPIATE FORFEND

WARDAGE WARTH

WARDEN ALCADE DIZDAR PORTER
RANGER REGENT ROLAND WARNER
ALCAIDE HOGMACE LEATMAN
ROWLAND CLAVIGER

WARDER PORTER GUARDER
HEIMDAL TURNKEY WATCHMAN
BEEFEATER

WARDROBE KAS CLOSET VESTRY
ALMIRAH ARMOIRE VESTUARY

WARE CLOTH GOODS SPEND
FABRICS SEAWEED SQUANDER
(CERAMIC —) SPODE
(ENAMELED —) BILSTON COALPORT
(INFERIOR —S) SLUM
(KIND OF —) RAKU MINTON
WHIELDON
(MAJOLICA —) DERUTA
(PORCELAIN —) CHINA BERLIN
(UNGLAZED —) BISQUE
(PL.) TROKE CHAFFER TROGGIN

WAREHOUSE GOLA GOLAH STORE
BODEGA FONDUK GODOWN STAITH
ALMACEN FUNDUCK SPICERY
STOWAGE ENTREPOT MAGAZINE
SERAGLIO

WARFARE WAR ARMS IRON ARMOR
BATTLE PSYWAR MILITIA CONFLICT

WAR-HORSE CHARGER COURSER
DESTRER TROOPER DESTRIER

WARILY TIPTOE GINGERLY

WARINESS CAUTEL CAUTION
DISTRUST WARESHIP WARIMENT

WARKLOOM TOOL WARKLUME

WARLIKE WARLY MARTIAL FIGHTING
MILITARY BELLICOSE
(NOT —) IMBELLIC

WARLOCK IMP WITCH SPRITE
WARLOW WIZARD CONJUROR
SORCERER

WARLORD TUCHUN

WARM HOT LEW LOO RUG BASK
BEEK KEEN LEWD MILD CALID
CHAFE EAGER FRESH MALMY
MUNGY SLACK TEPID TOAST
ACHAFE ARDENT DEVOUT DIGEST
FOSTER GENIAL HEARTY HEATED

RIZZLE TENDER CHERISH CLEMENT
CORDIAL GLOWING THERMAL
ZEALOUS FRIENDLY SANGUINE
(MODERATELY —) LEW SLACK
TEPID
(— UP) SCORE

WARMHEARTED KIND TENDER
FRIENDLY GENEROUS

WARMING FOVENT

WARMOUTH BIGMOUTH FLATFISH
SACALAIT

WARMTH GLOW HEAT LIFE ZEAL
ARDOR LEWTH ENERGY FERVOR
ARDENCY PASSION CALIDITY
FERVENCY
(INNER —) JUICE

WARN REDE WARD WERN ALERT
AREAD WEIRD ADVERT ADVISE
EXHORT INFORM CAUTION
COMMAND GARNISH PREVISE
ADMONISH THREATEN
(— OFF) FORBID

WARNING AHEM ITEM ALARM CHECK
KNELL CAVEAT LESSON NOTICE
OFFICE SAMPLE SIGNAL AVISION
CALLING CAUTION JIGGERS
MEMENTO MONITOR SUMMONS
DOCUMENT GARDYLOO MONITION
(— OF DISASTER) DIRE
(ARCHERY —) FAST

WARP CUP WEB BIAS CANE CAST
LIFT WARF WERP WIND ANGLE
CHAIN CHOKE CROOK GEYZE
KEDGE PORRY THRAW TWINE
WEAVE BUCKLE CHEESE DEFORM
WASHIN DEFLECT DISTORT SKELLER
(— IN WEAVING) CRAM

WARPED WRY BUCKLED GNARLED
HOUSING

WARPER BALLER

WARPING BOW PANDATION

WARRAGAL WILD DINGO HORSE
OUTLAW

WARRANT ABLE AMRIT BERAT FIANT
SANAD VOUCH AMRITA ASSERT
BRANCH BREVET DOCKET ENSURE
INSURE PARDON PERMIT PLEVIN
POLICY POTENT SUNNUD TICKET
BEHIGHT JUSTIFY PRECEPT
GUARANTY MITTIMUS

WARRAU GUARANO

WARREN CONYGER WARRANT

WARRIOR TOA WER EARL HERO
KEMP RINK WEER BERNE FREIK
FREKE HAGEN LLUDD SINGH THANE
THEGN OSSIAN WARMAN WEAPON
FIGHTER SOLDIER STARKAD
WARWOLF ZERBINO CHAMPION
RODOMONT SHARDANA STARKATH
SWORDMAN WARFARER
(— CLASS) MAGANI
(— OF NOBLE RANK) EARL
(AMERICAN INDIAN —) BRAVE
SANNUP
(BOASTFUL —) RODOMONT
(BRYTHONIC —) LLUDD
(BURGUNDIAN —) HAGEN
(FEMALE —) AMAZON SHIELDMAY
(IRISH —) FENIAN

(KAFFIR —S) IMPI
(MUSLIM —) GAZI GHAZI
(NOTED —) THANE THEGN
(SCANDINAVIAN —) BERSERK
(SCOTTISH —) ZERBINO
(TROJAN —) AGENOR
(VALIANT —) TOA
(VIRGIN —) CAMILLA
(PL.) CHIVALRY GAMMADIM
WARSHIP GUIDE WAFTER CRUISER
MONITOR SULTANA SULTANE
CORVETTE
WART RAT WRAT AMBURY ANBURY
PUSTULE VERRUCA VERRUGA
EPIDERMA PAPILOMA
(POTATO —) CANKER
WART HOG EMGALLA
WARTLIKE PYRENOID
WART SNAKE XENODERM
WARY SHY CAGY WISE CAGEY
CANNY DOWNY HOOLY LEERY
TENDER CAREFUL GUARDED
PRUDENT WAREFUL CAUTIOUS
SKITTISH VIGILANT WATCHFUL
WAS VAS WIS WUZ WYS PAST
WISSHE
(— ABLE) COULD
(— NOT) NAS
(I —) CHWAS
WASH DO BOG FEN LAG LAP NET
TUB BEER BUCK EDDY HOSE HUSH
LAVE SILT SUDS WADI BATHE
CLEAN CLEAR DOLLY DRAFF ERODE
MARSH RINSE SCRUB SLOSH SOUSE
SWILL BUDDLE CRADLE DOLLIE
LOTION PURIFY SLOOSH SLUICE
SOZZLE STREAM ALLUVIO CLEANSE
LAUNDER SHAMPOO ALLUVIUM
EYEWATER LAVAMENT LAVATORY
(— A GAS) SCRUB
(— AWAY) GULL
(— BY TREADING IN WATER) TRAMP
(— DOWN) SIND SOOGEE
(— FOR GOLD) PAN
(— GIVEN TO SWINE) DRAFF
(— GRAVEL) ROCK
(— IN LYE) BUCK
(— LIGHTLY) RINSE
(— OFF) DETERGE
(— ORE) TYE HUTCH BUDDLE
CRADLE STRAKE
(— OUT) SIND ELUTE FLUSH
LAVAGE
(— ROUGHLY) SLUSH
(— THOROUGHLY) SCOUR
(— VIGOROUSLY) SLOSH
(— WITH BROOM) TYE
(— WITH COSMETIC) SURFLE
SURPHUL
(DRY —) ARROYA ARROYO
WASHBASIN LAVER LAVABO
LAVATORY ALJOFAINA
WASHCLOTH FLANNEL
WASHED (— UP) SHOT THROUGH
WASHER BUR BURR DRUM ROVE
CLOUT BUTTON RONDEL SOURER
GROMMET LEATHER RACCOON
COTTEREL LAVENDER RONDELLE

WASHERMAN DHOBI DHOBIE
LAVANDERO
WASHERWOMAN LAUNDER
WASHING LAG BATH LAVAGE
SLOOSH LAUNDRY ABLUTION
LAVAMENT LAVATION
(PL.) ELUATE
WASHING MACHINE DASHWHEEL

WASHINGTON
CAPITAL: OLYMPIA
COLLEGE: WHITMAN
COUNTY: ASOTIN KITSAP SKAGIT
YAKIMA CLALLAM KITTITAS
DAM: COULEE
INDIAN: LUMMI MAKAH TWANA
SAMISH SKAGIT YAKIMA
CHINOOK CLALLAM COWLITZ
SANPOIL CHIMAKUM OKANAGON
LAKE: CHELAN
MOUNTAIN: JACK TUNK ADAMS
LEMEI LOGAN MOSES SLOAN
QUARTZ SIMCOE STUART
OLYMPUS RAINIER SHUKSAN
MOUNTAIN RANGE: KETTLE
CASCADE OLYMPIC
NICKNAME: EVERGREEN
RIVER: SNAKE YAKIMA COLUMBIA
SOUND: PUGET
STATE BIRD: GOLDFINCH
STATE FLOWER: RHODODENDRON
STATE TREE: HEMLOCK
TOWN: OMAK PASCO TACOMA
YAKIMA EPHRATA EVERETT
OTHELLO SEATTLE SPOKANE
LONGVIEW

WASHOUT FLOP STUMOR FAILURE
WASHROOM BASEMENT LAVATORY
WASHSTAND COMMODE
WASHTUB FLASKET
WASHY SOFT WEAK LOOSE MOIST
FEEBLE PALLID WATERY DILUTED
WASP MASON SPHEX WHAMP WOPSE
BEMBEX DAUBER DIGGER HORNET
TIPHIA TREMEX VESPID CYNIPID
DRYINID EUMENID MASARID SCOLIID
SERPHID SIRICID SPHECID STINGER
ACULEATE MUTILLID POMPILID
WASPISH TESTY FRETFUL PEEVISH
CHOLERIC SNAPPISH
WASSAIL TOAST PLEDGE CAROUSE
REVELRY CAROUSAL
WASTE EAT FUD GOB TED BURN
GNAW JUNK LOSS PASS ROSS SACK
TEAR TINE WEAR WILD DROSS
EXILE HAVOC SCRAP SLOOM SLOTH
SLOUM SPILL TABID THRUM BANGLE
BEZZLE COMMON DEBRIS DESERT
DEVOUR DIDDLE DRAFFY DRIVEL
ELAPSE EXPEND FOREST GARBLE
GOUSTY LAVISH MOLDER MUDDLE
PADDLE PERISH RAVAGE REFUSE
SPILTH WESTEN CONNACH
CONSUME EXHAUST FRITTER
GARBAGE MULLOCK RUBBISH
SLATTER CONFOUND DEMOLISH
SLATTERN SQUANDER

(— AWAY) BATE MELT DECAY
DWINE SWAIN SWEAL TRAIK TABEFY
WINDLE DWINDLE FORPINE MISLIKE
DISSOLVE EMACIATE FORSPEND
MACERATE
(— GRADUALLY) WEAR ABSUME
(— IN DRUNKENNESS) SOT
(— IN RIOT) BEZZLE
(— OF INK) INKSHED
(— OF SILK COCOONS) KNUB
(— TIME) FOOL FRIG IDLE DALLY
DEFER DRILL DAWDLE DIDDLE
FOOTER FOOTLE LOITER DRINGLE
FOOSTER GAUSTER
(COAL —) SLUDGE
(COTTON —) FLUKE SLASHER
SPOOLER
(FOOD —) SLOP
(LIQUID —) DRIPPING EFFLUENT
(MINING —) GOB GOAF
(WOOL —) FUD GARNETT
(YARN —) THRUM EYEBROW
WASTEBASKET HELL HELLBOX
WASTED IDLE FORWORN RAVAGED
DECREPIT
WASTEFUL LAVISH PROFUSE
DESOLATE PRODIGAL SPENDFUL
WASTEFULNESS WAIT UNTHRIFT
WASTELAND CURAGH CURRACH
WASTER THIEF LEISTER WASTREL
PRODIGAL
WASTING FRET DECAY LIGHT
AWASTE ATROPHY CACHEXY
EXEDENT MISLIKE PREYING TABIFIC
CACHEXIA PHTHISIS SYNTEXIS
(— AWAY) SYNTECTIC
WASTREL WAIF REFUSE WASTER
VAGABOND STROYGOOD
WATCH EYE FOB NIT SEE SPY TAB
DIAL ESPY GLIM GLOM HACK HEED
KEEP LOOK MARK MIND PIPE TOUT
TWIG VACH WAIK WAKE WARD
YARD CLOCK GUARD SCOUT SPIAL
SUPER TIMER VERGE VIGIL VIRGE
WAKEN WHEEL BEHOLD DEFEND
DIACLE FOLLOW HUNTER PERDUE
SENTRY SHADOW TICKER TICTIC
TURNIP WAKING YEMING OBSERVE
OVERSEE STRIKER THIMBLE
TOMPION HOROLOGE MEDITATE
SENTINEL SPECTATE TICKTICK
(— FOR) TENT ABIDE AWAIT
(— OF ARMY) BIVOUAC
(— ON THE SLY) FOX
(— OVER) HOLD KEEP TEND TENT
GUARD ATTEND OVERLOOK
(— PEOPLE EATING) GROAK
(— QUIETLY) HINT
(— THAT STRIKES) STRIKER
REPEATER
(— UNIT) LIGNE
(— WITH HINGED COVER) HUNTER
(ALARM —) TATLER TATTLER
(CLOSE —) SCRUTINY
(NAUTICAL —) HACK DOGWATCH
(NIGHT —) LICHWAKE LYKEWAKE
WATCHBAND WRISTER WRISTLET
WATCH CRYSTAL LUNET LUNETTE
WATCHDOG CUR GARM GARMR

MATIN BANDOG KRATIM CERBERUS

WATCHER VEIL WAKER VIEWER
WAITER MUSAHAR SPOTTER
WATCHMAN

WATCHFUL IRA ALERT AWARE
CANNY CHARY ERECT TENTY
WAKER TENTIE WACKER ANXIOUS
GUARDED JEALOUS LIDLESS
WAKEFUL VIGILANT WAKERIFE
WAUKRIFE

WATCHFULNESS OUTLOOK
JEALOUSY

WATCHMAN FLAG MINA WAIT
GUARD SCOUT VIGIL WATCH ASKARI
BANTAY GHAFIR SERENO SHOMER
TOOTER WAITER WARDEN WARDER
BELLMAN CHARLEY GUARDER
TALLIAR WAKEMAN CHOKIDAR
SENTINEL

(NIGHT —) SERENO CHARLIE

WATCHTOWER WARD BEACON
GARRET MIZPAH SENTRY ATALAYA
LOOKOUT MIRADOR SENTINEL
SPECCHIE

WATCHWORD CRY MAXIM ALERTA
ENSIGN PAROLE SIGNAL NAYWORD
PASSWORD

WATCH WORKS MOVEABLE

WATER EAU TJI AGUA AQUA BATH
BRIM BROO BURN LAGE LAKE POND
POOL TIDE WAVE ABYSS BILGE
FLUME LOUGH LYMPH RIVER TABBY
TEARS TUBIG BALLOW BAREGE
CAMLET CONGEE CONJEE PAWNEE
PHLEGM SALIVA STREAM VADOSE
WATHER AQUATIC CRYSTAL
JAVELLE IRRIGATE SNOWMELT

(— AFTER BOILING RICE) CONGEE
CONJEE

(— AS REFUGE FOR GAME) SOIL

(— AT THE MOUTH) DROOL

(— BY CALENDERING) TABBY

(— FOR BREWING) BURN

(— IN SOIL) HOLARD

(— IN WEIR) LASHER

(— REDDISH WITH IRON) RIDDAM

**(— RUNNING AGAINST MAIN
CURRENT)** EDDY

(— SPIRIT) KELPIE

(— SURROUNDED BY ICE) WAKE

(— UNDER PRESSURE) HUSH

(BAPTISMAL —) LAVER

(BOTTOM — OF SEA) ABYSS

(BUBBLING —) SPRUDEL

(DEEP —) BALLOW

(DIRTY —) SAUR PUDDLE

(FEN —) SUDS

(FROZEN —) ICE FROST

(HOLY —) HYSSOP

(HOT —) SOUP

(LIVING —) RASA

(MINERAL —) VICHY SELTER
SELTZER

(OPEN —) POLYNYA

(RED —) RESP RIDDAM

(ROUGH —) SEA

(SALT —) BRACK BRINE SEAWATER

(SOAPY —) SUDS GRAITH

(SPLASH OF —) FLASH

(STILL —) KELD LOGIN

(SULPHUR —) BAREGE

(SURFACE OF —) RYME

(SWEETENED —) AMRIT AMRITA

(WASHING —) LAVATION

(PL.) APSU

WATER ARUM DRAGON

WATER BAG CHAGUL MATARA
MUSSUK

WATERBIRD ALCATRAS

WATERBRAIN GID

WATERBUCK COB CHUZWI DEFASSA
WATERDOE

WATER BUFFALO KERBAU

WATER CARRIER BHISTI AGUADOR
BHEESTY

WATER CART DILLY

WATER CASK WINGER

WATER CHESTNUT LING CALTROP
SALIGOT

WATER CHINQUAPIN BONNET
NELUMBO WANKAPIN YONCOPIN
RATTLENUT

WATER CLOCK GHURRY
CLEPSYDRA

WATER CLOSET PETTY PRIVY
STOOL SANITARY NECESSARY

WATER COCK KORA

WATERCOLOR GRAPHIC

WATERCOURSE (ALSO SEE STREAM
AND RIVER) RUN URN AGOS DIKE
DYKE GOTE HAHR KHOR LADE LEAT
WADI WADY YORA AUWAI BAYOU
BROOK CANAL CANEL COWAL
DITCH DRAIN ARROYO CANNEL
COURSE FURROW GUTTER KENNEL
NULLAH TRINKET

WATERCRESS EKER KERS CARSE
KERSE BILDERS NOSESMART

WATER DOG OTTER WATERRUG

WATER DRINKER HYDROPOT

WATERED MOIRE

WATERFALL LIN LYN FALL FOSS
LINN SALT FORCE SAULT SPOUT
CATADUPE CATARACT OVERFALL

(FROZEN —) ICEFALL

WATER FENNEL EDGEWEED

WATER FLEA CYCLOPS DAPHNID

WATERFOWL WADER SWIMMER

WATERFRONT PRAYA

WATERGALL WINDDOG WINDGALL
JELLYFISH

WATER GERMANDER SCORDIUM

WATER HEMLOCK CICUTA DEATHIN
JELLICA

WATER HOG BUSHPIG CAPYBARA

WATER HOLE DUB CHARCO TINAJA
ALBERCA

WATER ICE SHERBET

WATERINESS AQUEITY AQUOSITY

WATERING EPIPHORA

WATER JUG GAMLA GOMLAH
GOOLAH

WATERLEAF SHAWNY

WATER LETTUCE QUIAPO

WATER LILY DUCK LOTOS LOTUS
WOCAS WOKAS BOBBIN CANDOCK
NELUMBO CAMALOTE NENUPHAR

WATERLOGGED SOGGY SWAMPY
EDEMATOUS

WATERMAN MERMAN QUENCH
OARSMAN

WATERMARK CROWN TIDEMARK

WATERMARKED LAID

WATERMELON PEPO GOURD MELON
TSAMA CITRUL SANDIA ANGURIA
MILLION CUCURBIT PEPONIDA
PEPONIUM SKIPJACK

WATER MOCCASIN CONGO

WATER NEWT ASK TRITON

WATER OPOSSUM YAPOK YAPOCK

WATER OUZEL PIET OOZEL OWZEL
DIPPER DUCKER

WATER PEPPER LAKEWEED

WATER PLANT LIMU AQUATIC

WATER PLANTAIN ALISMA
THRUMWORT

WATERPOT FONTAL

WATERPROOF RAINCOAT

(— MATERIAL) KERATOL

WATER RAIL RUNNER BILCOCK
MOORHEN OARCOCK

WATER RAT VOLE CRABER
MUSKRAT WATERRUG

WATER SCORPION NEPID

WATERSHED BROW DIVIDE DIVORT
SNOWSHED

WATER SHIELD FANWORT
DEERFOOD FROGLEAF

WATERSKIN MASHAK MATARA
MUSSUK MUSSACK MUSSICK

WATER SOLDIER PONDWORT

WATER SPIRIT ARIEL KELPY KELPIE
UNDINE

WATERSPOUT RONE CANAL SPATE
SPOUT VORTEX PRESTER TWISTER
CATARACT GARGOYLE

WATER STRIDER SKATER SKIMMER
SKIPPER SKETCHER

WATER THRUSH KICKUP WAGTAIL

WATER TIGER DYTISCID

WATERTIGHT THEAT THEET TIGHT
STANCH THIGHT STAUNCH

WATER WALLY BATAMOTE

WATERWAY GUT CASH DOCK HOLE
LODE DITCH INLET ARTERY SEAWAY
CULVERT FAIRWAY HIGHWAY
IGARAPE

(ARTIFICIAL —) LEAD CANAL

(PL.) SCUPPERS

WATERWHEEL NORIA SAGEER
SAKIEH DANAIDE SAKIYEH
TYMPANUM

WATERY WET LASH PALE SICK
WHEY BOGGY MOIST SAMMY
WASHY BLASHY FLASHY LIQUID
PALLID SEROSE SEROUS SWASHY
AQUATIC AQUEOUS CHOROUS
HYDROUS PHLEGMY HUMOROUS
ICHOROUS SKINKING

WATTLE GILL JOWL PLAT SALY TWIG
WAND BOREE COOBA FRITH MULGA
SALLY SALWE STAVE STICK HURDLE
JEWING JOLLOP LAPPET SALLOW
BLUEBUSH CARUNCLE

WATTLEBIRD IAO MOHO MINER
MANUAO MAOMAO GILLBIRD

WATTLE CROW KOKAKO
WAVE FAN FLY JAW SEA WAW BECK
FLAG FLAP GUST LUMP SUFF SULK
SWAY WAFF WAFT WAWE YTHE
BLESS CRIMP FLASH FLOAT PULSE
SHAKE SURGE SWELL SWING
BILLOW COMBER FLAUNT MARCEL
RIPPLE ROLLER WINNOW BREAKER
BRIMMER CRIMPLE FLICKER
FLUTTER TSUNAMI WHIFFLE
ARTEFACT BRANDISH FLOURISH
GRAYBACK UNDULATE UNIPULSE
WHISTLER WHITECAP
(— OF EXCITATION) IMPULSE
(— OF FLAG) DOT DASH
(— OF SHIP) BONE
(ELECTRIC —) STRAY CARRIER
(TIDAL —) EAGER
(PL.) SURF
WAVER HALT REEL SWAG SWAY
VARY CHECK DAKER DOUBT FLOAT
SWALE SWING WIVER DACKER
DAIKER DITHER FALTER MAMMER
QUIVER SWERVE TEETER TOTTER
WABBLE WOBBLE BALANCE FLICKER
FLITTER FLUTTER STAGGER
SWITHER VIBRATE HESITATE
WAVERING WAW WAVY WEAK
WAUCH WAUGH FICKLE GROGGY
WAVERY WIGGLY DUBIOUS
LAMBENT SHUTTLE DOUBTFUL
FLEXUOSE FLEXUOUS FLICKERY
HOVERING WAVEROUS
WAVINESS CRIMP
WAVING UNDE WAFT AWAVE OUNDY
UNDEE WAFTURE FLOURISH
WAVY ONDE UNDE UNDY CRISP
MOIRE SNAKY UNDEE FLECKY
SNAKEY UNDATE WIGGLY BUCKLED
CRINKLY CURVING ENDATED
ROLLING SINUATE UNDULAR
ENRIDGED FLEXUOUS ONDOYANT
SQUIGGLY UNDULATE
(PEOPLE WITH — HAIR) VEDDOID
WAWL HOWL WAIL WOWL SQUALL
WAX WOX CERE CODE GROW RAGE
WACE WOXE SCALE BECOME
CAPPING CERESIN KLISTER
CARNAUBA CERESINE CEROXYLE
COCCERIN EPILATOR INCREASE
(— IN HONEYCOMB) CAPPING
(— STRONG) PREVAIL
(CHINESE —) PELA
(COBBLER'S —) CODE
(KIND OF —) PINSANG
(SKI —) KLISTER
WAXBILL ASTRILD REDBILL
WAXEN WAX PALLID CEREOUS
WAXER GLAZER WAXMAN
WAXFLOWER EPIPHYTE
WAX MYRTLE ARRAYAN
WAX PLANT HOYA
WAXWING WAXBIRD RECOLLET
SILKTAIL
WAXY ANGRY VEXED PLIABLE
YIELDING
WAY LAW PAD TAO VIA WON WYE
FARE FORE FORM GAIT GANG GATE
KIND LANE LARK PACE PATH PAWK

RAKE ROAD SORT TOBY WISE
ALLEY CHANT FORTH GOING GUISE
HABIT MOYEN ROUTE SHEAR STEPS
STYLE TRACT TRADE ACCESS
AVENUE CAREER CHEMIN COURSE
MANNER METHOD STREET TRAJET
CHANNEL FASHION HIGHWAY
PASSAGE SKIDWAY APPROACH
CONTRADA DISTRICT FOOTPATH
THOROUGH VICINITY LAUNCHING
(— OF DEPARTURE) EXIT
(— OF LIFE) LARK TRACE
HEDONISM
(— OF SPEAKING) AMBAGE
(— OF THINKING) DIET
(— OF WALKING) JET
(— OUT) IT EXIT SALVO
(— THROUGH MINEFIELD) BREACH
(CLEVER —) KNACK
(INDIRECT —) AMBAGES
(LONG —) FAR
(MAJOR —) STEM
(NARROW —) DRANG
(ODD —S) JIMJAMS
(PLANK —) BRIDGE
(ROUNDABOUT —) DETOUR CIRCUIT
(SETTLED —) BIAS
(SIDE —) BRANCH
(SLOPING —) RAMP
(UNDEVIATING —) GROOVE
(PL.) DAPS
WAYBILL WILLIE
WAYFARER SHULER VIATOR PILGRIM
SHUILER TRAVELER
WAYFARING TREE WHITTEN
COTTONER VIBURNUM
WAYLAY BELAY BESET BLOCK
BRACE AMBUSH FORLAY FORSET
FORELAY OBSTRUCT SURPRISE
WAYLAYER WAIT
WAYMARK AHU
WEAK DIM LEW COOL DOWY FOND
LAME NESH NICE PALE PUNY SELI
SELY SOFT THIN WASH WAUF WOKE
BAUCH BAUGH CRIMP DICKY FAINT
FLASH FRAIL JERKY LIGHT NAISH
REEDY ROCKY SEELY SILLY SLACK
STANK WASHY WAUGH WEARY
WERSH YOUNG CADUKE DEBILE
DILUTE DOTISH FEEBLE FLABBY
FLAGGY FLIMSY FOIBLE GROGGY
INFIRM LIMBER LITTLE MARCID
SEMMIT SICKLY SINGLE SWASHY
TENDER UNSURE UNWISE WAIRCH
WATERY DWAIBLY DWEEBLE
FLACCID FOOLISH FRAGILE INSIPID
INVALID LANGUID PIMPING PUERILE
REGULAR RICKETY SAUGHEN
SHALLOW SHILPIT SLENDER
SPINDLY TOTTERY UNHARDY
UNLUSTY WEARISH ASTHENIC
CHILDISH DECREPIT DEFINITE
FECKLESS FEMININE FLAGGING
GRIPLESS HELPLESS IMBECILE
IMPOTENT LADYLIKE LANGUENT
PHTHISIC RESOLUTE RUSHLIKE
SACKLESS SCRANNEL UNMIGHTY
UNWIELDY
(— FROM FATIGUE) TANGLE

(— FROM HUNGER) LEER
(— IN RESOLUTION) FRAIL
(MENTALLY —) TOTTY
WEAKEN GO LAG SAP DAMP FAIL
HURT MELT SINK THIN ALLAY
BLUNT BREAK CRAZE DELAY QUAIL
SHAKE SPEND WATER APPALL
DEACON DEADEN DEFEAT DEJECT
DENUDE DILUTE FALTER IMPAIR
INFIRM LABEFY LESSEN REBATE
REDUCE SICKEN SOFTEN CORRODE
CORRUPT CRIPPLE DECLINE
DEPRESS DISABLE MOLLIFY
QUALIFY RESOLVE UNBRACE
UNNERVE CASTRATE DIMINISH
EMBEZZLE ENERVATE ENFEEBLE
ETIOLATE INFRINGE LABEFACT
UNSTRENG
WEAKENED GROGGY ANODYNE
INVALID SHOTTEN DECREPIT
LABEFACT STRAINED
WEAKENING CHRONIC FAILURE
FLAGGING
WEAKEST RECKLING
WEAKFISH DRUM TROUT ACOUPA
SALMON CORBINA CORVINA
DRUMMER SQUETEE TOTOABA
TOTUAVA BLUEFISH CHICKWIT
WEAKLY FEEBLY FEMALE SIMPLY
WEAKLING TOY WRIG DUGON
PULER SLINK SOFTIE RECKLING
SOFTLING
WEAK-MINDED DAFT DOTY DOTED
FOOLISH
WEAKNESS ATONY CRACK CRAZE
FAULT FOLLY TOUCH ATONIA
DEFECT FOIBLE ACRATIA FAILING
FISSURE FRAILTY DEBILITY
DELICACY FONDNESS
(CARNAL —) FLESH
WEAL WHEAL RICHES STRIPE
WEALTH WELFARE
WEALTH WAD WON DHAN GEAR
GOLD GOOD MUCK WONE THING
WORTH GRAITH MAMMON POCKET
PURPLE RICHES TALENT CASHBOX
FORTUNE RICHDOM WARISON
WELFARE CATALLUM OPULENCE
OPULENCY PROPERTY TREASURE
(— OF NATION) STOCK
(PATRON OF —) YAKSHA
WEALTHY FAT FULL OOFY RICH
WELI AMPLE PURSY TINNY OOFIER
COUTHIE MONEYED PURSIVE
ABUNDANT AFFLUENT
WEAN CHILD SPAIN SPANE WAYNE
INFANT ESTRANGE
WEAPON (ALSO SEE SPECIFIC TYPE
OF WEAPON) ARM BOW GUN BILL
BOLA BOLO CLUB COSH DART EDGE
EPEE FALX FOIL IRON MACE PATU
PIKE TOOL WIWI ADAGA ARROW
BILLY CAKRA DEATH FLAIL KNIFE
LANCE ONCIN SHARP SPEAR SQUID
STEEL SWORD VOUGE WAPIN
CANNON CHAKRA DAGGER GLAIVE
MACANA ARCHERY BAZOOKA
FIREARM GISARME HALBERD
HARPOON HURLBAT JAVELIN

LIANGLE POUNAMU SHOTGUN
SLASHER STICKER TICKLER
WHIFFLE ARBALEST BLOWBACK
BLUDGEON CROSSBOW FAUCHARD
HEDGEHOG LEEANGLE PARTISAN
TROMBASH
(DEADLY —) DEATH
(LINE OF —S) RIDGE
(PREHISTORIC —) CELT
(PL.) WAR TACKLE ARCHERY
WEAPONRY
WEAR KIT BEAR FRAY FRET GROW
HAVE PASS CHAFE GUARD SPEND
VOGUE WEARY ABRADE BATTER
BECOME BETHUMB CONSUME
DEFENSE DEGRADE FASHION
FATUGUE FRAZZLE PROCEED
WEATHER PROGRESS
(— AN OPENING) BREACH
(— AND TEAR) GAFF SLITE
GRUELING
(— AWAY) EAT FADE FRET GALL
GNAW GULL PINE ERODE GULLY
SCOUR SPEND ABRADE CORRADE
CORRODE CONTRIVE
(— CLOTHES) DRESS
(— DOWN) BRAY GRIND ABRASE
GRAVEL
(— FURROWS) GUTTER
(— IN PUBLIC) SPORT
(— OFF) FRAY ABRADE
(— OUT) DO BURN COOK FLOG
JADE TIRE TUCK BREAK SLAVE
SLITE SPEND BUGGER HATTER
MAGGLE PERUSE EXHAUST
FORWEAR FORWORK HACKNEY
INVALID SHACHLE OVERFRET
OVERWEAR
(— SHIP) CAST
(— SHOES OUT OF SHAPE)
SHACHLE SHACKLE
(— TIGHT CORSETS) LACE
WEARIED AWEARY FORGONE
FATIGUED WEARIFUL
WEARINESS TIRE FATIGUE
BRAINFAG SICKNESS VEXATION
WEARING DECAY SCUFF BURNING
CLOTHES ABRASION GARMENTS
GRINDING
WEARISOME DRY DULL HARD
WEARY MORTAL PROLIX SODDEN
IRKSOME TEDIOUS SAWDUSTY
TIRESOME TOILSOME
WEARISOMENESS TEDIUM
WEARY FAG IRK SAD BOEG BORE
MOIL PALL PUNY SADE TIRE TIRY
WEAK WORE WORN BORED BREAK
CURSE SPENT HARASS PLAGUE
SICKLY SQUEAL EXHAUST FATIGUE
IRKSOME FATIGATE FORCHASE
GRIEVOUS TIRESOME WRETCHED
FORJASKIT
(BECOME —) JADE
WEARY WILLIE TRAMP
WEASAND WISEN GULLET THROAT
WIZZEN TRACHEA WINDPIPE
WEASEL CANE VAIR VARE WARE
HULDA HURON SNEAK STOAT TAIRA
TAYRA ERMINE FERRET HULDAH

VERMIN ARCTOID VORMELA
FUTTERET MUISHOND MUSTELIN
WHITRACK
WEASEL CAT LINSANG
WEATHER SKY DIRT RAIN TIME
COLLA STORM WINDWARD
(— CONDITION) WHITEOUT
(FAIR —) SHINE
(HOT AND HUMID —) SIZZARD
(INCLEMENT —) SEASON
(INTERVAL OF FAIR —) SLATCH
(UNDER THE —) SEEDY
(VIOLENT —) ELEMENTS
WEATHERBEATEN SEAGOING
WEATHERCOCK COCK FANE VANE
FAINE FANACLE
WEAVE CANE HABI HUCK JOIN LACE
LENO LOOM REED ROCK SPIN WALE
WARP WIND WOOF DOBBY DRAPE
PLAIT TWINE UNITE BROCHE
DAMASK DEVISE DIAPER DOBBIE
FABRIC CANILLE ENTWINE FASHION
INDRAPE SATINET SHUTTLE
VANDYKE DIAGONAL DUCHESSE
OVERSHOT
(— PATTERNS INTO) BROCADE
(BASKET —) BARLEYCORN
(CARPET —) FLOSSA
(HERRINGBONE —) SUMAK SOUMAK
SHEMAKA
(LATTICE —) TEE
(OPEN —) LENO BAREGE
WEAVER KORI TANTI WEBBE
DRAWBOY WEBSTER WOBSTER
PENELOPE TAPESTER
WEAVERBIRD NUN BAYA MAYA
TAHA FINCH MUNIA VIDUA WEBBE
BISHOP CANARY OXBIRD WHIDAH
WHYDAH BENGALI AMADAVAT
AVADAVAT CARDINAL MANNIKIN
WEAVING TANIKO TEXTURE
WEBBING
(— OF WORDS) CONTEXT
(— TOGETHER) PLEXURE
WEAZEN WIZEN SHRINK WIZENED
WEB PLY WOB CAUL FELT MAZE
TENT TOIL VANE WARP WEFT
SNARE THROW TWIST FLEECE
TISSUE ENSNARE FEATHER LAYETTE
TEXTURE SNOWSHOE VEXILLUM
(— IN EYE) HAW
(CRANK —) THROW
WEBBED RINGED PALMATE
WEBBING MAT WEB PALAMA
WEB-FOOTED PALAMATE PALMIPED
WEB SPINNER EMBIID WEBWORM
WED GET BEWED BRIDE MARRY
STAKE WAGER ENGAGE PLEDGE
SPOUSE ESPOUSE WEDLOCK
WEDDING SPLICE NUPTIAL
WEDLOCK ESPOUSAL MARRIAGE
WEDGE KEY COIN FROE FROW GLUT
HORN KYLE PLUG STOB TRIP WAGE
CHOCK CHUCK CLEAT COIGN HACEK
HORSE QUINE SCOTE SLICE THROW
COTTER CUNEUS QUINET SCOTCH
EMBOLUS QUINNET SCHOCHE
VOUSSOIR
(— BETWEEN TWO FEATHERS) KEY

(— IN) JAM JAMB
(— OF OATMEAL) FARL FARLE
(— TO PREVENT MOTION) CHOCK
(CURVED —) CAM
(WOODEN —) COW GLUT JACK
WEDGER SPRINGER
WEDGE-SHAPED CUNEAL SPHENIC
CUNEATED SPHENOID
WEDLOCK WIFE SPOUSAL MARRIAGE
SPOUSAGE
WEDNESDAY MIDWEEK
WEE TINY EARLY SMALL TEENY
YOUNG LITTLE
WEED BUR HOE BURR CHOP CULL
DOCK FORB LOUK SHIM SIDA TARE
WEID CIGAR DRANK DRAWK DRESS
DROKE FLESH DARNEL JIMSON
KNAWEL RIPGUT SARCLE SPURGE
SPURRY STROIL ASHWORT COHITRE
CUCKOLD EGILOPS GARMENT
GOSMORE HOGWORT SANDBUR
TOBACCO VERVAIN VERVINE
CHADLOCK COCKSPUR COWWHEAT
PIRIPIRI PLANTAIN PURSLANE
TOADFLAX ALFILERÍA MARIJUANA
(MEXICAN —) BIRDEYE
(TROUBLESOME —) KEX TITTER
(PL.) FILTH WRACK DISMAL SPRING
WEEDAGE TRUMPERY
WEEDER SARCLER
WEEDY FOUL LANKY
WEEK OOK WOK OULK WOKE
SENNET STANZA HEBDOMAD
SENNIGHT
(TWO —S) FORTNIGHT
WEEKDAY FERIA WARDAY
WEEKLY AWEEK
WEEL LEAP POOL TRAP RIGHT
WHIRLPOOL
WEEN MEAN VENE WEND FANCY
GUESS EXPECT BELIEVE IMAGINE
SUPPOSE CONCEIVE
WEENY TINY SMALL WEESHY
WEEP CRY ORP SOB BAWL BEND
GIVE LEAK OOZE PIPE TEAR WAIL
GREET BEWAIL BEWEEP BOOHOO
LAMENT SHOWER BLUBBER
LAPWING SQUINNY COMPLAIN
WEEPER GREETER MOURNER
CAPUCHIN
(PL.) FLENTES
WEEPING WOP GREET MILCH RAINY
LAMENT OOZING PIPING MAUDLIN
TEARFUL DRIPPING LACRIMAL
MADIDANS PLORATION
WEEPING SINEW GANGLION
WEEVER JUGULAR STINGBULL
WEEVIL MAX BOUD POPE WHULE
PICUDO WEEBLE BILLBUG BRUCHUS
VAQUITA CURCULIO WOODWORM
(PLUM —) TURK
WEFT WEB PICK WOOF BLAST
FABRIC FILLING
WEIGH GO SIT HEFT PEIS TARE TELL
COUNT HEAVE HOIST PEIZE POISE
RAISE SCALE BURDEN PONDER
ANALYZE BALANCE DEPRESS
LIBRATE CONSIDER EVALUATE
MEDITATE MILITATE

(— **DOWN**) LADE SWAY SWEE
BESET HEAVY PEISE CADDLE
CHARGE CUMBER PESTER DEPRESS
FREIGHT INGRATE OPPRESS
OVERLAY ENCUMBER
(— **UPON**) SIT GRIEVE
WEIGHER BOXMAN PEISER SCALER
WEIGHING (— **MACHINE**) TRON
SCALE TRONE
WEIGHT (ALSO SEE MEASURE AND
UNIT) BOB FEN FOB MAN NET RAM
SER SIR TOM TUP ABAS ATOM BEEF
CLOG DROP GRAM HEFT IRON KITE
LEAD LOAD MACE MEAL NAIL ONUS
PEIS POND PORT ROTL SEAM SINK
WAIT ABBAS CLOVE CRITH GARCE
MAUND PEASE PEISE POISE POIZE
PRESS RIDER SCALE STAMP
AUNCEL BURDEN CHARGE HAMMER
IMPORT MOMENT MONKEY PASSIR
PONDER PONDUS SINKER STRESS
BALLAST DOLPHIN GRAVITY MILLIER
PLATINE PLUMMET POSIURE
CHALDRON DEMIMARK DUMBBELL
ENCUMBER FARASULA PRESSURE
QUINCUNX STANDARD STRENGTH
(— **AFTER TARE DEDUCTION**)
SUTTLE
(— **CARRIED BY HORSE**) IMPOST
(— **CLOTH**) FLOCK
(— **FOR HURLING**) HAMMER
(— **FOR LEAD**) FOTMAL
(— **FOR PRECIOUS STONE**) CARAT
(— **FOR WOOL**) TOD SARPLER
(— **FOR WOOL, CHEESE, ETC.**)
CLOVE
(— **OF 100 LBS.**) CENTAL CENTENA
CENTNER
(— **OF 1000 LIVRES**) MILLIER
(— **OF 20 OR 21 LBS.**) SCORE
(— **OF 40 BUSHELS**) WEY
(— **OF 5 UNCIAE**) QUINCUNX
(— **OF BROADSIDE**) GUNPOWER
(— **OF COAL**) KEEL
(— **OF COFFEE**) MAT
(— **OF HYDROGEN**) CRITH
(— **OF METAL**) JOURNEY
(— **OF ONE 100TH TAEL**) FEN
(— **OF ONE 10TH TAEL**) MACE
(— **OF PENDULUM**) BOB
(— **OF PILE DRIVER**) TUP
(— **OF RAW SILK**) PARI
(— **OF SILK OR RAYON**) DRAMMAGE
(— **ON MINE SWEEPER**) KITE
(— **ON STEELYARD**) PEA
(— **ON WATCH CHAIN**) FOB
(— **TO BEND HOT METAL**) DUMPER
(— **TO DETECT FALSE COINS**)
PASSIR
(— **TO HINDER MOTION**) CLOG
(— **WHICH VESSEL CAN CARRY**)
TONNAGE
(**ABYSSINIAN** —) FARASULA
(**CARAT** —) SILIQUA
(**CLOCK** —) PEISE
(**FALSE** —) SLANG
(**GREATLY VARYING** —) MAN MAUND
(**HEAVY** —) MONKEY
(**LIGHT** —) SUTTLE

(**MONEYER'S** —) DROIT
(**ORIENTAL** —) CATTY
(**SASHCORD** —) MOUSE
(**SHUFFLEBOARD** —) SHIP
(**SMALL** —) MITE GERAH RIDER
(**SPLINE** —) DOLPHIN
(**UNIT OF** —) SER VIS WEY LAST
ROTL SEER LIANG LIBRA LINGO
MINAL PECUL PERIT PIKOL KANTAR
LINGOE MISKAL POCKET LISPUND
PRICKLE QUINTAL ZOLOTNIK
WEIGHTED BIAS LOADED
WEIGHTER FULLER
WEIGHT-PRODUCING GRAVIFIC
WEIGHTY GRAVE GREAT HEAVY
HEFTY MASSY VALID COGENT
SOLEMN EARNEST MASSIVE
ONEROUS PEISANT SERIOUS
TELLING GRIEVOUS MATERIAL
POWERFUL PREGNANT
WEIR DAM CRIB KEEP LEAP STOP
CAULD DOACH GARTH GORCE
HATCH HEDGE STANK LASHER
WEIRD ODD EERY UNCO UNKO EERIE
UNCOW UNKID CREEPY ELDRICH
ELRITCH UNCANNY UNUSUAL
WIZARDLY
(— **SISTERS**) FATES
WEITSPEKAN YUROK
WEKA RAIL WOODHEN RAILBIRD
WELCOME SEE FAIN GOOD HAIL
ADOPT CHEER GREET RESET TREAT
ACCOIL INVITE SALUTE ACCLAIM
ACCUEIL AMBRACE GRATIFY
BIENVENU GREETING HAEREMAI
PLEASANT
WELD SHUT WELL SWAGE UNITE
WOALD ACACIA
WELDED SHOT
WELDING FUSION SHUTTING
WELFARE SEL GOOD HALE HEAL
SELE WEALTH BENISON BLESSING
WELKIN SKY HEAVENS WALKENE
WELL AIN EYE GAY PIT WEL BENE
FINE FLOW GOOD PANT PUIT PURE
RITE SAFE SINK WINK AWEEL
BOOLY BOWLY GREAT MUSHA
OILER QUELL WISHA BUCKET
CENOTE ENOUGH FAIRLY GASSER
NICELY OFFSET PUMPER TUNNEL
FALLWAY GRADELY HEALTHY
WILDCAT BOREHOLE FOUNTAIN
GRAITHLY POSTHOLE WATERPIT
WEALSOME
(— **AND STRONG**) BUNKUM
(— **THROUGH FLOORS OF
WAREHOUSE**) FALLWAY
(— **UP**) WALL WALM DIGHT
(**AS** —) ALSO
(**NONPRODUCTIVE** —) DUSTER
(**NOT** —) DONNY SOBER INVALID
(**OIL** —) OILER GASSER GUSHER
SPOUTER WILDCAT STRIPPER
(**RECTANGULAR** —) BOOLY BOWLY
(**SACRED** — **AT MECCA**) ZEMZEM
(**TOLERABLY** —) GAYLIES GEYLIES
(**VERY** —) BRAWLY CLEVER
WELL-BALANCED SOBER
WELL-BEHAVED GOOD NICE

MODEST MANNERED
WELL-BEING HEAL SKIN WEAL
HEALTH WEALTH COMFORT
EUCRASY WELFARE EUCRASIA
WELLBORN GENTLE EUGENIC
WELL-BRED GENTIL POLITE
GENTEEL REFINED CULTURED
LADYLIKE
WELL CASING STEANING
WELL-CHOSEN CHOICE
WELL-CONSIDERED THRIFTY
WELL CURB PUTEAL
WELL-DEFINED STRICT
WELL-DISPOSED SIB FAIN GOOD
VAIN
WELL DONE SHABASH
WELL-DRESSED BRAW GASH
BRAWLY
WELL-FED BLOWSY BLOWZY
CHUBBY GAWCEY GAWSIE
WELL-FORMED TIGHT DECENT
PROPER SEEMLY SHAPELY
WELL-FOUNDED FIRM GOOD JUST
SOUND WORTHY
WELL-GROOMED SMUG CRISP
SOIGNE SOIGNEE
WELL-GROUNDED VALID
WELL-GROWN THRODDY
WELL-HUSBANDED THRIFTY
WELL-INFORMED KNOWING
PERFECT
WELL-INTENTIONED AMIABLE
WELL-KEPT SMUG POLITE
WELL-KNIT WIRY
WELL-KNOWN BREEM BREME
BEATEN FAMOUS KENNED FAMILIAR
WELL-LIKED FANCIED POPULAR
WELL-MADE CLEVER
WELL-MANNERED POLITE
COURTEOUS
WELL-NIGH WELLY ALMOST NEARLY
WELLMOST
WELL-ORGANIZED SNOD
WELL-PLEASED FAIN VAIN
WELL-PROPORTIONED SUING
TRETIS HANDSOME
WELL-READ STUDIED LITERARY
WELL-ROUNDED CHUBBY
WELL-SHAPED CLEVER FEATOUS
WELL-TILLED NOT NOTT
WELL-TO-DO ABLE BEIN BIEN EASY
WARM PODDED
WELL-WISHER FRIEND FAVORER
WELS WALLER SHEATFISH
WELSH (ALSO SEE WALES) CYMRY
FUDGE TAFFY CYMRIC KYMRIC
CAMBRIAN
WELSHER QUITTER
WELSHMAN CELT KELT TAFFY
BRYTHON CAMBRIAN
WELSH ONION CIBOL CIBOULE
CHESBOLL
WELT RIDGE STRIP WHELP WELTING
BANDELET TURNOVER
(**SHOE** —**S**) WATTIS
WELTANSCHAUUNG FAITH
IDEOLOGY
WELTER REEL RIOT TOSS WILT
GROVEL TUMBLE WALLOW WRITHE

SMOTHER STAGGER SWELTER
(— OF SOUNDS) DIN
WELWITSCHIA TUMBOA
WEM FLAW SCAR SPOT STAIN
WEN CYST WYNN CLIER CLYER
TALPA TUMOR GOITER
WENCH DELL DILL DOXY DRAB GILL
GIRL JADE MAID MOLL PRIM TRUG
GOUGE KITTY MADAM QUEAN TRULL
WHORE AUDREY BLOUSE BLOWEN
BLOWZE DRAZEL JILLET KITTIE
MOTHER POPLET WOTLINK
POPLOLLY
(CLUMSY —) MODER MODDER
MOTHER MAUTHER
WENCHER DRABBER STRIKER
WEND BOW END SORB VEND STEER
BETAKE DEPART DIRECT TRAVEL
PROCEED SORBIAN LUSATIAN
(— ONE'S WAY) MARK
WENT GODE LANE ROAD YEDE
ALLEY PASSAGE
(— ABOUT) WOLK
WENTLETRAP SCALA
WENZEL JACK
WERE (— IT NOT) SAVE
WEREWOLF TURNSKIN VERSIPEL
WEST STY BEWEST PONENT
OCCIDENT
WESTERN PONENT SCAEAN
HESPERIC SANDWICH
WEST HIGHLAND KYLOE

WEST VIRGINIA
CAPITAL: CHARLESTON
COLLEGE: SALEM BETHANY
CONCORD MARSHALL
BLUEFIELD
COUNTY: MINGO ROANE UPSHUR
BARBOUR KANAWHA
INDIAN: MONETON
LAKE: LYNN
NICKNAME: MOUNTAIN
RIVER: ELK OHIO KANAWHA
POTOMAC GUYANDOT
STATE BIRD: CARDINAL
STATE FLOWER: RHODODENDRON
STATE TREE: MAPLE
TOWN: ELKINS KEYSER RIPLEY
VIENNA WESTON BECKLEY
GRAFTON SPENCER WEIRTON
FAIRMONT WHEELING

WESTWARD WESSEL OCCASIVE
WESTLINS
WET DEW DIP SOP WAT DAMP DANK
LASH MOIL SLOW SOAK SOFT UVID
BATHE DABBY DROOK DRUNK
HUMID JUICE JUICY LEACH MADID
MOIST MOOTH RAINY SLAKE SNAPY
SOBBY SOPPY SPEWY STEEP TIGHT
WEAKY CLASHY DABBLE DAGGLE
DAMPEN HUMECT IMBRUE JARBLE
LABBER MADEFY MARSHY MOISTY
QUASHY SHOWER SLABBY SOBBED
SPONGY SPOUTY SWASHY WATERY
ARROUSE BLUBBER DRABBLE
FLOTTER MOISTEN SLOPPED
SOBBING SPEWING SPRINGY

IRRIGATE SATURATE SLATTERY
SLOBBERY SLOTTERY WATERISH
(— AND STORMY) FOUL
(— LIGHTLY) SPRINKLE
(— THOROUGHLY) SOUSE DRENCH
(SOFTLY —) SQUASHY
(VERY —) SOPPY
WETHER PUR RAM HAMEL DINMAN
DINMONT
WETNESS DANK
WETTING SOUCE SOUSE SOWSE
MOILING
WHACK DAD LAM TRY BANG BELT
BIFF DEAL HACK SWAK TIME DRIVE
SHARE STATE SWACK WHANG
CHANCE DEFEAT STROKE THWACK
BARGAIN LAMBACK PORTION
WHACKING VERY WHALING
WHOPPING EXTREMELY
WHALE SEI CETE HUEL HULL LASH
ORCA WALL KOGIA POGGY SCRAG
SPERM STUNT BALEEN BELUGA
BLOWER FINNER GIBBAR KILLER
THRASH BOWHEAD DOLPHIN
FINBACK FINFISH GIBBERT
GRAMPUS RIPSACK RORQUAL
SPOUTER ZIPHIAN BALAENID
CACHALOT CETACEAN DOEGLING
GREYBACK HARDHEAD HUMPBACK
JUBARTES MUTILATE THRASHER
ZIPHIOID
(— BUTCHER) LEMMER
(— REFUSE) GURRY
(FINBACK —) GRASO
(SCHOOL OF —S) GAM POD
WHALEBONE BALEEN
WHALER HEADER BUSHMAN
SPOUTER SWAGMAN WHACKER
WHOPPER CETIDIDE
WHALESKIN MUKTUK
WHANG BEAT BLOW FLOG CHUNK
THONG WHACK THRASH RAWHIDE
WHARF KEY POW DOCK GARE PIER
QUAY SLIP BERTH JETTY STADE
STAITH STRAND LANDING PANTALAN
STELLING
WHARVE WARVE WHIRL WHORL
WHAT FAT HOT HOW WET WHO
HOOT HOTE WHEN STUFF WHICH
MATTER PARTLY
WHATA FUTTAH FUTTER
WHATNOT OMNIUM ETAGERE
WHATSOEVER MORTAL
WHEAL HIVE HUEL WALE WELT
URTICA POMPHUS
WHEAT WIT CORN CONES EMMER
FULTZ GRAIN SPELT SPICA TRIGO
BULGUR BURGUL CEREAL KANRED
STAPLE TURKEY EINKORN FORMITY
FRUMETY KUBANKA MARQUIS
POLLARD FRUMENTY SPELTOID
(— BOILED IN MILK) FURMITY
(— MEASURE) TRUG
(BEARDED —) RIVETS
(CRACKED —) GROATS
(GRANULATED —) SUJI SUJEE
(HARD —) DURUM
(PARCHED —) BULGUR
WHEATCAKE PURI

WHEATEAR CHACK ARLING WITTOL
CHACKER ORTOLAN SNORTER
WITTALL CHICKELL
WHEATGRASS BLUESTEM
WHEATLIKE VULGARE
WHEEDLE COG CANT CLAW COAX
CARNY FLUFF GLOSE GLOZE INGLE
JOLLY BANTER CAJOLE FLEECH
GLAVER RADDLE SMOOGE WHILLY
BLARNEY CUITTLE PALAVER
SMOODGE TWEEDLE COLLOGUE
SCROUNGE
WHEEDLING BUTTERY
WHEEL BOB BUR COG FAN NUT ORB
BEAD BUFF GEAR HELM HURL PURL
ROLL RULL STAR TIRL WYLE ATHEY
FLIER FLUFF FLYER IDLER NORIA
REWET RHOMB ROWEL SWING
TRUCK BILOBE CASTER CASTOR
CIRCLE DRIVEN DRIVER FANNER
HORRAL JAGGER KURUMA LEADER
PINION ROLLER ROTATE RUNDLE
RUNNER TRACER BALANCE BICYCLE
CHUKKER GUDGEON LANTERN
PEDRAIL PRICKER REVOLVE
STEPNEY TRAILER TRILOBE TRINDLE
TRUCKLE TRUNDLE UNILOBE
WILDCAT FOLLOWER ODOMETER
SPROCKET
(— A SKIN) FLUFF
(— CHARGED WITH DIAMOND DUST)
SLITTER
(— CONTROLLING RUDDER) HELM
(— FOR EXECUTIONS) RAT
(— IN KNITTING MACHINE) BUR
BURR
(— IN TIMEPIECE) BALANCE
(BUCKET —) LIFTER
(DIAMOND —) SKIVE
(GEAR —) DRIVEN HELICAL
(GRINDING —) SHELL
(GROOVED —) PULLEY SHEAVE
SHIVER
(INTERRUPTER —) TICKER TIKKER
(LOCOMOTIVE —) DRIVER
(METAL —) FILET FILLET
(MILL —) PIRN
(PAIR OF LOGGING —S) CATYDID
KATYDID
(POINTED —) TRACER
(POLISHING —) BOB BUFF SKAIF
SKEIF BUFFER SCAIFE
(POTTER'S —) LATHE THROW
(SPINNING —) TURN CHARKA
CHARKHA
(SPUR —) ROWEL
(TANK —) BOGY BOGEY BOGIE
(TOOTHED —) GEAR PINION
ROULETTE
(TURBINE —) ROTOR
(TWO PAIRS OF —S) CUTS CUTTS
(VANED —) FLIER FLYER
(WATER —) NORIA SAKIA SAKIEH
SAKIYEH TYMPANUM
(PL.) KATYDID
WHEELBARROW GURRY BARROW
CARRIAGE
WHEELER POLER PUSHER
WHEEL-SHAPED ROTATE ROTIFORM

WHEELWORK MOTION
WHEELWRIGHT WHEELER
WOODMAN WHEELMAN
WHEEZE JOKE HOOSE HOOZE TRICK
COGHLE
WHELK FILK GRUB WELT BUCKIE
MAGGOT PAPULE PIMPLE WINKLE
PUSTULE
WHELP CUB PUP SON CHIT FAWN
PUPPY YELPER KITLING SPROCKET
WHEMMEL UPSET FUMMEL FUMMLE
WHAMBLE OVERTURN
WHEN AS BUT FAN FRO GIN THO
WON THAN THEN THOA TILL SINCE
UNTIL ENOUGH ALTHOUGH
WHENEVER ONCE
WHERE AS FAR FUR FAUR FEAR
FERRE PLACE QUAIR THERE
WHITHER LOCATION
(— **ABOVE MENTIONED**) US
WHEREFORE WHY CAUSE FORWHY
REASON
WHERENESS UBIETY
WHEREVER THERE
WHEREWITHAL MEANS MONEY
RESOURCES
WHERRET BOX CUFF SLAP HURRY
TEASE WORRY TROUBLE WHIRRICK
WHERRY BARGE ROWBOAT WHIRREY
WHET WET GOAD HONE TIME TURN
GRIND POINT RIFLE ROUSE SLITE
WHILE EXCITE INCITE STROKE
QUICKEN SHARPEN APERITIF
EXACUATE
WHETHER IF GIF GIN WHAR WHERE
EITHER
WHETSTONE BUR RIP RUB BUHR
BURR SLIP STONE RUBBER STRAIK
SHARPER WASHITA WHITTLE
RUBSTONE STRICKLE
WHEY PALE QUAY WHIG SERUM
THRUST WATERY
WHIBA UEBA
WHICH AS THE WHO THAT QUILK
WHILK
(— **SEE**) QV QQV
WHICKER NEIGH WHINNY WIGHER
WHIDAH BIRD VEUVE WEAVER
WHYDAH REDBILL
WHIFF FAN GUF BLOW GUFF GUST
HINT PUFF TIFT WAFT WIFT FLUFF
QUIFF SMOKE EXHALE MAGRIM
MEGRIM WHIFFET
WHIFFLE FIFE SWAY FLICKER
FLUTTER
WHIFFLETREE HEELTREE
SWINGLEBAR
WHIG JOG QUIG WHEY
WHILE AS BIT GAM THO YET FILE
FYLE TIDE TILL WHEN WHET WOLE
FILIE PIECE SPACE STEAD STOUN
THROW UNTIL STOUND WHENAS
WHILOM BEGUILE TROUBLE
EXERTION OCCASION
(— **AWAY**) AMUSE FLEET DIVERT
DECEIVE
(**LITTLE** —) AWEE DRASS WHILEY
WHILEEN WHILOCK
WHILES UNTIL SOMETIMES

WHILLY GULL CAJOLE WHEEDLE
WHILST TILL UNTIL
WHIM BEE FAD GIG GIN TOY FIKE
FLAM KINK CRANK FANCY FLISK
FOLLY FREAK HUMOR QUIRK THRUM
FEGARY FITTEN MAGGOT MEGRIM
SPLEEN VAGARY WHIMSY BOUTADE
CAPRICE CONCEIT WRINKLE
CROTCHET
WHIMBREL JACK SPOW SPOWE
CURLEW MAYBIRD MAYFOWL
TITTEREL
WHIMPER GIRN MEWL PULE WAIL
WEAK BLEAT WHINE SIMPER
WHINGE YAMMER GRIZZLE SNIFFLE
SNUFFLE WHINDLE WHINNEL
WHITTER WHINNOCK
WHIMSICAL FANCY COCKLE FLISJY
NOTION QUAINT BIZARRE GIGGISH
BIZZARRO FANCIFUL FREAKISH
HUMOROUS NOTIONAL SINGULAR
WHIMSY WHIM FREAK VAGARY
CAPRICE WHIMWHAM
WHIN FUN ULEX FURZE WHINCOW
WOODWAX
WHINCHAT TICK UTICK WHEATEAR
WHINE WOW GIRN GOWL MEWL
PULE TIRM TOOT YARM YIRN BLEAT
CROON MEECH QUINE TWINE
WHAUP WHEWT SNIVEL TREBLE
WHINGE WINNEL YAMMER WHIMPER
WHINDLE
WHINNY HINNY NEIGH PLAIN
SNICKER WHICKER
WHINSTONE TRAP WHIN SCURDY
WHINYARD SWORD HANGER
POCHARD WHINGER SHOVELER
WHIP CAT EEL FAN GAD ROD TAW
BEAT CAST COIL DICK DUST FLOG
FOAM GOAD HIDE JERK LASH LICK
LOUK PLET TAWS URGE WHUP
ABUSE AZOTE BIRCH CRACK FLAIL
FLICK FLISK IMPEL KNOUT LEASH
PLETE QUILT ROMAL SLASH STRAP
SWEPE SWING SWISH TAWSE
THONG THUMP AROUSE BREECH
CHABUK DEFEAT FEAGUE INCITE
LAINER LARRUP LICKER MAIDEN
NETTLE PIZZLE QUIPPE SCUTCH
SNATCH SWITCH TICKLE CHABOUK
CHICOTE COWHIDE COWSKIN
CURBASH KURBASH LAMBAST
LAYOVER NAGAIKA RAWHIDE
SCOURGE SHINGLE SJAMBOK
SLASHER TICKLER CHAWBUCK
COACHMAN CONFOUND FLAGELLA
KOURBASH PEPPERER
(— **EGGS**) CAST
(— **HANDLE**) CROP
(— **IN PIANO ACTION**) WIPPEN
(— **WITH 3 LASHES**) PLET PLETE
(**HORSE** —) WAND
(**JOCKEY'S** —) BAT
(**RIDING** —) CROP DICK QUIRT
(**RUSSIAN** —) KNOUT
WHIPLASH COSAQUE CRACKER
WHIPPED BEATEN BROKEN
DEFEATED FOUETTEE CHANTILLY
WHIPPER TICKLER THONGMAN

THRASHER THREAPER
WHIPPER-IN PRICKER
WHIPPERSNAPPER SQUIRT
WHIFFET WHIPSTER
WHIPPING LICK TOCO TOKO HIDING
CLANKER FANNING SERVING
BIRCHING BROWSING SKELPING
WHIPPING POST FORK PILLAR
WHIP SCORPION GRAMPUS
PHRYNID PEDIPALP WHIPTAIL
WHIPSOCKET SNEAD
WHIPSTITCH MINUTE INSTANT
OVERCAST
WHIR BIRR ZIZZ WHIRRY
WHIRL BIRL EDDY FURL GYRE HURL
PURL RUSH SPIN TIRL DRILL GIDDY
SKIRL SQUIR SWIRL THIRL THROW
TWIRL TWIST WALTZ WHORL
BUSTLE CIRCLE GYRATE HURTLE
SWINGE VORTEX WHORLE WINDLE
WIRBLE MIZMAZE REVOLVE
TRUNDLE TURMOIL VERTICIL
(— **ABOUT**) DOZE GURGE
(— **IN THE AIR**) WARP
WHIRLIGIG GIG SPIN TURN WHEEL
FIZGIG FISHGIG
WHIRLING GIDDY WHEELY
GYRATION GYRATORY VORTICAL
WHIRLPOOL EDDY GULF SUCK WELL
WIEL GORCE GOURD BULLER
GORGES SWELTH VORTEX GURGLET
SWALLOW SWILKIE SUCKHOLE
MAELSTROM
WHIRLWIND OE DEVIL VORTEX
PRESTER TORNADO
WHISHT HUSH SILENCE
WHISK ZIP FISK TUFT WHID WHIP
WISP CAURI FLICK FLISK HURRY
SPEED SWISH CHAURI CHOWRY
SWITCH COWTAIL WHISKER
WHISKER HAIRLINE VIBRISSA
(**PL.**) BEARD ZIFFS WEEPER
GALWAYS VIBRISSA MOUSTACHE
SIDEBURNS
WHISKY RYE BOND CORN CIDER
IRISH USQUE POTEEN REDEYE
SCOTCH BOURBON BLOCKADE
BUSTHEAD CREATURE POPSKULL
USQUABAE
(**GLASS OF** —) RUBDOWN
(**RAW** —) DRUDGE
WHISPER BUZZ HARK HINT ROUN
RUNE ROUND RUMOR TRACE TUTEL
BREATH BREEZE HARKEN MURMUR
SUSURR TITTLE WHISHT HEARKEN
SUSURRUS
WHIST MORT VINT QUIET BOSTON
SILENT WHEESHT
WHISTLE BLOW CALL FUTE PIPE
WHEW QUILL WHAUP WHEEP WHUTE
BUZZER CUCKOO FUSSLE HOOTER
SIFFLE SISTLE SQUEAL YELPER
TWEEDLE BIRDCALL
WHISTLE FLUTE SIFFLOT
WHISTLER PIPER MARMOT ROARER
FLUTIST LAPWING SIFFLEUR
WHISTLING PIPY PIPEY ROARING
SIFFLET RHONCHUS
WHIT BIT JOT ATOM DOIT HATE

HOOT IOTA QUAT QUIT BODLE
GROAT POINT QUITE SPECK CIVITE
PARTICLE TWOPENNY
WHITE CUT WAN BAWN FITE HOAR
LILY PALE QUAT QUIT ASHEN
BLOND HOARY LABAN LINEN SNOWY
ALBINO ARGENT BLANCH BRIGHT
BUCKRA CANDID CIVITE ERMINE
SILVER WINTRY CANDENT LEUCOUS
NIVEOUS WHITTLE FAVORITE
INNOCENT LACTEOUS
(— AND SMOOTH) IVORINE
(— OF EGG) GLAIR ALBUMEN
(— PERSON) OFAY
(POOR —) YAHOO CRACKER
WHITE ALDER CLETHRA
WHITE ANT ANAY NASUTE TERMITE
WHITEBAIT SMELT ICEFISH
SALANGID SALMONID
WHITEBEAM ARIA SERVICE
MULBERRY
WHITEBOY PET LEVELER
WHITE BRYONY COWBIND
WHITE CEDAR JUNIPER
WHITE CLOVER SHAMROCK
WHITEFISH BLOAT CISCO PILOT
POWAN BELUGA CHIVEY POLLAN
TULIPI VENDIS BLOATER BOWBACK
LAVARET VENDACE BLACKFIN
GREYBACK HUMPBACK MENOMINI
SALMONID SCHNABEL TULLIBEE
WHITEFLY HOMOPTER MEALYWING
WHITE GUM TUART
WHITE-HEADED GOLDEN FAVORED
FORTUNATE
WHITE HELLEBORE ITCHREED
ITCHWEED
WHITE IPECAC ITOUBOU
WHITE LEAD CERUSE
WHITE MAPAU PIROPIRI
WHITE MUSTARD KEDLOCK SINAPIS
CRUCIFER
WHITEN SCURF ALBIFY BLANCH
BLANCO BLEACH BLENCH DEALBATE
EMBLANCH ETIOLATE
WHITENESS IVORY ALBEDO ARGENT
CANDOR PURITY CANITIES
PALENESS
WHITE OAK ROBLE
WHITE POPLAR ABELE ABELTREE
WHITE SNAKEROOT STEVIA
POOLWORT RICHWEED WHITETOP
WHITE STURGEON BELUGA
WHITETHROAT JACK MUFF MUFTY
MUGGY PEGGY EYSOGE MILLER
MUFFET WHISKY WINNEL HAYSUCK
WHEYBIRD
WHITEWASH LIME GLASS BLANCH
PARGET CHICAGO LIMEWASH
PALLIATE
WHITEWEED DAISY
WHITE WHALE BELUGA
WHITHER GUST HURL RUSH WHIZ
HURRY SHAKE WHERE FLURRY
BLUSTER WHERETO
WHITING BARB HAKE CORBINA
CORVINA KINGFISH MOONFISH
WHITING-POUT BIB KLEG BLENS

WHITISH BAWN PALE DILUTE
SUBALBID
WHITLOW FELON ANCOME FETLOW
BREEDER PANARIS RUNROUND
WHITLOW GRASS DRABA
NAILWORT SHADBLOW
WHITRACK WEASEL FUTTERET
WHITTRET
WHITSUNDAY TERM
WHITSUNTIDE PINXTER PINGSTER
PINKSTER
WHITTLE CUT PARE CARVE KNIFE
STEEL TWITE EXCITE MANTLE
THWITE BLANKET
WHIZ BUZZ DEAL GIRL PIRR QUIZ
SING WHIR ZIZZ SOUGH WHISH
WHIZZ WIZARD BARGAIN SWITHER
WHINNER
WHIZ-BANG EXPERT NOTABLE
WHO AS HOW THE WHA WHAT
WHICH
WHOA WO WAY WHO STOP
WHOEVER WHATSO EVERWHO
WHOLE ALL HOW SUM BODY COOL
EVEN HALE HALF HOLY HULL
BLOCK GREAT GROSS HAILL SOUND
TOTAL TOTUM TUTTA UNCUT
CORPSE ENTIRE HEALED INTACT
GENERAL INFRACT INTEGER
PERFECT SINCERE SOLIDUM
COMPLETE ENSEMBLE ENTIRETY
GLOBULAR INTEGRAL LIVELONG
OUTRIGHT UNBROKEN
(— OF ANY ORGANISM) SOMA
(— OF REALITY) ABSOLUTE
(ORGANIC —) SYSTEM
WHOLEHEARTED HEARTY SINCERE
ZESTFUL COMPLETE IMPLICIT
WHOLESALE MASSIVE SWEEPING
WHOLESALER JOBBER EXPORTER
WHOLESOME GOOD CLEAN SOUND
SWEET BENIGN SAVORY HEALTHY
PRUDENT CURATIVE HALESOME
HEALSOME HOMELIKE REMEDIAL
SALUTARY HEALTHFUL
WHOLE-SOULED SINCERE
WHOLLY ALL FAIR FLAT HALE ONLY
BLACK CLEAR FULLY QUITE STARK
ALGATE BODILY FLATLY HOLLOW
PURELY SOLELY ALGATES ROUNDLY
SOLIDLY TOTALLY DIRECTLY
ENTIRELY
WHOOP BOOM HOOP HOOT BOOST
RAISE SHOUT EXCITE HALLOO
HOOPOE
WHOOPING COUGH KINKHOST
CHINCOUGH PERTUSSIS
WHOP WAP BEAT THUD THUMP
STRIKE THRASH
WHOPPER LIE SIZER BOUNCER
CRUMPER SLAPPER SNAPPER
SWAPPER SWINGER STRAPPER
WALLOPER
WHOPPING VERY LARGE BANGING
RAPPING WAPPING WHALING
SWINGING WHACKING
WHORE DRAB JILT FILTH WENCH
HARLOT PUTAIN DEBAUCH
STRUMPET SUCCUBUS

WHOREMONGER HOLOUR
WHORL TURN CYCLE SPIRE SWIRL
WHIRL THWORL VOLUTE WHARVE
WREATH ANNULUS GYRATION
VERTICIL VOLUTION
WHORTLEBERRY HOT HURT FRAWN
HOOTE FRAGHAN BILBERRY
WHY HOW QUI ENIGMA FORWHY
WICK BAD EVIL FARM TOWN ANGLE
CREEK DAIRY MATCH QUICK SNAST
CORNER LIVING WICKED VILLAGE
FARMSTEAD
(— CLOGGED WITH TALLOW)
ROUGHIE
(LONG WAXED —) TAPER
WICKED BAD SAD DARK EVIL FAST
FOUL IRON LAZY LEWD MEAN PIKY
VILE BLACK CURST FELON SHREW
SORRY WRONG WROTH CURSED
GUILTY LITHER LUTHER NEFAST
PERDIT PITCHY SEVERE SHREWD
SINFUL UNHOLY UNJUST UNLEAD
UNLEDE UNWELL CAITIFF DARKSUM
GODLESS HEINOUS HELLISH
IMMORAL NAUGHTY NINETED
NOXIOUS PRAVOUS PROFANE
ROGUISH UNGODLY UNSEELY
UNSOUND UNWREST VICIOUS
VILLAIN CRIMINAL DARKSOME
DEPRAVED DEVILISH DIABOLIC
ENORMOUS FELONOUS FIENDISH
FLAGRANT MESCHANT OBDURATE
TERRIBLE UNKINDLY
WICKEDNESS ILL SIN EVIL HARM
VICE CRIME FOLLY GUILT BELIAL
FELONY NOUGHT UNGOOD ATHEISM
DEVILRY ILLNESS DARKNESS
DEVILTRY INIQUITY MISCHIEF
SATANISM WANGRACE
WICKERWORK WEB WEEL TWIGGEN
BASKETRY
WICKET GATE HOOP HATCH PITCH
STUMP GUICHET
(FALLING OF —S) ROT
WICKETKEEPER STUMP STUMPER
WICKIUP HUT WAKIUP SHELTER
WIDDRIM FIT FURY
WIDDY NOOSE WIDOW WITHY
HALTER
WIDE FAR LAX DEEP ROOM SIDE
AMPLE BROAD LARGE ROOMY
SHARP SLACK WRONG ASTRAY
ROOMWARD SPACEFUL SPACIOUS
(— OF THE MARK) AWRY ABROAD
(— OF) BESIDE
(LONG AND —) SIDE
WIDE-AWAKE FLY FOXY KEEN LIVE
ALERT FLASH LEERY SLIPPY
KNOWING WAKEFUL WATCHFUL
WIDELY FAR BROAD ABROAD
GREATLY LARGELY
WIDEN FLAN REAM DILATE EXPAND
EXTEND FLANGE FUNNEL BROADEN
WIDENESS WIDTH BREADTH
WIDESPREAD RIFE DIFFUSE
GENERAL CATHOLIC EXTENDED
SWEEPING
WIDGEON SMEE WHIM GOOSE
WHEWER ZUIZIN POACHER

POTCHER BALDPATE BLUEBILL
WHISTLER

WIDOW VID BALO DAME SKAT BLIND
KITTY VEUVE WEEDA WIDDY
MATRON RELICT TERCER DOWAGER
EMPRESS BARONESS DOWERESS
(PL.) VIDUAGE

WIDOWHOOD VIDUAGE VIDUITY

WIDTH GAPE SIDE RANGE SCOPE
BREADTH OPENING FRONTAGE
FULLNESS LARGEOUR LATITUDE
WIDENESS
(— OF CUT) KERF
(— OF HORSESHOE) COVER
(— OF PALM) HAND
(— OF PAPER) FILL
(— OF PULLEY) FACE
(— OF SHIP'S BAND) STRAKE
(— OF SHIP) BEAM
(— OF TYPE) SET
(— OF WEB) DECKLE

WIELD PLY RUN BEAR WALT WIND
EXERT SWING VELDE EMPLOY
GOVERN HANDLE MANAGE STRAIN
CONTROL

WIFE UX FEM HEN MRS RIB WYF
BABY BIBI DAME DORA ENID FEME
FERE FRAU FROW JAEL LADY MAKE
MATE RANI UXOR DIRCE DONNA
DUTCH FEMME LUCKY MATCH
MUJER SQUAW WOMAN ELMIRE
EMILIA GAMMER KEEPER MATRON
MISSIS MULIER SPOUSE VENDER
WAHINE BEDMATE DIONYZA
EMPRESS PARTNER WEDLOCK
DEIANIRA DEIDAMIA ERIPHYLE
HELPMATE HELPMEET MISTRESS
PECULIAR
(— OF COTTER) COTQUEAN
(— OF KNIGHT OR BARONET) DAME
(— OF MOHAMMEDAN) KHADIJA
(AFFIANCED —) FUTURE
(INDIAN'S —) WEBB
(OLD —) GAMMER
(PL.) PUNALUA

WIG BOB JIZ RUG TIE FRIZ GIZZ
JANE JIZZ LOCK TETE TOUR BUSBY
CAXON FLASH JASEY MAJOR SCALP
SCOLD ADONIS BRUTUS FROWZE
PERUKE REBUKE TOUPEE TOUPET
COMBING RAMILIE SCRATCH
SHEITEL SPENCER BOBJEROM
CHEDREUX CHEWELER NIGHTCAP
PERUKERY POSTICHE ROGERIAN
VALLANCY
(— WITH ROUGHLY CROPPED HAIR)
BRUTUS
(18TH CENTURY —) ADONIS
GEORGE
(BUSHY —) BUSBY
(GRAY —) GRIZZLE
(WORSTED —) JASEY

WIGGLE JET HOTCH JIGGLE WABBLE
WANGLE

WIGGLER PUPA LARVA WRYER

WIGHT MAN SWIFT STRONG VALIANT
CREATURE STALWART

WIGMAKER WIGGER PERUKER
PERUKIER

WIGWAG SIGNAL

WIGWAM LODGE WEEKWAM WICKIUP

WIKENO NIKENO HEILTSUK

WILD REE SHY FAST RUDE SCAR
WOWF CRAZY FANTI FELON FERAL
GIDDY MYALL RANDY RANTY
ROUGH ROYET SKEER WASTE
DESERT FANTEE FERINE FIERCE
LAVISH MADCAP NATIVE RAMAGE
RANDOM RENISH SAVAGE SHANDY
STORMY UNRULY BERSERK
BREACHY ERRATIC FRANTIC
GALLOUS GALLOWS HAGGARD
HOWLING MADDING OUTWARD
RIOTOUS SKADDLE SKEERED
WILDING ABERRANT AGRESTAL
BARBARIC DESOLATE FAROUCHE
FRENETIC HALUCKET HELLICAT
RECKLESS UNTILLED WARRAGAL
WILLYARD
(— CARD) FREAK

WILD ASS GOUR KIANG KULAN
COTULA KOULAN ONAGER QUAGGA
CHIGETAI

WILD BALSAM APPLE CREEPER

WILD BEE KARBI

WILD BOAR APER SUID TUSKER
SOUNDER SUIDIAN WILRONE
SANGLIER

WILD BUFFALO ARNA ARNEE

WILD BUSH BEAN PHASEMY

WILD CABBAGE YELLOWS

WILD CARDAMOM RUEWORT
KNOBWOOD

WILD CARROT DILL ELTROT FIDDLE
BIRDNEST HILLTROT

WILDCAT CAT BALU EYRA CHATI
CHAUS MANUL TIGER MARGAY
SERVAL WAGATI COLOCOLA

WILD CELERY ACHE ECHE
EELGRASS SMALLAGE

WILD CHERRY GEAN

WILD CHERVIL KECK COWWEED
HONEWORT MILKWEED

WILD CYCLAMEN SOWBREAD

WILD DOG ADJAG DHOLE DINGO
GUARA AGUARA AGOUARA
CIMARRON WARRAGAL

WILDEBEEST GNU

WILDERNESS BUSH WILD WASTE
DESERT FOREST WESTERN
SOLITUDE

WILD-EYED HAGGARD RADICAL

WILDFOWL VOLATILE

WILD GARLIC MOLY

WILD GERANIUM ALUMROOT
DOVEFOOT FLUXWEED

WILD GOAT TUR IBEX TAHR EVECK
PASAN MAZAME MARKHOR
AEGAGRUS MARKHOOR

WILD HORSE BRUMBY KUMRAH
TARPAN BRUMBIE WARRAGAL
WARRIGAL

WILD HYACINTH CUCKOO
CROWTOE GREGGLE BRODIAEA
CROWFOOT

WILD INDIGO SHOOFLY

WILD LETTUCE FIREWEED

WILD MAN SAVAGE WOODMAN
WOODSMAN

WILD MANGOSTEEN SANTOL

WILD MARJORAM ORGAN ORGAMY
ORGANY ORIGAN ORGAMENT

WILD MULBERRY YAWWEED

WILD MUSTARD CHARLOCK

WILDNESS FERITY HEYDAY HEYDEY
FEROCITY SAVAGERY SAVAGISM

WILD OAT DRANK DRAWK DROKE
HAVER HEVER EGILOPS

WILD ONION UMBEL UMBELLA

WILD OX BUF YAK ANOA BUFF REEM
UNICORN

WILD PARSLEY ELTROT HILLTROT

WILD PEAR DOGBERRY

WILD PLUM SLOE ISLAY

WILD POTATO MANROOT WAPATOO

WILD RADISH RUNCH

WILD RICE MANOMIN

WILD SAGE EYESEED

WILD SARSAPARILLA SHOTBUSH

WILD SERVICE TREE SORB
SORBUS

WILD SHEEP SHA URIAL AOUDAD
ARGALI BHARAL NAYAUR BIGHORN
MOUFLON

WILD SWAN ELK

WILD THYME HILLWORT SERPOLET

WILD TOBACCO GAGROOT
SOURBUSH MARIJUANA SALVADORA

WILD TURNIP NAVEW

WILD VANILLA LIATRIS

WILE PAUK PAWK RUSE FRAUD
GUILE TRICK ALLURE BLENCH
DECEIT ENGINE ENTICE BEGUILE
ARTIFICE TRICKERY

WILGA WILLOW

WILL EGO MAY ULL FATE LIST TEST
WISH LEAVE OUGHT SHALL WORST
ANIMUS CHOICE DESIRE DEVICE
DEVISE LEGATE LIKING QUETHE
SCRIPT APETITE CODICIL PASSION
WITWORD AMBITION BEQUEATH
PLEASING PLEASURE VOLITION
(— NOT) WONT WINNA WONNA
WUNNA WONNOT
(— OF DEITY) DECREE
(— OF GOD) LAW
(— OF LEGISLATURE) ACT
(— TO LIVE) TANGHA
(FREE —) ACCORD
(GOOD —) GREE
(I —) CHILL
(ILL —) ARR ENVY HEST ANIMUS
ENMITY UNTHANK AMBITION

WILLET TATLER TATTLER

WILLFUL HEADY WILLY FEISTY
UNRULY HAGGARD WAYWARD
WILSOME CAMSTRARY

WILLFULLY WOLDES SCIENTER

WILLIES JUMPS CREEPS

WILLING BAIN FAIN FREE GLAD LIEF
RATH PRONE READY MINDED
TOWARD CONTENT UNFORCED

WILLINGLY LIEF SOON FREELY
GLADLY LIEFLY FRANKLY READILY

WILLINGNESS HEART FREEDOM
FAINNESS

(— **TO FIGHT**) DEFIANCE
WILLIWAW STORM WOOLLY
TEMPEST
WILLOW DULY ITEA SALE WYLW
OSIER SALEW SALIX WIDDY WITHY
WOODY DUSTER SALLOW TEASER
TWILLY WITHEN WUDDIE
(— **FOR THATCHING**) SPRAYS
(— **IN TEXTILES**) WOLF
(**NATIVE** —) COOBA COOBAH
(**SIMPLE** —) WHIPPER
WILLOWER DULER DUSTER TEASER
WILLIER
WILLOW HERB WICOPY EPILOBE
FIRETOP PIGWEED ROSEBAY
BURNWEED FIREWEED
WILLOW WARBLER SMEU SMEUTH
MUDDLER TROCHIL OVENBIRD
WILLOW WREN PEGGY
WILLOWY SUPPLE SLIPPER
DELICATE
WILLY-NILLY PERFORCE
WILSON'S PLOVER COLLIER
WILSON'S SNIPE JACK SHADBIRD
WILSON'S TERN MEDRICK
WILSON'S THRUSH VEERY
WILT EBB SAG DROP FADE FLAG
WELK DROOP SUCCUMB COLLAPSE
WILTED EMARCID
WILY SLY FOXY CANNY SLICK
ARTFUL ASTUTE CLEVER CRAFTY
QUAINT SHREWD STALKY SUBTLE
CUNNING POLITIC VERSUTE
WINDING
WIMBLE BORE BRISK ACTIVE GIMLET
LIVELY NIMBLE WIBBLE WUMMEL
WIMPLE BEND WIND CURVE TWIST
GORGET RIPPLE MEANDER
WIMLUNGE
WIN BAG COP HIT DRAW GAIN HAVE
LAND LICK FORCE SCORE ATTACH
CLINCH OBTAIN ACHIEVE CONQUER
DESERVE HARVEST POSSESS
TRIUMPH DECISION OVERCOME
STRAIGHT
(— **AGAINST**) BREAK SCOOP
(— **AWAY**) STEAL DEBAUCH
(— **BACK**) RECOVER
(— **BY GUILE**) GET POT BEAR
CARRY RAISE TRAIN GATHER
CAPTURE INVEIGLE PROMERIT
(— **NARROWLY**) SQUEEZE
(— **OVER**) DEFEAT DISARM
(— **OVERWHELMINGLY**) SWEEP
WINCE KICK CHECK QUECH CRINGE
FLINCH QUATCH QUINCH QUITCH
RECOIL SHRINK
WINCH CRAB JACK REEL WINK
GIPSY WINZE ROLLER WHIMSY
WINDLE CATHEAD TRAVELER
VARIABLE WINDLASS
WIND AIR COP LAP BALL BIRR BISE
BIZE COIL CONE CURL EAST FIST
FLAW FOHN GALE GUST KINK PUFF
PUNO ROLL WEST WRAP BATCH
BLAST BLORE CRANK CREEK
CROOK FOEHN QUILL SPOOL
STORM TRADE TREND TWINE TWIST
WEAVE WITHE BOTTOM BOUGHT

BREEZE BUSTER CAURUS COLLAR
KECKLE SANSAR SHAMAL SPIRAL
SPIRIT SQUALL WAMPLE WESTER
ZEPHYR BREATHE CRANKLE
CRINKLE CYCLONE ENTWINE
EQUINOX ETESIAN GREGALE
INVOLVE MEANDER MISTRAL
SERPENT SINUATE TEMPEST
TWINGLE TWISTER WEATHER
WHIRLER WINDILL ARGESTES
DOWNWARD EASTERLY FAVONIUS
(— **ABEAM**) LASK
(— **ABOUT**) WIRE SNAKE
(— **AFTER DYEING**) BATCH
(— **FROM THE ANDES**) PAMPERO
(— **IN AND OUT**) INDENT WINGLE
(— **MAGNETS**) COMPOUND
(— **OF ARGENTINA**) ZONDA
PAMPERO
(— **OF HAWAII**) KONA
(— **OF OREGON AND WASHINGTON**)
CHINOOK
(— **OF TUNISIA**) CHILE CHILI CHILLI
(— **ROPE**) WORM WOOLD
(— **THREAD OR YARN**) QUILL
CHEESE
(— **TO PREVENT CHAFING**) KECKLE
(— **WOOL**) TREND
(— **YARN**) BEAM SERVE WINDLE
(—**S OF CHILE AND PERU**) SURES
(**ADRIATIC** —) BORA
(**BREAKING** —) FIST
(**BROKEN** —) HEAVES
(**COLD** —) BISE BIZE BORA SARSAR
BLIZZARD
(**COOLING** —) IMBAT
(**DEAD** —) NOSER
(**DESERT** —) SAMUM GIBLEH SAMIEL
SIMOOM SIMOON SIROCCO
(**DRYING** —) TRADE
(**EASTERLY** —) LEVANT LEVANTER
(**FIERCE** —) BUSTER
(**GUST OF** —) FLAN FLAW
(**HIGH** —) RIG
(**HOT** —) GIBLEH SOLANO CHAMSIN
KHAMSIN SIROCCO
(**LIGHT GENTLE** —) BREEZE
(**MOUNTAIN** —) PUNA
(**NORTH** —) BISE AQUILO BOREAS
AQUILON MISTRAL
(**NORTHEAST** —) BURAN GREGALE
(**NORTHWEST** —) CAURUS
(**PERIODICAL** —) ETESIAN MONSOON
(**PERSIAN GULF** —) SHAMAL SHARKI
SHIMAL
(**PERUVIAN** —) PUNO
(**ROARING** —) BLORE
(**SEVERE** —) SNIFTER
(**SOUTH** —) NOTUS AUSTER
(**SOUTHEAST** —) EURUS SOLANO
(**SOUTHEASTERLY** —) SHARKI
SHURGEE
(**SOUTHWEST** —) CHINOOK LIBECCIO
(**STRONG** —) BIRR
(**VIOLENT** —) BUSTER SQUALL
SNORTER
(**WARM** —) FOHN FOEHN CHINOOK
SANTANA

(**WEST** —) ZEPHYR FAVONIUS
ZEPHYRUS
WINDAGE DRIFT
WINDER REEL WINCH DRUMMER
PLUGGER SKEINER SPOOLER
TENDRIL
WINDFALL VAIL GRAVY MANNA
FALLING BLOWDOWN BUCKSHEE
WINDGALL PUFF WINDDOG
WINDING LINK MAZY CRANK LACET
SPIRE GYRATE SCREWY SPIRAL
TWISTY WANLAS CRINKLE DEVIOUS
MEANDER SINUOUS SNAKING
WRIGGLY WRINKLE
(**PL.**) RADDLINGS
WINDING-SHEET SHROUD SUDARY
CEREMENT
WINDING STAIR COCKLE COCLEA
WINDER COCHLEA
WINDLASS CRAB WINK FEARN
WINCH STOWCE STOWSE TACKLE
TURNEL WINDLE TWISTER WILDCAT
ARTIFICE DRAWBEAM MANEUVER
WINDMILL JUMBO MOTOR COPTER
PINWHEEL
(— **BAR**) UPLONG
(— **SAIL**) AWE EIE EIGHE FLIER
FLYER SWEEP SWIFT
WINDOW BAY EYE ROSE SASH SLIT
SLOT CHAFF GLAZE GRILL INLET
LIGHT SIGHT THURL AWNING
DORMER GRILLE LANCET PEEPER
SPLITE THURLE WICKET BALCONE
COUPLET DORMANT FENSTER
GUICHET LUTHERN MIRADOR
ORIFICE TRANSOM VENTANA
WINNOCK CASEMENT FANLIGHT
FENESTER FENESTRA JALOUSIE
VENETIAN
(— **OF TWO LIGHTS**) COUPLET
(**BAY** —) ORIEL MIRADOR
(**BLANK** —) ORB
(**DORMER** —) DORMANT LUCARNE
LUTHERN
(**HIGH NARROW** —) LANCET
(**OVAL** —) OXEYE
(**ROUND** —) OXEYE OCULUS
ROUNDEL
(**SEMICIRCULAR** —) FANLIGHT
(**TICKET** —) GRILLE GUICHET
(**TWIN** —) AJIMEZ
(**PL.**) STORMS
WINDOW DRESSING TRIM FRONT
FACADE
WINDOW FRAME SASH REVEAL
WINDOW OYSTER COPIS
WINDOWPANE LIGHT LOZEN QUIRK
LOZENGE
WINDOWSILL SOLE
WINDPIPE HALS ARBER ARBOR
ERBER HALSE WIZEN ARTERY
GUGGLE STROUP WEEZLE KEACORN
THACHEA WEASAND THRAPPLE
THROPPLE THROTTLE
WINDROW BANK HEAP RIDGE
SWATH SWATHE
WINDSOR CHAIR FANBACK
WINDSTORM BLOW BURA THUD
BURAN BOURRAN

WINDWARD ALOOF WEATHER
(— **SIDE**) KOOLAU
WINDY BLOWY EMPTY GASSY GUSTY
HUFFY PROUD STARK SWALE
FLIMSY STORMY WONDIE BREATHY
FEARFUL GUSTFUL NERVOUS
VENTOSE VIOLENT
(— **CITY**) CHICAGO
WINE CUP VIN BOIS BUAL CUIT CUTE
DEAL PALM PORT RAPE ROSE ROSY
TENT TYRE CAPRI GRAPE KRAMA
LUNEL PETER PORTO SCIAN SHRAB
TINTO VINUM WHITE BARSAC
CORTON COUTET GRAVES KIJAFA
LISBON MASDEU PIMENT ROCHET
SAUMUR SHIRAZ SOLERA TIVOLI
ALICANT AMBONNA BACCHUS
BANYULS BARBERA BASTARD
CATAWBA CHACOLI CHATEAU
DEZALEY FALERNO MARSALA
MISSION MOSELLE ORVIETO
PALERMO PIGMENT RHENISH
ROSOLIO SERCIAL SILLERY
VERNAGE VIDONIA VINTAGE
APERITIF BORDEAUX BURGUNDY
CHARNECO DELAWARE LACHRYMA
LIBATION MALVASIA MARSALLA
RIESLING ROCHELLE RULANDER
RUMBOOZE SPARKLER
(— **BOILED WITH HONEY**) MULSE
(— **CHEST**) TANTALUS
(— **FROM VINEGAR**) ESILL
(— **MIXED WITH WATER**) KRASIS
(— **OF EXCELLENT QUALITY**)
VINTAGE
(— **OF SACRAMENT**) BLOOD
(— **SELLER**) ABKAR BISTRO WINARE
(— **SERVING**) VOIDEE
(**AROMATIZED** —) DUBONNET
(**BULK** —) CUVEE
(**CONSECRATED** —) CUP
(**FIRST-GROWTH** —) LAFITE LAFITTE
(**FRANCONIAN** —) STEIN LEISTEN
(**GREEK** —) RUMNEY
(**HEATED** —) WHITEPOT
(**JAPANESE** —) SAKI
(**LIGHT** —) BUAL CAPRI BAROLO
CANARY
(**MULLED** —) GLUHWEIN
(**NEW — BOILED DOWN**) CUIT CUTE
(**NEW** —) MUST
(**PALM** —) SAGWIRE
(**RED** —) MACON TINTA BEAUNE
CLARET CHIANTI HOLLOCK
ALICANTE BURGUNDY CABERNET
FLORENCE
(**REVIVED** —) STUM
(**RHINE** —) HOCK SYLVANER
(**SPANISH** —) SACK TENT DULCE
OPORTO SHERRY ALIKANT BASTARD
(**STILL** —) PONTAC PONTACQ
(**SWEET** —) TYRE DULCE CANARY
BASTARD MALMSEY CHARNECO
MUSCATEL
(**TENT** —) TINTO
(**TOKAY** —) ESSENCE
(**TUSCAN** —) VERDEA CHIANTI
FLORENCE
(**WHITE** —) HOCK SACK CAPRI

CASEL FORST BARSAC MALAGA
BROMIAN CATAWBA CHABLIS
CONTHEY LANGOON BUCELLAS
RIESLING SAUTERNE VERMOUTH
(**PL.**) PALUS
WINEBERRY MAKO MAKOMAKO
WINEGLASS FLUTE
WINEGROWER WINER VIGNERON
WINESHOP BISTRO BODEGA
WINE-VAULT SHADE
WING ALA ARM ELL FAN FLY OAR
RIB VAN FORE JAMB SAIL TAIL
ALULA BLOCK FLANK JAMBE PINNA
POINT SHEAR VOLET BRANCH
FLETCH FLIGHT HALTER PENNON
PINION POISER DEMIVOL ELYTRON
ELYTRUM BALANCER DISPATCH
(— **OF ARMY**) HORN
(— **OF BUILDING**) ELL JAMB JAMBE
ALETTE FLANKER
(— **OF SHELL**) AURICLE
(— **OF THEATER**) COULISSE
TORMENTOR
(— **OF TRIPTYCH**) VOLET
(—**S DISPLAYED**) VOL
(**BASTARD** —) ALULA
(**BIRD'S** —) FLAG
(**PL.**) PENS FEATHERS
WINGED AILE ALATE LOFTY RAPID
SWIFT ALATED PENNED PENNATE
ELEVATED
WINGED DISK FEROHER
WING-FOOTED FLEET SWIFT ALIPED
WINGLESS APTERAL
WING-LIKE ALARY ALIFORM
PTEROID
WING SHELL STROMB ELYTRON
STROMBUS
WINK BAT NAP PINK BLINK DEATH
FLASH PRINK SLEEP TWINK
CONNIVE FLICKER INSTANT NICTATE
SPARKLE TWINKLE
WINKER EYE BLINKER EYELASH
WINKING BLINK
WINKLE PERIWIG TWINKLE
WINNER VICTOR FACEMAN
BANGSTER
WINNING GAIN SWEET PROFIT
GAINING VICTORY WINSOME
CHARMING
(— **OF ALL TRICKS**) CAPOT
SCHWARZ
(**PL.**) WIN VELVET
WINNOW FAN WIM CHAR SIFT WIND
DIGHT SIEVE DELETE REMOVE
SELECT WINDER SEPARATE
WINNOWER VAN WINDER DIGHTER
WINSOME GAY SWEET CHARMING
CHEERFUL PLEASANT
WINTER BISE SNOW YEAR HIEMS
DECEMBER HIBERNATE
(— **OVER**) HOG
WINTERBERRY PRINOS HOOPWOOD
WINTERBLOOM AZALEA
WINTERGREEN JINKS CHINKS
PYROLA DRUNKER BOXBERRY
DRUNKARD EYEBERRY GAYWINGS
IVYBERRY LIMONIUM RATSBANE
SHINLEAF TEABERRY

WINTERLIKE BRUMAL
WINTRY AGED COLD WHITE BOREAL
HIEMAL STORMY CHILLING
HIBERNAL
WINTUN COPEHAN
WINY VINOUS DRUNKEN
WIPE BEAT BLOW DRUB DUST GIBE
DIGHT SWIPE CANCEL SPONGE
SPUNGE STRIKE ABOLISH CLEANSE
SQUEEGEE
(— **BEAK OF HAWK**) FEAK
(— **NOSE**) SNITE
(— **OFF**) SCUFF
(— **OUT**) ERASE SCRUB SWEEP
EFFACE DESTROY
(— **UP**) SWAB SWOB
WIPER DUSTER TRIPPET
WIRE GUY TAP BINE CORE DENT
DRAG FILE FUSE PURL CABLE
OUTER RISER SNAKE SWEEP TAPER
BRIDGE FESCUE FINGER HEATER
JUMPER NEEDLE STAPLE STOLON
STRAND DROPPER HAYWIRE
LAMETTA LASHING PRICKER
SHIFTER SNUFFER FILAMENT
LIGATURE PALISADE PULLDOWN
STRINGER TELEGRAM
(— **BETWEEN TWO VESSELS**) SWEEP
(— **FOR CUTTING CLAY**) SLING
(— **FOR SUSTAINING HAIR**)
PALISADE
(— **IN BLASTING CAP**) BRIDGE
(— **IN CATHETER**) STYLET
(— **IN WEAVING LOOM**) DENT
(— **OF GOLD,SILVER OR BRASS**)
LAMETTA
(— **TO ADJUST WICK**) SNUFFER
(— **TO CLOSE A BREAK**) JUMPER
(— **TO REMOVE TUMORS**) LIGATURE
(— **USED AS POINTER**) FESCUE
(— **USED IN SPLICING CABLES**)
TAPER
(—**S BOUND TOGETHER**) SELVAGE
(**4** —**S TWISTED TOGETHER**) QUAD
(**ENAMELED** —) LITZ
(**FENCE** —) DROPPER
(**FRAYED** —) JAGGER
(**GOLD** —) KINSEN
(**PALLET** —) PULLDOWN
(**PRIMING** —) PICKER EPINGLETTE
(**SURGICAL** —) STYLET
(**TWISTED** —) HEADLE HEDDLE
(**VENT** —) PRICKER
WIRE CUTTER SECATEUR
WIREDRAW WREST OUTWIT
DEFRAUD DISTORT ELONGATE
WIREGLASS FLUTE
WIRE GRASS POA
WIRELESS RADIO
WIRE ROPE JACKSTAY
WIRETAP BUG
WIREWORM ELATER ELATRID
MILLIPEDE
WIRY THIN HARDY STIFF WITHY
FEEBLE KNOTTY SINEWY STRINGY
THREADY
WIS KNOW THINK SURELY SUPPOSE

WISCONSIN
CAPITAL: MADISON
COLLEGE: RIPON BELOIT ALVERNO CARROLL VITERBO CARTHAGE
COUNTY: DOOR VILAS JUNEAU CALUMET SHAWANO WAUSHARA
INDIAN: FOX SAUK KICKAPOO WINNEBAGO
LAKE: POYGAN MENDOTA WISSOTA
MOUNTAIN: TIMSHILL SUGARBUSH
NATIVE: BADGER
NICKNAME: BADGER
RIVER: FOX CHIPEWA STCROIX
STATE BIRD: ROBIN
STATE FLOWER: VIOLET
STATE TREE: MAPLE
TOWN: ANTIGO BELOIT RACINE WAUSAU ASHLAND BARABOO KENOSHA MADISON OSHKOSH PORTAGE SHAWANO LACROSSE SUPERIOR WAUKESHA MILWAUKEE

WISDOM WIT LORE SABE SABBY SAVEY SENSE SOPHY ADVICE GNOSIS HOKMAH POLICY SATTVA SOPHIA WISURE CUNNING MINERVA SAGESSE SLEIGHT AFTERWIT JUDGMENT PRUDENCE SAPIENCE
(DIVINE —) WORD THEOMAGY
(ESOTERIC —) GNOSIS
(SUPREME —) PRAJNA
WISE HEP SLY DEEP GASH GOOD KIND SAGE SANE SEND TURN CANNY FRESH GUIDE SMART SOUND WITTY ADVISE CRAFTY DIRECT QUAINT WITFUL WITTER ANCIENT ERUDITE GNOSTIC KNOWING LEARNED POLITIC PRUDENT SAPIENT THRIVEN PERSUADE PROFOUND SENSIBLE SPACIOUS
(— MAN) AMAUTA
WISEACRE SAGE DUNCE GOTHAM SOLONIST WISEHEAD WISELING
WISECRACK JOKE QUIP
WISENT BISON AUROCH UROCHS BONASUS
WISH CARE GIVE GOAL HOPE LIST LUST MIND VOTE WANT WILL BOSOM COVET CRAVE DREAM HEART TASTE VOICE DESIRE UTINAM FAREWELL GODSPEED PLEASURE
(DEATH —) DESTRUDO
(SLIGHT —) VELLEITY
WISHBONE FURCULA FOURCHET FURCULUM
WISHFUL EAGER HOPEFUL LONGING ALLURING
WISHING ANXIOUS DESIROUS
WISHY-WASHY PALE THIN WEAK BLAND VAPID FEEBLE DILUTED INSIPID SLIPSLOP
WISKET BASKET WHISKET
WISP WUSP SCRAP SHRED SKIFF

SKIFT TWIST RUMPLE CRUMPLE MASSAGE
(— OF HAY) RISP
(— OF STRAW) WAP WASE DOSSIL
(— OF THATCH) TIPPET
WISPY FRAIL NEBULOUS
WISTERIA FUJI KRAUNHIA
WISTFUL INTENT PENSIVE WISHFUL MOURNFUL YEARNING
WISTITI WISTIT MARMOSET
WIT VAT VYT WAG KNOW NOUS SALT BRAIN HUMOR IRONY SENSE THINK WHITE WOTTE ACUMEN ESPRIT POLICY SANITY SATIRE WISDOM CUNNING PICADOR SARCASM SUPPOSE THINKER WITWORM BADINAGE REPARTEE
(BITING —) DICACITY
(PL.) BUTTONS
WITCH ALP ANI HAG HEG HEX MARE SAGA TRAT WYCH BRUJA BUTCH GREBE LAMIA WIGHT ASUANG CARLEY CARLIN CUMMER DOWSER DUESSA HECATE KIMMER PILWIZ WIZARD AGANICE CANIDIA HAGGARD HELLCAT SYCORAX BABAJAGA CAROLINE ERICHTHO SORCERER SPAEWIFE VERSIERA WALKYRIE
(PL.) COVEN
WITCHCRAFT CHARM GOETY CUNNING HEXEREI SORCERY BRUJERIA DEVILTRY PISHOGUE WIZARDRY
WITCH DOCTOR BOCOR BOKOR GOOFER GUFFER
WITCHERY CHARM SPELL SORCERY SORTIARY
WITCHES'-BROOM STAGHEAD
WITCHGRASS COUCH PANIC PANICLE
WITE WAT BLAME FAULT WAYTE CENSURE REPROACH HAMESOKEN
WITH BY CUM MID MIT WUD AVEC CHEZ DOWN AMONG ANENT WIGHT AGAINST
(— HAND ON HIP) AKIMBO
(— REGARD TO) ABOUT
(— SPEED) TIVY
WITHDRAW GO COY DROP TAKE AVOID DEMIT LOOSE REVEL SHIFT START UNSAY CHANGE DECEDE DESERT DETACH DETRAY DEVOID EFFACE FLINCH MINISH RECALL RECANT RECEDE RETIRE REVOKE ROGATE SECEDE SHRINK SINGLE SYPHON ABSCOND CONCEAL DESCEND DETRACT FORSAKE INVEIGH RETRACT RETREAT SCRATCH SCUTTLE SECLUDE SUBDUCE SUBDUCT UNSCREW SEPARATE SUBTRACT
(— FROM POKER POT) DROP
(— FROM) VAIK
(— SUPPORT) ABANDON
WITHDRAWAL DRAIN FLIGHT HIDING OFFLAP RETIRE SHRINK ABSENCE PULLOUT REGRESS RETIRAL RETREAT SCUTTLE

(— OF BUILDING FACE) SETBACK
WITHDRAWN SHY ASOCIAL INGROWN SECLUSE DISTRAIT ISOLATED SECLUDED
WITHE HANK ROPE TIER TWIG WITHY WATTLE WICKER CRINGLE
WITHER BURN DAZE FADE MIFF PINE RUST SEAR STUN WARP WELK BLAST CLING DAVER DECAY QUAIL WIZEN COTTER SHRINK WALLOW WELTER WILTER WINDER AREFACT DECLINE FORWELK SENESCE SHRIVEL LANGUISH PARALYZE
WITHERED DRY ARID SEAR SERE CORKY SCRAM MARCID BLASTED UNGREEN WIZENED
WITHHELD DEFERRED SUSPENSE
WITHHOLD CURB DENY HIDE KEEP STOP CHECK SCANT ABSENT DEPORT DETAIN REFUSE ABSTAIN BOYCOTT DEFORCE FORBEAR OUTHOLD REPRESS RESERVE SUSPEND RESTRAIN SUBTRACT
(— CONSENT) DECLINE
WITHHOLDING DETAINER
(— OF DUES) CHECKOFF
WITHIN IN ON BEN BIN INBY INLY INTRA HEREIN INSIDE INWITH INDOORS ENCLOSED INCLUDED INWARDLY
WITHOUT EX BUT OUT SEN BOUT FREE OHNE SANS SINE MINUS SENZA FAILING OUTSIDE WANTING INNOCENT OUTDOORS
(— A FLANGE) BALD
(— A MATE) ODD
(— ACTION) DEEDLESS
(— BEGINNING OR END) ETERNAL
(— BLEMISH) CHOICE
(— CONTENTS) INANE
(— DELAY) AWAY FOOTHOT SUMMARY
(— DELIBERATION) HEADLONG
(— EMOTION) DRYLY DULLY
(— EXCEPTION) ALWAYS
(— FEET) APOD
(— FUNDS) CLEAN
(— HORNS) ACEROUS
(— INTEREST) BARREN
(— LIGHT) APHOTIC
(— LIMITS OF DURATION) AGELESS
(— ORDER) ANYHOW
(— POWER) ADRIFT
(— QUESTION) EASILY SECURELY
(— REALITY) AIRY
(— REASON) BLINDLY
(— REMEDY) BOOTLESS
(— ROADS) INVIOUS
(— RULE OR LAW) ANARCHIC
(— SADDLES) ASELLATE
(— TEETH, TONGUE OR CLAWS) MORNE
(— WINGS) APTEROUS
WITHSTAND BIDE DEFY TAKE ABIDE OPPOSE OPPUGN RESIST CONTAIN CONTEST FORBEAR SUSTAIN CONFRONT WITHSTAY
WITHY WIRY AGILE OSIER WOODY WILLOW WOODIE WINDING

WITLESS MAD GROSS INSANE STUPID FATUOUS FOOLISH UNWITTY HEEDLESS SLAPHAPPY
WITLOOF ENDIVE CHICORY
WITNESS SEE TAKE TEST PROOF ATTEST BEHOLD MARTYR RECORD TESTIS TESTOR CURATOR TESTATE TESTIFY EVIDENCE RECORDER SUFFRAGE
(FALSE —) JUROR
(PL.) SECTA
WITNESS-BOX STAND
WITOTO HUITOTE
WITTICISM WIT JEER JEST JOKE SLENT WHEEZE
WITTING NEWS TIDINGS
WITTOL FOOL CUCKOLD WITTALL
WITTY GASH WILY WISE DROLL LEPID SHARP SMART CLEVER FACETE JOCOSE JOCULAR KNOWING CONCEITY HUMOROUS
(NOT —) INFICETE
WIVERN DRAGON WYVERN
WIZARD SEER SHIZ FIEND DOCTOR EXPERT PELLAR WARLOW CHARMED MAGICAL SPAEMAN WARLOCK WISEMAN CONJUROR MAGICIAN SORCERER TROLLMAN WITCHMAN
(PL.) GOETAE
WIZARDRY SORCERY
WIZEN DRY WITHER SHRIVEL
WIZENED GIZZEN WEAZEN
WOAD DYE NIL ODE ANIL KERS NILL OADE CRESS ANILLA INDICO INDIGO PASTEL
WOADWAXEN ALLELUIA ALLELUJA
WOBBLE COCKLE COGGLE HOBBLE QUAVER TITTER WABBLE WIGGLE TREMBLE
WOBBLY LOOSE SHAKY COGGLY DRUNKEN DOUBTFUL
WOE WA WEI BALE BANE PAIN PINE WAWE GRIEF MISERY SORROW TROUBLE WILLAWA CALAMITY DISTRESS WELLADAY WELLAWAY
WOEBEGONE WAFF UNHAPPY DEJECTED DESOLATE DOWNCAST
WOEFUL MEAN DISMAL PALTRY RUEFUL DIREFUL DOLEFUL RUTHFUL DOLOROUS PITIABLE WRETCHED
WOLF GLUT LOBO CANID FREKI YABBI CHANCO COYOTE FAMINE FENRIR ISGRIN KABERU LOAFER MASHER SIGRIM THOOID POVERTY ISENGRIM
(FOX —) ZORRO
WOLFBERRY BUCKBUSH
WOLFHOUND ALAN BORZOI PSOVIE
WOLFISH LUPINE RAVENOUS
WOLFLIKE THOOID
WOLFRAMITE CAL TUNGSTEN
WOLFSBANE ACONITE DOGBANE FOXBANE
WOLF SPIDER HUNT JAGER HUNTER JAEGER JAYHAWK LYCOSID TARANTULA
WOLVERINE PIG GLUT GORB MIKER GLOTUM HELLUO GLUTTON GUTLING LURCHER MOOCHER

RAVENER SWILLER CARCAJOU DRAFFMAN GOURMAND GULLYGUT
(— STATE) MICHIGAN
WOMAN BIM DAM EVE HEN HER JUG MEG SHE TEG TIT BABE BABY BINT BOSS CONY DAME FAIR FEME FLAG FROW JADE JANE LADY MARY MORT PERI SLUT WIFE BIDDY BIMBO BLADE BROAD CHINA DONAH FEMME JATNI LUBRA LUCKY MUJER QUEAN SKIRT SMOCK SQUAW TAGGE TWIST UMMAN VROUW BURDIE CALICO CARLIN CUMMER FEMALE GIMMER HEIFER KIMMER LUCKIE MANESS SISTER TOMATO VIRAGO WAHINE CARLING CHANGAR DISTAFF PARTLET PINNACE PLACKET QUAEDAM MISTRESS
(— DESERTED BY HUSBAND) AGUNAH
(— OF CONSEQUENCE) HERSELF
(— OF LOW CASTE) DASI
(— OF RANK) DOMINA
(— OF UNSTEADY CHARACTER) FLAP
(— OF WEALTH) FORTUNE
(— WHO ACTS AS ADVISER) EGERIA
(— WITH 3 CHILDREN) TRIPARA
(— WITH ONE CHILD) UNIPARA
(ABORIGINAL —) GIN LUBRA
(ABUSIVE —) FISHWIFE
(ALLURING —) DISH
(ATHENIAN — OF HIGH RANK) GERARA GERAERA
(ATTRACTIVE —) DOLLY SHEBA DOLLIE CHARMER
(AUSTRALIAN —) BINT
(AWKWARD —) ROIL
(BEAUTIFUL —) HURI PERI BELLE HOURI SIREN SPARK CHERUB EYEFUL MUSIDORA
(BOISTEROUS —) HOYDEN
(BOLD —) RAMP
(CLEANING —) CHAR
(COARSE —) BEAST BLOWZE RULLION
(COOLIE —) CHANGAR
(COY —) HAGGARD
(CREMATED —) SATI SUTTEE
(DEAR —) PEAT
(DUTCH OR GERMAN —) FRAU FROW FROKIN FRAULEIN
(ENGAGED —) BONDAGER
(ENTICING —) SIREN
(EVIL OLD —) HAG HELLHAG
(FASHIONABLE —) MILADY GALLANT ELEGANTE
(FAT —) BOSS FUSTILUGS
(FINE —) SCREAMER
(FIRST —) EMBLA
(FLIRTING —) FIZGIG
(FORWARD —) STRAP
(GAUDY —) JAY
(GENTLE —) DOVE
(GOSSIPY —) HAIK HAKE BIDDY TABBY
(GROSS —) SOW
(GYPSY —) ROMI ROMNI GITANA
(ILL-TEMPERED —) VIXEN

(IMMORAL —) RIG GITCH FLAPPER HARLOTRY
(INDIAN —) SQUAW WENCH KLOOCH BUCKEEN
(INSPIRED —) PHOEBAD
(ITALIAN —) DONNA
(LASCIVIOUS —) GIGLET
(LEARNED —) PUNDITA CLERGESS
(LEWD —) REP SLUT BITCH HUSSY HUZZY BROTHEL
(LOOSE —) BAG BIM KIT TIB DRAB FLAP BIMBO TROLL GILLOT HARLOT LIMMER BAGGAGE FRANION TROLLOP
(LOUD-SPOKEN —) RANDY
(LOW OR WORTHLESS —) JADE JURR SLINGDUST
(MARRIED — OF LOWLY STATION) GOODY
(MASCULINE —) AMAZON RULLION CORQUEAN
(MEEK —) GRIZEL
(MYTHOLOGICAL —) HEROINE
(OLD —) GIB HEN BABA TROT CRONE FAGOT FRUMP TROUT BELDAM CARLIN GAMMER GEEZER GRANNY GRANDAM HARRIDAN
(OLD SHRIVELED —) FAGOT FAGGOT
(PEDANTIC —) BLUE
(PERT —) CHIT
(PORTUGESE —) SENHORA
(PREGNANT —) GRAVIDA
(PRIGGISH —) PRUDE
(RUSTIC —) JOAN
(SCOLDING —) SHREW
(SHORT OR STUMPY —) CUTTY
(SHREWISH —) JADE HARPY SKELLAT
(SLATTERNLY —) DRAB FLEABAG
(SLENDER GRACEFUL —) SYLPH
(SLIPSHOD —) MAUX CLATCH TROLLIMOG
(SLOVENLY —) BAG DAW SOW SLUT BESOM TAWPY TROLL TROLLOP SLATTERN
(SPANISH —) DONA GITANA
(SPANISH-INDIAN —) CHOLA
(SPITEFUL —) CAT FURY BITCH
(SQUAT —) TRUB
(SQUEAMISH —) COCKNEY
(STAID —) MATRON
(STATELY —) JUNO
(STORMY VIOLENT —) FURY
(TRACTABLE —) SHEEP
(UGLY —) HAG GORGON
(UNCHASTE —) JILT
(UNMARRIED —) DAME GIRL SPINSTER
(VIXENISH —) HARRIDAN
(WANTON —) MINX TRUB PARNEL
(WICKED —) JEZEBEL
(WISE —) VOLVA ALRUNA ALRUNE
(WITHERED —) CRONE
(YOUNG —) BIT BIRD BURD CHIT DAME DELL DOLL GIRL LASS PUSS BEAST CHICK FILLY FLUFF TOAST DAMSEL HEIFER PIGEON SHEILA SUBDEB BAGGAGE CHICKEN

DAMOZEL FLAPPER WINKLOT
BRISETTE DAUGHTER GRISETTE
WOMAN HATER MISOGYNIST
WOMANISH FEMALE FEMININE
LADYLIKE PETTICOAT
WOMANKIND WOMEN CALICO
MUSLIN FEMINIE
WOMAN'S TONGUE LEBBEK
WOMB BELLY CRADLE UTERUS
WOMBAT KOALA BADGER DIDELPH
VOMBATID
WOMEN DISTAFF
(— OF EARLY CHURCH) SETTERS
AGAPETAE
WON CITY LIVE ROOM ABIDE DWELL
REGION
WONDER AWE MUSE SELI SIGN
TROW UNCO UNKO VERY FARLY
FERLY SELLE SELLY UNCOW
ADMIRE MARVEL MIRATE MAGNALE
MIRABLE MIRACLE PORTENT
PRODIGY STRANGE UNCOUTH
AMERVEIL SELCOUTH SURPRISE
WONDERFUL KEEN SELI FERLY
GRAND GREAT SELLE SWELL
WAKON MIGHTY AMAZING GALLANT
MIRABLE MIRIFIC STRANGE
GLORIOUS MIRABILE WONDROUS
WONDERFULLY AMAZING
WONDER-WORKER THEURGIC
THEURGIST
WONG FIELD GROVE PLAIN MEADOW
WONKY AWRY SHAKY WRONG
UNSTEADY
WONT APT USE FAIN USED VAIN
HABIT USAGE CUSTOM INCLINED
WONTED USUAL HAUNTED
WOO SUE LOVE SEEK SUIT WALE
COURT SPARK SPOON ASSAIL
SPLUNT SUITOR ADDRESS
WOOD (ALSO SEE TREE AND TIMBER)
HAG KIP BOIS BOSK BOWL EKKI
HOLT KIRI MASS MOCK PALO SUPA
TREE WOLE CAHUY CHARK CROWD
EDDER FLOUR GROVE HURST
HYRST RESAK STICK STUFF WEALD
ALMOND ANGILI AUSUBO BRAZIL
EKHIMI FOREST ITAUBA JARANA
LUMBER PALING SPINNY TIMBER
APITONG AVODIRE COPPICE
DADDOCK DUDGEON HAYBOTE
SATINAY VENESIA BAGTIKAN
CRANTARA FIREBOOT
(— BURNT AS PERFUME) AGALLOCH
(— FOR CARPENTRY) STUFF
(— FOR REPAIRING HEDGE) TINING
HAYBOTE
(— OF SMALL EXTENT) GROVE
(— OF THE VERA) VENESIA
(— ON RAFTER) FUR
(— ROTATED ON STRING) ROMBOS
RHOMBOS
(— USEFUL FOR TINDER) PUNK
SPONK TOUCHWOOD
(— YIELDING PERFUME) LINALOA
(BABUL —) SUNT
(BLACK —) EBONY
(CONE-SHAPED PIECE OF —) ACORN
(DARK RED —) RATA

(DENSIFIED —) STAYPAK
(ELASTIC —) SYCAMORE
(FLAT ROUND PIECE OF —)
TRENCHER
(FLEXIBLE —) EDDER
(FOSSIL —) PINITE PEUCITES
(FRAGRANT —) CEDAR
(FUEL —) ESTOVERS
(HARD —) ASH DAO SAL BAKU IPIL
KARI LANA POON ANJAN EBONY
GIDYA KARRI KOKRA MAPLE ZANTE
BANUYO CAMARA FREIJO GIDGEE
KEMPAS SABICU WALNUT CURUPAY
DATTOCK HICKORY GUAIACUM
IRONBARK MAHOGANY
(HEAVY —) DAO EBON EBONY
CHENGAL GUAYABI SUCUPIRA
(LIGHT —) POON BALSA HEMLOCK
(LIMBA —) KORINA
(LOGGED —) CHIP
(LOST —) CHIPPAGE
(LUSTROUS —) LEZA BOARWOOD
(MATCHBOX —) SKILLET
(MOTTLED —) AMBOINA
(NARROW BAR OF —) SLAT
(NUMBER 1 —) DRIVER
(NUMBER 2 —) BRASSIE
(NUMBER 3 —) SPOON
(NUMBER 4 —) CLEEK
(OILY —) BATETE
(OLIVE —) COLLIE
(PETRIFIED —) LITHOXYL
ROCKWOOD
(PINKISH —) BOSSE
(POINTED PIECE OF —) TRIPPET
(REDDISH —) KOA KARI KARRI
ARANGA BANABA CHERRY DUNGON
SATINE KAMBALA
(REDDISH-YELLOW —) GUYO
(ROTTEN —) DADDOCK
(SANDARAC —) ALERCE
(SOFT —) KIRI GABUN GABOON
ELKWOOD AGALLOCH GUATAMBU
(SQUARE LOG OF —) NOG
(STICK OF —) BILLET
(STRIP OF —) LATH STAVE BATTEN
REEPER REGLET
(WATER RESISTING —) AMUBIS
(YELLOWISH —) HALDU FUSTIC
IDIGBO KADAMBA KAMASSI
GUATAMBU
WOOD ANEMONE CYME EMONY
BOWBELLA SNOWDROP
WOODBARK SABLE BLONDINE
WOODBINE BIND WIDBIN EGLATERE
WOODCARVER BODGER
WOODCHUCK CHUG CHUCK MONAX
MARMOT SUSLIK WEJACK MOONACK
GROUNDHOG
WOODCOCK QUIS PEWEE PEWIT
SNIPE SNITE SHRUPS BECASSE
SIMPLETON
WOODCUT BLOCK
WOODCUTTER AXEMAN LOGGER
WOODMAN WOODSMAN
WOOD DUCK SQUEALER BRANCHIER
WOODED BOSKY TREEY HYLEAN
SYLVAN FORESTED
WOODEN DRY DULL STIFF TREEN

CLUMSY STICKY STOLID TIMBER
AWKWARD DEADPAN TIMBERN
LIFELESS
WOOD GUM XYLAN
WOOD HEN WEKA
WOODHEWER PICUCULE
WOOD HOOPOE WHOOP WHOOPE
IRRISOR DUNGBIRD PICARIAN
WOOD HYACINTH SCILLA
CROWTOE GREGGLE HAREBELL
WOOD IBIS STORK GANNET JABIRU
IRONHEAD
WOODLAND DESERT MIOMBO
SPRING
(WASTE —) WEALD
WOODPECKER AWL CHAB JYNX
KATE PEEK ECCLE HECCO HEWEL
ICKLE SPEKT HECKLE NICKLE
PECKER PIANET PICULE SPRITE
TAPPER YAFFLE YUKKEL CLIMBER
CREEPER FLICKER HEWHOLE
HICKWAY LOGCOCK REDHEAD
SAPSUCK SNAPPER SPEIGHT
WHETILE WITWALL WRYNECK
DIRTBIRD KICKWALL PICARIAN
PICUCULE POPINJAY RAINBIRD
RAINFOWL WALLHICK
(LIKE A —) PICIFORM
WOODPILE STRAN STRAND
WOODRICK
WOOD ROBIN MIRO TOMTIT
WOODRUFF HAIROF MUGGET
MUGWET WOODROW HAIRHOOF
WOODS BOSK BUSH BOSQUE
WOODSMAN BUSHY SILVAN SYLVAN
BUSHMAN BUSHWACK
WOOD SORREL OCA COCKOO
HEARTS LUJULA OXALIS TREFOIL
ALLELUIA ALLELUJA SHAMROCK
STABWORT
WOOD THRUSH MAYBIRD
WOODTURNER BODGER
WOODWIND OBOE FLUTE CORNET
BASSOON PIBGORN PICCOLO
CLARINET
WOODWORK CEILING
WOODWORKER JOINER TURNER
MILLMAN
WOODWORM GRIBBLE
WOODY WITHY FRITHY STICKY
SYLVAN XYLOID LIGNOSE LIGNEOUS
WOOER BEAU LOVER WOWER
SUITOR COURTER WOOSTER
COURTIER PARAMOUR
WOOF WEFT WOUGH FILLING
TEXTURE
WOOING SUIT WOHLAC
WOOL OO COT DAG HOG VOL WOW
BEAT BLUE FRIB PULU ROCK FADGE
LAINE MUNGO STUFF TIPPY ALPACA
ARGALI BOTANY BREECH FLEECE
GREASE JACKET JERSEY KERSEY
LUSTER SLIVER WETHER COMBING
HASLOCK KASHMIR MORLING
STUBBLE WIGGING CASHMERE
CLOTHING COMEBACK MORTLING
PICKLOCK TOMENTUM
(— AS IT COMES FROM SHEEP)
GREASE

(— **FROM DEAD SHEEP**) MORLING MORTLING
(— **FROM LEOMINSTER**) ORE
(— **ON SHEEP'S LEG**) GARE BREECH
(— **ON SHEEP'S THROAT**) HASLOCK
(— **WEIGHT**) TOD
(**COARSE** —) ABB SHAG BRAID COWTAIL
(**COTTON** —) CADDIS CADDICE
(**DUNGY BIT OF** —) FRIB
(**FINE GRADE OF** —) PICKLOCK SPINNERS
(**GREASY** —) TIPPY
(**INFERIOR GRADE OF** —) HEAD
(**KNOT OF** —) NOIL
(**LAMB'S** —) WASSAIL
(**LOCK OF** —) FLOCK STAPLE
(**LONG** —) BLUE
(**LOW GRADE OF** —) LIVERY
(**MATTED** —) DAG SHAG
(**PULLED** —) SLIPE
(**RECLAIMED** —) MUNGO SHODDY
(**REFUSE** —) COT COTT FLOCK PINION
(**ROLL OF** —) CARDING
(**RUSSIAN** —) DONSKY
(**SMALL PIECE OF** —) TATE
(**SPUN** —) YARN
(**WOUND** —) TREND
WOOLCLOTH HODDEN
WOOLEN (ALSO SEE FABRIC) CADDIS CAMLET SUCLAT CADDICE PASHMINA
(PL.) LAINAGE
WOOL FAT LANOLIN
WOOLLY SHEEP LANATE LANOSE COTTONY FLOCCOSE PERONATE
WOOLLY BEAR WOUBIT
WOOLLY CROTON HOGWORT
WOOZY SICK DRUNK TIGHT VAGUE BLURRY WOOLLY
WORD GIG MOT EZEL GULE HAIT NEWS RAFF TERM VERB WHID WHUD ADNEX CHEEP COUCH DERRY DILLY FITCH GLOSS HAPAX HOKEY HYNDE LEMMA MAXIM ORDER PAROL RHEMA RUMOR SPELL ACCENT ADVERB AVOWAL BREATH ETYMON KIBBER LATIVE ONEYER PAROLE PLEDGE QUATCH REMARK REPORT SAYING ACCOUNT ADJUNCT BICCHED COMMAND COMMENT DICTION DUCDAME GENTILE GITTITH HOMONYM INCIPIT MESSAGE PALABRA PRAYFUL PRENZIE PROMISE PROVERB SYNONYM VOCABLE ACROSTIC CATCHCRY CHEVILLE COMPOUND ENCLITIC EQUIVOKE FRABJOUS FRINGENT IDEOGRAM ILLATIVE LATINISM SYLLABLE SYNTAGMA
(— **AS CALL TO DUCK**) DILLY
(— **EXPRESSING COMMAND**) JUSSIVE
(— **FORMED FROM VOWELS**) EUOUAE
(— **FROM INITIAL LETTERS**) ACRONYM
(— **IN A PUZZLE**) LIGHT

(— **MISPRONOUNCED**) BEARD
(— **OF CONCLUSION**) AMEN EXPLICIT
(— **OF HONOR**) PAROLE
(— **OF MOUTH**) FIDELITY
(— **OF OPPOSITE MEANING**) ANTONYM
(— **OF SECONDARY RANK**) ADNEX
(— **OF UNCERTAIN MEANING**) FRINGENT
(— **OF UNKNOWN MEANING**) KIBBER ONEYER PRAYFUL PRENZIE
(—**S IN LOW TONE**) ASIDE
(—**S OF OPERA**) LIBRETTO
(**BIBLICAL** — **OF DOUBTFUL MEANING**) EZEL FITCH GITTITH
(**CALL** —) JINGO
(**CHARACTERIZING** —) EPITHET
(**CODE** —) DOG FOX JIG ABLE EASY ECHO GOLF ITEM KING BRAVO DELTA HOTEL INDIA SUGAR GEORGE CHARLIE
(**GATHERING** —) SLOGAN
(**HONEYED** —S) MANNA
(**HYPHENATED** —) SOLID
(**IDENTIFYING** —) LABEL
(**LAST** — **OF SPEECH**) CUE
(**MEANINGLESS** —) DERRY
(**METAPHORICAL** —) KENNING
(**MNEMONIC** —) VIBGYOR
(**NONSENSE** —) RAFF RAFFE FRABJOUS
(**ORIGINAL** —) STEM
(**PARTING** —) ENVOI
(**QUOTED** —) CITATION
(**REDUNDANT** —) CHEVILLE
(**ROOT** —) ETYMON
(**SIGNAL** —) NAYWORD SECURITY
(**SINGLE** —) PHRASE
(**SOURCE** —) ETYMON
(**THIEVES' SLANG** —) TWAG WHID
(**UNEXPLAINED** —) DUCDAME
(**UTTERED** —S) SPEECH
(PL.) LIP TALK SPEECH LANGUAGE DISCOURSE
WORDBOOK LEXICON SPELLER LIBRETTO
WORDINESS VERBIAGE
WORDING LEGEND DICTION PHRASING
WORDLESS DUMB TACIT SILENT TACITURN
WORDPLAY EQUIVOKE
WORDY PROLIX VERBAL DIFFUSE VERBOSE WORDISH
WORK DO GO ACT FAG JOB DIKE DYKE FEND FRET NOTE OPUS TASK TEND TOIL GRAFT GRIND KARMA KNEAD LABOR PRESS YAKKA ARBEIT EFFECT HUSTLE OE1VRE REDUIT RESULT STRIVE THRIFT CALLING EXECUTE EXPLOIT FERMENT HEXAPLA LOUSTER MISSION OPERATE OPIFICE OPUSCLE OUVRAGE OVERAGE PICHERY PURSUIT TRAVAIL ADVOCACY AGENTING BUSINESS CAPONIER DEMILUNE DRUDGERY ENDEAVOR FUNCTION INDUSTRY

LABORAGE OPUSCULE PARERGON RETRENCH EXECUTION
(— **ACROSS GRAIN**) THURM
(— **ACTIVELY**) LOUSTER
(— **AGAINST**) KNIFE ATTACK COMBAT
(— **AIMLESSLY**) FIDDLE
(— **AS REPORTER**) HEEL
(— **BEYOND ONE'S POWERS**) OVERDO
(— **CARELESSLY**) RABBLE
(— **DILIGENTLY**) PEG STRIKE BELABOR
(— **DONE**) WRIHTE
(— **FOR**) LABOR SERVE BESWINK
(— **FREE**) START
(— **HARD**) TEW MOIL SLOG SWOT BULLOCK LEATHER
(— **HIDES**) BEAM
(— **INSIDUOUSLY**) WORM
(— **INTO A MASS**) KNEAD
(— **LAND**) FLOAT
(— **LEISURELY**) DAKER DAIKER
(— **OCCASIONALLY**) SMOOT SMOUT
(— **OF ACKNOWLEDGED EXCELLENCE**) CLASSIC
(— **OF ART**) GEM CRAFT ANTIQUE CAPRICE CREATION EPIPHANY EXERCISE
(— **OF FICTION**) SHOCKER
(— **OF HISTORY**) STORY
(— **OF MENIAL KIND**) DRUDGE
(— **ONE'S WAY**) WISE
(— **OUT IN ADVANCE**) FOREPLOT
(— **OUT**) FUDGE SOLVE DESIGN EVOLVE
(— **OVER**) DIGEST
(— **PAID FOR IN ADVANCE**) HORSE
(— **PERSISTENTLY**) HAMMER
(— **RESEMBLING PATCHWORK**) CENTO
(— **SLIPSHOD**) MULLOCK
(— **STEADILY**) PLY
(— **TO EXHAUSTION**) FAG
(— **TO WINDWARD**) CLAW
(— **TOGETHER**) COACT
(— **TRIFLINGLY**) PIDDLE
(— **UNDER ANOTHER NAME**) ALLONYM
(— **UNFAIRLY OR CRUELLY**) HORSE
(— **UP**) SPUNK
(— **UPON**) TILL LABOR
(— **UPWARD**) HIKE
(— **VIGOROUSLY**) BEND
(**ALLEGORICAL** —) BESTIARY
(**CANVAS** —) POINT
(**CLEANING** —) CHAR
(**CLUMSY** —) BOTCH
(**COMPLETED** —) TRAVAIL
(**CONTRACT** —) GYPPO
(**DAMASCENE** —) KOFTGARI
(**DAY'S** —) DARG DARGUE
(**DECORATIVE** —) FLOCKING
(**DIVINE** —) THEURGY
(**DULL** —) DRUDGERY
(**EMBOSSED** —) CELATURE
(**FRAUDULENT** —) JERRY
(**HAND** —) CAMAY
(**HARD** —) TEW MOIL MUCK SWOT

TWIG YERK SWEAT EFFORT
LEATHER SLAVERY SLOGGING
(JOINER —) FINISH
(LITERARY —) STUDY CHASER
SEQUEL SERIAL CLASSIC DIPTYCH
(LURID —) BLOOD
(MANUAL —) FATIGUE
(METAL —) NIELLO
(MOSAIC —) EMBLEM
(ORNAMENTAL —) BEADWORK
FILIGREE LEAFWORK
(PIECE OF —) JOB
(REFERENCE —) BIBLE SOURCE
(SACRED —) HIERURGY
(SCHOLASTIC —) SUMMA
(SKILLED MECHANICAL —) SLOJD
SLOYD
(SOCIAL —) ALMONING
(WOMAN'S —) DISTAFF
(PL.) CANON PLANT STODGE
FACTORY BUSINESS
WORKABLE YOUNG PLIANT
FEASIBLE
(EASILY —) SWEET
WORKADAY HUMDRUM PROSAIC
ORDINARY
WORKBASKET CABA
WORKBENCH SIEGE DONKEY
TEMPLATE
WORKED INWROUGHT
(— OUT) DEAD
(— UP) ANGRY EXCITED
WORKER (ALSO SEE WORKMAN AND
LABORER) AGER CARL DOER HAND
HIND ICER SCAB AXMAN BOXER
BUTTY DEMAS DRIER EDGER ENDER
FILER FIRER FIXER FLYER FOXER
GLUER GORER HOLER INKER JERRY
LINER LURER MAXIM MINIM NURSE
TAPER TOWER ASHMAN BACKER
BAILER BALLER BANDER BEADER
BENDER BINDER BINMAN BLADER
BLOWER BOILER BONDER BOOKER
BOSHER BRACER BUFFER BUMPER
BURNER BURRER CAPPER CARMAN
CASTER CASUAL CHASER COMBER
COOKER DAYMAN DIPPER DOCKER
DOGGER DOTTER DUMPER ETCHER
FACTOR FAGGER FANMAN FASHER
FEEDER FELLER FILLER FITTER
FLAKER FLAMER FLUTER FLUXER
FOILER FOLDER FORCER FORMER
FRAMER GASSER GOFFER GRADER
GUMMER GUTTER HASHER HEADER
HEELER HELPER HEMMER HOLDER
HOOKER HOOPER HOPPER HUNKIE
INKMAN JOGGER JOINER LEAFER
LEASER LEGGER NOILER PUGGER
READER REEDER SCORER SEAMAN
SEAMER SHAKER SKIVER SLAKER
SLICER SLIDER SLOPER STAVER
STAYER TOILER TOPPER BUILDER
CREATOR EMPLOYE FIELDER
LABORER
(— IN LEATHER) BEAMER CHUMAR
JACKER BLACKER CHUCKLER
(— IN METALS) SMITH FLAPPER
(ADDITIONAL —) EXTRA
(AGRICULTURAL —) ARKIE KISAN

(AIRCRAFT —) BOOTMAN
(ANT —) MAXIM ERGATES REPLETE
(ASBESTOS —) COBBER
(AUTO —) DISKER
(BAKERY —) BRAKER COOLER
DIVIDER BENCHMAN SPREADER
(BLUE-COLLAR —) STIFF
(BREWERY —) HOPPER STEEPER
STILLMAN
(BRICK —) DAUBER CROWDER
(CANNERY —) SLIMER SCALDER
SHEDMAN
(CLOCK —) STAKER
(COAL —) SUMPER GEORDIE
SPRAGGER
(DOCK —) BUNGS HOLDMAN
SHENANGO
(DOMESTIC —) HELP
(FELLOW —) CONFRERE
(FOUNDRY —) FLOGGER SNAGGER
(GARMENT —) FACER SLEEVER
ASSORTER INSEAMER
(GUN —) BLUER
(HARD —) SLOGGER
(HAT —) CURLER BRIMMER
(HIDE —) HEFTER COLORER
(HOSPITAL —) ALMONER
(HOTEL —) SCRUB
(ICEHOUSE —) AIRMAN
(JEWELRY —) ARBORER
(LOGGING —) SNIPER SKIDDER
(MATTRESS —) BEATER
(MIGRATORY —) HOBO
(MILL —) BILLER SPOUTER
(MINE —) BYEMAN FOOTER GOPHER
LANDER DROPPER FACEMAN
SLEDGER SWAMPER DRIFTMAN
(ORCHARD —) SMUDGER
(PACKINGHOUSE —) COOK
(PAPERMILL —) SIZER SIZEMAN
(PIANO —) BELLYMAN
(PLODDING —) GRUBBER
(POTTERY —) CASER BATTER
BEDDER FETTLER JOLLIER JUSTLER
(PRINTING —) FLY FLYBOY
(PUERTO RICAN —) GIBARO JIBARO
(QUARRY —) BREAKER
(RAILROAD —) JERRY HERDER
BRAKEMAN
(SAWMILL —) BOLTER SETTER
BOATMAN DECKMAN CHAINMAN
(SHOE —) CASER FOXER ARCHER
FUDGER HEELER CHALKER
BOTTOMER
(SKILLED —) ARTISTE
(SLAUGHTERHOUSE —) FATTER
SHOVER SINGER SLIMER CHEEKER
CHOPPER KNOCKER LIMEMAN
SCALPER SCRIBER STICKER
SNATCHER
(TANNERY —) GATER STONER
CROPPER CURRIER DELIMER
BEAMSMAN SEASONER
(TEXTILE —) DOFFER DOUPER
DRAWER GIGGER LAPPER LEASER
SINGER CREELER DOUBLER
JACKMAN KETTLER SKEINER
SPINNER SHUTTLER SOFTENER
SPLITTER TEASELER

(THEATER —) FLYMAN STAGEMAN
(TOBACCO —) BULKER SIFTER
STEMMER SCRAPMAN SPRIGGER
STICKMAN STRIPPER
(UNSKILLED —) HELPER DILUTEE
GREENER
(USELESS —) TOOL
(WHITE-COLLAR —) EFFENDI
(YARN —) SOURER CHAINER
(PL.) LABOR
WORKHORSE AVER AIVER TRESTLE
SAWHORSE
WORKHOUSE UNION FACTORY
WORKSHOP
WORKING PLAY GOING OPENCUT
FUNCTION LABORAGE OPENCAST
OPENWORK OPERATIC
(— ALONE) HATTING
(— HARD) HOPPING
(— OF MINE) GWAG CROSSCUT
(— ON) PRACTICE
(MINE —S) SPLIT
WORKMAN (ALSO SEE WORKER AND
LABORER) BOSS HAND MATE ROTO
CAGER CONER EXTRA FINER FLINT
FLUER FROCK LAYER MAJOR MIXER
POLER TONER TRIER TUBER
BLOUSE BOOMER BOWLER BUCKER
BUMMER COATER DIPPER DRIVER
FORKER GAGGER HANGER LASTER
LATHER MASTER NIPPER OILMAN
PUFFER RUNNER SAMMER SCORER
SHAKER SKIVER SLICER SLIDER
SOAKER SPIKER STAGER STAVER
TAPPER TARRER TEEMER TILTER
TIPMAN TIPPER TOPMAN WARMER
WASHER WETTER WRIGHT ARTISAN
DRUMMER HOTSHOT LUDDITE
SHOPMAN
(CHIEF —) BOSS
(CLUMSY —) BUNGLER
(FELLOW —) BULLY BUTTY
(PROFICIENT —) DEACON
(UNSKILLFUL —) BUTCHER
(PL.) VOLK
WORKMANLIKE DEFT ADEPT
SKILLFUL
WORKMANSHIP HAND FABRIC
OVERAGE ARTISANRY
WORKROOM DEN STUDY ATELIER
WORKS HACIENDA
(— OF CLOCK) WATCH
(SALT —) SALINA
WORKSHOP LAB SHED SHOP FORGE
LODGE SMITHY ATELIER BOTTEGA
HOSPITAL OFFICINA PLUMBERY
SKINNERY
WORKTABLE BENCH
WORLD ORB LOKA VALE WARD
EARTH WADRU WARDE CAREER
PUBLIC KINGDOM MONDIAL
CREATION CREATURE UNIVERSE
(— OF BOXING) FISTIANA
(— OF DARKNESS) SHEOL
(— OF DOGS) DOGDOM
(— OF FASHION) STYLEDOM
SWELLDOM
(— OF GODS) DEVALOKA
(— OF THE DEAD) DEEP

(— OF WOMEN) FEMINIE
(ACADEMIC —) CAMPUS
(EXTERNAL —) NONEGO
(LOWER —) ORCUS
(PRIVATE —) AUTOCOSM
(THE —) FOLD
(TWO-DIMENSIONAL —) FLATLAND
WORLDLING DIVES
WORLDLY LAY WARLY CARNAL
EARTHY MUNDAL EARTHLY FLESHLY
MUNDANE PROFANE SECULAR
SENSUAL TERRENE
(NOT —) INTERIOR
WORLD-WEARY BLASE
WORLDWIDE GLOBAL ECUMENIC
GLOBULAR PLANETAL
WORLD-WISE KNOWING
WORM BOB EEL ESS LOA MAD LURG
NAIS NEMA ARTER CADEW FLUKE
LYTTA PIPER SCREW SNAKE
DRAGON NEREID NEREIS PALMER
PALOLO SHAMIR SYLLID SYLLIS
TEREDO VERMIS WRETCH ANNELID
ASCARID CARBORA ENOPLAN
SABELLA SAGITTA SERPENT
SERPULA SETARID SHUFFLE SPIONID
TAGTAIL TRICLAD WRIGGLE
BRANDLIN CEPHALOB CERCARIA
CHETAPOD CHETOPOD GILTTAIL
HELMINTH LEODICID MEASURER
POLYCLAD STRONGYL TRICHINA
VERMICLE TOOTHACHE
(— USED FOR BAIT) TAGTAIL
(BLOODSUCKING —) LEECH
(CADDIS —) CADEW PIPER CADBAIT
(FLUKE —) PLAICE
(MEASURING —) LOOPER
(MUD —) IPO LOA
(SHIP —) BROMA COBRA
(PL.) APODA ENTOZOA
WORM-EATEN PITTED DECAYED
VERMOULU WERMETHE
WORMER JAG
WORMHOLE PIQURE
WORMLIKE VERMIAN
WORMSEED AMBROSIA
WORMWOOD MOXA ABSINTH
CUDWEED COMPOSIT MINGWORT
WORMY EARTHY
WORN SEAR SERE USED PASSE
TRITE MAGGED MIZPAH SHABBY
CONTRITE
(— NEXT TO SKIN) INTIMATE
(— OUT) SHOT BANAL JADED SEELY
SPENT STALE STANK BEATEN
BEDRID BLEARY EFFETE SCREWY
SHABBY CRIPPLE FORWORN
DECREPID FOUGHTEN HARASSED
OBSOLETE STRICKEN
(— SMOOTH) BEATEN
WORRICOW DEVIL BUGABOO
BUGBEAR HOBGOBLIN
WORRIED TOEY UNEASY ANXIOUS
FRETTED STREAKED
WORRIT VEX WORRY DISTRESS
WORRY DOG HOE HOW HOX LUG
NAG RUX TEW VEX BAIT BITE CARE
CARK FAZE FIKE FRAB FRET FUSS
HARE MOIL STEW ANNOY CHEVY

CHOKE FEEZE GALLY HARRY HURRY
LURRY PHASE SCALD SHAKE TEASE
TOUSE TOWSE BOTHER CADDLE
COTTER CUMBER FERRET FIDGET
GALLOW HARASS HATTER HECTOR
INFEST MOIDER PESTER PLAGUE
POTHER ANXIETY CHAGRIN
HATCHEL TROUBLE TURMOIL
WHERRET FASHERIE STRANGLE
WORRYING ANXIOUS
WORSE VER WAR SEAMY
WORSEN DESCEND
WORSHIP GOD CULT HERY RANK
ADORE DULIA HONOR NAMAZ
WURTH YAJNA CREDIT PRAISE
REPUTE REVERE BAALISM ELOHISM
ICONISM IDOLISM IDOLIZE IMAGERY
OBSERVE BLESSING HIERURGY
VENERATE
(— OF SHAKESPEARE) BARDOLATRY
(FORM OF —) RITUAL
(HIGHEST KIND OF —) LATRIA
(INFERIOR KIND OF —) DULIA
(SERPENT —) OPHISM
(STAR —) SABAISM
WORSHIPER ISIAC BHAKTA PRAISER
IDOLATER
(— OF STARS) AKKUM SABIAN
(FIRE —) PARSI GHEBER GUEBER
PARSEE
(SERPENT —) SETHIAN SETHITE
WORSHIPFUL GOOD PROUD
NOTABLE
WORST ACE GET BEST LAST OUTDO
SHEND WREST DEFEAT
WORSTED GARN JERRY SERGE
VESSES WHIPCORD
WORT GAIL GYLE SWAT PLANT
LENGTH TUTSAN FILLING KRAUSEN
POTHERB
(FERMENTED —) FEED WASH
(UNFERMENTED —) GROUT
WORTH FECK MEED CARAT MERIT
PRICE VALOR VALUE BECOME
BOUNTY DESERT ESTEEM REGARD
RICHES VALENT VIRTUE WEALTH
DIGNITY PRETIUM VALIANT WORSHIP
SPLENDOR TREASURE VALIDITY
VALLIDOM
(NET —) CAPITAL
WORTHINESS DESERT WORSHIP
WORTHLESS BAD LOW WAF BAFF
BALD BARE BASE EVIL IDLE LEWD
RACA SLIM VAIN VILE WAFF BLANK
BLOWN DUSTY FLASH FOUTY LOSEL
PUTID SLINK SORRY STRAW WASHY
CHAFFY CHEESY CRUMMY DRAFFY
DRASTY DROSSY HOLLOW LIMMER
LITHER LUTHER NAUGHT PALTRY
TRASHY WOODEN BAGGAGE
FUSTIAN NAUGHTY PIPERLY
RAFFISH RUBBISH SCABBED SHILPIT
USELESS FECKLESS HARLOTRY
NUGATORY PRECIOUS RASCALLY
RUBBISHY TRUMPERY VAGABOND
WANWORDY WRETCHED
(— THING) AMBSACE
WORTHLESSNESS BELIAL UNTHRIFT
WORTHWHILE TANTI

WORTHY BIG DEAR FAIR GOOD
HOLY TIDY AUGHT CANNY DIGNE
EXALT HONOR JELLY NOBLE PIOUS
GENTLE CONDIGN GRADELY
PAREGAL THRIFTY ELIGIBLE
VALUABLE WAUREGAN
(— OF BELIEF) CREDIBLE
(— OF DEVOTION) HOLY
(— OF PRAISE) LAUDABLE
WOULD WAD WID WANT WISH
COULD SHOULD
(— NOT) NOLD WADNA WADDENT
(I —) CHUD CHOLD
WOUND ARR CUT HEW WIN BITE
CALK CLAW DUNT FAKE FOIN GALL
GORE HARM HURT MAIM PAIN PINK
RASE RAZE RIST SCAR SKAG SORE
STAB TEAR VULN WING BLESS
BROKE GANCH GRIEF KNIFE KNOCK
SHOOT STICK STING SUGAT THIRL
TOUCH BREACH BRUISE CREASE
ENTAME GRIEVE HARROW INJURE
LAUNCH LESION MARTYR OFFEND
PIERCE PLAGUE SCOTCH TRAUMA
AFFLICT ATTAINT BLIGHTY DIACOPE
GUNSHOT SCRATCH DISTRESS
FLANKARD FLEABITE INCISION
LACERATE SPURGALL
(— FROM BOAR'S TUSK) GANCH
GAUNCH
(— FROM BULL'S HORN) CORNADA
(— FROM RUBBING) GALL
(— IN DEER'S SIDE) FLANKARD
(— MADE BY THRUST) FOIN
(— ON FOOT) FIKE
(— WITH POINTED WEAPON) STAB
SWORD
(DEEP —) DIACOPE
(MINUTE —) PRICK
(TRIFLING —) FLEABITE
(PL.) NOUNS
WOUNDED HURT WUND VULNED
WINGED VULNOSE STRICKEN
WOUNDWORT BETONY ALLHEAL
HERCULES
WOU-WOU WAWA WAWAH CAMPER
GIBBON
WOVEN BROCHE BROWDEN
DAMASSE
(— FULL WIDTH) SEAMLESS
(— WIDE) BROAD
(— WITH RIB) SOLEIL
WOW HIT MEW BARK HOWL RAVE
WAIL WHINE SUCCESS
WRACK KELP RACK RUIN CUTWEED
DESTROY DOWNFALL EELGRASS
WRECKAGE
WRAITH WAFT FETCH GHOST SPOOK
DOUBLE SHADOW SWARTH
SPECTRE
WRANGLE RAG YED CAMP MOIL
SPAR TIFT ARGLE ARGUE BRAWL
CHIDE DAFER FLITE JOWER PLEAD
STRUT ARGUFY BICKER CAFFLE
CAMPLE CANGLE DACKER FRAPLE
FRATCH HAGGLE HASSLE JANGLE
RAGGLE THREAP BRABBLE
BRANGLE DISPUTE PICKEER

QUARREL SCRAFFLE SQUABBLE TIRRWIRR

WRANGLER CAMPER COWBOY GRATER HAFTER WRAGER DEBATER DEFENDER OPPONENT

WRANGLING JANGLE

WRAP HAP LAP LOT WAP BIND FURL ROLL WHIP CLASP CLOAK LAMBA MANTA NUBIA SERVE TWINE WOOLD AFGHAN BURLAP CLOTHE COCOON COOLER DOLMAN EMBALE MOIDER MUFFLE PATTOO SWATHE WRIXLE ENVELOP INVOLVE SWADDLE UMBELAP BARRACAN
(— DEAD BODY) CERE
(— ONESELF) HUDDLE
(— UP HEAD) MOB MOP MOBLE
(— UP) HAP MAIL ENROL IMPLY
(— WIRE AROUND FISHING LINE) GANGE
(— WITH BANDAGE) SWATHE
(PL.) SECRECY RESTRAINT

WRAPPER APRON COVER MOTTO PILCH SHAWL SMOCK COUPON FARDEL JACKET ENVELOP OVERALL SARPLER COVERING MAHARMAH WOOLPACK
(— FOR BOOK) JACKET
(— FOR CUTLET) PAPILLOTE
(— WORN IN EGYPT) GALABIA GALABEAH

WRAPPING WAP PACK GELILAH LAPPING COVERING MANTLING
(— FOR DEAD) CEREMENT
(— OF HEBREW SCROLL) GELILAH
(— OF ROPE) SERVICE

WRASSE COOK BALLAN CONNER CUNNER LABRID HOGFISH PIGFISH SEAWIFE CORKWING DONCELLA JANIZARY LADYFISH SENORITA

WRATH IRE FURY GRIM ANGER WROTH FELONY PASSION VIOLENCE

WRATHFUL IRY EVIL HIGH ANGRY IRATE WROTH IREFUL RAGING FURIOUS JEALOUS CHOLERIC

WREAK CAUSE AVENGE EXPEND GRATIFY INDULGE INFLICT REVENGE
(— DESTRUCTION) ESTREPE

WREATH LEI ORLE PLAY CROWN GREEN LAURE LORRE OLIVE TORSE WHORL WRASE ANADEM CRANTS CREASE LAUREL POTONG TORTIL CHAPLET CORONET CROWNAL DOLPHIN FESTOON GARLAND WRINKLE KELYPHYTE
(SPIRAL —) VOLUTION

WREATHE BIND WIND CRISP TWINE TWIST INTORT WRITHE CONTORT ENTWINE INTWIST INVOLVE

WREATHED SPIRY TORTIVE WRITHED INTORTED TORTILLE

WRECK HULK RUIN BLAST CRACK SHOOT SMASH WRACK DESPOIL DESTROY FOUNDER GODSEND SHATTER TORPEDO DEMOLISH SABOTAGE SHAMBLES
(HUMAN —) DERELICT

WRECKAGE FINDAL FLOTSAM GODSEND WAVESON SHAMBLES

WRECKED NOUGHT

WREN GIRL STAG TOPE CUTTY JENNY KITTY PEGGY SALLY STAID TYDIE SCUTTY TIDIFE TIDLEY TINTIE TOMTIT WRANNY BLUECAP MALURINE WRANNOCK

WRENCH KEY PIN RUG PULL RACK RICK RUGG TEAR YERK CRICK CRINK FORCE THRAW THROW TWIST WRAMP WREST BEDKEY SPRAIN STRAIN TWEEZE DISTORT SPANNER SPANULE SQUINCH TORTURE TWISTLE

WREST REAR REND EXACT FORCE TWIST ARREST EXTORT WRENCH WRITHE ABSTORT WIREDRAW
(— AWAY) STRIP DESPOIL

WRESTLE PRAY RASSLE SQUIRM TUSSLE WRAXLE WRITHE GRAPPLE SCUFFLE THRIMBLE THRUMBLE

WRESTLER MATMAN WELTER CLICKER MATSTER GRAPPLER

WRESTLING SUMO PALESTRA WRAXLING
(— TECHNIQUE) GLIMA

WRETCH DOG MIX FILE WARY MISER SLAVE THING BUGGER PERSON SQUALL BRETHEL CAITIFF CAMOOCH CHINCHE GLUTTON HILDING SCROYLE CREATURE MESCHANT POLTROON RECREANT SCULLION

WRETCHED EVIL FOUL MEAN DAWNY DEENY GAUNT WISHT WOFUL YEMER CAITIF DISMAL MEAGER PALTRY SHABBY SICKLY UNLEAD UNLEDE WOEFUL ABYSMAL BENEATH FORLORN OUTWORN SQUALID UNSEELY MESCHANT
(— PERSON OR ANIMAL) MISERY

WRIGGLE REG RIG FRIG WIND WRIG SLIDE WRELE WRING SQUIRM WAMBLE WANGLE WARPLE WIDDLE WIMPLE WINTLE WRITHE EYEBROW SNIGGLE TWIDDLE TWINGLE WRABILL WRESTLE SCRIGGLE SQUIGGLE

WRIGGLING EELY SCRIGGLE SQUIGGLY

WRIGGLY SNAKY SNAKISH SQUIRMING

WRING RACK DRAIN EXACT SCREW TWIST WREST EXTORT OPPRESS SQUEEZE TORMENT TORTURE
(— THE NECK) SCRAG

WRINGER RUNG WRUNG SQUEEZER

WRINKLE RUT DRAW FOLD FURL HINT KNIT LIRK RUCK RUGA SEAM BREAK CRIMP CRISP DELVE FAULT FRILL REEVE RIVEL SNIRL BUCKLE COCKLE CRAVAT CREASE FURROW METHOD PUCKER RIMPLE RUMPLE RUNKLE SCRIMP WREATH BLEMISH CRINKLE CRUMPLE CRUNKLE FROUNCE FRUMPLE CONTRACT IRRUGATE RUGOSITY
(— OF FLESH) CRAVAT

WRINKLED PURFLY RUGATE RUGGED RUGOSE RUGOUS SEAMED

COCKLED SAVOYED CRUMPLED FURROWED PUCKERED WRIZZLED

WRINKLING KNIT KNOT FROWN

WRIST CARPUS SHACKLE

WRISTER MUFFETEE

WRISTLET WRISTER MUFFETEE

WRISTWATCH BAGUET BAGUETTE

WRIT AIEL CAPE MISE PONE TOLT ALIAS BREVE BRIEF ERROR RECTO UTRUM BRIEVE CAPIAS ELEGIT EXTENT VENIRE ACCOUNT DEDIMUS DETINUE EXIGENT LATITAT PLURIES PRECEPT PROCESS SUMMONS WARRANT CESSAVIT COSINAGE DETAINER DOCUMENT FORMEDON MANDAMUS MITTIMUS NOVERINT PRAECIPE QUOMINUS REPLEVIN SUBPOENA TESTATUM WARRANTY
(— FOR SUMMONING EXTRA JURORS) TALES

WRITE INK PEN BACK BOOK DITE DRAW READ CLERK DRAFT STYLE AUTHOR ENFACE INDITE SCRIBE SCRIVE ADDRESS COMPILE COMPOSE DICTATE EMPAPER EXARATE BIOGRAPH INSCRIBE
(— ADDRESS) BACK
(— BRIEFLY) JOT
(— CARELESSLY) DASH SCRAWL SCRIBBLE
(— DOWN) SIGN BREVE DENOTE RECORD AMORTIZE DESCRIBE
(— FURTHER) ADD
(— HASTILY) SCRATCH SCRIBBLE SQUIGGLE
(— IN A LARGE HAND) ENGROSS
(— IN LARGE CHARACTERS) TEXT
(— ON FRONT OF BILL) ENFACE
(— PASTORAL POEMS) PHILLIS
(— WHAT IS NOT TRUE) FABLE

WRITER PEN BARD HACK PUFF ALVAR GHOST ODIST SQUIB AUTHOR FATHER GLOZER HEROIC LAWYER LETTER MUNSHI NOTARY PENMAN PRABHU PROSER PURVOE SCRIBE TRAGIC YEOMAN ADAPTER ADSMITH ANALYST DIARIST ELOHIST ESSAYER GLOSSER GNOMIST HYMNIST IAMBIST JUVENAL LAUDIST MUNCHEE PENSTER PROPHET PROSAIC REVUIST SCRIVER STYLIST SUMMIST TEXTMAN AUGUSTAN BLURBIST COMEDIAN COMPOSER DECADENT DECADIST DIDACTIC EMBOSSER EPISTLER ESSAYIST FABLEIST FABULIST GROMATIC HUMORIST IDYLLIST MONODIST MOONSHEE NOVELIST PARODIST PENWOMAN PREFACER PRESSMAN PROSAIST PROSEMAN PSALMIST REVIEWER SCRIPTER VERSEMAN
(— OF BURLESQUE) GABBER
(FREE-LANCE —) CREEPER
(HACK —) PENSTER
(INCOMPETENT —) BOTCHER

WRITHE WRY WIND THROW TWIRL TWIST WRING SQUIRM TERVEE WAMBLE WRABBE WRENCH AGONIZE WRESTLE WRIGGLE

WRINGLE CONVOLVE
WRITHING EELY WRING WRITHY
WRITING BOOK FAIT PAGE POEM
KANJI LIBEL CADJAN GOSSIP
LEGEND LETTER PAGINE SCRIPT
SCRITE SCRIVE UNCIAL ARTICLE
DIPLOMA ESCRIPT SCREEVE
F.POCRYPH CONTRACT DOCUMENT
GRAVAMEN HARANGUE KAKEMONO
LETTRURE LIPOGRAM PAMPHLET
SCRIBING SONNETRY
(— OF LITTLE VALUE) STUFF
SCRIBBLE
(— ON PAPER SCROLL) MAKIMONO
(— ON SILK) KAKEMONO
(— UNDER SEAL) BOND
(BITTER —) DIATRIBE
(CARELESS —) SCRAWL
(CRAMPED —) NIGGLE
(CURSIVE —) JOINHAND
(HUMOROUS —S) FACETIAE
(ILLUMINATED —) FRACTUR
(MUSICAL —) GIMEL GYMEL
(PRETENTIOUS —) FUSTIAN
(SACRED —) ARANYAKA BRAHMANA
SCRIPTURE
(SHORT —) SCRIP
(SYLLABIC —) KANA
(VAPID —) WASH
(VERBOSE —) TOOTLE
(PL.) LEGENDA ARANYAKA
POSTHUMA
WRITING CASE STANDISH
WRITTEN KĘTIB KETHIB KTHIBH
GRAPHIC LITERAL

(— ABOVE) SS
(— AFTER) ADSCRIPT
(— HASTILY) STRAY
WROCLAW BRESLAU
WRONG BAD CAR ILL MIS OUT WET
AWRY HARM HURT SORE SOUR
TORT WITE AGATE AGLEE AGLEY
AMISS CRIME DUTCH FALSE GLEED
GRIEF MALUM UNFIT WATHE WOUGH
AGUILT ASTRAY BLOOEY FAULTY
INJURE INJURY NOUGHT OFFEND
SARAAD SINFUL UNTRUE WICKED
WONDER ABUSION DAMNIFY
DEFRAUD IMMORAL INJURIA
MISBEDE NAUGHTY UNRIGHT
VIOLATE AGGRIEVE COCKEYED
MISTAKEN PERVERSE UNLEEFUL
(CIVIL —) TORT
(IMAGINARY —) WINDMILL
WRONGDOER ACTOR SINNER
FAULTER MISDOER OFFENDER
WRONGDOING MISS CRIME FAULT
DEFAULT
WRONGHEADED WRY PERVERSE
WRONGFUL UNFAIR UNJUST
TORTIOUS TORTUOUS UNLAWFUL
WRONGLY AMISS BADLY FALSE
NOUGHT UNRICHT UNRIGHT
OVERWART
WROTH ANGRY IRATE IREFUL
WROUGHT BEATEN CARVEN
FORMED SHAPED VROCHT CREATED
HAMMERED
(ELABORATELY —) LABORED

WRY ASKEW AVERT TWIST WRING
WRONG WRITHE DEFLECT DISTORT
TWISTED WRITHEN SATURNINE
WRYNECK IYNX JYNX SLAB WEET
LOXIA PEABIRD WEETBIRD
WYCH ELM WITCH WITCHEN
WYLIECOAT WALYCOAT NIGHTGOWN
PETTICOAT
WYND HAW ALLEY CLOSE

WYOMING

CAPITAL: CHEYENNE
COUNTY: TETON UINTA GOSHEN
BIGHORN LARAMIE NIOBRARA
INDIAN: ARAPAHO
LAKE: JACKSON
MOUNTAIN: ELK CLOUD GANNET
HOBACK FREMONT ATLANTIC
SHERIDAN
MOUNTAIN RANGE: TETON
ABSARO BIGHORN LARAMIE
RATTLESNAKE
NICKNAME: EQUALITY
RIVER: GREEN SNAKE PLATTE
POWDER BIGHORN
STATE BIRD: MEADOWLARK
STATE FLOWER: PAINTBRUSH
STATE TREE: COTTONWOOD
TOWN: CODY LUSK CASPER
BUFFALO LARAMIE RAWLINS
WORLAND GREYBULL
KEMMERER SHERIDAN
SUNDANCE

X EX XRAY ERROR MISTAKE
XANTHIC YELLOW
XANTHIPPE (HUSBAND OF —) SOCRATES
XANTHIPPUS (SON OF —) PERICLES
XEBEC SHIP CHEBEC CHEBECK SHABEQUE
XENIUM GIFT DAINTY DELICACY
XERES JEREZ SHERRY

XHOSA KAFIR KAFFIR
(PL.) AMAKOSA AMAXOSA
XIPHISTERNUM XIFOID
XIPHOSURUS LIMULUS
X-RAY UROGRAM
XUREL SCAD SAUREL
XUTHUS (ADOPTED SON OF —) ION
(BROTHER OF —) DORUS AEOLUS
(FATHER OF —) HELLEN

(WIFE OF —) CREUSA
XYLEM HADROM HADROME XYLOGEN
XYLOID WOODY LIGNEOUS
XYLOPHONE REGAL SARON BALAFO GAMBANG GAMELAN MARIMBA BALAPHON GAMELANG GIGELIRA STICCADO
XYSTUS WALK XYST PORTICO TERRACE

Y WY YA WYE YOD YOKE YANKEE
- (— **CONNECTION**) SIAMESE
- (— **COORDINATE**) SINE

YABBER TALK JABBER LANGUAGE

YABBY CRAWLIE

YACARE CAIMAN CAYMAN JACARE

YACHT SAIL SCOW BRUTE YATCH
DINGHY SONDER YEAGHE KEELBOAT

YAFF YAP BARK YELP

YAFFLE ARMFUL YAFFIL

YAHOO BRUTE CLOWN ROWDY
BUMPKIN

YAHWEH GOD JAVE JAHVAH

YAHWIST JEHOVIST

YAK GAG JOKE LAUGH BULBUL
SARLAK SARLYK YAMMER CHATTER

YAKALA JAGA

YAKKA WORK LABOR

YAKUT SAKHA

YAM HOI UBE UBI UVE JAMB LIMA
RAIL TUGUI IGNAME INAMIA INHAME
POTATO BONIATA
- (**TARO** —) KOKO

YAM BEAN KAMAS JICAMA WAYAKA
SINCAMAS

YAMEN COURT YAMUN OFFICE

YAMEO LLAMEO

YAMMER CRY WAIL SCOLD WHINE
YEARN YOMER GRUMBLE WHIMPER

YAMP YAMPA SQUAWROOT

YANAN NOZI

YANG HONK GURJUN

YANK FLOG JERK SLAP HOICK
SNAKE BUFFET

YAP BARK YAWP YELP MOUTH
SCOLD WAFFLE BUMPKIN CHATTER
KYOODLE

YAPOK YAPOCK OPOSSUM OYAPOCK

YAQUI YAKI HIAQUI

YARD HAW YED CREW CROW DUMP
FOLD SKID SPAR TILT COURT
GARTH PATIO STICK CANCHA
HOPPET LOANIN CURTAIN GARSTON
KNACKERY OUTGARTH
- (— **OF SAWMILL**) DUMP
- (— **WHERE COWS ARE MILKED**)
LOANIN LOANING
- (**1-16TH OF A** —) NAIL
- (**1-3RD OF CUBIC** —) CARTLOAD
- (**20** —**S**) SCORE
- (**5 AND A HALF** —**S**) ROD
- (**FINAL** —) FELL
- (**GRASSY** —) GARSTON
- (**PAVED** —) CAUSEY
- (**POULTRY** —) BARTON
- (**SAIL** —) RAE

YARD GRASS ELEUSINE MANGRASS

YARDLAND VERGE VIRGATE

YARDMASTER DINGER

YARDSTICK VERGE YAIRD METRIC
MEASURE METWAND METEWAND
STANDARD

YARE YAR AYRE YORE BRISK READY
LIVELY NIMBLE PROMPT

YARETA LLARETA

YARM WAIL NOISE OUTCRY SHRIEK

YARN ABB END FOX CORD GARN
GIMP PIRN SILK SLIP WEFT WHIP
DYNEL FLOSS GRAIN INKLE PITCH
ALASKA ANGORA BERLIN BROACH
CADDIS COTTON CREWEL CUFFER
DACRON ESTRON FLORET FRIEZE
MERINO MOTTLE PEELER RATINE
SAXONY SINGLE STRAND THREAD
VINYON WOOLEN ZEPHYR ACETATE
CADDICE FILLING GENAPPE INGRAIN
MELANGE RACKING SCHAPPE
VIGOGNE WORSTED ASBESTOS
BOURETTE CHENILLE FORTISAN
ROUNDING SPINNING VIGOREUX
WHEELING
- (— **FOR WARP**) ABB
- (— **FROM FLOSS SILK**) FLORET
- (— **SIZE**) TYPP
- (**BALL OF** —) CLEW CLUE
- (**BITS OF ROPE** —) THRUMS
- (**BUNDLE OF** —) PAD
- (**CONICAL MASS OF** —) COP
- (**ELASTIC** —) LASTEX
- (**EXAGGERATED** —) STRETCHER
- (**FINE SOFT** —) ZEPHYR KASHMIR
CASHMERE
- (**LINEN** —) SPINEL
- (**ROLL OF** —) PRICK CHEESE
- (**ROPE** —**S**) SOOGEE
- (**SMALL PIECE OF SPUN** —) RABAND
ROBBIN ROPEBAND
- (**UNEVEN** —) BOUCLE
- (**PL.**) FOX MENDINGS

YARRAN GIDYA MYALL GIDGEA
GIDGEE

YARROW ALLHEAL CAMMOCK
MAUDLIN MILFOIL

YASHIRO SHA

YASHMAK VEIL ASMACK YAKMAK

YATAGHAN SABER ATAGHAN
SIMITAR

YATTER CHATTER PRATTLE

YAUD MARE YADE

YAUPON ASSI HOLLY YUPON CASINA
CASSINE

YAUTIA COCO TARO TANIA COCKER
TANIER MALANGA

YAW GAPE YAWN LURCH SHEER
BROACH SWERVE

YAWL HOWL DANDY MIZZEN SCREAM
SCHOKKER

YAWN GAP GALP GANE GANT GAPE
YANE ABYSM CHAUM CAVITY
TEDIUM DULLNESS

YAWNING HIANT CHASMA GAPING
OSCITANT

YAWP BAWL GAPE STARE SQUAWK
YAMMER COMPLAIN

YAWS TUBBA TUBBOE

YAWWEED RHUBARB

YAYA COPA

YEA YA YES YOY YIGH TRULY
ASSENT REALLY VERILY

YEAN EAN LAMB

YEANLING KID LAMB EANLING

YEAR EAR SUN AYRE HAAB TIME
ANNUS VAGUE WINTER ZODIAC
TOWMOND TZOLKIN BIRTHDAY
- (— **OF EMANCIPATION**) JUBILEE
- (**ACADEMIC** —) SESSION
- (**IN THIS** —) HA
- (**LAST** —) FERNYEAR
- (**MANY** —**S**) AGE
- (**MAYAN** —) TUN HAAB
- (**SABBATICAL** —) JUBILE JUBILEE
- (**PL.**) SEASONS

YEARBOOK ANNUAL SERIAL
ANNUARY

YEARLING COLT HORNOTINE

YEARLY ANNUAL SOLEMN

YEARN HO YEN ACHE BURN EARN
GAPE HONE IRNE LONG PANT PINE
SIGH CRAVE GREEN GRIEN ASPIRE
CURDLE GRIEVE HANKER YAMMER

YEARNING EROS DESIRE HANKER
RENNET CRAVING EARNFUL
HOMESICK

YEAST BEE EST BARM BEES EAST
KOJI SOTS FROTH SPUME LEAVEN
NEWING RISING SIZING TORULA
FERMENT SIZZING EMPTINGS
- (**FILM** —) FLOR

YEASTY LIGHT FROTHY TRIVIAL
RESTLESS

YEGG ROBBER BURGLAR

YELL CRY CALL GOWL HOWL ROAR
YARM YAUP YOWL YOWT GOLLY
SHOUT TIGER BELLOW GOLLAR
HOLLER SCREAM YAMMER YELLOCH
SCRONACH

YELLOW (ALSO SEE COLOR) OR
GULL AMBER BLAKE BLOND FAVEL
FLAVE JAUNE PALEW SHELL YELWE
ALMOND BANANA FLAVID MELINE
MIMOSA NUGGET OXGALL BISCUIT
JASMINE JONQUIL LEGHORN
MEXICAN MUSTARD NANKEEN
OATMEAL POPCORN SAFFRON
TILLEUL WHEATEN YUCATAN
AUREOLIN GENERALL ICTEROID
LUMINOUS MARIGOLD ORPIMENT
PRIMROSE
- (— **AS BUTTER**) BLAKE
- (**BROWNISH** —) FULVID FULVOUS
- (**GOLDEN** —) FLAVID
- (**GREENISH** —) ACACIA
- (**INDIAN** —) PURI PURREE
- (**LEMON** —) GENERALL

YELLOW ALDER SAGEROSE

YELLOW BEDSTRAW CRUDWORT
CURDWORT FLEAWEED

YELLOW BUGLE IVA IVE IVY

YELLOW CLINTONIA DOGBERRY

YELLOW FOXTAIL STICKERS

YELLOW GENTIAN FELWORT

YELLOWHAMMER SKYT YITE
AMMER GOWDY SKITE GLADDY
GOLDIE VERDIN YORLIN FLICKER
GLADEYE YELDRIN YOLDRING
- (— **STATE**) ALABAMA

YELLOW IRIS SEDGE LEVERS
DAGGERS

YELLOWISH SALLOW ICTERINE
SAFFRONY
- (— **GREEN**) GLAUCOUS
- (— **RED**) FALLOW

YELLOW JACKET VESPA VESPID

YELLOW JASMINE WOODBINE

YELLOWLEGS KILLCU TATLER
WINTER YELPER TATTLER

YELLOW MACKEREL CREVALLE

YELLOWNESS FLAVEDO
YELLOW POND LILY DUCK CLOTE
  CLOTS NUPHAR
YELLOW PRICKLE RUBIA
YELLOW RATTLE RATEL
  COCKSCOMB LOUSEWORT
YELLOW TOADFLAX RAMSTEAD
YELLOW WAGTAIL OATEAR
YELLOW WATER LILY KELP WOKAS
YELLOWWOOD FUSTIC FUSTOC
  MANGWE VIRGILIA
YELP CRY YAP YIP BAFF BARK KIYI
  WAFF YAFF YAUP YAWP BOAST
  YAMPH AVOCET SQUEAL YAFFLE
  YELLOW
YELPING CRY

YEMEN
ANCIENT KINGDOM: SABA SHEBA
CAPITAL: SANA SANAA
COIN: RIYAL
MUSLIM SECT: SHIA SUNNI
PEOPLE: ZAIDI SHAFAI
PORT: MOKA MOCHA
REGION: TIHAMA
RULER: IMAM
TOWN: MOKA DAMAR MOCHA
  TAIZZ HODEIDA

YEN EYES LONG URGE YEARN
  DESIRE SUCKER LONGING
YEOMAN CHURL CLERK WRITER
  GOODMAN GUIDMAN GRAYCOAT
  RETAINER BEEFEATER
YERBA SANTA TARBUSH
YERK BEAT GOAD HURL JERK KICK
  STAB YARK THUMP EXCITE THRASH
  LASHING
YES AY DA IS JA OC SI YA AYE ISS
  YAS YAW YEA YEP YIS YUH YUS
  YEAH TRULY
YESTERDAY YESTER YESTREEN
  (OF —) PRIDIAN
YET AND BUT YIT EVEN STILL
  ALGATE HOWEER THOUGH FINALLY
  HOWEVER HITHERTO
YETT GATE
YEUK EWK YUK ITCH YUCK ITCHING
YEW YO HEW UGH YOE YOW VIEW
  TAXUS TOPIARY CHINWOOD
YEX YOLK
YIDDISH JEWISH
YIELD GO BOW CUT ILD PLY BEAR
  BEND CAST CEDE CESS COME CROP
  DRAG FOLD GIVE HEAR HELD LOUT
  QUIT SELL VAIL WAGE AGREE
  ALLOW AMAIN AVALE AWALE BRING
  BUDGE CARRY CAUSE DEFER
  GRANT HEALD HIELD LEAVE OFFER
  SLAKE STOOP ACCEDE AFFORD
  BOUNTY BUCKLE COMPLY CONFER
  FOLLOW IMPART OUTPUT RELENT
  RENDER RETURN SUBMIT SUPPLY
  SWERVE UNGIVE UPGIVE ABANDON
  ANALYZE CONCEDE DELIVER
  FURNISH HARVEST KNUCKLE
  OUTTURN PRODUCE PROVIDE
  REDOUND RUCKSEY SUCCUMB

  BEGRUDGE FRUITAGE OVERGIVE
  UNDERLIE
  (— FRUIT) ADDLE GRAIN
  (— GRASS) GRAZE
  (— OF FIELD) BURDEN
  (— OF MINE) BONANZA
  (— ON BOND) BASIS
  (— TO TEMPTATION) FALL
  (— TO) INDULGE
  (— UP) LET FORLET FORLEIT
  (— WELL) HIT BLEED
YIELDING ABLE MEEK NESH SOFT
  TALL WAXY NAISH WAXEN BONAIR
  FACILE FEEBLE FLABBY LIMBER
  OUTPUT PLIANT QUAGGY SUPPLE
  BEARING CESSION FINGENT FLACCID
  DEDITION LADYLIKE RECREANT
  (— IRREGULARLY) BUNCHY
  (— OF HORSE) FLEXION
  (— STAGE) SEAR
  (— TO IMPULSES) ABANDON
YIN SHANG
YIRMILIK METALLIK
YODEL SONG JODEL WARBLE
  REFRAIN
YODH IOD JOD
YOGA JOG
YOGI JOGI FAKIR FAKEER
YOKE BOW YOK BAIL CROW DRAG
  FORK HOOP PAIR POKE SOLE
  BANGY FURCA SHEBA SPANG
  BANGHY COUPLE INSPAN DRAGBAR
  HARNESS OPPRESS ADJUGATE
  (— BAR) SKEY
  (— TO HOLD DRILL) CROW
  (— TO RAISE CANNON) BAIL
YOKEFELLOW MATE FELLOW
  PARTNER YOKEMATE
YOKEL YOB BOOR CLUB FARMER
  HAYSEED WAYBACK ABDERITE
  CHAWBACON
YOKING BOUT CONTEST MUGGING
YOLDRING YOWLEY
YOLK CENTER YELLOW ESSENCE
  LATEBRA VITELLUS
  (HAVING A —) LECITHAL
YON YONDER THITHER BACKWARD
YONDER THAT THERE THOSE
  THITHER
YORE PAST YARE YEARS
  (OF —) OLDEN
YORKER TICE
YORKSHIREMAN TIKE TYKE
  LEAROYD
YORUBA NAGO
YOU DU HE IT OW TA TU WE YA YO
  ONE OWE SHE SIE YOW YUH THOU
  YOUSE YOURSELF
YOUNG FRY JUV BIRD CALF DROP
  BIRTH BROOD FETUS FRUIT GREEN
  SMALL UNOLD JUNIOR KINDLE
  JUVENAL IMMATURE YEANLING
  YOUTHFUL
  (— OF ANY ANIMAL) FRY BABY
  CALF FOAL JOEY LAMB TOTO
  (— OF BEAST) SLINK
  (— OF BIRD) CHICK
  (— OF CAMEL) COLT
  (— OF DOG) WHELP

  (— OF FISH) FRY
  (— OF SEA TROUT) HERLING
  (VERY —) SUCKING NEPHIONIC
  SHIRTTAIL
YOUNGER KID LESS PUNEE JUNIOR
  PUISNE OFFSPRING
YOUNGEST (— OF BROOD)
  WALLYDRAG
YOUNGSTER KID BIRD COLT CHILD
  YOUTH BUTTON SHAVER URCHIN
  YONKER YOUNKER SPALPEEN
YOUNKER DUPE CHILD KNIGHT
  NOVICE SQUIRE YUNKER
YOUR OR YO THY YAR YER OURE
  OWRE YOURN
YOURSELF ITSELF HERSELF HIMSELF
  ONESELF
YOUTH BOY BUD IMP LAD CHAP
  PAGE BAHUR CHABO GROOM HYLAS
  POULT PRIME SPRIG SWAIN WHELP
  BOCHUR BURSCH EPHEBE HOYDEN
  INFANT JUVENT KOUROS MASTER
  SPRING SQUIRT YONKER CALLANT
  EPHEBOS GOSSOON JUVENAL
  PUBERTY SAPLING YOUDITH
  YOUNGTH ENDYMION JUVENILE
  SPRINGAL
  (— WHO SERVES LIQUORS)
  GANYMEDE
  (GODDESS OF —) HEBE
  (IMPUDENT —) SQUIRT
  (NON-JEWISH —) SHEGETZ
  (PERT —) PRINCOX
  (RUDE —) HOYDEN
  (RUSSIAN — ORGANIZATION)
  KOMSOMOL
  (SILLY —) CALF SLENDER
  (WELLBORN —) CHILD
YOUTHFUL RATH FRESH GREEN
  YOUNG BOYISH GOLDEN JUNIOR
  MAIDEN NEANIC VIRGIN YOUTHY
  LADDISH PUERILE YOUNGLY
  IMMATURE JUVENILE SPRINGAL
  VIGOROUS
YOUTHFULNESS JEUNESSE
YOWL GOWL HOWL WAIL YELL YELP
YUAN DOLLAR
YUAPIN YARURA
YUCCA LILY PITA YUCA DATIL IZOTE
  PALMA JOSHUA LILIAL LILIUM
  PALMITO SOAPWEED
YUGA KALI

YUGOSLAVIA
CAPITAL: BEOGRAD BELGRADE
COIN: PARA DINAR
GULF: KVARNER
LAKE: SCUTARI
MEASURE: RIF AKOV RALO DONUM
  KHVAT LANAZ STOPA MOTYKA
  PALAZE RALICO
MOUNTAIN: TRIGLAV DURMITOR
MOUNTAIN RANGE: DINARIC
PEOPLE: SERB CROAT SLOVENE
PORT: KOTOR SPLIT RIJEKA
  NOVISAD BELGRADE DUBROVNIK
REGION: BANAT BOSNIA SRBIJA
RIVER: DRIM IBAR KRKA SAVA

TISA BOSNA CAZMA DRAVA DRINA RASKA TAMIS VRBAS DANUBE MORAVA VARDER VELIKA NERETVA **TOWN:** NIS AGRAM BUDVA RTANJ SPLIT USKUB BITOLA MORAVA MOSTAR OSIJEK PRILEP

RAGUSA RIJEKA SKOPJE VARDAR ZAGREB CATTARO NOVISAD PRIZREN MONASTIR SARAJEVO SUBOTICA **WEIGHT:** OKA OKE DRAMM TOVAR WAGON SATLIJK

YULE NOEL CHRISTMAS
YUMA CUCHAN
YUMAN PATAYAN
YUNX WRYNECK
YURT TENT

Z ZAD ZED ZEE ZETA ZULU IZARD
ZEBRA IZZARD
(SHAPED LIKE A —) OPENBAND
ZABAGLIONE SABAYON
ZAFFER SMALT SAFFIOR ZAPHARA
ZAGREUS (FATHER OF —) JUPITER
(MOTHER OF —) PROSERPINE

ZAIRE

ALTERNATE NAME: CONGO
CAPITAL: KINSHASA
LAKE: KIVU MWERU
LANGUAGE: KIKONGO LINGALA
SWAHILI TSHILUBA
MONEY: ZAIRE
MOUNTAIN RANGE: MITUMBA
VIRUNGA RUWENZORI
PROVINCE: KIVU KASAI EQUATOR
KATANGA ORIENTAL
RIVER: RUKI CONGO DENGU IBINA
KASAI LINDI ZAIRE LIKATI
LOMAMI LUKUGA UBANGI
ARUWIMI LUALABA LULONGA
TOWN: BAYA BOMA LEBO AKETI
KAMINA KIKWIT BUTEMBO
KOLWEZI BAKWANGA YANGAMBI

ZAMBIA

CAPITAL: LUSAKA
COIN: KWACHA
FALLS: VICTORIA
LAKE: MWERU BANGWEULU
TANGANYIKA
LANGUAGE: LOZI BEMBA TONGA
LUVALE NYANJA AFRIKAANS
MOUNTAIN RANGE: MUCHINGA
RIVER: KAFUE LUANGWA LUAPULA
ZAMBEZI
TOWN: KITWE NDOLA LUAPULA
LUANSHYA MUFULIRA

ZAMBO CHINO SAMBO CAFUSO
CURIBOCA
ZAMIA BANGA CICAD CYCAD
COONTIE
ZAMINDAR MALIK
ZAMOUSE GAMOUS
ZAMPOGNA BAGPIPE PANPIPE
ZANDER ZANT PERCID SANDER
SANDRA
ZANTHOXYLUM FAGARA
ZANY FOOL CRAZY TOADY SAWNEY
BUFFOON IDIOTIC CLOWNISH
SCREWBALL
ZANZIBAR (SEE TANZANIA)
ZAPARO IQUITO
ZAPATEROL LIMA BOXWOOD
CERILLO
ZARAH KAZOO
ZEAL FIRE MOOD ARDOR FLAME
HEART FERVOR WARMTH DEVOTION
GOODWILL JEALOUSY
(WITH —) DINGDONG
ZEALOT BIGOT VOTARY VOTEEN

ZELANT DEVOTEE FANATIC
CANANEAN SERAPHIC SICARIUS
VOTARESS VOTARIST
ZEALOUS HOT HIGH ARDENT FERVID
STRING CORDIAL DEVOTED
EARNEST EMULOUS FERVENT
FORWARD JEALOUS PUSHFUL
VIGOROUS
(— ABOUT BEAUTY) ESTHETIC
ZEALOUSLY FAST INNERLY
HEARTILY
ZEBRA DAUW EQUID HORSE QUAGGA
SOLIPED
ZEBRAWOOD ARAROBA ZINGANA
ZEBU BRAMIN BRAGMAN BRAHMIN
(HYBRID OF — AND CATTLE)
CATTABU
(HYBRID OF — AND YAK) ZOBO
ZECCHINO SEQUIN
ZEN (— PARADOX) KOAN
(— QUESTIONS) MONDO
ZENANA HAREM HARIM SERAGLIO
ZENICK SURICATE
ZENITH ACME PEAK HIGHT HEIGHT
SUMMIT VERTEX
ZEOLITE ANALCIME ANALCITE
ZEPHYRUS FAVONIUS
(SON OF —) CARPOS
(WIFE OF —) CHLORIS
ZEPPELIN ZEP ZEPP AIRSHIP
ZERO OH NIL NUL BLOB DUCK NULL
AUGHT CLOSE EMPTY OUGHT TRAIN
ABSENT CIPHER NAUGHT LACKING
NOTHING NULLITY SCRATCH
NINETEEN
ZEST EDGE ELAN JASM GUSTO
FLAVOR RELISH STINGO PIQUANCY
ZESTFUL RACY SPICY BREEZY
ZETES (BROTHER OF —) CALAIS
(FATHER OF —) BOREAS
(MOTHER OF —) ORITHYIA
ZETHUS (BROTHER OF —) AMPHION
(FATHER OF —) JUPITER
(SE)(MOTHER OF —) ANTIOPE
ZEUS ZAN SOTER ALASTOR CRONION
KRONION POLIEUS CRONIDES
(BROTHER OF —) HADES POSEIDON
(FATHER OF —) KRONOS
(MOTHER OF —) RHEA
(SISTER OF —) HERA HESTIA
DEMETER
(SON OF —) ARES
(WIFE OF —) HERA JUNO METIS
THEMIS EURYNOME
ZEUXIS UNDERLAY
ZIGZAG BOYAU CRANK BROKEN
INDENT CRANKLE CHEVONRY
FLEXUOSE TRAVERSE
ZIMARRA CYMAR SIMAR CASSOCK
ZIMB FLY ZEBUB
ZINC FAR SPELT ZINCUM SPELTER
TUTENAG EXCLUDER
ZING PEP VIM ZIP DASH SNAP
ENERGY SPIRIT
ZINGEL PERCID
ZINKE CORNET

ZINNIA CRASSINA
ZION SION ISRAEL UTOPIA
ZIONIST IRGUNIST
ZIOSITE THULITE
ZIP VIM DASH SNAP FORCE WHISK
BUTTON ENERGY STINGO
ZIPPER FASTENER
ZIRCON JARGON AZORITE MALACON
HYACINTH STARLITE
ZITHER KIN CANON CANUN GUSLI
KANOON CITHARA GITERNE GITTERN
AUTOHARP GALEMPONG
(JAPANESE —) KOTO
ZITHER HARP KOTO
ZIZITH SISITH FRINGES TASSELS
TSITSITH
ZO DZO ZOH ZOBO
ZOARITE BIMMELER
ZOBO ZO DZO ZOH ZOBU
ZODIAC GIRDLE BALDRIC BAWDRICK
SIGNIFER
(SIGN OF —) LEO RAM BULL CRAB
FISH GOAT LION ARIES LIBRA SCALE
TWINS VIRGO ARCHER CANCER
GEMINI PISCES TAURUS SCORPIO
AQUARIUS CAPRICORN
ZONA ZOSTER
ZONE BED AREA BAND BEAM BELT
HALO PLAGE TRACT CIRCLE REGION
ZODIAC CLIMATE HORIZON
ZOMULET CINGULUM FRONTIER
HABENULA HISTOGEN STRINGER
(— OF CONFLICT) FRONT
(— OF FLAME) MANTLE
(— OF MINERALS) CORONA
(— OF VENUS) CEST CESTUS
(ABYSSAL —) BASSALIA
(PALEONTOLOGIC —S) ASSISE
(SAFETY —) ISLET ISLAND REFUGE
(STRATOGRAPHIC —) HEMERA
(WELDING —) ROOT
ZOOECIUM AUTOPORE
ZOOID PERSON SIPHON BRYOZOAN
HYDRANTH POLYPIDE ZOOTHOME
ZOOPHYTE CORAL SPONGE
HYDROID
ZOOSPORE MONAD SWARMER
ZOOCARP
ZORIL SKUNK POWCAT CHINCHE
POLECAT MUISHOND
ZOROASTRIAN GABAR PARSI
PARSEE
ZOROASTRIANISM MAZDAISM
ZOUAVE ZUZU SCALER ZOUZOU
ZOUNDS OONS WAUNS ZOONS
ZUCCETO CALOTTE SOLIDEO
SKULLCAP
ZUNI CIBOLAN SHALAKO
ZWINGLIAN TIGURINE
ZYGOMATIC JUGAL
ZYGOSPORE COPULA
ZYGOTE OOSPERM OOSPORE
SPORONT OOKINETE
ZYME YEAST ZYMIN ENZYME
FERMENT
ZYRIAN KOMI SYRYAN

The *Artificial* Kid

Bruce Sterling

THE ARTIFICIAL KID

HARPER & ROW, PUBLISHERS

NEW YORK

Cambridge
Hagerstown
Philadelphia
San Francisco

1817

London
Mexico City
São Paulo
Sydney

THE ARTIFICIAL KID. Copyright © 1980 by Bruce Sterling. All rights reserved. Printed in the United States of America. No part of this book may be used or reproduced in any manner whatsoever without written permission except in the case of brief quotations embodied in critical articles and reviews. For information address Harper & Row, Publishers, Inc., 10 East 53rd Street, New York, N.Y. 10022. Published simultaneously in Canada by Fitzhenry & Whiteside Limited, Toronto.

FIRST EDITION

Designer: Sidney Feinberg

Library of Congress Cataloging in Publication Data

Sterling, Bruce.
  The Artificial Kid.
  I. Title.
PZ4.S8377Re   [PS3569.T3876]   813 '.5'4
ISBN 0-06-014098-4   79-2661

80 81 82 83 84 10 9 8 7 6 5 4 3 2 1

The Artificial Kid

1

Reverie shines, the planet's edge lined in luminous atmospheric haze, her broad, shallow seas sparkling, her big coral-atoll continents brown and green and white through rifts in scattered clouds. The sky over Telset, my island city, is clear as glass as the camera zooms in; I was careful to check with the weather satellites before I did the taping. The effect is serene and hypnotic; and the camera accelerates downward and the gridwork of my city expands with nearness, to a single block, a single street, a single person, me, and my own image swells to fill the screen. The soundtrack says:

"Ladies and gentlemen, the Artificial Kid. This tape is made possible by Mr. Richer Money Manies and the Artificial Kid. Copyright C.R.Y. 499 by the Artificial Kid for Cognitive Dissonant Enterprises, Reverie."

Most of my audience are floaters, who circle our coraled planet in city-sized orbital oneills. I draw them down to the planet's surface, I involve them personally during those first thirty seconds of tape. Orbital Reverids think of Reverie as lovely, but remote, and surface dwellers like myself as rather quaint and sweet. I break down that distancing effect. I stare right into the descending camera, my slightly slanting eyes blacklined in kohl and as cold and mean as an adder's. I challenge the viewer. I believe in direct challenges; they're at the heart of combat artistry.

People used to ask me how I became a combat artist and why I'm called the Artificial Kid. People stopped asking such prying questions after I ruthlessly beat them up. Every formal interview I've given has ended with me "losing my temper" and soundly clubbing the journalist. Now, the days have passed when I found it necessary to establish a reputation for fury and volatile violence. Now, I intend to tell all.

Why, then, do people call me the Artificial Kid? My answer is that all combat artists must have a gimmick, and mine has always been my childishness and wild artificiality. "Kid," on Reverie, means a young person, but the word also has a certain raffish air of irreverent disrespect.

I'll explain further with an analysis of my tape image, an image I know well, an image, in fact, that obsesses me. Many times, I have risen at sunset and worked straight through the eighteen-hour Reverid night, editing and polishing my own tapes for Mr. Manies and the market. The image on the tape is that of a very young man. He is resiliently, but not heavily, muscled; his skin is suntanned dark brown under a thin, shiny film of green skin oil. He is short, about five feet four. He wears a thick armored leather surcoat over his torso, held up with two wide shoulder straps; a stiff, heavy collar shields the back of his neck. He wears a pair of gleaming metallic scale trousers with elastic waist and cuffs, and shiny black combat slippers. His head seems slightly oversized for the childish body; his face is unlined and beardless, with wide cheekbones, a pointed, narrow chin, and eyes with an epicanthic fold, heavily outlined in black. His hair is unusual; each strand of hair is separately laminated in plastic, forming a jackstraw array of stiff, black, pointed quills. Floating about him in the air are six small, silent camera modules, each with two lenses and sound recording equipment, each carefully programmed. These floating cameras are with him always.

In his right hand he casually grips his nunchuck. This weapon consists of two slightly tapering eighteen-inch clubs of blood-repellent padded black plastic, linked at their thin ends by eight inches of crystalline metal chain. He grips one club about half-way up its length and lets the other dangle. The solid metal core beneath the plastic assures a satisfying kinetic impact, while the slight malleability of the plastic provides stunning bruises rather than the actual mangling and spattering that a solid metal 'chuck would cause. Above all the Artificial Kid believes in theater. Theater is having opponents fall at your feet, stunned, numb, and nerveless. Theater is not gouging out great bloody chunks of flesh.

The Artificial Kid moves with resilient grace. He is aware at every moment of the exact position of every inch of his body, and his nunchuck moves like a living thing, absolutely obedient to his will because of his ninety-eight long years of practice. "Ninety-eight years, Kid?" I can hear my audience ask. "Isn't that seventy years longer than you've been alive?" So it is. And *that's* why I'm the Artificial Kid.

I happen to have the first moments of my "birth" on tape. They were taped by Professor Crossbow, my tutor and mentor for the first twenty years of my life, a person to whom I owe a profound debt. It was clever of it (Professor Crossbow is a neuter, so I will refer to it as "it," the pronoun it always preferred) to put the close-up on my face. In the first few minutes of the tape it is obvious that, despite the fact that he says nothing, we are looking at Rominuald Tanglin, my previous personality. He is two hundred and seventy-one standard years old and looks every day of it. The lines of madness are in his face; his eyes shift rapidly from side to side like hot black ball bearings; there is tension in the pale thinness of his grizzled lips. He is about to commit mental suicide. His hair is shoulder length and frivolously curled in the old style; there are half-a-dozen shaven spots where the metal contacts will touch his head, and they lend the proceedings a peculiarly makeshift air.

The machine that will kill him descends from above him, extruding six gleaming contacts. Tanglin still says nothing, but his throat moves visibly. The contacts touch; there is a discharge; Tanglin dies instantly and his eyes close. His face sags in total relaxation. The narrow jaw drops and a thread of drool forms at the corner of the lower lip; Crossbow's hand appears to touch it away with a sponge. The body, momentarily empty of any personality, sags in the chair, but transparent plastic braces, barely visible, keep the head upright. Tears form in the opened eye ducts and slide down across the broad cheeks. The memory eraser has done its work. Tanglin's mind is gone, his personality is scorched away. The machine rises from the head. Quickly, Crossbow touches away the tears and removes the head brace. Within seconds, consciousness returns, I am born, and I lift my head.

"Hello," Crossbow says gently. Wondering, I lift my hand and touch the cool dampness on my cheeks. "Hello," I say as I rub my eyes with two fingers.

CROSSBOW: Do you know who you are?

SELF: Yes. I'm R.T. [pause] R.T. Arti. [I move my mouth, tasting the words]

CROSSBOW: And do you know who I am?

SELF: Yes. You're my friend, Professor Crossbow. And we're in your house, on Reverie.

CROSSBOW: [with infinite gentleness] Very good! [I smile radiantly] Let's try to walk a little now, Arti, shall we? That's right. [I get up from the chair. Though I am newborn, my body has not forgotten its reflexes. I begin to pace around the room with the unnatural assurance and grace that comes from hundreds of years of experience. The camera follows us. The memory device looks ugly, bulky, and angular in Crossbow's room, amid its warm, tasteful driftwood panelling, its dangling mobiles and air chimes, its glass terraria and aquaria, its tape display screen.] There. How do you feel now, Arti?

SELF: I feel just fine, Professor.

CROSSBOW: Wonderful! Now drink this [it hands me a ceramic cup full of a thick dark liquid practically crystallizing with testosterone inhibitors] and then I'll take you for a swim out on the reef. After that we'll have a nice lunch, and then we'll start your lessons. You're not sleepy, are you?

SELF: [putting aside drained cup] No! [eagerly] Let's go swimming!

The tape ends when we go out the door. Crossbow was not especially enthusiastic about taping, except of course in its scientific work, where a rigorous recording of every step of scientific procedure is demanded by the Academy.

Not so Rominuald Tanglin. Tanglin, or "Old Dad" as my friends and I have come to refer to him, was a fanatical believer in the potency of tape. He was an image builder, at one time one of the planet Niwlind's most powerful politicians (and that on a world known for the maddening intricacy of its intrigue). I can't help but feel that I've inherited some of his remarkable abilities in this field.

It must have hurt Tanglin to erase the hundreds of years of taped memories in the personal computer I inherited from him, but he knew that the vast bulk of memory there would have crushed a young, developing personality. Even so, he left me the record of his last two years, severely edited, as his echoing, gesticulating legacy. This computer, a highly advanced Niwlindid model, was specially designed for Tanglin; he understood it far better than I ever will. He cunningly hid his last tapes in there somewhere, part of a virus program that resurrected them and played them at apparently random times. The tapes were addressed to me personally, usually by a full-faced, insanely earnest Old Dad. He always addressed me as "Kid" or "Son," so that not even my closest friends knew our true relationship.

How often have I been playing breathless tapes of my own combative exploits, only to have Old Dad pop up, raving? Dozens of times at least; in fact, his projected hologram was constantly haunting my house. He would lecture me on politics, or on the perfidy of his wife Crestillomeem, or on the lurking presence of the alien creatures he called "leeches." These "leeches" were his particular obsession during his last months. He claimed to have learned his nunchuck techniques to protect himself from "Them." "They" were degenerate survivors of the Elder Culture, he insisted; gray-skinned and rubber-boned, with brittle, hollow skulls lined inside with coarse black fiber. Of course, his insane assertions had no shred of backing evidence. Once I'd grown up, I no longer believed him.

There were hundreds of tapes. He must have done at least one a day during the two years of decontamination in the orbiting emigration oneill. During his last week, in Professor Crossbow's house off the Tethys Reef, sixty miles from Telset, he edited them. Some tapes, especially the ones where he gives the details of his paranoid theory regarding the Elder Culture, radiate an intense conviction that demonstrates how he managed to rise to the exalted position of First Secretary of the Niwlindid government.

Why did I become a combat artist? Well, what else was there? I was young, though I still had the habitual grace of age. My body still remembered its combat training. And combat art is a young person's pursuit; it takes the vitality of youth, its carelessness, its reckless self-assertion. This modern age is a hard one for the young. Our remote ancestors, and some contemporary humans dumb enough to live on low-technology planets, died early, sometimes before a single century of life. They didn't live on and on, smothering their sons and daughters with the weight of their centuries of power and experience. It's hard to find room to breathe when you're young; it's hard for someone two hundred years old to acknowledge the adulthood of someone eighteen. One answer on Reverie has been the Decriminalized Zone, an area freed of legal and social restraint.

When the Decriminalized Zone was first opened, twenty years ago, corporate citizens were shocked and titillated by the spontaneous anarchic violence that broke out among the small gangs of roving, idle, bored, and defiant delinquents. Their vicious activities aroused interest and sympathy among others suffering from a similar frustration. Bootleg tapes of people being savagely beaten up found a larger and larger audience, and not only among the young. Viewer money began to pour into the industry. Combat art forms sprang up, the original undisciplined hoodlums were quickly disposed of, and combat art became a profession.

In the Professor's house northeast of Telset on the shore of the continent Aeo, I was a devoted follower. The Professor disapproved at first, but it wisely left me to my own devices as I grew older. In fact, I saw less and less of the old neuter as it spent longer and longer hours exploring the reef and documenting its incredibly intricate Reverid ecology.

One day I simply left the Professor a note and took my sailboat to the city. In two weeks I was established and I came back for my computer. My note was gone, but so was the Professor. My departure had freed it of its last responsibility. I imagined that my old tutor had gone completely marine and simply moved under the surface of the Gulf of Memory.

I soon found that I loved Telset. She is an island, twelve miles long, five wide, set like a jewel in the shallow gleaming waters of the southern Gulf of Memory. She is shaped like the footprint of a pointed slipper. The northern tip is Prospect Point; the original city, Old Telset, is in the middle of the eastern shore. Orbiters can see the Gulf as a whole: an ocean-sized lagoon, almost completely encircled by the vast coral-crusted arms of the continent-sized atoll we call Aeo.

Five hundred years ago, the pioneer Reverids cooked Telset to a state of red-hot viscosity with powerful orbital lasers, killing all native life. When she cooled, they stocked her sterile soil with their own flora and fauna, mostly Niwlindid stock. The alien species did well, but as the centuries passed they began to succumb to highly evolved native species that were washed ashore or carried by birds. Now the island is a riotous scramble of species from a dozen planets, each seeking a niche in a chaotic, cosmopolitan ecosystem.

The boundaries of the city of Telset are vague; her modern villas, of limestone, travertine, marble, metal, and wood, are scattered throughout the island. They are hidden in the woods and half-buried in the reefs; they loom from the shoregrass, they nestle in dells and creeks and hollows. Telset is wired, which does away with the need for compactness. The primary recreation of her citizens is tape: drone tape, art tape, life tape, memory tape. That's the way we are.

I've explored all of Telset on foot or by drone. I know the dense-packed, thickwalled, deserted buildings of Old Telset like the back of my hand; most of Old Telset is now the Decriminalized Zone, my stage and arena. I know the channels of the Telset Reef well, too; I've sailed them all in my little skiff, the *Sea Whip*, and explored them while swimming or with aquatic drones. I've seen sea beavers, mudcumbers, skates, and rays; I've seen kittiwakes, skeiners, skimmers, and cormorants. I've seen great mud-belching holothurians, as big as houses, hauling their rubbery bulk to shore, and I've touched them with my hands. I've seen great crusted cylinders of Tower Coral, two stories high; I've climbed them and dived from the top. I've seen Telset, touched her, heard her, tasted her, and smelled the sharp brine of her ocean air. And best of all, I've known her people.

Those among my audience who have closely followed my career (and I've known some to have whole libraries of my tapes) know that I started my career as a junior gang member of the Cognitive Dissonants, a group led for the last eight years by that resplendent couple, Chill Factor and his Ice Lady. Chill and Icy were responsible for my development as an artist and tape craftsman. The fact that I have sometimes challenged and beaten up members of their gang (Six Fingers, Hammer, Million Masks, Happy Daze, Flying Bill Flatbeak, Chains, Brains, Sumo, Hobble, and Twinkles) should not blind anyone to the sincere affection I feel for all these extraordinary fighters and artists.

They bought me my first cameras. They gave me innumerable tips on the correct dramatic presentation. They bought me my first smuff, helped me find my first home. They taught me gang etiquette, and the rituals of combat art and the artists' Code. The Code rules our lives. If not for the Code, we would all have killed each other years ago.

Of course, that was eight standard years past. Since then I've climbed to the top of the bloody flagpole.

Combat artists, even in this day of technomedicine, spend a lot of time healing up. You can't fight all the time, there are limits: medical bills and smuff. Limits enough so that even the top ranks are only moderately well off by the standards of Reverid richesse. But money isn't everything; in fact, to my youthful mind, fame and a fearsome reputation meant much more. And I had enough money to live comfortably and securely in the Decriminalized Zone, thanks to computerized alarm systems, royalty payments, a steady supply of smuff, and my housekeeper, Quade Altman.

Why did I have a human housekeeper when I could have had all her not-very-onerous tasks done by machine? Not for sexual gratification, obviously; I've stayed on libido suppressants ever since Professor Crossbow first gave them to me. My hairless face and high-pitched voice attest to that. Nor was it an attempt to conform to the typical practices of status-conscious, dominance-conscious Reverids. No, I kept her because she begged me to.

I still have the tape of our first meeting. I just couldn't resist her plea when she knelt amid the rubble of her three-dimensional mosiacs to look me eye to eye. (I'm five feet four, while Quade approaches eight feet.) Two members of the Perfect Stranglers had broken into her Zone studio to hide from the Cognitive Dissonants during a gang clash. Being uncouth louts, they amused themselves by smashing her works of art—excellent three-dimensional mosaics, if you like that form of expression, which I do. Unfortunately for them, Quade's falsetto screams and the brittle crunching of the mosaics' multilucent panels alerted me and I broke in to gloriously beat them both to pulps. It was wonderful; the cameras caught everything, and Quade took her cue beautifully in an impromptu performance that had me gasping with admiration. She fell to her knees, threw her incredibly long, skinny arms around my neck, and begged, literally begged me to protect her and take her to safety. I hesitated; in those days I was obsessed with projecting an image of utter inhuman ruthlessness. Finally, reflecting that I could always edit the tapes for publication, I agreed, and she actually swooned with relief. I later learned that she swoons a lot anyway, due to various blood circulation problems caused by Reverid gravity, but it was a great performance and she's done some of her best mosaic work in my house.

She'd been with me two years. I was healing up from a fractured shin, watching a drone tape, doing a little nicotine. Quade came into my tape room, carrying a light nighttime brunch. "The stars are beautiful tonight," she said vaguely. Her face was flushed; her eyes were glazed, and the peculiar yellowness that sometimes filmed her eye-whites was gone. I didn't know what was wrong with Quade but I naturally assumed it had something to do with sex; she had no lover. I had been trying for two years to get her onto libido suppressants, but with sporadic success. "Rub your back?" she piped. "Shift your pillows? Help you rub on your skin goo? Bring you your weights?"

"Quade, you're spoiling me," I said. "But get me an apron. I don't like eating hot food without clothes." I lifted the cover of the tray; steam curled upward. It was diced roast ray with stir-fried marshgrass; none of your corporate-issue oneill-imported proteins for me. I like an idiosyncratic taste, even when it's far short of synthesized perfection. Some fanatics might blame me for eating wild game; but since we humans have already taken this island, why not enjoy it to the full? To do otherwise is to insult Reverie; we should partake of her bounty, with the appreciation she deserves.

Quade left the room with three incredibly long strides. I was about to dig in when I heard the ping-ping-ping of a personal communiqué. I cut into my personal channel to see the genial, froglike face of Mr. Richer Money Manies, my friend and patron.

"Hello, Money Manies," I said. "Nice to see you."

"So, Kid," said Manies, licking his everted lips. "Trying to tempt me with your atrophied, hairless link, are you? You've missed your true calling, dear fellow. You should have been in pornotapes."

"Sorry," I said, pulling a pillow over my loins. "I didn't intend to pander to your depraved tastes." Quade returned with an apron; I threw it over my body. "Quade, doll, stay and rub my feet," I told her, more to get to Manies than for any other reason. As she knelt at the end of the couch to adoringly rub my feet, I picked up a mouthful of crisp marshgrass on my chopsticks and offered it to her. She ate it gratefully. I checked my camera with one eye to make sure all this was registering on Manies. "Lovely sunset today, wasn't it, Money Manies? I was up in time to see it."

"Yes, lovely, lovely," agreed Manies distractedly, his blue eyes goggling a little. "I would have put in a trace more scarlet, myself. Listen, my dear. I intend to have another of my breakfasts in twelve hours. Shall we make it three hours before dawn? I really need a combat artist to round out the group, and you know you're my prize of prizes, Kid."

"I bet you tell that to all the fighters you can't seduce," I said. "Of course I'll be there. It would be futile to offer this shattered leg as an excuse." I lifted the leg in question, showing the transparent cast and the electrodes that were helping to regrow the bone. "It'll hold my weight already; I'll walk over."

Manies sniffed. "How mundane! Is this the Artificial Kid, my star of stars? Let me send over a quartet of my most luscious pornostars to transport you in a scented, canopied litter. Why risk meeting some brainless belligerent not fit to kiss the hem of your nunchuck? No, allow me to deal with transportation." He waved his pudgy fingers, dismissing the topic. "How have you been occupying your convalescence, dear Kid? Viewing?"

"Exactly."

"What channel?"

"Nothing special; a drone taping from the wilderness. Done by some floater; the computer work's excellent. Channel 85. One thing interests me; she's using a manipulative drone. She doesn't just passively observe—she picks things up and looks at them. She's an innovator." We cut off our visual and put on Channel 85 with our audio as voiceover. "Oh, I recognize this woman's work," Manies said. "That's Cewaynie Wetlock. She's very new—no older than you are."

I'd never heard of her. We proceeded to a minute criticism. We spent two hours on it. Manies got me to promise to do a tape for him for his critical broadcast (a broadcast that was eventually to reach the eyes and ears of Cewaynie Wetlock herself). Time means nothing to a three-hundred-year-old Reverid, but it was decent of the ugly old antique to make the effort to amuse me.

2

The third hour before dawn found me at the northern tip of the island, at Many Mansions, the sprawling, limestone, colonnaded dwelling place of my friend and patron, Mr. Manies. I marveled at my friend's stamina, his continued gusto for life amid such demanding surroundings. As usual, his beautiful seaside villa was stuffed with servants, clients, house guests, flatterers and sycophants, rising pornostars, and ambitious tape craftsmen, not to mention the usual unclassifiable oddities: Manies' surgically altered pets, the mutant and hybrid products of his huge, flourishing terraria and aquaria, grotesque wandering holograms, and at least one actual resident alien. Amid all this even his far-famed breakfasts must have been a relief to him. Certainly he seemed relaxed and completely at ease as he performed his hostly duties.

He had invited five of us—about the usual number. And, as usual, we were a markedly heterogeneous group. Alruddin Spinney, the poet, and "Ruffian Jack" Nimrod, the explorer, were already known to me; they were two of Manies' closest friends. But I had never before seen Professor Angeluce of the Academy or Saint Anne Twiceborn, a Niwlindid political refugee. Both had only recently made planetfall, after the long and painful decontamination process in an orbiting oneill.

Spinney was a small, scrawny man, with a prominent adam's apple and a thick shock of kinky red hair. With an air of quiet melancholy, he pulled a fist-sized gobbet of raw meat from his pocket and offered it to his pet mantis, a green, arm-long, chitinous monster that followed him everywhere. It accepted the gift with a gentleness and restraint that matched Spinney's own and began to nibble it, breathing audibly through spiracles as big around as my little finger.

"The Morning Star's beautifully bright tonight, isn't it?" said Ruffian Jack, looking off the airy balcony across the slow surf of the reef. "Did I ever tell you about the time I went there?"

"Come now, Ruffian," laughed Money Manies. Conversation was his element. "We mined the Morning Star four hundred years ago. We're all intelligent people here. Surely you won't try to hoodwink us with some grotesque and impossible brag about your longevity?"

"Who said anything about four hundred years?" demanded Jack. "I was there not fifty years back. My floater days, you know. The final detonations melted its entire crust; that's what gives it its high albedo." I liked Ruffian Jack; he could have been a good combat artist. I forgave him his constant habit of lying.

"Mr. Spinney," said Professor Angeluce in his penetrating, pedantic voice, "are you sure that that arthropod has been properly decontaminated? Might I ask its area of origin? Could it be the continental area known colloquially as the Mass?"

"I don't know, sir," said Spinney politely, patting his pet on the hard transparent case over one huge compound eye. "I found him washed up on the reef, half-drowned. I assure you that I have never probed his guts for protozoa, if that is your concern."

"What is your concern with the Mass, Professor?" asked Manies, his every syllable packed full of interest.

"My concern? My concern?" grated Angeluce. He gestured

irritably and one of his three cameras zoomed in for a close-up of his pale, pinched face. "I am a Scholar, sir. My doctorate is in the field of taxonomic microbiology, but I have a more than slight acquaintance with epidemiology. The Mass is this world's most fertile area for microorganisms, many of them potentially hostile to man. Insects often serve as vectors for such forms of life."

Annoyed and frightened, Spinney put one protective arm over his pet's narrow green shoulders. The mantis, its jaws ceaselessly working, twisted its sinewy neck to turn one jaundiced compound eye on Angeluce. Manies and Ruffian Jack laughed heartily; even Saint Anne Twiceborn allowed herself a smile. "No cause for worry, Professor," Ruffian Jack said. "My researches show that this particular species of mantis is native only to the eastern arm of Aeo. You notice the peculiar mottling on his inner forearms? We're quite safe."

"Indeed, sir," said Angeluce, visibly annoyed at their laughter. "You hold an Academic degree?"

Ruffian Jack scowled. "I'm an explorer," he said gruffly. "Even the Academy needs its legmen."

"Really, Professor," Manies said smoothly. "It's true that we are all laymen, but I think you underestimate us. My good friend Mr. Nimrod here has classified as many specimens as any Reverid alive, often at considerable risk to himself." All six of Manies' cameras flatteringly zoomed in on Ruffian Jack, and Jack immediately recovered his good humor. "Mr. Spinney is a noted historian as well as a distinguished poet. Even my very young friend the Artificial Kid has written several remarkable articles on chainlink weapons for the Reverid *Journal of Hoplology*, and is one of our planet's most accomplished camera programmers. It would be immodest of me to chronicle my own accomplishments, but I might mention in passing that I am the author of the Chemical Analogue Theory of the Body Politic. Saint Twiceborn is as yet a stranger to our shores, but I am sure she is as talented and intelligent as she is lovely. And here comes breakfast."

We left the railing of the balcony and moved to the oval wooden table. Manies' food programmer, Mr. Quizein, rolled through the door in his servochair, carrying the first course. Quizein was confined to his chair while he awaited the clone growth of a new pair of legs. He had recently lost both his legs to the attack of a ray while swimming on the reef. "Hello, Quizein," I said. "Haven't seen much of you lately."

Quizein pretended not to hear and served the first course, finger-sized breaded nerve clams with red sauce. I grabbed my chopsticks and dug in. They were delicious.

Saint Anne Twiceborn, her chopsticks idle, was staring at me, a bemused expression on her wide, freckled face. I had a camera follow her. Money Manies, whose alert, bulging eyes missed nothing, said: "My dear Saint Anne—do I detect the signs of homesickness on your lovely face? Even after two years in an oneill, the tug of one's homeland can be strong. Tell us, what brings you here? What force on Niwlind provoked your exile?"

Saint Anne reached up with an automatic gesture and smoothed a flat cluster of dark feathers pinned to her hair. She said softly, "I follow the path of righteousness wherever it leads. If to Reverie, so much the better. On Niwlind I was told that Reverie is a paradise—that no one has to work, and that the government is an invisible plutocracy. But I find that there is much work for me here. And it's true, Mr. Manies—I miss my poor flock. By now my government must have completed its policy of genocide, and my poor flock has been scattered and killed. I wish I would have done more for them. That's what makes me melancholy."

Said Manies, "You consider yourself, then, a force for good in our universe?" She nodded. Manies continued, "I have always found such doctrines very interesting. Tell us more about your work. It was with an alien species, am I right? The so-called moor moas—giant flightless birds, yes? And you consider them intelligent—you are convinced that they possess an intangible soul, essence, animus?"

Saint Anne touched the feathers in her hair again. "My heart tells me so," she said. "I freely admit that they are by no means as intelligent as humans, but they have their place in the cosmic scheme. That was why I organized demonstrations to protect their native moors from exploitation. Our government was callous and brutal, and many of my followers were driven to desperate, violent tactics. I was arrested and held to blame. The courts exiled me, so here I am."

Manies said, "Fascinating! I take it that the majority of your fellow Niwlindids did not concur with your estimation of the moas."

"Yes," said Saint Anne. "The moas have no language, they said. They have no hands, no tools, no history, no art. They devour their sick—they are given to mob stampedes—they attack and kill domestic animals as well as wild prey. They are irascible, warty-faced, ugly. Oh, they said many uncomplimentary things."

"All true, I take it," said Alruddin Spinney, pausing to tempt his mantis with a clam.

"Yes," said Saint Anne. "But they never lived with them on the moors. They never saw them dance."

"Can you tell me what inclined you to this friendship with the moas?" asked Manies. "Why did you do such an atypical thing?"

"All forms of life are sacred," said Saint Anne. "I felt the call, so I went."

"How did you prepare for this call? Was it prefaced by a long period of celibacy?" Again, she nodded. Manies' eyes lit up. "And I assume that you possess a fully functional reproductive system?" Another nod, this one rather hesitant.

"Such is my usual experience with such cases," said Manies with an airy gesture. "I suggest to you, dear Saint Anne, that your altruism and your repression of sexuality are intimately linked. I congratulate you on your adroit self-manipulation." He ate another clam.

"That's not so," Saint Anne said. "It's true that I have tried to purify myself with ascetic trials, but my innate goodness existed before that time."

"Really?" said Manies. "I suggest a trial. Let us determine how much of your goodness is natural, and how much cultural; how much you grow green and good from the heart, and how much you are twisted into predetermined shape like a human bonsai. Let us erase all traces of your sexual discipline. My Reverid pornostars are among the most accomplished sexualists in humanity. We could destroy your painful inhibitions with drugs, dear Saint Anne; and then you may fly with fiery wings into their embraces. I assure you that you would find your linkage entirely delightful. Many women would swear themselves into servitude for such an experience, but I offer it to you freely, in a spirit of liberating hedonism. Afterwards, we could see how many of your tenets you still held, and with what degree of firmness. Would you be willing to embark on such a voyage of self-discovery?"

Saint Anne hesitated. Finally she said, "I feel that you mean me no harm, Mr. Manies; so I control my disgust and repulsion. I must ask you not to make such an offer again."

Surprised, Manies said, "I meant no offense; my offer was quite sincere and grounded in a spirit of anthropological inquiry. Isn't that so, Jack?"

"Quite, quite," said Ruffian Jack, tugging playfully on the ends of his long drooping mustache. "The sexual attitudes of Niwlindids are endlessly fascinating. Take for instance the following case-history, which I can vouch for personally," and he told us a long and exceedingly improbable lie that lasted until Quizein came back in, took our plates, and left us with heaped bowls of saltgrass rice tastily fried with the savory meat of sandcrabs. From far away came the bright flash of a flying island detonating somewhere over the continent; we heard its hollow boom.

"It was our outrage at such decadence that gave our church its moral power," said Saint Anne. "I have always struggled against it; and I can see that this world, too, could use a thorough cleaning."

"You'll need a base for such an endeavor," said Manies hospitably. "Might I offer my home? I am willing to warn my many friends and guests about your predilections; I am sure they will make every effort not to offend you."

"No, thank you," said the saint. "I intend to see this planet's worst sink of depravity—the Decriminalized Zone. I saw tapes of the activities there while I was in decontamination. I think my efforts are most needed there."

"You're joking!" I said. "Why, you little ninny, you'll be beaten up and raped before you get twenty feet into the Zone. The Zone is the Zone—it's not a playground for crackbrained fanatics."

"Now I know where I've seen you before," she said. "I recognize your voice. You're that small spiky-headed fellow who beat up that great gross bellowing woman!"

"You saw my fight with Screamer?" I said. "Then you saw me win. My shin was fractured, but nowhere near as badly as her tapes showed. It's almost healed. Look at this cast." I swung my leg up onto the table and pulled up the loose leg of my fuzz-plastic formal pajamas. I was out of my fighting clothes, which may have accounted for her slowness to recognize me.

"And that weapon around your neck," she said. "It's just like the exercise device Secretary Tanglin used to carry. You even look like him!"

I was surprised at this reference to Tanglin. Put on my guard, I frowned. "I'm his son," I said slowly, telling my usual lie. "He came to Reverie thirty years ago."

"How horrible!" she said sadly. "To think of Rominuald Tanglin's blood and bone reduced to this! What a pity he's dead, and was unable to raise you, to give you some trace of his moral excellence!" She shook her head. "I pity you."

This made me angry. A small device on the back of my neck sensed this and sent a crackling rush of static electricity into my plasticized hair. It leapt up into bristling life. Money Manies, Spinney, and Ruffian Jack immediately pushed their chairs back from the table and got ready to retreat; my cameras took the cue and floated into combat formation around me. "What do you know about Rominuald Tanglin?" I said.

"Secretary Tanglin was my idol!" she said. "He was a great leader, a great man! At least, he was until his wife destroyed him and deliberately drove him mad. Why, he did more for the moas than any man alive!"

Suddenly Professor Angeluce, who had been placidly stuffing himself with rice, looked up angrily. "Rominuald Tanglin?"
he demanded. "*The* Rominuald Tanglin? Tanglin, the demagogue, the enemy of science? The man who backed that neuter
charlatan Crossbow in the Gestalt Dispute? Are you related to
Rominuald Tanglin, young man?"

"Yes," I said. I put both hands on my nunchuck and pulled
the chain down taut against the back of my neck. "Did I hear
you call Professor Crossbow a 'neuter charlatan'? Surely my
ears deceived me."

Angeluce went into a huff. "Are you attempting to threaten
me, youngster?" (I heard Jack groan, "Oh, God, now he's done
it.") "I am a Scholar, sir! I am here with the full backing of the
Cabal and I warn you that they will severely punish aggression!
My cameras are recording your every movement for a full report to the Academy as well as your own planetary government!"

I didn't say anything; I just stood up, whipped speed into my
nunchuck, and cracked all three of his cameras. It took about
two seconds. I sat down again. Angeluce was completely dumbstruck. I put my nunchuck back around my neck and released
its handles. Spinney, Ruffian Jack, and Money Manies all got
back into their chairs, from which they had leapt with alacrity
as soon as I pulled my 'chuck.

"Thanks, Kid," Manies said in relief. "We all appreciate your
restraint. Professor, tone down your rhetoric unless you want
the Kid to split your head. Kid, I apologize for him; he's an off-
worlder and doesn't know Reverid etiquette. Forgive him, for
my sake."

"All right, Mr. Manies," I said magnanimously. "For your
sake, I'll deprive my fans of the entertaining sight of Professor
Angeluce beaten to a bloody pulp." That remark about Professor Crossbow had roused my ire. I was familiar with the Tang-
lin-Crossbow alliance in the Gestalt Dispute, because Crossbow
had told me about it.

On the other hand, I was now much better disposed toward
Saint Anne. I had her pegged. She was one of the dozens, no,

hundreds of women overwhelmed at a distance by Tanglin's charisma. I even liked her some. We shared a common distaste for sex.

Angeluce was puce with rage, but he wisely refrained from saying anything. Alruddin Spinney spontaneously decided that something had to be done to break the tension. He picked up his pet mantis with both hands and set it on the table facing him, where it bobbed and weaved alertly on its thick, spiny legs. Spinney stuck a shred of raw meat between his lips. "Kiss kiss," he said. "Kiss kiss!"

The mantis leaned forward daintily and bit out the meat and a small piece of Spinney's lower lip. "Yau!" cried Spinney in pain. "Death take it! He did it right fifty times in practice!"

We all had a good laugh at Spinney's expense. Then I gave him just a trace of smuff to kill the pain and dabbed on a little quikclot. After he had covered the tiny wound with a scrap of skinseal he was as good as new. While I was ministering to Spinney his mantis leapt off the table with a rattle of wings, hopped into my chair, tipped over my bowl with one spiny forearm and started to pick out the bits of crab.

Quizein came in with the third course, a thick, creamy, skate's-egg omelet with kelp salad. It was so incredibly delicious that Angeluce's appetite apparently overcame his anger.

"I assume you've already prepared for next week's Quincentennial, dear Manies," Spinney said, lisping a little. Next week would usher in the five hundredth anniversary of the first settlement on Reverie, Corporate Reverid Year 500. It was an occasion that meant a great deal to surface-dwelling Reverids.

"Yes, of course," said Manies. "I'll be quite busy; I've made so many commitments that I'll have to be everywhere at once. It should prove very lively. The social consensus seems to favor a harlequinade."

I had heard the harlequinade rumor, but now that it was confirmed by Money Manies, a prime social arbiter, the rumor had become fact. "Harlequinade, harlequinade," I said irritably. "I'm sick of these stuffy harlequinades. Why can't we have a satyricon, or even a splashfest? Death, I'd settle for anything."

"A splashfest would hardly be suitable for a state occasion,"

Spinney said with a smile. "Even a harlequinade would have seemed awfully wild and extravagant five hundred years ago."

Ruffian Jack chuckled coarsely. "Moses Moses would spin in his grave, if he had a grave that wasn't blown to atoms."

"Tut tut, do these aged ears detect a crude defamation of the memory of the Corporate Founder?" asked Money Manies rhetorically, chiding Ruffian Jack with two minimal shakes of one pudgy forefinger. "Alas, Jack, your simple patriotism has been painfully tainted. You raise a blush to the cheek of Reverid modesty."

Jack rolled his eyes, but for the moment he seemed to accept Manies' humorous rebuke.

"Moses Moses wouldn't merely spin in his grave," Spinney said darkly. "It was no ordinary grave. Moses Moses was entombed alive, in a cryocoffin. Unfortunately he was posthumously assassinated three centuries ago by the Fox Day blast. His announced intention was to thaw and return to life in Corporate Reverid Year 500. Politically speaking his reappearance would mean disaster; but speaking as an historian, I would have loved a chance to talk to the man. In many ways he remains an enigma."

"Who cares?" boomed Jack callously. "The past is dead, Moses is dead. He's been dead since Fox Day, anyway, and that's three hundred years!"

"But I remember Fox Day," Money Manies said in a remote voice. "I was amazingly young then. No more than your age, Kid. Death, I haven't thought about it in ages. Ages. It was quite a commotion, really. We really thought that the whole world was going to collapse. After all, the entire Reverid Board of Directors was wiped out—the Chairman's Building smashed to rubble—Moses Moses' cryocrypt blown up! Suddenly we had no government! It amazed everyone. Of course, the Board of Directors was never very vigorous after Moses Moses had himself frozen, but once they were gone we had nowhere to turn. Everyone feared terrorism—anarchy! But it never developed."

"No, it didn't," said Spinney. "I've studied the history tapes. That three-week period of no government was the most amazing episode in our history, if you ask me. All our cities, even the oneills, were hotbeds of rumor. Why had the Board met in secret session, after years of idleness? Who was responsible for the explosion? Then the Rump Board assembled itself—a Board even more lax and meaningless than the first—and suddenly the word was on everybody's lips. Cabal. Cabal. Reverie was ruled by a conspirator's council. Faceless men and women. Everyone agreed that they were all rich, all immensely wealthy, but that was the limit of agreement.

"We knew that they were wealthy, because the Corporate limit on personal wealth was the major schism of the period, and the only cause for a coup d'etat. The progressive faction favored a relaxation of the strictures; the old Board of Directors insisted on the primacy of the word of Moses Moses. Destroying Moses Moses was the quickest way to destroy his hold on Reverid society, to loosen the puritanical discipline of the Mining Years. That was the Cabal's motive. They had assassinated the entire Board of Directors, destroyed the Founder of the Reverid Corporation, and assumed control. Their immense wealth gave them spies and assassins everywhere, so it was useless to resist. No one could stop such ruthless efficiency. No one even knew the names or faces of the enemy!"

"Crap," said Ruffian Jack. "It's common knowledge that there are thirteen Cabalists. Seven are men and six are women. The men are called Red, Orange, Yellow, Blue, Green, Indigo, and Violet. The women are called North, South, East, West, Up, and Down. They live in their own oneills, disguised as ordinary orbiters, and they appoint the Rump Board through their agents. Any ten-year-old could tell you that."

"Any ten-year-old surface dweller," Spinney said. "Oddly enough, most orbiters believe quite the opposite. They're convinced that the Cabal dwells on the surface."

"Mr. Spinney is right," said Professor Angeluce suddenly. "The agent of the Cabal who met me in orbit assured me that the Cabalists dwell here in Telset, and in Sylvain, Eros, and Jucklet, the four largest cities." As always, I winced at the mention of "Jucklet." Jucklet! What a tin ear that Moses Moses had for names!

"You met an actual agent of the Cabal?" Manies said with interest. "That's a rare privilege, Professor."

"Not so rare," said Angeluce. "In the oneills your own name is mentioned quite prominently in connection with the Cabal, as you, sir, are no doubt aware. Some allege that the Cabal stifled your political ambitions. Others hint that you yourself may be a member."

"Me, a Cabalist? Law forbid!" said Manies. "I have enough trouble managing this menagerie, much less the planet. As for my political ambitions, perish the thought! I am a simple entertainer. And editor. And antiquarian. And social theorist. Oh, I wear many hats, but the thorny wreath of politics has never encumbered my brow, sir, I assure you."

"Excellent," said Angeluce. "Would that I could say the same for some of my misguided rivals."

The hypocrisy of this covert reference to Professor Crossbow disgusted me. Crossbow had chosen a political ally, Rominuald Tanglin, for Crossbow's interstellar war of words with the cobwebbed reactionaries of the Academy. I was a little unsure about the issues involved in the so-called "Gestalt Dispute"—it was before my time, after all—but I knew which side had my sympathies.

"And what do you call your own alliance with the Cabal, sir, if not 'political'?" I said. "Surely you've demonstrated that you need its bloody-handed help in the promulgation of your own senile meanderings."

"Bloody-handed, sir?" said Angeluce, squaring his shoulders. "I should think that adjective better applied to yourself and your fellow hoodlums, rather than to your planetary government. As for my alliance with the Cabal, you may call it what you like. I care as little for your language as you do for ordinary standards of human decency."

My hair rose, crackling. Manies, Jack, and Spinney quickly ducked under the table. I stood up. Angeluce stood up. I said, "I think your alliance might be best described, sir, as a double buggery of truth and justice. Your rhetoric is as low and hypocritical as your mind is narrow and mean. You, sir, and your treacherous Academic faction are an immense fishbone in the throat of human enlightenment!" Angeluce was turning white. "There is more information in one strand of Professor Crossbow's DNA than there is in the entire rattling, desiccated husk you call your brain!"

Angeluce folded his arms. "Feel free to resort to your usual dastardly violence, sir! As you can see, I am unarmed and unable to resist! Don't let the presence of a decent human being stop you!" He nodded at Saint Anne Twiceborn, who immediately leapt up from her seat to interpose her body between us. I was getting all this on camera and, unwilling to let her upstage us, I quickly sapped her so that she fell onto the table in a heap.

"Sir," I said, "I am sure you would prove as inept in physical combat as you are in a battle of wits! If your lack of weaponry bothers you, feel free to borrow mine!" I threw him my nunchuck. He caught it and, fumbling with it, he cried, "I would not soil my hands with such things!" Clumsily, he flung it over the railing and into the sea.

"You lout!" I cried. "My favorite 'chuck!" Ignoring my injured leg, I leapt over the table, grabbed him by throat and crotch, and hurled him over the railing to fall screaming into the sea. I had a pair of cameras follow him to record his impotent splashing and wallowing until the servants fished him out. Dusting off my hands, I returned to the table.

My host and his two friends crawled out from under it. "He had it coming," Manies said.

"I'll say," said Spinney. He picked up his mantis, which had found a perch on the blunt-cut brown hair of Saint Anne's head. It picked curiously at the flat cluster of feathers there.

"A great performance, Kid," said Ruffian Jack. "Really makes me wish I'd brought my own cameras."

"I'll send you a copy after I edit it," I said. I opened the sleeve of my pajama and injected two cc's of tranquilizer into the plastic drugduct in my left forearm. It soon calmed me down. Spinney and I set Saint Anne back in her chair. I slipped a little smuff into her mouth, checked the bump on her head—a small one—and splashed water in her face. She came to immediately.

"What happened?" she said.

"You fainted," I said. "The excitement overwhelmed you."

She frowned hesitantly. "I feel very strange. Sort of numbtingly . . . all over."

"It'll pass," I said. "Why not relax and enjoy it?"

"Where's the Professor?" she asked vaguely.

"He left suddenly," Manies said. We all had a hearty laugh, and then Quizein brought in the fourth course.

At Manies' insistence, Dr. Kokokla, his personal physician, examined Saint Anne. He assured her that she was all right, gently pointed out that she had bumped her head, and offered her a sedative, which she refused. One of Manies' pornostars came onto the balcony, carrying my nunchuck, which she had carefully dried. I took it and thanked her; I felt uncomfortable without it.

"I've never fainted before in my life," said Saint Anne. "And I fail to see how I could have struck myself in the back of the head by falling face-forward. You can spare me your lying tact, sirs. I know that person struck me with that weapon!"

"Yes, so he did," admitted Manies. "Forgive me, dear Saint Anne; this spontaneous outbreak of violence was entirely my fault. I must own up to a miscalculation. I greatly enjoy the vigorous clash of disparate personalities, but I never thought that you would go so far as to fling yourself into the midst of a physical combat. Such grandiloquent gestures entail a certain risk!"

"Oh, stop groveling, Manies!" I said. "Yes, Anne, I slugged you. You upstaged me! As usual, our host is exquisitely considerate and polite; but don't expect the rest of us to conform to your bizarre notions! Now for heaven's sake, behave like a civilized person or I'll fling you over the balcony." A threat to severely pound Anne would only have roused her stubbornness, but the thought of being embarrassingly and disconcertingly thrown over a balcony made her reconsider. After looking at all of our faces, she took her social cue and sat down sulkily. After a moment she went back to her food. That's one thing about smuff—it seems to boost appetite and taste. It also completely kills pain, though it numbs, it disorients, it impairs coordination and sometimes hearing.

"Dear Saint Anne, thank you for being so reasonable," said Manies. "I give careful thought to picking the guests for these breakfasts, closely following the implied dictates of my Chemical Analogue Theory of the Body Politic—but sometimes I combine too sharp an acid, too bitter a base, and then I must deal with the following explosion! It's disconcerting, but often quite exhilarating! It keeps me young. I am a very old man, dear Saint; please allow me my quirks."

"I forgive you, Mr. Manies," said Saint Anne. "I believe that you have a good heart. And you have your own kind of wisdom, even if it be an ungodly one."

Manies beamed at this as if it were the most flattering compliment ever to touch his ears. Spinney and Ruffian Jack stifled smiles at her naïveté. "I am only fifty-two," Anne said. "You must have accumulated a lot of learning in such a long lifetime, even if you were never theologically trained. What is your Chemical Analogue Theory?"

Spinney and Jack rolled up their eyes, but the three of us were happy to hear it, as it gave us the chance to be silent and attack the main course, a tender roast tail of sea beaver that we ate with knives and forks.

"The Chemical Analogue Theory is, of course, an analogy," said Manies. He touched a stud on the heavy bracelet on his right wrist and in rushed his secretary Chalkwhistle, a neuter. Manies took pencil and slate from the neuter and began sketching as he talked. "As you are well aware, dear Saint Anne, the human body is an immensely complex system, in fact an ecosystem with its own flora and fauna. The same is true of the Body Politic, our human society. Their reactions, their structures are very similar. Now, the history of the human body is the history of its organic macromolecules, its linkages (pardon me) of separate atoms. Similarly, the history of the Body Politic is the history of many small groups and coteries, linked groups of friends. Of course, I would not go so far as to equate a single personality with a single atom. In most cases people would be better considered as small molecules; acids, bases, salts, et cetera. I often consider them atoms for simplicity's sake, however.

"Note that the effect of a single atom in the human body is almost negligible; but if that atom is included in the right molecule, its influence may be crucial! It does not matter which particular atom enters a molecule, you understand; the important thing is that it be the correct kind of atom, and attached in the correct molecular framework! It is the framework that counts, you see, just as the important thing is the relationships within groups of friends, rather than the friends themselves. Of course some atoms are comparatively rare, just as some personality types are comparatively rare, and they can exert a disproportionate influence; but it is the linkages that count.

"I regard myself as an enzyme, constantly endeavoring to link molecular groups into newer and more potent configurations. This breakfast is just such an attempt."

"In other words it's not who you are, it's who you know," Spinney said. Spinney, Jack, and I were shamelessly gorging ourselves; we had already heard Manies' ludicrous, disjointed theory several times. It was one of the most visible signs of his age. It was no stranger or crazier than other senile theories cooked up by people his age—Rominuald Tanglin, for instance.

"Correct! Such statements show an intuitive understanding of this principle," said Manies happily. "Let me offer a concrete example. Perhaps you recognize this molecule, delta-1 tetrahydrocannabinol." He held up his slate.

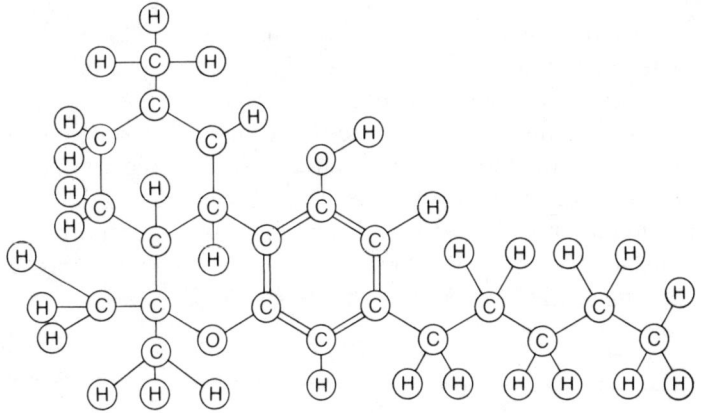

"This is a mild hallucinogen and euphoriant," said Manies. "As you can see, its structure is relatively simple; fifty-three atoms, all carbon, hydrogen, or oxygen, with no troublesome nitrogen or silicon as in so many drugs. I determined to deliberately replicate its structure as a Chemical Analogue, to determine its effect on the actions of the Body Politic. You may recall the occasion, dear Alruddin. It was the Mid-Year Satyricon, five years ago."

"Wau, do I!" said Spinney enthusiastically. "What a celebration! People were singing, shouting, laughing, crying, stripping off their costumes, linking right in the streets . . . howling at the Morning Star, diving off the Coral Towers . . . and at dawn there was a mass nude swim in Telset Bay! It was incredible, unbelievable!" He sobered. "You're not claiming you were responsible for that, Money Manies?"

"Responsible, my dear fellow?" said Manies with a cryptic smile. "You were one of the oxygens! It might have gone on indefinitely if one of my carbons had not eloped with someone else's hydrogen, breaking the structure down into a mere cannabinoid. . . . However, I consider the whole episode a strong point in favor of my theory. The experiment was well worth the effort of gathering together fifty-three hand-picked friends. Thank you, Chalkwhistle, that's all for now." Manies erased the slate with a touch of his thumb and handed it back to his secretary, who left. "Would anyone care for some sherbet?"

We all had sherbet, then had servants clear away the breakfast table and bring in lounge chairs. Manies passed around some mild after-breakfast drugs, and Spinney read us part of the new installment in his Telset Cycle. The eastern sky slowly reddened with dawn, and when the sun's vivid yellow rim touched the horizon we greeted it with shouts of acclaim. The placid waters of the great Gulf of Memory flamed up gold for an instant, then settled into the deep sapphire blue of daylight.

Breakfast was over; it was time to go home.

3

I now had one week to prepare for the Harlequinade, really an absolute minimum for a person in my status position. Most of the time I enjoyed status maneuvering—what Reverid doesn't?—but there were times when the endless minutiae and petty bickering made me sick, and this was one of them. I felt that it was aging me before my time.

The young can't begin to compete with the old in dominance games; the old have an overwhelming advantage in self-control, in experience, in knowledge of human motivation. But thanks to combat art and the Decriminalized Zone, the young now have their own social arena and their own rules of politesse. In fact, in many ways the combat art system has become a microcosm of the larger world outside. But it's our microcosm, where a young person at least has a chance at power—in the outside world you can only look forward to a hundred years of kindly, gentle, subtle slavery.

In this smaller world, I was a man to reckon with. Naturally I had my own client coterie, the Artificial Youth Faction. I restricted the membership to twelve, and the competition was intense, especially since I made it a point of honor never to beat up my clients unless they really deserved it.

The arrangements for the Harlequinade took time. First there was the problem of my costume. I made very little attempt to disguise myself, since the plasticized hair of myself and my twelve minions made disguise useless. Instead, I wore my usual fighting gear, barely camouflaged under a loose black-and-white smock and thin black flared pants vertically striped in scarlet. I also wore a simple black domino mask. Naturally I designed my own clothing.

Then there was the pressing matter of my palanquin. There was nothing wrong with the palanquin itself; Quade and I could easily unfold it, reassemble it, and redecorate it. The problem was choosing which six of my twelve clients would have the honor of bearing me about. The honored six would swagger intolerably, while the snubbed six would sulk. I had to arrange for everyone's rendezvous, and then go through the grapevine to establish a suitable location for my palanquin during the hologram display. I couldn't have cared less about the display, but socially speaking it was crucial that my palanquin be prominently placed.

I hated harlequinades.

Luckily, my good friend and fellow artist Chill Factor, co-head of the Cognitive Dissonants and chairman of C.D. Enterprises, was handling the details of the palanquin business. I got a call from him the day before the Harlequinade.

"Greetings, Arti, my little angel of violence!" said Chill. "How's the leg?"

"Cast comes off tomorrow," I told him. "What's on your mind, Chill?"

Chill looked harried; his sharp, narrow, glacially blue face had little puckers between his white, frost-brittle brows. There was a freezing beaded condensate on his cheeks and forehead and his icicle hair was half-an-inch thick in white rime. His status position was keeping him busy.

Behind him on the wall of his tape room was a map of the area in question, neatly marked off in a hexagonal grillwork. "I have you here," he said, rising from his console chair and pointing to the map. "You'll be next to Raphael of the Fourways and Todd Regewgaws of the Manglers. I'm just up the hillside a way, with Icy and a few of the Cogs—Twinkles, Hammer, Happy Daze—you know, the usual lot."

"I'll be there," I said. I was pleased at my position.

Chill looked relieved. He wiped his brow with the back of one ice-blue hand, cracking a thin layer of ice that had formed around his knuckles. Chill's refrigerated second skin was form fitted perfectly to his face, but there were a few small telltale bumps and wrinkles around his fingers. I still don't know how he supplied the necessary refrigerant power, but I suspect that it came from small engines hidden in his furry mukluks.

"You accept it, then?" he said. "Ah, that's my angel Arti. The status war this year has stricken me with grief, endless grief. Several areas are contested, including your own. I expect—well, not bloodshed, because fighting on holidays is gauche. But this will be the cause of many a bruise feud in the new year."

"I can hold my own territory," I said. "Call on me if you need help."

"Thoughtful, thoughtful," nodded Chill. "The Billy Club are the only ones on the Civic Detail, by the way."

I was disgusted. I despised police detail. The pay was great, but it was essentially a bribe from the Board of Directors to keep the combat gangs under control. Somehow the cunning old rascals had made the "Civic Detail" into a hotly contested honor. "Those bootlickers," I said. "What good are they? They couldn't punch their way out of a wet barrel. Crap, this could be serious."

"There was something else I meant to tell you," said Chill. He struck his forehead with the icy palm of his hand, then tore it loose with a shredding sound. "Ah yes. The mysterious gentleman in Red." He raised his voice. "Icy! Did I file that call under 'Grudges,' or under 'Threats'?"

"I think under grudges, darling," came Ice Lady's voice from off camera.

"Oh dear. I think the grudge file overflowed its capacity yesterday—you know these combat poseurs, Arti, taking a status demotion so, so personally—I must have lost the call. The man in question offered me five hundred fracs to beat you sense-less."

"Was it anyone you knew?"

"He wore a red mask. He seemed old, though. Hard to tell, of course. Obviously he knew very little about the art, or he would have called one of your enemies, rather than me. In fact, I'm sure he has asked someone else already. He seemed quite de-termined."

"Five hundred fracs isn't bad pay."

"For you, my angel Arti, I would have demanded at least five thousand."

"You flatter me, Chill." I cut off.

On New Year's Day, the Artificial Youth Faction gathered to-gether, to bear me in state through the Zone. The Decriminal-ized Zone was usually a lonely place. Most of the battered buildings were deserted.

Now, however, the Zone was clotted with people. As it al-ways did, the sight of such a large crowd gave me a creepy sen-sation of awe. For the first twenty years of my life, I had been alone on the reef except for Professor Crossbow and my tapes, and the occasional rare visitor. Even after eight years in Telset, crowds disturbed me.

There were all the expected costumes of Harlequinade, with a decided historical bent this time: floater costumes, the somber garb of the Mining Engineers, the black and nebular yellow of Confederate officials, the decadent six-hundred-year-old finery of the Niwlindid Directorate, combined, mutated, exaggerated, adulterated with every atom of a playful and cynical Reverid ingenuity. There were others dressed as historical figures— members of the Board of Directors, favorite artists, composers, and scientists, or drowned swimmers from Aquaria, Reverie's ill-fated underwater city, or maddened plutocrats from the first rash days of expansionism; and then, crowding thick as swarm-ing flies, the advocates of pure bizarrerie: people in fish cos-tumes, dressed as insects, as birds, as crustaceans and coelen-terates, people swathed in fur, or plated in skin-tight mirrors, people with no faces, or four arms, or eight legs; people in chains, in webs, in masses of bubbling froth; people dressed as the dead, the living, the not-yet-to-be, and the never-could-be. There were cameras everywhere.

It took a very special occasion to physically assemble Telset's scattered population, but this was it. The entire population was there: over three hundred thousand people. A crowd that large assumes an uncanny life of its own. Multicolored streams and filaments of people were pouring in and out of the crowd like the protoplasmic flow of an amoeba. Colored litters and palanquins were moving sluggishly above the heads of the crowd like food vacuoles. I rolled back the top of my palanquin and stood up as we neared the thickening edges of the crowd.

Cameras were drifting over the mass like hot droplets of grease over something frying. The crowd was making frying sounds; they were thousands of conversations, murmured propositions, shrieks of laughter, merging into an anonymous hiss and sputter like the sound from a blank tape, turned up far too high. Masked faces turned toward me; a murmur spread, because I had been recognized at once. Some people retreated from me, others advanced. I had a good view as the Artificial Youth Faction surged into the crowd.

I had delayed my arrival until midafternoon. The real fun would probably not begin until nightfall, anyway.

"You, sir! The gentleman in the black domino!" I looked down. I had been hailed by Emery Board, one of the minor members of the Billy Club. I recognized her despite her fish mask; she was wearing the rainbow armband of the Civic Detail. "This stranger has begged for an introduction." A huge lout in tasteless fringed leather clothing was standing at Emery's elbow. The stranger wore no mask. He was obviously not from Telset.

"You call yourself the Artificial Kid?" he bellowed, in a stupid breach of etiquette. He should have shown at least a token confusion over my disguise. I turned two cameras on him. "Why deny it?" I said easily.

"Why don't you hop out of that contraption and talk to me

man to man?" he demanded. "It makes my neck hurt to look up." Shocked titters arose from a rapidly growing group of spectators.

"My pleasure," I said. I leapt out of the palanquin and knocked him down with a kick in the chest.

He rolled with the kick and got up easily enough, dusting off his peculiar backwoods clothing with his rough, calloused hands.

"You're pretty clever with your feet," he said levelly. "In Jucklet we don't think much of feet fighters."

"In Jucklet you don't think much at all," I observed, winning a gratifying round of applause from the masked spectators. My cameras went into combat position. The six members of the Artificial Youth Faction set down the palanquin with sighs of relief and sat on it, grinning under their masks.

"I've seen you fight before, but I don't call that real fighting," the man said. "You don't feel pain. You use those chuka sticks. It's not man to man. It's opera stuff. It's faked! I'm more of a man than you, and I can prove it!"

The crowd was eating it up. Ribald suggestions flowed from their decadent lips. "Show us your manhood, then!" "Kiss 'im, Kid!" "Go on, Leather! Challenge him!"

I raised one hand for silence. From the corner of my eye I noticed that cameras were accumulating everywhere, which annoyed me; I hate bootleg tapes. "What do you propose?" I asked.

"Punch for punch," he said. "Man to man. No weapons. No dodging or defending. Last man to get back up loses. That's what I call an honest bout."

He knew as well as I did that those were impossible terms; it was my skill at dodging, defending, and blocking blows that made up for my lack of height and bulk. "Fine," I said. "You strike first." I dropped my candy-striped nunchuck and put my hands behind me.

As I expected, he swung for my chin. As the punch came in I leaned forward slightly and dropped my jaw. He punched me in the teeth. For anyone but myself it would have been a fatal gambit, but my teeth are a sturdy legacy from dear Old Dad.

They were all false, tooth-shaped white ceramic over a crystalline metal core, anchored solidly to one of the thin ceramic plates that armored my skull. He screamed and drew away his hand, dripping blood. I smiled evilly, skipped forward and hit him in the neck with the outside edge of the base of my hand. He fell down choking and soon lost consciousness. It was a nasty blow, but he was a nasty man.

I spoke quietly to Emery. "Get him to a doctor, Emery. You'd better hurry. I'll assume the charges." The man's neck already showed a dark stain; it was probably arterial hemorrhage.

I picked up my nunchuck and jumped back into the palanquin to a round of polite and somewhat intimidated applause from the spectators. If they had expected a long slugfest they were disappointed, but I wouldn't waste time being pounded for the sake of someone else's cameras. I pulled the cover of the palanquin up for privacy as the Artificial Youth Faction hoisted it with a grunt to their shoulders. I put salve on my lips to stop the swelling. My bravado in letting him strike first had cost me, but you don't win a reputation without taking risks.

Following the instructions that Chill had given me earlier, the Youth Faction made their way toward the area I had staked out for the hologram display. A nameless poseur had had the gall to park his palanquin in my place, and I had the Youth Faction dump him and stomp him soundly. We watched him crawl off as we broke his palanquin to pieces.

"Trouble, trouble, trouble, always trouble," observed a wry, vibrant voice. It was my best friend, the well-known combat artist, Armitrage. Armitrage had a lovely dark young woman on his left arm and a gentle, rather frightened-looking young man on his right. "These, sir, are my two new clients," he said, noticing my gaze. "For the time being you may address them as Jonquil and Coral." He struck a pose. "Have no fear, darling clients. I will protect you from this sinister ruffian." His two clients giggled shyly, cupping their hands over their mouths. I never learned which name fit which client.

Armitrage and I were so close that we merely played with the formalities of disguise. "Delighted to see both you and your complaisant lovelies, dear Stranger doll," I said. I invited him into my palanquin and offered him a flavored ice-stick. My housekeeper Quade, who had been faithfully tagging after me all this time, rushed up to offer sweetmeats to his two lovers.

"Where's your litter, 'Trage?" I asked.

He shrugged. "Left it behind," he said. "My aching death, these harlequinades bore the morals out of me." He sucked meditatively on his ice-stick. "It's as hot as the Morning Star out here. I can't remember when I've seen such a crowd, even on tape." I nodded. "I saw Money Manies a while ago," Armitrage said. "He had his Alien with him."

"Not again," I said.

"He never learns," Armitrage said sadly. "Even if he does learn, then he forgets."

"Yeah," I said. Even for an old man, Money Manies was unusually prone to peculiar lapses of memory. Most people thought that Manies was really forgetful, but I was convinced that it was one of his affectations. He was entirely too alert to be genuinely absent-minded.

"I understand the Clone Brothers are looking for you," Armitrage said. "I thought you'd settled with them."

"So did I," I said. "However, if they haven't learned, I'm always ready to administer another lesson."

"Want me to tag along today, in case there's trouble?"

"My gratitude, but no."

Armitrage shrugged again. "That's my proud Arti." He leaned gracefully back into the palanquin.

Most of the palanquins in the viewing area were down, and their tenants had left them to stroll about and socialize. The area just around us was crowded with combat artists and their young hangers-on. I spotted members of the Fourways, the Manglers, and the Perfect Stranglers.

Armitrage pried an artificial bubo from his neck and scratched under it. (I haven't mentioned as yet that Armitrage was disguised as an early Reverid settler suffering from a lymph infection.) "What are your plans now?" he asked. I shrugged. "Join me, then," he offered. "I'll keep you amused. You feel like some hot flashes? I've got some really nice Red Dust on me." Armitrage, besides being my best friend, also sold me my smuff. He was the drug supplier for many of the artists of the Zone—a very high-status occupation. "Maybe," I said. "I'd prefer something milder, though."

"Let's see what we can barter for, then." We dismissed our attendants and plunged into the crowd.

A man walked by us on stilts; Armitrage unobtrusively tripped him and sent him sprawling into a picnicking group of dancers from the third contingent of the Telset Ballet. Snickering, we ducked away behind the bearers of a litter. We detoured around a huge two-man pink palanquin belonging to a pair of lovers from the Perfect Stranglers, then almost stumbled over one of the Clone Brothers.

The Clone in question was squatting on the broken, weedgrown pavement with Jet Pink of the Stranglers, tossing polyhedral dice. He turned, saw me, and scrambled quickly to his feet. He was wearing a bright red bodysuit dotted with small metal studs. His mask was a stiff elongated band of white plastic that encircled his head; narrow red lenses hid his eyes. The plainness of this costume was strange for the tawdry Clones. It looked like livery, and its color could mean only one thing.

"Well," piped the Clone, recovering his composure. "It's the Mechanical Boy. How delightful to see you, Mechanical."

I looked him over, with contempt. "You shouldn't wear red, Clone doll," I told him. "It doesn't suit you."

"It hides the splatters of blood from those who offend their betters," said the Clone confidently. He stepped closer. I smelled the faint bitterness of cosmetic spices on his breath. He reached out slowly and laid his long, narrow palm across my cheek. "On behalf of my brothers and other selves, we challenge you, Artificial Kid. We challenge you! Bruise feud!" He slapped me.

I stepped back. "Tell your boss, the coward in red that hired you, that I will demolish him after I finish with his bootlicks."

The Clone pursed his lips. "Bootlick? Harsh words from the fawning pet of Money Manies."

My hair rose, crackling. Armitrage touched my wrist. "Don't hit him, Kid. He isn't armed."

"Right," I said. "I won't argue patronage with you, Clone.

Meet me in three days, midnight, at Rubble Plaza."

"Too late, too late," squeaked the Clone. "Haste is the essence of Red's request. No, we destroy you today, rash Kid."

"This is a holiday," Armitrage said indignantly. "Show some class, Clone!"

"See to your own health, officious and interfering Armitrage!" snapped the Clone. "The minor details of combat courtesy no longer concern us. Our new patron is powerful, and his commands predominate. Do not become his enemy!"

"If you attack the Kid today, you'll have to come through me first," Armitrage promised.

"Don't bother," I told Armitrage. "They can't force me to fight today. I'll pick my own ground and my own conditions."

"Think again, unwise Kid. You have ambushed and beaten us singly, but our corporate quartet will break you, tonight."

"All four of you intend to attack me, alone?"

"We have challenged you in accordance with the Code. Our techniques are our own business."

"In that case, I'll help the odds right now!" With a shriek of anger, I crushed the Clone's left instep with a heavy stamp kick and drove the handles of my nunchuck deep into his gut. He doubled over and I struck an overhand hammer-fist into the back of his neck. He fell in a heap.

As I administered smuff to the unconscious Clone, Jet Pink shook his head. "You attacked an unarmed man!" he said loudly, for the benefit of the crowd that had gathered during the argument. "Your arrogance calls for a heavy reprisal, Artificial Kid."

I gave him a deadly glare. "You know my communiqué line, Pink. For you, I'm ready any time." I pushed him aside and shoved my way through the crowd.

Armitrage caught up with me before I had left the palanquin grounds. By that time I had recovered my good humor. I clapped him on the back. "Come on, let's find old Oswald Pigment. I could use some White Light."

"Take it easy on the drugs today, Kid. That's my advice."

"Ha! I never thought I'd hear that from you, 'Trage!"

"You have a powerful enemy. You'll need your alertness."

"This is Harlequinade, dammit! No skinny little replica spoils my holiday. You saw how I disposed of him." I snapped my fingers. "Besides, no one fights today. How can they make me? I'll stay with friends."

Armitrage nodded slowly. "I'll see to that, anyway." Suddenly he grimaced. "Death, here comes my patron."

It was the lady Elspeth Milvain, Money Manies' closest rival, being borne in state in an immense flower-covered palanquin carried by a chain-gang of eight nude pornotapers.

"You there!" she crowed at Armitrage. "The ravishing gentleman with the disease! When can we tape that lovely body in action? We'll give you anything! Perhaps we'll even cure you!"

"Nothing can cure me but a healing kiss from the Queen of Beauty," cried Armitrage gallantly. He leapt athletically up onto her palanquin, sending the bearers staggering, grabbed Milvain by her feathered crown-mask and kissed her open mouth. Then he leapt back down and stripped the artificial bubos from the sides of his neck. "My recovery is complete!"

Elspeth Milvain laughed up into the higher reaches of hysteria and struck the side of her palanquin with her whip. Glaring blackly at Armitrage, her bearers shuffled off.

Armitrage watched them go. "The old bag," he muttered. "Here, Kid, see if you can help me tape these bubos back on."

Eventually we found our friend Oswald Pigment, surrounded by his aesthetic disciples, the Pigment Group of painters. He gave us some White Light, a drug which vastly intensifies visual imagery. From then on the day began to disintegrate.

To fully describe our drug-raddled wanderings would be tedious. There was one odd series of occurrences: we kept running into Money Manies, or people who looked like him. He was wearing a different costume every time we glimpsed him. I suspected that most of the multiple Moneys Manies were wandering holograms. Laughing, he admitted as much. "I told you I'd be everywhere at once, didn't I?" Somehow I got into a bizarre conversation with Money Manies' Alien, who was disguised as a human being. (There were those who claimed that Manies' Alien had actually once been a human being, but that was probably a slander.) The Alien was wearing a pair of infrared night-glasses that were fragmented into colored polygons like an insect's compound eyes. As usual, the Alien's face was hidden behind a thin white veil. Its false human skin looked rather dry and rubbery. "How good the crowd smells," the Alien observed. "I will never understand why people are not allowed to be eaten."

After night had fallen, Armitrage and I watched part of the hologram display from the beach, where members and hangers-on of the Cognitive Dissonants were roasting fresh-caught fish over a driftwood fire. I hadn't talked to any of the Cogs in weeks, and the occasion was pleasant. The food was good, the night was good, the drugs were fine. Even the hokey old holo-gram projections, stuffy, slow-paced stuff that only old people could enjoy, were fun to jeer at. From the beach, we could barely see the titanic, lumbering holos. Anyway, their color was off.

I hadn't planned on joining the Cogs on the shore, but Armi-trage had subtly steered me there—at some risk to himself, since he had a minor bruise feud going with Million Masks. It was all good will and camaraderie, however, until Armitrage began talking with Chains. I was close enough to listen in, since I had been staring in fascination at the links of Chains's light chain mail dress. Under the influence of White Light, her outfit was all splintered glittering.

"I talked to Brains today," Armitrage began, innocently enough.

Chains shrugged. "So what?"

"He was your man, Chains."

"Our breakup is no business of yours, friend." She hesitated, then said, "I couldn't live with him; he was analyzing us to death. He's too remote, too detached. He can't release himself. He's too smart for his own good—far too self-conscious. It drove me crazy."

"Words," said Armitrage. Slowly, he continued: "But love isn't words. Love is the other. It grows within you. It holds you. It warms you. It is its own being. It is a power, like fire. It cares nothing for the woman who thinks she owns it. It cares nothing for the man who thinks he can replace it. If you fight it, it will sour and poison you. If you suppress it, it will only sink deeper and destroy you."

"This tirade from you, Armitrage?" Chains laughed mockingly. "I know your promiscuity. You'll link with anything that moves. I've seen your tapes."

"Did I say that was love? Brains still loves you. If he didn't, he wouldn't seek his own destruction so ardently. I'm asking you to save him. He's too proud to ask for himself." He sighed. "Pride is the great vice of us Reverids."

"You're beginning to bore me, Armitrage. Shut up, I'm warning you."

"You are too proud to admit that you need him."

Reflex took over. Chains suddenly screamed at him and went for his face with a tiger-claw grip. Armitrage blocked the blow and knocked her down, blacking one of her eyes. Chains challenged him and they agreed to meet in a week's time, Armitrage and his combat staff against Chains and her weighted manrikigusari. Armitrage then left.

I stayed. Sumo and I had a good laugh over Armitrage's sentimental posturings. We agreed with Chains that he had been insufferable. It was true, but I liked him all the more for it. I didn't understand him, but friends are all the better for a touch of mystery.

I stuffed myself with fish, then wandered about twenty paces down the beach to lie down and listen to the surf. I pillowed my head on my padded nunchuck. I had fitted the padding myself, because this nunchuck was a special legacy from Old Dad. It had been built for him on Niwlind, during one of his peaks of paranoia. The bottom of each club unscrewed with a quick twist of the hand, revealing the muzzle of a single-shot projectile weapon.

I had tried the guns before on lonely beaches; either gun would blow a hole bigger than my head in wet, packed sand. Guns, however, were forbidden in the Zone by the combat Code, just like blade weapons, stilettos, explosives, and other immediately lethal arms. Even my good friends the Cognitive Dissonants would have been honor-bound to beat me to a pulp for carrying such a thing, if they had known about it. If I had actually used it on someone, they would have reefed me; weighted my feet with chains and dropped me off the reef to be food for rays.

But this candy-striped nunchuck was one of my favorites. I liked having something special in reserve; I liked having a final card to play. That, too, was a legacy from Tanglin.

"Pssst!" The hiss barely reached me. Torpid as a poolful of carp, I hardly stirred. The hiss came again, and this time I looked around.

It was Brains. He was lying prone in a spiky growth of marsh-grass, about four strides away. He was peeking out through a gap in the thick blades of tall grass, his gaudy costume well hidden.

"Brains!" I said.

"Not so loud!" he said. "Come down the beach a ways. I don't want to be seen."

I lurched to my feet and met Brains again in a sheltered spot out of earshot of the rest of the Cogs, who were doing a ritual dance anyway and paying absolutely no attention. "Get down, get down," insisted Brains, crouching in the sand. "I mustn't be seen here. She's just over there."

"Who cares?" I said. "You're being ridiculous, Brains doll."

Brains clapped the heel of his hand to the transparent window set into his skull. "This is the thanks I get? I've got important news, Kid. I wouldn't come within a mile of that woman otherwise."

"Well, what is it?"

"It's your housekeeper. The tall woman, with arms like pencils. She's been taken. Kidnapped by the Clone Brothers."

I stared at him. "My client? My servant? But that's a blood insult. Clients are sacred! They're asking for blood feud!"

Brains shook his head. "I heard about the way they challenged you today. Now they're just trying to force you to fight."

I stood upright. "I'll rally the Cogs. This is going too far. This kind of transgression involves all of us. At least Chill and Icy—"

"No, no!" Brains said hastily. "Don't tell them!" He motioned me back down again. "Come on, Arti. You don't need a lot of

Cogs to hog your glory. This is a great scenario! Master to the rescue and all that. And I'll help you track them down."

"You?" I said.

"Sure, why not? We always worked well together in the Cogs. Didn't I bring you the news? Don't you owe me one? Give me a break, Arti. I've left the Cogs, you know. I'm trying to make it solo. A tape with the Kid would help a lot. Come on, please?"

I looked at him skeptically. "Are you in condition to fight?"

"I'm always in condition," Brains said, offended, flexing his arms. He was a fanatic for fitness. Maybe it was his lack of humor that had kept him from reaching top rank. "There are only three of them. You practically crippled the fourth one today, if what I hear is true. The two of us can handle them. I've fought the Clones before. And I brought my tonfa." He held up his rotating club.

"Well...." I reached into my drugpak for my syringe and some stimulant. I injected a little into the plastic drugduct in my left forearm and breathed deeply as the rush cleared cobwebs from my head. Anger and confidence surged through me. "All right, Brains. You're on."

"Great! The Clones will never know what hit them."

"We have to find them first."

"Rubble Plaza, Kid. Their favorite turf. That's my guess." He was exultant. "Let's go, let's go! My new career is waiting in the wings. Come on, we'll redo the discovery scene." He shook himself. "Ready? One, two, three, four! 'Arti! Your servant! She's been stolen!' "

Once, Rubble Plaza had been the thriving center of Old Telset. Now it was the blasted, empty heart of the Decriminalized Zone. The transition had come in a single day, when the Fox Day bomb was smuggled into the Chairman's Building. Rumor said the bomb had been placed directly on the great black cryocoffin that was Moses Moses' resting place and living monument.

Now, at the center of the Plaza, stood the forty-foot bronze statue of Moses Moses, the Founder of the Corporation. White floodlights lit it from below tonight, and gave its immense metal face a sinister appearance. The titanic Founder seemed to be peering into the gutted five-story building that had once housed the Board of Distribution. The Fox Day blast had ripped the building's roof off and mashed its nearer wall into a shattered patchwork. The same for the Board of Records. The same for the Consular Library. I didn't know the names of the other broken buildings.

As for the Chairman's Building itself—once Telset's pride, stern and austere outside, but inside as rich and ornate as the Corporation's fantastic wealth could make it—it had been utterly leveled. Boulder-sized bits and pieces of it lay heaped everywhere, some with long jackstraw spars of metallic epoxy reinforcement jutting out. Chunks of the upper stories had been thrown as far as Telset Bay. Most of the building, however, had leapt out as a devastating wave of shrapnel that had knocked gaping holes even through the thick, solid, windowless walls of the surrounding structures.

It had never been restored. It would never be repaired. In itself, Rubble Plaza was a monument. For three hundred years it had been a place of silence. Now, part of the Zone, it was an artificial slum for the Zone's artificial thugs.

I liked Rubble Plaza. I felt at ease there. I had explored all the buildings, even the most hazardous, where the floors creaked ominously and the rotted ceilings were poised to mash you like a bug. Old people never went there. That was why I liked it.

Tonight, there were a few floating globes of light still left for the late stragglers or wanderers from the Harlequinade. Not many would come to this desolate place without a reason.

"They're not here," I said.

"They're probably lurking in one of the ruins hoping you'll show up," Brains said confidently. "Let's split up and flush them out."

I shook my head. "Better stay with me. You don't want to be caught alone."

Brains disagreed. "Nonsense. I can take care of myself." He whirled his tonfa efficiently. "Yell if you need help. I'll do the same if I have to. But I won't. Remember, they don't know I'm looking for them." He trotted off into the darkness.

"Hold on!" I said. When he replied, his voice was already eerily echoed from the tilted slab of a ruined wall. "Don't worry! I'll soon flush them out!"

This rashness was so unlike Brains that for the first time that night I stopped and soberly considered my situation. "This smells," I said, speaking aloud for the cameras. "This smells of a set-up." But it couldn't be. Brains had helped me too many times; we had fought back to back; we had guest-edited each other's tapes when I was a neophyte and he was already a hardened veteran. . . . Could it be that Brains so envied my success that he would betray me? Surely not if it meant helping the repellent Clone Brothers.

I would have plunged into the ruins myself in search of the Clones, but I had forgotten my infrared glasses. Stupidly, I had left them in my palanquin. I could see well enough to pick my way through the rubble, but fighting in the darkness was out of the question. If I met the Clones tonight, it would have to be by the statue of Moses Moses, in the glow from the floodlights.

I picked my way through the weeds and hip-high chunks of shattered masonry, looking for an area with good footing that was relatively clear. A floating orange light drifted over toward me, following its rudimentary programming, and my cameras switched lenses. About twenty feet from the statue's base, I found a clear area, about four strides square. The rubble there seemed to have been cleared deliberately. All the broken detritus had somehow been shoved off to one side, away from the statue, leaving scrape-marks in the gritty dust. No weeds grew there. The ruined scraps of heat-seared tile underfoot showed that this had once been the ornate floor of the Chairman's Building.

The Clone Brothers might have cleared this area themselves, knowing I would come here. It seemed suspicious. I checked the surrounding rubble for traps or hideyholes where the Clones might strike from ambush. I found nothing. The footing was solid and well-lit. Satisfied, I began pacing, stretching, clearing my lungs, doing my kata.

I heard a sound in the darkness. I leapt into a defensive position. A luminous white figure came toward me from the dimness, almost seeming to drift. My hair crackled and stood on end.

"Mr. Kid? It *is* you, isn't it?" I recognized the voice at once. It was Saint Anne Twiceborn. As she came into the light I saw that she was wearing her usual baggy white saint's garb, a shapeless sack that fastened tight around wrists, neck, and ankles.

I pulled off my flimsy Harlequinade domino mask. "Yes, it's me. What are you doing here? The Zone gets nasty again after Harlequinade. You're not even armed."

"We were hiding," said the Saint. "We saw a monstrous creature stalk by here, not long ago. It had great spiny jowls and a flattened pig's nose, and huge cruel arms with taloned fingers. It was naked, and it had no feet. It had hooves instead. Its legs bent backwards. It smelled awful. I've seen some horrible costumes today, but this was no costume, Mr. Kid. It was real!"

I laughed. "You make him sound terrifying! Why, that was just little Goaty, the gargoyle of the Zone. He's slow! He's stupid! Being heavily altered surgically—well, it slows you down. I could step on his neck as easy as crushing a bug." I considered. "Easier. I like bugs."

"He terrified us."

"What's this 'we' business?" I said impatiently. "Is there someone else with you, or do you have tapeworms?"

"I suppose you enjoy abusing those who have done you no harm," Saint Anne said tartly. "I've known people of that stripe before. Terrible things happen to them." She turned and called over her shoulder into the darkness. "Come on out, Mr. Whitcomb. It's safe now. I know this man."

A stranger walked gracefully out of the darkness. He was short, about my height, but broader in build, with a handsome, well-trimmed auburn beard. He was wearing an historical costume, a soberly cut black formal suit with white pinstripes, woven out of threads, in the antique style. He had no Harlequinade mask.

Whitcomb sat on a chunk of rubble at the edge of the small

cleared area. "Good evening, sir," he said politely. "I seem to have, ah, lost my way. This rubbled area here—" he waved one arm eloquently—"isn't this where the Chairman's Building once stood?"

"Yes, that's right," I said. For some reason, I took an instant liking to the old bearded man. I spoke to him kindly. "Listen, sir, you seem to be rather confused. Perhaps you're under the influence of some drug. That's all very well when the City's at play and the Zone is in truce. But the Harlequinade is over now. You shouldn't be in the Decriminalized Zone unarmed."

"Sir, I thank you for that warning," he said. For a long moment, he looked me over. Whitcomb's round, amber-colored eyes seemed to miss nothing. He said, "I feel that I should recognize you. Your face and that very tasteful hair seem familiar to me. You must pardon me for my apparent negligence. My memory has been affected—I suspect a breakdown in my computerized memory system. Perhaps I've seen you on tape before?"

"Very likely," I said. "Strangely, you look rather familiar to me, too, Mr. Whitcomb." I looked at him critically. "Maybe it's your costume. It looks like the sort of thing the old, pioneer Board of Directors used to wear." I stepped up close to him and touched the peculiar material of his sleeve. "A bit stern perhaps . . . stodgy . . . on you it looks good, however." I stepped back. "I tell you what, Mr. Whitcomb. You seem to be a man of substance, well worth bothering with. I'm sure you want to avoid the embarrassment of having your condition revealed publicly."

Whitcomb nodded quickly. "Yes. With all respect to Madame Twiceborn's suggestions, I'd like to avoid police involvement or any, ah, formal proceedings."

I nodded sympathetically. The old man's status was at stake. "These things can happen to anyone your age," I said airily. "What you need is competent, discreet treatment. My good friend Mr. Money Manies—you've heard of him of course—can help you recover your memory and restore you to yourself. There will be no charge. Mr. Manies is generosity itself."

"That's very kind of you, sir."

"People call me the Artificial Kid."

"Well, I'm very glad to make your acquaintance," he said. "My name is Amphine Whitcomb." He extended his hand. It took me a while to catch on, but I shook it. It's a custom you don't see much nowadays. He must have been very old.

"I'd like to take you home now, but other matters press," I said. "I could give you directions there, but my computer guards my house against intruders. Saint Anne, could I trust you with the password to the house? It's a bit complex—you never know when a spy camera might be watching or listening. . . ." I broke off as I saw Brains returning from the ruins, adroitly dodging through the rubble. "They're coming," he gasped, then drew up short. "Who are these people?"

"Friends," I said. "But not combatants. Call them clients for the time being. Yes, I declare them my clients."

"Well . . . Kid . . ." said Brains hesitantly, "I hate to imply that your ability to shelter clients is in question, but for the time being I'd suggest that they withdraw."

"Let them watch," I said. "I'm ready if you are. Did you see Quade?"

"She should be released soon. That's my understanding," said Brains. One by one, he began shutting off his cameras. The Clone Brothers had arrived.

"A lovely night to you, poisoned and foredoomed Kid," said one of the Clones, mincing up out of the shadows. A long chain dangled from his hand, clinking delicately on the ground. "A night you will long remember . . . a night that will make you wince henceforth at the mention of our name."

"He was supposed to be alone," another of the Clones told Brains accusingly.

Brains shrugged. "These are noncombatants. None of my doing. Our agreement still holds?"

"You will receive the rest of your recompense, helpful Brains. Our patron's resources are vast."

"Yes, so I've learned." Brains picked up his four dead cameras with a mournful look. He had already stepped carefully out of range of a surprise attack. "I can't bear to record this," he said. "Kid, I offer my regrets, but the reward was just too great.

My new lover's tastes are expensive. Call me when you get out of intensive care, and put the medical expenses on my tab. Believe me, I can afford it." He left.

"That's great, Brains," I shouted at his retreating back. "I hope to return the favor some time." I turned to Saint Anne and Whitcomb. "As you can see, I've been betrayed. I suggest that you run as fast and as far as you can." They exchanged glances, then began to back up rapidly, stumbling over rubble. Then they turned and fled into the darkness.

The Clones unlimbered their chains and drew nearer. They were all wearing infrared glasses, which gave them another advantage over me; otherwise I would have considered running and trying to out-dodge them in the rubble.

A peculiar hesitation gripped all four Clones. "Our tactics regarding your spindly client might seem provocative of blood feud, oh ignoble and much-outnumbered Kid," said the fourth Clone.

"And, indeed, we would enjoy your murder," said the first one, bravely.

"However, the loss of our best-known opponent would hurt our audience even if it helped our reputations. Therefore, you will be spared." This came from the Clone who was limping, badly.

"Your client is in the hands of Red, our puissant patron. She will be released when we deliver to him the tapes of your destruction. This occasion is imminent. Therefore, prepare to reap the whirlwind of our multiple wrath!"

I didn't wait. With a cry, I attacked the nearest Clone. I kicked him in the midriff with my steel-toed slipper, knocking him down in a tangle, and numbed another's arm with my chuck, but there were too many of them. A heavy iron chain hit my kneecap with crippling impact and I went down, squalling, kicking and gouging.

It was lucky for me that Old Dad had bequeathed me a tough, surgically altered body. My skull was sheathed with thin plates of ceramic reinforcement, and my teeth, all false, were white ceramic over a crystalline metal core. The leather body armor under my costume protected heart and kidneys, and my ribcage was reinforced. I needed it, because they gave me a terrible beating. My plastic hair helped a little with the blows to my head, but I felt the kiss of chains on legs and arms and chest and back and buttocks and padded groin. They turned me into a human drum that they beat in 4/4 time, chattering excitedly amongst themselves in the peculiar abbreviated vocabulary that they used with one another: "Pretty!" "Happy!" "Beat!" "Kick!"

As I lay there, battered and semiconscious, they slipped smuff into my mouth. True, they did it surreptitiously, but even the loathsome Clones were not devoid of this last shred of combat etiquette. Then they climbed with spiderlike agility up the great limestone pedestal of Moses Moses' statue. Hoisting me up by the arms and legs, they scuttled to the edge of the statue's base. "Kiddy off the statue, Kiddy off the statue!" they chanted happily, seizing me by the wrists and ankles. They swung me back and forth, gathering momentum: "One!" "Two!" "Threeee!" and they pitched me headfirst into space. I fell ten feet to land with a wet crunch on my back and shoulders. Magnanimously, they tossed down my nunchuck. I blacked out.

4

When I returned to consciousness my body was aflame with pain. With swollen fingers, I dug into the sealed pocket of my combat jacket and pulled out my smuff. Before I opened my eyes I swallowed it. The pain went far away and I sat up slowly.

I was not in my home, which surprised me. Usually, Quade came and got me if I had been severely beaten up. But of course, Quade had been taken. I saw that I was in an abandoned building with Saint Anne Twiceborn.

"Don't move!" Saint Anne cautioned. "Lie back down! You've been horribly beaten, Mr. Kid."

I snorted. "That should be obvious." I pulled off the thin, bloodied rags of my Harlequinade costume and looked myself over. It was ugly. "Feels like I broke my collarbone." I dug into the numbed flesh with my fingertips. "No, it's all right. What are you doing here, anyway? What am I doing here? I'm supposed to be at home being tenderly nursed in delicious luxury.

Why am I still out here in the ruins?" I looked at her suspiciously. "Did you drag me in here?"

"We found you unconscious and bleeding," she said indignantly. "What were we supposed to do?"

"How long have I been out?" I walked to the leaning, corroded door and looked outside. I checked the position of the stars. "Just past midnight. Where's my housekeeper? She should be released by now, unless the Clones have compounded their treachery." I checked the inner pockets of my combat jacket. "My locator is still on. She should have been able to find me by now if she's returned to my house." I turned my locator off and looked to see if I still had all six of my cameras. I still did. I turned to Saint Anne. "Have you seen my servant? Quade Altman?"

"I'm afraid not," Saint Anne said. "I've been hiding you in here for hours now. Please stop walking around so, Mr. Kid. You're a horribly sick man. Your pores are full of little black worms! They kept creeping into your wounds! If I hadn't found these tweezers in your pocket I could never have picked them out!"

"Little black worms?" I said, puzzled. Suddenly I realized what she had done. "Those were my follicle mites! You stupid fanatic! Those things *live* in wounds! They eat dead cells, they eat bacteria! Now it'll take forever to heal!" I clutched my head. "That was the worst thing you could have possibly done! I ought to pound you black and blue!" I snatched up my candy-striped nunchuck, but stopped when I saw her reaction of injured innocence. I looped the 'chuck into its usual position around my neck. I stared at her. "You're a very strange woman, Saint Anne. And you don't understand all this—this world of mine. Are you aware of the harm you've done?"

"I meant to help, Mr. Kid. We could have run away, but we stopped when we saw you suffering. I'm sorry, but how was I to know?"

"Did I ask for your interference?" I said rhetorically, but without much heat. She had deflated me again. "And stop calling me Mr. Kid, dammit. Call me Kid or Arti." I reached into my sealed jacket pocket for my drugpak and treated myself to a stimulant. The rush hit me harder than I had expected. I put my head between my knees and breathed shallowly until my head cleared. "There. That's better. Now let's have a look at me." I dug into a wound on my forearm and pulled back a flap of doubled-under skin. "At least you had the good sense to smear quikclot on some of these things."

"I saw you use it on Mr. Spinney a week ago."

"Pardon me while I strip." I pulled off my combat clothes and treated the wounds she hadn't touched. She averted her eyes. I laughed scornfully. "Some nurse you are! My death, with you around I'm lucky to be alive!"

I gestured her to her feet. "Here, make yourself useful for once. Help me smear on some of this skin oil." I brought out my spare packet of oil. "Come on, my skin won't burn your hands. This oil will feed the survivors among those poor mites you killed. You just smear it on my back. I'll do the threatening parts." I laughed, a little hysterically. The stimulant was getting to me.

"You need hardly regard me as a sexual threat, Saint doll. You could see that for yourself, without me telling you. I share your contempt for that silly, gross coupling." I smeared the oil all over myself. Luckily the mites multiplied rapidly in the right conditions and would soon be able to resume their healthful work. I put mite-permeable skinseal over the remaining open wounds. There was dried blood all over me, even inside my nostrils; I had lost a lot of it. My plastic hair was all clotted together; scalp wounds always bleed a lot. I felt dizzy, but it was probably just the smuff, and the stimulant would take care of that. I put my clothes back on.

"Let's go home," I said. "Where's your pinstriped friend?"

"Out in the Plaza," Anne said. "He's been wandering back and forth through the ruins for hours now. It seems to fascinate him. I warned him that it was dangerous, but he paid no heed."

"He's a strange one," I said. "I don't buy this amnesia story of his, either. It's no computer breakdown. He's too dazed for that. It's either drugs or suicide trauma."

Anne nodded slowly. "Something terrible has happened to him. He still needs my help."

"How did you run into him, anyway?"

"I met him for the first time early this morning. I was watching the Telset Ballet perform. I've always enjoyed watching dances. It's very wicked of me, of course, but if Telset's to be my home I'll have to accustom myself to seeing such things."

"How broad-minded of you."

"I wasn't wearing a mask, and had some difficulties because of it. I was standing quietly at the edge of the crowd. A man—Mr. Whitcomb—appeared at my elbow. I noticed that he wasn't wearing a mask either, so I smiled at him, and he said, 'I wonder if you can tell me, young lady—are most of the people in this crowd human?' Those were his exact words. I thought he was making a joke, but he was quite serious. He pointed out an eight-legged man nearby and swore the man was an alien. He said the man had tried to pull his face off."

"But mechanized legs show up at every Harlequinade," I objected. "In fact, they're kind of passé right now. And the man probably thought that Whitcomb was wearing some kind of incredibly detailed beard mask."

"We exchanged names, and then he asked me if I had anything to drink. He said he was afraid to ask the masqueraders for food or water. I gave him some juice. He seemed terribly thirsty. Then he began to ask me all kinds of strange questions—was I a corporate shareholder, was the Board of Directors still settled in Telset at the moment. He seemed bewildered. But he was very polite. Even charming."

"He's in a bad way," I said. "We'd better get him to my place in a hurry before he recovers. Money Manies loves little mysteries like this. Nothing pleases him more."

We crept out quietly into Rubble Plaza. Anne's hideaway bordered on it. We soon found Whitcomb sitting quietly under a tilted slab of shattered wall, staring at the titanic statue.

"Well, young citizen," Whitcomb said when he saw me. "Up again, I see. You certainly are of resilient fiber. I wonder if you could tell me—this is, of course, the famous statue of—?"

"Moses Moses," I said.

"Yes, I thought so," he said. He smiled and got to his feet. "I am at your service."

The buildings in the Decriminalized Zone, my own home included, are the oldest on Reverie. Most of them were abandoned painlessly; their peculiar starkness makes them repugnant to modern Reverid tastes. Modern Reverids prefer open, lavish, baroque homes, handcrafted out of native materials— Many Mansions, for instance. The buildings of the Zone were all constructed from orbit by drones, using the same techniques that had proven successful during the century-long Mining of the Morning Star.

First the island of Telset was fried with orbital lasers until sterile. Then orbital pods landed, laden with drones and raw materials. They were directed by the same tough-minded mining technicians who had enriched the Reverid Corporation with their manipulative skills. Their objective was to build a city capable of housing fifty thousand Reverids, about the population of one oneill.

The result was so uninspiring that most Reverids, who had already lived through one century in orbit and had made their big cylindrical oneills amazingly lavish and comfortable, simply decided to stay there. They could see all they wanted of the surface through their drones, which were often provided with a direct cerebral hookup and had reached a peak of development during the long and horribly complicated mining years.

We Reverids have no equals in our mastery of drones— "drone" meaning any one of several types of self-propelled mechanisms, piloted from a distance. We learned our mastery the hard way, mining the hostile, airless Morning Star by remote control. And when we settled Reverie, we put our knowledge to a thousand good uses—such as the floating cameras that make my lifestyle possible, and the computer-run armies of robots whose orbiting farms and factories make us continually richer.

The pioneer surface Reverids were much concerned with biocontamination; understandably, too, because Reverid protozoans are amazingly advanced. Most typical bacteria elsewhere, for instance, come in three shapes: spheres, rods, and spirals. There are plenty of those on Reverie, but there are also rings, spiral rings, T-shapes, snowflakes, and crosses. I know. I've seen them through Professor Crossbow's microscopes.

The old buildings of the Zone were built by those expecting plague. They have thick doors, carefully insulated ventilating systems, and a lack of frills and furbelows where dust and trash can build up. The walls are thick masonry, lavishly reinforced with metal (which the pioneers had in plenty, thanks to their mining operations). Joints and walls are sealed incredibly tight with metallic epoxy; in the destruction of a building the epoxy is always the last to go.

All this proved grossly unnecessary when computer simulation revealed that eighty-two different species of Reverid bacteria, carefully introduced into the body, would provide all the necessary vitamin-producing and digestive functions, while killing other bacterial intruders. Getting the bacterial ecosystem set up is a long and arduous process, but after that it works fine, provided that you don't foul it up with the wrong drugs. Freed of their fear of disease, Reverids gradually abandoned the old drone-built structures. When the Fox Day blast destroyed the Chairman's Building and damaged many others, it was the end. Old Telset echoed, empty, while open, breezy, hedonistic structures bloomed up all around like limestone flowers.

But I'm a combat artist. I loved those old drone-builts. They're built like forts. My home, for instance, was my literal castle. It had three stories, one of which was below ground. It looked completely anonymous from the outside, which pleased me. High ramparts surrounding the roof hid my terraria, Quade's little garden, and the pergola, where we sunbathed. The house had only one door, but I had cut a few holes in the walls to get decent-sized windows, paned with tough crystal quartz and protected with heavy shutters and eye-traps. I had my own generator, my own well, my own recycler. I even had the building's old ventilation system repaired, and could make the old place tight against even a gas attack.

I had the place completely wired and my computer handled the alarms. I felt secure against attack and had taken, I thought, all the necessary precautions; even a few unnecessary ones, in homage to Old Dad's paranoid spirit.

But they had never been put into practice, until today.

I smelled the tear-gas from the door-trap canisters a full block away from the house. I broke into a run, despite the smuff-muted whispers from my legs that should have been shouts of agonizing pain.

Most of the gas had been dispersed by the night breeze, but my eyes still ran freely when I reached the door. It had been tampered with. There were scratches around the jamb and the door's edge.

I shut the cunningly hinged flaps that had hidden the blunt copper muzzles of the gas canisters. I put three fingers on the door's pressure spots, muttered the password, and pushed my way in.

Armitrage was already inside. He leapt up from the couch, but lowered his quarterstaff when he saw me. "You're alive!" he said. "My death, you're pulped! But you're alive!"

Whitcomb and Saint Anne came in; Armitrage raised his staff. "They're with me, Armitrage," I said.

Armitrage pushed the door shut with the weighted end of his quarterstaff, then flung his arms wide, showing his embroidered shirt front and handsome green sleeves. "Arti, I swear I'd hug you to this bosom if you weren't drenched in your own gore. From the way you've been savaged today, I was sure it meant blood feud. I've been sitting here, convinced that your precious self was in a ray's belly."

"Hardly," I said. "What's going on here? Where's Quade? And who tried to break into my house?"

"One at a time." Armitrage held up one hand and began counting off points on his fingers.

"First, a group of men in colored bodysuits showed up in the Zone tonight and set your palanquin on fire. They soaked it in some kind of fluid first. It burned to the ground. That's what the witnesses said. Second, your housekeeper was stolen by the Clone Brothers in the middle of a crowd of witnesses. They yelled challenges addressed to you while they dragged her off. And they caught up with you, didn't they? I recognize the impact marks of their chains."

I held up my hand. "You warned me. I admit it. You warned me."

"Third, someone tried to break into your house, and your

house alarms called me and woke me out of a sound sleep. That was the latest development. I got here as soon as I could, of course, but I didn't see the assailants. In fact, I couldn't see anything for your damned tear gas."

"Sorry, 'Trage."

"That's all right," he said winningly. "I lied about the sound sleep, anyway. I was worried."

"How long have you been here?"

"Maybe an hour and a half. It's been bizarre. Your Old Dad has been in, raving, on and off."

"Yes, he always does that when the computer alarms are triggered," I said. "Even during drills. Damn, I'd hoped to find Quade here. Instead, I find I've been attacked on all fronts! This is a crisis!" I hesitated. "Obviously I'll want to look my best. The three of you must chat while I get out of these bloody rags and into a hot bath. Armitrage, meet my friends, Saint Anne and Mr. Whitcomb. You know where everything is . . . drinks, drugs, snacks, tapes . . . ." I hesitated in the doorway, then stepped aside as my Old Dad paced alertly into the room, looking to either side with glittering, rapacious eyes. "A time of attack is no time for half measures!" he thundered.

"Right," I said facetiously. "Saint Anne, Mr. Whitcomb: my father, Rominuald Tanglin. Dad, keep them amused a while, won't you?" I snickered mischievously when I saw Saint Anne turn white and grab the edge of the couch for support.

I left the room and went downstairs to bathe, emptying the tub and running in new water until it no longer turned crusty red at the touch of my body. I cleaned my hair, put on new skinseal, examined the wounds and found them all squirming with mites. I put a few temporary stitches in the larger wounds. Then I put on a second set of my full combat garb and slipped on a thin overrobe. I returned to my friends.

Armitrage was talking intently to Saint Anne, who kept looking sidelong at Tanglin's hologram. Whitcomb was standing in the corner listening to Tanglin's lecture and sipping a glass of water. It struck me suddenly that Whitcomb didn't realize that Tanglin was on tape.

"Now I'm prepared to take action," I said briskly. Anne

looked puzzled. "Style is a weapon," I explained. "I could never allow my enemies to blunt my style. I'd be two-thirds defeated already. That's what my Old Dad always told me. Isn't that so, Old Dad?" I walked up to the holo and put my hand through his torso. He vanished. Whitcomb raised his eyebrows.

"Anne has told me how you were betrayed by Brains," Armitrage said. "Let's go into your tape room for a minute and discuss some private strategy."

"All right," I said. We left Anne and Whitcomb and went into the soundproofed tape room. Armitrage shut the door unobtrusively.

"Who are those two spooks?" he said.

"You mean Anne and Whitcomb? They're harmless." I laughed. "They're both sort of borderline crazies. Anne's a Niwlindid, and Whitcomb is ... hmm ... come to think of it, I don't know what Whitcomb is. I like him, though. Don't you?"

"I like the woman," Armitrage said. "What does she have to do with your Old Dad?"

"She knew him on Niwlind. He was her patron, or whatever they call them there. Do you really think she's attractive, 'Trage?"

"Anyone who can wear clothes that ugly and look that good has to be more than just attractive," he said. "She's a real heartbreaker. A blind man couldn't miss the way she looked at Tanglin, though. As for this Whitcomb character ... you know, I have a suspicion that he may be behind all your troubles."

"Him? You think he is Red? Well, what grudge could he have? I've never even seen him before."

"Are you sure, Kid? He looks awfully familiar, somehow. I could swear I've seen him on tape."

"Well ... at least we have him where we can watch him. This has gone far enough. I look better now—haggard enough to be dramatic, but not absolutely demolished. I'm going to call Money Manies and Chill Factor. I'll try to hire some of the Cogs as my agents in a bruise feud against Red. Manies can provide the financial backing, so I can meet Red on his own terms."

"Let me in on this," Armitrage said. "I see this as the first major art event of the year. And you'll need my help."

"Do you work cheap?"

"No, but you can trust me."

"Good point." We went back into the living room and opened up my communiqué line. I tried to put a call through to Manies. There was a blur of static, and an image appeared on the screen.

It was a circular rainbow, surrounding a cluster of six directional arrows.

"What in death's name is that?" said Armitrage. "Looks like a test pattern."

I touched my selector. "It's on every channel," I said, amazed. "Someone's been at my wiring! What an insult! Great sweating death, I wouldn't have believed there'd be a Reverid alive who'd stoop so low!" I looked sidelong at Whitcomb, but he looked as surprised as the rest of us.

"Well, that tears it," I said. "Now I'll have to walk over to Many Mansions and have a long heart-to-heart with my patron." My hair was up; I glared fiercely at my companions.

"I'll go with you," Armitrage said. "The noncombatants will be safe enough here." He opened the door.

There were four men and a woman across the street in an alleyway. The men were all wearing simple skintight masks and bodytights. One was in red, one in yellow, one in orange, and one in blue. The woman was Quade Altman. She was gagged. Two of the men were holding her arms.

"Those must be the people who burned the palanquin," said Armitrage calmly. He shut the door.

"And they have my housekeeper hostage," I said. "Armitrage, do you remember where I keep my rifle? You were always better with it than I was."

"I can't just gun them down," Armitrage protested. "It just isn't done!"

"Never mind that! Just go up on the roof and keep an eye on them while I see what they want!"

Armitrage left. "Let me talk to them," Anne said. "I'll be your mediator; they won't hurt me."

I glared at her. "If you try to upstage me one more time, I'll rip your lungs out! Go sit on that couch and shut up!"

I pushed the door half open and let two of my cameras out. "How did you like a taste of my tear gas, you kidnapping miscreants?"

The figure in red put a small, compact bullhorn to his lips. "Do not seek to irritate us further," he said, in a conversational tone that rang through the empty night streets like the voice of a god. "Resistance is useless. We have the power of the entire planet marshaled behind us!"

I drew back from the door while the others looked out. "What is he talking about?" I said. "Am I dealing with a megalomaniac?"

"Why are they dressed like that?" Whitcomb asked. "Red, orange, yellow, and blue? Isn't that awfully conspicuous, such bright colors?"

Saint Anne said, "Mr. Nimrod told us that the members of the Cabal were named after colors. Do you remember, Kid?"

"I remember," I said. "But what would the Cabal want with me? I'm not political. I'm not even rich, not by plutocrat standards."

Saint Anne said, "They can't like you very much. After all, you did call them a pack of bloody-handed murderers. You said that they were a fishbone in the throat of human enlightenment."

"I said nothing of the kind," I said. "That was the Academy I was insulting, not the Cabal. Wait! The Academy!" I grabbed my head and felt a dull throb of pain; it was time for another dose of smuff.

I leaned out the door again. "You there! The impotent old geezer in red! I offer you two choices! Release my client at once and go your way; or tell me your name so that I can declare formal blood feud!"

"You are in no position to name terms," said the calm, magnified voice. "However, since your impudence has been properly punished, we are prepared to be lenient. We will exchange your client for the man you hold, the old man in black!"

"I thought it might come to this," Whitcomb said quietly.

"I don't trust you!" I shouted. "Release my client first."

"Not likely!" said Red. "Send us the old man, or we will destroy your house at once with explosives!"

"You're bluffing!" I yelled. "An explosion would bring every artist in the Zone! They'd rip you to shreds!"

"You stubborn child! You force this action on us!" Red hopped up into the air and ripped the gag out of Quade's mouth. At once, a thin, hideous wailing poured out of her. It was wordless, and mindless, like the cry of an animal. I had never heard such frantic pain from a human throat. Shocked fury galvanized me. I jumped through the door and ran toward them, snarling.

Suddenly, from nowhere, the man in blue produced a pistol. I didn't even see it. It was blind luck that made my swollen knee give way; I fell, and a bullet thwacked into the door behind me, jolting it farther open.

My enemies then unwisely decided to rush the house. Armitrage shot the man in blue, who was holding onto Quade Altman with his left arm; he fell down with a scream and the others scattered as he crawled for cover. I scrambled back to my feet, grabbed Quade's arm as she stood there dazed and howling, and hustled her into the house. There was the crack of another shot from the rooftop and a second scream.

Once inside the house, Quade suddenly lost her voice in a fit of convulsive choking. The tormented look in her yellowed eyes filled me with insane fury. I burst through the door, whipped my nunchuck around and prepared to kill one of the wounded men, but they had already been dragged away into the maze of the Zone. I went inside, slammed the door, and stood wheezing and snarling with rage.

Armitrage clattered down the stairs, half-dancing with exultation. "Was that shooting, or was that shooting?" He threw the rifle aside and embraced Quade. "You're rescued, my elegant, elongated friend! Why no smiles, no tears of joy. . . ." His voice trailed off vacantly and he suddenly released her as if he had been embracing a corpse. "My God, look at her head! Look at her arms and legs!"

With an effort, we got Quade to sit woodenly on the couch.

There were half-a-dozen ugly gouges in her scalp, and puckered red sear-marks on her thin arms and legs. "Those are burn marks," I said stupidly. "My God, she's been tortured." I shook her gently. "Who could have done this to you? You, my harmless innocent?"

Something in my tone seemed to reach her. Her eyes opened wide, showing eye-whites stained with yellow film, and she screamed again. Then she started thrashing, without co-ordination. Armitrage and I held her down and slipped smuff into her mouth. Soon her cries declined to whimpering and silence.

"She must be in shock," I said.

Armitrage shook his head. "I'm afraid not, Arti. Look at those eyes of hers. Are they often like that?"

"Yellow, you mean? Sometimes. I don't know why."

"Well, I do. She's a syncophine addict, and she's in withdrawal. I wonder where she keeps her stores. Syncophine's not on the market any more. She may have her own supply somewhere, but she'll have to go cold turkey now."

"Why? Why can't we ask her where she keeps her drug, and give her some?"

"Look. Look at those gouge-marks in her scalp. She's been memory-wiped. You've been talking to a new personality."

"But that's murder!" I hugged the unresisting, unresponsive Quade to me; she was like wood. Tears scalded my eyes. "I promised to protect her. I gave her shelter. She was *mine!* How dare they rob me of her life? This is it! Blood feud! I declare blood feud! Professor Angeluce, you are a dead man!"

Anne looked up, startled, from where she was pillowing Quade's head. "Professor Angeluce?"

"Yes," I said bitterly. "I'm certain that was him in the red costume. I recognized his voice and the way he moved. Now I'm going to kill him. Armitrage, will you help me?"

"Sure. Who is he?" After we had explained, Armitrage said, "Unless he's with the Cabal, then where did he get those hired bullies? Men like that don't work for a smile and a thank-you. But the Cabal has plenty of money. They must be backing him at least; otherwise, he wouldn't dare wear their livery. I don't like this, Kid. I'd be happy to spill the Professor's brains, whoever he is. But the planetary government . . . they're a little beyond the sticks and chains stage. They blew up the Chairman's Building. They killed the Board of Directors. They killed Moses Moses."

Whitcomb said, "The Cabal is the planetary government?" Amazed at his ignorance, we nodded. "They killed Moses Moses?" We nodded again. "This is all news to me," Whitcomb said. "I am Moses Moses."

Moses Moses took advantage of our dumbstruck silence to explain himself. His ornamental cryocrypt in the Chairman's Building had contained a dummy; the canny Moses had hidden his true cryocrypt beneath the building in a secret, heavily armored and completely automatic sanctum sanctorum. At precisely the stated date, he had been warmed up, stretched the stiffness out of his muscles, dressed himself, and come up through the rubble. That explained the cleared patch in the rubble at the base of the statue. "It's a good thing they didn't build the statue twenty feet further over," he said.

"You're Moses Moses?" I said at last. "Somehow I had always imagined you to be . . . well . . . *larger*. More mythic, somehow."

"Sorry, I'm flesh and blood," said Moses with a wry smile. "I expected a different world when I awoke, but I assure you I never expected *this*. I thought there would at least be someone to greet me. I never suspected that the center of my city would become a wasteland." He sighed. "It was a shock. I didn't know where to turn. And now it seems I've been recognized. I was recorded on the cameras of the men who beat you up, Artificial Kid. Their master must have recognized me and panicked. He tried to track you down to find me, even tortured your housekeeper to get her to help them break into your home. But she must have kept faith. Otherwise we would all be dead, I'm sure. They are obviously ruthless men. No doubt they wanted to wait here to ambush us."

"Yeah," I said. "The Cabal could hardly allow you to live. You must be the worst threat they could possibly face. You're a hero, you're the Founder of the Corporation. Holy Death, on Reverie you're the closest thing to God."

"I thought you looked familiar," Armitrage said wonderingly. "Excuse me, but . . . well . . . could I shake your hand? You've always been an idol of mine." Solemnly, they shook hands. Armitrage looked at the palm of his hand as if he expected it to glow with a sacred aura. "Wau," he said. "This is truly an unexpected privilege."

Except for poor Quade, we all shook his hand. Somehow the old ritual made us feel better.

"We'd better leave here," Armitrage said. "They're sure to return, and if they find us we'll be killed or brainwiped. Those portable brainwipers are terrible. You saw what it did to Quade. The Cabal protects its secrets."

"Yes, we've got to care for Quade somehow," I said. I looked at Armitrage. "You're the only one of us they haven't seen yet. You take Quade to the Cognitive Dissonants. Chill Factor can take care of her. Besides, he's the only one I can trust."

"How much should I tell him?" Armitrage said.

I shrugged. "I'll leave that to you. I'll take these two to Money Manies. He's the only person I can think of who could fight the Cabal on their own terms." I glanced at Saint Anne. "It's our only hope. Now that we've seen Moses Moses, our lives are forfeit, no matter what we do."

"But Professor Angeluce said that Mr. Manies was a Cabalist himself," Saint Anne objected. "Why don't we simply go to the streets and announce that Chairman Moses has Come Again? We'll soon have a crowd of loyal supporters around us, and we can get them to do what's best. Besides, we have the right on our side. The Cabal are usurpers. We shouldn't skulk around in the dark, like them. We should declare ourselves."

"Maybe so, but not in the middle of the Decriminalized Zone," I said. "They're armed, and they may have explosives. Besides, we should announce it to the whole world, not just a small group. Otherwise, they could kill us all, and then claim that the Second Coming was just a rumor. We need an announcement on tape, a released speech that six million Reverids can see at once. That way there'd be no way to stop us. Besides, if everyone knew, then the Cabal would have no reason to single us out—unless we got in the way while they were trying to kill Moses Moses, of course. And Money Manies can help us. He has access to more channels than any Reverid on Telset Isle. We have to have his help, or we can't survive. Armitrage, run upstairs to the storeroom and get us all some infrareds while I see to Quade. Get all my smuff, too. You know where I keep it."

I would have liked to take the rifle with us, but it would have attracted unwelcome attention outside my home. In any case, I still had my shotgun nunchuck. My arms and legs were stiffening up; they were blue and purple and swarming with mites. They felt hot to the touch. I didn't hurt, but the body has its own wisdom, and it wanted to be flat on its back. But there wasn't time to indulge it.

By the time I had finished ministering to Quade, Saint Anne and Armitrage were telling Moses Moses about the events of the past four hundred and twenty-five years, a process that was obviously going to take a very long time. They gestured excitedly and slapped their foreheads and backtracked and interrupted one another loudly. They all had infrareds on. Anne and Moses Moses had put on pairs of my night-party glasses, frivolous ornamented numbers that fit them very badly and looked completely ludicrous on them. Armitrage had Quade by the arm; he was tall and the top of his head came almost half-way up her forearm. I put on my infrareds and everything went black and white and shiny. "Ready?" I said. We left.

5

Armitrage and Quade left us at the door; Armitrage agreed to rejoin us at Many Mansions as soon as possible. Saint Anne, Moses Moses, and I walked quickly east. We reached the beach without meeting anyone of consequence, then headed south to the docks where I kept my little boat, the *Sea Whip*. I had half-expected it to be guarded, but the Cabal apparently hadn't had time to take that precaution. They must have been scrambling for some way to meet this unexpected emergency, and the long habit of sloth slowed them down. It's impossible to be both quick and secret.

I hadn't taken the *Sea Whip* out in two months, and there was a dense growth of weed on her hull. We got on board and cast off. She was sluggish; the night breeze off the reef was only mild. I took her down the channel and about half-a-mile offshore, where we wouldn't run the risk of holing the hull on coral.

By this time I was beginning to hurt quite badly. I took more smuff and heard the first telltale buzzing in my ears. I got off the little gunwale and stretched out on the deck so I wouldn't fall overboard; my equilibrium was shot. I was hungry, too, and the only food on board was four stale bars of oneill synthetic chocolate. I gobbled them down.

Saint Anne was giving Moses Moses her grossly biased view of Reverid history. Moses kept nodding and saying, "Really? Amazing, fantastic!" Moses Moses was at least three hundred subjective years old, probably closer to three-fifty, but he hadn't lost his zest for life. For him, his reawakening must have been a lot like a rebirth. He assured me that he could pilot the *Sea Whip*, and of course he knew where Prospect Point was, though in his day no one had lived there. I stretched out and went to sleep.

We reached Many Mansions about two hours past midnight. A Harlequinade party was still going on far down the western slope of Prospect Point, in one of the Mansions' beach outbuildings. At the top of the slope I saw a glow through one of the heavy one-way windows in Money Manies' private chambers, where no one was allowed to set foot but himself and his wife Annabella. Even his faithful secretary Chalkwhistle was excluded; Manies treasured that small three-roomed core of privacy. I was glad Manies was awake and separated from his usual horde of sycophants and hangers-on.

We tied up at Manies' dock, next to the *Albatross*. I glanced at Moses Moses and laughed. "No one could possibly recognize you behind those glasses," I said. "At least we're safe on that point." We left the *Sea Whip* and climbed up the slope to one of Many Mansions' numerous doors. I tried it; it was locked. I rang the bell and waited. Eventually Chalkwhistle answered it. "Hello, Kid," it said. "What happened to you?"

"Open up, Chalkwhistle," I told it brusquely. "I've got to talk to Manies."

Chalkwhistle looked apologetic. "Sorry," it said. "I've been told to admit no one. Why not go down the beach and join the party? Mr. Manies will be there some time before dawn."

"Sorry, Chalkwhistle," I said. "Emergency." I popped Chalkwhistle on the head with my 'chuck and it went down, its arms flailing. I stepped inside. We dragged Chalkwhistle aside onto a comfortable section of carpet, shut the door behind us, and locked it. We made our way through panelled corridors rich with mobiles and objets d'art to the door of Manies' private chamber. Manies must have been watching us through a house alarm system because he opened the massive, well-oiled door before we reached it.

"Kid!" he said. "What a peasant surplice." With an unsteady swing of his arm he gestured us into a richly decorated sitting room across the hall. Behind him, his wife Annabella came out, shut the door behind her, and ostentatiously locked it with a thumbprint. We heard heavy bolts and magnetic seals slide into place. Annabella was a slim, dark woman with enormous green eyes who had once been Manies' top pornostar, although she had never had a speaking role. She never spoke. She had the litheness of age but that was all I knew about her. Manies collapsed into a tapestry armchair. Annabella sat on the floor before him and wrapped her arms around one of his legs. Silently, she stared at us.

Manies' face was flushed and he kept nodding his head and tapping his fingers in rhythm. Saint Anne, Moses Moses, and I were too anxious to sit down. "Take off your glasses," I told Moses Moses. "Mr. Manies, do you recognize this man?"

Manies moved his head in Moses' direction, but his goggling eyes skimmed blankly over him. "My dear Kid," he said laboriously, "if it weren't for that lovely lovely hair I wouldn't even recognize you. And is this Saint Anne, your wife? Have you both discovered the happy happy joys of linking, at long last? I congratulate you. I felicitate you."

I sighed in heartfelt desperation. It was pitifully obvious that Money Manies had picked this night of all nights to take a powerful hallucinogen. He was completely wrecked. I addressed myself to his wife. "Annabella doll," I said, "I know you never speak, and I certainly wouldn't expect you to do it now, even though the political future of the planet is at stake. But this man is Moses Moses, the Father of the Corporation. He isn't dead, but the Cabal wants him that way, and they're sure to kill all three of us. We desperately need your husband's help." She stared at us stonily. "Can't you even nod, or anything?" She gave us all the lively response of a dead dugong.

Now Saint Anne tried. "Mr. Manies," she said. "We're your friends. Our lives are in terrible danger. Can't you help us?"

Manies blinked. He fidgeted uncomfortably and rubbed his nose. "My dear Saint Anne, how can I help you when you keep changing shape? Go to my pornostars. They understand your problem. I insist you enjoy yourself!"

Moses Moses said, "This man has taken a powerful drug. Look at his eye dilation."

I nodded. "I'm sorry, Mr. Chairman. I had no way of knowing. Neither did he. It's just an unhappy accident. He's a good man, and he would have helped us if he could, I'm sure of it."

"He's beyond helping us now," Moses said. "We'd better think of a new plan of action."

Manies nodded once and kept nodding, apparently unable to stop himself. "So you've guessed my little secret! My apologizing apologies. I didn't expect your visit."

"That's all right, Mr. Manies," I told him, forcing a smile. "I'll write you a note, and you can read it later when you're not having so much fun." I stepped to his desk, opened it, and took out a sheet of his creamy deluxe stationery. Like many of the older generations, Manies sometimes wrote letters, rather than bluntly stating things face to face over a communiqué line. I wrote Manies a quick note, explaining all the important details on a single sheet of paper. I folded it and handed it to Manies, and on the third try he managed to stuff it into the breast pocket of his red quilted drugging jacket.

"So you are the famous Moses Moses," said Manies hospitably. "You know, you died when I was only twenty-three, and that was a long long long time ago. Do you still read Riley?"

"Yes, Mr. Manies," Moses Moses said soothingly. I had to give him credit for presence of mind. He knew better than to press old Manies; had Manies fully grasped our situation it would very likely have sent him into a terrible panic fit. "He was my favorite author."

"Yes, I know," Manies said, going into his nodding routine again. "I have all his surviving works in my library—a complete edition of your first reissue. You saved him from oblivion."

"Yes," Moses Moses said. "I was very lucky to find that old microtape."

Manies smiled. "Like myself you are an antiquarian! Of course his *Flying Islands of the Night* is the longest surviving piece. Do you remember the verses that go:

> "O Prince divine! O Prince divine!
> Tempt thou me not with that sweet voice
> of thine!
> Though my proud brow bear the blaze of a
> crown,
> Lo, at thy feet must its glory bow down,
> That from the dust thou mayest lift me to
> shine,
> Heaven'd in thy heart's rapture, O Prince
> Divine!"

"How could I forget them?" asked Moses Moses with a sigh. "That's the confrontation scene between Queen Crestillomeem and her son Jucklet in Act One."

"Crestillomeem?" I said. "Jucklet?"

"Yes," Moses Moses said happily. "Wonderful names, aren't they? So evocative." Saint Anne and I traded amazed glances. The expression on Anne's face suggested that she had a mouthful of thick mush and was looking for some place to spit it out. Moses continued, "And what about those majestic verses in the beginning of Act One?

> "Lo, launched from the offended sight
> Of Aeo!—anguish infinite
> Is ours, O Sisterhood of Sin!
> Yet is thy service mine by right,
> And, sweet as I may rule it, thus
> Shall sin's myrrh-savor taste to us—
> Sin's Empress—let my reign begin!"

"It's marvelous," Manies said. "Crestillomeem, the prime creation of Lord Aeo, revolts from pride in her own beauty and is banished from heaven! What imagination! What a thundering cosmic scheme! I don't believe there's another work like it in the whole of literature."

"Did you say 'Aeo'?" I said. "I often wondered why anyone would give a name like that to a helpless, inoffensive continent."

Moses Moses frowned. "What do you mean? It's a perfect name. It rolls with superhuman majesty. Say it to yourself a few times. Aeo, Aeo, Aeo. It's perfect!"

I shrugged. "If I were a mass of land that big I think I would demand the dignity of at least one consonant."

"How it all comes back to me," Manies mused. "I haven't read Riley in a hundred years. Isn't it something how memories seize you in a state like this? As Riley says, 'All havoc hath been wrangled with the drugs!'"

"I must admit that I myself have neglected Riley," said Moses Moses with an introspective knitting of the brow. "I haven't read his work in twenty years, subjectively speaking. To think how his work inspired me in my youth, when the Corporation was myself and three men in a beer hall! I must say I'm glad to have met you, Mr. Manies, despite the circumstances. You have recalled me to myself."

"Think nothing of it," said Manies magnanimously, fidgeting in his chair. "Might I offer you an invitation to breakfast here next week? My guests would find you fascinating; they don't often meet the dead."

The usual slow ease of Reverid repartee was out of place in our predicament. "Listen," I said. "Let's give some thought to escape. It's only a matter of time before the Cabal thinks to look here for us."

"Where could we go?" said Saint Anne. "Besides, we promised to wait here for your friend Armitrage."

There was a pinging sound from the heavy bracelet on Money Manies' wrist. "Oho!" he said in annoyance, puffing out his cheeks. "Chalkwhistle should be taking my calls. I dislike disturbance!"

"Wait," I said. "It may be important. Answer it, I'll take the call." Manies fumbled with his bracelet and a holo of Chill Factor appeared in the room.

House cameras floated in to cover Manies. Irritated, he waved them to me. Chill looked haggard, but he brightened a little when he saw me. "Kid!"

"Has Armitrage reached you yet?"

"That's what I called about. He was here with your house-keeper. He gave us a really strange story, do you confirm it?"

"Yes, Chill, it's true."

Chill clutched his forehead. "Kid, you amaze me! Things like this can only happen to you! My little angel of intrigue, your news has stunned me like the blow of a hammer!"

"Spare us the histrionics, Chill; you can act them out and splice them in later. Quade all right?"

He nodded. "I got a strange call, Kid. From Instant Death himself. He's declared blood feud on all enemies of the Cabal in Telset. You in particular."

"That was quick," I said.

"They have some guns, Kid. They've transgressed the Code. The Cogs are completely outclassed. Instant Death has enough firepower to slaughter every artist in the Zone. He gave us a choice, Kid; stay with you and get shot, or throw in with them and take a cut from the Cabal. He's talking more fracs than any of us could earn in ten years."

I nodded. "I understand, Chill. Did he mention why I'm the Cabal's enemy all of a sudden?"

Chill looked guilty. He lowered his voice. "No, Kid. They didn't mention him. The Chairman."

"I've seen him, Chill. He's alive. Look." I waved one camera to Moses Moses, who looked into it and nodded once. "I know about him now; that's why they have to kill me. The Cabal will try to hush up the Second Coming for as long as they can; even if they can't, it won't matter much if they manage to kill the Chairman. Don't try to challenge them. Play along. Can you hide Quade?"

Chill started at the question; his eyes were fixed on Moses Moses in awe and amazement. "Hide her?" he said. "Sure. We'll take care of her, make sure no one sees her. But you'd better leave Telset. We can't protect you from guns. No one can. Go to Jucklet or Eros if you want to stay alive."

"Better cut off before someone can tap the line," I suggested. Chill waved once. "I'll spread the word," he said, and vanished.

Manies looked sick; the realities of the situation were beginning to percolate through to him. "Perhaps you should leave, Kid. I believe I am about to peak. I won't be good company."

"Right," I said. "Sorry, Mr. Manies. Perhaps we can get away before you're implicated."

An explosion shook the house. "I retract that statement," I said. I started unscrewing the base of one nunchuck handle.

It didn't take them long to find us. Saint Anne and Moses Moses had ducked down quickly behind the desk and an ottoman. When they came in they found Money Manies and I sitting in two armchairs, quietly conversing. Annabella Manies was still silently holding on to her husband's leg; he must have been the one oasis of certainty in her twisted universe.

There were two of them: the Stag, and Slummer. The Stag had a red pennant flying from one handsome antler; Slummer had a rag of red cloth twisted around one shabby arm. They were two of Instant Death's best men. Slummer had a small pistol, probably one of the few firearms the Cabal could scrape up on short notice. The Stag carried a heavy mace, his usual weapon. Slummer pointed the gun at me. "You're both under arrest in the name of the Cabal."

"Oh, I surrender, I surrender," said Manies cheerfully.

"Me too," I said. "We won't fight."

Stag and Slummer exchanged puzzled glances. "Well," said Stag. "I'm glad you're taking this so easily."

"Stag doll, what did you expect? I might fight the Instant Death, but the Cabal? Be reasonable. I don't buck the odds."

"But we've declared blood feud," Slummer said in his peculiar grating voice. Slummer had bent, rickety legs and always talked as if he were suffering from a lung disease. He dressed in filthy rags. "You've got to die, Kid."

"No," I said. "I'm betting the Cabal will change their minds when they see I've given myself up. I can probably get off with a partial brainwipe."

Stag looked around suspiciously, whacking one of his floating cameras with one antler. He was one of the rottenest camera programmers I've ever seen. "What exactly did you do, anyway? I can't figure out how a shrimp like you could do *anything* to bother the Cabal."

I gestured casually with my nunchuck. The base was unscrewed and ready to come off with a pull of my hand. "Why should I tell you?"

Slummer looked almost apologetic. "You might as well, Kid. This is blood feud. We've been ordered not to leave you alive. It's a dirty shame, too, if you ask me. I've got all of your tapes."

That saved his life for him. "Well," I said, "for one thing I've violated the gun code," and I blew off Slummer's left leg. He fell to the carpet, squalling. I jumped out of the armchair, evaded the hasty swing of Stag's mace, and whipped the chain of my nunchuck around one of his antlers. I yanked savagely and heard his neck crack. He fell, unconscious, but it didn't kill him.

Slummer had passed out. I ripped off some of his rags and put a tourniquet around his leg, just over the knee. I grimaced. His leg was still barely attached, and it was ugly.

"God," I said. "Guns really lack style." I picked up Slummer's little pistol and tucked it into my waistband. I screwed the nunchuck back together and dosed Stag and Slummer with their own smuff. Then I violated the artists' Code again; I stole some of their smuff. It deeply embarrassed me, but I needed it. I looked up at my cameras. "I'll have to cut this part later," I said.

Manies was staring transfixed at the thick pool of Slummer's blood on his carpet. "I'm sorry," he said. "I'm afraid I find this performance just too too strongly stated." He reached tremblingly into his drugging jacket and pulled out a small red bulb with a white jet nozzle. He squirted a puff of black dust or vapor into each nostril, inhaling sharply. He passed out not long afterward. Annabella Manies still said nothing, but she began to stroke her husband's knee with one hand, very slowly.

I gestured Moses Moses and Saint Anne to their feet. They got up, averting their eyes. "Come on," I said. "We'll all die if we stay in Telset. We'll take the *Albatross* out to sea. I hope Armitage has enough sense to hide himself."

Chalkwhistle was still unconscious when we got to the outside door; it had been blown to splinters, but the bulk of a chair had protected the neuter. We all put on our infrareds as we stepped outside. We heard shouts and thumps from the beach-house; they weren't party noises. Probably the Instant Death had looked there for us first.

A bullet ricocheted screaming across the paving stones outside Manies' doorstep and threw stinging powder into my shins. I jumped backward, crowding Anne and Moses back into the house. The bullet had left a long scar in the hard travertine; it had come from further up the hillside, to the east. This particular wall of Many Mansions faced north to the sea. The direction of the scar in the rock showed that the sniper would take a while to reach a position where he could shoot through the shattered doorway. We started piling up furniture as a barricade. We heard the rapid thumping of his footsteps as the sniper came sidling along the wall, and we took cover. He never made it. We heard a solid impact and the unmistakeable sound of a body falling to earth. In a moment I peeked outside.

I saw Armitrage leaning over the sniper's body. "Look," he said. "It's Orange."

"Good," I said. "How did you manage?"

Armitrage grinned. "I was up on the roof," he said. "When he came running along the wall, I just leaned over and gave him a nice thump in the head." He shook his weighted quarterstaff.

We dragged Orange back inside the house and peeled off his skintight mask. He had an anonymous, handsome face, the product of cosmetic surgery. His rifle was so complicated that none of us could figure out how to operate it; we couldn't even find the trigger. He also had a long, nasty knife attached to his belt. He wasn't carrying a memory wiper, which was too bad for him. My hair crackled. "Don't look," I said. I opened his jaw, put the tip of the blade against the roof of his mouth, and hit the pommel with my hand. It went in deep, so easily that his skull might almost have been hollow and held together with a kind of black fiber. At the thought of this I trembled with a long, sickening thrill.

Armitrage licked his lips. "Let's reef him," he said.

"There's no time," I said. "Besides, we don't have the weights. Let's get out of here." My hands wouldn't stop trembling. He was the first man I had ever killed.

We ran downhill back toward the docks. Two of the Clone

Brothers were there; they had found the *Sea Whip* and were busy demolishing her with their chains. They were making a lot of noise, but they stopped their high-pitched cries of excitement when they saw us at the docks.

They tried to climb out of the *Whip* and onto the dock. It would have been better theater to beat them up, but there wasn't time. I started shooting at them. Either Slummer's little gun was horribly inaccurate, or else the smuff had destroyed my aim; they jumped into the water and swam to safety under the dock. I think I may have winged one of them.

Armitrage, Moses Moses, and Saint Anne jumped aboard the *Albatross*. I stood guard while Armitrage and Moses Moses raised the mainsail. They were both shaken and it took them a long time, long enough for the Clone Brothers to work up courage and begin taunting us from beneath the dock. One of them sent out a camera to watch us and I wasted a bullet on it, which missed.

"Blood feud, Kiddy!" they called out. "Blood feud!" You would have thought they were having the time of their quadruple lives. "Red wants your red blood! Blue wants your blue veins! The Colors will cut you up and the directions will scatter the pieces!"

I cast off, so smuffed that I fell into the water and almost lost the little gun. As I pulled myself aboard, the joints in my elbows made weird popping sounds, giving eloquent testimony to tissues strained to their limits of endurance. My arms were swollen to twice their normal size, and I could feel a few of the wounds seeping up with blood beneath the skinseal.

A brisk breeze blew up off the reef and we put out to sea. In the light of the open doors of the beachhouse we could see innocent hedonists hustled out at gunpoint. The Cabal had probably made a bad mistake in hiring the Instant Death, but perhaps they were the best henchmen they could get on short notice. I was glad that we hadn't met Instant Death himself. He was one of the very few people on the planet who inspired me with real physical fear.

The *Albatross*'s sails were blue plastic and were soon lost in the darkness. No doubt the Clone Brothers gave the alarm as soon as they could, but by that time we were out of rifle range.

6

We put up the jib. Moses Moses took the tiller. It was three hours past midnight; I could tell by the position of the stars. As Telset dwindled to a dark lump on the horizon the four of us gradually relaxed. For a long time we said nothing, sunk in our private thoughts. I took a wound kit out of one of my sealed pockets and got out needle and thread. I stripped, pulled the skinseal off one of the larger wounds, and started sewing it up. It was black with mites, which were doing a wonderful job and would soon have the swelling down. I felt a rubbery stretching sensation as I stitched up a loose flap of skin; it always feels very odd, even when it doesn't hurt. I used a special thread; the mites would eat it after it had done its work. Armitrage helped me sew the wounds on my back. Like many multisexuals, he had a very gentle touch.

Finally Saint Anne said, "What do you think will happen to poor Mr. Manies?"

I shrugged. ("Don't do that!" Armitrage said.) "I don't know," I said. "There's never been a crisis like this before. Money

Manies is a pretty popular figure. He practically owns six channels and has access to dozens more. If his programming is disrupted, it'll change the lives of hundreds of thousands of viewers, floaters and grounders alike. I don't think the Cabal would want to do anything that obvious; they've always stayed in the background since Fox Day. I'd guess that they'd try to make some kind of deal with Manies. But I don't know what kind of terms he would demand."

"But what if Mr. Manies decides to fight?" Saint Anne said.

"Fight what?" I said. "The Cabal knows all about Manies. Where he lives, how he lives—he's published enough lifetapes so that everybody knows his habits. But the Cabal's a phantom. Sure, he could attack the Instant Death and get a lot of people killed, but he wouldn't have touched the Cabal itself. How could he prevent a Fox Day in his own home? It would be easy enough to smuggle explosives into Many Mansions and blow the whole place to atoms. He'll be forced to compromise with them."

"I think they made an error by hiring the Instant Death," Armitage said. "The Death have no class. They're louts and bullies. They're bound to rouse a lot of resentment. Besides, every time the Cabal gives an order there's a chance that someone will trace it back and discover their true identities. Then they'd be vulnerable. The temptation to strike back would be hard to resist. I know I would, if I could."

"Sure you would, now that they've attacked you personally," I said. "But I don't think the average Reverid would. After all, you could hardly call the Cabal an oppressive government. They've always been very careful to cover their tracks. They have the Rump Board to carry on the minutiae of government for them—distributing stock and the like. Besides, their real power is in their money. The Rump Board is just a sort of shell. The Cabal has always left well enough alone. They just want to be left in peace so that they can hoard millions of fracs. That's always been my understanding, anyway."

"Millions of fracs?" said Moses Moses, aghast. "How did they get into such a position? The Bill of Incorporation forbids any stockholder to hold more than three shares of stock. That was the very cornerstone of my social design! Why in death's name would anyone want so much money? One share of stock guarantees all the necessities of life, plus a nice discretionary income. Was pure greed so powerful?"

Armitrage had finished sewing up my back. He patted new skinseal into place, then turned to Moses Moses and spread his hands apologetically. "The Bill of Incorporation is a dead letter," he said. "Of course, your signature at the bottom makes it a sacred document, but it doesn't give it any more relevance. Besides, there was so much discretionary income! A thousand fracs a year, each, for millions of people! Naturally it started to accumulate in the hands of those who wanted it. Collecting money became a kind of game. And the Board of Directors was awfully lax. Their powers were so strictly limited that they had to depend on prestige, and when you left they lost a lot of it. They were trying to reassert their power when the Fox Day blast wiped them out. Then there was only the Rump."

"You could hardly call the Rump a government," I said. "They only handle routine matters, and most of that is done by computer anyway. I've seen tapes of the Rump in session. It's nothing but talk. Real mud-belching stuff. They only meet once a year."

Armitrage continued, "It's a ceremonial position. Some people say that the members of the Rump are directly appointed by the Cabal, but I don't think that's true any more. I think that the Board members retire when they get sick of it and sell the office to the highest bidder, or give it to a friend. There's not much turnover, though. They may be impotent, but they love to hear themselves talk."

"What about voting?" demanded Moses Moses. "The Board of Directors is supposed to be elected by shareholders! One share, one vote!"

"Oh, voting's outdated nowadays," Armitrage assured him. "Anyone with a complaint just calls up the central computer directly. It's programmed to respond to personal communiqués. Why get involved with the Rump Board?"

"But they're supposed to be your advocates! They're supposed to obey the will of the shareholders! Doesn't anyone ever complain about it?"

"Sure, you can complain to the computer if you want," I said. "But the computer's riddled with taps by now, and it keeps all its messages on permanent file. It'd be easy to find out who spoke up against the Cabal; then the Cabal could buy them off or arrange an 'accident,' if they thought it was necessary. But they're very tolerant. Except, of course, when their existence is directly threatened, like we threaten it."

"Doesn't it bother you at all to have lost your liberty?" Saint Anne said.

"Liberty?" I said. "Death, I don't know. The Cabal has ruled Reverie for three hundred years; that's longer than the Board of Directors ever did. I can tell you this much, though. I own four shares of stock. And if the old Board was still in power I wouldn't even have a profession. They would never have allowed combat art or a Decriminalized Zone. Or bet-slavery, or smuff, or personal servitude, or pornotapes, or the patronage system."

"Or multiple sexuality, or radical surgical alteration," Armitrage said. "Hell, we Reverids were used to the Cabal. They were like old shoes." Armitrage and I both sank into gloomy silence as we both realized how much we had lost, and how much more we stood to lose even if we survived. Moses Moses had returned and the Second Coming was bound to turn our world upside down.

We were trapped, too. Even if Armitrage and I clubbed Moses Moses and took him captive to the Cabal—a loathsome act of treason—we would still be killed, because we knew too much. Besides, a blood feud was on. I had sworn to kill Angeluce to avenge the murder of my servant Quade, and that meant war to the death with him and the Cabal. Any enemy of the Cabal would be a friend of ours, and their worst enemy—Moses Moses—would have to be our best ally. Armitrage and I both knew this.

We exchanged glances. Under his cheerful exterior, Armitrage was a moody, sensitive sort, and he seemed to be rapidly despairing. To cheer him up, I said, "Look at it this way, Armitrage. If the Cabal kills us, then that's it, zip. We're dead and it doesn't matter any more. Besides, everyone dies. But if we live, we'll be the heroes of the age. We'll be incredibly famous. It'll be the performance of our careers. This completely transcends anything we've ever done before, and just think, we're getting it all on tape." I gestured at his cameras; he had four of them, big clunky eyes with three lenses each and top-notch audio pick-ups.

"You're right," he said. "I have about two months' worth of tape left. Of course, I can always go back and erase what I've already recorded. It's mostly personal memory stuff—personal pornotapes and the like. There're a few good fights, too, but like you said, they pale compared to this. We're pretty lucky, really. We're in a privileged position. I just wish I'd been warned—I could have put everything in the computer and started off with clean, fresh, crisp tape." He looked up moodily at his cameras. Then he reached into the baggy sleeve of his fighting robe and pulled out his comb. He turned it on with a flick of his thumbnail and started to comb his long luxuriant black hair with practiced flicks of his wrist.

Armitrage was appallingly handsome, with his clear, sea-green eyes, his milk-white skin, his straight, surgically corrected nose (broken many times), his full lips and beardless face. But he was completely without vanity. What many others had mistaken for vanity was only a dedicated combat artist's concern for image. If he had a weakness it was his forthright, careless passion for sex. Like most multisexuals his bloodstream was a seething tide of hormones and libido stimulants. He had spent a year as a pornostar but quit because his hundreds of tapes were flooding the market. He then turned to combat art so that he could continue to support his personal entourage: two women, two men, and another multisexual. He always had at least five people around to minister to his personal needs, but his personnel were always changing because of his lecherous taste for novelty. Armitrage was a legend. He was only thirty.

"Say," he said suddenly, "I wonder what they're going to do about my new tapes. I had a great tape of a fight with Steam Engine that's supposed to premiere in four days. What about you, Kid?"

I shrugged. "The last thing I did was a tape critique for Cewaynie Wetlock. I was doing a gang tape but it fell through."

Armitrage smiled. "I saw that critique. Getting soft in your old age? You treated her a lot better than she deserved."

"Show some class," I told him. "Cewaynie Wetlock's great. You just don't understand Art with a Capital A." I was glad that Armitrage had cheered up enough to tease me. I let him do it because we both knew I could beat him up any time.

Armitrage leapt to his feet. "Hey, I bet Money Manies has some spare tapes here on board! Let's search the hold and see what we can find!"

The *Albatross* was a wooden catamaran, thirty-five feet long, fifteen across. Her two hulls were both sheathed in thin white ceramic to prevent the attack of teredos and boracles and to protect her against sharp coral. There was a wooden cabin on board that would sleep six, but I had already looked through it. It had Manies' old fishing equipment, which he no longer used, but kept for guests. It also had a dusty shelf full of vacuum-sealed provisions in glass jars, some with unhealthy-looking marbled streaks that suggested a choking death by poison for anyone unwise enough to eat them.

Money Manies was notorious for his reluctance to discard anything, which was unusual even among tidy, cycle-minded Reverids. It wasn't that Manies was methodically thrifty, far from it; he simply never threw anything away. He had seen so much of the past crumble and decay that it bothered him to see it happen to his own personal effects, to see entropy devouring his past even as he left it.

Though he seldom used her nowadays, the *Albatross* was still Manies' favorite boat. She was almost two hundred years old (though she had been repaired and refurbished so many times that hardly an atom remained of the original craft).

Armitrage opened the trap door to the port hull and climbed down the short stepladder into the darkness. "What do you see down there?" Saint Anne asked curiously.

"Junk," he said. "Wau, it smells down here. Looks like it hasn't been cleaned out in decades." We heard echoic clunking and scraping as he grabbed something below decks. Saint Anne went to the hatch to peer in and he handed her a collapsible, incredibly old-looking tapescreen. "There's a little generator to run it, too," he said. "But it looks broken. I'll have some trouble getting to it. Here, Anne, help me get some of these antiques out of the way." He began to hand her things through the hatch.

Moses Moses was still piloting; we were heading due north. He was a good pilot, relaxed yet alert and keeping an eye on the sonar. As usual, the Gulf was calm. Our course was north, not because we had a destination, but simply because it was the quickest way to put distance between ourselves and Telset.

Although Money Manies was one of my oldest friends, I had known him for only a fraction of his long, long lifetime. Succumbing to curiosity I began to pick through the heap of objects Anne and Armitrage were piling on the deck. There was a neatly folded bag full of spare sails and coils of spare line, a dusty case of handsome, spotless fishing knives, a plastic valise full of old navigation maps with a sextant and star guide. Their copyright date read C.R.Y. 380. Money Manies had been a mere two hundred and thirteen years old when they were published.

Armitrage handed Anne a square, black album. She opened it, looked inside for five seconds, then gasped and clapped it shut. She dropped it to the deck as if it had scalded her. I opened it. It was an album of porno stills, featuring an incredibly young-looking Money Manies. The nose and eyes were his, but the lips were thin and cruel and he was wearing a close-fitting tall red hat adorned with slick-looking swollen bulbs. He wore a pair of fetishistic thorny black bracelets around each ankle as well, but nothing else. I broke into helpless laughter at the next still, in which all three participants were fully clothed. It was like an essay on the history of Reverid fashions. Judging by the immense, jutting lapels, feathered sleeves, and elastic webwork of colored strings that crisscrossed their legs from waist to ankles, the picture was at least two centuries old. "Hey, Armitrage, come up and have a look at this," I said.

"Just a sec," he answered. Then he emerged from below decks, carrying a small generator crusted in old, dried-up grease. He dropped it to the deck with a crunch, and its starting handle snapped off with a pleasant metallic *sproingg* and fell into the Gulf.

"Crap," Armitrage said. "Oh well, it probably wouldn't have

worked anyway." He took the album, glanced at it briefly, then began to thumb through it avidly, with a critic's eye. "My word, look at that," he said, pointing at a picture of Money Manies and two friends suspended in harnesses above a parquet floor. "That's really hard to do. Takes a lot of technical skill, Kid."

"I wouldn't know," I said. "They look like idiots." I looked at him. "Did you ever try anything like that?"

"Well, of course. But never with anyone quite that large." He looked again and winced a little.

Anne had gone down into the hull. She emerged, smiling. "Look what I found!"

I looked at the peculiar object she had located, a squat, fluted cylinder of metal and glass with a thin wire handle. "What is it?"

"It's a lantern, of course! Haven't you ever seen one?"

I took it from her and looked it over. "I don't understand. Where's its lens? Where's its power source?"

"Here, silly, I'll show you." She took it back and shook it next to her ear. "It still has some oil in it. Now these little sticks here are called matches."

"Why?" said Armitrage. "What do they match to?"

She shook her head, shaking off his question with a peculiarly Niwlindid gesture. "I don't know. I haven't seen a lantern like this since I was a little girl. My great-great-grandfather, the Catechist, used to have one. He lent it to me sometimes. Now, you see, you pump this little rod like this to get pressure up— then you raise the chimney like this and light one of the matches." She rubbed the colored end of one of the sticks across the deck and with a pop and faint hiss it burst into flame. Surprised, Armitrage and I took a step back. The lantern lit with a whoosh and a dirty yellow light illuminated us. Anne replaced the chimney, and I heard four faint clicks as Armitrage's cameras switched lenses.

"It's a lighting device!" Armitrage said. "How bizarre! Look, Kid, it uses flame for light. How wasteful! Think of the waste heat." He clicked his tongue.

"Interesting lighting effect, though," I said. "Makes you look good, 'Trage."

"You think so?" he said, pleased. "Let's try the other hull and see what we can find there."

Happy now that action distracted us from our anxiety, Anne, Armitrage, and I immediately began to ransack the starboard hull. The first things we found were a dozen books, some spoiled by sea water. Armitrage tossed them aside incuriously, as he had never learned to read. He found a pocket autoharp, but unfortunately it was missing two strings. I found a hexagonal chessboard for three players, but Anne didn't know how to play.

Armitrage caressed the smooth top of a hip-high machine, cylindrical and studded with orifices and extrusible prongs. "Recognize this, Kid?"

"Sure, I've seen enough of them," I said. "Better make sure it's in working order if you want to use it. It's just about the oldest one I've ever seen. Sure is ugly."

"I think it looks sort of sweet," Armitrage said. "I might have known old Manies would have at least one of these on board. For those long solo voyages, you know." He bent over and briefly kissed its plastic top. Anne, who was carrying the lantern, looked at him curiously. She obviously didn't understand the machine's use at all.

"Can anyone tell me what these are?" she said. She showed us a metal cylinder with a connected ring-pull and a pair of lace-up plastic shoes with wheels attached to their soles.

"Good lord! Are those really shoes with wheels?" Armitrage said. With a wry expression he twirled their small metal wheels with the palm of his hand. The wheels whizzed along merrily on noisy ball bearings. The strangeness of the outré sight caused us all to break into loud, incredulous laughter that lasted almost five minutes.

Finally we threw the peculiar shoes aside. I tried pulling the ring-pull on the metal cylinder. An inflatable life raft, its fabric rotten and all its pressure gone, bloated its way flabbily out of the cylinder to lie in a blobby orange heap on the floor of the hold. We stared at it silently.

"Is that the only life raft on board?" Anne asked sepulchrally.

"I think I saw another one in the cabin," Armitrage said

doubtfully, but the carefree hilarity was gone from his voice. The sight of the musty-smelling orange raft, puffed and flabby like a gigantic slimemold, put a damper on our spirits. Petulantly, Armitrage kicked it with his pointed boot and it ripped loudly.

We continued to search the hold. We found other strange objects: a life-sized glass eyeball, a pair of crab gigs, a plastic tent, a glass bottle full of moldy white tablets, and a half-crushed wicker hamper containing two empty bottles, the fossilized crumbs of a meal, and a carefully folded, blood-stained handkerchief. There was also a square lacquered box full of small hook-shaped flanges of metal, of unknown function.

At last we found a heavy wooden trunk behind a dirty shroud. It proved to be full of clothes, musty, rustling antique clothes, many discolored with age, others actually woven out of threads of cloth fiber. We hauled the trunk up on deck.

At this point I offered to spell Moses Moses at the tiller, but he politely assured us that he was not tired. Armitrage and I stripped and started to try on the clothing. I saw Anne's eyes widen as she learned for the first time that Armitrage was a multisexual; even old Moses Moses seemed a little taken aback at Armitrage's surgically altered wealth of endowment.

All of the clothes were too large for me, which piqued me considerably. They fit Armitrage well, though. Particularly striking was an open-throated black one-piece, somber yet extravagant, adorned with dozens of soft, black, rubbery spines. Armitrage donned the accompanying wide-brimmed spined hat and studded, square-toed boots. It was impossible to resist his charm as he stretched and pirouetted, striking out briefly and precisely with his combat staff. Admiration and envy overcame me. "Armitrage, you amaze us all!" I cried. "Such antique majesty! Really, it touches me to the heart." I embraced him. Flattered and pleased, he hugged me close and kissed my forehead. "How marvelous to be praised, even by a captive audience," he said. "It is rather striking, isn't it? Anne, won't you try something on? You must be sick of that old white bag by now."

Anne stiffened. "This is the uniform of my order," she said.

"But you must've worn it for days now! Say, you'd look delightful in this." He pulled a sleek ankle-length gown thick with glimmering pink scales from the bottom of the trunk. "This would complement your eyes beautifully." He ran his hand across the smooth inner fabric. "Ah, its texture is delightful. Imagine this clinging deliciously to your skin. Here, just feel it." He handed it to her.

"It's regrettably thin," she said, holding it up with a frown. "Really, I have no need to flaunt my body in a garment of this kind. It promises actions I have no intention of fulfilling."

Armitrage smoothed the brim of his spiny hat. "Such rigorous self-discipline," he said mockingly. "Very well, I'll try it on myself." And he did. It looked marvelous on him.

Anne was visibly disturbed by Armitrage's graceful, ambivalent posturing. She turned her attention to the *Albatross's* old charts. "Perhaps it's time we plotted out a course for ourselves," she said. "Where do you think we should go, Kid?"

I examined the maps in the lantern light and frowned. "It's a good thing we have the sonar," I said. "The reefs have grown miles since this thing was printed. Let me see. I suppose it would be best if we headed for Jucklet. It's the only large city on the continent. Sylvain is way the hell on the other side of the planet and Eros wanders, of course, so it's out. It'd be safer to stay on water rather than going overland, so here's our course. We could head north and leave the Gulf through these gaps in the atoll here, the Straits of Circumstance. Then we'll be on the outside of Aeo, and we can sail along the reef, here, west, and then southwest, and then south, you see, paralleling the circular shore of the continent. By the time we dock here we can disguise ourselves, and the hunt for us will have cooled off a little. There's a little settlement on the edge of this bay, though it doesn't show on this old map. I forget the name of the place."

"Let me see," Moses Moses said eagerly. "Jucklet was just a village when I entered cryosleep." I showed him the map. "My, how it's grown."

"But Jucklet is far into the mountains here," Anne said. "What are they called? The Crater Mountains? That's a peculiar name."

"They're peculiar mountains," Moses Moses said. "They're

artificial. They date back about three billion years. They're bomb craters."

I looked at the map. "They're big craters."

"They were big bombs."

"They made a magnificent landscape, though," Armitrage said. "All lakes and woods and ridges. I've been there. There's no combat art, though."

I shrugged. "Jucklet's a hick town. The population's pretty well thinned and scattered through the mountains. That's good for us, because we won't attract too much attention when we enter town. If we just get smelly and hairy enough, we can pass ourselves off as backswoodsmen. Of course, then we're still faced with the problem of fighting the Cabal. But at least in Jucklet we'll have resources to draw on. We're completely harmless to them on this boat."

"Let's not get ahead of ourselves," Moses Moses said. "The Cabal is aware of our predicament too; they can follow our logic. We can't expect to sail there unmolested."

Armitrage sat down gracefully on the wooden deck. "What do you advise, then, Mr. Chairman?"

"Oh, a little patience," Moses Moses said. "It's my experience that, if you wait long enough, Time will drag your enemies, dead, past your door. The Cabal will expect us to land and begin agitating for their removal. Instead, we could put in at one of these hundreds of small offshore islands, and hide the boat. If we simply lie low for a little while, it'll drive them crazy. They will think one of two things: that we are dead, or that someone is harboring us. If they think we're dead, they'll stop looking for us, and we can return to Telset in safety. If they think we're being hidden, they'll intensify their search in the major cities. But don't you think that would arouse resentment against them?"

"Sure," I said eagerly. "Not only that, but it'll spread the rumor that you're alive. All Telset has probably heard by now. My friend Chill Factor knows the truth, and Telset is wired. Rumor moves at the speed of light."

Moses Moses was pleased. "There, you see?" he said. "By attacking an enemy who ducks aside, the Cabal will upset itself.

One should never strike at an enemy when he expects the blow and where he is braced for it. One should confuse the enemy first, so that his reactions are slow and inappropriate. They expect us to challenge them; so, we will duck that challenge. They will strike at us with all their force; they will miss us, and look like fools. Their morale will be hurt. They will not know where we are, or when we intend to strike. We will have turned the table on them. We will be the New Cabal. We will be hidden in the shadows; they will be open and vulnerable. By trying to protect themselves from all possible modes of attack, they will spread themselves thin."

Armitrage laughed incredulously. "You mean we can do all that just by disappearing? Without striking a blow?"

"Yes," said Moses Moses. "I think it would be the most disconcerting scheme we could hatch against them."

"Ha!" said Armitrage gleefully. "That really cracks me up! It seems so simple once it's explained! That's genius, Mr. Chairman. Pure genius!"

Moses Moses shook his head modestly. "No. Just elementary strategy."

"How long would we have to remain in hiding?" I said.

"Not too long," said Moses Moses. "Three, maybe four years."

"Four years!" I said, aghast. "My death, that's half my career! I'll be forgotten, washed-up, a has-been! Things move fast in combat art!"

"Four years is a big chunk of my lifetime!" Armitrage objected.

Moses Moses smiled indulgently. "When you get to be my age, you'll see four years for what they really are. An eye blink. A moment. A small interlude. And we're operating on the Cabal's time scale. The Cabalists are old. Aren't they?"

Armitrage and I traded disgusted glances. It was self-evident that the Cabalists were old. Only old people could have kept up such a long and elaborate charade. Of course, the original Cabalists must be dead by now, but we could rest assured that their successors were old as well.

"Well, Armitrage," I said, "once again we're buggered by ancients."

Armitrage nodded gloomily. Suddenly an idea occurred to him and an expression of sly glee touched his face. With naïve duplicity he suppressed it. "Four years isn't that bad," he said, with a judicious air of compromise that fooled no one. "Time passes quickly in pleasant company like this. It beats being dead, anyway."

"You've got no argument there," I said. I yawned. "But what about my house, my friends, my mobiles." The words sounded flat and pettish, even to me. Here we were, playing with the destinies of millions, and I was insisting on the primacy of my narrow, personal world. Embarrassed, I pretended a deeper fatigue than I felt. "I haven't slept in hours," I said. "Let's postpone any decisions until I've had some sleep. Is that agreeable, Mr. Chairman?"

"Of course," Moses Moses said kindly. "I only offer suggestions; I don't intend to dictate. All our lives are equally at stake, so each of us should have an equal voice. As for myself, I believe I'll stay awake until dawn. I've had such a long sleep that I hesitate to return to it."

I walked into the cabin and pulled aside the fresh, scented sheets on one of the two lowest bunks. It was dark, but I could see well enough with my infrareds, so I didn't turn on the light. As I stripped I felt an intolerable weariness settle over me; my battered body was finally taking its due. I took a little smuff to sweeten my dreams, slipped into bed, and slept, lulled to sleep by the comforting hum of my cameras, and the slap of waves on the hulls.

"Kid! Mr. Chairman! Wake up!" I swung my feet out of bed, focused blurry eyes on Armitrage's face, and felt a hot flush of pain course through me. I found my combat jacket and took some smuff. I felt better. "What time is it?"

"Four hours past dawn," Armitrage said. He was in his combat robe and was holding Slummer's tiny pistol in one hand. "You've slept almost ten hours."

I started to dress. Moses Moses, who had been sleeping perhaps an hour, pried open gummy eyes with a pitiful look of confusion on his bearded face. Old people often suffer such disorientation immediately after waking; their brains are so crowded with dreams. "What's the matter?" he asked vaguely.

"It's a glider," Armitrage said. "Anne saw it. I was snoozing out on deck." I saw that Armitrage's skin was slick with the anti-tan lotion he wore in sunlight; it kept his skin milk-white. "I thought I'd wake you up. It might mean trouble."

"I'll check, Mr. Chairman," I told Moses Moses. "You'd better sleep. We'll need you to pilot at night, anyway."

"No," Moses Moses said. "No, I can't sleep now. I'll go with you." He began to pull on his pinstriped suit; I saw that he slept in a white one-piece underall. His arms and legs were remarkably hairy, with reddish-brown hair the color of his beard.

With a touch I restored my cameras to full function, then adjusted my jacket, slipped into my pants and shoes, and looped my nunchuck around my neck. I went out on deck with Armitrage, wincing at the bright yellow sunlight. I shaded my eyes with one hand; my fingers were no longer swollen. "Where is it?" I asked Anne. She was at the tiller.

Without a word, she pointed. I saw a black speck silhouetted against the looming, faraway bulk of a morning thunderhead. It was a black sailplane with extremely long, thin wings; as I watched, she climbed, lifting on a thermal with the bright precision of a razor.

Armitrage looked at me seriously. "Here, try these," he said, handing me a pair of red plastic binoculars.

"Where did you find these?" I said.

"Under my bunk. Go ahead and look. You won't like it, though."

I looked at him sharply and then used the binoculars. I caught the long-winged sailplane just as she banked and I saw the white skull motif stenciled on her black wings. "It's the *Kite*," I said, lowering the binoculars. "Instant Death's sailplane."

"Yes, I recognized her, too," Armitrage said simply. "He's a very good pilot, isn't he?"

"He's the best," I said. "The best on Telset." I handed the binoculars to Moses Moses, who had joined us, his beard still half-crushed from the pillow. Moses watched the plane briefly, then turned to focus on the pale, white gasbag of a flying island, shrunken with distance, trailing its rooted burden of mud. His composure calmed us all.

"What do you think?" Armitrage asked me.

"He's come to kill us," I said. "I'd guess a bomb. That would be instant enough for his taste, don't you think?"

Armitrage nodded. "Yeah. We're about forty miles out. If he sank the boat, we'd drown for sure."

"He'll have to make a bombing run," I said. I hefted my nun-chuck. "Maybe he'll come within range of my scatter gun." I tried to color my voice with a hopeful vindictiveness, but I failed. The gun had a very short range.

"Let me try for him with the pistol," Armitrage said. "I might be lucky. The rest of you should stay in the cabin, in case he's using a rifle. Maybe he is. It would be much better theater that way. More elegant."

"I imagine that this tape is for a very exclusive audience," Moses Moses said drily. "I imagine that the Cabal favors effi-ciency over aesthetics."

"Let me fire at him, Armitrage," I said. "Why should you have the best role?"

"Ha," said Armitrage. "I've seen you fire this thing before. You couldn't hit a holothurian. Besides, I'm not smuffed."

"Well, I'm staying out here," I said. "If he swoops in low enough, I'll blast him."

Armitrage checked the gun. "Three bullets left. Not an overly generous allowance." He looked down at me, his eyes shining. "There are a lot of things I haven't expressed. Things I haven't accomplished. Projects I haven't tried." He looked up at the sailplane. "My brain teems with them."

With sincerity, almost with morbid gaiety, Saint Anne said, "The universe is kind to those who die in righteousness. I'm not afraid."

"Look," Armitrage said. Instant Death had gained all the height he wanted. Now he peeled away from the long spiral of his thermal climb and came toward us from the south. Briefly, he dipped his wings. "He's saluting us."

"A nice gesture," I said. Two of my cameras had already switched to telephoto, and they followed him in as he began his sleek and lethal dive.

"You should get into the cabin," Armitrage said. "Or better yet, into the holds. They've got that ceramic sheathing, you know. That would be some protection."

"No," said Saint Anne. "I want to see. It's rather pretty, really."

"Yes," said Moses Moses. "If this is death, let's savor it, as we savor all forms of experience." No one moved. The smell of the Gulf wind was sharp and briny and vital. It seemed to me that I had never really smelled it before. A small school of shiny fish skipped frantically across the ocean's surface, evading a predator. The sails flapped twice. No one said anything.

The *Kite* was beautiful. She had a wingspread of at least sixty feet. She was extremely lightweight, but perfectly rigid. It was almost a pleasure to be killed by a craft so elegantly engineered.

She came toward us, toward our stern, as if sliding down a chute. Armitrage braced his legs and lifted both arms, his left hand gripping his right wrist. I heard the pistol go pop . . . pop . . . pop. I threw myself overboard.

The explosion was jarring and I felt more than saw a chunk of wooden shrapnel tear into the water beside me, trailing sizzling bubbles. I held my breath. The weight of my metallic pants, my jacket, and nunchuck was slowly dragging me down. I heard pieces of the *Albatross* pancaking down into the sea all around me; then everything turned dark. For a moment I thought I was hit, but then I saw that the *Albatross*'s tattered mainsail had settled directly over me. I put my 'chuck around my neck and frogkicked my way out from under the sail. I came up for a welcome breath.

What was left of the *Albatross*'s deck was already awash. The explosion had dismasted her. Both hulls were shattered and shipping water. I saw a wicker hamper bob out of one hull, puffed out by a big rush of dirty bubbles. Quickly, I kicked off my metallic trousers, leaving myself in my padded combat groin-brace. After that I was able to tread water.

Wiping salt water from my eyes, I looked around and spotted Saint Anne. Her baggy white saint's garb was sealed by elastic at wrists and ankles; the air trapped inside was keeping her afloat. I swam over to her. "Are you all right?" She looked very strange with her blunt-cut hair plastered to her oval skull.

"Yes," she said. "But my legs. Something hit me across the backs of my knees. I can't feel much."

"Do you want some smuff?" I gasped out. A few yards away, Manies' shattered clothes chest sank, belching wet blobs of fabric.

"No," she said loudly. The explosion had apparently partly deafened her. "Where are the others?" She lifted her voice. "Mr. Chairman! Mr. Armitrage!"

There was no answer. I looked up. Instant Death had already caught another thermal and was gaining height for the long glide back to Telset and success. "Blood feud," I murmured to myself, but I felt disgust at my own dumb bravado. He had finished us.

I swam back to the wreckage of the *Albatross* and climbed onto the slippery top of the cabin, still a foot or two above sea level.

I was already numb with smuff, so I looked myself over quickly to make sure that I had no further injury. I was not worse off than I had already been.

Looking around, I saw the welcome sight of Moses Moses and Armitrage, both clinging to a splintery, ripped-up chunk of wooden deck. I signaled to Saint Anne and then dived off the cabin top to join them. Even as I left her, the *Albatross* blew air with a slurping, sucking sound, and began to glide easily, prow-first, to the bottom of the sea.

I swam to their chunk of wreckage. It barely kept them afloat, so I stayed away, treading water. They both looked severely shaken. Moses Moses started when I touched him. "I can't hear anything!" he shouted. "I think it deafened me!"

"Are you all right?" I shouted back. He read my lips and nodded. "It knocked the breath out of me! But I'm better now!"

I nodded and swam to Armitrage. I was alarmed when I saw the greenish, bloodless tint of his skin and his eyes, half-closed. I grabbed his cold, wet shoulder. "Armitrage!"

"I'm smuffed," he said. "I can barely hear, too. I took all the smuff I had. It was waterlogged."

"Where are you hurt?" I said. "Let me get skinseal over it."

He shook his head weakly, moving waterlogged black curls. "I didn't get him, did I?"

I glanced at the retreating sailplane. "No," I said. "But I think you scared him, 'Trage."

"I lost the gun," he said. "Couldn't hold on to it."

"It's all right," I said. I looked up. "Look, we still have all our cameras." It was true. Their tough casings had resisted the blast and they had come floating back to their masters, respecting their programming. For some reason it cheered me. I felt that I had not yet lost all my resources.

"I didn't want this to happen," Armitrage muttered. "There was supposed to be time. Time to win you to me." He looked at me, his green eyes stung with sea water and tears. "I have to tell you now. I love you, Kid. I always have. And you would have loved me back. I had plans. I would have been patient. It wouldn't have hurt you a bit, to love me back. It doesn't hurt to love. It just feels wonderful." A gout of blood filled his mouth and he spat it out, choking. In pity and horror I shouted, "No!" and tried to embrace him, to hold him up; and my right hand sank wrist-deep into the warm tangle of his guts. Bloody scum rose to the ocean's surface.

"You're dying," I said.

He said again, "It doesn't hurt. It just feels wonderful." He closed his eyes. His hands slipped from the broken deck and he started to sink; I caught his head in the crook of my elbow and held his face above the water. He said nothing. In a moment I heard his death rattle. Sobbing, I begged him not to die: "Armitrage, Armitrage, don't!"

Moses Moses swam up to help me. He looked into Armitrage's face and saw the blood on his mouth. "Is he dead?" he shouted.

I nodded, already raw-throated and racked with sobs. "I'm sorry," Moses yelled. "Let's get him onto the deck!"

We pushed the lax, unresisting body onto the splintered, floating boards. When I saw the way the explosion had ripped open his elegant body, I felt a tearing pain of revulsion and grief.

Anne approached, swimming clumsily toward us in her enveloping bag. It was easy to spot us now by the cloud of cameras. All four of Armitrage's cameras hovered around him, sucking up his gory image. Anne stopped at a distance, treading water. She seemed amazed to see me cry.

A minute passed. I ducked my over-heated face into the cool sea water, and stopped my tears. They I heard Anne shriek. "Something touched my legs!"

A broad black shadow rippled smoothly by us, just under the surface of the water. Moses Moses screamed, "Rays!" and we swam for our lives.

I had to turn to look. They were the big mid-ocean rays, dapplebacks, their broad leathery wings almost thirty feet across. There were at least three of them; I heard the explosive puff of air from their blowholes. The concussion and the scent of blood had brought them on us. I saw Armitrage's dead arms jerk upward as one of them snapped up his feet and dragged him beneath the surface. The water roiled, whipped to froth by their long, venomous tails. Another ray flopped up out of the water and crunched up two of his cameras with a single bite. After that I put my head down and swam after the others.

We were exhausted after two hundred yards. "My clothes," Moses gasped. "They're dragging me down!"

Anne helped him struggle out of his wet jacket; I pulled off his heavy, clinging trousers. I was about to let them sink when Anne panted, "Kid, wait!" While Moses floated on his back, exhausted, Anne took the trousers and knotted their cuffs. Then she put her head underwater and blew air into the waist. After several breaths, the legs puffed up taut, full of trapped air. By holding the waist underwater, Anne had turned the Chairman's trousers into a crude pair of water wings. Red-faced and wheezing, we all clung to them for support. The wet fabric held the air quite well, though we could see it slowly hissing out through the cloth in streams of tiny bubbles.

By floating on our backs and clinging to the air bags, we were able to float comfortably. Moses Moses had a coughing fit that cleared his lungs of sea water. "I can hear myself cough," he said loudly. "I'm not deaf then. Just stunned. Are you all right, Saint Anne?"

"Yes," she said. "I think a broken board hit me across the backs of my legs, but I'm all right. I'm just bruised, not bleeding."

"My ribs took a beating," Moses Moses said. "And I scratched my hands on that wreckage. It hurts, but I'm not bleeding either. How about you, Kid?"

"Not a linking scratch," I said bitterly. "If I'd stayed on board with him—"

Moses Moses laughed quietly. "Why feel guilt, Kid?" he asked gently. "He wouldn't have grudged us a few more hours of life. I don't care to spend my last moments in pain. Will you give me some of your drug?"

I was ashamed that I hadn't offered it sooner. "Of course," I said, pulling the watertight packet out of my combat jacket. "Don't spill any. Just a taste should be enough. You want some, Anne?"

Her face showed pain warring with taboo. "No," she said finally. "Not right now. But thank you, anyway."

I carefully resealed the packet and tucked it away. After a moment I said, "Do you think it's worth the effort to try to reach shore?"

Moses Moses shrugged. "I think I prefer the rays to exhaustion and drowning. But I'm open to suggestion."

"Perhaps we should try," said Anne. "It would be better morally to die fighting."

"The current is bearing us northward," Moses Moses pointed out. "Let's die comfortably instead. After all, who's to know?"

I looked up at my six faithful cameras, still hovering over us. "I wish I had some way to get my last tapes to an audience," I said. "But the cameras stay with me. What a shame. You know,

I almost regret that more than dying. After all, I've already died once."

"Really?" said Moses Moses. "A personality death?" I nodded. Moses smiled. "I thought so. I thought I recognized your age in the way you walked. It's hard to disguise."

"You're the first one to notice it," I said.

"Possibly," Moses Moses said. "Perhaps the others simply kept quiet about knowing. After all, it's your business, not theirs."

"Right," I said. Moses Moses took the hint. He stretched out his arms, his hairy fists loosely clenched. "Look at those clouds!" he said admiringly. "Their incredible height never ceases to astonish me. It's the depth of the atmosphere, and the length of the day here. So far, far superior to Niwlind. You children can hardly imagine it."

"I can," Saint Anne said. "I am a native Niwlindid. But you're right, Mr. Chairman, they're beautiful. So pure and white. The clouds on Niwlind are squat and gray. Over the moors, they are torn by the wind, knocked flat, scalloped. Like dark metal beaten flat with hammers. You can hear the wind all the time, the bleak wind. It's different here." She shivered and wiped wet bangs away from her forehead with one hand.

Moses said, "I haven't seen Niwlind in . . . let me see . . . it must be six hundred years now. Six hundred years. Two long lifetimes. Tell me, is it still ruled by the Directorate?"

"No," she said. "The Directorship still exists, but now it's a ceremonial office. Real political power has been taken over by the Director's First Secretary. The current Secretariat is held by a woman named Janet Decross, but she in turn is just the tool of another woman named Crestillomeem Tanglin."

Moses Moses nodded. "No surprises there. There's always been some power behind the throne, some damned courtier you have to buy off, sleep with, or blackmail. It's so rotten on Niwlind . . . rotten with age and inertia . . . I tried to start over, you know. Start over clean, with a new planet, a new society, a new world view, new morals and assumptions. I wanted to just sweep out all that choking garbage that was laying waste to people's lives, to give them a chance to find themselves, to express and explore themselves, beholden to no man. ..." His words sounded vaguely familiar. I recognized the strains of the Reverid Bill of Incorporation. "But it never works out like you hope. Just when you think you've pinned it down, it squirms away again. And people just don't understand! You point at the sun, and they'll spend years discussing your index finger! For years you build a monument, and when you lay the last brick the foundation shifts!" For a moment his face showed a titanic anger, but with a mercurial change of mood he laughed, mocking himself. "Listen to me talk! I had my chance. I gave it my best. I owned a planet, I led a people. How many men can say that much? I have no regrets. At least I die on my own world."

Impassively, he looked at us. He had an expression one often sees on the faces of the very old: as if they were looking at everything from a vast distance. Finally he said, "I've dragged you with me to death. I'm sorry, but frankly I'm glad I don't have to meet it alone. Since I have a captive audience, why shouldn't I tell you a story? After all, we may have hours left. We have to amuse ourselves somehow. If you like, I'll tell you the story of my life."

"I'd be honored to hear it," Saint Anne said simply. I nodded. "Why not?" I said. "It's just the three of us. We have no reason to hide anything from one another. If there's time, I'll tell my own story."

"So will I," said Anne.

"Good," said Moses. "Then I'll start."

7

"I was born ... let me see ... eight hundred and ten years ago, on Niwlind. I was probably bottled, but it may have been a natural birth, I don't know. I know that I was raised in a government crèche, but my earliest memories date back to when I was about nineteen or so." His heavy brows knotted painfully as he sifted through the detritus of centuries of memory. "This would be a lot easier if I had my computerized memory, but it's down in the basement with my cryocoffin, of course. Ah, I have it. Louise. Her name was Louise. My name wasn't Moses Moses then, I had some other name, I forget what. I had a job at the Bureau of Orbital Research and Assessment. We monitored the resources satellites. It was a pretty good job, really, for a nineteen-year-old, but I hated it. I was a bright youngster. Louise was my boss. She was about eighty years old. A child really, but I thought she was the ultimate in sophistication. I knew she slept around a lot, and that seemed very wicked and exciting.

"I don't know how I got her attention, I suppose I swaggered around a bit, making up for my height. In those days it bothered me to be short, I forget why. I imagine she thought I was cute. One day she called me into her office, and she gave me a demonstration of her skill, which was considerable. I was shattered, completely stunned. Naturally, I lost my head. I swore eternal constancy, begged her to be mine alone, told her that I loved her desperately, that I'd sacrifice my life to her pleasures, her tiniest whim. I was completely enslaved. It must have amused her.

"She toyed with me for a little while—two years, maybe. Of course, back then, two years seemed like forever to me. The other bureau workers were sick of my being the office favorite by then; on Niwlind sex was a very political thing, especially when you held a government post. Finally she told me we had to break up for the sake of the bureau.

"I threw tantrums. I ranted and raved, I threatened suicide. I had a hot temper and a lot of determination. I told her that I was destined for great things and I wouldn't let such minor, cheap crap destroy my happiness. If the government got in my way I'd crush the government; if society got in my way I'd build my own society. She couldn't help laughing at that, and her laughter wounded me deeply. I insulted her, maybe I even tried violence. She finished our affair then and there and had me fired from the bureau.

"The years after that were very hard. Hundreds of doors were closed in my face. I was denied any post in the government. My savings ran out—I had very little, because I spent most of my salary on gifts for Louise. Suddenly I was poor. I lived with the poor, and for the first time I saw their miserable, barren, hampered, dehumanized lives. Sometimes they actually starved, and the damned mechanized police were everywhere. The Confederacy complained about it. Planetary governments aren't supposed to allow their populations to starve. But what did the Directorate care? They never saw the poor. They literally thought that starvation—*which was a fact*—was a vile rumor. Of course they never checked for themselves. They never had time, they were too busy holding their posts and plotting against rivals. Life was stratified. And in its way, the life of the very powerful was as narrow and rigid as the life of the very poor.

"Slowly it dawned on me that our whole society was suffocating. We had locked ourselves into a closet, and we could only escape by breaking down the door.

"By the time I was thirty I had become completely radicalized." He paused, meditating. "Thirty—that's a good age. Imagine growing up to be thirty. Then imagine doing it eleven more times. You see? Now you know what it's like to be my age. I'm three hundred and seventy years old." He smiled distantly and went back to his story.

"By that time I had gotten over my affair with Louise. She was only the catalyst, after all. But I hadn't forgotten what I told her.

"I had learned to control my temper and hide my feelings. I realized that I must rigorously discipline myself before I could have even a chance of success. I thought of entering the Academy, but I realized that they gave no courses in revolution. I worked at a succession of odd jobs while I tried to educate myself. I was drawn inexorably to the greatest source of information on the planet—the Consular Library at the Confederate Consulate, which at that time was in the city of Miclo. Do you know that city, Anne?"

"I've never been there," she said.

Moses shrugged. "Planets are big places. At Miclo I took a job in industrial design, designing clock faces and digital readouts. Now came my first act of really consummate cunning. I swallowed my obsession, and for five years I applied the full force of my intelligence to my job, which I passionately hated. I lived a life of ruthless discipline. I unhesitatingly trampled and betrayed my fellow workers. I lived in a spartan cell, I had no friends, and no recreations. In my spare time I read textbooks on design. I was promoted by leaps and bounds. Finally only one man stood between myself and control of the enterprise. When my chance came, I unhesitatingly compromised him and ruined his career. Then I bled the company dry by embezzlement and finally sold it for far more than it was worth to a woman I controlled by blackmail. I was then forty-five years old, rich, and insane.

"I was literally and clinically insane. I heard voices, I felt that my limbs were detached from my body, and I knew that my many enemies were trying to kill me.

"I invested my wealth, but I had become so intensely paranoid that I couldn't bear the sight or smell of human beings. I fled to a very remote area in the planet's polar icecap, the farthest place I could think of. You, Kid, have probably never seen an icecap. They are harsh and terrible places, but not without their own weird beauty. I paid well for a prefabricated, self-sufficient retreat, which I built myself, alone, with my two hands and two primitive construction drones.

"I lived there for two years and went through a traumatic personality change. I adopted another name, and I returned to the Consular Library with my sanity restored but my resolve undiminished!

"I was looking for ways to design a whole society from scratch. There were plenty of examples—mostly miserable failures. Part of the problem was that it was impossible to start with brand-new human beings. The converts to the new society always brought along a cultural hangover from their areas of origin.

"Most of the very worst failures were those based on religions and airy moral convictions. I decided that mine would be based firmly on self-interest. I looked for a sound structural basis and I decided on the corporation. Citizens would be shareholders, so that everyone would profit equally from the collective endeavor.

"Since work had driven me mad, I decided to abolish it. For that I needed a get-rich-quick scheme, a corporate investment that would supply the revenue to support an entire society. Of course, you know what I eventually found." He pointed upward. "It was the Reverid Morning Star."

He stopped momentarily while Anne and I ducked underwater to blow more air into the flotation bags, which had gone flat.

"By this time I was fifty, still a youngster. I had reached full maturity, however. By the time I was sixty I had ingratiated myself with the Confederate Consul General and had taken a position as his Chief Archivist. It was then that I discovered the works of Riley. I had them reprinted at my own expense, in translation of course, and they were a planet-wide sensation. I was wealthier than ever and now famous as well. The usual seductions of fame offered themselves, but I refused them. Instead, I adopted a carefully calculated demeanor of modesty and common sense. I knew that I would need such a reputation when I offered my harebrained scheme to the public.

"During the next forty years I slowly laid the groundwork for my plans, never hinting them to a soul. I was offered a lucrative position with the planetary government, and I refused. This really electrified my contemporaries. When they demanded my reasons, I let it be known that I objected on moral grounds. I never polemicized, I never raised my voice; in fact, I never made my moral grounds exactly clear. I mentioned the plight of the poor of course, but mostly I just fed them with witty platitudes I had scraped up during decades of reading. Frankly, I kept a little notebook full of platitudes on my person at all times. They proved invaluable." He paused. "Men will give their lives for an idea, if it's large enough and not exactly clear to them.

"The real reason for my refusal was the fact that I had already thrown in my lot with the Confederacy. I needed the Confederacy badly, because they were in legal control of the planet I wanted, this very planet in fact. The Academy was investigating the planet for possible colonization at the time, and I knew from my sources that they would clear it. I could get it, for a price.

"Luckily the Academy was moving very slowly, as it always does, and the planet demanded a lot of investigation. There was quite a bit of concern over the microbial life.

"At the age of one hundred I married for the first time, and at one hundred and twenty I married again. Both times I married for money. My wives and I were still friends when we separated, and I jumped from moderate wealth to an immense fortune. I started my charitable works: preserving wildlife, endowing libraries, feeding people, housing and clothing them. This was another tactic I had learned from the past. That way I preserved my moral stature and my money. Was it hypocrisy? Was it schizophrenia? I've never decided." He shrugged again.

"I already knew that I would have to fight the Niwlindid Directorate tooth and nail. Naturally, they had grown to hate me, as they hated any power they couldn't corrupt or envelop. I knew that there were two sources of power I could turn against them: the Confederacy, and popular support." Suddenly a thought startled him. "The Confederacy still exists, doesn't it?"

"Of course," I said. "It's grown weaker since your time, though. Too much decentralization."

"Yes," Moses said. "I could see that coming. At any rate, it dawned on me that the time had come for popular agitation. I had to make myself such a nuisance to the government that they would be glad to see me go, no matter what the cost to their own resources. When I was one hundred and thirty, I changed my name to Moses Moses and started the Corporation.

"My plan was to mine the Morning Star. To strip a planet as it had never been stripped before. To blast it. To rip it. To turn it inside out and seize the metal of its core.

"I envisioned a cloud of oneills. Big, cylindrical orbital cities, the kinds the Confederates live in. I foresaw my people living in these cylinders, building drones, programming them to rip a planet. I knew there was a market for the metal, but the initial investment would be colossal. Ruinous. But Niwlind was ripe for ruin.

"I hired the best engineers I could find, and I paid to train others. I spent money like water. I was a man possessed. I got the necessary plans from the Confederacy, the documentation for oneills, and I paid them in the coin they liked best. Espionage. Yes, I committed treason—I confess it frankly. They joined me in plundering Niwlind, and many a Confederate official returned from my home planet rich. But I needed information only they could give me.

"The cost in human suffering was terrible, but it was blamed on the Confederacy and the Directorate, not me. Does that bother you, Kid, to know your life was based on the pain of the helpless?"

I shook my head. "That was six hundred years ago. They're all dead now, anyway."

Moses Moses smiled blandly. "It didn't bother me either. Their misery only drew them closer to me. I would have spared them their pain if I could, of course. I loved power, but I wasn't a sadist. Besides, I was offering them a chance to escape. They could never have had that chance without my genius. I could not afford to be hampered by useless guilt.

"Decades passed. I was battling the lethargy of the very old, and there's no lethargy like it. I started small. I endured twenty years of slander and ridicule, preaching, publishing, taping, testifying, pleading, arguing, begging, threatening, pimping, blackmailing. Then the young, the restless, the desperate began to flock around me. I picked good men and women for my apostles. You must have seen their names in your histories: Bowmarshay, Deeder, Quinn, Miniott, and all the others. The first members of the Reverid Board of Directors. They were all good people, the best I could find. They believed in me, and in return I gave them meaning for their lives.

"They had complete faith in the facade I had built for myself. And I had to stay within the facade, because I would have died rather than disappoint them. I had plenty of followers eager to do my dirty work, so I was able to retreat to a lofty moral eminence. Thanks to my long self-discipline, asceticism was very little effort for me, but it made an immense impression on people who were used to nothing but venality and greed. And this is the part you must believe . . . *my mask became my face*. I became Moses Moses, the prophet, the leader. I had started my people moving; now I was swept along by their tide. They had made me their lord and without hesitation I sacrificed everything for their happiness. . . .

"I had no private life, no selfishness, no will of my own, no *thoughts* of my own. In a very real, literal way I ceased to have an identity. I was the people's will made flesh. This seems bizarre and mystical, I know; it would have seemed so to me, if I had ever given myself time to think about it. But I never did. It absorbed me completely, like a dream, like a womb. I have memories of course: I gave speeches, I organized, I gave orders, I checked plans; I left the planet, I moved into the first oneills with the pioneers, I operated a mining drone like the rest, always like the rest. But it seems so vague to me now, as if I were entranced, as if I were someone else. It was a kind of madness, a kind of possession. I had built myself a role, and it swallowed me. I had burned away like the dross off molten tin; the only thing left of me was a shining tin god.

"I was like that for almost seventy years, until I was two hundred and twenty. We had already had the oneills operating for twenty-one years, and we had scraped up enough metal to begin to build our own oneills, to establish our independence from Niwlind. We had even begun to supply a trickle of money to the Confederacy; their lust for cash was incredible, and dammit, we were buying a planet, or at least the right to one. My plan was working. The long purgatory on the oneills was changing my Niwlindids into a people of their own, with their own customs, expressions, and ways of thought. Life on the oneills was grindingly hard at first; let no one tell you differently, I was there, and I *know*. Our supplies from Niwlind were grudging to say the least, and none of us were experts; we blundered time and again, and every time we blundered, people died. A life-support system is merciless; it knows nothing of pain, only the laws of mechanics. But we learned fast. We had to learn to stay alive. We went through the flame, and it tempered us. It made us what we were. It made you what *you* are.

"When I was two hundred and twenty-one, an accident occurred in my oneill, which was of course the center of government. It involved a newly constructed mining drone, which had not yet been dropped to the surface of the Morning Star. It was orbiting not far from the edge of the oneill when its laser malfunctioned briefly and sent a small pulse of pure light completely through the oneill outer wall; as it happened, right where I was speaking. This was not an assassination attempt as many people have claimed. It was only a deadly accident. My poor secretary, Madame Deeder, was killed immediately and the screams of the crowd were swallowed up by the roar of decompression. I looked and I saw naked space through the hole, which was no more than ten inches in diameter. Of course it would have taken weeks to empty all the air of the oneill through such a tiny hole, but my only thought was for the safety of my audience, who were trampling one another in panic. Naturally we kept the oneill spinning at Reverid gravity, since Reverie was to be our home; the zero-grav oneills came later. But I digress.

"To be brief, I saw them panicking; I heard the terrible roar, I saw it ripping up chairs, the podium itself, and I reacted quickly. I flung my body over the hole and blocked it with my chest. Of course I blacked out immediately under the crushing impact. I knew I was dead, because I knew I had given my life. But I wasn't dead.

"Things would have been different if I had died a martyr's death; they would have gone more to my plan. A dead man's hands can be crushingly strong. But I wasn't dead, because they healed me. It took them days to rebuild my body, but they succeeded, because they loved me. But when I opened my eyes again, I was no longer Moses Moses."

He sighed. We saw the lick of lightning against a distant thunderhead. Moses Moses' auburn hair had dried and was stiffened with brine. The skin of our hands had begun to wrinkle, as waterlogged as stewed fruit. It was almost noon and the glare off the sea was blinding.

"Oh, I kept the name," said Moses Moses. "I always kept the name. But I had lost that inspiration, that possessive zeitgeist. I knew my role, and I played it well, but now I was only the actor, not the man. Somehow they sensed it. I know this is the truth. No one ever spoke of it; maybe they never realized it consciously. Our lives went on, but they lacked luster, as if poisoned by anticlimax. That was it, the turning point. After that, the rot began to steal into my plans.

"I had lost it. Now that I think back on it, it amazes me to think how long I kept it. But now I was returned to myself, and the schemer had replaced the saint. It sickened me. When I tried to go on with the charade, it choked me; I felt that it was sucking out all of my life. I tried to delegate my authority to those I trusted, to go into retirement. It took me years. God, they were sickeningly coy. Oh, wonderful Moses Moses, they said, the heroic near-martyr, such statesmanlike modesty! As if we could go on without our very heart and soul! It cost me a tremendous effort to put power into the hands of the Board of Directors. When I picked them I had picked loyal followers, not statesmen. They were constantly deferring decisions to me. It lasted throughout the rest of the Mining Century, until I was three hundred miserable years old. God, what didn't I give for those people?

"One day I woke up and realized that we were rich. Fantastically rich! Our first concern had been to buy off the Confederacy; that came relatively quickly. Then, with their help and astronomical bribes, we were able to corrupt the Academic survey team and get the planet released to us before their study was complete. We were impatient; they'd already been studying it for two hundred years and they still weren't satisfied. We promised to take great care concerning the microbial life and I personally assured them that we would stay out of the Mass, which seemed to be the area they thought most dangerous. It's an ugly area anyway, all that mold and fungus, and who needs that when there are hundreds of thousands of beautiful, rich tropical islands? Then we turned our money back to Niwlind and paid off our investors; once that was done we declared our political independence. They didn't like it, of course. They called us traitors, but what could they do? The expenses of interstellar war are completely ruinous, and we had the support of the Confederacy who controlled the interstellar pilots. We were beyond their reach.

"And still the money kept pouring in, exponentially. We spent it on terraforming at first, building the big oneill gardens so that food would no longer be a problem. And I encouraged it, because we'd lived on green scum and yeast for years. Then we bought knowledge, trading metal for technology, so that we had the very best available food synthesis and vast orbital greenhouses tended by computer-run drones. Drone technology was our own, of course, we'd carried it as far as—or farther than—any other human people, so we placed the heaviest reliance on our own expertise. Drones were our slave labor force; we wanted a huge pyramid of drones to support a tiny apex of human aristocrats. So we built them in incredible numbers, until there were more drones than people, then twice as many, four times, six times, ten, twenty. And we built oneills to house them, for manufacturing, for energy, for food, communications, transportation. And as far as possible we kept them simple. We never allowed our computers to mock human sentience, because we'd learned from the lessons of the past.

"As money poured through our dwelling oneills, we were unable to resist making them beautiful. In my original plans they were only campgrounds, orbiting arks if you prefer. But after a century one feels differently; you learn to love the work of your own hands, to think of it as home. And oneills have their advantages; the lack of gravity at their cores for instance. That gave rise to hundreds of different pursuits from sports to sex, things that made us uniquely us, that people were loth to give up. Just as we started colonizing the planet, some oneills began canceling their centrifugal spin, going completely floater, like the Confederates themselves. They orbited Reverie, because it's such a beautiful planet, but they'd made their decision to stay in space and there was nothing I could do about it; it would have ripped the social fabric. I set an example by moving down to the planet, and I lived in those ugly drone-built fortresses that I'd helped to construct myself. They were uncomfortable and hideous, and every time a fresh wind blew in off the continent we would all come down with some minor ailment. We kept a close watch on our health, of course, and there weren't many fatalities, but we were constantly hampered by precautions. There were endless tests and inoculations and immunizations, and most of us were at a low level of illness much of the time—rotten little ailments like colds and diarrhea, stomach aches, low fevers, sticky eyes, peeling blisters on the hands and feet, bumps and itches—not dangerous things, not really challenging things, just trivial annoyances that sapped the will instead of strengthening it. After all, we were pioneers, and even with the full backing of a powerful technology, a pioneer faces difficulties. But the orbiters didn't see it that way. With a camera drone you can experience much of Reverie, sight and sound, without risking illness, from the lavish comfort of your oneill. You're not weighted down by gravity; you don't get sunburned, you don't get sand in your shoes. With a direct cerebral hookup you can even get good approximations of touch and scent. It was just too tempting to stay in orbit, to see the whole planet at a glance instead of a few acres through a tiny quartz window. They didn't want to struggle any more, and after the Mining Century, who could blame them? And oneills are close to self-sufficient, they have to be, since each is its own life-support system; an oneill naturally tends toward insularity, toward becoming a city-state. Our good communications prevented that, luckily, but nevertheless they were hard to control. . . .

"Things slowly got better as the decades passed, faster and faster, each one seeming to take less time than the last. The older settlers became immunized, we were able to see more, travel more, develop customs of our own, to take advantage of the incredible bounty of this planet. We grew to love it as a mother rather than fight it as an adversary. It's so beautiful, it's a gift. It had an intelligent race once. I often wonder what they were like. It was thoughtful of them to destroy themselves and leave their planet to us."

He grinned sardonically. "Death comes to us all, though not so quickly as it came to them. Death is rooted within me, it travels along every nerve. A man is lucky to live to three hundred. With a purpose in life, something to focus his will to survive, he may see three hundred and fifty. But the urge to die is as strong as the urge to live; it only manifests itself more subtly. After I passed three hundred, my death began to assert itself. Subtly at first, then more urgently. The degenerative process is peculiarly horrifying."

He looked at both of us, slowly, earnestly. "It started with the breakdown of memory. Distant memories had been blurred for a long time; I had depended on my computer to sort them out for me. But then I found myself prey to increasing absent-mindedness. I would forget the events of days or even mere hours past. I would forget if I had eaten a meal, forget errands and appointments, repeat myself in conversations. Then it became more intense. I suffered from the nightmarish feeling that I was living a single week over again; I began to suspect, insanely, that time had doubled back on itself, that I was trapped in an endless loop, like a tape.

"I felt that I was becoming thinner—stretched out into an intolerable, vulnerable state. I began to slip into the classic degenerative syndromes of extreme old age, the state we call Panan. Do you know what Panan is? Does it still exist?"

"Yes," I said. "I know what it is. It's pananesthesia—a sort of overall numbness."

"That's not half of it," Moses Moses said. "It involves physical numbness, of course. In its worst state, you can smash your fingers in a door and not even notice it until you see the dripping of blood. But it's a mental numbness too. Your strongest emotions, your deepest convictions run out of you like water from a broken jug. Apathy devours you. Black depression settles in, suddenly, without warning, and when you least expect it. You feel horribly distant from life, as if you were encased in glass, and other people seem like puppets. You can almost see the strings." He shuddered.

"God, it even hurts to talk about it! The pleasures that rooted you to life, that made it seem worth living, are leached away. Sex for example. I've been impotent for a long time now—decades. Aphrodisiacs would restore the function of my body, but it was as if it were happening to someone else. You feel out of phase with your body, as if you had drifted away from it. That's the very worst part of it. It's madness, a madness peculiar to the old. You begin to suspect that your body is useless, that it drags you down. You begin to hate your body, you begin to hate yourself. Your catch yourself inflicting small punishments on the body; you become accident prone. Most old people die by accidents, by indirect suicide. Only a few have the nerve to confront death directly and take their own lives.

"I didn't want to die. Consciously, I hated the idea of death. Unconsciously, I planned my own destruction. I convinced myself that a shock would restore my appetite for living; I took up mountain climbing, gliding, diving. I confronted these natural risks, and I manufactured more of my own. It didn't work, but it did show me the opposite side of the coin. It's called Hyperas. From hyperasthesia, of course.

"In many ways Hyperas is worse then Panan. Instead of being distanced, you feel suffocatingly close. Instead of feeling numb, you are hideously sensitive. Whispers sound like shouts and shouts like earthquakes. The softest clothing chafes you. The tastiest food is cloying, sickeningly rich. You notice everything, even the tiniest things that you never realized existed. Not merely people's faces, but the dirt in their clogged pores, the stubble in their follicles, the split ends in individual hairs. You notice the smallest, most fleeting expressions; people behave like slapstick clowns, mugging everything. You can tell what they say before they say it, what they'll do before they do it. Actually this is true for most old people; it's a matter of experience. But in Hyperas, your perceptions become so acute that it dehumanizes people. They seem like programmed drones. You rob them of their free will, and suddenly it seems that they never had any.

"You notice so many tiny details that you smother under the rush of information. It drives you frantic. It forces you to retreat from your usual haunts into a less cluttered environment; a bare room, for instance. I tried that, but I became painfully fascinated by the texture of the wall, by the weaving of the sheets on my cot, by the dust motes in the air, even by self-induced ringing in my ears. During my worst attack I retreated to a sensory deprivation tank; warm water, silence, darkness. It seemed to work; I calmed down. But when I finally came out, I was completely engulfed by Panan. From then on, the two states alternated, sometimes in a single day. When I realized that I was being driven to suicide, I decided to postpone my final confrontation with death by putting myself under ice. I started preparing my cryocoffin. When I had this task to distract me, my sanity was restored. I suppose the cryosleep was close enough to death to satisfy my destructive urge, so it granted me a respite from my self-torment. I picked what I thought would be a significant date for my reawakening; I thought that the marvels of the distant future would distract me long enough to provide a few more decades of life. If the Panan returned, I would kill myself, or go back under ice again. That way I could extend my life almost indefinitely.

"Also, there was an element of vanity. Naturally I wanted to see how long my social handiwork would last. Curiosity was a good enough reason to live. It aroused my interest, it broke the shell of apathy. So I did it. I never thought it would end in this, though I was prepared for disaster. I carefully hid my coffin, you remember. But I never anticipated this." He shook his head. "At least it relieves me from the moral effort of suicide. People tell me that suicide, deliberate, self-conscious self-destruction, is the only way to die with dignity. But I never believed that. The perfect death, for me, would have come quickly, without warning, as it did when the drone pierced my oneill. But death had his chance then, and he failed to get me. Since, then, I've resolved on life. When the rays come to get us, I suppose I'll fight them! That should be a sight to see."

He laughed lightly, mocking himself, but without bitterness. "I've said enough. Who'll be next to tell their story?"

Anne and I exchanged glances. Anne's freckled face was sunburned; it was noon and the burn would get much worse if we lived until sundown, nine hours away. "I'll go next," she said.

"All right," I said. I looked overhead. A flock of dark, long-winged birds were flying west in a V formation. Perhaps one of the towering, white-piled thunderclouds would drift over us and shade us. Perhaps it would even rain on us. Although we were neck-deep in water, I was getting thirsty. I tried not to think about it. The hunger was worse, anyway; as usual, the smuff stirred my appetite.

8

Anne said, "I believe in God, the catalyst of life, the core of the universe, the essence of good. I believe in good, and I believe in evil, and I have sworn to support the first and destroy the second. I believe in a soul, which is manifested in matter, but is different from matter and superior to it. God breathed life into matter, because God is pure soul, and the souls of all living things return to God when their stay in the realm of matter is dissolved by death. Evil comes when the pure and passionless soul is polluted by material lust and greed. The way of salvation is to purge the soul of evil and return to the good. All forms of life contain some good, because they all come from God; therefore all life is sacred and not to be wantonly destroyed. Such is the creed of my Church; such is my creed; such is my faith."

After this strange statement she fell silent for so long that I thought she had finished. I was annoyed and amused. "That's it, then?" I said mockingly. "That's your life story?"

"That is the core of it," she said. "The rest is only personal details."

"Well," said Moses Moses with an air of humorous restraint, "perhaps you should go ahead and tell us a few of them. Maybe you'll find it easier if you start with the history of your Church."

"The history of my Church is the history of my life," said Anne with a quiet womanly dignity quite amazing for one sunk to her neck in sea water. "I was born into the Church, because I am the great-granddaughter of the Mysteriarch. She is the leader of our Church, and her father is our greatest theologian, the wisest man alive. He is five hundred years old."

"Impossible," said Moses Moses and I, together.

She shook her head. "It's the truth."

"Then he's had a memory wipe, probably several," I said. "How do you know he's that old? What proof can he offer?"

"Church leaders never lie," Anne said indignantly. "Sometimes they prefer to meet questions with silence, but they never lie. Men and women are not born to destroy themselves; that idea is the lie. Those outside the faith die early, because they tear themselves apart with frustration and despair. Their lives are pointless; they have nowhere to turn; they have no goals in life nobler than the gratification of their own vanity. Their lives are empty! Hollow, echoing, empty! They have nothing to live for! They have nothing beyond themselves! Is it any wonder that they die? No. The wonder is that they manage to live so long. God put no limitation on life. Those who follow the path of righteousness can live indefinitely, because they dedicate their lives to God.

"Their lives are healthy, because they are dedicated to a noble purpose, the noblest there is: they do good. They do good, and they avoid the black paths of suicidal evil: Hate. Envy. Greed. Luxury. Sloth. The dissolutions of the flesh. They avoid all those things. They avoid all those things and they focus their eyes on the sublime." She looked piously upward. "That's why our creed has spread, slowly but surely. Now there are over a million men and women in our Church family. We are a force to be reckoned with on Niwlind."

I said, "What's Niwlind's current population? About six billion, right?"

"Six point two billion," she said. "But our million are the best among them, and the rest will see the light in time."

Moses Moses was aghast. "Are there that many people now? How did it get so overcrowded? There were only three billion when I left."

"It was evasion of the population laws," Anne said calmly. "Everyone does it. People need children, you know; it's a very deep-seated need. I intend—well, I intended to have children someday. It's too late now, of course."

I was interested. "Really?" I said. "Do you favor artificial insemination, or were you going to give yourself to some man's sweaty fleshy embraces?"

Anne looked at me coldly. "Marriage is a sacrament. It is a meeting of souls. Marriage in the Church transcends carnal lusts." I nodded skeptically. She frowned. "I didn't expect you to understand that. Obviously it's completely beyond you."

I was annoyed. "I don't pretend to understand sex, but I know hypocrisy when I see it."

"That doesn't suprise me," she said cuttingly. "You claimed to be Tanglin's young son when you're really hundreds of years old. Obviously you're an old hand at hypocrisy."

"Why, you mudbrained idiot," I began, but Moses Moses interrupted. "Children, please," he said smoothly. "Let's avoid squabbling. These are my last hours. Let me live them in peace. You'll have your chance to explain yourself, Kid. Let Anne have hers."

My anger evaporated. "Yes, of course," I said. "Go ahead, Anne." I relished the thought that she would soon know the full truth about Tanglin, and our relationship.

Anne said, "The Uplands on Niwlind are one of the planet's oldest areas. They are a high plateau. The air is thin and it is cold and windy, especially in winter. It has never been heavily populated. Even now most of the development is in mining camps. But that is where the Mysteriarch founded our Church Sanctuary, and that is where I was born, fifty-two years ago.

"Only the initiates know the full extent of Sanctuary. Visitors only see the domes and churches that cling to the side of the rock. Sometimes rumors are heard about the tunnels in the valley cliff wall. They do not realize that there are miles of tunnels. And not all the tunnels were built by men.

"The Upland Plateau itself is grassy and arid. We chose to dwell in the canyons, great, deep river canyons that the water carved over millions of years. The rock is the continental shield itself—there is no sedimentation, no colorful layering in it. It is black and gray and sometimes, rarely, dark red. The canyons are thousands of feet deep and sometimes miles wide. The rivers are thin and sinuous and in some places they are blocked by falls of rubble. Then thin, deep little fjords appear, and there are rapids. The water is dark and very cold.

"Every morning and every evening, with sunrise and sunset, winds whip through the canyon, and they howl. If you listen carefully you can hear voices in the howling, but it is best not to listen to them. The wind tears at everything it touches—that's why the plants of the valley floor are almost all roots. They are small and gnarled and tough, but if their seeds land behind a windbreak then they grow tall and put out hard stiff colorful flowers whose petals can scratch glass.

"Even as a little girl I didn't like the valley floor—it is too dark, the walls are too high. I wanted to live on the moors instead. The moors are windy too, it blows all the time. But it blows steadily, not with the brief killing violence of the morning and evening valleywinds. And it is open. You can see the sun and the dark battered clouds and the knee-high grass and smell the little flowers and see the little denizens of the plains. There are beetles and grasshoppers and flutterbys, and little marmots and rabbits and goats, and of course moas. The moas are best." Anne reached up slowly and touched the sodden cluster of dark feathers pinned to her hair.

"I was a good girl and I understood the truth of the catechism almost from the first, and I was better even than they expected me to be. Until I was ten I stayed almost all the time in Sanctuary, because I was an illegal child and the old habits of caution die hard. But after a while I was given a forged identity and I went through my Borning and I took my adult name, Anne.

"Then I was allowed to go up the steep trail from the valley floor up to the moors, where I worked in the gardening domes with my uncle and cousins. During prayertime in the mornings and evenings, when the valleywinds blew, I was able to go out on the moors to meditate. I saw my first moa when I was twelve. It was an old moa—an old female with dirty feathers and big pendulous wattles on her neck. I was wandering, and so was she. I wasn't frightened, although mother had told me that in the first days of Sanctuary a child had been pecked to death by big rogue moas. The old moa wasn't frightened either. She just backed away slowly and then ran off over the grass on her great thick scaly legs.

"That night I dreamed that I was wandering over the moors and I came into a depression like a grassy bowl. And I dreamed that in the middle of the depression was a big circular track of beaten earth, like a big wheel, with eight dirt tracks like spokes. And in the dream something called me to step into the center of the wheel, but when I stepped over the boundary of the circle I woke up.

"In the morning I told my uncle about the dream. We of the Church know about dreams; they come from the depths of the soul, and therefore they are close to the Great Soul that is the author of consciousness and dreams alike. We put on our plains boots, and we took our hiking staves, and we went out into the moors to look for the wheel, and on the second day we found it. It was a dancing ground of the moas, such as few human beings had ever seen. We could see their big three-toed tracks in the beaten dirt, and we saw the strange flat mushrooms that grow in the dung of moas all around its rim.

" 'I knew we would find it,' my uncle told me. 'The Catechist, your great-great-grandfather, dreamed the site of Sanctuary long before we found it, and your grandmother, my mother, dreamed the site of the Iron Caves before the landslide exposed them. Look into your heart now, child, and tell me what we must do.'

"For a little while I knelt in the blowing grass and prayed, and the answer came to me. And I said, 'Uncle, you must leave me, and I must stay here. Something calls me to this spot and I must answer the call as best I hear it.' So my uncle left me."

"But moas are dangerous," Moses Moses objected. "They're carnivorous; I've seen them fed in zoos. Those big beaks could rip off a man's arm."

Anne nodded. "Yes. I've seen them tear moor goats to pieces in less time than it takes to breathe. But I wasn't afraid, although I trembled. I pulled my hood over my head and laced my gray cape around my shoulders and pulled on my gray gloves and leaned on my staff of gray stonewood. I stared for a long time at the wheel with the eight spokes.

"The sun began to set and it grew colder, and when the first pale star shone on the eastern horizon the moas began to appear. There were big blue-wattled males, and big red-wattled females, and little moa chicks no higher than my knee. They came in utter silence, because they are mute. I didn't move at all, and none of them seemed to notice me. Then they danced. They ran around the circle, and they danced across the spokes, dipping their heavy heads, and spreading their wings, and leaping in the air. They danced until it was dark and I could not see them moving but only heard the thump of their feet in the dirt. After a while even that sound faded, and I sat down in the grass and drew my knees to my chest and covered up in my cloak and slept and dreamed. I dreamed that I danced with the moas in the form of a moa. In the morning I walked back to the gardening domes, which took all day. In the evening my stomach began to cramp and hurt and I bled for the first time.

"I went to the dancing-ground many times after that, but I did not see any moas. When I was fifteen a mining expedition came to Sanctuary and the illegal population retreated into the tunnels. Everyone circumvented the population laws, and, until Rominuald Tanglin legitimized the illegal population, any of us could have been arrested and our parents heavily fined. And illegal people were denied the protection of the law as well—we could be robbed or beaten or raped and we wouldn't have dared go to the police. Of course there were no such criminal problems within Sanctuary. Our Church family was well disciplined—we all knew one another and did not tolerate crime. But the miners were terrible. They wouldn't have come to prospect if the Reverid Emigration hadn't taken so much of our metals, by the way—that was one of the legacies you left us. But I don't blame you for struggling to leave such corruption. The police had their agents among the miners. The Directorate didn't like the idea of a powerful religious group with their own city and they sent their census takers to harass us.

"But we were not helpless. We had the right on our side, of

course. We appealed for the help of Rominuald Tanglin and put what power we had into his coalition. We had many Church brothers and sisters all over Niwlind, though Sanctuary was our holy city and our headquarters.

"Naturally I personally had very little to do with this—I was in my teens when the mining controversy first began. But I followed the controversy avidly, we all did. We hated the miners, who brought vice and brutality with them and tried to exploit Church members for sexual purposes. We tried to expel them, but the demand for the metal was great and we were overruled politically.

"I was still fascinated by the moas. When the Legitimation Act came through and I was granted my own identity, I was free to study them without harassment—thanks to Rominuald Tanglin, of course. Since we Church folk and the miners were the only people on the Upland Plateau, and since that was the moas' only habitat, I became one of the planet's top specialists on moas. I was very patient. I followed them on foot, I made no threatening gestures, and when I could I left them food. They grew used to my scent, to my presence. I often roamed with them for days. I had my own flock. I gave them names.

"But the mining went on at a redoubled pace, and foreign Niwlindids poured in from all over the planet in a rush. More than once I found moas shot dead or caught in cruel traps. The moas were not entirely innocent, of course, but it was their land. The intruders were ruthlessly developing their sacred places. Yes, sacred places, you needn't look so surprised—why should they dance so, if not to worship?

"The intruders were afraid of the moas, and with good reason. More than one wanderer on the moors was found with beak-marks on his bones. I can only say that my flock never killed a human—they lived near Sanctuary, where Church folk defended native life with their own bodies if need be. The miners were anxious to exterminate the moas, and they started the bureaucratic process that would have granted them that right— or that wrong, I should say. But thank God for Rominuald Tanglin! He got wind of this evil procedure. His upright soul was filled with righteous indignation.

"He visited Sanctuary in person. We gave him the finest reception we could—after all, by this time he was First Secretary, though his position was shaky. He seemed pleased by our acclaim, but it was hard to judge for sure, as he was in many ways a peculiar man. Those strange sticks linked with a chain—the weapon you use, Kid—he kept them with him at all times. He never let them get farther away than his fingers' ends. He, of course, never put them to the ignoble uses of violence, though. He used them only for healthful exercise, I can assure you.

"Secretary Tanglin spent several hours in close conference with our Mysteriarch. They got along famously, which very much pleased and surprised us, as the Mysteriarch usually had a short way with outsiders. She was over four hundred years old and did not tolerate sin easily, but apparently she found the Secretary to be morally sound. Or maybe it was the Secretary's famous ability to charm.

"You can imagine my shock and surprise when I, myself, Anne Twiceborn, was called to their conference chamber. Of course I had no right to be in such a place. I had not even been canonized yet—in fact I was only twenty years old.

"It was the most exciting thing that had ever happened to me. Never in my most cryptic dreams had I had a hint of such a thing—meeting the planet's First Secretary in person! And not merely a First Secretary, though they are rare enough, but Rominuald Tanglin! I was so excited that I actually cried. I must have committed fifty sins of vanity that day—it was shameful.

"I can remember every word the Secretary said. It was very strange. I had never moved in such exalted circles, so I didn't know what to expect; but it was very odd even so.

"The first thing I noticed was the strange way the Mysteriarch was behaving. She and Secretary Tanglin were both sitting in formal armchairs, and he was in his usual position, the one you always see in the tapes: with his right leg hooked over his left knee. And she was in the same position! It was so unusual for her that I gasped a little. And he said smoothly, in that famous voice that I had heard a thousand times, "This is her? Well, Alice! That's more like it! Oh, she should do famously!" Then he did something very peculiar. He held out his hands in front of him and made a little square with his thumbs and fore-fingers. Then he looked at me through the little square, moving his hands around so that he framed my face.

" 'She's marvelous,' he said to the Mysteriarch. 'You say she's your great-grandchild? Well, it's easy to see where she got her looks.' He grinned, and the Mysteriarch smiled and said, 'Thank you, Rominuald.'

"I was amazed. I couldn't have been more surprised if the sun had changed color. They were calling one another by their first names! Perhaps it wasn't so surprising in the Secretary—he was called the People's Friend, after all, and he was known for his informality. But the Mysteriarch! Crossing her legs under her black robe! Smiling! Answering to the name Alice! I hadn't even known her name *was* Alice. She'd always been just the Mysteriarch to us. I couldn't imagine what had made her do it.

"Then the Secretary spoke to me. 'I'm very pleased to meet you, child. I am Rominuald Tanglin. And your name is . . . ?'

"After an embarrassing pause I stuttered, 'Anne, Mr. Secretary. Anne Twiceborn.'

" 'Anne,' he said musingly. Suddenly he nodded. 'Anne. A fine name. Couldn't have thought of a better one myself. Marvelous, be sure you keep that name. How old are you, Anne?'

" 'Twenty, sir,' I said.

" 'Twenty!' he said. 'In many ways still our mental peak! Marvelous! Turn a little and show me your profile, dear. Have you ever been on tape before? Have you used tape?'

" 'A little,' I said. 'I've taped the moas in their native habitat.'

" 'Excellent. Then you'll be a new face. Your delightful ancestress here informs me that you know the moas very well indeed. How many years have you studied them so far?'

" 'Five, Mr. Secretary. Three years full-time.'

" 'That's all?' he said, frowning. 'Still, that's remarkable for one so young. I just wish they were better known before I. . . . You have a lovely skin considering the time you've spent outside, child. Those freckles would melt the heart of a man on ice. Do you like moas, child? What would you do to save them from their persecutors?'

" 'Anything,' I said.

"The Secretary turned to my great-grandmother. 'I like this child of yours,' he said. 'She gets to the point with alacrity. I think she'll do just fine. Are we still agreed, then?'

"The Mysteriarch nodded. 'Yes, Mr. Secretary.'

"'Excellent.' He lifted both hands and fluffed up the curls in his hair. He really was very handsome—it wasn't just the make-up.

"'Anne,' he said, 'will you come with me to the capital? I can't offer you anything but work and suffering—and this at your tender age, as well. But I need you and that means the planet needs you. I want you to speak for the moas, since they have no voices. You may be the only person on the planet who can save them. It will destroy your privacy and your peace of mind and change you forever. But your help is crucial to their cause and my cause and the cause of all of us. Will you do it?'

"I looked at the Mysteriarch and she nodded slightly, and I said, 'Yes, Mr. Secretary.'

"He said, 'Good. I knew you wouldn't fail me. I could tell it just by looking at your face. A lot of people will be looking at that face of yours in the months to come, Anne. And I know they'll see the simple honesty and goodness that I myself see in it. Ah, these Uplands are a stern land, but they breed fine, sturdy women. You'll carry quite a burden on those square little shoulders of yours, child—the kind I carry myself. Such burdens can be galling. Sometimes they'll make you weep. But they'll make you strong.' He turned his head to my great-grandmother. 'When can she leave for Peitho?'

"'As soon as you like, Rominuald,' she said." Anne broke off suddenly and said to Moses Moses, "Peitho is the planetary capital now. In your day it was Miclo."

Moses Moses nodded. "I've never heard of it. Built after my time, I suppose."

Anne nodded absently and drew in a deep breath. "Then the First Secretary got up from his armchair and stepped off the dais and to my side. He put both his hands on my shoulders and looked down into my eyes. He was tall—taller than you, Kid, by three or four inches."

"He must have been wearing block heels," I said.

"He said, 'This is sudden, Anne, I know. We'll be leaving to-morrow, and I'll be taking you from all you love best. You may not see this land again for months—maybe longer. You'll move into a new world—a complicated world, full of danger and ruthless sin. It will confuse you, and hurt you terribly if you are not careful. I'll have to guide your steps at first—you'll have to depend on my advice, and obey it, even if you don't understand all the reasons behind it. You see the sense in this, don't you?' And he looked into my eyes with his wise old eyes—like yours, Kid, but bigger and shinier, like black whirlpools.

"And I said, 'Yes, Mr. Secretary. I'll follow your advice. You will guide me.' And I looked away, because his stare was so intense. I couldn't meet his eyes.

"'Good,' he said. 'When we leave tomorrow we'll have a long talk together on the way to the capital. There will be cameras and lights and noise and more people than you've ever seen in your life. But Anne, you won't be afraid, because your cause is just and *I will support you*. Do you follow me?'

"'Yes, I follow you,' I said, but I only whispered because I was about to cry. He embraced me for a moment, and then he turned and bowed to the Mysteriarch, so low that the two sticks leaned down from his neck and touched the floor. Then he left the room without another word. When the door closed behind him I couldn't hold back my tears. I flung myself at great-grand-mother's feet and cried into her lap.

"She said nothing but only waited patiently until I had recovered myself, and she dried my eyes with her black skirt. 'I'm glad you cried, my child,' she said, 'because those tears will have to last you for a long time. They must be your last tears, do you understand? You will have to be brave from now on.'

"'Oh, Madame, what shall I do?' I asked her.

"She was quiet for a few minutes as she tapped the deep waters of her holy intuition. 'Do as he says,' she said at last. 'Ah, I hate to trust you to him, a man with as many sins as he has hairs. But I must. I've spoken with him, dear, and without meaning to, he has opened his heart to me. He is mad. He is the only one who can help us, but he is mad. He has many enemies but he has built others from the ghosts of the past, the far, far past. His fears obsess him, and his end must be near because death has already set his seal in the lines of that man's face. And yet I must trust you to him.

"'It may be that he will try to corrupt you. He might find that an amusement for an idle hour, and he is a charmer, isn't he? Repulse him if you can, but do not anger him. Give in to him rather than risk his anger. The survival of our faith outweighs one young woman's personal modesty. Child, you cannot sin if your heart remains pure. Remember that.'

"'I will, Madame,' I said.

"'Then I have one last word of advice,' she told me. 'Beware of his wife! He trusts her absolutely, and that worries me. Stay away from her!'

"'Yes, I will,' I said, and that was all she said." Anne sighed wistfully. "That was the strangest day of my life. It meant more to me than any days that followed, even the last day of my trial, when I was sentenced to exile. I was famous for a while, you know—more famous than you, Kid, because six billion people knew my name. I won't bore you with the political side of my life—I hated it anyway, and I only did it out of duty. And it certainly wouldn't have meant much to you, Mr. Chairman—a man who could buy and sell a whole planet. I only wanted to save a small patch of land and a few of its birds from the great devouring mouths of the six billion. And in the long run I failed even in that.

"If the First Secretary had lived longer we might have won. I thought we had won at first, when Mr. Tanglin passed the Biome Preservation Act. But he declined rapidly as his wife undermined his sanity with subtle hints and horrible skill and probably drugs and poison too, I wouldn't doubt it. Too many of her enemies have died convenient deaths. She is a devil.

"He left for Reverie just two years after we met. He taught me everything I knew about taping and testifying and talking to crowds, huge crowds sometimes, hundreds of thousands. And after his madness seized him then his enemies tried to blacken his memory, claiming that he'd done all kinds of horrible things. It was typical of those cowards, slandering him when he was unable to fight back. Later we learned that he had killed himself. I cried for days. I loved him. Purely. And he never said an impure word to me, or made an unclean suggestion. He always treated me with pure affection and respect."

I smiled sadly at these last words. All the dignity and conviction in the world couldn't have masked that tiny undertone of regret. I looked at Moses Moses; his face was grave and impassive, but he must have caught it too.

"Thirty years have passed since I last saw Secretary Tanglin," Anne said. "A great deal happened, of course. For the first five years I agitated. Those were the days of my finest commitment, when I felt most exalted in the right. When I thought we had firmly defeated the opposition, I went back to Sanctuary. But I had changed, of course, as the Secretary warned me, and I found Sanctuary very constricting. I returned to the moas and followed them for ten years. I taped their dance, and I learned bits and pieces of their peculiar language. It is all gestures of course, movements of the head and wings and feet, and some other element—scent probably, but I'm not sure. They hurt me several times, but I had the scars removed when I returned to public life after the repeal of the Preservation Act.

"That was when the slaughter began. We preservationists joined together in a united front. The preservation issue attracted many followers other than Church members. In fact we Church folk were greatly outnumbered, but we led the others because of our firm moral stance and strict ideology. We were considered the movement's most radical elements until the violence began. It was about this time that I was canonized.

"I was arrested several times during nonviolent resistance sessions. I was jailed for almost two years. I saw people killed in riots and I threw my body between combatants sometimes and I was beaten with the rest. I saw injustice and violence and hatred. And it was real violence, with real pain." Anne looked at me with a frown.

"My trial lasted two years. I'm certain that Madame Tanglin had something to do with it, though that could never be proved, of course; she was much too clever. The movement put its whole force into the trial. We wanted to bring the persecutors to their knees. And we lost. The sentence was supposedly very light. As if they didn't know that the death of the moas would be the cruelest punishment they could inflict on me.

"They sent me here. The Confederacy has no love for Niwlind, so news is scarce. And I can never return, so I'm dead to Niwlind, and it to me."

She sighed. "I never thought I could love any place but the moors, but these islands, this beautiful sea. . . . I think I could have been happy here, if circumstance had let me. I'm not sorry to die, but I'm sorry not to have seen it all." She fell silent as a cloud drifted mercifully over us, plunging us into cool shadow. "I guess that's all I have to say."

Moses Moses and I said nothing; we were both touched by the simple sincerity of her story, but for different reasons. I felt sorry for Anne. I did not doubt for a moment that Crestillomeem Tanglin had destroyed her career and had her exiled. What chance did poor Anne, Tanglin's pawn, have against the malignant woman who had destroyed Old Dad himself? It would have been like a five-year-old child clenching her tiny fists to fight a combat artist.

A bathetic rush of mingled emotions washed through me like the synergetic effect of a dozen different drugs. Despair at our situation, grief at the death of my best friend Armitrage (I felt a sharp pain of loss—how he would have loved to hear what I had just heard), pity for Anne, the bitterness of irony and my own flinty self-possession, and above it all, a peculiar cosmic humor that was beyond all this and beyond all self. I smiled, turning by long habit so that the cameras could catch me at my best angle.

"Anne, you're getting sunburned," I said. "Let me give you my combat jacket. You can use it for shade." Treading water, I unlaced it and pulled it off. "Don't lose it," I said. "It has all my smuff and my camera controls."

I adjusted the jacket so that the stiff collar shaded her face while the back of the jacket was supported by her oblong head. "Thank you, Kid," she said. "I'll take good care of it." She seemed glad that I hadn't mocked her. Her gratitude embarrassed me. I reached unobtrusively inside the jacket and touch-set the controls so that they would continue to follow me rather than the jacket. I needed the comforting presence of their attentive lenses as I told Anne and Moses my story.

9

"I'm sure it will be no surprise to you, Mr. Chairman, to realize that I am Rominuald Tanglin. Or rather, I was once Rominuald Tanglin. Our relationship is a peculiar one, rare enough so that there are very few terms for it. At any rate, Secretary Tanglin underwent terminal personality disruption and I now inhabit his body. You can call me his son, his clone, his successor, or anything you please.

"This happened twenty-eight years ago, so you might call that my age. That makes me the youngest of the three of us by far, and I have the tastes and appetites of the young—well, some of them, anyway. I have what old people call the vices of the young—impatience, impetuousness, carelessness, cruelty. No doubt you could name several more, Anne. I've had mine named often enough. Named to me by old people, of course, old people who slaver at the idea of a young man following his own pursuits instead of their fossilized scheming. Since they deprived the young of any chance of making a mark in the world, we chose our own ways; is that so bad? And if it is, can you stop me? I have power and vitality, you see that I have no patience with argument, because words are the nets of the old, and old people are stuck waist-deep in their own approaching deaths and they long to lure the young into the mire as well. . . ." My voice died away and I shook my head in frustration. Long oratory didn't suit me; I shared Rominuald Tanglin's contempt for long-winded formal apostrophes. My best efforts were in the exchange of stinging insults, followed by the cry of combat, the sizzling crunch of impact. I was no orator, no politician. I preferred to make my point with a blunt edge.

"You'll be old yourself one day. Or you would have been," Anne said.

"I've been old! I've seen what happens to me—to him, that is." I looked at them suspiciously. "He went insane. You probably think that I'm afraid that the same thing will happen to me, that I'm afraid of age because I know I share his weaknesses. Well, it's not so! I'm independent of him, completely independent, I assure you. I don't share his vices, his weakness, or his madness. I've never met him, of course, but he left me an extensive collection of tapes, so I've seen him at his worst, and I know him well. His last madness took the form of a persecution mania. He claimed that humanity was riddled with cunning aliens impersonating people, who preyed on human vitality. He claimed his own wife was one of them. Leeches, he called them. I won't bore you with the details.

"I was born an adult, you know. Into an adult body. I was born able to speak and with a knowledge of basic trained behavior, table manners, hygiene, how to walk, run, swim, operate a keyboard. I was never a child, not really. I suppose that's why I chose to live in an artificially childlike body. As you can see, it's nothing like Tanglin's body; it's my own, dammit, mine! But although I was born an adult physically, I shared certain traits with other children. Innocence. Sensitivity. I was very impressionable. So when I saw Tanglin's tapes I was terrified. I've always thought of him as my father. Strong, cold, remote. And I could tell that he was tormented by exhaustion and fear. Oh, I believed in Leeches, very strongly. There were days when I trembled in terror in my bed. Nights when I could swear I saw withered hungry faces at the window. The fear was worse because I was so isolated. I lived on the continent, you know, on the eastern edge of the Gulf, northeast of Telset. Not far from here, in fact; only thirty miles or so. I rarely saw people except in tapes and broadcasts. It was just me and my tutor, Professor Crossbow."

"Professor Crossbow!" Anne said.

"Yes. Do you know it?"

"Of course I do, it was world-famous. So it's true. You were telling the truth." Tears came to her eyes. "I'm sorry, Rominuald."

"Don't call me that!" I shouted. "I'm not your lover, you dumb cow! Do I look like him? Do I talk like him? No, no, no! I'm my own person, I've proved that!" A weighty silence fell. Anne turned her face from me and wept quietly. Moses Moses looked on with an expression of cool remoteness.

I shrugged helplessly. "All right, so it makes me anxious. Put yourself in my place. It's like living in a house whose builder died mad. It's like having a ghost at your elbow. I'm his heir. I have his legacy. His reflexes, his speed, his altered body, his cunning. But what else did he leave me? What guarantee do I have that he will stay dead? How do I know that he's not still in here—" I tapped my head—"hiding and biding his time? It would be just like him, you know. A masterstroke of horrible cunning. And it would make him a Leech. Disguising himself as me. I'm sure the thought occurred to him just as it occurred to me, because our thoughts run in the same channels, how could they help it? But I don't believe this. I've overcome those childhood fears. A man like Tanglin casts a long shadow, but I'm out of it now. I have my own friends, my own reputation, my own fame. I don't owe it to him. Oh, I used his fighting skills, but his were academic. Gymnasium fighting. The act of a paranoiac. I put the edge on it. I made it a marketable commodity. If I met Tanglin man to man I could break his back in ten seconds." I was quiet for a while. The weight of my nunchuck was dragging me down a little, despite the buoyancy of our makeshift airfloat. I had been treading water for hours now and a rubbery fatigue was invading my legs through the tingly numbness of smuff.

"I've never told this to anyone before," I said at last. "Professor Crossbow was the only one to know, and I haven't seen it in years. It may be dead. It was old, as old as Tanglin. And it was a hermit at heart. Its studies meant more to it than anything, even its friendship with Tanglin. I loved that old neuter. It was probably the only friend Tanglin had. It could have destroyed me so easily—turned me into another Tanglin. But it let me go my own way, at my own speed. It took away the burden of sex. Sex destroyed Tanglin. It made him his wife's dupe. I know better. I have no wife. I have no lovers. . . ." I choked on my words as I remembered Armitrage's last declaration. There hadn't been time to think about it. Now the memory was like a kick in the stomach.

"*He* loved you," Moses Moses said. Anne looked puzzled. "You overheard?" I said.

"No," Moses said. "But I could tell by the way he looked at you. And that woman in your apartments—the tall, frail one, that the Cabal murdered. . . ."

"Quade."

"Yes, Quade. She loved you too."

"No," I said. "She never told me so. She knew it was impossible. She was loyal, that's all. Loyal and stubborn."

Moses smiled ironically at my naïveté. "Do you think she stood the torture because she was stubborn, Kid? Do you really believe that? Or did you know all along that she loved you? Did you know how she longed to hold you, to touch you, to mend your wounds?" I jerked my face up to look at him and we locked eyes. His ancient yellow gaze pierced me with its insight; he seemed to suck up the thoughts from my head. "Ah, now you remember," he said softly. "You remember how she tended to you, worked for you, obeyed your least whims. And your response, Kid?" He nodded, sucking in his lower lip. "Yes. You knew she loved you. You knew she burned for your embrace and you lorded it over her. You threw her scraps of your affection, you flattered her, you led her on. You won her heart and you kept your own cool and shielded. Just as Tanglin did with this poor girl." He waved one finger-wrinkled hand at Saint Anne.

Anne cried indignantly, "No! You don't know that. You weren't there, so how can you say such a thing?"

Moses Moses turned his calm gaze on her and she withered instantly. She almost cowered and I shuddered at the way he had dropped his mask, at the way he spared us nothing. The old are powerful. They see too much. Maybe that is what drives them mad. "I can guess," he said gently. "It's not for nothing that we say the young are cruel. The old are cruel too sometimes, cruel in their madness and their desperation to live; but the young are cruel naturally, like trees that grow and crowd out their brothers. They cause pain because they don't understand, because they love themselves wholeheartedly. They have not yet developed the self-contempt that poisons all our enjoyment, the wisdom that comprehends our own weaknesses. And when you first begin to gain that wisdom, then you'll look back on your youth, and you'll see all the pain you have caused. But," and he smiled, "those who die young are spared that. So you are both fortunate."

After that there was little to say. Anne and I traded glances and we saw the wariness and fear that the old man had inspired in both of us. For the first time I realized that Anne was warm and human. I felt a surge of friendliness toward her. "Anne, I'm sorry," I said. "I'll be your friend from now to the end, I swear."

"I'm sorry, too," she said. "I had no right to judge you. I'm just a fool, I suppose. A dupe." She shook her head bitterly.

"Don't say that," said Moses Moses kindly. "It's no sin to be young. It happens to all of us once." He smiled at me. "Sometimes twice!"

We heard splashing and turned to see a large school of fish swimming toward us, leaping above the water. They were skipperjacks, foot-long, yellow-backed, elegant fish. As they drew nearer we saw that they were a whole shoal; dozens leapt above the water, but there were hundreds, perhaps thousands, swimming beneath the surface in gleaming phalanxes.

"Will they hurt us?" Anne said. "What shall we do?"

"No, they won't hurt us," I said. "They're only skipperjacks. I guess they're migrating."

"They look to me like they're running from something," Moses Moses said. They were coming from the north. The current was drawing us in that direction.

"Here they come!" I said. In moments they were all around us. One of them leapt by and rattled my hair as I ducked. I felt their fins and scaly sides brush slickly against my bare legs. Anne shrieked. They were making no special effort to avoid us, and their fishy intimacies made us laugh in embarrassed half-revulsion. In half a minute it was over; they were gone.

"I wonder what that was all about?" Anne said.

"I don't know, but they've provided lunch," said Moses equably. He held up a large skipperjack which he had somehow snagged with his bare hands. It was still struggling weakly.

"Ugh," said Anne. "Do you expect us to eat raw fish? Take my share. I'd rather go hungry."

"How will we gut it?" I said. "We've got no blades."

"And the blood may attract rays," Anne said practically. "Maybe you should let the poor thing go."

"Let it go?" said Moses indignantly. I could see that he had slipped back into his shell, and I was glad to see it; his frankness had deeply disturbed me. "After the trouble it took me to catch it! I'm thirsty, aren't you? This sea water is far too briny to drink, but the juice from this fish would be—"

"Holy death, look at that!" I shouted. Something was approaching us from the north. It was deep under the water, twenty or thirty feet down, at the limit of clarity. But it was huge. It was hard to tell its exact size because of the distance, but it was at least fifty feet across, I would swear to that. The cameras back me up on this. They show that it was an oblong, black oval, and there is a suggestion that it undulated slowly. We drew up our feet in silent terror. It seemed to take forever to pass under us. When it was gone we felt the chill of an icy upgush of deep water.

Half a minute passed before we dared to speak. "What *was* that?" Anne said. Moses and I shook our heads; it was impossible to tell, and the placid seas of Reverie hold many secrets. "I lost my fish," Moses said sadly.

The afternoon passed slowly. We grew bored. Moses Moses had not slept much, so we stuck the back of his head into the crotch of the air-float and let him sleep as we floated on our backs. I kicked off my shoes, but I still kept my nunchuck; I couldn't bear to part with it. Besides, its explosive charge offered a quick, clean death if the rays were tardy.

After Moses had slept, Anne slept; then it was my turn. It was not very restful. I never liked to sleep on my back and the gentle swell of the water was not soothing. I was forced to sneeze brine several times and when I finally gave up the attempt to sleep I was crotchety and miserable. My wounds were beginning to ache again, and it was not wise to take smuff on an empty stomach.

By the time the sun went down we were in terrible shape. All three of us were sunburned, especially on our faces. Anne's was worst. If she lived, she would lose all the skin on her face. Her eyes were swollen and her lips were chapped. We were all horribly thirsty. Anne and I had washed out our mouths with the bitter sea water, though we hadn't dared to drink it, following Moses' warning. Even so, it had made our thirst worse. Anne's hair was a mess; even the feather ornament in her hair looked drab and soaked. My plastic hair had crusted up considerably with brine.

After sundown I put my combat jacket back on and reset my cameras. I even reattached the electrical charge to my hair, but the sea water had shorted it out. Luckily the camera controls were rugged. They were designed to resist heavy impact and soaking with blood, so the water hadn't damaged them.

"I wish it were over with," Anne said at last, as the first stars showed after a magnificent sunset. "Why are we going on? Is there any chance of rescue at all? Ocean liners? Airplanes that might spot us?"

"No, of course not," I said. "I know this area well; I used to sail out here when I lived off the Tethys Reef with Professor Crossbow. This is wilderness. I suppose there's a chance in a million that someone's pleasure yacht might spot us, but certainly not at night. The only other things that come out here are camera drones. We might stumble over one of them, but they're pretty rare, and who would want to tape the middle of the ocean? There are aquatic drones, but they stay underwater. And their range is limited. They can only see as far as their lights can reach."

"Well, why haven't the rays gotten us?" Anne said fretfully.

"How should I know?" I said petulantly. "Maybe they're just not very fond of human flesh. It probably tastes funny. We're alien to this planet. You know. Biochemically."

"I can't understand why the first rays didn't get us," Moses said.

"Armitrage was full of smuff," I said bitterly. "Maybe it poisoned them. 'The Effect of Smuff on Rays.' That sounds like one of Professor Crossbow's experiments."

Hours passed. A flying island blew up over the continent. None of us talked; our mouths were too parched.

At midnight it was my turn to blow up the float again. When I put my head underwater, I heard the incredible: a dull, resonant boom from deep below.

I surfaced and said, "Listen. Did you hear that? Put your ears underwater."

We all heard it. Loud booming, like the taut skin of a drum. "What could it be?" Anne asked wearily. None of us knew. "Fish, maybe," croaked Moses. "Some kind of sonar."

It meant nothing to us, but the fish knew better. We heard flopping and splashing all around us as fish fled in panic. It was too dark to see them. The booming grew louder and more urgent; we could hear it faintly even with our ears above the water. Several times we felt backwash as big animals swam past us. "The water's getting warmer!" Anne said. She was too tired to resist her fright; we were all on edge.

"Look!" Moses said hoarsely. "Look down into the water; do you see it?"

We all saw it; a scattering of dim phosphorescence, deep beneath us; it was impossible to tell how far. It seemed to be murky nodes or lumps scattered across the back of some huge animal.

"Is that the ocean floor?" Anne asked. "Is the water that shallow here?"

"It's too big to be an animal," Moses said. "It looks like some kind of web. See how the glowing spots spread out. Are they moving?"

"No," I said. "We're moving." We heard another series of mellow booms. "They're coming from those spots of light," Anne said.

"I think I'll swim down for a closer look," I said.

Anne said, "No, Kid! What if it's dangerous?" Moses and I both laughed hollowly; it made no difference, of course.

"Here, Mr. Chairman; hold my weapon, if you please." I handed him my nunchuck and began to hyperventilate. I reset my cameras. When I had taken a dozen deep breaths I felt the peculiar effects of excess oxygen in dizziness and tingling fingers. I half-emptied my lungs, doubled over to dive down headfirst and began swimming strongly. My ears popped; I held my nose and blew to equalize the pressure. My ears shrieked. At twenty feet I lost my buoyancy as the pressure compressed my lungs; I began sinking slowly, then more rapidly. Quickly, I cupped both hands over my brows and blew out a little air, to form a shallow air pocket over my eyes. The phosphorescent spots leapt into sharp focus; they were below me, about a dozen feet. I could see now that the glowing green blobs were spots on a tense web or skein of some dim, filmy material. The structure, or whatever it was, was huge. Even the spots looked five or six feet across, and there were dozens of them. Bubbles escaped from my fingers and sea water stung my eyes. The water was strangely warm and my lungs felt crushed. I struck out for the surface. It was a lot farther away than I had thought, but I made it anyway. I had to call out for Anne and Moses and follow their voices in the darkness.

"Well, what was it? What did you see?" she asked eagerly.

I shook my head. "I don't know. It looks like some kind of titanic jellyfish. It was odd—as I got closer the water seemed to get a little warmer. I could feel currents moving over it. I only saw a piece of it. I got the impression that it covers whole acres. An incredible area."

"Is it some kind of undersea mountain, then? A guyot, or something?"

"No, it looked like skin," I said. There came another rush of booms, the loudest yet. A stream of immense dirty bubbles that smelled like muck burst through the dark water around us.

"God, is it breathing?" Anne shouted. "It smells awful!" The booms merged into a crescendo. We could hear bubbles geysering up all around us. We seemed to hear a sort of strumming and straining and rumbling, half-muffled by water. We looked into the sea. The phosphorescent spots were moving in unison, shifting back and forth in a sort of straining undulation, and of a sudden they seemed to break free and began to float up toward us with a slow, horrible purposefulness.

"Here it comes!" Moses shouted. "Swim for it!"

"Stop!" I said. "It's too big for us, it's all around us!" And it was true. The bulk of the thing was unbelievable. We grabbed one another's arms and waited for the end.

We drew up our feet in panic but it came to get us anyway. We all cried out at once when the hot fabric touched us; and then it was lifting us up. We sprawled out on the hot webby surface like beached whales, and our pitiful little float collapsed like a burst bladder. We heard the thing below us popping and snapping and making sounds like damp sails flapping full of wind as it carried us up, and up, and up into the dark Reverid night. By that time we had stopped screaming and were merely clinging to the taut pale seaweed membrane with hands and feet. We had risen at least a thousand feet above the sea when a breeze blew up. Slowly, the immense bulk beneath us began to drift to the west, with the wind. Then we realized what had happened.

We were beached on a flying island.

10

We could see our surroundings fairly well, because of the yellow-green glow from the round patches of phosphorescence on the island's skin. The island's titanic flotation bag was made of hundreds of cells of thin, taut skin, clustered tightly together like a compressed froth of bubbles or the pips of a mulberry. Each of the dozens of outer gas-cells had its own broad, glowing node.

The three of us had slid half-into the dimpled margin between two large gas cells. The seaweed membrane of the cells was very taut and still slick with sea water; it was difficult to hold. We were not quite at the apex of the great dredge-balloon, but we were in no danger of sliding off. In fact, for the moment we were in no danger at all. The relief was incredible.

"It's a flying island," I heard Moses mutter. "A flying island," and I heard him dig his blunt fingers into the skin with a wet squeak, as if he couldn't trust the evidence of his senses.

"Yes," I said hoarsely. "We're safe! We're up in the air and we're safe!" A great wash of release from tension swept through me. My spirits rose up like the island itself and I burst into hysterical laughter. My throat was so dry and sore, though, that I heard a weak, wretched cackling that alarmed me.

"Oh, it's real water!" I heard Anne say in a voice of rapture. "Look, water oozing out!"

Moses and I both immediately scrambled to the spot with pitiful haste. It was true. A wet, sappy-tasting, brownish moisture was oozing up from the juncture of the membranes of two gas-cells. All three of us stuck our faces into it and lapped and sucked it up with a complete lack of dignity. There wasn't much of it. We had to run our noses along the trough, slurping vigorously, for several feet to get enough to fill our mouths. But it was wonderful.

After a minute or so I had soothed my tortured throat with the vented sap and I stood up. My legs wouldn't support me. After several efforts I managed to stand, and I felt the taut, hot skin of the balloon dimpling under my feet. I took a few springy steps and reached one of the glowing, phosphorescent spots.

The glowing node in the center of the cell was about six feet across. The gas-cell itself was roughly hexagonal and about twenty or twenty-five feet across. I prodded the glowing spot with the handle of my nunchuck. It broke through a thin crust and came up glittering with yellow-green paste. There was a sharp chemical reek and a slight sensation of heat when I held it up to my face. I showed it to one of my cameras and then wiped it off on the pale white cell-skin.

Standing up, I could get a rough estimate of the island's size. I could see a horizon all around me, about three hundred yards away in every direction. There were hundreds upon hundreds of glowing disks, one in every cell. It reminded me strongly of some of the round, multicellular organisms I had seen in Professor Crossbow's microscopes—"volvoids," he had called them. They had floated as serenely in their drops of water as this dredge balloon did in its ocean of air.

Moses Moses and Saint Anne were still worming their way across the juncture of membranes with their heads down and their haunches up. It would be hard to conceive of a posture less fitting for the Founder of the Corporation, or for a saint. I made sure that I caught both of them with my cameras.

"We're safe," I said. "And I've got it all on tape." My knees grew weak and I collapsed with a springy rebound onto my back, then slid slowly down to the broad crevice between membranes. The hydrogen beneath me was deliciously warm. I spread out my arms in sybaritic ease, pillowed up by the thin skin over the hot, explosive gas. I pulled off my combat jacket and padded, sopping groin-brace. A warm breeze curled over my naked skin. I yawned, helplessly, looking at the stars. Instant Death had failed. Angeluce had failed. The Cabal had failed. My vengeance would be terrible. I slept the smug and peaceful sleep of hopeful, murderous ambition.

I awoke at dawn, after eight hours of chaotic dreaming. The air was cold and noticeably thinner, but the balloon was still warm. I sat up. I was thirsty and terribly hungry and my pounded muscles ached abominably. The incredible panorama of fleecy sea-clouds far below us distracted me, but only for a moment.

Moses Moses was sitting nearby. "I'm starving," I said. "What's for breakfast?"

He laughed hollowly and my growling stomach sank. "What do you think?" he said. "I tried a taste of the glowing paste in those phosphor dots. I should have known better. It burned my tongue. As for water, there's still a little sap left, but it's been drying out all night. The island is venting its ballast." He shrugged. "I explored a little last night. The balloon's about two thousand feet across. There's probably something edible down in the mud it's carrying. Starfish maybe. But how can we get to it? We can't cling to the membrane. We can't climb down. We'd slip, and it's a long way down to the sea. We're marooned on the top of this thing."

I shook my head impatiently. "What do we do, then? Sit here and starve to death?"

"Not so loud," he said. "Anne's asleep, poor girl. She's exhausted." He considered. "I've thought of one possibility. We could rupture some of the cells and try to break our way through the center of the balloon down to the bottom. However, if we don't blow up, we'll probably smother in the hydrogen, or get squashed between two expanding cells when we're in the balloon's center. It doesn't look good, Kid."

"What about the cell walls?" I said. "Have you tried eating them?"

"Too tough," he said. "It'd be like chewing cloth. I admit I haven't tried it yet. I'm afraid to rupture one of the cells for fear of a detonation."

"So what?" I said. "The thing's going to blow up eventually anyway; they're built to blow up so they can drop their mud on the continent. I'm willing to give it a try." I yawned and prodded experimentally at the cell-skin with the handle of my 'chuck. "Wish I had a knife."

Moses Moses looked speculatively at one of my cameras. "You might smash one of your cameras," he said. "We could probably batter some of the metal into a crude edge."

"Smash my cameras?" I yelled. "Forget it, doll! Over my smuffed-out body!"

Moses spread his hands apologetically. "Just a suggestion, Kid."

"Well, maybe if it was life and death." I looked up at my cameras with a protective frown. The very idea of breaking them unsettled me. I'd rather break an arm, any day.

"I'll give it a try with my nunchuck," I said. "Maybe you'd better stand well back."

"Wait!" Moses yelped. "Get those cameras out of the way first, for death's sake! They might ignite the gas!"

"No, they're airtight," I said. I stood up, grabbed both handles in a reverse grip, and fell to my knees, stabbing into the fabric with both swivel-heads. The skin dimpled. I pushed down with all my strength. Suddenly it ripped open and I fell through the opened slash. I dropped thirty feet to bound resiliently off an interior cell. Hot gas whooshed out. I coughed convulsively. "God, it stinks!" I said, my voice squeaking.

"It's not pure," I heard Moses shout. "Smells like something rotting! Are you all right, Kid?"

I had no time to answer. The walls of the other cells were bulging in toward me as the broken cell deflated. I dropped my 'chuck around my neck and with a scramble and lunge I managed to grab an edge of trailing skin. I pulled myself hand over hand toward the surface of the balloon again, pushing away at the encroaching walls with my bare feet.

After a few moments the other cells reached the limit of their expansion, and a pit ten feet deep was left where the first cell had burst. I heard shredding sounds as the sealed junctions between the surrounding membranes adjusted themselves. I pulled my legs up as the interior cell membranes rejoined stickily just beneath my feet. I was now at the bottom of the pit, but I could climb out easily enough once I gathered the strength. The hunger and thirst had badly weakened me.

Moses cautiously approached the edge of the pit. "So much for that idea," I said.

"Oh, it wasn't wasted," he said. "With this skin from the burst cell we can make a kind of shelter out of this pit. It'll keep us out of the sun, at least. Anne needs that badly. Come on out, Kid, and help me spread it out."

I climbed sluggishly out of the dimple and helped Moses stretch out a section of the ruptured skin to serve as a crude tent or cave. The lightweight stretched skin felt peculiarly damp and elastic in my fingers. "Nice place to starve," I said.

"Nonsense," said Moses. "If worse comes to worst, you can fire your gun into the bulk of the island. We'll die painlessly in a second or two. And we're not without hope. Birds may roost here. I'm very hungry. My word, do you realize how long it's been since I last had a meal?"

"The last things I ate were some moldy bars of chocolate," I said wistfully. My mouth watered uncontrollably at the thought.

"Let's go wake Anne," Moses said. "She'll sleep more comfortably in there. The sun is fierce at this height; less cloud, you know. If she doesn't get shade she'll blister."

We found Anne sprawled out at the dimpled junction of three cells. Her face was vivid red and her eyes were almost swollen shut.

Moses shook the scorched fingers of one of her outstretched hands. "Anne, wake up."

Anne forced her eyes open and frowned painfully. "I had the oddest dream," she said. "I dreamed I heard something bouncing and thumping around beneath me. Inside the island."

"Oh?" Moses said. He looked down at the cell beneath his feet, but the white film was opaque.

"Kid! You're naked!" She averted her face.

"Get used to it," I said.

"He's right, Anne," Moses said. With an effort, he stripped off his one-piece underall and flung it aside. "The salt in our clothes will abrade our skins. You'd burn badly without your clothes, but the Kid and I have made a sort of shelter for you."

"I won't take off my clothes," she said with determination. "Not much water got inside, actually. I'm perfectly all right as I am." The dried brine in her saint's garb must have made it horribly scratchy and uncomfortable, but Anne's bizarre modesty had martyred her. Moses looked at her doubtfully, then said, "Well, at least have a look at our tent. The sun's already up. Doesn't it hurt your face?"

Still unwilling to look at our nudity, Anne hurried ahead of us, falling down once or twice but bounding back onto her white-slippered feet. She stopped at the pit.

"Oh! This is fine!" she said. "Look at all this extra film. Why, we can make clothes from it. Hoods. Umbrellas."

"Good trick without any tools," I said sourly. "Anyway, you won't get me to wear any of that stuff. I have a tan."

"Stop taunting her and let her go back to sleep," Moses said patiently. "Let's go to the top of the balloon, Kid. We'll get the best view there. I'd like to see it while it's still cool, and while I still have the strength to walk around." At this depressing note Moses and I struck out for the apex of the balloon. The phosphorescent spots on the flotation cells were still glowing, but the stronger sun had made them pale. It looked as if they would soon flicker out entirely and begin sucking up sunlight for another eighteen-hour night.

The view from the top was incredible. There was no breeze, for we were being borne along at the same speed as the tradewind. "We're at least a mile up," Moses said analytically.

"Look," I said. "You can see Telset through those clouds." I pointed and a twinge of pain ran up my battered arm.

We could see the Gulf far below us, faintly wrinkled with

waves, and a white, tenuous plateau of morning clouds over the water. Sunlight glittered off the sea to the east, blinding us. To the west, perhaps a hundred miles away, we could barely make out the dark smudge of the continental arm. "That's our destination," Moses said calmly. "I imagine we'll reach it in four days. Maybe five."

"Plenty of time left to die of thirst, then," I observed.

"It may rain on us," Moses said. "We're still rising, and we should go higher and higher as the sun heats the balloon. But we're still not as high as a thunderhead. They go all the way to the troposphere."

"I've heard of flying islands destroyed by storms before," I said.

"Maybe we can collect some dew on the extra fabric," he said.

We heard a peculiar popping sound from the cell beneath our feet and we hurriedly retreated from its surface. "We'd better not put all our weight on one spot," Moses said. "The balloon may be weaker in places."

"Look out, it's ripping open!" I shouted. Before our eyes, the very topmost cell broke open in a neat slash, five feet long. We lifted our arms to shield our faces and pinched our noses shut, but there was no outrush of smelly, unbreathable air. Instead, a shaggy blond head and a pair of narrow shoulders pushed their way out of the opened slash, and their owner climbed out onto the top of the cell, clumsily, like a beached dugong. I would have recognized that red, gill-clad neck and those sleek swimmer's muscles anywhere, even in a place as strange as this.

It was my oldest friend, my tutor, my mentor, my only parent. I called out in stunned amazement and incredulous delight. "Professor! Professor Crossbow!"

Crossbow started violently and scrambled back a couple of paces on its hands and knees. Its fingers were webbed. It squinted at us hesitantly and rubbed its bloodshot eyes with one long-fingered, webby fist. "How did you get here?" it said in a breathy, asthmatic voice. "How do you know my name?"

"Professor!" I chided it. "It's me, Arti! Don't you recognize me?"

"Arti?" it said. "My old ward, Arti? It *is* you, isn't it? But what have you done to your hair?"

I reached for my plasticized hair self-consciously but recovered at the last moment. Hearing the Professor's voice had stirred many long-buried memories. "For death's sake, Professor, never mind that now! What are you doing on this island? I can't believe I'm actually seeing you! How did you get here?"

Crossbow got to its feet uneasily, as if it had not done so for months or years. "*I've* been here all along," it said. "Why did you come to my island? How did you know where to find me? This place is miles from the house. I haven't even been to the house in ages!"

"Professor, I'm overjoyed to see you, but I wasn't looking for you, I swear! We were marooned here by accident! We were shipwrecked!"

Crossbow's almost hairless brows drew together and it looked at us querulously. "Arti, you wouldn't trick your old professor, would you?"

"It's true, Professor, really! Tell him, Mr. Chairman." I turned to Moses Moses, who had unobtrusively stepped behind me. He had half-pursed his bearded lips and I realized that his nudity embarrassed him. "Yes, it's quite true," Moses mumbled indistinctly. I understood his chagrin. He and I both looked like naked ragamuffins while Crossbow was quite spruce in an iridescent blue bodytight and slim, embroidered belt hung with pouches and waterproof metallic instruments. It looked well enough, but there were lines in its face that alarmed me. The neuter looked old and worn. Years had passed since its last age treatment. Some of its bushy blond hair was threaded with white and gray.

"Now, Arti," Crossbow said patiently. "You wouldn't persist in a practical joke, certainly? This means a great deal to me; it's my scientific work. You shouldn't have interfered unless it was absolutely necessary."

"Professor, please!" I said. "Can't you see that I'm stripped right down to my cameras? Can't you see our sunburns? Can't you hear our rumbling bellies? Good God, we're collapsing of hunger and thirst!"

"We're in desperate straits, sir," Moses said politely. "Your presence here is a godsend. We beg your assistance for ourselves and our companion. We had no intention of interfering, I assure you."

Crossbow looked flustered. "Well," it said. "I must take you to my study station, then. There's water there, a few medical supplies. . . . Of course I wasn't expecting visitors, the place is . . . well . . ."

"Oh, no need for apologies from you, sir," Moses said winningly. "We are entirely at fault. Let me fetch our companion and we'll go there at once; we're at your orders." He turned and raced away over the rounded, inflated landscape.

Crossbow folded its arms and ran its tongue along the inside of its left cheek. It was a typical gesture that brought back the eight-years-past as if it were yesterday. "Now Arti, we're alone now," it said with a martyr's patience. "You know I can always tell when you fib. Now what are you really doing here? And where are your clothes?"

I brushed its doubt away with an impatient gesture of my hand. "I told the truth, Professor."

It blinked once or twice. "Really? How can I believe that? What are you doing shipwrecked, anyway? And who are these people with you? Now confess, Arti. Are you sure this has nothing to do with the Academy? Nothing at all?" It looked at me keenly. "Perhaps not you, but your friends then. Have they never spoken of me? Never asked you to help them find me?"

"No, Professor, of course not. Believe me, I'm really astonished to find you here. We were sure that we were going to starve to death. And I haven't seen anything of you in eight years. Not a note. Not even a whisper." I looked up at it curiously. "Haven't you heard anything about me, Professor? Seen my pictures in the gossip tapes? Or my combat art? Or read my work in the journals?"

"I'm afraid I haven't had much leisure time for amusement tapes," Crossbow said.

"I'm pretty well known now, Professor. Famous even."

"That's fine, Arti. I'm glad for you."

"Maybe you've heard of me by the name 'Artificial Kid.' That mean anything to you?"

"I wish I could say it did," Crossbow said. "I haven't seen much of people lately, these last, well, six or seven years. I don't spend much time above the surface. Not much time at all. Just my reports to the Academy. My own tapes, you know . . . that's a nice set of cameras you have, by the way."

"Thanks, Professor. Luckily, I can afford the best."

"I'm afraid my new reports may have re-opened some old wounds. The Gestalt Dispute was never quite settled, you know. At least, not to my satisfaction. Or your father's."

"Really?" I said. "Well, I'm in a position to help you politically, again. I'm running in pretty exalted circles now. In fact, that naked man you saw is the . . ." I hesitated, not wanting to further strain my old tutor's credulity. "Well, I'll let him tell his own story. It's pretty incredible. But it's true." I looked at him earnestly. "It's no trick, Professor. I'm mature now. I'm beyond that sort of thing. I have my reputation to uphold."

"Then you no longer put crabs in people's beds? Or tie them down with seaweed while they sleep? Or make fake insects out of glue and thread and leftover wings and legs?"

I laughed with forced casualness. "No, Professor, I've changed a lot, seriously. I'm the Artificial Kid now. I have hundreds of fans. Thousands. I have my own house. I own four shares." I hesitated again. "Of course, the situation's changed a little recently. In fact it's changed a lot." I coughed drily. "Let me have a little water and I'll tell you all about it."

"Of course. But here come your friends. Introduce us, Arti, do."

"Of course, Professor. The lady in white is Saint Anne Twiceborn."

"*The* Anne Twiceborn?" Crossbow said. "Incredible! But it is! It is she!" He started to walk clumsily toward them, holding his arms out a little to balance himself in the unfamiliar medium of air. I was glad that he had spared me the trouble of introducing the Founder of the Corporation. It would have been too much.

I saw that Moses Moses had slipped painfully back into his one-piece.

"You're Anne Twiceborn," Crossbow said. "Do you remember me? We met once briefly many years ago. At a reception in Peitho."

Anne shook her head. "I'm sorry, I don't remember. But I've heard about you, Professor, of course. And I'm so glad you're here."

Crossbow smiled shyly. "This is the least expected pleasure in my long lifetime, I must say. And you, sir?"

"I'm travelling under the name of Amphine Whitcomb," Moses Moses said with bland caution. "I'm very glad to meet a person so well known in the field of learning. The pursuit of knowledge is the one truly preeminent human endeavor. As was once said, 'The pen is mightier than the sword.' "

All three of us looked at Moses, impressed. "The pen is mightier than the sword." It was the kind of blunt, pithy aphorism that had made his perception and wisdom famous on two planets.

Professor Crossbow looked pleased and flattered. "I thank you, sir. Let's waste no more time, but hurry to your rescue and sustenance. I can see that you are all fatigued." It looked at us kindly. The sight of Saint Anne seemed to have temporarily relieved its suspicions.

Anne was no longer wearing her saint's garb. Instead, using no other tools than her hands and teeth, she had ripped a kind of crude poncho out of the pale, striated balloon fabric. She had stuck her head through it and cinched it around the waist with a long, ragged belt. It should have looked ludicrous, but she wore it with a kind of brazen dignity that made me stifle my smiles. When she walked it unveiled her pale, unshaven legs almost to the knee.

"Come along this way and we'll slip through the airlock," Crossbow said, walking unsteadily to the very top of the balloon. "I believe that two of us can fit through at one time, if we squeeze. I'm trying to conserve air pressure. Mr. Whitcomb, will you accompany me?"

"A privilege," Moses said quickly. The two of them squirmed through the long slash in the top of the cell and into a small, fabric antechamber just beneath it. Crossbow reached out, accidentally jabbing Moses with his elbow, and pulled the long slash shut. It was zippered. He must have opened another zipper inside, for the flaccid fabric blew out tight with a snap. We heard thumping and bumping.

"So that's what it was," Anne said dreamily. "I heard that while I was asleep."

"I've got to get my camera controls," I said.

"Oh," she said. "Here they are, I brought them for you." She produced my combat jacket from beneath the voluminous folds of her poncho.

Surprised, I took it from her. "You needn't have done that for me. Thank you."

She smiled tentatively. "Why not? It's as easy for us to be friends as enemies, isn't it?"

"Of course it is," I agreed.

She persisted. "And it's as easy to please people as it is to hurt them."

"Now you're gilding the lily," I said. I turned off the cameras and they fell, bouncing off the pale stretched fabric and rolling and tumbling off for quite a distance. We chased them down and gathered all six of them up like ripe fruit. Then we unzipped the airlock and slithered into the little fabric cul-de-sac. I zipped it shut behind us.

Anne drew a deep breath. "It's rather nice in here," she said cheerfully. "Like a womb, almost."

"I wouldn't know, I've never been in one," I said. I unzipped the long slash in the tight fabric beneath us and air rushed in. It was quite breathable. I peeked out.

The industrious Crossbow had burst through all the central cells of the balloon, evacuated the hydrogen, and replaced it with fishy-smelling, slightly stale air. I had no idea how he had managed this while the balloon was growing underwater.

Crossbow and Moses were already thirty or forty yards down a long, swaying rope ladder. The top of the ladder was glued securely to a long section of fabric. Tightened ropes attached the ladder to connecting cells every thirty or forty feet, and kept the ladder from swaying too violently.

The ladder itself was slightly twisted, like a DNA chain. In several places down this long, long central chamber, there were safety membranes, also equipped with air locks, that blocked our descent temporarily. They were obviously there to prevent the whole chamber from evacuating at once in case of an accident. They also made good places to sprawl out, sweating, and rest.

I turned on my cameras as soon as Anne and I began our descent. Anne went first, as she insisted on it. After forty feet of descent the pain in my pounded muscles was simply too great and I took some smuff. Buzzing filled my head. After managing a few more rungs I lost my grip and fell with a scream, almost knocking Anne from the ladder and narrowly missing both Moses and Crossbow. I hit the first safety membrane, which bowed deeply under my impact and then snapped back, flinging me into the air again. After some smaller subsidiary bounces I got to my hands and knees and dry-retched. My cameras, floating along sedately, caught up with me about this time, and I hid my face in my arms so that I would appear to be merely stunned. I had fallen almost two hundred feet.

I reached into my drugpak and injected the last of my stimulant. Sea water had somehow seeped inside my combat jacket and ruined my tranquilizers and some really good, mild, social hallucinogens that I habitually carried. All I had left was my smuff, a little quikclot, a packet of skinseal, and some pellets of powdered nicotine that Chill Factor had given me over a year ago. The rest was a pasty mess. "Well, death sucks it dry," I said with bitter profanity.

By the time the others had climbed down to me, my teeth were chattering with stimulant. Nodding uncontrollably I assured them that I was all right and raced through the airlock and down the ladder ahead of them. I went through four more airlocks at a tremendous pace and through a final skein to the Professor's study chamber, where I collapsed on the fabric floor with my heart racing and pulsating black spots devouring my vision. I couldn't even sit up until the Professor arrived and gave me water. All three of us castaways drank with many a gasp for breath. We then took salt tablets and ate some leftover fish that the Professor had prepared in his little pressure cooker. The food took the sharp biting edge off the stimulant and I stopped trembling and was able to look around without seeing spots.

With truly Reverid ingenuity—for Crossbow had been cloned on Reverie—the Professor had adapted itself to its surroundings without damaging their peculiar charm.

The cells were smaller on the underside of the flying island and the little cell that held the Professor's living quarters was no more than fifteen feet across. It smelled strongly of fish and sea water. The walls were of triply-reinforced fabric, neatly sewn together, and the room was cooled by a small fan set in the floor with a conduit to the outside. It was much cooler in the room than it had been in the long passageway through the balloon.

The Professor had not been expecting visitors. Fish scales and bits of cast-aside edible kelp were everywhere. The walls were decorated with frightening photomicrographs blown up big as doors: the immense slavering jaws of sand fleas, the spiny threatening elbows of water beetles, the cruel, jagged feet of barnacles. Two of the Professor's favorite mobiles dangled from the fabric ceiling.

Another wall held a mounting board with a number of specimens preserved in little square blocks of transparent plastic. The rest of the small round room was crowded with the Professor's machines: a generator, a refrigerator, a pressure cooker, a compressor, a small sewage recycler, a distillery with a large water tank, a microscope, an old tape screen and its antique cameras. The machines sat on tough mats of woven seaweed that prevented them from ripping through the layers of fabric in the floor.

There were other miscellaneous items about. There were kitchen knives and a cutting block, the Professor's foot fins and speargun, a few books and journals, no more than a couple of dozen; his clothing, his hammock, and suspended from the ceiling, an incredibly intricate framework of hundreds of thousands of colored beads linked with wire, glistening in the mellow light from a number of small yellow bulbs. The bulbs looked like transparent fish bladders stuffed with phosphorescent plankton.

Moses Moses looked up at the torus-shaped wire sculpture, then looked around the disconnected tangles of beaded wire on the floor; some with hundreds of linked beads, others with as few as five or six.

"I've seen a structure like that once before," he said politely. "You'll pardon my asking, but is it an Elder Culture space sculpture, or perhaps a replica of one?"

"No, Mr. Whitcomb," said the Professor with an uneasy smile. "But it does resemble one, doesn't it? How perceptive of you to point that out. The similarity had occurred to me before. But I doubt if there was an influence."

"I thought perhaps you had tackled the old problem concerning their reason for existence," Moses said. Naturally, he had no way of knowing the Professor's involvement in this problem.

"What do you mean?" said Crossbow warily. "I thought that question had been explored long enough to sicken everyone."

"You're in luck, Professor," I said, hoping to cover Moses' slip. "You're in the presence of a man who has never heard of the Gestalt Dispute."

"Indeed," Crossbow said. It ran its tongue along the inside of its left cheek again. "I take it that you don't closely follow Academic controversies."

"Not recently, no."

Crossbow shrugged its muscular shoulders. "I won't burden you with it, then. I'm hardly a dispassionate witness, as has been pointed out many times."

"No need for modesty here, sir," said Moses alertly. "If you have a theory regarding those mysterious objects, I'd be delighted to hear it." He squeezed water into his mouth from the nozzle of a compressible bulb. We had all been drinking out of them. I think they were fish bladders.

Crossbow shrugged again with feigned indifference, but I could tell it was pleased.

"It's been generally accepted that these sculptures had a religious function," Professor Crossbow said. "Most Academic archaeologists declined to speculate any further, but I did, and I suffered for it." With a heavy sigh the old neuter seated itself on a square canvas pack on the bowed floor. With a start I realized that the pack was a parachute.

"My field of expertise is taxonomic microbiology, but I have a more than slight acquaintance with reductionist doctrine," Crossbow said. It slipped with ease into its lecturing attitude. "Reductionism has been the gospel of the Academy for many centuries. Essentially, this doctrine states that all mental and physical actions, no matter how grandiose or subtle, can be broken down into a set of simple chemical interactions. Thoughts, for instance, are electrochemical interchanges between groups of neurons, and nothing more. Life is a series of biological tropisms which can be reduced to the simple terms of physics. It is a very beautiful and elegant theory. It was the belief of our ancestors, so it is hallowed by custom; for centuries it was held by all men of learning. I believed it to be quite solidly established; as solid as, say, evolution, on which all thinking men agree. A doctrine which seems almost self-evident, even though our language still holds remnants from earlier beliefs."

Crossbow lodged its ankle on top of one knee and brushed adhering fish scales from the sole of its naked foot. "My researches here on Reverie, however, seemed to hint at a flaw in our theory. I found that flaw in the behavior of the Reverid ecosystem. It doesn't behave like other ecosystems elsewhere. For one thing, it is vastly older. Life has existed on this planet for almost eight billion years. Life has even outlasted the planet's era of geological activity. Continents here are artificially created—huge ring-shaped atolls. The sea long ago eroded away the original continents. All the dry land on Reverie is the work of organisms, like tower coral, mudcumbers, sea beavers, even flying islands, like this one." It thumped the fabric floor beneath it with one webby hand.

"I found it hard to account for this kind of behavior. Why didn't life simply adapt to oceanic conditions, and let the shallow sea cover all the land? Why this apparent altruism of marine organisms for those on land? What genetic purpose did it serve?

"I found these questions unanswerable, so I appealed to my superiors in the Academy for help in my research. I was called to one of the Academy's deep-space oneill clusters to testify. I presented my evidence and a research team was sent to verify my findings. They took their time, of course; there is no rushing true scientific research. In the meantime I began to search for possible alternatives to a strictly reductionist world-view and it was then that I discovered the doctrines of Gestalt.

"Gestalt means that there is a hidden force in wholeness. It means that the totality of the bits and pieces of a whole are greater than their mere sum. There is a mystic force in a whole system, there is something else lurking in that web of interactions, those chains of feedback. The greater the system's complexity, the greater its gestalt! Man is vastly complex, and that complexity makes itself known in the phenomenon we call consciousness. This element of self-awareness is something that has always troubled reductionists, but they have tried to sideslip its intuitive evidence. They have built artificial consciousnesses for machines, though we all know how that turned out." Anne shuddered delicately.

"They have even demonstrated that consciousness is tied to matter by altering the brain and showing that this causes altered mental states. This was done centuries ago, and that destroyed the old, old doctrine of mind-body dualism. But I never espoused *that* doctrine, and the idea of gestalt is entirely different! The idea of gestalt acknowledges the presence of matter in mind, the presence of those physical actions and interactions. The only supposition it makes is that we do not fully understand the nature of these apparently simple events. A reasonable supposition, one would think. A theory that at least deserved a good hearing. At least I thought so." It buried the tips of its webbed fingers in its unruly yellow hair.

There was a long silence. I got up, poured some water into a dead sponge, and began to sponge the crusted salt from my skin.

The Professor looked up suddenly. "Oh yes, you asked about

the bead sculptures. I saw my first sculpture there in the University, while I was giving my testimony. Its peculiar beauty entranced me; they had several of them, and data on a great many others. They are found occasionally, but only in deep space, always looking as perfect as they did the hour they were launched, so many millennia ago. That struck me immediately—their element of permanence. They were not meant to be on display. They were not meant to be found or seen. They were meant to be permanent, untouched by time. And they were obviously constructed with extreme care—the relationship of every bead to every bead was so sinuously perfect, the angles of the connecting wires were so incredibly exact. The entire sculpture was a system, and since it was a system it must contain gestalt. And since it was so carefully protected—meant to outlast even the Elder Culture itself—it must be something very precious.

"I arrived at the theory that it contained a soul. Probably the soul of the person who built it. I'm convinced that they still hold souls, the souls of members of the Elder Culture. I wouldn't claim that these sculptures are conscious, of course. They've been extensively monitored, even cut apart bit by bit, and there is no transfer of energy within the structure, at least none that our instruments can monitor. But they live. I could sense it somehow. I have no proof of this. It simply made sense to me. It was an elegant theory. It accounted for both the great amount of effort invested in the sculptures and the fact that they were abandoned in the quietest wastes of interstellar space. But I kept this theory to myself, having no firm evidence to back it. I only brought it out, as a theory, in the worst heat of the Gestalt Dispute, and only then because Rominuald Tanglin urged it strongly on me. He had his own theories concerning the Elder Culture and they meshed to a degree with mine. But only to a degree. I take no responsibility for his doctrines during his final delirium."

"I thought one of the criteria of a scientific theory involved its being tested empirically," Moses Moses said. "Did you try that, Professor?"

The Professor made a peculiar quick fiddling movement with

its fingers, a typical gesture that expressed its frustration. "How could I, when Gestalt could not be monitored or quantified? What is it, actually, that makes a system a system? Oh, I made tentative experiments, of course. There was my ten-year involvement with the Reverid slimemold. It is a creature that begins as a cluster or grouping of amoeboid protozoa and slowly develops into a crude salamander-like form with an interior skeleton and a circulatory system. Later the salamander develops a cancer-like fruiting body and bursts into millions of protozoa again. I attempted to find the lowest threshold of interconnections—to tabulate the relationships between the original amoeboid bits that triggered the rapid development of the salamander—the lowest possible number of webbed interactions that each contributed gestalt to the living system, you see?"

Anne and Moses looked at him blankly. Crossbow shook its head. "It's been such a long time since I tried to express it to laymen," it said. "My friend Tanglin was always much better at it. If he were here he could make you understand."

"I've seen the tapes he made during the Dispute," Anne said slowly, "but I must confess that they didn't mean very much to me. The worst of the Dispute was well before my time. I heard other Church members refer to it at times, not very flatteringly, I'm afraid."

Crossbow nodded. "Yes, churches of all kinds are usually opposed to the Academy on principle. They follow their own dogma too closely to concern themselves with the dispassionate search for truth."

Anne looked none too pleased at this and it was then that I first noted the peculiar rapport that had sprung up between Moses Moses and Professor Crossbow. Obviously Crossbow was in a wary, suspicious state, and its suspicion should have focused on Moses, the only one of the three of us whom Crossbow did not know. But this was not the case. I noticed that the two of them kept exchanging brief glances, little two-second moments of eye contact. It was as if they spoke some private code of the very old, some intense rapport beyond the youthful crudities of speech. I had never seen anything quite like it and it bothered me at once.

"I have some ointment for that sunburn of yours," Crossbow said to Anne. It got up from its seat on the parachute and popped open the lock on a small waterproof case made of wood and green plastic. There was a little compartmented case inside. Crossbow produced a transparent collapsible tube full of gooey white paste. "Shall I put it on for you?" asked the neuter politely. "It may burn a bit at first."

"Thank you, no," Anne said. She squeezed out a small blob of paste, sniffed it, and made a face. Then she began to spread it on her cheeks.

Crossbow, as usual, was generous to a fault. It provided Moses and me with new clothing, two pairs of blue bodytights. Anne refused to wear clothing that clung so tightly to the body, so Crossbow tolerantly gave her needle and thread so that she could stitch her own clothes out of balloon fabric. He then warmed up his pressure cooker and shared with us his hardy wilderness fare: steaks of deep-sea fish, plankton puree, minced kelp, and sweet seaweed gelatin.

The three of us ate ravenously, but Crossbow merely toyed with its chopsticks. Finally it spoke in a low voice, its words obviously directed to Moses Moses. "I would like to make an appeal to frankness."

"Do you think that's wise?" Moses said. Anne and I traded worried glances.

Crossbow lowered its head and mumbled almost incoherently, "Perils of personal dominance. The mask becomes the face. Sieges of panan. Too many steps back ... do you follow me?"

"Yes, of course," Moses said with deep, tender sympathy. The words meant absolutely nothing to us and Anne and I were alarmed. It obviously meant something to the neuter, however, for it actually blushed. I had never seen it blush before and I had thought that it was impossible.

"It's been a long time," Crossbow said. "Very well, all masks off then. A pact between us. You agree? We'll seal hands then." Moses put down his platter and took the neuter's slim, webbed hands into his own.

They were silent, staring into one another's eyes. Anne put down her chopsticks and I stopped wolfing down the gelatin.

She shivered. I was frightened too. It seemed to have grown colder inside our snug little bubble. For a long moment we heard only the impersonal hum of the generator and the quiet breathing of the two old people. Their breathing seemed to be synchronized. They were going through something that we didn't understand, that we had never seen before. They were both so incredibly old. Anne and I couldn't help it. We were overcome by a sort of superstitious dread. I felt that there was some sort of tainted power at work; an old, cold, strong power that could eat us up like a viper eats young birds. Moses had dropped his facade again, just as he had when we were floating in the water, convinced that we would die. His face seemed to shine and there was a look in his round yellow eyes that terrified me. A glance at Anne showed that she felt the same way. I wanted to beg them to stop, but I was afraid to break their eerie concentration.

At last they released one another's hands and Anne and I both drew a sigh of relief. I was deeply glad that she had been with me to share that peculiar ordeal, and her look at me showed that she was also grateful. It had lasted only twenty seconds but it had drawn us much closer to one another. I wanted to embrace her and sit and breathe in the warmth of young, human contact, but I didn't, for Crossbow spoke.

"You are Moses Moses."

Moses nodded. "Yes, Crossbow. I slipped past death and ran for the light with destruction gnawing at my heels. And I lived. I have nothing beneath me but a shell, but I live. It rasps away inside me until I echo with hollowness, but it has never caught me."

Crossbow nodded. "Yes, we are members of the same brotherhood. You have seen how my old friend compromised with death." It nodded sharply at me. "I found an anchor. He thought he had found one too, but she destroyed him. And even now my enemies pull at me. They seek to tug me from the sea bottom just as this flying island tugged itself from its rooted moorings and floated up into the airy thinness of despair. But they won't succeed. You can help me."

Moses shook his head. "I haven't the strength. I haven't your conviction. Ask the young people. They have the vitality you need, not me. I haven't anything—I even envy you what you have. You've studied life. You understand it. You have meaning. I have nothing."

"There is a way, Moses."

"You're mad."

"No! Did you see madness within me? No. Think, Moses. It is awful, it is dreadful, as all things of great power contain an element of dread. But it can be ours. It is immortality. It may be tainted. Tainted with great age. But we are tainted. How could we live but with a tainted life?"

The terrible intensity of their rapport seemed to scorch us. Anne could not bear it any longer. "Stop! Please stop!" She folded her small hands over her sunburned ears, and shrank into a ball, drawing up her arms and legs.

Moses and Crossbow jerked up their heads, the thread of their rapport broken by her cry. In an instant their friendly, genial masks were back on; they seemed to drop over the two of them like flesh shrouds naked bone. They stopped leaning toward one another; they broke their eye contact. Moses reached down and picked up his platter. Crossbow stood up and smiled its old parental, protective smile at me. It seemed to drape it over me as if it were an old, warm blanket. It seemed intolerably artificial; I just stared.

"I still haven't told you what I'm doing on this island," said Crossbow brightly, leaping to a new subject with the agility of a mountain goat. "My presence here must have shocked you as much as yours shocked me!" It chuckled genially but without much conviction. Anne uncurled and moved closer to me; we sat together on the floor, touching hips and shoulders. I felt the warmth of her shoulder through the fabric we wore. Moses Moses was eating stoically and apparently ignoring the neuter, but I could sense him vibrating inside like the plucked strings of an autoharp. I slipped my fingers around Anne's naked wrist and the touch seemed to calm us both.

"I discovered this island in its bud stage three years ago," Crossbow said. "I found it on a tape while I was mapping the sea bottom near my house, with undersea drones. I had tracked the life cycle of the flying islands before, with drones and tracers, but I had always wanted to observe one personally and do a great deal of necessary detail work. I was able to estimate this island's eventual destination by calculating the trade winds and the paths of other islands; in fact, to be frank, I chose this island because of its destination."

"The Mass," Moses Moses said.

Crossbow nodded. "The Mass." It seemed pleased that Moses Moses had guessed correctly.

"But we can't go there," Anne said in alarm. "That's a horrible place."

"The Corporate terms of settlement are supposed to forbid human exploration," I said, trying to keep my voice neutral. I didn't disapprove; I merely wanted to point it out. "And the drone tapes I've seen of the Mass . . . well . . . they didn't look promising." In my mind's eye I saw the nightmare landscape of the Mass: sticky pools slimed with white muck, leafless trees furred inches deep in bright mold, crawling things bristling with damp ridges of shelf fungus, breathless stillness broken only by dripping . . . a landscape not of death but of fervid, fetid life.

"I've been there before," Crossbow said. "I wasn't able to stay as long as I liked. But I had time to make a crucial discovery." It looked at Anne and me, then it shrugged and smiled shyly. "I might as well tell you; there's no call for false modesty, as my friend Tanglin used to say. It was this thing—this organism." It pointed with one slim webbed finger at the tangled wiring overhead. "This is a model of its molecular structure—a very limited one of course, though the torus shape seems to be well established. You'll notice the helical gaps within the structure; there are twenty-three of them, though why that number I can't say. Notice the peculiar arrangement here at these genomes; you can see that by faulting and folding this long double chain is moved shut almost like a trap door." The neuter stood up and began crimping and bending a section of wire with its thin but powerful fingers. Anne and I watched nonplussed as a long chain of linked beads moved up over a gap in the structure, like jaws closing. A section of fatigued wire popped with the strain and half-a-dozen beads of varying color spilled to the fabric floor and rolled off drunkenly under the generator, but Crossbow didn't seem to notice.

"See how it covers up that helical gap!" said Crossbow, filled with admiration. "It can trap an entire chain of genes in there—a whole half-helix. You probably wonder why it doesn't hold them there by chemical means—why it uses this mechanical arrangement instead. Well, it does use chemical linkage to a certain extent. Of course it has to have a chemical catalyst to trigger this crimping movement. But if it used a completely chemical linkage it would induce too many mutations. A half-chain of DNA is very volatile chemically, you know! There are all those open-ended linkages, just looking for adenine, thymosine, guanine, to complete itself and initiate a new being! It's like a little box, you see? A little torus-shaped box to hold life itself!" The neuter's face shone with a saintly radiance as it prodded eagerly at the tangled mess.

"I call it the Crossbow Body—that's the name the Academy gave it. I'm still uncertain whether or not it lives. It seems to be as much a construct as a being. I can't decide how it reproduces. I'm not sure that it does reproduce. It seems to be immortal, like an amoeba, barring accident of course, barring dissection. . . . And yet it can't be sterile—there must be some mode of reproduction, or perhaps reconstruction is a better word. And as for the problem of its origin—well, I'm convinced that it is natural. I'm convinced that it is the product of a Gestalt agency that is not intelligence—that is not consciousness—that is an attribute of a world-spanning gestalt that transcends intelligence as completely as intelligence itself transcends instinct. It is a teleology! It has a purpose that transcends determinism! It has slipped free of the iron chains of evolution! And it is evolution that demands death! It demands all death so that the old can give way to the new! But the Crossbow Body escapes death. The Crossbow Body destroys the motive for competition between species. It destroys competition between the old and the new."

Trembling with excitement, the old neuter sat down with a sigh on the single parachute. Then it looked at me with reproachful amusement. "Arti, you don't believe me! Don't worry. You'll see the truth soon enough."

I smiled falsely. Crossbow's speech had sounded very familiar, in form if not in content. It sounded very much like the senile ravings of my old patron, Mr. Money Manies. And a similar motivation had triggered it, I felt sure. Members of the Academy were no more immune from aging than were laymen. It sounded like poor Crossbow was cloaking its obsession with death in a thick blanket of pseudo-scientific patter. Its critical faculties had been distorted by the bright promise of personal immortality.

Obsessions with the molecular workings of life seemed to be in the air among the oldsters of Reverie. No doubt it was our peculiar zeitgeist.

"Have you already sent your findings to the Academy, Professor?" I asked.

Crossbow nodded eagerly. "Yes. Three years ago."

I nodded resignedly. "Well, that explains the presence of Professor Angeluce, then. It just struck me. Taxonomic microbiology—that was his specialty, too, wasn't it, Anne?"

"Yes, I remember," Anne said, nodding.

Crossbow shrieked and convulsively grabbed the sides of its head with both hands. "Angeluce! They didn't send him, certainly!"

"They certainly did," I said grimly. "And a most unpleasant little bugger he is, too. I've sworn to kill him. If I live through this, I will."

"Yes," Anne said musically. "He called you a 'neuter charlatan,' Professor. After that the Kid criminally assaulted him—didn't you, Kid?"

"How do you know?" I said testily. "You were unconscious at the time." It had struck me suddenly that Crossbow's mad meddlings had been the root cause of the disruption of my idyllic existence. If it hadn't stirred up the embers of the old Gestalt Dispute, Angeluce would never have come to Reverie. I would never have insulted him and thrown him off Money Manies' balcony. He would never have attacked me and poisoned the minds of the Cabal against me. Quade Altman would never have been mind-killed. The Instant Death would not have declared blood feud on me. Armitrage would not have died. Sulkily, I ate the rest of my gelatin, darting occasional black looks at my old tutor. I felt like beating it up, but it was my oldest friend, and my Old Dad's last and best friend. I restrained the impulse. As the last of the stimulant I had taken wore off, I somehow found it in my heart to forgive the old neuter. After all, it was our host, and it had meant no harm.

The news about Angeluce had devastated poor Crossbow. It sat with its head in its hands, groaning a little from time to time. Moses Moses helped himself to more fish. I had finished eating. I got out Crossbow's old tape screen.

"Here, Professor, I'd like to show you a few things," I said.

We spent the rest of the day examining my tapes and explaining our horrible difficulties. We cheered when Angeluce fell in the water; we sobbed unashamedly at Armitrage's death, which was his final tape appearance but undoubtedly the very best of his career. My spirits soared when I saw the quality of the recordings. They were the finest I had ever done.

It did me good to be working in tape again; it reaffirmed my self-image. Crossbow's equipment, however, was so old-fashioned that I hesitated to do any real editing. I had plenty of tape time left—six months' worth of thin metallic image ribbon, so I didn't erase anything. I spent several happy hours, however, cleaning and oiling my cameras.

We fell asleep at sunset after eighteen exhausting hours of wakefulness. I woke up at about two hours past midnight. I took some smuff, and when I got up for some water I noticed that Crossbow and Moses Moses were gone.

"Anne," I said. She threw off her thin fabric coverlet and sat up on the floor. She yawned. "What is it?"

"They're gone," I said, waving my hand at Crossbow's empty hammock. Crossbow had taken down some of its phosphorescent bulbs before we slept and there were peculiar multiple shadows in the little cell. My cameras resumed full activity as I touched the controls in my jacket. I put the jacket on and began to lace it up; I had already sponged the brine off of it.

"Yes," she said sleepily. "I saw them creeping out through a hole in the floor a while ago. They woke me up. Didn't you feel the wind?"

I shook my head. I always slept deeply when I was wounded; my body knew best. I was healing very rapidly, thanks to the actions of my follicle mites, which had struggled on manfully despite sunburn and prolonged soaking in sea water. The wounds that had required stitches were gummily sealed up and the big splotches of rainbow-colored bruises were turning paler.

I looked at the floor and noticed a thin zipper in the heavy fabric. It was another airlock, still damp inside with sea water. The new ventilation hole in the floor of the cell had been cut very recently, after the flying island had risen up from the Gulf; the old zippered airlock had been Crossbow's entryway into the balloon while it was still underwater. I opened up both sides of the lock and a heavy draft of wind swept through the cell. I turned off the ventilation fan, but not before a small cloud of dried fish scales, bits of seaweed, and fragments of beaded wire modelling had been swept out through the old airlock.

I slid onto my stomach and looked down through the hole in the loose flapping fabric of the airlock. It was dark outside. There was a short rope ladder, no more than twenty feet long, leading down into the darkness. Below it was an expanse of rich, black, smelly bottom mud, laced together with roots and cables—the island's payload. Seventeen thousand tons of it, the Professor had said. A forest of thick cables attached it in hundreds of places to the fabric of the balloon, distributing the strain of the immense burden. It was slowly drying out, at a rate that offset the loss of lift as hydrogen slowly seeped out of the balloon.

"Hey, look, it's the island itself!" I said. "Let's go down and see what the bag dragged up."

"Here, take one of the bulbs," Anne said, handing me one. "You go ahead, I'll come down in a moment." I attached the sticky side of the bulb to the fabric of my bodytight, at the sleeve. Then I went down the ladder, grinning secretly. Poor Anne, she was so embarrassed at her own natural functions that she couldn't bear to perform them with me in the room.

I climbed hand over hand down the ladder, carefully, for I

was a little dizzy with smuff. A crumbly, dried crust, interlaced with fibrous white roots, had formed in the sun-baked mud. It was thick enough to bear my weight, and I soon grew used to the pungent smell.

The Professor had told us that these seventeen thousand tons of rich black mud were grasped by roots into the shape of an inverted cone, roughly round and deepest in the center where it followed the island's tap root. The expanse of mud was about sixty feet across, and at its thickest it was eighteen or twenty feet deep. The entire mass had been wrenched up from the sea bottom, leaving a wide crater in the silent, black deeps now far behind us. Some of the island's volume was made up of the porous network of roots, but the rest was rich, prime mud, stolen by erosion and now returned, with interest.

I crouched down to examine the mud, digging into it gingerly with the end of my 'chuck. The white rootlets were incredibly tough. Trapped beneath their tendrils were tons of chipped shell, yellowed fish bone, and greasy mud half-turned to squashy slate. I dug up a long, ragged, broken ray's tooth and knocked the mud from it; it was as long as the width of my hand.

There were a few bottom animals scattered about, too weak, slow, or stupid to escape the island as it began its ascent: sea stars, thick, gut-colored bottom worms with armored heads, some tiny skates, some big-eyed flounders puffed up to bursting. I kicked one of the flounders over and a host of tiny crabs the color of roots ran out from under it, their minuscule pincers rich with rotting flesh. I wondered how the little scavengers expected to survive the detonation. Perhaps they would simply leap off the island once they had eaten their fill.

A few paces later I stepped into the mouth of something's burrow and almost tripped. I don't know what made the burrow but it hissed in annoyance as I skipped away.

It was Reverie herself at work. Even in this temporary ecosystem, life was stuffing itself into every available niche.

I saw Anne come rapidly down the ladder, her white garments floating out around her like a nimbus as she descended. She had given up wearing her saint's garb, because we couldn't spare the water to wash its coarse fabric. She stepped daintily off the end of the ladder, her feet scarcely denting the crusted mud. She had a phosphorescent bulb attached to each shoulder.

"Oh, it's like a fairyland," she said, looking around wide-eyed.

"This filthy wasteland?" I almost said, but I bit back the words. Looking around, I made a conscious effort to see it through her eyes. I became aware of its peculiar beauty. It was the light that had done it; the pale yellow light of our bulbs, the wan greenish lights from the phosphorescent spots dotting the cells of the balloon, the weak bluish glow from clustered stars around the horizon. The jackstraw verticals of the hundreds of supporting cables gave the scene an eerie unreality, and if it weren't for the smell of the mud, you would swear that it was a mosaic—it was a broken jigsaw of shrunken plates of crumbly mud, linked by roots, touched with phosphorescent green amid the shadowed black of its interstices.

"It's pretty," I said. "I wonder where the Professor and Moses are."

Anne looked at me anxiously. "Kid, do you really want to see them? I'd rather be alone. With you."

I was touched. "Really? I thought you hated me."

She shook her head. "No, Kid, of course not. But Moses and Professor Crossbow are acting so strangely, and we're stuck here alone with them."

I smiled cynically. "You want me to protect you, then, is that it? How could I? If they wanted to kill us all, all they'd have to do is touch one little flame to that hydrogen up there and we'd all be tumbling lumps of charcoal." I enjoyed the look of horror that appeared on her face after this sadistic bit of teasing. "We'd be helpless. How could I possibly stop them?" Anne looked so unhappy that I repented.

"Oh, Anne, don't be so soft-headed. Crossbow's a gentle soul. When that precious hero of yours, Tanglin, was betrayed by all around him and sunk neck-deep in madness, Crossbow was the last friend he had. Crossbow was the person he chose to trust right up to death and through to the other side. Crossbow was the person he chose to raise him, to tutor him, to be his parent. No need to be afraid of it or of Moses either. They're old people. You have to allow them their quirks. They allow us ours."

"Kid, Tanglin was a great man. You should respect him. After all, you were him once."

"No. Never."

"You say that, but I see it differently. Now that I know, I can see the resemblance. You don't talk like him, but the way you walk, the way you . . . well . . . move your eyebrows, move your hands. I can tell. It's very strange. I think you're the strangest man I've ever met."

I shook my head. "Anne, you're so innocent! You're so full of silly delusions! When will you give up this dumb fixation about Tanglin? Do you think you were the only woman in his life? For death's sake, he had hundreds of followers like you. He charmed them. He made a science of it. It wasn't respect that made him treat you the way he did. When he first saw you he summed you up in fifteen seconds. Then he did whatever was necessary to make you obey him."

"That's cruel, Kid. And it's not true."

"Isn't it, though? You weren't even a warm body to him. You were a tool, a statistic. He couldn't even find the time to seduce you. You should thank your God that Crestillomeem Tanglin kept him busy, or your precious chastity would be just a memory now."

At last she was angry. "I didn't expect a lecture on sex from you! What makes you the expert? Do you think I know nothing about it, just because I restrain myself? I've been approached by experts in seduction—by wealthy, powerful, handsome men, and women, who would have offered me anything to sin. You forget that I was famous—that my seduction would have made any man's reputation. I've seen the temptations and I've turned away from them, which is a great deal more than you can say."

The justice in her retort annoyed me. "I've seen the gamut too—don't forget I'm a Reverid, and Money Manies' friend! I stay cool and detached, like Crossbow, because it's easier that way—and because sex ruined me once. It destroyed Tanglin.

He trusted his lover, and she ripped his insides out. I've learned by his mistake. It's just a complication. It's a lure I'd rather avoid."

"We're in agreement there, then," Anne said. She looked at me speculatively. "I like you for your frankness, Kid. I'd much rather hear that than the guile of some seducer, some deceiver. I've never had any patience with such people. They are uncaring. They cause pain and humiliation and exult in it. The best any such person can offer is a few moments of sterile pleasure that only detract from discipline and good works."

She looked at me again to see how I was taking it. I nodded a little, thoughtfully. She soon warmed to her topic.

"Our Church has a very common-sensical attitude, I think. They accept the role of sex in marriage, and the role of marriage in life. We marry only once. That is why we insist on a long betrothal period—ten years at least. If my cause had been successful . . ." Reflexively, she touched the feathers in her hair, lightly, as if she were touching a bruise. ". . . I might be betrothed now. I've always meant to marry and have children, so that I could continue the lineage of the Catechist. Now that duty falls to my cousins. I had other duties . . . too many other duties. Now that I live on Reverie, marriage is out of the question."

"You're still alive," I said.

"Yes, but I could never bring up a child in Telset. The moral atmosphere is too corrupt. A child is a sacred responsibility. It's no light decision, to create a life. And I am severed from the chain of descent. My child would be born outside the Church." She paused. "If I had this planet all to myself, just myself and the child's father, then things would be different." The fancy seemed to please her; she smiled. "I believe in life. I want life to go on, the life that came to me through my mother and her mother and her mother in a long chain back to the beginning of Life itself. But I'm not alone on this planet. I'm only isolated. And Church members marry only once. What Reverid would spend his life with me? Better to forget such things and devote my life and strength to my moral duties. You're a Reverid, so I

doubt if you understand. But what do you think of that, Kid?"
She looked at me. "I'm surprised you're not laughing."

"No, of course I'm not, but it sounds very odd," I said. "But
knowing you as I do now I think it's about what I expected."
Her little speech had roused an odd feeling in me—a sort of
fascination mixed with distaste. It sounded so earthy, so primeval—especially that remark about the chain of descent to the
beginning of time. I had a sudden quick-flash vision of Anne,
apelike, filthy, covered in skins, suckling a naked brat at one
discolored breast. I shook it off with a rattle of plastic hair.

Anne looked at me curiously. "So now I've told you," she
said. "But what about you, Kid? What about your ideas for the
future, your ambitions?"

I shrugged. "Hadn't thought of it. Besides, all plans are off
now. Now I just want to survive long enough to bash the brains
out of Angeluce and Instant Death."

"But didn't you have plans before all of this started? What
were they? Tell me, I'm interested, really."

I considered. "Well," I said slowly, "I'm still young, and still
top dog in my profession. I thought I'd fight a few years more,
accumulate a few more shares of stock, and then get out of active combat art while I was still at my peak. I wouldn't wait for
brain damage or spine damage to put me out of it. And I'd stay
in trim so I'd never have to refuse an honest challenge. And I'd
probably run with the Cogs every once in a while, for old times'
sake." I looked at Anne. She seemed to be drinking in every
word, so I went on with a little more enthusiasm.

"Then I'd like to have my own channel," I said. "I'd edit everything that went on it, personally, so that it was really top-
drawer stuff. Then I'd become a patron, and get myself a talented group of proteges to do all the hard work—you know, like
Money Manies does. I'd just do the fun stuff—a little light editing here and there, a few art tapes. I've always wanted to work
with video mandalas, for instance. Then I'd get a few more
channels, build myself an industry. The sort of thing you can
run on an income of twenty-five or thirty shares. That's as rich
as I'd ever like to be, really; anything more would be ridiculous.

Oh, and I'd move out of the Decriminalized Zone, and build myself a fine villa on the shoreline somewhere, half-buried in the reef, like Crossbow's old house where I grew up. With a dock, and an airlock, and a big stand of Tower Coral. Then I'd get a nice household going, with lots of parties and celebrations, and lots of interesting people to call me their patron, and lots of good art going—the kind of art that'll make a name for you. And everyone would toe the line, because they knew if they didn't their patron would beat them black and blue. And I wouldn't grow old, either; if I felt myself going batty I'd just kill myself at once and put an end to it. Clean. Efficient. Straight-from-the-shoulder. That's the kind of life I'd like to lead."

Anne looked at me doubtfully. "It sounds rather sterile."

"Yes. Right," I said enthusiastically. "Sterile."

Anne slowly nodded, then looked away absently as if she had lost all interest. "Let's explore the island and see if we can find the others."

"Fine," I said cheerfully. "Let's. I could use some breakfast." I walked along lightly at Anne's shoulder, content to let her lead while I looked for interesting bits and pieces of stuff from the sea bottom. I had picked up a few shells and was crumbling the mud from them when Anne stopped suddenly and I bumped into her. "Hey," I said, and then fell silent at the tableau before us.

Crossbow and Moses were sitting on a spread-out section of balloon fabric, in a small clearing where the long support cables were especially numerous. They were sitting in the dark. I didn't see any of the glowing bulbs they had taken with them. Crossbow probably knew the whole area by heart, anyway. They sat cross-legged, silent; their eyes were closed. Their hands were palm to palm—Crossbow's webby ones to Moses' hairy ones. It was dark and it was hard to tell, but there was a hypnotic rigidity to their arms and a certain compression about the interfaces of their hands that suggested that the flesh was blurring—that their hands were stickily adhering—that their palms had blobbed together somehow like two bacteria exchanging genes.

Anne backed up quickly, nearly trampling me, then turned and ran. I stayed a little longer, curious, making sure that my cameras got it all. The two of them didn't move, they hardly seemed to breathe. It was eerie. As I stood and watched, a feeling of sickly nausea welled up in me from some place deep in my being, like a cold upwash of murky water from the ocean's bottom. I left too.

The rope ladder was still swaying when I reached it; I found Anne back up in Crossbow's dwelling quarters. She was pale, but seemed to have reasserted her self-control.

"Look at these shells," I said.

She didn't spare them a glance. "Never mind the bravado," she said. "What were they doing?"

I shrugged. "Ask them. I never saw anything like it. You want something to eat? I'm going to fix something." I opened the refrigerator.

"Are you going to eat at a time like this? Aren't you worried?"

"Yes, I'm worried, but smuff gives me an appetite," I said patiently. "How about some of these prawns? They look really good."

I was bolting down hot prawns in tangy white sauce when Moses Moses and Professor Crossbow came up through the airlock.

"It's a lovely night," Crossbow offered.

I looked at Anne; she was tight-lipped. I decided I'd better talk for the both of us. "Yes, I noticed," I said. "Have you eaten? I cooked some prawns."

"You look worried, Anne," Moses said perceptively. I decided to take the plunge. "Yes," I said. "There's something unspoken between the four of us."

"Oh," said Crossbow. "You noticed the problem with the parachute." There was an uncomfortable silence.

"The parachute?" Anne said in a small voice.

"Yes, of course," Crossbow said bluffly. "Moses and I had a chance to talk it over this morning, and there is no cause for alarm. It's true that we have only one parachute. And it's true that we haven't the slightest idea how to make another one—

not one that would work, anyway. But if we begin work today, with luck, we can cut one of the flotation cells free and use it to float down to earth well ahead of the detonation."

"Yes," Moses chimed in. "The island will lose some lift, but probably not enough to make it explode prematurely. On the other hand, if we wait until the last moment, when the island has dried out and is primed to explode, then our meddling will almost certainly blow us all sky-high—or perhaps I should say ground-low." He smiled charmingly. Both of them looked quite hearty. Their palms were brick-red, but it could have been the effort of climbing the rope ladder that had done it. Not likely, though.

"Luckily I have some hunting harpoons, some knives, and some spare glue," Crossbow said. "Under my direction, we should be able to do the work with a minimum of risk. However, we'll have to start work at sunrise. We can sleep through the hottest part of the day and start work again in the evening."

"There's not much time to lose," Moses said. "As the balloon fabric dries out and ages in the sun, it becomes brittle and volatile. And the balloon will be over the Mass in four days, according to the Professor's calculations."

"Right," said Crossbow. "And we ought to have the flotation cell cut loose from the island before the phoenixes come to attack it. Hopefully the phoenixes will ignore a target as small as a single cell, and I suppose it's possible that there might not even be phoenixes around the Mass. But I would imagine that there are."

"What are phoenixes?" Anne said.

"They're just small birds, about the size of a sandpiper—very pretty birds too, all orange and vermilion. Not much is known about them; I'd meant to capture a few specimens on this trip. Each bird carries a number of tiny eggs within its body, and the eggs become fully fertile only when the parent bird's body is charred by intense heat. The eggs incubate in mud. These phoenixes fly very swiftly, and they have sharp beaks. They dive at the island, fold down their wings, and punch right through the balloon fabric. That alone might generate an explosion, but I suspect that they have some other method of producing flame—perhaps by striking sparks off certain rough scales on their legs. We should see a great many other birds in the next few days, too. I believe I've already seen a few nightkites circling the island—I glimpsed their silhouettes against the stars. And by morning there will be seabirds in to search for crabs and carrion and insects. Many of them will carry the seeds of certain symbiotic plants, which they will bury in the mud. Oh, it's all very complex, and should be completely fascinating."

And that was that. For some reason, Anne and I couldn't bring ourselves to challenge them over their odd behavior, perhaps from fear of provoking something worse. Dawn found us on the top of the balloon, bristling with knives and harpoons, shivering in the cold predawn air of the altitudes.

Crossbow was tramping around one particularly large cell. "Here, this one looks good," it said. "I won't guarantee that it will be an easy landing, but it should slow down the three of us considerably."

"The three of us?" Anne said. She hugged her elbows and shivered. Her pleasant, broad-cheeked, freckled face was peeling horribly, skin shredding off in thin, dirty, tenuous sheets.

"Yes," Crossbow said. "I think the Chairman should take the parachute, don't you?" Anne nodded at once, self-sacrificing to the point of masochism, and I was willing to go along.

"Let's start by scraping off this luminescent gel," Crossbow suggested. "It seems to generate heat as well as light, and it probably has something to do with the detonation."

Anne, Crossbow, and I went to our hands and knees and began to scrape the yellow-greenish crust away with the blunt backs of our kitchen knives. We wrinkled our noses at the sharp chemical reek of the glowing paste. Moses collected it in a broad scrap of fabric, then walked to our balloon horizon to fling it over the edge and down to the mist-shrouded sea a mile below.

We soaked down the fabric with a little of the precious fresh water from a fish-bladder squeeze-bulb. "I hope this helps," Crossbow said. "All right, now let's attach the tethers."

The tethers were long reins of knotted balloon fabric, braided for extra strength by our dexterous saint. We glued them to the fabric of the cell we had chosen, using the glue sparingly, as there wasn't much left. The free ends of the tethers were attached to nearby cells.

"We'll open small slashes in the neighboring cells," Crossbow said. "We'll let them deflate slowly, to minimize the risk, Then one of us will have to crawl down through a deflated cell and cut through the attachments to the interior cells. With luck, some of the fabric may peel away spontaneously when the other cells expand to take up the deflated space. If we pull on the tethers, we may be able to peel it loose without having to break all of the connecting cells. We'll have to break at least six, and that represents a lot of lift. If we begin to sink too drastically we may have to go down to the island's payload and try to lighten it by cutting cables and dumping off mud."

"That won't be easy," I objected. "Those connective roots have it all webbed together into one big lump."

"We'll just have to make the effort," the neuter said. It stroked its red, feathery gills, which hung limp and moist at its neck. "Let's put it this way, Arti. If I hit the water, I won't drown. But I can't vouch for the rest of you."

"Do you have any spare gills?" Anne asked hopefully.

"Yes, but I can't do the necessary surgery," said Crossbow with a smile. We all laughed. Poor Anne knew very little about amphibious life.

Shading his eyes, Moses pointed into the sunrise. "Look, kittiwakes." We all turned to look, squinting. A flock of kittiwakes were coming in; we could faintly hear their grating, high-pitched cries.

They circled the top of the balloon once, screeching. Their blade-like black wings and long, elegant scissor tails flashed in the yellow morning sunlight. "They've come to search the mud for carrion," Moses said.

I looked at him, surprised. He seemed to have adopted the Professor's detached, Academic tone. Crossbow, on the other hand, paid little attention to the birds but stood with its chin in its hand, vigorously contemplating the problem before it, quite the resolved person of action. It took one of the instruments from its embroidered belt, knelt, and punctured the skin of a neighboring cell. We smelled the escaping gas at once.

"We'll see how this one goes before we attempt the others," it said authoritatively. Moses, nodding, stepped tentatively off to one side.

The first deflation went well and Crossbow quickly punctured the skins of the other five surrounding cells. The cells were naturally spherical; it was only their close packing that had forced them to assume a hexagonal shape.

The central cell expanded with the loss of external pressure and slowly rose upward, tugging at the slackened skins of the flabby adjoining cells. We heard a long, muffled shredding sound as the force of its lift began to peel it free from the sticky, clinging skins of the other cells.

"Excellent!" Crossbow cried. "I believe it will rip free of the cells beneath it without our having to cut. Quickly, Arti, help me slash it free of these others."

Crossbow and I leapt onto the collapsing fabric of the other cells and began slashing for all we were worth. My section of the fabric ripped completely and once again I tumbled downward into the balloon. I bounced off the resilient interior cells, keeping the presence of mind not to puncture one accidentally with my knife. It smelled terrible. I held my breath and cut away wherever I detected a strain on the fabric.

Two of my cameras were caught under the shroud, and my foot was trapped momentarily between the bulging edges of two expanding cells. I wrenched myself free, though, and had the satisfaction of seeing our savior cell rise up slowly from the body of the balloon, held only by shreds of white skin and our four tether lines.

I retrieved my cameras and, dancing adroitly so as not to get trapped again, I managed to scramble out of the deep, deflated pit. We heard muffled popping and peeling sounds all around us as the cells rearranged themselves beneath our feet. Anne and Moses were both knocked down.

Crossbow cut its way through a thin, flabby shroud and clambered out of the pit to join us. "There," it said. "That's fine. We'll leave what's left of the skin on it for now. When we cut the rest of the skin the cell will turn upside down, because we've attached the tethers to the top. Also, the remaining skin will help distribute the strain. I don't want to put too much of a strain on our glue bonds. I don't think it will rip free, but the tension might make the cell lose too much hydrogen."

"I thought I saw something slithering around in the bottom of the pit," Anne said.

Moses nodded. "Ah, yes. That would be the cell slugs. They live in the lining between cells. They eat sap. Isn't that so, Professor?"

Crossbow nodded briefly.

"I wish we could have caught a specimen," Moses said. I looked at Moses sharply. This was too much. The intonation was Crossbow's, syllable for syllable. Crossbow must have been aware of the mimicry, but it said nothing about it.

"Well, that's that," Crossbow said cheerily. "It went much more smoothly than I expected."

My ears popped. "Hey, we're descending," I said.

"Let's go back to our study," Crossbow said. "We'll go down to the island's payload. We can judge our rate of descent from there, and if necessary we'll cut a few cables and hope for the best."

Once again, we made the tiresome descent through the center of the balloon. The hundreds of rungs were a trial; they blistered Anne's hands, and I almost fell again.

We grouped together down on the crunchy, crusted mud. The morning sunbeams slanted in, cool under the balloon's immense bulk. Kittiwakes and shrikes were everywhere, perching on the cables, squabbling over the bodies of parched, bursting fish and filling the air with their cries. A few of them darted curiously over our heads, but most of them ignored us. Probably they had never before seen a human being.

Drifting with the tradewind, the balloon sank within fifteen hundred feet of the sea, low enough for us to see gentle swells chasing one another across its gilded surface. Then the heat of the sun inflated the balloon and it rose a little, up to perhaps two thousand feet. We drifted into a thin cloudbank, and dew began to collect on the island's support cables.

Moses Moses dropped to his knees and stared intently at the cracked mud. "Look at this mold growing," he said. Furry, greenish patches of some kind of mold were growing in the wet valleys between the cracked plates of mud. "Look," he said wonderingly. "This is life itself. This mold has seized the chance to live, if only for four days. Look how it accepts life, so completely, so gratefully. It has a great deal to teach us, if we will only deign to listen." He sighed. "When I look at this I feel that I have foolishly wasted my life. I've squandered so many years in pointless, useless strife, and all along, all these centuries, the secret has been here." He looked at us with tears in his eyes. "I want a chance to live again."

I looked at Crossbow. "Crossbow, this is your doing."

Crossbow shrugged. It had caught Moses' characteristic shrug perfectly; it was uncanny. "I need someone to complete my work," it said. "He needs someone to complete his. What could be more natural? By exchanging lives, we can revitalize one another."

"So that's what you intend to do?" asked Anne. "Trade lives?"

"We must," Moses said. "I can't go on the way I was, with madness nibbling at me day by day. And Crossbow's work is vital. I can lose myself in it."

"And I've given it the best years of my life," the neuter said bitterly. "But I've seen the truth I dedicated my life to, mocked by charlatans. I trusted the Academy. I trusted in the disinterested search for truth. I sincerely thought that they would want the truth revealed. I thought that they would rejoice in my discovery, just as I did. But I've been cheated by political maneuverings. The arrival of Angeluce has opened my eyes to their true motivations. I can't let him ruin my hopes as he did fifty years ago. And since he has the Cabal on his side, he has made them my enemy as well as Moses's. Death take him! I'll fight them all to my last drop of blood!" It clenched its thin, webby fists.

"Wait a minute, wait!" I shouted. "This is ridiculous! Listen to what you're saying! Moses, you can't do Crossbow's work. You've never been scientifically trained." I was furious. I shook my head, but my hair wouldn't stand up. For some quirky reason, that annoyed me even more than did their calmly stated madness. "You don't know a microscope from a micrometer. You don't know gram-positive from gram-negative!

"And as for you, Crossbow—my death, I never heard such idiocy! You? Politics?" My voice rose to a squeak. "What do you think you can do? What do you think will happen when we reach Telset? Do you think that the citizens are going to rush out, saying, 'Hurray, it's not Moses Moses, but it's the next best thing!'?" I grabbed his muscular arm. "Professor, you're a complete political nonentity! You haven't even been seen in seven years, and the Gestalt Dispute is completely forgotten! Do you think a wire model is going to topple the Cabal? We don't have a chance without the prestige of Moses Moses! He's the only rallying point we could possibly have! Good God, I don't know much about politics, but any child could tell you that much! You shouldn't need me to tell you this!" I lowered my voice. "Now, Professor, talk sense. Don't joke with us. It's easy to belittle Anne and me because we're young, but our lives are at stake. We're worried. Don't say such things, even in jest."

"I knew it was something suspicious even from the beginning," Anne said shrewishly, looking at the two of them through narrowed, puffy eyes. "Be serious. You can't just abdicate your responsibilities like this. None of us ever can. Mr. Chairman, this is your society whose future is at stake. You can squirm all you like, but it's your moral responsibility, and that's a fact. You can't just hide and get this—this person to rush out and lead all three of us to our deaths. You saw the kind of hoodlums that were pursuing us. What chance would we have against them, without you to help us? Are we supposed to live under the tyranny of the Cabal forever, as hunted fugitives? You know they'll kill us, just because we once saw you!"

"They might even turn it around," I said. "They might say we kidnapped you, took you from the island, and killed you ourselves. Without you there to prove otherwise, we haven't a chance. Now, be sensible. You can study biology anytime. The Professor can give you lessons. And Professor, you can study politics. You could help us by defaming Angeluce, and giving us a chance to kill him legally—if I can wait that long, which I doubt. Doesn't that make sense? Isn't that what you planned?"

"Frankly, no," said Moses. "My work here is too important to be interrupted by a political squabble. Politics is ephemeral. I'm dealing with eternal truths." He got up and brushed mud from the knees of his bodytight.

"And you underestimate me," Crossbow said loftily. "Even fifty years ago I gave them the fight of their lives, and I know better now. With the intuition of Moses Moses to help me, I'll turn the lot of them inside out. I'll make them wish they'd never been born. Besides, they'll be looking for Moses Moses. They won't expect me. When we get back to Telset, I'll burrow from within like a deadly parasite. I'll find Angeluce and destroy him. He couldn't escape me if he hid at the bottom of the ocean."

"That's the spirit," Moses said, but with the detached coolness of a spectator rather than the fervid warmth of a participant. "I'll drop the three of you off at the shoreline. You can make your way south along the coast until you are west of Telset, then float across the Gulf by boat. You're both accomplished sailors. You could manage the Gulf even in a homemade craft. I can lend you the tools. They'll be abandoned when the island detonates, anyway."

"And what will you do then?" I demanded angrily. "You'll parachute alone into the wilderness, right?"

"Right. But with Crossbow's insight to guide me, I'll be able to survive quite handily. After all, that's what it intended to do in the first place, right, Professor?"

"Yes, certainly."

"How do you expect to have Crossbow's insight when Crossbow is miles away, with us?" Anne demanded scornfully. Her answer was identical smiles from the two of them, smiles that chilled us both.

"When the transference is complete," said Crossbow bleakly, "I intend to adopt the name of Crossbow Moses. The Chairman will rejoice in the name of Moses Crossbow. Thus our internal exchange will be perfectly mirrored externally, as is only right."

"But you can't do this," insisted Anne, close to tears. "It'll ruin everything."

Moses shrugged. "As you may have guessed," he said, "it's already too late."

11

The next four days were hell for Anne and me. Moses and Crossbow gave up all pretense of normal behavior. They spent every spare moment in their strange communion. They ignored us completely whenever possible; when we forced them to confront us, they faced us as blankly as men in a trance. They refused to answer our most earnest pleas, our begging, our frenzied denunciations.

I regarded their insane behavior as a betrayal of all our hopes. Anne and I pointed out their folly in terms that a three-year-old could understand, but no; they were rapt in one another. I was ready to beat them both up, and, if that failed, to tie them up and threaten to drop them off the island. But Anne dissuaded me, and it would have looked rather mean and paltry on tape. After all, the two of them were obviously in no condition to fight. They ate almost nothing. They slept little. They looked pasty-faced and anaemic and both of them were given to fits of inexplicable trembling. We heard the two of them mumbling in their sleep at times: bits and pieces of garbled stuff, recited most horribly in one another's voices.

We took to sleeping on different shifts. Anne and I stayed up far into the day after Moses and Crossbow announced their decision, holding long fruitless discussions on how to get them to reverse the process. I blamed Crossbow for it; I was sure that the actual transferral mechanism was Crossbow's invention. Its knowledge of the chemical basis of mental processes was vast. For instance, it had programmed Tanglin's memory eraser. I was sure that this mind-exchange was something much deeper than mutual hypnosis, or mutual suggestion. It had something to do with the mysterious Crossbow Body, I was certain. If the Body could capture chains of DNA, as Crossbow said, then why not RNA, which was the basis of memory? Crossbow must have found some way to activate the Body, to make it behave as Crossbow wished. And who was better qualified to do this than its discoverer?

It was a risky and unprecedented venture. Only the looming specters of their own deaths could have driven them to it. Moses and Crossbow were old and exhausted. They faced the worst challenges of their lives without the confidence and energy to meet them. But they were too proud, cunning, and stubborn to die. There was one chance left to regain their lost vigor, and that was in an amalgamation of personalities. Their new composite selves would see the world with fresher eyes, defeating the weary staleness of extreme old age.

It would mean a descent into madness, with no guarantee of success. But Crossbow and Moses insisted on taking that risk, not caring if they gambled away our futures as well.

Without speaking to them, without making any formal arrangement, the four of us separated. Crossbow and Moses took over the study room, except for the brief moments when Anne and I heated our meals, and that usually occurred while they slept. Anne and I moved down to the island's payload, where we could escape the intolerable burden of their presence.

In two days, life had swept over the island like wildfire. It was a brief, ephemeral life, frantic and delicate. Perhaps most remarkable were the mosses and molds. Most of them must have been carried by airborne spores, but at least a few of them were borne in on the feet of birds; Anne and I found the muddy tracks of three-toed shrikes filled up within hours by bright orange fur. By the evening of the second day, a carpet of green mold covered the mud, giving the illusion of grass without its substance. It burst into powder under our feet. Curly red mosses appeared in clumps on the thickest support cables, and tiny bluish-white mushrooms sprouted in profusion, spreading out day by day into wider and wider fairy rings, like atolls. They too were tenuous; they crumbled at a touch.

Insects arrived in profusion, starting with a plague of tiny, lace-winged midges. For a few hours on the third day they were everywhere, "like snow," Anne said; by sunset they had vanished without a trace. There were a number of larger flies as well, and a large population of small, round, iridescent beetles, no larger than the nails of my little fingers. There were a few dragonflies, too, of the large, ocean-going size, big as forearms; and once I saw a small mantis, though how it reached that dizzy height on its filmy little wings I'll never know.

On the evening of the third day Anne discovered a series of damp footmarks in the dried mud. It was some large, four-footed animal; the marks of its blunt flippers were spread as wide as my hand. The tracks led to the edge of the island. They did not return.

Just before dawn on the fourth day, Crossbow Moses, as it was now calling itself, came to wake us. It did so by the simple expedient of shaking the cables on which Anne and I had strung our hammocks. I sat up and turned on my cameras. I looked at it bleakly. "So," I said sourly. "Back in the land of the living, are we?"

"No need for pointless recriminations, Kid," said the neuter tolerantly, its voice a distorted echo of Moses Moses's. It had never called me Kid before. It was then, bleary-eyed with sleep, feeling faintly sick, that I realized that my old tutor was dead. "What's done is done," it said. It had slipped past death, but at a price. Its old self had been destroyed; the old, muscular body was now animated by a strange, conglomerate personality. It looked weak, but whole, as if it had recovered from a long illness.

"Listen," it said. "Do you hear the roar of the breakers?"

I listened. I heard the murmur, far beneath us, carrying me back in memory to the beach at Telset. "Yes," I said. I hopped out of my hammock. Anne sat up, rubbing her eyes.

"Are we going to do the jump?" I said. "Is everything ready?"

"It's ready, but a new contingency has come up," said Crossbow Moses. "There's a heavy cloud layer lying low over the shoreline. We can't jump blind. We might land in coral. The surf would catch us and dash us to ribbons against it."

"Then what happens now?" Anne asked.

"We'll be borne inland," Crossbow said. "We might as well go up to the top of the balloon. If we see a momentary break in the cloud cover, we should go for it. Moses Crossbow did a star sighting an hour ago—we'll soon be over the eastern fringe of the Mass."

"Maybe the morning sun will burn off the clouds," Anne said hopefully.

"Maybe," Crossbow said.

Following the neuter, we climbed up the rope ladder into the study chamber. Moses Crossbow was there, twiddling bits of beaded wire in his blunt fingers and studying the convoluted, glistening web of the Body before him. The little room had been carefully swept and put into meticulous order. It was as if a demon of energy and neatness had invaded the room. Even Moses Crossbow himself looked unusually polished and trimmed. He was wearing an embroidered belt hung with instruments, his bodytight had been brushed until it shone, and he had trimmed his beard. Even his round yellow eyes had an unnatural twinkle; they were filled with a sprightly, ingenuous alertness that made me feel rather sick. One of Crossbow's books lay half-open near at hand; its spine showed a forty- or fifty-letter title that was all hexa-dexa-chloro-silico's. Moses had been reading it.

"Look at this, my dear fellow," said Moses Crossbow. Twisting a small chain of a dozen beads, he slipped it adroitly into a small space in the web of the Crossbow Body. "There, you see?" he said. "It was inverted, levo rather than dextro! Now it fits perfectly. The data is confirmed!"

"Why, how marvelous," said Crossbow Moses, but its voice had a polite congratulatory tone rather than a genuine interest. "Be sure to fit that into the micronotes—you know where to find them. The three of us will make ready for the descent; with any luck, we'll be gone indefinitely."

"Well, I wish you luck," said Moses Crossbow, leaping with nervous grace to his feet. "I'd come along to see you off, but you well understand that time presses. I haven't had much time during the transfer for note-taking, and my ecological records are in a frightful state. I must see to the Petri dishes; there are a number of molds that will expire at any time; specimens must be taken. And I've neglected my taping sessions. I'll be very busy; delightfully busy, every moment."

"This is farewell, then," said Anne. "We'll see you no more. You'll be alone."

"Oh, not alone, my dear," said Moses Crossbow distractedly, picking a bit of lint from one sleeve. "I'll be surrounded by life, you see. The whole planet hums with life. I will contribute my own small note to that vast orchestra." Suddenly he embraced her and gave her a light social kiss on her peeling forehead.

"Goodbye." He shook my hand, then embraced me as well; I could feel a light, tense trembling in his thick arms. He seemed to be keyed up to fever pitch. "Goodbye, my dear Kid," he said. "No doubt I will see the two of you again; you are destined for fame, and if you deign to visit a humble professor, I will be very happy to see you. Goodbye, Mr. Chairman."

"I won't fail you, Professor," the neuter said, an iron resolution stiffening its beardless jaw.

Moses Crossbow nodded. He folded his arms and ran his tongue along the inside of his left cheek. "Be so good as to put on these packs I've made," he said. "I've doublestitched the seams, but if they fail to hold I've put extra needle and thread in your own pack, Mr. Chairman."

"Thank you, Professor, you are thoughtful as always," said Crossbow Moses. It shrugged a heavy pack made of thick green plastic onto its muscular swimmer's shoulders. Anne and I struggled into smaller packs made of white island fabric. They were heavy. "What's in this thing?" I asked peevishly.

"Provisions. Supplies." said the neuter. "I've packed everything."

"Then I guess there's nothing left for us, but to leave," I said. I looked at the person who had once been Moses Moses. "Mr. Chairman," I began.

"Professor, please," said Moses with a polite smile.

I shrugged irritably. "Professor, then. I'm not sure why you did this, but I do have a parting word of advice, if you're willing to listen. Don't let anyone find you. Don't use the name Moses or the name Crossbow. Both will be your death warrant, if I know the Cabal. Change your name. Change your face. Hide for as long as you can."

"Oh, my intentions exactly," said Moses Crossbow, nodding blandly. "Don't think I've forgotten the rules of strategy. I'm not so rash as to confront our enemy directly, you can be sure of that. I'll disguise myself. And mind you follow your own advice, Arti, for your own transformation will soon be upon you."

With this last cryptic announcement, the ex-Founder of the Corporation turned away, dismissing us from his attention. Crossbow Moses leapt vigorously for the bottom of the rope ladder and we began the long, exhausting climb up through the bulk of the balloon. Anne used the sleeves of her fabric poncho to protect her blistered hands. My arms ached horribly, but I waited until we reached the top of the island before I took any smuff.

As we collapsed, panting, on the bulging cells, it dawned. The rim of Reverie's butter-yellow sun appeared on the horizon and we heard, faintly, screams of delight from the hundreds of birds resting amid the mud and cables of the payload below.

Crossbow Moses was the first to sit up. "We must have a look at the cloud cover below us," it said energetically. "I'll have to peek over the edge of the balloon. The two of you will have to serve as my anchor, once I have this rope tied around me." It slipped off its pack and pulled out a length of braided ceramic fiber. It tied the rope tightly but comfortably around its waist and we set off for the edge of the balloon.

When the curvature grew steep Anne and I braced ourselves in the crevice between two cells and began to pay out line to the neuter, who continued descending. I sent a camera after it.

"We're definitely inland!" we heard it cry out faintly. "At least two miles!" This surprised me. Since we moved with the wind, it was hard to estimate our speed without seeing the ground. There was no sensation of movement at all.

"How are the clouds?" I yelled at the top of my voice. Anne, sitting next to me, winced. "Terrible!" it answered. "We can't possibly go through this. Perhaps they'll get thinner overland." There was a long silence. Anne and I wondered aloud how fast we were moving. We made ourselves comfortable and paid out more line. An hour passed. Finally we called out again.

There was no answer. "Pull me up!" we heard it call at last. We did so; it came scrambling toward us as soon as it could get to its feet.

"Hurry!" it shouted. "Phoenixes!"

Anne and I leapt to our feet. "What shall we do?" she said. "The Chairman...."

"There's no time for that," the neuter snapped. It was quite the brusque, hard-headed commander; my gentle old tutor was truly dead. "We've got to get to the mooring cables and cut free our descent cell. The whole island could detonate at any time!"

"But we can't just abandon him to die!" Anne insisted.

"Don't be a fool," snapped Crossbow Moses. "It'll take twenty minutes to get down the ladder; we'll all burn. He should be out on the payload by now; he can recognize a phoenix if he sees one. We've got to jump now, despite the clouds. We've gone miles inland, anyway."

Anne hesitated, then made up her mind. "You go," she said firmly. "I'll go to warn him." She set off at a run for the top of the balloon.

Crossbow Moses and I ran after her. When we reached the moored descent cell, it gestured unmistakeably with one hand. "Kid!"

I ran Anne down and hit her in the back of the head. Then I dragged her unconscious body to the mooring cables. "Good work, Kid," it said. "Make her fast to the cable with the hooks you'll find in the straps of the pack." Following its example as it attached itself, I did so. "Now take this knife and cut her free."

I did that, too. The single-cell balloon rose a little, Anne dangling free and swaying like a pendulum.

"Now attach yourself. Hurry! When I give the word, we'll sever our lines together!" With our frantic haste, it was the work of a minute.

"Go!" said Crossbow Moses. We slashed through the last mooring lines. For a moment we rose into the air, then, with agonizing slowness, we dropped down again to the surface of the balloon. Crossbow, who weighed most, was the first to touch down. It scrambled along daintily on the ends of its slippered toes, frantically trying to get us over the edge of the balloon. Wriggling desperately, I was just able to help.

"Hurry, hurry," gasped Crossbow. The cell's lift deprived us of the traction we needed to get up speed. We went through all kinds of panicked antics, which my cameras caught to embarrassing perfection. At least ten minutes passed before we reached the edge of the balloon. Anne began to come to just before we reached the steep, circular edge, but it took her a few minutes to gather her wits.

"You hit me again," she accused me groggily.

"It's too late to sacrifice yourself, so shut up and help us," I wheezed. Crossbow and I kicked away at the edge of the balloon for all we were worth, trying to push ourselves away from it. The curvature was such that we would kick away, descend a little ways, kick again, descend some more, and gain perhaps ten feet each time. It seemed to take forever, and all this time we were being borne relentlessly inland. At last we drifted down past the balloon's equator, and from then on we were free of it. However, we were still close enough to be engulfed in the fireball if the island went up.

"Look!" Crossbow screeched. Anne and I both flinched in terror as a bullet-like flash of red zipped past us, banking just at the edge of the island and careening off at astonishing speed. Flocks of seabirds burst up like fireworks from the island, diving toward the clouds below in noisy panic flight.

We also screamed a warning to the ex-Founder as we drifted past the bottom of the island, but we didn't see him anywhere. For the first time we saw the bottom of the payload, a titanic mud-black mass of tangled roots and dripping slime. Immense toadstools as big as beds had sprouted on its undersurface.

We continued to descend in a leisurely way, drifting farther from the island as we descended into a slightly slower wind. There was still no explosion. Minutes passed. Still nothing. We fell into a bank of clouds that shrouded us in white tenuous dampness. It was then that the explosion came, a flash that lit the cottony dimness followed by a deafening roar and a hot shock wave that half-flattened our little balloon and jerked us like puppets on strings. Our jaws dropped open as our whole bodies shuddered with the blast. We were too deaf to hear the squashy impact as the mud splattered to earth far below.

My ears rang as if I was stuffed with smuff. The two others were dim forms in the fog; I yelled at them, but could barely hear my own voice. My cameras, brushed aside by the rush of hot wind, floated back to me. I thought of swinging over to Anne, but decided against it. The tension might rip my tether line.

We continued to descend. It was impossible to judge our speed inside the cloud; we barely seemed to move, though I had to swallow several times to depressurize my ringing ears.

Suddenly we began to fall faster. The balloon may have cooled, or a tiny rip may have opened it. After a few moments we dropped through the bottom of the cloud layer.

A dizzying spread of land was beneath our feet, white and brown and green to my painfully contracted eyes. The sunlight was bright with morning and the sea was nowhere in sight. We couldn't even see the splashdown point of the flying island.

We were moving quite rapidly with a brisk wind, I could see that now. The tops of jungle trees were moving in the warm breeze, sweeping past under our feet. They were two hundred feet below us, and they looked tall.

I heard an indistinct mumble; I turned to see Crossbow Moses shouting and pointing at the trees below us. It made grabbing and hugging motions with its slender, webbed hands. It wanted us to seize the branches of the trees when we were swept into the forest canopy. I nodded violently to show I understood.

There were no signs of clearings or landmarks beneath us. This was part of the Mass; I could tell by the peculiar white blotchiness on some of the trees. The usual continental forests were every shade of green, but never white. As far as I could tell from our dizzy descent, the trees were otherwise normal.

Crossbow Moses dangled down farthest among the three of us; its feet rattled through the thinnest top branches of a tree as we were swept over it. It grabbed at a branch but the leaves stripped off in its hand. We crashed solidly into the next one and grabbed branches. The balloon tugged mightily at us and ripped Anne free, but she caught another branch further down. Crossbow and I gripped our branches like demons. I still had Crossbow's knife; I could have cut myself free, but that would only have increased the strain on the others.

Suddenly a gust of warm wind drove the balloon down into the tree and we heard the fabric rip. The balloon went flaccid almost at once, but it did not explode, and we were grateful for that. The strain abated at once. Crossbow and I cut ourselves loose.

The immense tree whose branches we gripped seemed perfectly normal; the whiteness of the Mass did not show on it anywhere. Its bark was smooth and gray; its waxy green leaves were as broad as two hands set side by side. The leaves were tri-lobed and smelled faintly of cinnamon. Smelly pale sap showed where our impact had broken and twisted some of the smaller branches.

"Ants!" Crossbow yelled suddenly. I could barely hear him. "Ants! Climb down, climb down! They're all over me!"

Suddenly I too felt a tickling on my feet and exposed neck. Tiny black ants were pouring out of large wooden galls attached to some of the twigs. I saw them doubled up, biting my feet vigorously, but the pain was very slight. It felt a little like a stiff hairbrush laid lightly on the skin. The ferocity of their painless attack alarmed me, however, and I descended as rapidly as I could, burdened as I was with the heavy pack. I crushed some of the ants on my way down, but that was a mistake, for they smelled horrible.

I could see as I descended that the jungle was divided into

three distinct vertical layers; a sunny canopy, where we had landed, a denser middle layer, crowded with the green crowns of the shorter trees, and, far below, a dappled jungle floor.

With my agility I easily outdistanced Anne and Crossbow and dropped the last ten feet to the ground. Satisfied that I would no longer annoy their beloved tree, the ants flowed off me in dense black streams.

My hearing improved with every passing minute and I became aware of the Reverid jungle cacaphony. The entire aural spectrum was as crowded with sounds as the jungle was crowded with life. I had heard these sounds before in drone tapings, but it was different to stand there, to feel the faint cool breeze, smell the odors, feel the leaf-crowded black humus under my feet. Prominent among the sounds was a piercing, rather oily-sounding double creak, endlessly repeated; insects without a doubt. It was interrupted occasionally by a mellow booming like an iron drum half-filled with water, and by low, almost subsonic, rumbles, like slowly moving doors with rusty hinges. In the upper register I heard the whine of passing bugs, the querulous, lean-throated cries of treetop animals, the warble and cackle of birds. There were other sounds, too; rustling, dripping, scraping. And these were only the usual ones; sounds you heard so often that they immediately faded into the background. The unusual sounds: roars, cries of alarm, territorial signals perhaps—were remarkable for their elaborateness. Where another animal would have settled for a simple bellow, a sonic-conscious Reverid beast had to introduce some arpeggio, some arresting variation.

Anne and Crossbow joined me on the ground; Crossbow was sucking a small scratch on one of its webs. "Those ants are so strange!" Anne said. "Why didn't they sting?"

"Oh, they stung, all right," Crossbow said. "But their venom has no effect on our metabolism. If you look carefully you can see the bites, but they're not at all inflamed."

Anne brushed leaves from her loose, balloon-cloth garment. "It's delightfully cool down here," she said. "I thought jungles were supposed to be steamy and sticky."

"That may be true on other planets, but Reverie is always a

special case," Crossbow said. "This jungle is the product of advanced evolution, not tropical circumstances. Reverid photosynthesis is very efficient. Because it traps more of the sun's energy, plants here can support a much larger population than plants on other worlds. And a jungle is more stable ecologically than other environments, because there is room in it for a vast variety of species. The stability of an ecosystem depends on its diversity; that is an elementary law. This jungle is billions of years old."

Anne laughed gaily. "I had thought this would be a horrible place. But it's beautiful, like a park! Look at those majestic trees! Why, it's marvelous down here. I like this much better than the balloon."

"Don't depend on a snap judgment," Crossbow said. "We still have the Mass to deal with before we can reach the shore again."

"I'm starving," I said. "Let's have something to eat before we start our hike. Smuff gives me an appetite."

Crossbow Moses looked at me reproachfully. "Are you still taking that drug? Why, you're almost healed. Your bruises are practically gone."

"Those are just the ones that show," I said. "Anyway, I hate pain."

"Very well," Crossbow said. It shrugged off its pack. "But we'll have to make our provisions last. Otherwise we'll have to live off the land, and in the middle of the Mass that entails some risks. The venom of the ants didn't affect us, but there are things harmless to Reverid organisms that will kill us as dead as sea shells. At one time I knew most of these things, but now my memory. . . . And in the Mass it's often hard to tell, as you'll soon see."

It dug into its pack and drew out three tasty seaweed cakes, part of the stock of travelling food it had saved for itself. "We'll have to eat sparingly, so you get only one," it said, passing them out. "The island was provisioned for one, not four." We bit eagerly into the dense green cakes. We had hardly downed the first swallow when we were assaulted by a horde of bright yellow butterflies. "Holy Death, what are these things?" I demand-

ed, for I had never seen a butterfly before. I swatted at them in-
effectually. The smell of the food seemed to drive the insects
wild; they kept alighting on my cake. Crossbow mumbled something that I didn't catch, for it had wisely stuffed the entire cake
into its mouth. I did the same, but I had to spit out bitter butterfly bodies and lost a good chunk of my cake, which fell to the
jungle floor followed by a swarm of insects. Crossbow guarded
its mouth with both hands as it chewed and swallowed. Our
heads and shoulders were covered with them.

More and more of them poured in from the depths of the jungle. We couldn't even see one another, especially as they insisted on settling on our eyelids, even on my cameras. I went into a
wild capering dance, but they clung to me as if I were a tree
trunk. Finally I danced my way out of the enveloping cloud of
insects and swallowed what was left of my cake. Then I pried a
wetly adhering butterfly wing from the roof of my mouth. Bugs
followed the scent on my breath, so I breathed through my
nose.

Once we had swallowed the cakes, we were able to escape
most of them. But a large number stayed with us tenaciously,
clustering on our heads and around the flaps of our packs,
which held more of the cakes.

"These are butterflies. Harmless," said Crossbow through
gritted teeth, brushing them away as they sought to cling to his
lips. "You won't see them on Telset, but they're common here.
Come on, let's run."

We eventually outdistanced most of the butterflies, though at
least a dozen of them clung to the strands of my plasticized
hair. We sat down to rest on the lumpy knees of a huge tree
with thin, light-red bark.

"It's the scent of the sea that does it, I suppose," Crossbow
said mournfully. "Normally, when they follow that scent, it
leads them to the site of an island splashdown. From now on
we can eat inside the tent, if need be. By the way, the tent is in
your pack, Kid, so don't lose it."

A number of the small yellow butterflies were climbing dog-
gedly about in Crossbow Moses' bushy blond hair. Others sat
sedately like little jewels on Anne's smooth, blunt-cut brown

hair and her feather barette. I laughed at the sight they made; Anne looked at me and laughed back.

"Your hair looks different now, Kid," she said. "It lies down flat now instead of standing up all prickly."

I brushed my hair self-consciously, dislodging a number of flutterers. "It's growing," I said. "It's not plastic down to the roots any more, and it's bending on a hinge of normal hair. I have to re-do it every week, when I take my hormone treatment." I paused. "*Uh-oh.*"

There was a weighty silence. Crossbow said, "You didn't take any treatment with you, Kid?"

"How could I?" I said. "I didn't plan this trip. I left with an escort of bullets."

There was a second weighty silence as each of us considered the implications of this peculiar predicament.

"Well," said Crossbow at last, "there's no help for it, then. You'll have to go through a forced adolescence. You're in for a strange experience, I'm afraid."

"But I've been on suppressants for almost thirty years now," I said. "Who knows what the effect on my body will be?"

"The effects will be serious, no doubt about that," Crossbow said. "But almost all young males go through the process, and without the calmness of maturity to help them endure it. You'll just have to manage with the inconvenience until we get back to civilization. I'm sure you can deal with it."

"I don't suppose I have any choice," I said morosely. I snatched a butterfly out of midair, reacting absently as it fluttered too close.

"Don't kill it!" Anne said. Surprised, I shrugged and let the butterfly go. She looked embarrassed. "Look at the bright side," she suggested tentatively. "Your voice will change. You'll probably grow a beard. And when you cut off that plastic coating from your hair, you'll be unrecognizable. Already your skin color has changed—you're darker, and it doesn't have the greenish tint it used to have from that oil you used. The cosmetics are gone from around your eyes. If it weren't for your chain weapon and your cameras, no one would possibly guess that you were the Artificial Kid."

"Holy death, a beard!" I said, clutching at my face. Was there already a trace of stubble under my panicked fingers? "Good God, my image will be ruined!" My voice climbed into its higher registers. "I'll be finished! Washed up! The Cabal has probably already revoked my shares, burned down my house—how will I get the money for new treatments? Death, that stuff's expensive, it costs as much as smuff! And—oh no, what's even worse—I'll look just like Tanglin!" Clutching my head, I reeled back, looking straight into one of my cameras and making sure that another got a good side shot. "Just like Old Dad! My best friends won't know me! Poor Quade will scream and run when she sees me! What a catastrophe! Is this the end of the Artificial Kid?" I hadn't thought of poor Quade in a long time—a tear trickled down my cheek.

Anne looked at me, upset. "Don't take it so hard, poor Arti! Your career's not so important, is it? After all, when we reach Telset, we'll still have to stay in hiding. You'll have to give up fighting anyway, give up your fame. You should be thankful that you have such a good disguise!"

She had upstaged me again. Amazed at her gall, I dropped my hands and looked at her nonplussed. She looked back at me innocently, surprised at my sudden change of mood. "Right, right," I muttered in disgust. "Belittle my difficulties. Never mind, I'll probably have to edit all this anyway—it would never do to be seen with these linking butterflies in my hair." I stood up, washing my hands of the whole business. "Come on, let's get a move on."

Crossbow Moses got to its feet. "We're faced with a choice now," it said. "We can try to detour around the Mass, or we can plunge directly through it. If we detour it will take us much longer—weeks, perhaps. Our provisions will soon be exhausted. We could try to live off the land, but we risk death by poison. If we were at the shore, I could feed the three of us indefinitely, but the forest is not my area of expertise."

"Let's get to the shore as soon as possible, then," I said.

Crossbow nodded. "Water would be our worst problem if we took the forest route. But the Mass has plenty of water. It is riddled with stagnant karst pools, of course, and I wouldn't advise drinking from those, but it has a number of streams and a major river. If we can reach the river our difficulties are over; we can reach the sea easily, just by walking down the riverbank."

"What about the molds and bacteria?" Anne said. "The chances of illness?"

"It's true that the Mass is especially rich in microfauna, but if we keep up a good pace our exposure will be brief," Crossbow said. "We'll have to depend on our bacterial ecosystems to protect us. Besides, the forest itself is rich in bacteria. Our chances of infection would actually be worse if we were weakened by short rations and a long trek."

I looked at it through narrowed eyes. "You're hiding something, Professor. Chairman, I mean. You want us to go through the Mass. Why?"

Crossbow looked innocent. "I know the Mass better than the forest. That's all. Besides, I'd like you to see the Crossbow Body at work. You patently doubt my theories. What better proof can I offer?"

I shook my head. "If the Mass is so harmless, why has it been off-limits all these years? Why is its reputation so foul? They call it 'a thousand square miles of disease.' "

"Academy propaganda," Crossbow said confidently. "The Mass has only one disease, and that's the Crossbow Body. And that's no disease, that's a benefit. Trust me, Arti. Have I ever deceived you?"

"No," I admitted. I turned to Anne. "What do you think?"

Anne tore her eyes away from a small yellow butterfly sitting, tamed, on her forefinger. "We haven't any other guide or expert," she said. "We'd better accept its advice." And so we did.

12

We adjusted our packs. The heavy clouds that had been above us all day were descending through the upper reaches of the forest canopy. A silvery mist began slowly drizzling around us, not so much falling as drifting. We felt dazed and lost as we meandered among the shadowy columns of immense trees. The underbrush was not heavy, mostly shade-tolerant herbs and ferns, heavy with dew, with occasional lacework bushes dotted with flowers. Fallen tree trunks were our largest obstacles. The process of rotting was fast and riotous, and the fallen trunks were slippery with orange shelf-fungus, fat-bodied slug-like slimemolds with wet skins as varicolored as oil slicks, heavy green carpet mosses, ferns with entangling stems as tough as ceramic fiber, and blood-colored puffballs that ruptured at a touch to fill the air with stinking, choking spores.

We detoured when we could to avoid the fallen forest giants, but it was difficult. The hole left in the forest canopy spurred the growth of lush bamboos that crawled with fat, furry sapsuckers and chitinous marmosets. Immense dragonflies flitted past us, snapping up mosquitoes that Crossbow would not let us swat. "They don't give diseases," he said. "They inject vaccines. After all, it's in their best interest to keep us healthy, so that we'll have plenty of blood." Their bites left no welts.

Sometimes we left the ground to clamber over rough-barked lianas that webbed whole groves together, their saprophytic roots sunk deep into the wood. Twice I had to fight off hives of hairy spiders that had caught my cameras in their tough, dense nets.

At noon we slept, slinging our light, balloon-cloth hammocks from low branches. After three hours Anne and I were awakened by a loud rip and a crash as Crossbow fell to the forest floor.

Mildew was devouring our packs and hammocks, and Anne's dress. Crossbow gave her a bodytight that was much too large. We repacked what we could into the tough synthetic fabric of our tent and slept, cramped and miserable, in the crotches of trees.

When we awoke, we slung the tent from a long wooden pole that Anne and I carried over our shoulders.

We marched until sunset. The terrain, which had been gently sloping, grew more difficult. We began to find immense lumps of primordial limestone, like gigantic toadstools, thrusting their rounded heads up through the thick forest humus. They were thickly crusted with fossilized shells and bones, and were densely festooned with creepers, ferns, tough bushes, and small trees whose naked brown roots gripped the rock like stiff snakes.

When night fell the forest grew incredibly raucous. From above our tiny campsite under the shelter of a weathered, crumbling knoll came rich howls of glee and showers of dead twigs and excrement. Booms and metallic screeches that seemed to come from everywhere and nowhere added a stirring counterpoint. We choked down wads of seaweed cake that already had the first lingering aftertaste of rancidness. Phosphorescent globes as big as eyeballs meandered through the branches above us, glowing red and blue and green, sometimes casting reflected pinpoints of light from the eyes of treetop animals.

When something large came thudding and snuffling past us, I decided I had had enough. "Let's build a fire," I said. Anne nodded eagerly; Crossbow said nothing but handed me a small flashlight from its pack.

I advanced on a nearby bush. It retreated warily. With a shriek of terror I attacked the bush and it exploded into its component elements: long, brown, multi-limbed twigs, fluttering, green-winged leaves, even feeble, tiny-legged flowers.

"Don't hurt them!" Crossbow called out. I retreated to the shelter of our limestone overhang, trembling a little. Crossbow was squatting on its haunches, a melancholy expression on its face; the long walk had been hard on its aquatic legs. "It might have unforeseen repercussions," it said. "Everything is connected to everything else."

I looked at the other bushes warily. "Are they all like that?" Crossbow shrugged. "Some of them," it said. "Mimicry is very advanced here." With a sigh, it sat on a patch of moss and propped up its tired feet on a fallen limestone boulder. It began to rub its legs with its webbed hands. "Actually, that particular adaptation was camouflage, not mimicry proper," it said.

After a more successful search, I returned to the fire with an armload of dry leaves, twigs, and branches that had been sheltered from the mist. Unfortunately we had no lighter—Crossbow hadn't had much use for one in its aquatic existence—but Anne explained to us the principle of the bow-drill. By chafing away at dry, rotten wood till our fingers blistered, Anne and I produced a few feeble sparks that we fanned to a flame. As the dry leaves ignited with a bright flaring we heard a startled snort from perhaps six feet away. A small, burly, bear-like animal got up on oddly-jointed legs and stalked off into the forest.

"And take your bug-trees with you!" I yelled after it, heaping branches onto the fire.

We took turns keeping watch, Anne first. Insects were attracted by the light from our fire, but did not fly into it; they were precision navigators. As night's darkness grew denser, we heard rustling in the branches, and small furry animals with the tired, wrinkled eyes of debauchees ambled up out of the darkness to look us over. Occasionally these animals, which Crossbow called "squirrels," would catch a moth and eat it, but with an abstracted, bored air that suggested that they were doing us a favor.

During my watch, the last one, the fire burned low again. To save effort I dragged in a large log and heaped it on the fire, and a horde of ants large as crickets poured out of the log. The warrior ants had long nozzles in their heads and they assaulted us with spurts of glue and formic acid, so that we were forced to retreat to the top of the limestone crag that sheltered us.

We dumped our provisions out of the tent and pegged it to the top of the crag. We slept uncomfortably, painfully gouged by hard limestone lumps under the tent floor. We awoke well before dawn and sat up in the darkness, stiff with boredom. When it finally dawned we found that most of our shiny objects, including our knives and hatchets, had been stolen during the night. We also found that our seaweed cakes were riddled with tiny weevils.

"Oh well, they add protein," said Crossbow nonchalantly, and he ate them. Anne and I forced ourselves to follow his example. They had a nutlike, slightly bitter flavor.

We marched on. As the terrain continued to descend, springs grew more frequent, but the going was much rougher. The chunks of limestone appeared more often; the trees declined in height, and we began to see increasing signs of the presence of the Mass. Green tree-leaves were splotched with faintly furred patches of white. Damp furred masses like thin white throw-rugs clung to the trunks of trees. The ground grew noticeably damper underfoot, and some of the trees showed heavy knees and buttresses for support in the wet soil.

We began to spot pools and sinkholes. With a sigh of relief, Crossbow flung itself into a wide pool, sank beneath the surface, and did not return for half an hour. Then it came back, its ribs convulsing as it choked out a lungful of water, exulting over the network of water-caves it had found beneath the surface. While I climbed a tree in search of dead branches for a fire, Crossbow paddled around the pond, catching aquatic game with its long, agile fingers. We built a fire in a natural depression in a limestone slab and had roast turtle and fish steamed in bladdered pondweed. It tasted marvelous in our famished mouths, and we napped for three hours in the afternoon while Crossbow snoozed comfortably at the pond's weedy margin. Mosquitoes bit us, and I swatted one whose hair-thin legs were suspiciously furred.

We had to force ourselves awake again, but we could not afford to waste the daylight hours. Violating our natural circadian rhythms, we staggered to our feet and plodded on as if dosed with depressants. I took a little smuff for the soreness in my legs. The wounds in my arms and torso were already almost healed, and the busy follicle mites were devouring the edible stitches still sunk in the pink new flesh.

The forest was giving way to swamp. The trees were shorter and broader in the base, with thicker bark, and we found larger and larger areas where the earth squelched messily under our tired feet. We had to skirt more sinkholes and broad marshes where the shimmering water was half-hidden under the thick leaves of fleshy aquatic plants. Many of the plants were white, and there were areas where different species of plants were gummed together by a surface froth of sticky Mass material. The forest canopy overhead grew thinner and thinner and finally disappeared altogether in places, leaving the afternoon sun shining almost blindingly off glittering expanses of shallow marshwater.

Crossbow dealt easily with the water in our path; it simply plunged in and swam, leaving us to wade along as best we could, our feet wrinkling up in our shoes like stewed fruit. Sometimes we sank neck deep and paddled after the neuter, clinging to the airtight tent for support.

Finally we discovered that the wet ground beneath us had degenerated into the "trembling earth" of a true marsh. There was no honest dirt in it. Instead, we walked bent-kneed on wadded mats of decaying vegetation, some of them rooted in squashy mud but others floating free, buoyed up by pockets of trapped gas from decomposition. Luckily there were still many firm islands that had collected around the roots of groves of mighty aquatic trees. We dried off at the islands when we could, eating sparingly of berries from thorny marsh vines, weaving mats to sit on from the green waxy stalks of pliant rushes. Blobs of wet white moss dangled from the tree branches. We found several trees that were almost devoured with fur, but they seemed healthy; the cranes and egrets of the marsh nested in them without fear, and even thatched their nests with bits of fuzz.

When night fell we camped on the largest island we could find. While I looked for firewood I killed three snakes with my nunchuck. Crossbow had throttled an immense snapping turtle; he assured us that the turtles were safe to eat, while some of the most innocuous-looking fish were full of subtle poisons. We picked pink leeches from Crossbow's back while it cleaned the turtle with a tiny dissection scalpel, the only knife we had left.

Day in the marsh had been full of the cries of birds, but with night they slept and the night was alive with ghastly roars from furry mammalian crocodiles. Glowing blobs of swamp gas drifted over the waters. A few yards from our campsite we heard something huge emerge from the water, splashing and washing. We sat quietly until we heard it blunder off into the trees.

"The marsh drains into a major river a few miles from this spot," said Crossbow cheerfully. Its long immersion in the water had done wonders for its morale. "By late tomorrow we'll be strolling down the river to the sea."

We ate the turtle and fell into an exhausted stupor, trusting to our large bonfire to keep predators away. We slept almost twelve hours and awoke about six hours before dawn. We whiled away the time curing what was left of the turtle meat in the smoke. Anne cut my hair with the scalpel, leaving me with close-cropped stubs of rattling plastic.

Just after dawn I climbed to the top of the largest tree on the island, hoping to get an overview that would help us avoid the worst of the swamp. From above, the swamp was a shattered mosaic of green sawgrass, dark peaty water, and white splotches of Mass material, pitted and threaded by sinkholes and canals. As my eyes followed a morning flock of white egrets, I saw something that shocked me. It was the glint of sunlight off the metallic sides of a pair of huge camera drones. There was no mistaking their silhouettes; they were blunt cylinders studded with audio pickups and trailing jointed manipulative arms.

They were big ones; ten feet long at least. They were less than a mile away, cruising in a purposeful way over the swamp.

I drew my own cameras in close, fearful lest it should spot them with a telephoto. After a moment my surprise and dread faded into curiosity. The drones glided noiselessly off to the west, and I relaxed. I climbed down the tree and told Anne and Crossbow about the drones. Anne was interested. "Are they common here?"

"Hardly," I said. "But drones are the only legal way to view the Mass. I wish I'd known who their operator was. It could mean plenty of trouble for us. The drones themselves may be harmless, but they could track us and inform on us. We'd better try to hide if we spot them again." I hesitated. "Good God, what would happen if they caught me with my hair like this?"

"What about your own cameras?" said Crossbow.

"You don't understand, Professor. Chairman, I mean. I can edit my own tapes. I mean, here I am—covered with mud—cropped to the scalp—dirt under the fingernails—an unsympathetic editor could make me look like a buffoon! It could damage me professionally! It'll take an editor of genius to present this fiasco as the soul-stirring adventure I mean it to be." I looked around quickly and reflexively, making sure that all my lenses were clean.

We bolted down some chewy turtle meat and started slogging through the swamp again. While Crossbow wallowed unashamedly in the brackish water, Anne and I tried to pick our way through the firmest spots. Sawgrass cut us. Leeches nibbled our legs. Fetterbushes stuck their hooks in our skin and clothing. Broken milkworts drenched us with sweet greenish sap. Frogs clung to our heads. Algae plugged our nostrils. Silver darters tickled us and waterbirds flew at our heads, squawking, when we neared their nests. Our progress was maddeningly slow. Crossbow encouraged us, lolling on its back in the water, offering us the amused, confident advice that one gives to people without one's natural advantages.

Finally, when our legs trembled with exhaustion and our clothes and hair were caked with mud and pondweed, we discovered that the land was rising. The ponds grew shallower and were easily waded. Dry-earth trees, whitely blighted with Mass fur, appeared again. We found dirt that would support our weight.

"We must have made a mistake," Crossbow said, dragging itself out of the water with a reluctant frown. "The terrain should be falling, not rising. The swamp is supposed to drain here. Water can't run uphill."

"Spare us, Professor," I said, and Anne said, "It's so lovely to be on dry land again. This is the right direction, isn't it? It'll get us to the sea, won't it?"

"I suppose so," said Crossbow, "but it's peculiar all the same." We started walking overland, gaining our second wind now that the long frustration of the swamp was over. We had gone perhaps a mile through a small forest ("Intermediate growth," sniffed Crossbow, "not full climax. Couldn't be more than two hundred years old.") when we heard a wind blowing and noticed the movement of the treetops. The trees stopped in a broken chaos of white limestone rocks, and when we clambered over the rocks we realized that we had come to the edge of a long escarpment.

In the plain below us festered the center of the Mass. It was almost solid white, and resembled nothing else alive. We saw a nightmare landscape, twisted, contorted, visibly gummy and sticky, filled with lumpy spirals, convolutions, writhings of thick flabby fibers yards across. There were towers in it that might once have been trees, but they were draped with mangled, twisted strips and straps of sticky Mass fibers, as broad as highways. Parts of it seemed to seethe visibly even as we watched, like cells undergoing mitosis. Other areas were as wrinkled as the surface of a brain.

Half a mile to the east the swamp drained out through a gap in the escarpment in a low waterfall. Mist shrouded the bottom of the fall, but we could see where the stream from the swamp met the sluggish river, and, miles to the east, we saw the glint of the sea.

"This escarpment is a fault line," Crossbow said. "Fairly recent, too; a matter of two or three centuries. This explains the peculiar geology of the swamp." It leaned out precariously to examine the escarpment wall.

"Do you expect us to march through *that?*" I said.

Crossbow pretended not to hear me. "Look at those slicken-sides," it mused. "And look at that dark cluster of cave openings in the escarpment wall. I think I can state what happened here. It was the immense weight of the Mass. It caused the underlying network of caves to collapse. This whole continent is riddled with caves, you know. Limestone dissolves very easily."

"Listen, I'm not trekking through that mess unless there's absolutely no other possibility," I said. "Just look at it! It's ghastly! It's moldy! It looks like Death's cesspool! Isn't there some way we can skirt around it?"

Crossbow looked at me patiently. "Do you want to go back through the swamp? Look, we can descend by the falls, and then follow the river quite easily. It will be downhill all the way to the sea."

"How do we know it won't collapse on us? What if we get stuck in it, knee deep? What if we're eaten away by some kind of ravenous fungus? What if it eats our skin away and we sprout white fuzz all over our bodies...."

"Look at that!" said Anne, pointing.

We looked and then leapt for the cover of a jumble of limestone boulders. It was a camera drone, almost certainly one of the two I had spotted above the swamp. It had the same tapered cylindrical body, the clusters of audio pickups, the pair of manipulative arms, cocked in a position of readiness like the arms of a preying mantis. It stalled momentarily in its patrol over the Mass, and then descended smoothly into one of the Mass's irregular corrugations. Cautiously, we crept out from behind our cover.

"I hope it didn't spot us," I said. "Those big drones have telephoto lenses and automatic tracking systems like you wouldn't believe. And that one's really big, it has room for all kinds of equipment. Infrareds, satellite hookups, odor analysis even."

"But could it possibly be looking for us?" said Anne.

"Professor Angeluce has an interest in the Mass," I said grimly. "And don't think that a drone is helpless. Those manipulative arms are computer-controlled. They move fast and they don't make mistakes. I wouldn't care to trade punches with a drone."

"Don't worry," said Crossbow Moses. "Once we are inside the Mass it'll be the merest good luck if it should find us."

"Hold on!" I said. "It's obvious that you want to hustle us into the Mass, but you might at least take the time to think up a good reason for it. Stop treating us like children. I told you that I'm not going into that poisonous dump unless there's no other choice."

Crossbow stuck its tongue into its cheek and crossed its arms. "Really, Arti, is this melodrama necessary? Your physical bravery should be beyond question. You've seen Mass material before. Did it bite you? Did it sting? What are you worried about? I've dealt with the Mass before. I give you my word as a microbiologist, and as an Academic, that you'll come to no harm." It hesitated at the look of open skepticism on my face. "Come now, Arti. The only reason for your fear is ignorance. It looks very impressive from this height, I know. Let me demystify it for you."

With a studied gesture it slipped into its lecturing attitude. "The Mass itself is made up of the Crossbow Body, its attendant micro-organisms, and elements of the Reverid gene pool. The micro-organisms are mostly advanced species of molds and yeasts, and they serve as a binder and an incredibly rich reserve of nutrients. The Crossbow Body traps genes, preserves them, and recombines them. It's like a gigantic Petri dish, that covers whole square miles. When the genes are recombined, they form a new organism, which is nurtured by the nutrients in molds and yeasts. And it spawns not just simple mold cultures, but species of all kinds: insects, mammals, birds. It's like a gene bank. And it's a permanent guarantee against extinction. It is the ultimate advance in the evolutionary battle against death."

"You're saying that birds grow in there?" I said incredulously. "Animals too? Without wombs to grow in? Without sperm cells or egg cells? And they grow to full maturity?"

"Well, rarely," admitted Crossbow. "Mostly they grow in little pockets of undifferentiated tissue, and then are broken down again by the Crossbow Body. But the number of captured genes is vastly increased every time that happens. When the concentration of genes of a single species reaches a certain critical point, then a full organism is sometimes produced. Of course its tissue is full of the Crossbow Body, and it serves as a vector for the distribution of the Body. And of course, if it dies, then the cells are broken down again and preserved in a new growth of the Body. It evades death, because its genetic constituents are preserved. The genes are the heart of life. The tissue is just an expression of the genes."

I looked out across the white, festering landscape. "I don't see many 'full-grown organisms' down there. There are a few things that look like trees, or things that might have been trees. . . ."

Crossbow shrugged. "Well, the growth of full organisms is a bit of an anachronism, anyway, isn't it? There is no need for adult organisms when reproduction is handled by the Mass. The only real purpose they serve is to spread the Mass by wandering. And once the Mass has taken over the planet, there'll be no need for that either."

"Taken over the planet!" said Anne and I in unison.

"An event in the distant future," Crossbow assured us. "The Mass is in no hurry. For one thing, it will have to produce an aquatic form before it can move into the seas."

"But that's horrible!" I said. "You call that living? Little bits of broken cells, trapped in white mush? No forests? No animals? No dance of predator and prey? No intricacy? No sensation? No intelligence?"

"I tell you that the Mass transcends intelligence! Do you think it has no intricacy, because your great gross eyes can't see it? On a molecular level, it is the most intricate creation in the known universe!"

"But it's just a mindless, devouring fungus!"

"Mindless? Remember that the basis of thought and memory is molecular. RNA is the sister of DNA. The transfer of genetic material from unit to unit of the Crossbow Body is incredibly complex. Think of the amount of gestalt implied in such an intricate system! Think of the powerful bulwark it presents against the forces of disorder! I'm not saying that its function is perfect as yet—there are accidents, admittedly there are accidents. But intelligence is a function of gestalt—a very weak function, from a very small system! But the complexity here has produced a gestalt function that surpasses intelligence like a bonfire surpasses a spark! Don't you realize—the Mass has defeated determinism! It has broken the rigid chains of evolution! It has become teleological! It is the quintessence of life—it is the enemy of entropy!" Crossbow looked searchingly into our faces. "How could words ever convince you?" it said. "I knew you could not be convinced until you had seen its power with your own eyes. That's why we must march through it."

"How do we know it won't grow on us and dissolve us?" I said.

"I am a vector of the Crossbow Body. So is Moses Crossbow. Did we dissolve?"

"You mean, if you die, you'll turn into a mess of white pudding, like that stuff?"

"The Body would dismantle my cells, yes. But that does not constitute death. My genetic content would be preserved. In all likelihood I would eventually be recreated. Whether I would be re-born in the full sense of the word depends on your definition of identity. I would be a clone. But all neuters are clones, of course."

"And if we're contaminated by the Crossbow Body while we're marching through the Mass, and we die, then we'll also be dissolved into white goo? That's what you're saying?"

"What's so terrible about that?" Crossbow demanded. "If you died in the forest, you'd be eaten by beetles and toadstools. If you died in Telset, you'd be cremated, or—what do they call it? Reefed? Eaten by sharks and rays? Is that any better?"

"Of course it isn't," Anne said vehemently. "What does it matter what happens to us if we have the misfortune to die? Our souls will be reabsorbed into the Infinite—these bodily shells will no longer be our concern. As long as it doesn't attack us while we're living, there's no danger. Isn't that so, Professor? Mr. Chairman, I mean?"

"Exactly," said Crossbow. "Come, we've wasted enough time in idle palaver. Let's find a way to descend the escarpment. No doubt the water draining from the marsh has carved a descendible channel. Let's try it." Crossbow got to its feet and began marching along the lip of the escarpment.

"I don't like this," I called after its retreating back, but it did not stop. After a moment Anne hurried after it. I had to choose between following Crossbow Moses, or plunging alone back into the swamp. That was no choice at all.

On our way to the waterfall it rained hard, soaking us through. Crossbow would not seek shelter; it merely fluffed out its dry gills in a self-satisfied way and trudged on.

The land sloped by the channel of the waterfall. The way was steep and slick. Mist from the last tumbling of the waterfall soaked us in an explosion of rainbows.

We stopped at the gushing, roaring pool at the foot of the fall. Long knotted white extensions of Mass fiber, like crippled stems of thick ivy, clung to the limestone base of the escarpment, white against white. "I can't go on," I said. "Let's pitch camp and catch a few hours' sleep before we plunge into the worst of it."

"Not here," Crossbow said. "Too scenic. It's a natural place for a camera drone. Let's seek shelter under that tree."

"Call that a tree?" I said, too tired even for derision. The object in question was tall, and it had a central column that might be considered a trunk, but its branches were long cable-like ribbon extensions that arced from the trunk to the ground. And the ground itself was bizarre. It had a certain granular quality—it was relatively dry—but it was not soil. It was milk-white crystals, loosely clumped, with puffs and domes of white fungus emerging from it. There were areas of round white lichen, like splashes of thick white paint.

We hid ourselves in a small, shadowy area under the tangle of branches. They would shelter us from prying eyes.

Anne and I pitched the tent. Crossbow dug its webbed fingers into one of the domes of white fungus. Crossbow tugged and twisted and the dome broke apart laterally like a splitting plate of mica. "Here, look," Crossbow said.

The dome was full of leaves. They looked like fossils, or more exactly, like plant specimens pressed flat between the pages of a book. Most of the leaves were ferns. They were perfectly formed, except for their whiteness and a touch of fuzziness.

Anne looked at the leaves and then looked at Crossbow. "Why, it's full of leaves, how marvelous," she said, but her intonation suggested that the sight had given her a turn.

I looked at the leaves. They gave me a crawly feeling. "What good does it do them to grow inside this pasty-looking lump?" I said. "They can't see the light. Look how pale they are."

"Oh, they don't need their chlorophyll, or any light," Crossbow said. "The nutrients in the fungus supply all their needs. Notice how perfect they are—without blemish or disease. They stay like this until they either emerge as full specimens or are genetically dismantled and reabsorbed into the Crossbow Body. And if we dig a little deeper—" The neuter shredded its way into the bulk of the dome. "Look. There's an insect."

A brown cricket, furred with white, crawled feebly out of a little pocket inside the white fungoid mass. It cleaned its feelers with its mandibles, then perked up and hopped off. "You'll find other insects, too. Mantises. Centipedes. Even predators, produced without the necessity of killing their prey. Killing is wasteful. The Mass produces life without the necessity of death."

"But what happens when they get loose?" I said. "There's nothing to eat here."

"Well, if they are born at the edge of the Mass, then they can sometimes enter the bordering ecosystem. Otherwise, they eat Mass material. They generally disintegrate then. If we're lucky, we'll find an animal in the process of disintegration. It's a fascinating thing to watch. Often the Crossbow Bodies within them carry the seeds of other forms of life. Even as the old host breaks down, another species spontaneously takes form within its tissues and breaks free. It's not painful. At least, it doesn't seem to be."

"I can't wait," I said sourly. We slept the sleep of total exhaustion and awoke about three hours before sunset.

We packed up and returned to the waterfall, then walked down the brook. The running water was full of green clumps of moss, small fish, and crustaceans, nibbling at the occasional blobs of Mass material washed in from the brook's stagnant bywaters. The running water seemed to protect them, but the stagnant pools at the brook's margin were scummed over with white. The bulging domes of fungus on the banks of the brook were full of Mass-grown pondweed and moss, as Crossbow proved by ripping one open. Others had been broken open from the inside by escaping animals.

We waded down the brook, preferring the algae-slick rocks to the clammy touch of Mass material. Crossbow swam as usual, leaving Anne and I to flounder along as best we could. Bridges of mold arched over the brook, casting shadows on the rippling water, and there were small gravel islands, no bigger than stepping-stones, where the Mass had established a beachhead and sent up clusters of fuzz.

When I could, I stopped to wash off the powder of spores. The touch of the Crossbow Body on my skin seemed to be driving my follicle mites wild with hunger. They were not native Reverid organisms—they were genetically altered, specially bred to protect my body from infection. They were devouring the Mass material wherever it touched me. They were fierce little creatures, and their digestive acids might be breaking down the Crossbow Body. I hoped so, anyway.

The texture of the Mass material was, surprisingly, rather pleasant. The tops of the life-containing fungus domes, for instance, were rather rough, dry, and pebbly, like reptile leather. Even the white fuzz that was so typical of the Mass showed a surprisingly intricate configuration when viewed from close range: the ghostly outlines of leaves and branches, the pointillistic silhouettes of animals. Still, I touched it only when absolutely necessary. Anne shared my caution, but Crossbow was recklessly indifferent.

Our quiet, wadeable stream ended at the white-mossed banks of a major river. It was sunset, so we decided to camp. We retreated to a dim nook in a lumpy, tortuous upheaval of Mass material; it was our only choice of shelter. Crossbow intended to sleep in the river, but changed its mind. Protruding from the brown water were the brow and bulging yellow eyes of some amphibious behemoth. The eyes were as wide across as the outstretched fingers of my hand. The body was hidden beneath the opaque peaty waters and its size was impossible to determine.

"Should we keep watch?" I said as we set up the tent on a furry flat space between two wrinkled white knolls. "There'll be no campfire tonight. There's nothing to burn."

"It's not likely that we'll meet anything on land large enough to menace us," Crossbow said. "The largest animals generally are disintegrated quickly. Besides, they don't learn the mechanics of predation because prey is scarce and they have no parents to teach them. If one comes blundering by, we'll hear it and wake up." So we went to sleep.

I woke up before midnight with a crawling sense of unease. I looked at Anne and Crossbow in the darkness inside the tent. Their breathing was quiet and even. I restored my cameras to full function and sat up. Anne stirred; it was crowded in the little tent, but I crept out without waking her. Crossbow always slept heavily, its old brain a riot of dreams.

I looked up at the stars and saw an immense shape blocking them. It was a drone.

It didn't move. It had been watching our tent, perhaps for hours.

The drone descended in absolute silence, its arms cocked in readiness. I readied my nunchuck to blast it, wondering whether I should cry out in alarm and reveal the presence of the others. With its infrared detectors it probably knew of them already.

Its arm moved with blinding speed and snatched up one of my cameras. I howled in rage and blasted it at point blank range.

A hole as big as my fist appeared in the thin metal of its underbelly. It sagged and listed to one side, but its arms were moving like lightning. It caught all my cameras with its jointed claws, one after another, as if it were plucking berries. I screamed piercingly and struck it as hard as I could on the elbow joint of one of its arms; the drone rocked slightly, and stuffed my last camera into a yawning storage aperture in its back.

"You linking thief! Give them back!" I screamed, and for the first time I heard my voice crack and shriek alarmingly in its upper registers. I leapt into the air and smashed one of its sound pickups; shattered plastic flew in every direction, but the drone did not try to fight back. Instead, it began to rise, tilting visibly and making, for the first time, a faint, strained humming. But it rose steadily and began to drift off toward the east.

"Leave me one, at least!" I begged, helpless now that it was out of my reach. I ran after it, hoping that its engines would fail, recklessly thrashing my way in the darkness through the knolls and walls and tendrils of the Mass. I could hear my cameras, faintly, complaining and buzzing as they tried to return to their master. A puffball burst under my hand and almost blinded me with spores; a few steps later, my feet caught in an ankle-high tangle of green vines and I went down on my face. In the half-second before I hit the ground I twisted and tried to roll, and the top of my head hit the ground and broke through a brittle white crust into a shallow pool of heavy, viscous fluid. A sharp, faintly pleasant chemical reek bit my nostrils. My scalp tingled where the fluid had touched it.

Anne and Crossbow caught up with me and helped me to my feet, out of the litter of green vines and broken fungus domes. They half-supported me as I sobbed uncontrollably. I looked around, half-blinded with tears, and for the first time in seven years the familiar, cheery presence of my cameras was gone. Gone. They were all gone. I made a motion to tear my hair; not only was it cut short, but the top of my head was crusted with thick white goo that was already dripping over my brow and ears. I screamed in rage, my voice cracking again, and looked around red-eyed for something to kill. I whipped my nunchuck around, but then slowed it and dropped it as I came to a stunning realization: why should I bother? The gesture would be lost forever. No one would see it but Anne and Crossbow, and they were not able to appreciate it; besides, they would forget. I was reduced to the ephemeral impermanence of the uncameraed. All my actions had been robbed of their true content, their true meaning. I slumped to the ground, sobbing apathetically.

I ignored Anne and Crossbow's querulous attempts to console

me; their words sounded like dry puppet voices. I said nothing. Crossbow went back to sleep, but Anne led me to the river, where she washed the crusted mush from my head. It stuck tenaciously. Some of it seemed to have soaked into the plastic coating on my hair. I washed my burning face in the murky water and stopped weeping. I could feel the muscles of my face growing rigid with bitterness. A fierce sulk came bubbling up like hot black oil from the cores of my bones. My face grew dark with congested blood. I trembled. "It'll be all right," Anne said. I turned on her, snarling, and she retreated to the tent.

I stayed awake until morning, while my furious anger declined into despondent worthlessness. Sniffing back tears, sunk in a slough of self-pity, I seriously considered flinging myself into the river to drown. Only the fact that the gesture would be wasted caused me to hesitate and abandon the idea.

By the time the first pale edge of morning lightened the sky, I had been awake ten hours straight, and I was exhausted and sick. My scalp tingled, and for the first time I felt the borderline nausea of hormone changeover. My suppressants had worn off, and a whole dancing, capering Harlequinade of male biochemicals were washing through my bloodstream, charging into hair follicles at lip and jaw and groin and armpit, triggering neotenic growth in my vocal cords, even badgering the pituitary into an atavistic state of alertness. I was too sick to notice the erotic effects, at least for the time being.

Anne and Crossbow had been awake for several hours. At dawn they came down to the river to get me. "We must be on our way," Crossbow said. "Now that the drone has located us, speed is of the essence."

"I'm sick," I said. "Go on without me."

"A ridiculous attitude," sniffed Crossbow. "Neither of us have cameras, but our zest for life is unimpaired. Consider how much worse things could be. The drone could have crushed us in our tent while we slept. Instead, it merely took your cameras. No doubt it was seeking news of the man it believes to be the Chairman. The drone's operator knew that your cameras must have news on Moses Moses. If its intentions had been hostile, it could have attacked us. I believe it was controlled by a friend.

One of your fellow tape craftsmen. Perhaps someone you know."

"You don't understand," I said. "My *cameras* are gone. It *blinded* me." My voice croaked horribly. I put my face in my hands.

"Arti, your forehead is blistered," Anne said. "You need medical attention. Besides, once we get to Telset you can get more cameras."

I shook my head. "You don't want to go with me, Anne. My suppressants have worn off. Hormones are turning me into an animal. I don't know what's happening to me. Besides, I'm worthless to you now. I've lost my cameras. I'm losing my identity, and that means I'll lose my following and my fame. No one will recognize me. I'm a liability. Not an asset."

Anne shook her head. "You should never be ashamed of something you can't help. Besides, there are just the three of us, now. We won't tell anyone."

Crossbow folded its arms. "Why give up now? We're on the riverbank! It's just an easy day's stroll to the seashore. Our difficulties are over. Stop sulking, Arti, it's beneath you. Just get on your feet and follow my lead."

Anne helped me up as Crossbow ambled downstream, its feet sending up thin puffs of spores from the thick Mass fuzz blanketing the riverbank. It had gone less than ten strides when a thick crust collapsed beneath its weight and it fell with a heavy splash into a corrosive pool of thick white liquid.

We rushed to the spot and started probing for Crossbow with the wooden pole we used to carry our tent and baggage. Minutes passed. We were about to despair when we felt a tug on the end of the pole. We pulled mightily and slowly dredged the neuter out of the thick, clinging fluid. Crossbow was clutching with both hands to the very end of the pole. It crawled out onto the pool's margin on its hands and knees, completely drenched in a thick coat of the reeking stuff. It retched fluid, forcing it out of its stomach and lungs and gills, then began crawling feebly toward the river, coughing. It half-fell into the murky water and disappeared beneath the surface. White scum floated up behind it.

The smell of the curdled white Mass fluid made my scalp start tingling again. There was already a network of tiny blisters across my brow and around my head, like a crown. Surprisingly, they didn't hurt, although the skin was red and swollen and swarming with follicle mites.

I sat on a shelf of Mass fiber to wait for the neuter to resurface. For several minutes Anne stood by herself, staring thoughtfully into the white pool where the neuter had sunk. Then she came to sit beside me, but said nothing. We ate the last of our stores, and my hormone nausea subsided a little. Half an hour passed. Finally there was a burst of murky bubbles near the shore and Crossbow came slogging out.

Its skin had bubbled up all over and detached itself in pockets from Crossbow's flesh. The poor neuter's skin was visibly waterlogged, and brown river water was seeping out of the blisters. Anne and I shrank back in horror. Crossbow coughed convulsively and spat out a thick white mouthful of mush. "I'm all right," it croaked. "It doesn't hurt."

"You're dying!" I yelled. "It looks like third-degree burns!"

"Just crust," it replied. "Look, it peels right off." It tugged at one of the blisters with webby, crusted hands and a wide strip of skin shredded off, revealing puffy white endodermis. "The only thing that hurts is these splinters in my hands. No, Anne, don't touch them. I'll be all right." It drew in a deep breath of air. The expression on its face might have been resignation. The blisters made it hard to tell. "Don't either of you touch me. I've ingested a great deal of the Crossbow Body. I don't know the effects. They may be serious."

"Is there anything we can do?" Anne said sadly.

"Of course. Follow me," Crossbow said, and kept walking.

Anne insisted that she lead the way, testing the firmness of the ground with our baggage pole, which she had washed clean. I carried our provisions on my shoulders while Anne probed the ground. Our progress was slow. Crossbow swam when it could, and the water seemed to help it. Most of the brown, blistered skin came off, but by noon the skin under the blisters was covered with little white bumpy colonies of Mass fur.

We pitched our tent and rested. Crossbow was delirious. It kept mumbling things, little evocative fragments that made me weep for my recorder. Things like: "She loves power, not you. And you must say the same for her," and, "Louise, you can't mean that," and, "But they're all dead. They've been dead for centuries," interspersed with bits and pieces of poetry and legal documents and scientific monographs. I was gray with exhaustion, nauseated with hormones and the sight of Crossbow's skin. I vomited twice. Anne kept us alive. She led Crossbow to the water; its eyelids were heavy with fuzz and it was almost blind. She bathed my blistered forehead and didn't flinch when a pocket of skin peeled away and revealed a tiny bud of green ivy, rooted in my skull.

We slept and then trudged on. Buds of ivy popped through my skin around my head in a dozen places. Crossbow's joints grew so stiff that it was hardly able to walk. Finally we attached ropes to it and towed it along in the water like a log.

By late afternoon the Mass was slowly being replaced by tough shrubs, then small trees, then riverside ferns and weeds and birds and, more and more often, mangroves. We could smell the sea. It was the heavy, dense-rooted mangrove so typical of the continental shore. When sunset began, we were wading around and through a network of thick round roots, scolded by aquatic birds and small, armored sapsuckers. We heard the roar of the surf, and it led us on. We were just in time to catch the last glimmer of the yellow sun on the blessed Gulf of Memory.

Anne explored for two days and found us a small patch of white beach amid the miles of tangled mangroves, where we camped to await Crossbow's death. There was a small freshet of water there, and the banks of the little creek were rich with deep black dirt. That was where Crossbow chose to stay. Its eyes and mouth were already webbed shut, and its joints were as stiff as wood. It had never removed the splinters from its palms, and that was where its transformation began.

It started slowly, as slowly as the growth of ivy around my head. It took whole months. The leaves grew in the damp spaces under the blisters on Crossbow's hands; when they were fully formed, they burst through the skin. We could do very little for Crossbow, but we heaped up dirt around the brown barky knobs that had been its ankles and made sure that it got plenty of water. Its fingers shrivelled into pliant twigs, bark crept up its calves, seaming its legs together, and its skull dissolved as strong, vigorous branches broke out through eyes and ears and mouth.

Anne and I lived on fish and crabs and clams and seaweed. We lived well. Even the ivy growing from my scalp seemed to thrive. Anne cut it for me when it dangled down into my eyes. My follicle mites prevented it from spreading any farther; it was confined to the areas where my head had been soaked in the thick Mass fluid. It didn't hurt, thought it bled red sap if Anne pruned it too close to the scalp.

I was growing, too. I grew three inches in a month, and it ruined three hundred years' worth of ingrained reflexes. I lost my smooth, fluid, self-aware grace, and it was replaced with adolescent gawkiness. For the first time in my life I found myself stumbling, stubbing my toes, dropping things. I even cut myself when I tried to shave with Crossbow's tiny scalpel. My career was ruined. It was useless to even think of resuming it.

We had no reason to return to Telset. Since my cameras were gone, we had no way to support our testimony. We had no political advisor, no leader who could rally resistance to the Cabal. We had no reason to risk our lives voyaging to Telset in a homemade boat. Even if we reached Telset, we had no guarantee that we would not be shot on sight.

Survival occupied our energies. When our tent wore out, we built a snug thatched shack out of mangrove wood and foliage, with my leather combat jacket for a door. We wove nets out of vines and bark and built fishtraps out of rocks and driftwood. We kept a hearthfire burning. We grew brown and lean and tough.

I had expected Anne to argue about our moral obligation to return to Telset. But Anne had changed, just as I had. One night in our third month, I looked at her curiously as we sat beside our driftwood fire. She had changed. It was not merely the long wisps and curls of tangled hair over her ears and the base of her neck. It wasn't the explosion of freckles under her sunburn, or her ragged bodytight, torn and stained. Something was missing. An element of tension in her face, a certain grimness around her mouth, was gone. She looked—not determined—only calm.

"You've looked different ever since you lost your feather brooch," I said. "The little ornament you wore in your hair. You never told me what happened to it."

"It was no ornament," Anne said. "It was a badge. I never wear ornaments."

"Did you lose it?"

"No. I gave it away." She hesitated for a long time, looking up at the night sky. Then, slowly, the words came to her. "Rominuald Tanglin gave me that brooch. He asked me to wear it for him, to wear it always. Especially on camera. It was supposed to identify me to the public. It was made of moa feathers, shed by the favorite birds in my flock. I wore it for thirty years." She looked at me intensely. "But its age doesn't matter. It was still made up of cells, the cells of the birds that grew the feathers, and cells have genes, and the genes are the heart of life. Some of the genes must have still been viable. I threw it away! I threw it into the pool that Crossbow fell in. It's been broken up and preserved in the Crossbow Body, forever. My birds can never die now. No matter what anyone does. I've saved them. I did it, no one else."

"That was clever," I said. I looked up at her with genuine admiration. The months with Anne had wrought a bizarre and drastic change in my way of expressing and feeling. She was the only audience I had left, so I played to her. At first, it had seemed a waste to feel *anything* without an audience to share it, but the deadly apathy wouldn't cling to me; there was too much else to do. There was the task of staying alive, there was the wind, there was the sun, there was the wet green ivy that circled my head and haunted my dreams . . . .

I couldn't have hidden the effects of my puberty from Anne, even if I'd wanted to. Hair was appearing all over me, like the rank, coarse fur of an animal, long-buried in my flesh, but awake now and moving with irresistible, lazy power. It was the

Other, the Other Thing that Armitrage had spoke of; I was abandoned to it, and it grew inside me, wet and green and strong like ivy. I had dreams of flying, dreams of burning; even broken dreams of Tanglin's adult flesh, touched by ghost fingers of the women of the past. Anne was among the women.

Anne was the only woman. I saw her with new eyes, not the calm blackrimmed eyes of the Artificial Kid, but older, hotter eyes that showed slow heat shimmering just above the surface of her skin. I had never seen that the lines of a woman's body were curves; that they were not static, not just the outside layer of skin over muscle and tendon, but flowing and living. Before, I had seen proportion; now, I saw grace. When I had seen Anne's face before, I had seen her features; now, I saw a woman.

"I did it alone," Anne said. "No church could have helped me. I didn't need any church. I didn't even need Tanglin. It was Tanglin that put that badge on my head. It was only feathers, but Arti, it weighed so much! I fought so long to keep it there, even when the weight of it was crushing me. While my flock lived, I couldn't fail them; when I failed them, there was nothing left for me but shame.

"But how can I feel shame when there are only the two of us? We're marooned here. Reverie is a big world, but we only need a piece of it. This beach is our world, and we're the only people on it. You don't care what I did in the past. You don't care about me and the Church, or about me and Tanglin. That's what I've learned from you, Arti. I've learned not to care."

"I care, Anne. Without you here, I'd have died. You are the only person I've ever really known. . . . You are my audience, Anne, but you're more than audience. . . . Another person can be like a whole world, can't she? And we're all the world that's here."

"Yes, that's it!" Anne laughed then. It was a brittle, high-pitched laugh, with a cutting edge of hysteria in it; it sounded like chains breaking. She scrambled to her feet and ran down the beach. Sand scattered with each footstep. "There's no one to see us!" she shouted. "There's no one left to care! I'm dead to the old world, to the old things!" She spun around suddenly, looked at the sky, and stabbed her finger accusingly at one of the stars. "I'm dead to you, do you hear? I did everything you wanted, and now I've thrown you away! I'm my own world now. I'm my own people! I'm reborn! I declare myself reborn, right now! No one else can do it for me!" She sprinted suddenly for the foamy line of surf and threw herself into the sea. She poured briny sea water over her tousled head, three times, carefully, with cupped hands.

The shock of the cool water seemed to calm her. She came out of the water, dripping, and threw aside her wet clothing to stand naked, ankle deep in the foam.

"I am newborn," she said quietly. "Did you understand the ritual?"

"It's happened to me before," I said. "I wish it had been that clean and that easy."

"I suppose I'll keep the name Anne," she said musingly, digging into the sand with one naked toe. "I like the name Anne. Why shouldn't I keep it? From now on I'll do what I want."

"What do you want to do, then?" I said. Something awful was happening to me. My mouth was dry and my heart was pounding at my ribs like a madman at a prison door.

"I want to dance."

I got to my feet. "All right. I'll teach you."

"No," she said. "I'll teach you. First we draw the eight-spoked wheel in the sand, like this." She stooped over gracefully and began to scrape a wide circle in the damp sand. Trembling, I closed my eyes. I didn't want to see, for fear it would happen too soon. I pulled off the rags of my bodytight and dropped them in the sand. "The males go on this side, the females on the other. There seem to be only two of us, but there are really four: you and your older self, and me and mine. So, we begin."

The dance did not last long. Instead, we made love in the sand, like gods. "Rominuald," she said, and I shuddered in her embrace because the name sounded so right.

There came a day when we had been on the beach for five months. We had caught a huge ray with one of our heavy bone fishhooks and we were roasting it over a bonfire. They told us later that it was the dark pencil of smoke that had attracted them.

We heard the boat coming and we hid in the mangroves. They would never have found us if I hadn't recognized the boat as Ruffian Jack's exploring hydrofoil, the *Ruffian's Delight*.

Even then we were cautious. We didn't come out until we saw Ruffian Jack and Alruddin Spinney wade ashore, surrounded by clouds of cameras. When we came out of the brush we received a standing ovation and a round of cheers from Jack, Spinney, and their five-man crew.

Jack and Spinney ran toward us, grinning broadly. Jack embraced me. Spinney and his mantis embraced Anne. Even the crew jumped ship and slogged in toward shore, with more cameras, narrating the historic moment with off-satellite transmitters.

"A beard! I can't believe it," bellowed Jack, holding me at arm's length. "Is it really you, Kid? Or should I be calling you Mr. Tanglin now?" There were cameras all around us—a dozen of them at least. I looked into their lenses nonplussed. "What do you know about Tanglin?" I asked cautiously.

Jack laughed. "God's Death, boy, we've got all your tapes! Alruddin, look, he doesn't know! Kid—Arti my lad—they were beautiful! You're a hero! Anne's a heroine! A cult idol! And what about Crossbow, eh? What about its amazing discovery? Where is our sexless savant? I swear it's more of a man than any of us!"

I pointed to the tree. Jack looked. Cameras trained their lenses on it. "*Sylvaticum pinnatus*," said Jack absently. "Not native here. What's it doing this close to shore, eh? Lovely tree."

"It's Crossbow's grave," I said soberly. "We planted it there. It would have wanted it that way."

"You mean he's died?" said Spinney, letting go of Anne for the first time.

"It was an accident," Anne said, catching on fast. "In the Mass. A terrible illness. The long trek was too much for it."

"It was a martyr to the Cause," said Spinney sadly, tears coming to his eyes. It was the first line of what was to become Spinney's lyric masterpiece, "Martyr to the Cause."

"What's the situation like in Telset these days?" I said.

"Why, we've won! The Old Cabal has been annihilated! The New Cabal and the Reformed Board have everything under control. It was your tapes that did it, Kid. Tanglin, I mean. Angeluce is dead. Instant Death surrendered! Your tapes caused a planet-wide riot, a full-fledged Revolution! It's the greatest tape accomplishment in history!" Ruffian Jack waved his arms wildly. "Back on board, crew! It's back to Telset and a hero's welcome!"

Half-ushered, half-dragged by Jack's crew, Anne and I were heaved on board and surrounded by yelling, cheering sailors, who ripped bits of our tattered bodytights off for souvenirs and demanded autographs and statements for the planet-wide live broadcast. Jack gunned the engines wildly and the backwash from his craft's powerful engines nearly swamped the little hut Anne and I had built. We were in Telset in an hour and a half.

13

Our reception was half power-fantasy, half baroque nightmare. The entire population of Telset met us on the docks. The shore was black with people and packed so tight that citizens were being forced chest-deep into the sea by the pressure of crowding. Every man, woman, and clone in the city was screaming his, her, or its lungs out and setting off powerful, dangerously haphazard fireworks that rained red-hot cinders on unprotected necks and heads. They were chanting, too. "*Tang-lin, Tang-lin, Tang-lin!*"

"Merciful God, I haven't seen anything like this since Peitho," yelled Anne.

"Whose idea was this?" I screamed in Jack's ear.

"Money Manies', who else?" he said.

The screaming, billowing crowd was on the hair-trigger edge of mass hysteria. Members of the Cognitive Dissonants and the Fourways were trying to keep order. I noticed that they were wearing new armbands, not the rainbow armbands of the Civic Detail, but thick bracelets of linked beads.

"Go up to the bow and wave to them," Jack howled. "Go on, or they'll tear the city apart!"

Anne and I walked to the bow, joined hands, and waved. The crowd went absolutely out of their minds. In seconds we were in the middle of a maelstrom of cameras, bashing each other, cracking their lenses, spinning around in tight circles, going completely out of control as the drone wavelengths were overloaded with contradictory signals. When one of them knocked Anne down, I went berserk and started whacking them to rubble with my nunchuck. They were so thick that we couldn't see the crowd, could barely see each other.

Jack reacted quickly, gunning the engines and pulling us out of the dock, so rapidly that I was almost thrown overboard and Anne saved herself only by grabbing the brass railing on the bow.

Coral grated under the hydrofoils as Jack ran the *Delight* out to sea, ignoring the usual navigation channels. We zipped out of sight of the island, waiting for the cover of darkness while we monitored the riot on four channels, all of them Money Manies'. "My aching death, look at Hammer whacking the daylights out of that noncombatant!" I marveled. "Look, Ice Lady's whipping that man half to death! The Cognitive Dissonants are really beating the crap out of unarmed civilians! What in creation is happening here?"

"Oh, Chill Factor, your old friend, is part of the New Cabal now," Jack assured me. "He's in charge of keeping order, and he's doing it. Without guns, too. It hasn't been easy in Telset these last few months. Angeluce had a purge, you know. Eighty people were executed. Then there were the fatalities in the Decriminalized Zone—look, what's left of the Zone is coming up on screen four now."

"Good God, it's been leveled!" I cried.

"Yes. It was the scene of the first pitched battle between Old Cabal and revolutionary forces. It came just two weeks after you left—an abortive uprising in favor of Moses Moses. Word of the Second Coming got out almost immediately, of course. Angeluce lured them into the Decriminalized Zone and blew them sky-high. We learned later that he had been manufacturing explosives in an orbital oneill for almost two years."

"And my house?"

"Rubble. We saved a few of your tapes. Your computer's gone, though. I'm sorry."

"So am I. Poor Old Dad."

Jack smiled. "Oh, don't worry about *him*. His reputation's made. Imagine, all this time, and I never knew you were really Tanglin! Why, the news set all Telset on its ear. Look, that's where work is progressing on the new statue of Moses Moses. There's been no word on Crossbow Moses, by the way. Or Moses Crossbow, whatever you call him. You know, the one with the beard."

"Right," I said.

"At any rate, the true, original Moses is safely dead now, so we can deify him like a hero deserves." Jack guffawed. "I really liked the old gaffer. I'd like to shake his hand, or his successor's hand—whatever you call the guy who went down with the balloon. He was okay in my book. Shook the place up a little, through no fault of his own. Maybe it needed some shaking. Look, they're chasing the crowd back from the docks. Oooh, *that* was a shrewd blow. Looks like the worst is over now." He turned off the tapescreens from a central switch. "It'll be dark soon. I'll take you in to see old Manies. He's been anxious to have a good talk with the both of you. Congratulations. Celebrations. Parties all night. You know, the usual stuff."

"Right," I said again.

Money Manies did us the signal honor of meeting us at his private dock. "Darling Kid! You don't know how much this cheers an old man's heart!" he cried, embracing me and printing a wet social kiss on my forehead. "The days and nights I've spent, consumed with worry! But come in, come in! I'm just starting breakfast."

Manies touched his bracelet and the door of his mansion swung open. There were still a few raw bullet pock-marks on the wall that faced the sea. "Mementos," smiled Manies. He hurried us inside.

"You're looking well, Mr. Manies," I said.

"Thank you!" Manies said brightly, ushering us down the hall. "I've lost twenty pounds in weight, and I seem to have shed eighty years." He led us through a heavy, inlaid door into an interior dining room, lit by a glistening chandelier mobile. Wooden chairs thickly upholstered in dark red velvet rolled up to meet us, and then bore us to the table.

"Just a very small breakfast this time, with a few very close friends and allies," said Manies with a smile. "Let me have another look at the guest list." With a flourish, he pulled a roll of paper from a small pocket in one of his elaborate cream-colored lace cuffs.

"Let me see, let me see. . . . Are the place-cards out yet? I see they are. Well. We have my dear wife Annabella Manies, Mr. Richer Money Manies. . . ." He coughed self-consciously. "Arthur Tanglin—I understand that's the name you are going by now, Kid."

I shrugged. "I don't know how the rumor got started, but so be it. Obviously I'm not the Artificial Kid any more." I reached up to tug a lock of soft black hair and a leaf of ivy. Manies looked interested. "I've been meaning to mention that delightful headgear of yours. It's a far cry from the old spikes, but I find the change refreshing."

"Thanks," I said. "I've grown used to it by now, of course."

"My sagacious Arti. You certainly picked the right moment to change your image, I must say. You must let me supply you with some cameras before you leave. I'll have the house cameras record you at breakfast and give you the tapes."

"Thanks."

Manies looked back at his list. "Saint Anne Twiceborn — you haven't renounced your title, by any chance?"

"I am three times born, Mr. Manies." Anne and I were both suspicious. We traded glances of mutual reassurance.

"Professor Crossbow—I'm afraid we shall have to leave a seat empty, in its memory. A very great loss to science. How I regret never having met it. Ruffian Jack Nimrod. Alruddin Spinney, if he can tear himself away from his composing desk. He's working on a history of the Revolution, you know. Chill Factor and his Ice Lady. Your client Quade is fine, by the way;

they're still teaching her table manners, so she won't be here, but she survived the purge quite handily, thank goodness. Plus my very good friend Cewaynie Wetlock, down from orbit, and my Alien."

"Cewaynie Wetlock?" I said. "I remember her. I did a critique on one of her tapes just before I was chased out of Telset."

"Yes. She owned the big drone that discovered your cameras. She edited the tapes for publication, too. You'll love her. She's a very talented and sweet young lady, and very anxious to meet both of you."

Manies touched one of the studs on his heavy bracelet. "How long will it be, Quizein?"

"Another thirty minutes, sir. I'm having a bit of a time with the Alien's main dish."

"Oh." Manies chuckled. "That Alien of mine! Its biochemistry requires a special diet, you know."

"Who's your surprise guest?" said Anne.

"What, my dear?"

"You mentioned eleven guests. Even counting the empty seat for Crossbow, I see twelve chairs here."

Manies looked distressed. "You've spoiled it! Well, don't worry, he'll be here very soon. In the meanwhile, shall we beguile the time with a few tapes? I want you to see some of these, Mr. Tanglin. I want your comment on their technique."

Manies busied himself with his bracelet. A tapescreen appeared, sliding down out of the ceiling near the opposite wall. I leaned forward and rested my elbows on the table, which was round—one of Manies' affected bits of egalitarianism.

"I'm going to run this first one without the soundtrack, which was quite vile. This took place just after the massacre in the Decriminalized Zone after the first uprising." He ran the tape.

"It's Professor Angeluce!" I said.

"The late Professor Angeluce, yes."

"Who's the poor man tied up in the chair with the bag over his head?" said Anne.

"You'll see that very soon, as soon as he finishes his harangue—there!" Angeluce whipped the black bag from the head of his trussed-up victim. It was none other than Richer Money Manies.

Manies chuckled at our surprise. "Yes, it's me all right. Look at that expression of total fear on my face—maximum audience impact, eh? I had been arrested for 'collaboration,' just after you had made good your escape. My vocal cords were paralyzed, of course; otherwise, I would have protested quite violently, let me assure you. Now watch what he does with the gun."

Angeluce jammed the muzzle of a handgun into Manies' fat cheek and pulled the trigger. Manies' head burst apart, and wet chunks of it tumbled into the air.

"Very effective, eh?" said Manies grimly. "Those were raw terror tactics. A very sad and unsavory episode in our history, I'm afraid. Shall I run it over again?"

"God, no!" we said.

"Fine," said Manies. He touched his bracelet again. "You might as well come in now; I've run our brother's execution."

A few seconds passed. A second Money Manies ambled into the room.

"There were three of us," said the new Money Manies.

"Yes," said the first Money Manies, smiling at our manifest amazement. "There've been three of us for almost eighty years now. Luckily, the man who was caught and executed was my youngest clone. I suppose I can call that lucky, being the oldest clone. Though you would hardly agree, brother?"

"Don't we always agree?" said the new Money Manies with a smile.

The first Manies nodded. "Yes. The two of us were hidden in my privacy chambers when the Instant Death arrested our poor dead brother. We've spent most of our lives there, anyway, since we only appear in shifts. You must have known about my reputation for forgetfulness. Actually, my memory is excellent, but even with lifetapes it was hard to keep track of all three of me sometimes. Oh, we came out in force occasionally. At the last Harlequinade, for instance."

"We were everywhere at once," said the second Money Manies, chuckling genially. "I was the surprise guest of today's breakfast, by the way. It was a surprise for you and Anne. Everyone else knows by now. I had to reveal the truth when I staged my coup."

"My darling wife knew, of course," said the first Manies, "but she's a girl who knows how to keep her own counsel." He winked. "I married her because she had the skill to satisfy all three of us at once."

"Don't look so crestfallen, Arti," said the second Manies. "There was no way you could have guessed. We put all the talent we possessed into the deception."

"And it paid off, of course. I have another tape now. This is the tape of Angeluce being run down and torn to pieces by the Telset mob. It took place about two hours after I managed to release Cewaynie Wetlock's version of your tapes."

"Wait," I said. "I don't think either one of us wants to see it. We'll take your word for it."

Both of the Moneys Manies rubbed their chins with an identical gesture. "You've changed, Arti. There was a time when you'd be clamoring for a sight of such a splendid vengeance."

"Yes, I've changed," I said.

"Well, rest assured that the unpleasant Professor got everything he deserved. We found most of his body afterwards. The missing portions seem to have been taken for souvenirs by righteously outraged citizens. The death of two hundred of us left many with scores to settle." They sighed heavily. "It was the painful and bloody birth of a new age. I can't say how much I admire that ivy of yours, by the way—it looks so green and young and vigorous. You know, it would make a splendid symbol for the New Cabal. You wouldn't mind if we appropriated it?"

"Tell me what happened to the Old Cabal, first," I said. "That's the core of the matter. Angeluce was just their tool."

"Oh yes, the Old Cabal, the Old Cabal," said the elder Manies, nodding. "Well, the two of us have been working with Cewaynie Wetlock on that. A delightful girl, I can't tell you how much I admire her talent, especially in computer simulation. Could you believe she is only eighteen? She has genius, plus all the vigor and audacity of youth. I swear you'll love her, Kid."

"Tanglin."

"Yes, Tanglin, of course. Well, brother, let's run the first tape. Watch this closely, Arthur, I'll want your professional opinion on this."

The tape opened with an orbital shot of the glowing rim of Reverie. "Very effective, eh, Arti? She stole it from the beginnings of your combat tapes. She's your biggest fan. Yes, here it comes, just over the horizon—look at that! Can you believe it's simulated?"

"It's an oneill. One of the old-style models," I said.

"Yes, being an orbiter, Cewaynie knows them well. Now look at that rainbow insignia! It's the Cabal's oneill, where they're meeting in secret session! We'll put all this in the soundtrack, of course. We were hoping we could get you to narrate it."

"I see," I said.

"Of course, your voice has changed now. Oh, here comes the good part." A fat, glimmering yellow spacecraft lumbered onto the screen. It bore an insignia of linked beads. "These are the good guys—our side. Now watch them open up on that oneill. Bang! Wham!" The Moneys Manies gripped the arms of their chairs in excitement. "Look at the atmosphere gush out! Look at those pieces of debris! But it's not over yet! The oneill fights back! Lasers rake the vacuum! Wau, that was close, wasn't it? But now we fire again! The oneill splits open, it's a direct hit! They're abandoning ship. Count those little lifeboats, Arti—there are thirteen of them, no mistake there! But it's too late for the wicked Cabalists! The mighty hand of vengeance is upon them!"

The other Manies took up the narration. "These close-ups are marvelous, aren't they? Pow! There goes the first one. That was Red. You've noticed the crafts with the little directional arrows on them, I'm sure. Pow! Pow! Look at that one wobbling—we had to have a few misses for verisimilitude, you know—Pow! Pow! PowPowPow, two with one shot! Her technique is incredible, isn't it? I've never seen anything like it! Now watch her pursue them to the limits of the atmosphere. Look at those re-entry glows from atmospheric friction. That just slows them up, though—Zap! They're helpless! Well, that's the last of them. Wonderful, wasn't it?"

"Very exciting," I said stonily. "Good theater."

"Ah, I knew you'd say that. Cewaynie will be so pleased. That was just the surface-dwellers' version, though. We've done another one for consumption up in the oneills. As you recall, they believe that the Cabal had its headquarters on the planet's surface. All right, brother, run the tape.

"Now look at this. It's all done *underwater!* All with studio techniques, too, and by a woman who's never gone diving in her life—except with drones, of course. Notice the bead bracelets on the arms of these valiant frogmen. Those big guns they have are torpedo launchers. The design is authentic, too; I took it from the Confederate archives. Here we go, it's just past this rill in the ocean's bottom—look at that! The Cabal's secret headquarters, whole fathoms deep! No wonder we never found it, eh? It's wonderfully squat and evil-looking, isn't it? We were going to have some enemy frogmen come out of that airlock there, get in some exciting underwater hand-to-hand combat. But we thought that would be gilding the lily. You agree, of course."

"Right," I said.

"I knew you would. Now watch them firing their torpedoes. Boom! Blam! We'll put the sound effects in when we do the soundtrack, of course. Water carries sound quite well. I'm doing the soundtrack myself, since it's not Cewaynie's specialty. All right, here they come, puttering out in their little underwater lifeboats. You notice the insignia again. Too late for them, the hand of vengeance, et cetera et cetera. There goes the first one. Those rushes of bubbles are very dramatic, aren't they? Very visually exciting. Boom. Boom." Manies seemed to be losing interest. "Right, there goes the next one and the next one. Now, look at this, Orange pulls out of the way of the torpedo but it goes right on to hit Green. Bit of unconscious humor there, perhaps. Boom. Yes. Well, there goes the last of them."

"You're being very audacious," Anne said. "What happens when a floater and a surface dweller get together to compare notes on your stories?"

"Oh, each one will believe he's seen the truth, while the other has been suckered in by the official line. No? You don't believe so? Well, perhaps we'll release just one of them, then. It seems a shame. Which one do you think is better?"

"How about showing the truth instead?" I said bluntly.

"The truth? Oh. Well. The Corporation isn't quite ready for that as yet. The Gestalt Theory and everything. The Chemical Analogue Theory of the Body Politic. It's a very volatile situation politically. The Academy has disowned Angeluce of course—I saw to that. Even so, they were behind Angeluce all along. At least, they supplied his huge financial backing. They were determined to destroy Crossbow and all his evidence once and for all. But if the Reverid government embraced Crossbow's anti-Determinist theories, there would still be trouble. Reverie is just one planet after all, and the Academy is a very large enemy."

"That didn't stop Rominuald Tanglin," Anne said.

"Yes, and you see where it got him, begging your pardon, Arti."

"Well, privately then," I insisted. "Let's hear the real story, Manies. The truth."

"Well. Yes. The truth. Well, that's a bit of a ticklish situation, isn't it? A question of definition. Of perception. Of subjective interpretation." There was a double pinging from the bracelets on the wrists of the Moneys Manies. They looked up in some relief. "Ah, I see it's a topic that will have to wait till breakfast. Here come our guests."

Manies' wife appeared at the doorway and glided up silently to her husbands. She was wearing a remarkable dress of linked beads, but it was the wreath of fresh ivy in her black hair that caught my attention. A chair rolled up to her and she took it. It bore her to the table, between the two Manies.

Ruffian Jack came in, patently drunk. Spinney was behind him, carrying his mantis on his shoulder with a thin wire leash. Jack rumbled a greeting as they took their seats. They were both wearing wreaths in their hair.

Then Chill Factor and Ice Lady came in, smiling broadly, dressed very prosperously, almost to the point of bad taste. Chill had taken off his skin-tight, ice-blue mask, because there was a long, hastily stitched slash in his forehead. I saw that they both had new sets of cameras, big ones, almost small drones.

"Arti, our little angel, our star pupil, our salvation!" crowed Chill. "Let these arms embrace you, let this heart almost reach its melting point with gratified pride and joy!"

He embraced me cautiously, careful not to freeze my unprotected skin. Parts of the bodytight I had borrowed from Ruffian Jack stuck to his icy forearms.

"Anne, darling," said Ice Lady, swaying up to Anne and laying her whip gently and caressingly aginst Anne's cheek, "we've never met, but I'd like to thank you from the bottom of my heart for taking care of our little Arti, who's more than a son to us but our beautiful vicious brute and one freezing hell of a fine actor. You're welcome in our gang, anytime."

It was the highest compliment she could offer. Anne seemed to sense this. "Thank you, Ice Lady," she said.

"We've taken good care of your Quade," Ice Lady told me. "It was the least we could do for you, Kid. She's just fine, and dying to meet you. We've told her all about you. Is it true you've changed your name?"

"Yes, it's true," I said.

"Everything seems to be changing," sighed Chill Factor. "The Zone's rubble now. We meet on the beaches to fight, when we can. Mostly, we've got our hands full with the Civic Detail. Look at this rip in my forehead. Who would have thought a noncombatant could do that, eh? I tell you, the Revolution has got these people's blood up." He shook his head sadly. "The Instant Death's disbanded, too. Our best enemies."

Then Cewaynie Wetlock came in. She walked tentatively, with the hesitant, stiff-legged stride of an orbiter newly come to gravity. She was wearing a floater's blue overalls. She was painfully young, pale, and slender, with light blonde hair swept back from her forehead and caught in a beaded barette. Like everyone else, she was wearing an ivy wreath.

"You're the *Kid*," she said worshipfully, walking carefully up and seizing my arm for balance, with both hands. "I'm Cewaynie Wetlock. Gosh, can you ever forgive me for taking your cameras? I did it sort of on impulse—I was afraid Angeluce would find out I was exploring the Mass, and I was afraid I'd lose the chance. My telephoto picked you up almost at once.

If only my drone had had a voder unit! But I hadn't expected to find anyone in the Mass. Least of all you, Kid."

"Tanglin," Anne said.

The Alien came in, carrying a heavy tray with a hinged metal lid. Steam curled up around its edges. "Let's eat!" said the Alien from behind its filmy white veil.

The moving chairs predetermined our seating arrangement. Annabella Manies had her slim back to the tape screen. To her left sat the elder Manies, then Cewaynie Wetlock, Ruffian Jack, Alruddin Spinney, Crossbow's empty chair, the Alien, Ice Lady, Chill Factor, Anne, myself, and, finally, the younger Manies on Annabella's right.

Quizein, on his own two good legs this time, came in and deftly distributed plates, chopsticks, knives, and forks to all the humans present. To the Alien, he gave a round dish with steeply sloping edges and two pincerlike utensils that the Alien gripped with double-jointed fingers. The Alien had the covered dish to itself. Ignoring etiquette, it eagerly lifted the hinged cover a bit, snaked in a pincer, and nipped out a fatty-looking gobbet of some unidentifiable food. Heavy mandibular crunching came from behind its veil.

"This informal meeting of the New Cabal will come to order!" said the elder Manies with a smile, rapping the wooden table with the back of his fork. "Quizein, serve the first course, if you please."

Quizein brought in tiny cups of highly spiced soup, which we drank hot. Ruffian Jack coughed and reached into his brocaded coat for a plastic flask.

Manies belted down his soup. "Now," said the younger Manies, "I propose today's topic: The Truth!"

"Hear, hear!" said the company.

"I heard a true story once," said Jack with a hiccup.

"Quiet, Jack." The elder Manies looked around, beaming. "As you know, I've been preparing this presentation for some time. Now I know—and don't try to deny it—I know that some of you have an unhealthy skepticism concerning my Chemical Analogue Theory of the Body Politic."

"Aw, for Law's sake, Manies!" cried Jack. "Can't we postpone this till the second course, at least? If we gotta keep our mouths shut, we might as well have something in 'em."

"Really, Jack! These outbursts will cease or the New Cabal will have your shares declared forfeit." There was a derisive outburst of spirited hooting from the guests, especially the Alien, who caught on slowly but went on hooting long after all the other guests had stopped.

Both Manies waited tolerantly until the Alien grew tired and the second course had been served. "First," said Manies, "we must deal with the thorny problem of the existence of the Old Cabal. Put simply, our problem is this. How could one deal with an entity, or purported number of entities, who were universally acknowledged to exist, but could not be seen, touched, heard, smelled, or tasted?"

"There is only one such Entity," Anne said.

Manies smiled. "I think we can rule out theological implications for the time being. Here is our one solid piece of evidence: the destruction of the Chairman's Building, and the attempted assassination of Moses Moses. It is from this single piece of evidence—an occurrence three hundred years ago—that the vast mythology of the Cabal grew. Who was responsible for the Fox Day bomb? A long-neglected mystery. Many possibilities suggest themselves. A conspiracy is one. Perhaps it was a conspiracy, rather than, say, a suicide attempt by a deranged government official. But conspiracies are not long-lived. They dissolve once they have served their purpose. There may have been a Cabal once. Three hundred years ago. But does it still exist? It gives no evidence of persistence. I move that we dismiss the idea entirely!"

"But who rules Reverie, then? Who's been running things all this time?" I said.

"Ah, now we come to the crux of the matter," Manies said. He touched his bracelet. "Chalkwhistle, run the diagram, please."

An immense beaded network appeared on the tapescreen behind the two Moneys Manies and their wife. It was torus-shaped, and made of millions of varicolored beads.

"Thanks to your excellent camera work, Arthur, we were

able to reconstruct this and thus prevent a tragic loss to science," said the elder Manies sententiously. "This, of course, is the Crossbow Body, that marvelous, mystic construct that defies the laws of determinism. Naturally, due to the ticklish situation vis-a-vis the Academy, this information must not leave this room." Both Manies looked us over, jutting out their lower jaws with identical determined expressions. "Very well. Chalkwhistle, run the second diagram, if you would be so good. Ah yes, now we see it."

An identical diagram—I would swear it was the same one—flashed onto the screen. "Thanks to the splendid help of the Reformed Board and the help of certain very cooperative computer technicians, We, Richer Money Manies, have constructed this Chemical Analogue of the *entire population of Reverie!* It includes social, economic, and personal dominance factors. A remarkable resemblance, wouldn't you say? And the implications are unescapable! Reverie has been running herself! Reverie has been plotting her own historical evolution, just as the Crossbow Body fulfills the evolution of life on this planet! I should have reached this conclusion long ago, but my assumption that a Cabal existed had completely warped my calculations! Here, Chalkwhistle, run that pitiful tissue of errors that was my first reconstruction—mind you, friends, you must promise not to laugh. Ah, there it is. A wretched thing, isn't it? A mere circular tangle of beads! But remove the assumption of the Cabal, thusly . . . and you see that our social structure now has *twenty-three* specific gaps, corresponding exactly to the twenty-three storage gaps in the Crossbow Body! Friends, this is more than coincidence. I rest my case."

"You expect us to believe that?" I demanded.

"Arti, you are welcome to check the figures yourself. I warn you, however, that it will take you at least one hundred and eighty years to learn the mathematics. It took me two hundred, and I had the help of skilled tutors."

"Then where did Professor Angeluce fit in?"

"Angeluce," said Manies, "was merely a shrewd and unscrupulous manipulator. He had guessed the truth about the Cabal, and used our own mythos against us. His long-range goal was to annihilate the Mass and all traces of the Crossbow Body, thus liquidating the anti-Determinist evidence. I assume that he meant to use orbital lasers to fry the Mass. He meant to turn the greatest triumph of Reverid technology against us. He knew we Reverids would never freely agree to such a massive assault on our planetary ecosystem, so he concluded that he would have to force us by taking over our government. When Moses Moses reappeared, he realized that he would soon have a very serious rival, and took steps to eliminate him—steps that soon got completely out of hand."

"That's very interesting," I said. "I have an alternate theory, though."

Manies stared. "Wonderful," he said at last. "Let's hear it, by all means."

"Very well," I said. "Imagine a very old, very powerful, and very intelligent man, a member of an organization, not a Cabal exactly, but a loose alliance of the very old whose age and experience give them a piercing insight into human affairs. Imagine this man in a position of power, not crushing, overwhelming power, but behind-the-scenes control. It is not a lust for power and fame that motivates him. He is far beyond that. He is merely bored enough, and skilled enough, to enjoy playing the ultimate dominance game. Suddenly, two rivals present themselves. He uses the first rival to neutralize the second, then gives the first enough rope to hang himself. He operates with incredible, even self-destructive subtlety. When the fracas is over, he returns to his old position, and his old power, merely changing names and symbols to protect himself."

Both Manies looked shocked, then deeply pained. "Kid," said the older one pleadingly. "These suspicions are truly beneath you. Why, they're like Rominuald Tanglin's last days. Ah, I know what bothers you—stalwart freedom fighter that you are—how tactless of me not to mention this first of all. This is the deepest, most vital secret of them all—the existence of the New Cabal. I can tell that you dislike the sound of that title. Well, these people are the members of the Cabal. All of them. Your best friends. Oh, that's certainly not what we've told the public. They believe that we, Money Manies, are only the front man for a new group of conspirators, who have overthrown the old group and instituted a similar despotic rule. *It is vital that they believe that.* You remember those helical gaps in the structure? They would be filled if a true Cabal existed. *We must not be allowed to plot our own destiny.* The Crossbow Body does that for us. We are guided by the deepest forces inherent in life itself. A great new age beckons to us Reverids—salvation by a mighty force that transcends intelligence. If people began making plans to govern themselves—to resist the will of the Body— there might be another social upheaval like the one caused by Professor Angeluce. No one wants that. That's our secret power, we members of the Cabal—*we do nothing.* We will allow every man and woman and neuter to go their own ways in peace, to express themselves freely, beholden to no man."

I got up from my chair. "Crap, Manies. These are young people. They can't see through your subtleties. I'm not sure how you'll do it, but you'll arrange things to suit yourselves. You Cabalists always have."

Manies sat up and said with dignity, "My friends are young. Money Manies is the friend of all young people. Is there something wrong with that?"

"Don't get me wrong, old patron mine. I'm not your enemy. Rule Reverie if you want to. Play your games. Keep your last toe hold on life. If I were as old and wretched and desperate as you, I might do the same thing. Your pursuits don't concern me, as long as you don't cross me. There's only one thing I want you to tell me—an old score I have to settle. Where is Instant Death?"

Manies looked gravely concerned. Even Chill Factor and Ice Lady made sour faces. "He's left Telset," Manies said. "His gang has been dissolved. I know about the customs of blood feud, Tanglin, but you'll have to content yourself with that. Instant Death could have fought us to the bitter end, but he deserted Angeluce as soon as your tapes were shown and he learned the truth. We've granted him amnesty. We can't allow you to murder him. By his own lights, he was doing his duty to his government."

I pulled my nunchuck. It felt oddly slick in my hands; my

palms were sweating. "Don't make me angry, Manies," I said. "You disposed of Angeluce easily enough, but I saw that welcoming crowd on the docks. I'm not without power of my own, and I learned enough from Old Dad to know how to use it if I have to. Make things easy for yourselves, and tell me where he is. Don't force me to take drastic steps."

Manies blew out his cheeks. "I hardly expected this. Arthur, no doubt your analogous chemical make-up has changed. I see that we are reduced to a vulgar contest of will." He touched his bracelets. "Chalkwhistle, would you step in for a moment? Bring the weapon."

A few seconds passed. Anne got up and stood beside me, ignoring the plaintive attempts of her chair to persuade her to sit. Chalkwhistle came in, bearing a high-powered, oiled, and polished pistol on a small red pillow. Chalkwhistle gave me a black look. I had forgotten that I had knocked it down without warning, all those months ago.

Both the Manies pointed at the pistol. "There, you see, a deadly weapon, obviously in operating condition. We have ammunition for it, too, somewhere or other."

"In the desk drawer," the younger Manies said.

"Right, the desk drawer," nodded his twin. "There, that should convince you. Obviously, we possess overwhelming might. Needless to say, through the Reformed Board, all good friends of mine, we control all the ammunition stocks in Telset. If it comes to a showdown, we possess the power. You are helpless."

"Don't underestimate me," I said. "I have my own ways. I needn't resort to violence." I threw the nunchuck on the table with a clatter. "I can fight a social battle. Your charisma versus mine, Manies dolls."

"Would you really go that far for the sake of empty vengeance?" said Manies with a painful smile. "Kid, I love you like a son, but if you resist the will of the Body Politic, a thunderbolt will strike you. I'll have you assassinated."

"You wouldn't dare," I said.

"You think I lack the will and the ruthlessness." He sighed. "I regret that I have to make this demonstration." The older

Manies stood up. "Guests, friends, I apologize for this piece of rudeness, an unpleasantness which I would prefer that you not witness. I must ask you, as a personal favor, to turn your chairs and close your eyes. I assure you that no harm will come to Arti."

This was the true measure of Manies' control over them. They all did it. They did it without question or hesitation. All of them turned around, leaving only the two Manies, Annabella Manies, Anne, myself, and the Alien facing the table.

Manies gestured to the Alien. "And now, if you would."

The Alien turned its tray around and pulled it wide open. Despite the fact that it had been cleaned, steamed, and partially eaten, I recognized the object at once. It was Professor Angeluce's head.

The Alien closed the tray again, still chewing.

"I think you understand the depth of my conviction now," Manies said evenly. "Friends, you may return to the table. Again, I apologize."

"I'm leaving," Anne said. She walked quickly from the room.

"So am I," I said. "But I have one question for you, Alien. If I broke your head open, would it be hollow and held together with thick black fiber?"

The Alien only winked, and kept chewing.

I left the room. "Chalkwhistle will give you new cameras, and fresh tape," Manies called out. "Send me anything you do! It's always welcome!"

I slammed the door behind me and rejoined Anne in the hall. "It was horrible," she said, shuddering. "But Arti—I don't believe you should fight him. Not for vengeance. I've never believed in vengeance."

"I'm swearing off blood feud," I muttered. "I can't live that life any more. I can't compete with that. Oh bloody death—he had me so rattled that I walked off and left my nunchuck behind for the first time in thirty years."

As if they were listening in, Cewaynie Wetlock appeared at the door with my nunchuck in hand. "You left this," she said shyly. "Kid—Mr. Tanglin—I'm very sorry you argued with Mr. Manies, and I think he treated you *cruelly*. I know about your love for Armitrage—I edited it, remember? It's a legend already! I don't want to stay at some stuffy banquet. Listen. I want to show you all your tapes—what I did with them, how I handled it. I've seen every single tape you've ever done, I swear I have. I did it just like you would have. Won't you come to my house? I have a beautiful place, it used to belong to a member of the Rump Board, before Angeluce purged her. Oh, it's wonderful, and ... well ... you're not a child any more are you? Neither am I. I want to show you all the tapes. Then we'll make some of our own. I have a whole library of tapes. Armitrage's too. Even the weirdest ones. If you'll only say yes, then we could do all of the wonderful things on those tapes. Whatever you like. Or if you don't want to, then you don't have to. But come with me. Please?"

"I'm sorry," I said. "I'm leaving Telset immediately."

"Oh, but that would be tragic! Can't you spare even a few hours? It's night already!"

"Madame Wetlock," said Anne with strained patience, "don't you think you're assuming a lot?"

"Oh Anne," said Cewaynie Wetlock, putting her hands on her hips, "I love you like a sister, and you're a real heroine that everyone in Telset is crazy about, but there's a lot you don't know about men, and especially not Reverid men, and super-specially not about the *Kid*. Remember, I've gone through all of your hours together, and I know, well, everything about the two of you. Except what happened on the beach, of course. But I know you, and I know your weird moral code. After fifty-two years of celibacy, six short months on a beach can't have meant that much." She looked into Anne's face. "Nothing happened!"

"I see you have great confidence in your own appeal," Anne said stiffly.

"Anne, you're wonderful, and I admire you in a crazy sort of way, but you had your chance at Tanglin and you blew it! He's a man now! He's not a life-sized doll! I can give Arti things that you couldn't dream of giving—"

Then Cewaynie Wetlock sagged to the floor, wheezing. The incredible had happened. Anne had struck Cewaynie Wetlock in the solar plexus with the full power of a clenched combat fist.

I looked at her, amazed. "Don't say it," she said hoarsely, tears coming to her eyes. "I've struck her. I had no right to. What do you and I really know of each other? Our little world's been shattered now—"

"Anne," I said, "I'm leaving Telset and I'm going back to Crossbow's old house on the continent. I'm going to change my whole life, and I swear, if you don't help me do it, if you don't come with me, I'll kill myself."

"I'll come with you," she said. "I want to more than anything in this world."

We broke out of Manies' huge and suffocating mansion. Then we borrowed Ruffian Jack's hydrofoil. We picked up Quade and left Telset for good.

Crossbow's house was a shambles, but the three of us made it beautiful again. Quade is our daughter now, and she and Anne have taught me more about love and caring than most Reverids ever bother to learn. We'll have another daughter soon, if Anne's delivery is normal, and the doctors assure us it will be, even as they shake their heads at the eccentricity of a natural birth.

I'm happy here. It doesn't matter if my hair is long and curled, if I wear Tanglin's brocades and heels instead of leather. I do what makes Anne happy. And Quade is much happier, on suppressants. It's the only way to be a child. Just a few days ago she was playing on the beach, and when I joined her I found that she had made a little mosaic of seashells in the wet sand. "It's pretty, isn't it, Daddy?" she said, looking at me eye to eye from where she knelt, and as tears came to my eyes I said, "Yes, darling, it's beautiful," and I made a tape out of it that was a smash hit and took Telset, Jucklet, Sylvain, and Eros by storm. My new tapes, of my new life, have a vast appeal. I number my fans in the millions.

It's peaceful here. Money Manies is vastly supportive, and money pours to us from his networks. My position is perfect for him and his Cabal, since, like Moses Moses, I am a national hero safely retired to a pedestal.

Moses Crossbow's body has never been found. Perhaps he is waiting, like I am.

Just wait till the Kid grows up.